ALBUQUERQUE ACADEMY
1955

This book was donated
to honor
the birthday of

Carlin Venaglia

by

Fred F. Venaglia

1998

DATE

BAKER'S Dictionary of *Music*

BAKER'S

Dictionary of *Music*

Nicolas Slonimsky

EDITED BY RICHARD KASSEL

SCHIRMER BOOKS
An Imprint of Simon & Schuster Macmillan
New York

PRENTICE HALL INTERNATIONAL
London   Mexico City   New Delhi   Singapore   Sydney   Toronto

Schirmer Boooks
An imprint of Simon & Schuster Macmillan
1633 Broadway, 5th Floor
New York, NY 10019

Manufactured in the United States of America.

printing number
1 2 3 4 5 6 7 8 9 10

Library of Congress Cataloging-in-Publication Data

Slonimsky, Nicolas, 1894-
     Baker's dictionary of music / by Nicolas Slonimsky : edited by
Richard Kassel.
         p.   cm.
     ISBN 0-02-864791-2
     1. Music—Dictionaries.   I. Kassel, Richard.   II. Title.
ML100.S635 1997
780'.3—dc21   97-21923
                                        CIP
                                        MN

This paper meets the requirements of ANSI/NISO Z39.48-1992
(Permanence of Paper).

Contents

Publisher's Note

Nicolas Slonimsky (1894–1995) was one of this century's greatest dictionary makers and perhaps one of the greatest lexicographers of all time. Born in St. Petersburg, Russia, he emigrated to Turkey, Bulgaria, Paris, and, in 1923, the United States, landing first in Rochester, New York, and then settling in Boston. Within a year or two of his arrival he had taught himself English and was writing regularly for the *Boston Evening Transcript* and the *Christian Science Monitor*. He became assistant to Serge Koussevitzky, who was then conductor of the Boston Symphony Orchestra, but he also organized his own chamber orchestra for the performance of works by contemporary composers like Charles Ives, Edgard Varèse, Henry Cowell, among others. Slonimsky's position as conductor and champion of modern music culminated in a famous concert in the Hollywood Bowl in 1933, a concert so controversial that it brought his conducting career to a virtual standstill. But he remained a champion of the new throughout his life.

Slonimsky began his lexicographic work in 1937 with the first edition of the monumental *Music Since 1900*, a selective chronology of musical events large and small rendered in an unusual literary format. The work went through five editions. He next edited *Thompson's International Cyclopedia of Music and Musicians* (4th to 8th editions, 1946–58) and then embarked on his major work, the remaking of *Baker's Biographical Dictionary of Musicians*, which he took from the 5th through the 8th editions, completely rewriting its entries in his peerless style. The 8th edition, published in 1992, contains more than three and a half million words.

His hilarious and sobering *Lexicon of Musical Invective* (1952) collected bad reviews of famous composers' music and is a perennial favorite, especially amongst creative people. He completely revised the *Schirmer Pronouncing Pocket Manual of Musical Terms* in 1978. Finally, in 1988, his long-awaited autobiography, *Perfect Pitch*, appeared and was widely read and admired.

Not long afterward, Slonimsky published his *Lectionary of Music*, a narrative approach to musical lexicography, covering usual and unusual musical topics and designed to be read for pleasure and general information. The published version, however, did not include the entire original manuscript as written, the editors having decided to limit the book's coverage and size. After Nicolas's death we examined the unpublished drafts and, working with his daughter Electra Yourke, were able to reassemble the complete work. We also drew material from the immense archive of his voluminous writings, produced over more than seventy active years, including hundreds of articles, program notes, and liner notes, as well as entries from the *Pocket Manual* and *Baker's 8th*. In sum, a new, comprehensive introductory music dictionary could be derived from this mass of work.

An initial concern was covering contemporary musicians who have emerged since Nicolas wrote the last edition of *Baker's* or whose entries require updating. He had, of course, covered important groups like the Beatles and the Rolling Stones, and we were able to complete those entries, hopefully in a style that approaches his standard. In all his reference works Nicolas relied on the help of scholars, amateur musical sleuths, and his own tireless assistants. Often they drafted entries that he would then carefully craft in his own style. For the present work we have had to rely on Nicolas's ghost to help us to completion, and we have quietly corrected a few errors that somehow escaped his vigilant eye, as he would wish. But virtually in its entirety this work is as Nicolas wrote it, and we are proud to introduce it in a new, expanded, and updated version.

Rather than call the present volume a 2nd edition of the *Lectionary*, we have rebaptized it *Baker's Dictionary of Music*. Thus it takes its place in the royal family of music dictionaries and expands our line of offerings under the Baker name.

Schirmer Books

Preface and Acknowledgments

I have attempted to put Mr. Slonimsky's innumerable thoughts and words into perspective, balancing his knowledge, personal experience, lively and opinionated outlook, humor, and sheer love of language (especially the less familiar aspects of it) with the needs of a music dictionary written for individuals new to the richness of music—its variegated history, major participants, and seemingly overwhelming vocabulary. To the extent that I have been able to reach a meeting of the minds with the indomitable Mr. Slonimsky is a tribute to his acuity and remarkable productivity.

I am grateful to the people at Schirmer Books who have given their all to make this volume a welcome addition to the music reference shelf (or, for that matter, any bookshelf), in particular Richard Carlin, longtime friend, fine musician, and an editor's editor. I have enjoyed the privilege of working with Mr. Slonimsky's daughter Electra Yourke, who has maintained and expanded her father's legacy with distinction.

To accomplish such a task as this, I have drawn upon the knowledge, encouragement, and love of many people: teachers such as Professor Janet Knapp, colleagues such as Herr Professor Doktor Albin Zak III, friends and lovers past and present, an amazing family that remains remarkably close and supportive despite life's sometimes painful distractions, and even those who, by example, have taught me how (and how not) to treat others, and how to withstand the natural shocks that flesh is heir to.

I hope that you find Mr. Slonimsky's way of expressing the pleasures of music salutiferous.

Richard Kassel

Introduction: Lexicographis Secundus Post Herculem Labor

By Nicolas Slonimsky

Lexicographis secundus post Herculem Labor. This was the judgment pronounced by Joseph Justus Scaliger (1540–1609), himself a formidable lexicographer; the Herculean labor to which he compared his lexicographical task was that of cleaning up the manure-filled stables of King Augeus, son of the sun god Helius. Hercules performed the job in twenty-four hours.

Dr. Johnson was egregiously wrong when he described a lexicographer as a harmless drudge. The job might well be hazardous to the lexicographer's health. *Baker's Biographical Dictionary of Musicians*, which I was hired to sanitize, reports the melancholy case of John Wall Callcott (1766–1821): His mind gave way from overwork on a projected but unrealized music dictionary. He recovered but not sufficiently to continue his work. In his biographical dictionary Callcott reached the letter *Q*, associated with such malevolent concepts as queer, quagmire, and quaquaversal quirks, and proceeded no further. Dictionary makers of my own time experience a similar sort of malaise. One of the editors of the 4th edition of *Baker's* wrote on the margins of the galley proofs: "I will go mad if I have to continue this for a long time." When a distinguished British musicologist ("nomina sunt odiosa") took over provisionally the editorship of the 6th edition of *Grove's Dictionary*, he wrote me from his temporary retreat in Pennsylvania that he deliberately took his lodgings on the ground floor of an apartment house just in case he would be tempted to commit the act of defenestration after reading pages and pages of *Grove 5*—and he proceeded to quote lengthy paragraphs from that edition to prove they were conducive to disorientation and ultimately madness.

I recall with fond memories my voluminous correspondence with two great dictionary makers, Percy A. Scholes (pronounced *Skoles*, as he never failed to point out) and Eric Blom, whose letters I handed over to the Library of Congress for safekeeping, just in time to receive a generous tax deduction for my gift (which also included a lot of other letters, manuscripts, and a mass of birth and death certificates). Scholes was peculiarly obdurate when it came to American musical terms. He claimed, for instance, that Americans used *bar* only in the sense of barline. In vain did I send him numerous clippings from American publications that used the term *bar* in the sense of rhythmic content of a measure, just as the British do. He yielded the point only after I sent him a copy of the boogie-woogie classic "Beat Me, Daddy, Eight to the Bar." In the subsequent edition of his *Oxford Companion to Music* he inserted this paragraph in the entry on American Musical Terminology: "It may be added that recent American usage seems to tend to the use of *bar* for the rhythmic period and of *barline* for the sign, as in the common British usage." He also claimed that Americans used the term *cancel* for "natural," as in "C cancel," to indicate the cancellation of a previous sharp or a flat. He brushed aside my quotations from American music-school books, which used the term *natural*. "You Americans don't know your own common usage!" he wrote me during one of our heated exchanges about the subject. To settle the matter I sent a questionnaire to eminent American composers, music critics, and teachers around Boston where I lived at the time, among them Arthur Shepherd and Walter Piston, inquiring whether they ever used the term *cancel*. None did. But then a postcard arrived from Warren Storey Smith amending his previous disavowal. "Doggone it," he wrote, "I remembered that in high school we did use the word 'cancel,' even though the teacher always said that natural was the proper term." Swallowing my pride, I forwarded Smith's postcard to Scholes. His response was characteristic. "What's doggone?" he asked.

Conscientiously, Scholes changed clause four in the entry on American Musical Terminology in the *Oxford*

Companion to Music to read: "The substitution in some parts of the country of *cancel* for 'natural' (after a sharp or flat) is sometimes seen and is certainly logical." Dear irreplaceable Scholes! He invariably sent me his publications; among them was *The Mirror of Music*, a centennial compilation, with commentaries, of articles in *The Musical Times* of London. Browsing one day in the basement of Goodspeed's book store near the old State House in Boston, I found an old music book published about 1850 with the very same title, *The Mirror of Music*. Delighted by my discovery, I purchased the book and mailed it to Scholes. His reply was priceless: "Thank you for sending me the book. How dares the author anticipate my own title!"

Scholes could be quite beastly to his colleagues. He commented on the demise of Arthur Eaglefield Hull: "Hull's suicide was the result of my exposure of his thefts in his book *Music: Classical, Romantic and Modern*. He threw himself under a train."

My epistolary exchange with Eric Blom formed a florid counterpoint to that with Scholes. There was not mutual admiration between these two great arbiters of musical facts and musical values. When I pointed out a bit of misinformation in *Grove 5* that misled me, and apparently misled Scholes as well, to judge by the inclusion of some dubious data in the *Oxford Companion to Music*, Blom wrote me: "I am indeed sorry for having misled you; not so sorry for having misled Scholes."

Both Scholes and Blom gave generous space to pandiatonicism, which was my own brainchild. Scholes frankly told me that he could not understand what pandiatonicism was all about. I sent him a suitable text, and he included it in his *Oxford Companion to Music*, dutifully enclosed between quotation marks. I sent a practically identical statement to Blom. He thought that the term should be *pandiatonism*. I retorted by an analogy with chromaticism vs. chromatism. The dilemma was resolved by having the article in *Grove 5* inserted under the heading Pandiaton(ic)ism. (Years later I read a biography of the American philosopher Charles Sanders Peirce, who introduced the term *pragmatism* into philosophical usage, only to have William James pick it up and make it his own. Peirce was quite upset about this, and to regain his priority he changed it to *pragmaticism*, which, he said, "was ugly enough to be safe from kidnappers.")

In one instance I unintentionally caused Blom a lot of trouble. In the entry on the violinist Marie Hall, *Grove 5* said that she died in October 1947. I could not find any reference to her demise in obituary columns; yet she was a famous person. When she arrived in New York for a concert in November 1905, she was met by an admiring crowd in New York Harbor, and her pictures adorned the covers of commercial music periodicals (yes, there were lavishly illustrated music magazines in those days). Could she have departed this life unnoticed and unmourned, I asked Blom. He replied, with his usual show of baffled insouciance: "I do not keep references to my sources of information. Do you?" So I wrote to the editor of *The Strad*, the British violin magazine, asking for information. No, the editor wrote back, he did not know that Marie Hall had died; nor could he assert that she hadnt died. He proposed to print my letter. The response to it was quite startling: eleven letters arrived from friends, associates, students, and relatives of Marie Hall assuring me that not only was she very much alive, but that she had a couple of years after her Grove-conducted funeral played a successful concert in London. I forwarded the information to Blom. He was quite taken aback by Marie Hall's resurrection, and said he remembered vaguely that it was the English music scholar Edmund Horace Fellowes who told him that Marie Hall was dead. And Fellowes was definitely dead, Blom added, for he, Blom, had attended his funeral. The affair had unpleasant consequences. English law does not accept the excuse of innocent error. The publishers and Blom himself received ominous writs from solicitors with Dickensian last names, asking for redress. I never found out how the affair was finally settled, and I felt badly about starting the whole ruckus. In a few years Marie Hall was really dead; she passed on in Cheltenham on November 11, 1956.

Noble, honorable Blom! He had his pet aversions, among them Mascagni, Offenbach, Rachmaninoff, and Dohnányi, and he could be beastly to them. By a stroke of funereal irony, when an organist officiating at Blom's own funeral asked an intimate of the family what to play during the service, he suggested a Bach chorale. The organist thought he said barcarolle, and launched into the one from *The Tales of Hoffmann*, Bloms bête noire.

Among the most nightmarish recollections of lexicographic horrors was my bout with *Thompson's International Cyclopedia of Music and Musicians*, indelibly etched in the corrugations of my medulla oblongata. I got involved with it when Oscar Thompson sold the idea of a huge one-volume encyclopedia to Dodd, Mead, Inc., in 1938, only to find that the ineffable A. E. ("Weird") Wier had sold a similar project to Macmillan. A race ensued between the two giant publishing houses. At the time Oscar Thompson was the editor of *Musical America*. One spring morning I dropped in on Thompson's office where two female secretaries were busily copying something from the 1926 edition of *Grove*, and a graduate student was struggling with the tenebrous impenetrabilities of *Riemann's Musik Lexikon*. Thompson emerged from his editorial cubicle and asked me, somewhat sheepishly, whether I could read the galley proofs for the letter *R*, fresh from the typesetter. I asked him how much time I would have. He averted his gaze and said, "Until two oclock." The office clock showed 12:30. The mention of the letter *R* produced a strange illumination in my psyche and I exclaimed inwardly: "Rybner!" Rybner was a Danish pianist and a composer of sorts who studied at the Leipzig Conservatory, and in 1904 emigrated to America. His original name was Rubner, with a little cipher over *u*, which palatalized the vowel. In Germany he replaced the cipher by an umlaut, and most of his published works bear the German spelling Rübner. When he came to America he experimented with Ruebner, but eventually adopted the spelling Rybner. I knew that various music dictionaries used different spellings, and realizing that Thompson's assistants were innocent of the intricacies of diacritical signs, I looked up all the possible spellings of the name in the galley proofs. Sure enough, there was Ruebner, and Rübner, and Rybner, all with divergent dates and different misspellings of the Danish titles of his works. Quickly, I destroyed Ruebner and Rübner, leaving the Americanized Rybner to face the music. I did what I could for the other *R*'s in time for the printer to collect the galleys. But my misgivings for the fate of the rest of the alphabet were greatly increased by the state of the *R*'s.

Not surprisingly, when the volume was out I found unspeakable horrors all over the place. According to this early tome, Mozart was influenced by Schubert in composing polonaises; of course it was Schobert whose influence Mozart may or may not have experienced, but someone around the office must have thought it was a misprint and changed Schobert to Schubert. There was a trinity of Philippes de Vitry, one under Philippe, one under De, and one under Vitry, all with different dates. And there was some horrifying mix-up in the listings of the members of the German Danish musical dynasty of Hartmanns. In *Grove* they were all listed in chronological order, beginning with grand old Johann Ernst Hartmann, who was born in Silesia, in 1726, went to Copenhagen and died there in 1793; his son August Wilhelm Hartmann, born in Copenhagen in 1775, who died there in 1850; his son Johan Peder Emilius, already quite Danified, with one *n* in Johan, whose dates were 1805–1900. Well, it said in *Grove* that Johan Peder was the "son and pupil of the preceding," the preceding being August Wilhelm. Although an inveterate Grove-digger, Thompson departed from *Grove*'s format and split the

Hartmanns alphabetically without altering the *Grove* context; in such an arrangement the one who preceded J. P. was J. E.; but J. E. died in 1793, twelve years before the birth of J. P. I informed Thompson of the genetic mix-up, adding facetiously that posthumous artificial insemination had not been perfected in the eighteenth century. Thompson had his laugh, and in the next edition the entry on J. P. Hartmann (1805–1900) read, "*grandson and pupil* of the preceding." That made it a case of prenatal study. By the time I was ready to write Thompson another funny letter, he was dead, and I inherited the whole lexicographical kit-and-caboodle.

There was an even more spectacular case of prenatal activities among composers, also due to the reckless zeal of the Grove-diggers. Marion Bauer, in one of her cooperative books bearing the incredibly ugly title *How Music Grew*, had a paragraph about Bach's famous walk to Lübeck to hear Buxtehude play. *Grove* lists Buxtehude senior and Buxtehude junior in the same article, first the father, second the son. Bauer, an earnest Grove-digger, took the dates of Buxtehude, Sr., 1602–1674, and wrote as follows: "Bach, who must have been a prodigious walker, walked three hundred miles to hear Johann Buxtehude (1602–1674) play the organ." Bach must have been indeed quite prodigious to hear someone play who died eleven years before Bach saw the light of day. Of course, if anyone had asked Marion Bauer, who after all was a music teacher, the date of Bach's birth, she would have answered without a moment's hesitation, 1685. But such is the stultification wrought upon Grove-diggers that apparently neither she nor any of her editors noticed that she got the wrong Buxtehude to play for Bach, even though the dates of Bach's real Buxtehude (1637–1707) were right there in the *Grove* article for anyone to see. I spoiled the fun by babbling about Bach's prenatal walk in public places; Bauer got wind of it and corrected the error in the new edition of her book; she even thanked me personally for calling attention to it. (Incidentally, it is doubtful whether Bach walked to Lübeck at all; the weight of probability is that he hired himself as a student valet to a paying passenger on the stagecoach—but this something else again.)

That Oscar Thompson's assistants were faithful Grove-diggers was to be expected; but they were also conscientious garbage collectors, picking up refuse from the *Dictionary of Modern Music and Musicians* by Eaglefield Hull. In it one reads that Gustav Mahler married Alma Mahler in 1904, while she married him in the adjoining entry two years earlier. Prenatal cello recitals were given by David Popper, who is said to have been born in 1876 but traveled in Europe as a cello virtuoso from 1868 to 1873. Hull had also an entry on a quite unnecessary Australian composer listed as R. G. Davy. Thompson's volume dutifully incorporated Davy, but fleshed out the curt sentences in the entry and specified the personal masculine pronoun *he*, absent in the Hull entry. The trouble is that Davy was a woman. Her true sex was not restored until the 9th edition of Thompson's volume.

In the course of my Augean labors I was confronted with the Cobbett *Cyclopedia of Chamber Music*, which I was asked to revise and supplement. It was a lexicographical garden overgrown with strange flowers. Who was D. Michaud who wrote a trio in 1921, published by Durand? No such name was to be found in any French music reference work. I nearly gave up, when I realized that Michaud was a misprint for Milhaud, who indeed composed a trio in 1921. An even harder nut to crack was Marcel Babey. I inquired at the Société des Compositeurs in Paris, without result. But as I was perusing the entries in the letter L in my own dictionary, I was stopped in my tracks by Marcel Labey, whose doppelgänger was the aforesaid Marcel Babey in Cobbett. Then there was a famous violinist Heinrich Wehtan, mentioned in the article on Russian chamber music by Findeisen. In the Cobbett volume he was said to have organized a quartet in the middle of the nineteenth century. It took me weeks of free association before I arrived at the conclusion that Heinrich Wehtan was none other than Henri Vieuxtemps. Apparently the Findeisen article was translated from the original Russian into German, and from German into English. The Russian spelling of Vieuxtemps in Cyrillic letters, BbETAH, was phonetically transcribed as Wehtan in German, and was incorporated without change in Cobbett.

Robert Eitner is a name of awesome authority, the man who compiled a monumental encyclopedia of musical sources. He spent a lifetime in the dusty libraries of Europe collecting his materials. In the course of his research he came upon a pile of anonymous eighteenth-century French songs. Ignorant of the French language, Eitner apparently decided that the nouns in the titles were the names of the composers. Thus we learn from Eitner that "La Chanson dun gai Berger" was a work by Ungay Berger, and "La Chanson de l'Auberge Isolée" was written by Mlle Isolée L'Auberge. There must be a number of desperate lexicographers who are trying to find out something more about the lives of Mr. Gay Shepherd and Miss Isolated Tavern.

Musical autobiographies are suspect. Few musicians have the literary skill enabling them to organize the events of their lives into a coherent narrative, and vanity often compels them to convert an autobiography into an auto-hagiography. Family tales, recounting the marvels of a child who eventually became a celebrated artist, are taken on faith, and creep into an autobiography or an authorized interview. Ethel Leginska tried to persuade me to write her autobiography. She was English, but upon advice of well-wishers she changed her real name Liggins to Leginska to lend it a Slavic flavor essential for artistic success. She told me that she had many interesting experiences in her life. For instance, she said, as a small child she was bounced on his knee by Winston Churchill when he returned a hero from the Boer War and stood for Parliament. She volunteered her own date of birth, April 13, 1886, and I verified it by securing a birth certificate. Now, Winston Churchill came home to England in glory in 1899, and since it is unlikely that he proceeded right away to bounce Leginska on his knee, she would have reached a nubile adolescence at the time, and the whole scene would have assumed a different complexion. "Botheration!" Leginska exclaimed when I pointed out the mixed chronology to her. "How do you know when Churchill returned from South Africa? You are not British!"

Surmised chronology is a treacherous thing. Casals told me that the string quartet opus 67 in B-flat major of Brahms was peculiarly his own; he owned the manuscript of the work which was presented to him by an admirer in Vienna and, which is most beguiling, he, Casals, was conceived when Brahms began the quartet and was born when Brahms finished it. A fascinating tale, leaving aside the question as to how anyone could have known the exact date of his own conception, but it is ruined in chronology: Brahms completed the quartet in 1875, and it was first performed in that year; Casals was not born until December 29, 1876, and therefore was not conceived until about April.

When Ponce de León embarked on his search for the Fountain of Youth in the Bahamas and in Florida, he was stimulated by the eternal desire to save oneself from the advent of old age and to preserve or enhance his virility. Faust sold his soul to the devil in return for youth. One Dr. Woronoff, who made a meteoric appearance in Paris in the 1920s, held up the promise of rejuvenation by the transplantation of monkey glands to old men's testicles. Rumor had it that Clemenceau, the hero of 1870 and 1914, was among Dr. Woronoff's clients, as were many artists and musicians—alas, all without avail. But what satisfaction can one derive from a chronological rejuvenation by advancing ones date of birth on paper? Such falsifications are usually paltry, making oneself a year or two younger. Still, it is amazing what rational people will not do to gain a couple of years of nominal life expectancy. When I met the Spanish composer

Oscar Esplá in Brussels, in 1949 (he was then in exile), he complained that his date of birth was wrong in one of my reference works. He was born in 1888, not in 1886, as my dictionary said, and he actually produced a passport to prove it. But I was aware only too well that dates given in the passport are taken from oral statements of the bearer, and just to play safe, I obtained Esplá's birth certificate. Sure enough, he was born in 1886, just as most dictionaries have it.

Sometimes denying the reality of years is justified by practical considerations. Parents of child prodigies often make time stand still. Leopold Mozart advertised annual appearances of Wolfgang Amadeus in the capitals of Europe by declaring a sort of moratorium on the age of the genius child. In a promotional biography of a much lesser child prodigy, Raoul Koczalski, the subject ceased to grow from one chapter to the next. At first it appeared that he was born in 1884, which is the right date; then imperceptibly his birth is shifted to 1885, the wrong date that survived in the latest edition of *Riemann's* and was corrected only in the 1974 Supplement. Unadulterated vanity plays the determining role when a grown-up musician insists on giving the rejuvenated date of birth. Beethoven made several attempts to have his date of birth changed from 1770 to 1772, arguing that there was another Ludwig van Beethoven who was born in 1770 and who died in infancy. The 1772 date is found in several old books of reference.

In compiling lists of corrections in birthdates, I could find very few instances when the dates had to be revised upward. Mussorgsky's year of birth was given as 1835 (instead of the correct 1839) in the 1906 edition of *Grove*, and it was copied in the Mussorgsky article in Hull's *Dictionary of Modern Music and Musicians* under the signature of the respected authority on Russian music M. D. Calvocoressi. I pointed out this egregious error in the 1st edition of my book *Music Since 1900*. In a review of my book, Calvocoressi exculpated himself by saying that he had the right date in his manuscript but it was changed to 1835 by some Grove-digger in the editorial office. In fact, I myself was not without blame, for when the supposed centennial of Mussorgsky rolled along in 1935, I blithely gave a special lecture on the occasion at the Boston Public Library. I was a Grove-digger, too, at the time.

Another advanced date of birth was that of Alessandro Scarlatti, who was born in 1660, not in 1659, as stated in old *Grove*. I could not conceal my embarrassment when one day in 1959 I walked into a sumptuous tercentennial exhibit of Alessandro Scarlatti's works in the Music Division of the New York Public Library, then housed in its old location on 42nd Street. I had to break the news to the curator of the exhibition, and suggested facetiously that he repeat the exhibit in 1960 to make amends for the premature homage.

The bicentennial of Viotti was widely celebrated in 1953, honoring, as it turned out, not the composer but his infant brother who died a year before the birth of the composer Viotti. The famous Viotti was born in 1755.

That centennials of even greatly celebrated musicians should be observed on the wrong dates in their own countries seems incredible. Yet Weber's centennial was observed all over Germany a month late, on December 18, 1886, instead of November 18. *Grove 5* gives me credit for the discovery of the right date, but actually it was known long before.

It is astounding to what lengths a cultured and intelligent person will go to steal a year from a long life. Mabel Daniels insisted that she was born in 1879, not in 1878, as I had it in my dictionary. I had the date from the registrar of Radcliffe College, of which she was a distinguished alumna. "Dear Nicolas," she wrote me, "You are no gentleman. And anyway, I was born in late November, just a few weeks short of 1879." Poor Mabel! She lived into her tenth decade, dying in 1971.

In one famous instance the difference of a few weeks in the date of birth was literally a question of life or death. On June 28, 1914, in Sarajevo, Serbia, Gavrilo Princip assassinated Franz Ferdinand, the heir to the throne of the Austro-Hungarian Empire. His act precipitated World War I, which precipitated the Russian Revolution, which precipitated the rise of Hitler, which precipitated World War II, which precipitated, etc., etc., etc. Now, according to the Austrian laws, no person less than twenty years of age could be executed for a capital crime. Princip was born on July 25, 1894, according to the Gregorian calendar, and was not quite twenty when he turned the world upside down. This saved him from execution, and he died in prison of tuberculosis of the bone on April 28, 1918, following the amputation of an arm. He became a national hero of Yugoslavia, the formation of which was the aim of the terrorist activities of his revolutionary group.

Oscar Wilde was not so lucky about his own chronology. Being exquisitely vain, he whittled two years off his true age, claiming that he was born in 1856, whereas his real year of birth was 1854. Because of a quirk in nineteenth-century English law, persons under forty were treated as immature in cases involving immorality. Oscar Wilde was arrested for sodomy in 1895, and would have benefited by this law had it not been for a conscientious court clerk who obtained Wilde's birth certificate, proving him to be over forty at the time of indictment. This precluded leniency, and he got a severe sentence. Yet despite the availability of the correct date, the *Encyclopaedia Britannica* carried the 1856 date in its article on Oscar Wilde right through its 13th edition. The *Century Cyclopedia* and several other reference works still list Oscar Wilde as born in 1856.

Historical sayings are notoriously unverifiable, and the more eloquent such utterances are the more are they subject to doubt. One of the most famous is the exclamation of Madame Roland on her way to the guillotine, "Liberty, how many crimes are committed in thy name!" The earliest reference to this phrase is listed by Bartlett's *Familiar Quotations* as occurring in Lamartine's *Histoire de la Révolution*, published in 1848. But browsing through the 1793 issue of *The Annual Register* of London, I came upon a dispatch from Paris quoting the famous phrase. So its authenticity depends entirely on the reliability of that particular Paris correspondent. The question inevitably arises: Did he actually follow the cart taking the unfortunate lady to her execution, and did he actually hear her make that exclamation? Not bloody likely.

But, "revenons à nos moutons," i.e., musicians. To a sober-minded reporter of musical facts it is a matter of constant frustration to realize that the re-creations in a musicians mind of the circumstances of composing this or that work become hopelessly clouded by later conscious or unconscious revisions. Mahler systematically denied the programmatic intent of his symphonies, and yet descriptive titles appear in the original manuscripts. In other instances a composer may put a fanciful title to a new edition of a work that was originally written as a piece of absolute music. Even Schoenberg, who was ideologically opposed to musical pictorialism, yielded to the importunities of his publisher, and appended romantic titles to his *Five Orchestral Pieces* for a later printing. On the other side of the ledger is Beethoven's careful disavowal of the literal pictorialism of the *Pastorale*, with its birdcalls and electrical storm, as an "impression" rather than a "description."

By and large, composers of all times prefer to have their works judged as absolute music regardless of the psychological or representational intent. In the published score of Stravinsky's early *Scherzo fantastique* appears the following prefatory note: "This piece was inspired by an episode in Maeterlinck's *Vie des Abeilles*. The first part describes the busy life of the hive, etc., etc." Robert Craft asked Stravinsky about this apiary connection, and he reports in *Conversations with Igor Stravinsky* (1959) the old man's reply: "No, I wrote the Scherzo as a piece of pure symphonic music. The bees were a choreographer's idea. . . . My Scherzo had been titled *Les Abeilles* and made the subject of

a ballet. . . . Some bad literature about bees was published on the fly-leaf of the score, to satisfy my publisher, who thought a 'story' would help to sell the music."

Stravinsky's elaborate explanations are disingenuous and are belied by his own old letters to Rimsky-Korsakov, published in a collection, *Stravinsky: Articles and Materials* (Moscow, 1973). In a letter dated June 18 (July 1), 1907, from his summer home in Ustilug, in Volynia, Stravinsky writes:

> I intended to write a Scherzo already in St. Petersburg, but I had no subject. It so happened that I was reading *La Vie des Abeilles* of Maeterlinck, a half-philosophical, half-poetic work, which captivated me completely. At first I had the idea of using direct quotations so as to make the program of my piece clear, but I realized that it would not work because in the book the scientific and poetic elements are interwoven too closely. I therefore decided to guide myself by a definite programmatic design, without using actual quotations, and to entitle the work simply *The Bees, After Maeterlinck, Fantastic Scherzo.*

Throughout his life Stravinsky was rigidly authoritarian in his pronouncements regarding himself and his music. When Alfredo Casella pointed out to him a number of errors in the published edition of *Les Noces* and asked him to check on them with him, Stravinsky refused, and declared simply: "Ce qui est imprimé est juste." The errors, some of them of importance, are still found in the score of *Les Noces*. Stravinsky's declaration to a French critic that his music was no more to be criticized than his nose, because it is an objective phenomenon, to be observed but not judged, is typical. Among other articles of faith, Stravinsky decreed that his birthday should be celebrated on June 18 rather than June 17, which date corresponds to the date of his Russian birth, June 5, 1882. (The difference between the Russian and Western calendars increased from 12 to 13 days in 1900, which was a leap year in Russia but not in the West.)

I became unwittingly involved in this quibble during my Boston days. John N. Burk, the scholarly annotator of the Boston Symphony program books, used the date June 17 in Stravinsky's biographical sketch for a program Stravinsky conducted with the Boston Symphony in 1942. Burk was quite shocked when Stravinsky rudely berated him for not checking on the date with him personally, and even said to Burk (in French), "Cest idiot!" Burk called me back for further enlightenment, which I willingly provided; he in turn notified Stravinsky for the reasons of the discrepancy. Apparently Stravinsky was convinced, for he told about his discovery of his true birthday, June 5 (17), to a Russian Memorial violinist of the Boston Symphony, who wasted no time to report to me his conversation with Stravinsky for use in my lexicographical annotations. But the controversy exploded all over again in 1962, on the occasion of Stravinsky's eightieth birthday. The *New York Times* published an article saying that the faces of some lexicographers would be red on June 18, Stravinsky's preferred date of birth, whereas most dictionaries, my own included, list it as June 17. I sent a letter to the editor of the paper, explaining the origin of the discrepancy, and it was published under the heading "It Is All Clear Now." This aroused Stravinsky's ire, and he dispatched an angry telegram to the *Times*, asserting his right to celebrate his birthday at his own discretion, and adding that in the 21st century he proposed to observe it on June 19, expecting the difference between the two calendars to increase by another day, as in the previous centuries. He overlooked, or ignored, the fact that the year 2,000 A.D. will be a leap year according to both the Gregorian calendar in the West and the Julian calendar adopted by the Russian Orthodox Church. He would have to wait another century for the difference to increase again.

Musicians are people, and they share with the rest of humanity the peculiarities of sexual aberrations. Arthur Cohn once planned to compile a dictionary of composers according to their sexual drives and hang-ups. The time for such candor may have come. After all, writers and movie actors freely discuss their once hidden vices on the pages of popular magazines. But it is only recently that Tchaikovsky's homosexuality became a matter of comment in print. I guardedly alluded to it in the 1958 edition of *Baker's* as a "deviation," and was castigated for this description by a member of the then emerging gay group as a demeaning and inaccurate reference. Deviation from what, pray? I explained to the writer, who signed his full name and gave me his address, that it was a deviation from the mores of Tchaikovsky's time, and that Tchaikovsky desperately tried to conceal it, even to the point of marrying a female, only to flee from her in horror when she tried to sit on his lap on their wedding night. The first time any reference to Tchaikovsky's homosexuality appeared in Russia was in the commentaries to the 1934 edition of his correspondence with Madame von Meck. In 1940 a collection of Tchaikovsky's letters to his family, including his brother and biographer Modest, who was also a homosexual, was pub-

lished, containing even more explicit references to his predilections in sex. But the ax went down on such disclosures in 1948 when the monstrous Soviet bureaucrat Zhdanov held the reins as cultural dictator. Either by coincidence or by order, all books on Tchaikovsky dealing with his sexual inclinations became "nonbooks," which were replaced in due time by new expurgated editions. In East Germany a serial publication of a book on Tchaikovsky mentioning the unmentionable was stopped in midstream. The mythical Armenian Radio Station reported this question-and-answer exchange: *Q. Is it true that Tchaikovsky was a pederast? A.* Yes, but this is not the only reason that we admire him.

Because of this suppression of known facts, a demonological rumor spread in the Soviet Union, exceeding all flights of fancy indulged by biographical fiction. Rumors that Tchaikovsky committed suicide by drinking water contaminated by cholera bacilli were reported in the Western press shortly after his death. It took me a lot of effort to persuade Scholes to take this fantastic supposition out of his *Oxford Companion to Music*. There were letters exchanged between Tchaikovsky's family physician, Dr. Bertenson, and Modest Tchaikovsky during Tchaikovsky's sickness that trace in detail the etiology of his illness. This documentary evidence did not preclude some Soviet demonologists from concocting an even more fantastic story. Tchaikovsky, they claimed, became implicated in an affair with a young member of the Russian Imperial family. Czar Alexander III, father of the last Romanov Czar, got wind of the affair, and served the Tchaikovsky family an ultimatum: have Tchaikovsky take poison, or have him tried for sodomy. Modest Tchaikovsky, Dr. Bertenson, and other intimates, so the story went, took counsel and decided to obey the Czar's command. Tchaikovsky was given a drink containing a strong dose of intestinal poison producing symptoms similar to those of the deadly comma-shaped bacillus, and since a cholera epidemic was raging in St. Petersburg at the time, Tchaikovsky's death was declared to be caused by the disease. Dr. Bertenson drew ex post facto the letters descriptive of the course of the sickness, so the tale ran, and the affair was closed. As proof that Tchaikovsky did not die of cholera, the proponents of the theory of conspiracy point out that all victims of the epidemic were buried in zinc-lined sealed coffins, whereas Tchaikovsky's body was allowed to lie in state for the ritual three days (to allow for resurrection), and that many of his intimates kissed the body on the mouth.

By far the most extraordinary experience I had with tracking down a musician whose name was listed in one of my dictionaries was that vouchsafed by the German writer on music named Walter Dahms. When I undertook the job of revising the 5th edition of *Baker's*, I was determined to find out what happened to a lot of obscure individuals who infested the earlier editions of the book. Among them was Dahms, about whom the last unverified report was that he went to Rome in 1922. What happened to him afterward? I used to mention his case whenever I had an occasion to discuss lexicographical vagaries, until a Central European lady musicologist told me that she had actually met Dahms in Lisbon, Portugal. He adopted a Portuguese-sounding name and continued to publish books on music. I inserted this seemingly innocuous bit of information in my 1965 Supplement to *Baker's*. This unleashed a fantastic chain of events. The editors of the Supplement to *Riemann's*, who were also interested in finding out what happened to Dahms, asked Santiago Kastner, a German musician resident in Lisbon for many years, to check on Dahms. Kastner conscientiously inquired around the German colony in Lisbon, but no one seemed to know Dahms. The acting editor persisted in his inquiry. I must again importune you in regard to Dahms, he wrote to Kastner on November 10, 1969. "*Baker's* Supplement of 1965 asserts plainly but positively: 'Went to Lisbon about 1935, where he was still living in 1960.' This could not have come out of the thin air. May I ask you therefore to make renewed démarches in this direction?" Kastner obliged, but again had to reply in the negative. "No one here knows who Dahms is," he communicated in a letter of November 18, 1969. "Yesterday, I asked the Cultural Attaché of the German Embassy and also the Director of the German Cultural Institute who was stationed in Portugal since the 1930s. Neither has ever heard of Dahms. Can it be that your Walter Dahms is identical with a certain Gualterio Armando who came here as a German refugee in the 1930s? I will investigate further, although without much hope." *Riemann's* to Kastner, November 26, 1969: "*Baker's* (really, Slonimsky) is greatly prized here because of its general reliability. I would think that behind the bland declaration, 'was still in Lisbon in 1960,' is hidden a lot of painstaking research. Kastner then decided to ask Gualterio Armando point-blank whether he was really Dahms. "The editors of *Riemann's Musik Lexikon* have asked me repeatedly to obtain biographical information about Walter Dahms, reportedly resident in Lisbon," he wrote to Armando on December 11, 1969. "I was compelled to answer each time that I did not know anyone by that name, but the editors insisted that this Dahms is mentioned in *Baker's Dictionary* as living in Lisbon. All other attempts

to clear the case have failed. But the German publishers Rutten & Luening and Bertelsmann have referred to you as Walter Gualterio Armando (Walter and Gualterio are after all the same names), which leads me to surmise that you, esteemed Herr Armando, may be identical with Walter Dahms. If this is indeed so, I would be most grateful to you if you would write directly to the editors of *Riemann's Musik Lexikon* and clear up the matter." All hell broke loose thereafter. "I see to my astonishment," Dahms-Armando wrote Kastner on January 15, 1970, "that in your zeal you went so far as to conduct correspondence behind my back with my publishers, with whom I maintain an excellent relationship. I have no idea what your motive is in all this, and I am at a loss to find the right word to characterize your actions. I am not identical with anyone but myself. I have absolutely nothing to say about Herr W. D. mentioned by you because I know nothing about him. I hope that this will put an end to it once and for all."

Kastner to Armando, dated January 17, 1970: "I acknowledge the receipt of your letter. I can assure you that the editors of *Riemann's Musik Lexikon* turned to me as a collaborator with a request to obtain information about Walter Dahms, and I had to say that I knew no one in Lisbon under this name. The editors could refer only to *Baker's Dictionary*, which I have never seen. This ought to be sufficient to demonstrate that there is nothing objectionable in my actions." On the same date Kastner wrote to *Riemann's*: "I am forwarding to you an impudent letter I received from G. Armando, and a copy of my answer. This suspicious, low scoundrel does not deserve any courtesy. I knew in advance that he would raise a stink when cornered. Yet the very fact that he got so excited about it proves that he must have something to hide." Kastner wrote to *Riemann's* again on April 7, 1970: "As far as Dahms is concerned, I must abandon his track. I imagine that he is identical with that asshole Gualterio Armando after all."

There was a lot of additional circumstantial evidence pointing out the identity of Dahms and Armando. Dahms was born in Berlin on June 9, 1887. He studied violin, piano, and composition, and was active as choral conductor and music critic. When the editors of *Riemann's Musik Lexikon* sent a questionnaire to Armando in Portugal, he dutifully filled it in but advanced his date of birth by 10 years; other details in the biographies of Dahms and Armando were similar. Dahms published monographs on composers before he vanished; Armando surfaced in Portugal shortly after the disappearance of Dahms and picked up where Dahms left off, continuing to publish biographies of composers in the

German language. One more detail: The editors of *Die Musik in Geschichte und Gegenwart* also asked an intermediary to contact Dahms-Armando in Lisbon, but he flew into a rage and declared that he would rather remove his person from the pages of the encyclopedia if this interrogation continued. The editors complied, and the name of Dahms does not figure in *Die Musik in Geschichte und Gegenwart*.

I recounted this whole fantastic story to Hans Heinsheimer, then director of publications of G. Schirmer, Inc., publisher of *Baker's*. "But you can't publish this," Heinsheimer exclaimed, "Dahms will sue us for a million dollars!" His argument seemed valid, and I decided to resort to a polysyllabic circumlocution. In the 1971 Supplement to *Baker's*, which was then being readied for publication, I said about Dahms that he went to Lisbon, "adopted an operatic sounding lusitanized *nom de machine à écrire*, making use of 60 percent of the letters in his original surname, chopped two lustra off his age, while steadfastly declining to admit his true identity." Since I did not mention the name Armando, he could not sue Schirmer for identifying him with Dahms; on the other hand I was obviously free to write anything I wanted about Dahms since Armando disclaimed all knowledge of any such person. The editors of *Riemann's* were bolder. The "Personenteil" of the Ergänzungsband published in 1972 states in its entry on Dahms that he went to Lisbon in the 1930s and published several biographies under the name Gualterio Armando. On October 5, 1973, Dahms-Armando died, carrying to his grave the secret of what compelled him to deny so vehemently his true identity.

Among thousands of musical biographies it is inevitable that there must be changes of last names. A case in point is that of Werner Egk. For a number of years a rumor went around that it was a manufactured name, an acronym for "ein guter Künstler," and even "ein genialer Künstler," and that Egk himself adopted this flattering identification. To find out his real name, I wrote to the director of the archives of the City of Augsburg, in the district where Egk was born. In due time I received a courteous reply stating that Egk was indeed the legal name of the composer; further inquiries elicited information that Egk's real name was Mayer. If so, whence Egk? The composer himself finally came forward with the extraordinary explanation, which, *faute de mieux*, must be accepted at its face value: the outer letters of the name (which he assumed upon his marriage) are the initials of his wife Elisabeth Karl, and the middle letter in Egk was inserted "for euphony."

A rumor that will not be squelched is that Leopold Stokowski's last name was really Stokes, a not unreasonable assumption since so many English and American musicians added Russian or Polish suffixes to their names as a veneer for artistic success. Not so. Stokowski was a son of a Polish cabinetmaker named Kopernik Joseph Boleslaw Stokowski, and an Irish woman, Annie Marion Moore-Stokowski, of whom he was born in London on April 18, 1882. Stokowski himself must be held responsible for much of this confusion, seeing that he liked to tell interviewers that he was born in Cracow, and that his full name was Leopold Boleslawowicz, which is all right in Russian but impossible in Polish. This bit of fantasy appears in the basic volume of *Riemann's*; when I sounded alarm, the editors sent me a photostat copy of the original questionnaire in Stokowski's own handwriting and containing not only the fantastic patronymic but also the wrong place of birth, Cracow instead of London, and the wrong year of birth, 1887 instead of 1882. By way of rebuttal I sent to the *Riemann's* editor a copy of Stokowski's birth certificate, which I had long ago obtained from London and which leaves no doubt whatever as to the correctness of the date and place of Stokowski's birth. The *Riemann's* editors inserted a corresponding correction in the 1975 Supplement.

Somehow I acquired the reputation of a musical sleuth, expert in tracking down missing persons lost in the music world. One of the more beguiling queries I received was this: Was François Servais really a *bâtard* of Liszt and the Princess Sayn-Wittgenstein, as is asserted in *Baker's* and elsewhere? He was born in St. Petersburg in 1846, a date that would fit into the chronology of Liszt's dalliance with the married Princess. Her dealings with Liszt and with her husband were entangled in such a web of mutual contradictions that even affidavits from them or from Servais himself would be suspect. Besides, Romantic nineteenth-century musicians liked to provide themselves with an illegitimate origin, preferably from famous or titled persons. Witness the extraordinary case of Sigismund Thalberg who abetted a story that his father was a Count Dietrichstein and his mother a baroness; there was even a letter in circulation, allegedly written by his mother to the Count, suggesting that the happy *bâtard* be given the name of Thalberg, so that he would grow up as peaceful as a Thal (valley), and would tower as a Berg (mountain) over those less favored by fortune.

The "mystery" of Thalberg's birth was further reinforced by a footnote in *Grove*, asserting that his birth certificate was unobtainable from the registries of Geneva where he was born. Faithful Grove-diggers never tried to check on this bit of negativism, and yet the document was available for the asking. I got a copy in a matter of days by airmail, and I have since discovered that the document had been previously published in a Belgian magazine on the occasion of Thalberg's centenary in 1912. And the name of Thalberg's father was indeed Thalberg, so all this business of its symbolic significance was a complete fabrication. *Riemann's* set things right in its 1975 Supplement, with an intriguing addition that Thalberg was indeed adopted by Count Dietrichstein.

The strange lure of aristocratic birth seems to continue even in our own century. An English singer who had appeared in England and America under the name of Louis Graveure declared in an interview published in the *New York Times* in 1947 that he had no idea where and when he was born, and hinted darkly that the story of his origin would be worth a fortune in publicity value to him if it could be substantiated. Well, the mystery was self-propelled; for the modest sum of two shillings and sixpence I obtained from London a copy of his birth certificate. His real name was Wilfrid Douthitt; Graveure was his mother's maiden name, which he assumed for his career as a singer.

Some years ago I received a letter from a Russian woman who lived in Rome, Italy, asking me to find out if her father, the violinist Vassili Bezekirsky who settled in America when she was a child, was still living. After a series of inquiries at various American music schools where he taught violin playing, I finally found out that he was retired in a small town in upstate New York. I announced the happy tidings to both father and daughter, smugly content with my good deed. But I had a rude reawakening when I received a curt missive from Bezekirsky, in which he wrote: "Your mission was successful, if you call several unpleasant and demanding letters from my daughter a success. I am in no position to help her in any way." I never heard from the daughter.

If I were to name one discovery in my lexicographical labors that gave me the greatest joy, I would say Minkus. For years I have been haunted by his elusive ghost. A mediocre Austrian composer of operas and ballets, he for some reason became a favorite of the Russian ballet masters. For a hundred years, under the Czars and under the Soviets, his ballets *Don Quixote* and *La Bayadère* were the mainstays of the Russian ballet repertoire. And yet the fate of Minkus, the person, remained an enigma. After a successful career in Russia between 1866 and 1891, he simply vanished. According to Russian dictionaries he died in 1907, with the date usually accompanied by a question mark in parentheses; other dictionaries prefer to terminate his life in 1891, when he left Russia. Not a year passed without my receiving an anguished inquiry from some ballet company, or from some beleaguered librarian, asking me about Minkus. I

myself must have written a dozen letters to municipal registries of vital statistics in Vienna in the hope of obtaining his death certificate. I was able to ascertain that he was born March 23, 1826, rather than 1827 as most dictionaries have it, but as to his date of death the Vienna archivists could tell me nothing. Then, in the summer of 1976, I got a clue from an unpublished manuscript on Austrian composers that a correspondent sent me from Vienna. And there he was, the much sought after Alois Minkus. He died in Vienna on December 7, 1917, in the ninety-second year of his life, from pneumonia. But if so, then why did all my letters to the Wiener Stadtarchiv, to the Landesarchiv, to the Vienna Rathaus and its numerous subdivisions fail to elicit this information through the years? The explanation, according to the Archivrat, was that all death notices before 1939 were kept in the corresponding church registries. There was one obvious clue that I and all other Minkus chasers overlooked: namely, the Vienna City Directory, which in its volume for 1917, the last year of Minkus's life, listed his domicile at Gentzgasse 92. And had I written to the registry of burials in Vienna I would have discovered that he was laid to rest at the cemetery of Döbling. "Sapienti sat," and all that jazz.

The 1965 and 1971 Supplements to *Baker's* are penitential documents insofar as avoidable errors are corrected therein. Naturally I got numerous letters from offended parties, and all I could say was "Peccavi!" In an exceptional manifestation of charity and compassion, Ezra Sims decided to correct my erroneous listing in his entry of a nonexistent second string quartet, which I dated 1962, by retroactively composing a piece in 1974 entitled *String Quartet No. 2 (1962)* and graciously dedicated "to Nicolas Slonimsky, that he may be now less in error."

Generally speaking, I welcome specific corrections to my dictionaries and other writings, but I must admit that I was startled when in August 1972 I received a letter from one Stephen W. Ellis of Glenview, Illinois, in which he raked me over the coals for numerous errors of commission and omission in my edition of *Baker's*. His emendations ranged widely and included musicians from such remote countries (remote, that is, to American musicologists) as Iceland, Bulgaria, Denmark, and Romania. He showed shocking disregard for my supposedly high standing in the field of musical lexicography, using such terms as "grossly incomplete," "flagrantly inaccurate," "absurd," "shockingly out of date," "sadly inadequate," "ridiculous," "disgraceful," and even "criminal." The last epithet he applied to my failure to list recent works composed by Mihalovici after 1952. Was I not aware that in the 1970 edition of his

Muzicieni Români, Viorel Cosma has a list of Mihalovici's works three pages long? In reply to such a massive assault, I could have pulled my rank on Ellis, by exploding in wrathful indignation: "Sirrah! How dare you? Do you realize that you are addressing one of whom *The Oxford Companion to Music* said that 'on the chronology of the subject of music nobody in the world is so great an authority as he,' whom *The Penguin Dictionary of Music* called 'a modern prince of musical lexicography,' and for whom Percy Scholes invoked, in a personal letter (*rubesco referens*), the famous lines of Goldsmith, 'and still the wonder grew that one small head could carry all he knew'?" I cooled down very quickly, however, and pleaded guilty on all counts. But who was Stephen Ellis, I wanted to know. I ventured a guess that he was not a professional musicologist (professional musicologists simply don't have such a variety of knowledge), that he was probably a record collector and a reader of musical periodicals from all over the world, that he was about forty-two years old and had two children. Well, he turned out to be only thirty years old with only one child (another came shortly afterward), but, indeed, he was a record collector. By profession he was a copyreader for a small publishing house. This was the beginning of a most fruitful correspondence, in the process of which Ellis helped me enormously in the biographics of "dii minores" of Scandinavian, Finnish, Hungarian, Belgian, and Dutch musicians. Much of this material will be included in the 6th edition of *Baker's*, now in preparation.

In praising Ellis I must not forget others who solved for me some problems that seemed beyond human powers to tackle. First and foremost among them is Bill Lichtenwanger, a veritable magician of musical lexicography and bibliography. I cannot refrain from reporting ever so briefly how he managed to locate Heinrich Hammer, a German musician who migrated to California, married one of his young violin pupils at the age of ninety, and then disappeared. Lichtenwanger contacted Hammer's son, a telephone lineman, literally while he was working on the telephone pole, and found out from him the date of his father's death in Phoenix, Arizona, in 1954.

A biographical dictionary does not consist exclusively of dates and lists of accomplishments. The musicians in *Baker's Dictionary* were people, whose lives ought to be described in human terms. It is quite proper, of course, to list loves and marriages of famous men and women of music, but only if the facts are ascertained with a considerable degree of probability. One should not follow the example of a Goethe biographer who took exception to Goethe's statement that he had never loved anyone as much as Lili Schönemann: "Here the great Goethe errs," he footnoted: "his greatest love was Frederike Drion."

And for the end, let me once more recall my favorite quotation from a letter that Alfred Einstein wrote me shortly before his death, wondering "ob wir, und natürlich vor allem Sie, im Himmel einmal dafür belohnt werden, dass wir einige Ungenauigkeiten aus der Welt geschafft haben. . . ." Onward to a heavenly reward!

Introduction to Musical Terminology

Elements of Notation

Notation is a system of signs used in writing music. The written signs for the time value (length, duration) of musical tones are called *notes;* the written signs for pauses (intervals of silence) between the tones are called *rests.*

Notes and Rests

Whole note o Half note ♩ Quarter note ♩

Whole rest ▬ Half rest ▬ Quarter rest ᶚ

Eighth note ♪ 16th note ♬ 32nd note ♬ 64th note ♬

Eighth rest ᶚ 16th rest ᶚ 32nd rest ᶚ 64th rest ᶚ

Whole note o = 2 ♩, or 4 ♩, or 8 ♪, or 16 ♬, or 32 ♬, or 64 ♬

Half note ♩ = 2 ♩, or 4 ♪, or 8 ♬, or 16 ♬, or 32 ♬

Quarter note ♩ = 2 ♪, or 4 ♬, or 8 ♬, or 16 ♬

Eighth note ♪ = 2 ♬, or 4 ♬, or 8 ♬

Sixteenth note ♬ = 2 ♬, or 4 ♬

Thirty-second note ♬ = 2 ♬

The Staff

The staff consists of five parallel horizontal lines. Notes are written on the lines, or in the spaces between. For higher

or lower tones, additional short lines are provided, called *ledger lines.*

The Clefs

A *clef* is a sign written at the head (beginning) of the staff to fix the position of one note. The most common clefs are

the *G* clef (Treble Clef) ![treble clef] fixing the place of the note g¹

the *F* clef (Bass Clef) ![bass clef] fixing the place of the note f;

and

the *C* clef, which designates a line on the staff as c¹ (middle C); it acquires a different name according to the line used:

Tenor Clef Alto Clef Soprano Clef

The Scales

The staff and clefs together fix the pitch of the notes, showing whether they are high or low. A series of eight successive notes on the staff forms what is called a *scale*. To name the notes of the scale, we use the first seven letters of the alphabet, *A B C D E F G*. Scales are named after the notes on which they begin, which is called the *keynote*. The scale of *C,* written in whole notes, in the bass and treble clefs, is as follows:

The *C* written on the ledger line just below the treble staff and just above the bass staff is called middle C.

The notes in the same vertical line are of the same pitch and have the same name. For ordinary purposes, any note marked *C (c)* is called simply "*C.*" But, in order to fix the place which any given note occupies among all the others (that is, to fix its "absolute pitch"), the whole range of musical tones is divided into sections of seven notes each, called "octaves," and lettered and named as shown:

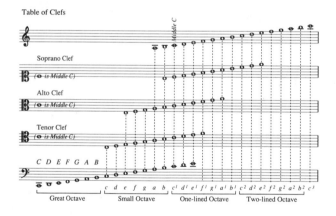

Pitch Registers

In order to indicate the exact location of a note in the total gamut, the following system is used in this dictionary:

Chromatic Signs

The *chromatic signs* are set before notes to raise and lower their pitch.

The *sharp* ♯ raises its note a semitone;

The *flat* ♭ lowers its note a semitone;

The *natural* ♮ restores its note to the natural pitch on the staff (without chromatic signs);

The *double sharp* 𝄪 raises its note two semitones;

The *double flat* ♭♭ lowers its note two semitones;

The sign ♮♯ restores a double sharped note to a sharped note;

The sign ♮♭ restores a double flatted note to a flatted note.

The Intervals

An *interval* is the difference in pitch between two notes. In measuring an interval, it is customary to take the lower note as the basis, and to measure up to the higher note. When the two notes are exchanged and the measurement is made downward, the interval is called "inverted."

Diatonic Intervals of the Major Scale

All Standard Intervals and Their Inversions

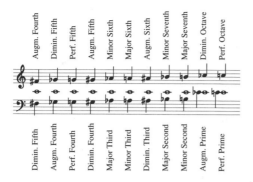

The Keys

A *key* is a scale employed harmonically, that is, employed to form chords and successions of chords. On the keynote *C*, or on any other note, two different species of scale or key may be built up:

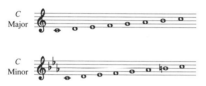

Such a key or scale is called *major* when its third and sixth are major intervals; it is *minor* when its third and sixth are minor intervals. The succession of intervals in every major key is the same as that in *C* major; in every minor key, as in *C* minor. To adjust the intervals properly, chromatic signs are employed.

Table of Major Keys

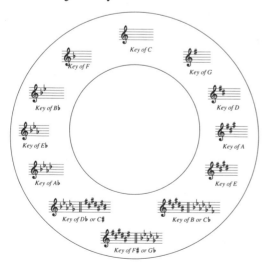

It will be seen, on passing around the circle in either direction, that the keynotes of the successive keys always follow each other at the interval of a perfect fifth; hence, this circle of keys, ending where it began, is called the circle of fifths.

Chords

A *chord* is formed by a succession of from three to five different tones, built up in intervals of diatonic thirds from a given tone, or *root*. A three-tone chord is a triad; a four-tone chord is a *seventh chord* (chord of the *seventh*); a five-tone chord is a *ninth chord* (chord of the *ninth*).

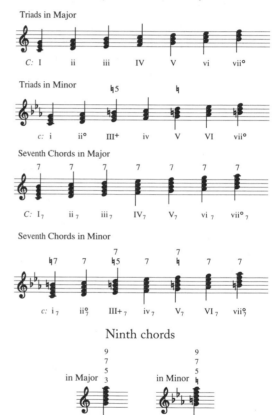

When the root of the chord is the lowest tone, the chord is in the fundamental position; when some other tone is the lowest, the chord is inverted. Each triad has two inversions; each seventh chord has three.

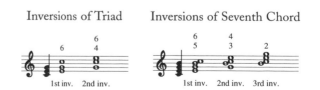

xxv

The first inversion of a triad is called a 6 chord.

The second inversion of a triad is called a $^6_4$ chord.

The first inversion of a seventh chord is called a $^6_5$ chord.

The second inversion of a seventh chord is called a $^4_3$ chord.

The third inversion of a seventh chord is called a 2 chord.

Time Signatures

The *time signature* appears after the clef, at the beginning of the staff; the lower figure shows the *kind* of notes taken as the unit of measure, while the upper figure shows the number of these notes that can fit in a measure, and the groupings of beats.

For instance $\frac{3}{4}$ (3/4 time) means "three quarter-notes to the measure": | ♩ ♩ ♩ |

$\frac{12}{16}$ (12/16 time) means "twelve sixteenth-notes to the measure": | ♫♫♫ ♫♫♫ |

Comparative Table of Tempo Marks

CLASS I
INDICATING A STEADY RATE OF SPEED

Largo (broad, stately)
 Largamente
 Larghetto
Grave (heavy, dragging)
Lento (slow)
 Adagissimo
Adagio (slow, tranquil)
 Adagietto
 Andantino

Group I.
General
signification
of terms is
SLOW.

Andante (moving, going along)
Moderato
 Allegretto
 Allegramente
Allegro (brisk, lively) [con moto, vivace] [agitato, appassionato]
Presto (rapid) [con fuoco, veloce]
 Prestissimo

Group II.
General
signification
of terms is
FAST.

CLASS II
INDICATING ACCELERATION

Accelerando	(with increasing rapidity)
Stringendo	(swiftly accelerating, usually
Affrettando	with a *crescendo*)
Incalzando	
Doppio movimento	(twice as fast)
Più mosso	(a steady rate of speed,
Più moto	*faster* than preceding
Veloce	movement)

CLASS III
INDICATING A SLACKENING IN SPEED

Rallentando	
Ritardando	
Allargando	(gradually growing slower)
Tardando	
Slentando	
Strascinando	
Molto meno mosso	(♩ = ♩ del movimento precedente) (half as fast)
Ritenuto	(a steady rate of speed,
Meno mosso	*slower* than preceding
Meno moto	movement)
Calando	
Deficiendo	
Mancando	(growing slower
Morendo	and softer)
Sminuendo	
Smorzando	

Aa

A. The initial note of the alphabetical scale in German and English terminology; *A* corresponds to the note *La* of France, Italy, Spain, Portugal, Latin America, and Russia. Its alphabetical primacy was established in the 16th century when GLAREANUS, in his *Dodecachordon* (1547), fixed *A* as the tonic of the Aeolian mode. However, in 1571 ZARLINO elevated the Ionian mode to primacy, relegating *A* to the 6th step of our C-major scale. In some methods of musical analysis, capital *A* stands for the A-major triad, small *a* for the a-minor triad. *A* is the note used for tuning an orch.; it is usually given out by the oboe because the oboe is the least affected by humidity or other weather conditions of all pitched instruments. The frequency for A above middle C is 440 cycles (vibrations) per second.

a (It. preposition); **à** (Fr. preposition). By, at, in, with, for.

a cappella (It., as in chapel). Performed in the church style; choral singing without instrumental accompaniment. Generally, any unaccompanied vocal performance.

A major. A key often associated with springtime. Mendelssohn's *Spring Song*, from the *Songs Without Words* (op. 62), is cast in the key of A major, although the title is not the composer's (it was probably invented by one of his publishers). His "Italian" sym. (No. 4) is in A major, as is Tchaikovsky's *Italian Capriccio*, for Italy was poetically associated in the minds of men of the North with sun and spirit. Beethoven's most joyful sym., No. 7, is in A major; Wagner grandiloquently described it as "the apotheosis of the dance." Many classical works catalogued as A minor end in A major; among them are the Piano Concerto of Schumann and the Violin Concerto of Glazunov, with their tonally assertive fanfares in the finale suggesting the triumph of the glow of optimism.

a mezza voce (It., half voice). With half the power of the voice (or instrument).

A minor. The key of resignation. Few symphonies are set in it, although A minor is technically advantageous for string instruments, with the upper violin strings providing for the tonic and the dominant of A minor and the upper strings of the viola and cello offering the tonic and the subdominant. Mozart avoids A minor as a principal key, as does Beethoven, although the opening movement of the *Kreutzer Sonata* mixes A minor and major effectively. Mahler's Sym. No. 6, a work of mental depression in which Mahler wrestles with Fate, is in A minor, as is Sibelius's Sym. No. 4, a work so unlike the robust Sibelius of Finnish inspiration that it must be regarded as exceptional. It is especially difficult to explain the lack of violin concertos in this eminently violinistic key. Glazunov wrote a violin concerto in A minor, as did Bloch and Dvořák. Two great piano concertos are in A minor, 1 by Schumann and 1 by Grieg. This introspective and essentially pessimistic key suits Tchaikovsky perfectly. His Piano Trio opens with a phrase on the cello in A minor, and it comes nearest to the sound of sobbing in music; Tchaikovsky dedicated the work to the memory of his friend Nicholas Rubinstein, director of the Moscow Conservatory.

a poco a poco (It., little by little). Gradually. Correct adverbial form for *poco a poco*, but seldom used.

A Quiet Place. Opera by Leonard Bernstein, 1983. A flashback within the work yields a performance of Bernstein's earlier 1-act opera, *Trouble in Tahiti.*

A string. The 2nd string (2nd highest) of a violin; the 1st of a viola or cello; the 3rd of a double bass; the 5th of a guitar.

A tempo (It., in time). Return to the preceding rate of speed.

Ab (Ger., off). In organ music, remove a stop or coupler.

ABA. A symbolic representation of TERNARY FORM, in which the 1st section (A) is repeated after the 2nd (B). Many classical songs and arias follow this formula; ABA is therefore also known as SONG FORM.

Abbado, Claudio, outstanding Italian conductor; b. Milan, June 26, 1933. Abbado received his early music training from his father, then enrolled in the Milan Cons., graduating in 1955 in piano. He made his conducting debut in Trieste (1958); won the Koussevitzky conducting prize at Tanglewood; was a winner of the Mitropoulos Competition, N.Y. (1963). He made his American conducting debut with the N.Y. Phil. on Apr. 7, 1963; subsequently conducted at La Scala, Milan; the Vienna Phil; the London Sym. Orch.; Chamber Orch. of Europe; Chicago Sym. Orch.; Vienna State Opera. In 1989 he was named artistic director of the Berlin Phil., succeeding Karajan. He also founded the European Community Youth Orch.; La Filarmonica della Scala in Milan; and Vienna's Mahler Orch. A fine technician, Abbado is capable of producing distinguished performances ranging from the Classical era to the cosmopolitan avant-garde.

abdampfen (Ger., evaporate). Deaden the sound, e.g., place hand on timpani; release piano damper pedal.

Abduction from the Seraglio, The (*Die Entführung aus dem Serail*). Opera by Mozart, 1782. A young woman is captured by a Turkish pasha. A youth in love with her tries to rescue her, but his attempt is foiled by the wily pasha, who yields in the finale to a sudden magnanimous impulse and lets her go with her lover. Apart from the treasure of Mozartean melos, the score stylizes "Turkish" tunes and rhythms—movements *alla turca* in slightly syncopated 2/4 time—with added exotic percussion.

Abecedarianism (A-B-C-D-arianism). A reference to anything alphabetarian in its essence. But *Abecedarianism* is not necessarily a pejorative term. It takes a highly trained intellect and technical skill to create an Abecedarian masterpiece, e.g., the self-inverted redundant prose of Gertrude Stein. Musical Abecedarianism is far from tonal INFANTIL-OQUY. Stravinsky's *Piano Pieces for 5 Fingers*, Bartók's *Mikrokosmos*, and Casella's *Valse diatonique* from his *Pezzi infantili* are illustrations of sophisticated Abecedarianism. Abecedarian effects are naturally produced by small children banging at random on the white keys of the piano keyboard at the level of their heads, often resulting in the unintentional formation of interesting pandiatonic patterns vivified by asymmetrical rhythms. The walk across the keys by Domenico Scarlatti's cat provided the inspiration for a fugue; critics who describe music they dislike as "cat music" have an imperfect understanding of the constructivist potential of random tonal juxtaposition.

ablation. A decadent overuse of decorative and ornamental elaborations in the post-Romantic period of early 20th-century music resulted in a profound repugnance to such practices. An inevitable consequence was a drastic ablation of all nonessential thematic excrescences and protuberances from a finished composition. A process of subjective ablation impelled some modern composers to revise their early works and reduce their instrumental luxuriance to an economically functional organization. A very striking instance of such ablation is Stravinsky's reorchestration of the score of his ballet *The Firebird*, removing some supernumerary instruments, excising florid cadenzas, and in effect plucking the fiery bird of its iridescent plumage. Most audiences prefer the original luxuriant version to this later parsimonious arrangement. In his mature years Hindemith devised a harmonic theory so self-sufficient that he "corrected" several earlier works according to its principles, not unlike straining cheese through cloth.

Abraham and Isaac. Sacred ballad for baritone and small orch. by Igor Stravinsky, based on Genesis, 1964.

Abravanel, Maurice, distinguished Greek-born American conductor; b. Saloniki, Jan. 6, 1903. He was taken to Switzerland at the age of 6, then to Berlin, where he took composition lessons with Weill. With the advent of the Nazis in 1933, Abravanel moved to Paris and conducted ballet; in 1934–35 he toured Australia. In 1936 he joined the Metropolitan Opera in N.Y.; generally adverse reviews compelled him to resign in 1938. He turned to leading Broadway musicals; conducted a season with the Chicago Opera Co. (1940–41). In 1947 he became conductor of the Utah Sym. Orch. at Salt Lake City; in the 32 years of his tenure he built it into one of the finest sym. orchs. in the U.S.; he introduced many modern works into its repertoire. In 1976 he underwent open-heart surgery; he retired in 1979.

Abschnitt (Ger.). Section.

absolute music. Music without extramusical connotation. The term is applied to music that is free from programmatic designs, psychological affiliations, or illustrative associations; its Latin etymology connotes independence. In its function absolute music is nearly synonymous with ABSTRACT MUSIC, but the 2 terms differ in their temporal points of reference. The concept of absolute music is of ancient heritage, while abstract music is a relatively recent phenomenon, marked by structural athematism in an atonal context. See PROGRAM MUSIC.

absolute pitch. PERFECT PITCH.

abstract music. A separation of sonic structures from representational images, whether pictorial or psychological. Abstract music is the antonym of all musical styles that are concrete or naturalistic; abstract works are usually short, athematic, and rhythmically asymmetric. Intellectual fantasy, rather than sensual excitation, is the generating impulse of abstract music; its titles are often derived from constructivistic and scientific concepts: *Structures, Projections, Extensions, Frequencies, Synchronisms.* The German composer Boris Blacher even developed a successful form of abstract opera, lacking nearly all reference points to the genre. Abstract expressionism, a term applied to nonobjective painting, is sometimes used to describe musical works of abstract quality with expressionistic connotations. A subsidiary genre of abstract music is ALEATORY MUSIC, in which the process of musical cerebration is replaced by a random interplay of sounds and rhythms. An earlier but similar concept is known as ABSOLUTE MUSIC.

absurd music (Eng., away from + irrational). The validity of absurd logic was enunciated by Tertullian when he said: "Credo quia absurdum est" (I believe in that which is absurd). Oxymoronic pairs, such as "passionate indifference" or "glacial fire," are intrinsically absurd and yet eloquent in their self-contradiction. Absurd music cultivates analogous incompatibilities. It is particularly effective in modern opera, where a scene of horror may be illustrated by a frivolous waltz, or a festive celebration by the sombre strains of a funereal march. The scherzo in Mahler's 1st sym. is a fine instrumental example. The modern techniques of POLYTONALITY and ATONALITY represent absurd music (and worse) to the withered sensitivity of an old-fashioned ear.

Abteilung (Ger.). A division or portion of a composition.

Academic Festival Overture. A musical acknowledgment by Brahms of the honorary doctoral degree conferred upon him by the University of Breslau in 1879. The overture is not academic in the deadly sense of the word. It is based on student songs, some of them frivolous. Its finale is a brilliant orchestration of the lugubrious university song GAUDEAMUS IGITUR. It was 1st performed in Breslau on Jan. 4, 1881, with Brahms conducting.

Accardo, Salvatore, outstanding Italian violinist; b. Turin, Sept. 26, 1941. He won the Vercelli (1955), Geneva (1956), and Paganini (Genoa, 1958) competitions, then pursued a career as orch.l soloist and as recitalist. He has also been active in later years as a conductor. As a violin virtuoso he excels in a vast repertoire; in addition to the standard literature, he performs many rarely heard works, including those by Paganini. His playing is marked by a fidelity to the classical school of violin playing, in which virtuosity is subordinated to stylistic propriety.

accelerando (It., accelerating). Gradually growing faster. Abbr. *accel.* or *acc.,* followed by dots or lines to indicate the continuity of the acceleration.

accelerato (It., accelerated). Livelier, faster.

accent. A stress, such as an increase in dynamic level.

acciaccatura (It.). 1. A short accented appoggiatura. 2. A note a 2nd above, and struck with, the principal note, and instantly released.

accidental

A chromatic sign not found in the key signature but placed in front of a note to alter its pitch in the course of a piece. Sharps, flats, naturals, double sharps, and double flats are the accidentals commonly used. Triple sharps and triple flats are theoretically conceivable, but are unnecessary in equal temperament.

The flat sign (♭) lowers the note, following it by a semitone. It takes its origin from the small *b*; it was introduced as early as the 11th century to provide the perfect 4th over the major tetrachord on F, to avoid the forbidden tritone, considered by medieval scholars the DIABOLUS IN MUSICA (devil in music). The flatting of B in the F tetrachord was regarded as such an obvious necessity that the ♭ was dubbed *signum asininum* (mark of the ass), for only hopelessly stupid students had to be told to put this sign in. (To this day, B-flat is designated in the German musical alphabet simply as *B*.) In medieval Latin music books this B-flat was called *b rotundum*, a round *B*, or *b mollis*, a soft *B*. (Thus the French term *bémol* for "flat.") When it became necessary to devise a symbol for B natural, a square was substituted for the gentle oval of *b*. This note received the name *b quadratum*, a square *b*, or *b durum*, a hard *b*. Because in Gothic script the square *b* looked like the letter *h*, the square *b* was eventually substituted for the sign of B natural. As a result, the German musical scale was extended to 8 letters of the alphabet, where *H* stands for B-natural. (Thus the musical theme for BACH is B-flat, A, C, B.) A double flat is marked simply by 2 flats (♭♭).

The origin of the sharp (♯) is more complicated. Sharps originally appeared in medieval notation to cancel previously used flats; a sharp was therefore called *signum cancellatum*, sign of cancellation. (In French this canceling sign was called *b carré*, squared *b*, so the French term *bécarre* came to mean a natural sign.) Further modifications of the signs for a sharp (raising a note by a semitone) and a natural (canceling a previous sharp or flat) were necessary to differentiate between them. The sharp assumed the shape of a crisscrossed lattice (♯), and the natural was represented by a rhombus with an upward stem to the left and a downward stem to the right (♮). Some old American music manuals simply used the term *cancel* for a natural. Double sharps are represented by a cross resembling the letter *x* (×).

Accidentals usually retain their validity throughout 1 bar, but the rules are not absolute, especially in the 20th century. To add to the uncertainty, flats and sharps in Baroque scores were sometimes retroactive; the player was expected to know or guess where the leading tone led or a passing note passed, taking a hint from the future accidentals. In fact, Baroque composers and copyists often omitted self-evident accidentals that the player was supposed to supply, relying on general usage.

Modern composers are not always strictly logical in their use of accidentals. Charles Ives upbraided a conscientious copyist for trying to correct a seemingly wrong accidental by scribbling in the margin of his manuscript: "Please don't correct the wrong notes. The wrong notes are right." But Rimsky-Korsakov took offense when his Russian copyist put a question mark over a patently wrong accidental: "I am not somebody like Richard Strauss or Debussy, to put in wrong notes deliberately. So fix it!" Schoenberg sacrificed logic in bar 22 of his piano piece, op. 33a, where an irregular A-natural appears instead of the dodecaphonically correct A-flat. Yet Schoenberg most definitely put down an A-natural, allowing, *horribile dictu*, an improper recurrence of a note within the tone row for the sake of euphony. After a brief skirmish in the correspondence columns of a British publication, an advocate of the strict dodecaphonic orthodoxy recognized Schoenberg's right to disrupt the continuity of his own tone row and withdrew a proposed correction.

In atonal music and 12-tone works, double sharps or double flats have no raison d'être, because only the absolute pitch counts, not its notation. Still, there are some preferences. Just as in tonal music B-flat and F-sharp are the harbingers of keyed tonality, so in atonal music B-flat is used more often than its enharmonic equivalent A-sharp, and F-sharp is used in preference to G-flat.

accompaniment. Any part or parts (chords, other harmonic units) that attend or support the voices or instruments bearing the principal part or parts in a composition. It is *ad libitum* when the piece can be performed without it, and *obbligato* when it is necessary. Accompaniment can be added to a composition by some other person than its original composer. Accompaniment of the scale is a series of chords used to harmonize the ascending or descending diatonic scale. In modern music, accompaniment transcends its traditional ancillary function and becomes an integral part of the entire composition. The simplest form of modern accompaniment is that of POLYTONALITY, in which the melody is set in one key and the harmony in another. Rhythmically, the modern accompaniment rarely follows the inflections of the melody; deliberate oxymoronic usages are enhanced by translocated accents.

accordion. A free-reed instrument patented by Cyrillus Demian of Vienna in 1829. The elongated body serves as a bellows, to be drawn out and pushed together; the bellows is closed at either end by a keyboard. In older types the right hand plays a set of buttons having a diatonic or incomplete chromatic treble scale; the later models have a pianolike chromatic keyboard. The left hand has up to 120 keys for harmonic bass tones. See CONCERTINA.

Ach, du lieber Augustin. Popular Viennese tune from the late 18th century. It is in waltz time and associated with

PHOTOGRAPH BY EDMUND SHEA, COURTESY ARHOOLIE RECORDS

Clifton Chenier, Cajun accordionist

middle-class *Gemütlichkeit*. The tune was made into a children's rhyme with the words "Did you ever see a lassie?"

acid rock. A heavier form of rock, developed in the California music scene in the later 1960s, with a relatively light contrapuntal texture, emphasis on feedback guitar solos, and powerful amplification. Often, cryptic references to drugs such as LSD ("acid") are made in the lyrics. See ROCK.

Ackerman, William, German-born American composer, guitarist, and entrepreneur; b. in Germany, Nov. 16, 1949. An orphan, he was adopted at age 9 by a Stanford Univ. (Palo Alto, Calif.) prof.; mastered folk, classical, and rock guitar styles. Studied at Stanford, dropped out to become a carpenter; composed guitar pieces for theater productions. He eventually invested $300 to make a record, initiating a business that eventually became the very successful Windham Hill Records label. He is one of the best composers in the "new age" style, most closely associated with his record company; termed *neoimpressionism,* it generally involves folk and modal elements performed by guitar, piano, or electronics.

acousma. An auricular disturbance induced in hostile audiences by ultramodern music. Music critics, even those not suffering from professional indigestion, are chronically prone to acousma, and their discomfort is often reflected in their reviews.

acoustics

The physics of sound; the laws of the vibrations of strings and other solid materials, the transmission of air movement in the organ and wind instruments, and the effect of the superposition of the resulting sound waves on consonant or dissonant intervals and harmonies. Acoustics (Grk., audible) also establishes the causes of different tone colors and related problems, such as noise. This science of sound has come to be the connecting link between physics and musical aesthetics.

It has long been known that pitch depends on the length and tension of a vibrating string, the length and diameter of the air column in a pipe of the organ, or the size of a bell or a drum. The height of pitch is proportionate to the frequency of vibrations. If the thickness of a string remains the same, the frequency of vibrations decreases with its length. If a string is set in motion with a greater force so that the amplitude of its vibrations is increased, then the resulting sound becomes louder without changing the actual pitch. The range of audible sounds for the human ear is between 16 and 25,000 cycles per second (cps), a cycle being a complete vibration of a string oscillating up and down. Dogs hear sounds far above the human range; high-pitched whistles, inaudible to humans, are used by handlers to summon dogs.

Each string or air column naturally divides itself into component parts to produce overtones, or PARTIALS. Theoretically, each complete vibration produces also 2 vibrations of one-half that of the sounding body, 3 vibrations of one-third that of the sounding body, and so on; these partials have the potential to be audible. Generally, the simpler the fraction produced by the divided string, the more euphonious is the interval created by such overtones. Thus the perfect octave produced by the division of a string into 2 equal parts (1/2, or 2:1) is the most consonant interval; the interval between one-third of the string and one-half of the string produces the interval of the perfect 5th (2/3); the interval between the division of the string into 3 parts and 4 parts produces the interval of the perfect 4th (3/4); the interval between the division of the string into 4 parts and 5 parts produces the major 3rd (4/5). These intervals together constitute the major triad, which is acoustically the most natural consonant triad. This theoretically infinite group of intervals comprises the HARMONIC SERIES of intervals.

To the panoply of humanly audible sounds must be added a whole series of COMBINATION SOUNDS produced by either the difference or the summation of 2 tones, particularly those sounded in perfect tuning (JUST INTONATION). A violinist playing the double stop e^2 and g^2 on the 2 upper strings in the perfect acoustical ratio of a minor 3rd (5/6) will hear an unwelcome DIFFERENCE TONE, C below the G string. These intrusive sounds are also called TARTINI TONES, after the 18th-century violinist who 1st described them in detail. Furthermore, combinational tones form between the overtones of the individual sounds; fortunately, they cannot be heard in performances. Aware of this parasitic phenomenon, string players instinctively avoid using such acoustically perfect double stops. Indeed, a veritable pandemonium would result if musicians could match pitch precisely. The combinational tones would then cling to the basses of the harmony like barnacles to the bottom of a ship, and an additional maze of nonharmonic sounds would plunge the orch. into a sonic fog. Thus it is the very imperfection of manufactured instruments and the limitations of the human performers to play in perfect tuning that saves music from chaos.

For more than 2,000 years theorists have wrestled with the problem of equalizing the perfect octave by having its ratio of vibrations 2:1 commensurate with that of a 5th that has a ratio of vibrations 3:2. In the traditional cycle of 5ths, 12 perfect 5ths on the keyboard of the piano (or any instrument built on the tempered scale) is supposed to be identical to 7 octaves. But this is an impossible equation, because 2 to the 7th power (2^7) equals 3:2 to the 12th ($3/2^{12}$). Therefore, the acoustic perfection of the perfect 5th was sacrificed in order to fit 12 3:2's into the compass of 7 octaves; a similar adjustment was made in other intervals. When the piano tuner tunes a "perfect 5th," it is actually slightly flat. Violinists and players of other string instruments, however, tune their strings in nontempered perfect 5ths. If a violinist plays a 5th on the open strings and the piano accompanist plays the same 5th, a disagreeable discrepancy results. It was not until the late Classic period that acousticians finally abandoned all hope of reconciling the pure harmonic series with practical instruments, and EQUAL TEMPERAMENT became generally accepted. The result is that the major chord is not a nontempered triad in JUST INTONATION but an artificially adjusted, tempered harmony.

In the 20th century the prevalence of dissonance has forced reconsideration of the OVERTONE SERIES, interpreted nominally as its source. The tritone, deprecated by medieval scholiasts, is a foundation of atonality, polytonality, and other modern techniques. Acoustically it resembles the 45th partial, some 6 1/2 octaves from the fundamental note, with which it theoretically forms a concord. Scriabin, theorizing ex post facto, regarded his MYSTIC CHORD as a consonance, as its constituents approximate higher partials. In Ravel's *Bolero* the melody is at 1 point accompanied by a group of flutes and piccolos constituting the 6th, 8th, 10th, and 12th overtones progressing in parallel formations. In the score, Ravel marks the gradually decreasing dynamics of these progressively higher notes, corresponding to a natural tapering of their strength. This calculated enhancement of natural overtones affects the timbre of the solo instrument, whose tone color changes of its own accord.

Rhythms can be combined in special proportions with the overtone series. In 1932 Cowell, in collaboration with Theremin, constructed the RHYTHMICON, an instrument that generated a series of rhythmic beats analogous to the overtone series, the number of beats being proportional to the position of each overtone. This arrangement made it possible to devise polyrhythmic counterpoint of great variety and unique sonority. The instrument did not gain a foothold; similar results can now be effected by digital technology.

acoustics, architectural. Acoustical innovations and improvements in the purity of intonation are not without musical perils. The desire of modern architects to attain acoustical perfection often leads to orch.l pollution in the concert hall. Old-fashioned rococo architecture, with its ornate brocades and heavy curtains, contributed the necessary dampening of sounds and echoes that secured harmonious euphony. Modern acousticians eliminated the decorations, removed the tasseled seat covers and cushioned surfaces, replacing them with plywood and plastic, and added an array of mobiles suspended from the ceiling to eliminate microsonic impurities. But these elaborations resulted in some unwelcome side effects. While parasitical noises were neutralized, a slew of unanticipated musical microorganisms, overtones, and combination tones arose from the instruments themselves, flooding the hall in a harmonious plasma that all but destroyed the natural equilibrium of tonal imperfections and mutual reverberations that were responsible for the rich resonance intuitively achieved by the musical architects of the past.

The consequences of such modernization were painfully evident in the scientifically designed Phil. (now Avery Fisher) Hall at Lincoln Center, N.Y. When George Szell was invited to make suggestions to improve the hall, he is said to have recommended tearing the whole thing down and starting over. Many years later the equivalent action was taken; the aforementioned acoustical anarchy was corrected by an ingenious rearrangement of the physical properties of the auditorium and the stage, so that the natural heterogeneity of sonic euphony was restored.

act. A primary division of an opera or scenic cantata. In opera each act may be subdivided into several scenes or tableaux.

action. In keyboard instruments, the mechanism set in motion by the fingers, or by the feet (organ pedals). In the harp the "action" (a set of pedals) does not directly produce the sound, but changes the key by shortening the strings by a semitone or whole tone.

action music. Developing in the late 1950s and early 1960s, a manifestation in MIXED MEDIA, HAPPENINGS with audience participation, or PERFORMANCE ART in which spontaneous psychological and physiological excitations determine the course of events. Composers of action music may provide a set of instructions, leaving specific decisions to the performers. The actions of the performers are generally equal in importance to the sounds they make.

Like IMPRESSIONISM, the term itself arose by analogy with painting. Action painting implies a free wielding of the brush in which the unpremeditated splash of color becomes a creative enzyme for the next projection. In action music there is no calculated design goal; the initial reflex generates a successive series of secondary reflexes in a network of musico-neural synapses, resulting in the formation of dynamically propelled sounds.

action song. A children's song in which bodily movements depict the action of the words, such as folding the hands and closing the eyes to represent sleep, fluttering of the fingers downward to represent rain, crossing the arms in a circular movement to represent the sun, flapping the hands to imitate a bird in flight, etc. An example of this genre is *The Itsy Bitsy Spider*.

Acuff, Roy (Claxton), American country-music singer, guitarist, and songwriter; b. Maynardville, Tenn., Sept. 15, 1903; d. Nashville, Tenn., Dec. 23, 1992. He learned to play the fiddle, and later appeared as a singer and guitarist. In 1938 he and his Smoky Mountain Boys became featured artists on the Grand Ole Opry radio program in Nashville; he became famous with his renditions of *The Great Speckled*

Bird, *Wabash Cannonball*, and *Wreck on the Highway*. He also composed *Precious Jewel* and was active as a music publisher. In 1962 he became the 1st living musician to be elected to the Country Music Hall of Fame. In 1988 he celebrated his 50th anniversary at the Grand Ole Opry.

ad libitum (Lat., at will; abbr. *ad lib.*). 1. Employ the tempo or expression freely; 2. An indication that a vocal or instrumental part may be left out. *Cadenza ad libitum*, a cadenza that may be performed or not, have another substituted for it or improvised, at the performer's will.

adagietto (It.). 1. A tempo or movement slightly faster than adagio. 2. A short adagio movement.

adagio (It., at ease). Quite slowly, leisurely; a slow movement; similar to LARGO. Often used for slow introductions to SONATA ALLEGRO movements.

adagio adagio. Very slow.

adagio assai. Very slow.

adagio (ma) non tanto. Not too slow.

adagio molto. Very slow; *Adagio non molto*, not too slow.

Adagio for Strings. A transcription of the slow movement of Samuel Barber's String Quartet, made by the composer for Toscanini and the NBC Sym. It was performed for the 1st time in N.Y. on Nov. 5, 1938. It has become Barber's best-known piece and probably the most frequently played short work by any American. Because of its finely sustained mood of modal harmonies, it is often performed at funeral occasions, including the services for Franklin Delano Roosevelt in Apr. 1945 as well as Barber's own funeral in 1981.

adagissimo (It.). Extremely slow.

Adam, Adolphe (-Charles), celebrated French opera composer; b. Paris, July 24, 1803; d. there, May 3, 1856. He studied piano, then went to the Paris Cons. Adam devoted his entire career exclusively to the music of the theater; he obtained his 1st success with a short comic opera, *Le Chalet* (1834), which held the stage for 1,400 performances through the years; an even greater success was *Le Postillon de Longjumeau* (1836), an opera that achieved permanence in the operatic repertoire all over the world. There followed a long series of stage works; at times Adam produced 2 or more operas in a single season. In the process of inevitable triage, most of them went by the board, but a considerable number remained in the repertoire; among these was the comic opera *Si j'étais roi* (1852). Adam wrote 53 operas in all, but his most durable work is probably the ballet *Giselle* (1841), a perennial favorite to this day. The song *Cantique de Noël* also became popular. Unfortunately, Adam was a poor businessman; in 1847 he ventured into the field of management with the Opéra-National, which failed miserably and brought him to the brink of financial ruin. In 1849 he was appointed prof. at the Paris Cons.; he also traveled widely in Europe, visiting London, Berlin, and St. Petersburg. As one of the creators of French opera, Adam ranks with Auber and Boieldieu in the expressive power of his melodic material and a sense of dramatic development.

Adam (Adan) **de la Halle** (Hale), called "Le Bossu d'Arras" (Hunchback of Arras); b. Arras, *c.* 1237; d. Naples, *c.* 1287. Adam was a famous trouvère, many of whose works have been preserved; the most interesting is a dramatic pastoral, *Le Jeu de Robin et de Marion* (1285), written for the Anjou court at Naples and resembling an OPÉRA COMIQUE in its plan. He was gifted in the dual capacity of poet and composer. Both monodic and polyphonic works of his survive.

Adams, John (Coolidge), prominent American composer; b. Worcester, Mass., Feb. 15, 1947. Minimalist composer best known for his topical operas *Nixon in China* (1987) and *The Death of Klinghoffer* (1991). His music covers a wide spectrum of media, including works for video, tape, film scores, and live electronics.

adaptation. An ARRANGEMENT.

added seventh. A minor or major 7th added to the major triad. In jazz, the minor 7th (e.g., in the chord C, E, G, B♭) is one of the BLUE NOTES (along with the minor 3rd). Depending on the context, the major 7th can be more or less acrid when added to a tonic major triad at the end of a piece.

added sixth. A 6th added to the major tonic triad, often at the end of a phrase, and treated as a consonance. 1st used by Debussy and others early in the 20th century, the added 6th chord (e.g., C, E, G, A) became extremely popular in jazz piano playing.

Adderley, "Cannonball" (Julian Edwin), African-American jazz alto saxophone player; b. Tampa, Fla., Sept. 15, 1928; d. Gary, Ind., Aug. 8, 1975. He owes his nickname to a mispronunciation of "cannibal," a reference to his voracious eating habits. After receiving his B.A., he was a band director in Fort Lauderdale (1948-50). His jazz career began in a combo at a Greenwich Village (N.Y.) club; in 1956 formed a group with his brother Nat Adderley (b. Tampa, Nov. 25, 1931), a cornetist. He achieved fame through his recordings, beginning with *African Waltz* (1961); others include *Dis Here, Sermonette, Work Song, Jive Samba, Mercy Mercy Mercy, Walk Tall,* and *Suite Cannon.* He suffered a stroke during a concert engagement and subsequently died.

Adeste Fideles. The Latin words of this hymn are usually attributed to St. Bonaventura, who lived in the 13th century. The musical setting is dated much later and variously ascribed to Marcos Portugal and King John IV of Portugal. The English text *O Come All Ye Faithful* was 1st published in London in 1760.

Adieux, Les. Beethoven's Piano Sonata in E-flat Major, op. 81a. The full title is *Les Adieux, l'Absence et le Retour.* The French titles were given by Beethoven himself, who even added an alternative title, *Sonate caractéristique.* The title refers to a vacation taken by Archduke Rudolph, a friend of Beethoven. The opening theme imitates the postillion horn (descending major 3rd, perfect 5th, and minor 6th, harmonizing the melodic mediant, supertonic, and the tonic). The 2nd movement leads into the 3rd without pause.

Adler, Richard, American composer of popular music; b. N.Y., Aug. 3, 1921. He was educated at the Univ. of North Carolina; served in the U.S. Navy (1943–46); became a producer; staged shows at the White House during the Kennedy and Johnson administrations. He wrote musicals in collaboration with Jerry Ross. The most popular were *The Pajama Game* (1954), with its striking hit song *Hernando's Hideaway,* and *Damn Yankees* (1955). He also wrote *The Lady Remembers (The Statue of Liberty Suite)* for soprano and orch. (1985).

Adorno (born Wiesengrund), **Theodor,** significant German musician and philosopher; b. Frankfurt am Main, Sept. 11, 1903; d. Visp, Switzerland, Aug. 6, 1969. He studied with Sekles in Frankfurt and Berg in Vienna; for several years he was a prof. at the Univ. of Frankfurt.

Devoting himself mainly to music criticism, he was ed. of the progressive music journal *Anbruch* in Vienna (1928–31). In 1934 he went to Oxford; later emigrated to the U.S., where he became connected with radio research at Princeton Univ. (1938–41); subsequently lived in Calif. He returned to Germany in 1949 and became director of the Institut für Sozialforschung, Frankfurt. He publ. numerous essays dealing with the sociology of music, among them *Philosophy of the New Music* (1949); *Dissonances: Music in the Bureaucratic World* (1956); *Arnold Schönberg* (1957); *Form in New Music* (1966); *Alban Berg, Master of the Smallest Passages* (1968). In his early writings he used the hyphenated name Wiesengrund-Adorno. He advised Thomas Mann on the musical parts of his novel *Doktor Faustus.* He exercised a deep influence on the trends in musical philosophy and general esthetics, applying the sociological tenets of Karl Marx and the psychoanalytic techniques of Freud. In his speculative writings he introduced the concept of cultural industry, embracing all types of musical techniques, from dodecaphony to jazz.

Adriana Lecouvreur. Opera by Cilèa, 1903, dealing with a historical figure, an 18th-century Parisian tragedienne engaged in crisscrossed amours. She is poisoned by a bouquet of lethal violets. It is Cilèa's most famous opera.

Adventures in a Perambulator. Orch.1 suite by John Alden Carpenter, 1915. The normal orch. is supplemented by tinkling, jingling, and jangling percussion instruments such as triangle, xylophone, glockenspiel, and bells. The 6 movements represent a child's view of the world while being wheeled around in a baby carriage; the most spectacular of these impressions are a policeman and a dog. Its cuteness soon became too fulsome for sophisticated consumption; it has become a seldom-revived period piece.

aeolian harp or lyre (from Grk. *Aeolus,* god of wind). A stringed instrument sounded by the wind. It is a narrow, oblong wooden box with low bridges at either end, across which are stretched a number of gut strings. The harp is placed in an open window or some other aperture where a draft of air will sweep the strings.

Aeolian mode. A church mode, codified in Glareanus's *Dodecachordon,* corresponding to the modern natural minor scale. Using the piano's white keys, the mode ranges from A to A (A–B–C–D–E–F–G–A).

aerophones (Grk. *aeros* + *phonos*, air sound). An older classification of music instruments that produce their sounds by the vibration of air, including the accordion, pipe and reed organ families, flutes, and mouth-blown reed instruments.

Affects, Doctrine of

A protopsychomusical theory treating the relationship between music and emotions. The affects doctrine (Lat. *affectus*, state of the soul) dates back to Greek antiquity, when the correlation between music and soul was accepted as a scientific fact. The Greek word for *affectus* is *pathos*, which conveys the meaning of deep emotion. (The adjective *pathétique* still retains that meaning, as it is used in the subtitle of Tchaikovsky's Sym. No. 6.)

St. Augustine wrote, "Musica movet affectus." In medieval Latin treatises, the term *musica pathetica* was attached to music that represents emotions. The medieval description of the TRITONE as *diabolus in musica* is an early precursor of the Doctrine of Affects. In his *Musica practica* (1482), Ramos de Pareia draws a correspondence between the 4 temperaments of human condition and the 4 authentic church modes. An even more "scientific" tract is *Istitutioni harmoniche* by Zarlino (1558), in which all consonant intervals are divided into 2 categories: those consisting of whole tones (major 2nds, major 3rds, and their inversions) reflect the feeling of joy, and those containing fractional tones (minor 2nds, minor 3rds, and their inversions) express sadness.

The theorists of the Renaissance expanded the affects doctrine to include tempo, rhythm, registers, and dynamics. If some of these scholastic applications have retained their validity, it is because they generally correspond to observable physiological or psychological conditions. Rapid passages do not readily portray illness or death, and slow progressions in static harmonies do not easily evoke anger.

The establishment of major and minor tonality brought about the most durable affectus, associating major keys with joy and minor keys with sorrow; this dichotomy persists even today. One cannot imagine Schumann's *The Happy Farmer* in a minor key, or Chopin's *Funeral March* (from the op. 35 sonata) in a major key.

The Doctrine of Affects greatly influenced the melodic structure of vocal works. The symbolism of states of mind is evident in the works of Bach. Thus the verbal injunction "Get up, Get up!" is expressed by an ascending major arpeggio; the phrase "Follow me" is illustrated by a very long ascending-scale passage; suffering is depicted by narrow chromatic configurations; the fall into Hell is punctuated by a drop of the diminished 7th.

During the Baroque period some musical philosophers actually drew comparative tables between states of mind and corresponding intervals, chords, tempos, and the like. The famous 18th-century lexicographer Mattheson stated in his treatise *Die neueste Untersuchung der Singspiele* (1744) that "it is possible to give a perfect representation of the nobility of soul, love, and jealousy with simple chords and their progressions." This exaggerated notion of the precise correspondence between emotions and musical progressions was tenaciously upheld in the annotations, mostly by German writers, of programmatic works. One such literal analyst even found in a perfectly innocuous descending interval near the end of Beethoven's Overture to *Egmont* the representation of the beheading of the historical Egmont. The diminished-7th chord, often used to enhance the dramatic tension in opera, received the nickname of ACCORDE DI STUPEFAZIONE, a designation related to the Doctrine of Affects. The selection of registers by Romantic composers also frequently follows these psychological associations. The preference of Sibelius for the somber sonorities of the lower registers may reflect the severity of the Finnish landscape. Indeed it can be hypothesized that the music of the North tends toward a greater exploitation of low registers, slower tempos, and minor modes, whereas the music of the South cultivates high registers and fast tempos.

The elaborate enumerations of leading motives and the analysis of their intervallic content by annotators of

Wagner's music dramas and the symphonic poems of Richard Strauss are remnants of the affects doctrine. Even Schoenberg, who rejected programmatic interpretations of musical tones, yielded to the temptation of writing descriptive music in his score *Accompaniment to a Cinema Scene*, in which the subsections (Imminent Danger, Anxiety, and Catastrophe) follow in their dynamic content the precepts of the affects doctrine. In the 20th century the Doctrine of Affects has practically disappeared and been replaced by a structural analysis unconnected with emotional content.

affettuoso (It., with affect). Passionately, emotionally, with great feeling, very expressively.

A-flat major. A key of joyous celebration and human devotion; also, an eminently pianistic tonality having 4 black keys and 3 white keys, a convenient digital disposition for melodies and harmonies. It lies uneasily for string instruments, however, and is therefore rarely if ever selected as the principal key for a large orch.l work; among individual symphonic movements in A-flat major, the 3rd movement of the Sym. No. 1 of Brahms is notable. A-flat major describes a festival mood in Schumann's *Carnaval*, and it is a romantic invocation in Liszt's *Liebestraum*.

Africaine, L'. Meyerbeer's last opera, premiered posthumously, 1865. The African of the title is Selika, the Malagasy whom Vasco da Gama brings back to his native Portugal from his African adventures. Becoming aware of the racial barrier, she sacrifices her life so that Vasco da Gama can marry his white former mistress. The opera takes nearly 6 hours to perform, but it attained tremendous popularity with sentimental audiences of the last 3rd of the 19th century. It has exotic flavor, Italianate bel canto, thunderous sunderings of love, and loud orchestration, all qualities that made Meyerbeer the idol of his time.

African music

To the white people of Europe and America during the centuries of colonialism, Africa was the Dark Continent; Stanley, who "found" Livingstone and extended his famous superfluously genteel salutation, entitled his book *In Darkest Africa*. Joseph Conrad, who actually traveled in central Africa, summarized his experience in his novel *Heart of Darkness* with the words of its central character, "The Horror! The Horror!" In colonial times, European opera composers eagerly exploited reports from the mysterious continent as material for exotic libretti. Verdi's *Aida* is a prime example of a melodramatic story of the collision of 2 civilizations. In Meyerbeer's opera *L'Africaine*, the woman of the title is a Malagasy beauty. Composers of such operas did not even attempt to find out what real African music was. Rather, the peoples of the African coastal regions absorbed the cultures, including music, of the various European and Asian powers. On its Mediterranean coast, Arabian modalities in song and dance held sway. The British influence was paramount on the coast of the Indian Ocean; the Portuguese were the colonial powers in Mozambique and Angola. Both the Dutch and the English established their artistic influence in South Africa. France and Belgium spread their cultures in western Africa and the Congo. The islands in the Indian Ocean, Madagascar and St. Mauritius, developed a unique mixture of European and Arabian musical cultures.

With the availability of modern transportation and the development of ethnological research, it became possible to examine the reality of Africa beyond the archetypal figures of witch doctors and local chiefs holding court under an umbrella. One could now notate and record the indigenous music of Africa. Such knowledge could be exploited; the motion picture *The African Queen* includes a large section in which the indigenous people play drums and chant authentic music. But Europeans and Americans could not easily understand the powerful role of singing and drumming in African life, e.g., that plaintiffs are known to submit their claims in court by chanting and the judges deliver their sentences to the accompaniment of gongs and drums: the truth of the briefs is measured by the expressiveness of the lilting phrase.

The diversity of African chants and rhythms is extraordinary. The tonal progressions allow a great variety of pitch, quasi-diatonic and ultrachromatic scales alternating with wide intervals but rarely exceeding a 5th. Remarkably, the TRITONE, once anathematic in European music, is freely used in African song cadences. The rhythmic figures are regular in meter, with some asymmetry and syncopation; in ensemble, however, they combine to form complex polyrhythmic designs with a feeling of absolute spontaneity and improvisatory freedom. The strong beat may be emphasized by loud claps. Chant texts are invocations to the gods of the village, laments when disaster strikes, and celebrations for important local events, marriages, or the inauguration of a new chief.

Griot playing the kora (harp), Bamana tribe, Mali

There are hundreds of dialects among African tribes, and the language itself serves as a dynamic means of communication. Thus the unique click of the Bushmen and others may serve to mark the ending of a musical phrase. Intonation is of prime significance; a slight rise or drop in pitch may change the meaning of the phrase.

The most common African ensemble contains drums of various sizes, gourds with rattling beads attached as shakers, metal bells, slit-log drums, and various manufactured products. One interesting drum, known as the TALKING DRUM, is in the form of an hourglass with long strips of leather stretching down the sides from the head so that when the drum is squeezed under the arm it changes pitch; it is played with bent sticks. Another native instrument is the thumb piano, or MBIRA, a small wooden box with flexible nails or prongs of various lengths that are thumbed to produce sounds. For a larger gamut, harp-lutes are widely used, the largest being the KORA with 21 strings. The KORA has a notched bridge to help tune the instrument and to which freely vibrating metal jingles are attached. Animal horns are the most prominent aerophones.

There is much dispute as to the influence of the African diaspora on black and black-influenced musics of the Western hemisphere. The rhythmic element seems the most incontrovertible, with the drum kit of popular music and jazz a modern adaptation of African polyrhythmic drumming. Dance music is especially receptive to African rhythmic patterns. In addition to percussion, the BANJO is a descendent of West African models. Less convincing are arguments supporting the presence of blues and pentatonic scale elements in African sources; given the lack of examples of pre-20th-century traditional African music and the intense confluence of white and black stylistic elements, such claims will probably remain speculative.

At this time—toward the end of the 20th century—Africa is no longer an unwilling receptacle of the colonials' music in lieu of their own; it has become the source of a new musical art with great influence upon grateful European and American musicians. Earlier in the century, Cuban avant-garde composers such as Caturla (*Bembé*) and

PHOTOGRAPH BY ELIOT ELISOFON, COURTESY NATIONAL MUSEUM OF AFRICAN ART, ELIOT ELISOFON ARCHIVES, SMITHSONIAN INSTITUTION

Roldán (*La Rebambaramba*) borrowed extensively from African music, as did Brazilians such as Villa-Lobos and Nobre. Western musicians now go to Africa to learn their music. The American composer Steve Reich took a summer course in African percussion techniques at the Univ. of Ghana and upon return to the U.S. wrote a piece for voices and drums entitled *Drumming*. Conversely, African popular music has flourished with distinctive national and group-associated styles, incorporating a large dose of Western popular music and contributing significantly to WORLD MUSIC.

Age of Anxiety, The. Sym. No 2 by Leonard Bernstein, for piano and orch.; the title is from a poem by W. H. Auden. The work summarizes the unquiet mid-20th century musically, with a variety of techniques and styles—jazz, neo-Baroque commotion, occasional episodes of dodecaphony—all enlivened by pungent rhythms. The work was 1st performed by the Boston Sym. Orch. on Apr. 8, 1949, with Serge Koussevitzky conducting and Bernstein playing the piano part.

Age of Gold, The. Ballet by Shostakovich, 1st performed in Leningrad on Oct. 26, 1930. At a festival, soccer teams of the Soviet Union and an unnamed capitalist nation participate; it ends in a triumphant procession of all workers of the world united in a common cause. A polka ridicules a 1920 disarmament conference in Geneva; it has become a celebrated piano piece.

aggregate. 1. The collected notes in a serial composition representing 1 instance of a pitch class. 2. A collection of notes heard at the same time.

agitato (It.). Agitated. *Mosso agitato*, very agitated; *agitato con passione* (It.), passionately agitated; *agitazione, con* (It.), with agitation, agitatedly.

Agnus Dei. The 5th and usually last section of the Catholic High Mass ORDINARY, divided into 2 parts: *Agnus Dei* (Lamb of God) and *Dona nobis pacem* (Give Us Peace).

agogic (Grk., to lead). A slight deviation from the main rhythm for the purposes of accentuation. This legitimate performing practice may allow melodically important notes to linger without disruption of the musical phrase. RUBATO is an agogical practice. The term was introduced by Riemann in 1884. In musical rhetoric, it is opposed to the concept of DYNAMICS, which provides accentuation by varying the degree of intensity.

Agon (Grk., competition). Ballet by Stravinsky, with choreography by George Balanchine, 1957. A highly abstract contest between groups of players matches the cleanly edged choreography. Stravinsky uses thematic serial techniques.

agony pipe. American slang for the clarinet during the swing era (1930s).

aguinaldo. Spiritual Spanish song glorifying Jesus and the saints, almost invariably in ternary form. Also called an *adoración*.

Ägyptische Helena, Die. Opera by Richard Strauss to a Hofmannsthal libretto, parodying the Greek myths concerning Helen of Troy, 1928. This was their last collaboration; Hofmannsthal died the following year.

Aida. Opera by Verdi, 1871; one of the most melodramatic operas, written to the most tragic and most implausible of all librettos ever contrived. Radames, commander of the ancient Egyptian army, falls in love with a captive Ethiopian princess, Aida, and inadvertently reveals a crucial military secret to her while her father, the king of Ethiopia, also captured anonymously, listens from behind the bushes. Amneris, the Egyptian king's daughter, who is affianced to Radames, discovers the treachery but is willing to save Radames if he relinquishes Aida. Radames refuses and, joined by Aida, is buried alive in a stone crypt. *Aida* was commissioned for the inauguration of the Cairo Opera House; the outbreak of the Franco-Prussian War delayed the delivery of the costumes from Paris; the production was postponed until Christmas Eve, 1871. The premiere was spectacular, with shiploads of notables and music critics converging on Cairo. But the ever-unsocial Verdi declined the invitation to attend. Egyptian scholars regarded *Aida* as quite inauthentic in its story and music, and it didn't enter the repertoire of the Cairo Opera House. But on May 3,

1987, it was lavishly staged in ancient Luxor, with the participation of some 150,000 Egyptian soldiers and hundreds of singers in the chorus, not to mention horses. The role of Radames was performed by Placido Domingo. The price of a single ticket was $750, and several supersonic Concorde planes were rented to transport wealthy opera lovers. Note: *Aida* does not have a diaeresis in Italian: *Aïda* with the diaeresis is the French spelling.

Aida trumpet. A long trumpet specially constructed for use in Verdi's opera *Aida*. The original, manufactured in France, was called *trompette thébaine*, trumpet of Thebes. It produced only 4 notes: A-flat, B-flat, B-natural, and C.

Ain't She Sweet? Song by Milton Ager, 1927; the words were added later.

air. Tune, melody; a song.

Air on the G String. Nickname of Bach's *Air* from the Orch.1 Suite No. 3, BWV 1068.

air varié (Fr.). TEMA CON VARIAZIONI.

Ais (Ger.). A sharp.

Aisis (Ger.). A double sharp.

al fine (It., to the end). Used in phrases like *Dal segno al fine*, an instruction for the performer to play "from the sign to the place marked *fine*," or *Da capo al fine*, "from the beginning (*capo*, head) of the piece to the place marked *fine*." The latter instruction is associated with pieces in TERNARY FORM (ABA).

al fresco (It., in the open air). A description of outdoor concerts, operatic performances, and other events, usually free of charge.

al segno (It., to the sign). A direction to play until the appearance of a sign ℅, usually indicating the end of a repeated section.

al tallone (It., at the heel). To play near the nut of the bow.

Alba (Prov., light of dawn). A Provençal morning song, very popular with the TROUBADOURS, that corresponds to the serenade, or evening song. See ALBORADO, AUBADE.

Albéniz, Isaac (Manuel Francisco), eminent Spanish composer; b. Camprodon, May 29, 1860; d. Cambo-les-Bains (Pyrenees), May 18, 1909. Exceptionally precocious, he was exhibited as a child pianist and soon began taking piano with Narciso Oliveros. When he was 7 he was taken to Paris, where he studied with Marmontel, teacher of Bizet and Debussy. Returning to Spain, he studied at the Madrid Cons.; possessed by the spirit of adventure, he stowed away on a ship bound for Puerto Rico; made his way to the southern U.S.; earned a living by playing at places of entertainment. He returned to Spain and traveled in Europe; in 1880 he met Liszt in Budapest. After a trip to South America he settled in Barcelona in 1883; married Rosina Jordana; one of their daughters, Laura Albeniz, became a well-known painter. Met Pedrell, who influenced him in the direction of national Spanish music; went to Paris for composition studies. Abandoned career as concert pianist; lived in London (1890–93); Paris (1894–99); returned to Barcelona (1900–1902), then again to Paris. In 1903 he moved to Nice; later went to Cambo-les-Bains (Pyrenees), where he died.

Almost all of his works are for piano; all inspired by Spanish folklore. He established the modern school of Spanish piano literature, derived from orig. rhythms and melodic patterns rather than by imitating the imitations of national Spanish music by French and Russian composers. His piano suite *Iberia* (1906–1909) is a brilliant display of piano virtuosity.

Albert Herring. Opera by Britten, based on a Maupassant story centering on a contest in a small village for the most virtuous young woman. With none available, the contest is won by Albert, but his immaculate virginity is immediately undermined by alcohol and he goes morally berserk. The opera was produced at the Glyndebourne Festival in England on June 20, 1947, with the composer conducting.

Alberti bass. A type of arpeggiated tonal accompaniment in an even tempo, traditionally for the left hand on the keyboard. Popularized (if not invented) by Domenico Alberti (Italian singer, harpsichordist, and composer; b. Venice, 1710; d. Rome, *c.* 1740) early in the 18th century, it was used extensively by Haydn, Mozart, and Beethoven, among others.

Albinoni, Tomaso (Giovanni), Italian violinist and composer; b. Venice, June 8, 1671; d. there, Jan. 17, 1751. Between 1694 and 1740 he produced 53 operas, mostly in Venice. However, his historical significance lies with his concertos, sonatas, and trio sonatas. Bach admired Albinoni's music, and made arrangements of 2 fugues taken from trio sonatas. However, the famous *Adagio* for strings and organ is almost totally the work of R. Giazotto, an Italian musicologist.

albisifono (It.). Bass flute, an octave plus the pedal B below the standard flute, invented by Albisi, 1910.

alborada (Sp.). Spanish morning song, orig. performed on a primitive oboe with drum accompaniment as a morning serenade. See ALBA, AUBADE.

Albumblatt (Ger.). A short and (usually) simple vocal or instrumental piece, often intended as a musical autograph or offering; album-leaf.

Alceste. Opera by Gluck, based on the tragedy of Euripides, 1767. The mythological story deals with Alcestis, who volunteers to enter Hades in place of her dead husband; in a LIETO FINE, however, she is saved from the nether region by Hercules. Handel wrote an opera on the same story, and Lully even earlier, but Gluck's opera remains the most important historically, largely because of the preface to the published score, in which Gluck criticizes the emphasis given to performers, scenery, and costumery, maintaining that the dramatic and poetic content should be a paramount consideration in any artistic stage work. Gluck's approach resulted in "reform opera," the heart of the QUERELLE DES BUFFONS debate.

Alceste, ou Le Triomphe d'Alcide (Triumph of the Alcead). Opera by Lully, 1674, based on Euripides's tragedy, with the same happy ending as Gluck's *Alceste*.

Alcina. Opera by Handel, based on Ariosto's *Orlando Furioso*, with an archetypal plot concerning a woman's loss of power through love, 1735.

alcuno, -a (It.). Some; certain.

aleatory music (from Lat. *alea*, a die or dice game). Chance music, either in the compositional process or the performer's realization. Random composition can be gener- ated by the throw of dice or some other way of producing numbers by chance. By drawing an arbitrary table of correspondences between numbers and musical parameters (pitch, duration, rests) it is possible to derive a number of desirable melorhythmic curves. In realizing aleatory scores, rhythmic values and pitches are subject to multiple choices by the performer; sometimes only duration is specified by the composer; in extreme cases even the length of the piece itself is aleatory.

Chance music is nothing new, having been practiced as early as the 18th century. Mozart amused himself by writing a piece with numbered bars that could be put together by throwing dice. Aleatory music in modern times, however, is a more serious business, especially as cultivated by Cage, who often used numbers derived from the Chinese *I Ching*. His classic aleatory works include *Music of Changes* for piano and the *Piano Concert*. Stockhausen wrote numerous aleatory pieces for piano and chamber ensembles, as did his many disciples and followers in Europe and Japan. The term *aleatoric* is sometimes used.

Human or animal phenomena may also serve as primary data. Configurations of fly specks on paper, curves and parabolas produced by geometry and trigonometry, flight patterns of birds over a specific location, etc. are possible materials for aleatory music. Kagel has made use of partially exposed photographic film for aleatory composition. Xenakis organizes aleatory music in stochastic terms, providing the teleological quality absent in pure aleatory pursuits. Among related subjects of aleatory music are PROBABILITY, INFORMATION THEORY, STOCHASTIC COMPOSITION, CYBERNETICS, EXPERIMENTAL MUSIC, COMPUTER MUSIC, EMPIRICAL MUSIC, and INDETERMINACY.

Alexander Nevsky. Cantata by Prokofiev, 1st performed in Moscow on May 17, 1939. The score is based on the music Prokofiev wrote for a Sergei Eisenstein film depicting the Russian hero who routed the German invaders in 1242. The production was a gentle caution to the Nazis not to tempt fate by attempting another such invasion. As history shows, the warning was entirely prophetic.

Alexander's Feast, or The Power of Music. An oratorio by Handel, 1736. The text is derived from the famous ode by John Dryden. The oratorio would have been forgotten were it not for Handel's decision to add the Concerto Grosso in C Major to the score; this work became known as *The Celebrated Concerto from Alexander's Feast*.

Alexander's Ragtime Band. Song by Irving Berlin, 1910. The piece is not in ragtime but is a march; there was no bandleader named Alexander; nonetheless, it popularized "ragtime" as a musical genre, particularly introducing syncopated rhythms into popular song.

Alexander, Roberta, African-American soprano; b. Lynchburg, Va., Mar. 3, 1949. She studied at the Univ. of Mich., Ann Arbor (1969–71; M.Mus.). She appeared as Pamina (Houston Grand Opera, 1980), Daphne (Santa Fe, 1981), and Elettra in *Idomeneo* in Zurich (1982). Following a tour of Europe, made a successful debut at the Metropolitan Opera, N.Y., as Zerlina (Nov. 3, 1983); later sang Bess and Jenufa there. Subsequently appeared throughout the world.

Alfonso und Estrella. Opera by Schubert, 1822, not performed until 1854.

Alkan (born Morhange), **Charles-Valentin,** eccentric French pianist and composer; b. Paris, Nov. 30, 1813; d. there, Mar. 29, 1888. His father, Alkan Morhange (1780–1855), operated a Parisian music school; he and his 4 brothers became well-known musicians who adopted their father's 1st name as their surname. Charles-Valentin entered the Paris Cons. in 1819; he made his public debut as pianist and composer in Paris in 1826. He visited London twice (1833, 1835), the only times he left Paris; at home developed friendships with Dumas *père*, Hugo, George Sand, Delacroix, and his neighbor Chopin. In 1838 he appeared in a concert with Chopin; despite the favorable reception, did not appear again until 1844. Following concerts in 1845, again interrupted his playing career, now for 28 years. His piano work, *Le Chemin de fer*, op. 27 (1844), is the 1st work to describe a railroad. In 1848 Zimmerman retired as piano prof. at the Paris Cons. and suggested Alkan as his successor. Despite intercessions by Sand, the position went to Marmontel, propelling Alkan even further into seclusion. After Chopin's death Alkan abandoned his circle of artistic friends and became a virtual recluse. In 1857 several of his piano compositions were publ., including the remarkable *12 études dans les tons mineurs*, op. 39; études 4–7 constitute a sym., études 8–10 a concerto without orch. In 1859 one of his few nonpianistic works, the grotesque *Marche funèbre sulla morte d'un papagallo* for Voices and Double Reeds, appeared. About this time he also became interested in the PEDALIER, a pedal board that attaches to a piano, on which he played organ works of Bach and for which he wrote compositions, including the unique *Bombardo-carillon* for 4 Feet Alone.

During his lifetime, Alkan was an enigma; his pianistic skills were highly praised, compared to those of Chopin and Liszt, and yet his aberrant behavior and misanthropy caused his name to fade into the foreground. Judging from the difficulty of his works, his skills must have been formidable. Since his death several pianists—notably Busoni, Petri, Lewenthal, and Ronald Smith—have kept his works alive.

all', alla (It.). To the, in the, at the; in the style of; like.

alla breve (It.). In modern music, a 2/2 meter, i.e., 2 beats per measure with the half note carrying the beat; also called *cut time* (from medieval terminology). Implies a faster tempo than 4/4.

all' ottava (It., at the octave). Play the notes an octave higher than written. The sign 8va————————— or 8————————— is usually employed.

alla siciliana (It.). In Sicilian style; like a SICILIANA.

alla stretta (It., narrow, close together). 1. Growing ever faster. 2. In the style of a STRETTO (*stretta*).

alla turca (It.). In Turkish style.

all'unisono (It.). In unison (or octaves).

allargando (It., widening). Growing slower; usually presages an ending.

allegretto (It., quite lively). Moderately fast; faster than ANDANTE, slower than ALLEGRO. Light; almost dancelike.

allegro (It., joyful). Fast, lively, brisk, rapid. Allegro is not as fast as PRESTO. *Sonata allegro*, a formal structure found in many movements of Classic and Romantic music; the tempo is not necessarily allegro.

Allegro. Musical by Richard Rodgers and Oscar Hammerstein, 1947. A small-town doctor and his spouse discover the ups and downs of life in the big city. Includes *A Fellow Needs a Girl*.

allein (Ger.). Alone; only.

alleluia. The Latin form of the Hebrew *Hallelujah* (Praise the Lord!), an acclamation found throughout the Roman

Catholic liturgy. In the High Mass the alleluia chant follows the GRADUAL. It is in ternary form, with a verse in the middle; the alleluia section ends with a lengthy melisma called a *jubilus*. When joy is not called for (e.g., the REQUIEM MASS), the alleluia is replaced by the TRACT.

Alleluia. Nickname for Haydn's Sym. No. 30 in C Major.

allemanda (It.); **Allemande** (Fr.). 1. In the Renaissance, a German dance in 2/4. 2. In the Classic period, a German dance in 3/4 time, similar to the Ländler. 3. A movement in the Baroque suite (usually the 1st or following a prelude) in 4/4 time and moderate tempo (ANDANTINO). It is as much French in style as German.

Allison, Mose, American singer, songwriter, and pianist; b. Tippo, Miss., Nov. 11, 1927. After serving in the U.S. Army he formed his own trio; then played with Stan Getz and Gerry Mulligan. His earlier songs were heavily blues-influenced; his mature songs, often marked by satirical and cynical lyrics, have been performed by such notables as Van Morrison, the Who, John Mayall, Georgie Fame, and Bonnie Raitt. Some of his best-known songs include *7th Son* (a hit for Johnny Rivers), *One of These Days*, *Parchman Farm*, *Tell Me Something*, *I Don't Want Much*, and *Perfect Moment*.

Almeida, Laurindo, Brazilian guitarist; b. São Paulo, Sept. 2, 1917; d. Van Nuys, Calif., July 26, 1995. After mastering the guitar he settled in Rio de Janeiro and made appearances on the radio; led his own orch. at the Casino da Urca. In 1947 he moved to the U.S.; was a soloist with Stan Kenton's band; later led his own small groups. He gave numerous recitals and was a soloist with sym. orchs.; also appeared with his wife, the soprano Deltra Eamon. Almeida brought the Brazilian style of jazz, with its dance rhythms and modalities, into greater prominence, preparing the way for its burst of popularity in the 1960s.

Almira. Opera by Handel, his 1st, 1705. It is actually a medley of German and Italian arias and recitatives.

Aloha Oe. Song composed by Liliuokalani, the Princess Regent of Hawaii, in 1898, while she was imprisoned by the Republican government of the island. The melody of the refrain is taken from an 1847 George F. Root ballad, *There's Music in the Air*.

alphorn (Ger.). A long wooden natural horn able to produce up to the 12th partial, used by shepherds in the Alps to call the sheep back home at sunset. Brahms notated an Alpine horn tune on a postcard he sent to Clara Schumann in 1868 with the words "Hoch auf 'm Berg, tief im Tal, grüss' ich dich viel tausendmal!" (High on the mountain, deep in the valley, I greet you many thousand times.) Eight years later he made use of it in the famous horn solo in the last movement of his Sym. No. 1, which contains an approximation (F♯, 3–1/2 octaves above the fundamental C) of the 11th partial note.

Alpine Symphony. A panoramic work by Richard Strauss, 1915. It depicts the ascent of an Alpine peak and a fearful thunderstorm near the summit, conglomerating into chords containing all 7 notes of the diatonic scale. A thunder machine and a wind machine for realistic effect are included in the huge score.

Also sprach Zarathustra (Thus Spake Zarathustra). Symphonic poem by Richard Strauss, 1896, inspired by the philosophical poem by Nietzsche. The opening is set in a proclamatory C major. There follow sections on religion, passions, science, and other matters. The fugal theme of science is an interesting anticipation of 12-tone composition; the coda, combining the basic key of C major with a B-major triad in the highest treble, ventures into polytonality in order to represent Nietzsche's "world riddle." The musical solution of this riddle lies in the fact that a very high B-major triad is actually composed of very high partials of the fundamental low C. Although damned by critics as chaotic in its early history, the work gained renown when its opening theme was used as a thematic signature for the celebrated film *2001: A Space Odyssey*.

Alt (Ger.). ALTO.

alt, in (*alto*; It.). Notes in the octave from f² to f³:

Notes in the octave above this are said to be *in altissimo*.

alteration. 1. A generic term for raising or lowering a note's pitch by means of an ACCIDENTAL. 2. In mensural notation, the doubling of the value of the 2nd semibreve in duple time, thus converting it into triple ("perfect") time.

altered chords. Chords containing chromatic alterations of harmonies normally expected within the tonality of the music; also called chromatic chords.

alternativo (It.). A contrasting section in dance forms, such as a trio in a minuet; a substitute for such a section.

althorn (U.S. Eng., Ger.). The B♭ alto saxhorn, patented by Sax in 1845 and perfected by the Bohemian maker Václav Nervenv in 1859; the orig. Fr. name was *saxhorn ténor*.

alti naturali (It., naturally high ones). In the Middle Ages, male falsetto singers, as opposed to *voci artificiali*, the castratos.

altissimo, in (It., in the highest). Range of voices from g³ (an octave above the treble staff) to g⁴. Some medieval singers are reputed to have been able to sing in this range without falsetto. See ALTO.

alto (It., from Lat. *altus*, high). 1. The deeper of the 2 main divisions of women's or boys' voices, the SOPRANO being the higher; the standard alto gamut ranges from g to c²; in voices of great range, down to d and up to f² or even higher. Alto singers possess resonant chest voices. In opera the parts of young swains who unsuccessfully court the heroine are often given to altos (TROUSER ROLES), e.g., Siebel in Gounod's *Faust*. Also called *contralto*. 2. An instrument of similar compass, such as the alto saxhorn, alto saxophone, alto recorder, alto flute, and alto clarinet (basset horn). 3. The counter-tenor voice. 4. (Fr.) The viola; tenor violin.

alto, -a (It.). High. *Alta viola*, tenor violin; *ottava alta*, an octave higher.

alto clef. A C-clef placing middle C on the 3rd line.

amabile (It.). Sweet, tender, gentle, amiably.

Amahl and the Night Visitors. Opera by Menotti to his own libretto, broadcast on Christmas Eve, 1951, by NBC Television; it is the 1st operatic work written for television, and its success was such that it became an annual Christmas presentation. Suggested by Bosch's painting *The Adoration of the Magi*, the story deals with the crippled boy Amahl, who is miraculously healed when he gives his crutches to the visiting 3 Wise Men as a gift for the Christ child.

amateur

An art lover who, while possessing an understanding for and a certain practical knowledge of it, does not pursue it as a profession. A noble word degraded during the past couple of centuries to connote persons who dabble in the arts without requisite skill or understanding, *amateur* (from Fr., one who loves) is often synonymous with *dilettante* (from It., one who delights), which itself has been unjustly degraded from its original meaning. In the 18th century the word *amateur* had a complimentary meaning. There was a flourishing society in Paris called Concerts des Amateurs. Composers dedicated their works to persons described as amateurs in the dedication. Such publications could also be directed at a specific market; C. P. E. Bach entitled a set of clavier sonatas "à l'usage des dames." In the 19th century the salon genres of instrumental and vocal chamber music were the true popular music of their day, along with the most successful operatic arias. By the next century the cultivated and vernacular traditions were more or less irreconcilable; classical composers wrote primarily pedagogical pieces, while most audiences turned to the succession of popular music styles that filled the air.

Of all professions, medical doctors are probably the most enthusiastic amateurs of music. There are doctors' sym. orchs. in several major cities of the U.S. and in other countries. A story is told about a famous pianist who played a concerto with a doctors' orch. Shortly afterward he suffered an attack of appendicitis; several surgeons from the orch. volunteered to operate on him, but he declined. "I prefer to have my appendix removed by a member of the New York Philharmonic," he declared in all solemnity. Mathematicians and physicists like to play chamber music. Albert Einstein was quite proficient on the violin, although an anecdote suggests that when he played a Mozart sonata with the famous pianist Schnabel, he could not keep time. "For pity's sake, Albert," his partner exclaimed, "can't you count?" Chess players love music. The 18th-century composer Philidor earned a place in chess history by his opening known as Philidor's Defense. Prokofiev reached the rank of a top chess player in Russia. Painters, too, are often musical. The famous French artist Ingres loved to play the violin, even though he could never quite master it. Hence the expression "violon d'Ingres" is applied to a passionate but inefficient amateur. Conversely, many musicians show a respectable talent for painting; Schoenberg, Gershwin, and Robert Moran have had public exhibitions of their art. The Italian futurists, among them Russolo, painted canvases in an expressionistic manner that fetched high prices after their deaths. Ruggles devoted himself entirely to painting and stopped writing music during the last 40 years of his very long life. Rudhyar painted hundreds of pictures symbolic of his mystical beliefs.

Some statesmen were accomplished music amateurs. Many royal personages were amateurs in the best sense of the word, among them Frederick the Great of Prussia (who performed regularly with C. P. E. Bach and Quantz) and Albert, Prince Consort of England. Francis Hopkinson, a signer of the Declaration of Independence, claimed the distinction of being the 1st American to produce a musical composition. Thomas Jefferson played the harpsichord, violin, and recorder; Benjamin Franklin perfected the glass harmonica. Presidents Harry Truman and Richard Nixon played the piano, but their repertory was limited; Bill Clinton is the finest presidential saxophonist the U.S. has ever had. On the other hand, the great Polish patriot Paderewski was a pianist 1st, a statesman 2nd. It is said that when he met the French prime minister Clemenceau at the Versailles Peace Conference following World War I, Clemenceau exclaimed, "So you are the famous pianist, and now you are Prime Minister! What a comedown!" Even Verdi was a member of the 1st Italian parliament.

Amati. Renowned Italian family of violin makers working at Cremona. (1) Andrea (b. between 1500 and 1505; d. before 1580) was the 1st violin maker of the family; established the prototype of Italian instruments, with characteristics found in modern violins. His sons were (2) Antonio (b. *c.* 1538; d. *c.* 1595), who built violins of varying sizes, and (3) Girolamo (b. *c.* 1561; d. Nov. 2, 1630), who continued the tradition established by his father, working together with his brother. (4) Nicola (Niccolò) (b. Dec. 3, 1596; d. Apr. 12, 1684) was the most illustrious of the family. Son of Girolamo, he built some of the "grand Amatis," large violins of powerful tone surpassing in clarity and purity those made by his father and grandfather. In Nicola's workshop both Andrea Guarneri and Antonio Stradivari received their training. (5) Girolamo (b. Feb. 26, 1649; d. Feb. 21, 1740), son of Nicola and the last of the family, produced violins inferior to those of his predecessors; he departed from the family tradition in many respects, seemingly influenced by Stradivari's method without equaling his superb workmanship.

ambitus. 1. In church mode theory, the range of scale degrees comprising a given mode. The determination of the ambitus can depend on the mode's being authentic, plagal, or mixed. 2. The range of a voice, instrument, or piece.

Ambrosian chant. A system of plainchant associated with the 4th-century bishop of Milan, St. Ambrose (b. Trier [Treves], *c.* 333; d. Milan, Apr. 4, 397). It preceded by 2 centuries the codification of Gregorian chant. There are many musicological views of Ambrosian chant: as an inchoate predecessor of Gregorian chant; as a refreshing style free from the stricter Gregorian doctrine; as an extension of Eastern liturgical sources. The last interpretation is supported by its use of florid quasi-exotic melismas that adorn its melodies and move freely between modes; some such fio+ituras comprise more than 100 notes. Perhaps the most rational theory about the historical place of the Ambrosian chant is its being a Milanese branch of the liturgical ritual; the other main branches are the Gregorian of Rome, the Gallican of France, and the Mozarabic of Moorish Spain. This division is analogous with the emergence of Romance languages from their common Latin source.

ambulation. The indicated movement of performers in the process of playing a piece. This is an example of SPATIAL DISTRIBUTION, in which the player's position in physical space is treated as an independent parameter. Ambulation is related to VECTORIALISM, in that the direction of the sound source depends on the placement, stationary or kinetic, of the performers. In an ambulatory composition the players may be instructed to make their entrances on, or exits off, the stage while playing their instruments; they may utilize the concert hall; they may be suspended from the flies or rise from beneath the stage; they may move during the piece, in random or specified directions; they may "interact" with each other, with varying degrees of improvisatory freedom; percussionists may have more than one setup on stage, and are required to move between them, sometimes quite rapidly.

Amelia al Ballo (Amelia Goes to the Ball). Opera buffa by Menotti, to his own libretto in Italian, 1937. The ambitious Amelia is eager to get to the ball on time but is delayed by a violent encounter between her husband and her lover. She finally is escorted to the ball by a friendly policeman.

Ameling, Elly (Elisabeth Sara), outstanding Dutch soprano; b. Rotterdam, Feb. 8, 1934. After studies in Rotterdam and the Hague, she completed her training with Bernac in Paris; won the Hertogenbosch (1956) and Geneva (1958) competitions; made her formal recital debut in Amsterdam (1961); appeared with the Concertgebouw Orch., Amsterdam, and the Rotterdam Phil.; made her London (1966) and N.Y. (1968) debuts. Her 1st operatic appearance was as Ilia in *Idomeneo* (Amsterdam, 1973), but she chose to concentrate on a concert career. She gave numerous lieder recitals and appeared with many major European orchs. In 1971 she was made a Knight of the Order of Oranje Nassau by the Dutch government; established a prize to be awarded at 's Hertogenbosch.

Amen (Heb.). The concluding word in a Jewish or Christian prayer, as an expression of faith. Sometimes an Amen section in an oratorio is extended so as to become a concluding chorus of considerable length.

Amen cadence. A popular term for PLAGAL CADENCE, to which the word *Amen* is often sung.

America. Patriotic song to words written by Samuel Francis Smith in 1832. Commissioned to write a chorus for children, he selected a German song with the 1st line "Heil, dir im Siegerkranz." Smith's version, which began with "My country 'tis of Thee," became widely popular. It was not chosen as the American national anthem because its tune is identical to that of England's *God Save the King*. *America* was 1st performed by a children's choir at the Park Street Church, Boston, on July 4, 1832.

America. Symphonic rhapsody by Ernest Bloch, 1928. It traces the history of the U.S. from the landing of the Pilgrims to the dawn of the 20th century. Bloch used all kinds of American melodies, ending with a newly composed hymn to his adoptive land; the work sank into oblivion despite its patriotic proclamations.

America the Beautiful. Patriotic song to words written by Katherine Lee Bates, prof. of English at Wellesley College. She was inspired by the view from Pikes Peak, Colo. Her poem was publ. to great acclaim on July 4, 1895; songwriters vied to set the words to divinely inspired music, but no one conjured a sufficiently powerful melody. Finally, an unknown seeker set the words to *O Mother Dear Jerusalem* (*Materna*) by Samuel Augustus Ward (1882), and the hymn became an obligatory effusion at patriotic gatherings. Bates lived long enough (until 1929) to see her work enshrined as an American classic.

American Festival Overture. Concert overture by Schuman, 1939. The work incorporates the vernacular and provocative calls of small American boys at play.

An American in Paris. Symphonic poem by Gershwin, 1928, in which he introduces realistic sounds such as taxi horns and Parisian popular songs of the time.

American Quartet. A nickname for Dvořák's String Quartet in F Major, op. 96, written during his sojourn in the U.S. Its original racist nickname referred to its syncopated themes, which suggested Negro spirituals. This familiar title was not changed until the 1930s, when such epithets became unacceptable in the lingua franca.

Amériques. Symphonic poem by Varèse, 1926, composed in the U.S. (1918–22). The score, a panorama of North and South America, abounds in resonant discords and is built on a gargantuan scale of instrumental sonorities; it was received with typical critical incomprehension.

ametric. Without meter; lacking a regular, sustained pulse.

Amico Fritz, L'. Opera by Mascagni, 1891, in which a wealthy bachelor landowner succumbs to the charms of the daughter of one of his tenants.

Amirkhanian, Charles (Benjamin), American avant-garde composer and influential radio producer of Armenian extraction; b. Fresno, Calif., Jan. 19, 1945. His early percussion compositions experimented with sound phenomena independent of traditional musical content, as in the 1965 Sym. I, scored for 12 players and 200-odd objects ranging from pitch pipes to pitchforks. With painter Ted Greer he developed a radical notational system based on visual images transduced by performers into sound events. He is perhaps best known for his developments in TEXT-SOUND COMPOSITION, featuring a voice percussively intoning and articulating decontextualized words and phrases; an especially difficult but rewarding example is *Dutiful Ducks* (1977). Since the early 1980s his works have used sampled ambient sounds manipulated by a SYNCLAVIER digital synthesizer.

Amor brujo, El (Love, the Magician). Ballet by Falla, 1915; a successful symphonic suite was drawn from it. The romantic scenario deals with the posthumous pressure of a dead gypsy lover upon his surviving beloved not to yield to any living human; but a new lover conquers the spectral prohibition.

Amore dei tre re, L' (Love of Three Kings). Opera by Montemezzi, 1913, involving a king who manages to kill his daughter-in-law and her lover (intentionally) and his own son (unintentionally).

amoroso (It.). Amorous; loving, fond, tender.

amplifier. Electronic device used in all reproducing sound systems to control and heighten volume.

amplitude. The widest disturbance in a vibration; the scientific correlate to the sensation of loudness. *Amplitude modulation*, change made to the amplitude of a sound wave enabling information transfer to electromagnetic wave (AM).

Amram, David (Werner, III), American instrumentalist, conductor, and composer; b. Philadelphia, Nov. 17, 1930. Amram is best known for his cross-cultural experiments, combining jazz, world, and classical musical styles in his compositions and performances. He has also composed film scores, radio works, for the theater, and for orch. and smaller ensembles.

anacrusis (Gk., upbeat). Unaccented syllables beginning a verse of poetry. In music, the weak beat, or weak part of a measure, with which a piece or phrase may begin. See AUFTAKT.

anagrams. The rearrangement of notes of a subject to generate plausible thematic variations; analogous with literary anagrams, in which words and sentences are derived from a given meaningful matrix (e.g., "Flit on, cheering angel" from *Florence Nightingale*). The 12 notes of the chromatic scale yield 479,001,600 possible permutations suitable for dodecaphonic usages. Polyanagrams, formed by linear (melodic), vertical (harmonic), and oblique (fugal) parameters, are comprised in the generic term COMBINATORIALITY, introduced by Babbitt. The remarkably intricate *Anagrama* by Kagel, scored for speaking chorus, 4 vocalists, and instruments, to a text derived from Dante's *Divina Commedia*, executes a number of permutations forming plausible sentences in different languages.

analysis

〜〜 〜〜 〜〜 〜〜 〜〜

The study of musical structure and form. Description of a musical composition in verbal terms offers 2 alternatives: to paint a word picture with poetic metaphors and psychological excursions, or to confine oneself to the methodical compilation of an inventory of melodic phrases, rhythmic terms, harmonic progressions, contrapuntal combinations, and formal designs. The obvious defect of the 1st method is the impossibility of forming any idea of style or technique. The nickname "Moonlight" given to Beethoven's Piano Sonata "quasi una fantasia" (No. 2, op. 27) by a literary critic communicates little or nothing about the work's structure. Emotional similes such as *romantic*, *stormy*, *wistful*, and *fantastic* are no better. Stylistic designations can be a little more informative, if one knows their meaning (e.g., Baroque, rococo, traditional).

Moving to the 2nd alternative, the next level involves the bar-by-bar description of the music in its melodic, rhythmic, and harmonic content within a composer-selected form of composition. Finally there is the presumption of a working hypothesis, where the analyst proposes a widely ranging specific notion, e.g., that all of Beethoven's main themes are based on an interval of a falling 3rd, either major or minor. However, the elaboration of such a thesis, starting from an example as famous as the opening of his 5th Sym., requires either the avoidance of instances where the thesis does not apply or the derivation of "alternative" 3rds, such as a 6th (an inverted 3rd) or a 4th (an expanded 3rd).

Global hypotheses are made more impressive through the invention of their own nomenclatures and rationalizations. Several theories are based on the natural system of HARMONICS (overtones), which has the advantage of an empirically studied structure and demonstrable import in melody and harmony throughout music's recorded history. Schenker's system outlines a scientific looking terminology, of which URLINIE (primordial line) promises to trace any tonal melody of the Baroque, Classic, and Romantic periods (Common Practice Period) to its component elements; inversely, the fundamental presence of the triad makes it possible to reconstruct any tonal melody through an arbitrary process of interpolation and extrapolation of melodic notes. Any musical phrase, rhythm, and harmonic accompaniment can be reduced to a preselected form, in a process related to topological congruence.

But if the metaphorical, mechanical, or theoretical approach are by themselves ineffective, analysts could attempt to combine all these methods. Elements may include the use of musical examples, although space limits their number; the use of applicable musical metaphors (accelerating, contrasting, harmonious) and traditional expression marks; and references to a composer's choice of musical devices, particularly quotation. The recurrence of motives within a composer's oeuvre and among several composers' works can be treated as a stylistic hallmark: Beethoven's so-called fate motive in the 5th Sym. and its presence in several of his works; the appearance of Wagner's "Tristan motive" in a Liszt song 10 years earlier; and the numerous borrowings by Handel, Bach, and other Baroque composers from others.

Unfortunately, composers' own comments are often unenlightening or even misleading, e.g., Beethoven's "Pastoral" Sym., Mahler's early programmatic symphonies, Schoenberg's postdated titles for the 5 Orch.1 Pieces (op. 16), and Tchaikovsky's 4th Sym. as described to Madame von Meck. Indeed, taking a composer's biography, personal observations, and psychological profile as the basis of musical analysis mistakes rhetoric and "inner meaning" for musical style and technique. The problem of analytical description of musical works remains unsolved.

anamnesis. In music, an unexpected appearance of a theme or motive amid otherwise irrelevant melorhythmic events.

anapest (Grk.). A metrical foot of 3 syllables, 2 short (unstressed) and 1 long (stressed); in music, corresponds to an upbeat of 2 quick notes followed by a long note in 4/8 time.

Anchors Aweigh. A marching song of the U.S. Navy, 1907, composed by Charles Zimmerman, musical director of the Naval Academy at Annapolis; Alfred H. Miles is sometimes credited with joint authorship.

ancor (from It. *ancora*). Again, also, yet, still, ever.

ancora piano (It.). Continue singing (or playing) softly. *Ancora più piano* (It.), still softer.

andante (It., going, moving, walking). A tempo mark indicating a moderately slow, easily flowing pace between ADAGIO and ALLEGRETTO. Often used ambiguously, its speed depends on other factors, such as the type of accompaniment.

andante con moto (It.). Flowing and rather more animated.

andante mosso (It.). Flowing and rather more animated.

andante un poco allegretto (It.). Flowing and rather more animated.

andantino (It.). A diminutive of ANDANTE, used ambiguously; it literally means "a little slower than andante," but it is generally used to mean "a little faster than andante."

Anderson, Laurie, composer and violinist, imaginative representative of American performance art; b. Chicago, June 5, 1947. Renouncing the tradition of conventional modernism, her goal is to unite all arts as they once existed in ancient theatrical practice; she makes use of all available styles and technologies, from topical pop to electronics, incorporating images of herself projected on a screen. She also uses a variety of instrumentation, including a home-made violin activated by a luminous bow made of electronic tape. She has become particularly famous for her multimedia cyberpunk projections, extending the principles of cybernetics to deliberately commonplace movements, behavior, and language. Her performances combine speech, song, and bodily exertions, her programmed compositions mostly improvisations in which she alters her natural voice electronically, making use of vocal glissando, crooning, panting, and heavy aspiration. Her 1st popular success was the minimalist *O Superman*, built on a repeating phrase. In 1983 she produced the large-scale collage epic *United States* on themes of travel, politics, money, and love.

Anderson, Marian, celebrated African-American contralto; b. Philadelphia, Feb. 17, 1897, in impoverished circumstances; d. Portland, Oreg., Apr. 8, 1993. She sang in the choir of the Union Baptist Church, South Philadelphia. Funds were raised for her to study voice with Giuseppe Boghetti. In 1923 she won 1st prize at a Philadelphia singing contest; in 1925 received top honors at a contest held by the N.Y. Phil. at Lewisohn Stadium, winning for a solo appearance. In 1929 she gave a recital at Carnegie Hall; made her 1st European appearance in London (1930); and subsequently toured Europe and the Soviet Union; her singing of Negro spirituals produced a sensation. In Feb. 1939 she gained national attention when the Daughters of the American Revolution (DAR) refused to let her appear at their Constitution Hall in Washington, D.C., citing the organization's policy of racial segregation. The resulting publicity led to Eleanor Roosevelt's resigning from the DAR and an invitation to sing at the Lincoln Memorial on Easter Sunday, Apr. 9, 1939; a huge audience attended, and the concert was broadcast. Another landmark occurred when she sang the role of Ulrica in *Un ballo in maschera* at the Metropolitan Opera, N.Y., on Jan. 7, 1955, the 1st black singer to appear there. (Unfortunately, the opportunity came too late in her career.) Her remaining years were filled with a seemingly unending list of honors.

Andrea Chénier. Opera by Giordano, 1896. The libretto by Illica deals with the historical fate of a poet condemned to the guillotine by the French revolutionary tribunal in 1793. His beloved contrives to incriminate herself in order to die with him.

Andrews, Julie (born Julia Elizabeth Wells), English singer of popular music and an actress; b. Walton-on-Thames, Oct. 1, 1935. Her mother was a pianist and her stepfather, whose surname she adopted, was a music-hall singer. She was praised for her performance in the Broadway musical *The Boy Friend* (1954), displaying considerable vocal range and technique; followed with her outstanding portrayal of Eliza Doolittle in *My Fair Lady* (1956-60), for which she received the Drama Critics Award; subsequently appeared in *Camelot* (1960-62). Turning her attention to films, she appeared in the whimsical *Mary Poppins* (1964), for which she won an Academy Award for best actress, and *The Sound of Music* (1966). In later years she appeared in several films directed by her husband, Blake Edwards, by which she hoped to alter her squeaky clean image. Their biggest success was *Victor, Victoria,* a farce on gender role-playing, made into a musical (1995) with Andrews in the lead.

Andrews Sisters, American popular singing group. (Members: LaVerne, b. Minneapolis, Minn., July 6, 1915; d. Brentwood, Calif., May 8, 1967; Maxene, b. Minneapolis, Jan. 3, 1918; and Patricia [Patti], b. Minneapolis, Feb. 16, 1920.) They formed the Andrews Sisters, the most successful "girl group" in history, selling over 60 million records. Among their most popular songs were *Bei Mir Bist Du Schoen* (1937), *Rum and Coca Cola* (1944), and *Winter Wonderland* (1947). They were excellent at boogie-woogie renditions, performed in close 3-part harmony, including *Beat Me Daddy 8 to the Bar* and *Boogie Woogie Bugle Boy*; the latter was reinterpreted by Bette Midler in 1973 (with Midler doing all 3 vocal parts), setting off a resurgence of interest in their music.

Andriessen, Louis, prominent Dutch composer; b. Utrecht, June 6, 1939. He 1st studied with his father (the composer Hendrik Andriessen, 1892–1981) and van Baaren at the Royal Cons. in the Hague (1957–62); also studied with Berio in Milan (1962–63). He was a cofounder of a Charles Ives Soc. in Amsterdam. His works are conceived in an advanced idiom, extending minimalist concepts into complex sonority (*De Tijd*) or emphatic, iconoclastic expression (*Hoketus, De Materie*). His brother Jurriaan (1925–) is also a leading Dutch composer.

Andromache's Farewell. Lament for soprano and orch. by Barber, inspired by Euripides's *Trojan Women*, 1963.

Angeles, Victoria de los (born Victoria Gómez Cima), famous Spanish soprano; b. Barcelona, Nov. 1, 1923. Made her concert debut in Barcelona in 1944, and her 1st operatic appearance there in 1946; in 1947 won the Geneva Competition. In 1949 she performed at the Paris Opera as Marguerite; in 1950 at Covent Garden, London, as Mimi. On Mar. 17, 1951, she appeared at the Metropolitan Opera, N.Y., once more as Marguerite; she sang at the Metropolitan until 1961. She retired from the stage in 1969; continued to give occasional recitals, excelling particularly in Spanish and French songs. Her extensive operatic repertoire included Manon, Donna Anna, Nedda, Melisande, Cio-Cio-San, and Carmen.

Anglican chant. Liturgical singing generally adopted in English-speaking Protestant liturgy; it is usually harmonized with simple chords.

ängstlich (Ger.). Anxiously, fearfully.

Anhang (Ger.). 1. Coda, codetta. 2. Supplement, as in a GESAMTAUSGABE.

Aniara. Opera by Karl-Birger Blomdahl, 1959, after the novel by Harry Martinson; it is described as "a revue of mankind, in space-time." After an atomic war, survivors from Earth emigrate to Mars in the spaceship *Aniara*. They become demoralized during the long journey and fail to achieve the new way of life that they seek. The score employs electronic sounds, but its tonal fabric is derived from the GROSSMUTTERAKKORD, consisting of 12 different notes separated from each other by 11 different intervals.

animals and animal music

Because birds are the primordial music-makers of the animal world, it is not surprising that composers have for centuries imitated birdcalls in their works. The cuckoo has the most immediately identifiable leitmotif: a falling major 3rd. Beethoven immortalized it, along with the trilling nightingale and the repetitive quail, in his *Pastoral Sym.* The 18th-century French composer Daquin wrote a harpsichord piece entitled *The Cuckoo*, which became a universal favorite. The contemporary French composer Messiaen expanded the musical aviary by filling his compositions with painstakingly notated exotic birdcalls. The rooster is glorified in Rimsky-Korsakov's opera *Le Coq d'or*, sounding his call on the muted trumpet. Villa-Lobos reproduces the piercing cry of the araponga on high B-flat in one of his *Bachianas Brasileiras*.

Non-avian creatures are represented as well. Buzzing insects provide an obvious source of animal onomatopoeia. Rimsky-Korsakov's *Flight of the Bumble Bee* is a famous example; a more esoteric illustration is Bartók's *Diary of a Fly* from his *Mikrokosmos*. In the score of his opera *L'Enfant et les sortilèges*, Ravel includes a couple of meowing amorous cats. The bleating of sheep is imitated by a cacophonous ensemble of wind instruments in R. Strauss's *Don Quixote*. In the *Duet for 2 Cats* traditionally attributed to Rossini, 2 sopranos sing their parts to the most familiar phrase associated with felines. Saint-Saëns has a whole menagerie in his *Carnival of the Animals*.

Sometimes instruments are invented to imitate animal sounds; such as the toy cuckoo used in Leopold Mozart's *Toy Sym.* Actual reproductions of animal noises on a phonograph disc or tape are used in some modern scores: Respighi introduced a recording of a nightingale in his symphonic poem *The Pines of Rome*. The American composers Crumb and Hovhaness have used recordings of the sounds of humpback whales. These giant marine animals have no vocal cords but are capable of producing tones covering the entire human range; furthermore, the whale voice has a tremendous endurance and can carry a tone as long as 18 minutes. When a dog incidentally barked during a recording of Piston's ballet suite *The Incredible Flutist*, the conductor decided to keep it in the final recording. In Kirk Nurock's *Sonata for Dog and Piano* the canine performer's role is obbligato and totally improvised.

Are animals themselves sensitive to music in any selective way? Experiments conducted on dairy farms in New Zealand in 1947 seemed to show that cows produce more milk when jazz is played. On a New Jersey farm 2,500 pigs were exposed to a constant flood of jazz in 1950, and they put on weight faster than pigs not so favored. A farmer in Surrey, England, wrote to the British Broadcasting Corp. that his cows gave their highest milk yield when Haydn's string quartets were played for them. The curator of reptiles at the Brookfield Zoo in Chicago noted that the alligator mating calls approximated the pitch of B-flat below middle C. He hired 4 French horn players and instructed them to play B-flat in unison, but no visible mating ensued. All these and numerous other attempts to connect music with physiological processes in animals have failed in the end, proving, as if proof were needed, that animals lack a talent for music appreciation. Perhaps the most vocal animal is the Siamang (*Symphalangus syndactylus*), a large gibbon of Sumatra. Its throat sac swells like a red balloon during vocalization, and it has the loudest voice among primates, not excluding sopranos.

animando (It.). With increasing animation; growing livelier.

animando un poco (It.). Somewhat more animatedly.

animato (It.). With spirit, spiritedly, vivaciously.

Anna Magdalena Book. A common name for Bach's *Clavierbüchlein* (Little Clavier Book), a collection of keyboard music that Bach composed for his young 2nd wife, Anna Magdalena.

Années de pèlerinage (Years of Wandering). Three series of piano works by Liszt, begun in 1837 (1855, 1858, 1883); each piece bears a descriptive title. Pieces include: *Sposalizio*, inspired by Raphael's painting of the wedding of Joseph and Mary; *Il Pensieroso*, inspired by Michelangelo's monuments to Lorenzo de' Medici in Florence; *Après une lecture de Dante* (Upon Reading Dante); *Au bord d'une source* (By the Bank of a Brook); 3 *Sonnets of Petrarca; Venezia e Napoli; Les Jeux d'eau à la Villa d'Este* (Fountains at the Villa d'Este); and *Aux Cyprès de la Villa d'Este* (Cypresses at the Villa d'Este).

Annie Get Your Gun. Musical by I. Berlin about Annie Oakley and Wild Bill Hickok, 1946, starring Ethel Merman. Includes *There's No Business Like Show Business, Anything You Can Do, I Can Do Better*, and *Doin' What Comes Natur'lly*, whose unpublished verses are more risqué than the published ones of this song of modest sexual innuendo.

Annie Laurie. A Scottish song composed by Lady John Scott in 1835. Annie Laurie may have been a real person whose unhappy romance with a member of a rival Scottish clan was the subject of the poem reputedly written by her lover.

Anon. Abbr. for *Anonymous*, used in the attribution of religious music of the Middle Ages, traditional music, and many other pieces. Most ecclesiastical chants are anonymous.

Ansatz (Ger.). 1. Proper adjustment of the lips in wind playing; EMBOUCHURE. 2. Precise attack at the beginning of a phrase in string playing.

Anstimmen (Ger.). Tune; begin singing.

Anstimmung (Ger.). Tuning, intonation.

answer. In a fugue, the 2nd voice or part (COMES), which takes up (starting at a different pitch) the subject (DUX, fugal theme) given in the 1st voice or part. A *real answer* is derived from the subject by transposing it exactly to the dominant. A *tonal answer* requires a modification, replacing the tonic with the supertonic, to fulfill certain harmonic requirements.

antecedent. The theme or subject of a canon or fugue, as proposed by the 1st part; the DUX. Also, any theme or motive proposed for imitation, or imitated further on.

Antheil, George (Georg Johann Carl), American modern composer; b. Trenton, N.J., July 8, 1900; d. N.Y., Feb. 12, 1959. Antheil was famous in his day for composing music that glorified the age of the machine. He went to Europe in 1922; gave several concerts featuring his compositions as well as impressionist music; spent a year in Berlin, then went to Paris, his domicile for several years; he was one of the 1st American students of the legendary Nadia Boulanger, the *nourrice* of more than one generation of modernistically minded Americans. In Paris he made contact with Joyce and Pound; in the course of events became the self-styled *enfant terrible* of modern music; naively infatuated with the world of the modern machine, composed the *Ballet mécanique* with the avowed intention to "épater les bourgeoisie"; collaborated with Fernand Léger on a film to be synchronized with the music; this proved impossible, so the music's 1926 premiere was noncinematic. He returned to America, staging a spectacular production of the *Ballet mécanique* in N.Y. in 1927, employing airplane propellers, 8 pianos, and a large percussion battery, creating an uproar in the audience and much publicity in the newspapers.

His subsequent works were less successful, and Antheil moved to Hollywood (1936), where he wrote some film music and ran a syndicated lonely-hearts column. He continued to write syms., operas, and other works, but reduced his musical idiom to accessible masses of sound; these works were rarely performed until recently; nevertheless, he remains a herald of the AVANT-GARDE of yesterday.

anthem (Mid. Eng. *antem*). A hymnal song performed by a chorus, with or without accompaniment and of moderate

George Antheil, 1930

COURTESY FRANK DRIGGS COLLECTION

length. Many anthem texts are based on Scripture, but others are newly composed. Liturgically the form corresponds to the Roman Catholic MOTET. Anthem-singing arose in the Reformation; consequently, it had its most fruitful development in the Lutheran and Anglican churches. More widely the term came to signify any solemn song performed by a community. *National anthems* are the patriotic extensions of the prayerful religious anthems.

anticipation. Resolution of a dissonant melodic note on the upbeat, without resolving other parts of the HARMONY; most commonly applied to the LEADING TONE, moving to the TONIC, thereby preempting its resolution. Such an anticipation forms a highly dissonant chord combining elements of the DOMINANT and tonic harmonies; thus the anticipatory element is enhanced.

antiphon(e) (from Grk. *anti* + *phōnæ*, countersound). 1. Orig., a responsive system of singing by 2 choirs (or divided choir), an early feature in the Catholic service of song, where the same phrase would be repeated an octave higher by a 2nd chorus composed of women and boys. 2. Responsive or alternate singing, chanting, or intonation in general, as practiced in the Greek, Roman, Anglican, and Lutheran churches. 3. A choral response after the singing of a psalm, usually sung in a plain syllabic manner. In large polyphonic compositions an antiphon may become an elaborate setting, vying in importance with the main section. 4. A short sentence, generally from Holy Scripture, sung before and after the psalms for the day.

antiphonal. 1. A liturgical book containing most of the DIVINE OFFICE; antiphonary; antiphoner. 2. In the style of an antiphon; responsive, alternating.

antique cymbals. Small hollow-sphere brass cymbals, orig. used in accompanying dances in ancient Greece. They are used in modern scores for special effects. Also called crotales (Fr., from Lat. *crotalum*).

Antony and Cleopatra. Opera by Barber, based on Shakespeare's play, 1966. The work was commissioned by the Metropolitan Opera for the inauguration of its new house at N.Y.'s Lincoln Center for the Performing Arts. Despite, or perhaps because of, the unabashed romantic flow of operatic cantilena, *Antony and Cleopatra* was generally damned by the critics; but major problems with the stage machinery must also be blamed. Barber revised the score in 1975.

anvil. A metal bar struck by a hammer, 1st used in Auber's *Le Maçon*, 1825, and made famous in the so-called ANVIL CHORUS in Verdi's *Il Trovatore*, 1853. In *Das Rheingold* Wagner introduces 18 anvils to illustrate the forging of the ring of the Nibelung. The anvil is also used by Varèse (*Ionisation*, 1931) and Orff (*Antigonae*, 1949).

Anvil Chorus. Popular designation of the scene in act 2 of Verdi's *Il Trovatore*, in which gypsy camp blacksmiths strike anvils in time with the chorus. Nowhere in Verdi's MS does the indication "Anvil Chorus" appear, however. It is 1 of the most celebrated single passages in all opera; for the Peace Jubilee in Boston in 1872, 100 city firemen beat anvils during a performance of this number.

Anything Goes. Musical by Cole Porter concerning the denizens of a transatlantic boat journey. Includes several hits, including the title song, *Blow Gabriel Blow*, *You're the Top*, and *I Get a Kick Out of You*. The show has often been revived, although rarely with its original book or song selection.

aperiodicity. Nonrecurrence of musical time, with formants distributed unpredictably.

Apocalyptic Symphony. 1. The nickname of Bruckner's Sym. No. 8 in C Minor, to point out its religious depth and expectations of eternity. Actually it is neither overly long nor too demanding of an unprejudiced listener. It was premiered in 1892; a newly edited version premiered in 1973. 2. H. Rosenberg's name for his 4th Sym., 1940.

Apollon musagète (Apollo, Leader of the Muses). Ballet with string orch. by Stravinsky, 1st performed in Washington, D.C. (1928). This work confirms Stravinsky's transition to a neoclassical style: the score is emphatically diatonic in texture, and all attempts at purely coloristic effects are abandoned.

Appalachian Spring. Ballet by Copland, with choreography by Martha Graham, 1st performed in Washington, D.C., 1944. The title is from a poem by Hart Crane; the music is only peripherally related to its text. There are 8 sections, descriptive of a wedding celebration on a farm in the Appalachian hills. As with most of his ballet scores, Copland drew an orch.l suite from it, 1st performed in N.Y., 1945.

Appassionata. The title given by Beethoven's publisher to his Piano Sonata in F Minor, op. 57. Beethoven entitled it simply "Grande Sonate pour piano." There is certainly enough passion in the work—somber and unpredictable in the 1st movement, stormy and unrestrained in the 3rd, with a lyrical 2nd in-between—to justify the nickname.

appassionatamente (It.); **appassionato, -a** (It.). Passionately, ardently.

applause

A culturally determined, seemingly instinctive reaction to an excellent artistic performance. Shouts of "Bravo!" often join the applause (from Lat. *plaudere*, to clap hands); outside Italy, "Bravo!" is shouted equally at men and women performers, although the proper grammatical form for a female artist is "Brava!"

(Kudos addressed to more than 1 performer take the form "Bravi!") In Islamic countries audiences cry out "Allah, Allah!" to commend a singer; in Spain it is "Olé, olé!"

At the opera, applause often greets the entrance of a favorite singer. When there is an orch.1 coda after a particularly successful aria, it is often drowned out by intemperate applause, as in the case of the soft instrumental conclusion to the famous tenor's aria in Leoncavallo's *Pagliacci*. A tug-of-war can ensue when the conductor makes a serious effort to proceed with the music while the singer is eager to prolong the applause. In the heyday of opera, a singer expiring at the end of an aria might have been forced to rise again and bow to the public. Cries of "Bis!" (twice, encore) can bring a repetition of the aria. It was once a common practice among opera singers, especially in the 19th century, to hire people to applaud them. The hired group was known as a CLAQUE.

A peculiar type of responsorial applause emerged in Russia toward the middle of the 20th century, when the artists themselves applauded the audience, usually in a rhythmic measure of 1 long and 2 short claps. The origin of this custom can be traced to the practice of political leaders returning the applause of an enthusiastic audience. It is interesting that whistling, an expression of passionate pleasure at a performance in England and America, is equivalent to hissing or booing in France and Russia. Shortly after the conclusion of World War II, American soldiers greeted the Russian dancers in Berlin with whistling; the performers were in tears, believing that they had been roundly dismissed. The so-called Bronx cheer, produced by sticking out the tongue between closed lips and exhaling vigorously, is the most emphatic American way of expressing displeasure at the quality of performance, short of physical violence.

In commercial musical programs on radio and television, for which timing is essential, the amount and the loudness of applause is precisely proportioned by signs passed in front of the audience; an even safer practice is "canned applause," the time and volume of which can be controlled by the studio engineers. However, unrestrained outbursts of adulation are usually preferred by highly paid popular performers.

appoggiatura (It., leaning note). 1. A dissonant note to be performed on the beat and immediately resolved. It is usually indicated by a note printed in small type before the principal note. In binary time it borrows half the value of the principal note; in ternary time it may borrow two-thirds of the principal dotted note. Its usage can be uncertain and therefore frustrating for scholars, editors, and performers.

An *accented appoggiatura* is a grace note which takes the accent and part of the time-value of the following principal note.

The *long appoggiatura* performed  is seldom written now.

The *short appoggiatura* is performed .

The *unaccented appoggiatura* is performed ,

taking its time value from the preceding principal note, to which it is smoothly bound.

2. In analysis, any note that functions like an ornamental appoggiatura but is written out fully.

April in Paris. Vernon Duke's most famous song, to words by Yip Harburg; 1st heard in the musical *Walk a Little Faster* (1932). The phrase was supposedly taken from a remark made by Dorothy Parker during a bleak and cold N.Y. December: "I wish I were in April in Paris." It is said that a N.Y. dandy, inspired by the song, went to Paris in April, found it damp and chilly, and reported his disillusion to Duke, who said, "Okay, so Paris is miserable in April. It is lovely in May, but I needed a word with 2 syllables for the rhythm."

Arab music

〜〜 〜〜 〜〜 〜〜 〜〜

The traditional music of Arab nations of the Mediterranean and Persian Gulf basins differs so greatly from the nature of Western music that transcription with any degree of fidelity into Western notation is fraught with difficulties. Arab musical meters and rhythms lack the regular quality of Western songs; its melodic structure is incommensurable with the tempered scale. Form is not divisible into even periods. The melodic range is narrow; the only development of the principal theme consists in florid melodic variations and embellishments (see ARABESQUE). The melodies themselves register to a Western-trained ear as progressions of quarter tones, semitones, and other divisions of a whole tone.

The tuning of Arab music rarely coincides with the Western system of tetrachords; major and minor tonalities are nonexistent in the Western sense of those terms. There are 12 basic modes (each called MAQĀM) in Arab music, which tend to emphasize the minor 3rd. Harmonization and polyphony in the Western sense of the word are nonexistent; the only combination of tones in Arab music results from simultaneous accompaniments on Arab instruments to a singing voice, sometimes producing a quasi-heterophonic texture.

A considerable number of medieval theoretical treatises by Arab mathematicians and philosophers have survived. Notation of Arab chants and rhythmic modes usually gives the hand positions on indigenous instruments, which have undergone practically no changes in their construction and tuning throughout the centuries. In addition to the Arab lute (ūnd), musicians typically use a variety of vertical flute (nāy), 1-string fiddle (rabāb), vase-shaped drum (darabukka), and tambourine (ṭār).

Several Russian and French composers wrote pieces purporting to be of Arabian inspiration, and their melodies invariably emphasize the melodic augmented 2nd and other intervallic progressions. Tchaikovsky included a *Danse Arabe* in his *Nutcracker*, in which the only suggestion of an exotic atmosphere is the avoidance of a perfect cadence and a continuous organ point on the tonic and dominant in a minor mode. The most famous Arabian tale in Western music is Rimsky-Korsakov's symphonic suite *Scheherazade*, inspired by the Arabian Nights; but there is no ersatz Arab modality.

Arabella. Opera by R. Strauss to a Hofmannsthal libretto, 1923; a Viennese version of a daughter's true love triumphing over a father's mercenary motives.

arabesque. A type of character piece for piano, featuring ornamental passages accompanying or varying a melody, usually in a pronounced rhythmic manner in 2/4 time. The etymological reference to Arab design reflects the Romantic infatuation with exotica, in this case nonrepresentational Islamic art. Schumann, Tchaikovsky, Debussy, and others wrote arabesques.

Arbeau, Thoinot (anagram of birth name Jehan Tabourot), French writer; b. Dijon, Mar. 17, 1520; d. Langres, July 23, 1595. He owes his fame to his *Orchésographie* (Langres, 1588; 2nd ed., 1589), a "manual in dialogue form so that everyone might learn and practice the virtuous activity of dancing." In addition to the dance instructions (based on a simple system of initial letters), it contains invaluable observations on contemporaneous dance music.

Arcana. Symphonic poem by Edgard Varèse, 1927. The title ("mysteries") is inspired by the hermetic philosophy of Paracelsus. The score uses 40 percussion instruments besides a huge orch. It was received with a critical torrent of invectives; a quarter of a century later it had become an acknowledged modern classic.

Archduke Trio. Beethoven's last piano trio, in D-flat major, op. 97 (1811), taking its name from the dedication to the composer's pupil and patron, Archduke Rudolph of Austria.

arciorgano. An organ, described by Vicentino (1561), with manuals or divided keys, designed to incorporate the diatonic, chromatic, and enharmonic GENERA of ancient Greek theory, so that modulation could occur in all keys without the necessity for temperament.

arco (It., bow). Return to the normal use of the bow; follows PIZZICATO or COL LEGNO passages.

Argento, Dominick, greatly talented American composer excelling in opera; b. York, Pa., Oct. 27, 1927. In the pantheon of American composers, Argento occupies a distinct individual category, outside any certifiable modernistic trend or technical idiom. He writes melodious music in a harmonious treatment so deliberate in intent that even his apologists profess embarrassment at its unimpeded flow; there is also a perceptible ancestral strain in the BEL CANTO style of his Italianate opera scores; most important, audiences and an increasing number of sophisticated critics profess their admiration for his unusual songfulness. Yet an analysis of Argento's productions reveals the presence of acerbic harmonies and artfully acidulated melismas.

He has long been associated with the Minnesota Opera, which he helped to found, and most of his works have premiered there. Among his many operas are *Christopher Sly*, a scene from Shakespeare's *The Taming of the Shrew* (1963); *Postcard from Morocco* (1971); *The Voyage of Edgar Allan Poe*, which achieved great critical acclaim (1976); *Miss Havisham's Fire*, after Dickens's *Great Expectations* (1979); *Casanova's Homecoming*, opera buffa (1985); and *The Aspern Papers* (1988). He has written many other vocal works.

ärgerlich (Ger.). Angrily.

arhythmic. Without rhythm; lacking a regular, sustained beat or pulse.

aria (It.; from Lat. *aer*; plural *arie*). An air, song, tune, or melody. A word, common to all European languages, signifying a manner or model of performance or composition. In 17th-century England the spelling *ayre* designated a wide variety of songs, whether serious or popular. Baroque instrumental pieces of a songful character were often called arias. The most common association of *aria* is with a solo song in opera. Specialized categories of such arias came to be used in Italian opera; several are defined below.

aria buffa (It.). A comic or burlesque aria.

aria cantabile (It.). A "songful" aria, expressing sorrow or yearning.

aria da capo (It., to the head). An aria in symmetric ternary form with the 3rd part being the exact repetition or slight variation of the 1st part (ABA, ABA[1]). This type, also called a *da capo aria*, was popularized by the composers of the Neapolitan school in the 2nd half of the 17th century. It became the most common form of the operatic aria, especially among Italian and Italianate composers of the 18th and 19th centuries. In Romantic opera this type evolved into the *grand aria* (It., *aria grande*), divided into (1) the main theme, fully developed; (2) a more tranquil and richly harmonized 2nd section; and (3) a repetition *da capo* of the 1st, with more florid ornamentation.

aria da chiesa (It.). Church aria, as opposed to a secular operatic aria.

aria da concerto (It.). An aria for concert singing.

aria d'entrata (It.). An aria sung by any operatic character upon her or his 1st entrance.

aria di bravura (It.). A rapid virtuosic song expressing violent passion through florid ornamentation.

aria parlante (It.). A "talking aria," in a declamatory manner.

Ariadne auf Naxos. Opera by R. Strauss to a libretto by Hofmannsthal. The 1st version, 1912, as the 2nd half of a bill with Molière's *Le bourgeois gentilhomme*; expanded 2nd version without the Molière play, 1916. The extremely involved story consists of 3 superimposed worlds: a nonsinging bourgeois refugee from Molière's play engages an OPERA SERIA company and a COMMEDIA DELL'ARTE troupe. A philosophical, methodological, and aesthetic imbroglio ensues in which the idealistic composer (a TROUSER ROLE) is forced to perform his opera seria simultaneously with the commedia play. The opera centers on the mythical Ariadne, abandoned on the island of Naxos, praying for death to release her; she is often interrupted by the commedia players. Bacchus arrives opportunely and takes Ariadne with him to the heavens, to the approval of the onstage spectators.

Arie (Ger.). Aria.

arietta (It.). A short aria, lacking the da capo repeat; similar to the CAVATINA found in Baroque Italian opera.

ariette (Fr.). A short aria or song; usually an insertion into French DIVERTISSEMENT rather than opera.

arioso (It., like an aria). 1. In vocal music, a style between full aria and lyric recitative; a short melodious strain interrupted by or ending in a recitative. Invented by the Florentine opera inventors, who called it *recitativo arioso*. 2. An impressive, dramatic style suitable for the *aria grande*; hence, a vocal piece in that style. 3. In instrumental music, the same as CANTABILE.

Arkansas Traveler. An American dancing song of 1847. Its composer is unknown; the attribution to Colonel Sanford D. Faulkner of Arkansas is highly dubious. *Arkansas Traveler* is also an American square dance of unknown origin that acquired popularity in the middle of the 19th century. Its syncopated design, like that of the dancing song that shares its name, presages ragtime rhythms.

Arlecchino (It.). Harlequin. In COMMEDIA DELL'ARTE, the character of a buffoon, usually wearing a mask. Arlecchino is often the lover of Colombina (Columbine).

Arlen, Harold (born Hyman Arluck), American composer of popular songs, Broadway musicals, and Hollywood film scores; b. Buffalo, Feb. 15, 1905; d. N.Y., Apr. 23, 1986. His collaborators included Ira Gershwin (the 1954 film *A Star is Born*, including *The Man That Got Away*); Johnny Mercer (the musicals *St. Louis Woman*, 1946, and *Saratoga*, 1959; several films, among them the 1944 *Here Comes the Waves*, including *Ac-cent-tchu-ate the Positive*), Truman Capote (the 1954 musical *House of Flowers*), Ted Koehler (songs for Harlem's Cotton Club revues, 1930–34, including *Get Happy, Between the Devil and the Deep Blue Sea, I Love a Parade, I Gotta Right to Sing the Blues*, and *Stormy Weather*); and his most frequent partner, E. Y. Harburg, with whom he wrote 3 musicals, several films (particularly the legendary *The Wizard of Oz*, 1939, including the revered *Over the Rainbow* sung by Judy Garland), and songs such as *Satan's Li'l Lamb, It's Only a Paper Moon*, and *Happiness Is a Thing Called Joe* (used in the film *Cabin in the Sky*, 1943).

Armatrading, Joan, West Indies–born English singer and songwriter; b. St. Kitts, Dec. 9, 1950. Her family moved to Birmingham in 1956; relocating to London in the early 1970s, she paired up with Pam Nestor, producing 2 moderately successful albums, *Whatever's for Us* (1974) and *Back to the Night* (1975); her subsequent solo album, *Joan Armatrading* (1976), was extremely well received. With the lessening interest in the singer/songwriter genre in the 1980s, Armatrading's popularity declined; she has retained a coterie of fans, however, and many of her songs, with their acoustic sound, jazz inflections, and mature, often feminist lyrics, have had lasting appeal.

Armide. Opera by Gluck, 1777, based on Tasso's *Gerusalemme liberata.* A medieval crusader is bewitched by a magic love garden and its owner; after a lengthy dalliance, he abandons her for other conquests, leaving her to destroy the garden with its memories of love. This plot is shared by Lully's *Armide et Renaud* and many other operas.

Armstrong, Louis, famous African-American jazz trumpeter, cornetist, singer, bandleader, and entertainer; b. New Orleans, *c.* 1898; d. N.Y., July 6, 1971. Armstrong was known familiarly as Satchmo, Satchelmouth, Dippermouth, and Pops. The long-held belief that he was born on July 4, 1900, now seems dubious. He grew up in Storyville, New Orleans's brothel district; as a juvenile delinquent he was placed in the Home for Colored Waifs, where he played cornet in its brass band, with its repertoire of marches, rags, and songs; after his release he learned jazz style in blues bands in local honky-tonks; played in "Kid" Ory's band (1918-19). In 1922 he went to Chicago to play in "King" Oliver's Creole Jazz Band; made his 1st recordings (1923); joined Fletcher Henderson's band in N.Y. (1924–25). Returning to Chicago, he organized his own jazz combo, the Hot 5, in 1925; made a series of now-historic recordings with it, the Hot 7, and other groups he led until 1928; from about 1926 the trumpet was his principal instrument. In 1929 he returned to N.Y.; became notably successful through appearances on Broadway, in films, and on radio; led his own big band (1935–47); organized his All Stars ensemble (1947). In succeeding years he made innumerable tours of the U.S. and abroad; became enormously successful as an entertainer; made television appearances and hit recordings, including his celebrated version of *Hello, Dolly* (1964). Although he suffered a severe heart attack in 1959, he made appearances until his death.

Armstrong was one of the greatest figures in the history of JAZZ, and one of the most popular entertainers of his time. His revolutionary "hot" style of improvisation moved jazz irrevocably away from the New Orleans style in the

1920s. His unique gravelly voiced scat-singing and song renditions became as celebrated as his trumpet virtuosity. Married 4 times, his 2nd wife was the jazz pianist and composer Lil(lian) Hardin (b. Memphis, Tenn., Feb. 3, 1898; d. while playing in a memorial concert for Armstrong, Chicago, Aug. 27, 1971), who played for both Oliver and Armstrong in Chicago; their marriage lasted from 1924 to 1938.

Arne, Thomas Augustine, famous English dramatic composer; b. London, Mar. 12, 1710; d. there, Mar. 5, 1778. He schooled at Eton; spent 3 years in a solicitor's office; at the same time studied music and acquired considerable skill on the violin. He began to write musical settings "after the Italian manner" to various plays. His most important work was *Comus* (1738); in 1740 he produced the masque *Alfred*; the finale contains the celebrated song *Rule Britannia*, which became a patriotic song of Britons everywhere. In 1737 Arne married Cecilia Young, a singer who performed with Arne's company until 1754.

In addition to nearly 100 dramatic works, he contributed separate numbers to 28 theatrical productions and composed 2 oratorios, many secular vocal pieces, and miscellaneous instrumental music. His sister was the celebrated actress Mrs. Cibber; his natural son, Michael (b. *c.* 1740; d. Lambeth, Jan. 14, 1786), wrote dramatic works and songs.

Arnold, Malcolm, prolific and versatile English composer; b. Northampton, Oct. 21, 1921. He studied trumpet, conducting, and composition at the Royal College of Music, London (1938–40); played 1st trumpet with the London Phil. (1941–42; 1946–48); then devoted himself chiefly to composition, developing a melodious and harmonious style of writing that possessed the quality of immediate appeal to the general public while avoiding obvious banality; many of his works reveal modalities common to English folk songs, often invested in acridly pleasing harmonies. His experience as a trumpeter and conductor of popular concerts provided a secure feeling for propulsive rhythms and brilliant sonorities. He had a knack for composing effective background music for films. In 1970 Arnold was made a Commander of the Order of the British Empire.

arpa (It.). 1. Harp. 2. Play arpeggio.

arpeggiando; arpeggiato (It., playing like a harp). Sounding a chord's notes in steady succession; playing broken chords.

arpeggio (It., play like a harp; plural, *arpeggi*). 1. Play the notes of a chord in steady succession; playing broken chords. Usually played from lowest to highest note. 2. A chord so played; a broken or spread chord, or chord passage.

arpeggione. A string instrument about the size of a cello, having 6 strings and a guitarlike shape. Invented by Johann Georg Staufer of Vienna in 1824, its vogue was of a short duration; Schubert wrote a sonata for it, now usually played on cello.

Louis Armstrong, c. 1960s

COURTESY FRANK DRIGGS COLLECTION

arrangement

~~ ~~ ~~ ~~ ~~

The adaptation, transcription, or reduction of a composition for performance on an instrument, or by any vocal or instrumental combination, for which it was not originally written. Also, any composition so adapted or arranged.

Reductions of classical symphonies for piano 4-hands that proliferated in the 19th century made it possible for amateurs to become acquainted with sym. literature when mechanical recordings did not exist. Piano albums published under such ingratiating titles as *Brother and Sister* made it possible to acquaint pianistic youth with popular arias of the operatic repertoire as well. Professional composers were called upon to make such arrangements, and they did not regard it as beneath their dignity to do so.

With the advent of the phonograph this practice declined; composers wrote 4-hand music primarily for their own purposes. Stravinsky arranged *Le Sacre du Printemps* for his own convenience; Grieg arranged Mozart piano sonatas for 2 pianos, while remaining faithful to the originals. Debussy and Ravel wrote 4-hand works for children. Rimsky-Korsakov arranged music by Mussorgsky, Borodin, and many other composers, popularizing many works while introducing bowdlerized elements. Ravel was probably the most active composer/arranger of his own piano music, including *Rapsodie Espagnole, Ma Mère L'Oye, Le Tombeau de Couperin*, and *Valses Nobles et Sentimentales*. When Rachmaninoff played his Piano Concerto No. 2 in Los Angeles, a lady rushed to him after the show, exclaiming, "Beautiful! Who is your arranger?" "Madam," Rachmaninoff replied, "in Russia, we composers were so poor we had to write our own music." Busoni's famous version for piano solo of Bach's *Chaconne* has become an independent virtuoso piece; Brahms arranged the Bach for piano left-hand.

A special form of reduction was the so-called theater arrangement, adaptations of symphonic works for small amateur productions. Theater arrangements usually contained indications for optional substitutions of one instrument by another, with the piano part filling in the harmonic vacuum. This practice is comparable to the Baroque's interchangeable scoring.

Musical literature abounds with melodic theft, but publishers must be careful not to infringe on the copyright protection of popular pieces. An American publisher issued a song called *Avalon*, based on Cavaradossi's aria from *Tosca*; as the Puccini was protected, the publ. was obliged to pay a heavy fine. On the other hand, nothing could be done to the perpetrators of the song *I'm Forever Chasing Rainbows*, based on the middle section of Chopin's posthumous *Fantaisie-Impromptu*, because the original was not protected. For the same reason, Mozart was not spared the depredation of his C-major Piano Sonata (K. 545) in a song entitled *In an 18th-Century Drawing Room*, nor could Tchaikovsky stop the transmogrification of his Piano Concerto No. 1 into *Tonight We Love*. Rachmaninoff, on the other hand, enjoyed the *Russian Rag* based on his celebrated C-sharp minor Prelude (No. 2, op. 3).

The terminology surrounding arrangements is imprecise; works labeled transcriptions tend to be grander and freer, approaching a fantasy. Paraphrases may be said to be even freer, more inspired by than translating their models, such as Liszt's many lied and operatic paraphrases.

Arrau, Claudio, eminent Chilean-born American pianist; b. Chillan, Feb. 6, 1903; d. Murzzuschlag, Austria, June 9, 1991. He received his early training from his mother; as a child, played publicly in Santiago. In 1910 he was sent to Berlin, and he gave piano recitals in Germany and Scandinavia (1914–15), attracting attention by his precocious talent. In 1921 he returned to Chile; in 1924 he made his 1st American tour as a concerto soloist, and he was appointed to the faculty of the Stern Cons., Berlin. In the period 1928–40 he toured Russia several times and performed in Europe, Latin America, and the U.S. In 1941 he settled permanently in N.Y. and continued performing, teaching, and touring. From 1962 to 1969 he recorded the complete Beethoven sonatas; supervised an urtext ed. of those works. In 1978 he gave up his Chilean citizenship in protest against the Pinochet regime, becoming a naturalized

U.S. citizen in 1979; nevertheless remained a revered figure in Chile; awarded the Chilean National Arts Prize (1983); toured Chile in 1984, after an absence of 17 years. In his playing, Arrau combined a Classical purity and precision of style with a rhapsodic éclat.

ars antiqua (Lat., old art). A designation applied by historians to polyphonic musical developments of the 12th and early 13th centuries. *Ars antiqua* had its inception in France; its great early representatives were the masters of the Notre Dame or Paris school. Leoninus was called *optimus organista*, "best composer of the ORGANUM," polyphonic music with a slow moving CANTUS FIRMUS in the lower voice and a florid melismatic upper voice with chantlike rhythm. The younger Perotinus was described as *optimus discantor*, "best composer of DISCANT," a style that used more durationally similar lower and upper voices, producing a somewhat note-against-note effect, and that used modal rhythms; an intermediate system between organum and discant was COPULA, although the term seems to refer to text rather than musical structure. The organa eventually engendered the CLAUSULA, a short piece à 2 serving as flexible interludes within the organa. When a liturgical text in Latin was added to the upper voice of the clausula, it evolved into the motet; when this process was applied to secular music, the seemingly chaotic practice emerged of appending different texts, in French as well as Latin, to the upper voices; the cantus firmus voice became an instrumental part. It was a striking departure from earlier polyphonic forms, but it proved the most fertile development in medieval music. The cantus firmus retained its dominant role in all musical forms during the ars antiqua, with the exception of the freely composed CONDUCTUS.

The metrical system of ars antiqua is confined almost exclusively to ternary groupings in the TEMPUS PERFECTUM. Binary meters were used in the TEMPUS IMPERFECTUM, more incomplete than imperfect. This preference had a theological significance for medieval theorists, to whom triple time symbolized the perfection of the Holy Trinity. The theoretical doctrine of ars antiqua was best expressed by Franco of Cologne, active in the 13th century, in his treatise ARS CANTUS MENSURABILIS, in which he codified the rhythmic modes of ars antiqua, indicating the relative note values of mensural notation.

ars musica. The art of music. In medieval universities, music was regarded as one of the *septem artes* (7 liberal arts), taught like most subjects in the Latin language. It was a part of the *quadrivium*-arithmetica, geometria, musica, and astronomia. The remaining *trivium* of the *septem artes* included *grammatica*, *rhetorica*, and *dicilectica*. In medieval Latin, *ars* fell in between the more elevated concept of *scientia* (science), and above the more common category of *usus* (use). When Guido d'Arezzo taught singers with the aid of the GUIDONIAN HAND in the 11th century, he was following the precepts of practical *usus*. When he introduced *neumes*, 1st without lines (*neumae usuales*) and later with lines (*neumae regulares*, from *regula*, line), he elevated the ars musica to the point of *scientia canendi*, the science of singing. This innovation marked the beginning of musical notation, which received its culmination in the treatise *Ars nova*, compiled *c.* 1320 by Philippe de Vitry and subtitled *Ars nova notandi* (The New Art of Notating Music). As this "scientific" aspect of music began developing further in medieval universities, it was subdivided into branches, such as *ars cantus plani*, the art of plainchant, and *ars componendi*, the art of composing. Bach subtitled his *Musikalisches Opfer* "*ars canonica*," the art of writing canons.

ars nova (Lat., new art). The period of 14th-century music that contrasted with the ARS ANTIQUA by its more complex and controlled counterpoint and by a return to lighter textures, even monophony, in secular music. The name stems from the eponymous treatise of Philippe de Vitry, compiled *c.* 1320, and from a work by Johannes de Muris, *Ars novae musicae*, dating from 1321. Actually, the new art originally had more modest aspirations, as its subtitle suggests: to serve as a new method of notating music (*Ars nova notandi*). By themselves the 2 theorists' innovations were historically important: the extension of mensural notation to include small note values, down to the SEMIMINIMA; the formal acceptance of the binary division of the measure, as contrasted with the previous designation of ternary division as the sole *tempus perfectum*. The composers of ars nova, on the other hand, went even further; they dismissed music in ternary division as ars antiqua, old-fashioned and, by implication, inferior art.

Besides raising *tempus imperfectum* to equal status with the *tempus perfectum*, the ars nova introduced other innovations. Of these the most significant was the acceptance of 3rds and 6ths as consonances and the resulting toleration of FABURDEN and FAUXBOURDON, the use of 6th chords as concords in parallel motion. These "novelties" aroused opposition by adherents of *ars antiqua*; thus Jacques de Liège, in his treatise *Speculum musicae* (Mirror of Music, early 14th century) declares ruefully, "Regnat nova ars, exulat antiqua" (New art reigns, old art is exiled), and then proceeds to excoriate the "unnatural" novelties of the modernists.

The most important representatives of the ars nova were Machaut and Landini. The great accomplishment of Machaut was his skillful use of the rhythms and melos of popular dances and song forms, including ballades, rondeaux, and virelais. The fluid, direct works of Landini were notated in a manner strikingly close to modern notation (but with no subsequent influence); he is known for the LANDINI CADENCE which, however, he did not invent. Ciconia, a Flemish composer who was active in Italy at the end of the 14th century, helped reverse the trend of ars nova toward further simplification and engaged in the exploration of a new polyphony. In this sense he was a forerunner of the great Netherlandish contrapuntal school that reached its height in the Renaissance. Ars nova, which began as a movement of simplification, transformed into a harbinger of new complexity, which in turn reached the saturation point and precipitated another simplification, that of the Florentine school of *c.* 1600.

To modern ears the music of the ars antiqua, with its quartal harmonies, sounds more progressive than the ars nova, with its peculiar fauxbourdon. In rhythmic patterns, too, ars antiqua cultivates the more "modern" syncopated iambic prosody (short-long), whereas ars nova uses the more "natural" trochaic rhythmic figure (long-short).

Art of the Fugue, The (Ger. *Die Kunst der Fuge*). The last great work of Johann Sebastian Bach, which remained unfinished. It was ed. and publ. by Bach's son Wilhelm Friedemann, who inscribed these words after the last fugue, based on Bach's own name, B–A–C–H: "During the composition of this fugue the author died"; he gave the work its title, not the composer. Bach's original was set simply as a collection of *contrapuncti*-canonic and fugal examples all based on the same subject in D minor. It seems more a manual of contrapuntal composition than a work for performance; but inevitably the work has become the plaything of experimenters, theorists, and scholars who have tried to read Bach's mind and decide for him in what form his contrapuncti should be understood.

articulation. By analogy to speech, the manner in which notes are joined one to another by the performer; a principal component of phrasing. Specifically, the art of clear enunciation in singing and precise rhythmic accentuation in instrumental playing.

artificial harmonics. Harmonics produced on a stopped string rather than on an open string (as on the vio-

lin). Two fingers of the left hand are required to perform these notes: the finger nearer the neck presses the string (establishing the fundamental), and the finger nearer the bridge lightly touches the string to produce the harmonic relative to the fundamental; e.g., a perfect 4th above the stopped fundamental produces a note 2 octaves higher than that fundamental.

As (Ger.). A-flat (A♭).

As Time Goes By. A song by Herman Hupfeld written in 1931 for the musical *Everybody's Welcome*. Its popularity was boosted when it was used in the 1942 movie *Casablanca*.

L'Ascension. Orch.l suite by Messiaen, subtitled *4 Méditations symphoniques*, 1935.

Ashkenazy, Vladimir (Davidovich), greatly gifted Russian pianist and conductor; b. Gorki, July 6, 1937. His parents were professional pianists who taught him at an early age; subsequently took lessons at the Central Music School and the Moscow Cons.; won 2nd prize at the International Chopin Competition, Warsaw, in 1955. A turning point in his career occurred when, in 1956, he won 1st prize in the Queen Elisabeth of Belgium International Competition, Brussels; made his 1st U.S. tour in 1958; in 1962 he and John Ogdon shared 1st prizes in the Tchaikovsky International Competition, Moscow. In 1961 he married a young Icelandic pianist, Sofia Johannsdottir; they moved to England, retaining their Soviet citizenship (1963); moved to Reykjavík (1968); Ashkenazy became a citizen of Iceland (1972). He has also served as a conductor for various orchs. As a piano virtuoso he has gained an international reputation for his penetrating insight and superlative technique; his mastery extends from Haydn to early 20th-century composers; known for his superb performances of the Rachmaninoff concertos; has stated a general antipathy toward avant-garde music. As a conductor he has demonstrated an affinity for the 19th- and 20th-century repertoire; prepared and conducted his own effective orchestration of Mussorgsky's *Pictures at an Exhibition.*

Ashley, Robert (Reynolds), avant-garde American composer; b. Ann Arbor, Mich., Mar. 28, 1930. He was active with Milton Cohen's Space Theater (1957–64), the ONCE Festival and ONCE Group (1958–69), and the Sonic Arts Union (1966-76), touring with them in the U.S. and Europe; directed the Center for Contemporary Music at

Mills College in Oakland, Calif. (1969–81). In his independent compositions he pursues the ideal of "total musical events," absorbing gesticulation, natural human noises, and the entire planetary environment; known particularly for his highly original video operas, including *Music with Roots in the Aether* (1976), *Perfect Lives (Private Parts)* (1977–83), *Atalanta (Acts of God)* (1982), and *Improvement.*

aspramente (It.). Sternly, even cruelly (Verdi, *Otello*).

assai (It.). Very.

assez doux (mais d'une sonorité large) (Fr.). Rather soft, but with ample sonority (Ravel, *Pavane pour une infante défunte*).

Astaire, Fred (born Frederick Austerlitz), charismatic American dancer, choreographer, singer, and actor; b. Omaha, May 10, 1899; d. Los Angeles, June 22, 1987. With his sister Adele (b. Omaha, Sept. 10, 1897; d. Phoenix, Jan. 25, 1981) he appeared in dance and comedy routines from the age of 7; they worked on the vaudeville circuit, then starred in revues and musicals. Following his sister's retirement he went to Hollywood; teamed up with the dancer Ginger Rogers and gained renown through such films as *The Gay Divorcée* (1934), *Roberta* (1935), *Top Hat* (1935), *Swing Time* (1936), and *Shall We Dance* (1937). His mastery of the dance, ably abetted by an insouciant singing style, contributed greatly to the development of the musical film, earning him a special Academy Award in 1949.

asymmetry. A departure from the customary binary or ternary rhythm. Asymmetry is common outside of Western European and related music. Compound meters are intrinsically asymmetric, as are the subdivisions of binary and ternary meters into unequal groups. Such subdivisions are typical of Serbian, Croatian, Bulgarian, Macedonian, and Rumanian folk music. The ethnomusicologist Bartók used such meters, derived from the multiethnic folkways of his native Transylvania, in his own music. In modern primitivist music, asymmetry is artificially imposed; a clear illustration is provided by Stravinsky's *L'Histoire du soldat*, in which an asymmetrical melodic line is projected upon a steady bass, creating a constant arhythmia and suggesting a missed heartbeat. The opponent situation, where an easily apprehended melody is deliberately thrown out of symmetry by the addition or elision of a rhythmic unit while the

accompanying figure continues its preordained course, is also possible.

Atempause (Ger., pause in breath). A slight break to catch breath before a strong beat.

athematic. Without theme; lacking a discernible subject or melody.

athematic composition. A deliberate effort to separate the melodic line into segregated groups of phrases and motives bearing no relation to one another. Athematic music does not adhere to any formal organization; such music can therefore start and end at any point. Stockhausen (*Klavierstück XI*), Haubenstock-Ramati, and others organize some works in segments (MOBILE FORM) playable in any order whatsoever, with the stipulation that when a performer, accidentally or intentionally, arrives at an already-performed segment, the piece ends. Athematic composition tends toward atonality, where the nonrepetitive principle of melodic material is paramount. An athematic work need not be incoherent or inchoate; successive melodic statements may be related by a preferential use of a certain interval or rhythmic configuration. In this sense it may be said that an athematic composition has either zero or an indefinitely large number of themes.

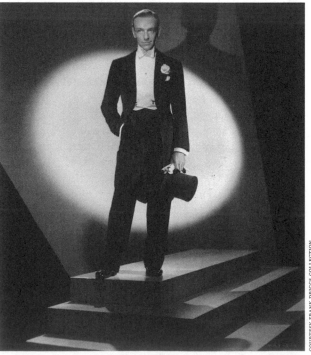

Fred Astaire, c. 1933

At(h)emlos (Ger.). Breathlessly.

A-Tisket, A-Tasket. Ironic nursery rhyme by Ella Fitzgerald and Al Feldman, 1938.

Atkins, Chet (Chester Burton), American country guitarist and producer; b. Luttrell, Tenn., June 20, 1924. He began playing the guitar as a child, mastering it without formal instruction; from 1941 he appeared on radio, including the *Grand Ole Opry*, Nashville; in 1957 he became an executive for RCA Victor, managing its recording studio in Nashville; became a leader in the movement toward popular country-western music (Nashville sound), using electric instruments and modern techniques. A versatile guitarist, he felt at ease in many popular genres; played jazz and toured Europe, the Far East, and Africa. He was elected to the Country Music Hall of Fame in 1973.

Atlantide, L'. Lyric opera by Tomasi, 1954, centered on the queen of Atlantis (played by a dancer).

atonality

The absence of tonality, avoiding the historic relationships between members of major and minor scales; traditional tonal structures are abandoned and the key signature is absent. The technique of atonal writing derives from the chromatic scale but resolutely shuns the use of consecutive semitones; Rimsky-Korsakov's *Flight of the Bumblebee* is not an example of atonality. The term *atonality* became current among progressive musicians in Vienna at the turn of the century. Schoenberg is generally credited (or blamed) for the invention of atonal composition, but he expressly denied this honor (or dishonor). But his posttonal music avoided triadic constructions and harmonic relationships, letting the melody flow freely, unconstrained by the rigid laws of modulation, cadence, sequence, and other time-honored devices of tonal writing. It was not until 1924 that he reached the theoretical apogee of his compositional approach, the 12-tone technique (DODE-CAPHONY), in which all semitones (and melodies) are related to each other without reference to a tonal center or epicenter.

Atonal composers avoid the repetition of a particular tone to avoid any implication of a tonic. Atonal melodies cultivate wide intervallic leaps, avoiding the monotony of consecutive small intervals. Although individual phrases in atonal music are usually short, the cumulative melodic curve appears long and sustained. Moreover, there is a singular sense of equilibrium inherent in a good atonal melody, in which the incidence of high notes is balanced by a countervailing group of low notes, with the solid central range representing a majority of essential notes. Such melodies invite dissonant harmonization; the overwhelming desire to obviate the tonic-dominant relationship in atonality requires the replacement of the perfect 5th by the tritone and of the octave by a major 7th; it is noteworthy that the tritone divides the octave in half and is in a sense neutral. Tertian melodies and harmonies—affiliated with triadic structures—gave way to quartal and quintal progressions; melodic 4ths became a hallmark of atonal writing, potentially evolving into a chord comprising 12 perfect 4ths.

At 1st the musical notation of atonal music bristled with double sharps and double flats. The use of accidentals has been functionally simplified; double sharps, double flats, and tonal symbols like E-sharp, B-sharp, F-flat, and C-flat were replaced by their enharmonic equivalents. Other systems of atonal notation have been proposed in which accidentals are replaced by special symbols or eliminated altogether. Hauer suggested a multilineal staff. Jefim Golvscheff, a Russian composer and painter, notated sharps with a cross inside a white circle and designated note values by stems; a similar notation was adopted by the Russian composer Nicolas Obouhov, which he called "absolute harmony."

Schoenberg and Berg deprecated the use of the term *atonality*. Berg concluded a 1930 radio talk on the subject with these words: "Antichrist himself could not have thought up a more diabolical appellation than atonal!" A negative concept etymologically, the term was 1st applied by hostile critics as a derisive description of this new style, but a perjorative term became the accepted one.

attacca (It., attack). 1. Begin what follows without pause or with a very short pause. 2. In singing, a stroke of the glottis.

attack. The act (or style) of beginning a phrase, passage, or piece.

Attila. An opera by Verdi, 1846. The libretto draws its subject from the final struggle of Rome against the invading hordes of Attila and his Huns. Contemporaneous audiences found a parallel with the subjugation of Italy by Austria in the middle of the 19th century, contributing to the opera's temporary success.

atto (It.). Act in an opera.

au mouvement (Fr.). A TEMPO.

aubade (from Fr. *aube*, dawn). Morning music, as contrasted with SERENADE, evening music. Aubades were popular in the 17th and 18th centuries, when they were played by military and municipal ensembles on special occasions. The aubade corresponds to the Spanish *alborada*. Several 20th-century composers have written aubades as a sophisticated or nostalgic evocation of the past. See also ALBA.

Auber, Daniel-François-Esprit, prolific French composer of comic operas; b. Caen, Normandy, Jan. 29, 1782; d. Paris, May 12, 1871. His father, a Parisian art dealer, sent him to London to acquire knowledge of the field; Auber studied music and wrote songs for social entertainment there. Political tension between France and England forced his return to Paris (1803); he devoted himself exclusively to music. His pasticcio *L'Erreur d'un moment* was produced by an amateur group (1806); his next theatrical work, *Julie*, was performed privately (1811). Auber's 1st opera to be given a public Parisian performance was *Le Séjour militaire* (1813); *La Bergère châtelaine* (1820) was his 1st success. From then on hardly a year elapsed without the production of a new Auber opera; 45 operas were staged professionally in Paris between 1813 and 1869. He was fortunate in his collaboration with the best French librettist of the time, Scribe, who wrote (alone or with others) no fewer than 37 librettos for him. Auber's greatest success was *Masaniello, ou La Muette de Portici* (1828); historically it laid the foundation of French grand opera along with Meyerbeer's *Robert le diable* and Rossini's *Guillaume Tell*. Its vivid portrayal of nationalist fury stirred French and Belgian audiences; anti-Dutch riots followed its performance in Brussels (1830). Another popular success was *Fra Diavolo* (1830), which became a repertory standard.

Despite his successes with grand opera, Auber is best seen as a founder of later French *opéra comique*, a worthy successor to Boïeldieu and at least an equal of Adam and Hérold; Rossini and Wagner valued his music. He lived most of his life in Paris, even during the Franco-Prussian War and the German siege; he died during the days of the Paris Commune. Among his other operas are *Le Cheval de bronze* (1835); *Le Domino noir* (1837); and *Manon Lescaut* (1856).

Aucassin et Nicolette. A French CHANSON DE GESTE of the 13th century, illustrating the tale of a young Provençal prince who falls in love with a slave girl captured by the Saracens. The lovers are united after many vicissitudes when Nicolette is revealed to be of noble blood. Several modern composers have used this subject to evoke the medieval period.

audiences

As classical music's tendency toward formalization has limited audience participation to communal church singing, folk festivals, or GEBRAUCHSMUSIK, the primary role for the audience is its reception of works and performances. The response of an audience to a new work or to an artist's debut is of crucial significance to public success. Yet there are numerous cases in which the 1st performance of a famous work was a fiasco: THE BARBER OF SEVILLE, TOSCA, PELLÉAS ET MÉLISANDE, and TANNHÄUSER. On the other hand, rapturous applause has greeted many an artistic failure.

The reaction of music critics has been even less indicative of final judgment than that of the audience. Generally speaking, audiences in England, America, and Germany are restrained in their vocal expression of disapproval; in France, audience reaction, particularly to opera, is more pronounced; most exuberant and uninhibited of all are the audiences of Italy. Because Italian operagoers often know the music as well as, or better than, the singers themselves, they often shout encouragement or condemnation. When a tenor sang flat at a Naples performance, a listener pointed his index finger upward and shouted: "Su! Su!" (higher, higher). When in a scene of romantic discovery the weighty leader of brigands warned his followers not to attack the demure lady of the castle whom he recognized as his half-sister by saying, "Desist! On the same milk were we nurtured!" a member of the audience shouted, "You bastard! You must have lapped up all the cream!" In an inverted situation, when the male singer was slight and the prima donna ample, the scenario required him to carry her off the stage; someone in the audience suggested, "Make it in 2 trips!" At a futurist concert in Paris in 1913, several people actually mounted the stage and attacked the performers physically. The futurists, however, fought back; a dozen members of the audience had to be hospitalized.

Enthusiasm for popular pianists, violinists, and (especially) singers often carried the audience away to extremes. At the height of the golden age of opera, admirers were known to unharness the carriage of a prima donna and pull her and it to her home or hotel. In the 1890s young girls with scissors invaded the stage after a Paderewski concert, intent on cutting off a lock of his flowing hair. The adulation for serious artists in Russia was extraordinary both before and after the Revolution. Music lovers used to stand in line all night to get a ticket for a recital by Chaliapin, and were known as Chaliapinists. One crooked entrepreneur in Leningrad collected a considerable number of rubles in the 1920s by selling tickets for a phantom piano recital by Josef Hofmann. Russian audiences, insatiable in demands for encores, sometimes refuse to leave the hall until the lights are turned off.

None of these revelations of enthusiasm can approach the frenzy of rock concert fans, who have been known to abandon themselves to orgies of animal delight. Other groups of fans have been known to follow their favorite band literally, such as the Deadheads who traveled with their beloved Grateful Dead until its demise. While symphonic, operatic, and recital audiences are limited by the size of the hall, rock festivals have been taking place in the open air since the 1960s, most notably the 1969 Woodstock festival in N.Y. State, attended by half a million people.

audition. A performance test given to an aspiring actor, singer, instrumentalist, or sym. conductor, preliminary to the offer of a place in a cons. or contract. In the professional world, the fate of a trembling (or arrogant) hopeful usually lies in the hands of an all-powerful manager, casting director, or talent scout. At its worst, a theatrical or film audition depends on the applicant's willingness to share the "casting couch" with their interrogator. In more "humane" classical auditions, a jury of professional musicians, usually consisting of retired concert players or obsolete opera singers, is engaged to sit in judgment. The greatest nightmare for an auditioning performer is to be suddenly interrupted while playing by a jury member who exercises his or her temporary power with a curt "thank you," 1st flashing a glance at jury colleagues for anticipated approbation of the verdict. It is comforting to realize that the annals of the opera and concert hall are full of stories about budding celebrities ignominiously cast aside, only to rise to the heights as critically acclaimed artists and commercially successful stars.

auf (Ger.). On. *Sordinen auf*, put mutes on.

Aufführung (Ger.). Performance.

aufgeregt (Ger.). Agitated, excited.

aufhalten (Ger.). Stop, retard.

Aufstieg und Fall der Stadt Mahagonny (The Rise and Fall of the City of Mahagonny). Opera by Weill to Brecht's libretto, 1930. Four workers contend with a Miami-like city in which justice is meted out according to an extreme capitalistic creed, with murder and rape punished lightly and crimes against property penalized by execution. The score includes the pidgin English lament *Alabama Song*. The 1st production was accompanied by shouts from the audience, "Es stinkt!" and "Schweinerei!"

Auftakt (Ger.). Upbeat, ANACRUSIS; a fractional measure beginning a movement, piece, or theme.

Auftritt (Ger.). A scene of an opera.

Aufzug (Ger.). An act of an opera.

Augenmusik. EYE MUSIC.

augmentation. Doubling (or otherwise multiplying) the duration of the notes of a theme or motive; the subject is thereby presented at half speed. This simple arithmetical device looms large in contrapuntal and fugal writing; in Bach's fugues, augmentation is employed with a didactic purpose to illustrate resources of tonal counterpoint. In his C-minor fugue in book II of *The Well-Tempered Clavier*, Bach combines the original theme with itself at half the speed. Augmentation lends itself naturally to the expression of Gothic grandiloquence, particularly in the concluding section of a work; Reger and Bruckner produced fine effects of this type. In organ works, augmentation can be used impressively in the bass register of the pedals. A rather unusual type of augmentation occurs in the coda of the 1st movement of Debussy's *La Mer*, where the pervading whole-tone harmonies secure a needed euphony. The reciprocal (opposite) device is called DIMINUTION.

augmented fourth. The interval an enharmonic semitone larger than the perfect 4th, as from C to F-sharp (not G-flat).

augmented second. An interval an enharmonic semitone larger than a major 2nd. It is found between the 6th and 7th degrees of the harmonic minor scale, such as F and G-sharp in the a-minor scale. It is characteristic of Eastern melodies.

augmented sixth. An interval an enharmonic semitone larger than a major 6th, as from C to A-sharp (not B-flat). It is the framing interval of the so-called FRENCH 6TH, GERMAN 6TH, and ITALIAN 6TH chords.

augmented triad. A triad consisting of 2 major 3rds, as in C, E, G-sharp.

Auld Lang Syne (Scot., old long since). A famous valedictory song with words by the Scottish poet Robert Burns. The melody, of unknown origin, underwent many changes until it assumed its present form.

aulos (Grk., reed, pipe). An ancient Greek wind instrument presaging the oboe. It usually had 2 connected pipes branching out in the shape of the letter *V*, blown simultaneously through a bulbous mouthpiece holding a single, sometimes double reed. The aulos could be made of reed, wood, ivory, or bone; both pipes had an equal number of symmetrically placed holes. While fingers of both hands could play either pipe, it seems possible that one of the pipes functioned as a drone. The aulos is associated with the corybantic dances of Dionysian worship, as opposed to the Apollonian music on the KITHARA.

Auric, Georges, notable French composer; b. Lodève, Hérault, Feb. 15, 1899; d. Paris, July 23, 1983. He studied music at the Montpellier Cons.; went to Paris; studied at the Cons. and at the Schola Cantorum. By age 20 he had composed around 300 songs and piano pieces, a ballet, and a comic opera. In the aftermath of continental disillusion following World War I, he joined the anti-Romantic movement in France, led by the apostles of this disenchanted age, Satie and Cocteau; Satie urged young composers to produce "auditory pleasure without demanding disproportionate attention from the listener," while Cocteau elevated artistic ugliness to an aesthetic ideal. Under Satie's aegis, Auric joined 5 composers of his generation in a group 1st described as Les Nouveaux Jeunes, later LES SIX (the others were Milhaud, Honegger, Poulenc, Durey, and Tailleferre). He established a connection with Diaghilev, who commissioned him to write ballets for his Ballets Russes; Auric's facile yet felicitous manner of composing, with mock-Romantic connotations, fit perfectly into Diaghilev's scheme; particularly successful were LES FACHEUX (1924) and LES MATELOTS (1925). He wrote music for numerous films, among them *Le Sang d'un poète* (1930), *A nous la liberté* (1932), *La Belle et la Bête* (1946), *Orphée* (1949), and *Lola Montes* (1955). His theatrical experience earned him important administrative posts; acted as general administrator of both the Paris Opéra and the Opéra-Comique (1962–68); served as president of the French Union of Composers and Authors (1954–77); elected to the Academie (1962).

Aus Italien. An early symphonic fantasy by R. Strauss, 1887. The score contains the tune of *Funiculì, Funiculà,* which Strauss believed to be a Neapolitan folk song; it was actually the composition of one Luigi Denza.

Ausdruck, mit (Ger.). With expression.

Ausdruck, mit innigem (Ger.). With heartfelt expression.

Ausdrucklos (Ger.). Without expression (Berg, *Wozzeck*).

Ausgabe (Ger.). Edition. *Ausgabe, neue,* new edition. *Ausgabe, revidierte,* revised edition.

Auszierungen (Ger.). Ornaments, ornamentations.

Auszug (Ger.). Arrangement or reduction, as in KLAVIERAUSZUG, a piano reduction from a full score.

authentic mode. One in which the lower tonic or final is the lowest note of the mode; in a PLAGAL MODE the lowest note is the dominant a perfect 4th below the final. In Gregorian chant the 4 most frequently used modes are the Dorian , Phrygian, Lydian, and Mixolydian, with finals D, E, F, and G, respectively. The 1-octave gamut of authentic modes ranges from the lower tonic (final) to upper tonic (D to D, E to E, etc.). These modes use the equivalent of the piano's white keys, although contrapuntal rules demand flexibility between B and B♭. In early church singing and theory the modes were called Protus, Deuterus, Tritus, and Tetradus; later a system of tonoi (modes) emerged, numbering authentic modes with odd numbers (1, 3, 5, 7) and plagal modes with even numbers. In the 16th century Glarean (Dodecachordon) added 4 more modes to reflect late Renaissance practice; the authentic modes were Aeolian (A to A) and Ionian (C to C).

autoharp. A 19th-century zither invented by Charles Zimmerman, with devices for playing preset chords; used to demonstrate harmonic progressions and to accompany

Bryan Bowers, autoharp player

PHOTOGRAPH BY JENNIFER GIRARD, COURTESY FLYING FISH RECORDS

simple songs. The instrument has special harmony buttons that dampen all strings except the ones needed for the desired chord, so that the player can strum arpeggios freely with the fingers or a plectrum. The autoharp was also used in U.S. Appalachian traditional music.

automatic composition. The creative generation of sounds by computer or other technological device capable of either random processes or responses to a set of instructions. The 1st such work was the *ILLIAC Suite* for String Quartet (1955–56), a score generated by a computer at the Univ. of Illinois under the supervision of Lejaren Hiller. As digital synthesis has grown in sophistication, interactivity between performer (or audience) and machine has received the most attention.

automatic writing. A means of communication from beyond the grave, as employed by spiritualists. A British housewife, Rosemary Brown, appeared on television in the summer of 1969 and claimed that her diluted imitations of works by Schubert and Liszt were dictated to her by them, and that she wrote them down automatically. Her claims were never subjected to controlled examination, but if substantiated they would prove that a prolonged state of death fatally affects the ability to compose even among celebrated musicians.

authentic cadence. A cadence in which the penultimate chord is the dominant, followed by the final tonic.

authentic modes. In Gregorian chant, the 4 modes whose gamuts range from the lower tonic (final) to the upper tonic: DORIAN, PHRYGIAN, LYDIAN, and MIXOLYDIAN. The complements of the authentic modes are the PLAGAL MODES, whose gamuts range from the lower dominant, a 4th below the tonic final, to the upper dominant; the prefix *hypo,* as in Hypodorian, indicates that it lies "below" the corresponding authentic mode.

In the early practice of church singing and music theory, authentic modes were named by Latinized quasi-Greek ordinal numbers: Protus, Deuterus, Tritus, and Tetrardus. Later, authentic and plagal modes were incorporated into a system that became standard. The 4 authentic and 4 plagal modes were originally called *tonoi*, with the old terminology translated into accurate Latin: *Primus tonus, Secundus tonus*, etc., corresponding to *Protus authentic, Protus plagal*, etc. In the 16th century Glareanus recognized 4 more modes— AEOLIAN, Hypoaeolian, IONIAN, and Hypoionian—for a total of 12 church modes.

auxiliary note. A nonharmonic melodic note approached by step in one direction and left by step in the opposite direction; NEIGHBOR NOTE.

avant-garde (Fr. *vanguard*, in advance). A term, dating from 1910, referring to radical or incomprehensible art as viewed in its own time; generally, yesterday's avant-garde becomes today's commonplace. The term *avant-garde* is the heir to a long series of terms descriptive of progressive art: *modern, ultra-modern, new, modernistic, experimental, empiric*. Its unfortunate derivation from military vocabulary does not seem to dismay progressive composers, who accept the term as an honorable profession of artistic faith. At present the term usually denotes the musical ideas and practices of Europeans such as Boulez, Stockhausen, or Berio, as distinct from those of the American experimental school or tradition, e.g., Cage, Feldman, or Wolff. See EXPERIMENTAL MUSIC.

Ave Maria. One of the most celebrated religious songs, adapted by Gounod to the C-major prelude of Bach's *Well-Tempered Clavier*, book I. Its original version (1853) was an instrumental *Méditation*; the texted version was publ. in 1859.

avec (Fr.). With: *emphase, energie, sécheresse*. Some of the most imaginative directions beginning with this word are found in the works of Scriabin.

avec abandon (Fr., with abandon). Emotionally; passionately; carried away by feeling.

avec âme (Fr.). CON ANIMA.

avec charme (Fr., with charm). Gracefully.

avec élan (Fr.). Dashingly; CON ISLANCIO.

avec emphase (Fr.). With emphasis.

avec énergie (Fr.). With energy, energetically; accent vigorously and phrase distinctly.

avec le chant (Fr.). See COL CANTO.

Avison, Charles, English organist and composer; b. Newcastle-upon-Tyne, 1709 (old style; baptized Feb. 16); d. there, May 9, 1770. He wrote concertos employing various combinations of strings with basso continuo; sonatas in which the keyboard instrument is predominant; concertos for strings *à* 7 (4 violins, viola, cello, bass), with harpsichord; keyboard concertos with string quartet, quartets for keyboard with 2 violins and cello, and trio sonatas for keyboard with 2 violins. His *Essay on Musical Expression* (London, 1752) is historically important as an early exposition of relative musical values by an English musician.

Ax, Emanuel, outstanding Polish-born American pianist; b. Lwów, June 8, 1949. He began playing the violin at age 6; studied piano with his father; moved to Warsaw when he was 8, to Winnipeg when he was 10; in 1961 settled in N.Y.; enrolled at the Juilliard School of Music. He toured South America in 1969; became a U.S. citizen in 1970; made his N.Y. debut (1973). After many frustrations he won 1st place in the Rubinstein International Piano Master Competition, Tel Aviv; among its awards was an American concert tour; he also appeared throughout Europe. He was awarded the Avery Fisher Prize in 1979. In addition to his fine interpretations of the standard repertoire, he has also distinguished himself as a champion of contemporary music.

ayre. An English court song of the 16th and 17th centuries, usually accompanied on the lute. The word is an old English spelling of AIR.

Aznavour (born Aznavurian), **Charles,** French chansonnier; b. Paris, May 22, 1924. A son of an Armenian baritone from Tiflis, he received his early musical training at home; acted in Paris variety shows at age 5; learned to play the guitar. His songs became popular in the 1940s; championed by Mistinguette, Chevalier, and Piaf. He made several American tours as a nightclub entertainer; also acted in several films. He composed a great number of songs, of the genre of *tristesse chansons* and frustration ballads. His best-known songs in translation include *Yesterday When I Was Young, All the Pretty Girls, The Old-Fashioned Way*, and *She*. His operetta *Monsieur Carnaval* was produced in Paris (1965).

B♭

B (Ger. *H*; Fr., It., Rus., Sp. *Si*). 1. The 7th tone and degree in the diatonic scale of C major. 2. In musical theory, uppercase *B* designates the B-major triad, while lowercase *b* indicates the b-minor triad. 3. In Ger., B-flat. This unique usage makes it possible to render Bach's name in musical notes, since the Ger. *H* corresponds to B-natural (see B–A–C–H). 4. (Abbr.) Bass, basso; *c.B.*, COL BASSO; *b.c.*, BASSO CONTINUO).

B dur (Ger.). B-flat major.

B major. A key of velvety warmth, rich in texture and emotionally ingratiating. The scale of B major, numbering all 5 black keys (F♯, C♯, G♯, D♯, A♯) and 2 white keys (B, E), is eminently pianistic, but the tonality is not suited for orch.l works. Only the subdominant of B major is represented by an open string on the violin and double bass. As for brass instruments, they are easier to play in flat keys, which B major certainly is not. Its ENHARMONIC EQUIVALENT, C-flat major, with 7 flats in the key signature, has a certain affinity with the standard tuning of transposing wind instruments; Stravinsky's ballet *The Firebird* has a section in C-flat major, a rarity in orch.l music.

B minor. As described by the 17th-century French composer Charpentier, a *solitaire et mélancolique* key. The description has held true, as composers have demonstrated. Tchaikovsky's *Pathétique Sym.*, certainly one of the most melancholy pieces ever written, is in B minor, as are Mendelssohn's overture *Fingal's Cave* (suggesting aloofness and remoteness) and the bassoon solo in the 2nd movement of Rimsky-Korsakov's *Scheherazade*. Perhaps the epitome of dolor is achieved in the 1st movement of Schubert's *Unfinished Sym.*

B moll (Ger.). B-flat minor.

Babbitt, Milton (Byron), prominent American composer, teacher, and theorist; b. Philadelphia, May 10, 1916. He received his 1st musical training in Jackson, Miss.; revealed an acute flair for mathematical reasoning as well. He studied with Philip James, Marion Bauer, and Roger Sessions. He taught mathematics at Princeton Univ. (1942–45), then music (1948–84); taught at Juilliard School, N.Y. (from 1973); elected a member of the National Inst. of Arts and Letters (1965). For Princeton and Columbia Univs. he inaugurated a Center for Electronic Music with a newly constructed mainframe synthesizer.

Babbitt promulgated a system of melodic and rhythmic sets ultimately leading to (integral) TOTAL SERIALISM. He extended Schoenberg's serial principle to embrace 12 different note values, time intervals between instrumental entries, dynamic levels, and instrumental timbres. In order to describe the potential combinations of the 4 basic aspects of a tone-row, he introduced the term COMBINATORIALITY, with symmetrical parts of a tone-row designated as *derivations*. Among his theoretical writings are *12-Tone Invariants as Compositional Determinants* (*Musical Quarterly*, 1960) and *12-Tone Rhythmic Structure and the Electronic Medium* (*Perspectives of New Music*, 1962). His mathematically based theories have profoundly influenced the musical thinking of young American composers; a considerable literature, both intelligible and unintelligible, arose in special publications to penetrate and attempt illuminating Babbitt's mind-boggling speculations. His original music, some of it aurally beguiling, can be fully understood only after a preliminary study of its underlying compositional plan. In 1982 he won a special citation of the Pulitzer Committee for "his life's work as a distinguished and seminal American composer."

Babes in Arms. Musical by Rodgers and Hart, 1937. The plot involves thespian adolescents stranded on Long Island and a transatlantic aviator who rescues them. Includes *My Funny Valentine* and *The Lady Is a Tramp*.

Baby Face. Popular flapper song by Harry Akst, 1926.

baby grand. The smallest size of the grand piano.

Baby, It's Cold Outside. Song by Frank Loesser from the film *Neptune's Daughter*, 1949.

baccheta di legno (It.). Wooden drumstick used for a dry (nonresonant) beat. *Baccheta di tamburo* (It.), a larger drumstick. *Bacchetto* (It.), a smaller drumstick.

bacchetta (It.). Conductor's baton.

Bacchus et Ariane. Ballet by Roussel, 1935, based on the Ariadne myth used by R. Strauss, Monteverdi, and many others. Roussel drew two orch.l suites from the ballet.

B–A–C–H. The letters of Bach's name, which in German pitch nomenclature generate the notes B-flat, A, C, and B-natural. Bach used this chromatic theme in the unfinished last fugue of *The Art of the Fugue*, and many composers have since paid tribute to him by writing pieces based on the same 4 notes.

Bach, Carl Philipp Emanuel, the "Berlin" or "Hamburg" Bach, 3rd son of Johann Sebastian Bach; b. Weimar, Mar. 8, 1714; d. Hamburg, Dec. 14, 1788. He studied with his father at the Thomasschule, Leipzig; studied jurisprudence at the Univs. of Leipzig and Frankfurt-an-der-Oder. He went to Berlin (1738); became chamber musician to Frederick the Great of Prussia (1740); arranged his father's visit to Potsdam (1747). In 1768 he became cantor at the Johanneum, Hamburg; directed the music for the 5 major churches; held these posts until his death. Abandoning the strict polyphonic style of composition of his father, he became a leader of the new school of piano writing, a master of *Empfindsamkeit* (inner expressivity), the North German counterpart of the French ROCOCO but with stronger affect. His *Essay on the True Art of Playing the Clavier* (2 parts, 1753–62) has been very influential and has yielded much authentic information about musical practices of the latter 18th century.

Bach, Johann (John) **Christian,** the "London" Bach, noted German composer, 11th surviving son of Johann Sebastian Bach; b. Leipzig, Sept. 5, 1735; d. London, Jan. 1, 1782. He studied with his father and, after 1750, with his stepbrother C. P. E. Bach in Berlin. In 1754 he went to Italy; studied with Padre Martini; converted to Roman Catholicism for work purposes; served as organist at the Milan Cathedral (1760–62); traveled throughout Italy; composed several successful operas there. In 1762 he moved to London; his acclaimed opera *Orione, ossia Diana vendicata* was premiered there (1763); appointed music master to the Queen (1764); gave, together with C. F. Abel, a famous series of London concerts (1764–81).

When young Mozart came to London in 1764, Bach took interest in him and improvised with him at the keyboard. Mozart retained a lifelong affection for him; he used 3 of Bach's keyboard sonatas as models for his earliest piano concertos. Bach was highly prolific; he wrote syms., keyboard concertos, chamber music, violin sonatas, and piano sonatas. His music exhibited the GALANT STYLE of the 2nd half of the 18th century, with an emphasis on expressive AFFECTS and brilliance of instrumental display. He totally departed from his father's ideals; his music became an important influence on the classical era. Although he was best known as an instrumental composer, Bach also wrote successful operas, most of them to Italian librettos, including *Catone in Utica* (1761); *Temistocle* (1772); *Lucio Silla* (based on the libretto used by Mozart, 1774); *La clemenza di Scipione* (1778); and *Amadis de Gaule* (1779).

Bach, Johann Christoph, 2nd cousin of Johann Sebastian Bach, organist and composer of the highest distinction among the earlier Bachs; b. Arnstadt, Dec. 3, 1642; d. Eisenach, Mar. 31, 1703. He was organist in Arnstadt (1663–65); then in Eisenach (from 1665); appointed court musician there (from 1700). C. P. E. Bach described him as a "great and expressive composer"; his works include motets, sacred concertos, and organ music.

Bach, Johann Christoph Friedrich, the "Bückeburg" Bach, 9th son of Johann Sebastian Bach; b. Leipzig, June 21, 1732; d. Bückeburg, Jan. 26, 1795. He studied music with his father; attended the Univ. of Leipzig in jurisprudence. He became chamber musician to Count Wilhelm of Schaumburg-Lippe of Bückeburg (1750); became "Concert-Meister" (1759), which he remained until his death. He was a virtuoso musician, although less known as a composer than his brothers and stepbrothers; he wrote sym., concertos, oratorios, cantatas, and a great deal of keyboard music in the STYLE GALANT.

Bach, Johann Sebastian

Supreme arbiter and lawgiver of music, a master comparable in greatness of stature with Aristotle in philosophy and Leonardo da Vinci in art; b. Eisenach, Mar. 21 (baptized Mar. 23), 1685; d. Leipzig, July 28, 1750. He was a member of an illustrious family of musicians who were active in various capacities as performing artists, composers, and teachers. The word Bach is German for "stream"; thus the rhetorical phrase that J. S. Bach was not a mere stream but a whole ocean of music ("Nicht Bach aber Meer haben wir hier"), epitomizing his encompassing magnitude.

Bach's biography is singularly lacking in dramatic events. He attended the Latin school in Eisenach and apparently was a good student. His mother died in 1694; his father remarried but died soon afterward. Bach began attending the Lyceum, Ohrdruf (1695); he lived with his brother Johann Christoph (1671–1721), who supported him in his musical studies. He was admitted to the Mettenchor of the Michaeliskirche, Lüneburg (1700). In 1703 he won a position in Weimar but was prevented from taking the post.

In the meantime he was appointed organist at the Neukirche, Arnstadt (1703). In 1705 he obtained a leave of absence to travel to Lübeck to hear the famous organist Buxtehude. It is physically impossible for Bach to have made this journey by foot; he may have hired himself out as a valet to a coach passenger, a not uncommon practice among young men of the time. The reason for his trip was presumably his hope of obtaining Buxtehude's position as organist upon his retirement, but there was a catch: having 5 unmarried daughters, Buxtehude expected his successor to marry the eldest of them. Bach apparently was not prepared for matrimony under such circumstances and returned to Arnstadt.

In 1707 Bach became organist at the Blasiuskirche, Mühlhausen; that year, he married his cousin Maria Barbara (1684–1720). In 1708 Bach presented his cantata *Gott ist mein König* (BWV 71) for the installation of a new Mühlhausen town council; this was Bach's 1st public work. Although his employment in Mühlhausen was satisfactory, he resigned that summer after receiving the better-paid post of court organist to Duke Wilhelm Ernst of Weimar. In 1714 the Duke gave Bach the position of KONZERTMEISTER, at a time when Bach considered taking a position in Halle. J. S. Drese, the Weimar KAPELLMEISTER, died on Dec. 1, 1716; Bach hoped to succeed him, but the post went to Drese's son. In response, Bach accepted the position of Kapellmeister and music director to Prince Leopold of Anhalt in Cöthen (1717), but his request to be released from his Weimar obligations was at 1st refused by Wilhelm Ernst, who imprisoned Bach for a month in late 1717 before releasing him from his duties.

The Cöthen period was one of the most productive and least troubled in Bach's life, with an emphasis on instrumental music: the set of *Brandenburg Concertos*, *Clavierbüchlein für Wilhelm Friedemann Bach*, book I of *Das Wohltemperierte Clavier*, and the solo violin and cello works. In 1720 Bach accompanied Prince Leopold to Karlsbad; while he was away, his wife Maria Barbara took ill and died, leaving Bach to care for their 7 children. He remained a widower for nearly a year and a half before he married his 2nd wife, Anna Magdalena Wilcken (1701–60), a daughter of a Weissenfels court trumpeter. They had 13 children during their happy marital life.

As Prince Leopold married a woman who had no interest in music, Bach was ready to consider a job change. When Kuhnau, the cantor of Leipzig, died (1722), Bach applied for the post. The Leipzig authorities offered it 1st to Telemann and, when he declined, to Christoph Graupner; when Graupner could not obtain a release from his Darmstadt position, Bach was elected cantor of the city of Leipzig and officially installed in 1723.

As director of church music, Bach supervised musicians in 4 churches, provided music for performance at 2 of them, and taught at the Thomasschule. There were more mundane obligations that Bach was expected to discharge (e.g., gathering firewood for the Thomasschule), about which Bach had recurrent disputes with the rector. It was in Leipzig that Bach created his greatest sacred works: the *St. Matthew Passion* (BWV 244), *St. John Passion* (BWV 245), the B-minor Mass (BWV 232), *Magnificat* (BWV 243), the holiday oratorios, and most of the church cantatas. In 1729 he organized the famous Collegium Musicum, made up of professional musicians and univ. students with whom he gave regular weekly concerts; he led this group until 1737 and again from 1739 to 1741. He made several visits to Dresden, where his son Wilhelm Friedemann was organist at the Sophienkirche.

In June 1747 Bach joined Leipzig's Soc. der musikalischen Wissenschaften, a scholarly organization founded by a former member of the Collegium Musicum. The rules of the society required an applicant to submit a sampling of works; Bach contributed a triple canon *à* 6 (BWV 1076) and the canonic variations on *Vom Himmel hoch da komm' ich her* (BWV 769). He suffered from a cataract that was gradually darkening his vision. An operation on Bach's eyes in 1749, performed with the crude tools of the time, left Bach almost totally blind. The etiology of Bach's last illness is unclear. It is said that his vision suddenly returned (possibly when the cataract receded spontaneously), but a cerebral hemorrhage supervened, and a few days later Bach was dead. Bach's great contrapuntal work, *Die Kunst der Fuge,* remained unfinished. The final page bears this inscription by Wilhelm Friedemann: "Upon this fugue, in which the name B–A–C–H is applied as a countersubject, the author died."

Despite the grandeur of the phenomenon of Bach, he was not an isolated figure dwelling in the splendor of his genius apart from the zeitgeist of his time; he was a mentor to young students, a master organist and instructor who spent his life within the confines of his native Thuringia whose compositions were designed for immediate performance in church and in the schoolroom. Indeed, the text of the dedication of his epoch-making *Das wohltemperierte Clavier oder Praeludia und Fügen* emphasizes its pedagogical aspect: "The Well-Tempered Clavier, or Preludes and Fugues in all tones and semitones, both with the major 3rd of Ut Re Mi [C D E], and the minor 3rd of Re Mi Fa [D E F], composed and notated for the benefit and exercise of musical young people eager to learn, as well as for a special practice for those who have already achieved proficiency and skill in this study." The MS of book I is dated 1722 (BWV 846–69); book II was compiled in 1742 (BWV 870–93).

While equal temperament was considered theoretically viable at the time, Bach's title indicates WELL TEM-PERAMENT, any of a family of subtly altered tunings that lie somewhere between the MEANTONE tunings of the Baroque and EQUAL TEMPERAMENT. Bach was not the 1st to attempt such a cycle, however; J. C. F. Fischer anticipated him in his 1702 collection *Ariadne musica*, comprising 20 preludes and fugues in 20 different keys. Undoubtedly Bach was aware of this work, as the subjects of several of Bach's pieces are similar to the point of identity to the themes of Fischer's work. These coincidences do not detract from the significance of Bach's accomplishment, for it is the beauty and totality of development that makes Bach's work vastly superior to those of any of his putative predecessors.

In the art of variations, Bach was supreme. A superb example is the set known as the *Goldberg Variations* (BWV 988), so named because it was commissioned by the Russian diplomat Kayserling through the mediation of Bach's pupil J. G. Goldberg (1727–56), who was in Kayserling's service as a harpsichordist. This work is listed by Bach as the 4th part of the *Clavier-Übung*, another typically didactic title. A different type of Bach's great musical projections is exemplified by his *Concerts à plusieurs instruments*, known as the *Brandenburg Concertos* (BWV 1046–51) because of their dedication to Christian Ludwig, margrave of Brandenburg (possibly as a petition for an appointment). They represent the crowning achievement of the secular Baroque. Nos. 2, 4, and 5 of the Brandenburg Concertos are examples of CONCERTO GROSSO, in which a group of solo instruments—the CONCERTINO—is contrasted with the accompanying string orch. (RIPIENO).

Die Kunst der Fuge (The Art of Fugue; BWV 1080), Bach's last composition (begun in 1749), provides an encyclopedia of fugues, canons, and various counterpoints based on the same theme: inversion, canon, augmentation, diminution, double fugue, triple fugue, at times appearing in fantastic optical symmetry so that the written music itself forms a balanced design. Here Bach's art is calculated to instruct the musical mind as well as delight the aural sense. Of these constructions, the most extraordinary is *Das Musikalische Opfer* (Musical Offering, BWV 1079), composed for Frederick the Great of Prussia. Carl Philipp Emanuel, who was serving Frederick, arranged for his father to visit Frederick's palace in Potsdam; Bach arrived there, accompanied by Wilhelm Friedemann, in 1747. The ostensible purpose of Bach's visit was to test the Silbermann pianos installed in the palace. The King, who liked to flaunt his musical awareness, gave Bach a subject (allegedly of his own invention) and asked him to improvise a fugue upon it (which Bach did). He later improvised a fugue *à* 6 on his own theme. Upon his return to Leipzig, Bach composed a set of pieces based on the King's theme. The work is subdivided into 13 sections; it includes a puzzle canon in 2 parts, marked "quaerendo invenietis" ("you will find it by seeking"). Bach had the score engraved, and sent it to the King.

Although Bach wrote most of his contrapuntal works as didactic exercises, there are in his music extraordinary looks into the future; consider, for instance, the A-minor fugue of book I of the *Well-Tempered Clavier*, where the inversion of the subject seems to violate all the rules of proper voice-leading in its bold leap from the tonic upward to the 7th of the scale and then up a 3rd. The answer to the subject of the F-minor fugue of book I suggests the chromatic usages of later centuries.

Of Bach's 20 children, 10 reached maturity. His sons Wilhelm Friedemann, Carl Philipp Emanuel, Johann Christoph Friedrich, and Johann (John) Christian made their mark as independent composers. Among Bach's notable pupils were Goldberg, J. C. Altnikol, G. A. Homilius, J. P. Kirnberger, J. T. Krebs, and J. L. Krebs. Contrary to received wisdom, Bach was not unappreciated by his contemporaries; his sons kept his legacy alive for a generation after Bach's death, however much their own styles might have differed. Mozart and Beethoven studied the preludes and fugues; Chopin followed their example. While Mendelssohn's Berlin

Johann Sebastian Bach

COURTESY FRANK DRIGGS COLLECTION

revival of the *St. Matthew Passion* (1829) was an important event, Bach's genius had never been dimmed; he was never a prophet without a world. The advent of Bach marked the greatest flowering of Baroque music; his name became a synonym for perfection.

Modern composers, even those who champion the total abandonment of all conventional methods and the abolition of musical notation, are irresistibly drawn to Bach as a precursor; suffice it to mention Berg's use of Bach's chorale *Es ist genug* (from the cantata *O Ewigkeit, du Donnerwort*, BWV 60) in the concluding section of his violin concerto (1935), dedicated to the memory of Alma Mahler Werfel's young daughter. It is interesting to note also that Bach's famous acronym B–A–C–H (i.e., B-flat, A, C, B) consists of four adjacent chromatic notes in alternation, thus making it possible to use it as an element of a 12-tone row. Reger was told by Riemann that he could be the 2nd Bach, and his skill in composition almost justified his aspiration; Busoni was described by his admirers as the Bach of the modern era; a similar honor was claimed for Hindemith by his disciples. The slogan "Back to Bach," adopted by composers of the early 20th century, seems to hold true for every musical era; yet the art of Bach remains unconquerable.

The standard Bach thematic catalogue is W. Schmieder's *Thematisch-systematisches Verzeichnis der musikalischen Werke von J. S. B. (Bach-Werke-Verzeichnis)* (Leipzig, 1950; 3rd ed., 1961); it includes bibliographical information on each composition. The catalogue arranges works generically rather than chronologically; numerous Bach compositions are difficult to date precisely.

Bach, P. D. Q. See SCHICKELE, PETER.

Bach, Wilhelm Friedemann, the "Halle" Bach, eldest son of Johann Sebastian Bach; b. Weimar, Nov. 22, 1710; d. Berlin, July 1, 1784. He studied with his father at the Thomasschule (1723–29) and violin with J. G. Graun in Merseburg (1726); enrolled at the Univ. of Leipzig in mathematics, philosophy, and law (1729). In 1733 he became organ-

ist at the Sophienkirche, Dresden, then the Liebfrauenkirche, Halle (1746); offered the KAPELLMEISTER position in Darmstadt, but somehow lost it (1762); walked out on the Halle position (1764); moved to Brunswick (1770), then Berlin (1774), where he taught Mendelssohn's great-aunt and gained favor at Anna Amalia's court; his own intrigues there backfired; died in poverty. He was a highly gifted composer, alternating between his father's style and the

EMPFINDSAMKEIT favored by Carl Philipp Emanuel. His career was flawed by personal instability; his custodianship of part of Johann Sebastian's MSS was incompetent, if not criminal; at the end he claimed some of his father's music for his own, and he forged the older Bach's signature on at least 1 of his own pieces.

Bacharach, Burt, American composer of popular songs; b. Kansas City, May 12, 1928. He played jazz piano in nightclubs; studied at McGill Univ., Montreal; took courses with Darius Milhaud and Henry Cowell at the New School for Social Research, N.Y. He toured with Marlene Dietrich as her accompanist (1958–61). In 1962 he joined forces with lyricist Hal David; they produced such songs as *Reach Out for Me, Trains and Boats and Planes, Make It Easy on Yourself, Blue on Blue, Walk on By, Always Something There to Remind Me, What the World Needs Now Is Love, Do You Know the Way to San Jose?, Raindrops Keep Fallin' on My Head, The Look of Love,* and *I'll Never Fall in Love Again*; they produced the successful Broadway musical *Promises, Promises* (1968). He wrote songs for the films *What's New Pussycat?, Wives and Lovers, Alfie, Send Me No Flowers, Promise Her Anything,* and *Butch Cassidy and the Sundance Kid.* The singer Dionne Warwick (b. 1941) was his best-known interpreter.

Bachianas Brasileiras. Nine pieces for various combinations by Villa-Lobos (1930-45), who had a whimsical but fruitful idea of a link between Brazilian folk rhythms and Bach counterpoint. This creative fusion led to works involving orch., piano, chorus, woodwinds, and 2 works involving cello ensembles, including the engaging No. 5, with soprano (1938–45).

background music. Orig., music accompanying dramatic scenes in a play; now any music that functions as an atmospheric element in any setting.

Backhaus, Wilhelm, eminent German-born Swiss pianist and pedagogue; b. Leipzig, Mar. 26, 1884; d. Villach, Austria, July 5, 1969. He studied with Reckendorf (1891–99) and briefly with d'Albert; went on a major tour in 1900; acquired a fine European reputation as pianist and teacher. He made his U.S. debut as soloist in Beethoven's *Emperor Concerto* under Walter Damrosch in N.Y. (1912). In 1930 he settled in Lugano; continuing to teach, he became a Swiss citizen. Following World War II he resumed his concert tours; made his last U.S. appearance at a N.Y. recital in 1962, displaying undiminished virtuosic vigor. He

was particularly distinguished in his interpretations of the works of Beethoven and Brahms.

Baez, Joan (Chandos), politically active American folksinger, guitarist, and songwriter of English, Irish, and Mexican descent; b. Staten Island, N.Y., Jan. 9, 1941. She learned the guitar by ear; studied drama at Boston Univ.; made her 1st important appearance at the Newport Folk Festival (1959). In 1965 she founded the Inst. for the Study of Non-Violence; joined the anti-Vietnam War movement and supported the organizing fight of the United Farm Workers' Union; appeared at concerts promoting topical humanitarian causes. She was associated with Bob Dylan in the 1960s and 1970s, and followed his lead into folk-rock; but her most recognizable trademark is her beautiful and rich voice, combined with superb diction.

bagatelle (Fr., trifle). A short, lighter piece with no specific form, usually for keyboard; the term was 1st used by Couperin for a RONDEAU (*Les Bagatelles*, 10th *ordre*, 2nd Book of Harpsichord Pieces, 1717); Beethoven wrote 3 sets for piano (opp. 33, 119, 126), many of which are far from trifling. Other composers to use the term are Smetana, Saint-Saëns, Sibelius, and Bartók; it is also found in works by Dvořák, Poulenc, and Webern. Liszt's *Bagatelle ohne Tonart*, written *c.* 1880 and publ. posth., is remarkable because of its explicit indication, "without key"; it lacks a key signature, and it cultivates tritones, major 7ths, and other "atonal" intervals.

bagpipe(s). An ancient wind instrument of Eastern origin, still popular in Great Britain, Ireland, and many European cultures. Basically the instrument comprises an air-holding bag and pipes. The Scottish highland bagpipe is typical with its 4 pipes: 3 drone-pipes, single- or double-reed pipes tuned to a tone, its 5th, and its octave; and 1 chanter (melody-pipe), a single- or double-reed pipe with 6 or 8 holes. The bag is a leather sack filled with wind either from the mouth (through a blowpipe) or from small bellows worked by the player's arm; the sounding pipes are inserted in and receive wind from the bag.

Scotland has several varieties of bagpipe; the best known is the highland pipe, a mouth-blown military instrument held upright, covered in plaid, and played by men in skirts. The most familiar Irish pipe is the union or UILLEANN PIPE, which is smaller, bellows-blown, lap-held, and adds regulator pipes, with keys played with the heel of the hand, permitting chords to be played.

Although the bagpipe is the national instrument of Scotland and Ireland, many similar instruments are found in Europe: Northumbrian small-pipe (England); musette, cornemuse, and biniou (France); gaita and zampoña (Spain, Portugal); Dudelsack (Germany); zampogna and cornamusa (Italy); gadje (Yugoslavia, Macedonia, Bulgaria); duda (Hungary, Belarus); cimpoi (Rumania); dudy (Czech Republic); gajdy (Slovakia); dudy and koziol (Poland); and mashq (India). The *bag-hornpipe* is a family of instruments found from Crete and Turkey to the Caucasus and Volga regions and in northern Africa; these lack drones, and have double-chanter pipes (canes).

baguette (Fr.). Conductor's baton; also, a drumstick. *Baguette de bois* (Fr.), wooden drumstick; *baguette d'eponge* (Fr.), drumstick with a sponge head.

Baiser de la fée, Le (The Kiss of the Fairy). Allegorical ballet by Stravinsky, 1928, on melodies of Tchaikovsky, choreography by Ida Rubinstein; the premiere was led by the composer. The scenario, adapted from Andersen's *The Snow Maiden*, involves a fairy who kisses a stolen baby boy, then leaves him to be found by villagers; when he grows up and plans to wed, she disguises herself as his fiancée and reclaims him, sealing their union with another kiss. Stravinsky restructured assorted pieces by Tchaikovsky, changing the meter and the harmony but preserving the original's essence; so great is Stravinsky's mastery that the melodies are transmuted into something wondrous and new.

Baker, David (Nathaniel), African-American composer and jazz musician; b. Indianapolis, Ind., Dec. 21, 1931. He studied with G. Schuller, B. Heiden, J. Orrego-Salas, W. Russo, and G. Russell; after teaching in small colleges and public school, became chairman of jazz studies at Indiana Univ. (1966). He played trombone with S. Kenton, L. Hampton, and Q. Jones. His compositions fuse jazz improvisation with ultramodern devices, including serial procedures; he has composed extensively in most genres. Among his books are *Jazz Improvisation: A Comprehensive Method of Study for All Players* (1969) and *Techniques of Improvisation* (1971); he co-ed. *The Black Composer Speaks* (1978).

Baker, Dame Janet (Abbott), celebrated English mezzo-soprano; b. Hatfield, Yorkshire, Aug. 21, 1933. She began singing lessons in London with H. Isepp and M. St. Clair. She attended classes at the Mozarteum, Salzburg (1956); enrolled in Lotte Lehmann's London master class. A decisive career turn came with her joining Britten's English Opera Group; created the role of Kate Julian in Britten's television opera *Owen Wingrave* (1971). She made her American debut with the San Francisco Sym. in Mahler's *Das Lied von der Erde* and presented a solo recital in N.Y. (1966), both with excellent reviews; subsequent engagements took her all over Europe. Queen Elizabeth II made her a Dame Commander of the Order of the British Empire (1976); gave her operatic farewell in 1982. Baker was an outstanding artist of intellectual brilliance; her extensive operatic repertoire ranged from Monteverdi and Handel to R. Strauss and Britten. She was also one of the great lieder artists of her day, excelling in Schubert and Schumann.

Baker, Josephine, African-American-born French dancer, singer, and actress; b. St. Louis, June 3, 1906; d. Paris, Apr. 12, 1979. She was a street musician by age 13; toured on the vaudeville circuit; gained recognition in the show *Chocolate Dandies* (1924). Making her way to Paris, she starred in *La Revue nègre*, then the Folies-Bergère (1925), where her bracelets-and-bananas costume was introduced. Her exotic, highly erotic, quixotic stage persona gained her fame; she starred in a revival of Offenbach's *La Créole* (1934); became a naturalized French citizen (1937); enter-

Josephine Baker, Paris, c. 1928

COURTESY FRANK DRIGGS COLLECTION

tained troops and assisted in the French Resistance during the Nazi occupation (1940–44). After the war she turned to humanitarian causes, adopting orphans from various countries. She was also active in the U.S. civil rights movement.

Baker, Theodore, American lexicographer and writer on music, for whom the present work is named; b. N.Y., June 3, 1851; d. Dresden, Oct. 13, 1934. Although trained for business employment, he decided to devote himself to music; went to Leipzig (1874); took a Ph.D. by writing the 1st serious study of Native American music (1882). He returned to the U.S. (1890); became literary ed. and trans. for G. Schirmer (1892); retired and returned to Germany (1926). In 1895 he publ. *A Dictionary of Musical Terms*; other valuable works were *A Pronouncing Pocket Manual of Musical Terms* (1905) and *The Musician's Calendar and Birthday Book* (1915–17). In 1900 he publ. *Baker's Biographical Dictionary of Musicians*, his imperishable monument. The 1st ed. rectified the lack of American musicians in reference works at the time; he publ. a 2nd ed. (1905). Subsequent eds. were rev. by Alfred Remy (3rd ed., 1919); Carl Engel (4th ed., 1940); and Nicolas Slonimsky, who undertook the 1949 Supplement, a completely rev. 5th ed. (1958), the Supplements of 1965 and 1971, the 6th ed. (1978), the 7th ed. (1984), and the 8th ed. (1991).

Balakirev, Mily (Alexeievich), significant Russian composer, protagonist of the Russian national school, member of the "Mighty 5"; b. Nizhny-Novgorod, Jan. 2, 1837 (new style; Dec. 21, 1836, old style); d. St. Petersburg, May 29, 1910. He went to Moscow; studied piano with A. Dubuque and theory with K. Eisrich, who introduced him to A. Oulibishev, author and owner of an estate in Nizhny-Novgorod; Balakirev played piano in private musical evenings there. In 1853–54 he attended the Univ. of Kazan in mathematics; in 1855 went to St. Petersburg and met Glinka, who encouraged his musical interests. In 1856 he made his compositional debut there, playing the solo part in the 1st movement of his Piano Concerto (never completed); his *Overture on the Theme of 3 Russian Songs* was performed in Moscow in 1859, his *Overture to King Lear* in St. Petersburg later that year.

In 1860 Balakirev took a boat ride down the Volga River from Nizhny-Novgorod to the Caspian Sea delta; while traveling he collected, notated, and harmonized Russian folk songs; his 1866 collection included the ever-popular *Song of the Volga Boatmen*, also known as *Song of the Burlaks* (peasants who pulled large grain boats upstream on the

Volga). In 1863 Balakirev organized a St. Petersburg group that became known as the Balakirev Circle, to promote nationalist Russian music and to oppose the passive imitation of classical German compositions, then a dominant influence in Russia; founded the Free Music School in St. Petersburg; gave concerts of Russian and German compositions. These activities coincided with a Slavophile movement among patriotic Russian writers and artists; a dream of uniting all Slavic nations under the loving gaze of Mother Russia animated Balakirev and others.

In 1867 Balakirev went to Prague to conduct Glinka's operas there; organized a concert of Russian and Czech works at his Free Music School later that year; the program included pieces by Borodin, Cui, Mussorgsky, Rimsky-Korsakov, and himself. The occasion moved the critic Vladimir Stasov to declare that Russia, too, had its "mighty little company" (*moguchaya kuchka*) of fine musicians; the phrase became a catchword of Russian musical nationalism; in English-language music histories it became known as the "Mighty 5." In addition to the spiritual union of Slavic nations, the Mighty 5 looked to the exotic Moslem lands through the Caucasus to Persia in the south and to Central Asia in the east. Balakirev became fascinated with the quasi-oriental melodies and rhythms of the Caucasus during several trips there. In 1869 he wrote a brilliant oriental fantasy for piano entitled ISLAMEY; its technical difficulties rival Liszt's études.

Among his comrades Balakirev was always a leader; when Rimsky-Korsakov shipped out as a midshipman in the Russian Imperial Navy, he maintained a remarkable correspondence with Balakirev, who gave him specific advice in composition. However, Balakirev slackened the tempo of his work as a composer, conductor, and teacher; he consistently had trouble completing his scores. In 1872 he discontinued his concerts at the Free Music School; worked for the railroad transport; became an administrator in 2 women's educational insts. in St. Petersburg.

In 1881 he returned to musical activities; conducted the premiere of the Sym. No. 1 by the 16-year-old Glazunov (1882); rev. and completed earlier scores, including the *2nd Overture on Russian Themes*, renamed *Russia* (1864–82); the symphonic poem *Tamara* (1867–82); and the Sym. No. 1 in C Major (1864–97). He composed his 2nd Sym. in D Minor (1909); took up the 2nd Piano Concerto (begun 1861) but left it unfinished (completed by Liapunov). His long-strained relationship with Rimsky-Korsakov came to a breaking point in 1890; thereafter they would not even greet each other in public; still, Rimsky-Korsakov performed

Balakirev's music at his concerts. Balakirev retired in 1894 and spent his remaining years composing.

Balakirev made a tremendous impact on the destinies of Russian music, particularly because of his patriotic conviction that Russia could rival Germany and other nations in the art of music. If his output seems relatively small, it can be attributed to illnesses, among them encephalitis and severe depression. Nonetheless, he left powerful and exotically colored works; they deserve more performances.

balalaika (Rus.). Popular Russian instrument of the guitar type, with a triangular body, long neck, and 3 strings. It became popular in the 18th century. Toward the end of the 19th century serious Russian musicians became interested in constructing differently sized balalaikas and combining with the more ancient DOMRA in ethnic Russian ensembles.

Balanchine, George (born Gyorgy Melitonovich Balanchivadze), celebrated Russian-American choreographer; b. St. Petersburg, Jan. 22, 1904; d. N.Y., Apr. 30, 1983. He attended the Imperial Ballet School, St. Petersburg; studied music at the Petrograd Cons.; founded the Young Ballet; joined Diaghilev's *Ballets Russes*, Paris (1924–29) and created works for it. At the invitation of the American dance specialist Lincoln Kirstein, he went to N.Y. (1933); they formed the School of American Ballet (1934), which went through several metamorphoses: American Ballet (1935–38), Ballet Caravan (1941), Ballet Soc. (1946–48), and the N.Y. Ballet (from 1948). In 1962 he toured Russia with the company.

Balanchine was distinguished for his modern innovations in ballet, with music by old and new composers, most memorably Stravinsky, beginning with the rev. *Le Chant du Rossignol* (1925) and culminating in *Agon* (1957). He retained his connections with Europe (Hindemith's Kammermusik No. 2, Mozart's Divertimento No. 15) but was able to adapt quickly to the American landscape, with his dances to works by K. Swift, M. Gould, H. Kay, Sousa, Gershwin, and R. Rodgers (4 musicals). In 1983 he received the Presidential Medal of Freedom, but he died shortly thereafter of the consequences of "progressive cerebral disintegration." He was married 5 times; as all of his brides were dancers, it is said that his marriages were more like collaborations. In his long career he created nearly 200 ballets to musical scores ranging from the Baroque to the avant-garde; he once said, "Music must be seen, and dance must be heard."

ballad (from Lat. *ballare*, to dance). 1. Orig., a song intended for dance accompaniment; hence the air of such a song. 2. In modern usage, a simple narrative poem, often sentimental or dramatic, generally meant to be sung. The ballad has been an especially fruitful genre in English-speaking countries, acquiring Romantic connotations in the choice of mysterious legends or horror stories as subject matter. 3. Orig., a short, simple vocal melody set to 1 or more symmetrical stanzas, with a light instrumental accompaniment; the term now includes instrumental melodies of a similar character. 4. Compositions for single instruments or orch., embodying the idea of a narrative. 5. In the U.S., any folk song, regardless of content.

Ballad of Davy Crockett, The. Song by George Bruns, introduced by Fess Parker in a Disney television program in 1954. Along with the recording, coonskin caps sold exceptionally well as a result; however, the number of bears killed by infants did not rise significantly.

ballad opera. A musical stage work primarily made up of extant ballads and folk songs, or at least their tunes; spoken dialogue is a component. A genre popular in 18th-century England and its northern colonies, it is stylistically close to the French VAUDEVILLE. The work that precipitated the genre's heyday was *The Beggar's Opera*, 1728, by John Gay, with music arranged by John Christopher (Johann Christoph) Pepusch (1667–1752). Subsequent English ballad operas drew freely on arias and choruses of past composers. The genre exhausted itself toward the end of the 18th century and gave way to the fertile development of the German SINGSPIEL. More than a century later the ballad opera was revived in Germany by Weill and others who used the mixed English-German designation *Songspiel* (the English *song* having acquired the German meaning for musical entertainment of any kind); the primary difference was that the 20th-century model was usually newly composed.

ballade (Fr., from Lat. *ballare*, dance; Ger.). A term of widely ranging connotations. It 1st applied to vocal compositions of the masters of the ARS NOVA and to TROUBADOUR songs. Despite the word's derivation, the choreographic aspect of this genre had disappeared by this time. Among the most significant ballades in a polyphonic vocal form are those by Machaut; later development of the French genre were BERGERETTES (from *bergère*, a shepherdess) and pastoral songs of the 18th century.

In the Romantic period the ballade had become either a balladlike art song or an instrumental solo piece, as applied by German-speaking composers. Ballades were now strophic poems of the type popularized by Goethe and Schiller. Schubert and Schumann were particularly fond of these poems and set a multitude of strophic songs in which all stanzas were sung to the same music. The most prolific composer of German ballades was Loewe, who published 17 vols. of mostly strophic songs. A more elaborate type of ballade was *durchkomponiert* (THROUGH-COMPOSED), in which each stanza could be set to different music.

Instrumental ballades were designed as wordless narratives. Chopin's ballades for piano are the greatest examples of this genre. Piano ballades were also written by Liszt, Brahms, and Grieg. The Russian composer Medtner introduced a combined sonata-ballade for piano; orch.l ballades were also composed, e.g., Glazunov composed the *Concerto Ballata* for Cello and Orch. (op. 108, 1931).

ballata (It.). The most popular song form of the early Italian Renaissance, close in function and spirit to the French VIRELAI and the Spanish VILLANCICO. It has several stanzas, each followed by a *ripresa* (refrain). While the word may be derived from the Lat. *ballare* (dance), no dance-related ballatas have been found. In the Trecento (14th century), many composers produced masterpieces in this genre, particularly Landini.

ballet (Fr.; Ger. *Ballett*). 1. An integral dance work, or dance introduced in an opera or other stage work. 2. A pantomime, with music and dances setting forth the thread of the story.

balletto (It.). 1. A ballet. 2. The title of an allegretto by Bach, in common time. 3. In the 17th century, a dramatic madrigal for voices and instruments written in a free manner, with some passages suited for dance. 4. Purely instrumental compositions with no dance associations.

ballo (It.). 1. A dance. 2. A short theatrical work with dance. 3. A dramatic musical work with dance, e.g., Monteverdi's *Il Ballo delle ingrate*.

ballet de cour (Fr.). A court dance genre of French royalty, from Henry III to Louis XIV, with court members, including the King, participating in the performance. Subject matter included mythology, non-Christian "primitives and savages," and the glory of the royal state. Stylistically, the genre borrowed from the Italian MASCHERATA and INTERMEDIO and French courtly pantomimes and fetes; it was similar to the English MASQUE. Louis XIV danced from 1651 (at age 13) until 1670; thereafter the genre began a decline that, excepting a brief revival under Louis XV, saw its extinction by the mid-18th century. Composers of music for *ballets de cour* included P. Guérdon, Lully, de Lalande, Destouches, Campra, and Mouret.

Ballet mécanique. Quasi-symphonic poem by George Antheil, a celebrated work for percussion ensemble that shocked Paris at its 1st performance (1926). It shocked the American public even more the following year in N.Y., where Antheil added airplane propellers, buzz saws, and loud drums to the orch. Several revivals of *Ballet mécanique* have occurred over the years, but it has become a period piece; the only shock that recent audiences experienced was from the knowledge that this music ever shocked anyone at all.

Ballo in maschera, Un (The Masked Ball). Opera by Verdi, 1859, adapted from a Scribe libretto based on the assassination of King Gustavus III of Sweden (1792). Regicide was not regarded as appropriate by the stage censors when Verdi's opera was premiered in Rome, so the locale was changed to America and the victim of the plot to the "governor of Boston," a nonexistent title (and therefore a safe choice). He consults a fortune teller for a reading of his future and she tells him that he will be murdered. Operatic fortune tellers are never wrong, and the unfortunate governor is stabbed to death at a masked ball by his male secretary with whose wife the governor had been consorting. In 20th-century productions, when royal personages were no longer banned, attempts have been made to restore the orig. libretto, but they are rarely successful. Opera audiences prefer Romantic invention to historic truth.

band. 1. An instrumental ensemble consisting of brass, woodwind, and percussion instruments to the exclusion of string instruments. The term is used for such groups as military bands, jazz bands, dance bands, and brass bands; in jazz a stylistic distinction exists between big bands (orch.) and small bands (combos, groups). In the hierarchy of musical ensembles, the band occupies a lower position than an orch.; a band leader who has symphonic ambitions prefers to be called conductor, and the terms *wind orch.* or SYMPHONIC BAND are found. However, English and other kings had their royal bands, with no suggestion of condescension in this designation. Lully's group of 24 VIOLONS DU ROY was called

LA GRANDE BANDE. 2. A company of musicians playing military or sports-oriented music. 3. A section of the orch. playing instruments of the same family (BRASS BAND, STRING BAND, WIND BAND, WOOD BAND).

Band Played On, The. Ballad in waltz time by John E. Palmer, 1895; the song's copyright was bought by vaudevillian Charles R. Ward, to Palmer's subsequent and great regret.

band, big. BIG BAND.

band, brass. 1. Large ensemble consisting of brass instruments, with tubas of various sizes; mostly used for military and sports displays or municipal entertainments, brass bands sometimes present concerts of classical music or specially commissioned works by modern composers. 2. The brass section of the orch.

band, marching. A military band used in more pacific pursuits, such as holiday parades and sporting events.

band, military. A large, mobile ensemble designed to accompany military activities. Since time immemorial, military activities have been accompanied by brass instruments, drums, and cymbals; as the apostle Paul asks rhetorically (I Corinthians 14:8), "If the trumpet gives an uncertain sound, who shall prepare himself to the battle?" Military bands, dominated by brass and percussion, arose in Europe during the Middle Ages; Frederick the Great added other melody instruments such as oboes and clarinets to them. In the latter 18th century the instrumentation of military bands included the sound of JANISSARY MUSIC, with drums, cymbals, and bells. About the middle of the 19th century Adolph Sax enriched the sonority of French military bands by creating the instruments later known as saxophones.

As a rule, each branch of the military service has its own band. In the U.S. the bands of the Marines, the Army, the Navy, and the Air Force maintain a high professional standard of performance. In Great Britain there are several excellent military bands, notably that of the Scots Guard Royal Artillery, with its signature bagpipes. In France the Garde Républicaine still presents regular concerts.

band, string. 1. An American traditional music ensemble of the Appalachian and southern regions, evolved in the 19th century from black minstrelsy, work songs, and Anglo-Irish balladry. The instrumentation generally included banjo, fiddle, and guitar. See OLD-TIME. 2. The string section of the orch.

band, symphonic. A British or American ensemble capable of playing music on a symphonic scale. An American univ., college, or high school band includes more wind instruments than a regular sym. orch.; a large symphonic band may have up to 2 dozen clarinets, numerous brass and saxophones, and an impressive contingent of percussion; double basses may also be included. A considerable literature for symphonic band exists, beginning with the HARMONIEMUSIK Haydn wrote for Prussian regimental bands, the predecessors of the sym. band. Among modern composers, Holst, Vaughan Williams, Hindemith, Stravinsky, Prokofiev, and Milhaud contributed to the repertoire; Schoenberg made a significant departure from his 12-tone method by composing a perfectly tonal piece for an American school band. The activity and music of the American symphonic band (also called concert band or wind orch.) is one of music's best-kept secrets.

band, wind. The wind section of the orch.

band, wood. The woodwind section of the orch.

banda (It.). 1. Military band. 2. The brass instruments and percussion in the orch. 3. An ensemble playing onstage in an opera.

bandmaster. Conductor of a military band.

bandola (Sp.). 1. A Latin American relative of the Spanish BANDURRIA, with a teardrop shape and concave back; *bandolón* (Sp.), a larger BANDURRIA, with 6 sets of 3 or 4 strings.

bandonéon (Sp., from Ger. *Bandoneon, Bandonion*). A large square concertina with single or double action, invented by the German instrument manufacturer Heinrich Band in the 1840s. The instrument has become a staple of South American tango music.

bandora (Sp.). PANDORA.

bandoura (Ukr.). 1. An Ukrainian ARCHLUTE. 2. A hybrid Ukrainian PSALTERY with an unfretted lute, tuned chromatically and played with a plectrum. Found in Russia, it is sometimes used in homogenous ensembles. Also called *bandura*.

bandurria (Sp.). A flat-backed member of the lute family from Spain, with 6 pairs of steel or gut strings and fretted short neck, and played in tremolo style with a plectrum; very similar to the mandolin. See BANDOLA.

banjo. African-American traditional string instrument, strummed or picked with a plectrum, with a long neck connected to a tambourinelike, open-backed wooden body; the striking of strings against the head is one of the timbral effects available. The standard instrument has 5 strings; the 5th, added in the 1830s, is the thumb string (*drone chanterelle*), about half the others' length. The tenor banjo has a shorter neck and no thumb string.

The 1st written references to a banjo forerunner occur in the 17th century, with references to a *strum-strum* and *banza*; later names include *banjer* and *banjar*. A nearly identical similar instrument called the *ramkie* was in use in southern Africa by the early 18th century. Undoubtedly similar instruments existed long before these. In the U.S. the banjo was an ingredient of blackface minstrelsy, Appalachian and southern old-time string-band music (played in a strummed style called variously "frailing," "rapping," or "knocking"), bluegrass (in a style developed 1st by Earl Scruggs, in which the player picks the strings with his 3 fingers), and early jazz (using the tenor banjo).

Bànk Bàn. Opera by Erkel, 1861, in which the contemporaneous political situation is reflected in an allegory of 13th-century German wickedness and patriotic Hungarian vengeance; considered the national opera of Hungary.

bar. 1. A vertical line dividing measures on the staff, indicating where the strong downbeat falls; barline. The 1st regular usage of the bar occurs in 15th-century TABLATURES; the downbeat and upbeat were not consistently notated until the Baroque. 2. An American name for measure; thus, the notes and rests contained between 2 bars.

Barber of Seville, The (Il Barbiere di Siviglia). Opera by Rossini, 1816, after Beaumarchais's *Le Barbier de Séville*. The opera's original name was *Almaviva, ossia L'Inutile precauzione* (Almaviva, or The Futile Precaution). Count Almaviva is in love with Rosina, ward of Dr. Bartolo, who plans to marry her. The versatile barber Figaro arranges various disguises for Almaviva to pursue his quest. After much chicanery, the lovers are united by Bartolo's own notary. Rossini's setting was preceded by that of Giovanni Paisiello (1740-1816), which enjoyed considerable success (1782).

Barber, Samuel, American composer of superlative gifts; b. West Chester, Pa., Mar. 9, 1910; d. N.Y., Jan. 23, 1981. His aunt was the esteemed operatic contralto Louise Homer (b. Shadyside, near Pittsburgh, Apr. 30, 1871; d. Winter Park, Fla., May 6, 1947), her husband the composer Sidney Homer (b. Boston, Dec. 9, 1864; d. Winter Park, July 10, 1953). Barber began composing at age 7; played piano at school functions and organ in church; enrolled at age 14 in the newly founded Curtis Inst. of Music, Philadelphia; studied with I. Vengerova, R. Scalero, E. de Gogorza, and Fritz Reiner. A baritone, he sang successfully in public; however, composition became his main interest. Barber avoided facile, fashionable modernism; he adopted a lyrical and Romantic idiom with a distinct originality in its melodic and harmonic aspects. His early successes included the *Overture to "The School for Scandal,"* after Sheridan (1933); *Dover Beach* for Baritone and String Quartet, after Arnold, premiered that same year and was recorded by Barber 2 years later; *Music for a Scene from Shelley* (1935); and the 1-movement Sym. No. 1 (1937). In 1938 the *1st Essay for Orchestra* and *Adagio for Strings*

The Princeton Banjo Club, c. 1890

(arranged from his 1936 String Quartet) were performed by Toscanini; the passionately serene *Adagio* became one of the most popular American works.

Barber taught intermittently at the Curtis Inst. (1939–42); joined the Army Air Force (1942), which commissioned him to write his 2nd Sym. The orig. score, with an electronic instrument imitating the sound of radio signals, was performed by Koussevitzky (1944); after the war he eliminated such incidental intercalations; this demilitarized version was performed by the Philadelphia Orch. (1948); still dissatisfied, he discarded the work except for the 2nd movement, rev. as *Night Flight* (1964). (The complete work was rediscovered and revived after his death.) He was discharged (1945) and settled in Mount Kisco, N.Y., in a house (named "Capricorn") purchased jointly with Menotti (1943).

Barber was always devoted to the theater. He wrote a ballet, *Medea (The Serpent Heart)*, for Martha Graham (1946): rev. and danced by her group as *Cave of the Heart* (1947); arr. as an orch.l suite (1947); a final extrapolation was *Medea's Meditation and Dance of Vengeance* (1956). As a preparation for greater challenges, he produced a light operatic sketch, *A Hand of Bridge*, to a Menotti libretto (composed 1953; 1959); it is a staple of the opera workshop repertory. In *Prayers of Kierkegaard* for Soprano, Chorus, and Orch. (1954) he experimented with the modern oratorio; but only in 1957 did he write his 1st full opera, *Vanessa*, to a Romantic libretto by Menotti; it was successfully produced by the Metropolitan Opera, N.Y., in 1958, and earned Barber his 1st Pulitzer Prize in music; a rev. version was produced at the Spoleto Festival U.S., Charleston (1978). A more ambitious opera, commissioned by the Metropolitan, was *Antony and Cleopatra*, after Shakespeare, produced with great expectations at the opening of the new Metropolitan Opera House (1966). Unfortunately, the production was haunted by mechanical mishaps: a revolving stage did not rotate properly, the acoustics were faulty, and the annoyed newspaper critics damned the music along with the staging. Barber rev. the libretto and music; the new version (1975) received a more positive response.

Despite these difficulties, Barber emerged as a composer of fine instrumental works: the Piano Concerto (1962), a striking work in an original modern idiom, winning him his 2nd Pulitzer Prize; the Piano Sonata, introduced by Horowitz (1949), which uses modernistic resources, including applications of 12-tone writing; and his witty piano suite *Excursions* (1945). Barber excelled as a melodist in vocal works, among them *Knoxville: Summer of 1915* (1948);

Hermit Songs (1953); *Andromache's Farewell* (1963); and numerous songs and song cycles. Although the harmonic structures of his music remained fundamentally tonal, he made free use of chromatic techniques, verging on atonality and polytonality; his mastery of modern counterpoint enabled him to write canons and fugues in effective neo-Baroque sequences. His orchestration was opulent without being turgid; his treatment of solo instruments was unfailingly idiomatic, even though requiring a virtuoso technique.

barbershop harmony. A type of A CAPPELLA close harmony singing, replete with chromatic passing notes. It developed in the late 19th century when men waiting for haircuts crooned favorite songs. Professional and amateur groups were very popular in the 1st quarter of the 20th century. In modern performances this type of arrangement is usually presented satirically, with appropriately costumed singers gesticulating in mock eloquence.

Barbirolli, (Sir) **John** (Giovanni Battista), eminent English conductor; b. London, Dec. 2, 1899, of Italian-French parentage; d. there, July 29, 1970. He made his 1st appearance as a cellist at the Queen's Hall (1911), then joined the Queen's Hall Orch. (1916); after serving in the British Army (1918–19) he resumed his musical career. In 1924 he organized a chamber orch. in Chelsea, which he conducted for several years; served as a staff conductor with Sadler's Wells, London (1926–29); substituted for Beecham at a London Sym. Orch. concert (1927); guest conducted at Covent Garden, London (1929–33); in 1933 was named conductor of both the Scottish Orch., Glasgow, and the Leeds Sym. Orch. He made his American debut as a guest conductor with the N.Y. Phil. (1936–37); was engaged as its permanent conductor (1937–42). He returned to England, where he was named conductor of the Hallé Orch., Manchester (1943), its conductor-in-chief (1958), and its conductor laureate for life (1968). He returned to guest conducting at Covent Garden; led the Houston Sym. (1961–67) while continuing at the Hallé. He was knighted (1949) and made a Companion of Honour (1969).

Barbirolli was distinguished primarily in the Romantic repertoire; his interpretations were marked by nobility, expressive power, and brilliance. He had a fine pragmatic sense of shaping the music according to its inward style, without projecting his own personality upon it. However, this very objectivity tempered his success with American audiences, accustomed to charismatic flamboyance in music making. He had a special affinity for English music and performed many works of Elgar, Delius, and Britten; conducted the 1st performances of the 7th and 8th Syms. of Vaughan Williams; later developed a fondness for Mahler but had little use for most modern music. He composed an Oboe Concerto on themes by Pergolesi for his 2nd wife, the oboist Evelyn Rothwell.

Barbiere di Siviglia, Il. BARBER OF SEVILLE, THE.

Barbosa-Lima, Carlos, Brazilian guitarist; b. São Paulo, Dec. 17, 1944. He began guitar study at age 7; his principal teachers were Isaias Savio and Andrés Segovia. He made his 1st U.S. tour (1967); toured South America, Europe, and Israel; commissioned works for guitar from Ginastera, Balada, and Mignone; transcribed works by Bach, Handel, and other composers. He combined his concert career with teaching at the Manhattan School of Music, N.Y.

barcarolle (*barcarole*; Fr., from It. *barce* + *rollo*, bark-rower; It., *barcarola, barcarole*; Ger. *Barcarole*). 1. A song of the Venetian gondoliers. The genre is inseparably associated with the taxi-boaters who entertained and delighted tourists in the 19th century. The barcarolle is usually set in 6/8 or 12/8 time, suggesting a lulling motion of the waters in the Venetian canals. The most famous operatic barcarolle is in Offenbach's *Tales of Hoffmann.* Gilbert and Sullivan turned the gondoliers into sentimental lovers in their operetta *The Gondoliers.* Also called *gondoliera.* 2. A vocal, instrumental, or concerted piece imitating the Venetian gondoliers' songs. Chopin wrote a poetic barcarolle for piano (op. 60, 1845), in which the accompaniment maintains a constant movement from the tonic to the dominant while the melody engages in artful fiorituras; Mendelssohn has 3 gondola pieces in his *Songs Without Words* for piano.

bard. A name given to Celtic epic poets and musicians. The activities of the bards were 1st described in ancient Greek and Roman sources, but the tradition dates to the pre-Christian British Isles when they were dominated by Celtic peoples. By the later Middle Ages, bards were included in a caste system which included the *filidh*, a higher ranking type of bard. The use of an elaborate metric system and classical Gaelic persisted into the 17th century in Ireland and the 18th century in Scotland (where *bard* still means "poet" in Scots Gaelic). Bards were accompanied by (or accompanied themselves on) the Irish harp or the CRWTH (Welsh lyre). The medieval Welsh bards established an annual festival, the EISTEDDFOD, which was revived in 1880 as a choral festival.

Barenboim, Daniel, greatly talented Israeli pianist and conductor; b. Buenos Aires, Nov. 15, 1942. He studied and played piano publicly in Buenos Aires; in 1952 the family moved to Israel. During the summers of 1954–55 he studied with Edwin Fischer, Markevitch, and Enrico Mainardi in Salzburg; studied with Nadia Boulanger in Paris (1954–56), then Carlo Zecchi in Siena. He performed in Paris (1955) and London (1956); in N.Y., played Prokofiev's First Piano Concerto under Stokowski (1957); gave 1st U.S. solo recital there (1958).

Barenboim played all 32 Beethoven sonatas in a concert series in Tel Aviv (1960); repeated this cycle in N.Y. He made his conducting debut in Haifa (1957); toured with the Israel Phil. in the U.S. (1967); led the London Sym. Orch. in N.Y., then filled engagements throughout the U.S. In 1967 he married the English cellist Jacqueline DuPré; they appeared in numerous sonata programs until she was stricken in 1972 with multiple sclerosis and had to abandon her career. He made his debut as an opera conductor at the Edinburgh Festival (1973); named music director of the Orch. de Paris (1975). In 1988 Barenboim was named artistic director of the new Bastille Opéra, Paris; disagreements over artistic policy and remuneration led to Barenboim's abrupt dismissal (1989). That same month he was appointed Solti's successor as music director of the Chicago Sym. Orch.

As a pianist he sometimes emphasized Romantic flexibility over Classic balance of form and thematic content. As a conductor he gave congenial performances of the masterpieces of Romantic music; became particularly engrossed in the music of Tchaikovsky, Elgar, and Bruckner. His early performances of Mozart were accused of sentimentality and excessive attention to detail, but his interpretations have gained in perspective and maturity.

barform (Ger.). A medieval German strophic structure; each stanza is divided into 2 sections, the *Aufgesang* (on song), followed by an *Abgesang* (off song). In musical settings, the 1st section is repeated before moving to the 2nd (which is not repeated); thus AAB. The term would have been long relegated to limbo had it not been for Wagner, who provides a surprisingly logical definition of barform in *Die Meistersinger von Nürnberg.* In a once famous series of analyses, Alfred Lorenz found Wagner's operas to consist of a string of barforms.

baritone (Grk., deep sound). 1. The medium-range male voice, lower than the tenor and higher than the bass. The compass of the baritone voice is from A to about f¹. An ideal baritone voice possesses the character of lyric masculinity. Baritones are rarely given leading operatic roles, usually the property of tenors; yet Mozart entrusted the role of Don Giovanni to a baritone. Character baritones range from villainy to piety, from nefarious Scarpia in *Tosca* to saintly Amfortas in *Parsifal*. The imperious Wotan in Wagner's *Der Ring des Nibelungen* is a bass baritone. The most famous dramatic baritone part is the toreador Escamillo in *Carmen*. Baritones are often given comic parts, e.g., Mr. Lavender-Gas, a professor of literature in Menotti's satirical opera, *Help! Help! The Globolinks!*

2. A valved brass instrument in B♭, with the range of the trombone and a narrower bore than the euphonium. The baritone serves to fill harmony rather than play solo. The distinction between baritone and euphonium is maintained in the U.K., France, and Germany (*Tenorhorn* and *Bariton*, respectively); in the U.S. *baritone* tends to be used for either instrument.

baritone clef. The obsolete F clef on the 3rd line:

barline. See BAR.

Baroque music

T he classical music developed between around 1600 and 1750. Although the term *Baroque* (from Port. *barroco*, irregularly shaped jewel) originally implied a bizarre and even crude quality, it has acquired the opposite meaning of dignity and precise craftsmanship. The concept originated with French critics and was used in a derogatory sense; in his *Dictionnaire de Musique* (1768) Rousseau wrote that "a Baroque music is one in which harmony is confused, charged with modulations and dissonances; the melody is harsh and hardly natural; the intonation difficult; and the movement constrained." For the 18th century and early 19th century the expression *goût baroque* came to mean having a taste for fanciful design in architecture and painting. A change of attitude came about in 19th-century Germany with the rehabilitation of the Baroque style as a technically advanced art. Curt Sachs applied the term to music in 1919; despite some disagreement, the term came to refer to the era of the greatest flowering of contrapuntal, instrumental, and vocal art.

In this period a symbolic link was drawn between tonalities and musical intervals with the words in the text; major keys became the expressions of joy, fortitude, and determination, whereas minor keys expressed melancholy, dejection, and depression; melodic intervals conveyed the meaning of the text even when words themselves could not be clearly understood. For example, in Bach's cantatas words describing the act of rising to heaven were set to ascending passages in a major key; a descent into the nether regions was illustrated by a mournful falling figuration; acute agony was invariably rendered by chromatic ornamentation.

The inception of the Baroque coincided with the birth of opera, a genre that challenged the highly intricate polyphony of the late Renaissance. Baroque opera grew out of the rudimentary form envisioned by the Florentine Camerata, where the melodic content of operatic recitative, arioso, and aria was essentially monodic; the voice and text were determining factors of rhythm. By the mid-18th century the 1st wave of Italian bel canto vocal virtuosity had overwhelmed monodic intelligibility. In other vocal genres the madrigal evolved into the cantata; unstaged religious operas called oratorios were written to sidestep the theatrical bans during Lent; and in all vocal music the da capo aria became the primary formal structure.

Even more dramatic developments occurred in instrumental music, which developed an independent identity from the vocal music it had mostly accompanied. In addition to the solo keyboards, brass ensembles, and string consorts that had existed before 1600, the orch. and mixed chamber ensembles became extremely popular; important instrumental genres during this period included the sonata, concerto, suite, prelude and fugue, theme and variations, and sinfonia (the predecessor of the sym.). Another major development was that of the BASSO CON-

TINUO, by which figures (i.e., ciphers) indicated the intervals from the bass note up, thus determining the harmonic progressions and (in the later Baroque) modulations. By that time German composers had revitalized the polyphonic style with the fugue, within or without the basso continuo framework.

Another great accomplishment of Baroque music was the decisive retreat from the ambiguous modality of the period to definitive tonality, culminating in the creation of Bach's *Well-Tempered Clavier*. The prevailing techniques of the Baroque era were derived not from postmedieval polyphonic modalities, but from the new principles of symmetry and self-consistency, allowing unlimited diversity of thematic transformation within a firm tonal system.

The popular notion that Baroque music is analogous to architecture—with the metrical units in a melody corresponding to the severe proportions of a Doric column, and the melodic ornaments of a Baroque phrase measured as precisely as the fanciful incrustations of a Gothic cathedral—is belied by contemporaneous descriptions of the state of mind and bodily actions of performers of this music. In *Principles of Musick* (London, 1636) Charles Butler commented: "The composer is transported as it were with some musical fury, so that he himself scarce knoweth what he doth nor can presently give a reason for his doing." In *Musick's Monument* (London, 1676) Thomas Mace described the mental state of the Baroque listener: "Sensibly, fervently, and zealously captivated, we are drawn into raptures and contemplations by those unexpressible rhetorical, uncontrollable persuasions and instructions of musick's divine language, to quietness, joy, and peace; absolute tranquility." The anonymous English translator of a 1702 French treatise described his impression of Corelli: "I never met with any man that suffered his passions to hurry him away so much whilst he was playing on the violin…. His eyes will sometimes turn as red as fire; his countenance will be distorted; his eyeballs roll as in an agony; and he gives in so much to what he is doing that he doth not look like the same man." This was the same Corelli to whom a German musician said, after he heard him play, "Your 1st name may be archangel, but you play like an archdevil."

In light of these reports it seems ironic that the 20th-century standard of "authentic" performance of Baroque music should be commanded by the rigorous observations of the written notation with no tolerance for deviation from the mathematical precision of meters and rhythms unless specifically indicated in Baroque writings, and that no personal or collective emotions should intrude into the immutable music of Baroque masters.

Several generations of earnest musicians have devoted themselves to the worship of the Baroque musical deities—Monteverdi, Bach, Handel, and their lesser contemporaries Vivaldi, Telemann, Buxtehude, Purcell, and the 2 Scarlattis—with a singleness of purpose worthy of Torquemada. Bach became the Jehovah of music; to alter a single note in his music was a blasphemy. Inevitably, conflicting factions arose among the specialists; no 2 music editors agreed on the proper execution of trills, mordents, and other ornaments in Bach's works. Yet diversity ruled the performance of Baroque music in its own time; one suspects the "truth" to be less marmoreal, if there be a single truth.

The forms of sonata and sym. were still undifferentiated at the middle of the 18th century, when the Baroque era was coming to an end. The STYLE GALANT and EMPFINDSAMER STIL introduced a less monumental and polyphonic music, with an at times idiosyncratic attention to the smallest affect. Learning from the music of these style's proponents (e.g., Bach's sons, the MANNHEIM SCHOOL), Haydn and Mozart brought these forms to perfection. Mozart was born 6 years after the death of Bach and while Handel and Telemann were still alive. Haydn began his career during the Baroque era, but he mostly relinquished the monody of the early Classic style in favor of a new type of enlightened polyphony. With Mozart and Haydn, music entered the mature Classic period.

Baroque organ. A highly developed Gothic organ with several manuals and a variety of stops, as used by Bach.

Baroque suite. See SUITE.

barré (Fr.). In lute or guitar playing, the stopping of several or all the strings with the left-hand forefinger.

barré, grand. GRAND BARRÉ.

barrel organ. A species of mechanical organ in which a wooden cylinder (or barrel) is mounted on a metal spindle attached to a board; the cylinder is slid into position and rotated with a hand crank; the brass staples or pins on the cylinder's circumference trigger the desired pitches. The wind required to produce sound is generated by a bellows operated by the same hand crank. The whole action is encased according to the purchaser's means. The instrument had its origins in antiquity, with a variety of instruments evolving over centuries. The most salient use of the barrel organ was as a church instrument in parishes unable to afford or find organists; it also found its way onto the streets, where it received the erroneous moniker of HURDY-GURDY. The instrument's popularity died out in the mid-19th century; a substantial number of instruments have survived in playable condition, attesting to their practical and durable designs. Related examples include the ORCHESTRION and Maelzel's PANHARMONICON.

barrelhouse. A style of piano playing related to BOOGIE-WOOGIE, using ragtime, stomping, or walking basses, 4/4 meter, and blues-based melodies. Barrelhouse was in vogue in the 1920s and 1930s, beginning in the South and then moving north.

Barrett, "Syd" (Roger). See PINK FLOYD.

Bartered Bride, The (Cz. *Prodaná nevěsta*, The Bride Who Is Sold). Opera by Smetana, 1866. In early 19th-century Bohemia the parents of a young woman intend to give her in marriage to a rich man's son, but she loves another. The wily marriage broker attempts to bribe the woman's lover, but he indignantly refuses to trade love for money. All ends well when the lover reveals that he is himself wealthy, a prodigal son of the village headmaster.

Bartók, Béla

Great Hungarian composer whose style was intimately welded to his pioneering folk music research; b. Nagyszentmiklós (now Sinnicolau Mare, Rumania), Mar. 25, 1881; d. N.Y., Sept. 26, 1945. His mother gave him his 1st piano lesson. After his father's death (1888) and several itinerant years (during which he began composing), the family settled in Pozsony, where he studied with László Erkel (son of Ferenc) and Hyrtl. In 1899 he enrolled at the Budapest Academy of Music; studied with István Thomán, a Liszt pupil, and J. Koessler. In his early career he was best known as a pianist; his early compositions reveal the accumulating influences of Liszt, Brahms, R. Strauss, and anti-German Hungarian nationalism; his 1st public success was the symphonic poem *Kossuth* (1903).

In 1904 he began exploring the resources of genuine traditional music, including Hungarian, Rumanian, Slovak, and other ethnic strains found in his native Transylvania. He formed a scholarly and personal friendship with Kodály; they traveled throughout Hungary collecting folk songs and publ. *Magyar Népdalok* (1906). From then on Bartók journeyed all over Hungary, doing fieldwork and making recordings; his writings helped changed the long-held notion that Hungarian music was a bastardized version of Gypsy music.

In 1907 Bartók succeeded Thomán at the Academy of Music; collected traditional music in North Africa (1913); planned (with Kodály) the monumental *Corpus Musicae Popularis Hungaricae*; was a member of the musical directorate (with Dohnányi and Kodály) of the short-lived Hungarian Democratic Republic (1919). A brilliant pianist, he limited his recitals primarily to his own compositions; regularly toured throughout Europe; gave 2-piano concerts with his 2nd wife, Ditta Pásztory (b. *c.* 1902; d. Budapest, Nov. 21, 1982), whom he married in 1923.

In his own compositions Bartók was now influenced by tonal colors and impressionistic harmonies as cultivated by Debussy and other modern French composers; his successful ballet *The Wooden Prince* (1917) and opera *Bluebeard's Castle* (1918) made him an international figure. The harmonic sonority of his music remained true to tonality, but he expanded it to embrace chromatic polymodal structures and unremittingly dissonant chordal combinations; in his piano works he exploited the extreme registers of the keyboard, often in the form of tone clusters to simulate pitchless drumbeats (*Allegro Barbaro*, 1911). He made use of strong asymmetrical rhythmic figures derived from Slavic folk music, a usage that imparted a non-Western coloring to his music. The melodic line of his works sometimes veered toward atonality in its chromatic involutions, but the impact of folk song on his music grew pronounced; in some instances he employed melodic figures comprising the 12 different notes of the chromatic scale; however, he never adopted the integral techniques of the 12-tone method.

Bartók toured as a pianist in the U.S. (1927–28) and the Soviet Union (1929). He resigned from the Academy of Music (1934) but continued ethnomusicological research as a member of the Hungarian Academy of Sciences. He realized the long-planned *Corpus Musicae Popularis Hungaricae*, cataloguing 13,000 Hungarian and 2,500 Rumanian items, and explored relationships between these and Slovak, Ruthenian, and Serbo-Croatian music.

The shadow of Nazism gradually made life intolerable, even as Bartók composed some of his most important works. With increasing press attacks and his withdrawal from public musical life, he awaited his mother's death (1939) and the outbreak of war to make his final voyage to the U.S. (1940). He had many setbacks: unsuccessful duo-recitals, rejected MSS on Rumanian and Turkish music, declining health; but he worked on 2,600 discs of Yugoslav traditional music in a Harvard Univ. collection (1941–42). ASCAP helped support the Bartóks in his last years; the Concerto for Orch. (1944), commissioned by Koussevitzky at Szigeti and Reiner's behest, proved to be his most popular work (and last completed score). He succumbed to polycythemia and was buried in N.Y. State. His 3rd Piano Concerto was virtually complete, except for the last 17 bars; the Viola Concerto was a sketch; his pupil Tibor Serly finished the 1st and realized the 2nd. Ironically but typically, perfor-

mances and recordings of his music increased enormously after his death; 43 years after his death his remains were taken to Budapest (as he had requested) for a state funeral (1988).

Far from being a cerebral purveyor of abstract musical designs, Bartók was an ardent student of folkways, seeking the roots of meters, rhythms, and modalities in the spontaneous songs and dances of the people. Indeed, he regarded his analytical studies of popular melodies as his most important contribution to music. He was similarly interested in the natural musical expression of children, firmly believing them capable of absorbing modalities and asymmetrical rhythmic structures with greater ease than adults trained in the rigid disciplines of established music schools. His remarkable collection of piano pieces, *Mikrokosmos* (6 vols., 1940), was intended as a method to initiate beginners into the world of unfamiliar tonal and rhythmic combinations; in this he provided a parallel means of instruction to the Kodály method of musical training.

For the grownups Bartók left a considerable legacy: the trio of stage works (adding the pantomime *The Miraculous Mandarin*, 1926); choral music, a cappella and accompanied, notably the *Cantata Profana* (1934); numerous songs, mostly related to folk melodies; orch.l music, including suites, folk music transcriptions, violin concertos and rhapsodies (2 apiece), and the powerful *Music for Strings, Percussion and Celesta* (1937); piano music, including lively folk melody arrangements and more abstract works, e.g., *14 Bagatelles* (1908), Sonata (1926), *Out of Doors* (1926), Sonata for 2 Pianos and Percussion (1937); and chamber music, featuring several violin and piano works, the Sonata for Solo Violin (1944), the quirky *Contrasts* written for Szigeti and Benny Goodman (1938), and, most importantly, the 6 string quartets, written between 1908 and 1939; in their breadth and depth these are the most important works in this genre since Beethoven, and one wishes that Bartók had lived to write his planned 7th quartet.

Béla Bartók, c. 1940.

baryton. A now-archaic string instrument developed from the VIOLA BASTARDA. It is about the size of the VIOLA DA GAMBA, with 6 or 7 gut strings and up to 20 wire sympathetic strings that could with difficulty be plucked. Josef Haydn wrote around 175 chamber works with baryton for his patron Count Nikolaus Esterházy, an avid amateur player. Somewhat popular in the 18th century, the instrument sank into oblivion thereafter.

Basie, "Count" (William), eminent African-American jazz pianist and bandleader in the big band era; b. Red Bank, N.J., Aug. 21, 1904; d. Hollywood, Fla., Apr. 26, 1984. After studying with his mother he met and learned from important stride pianists (J. P. Johnson, "Fats" Waller); toured on the vaudeville circuit; played for various bands in N.Y. (1923–26). While touring the country he was stranded in Kansas City and began playing for local bands (1927); joined Bennie Moten's Kansas City Orch., one of the pioneering swing bands. After Moten's death (1935) Basie formed a new band with old and new colleagues (including saxophonist Lester Young, its most important soloist); in a few years it had gained fame, recording contracts, and a new name: the Count Basie Orch.

Basie attracted attention by his peculiar piano technique, emphasizing passages played by a single finger while directing his band with a glance or a movement of the eyebrow. He adopted Waller's discursive brilliance on the keys but altered it in the direction of rich economy of means. He fulfilled big band engagements, with a break for financial reasons when he formed an octet (1950–51); however, he soon organized a new big band; toured Europe successfully several times; played a command performance for the Queen of England (1957). In 1976 he suffered a heart attack; he recuperated and returned to an active career. He received the Kennedy Center Award for achievement in the performing arts (1981) and the Medal of Freedom (posth., 1985). Among his greatest hits were *1 O'Clock Jump* (which became his theme song), *Jumpin' at the Woodside*, *Goin' to Chicago*, *Lester Leaps In*, *Broadway*, *April in Paris*, and *L'il Darlin'*.

bass (Eng., Ger.; It. *basso*). 1. The lowest male voice, with an ordinary compass from F to e¹; its extreme compass from C to f¹. Bass parts are usually assigned to the roles of sinners or devils, e.g., Mephistopheles in *Faust*, the villainous usurper Boris Godunov in Mussorgsky's opera, and the treacherous but victimized Hunding in *Die Walküre*. 2. A singer having such a voice. There have been exceptional bass singers, particularly Russian, who could go below this range. In his drama *The Sea Gull*, Chekhov tells of an Italian bass singer who sang at the Imperial Opera in St. Petersburg, rousing the audience to admiring frenzy when he reached low C, whereupon a choir bass singer in the audience shouted "Bravo" an octave lower (C¹). Some speculate that the vast expanse of the Russian landscape somehow contributes to the formation of powerful chest cavities, whereas the cerulean waters of the Bay of Naples favor the development of the lyric tenor voice in Italy. 3. The lowest tone in a chord, or the lowest part in a composition. 4. The double bass or electric bass. 5. The antiquated bass VIOLA DA GAMBA. 6. A family of organ stops on the pedals, e.g., GEMSHORNBASS. 7. A valved brass instrument used in brass and military bands with a range similar to the tuba.

bass clarinet. A B-flat instrument an octave below the standard (soprano) clarinet. Like other members of the clarinet family, it evolved from the now obsolete CHALUMEAU. The 1st extant instruments date from the end of the 18th century; the modern form was patented by Sax in 1838. The bass clarinet, like other orig. "adjunct" woodwinds, has been very popular among 20th-century composers.

bass clef. F clef on the 4th line:

bass drum. A large cylindrical drum of indefinite pitch with heads on both sides; the orch.l instrument is at least 32 inches in diameter. The bass drum entered the classical orch. with Gluck and Mozart (*The Abduction from the Seraglio*); Beethoven introduced it in the finale of his Sym. No. 9. The dramatic and often ominous sound of the bass drum was used dramatically by R. Strauss and Mahler, who punctuated his symphonies with single drum strokes. In *Pagliacci* the bass drum is one of the props used by the clown who is tormented by jealousy. In Litolff's overture *Robespierre* it illustrates Robespierre's beheading. The instrument is commonly found in military bands.

bass flute. The lowest member of the flute family, requiring a wide cylinder and wound tubing. The range starts at c, an octave below the standard (soprano) flute. The bass flute requires considerable lung power to blow and superlative lip technique to articulate. Although the instrument is reported in the 16th century, a truly usable version did not appear until early in the 20th century (see ALBISIFONO).

bass guitar. The bass guitar has a guitar-shaped body, 4 strings, and is held against the body like the guitar. Most electric basses are solid-bodied, like electric guitars. It used to provide the rhythmic and harmonic underpinnings in a standard rock band.

bass line. Since the Renaissance, the lowest voice; since the Baroque period, the determinant of the melody and essential factor in the harmony. The bass line is often and incorrectly regarded as a subsidiary component of a musical work, but each of its notes serves as the lowest pitch in a series of progressive harmonies, determining the position of each chord. The melody and the bass line are the most exposed, so that the counterpoint between them must be absolutely correct according to the rules of the stylistic period.

bass-baritone. High bass voice.

basse danse (Fr., flat or low dance; It. *bassadanza*). The principal court dance of the late Middle Ages and Renaissance. The word *basse* describes the nature of the dance, in which partners move with striding steps without leaving the floor. The basse danse was usually accompanied by wind instruments, with a 3/2 meter and a slow and stately tempo. The dance was 1st cited by a troubadour in 1340; the earliest extant choreography dates from the late 15th century; the CANTUS FIRMUS technique was used, with improvisation being the means of realization.

basset horn (Fr. *cor de basset*; Ger. *Bassetthorn*; It. *corno di bassetto*). A relative of the clarinet and chalumeau, now pitched in F, with a bent or curved tube and a mellow, sombre timbre. The range has varied, with a present compass from F to c³; this later instrument, with its larger bore, makes it virtually identical with the 19th-century alto clarinet. But the orig. basset horn in G, with a narrow bore, was developed in the late 18th century; this instrument was the one favored by Mozart for his Masonic music, Serenade K. 361, Requiem, 3 operas, divertimentos, vocal and wind ensemble pieces, and in his orig. plan for the Concerto K. 622. Beethoven, Mendelssohn, and R. Strauss also composed for this Classic-period instrument.

basso buffo (It.). A comic bass, such as the music master Don Basilio in Rossini's *The Barber of Seville*.

basso cantante (It.). A bass-baritone.

basso continuo (It., continuous bass; Eng. *figured bass*, *thoroughbass*; Fr. *basse continue*, *chifrée*, *figurée*; Ger. *Generalbass*, *bezifferter Bass*; abbr. *continuo*). In Baroque ensemble music, the part played by 2 instruments: a keyboard or fretted string instrument (harpsichord, organ, lute) and a low-pitched instrument (cello, viola da gamba, bassoon); also, the notational system used for it. Only the bass line is given; the numerical figures located below it indicate the intervals above it to be played, thus spelling out stenographically the harmony within a given tonality. The number of notes or the position of the voices is not specifically marked.

Historically the basso continuo developed as an aid to improvisation and as an indicator of the main harmony in the keyboard part, which supplied the accompaniment. Thus 6/4/2 over the bass D in the key of A major or minor would indicate the notes D, E, G-sharp, and B, whether in closed or open harmony, and with any number of duplications of these notes. Ornamentation and contrapuntal writing could be included in the improvisation, depending on the ability and taste of the player. This method was widely used in the educational system in Baroque music and retained in musical training through the 19th century.

basso obbligato (It.). An indispensable bass part or accompaniment.

basso ostinato (It., obstinate bass). A bass line consisting of a repeated motive or phrase that serves as the foundation for variations in the upper voices. A basso ostinato can be greatly diversified as a composition, or it can also approach the more static quality of the English GROUND BASS. The PASSACAGLIA and CHACONNE are musical forms that use a basso ostinato.

basso profondo (It., profound bass). The lowest bass voice; often misspelled *basso profundo*.

bassoon (It. *bassone*, *fagotto*; Fr. *basson*; Ger. *Fagotte*). A low-pitched woodwind instrument of the oboe family; its double reed is attached via a curved metal mouthpiece to the conical double bore, which consists of 4 joints wrapped vertically, ending in a slightly flared bell. The cognates *fagotto* and *Fagott* mean "a bundle of sticks," a description of its shape; traditionally pearlwood is used in its manufacture. The normal range is from B♭₁ to f², sometimes higher. The bassoon's tone is soft and mellow, with the nasal quality associated with double-reed instruments. It developed from the curtal in the mid-1600s, with gradual expansions of range and keys until the 19th century, when 2 schools of bassoon making—French and German—were distinct. At 1st used for BASSO CONTINUO, the bassoon was given independent parts from the mid-18th century on, as well as concertos (Mozart, K. 191, 1774); the opening of Stravinsky's *The Rite of Spring* (1913) gives the bassoon a solo in its upper register, producing an unusual but memorable effect. See also CONTRABASSOON, OBOE.

Bastien und Bastienne. A Singspiel by Mozart, 1768, with a simple tale of young love for a plot. It was produced in Vienna when Mozart was only 12 years old, at the home of Dr. Franz Mesmer, the protagonist of the therapeutic method known as mesmerism.

baton (Fr. *bâton*, stick, roll). 1. A conductor's stick; oddly enough, the French word for the conductor's baton is *baguette*. The device was in place by the mid-18th century, although it had several predecessors. 2. In the U.S. the term is used, in a less exalted way, for the twirling stick of a drum major or majorette in a marching band.

battaglia (It., battle; Eng. *battle piece*). In musical usage, compositions featuring imitations of trumpet flourishes, fanfares, drum rolls, and similar explosions of sound; the genre evolved in the 14th century. Battle pieces were invariably in march time, with a typical rhythmic figure consisting of a half note followed by 2 quarter notes. A characteristic piece of Renaissance battle music is *La Guerre de Marignan*, a 4-part chanson by Jannequin (1528). Instrumental battaglias were written by Byrd, Sweelinck, Frescobaldi, and Couperin. Monteverdi introduced the STILE CONCITATO in the *canto guerriero Combattimento di Tancredi et Clorinda* (1624). Possibly the most durable battaglia is the representation of the combat between David and Goliath in the *Biblische Historien* keyboard sonata No. 1 by Kuhnau (1700). During the Baroque period, battaglias were favored in operas and oratorios.

Of later works of the battaglia type *The Battle of Prague* for Piano by the Czech composer F. Koczwara still furnishes its element of bland amusement. Beethoven's notorious *Wellington's Victory*, originally written for a mechanical instrument, is often cited as a paradigm of exceptionally bad music written by an exceptionally great composer. Tchaikovsky wrote a celebrated symphonic battle piece, *Overture: 1812*, commemorating the Russian victory over

Napoleon. One of the best operatic battaglias is the orch.l interlude in Rimsky-Korsakov's *The Legend of the Invisible City of Kitezh*, describing the battle between Russians and Mongols.

Battaglia di Legnano, La. Opera by Verdi, 1849. The Italian struggle for independence was mirrored in its historical plot describing the defeat of the Emperor Frederick Barbarossa by the Lombards in 1176.

battery (Fr. *batterie*). 1. The group of percussion instruments. 2. A drum roll. 3. An 18th-century term for arpeggiated figures; also, the RASGUEADO. 4. A SONNERIE.

Battle Cry of Freedom, The. A Civil War ballad composed by George Frederick Root in 1863 that became a rallying song in the Union (Northern) camp. President Lincoln wrote to Root saying that his song had done more for the cause of the Union than 100 generals and 1,000 orators.

Battle Hymn of the Republic, The. A song with words written by Julia Ward Howe (1862), to the well-known tune of *Glory, Glory, Hallelulah!* The composer of the music is unknown. Another set of words to the same tune is *John Brown's Body Lies a-Mouldering in the Grave*, referring to the martyred abolitionist. Both were popular in the Civil War era and remain well-known folk songs.

Battle, Kathleen, outstanding black American soprano; b. Portsmouth, Ohio, Aug. 13, 1948. She studied voice with Franklin Bens; made her debut at the Spoleto Festival in the Brahms Requiem (1972); subsequently sang with the N.Y. Phil., Cleveland Orch., Los Angeles Phil., and other leading American orchs. She made her Metropolitan Opera, N.Y., debut as the Shepherd in *Tannhäuser* in 1978; in 1985 she appeared for the 1st time at Covent Garden, London, as Zerbinetta. Karajan chose her as soloist for the New Year's Day concert of the Vienna Phil. in 1987, telecast throughout the world. A dispute with management led to her departure from the Metropolitan in January 1993; nonetheless, she continues to perform widely, excelling in the light, lyric soprano repertoire; she is particularly acclaimed for her portrayals of Sophie, Despina, Blonde, Zerlina, Nanetta, and Adina. She has also established a concert and recital career.

battuta (It., beat). Downbeat; measure; also, a return to strict time after a deviation.

Bax, (Sir) **Arnold** (Edward Trevor), outstanding English composer; b. London, Nov. 8, 1883; d. Cork, Ireland, Oct. 3, 1953. He studied with Matthay and Corder at the Royal Academy; visited Dresden (1905), then went to Ireland; became profoundly interested in ancient Irish folklore after reading Yeats; wrote poetry and prose under the pseudonym Dermot O'Byrne; found inspiration in Celtic legends for his compositions. In 1910 he returned to England; that year he visited Russia, composing a series of piano pieces in a pseudo-Russian style; wrote music for J. M. Barrie's skit *The Truth about the Russian Dancers.* The rest of his career was spent living in Britain and visiting Ireland. By the 1930s he was receiving frequent official acknowledgments (knighthood, 1937; Master of the King's Musick, 1941); but the days of his greatest creativity were over, and personal depression set in.

Bax was an extremely prolific composer; his style is rooted in neo-Romanticism, but impressionistic elements are much in evidence in his instrumental compositions; his harmony is elaborate and rich in chromatic progressions; his contrapuntal fabric is free and emphasizes complete independence of component melodies. In his many settings of folk songs, he succeeded in adapting simple melodies to effective accompaniments in modern harmonies; in his reinterpretations of Celtic moods, he successfully re-created the archaic style of the epoch. In addition to 7 syms., concert overtures, and many chamber and piano works, he composed many orch.l works with Celtic inspiration, among them *In the Faery Hills* (1909), *Spring Fire* (1913), *The Garden of Fand* (1916), *November Woods* (1917), *Tintagel* (1919), *The Happy Forest* (1921), *Winter Legends* 1930), and *A Legend* (1944). He was an excellent pianist but was reluctant to play in public; he never appeared as a conductor of his own works. He recorded the story of his life and travels in his candid autobiography, *Farewell, My Youth* (London, 1943).

Be (Ger.). The flat sign ♭.

Beach, Amy Marcy Cheney (Mrs. H.H.A.), eminent American composer; b. Henniker, N.H., Sept. 5, 1867; d. N.Y., Dec. 27, 1944. She studied with Ernest Perabo, Carl Baermann, and J. W. Hill. She made her debut as a pianist in Boston, on Oct. 24, 1883, playing a concerto by Moscheles (1883). In 1885 she married Dr. H. H. A. Beach, a Boston surgeon, a quarter of a century older than she was; the marriage was a happy one, and she used as her professional name Mrs. H. H. A. Beach. She began to compose modestly, mostly for piano, but then completed a Mass in E-flat, performed by the Handel and Haydn Soc. in Boston (1892). In 1896 her GAELIC SYMPHONY, based on Irish folk tunes, was performed by the Boston Sym. with exceptional success; this was probably the 1st performance of a female composer's sym. in the U.S. She premiered her Violin Sonata with Franz Kneisel (1897), then appeared as soloist with the Boston Sym. in the 1st performance of her Piano Concerto in C-sharp Minor (1900). She also wrote a great many songs in Romantic manner. After her husband died in 1910 she traveled to Europe; played her works in Berlin, Leipzig, and Hamburg; attracted considerable attention as the 1st of her sex and national origin to compose music at a European level of excellence. She returned to the U.S. in 1914 and lived in N.Y. Her music, unpretentious in its idiom and epigonic in its historical aspect, retains its importance as the work of a pioneer woman composer in America. Her opera *Cabildo* (1932) has received attention in recent years.

Beach Boys, The. (Leader/bass/vocal: Brian Wilson, b. Hawthorne, Calif., June 20, 1942; guitar/vocal: Carl Wilson, b. Hawthorne, Dec. 21, 1946; drums/vocal: Dennis Wilson, b. Hawthorne, Dec. 4, 1944; d. Dec. 28, 1973, Marina del Rey, Calif.; guitar/vocal: Al Jardine, b. Los Angeles, Sept. 3, 1942; lead vocal: Mike Love, b. Los Angeles, Mar. 15, 1941.) Surf-and-sun harmony group of the 1960s. Formed around the musical Wilson family, the group was led by the talented, although troubled, teenager, Brian Wilson, who wrote and arranged most of their material. They 1st scored hits with surf-oriented material, and then expanded into the general Calif. teen lifestyle (*Surfer Girl, Fun Fun Fun, California Girls*). Wilson's studio skills grew to such an extent that he was able to create dense arrangements, both vocal and instrumental, influenced by producer Phil Spector. He reached the zenith of his creativity with the album *Pet Sounds* and the hit *Good Vibrations* (1967). Increasing drug use, mental problems, and tensions within the group led Brian to withdraw from performing and composing after this

Mrs. H. H. A. Beach

time, and the quality of the group's work dropped. They have survived primarily as a nostalgia band, although occasionally Brian has returned to recording, writing, and performing, with mixed results.

beam. Horizontal lines connecting adjacent notes.

Bear, The (Fr. *L'ours*). Sym. No. 82 in C Major by Haydn, written in 1786. The nickname may derive from the imitation bagpipe passage, as circus bears were often made to dance to the accompaniment of Scottish bagpipes. The sym. is 1 of the 6 "Paris" syms., written for performances there; thus the frequent listing under its French nickname.

Beardslee, Bethany, American soprano, specialist in modern music; b. Lansing, Mich., Dec. 25, 1927. She made her N.Y. debut in 1949. She became known as a specialist in modern music, evolving an extraordinary technique with a flutelike ability to sound impeccably precise intonation; mastered the art of SPRECHSTIMME, enabling her to give classic renditions of such works as Schoenberg's *Pierrot Lunaire*; was also a brilliant performer of vocal music by Berg, Webern, Babbitt, and Stravinsky; gave fine recitals. She has taught at the Westminster Choir College and Univ. of Tex., Austin.

beat. 1. A division or unit of musical time in a measure. 2. A movement of the hand in marking ("beating") time. 3. In a trill, the pulsation of 2 consecutive tones. 4. An APPOGGIATURA. 5. A throbbing caused by the interfering tone waves of 2 tones of different pitch. Beats are used to tune instruments correctly.

Beat Me, Daddy, 8 to the Bar. A 1940 boogie-woogie song of immense and lasting popularity, originally a hit by the Andrews Sisters and revived by Bette Midler among others.

Beatles, The. (Leader/guitar/vocal: John [Winston] Lennon, b. Liverpool, Oct. 9, 1940; d. N.Y., Dec. 8, 1980; vocal/bass/piano: [John] Paul McCartney, b. Liverpool, June 18, 1942; lead guitar/vocal: George Harrison, b. Feb. 25, 1943; drums/vocal: Ringo Starr [Richard Starkey], b. Liverpool, July 7, 1940.) Original, innovative, and highly influential rock band of the 1960s. Influenced by the skiffle movement in England, Lennon formed his 1st band with art-school friends when he was a teenager; named for their school, the Quarry Men 1st played in 1957 at church bazaars

and local events. Paul McCartney joined the band originally as a guitarist and brought on board a younger school friend, George Harrison; Lennon brought his friend Stu Sutcliffe, an art student who tried (not too successfully) to play the bass. The group was known 1st as the Silver Beatles, and then simply the Beatles. (Inspired by Buddy Holly and the Crickets, Lennon hit upon the Beatles name, which possessed the acoustical ring of the coleopterous insect and the rock-associated "beat.") The Beatles opened at the pseudo-exotic Casbah Club in Liverpool in 1959; they soon moved to the more prestigious Cavern Club (1961), where they co-opted Pete Best as drummer. In 1960 they played in Hamburg's Star Club, scoring a gratifyingly vulgar success with the beer-sodden customers by their loud, electrically amplified sound. Back in England the Beatles crept on to fame. In 1961 they were taken up by the perspicacious promoter Brian Epstein, who owned a local record shop and launched an extensive publicity campaign to put them over the footlights. Sutcliffe died of a brain hemorrhage in 1962. Best was forced out of the group after their 1st audition tapes were made for the British Decca label; he was replaced by local drummer Richard Starkey, aka Ringo Starr.

The quartet opened at the London Palladium in 1963 and drove the youthful audience to a frenzy, a scene that was to be repeated elsewhere in Europe, in America, in Japan, and in Australia. Although American in origin, the type of popular music plied by the Beatles had an indefinably British lilt. The meter was square; the main beat was accentuated; syncopation was at a minimum; the harmony was modal, with a lowered submediant in major keys as a constantly present feature; a propensity for plagal cadences and a proclivity for consecutive triadic progressions created at times a curiously hymnal mood. They lyrics, most of them written by Lennon and McCartney, were distinguished by suggestive allusions, sensuous but not flagrantly erotic, anarchistic but not destructive, cynical but also humane. Early hits began with *Love Me Do* and *Please Please Me*, through *I Want to Hold Your Hand, Can't Buy Me Love, All My Loving, 8 Days a Week, Ticket to Ride*, and *Day Tripper*. The Beatles produced the highly original films *A Hard Day's Night, Help!, Yellow Submarine*, and *Let It Be*. The group abandoned touring with much fanfare in 1966 to devote themselves to their recording activities; the 1st result was the innovative single *Penny Lane* and *Strawberry Fields Forever*, both sound portraits of their Liverpool childhood. They produced one of the 1st, and best, concept albums with 1967's *Sergeant Pepper's Lonely Hearts Club Band*, featuring the song *A Day in the Life* that was originally banned by British radio. After manager Brian Epstein died in 1967, the band members turned to Transcendental Meditation, spending some months in India, resulting in the songs that were recorded on the famous *White Album*. However, strains in the group were beginning to show, and eventually they acrimoniously split up in 1969-70.

For their subsequent careers, see also JOHN LENNON and PAUL MCCARTNEY.

Beatrice di Tenda. Opera by Bellini, 1833, in which a Renaissance woman falsely accused of adultery is put to death by her husband.

Béatrice et Bénédict. Opera by Berlioz, 1862, after the comic romantic subplot in Shakespeare's *Much Ado About Nothing*.

Beautiful Dreamer. S. Foster's last song, 1864.

bebop. A type of jazz that emerged in America in the 1940s, associated most strongly with Charlie Parker, Dizzy Gillespie, Thelonious Monk, and Bud Powell. The name derives from one of the many onomatopoeic vocables (*bebop, rebop, bop*) descriptive of jazz techniques. The invention of the term and the technique is generally attributed to Gillespie.

The most striking characteristic of bebop is its maximal velocity, sometimes reaching 20 notes a second in clear articulation, with a strong off-beat stress. Bebop is marked by irregular syncopation, a widely ranging melody of quasi-atonal configurations, and an accompaniment in rapidly changing modernistic harmonies, making use of unresolved dissonances and polytonal combinations. The improvisational element far outweighs the precompositional; bebop structures are almost invariably repetitions of 32-bar sections, and there is a fair amount of blues-based or borrowed composition.

bebung (Ger., trembling). A vibrato effect on stringed instruments or on a clavichord, the latter produced by pressing the key repeatedly so that the tangent vibrates the string slightly without releasing it.

bécarre (Fr.). Natural sign (♮).

Bechet, Sidney (Joseph), famous Creole-American jazz clarinetist and soprano saxophonist; b. New Orleans, May 14, 1897; d. Garches, France, May 14, 1959. He learned to play blues and rags on clarinet in HONKY-TONKS in Storyville, the brothel district of New Orleans; played with leading jazz

musicians in New Orleans, Chicago, and on tour; purchased a soprano saxophone in London (*c.* 1919). In addition to making frequent trips to Europe throughout the 1920s, he worked with Armstrong (as part of Clarence Williams's Blue Five and the Red Onion Jazz Babies), Ellington, Noble Sissle, Johnny Hodges, Tommy Ladnier, and Zutty Singleton. The 1930s saw a decline in his fortunes, but the Dixieland revival brought him to the forefront once more. During the 1940s he led his own jazz groups in N.Y.; made recordings with Mezz Mezzrow; settled in Paris (1951). He was one of the most important jazz musicians of his era, unchallenged on the soprano saxophone, admired for his passionate playing and unbridled freedom of expression. His autobiography, *Treat It Gentle*, was publ. posth. (N.Y., 1960).

becken (Ger.). Cymbal (singular); cymbals (plural).

Becker, John J(oseph), remarkable American composer; b. Henderson, Ky., Jan. 22, 1886; d. Wilmette, Ill., Jan. 21, 1961. He studied with Alexander von Fielitz, Carl Busch, and Wilhelm Middleschulte. He taught at Notre Dame Univ. (1917–27), the College of St. Thomas, St. Paul (1929–35), Barat College of the Sacred Heart, Lake Forest (1943–57), and sporadically at the Chicago Musical College; also served as Minn. State Director for the Federal Music Project (1935-41). His early works are characterized by romantic moods in a somewhat Germanic manner. About 1930 he was drawn into the circle of modern American music; was on the editorial board of *New Music Quarterly* (founded by Cowell); became associated with Ives (Becker scored his *General William Booth's Entrance into Heaven* for Chamber Orch. in 1934). He conducted modern American works with various groups in St. Paul. Striving to form a style that would combine modernity and Americanism, he wrote 8 works for various instrumental groups called "Soundpieces." He also developed a type of dramatic work connecting theatrical action with music. Becker's mature music is marked by sparse sonorities of an incisive rhythmic character contrasted with dissonant conglomerates of massive harmonies.

bedächtig (Ger.). Meditatively.

bedeutungsvoll (Ger.). Full of meaning; significantly.

bedrohlich (Ger.). Menacing.

Beecham, (Sir) **Thomas,** celebrated English conductor; b. St. Helens, near Liverpool, Apr. 29, 1879; d. London,

Mar. 8, 1961. His father was a man of great wealth, derived from the manufacture of the once-famous Beecham pills, which worked wonders on anemic people; thanks to this, young Thomas could engage in life's pleasures and the arts without troublesome regard for economic limitations. After early studies, he organized an amateur orch. soc.; conducted a performance with the prestigious Hallé Orch. in Manchester (both in 1899). In 1902 he got a conducting job with a traveling opera company, giving him valuable practical experience in theater music; settling in London, he gave his 1st professional sym. concert there (1905); assembled and led the New Sym. Orch. (1906–1908); formed the Beecham Sym. Orch., which presented its 1st concert in 1909. In 1910 Beecham appeared in a new role, that of operatic impresario; from then until 1913 he worked at Covent Garden and at His Majesty's Theatre. During this period he boldly invited R. Strauss to Covent Garden to conduct his own operas. Beecham conducted at the Theatre Royal at Drury Lane; became conductor of the Royal Phil. Soc. concerts (1916); gave operatic performances with the Beecham Opera Co.

By that time his reputation as a forceful and charismatic conductor was securely established in England. His audiences grew; many critics, impressed by his imperious ways and his unquestioned ability to bring out spectacular operatic productions, sang his praise; however, other commentators criticized his somewhat cavalier treatment of the classics. In appreciation of his services to British music, Beecham was knighted in 1916; at the death of his father, succeeded to the title of baronet; his inherited money was insufficient to pay for exorbitant financial disbursements in his ambitious enterprises; was declared bankrupt in 1919; rebounded a few years later and continued his extraordinary career.

In 1928 Beecham made his American debut conducting the N.Y. Phil.; organized and conducted the Delius Festival in London (1929), to which Delius, racked by tertiary syphilitic affliction, paralyzed and blind, was brought from France to attend; organized the London Phil. Orch. (1932); contemptuous of general distaste for the Nazi regime in Germany, he took the London Phil. to Berlin for a concert attended personally by the Führer (1936). Returning to England, he continued his activities; as the Allied war situation deteriorated on the Continent, he went to the U.S. in 1940, and toured Australia; engaged as music director and conductor of the Seattle Sym. Orch. (1941–43); filled guest engagements at the Metropolitan Opera, N.Y. (1942–44). In America he was not exempt from sharp criticism, which he haughtily dismissed as philistine complaints. On his part he was outspoken in his snobbish disdain for the cultural inferiority of England's wartime allies, often spicing his comments with mild obscenities, usually of a scatological nature. Returning to England, he founded yet another orch., the Royal Phil. (1946); resumed his post as conductor at Covent Garden (1951). In 1957 Queen Elizabeth II made him a Companion of Honour. He publ. an autobiography, *A Mingled Chime* (London, 1944) and an extensive biography of *Frederick Delius* (London, 1958).

Beer, Jacob Liebmann. See MEYERBEER, GIACOMO.

Beeson, Jack Hamilton, American composer; b. Muncie, Ind., July 15, 1921. He studied with B. Phillips, B. Rogers, H. Hanson, and Bartók. In 1945 Beeson joined the staff of Columbia Univ.; was made a prof. there in 1965; chairman of the music dept. (1968–72); named MacDowell Prof. of Music (1967). His music is marked by enlightened utilitarianism; particularly forceful are his operatic compositions, which seem to grow out of the lyrical aesthetic of Douglas Moore's many operas and also rely on American subject manner.

Beethoven, Ludwig van

〜〜 〜〜 〜〜 〜〜 〜〜

The great German composer whose unsurpassed genius, expressed with supreme mastery in his syms., chamber music, concertos, and piano sonatas, revealed an extraordinary power of invention and marked a historic turn in the art of composition; b. Bonn, Dec. 15 or 16 (baptized Dec. 17), 1770; d. Vienna, Mar. 26, 1827. (Beethoven himself maintained that he was born in 1772, and that the 1770 date referred to an older brother, deceased in infancy, whose name was also Ludwig but who in fact was born in 1769.) The family was of Dutch extraction (the name means "beet garden"). Beethoven's grandfather, also named Ludwig van Beethoven (b. Malines, Belgium, Jan. 5, 1712; d. Bonn, Dec. 24, 1773), served as choir director of St. Pierre, Louvain, in 1731; went to Liège, where he sang bass in the cathedral choir of St.-Lambert (1732); became a member of the choir in Bonn, where he married Maria Poll (1733). The couple's only surviving child was Johann van Beethoven (b. Bonn, c. 1740; d., Bonn, Dec. 18, 1792), who worked for the Elector (from 1752); he married a young widow, Maria Magdalena Leym (1767); they were the composer's parents.

Beethoven's father gave him rudimentary instruction in music; he also studied with T. F. Pfeiffer, G. van Eeden, F. Rovantini, Franz Anton Ries, and Nikolaus Simrock. His 1st important composition teacher was Christian Gottlob Neefe (1748–98), a thorough musician who understood his young pupil's great potential; he guided Beethoven through the study of Bach and keyboard improvisation. His *9 Variations for Piano on a March of Dressler* was the 1st to be publ. (1783); the Bonn Elector Maximilian Franz appointed him to the post of deputy court organist (1784–92); also served as a violist in theater orchs. In 1787 the Elector sent him to Vienna, where he stayed briefly; the report that he met and played for Mozart and that Mozart pronounced him a future great composer may be a figment of somebody's eager imagination. Beethoven returned to Bonn in time to watch his mother die of tuberculosis; was obliged to provide sustenance for his 2 younger brothers, as his father, who drank in excess, could not meet his obligations; Ludwig successfully petitioned for half of his father's salary (1789). He supplemented his income by giving piano lessons; he met several wealthy patrons, and continued to compose.

In 1790 Haydn was honored in Bonn by the Elector on his way to London; it is likely that Beethoven was introduced to him, and that Haydn encouraged him to come to Vienna to study with him. Beethoven went to Vienna in Nov. 1792 and began his studies with Haydn. Haydn was a kindly but somewhat careless teacher; when Haydn had to go to London again (early 1794), Beethoven began a formal study of counterpoint with Johann Georg Albrechtsberger (1736–1809), a learned musician and knowledgeable pedagogue; these studies continued for about a year, until 1795. Beethoven also took lessons in vocal composition with Salieri, the Imperial Kapellmeister at the Austrian court.

Beethoven was fortunate to find a generous benefactor in Prince Karl Lichnowsky, who awarded him an annual stipend about 1800; he was amply repaid by entering the pantheon of music history through Beethoven's dedications to him of the *Sonate Pathétique* (op. 13), the op. 1 piano trios, and other works. Other aristocratic patrons of Vienna similarly honored were Prince Franz Joseph Lobkowitz, whose name adorns the title pages of the 6 String Quartets, op. 18; the *Eroica Sym.* (after Beethoven dropped the dedication to Napoleon); the Triple Concerto, op. 56; and (in conjunction with Prince Andrei Razumovsky) the 5th and 6th syms. Prince Razumovsky, the Russian ambassador to Vienna, maintained in his residence a string quartet (1808–14) in which he himself played the 2nd violin (the leader was Beethoven's friend Ignaz Schuppanzigh). It was to Razumovsky that Beethoven dedicated his 3 string quartets (op. 59), in which he used an authentic Russian folk melody in 2 of the quartets. Another Russian patron was Prince Nikolai Golitzyn, for whom Beethoven wrote his great string quartets opp. 127, 130, and 132.

Beethoven made his 1st public appearance in Vienna on Mar. 29, 1795, as soloist in one of his piano concertos (probably the B-flat Major Concerto, op. 19); played in Prague, Dresden, Leipzig, and Berlin (1796); participated in fashionable "competitions" with other pianists, including Joseph Wolffl (1799) and Daniel Steibelt (1800). At the threshold of the 19th century, new compositions included the 1st and 2nd Syms.; 5 piano sonatas, including the "Moonlight" and "Pastoral" (opp. 22, 36, 27/1–2, 28); the 4th and 5th violin sonatas (opp. 23–24); the variations on Mozart's *Bei Männern, welche Liebe fühle* for cello and piano; 6 string quartets (op. 18); the Septet in E-flat Major (op. 20); the String Quintet (op. 29); and a number of songs.

Beethoven's early career in Vienna was marked by fine success; he was popular not only as a virtuoso pianist and a composer, but also as a social figure who was welcome in the aristocratic circles of Vienna; Beethoven's students included society ladies and even royal personages, such as Archduke Rudolf of Austria, to whom Beethoven dedicated the so-called *Archduke Trio* (op. 97, 1811). But Beethoven's progress was fatefully affected by a mysteriously growing deafness, which reached a crisis in 1802. In Oct. 1802 he wrote a poignant document known as the "Heiligenstadt Testament," after the village in which he resided at the time. The document, discovered after Beethoven's death, voiced his despair at the realization that the most important sense of his being, the sense of hearing, was inexorably failing. He implored his brothers, in case of his early death, to consult his physician, who knew the secret of his "lasting malady" contracted 6 years before he wrote the *Testament*, in 1796. The etiology of his illness leaves little doubt that the malady was syphilis. However, the impairment of his hearing may have had an independent cause: an otosclerosis, resulting in the shriveling of the auditory nerves and concomitant dilation of the accompanying arteries. Externally there were signs of tinnitus, a constant buzzing in the ears, about which he complained. To the end of his life Beethoven had hoped to find a remedy for his deafness among the latest "scientific" medications. His *Konversationshefte* (conservation books) bear a pathetic testimony to these hopes; in one, dated 1819, he notes down the address of a doctor who treated deafness by "sulphur vapor" and a vibration machine.

By tragic irony Beethoven's deafness greatly contributed to the study of his personality, thanks to the existence of the conversation books in which his interlocutors wrote down their questions and Beethoven replied, a method of communication that became a way of his life after 1818. Unfortunately, Beethoven's friend and amanuensis, Anton Schindler, altered or deleted many of these; it seems also likely that he destroyed Beethoven's correspondence with his doctors, as well as the recipes which apparently contained indications of treatment by mercury, the universal medication against venereal and other diseases at the time.

Remarkably, Beethoven was able to continue his creative work with his usual energy; there were few periods of interruption in the chronology of his works, and similarly there was no apparent influence of his health or moods of depression on the content of his music; tragic and joyful musical passages had equal shares in his inexhaustible flow of varied works. In Apr. 1803 Beethoven presented a concert of his compositions in Vienna at which he was soloist in his 3rd Piano Concerto (op. 37); the program also contained performances of his 2nd Sym. and the oratorio *Christus am Oelberge* (op. 85). In May 1803 he played the Violin Sonata, op. 47, accompanying the mulatto virtuoso George Polgreen Bridgetower (*c.* 1779–1860). The dedication would doubtless have gone to him; but a dispute ended their relationship, and

Beethoven chose to honor the violinist Rodolphe Kreutzer (1766–1831). *The Kreutzer Sonata* (1889) was the title of a Tolstoy novella concerning the moral risks of the unrestrained and adulterous emotions "inspired" by the Romantic Beethoven.

During 1803–1805 Beethoven composed his great Sym. No. 3 in E-flat Major, op. 55, the *Eroica*. According to Beethoven's student Ferdinand Ries, Beethoven tore off the title page of the MS of the score, orig. dedicated to Napoleon, after learning of his self-proclamation as Emperor of France in 1804; Beethoven supposedly exclaimed, "So he is a tyrant like all the others after all!" Ries reported this story shortly before his death, some 34 years after the work's composition, which throws some doubt on its credibility. In fact, an 1804 letter to the publishing firm of Breitkopf & Härtel, long after Napoleon's proclamation of Empire, has Beethoven's reference to the title of the work as "really Bonaparte." His own copy of the score shows that he crossed out the designation "Inttitulata Bonaparte" but allowed the words written in pencil, "Geschrieben auf Bonaparte," to stand. In Oct. 1806, when the 1st ed. of the orch.l parts was publ. in Vienna, the sym. received the title *Sinfonia eroica composta per festeggiare il souvenire d'un grand' uomo* (Heroic sym. composed to celebrate the memory of a great man). But who was the great man whose memory was being celebrated in Beethoven's masterpiece? Napoleon was very much alive and was leading his Grande Armée to new conquests (his forces entered Vienna in 1805). Yet the famous funeral march (2nd movement) expressed a sense of loss and mourning. Is the tribute now a generalized one? Or is Beethoven mourning the passing of Napoleon, First Consul? The mystery remains.

In 1803 Schikaneder, still the manager of Theater an der Wien, asked Beethoven to compose an opera to a libretto he had prepared, but Beethoven soon lost interest and instead began work on another opera, based on J. N. Bouilly's *Leonore, ou L'Amour conjugal*. The completed opera was named *Fidelio, oder Die eheliche Liebe*; Fidelio is the heroine's assumed name in her successful efforts to save her imprisoned husband. Elements of German Singspiel persist through this otherwise serious work. The opera was given at the Theater an der Wien in late 1805, under difficult circumstances, a few days after the French army entered Vienna. There were only 3 performances before the opera was rescheduled for the spring of

1806; after another long hiatus a final and greatly rev. version was produced in 1814. Beethoven wrote 3 overtures for the earlier versions (now known as LEONORE 1, 2, and 3); for the final version he wrote a 4th overture, now known as FIDELIO.

An extraordinary profusion of creative masterpieces marked the years 1802–1808 in Beethoven's life. During these years he brought out the 3 String Quartets, op. 59, dedicated to Count Razumovsky; the 4th, 5th, and 6th Syms.; the Violin Concerto; the 4th Piano Concerto; the Triple Concerto; the Coriolan Overture; and 6 piano sonatas, including the *Tempest* (D minor, op. 31/2); the *Waldstein* (C major, op. 53); and the *Appassionata* (F minor, op. 57). Financial difficulties beset Beethoven: the various annuities from patrons were uncertain, and the devaluation of Austrian currency played havoc with his calculations. In Oct. 1808 King Jerome Bonaparte of Westphalia offered the composer the post of Kapellmeister of Kassel at a substantial salary, but Beethoven decided to remain in Vienna.

Between 1809 and 1812 Beethoven wrote his 5th Piano Concerto; the String Quartet in E-flat Major, op. 74 ("Harp"); the incidental music to Goethe's drama *Egmont*; the 7th and 8th Syms.; and 3 Piano Sonatas, including the E-flat Major, op. 81a, whimsically subtitled *Das Lebewohl, Abwesenheit, und Wiedersehn* (also known by its French subtitle, *Les Adieux, l'absence, et le retour*). He provided a specific description for this "sonate caracteristique." Such explicit characterization was rare with Beethoven; he usually avoided programmatic descriptions, preferring to have his music stand by itself. Even in his 6th Sym., the *Pastoral*, which bore specific subtitles for each movement and had the famous imitations of birds singing and the realistic portrayal of a storm, Beethoven appended a cautionary phrase: "More as an expression of one's feelings than a picture." He specifically denied that the famous introductory call in the 5th Sym. represented the knock of Fate at his door, but the symbolic association was too powerful to be removed from the legend; yet the characteristic iambic tetrameter was anticipated in several of Beethoven's works. Czerny, a Beethoven student and friend, claimed that Beethoven derived the theme from the cry of a songbird (*Emberiza*, European bunting), which was piercing enough to compensate for Beethoven's increasing deafness as he took one of his frequent walks in the Vienna woods. However it may be, the 4-note motif became inexorably connected with the voice of doom for enemies and the exultation of the victor in battle. It was used as a victory call by the Allies in World War II; that 3 short beats followed by 1 long beat spelled *V* for *Victory* in Morse code reinforced its effectiveness. The Germans could not very well jail people for whistling a Beethoven tune, so they took it over themselves as the 1st letter of the archaic German word *Viktoria* and trumpeted it blithely over their radios.

Another famous nicknamed work by Beethoven was the *Emperor* Concerto, op. 73. He wrote it in 1809, when Napoleon's star was still high in the European firmament; some publicist decided that the martial strains of the music, with its sonorous fanfares, were a tribute to the French Emperor; Francis I, emperor of Austria, could also have been intended, as the work was dedicated to his brother, Archduke Rudolf. Political reasons seemed to underlie Beethoven's designation of his Piano Sonata, op. 106, as the *Hammerklavier Sonata*, i.e., a work written for a "hammer keyboard," or fortepiano, as distinct from harpsichord. But all of Beethoven's piano sonatas were for fortepiano; moreover, he assigned the title *Hammerklavier* to 4 late sonatas (opp. 101, 106, 109, and 110); by so doing he was expressing his patriotic consciousness of being a German.

Like many professional musicians, Beethoven was occasionally called upon to write a work glorifying an important event or a famous personage. Pieces of this kind seldom achieve validity and usually produce bombast. Such a work was Beethoven's *Wellingtons Sieg, oder Die Schlacht bei Vittoria*, celebrating the British victory over Joseph Bonaparte, Napoleon's brother who was briefly on the Spanish throne. In 1814 Beethoven wrote a cantata entitled *Der glorreiche Augenblick*, intended to mark the "glorious moment" when his erstwhile idol, Napoleon, was defeated.

Personal misfortunes, chronic ailments, and intermittent quarrels with friends and relatives preoccupied Beethoven's entire life. He ardently called for peace among men but he never achieved peace with himself. Yet he could afford to disdain the attacks in the press; on the margin of a critical but justified review of his *Wellington's Victory*, he wrote to the writer: "You wretched scoundrel! What I shit is better than anything you could ever think up!" Beethoven was overly suspicious; he exaggerated his poverty; he was untidy in personal habits, often using preliminary drafts of his compositions to cover the soup and the chamber pots, leaving telltale circles on the MSS. He studiously examined the winning numbers of the Austrian government lottery, hoping to find a numerological clue to a fortune for himself.

His handwriting was all but indecipherable. An earnest Beethoveniac spent time with a microscope trying to figure out what kind of soap Beethoven wanted his housekeeper to purchase for him; the scholar's efforts were crowned with triumphant success: the word was *gelbe*—Beethoven had wanted a piece of yellow soap. The copying of his MSS presented difficulties; not only were the notes smudged, but sometimes Beethoven even failed to mark a crucial accidental. A copyist said that he would rather copy 20 pages of Rossini than a single page of Beethoven. On the other hand, Beethoven's sketchbooks, containing many alternative drafts, are extremely valuable, for they allow one to peek into the inner sanctum of Beethoven's creative process.

Beethoven had many devoted friends and admirers in Vienna, but he spent most of his life in solitude. Czerny reports in his diary that Beethoven once asked him to let him lodge in his house, but Czerny declined, explaining that his aged parents lived with him and he had no room for Beethoven. Deprived of the pleasures and comforts of family life, Beethoven sought to find a surrogate in his nephew Karl, son of his brother Caspar Carl, who died in 1815. Beethoven regarded his sister-in-law Johanna as an unfit mother; he went to court to gain sole guardianship over the boy, pouring torrents of vilification upon the woman, implying that she was engaged in prostitution. In 1820 he won custody; he proceeded to make his nephew's life very difficult, particularly by banning visits to his mother. In 1826 Karl attempted suicide; it would not be unreasonable to blame this act in large part to Beethoven's stifling avuncular affection. Karl survived, went into the army, was the sole inheritor of his uncle's estate, and enjoyed a normal life.

That Beethoven dreamed of an ideal life companion is clear from his numerous utterances and candid letters to friends, in which he often asked them to find a suitable bride for him. But he never kept company with any particular woman in Vienna. Beethoven lacked social graces; he could not dance; he was unable to carry on a light conversation; and behind it all there was the dreadful reality of his deafness. There were several objects of his secret

COURTESY OF THE NEW YORK PUBLIC LIBRARY

Ludwig van Beethoven

passions, among his pupils or the society ladies to whom he dedicated his works. But he either didn't propose marriage or chose unsuitable women; most married less hesitant or more conventional suitors. It was inevitable that Beethoven should seek escape in such illusions. The best-known of these was the famous letter addressed to an "unsterbliche Geliebte" (Immortal Beloved), couched in exuberant emotional tones characteristic of the sentimental romances of the time and strangely reminiscent of Goethe's novel *The Sorrows of Young Werther* (1774). The letter was never mailed; it was discovered in the secret compartment of Beethoven's writing desk after his death. Clues to the identity of the object of his passion are maddeningly few. He voiced his fervid anticipation of an impending meeting at a place indicated only by the letter *K*; he dated his letter "Monday, the 6th of July," without specifying the year; eager Beethoveniacs readily established the most likely year as 1812. Then a complete inventory of ladies of Beethoven's acquaintance from 14 to 40 years of age was laid out, and the lengthy charade unfolded, lasting one and a half centuries. The most likely "Immortal Beloved" now seems to be Antonie Brentano, the wife of a merchant and mother of 1 daughter. Beethoven was a frequent visitor at their house (1810–12), and he dedicated works to all 3 Bretanos. His letters to Antonie and her replies express mutual devotion, but they could not be stylistically reconciled with the torrid protestation of undying love in the unmailed letter. And if indeed Frau Brentano was the "Immortal Beloved," why could not a tryst have been arranged in Vienna when her husband was away on business? There were other candidates; one researcher established, from consulting the town records of arrivals and departures, that Beethoven and a certain lady of his Vienna circle were in Prague on the same day, and that about 9 months later she bore a child who seemed to bear a remarkable resemblance to Beethoven. Another researcher, exploring the limits of the incredible, concluded that Beethoven had sexual relations with his sister-in-law Johanna and that his execration of her stemmed from this relationship (a view explored in the recent film *Immortal Beloved*). Other speculation regarding his consorting with prostitutes and alleged repressed homosexuality have also caused ink to be spilt.

The so-called 3rd style of Beethoven is generally assigned to the last 10 or 15 years of his life. It included the composition of his monumental 9th Sym. (op. 125), completed and 1st performed in Vienna (1824); the program also included excerpts from the Missa Solemnis (op. 123) and *Die Weihe des Hauses* (The Consecration of the House, 1815). It is reported that Caroline Unger, the alto soloist in the Missa Solemnis, had to pull Beethoven by the sleeve at the end of the 2nd movement so that he would acknowledge the applause he could not hear. With the 9th Sym., Beethoven completed the evolution of the symphonic form as he envisioned it. The choral finale, with its reminiscences of the previous 3 movements, was his manifesto addressed to the world at large, using the text from Schiller's ode *An die Freude* (To Joy). In it, Beethoven, through Schiller, appealed to all humanity to unite in universal love; a musical work was serving a sociopolitical ideal.

Beethoven's last 5 string quartets (opp. 127, 130, 131, 132, and 135) served as counterparts to his 9th Sym. in their striking innovations, dramatic pauses, and novel instrumental tone colors. Other works of importance were the 10th violin sonata (op. 96); the 6 late piano sonatas, as original as the string quartets; the monumental *33 Variations on a Waltz by Diabelli* (op. 120); 2 sets of bagatelles (opp. 119 and 126); and numerous English-language folk song arrangements.

In Dec. 1826, on his way back to Vienna from a visit in Gneixendorf, Beethoven was stricken with a fever that developed into a mortal pleurisy; dropsy and jaundice supervened to this condition; surgery to relieve the accumulated fluid in his organism was unsuccessful, and he died on the afternoon of Mar. 26, 1827. It was widely reported that an electric storm struck Vienna as Beethoven lay dying; this fact has been confirmed by the contemporaneous Viennese weather bureau. But the story that he raised his clenched fist aloft as a gesture of defiance to an overbearing Heaven must be relegated to fantasy. The funeral of Beethoven was held in all solemnity; his life and work has been honored on many occasions and in many ways.

Beethoven's music marks a division between the Classical period of the 18th century, exemplified by the great names of Mozart and Haydn, and the new spirit of Romantic music that characterized the entire course of the 19th century. There are certain purely external factors that distinguish these 2 periods of musical evolution; one of them pertains to sartorial matters. Music before Beethoven was *Zopfmusik*, pigtail music. Haydn and Mozart are familiar to us by portraits in which their heads are crowned by elaborate wigs; Beethoven's hair was by contrast luxuriant in its unkempt splendor.

The music of the 18th century possessed the magnitude of mass production. The accepted number of Haydn's syms., according to his own count, is 104; Mozart wrote about 45 syms. during his short lifetime. Haydn's syms. were constructed according to an easily defined formal structure; while Mozart's last syms. show greater depth of penetration, they do not depart from the Classical convention. Besides, both Haydn and Mozart wrote other multimovement instrumental works variously entitled cassations, serenades, divertimentos, and suites. Beethoven's syms. were few in number and mutually different. The 1st and 2nd Syms. may still be classified as *Zopfmusik*, but with the 3rd Sym. he entered a new world of music: it was on a grander scale than previous syms., contained the intense contrast of a funeral march movement, and merged the scherzo with the finale. Although the 5th Sym. had no designated program, it lent itself easily to programmatic interpretation; its thematic unity was unprecedented. Wagner attached a bombastic label, "Apotheosis of the Dance," to the 7th Sym., with the memorably economical slow march movement. Beethoven called the 8th Sym. his "little sym."; the 9th is usually known as the Choral Sym. With the advent of Beethoven, the manufacture of syms. en masse ceased; Schumann, Brahms, Tchaikovsky, and their contemporaries wrote a few syms. apiece, each with a distinctive physiognomy, or turned to the concert overture or symphonic poem for orch. music. (The exceptions were Dvořák, Bruckner, and Mahler, who equaled Beethoven's total.)

Similarly novel were Beethoven's string quartets; a musical abyss separated his last string quartets from his early essays in the same form. Trios, violin sonatas, cello sonatas, and the 32 great piano sonatas also represent evolutionary concepts. Yet Beethoven's melody and harmony did not diverge from the sacrosanct laws of euphony and tonality. The famous dissonant chord introducing the last movement of the 9th Sym. resolves naturally into the tonic, giving only a moment's pause to the ear. Beethoven's favorite device of pairing the melody in the high treble with triadic chords in close harmony in the deep bass was a peculiarity of his style but not necessarily an infringement of the Classical rules. Yet contemporaneous critics found some of these practices repugnant and described Beethoven as an eccentric bent on creating unconventional sonorities. Equally strange to the untutored ear were pregnant pauses and sudden modulations in his instrumental works.

Beethoven was not a natural contrapuntist, but like Haydn in his middle years he began to use fugal finals; his monumental *Grosse Fuge*, originally composed as the finale of the String Quartet, op. 130, was separated and publ. as op. 133. His fugal movements were usually free canonic imitations, with the structure but not the essence of the Baroque masters. But he was a master of instrumental variation, deriving extraordinary transformations through melodic and rhythmic alterations of a given theme. His *Diabelli Variations* (op. 120) represents one of the greatest achievements in the art.

J. A. Schlosser (1828) was the 1st to suggest the division of Beethoven's compositions into 3 stylistic periods; Fétis followed in 1837. Wilhelm von Lenz fully elucidated this approach in *Beethoven et ses 3 styles* (St. Petersburg, 1852). Despite this seemingly arbitrary chronological division, the concept became the norm in Beethoven literature; a 4th period, the time spent in Bonn, has been proposed. When von Bülow was asked for his favorite key signature, he replied that it was E-flat major, the tonality of the *Eroica*, for it had 3 flats—1 apiece for Bach, Beethoven, and Brahms. Beethoven became forever the "2nd B" in popular music books.

The basic works catalogues are those by G. Kinsky and H. Halm, *Beethoven's Works. Thematic-bibliographical Catalogue of His Collected Completed Compositions* (Munich and Duisburg, 1955), and by W. Hess, *Catalogue of Works Missing from the Gesamtausgabe of Ludwig van Beethoven's Publ. Compositions* (Wiesbaden, 1957). Beethoven attached opus numbers to most of his works, and they are essential in a catalogue of his works. Other works are catalogued as WoO (without op. number) and Hess (those appearing for the 1st time in the Hess catalogue).

begeisterung, mit (Ger.). With enthusiasm, spirit, inspiration.

Beggar's Opera, The. A satirical BALLAD OPERA to the text by John Gay, with music collated in the manner of pasticcio by the German-born composer John Pepusch. The spectacle was usually introduced by an actor dressed as a beggar announcing the wedding of 2 popular ballad singers. The musical score mixed street tunes with French airs, while the text contained undisguised persiflage of British political figures along with highwaymen and other common criminals. The 1st production took place in London on January 29, 1728, and was staged in a theater frequented by the poor rather than the aristocracy that patronized performances of Italian opera. Its tremendous success brought forth countless imitations and established the popularity of the ballad opera genre in Britain. The satirical impact of the opera moved the Lord Chamberlain to forbid the production of its sequel, POLLY. The music historian Sir John Hawkins wrote in all solemnity, "Rapine and violence have been gradually increasing ever since the 1st representation of *The Beggar's Opera*," while Dr. Jonson opined that there was in the work "such a labefactation of all principles as might be injurious to morality." The idea of mixing rogues and politicians in a play accompanied by light music was attractive in the 20th century as well as the 18th, for Kurt Weill, in collaboration with the radical dramatist Bertolt Brecht, adapted *The Beggar's Opera* to a satire on the world conditions in 1928, under the title DIE DREIGROSCHENOPER. The American composer Marc Bliztstein made an adaptation of the opera into the colloquial American, called THE THREEPENNY OPERA.

Begin the Beguine. See BEGUINE.

begleitung (Ger.). Accompaniment.

beguine. A Latin American dance in a lively syncopated rhythm. Cole Porter made a brilliant play on words in his *Begin the Beguine* (from *Jubilee*, 1935), a song imitative of Latin rhythms. He composed it after hearing the beguine during a cruise in the West Indies.

behaglich (Ger.). Easily, comfortably; COMODO.

Beiderbecke, (Leon) **Bix,** American jazz cornet player; b. Davenport, Iowa, Mar. 10, 1903; d. N.Y., Aug. 6, 1931. He began to play music as a small child; developed a flair for ragtime and jazz. He played cornet in various jazz groups in Chicago and St. Louis, and developed his distinctive style of rhythmic lyricism; joined the Paul Whiteman band (1927). His closest musical associate was saxophonist Frank Trumbauer. Although lacking formal musical education, he wrote a few beguilingly attractive piano pieces of an impressionistic coloring (*In a Mist*). He succumbed to severe alcoholism. His musical legacy was preserved in recordings; although the settings were conventional, his unique tone and improvisational sensitivity to pitch choice and rhythm transcended the ordinary harmonic progressions. He was one of the 1st white jazz musicians to be admired by black performers; after his death a cult was formed around him and his tantalizingly small legacy.

Beinum, Eduard van, eminent Dutch conductor; b. Arnhem, Sept. 3, 1900; d. Amsterdam, Apr. 13, 1959. He studied with J. B. de Pauw and Sem Dresden. He 1st appeared as a pianist with the Concertgebouw Orch., Amsterdam (1920); thereafter devoted himself to choral conducting. In 1931 he was appointed associate conductor of the Concertgebouw Orch.; in 1945 he became principal conductor, succeeding Mengelberg (who had been disfranchised for his collaboration with the Germans during their occupation of the Netherlands). He was a guest conductor of various European orchs.; made his American debut with the Philadelphia Orch. (1954); later that year toured the U.S. with the Concertgebouw Orch. From 1957 until shortly before his death he was the principal guest conductor with the Los Angeles Phil. Beinum was regarded by most critics as an intellectual conductor whose chief concern was the projection of the music itself rather than the expression of his own musical personality. He was equally capable in Classical, Romantic, and modern works.

bel canto (It., beautiful song). 1. The art of lyrical and virtuosic performance as exemplified by the finest Italian singers of the 18th and 19th centuries, in contrast to recitative and the declamatory singing style brought into such prominence by Wagner. The term representing the once glorious tradition of vocal perfection for beauty's sake. The secret of bel canto was exclusively the property of Italian singing teachers who spread the technique to Russia, to England, and to America. It was, above all, applied to lyric singing, particularly in opera. The art of bel canto is still being taught in conservatories and music schools as a necessary precondition for an operatic career. 2. The operatic repertoire composed to highlight bel canto singers, notably late Baroque and early Romantic Italian opera. The repertoire fell into disuse until after World War II, when singers such as Callas, Sutherland, and Sills brought new life to the works of Bellini, Donizetti, Handel, and others.

belebt (Ger.). Animated, brisk.

bell. 1. A hollow metallic percussion instrument sounded by a clapper hanging inside or by a hammer outside. See BELLS. 2. The flaring, open end of wind instruments such as the trumpet, trombone, or English horn. The instruction "bells up" signifies that the player should hold his or her instrument upward for a louder sound.

Bell Song. The memorable aria for coloratura soprano in Delibes's opera LAKMÉ, in which the heroine, a daughter of a Brahman priest but unhappily in love with a British officer in colonial India, sings to the resonant accompaniment of temple bells. The necessary purity of intonation in performing the song is underlined by the American author Raymond Chandler, when he alludes to the piece in a spoof on a typical British murder mystery in which the soprano is stabbed with a solid platinum poniard when she sings flat on the top note of the *Bell Song*.

Bell, Joshua, talented American violinist; b. Bloomington, Ind., Dec. 9, 1967. He studied with Mimi Zweig, Josef

Gingold, Ivan Galamian, and Henryk Szeryng. After winning a competition, he appeared with the Philadelphia Orch. under Riccardo Muti, thus becoming the youngest soloist to appear with it on a subscription concert. In 1985 he made his Carnegie Hall debut in N.Y. as soloist with the St. Louis Sym. Orch.

Belle Hélène, La. Operetta by Offenbach, 1864, a farce on the Paris-Helen encounter in Homer's *Iliad*.

bellicoso (It., bellicose). In a martial, warlike manner.

Bellini, Vincenzo, famous Italian opera composer and a master of operatic bel canto; b. Catania, Sicily, Nov. 3, 1801; d. Puteaux, near Paris, Sept. 23, 1835. Bellini's grandfather and father were maestri di cappella in Catania; after studying with them he entered the Real Collegio di Musica di San Sebastiano (Naples), where he was instructed by Giovanni Furno, Giacomo Tritto, Carlo Conti, Girolamo Crescentini, and Nicola Zingarelli; he wrote several sinfonias, 2 Masses, and the cantata *Ismene* (1824). His 1st opera, *Adelson e Salvini*, was given at the Collegio in 1825, followed by a production at the Teatro San Carlo in Naples of his 2nd opera, *Bianca e Gernando* (1826; rev. as *Bianca e Fernando*, 1828). He went to Milan and wrote an opera seria, *Il Pirata*, for the Teatro alla Scala, where it was successfully produced (1827); this was his 1st setting of a libretto by the noted Felice Romani (1788–1865). It was followed by another successful opera seria, *La Straniera*, (La Scala, 1829); he also produced *Zaira* that year, with less success (Parma). He was then commissioned to write an opera for the Teatro La Fenice, Venice; the result, the Shakespearean *I Capuleti ed i Montecchi* (1830), had a decisive success; even more successful was his *La Sonnambula* (Milan, 1831), with the celebrated soprano Giuditta Pasta as Amina; she also appeared in the title role of his most famous opera, *Norma* (La Scala, 1831), which gradually established Bellini's reputation as a master of the Italian operatic bel canto. *Beatrice di Tenda*, produced in Venice (1833), failed to sustain his series of successes; it was his last collaboration with Romani. He then traveled to London and Paris, where he produced his last opera, *I Puritani* (1835), which fully justified the admirer's expectations, thanks in part to its superb cast (Grisi, Rubini, Tamburini, and Lablache). Bellini was contemplating future productions and marriage when he was stricken with an attack of amebiasis and died 6 weeks before his 34th birthday. His remains were reverently removed to his native Catania in 1876.

Bellini's music represents the Italian operatic school at its most glorious melodiousness, truly representative of BEL CANTO. In his writing, the words, the rhythm, the melody, the harmony, and the instrumental accompaniment unite in mutual perfection. The lyric flow and dramatic expressiveness of his music provide a natural medium for singers in the Italian language, with the result that his greatest masterpieces, *La Sonnambula* and *Norma*, remain in the active repertoire of opera houses throughout the world, repeatedly performed by touring Italian opera companies and by native forces everywhere.

Bellini wrote exclusively in the opera seria and semiseria genres. He selected melodramatic subjects possessing a natural appeal to the public, with Romantic female figures in the center of the action. In *Il Pirata* the heroine loses her reason when her lover is condemned to death for killing her unloved husband; in *La Sonnambula* the sleepwalker innocently wanders into the bedroom of a lord and is suspected of infidelity by her lover but is exonerated when she is observed again walking in her sleep; in *Norma* a Druid priestess sacrifices herself when she ascends a funeral pyre with her Roman lover as a penalty for her betrayal of her sacred duty; in *I Puritani*, set in the period of the civil war in Britain, the heroine goes mad when she believes she has been betrayed by her beloved, but she regains her reason when he accounts for his essentially noble actions.

bells. A generic name for church bells, carillons, tubular chimes, and other types. In the case of church bells, the collective name is a *ring*, and the sound they make together is a *peal*; thus, "the peal of a ring of 5 bells" is a typical phrase. The largest church bell was the Czar's Bell, which was cast in Moscow in 1733 but fell and cracked. It weighed nearly 500,000 pounds and was about 20 feet in diameter. The Liberty Bell in Philadelphia is far smaller, but it is etched in American memories as a patriotic symbol of the early days of the U.S.; it too is cracked. Church bells are rarely used in musical scores; their sounds are often produced by imitation.

Other bells: tubular bells (also called tubular chimes or simply chimes), suspended from a horizontal bar and struck with a hammer; sleighbells, such as are attached to the harness of a horse-drawn sleigh, included in the scores of Mozart, Mahler, and Varèse; cowbells, heavier bells with a clapper, found in a few classical scores but very common in popular music; domestic handbells, used for special effects in some operas; handbell orchs., consisting of a number of handbells of varying pitches, popular in churches in the U.K. and U.S., played using the CHANGE-RINGING system; glockenspiel, a set of bells in the form of metal bars; carillon, a tower of stationary bells (inside or outside churches), played on a large keyboard. The science of making and playing bells is called campanology (It. *campana*, bell).

Bells Are Ringing. Musical by Jule Styne, Comden, and Green, 1956, in which Judy Holliday played a telephone answering service operator who helps men in distress and foils an illicit betting ring. Includes *Just in Time, Drop That Name*, and *The Party's Over*.

Belshazzar's Feast. Oratorio by Walton, 1931, based on a Biblical text (Daniel 5) concerning Daniel's interpretation of the handwriting on the wall. The work begins with the powerful choral lament *By the Waters of Babylon We Sat Down and Wept*. The oratorio is in a neo-Handelian manner.

Belshazzar's Feast. Orch.l suite by Sibelius, 1907, taken from incidental music for a play by Procopé, 1906.

bémol (Fr.). The flat sign (♭).

ben (It.). Well, good, very.

ben articolato (It., very articulated). Clearly and neatly pronounced and phrased.

ben marcato (It.). Well marked.

ben pronunziato (It.). Clearly enunciated.

ben ritmato (It.). Observe the rhythm carefully and precisely.

ben sostenuto (It.). Very sustained.

ben tenuto (It.). Very sustained.

benedictus (Lat., blessed). The concluding portion of the Sanctus in the Roman Catholic Mass. In nonmonophonic settings it often appears as a separate movement.

benefit. A special performance whose proceeds go to the singer or director of an opera performance. This was a common practice in the 18th and 19th centuries but declined toward the middle of the 20th century, when benefits were usually given for charitable or patriotic purposes.

Bennett, Richard Rodney, prolific and successful English composer; b. Broadstairs, Kent, Mar. 29, 1936. He studied with Lennox Berkeley, Howard Ferguson, and Boulez. He taught at the Royal Academy of Music, London (1963–65); was a visiting prof. at the Peabody Cons., Baltimore (1970–71); made a Commander of the Order of the British Empire (1977). He composes in a typically British neoclassicism, with a more dissonant harmonic pallette. He is also an excellent pianist. Among his many works are operas (*The Mines of Sulphur*, 1965; *Victory*, after the Conrad novel, 1970); ballets (*A Jazz Calendar*, 1968; *Isadora*, 1981); concertos for horn, flute, oboe, guitar, violin, viola, cello, double bass, harpsichord, piano; pieces for chamber and full orchs. (*London Pastoral*, 1961; *Aubade*, 1964; 2 syms., 1966, 1968; *Zodiac*, 1976; *Moving into Aquarius*, 1985; *Dream Dancing*, 1986); vocal music, including choruses; piano and chamber music; and film scores such as *The Nanny* (1965), *Billion Dollar Brain* (1967), *Nicholas and Alexandra* (1971); *Murder on the Orient Express* (1974); and *Equus* (1977).

Benvenuto Cellini. Opera by Berlioz, 1838, on the life of the Italian sculptor and libertine. Berlioz later used some of the music for his *Roman Carnival Overture*.

Berberian, Cathy, versatile American mezzo-soprano; b. Attleboro, Mass., July 4, 1925; d. Rome, Mar. 6, 1983. She studied singing, dancing, and pantomime; traveled to Italy; attracted wide attention in 1958 when she performed the ultrasurrealist *Fontana Mix* by Cage, which demanded a fantastic variety of sound effects. Her vocal range extended to 3 octaves, causing one bewildered music critic to remark that she could sing both Tristan and Isolde. Thanks to her uncanny ability to produce ultrahuman (and subhuman) tones, and her willingness to incorporate into her professional vocalization a variety of animal noises, guttural sounds, grunts and growls, squeals, squeaks and squawks, clicks and clucks, shrieks and screeches, hisses, hoots, and hollers, she instantly became the darling of inventive composers of the AVANT-GARDE, who eagerly dedicated to her their nearly unperformable works.

She married Berio (1950), but they were separated (1966) and divorced (1968); by then he had written *Circles, Epifanie, Visage, Sequenza, Recital I (for Cathy)*, and *Folk Songs* for her. She could also intone earlier music, and made a favorable impression with her recording of Monteverdi pieces. Shortly before her death she sang her own version of the *Internationale* for an Italian television program commemorating the centennial of the death of Karl Marx (1983). She was a composer in her own right, writing multimedia works such as *Stripsody*, an arresting soliloquy of labial and laryngeal sounds, and a piano piece, *Morsicat(h)y*. She resented being regarded as a freak, insisting that her objective was merely to meet the challenge of the new art of her time.

berceuse (Fr. *berceau*, cradle). A cradle song or lullaby. It is usually set in 6/8 time, suggesting the rocking of a cradle, with an ostinato accompaniment on the tonic and the dominant. Chopin's famous Berceuse (op. 57) for piano has an ingeniously variegated melody against a steady accompaniment on a pedal point. Composers such as Balakirev, Debussy, Ravel, Busoni, and Stravinsky wrote berceuses.

Berg, Alban (Maria Johannes), greatly significant Austrian composer, celebrated pupil of Schoenberg, whose music combined classical clarity of design and highly original melodic and harmonic techniques; b. Vienna, Feb. 9, 1885; d. there, Dec. 24, 1935 (of an abscess that could have been cured by sulfa drugs only 2 years later). He played piano and composed songs without formal training. In 1904 he met Schoenberg, who became his teacher, mentor, and close friend; he remained Schoenberg's pupil for 6 years. Webern was a fellow classmate; the 3 initiated the radical movement known as the 2nd Vienna school of composition. Berg assisted Schoenberg in organizing Vienna's Soc. for Private Musical Performances (Verein für Musikalische Privataufführungen, 1918–22) with the purpose of performing works unacceptable to established musical society; in 1925 Berg joined the newly created ISCM, which continued in an open arena the promotion of fresh musical ideas.

Berg's early works reflected the Romantic style of Wagner, Hugo Wolf, and Mahler; typical of this period were numerous songs and the *Piano Sonata* (1908, premiered 1911); an aphoristic quality soon entered his style, as seen in the *5 Orchestral Songs on Postcard Texts* (1912, premiered 1952), the *4 Pieces for Clarinet* (1913, premiered 1919), and his *3 Pieces for Orchestra* (1915, premiered 1930).

In 1917 Berg began work on his opera *Wozzeck* (based on Georg Büchner's fragmentary play), which became a masterpiece. The score represents an ingenious synthesis of Classical forms and modern techniques; organized as a series of purely symphonic sections in traditional forms, the 3 acts (each 5 scenes long) comprise an exposition of character-pieces, a sym. of increasing despair, and a dénouement of inventions on different ostinatos, respectively. Its 1st production at the Berlin State Opera (1925) precipitated a storm of protests and press reviews of extreme violence; a similarly critical reception was accorded in Prague (1926). Undismayed, Berg and his friends responded by publ. a brochure incorporating the most vehement of these reviews so as to shame and denounce the critics. Stokowski, ever eager to defy convention, gave the 1st American performance of *Wozzeck* in Philadelphia (1931); it aroused a great deal of interest and was received with cultured equanimity. Thereafter, performances multiplied in Europe (including Russia); in due time it became recognized as the modern masterpiece that it is.

Berg then wrote the *Lyric Suite* for string quartet in 6 movements; it was premiered in Vienna by the Kolisch Quartet (1927). Rumors of a suppressed vocal part for the suite's finale, bespeaking Berg's secret affection for a married woman, Hanna Fuchs-Robettin, proved true, as American scholars found an annotated copy of the score in a Viennese library (1976); Berg's widow Helene, understandably reluctant to perpetuate her husband's emotional aberrations, had donated it. The text proved to be Stefan Georg's translation of Baudelaire's *De Profundis clamavi* from *Les Fleurs du mal*. Berg also inserted all kinds of semiotical and numerological clues to his feelings in a sort of symbolical synthesis. The *Lyric Suite* with vocal finale was performed for the 1st time in N.Y. (1979).

Berg's 2nd opera, *Lulu* (1928–35), to a libretto derived from 2 plays by Wedekind, was left unfinished at Berg's death; the 2 completed acts and music from the *Symphonische Stücke aus der Oper "Lulu"* (1934) were performed posth. in Zurich (1937). Again Helene Berg forestalled any attempt to have the work reconstituted by another musician. However, Berg's publishers, asserting their legal rights, secretly commissioned the Viennese composer Friedrich Cerha (b. 1926) to re-create the 3rd act from the *Symphonische Stücke*, Erwin Stein's unpubl. vocal score (1936), and other authentic sources. Cerha's task required 12 years (1962–74); after Berg's widow died (1976), several opera houses competed for 1st performance rights; the premiere of the complete opera was given at the Paris Opéra, with Stratas as Lulu and Boulez conducting (1979); the 1st American performance followed in Santa Fe later that year. As in *Wozzeck*, so in Lulu, Berg organized Lulu in a series of Classical forms; but while *Wozzeck* was written before Schoenberg's formulation of the 12-tone method of composition, *Lulu* was set in full-fledged dodecaphonic techniques; even so, Berg allowed himself frequent divagations from the dodecaphonic code, permitting triadic tonal harmonies.

Berg's last completed work was the Violin Concerto, commissioned by the American violinist Louis Krasner, who gave its 1st performance at the Festival of the ISCM in Barcelona (1936). The score bears the inscription "Dem Andenken eines Engels" (To the memory of an angel), a reference to Manon, the daughter of Alma Mahler and Walter Gropius, who had just died of consumption at an early age. The work is couched in the 12-tone technique, with free and frequent interludes of passing tonality and quotations from a Carinthian folksong and the Bach chorale *Es ist genug* (from *O Ewigkeit, du Donnerwort*, BWV 60).

bergerette (Fr. *berger*, shepherd). 1. A pastoral or rustic song popular in 18th-century France, and the poetry associated with it. 2. An instrumental dance of the 16th century.

Bergonzi, Carlo, noted Italian tenor; b. Polisene, near Parma, July 13, 1924. He studied with Grandini; made his operatic debut as a baritone in Lecce, singing Figaro in *The Barber of Seville* (1948); switched to tenor, singing Andrea Chénier in Bari (1951); appeared at La Scala, Milan, with much success (1953); sang in London (from 1953). He made his U.S. debut with the Chicago Lyric Opera as Luigi in *Il Tabarro* (1955); made his 1st appearance at the Metropolitan Opera, N.Y., as Radames (1956), and remained on its roster until 1974. His voice had well-modulated and beautiful tone; he possessed an elegant and lively sense of line and taste. He was particularly distinguished in Italian lyric dramatic operatic roles, such as Canio, Turiddu, Des Greux, Manrico, Riccardo (*Un Ballo in Mascera*), Cavaradossi, and Boito's *Faust*.

Berio, Luciano, outstanding Italian composer of extreme musicoscientific tendencies; b. Oneglia, Oct. 24, 1925. He studied music with his father, then with Ghedini, Giulini, and (in the U.S.) Dallapiccola. He married an extraordinary singer, Cathy Berberian, who was willing and able to sing his most excruciating soprano parts; they were divorced in 1968, but she magnanimously continued to sing his music after their separation. He returned to Italy and joined the staff of the Italian Radio; founded the Studio di Fonologia Musicale (1955) for experimental work on acoustics; ed. the progressive magazine *Incontri Musicali* (1956–60). He joined the faculty of the Juilliard School of Music, N.Y. (1965–71), providing an alternative to its traditionally conservative atmosphere; subsequently maintained an infrequent but important connection with America. In the mid-1970s he joined the Inst. de Recherche et de Coordination Acoustique/Musique (IRCAM) in Paris, working closely with its director, Boulez; became the director of the Accademia Filarmonica Romana (1976). In 1989 he was awarded Germany's Siemens Prize for his contributions to contemporary music.

Perhaps the most unusual characteristic of his creative philosophy is his impartial eclecticism, by which he permits himself to use the widest variety of resources, from Croatian folk songs to objets trouvés. He is equally liberal in his use of graphic notation; some of his scores look like expressionist drawings. He is one of the few contemporary composers who can touch the nerve endings of sensitive listeners and music critics, one of whom described his *Sinfonia* (1968–69, his best-known work) with ultimate brevity: "It stinks." (The last traceable use of the word was Hanslick's 1881 response to Tchaikovsky's Violin Concerto.) But if *Sinfonia* stank, then by implication so did the ample quotes from Mahler, Ravel, and Richard Strauss used as found musical objects in this work. Apart from "pure" music, many of Berio's works use all manner of artifacts and artifices of popular pageants, including mimodrama, choreodrama, concrete noises, acrobats, clowns, jugglers, and organ grinders (*Opera*, 1970). See also BERBERIAN, CATHY.

Berlin, Irving (born Israel Balin), fabulously popular Russian-born American composer of hundreds of songs that became the musical conscience of the U.S.; b. Mogilev, May 11, 1888; d. N.Y., Sept. 22, 1989, at the incredible age of 101. Fearing anti-Semitic pogroms, his family emigrated when he was 5 years old and landed in N.Y. His father was a synagogue cantor; he worked as a newsboy, a busboy, and a singing waiter. He improvised on the bar piano and wrote the lyrics to a song, *Marie from Sunny Italy*; when the song was publ. (1907), his name appeared as Berlin instead of Balin. He soon acquired the American vernacular and throughout his career never tried to experiment with sophisticated language, thus distancing himself from his younger contemporaries, such as Ira Gershwin and Cole Porter. He never learned to read or write music, and he composed most of his songs in F-sharp major for the convenience of fingering the black keys of the scale. To modulate into other keys he had a special hand clutch built at the piano keyboard, so that his later songs acquired an air of tonal variety. This piano is now installed at the Smithsonian Institution, Washington, D.C.

Berlin worked as a song-plugger and performer of his own songs. His 1st big hit was *Alexander's Ragtime Band* (1911). His 1st wife died of typhoid fever, contracted during their honeymoon in Havana (1912); wrote his 1st ballad in her memory, *When I Lost You*, which sold a million copies. His 1st complete score was written for *Watch Your Step*, a musical comedy featuring Vernon and Irene Castle (1914). Berlin was drafted into the U.S. Army (1917) but did not serve in military action; instead wrote a revue, *Yip, Yip, Yaphank*, which orig. included the 1st version of *God Bless America*; it was omitted from the show, but Berlin revised it for singer Kate Smith (1938); the song, patriotic to the core, became an unofficial American anthem.

After the war ended Berlin helped produce the *Music Box Revues* (1921–25); the best-known song was *Say It With Music*. In 1925 he met Ellin Mackay, the daughter of the millionaire head of the Postal Telegaph Cable Co., and proposed to her; she accepted; her father threatened to disinherit her if she married a Jewish immigrant. As money was not the object (Berlin was by now a contented millionaire), the 2 eventually married in a civil ceremony. The marriage proved to be happy, lasting 62 years until Ellin's death in 1988.

Beginning in 1935, Berlin turned his attention to films and musicals. His most successful films were *Top Hat*, with Astaire and Rogers (1935); *Follow the Fleet* (1936); *On the Avenue* (1937); *Holiday Inn*, with Bing Crosby singing *White Christmas* (1942); and *Easter Parade* (1948). His 1st musical was *Louisiana Purchase* (1940); the most successful of them were *Annie Get Your Gun* (1946) and *Call Me Madam* (1950); his last musical was *Mr. President* (1962).

Irving Berlin, 1928

COURTESY FRANK DRIGGS COLLECTION

Berlin's 1st biographer, Alexander Woollcott, referred to him as a "creative ignoramus," meaning it as a compliment. Victor Herbert specifically discouraged Irving Berlin from learning harmony for fear that he would lose his natural genius for melody; indeed, despite his lack of formal training, he composed songs with unusual tonal and harmonic progressions, unlikely formal structures, and uneven phrase lengths.

Herbert also encouraged him to join the American Soc. of Composers, Authors, and Publishers (ASCAP) as a charter member, a position that became the source of his fantastically prosperous commercial success. Berlin was extremely generous with his enormous earnings. All of *God Bless America's* royalties were donated to the Boy and Girl Scouts of America. Another great song, *White Christmas*, became a sentimental hit among American troops stationed in Pacific bases in the Pacific during World War II. His financial interests were taken care of by his publ. enterprise, Irving Berlin Music, Inc., founded in 1919, and also by ASCAP. According to some records, his income tax amounted to 91% of his total earnings.

In 1954 Berlin received the Congressional Medal of Honor for his patriotic songs. But he was reclusive in his last years; he even avoided making a personal appearance when members of ASCAP gathered before his house to serenade him on his 100th birthday.

Berlioz, (Louis-) Hector

〰〰 〰〰 〰〰 〰〰 〰〰

Great French composer and master of orchestration who exercised profound influence on the course of modern music in the direction of sonorous grandiosity, and who propagated the Romantic ideal of literary program music; b. La Côte-Saint-André, Isère, Dec. 11, 1803; d. Paris, Mar. 8, 1869. Berlioz played the flute and guitar; went to Paris and entered the École de Médecine; studied composition with J.-F. Le Sueur (1822). He abandoned his medical studies to compose (1824); his 1st important work was a *Messe solennelle* (1825; MS lost until recently). He resumed studies with Le Sueur and Reicha (1826); wrote an opera, *Les*

Francs-juges, never given a complete performance (partially extant). In 1828 he presented a concert of his works at the Paris Cons., including the Resurrexit from the *Messe solennelle*, the heroic scene *La Révolution grecque*, and the overtures *Les Francs-juges* and *Waverley*. In 1828–29 he wrote *Huit scènes de Faust*, after Goethe; this score was eventually revised and produced as *La Damnation de Faust* (1845–46).

In 1827 he began a yearly attempt to win the Prix de Rome awarded to the composer of the "best" cantata, all candidates setting the same text. After 3 years of failure he finally won with *La Mort de Sardanapale* (1830). In the meantime he became hopelessly infatuated with the Irish actress Harriet Smithson after attending her portrayal of Ophelia in Shakespeare's *Hamlet*, given by a British drama troupe in Paris (1827). He knew no English and Miss Smithson spoke no French; he made no effort to engage her attention personally; conveniently, he found a surrogate for his passion in the person of Camille Moke, a young pianist. Romantically absorbed in the ideal of love through music, Berlioz began to write his most ambitious and enduring work, the *Sym. fantastique*, which was to be an offering of adoration and devotion to Miss Smithson. In the 5-movement work the object of the hero's passion haunts him through the device of the IDÉE FIXE; she appears 1st as an entrancing but unattainable vision; as an enticing dancer at a ball; then as a deceptive pastoral image. He penetrates her disguise and kills her, a crime for which he is led to the gallows. At the end she reveals herself as a wicked witch at a Sabbath orgy. The fantastic program design does not interfere, however, with an orderly organization of the score, and the wild fervor of the music is astutely subordinated to the symphonic form. The idée fixe itself serves merely as a recurring motif, not unlike similar musical reminiscences in Classic syms. The 4th movement (*March to the Scaffold*) makes use of a section from *Les Francs-juges*, with a few bars of the idée fixe to justify its use. No matter; the *Sym. fantastique* emerges as a magnificent tapestry of sound; its unflagging popularity for a century and a half since its composition testifies to its evocative power. The work was 1st performed at the Paris Cons. in 1830, with considerable success; Cherubini, who failed to attend the performance, spoke disdainfully of it from a cursory examination of the score; nor did Miss Smithson herself grace the occasion by her physical presence.

Berlioz followed the *Sym. fantastique* with a sequel entitled *Lélio, ou Le Retour à la vie*, supposedly signaling the hero's renunciation of his morbid obsessions; the work is a collection of earlier pieces and excerpts. Both works were performed at a single concert in Paris (1832); Smithson finally made an appearance. Music proved to be the food of love; Berlioz and Smithson soon became emotionally involved, and they were married in 1833. Alas, their marriage proved happy for no more than 6 years; they had 1 son, Louis; throughout their life together she was beset by debilitating illnesses. Berlioz found a more convenient woman companion, the singer Marie Recio, whom he married shortly after Smithson's death in 1854. Berlioz survived his 2nd wife too; she died in 1862.

Whatever the peripeteias of his personal life, Berlioz never lost the lust for music. During his Prix de Rome sojourn in Italy he produced the overtures *Le Roi Lear* and *Rob Roy* (both 1831). His next important work was *Harold en Italie* for Solo Viola with Orch., based on Byron's *Childe Harold* (1834); commissioned by Paganini, it had too little solo viola writing to satisfy him (he let Berlioz keep the fee). Berlioz followed it with an opera semiseria, *Benvenuto Cellini* (1834–37), which had its 1st performance at the Paris Opéra (1838); it was not successful, and Berlioz revised the score; the new version had its 1st performance in Weimar, conducted by Liszt (1852). About the same time, Berlioz became a highly active music critic and *feuilleoniste*; in 1835 he began a career as a conductor.

Now entrenched in the Parisian cultural world, Berlioz composed the *Grande messe des morts* (Requiem; 1837), for which he demanded a huge chorus and revived the tradition of spatially divided forces. In late 1838 he conducted a successful concert of his works; legend has it that Paganini came forth after the concert, knelt in homage to Berlioz, and (if Berlioz is to be trusted) subsequently gave Berlioz 20,000 francs. In 1839 Berlioz conducted the 1st performance of his dramatic sym. *Romeo et Juliette*, after Shakespeare; the work is one of the most moving lyrical invocations of Shakespeare's tragedy, rich in melodic invention and instrumental interplay. In 1840 Berlioz premiered the *Grande symphonie funèbre et triomphale*, commemorating the soldiers fallen in the fight for Algeria; he exploits the military band sonority to the fullest; if contemporaneous reports can be taken literally, he conducted it with a drawn sword through the streets of

Paris, accompanying the ashes of the military heroes to their interment in the Bastille column.

The spirit of grandiosity took possession of Berlioz; at an 1844 concert after the Exhibition of Industrial Products, he conducted Beethoven's 5th Sym. with 36 double basses, Weber's overture to *Der Freischütz* with 24 French horns, and the Prayer of Moses from Rossini's *Mosè in Egitto* with 25 harps. He boasted that his 1,022 performers achieved an ensemble worthy of the finest string quartet. For his *L'Imperiale*, performed after the 1855 version of the same exhibition, he had 1,200 performers, augmented by huge choruses and a military band. Anticipating the modus operandi of a century later, he installed 5 semiconductors and, to keep them in time, activated an "electric metronome" with his left hand while holding the conducting baton in his right. Such indulgences generated a chorus of derision on the part of classical musicians and skeptical music critics; caricatures represented Berlioz as a madman commanding a heterogeneous mass of instrumentalists and singers driven to distraction by the music. Berlioz deeply resented these attacks and bitterly complained about the uncongenial artistic environment in Paris.

But whatever obloquy he suffered, he also found satisfaction in the pervasive influence he had on his contemporaries, among them Wagner, Liszt, and the Russian school of composers. His grandiosity gradually attained true grandeur; he no longer needed huge ensembles to project the magic of his music. He publ. his *Grand traité d'instrumentation et d'orchestration modernes* (Paris, 1843), which became a standard text in orchestration. In 1844 he wrote the *Roman Carnival Overture*, partially based on music from *Benvenuto Cellini*. There followed the overture *La Tour de Nice* (later rev. as *Le Corsaire*). In 1846 he completed the revision of his earlier Faust work as an oratorio-like dramatic legend, *La Damnation de Faust*; the score included an arrangement of the Rákóczy March, in which he took the liberty of conveying Goethe's Faust to Hungary; the march became extremely popular as a concert piece.

Berlioz undertook successful tours of Russia and England (1847–48). In 1849 he composed his grand Te Deum (premiered 1855). In 1852 he traveled to Weimar at the invitation of Liszt, who organized a festival of Berlioz's music (including the revised *Benvenuto Cellini*). He wrote the uncharacteristically gentle oratorio *L'Enfance du Christ* (1854). Despite past failures with operatic productions, he returned to composing for the stage; chose the *Aeneid* of Virgil, selecting the episodes concerning the Trojan War and Aeneas's visit to Carthage; titled this grand opera *Les Troyens* (1856–60). He was never able to produce the work in its entirety, and so divided the score into 2 parts: *La Prise de Troie* and *Les Troyens à Carthage*. Only the 2nd part was produced in his lifetime, at the Théâtre-Lyrique, Paris (1863); the opera's financial returns made it possible for Berlioz to abandon his occupation as a newspaper music critic. His next operatic project was *Béatrice et Bénédict*, after Shakespeare's play *Much Ado About Nothing*; conducted its 1st performance in Baden-Baden (1862).

Despite frail health and a state of depression generated by his imaginary failure as composer and conductor in France, he achieved a series of successes abroad. He conducted *La Damnation de Faust* in Vienna (1866); went to Russia during the 1867–68 season, where he had a most enthusiastic reception among Russian musicians, who welcomed him as a true prophet of the new era in music. But the death of his beloved son Louis, who was serving in the military (1867), was a final blow to his well-being.

Posth. recognition came slowly to Berlioz; long after his death some conservative critics still referred to his music as bizarre and willfully dissonant. No cult comparable to the ones around the names of Wagner and Liszt was formed to glorify Berlioz's legacy; only the overtures, the *Sym. fantastique*, and the songs (particularly the beautiful *Les nuits d'été*, 1841) entered the repertory. Performances of his operas were extremely rare; since he did not write solo works for any instrument, concert recitals could not include his name in the program. However, literature about and recordings of his legacy mushroomed after World War II, particularly in the English language and by British artists; these have now secured his rightful place in music history.

Berman, Lazar (Naumovich), brilliant Soviet pianist; b. Leningrad, Feb. 26, 1930. He studied with Goldenweiser. After a modest beginning, he made a highly successful tour of Italy (1970); toured the U.S. with tremendous acclaim (1976). In his repertoire he showed a distinct predilection for the Romantic period; among modern composers his favorites were Scriabin and Prokofiev. His titanic technique, astounding in the facility of bravura passages, did not preclude the excellence of his poetic evocation of lyric moods.

Bernac (born Bertin), **Pierre,** eminent French baritone; b. Paris, Jan. 12, 1899; d. Villeneuve-les-Avignon, Oct. 17, 1979. He started his singing career late in life, studying with Walter Straram; gave a recital in Paris, offering songs by Poulenc and Auric (1926); at other concerts he sang works by Debussy, Ravel, Honegger, and Milhaud. Eager to learn the art of German lieder, he studied with Reinhold von Warlich; returning to Paris, devoted himself to concerts and teaching. He became a lifelong friend to Poulenc, who wrote many songs and song cycles for him and acted as his accompanist in many of their tours through Europe and America. Younger composers such as Daniel-Lesur, Jolivet, Sauguet, and Françaix also wrote for him. He conducted master classes in the U.S. and taught at the American Cons., Fontainebleau; publ. a valuable manual, *The Interpretation of French Song* (N.Y., 1970), and a monograph, *Francis Poulenc: The Man and His Songs* (N.Y., 1977).

Bernstein, Elmer, talented American composer of film music; b. N.Y., Apr. 4, 1922. He studied with Sessions and Wolpe; served in the U.S. Air Force during World War II; then settled in Hollywood and became a highly successful and versatile composer of background scores, particularly in dramatic films; of these the most effective were *The Man with the Golden Arm* (1955), *The 10 Commandments* (1956), *Desire under the Elms* (1958), *The Magnificent 7* (1960), *Summer and Smoke* (1958), *Walk on the Wild Side* (1962), *To Kill a Mockingbird* (1963), *The Great Escape* (1963), *Hawaii* (1966), *True Grit* (1969), *The Shootist* (1976), *Airplane!* (1980), and *Ghostbusters* (1984). He has also composed chamber music, the musical *How Now Dow Jones* (1967), 3 orch.l suites, chamber music, and songs.

Bernstein, Leonard (born Louis), prodigiously gifted American conductor and composer, equally successful in writing symphonic music of profound content and striking-

COURTESY FRANK DRIGGS COLLECTION

Leonard Bernstein, c. 1965

ly effective Broadway shows, and, in the field of performance, an interpreter of magnetic powers, exercising a charismatic spell on audiences in America and the world; b. Lawrence, Mass., Aug. 25, 1918, of a family of Russian Jewish immigrants; d. N.Y., Oct. 14, 1990. He studied piano with Helen Coates and Heinrich Gebhard; entered Harvard Univ. (1935) and studied with Piston, A. Tillman Merritt, and E. B. Hill; moved to Philadelphia (1939) and studied with Reiner, R. Thompson, and I. Vengerova. In 1940–41 he attended Tanglewood, where he worked with Koussevitzky.

In 1943 he became assistant conductor to Artur Rodzinski, director of the N.Y. Phil. Bernstein's break came on Nov. 14, 1943, when he replaced Bruno Walter on short notice in a N.Y. Phil. concert; acquitted himself magnificently and was roundly praised in the press. He became the N.Y. Phil.'s 1st American-born music director (1958); over the next several years he toured with the orch. in South America, Russia, and 16 other European and Near Eastern countries, and Japan, Alaska, and Canada.

Bernstein was the 1st American conductor to lead a regular performance at La Scala, Milan (Cherubini's *Medea*, 1953); made his Metropolitan Opera, N.Y., debut (1964), conducting *Falstaff*, the work chosen for his debut with the Vienna State Opera (1966). In 1969 he resigned his directorship at the N.Y. Phil. in order to devote more time to composition and other projects; the orch. bestowed upon him the unprecedented title of "laureate conductor"; in 1976 he took the orch. on a Bicentennial tour of 11 European cities, giving 13 concerts in 17 days.

Ebullient with communicative talents, Bernstein initiated in 1958 a televised series of "Young People's Concerts" in which he served as an astute and self-confident commentator; these concerts became popular with audiences of all ages. He also arranged a series of educational music programs for television; taught at Brandeis Univ. (1951–55) and, concurrently, in Tanglewood; served as the prestigious Charles Eliot Norton Prof. in Poetry at Harvard Univ. (1973); lectured at M.I.T. He was the recipient of many honors throughout Europe; elected to the American Academy of Arts and Letters (1981); made president of the London Sym. Orch. (1987) and laureate conductor of the Israel Phil. (1988). As an interpreter and program maker he showed a unique affinity with the music of Mahler, whose syms. he repeatedly performed in special cycles. In late 1989 he conducted celebratory performances of Beethoven's 9th Sym. on both sides of the Berlin Wall; the orch. was made up of members from the Bavarian Radio Sym. Orch., Munich, augmented by players from N.Y., London, Paris, Dresden, and Leningrad.

An excellent pianist in his own right, Bernstein often appeared as a soloist in classical or modern concerts, occasionally conducting the orch. from the keyboard. An intellectual by nature, and a *litterateur* and modernistically inclined poet by aspiration, he publ. some excellent sonnets. He was outspoken on behalf of liberal causes and was once dubbed by a columnist as a member of the "radical chic." His tremendous overflow of spiritual and purely animal energy impelled him to display certain histrionic mannerisms on the podium that elicited on the part of some critics derisive comments about his "choreography."

Musical history knows of a number of composers who were also excellent conductors, but few professional conductors who were also significant composers. Bernstein seemed unique in his protean power to be equally proficient as a symphonic and operatic conductor as well a composer of complex musical works and original and enormously popular stage productions. In his *West Side Story* (1957) he created a significant social drama, abounding in memorable tunes; other successful shows were *On the Town* (1944) and *Candide* (1956). In his 2nd Sym., *The Age of Anxiety* (1949; rev. 1965), he reflected the turbulence of modern life. Ever true to his Jewish heritage, Bernstein wrote a devout choral sym., *Kaddish* (1963; rev. 1977). As a testimony to his ecu-

menical religious feelings, he produced the semidramatic *Mass* (1971), with numerous departures from the Roman Catholic liturgy.

Bernstein's death (of progressive emphysema, complicated by a chronic pleurisy, leading to a fatal heart attack) shocked the music world and hundreds of his personal friends, particularly since he had been so amazingly active as a world-renowned conductor and as the composer of lasting works for the stage and concert hall until his final days.

Berry, Chuck (Charles Edward Anderson), African-American rock singer, guitarist, and songwriter; b. San Jose, Calif., Jan. 15, 1926. He received his musical training as a chorister at the Antioch Baptist Church, St. Louis; learned to play guitar and improvised tunes in a then-current jazz manner. In 1955 he went to Chicago and recorded his song *Maybellene* for the Chess record company; it quickly climbed the charts in all 3 major categories: rhythm-and-blues, country-and-western, and popular. He scored many more hits with his own compositions through the late '50s, including *Brown-Eyed Handsome Man, Roll Over Beethoven, Rock and Roll Music, Johnny B. Goode, Sweet Little 16,* and *Memphis, Tennessee*.

Around this time Berry opened the Chuck Berry Club Bandstand in St. Louis; it prospered, but he ran into trouble when a 14-year-old hatcheck girl employed in the club brought charges that he had transported her across state lines for immoral purposes. He was found guilty of violating the Mann Act and served 2 years in the federal penitentiary in Terre Haute (1961–63). Jail made him bitter, but he maintained his onstage spirit of happy-go-lucky insouciance, and he rebounded with *Nadine, No Particular Place to Go,* and *My Ding-a-Ling,* his last big hit. Other than a tax-evasion conviction that put him back in prison briefly in 1979, he maintained an active career as a lively oldie-but-goodie, still doing his patented "duckwalk" across the stage.

Berry's guitar style was based on rapid rhythm-and-blues riffs, showing also country influences; he exploited the electric guitar's potential for highly rhythmic chording (perhaps the most distinctive feature of his playing) and ringing overtones. His songs were primarily of the blues type, with strong emphasis on "a backbeat [so that] you can't lose it/Any old time you use it." He was probably the most influential musical artist of the 1950s on later musicians.

beruhigend (Ger.). Becoming calmer, gradually calming down.

Berwald, Franz (Adolf), foremost Swedish composer of the 19th century; b. Stockholm, July 23, 1796; d. there, Apr. 3, 1868. Franz studied with his father, his cousin, and J. B. E. du Puy. He played violin and viola in the orch. of the Royal Chapel, Stockholm (1812-28); toured Finland and Russia with his brother, Christian August (1819); moved to Berlin (1829) and opened an orthopedic establishment (1835), which flourished; went to Vienna (1841), where he obtained some success as a composer of symphonic poems and was highly productive. He then returned to Stockholm (1842); secured a foothold with his operettas and cantatas; in late 1843 his cousin Johan Fredrik conducted the premiere of his *Sinfonie sérieuse* (the only 1 of 4 syms. performed in his lifetime), but a poor performance did little to further his cause.

He returned to Vienna, where Jenny Lind sang in his stage cantata *Ein ländliches Verlobungsfest in Schweden* at the Theater an der Wien (1846); in 1847 he was elected an honorary member of the Salzburg Mozarteum. In 1849 he returned to his homeland in hopes of securing a position; hopes dashed, he became manager of a glassworks in Sandö (1850–58), part owner of a sawmill (1853), and operator of a brick factory. Berwald was shunned by the Swedish musical establishment (which he disdained), and his extraordinary gifts as a composer went almost totally unrecognized in his lifetime. Finally, in 1864, he was made a member of the Swedish Royal Academy of Music, Stockholm. In 1867 he was named to its composition chair, despite an attempt to unseat him.

Berwald's masterpiece is his *Sinfonie singulière* (1845), an original and even forward-looking work not performed until 60 years after its composition. He also wrote 3 other fine syms., worthwhile chamber music, and at least 1 fine opera (*Estrella de Soria*). His output reveals the influence of the early German Romantic school in general, but with an unmistakably individual voice, notable for modulatory audacity.

beschwingt (Ger.). Winged. *Leicht beschwingt*, lightly and swiftly, VOLANTE.

besetzung (Ger.). The scoring of a work, enumerating the voices and instruments employed.

Bethune, "Blind Tom" (Thomas Greene), black American pianist and composer; b. Columbus, Ga., May 25, 1849; d. Hoboken, N.J., June 13, 1908. Born blind and into slavery, he was purchased, along with his parents (Charity and Mingo Wiggins), by James N. Bethune (1850); he was taught by J. N. Bethune's daughter when he showed great aptitude and retentive ability. The exploitation of his musical abilities began when J. N. Bethune "exhibited" him throughout Ga. (1857), then "leased" him for 3 years to Perry Oliver, a Savannah planter, who arranged concert appearances for him throughout the southern states as well as performances in Washington, D.C. With the outbreak of the Civil War, J. N. Bethune took full charge of Tom's career, touring around the Confederacy to raise money for the war cause; he obtained legal custody and a major part of Tom's earnings (1865). Tom Bethune spent the rest of his career playing in Europe and North America; he was never able to escape the grip of the Bethune family; a court upheld their "guardianship" in 1887; by the end of his public performing days he was working the vaudeville circuit.

Tom Bethune was an excellent pianist; his programs usually included Bach, Beethoven, Liszt, Chopin, Thalberg, Gottschalk, and his own compositions, mostly improvised character pieces in salon manner, arranged, publ., and supplied with appropriate titles by his managers, e.g., *Rainstorm* (1865); *The Battle of Manassas* (1866); *Wellenlänge* (Wavelength, 1882); *Imitation of the Sewing Machine* (1889). He also improvised on themes given by members of the audience.

Bestiaire, Le (The Menagerie). Song cycle by Poulenc, 1919, for baritone and chamber ensemble; 6 animals, from a dromedary to a crayfish, are depicted.

bestimmt (Ger.). Decisively, with energy.

betont (Ger.). Accented, marked. *Betonung, mit*, accented, with emphasis.

betrübt (Ger.). Grieved, afflicted.

Bettelstudent, Der (The Beggar Student). Operetta by Millöcker, 1882, in which a seemingly impecunious student is revealed as a foreign prince.

bewegt (Ger.). Moved, agitated., animated. *Bewegter*, faster; *più mosso*, movement; *Bewegung*, agitation.

Bewitched, Bothered and Bewildered. See PAL JOEY.

Beyer, Johanna Magdalena, German-American composer and musicologist; b. Leipzig, July 11, 1888; d. N.Y., Jan. 9, 1944. After studies in Germany, she emigrated to the

U.S. (1924), earning a teacher's certificate (1928); studied with Rudhyar, Crawford Seeger, and Cowell; wrote music and several plays for various N.Y. projects. During Cowell's term in San Quentin prison (1937–41), Beyer acted as his secretary and cared for his scores. Her compositional style is dissonant counterpoint; composed much chamber music; among her most interesting works are 4 string quartets (1934, 1936, 1938, 1943), *Cyrnab* for Chamber Orch. (1937), *Reverence* for Wind Ensemble (1938), and *Music of the Spheres* for 3 Electrical Instruments or Strings (1938; from the unfinished opera *Status Quo*).

bezifferter bass (Ger., figured bass). BASSO CONTINUO.

B-flat major. If any key can claim to be the key of the universe, it is B-flat major. Most machines of modern industry—such as electric motors, fans, and washing machines—buzz, whir, and hum on the 60-cycle B-flat, corresponding to the lowest note of the bassoon, with its natural overtones forming the triadic complex of B-flat major. The transposing instruments of the orch., particularly the trumpets and the clarinets, are most often in B-flat. This tuning enables them to be played in the key of B-flat major with the same digital facility that C major gives pianists. B-flat major is the key of fanfares and of festival and military marches, in which natural trumpets in B-flat play such an overwhelming role. The march of the soldiers in *Faust*, the return of Radames from the conquest of Ethiopia in *Aida*, and the march of the children and the signal call summoning Don José back to the barracks in *Carmen* are all in B-flat major. The dramatic trumpet call in *Fidelio*, announcing the arrival of the governor, is in B-flat major. In the purely symphonic repertory, Schubert's romantic Sym. No. 5 is in B-flat major; in a more introspective mood, Bruckner's Sym. No. 5. Beethoven selected this key for his unpretentious Sym. No. 4, but for Schumann the key must have signified the joy of life, for he wrote his Sym. No. 1, which he called the *Spring*, in this key. Prokofiev described the blinding pagan sunrise at the end of his *Scythian Suite* in blazing B-flat major. Standard arrangements of national anthems, including *The Star-Spangled Banner* and the *Marseillaise*, are in B-flat major. The song *Over There*, imitating the bugle calls of the doughboys of World War I, is in B-flat major, as is the bugle call that announces the opening of horse races. And then there is that gloriously uninhibited upward sweep of the clarinet (a B-flat clarinet, of course) that opens Gershwin's *Rhapsody in Blue*. Can there be a special psychological reason in Mahler's exclusion of B-flat major as the principal tonality in any of his symphonies? Was he inhibited by its aggressive character? Was he subconsciously concealing his darksome inner self from the intrusion of the brilliant illumination of B-flat major? It might be a subject for psychomusical study.

B-flat minor. The key of B-flat minor is pianistically desirable as the relative key of D-flat major, both scales having 5 flats in the key signature. Tchaikovsky's famous Piano Concerto No. 1 is nominally in the key of B-flat minor, but after a few perfunctory measures in the principal key it explodes into action with the famous optimistic D-flat major theme. Chopin favored B-flat minor, as he wrote a scherzo (op. 31) and a piano sonata (op. 35) in this key; the sonata's slow movement is the well-known, solemn, but ultimately depressing *Marche funèbre*. It is difficult to find any symphonic works unambiguously set in B-flat minor. A good example is the *Alpine* Sym. by R. Strauss, in which the ascent and the descent to and from the summit are illustrated by the correspondingly ascending and descending scales of B-flat minor. Miaskovsky assigned the key of B-flat minor to his Sym. No. 11, but then he wrote syms. in virtually every key.

Biber, Heinrich (Ignaz Franz von), famous Bohemian violinist and composer; b. Wartenberg, Bohemia, Aug. 12, 1644; d. Salzburg, May 3, 1704. After employment in smaller cities, he became a member of the royal chapel at Salzburg (1670); appointed vice-Kapellmeister (1679) and Kapellmeister (1684). He was in the service of the Emperor Leopold I, who ennobled him in 1690; the archbishops of Salzburg were his patrons. Biber was a founder of the German school of violin playing and was among the 1st to employ SCORDATURA, a system of artificial mistuning to facilitate performance; the best-known collections are his so-called Mystery Sonatas and Passacaglia for Violin (*c.* 1676; publ. 1905) and the trios publ. as *Harmonia artificiosa* (1712). He composed 3 operas, only 1 of which, *Chi la dura la vince* (1687), has survived; sacred music, including a Mass and a Requiem; and chamber music.

Biches, Les (The Does). Ballet by Poulenc, 1924, with chorus, orig. for Diaghilev's Ballets Russes. The work combines pastoral innocence with clarity and lightness, a mock-Wagnerian passage satirizing musical symbolism.

bicinium (Lat., double song). A 16th-century term for a composition for 2 voices or instruments. The 1st significant collection of such compositions was *Bicinia Gallica, Latina,*

Germanica, publ. by Georg Rhau (1545); other collections followed. The popularity of bicinium rose, primarily in reaction to the polyphonic structures of the Flemish school of the Renaissance. Bicinia also served as teaching devices in theoretical textbooks. The genre remained popular until the early Baroque, with Lassus the greatest practitioner. A revival took place in the early 20th century, when Bartók and Hindemith composed pieces of this type, using dissonant harmony.

Bicycle Built for Two, A. Song by Harry Dacre, 1892, orig. entitled *Daisy Bell*. It has a continuing nostalgic caché and serves as the last verbal emission of the computer HAL in *2001: A Space Odyssey*.

Biedermeier. A genre of domestic furniture that became standard in petit bourgeois homes in Germany in the middle of the 19th century. The term subsequently expanded in its meaning to include sentimental literature, painting, and music; as such, it acquired derogatory implications. The name was the pseudonym of the writer of ostensibly naive and implicitly satirical stories publ. in the German humor magazine *Fliegende Blätter*, written in the voice of the fictional Gottlieb Biedermeier.

big band. The primary ensemble of the swing era of American jazz and popular music of the 1930s and 1940s. Big band music is scored for multiple trumpets, trombones, clarinets, and saxophones (melody group) while small groups usually employ at most 1 of each instrument. In both big and small bands the rhythm section is the same (piano and/or guitar, drum kit, and double bass). As a style of orchestration, melody instruments are often reinforced in unison. Big band nomenclature includes *front line*, *sidemen*, and the *signature tune* (the musical motto of a particular band).

Bigard, "Barney" (Alban Leon), African-American jazz clarinetist; b. New Orleans, Mar. 3, 1906; d. Culver City, Calif., June 27, 1980. He played E-flat clarinet, then tenor saxophone in local New Orleans bands; went to Chicago, where he worked with King Oliver (1925–27); recorded with Armstrong, Morton, and Johnny Dodds; began playing clarinet again. In 1927 he joined Ellington's band, with which he played until 1942; collaborated on *Clarinet Lament*, *Mood Indigo*, *Ducky Wucky*, and *Saturday Night Function*. He later formed small bands of his own,

working mostly in Los Angeles and N.Y.; played intermittently with Armstrong's All Stars (1947–61). He acquired a reputation as one of the best jazz clarinet players, known for warm tone and a capacity for smooth glissandos and chromatic runs.

Biggs, E(dward George) Power, eminent English-born American concert organist; b. Westcliff, Mar. 29, 1906; d. Boston, Mar. 10, 1977. After studies and performances in the U.K., he went to the U.S. (1930), becoming a naturalized citizen (1937); made his N.Y. debut at the Wanamaker Auditorium (1932). He was an organist in Newport, R.I. (1930–31); moved to Cambridge, Mass.; served as organist at Christ Church; became music director of the Harvard Church, Brookline. He toured Europe; surveyed old church organs throughout Europe in search of the type of organ that Bach and Handel played. His repertoire consisted mostly of the Baroque masters, but he also commissioned works from American composers (Piston, Harris, Hanson, Porter); Britten also wrote for him. Biggs became well known to American music lovers through his weekly organ recitals broadcast over the CBS network (1942–58); continued to concertize until arthritis forced him to reduce his concert activities; continued recording organ music; ed. organ works for publ. Biggs refused to perform on electronic instruments, which in his opinion vulgarized and distorted the classical organ sound. His style of performance had an austerity inspired by the Baroque school of organ playing.

Bill Bailey, Won't You Please Come Home? Ragtime song by Hughie Cannon, 1902. Bailey was a real person, a vaudevillian, but the text concerned a fictitious story of his being locked out of his house for a night by his temperamental wife.

Billings, William, pioneer American composer of hymns and anthems and popularizer of "fuging tunes"; b. Boston, Oct. 7, 1746; d. there, Sept. 26, 1800. A tanner's apprentice, he learned musical rudiments from treatises by William Tans'ur (*c.* 1700–83) and other British psalmodists; compensated for his lack of training by a wealth of original ideas and a determination to put them into practice. His 1st collection of choral music, *The New England Psalm Singer* (Boston, 1770), contained what he later described as "fuging pieces . . . more than 20 times as powerful as the old slow tunes." These pieces were freely canonic, with "each part striving for mastery and victory." His other publ. books were *The Singing Master's Assistant* (1778); *Music in Miniature* (1779); *The Psalm Singer's Amusement* (1781); *The Suffolk Harmony* (1786); and *The Continental Harmony* (1794). His sense of humor is evident in *Jargon*, harmonized entirely in dissonances and prefaced by a "manifesto" to the Goddess of Discord. Another work, *Modern Music*, has its express aim stated in the opening lines: "We are met for a concert of modern invention/To tickle the ear is our present intention." Several of his religious works became popular, particularly *Chester* and *the Rose of Sharon*; an interesting work historically is his *Lamentation over Boston*, written in Watertown while Boston was occupied by the British.

Despite his skill, he could not earn a living by his music or as a singing-master; physical handicaps limited his opportunities, although he held various minor municipal positions. Appeals made to provide him and his large family with funds bore little fruit, and Billings died in poverty. The combination of reverence and solemnity with humor makes the songs of Billings unique in the annals of American music, and aroused the curiosity of many modern American musicians; Cowell wrote a series of "fuging tunes," and Schuman's *New England Triptych* is based on 3 Billings tunes.

Billy Budd. Opera by Britten, 1951, after Melville's highly symbolic novella, describing a mutiny on the British war ship *Nore* in 1797, during which the young sailor Billy Budd kills his brutal superior officer and is hanged for it. The work is almost unique as a large-scale opera written for men's voices exclusively.

Billy the Kid. Ballet by Copland, 1938, with choreography by Eugene Loring, tracing the brief career of the famous Western outlaw while incorporating several cowboy songs; Copland later derived a popular orch.l suite from the ballet (1940).

binary. Dual; 2-part; in music, twofold form or rhythm. *Binary form*, a structural form founded on 2 principal themes (see SONATA FORM), or divided into 2 distinct or contrasted sections. Binary forms are represented in songs and dances of the Baroque period that lack a contrasting middle section. The harmonic plan in binary composition is symmetrical. The 1st section proceeds from the tonic to the dominant, and the 2nd section begins on the dominant and ends on the tonic. The ALLEMANDE is typical of binary form. Although a large number of compositions are set in ternary forms, the nucleus is always binary, with the 3rd section being the repetition, either literal, as in DA CAPO songs, or oblique, as in the sonata form where the recapitulation differs in tonality and sometimes in structure from the exposition.

It is always possible to convert a composition in binary form to one in ternary form by repeating, with or without variations, the 1st section and adding a cadence leading back to the tonic. It is difficult, if not impossible, however, to shorten a ternary composition to the binary without performing major surgery. Stravinsky is quoted as saying, perhaps apocryphally, that Mozart's music would gain if the contrasting middle sections were removed from all his works to reduce them to the binary structure; *binary measure*, common time, where the 1st of every 2 components takes the accent (regular and equal alternation between downbeat and upbeat). Binary rhythms may contain 2 subdivisions per beat. In medieval music, binary division in metrical time was called *tempus imperfectum*, "incomplete rhythm," the ternary division being *tempus perfectum*, "complete rhythm."

Binchois (Binch, Binche), **Gilles (de),** important Franco-Flemish composer; b. probably in Mons, Hainaut, *c.* 1400; d. Soignies, near Mons, Sept. 20, 1460. After training as a chorister, he was an "honorably chivalrous soldier," probably in the service of the Earl of Suffolk, who was among the English occupying France (1424); joined the Burgundian court (by 1427), where he advanced from 5th chaplain (1436) to 2nd, retaining the latter position until his death; also held several prebends and titles. He knew his great contemporary, Dufay. Binchois greatly distinguished himself as a composer of both sacred and secular works, noted for organic melodic constructions, characteristic rhythms, and contrapuntal independence; his style is considered traditional when compared to Dufay's.

Bing, Sir Rudolf (Franz Joseph), Austrian-born English operatic impresario; b. Vienna, Jan. 9, 1902. He studied at the Univ. of Vienna; took singing lessons; worked for opera houses in Darmstadt (1928–30) and Berlin (1930–33). He went to England (1934); became general manager at Glyndebourne (1936–49); became a British subject (1946). He was an active organizer of the Edinburgh Festival; was its artistic director (1947–50). In 1950 he was appointed general manager of the Metropolitan Opera, N.Y., inaugurating one of the most eventful and at times turbulent periods in the history of the Metropolitan; his controversial dealings with prima donnas were legendary. In 1971 Queen Elizabeth II of England conferred on him the title of Knight Commander of the Order of the British Empire; resigned from the Metropolitan in 1972. He later acted a nonspeaking part in Henze's *The Young Lord* at the N.Y. City Opera.

Bingen, Hildegard von. Hildegard von Bingen.

Binkley, Thomas (Eden), American lutenist, wind player, and music scholar; b. Cleveland, Dec. 26, 1931; d. Bloomington, Ind., Apr. 28, 1995. He studied at the Univ. of Ill. (B.M., 1956), then pursued postgraduate studies at the Univ. of Munich, and finally returned to the Univ. of Ill. From 1960 to 1980 he directed the Studio der frühen Musik, Munich; taught and performed in the medieval program at the Schola Cantorum Basiliensis, Basel (1973–77). In 1979 he became prof. of music and director of the Early Music Inst. at the Indiana Univ. School of Music, Bloomington. The Studio der frühen Musik quartet included Andrea von Ramm (mezzo-soprano), Sterling Jones (bowed strings), and a succession of tenors (Nigel Rogers, Willard Cobb, Richard Levitt) along with Binkley; their performances and recordings redefined early music realization through an improvisatory and free approach, tinged with an Arab flavor, and an innovative approach to instrumentation. Many performers gained from their experiences with Binkley, most notably Benjamin Bagby of Sequentia.

biomusic. Biological events are electrochemical in nature. Because energy in any form can be transmuted into sound waves, musically inclined biologists have experimented in converting the electrical energy in the brain, heart, lungs, eyeballs, and blood into signals that can be perceived through the auditory nerve. The brain activity, as recorded in an electroencephalogram, can be electronically metamorphosed into sounds. The brain as a musical composer is a fascinating notion for musicians who hope that their art can be scientifically reduced without losing its human quality. Brain signals, and consequently brain music, are transmitted through electrodes attached to the skull and at best reflect cranial rather than cerebral states. Indeed, the Parisian music-hall artist Jacques Perrot, known as "Tête de bois," composed and performed in 1962 a concerto for the cranium, producing the scale by tapping different parts of his skull bones with a mallet, using his mouth cavity as a resonator. The Aztecs had percussion ensembles consisting of the skulls of their defeated enemies. Catgut is used for violin strings, horsehair for the violin bow, and animal hides for the membrane of a drum. All these forms may be described as biomusical.

In a modern sense, biomusical experimentation is concerned with measuring the stimuli of sounds upon the auditory organs and the electrical signals produced by the organs of the body, whether human or animal. The ultimate aim of these studies is to connect emotional states with the sound waves produced by electronic transformation of the original biological impulses. The acceleration of the pulse under the influence of a powerful emotion has an obvious counterpart in music as accelerando and crescendo, and the reduction in pulse rate can be likened to a ritenuto and diminuendo.

Birtwistle, (Sir) **Harrison** (Paul), noted English composer; b. Accrington, Lancashire, July 15, 1934. He studied clarinet; entered the Royal Manchester College of Music (1952), where he studied composition and formed the New Music Manchester Group with P. M. Davies, Goehr, and Ogdon; studied clarinet with R. Kell in London. In 1966 he was visiting fellow at Princeton Univ. (1966) and visiting prof. at Swarthmore College (1973). In 1975 he became music director at the National Theatre, South Bank, London; he received the Grawemeyer Award (1987); knighted (1988).

In his compositions he departed completely from the folkloric trends once popular in British modern music and adopted an abstract, complex idiom, often with satirical overtones in his stage works, including *Punch and Judy* (1968), *Down by the Greenwood Side* (1969), *Bow Down* (1977), *Yan Tan Tethera* (1984), *The Mask of Orpheus* (1971–84; premiered 1986), and *Gawain* (1991). Important orch.l works include *The Triumph of Time* (1972) and *Silbury Air* (1977). Among his chamber vocal works are *Ring a Dumb Carillon* (1965) and *Nenia on the Death of Orpheus* (1970); instrumental works include *Refrains and Choruses* (1957), *Verses for Ensembles* and *Tragoedia* (both 1965), and *Secret Theater* (1984).

bis (Lat., twice). 1. An accolade used by European audiences to request an encore. 2. In printed music indicates that a passage is to be repeated.

bitonality

〜〜 〜〜 〜〜 〜〜 〜〜

The simultaneous presence of 2 different tonalities. The employment of 2 keys simultaneously is often termed POLYTONALITY, but bitonality is a more accurate description. Before the advent of modern music in the 20th century, playing in 2 different keys at the same time could be regarded only as a joke. Mozart wrote a piece entitled *Ein musikalischer Spass* (A Musical Joke, K. 522) that uses bitonal writing; but the subtitle of the piece, *Dorfmusikanten* (Village Musicians), betrays his sly purpose to ridicule the inability of rustic players to perform music correctly.

Bitonality is no longer a joke in the 20th century, but a well-established practice calculated to add spice and sparkle to singular tonality. The most effective type of bitonality is the combination of 2 major triads whose tonics form the interval of a tritone. The sum of the absolute values of sharps or flats in the key signatures of such triads is always 6 (e.g., C major and F-sharp major, with no sharps and 6 sharps respectively, or A-flat major and D major with key signatures of 4 flats and 2 sharps). The complex of C major and F-sharp major triads forms the harmonic foundation of Stravinsky's *Petrouchka*, and is often called the "Petrouchka chord." Acoustically the most advantageous position of these 2 chords is the spacing of 1 in open harmony, in root position in the low register, and

of the other in close harmony in the 1st inversion of the triad (e.g., C, G, E, A-sharp, C-sharp, F-sharp). In this disposition the outer voices, the middle voices, and the inner voices are all in the relationship of a tritone. Bitonality of minor triads is encountered more seldom, owing to the poor acoustical balance of such combinations.

In neoclassical music a modal type of bitonality has come into existence, as exemplified by such complexes as C major and D major falling within the Lydian mode. Another type of bitonality is a combination of 2 major or minor triads with a tone in common; for instance, C major combined with E major or E-flat major, favored particularly by composers exploring ethnic associations, among them Vaughan Williams and Harris. A very important noneuphonious type of bitonality is the homonymous complex of major and minor triads in close harmony (e.g., C, E, G, C, E-flat, G), with a friction point at a semitone between the major and the minor 3rd above the same tonic. It was cultivated assiduously by Stravinsky from his earliest period; in its linear devolution it offers a stimulating quasi-atonal melodic design. In his variations on the tune of *America*, reportedly written in 1891, Ives combines F major with A-flat major. In order to bring out the bitonal resonance, he marks one of the tonalities pianississimo and the other fortissimo.

biwa. A Japanese plucked flat lute, usually with 4 strings, played upright in a sitting position. The Chinese equivalent is the pip'a.

Bizet, Georges (Alexandre-Cesar-Leopold), great French opera composer; b. Paris, Oct. 25, 1838; d. Bougival, June 3, 1875. His father was a singing teacher and composer; his mother, an excellent pianist. At age 9 he entered the Paris Cons., studying with Marmontel, Benoist, Zimmerman, and Halévy, whose daughter, Geneviève, married Bizet in 1869. In 1857 he won the Grand Prix de Rome; shared (with Lecocq) a prize offered by Offenbach for a 1-act opéra comique, *Le Docteur Miracle* (1857). While in Rome he

composed a 2-act Italian opera buffa, *Don Procopio* (composed 1858–59; premiered 1906). Another 1-act opera was composed in Rome (*La Guzla de l'Emir*; accepted for production, but withdrawn by Bizet).

Returning to Paris, he produced a grand opera, *Les Pêcheurs de perles* (Théâtre-Lyrique, 1863); but this work, like *La Jolie Fille de Perth* (Théâtre-Lyrique, 1867), failed to win popular approval. A 1-act opera, *Djamileh* (Opéra-Comique, 1872), fared no better. Bizet's incidental music for Daudet's play *L'Arlèsienne* (1872) was ignored by audiences and critics; it received more attention at its revival (1885), and an orch.l suite brought out by Pasdeloup (1872) was acclaimed (a 2nd suite was made by Guiraud after Bizet's death).

Bizet's next major work was his masterpiece, *Carmen*, based on an 1845 novel by Mérimée and produced, after many difficulties with the management and the cast, at the Opéra-Comique (1875). The reception of the public was not enthusiastic; several critics attacked the opera for its lurid subject, and the music for its supposed adoption of Wagner's methods. Although the attendance was not high, the opera was maintained in the repertoire; there were 37 performances before the end of the season; Bizet was chagrined by the controversial reception of the opera, but it is a melodramatic invention to claim, as some biographers have, that the alleged failure of *Carmen* precipitated the composer's death (he died on the night of the 33 perf. of the opera, of a heart attack resulting from years of quinsy attacks). *Carmen* soon became a triumphant success all over the world, receiving stagings in London (in Italian), St. Petersburg, Vienna, Brussels, Naples, Florence, Mainz, and N.Y. The Metropolitan Opera 1st produced Carmen in Italian (1884), then in French (1893). It should be noted that the famous act 1 habanera is not Bizet's own, but a melody by the Spanish composer Yradier; he inserted it in *Carmen* (with alterations), mistaking it for a folk song. Bizet also wrote or planned several other stage works, composed a few notable orch.l works (Sym. in C Major, *Roma*, *Patrie*), piano music (including the fine suite *Jeux d'enfants* for piano duet), choral works (notably *Vasco da Gama*, an "ode-sym."), and songs.

Björling, Jussi (Johan Jonatan), eminent Swedish tenor; b. Stora Tuna, Feb. 5, 1911; d. Siaro, near Stockholm, Sept. 9, 1960. He studied singing with his father; joined the vocal Björling Male Quartet (1916–21); toured the U.S. He studied with John Forsell and Joseph Hislop in Stockholm (from 1928); made his operatic debut at the Royal Swedish Opera, Stockholm, as the Lamplighter in *Manon Lescaut* (1930); remained a company member until 1938; sang with the Vienna State Opera, the Dresden State Opera, and at the Salzburg Festival. He made his professional U.S. debut in a concert broadcast from Carnegie Hall, N.Y., in 1937; made his 1st appearance with the Metropolitan Opera as Rodolfo (1938); continued to sing there until 1941, when he went to Sweden. He returned to the Metropolitan Opera (1945–54, 1956–57, 1959). In early 1960 he suffered a heart attack as he was preparing to sing Rodolfo at Covent Garden, London; in spite of his great discomfort he went through with the performance; appeared for the last time in a Stockholm concert later that year.

Björling was highly regarded for the purity of his fine vocal technique, with its consistency throughout his register and his interpretative restraint and sense of style. He excelled in Puccini, Verdi, and Gounod roles, and also essayed some Russian operas.

Blacher, Boris, remarkable German composer; b. Newchwang, China (of half-German, quarter-Russian, and quarter-Jewish ancestry), Jan. 19 (Jan. 6 according to the Russian old-style calendar), 1903; d. Berlin, Jan. 30, 1975. His family moved to Irkutsk, Siberia (1914–20); in 1922 Blacher went to Berlin; studied architecture, and then studied composition with F. E. Koch. From 1948 until 1970 he was prof. at the Hochschule für Musik, Berlin (director, 1953–70). An exceptionally prolific composer, Blacher was equally adept in classical forms and in experimental procedures. He initiated a system of "variable meters," with time signatures following the arithmetical progression, alternatively increasing and decreasing, with permutations contributing to metrical variety. For the theater he developed a sui generis "abstract opera," incorporating an element of organized improvisation. In 1960 he was appointed director of the Seminar of Electronic Composition at the Technological Univ. in Berlin, and he subsequently made ample use of electronic resources in his own compositions.

Black Crook, The. A musical extravaganza put together from miscellaneous popular numbers, 1st produced in N.Y. on Sept. 12, 1866. The overly Gothic plot concerns an earthly demon who is endowed by the devil with preternatural powers but fails to deliver the Christian soul required of him, thanks to a dove who turns into a fairy queen. It served as an excuse for incredible stage effects and a daring display of uncovered female skin; the enterprise flourished despite the thundering from the pulpit and press demanding its suppression. At one point the producers "assuaged" the clamor by substituting "baby ballets" (requiring several hundred infants) for the women.

Blackbirds of 1928. An African-American revue, 1928, with music by Jimmy McHugh. Successfully produced in N.Y., the revue is a series of topical skits. The score includes the famous madrigal *I Can't Give You Anything but Love, Baby*.

Blades, Rubén, Panamanian singer and songwriter; b. Panama City, July 16, 1948. He was self-taught in music; despite receiving a law degree at the Univ. Nacional de Panama (1974), went to work for Fania Records in N.Y. Discovered by Ray Barretto, he made his singing debut at Madison Square Garden; collaborated with Willie Colon and gained a reputation as a fine performer and songwriter whose lyrics were highly charged with social and political significance and undergirded by salsa rhythms. Organizing his own band, Seis del Solar, he produced the successful album *Buscando America* (1984). He wrote the score for and starred in the film *Crossover Dreams* (1985), and also acted in Spike Lee's *Mo' Better Blues* (1990).

Blake, Eubie (James Herbert), African-American jazz piano player, dancer, vaudevillian, and composer of popular music; b. Baltimore, Feb. 7, 1883; d. N.Y., Feb. 12, 1983, 5 days after reaching his 100th birthday. He grew up in an atmosphere of syncopated music and sentimental ballads played on music boxes; had piano lessons from a church organist. At age 15 he got a regular job as a pianist in a "hookshop" (bordello), which provided him with tips from both the inmates and their customers. He improvised rag music (his long fingers could stretch to 12 keys on the keyboard) and soon began to compose in earnest. In 1899 he wrote his *Charleston Rag*, which became a hit. In 1915 he joined a singer named Noble Sissle, and they appeared on the vaudeville circuit together, advertised as the Dixie Duo. They broke the tradition of blackface comedians (white and black) and devised an all-black musical, *Shuffle Along*, which opened in N.Y. in 1921, billed as "a musical melange;" the score included *I'm Just Wild About Harry*, which became a hit and was used as a campaign song for Harry Truman in 1948. Another hit song was *Memories of You*, which Blake wrote for the musical *Blackbirds of 1930*. He was moved by a purely scholarly interest in music and, as late as 1949, took courses in the Schillinger system of composition at N.Y. Univ. In 1969 he recorded the album *The 86 Years of Eubie Blake*, which launched a revival of interest in his music and himself as a musical performer; in 1972 he formed his own record company.

As his centennial approached there was a growing appreciation of his legacy, and a Broadway revue billed simply *Eubie!* was produced with resounding success. In 1981 he received the Medal of Freedom from President Reagan. He made his last public appearance at the age of 99, at Lincoln Center in N.Y., on June 19, 1982. During his career he composed musicals, rags, études, boogies, novelties, waltzes, and a plethora of miscellaneous popular numbers; among his songs were *Love Will Find a Way*, *That Charleston Dance*, *Memories of You*, *Roll Jordan*, *Harlem Moon*, and *Ain't We Got Love.*

Blake, Rockwell (Robert), gifted American tenor; b. Plattsburgh, N.Y., Jan. 10, 1951. He sang with various small opera companies, attracting notice when he appeared as Lindoro with the Washington (D.C.) Opera (1976); sang with the Hamburg State Opera (1977–79) and the Vienna State Opera (1978). He made his N.Y. City Opera debut as Count Ory (1979), and his Metropolitan Opera, N.Y., debut as Lindoro (1981). He sang at the Chicago Lyric Opera (1983), the Rossini Opera Festival, Pesaro (1983), San Francisco Opera (1984), Paris Opéra (1985), Paris Opéra-Comique (1987), Bavarian State Opera, Munich (1987), Montreal (1989), and the Salzburg Festival (1989). In 1990 he appeared in the leading tenor role in Pergolesi's *Annibal* in Turin. He also sang widely in concerts. Blessed with a remarkable coloratura, Blake won notable distinction as a true *tenore di grazia*, excelling in Mozart and Rossini.

Blakey, Art (called Abdullah Ibn Buhaina), African-American jazz drummer; b. Pittsburgh, Oct. 11, 1919; d. N.Y., Oct. 16, 1990. He 1st studied piano, then turned to drums. He played with Mary Lou Williams (1942), then joined Fletcher Henderson (1942–43), Billy Eckstine (1944–47), and Buddy de Franco's quartet (1952–53). In 1947 he formed a group, the Jazz Messengers, which went through several transformations over the years. In his Eckstine years he worked with M. Davies, D. Gordon, F. Navarro, and T. Monk; in the early 1950s, C. Parker, C. Brown, and Horace Silver. Silver joined with Blakey in the Jazz Messengers of 1955; Silver left the following year, and Blakey took full control. Numerous important musicians have jumped from the Blakey springboard into the spotlight. Blakey participated in the "Giants of Jazz" tour with Gillespie and Monk (1971–72), and in a memorable drum battle with M. Roach, E. Jones, and B. Rich (Newport, 1974). In 1984 the Jazz Messengers won a Grammy Award for their album *New York Scene*. Blakey's driving, freewheeling style was quintessential in the hard-bop period of jazz.

Blaník. The 6th and last symphonic poem from Smetana's *Ma Vlast.* It depicts the same legend described in Fibich's opera *Blaník*, 1881.

Bläser (Ger.). Wind instruments. Also *Blasinstrumente*.

Blasquartett (Ger.). Wind quartet.

Blech (Ger.). Brass. *Blechinstrumente*, brass instruments.

Blechmusik (Ger.). Brass music.

blindness. It is well known that musically gifted blind children develop more rapidly than normal children as performers on a musical instrument; blind organists in particular often achieve great distinction in their profession (Helmut Walcha). The blind pianist Alec Templeton made a lucrative career as an entertainer. The jazz pianists Ray Charles and George Shearing are blind. The British composer Frederick Delius lost his sight because of a syphilitic infection but continued to compose by dictating music, note by note, to Eric Fenby. The Spanish musician Joaquín Rodrigo became blind early in his childhood but was able to compose for guitar, as does José Feliciano. Rahsaan Roland Kirk extended bop saxophone playing by inventing instruments. Stevie Wonder has been a significant force in popular music for more than a quarter century.

A curious case of a blind musical genius was a former Negro slave known as "Blind Tom" Bethune, whose pianistic talent was discovered when he was a small child. He was exploited for most of his life by his former owner and his family, who gained custody and toured him throughout the U.S. and Europe for half a century.

Bliss, (Sir) **Arthur** (Edward Drummond), significant English composer; b. London, Aug. 2, 1891; d. there, Mar. 27, 1975. He studied with Stanford, Vaughan Williams, and Holst. He served in the British Army during World War I; was wounded in 1916, and gassed in 1918. He resumed his musical studies after the Armistice; 2 early works, *Madam Noy* for Soprano and 6 Instruments (1918) and *Rout* for Soprano and Orch. (setting nonsense syllables, 1922), were highly successful, establishing Bliss as a leading modernist. He taught in California (1923–25); returning to London, he wrote the score for the film *Things to Come*, after H. G. Wells (1935); a succession of important ballets followed: *Checkmate* (1937), *Miracle in the Gorbals* (1944), and *Adam Zero* (1946). His most ambitious work is the opera *The Olympian*, after J. B. Priestly (1949). During World War II he was music director of the BBC (1942–44); was knighted (1950); named Master of the Queen's Musick as the successor to Sir Arnold Bax (1953).

Blitzstein, Marc, important American composer of socially conscious theater music; b. Philadelphia, Mar. 2, 1905; d. Fort-de-France, Martinique, Jan. 22, 1964, from a brain injury sustained after a political altercation with a group of men in a bar. He studied with R. Scalero, Siloti, N. Boulanger, and Schoenberg. Back in the U.S. he devoted himself chiefly to the cultivation of stage works of "social consciousness," the type created in Germany by Bertolt Brecht and Kurt Weill; accordingly he wrote his stage works for performances in small theaters of the cabaret type. *The Cradle Will Rock*, a 1-act opera of "social significance," became a succès du scandale when its sponsor, the Federal Theatre Project, withdrew because of its theme (steel-union organization); instead, John Houseman and Orson Welles produced it under the auspices of the Mercury Theatre (N.Y., 1937, with the composer at the piano).

In 1940 he received a Guggenheim fellowship; during World War II he was stationed with the U.S. Armed Forces in England, where he composed *The Airborne Sym.* for Narrator and Orch. (N.Y., 1946). In 1952 he had his biggest success—as a translator of Brecht and Weill's *Der Dreigroschenoper* into *The Threepenny Opera*. The most successful of his own works after World War II were the opera *Regina*, after Hellman's play *The Little Foxes* (1949), and 2 musicals: *Reuben Reuben* (1955) and *Juno*, after O'Casey's *Juno and the Paycock* (1959). Unfortunately, an opera commissioned by the Ford Foundation on the subject of Sacco and Vanzetti was never finished.

Bloch, Ernest, remarkable Swiss-born American composer of Jewish ancestry; b. Geneva, July 24, 1880; d. Portland, Oreg., July 15, 1959. He studied with Jaques-Dalcroze and L. Rey in Geneva (1894–97); then with Ysaÿe and Rasse in Brussels (1897–99); his earliest works demonstrated his natural attraction to non-European cultures and coloristic melos. In 1900 he went to Munich to study with Iwan Knorr and Ludwig Thuille; began the composition of his 1st Sym., in C-sharp minor (1910), with its 4 movements orig. bearing titles expressive of changing moods. He spent a year in Paris, where he met Debussy; his 1st publ. work, the song cycle *Historiettes au crépuscule* (1903), shows Debussy's influence. In 1904 he returned to Geneva, where he began the composition of his only opera, *Macbeth*, after Shakespeare (1910). As a tribute to his homeland he outlined the orch.1 work *Helvetia*, based on Swiss motifs, as early as 1900, but the full score was not completed until 1928. During the 1909–10 season Bloch conducted symphonic concerts in Lausanne and Neuchâtel. During World War I Bloch began to express himself musically as an inheritor of Jewish identity, in works such as *3 Jewish Poems*, *Israel* for Soloists, Chorus, and Orch.), and *Schelomo*, a "Hebrew rhapsody" for Cello and Orch., mark the height of Bloch's greatness as a Jewish composer; long after his death, *Schelomo* retains its popularity.

In 1916 Bloch toured the U.S. as conductor for dancer Maud Allan's troupe; the tour was not successful, however, and Bloch returned to Geneva; he came back to teach at the David Mannes School of Music, N.Y. (1917–20) and became an American citizen (1924). In America he found sincere admirers and formed a group of greatly talented students, among them Sessions, Bacon, Antheil, Moore, B. Rogers, R. Thompson, Porter, Stevens, Elwell, I. Freed, F. Jacobi, and Kirchner. He directed the Inst. of Music, Cleveland (1920–25), and the San Francisco Cons. (1925–30). In 1927 Bloch won 1st prize in a *Musical America* competition for his epic rhapsody entitled *America*; the work was performed with a great outpouring of publicity in 5 cities, but as happens often with prizewinning works, it failed to strike the critics and the audiences as truly great, and in the end remained a mere by-product of his genius. He returned to Switzerland (1930–39), then resettled in the U.S. and taught at the Univ. of Calif., Berkeley (1940–52); retired to his newly purchased house at Agate Beach, Oreg.

In general, Bloch's aesthetic shifted from a somewhat expressionist quality to a neoclassic approach. In his harmonic idiom he favored sonorities formed by the bitonal relationship of 2 major triads with the tonics standing at the distance of a tritone, but even the dissonances he employed were euphonious. In his last works of chamber music he experimented for the 1st time with thematic statements of 12 different notes, but he never adopted the strict dodecaphonic technique. In his early Piano Quintet Bloch made expressive use of quarter tones in the string parts. In his Jewish works he emphasized the interval of the augmented 2nd, without a literal imitation of Hebrew chants.

block chords, block harmony. A modern type of harmony in which the component chords move in parallel formation, whether triads, 7th chords, 9th chords, or more dissonant combinations.

Blockflöte (*Blochflöte*; Ger.). 1. The recorder; an old kind of *flute à bec*. 2. An organ stop having pyramid-shaped flue pipes of 2', 4', 8', or 16' pitch, sometimes stopped.

Blomdahl, Karl-Birger, significant Swedish composer; b. Växjö, Oct. 19, 1916; d. Kungsängen, near Stockholm, June 14, 1968. He studied with Rosenberg, Wöldike, and Tor Mann in Stockholm; traveled in France and Italy (1946); began teaching students, including Pettersson, Bucht, and Karkoff; attended a seminar at Tanglewood (1954–55). Returning to Stockholm, he taught at the Royal Academy of Music (students included Rabe and Mellnäs, 1960–64); was appointed music director at the Swedish Radio (1964).

In the 1940s Blomdahl was an organizer (with Bäck, Carlid, Johanson, and Lidholm) of the "Monday Group" in Stockholm, dedicated to the propagation of an objective and abstract idiom as distinct from the prevalent type of Scandinavian Romanticism. Blomdahl's early works are cast in a neoclassic idiom influenced by Hindemith, but he then turned to advanced techniques, including the application of ELECTRONIC MUSIC. He composed several major orch.1 works and ballets; his 3rd Sym., subtitled *Facetter* (Facets), utilizes DODECAPHONIC techniques. In 1959 he brought out his opera *Aniara*, which made him internationally famous; it pictures a pessimistic future when the remnants of the inhabitants of the planet Earth, devastated by atomic wars and polluted by radiation, are forced to emigrate to saner worlds in the galaxy; the score employs electronic sounds, and its thematic foundation is derived from a series of 12 different notes and 11 different intervals. At the time of his death Blomdahl was working on an opera entitled *The Saga of the Great Computer*, incorporating electronic and concrete sounds and synthetic speech.

Bloomer Girl. Musical by Arlen and Harburg, 1944, focusing on the 19th-century American feminist Amelia Jenks Bloomer, her trousers, the resulting conflicts with her family, and her participation in the "underground railroad" movement of the abolitionists.

Blow, John, great English composer and organist; b. Newark-on-Trent, Nottinghamshire (baptized), Feb. 23, 1649 (1648, Julian calendar); d. Westminster (London), Oct. 1, 1708. In 1660–61 he was a chorister at the Chapel Royal under H. Cooke; studied organ with Christopher Gibbons; appointed organist of Westminster Abbey (1668). In 1679 he left this post; Purcell, who had been Blow's student, succeeded him; after Purcell's untimely death, Blow was reappointed (1695), and he remained at Westminster Abbey until his death; he is buried in the north aisle. He married Elizabeth Braddock in 1674; she died in 1683 in childbirth, leaving 5 children. Blow held the rank of Gentleman of the Chapel Royal (from 1674); succeeded Humfrey as Master of the Children of the Chapel Royal (1674); appointed Master of the Choristers at St. Paul's (1687–1703); appointed Composer of the Chapel Royal (1699).

While still a young chorister of the Chapel Royal, Blow began to compose church music; his oeuvre includes Anglican services, secular part-songs, catches, and organ and instrumental music. In collaboration with Humfrey and William Turner he wrote the Club Anthem (*I Will Always*

Give Thanks, c. 1664); at the behest of Charles II he wrote a 2-part song on Herrick's poem *Go, Perjur'd Man* (publ. 1700). He wrote odes for many occasions, among them an ode for New Year's Day, 1682, *Great Sir, the Joy of All Our Hearts*, and 5 odes for St. Cecilia; numerous anthems, including 2 for the coronation of James II; *Epicedium for Queen Mary* (1695); *Ode on the Death of Purcell* (1696). Blow's collection of 50 songs, *Amphion Anglicus*, was publ. in 1700. His best-known work the MASQUE *Venus and Adonis* (*c.* 1685); this is his only complete score for the stage, but he contributed separate songs for numerous dramatic plays. Purcell regarded Blow as "one of the greatest masters in the world."

blue note. Pitches approximating the lowered 3rd and 7th degrees in a major scale, as B-flat and E-flat in the C-major scale; the blue note is characteristic in jazz and blues melodies. While fixed instruments must allow blue notes to fall "between the cracks," string and wind instruments (including the voice) can bend pitch and thus produce the highly emotive tonal effects associated with blue notes.

Blue Tango. An orch.l novelty by L. Anderson, the 1st of its kind to top the U.S. popular charts, 1952. Lyrics were added later.

Bluebeard's Castle. An opera by Béla Bartók, produced in Budapest on May 24, 1918. The justly infamous Bluebeard (possibly a historic character) lets his last bride open 7 secret doors of his castle that conceal torture chambers and the dead bodies of his previous wives. As Bluebeard protests his love for his last bride, she joins the dead wives behind the last door. The music is lyrically dissonant, stressing the cumulative melodramatic events.

bluegrass. A musical style pioneered by mandolinist Bill Monroe with his famous group the Blue Grass Boys (named for his home state of Ky.). Monroe's aggressive mandolin style, high vocal harmonies, and bluesy compositions all became standard ingredients for the bluegrass style. The instrumentation of his most successful band—guitar, mandolin, banjo, fiddle, and bass—became the model for the standard bluegrass lineup. Two key musicians in Monroe's 1945–48 group, Lester Flatt and Earl Scruggs, separated from the master and formed their own successful band, most notably providing the music for the 1967 film *Bonnie and Clyde*, which did much to popularize the style. More recent bluegrass (known as newgrass) exhibits harmonic, melodic, and formal experimentation as well as the influence of other styles, primarily jazz and progressive rock.

blues

A traditional black American ballad style. It is in 4/4 time, is based on major tonality with a melody characterized by lowered 3rd and 7th ("blue") notes, and has developed into a stereotyped, 12-measure harmonic pattern: I (x4)-IV (x2)-I (x2)-V (x1)-IV (x1)-I (x2). The colloquialism "blues" (sadness) dates back to at least the early 19th century, but the musical form evolved from Negro spirituals, work songs, field hollers, and ballads, both Anglo- and African-American.

The country blues style seems to have existed by the 1890s, with a singer who was self-accompanied by a banjo, later a guitar. The genre was associated with the southern states, going as far west as Texas. Already then, the standard and relatively unusual strophe scheme was in place: line A, repeat line A, then a rhyming line B (like the medieval German BARFORM). The country genre was popularized 1st by the songsters, itinerant performers on the medicine-show circuit; by the 1920s the pure blues performer began to replace the songster.

At the same time, the black composer and trumpet player W. C. Handy claimed to be the discoverer of the blues; he publ. his *Memphis Blues* (1911) and *St. Louis Blues* (1914), aimed at an urban clientele. The marketing approach worked, and Handy became a wealthy man. In the 1920s the style known as urban or city blues emerged: either the 12-measure or the 16- or 32-measure strophic-harmonic pattern (A–A–B–A) became standard; the supporting instrumentation drew upon the piano, trombone, cornet, saxophone, and drum kit, i.e., a jazz ensemble; the harmonica became a significant component in the 1930s.

Urban blues reached its 1st level in N.Y. and other northern cities, growing out of the "chitlin circuit" tours in the South. Many female urban blues singers became stars: Ma Rainey, Mamie Smith, Alberta Hunter, Ida Cox, and the great Bessie Smith. Meanwhile, numerous performers continued and expanded the traditional blues horizon: Charley Patton, Blind Lemon Jefferson, Son House, Blind Boy Fuller, Bukka White, Texas Alexander, Bo Carter, Blind Willie McTell, Memphis Minnie, and the last great traditional blues musician, Robert Johnson. After the 2nd World War John Lee Hooker, Lightnin' Hopkins, Fred McDowell, Sonny Terry and Brownie McGhee, and Mance Lipscomb contributed to the style. A blues revival in the 1960s (paralleling the folk revival) led to the rediscovery of long-unrecorded musicians: House, White, Sleepy John Estes, and Mississippi John Hurt.

Mance Lipscomb, Texas blues singer

PHOTOGRAPH BY CHRIS STRACHWITZ, COURTESY ARHOOLIE RECORDS

The urban wing of blues became dominant, and the scene shifted to Chicago after a period of important BARRELHOUSE and BOOGIE-WOOGIE piano playing throughout the country. Blues bands began to produce important music (Tampa Red, Big Bill Broonzy, Washboard Sam, the 1st Sonny Boy Williamson). After World War II the electrification of the guitar led to the development of rhythm and blues, combining elements of blues, swing, and boogie-woogie; but the urban blues developed into the electric blues known as Chicago style in the hands of Muddy Waters, Howlin' Wolf, James Cotton, Otis Spann, Little Walter, the 2nd Sonny Boy Williamson. This style, with its strong emphasis on improvisation, offered white musicians an opportunity to explore the blues: Paul Butterfield, Mike Bloomfield, Eric Clapton, the Yardbirds, and Canned Heat.

BMI (Broadcast Music Incorporated). A music licensing organization founded in N.Y. in 1940 as an alternative collecting agency to ASCAP. It operates by granting licenses to entertainment businesses, including radio and television stations, hotels, restaurants, ballrooms, airlines, even circuses—wherever music is performed. BMI purchases the rights from publishers, who in turn pay royalties to composers and lyricists. In other words, BMI serves as an intermediary between the composer of music, or writer of words used with music, and the public users of such productions.

Since BMI started out as a rival organization to ASCAP, it naturally tried to attract composers with prestigious names but who did not command a decent income from royalties for performances. In its early years BMI offered large sums of money to such composers—up to $10,000 a year. BMI was also more adventurous than its rival in attracting rock and other postwar composers of popular music. The 2 organizations have reached a professional truce.

boat song. See BARCAROLLE.

bocca (It.). Mouth. *Bocca chiusa, con*, with closed mouth; *Brummstimmen* (Ger.), humming.

Boccherini, (Ridolfo) **Luigi,** famous Italian composer and cellist; b. Lucca, Feb. 19, 1743; d. Madrid, May 28, 1805. In 1757 he was engaged as a cellist in the orch. of the Court Theater, Vienna. He spent most of the next decade in his birthplace (1761–66); then undertook a concert tour with the violinist Filippo Manfredi, arriving in Paris, where he appeared at the Concert Spirituel (1768). He became exceedingly popular as a performer; his 1st publications were 6 string quartets and 2 books of string trios (Paris, 1767). In 1769 he became chamber composer to the Infante Luis at Madrid; after the latter's death (1785), remained in Spain and received a pension; appointed court composer *in absentia* to Friedrich Wilhelm II of Prussia (1786). After the death of the King (1797), he concentrated fully on his Spanish opportunities. In 1800 he enjoyed the patronage of Napoleon's brother, Lucien Bonaparte, who served as French ambassador to Madrid (1800–1801). Despite his successes at European courts, Boccherini lost his appeal to his patrons and to the public. He supposedly died in poverty; in a belated tribute to a native son, the authorities in Lucca had his remains transferred there and reinterred with great solemnity in 1927.

Boccherini had profound admiration for Haydn; indeed, so close was Boccherini's style to Haydn's that this affinity gave rise to the saying, "Boccherini is the wife of Haydn." He was an exceptionally fecund composer, specializing almost exclusively in chamber music. A list of his works includes 26 chamber syms.; 2 octets; 16 sextets; 125 string quintets; 12 piano quintets; 24 quintets for strings and flute (or oboe); 91 string quartets; 48 string trios; 21 violin sonatas; 6 cello sonatas; and 11 cello concertos. He further wrote secular and sacred vocal music, including a Christmas cantata.

Bock, Jerry (Jerrold Lewis), American songwriter of popular music; b. New Haven, Conn., Nov. 23, 1928. He studied at the Univ. of Wis.; settled in N.Y.; composed for revues (*Catch a Star!*, 1955) and television's *Your Show of Shows*. He gained wide recognition with his Broadway musicals *Mr. Wonderful* (1956), *The Body Beautiful* (1958), *Fiorello!* (based on the life of N.Y. mayor LaGuardia, 1959), and *She Loves Me* (1963). His greatest success was *Fiddler on the Roof* (1964), also made into a movie.

Bockstriller (Ger.). GOAT'S TRILL.

bodhran (Gael.). Traditional Irish drum with a goat hide stretched over a circular shallow frame, played with a 2-headed beater. Used in uptempo dance pieces, the bodhran sets a steady fast beat, with accents and timbral changes interwoven.

Boehm system. A system of playing the flute with keys replacing the holes in the old instruments, making it more convenient to play; named after the 19th-century German inventor Theobald Boehm (1794–1881). Boehm, one of the greatest flute players of his time, sought to produce a more acoustically correct instrument. He fixed the position and size of the holes so as to obtain purity and fullness of tone; all holes were covered by keys, whereby prompt and accurate "speaking" was assured; the bore was modified, rendering the tone much fuller and mellower. He publ. *On Flute-Making and its Latest Innovations* (Mainz, 1847; Eng. trans., 1982) and *The Flute and Flute-Playing* (Munich, 1871).

Boethius (Anicius Manlius Torquatus Severinus Boetius), Roman philosopher and mathematician; b. Rome, A.D. *c.* 480; d. 524, executed on suspicion of treason by the Emperor Theodoric, whose counselor he had been for many years. Boethius wrote a treatise in 5 books, *De Institutione Musica*, which became the chief sourcebook for the theorizing monks of the Middle Ages; this treatise was publ. in Venice (1491, 1499), Basel (1570), Leipzig (1867), and in a German trans. (Leipzig, 1872); a French trans. by Fétis is unpubl. Whether the notation commonly called "Boethian" (using Latin indices to denote traditional Grk. notation) is properly attributable to him has been questioned for about 3 centuries.

Boeuf sur le toit, Le (The Bull on the Roof). A pantomime by Milhaud, 1920, with the music derived mainly from Brazilian dances (Milhaud served as an attaché to the French Embassy in Rio de Janeiro during World War I); the original score was for 2 pianos. Milhaud later transformed the work into an orch.1 ballet. The elements of jazz are among the 1st found in classical music. So popular did the piece become that a Paris bartender named his establishment Le Boeuf sur le Toit.

Bogen (Ger.). 1. A bow. 2. A slur or tie.

Bohème, La. An opera by Puccini, 1896, that depicts the life of 2 impoverished but amorous Paris artists (known as Bohemians in the 19th century). One befriends a neighboring girl; they fall in love, but are separated 1st by poverty and then by her death from consumption. The realism of the subject and the relative modernity of the score made *La Bohème* a scandalous landmark in opera. Leoncavallo produced an opera on the same subject with the same French title in Venice (1897); although meritorious, his *La Bohème* was eclipsed by Puccini's masterpiece.

Bohemian Girl, The. Opera (1843) by the Irish composer Michael William Balfe (1808–70), on a subject ultimately derived from *La Gitanella* by Cervantes. The much-revised libretto deals with a girl abducted by gypsies from her socially important father but finally restored to him and allowed to marry her Polish lover. The opera was 1st produced in London; it was by far Balfe's greatest success, and has clung onto the British stage ever since. It includes the famous nostalgic aria *I Dreamt That I Dwelt in Marble Halls.*

Böhm, Karl, Austrian conductor of great renown; b. Graz, Aug. 28, 1894; d. Salzburg, Aug. 14, 1981. He studied law (Dr.Jur., 1919), then music with Mandyczewski and G.

Adler at the Vienna Cons. After service in the Austrian army during World War I, he was appointed conductor at the Municipal Theater, Graz (1917–21); conducted at the Bavarian State Opera, Munich (1921–27); appointed Generalmusikdirektor in Darmstadt (1927–31). Having already mastered a number of works by Mozart, Wagner, and R. Strauss, he added to his repertoire operas by Krenek and Hindemith; conducted Berg's *Wozzeck*, a performance praised by the composer (1931).

From 1931 to 1933 Böhm served as General Musikdirektor of the Hamburg Opera (1931–33); from 1934 to 1943 he was music director of the Dresden State Opera, where he gave the 1st performances of 2 operas by R. Strauss: *Die Schweigsame Frau* (1935) and *Daphne* (1938), which Strauss dedicated to him. During the last 2 years of the raging war he was conductor at the Vienna State Opera (1943–45). After the war he was not allowed by the Allied authorities to give performances pending an investigation of his political past; he was cleared and resumed his career in 1947. He went to Buenos Aires, where he organized and conducted German opera seasons at the Teatro Colón (1950–53); returned to the Vienna State Opera (1954–56); conducted *Fidelio* at the opening of the reconstructed Vienna State Opera House (1955). He made his 1st U.S. appearance with the Chicago Sym. Orch. (1956); gave his debut at the Metropolitan Opera, N.Y., with *Don Giovanni* (1957); continued to conduct occasional performances there until 1974. In 1961 he took the Berlin Phil. to the U.S.; toured Japan with it (1963–64); led a U.S. tour with the Deutsche Oper, Berlin; took the Vienna State Opera for its 1st U.S. tour (1979). He also conducted radio and television performances.

In the annals of the art of conducting, Böhm may well be regarded as a worthy successor of the glorious pleiad of German and Austrian conductors such as Muck, Walter, and Furtwängler. He was admired for his impeccable rendition of classical opera scores, particularly those of Mozart, in which he scrupulously avoided any suggestion of improper romanticization; he was equally extolled for his productions of the operas of Wagner and Strauss, and he earned additional respect for his audacious espousal of modern music.

Boieldieu, François-Adrien, celebrated French opera composer; b. Rouen, Dec. 16, 1775; d. Jarcy, near Grosbois, Oct. 8, 1834. Boieldieu received his musical instruction from Charles Broche, who made him an assistant organist at St. André, Rouen. His 1st opéra-comique, *La Fille coupable*, was produced in Rouen (1793); his next work, *Rosalie et Myrza*, was also staged in Rouen (1795). He was befriended by Cherubini, Méhul, L. E. Jadin, and Erard. His romances (songs of a popular nature) were printed in Paris (16 vols., 1794–1811), as were his 9 piano sonatas (1795–1800). A facile composer, he produced one opera after another and had no difficulties getting them Parisian performances; particularly successful was his opéra-comique *Le Calife de Bagdad* (1800), which appealed to the public because of its exotic subject and pseudo-oriental arias.

In 1802 Boieldieu married the dancer Clotilde Mafleurai; sadly he separated from her the following year. Opportunely, he was invited to write operas for the Imperial theaters in St. Petersburg for a handsome salary; attended to his duties conscientiously, and produced at least 1 opera annually; was admired by Czar Alexander I. Despite a salary increase and a comfortable life, Boieldieu decided to leave Russia in 1811 and return to Paris. His estranged wife died in 1826, and he married the singer Jenny Phillis-Bertin the following year.

True to his custom, Boieldieu resumed composing operas for the Paris theaters. He was appointed prof. of composition at the Paris Cons. (1817–26); named a Chevalier of the Legion of Honor (1821). After a number of insignificant productions, he achieved his greatest success with his opéra-comique *La Dame blanche*, to a Scribe libretto after Walter Scott; the suspenseful story and the effective and atmospheric musical setting corresponded precisely to the tastes of the public of the time. It was produced at the Opéra-Comique, Paris (1825), and became a perennial success in Paris and elsewhere. In 1833 he received a grant of 6,000 francs from the French government and retired to his country house at Jarcy, where he died. During the last years of his life he became interested in painting; his pictures show a modest talent in landscape. He was also successful as a teacher; among his pupils were Fétis, Adam, and P. J. G. Zimmerman.

Boieldieu composed about 40 operas, of which several were written in collaboration with Méhul, Berton, Hérold, Cherubini, Catel, Paer, Isouard, Kreutzer, and Auber; 9 operas are lost. Boieldieu's significance in the history of French opera is great, even though the nationalistic hopes of the French music critics and others that he would rival Rossini (whom he admired) did not materialize; he simply lacked the tremendous power of invention, both in dramatic and comic aspects, that made Rossini a magician of 19th-century opera. Boieldieu's natural son, Adrien-Louis-Victor Boieldieu (1815–83), was also a composer; his mother was Thérèse Louise Antoinette Regnault, an Opéra-Comique singer. He wrote 10 operas, including *Marguerite* (libretto by Scribe), sketched by his father but left incomplete, and *L'Aïeule*.

bois (Fr., wood). Woodwinds.

Boismortier, Joseph Bodin de, French composer; b. Thionville, Moselle, Dec. 23, 1689; d. Roissy-en-Brie, Oct. 28, 1755. After living in Metz and Perpignan he settled in Paris in 1724. Very little is known about his career; he publ. 102 works between 1724 and 1747. A prolific composer of instrumental music, he wrote works for recorders and transverse flutes; 2 clavecin suites; trio sonatas, among them 1 set including the viola da gamba (1732); pieces designed for amateurs (in the positive sense), scored with a drone instrument, either a musette or a vielle, and publ. under such coaxing titles as *Gentillesses* (1731, etc.) or *Divertissemens de campagne* (1734). He also wrote 3 ballet-operas—*Les Voyages de l'Amour* (1736), *Don Quichotte* (1743), and *Daphnis et Chloé* (1747)—and a number of cantatas.

boîte à musique (Fr.). Music box.

Boito, Arrigo (birth name, Enrico), important Italian librettist and composer; b. Padua, Feb. 24, 1842; d. Milan, June 10, 1918. He studied with Alberto Mazzucato and Ronchetti-Monteviti; his 2 cantatas, *Il 4 Giugno* (1860) and *Le Sorelle d'Italia* (1861), written with Franco Faccio, attracted favorable attention; the Italian government granted them a gold medal and a 2-year foreign travel stipend. Boito visited Paris, Poland (to meet his father's family), Germany, Belgium, and England. He was strongly influenced by new French and German music; upon his return to Milan he undertook the composition of his 1st opera and most significant work, *Mefistofele*, which contains elements of conventional Italian opera and dramatic ideas stemming from Beethoven and Wagner; performed for the 1st time at La Scala (1868). The premiere was a disaster, with factions—for and against the unusual treatment of the subject—interrupting an already-long work (prologue and 5 acts) and the inept conducting by the composer. After a 2nd performance the opera was withdrawn; Boito undertook a revision with 1 less act, which successfully premiered in Bologna (1875). It appears in the repertory of leading opera houses, but—although it is truer to Goethe—its success has never matched that of Gounod's *Faust*. Boito never completed his 2nd opera, *Nerone*, on which he worked for more than half a century (from 1862 to 1916). The score was heavily revised by Tommasini and Toscanini (including the elimination of the important 5th act) and premiered by the latter at La Scala (1924). An early attempt at an opera, *Ero e Leandro*, was relinquished by 1879 and the libretto given to other composers.

Boito's gift as a lyric poet is equal to his as a composer. He publ. a book of verses under the anagrammatic pen name of Tobia Gorrio (Turin, 1877); he wrote his own operas' librettos and made admirable trans. of foreign works (*Armide*, *Der Freischütz*, *Rienzi*, *Russlan and Ludmilla*, the Wesendonk Lieder); wrote the librettos of *Otello* and *Falstaff* and revised *Simon Boccanegra* for Verdi; also wrote *La Gioconda* for Ponchielli, *Amleto* for Faccio, etc. He also publ. novels. He held many honorary titles from the King of Italy; in 1912 he followed in Verdi's footsteps and was made a senator.

Bolcom, William (Elden), American pianist and composer; b. Seattle, May 26, 1938. He studied with John Verrall, Milhaud, and Leland Smith. He taught at the Univ. of Washington, Seattle (1965–66), Queens College, CUNY (1966–68), and the N.Y. Univ. School of the Arts (1969–70). He joined the faculty of the Univ. of Mich.'s school of music (1973); made a full prof. (1983). He was composer-in-residence of the Detroit Sym. Orch. (from 1987). In 1988 he won the Pulitzer Prize in music for his *12 New Études* for Piano. After absorbing a variety of techniques, he experimented widely and wildly in serial thematics, musical collage, sophisticated intentional plagiarism, and microtonal electronics. He was also active as a pianist, recording and giving recitals of ragtime piano; with his wife, the singer Joan Morris, he gave concerts of popular American songs from olden times.

Bolcolm's compositions include 5 syms., the actors' opera *Dynamite Tonight* (1963), *Commedia* for Chamber Orch. (1971), *Frescoes* for 2 Keyboardists (1971), the secular oratorio *Songs of Innocence and of Experience* (1981), the theater piece *Casino Paradise* (1990), and *McTeague* (1992). He publ., with Robert Kimbass, *Reminiscing with Sissle and Blake* (N.Y., 1973); ed. the collected essays of George Rochberg, under the title *The Aesthetics of Survival: A Composer's View of 20th Century Music* (Ann Arbor, Mich., 1984).

Bolden, "Buddy" (Charles Joseph), African-American jazz cornetist; b. New Orleans, Sept. 6, 1877; d. Jackson, La., Nov. 4, 1931. He was a pioneering figure in early jazz, active in New Orleans. By 1901 he had a 6-piece unit and was playing in the honky-tonks and dives of Storyville. His career was broken by a cerebral dysfunction and alcoholism; confined to a state hospital in Jackson in 1906, he lingered there for many years before succumbing. While Bolden's life and contributions are clouded in legend and spurious anecdote, his tone, rhythmic power, and emotional slow-blues playing separated him from more mellow early jazz bands. His playing was not so much improvisatory as ornamented; he influenced the next generation of New Orleans cornetists (Keppard, Bunk Johnson) and helped standardize the ensemble and repertory of early jazz.

bolero (Sp.). 1. A Spanish national dance in syncopated 3/4 time and lively tempo (allegretto), the dancers accompanying their steps with castanets. It evolved from either the FANDANGO or SEGUIDILLA. It resembles the Andalusian cachucha. 2. A Cuban dance in 2/4 time, close to the HABANERA. 3. A composition in bolero style, such as Chopin's piano piece (op. 19) and Ravel's orch.l work (see below). Other examples of boleros or bolero rhythms in classical music are found in Beethoven, Weber, Méhul, Auber, Berlioz, and Moszkowski.

Boléro. A celebrated ballet by Ravel, 1928, inspired by the Spanish popular dance and written for the dancer Ida Rubinstein. Two alternating sections repeat several times; the insistent rhythm, melody, and harmony never change. An extraordinary variety and buildup is created by diversified instrumentation and colorful dynamics. With the exception of a brief deviation to E major before the coda, the entire piece is maintained in C major, a veritable tour de force of modernity made simple. Ravel grew to despise the piece; unfortunately for him, it was the last orig. orch.l work he was to compose, save the 2 piano concertos.

Bolling, Claude, outstanding French jazz pianist, bandleader, composer, and arranger; b. Cannes, Apr. 10, 1930. He received grounding in piano, classical repertoire, and the jazz idiom; studied with Duruflé in Paris; immersed himself in the jazz scene. He became a prominent crossover figure when he composed his *Sonata for 2 Pianists* (1970) for Jean-Bernard Pommier. His *Suite for Flute and Jazz Piano Trio*, written for Rampal (1975), became an internationally successful recording, attaining gold-record status (1981). He also wrote *California Suite* (film score, 1976), *Suite for Violin and Jazz Piano Trio* (for P. Zukerman; 1978), *Suite for Chamber Orch. and Jazz Piano Trio* (1983), and *Suite for Cello and Jazz Piano Trio* (for Yo-Yo Ma; 1984).

bombard (Eng., Ger.; It. *bombardo*; Fr. *bombarde*). 1. A low-pitched member of the SHAWM family, used during the 14th to 16th centuries, now obsolete. See also POSAUNE. 2. A 32', 16', or 8' organ reed stop, popular in France.

bombardon (Eng., Ger., Fr.; It. *bombardone*). 1. Bass bombard. 2. A 3- or 4-valve bass tuba, invented in the 1840s. 3. A 32' or 16' organ reed stop, popular in France.

bomba. A traditional dance of Puerto Rico; also its music, which was a significant predecessor of salsa.

Bombo. Musical extravaganza, 1921, featuring Al Jolson in blackface in a farce about Christopher Columbus. Includes the prototypical *My Mammy* as well as *April Showers*, *Yoo Hoo*, and *California Here I Come.*

bones. A primitive rhythm instrument of 2 bones or pieces of wood clicked together by the fingers of 1 hand; used in Irish traditional music, American blackface minstrelsy, and old-time Appalachian music.

bongos. Paired, knee-held Cuban drums, struck by the fingertips. Their sonority is weak, but they furnish a distinct percussive sound that stands out in percussive ensembles. Bongos have also been adopted by many symphonic composers.

Bonynge, Richard (Alan), noted Australian conductor; b. Sydney, Sept. 29, 1930. He began his career as a pianist; after marrying the soprano Joan Sutherland (1954) he devoted himself to helping her master the BEL CANTO operatic repertoire. He made his conducting debut in a concert with Sutherland in Rome (1962); made his operatic debut conducting *Faust* in Vancouver (1963); led *I Puritani* at Covent Garden, London (1964). In 1966 he made his Metropolitan Opera, N.Y., debut, conducting *Lucia di Lammermoor* with his wife in the title role. In subsequent years he conducted concerts and operas throughout the world. He was music director of the Australian Opera, Sydney (1976–86); made a Commander of the Order of the British Empire (1977).

boogie-woogie. A piano-based jazz style that developed in the late 1920s, beginning in Chicago and quickly spreading to N.Y. and elsewhere. Like many jazz terms, *boogie-woogie* is an onomatopoeic alliterative word suggesting a certain type of rhythmic beat. Its characteristic features are found in the ostinato accompaniment: rapid 8th notes in broken octaves, following the WALKING BASS pattern; or the so-called doubled blues bass, following the standard harmonic pattern (see BLUES). In the late 1930s a boogie-woogie craze swept the U.S.; as a result, many important pianists received due attention: Albert Ammons, Meade "Lux" Pete

Johnson, Jimmy Yancey, and "Cripple" Clarence Lofton. The style was adopted or transmogrified by swing bands and songs, most notably *Boogie Woogie Bugle Boy* by the Andrews Sisters (1941).

After World War II, boogie-woogie was incorporated into the blues, particularly as practiced by Chicago pianists. The Dutch painter Mondrian, who lived in N.Y., drew an abstract painting in straight lines that are interrupted by blank spaces crossing at right angles another set of broken straight lines; he called it *Broadway Boogie-Woogie*.

bop. BEBOP.

bore. The shape of the body of woodwind and brass instruments, beginning with the diameter of the cylinder.

Borge, Victor (born Borge Rosenbaum), variously talented Danish pianist and inborn humorist who, in his American avatar, carved for himself a unique niche as a provider of "comedy in music"; b. Copenhagen, Jan. 3, 1909, of Russian Jewish extraction (his father having left Russia to avoid being drafted into the Imperial Army). He developed a remarkable facility and prestidigital velocity on the keys; took theory courses at the Copenhagen Cons.; went to Berlin; became a pupil of a pupil of Liszt, then a pupil of a pupil of Busoni. His plans for a Swedish tour were prevented by the Nazi invasion of Denmark; emigrated (1940); became a U.S. citizen (1948).

In America he changed his name and inaugurated a show under the rubric *Comedy in Music* (1953), giving a total of 849 performances—then unprecedented in Broadway annals for a 1-man show. As a diversion he also started a poultry farm on his rural estate, specializing in Rock Cornish game hens; mastered idiomatic English to such an extent that he could improvise jokes that invariably elicited chuckles. He developed a sepulchral voice imitating bass singers and an ornithological coloratura à la Jenny Lind. Thus equipped, he made a career on television, continuing his solo appearances well into his 80s.

Boris Godunov. Music drama in 4 acts by Mussorgsky (composed 1868–69; rev. version, 1871–72, premiere with cuts, 1874), based on the historical tragedy of Pushkin. The action takes place during the Russian interregnum of 1598–1605. After his coronation Boris is tormented by the murder of the young Czarevitch Dmitri, lawful heir to the Russian throne, perpetrated on his behalf by assassins. A young monk, Gregory, decides to pretend that he is the "true Dmitri," miraculously saved from Boris's assassins. The Polish government backs the claim and leads its army to Moscow with Gregory as the pretender to the throne. Boris begins to go mad, and demands proof from his henchmen that it was the child Dmitri who was actually slain. The opera ends with Boris's death (after placing his young son Fyodor on the throne), and the expectation of the pretender's entry into Moscow.

In its orig. form, *Boris Godunov* has 7 scenes and no act subdivisions; in the 4-act rev. version, Mussorgsky eliminated 1 scene, added 3 new scenes, and altered extant scenes. After his death it was radically revised by Rimsky-Korsakov (1891–1906), and it was in this version that the opera became internationally famous. From the late 1920s various attempts to restore Mussorgsky's version began, sometimes in a mixture with the Rimsky-Korsakov; others returned to Mussorgsky's notes but altered the orchestration (K. Rathaus, Shostakovich), to answer the traditional charges against Mussorgsky's orchestrating abilities. Orig. score was republ. in 1928 and 1975, and some recent performances have combined the 2 Mussorgsky versions into a *Gesamtausführungausgabe*.

Borodin, Alexander (Porfirievich), celebrated Russian composer; b. St. Petersburg, Nov. 12, 1833; d. there, Feb. 27, 1887. The illegitimate son of a Georgian prince, he received an excellent education; learned several foreign languages; learned to play the flute. He played 4-hand arrangements of Haydn and Beethoven syms. with his friend M. Shchiglev. At age 14 he wrote a piece for flute and piano and a String Trio on themes from *Robert le Diable*. He became a student of the Academy of Medicine, St. Petersburg (1850); developed a great interest in chemistry; graduated with honors and joined the staff as assistant prof. (1856); contributed important scientific papers to the Russian Academy of Sciences' bulletin; traveled in Europe to continue studies (1859–62). Although mainly preoccupied with his scientific pursuits, Borodin continued to compose. In 1863 he married Ekterina Protopopova, an accomplished pianist who shared her appreciation of Chopin, Liszt, and Schumann with him; they remained each other's faithful companion and musical partner; his letters to her from Germany (1877), describing his visit to Liszt in Weimar, are of great interest.

A decisive influence on his compositional progress was his meeting with Balakirev in 1862; later he formed friendships with the critic Stasov (who included him in the "Mighty 5"), Mussorgsky, and other musicians of the Russian national school. He adopted a style of composition in conformity with their new ideas; particularly excelled in a type of Russian orientalism which had a great attraction for Russian musicians at the time; never became a consummate craftsman, like Rimsky-Korsakov; although quite proficient in counterpoint, he avoided purely contrapuntal writing. His feeling for rhythm and orch.l color was extraordinary, and his evocation of exotic scenes in his orch.l works and his masterpiece, the opera *Prince Igor* (1869–87; premiered 1890) is superb.

Composition was a very slow process for Borodin; several of his works (e.g., *Prince Igor*) remained incomplete and were ed. after his death by Rimsky-Korsakov and Glazunov. Other major works include the 4th act of MLADA, a group project with other members of the "Mighty 5"; 2 syms., and part of a 3rd; *In Central Asia*, a symphonic poem; 2 string quartets; a piano quintet; *Petite Suite* for Piano; several songs; several pieces based on others' music; and a large number of unfinished and fragmentary works, especially chamber music.

bossa nova (Port., new beat). Popular Brazilian song and dance music in diversely syncopated 2/4 time, derived from samba and influenced by jazz. In its purest form the vocal part is mostly improvised to rhythmic accompaniment, including a musical bow called the *marimban*. Bossa nova became internationally popular in the late 1950s and 1960s, thanks largely to Antonio Carlos Jobim (*Desafinado*, 1959), Stan Getz, Baden Powell, Astrud Gilberto, and others; it gradually became submerged in other popular styles.

Boston (*Valse Boston*). HESITATION WALTZ.

Bottesini, Giovanni, Italian double-bass virtuoso, conductor, and composer; b. Crema, Dec. 22, 1821; d. Parma, July 7, 1889. He studied double bass with Rossi at the Milan Cons. (1835–39); played in various orchs.; visited the U.S. (1847); went to England (1848), where he appeared as a cello soloist; made his independent concert debut in London (1849). In 1853 he was once more in America; also active as a conductor in Paris, Russia, and the Scandinavian countries. He was invited by Verdi to conduct the world premiere of *Aida* in Cairo (1871); eventually retired to Parma as cons. director.

Bottesini was the 1st great virtuoso on the double bass (3-stringed), usually regarded as an unwieldy instrument, and thus became a legendary paragon for the relatively few artists who essayed that instrument after him; thus Koussevitzky was often described as the "Russian Bottesini" during his early career as a double-bass player. Bottesini was

the composer of a number of passable operas which had several performances in his lifetime.

bouche (Fr.). Mouth.

bouche fermée (Fr., with mouth closed; It. *bocca chiusa*). Humming. An effective device used in choral singing and in opera. A famous example occurs in act 4 of Verdi's *Rigoletto*, where it is used with great dramatic effect; other examples include Puccini's *Madama Butterfly* and Debussy's *Sirènes* (*Nocturnes*). This technique differs from vocalise, sung without words but with the mouth open.

bouffe (Fr.). Comic, burlesque. *Opéra bouffe*, comic opera.

bouffon (Fr., jester, comedian). Mime-dancers who performed exotic dances at French courts in the 16th century. The famous polemical exchange between adherents of Italian and French opera in mid-18th-century Paris became known as the GUERRE DES BOUFFONS.

Boulanger, Lili (Juliette Marie Olga), talented French composer, sister of Nadia (Juliette) Boulanger; b. Paris, Aug. 21, 1893; d. Mezy, Seine-et-Oise, Mar. 15, 1918. She studied composition with Vidal at the Paris Cons. (1909–13); attracted considerable attention when she won the Grand Prix de Rome with her cantata *Faust et Hélène*, the 1st woman to receive this distinction. Her death less than 5 years later was lamented by French musicians as a great loss. Her talent, delicate and poetic, continued the tradition of French Romanticism on the borderline of Impressionism.

Besides her prizewinning cantata she wrote 2 symphonic poems, *D'un soir triste* and *D'un matin de printemps*; piano pieces; violin pieces. She left far more choral and vocal music, although her opera to Maeterlinck's *La Princesse Maleine* remained incomplete. She wrote several choral works with orch.: *Soir sur la plaine*; *Hymne au soleil*; *La Tempête*; *Les Sirènes*; *Sous-bois*; *Du fond de l'abîme*; *La Source*; *Pour les funérailles d'un soldat*; *6 Psaumes*; *Vieille prière bouddhique*; *Pie Jesu*, sacred chorus for mezzo, string quartet, harp, and organ; *Clairières dans le ciel*, a beautiful cycle of 13 songs to texts of F. Jammes; individual songs.

Boulanger, Nadia (Juliette), illustrious French composition teacher, sister of Lili (Juliette Marie Olga) Boulanger; b. Paris, Sept. 16, 1887; d. there, Oct. 22, 1979. Her grandmother, father, and mother were professional musicians; her mother was her 1st teacher. At the Paris Cons. she studied with Guilmant, Vierne, Vidal, Widor, and Fauré; in 1908 she received the 2nd Prix de Rome for her cantata *La Sirène*; she collaborated with Raoul Pugno on compositions, and completed his opera *La Ville Morte* after his death. She composed other works but, realizing that she could not compare with her sister Lili's compositional talent, devoted herself to teaching, a profession in which she found her finest vocation and greatest fame. She assisted in a harmony class at the Paris Cons. (1909–24); was engaged as a teacher at the École Normale de Musique (1920–39); when the American Cons. was founded at Fontainebleau (1921) she joined its faculty as a teacher of composition and orchestration; became its director in 1950. She also had a large class of private pupils from all parts of the world; among the many Americans who studied with her were Copland, Harris, Piston, Thomson, Carter, Diamond, Siegmeister, I. Fine, Blackwood, Berger, J. Vincent, Shapero, and Glass; others were Markevitch, Françaix, L. Berkeley, and Lipatti. Not all of her students were enthusiastic about her methods; some of them complained about the strict, and even restrictive, discipline she imposed on them; but all admired her insistence on perfection of form and accuracy of technique.

Her tastes were far from catholic; a great admirer of Stravinsky, Debussy, and Ravel, she had little appreciation of Schoenberg and the modern Vienna School. She visited the U.S. several times; played the organ part in Copland's Organ Sym. (which she advised him to compose) with the N.Y. Sym. Orch., under W. Damrosch's direction (1925). She was also a fine conductor; led the premiere of Stravinsky's *Dumbarton Oaks Concerto*; was the 1st woman to conduct subscription concerts of the Boston Sym. Orch. (1938) and any concert of the N.Y. Phil. (1939) or any London orch. (Royal Phil. Soc., 1937). During World War II she stayed in America; taught classes at Radcliffe College, Wellesley College, and the Juilliard School of Music, N.Y.; returning to Paris (1946), took over a class in piano accompaniment at the Paris Cons.; continued her private teaching as long as her frail health permitted; her 90th birthday was celebrated in 1977, with sincere tributes from her many students in Europe and America.

Boulez, Pierre, celebrated French composer and conductor; b. Montbrison, Mar. 26, 1925. He studied composition with Messiaen and R. Leibowitz, who initiated him into the procedures of serial music. In 1948 he became a theater conductor in Paris, and made a tour of the U.S. with a French ballet troupe (1952). In 1954 he organized in Paris a series of concerts, called "Domaine Musical," devoted mainly to avant-garde music; went to Germany, where he gave courses at the International Festivals for New Music in Darmstadt (1958). He delivered a course of lectures on music at Harvard Univ. (1963); made his American debut as conductor in N.Y. (1964); engaged as a guest conductor with the Cleveland Orch. In 1971 he was engaged as music director of the N.Y. Phil., a choice that surprised many and delighted many more.

From the outset he asserted complete independence from public and managerial tastes, and proceeded to feature on his programs works by Schoenberg, Berg, Webern, Varèse, and other modernists, giving a relatively small place to Romantic composers. This policy provoked the expected opposition on the part of many subscribers, but the management decided not to oppose Boulez. The musicians themselves voiced their full appreciation of his remarkable qualities as a professional of high caliber; they described him as a "French correction," with reference to his extraordinary sense of rhythm, perfect pitch, and memory but also a signal lack of emotional participation in the music. In America Boulez showed little interest in social amenities and made no effort to ingratiate himself with men and women of power. His departure in 1977 and the accession of the worldly Zubin Mehta as his successor were greeted with a sigh of relief, as an antidote to Boulez's stern regimen.

While attending to his duties at the helm of the N.Y. Phil., Boulez accepted outside obligations; from 1971 to 1975 served as chief conductor of the BBC Sym. Orch., London; as a perfect Wagnerite, he gave exemplary performances of Wagner's operas both in Germany and elsewhere. It was in Germany that he had orig. gained experience as an operatic conductor; was one of the few Frenchmen to conduct *Parsifal* in Germany; was engaged to conduct the Ring cycle in Bayreuth (1976). The precision of his leadership and his knowledge of the score produced a profound impression on both the audience and the critics.

He established his residence in Paris, where he had founded the Inst. de Recherche et Coordination Acoustique/Musique (IRCAM), a futuristic establishment generously subsidized by the French government (1974); in this post he and others could freely carry out experiments with electronic compositional techniques aided by digital synthesizers and a complex set of computers capable of acoustical feedback. Boulez's music is an embodiment of such futuristic techniques; it is fiendishly difficult to perform and even more difficult to describe in the familiar terms of dissonant counterpoint, free serialism, or indeterminism. He was one of the 1st composers to pursue total serialism and electroacoustic technology. He specifically disassociated himself from any particular modern school of music. He even publ. a pamphlet with the shocking title *Schoenberg est mort*, shortly after Schoenberg's actual physical death; he similarly distanced himself from other current trends.

Boult, (Sir) **Adrian** (Cedric), eminent English conductor; b. Chester, Apr. 8, 1889; d. London, Feb. 22, 1983. His mother and a science teacher gave him his 1st music instruction; sang in the Oxford Bach Choir; studied with Hans Sitt at the Leipzig Cons. (1912–13); attended rehearsals and concerts of the Gewandhaus Orch. under Nikisch and sang in its choir. He returned to England; joined the staff of Covent Garden, London (1914); appeared as guest conductor with the Liverpool Phil. (1916) and the London Sym. Orch. (1918). He was principal conductor of Ballets Russes's 1919 London season; conducted the British Sym. Orch., an ensemble made up of former British army soldiers (1919–24). He taught conducting at the Royal College of Music, London (1919–30); was music director of the City of Birmingham Orch. (1924–30); was music director of the Bach Choir (1928–31).

Boult's busy professional life continued in the 1930s, when he was appointed director of music for the BBC, London (1930–42). He organized the BBC Sym. Orch., which he led in its 1st concert (1930), serving as its chief conductor until 1950. He led it on several tours abroad, including a notably successful one to Paris, Vienna, Zurich, and Budapest (1936); appeared as guest conductor with the Vienna Phil. (1933), the Boston Sym. Orch. (1935), the NBC Sym. Orch., N.Y. (1938), the N.Y. Phil. (conducting the premieres of Bax's 7th Sym. and Bliss's Piano Concerto, 1939), the Chicago Sym. Orch. (1939), and the Concertgebouw Orch., Amsterdam (1945). From 1942 to 1950 he was associate conductor of the Henry Wood Promenade Concerts in London; was music director of the London Phil. (1950–57) and toured with it in the Soviet Union (1956). In 1959–60 he was again music director of the City of Birmingham Sym. Orch. (1959–60); taught once more at the Royal College (1962–66). In addition to his knighthood (1937) and many other honors, he conducted at the coronations of King George VI (1937) and Queen Elizabeth II (1953).

Boult's style of conducting was devoid of glamorous self-assertion; rather, his ideal was to serve the music with a minimum of display, and for this he was greatly respected by the musicians of the orchs. he conducted. Throughout his long and distinguished career he championed the cause of British music. He was particularly esteemed for his performances of the works of Vaughan Williams, whose Pastoral Sym. (1922), 4th Sym. (1935), and 6th Sym. (1948) received their premiere performances under his direction in London.

bourdon (Fr., bumblebee; Lat. *vox obtusa*; Ger. *Gedackt*). 1. An organ stop of 32' or 16' pitch, having stopped wooden pipes, sometimes with metallic tops; French organs also have open bourdons of 8' and 4' pitch. 2. A great bell, as the bourdon of Notre Dame. 3. Sustained pedal tone or drone, as played on the bagpipes, hurdy-gurdy, lute, or bowed strings.

Bourgogne. Symphonic poem by Varèse describing the French province where he lived before coming to the U.S., 1910. Completely different stylistically from his later work, it was destroyed by the composer in 1962.

bourrée (Fr.). 1. A dance of French or Spanish origin, in rapid tempo, having 2 sections of 8 measures each, and in 2/4 or 4/4 time. 2. An optional movement in the Baroque instrumental suite, in alla breve time.

bow (Fr. *archet*, Ger. *Bogen*; Sp., It. *arco*). 1. A long and slender piece of subtle and flexible wood strung with a length of horsehair, used to play string instruments such as the violin or cello. The hair is attached to the stick by a bent point or head and drawn into proper tension by the sliding nut, which is worked by the screw. Originally the bow was curved, like the bow used in archery; this derivation is reflected in the terms for the bow in all languages. The modern type of bow was standardized early in the 19th century; earlier bows were shorter and had a greater distance between the bow itself and the hair. The cello and double-bass bows are usually heavier and shorter than the violin and viola bows. 2. Execute with a bow; mark a piece with signs indicating the bowing.

bow-arm or -hand. The right arm or hand.

bowed guitar. A kind of violin with a guitar-shaped body.

bowed instrument. Any instrument played with a bow.

bowed zither. A heart-shaped, 3-stringed instrument developed in Bavaria around 1823. Another type, the 4-

stringed, viol-shaped *Breitoline*, was developed about 30 years later in Moravia and fingered like a viol.

Bowie, David (born David Jones), British rock musician, master of image manipulation; b. South London, Jan. 8, 1947. He changed his name to avoid confusion with the British singer Davy Jones of the Monkees. After several failed attempts he scored his 1st hit with *Space Oddity* (1969), associated with extraterrestrial visions. Dissatisfied with his direction, he opened the innovative Arts Lab, but was talked into returning to rock. With the guitarist Mick Ronson and the drummer Woody Woodmansey he put out a record, *The Man Who Sold the World* (1970), with the cover showing him in drag; it gave the impetus to a subdivision of rock known as "glitter rock." (The cover was banned in the U.S. because of his uncanny resemblance to movie star Lauren Bacall.) Carrying on his space obsession, Bowie released several "conceptual" albums, including the very successful *Ziggy Stardust* (1972); in it he paid tribute to drug society in *Rock 'n' Roll Suicide* and offered the powerful *Suffragette City*. Subsequent avatars were found in the problematic *Diamond Dogs* (1974), with the anthemic *Rebel, Rebel*; and *Young Americans* (1975), with the title song and the soul-influenced hit *Fame*.

He decided to try his luck in the movies, and starred in the space fantasy *The Man Who Fell to Earth* (1976), in which his somewhat introspective image and emaciated appearance fitted the alien hero's image; he took the title role in the stage play *Elephant Man* (1980), depicting an actual case of a man afflicted by filariasis, a disease characterized by granulomatous lesions and resulting in gross expansion of the tissues of the face and scrotum; also performed on stage in Brecht's *Baal* (1982); other important film roles in *Christian F.*, *Merry Christmas Mr. Lawrence*, *Absolute Beginners*, and the role of Andy Warhol in Julian Schnabel's film *Basquiat*. Bowie has also produced many other artists' albums, and written film songs and soundtracks. His most significant musical contributions in the last 2 decades include 3 moody synthesizer albums made with Brian Eno (1977–79); *Let's Dance*, with 4 hit singles; and several collections.

Bowie, Lester, American jazz trumpeter and composer; b. Frederick, Md., Oct. 11, 1941. He began playing in St. Louis in the rhythm-and-blues bands of Albert King and Little Milton; in 1965 moved to Chicago, where he helped found the Assoc. for the Advancement of Creative Musicians (AACM), an organization composed of young, avant-garde black jazz players. In 1969 he became a founding member of the Art Ensemble of Chicago; his performances, aside from those with the Ensemble, range from solo concerts to ones with his own bands, From the Root to the Source and Lester Bowie's Brass Fantasy. His most popular recordings include *Fast Last* (1974), *The 5th Power* (1978), and *All the Magic* (1982). His *23 Facts in 2 Acts* for musicians, dancers, chorus, and actors was premiered at the Brooklyn Academy of Music (1989).

bowing. The art of playing with the bow on string instruments; a player's method or style, depending on the manner of applying the bow to the strings. Because a bow is of a finite length, a melody must be played alternately with up-bows and down-bows. Up-bows move against gravity, therefore more effort must be applied to the movement than to a down-bow, which follows the direction of gravity. When a composer wishes to produce a succession of strong sounds, down-bows are indicated by a specific sign that looks like a square bracket turned 90 degrees to the right (⌐). A succession of up-bows, used to produce lighter sounds, is indicated by a capital letter *V* above the note.

When several notes are used in the same stroke of a bow, the 1st and last notes are connected by a curved line. It is not generally realized that because of the need to change direction of the bow, rhythmic figures such as a quarter note followed by an 8th note, when not played by the same type of bowing, cannot be performed evenly with the same amount of pressure and consequently with the same amount of tone. In actual performance, therefore, a string player automatically changes such rhythmic figures to 2 8th notes separated by an 8th-note rest, making legato quite impractical.

Apart from LEGATO, which in theory should not have any interruption of the sound, the most common stroke is STACCATO, Italian for "detached." For special effects the player is instructed to bow *sul ponticello*, close to the bridge; *sul tasto*, on the fingerboard; or *col legno*, with the wooden part of the bow.

Bowles, Paul (Frederic), American composer and novelist; b. Jamaica, N.Y., Dec. 30, 1910. As a youth he became fascinated with pictorial arts, belles lettres, and vocal projection of poetry. After a sojourn in Paris he returned to N.Y., where he worked as a bookshop clerk and composed. He impressed Copland by his early vocal pieces, and studied with him privately. He returned to Paris; befriended Thomson and studied with Boulanger; became a habitué of the dadaist circles on the left bank of the Seine; composed the cantata *Par le détroit* (1933), and the pseudo-Grecian *Scènes d'Anabase* for tenor, oboe, and piano (1932). In 1936 he returned to the U.S.; wrote his 1st stage work, the ballet *Yankee Clipper* (1937); wrote incidental music for theatrical productions as well as a short opera, *The Wind Remains*, to a text by Lorca, produced in N.Y. with L. Bernstein conducting (1943). A total change in artistic orientation occurred in 1949 when he publ. the novel *The Sheltering Sky*, the 1st of many bone-chilling novels, short stories, and translations of Moroccan literature. Although he completed his 3rd opera, *Yerma*, based on the Lorca play (1955), the N.Y. scene no longer satisfied his needs, and he moved permanently to Tangier (1959).

While his writings are dark, even grim, his musical works recall those of the French neoclassical school, with a fair amount of nostalgia, wit, and evocations of jazz, Mexican, and Moroccan traditional music. He composed 16 film scores; the Concerto for 2 Pianos and Ensemble (1947); chamber and piano music; and the genteel *A Picnic Cantata* for Women's Voices, 2 Pianos, and Percussion (N.Y., 1954). Bowles was intermittently united in marriage to Jane Auer Bowles, who was a fine novelist in her own right; she died in 1973.

boy (boys') choir. Especially in the Anglican church, a group of prepubescent males singing soprano parts, with the alto parts sung by countertenors or older boys.

boy soprano. A prepubescent male singing in the upper register. In religious settings that banned female participation, the boy soprano was an essential part of the chapel choir. Many Renaissance, Baroque, and early Classic composers started their careers in this capacity, losing those jobs when their voices broke.

Boyce, William, significant English organist and composer; b. London (baptized), Sept. 11, 1711; d. Kensington, Feb. 7, 1779. As a youth he was a chorister in St. Paul's Cathedral under Charles King; studied with Maurice Greene, the cathedral organist; was organist at the Earl of Oxford's chapel (1734–36), then at St. Michael's, Cornhill (1736–68); also named composer to the Chapel Royal (1736). His main task consisted in providing sacred music; also contributed incidental music to theatrical productions; conducted the Festivals of the 3 Choirs (Gloucester, Worcester, Hereford, 1737); served as Master of the Royal Band in 1755. In 1757 he became Master of the King's Musick, succeeding Greene; but increasing deafness forced him to abandon active musical duties after 1769.

In his last years he compiled the remarkable collection *Cathedral Music* (3 vols., 1760, 1768, and 1773). This anthology comprises morning and evening services, anthems, and other church music by a number of British composers, including Blow, Bull, Byrd, Clarke, Croft, Gibbons, Henry VIII, Humfrey, Lawes, Locke, Morley, Mundy, Purcell, Tallis, and Tye. His compositions were nearly all vocal music: numerous anthems, odes, cantatas, and more than 15 stage works. But it is his remarkable instrumental works that maintain his reputation: 12 sonatas for 2 Violins and Bass (London, 1747); 8 syms. (London, 1760); 12 overtures (London, 1770); and 10 voluntaries for organ or harpsichord (London, 1779).

Boys from Syracuse, The. Musical by Rodgers and Hart, 1938, paraphrasing Shakespeare's *A Comedy of Errors*, on the perennial theme of confused identity. Includes *Falling in Love with Love*.

brace. 1. The character { that connects 2 or more staves indicating that the parts on these staves are to be played simultaneously. 2. The group of staves so connected, as the *upper brace.*

Brahms, Johannes

〜〜〜 〜〜〜 〜〜〜 〜〜〜 〜〜〜

Great German composer; b. Hamburg, May 7, 1833; d. Vienna, Apr. 3, 1897. His father, a double bassist in the Hamburg Phil. Soc., taught Brahms the rudiments of music; he then studied with Otto F. W. Cossel and Eduard Marxsen. Brahms, on his own, eked out his subsistence by playing piano in taverns, restaurants, and other establishments (but not in brothels). In 1848 he gave a solo concert in Hamburg under an assumed name; met the Hungarian violinist Eduard Reményi (born Hoffmann), who taught him the fine points of the ALLA ZINGARESE style, and with whom he made a successful concert tour (1853). In Göttingen Brahms formed a friendship with Joachim, who gave him an introduction to Liszt in Weimar; he came to see the differences in his own aesthetic from the "new German school." Of greater significance was his meeting with the Schumanns in Düsseldorf. Robert called him a "young eagle" and reiterated his positive appraisal in his article "Neue Bahnen" (New Paths), which appeared in the *Neue Zeitschrift für Musik* (1853); in it he described young Brahms as having come into life as Minerva sprang in full armor from the brow of Jupiter. Later that year, Breitkopf & Härtel publ. 2 piano sonatas and his op. 3 songs.

Johannes Brahms

COURTESY OF THE NEW YORK PUBLIC LIBRARY

Schumann's death in 1856, after years of agonizing mental illness, deeply affected Brahms. He remained a devoted friend of Schumann's family; his correspondence with Clara (14 years his senior) reveals a deep affection and spiritual intimacy, but if there were more romantic feelings in their relationship, it was apparently only on his part; any speculation about their friendship entering a more physical phase exists solely in the fevered imaginations of wishful biographers. Objectively judged, the private life of Brahms was that of a middle-class bourgeois who worked systematically and diligently on his current tasks while maintaining a fairly active social life. There was a pattern of relationships with eligible women and contemplations of marriage; but, like Beethoven, he never surrendered his bachelorhood.

From 1857 to 1859 Brahms was employed in Detmold as court pianist, chamber musician, and choir director; completed and performed his 1st piano concerto in Hannover, with Joachim as conductor (1859); returning to Hamburg, formed a women's chorus (1859–62). Other important works of the period were the 2 orch.l serenades and the 1st string sextet. He hoped to be named conductor of the Hamburg Phil. Soc., but the directoriat engaged the singer Julius Stockhausen in that capacity (1863). Brahms became conductor of the Viennese Singakademie (1863–64); for financial reasons, focused on *a cappella* works, giving him the opportunity to study Baroque music; he left to avoid political intrigue.

As early as 1857 Brahms began work on his choral masterpiece, *Ein deutsches Requiem*; deeply saddened by his mother's death (1865), he now concentrated on and completed the score (1868); the 1st performance of the final version was given in Leipzig (1869). The title "German Requiem" has no nationalistic connotations; it indicates that the text is in German rather than Latin and that the texts are drawn from Luther's Bible. Among his other important vocal scores are *Rinaldo*, a cantata (1868); the *Liebeslieder* and *Zigeunerlieder* for Vocal Quartet and Piano (2 or 4 hands); the *Alto Rhapsody* (1869); the *Schicksalslied* (1871); *Nänie* (1881); and many lieder. He publ. 2 vols. of *Hungarian Dances* for Piano 4-hands (1869–80); these were extremely successful. Among his chamber music works, the Piano Quintet, op. 34 (1864); the String Sextet No. 2, op. 36 (1865); the Trio for French Horn, Violin, and piano, op. 40 (1865); the 2 String Quartets, op. 51 (1873); and the 3rd String Quartet, op. 67 (1876) are exemplary works of their kind.

In 1872 Brahms was named artistic director of the concerts of Vienna's famed Gesellschaft der Musikfreunde; he held this post until 1875. During this time he composed the *Variations on a Theme by Joseph Haydn*, op. 56a (1873). The title was an unintentional misnomer; the theme occurs in a *Feld-partita* for military band by Haydn, but it is not Haydn's own (the composer is unknown). For many years friends and admirers of Brahms urged him to write a sym. His piano concertos were symphonic in outline and thematic development. As early as 1855 he began work on a full-fledged sym.; in 1862 he nearly completed the 1st movement of what was to be his 1st Sym. The famous horn solo in the finale of the 1st Sym. was jotted down by Brahms on a picture postcard to Clara (1868) from his summer place in the Tyrol; he heard the tune played by a shepherd on an Alpine horn. Yet Brahms was still unsure about his symphonic capacity; finally, the great C-minor Sym. (op. 68) was completed and premiered in Karlsruhe, conducted by Dessoff (1876). Von Bülow, the German master of the telling phrase, called it "The 10th," thus placing Brahms on a direct line from Beethoven. Brahms was both aware of his debt to the older composer and, like many of his contemporaries, haunted by it.

Brahms composed his 2nd Sym., op. 73, premiered by the Vienna Phil. under the direction of H. Richter (1877). He wrote his Violin Concerto, op. 77, dedicated to Joachim, who gave its premiere with the Gewandhaus Orch. (1879). The 2nd Piano Concerto, op. 83, came next; Brahms was its soloist at the premiere in Budapest (1881). Then followed the 3rd Sym., op. 90, 1st performed by the Vienna Phil., under Richter (1883); the 4th Sym., op. 98, premiered in Meiningen (1885). Brahms's symphonic cycle was completed in less than a decade; there are fewer departures from the formal scheme than in Beethoven, and no extraneous episodes interfering with the grand general line. He wrote music pure in design and eloquent in sonorous projection; he was a true Classicist, a quality that endeared him to the critics who were repelled by Wagnerian streams of sound, and by the same token alienated those who sought something more than a surface geometry of thematic configurations from a musical composition.

The chamber music of Brahms possesses similar symphonic qualities; when Schoenberg made an orch.l arrangement of the op. 25 Piano Quartet in 1937, he only had to expand the sonorities and tone colors already present in the original. The string quartets of Brahms are edifices of Gothic perfection; his 3 violin sonatas and op. 8 Piano Trio (1854, rev. 1889) all contribute to a permanent treasure of musical Classicism. The piano writing of Brahms is severe in its contrapuntal texture, but pianists have always kept his rhapsodies, intermezzos, and other character pieces in their repertoire. He was able to impart sheer delight in his Hungarian rhapsodies and waltzes; they represented the Viennese side of his character, as contrasted with the profound Germanic quality of his syms. The song cycles of Brahms continued the evolution of the art of the lieder, a natural continuation of the song cycles of Schubert and Schumann, culminated in the starkly beautiful *4 Serious Songs* (op. 121, 1896).

Brahms was sociable and made friends easily; he traveled to Italy, and liked to spend his summers in the solitude of the Austrian Alps. But he was essentially reserved, unsentimental, at times even callous, someone who needed his privacy for artistic and personal reasons. Even Clara wrote in 1880 that she considered him "as much a riddle—I might almost say as much a stranger—as he was 25 years ago." But he was also a selfless family member who tried to save his parents' marriage and helped support his stepmother and stepbrother after his father's death. He was always ready and willing to help others, especially young composers (his earnest efforts on behalf of Dvořák were notable). At 1st he was reluctant to appear as a center of attention, turning down the honorary degree of Mus.D. from Cambridge Univ. (1876), but then he accepted the Gold Medal of the Phil. Soc., London (1877). Two years later he received an honorary Ph.D. from the Univ. of Breslau; as a gesture of appreciation and gratitude he wrote an *Acadmic Festival Overture* (1881).

With Brahms's success and fame came a sense of self-sufficiency, which found its external expression in the corpulence of his appearance, familiar to all from photographs and drawings of Brahms conducting or playing the piano. Even during his Viennese period Brahms remained a sturdy Prussian; his ideal was to see Germany a dominant force in Europe philosophically and militarily. In his workroom he kept a bronze relief of Bismarck, the "Iron Chancellor," crowned with laurel. He was extremely meticulous in his working habits (his MSS were clean and legible), but he avoided wearing formal dress, preferring a loosely fitting flannel shirt and a detachable white collar but no cravat. He liked to dine in simple restaurants, and he drank a great deal of beer.

Brahms was indifferent to hostile criticism and entirely free of professional jealousy; his differences with Wagner were those of style. Wagner was an opera composer, whereas Brahms never wrote for the stage (although he sought librettos). Some ardent admirers of Wagner (such as Hugo Wolf) found little of value in the music of Brahms, while admirers of Brahms (such as Hanslick) were sharp critics of Wagner. Still, it is amazing to read the outpouring of invective against Brahms by G. B. Shaw and by American critics; the usual accusations were of dullness and turgidity. Yet at the hands of successive Austro-German conductors, Brahms became a standard symphonist in N.Y., Boston, Philadelphia, and Baltimore. He lived a good life, but died a painful death, stricken with cancer of the liver.

From the perspective of over a century, Brahms appears as the greatest master of counterpoint after Bach; one can learn polyphony from a studious analysis of the chamber music and piano works of Brahms; he excelled in variation forms; his piano variations on a theme of Paganini are exemplars of contrapuntal learning, and they are also among the most difficult piano works of the 19th century. Posterity gave him a full measure of recognition; Hamburg, which had never treated him well, celebrated his sesquicentennial in 1983 with great pomp.

Brain, Dennis, English French-horn virtuoso; b. London, May 17, 1921; d. in an automobile accident, Hatfield, Hertfordshire, Sept. 1, 1957. He studied with his father, Aubrey (Harold) Brain, who had been a hornist with the London Sym. and BBC Sym. Orch. (1893–1955); served as 1st horn player in the Royal Phil. and later with the Philharmonia Orch. He rapidly acquired the reputation of a foremost performer on his instrument. Britten's *Serenade for Tenor, Horn, and Strings* was written for him. He was killed when he drove at a high speed, at night, from Edinburgh to London, and hit a tree. His death caused a profound shock among English musicians. His grandfather and uncle (Alfred, 1885–1966) were hornists, while his brother Leonard (1915–75) chose to be an oboist.

Branca, Glenn, art-rock composer and performer; b. Harrisburg, Pa., Oct. 6, 1948. After drama studies, he moved to N.Y. (1976), where he cofounded the experimental group Theoretical Girls. Later in the decade, Branca began composing works for massed, overamplified electric guitars, later adding brass, percussion, and other electric instruments. Most of his works are called syms., in the orig. sense (concordance of sound); his music is generally extremely loud and works best in a live setting. Stylistically the syms. can evoke Varèse, the futurists, 1930s percussion pieces, instrumental art-rock, and the 2nd minimalist school; but Branca's music is totally distinctive. He received considerable publicity in 1982 when Cage responded to a Branca performance by calling the piece "fascist."

Brandenburg Concertos. The popular name of a set of 6 concertos by Bach (BWV 1046–51), for various instrumental combinations, gathered in 1721 and fulsomely dedicated to the Margrave of Brandenberg. Strictly, only 3 of the pieces belong to the category of the concerto grosso, characterized by contrasts between the *concertino*, a small group of solo instruments, and *ripieno*, "replenishing instruments" (i.e., the main ensemble). Although the dedication does not seem to have been very efficacious, the concertos remain among Bach's most popular works.

Brandenburgers in Bohemia, The (*Braniboři v Čechách*). Opera by Smetana, 1866, grounded in nationalistic sentiments and involving a lecherous 13th-century German official, the 3 Czech sisters he kidnaps, and the Czech patriot he accuses of the crime.

branle, bransle (Fr.; Eng. *brangle*, brawl). Popular 16th-century French dance in which several persons joined hands and took the lead in turn. Derived from the generic BASSE DANSE type, there were several varieties of branle, in both binary and ternary meters; the latter is the putative predecessor of the minuet.

Brant, Henry, Canadian-born American ultramodern composer and pioneer of SPATIAL MUSIC; b. Montreal (of American parents), Sept. 15, 1913. He learned musical rudiments from his father; moved to N.Y. (1929); studied with L. Mannes, Riegger, Antheil, and Fritz Mahler (Gustav's nephew). He taught at Columbia Univ., the Juilliard School, and Bennington College; settled in Santa Barbara, Calif. (1982). An audacious explorer of sonic potentialities, he drew without prejudice upon resources ranging from kitchen utensils to tin cans in search of superior cacophony.

He was a 20th-century pioneer in the field of spatial music, in which the participating instruments were to be placed at specified points in space, on the stage, in the balcony, and in the aisles; almost all of his music since the early 1950s has used spatial technique. In conducting spatial music he developed an appropriate body language, turning at 90°, 135°, and 180° angles to address his instrumentalists. He gave cues by actually imitating the appearance of the entering instruments, miming the violin bow, a trombone valve, a piccolo, or a drum by the movement of his body or by facial movements. He also proposed to construct a concert hall with movable plywood partitions, changing configurations according to acoustical requirements; the closest (but unrelated) realization of this plan, at the Calif. Institute of the Arts, Valencia, is not designed for musical acoustics; Brant's plan will have to be relegated to a later century.

Among his many works: *Angels and Devils*, concerto for flute accompanied by 10 members of the flute family (1st version, 1931); *Signs and Alarms* for Chamber Ensemble (1953); *Kingdom Come*, spatial work for orch., circus band, organ (1970); *Meteor Farm*, spatial work for Javanese, West African, southern Indian, Western orch., jazz, and 2 choral ensembles (1982); and *Western Springs* for 2 Orchs., 2 Choruses, and 2 Jazz Groups (1984).

brass band. BAND, BRASS.

brass instruments. Wind instruments made of metal, forming one of the Western orch.l instrument families. The 4 orch.l brass instruments today are the French horn, trumpet, trombone (the only modern unvalved brass instrument), and tuba. Most other brass instruments are or were found in brass, military, and wind bands: cornet, bugle, tenor horn, flugelhorn, baritone, euphonium, bombardon, saxhorn, ophicleide, and serpent. A refinement of the definition of a brass instrument involves the size of the mouthpiece and shape of the bore; so the saxophone, found in most bands, is technically a woodwind made of metal; while the serpent, popular in bands until the early 19th century, was made of wood.

Bratsche (Ger.). The viola.

bravo, -a (It.). A shout of acclaim for the performer, commonly a male or female opera singer, respectively. *Bravi*, acclaim for more than one performer.

Bravour (Ger.). Bravura. *Bravourstück*, a vocal or instrumental piece of a brilliant and difficult character.

bravoure (Fr.). Bravura. *Valse de bravoure*, an instrumental waltz in brilliant, showy style.

bravura (It.). Boldness, spirit, dash, brilliancy; a resounding display of technical virtuosity.

bravura, aria di (It., Fr. *bravourarie*). ARIA DI BRAVURA.

bravura, con (It.). With boldness; brilliantly; with swaggering confidence.

Braxton, Anthony, black American jazz alto saxophonist, contrabass clarinetist, and composer; b. Chicago, June 4, 1945. After early studies in both jazz and classical music, he joined the Assoc. for the Advancement of Creative Musicians (AACM; 1966); formed the Creative Construction Co. with Leroy Jenkins and Wadada Leo Smith (1967). He later went to N.Y., where he played in the improvisation ensemble Musica Elettronica Viva (1970) and Chick Corea's free-jazz quartet, Circle (1970–71). Although his activities and influence have been most visible in avant-garde jazz improvisation based on graphic and other nontraditional notation, his output in the 1970s included compositions for band and piano. His album *For Alto* (1968) was the 1st recording for unaccompanied saxophone.

break (1). A short and lively improvised instrumental solo in jazz that momentarily disrupts the continuity of the tune without upsetting the symmetric period of the whole, usually in prearranged harmonic changes. Breaks can be of various lengths, can be improvised by 1 instrumentalist or by several solo instruments, and can result in extremely ingenious and even complex contrapuntal settings.

break (2). 1. The point where one register of a voice or instrument passes over into another: in the voice, the junction of the head and chest registers; in the clarinet, between the 4 registers. 2. A false or imperfect tone produced by incorrect lipping of a horn or trumpet; or by some difficulty with the reed of the clarinet (called "the goose"); in singing, by some defect in the vocal organs. 3. In an organ stop, when playing up the scale, the sudden return to the lower octave (caused by an incomplete set of pipes); in compound stops, any point in their scale where the relative pitch of the pipes changes.

breakdown. A lively white-American traditional dance music in 4/4, associated with the old-time fiddle and banjo style, dating from the late 19th century. In bluegrass, the breakdown became the genre for friendly rapid-finger competition between players.

breaking of the voice. See MUTATION.

Bream, Julian (Alexander), noted English guitarist and lutenist; b. London, July 15, 1933. He was educated at the Royal College of Music in London; made his debut at the age of 17. In 1960 he founded the Julian Bream Consort; also directed the Semley Festival of Music and Poetry from 1971. Through his numerous concerts and recordings he has helped to revive interest in Elizabethan lute music. He was named an Officer of the Order of the British Empire in

1964, and a Commander of the Order of the British Empire in 1985. Several works have been written for him.

breath/ing mark. A sign (', *, ^, v, or ") inserted in a vocal part to show that the singer may (or must) take breath at that point, rather than elsewhere.

Breit (Ger.). In a broad tempo.

Breiten Strich (Ger.). Use a broad stroke of the bow (when playing a string instrument).

Brel, Jacques, Belgian-born French singer and songwriter; b. Brussels, Apr. 8, 1929; d. Paris, Oct. 9, 1978. He rose to fame in France in the 1950s as a singer and writer of popular songs, which emphasized such themes as unrequited love, loneliness, death, and war. In 1967 he quit the concert stage and turned to the theater, as a producer, director, and actor. In 1968 the composer Mort Shuman brought Brel's songs to Broadway in his musical *Jacques Brel Is Alive and Well and Living in Paris.* The title proved ironic; stricken with cancer, Brel abandoned his career in 1974 and made his home in the Marquesas Islands; in 1977 he returned to Paris to record his final album, *Brel.*

Brendel, Alfred, eminent Austrian pianist; b. Wiesenberg, Moravia, Jan. 5, 1931. His teachers were E. Fischer, Paul Baumgartner, Steuermann, and Michl. He made his concert debut in Graz (1948); then began a successful career in Europe. He played for the 1st time in America (1963); also toured in South America, Japan, and Australia. He is particularly distinguished as an interpreter of the Vienna classics, but he also included in his active repertoire Schoenberg's difficult Piano Concerto. In 1983 he presented in N.Y. a cycle of 7 concerts of the complete piano sonatas of Beethoven. In 1989 he received knighthood from Queen Elizabeth II of England.

Brendel, Wolfgang, German baritone; b. Munich, Oct. 20, 1947. He joined the Bavarian State Opera, Munich (1971); became Kammersänger (1977). In 1975 he made his Metropolitan Opera, N.Y., debut as Count Almaviva in *Le nozze di Figaro,* at the San Francisco Opera as Rodrigo in *Don Carlo* (1979), Milan's La Scala as Count Almaviva (1981), Chicago Lyric Opera as Miller in *Luisa Miller* (1982), and at the Bayreuth Festival as Wolfram (1985). He made his debut at London's Covent Garden as Conte Di Luna in *Il Trovatore* in 1985. He appeared in opera centers throughout Europe and the U.S.; his most noted roles include Rossini's Figaro, Papageno, Eugene Onegin, Amfortas, Silvio, and Pelleas.

breve (Lat. *brevis*; *nota brevis*, short note). A short note value that in medieval mensural notation was indicated by a black or open square; its value was half of a LONGA. However, a whole generation of shorter notes made their appearance, and as a result the breve became incongruously the longest note in modern notation. This unnatural terminology is retained in contemporary British usage: the breve equals 2 whole notes and can be used only in the time signature of 8/4. It is written as an oblong, not blackened in.

Brian, Havergal, English composer of extraordinary fecundity and longevity; b. Dresden, Staffordshire, Jan. 29, 1876; d. Shoreham-by-the-Sea, Sussex, Nov. 28, 1972. He studied instruments with local teachers; taught himself elementary music theory, French, and German. From 1904 to 1949 he engaged in musical journalism. He attained a reputation in England as a harmless eccentric possessed by inordinate ambitions to become a composer; he attracted supporters among English musicians, who in turn were derided as gullible admirers of a patent amateur. Brian continued to write music in large symphonic forms; some of his works were performed, mostly by nonprofessional organizations and often many years after their composition, e.g., Sym. No. 1, the *Gothic* for Solo Voices, Chorus, Children's Chorus, Brass Bands, and Orch., composed in the 1920s, 1st complete performance in the 1970s. Amazingly enough he increased his productivity with age; he wrote 22 syms. after reaching the age of 80, and 7 more after the age of 90. The total number of syms. at the time of his death was 32.

Finally, English musicians, critics, conductors, and concert organizations became aware of the Brian phenomenon, and performances, mostly posthumous, followed. A Havergal Brian Soc. was formed in London, and there were a few timorous attempts to further the Brian cause outside of England. The slow acceptance of Brian's music was not due to his overindulgence in dissonance. Quite the contrary is true; Brian was not an innovator; he followed the Germanic traditions of R. Strauss and Mahler in the spirit of unbridled grandiosity, architectural formidability, and rhapsodically quaquaversal thematicism. Brian's modernism tended to be programmatic, as in the ominous whole-tone progressions in his opera *The Tigers* (1918), illustrating the aerial attacks on London by zeppelins during World War I. Brian's readiness to lend his MSS to anyone showing interest in his music resulted in the loss of several of his works; a few of them were retrieved after years of search.

Brice, Fanny (born Fannie Borach), American comedienne and singer; b. N.Y., Oct. 29, 1891; d. Los Angeles, May 29, 1951. After singing in her parents' tavern, she toured the burlesque circuit; there she was discovered by Florenz Ziegfeld, who featured her in his Follies of 1910. Subsequently she appeared in other eds. of the Follies and in Broadway musicals. Her most notable film role was her self-portrayal in *The Great Ziegfeld* (1936); in the Ziegfeld Follies of 1934 she created the role of little Baby Snooks, a character she continued to portray on radio from 1938 until her death. Her 3rd husband was Billy Rose, the producer and songwriter (married 1929; divorced 1938). Her career was the subject of the 1964 Broadway musical *Funny Girl*, which was later made into a film starring Barbra Streisand (1968).

Brico, Antonia, Dutch-born American pianist, teacher, and conductor; b. Rotterdam, June 26, 1902; d. Denver, Aug. 3, 1989. She moved to California in 1906 and took courses at the Univ. of Calif., Berkeley, graduating in music in 1923; she then went to Berlin, where she took conducting lessons with Karl Muck at the State Academy of Music. She also studied piano with Sigismund Stojowski. She played piano recitals in Europe, but her main interest was in conducting. Overcoming the general skepticism about feminine conductorship, she raised funds to conduct a special concert with the Berlin Phil. in 1930, which aroused some curiosity in music circles. She then received a conducting engagement in Finland, which gained her a commendation from Sibelius. She later became associated with Albert Schweitzer, visiting his hospital in South Africa and receiving from him some suggestions for performing the works of Bach.

In 1974 she was the subject of a film documentary entitled simply *Antonia*, in which she eloquently pleaded for the feminist cause in music and especially in conducting. On the strength of this film she obtained some engagements, among them an appearance at the Hollywood Bowl in a program of common favorites. She returned to Denver, where she maintained a studio as a piano teacher.

bridge. 1. In bowed instruments, a thin, arching piece of wood set upright on the belly to raise and stretch the strings above the resonance box, to which the bridge communicates the vibrations of the strings. 2. In the piano and other stringed instruments, a rail of wood or steel over which the strings are stretched.

Bridge, Frank, distinguished English composer and teacher of Benjamin Britten; b. Brighton, Feb. 26, 1879; d. Eastbourne, Jan. 10, 1941. He took violin lessons from his father; entered the Royal College of Music in 1899 and studied composition with Stanford, graduating in 1904. He specialized in viola playing; was a member of the Joachim String Quartet in 1906 and later of the English String Quartet. He also appeared as a conductor; was in charge of the New Sym. Orch. during Marie Brema's season (1910–11) at the Savoy Theatre in London; then conducted at Covent Garden during the seasons of Raymond Roze and Beecham; also appeared as conductor at the Promenade Concerts. He toured the U.S. in 1923, conducting his own works with the orchs. of Rochester, Boston, Detroit,

Fanny Brice, 1929

COURTESY FRANK DRIGGS COLLECTION

Cleveland, and N.Y.; he revisited the U.S. in 1934 and 1938. As a composer he received a belated recognition toward the end of his life, and posthumously; although he wrote a great deal of instrumental music, his name appeared but rarely in the programs of modern music festivals.

Much of his music is generated by passionate emotionalism, soaring in the harmonic realms of euphonious dissonances, while most of his chamber music maintains a classical spirit of Baroque construction. Although he was greatly impressed by the works of the 2nd Vienna School, he never embraced serial methods of composition. Most remarkable of these advanced works was his 4th String Quartet, written in 1937. Britten, who was an ardent student and admirer of Bridge's, wrote his *Variations on a Theme of Frank Bridge* (1937) based on the Idyll No. 2 for string quartet (1906).

Brigadoon. Musical by Lerner and Loewe, 1947, about a supernatural Scottish town visible for only one day per century, visited by an American tourist who chooses between staying with a woman in Brigadoon or returning to the natural world. Includes the title tune, *Come to Me Bend to Me*, *The Heather on the Hill*, and *Almost Like Being in Love*.

brillante (It.). Brilliant, showy, sparkling.

Brindisi (It., from Ger. *bring' dir's*, I bring it to you). A salutatory drinking song or toast. It is not connected to the Italian city of Brindisi. The earliest known operatic Brindisi is in Donizetti's *Lucrezia Borgia*; the best known is in *La Traviata* (*Labiamo!*).

brio, con (It., with noise). With gusto; spiritedly; vigorously, brilliantly; *brioso*.

brisé (Fr., broken). 1. In string playing, short, detached strokes of the bow. 2. Arpeggiate a chord. 3. In the 18th century, a FIORITURA.

Britten, (Edward) Benjamin

Lord Britten of Aldeburgh, one of the most remarkable composers of England; b. Lowestoft, Suffolk, Nov. 22, 1913; d. Aldeburgh, Dec. 4, 1976. He grew up in moderately prosperous circumstances; his father was an orthodontist, his mother an amateur singer. He played the piano and improvised facile tunes; many years later he used these youthful inspirations in a symphonic work which he named *Simple Sym*. In addition to piano he began taking viola lessons with Audrey Alston. At the age of 13 he was accepted as a pupil in composition by Bridge, whose influence was decisive on Britten's development as a composer. In 1930 he entered the Royal College of Music in London, where he studied piano with A. Benjamin and H. Samuel and composition with J. Ireland.

He progressed rapidly; even his earliest works showed a mature mastery of technique and a fine lyrical talent of expression. His *Fantasy Quartet* for Oboe and Strings was performed at the Festival of the ISCM in Florence in 1934. He became associated with the theater and the cinema and began composing background music for films. He was in the U.S. at the outbreak of World War II; returned to England in the spring of 1942; was exempted from military service as a conscientious objector. After the war he organized the English Opera Group (1947), and in 1948 he founded the Aldeburgh Festival, in collaboration with Eric Crozier and the singer Peter Pears; this festival, devoted mainly to production of short operas by English composers, became an important cultural institution in England; many of Britten's own works were performed for the 1st time at the Aldeburgh Festivals, often under his own direction; he also had productions at the Glyndebourne Festival.

In his operas Britten observed the economic necessity of reducing the orch.l contingent to 12 performers, with the piano part serving as a modern version of the Baroque ripieno. This economy of means made it possible for small opera groups and univ. workshops to perform

Britten's works; yet he succeeded in creating a rich spectrum of instrumental colors, in an idiom ranging from simple triadic progressions, often in parallel motions, to ultrachromatic dissonant harmonies; upon occasion he applied dodecaphonic procedures, with thematic materials based on 12 different notes; however, he never employed the formal design of the 12-tone method of composition. A sui generis dodecaphonic device is illustrated by the modulatory scheme in Britten's opera *The Turn of the Screw* (1954), in which each successive scene begins in a different key, with the totality of tonics aggregating to a series of 12 different notes. A characteristic feature in Britten's operas is the inclusion of orch.l interludes, which become independent symphonic poems in an impressionistic vein related to the dramatic action of the work. The cries of seagulls in Britten's most popular and musically most striking opera, *Peter Grimes* (1945), create a fantastic quasi-surrealistic imagery. Britten was equally successful in treating tragic subjects, as in *Peter Grimes* and *Billy Budd* (1951); comic subjects, exemplified

by his *Albert Herring* (1947); and mystical evocation, as in *The Turn of the Screw*. He was also successful in depicting patriotic subjects, as in *Gloriana* (1953), composed for the coronation of Queen Elizabeth II. He possessed a flair for writing music for children, in which he managed to present a degree of sophistication and artistic simplicity without condescension.

Britten was an adaptable composer who could perform a given task according to the specific requirements of the occasion. He composed a realization of Gay's *Beggar's Opera*. He also wrote modern parables for church performance and produced a contemporary counterpart of the medieval English miracle play *Noye's Fludde* (1958). Among his other works perhaps the most remarkable is the *War Requiem* (1962), a profound tribute to the war dead, mixing the Latin Requiem with Wilfrid Owen's poetry. In 1952 Britten was made a Companion of Honour; in 1965 he received the Order of Merit. In June 1976 he was created a life peer of Great Britain by Queen Elizabeth II, the 1st composer to be so honored.

broken chords. Harmonic units (chords) whose tones are sounded in succession instead of together, whether as self-contained progression or accompaniment. See ARPEGGIO.

broken consort. An old description of a Renaissance ensemble having both strings and wind instruments; contrasted in Shakespeare with *whole consort*, where all the instruments were of the same family. *Broken music*, music for a broken consort.

broken octaves. 1. Series of octaves in which the higher tones alternate with the lower. 2. Short octave, the lowest octave in keyboard instruments before 1700, in which rarely used chromatic bass notes were left out, leaving only 8 notes in that octave.

Broonzy, "Big Bill" (born William Lee Conley), African-American blues singer; b. Scott, Miss., June 26, 1893; d. Chicago, Aug. 14, 1958. He 1st took up the fiddle; after making his way to Chicago in 1920, he learned to play the guitar and subsequently began his career as a blues singer. He was as popular in Europe as in the U.S., making tours in 1951, 1955, and 1957. He was an important participant in the transition to the Chicago blues style.

Broschi, Carlo. See FARINELLI.

Broschi, Riccardo. See FARINELLI.

Brown, Clifford ("Brownie"), African-American jazz trumpeter; b. Wilmington, Del., Oct. 30, 1930; d. in an automobile accident on the turnpike near Bedford, Pa., June 26, 1956. He studied at Del. State College and Md. State College; gained experience playing in college jazz bands; later joined Tadd Dameron's group; toured Europe in 1953 with Lionel Hampton's orch.; returning to the U.S., worked with Art Blakey; subsequently formed the Brown-Roach Quintet with Max Roach. Brown was particularly successful as a master of improvisation.

Brown, Earle (Appleton, Jr.), American composer of the avant-garde; b. Lunenburg, Mass., Dec. 26, 1926. He played trumpet in school bands, then enrolled in Northeastern Univ., Boston, to study engineering; played trumpet in the U.S. Army Air Force Band; also served as a substitute trumpet player with the San Antonio Sym. Returning to Boston, he began to study the Schillinger system of composition; also took private lessons in music theory with Rosalyn Brogue Henning. He soon adopted the most advanced types of techniques in composition, experimenting in serial methods as well as in aleatory improvisation. He was fascinated by the parallelism existing in abstract expressionism in painting, mobile sculptures, and free musical forms; to draw these contiguities together he initiated the idea of open forms, using graphic notation with visual signs in musical terms. The titles of his works give clues to their contents: *Folio* (1952–53) is a group of 6 compositions in which the performer is free to vary the duration, pitch, and rhythm; *25 Pages* (1953) is to be played by any number of pianists up to 25, reading the actual pages in any desired order, and playing the notes upside down or right side up. Further development is represented by *Available Forms I* for 18 Instruments, consisting of musical "events" happening in accordance with guiding marginal arrows. Brown made much use of magnetic tape in his works, both in open and closed forms.

Apart from his creative endeavors, he had numerous lecturing engagements in Europe and the U.S. He was composer-in-residence with the Rotterdam Phil. in the Netherlands in 1947, and guest prof. at the Basel Cons. in Switzerland in 1975; also served as visiting prof. at the Univ. of Southern Calif. in Los Angeles (1978), and at Yale Univ. (1980–81; 1986–87). He was composer-in-residence at the American Academy in Rome (1987), and from 1986 to 1989 served as president of the American Music Center. He professes no *parti pris* in his approach to techniques and idioms of composition, whether dissonantly contrapuntal or serenely triadic; rather, his music represents a mobile assembly of plastic elements, in open-ended or closed forms. As a result, his usages range from astute asceticism and constrained constructivism to soaring sonorism and lush lyricism.

Brown, James, African-American gospel-soul singer and composer; b. Barnwell, Ga., May 3, 1928. He originally played keyboards and drums, and plucked the string bass; then formed a group which he called the Famous Flames. In 1956 he produced a triply emphatic song, *Please, Please, Please*, which made the top of the charts. Other big-time hits were *Try Me, Prisoner of Love, It's a Man's World, Out of Sight,* and *Papa's Got a Brand New Bag.* He then formed the James Brown Revue and produced stage shows. His songs acquired a political flavor, such as his militant proclamation *Black Is Beautiful, Say It Loud, I'm Black and I'm Proud,* and *Living in America.* He cultivated vocal sex motifs in such songs as *I Got Ants in My Pants, Hot Pants, Body Heat,* and *Sex Machine.* He also made an admonitory gesture to junkies in his song *King Heroin.* At the height of his fame as a soul singer he was called "Soul Brother Number 1," "Godfather of Soul," and "King of Soul."

Brown, Rosemary, British musical medium; b. London, July 27, 1917. She led a middle-class life as a housewife, and liked to improvise at the piano. Possessed of a certain type of musical mimicry, she began playing passages in the manner of her favorite compositions by Mozart, Beethoven, Schubert, Chopin, or Liszt; they usually consisted of short melodies invariably accompanied by broken triads and 7th-chords. Under the influence of popular literature dealing with communication with ghosts, she became convinced that the music she played was actually dictated to her by departed composers, and she willingly recited stories about their human kindness to her (Chopin warned her to turn off the leaking faucet in the bathtub to prevent flooding). On an errand to a grocery store as a small child, she was approached by a tall, gray-haired gentleman who, observing that she carried a music book, introduced himself as Franz Liszt and volunteered to teach her piano without remuneration. She had similar happy encounters with other famous composers, and soon arranged to take dictation of posthumous works from them. She appeared on British television writing down notes under the dictation of Beethoven, but Beethoven's image failed to materialize on the screen, owing no doubt to some last-moment scruples on the part of the producers. She put out a couple of maudlin, maundering, meandering pamphlets dealing with her transcendental experiences, and a professional journalist publ. the story of her contacts with dead composers. Also transmitted were some postmortem essays by Tovey, well-known for his belief in spooks.

Brubeck, Dave (David Warren), prominent American jazz pianist, bandleader, and composer, brother of Howard R(engstorff) Brubeck; b. Concord, Calif., Dec. 6, 1920. He received classical piano training from his mother, and played in local jazz groups from age 13. He also studied music at the College of the Pacific in Stockton, Calif. (1941–42), and received instruction in composition from Milhaud at Mills College in Oakland, Calif., and from Schoenberg in Los Angeles. During military service in World War II he led a band in Europe; he then founded his own octet and trio (1949). Subsequently, in 1951, he organized the Dave Brubeck Quartet, which acquired a reputation as one of the leading jazz groups of the era, known for its metric experiments and stylistic borrowings from Classical sources.

His sons Darius (b. San Francisco, June 14, 1947), a keyboard player; Chris (b. Los Angeles, Mar. 19, 1953), a bass-guitar and bass-trombone player; and Danny (b. Oakland, May 5, 1955), a drummer, often performed with him. His works include 2 ballets, *A Maiden in the Tower* (1956) and *Points on Jazz* (1961); a musical, *The Real Ambassador* (1962); 2 oratorios: *The Light in the Wilderness* (1968) and *Beloved Son* (1978); 3 cantatas: *The Gates of Justice* (1969), *Truth Is Fallen* (1971), and *La fiesta de la posada* (1975); *Festival Mass to Hope* (1980); and piano pieces. His brother, Howard R(engstorff) Brubeck (b. Concord, Calif., July 11, 1916), was a composer; served as chairman of the music dept. at Palomar Junior College, San Marcos, Calif. (1953–78).

Bruch, Max, celebrated German composer; b. Cologne, Jan. 6, 1838; d. Friedenau, near Berlin, Oct. 2, 1920. His mother, a professional singer, was his 1st teacher. He afterward studied theory with Breidenstein in Bonn; in 1852 he won a scholarship of the Mozart Foundation in Frankfurt for 4 years, and became a pupil of Hiller, Reinecke, and Breuning. At the age of 14 he brought out a sym. at Cologne, and at 20 produced his 1st stage work, *Scherz, List und Rache*, adapted from Goethe's singspiel (Cologne, 1858). Between 1858 and 1861 he taught music in Cologne; also made prolonged visits to Berlin, Leipzig, Dresden, and Munich; in 1863 he was in Mannheim, where he produced his 1st full-fledged opera, *Die Loreley* (1863), to the libretto by Geibel, orig. intended for Mendelssohn. About the same time he wrote an effective choral work, *Frithjof*, which was presented with great success in various German towns, and in Vienna.

From 1865 to 1867 Bruch was music director of a concert organization in Koblenz; there he wrote his 1st Violin Concerto (in G minor), which became a great favorite among violinists; then was court Kapellmeister in Sonderhausen. In 1870 he went to Berlin; his last opera, *Hermione*, based on Shakespeare's *The Winter's Tale*, was produced at the Berlin Opera in 1872. In 1880 he accepted the post of conductor of the Liverpool Phil., and remained in England for 3 years; in 1883 he visited the U.S. and conducted his choral work *Arminius* in Boston. From 1883 to 1890 he was music director of an orch. society in Breslau; in 1891 he became a prof. of composition at the Hochschule für Musik in Berlin, retiring in 1910. Bruch was married to the singer Clara Tuczek (d. 1919). Cambridge Univ. conferred upon him the honorary degree of D.Mus. (1893); the French Academy elected him corresponding member; in 1918 the Univ. of Berlin gave him the honorary degree of Dr.Phil.

Bruch's music, although imitative in its essence and even in its melodic and harmonic procedures, has a great eclectic charm; he was a master of harmony, counterpoint, and instrumentation; he was equally adept at handling vocal masses. He contributed a great deal to the development of the secular oratorio, using soloists, chorus, and orch. In this genre he wrote *Odysseus*, *Arminius*, *Das Lied von der Glocke*, and *Achilleus*; *Normannenzug* for baritone, male chorus, and orch.; and several other works for various vocal ensembles. Among his instrumental works the so-called *Scottish Fantasy* for Violin and Orch. (1880) was extremely successful when Sarasate (to whom the work was dedicated) performed it all over Europe; but the most popular of all works by Bruch is his *Kol Nidrei*, a Hebrew melody for Cello and Orch., composed for the Jewish community of Liverpool in 1880; its success led to the erroneous assumption that Bruch himself was Jewish (he was, in fact, of a clerical Protestant family). His Concerto for 2 Pianos and Orch. was commissioned by the American duo-piano team Ottilie and Rose Sutro; when they performed it for the 1st time (Philadelphia Orch., Stokowski conducting, 1916), they drastically revised the original. In 1971 the authentic version was discovered in Berlin, and it was given its 1st performance by Nathan Twining and Mer Berkofsky with the London Sym., Dorati conducting (1974).

Bruckner, (Josef) Anton

〰 〰 〰 〰 〰

Inspired Austrian composer; b. Ansfelden, Sept. 4, 1824; d. Vienna, Oct. 11, 1896. He studied music with his father, a village schoolmaster and church organist; also took music lessons at Hörsching with his cousin Johann Baptist Weiss. After his father's death in 1837, Bruckner enrolled as a chorister at St. Florian, where he attended classes in organ, piano, violin, and music theory. In 1840–41 he entered the special school for educational training in Linz, where he received instruction from J. N. A. Dürrnberger; he also studied music theory with Leopold Edler von Zenetti in Enns.

While in his early youth, Bruckner held teaching positions in elementary public schools in Windhaag (1841–43) and Kronstorf (1843–45); later he occupied a responsible position as a schoolteacher at St. Florian (1845–55); also served as provisional organist there (1848–51). Despite his professional advance, he felt a lack of basic techniques in musical composition, and at the age of 31 went to Vienna to study harmony and counterpoint with the renowned pedagogue Sechter; he continued his studies with him off and on until 1861. In 1856 he became cathedral organist in Linz, having successfully competed for this position against several applicants. Determined to acquire still more technical knowledge, he sought further instruction and began taking lessons in orchestration with Otto Kitzler, 1st cellist of the Linz municipal theater (1861–63). In the meantime he undertook an assiduous study of the Italian polyphonic school, and of masters of German polyphony, especially Bach. These tasks preoccupied him so completely that he did not engage in free composition until he was nearly 40 years old. Then he fell under the powerful influence of Wagner's music, an infatuation that diverted him from his study of classical polyphony.

In 1865 he attended the premiere of *Tristan und Isolde* in Munich and met Wagner. He also made the acquaintance of Liszt in Pest, and of Berlioz during his visit in Vienna. His adulation of Wagner was extreme; the dedication of his 3rd Sym. to Wagner reads: "To the eminent Excellency Richard Wagner the Unattainable, World-Famous, and Exalted Master of Poetry and Music, in Deepest Reverence Dedicated by Anton Bruckner." Strangely enough, in his own music Bruckner never embraced the tenets and practices of Wagner, but followed the sanctified tradition of Germanic polyphony. Whereas Wagner strove toward the ideal union of drama, text, and music in a new type of operatic production, Bruckner kept away from the musical theater, confining himself to symphonic and choral music. Even in his harmonic techniques, Bruckner seldom followed Wagner's chromatic style of writing, and he never tried to emulate the passionate rise and fall of Wagnerian "endless" melodies depicting the characters of his operatic creations.

To Bruckner, music was an apotheosis of symmetry; his syms. were cathedrals of Gothic grandeur; he never

hesitated to repeat a musical phrase several times in succession so as to establish the thematic foundation of a work. The personal differences between Wagner and Bruckner could not be more striking: Wagner was a man of the world who devoted his whole life to the promotion of his artistic and human affairs, while Bruckner was unsure of his abilities and desperately sought recognition. Devoid of social graces, being a person of humble peasant origin, Bruckner was unable to secure the position of respect and honor that he craved. A signal testimony to this lack of self-confidence was Bruckner's willingness to revise his works repeatedly, not always to their betterment, taking advice from conductors and ostensible well-wishers. He suffered from periodic attacks of depression; his entire life seems to have been a study of unhappiness, most particularly in his numerous attempts to find a woman who would become his life companion. In his desperation he made halfhearted proposals in marriage to women of the people; the older he grew, the younger were the objects of his misguided affections; a notorious episode was his proposal of marriage to a chambermaid at a hotel in Berlin. Bruckner died a virgin.

A commanding trait of Bruckner's personality was his devout religiosity. To him the faith and the sacraments of the Roman Catholic Church were not mere rituals but profound psychological experiences. Following the practice of Haydn, he signed most of his works with the words "Omnia ad majorem Dei gloriam"; indeed, he must have felt that every piece of music he composed redounded to the greater glory of God. His original dedication of his Te Deum was actually inscribed "an dem lieben Gott." From reports of his friends and contemporaries, it appears that he regarded each happy event of his life as a gift of God, and each disaster as an act of divine wrath. His yearning for secular honors was none the less acute for that.

He was tremendously gratified upon receiving an honorary doctorate from the Univ. of Vienna in 1891; he was the 1st musician to be so honored there. He unsuccessfully solicited similar degrees from the Univs. of Cambridge, Philadelphia, and even Cincinnati. He eagerly sought approval in the public press. When Emperor Franz Josef presented him with a snuffbox as a sign of Imperial favor, it is said that Bruckner pathetically begged the Emperor to order Hanslick to stop attacking him. Indeed, Hanslick was the nemesis of the so-called New German School of composition exemplified by Wagner and Liszt, and to a lesser extent also by Bruckner. Wagner could respond to Hanslick's hostility by caricaturing him in the role of Beckmesser (whom he had originally intended to name Hanslick), and Liszt, immensely successful as a virtuoso pianist, was largely immune to critical attacks. But Bruckner was highly vulnerable. It was not until the end of his unhappy life that, thanks to a group of devoted friends among conductors, Bruckner finally achieved a full recognition of his greatness.

Bruckner himself was an inadequate conductor, but he was a master organist. In 1869 he appeared in organ recitals in France, and in 1871 he visited England, giving performances in the Royal Albert Hall and the Crystal Palace in London. He was also esteemed as a pedagogue. In 1868 he succeeded Sechter as prof. of harmony, counterpoint, and organ at the Vienna Cons.; also in 1868 he was named provisional court organist, an appointment formally confirmed in 1878. Concurrently he taught piano, organ, and music theory at St. Anna College, Vienna (1870–74). In 1875 he was appointed lecturer in harmony and counterpoint at the Univ. of Vienna. In failing health, Bruckner retired from the Vienna Cons. in 1891 and a year later relinquished his post as court organist; in 1894 he resigned his lecturer's position at the Univ. of Vienna. The remaining years of his life he devoted to the composition of his 9th Sym., which, however, remained unfinished at his death.

Bruckner's syms. constitute a monumental achievement; they are characterized by a striking display of originality and a profound spiritual quality. His sacred works are similarly expressive of his latent genius. Bruckner is usually paired with Mahler, who was a generation younger but whose music embodied qualities of grandeur akin to those that permeated the symphonic and choral works of Bruckner. Accordingly, Bruckner and Mahler societies sprouted in several countries, with the express purpose of elucidating, analyzing, and promoting their music.

The textual problems concerning Bruckner's works are numerous and complex. He made many revisions of his scores, and dejectedly acquiesced in alterations suggested by conductors who expressed interest in his music. As a result, conflicting versions of his syms. appeared in circulation. With the founding of the International Bruckner Soc., a movement was begun to publ. the original versions of his MSS, the majority of which he bequeathed to the Hofbibliothek, Vienna. A complete ed. of Bruckner's works, under the supervision of Robert Haas and Alfred Orel, began to appear in 1930; in 1945 Leopold Nowak was named its editor in chief.

Bruggen, Frans, distinguished Dutch recorder player, flutist, and conductor; b. Amsterdam, Oct. 30, 1934. He studied the recorder with Kees Otten and flute at the Amsterdam Muzieklyceum; in addition, took courses in musicology at the Univ. of Amsterdam; then launched a major career as a virtuoso performer of music for the recorder. As a flute soloist he was equally at home in performances of the Baroque masters and contemporary avant-garde composers; also gave informative lectures and illustrative performances of recorder music in Europe, and taught at the Royal Cons. in the Hague. In 1981 he founded the Orch. of the 18th Century, which he conducted with fine success on both sides of the Atlantic.

bruitism (Fr. *bruitisme*; *bruit* = noise). A term, originally derogatory, denoting the use of noise as a compositional element. The pioneer work of bruitism was *Arte dei Rumori* by the Italian futurist Luigi Russolo, in which he codified the noises of friction, attrition, sibilation, percussion, and concussion, and for which he created his noise-producers (*intonaru-* *mori*). Varèse elevated the inchoate bruitistic scheme to a purely musical form in his epoch-making work *Ionisation*.

Brummstimmen (Ger., humming voices; It. *bocca chiusa*). Vocal production of the tone without words, through the nose, and with closed mouth.

brunette (Fr., dark-haired woman). French song genre of the 17th and 18th centuries, similar to the bergerette, containing both authentic traditional and street ballad motives. Lully and Rameau wrote brunettes into their operas.

bruscamente (It.). Brusquely or forcibly accented; *brusco* (It.), brusque.

Brustregister (Ger.). Chest voice production.

Brustwerk (Ger., chest work). A group of pipes in front of the organ, usually played on the 2nd manual and having a softer sound than the larger main organ.

Bryars, Gavin, English composer and teacher; b. Goole, Yorkshire, Jan. 16, 1943. He studied philosophy at Sheffield Univ. and composition with Cyril Ramsey and George Linstead, then began his career as a bassist, turning in 1966 to composition and quickly emerging as one of England's most influential experimental composers. His academic appointments have included Portsmouth College of Art, where he founded the Portsmouth Sinfonia (made up of amateurs), and Leicester Polytechnic (from 1970); he also ed. the *Experimental Music Catalogue* (1972–81) and is official biographer of the eccentric English composer, novelist, and painter Lord Berners. His compositions, indeterminate and replete with repetition, often utilize electronic means. His warmth and humor is evidenced in his *The Sinking of the Titanic* (1969), a multimedia, meditative collage work composed of excerpts from pieces the drowning orch. might have been playing. Other compositions include *Jesus' Blood Never Failed Me Yet* (1971), *Out of Laeski's Gazebo* (1977), *My 1st Homage* (1978), *The Vespertine Park* (1980), and *Effarene* (1984).

He has collaborated with a number of well-known musicians, including Eno, Reich, and Cardew; a number of his pieces have been choreographed by Lucinda Childs. In 1984 his opera *Medea*, in collaboration with Robert Wilson, was premiered at the Opera de Lyon.

buccina. Ancient Roman semicircular metal horn used during festivals, usually adorned with a metal ornament in the shape of an animal horn; similar to a shepherd's horn.

Buchla, Donald (Frederick), American electronic-instrument designer and builder, composer, and performer; b. Southgate, Calif., Apr. 17, 1937. After studying physics at the Univ. of Calif., Berkeley, he became active with the San Francisco Tape Music Center, where in 1966 he installed the 1st Buchla synthesizer. That same year he founded Buchla Associates in Berkeley for the manufacture of synthesizers. In addition to designing and manufacturing electronic instruments, he also installed electronic-music studios at the Royal Academy of Music, Stockholm, and at IRCAM, Paris, among other institutions. In 1975 he became cofounder of the Electric Weasel Ensemble, a live electronic-music group; in 1978 he became codirector of the Artists' Research Collective in Berkeley. He held a Guggenheim fellowship in 1978.

Buffalo Springfield. (Leader/guitar/vocal: Stephen Stills, b. Dallas, Tex., Jan. 3, 1945; lead guitar/vocal: Neil Young, b. Toronto, Canada, Nov. 12, 1945; rhythm guitar/vocal: Richie Furay, b. Yellow Springs, Ohio, May 9, 1944; bass: Bruce Palmer, b. Liverpool, Ontario, Canada, 1946; drums: Dewey Martin, b. Chesterville, Ontario, Canada, Sept. 30, 1942. Jim Messina, b. Maywood, Calif., Dec. 5, 1947, replaced Palmer in late 1967.) Popular rock band of the 1960s, which took its name from a brand of steamroller, whose various members have gone on to illustrious careers. The original band was shortlived (*c.* 1965–68), with 1 minor hit, Stephen Stills's social-protest song *For What It's Worth*. The band combined various influences, from folk and country to progressive rock. Stills went on to form the "supergroup" Crosby, Stills and Nash; Young undertook a solo career and also performed from time to time with CSN; Furay and Messina formed Poco.

buffa (It.). Comic, burlesque.

buffa, aria. ARIA BUFFA.

buffa, opera. OPERA BUFFA.

buffo (buffo-singer; It. *buffone*, jester). Comic actor or operatic singer.

bugaku. Japanese masked dances derived from Chinese and Korean court traditions. The musical accompaniment is slow and stately, emphasizing the woodwinds and the drums.

bugle. 1. A wind instrument of brass or copper, with cupped mouthpiece, used for military calls and infantry signals; a trumpet without keys. 2. The key-bugle, with 6 keys, and a compass of over 2 octaves. 3. The valve-bugle. See SAXHORN.

Bühnenmusik (Ger., stage music). Incidental music for plays or music performed on the stage, such as the 2nd-act finale of *Don Giovanni*.

buisine (from Lat. *buccina*, semicircular metal horn). A long straight slender Roman military trumpet, spread throughout Europe by the conquering Roman armies.

Bull, John, famous English organist and composer; b. probably in Old Radnor, Radnorshire, *c.* 1562; d. Antwerp, Mar. 12, 1628. He was a pupil of William Blitheman in the Chapel Royal; received his Mus.B. from Oxford in 1586. He was sworn in as a Gentleman of the

Chapel Royal in 1586, becoming its organist in 1591. In 1596, on Queen Elizabeth's recommendation, he was appointed prof. of music at Gresham College, and in 1597 he was elected 1st public lecturer there. He got into difficulties with Gresham College when he impregnated premaritally a maiden named Elizabeth Walter; he was forced to resign in 1607, and he hastened to take a marriage license 2 days later. In 1610 he entered the service of Prince Henry, but in 1613 was charged with adultery and had to flee England. In Sept. 1615 he became assistant organist at the Antwerp Cathedral in Belgium, and he was named its principal organist in 1617. In the Netherlands he became acquainted with the great Dutch organist and composer Sweelinck; both he and Bull exerted considerable influence on the development of contrapuntal keyboard music of the time. Bull also composed many canons and anthems. Various works previously attributed to him are now considered doubtful.

bull-roarer. Aerophone consisting of a rhomboid piece of wood attached to a string passed through a small hole, pierced at one end and whirled through the air. The string may be held by the player's hand or on a stick.

Bülow, Hans (Guido) **von,** celebrated German pianist and conductor; b. Dresden, Jan. 8, 1830; d. Cairo, Feb. 12, 1894. At the age of 9 he began to study piano with Friedrich Wieck and theory with Max Eberwein; then went to Leipzig, where he studied law at the univ. and took a music course with Moritz Hauptmann; he also studied piano with Plaidy. From 1846 to 1848 he lived in Stuttgart, where he made his debut as a pianist. In 1849 he attended the Univ. of Berlin; there he joined radical social groups; shortly afterward he went to Zurich and met Wagner, who was there in exile. After a year in Switzerland, where he conducted theater music, Bülow proceeded to Weimar, where he began to study with Liszt. In 1853 he made a tour through Germany and Austria as a pianist. In 1855 he was appointed head of the piano dept. at the Stern Cons. in Berlin, retaining this post until 1864. He married Liszt's natural daughter, Cosima, in 1857.

In 1864 he was called by Ludwig II to Munich as court pianist and conductor; the King, who was a great admirer of Wagner, summoned Wagner to Munich from exile. Bülow himself became Wagner's ardent champion; on June 10, 1865, he conducted at the Court Opera in Munich the 1st performance of *Tristan und Isolde*, and on June 21, 1868, he led the premiere of *Die Meistersinger von Nürnberg*. It was about this time that Wagner became intimate with Cosima; after her divorce she married Wagner, in 1870. Despite this betrayal, Bülow continued to conduct Wagner's music; his growing admiration for Brahms cannot be construed as his pique against Wagner. It was Bülow who dubbed Brahms "the 3rd B of music," the 1st being Bach, the 2nd Beethoven. When he was asked why he did not instead nominate Bruckner for the 3rd B, he is supposed to have replied that Bruckner was too much of a Wagnerian for him.

Bülow was indeed renowned for his wit and his aptitude for alliterative punning; his writings are of elevated literary quality. In 1872 Bülow lived in Florence; then resumed his career as a pianist, winning triumphant successes in England and Russia; during his American tour in 1875–76 he gave 139 concerts; he revisited America in 1889 and 1890. An important chapter in his career was his conductorship in Meiningen (1880–85). In 1882 he married a Meiningen actress, Marie Schanzer. He was conductor of the Berlin Phil. from 1887 to 1893, when a lung ailment forced him to seek a cure in Egypt. He died shortly after his arrival in Cairo.

As a conductor Bülow was an uncompromising disciplinarian; he insisted on perfection of detail, and he was also able to project considerable emotional power on the music. He was one of the 1st conductors to dispense with the use of the score. His memory was fabulous; it was said that he could memorize a piano concerto by just reading the score, sometimes while riding in a train. The mainstay of his repertoire was Classic and Romantic music, but he was also receptive toward composers of the new school. When Tchaikovsky, unable to secure a performance of his 1st Piano Concerto in Russia, offered the score to Bülow, he accepted it, and gave its world premiere as soloist with a pickup orch. in Boston (1875); however, the music was too new and too strange to American ears of the time, and the critical reactions were ambiguous.

Bülow encouraged the young Richard Strauss, and gave him his 1st position as conductor. Bülow was a composer himself, but his works belong to the category of "Kapellmeister Musik": competent, well structured, but devoid of originality. He made masterly transcriptions, and he annotated and ed. Beethoven's piano sonatas; these eds. were widely used by piano teachers, even though criticism was voiced against his cavalier treatment of some passages and his occasional alterations of Beethoven's original to enhance the resonance.

Bumbry, Grace (Melzia Ann), greatly talented African-American mezzo-soprano; b. St. Louis, Jan. 4, 1937. She sang in church choirs as a child; in 1955 went to Northwestern Univ. to study voice with Lotte Lehmann, and continued lessons with her at the Music Academy of the West, Santa Barbara. She made her professional debut in a concert in London in 1959; then made a spectacular operatic appearance as Amneris at the Paris Opera in 1960. In a lucky strike, Wieland Wagner engaged her to sing Venus in *Tannhäuser* at the Bayreuth Festival on July 23, 1961; she was the 1st African-American to be featured in the role of a goddess. This event created immediate repercussions in liberal circles, and she was invited by Jacqueline Kennedy to sing at the White House in 1961. She then undertook a grand tour of concerts in the U.S.; in 1963 she performed the role of Venus again at the Chicago Lyric Opera, and also sang it at Lyons, France.

In 1965 she made her Metropolitan Opera debut in N.Y. as Princess Eboli in *Don Carlos*. In 1966 she sang Carmen at the Salzburg Festival under the direction of Karajan; she repeated this role at the Metropolitan with extraordinary success. The sensational element of her race was no longer the exclusive attraction; the public and the press judged her impartially as a great artist. In 1970 she sang Salome at Covent Garden, London, and she sang it again, in German, at the Metropolitan Opera in 1973. She proved her ability to perform mezzo-soprano and soprano roles with equal brilliance by singing both Aida and Amneris, and both Venus and Elisabeth. In 1963 she married the Polish tenor Erwin Jaeckel, who also became her business manager.

Burgundian cadence. See LANDINI CADENCE, DOUBLE LEADING-TONE CADENCE.

Burgundian school

The ill-defined name of the school of composition that formed a natural transition from the ARS NOVA—in which the motet was the crowning achievement—to the great Flemish school, which achieved its luxuriant polyphonic flowering during the late Renaissance.

The justification for the term *Burgundian* is that most of the musicians who created this intermediary style of composition served at the various courts in the large geographical dominion that comprised, under the benevolent rule of the Dukes of Burgundy, Philip the Good and Charles the Bold, much of the Netherlands and Belgium, as well as Burgundy proper in central France. Against this stood the embarrassing fact that not 1 of the masters of the Burgundian school was born in Burgundy. To mitigate this ambiguity, some music historians designated the entire 15th century, in which the Burgundian school flourished, as the Burgundian epoch. To emphasize its role in the inception of the Flemish school, other historians suggested replacing the term *Burgundian school* by *1st Flemish school*. Still others, particularly Belgian musicologists, felt that the contribution of the French-speaking Walloons of Belgium should be noted, and they suggest-

ed the name *École franco-flamande*. To point out the important role played in the development of the Burgundian school by Italian musicians, it was also proposed to describe the Burgundian school as "Italo-Burgundian." Finally, a compromise was achieved by retaining the name Burgundian school, or Burgundian music, to denote the art of the courtly chanson, which was indeed cultivated primarily at the various courts of the sprawling Duchy of Burgundy, and by restoring the general description of the Netherlands or Flemish school for other musical forms that were developed under the aegis of Burgundy, such as the Mass with a definite cantus firmus, and the peripheral secular forms of the narrative ballade and the popular virelai. Perhaps the most practical means of resolving this problem of nomenclature would be to call the period in question the Quattrocento school, that is, the 1400s, the school of the 15th century.

The greatest masters of this period were Guillaume Dufay, whose life covered the 1st three-quarters of the Quattrocento, and Gilles Binchois, whose lifetime embraced the 1st 60 years. Dufay was known as "Cantor illustrissimi ducis burgundie" (court musician of the illustrious Duke of Burgundy), although his term of tenure at the duchy was relatively short. The Burgundian school had many features in common with the developing style of English polyphonic music; it was during this cosmopolitan Quattrocento that 3ds and 6ths were definitely accepted as consonant intervals, parallel to the acceptance of the FAUXBOURDON. The tonic and dominant triads became the mainstays of the harmonic texture, particularly in cadences. Also the major key, described a century before by the pejorative term MODUS LASCIVUS, now became frequently used, particularly in secular music.

Generally speaking, the Burgundian school contributed much to the relaxation of the rigid theological rule that hampered the natural development of musical composition. This was invariably accompanied by the simplification of the prevalent contrapuntal idiom to clear the way for the advent of the new art of the great polyphonic school of the Netherlands in the Renaissance.

burla (It.). BURLESCA.

burlando (It.). Joking, jesting, romping.

burlesca (It., jest). A short piece, usually for keyboard, in a lighter mood. Bach was one of the 1st to write a burlesca.

burlescamente (It.). In burlesque style.

burlesque. A dramatic extravaganza, or farcical travesty of some serious subject, with more or less music. A popular type of theatrical entertainment that flourished in the 18th century parallel to the ballad opera; it usually included comic recitatives and songs with original texts set to preexisting popular tunes. In the 19th century the genre of burlesque was lifted from its vulgar connotations and became a dignified instrumental or vocal form. R. Strauss wrote a *Burleske* for Piano and Orch., as did Bartók and other modern composers. Stravinsky's ballet *Petrouchka* is subtitled *Scènes burlesques*. In the late 19th and 20th century burlesque devolved into the BURLESQUE SHOW.

burlesque show. A popular type of entertainment which became the staple of American musical theater in the 2nd half of the 19th century. Imported from England, the 1st true burlesque show was an exhibition called *British Blondes*. The burlesque differed from the minstrel show in its emphasis on "sensuality," mostly in the form of (relatively) scantily clad young women (hence the synonym "girlie show"); the burlesque had much in common with the musicals of the period, which were more like revues and featured chorus lines. Striptease was added to the burlesque in the 20th century, and one famous club was the subject of a film (*The Night They Raided Minsky's*). The "sexual revolution" of the 1960s killed off the burlesque show.

burletta (It., little joke). A burlesque; a musical farce; short comic opera.

burlevole (It.). Like a burlesque.

Burney, Charles, celebrated English music historian; b. Shrewsbury, Apr. 7, 1726; d. Chelsea, Apr. 12, 1814. He was a pupil of Edmund Baker (organist of Chester Cathedral), of his eldest half brother, James Burney, and, from 1744 to 1747, of Arne in London. In 1749 he became organist of St. Dionis-Backchurch and harpsichord player at the subscription concerts in the King's Arms, Cornhill; resigned these posts in 1751, and until 1760 was organist at King's Lynn, Norfolk, where he planned and began work on his *General History of Music*. He returned to London in 1760; having begun and then exhausted such material as was available in London for his *History of Music*, he visited France, Switzerland, and Italy in 1770 and Germany, the Netherlands, and Austria in 1772, consulting libraries, attending concerts of sacred and secular music, and forming contacts with the leading musicians and scholars of the period (Gluck, Hasse, Metastasio, Voltaire et al.). The immediate result of these journeys was the publication of *The Present State of Music in France and Italy* (1771, in diary form) and *The Present State of Music in Germany, the Netherlands* (1773). His *General History of Music* appeared in 4 vols. (1776–89; the 1st volume was publ. concurrently with the complete work of his rival, Sir John Hawkins). From 1806 he received a government pension. In addition to other musicological publ., he composed for the stage and for small ensembles.

Burning Fiery Furnace, The. Church parable by Britten, 1966, taken from the Book of Daniel incident concerning the 3 Hebrews surviving a Babylonian death chamber.

Burns, Robert, great Scottish poet and songwriter, b. Alloway, Jan. 25, 1759; d. Dumfries, July 21, 1796. He collected traditional songs, completed fragmentary songs, and wrote lyrics in traditional style, matching them to folk melodies. His major publication in this field was *The Scots Musical Museum* (6 vols, 1787–1803).

Busoni, Ferruccio (Dante Michelangiolo Benvenuto), influential Italian-German composer, greatly admired pianist, and writer on modern aesthetics; b. Empoli, near Florence, Apr. 1, 1866; d. Berlin, July 27, 1924. His father played the clarinet; his mother, Anna Weiss, was an amateur pianist; Busoni grew up in an artistic atmosphere, and learned to play the piano as a child; at the age of 8 he played in public in Trieste. He gave a piano recital in Vienna when he was 10, and included in his program some of his own compositions. In 1877 the family moved to Graz, where Busoni took piano lessons with W. Mayer. He conducted his *Stabat Mater* in Graz at the age of 12. At 15 he was accepted as a member of the Accademia Filarmonica in Bologna; he performed there his *oratorio Il sabato del villaggio* in 1883. In 1886 he went to Leipzig; there he undertook a profound study of Bach's music. In 1889 he was appointed a prof. of piano at the Helsingfors Cons., where among his students was Sibelius (who was actually a few months older than his teacher). At that time Busoni married Gerda Sjostrand, whose father was a celebrated Swedish sculptor; they had 2 sons, both of whom became well-known artists.

In 1890 Busoni participated in the Rubinstein Competition in St. Petersburg and won 1st prize with his *Konzertstück* for Piano and Orch. On the strength of this achievement he was engaged to teach piano at the Moscow Cons. (1890–91). He then accepted the post of prof. at the New England Cons. of Music in Boston (1891–94); however, he had enough leisure to make several tours, maintaining his principal residence in Berlin. During the season of 1912–13 he made a triumphant tour of Russia. In 1913 he was appointed director of the Liceo Musicale in Bologna. The outbreak of the war in 1914 forced him to move to neutral Switzerland; he stayed in Zurich until 1923; went to Paris, then returned to Berlin, remaining there until his death in 1924. In various cities, at various times, he taught piano in music schools; among his piano students were Brailowsky, Ganz, Petri, Mitropoulos, and Grainger. Busoni also taught composition; Weill, Jarnach, and Vogel were his pupils. He exercised great influence on Varèse, who was living in Berlin when Busoni was there; Varèse greatly prized Busoni's advanced theories of composition.

Busoni was a philosopher of music who tried to formulate a universe of related arts; he issued grandiloquent manifestos urging a return to classical ideals in modern forms; he sought to establish a unifying link between architecture and composition; in his eds. of Bach's works he included drawings illustrating the architectonic plan of Bach's fugues. He incorporated his innovations in his grandiose piano work *Fantasia contrappuntistica*, which opens with a prelude based on a Bach chorale and closes with a set of variations on Bach's acronym, B–A–C–H (i.e., B-flat, A, C, B-natural). In his theoretical writings Busoni proposed a system of 113 different heptatonic modes, and also suggested the possibility of writing music in exotic scales and subchromatic intervals; he expounded those ideas in his influential essay *Entwurf einer neuen Aesthetik der Tonkunst* (Trieste, 1907; Eng. trans., 1911). Busoni's other publications of significance were *Von der Einheit der Musik* (1923; Eng. trans., 1957) and *Über die Möglichkeiten der Oper* (Leipzig, 1926).

But despite Busoni's great innovations in his own compositions and his theoretical writing, the Busoni legend is kept alive not through his music but mainly through his sovereign virtuosity as a pianist. In his performances he introduced a concept of piano sonority as an orch.l medium; indeed, some listeners reported having heard simulations of trumpets and French horns sounded at Busoni's hands. The few extant recordings of his playing transmit a measure of the grandeur of his style, but they also betray a tendency, common to Busoni's era, toward a free treatment of the musical text; surprising, since Busoni preached an absolute fidelity to the written notes. On concert programs Busoni's name appears most often as the author of magisterial and eloquent transcriptions of Bach's works. His gothic transfiguration for piano of Bach's *Chaconne for Unaccompanied Violin* became a perennial favorite of pianists all over the world.

Butterfly Étude. Chopin's Étude in G-flat Major, op. 25; not so named by the composer.

Buxtehude, Dietrich (Didericus), significant Danish-born German organist and composer; b. probably in Helsingborg, *c.* 1637; d. Lübeck, May 9, 1707. His father, Johannes Buxtehude (1601–74), an organist of German extraction, was active in Holstein, which was under Danish rule. After receiving a thorough education, in all probability from his father, Dietrich became organist at St. Mary's in Helsingborg (1657 or 1658), and then at St. Mary's in

Helsingør (1660). In 1668 he was appointed organist and Werkmeister in succession to the recently deceased Franz Tunder at St. Mary's in Lübeck, subject to the condition that he would abide by the custom of marrying the predecessor's unmarried daughter; he did so, marrying Anna Margaretha later that year. He continued the *Abendmusiken*—concerts consisting of organ music and concerted pieces for chorus and orch.—held annually in Lübeck in late afternoon on 5 of the 6 Sundays immediately preceding Christmas.

William Byrd

COURTESY OF THE NEW YORK PUBLIC LIBRARY

Mattheson and Handel visited Buxtehude in 1703, with the ostensible purpose of being considered as his successor; but it is a valid surmise that the notorious marriage clause, which would have compelled the chosen one to marry Buxtehude's daughter, allegedly lacking in feminine charm, deterred them from further negotiations. In 1705 J. S. Bach made a pilgrimage allegedly to hear the *Abendmusik*, to study with Buxtehude, and possibly to investigate the impending opening; though details of Bach's trip are subject to speculation, there can be no doubt that Buxtehude exercised a profound influence on Bach, as both organist and composer. (Buxtehude's daughter, 1 of 7, eventually married her father's successor, Johann Christian Schieferdecker, in 1707.)

Buxtehude exerted a major influence on the organists who followed him by virtue of the significant role he played in the transitional period of music history from Froberger to the contrapuntal mastery of Bach. Though little of his music exists in MS, many composers were known to have made copies of his works for their own study. His major student was Nicolaus Bruhns. Buxtehude appears prominently in the painting *Domestic Music Scene* (1674) by Johannes Voorhout.

Bye Bye Birdie. Musical by Strouse, 1960, satirizing the 1st generation of rock 'n' roll groupies; includes *Put On a Happy Face.*

Byrd, Henry Roeland ("Professor Longhair"), American blues pianist; b. Bogalusa, La., Dec. 19, 1918; d. New Orleans, Jan. 30, 1980. He received rudimentary instruction in music from his mother; subsequently developed an individual style of playing which utilized blues, New Orleans, and Caribbean elements; such musicians as Fats Domino, Huey Smith, and Allen Toussaint made his

style popular outside New Orleans. His erudite synthetic techniques earned him his nickname.

Byrd (Byrde, Bird), **William,** great English composer and organist; b. probably in Lincoln, 1543; d. Stondon Massey, Essex, July 4, 1623. There are indications that Byrd studied music with Tallis. In 1563 Byrd was appointed organist of Lincoln Cathedral; in 1568 he married Juliana Birley; in 1570 he was sworn in as a Gentleman of the Chapel Royal while retaining his post at Lincoln Cathedral until 1572; he then assumed his duties, together with Tallis, as organist of the Chapel Royal. In 1575 Byrd and Tallis were granted a patent by Queen Elizabeth I for the exclusive privilege of printing music and selling music paper for a term of 21 years; however, the license proved unprofitable and they successfully petitioned the Queen in 1577 to give them an annuity in the form of a lease. In 1585, after the death of Tallis, the license passed wholly into Byrd's hands.

The earliest publication of the printing press of Byrd and Tallis was the 1st set of *Cantiones sacrae* for 5 to 8 voices (1575), printed for them by Vautrollier and dedicated to the Queen; works issued by Byrd alone under his exclusive license were *Psalmes, Sonets and Songs* (1588), *Songs of Sundrie Natures* (1589), and 2 further vols. of *Cantiones sacrae* (1589, 1591). Many of his keyboard pieces appeared in the MS collection *My Ladye Nevells Booke* (1591) and in Francis Tregian's collection *Fitzwilliam Virginal Book* (c. 1612–19), among others. During the winter of 1592–93 he moved to Stondon Massey, Essex. He subsequently was involved in various litigations and disputes concerning the ownership of the property. Between 1592 and 1595 he publ. 3 masses, and between 1605 and 1607 he brought out 2 vols. of *Gradualia*. His last collection, *Psalmes, Songs and Sonnets*, was publ. in 1611.

Byrd was unsurpassed in his time in compositional versatility. His masterly technique is revealed in his ecclesiastical works, instrumental music, madrigals, and solo songs.

Byrds, The. (Leader/guitar/vocal: Jim [later Roger] McGuinn, b. Chicago, Ill., July 13, 1942; guitar/vocal: David Crosby, b. Los Angeles, Calif., Aug. 14, 1941; guitar/vocal: Gene Clark, b. Tipton, Mo., Nov. 17 1941; d. Sherman Oaks, Calif., May 24, 1991; bass/vocal: Chris

Hillman, b. Los Angeles, Dec. 4, 1942; drums: Mike Clarke, b. New York, June 3, 1944; d. Treasure Island, Fla., Dec. 19, 1993.) Harmonious American folk-rock group of the 1960s. They 1st scored hits with their sunny harmonies on folk/social-protest songs like Bob Dylan's *Mr. Tambourine Man* (1965), introduced by McGuinn's jangly electric 12-string guitar and Pete Seeger's *Turn Turn Turn*. They next went psychedelic with extended improvisations on *8 Miles High* (1966), thought to refer to a drug experience (although McGuinn claimed it had to do with an airplane flight). The group dropped to a quartet when Clark left, and then a trio when Crosby bailed out; subsequently McGuinn led a new lineup of Byrds through 1973.

Byrne, David, Scottish-born American musician; b. Dumbarton, May 14, 1952. He went to the U.S. in his tender years and entered the Rhode Island School of Design, where he developed his dominant conviction that dance, song, instrumental music, drama, and cinema were parts of a total art. As his own medium he selected modern dance music and vocal works, stretching in style from folk music to rock. He frequented the popular cabarets and dance halls of N.Y., where he absorbed the essence of urban folklore and the rhythmic ways of natural musicians. He joined the group Talking Heads, which made a specialty of exotic rhythms, especially Caribbean dance tunes, merengue, salsa, bomba, and cha-cha; from Colombia the Talking Heads took cambia; from Brazil, the classical samba. Much of the music that Byrne concocts of these elements is multilingual; one of his albums is titled *Speaking in Tongues*. Byrne also favors African sounds, such as that of the Nigerian juju. The titles of his own songs are fashionably nonsensical, e.g., *Stop Making Sense*, which seems to make plenty of sense to his public. He is an accomplished guitarist, and as a performer displays unbounded physical energy, allowing himself a free voice that ranges from a hiccup to a cry, while urging the accompanying chorus to intone such anarchistic declarations as "don't want to be part of your world."

The devotion that Byrne has for modern dance is exemplified by the remarkable score he wrote for *The Catherine Wheel*, choreographed by Twyla Tharp; it possesses the widely differing ingredients of new-wave rock and spiritual soul music, masculine and rough on the one hand and elegiac and devotional on the other. The resulting complex has also the additional element of African percussion. Taken as a whole, it represents a synthesis of urban beat and a largely unrelated Eastern rhythm. His 1989 album, *Rei Momo* (promoted in concert at the Brooklyn Academy of Music as part of the New Music America Festival), consists of songs that, backed by a 16-piece band, combine Latin and pop styles. There is a hypnopompic quality in his inspiration as a composer, asymptotically lying in both reality and irreality, like a half-waking state.

Byzantine chant. The church system of modes as established in the Byzantine Empire of Constantine the Great in A.D. 330 and continued until the fall of Constantinople to the Turks in 1453. Byzantine hymnody is similar to Gregorian chant in its monophonic melos, diatonic structures, and asymmetrical sequences unsubordinated to a generic meter. The development of Byzantine chant can be summarized by considering the successive emergence of various types of hymns: *kontakion* in the 6th century, *troparia* in the 7th century, and *kanons* in the 8th century. The essentially syllabic chant began to be adorned with flowery melodic elaborations, but even these embellishments were sung to syllabic verbal formations, having no meaning in themselves.

Byzantine music masters outlined a system of modes, or *echoi*, that paralleled the system of modes in the Western church. The language of Byzantine chant from its inception to its decline remained Grk., but there is no formal, tonal, or structural link between the Byzantine *echoi* and the ancient Greek modes. It is, rather, an autochthonous Christian type of hymnody. Its dependence on Oriental rites, particularly Jewish, has been a matter of speculation among scholars.

C (Eng., Ger.; Fr. *ut*; It. *do*). 1. The 1st tone and degree of the C-major or C-minor scale, thus the tonic of the 1st scale in the cycle of scales; it has neither sharps nor flats in the key signature. C is *ut*, the syllable assigned to it in the hymn of Guido d'Arezzo; in other Romance languages and Russian it is *do*. In our musical C-bound universe, C major is a "white" scale on the piano keyboard (i.e., lacking black keys), beloved by such pianistically minded composers as Chopin, Rachmaninoff, and Prokofiev; it is also the generating point of "white" pandiatonic harmonies. The primacy of C in medieval notation is suggested by the term CLAVIS SIGNATA attached to middle C. Browning referred to his permanent abode as "the C major of this life." 2. In musical theory, capital *C* designates the C-major triad, small *c* the c-minor triad. 3. *Middle C* is the note c^1 on the piano keyboard:

Tenor C is the lowest note in the tenor voice, *c*:

The tenor-C time signature symbol (𝄴) indicates 4/4 and is not, as is sometimes suggested, the phonetic sign for the Spanish *cuatro*, Italian *quattuor*, French *quatre*, or English *common time*, but is actually a relic of the medieval half circle, meaning "imperfect" time, "perfect" time being triple meter.

The *cut-time* time signature (𝄵) designates the tempo ALLA BREVE (It., quickened), corresponding to 2/2 or 2/4 time.

C clef. A clef indicating the position of middle C on the staff; its visual form varies, but a shape suggestive of a Gothic letter *K* is the most common. Historically the standard types are the soprano, mezzo-soprano, alto, tenor, and baritone (see "The Clefs," p. xxiii).

The tenor clef is still used for bassoon and cello parts; the alto is the standard viola clef. Tenor vocal parts are now written on the treble clef, sounding an octave below written pitch; this is sometimes indicated by a double treble clef or a hybrid superimposition of the C clef onto the treble clef. Bach used C clefs even for keyboard compositions, e.g., his 2-Part Invention No. 15 in F Major (BWV 786) is notated in the MS with the soprano clef in the right hand and the tenor clef for the left hand.

C dur (Ger.). C major.

C major. In common musical association this is the key of exultant joy, triumphant jubilation, and communal celebration. Multitudes of piano studies of Czerny and by Hanon are set in C major. Beethoven selected the key of C major for his 1st Sym. and his 1st Piano Concerto, as well as the finale of his 5th Sym. The most Olympian of all of Mozart's syms., No. 41 (the JUPITER SYMPHONY) is also in C major. When Schumann completed his own C-major sym. he must have been aware of the splendors of Mozart's sym. in that key, for he remarked to a friend, "Yes, I think it will be a regular *Jupiter*." Wagner set the prelude to his only comic opera, *Die Meistersinger von Nürnberg*, in C major. The key of C major may be solemn and proclamatory, as it is in the opening of *Also sprach Zarathustra* of R. Strauss. Scriabin ended his *Poem of Ecstasy* with 53 measures of C major. Prokofiev was fond of C major. His most popular piano concerto, No. 3, goes on for pages of music on white keys before modulating; in his fairy tale *Peter and the Wolf* Peter's opening theme is set in undiluted C major; the coda of the march from his opera *Love for 3 Oranges* ends on a loud C-major triad.

It is natural that pianists should be addicted to C major, for it is the 1st scale they practice when they begin their lessons, being innocently free from bothering with black keys. And, naturally, pianists who become composers are apt to make full use of their familiar white keys. On the other hand, composers of atonal music are apt to exclude C-major associations from their musical vocabulary. Schoenberg used occasional triadic formations, but it would be difficult to find a single instance of his employment of an unadulterated C-major chord during his atonal and dodecaphonic period. Yet Schoenberg's faithful disciple Berg did not hesitate to use C major in his atonal masterpiece, *Wozzeck*, in the recitative "Da wieder ist Geld, Marie" (Here is money again, Marie) to underline, as it were, the vulgar essence of money. Curiously enough, the C-major string quartet of Mozart (K. 465) acquired the sobriquet of *Dissonance Quartet*, owing to the presence of some perfectly innocent and plainly resolvable melodious ornaments in its introduction.

C minor. This is the key of concentration in solemnity, a key of philosophical introspection, quite different from its major homonym, C major. But the 2 are intimately related, not through the traditional cycle of scales, but by the virtue of the TIERCE DE PICARDIE, in which the minor 3rd at the root of a minor triad is replaced by a major 3rd. Thus no matter how sepulchral, how lugubrious, how morbid an opening C minor can be, there is always a promise of C major in the finale. The most famous sym. in C minor is unquestionably Beethoven's 5th, with its "fateful" opening of 4 notes falling from the dominant to the mediant in C minor. But we can confidently expect, even if we banish all previous knowledge of the work from our memory, the glorious explosion of a C-major finale. Perhaps less predictable is the last movement in C major of the 1st Sym. of Brahms in C minor, but the apotheosis is nonetheless redeeming.

For Mozart the key of C minor had tragic connotations, or so we are inclined to think by observing the angular convolutions of the opening theme of the 1st movement of his Piano Concerto in that key, which travels into the alien region of chromatic modulations. Beethoven's *Pathétique Sonata* is in C minor, and the tragic connotations of its slow

opening are unmistakable. Schubert's 4th Sym. bore the designation *Tragic* in the MS and is set in the key of C minor. Bruckner must have been possessed by the key of C minor; his 1st and 2nd Syms. are in C minor, as is his 8th, which, paraphrasing what Schumann said about Schubert's "sym. of heavenly length" (No. 9), may be called the "sym. of infernal length." Mahler was also partial to C minor. His 2nd Sym., which rivals in length the interminably revolving syms. of Bruckner, is in the key of C minor. And it is little consolation to the listener that the choral finale of that sym. proclaims the dubious promise, "You must die to live."

Scriabin selected the key of C minor for 2 syms., the 2nd and the 3rd, which he named *Divine Poem*; both end in redeeming C major. The most frequently performed Saint-Saëns sym., his 3rd, with organ, is in C minor; but this sym. teleologically directs itself toward a C-major finale, with the organ literally pulling out all the stops. The key of C minor is eminently pianistic: Beethoven's great 3rd Piano Concerto is set in that key. And can one speak of C minor without mentioning the most popular piano concerto of modern times, the 2nd by Rachmaninoff, with its overwhelming C-major finale? *Tod und Verklärung* by R. Strauss is in the key of C minor, representing the corruption of death, but concluding in triumphant C major, depicting transfiguration.

C moll (Ger.). C minor.

cabaletta (It., rhythmic verse). In 18th-century Italian opera, a cavatinalike form; later, the concluding section of an aria or duet, forming a summary in rapid tempo and with heightened intensity.

Caballé, Montserrat, celebrated Spanish soprano; b. Barcelona, Apr. 12, 1933. She learned to sing at a convent which she attended as a child; at the age of 8 she was accepted at the Cons. del Liceo in Barcelona; her teachers there were Eugenie Kemini, Conchita Badia, and Napoleone Annovazzi. She graduated in 1953, then went to Italy, where she sang some minor roles. After a successful appearance as Mimi at the Basel Opera, she advanced rapidly, singing Tosca, Aida, Violetta, and other standard opera parts; she also proved her ability to master such modern and difficult parts as Salome, Elektra, and Marie in *Wozzeck*. She filled guest engagements at the Vienna State Opera, then made a grand tour through Germany. In 1964 she sang Manon in Mexico City.

She made a triumphant American debut in 1965, when she was summoned to substitute for Marilyn Horne in the title role of Donizetti's *Lucrezia Borgia* in a concert performance at Carnegie Hall in N.Y.; the usually restrained N.Y. critics praised her without reservation for the beauty of her voice and expressiveness of her dramatic interpretation. There followed several other American appearances, all of which were highly successful. She made her debut at the Metropolitan Opera in N.Y. as Marguerite in 1965; she continued her appearances with the Metropolitan Opera; among her most significant roles were Violetta, Mimi, Aida, Norma, Donna Anna, and other roles of the standard operatic repertoire. In 1989 she created the role of Queen Isabella in Balada's *Cristobal Colón* in Barcelona. In 1964 she married Bernabé Marti, a Spanish tenor. Subsequently they appeared together in joint recitals.

cabaret. A form of nightclub entertainment dating from *c.* 1880 to the 1930s; especially popular in Paris and Berlin. Many cabarets sprung to life, including the famous Chat Noir and Le Boeuf sur le Toit (Paris) and Überbrettl (Berlin). The French cabaret featured numerous witty and slyly ironic songs and artists such as Yvette Guilbert (1885–1944), who inspired a host of 20th-century *chanteurs* and *chanteuses*; the Berlin cabaret world continued until the Nazi succession in the 1930s, having inspired the political music of Weill, Eisler, and Dessau.

Cabaret. Musical by Kander and Ebb, 1966, based on Christopher Isherwood's *Berlin Stories*, featuring an American writer who records the murky and ominous atmosphere in pre-Hitler Berlin, especially the denizens of a Berlin cabaret. Includes the title song, *Willkommen, Meeskeit, Don't Tell Mama, Two Ladies, If You Could See Her Through My Eyes*, and the haunting and prophetic *Tomorrow Belongs to Me.*

Cabin in the Sky. Musical fantasy by V. Duke, 1940, uses an all-black cast (a common production premise of the era) to retell the story of the Devil and the Lord battling over a soul. Includes the title song and *Taking a Chance on Love.*

caccia (It., chase, hunt). Italian medieval musical form originating in Florence in the 14th century. Initially the caccia used words concerned with hunting, and therefore was often arranged in the form of a canon in which one voice chased another. The popularity of the caccia grew when renowned composers wrote vocal works in this form. It often combined with a madrigal; such compound forms became known as canonic madrigals. Motets containing canonic imitation were called *caccia motets. Alla caccia*, in hunting style, thus accompanied by horns.

Caccia, La. Violin Concerto in B-flat Major by Vivaldi, *c.* 1725, No. 10, op. 8.

Caccini, Francesca "La Cecchina," Italian composer, daughter of Giulio Caccini; b. Florence, Sept. 18, 1587; d. ?, Florence, *c.* 1640. She was probably the 1st woman composer of operas. Her opera-ballet *La liberazione di Ruggiero dall'isola d'Alcina* was produced at a palace near Florence in 1625, and a book of songs from it was publ. that same year. Caccini wrote a *Ballo delle zingare* (Florence, 1615) in which she acted as one of the gypsies. Her sacred drama *Il martirio di Sant'Agata* was produced in Florence (1622).

Caccini, Giulio "Romano," important Italian composer of monody, an originator of opera, teacher, and father of Francesca Caccini; b. probably in Tivoli, Oct. 8, 1551; d. Florence (buried), Dec. 10, 1618. He is nicknamed "Romano" in token of the time he spent in Rome; but he is not the same person as Romano, a monodist of the early 17th century. Caccini was a pupil of Scipione delle Palla in singing and lute playing. His 1st compositions were madrigals in the traditional polyphonic style, but the new ideas generated in the discussions of the artists and literati of the Camerata, in the houses of Bardi and Corsi at Florence, inspired him to write vocal soli in recitative form (then termed *musica in stile rappresentativo*), which he sang with consummate skill to his own accompaniment on the theorbo. These 1st compositions in a dramatic idiom were followed by his settings of separate scenes written by Bardi, including *Il combattimento d'Apolline col serpente*; next were 2 collaborations, *Euridice* (libretto by Rinuccini, 1600) and *Il rapimento di Cefalo* (libretto by Chiabrera, 1600); he later composed the *Euridice* as his own (1602).

He is best known for 2 vols. of *Le nuove musiche*, sets of madrigals for solo voice with bass, or monodies (Florence, 1601, 1614). The song *Amarilli mia bella* from vol. 1 became very popular. From the mid-1560s Caccini lived in Florence as a singer at the Tuscan court. He was called "the father of a new style of music" (Angelo Grillo); Bardi said of him that he had "attained the goal of perfect music." But his claim to priority in writing vocal music in the *stile rappresentativo* is not clearly supported by known chronology.

cachua. A traditional dance of the Quechua people of Peru, usually performed on indigenous flutes with the accompaniment of a small drum. The meter is usually binary.

Cäcilienmesse. Mass in C Major by Haydn, 1766.

Cacioppo, George (Emanuel), American composer of the avant-garde; b. Monroe, Mich., Sept. 24, 1927; d. Ann Arbor, Mich., Apr. 4, 1984. He studied with Ross Lee Finney at the Univ. of Mich. (M.A., 1952) and with Leon Kirchner in Tanglewood; subsequently cofounded the ONCE Festival concerts in Ann Arbor (1960). His technique of composition is basically dodecaphonic; however, he allowed himself to deviate with all necessary caution from total serialism. He also experimented with "open end" forms of composition according to the fashionable aleatory principles. In that manner he produced *Piano Pieces* (1962–70) for any number of pianos, with their realization on tape sounding synchronously or nonsynchronously and lasting any practical (or impractical) length of time. Other works include *Time on Time in Miracles* for Soprano, 2 Horns, 2 Trombones, Cello, Piano, and Percussion (1964); *Holy Ghost Vacuum, or America Faints* for Electric Organ (Ann Arbor, Mar. 29, 1966, composer at the manuals); and *Dream Concert* for Organ, Voice, and Percussion (1976).

cacophony (Grk., bad sound). A raucous conglomeration of sound. This pejorative is often applied by baffled or conservative music critics (whose untutored ears are incapable of comprehending innovative concords) to any new music. Thus an English writer reviewing Chopin's recital in London in 1842 described his music as "excruciating cacophony." Nikita Khrushchev, expressing an opinion on 12-tone music, said, "To you it may be dodecaphony, but to me it's plain cacophony." (*Dodecaphony* and *cacophony* also rhyme in Russian.) Other favorite targets of this accusation were Wagner, Debussy, R. Strauss, Schoenberg, Stravinsky, Bartók, and Prokofiev.

cadence

A generic term denoting the conclusion of a melody or harmonized movement, the close or ending of a phrase, section, or movement; many of these categories overlap. The purpose of a cadence (Lat. *cadere*, fall) is to establish the terminal key of a musical composition.

At the minimum, a cadence contains the dominant triad followed by the tonic triad (V–I); such a cadence is called an *authentic cadence*. A cadence consisting of a subdominant triad leading to a tonic triad (IV–I) is called a *plagal cadence* (also called *amen* or *oblique*). In order to circumscribe the tonality more fully, 3 chords are used: the subdominant, the dominant, and the concluding tonic triads. This is a *full authentic cadence* (complete, full, perfect), which includes all 7 notes of the scale, thus outlining the key unambiguously. To enhance the tonality in a cadence, the 2nd inversion of the tonic triad ($I^6/_4$) is inserted between the subdominant and the dominant triad ($I–IV–I^6/_4–V–I$). Various surrogates of these fundamental chords are commonly adopted. Thus the subdominant harmony can be substituted by the use of the 1st inversion of the supertonic triad ($II^6/_3$), which has the same bass as the root of the subdominant triad. In the so-called *Neapolitan cadence*, the subdominant is replaced by a 1st-inversion triad in which supertonic and the submediant are flatted ($♭II^6/_3$); this chord then moves through the dominant to the tonic. The dominant triad can be extended by adding the 7th, forming the dominant-7th triad (V^7), or else be replaced by the 1st inversion of the leading-tone triad ($VII^6/_3$), which contains 3 ingredients of the dominant 7th chord; this substitution would not be used in the final cadence of a piece.

Cadences that do not end on the tonic are an important feature of tonal music. The most common is the *half cadence* (imperfect), where the harmonic progression ends without difficulty on the dominant chord, approached from any number of chords. An important type of irregular cadence is the *deceptive cadence* (evaded, interrupted), in which the dominant-7th chord leads into the submediant triad instead of the tonic triad, thus "deceiving" the expectations of the ear. In the major keys such a deceptive submediant is a minor triad (e.g., in C major, the A-minor chord); in the minor keys the submediant triad is major (e.g., in C minor, A-flat major). A great variety of melodic embellishments can be used in actual composition. During the period of the ARS NOVA the Italian composer Landini was among the most consistent users of a cadence that now bears his name; in it the leading tone in the melody is diverted to the submediant, a degree below, before resolving into the tonic (7–6–8). To modern ears this melodic divagation creates a momentary impression of a plagal cadence; it is usually a component of the DOUBLE-LEADING-TONE CADENCE.

Cadences can be endlessly ornamented—and the final resolution into the tonic chord tantalizingly delayed—creating harmonic suspense. A common delaying device is the insertion of a florid cadenza over the $I^6/_4$ chord, in anticipation of the inevitable arrival of the dominant harmony prior to the final resting point of the tonic. The concluding tonic chord is then repeated several times, in varying rhythmic figures and harmonic positions, so that the melody may be traversing through the 3rd or the 5th note of the tonic triad before arriving at the fundamental note of the key in the melody. It is most instructive to compile a statistical table of the number of such tonic chords in classical syms. In the resonant C-major coda of Beethoven's 5th Sym., the tonic chord is repeated after alternating with the dominant triad, 15 times; his 8th Sym., 24 times.

In modern compositions, cadences are apt to be abrupt. Prokofiev's March from his opera *Love for 3 Oranges* ends in a single C-major chord preceded by the briefest appearance of the dominant. While in Classical and Romantic music the final chord cannot possibly consist of more than 3 notes of the tonic harmony, 20th-century composers have introduced a pandiatonic type of a cadence in which the tonic triad is supplemented by the submediant, supertonic, or tonic 7th in a major key, so that the C-major triad blossoms out into a chord of C–E–G–A, C–E–G–B, or C–G–E–A–D, or other combinations of those ingredients, comprising every degree of the scale except the subdominant. (This exclusion could be explained by the fact that the subdominant cannot be derived from the fundamental tone by an expansion of the overtone series.) Jazz musicians popularized harmonies with "added notes," culminating in final chords with added 6ths, 7ths (natural or flatted), 9ths, 11ths (often sharped), and 13ths, all technically classified in academic harmony as dissonances, but all sounding to the modern ear as more satisfyingly concordant than undiluted sterile triadic tonic harmony.

cadence. 1. CADENZA. 2. The rhythm and/or tempo of a piece.

cadenza (It., cadence; from *cadere*, fall; Ger. *Kadenz*; Rus. *Kadentsia*). 1. In an aria or other accompanied vocal piece, a brilliant improvisatory passage for the soloist in free time, usually near the end. During the Golden Age of Opera (18th and early 19th centuries) COLORATURA singers were expected to roll out a formidable line of trills and arpeggios; composers began to rebel against this sometimes indulgent artistic freedom, and composers like Berlioz, Wagner, and Verdi did everything they could to prohibit such improvisation. By the 20th century the vocal cadenza is extinct per se, utilized only at the specific self-conscious direction of the composer. 2. An elaborate passage or fantasia at the end of the 1st or last movement of a concerto, played by the solo instrument. In its orig. conception *cadenza* signified an improvisatory interpolation in an instrumental vocal work, mainly intended to demonstrate the technical brilliance of the virtuoso performer. Solo cadenzas in classical concertos were rarely written by the composer himself, but were contributed by performers.

Among writers of cadenzas the most notable were Hummel, Moscheles, and Reinecke for piano concertos and Joachim for violin concertos. Still, their products were not always compatible with the style of the original work, and the emphasis on technical display sometimes jarred with the style of the unornamented original. Beethoven wrote his own cadenzas in his piano concertos, as did Schumann and Brahms. Chopin and Liszt avoided long cadenzas in their concertos and preferred to interpolate brief fiorituras or amplified embellishments: Schumann's piano concerto features a middle movement of a quasi-improvisatory quality.

Most 20th-century composers have abandoned the cadenza as a virtuoso exercise. As a working rule, a competently written cadenza should incorporate the main themes of the orig.; in Romantic concertos the device of continued sequences and modulations into relative keys are common. Cadenzas are usually announced by a sustained tonic 2nd-inversion chord ($I^6/_4$), with the pedal point on the dominant in the bass.

cadenza (It.). 1. CADENCE. 2. *Cadenza ad libitum*, the performer is to choose whether to perform the written cadenza, substitute another cadenza, or improvise a cadenza.

cæsura. CESURA.

café chantant (Fr., singing cafe). A predecessor of the cabaret that flourished during the 2nd Empire in Paris between 1852 and 1870, more like a nonsmoking saloon than the cabaret world painted by Toulouse-Lautrec. The repertoire usually consisted of sentimental ballads. It eventually evolved into larger places of entertainment of which the most celebrated was the Folies-Bergère (follies of the Bergere district) where increasingly explicit sexuality reigned. When the café chantant was transferred to England it assumed the name MUSIC HALL, but it was scorned by Victorian society as a shocking institution of sensuality.

Cage, John

Outstanding American composer, writer, philosopher, and visual artist of the experimental school, whose ideas about sound and silence and whose use of chance operations radically changed the course of 20th-century music; b. John Milton Cage, Jr., Los Angeles, Sept. 5, 1912; d. N.Y., Aug. 12, 1992. So important did Cage's work eventually become in music history that even the *Encyclopedia Britannica* described him as a "composer whose work and revolutionary ideas profoundly influenced mid-20th-century music." His father, John Milton Cage, Sr., was an inventor, his mother active as a clubwoman in California. He studied piano with Fannie Dillon and Richard Buhlig in Los Angeles and with Lazare Levy in Paris; returning to the U.S., he studied composition in California with A. Weiss and Schoenberg, and with Cowell in N.Y. On June 7, 1935, Cage married, in Los Angeles, Xenia Kashevaroff; they were divorced in 1945. In 1938–39 he was employed as a dance accompanist at the Cornish School in Seattle, where he also organized a percussion group. He developed Cowell's piano technique, making use of tone clusters and playing directly on the strings, and initiated a type of procedure to be called prepared piano, which consists of placing on the piano strings a variety of objects, such as screws, copper coins, and rubber bands, which alter the tone color of individual keys. Eventually the term and procedure gained acceptance among avant-garde composers and was listed as a legitimate method in several music dictionaries.

Cage taught for a season at the School of Design in Chicago (1941–42); he then moved to N.Y., where he began a fruitful association with the dancer Merce Cunningham, with whom he collaborated on a number of works that introduced radical innovations in musical and choreographic composition. He served as musical adviser to the Merce Cunningham Dance Co. until 1987. Another important association was his collaboration with the pianist David Tudor, who was able to reify Cage's exotic inspirations, works in which the performer shares the composer's creative role. In 1952, at Black Mountain College, he presented a theatrical event historically marked as the earliest musical happening.

With the passing years, Cage departed from the pragmatism of precise musical notation and definite ways of performance, electing instead to mark his creative intentions in graphic symbols and pictorial representations. He established the principle of indeterminacy in musical composition, producing works any 2 performances of which can never be identical. In the meantime, he became immersed in an earnest study of mushrooms, acquiring formidable expertise and winning a prize in Italy in competition with professional mycologists. He also became interested in chess, and played demonstration games with Marcel Duchamp, the famous painter turned chessmaster, on a chessboard designed by Lowell Cross to operate on aleatory principles with the aid of a computer and a system of laser rays.

In his endeavor to achieve ultimate freedom in musical expression, Cage produced a piece entitled *4′33″*, in 3 movements, during which no sounds are intentionally produced. It was performed in Woodstock, N.Y., in 1952, by Tudor, who sat at the piano playing nothing for the length of time stipulated in the title. This was followed by another "silent" piece, *0'00"*, an idempotent "to be played in any way by anyone," presented for the 1st time in Tokyo (1962). Any sounds, noises, coughs, chuckles, groans, and growls produced by the listeners are automatically regarded as integral to the piece itself, so that the wisecrack about the impossibility of arriving at a fair judgment of a silent piece, since one cannot tell what music is not being played, is invalidated by the uniqueness of Cage's art.

Cage was a consummate showman, and his exhibitions invariably attract music lovers and music haters alike, expecting to be exhilarated or outraged, as the case may be. In many such public happenings he departed from musical, unmusical, or even antimusical programs in favor of a free exercise of surrealist imagination, often instructing the audience to participate actively: for instance, to go out into the street and bring in garbage pails needed for percussion effects, with or without garbage. His music is publ. by C. F. Peters Corp. and has been recorded on many labels. In view of the indeterminacy of so many of Cage's works, the catalog publ. by Peters in 1969 can only serve as a list of titles and suggestions of contents.

In order to eliminate the subjective element in composition, Cage resorted to a method of selecting the components of his pieces by dice throwing, suggested by the Confucian classic *I Ching*, an ancient Chinese oracle book; the result was a system of total serialism, in which all elements pertaining to acoustical pulses, pitch, noise, duration, relative loudness, tempi, combinatory superpositions, etc. were determined by previously drawn charts. His stage work *Europeras 1 & 2* (1987), which he wrote, designed, staged, and directed, is a sophisticated example, a collage comprised of excerpts from extant operas selected and manipulated by a computer software program, IC (short for *I Ching*), designed by Cage's assistant Andrew Culver. The scheduled opening of *Europeras 1 & 2*, which was to take place on Nov. 15, 1987, was delayed and its location changed due to a fire, reportedly set by a vagrant in search of food, which devastated the Frankfurt Opera House just a few days before the opening. Cage later composed 3 more *Europeras*.

Cage was also a brilliant writer, much influenced by the manner, grammar, syntax, and glorified illogic of

Gertrude Stein. Among his works are *Silence* (1961), *A Year from Monday* (1967), *M* (1973), *Empty Words* (1979), and *X* (1983). He developed a style of poetry called mesostic, which uses an anchoring string of letters down the center of the page that spell a name, a word, or even a line of text relating to the subject matter of the poem. Mesostic poems are composed by computer, the "source material" pulverized and later enhanced by Cage into a semicoherent, highly evocative poetic text. He also collaborated on a number of other projects, including *The 1st Meeting of the Satie Society*, with illustrations by Johns, Twombly, Rauschenberg, LeWitt, Daniel, Thoreau, and Cage himself, prepared by the Limited Editions Club. Since Cage's works are multigenetic, his scores have been exhibited in galleries and museums; he returned annually to Crown Point Press in San Francisco to make etchings. A series of 52 paintings, the New River Watercolors, executed in 1987 at the Miles C. Horton Center at the Virginia Polytechnic Inst. and State Univ., were shown at the Phillips Collection in Washington, D.C. (1990).

John Cage preparing a piano, c. 1960s

Cage was elected to the American Academy and Inst. of Arts and Letters in 1968, and to the American Academy of Arts and Sciences in 1978; he was inducted into the 50-member American Academy of Arts and Letters in 1989. In 1981 he received the Mayor's Award of Honor in N.Y. He was named Commander of the Order of Arts and Letters by the French Minister of Culture in 1982, and received an Honorary Doctorate of Performing Arts from the Calif. Inst. of the Arts in 1986. In 1988–89 Cage was Charles Eliot Norton Prof. of Poetry at Harvard Univ., for which he prepared a series of lengthy mesostic poems incorporating the writings of R. Buckminster Fuller, Thoreau, Marshall McLuhan, and others. In the summer of 1989 he was guest artist at the International Festivals in Leningrad and Moscow, at which he presented works characteristically entitled *Music for . . .*, which he conducted cheironomically by pointing out instruments that were to enter. In late 1989 he traveled to Japan to receive the prestigious and lucrative Kyoto Prize.

Cahn (Kahn), Sammy (born Samuel Cohen), American song lyricist; b. N.Y., June 18, 1913. He played violin in variety shows and organized a dance band; in 1940 he went to Hollywood and wrote songs with Jule Styne for several films: *Youth on Parade* (1942), *Carolina Blues* (1944), *Anchors Aweigh* (1945), *It Happened in Brooklyn* (1947), *Romance on the High Seas* (1948). In 1955 he started a music publ. company. Among his best-known songs are *Bei Mir Bist Du Schoen, I Should Care, 3 Coins in the Fountain, I'll Never Stop Loving You, The Tender Trap,* and *High Hopes* (which became John Kennedy's 1960 campaign song). He publ. *The Songwriter's Rhyming Dictionary* (N.Y., 1983).

caisse (Fr.). Drum. *Caisse à timbre, caisse claire,* snare drum; *grosse caisse,* bass drum; *caisse roulante* (Fr., rolling drum), tenor drum; *caisse sourde* (Fr., muffled drum), tenor drum.

Caissons Go Rolling Along, The. Song composed by Edmund Gruber, 1907, for the 5th U.S. Artillery in the Philippine Islands. Sousa arranged it for band. Eventually the song became a semi-official march for the Artillery.

cakewalk. An African-American dance in quick 2/4 time which became popular in blackface minstrelsy in the latter 19th century; its vogue soon spread all over the world. The cakewalk was used in the WALK-AROUND FINALE in the minstrel show (and, later, vaudeville and burlesque). Its syncopated rhythm is essentially that of ragtime; Debussy included a cakewalk in his piano suite *Children's Corner* with the politically incorrect title of *Golliwog's Cakewalk*.

calando (It.). Decreasing in loudness and (usually) tempo.

Caldwell, Sarah, remarkable American operatic conductor, director, and impresario; b. Maryville, Mo., Mar. 6, 1924. She learned to play violin at home and appeared at local events as a child; enrolled as a psychology student at the Univ. of Arkansas. She undertook serious violin study at the New England Cons. in Boston with Richard Burgin, concertmaster of the Boston Sym. Orch.; also studied viola with Georges Fourel. In 1947 she was engaged by Boris Goldovsky, head of the opera dept. at the New England Cons., as his assistant, which proved a valuable apprenticeship for her. In 1952 she was engaged as head of the Boston Univ. opera workshop. In 1958 she formed her own opera company in Boston, called the Opera Group; this was the beginning of an extraordinary career, in which she displayed her peculiar acumen in building up an operatic enterprise with scant musical and financial resources. In 1965 she changed the name of her enterprise to the Opera Co. of Boston, making use of a former vaudeville theater for her performances. In most of her productions she acts as producer, conductor, administrator, stage director, scenery designer, and publicity manager.

Among her productions were *La Traviata, Falstaff, Benvenuto Cellini* by Berlioz, *Don Quichotte, I Capuletti ed i Montecchi,* and several modern operas, among them *War and Peace, Moses und Aron, Lulu, Intolleranza,* and *Montezuma.* She produced the American premieres of *The Ice Break* by Tippett and *The Soldiers* by Zimmermann. She was able to induce famous singers to lend their participation, among them Sills, Horne, Gobbi, Gedda, and Domingo. Soberminded critics heap praise on Caldwell for her musicianship, physical and mental energy, imagination, and a sort of genius for opera productions. In 1976 she became the 1st woman to conduct at the Metropolitan Opera, N.Y. (*La Traviata*).

Cale, John. See VELVET UNDERGROUND.

California Girls. Ode to sun, fun, and surf by Brian Wilson of the Beach Boys, a major hit in 1965.

call and response. A synonym for ANTIPHONY, used in English-speaking religious contexts.

Call Me Madam. Musical by I. Berlin, 1950, a satire on a Washington hostess's being chosen as American ambassador to "Lichtenburg"; includes songs about hostessing and Eisenhower, *The Best Thing for You, It's a Lovely Day Today, Marrying for Love,* and *You're Just In Love.*

Callas, Maria (born Maria Anna Sofia Cecilia Kalogeropoulos), celebrated American soprano; b. N.Y., Dec. 3, 1923; d. Paris, Sept. 16, 1977. Her father was a Greek immigrant; the family went back to Greece when she was 13; she studied voice at the Royal Academy of Music in Athens with the Spanish soprano Elvira de Hidalgo, and made her debut as Santuzza in a school production of *Cavalleria rusticana* (1938). Her 1st professional appearance was in a minor role in Suppe's *Boccaccio* at the Royal Opera in Athens when she was 16; her 1st major role, as Tosca, was there in 1942. She went back to N.Y. in 1945; auditioned for the Metropolitan Opera Co. and was offered a contract, but decided to go to Italy, where she made her operatic debut in the title role of *La Gioconda* (Verona, 1947).

She was encouraged in her career by the famous conductor Tullio Serafin, who engaged her to sing Isolde and Aida in various Italian productions. In 1951 she became a member of La Scala, Milan. She was handicapped by her excessive weight; in a supreme effort of will she slimmed down (from 210 to 135 pounds); with her classical Greek profile and penetrating eyes, she made a striking impression on the stage; in the tragic role of Medea in Cherubini's opera she mesmerized the audience by her dramatic representation of pity and terror. Some critics opined that she lacked a true BEL CANTO quality in her voice, and that her technique was defective in COLORATURA, but her power of interpretation was such that she was soon acknowledged to be one of the greatest dramatic singers of the century.

Her professional and personal life was as tempestuous as that of any prima donna of the bygone era. In 1949 she married the Italian industrialist G. B. Meneghini (d. 1981), who became her manager, but they separated 10 years later. Her romance with the Greek shipping magnate Aristotle Onassis was a recurrent topic of sensational gossip. Given to outbursts of temper, she regularly made newspaper headlines when she walked off the stage following some altercation, or failed to appear altogether at scheduled performances, but her eventual return to the stage would be all the more eagerly welcomed by her legion of admirers.

After leaving La Scala in 1958, she returned there from 1960 to 1962. From 1952 to 1959 she sang at Covent Garden, London, the Chicago Lyric Opera, and the Dallas Opera. Perhaps the peak of her success was her brilliant debut at the Metropolitan Opera in N.Y. as Norma (1956). Following a well-publicized disagreement with its management, she quit the company only to reach an uneasy accommodation with it to return as Violetta in 1958; that same year she left the company again, returning only in 1965 to sing Tosca before abandoning the operatic stage altogether. In 1971 she gave a seminar on opera at the Juilliard School of Music, and her magic worked even in her 1st attempt at teaching; her classes were enthusiastically received by the students. In 1974 she went on a concert tour with Di Stefano; any hopes of a comeback were forever dashed.

She retired to Europe; she died suddenly of a heart attack in her Paris apartment. Her body was cremated and her ashes were scattered on the Aegean Sea. A radio commentator's characterization of her artistry: "If an orgasm could sing, it would sound like Maria Callas." Pleonastically speaking, she was an incarnation of carnality.

calliope. A circus pipe organ with very loud whistles activated by steam. Raucous and vulgar, the calliope became a musical symbol of the swashbuckling and aggressive late 19th century. It went into a limbo of nostalgia with the advent of the modern sophisticated age. Calliope is the Muse of Eloquence.

Calloway, Cab(ell), noted African-American jazz singer and bandleader; b. Rochester, N.Y., Dec. 25, 1907; d. Cokebury Village, Del., Nov. 8, 1994. After making his way to Chicago he began his career as a singer and dancer; led the Alabamians (1928–29); took over the leadership of the Missourians, with which he established himself in N.Y. (1929–30); appeared in the revue *Hot Chocolates* (1929); subsequently led various other groups, becoming house band at the Cotton Club; later performed on Broadway and in film. He was a proponent of scat singing, characterized by nonsense syllabification and rapid glossolalia with the melodic line largely submerged under an asymmetric inundation of rhythmic heterophony; he was known as the Hi-de-ho Man. His biggest and most enduring hit was *Minnie the Moocher* (1931). He compiled the *Hepster's Dictionary,* listing jazz terms (1938).

calma, con (It.). With calm; calmly, tranquilly. *Calmando(si)* (It.), growing calm, becoming tranquil; *calmato,* calming down.

calypso. Popular music of the West Indies, originating in Trinidad in the 1920s. Much influenced by American jazz, its meter is 4/4 with sharp syncopations. The mostly English lyrics often reflect topical subjects. Accompaniment may include drums, maracas, kitchen utensils, and bottles. Calypso is the wellspring from which many Caribbean dance and song genres have arisen.

Calzabigi, Ranieri (Raniero Simone Francesco Maria) **di,** Italian poet and music theorist; b. Livorno, Dec. 23, 1714; d. Naples, July 1795. In 1750 he went to Paris, then proceeded to Brussels (1760); lived in Vienna (1761–72); was in Pisa by 1775. He engaged in polemics regarding the relative merits of French and Italian operas; lent energetic support to Gluck in his ideas of operatic reform; wrote for Gluck the librettos of *Orfeo ed Euridice*, *Alceste*, and *Paride ed Elena*; broke with Gluck when the latter handed over one of his librettos to another composer. Salieri and Paisiello were other important composers of his librettos. He publ. *Dissertazione su le poesie drammatiche del Sig. Abate Pietro Metastasio* (1755), a controversial work concerning Metastasio and Hasse.

Cambiale di Matrimonio, La (The Marital Bill of Exchange). Farce by Rossini, 1810. The daughter of a British banker is traded without her consent to a Canadian merchant, but she loves a young employee of her father. When the Canadian, improbably named Slook, arrives in Europe to claim her hand, she explains to him that she is already "mortgaged." Moved, he writes off his own capital to her and her lover as a matrimonial "bill of exchange" (*la cambiale*). The work is full of jollity and has been revived to considerable acclaim.

cambiata (It., changed; Eng. *changing note*). Common abbrev. for *nota cambiata*. Formerly, an accented passing tone; now, an auxiliary note placed on the weak beat below or above the principal note and left by a skip of a 3rd in a diatonic melody:

In the 1st half of the example the c^2 is the cambiata, auxiliary to the overall upper-neighbor motion (d^2–e^2–d^2); in the 2nd half of the example the d^2 is the cambiata, auxiliary to the overall passing-note motion (e^2–d^2–c^2). In either case, a pleasing dissonance against the main harmony is formed.

Unlike the ECHAPPÉE, the harmony does not change during this ornament.

Camelot. Musical by Lerner and Loewe, 1960. The plot is derived from the legend of King Arthur, the founder of the Round Table at Camelot, Queen Guinevere, and her youthful lover Sir Lancelot. The King magnanimously forgives them their transgressions. Includes the title song, *The Lusty Month of May, If Ever I Would Leave You, How to Handle a Woman*, and *What Do the Simple Folk Do?*

camera (It.). Chamber, room, small hall. *Alla camera*, in the style of chamber music; *musica da camera*, chamber music.

Camerata. Historically important Florentine intellectual and artistic group organized by Giovanni de' Bardi (*c.* 1573–87), including aristocratic poets, philosophers, and music lovers. Besides functioning as a musical salon, its aim was to reinstate a "pure" singing manner without accompaniment as it was believed to have been practiced in ancient Greek drama; it was thus philosophically allied to the Renaissance. Renouncing the florid art of polyphonic writing, the Camerata cultivated lyric melody and homophonic monody, the basis for the imminent genesis of opera.

Camp Meeting. Sym. No. 3 by Ives, 1901–1904.

campana (It.). A bell. *Campanella, -o,* a small bell.

Campanella, La. Brilliant piano composition by Liszt, 1832, arranged by him from the Violin Concerto No. 2 by Paganini. Liszt expanded the tune into a veritable feast of tintinnabulations in high treble.

campanology. The science of bell making and ringing.

campestre (It.). Pastoral, rural, idyllic.

Camptown Races. The popular name for a dialect song by Foster, 1850, orig. titled *Gwine to Run All Night.* The opening is often sung to the words "The Camptown Ladies sing this song . . ."; the orig. lyrics are even more politically incorrect than the standard ones.

canary (Fr. *canarie*; Sp. *canario*). A European dance popular in the 16th and 17th centuries, derived from an old dance of the Canary Islands. Most composers expressed the rhythm in triple (3/8, 3/4) or compound meters (6/4, 6/8); however, there are examples of duple-meter canaries. The music resembles that of the sarabande or passamezzo moderno; Quantz distinguishes the canary from the gigue, which "have the same movement, [by the fact that] the Gigue is played with a short and light bow, but in the Canarie, which consists always of dotted notes, the bowing is short and sharp."

cancan. A lively and somewhat salacious dance that arrived in Paris from Algeria about 1830; set in rapid 2/4 time, it is musically similar to a GALOP or QUADRILLE. At the height of its popularity under the 2nd Empire, the cancan, as danced by young women on the vaudeville stage, shocked the sensitivities of conservative French audiences of the time because the beskirted choristers used to kick their legs above their waists in time with the music and perform leg splits. Early editions of the *Oxford Companion to Music* characterized the cancan as "a boisterous and latterly indecorous dance, of the quadrille order and including high kicking," and demurred at further elucidation by stating that "its exact nature is unknown to anyone connected with this *Companion*." It is still performed as a show dance.

cancel. The natural sign (♮); a term current in American schools in the 2nd half of the 19th century.

canción (Sp.). Song, applied specifically to the poetic type of 15th-century Spanish popular ballad but semantically given a more dignified standing than the rustic VILLANCICO. The verse is usually strophic, and the musical setting strictly symmetrical. *Cancionero*, a gathered or published collection of Spanish-language songs. For example, many cancioneros of Spanish Renaissance secular music are preserved in Spanish archives; there are also numerous collections of sacred music surviving in Mexico.

cancrizans (Lat., crabwise). Retrogressive, moving backward. See CANON CANCRIZANS.

Candide. Musical by Bernstein, 1956, with text by, among others, Lillian Hellman, Richard Wilbur, and Dorothy Parker. It is derived from Voltaire's famous story of a Westphalian youth learning the sordid side of the *Best of All Possible Worlds*. Also includes *It Must Be So, Glitter and Be Gay, You Were Dead You Know, I Am Easily Assimilated,* and *Make Our Garden Grow.* Bernstein later revised the orchestration and text into an "opera-house version" which was produced in N.Y. (1982).

canon. 1. A contrapuntal composition of 2 or more voices in which a subject (theme) introduced by 1 of the voices is strictly imitated by another voice, while the 1st voice continues with a suitable contrapuntal part. The most common type of canon is imitation on the same pitch or an octave higher; it is called *canon at the (in) unison*. A more difficult imitation is the *canon at the 5th*, which gave rise to the fugue. In a Classical fugue the imitating voice is in the key of the dominant, and it may enter either a 5th higher or a 4th lower than the initial subject.

The most popular canons are in 2 voices, but the earliest canon ever written, *Sumer is icumen in*, is set for 4 voices. Examples are known of canons in 8, 16, 32, and even more voices, but the subjects of such canons are inevitably reduced to a series of broken tonic triads, with few auxiliary notes, and so contribute little to the contrapuntal essence of the form. There are also canons in which the subject is imitated by AUGMENTATION, that is, by doubling the note values of the original theme, or by DIMINUTION, that is, by halving the note values. In *canon by inversion*, the imitating voice inverts the melodic intervals of the subject; canons by inversion are also called "mirror canons" because they form the mirror image of the subject. The most ingenious, the most artificial, and the most difficult to compose is the *canon cancrizans*, that is, crab-walking canon, in which the melody is imitated by playing it backward. (Actually, crabs do not walk backward; they walk sideways, but the old contrapuntists were not acquainted with the walking modes of crabs.) If the crab-walking voice is inverted, the result is *imitation by retrograde inversion* (or, by inverted retrograde). Most canons are furnished with an ending by way of an *authentic cadence.* Canons that return to the beginning, called *perpetual canons*, or rounds, are very popular types of group songs.

Composers of the Baroque period found pleasure in asking the performer or the person to whom the canon is dedicated to decide at what particular beat the imitating voice should enter, with a suitable Latin quotation, such as "seek, and ye shall find." Bach's *Musikalisches Opfer* (Musical Offering), which he wrote for Frederick the Great of Prussia, is full of such verbal riddles, e.g., "Ascenden teque modulatione ascendat gloria regis" (With an ascending modulation, let the King's glory ascend also), meaning that the canon must modulate by ascending degrees. This type of canon is fittingly called a *riddle canon*. The masters of the Baroque developed fantastic ingenuity in writing canons in all conceivable forms, and in carefully attending to the proper resolution of dissonances without breaking the established rules of harmony and counterpoint.

The art of canon suffered an inevitable decline in 20th-century music when dissonances became emancipated and canons could be written at any interval and in any form of inversion, retrograde, or the inversion of the retrograde, without fear of violating harmonic conventions. Yet composers such as Schoenberg, Webern, and Bartók have written well-constructed canons, and the technique itself has been revived in larger dodecaphonic contexts. 2. Established repertoire for a particular genre.

canon à l'écrivisse (Fr.). CANON CANCRIZANS.

canon ad infinitum (Lat.). Infinite canon; a round.

canon al rovescio (It.). CANON CANCRIZANS or by inversion.

canon by inversion. See CANON.

canon cancrizans (Lat., crab canon). Canon in which the imitating voice is retrograde (reverse) of subject.

canon enigmaticus (Lat.). Riddle canon, requiring verbal instruction. See CANON.

canon per arsin et thesin (Lat., canon by upbeat and downbeat). 1. CANON AL ROVESCIO. 2. Canon where the imitating voice shifts the melody over by 1 beat.

canon per augmentationem (Lat.). Canon by augmentation. See CANON.

canon per diminutionem (Lat.). Canon by diminution. See CANON.

canon per recte et retro (Lat.). CANON CANCRIZANS.

canon perpetuus (Lat.). Perpetual canon; a round. See CANON.

canonic imitation. Use of canonic procedure; imitation of the subject in another voice.

Canonical Hours. The Divine Office established times for daily prayer within the Roman Catholic Church. Beginning in the morning, the present cycle (adopted in 1971) comprises *Lauds, Terce, Sext, Nones, Vespers,* and *Compline*; the old night Office, *Matins/Vigils,* is now an *Office of Readings*, which may be said at any time.

canso (Prov.). Song.

cantabile (It.). In a songful manner, songfully. This Italian term received its currency in the 18th century when it became an aesthetic criterion of beauty in music. As applied to vocal compositions, cantabile appears redundant, for it is obvious that a singer ought to sing singingly, but it became of aesthetic importance as an expression mark in instrumental writing. Often a cantabile was part of the name of the movement itself, as in Mozart's Andante cantabile *con espressionione* in his A-minor Piano Sonata (K. 310) and in Beethoven's Adagio cantabile in his 2nd Violin Sonata (op. 12/2). Romantic composers made use of the term with increasing frequency, as Tchaikovsky did in the Andante cantabile of his 1st String Quartet (op. 11). In the piano music of Chopin, Schumann, and other romantic composers, cantabile is in effect synonymous with LEGATO.

cantando (*cantante*; It.). Singingly; smooth and flowing.

cantata (It., work to be sung). A vocal work with instrumental accompaniment, eventually written for solo voices (singing recitatives, arias, duets, etc.), chorus, and instruments, which developed parallel to the emergence of opera and oratorio at the threshold of the 17th century. The cantata genre is distinguished from the SONATA, "a work to be sounded, or played."

In contrast to the ORATORIO, of religious origin, the cantata appeared 1st as a secular composition, as a series of vocal stanzas in strophic form; only later, growing out of German 17th-century SACRED CONCERTOS through the works of Bach, did the cantata become primarily a medium of religious composition. The early type of cantata embodied varied characteristics, making use of both polyphonic and monodic construction. A cantata is usually of a shorter duration than an oratorio; its form is flexible, so that it can admit both lyrical and dramatic elements and appear as a series of extended arias or else as an operatic scene with recitatives.

Bach's cantatas contributed decisively to this standardization of the form; at his hands the common type of monodic cantata grew to dimensions of fervent religious devotion and dramatic grandeur within a polyphonic framework of incomparable mastery. Bach was not averse to writing cantatas of a topical nature, such as in his justly celebrated *Coffee Cantata*. Beginning early in the 19th century the composition of secular cantatas to prechosen texts was prescribed in order to obtain the Prix de Rome at the Paris Cons. Since practically all French composers worth their bouillabaisse competed for the Prix de Rome, the number of prize-winning and prize-losing French cantatas reached tens of thousands of MSS. Mozart wrote a Masonic cantata; one aria from it became the Austrian national hymn after World War I, when all other proposed tunes were judged suspect of having monarchical associations.

In the 20th century the borderline between an oratorio and a cantata became more difficult to trace. Prokofiev's patriotic film suite *Alexander Nevsky* partakes of the features of both oratorio in the solemnity of its invocation and of a cantata in the brevity of its individual numbers. Generally, modern composers resorted to the writing of cantatas when a festive occasion demanded it. Britten wrote 2 particularly memorable cantatas: *Cantata Accademica* (1960), based on the *Carmen basiliense*, and *Cantata Misericordium*, commemorating the centennial of the International Red Cross (1963). Bartók's *Cantata Profana* (*The Enchanted Stags*, 1934) is a choral work with orch., with text and musical themes borrowed from Rumanian folklore. Alberto Ginastera wrote an effective cantata, *Cantata para América Mágica*, to pseudo-Indian texts and based on traditional South American melodies, 1961.

cantatore (It.). Singer (male); *cantatrice* (Fr.), singer (female).

cante chico (Sp., small song). A lesser genre of FLAMENCO singing, as distinct from the more developed CANTE JONDO.

cante jondo (Andal., deep song; Sp. *cante hondo*). Chief genre of flamenco singing, as opposed to CANTE CHICO.

Canteloube (de Malaret), **(Marie-) Joseph,** French pianist, composer, and writer on music; b. Annonay, near Tournon, Oct. 21, 1879; d. Grigny, Seine-et-Oise, Nov. 4, 1957. He studied piano in Paris with Amelie Doetzer, a pupil of Chopin, and composition with d'Indy at the Schola Cantorum. He became an ardent collector of French folk songs and arranged and publ. many of them for voice with instrumental accompaniment. His *Chants d'Auvergne* for Voice and Piano/Orch. (4 vols., 1923–30) are frequently heard. Among his other albums, *Anthologie des chants populaires français* (4 vols., 1939–44) is a comprehensive collection of regional folk songs. He also publ. a biography of d'Indy (Paris, 1949).

canti carnascialeschi (It., carnival songs). Polyphonic songs performed at Florentine festivals that flourished during the reign of the murderous but artistically minded Medicis in the 15th century. Canti carnascialeschi are historically important because of their inclusion of work songs, such as those of tailors, scribes, and perfume makers. Their form approximates that of the frottola.

canticle (Lat. *canticum*, a song). Christian hymns whose texts are in the nature of psalms, taken from the Bible, but not from the Book of Psalms itself; the term is sometimes extended to include nonscriptural texts and certain psalms. Canticles are called major when they are taken from the New Testament, minor when they are from the Old Testament; texts from the Song of Solomon are often set. In the 20th century Britten composed 5 canticles (1947–75).

canticum (Lat., song). CANTICLE.

Canticum sacrum ad honorem Sancti Marci nominis. Sacred cantata by Stravinsky, 1956. The text is in Latin, the prosody Gregorian. Stravinsky conducted its premiere in the Basilica of San Marco, Venice. This is the 1st work of Stravinsky in which he makes explicit use of Schoenberg's 12-tone system of composition.

cantiga. A medieval Sp. or Port. song, to texts in the vernacular. Secular cantigas were subdivided into several categories according to their content, such as *cantigas de amor* (sung by a woman), *cantigas de amigo, cantigas de escarnio* (satires), and *cantigas de gesta* (narrative and epic songs). Religious cantigas were most often sung in praise of the Virgin Mary. The theory that they were of Arabic origin and were brought to Spain by the Moors is unfounded; most probably they are varieties of villancicos, with some influence from French and Provençal singers. Only 2 sets of cantigas have survived, the 6 secular love songs by the Galician Martin Codax (*c.* 1230) and the voluminous *Cantigas de Santa Maria* (*c.* 1250–80), more than 400 religious songs collected and illuminated by employees of King Alfonso X ("el Sabio," the Wise) of Castile and León.

cantilena (It., little song; Ger. *cantilene*; Fr. *cantilène*). 1. Orig., plainchant. 2. Medieval secular monophony. 3. An English polyphonic song genre of the late 13th and 14th centuries. There was a strong tendency toward homorhythm, and therefore an ideal opportunity for the *contenance angloise* (frequent use of parallel 1st-inversion chords) to flourish; however, more typical free medieval counterpoint is present also. 4. From the 19th century on, a flowing, songlike passage on an instrument.

cantillation (Lat. *cantillare*, to sing softly). Religious chanting in the Jewish synagogue service, usually a recitative with a text from the Jewish liturgy. The manner of the cantillation is peculiarly rhapsodic, and is often set in the style of a lamentation. Its rhythm follows the natural accents of the text.

cantique (Fr.). HYMN.

canto (It.). 1. A melody, song, chant. 2. The soprano, i.e., highest vocal or instrumental part. *Canto a cappella*, sacred song performed without accompaniment; canto fermo, CANTUS FIRMUS; *canto figurato*, florid polyphonic writing rich in melodic figuration.

canto, col (It., with the melody). A direction to accompanists to follow the solo part in tempo and expression.

cantor (Lat. *cantare*, sing). 1. In the Roman Catholic Church, the soloist in the liturgical chants, while the chorus is called *schola*. 2. In Lutheran liturgy, the music director (as Bach was in Leipzig). 3. In the Jewish synagogue, the soloist who sings the cantillation.

cantus ambrosianus (Lat.). AMBROSIAN CHANT.

cantus choralis (Lat., choral chant). GREGORIAN CHANT performed as notes of equal length.

cantus firmus (Lat., firm song). A fixed or given melody used in contrapuntal music and to which other parts are to be set correctly. Historically it was the term for the main musical subject in medieval and Renaissance polyphonic music, traditionally a plainchant melody. The practice dates back to the organum of the Parisian Notre Dame school in the 12th century and continued to appear in the religious music of the Renaissance. In the quattrocento masses the melody of the cantus firmus was often taken from secular popular songs, such as *L'homme armé*. A cantus firmus was usually given to the tenor part and consisted of long notes of even values; however, later Renaissance composers used the cantus firmus as thematic material (e.g., Des Prez's *Missa Pange lingua*). In the Baroque the cantus firmus was often placed in the bass, as in organ chorales, where it was played by the pedals. In such applications the bass cantus firmus seems related to the passacaglia.

cantus fractus. A chant with subdivisions of long notes; thus a chant consisting of notes of different metrical value, as distinct from CANTUS PLANUS with notes of even values.

cantus gemellus (Lat., twin song; Eng. *gymel*). A type of 2-part writing in parallel 3rds or 6ths.

cantus gregorianus (Lat.). Gregorian chant.

cantus mensuratus (Lat., measured song). A chant consisting of precisely measured notes, usually of equal duration.

cantus planus (Lat., plain chant). GREGORIAN CHANT with notes of equal duration.

cantus transpositus (Lat., transformed song). In the theory of mensural notation, an indication to alter a given meter.

canzona (It.). An Italian term with several meanings, a cognate of the French CHANSON. 1. A song or folk song; a vocal genre. In Dante's time, a lyrical poem consisting of several stanzas; also, settings of such poems. During the Renaissance period the canzona acquired traits of a folk song melody, in monodic settings; such a canzona became known as a CANZONA ALLA NAPOLETANA, a designation applied to a lyric ballad. The term was frequently applied to a madrigal-style PART SONG. 2. An instrumental piece; the term was 1st used for lute or keyboard works. During the Renaissance period the instrumental canzona became differentiated into the form of CANZONA FRANCESE (CANZONA ALLA FRANCESE)—that is, a canzona in which musical differentiation of sections became significant. An instrumental canzona for ensemble was called CANZONA DA SONAR—that is, a canzona to be played rather than sung. As canzonas became more complex in contrapuntal settings, they came to be identified with the RICERCAR, eventually giving rise to a hybrid form of variation canzona, with a single theme followed by a free fantasy in variation form.

By the Baroque, canzona began to be identified with SONATA, in the sense of an instrumental piece without any connotation of the Classic sonata form. Some German editors even equated the canzona with the fugue. This terminological proliferation led to such semantic oversaturation that the canzona became a PASSE-PARTOUT word for any melodious vocal or instrumental work. It is in this sense that Tchaikovsky designated the slow movement of his 4th Sym. as "in modo di canzona." With the advent of neoclassicism in the 2nd quarter of the 20th century, the canzona was artificially revived as an instrumental form of a neo-Baroque type.

The plural of *canzona* is *canzone*, but *canzone* is also used as a singular noun, in which case the plural is *canzoni*.

canzonet (It. *canzonetta*, a little canzona). A solo song or part song; a brief instrumental piece.

Capitan, El. Comic opera by Sousa, 1896, the most successful of his 10 comic operas. The Viceroy of Peru foils a conspiracy against him by joining it in disguise as El Capitan, a legendary bandit. When he reveals his real identity, the plot against him collapses. Besides the marching chorus *El Capitan*, there is the song *A Typical Tune of Zanzibar*.

capo (It.). Chief, head, beginning. *Da capo*, from the beginning.

capo tasto (It. *capotasto*, *capo*, head fret). 1. A wood, ivory, or metal bar placed on the fingerboard of guitars or lutes to shorten the length of all strings and thus raise their pitch. This enables a player to transpose to other keys without changing the fingering. 2. The nut of stringed instruments having a fingerboard.

cappella (Lat., It., chapel). A chorus; an orch.; court or chapel ensemble. Through the centuries the word was used in 2 senses: as the place of worship, and as persons participating in the church service. *A* (or *alla*) *cappella* (It., as in chapel), without instrumental accompaniment; music, mostly polyphonic choral works, composed and performed according to the way it was done in chapel, beginning with the Renaissance.

capriccio (It., from Lat. caper, goat). A caprice; a musical caper. The capriccio originated in the Renaissance as a live-

ly instrumental composition in a free improvisatory style; the term was interchangeably used for such varied forms as RICERCAR, CANZONE, or TOCCATA. In the 19th century the capriccio reasserted its capricious character.

Beethoven, Weber, Mendelssohn, Brahms, Reger, Dvořák, Tchaikovsky, Rimsky-Korsakov, Saint-Saëns, and R. Strauss wrote instrumental capriccios. Paganini composed 24 capriccios for solo violin, arranged by other composers for various instruments. Bach entitled one of his few pieces frankly expressing a sentiment *Capriccio on the Departure of His Beloved Brother*. Beethoven notated his rondo op. 129, nicknamed *Rage Over a Lost Penny*, "quasi un capriccio." The free form of capriccio makes it especially suitable for works of national colors. Tchaikovsky wrote a *Capriccio Italien*; Rimsky-Korsakov a *Capriccio Espagnol*; Saint-Saëns a *Capriccio Arabe*; and Strauss an opera he called *Capriccio* (see below).

With the accentuation of a neoclassical trend in the 20th century, the term *capriccio* regained its original meaning as a contrapuntal instrumental piece in the manner of a ricercar. Stravinsky's 1929 *Capriccio* for piano and orch. is an example of a modern use of the term. The proper Italian plural of *capriccio* is *capricci*.

Capriccio. Opera by R. Strauss, 1942. An 18th-century musical play-within-a-play, with various theatrical and operatic characters discussing the problem of whether words or music are more important. The title seems to denote a form of uninhibited whimsical production.

Capriccio brillante. Concert piece by Mendelssohn for piano and orch., 1st performed in 1835; the soloist was Clara Wieck, future wife of Schumann. The adjective *brillante* describes the nature of the work, but the noun *capriccio* does not necessarily imply any capriciousness in the music; on the contrary, the piece is highly organized in a symmetric formal fashion.

Capriccio Espagnol. Symphonic suite on Spanish themes by Rimsky-Korsakov, 1887. Rimsky-Korsakov borrowed the themes and harmonies from a collection of authentic Spanish songs and dressed them up in a multicolored panoply of instrumental timbres. The result was a triumph of sonorous orchestration.

Capriccio Italien. Symphonic fantasy by Tchaikovsky, 1880, based on authentic Italian songs that Tchaikovsky heard during his sojourn in Italy. There is a bolero, a Neapolitan ballad, and a tarantella.

capriccioso (It.). In a capricious, fanciful, whimsical, fantastic style.

Capricieuse. Sym. No. 2 in D Major by Berwald, 1842.

Capricorn Concerto. Concerto grosso by Barber, 1944, with flute, oboe, and trumpet the concertante instruments. It is, in 3 sections, alternately meditative and playful. He named it after the home he co-owned in Mt. Kisco, N.Y., with his great friend and fellow composer Menotti.

Capuleti ed i Montecchi, I. Opera by Bellini, 1830, derived from Shakespeare's tragedy *Romeo and Juliet.* Bel canto arias and conventional Italian recitatives being adaptable to different words and lyrico-dramatic situations, Bellini made use in the score of portions from his earlier unsuccessful operas, *Adelson et Salvini* and *Zaira.* The part of Romeo was written for a female alto, a surrogate for the quondam male CASTRATO of the Baroque opera. The spectacle of a richly bosomed female making like Romeo jarred on the eyes and ears of literal-minded operagoers of the 19th century, and eventually the part of Romeo had to be given to a tenor. The result was a misalliance of registers, unisons becoming octaves, and, worse still, consecutive 3rds being stretched to 10ths. Attempts to return to the nonrealistic but melodically superior original were made during the last quarter of the 20th century.

Cardillac. Opera by Hindemith, 1926, after a story by the fabulist E. T. A. Hoffmann, in which a wily craftsman murders his customers after they buy his jewels. It was subsequently revised according to the composer's later harmonic theory.

Cardew, Cornelius, English composer of extreme avant-garde tendencies; b. Winchcombe, Gloucester, May 7, 1936; d. after being hit by a car, London, Dec. 13, 1981. He sang in the chorus at Canterbury Cathedral until puberty; then studied composition with Howard Ferguson at the Royal Academy of Music in London (1953–57); in 1957 he went to Cologne and worked at the electronic studio there as an assistant to Karlheinz Stockhausen (1958–60). Returning to England, he organized concerts of experimental music; from 1963 to 1965 he was in Italy, where he had some private lessons with Goffredo Petrassi in Rome. In 1967 he was appointed to the faculty of the Royal Academy of Music in London. In 1969, together with Michael Parsons and Howard Skempton, he organized the Scratch Orch., a heterogeneous group for performances of new music, militantly latitudinarian and disestablishmentarian.

Under the influence of the teachings of Mao Zedong, Cardew renounced his modernistic past as a bourgeois deviation detrimental to pure Marxism, and subsequently attacked his former associate in a book ominously entitled *Stockhausen Serves Imperialism* (London, 1974). He also repudiated his own magnum opus, *The Great Learning,* orig. performed at the 1968 Cheltenham Festival, scored for a nonsinging chorus to the words of Ezra Pound's trans. of Confucius, a chorus which was admonished to bang on tapped stones, to whistle and shriek, but never to stoop to vocalizing. In the revised version of the work he appended to the title the slogan, "Apply Marxism-Leninism-Mao Zedong Thought in a living way to the problems of the present." This version was 1st performed by the Scratch Orch. in the Promenade Concert in London (1972).

His other works include *Volo Solo* for any handy musical instrument (1965); *3 Winter Potatoes* for piano and various assorted concrete sounds, as well as for newspapers, balloons, noise, and people working (Focus Opera Groups, London, 1968). He also publ. several pamphlets containing some confusing confutations of Confucius. In addition, he compiled a seminal manual, *Scratch Music* (London, 1970).

carezzevole (It.; Fr. *caressant*). Caressingly, soothingly.

carillon (Fr.; Ger. *Glockenspiel*). 1. A set of church bells suspended from a beam in the belfry, operated either by swinging them or playing them from a keyboard, with the keys connected to the clappers of the bells. Modern carillons may have as many as 50 bells and are capable of playing rapid scales, complete harmonies, and trills. 2. A tune played on this instrument; an instrumental piece imitating its effect. 3. A mixture organ stop.

carioca. Brazilian dance in a fast 4/4 time, derived from the rhythm of the samba, originating in the vicinity of Rio de Janeiro (*carioca* is a colloquial term for an inhabitant of that city).

Carissimi, Giacomo, important Italian composer; b. Marino, near Rome (baptized), Apr. 18, 1605; d. Rome, Jan. 12, 1674. From 1625 to 1627 he was organist at the Cathedral of Tivoli; from 1628 to his death, maestro di cappella in the Church of S. Apollinare in Rome; he also served as maestro di cappella of the Collegio Germanico in Rome. A prolific and original composer, he broke with the

Scene from Carmen

took courses with Vladimir Ussachevsky. At the same time he began working with the electronic engineer Robert Moog in perfecting the Moog Synthesizer. The result of their experiments with versified tone colors was a record album under the title *Switched On Bach* (1968), which became unexpectedly successful, especially among the wide-eyed, susceptible American youth, selling some million copies. This was followed in 1969 by *The Well-Tempered Synthesizer*, engineered entirely by Carlos. Then, at the age of 32, he accepted his sexual duality, a woman's psyche imprisoned in a man's body; he underwent a transsexual operation and, on St. Valentine's Day, 1979, he officially changed his 1st name from Walter to Wendy. She produced the film scores for *A Clockwork Orange*, *The Shining*, and *TRON*.

carmen (Lat.). In the Middle Ages, a song, lyric poem, or melody in a vocal composition.

Carmen. Opera by Bizet, 1875. The oft-repeated story that *Carmen* was a fiasco, and that Bizet expired of chagrin over it, is contradicted by chronology. Bizet died on the night of its 33rd performance, 3 months after its premiere, surely a very satisfactory run. With Gounod's *Faust* and Verdi's *Aida*, *Carmen* became one of the most successful operas in the repertory, continually produced all over the world. Nietzsche counterposed the spirit of *Carmen*, with its Mediterranean gaiety, passion, and drama, to the somber creations of the Nordic Wagner, once his idol. The action of *Carmen* takes place in Seville around 1820. Don José, a soldier, falls in love at 1st sight with a gypsy cigarette girl, Carmen, and deserts the army: all in vain, for Carmen abandons him for a bullfighter. Distraught, Don José stabs her to death. The most famous arias in Carmen are the bullfighter's victory song, *Toreador* (from Sp. *torero*), and Carmen's song, *Habanera* (often misspelled *Habañera*), borrowed unintentionally by Bizet from

Palestrina tradition, devoting himself to perfecting the monodic style, as is evidenced by his highly developed recitative and more pleasing and varied instrumental accompaniments. His MSS were dispersed at the sale of the library of the Collegio Germanico, and many are lost, but some printed works are still extant. There are oratorios (*Jephte*—his masterpiece, *Judicium Salomonis, Jonas, Balthazar*); 2 collections of motets à 2, 3, and 4 (Rome, 1664, 1667); masses à 5 and 9 (Cologne, 1663, 1667); cantatas; and individual pieces in several collections.

Carlos, Wendy (born Walter), American organist, composer, and electronics virtuoso; b. Pawtucket, R.I., Nov. 14, 1939. He played piano as a child; then studied music and physics at Brown Univ. and at Columbia Univ., where he a song by the Cuban Sebastian Yradier. Just how a Cuban song got into an opera with the action taking place in Seville remains a mystery.

Carmen Jones. Musical play, 1943, with a text by Hammerstein and a score preserved almost intact from Bizet's *Carmen*. In his modern version Hammerstein shifted the scene from Seville to a southern American town during World War II. Carmen is a worker in a parachute factory, Don José is a black corporal, and the toreador is a prize fighter. Don José kills Carmen outside a Chicago arena during her lover's fight for the heavyweight championship.

Carmichael, Hoagy (Hoagland Howard), American pianist and composer of popular music; b. Bloomington, Ind., Nov. 22, 1899; d. Rancho Mirage, Calif., Dec. 27, 1981. His ambition as a youth was to become a lawyer, and in fact he graduated from the Ind. Univ. Law School and played the piano only for relaxation. In 1929 he went to Hollywood but failed to obtain work as a musician. Working on his own he organized a swing band and composed songs for it. Although unable to write music professionally, he revealed a natural gift for melody and soon had success with such songs as *Riverboat Shuffle* and *Washboard Blues*. He made a hit with the song *Stardust*, which became the foundation of his fame and fortune. Among his other popular tunes were *Georgia On My Mind* (brought to the height of its popularity by Ray Charles), *Ivy*, *I Get Along Without You Very Well*, *Heart and Soul*, and *In the Cool, Cool, Cool of the Evening*, which won the Academy Award as the best movie song for 1951. He was also active as an actor in films and on television.

Carmina Burana. Scenic cantata by Orff, 1937, 1st performed in Frankfurt. The texts, in rhymed verse in a variety of dialects—Latin, French, and Provençal—date back to the 12th and 13th centuries. They were discovered in the Benediktbeuren Cloister in Bavaria, and the collection became known under the Latin name *Burana Sancti Benedicti*. Despite linguistic difficulty and occasional profanity in the selected texts, *Carmina Burana* became extremely popular; Orff later combined this work with *Catulli Carmina* (1943) and *Trionfi d'Afrodite* (1953) into the trilogy *Trionfi*.

Carnaval. Piano cycle by Schumann, op. 9 (1835). Schumann subtitled the work *Scènes mignonnes sur quatre notes*. Taking into consideration the work's extraordinary

popularity, it is mind-boggling that all this romantic display is manufactured artificially on the thematic foundation of 4 notes that spell the name of the town (Asch) where Schumann had a girlfriend. These thematic notes spell, in the German musical alphabet, A, S (*Es*, German for E-flat), C, and H (German for B-natural). The same town can also be spelled in 3 letter notes: AS (*As*, or A-flat), C, and H. Schumann weaves a colorful tapestry out of these letter-notes, creating 21 sections that include musical portraits of Chopin, Paganini, and Schumann's future wife, Clara. There is also a "silent" section entitled *Sphinxes*, which notates the "riddle" of the piece; that is, the 4 notes of the subtitle.

Carnaval des Animaux, Le. CARNIVAL OF THE ANIMALS, THE.

Carnaval Romain, Le. ROMAN CARNIVAL OVERTURE.

Carnegie Hall. The most famous concert hall in the U.S., opened in N.Y. in 1891 through endowment from the wealthy English-born magnate Andrew Carnegie (1835–1919), who built an immense fortune from successful investments in steel and oil. Before becoming a multi-millionaire, Carnegie publ. an essay, *Gospel of Wealth*, in which he outlined his philanthropic program of supporting education and art by establishing financial foundations. Tchaikovsky was the guest conductor at the opening of Carnegie Hall, 1st called Music Hall. Carnegie Hall is beloved by concert performers for its remarkable acoustics, although recent adjustments have been controversial. In the subculture of movies and rock, the name Carnegie Hall has assumed a magical aura as a passport to greatness in music.

Carnival (from Lat. *carne*, meat; + *vale*, from Lat. *levare*, abandon). Carnival is the occasion for eating meat for the last time before Lent. Many composers wrote pieces glorifying the carnival season: Berlioz produced an orch. work, *Roman Carnival Overture*; Liszt's 9th Hungarian Rhapsody is subtitled *Carnaval de Pest*; Saint-Saëns presented an ingenious suite, *The Carnival of the Animals*; and Schumann wrote a piano suite, *Carnaval*, subtitled *Scenes mignonnes sur quatre notes*.

Carnival. Musical by Bob Merrill, 1961, based on the motion picture *Lily*, about an orphan who falls in with a circus. Includes *Love Makes the World Go Round* and *Mira*.

carnival songs. A generic description of festive songs that mark Mardi Gras celebrations in Europe and South America. For the Florentine variety, see CANTI CARNASCIALESCHI.

Carnival of the Animals, The (*Carnaval des animaux, Le*). A "grand zoological fantasy" by Saint-Saëns, 1886 (premiered posthumously, 1922), marvelously witty and musically enchanting, scored for orch., piano, xylophone, and metal plates struck with a mallet. There are 14 pieces, making delicious fun of animals (and others), among which the composer includes pianists playing asinine scales. The cello solo for the 13th piece, entitled *The Swan*, has become a celebrated concert piece; it serves as accompaniment for a Pavlova dance, *The Dying Swan*. Although he completed the score in 1886, Saint-Saëns did not allow it to be performed publicly or publ. during his lifetime.

carol. A joyous Christmas song; the name may be derived from the French medieval *carole*, a round dance often accompanied by singing. The most common type, established in the 19th century, is in 4-part harmony, symmetrical in structure, and most often in a major key. More ancient forms preserve the style of polyphonic modality.

Carolan (O'Carolan), **Turlough,** Irish harper and song composer; b. near Nobber, County Meath, *c.* 1670; d. near Kilronan, Mar. 25, 1738. He was an itinerant harper who improvised Irish verses and tunes; these were publ. in various 18th-century collections of Irish music. He wrote around 220 orig. tunes.

Carousel. Musical play by Rodgers and Hammerstein, 1945; a fantasy in which a young man turns to crime, is killed, goes to purgatory, and returns to earth for a day to be redeemed by love. Includes *June Is Bustin' Out All Over*, *If I Loved You*, and *You'll Never Walk Alone*.

Carpenter, John Alden, American composer; b. Park Ridge, Chicago, Feb. 28, 1876; d. Chicago, Apr. 26, 1951. He received his B.A. degree from Harvard Univ. in 1897; studied music there with John K. Paine; entered his father's shipping supply business and from 1909 to 1936 was vice president of the firm. During his earlier years in business he continued his musical studies in Rome (1906) and in Chicago with Bernard Ziehn (1908–12); was made a Knight of the French Legion of Honor (1921); received an honorary M.A. from Harvard Univ. (1922) and an honorary Mus.Doc

from the Univ. of Wisconsin (1933). After his retirement from business in 1936 he devoted himself entirely to composing; in 1947 was awarded the Gold Medal of the National Inst. of Arts and Letters.

His 1st well-known work was the orch. suite *Adventures in a Perambulator* (1915). From his musical contacts abroad he absorbed mildly modernistic and impressionistic techniques and applied them to his music based on American urban subjects, adding the resources of jazz rhythms. His 1st work in this American idiom was a "jazz pantomime," *Krazy Kat*, after a well-known cartoon series (1921); he then wrote a large-scale musical panorama, *Skyscrapers* (1926), performed as a ballet and an orch. suite in America and abroad, attracting much critical comment as the 1st symphonic work descriptive of modern American civilization; as such, the score has historical significance.

Carreño, (Maria) **Teresa,** famous Venezuelan pianist, singer, and composer; b. Caracas, Dec. 22, 1853; d. N.Y., June 12, 1917. As a child she studied with her father, an excellent pianist; driven from home by a revolution, the family in 1862 settled in N.Y., where she studied with Gottschalk. At the age of 8 she gave a public recital in N.Y. She began her career in 1866, after studying with G. Mathias in Paris and A. Rubinstein. She lived mainly in Paris from 1866 to 1870; then in England. She developed a singing voice and made an unexpected appearance in opera in Edinburgh as the Queen in *Les Huguenots* (1872); was again in the U.S. in 1876, when she studied singing in Boston. For the Bolivar centenary celebration in Caracas (1885), she appeared as singer, pianist, and composer of the festival hymn, written at the request of the Venezuelan government; hence the frequent but erroneous attribution to Carreño of the national hymn of Venezuela, *Gloria al bravo pueblo* (actually composed in 1811 by J. Landaeta, and officially adopted as the Venezuelan national anthem in 1881). In Caracas she once again demonstrated her versatility, when for the last 3 weeks of the season she conducted the opera company managed by her husband, the baritone Giovanni Tagliapietra. After these musical experiments she resumed her career as a pianist; made her German debut in Berlin (1889); and in 1907 toured Australia. Her last appearance with an orch. was with the N.Y. Phil. (1916); her last recital was in Havana (1917).

She impressed her audiences by the impetuous élan of her playing, and was described as "the Valkyrie of the piano." She was married 4 times: to the violinist Emile Sauret (1873), Tagliapietra (1876), Eugene d'Albert (1892–95), and to Arturo Tagliapietra, a younger brother of Giovanni (1902). Early in her career she wrote a number of compositions, some of which were publ.: a string quartet; *Petite danse tsigane* for orch.; 39 concert pieces for piano; a waltz, *Mi Teresita*, which enjoyed considerable popularity; and other small pieces. She was one of the 1st pianists to play MacDowell's compositions in public; MacDowell took lessons from her in N.Y. She was greatly venerated in Venezuela; her mortal remains were solemnly transferred from N.Y., where she died, and reburied in Caracas, in 1938.

Carreras, José (Maria), prominent Spanish tenor; b. Barcelona, Dec. 5, 1946. He was a pupil of Jaime Francesco Puig at the Barcelona Cons. In 1970 he sang Gennaro opposite Caballé's portrayal of Lucrezia Borgia in Barcelona, and in 1971 made his Italian debut as Rodolfo in Parma, as well as his 1st appearance in London, in a concert performance of *Maria Stuarda* as Leicester. In 1972 he made his N.Y. City Opera debut as Pinkerton; he continued to sing there until 1975. He made his Metropolitan Opera debut in N.Y. as Cavaradossi in 1974; later that year he made his 1st appearance at Covent Garden, London, and in 1975 at La Scala, Milan.

In 1987 he was stricken with acute lymphocytic leukemia; after exhaustive medical treatment he appeared at a special Barcelona outdoor concert in 1988 that drew an audience of 150,000 admirers; that same year he founded the José Carreras Leukemia Foundation. In 1989 he sang in recital in Seattle and N.Y. and also returned to the operatic stage, singing the role of Jason in Cherubini's *Medea* in Mérida, Spain. On Sept. 24, 1989, he created the title role of Balada's *Cristobal Colón* in Barcelona. Among his other fine roles are Alfredo, Edgardo, Nemorino, Don Jose, Andrea Chenier, the Duke of Mantua, and Don Carlos. He is a member of the "3 Tenors" tour, with Domingo and Pavarotti.

Carry Me Back to Old Virginny. Song by James A. Bland (1854–1911), 1878. Influenced by Negro spirituals, it was until recently the official song of the state of Virginia. The African-American Bland learned to play the banjo and joined a minstrel troupe, improvising songs in the manner of Negro spirituals. From 1881 to 1901 Bland lived in England, enjoying excellent success, including a command performance for Queen Victoria, but he dissipated his savings and died in abject poverty. Ironically, although written by an African-American, the song has been attacked for its racial stereotypes and offensive language.

Carry Nation. Opera by D. Moore, 1966, 1st performed in the home state of the eponymous heroine. Carry Nation was a temperance fanatic who devoted her life to the fight against the "demon rum," carrying a small axe with which she bashed in the glass doors of saloons in her native Kansas. The libretto invents an episode about her marrying an unregenerate alcoholic.

Carte, Richard D'Oyly, English impresario; b. London, May 3, 1844; d. there, Apr. 3, 1901. He studied at Univ. College in London; wrote an opera, *Dr. Ambrosias*, and songs; later turned to music management; he represented, among others, Gounod, Adelina Patti, and the tenor Mario. He then became interested in light opera and introduced in England Lecocq's *Giroflé-Girofla*, Offenbach's *La Périchole*, and other popular French operettas. His greatest achievement was the launching of comic operas by Gilbert and Sullivan; he commissioned and produced at the Royalty Theatre their *Trial by Jury* (1875) and then formed a syndicate to stage other productions of works by Gilbert and Sullivan at the London Opéra-Comique Theatre. Dissension within the syndicate induced him to build the Savoy Theatre (1881), which subsequently became celebrated as the home of Gilbert and Sullivan productions, with Carte himself as the leading "Savoyard." He successfully operated the Savoy until his death; the enterprise was continued by his wife (Helen Lenoir) until her death in 1913; thereafter by his sons, and finally by his granddaughter; it was disbanded in 1982.

In 1887 Carte attempted to establish serious English opera through the building of a special theater (now known as the Palace Theatre), and the production in 1891 of Sullivan's grand opera *Ivanhoe*, followed by commissions to other English composers to write operas. Carte introduced many improvements in theatrical management, including the replacement of gaslight by electric illumination.

Carter, Benny (Bennett Lester), outstanding African-American jazz instrumentalist, bandleader, arranger, and composer; b. N.Y., Aug. 8, 1907. He was mainly autodidact as a musician; after learning to play the piano as a child, he took up the trumpet and the alto saxophone. He worked with various bands (1923–28) before gaining wide recognition as a leading arranger. He led his own band (1932–34), then went to London, where he was an arranger for the BBC dance orch. (1936–38); concurrently he was active as an instrumentalist, a bandleader, and a recording artist. Upon his return to the U.S. in 1938 he led his own orch. in N.Y. (until 1940); he then organized a big band and settled in Los Angeles (1942). After 1946 he devoted himself mainly to composing and arranging scores for films and television, and also worked as an arranger for major jazz singers.

He made occasional appearances as an instrumentalist in later years, including tours abroad, and made a number of recordings. He also assumed a new role as a teacher, giving lectures at various univs. and colleges. One of the outstanding jazz alto saxophonists of his day, Carter also shone as a trumpeter, trombonist, clarinetist, and pianist. In 1974 he was awarded an honorary doctorate from Princeton Univ.

Carter, Elliott (Cook, Jr.), highly respected American composer, innovator of metric modulation; b. N.Y., Dec. 11, 1908. After graduating from Horace Mann High School in 1926, Carter entered Harvard Univ., majoring in literature and languages; at the same time he studied piano at the Longy School of Music in Cambridge, Mass. In 1930 he devoted himself exclusively to music, taking up harmony and counterpoint with Walter Piston and orchestration with Edward Burlingame Hill; also attended in 1932 a course given at Harvard Univ. by Gustav Holst. He obtained his M.A. in 1932 and then went to Paris, where he studied with Nadia Boulanger at the Ecole Normale de Musique, receiving there a "licence de contrepoint"; in the interim he learned mathematics, Latin, and Greek.

In 1935 he returned to America; was music director of the Ballet Caravan (1937–39); gave courses in music and also in mathematics, physics, and classical Greek at St. John's College in Annapolis, Md. (1939–41); then taught at the Peabody Cons. in Baltimore (1946–48). He was appointed to the faculty of Columbia Univ. (1948–50) and taught at Yale Univ. from 1958 to 1962. In 1962 he was the American delegate at the East-West Encounter in Tokyo; in 1963 was composer-in-residence at the American Academy in Rome, and in 1964 held a similar post in West Berlin. In 1967–68 he was a professor-at-large at Cornell Univ. He held Guggenheim fellowships in 1945 and 1950, and the American Prix de Rome in 1953. In 1965 he received the Creative Arts Award from Brandeis Univ. In 1953 he received 1st prize in the Concours International de Composition pour Quatuor a Cordes in Liège for his 1st String Quartet; in 1960 he received the Pulitzer Prize for his 2nd String Quartet, which also received the N.Y. Music Critics' Circle Award and was further elected as the most important work of the year by the International Rostrum of Composers. He again won the Pulitzer, for his 3rd String

Quartet, in 1973. In 1985 he was awarded the National Medal of Arts by President Reagan.

His reputation as one of the most important American composers grew with every new work he produced; Stravinsky was quoted as saying that Carter's Double Concerto was the 1st true American masterpiece. The evolution of Carter's style of composition is marked by his constant preoccupation with taxonomic considerations. His early works are set in a neo-Classical style. He later absorbed the Schoenbergian method of composition with 12 tones; finally he developed a system of serial organization in which all parameters, including intervals, metric divisions, rhythm, counterpoint, harmony, and instrumental timbres, become parts of the total conception of each individual work. In this connection he introduced the term *metric modulation*, in which secondary rhythms in a polyrhythmic section assume dominance expressed in constantly changing meters, often in such unusual time signatures as 10/16, 21/8, etc. Furthermore, he assigns to each participating instrument in a polyphonic work a special interval, a distinctive rhythmic figure, and a selective register, so that the individuality of each part is clearly outlined, a distribution which is often reinforced by placing the players at a specified distance from one another.

Carter Family, The. (Guitar/autoharp/vocal: "Mother" Maybelle [Addington]; b. Nickelsville, Va., May 10, 1909; d. Nashville, Tenn., Oct. 23, 1978; vocal: A[lvin]. P[leasant]. Delaney Carter, b. Maces Spring, Va., Apr. 15, 1891; d. there, Nov. 7, 1960; autoharp/vocal: Sara Dougherty Carter, b. Flat Woods, Va., July 21, 1898; d. Lodi, Calif., Jan. 8, 1979.) Well-known country singing group, formed in 1927 by A. P. Carter, his wife, and his wife's cousin. Through recordings and radio broadcasts (1927–43) they led the way to the widespread popularity of mountain folk and country music; among their greatest successes were their versions of *Wildwood Flower, It Takes a Worried Man to Sing a Worried Song, Will the Circle Be Unbroken, Wabash Cannonball,* and *Amazing Grace.* In later years Maybelle appeared with her 3 daughters at the Grand Ole Opry in Nashville, where she displayed her talents as a guitarist, autoharpist, and songwriter. She also made appearances with her son-in-law, the singer Johnny Cash.

Carter, Ron(ald Levin), African-American jazz double-bass player; b. Ferndale, Mich., May 4, 1937. He took up the cello at 10 and the double bass at 17; then studied formally at the Eastman School of Music in Rochester, N.Y.

(B.Mus., 1959), where he played in its Philharmonia Orch., and at the Manhattan School of Music in N.Y. (M.Mus., 1961). After playing in the Chico Hamilton quintet, he did stints with Cannonball Adderley, Thelonious Monk, and others; he then was a member of Miles Davis's quintet (1963–68). In subsequent years he worked with the N.Y. Jazz Quartet and led his own quartet. He has explored bowing techniques in addition to the more typical jazz pizzicato. He publ. a method book for his instrument, *Building a Jazz Bass Line* (1966; 2nd ed., 1970).

Caruso, Enrico (Errico), legendary Italian tenor; b. Naples, Feb. 25, 1873; d. there, Aug. 2, 1921. He sang Neapolitan ballads by ear; as a youth he applied for a part in *Mignon* at the Teatro Fondo in Naples, but was unable to follow the orch. at the rehearsal and had to be replaced by another singer. His 1st serious study was with Guglielmo Vergine (1891–94); he continued with Vincenzo Lombardi. His operatic debut took place at the Teatro Nuovo in Naples (1894), in *L'Amico Francesco*, by an amateur composer, Mario Morelli. In 1895 he appeared at the Teatro Fondo in *La Traviata*, *La Favorita*, and *Rigoletto*; during the following few seasons he added *Aida*, *Faust*, *Carmen*, *La Bohème*, and *Tosca* to his repertoire.

The decisive turn in his career came when he was chosen to appear as leading tenor in the 1st performance of Giordano's *Fedora* (Teatro Lirico, Milan, 1898), in which he made a great impression. Several important engagements followed. In 1899 and 1900 he sang in St. Petersburg and Moscow; between 1899 and 1903 he appeared in 4 summer seasons in Buenos Aires. The culmination of these successes was the coveted opportunity to sing at La Scala; he sang there in *La Bohème* (1900), and in the 1st performance of Mascagni's *Le Maschere* (1901).

At the Teatro Lirico in Milan he took part in the 1st performances of Franchetti's *Germania* (1902) and Cilèa's *Adriana Lecouvreur* (1902). In the spring season of 1902 he appeared (with Melba) in Monte Carlo, and was re-engaged there for 3 more seasons. He made his London debut as the Duke in *Rigoletto* (Covent Garden, 1902) and was immediately successful with the British public and press. He gave 25 performances in London until 1902, appearing with Melba, Nordica, and Calvé. In the season of 1902–1903 Caruso sang in Rome and Lisbon; during the summer of 1903 he was in South America. Finally, in 1903, he made his American debut at the Metropolitan Opera, N.Y., in *Rigoletto*. After that memorable occasion, Caruso was connected with the Metropolitan to the end of his life. He trav-

eled with various American opera companies from coast to coast; he happened to be performing in San Francisco when the 1906 earthquake nearly destroyed the city. He achieved his most spectacular successes in America, attended by enormous publicity. In 1907 Caruso sang in Germany (Leipzig, Hamburg, Berlin) and in Vienna; he was acclaimed there as enthusiastically as in the Anglo-Saxon and Latin countries. (A complete list of his appearances is found in the biography by Key and Zirato, 1922.)

Caruso's fees soared from $2 as a boy in Italy in 1891 to the fabulous sum of $15,000 for a single performance in Mexico City in 1920. He made recordings in the U.S. as early as 1902; his annual income from this source alone netted him $115,000 at the peak of his career. He excelled in realistic Italian operas; his Cavaradossi and Canio became models which every singer emulated. He sang several French operas; the German repertoire remained completely alien to him; his only appearances in Wagnerian roles were 3 performances of *Lohengrin* in Buenos Aires (1901).

His voice possessed such natural warmth and great strength in the middle register that as a youth he was believed to be a baritone. The sustained quality of his BEL CANTO was exceptional and enabled him to give superb interpretations of lyrical parts. For dramatic effect he often resorted to the "coup de glotte" (which became known as the "Caruso sob"); here the singing gave way to intermittent vocalization without tonal precision. While Caruso was criticized for such usages from the musical standpoint, his characterizations on the stage were overwhelmingly impressive.

Although of robust health, he abused it by unceasing activity. He was stricken with a throat hemorrhage during a performance at the Brooklyn Academy of Music (1920), but was able to sing in N.Y. one last time, later that year. Several surgical operations were performed in an effort to arrest a pleurisy; Caruso was taken to Italy, but succumbed to the illness after several months of remission. He was known as a convivial person and a lover of fine food (a brand of macaroni was named after him). He possessed a gift for caricature; a collection of his drawings was publ. in N.Y. in 1922.

His private life was turbulent; a liaison (never legalized) with Ada Giachetti, by whom he had 2 sons, was painfully resolved by court proceedings in 1912, creating much disagreeable publicity; there were also suits brought against him by 2 American women. In 1906 the celebrated "monkey-house case" (in which Caruso was accused of improper behavior toward a lady while viewing the animals in Central Park) threatened for a while his continued success in America. In 1918 he married Dorothy Park Benjamin of

N.Y., over the strong opposition of her father, a rich industrialist. Caruso received numerous decorations from European governments, among them the Order of Commendatore of the Crown of Italy; the Legion d'honneur; and the Order of the Crown Eagle of Prussia.

Casals, Pablo (Pau Carlos Salvador Defilló), outstanding Catalan cellist and conductor; b. Vendrell, Catalonia, Dec. 29, 1876; d. San Juan, Puerto Rico, Oct. 22, 1973. He was the 2nd child of a progeny orig. numbering 11, 7 of whom died at birth. Legend has it that Casals barely escaped the same fate when the umbilical cord became entangled around his neck and nearly choked him to death; another legend (supported by Casals himself) is that he was conceived when Brahms began his B-flat-Major Quartet, op. 67 (of which Casals owned the original MS), and that he was born when Brahms completed its composition. (This legend is rendered moot by the fact that the quartet in question was completed and performed before Casals was born.) But even the ascertainable facts of the life of Casals make it a glorious legend.

His father, the parish organist and choirmaster in Vendrell, gave Casals instruction in piano, violin, and organ. When Casals was 11 he 1st heard the cello performed by a group of traveling musicians, and decided to study the instrument. In 1888 his mother took him to Barcelona, where he enrolled in the Escuela Municipal de Música. There he studied cello with José Garcia, music theory with José Rodoreda, and piano with Joaquin Malats and Francisco Costa Llobera. His progress as a cellist was nothing short of prodigious, and he was able to give a solo recital in Barcelona at the age of 14, in 1891; he graduated with honors in 1893. Albéniz, who heard him play in a cafe trio, gave him a letter of introduction to Count Morphy, the private secretary to Maria Cristina, the Queen Regent, in Madrid. Casals was asked to play at informal concerts in the palace, and was granted a royal stipend for study in composition with Tomas Bretón.

In 1893 he entered the Cons. de Musica y Declamación in Madrid, where he attended chamber music classes of Jesus de Monasterio. He also played in the newly organized Quartet Soc. there (1894–95). In 1895 he went

to Paris and, deprived of his stipend from Spain, earned a living by playing the 2nd cello in the theater orch. of the Folies Marigny. He decided to return to Spain, where he received, in 1896, an appointment to the faculty of the Escuela Municipal de Música in Barcelona; he was also principal cellist in the orch. of the Gran Teatro del Liceo. In 1897 he appeared as soloist with the Madrid Sym. Orch. and was awarded the Order of Carlos III from the Queen. His career as a cello virtuoso was now assured.

In 1899 he played at the Crystal Palace in London, and he was later given the honor of playing for Queen Victoria at her summer residence at Cowes, Isle of Wight. In 1899 he appeared as a soloist at a prestigious Lamoureux Concert in Paris; he played with Lamoureux again later that year, obtaining exceptional success with both the public and the press. He toured Spain and the Netherlands with the pianist Harold Bauer (1900–1901), then made his 1st tour of the U.S. (1901–1902). In 1903 he made a grand tour of South America; in 1904 he was invited to play at the White House for President Theodore Roosevelt. In 1906 he became associated with the talented young Portuguese cellist Guilhermina Suggia, who studied with him and began to appear in concerts as Mme. P. Casals-Suggia, although they were not legally married. Their liaison was dissolved in 1912; in 1914 Casals married the American socialite and singer Susan Metcalfe; they separated in 1928 but were not divorced until 1957.

Continuing his brilliant career, Casals organized, in Paris, a concert trio with the pianist Cortot and the violinist Thibaud; they played concerts together until 1937. Casals also became interested in conducting, and in 1919 he organized, in Barcelona, the Orquesta Pau Casals and led its 1st concert in 1920. With the outbreak of the Spanish Civil War in 1936, the Orquesta Pau Casals ceased its activities. Casals was an ardent supporter of the Spanish Republican government, and after its defeat vowed never to return to Spain until democracy was restored there. He settled in the French village of Prades, on the Spanish frontier; between 1939 and 1942 he made sporadic appearances as a cellist in the unoccupied zone of southern France and in Switzerland. So fierce was his opposition to the Franco regime in Spain that he declined to appear in

Pablo Casals, c. 1930s

COURTESY FRANK DRIGGS COLLECTION

countries that recognized the totalitarian Spanish government, making an exception when he took part in a concert of chamber music in the White House in 1961, at the invitation of President Kennedy, whom he admired.

In June 1950 he resumed his career as conductor and cellist at the Prades Festival, organized in commemoration of the bicentennial of the death of Bach; he continued leading the Prades Festivals until 1966. He made his permanent residence in 1956, when he settled in San Juan, Puerto Rico (his mother was born there when the island was still under Spanish rule). In 1957 an annual Festival Casals was inaugurated there. During all these years he developed energetic activities as a pedagogue, leading master classes in Switzerland, Italy, Berkeley, Calif., and Marlboro, Vt.; some of these sessions were televised. Casals was also a composer; perhaps his most effective work is *La sardana*, for an ensemble of cellos, which he composed in 1926.

His oratorio *El pessebre* (The Manger) was performed for the 1st time in Acapulco, Mexico, in 1960; in subsequent years he conducted numerous performances of the score. One of his last compositions was the *Himno a las Naciónes Unidas* (Hymn of the United Nations); he conducted its 1st performance in a special concert at the United Nations in 1971, 2 months before his 95th birthday. In 1957, at the age of 80, Casals married his young pupil Marta Montañez; following his death, she married the pianist Eugene Istomin (1975). Casals did not live to see the liberation of Spain from the Franco dictatorship, but he was posth. honored by the Spanish government of King Juan Carlos I, which issued in 1976 a commemorative postage stamp in honor of his 100th birthday.

Casella, Alfredo, significant Italian composer; b. Turin, July 25, 1883; d. Rome, Mar. 5, 1947. He began to play the piano at the age of 4 and received his early instruction from his mother; in 1896 he went to Paris, and studied with Diemer and Fauré at the Paris Cons.; won 1st prize in piano in 1899. He made concert tours as pianist in Europe, including Russia; appeared as guest conductor with European orchs.; in 1912 conducted the Concerts Populaires at the Trocadero; taught piano classes at the Paris Cons. from 1912 to 1915; returned to Rome and was appointed a prof. of piano at the Accademia di Santa Cecilia, as successor to Sgambati. In 1917 he founded the Soc. Nazionale di Musica (later the Soc. Italiana di Musica Moderna; since 1923 the Corporazione delle Musiche Nuove, Italian section of the ISCM).

In 1921 Casella made his American debut with the Philadelphia Orch. in the triple capacity of composer, con-

ductor, and piano soloist; he also appeared as a guest conductor in Chicago, Detroit, Cincinnati, Cleveland, and Los Angeles. He was conductor of the Boston Pops from 1927 to 1929, introducing a number of modern works but failing to please the public. In 1928 he was awarded the 1st prize of $3,000 given by the Musical Fund Soc. in Philadelphia; in 1934 won the Coolidge Prize.

In 1938 he returned to Italy, where he remained until his death. Apart from his activities as pianist, conductor, and composer, he was a prolific writer on music and contributed numerous articles to various publications in Italy, France, Russia, Germany, and America; he possessed an enlightened cosmopolitan mind, which enabled him to penetrate the musical cultures of various nations; at the same time he steadfastly proclaimed his adherence to the ideals of Italian art. In his music he applied modernistic techniques to the old forms; his style may be termed neo-Classical, but in his early years he cultivated extreme modernism.

Casey Jones. American railroad ballad, authorship disputed, composed after 1900. Based on an actual event that occurred in 1900, in which John Luther "Casey" Jones (1864–1900), a daring railroad engineer on the Cannonball Limited, told his stoker to jump before an impending fatal crash; in the collision he was either crushed or scalded to death. The song was popular in the vaudeville circuit.

Cash, Johnny, popular American country singer, guitarist, and songwriter of partly Indian descent (one-quarter Cherokee); b. in a railroad shack near Kingsland, Ark., Feb. 26, 1932. He worked as a water boy in a farmer's family; sang Baptist hymns in church; at the age of 17 won $5 at a local amateur talent contest. In 1950 he enlisted in the U.S. Air Force; served in Germany, returning to the U.S. in 1954. He learned to play the guitar while in the service; in 1955 began a series of appearances on the radio and various country circuits specializing in country-western music, and soon began to compose his own songs, both lyrics and tunes. He could never learn to read the notes, a fact of no importance in his professional life.

The subjects of his songs include the miseries of common folks as well as prison life. His most popular recordings include *Folsom Prison Blues* (inspired by his imprisonment overnight in El Paso on the charge of smuggling tranquilizer tablets from Mexico), *Ring of Fire*, *A Boy Named Sue*, *The Ballad of Ira Hayes, Understand Your Man*, and *I Walk the Line*. In 1968 he married the well-known country-music singer June Carter Cash (b. Maces Spring, Va., June 23,

1929). His daughter by an earlier marriage, Rosanne Cash (b. Memphis, Tenn., May 24, 1955), is a new-country singer and composer.

cassa (It.). Drum. Unless otherwise specified, the cassa is the snare drum. *Cassa chiara*, snare drum; *cassa grande* (*cassa, gran*), bass drum; *cassa rullante*, tenor drum.

cassation. An 18th-century instrumental form which combines the contiguous traits of a serenade, suite, divertimento, and sinfonia. There are many etymological theories regarding the term: from the It. *cassare*, dismiss, release; Fr. *casser*, break; *cassa*, drum; Ger. *gassatim gehen*, perform in the streets (18th century). The multimovement cassation had an extremely brief currency, limited to the latter 18th century.

castanets (Sp. *castaña*, chestnut). A pair of small concave pieces of wood or ivory, attached by a cord to a dancer's thumb and forefinger and struck together in time with the music. Of Spanish origin, the name refers to the wood traditionally used for the instrument. In the orch. version of the castanets, the small concave pieces are attached to a central piece of wood ending in a handle, by which they are held and shaken or struck against the palm.

Castelnuovo-Tedesco, Mario, greatly significant Italian-born American composer; b. Florence, Apr. 3, 1895; d. Los Angeles, Mar. 16, 1968. He studied at the Cherubini Inst. with del Valle (piano) and Pizzetti (composition); he began to compose at an early age; his 1st organized composition, *Cielo di settembre* for Piano, revealed impressionistic tendencies. He wrote a patriotic song, *Fuori i barbari*, during World War I. He attained considerable eminence in Italy between the 2 wars, and his music was often heard at European festivals. Political events forced him to leave Italy; in 1939 he settled in the U.S. In 1946 he became a naturalized citizen. He became active as a composer for films in Hollywood but continued to write large amounts of orch. and chamber music. His style is remarkably fluent and adaptable to the various moods evoked in his music, often reaching rhapsodic eloquence.

Castor et Pollux. Tragédie en musique by Rameau, 1737, concerning the mythical twins, brothers of Helen and Clytamnestra, who ended their days as a constellation.

castrato (It.; plur. *castratos, castrati*). A castrated adult male singer with soprano or alto voice. Young males were castrated at puberty in order to inhibit the maturation of their sexual glands, thereby preserving their high voices. This barbarous practice originated in the 16th century, not long before the development of opera, which created the demand for "angelic" voices in certain mythological roles such as Orpheus. In the 18th century the castratos became so famous that they could command large fees to sing in opera houses. Handel wrote special parts for the famous castratos Senesino and Nicolini. Perhaps the most celebrated castrato singer was Carlo Broschi, called Farinelli, who was engaged by the court of Philip II of Spain, who suffered from melancholy; Farinelli sang for him the same 4 songs every night for 25 years.

After 1750 the production of castrato singers became an increasingly hidden affair; it was finally completely forbidden in the latter 19th century. The story is often told of a pharmacy in Naples around 1820 which bore the sign "Qui si castrati ragazzi" (Boys are castrated here). A famous case of incomplete castration was that of the Italian singer G. F. Tenducci, who may have been a triorchis. So manly did he become that he managed to elope with an Irish mayor's daughter. She allegedly wrote a memoir in which she described her family life (they had children, too). The last castrato singer was Alessandro Moreschi (1858–1922) and who was known as the "Angelo di Roma" because of his celestially pure voice. There are recordings extant of Moreschi's singing made in 1903.

Cat and the Fiddle, The. Musical by Kern, 1931, in which a Rumanian composer inserts popular songs into his opera in order to woo an American woman. Includes *The Night Was Made for Love* and *She Didn't Say Yes*.

Catalani, Alfredo, greatly talented Italian composer; b. Lucca, June 19, 1854; d. Milan, Aug. 7, 1893. He studied music with his father, a church organist; in 1872 studied with Fortunato Magi and Bazzini at the Inst. Musicale Pacini in Lucca; then went to Paris, where he attended classes of Bazin (composition) and Marmontel (piano). He returned to Italy in 1873; in 1886 became the successor of Ponchielli as prof. of composition at the Milan Cons. It was in Milan that he became acquainted with Boito, who encouraged him in his composition; he also met young Toscanini, who became a champion of his music.

Catalani was determined to create a Wagnerian counterpart in the field of Italian opera, and he selected for his librettos fantastic subjects suitable for dramatic action. After several unsuccessful productions he finally achieved his ideal in his last opera, *La Wally*; he died of tuberculosis the year after its production.

catcalls. Derogatory hissing at a performance. The term is unfair to cats, who never meow derogatorily.

catch. A popular type of English social song, for 3 or more male parts and in the form of a canon or round; thus the need for each singer to "catch" or take up his part at the right instant. Catches were favorite songs in the aristocratic clubs of London in the late 16th, 17th, and 18th centuries, along with the GLEE. Such clubs often commissioned celebrated composers to write catches for them; they were usually collected and publ. in anthologies (by Ravenscroft, Hilton, Benson & Playford, Walsh & Hare).

Purcell, Blow, and Handel were among the many who composed catches. Among the earliest catches was *Three Blind Mice*; another begins with the famous line "Catch that catch can." The texts often contained humorous allusions to topical events, puns, and even mild obscenities, usually of a scatological character. The word *catch* itself is probably derived from the Italian CACCIA, or chase, because one voice "chases" another as in a canon.

catgut. Common but misleading name for gut strings, which are generally made from lamb intestines.

cats. 1. KATZENMUSIK (Ger., cat music) was the ultimate term of opprobrium used by ailurophobic critics; cat lovers were alienated by such comparisons. In his singing ballet L'ENFANT ET LES SORTILÈGES, Ravel introduces an amorous baritone tomcat and a nubile mezzo soprano kitten singing a fine atonal duet. In a modern piece, *Anatomy of Melancholy*, an anonymous composer has a cat solo; the cat player is instructed to pull the animal's tail at climactic moments. 2. *Cats* is also a 20th-century Americanism for musicians in popular bands and by extension can be applied to any human, mostly of the masculine gender. The term carries a bantering but friendly and even affectionate connotation.

Cat's Fugue. Harpsichord piece in G minor by Domenico Scarlatti, with a theme based on curiously unrelated rising intervals. According to a common but unverifiable story, this theme was inspired by a domestic cat walking up Scarlatti's keyboard. The British prof. Edward Dent tried to coax his cat to walk up Scarlatti's scale—but failed.

Catulli Carmina. A scenic cantata by Orff based on the poems of Catullus. It was 1st performed in Leipzig (1943) and was later incorporated into a triptych, *Trionfi* (1953).

Caturla, Alejandro García, Cuban composer and government official; b. Remedios, Mar. 7, 1906; d. assassinated there, Nov. 12, 1940. He studied with Pedro Sanjuán in Havana; then with Nadia Boulanger in Paris (1928); was founder (1932) and conductor of the Orquesta de Conciertos de Caibarién in Cuba; served as district judge in Remedios. His works have been performed in Cuba, Europe, and the U.S. In Caturla's music, primitive Afro-Cuban rhythms and themes are treated with modern techniques and a free utilization of dissonance, in works such as the *Suite of 3 Cuban Dances* (1928); *Bembé* for 14 Instruments (1929); *Dos poemas Afro-Cubanos* for Voice and Piano (1929; also orch.); *Yambo-O*, Afro-Cuban oratorio (1931); *Rumba for Orch.* (1931); *Primera suite cubana* for Piano and 8 Wind Instruments (1930); *Manita en el Suelo*, "mitologia bufa Afro-Cubana" for Narrator, Marionettes, and Chamber Orch., to a text by Alejo Carpentier (1934).

Cavalleria rusticana. Opera by Mascagni, 1890. The title means "rustic chivalry," not rural cavalry. The drama takes place in Sicily and is based on an actual event. A young villager is emotionally torn between his attachment to a local girl and his passion for a married woman. The unfortunate lover is confronted by the husband; a duel ensues, and he is killed. *Cavalleria rusticana* launched the vogue of the operatic verismo after its 1st production in Rome. Because *Cavalleria rusticana* is unusually short, it is often paired on the same evening with Leoncavallo's *Pagliacci*; in America the 2 are affectionately referred to as *Cav* and *Pag*.

Cavalli (Caletti), **Pier Francesco,** historically significant Italian opera composer; b. Crema, Feb. 14, 1602; d. Venice, Jan. 14, 1676. His father, Giovanni Battista Caletti (known also as Bruni), was maestro di cappella at the Cathedral in Crema; he gave him his 1st instruction in music; as a youth he sang under his father's direction in the choir of the Cathedral. The Venetian nobleman Federico Cavalli, who was also mayor of Crema, took him to Venice for further musical training; and as it was a custom, he adopted his sponsor's surname. In Dec. 1616 he entered the choir of S. Marco in Venice, beginning an association there which continued for the rest of his life; he sang there under Monteverdi; also served as an organist at Ss. Giovanni e

Paolo (1620–30). In 1638 he turned his attention to the new art form of opera, and helped to organize an opera company at the Teatro San Cassiano. His 1st opera, *Le nozze di Teti e di Peleo*, was performed there (1639); 9 more were to follow within the next decade.

In 1639 he successfully competed against 3 others for the post of 2nd organist at S. Marco. In 1660 Cardinal Mazarin invited him to Paris, where he presented a restructured version of his opera *Serse* for the marriage festivities of Louis XIV and Maria Theresa. He also composed the opera *Ercole amante* while there, which was given at the Tuileries (1662). He returned to Venice in 1662; in 1665 he was officially appointed 1st organist at S. Marco; became maestro di cappella there (1668).

After Monteverdi, Cavalli stands as one of the most important Venetian composers of opera in the mid-17th century. Cavalli also composed much sacred music; several works are available in modern eds.

cavata (It., extraction). An operatic arioso epitomizing the sentiment of a scene, in a regular meter and placed at the end of a recitative (*recitativo con cavata*). It eventually evolved into the CAVATINA.

cavatina (It.). A short song; an operatic aria without a 2nd section or DA CAPO. It is often preceded by an instrumental introduction and concludes with a CABALETTA.

CD. COMPACT DISC.

CD-ROM (Compact Disc with Read-Only Memory). A system of data storage that preserves an impressive amount of aural, written, and/or visual information on a CD-sized disk. The CD-ROM may be used on a properly equipped personal computer or through a MIDI into a synthesizer or sampler in order to access a large number of pre-recorded sounds.

Ce qu'on entend sur la montagne (What One Hears on the Mountain). Symphonic poem by Liszt, 1857, after a poem by Hugo. The 2 principal voices heard on the mountain represent the joyous song of nature and the depressed lament of man.

Cecilianism (after St. Cecilia, patron saint of music). A reform movement in Roman Catholic church music, intended to restore Roman Catholic choral polyphony in all its purity, as opposed to the romantic treatment of religious themes. The Cecilian movement had its inception in Germany in the 19th century, where numerous choral organizations were founded; later in the century Cecilianism spread to the U.S., cultivated mostly by German emigré societies and their publications.

cedendo (It.). Gradually growing slower, receding. *Céder* (Fr.), recede, slow down; *cédez* (Fr.), go slower.

celesta (Fr. *céleste*, heavenly). A keyboard instrument built on the principle of a glockenspiel, with keys activating hammers which strike the steel bars in its mechanism. Its keyboard, once limited to 4 octaves, has been expanded to 5, and has a soft ingratiating sound, which explains the name given it by its Parisian inventor, Auguste Mustel, in 1886. Tchaikovsky discovered the celesta during his visit in Paris; he was so enchanted with its sound that he warned his publisher not to tell any composers about its existence, specifically naming Rimsky-Korsakov and Glazunov as those who might use it before him. Tchaikovsky himself included a part for celesta in the movement describing the fairy chocolate-covered candy in his ballet *The Nutcracker*. Another type of celesta is the dulcitone, probably dating from the 1860s, which uses tuning forks instead of steel bars to produce sound.

céleste (Fr.). Celestial.

cell. A small group of notes, indicative of pitch or rhythm, serving as an organizing device. The term is usually applied to ATONAL or DODECAPHONIC MUSIC.

cello (It.; plur. *cellos, celli*). Abbrev. of VIOLONCELLO.

Cello Symphony. Concerto-like work by Britten, 1964, written for Rostropovich.

cembalo (It.). Harpsichord; pianoforte, clavier; formerly, dulcimer. The term was often used interchangeably with BASSO CONTINUO.

cencerros (Sp., lead-mule bell). Cuban cowbells, heard often in Latin American dance music and also used by Messiaen.

Cenerentola, La, o La Bontà in Trionfo (Cinderella, or the Triumph of Goodness). Opera by Rossini, 1817, based on the classic fairy tale.

cercar la nota (It., seek the note). A vocal practice in which the principal note is arrived at through a soft anticipatory grace note, thus achieving a better projection of the voice.

Ceremony of Carols, A. Choral cantata by Britten, 1942, for treble voices and harp. There are 9 carols (including *Deo Gratias*), a harp solo, and a "recession," a repetition of the opening "procession." The melodies all come from medieval chants.

Cerha, Friedrich, Austrian composer of the avant-garde; b. Vienna, Feb. 17, 1926. He studied violin with Vasa Prihoda and composition with Alfred Uhl at the Vienna Academy of Music (1946–51); also studied musicology and philosophy at the Univ. of Vienna (Ph.D., 1950). Upon graduation he became active in the modernistic movement as a violinist, conductor, and composer. In 1958 he organized (with Kurt Schwertsik) the Vienna concert ensemble Die Reihe, devoted to NEW MUSIC. In 1960 he became director of the electronic-music studio and a lecturer at the Vienna Academy, becoming a prof. in 1969. He was commissioned by the publisher of Alban Berg to complete the 3rd act of *Lulu* (1962–74); it was 1st performed at the Paris Opéra (1979). His own music pursues the aim of "atomization of thematic materials" as a means toward total integration of infinitesimal compositional quantities, with minimal variations of successive temporal units. His best-known work is the opera *Baal*, after Brecht (1973–81).

Čert a Káča. DEVIL AND KATE, THE.

Ces (Ger.). C-flat.

Ceses (Ger.). C double-flat.

Cesti, Antonio (born Pietro), renowned Italian composer; b. Arezzo (baptized), Aug. 5, 1623; d. Florence, Oct. 14, 1669. Although earlier reference works give his 1st name as Marc Antonio, this rendering is incorrect; he adopted the name Antonio when he joined the Franciscan order. He was a choirboy in Arezzo before joining the Franciscan order in Volterra in 1637; he served his novitiate at S. Croce in Florence and then was assigned to the Arezzo monastery. He is reported to have received his musical training from Abbatini in Rome and Citta di Castello (1637–40) and from Carissimi in Rome (1640–45). While in Volterra he was accorded the patronage of the Medici family.

His 1st opera, *Orontea* (Venice, 1649), was highly successful. He was active at the court of Archduke Ferdinand Karl in Innsbruck from 1652 to 1657; then was a tenor in the Papal Choir in Rome (1659–60). After being released from his vows, he quit the Papal Choir with the intention of returning to his court duties in Innsbruck. In spite of a threat of excommunication, he went to Innsbruck until the death of the Archduke in 1665 led to the removal of its musical entourage to Vienna in 1666. He was made assistant Kapellmeister at the Vienna court in 1666, and in 1668 he returned to Italy and served as maestro di cappella at the Tuscan court in Florence during the last years of his life.

Cesti was one of the most important composers of secular vocal music of his time. He composed mostly operas and cantatas; his most notorious work was his last opera, *Il pomo d'oro* (1668).

cesura (*caesura*; from Lat. *caedere*, cut). The dividing line between 2 melodic and rhythmical phrases within a period; called *masculine* or *feminine* dependent upon whether it occurs after a strong or weak beat.

Cetra, La. Set of violin concertos by Vivaldi, 1727 (op. 12).

Chabrier, (Alexis-) Emmanuel, famous French composer; b. Ambert, Puy de Dome, Jan. 18, 1841; d. Paris, Sept. 13, 1894. He studied law in Paris (1858–61); also studied composition with Semet and Hignard, piano with Edouard Wolff, and violin with Hammer. He served in the government from 1861; at the same time cultivated his musical tastes; with Duparc, d'Indy, and others he formed a private group of music lovers, and he was an enthusiastic admirer of Wagner. He began to compose in earnest and produced 2 light operas: *L'Etoile* (1877) and *Une éducation manquée* (1879).

In 1879 he went to Germany with Duparc to hear Wagner's operas; returning to Paris, he publ. some piano pieces; then traveled to Spain; the fruit of this journey was his most famous work, the rhapsody *España* (1883), which produced a sensation when performed by Lamoureux in 1884. Another work of Spanish inspiration was the *Habanera* for Piano (1885). In the meantime he served as chorus master for Lamoureux; this experience developed his knowledge of vocal writing; he wrote a brief cantata for mezzo-soprano and women's chorus, *La Sulamite* (1885), and his operas *Gwendoline* (1886), *Le Roi malgré lui* (1887), and *Briséïs* (concert performance, 1897; stage performance, 1899).

In his operas Chabrier attempted a grand style; his idiom oscillated between passionate Wagnerianism and a more conventional type of French stage music; although these operas enjoyed a succès d'estime, they never became popular, and Chabrier's place in music history is secured exclusively by his *España* and piano pieces such as *Bourrée fantasque* (1891); his *Joyeuse Marche* for orch. (orig. entitled *Marche française*, 1888) is also popular.

cha-cha. Latin American dance in an insistent binary rhythm, a variant of the mambo; sometimes called more emphatically *cha-cha-cha*. It had a wave of popularity in Europe and the U.S. in the 1950s.

chaconne (Fr.; Sp. *chacona*; It. *ciaccona*). 1. A Spanish dance in triple meter, imported from Latin America in the early 17th century. 2. An instrumental piece, derived from the dance of the same name, consisting of a series of variations above a ground bass not over 8 measures in length, in 3/4 time and slow tempo; a contrapuntal form of composition consisting of a series of variations on a theme in a definite harmonic progression. The chaconne is close in structure to and often difficult to distinguish from the PASSACAGLIA.

Chaconne

Chaliapin, Feodor (Ivanovich), celebrated Russian bass; b. Kazan, Feb. 13, 1873; d. Paris, Apr. 12, 1938. He was of humble origin; at the age of 10 he was apprenticed to a cobbler; at 14 he got a job singing in a chorus in a traveling opera co.; his companion was the famous writer Maxim Gorky, who also sang in a chorus; together they made their way through the Russian provinces, often forced to walk the railroad tracks when they could not afford the fare. Chaliapin's wanderings brought him to Tiflis, in the Caucasus, where he was introduced to the singing teacher Dimitri Usatov (1847–1913), who immediately recognized Chaliapin's extraordinary gifts and taught him free of charge, helping him besides with board and lodgings. In 1894 Chaliapin received employment in a summer opera company in St. Petersburg, and shortly afterward he was accepted at the Imperial Opera during the regular season. In 1896 he sang in Moscow with a private opera company and produced a great impression by his dramatic interpretation of the bass parts in Russian operas. He also gave numerous solo concerts, which were sold out almost immediately; young music lovers were willing to stand in line all night long to obtain tickets.

Chaliapin's 1st engagement outside Russia was in 1901, at La Scala in Milan, where he sang the title role in Boito's *Mefistofele*; he returned to La Scala in 1904 and again in 1908. In 1907 he made his American debut at the Metropolitan Opera, N.Y., as Mefistofele; then sang Méphistophélès in *Faust* and Leporello in 1908. He did not return to America until 1921, when he sang one of his greatest roles, Boris Godunov (1921); he continued to appear at the Metropolitan until 1929. He sang in Russian opera roles at Covent Garden, London, in 1913; returned to Russia in 1914 and remained there during World War I and the Revolution. He was given the rank of People's Artist by the Soviet government, but this title was withdrawn after Chaliapin emigrated in 1922 to Paris, where he remained until his death, except for appearances in England and America.

The critical attitude toward Chaliapin in Russia on account of his emigration changed when he was recognized as a great Russian artist who elevated the art of Russian opera to the summit of expressive perfection; numerous articles dealing with Chaliapin's life and career were publ. in the Russian language. He was indeed one of the greatest singing actors of all time; he dominated every scene in which he appeared, and to the last he never failed in his ability to move audiences, even though his vocal powers declined considerably during his last years. He was especially famed for his interpretation of the role of Boris Godunov; both dramatically and vocally he created an imperishable image. He was equally great as Méphistophélès and in the buffo roles of Don Basilio and Leporello. He also played the title role in a film version of *Don Quixote*. His last American recital took place in N.Y. in 1935.

chalumeau. 1. A single-reed, cylindrical-bore woodwind, related to the clarinet. The chalumeau was developed in the 17th century, orig. with no keys; these were added in the 18th century. While many view the chalumeau as the progenitor of the clarinet, the 2 instruments coexisted in the 18th century; the chalumeau was stronger in the lowest register than the clarinet of the era. By the end of the century the chalumeau had been superseded, but not before influencing the construction of the bass clarinet. 2. The lowest register of the clarinet.

chamber music. Vocal or instrumental music suitable for performance in a room or small hall; especially, quartets and similar concerted pieces for solo instrument ensembles.

chamber opera. An opera suitable for performance in a small hall, with a limited number of performers and accompanied by a chamber orch.

chamber orchestra. A small orch., with a much reduced string section and fewer winds and percussion.

chamber symphony. A sym. for a smaller orch., usually of lesser musical scale.

champagne aria. Don Giovanni's aria in act I of Mozart's eponymous opera, in which he orders Leporello to make preparations for the masked ball he's having. Giovanni probably drank sherry, however.

chance music. See CHANCE OPERATIONS; ALEATORY.

chance operations. The practice, highly developed by Cage, of composing music via chance means (throwing dice, consulting the *I Ching*, making use of random-number generators, etc.), resulting in works devoid of compositional taste or intentions.

Chandos Anthems. Anthems by Handel, 1717–18, written for the Duke of Chandos.

change. 1. In harmony, MODULATION. 2. In the voice, MUTATION. 3. Any melodic phrase or figure played on a chime of bells.

change-ringing. The art and practice of ringing a peal of bells in varying and systematic order.

changing note. CAMBIATA.

chanson (Fr.). 1. Song; used as a generic term for songs of any description, but specifically to describe the polyphonic type cultivated during the 15th and 16th centuries in France and the Netherlands. Such chansons were usually strophic in structure, with the same melody repeated for different stanzas. 2. A French equivalent to the LIED; also called MÉLODIE. 3. French popular song genres from the 17th century on.

chanson de geste (Fr., heroic song). A medieval lyric genre, of which *Chanson de Roland* is the most famous example. Such poems are fantastically long, sometimes numbering more than 20,000 lines in an unchanging meter. They were usually sung to monotonous melodic phrases, intoned by professional minstrels. Improvisation was apparently an integral feature of the CHANSON DE GESTS. Some melodic lines are preserved through quotations in *Jeu de Robin et Marion* by Adam de la Halle and *Aucassin et Nicolette*.

chansonette (Fr., small song). A French song of a light nature, often containing scabrous verses. The genre of chansonette flourished in France in the 19th century, in CAFÉS CHANTANTS.

Chansons de Bilitis. Song cycle by Debussy, 1897, to the sensuous poems by the French poet Pierre Louÿs, in imitation of Greek lyric poetry. Debussy wrote these songs using neo-Grecian modalities. Another work of the same title by Debussy is a melodrama for a reciting voice and a small ensemble which he composed in 1901.

chant. 1. A sacred song. 2. Anglican song, adapted to the Canticles and Psalms, consists of 7 measures, harmonized, the time-value of the single note constituting the 1st and 4th measures being lengthened or shortened to fit the words, whereas the others are sung in strict time. Each of its 2 divisions (of 3 and 4 measures, respectively) begins on a reciting-note and ends with a final. 3. Gregorian song, with a melody repeated with the several verses of biblical prose text; it has 5 divisions: (1) the intonation, (2) the 1st dominant, or reciting-note, (3) the mediation, (4) the 2nd dominant, or reciting-note, and (5) the final. 4. (Fr.). Song; singing; melody; tune. 5. The vocal part, as distinguished from the accompaniment.

Chant de Rossignol, Le (The Song of the Nightingale). Symphonic poem by Stravinsky, 1917, based on his opera *Le Rossignol*.

chanter. The melody-pipe of the BAGPIPE.

chanteur (Fr.). Singer (male); *chanteuse*, singer (female).

chantey (chanty). SHANTY.

Chantilly Lace. A 1958 hit by J. P. Richardson, aka "The Big Bopper," who died in the same airplane crash that took the life of Buddy Holly.

chapel (Fr. *chapelle*). 1. A church building or assembly room where congregants worship. 2. A company of musicians attached to the establishment of any distinguished personage, as in the Chapel Royal of England.

character piece (Ger. *Charakterstück*). A musical genre cultivated in the 19th century, usually applied to piano pieces and furnished with titles suggesting a mood, impression, scene, event, landscape, or pictorial subject. Among typical titles are *bagatelles, impromptus, moments musicaux, Lieder ohne Worte,* and *Albumblätter.* Schumann composed a number of character pieces under the titles *Fantasiestücke, Nachtstücke, Kinderszenen, Waldszenen,* and *Carnaval.* The genre was anticipated by Couperin and Rameau, who used such descriptive titles as *Les langueurs-tendres, La triomphante,* etc. Character pieces are usually short, symmetrically constructed, and not too difficult to perform. Modern composers abandoned the German model of character pieces but were not averse to using imaginative titles, as illustrated by Prokofiev's *Visions fugitives.* Scriabin appended titles of a mystical nature to some of his short piano pieces, *Flammes sombres, Desir,* and even *Poème satanique.*

charango (Sp.). Peruvian guitar, usually with 10 strings, many of which are tuned to the same note for greater sonority.

charivari. A raucous and cacophonous serenade calculated to ridicule or upset a pompous official or a honeymooning couple, a type of entertainment that arose in France in medieval times. The word itself is onomatopoeic, and its etymology is uncertain; its pronunciation is "shivaree."

Charles, Ray (born Ray Charles Robinson), outstanding African-American rhythm-and-blues and soul singer, pianist, arranger, and songwriter; b. Albany, Ga., Sept. 23, 1930. Born to impoverished parents, he was stricken with glaucoma and became totally blind at the age of 6; nevertheless, he began playing the piano and was sent to the St. Augustine (Fla.) School for the Deaf and Blind, where he received instruction in composition and learned to compose in Braille; he also learned to play the trumpet, alto saxophone, clarinet, and organ. He quit school when he was 15 and formed his own combo; he settled in Seattle, where he acquired a popular following. Shortening his name to Ray Charles to avoid confusion with the boxer Sugar Ray Robinson, he scored his 1st hit recording with *Baby Let Me Hold Your Hand* (1951). It was followed by *I've Got a Woman* (1955), *Hallelujah, I Love Her So* (1956), *The Right Time* (1959), *What'd I Say* (1959), *Hit the Road Jack* (1961), *1 Mint Julep* (1961), and *I Can't Stop Loving You* (1962); among his notable albums were *The Genius of Charles* (1960) and *Modern Sounds in Country and Western Music* (1962). He also toured widely and frequently performed on radio and television.

Charleston (after city in South Carolina). A syncopated binary dance tune, orig. in the all-African-American revue *Runnin' Wild* (1923), which launched one of the most obsessive dance fads in American history. The dance involves twisting knees and heels while hands and arms follow in alternation.

charme, avec (Fr.). With charm; gracefully.

Charpentier, Gustave, famous French opera composer; b. Dieuze, Lorraine, June 25, 1860; d. Paris, Feb. 18, 1956. He studied at the Paris Cons. (1881–87), where he was a pupil of Massart (violin), Pessard (harmony), and Massenet (composition). He received the Grand Prix de Rome in 1887 with the cantata *Didon*. Charpentier evinced great interest in social problems of the working classes, and in 1900 formed the society L'Oeuvre de Mimi Pinson, devoted to the welfare of the poor, which he reorganized during World War I as an auxiliary Red Cross society. He owes his fame to 1 amazingly successful opera, *Louise*, a "roman musical" to his own libretto (his mistress at the time was also named Louise, and, like the heroine of his opera, was employed in a dressmaking shop), produced at the Opéra-Comique in Paris (1900). The score is written in the spirit of naturalism and includes such realistic touches as the street cries of Paris vendors. Its success was immediate, and it entered the repertoire of opera houses all over the world; its 1st American production, at the Metropolitan Opera, N.Y., took place in 1921. Encouraged by this success, Charpentier wrote a sequel under the title *Julien* (1913), but it failed to arouse interest comparable to that of *Louise*.

Charpentier, Marc-Antoine, significant French composer; b. Paris, *c.* 1645–50; d. there, Feb. 24, 1704. He studied with Carissimi in Italy; after returning to Paris he became active as a composer to Molière's acting troupe; he was also in the service of Marie de Lorraine, the Duchess of Guise, later serving as her *haute-contre*, and finally as her *maître de musique* until her death (1688); likewise he was in the service of the grand Dauphin. Louis XIV granted him a pension (1683); he subsequently served as music teacher to Philippe, Duke of Chartres, was *maître de musique* to the Jesuit church of St. Louis, and finally held that post at Sainte-Chapelle (1698–1704). Charpentier was one of the leading French composers of his era, distinguishing himself in both sacred and secular works. His extensive output of sacred music includes 11 masses, 10 Magnificats, 4 Te Deums, 37 antiphons, 19 hymns, 84 psalms, and over 200 motets, many of which are akin to oratorios; he also composed sacred instrumental works. He wrote some 30 works for the stage, including the *Tragédies lyriques David et Jonathas* (1688) and *Medée* (1693), cantatas, overtures, ballet airs, pastorals, incidental pieces, *airs serieux*, *airs a boire*, etc.; he also composed secular instrumental pieces, including dances for strings.

Chasse, La. This is a nickname frequently used for pieces depicting the hunt. Among them are Haydn's 1st string quartet (No. 1, op. 1), Mozart's *Jagd Quartett* (K. 458), and Beethoven's Piano Sonata No. 3, op. 31. Both are in the key of B-flat major, the tonality of the natural horn used in the hunt and military exercises, and both have melodic and harmonic figures evoking hunting horns.

Chattanooga Choo Choo Song. Song by Harry Warren, 1941, from the film *Sun Valley Serenade*, made famous by Glen Miller's band.

Chausseur maudit, La (The Accursed Hunter). Symphonic poem by Franck, 1882, inspired by Bürger's German ballad in which a man hunts on a Sunday, misses church, and is himself hunted by demons.

Chausson, (Amedee-) Ernest, distinguished French composer; b. Paris, Jan. 20, 1855; d. Limay, near Mantes, June 10, 1899 (in a bicycle accident). He studied with Massenet at the Paris Cons., then took private lessons with César Franck and began to compose. The influence of Wagner as well as that of Franck determined the harmonic and melodic elements in Chausson's music; but despite these derivations, he succeeded in establishing an individual style, tense in its chromaticism and somewhat flamboyant in its melodic expansion. The French character of his music is unmistakable in the elegance and clarity of its structural plan. He was active in musical society in Paris and was secretary of the Soc. Nationale de Musique. He composed relatively little music; possessing private means, he was not compelled to seek employment as a professional musician.

Chávez (y Ramírez), Carlos (Antonio de Padua), distinguished Mexican composer and conductor; b. Calzada de Tacube, near Mexico City, June 13, 1899; d. Mexico City, Aug. 2, 1978. He studied piano as a child with Pedro Luis Ogazon; studied harmony with Juan B. Fuentes and Manuel Ponce. He began to compose very early in life; wrote a sym. at the age of 16; made effective piano arrangements of popular Mexican songs and also wrote many piano pieces of his own. His 1st important work was a ballet on an Aztec subject, *El fuego nuevo*, which he wrote in 1921, commissioned by the Secretariat of Public Education of Mexico. Historical and national Mexican subject matter remained the primary source of inspiration in many works of Chávez, but he rarely resorted to literal quotations from authentic folk melodies in his works; rather, he sublimated and distilled the melorhythmic Mexican elements, resulting in a sui generis style of composition.

In 1922–23 he traveled in France, Austria, and Germany, and became acquainted with the modern developments in composition. The influence of this period on his evolution as a composer is reflected in the abstract titles of his piano works, such as *Aspectos, Energia, Unidad.* Returning to Mexico, he organized and conducted a series of concerts of new music, giving the 1st Mexican performances of works by Stravinsky, Schoenberg, Satie, Milhaud, and Varèse. From 1926 to 1928 he lived in N.Y. In the summer of 1928 he organized the Orquesta Sinfónica de Mexico, of which he remained the principal conductor until 1949.

Works of modern music occupied an important part in the program of this orch., including 82 1st performances of works by Mexican composers, many of them commissioned by Chávez; Revueltas was among those encouraged by Chávez to compose. During his tenure as conductor Chávez engaged a number of famous foreign musicians as guest conductors, as well as numerous soloists. In 1948 the orch. was renamed Orquesta Sinfónica Nacional; it remains a permanent institution. Chávez served as director of the Cons. Nacional de Música from 1928 to 1933 and again in 1934; he was general director of the Inst. Nacional de Bellas Artes from 1946 to 1952.

Beginning in 1936 Chávez conducted a great number of concerts with major American orchs., and also conducted concerts in Europe and South America. Culturally Chávez maintained a close connection with progressive artists and authors of Mexico, particularly the painter Diego Rivera; his *Sinfonía proletaria* for chorus and orch. reflects his political commitment. In 1958–59 Chávez was Charles Eliot Norton Lecturer at Harvard Univ.; these lectures were publ. under the title *Musical Thought* (Cambridge, Mass., 1960); Chávez also publ. a book of essays, *Toward a New Music* (N.Y., 1937). Chávez is best known for his ballets—*El fuego nuevo, Los cuatro soles, Caballos de Vapor/HP, Antigona, La hija de Colquide,* and *Piramide*—and his syms., including *Sinfonía India,* Sym. No. 2 (1935), and *Sinfonía romántica,* Sym. No. 4 (1952).

Checker, Chubby (born Ernest Evans), African-American rock 'n' roll singer and dancer; b. Philadelphia, Oct. 3, 1941. Adopting the name Chubby Checker as a takeoff on Fats Domino, he first attracted a following with his recording of *The Class* (1959). Fame, however brief, was achieved with his recording of Hank Ballard's *The Twist* (1960); he then toured the U.S. to exploit the new dance craze. With the invasion of the Beatles in 1964, his career was aborted; in later years his performances were relegated to the U.S. nostalgia circuit.

Checkmate. Ballet by Bliss, 1937; a match between love and death; love loses; choreographed by Ninette de Valois.

Chef d'attaque (Fr., chief of the start). A term occasionally used by orch. players for the concertmaster; a more common French term is *premier violon.*

chef d'orchestre (Fr., chief of the orch.). Conductor. It is occasionally abbrev. *chef.*

cheironomy (Grk., law of the hand). An ancient system of leading the choir with the aid of a sign language, in which movements of the fingers indicate the tempo, intervals, and rhythm. Pictorial representations indicate the use of cheironomy in ancient Egypt, Coptic Christian, India, Israel, and Byzantine and Roman chant.

cheng. ZHENG.

Cherevichki (The Little Shoes). Opera by Tchaikovsky, 1887, the revised version of *Vakula, the Smith.*

Cherry, Don(ald), African-American jazz cornetist, trumpeter, and pianist; b. Oklahoma City, Nov. 18, 1936; d. Malaga, Spain, Oct. 19, 1995. He studied trumpet and harmony while attending high school in Los Angeles; began his career in 1951, appearing with Red Mitchell, Dexter Gordon, and other jazz musicians; he then went to N.Y., where he worked and recorded with Ornette Coleman; after 1963 he toured extensively in Europe, and also in Africa. A proponent of free jazz, he adopted instruments of other folk cultures in his performances. His stepdaughter, Neneh (b. Stockholm, Sweden, Mar. 10, 1964), enjoyed brief success with 1989's dance hit *Buffalo Stance.*

Cherubini, (Maria) Luigi (Carlo Zenobio Salvatore), famous Italian composer and teacher; b. Florence, Sept. 14, 1760; d. Paris, Mar. 15, 1842. He 1st studied music with his father, the *maestro al cembalo* at the Teatro della Pergola in Florence, and then composition with Bartolomeo Felici and his son Alessandro and with Bizarri and Castrucci. In 1778 he received a grant from the Grand Duke Leopold of Tuscany, which enabled him to continue his studies with Sarti in Milan. By this time he had composed a number of works for the church and also several stage intermezzi.

While studying with Sarti he wrote arias for his teacher's operas as well as exercises in the early contrapuntal style. His 1st operatic success came with *Armida abbandonata* (1782).

In the autumn of 1784 he set out for London, where he was commissioned to write an opera for the King's Theatre. *La finta principessa* was given there in 1785, followed by *Il Giulio Sabino* (1786), which brought him public acceptance and the admiration of the Prince of Wales. He made his 1st visit to Paris in the summer of 1785; there he was introduced to Marie Antoinette by the court musician Giovanni Battista Viotti; in the spring of 1786 he made Paris his home. He made 1 last visit to Italy to oversee the production of his opera *Ifigenia in Aulide* (1788). His 1st opera for Paris, *Démophon* (1788), was a failure, due largely to J. F. Marmontel's inept libretto and Cherubini's less than total command of French prosody.

In 1789 Leonard, a member of the Queen's household, assisted by Viotti, obtained a license to establish an Italian opera company at the Tuileries; Cherubini became its music director and conductor. After the company moved to a new theater in the rue Feydeau, he produced his opera *Lodoïska* (1791), with notable success; with this score he effectively developed a new dramatic style, destined to have profound impact on the course of French opera. The increased breadth and force of its ensemble numbers, its novel and rich orch.l combinations, and its generally heightened dramatic effect inspired other composers to follow his lead, particularly Mehul and Le Sueur.

With the French Revolution in full swing, the Italian Opera was disbanded (1792). Cherubini then went to Normandy, but returned to Paris in 1793 to become an inspector at the new Inst. National de Musique (later the Cons.). His opera *Medée* (1797), noteworthy for its startling characterization of Medea and for the mastery of its orchestration, proved a major step in his development as a dramatic composer. With *Les Deux Journées, ou Le Porteur d'eau* (1800) he scored his greatest triumph with the public as a composer for the theater; the opera was soon performed throughout Europe to much acclaim.

In 1805 Cherubini received an invitation to visit Vienna, where he was honored at the court. He also met the foremost musicians of the day, including Haydn and Beethoven. He composed the opera *Faniska*, which was successfully premiered at the Kärnthnertortheater (1806). After Napoleon captured Vienna, Cherubini was extended royal favor by the French emperor, who expressed his desire that Cherubini return to Paris. When Cherubini's opera *Pimmalione* (Nov. 30, 1809) failed to please the Parisians, Cherubini retired to the château of the Prince of Chimay, occupying himself with botanizing and painting.

At the request to compose a Mass for the church of Chimay, he produced the celebrated 3-part Mass in F Major. He subsequently devoted much time to composing sacred music. In 1815 he was commissioned by the Phil. Soc of London to compose a sym., a cantata, and an overture; he visited London that summer for their performances. In 1816 he was appointed cosuperintendent (with Le Sueur) of the Royal Chapel, and in 1822 became director of the Paris Cons., a position he held until a month before his death. During the last years of his life he composed 6 fine string quartets. In 1814 he was made a member of the Inst. and a Chevalier of the Legion d'honneur, and in 1841 he was made a Commander of the Legion d'honneur, the 1st musician to be so honored. He was accorded a state funeral, during which ceremony his Requiem in D Minor (1836) was performed.

Cherubini was an important figure in the transitional period from the Classic to the Romantic eras in music. His influence on the development of French opera was of great historical significance. Although his operas have not found a permanent place in the repertoire, several have been revived in modern times. His Sym. in D Major (1815) is still performed by enterprising conductors. He also played a predominant role in music education in France during his long directorship of the Paris Cons. His influence extended beyond the borders of his adoptive homeland through his valuable treatise *Cours de contrepoint et de fugue* (written with Halévy; Paris, 1835; Eng. trans., 1837).

As the all-powerful director of the Paris Cons., Cherubini established an authoritarian regimen; in most of his instruction of the faculty he pursued the Italian type of composition. He rejected any novel deviations from strict form, harmony, counterpoint, or orchestration; he regarded Beethoven's 9th Sym. as an aberration of a great composer's mind. He rejected descriptive music and demonstratively refused to attend rehearsals or performances of the *Sym. fantastique* by Berlioz, who was then a student at the Paris Cons. But his insistence on the letter of the musical law was nonetheless a positive factor; his treatise on counterpoint remained for many years a fundamental study of the art of composition.

chest register. The lower register of the male or female voice, the tones of which produce sympathetic vibration in the chest.

chest tone (chest voice). 1. Vocal quality of the chest register. 2. A manner of voice production recommended by Italian teachers for tenors and basses, subjectively felt as though traveling into the chest from the larynx; the corresponding expansion of the lungs produces a richer tone.

Chester. An American Revolutionary song by Billings, 1778. Although the tune is of a hymnal nature, it was adapted to the ringing revolutionary words, "Let tyrants shake their iron rod." It serves as the basis for a movement in Schuman's *New England Triptych*.

Cheval de bronze, Le (The Bronze Horse). Opera by Auber, 1835, a fantasy in which a prince on a bronze steed prevents a marriage between an elderly Mandarin and an unwilling Chinese maiden by taking the Mandarin into the heavens and transforming him into a statue, a state he is freed from only when he relinquishes his marital plans.

Chevalier, Maurice, popular French *chansonnier*, b. Paris, Sept. 12, 1888; d. there, Jan. 1, 1972. He began his career as a singer in Parisian cafés and music halls; then acted in films. In 1929 he went to Hollywood, and he soon established himself as one of the foremost musical comedy stars, speaking and singing in English with an ingratiating French accent, affecting a debonair mien, carrying a cane, and wearing a straw hat. His early films included *The Innocents of Paris* (1929), *Love Me Tonight* (1932), and *The Merry Widow* (1934). He remained in France during the German occupation and gave shows for French prisoners of war in Germany. This activity led to accusations of collaboration with the enemy, but Chevalier was able to explain his conduct as a desire to maintain the public spirit among Frenchmen, and he was exonerated. His later films included *Gigi* (1958), *Can-Can* (1960), and *Fanny* (1961). A special Academy Award was presented to him in 1958 in appreciation of his contributions to popular entertainment.

chevrotement (Fr., like a goat; Ger. *Bockstriller*). A rather uncomplimentary reference to a singer performing a goat trill. Chevrotement is occasionally used for special comic effects in opera.

chiarezza, con (It.). Clearly, distinctly, limpidly. *Chiaro,* clear.

chiave (It.). Clef. *Chiavette* (It.), little clefs. They were commonly used in the 16th and 17th centuries to change the range of the standard clef in order to avoid the use of extra lines above or below the staff. The baritone F clef, with the F on the 3rd line instead of the more common position of the 4th line, is an example. However, the C clefs placed on different lines of the staff are standard and are therefore not considered chiavette.

Chicago. Song by Fred Fisher, 1922.

Chichester Psalms. Work for chorus and orch. by Bernstein, 1965.

chiesa (It.). Church. *Sonata da chiesa,* an instrumental piece suitable for church performance.

A Child of Our Time. Oratorio by Tippett, 1944, to his own text, inspired by a tragic episode when a young Jew killed a Nazi diplomat in Paris shortly before World War II. To underline the theme of racial persecution, Tippett included in the score several quotations from Negro spirituals; it was 1st performed in London. During the war itself, Tippett served a brief prison term as a conscientious objector.

child prodigies. The idea of a child who possesses great musical talents was a popular one in the Romantic era, when childhood itself was revered as a time of behavior unspoiled by the hand of civilization. The files of old music magazines are strewn with erstwhile music prodigies. The *Musical Courier* of June 4, 1884, published this item: "A Boston Musical Wonder, Master Herbert Bitswell, is only 5 years old and yet has excited great astonishment by his remarkable performance of a Bach gavotte. He is considered a prodigy." Where is Master Bitswell now?

About 10 percent of child prodigies make good and become adult virtuosos. Jascha Heifetz was a child prodigy with flowing locks of hair, and he certainly did make good. So did Mischa Elman and Yehudi Menuhin. Among piano prodigies of our time, Josef Hofmann was undoubtedly the greatest. His American tour in 1887–88 was sensational. He also ran into trouble with the Soc. for the Prevention of Cruelty to Children, who objected to his heavy concert schedule. As a result of this agitation the artistic tours of Josef Hofmann were interrupted for a period of several years and he was given full opportunity to study and relax. He returned to America as an adult virtuoso at the age of 22.

While child violinists and child pianists are practically common occurrences in the musical-prodigy market, child composers are relatively rare. After all, it takes more ability and mature concentration to compose an organized piece of music than to play through a piano sonata or a violin concerto. Mozart's music composed at 15 shows unmistakable genius. Schubert wrote some of his greatest songs at 17.

Child conductors enjoyed a vogue in the 1940s. Among them only 1 continued a career in music: Lorin Maazel, who made several appearances with the N.Y. Phil. Orch. when he was just 11 years old. The newspaper *PM*, in its issue of July 6, 1941, succinctly described the event in the headline: "11-Year-Old Wrings Zing Out of Toscanini's Band." The boy showed considerable musical understanding and rhythmical vivacity as he led the orch. through a series of standard symphonies and overtures, and the orch. musicians were joking among themselves that their next conductor would probably be a trained seal. Maazel has had a distinguished career in conducting, but his story is unusual in the world of prodigies, most of whom never mature into concert artists.

Child, Francis, ballad collector and scholar; b. Boston, Feb. 1, 1825; d. there, Sep. 16, 1896. He is remembered for his *English and Scottish Popular Ballads* (1882), in which he collected more than 300 song texts, codified folklore, and compared variants. Although he is criticized for some of his editorial choices, particularly a Victorian attitude toward bawdiness, his collection is still the starting point for any serious student of this repertoire.

children's chorus. A choir of boys and girls, all singing treble parts, often called for in opera (*Carmen*) and less often in symphonic works.

Children's Corner. Suite of piano pieces by Debussy, 1908, written for his little daughter; the English title is explained by the fact that she had an English governess. There are 6 movements: the 1st, *Doctor Gradus ad Parnassum*, parodies Clementi's famous piano studies; the last, *Golliwog's Cakewalk*, is a rollicking pseudo-American ragtime, with a quotation from *Tristan und Isolde* thrown in.

Childs, Barney (Sanford), American composer; b. Spokane, Wash., Feb. 13, 1926. He studied intermittently with Leonard Ratner, Carlos Chávez, Aaron Copland, and Elliott Carter; obtained a B.A. degree in English from the Univ. of Nevada (1949), an M.A. from Oxford Univ. as a Rhodes Scholar (1955), and a Ph.D. in literature from Stanford Univ. (1959). He taught English at the Univ. of Arizona (1956–65); then served as dean of Deep Springs College in Calif. (1965–69). From 1969 to 1971 he taught

music theory at Wisconsin College-Cons. in Milwaukee; in 1971 joined the faculty at Johnston College of the Univ. of Redlands in Calif.; became a prof. there in 1973. Not overly concerned with public tastes and current fashions of cosmopolitan styles, he cultivates indeterminate structures. He ed., with Elliott Schwarz, *Contemporary Composers on Contemporary Music* (N.Y., 1967).

chimes. 1. A set of between 5 and 12 bells tuned to the scale, played by swinging either the bells themselves or clappers hung within them; also, a tune so played. 2. A set of bells and hammers played by a keyboard; a CARILLON 3. Tubular bells.

ch'in. QIN.

COURTESY OF K. H. HAN

Ch'in

chin rest. An oval plate of ebony attached to the edge of the violin or viola, to the left of the tailpiece.

Chinese blocks. Hollowed out polished boxes of resonant wood. When struck with a drumstick or mallet they produce a xylophonelike tone. Chinese blocks, which are actually Caribbean in origin, are popular in jazz and popular percussion; they can also be arranged in a set approximating a scale. Also called Chinese temple blocks, temple blocks, or woodblocks.

chirality. The etymology of *chirality* (from Grk. *heir*, hand) connotes the symmetry of human hands. Lord Kelvin, who coined the term, proposed the following definition: "I call any geometrical figure, or a group of points, 'chiral,' and say it has chirality if its image in a plane mirror, ideally realized, cannot be brought to coincide with itself."

Since music evolves in time and not in space, a composition that possesses chirality must consist of 2 symmetrical halves, the 1st note or chord being identical with the last, the 2nd with the penultimate, the 3rd with the antepenultimate, etc. In other words, musical chirality is achieved by the technique of specular reflection, or retrograde imitation. In spatial terms of musical performance, chirality exists between the 1st violin and 2nd violin sections in an orch., if they are placed in the once-standard positions to the left and to the right of the conductor.

chitarra (It.). A guitar. *Chitarrina*, small Neapolitan guitar.

chitarrone (It.). A large double-necked archlute.

chiuso, -a (It.). Closed. *A bocca chiusa* (It., with closed mouth), humming. Opposite: *aperto*, open.

chocalho (*kocalho*; Port.). Brazilian tube rattle in the form of a long cylinder filled with seeds or buckshot, held horizontally between the fingers of both hands and shaken rhythmically. The sound is similar to that of maracas. The chocalho accompanies the samba and other Brazilian dances.

Choëphores, Les (The Cup Bearers). Incidental music by Milhaud, 1935, to Claudel's libretto based on the 2nd part of Aeschylus's *Oresteia*.

choeur (Fr.). Chorus.

choir. 1. A company of singers, especially in a church. 2. A choral society. 3. In the Anglican church, the singers of the daily choral service, who sit divided on the *decani* and *cantoris* sides of the chancel. 4. A subdivision of a chorus; for example, the 1st and 2nd choirs in 8-part music. 5. Instrumental groups, such as a brass choir.

choirmaster. Leader of a choir.

Chopin, Frédéric

Incomparable Polish composer and genius of the piano who created a unique romantic style of keyboard music; b. Zelazowa Wola, near Warsaw, probably Mar. 1, 1810 (his certificate of baptism gives the date Feb. 22, 1810); d. Paris, Oct. 17, 1849. His father, Nicolas Chopin, was a native of Marainville, France, who went to Warsaw as a teacher of French; his mother, Tekla-Justyna Krzyżanowska, was Polish; he was orig. Fryderyk Franciszek. Chopin's talent was manifested in early childhood; at the age of 8 he played in public a piano concerto by Gyrowetz, and he had already begun to compose polonaises, mazurkas, and waltzes. He received his primary musical instruction from the Bohemian pianist Adalbert Żiwny, who resided in Warsaw at the time. A much more important teacher was Józef Elsner, director of the Warsaw School of Music, who gave him a thorough instruction in music theory and form.

Chopin was 15 years old when his Rondo for piano was publ. in Warsaw (op. 1). In the summer of 1829 he set out for Vienna, where he gave 2 highly successful concerts. While in Vienna he made arrangements to have his variations on Mozart's *Là ci darem la mano* (from *Don Giovanni*) for piano and orch. publ. by Haslinger (op. 2). It was this work that attracted the attention of Schumann, who saluted Chopin in his famous article publ. in the *Allgemeine Musikalische Zeitung* of late 1831, in which Schumann's alter ego, Eusebius, is represented as exclaiming, "Hats off, gentlemen! A genius!" The common assumption in many biographies that Schumann "launched" Chopin on his career is deceptive; actually Schumann was some months younger than Chopin and was referred to editorially merely as a student of Prof. Wieck.

Returning to Warsaw, Chopin gave the 1st public performance of his Piano Concerto in F Minor, op. 21, in 1830; later that year he was soloist in his Piano Concerto in E Minor, op. 11. Contrary to the usual listing of the E-minor Concerto as 1st and the F-minor Concerto as his

2nd, the composition of the F-minor Concerto preceded the E Minor. He spent the winter of 1830–31 in Vienna.

The Polish rebellion against Russian domination, which ended in defeat, determined Chopin's further course of action, and he proceeded to Paris, visiting Linz, Salzburg, Dresden, and Stuttgart on the way. He arrived in Paris in 1831 and was introduced to Rossini, Cherubini, and Paer. He also met Bellini, Meyerbeer, Berlioz, Alkan, Hugo, and Heine; he became particularly friendly with Liszt. Paris was then the center of Polish emigration, and Chopin maintained his contacts with the Polish circle there. He presented his 1st Paris concert in early 1832. He also taught the piano. The Paris critics found an apt Shakespearean epithet for him, calling him "the Ariel of the piano." In 1834 he went with Hiller to Germany, where he met Mendelssohn, Clara Wieck, and Robert Schumann. In July 1837 he went with Camille Pleyel to London.

In 1836 Chopin met the famous novelist Amandine Aurore Lucie Dupin Dudevant, who publ. her works under the affected masculine English name George Sand. They became intimate, even though they were quite incompatible in character and interests. Sand was involved in social affairs and held radical views; Chopin was a poet confined within his inner world; it has been said that she was the masculine and he the feminine partner in their companionship. In the winter of 1838–39 Chopin accompanied Sand to the island of Majorca, where she attended to him with total devotion; yet she portrayed him in her novel *Lucrezia Floriani* as a weakling. Indeed, she was quite overt in her reference to him as a lover; in a personal letter dated 1838 she said that she had difficulty in inducing him to submit to a sensual

Frédéric Chopin

COURTESY OF THE NEW YORK PUBLIC LIBRARY

embrace, and implied that she lived as an immaculate virgin most of the time they were together. They parted in 1847; by that time he was quite ill with tuberculosis; a daguerreotype taken of him represents a prematurely aged man with facial features showing sickness and exhaustion, with locks of black hair partly covering his forehead. Yet he continued his concert career.

He undertook a tour as pianist in England and Scotland in 1848; he gave his last concert in Paris in early 1848. *La Revue et Gazette Musicale* gives a precious account of the occasion: "The finest flower of feminine aristocracy in the most elegant attire filled the Salle Pleyel," the paper reported, "to catch this musical sylph on the wing." Chopin played his last concert in London, a benefit for Polish émigrés, in late 1848. He died the following year; Mozart's Requiem was performed at Chopin's funeral at the Madeleine, with Habeneck conducting the orch. and chorus of the Paris Cons. and Pauline Viardot and Lablache singing the solo parts. He was buried at Père-Lachaise between the graves of Cherubini and Bellini; however, at his own request his heart was sent to Warsaw for entombment in his homeland.

Chopin represents the full liberation of the piano from traditional orch.l and choral influences, the authoritative assumption of its role as a solo instrument. Not seeking orch.l sonorities, he may have paled as a virtuoso beside the titanic Liszt, but the poesy of his pianism, its fervor of expression, the pervading melancholy in his nocturnes and ballades, and the bounding exultation of his scherzos and études were never equaled. And, from a purely technical standpoint, Chopin's figurations and bold modulatory transitions seem to presage the elaborate transtonal developments of modern music.

Chopsticks. This celebrated children's piano exercise is played by 2 hands, each using a single finger, or else with both hands turned sideways imitating the chopping of wood, which explains the origin of the name. The piece evolved from a binary polka to a ternary waltz and was 1st published in England in 1877 under the title *The Celebrated Chop Waltz*, without an inkling of the composer's name; no research has found out the name of the perpetrator. The piece was known in Germany as *Koteletten Walzer*, in France *Cotelettes*, that is, cutlets. Several Russian composers published a set of variations on *Chopsticks*, and Liszt added a variation of his own. The story that a young female ward of Borodin's introduced him to the tune is charming, if perhaps fanciful.

choral. Relating or pertaining to a chorus, or to vocal concerted music. *Choral notes*, the square notes used for writing plainsong; *choral service*, a church service with music by the choir.

Choral Symphony. The popular name for Beethoven's mighty 9th Sym. in D Minor, op. 125, with a final chorus on Schiller's *Ode to Joy*. Beethoven worked on this sym. for nearly 10 years and completed it barely in time for the scheduled 1st performance in Vienna, 1824. It is easy to call the work a sublime masterpiece a century and a half after its creation, but at the time, it appeared as a curious challenge to an established tradition: a choral ending seemed unfit for an instrumental work. And what an ending! Beethoven forced the singers into the upper region of their ranges with a massive accompaniment of the orch. In fact, the entire sym. seems to partake of the spirit of a solemn oratorio. It opens with a series of open 5ths as if Beethoven hesitated to commit himself to a definite tonality.

There is another departure from tradition: Beethoven places the scherzo as the 2nd, instead of the 3rd, movement, as in his previous syms.; however, he had used such an alteration in his late piano sonatas. There follows the slow movement, leading to the choral finale which opens with a horrendously dissonant chord containing all seven notes of the D harmonic minor scale. Academic music analysts should not interpret this chord, however, as Beethoven's anticipation of total dissonance, for it is nothing more than a suspended in midair diminished-7th chord on the 7th degree of the scale resolving to everyone's satisfaction into the tonic.

Choral Symphony. Work by Holst, 1925, for soprano, chorus, and orch. The texts are taken from Keats.

chorale (Lat. *choralis*, of the chorus). Generic term for religious choral compositions employed in German Protestant churches. The historical development of the chorale within the German Protestant service is intimately connected with the activities of Luther himself, who had the Latin hymns of the Roman Catholic Church translated into the vernacular and made it possible for the congregation to take part in the singing. Most of these texts were direct translations from Latin, so that *Te deum laudamus* became

Herr Gott, Dich loben wir, and the CREDO opening became *Wir glauben all' an einen Gott*. But the Lutheran Church also boldly borrowed the melodies from secular songs of the people; one of the most popular was *Durch Adams Fall ist ganz verderbt* (Through Adam's Fall We Sinned All).

Collections of Lutheran chorales were published in Germany as early as 1524, when the Protestant movement was still fighting the stigma of heresy. Soon these chorales became the sources for polyphonic compositions, thus effectuating a link between chorale and instrumental music. The chorale reached its peak in the works of Bach, who harmonized hundreds of known chorale melodies and composed many more. Thus the purely practical movement of the Protestant chorale, begun in the early 16th century with the purpose of forming a repertory of songs in the German tongue in order to bring sacred music closer to the people, grew into a great art, embracing all genres of sacred and secular music.

chorale cantata. Any cantata in which harmonized chorales are used in some or all sections of the cantata, along with free recitatives and homophonic arias. Most of Bach's cantatas are of this type.

chorale prelude. An organ composition based on a chorale or hymn tune. The chorale prelude opens Protestant church services; in Roman Catholic usage this genre corresponds to the organ hymn.

chorale variations. A common term for variations on a chorale tune. Such variations proliferated, particularly in the 17th and 18th centuries, in the form of keyboard compositions. The rhythms of the variations can derive from the movements of the Baroque instrumental suite.

Choralmässig (Ger.). In the style of a chorale.

chord. 1. All tonal combinations containing 3 or more different notes. The major TRIAD (3-note chord) is colloquially described as a common chord; this does not mean that other chords are uncommon. Before the advent of modern music in the 20th century, triadic chords (chords derived from triads by inversion and distribution in various registers) constituted a statistical majority in all Classic and Romantic music. The final chords in a CADENCE in every composition written before 1900 are necessarily tonic triads or a unison, discounting duplications in octaves. Any chord that contains more than 3 different notes was regarded as a DISSONANCE, requiring resolution into a CONSONANCE according to traditional academic rules. Discrimination against unrestricted use of dissonant chords has been abolished in the music of the 20th century. 2. A harmony of from 3 to 7 tones forming an ascending series of diatonic 3rds (see "Chords," p. xxv). *Block, flat, or solid chord,* one whose notes are played simultaneously; *broken or rolled chord,* arpeggiated chord.

chord organ. An electronic keyboard instrument invented by Laurens Hammond and introduced in 1950 which allows harmonies to be produced by pressing the appropriate button.

chordophones (Grk., string sound). Older classification of instruments that produce their sound by means of vibrating strings stretched between fixed points.

chorea (Grk., row of dancers). A medieval term for a dancing melody, or dance in general.

choree (Grk.; Lat. *chorea*). In Greek prosody, a foot of 2 syllables in which the 1st is accented; also called TROCHEE. Modern examples include the polka and galop.

choreography (Grk. *choreo* + Fr. *graphie*). 1. The composition and arrangement of dances, particularly ballet and modern types. 2. Notation of such a composition, indicating the position and movement of the dancer(s).

choro. A generic term used in Brazil to describe urban instrumental music beginning in the 1870s; the music performed is played by an ensemble with a soloist. All kinds of music have been performed by choro groups: polka, waltz, modinha, samba, maxixe, and the Brazilian tango.

Chôros. Music written in a Brazilian style. The term is most closely associated with Villa-Lobos, who wrote 14 works for various instrumental groups under this name. The most engaging of the Chôros is No. 5 for Piano (1926), subtitled *Alma Brasileira* (Brazilian Soul).

chorus. 1. Ensemble of voices, consisting of sopranos, altos, tenors, and basses, abbreviated SATB. A female or boys' chorus consists of sopranos and altos; a male chorus consists of tenors, baritones, and basses. A double chorus often involves a spatially separated ensemble. In any case, there are usually several singers to a part. 2. A refrain in traditional music, popular songs, show tunes, jazz, and similar music.

chorus master. CHOIRMASTER.

Chou Wen-chung, remarkable Chinese-born American composer; b. Chefoo, June 29, 1923 (corresponding to May 16, 1923, using the lunar calendar in the Chinese Year of the Bear). He studied civil engineering at the National Univ. in Chungking (1941–45), then went to the U.S. on a scholarship to study architecture. Turning his attention to music, he studied composition with Slonimsky in Boston (1946–49), Luening at Columbia Univ. (M.A., 1954), and Varèse in N.Y. (1949–54); he also held 2 Guggenheim fellowships (1957, 1959). In 1958 he became a naturalized U.S. citizen. He was composer-in-residence at the Univ. of Illinois in Urbana (1958) and on the faculties of Brooklyn College (1961–62), Hunter College (1963–64), and Columbia Univ. (from 1964). In 1982 he became an elected member of the Inst. of the American Academy and Inst. of Arts and Letters. He ed. several Varèse works.

His music combines Chinese elements of structure and scale formation with free dissonant counterpoint related to Varèse's theory of "organized sound." He has written 3 orch.l works: *Landscapes* (1949, premiered 1953); *All in the Spring Wind* (1952–53); *And the Fallen Petals* (1955); *In the Mode of Shang* for Chamber Orch. (1956); *Metaphors* for Winds (1960–61); *Riding the Wind* for Winds (1964); *Pien,* chamber concerto for piano, percussion, and winds (1966); Suite for Harp and Wind Quintet (1950); *2 Miniatures from the T'ang Dynasty* for 10 Instruments (1957); *To a Wayfarer* for Clarinet, Harp, Percussion, and Strings (1958); *Soliloquy of a Bhiksuni* for Trumpet, Brass, and Percussion (1958); *The Dark and the Light* for Piano, Percussion, and Strings (1964); *Yü Ko* for 9 Instruments (1965); *Ceremonial* for 3 Trumpets and 3 Trombones (1968); *Yün* for 2 Pianos, 2 Percussion, and Wind Sextet (1969); vocal, choral, duo, and piano works; film scores.

Chout (The Buffoon). Ballet by Prokofiev, 1921, produced by the Ballets Russes in Paris. The complete and very long title is *A Tale of a Buffoon Who Outwitted 7 Other Buffoons.* To attempt to report that the plot derived from a Russian fairy tale in any rational manner would be futile, but the music is very exciting and provocative, with rhythms pushing and pulling in different directions and lyric passages full of poetic self-ridicule.

Christe eleison (Grk., Christ have mercy). Part of the Kyrie. See MASS.

Christian, Charlie, African-American guitarist; b. Bonham, Tex., July 29, 1916; d. N.Y., Mar. 2, 1942. His parents and his 4 brothers were musicians; as a child he played in the family band; at maturity he began playing an amplified guitar; from 1939 to 1941 he played in Benny Goodman's Sextet; later played with Gillespie and Monk. Christian was among the first jazz musicians to adopt the electric guitar, and his single-string leads were much admired and copied by other musicians. He was one of the finest early bebop performers; but he was stricken with tuberculosis and died at the age of 25.

Christie, William (Lincoln), harpsichordist and early music conductor, b. Buffalo, N.Y., Dec. 19, 1944. He studied with Igor Kipnis, Ralph Kirkpatrick, Palisca, Krigbaum, and Temperley. Moving to France in 1971, he performed with the Concerto Vocale, a Renaissance and Baroque ensemble; in 1978 he formed Les Arts Florissants (named after a M.-A. Charpentier opera), an ensemble dedicated to Baroque French and Italian repertory. His performances and recordings of works by Charpentier, Lambert, Lully, Monteverdi, Purcell, Rameau, Rossi, Gesualdo, Montéclair, and Bouzignac have been enthusiastically received in Europe and on the relatively few occasions his company has come to the U.S.

Christmas Concerto. Concerto Grosso in G Minor by Corelli, 1714, op. 12, No. 8.

Christmas Eve. Opera by Rimsky-Korsakov, 1895, on the same story as Tchaikovsky's *Vakula the Smith.* The village smith meets the marital precondition of his beloved by getting her a pair of the Czarina's slippers, thanks in part to his mother, a part-time witch.

Christmas Oratorio. A cycle of 6 cantatas by Bach, 1734–35, for performance on 6 separate days after Christmas Day (BWV 248).

Christoff, Boris (Kirilov), celebrated Bulgarian bass; b. Plovdiv, May 18, 1914; d. Rome, June 28, 1993. He sang in the Gusla Choir in Sofia, where he was heard by King Boris, who made it possible for him to go to Rome to study with Stracciari; he later studied in Salzburg with Muratti. He made his debut in a concert in Rome in 1946; that same year he made his opera debut there at the Teatro Argentina as Colline in *La Bohème.* He made his 1st appearance at La Scala in Milan in 1947, at Covent Garden in London in 1949, and his U.S. debut as Boris Godunov with the San Francisco Opera in 1956.

During his distinguished career he appeared at many leading opera houses, singing most of the principal bass roles in the operas of Verdi as well as such roles as Gurnemanz, Ivan Susanin, Hagen, Rocco, Konchak, and King Mark. He was most renowned for his dramatic portrayal of Boris, which recalled the interpretation of Chaliapin. His brother-in-law was Tito Gobbi.

Christophe Colomb. Opera by Milhaud, 1930, to a Claudel text. This 2-act extravaganza contains 27 scenes.

chromatic (Grk. *chroma,* color). 1. A progression of notes by semitone, or half step. 2. Tones foreign to a given diatonic scale or harmony.

chromatic signs. Accidentals; the sharp (♯), flat (♭), natural (♮), double sharp (𝄪), and double flat (𝄫).

chromatic torsion. Chromatic melodies are most effective when they are involuted toward a central tone in a spiral. The effect of constant vectorial changes during which such a central tone is approached alternately from above and from below may be described as chromatic torsion. An interesting example is the theme of the Queen of Shemaha in Rimsky-Korsakov's opera *Le Coq d'or,* in which chromatic torsion (and contortion) is effectively applied along the stems of diminished-7th chord harmonies.

chromaticism. A consistent and frequent use of chromatic progressions; the systematic insertion of intermediary notes between two diatonic degrees. In the key of C major every sharp and every flat would constitute a chromatic note, which is a semitone apart from the preceding diatonic degree or the following one. A distinction is made between a chromatic and a diatonic semitone. The interval from E to F is a diatonic semitone, but the interval between F and F-sharp is a chromatic one, because the same letter-note F is used twice, 1st as a diatonic degree of the scale and then as a chromatic note, F-sharp. In the progression F, F-sharp, G, the F-sharp constitutes a chromatic passing note. Ascending appoggiaturas, as represented by such embellishments as D-sharp going to E, or F-sharp going to G, or G-sharp going to A, are not necessarily chromatic if they occur in isolation. But if every note of the ascending C-major scale is embellished by an appoggiatura from below, the effect is considered chromatic.

In analyzing a musical composition from the viewpoint of chromaticism, it is necessary to consider the prevalence of diatonic melody and harmony relative to the frequency of chromatic passages. A convoluted melody weaving its way around principal triadic tones impresses the ear as highly chromatic, even when 2 consecutive semitones do not occur. On the other hand, a clearly tonal melody with a plethora of chromatic passage notes will register as diatonic if such a melody is harmonized in triads or 7th chords belonging to the principal key. Even such an obvious chromatic run as in Rimsky-Korsakov's *Flight of the Bumblebee* cannot be classified under the rubric of chromaticism because the underlying harmonies are triadic. But there can be no question as to the chromatic nature of the prelude to Wagner's *Tristan und Isolde*, for the harmonies proceed by semitones. In Bach's *Chromatic Fantasy*, the bass line moves upward in chromatic semitones, but because triadic harmonies occur on the strong beats of each measure, the feeling of tonality persists.

The music of the post-Wagnerian era was swept by a tidal wave of chromaticism; many composers abandoned key signatures altogether because the triadic resting point occurred too infrequently to justify their use. Chromatic melody and chromatic harmony achieved their ultimate development in the method of composition with 12 different notes of the chromatic scale related to one another, as formulated by Schoenberg. As a coup de grâce to diatonicism, and particularly triadic diatonicism, Schoenberg avoided using triads and their inversions, particularly the major triads. Still, chromaticism was not Schoenberg's aim; having rejected tonality as a governing principle, he organized both harmony and melody according to the new dodecaphonic principle uniting both melody and harmony within the framework of the 12 chromatic tones. A reaction to chromaticism developed in the 2nd quarter of the 20th century when diatonicism returned in the postmodern wave of neoclassicism.

Chronochromie (Color of Time). Orch.l work by Messiaen, 1960. Instrumental sonorities represent the color, and the rhythms represent time.

Chung, Kyung-Wha, brilliant Korean violinist, sister of Myung-Wha and Myung-Whun Chung; b. Seoul, Mar. 26, 1948. She began to study the violin as a small child; made her orch. debut in Seoul at the age of 9, playing the Mendelssohn Concerto; in 1961 she went to the U.S., where she studied with Ivan Galamian at the Juilliard School of

Music, N.Y. In 1967 she shared 1st prize with Pinchas Zukerman in the Leventritt Competition. In 1968 she appeared as soloist with the N.Y. Phil.; made her European debut in 1970 with the London Sym. Orch. She then embarked upon a wide-flung concert tour in Europe and Asia. She gave numerous trio concerts with her sister and brother, and also appeared as a soloist with her brother acting as conductor.

Chung, Myung-Wha, Korean-born American cellist, sister of Kyung-Wha and Myung-Whun Chung; b. Seoul, Mar. 19, 1944. She studied cello in Seoul; made her orch. debut there in 1957; in 1961 she went to the U.S., where she studied with Rose at the Juilliard School of Music, N.Y.; then attended a master class given by Gregor Piatigorsky at the Univ. of Southern Calif. in Los Angeles. She made her U.S. debut in San Francisco (1967) and her European debut in Spoleto (1969); she won 1st prize in the Geneva Competition (1971) the same year she became a naturalized U.S. citizen. She appeared as soloist with orchs. in Europe and America; also played trio concerts with her sister and brother.

Chung, Myung-Whun, Korean-born American pianist and conductor, brother of Myung-Wha and Kyung-Wha Chung; b. Seoul, Jan. 22, 1953. He played piano as a child, making his debut as soloist with the Seoul Phil. when he was 7; he then went to the U.S., where he studied with Nadia Reisenberg (piano) and Carl Bamberger (conducting) at the Mannes College of Music in N.Y., and at the Juilliard School (diplomas in piano and conducting, 1974); he received additional tutelage in conducting there from Sixten Ehrling (1975–78). He made his conducting debut in Seoul (1971), subsequently winning 2nd prize in piano at the Tchaikovsky Competition in Moscow (1974); he became a naturalized U.S. citizen in 1973.

He pursued a dual career as a pianist and conductor, and gave trio concerts with his sisters; was assistant conductor of the Los Angeles Phil. (1978–81) and chief conductor of the Saarland Radio Sym. Orch., Saarbrucken (1984–90). In 1986 he made his Metropolitan Opera debut in N.Y. conducting *Simon Boccanegra*. In 1989 he became music director-designate and in 1990 was confirmed in the most prestigious position, as music director of the new Bastille Opéra, Paris. This appointment, considering his relative youth and his absence from the customary engagements at European musical centers, created a sensation among impresarios and the press.

church modes. The octave scales employed in medieval and Renaissance church music. See AUTHENTIC MODES, PLAGAL MODES.

church sonata. SONATA DA CHIESA.

ciaccona (It.). CHACONNE.

Ciconia, Jean (Johannes), Walloon music theorist and composer; b. Liège, *c.* 1335; d. Padua, between Dec. 11 and Dec. 24, 1411. Little is known about his life; he was in Italy from 1358 to 1367; was in Liège from 1372 until 1401. In 1402 he went to Padua, where he was a canon. He wrote the treatise *De proportionibus musicae* (latter 14th century). Ciconia's significance lies in his early use of musical devices that did not become current until much later; he applied the technique of French isorhythmic style as well as canonic imitation.

Cid, Le. Opera by Massenet, 1885, after Corneille's play, based on the legendary 11th-century Spanish hero Rodrigo, victor over the Moors.

Cielito Lindo (Sp., beautiful little heaven). Popular Latin American song, stylistically Mexican, possibly written by Quirino Mendoza.

Cilèa, Francesco, Italian composer; b. Palmi, Calabria, July 23, 1866; d. Varazze, Nov. 20, 1950. He studied at the Naples Cons. (1881–89) with Cesi (piano) and Serrao (composition); taught piano there (1894–96), then harmony at the Istituto Musicale in Florence (1896–1904); was head of the Palermo Cons. (1913–16), then director of the Cons. di San Pietro a Majella in Naples (1916–35). He was a member of the Reale Accademia Musicale in Florence (1898) and a knight of the Order of the Crown of Italy (1893). He wrote relatively few works, most of them operas; his most famous is *Adriana Lecouvreur*, after Scribe (Milan, 1902).

Cimarosa, Domenico, famous Italian composer; b. Aversa, near Naples, Dec. 17, 1749; d. Venice, Jan. 11, 1801. He was the son of a stonemason. After his father's death, his mother placed him in the monastery school of the church of S. Severo dei Padri Conventuali in Naples, where he began his musical training with Father Polcano, the monastery organist. He then enrolled at the Cons. di S. Maria di Loreto (1761), where he studied voice, violin, and keyboard playing with Fenaroli, P. A. Gallo, and Carcais. Following his gradu-

ation in 1771 he studied voice with the castratro Giuseppe Aprile. His 1st opera, *Le stravaganze del conte*, was staged in Naples in 1772. From 1776 he composed operas at a prolific rate, producing about 65 works for the major Italian opera centers as well as those abroad. In 1779 he was named supernumerary organist of the Royal Chapel in Naples; in 1785 he became its 2nd organist. He also served for a time as maestro of the Ospedaletto, a cons. for girls in Venice.

In 1787 he was given the post of maestro di cappella to the court of Catherine the Great in St. Petersburg. During his Russian sojourn he wrote 3 operas and various other works for the court and the nobility. However, the court cut back on its funding of music and Cimarosa's contract was allowed to lapse in 1791. He proceeded to Vienna, where Emperor Leopold II appointed him *Kapellmeister*. He then composed his masterpiece, *Il matrimonio segreto*, which was premiered with great acclaim at the Burgtheater on Feb. 7, 1792. The Emperor was so taken by the opera that he ordered it to be repeated that evening, undoubtedly the most elaborate encore in operatic annals. The opera's fame spread throughout Europe, and Cimarosa returned to Italy in 1793 as one of the most celebrated musicians of the age. In 1796 he was appointed 1st organist of the Royal Chapel in Naples.

In 1799 he welcomed the republican movement in Naples by composing a patriotic hymn for the burning of the royal flag; however, the monarchy was restored later that year and Cimarosa's efforts miscarried. In consequence of this he was arrested in Dec. 1799 and sent to prison for 4 months. He was released only after the intervention of several prominent individuals. He then went to Venice, where he died while working on his opera *Artemisia*. It was rumored abroad that he had been poisoned by order of Queen Caroline of Naples; the rumor was so persistent— and popular feelings so pronounced—that the Pope's personal physician, Piccioli, was sent to Venice to make an examination; according to his sworn statement (Apr. 5, 1801), Cimarosa died of a gangrenous abdominal tumor.

Cimarosa was an outstanding composer of Italian opera buffa in his day. His melodic inventiveness, command of form, superb vocal writing, and masterly orchestration were unexcelled until Rossini arrived upon the scene.

cimbalom. A large dulcimer, typical of Hungarian and other Gypsy bands; the range is 4 octaves (from E to e^3). In the form of a trapezoid it is laid out on a table or other flat surface and is played with two mallets. A type with a chromatic scale and damper pedal was developed in the 1870s. Kodály uses the cimbalom in his orch.1 work *Háry János*;

Stravinsky employs it in his *Renard* and a provisional version of *Les Noces*. Liszt imitates the sound of the cimbalom in his Hungarian Rhapsody No. 11 for piano, specifically indicating the passage as *quasi-Zimbalo* (like a cimbalom).

Cimento dell'armonia e dell'inventione, Il (The Challenge Between Harmony and Invention). Set of violin concertos by Vivaldi, 1725.

Cinderella. Ballet by Prokofiev, 1945, based on the classic fairy tale.

Cinderella, or The Triumph of Goodness. Cenerentola, La, o La Bontà in Trionfo.

cinelli (It.). Cymbals.

Cinq Doigts, Les (5 Fingers). A group of 8 piano pieces by Stravinsky, 1921. Ostensibly written for little children, the pieces are dissonant and rhythmically difficult to play. The object is that once the 5 fingers are set on 5 keys of the piano, they don't have to be moved. They illustrate Stravinsky's desire to create a new simplicity in music without sacrificing its novel content.

cipher. 1. The practice of basing a composition on pitches that are tonal equivalents to letters of the alphabet; e.g., see B–A–C–H. 2. On the organ, a note that, owing to some derangement of the action, persists in sounding.

circatonalitarianism. The employment, whether successive or quaquaversal, of all 24 minor and major modalities in a single composition, by analogy with the biological term *circadian*. Circatonalitarianism structures are present literally in polytetrachords, which traverse 12 major or minor tetrachords.

circle of fifths (cycle of fifths). 1. A series of 5ths tuned (as on the piano) in equal temperament, so that the 12th 5th in the series has the same letter name as the 1st note. 2. A chart showing the 12 major and 12 minor keys, arranged by ascending 5ths and represented graphically by the face of a clock beginning at 12 o'clock with C major and A minor, each having no sharps or flats. The direction of sharp keys is clockwise, while the direction of flat keys moves counterclockwise. When the 6 o'clock position is reached, going in the sharp direction, the key of F-sharp major enharmonically meets G-flat major; similarly, its relative key—D-sharp minor—is changed to E-flat minor.

Of course it is theoretically possible to continue the accumulation of sharps in key signatures, moving clockwise, reaching the key of B-sharp major at the 12 o'clock position, with 12 sharps in the key signature. Similarly it is possible to continue accumulating flats in key signatures moving counterclockwise, making a full circle at the position of 12 o'clock in the key of D-double-flat major, with 12 flats in the signature. But key signatures of more than 7 sharps or flats are totally impractical and are never found in actual usage. Among exceptions are the scale passages in B-sharp major, enharmonically equal to C major, in the 4-hand piano arrangement of Stravinsky's *Le Sacre du printemps*; Ravel has a D-double-flat major scale outlined in the piano part of his Piano Trio. And in 1 amazing instance, in the score of his opera *The Legend of the Invisible City of Kitezh*, Rimsky-Korsakov allows himself to modulate clockwise until he is forced to use an accidental triple-sharp. See "The Keys," p. xxv.

circuitry. The stipulation of spatial, visual, or lighting requirements. Modern scores for mixed-media performances often have the appearance of blueprints for the electric circuits in scientific instruments and digital computers. An early example of musical circuitry is the part marked *Luce* in Scriabin's *Prometheus*, intended to fill the concert hall with changing colors corresponding to fluctuations in instrumental timbre. The detailed directions as to lighting given by Schoenberg in his monodrama *Erwartung* are in the same category. The Russian composer Nikolai Obouhov (1892–1954), who called himself "Nicolas L'illumine," designed an electronic instrument in the form of a cross, the *croix sonore*. In the circuitry of some ultramodern scores, the spatial distribution of instruments becomes a musical parameter. Carter, Foss, Penderecki, Christou, Bussoti, Xenakis, Cage and others wrote works stipulating the position of each instrument in relation to the rest of the ensemble.

circular breathing. Modern technique, primarily among vocalists and wind players, where the performer inhales breath through the nose while simultaneously exhaling breath through the mouth, thus sustaining sound for an indefinite length of time.

circular canon. A canon closing in the key a semitone above that in which it begins; 12 repetitions would thus carry it through the "circle" of 12 keys.

circus music. A type of band music associated with circuses; early on with fiddles and drums, later with bands of up to 36 players, mostly brass and timpani. The repertoire, like early extemporized accompaniment to silent film, is determined by the character of the acts being supported.

Circus Polka. An orch.l sketch by Stravinsky originally written for piano, commissioned by the Ringling Brothers' Circus to accompany the entrance of the elephants. It was arranged for band by David Raksin in 1942. Stravinsky conducted its 1st performance for sym. orch. in Cambridge, Mass. (1944).

Cis (Ger.). C-sharp.

Cis dur (Ger.). C-sharp major.

Cis moll (Ger.). C-sharp minor.

Cisis (Ger.). C-double-sharp.

citole (Ger. *Citole, Zitole*; It. *cetula*). A medieval and early Renaissance fretted string instrument with a body in 1 piece and 4 strings; plucked with a quill.

cittern (*cithern, cithren*; Fr. *cistre*; Ger. *Cister, Cither, Zitter*). A fretted string instrument with a pear-shaped body, strung with wire and played with a plectrum; used in the 16th and 17th centuries. There were many variants in the construction, but the most common instruments had 4 to 6 double-strung courses and a neck cut half away from behind the fingerboard; there are diatonic and chromatic models.

Čiurlionis, Mikolajus Konstantinas, Lithuanian composer and painter; b. Varena, Oct. 4, 1875; d. Pustelnik, near Warsaw, Apr. 10, 1911. He studied composition with Noskowski, and at the Leipzig Cons. with Carl Reinecke and Jadassohn. From 1902 till 1909 he was active in Warsaw as a choral conductor. His music reflects the Germanic Romantic tendencies, but he also developed interesting theories of so-called *tonal ground formations*, anticipating the serial methods of Schoenberg and Hauer. Čiurlionis was also a remarkable painter, in an abstract expressionist manner; many of his paintings carry musical titles, such as *Prelude and Fugue, Spring Sonata,* etc. His musical works include the symphonic poems *In the Forest* (1901) and *The Ocean* (1907); cantata, De profundis (1899); String Quartet; numerous piano pieces and songs.

clair (Fr.). Clearly, transparently.

Clair de lune. See SUITE BERGAMASQUE.

clang (Ger. *Klang*). A fundamental tone with its harmonics. *Clang-color, clang-tint,* tone color or timbre in relation to the harmonic spectrum.

clappers. A pair of wooden or metal disks or sticks held between the fingers and struck together to mark the beat in a dance; a rudimentary type of castanets, perhaps the most ancient percussion instrument.

Clapton, Eric (Patrick), also called "Slowhand"; prominent English electric blues and rock guitarist; b. Ripley, Surrey, Mar. 30, 1945. He played guitar as a youth; at 18 he joined the Metropolis Blues Quartet, a group which later changed its name to the Yardbirds. Clapton played with it for a short time but was turned off by its turn toward commercialism; in 1965 he joined John Mayall's Bluesbreakers; in another year he organized a trio named Cream, with bassist Jack Bruce and drummer Ginger Baker; the group turned the rock world upside down by introducing prolonged improvisational jams. When in the course of human events Cream soured, Clapton organized a "supergroup"— Blind Faith, with Baker, Stevie Winwood, and Rick Grech—but like so many men of little faith, Blind Faith soon gave up the ghost; Clapton's spiritual hymn *In the Presence of the Lord* helped maintain the flame briefly. After a brief fling with Delaney and Bonnie, Clapton formed Derek and the Dominoes, which received a certified Gold Award in 1971 with its album *Layla.* The group disbanded after a year or so of feverish activity. Depressed by these recurrent failures, Clapton went into crooning, fully aware that he was no Mick Jagger. His album titles expressed his pessimism, as in *E.C. Was Here, There's 1 in Every Crowd,* and *No Reason to Cry.* In 1979, after a long period of doldrums, he hit the jackpot with *Lay Down Sally.* He also paid a debt to the middle-class fascination with coke by covering the tunes *Tulsa Time* and *Cocaine;* he was eventually able to kick his own drug habit. In 1980 he finally found his niche with the album *Just One Night;* subsequent successful albums include *Another Ticket* (1981), *Money and Cigarettes* (1983), *August* (1986), and *Unplugged* (1992). In 1995 he scored a hit with *Tears in Heaven,* a song partially inspired by the death of his son, who fell from an apartment window.

claque (Fr., clapping). Mercenary applause, hired by operatic stars, bosomy prima donnas, self-inflated tenors, and occasionally even seemingly normal pianists and some desperate violinists. The practice of engaging a claque began in the early 19th century in Italy; it rapidly spread into France, even into otherwise snotty Victorian England, and by international infection caught on in America. Claques failed to prosper in Germany, perhaps because Germany regarded its music seriously. Occasionally an ambitious opera star would engage an anticlaque to drown out a rival's claque. Well-paid enthusiasm might spill out onto the street, with opera lovers unharnessing the horses of a prima donna's carriage and pulling the carriage to the artist's home by manpower. A list for services circulating Paris in the middle of the 19th century quoted the following prices:

Applause sufficient for a
single curtain call . . . . 150 francs

Overwhelming applause. . . . . 225 francs

Hissing a rival singer. . . . . 250 francs

Ovation after the last act, serenading before the window of the artist's home, price by special arrangement.

The claquers were officially banned at the Metropolitan Opera House in N.Y. in 1935 but apparently still prospered as late as 1960, at the cost of up to $100 for a group of vociferous young males on Saturday afternoons.

clarinet

〰〰 〰〰 〰〰 〰〰 〰〰

A transposing woodwind instrument derived from the 18th-century CHALUMEAU, and a standard member of the classical orch. since the latter part of the 18th century. The instrument is 1st mentioned in 1710. It has a cylindrical tube of African blackwood pierced by 18 holes, 13 being closed by keys. Its compass comprises 3 octaves in 4 different registers: low (chalumeau), medium (throat, break), high (clarinetto), and extreme. The clarinet (It. *clarinetto, clarino*; from Lat. *claro, clear*; Ger. *Klarinette*; Fr. *clarinette*) is a single-reed instrument, as contrasted with the oboe and the bassoon, both double-reed woodwind instruments. It is a vertical pipe that has a beak at one end and a bell-shaped aperture at the other. The player blows into the beak; a number of holes vary the length of the instrument, enabling it to change pitch. Unique among wind instruments, the acoustic spectrum of clarinet tone reveals only the odd-numbered harmonics, producing both its special timbre and the difficulties in constructing an instrument capable of overblowing the higher pitches in tune.

The modern clarinet is a rather late addition to the family of woodwind instruments; as an orch.l instrument it did not come into usage until the middle of the 18th century. The Bohemian composer Johann Stamitz was the 1st to include a clarinet part in an orch.l score; in 1755 he wrote a "sym. with a clarinet and double basses." The clarinet is the most expressive and the most versatile instrument of the woodwinds; it is capable of attaining a zephyrlike waft in the low and middle registers, and an overwhelming fortissimo in the upper register.

The written range of the clarinet is from E below the treble clef to the high G or beyond above the treble clef (i.e., $e–g^3$). It is a transposing instrument, which means that the written note is automatically raised or lowered; the most commonly used clarinet is the soprano in B-flat, so that the written note C sounds B-flat (for the A clarinet, the written C sounds A, etc.). A clarinet in C was formerly much in use, but because of the technical arrangement of the instrument, it was awkward to play in tonalities which have several sharps or flats in the key signature. The modern clarinet avoids these technical difficulties, for the B-flat clarinet automatically provides 2 flats in the key signature and the A clarinet provides 3 sharps in the key signature. Thus the player uses the B-flat clarinet for scores that have flats and the A clarinet for those that have sharps. As with other transposing instruments, the key signatures are affected; e.g., if a work is written in the key signature of 5 flats, the clarinet in B flat needs only 3 flats; on the other hand, when a clarinet player has to play a work written in a key of 4 sharps, the clarinet in A will automatically deduct 3 sharps and leave the clarinet player with only 1 sharp in the key signature. That is why in orch.l scores key signatures in the clarinet parts differ from those in the strings. Some modern composers prefer to write orch.l clarinet parts in the conductor's score without transposition, while writing the individual clarinet parts in B flat and A. This saves the conductor the trouble of figuring out the proper transposition but still provides the correct transpositions to clarinet players themselves.

The clarinet family includes 2 small (sopranino) clarinets, tuned in D and E-flat, which transpose, respectively, a major 2nd and a minor 3rd up. The most striking example of the clarinet in D appears in the score of *Till Eulenspiegels* by Strauss, where it portrays the famous prankster of the title. The B-flat clarinet is more common than the A clarinet, especially as modern clarinet virtuosos are able to transpose without much difficulty. Similarly, parts for the small clarinet in D are often played on the more common clarinet in E-flat. The clarinet in F transposing down a 5th was originally called the basset horn; in later years the alto clarinet in F, or Heckelphone, was developed; it appears rarely in orch.l scores. The bass clarinet in B-flat transposes an octave below the common clarinet. There also exists a contrabass clarinet

Clarinet

which transposes 2 octaves lower than either of the common clarinets in B-flat and A. Playing on the contrabass requires exceptionally strong lungs, and, on the rare occasions that it is required, there is usually a special pedal provided that blows in additional air. Ironically, the standard instrument is known as the Boehm clarinet, although the modern clarinet was cocreated (early 1840s) by the clarinetist Klosé and the maker Buffet *jeune*, and the German flutist had nothing to do with clarinets.

A large repertory of music written for the clarinet exists. Stamitz was only one of the Mannheim composers to write for the new instrument; Mozart bemoaned the absence of clarinets at Salzburg in 1778. He soon had 2 fine clarinets (the Stadler brothers) and wrote the 1st significant corpus of clarinet music. Among the most popular clarinet concertos are those by Mozart, Weber, Spohr, Nielsen, Debussy (*Première rapsodie*), Hindemith, Copland, and Musgrave. Gershwin's *Rhapsody in Blue* is practically a double concerto for clarinet and piano; the opening clarinet solo reaches a high B-flat, approached by a glissando, an effect that only modern virtuosos are capable of achieving. The clarinet was an essential instrument in jazz ensembles through the Dixieland/New Orleans, Chicago/ "hot," and the swing/big band eras. Stravinsky wrote his EBONY CONCERTO for the clarinetist Woody Herman; the title uses the slang term for clarinet, *ebony stick*.

clarinet stop. See CRUMHORN.

clarino. 1. The high register of the trumpet, where it is possible to produce a complete diatonic scale in natural harmonics. 2. The long-tubed Baroque high trumpet, capable of fast tempo and clear articulation, made obsolete by the modern trumpet. 3. A 4' reed organ stop of shrill, piercing tone; clarion stop.

Clarke, Rebecca (Thacher), English-born American composer and violist; b. Harrow, Aug. 27, 1886; d. N.Y.,

Oct. 13, 1979. She studied violin with Hans Wessely at the Royal Academy of Music (1902–1904) and composition with Stanford at the Royal College of Music (1904–10) in London; she then switched to the viola, taking a few private lessons from Tertis and becoming the 1st female member of Henry Wood's Queen Hall Orch. (1912). In 1928 she formed the English Ensemble, with which she played until 1929. She married James Friskin in 1944; she then lived in N.Y. Her fine music, comprising entirely chamber works, was quite advanced, being on the fringe of atonality in outline but remaining firmly rooted in English

Impressionism. For some of her compositions she used the name Anthony Trent.

Her greatest fame came from tying for 1st place with E. Bloch for the 1919 Coolidge Competition (Viola Sonata); the award eventually went to Bloch, due in large part to Mrs. Coolidge's discomfort with the notion of a woman composer equal to any man. Clarke's works include: String Quartet (1924); *Three Irish Country Songs* for Voice and Violin (1926); *Prelude, Allegro, and Pastorale* for Clarinet and Viola (1942); *Combined Carols* for String Quartet and Strings (1941). Works with piano: Sonata for Violin (1909); *Morpheus* for Viola (1917); Sonata for Viola (1919); Piano Trio (1921); *Epilogue* for Cello (1921); *Rhapsody* for Cello (1923); *Midsummer Moon* for Violin (1924); *Passacaglia on an Old English Tune* for Viola (1941); over 60 songs.

clarsach (Gael.). IRISH HARP.

Classic era (from Lat. *classicus*, of the highest rank). The classical music style dating *c.* 1750–1825. It was preceded by the ornate Baroque style and ended with the expansion of the Romantic period of composition. Stylistically, Classic music is distinguished by the symmetry of form, set in either binary or ternary structures, strict observance of the proper sequence of tonalities in modulation, incisive but relatively simple rhythms, articulate polyphony, and harmonic euphony. Instrumental technique in the Classic era was conservative; virtuosity was encouraged as long as it served the dignified formality of the general design. The Romantic period that followed shifted the emphasis from clarity of form to a humanistic concern for emotional expression. Since the formulas of Classic harmony, melody, and rhythm were standardized to a considerable degree, composers of the period were able to turn out hundreds of syms., concertos, sonatas, and dozens of operas, cantatas, and other works, all tailored to a fairly uniform model, no matter how different were their stylistic contents.

The external attire of men of the 18th century was an aspect of their artistic uniformity. Portraits of 18th-century composers show them invariably adorned with wigs; the Classic era itself has become known derisively as the *Zopf* (wig) era. Wigs, perukes, and pigtails disappeared early in the 19th century. The paintings of Beethoven show his tousled hair, which he did not try to cover with a queue. Like all historical concepts, the Classic era does not yield to temporal delimitation. The roots of Beethoven's music were firmly lodged in the spirit of the Classic, while his last period bears the traits of Romanticism; a similar dichotomy

applies to the music of Schubert. To account for this historic indeterminacy, the term *Vienna Classicism* was introduced to describe the productions of composers active in Vienna between 1800 and 1830. Inevitably, composers of the 20th century, weary of the endless self-projections of the Romantic composers, turned for relief to the clear, unambiguous, and, in some respects, impersonal ways of the 18th century. A modern version of the Classic era arose under the guise of NEOCLASSICISM.

classical music. Colloquially, any highly evolved music where a significant written element has helped to preserve it, as opposed to popular or folk music, whose survival has depended on some form of oral tradition. For better or worse, classical music is also called *serious music, highbrow music, cultivated music,* or *art music.* As a stylistic concept it derives from the ancient Roman notion of *classis* (Lat., aristocratic pedigree), suggesting order, purposeful behavior, high morality, aesthetic perfection, productivity, efficiency, and the ability to create attractive artifacts. Renaissance scholars applied the term to the arts, emphasizing those sought-after qualities, as they found in the surviving literature, architecture, and statuary of ancient Greece and Rome. However, the term *classical music* does not apply exclusively to the period of Haydn, Mozart, and Beethoven (*c.* 1750–*c.* 1825), which in this dictionary is called the Classic period. (Similarly, "romantic" is a qualitative assessment; "Romantic" is a 19th-century style period.)

classical suite. See SUITE.

Classical Symphony. Sym. No. 1 in D Major by Prokofiev, 1917, one of the earliest and most popular neoclassical works.

classicism. A historically recurring aesthetic emphasizing purity of design, perfection of form, and the meeting of the highest cultivated demands, applied to literature, art, and music. These qualities were connected in the minds of historians with the remote ages, particularly of Greece and Rome. Negative aspects of ancient society were overlooked, so as not to detract from the artistic glory that was Greece and the grandeur that was Rome. The flowering of the arts in the middle of the 2nd millennium, during the Renaissance, was marked by the renascence of interest in the Greek and Roman cultures. The emergence of the art of opera at the threshold of the 17th century was the intellectual outgrowth of the search for the artistic essence of Greek tragedy. Since the dramatic performances in ancient Greece were accompanied by music, the theorists of opera urged a return to monodic simplicity in melody and rhythm and the abandonment of the intricate polyphony of the period prior to the birth of opera. See also NEOCLASSICISM.

clausula (Lat. *claudere*, conclude). Certain formalized endings in medieval vocal polyphony. Clausulae are usually sung to a single vowel or syllable derived from a melisma of a sacred chant such as Alleluia. The singing of a clausula signalized the termination of a chant or a polyphonic work and thus served a definite function in performance. During the Renaissance period the distinction between the clausula and the cadence tended to disappear. Yet there is a distinction, namely that the cadence signifies a homophonic, rather than a polyphonic, ending in a harmonic setting. During the Renaissance the distinction between the cadence and clausula tended to disappear.

clavecin (Fr.; It. *clavicembalo*). A harpsichord or virginal.

claves (Sp.). A percussion instrument with a sharp sound produced by a pair of sticks of resonant polished hardwood struck 1 against the other; used in much Latin American popular music.

clavichord (Lat. *clavis*, key + Grk. *chorda*, string). A keyboard instrument popular during the Renaissance and Baroque periods, particularly in Germany, where it was the favored domestic instrument. A precursor of the pianoforte, it differs in action from the latter in having, instead of hammers, upright brass wedges called tangents on the rear end of the keys; upon pressing a key, the tangent strikes the wire and remains pressed against it until the finger is lifted, causing only 1 section of the string to vibrate. It thus differs in construction from its musical siblings, the harpsichord and the virginal, in that the strings are not plucked but struck; it is therefore closer to the sound production of a modern piano.

The clavichord has a delicate intimate sound much softer than that of the harpsichord, and it possesses the unique capacity of producing a peculiar vibrato that can be governed by varying the pressure on the keys even after they are depressed (BEBUNG). Its range was between 3 and 5 octaves. During the Baroque era composers designated strung keyboard music as being for CLAVIER; in some cases the term may have been valid for both harpsichord and clavichord; the 18th century seems to have used the term primarily for

the clavichord. The problem of precise attribution remains ambiguous. While the harpsichord has retained its significance in performance contexts, the clavichord has retreated to the sidelines.

clavier. 1. The keyboard or manual of any keyboard instrument; used in this way from the early 16th century. 2. Any strung keyboard instrument. This spelling was used in the late 17th and 18th centuries; in the 19th century *clavier* generally referred to the piano; in 20th-century Germany the spelling was changed to *Klavier*.

clavier de récit (Fr.). Swell manual.

clef (Fr., key). A character set in the staff at the beginning of a composition to fix the pitch or position of 1 note, and thus of the rest.

Two clefs are used in piano music, the G clef (🎼), indicating the position of the note G above middle C on the 2nd line, and the F clef (𝄢), indicating the position of the note F below middle C on the 4th line. The G clef is also called treble or violin clef, because it is the only clef used by the violin; the F clef is called bass clef, because it covers the bass register. The present shape of the G clef evolved from the Gothic capital letter *G* (𝕲); the F clef was 1st indicated as a red line; it later evolved from the capital letter *F*.

There is also a group of clefs which indicate the position of middle C on the staff. The present shape of the C clef (𝄡) evolved from the letter *C*. The most common C clefs are the viola clef, placing middle C on the 3rd line, and the tenor clef, with middle C on the 4th line. The viola clef is used in viola parts and occasionally in trombone parts; the tenor clef is occasionally used in cello and bassoon parts. Several C clefs are obsolete, among them the soprano clef, with middle C on the 1st line, and the baritone clef, with middle C on the 5th line of the staff.

Obviously the lower the clef is posted the more room it affords to high notes; conversely, when a clef is placed high on the staff the available range lies in the low register. A combined form of the tenor clef and the treble clef is sometimes used in the tenor parts of operatic scores to replace the inaccurate G clef, which covers the register an octave above the common tenor range and is best suited to soprano parts. Bach made use of various C clefs even in his keyboard compositions. His Invention No. 15 in F Major is notated in the soprano clef for the right hand and in the tenor clef for the left. This notation is apt to startle a piano-minded clef reader who happens to come upon Bach's Inventions in the facsimile edition. See also "The Clefs," p. xxiii.

Clementi, Muzio (baptized Mutius Philippus Vincentius Franciscus Xaverius), celebrated Italian pianist and composer; b. Rome, Jan. 23, 1752; d. Evesham, Worcestershire, England, Mar. 10, 1832. He began to study music as a child with Antonio Buroni, and at the age of 7 commenced studies with the organist Cordicelli. He later studied voice with Giuseppe Santarelli. By Jan. 1766 he was organist of the parish San Lorenzo in Damaso. About this time Peter Beckford, cousin of the English novelist William Beckford, visited Rome; he was struck by Clementi's youthful talent and, with the permission of Clementi's father, took the boy to England. For the next 7 years Clementi lived, performed, and studied at his patron's estate of Stepleton Iwerne in Dorset.

During the winter of 1774–75 Clementi settled in London, making his 1st appearance as a harpsichordist in a benefit concert (1775). He then appears to have spent most of his time as harpsichordist at the King's Theatre, where he conducted operatic performances. In 1779 his 6 sonatas, op. 2, were publ., which brought him his 1st public success, both in England and on the Continent. In 1780 he embarked on a tour of the Continent, giving a series of piano concerts in Paris; in 1781 he continued his tour with appearances in Strasbourg, Munich, and Vienna. It was during his stay in Vienna that the famous piano contest with Mozart took place at court before Emperor Joseph II (1781). In 1786 several of his syms. were performed in London, only to be eclipsed by the great syms. of Haydn. In 1790 he retired from public performances as a pianist, but he continued to conduct orch. concerts from the keyboard. After 1796 he appears to have withdrawn from all public performances, devoting himself to teaching, collecting large fees. He lost part of his fortune through the bankruptcy of Longman and Broderip in 1798; however, with John Longman he formed a partnership on the ruins of the old company and became highly successful as a music publisher and piano manufacturer; his business acumen was keen, and he remained most successful with subsequent partners during the next 3 decades.

From 1802 to 1810 he traveled extensively on the Continent, pursuing business interests, teaching, composing, and giving private concerts. While in Vienna in 1807 he met Beethoven and arranged to become his major English publisher. He returned to England in 1810, and in 1813 helped organize the Phil. Soc. of London, with which he appeared

as a conductor. In 1816–17 he conducted his syms. in Paris, followed by engagements in Frankfurt in 1817–18. He again visited Paris in 1821, and was in Munich in 1821–22. In Jan. 1822 he conducted his works with the Gewandhaus Orch. in Leipzig. Returning to England, he made several more conducting appearances with the Phil. Soc. until 1824; however, his syms. were soon dropped from the repertoire as Beethoven's masterpieces eclipsed his own efforts. In 1830 he retired from his mercantile ventures, and he eventually made his home at Evesham, Worcestershire. As a teacher, Clementi had many distinguished pupils, including Johann Baptist Cramer, John Field, Karl Zeuner, Alexander Klengel, Friedrich Kalkbrenner, and Ludwig Berger.

Clementine. A sentimental American song of uncertain authorship, originally published as *Oh My Darling, Clementine.*

Clemenza di Tito, La. Opera seria by Mozart, his last, 1791. The libretto by Metastasio deals with the generous clemency granted by the Roman Emperor Titus to those who plotted against him. The same libretto was set to music by numerous composers, before and after Mozart.

Cleveland, James, African-American gospel singer and composer; b. Chicago, Dec. 5, 1931; d. Los Angeles, Feb. 9, 1991. He was reared in a gospel milieu in which he was encouraged to develop his natural talent for music by the pianist Roberta Martin. He was a pianist and singer with the group known as the Caravans, and then formed his own Gospel Chimes in 1959; he also became a licensed minister of the Church of God in Christ. His song *Grace Is Sufficient* (1948) became a gospel standard, and his album *Peace Be Still* (1963) added further to his renown. In 1970 he founded the Cornerstone Institutional Baptist Church, for which he also served as pastor.

Cliburn, Van (Harvey Lavan, Jr.), brilliant American pianist; b. Shreveport, La., July 12, 1934. His mother, Rildia Bee Cliburn, was a pupil of Arthur Friedheim; she was his only teacher until 1951, when he entered the Juilliard School of Music in N.Y. as a student of Rosina Lhevinne, graduating in 1954. He was 4 when he made his 1st appearance in public in Shreveport; after winning the Texas State Prize in 1947, he appeared as a soloist with the Houston Sym. Orch. In 1948 he won the National Music Festival Award, in 1952 the Dealy Award and the Kosciuszko Foundation Chopin prize, in 1953 the Juilliard School of

Music concerto competition, and in 1954 the Roeder Award and the Leventritt competition in N.Y.; that same year he appeared as a soloist with the N.Y. Phil. In 1958 he captured 1st prize at the Tchaikovsky Competition in Moscow, the 1st American to achieve this feat; upon his return to N.Y. he received a hero's welcome and a ticker tape parade. In subsequent years he toured extensively, appearing as a soloist with leading orchs. and as a recitalist. In 1978 he withdrew from public performances, but he appeared again in 1987 as a recitalist in a concert for President Reagan and Soviet General Secretary Gorbachev at the White House in Washington, D.C. In 1989 he appeared as soloist in the Liszt and Tchaikovsky 1st piano concertos with the Philadelphia Orch.; that same year he accepted Gorbachev's invitation to perform in Moscow and was the soloist with Eduardo Mata and the Dallas Sym. Orch. in the gala opening of the Morton H. Meyerson Sym. Center.

Cliburn's playing combines a superlative technique with a genuine Romantic sentiment, particularly effective in the music of Tchaikovsky and Rachmaninoff. The Van Cliburn International Piano Competition was organized in 1962 and is held quadrennially in Fort Worth, Tex., the home of the Van Cliburn Foundation.

Cline, Patsy (born Virginia Patterson Hensley), American country-music singer; b. Winchester, Va., Sept. 8, 1932; d. in an airplane crash, Camden, Tenn., Mar. 5, 1963. She became an accomplished singer of country music; in 1957 she won national recognition on Arthur Godfrey's *Talent Scouts* television program with her rendition of *Walkin' After Midnight*; among her hits were *Heartaches, I Fall to Pieces,* and *Sweet Dreams of You.* In 1973 she was elected to the Country Music Hall of Fame. She was at the peak of her popularity when she met her untimely death.

cloche (Fr.). Bell. *Cloches,* chimes; *clochette,* a small bell.

Cloches de Corneville, Les. Operetta, 1877, by Robert Planquette (1848–1903).

Clock, The (Ger. *Die Uhr*). Sym. No. 101 by Haydn, 1794, in D major; it is listed as the 11th of Haydn's 12 syms. (*Salomon*) written for his London tours. The nickname comes from the pendulumlike accompanying figure in the slow movement.

clog box. CHINESE BLOCK.

Clooney, Rosemary, American singer of popular music; b. Maysville, Ky., May 23, 1928. She sang on a Cincinnati radio station when she was 13, later touring as a soloist with Tony Pastor's Orch. (1945–49). She acquired popular success with her recording of *Come On-a My House* (1951), subsequently pursuing a lively career as a singer in nightclubs and on recordings, radio, and television. A long-standing dependence on drugs resulted in a mental collapse in 1968; however, she was able to resume her career in 1976.

close. A cadential ending of a section, movement, or piece.

close harmony. A 4-voice arrangement in which the 3 upper voices are confined within an octave.

cluster. TONE CLUSTER.

Cockaigne Overture ("In London Town"). Concert overture by Elgar, 1901, depicting a mythical paradise in the north, associated with London, the "city of Cockneys."

Coco. Musical by A. Previn, 1969, based on the life of the Parisian *courtière* Gabrielle Chanel. The show's success was in part due to Katharine Hepburn's playing the lead.

coda (It., tail). A closing passage after the formal structure of a movement has been fulfilled. The imminent arrival of a coda is usually signalized by a deep pedal point on the dominant in the bass; other ways to announce the coming of a coda are a rapid acceleration followed by a prolonged retardation, a forceful crescendo, or an equally eloquent diminuendo. In fugal writing the coda often annexes additional voices, forming a harmonic section, with the pedal point on the tonic. Bach's fugue in C minor in the 1st book of the *Well-Tempered Clavier* is an example.

codetta (It., little tail). A short coda.

Coffee Cantata. Secular cantata by Bach, 1732, unique among his works in being a vocal composition in a style approaching that of opera buffa. When it was written, coffee was still regarded, along with tobacco, as a dangerous exotic product. The cantata deals with an attempt of the father of a willful young woman to persuade her to abandon her addiction. As a reward he promises to find her a personable husband, and actually produces a candidate. She likes his looks, but she likes drinking coffee even more. Bach's score is set in an elevated style. Indeed, if the text were to be rewritten, the music could be appropriate for a solemn, although occasionally vivacious, oratorio.

Cohan, George M(ichael), celebrated American composer of musicals and popular songs; b. Providence, R.I., July 3, 1878 (Cohan believed that he was born on July 4, but his birth certificate proves July 3 to be correct); d. N.Y., Nov. 5, 1942. He was a vaudeville performer and had a natural talent for writing verses and simple melodies in the ballad style. His greatest song, *Over There* (1917), became sweepingly popular during World War I. A congressional medal was given to him for this song. The film *Yankee Doodle Dandy* (1942) and the Broadway musical *George M!* (1968) were both based on his life.

col legno (It., with the wood). In string-instrument playing, strike the strings with the wooden part of the bow rather than with the horsehair.

col pugno (It., with the fist). A percussive effect on the piano keyboard. Prokofiev marked *col pugno* in an episode in his 6th Piano Sonata, and it is probably the sole example of fist pounding in concert literature for piano before the 1950s. This effect is similar to the TONE CLUSTERS introduced by Henry Cowell which are played with forearms or fists.

Cole, "Cozy" (William Randolph), African-American jazz drummer; b. East Orange, N.J., Oct. 17, 1906; d. Columbus, Ohio, Jan. 29, 1981. After taking up the drums while young, he began his career in 1928; he played with Jelly Roll Morton, Stuff Smith, and others before joining Cab Calloway's band in 1938; then appeared on radio; he played on Broadway in 1943 in the musical *Carmen Jones*, displaying his expertise in the number *Beat Out Dat Rhythm on a Drum*; also appeared in the 1945 production of *The 7 Lively Arts* with Benny Goodman's Quintet. He later played with Louis Armstrong; then formed his own band, which toured Africa in 1962; was also a member of the Jonah Jones Quintet (1969–76); then was artist-in-residence at Capital Univ. in Columbus, Ohio.

Cole, Nat "King" (born Nathaniel Adams Coles), beloved African-American pianist and singer; b. Montgomery, Ala., Mar. 17, 1917; d. Santa Monica, Calif., Feb. 15, 1965. He worked as a jazz pianist in Los Angeles nightclubs; in 1939 formed the original King Cole Trio (piano, guitar, bass); then turned to singing. He was the 1st black artist to acquire a sponsor on a radio program; also had

a brief series on television. He created a distinct style of velvet vocalization and satin softness in the rendition of intimate, brooding, sentimental songs. His appeal was universal; his tours in South America, Europe, the Middle East, and the Orient attracted great multitudes of admirers who knew him by his recordings. The sole exception was his native state; at his concert in Birmingham, Ala., on Apr. 10, 1956, he was attacked by 6 white men and suffered a minor back injury.

Coleman, Cy (born Seymour Kaufman), American composer of popular music; b. N.Y., June 14, 1929. He studied at the N.Y. College of Music, and began his career as a composer for radio and television. With the lyricist Joseph A. McCarthy, he composed the songs *I'm Gonna Laugh You Out of My Life* and *Why Try to Change Me Now?* To the words of Carolyn Leigh he wrote the song *Witchcraft*; as propelled through the pharynx and larynx of Frank Sinatra it became a hit. He also wrote the musical *Wildcat* (1960), best remembered for the song *Hey, Look Me Over*, *Little Me* followed in 1962. He achieved further success with *Sweet Charity*, composed in 1966, to the lyrics of Dorothy Fields. He also used her lyrics for *Seesaw* (1973). Among his later works were *I Love My Wife* (1977), *On the 20th Century* (1978), *Barnum* (1980), and *City of Angels* (1989).

Coleman, Ornette, African-American jazz alto saxophonist and composer, innovator of a radically new freestyle form of improvisation; b. Fort Worth, Tex., Mar. 9, 1930. He was largely autodidact; served his apprenticeship playing in carnival and rhythm-and-blues bands. His own studies of harmony and theory led him to develop a distinctive style in which the improvisational melodic line is independent of the preassigned harmonic scheme. He also writes concert music in a respectable modernistic idiom; among his works are *Forms and Sounds* for woodwind quintet (1965), *Skies of America* for orch. (1972), and *Sex Spy* (1977).

Coleridge-Taylor, Samuel, esteemed English composer of African descent (his father was a native of Sierra Leone; his mother English); b. London, Aug. 15, 1875; d. Croydon, Sept. 1, 1912. He studied violin at the Royal College of Music (1890); won a composition scholarship (1893); studied under Stanford until 1896. In 1903 he founded at Croydon an amateur string orch. which was very successful; later he added professional woodwind and brass; was appointed a violin teacher at the Royal Academy of Music (1898); became a prof. of composition at Trinity College in London (1903) and at the Guildhall

School (1910); was conductor of the London Handel Soc. (1904–12); lived as a composer and teacher in Croydon. He made 3 concert tours of the U.S., in 1904, 1906, and 1910, conducting his own works. From the very beginning his compositions showed an individuality that rapidly won them recognition, and his short career was watched with interest. His most successful work was the trilogy *The Song of Hiawatha*, including *Hiawatha's Wedding Feast* (London, 1898), *The Death of Minnehaha* (North Staffordshire, 1899), and *Hiawatha's Departure* (London, 1900); the 1st complete performance was presented in Washington, D.C. (1904).

colla parte (It.). Yield to and follow discreetly the solo part or voice.

colla punta dell'arco (It.). At the point (tip) of the bow.

colla sinistra (It.). With the left hand.

colla voce (It., with the voice). COL CANTO.

collage. As in the visual arts, heterogeneous compositions in which unexpected or inharmonious elements are juxtaposed, frequently with reference to other, earlier musics.

collective composition. The practice of parceling the composition of an opera or another large work among several composers. Handel, Bononcini, and Amadei wrote 1 act each for the opera *Muzio Scevola* for a London performance in 1721; it served also as a test of excellence which Handel apparently won. The brothers Paul and Lucien Hillemacher collaborated on a number of operas and even adopted a joint signature, P. L. Hillemacher. Collective composition is frequently the modus operandi of writers of popular musical comedies. Sometimes several names are given as composer of a successful song.

During the early years of the Soviet ragtime the idea of musical collectivism fascinated student composers at the Moscow Conservatory, and they formed the Productive Collective of Student Composers of the Moscow Cons. (PROCOLL). Its announced aim was to represent the collectivism of the masses. Chinese musicians have also contributed to musical collectivism. *The Yellow River Concerto for Piano and Orch.*, produced by the Peking Opera Troupe in Shanghai, was purportedly written by a committee, but only 4 musicians, presumably members of the committee, acknowledged the applause after its production. Several Chinese revolutionary operas have been produced without giving credit to their composers. See also PASTICCIO.

collective nouns. Singular nouns referring to groups of like animals or things. The following are suggestions for collective nouns to designate groups of musical instruments: a fluviality of flutes, an exhalation of piccolos, a conviviality of clarinets, a scabrosity of bassoons, a promiscuity of saxophones, an oriflamme of French horns, a plangency of oboes, an ambrosia of harps, a flourish of trumpets, a pomposity of trombones, a phlogiston of tubas, a circumspection of pianos, an enfilade of violins, a reticence of violas, an elegance of cellos, a teratology of double basses, a titillation of triangles, and the Brobdingnagian borborygmuses of bass drums.

Collegium musicum (Lat.). A group organized to make music for pleasure. The 1st Collegium musicum was formed in 1616 in Prague; a similar group was organized by Bach in Leipzig. A contemporary description of the Collegium musicum in Frankfurt in 1718 stated that its purpose was "to quicken the spirit after a day of work by providing innocent pastime." At such gatherings amateur musicians were given an opportunity to play instrumental music and also discuss musical matters. The practice was revived in colleges and universities in Europe and America in the 20th century, primarily with the purpose of studying and reviving early music.

coll'ottava (It.). Play in octaves; double at the octave.

Colombina (It., Fr. *Columbine*). A stock female character in the commedia dell'arte, the sweetheart of Arlecchino (Harlequin).

Colonel Bogey. Mar. 1914, by the English band composer Kenneth J. Alford (born Frederick Joseph Ricketts, 1881–1945). Its greatest popularity stems from its use in the 1958 film *The Bridge on the River Kwai*.

colophane. Rosin applied to the hair of string instrument bows to make them more prehensile.

colophon. Inscription at the end of a MS giving information regarding its production.

color. 1. Timbre. 2. In 14th- and 15th-century isorhythmic music, a repeated pitch pattern.

color hearing. The psychological and aesthetic association between sound and color. The 1st scientific (or pseudo-scientific) treatment of this supposed association was given by the English rationalist philosopher John Locke in *An Essay Concerning Human Understanding*, published in 1690. An English ophthalmologist, Theodore Woolhouse, drew an arbitrary comparative table of sounds and colors, asserting, for instance, that the sound of a trumpet is red. But mostly the parallelism of hearing and seeing arose from speculation about the unity of the senses. Mathematical symbolism also played a part. The magic number 7 determined both the number of degrees in the diatonic scale and the number of colors of the spectrum as outlined by Isaac Newton. Scriabin, who was a profound believer in the unity of all senses, inserted a part for a color organ in the score of his last orch.l work, PROMETHÉE. It was to inundate a concert hall with changing colors correlating to keys struck on the organ manual.

It is notable that the dual sense of sound and color is possessed mainly by musicians who possess perfect pitch. Indeed, it cannot be otherwise, for how can one perceive a definite color for a note or tonality without being able to identify the note as immediately and unhesitatingly as one does in perceiving a color? Random testing of color hearing among persons having perfect pitch shows no demonstrable coincidences in color designation. There is one exception, however. Most pianists perceive the key of C major as white, and the key of F-sharp major as black. But, obviously, this association is due to the fact that the C-major scale is played on the white keys and the F-sharp major scale is played on the black keys, with white keys used only for 2 notes. It would be interesting if such an association were valid on harpsichords on which the white keys are manufactured in color, and the black keys are actually painted white.

If a true correspondence existed between tones and sounds, then the ascending chromatic scale should register as the spectrum from red to violet, from low to high frequency of vibrations, which is not the case. It follows, therefore, that color hearing is a purely subjective impression, similar to color perception by sensitive persons (particularly children) who are apt to describe natural sound phenomena in terms of color (thunder is gray, crying is red). In Tolstoy's *War and Peace* the sensitive young Natasha describes Pierre and other friends in terms of color. Such psychological coloring is akin to color hearing; the voice of a child may be associated with yellow; the wrinkled face of an old man with brown; the meow of a cat with silver blue.

coloratura (It.). 1. An ornamental passage in opera, consisting of diversified, rapid runs and trills, often applied in cadenzas and occurring in the highest register; it is intended to enhance the brilliancy of a composition and display the singer's skill. A coloratura soprano is a soprano singer capable of performing virtuoso passages in high treble. Famous examples are in the aria of the Queen of the Night in Mozart's *The Magic Flute*, and in Verdi's *Rigoletto*. In modern times Rimsky-Korsakov wrote a highly chromatic coloratura part for the Queen of Shemaha in his opera *Le Coq d'Or*. Tenor roles may also fall into this category. 2. A similar passage in instrumental music.

Colorines (Sp., colored beads worn by Mexican Indian women). Symphonic poem by Revueltas, 1932.

Colour Symphony. Orch. work by Bliss, 1922. The colors of the title are heraldic, not instrumental. There are 4 movements: *Purple*, *Red*, *Blue*, and *Green*.

colpo (It.). A blow. *Di colpo*, suddenly.

Coltrane, John (William), remarkable African-American jazz musician, a virtuoso on the tenor saxophone; b. Hamlet, N.C., Sept. 23, 1926; d. Huntington, Long Island, N.Y., July 17, 1967. He studied at the Ornstein School of Music in Philadelphia; played in the bands of Dizzy Gillespie, Johnny Hodges, Miles Davis, and Thelonious Monk. As a leader and soloist he enhanced the resources of his style by studying ancestral African and kindred Asian music, absorbing the fascinating modalities of these ancient cultures. Coltrane was a master musician, whose theory and practice stimulated the creation of sophisticated jazz performance. Although a controversial figure, he was duly recognized as a major contributor to the avant-garde jazz movement of his era. Among his many albums are

John Coltrane, c. 1960

COURTESY OF THE NEW YORK PUBLIC LIBRARY

178

Giant Steps, My Favorite Things, Live at the Village Vanguard, A Love Supreme, Om, and *Expression.*

Columbia, the Gem of the Ocean. Song of uncertain ancestry, dating from the mid-19th century. It is remarkable that a song as popular as this one, so full of patriotic pride, should be an orphan, contested by 2 English-speaking nations and with several claimants for paternity. It is known in England under the title *Britannia, the Pride of the Ocean,* but several editions of the song were published under the title, *Red, White and Blue,* which are, of course, the colors of both the American and British flags. Ives often quoted this melody in his music.

Colvig, William. See HARRISON, LOU.

Combattimento di Tancredi e Clorinda, Il (The Combat Between Tancredi and Clorinda). Dramatic "madrigal of war" by Monteverdi, 1624, based on the episode from Tasso's *Gerusalemme liberata* where a Christian crusader unintentionally kills his fully armored non-Christian Persian lover; he then bemoans their fates. The work introduced the STILE CONCITATO (agitated style) in a meter of 2 short syllables; it was 1st published in a collection called *Madrigali guerrieri ed amorosi* (Madrigals of War and Love), using early Baroque basso continuo.

combination pedal. A metal foot-lever above the organ pedals; the *forte pedal* draws all the stops of its keyboard; the *mezzo pedal,* the chief 8- and 4-foot stops of its keyboard; the *piano pedal* pushes in all but a few of the softest stops.

combinational tones. These are parasitic tones that are generated when 2 notes are played simultaneously very loudly. They are known as differential (difference) tones if the result is the emergence of a sound the frequency of which is the difference of the frequencies of the 2 original sounds, and as summation (sum) tones if the resulting parasitic sound has the frequency of the sum of the 2 original sounds. The differential tones are heard with particular distinction when a consonant interval is sounded in a near perfect tuning. Such differential tones are known also under the name Tartini tones, because Giuseppe Tartini is reputed to have been the 1st to describe them.

Since, theoretically at least, differential tones form a secondary relationship with summation tones, yet another level of parasitic tone may emerge from this interference. The overtones which are the natural extension of a single sound also enter into this multilateral combination. If all these parasitic tones were to materialize audibly, even the simplest piece of music would degenerate into a monstrous jungle of mutually discordant sounds. Fortunately the principal tones are so clear and loud in comparison with their combinational sounds that musical pollution is not a real threat.

combinatoriality. A characteristic of a set that its elements can be found in combination in other segments. Specifically, a serial (12-tone) set comprising 2 subsets of 6 notes apiece (hexachords) which are both transpositions and complements of each other. The chromatic hexachords C–F and F♯–B are mutually combinatorial, as are the 2 whole-tone scales; a more subtle example are the hexachords C–F–C♯–E–D–E♭ and F♯–B–G–B♭–G♯–A. Each hexachord can be inverted or used in retrograde without disrupting combinatoriality.

In general topology the concept of combinatoriality applies to the functional congruence of geometrical figures of the same order of continuity. Thus a square can be brought into topological congruence with a circle because all the points of the former are in an enumerable correspondence of the other. On the other hand the geometry of figure 8 cannot be made congruent with a square or a circle without cutting. Babbitt extended the term to serial techniques. The parameter of continuity in dodecaphonic writing is the order of succession of the 12 thematic notes in their 4 forms—basic, retrograde, inversion, and inverted retrograde—all of which are combinatorially congruent. Furthermore, the tone-row can be functionally divided into 2 potentially congruent groups of 6 notes each, or 3 groups of 4 notes each, or 4 groups of 3 notes each, with each such group becoming a generating serial nucleus possessing a degree of subsidiary combinatoriality.

Extending the concept of combinatoriality to other parameters of serial music, a state of TOTAL SERIALISM is attained, in which not only the actual notes of a series, but also meter, rhythm, intervallic configurations, dynamics, and instrumental timbres are organized in sets and subsets. The subsets in turn are organized as combinatorial derivations, possessing their own order of continuity and congruence. One fruitful approach is the principle of rotation, in which each successive set is obtained by the transposition of the 1st note of the series to the end of a derived set. Thus the 1st set, 1, 2, 3, . . . 12, appears after rotation as subset 2, 3, 4, 5, . . . 12, 1, or as 3, 4, 5, 6, . . . 12, 1, 2, etc. This technique was favored by Stravinsky.

Inversion, retrograde, and inverted retrograde can be subjected to a similar type of rotation. The additive Fibonacci series, in which each number equals the sum of the 2 preceding numbers, as in 1, 1, 2, 3, 5, 8, 13, 21, etc., is another fertile resource for the formation of sets, subsets, and other derivations. The Fibonacci numbers can be used for building nondodecaphonic tone-rows, in which case the numbers will indicate the distance from the central tone in semitones, modulo 12, so that 13 becomes functionally identical with 1, 21 with 9, etc. The numerical field of combinatoriality is circumscribed by 12 different notes. But experiments have been conducted, notably by Krenek, with artificial scales of 13 equal degrees, obtained with the aid of electronic instruments. Potential uses of combinatoriality operating with sets of more than 12 notes in an octave are limitless.

combo (from *combination*). A once-common term for a jazz or popular small group; corresponds to classical chamber music.

Comden and Green, Betty Comden, American musician, lyricist, and dramatist; b. N.Y., May 3, 1915; and Adolph Green, American musician, playwright, and lyricist; b. N.Y., Dec. 2, 1915. After performing with the Revuers, they entered a long-standing and highly successful collaboration in the 1940s; their 1st success came with *On the Town* (1944, music by Bernstein), followed by *Two on the Aisle* (1951, Styne), *Wonderful Town* (1953, Bernstein), *Peter Pan* (1954, Styne), *Bells Are Ringing* (1956, Styne), *Say Darling* (1958, Styne), *Do Re Mi* (1960, Styne), *Subways Are for Sleeping* (1961, Styne), *Fade Out-Fade In* (1964, Styne), *Hallelujah, Baby!* (1967, Styne), *Applause* (1970, Strouse; Tony Award) and *On the 20th Century* (1978, Coleman; Tony Award). They wrote the screenplays for *Singin' in the Rain* (1952) and *The Band Wagon* (1953).

come (It.). As, like.

come eco (It.). Like an echo.

Come Home, Father. A temperance song by Henry Clay Work, 1864, in which a dying child begs his dad to come home from an extended drinking bout. It was featured in the expressively titled melodrama *Ten Nights in a Barroom*.

come prima (It., as before). Resume the tempo and expression of a previous section of the same character.

come retro (It.). As before.

come sopra (It.). As above.

come sta (It.). As it stands, as written.

Comedians, The. Orch.l suite by Kabalevsky, 1946, drawn from incidental music for a children's theater play, *The Inventor and Comedians*.

comédie-ballet. A type of scenic performance cultivated by Lully and Molière for the court of Louis XIV, e.g., *Les plaisirs de l'île enchantée* (1664) and *Le bourgeois gentilhomme* (1670). The comédie-ballet included, besides the dialogue and ballet, arias and choral pieces.

comes (from *companion*). Answer to the subject (DUX) in a fugue or canon; RIPOSTA.

comic opera. Opera with a comic subject; in French opéra-comique, opera with spoken dialogue. Comic opera does not connote humorous content in the modern sense, but refers to a play in the sense of the Italian commedia dell'arte or even Dante's *Commedia divina*; it is applicable to any scenic representation, even a tragedy. In the French opéra-comique a famous example is Bizet's *Carmen*, which, in its orig. version, included spoken, unaccompanied dialogue, thus fulfilling the requirements of the Opéra-Comique theater in Paris; its repertory includes tragic operas as well as the type of opera buffa or operetta. In contemporary usage comic operas must necessarily include elements of comedy. The comic operas of Gilbert and Sullivan are typical in this respect. Historically comic opera was the opposite of OPERA SERIA, or serious opera par excellence. Composers through the centuries were not consistent in attaching the description of comic opera or opera seria to their works, so that even such an unquestionably tragic opera as Mozart's *Don Giovanni* bore the description *dramma giocoso* (jocose drama).

Comin' Thro the Rye. A Scottish song, to a Burns text, publ. in the collection *The Merry Muses of Caledonia* (*c.* 1800), in which the text was much more sexually licentious than the commonly accepted version. The song was the source for the title of J. D. Salinger's novel *The Catcher in the Rye*.

comma. 1. A small interval in Pythagorean (ditonic) tuning, resulting from the difference between 7 octaves and 12 perfect 5ths, equal to a little more than 1/8 of a whole tone (23.4 cents). In tempered tuning the 5ths are adjusted so as to become commensurate with octaves, avoiding the difficulty of handling the comma. 2. A small interval (comma of Didymus) in syntonic (Ptolemaic) tuning, resulting from the difference between a just-major 3rd and 4 just-perfect 5ths (minus 2 octaves), equal to a little less than 1/10 of a whole tone (21.5 cents).

comme (Fr.). As, like; used in some expression marks, particularly by Debussy and Scriabin.

comme sopra (Fr.). As above.

commedia dell'arte (It., artistic play). An Italian genre of theatrical performance which emerged at the time of the Renaissance and incorporated versatile elements of pantomime, acrobatics, masks, music, and dance. Most of the action was improvisational, but the main characters were clearly delineated. They usually included a cuckolded husband, a handsome gallant, an accommodating servant, a wily lawyer, an incompetent doctor, etc. Later on the stock characters received definite names: a grumbling old Pantalone (Pantalon); his beautiful daughter or ward Columbina (Columbine), her lover Arlecchino (Harlequin); a grotesque clown adorned with a long nose, Pulcinella (Punchinello); and the braggart warrior Scamarella (Scaramouche). Some composers have used these characters in their own operas, pantomimes, and plays. Leoncavallo built his opera *Pagliacci* as a play within a play, in which a circus clown discovers that his wife, performing the part of Columbina, has a lover. Stravinsky emulated commedia dell'arte in his ballets *Petrouchka* and *Pulcinella*, and partly in his *L'Histoire du Soldat*.

commedia per musica (It., play with music). Early designation for opera, not necessary comic.

commercials, singing. Short melodic phrases used in the marketing of crass consumer products. These jingles which used to drive people up the wall by their faulty grammar ("Winston tastes good like a cigarette should") or by promises of instant success in love (for men by using a certain brand of toothpaste and for women by putting on aphrodisiac perfume).

As a subgenre the composer Nicolas Slonimsky also composed, in 1925, 5 art songs with texts drawn from chunks of advertisements from *The Saturday Evening Post* and other purveyors of American culture. The texts were wisely selected for their lyric poetry, dramatic rhetoric, and persuasive power. There were 5 of them: 1 for a toothpaste, 1 for a mild laxative, 1 for bed linen, 1 for nose powder, and, the most expressive 1 of all, for Castoria. They were couched in melodramatic idiom, suitable for such climactic points as the appeal, "Mother, relieve your constipated child!" in the Castoria song, or, with an ominous quotation from Rachmaninoff's C-sharp minor Prelude, in the warning, "And then her doctor told her . . ."

commodious nomenclature. The musical avantgarde does not oppose euphony on general principle. Harmonious progressions are tolerated in modern music. The compromise between the prospective music of the future and the modality of the past is often achieved by resorting to commodious nomenclature, as exemplified by the neologisms NEOCLASSICAL, NEO-BAROQUE, NEOROMANTIC, and beyond that by the exotic terms VECTORIALISM, LIPOGRAMMATICISM, and SPATIAL SERIALISM. New music, modern music, contemporary music, etc., once progressive slogans, have long been overgrown with a fungus of obsolescence. Futurism itself, a rebellious cry of the dawn of the century, is now an academic object of historical study.

commodo (It.). COMODO.

common chord. A major or minor triad.

common hallelujah meter. See METER.

common long meter. See METER.

common measure. COMMON TIME.

common meter. See METER.

common particular meter. See METER.

common time. A meter in which one measure contains 2 half notes or 4 quarter notes; duple or quadruple time. Ordinarily common time is understood to mean 4 quarter notes, and as many beats, to the measure. The time signature may be represented by a capital *C*, derived from the semicircle that served as the medieval symbol for duple time.

comodo (It.; *commodo*, wrong sp.). Easy, leisurely, at a convenient pace, in a relaxed manner, accommodatingly.

comp (Abbrev. *accompany*). In jazz, accompany a soloist with chords.

compact disk (abbrev. *CD*, *disk*). A revolutionary, noninteractive, digital recording; in circulation since the 1980s.

Company. Musical by Sondheim, 1970. A bachelor confronts both the marital woes of his friends and his ambivalent feelings toward singlehood. Includes the title song, *Side by Side by Side*, *What Would We Do Without You?*, *Ladies Who Lunch*, *Being Alive*, and *I'm Not Getting Married*.

comparative musicology (Ger. *vergleichende Musikwissenschaft*). The orig. term for the study of world musics, with a particular focus on folk modalities. As the practitioners were primarily European and Euro-American, there was usually cultural bias in the analysis, borrowed in part from the ethnological concept of the "primitive" or "savage" and in part from the application of social Darwinism. By the mid-20th century the term had been changed to ETHNOMUSICOLOGY (i.e., moving from comparison to integral study); the discipline continues to spread throughout the academic world, not without its problems.

compass. The range of a voice or instrument, i.e., the scale of all the tones it can produce, from the lowest to the highest.

compensation. The proportion between the relative complexity or simplicity of the principal elements in a musical composition: melody, harmony, rhythm, dynamics, form, and instrumental arrangement. As music history evolved toward a greater complexity, only 1 of these at a time tended toward a maximum of technical involvement. When modern melody abandoned tonality and gradually assumed an atonal aspect, the elements of rhythm, harmony, and orchestration remained relatively stable. In dodecaphonic composition, harmony is a function of the tone-row, incorporating the horizontal melodic elements in a vertical dimension; but rhythm, meter, and form are restrained in their developments. It is indeed remarkable that composers of the dodecaphonic school are very conservative in the matter of form, sometimes prescribing classical repeats in dance movements. Berg maintained the form of a classical instrumental suite even in his operas. When rhythm is paramount, and metrical exchanges are frequent, as in Stravinsky's *Le Sacre du printemps*, the melody and harmony become remarkably static, even in highly dissonant settings.

The law of compensation is at work in canonic movements, when the orderly procession of voices in mutual imitation creates at times surprisingly dissonant combinations. It is sufficient to play the development section of some of Bach's fugues in a very slow tempo to realize how many vertical discords are created in the canonic process. Here the formal dissonances are justified by the strong linear counterpoint. The unifying strength of the pedal point on the dominant in the deep bass register gives license to modulation into remote keys without discomfort. In the wedding procession in Rimsky-Korsakov's opera, *Le Coq d'or*, with the dominant pedal point on G in the bass, there are modulations into the keys of A-flat major and D-flat major. An exception to the law of compensation is exemplified by totally serial works, in which rhythm, dynamics, melody, harmony, instrumentation, and form are organized so as to prevent any compensation for unrelieved diversification. But, paradoxically, this exclusion of compensation leads to a unification sui generis, with the totality of musical elements regarded as a single entity.

complement (complementary interval). An interval which, added to any given interval not wider than an octave, completes the octave; a perfect 4th is the complement of a perfect 5th, a minor 3rd of a major 6th, etc.

complete cadence. See CADENCE.

complin(e) (from Lat. *completorium*, completion). A short, early evening service, one of the CANONICAL HOURS of the Roman Catholic liturgy. In addition to 4 Mary antiphons and a hymn, the most significant portion is the dismissory canticle of Simeon, Nunc dimittis.

composer (from Lat. *componere*, put things together). A man or woman who writes music and transmits it by written or oral means. The musical sense of the term is at least 1,000 years old; Guido d'Arezzo includes it in his Latin treatise *Micrologus*, establishing the necessary properties for a melody to be well "put together" (*componenda*). The medieval Latin term for composer was *compositor*, the word which is now reserved in English for typesetters. The designation *compositor* is preserved in Spanish in its original Latin sense, that is, composer. Tinctoris, the author of the 1st dictionary of music, describes the composer as a writer of a new melody. Later theorists drew the distinction between *compositio*, a conscious act of composing, and *sortisatio*, a random improvisation.

The rules for composition vary enormously through the centuries. Dissonances of yore are acceptable to modern ears (e.g., the interval of a 3rd, not permissible in a cadential final chord until the 16th century), but changes, however momentous, have not altered the basic definition of a composer as a person who puts notes together in a more or less logical and coherent manner.

composition. The broadest term for writing music in any form for any instruments or voices.

composition pedal. In the organ, a pedal which draws out or pushes in several stops at once.

compound interval. An interval greater than an octave.

compound meters. Time signatures with the numerator in prime numbers (except 1, 2, or 3), representing the sum of commonly used meters; 5/4, 7/4, 11/4, and 13/4 are compound meters. Ideally there should be only a single accent on the 1st beat, but in practical usage compound meters are divided into 2 simple meters. Thus 5/4 is perceived as 3/4 + 2/4 or 2/4 + 3/4; 7/4, as 4/4 + 3/4 or 3/4 + 4/4, etc. It has been asserted, on inadequate evidence, that a bar of 5 beats is a natural metrical unit in Russian folksong; but it is true that Russian composers introduced whole sections in 5/4 into their works, the most famous example being the "waltz in 5/4 time" in the 2nd movement of Tchaikovsky's *Pathétique Sym.*; 11/4 is used in Rimsky-Korsakov's opera *Sadko*; Russian chorus singers used to sing the 11-syllable equivalent of the sentence "Rimsky-Korsakov is altogether mad," to cope with the unusual count. Mussorgsky used the equivalent of 11/4 in the *Promenade* in his *Pictures at an Exhibition*, but he notated it by alternating bars of 5/4 and 6/4.

Early in the 20th century compound meters were used by numerous composers as novelties. This tendency was particularly enhanced by the great diversification of time signatures in Stravinsky's works, especially in *Le Sacre du printemps*. An important category of compound meters is represented by the asymmetric division of traditional time signatures, as for instance, the sum of 2/8, 3/8, 2/8, and 2/8, aggregating to 9/8 which was used by Rimsky-Korsakov, or time signatures in 10/8, being simply the coalescence of 2 bars of 5/8. Bartók utilizes asymmetric meters in his many folk-influenced works (e.g., *6 Dances in Bulgarian Rhythm* from *Mikrokosmos*, vol. 6); the Dave Brubeck Quartet became very popular through its asymmetric pieces (*Blue Rondo à la Turk*).

Compound meters are sometimes masked by the use of dotted notes and rests within a traditional time signature. An interesting example of this metrical distribution is George Gershwin's *I Got Rhythm*, which is notated in 4/4 time, with four dotted 8th notes flanked by 2 8th-note rests. When written out the measure could be differentiated into 1 bar of 2/16, 4 bars of 3/16, and 1 bar of 2/16. The value of the denominator, which is always a power of 2 for all time signatures, has no bearing on the nature of the compound meter, because by doubling or halving the duration of the note value in the denominator the resulting measures would be equal to the ear. Thus 3/4, with a metronome mark of a quarter note equaling 60, would sound the same as 3/8 with an 8th note equaling 120.

computer. A programmable, digitally based electronic device that stores, retrieves, and processes data. Computers can be used by composers to calculate details of compositions, store information for subsequent use, or generate new sounds (or transform existing ones). Computer technology has led to specific devices to create an interaction between live performance and digital realization.

computer music

〜〜　〜〜　〜〜　〜〜　〜〜

Music generated by COMPUTER, whether directly, through interaction with live instruments, or as the product of precompositional data.

For many centuries music theorists and composers cherished the notion that beautiful melodies and wonderful harmonies could be produced by mathematical means.

Such musical alchemy fascinated the masters of polyphonic music of the Renaissance who eagerly experimented with the techniques of inversion, retrograde movement, interval extension, rhythmical expansion, and other basically mathematical concepts. It was only natural that when digital computers were perfected in the middle of the 20th century, musicians began to explore electronic resources for the creation of scientific "music of the spheres" which would provide composers with new resources.

Digital computers and other electronic devices could not produce any output more valuable than the input fed into the computer by the human programmers. Programming a computer by a series of numbers is no different from the process of writing notes on paper. In one of the earliest computerized compositions, with a relatively primitive computer called Illiac, 2 programmers (including Lejaren Hiller) produced an *Illiac Suite*, which ended with a lengthy coda in C major. Obviously the Illiac did not select C major in preference to some other chord. Digital computers are ideal purveyors of random numbers, which in turn can be converted into musical parameters, furnishing the natural sources for aleatory music. Care should be taken, however, not to program computer music excessively, for such input would amount to the dictation of the programmer's own musical ideas, which are often lamentable.

But if a digital computer is helpless without a programmer, it still can become a fascinating resource for the composition of instantaneous canons or similar contrapuntal forms. The computer is given a subject and instructed to cause it to enter after a given time lapse in another voice, at an octave or another interval. The result can be tested by immediate playback. Computers can also solve specific problems, such as the possibility of forming a dodecaphonic series consisting of two major and minor triads consecutively arrayed with either a minor or a major 3rd separating these triads from one another. The answer to the problem is in the affirmative, but while a human must wrack his brain for days to find a solution, a computer can give an answer within microseconds: F♯, A♯, C♯, E, G♯, B, D, F, A, C, E♭, G.

In musical analysis a computer can be most useful. Suppose a music scholar undertakes the task of comparing the main subjects of a number of sonatas and syms. of the Baroque period, to prove a certain point and to trace coincidences and unconscious borrowings. By devising a relatively simple code, indicating duration of each note in the melody with the plus and minus signs respectively for ascending and descending intervals using the semitone as a unit, the motives can be tabulated and the degree of similarity among them determined by statistics. A criterion of similarity can be measured by the number of steps necessary to convert one melody into another, with each semitone of alteration counted as a melodic unit, and each difference in an assigned note value as a rhythmic unit. Such an anamorphic alteration is a basic principle in the science of topology. Such scientific checks would be particularly valuable to composers of popular songs who are periodically sued for pilfering someone else's tunes.

If all popular songs were to be stored away in code in a digital computer's memory bank, composers with retentive memories of other tunes would be saved a lot of work. On the other hand, such a computerized memory bank may turn out to be a Frankenstein monster. The number of tunes and rhythms, many of them revolving around the major triad, with rhythms kept to the simplest proportions of relative note values, is limited, and time may not be far away from the Doomsday of popular music, predicted by John Stuart Mill more than a century ago: "I was seriously tormented by the thought of the exhaustibility of musical combinations. The octave consists only of 5 tones and 2 semitones, which can be put together in only a limited number of ways of which but a small proportion are beautiful; most of these, it seemed to me, must have been already discovered."

comprimario (It., with the primary). A secondary operatic role; in *Faust*, Valentin (a baritone) is an example.

Comte Ory, Le (Count Ory). Opera by Rossini, 1828, produced in Paris. It was the 1st of Rossini's 2 operas to French texts. The story deals with a licentious count's attempt to seduce a woman whose husband is out on a Crusade.

con (It.). With; in a style expressive of; for definitions of phrases beginning with *con*, see the 2nd word in the given phrase.

concert. A musical performance in the presence of an audience. Public concerts were 1st organized in Italy in the early 17th century; solo performances and chamber ensemble concerts were popular in London in the 18th century. In France a series of concerts was organized in 1725 under the name Concert Spirituel; in the 19th century concerts became part of cultural life in every part of the world. The word RECITAL for a solo concert came into vogue in the middle of the 19th century; it was invented by the London manager of Liszt. Regular sym. concerts were organized in Paris (1828); later they spread to England, Russia, and all over Europe. America became the *El Dorado* of concert artists in the 2nd half of the 19th century.

Concert Champêtre. Work for harpsichord and orch. by Poulenc, 1929, written for Landowska.

concert grand. The largest type of GRAND PIANO.

concert overture. An overture for full orch., sometimes programmatic, performed as an independent composition at a sym. concert.

concert pitch. The actual sound produced by an instrument, as distinct from a written note in transposing instruments. Thus in the B-flat clarinet the written note C sounds B-flat. As for the pitch itself, the A = 440Hz now considered standard has not always been so; pitch has been consistently on the rise for more than a century. If Mozart were to come back to life and hear his C-major *Jupiter Sym.,* he would hear it as being in D-flat. In any case, many orchs. today do not use A = 440Hz as their tuning basis.

Concert Spirituel. A famous series of concerts in Paris, 1725. They were usually given on religious holidays when the opera house was closed; the programs featured secular and sacred music.

concertante (It.). 1. A concert piece. 2. A composition or section of a composition for 2 or more solo voices or instruments with accompaniment by orch. or organ, in which each solo part is in turn brought into prominence. 3. A composition for 2 or more unaccompanied solo

instruments in orch.l music, often called a SINFONIE CONCERTANTE. *Concertante style*, a style of composition admitting of a brilliant display of skill on the soloist's part.

concerted music. Music written in parts for several instruments or voices, i.e., trios, quartets, etc.

concerti (It.). CONCERTOS (the plural used in this book).

concertina. A free-reed instrument with 2 hexagonal heads, each with a button keyboard and handle, connected by expandable bellows; the instrument was patented by Charles Wheatstone in 1829. The 2 basic systems are the English, fully chromatic, where each button produces the same note on the extension and compression of the bellows; and the German-Anglo, diatonic in conception, where each button produces different pitches on the extension and compression of the bellows. It comes in registers ranging from soprano to double bass. The repertory has included classical, light classical, novelty, and traditional music.

concertino (It., Ger. *Konzertstück*). 1. A small concerto, scored for a small ensemble. 2. The group of soloists in a CONCERTO GROSSO.

Harry and Neville Crabb in their concertina workshop

COURTESY H. CRABB & SON

concertmaster. In the U.S., the 1st violin player in an orch.; the word is a translation from the German KONZERTMEISTER. In England the 1st violinist in the orch. is called LEADER; in France it is PREMIER VIOLON or CHEF D'ATTAQUE; in Italy, VIOLINO PRIMO; in Spain, CONCERTINO.

concerto

〜〜〜 〜〜〜 〜〜〜 〜〜〜 〜〜〜

An extended composition for a solo instrument (or instruments) and orch., frequently in a (modified) sonata form. A concerto (It.) for orch. without a soloist is called CONCERTO GROSSO, a grand concerto. The etymological derivation of the word *concerto* is subject to debate: the most logical origin is from the Latin verb *concertare* (compete, contend with one another); but the word also appears in Italian as a cognate of *concerto* (agreement). Another conjecture is that *concerto* comes from the Latin verb *conserere* (come together); in fact, the spelling *conserto* is found in some Italian MSS of the 17th century.

The form of the classical concerto is similar to that of a sonata. Most concertos are in 3 movements, most commonly marked *Allegro, Andante, Allegro.* A Minuet can be inserted after the 2nd movement; in later works it can be replaced by a Scherzo. The chief characteristic of a concerto is ANTIPHONY, with the soloist and the orch. alternating in presenting the main themes. Classical concertos usually feature a CADENZA for the solo instrument, inserted in a cadence between the tonic 6/4 chord and the dominant. A good cadenza should confine itself to the tonic harmony with the bass on the dominant, so as not to interfere with the sense of an interrupted cadence, and any intervening modulations ought to be handled with caution.

The length of an orch.l introduction to a concerto varies widely. A story is told about a near disaster that befell the famous violinist Mischa Elman during one of his concert tours. Mistakenly believing that the Beethoven concerto was the one scheduled on the program, he relaxed, letting his violin rest loose on his left arm in the expectation of a long orch.l opening TUTTI, and was rudely jolted out of his siesta when the orch. struck the opening chord of the Mendelssohn Concerto, which has only a brief introduction. Conditioned by countless performances of this work, he launched into the concerto by automatic reflex. Piano concertos often begin with a solo passage; a striking example is Beethoven's 4th Piano Concerto in G Major. Rachmaninoff's 2nd Piano Concerto opens with a short prelude in the solo part, letting the orch. present the main theme.

Numerically, piano concertos are in the majority. Composers who are pianists themselves naturally give preference to their own instrument in writing concertos. Among piano concertos that have been permanently enshrined in the repertory are those of Mozart, Beethoven, Chopin, Schumann, Mendelssohn, Liszt, Saint-Saëns, Brahms, Tchaikovsky, Grieg, and Rachmaninoff. The piano concertos by Anton Rubinstein, which enjoyed great popularity in the 19th century, owing to Rubinstein's own virtuoso performances, went into limbo in the 20th century, except in Russia. Piano concertos by Dvořák, MacDowell, and such minor figures as Thalberg, Moscheles, or Litolff occasionally appear on concert programs. Modern piano concertos tend to be less discursive and more compact than their Romantic predecessors; following the example of Liszt, they are often compressed into a single movement subdivided into several sections that allow changes of tempo and character. Piano concertos by Ravel, Prokofiev, and Bartók have become firmly established in the modern piano repertoire. Schoenberg's Piano Concerto is slowly gaining ground despite the unfamiliarity of its idiom and its tremendous technical difficulties. A special type of piano concerto is represented by those for left hand alone, many of which were commissioned by the Austrian pianist Paul Wittgenstein (1887–1961), who lost his right arm on the Russian front in World War I. Ravel, R. Strauss, Prokofiev, Korngold, and several other composers obliged him with one-armed works.

The number of violin concertos written during the 3 centuries of the violin as a virtuoso instrument is almost as large as that of piano concertos. Vivaldi and other Baroque composers wrote hundreds of them. Among the most celebrated violin concertos are those by Mozart, Beethoven, Mendelssohn, Brahms, Tchaikovsky, and Sibelius; Paganini's concertos are brilliant virtuoso pieces. Glazunov's Violin Concerto enjoys an unabated popularity in Russia; concertos by the violin virtuosos Wieniawski, Vieuxtemps, and Bruch are also popular. Among modern violin concertos, those of Prokofiev, Bartók, and Khachaturian are often heard. Berg's Violin Concerto has achieved a permanent place in the repertory of modern violinists. Schoenberg's Violin Concerto has yet to achieve a comparable public acceptance. Stravinsky's Violin Concerto enjoys respectability but offers little attraction to performers. Among cello concertos of the Classic period, those by Haydn and Boccherini are well established; the best-known 19th-century cello concertos are those by Saint-Saëns and Dvořák. Tchaikovsky's *Variations on a Rococo Theme* for cello and orch. can be classified as a concerto; equally qualified is Ernest Bloch's *Schelomo* for cello and orch. The character of Don Quixote in the tone poem of R. Strauss is portrayed by the cello solo, but the work is more a programmatic tone poem rather than a true solo concerto. The viola is the orphan of the string family; there are few composers who are charitable enough to write concertos for the instrument. Berlioz assigned a concertizing part to the viola in his *Harold in Italy*; the work may be classified as a sym. with viola OBLIGGATO. In modern times, Hindemith and William Walton contributed viola concertos. Bartók worked on a viola concerto but did not finish it by the time he died; his faithful disciple Tibor Serly completed the score. Koussevitzky wrote a concerto for double bass, an instrument on which he was a virtuoso.

In the woodwind department, there are concertos for practically every instrument. Quantz, who was the court flutist for Frederick the Great, wrote a plethora of flute concertos for himself and for his sovereign to play. There is an oboe concerto by Eugene Goossens which he wrote for his brother, an oboe virtuoso, and one by R. Strauss, written in his later years. Clarinet concertos are not lacking in quantity; there are some by Mozart, Weber, Carl Nielsen, and one by the 20th-century composer Thea Musgrave, written in an ultramodern idiom. Stravinsky composed an *Ebony Concerto* for clarinet and jazz ensemble. There are several bassoon concertos available for ambitious performers, beginning in the Baroque. Glazunov composed a saxophone concerto. Haydn's *Trumpet Concerto* is a brilliant virtuoso piece. Strauss wrote 2 concertos for horn and orch. (his father was a renowned horn player). There are a few scattered trombone concertos. Vaughan Williams wrote a concerto for tuba.

Concertos for harp and orch. are not too numerous, but Ravel's *Introduction et Allegro* for harp and instruments is in effect a harp concerto. The modern harpist Carlos Salzedo wrote a harp concerto accompanied by wind instruments. Guitar concertos have been written by Ponce, Castelnuovo-Tedesco, and Rodrigo. Glière wrote a concerto for voice and orch. Henry Cowell composed a concerto for a Japanese string instrument, koto. There is even a concerto for kazoo with orch., concocted by the American composer Mark Bucci.

Double concertos are those in which 2 instruments are soloists on an equal standing. The Concerto for Violin, Cello, and Orch. by Brahms is an example. Bartók orchestrated his Sonata for 2 Pianos and Percussion into a Concerto for 2 Pianos and Orch. The category of triple concerto is represented by Bach's mighty Concerto for 3 Harpsichords and Orch., and by Beethoven's Concerto for Violin, Cello, and Piano with Orch. Spohr wrote a quadruple concerto for string quartet and orch. Such multiple concertos effectively cross the line of demarcation separating solo concertos from the class of CONCERTO GROSSO.

concerto, sacred. SACRED CONCERTO.

concerto for orchestra. A symphonic work in which the orch.l instruments play the role of soloists in free rotation; the pioneering work of this type is Bartók's (1943).

concerto grosso (It., grand concerto). An instrumental composition employing a small group of solo instruments (CONCERTINO, little group) within a larger group or full orch. (RIPIENO, filling up). This essentially Baroque genre differs from a solo concerto because of the nature of the concertino, functioning as a multiple soloist, alternating with and antiphonally supported by the ripieno, also designated by the Italian term TUTTI (all; every instrument). The concertino usually comprises 2 violins and a cello, with the harpsichord furnishing the harmony indicated by BASSO CONTINUO. The tutti consist of a fairly large ensemble of strings supplemented by trumpets, flutes, oboes, and horns. The earliest works in this genre were Corelli's *Concerti Grossi con duoi violini e violoncello di concertino obbligati e duoi altri violini, e viola, e basso di concerto grosso ad arbitrio*, probably composed in 1680 but not published until much later; Torelli wrote a group of concerti grossi about 1690.

The concerto grosso was standardized by Vivaldi; it consisted of 3 cyclic movements: Allegro, Adagio, Allegro. Bach's Brandenburg Concertos are basically of the concerto grosso type, but Bach often diversified the concertino parts in the manner of a solo concerto. Handel's concerti grossi observed the formal elements of the type more strictly than Bach. In the 2nd half of the 18th century, with the growing tendency toward Classical symphonic forms, the concerto grosso evolved into the SYMPHONIE CONCERTANTE and eventually into a full-fledged SYMPHONY without individual solo groups. In the 19th century the concerto grosso was virtually obsolete, and it was left to the 20th century to revive the concerto grosso in the original Baroque form. A typical example is Max Reger's *Konzert im alten Stil* (Concerto in the Old Style), in which the Baroque structure is tinted with Romantic colors.

Concerto in F. Piano concerto by Gershwin, 1925, in 3 movements, full of jazz rhythms and harmonies.

Concertstück (*Konzertstück*; Ger., concert piece). One-movement concerto; CONCERTINO.

concitato (It.). Moved, excited, agitated.

concord. Euphony; harmony; consonance.

Concord Sonata. The 2nd multimovement piano sonata by Ives, 1915, subtitled *Concord, Mass.: 1840–60*. Its 4 movements are named after the Concord transcendentalist writers, *Emerson, Hawthorne, The Alcotts,* and *Thoreau.* Ives published the *Concord Sonata* at his own expense in 1920. The difficulties of the music were insurmountable to ordinary piano virtuosi, and it took the stamina and perseverance of John Kirkpatrick to give its 1st complete performance in New York (1939). Eventually the work became a standard of pianistic technology, performed by a number of pianists in America and in Europe. As with many Ives works, there is no definitive edition of the *Concord Sonata*; Kirkpatrick had hoped to create a variorum edition, but he died before he could complete the project.

concrete music. MUSIQUE CONCRÈTE.

conduct. Rehearse and direct an orch., band, or chorus.

conducting

The art of rehearsing and directing a large ensemble. When a number of singers or instrumentalists perform together, it is convenient to have a leader whose function is to give the signal to begin the music and to indicate the tempo. In Baroque practice it was usually up to the MAESTRO AL CEMBALO (master at the keyboard) to give these directions. When performing groups evolved into multimusical bodies, the 1st violinist usually initiated the proceedings with a motion of his violin bow. An alternative was for the composer-conductor to beat time on the desk with a small stick or a roll of paper, occasionally emphasizing the beat by stamping his foot on the floor, or by using a long cane to accomplish the same effect. It is believed that Lully, who was the leader of the PETITS VIOLONS DU ROI for Louis XIV, struck his foot with the sharp point of his conducting baton, leading to a fatal gangrene.

The present tradition of conducting with a wooden baton originated early in the 19th century. Mendelssohn mentions in one of his letters that he conducted an orch. in London "with a white stick." Although the baton is the scepter of conductorial authority and the emblem of the art of conducting, some conductors found it convenient to dispense with it and lead an orch. with their bare hands. The Russian conductor Wassily Safonoff was the 1st to become batonless; he said that in abandoning the baton, he acquired 10 batons with his fingers. Leopold Stokowski did away with the baton during his entire U.S. career and made an eloquent use of his aristocratic fingers.

In the early days of professional conducting it was a general custom for conductors to face the audience rather than the orch., and indeed it would have been regarded uncivil to turn one's back to the public. But since such a fashion of polite conducting made it virtually impossible for the conductor to control his players, the orch.l leaders gradually decided to "face the music." Yet as late as 1925 Walter Damrosch would turn toward the public for the grand finale in Beethoven's 5th Sym.

Beards on conductors were common in the 19th century, and some also sported flowing hair. Such adornments disappeared in the 1st half of the 20th century, but the hirsute fashions had a revival later on. Natural hair, whether groomed or flowing, seemed to be a condition sine qua non for conductors; sartorial elegance was also de rigueur. With the advent of the age of functional efficiency, capable conductors were often bald or, more significantly, female.

As with many branches of music it was in Germany that the art of conducting was formalized. A whole generation of impeccably tailored conductors set the tradition of "dictators of the baton," commanding their players in the manner of a feudal lord ordering about his vassals. Hans von Bülow in particular was as famous for his superior musicianship as for his Prussian brutality toward the players. A typical anecdote deals with his dislike of 2 members of his orch. named Schulz and Schmidt. One day the manager announced to him that Schmidt had died. "And Schultz?" Bülow asked coldly. Another time he remarked to his soprano soloist that she was not pretty enough to sing so badly out of tune. When major sym. orchs. organized themselves into unions, the orch. men also began to assert their human dignity. Toscanini was probably the last conductor who could afford to hurl insulting epithets to orch. members with impunity. At the last rehearsal for his last concert he shouted at his men: "Imbecili! Tutto è scritto. La più bella musica del mondo!" In deference to Toscanini's great age and supreme musicianship, the orch. fell silent at his imprecations, and Toscanini walked slowly off the podium.

The art of conducting is the most elusive of musical professions. Ideally it requires a total mastery of the musical score and an ability to coordinate the players and singers so that they would create a euphonious ensemble.

The tempo must be established with a wave of the hand that is clear without being obtrusive. The subtlest nuances must be communicated to the players with a gentle motion of the fingers or a suitable facial expression. A common gesture (often immortalized on professional photographs) is to put the index finger of a right hand on the lips to indicate PIANISSIMO. An imperious thrust of the right hand toward the brass section indicates FORTISSIMO. Conductors of the Romantic type, such as Arthur Nikisch and Serge Koussevitzky, used to address the orch. with a great expenditure of bodily motion, often changing their angle of direction. Toscanini usually bent his left arm and kept it almost immobile pressed against his left side. Idiosyncrasies are many. Some conductors move their lips as if trying to speak; others hum with the melody, often out of tune. While histrionic conductors were the most successful in earlier times, remarkably ungainly orch. leaders have attained great renown. Old-fashioned conductors were often moved to explain the imaginary meaning of the music. When the famous Willem Mengelberg exhorted the solo cellist, pointing out that the music expressed the yearning of the soul for happiness and redemption, the cellist looked at him quizzically and said, "You mean mezzoforte?"

While a pianist or a violinist must practice for years to build even a passable technique, a conductor may begin his career without any preparation, for his instrument is an orch. on which he cannot practice at home. The basic technique of conducting can be learned in a few lessons. As traditionally established, conductors must give the downbeat on the 1st beat of the measure, and an upbeat on the 2nd beat, when the measure is 2/4; in 3/4 his stick must describe a triangle with its lowest apex always downward. In 4/4, after the mandatory downbeat the hand moves northwest, then across to northeast, then at an angle to north, and down south for the next downbeat. Compound measures combine these fundamental motions. Time was when apprentice conductors had trouble with the 5/4 movement in Tchaikovsky's *Pathétique Sym.* A tale is told about a French conductor who counted the time allowed as "un, deux, trois, quatre, cin, -que," thus converting the 5/4 measure into one of 6/4. He could not understand why the orch. stopped and waited for his next downbeat. Some would-be conductors do not realize that in order to give the downbeat, one must 1st lift the conducting hand in an anticipatory upbeat which also sets the tempo. However, some very great conductors allow themselves the luxury of starting a pianissimo movement by gradually lowering the hand without a discernible upbeat.

If the orch. cooperates with a nervous or hesitant conductor, then even the rankest amateur can get through an overture or a movement from a sym. without suffering a major disaster. Danny Kaye, the talented American comedian who could not read music, managed to lead a whole symphonic movement with an impressive and humorous show of command. Mayor Fiorello LaGuardia of New York liked to conduct *The Star-Spangled Banner* during World War II, but he could not master the trick of beating triple time, and conducted the national anthem in 2/4, with the result that his downbeat was coming successively on the 3rd beat of the 1st bar and on the 2nd beat of the 2nd bar. Hans Richter, the celebrated Wagnerian conductor, was once asked how he succeeded in maintaining the tempo with such metronomic precision. "Simple," he said. "My upbeat always equals my downbeat."

Some conductors prefer imperceptible movements, and sometimes stop beating time altogether to demonstrate their full control of the orch. Such ventures, however, only strengthen the cynical notion that conductors are useless at best and nuisances at worst. An interesting experiment was made in Russia after the Revolution to dispense with a conductor as an undemocratic vestige of musical imperialism. Indeed, a conductorless orch. of Moscow lasted for 10 seasons until it was abandoned as a perverse distortion of socialism and the conductors returned to the Soviet podium to exercise their authoritarian power over the downtrodden musical masses. Groups such as the Orpheus Chamber Ensemble have revived the conductorless orch. But even the most vocal skeptics about the role of conductors agree that a musical coordinator is necessary to lead the highly complex orch.l scores of 20th-century (and earlier) works, with their technical demands and polytextures.

Whatever the technique used by a professional conductor, his or her prime duty is to translate the written notes in an orch.l score into an effective panorama of sound, faithfully rendering the composer's creative designs. The art of conducting is unique in that it requires the musical, psychological, and intellectual ability to coordinate the instruments and voices in such a way as to create a perfect euphony of the ensemble incorporating a great variety of dynamic nuances and timbres, and to maintain a balance of contrapuntal components within the general harmonic framework and the animating flow of propulsive rhythm.

Paradoxically, composers are rarely the best interpreters of their own works. Perhaps only Wagner, Berlioz, Mahler, and Bernstein, all excellent conductors in their own right, gave full justice to their own masterpieces. Tchaikovsky conducted his passionate music in a singularly pedestrian manner. Rimsky-Korsakov never knew how to bring out the brilliant sounds of his operatic suites in actual performance. Debussy lacked the sensitivity required to project the impressionistic colors of his scores when he was called upon to act as composer-conductor. Ravel was so uncertain on the podium that he was content with just managing to finish beating time when the orch. played the last bar of his score. No wonder then that composers had to have their interpreters, much as presidents must have their speechwriters. It is in this sense that one talks about "Toscanini's Beethoven," "Walter's Mozart," or "Furtwängler's Brahms."

Considering the tremendous difficulties in controlling a large body of musicians by the wave of a hand, it would seem hazardous to conduct without a score. Toscanini was the 1st to lead operas and symphonic works from memory; he was compelled to do so, it is said, because of his poor eyesight. But Toscanini's repertory was limited to Classical and Romantic works which he absorbed by musical osmosis; when he attempted to conduct Stravinsky's *Petrouchka*, he had several memory lapses. The pioneer in conducting from memory was Dimitri Mitropoulos, who led rehearsals as well as concerts without a score. Now that such feats of memory have become a matter of routine, reviewers do not, as a rule, mention such accomplishments.

In the 19th century the majority of conductors were Germans. They filled the ranks not only in Germany and central Europe, but also in Scandinavia, Russia, England, and the U.S. When Major Henry Lee Higginson decided to finance the Boston Sym. Orch. in 1881, he stipulated that conductors must be German by origin. It was a profound shock when, at the outset of World War I, the great German conductor of the Boston Sym. Orch., Karl Muck, was arrested and interned as an enemy alien. Similar fates befell most German-born conductors of American orchs. during the war. A few who had become American citizens, among them Walter Damrosch, were spared the disgrace of an internment and continued in their profession, although they were warned not to play German music French, British, and Russian conductors filled the vacated posts.

Another wave of political discrimination arose in 1933 when some great German conductors such as Furtwängler were unable to obtain American engagements because of their alleged collaboration with the Nazi government; this de facto ban persisted after the war. However, German conductors of Jewish origin, victimized by the Hitler regime, were welcome in the U.S. An extraordinary development ensued in later decades of the century when 2 of the most important conducting positions in the U.S. were entrusted to Asians: the Indian Zubin Mehta, conductor of the Los Angeles Philharmonic, was appointed music director of the N.Y. Phil., and Seiji Ozawa of Japan became head of the Boston Sym. Orch.. Gradually racial and gender barriers gave way, and African-American and female conductors began to hold directorships at some of the smaller city orchs. and chamber orchs.

conductor. Leader or director of an orch., band, or chorus.

conductus (Lat., procession). A secular song genre of the ARS NOVA, by contrast to the sacred motet. Most conductus are monophonic, sung in unison or octave. A polyphonic conductus developed in the 13th century; the 2nd (added) part was also called the conductus. Some conductus were derived from liturgical melodies, others freely composed. The typical contrapuntal rhythmic structure is note against note. In the 15th century the conductus, especially in Italian, adopted florid ornamentation of a madrigal type.

confinalis. The secondary final tone, usually the dominant, in ecclesiastical modes. The confinalis of the Dorian mode is particularly important because it corresponds to A, which in the 16th century became the primary tone of the alphabetical scale.

conga. An Afro-Cuban ballroom dance, in duple time, with a rhythmic anticipation at every 2nd beat.

conical mouthpiece. The deeper, cone-shaped form of mouthpiece for brass wind instruments, as opposed to the shallower cupped mouthpiece.

conical tube. An instrument tube that tapers very gradually; the opposite of the CYLINDRICAL TUBE, which does not taper.

conjugated counterpoint. Polyphony in which contrapuntal considerations outweigh harmonic ones. By definition, counterpoint is a conjugation of 2 or several melodic parts, but too often in common practice contrapuntal techniques follow harmonic formulas, to the detriment of the interdependence of component voices. It is therefore useful to introduce the term conjugated counterpoint in its etymological sense of "opposite notes yoked together." The locus classicus of conjugated counterpoint is the 2nd movement of Bartók's Concerto for Orch., in which conjugated pairs of wind instruments are arrayed in succession and intussusception.

conjunct degree. The nearest degree in the scale (chromatic or diatonic) to the given degree. *Conjunct motion,* progression by conjunct degrees or intervals.

Connecticut Yankee, A. Musical by Rodgers and Hart, 1927. A reworking of Mark Twain's social satire about a time traveler ending up in King Arthur's Camelot. Includes *Thou Swell* and *My Heart Stood Still.*

Connotations. Orch. work by Copland, 1962, written for the opening of Phil. Hall at Lincoln Center for the Performing Arts, N.Y. This was Copland's 1st work in which he used an explicit technique of 12-tone composition.

consecutive intervals. The progression of 2 voices moving in the same direction at the distance of a perfect 5th, strictly forbidden in conventional harmony. The importance attached to this prohibition among academic teachers was paramount. Rimsky-Korsakov was extremely careful in this respect, and he used to double-check his students' exercises by handing them over to his trusted pupil and assistant Glazunov, who enjoyed the reputation of an expert in ferreting out such 5ths. There are consecutive 5ths in the coda of Liszt's *Liebestraum;* to "correct" it, some editors removed one of the voices, even though the customary 4-voice harmony was left incomplete.

The progression of consecutive 4ths is also not allowed in 2-part counterpoint, unless it is protected by overlapping consecutive 6ths, in which case the result becomes a progression of 2 6–3 chords (⁶/₃, 1st inversion) in 3-part harmony. Likewise, consecutive octaves, particularly between the 2 outer voices, are strictly prohibited, with the exception of course if 2 voices are mere duplications of one another. By the early 20th century the prohibition of these consecutive intervals in free composition had been quietly dropped; indeed, they were a major component of the impressionist and symbolist styles.

consequent. In a canon, the COMES (follower); the part imitating the antecedent or DUX (leader).

conservatoire (Fr.); conservatorium (Lat.); conservatory (abbrev. *cons.*). A public or private institution for providing practical and theoretical instruction in music.

consolations. A cycle of 6 piano pieces by Liszt, inspired by the romantic musings of the French literary critic Sainte-Beuve and composed in 1850. The characteristic epigraph of the cycle is "Notre bonheur n'est qu'un malheur plus ou moins consolé" (Our happiness is nothing but sorrow which is more or less consoled). The symbolism of the tonalities is interesting; 4 numbers are in E major and 2 are in D-flat major, which for Liszt symbolized, respectively, the concepts of love and meditation, respectively.

console. 1. A structure or table supporting the entire apparatus of a large organ: keyboard, stops, and pedals. 2. A piece of furniture containing an "entertainment center," which can include a radio, phonograph, tape player, CD player, and television.

consonance

A combination of 2 or more tones, harmonious and pleasing in itself and requiring no further progression to make it satisfactory; in common practice period tonality, the major and minor 3rds and 6ths, and the perfect octave, 5th, and 4th. Consonance is the opposite of DISSONANCE, a combination presumably unpleasant to the ear. The Latin etymology of *consonance* corresponds precisely to the Greek SYMPHONIA (*con = sym*, together; *sonance = phonos*, sounding). A more poetic synonym of consonance is concord, the "agreement of hearts," as opposed to discord, "disagreement of hearts."

Consonant intervals are those pairs of tones that correspond to the contemporaneous definition of harmonious sound. Early in Western musical history only the PERFECT CONSONANCES of the octave, the 5th, and the 4th were considered consonant; 3rds and 6ths were cast out as dissonances, and were not accepted as IMPERFECT CONSONANCES until well into the 13th century. The separation of consonances from dissonances is not entirely frivolous. The concept of harmonious consonance is based on the laws of acoustics. According to historical practice and Renaissance theory, consonances were those combinations of tones whose mutual ratios of vibrations do not

exceed the fractions formed by numbers 2 to 6 in the numerator and the denominator. The smaller these numbers are, the more perfect is the consonance formed by such fractions. Thus the octave is the most perfect consonance, representing the frequencies in the ratio of vibrations 2/1. The 5th corresponds to the ratio of 3/2; the 4th is represented by the fraction 4/3; the major 3rd has the ratio of 5/4; the minor 3rd, 6/5. The frequency of vibrations 5/3 corresponds to a major 6th, also a consonance. The acoustical point of these ratios is that consonant intervals were found among the 1st 6 tones of the overtone series. It is significant that its 1st 5 partial tones form a major triad, which may therefore be quite properly described as "a true chord of nature."

There are paradoxes aplenty inherent in the overtone series, for indeed, all intervals found in the series theoretically form a consonance with the fundamental note as long as the notes involved are in their proper place in the series. Consider, for example, the demonstrable fact that if we play the C-major scale in the lowest register of the piano simultaneously with the B-major scale in high treble, the 2 scales will form consonances. The reason? B in the middle octave of the piano forms the 15th partial tone of the lowest available C; B an octave higher is the 30th partial, and 1 more octave higher constitutes the 60th partial.

Ragtime and jazz pianists who introduced unresolved dissonances into harmony did so spontaneously in blissful ignorance of the overtone series, but they invariably and instinctively placed dissonant notes higher in the treble where they became acoustically consonant with the bass note. The so-called added 6th over the major triad forms the 27th overtone from the fundamental bass note. The tonic 7th-chord is a favorite among jazz pianists for the final cadence; when the 7th is placed in the high treble at a distance of nearly 4 octaves, it is the 15th overtone of the fundamental bass note. Other cadential chords employed by popular musicians contain the 9th overtone, which is the supertonic of the major scale counting from the fundamental tone. But no jazz player avoided putting a perfect 4th on top of the harmonic pile. Why not? Because no matter how high we go in the overtone series, we will never reach a perfect 4th from the bass. Other unavailable intervals from the bass in the overtone series are a minor 2nd and a minor 3rd, and their inversions, the major 7th and major 6th. However, the dissonant interval of the augmented 4th is, *mirabile dictu*, a part of the overtone series; it is the 45th partial tone. If we play the C-major scale in the low bass register and the F-sharp major scale in the highest treble, the effect will be a progression of theoretical parallel consonances.

consonant chord. A harmony containing no dissonant interval.

consort (Lat. *consortium*, congregation). An Old English term for an instrumental ensemble; a *whole consort* consisted of either all wind or all string instruments (e.g., recorders, viols), while a *broken consort* was a mixed group of wind and string instruments; Shakespeare called the latter BROKEN MUSIC.

consort song. Vocal ensemble, usually a quartet, sometimes accompanied by a BROKEN CONSORT.

constructivism. Early 20th-century Russian aesthetic movement in which the artwork exhibits a high degree of visible structure, based on geometric or (in music) industrial principles.

Consul, The. Opera by Menotti, 1950, to his own libretto, 1st produced in Philadelphia. This is Menotti's most dramatically powerful work, focused on the desperate effort of a man and his wife trying to escape from an unidentified fascist country. They are doomed when the Consul (who never appears on stage) of an unnamed great transoceanic nation refuses to grant them a visa.

contenu (Fr.). Restrained, under control.

Contes d'Hoffmann, Les. TALES OF HOFFMANN, THE.

continuo (It.). BASSO CONTINUO; often interchangeable with CEMBALO.

contra (Lat., It., against). Prefixed to instrument names, a larger instrument sounding an octave below the standard size.

contrabass (It. *contrabasso*; Fr. *contrebasse*; Ger. *Kontrabass*). DOUBLE BASS.

contrabassoon (Brit. *double bassoon*; Fr. *contre-basson*; It. *contrafagotto*; Ger. *Kontrafagott*). A lower-pitched member of the BASSOON family, sounding an octave lower than the standard instrument. Like the bassoon, the contrabassoon is bent back on itself; in its present form (established in the 19th century) the tube is 16 feet long when laid straight. The 1st references to the instrument date to the early Baroque; except for French makers who continue to use wood, metal is the material of choice. Possessed of the same nasal quality as the bassoon, the contrabassoon functioned as a bass instrument in military bands. It is probably for this reason that Beethoven gave the contrabassoon its most famous orch.l moment: the beginning of the military variation in the chorale finale of Sym. No. 9.

contradanza (It.). CONTREDANSE.

Contrafagott (*Kontrafagott*; Ger.). 1. CONTRABASSOON. 2. A 16' reed organ stop.

contrafactum (from Lat. *contrafacere*, counterfeit, imitate). The fitting of a new text to a preexistent melody. A technique begun in the Middle Ages, it applied more commonly to secular texts grafted to sacred melodies. In the 17th century the practice became known as parody, not in the current sense of caricature, but as a "near song" (*para-ode*).

contralto (It.). ALTO.

contra-octave. The 16' octave (C_1), 1 octave below the GREAT OCTAVE.

contrapuntal. Pertaining to the art or practice of counterpoint.

contrapuntal intussusception. The accumulation of contrapuntal parts using registral space. In many modern scores contrapuntal groups are arranged in pairs, and each pair becomes an individual entity which is subsequently combined with another prefabricated pair, and yet another. When 2 such pairs are widely separated in their ranges, an opportunity is presented for an intussusception of a new pair, forming a structure of 6 contrapuntal voices in 3 subdivisions. Alexander Tcherepnin made systematic use of this technique in his method of "interpoint" (*contrapunctus inter punctum*).

contrary motion. Counterpoint wherein one part moves upward while the other part moves downward; in academic terms, the preferred type of motion.

contratenor. COUNTERTENOR.

contre (It., contra). Against.

contredanse (Fr.; Ger. *Contratanz, Kontretanz*; It. *contradanza*). A Baroque French salon dance similar to the quadrille and related to the English COUNTRY DANCE, usually in duple or compound duple meter (6/8). It is conjectured that a contredanse is not a "counter-dance," but a corrupted form of "country dance"; indeed, there are in existence collections of CONTREDANSES ANGLAISES, published in France in the 17th century. Beethoven wrote several contredanses, and used 1 of them in the finale of the *Eroica Sym.*

controlled improvisation. An arrangement of available thematic elements following a definite formal design and confined within a specified period of time. Accordingly, the performer selects attractive or significant motives and phrases of an otherwise nonintegrated work, as though drawing preset lines from a printer's tray, resetting them at will, duplicated, fragmented, or upside down. Stockhausen, Foss, Brown, and others have availed themselves of this manner of composition.

Cook, Will Marion, African-American conductor and composer; b. Washington, D.C., Jan. 27, 1869; d. N.Y., July 19, 1944. He entered the Oberlin (Ohio) Cons. to study violin when he was 13, continuing his studies with Joachim in Germany and at the National Cons. in N.Y. He had a brief career as a concert violinist before devoting himself to composition for the black musical theater in N.Y.; he was director and composer for the Bert Williams-George Walker productions (1900–1908) and founded his own "syncopated" sym. orch. (1918), with which he toured extensively. In his later years he was active mainly as a conductor and teacher in N.Y. His best-known musicals are *Clorindy, or The Origin of the Cakewalk* (1898) and *Swing Along* (1929; in collaboration with W. Vodery).

Cooke, Sam (born Samuel Cook), African-American balladeer; b. Chicago, Jan. 22, 1931; shot to death in Los Angeles, Dec. 11, 1964. He sang in a lyric tenor voice, avoiding the shouts and the screams that often suggested vocal incompetence among so many popular singers. His songs recalled the Negro spirituals and the texts reflected religious sentiments; later, he reached a broad audience with his rhythm-and-blues hymns to the woes of unrequited love and other traumas. Among his big hits were *You Send Me, Chain Gang, Wonderful World, Twistin' the Night Away,* and *Cupid.* As a gospel performer with the Soul Stirrers, he sang gospel hymns such as *Nearer to Thee, Touch the Hem of His Garment, Wonderful (God Is So Wonderful),* and *Jesus, Wash Away My Troubles.*

cool jazz. 1. In general, any style with a more restrained or precomposed quality, as with the swing/big band, 1950s, and fusion periods. 2. A jazz style of the 1950s, characterized by a less "hot" atmosphere than earlier styles, use of unusual instruments (baritone saxophone, flute, French horn), and adoption of classical techniques (i.e., fugue, mixed orchestration). In general, cool jazz cultivates an evenly flowing mood of relaxation, in serene legatissimo, replacing the frenetic syncopated beat of earlier jazz by an emphasis on the strong parts of the measure; for musical and economic reasons, cool jazz musicians preferred smaller ensembles, which offered greater freedom for individual solo improvisations. Among the most famous cool jazz musicians was Miles Davis, who defined the style in his 1948 collaboration with Gil Evans, *Birth of the Cool*; Gerry Mulligan, who established a pianoless quartet with Chet Baker; the Modern Jazz Quartet (with John Lewis and Milt Jackson), who collaborated with Gunther Schuller on the 3rd Stream, music combining classical composition and jazz improvisation; and the Dave Brubeck Quartet.

coperto (It.). Covered, muffled. Applied to mutes in horns, trumpets, and kettledrums.

Copland, Aaron

Greatly distinguished and exceptionally gifted American composer; b. N.Y., Nov. 14, 1900; d. North Tarrytown, N.Y., Dec. 2, 1990. He was educated at the Boys' High School in Brooklyn; began to study piano with Victor Wittgenstein and Clarence Adler as a young child. In 1917 he took lessons in harmony and counterpoint with Rubin Goldmark in N.Y., and soon began to compose. His 1st publ. piece, *The Cat and the Mouse* for Piano (1920), subtitled *Scherzo humoristique*, shows the influence of Debussy. In 1920 he entered the American Cons. in Fontainebleau, near Paris, where he studied composition and orchestration with Nadia Boulanger. Returning to America in 1924, he lived mostly in N.Y.; became active in many musical activities, not only as a composer but also as a lecturer, pianist, and organizer in various musical societies. He attracted the attention of Koussevitzky, who gave the 1st performance of his early score *Music for the Theater* with the Boston Sym. Orch. in 1925; then engaged Copland as soloist in his Concerto for Piano and Orch. in 1927; the work produced a considerable sensation because of the jazz elements incorporated in the score, and there was some subterranean grumbling among the staid subscribers to the Boston Sym. concerts. Koussevitzky remained Copland's steadfast supporter throughout his tenure as conductor of the Boston Sym., and later as the founder of the Koussevitzky Music Foundation. In the meantime Walter Damrosch conducted in N.Y. Copland's Sym. for Organ and Orch., with Nadia Boulanger as soloist.

Other orchs. and their conductors also performed his music, which gained increasing recognition. Particularly popular were Copland's works based on folk motifs; of these the most remarkable are *El Salón México* (1933–36) and the American ballets *Billy the Kid* (1938), *Rodeo* (1942), and *Appalachian Spring* (1944). A place apart is occupied by Copland's *Lincoln Portrait* for narrator and orch. (1942), with the texts arranged by the composer from speeches and letters of Abraham Lincoln; this work has had a great many performances, with the role of the narrator performed by such notables as Adlai Stevenson and Eleanor Roosevelt. His patriotic *Fanfare for the Common Man* (1942) achieved tremendous popularity and continued to be played on various occasions for decades; Copland incorporated it in toto into the score of his 3rd Sym. He was for many years a member of the board of directors of the League of Composers in N.Y.; with Roger Sessions he organized the Copland-Sessions Concerts (1928–31), and he was also a founder of the Yaddo Festivals (1932) and of the American Composers' Alliance (1937); was a participant in such organizations as the Koussevitzky Music Foundation, the Composers Forum, the Cos Cob Press, etc. He was head of the composition dept. at the Berkshire Music Center at Tanglewood from 1940 to 1965, and from 1957 to 1965 was chairman of the faculty.

He lectured extensively and gave courses at the New School for Social Research in N.Y. and at Harvard Univ. (1935 and 1944); was the Charles Eliot Norton Lecturer at Harvard in 1951–52. He was the recipient of many awards: Guggenheim fellowship (1925–27); RCA Victor award of $5,000 for his *Dance Sym.*; Pulitzer Prize and N.Y. Music Critics' Circle Award for *Appalachian Spring* (1945); N.Y. Music Critics' Circle Award for the 3rd Sym. (1947); Oscar award for the film score *The Heiress* from the Academy of Motion Picture Arts and Sciences (1950); Gold Medal for Music from the American Academy of Arts and Letters (1956); Presidential Medal of Freedom (1964); Howland Memorial Prize of Yale

Univ. (1970); was also decorated with a Commander's Cross of the Order of Merit in West Germany; was elected to honorary membership of the Accademia di Santa Cecilia in Rome. He held numerous honorary doctor's degrees: Princeton Univ. (1956); Brandeis Univ. (1957); Wesleyan Univ. (1958); Temple Univ. (1959); Harvard Univ. (1961); Rutgers Univ. (1967); Ohio State Univ. (1970); N.Y. Univ. (1970); Columbia Univ. (1971); also York Univ. in England (1971).

About 1955 Copland developed a successful career as a conductor; he led major sym. orchs. in Europe, the U.S., South America, and Mexico; he also traveled to Russia under the auspices of the State Dept. In 1982 the Aaron Copland School of Music was created at Queens College of the City Univ. of N.Y. In 1983 he made his last appearance as a conductor in N.Y. His 85th birthday was widely celebrated; Copland attended a special concert given in his honor by Zubin Mehta and the N.Y. Phil., which was televised live by PBS. He was awarded the National Medal of Arts (1986). As a composer Copland made use of a broad variety of idioms and techniques, tempering dissonant textures by a strong sense of tonality. He enlivened his musical textures by ingenious applications of syncopation and polyrhythmic combinations; but in such works as the Piano Variations he adopted an austere method of musical constructivism. He used a modified 12-tone technique in his Piano Quartet (1950) and an integral dodecaphonic idiom in the score of *Connotations* (1962). He wrote several musical appreciation books: *What to Listen for in Music* (N.Y., 1939; 2nd ed., 1957); *Our New Music* (N.Y., 1941; 2nd ed., rev. and enl. as *The New Music, 1900–1960*, N.Y., 1968); *Music and Imagination*, the Norton Lectures delivered at Harvard, 1951–52 (Cambridge, Mass., 1952); *Copland on Music* (N.Y., 1960).

Coppélia. Ballet by Delibes, 1870, produced for the 1st time in Paris. Its subtitle was *La fille aux yeux d'émail* (The Girl with Enamel Eyes). The story is derived from a fantastic tale by E. T. A. Hoffmann dealing with the toymaker Coppelius, whose creations are magically lifelike; of these the most entrancing is the doll Coppélia. A village youth is so struck with her beauty that he abandons his warm-fleshed human girlfriend Swanhilda, who in a fit of jealousy intrudes into the house of Coppelius and accuses Coppélia of alienation of affection before she realizes that Coppélia is a doll. Swanhilda marries her suitor, and Coppélia and her fellow dolls arrange a celebration.

The 1st Swanhilda was a 16-year-old ballerina named Giuseppina Bozacchi. Tragically, she fell victim to malaria after a few performances, and even more tragically, the Prussians laid siege to Paris a few weeks after that. But *Coppélia* survived both disasters and became one of the most celebrated ballets of all time. Among separate numbers there is an energetic mazurka, an entrancing waltz, an intoxicating CSÁRDÁS, and an impetuous galop. When Tchaikovsky heard the performance of *Coppélia* in Paris, he wrote to a friend that he felt ashamed of his own ballets when compared to the glorious music of Delibes.

copula. In medieval music theory, a connecting passage, ranging from a single note and a part of a ligature to a protracted melisma. A common trait among all varieties of copulae is a quickened tempo, notated in smaller values.

copyright. The legal ownership right to an individual production. It applies to musical compositions and is recognized by the laws of most nations. The oldest performing rights society is the French Soc. des auteurs, compositeurs, et éditeurs de musique, formed in 1851. Although Great Britain passed its 1st copyright act in 1709, musical works came under its protection much later. In the U.S., copyright was 1st based on English common law; then purely American laws were passed in 1790 (revised 1802, 1829); 1831 (the 1st to mention musical works, revised 1870, 1891, 1909); and the all-new 1976 law.

Russia did not join the international copyright convention until 1914. The Soviet government abolished all international copyright law after the Revolution, but joined the International Copyright Convention in 1972. As a result of these delays, many celebrated Russian works were published and performed without any payment to the composers; Rachmaninoff never collected a penny for his Prelude in C-sharp Minor and his 1st 3 piano concertos; Prokofiev's *Classical Sym.* was pirated freely. No protection existed for Shostakovich and other Soviet composers, but a gentleman's agreement was made with publishers to collect fees for performances of major works by Soviet composers. In order to regain copyright for his most popular works, published but not properly copyrighted before the Revolution, Stravinsky revised his ballet *The Firebird* and other scores, but many conductors make use of the original uncopyrighted editions, not necessarily in order to avoid payments but out of musical preference or historical imperative.

The Mexican composer Manuel Ponce failed to copyright his popular song *Estrellita*, thus losing substantial income. Numerous lawsuits were fought over popular American songs pirated because of inadequate copyright protection. A rather celebrated case is that of the song *Happy Birthday to You*, freely used until a clerk in a Chicago music company discovered that the tune was written by two sisters, Patty and Mildred Hill, to a different set of words ("Good morning, dear teacher"). The Western Union Company, which made use of the tune for its singing birthday telegrams, had to pay a substantial sum of money for the newly discovered copyright. A movie depicting a father whose family forgot his birthday, and who sings *Happy Birthday to Me* all alone, had to change the words and the tune to *For He's a Jolly Good Fellow*, an uncopyrighted song, to escape the penalty for infringement of a valid copyright. Once a copyright lapses, whether by intent, accident, or legal limit, a composition enters public domain and may be performed without copyright payment; thus a Wagner opera has the same legal status as *3 Blind Mice*.

Coq d'or, Le (The Golden Cockerel). Opera in 3 acts by Rimsky-Korsakov, 1909, produced posthumously in Moscow. The libretto is drawn from a fairy tale by Pushkin involving an indolent Czar, his falsetto-singing (but virile) astrologer, the astrologer's magical bird that warns the Czar of invading armies, and the exotic queen the 2 men fight over; she sings a famous COLORATURA hymn to the sun. After the Czar angrily murders the astrologer, he is pecked to death. The Czarist censor prescribed some modifications in the text to soften the resemblance between the bumbling ruler of the fairy tale and the bungling reigning Czar Nicolas II, who had just lost a war with Japan. Rimsky-Korsakov refused to submit, and the opera was not performed during his lifetime.

cor (Fr.). A horn.

cor anglais (Fr.). ENGLISH HORN.

cor de basset (Fr.). BASSETT HORN.

cor de chasse (Fr.). Hunting horn.

coranto (It.). 1. COURANTE. 2. Country dance.

corda (It.; plural *corde*). String. *Due corde* (It.), 2 strings. 1. Release soft pedal on piano. 2. Depress the soft pedal halfway on piano. 3. Play the notes on 2 strings, NON DIVISI; *tre corde*, release soft pedal on piano; *corda vuoto*, open string.

Corea, "Chick" (Armando Anthony), American jazz pianist and composer; b. Chelsea, Mass., June 12, 1941. He began his career as a sideman with Mongo Santamaria, Willie Bobo, Blue Mitchell, and Herbie Mann; also worked with Miles Davis. After leading a group known as Circle (1970–71), he worked with Stan Getz. His popularity grew as he turned to jazz rock, playing with Return to Forever (with Al DiMeola, Stanley Clarke, and Flora Purim). He later led his Elektric Band and Acoustik Band and has made other group and solo recordings (*Piano Improvisations*, 1970–71).

Corelli Fugue. Organ fugue in B minor by Bach, BWV 579.

Corelli, Arcangelo, famous Italian violinist and composer; b. Fusignano, near Imola, Feb. 17, 1653; d. Rome, Jan. 8, 1713. His violin teacher was G. Benvenuti in Bologna; he learned counterpoint with Matteo Simonelli. Little is known of his early life; about 1671 he went to Rome, where he was a violinist at the French Church (1675); in the beginning of 1679 he played in the orch. of the Teatro Capranica; Rome remained his chief residence to the end of his life, except for visits to Modena (1689–90) and Naples (1702). There is no substance to the story that in 1672 he went to Paris and was driven out by the intrigues of Lully; biographers mention also his stay at the court of the Elector of Bavaria in Munich about 1680, but there is no documentary evidence of this stay. Equally unfounded is the story that while he was in Naples, a mediocre violinist, Giuseppe Valentini, won the favor of the Roman public so that Corelli returned to Rome a broken man and died shortly afterward. Quite contrary to these fanciful legends, Corelli enjoyed respect, security, and fame. In Rome he had a powerful protector in Cardinal Benedetto Pamphili; later he lived in the palace of Cardinal Pietro Ottoboni, conducting weekly concerts which were attended by the elite of Roman society. One of Corelli's admirers was Queen Christina of Sweden, who lived in Rome at the time. Among his pupils were Baptiste Anet, Geminiani, Locatelli, and Giovanni Somis.

Corelli was famous as a virtuoso on the violin and may be regarded as the founder of modern violin technique; he systematized the art of proper bowing, and was one of the 1st to use double stops and chords on the violin. His role in music history is very great, despite the fact that he wrote but few works; only 6 opus numbers can be definitely attributed to him. His greatest achievement was the creation of the CONCERTO GROSSO, especially the 12 concertos of op. 6 (1714), which includes the *Christmas Concerto* in G Minor. Handel, who as a young man met Corelli in Rome, was undoubtedly influenced by Corelli's instrumental writing. Corelli was buried in the Pantheon in Rome.

Corigliano, John (Paul), American composer; b. N.Y., Feb. 16, 1938. He was the son of John Corigliano (1901–75), concertmaster of the N.Y. Phil. Orch. (1943–66) and the San Antonio Sym. The younger Corigliano studied at Columbia Univ. with Otto Luening (B.A., 1959), with Vittorio Giannini at the Manhattan School of Music, and privately with Paul Creston. He was subsequently employed at the radio stations WBAI and WQXR in N.Y. and as assistant director for CBS-TV (1961–72). He held a Guggenheim fellowship in 1968–69. In 1971 he joined the faculty of the Manhattan School of Music, and from 1973 taught at Lehman College. From 1987 to 1990 he was composer-in-residence of the Chicago Sym. Orch. His style of composition shows a fine capacity for lyrical expression, and an incisive sense of rhythm, in the generic tradition of Bartók and Prokofiev. Despite the dissonant freedom of his polyphonic writing, his music retains a firm tonal anchorage.

cornemuse (Fr.). BAGPIPE, with 2 drones sounding an octave apart.

cornet. 1. A brass instrument of the trumpet family, with a smaller conical tube and larger cupped mouthpiece than the trumpet; the result is a mellower tone and greater technical facility. It evolved from the old post horn by the addition of 3 valves; its range covers 2 octaves and 3 tones: It is usually tuned in B-flat, so that a written C sounds a whole step lower. It is primarily found in military bands, although early jazz performers like Armstrong and Oliver played it in their small groups. 2. Organ stops: *a.* reed stops of 2', 4', 8', and 16' pitch; *b.* the German *Kornett*, of 2' or 4' pitch, on the pedal; *c.* a com-

Arcangelo Corelli

COURTESY OF THE FREE LIBRARY OF PHILADELPHIA

pound stop having from 3 to 5 ranks; *d.* the *echo-cornet*, a soft-toned cornet stop enclosed in a wooden box; *e.* the *mounted cornet*, mounted on a separate soundboard to render its tone louder.

cornet à pistons (Fr.). The modern valve cornet.

cornet (It. *cornetto*; Ger. *Zink*). An early brass family instrument of noble lineage and multiple mutations. It is shaped like a straight pipe and is made of ivory or strong wood. Some cornets are bent to provide a more convenient placement of fingerholes. During the Renaissance there were cornets of different registers, one for soprano, called *cornettino*, that is, a little cornet, and one of the tenor pitch, called in Italian *cornone*, that is, a big cornet.

The bass size, which was added to the cornet family in the 16th century, was bent in the shape of a snake to enable the player to reach the appropriate holes; it acquired the majestic and awesome appellation "serpent," but it had a melodious tone that was anything but reptilian. Disregarding the curse put on the serpent in the Book of Genesis, the instrument made regular appearances in church music. In France, it bore an explicit designation, *serpent d'Église.* The serpent underwent another change of shape in the 18th century when a section of it was bent back so as to form 2 adjacent tubes. In this shape it became known as the Russian bassoon. Other varieties of the serpent were the English bass horn and OPHICLEIDE. Eventually all these quaint instruments lapsed into innocuous desuetude.

corno (It.; plural *corni*). HORN.

corno a macchina (It.). Valve horn, capable of playing entire chromatic scales.

corno da caccia (It.). Hunting horn.

corno di bassetto. BASSETT HORN; alto clarinet. This Italian term would have long become obsolete were it not for George Bernard Shaw, who whimsically elected to use it as a nom de plume for his music criticism in London papers in the late 19th century, undoubtedly with the intent of comparing the rarity and the unconventional quality of the instrument with his style of writing.

cornon (Fr.). 1. A cornet stop. 2. Wide-bore FRENCH HORN invented by V. F. Červený in 1846. By 1872 he had produced a family of cornons. The instrument has been described as a "pre-Wagnerian Wagner tuba."

cornu. A tremendously impressive metal horn of ancient Rome, more than 3 meters in length, curved in the shape of the capital letter *G*, and for this reason known also as *tuba curva*. Two authentic specimens were found in the excavations in Pompeii. The cornu was used in Rome at ceremonial occasions, and was revived during the classically obsessed French Revolution. When Voltaire was solemnly reburied in the Pantheon (he died before the Revolution), Grétry wrote a special fanfare to be played on a modernized recreation of the cornu.

coro spezzato (It., fragmented chorus; plural *cori spezzati*). A divided chorus, originating in the 16th century when Zarlino referred to choral ensembles that had been divided into 2, 3, or 4 self-contained units. These cori spezzati were used antiphonally, in partial or total congruence. The compositional style for this music is often labeled polychoral. The technique persisted (e.g., Berlioz's Requiem) and continues to this day, although composers are often not concerned with achieving a harmonically diatonic vista (e.g., Henry Brant).

Coronation Mass. 1. Mass in D Minor by Haydn, 1798; also known as the *Lord Nelson Mass*. 2. Mass in C Major by Mozart, 1779 (K. 317), written for the unveiling of the statue of the Virgin Mary near Salzburg.

Coronation Concerto. Piano Concerto in D Major by Mozart, 1788 (K. 537), premiered by him on the coronation of the Austrian Emperor Joseph II (1790).

Corregidor, Der (The Magistrate). Opera by Wolf, 1896; a comedy about intentional and unintentional spouse-swapping.

corrente (It.). An Italian variant of the French COURANTE, marked by a faster tempo and less florid ornamentation. *Corrente alla francese*, the Italian equivalent of the French COURANTE, with all of its characteristics.

corrido (from Sp. *correr*, run). Twentieth-century Mexican topical ballad. It is usually sung in mariachi style, in 6/8 or 9/8 measure, with melodies consistently doubled at the 3rd.

Corsaire, Le. Concert overture by Berlioz, 1845, 1st performed in Paris with the composer conducting. Ostensibly the work was inspired by the Byron poem *The Corsair*, depicting the picaresque adventures of a gentleman pirate. But, disconcertingly, Berlioz 1st entitled the work *La Tour de Nice*, then changed it to *Le Corsaire rouge*, finally abbreviating the title to *Le Corsaire*. The listener can therefore fit his impressions of the Romantic score into either a tourist's trip through the Riviera or the tempestuous travels on the Mediterranean.

Corsaro, Il. Opera by Verdi, 1848, based on Byron's poem *The Corsair*.

Cortot, Alfred (Denis), famous French pianist; b. Nyon, Switzerland (of a French father and a Swiss mother), Sept. 26, 1877; d. Lausanne, June 15, 1962. He was a pupil at the Paris Cons. and studied with Decambes, Rouquou, and Diémer; he won the 1st prize for piano in 1896; the same year he made his debut in Paris, playing Beethoven's C-minor Concerto at 1 of the Colonne concerts, and won signal success; he went to Bayreuth (1898) and studied Wagner's works with J. Kniese, acting as repetiteur at the festivals from 1898 to 1901. Returning to Paris, he began a most active propaganda for Wagner; in 1902 he conducted the French premiere of *Götterdämmerung* at the Theatre du Château d'Eau, and in the same year he established the Association des Concerts A. Cortot, which he directed for 2 years, educating the public to an appreciation of Wagner; in 1904 he became conductor of the orch. concerts of the Soc. Nationale and of the Concerts Populaires at Lille (to 1908). In 1905, together with Thibaud (violin) and Casals (cello), he formed a trio which soon gained a great European reputation. He founded, with A. Mangeot, the École Normale de Musique (1919), and became its director, also giving a summer course in piano interpretation there annually; gave many lecture recitals and appeared as a guest conductor with various orchs. He authored *Principes rationnels de la technique pianistique* (Paris, 1928); *La Musique française de piano* (2 vols., 1930–48); *Cours d'interpretation* (Paris, 1934); *Aspects de Chopin* (Paris, 1949).

cosa rara os sia Bellezza ed onestà, Una. Opera, 1786, by Vicente Martín y Soler (b. Valencia, May 2, 1754; d. St. Petersburg, Jan. 30, 1806), to a libretto by Da Ponte, 1st performed in Vienna. The score reflects the contemporaneous fascination with exotic subjects; its libretto is drawn from the history of the Ottoman Empire. The opera was probably the 1st to include a Viennese waltz in the score; another distinction is the use of the mandolin as an accompanying instrument in a serenade. Mozart quoted an aria from *Una cosa rara* in *Don Giovanni*.

Così fan tutte (Thus Do All Women). Opera buffa by Mozart, 1790, 1st produced in Vienna. Da Ponte's libretto treats the testing of romantic fidelity through 2 disguised soldiers pursuing each other's sweethearts.

Costello, Elvis (born Declan Patrick McManus), English rocker and songwriter; b. London, Aug. 25, 1955. He spent his childhood in Liverpool, the city of the Beatles. When he was quite young he managed to get a contract with a company called Stiff Records. His well-written songs were permeated with the feeling of doom, personal as well as universal; he also challenged conservatism and fascism at every opportunity. Among his 1st hits were *Less than Zero*, *Watching the Detectives*, *Red Shoes*, and a love ballad, *Alison*, all on his album *My Aim Is True* (1977). His next album, *This Year's Model* (1978), increased his popularity with *Chelsea*, *Pump It Up*, *No Action*; the 3rd album, *Armed Forces* (1979), included *Oliver's Army*, *Accidents Will Happen*, and *Green Shirt*. From then on Costello continued to be prolific, if not always consistent; while he has recorded a majority of his albums with the Attractions (keyboards, bass, drums), he will shift his style of repertoire, production values, and instrumentation where it suits him. Among his more interesting albums are *Get Happy* (1980), influenced by soul; *Almost Blue* (1981), an album of country-western covers; *Imperial Bedroom* (1982), a successful concept recording; *King of America* (1986), with a varied cast of backup musicians; and *The Juliet Letters* (1993), with the Brodsky String Quartet.

cotillion (Fr.). An 18th–19th century French dance, in 3/4 time, to quadrillelike music.

coulé (Fr.). LEGATO, slurred; also, a harpsichord grace note.

Council of Trent. A gathering of dignitaries of the Roman Catholic Church held in Trent from 1545 to 1563, part of which was devoted to the condemnation of the practice of using secular melodies and rhythms in sacred works. A decree was issued under the title *Abusus in sacrificio missae* (Abuse in the sacred mass). Some members of the Council advocated a total elimination of polyphony from the Mass and a return to plainchant, but the final verdict was to recommend that the Mass be primarily free from popular motives. Palestrina composed his celebrated *Missa Papae Marcelli* (c. 1555–62) in a purified type of polyphony as a demonstration of a possible reform without destroying its underlying structure. Exuberant music historians describe Palestrina's accomplishment as the "salvation of church music" from obscurantist forces, but this was an extravagant exaggeration.

count. An accent, beat, or pulse of a measure.

counter. Any vocal part set to contrast in some manner with the principal part or melody, i.e., *bass counter*, a 2nd bass part, or *countertenor*, a voice usually developed from the head-tones and falsetto of a bass voice, compass from g to c^2. Also, *counter-exposition*, reentrance of a fugue-subject; *counter-subject*, a fugal theme following the subject in the same part; *counter-tenor clef*, the C clef on the 2nd line (now obsolete).

counterculture. In modern sociology, counterculture embraces all manifestations of the rebellious young generation counterposing their own concept of social behavior, art, and even science in opposition to the establishment. In music, counterculture uses the techniques of the avant-garde calculated to irritate, exasperate, and stupefy the bourgeoisie and academic listeners (*épater le bourgeoisie*). Counterculture may express itself by the lowest audible sounds in deep bass. The most violent expressions of counterculture, reaching its climax in the 1960s, included the physical destruction of musical instruments, exemplified by forcible burning of an upright piano, drowning it, or dropping it from a helicopter at the altitude of 300 feet (as was actually done near Detroit under the auspices of the radio program *Detroit Listener's Digest*).

counterpoint (from Lat. *punctum contra punctum*, point against point, note against note). 1. The art of polyphonic composition. It did not take long before 2, 3, or more "points" (notes) were used against 1 point, and that principal point became CANTUS (song) and, by extension, CANTUS FIRMUS (a firm singing line). This terminology found its source in the hymns of the Christian Church. It was also in the tenets of the Church that the domination of perfect intervals—the octave, 4th, and 5th—was firmly established.

Early contrapuntal usages, such as those of the Parisian Notre Dame masters Leoninus and Perotinus, who flourished in the early centuries of the 2nd millennium of our era, introduced the dissonant ornament on the basic cantus. However, the interval of the 3rd, fundamental in common chords, was regarded as a dissonance and was used only as a concession to advanced tastes in the so-called FAUXBOURDON (false bass). The early stage of counterpoint was the tool of ARS ANTIQUA, as it was described by the later "enlightened" theorists of the ARS NOVA. But even ars nova was a body of composition abounding in contradictions.

True counterpoint, as we understand it from our study of the music of Bach, belongs to the great age of the Baroque. What are the foundations of this mighty art? These can be summarized as follows: several voices, above or below the basic theme, engage in a dance of mutually-consistent figurations; consonant intervals, the octave, 5th, major and minor 3rds and 6ths, form a tonal fabric of extraordinary variety, and yet all aim at the foreseeable cadence and the final triadic chord; rhythmic imitation among several interconnected voices creates a sense of unity in variety; dissonant intervals which participate in a pattern of intermingling voices must be resolved into consonances, even though such resolutions can be delayed by the introduction of numerous passing notes or ornamentation; the bass plays a commanding role establishing the fundamental tonality of the whole composition. Compositions with 2 or more simultaneous melodies form a polyphonic web of considerable intricacy. *Double counterpoint* is written so that the upper part can become the lower part, and vice versa; in *triple* and *quadruple counterpoint*, 3 and 4 parts are written so that they can be mutually exchanged.

Bach's great collections, *The Well-Tempered Clavier* and *The Art of the Fugue*, were designed as didactic works, specifically described as an aid to study. They summarized the practice of counterpoint as well as its development in mutual imitation of its component parts. By that time a number of scholastic works were published by various theorists establishing the rules of counterpoint in 5 species: note against note; 2 notes against note; 3 or more notes against note; syncopated counterpoint; and, finally, florid counterpoint. These species became fundamental to music courses in conservatories until the most recent times. Simultaneously, several attempts were made to unite counterpoint with harmony by means of figured bass. In the 19th century a number of learned professors of music, ensconced mainly at the German cons., spread their prehensile grasp throughout educational institutions of Europe, including Russia and America (German education in music soon became ubiquitous), inaugurating what may be called the Art of Pedantry, with the harmonic rules, by way of figured bass, being paramount. The British music theorist Ebenezer Prout introduced the principle of assumed fundamental bass, so as to prove that all counterpoint, and indeed all harmony, should be derived from the tonic and dominant. Thus, a chord of the supertonic 7th was indicated in such a treatise as the dominant-11th chord ($II^7 = V^{11}$).

countertenor. A very high male voice. Ideally, a countertenor sings in the contralto or soprano range, while retaining a masculine tone quality. Highly praised in the Middle Ages, countertenors were replaced in the Baroque era and their function was taken over by the castrati. But when the practice of emasculation came to an end in the 19th century, composers resumed the use of countertenors. They remain in fashion, thanks primarily to the early music movement.

country dance. A dance in 2/4 or 3/4 time in which the partners form 2 opposing lines which advance and retreat, the couples also dancing down the lines and returning to their places. See also CONTREDANSE.

country-western (country-and-western music). A symbiosis of American rural and cowboy song styles, producing a post-World War II mixture of traditional and popular musical Americana. Sources include Appalachian OLD-TIME ballads, fiddle tunes, and BLUEGRASS, jazz-influenced WESTERN SWING, the prewar Hawaiian guitar craze, and mainstream popular music. The geographic center of modern country-western music is Nashville, Tenn., where an unabashedly commercial agenda produced songs in which men missed their women, their whiskey, or their wandering; women were left holding the bag and pouring out their hearts. Beginning in the 1960s, country-western lyrics became more socially or politically topical, with the cultural changes of the U.S. reflected, albeit not immediately. The country-western world has since been splintered into several genres, including outlaw country, countrypolitan, folk revival, country-rock, and new country.

The songs are usually set in square time (4/4), although the waltz of the French Acadians (Cajuns) influences some of the repertoire. The simple melodies are characterized by an accented appoggiatura, moving from the 2nd to the 3rd scale step (e.g., in C major, D–E); country-western singers are happily free of academic restrictions and rich in artless syncopation, enlivened by plagal harmonic progressions. The classic country-western instrumentation includes acoustic, electric, and bass guitars; pedal steel guitar, a horizontal version of the Hawaiian steel guitar; and drums. Other traditional and modern instruments are added as needed.

coup de glotte (Fr., stroke of the glottis). A highly dramatic way of interrupted breath in singing, very popular among Italian singers but now regarded as old-fashioned stylistically. However, Caruso's coup de glotte in the aria *Ridi, pagliaccio* (from *Pagliacci*) moved audiences to tears.

couper sec et bref (Fr.). Cut off abruptly and quickly.

Couperin. Renowned family of French musicians. Its musical prominence dates from the 3 sons of Charles Couperin, merchant and organist of Chaume, in the dept. of Brie (now part of the dept. of Seine et Marne), and his wife, Marie Andry. The eldest of these, Louis (son #1), established the family in Paris, where it remained until the extinction of the male line in 1826. He was also the 1st of his name to hold the post of organist at St.-Gervais in Paris. He was followed in this position by his youngest brother, Charles (#2); François le Grand, son of Charles, and the family's most illustrious representative; Nicolas, son of François (son #3); Armand-Louis, son of Nicolas; and by the 2 sons of Armand-Louis, Pierre-Louis and Gervais-François. The following articles, arranged alphabetically, give the individual histories of some members of the Couperin family:

Couperin, Armand-Louis, organist and composer, son of Nicolas Couperin; b. Paris, Feb. 25, 1727; d. there, Feb. 2, 1789. His virtuosity on the organ was extraordinary; in 1748 he succeeded his father as organist at St.-Gervais; was also organist to the King (1770–89), and held appointments at St.-Barthelemy, Ste.-Marguerite, Ste.-Chapelle, St.-Jean-en-Greve, etc. He was one of the 4 organists of Notre Dame. He died a violent death, having been knocked down by a runaway horse. His compositions include sonatas, a trio, motets, and other church music. His wife, Elisabeth-Antoinette (born Blanchet; b. Paris, Jan. 14, 1729), was also a remarkable organist and clavecinist, still playing in public at the age of 81 (in 1810). She was the daughter of Blanchet, the famous clavecin maker, and sister-in-law to Pascal Joseph Taskin, the court instrument keeper under Louis XV.

Couperin, Charles, organist; b. Chaumes (baptized), Apr. 9, 1638; d. Paris, between Jan. 15 and Feb. 26, 1679. He succeeded his brother Louis as organist at St.-Gervais in 1661. He married Marie Guerin (Feb. 20, 1662), and is principally remembered as being the father of the celebrated François le Grand.

Couperin, François, organist and teacher; b. Chaumes, *c.* 1631; d. Paris, after 1708. He was a pupil of Chambonnières in harmony and clavecin playing; was active as a music teacher and organist. His claim to the appellation "Sieur de Crouilly" has been disproved. His daughter, Marguerite Louise (b. Paris, 1676; d. Versailles, May 30, 1728), was a well-known singer and harpsichordist. She was a fellow member of the Chambre du Roi with her cousin François le Grand, who wrote for her the verset *Qui dat nivem* and other pieces. Uncle of François "le Grand."

Couperin, François (surnamed "le Grand" for his superiority in organ playing), the most illustrious member of a distinguished family and 1 of the greatest of early French composers, son of Charles Couperin; b. Paris, Nov. 10, 1668; d. there, Sept. 11, 1733. He studied with his father; later was a pupil of Jacques-Denis Thomelin, organist of the King's chapel; in 1685 he became organist of St.-Gervais, which post he held until his death; on Dec. 26, 1693, after a successful competition, he succeeded Thomelin as organist of the Chapelle Royale, receiving the title of "organiste du roi"; in 1701 he was appointed "claveciniste de la chambre du roi, et organiste de sa chapelle," and in 1717 he received the title "Ordinaire de la musique de la chambre du roi"; also was made a chevalier of the Order of Latran. He was music master to the Dauphin and other members of the royal family, and ranked high in the favor of Louis XIV, for whom he composed the Concerts royaux, which, during 1714–15, were played in Sunday concerts in the royal apartments. He married Marie-Anne Ansault (Apr. 26, 1689), by whom he had 2 daughters: Marie-Madeleine (b. Paris, Mar. 9, 1690; d. Montbuisson, Apr. 16, 1742), who became organist of the Abbey of Montbuisson, and Marguerite-Antoinette (b. Paris, Sept. 19, 1705; d. there, 1778), who was a talented clavecin player; from 1731 to 1733, she substituted for her father as clavecinist to the King, being the 1st woman to hold this position; there were also 2 sons, Nicolas-Louis (b. July 24, 1707), who died young, and François-Laurent (b. c1708). Famed as an organist, Couperin also acquired a high reputation for his remarkable ability as a performer on the clavecin.

His compositions may be conveniently divided into 3 categories: those written for the church, those for the King, and those for the general public. More than half of his creative life was taken up with the religious compositions of the 1st 2 periods. These include *Pieces d'orgue consistantes en deux Messes* (1690, a total of 42 pieces), formerly attributed to his uncle François; motets; *Elevations*; *Leçons de tenébres*, etc. Couperin's last and most prolific period was concerned exclusively with instrumental works, and in this field he achieved his greatest and most enduring distinction. In 1713, 1716, 1722, and 1730 he publ. the 4 vols. of his *Pieces de clavecin*, consisting of about 230 pieces in 27 *ordres* (suites), each suite being a series of dance forms, programmatic in title and content (*Les Baccanales, La Nanète, Les Petits Moulins à vent, Le Carillon de Cythère, Les Baricades Mistérieuses, Les Tic-Toc-Choc ou Les Maillotins,* etc.). In 1716 he publ. an expository work pertaining to the execution of his clavecin pieces, *L'Art de toucher le clavecin,* which attained wide celebrity, and which influenced the keyboard style of Couperin's great contemporary, Bach. Couperin also introduced the trio sonata to France, his 1st works in this form being an imitation of Corelli. Later, in 1726, he publ. 4 sonatas, *Les Nations,* described as "sonades" or "suites de symphonies en trio," 3 of which are partial reworkings of earlier pieces. They are composed alternately in the strict primitive form, SONATA DA CHIESA, and the more flexible composite of dance forms, SONATA DA CAMERA. The 3rd of the series, *L'Imperiale,* perhaps represents his most mature and inspired style. Living at a time during which the rivalry between French and Italian music reached its climax, Couperin sought to adapt the new Italian forms to his own personal, and essentially French, style. In his *Les goûts-réünis* (1724), a series of concerted pieces with strings very similar in form and spirit to the *Pieces de clavecin,* one finds titles such as *Sicilienne* and *Ritratto dell' amore.* In the following year he publ. an *Apothéose de Lully,* in which the rivals Lully and Corelli are made to unite for the furtherance of art.

Couperin's style of composition was based on the BASSO CONTINUO, the most important voices usually being the uppermost, carrying the melody, and the bass. Nevertheless, his music sometimes attains considerable complexity (on

François Couperin

occasion requiring as many as 3 harpsichordists for its proper execution). His melodic invention, particularly in his use of the rondeau, was virtually inexhaustible, his themes swift and expressive. An outstanding feature was his inventive mode of ornamentation, in the gallant style of the period.

Couperin, Gervais-François, organist and composer, 2nd son of Armand-Louis Couperin; b. Paris, May 22, 1759; d. there, Mar. 11, 1826. He succeeded his brother, Pierre-Louis, as organist at St.-Gervais in 1789, also taking over his other appointments. He composed sonatas, variations, etc. He was the last of the Couperins to serve as organist at St.-Gervais, although his daughter, Celeste (b. 1793; d. Belleville, Feb. 14, 1860), played there at the time of her father's death. She was a teacher of singing and piano at Beauvais for about 10 years.

Couperin, Louis, organist, violinist, violist, and composer; b. Chaumes, *c.* 1626; d. Paris, Aug. 29, 1661. He went to Paris with Chambonnières, whose pupil he was; in 1653 became organist of St.-Gervais, a post in which he was succeeded, without interruption, by other members and descendants of the Couperin family until 1826; from 1656 he was a violinist and violist in the orchs. of the court ballets, and musician of the Chambre du Roi. He composed Pieces de clavecin, Carillons for Organ, violin pieces, etc. He was one of the earliest of French composers for the harpsichord in the new harmonic style employing the basso continuo, possibly being preceded only by his teacher, Chambonnières.

Couperin, Nicolas, organist, son of François; b. Paris, Dec. 20, 1680; d. there, July 25, 1748. In 1733 he succeeded his cousin François le Grand as organist at St.-Gervais.

Couperin, Pierre-Louis, organist and composer, known as M. Couperin *l'aine* or Couperin *fils,* son of Armand-Louis Couperin; b. Paris, Mar. 14, 1755; d. there, Oct. 10, 1789. He was organist to the King, later at Notre Dame, St.-Jean, St.-Merry, and St.-Gervais (succeeded his father early in 1789; died 8 months later).

coupler. A mechanical organ stop acting to connect 2 manuals, or pedal with manual, so that when 1 is played on, the other is combined with it. *Coupler-pedal*, a coupler worked by foot.

couplet. 1. Two successive poetic lines forming a pair, usually rhymed. 2. In triple time, 2 equal notes occupying the time of 3 such notes in the established rhythm, thus:

courant. COURANTE.

courante (Fr.). A stately and courtly old French dance in triple meter, of moderate tempo, with considerable melodic ornamentation. In the 18th century the courante became an integral part of the Baroque; hence, the instrumental piece so called.

courtship and music. Darwin wrote in *The Expression of the Emotions in Man and Animals*: "Music has a wonderful power of recalling in a vague and indefinite manner those strong emotions which were felt during long-past ages, when, as is probable, our early progenitors courted each other by the aid of vocal tones." Literature and art abound in stories of courtship and love engendered and encouraged by music making. Winged cupids anachronistically play the lute to speed Venus and Adonis on the road to erotic consumption. Apollo plays the lyre to win the hearts of nymphs. Orpheus, son of Apollo, enchanted nymphs by his lyre, and even reclaimed Eurydice from the nether regions by singing. But when he refused to make love to the multitudes of furiously inflamed Bacchantes, he was torn to pieces by them and his dismembered limbs were sent down the river. The forest god Pan used his vocal powers to attract the reluctant nymph Syrinx, and she sought refuge in a pond where she was metamorphosed into a field of reeds. Frustrated, Pan collected the reeds and made a panpipe out of them.

Composers of historical times wrote syms. to attract their distant objects of adoration. Berlioz wrote his *Sym. fantastique* as an offering of love to the Shakespearian actress Harriet Smithson. But he could not speak English and she could not speak French, so they had to wait. He finally married her, but their life together was fairly miserable, and she died young. Schumann paid tribute to his love for Clara Wieck by inserting a brief elegy to her under the Italian form of her name "Chiara" in his piano work,

CARNAVAL. Tolstoy, who in his old age came to regard art, literature, and music as conduits of immorality, drew a horrendous picture of the aphrodisiac power of the last movement of Beethoven's *Kreutzer Sonata* by throwing together the female pianist and the male violinist. A famous 19th-century French painting, representing a similar outburst of passion between a mustachioed violinist and a fragile girl pianist, has been used commercially to advertise perfume. A painting by the British artist William Holman Hunt, entitled *The Awakening Conscience*, shows a well-petticoated Victorian damsel rising distractedly from the lap of her piano teacher. A great number of male piano teachers married their pupils; Theodore Leschetizky married at least 4. Many more music teachers took their nubile pupils as outlets for their artistic passions, most notably Fibich, who wrote hundreds of piano pieces as a diary of his relationship with a beloved piano student (who was also his librettist).

Coussemaker, (Charles-) Edmond (-Henri) de, French music scholar; b. Bailleul, Nord, Apr. 19, 1805; d. Bourbourg, Jan. 10, 1876. He studied music as a child. His main profession was the law; while studying law at the Univ. of Paris he took private lessons with Pellegrini in singing and Anton Reicha in harmony. He continued his studies with Lefebvre in Douai, after becoming a practicing lawyer. At this time (1831–35) he found leisure to compose music of the most varied description, all of which, with the exception of a few romances and 2 sets of songs, is unpubl., and apparently lost. His interest in history and archaeology led him to the study of the authentic documents of music; he was also influenced by the scholarly articles in *La Gazette et Revue Musicale* (then ed. by Fétis). During successive terms as judge in Hazebrouck, Dunkirk, and Lille, he continued to accumulate knowledge of musical documentation; he assembled a vast library; 1,075 items in his library are listed in the *Catalogue des livres, manuscrits et instruments de musique du feu M. Ch. Edm. de Coussemaker* (Brussels, 1877; issued for an auction).

covered. See OCTAVE.

covered strings. Strings of silk, wire, or gut, covered with spiral turns of fine silver or copper wire.

Coward, (Sir) Noël, English playwright and author of musical comedies; b. Teddington, Middlesex, Dec. 16, 1899; d. Port Maria, Jamaica, Mar. 25, 1973. At the age of 11 he appeared on the stage and was associated with the theater ever after, in the triple capacity of actor, playwright, and producer. Having had no formal education in music, he dictated his songs to a musical amanuensis. Among the musical comedies for which he wrote both words and music are *This Year of Grace* (N.Y., 1928); the operetta *Bittersweet* (London, 1929); *Conversation Piece* (London, 1934); *Pacific 1860* (London, 1946); *Ace of Clubs* (London, 1950); *After the Ball*, to Wilde's *Lady Windermere's Fan* (London, 1954); 51 songs from his musical plays are publ. in the *Noël Coward Song Book* (N.Y., 1953) with the author's introduction.

cowbell. Large metal bell with heavy clappers worn around the neck of a cow or bellwether. In the modern era, scores by Webern and Mahler have included the instrument; it is commonly found in Latin American, jazz, and other popular music.

Cowell, Henry Dixon

Remarkable, innovative American composer; b. Menlo Park, Calif., Mar. 11, 1897; d. Shady, N.Y., Dec. 10, 1965. His father, of Irish birth, was a member of a clergyman's family in Kildare; his mother was an American of progressive persuasion. Cowell studied violin with Henry Holmes in San Francisco; after the earthquake of 1906, his mother took him to N.Y., where they were compelled to seek support from the Soc. for the Improvement of the Condition of the Poor; they returned to Menlo Park, where Cowell was able to save enough money, earned from menial jobs, to buy a piano.

He began to experiment with the keyboard by striking the keys with fists and forearms; he named such chords TONE CLUSTERS and at the age of 13 composed a piece called *Adventures in Harmony*, containing such chords. Later he began experimenting in altering the sound of the piano by placing various objects on the strings, and also by playing directly under the lid of the piano pizzicato and glissando. He 1st exhibited these startling innovations on Mar. 5, 1914, at the San Francisco Musical Soc. at the St. Francis Hotel, much to the consternation of its members, no doubt. The tone clusters per se were not new; they were used for special sound effects by composers in the 18th century to imitate thunder or cannon fire. The Russian composer Rebikov applied them in his piano piece *Hymn to Inca*, and Ives used them in his *Concord Sonata* to be sounded by covering a set of white or black keys with a wooden board. However, Cowell had a priority by systematizing tone clusters as harmonic amplifications of tonal chords, and he devised logical notation for them. The tone clusters eventually acquired legitimacy in the works of many European and American composers.

Cowell also extended the sonorities of tone clusters to instrumental combinations and applied them in several of his symphonic works. In the meantime Cowell began taking lessons in composition with E. G. Strickland and Wallace Sabin at the Univ. of Calif., Berkeley, and later with Frank Damrosch at the Inst. of Musical Art, N.Y., and, privately, with Charles Seeger (1914–16). After brief service in the U.S. Army in 1918, where he was employed 1st as a cook and later as arranger for the U.S. Army Band, he became engaged professionally to give a series of lectures on new music, illustrated by his playing his own works on the piano. In 1928 he went to Russia, where he attracted considerable attention as the 1st American composer to visit there; some of his pieces were publ. in a Russian ed., the 1st such publications by an American. Upon return to the U.S. he was appointed lecturer on music at the New School in N.Y.

In 1931 he received a Guggenheim fellowship grant, and went to Berlin to study ethnomusicology with Hornbostel. This was the beginning of his serious study of ethnic musical materials. He had already experimented with some Indian and Chinese devices in some of his works; in his *Ensemble for Strings* (1924) he included Indian thundersticks. The piece naturally aroused considerable curiosity. In 1931 he formed a collaboration with the Russian electrical engineer Theremin, then visiting the U.S.; with his aid he constructed an ingenious instrument which he called the Rhythmicon; it made possible the simultaneous production of 16 different rhythms on 16 different pitch levels of the harmonic series. He demonstrated the Rhythmicon at a lecture-concert in San Francisco in 1932. He also composed an extensive work entitled *Rhythmicana*, but it did not receive a performance until 1971, at Stanford Univ., using advanced electronic techniques. In 1927 Cowell founded the *New Music Quarterly* for publication of ultramodern music, mainly by American composers.

Cowell's career was brutally interrupted in 1936, when he was arrested in Calif. on charges of homosexuality (then a heinous offense in that state) involving the impairment of the morals of a minor. Lulled by the deceptive promises of a wily district attorney of a brief confinement in a sanatorium, Cowell pleaded guilty to a limited offense, but he was vengefully given a maximum sentence of imprisonment, up to 15 years. Incarcerated at San Quentin, he was assigned to work in a jute mill, but indomitably continued to write music in prison. Thanks to interventions in his behalf by a number of eminent musicians, he was paroled in 1940 with Percy Grainger as a guarantor of his good conduct; he obtained a full pardon in 1942, from the governor of Calif., Earl Warren,

after it was discovered that the evidence against him was largely contrived.

In 1941 he married Sidney Robertson, a noted ethnomusicologist. He was then able to resume his full activities as ed. and instructor; he held teaching positions at the New School for Social Research in N.Y. (1940–62), the Univ. of Southern Calif., Mills College, and the Peabody Cons. of Music in Baltimore (1951–56); was also appointed adjunct prof. at summer classes at Columbia Univ. (1951–65). In 1951 Cowell was elected a member of the National Academy of Arts and Letters; received an honorary Mus.D. from Wilmington College (1953) and from Monmouth (Ill.) College (1963). In 1956–57 he undertook a world tour with his wife through the Near East, India, and Japan, collecting rich prime materials for his compositions, which by now had acquired a decisive turn toward the use of ethnomusicological melodic and rhythmic materials, without abandoning, however, the experimental devices which were the signposts of most of his works. In addition to his symphonic and chamber music, Cowell publ. in 1930 an important book, *New Musical Resources*. He also ed. a symposium, *American Composers on American Music*; in collaboration with his wife he wrote the 1st biography of Ives (1955).

crab canon. A canon in which the imitating voice proceeds in reverse, i.e., from the last to the 1st notes of the subject. *Crab movement*, backward movement of a melody.

Cradle Will Rock, The. Musical play by Blitzstein, 1937, a proletarian drama concerning the formation of a steelworkers' union.

Craft, Robert (Lawson), American conductor and brilliant writer on music; b. Kingston, N.Y., Oct. 20, 1923. He studied at the Juilliard School of Music (B.A., 1946) and the Berkshire Music Center; took courses in conducting with Monteux. During World War II he was in the U.S. Army Medical Corps. In 1947 he conducted the N.Y. Brass and Woodwind Ensemble. He was conductor of the Evenings-on-the-Roof and the Monday Evening Concerts in Los Angeles (1950–68). A decisive turn in his career was his encounter in 1948 with Stravinsky, whom he greatly impressed by his precise knowledge of Stravinsky's music; gradually he became Stravinsky's closest associate. He was also instrumental in persuading Stravinsky to adopt the 12-

tone method of composition, a momentous turn in Stravinsky's creative path. He collaborated with Stravinsky on 6 vols. of a catechumenical and discursive nature: *Conversations with Igor Stravinsky* (N.Y., 1959); *Memories and Commentaries* (N.Y., 1960); *Expositions and Developments* (N.Y., 1962); *Dialogues and a Diary* (N.Y., 1963); *Themes and Episodes* (N.Y., 1967); *Retrospections and Conclusions* (N.Y., 1969). Resentful of frequent referral to him as a musical Boswell, Craft insists that his collaboration with Stravinsky was more akin to that between the Goncourt brothers, both acting and reacting to an emerging topic of discussion, with Stravinsky evoking his ancient memories in his careful English, or fluent French, spiced with unrestrained discourtesies toward professional colleagues on the American scene, and Craft reifying the material with an analeptic bulimia of quaquaversal literary, psychological, physiological, and culinary references in a flow of finely ordered dialogue.

Crawford (Seeger), **Ruth Porter,** remarkable American composer; b. East Liverpool, Ohio, July 3, 1901; d. Chevy

Chase, Md., Nov. 18, 1953. She studied composition with Charles Seeger, whom she later married; her principal piano teacher was Heniot Levy. She dedicated herself to teaching and to collecting American folk songs; when still very young she taught at the School of Musical Arts, Jacksonville, Fla. (1918–21); then gave courses at the American Cons., Chicago (1925–29) and at the Elmhurst College of Music, Ill. (1926–29). In 1930 she received a Guggenheim fellowship. She became known mainly as a compiler of American folk songs; publ. *American Folk Songs for Children* (1948), *Animal Folk Songs for Children* (1950), and *American Folk Songs for Christmas* (1953). Her own compositions, astonishingly bold in their experimental aperçus and insights, often anticipated many techniques of the future avant-garde; while rarely performed during her lifetime, they had a remarkable revival in subsequent decades, most notably the 1931 String Quartet.

Creation Mass. Mass in B-flat Major by Haydn, 1801.

Creation, The (*Die Schöpfung*). Oratorio by Haydn, 1798, who conducted its 1st performance in Vienna. The orig. text was in English, compiled mainly from Genesis and Milton's epic poem, *Paradise Lost,* by an obscure writer; it was trans. into German by Gottfried van Swieten. It is grandiose in conception; the section entitled *Representation of Chaos* is particularly remarkable in its orch.1 coloring.

Création du monde, La (Creation of the World). Ballet by Milhaud, 1923, 1st performed in Paris. The music was inspired by Milhaud's visit to Harlem, N.Y. (1922); the jazz bands he heard there impressed him greatly. *La Création du monde* is a reinterpretation of Genesis. The score is historically important as the 1st example of "symphonic jazz," a full year before Gershwin's *Rhapsody in Blue.*

creativity

The musical profession is sharply divided into 2 categories: creative work, that is, individual composition, and performing interpretation. Since the interpreter is only a servant of the composer, it is natural that performing artists are placed lower in the philosophical estimate of music than creative musicians. But as far as worldly success is concerned, famous interpreters gain by and large greater fame and a much greater fortune. But it is the composers who enter their names in gold letters on the illuminated pages of music history, not the interpreters.

Fortunately for the cause of music, many composers are also great artists who can perform their own works as pianists, violinists, or conductors. In rare instances the composer's talent as an interpreter matches his genius as a composer. Chopin, Liszt, and Paganini were such complete men of music. In the 20th century perhaps the only composers who were also great performers were Rachmaninoff and Bernstein. Most composers can play only their own compositions, avoiding the careers of performing artists. Such were Scriabin, Debussy, and Bartók, as interpreters of their piano works. Stravinsky played the piano in some of his works, but he was not a professional pianist.

Many musicians known chiefly as interpreters also compose music on the side, but this music is generally of a fairly low quality. Symphonies written by professional conductors are often derisively described as KAPELLMEISTERMUSIK, a conductor's music. Some pianists have written technical studies and minor pieces of excellent value and of great popular appeal. The case of Anton Rubinstein is curious. He was undoubtedly one of the greatest pianists who ever lived, but in his lifetime he was also an extremely successful composer of operas, syms., and concertos. The judgment of posterity greatly devaluated his importance as a composer; his name is rarely even mentioned in histories of composition. He remains a disembodied phantom of great pianism, for he died before the advent of the phonograph; only his solo piano pieces escaped the dustbin of music history.

The question of whether the art of composition is superior to the interpretive art has been at least partly answered by recent investigations in the physiology of the brain. In normal right-handed individuals, the left hemisphere of the brain is the seat of higher intellectual qualities, governing speech, analytical reasoning, and other attributes of the active intellect, whereas the right hemisphere controls emotions, gestures, and the passive appreciation of the arts. It is, therefore, in the right hemisphere that the performing ability has its nervous center, and if it is damaged, the artist can no longer express himself in music and would be unable even to remember the simplest melodies. But if his musical intellect, located in the left side of the brain, is untouched, he will be able to compose music even if he cannot remember the notes he writes down.

The process of musical invention remains mysterious. Although it has been established that the musical impulses generate in the right hemisphere of the brain, which governs emotion and the fine arts and other nonverbal capacities, it is the intellectual left side that must arrange and organize the raw creative material. This process probably underlies the nature of inspiration. If this analysis is correct, as recent physiological studies of the brain suggest, then inspiration, or creative impulse, is generated vaguely and almost unconsciously in the right side of the brain, and is then "brained over" to the rational left side. It is then the right side that figuratively exclaims "Eureka!" and the left side is the one that develops this stroke of genius, rationally and intellectually. But even the development of an idea needs periodical impulses of creativity at important points.

Every person working in the abstract field experiences a series of such spurts of inspiration, following the primary "eureka"-type impulse. It is not inconceivable that these impulses can eventually be measured in terms of electrical units and that the chemical changes that are effected by them can be analyzed. It will then be possible to draw an electroencephalograph of inspiration. Such a drawing of inspiration may not be inspiring per se as a design, and *a priori* it seems probable that there is no quantitative, or qualitative, difference between the inspirational impulse of a Beethoven and a Malotte. It is interesting to note that in German, inspiration is *Einfall*, a "falling in." The remaining mystery involves the peculiar nature of the electro-chemical condition that creates favorable circumstances for the incidence of a "eureka" in the right hemisphere of the brain.

Credo (Lat., I believe). The Nicene Creed, part of the Roman Catholic High Mass Ordinary. The longest portion of the Ordinary, the Credo can be broken down into sections for compositional purposes: *Credo in unum deum* (I believe in one God); *Patrem omnipotentem* (Father almighty); *Et in unum Dominum* (and in one Lord); *Et incarnatus est* (and was incarnate); *Crucifixus* (Crucified); *Et resurrexit* (and was resurrected); *Et in Spiritum sanctum* (and in the Holy Spirit); *Confiteor unum baptisma* (I confess one baptism).

Credo Mass. Mass in C Major by Mozart, 1776 (K. 257).

Creedence Clearwater Revival. (Leader/guitar/vocal/songwriter: John Fogerty, b. Berkeley, Calif., May 28, 1945; guitar/piano/vocal: Tom Fogerty, b. Berkeley, Nov. 9, 1941; d. Scottsdale, Ariz., Sept. 6, 1990; bass: Stu Clark, b. Oakland, Calif., Apr. 24, 1946; drums: Doug Clifford, b. Palo Alto, Calif., Apr. 24, 1945.) Roots-revival rock band of the late 1960s noted for the pungent songs and vocals of John Fogerty. Growing out of a series of amateur high school bands, the band was signed to a local Calif. jazz label, Fantasy, in 1967. The group soon had major hits with Fogerty's *Proud Mary* (later covered by Ike and Tina Turner), *Born on the Bayou, Bad Moon Rising, Fortunate Son, Who'll Stop the Rain?, Run through the Jungle,* and *Lookin' Out My Backdoor.* Most of Fogerty's songs drew on American folk themes, getting inspiration from early rock and rockabilly styles. In early 1971 Fogerty left the group, and they struggled on for about a year before disbanding. Fogerty unsuccessfully pursued a solo career, staging a successful comeback in the mid-'80s with a couple of hits from his album, *Centerfield.* He made yet another comeback in 1997 with a new album and tour.

crescendo (It., growing). A gradual increase in loudness. The abbreviation is *cresc.*, followed by lines or dots to indicate the duration: cresc......... The word itself can also be broken up by several dots or hyphens: cre....scen....do. The effect of gradual swelling up of the sound was primarily cultivated by the Mannheim school in the 18th century. A musician who heard the Mannheim musicians perform wrote that the power of their crescendo made the audience rise from their seats in response to the music. A brief outburst of crescendo may be indicated by two lines diverging at an acute angle from a point: ◁ .

Crescendo may begin from any dynamic level, including forte.

Crescendo il forte (It.). Increase the loudness (found in Baroque scores). *Crescendo molto molto*, increase the loudness quickly; *crescendo pedal*, a pedal mechanism drawing all stops successively up to *full organ*; the swell-pedal.

Crescent (Chinese crescent, Chinese Pavilion). An instrument of Turkish origin, used in military music; it has crescent-shaped brass plates hung around a staff and surmounted by a cap or pavilion; around the plates little bells are hung, which are jingled in time with the music.

Crespin, Régine, outstanding French soprano, later mezzo-soprano; b. Marseilles, Feb. 23, 1927. She studied pharmacology; then began taking voice lessons with Suzanne Cesbron-Viseur and Georges Jouatte in Paris. She made her debut in Mulhouse as Elsa in 1950 and then sang at the Paris Opéra. She acquired a European reputation as one of the best Wagnerian singers; she sang Kundry at the Bayreuth Festivals (1958–60); appeared also at La Scala in Milan, at Covent Garden in London, and made her debut with the Metropolitan Opera, N.Y., as the Marschallin (1962); she remained with the Metropolitan until her farewell appearance as Mme. De Croissy in *Dialogues of the Carmelites* in 1987. She also sang Sieglinde and Amelia in *Un ballo in maschera*; also appeared as a concert singer. Her sonorous, somewhat somber voice suited dramatic parts excellently.

Cristofori, Bartolomeo, celebrated Italian instrument maker; b. Padua, May 4, 1655; d. Florence, Jan. 27, 1731. He was the inventor of the 1st practical piano as opposed to the clavichord (which also employs a type of hammer action), although 2-keyed instruments called "Piano e Forte" are known to have existed in Modena in 1598, and a 4-octave keyboard instrument shaped like a dulcimer, with small hammers and no dampers, dating from 1610, is still in existence. He was a leading maker of clavicembalos in Padua; about 1690 went to Florence, where he was instrument maker to Ferdinando de' Medici; on the latter's death in 1713, he was made custodian of the court collection of instruments by Cosimo III. According to an article by Maffei (1711), Cristofori had up to that year made 3 "gravecembali col piano e forte," these having, instead of the usual jacks plucking the strings with quills, a row of little hammers striking the strings from below. The principle of this hammer action was adopted, in the main, by Gottfried Silbermann, the Streichers, and Broadwood (hence called the "English action"). Following the designation by its inventor, the new instrument was named piano-forte. A piano of Cristofori's making is in the possession of the Metropolitan Museum of Art, N.Y.

croche (Fr., crooked). Eighth note. Its black mensural equivalent, the semiminim, was notated by a perpendicular stem with a drooping flag attached to it.

Crociato in Egitto, Il (The Crusader in Egypt). Opera by Meyerbeer, 1824.

croma (It.). 8th note.

cromatico (It.). Chromatic.

cromorne (Eng., obsolete). CRUMHORN.

crook. A short tube, bent or straight, which can be fitted to the main tube of a horn, trumpet, or cornet to lower its

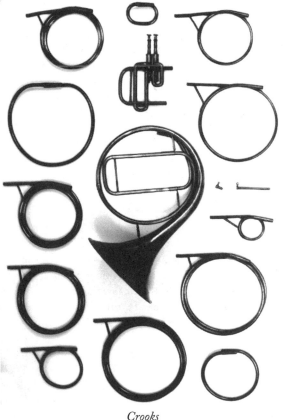

Crooks

fundamental pitch. This method was widely used in the 18th and 19th centuries but became obsolete with the invention of chromatic valve trumpets and horns.

crooner. A popular singer who intones his songs in a soft, seductive manner.

cross flute. Transverse flute; that is, one held across the mouth and blown from the side.

cross relation. The chromatic contradiction of a tone in one part by another; it consists in sounding, either together or in succession, a tone and its chromatically altered octave. This progression may also be viewed as a chromatic passing tone occurring not in the same voice but in another. This modus operandi is strictly verboten in proper scholastic exercises. But English consort music of the latter 17th century is replete with such progressions. Even in the very opening of his 3rd Sym. in F Major, Brahms violates the pedantic prohibition by having the melody descend via F major—F–C–A–G–F—while the bass defiantly rises from the low F to A-flat, a minor 3rd above it.

cross rhythm. Simultaneous use of 2 or more different meters while observing the least common denominator of the measure. For example, the Spanish polymeter, placing 3/4 against 6/8, produces a distinctive cross rhythm in which the strong beats of the meters alternate; they fall together only on the downbeat, the 1st of 6 beats:

Jazz syncopation thrives on cross rhythm; much world music depends on it. But European classical music tends to be dominated by the main beat or beats of the chosen meter, so that the cross rhythm functions in a momentary or ornamental manner. Brahms was probably the most consistent of pre-20th-century composers to use the device, e.g., the piano *Capriccio* in C-sharp Minor (No. 5, op. 76).

crossover. This term evolved in mainstream popular circles to describe the phenomenon of a recording in one style of music becoming highly successful with a very different audience; typical examples are classical music recordings of performers such as Horowitz, Cliburn, Pavarotti, Perlman,

and Domingo that have soared to or near the top of the hit parade; sometimes specific pieces become popular. The other principal crossover situation is when a performer records in an unexpected style, such as Streisand's classical album or Mark O'Connor's Concerto for fiddle and orch. See also FUSION.

crotales (Fr., from Lat. *crotalum*, hand clappers). Small hollow-sphere cymbals of definite pitch, played with a small mallet; antique cymbals.

crotalum (Lat., from Grk. *crotalon*). A clapper used in ancient Greek dances and choruses to punctuate stressed beats.

crotchet (U.K.). Quarter note. *Crotchet-rest*, a quarter rest.

Crucifixus (Lat.). A section of the CREDO, from the Roman Catholic High Mass.

Crumb, George (Henry, Jr.), distinguished and innovative American composer; b. Charleston, W.V., Oct. 24, 1929. He was brought up in a musical environment; his father played the clarinet and his mother was a cellist; he studied music at home; began composing while in school, and had some of his pieces performed by the Charleston Sym. Orch. He then took courses in composition at Mason College in Charleston (B.M., 1950); later enrolled at the Univ. of Ill. (M.M., 1952) and continued his studies in composition with Ross Lee Finney at the Univ. of Mich. (D.M.A., 1959); in 1955 he received a Fulbright fellowship for travel to Germany, where he studied with Boris Blacher at the Berlin Hochschule für Musik. He further received grants from the Rockefeller (1964), Koussevitzky (1965), and Coolidge (1970) foundations; in 1967 held a Guggenheim fellowship, and also was given the National Inst. of Arts and Letters Award. In 1968 he was awarded the Pulitzer Prize in music for his *Echoes of Time and the River*. Parallel to working on his compositions, he was active as a music teacher. From 1959 to 1964 he taught piano and occasional classes in composition at the Univ. of Colo. at Boulder; in 1965 he joined the music dept. of the Univ. of Pa.; in 1983 he was named Annenberg Prof. of the Humanities there.

In his music Crumb is a universalist. Nothing in the realm of sound is alien to him; no method of composition is unsuited to his artistic purposes; accordingly, his music can sing as sweetly as the proverbial nightingale, and it can be as rough, rude, and crude as a primitive man of the mountains.

The vocal parts especially demand extraordinary skills of lungs, lips, tongue, and larynx to produce such sound effects as percussive tongue clicks, explosive shrieks, hissing, whistling, whispering, and sudden shouting of verbal irrelevancies, interspersed with portentous syllabification, disparate phonemes, and rhetorical logorrhea. In startling contrast Crumb injects into his sonorous kaleidoscope citations from popular works, such as the middle section of Chopin's *Fantaisie-Impromptu*, Ravel's *Boléro*, or some other "objet trouvé," a procedure 1st introduced facetiously by Satie. In his instrumentation Crumb is no less unconventional. Among the unusual effects in his scores is instructing the percussion player to immerse the loudly sounding gong into a tub of water, having an electric guitar played with glass rods over the frets, or telling wind instrumentalists to blow soundlessly through their tubes. Spatial distribution also plays a role: instrumentalists and singers are assigned their reciprocal locations on the podium or in the hall. All this is, of course, but an illustrative decor; the music is of the essence.

Like most composers who began their work around the middle of the 20th century, Crumb adopted the Schoenbergian idiom, seasoned with pointillistic devices. After these preliminaries he wrote his unmistakably individual *Madrigals*, to words by the martyred poet Federico García Lorca, scored for voice and instrumental groups. There followed the most extraordinary work, *Ancient Voices of Children*, performed for the 1st time at a chamber music festival in Washington, D.C., in 1970; the text is again by Lorca; a female singer intones into the space under the lid of an amplified grand piano; a boy's voice responds in anguish; the accompaniment is supplied by an orch. group and an assortment of exotic percussion instruments, such as Tibetan prayer stones, Japanese temple bells, a musical saw, and a toy piano. A remarkable group of 4 pieces, entitled *Makrokosmos*, calls for unusual effects; in one of these, the pianist is ordered to shout at specified points of time.

Crumb's most grandiose creation is *Star-Child*, representing, in his imaginative scheme, a progression from tenebrous despair to the exaltation of luminous joy. The score calls for a huge orch., which includes 2 children's choruses and 8 percussion players performing on all kinds of utensils, such as pot

Crumhorn

lids, and also iron chains and metal sheets, as well as ordinary drums; it had its 1st performance under the direction of Pierre Boulez with the N.Y. Phil. in 1977.

crumhorn. An obsolete double-reed WINDCAP INSTRUMENT of the oboe family, gently curved upward at the bell; its greatest prominence was in the late 15th, 16th, and the 1st half of the 17th centuries. Its sound was angelically pure and sweet; angels in Renaissance paintings were often shown playing crumhorns. However, its range was not much greater than an octave, and its dynamic range was limited. *Crumhorn* is a common English spelling; an alternative form is *cromorne*. In German, it is *Krummhorn* (crooked horn); in French, *tourebout* (turned-up end); in Italian, *cornamuto toto* (twisted horn).

crwth (crouth, crouch; Welsh, Middle Eng.; pronounced "crowd"). An ancient plucked or bowed lyre, probably the earliest European instrument of this type; the national instrument of Wales. In its modern form it has a fingerboard and 6 (formerly 3) strings. It is rectangular in shape and is topped by a wooden board. The body is carved out of a single piece of wood; it was terminated by 2 parallel arms joined at the end by a crossbar, the center of which supported the fingerboard.

csárdás (Hung.; misspelled *czárdás*). A stylized Hungarian folk dance in 2/4 time that became popular in the 1st half of the 19th century. The term comes from the word *csárda*, Hungarian for a village inn. The dance consists of 2 parts, a slow introduction, called *lassu*, which is danced by men only, and the csárdás proper, also called *friss* or *friszka*, a lively dance for both men and women, in accentuated 2/4 or 4/4 time. The csárdás became popular in

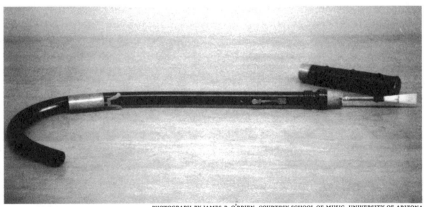

PHOTOGRAPH BY JAMES P. O'BRIEN, COURTESY SCHOOL OF MUSIC, UNIVERSITY OF ARIZONA

Hungary as a salon dance toward the middle of the 19th century. Csárdás numbers are often included in ballets; one of the best known is the csárdás in *Coppélia* by Delibes.

C-sharp minor. This key, to judge from its use by composers, particularly in piano pieces, possesses a meditative, somewhat somber nature. Typical in this regard is the 1st movement of Beethoven's *Moonlight Sonata*, (No. 2, op. 27) which suggested to an imaginative critic the surface of a moonlit lake in Switzerland. The famous Prelude in C-sharp Minor by Rachmaninoff (No. 2, op. 3) is an example of the use of this key for solemn evocation of old Russia, with bells ringing over the resonant harmonies. Schumann's *Études symphoniques*, also in C-sharp minor, fit into the description of meditative recollection. There is an evocative Tchaikovsky Nocturne in C-sharp Minor (No. 4, op. 19).

This tonality is rarely encountered as the principal key of a symphonic work; the most outstanding example is Mahler's 5th Sym., which begins with the funereal measures of doom; but modulations are frequent in the score. Prokofiev set his last sym., the 7th, in C-sharp minor; he called the work a *Youth Sym.*, glorifying the spirit of the young Soviet generation. The finale is in the major tonic of the key, enharmonically notated as D-flat major. But what is most intriguing in this work is that its opus number is 131, which is the opus number also of one of Beethoven's last string quartets, also in C-sharp minor. Prokofiev, ever alert to numerical parallels and contrived coincidences, could not have been unaware of this double identity of key and opus number, but apparently he decided to enjoy the joke in private; not anyone of the usually alert Soviet analysts of Prokofiev's works has noted this similarity.

Cuatro Soles, Los. Indigenous ballet by Chávez, 1930. The 4 suns each represent 1 of the 4 elements of heaven and earth.

Cuauhnahuac. Symphonic poem by Revueltas, 1933, in which Mexican percussion instruments play a dominant role. Cuauhnahuac is the Indian name for Cuernavaca, a Mexican tourist resort. Revueltas described this piece as "music without tourism" and said that it represents "anticapitalist agitation." It was 1st performed in Mexico City.

Cuban Overture. Concert overture by Gershwin, 1932, with many Cuban instruments and influences, originally entitled *Rhumba*.

cubism. The musical counterpart of cubism in art is the erection of massive sonorous complexes moving at different speeds and angular motion. Such harmonic boulders produce the best effect in polytriadic structures. Cubistic music must be static, with a low potential. There should be no intermediate melodic or harmonic shifts between cubistic complexes, but tremolo effects within each unit may contribute to resonant power congruent with massive sonic structures.

Cucaracha, La (The Cockroach). Famous Mexican song which became popular about the time of the Mexican revolution of 1910. "La Cucaracha" was the nickname of the girl in the song; the words vary, those of the modern version complaining that La Cucaracha would not go out because she had no marijuana to smoke.

Cuckoo and the Nightingale, The. Organ concerto in F major by Handel, 1739, publ in the "2nd set," 1740. The nickname is suggested by falling 3rds and trills.

cue. A phrase, from a vocal or instrumental part, occurring near the end of a long pause in another part, and inserted in small notes in the latter to serve as a guide in timing its reentrance.

Cui, César (Antonovich), significant Russian composer, 1 of the "Mighty Five"; b. Vilnius, Jan. 18, 1835; d. Petrograd, Mar. 26, 1918. He was the son of a soldier in Napoleon's army who remained in Russia, married a Lithuanian noblewoman, and settled as a teacher of French in Vilnius. Cui learned musical notation by copying Chopin's mazurkas and various Italian operas, then tried his hand at composition on his own. In 1849 he took lessons with Moniuszko in Vilnius. In 1850 he went to St. Petersburg, where he entered the Engineering School in 1851 and later the Academy of Military Engineering (1855). After graduation in 1857, he became a topographer and later an expert in fortification. He participated in the Russo-Turkish War of 1877; in 1878 he became a prof. at the Engineering School and was tutor in military fortification to Czar Nicholas II. In 1856 Cui met Balakirev, who helped him master the technique of composition. In 1858 he married Malvina Bamberg; for her he wrote a scherzo on the theme BABEG (for the letters in her name) and CC (his own initials). In 1864 he began writing music criticism in the St. Petersburg *Vedomosti* and later in other newspapers, continuing as music critic until 1900.

Cui's musical tastes were conditioned by his early admiration for Schumann; he opposed Wagner, against whom he wrote vitriolic articles; he attacked Strauss and Reger with even greater violence. He was an ardent propagandist of Glinka and the Russian national school, but was somewhat critical toward Tchaikovsky. He publ. the 1st comprehensive book on Russian music, *Musique en Russie* (Paris, 1880). Cui was grouped with Rimsky-Korsakov, Mussorgsky, Borodin, and Balakirev as one of the *Moguchaya Kuchka* (Mighty Five); the adjective in his case, however, is not very appropriate, for his music lacks grandeur; he was at his best in delicate miniatures, e.g., *Orientale*, from the suite *Kaleidoscope*, op. 50. A vol. of his Selected Articles (1864–1917) was publ. in Leningrad in 1953.

cuivré (Fr., metal-covered). With a brassy tone, especially on the French horn, when a hand is inserted into the bell, partially closing it, and thus producing a forced sound. If the bell is closed more completely, the pitch is raised a semitone; the notation for this effect is the desired pitch with a plus sign (+) over the note.

cuivres (Fr., metal-covered instruments). Brass instruments.

Cunning Little Vixen, The. Opera by Janáček, 1924, based on a newspaper serial depicting the natural world anthropomorphically, so as to make social commentary.

cupo, -a (It., gloomy). Dark, deep, obscure; reserved. *Con voce cupa*, with a veiled, intense tone.

cupped mouthpiece. The shallower, cup-shaped form of mouthpiece for brass wind instruments, as opposed to the deeper CONICAL (cone-shaped) MOUTHPIECE.

Curlew River. Church parable by Britten, 1964, 1st performed at the Aldeburgh Festival in England, 1964. The libretto is derived from a Japanese Noh play in which a mother searches for her son who was taken away from her on the Curlew River; he is dead, but his grave becomes an object of pilgrimage.

Curran, Alvin, important American composer of the experimental school; b. Providence, R.I., Dec. 13, 1938. He studied piano and trombone in his youth, later receiving training in composition from Ron Nelson at Brown Univ. (B.A., 1960) and from Elliott Carter and Mel Powell at Yale Univ. (M.Mus., 1963). He went to Rome (1965), where he founded the Musica Elettronica Viva ensemble for the performance of live electronic music with Richard Teitelbaum and Frederic Rzewski; the ensemble later evolved to include all manner of avant-garde performance practices. His compositions range from tape works to experimental pieces using the natural environment.

cursus (Lat.). Generically, the type of prosody used at the end of a sentence. The type of cursus depends on the relative length of certain syllables. Some scholars maintain that a metrical cursus developed in church singing into a rhythmic cursus, in which the long syllables are sung at a higher pitch.

curtal. An obsolete dulcian- or bassoon-type instrument, used in the 16th to mid-18th centuries. It is known in other languages by the term eventually applied to the modern bassoon.

cut time. ALLA BREVE.

cybernetics (from Grk. *kybernan*, govern). The exercise of human control over mechanical and electrical apparatus, especially in the field of communication. In music, cybernetical data are collected by various aleatory, intuitive, or other means; the resulting materials are translated into a system of musical parameters, and a viable outline is drawn. It is in the selection and the programming of cybernetical elements that a composer can assert his personality. In music, cybernetical serendipity plays a beneficial part. Novel ideas often suggest themselves during the process of mutation and permutation of thematic elements, contributing to the all-important problem of musical communication.

cyclical forms. Forms which embrace a cycle or set of movements, such as the SUITE or PARTITA, the SONATA, SYMPHONY, and CONCERTO.

cylindrical tube. An instrument tube that does not taper; as opposed to the CONICAL TUBE, which tapers very gradually.

cymbales antiques (Fr.). Antique cymbals. See CROTALES.

cymbals. Orch. percussion instrument, consisting of a pair of concave plates of brass or bronze, with broad, flat rims and holes for the straps by which they are held; used to make strong accents, or to produce peculiar effects.

Cyrenaic hedonism. Hedonistic traits in modern music developed as a natural psychological reaction to the cataclysm of World War I. Composers and the public sought relaxation in hedonistic dalliance, cyrenaic in its complete orgiastic abandon and sybaritic in its quest for mindless comforts. The center of this cult of music for pleasure was France; it enjoyed a particular vogue between 1920 and 1935, when the slogan of NEW SIMPLICITY was launched as an antidote to post-Romantic solipsism. In form and content this new music cultivated the elegant conceits of the French rococo period, with an emphasis on epicurean qualities designed to please the palate. Historically it was the long-delayed fruition of the musical cuisine of Rossini, with occasional polyharmonies and asymmetric rhythms used for modern seasoning.

Cythara. KITHARA.

Czerny, Carl, composer, pianist, and influential pedagogue; b. Vienna, Feb. 20, 1791; d. there July 15, 1857. Of Czech extraction (*černý* means "black" in Czech), he was trained as a pianist by his stern father whose rule of life was work without any distraction. When Czerny himself became a teacher he demanded a similar dedication from his pupils. His day began at 7 o'clock in the morning and included a single meal before going to bed. Czerny was fortunate in gaining Beethoven's friendship; his only Piano Sonata, op. 7, bears a striking resemblance to Beethoven's style. Among Czerny's own students was Liszt.

Czerny's name is everlastingly connected with the enormous compounds of piano studies under such names as *School of Velocity* or *School of Finger Dexterity*, the exercises that continued to inflict pianistic torture upon generations of students after him. Czerny declared that he had no time to get married because of his heavy teaching schedule, but nature took vengeance on him when at the age of 50 he confessed in a secret diary his adoration of a youthful pupil to whom he never dared to admit his sentimental attraction.

D. 1. Fourth note of the alphabetical scale. In French, Spanish, Italian, and Russian nomenclature, this note retains the name Re, derived from the 1st syllable of the 2nd line of the millennian hymn *Ut queant laxis*: "Resonare libris." 2. (Ger. *D*; Fr. *ré*; It. *re*) The 2nd tone and degree in the typical diatonic scale of C major. In musical theory capital *D* designates the D-major triad, small *d* the d-minor triad. *D* also stands for Da (D.C. = da capo) and Dal (D.S. = dal segno).

D dur (Ger.). D major.

D major. This is the key of classical vigor and clarity of expression, particularly suitable for works written for string instruments, for the tonic and the dominant are available in D major on open strings in the violin, viola, and cello. Triadic and scale passages in D major can be executed with natural facility in rapid tempo on string instruments, with open strings serving as convenient signposts. The greatest majority of violin concertos are written in D major: those by Beethoven, Brahms, and Tchaikovsky are the most famous examples. Mozart set his *Prague Sym.* and the endearing Haffner Serenade in D Major, both works exuding the joy of music-making. One of the most frequently played Haydn syms., written for his London concerts and catalogued as no. 104, is in D major. An American music critic who once opined that the fire exit signs in the then newly built Sym. Hall in Boston should be marked "Exit in Case of Brahms" qualified his anti-Brahms sentiment when he wrote that the 2nd Sym. of Brahms—in the key of D major—is "the most genial of the 4, and the most easily accepted by an audience." When Prokofiev determined to show to the world that he could emulate Haydn à la moderne, he wrote his *Classical Sym.* in the key of D major.

D minor. This is the key of repressed passion. The greatest of all works written in D minor, Beethoven's 9th Sym., opens with an allusion rather than an overt declaration, exposing vacant 5ths, with the full triadic conjunction disclosed only after the listening ear can no longer endure the ambiguity. The last sym. of Schumann is also in D minor, but, strangely enough, he let it lie fallow for many years before completing it. Bruckner selected the key of D minor for his most lugubrious inspiration, his 3rd Sym. Yet Mahler's 3rd Sym. (and Mahler is commonly regarded as a kindred spirit to Bruckner), also set in D minor, expresses joy in the presence of nature; its separate movements describe in musical tones what the flowers tell us in perfume, and what the angels tell us in their cherubic language. Franck's Sym. in D Minor is philosophically restrained; the use of an English horn, never regarded as a "symphonic" instrument, reveals an emotional strain. In his popular Piano Trio, op. 49, Mendelssohn represses his passion almost to the point of rupture.

Why is the D-minor triad commonly used by pianists to tune up string instruments in playing chamber music? Why not D major? The explanation may be in the neutral character of the sound of D minor, which is more suitable to the nontempered natural pitch of the violin and the cello.

D moll (Ger.). D minor.

D string. The 3rd string on the violin; 2nd on the viola, cello, and double bass.

da (It.). By, from, for, of.

da braccio (It.). Describing string instruments held "at the arm."

da camera (It.). In the Baroque, secular chamber music.

da capo (It., from the head). Repeat from the beginning. *Da capo al fine*, repeat from beginning to end (that is, to the word *fine* or a fermata); *da capo al segno*, from the beginning to the sign ⅍; *da capo al segno, poi (segue) la coda*, from the beginning to the sign, then play the coda.

da capo aria. ARIA DA CAPO.

da capo senza replica (senza ripetizione; It.). Play through from the beginning, ignoring the repeats.

da chiesa (It., of the church). Music intended for church performance.

da eseguirsi (It.). To be executed.

da Ponte, Lorenzo (born Emanuele Conegliano), famous Italian librettist; b. Ceneda, near Venice, Mar. 10, 1749; d. N.Y., Aug. 17, 1838. He was of a Jewish family; was converted to Christianity at the age of 14, and assumed the name of his patron, Lorenzo da Ponte, Bishop of Ceneda. He then studied at the Ceneda Seminary and at the Portogruaro Seminary, where he taught from 1770 to 1773; in 1774 obtained a post as prof. of rhetoric at Treviso, but he was dismissed in 1776 for his beliefs concerning natural laws. He then went to Venice, where he led an adventurous life, and was banished in 1779 for adultery; subsequently lived in Austria and in Dresden; in 1782 he settled in Vienna and became official poet to the Imperial Theater; met Mozart and became his friend and librettist of his most famous operas, *Le nozze di Figaro*, *Don Giovanni*, and *Così fan tutte*. From 1792 to 1798 he was in London; traveled in Europe; then went to N.Y. in 1805. After disastrous business ventures, with intervals of teaching, he became interested in various operatic enterprises. In his last years he was a teacher of Italian at Columbia College.

da seguirsi (It.). To be executed.

dactyl(e) (Lat., *dactylus*, finger, in reference to the layout of the joints). A metrical foot with syllables arranged as 1 long accented syllable followed by 2 short unaccented ones. A rapid waltz without strong upbeat represents a musical equivalent.

dadaism. A word invented by Tristan Tzara in 1916 at a congenial gathering of friends in a Zurich café. According to one of the many versions, the word *dada* owes its origin to French infantiloquy as a sort of dental lallation. Aesthetically dadaism was the product of the frustrations endured during World War I. Its philosophy was entirely negative. Derived from the vociferously proclaimed detestation of all art, music, and poetry, dadaism stood close to FUTURISM in its furious onslaught on all established values, but failed to offer a new art to replace the old. Despite its violently negative code, dadaism prepared a well-manured ground for the flowering of such fertile stylistic vegetation as surrealism. Dadaism also cast its proleptic shadow on the avant-garde of the 1920s and the improvisatory art of the HAPPENINGS.

Dafne. Opera by Peri, 1597, text by Rinuccini, considered the 1st opera to be composed. The music is lost.

dagli (dai, dal, dall', dalla, dalle, dallo; It.). To the, by the, for the, from the, etc.

Dahl, Ingolf, distinguished Swedish-born American composer, conductor, pianist, and teacher; b. Hamburg (of Swedish parents), June 9, 1912; d. Frutigen, near Bern, Switzerland, Aug. 6, 1970. He studied composition with Jarnach at the Cons. of Cologne (1930–32) and musicology at the Univ. of Zurich (1932–36), where he received instruction in conducting from Andreae. He went to the U.S. in 1938; settled in Calif., where he became active as a conductor and composer; was appointed an assistant prof. at the Univ. of Southern Calif. (1945); received 2 Guggenheim fellowships (1952 and 1960). He taught at the Berkshire Music Center, Tanglewood, in the summers of 1952–55. As a composer he adhered to an advanced polyphonic style in free dissonant counterpoint.

dal segno (It.). From the sign. *Dal segno al fine*, from the sign to the end.

Dale, Clamma, African-American soprano; b. Chester, Pa., July 4, 1948. She began to study piano as a child; later studied clarinet and singing; at 14 she began to study voice at Philadelphia's Settlement Music School; subsequently enrolled at the Juilliard School of Music in N.Y. (B.Mus., 1970; M.S., 1975); her teachers were Hans Heinz, Alice Howland, and Cornelius Reed. She made her debut with the N.Y. Opera as Antonia in *Les Contes d'Hoffmann* in 1975;

her other roles were Nedda, Musetta, the Countess in *Le nozze di Figaro*, Pamina, and Bess.

Dalibor. Opera by Smetana, 1868, based on a historical rebellion of Bohemian peasants led by the eponymous hero. He is captured, but a noblewoman who loves him attempts to free him from prison through male disguise. Unlike Beethoven's *Fidelio*, however, the scheme is unsuccessful; Smetana wrote 3 endings, all ending tragically for the lovers.

Dallapiccola, Luigi, distinguished Italian composer and pedagogue; b. Pisino, Istria, Feb. 3, 1904; d. Florence, Feb. 19, 1975. He took piano lessons at an early age; went to school at the Pisino Gymnasium (1914–21), except in 1917–18, when his family was politically exiled in Graz; studied piano and harmony in nearby Trieste (1919–21); in 1922 moved to Florence, where he took courses at the Cherubini Cons., studying piano with Ernesto Consolo (graduated 1924) and composition with Vito Frazzi (graduated 1931); was active in the Italian section of the ISCM from the early 1930s. In 1934 Dallapiccola was appointed to the faculty of the Cherubini Cons., where he stayed until 1967.

As a composer Dallapiccola became interested from the very 1st in the melodic application of atonal writing; in 1939 he adopted the dodecaphonic method of Schoenberg, with considerable innovations of his own (for example, the use of mutually exclusive triads in thematic structure and harmonic progressions). He particularly excelled in his handling of vocal lines in a difficult modern idiom. He visited London in 1946 and traveled on the Continent; taught several courses in American colleges: Berkshire Music Center, Tanglewood, Mass. (1951); Queens College, N.Y. (1956, 1959); the Univ. of Calif., Berkeley (1962); Dartmouth College (summer, 1969); Aspen Music School (1969); and Marlboro (1969). A collection of his essays was publ. under the title *Appunti incontri meditazioni* (1970).

Dame blanche, La (The Woman in White). Opera by Boieldieu, 1825, after Walter Scott. A woman pretends to be a ghost haunting a Scottish castle—hence the title.

Dameron, Tadd (Tadley Ewing), African-American jazz pianist, bandleader, arranger, and composer; b. Cleveland, Feb. 21, 1917; d. N.Y., Mar. 8, 1965. He was inspired to follow a career as a jazz musician by his brother Caesar, a saxophone player; he subsequently played piano with Freddie Webster, Zack White, and Blanche Calloway. In the 1940s and 1950s Dameron played with Gillespie,

Davis, and Clifford Brown. He became an accomplished composer and arranger, working in Chicago and N.Y. His career was plagued by his addiction to narcotics, as a result of which he served time in the federal prison in Lexington, Ky. (1958–60).

Damn Yankees. Musical by Richard Adler and Jerry Ross (the last work of the latter), 1955, based on Douglass Wallop's novel *The Year the Yankees Lost the Pennant*. With the aid of the Devil an aging baseball fan is transformed into a superstar who helps the lowly Washington Senator team defeat the perennially winning N.Y. Yankees. The fan gets out of the Devil's hold through a technicality. Includes *You've Got to Have Heart* and *Whatever Lola Wants*.

Damnation de Faust, La. Dramatic legend by Berlioz, 1846, based on part I of Goethe's *Faust*, 1st performed in Paris. Berlioz added a sequence placed in Hungary, which includes the celebrated *Rakoczy March*; an effective choral pandemonium in which minor devils converse in an agglutinative nonsense language; and, while Gretchen goes to Heaven, Faust is sent straight to Hell. The reinterpretation of Goethe (found also in Gounod's opera) is considered blasphemous by certain German cultural patriots. The Berlioz work is an oratorio, although there have been staged performances.

Damoiselle élue, La. Cantata by Debussy, 1893, based on a poem by D. G. Rossetti, for soprano, female chorus, and orch.

damper (Ger. *Dämpfer*). 1. A set of mechanical devices placed over piano strings; it goes into operation when the key of a note is released by the finger; this triggers the damper to stop the string, thus causing the string's vibration (i.e., sound) to end. 2. The mute of a brass instrument.

damper pedal. The right, or loud, piano pedal. When pressed, the DAMPERS are lifted from the strings, allowing them to vibrate freely and resonantly.

Dämpfer (Ger.). 1. DAMPER. 2. MUTE.

dance band. An instrumental ensemble accompanying ballroom dancing, composed of saxophones, trumpets, trombones, and percussion.

Dance in the Place Congo, The. Symphonic poem, 1918, by the American composer Henry F. Gilbert (1868–1928). Place Congo is a New Orleans square, once a hangout for African-Americans; the borrowing of local tunes signified Gilbert's pioneering attempt to integrate classical and world musics.

Dance of the Hours. See LA GIOCONDA.

Dancing in the Streets. Martha and the Vandellas' 1964 hit that became an anthem for 1960s inner-city youth. Later covered by Van Halen and Mick Jagger and David Bowie.

Danican-Philidor. PHILIDOR.

Danny Boy. Text added to the *Londonderry Aire* by Frederick Weatherly, 1913.

danse (Fr.). Dance.

Danse des Morts, La. Oratorio by Honegger, 1940, to a text by Claudel, based on the traditional image of the Dance of Death, including a quotation of the Dies Irae.

Danse macabre. Symphonic poem by Saint-Saëns, 1875, depicting an orgiastic Halloween-like evening, with ghostly violin apparitions, coming to an end with the rooster's crow.

Danse sacrée et danse profane. A work by Debussy, 1904, for harp and strings. The Sacred Dance is pentatonic and rhythmically static; the Profane Dance is set in mundane syncopation.

Danse Sauvage. Piano piece, 1913, by the American composer-pianist Leo Ornstein (1892–?). Its savagery is expressed by a series of rhythmic, dissonant chords. Amazingly enough, the piece shocked listeners when Ornstein played it in N.Y. and London on the eve of World War I, causing one bewildered English critic to describe Ornstein as "a new star in the musical sky that effectually pales the fires of Schoenberg and Stravinsky."

Danses concertantes. Orch.l suite by Stravinsky, 1942.

Dantons Tod. Opera by Einem, 1947, based on the life and death of a prime mover of the French revolution. The *Marseillaise* and other revolutionary songs are quoted.

danza (It., Sp.). Dance.

Danzón Cubano. A work by Copland, 1946, originally for 2 pianos and later orchestrated. It is similar in concept to his earlier *El Salón Mexico*.

Daphne. Bucolic tragedy by R. Strauss, 1938, on a subject found in the earliest operas: the eponymous nymph who eludes the amorous Apollo by transforming herself into a laurel tree. In his unhappiness he consecrates the tree.

Daphnis et Chloé. Ballet by Ravel, 1912, recounting in sensuous instrumental colors the mutual love of Daphnis and Chloé, who tend sheep. It was 1st performed by Diaghilev's Ballets Russes. Ravel later drew 2 orch.l suites from the ballet.

Dardanus. TRAGÉDIE EN MUSIQUE by Rameau, 1739, about a son of Jupiter who wins over a beloved princess of Phrygia and gets close to Venus as well.

dargason. An English country dance from the 16th century, also used in balladry, with an 8-measure melody that lacks a tonic final cadence, hence the description "circular." It is found in works or publications by Ravenscroft, Dowland, Playford, and Holst; Ben Jonson refers to it in his *Tale of a Tub*.

Dargomyzhsky, Alexander (Sergeievich), outstanding Russian composer; b. Troitskoye, Tula district, Feb. 14, 1813; d. St. Petersburg, Jan. 17, 1869. From 1817 he lived in St. Petersburg; studied piano with Schoberlechner and Danilevsky, and violin with Vorontsov. At 20 he was a brilliant pianist; from 1827 to 1843 he held a government position, but then devoted himself exclusively to music, studying assiduously for 8 years; visited Germany, Brussels, and Paris in 1845; in Moscow, produced an opera, *Esmeralda* (after Victor Hugo's *Notre-Dame de Paris*, 1847), with great success (excerpts publ. in piano score, Moscow, 1948). From 1845 to 1855 he publ. over 100 minor works (vocal romances, ballads, airs, and duos; waltzes, fantasies, etc.); in 1856 he brought out his best opera, *Rusalka*, at St. Petersburg (vocal score, with indications of instruments, publ. at Moscow, 1937); in 1867, an opera-ballet, *The Triumph of Bacchus* (written in 1845; perf. 1867); a posthumous opera, *The Stone Guest* (*Kamennyi gost*, after Pushkin's eponymous poem), was scored by Rimsky-Korsakov and produced at St. Petersburg in 1872; of *Rogdana*, a fantasy-opera, only a few scenes were sketched. At 1st a follower of Rossini and Auber, Dargomyzhsky gradually became convinced that dramatic realism with nationalistic connotations was the destiny of Russian music; he applied this realistic method in treating the recitative in his opera *The Stone Guest* and in his songs (several of these to satirical words). His orch.l works (*Finnish Fantasia, Cossack Dance, Baba-Yaga,* etc.) enjoyed wide popularity. In 1867 he was elected president of the Russian Music Soc.

dark (Fr., *relâche*). In theatrical jargon, no performance.

Daughter of the Regiment, The. FILLE DU RÉGIMENT, LA.

David. Opera by Milhaud, 1954, commemorating the city of Jerusalem and its greatest king.

David, Hal, American lyricist, brother of Mack David; b. N.Y., May 25, 1921. He studied journalism at N.Y. Univ.; then became collaborator with Bacharach and other composers of popular songs. His lyrics for *Raindrops Keep Falling on My Head* (1969) won an Academy Award. The lyrics he wrote for Bacharach include *Here Am I, Magic Moments, My Little Red Book, Love Can Break a Heart, Send Me No Flowers, The Story of My Life, What's New, Pussycat?,* and *Wives and Lovers.* They wrote the popular Broadway musical *Promises, Promises* (1968). He also contributed lyrics to several films, among them *Lost Horizon, Butch Cassidy and the Sundance Kid,* and *Moonraker.* From 1980 to 1986 he served as president of ASCAP.

David, Mack, American lyricist and composer, brother of Hal David; b. N.Y., July 5, 1912. He studied at Cornell Univ. and at St. John's Univ. Law School. Turning to writing for Broadway and for films, he collaborated with Count Basie, Burt Bacharach, Ernest Gold, Elmer Bernstein, David Raksin, Henry Mancini, and other composers. Among his best-known songs are *Bibbidi, Bobbidi, Boo* (1948); *Cat Ballou* (1965); *The Hanging Tree* (1959); *It's a Mad, Mad, Mad, Mad World* (1963); *My Own True Love* (1954). David filed a spectacular lawsuit for copyright infringement of his song *Sunflower* (1948), which he claimed was plagiarized by Jerry Herman for the latter's sensationally popular song *Hello, Dolly* (1964). The sum paid in an out-of-court settlement to David was in excess of half a million dollars.

Davidovich, Bella, esteemed Russian-born American pianist and pedagogue, mother of Dmitry Sitkovetsky; b. Baku, July 16, 1928. Her maternal grandfather was concertmaster of the Baku opera orch. and her mother was a pianist.

She began formal piano training when she was 6; at age 9 she appeared as soloist in the Beethoven 1st Piano Concerto in Baku. In 1939 she was sent to Moscow to pursue her studies with Konstantin Igumnov, with whom she subsequently also studied at the Moscow Cons. (1946–48), where she completed her training with Yakov Flier (1948–54). In 1949 she captured joint 1st prize at the Chopin Competition in Warsaw, which launched her upon a highly successful career in Russia and Eastern Europe; she was a soloist each season with the Leningrad Phil. (1950–78) and also taught at the Moscow Cons. (1962–78). In 1967 she made her 1st appearance outside Russia, playing in Amsterdam; in 1971 she made a tour of Italy.

Following the defection of her son to the West in 1977, she was refused permission to perform there by the Soviet government. In 1978 she emigrated to the U.S., becoming a naturalized U.S. citizen in 1984. In 1979 she made an acclaimed debut in a recital at N.Y.'s Carnegie Hall. In 1982 she joined the faculty of the Juilliard School in N.Y. but continued to pursue an international career. In 1988 she and her son returned to Russia, being the 1st émigrés to be invited to perform there by Goskontsert since the Gorbachev era of reform was launched.

Davidovsky, Mario, Argentine composer; b. Buenos Aires, Mar. 4, 1934. He studied composition and theory with Guillermo Graetzer in Buenos Aires and also took courses with Teodor Fuchs, Erwin Leuchter, and Ernesto Epstein. He continued his training with Milton Babbitt at the Berkshire Music Center, Tanglewood (summer 1958). He worked at the Columbia-Princeton Electronic Music Center (from 1960) and taught at the Univ. of Mich. (1964), the Di Tella Inst. of Buenos Aires (1965), the Manhattan School of Music in N.Y. (1968–69), Yale Univ. (1969–70), City College of the City Univ. of N.Y. (1968–80), and Columbia Univ. (from 1981), where he served as director of the Columbia-Princeton Electronic Music Center. He held 2 Guggenheim fellowships (1960, 1971) and in 1971 received the Pulitzer Prize in music for his *Synchronisms No. 6* for Piano and Electronics. In 1982 he was elected a member of the Inst. of the American Academy and Inst. of Arts and Letters. His method of composition tends toward mathematical parameters, as evidenced in his series of 8 electroacoustic compositions entitled *Synchronisms* (1963–74); electronic sound is integral to most of his work.

Davidsbündler-Tänze. Piano suite by Schumann, 1837, containing 18 pieces. The Davidsbund, the imaginary

"David's band," is dedicated to the overcoming of the Philistines in the musical world. The cryptic initials E. and F., which appear as signatures after each piece, stand for Eusebius and Florestan, representing the dual personalities of Schumann's nature, Eusebius as an earnest student of music and Florestan as a romantic youth.

Davies, Dennis Russell, American conductor; b. Toledo, Ohio, Apr. 16, 1944. He studied piano with Lonny Epstein and Sascha Gorodnitzki, and conducted with Jean Morel and Jorge Mester at the Juilliard School of Music in N.Y. (B.Mus., 1966; M.S., 1968; D.M.A., 1972), where he also taught (1968–71) and was cofounder (with Luciano Berio) of the Juilliard Ensemble (1968–74). He was music director of the Norwalk (Conn.) Sym. Orch. (1968–73), the St. Paul (Minn.) Chamber Orch. (1972–80), the Cabrillo (Calif.) Music Festival (from 1974), and the American Composers Orch. in N.Y. (from 1977). In 1978 he made his 1st appearance at the Bayreuth Festival, conducting *Der fliegende Holländer.* He was Generalmusikdirektor of the Württemberg State Theater in Stuttgart (1980–87), principal conductor and director of classical music programming at the Saratoga (N.Y.) Performing Arts Center (1985–88), and Generalmusikdirektor of Bonn (from 1987). In 1991 he assumed the posts of music director of the Brooklyn Academy of Music and principal conductor of the Brooklyn Phil. In 1987 he received the Alice M. Ditson conductor's award. Davies has acquired a notable reputation as a champion of contemporary music. He has conducted numerous premieres in the U.S. and Europe.

Davies, (Sir) **Peter Maxwell,** remarkable English composer and conductor; b. Manchester, Sept. 8, 1934. He went to Leigh Grammar School and then to the Royal Manchester College of Music and Manchester Univ. In 1957 he won a scholarship from the Italian government and proceeded to Rome, where he studied with Goffredo Petrassi; his orch.l work *Prolation* (named after the medieval metrical division) received the Olivetti Prize in 1958 and was performed at the festival of the ISCM in Rome on June 10, 1959. Returning to England, he served as director of music at Cirencester Grammar School (1959–62); it was there that he introduced for the 1st time his neo-Socratic method of schooling, encouraging his students to exercise their curiosity.

In 1962 he went to the U.S. on a Harkness fellowship and took a fruitful succession of sessions at Princeton Univ. In 1965 he joined the UNESCO Conference on Music in Education and traveled around the world on a lecture tour. In 1966–67 he served as composer-in-residence at the Univ. of Adelaide in Australia. In 1967 he organized with Harrison Birtwistle in London an ensemble called the Pierrot Players; in 1970 they decided to rename it the Fires of London, with programs of provocative modernistic works. In 1970 Davies made his home in the Orkney Islands; in 1977 he organized there the annual St. Magnus Festival, which gave its presentations at the Norse Cathedral of St. Magnus; there he also staged many of his own compositions, inspired by medieval chants. Despite the remoteness of the Orkney Islands from musical centers, the festival attracted attention. In 1979 Davies was awarded an honorary doctorate of music at Edinburgh Univ.; he was also appointed successor to Sir William Glock as director of music at Dartington Summer School and was named Composer of the Year by the Composers' Guild of Great Britain. He was commissioned to write a sym. for the Boston Sym. Orch. on the occasion of its centennial in 1981. In 1985 he was named composer-in-residence and associate conductor of the Scottish Chamber Orch. in Glasgow, with which he toured. In 1987 he was knighted.

In his works Davies combines seemingly incongruous elements, which include reverential evocations of medieval hymnody, surrealistic depictions of historical personages, and hedonistic musical theatrics. His most arresting work in this synthetic manner is a set of *8 Songs for a Mad King* for Male Voice and Instruments, a fantastic suite of heterogeneously arranged pieces representing the etiology of the madness of King George III (1969); at the other end of the spectrum is *Vesalii Icones* for Dancer, Solo Cello, and Instruments, in 14 movements, after 14 anatomical drawings by Andreas Vesalius depicting Christ's Passion and Resurrection. Davies is a fervent political activist, a participant in the movement combating the spread of nuclear weapons, and a staunch defender of the planetary environment against industrial pollution.

Davis, Anthony, African-American composer and pianist; b. Paterson, N.J., Feb. 20, 1951. He studied at Yale Univ. (B.A., 1975), proving himself to be an extremely facile jazz pianist; was cofounder of Advent (1973), a free jazz ensemble that included trombonist George Lewis; then played in trumpeter Wadada Leo Smith's New Delta Ahkri band (1974–77). He also played in N.Y. with violinist Leroy Jenkins (1977–79) and with flutist James Newton, both active proponents of the Assoc. for the Advancement of Creative Musicians. His compositions, while strictly notated, are improvisational in tone. His opera *X, The Life and Times of Malcolm X* was produced in Philadelphia (1985) and at N.Y.'s Lincoln Center (1989). Other works include *The Ghost Factory—MAPS* for solo violin, strings, harp, and percussion; *Lost Moon Sisters* for soprano, violin, keyboards, marimba, and vibraphone (1990); and *Hemispheres*, a 5-part dance work for Molissa Fenley (1983). Among his many recordings are *Of Blues and Dreams* (1978), *Hidden Voices* (with J. Newton; 1979), and *Under the Double Moon* (with J. Hoggard; 1982).

Davis, (Sir) **Colin** (Rex), eminent English conductor; b. Weybridge, Sept. 25, 1927. He studied the clarinet at the Royal College of Music in London, and played in the band of the Houschold Cavalry while serving in the army. He began his conducting career with the semiprofessional Chelsea Opera Group; in 1958 he conducted a performance of *The Abduction from the Seraglio* in London; from 1961 to 1965 he served as music director of Sadler's Wells. He made his U.S. debut as a guest conductor with the Minneapolis Sym. Orch. in 1960; subsequently had engagements with the N.Y. Phil., the Philadelphia Orch., and the Los Angeles Phil. From 1972 to 1983 he served as principal guest conductor of the Boston Sym. Orch. In 1967 he made his Metropolitan Opera, N.Y., debut, conducting Peter Grimes. From 1967 to 1971 he was chief conductor of the BBC Sym. Orch. in London. In 1965 he conducted at the Royal Opera at Covent Garden; he succeeded Solti as its music director in 1971.

Among his notable achievements was the production at Covent Garden of the entire cycle of *Der Ring des Nibelungen* in 1974–76; in 1977 he became the 1st British conductor to appear at the Bayreuth Festival, conducting *Tannhäuser*. He conducted the Royal Opera during its tours in South Korea and Japan in 1979, and in the U.S. in 1984. In 1983 he was appointed chief conductor of the Bavarian Radio Sym. Orch. in Munich, which he led on a tour of North America in 1986. In 1986 he stepped down as music director at Covent Garden to devote himself fully to his duties in Munich and to pursue far-flung engagements as a guest conductor with the major orchs. and opera houses of the world. He was made a Commander of the Order of the British Empire in 1965, and was knighted in 1980.

Davis, Miles (Dewey, III), outstanding African-American jazz trumpeter and bandleader; b. Alton, Ill., May 25, 1926; d. N.Y., Sept. 21, 1991. He learned to play trumpet while attending elementary school in East St. Louis, Ill., then continued his studies in high school, where he played in the band; even before his graduation he made professional appearances. In 1944 he went to N.Y. and entered the Juilliard School of Music; he frequented the jazz spots in the city. After deciding upon a full-time career as a jazz musician, he quit Juilliard in 1945 and commenced working with Charlie Parker, Coleman Hawkins, Benny Carter, and Billy Eckstine. His bebop style was modified in 1948, when a band he led included such an untypical jazz instrument as the horn (played by Gunther Schuller), and was exemplified by such numbers as *Boplicity*.

Miles Davis, at Birdland, 1955, with Paul Chambers on bass and John Coltrane on tenor sax

He introduced a "cool" manner of playing, as contrasted with the frantic "hot" bebop. His arranger was Gil Evans; he had John Coltrane on the saxophone and Philly Joe Jones on the drums. In his own numbers he introduced the lyrical and quiet modal type of setting, favoring the Lydian scale with its enervating tritone base, and he found suitable harmonies for it. By 1958 he abandoned standard pop practices and plunged into the mystical depths of exotic jazz in such far-out numbers as *Nefertiti* and *Sorcerer*. He then annexed electronics, forming a fusion style with hard rock (*Bitches' Brew*). To emphasize his departure from his native territory, he affected pseudo-African vestments at his public appearances. He began to use hallucinogenic drugs, and had some close encounters with unfeeling law enforcers.

As he prospered from megamillion sales of recordings, he became the target of extortionists eager to muscle in on the action; some inartistic malefactors peppered his snazzy Ferrari car with machine-gun bullets; he suffered a hip injury that required the implantation of an artificial bone. After a hiatus from 1975 to 1981 he returned to center stage with his album *The Man with the Horn* (1981). In 1982 he made an extensive tour of Europe. Always searching for new avenues of expression, he adapted the songs of such rock artists as Michael Jackson and Cyndi Lauper for use in his concerts. In 1986 he collaborated on a recording project with Prince. He also tried his skill at painting and appeared on television as an actor. In 1981 he married the actress Cicely Tyson; they divorced in 1988.

davul (*dawūl*). Cylindrical Turkish drum with a double head, closely associated with the ZURNĀ, a Turkish oboe.

Dawson, William Levi, African-American composer; b. Anniston, Ala., Sept. 26, 1898; d. Tuskegee, Ala., May 2, 1990. He ran away from home at 13 to enter the Tuskegee Inst.; later played trombone on the Redpath Chautauqua Circuit; graduated from the Tuskegee Inst. in 1921; studied with Carl Busch in Kansas City and at the American Cons. in Chicago (M.A., 1927). He played 1st trombone in the Chicago Civic Orch. (1926–30); then conducted the Tuskegee Choir. His best-known work is the *Negro Folk Sym.* in 3 movements (1934).

De Franco, "Buddy" (Boniface Ferdinand Leonardo), American jazz clarinetist; b. Camden, N.J., Feb. 17, 1923. He took up the clarinet at the age of 12; worked with many leading jazz musicians, including Gene Krupa (1941–42), Charlie Barnet (1943–44), Tommy Dorsey

(1944–46), and Count Basie (1950); then organized his own big band (1951) and quartet (1952), appearing with the latter for many years with much success. He led the Glenn Miller Orch. from 1966 to 1974, then resumed touring on his own.

De Koven, (Henry Louis) **Reginald,** American composer; b. Middletown, Conn., Apr. 3, 1859; d. Chicago, Jan. 16, 1920. He was educated in Europe from 1870, taking his degree at St. John's College, Oxford, in 1879. Before this he studied piano under W. Speidel at Stuttgart, and after graduation studied there another year under Lebert (piano) and Pruckner (harmony). After a 6-month course in Frankfurt under Hauff (composition), he studied singing with Vannuccini at Florence, and operatic composition under Genee in Vienna and Delibes in Paris. In 1902 he organized the Phil. Orch. at Washington, D.C., which he conducted for 3 seasons. He was music critic for the *Chicago Evening Post* (1889–90), *Harper's Weekly* (1895–97), N.Y. *World* (1898–1900; 1907–12), and later for the N.Y. *Herald*. Of the 30 stage works De Koven produced over a 33-year span, his best-known operetta *Robin Hood* (Chicago, 1890), the celebrated song *O, Promise Me* was introduced into the score shortly after its 1st perf., having originally been publ. as a separate song in 1889.

deaconing. In English and American colonial parish churches, the preliminary reading by a deacon, or another lay singer, of a line from a hymn before the entire congregation sings it; the practice was also called LINING OUT.

deafness. No greater misfortune can befall a musician than the loss of hearing. Beethoven gave an eloquent expression of this horror in his famous "Heiligenstadt Testament." He was willing to consult every Viennese quack who promised a cure. In his conversation books there is this pathetic notation: "There is in Vienna a Dr. Mayer who is employed by a sulphur vapor company which uses vibrations to cure sufferers from hearing impediments when no organic fault is found in the tissues. His electro-vibratory machine works by strengthening rheumatic ear infections, hardness of hearing and deafness." Some critics of Beethoven's last works explained their strangeness by Beethoven's deafness. "Beethoven's imagination seems to have fed upon the ruins of his sensitive organs," wrote William Gardiner of London in 1837.

Among other victims of ear ailments was Smetana. Pressure on the auditory nerve made him hear a constant drone on a high E; he memorialized this affliction in his 1st

String Quartet, entitled *From my Life*, in which he has the violin play a persistent high E. Schumann suffered from a similar disturbance technically known as tinnitus; during his last years he heard a constant A-flat. Fauré became almost totally deaf toward the end of his life, but he succeeded in hiding this condition sufficiently long to continue in his office as director of the Paris Cons.

Dearest Enemy. Musical by Rodgers and Hart, 1925, based on a historical moment during the American Revolution when a Manhattan woman entertained a group of British officers at her home long enough to allow an American battalion to escape from Harlem Heights. Includes *Bye and Bye* and *Here in My Arms*.

Death and the Maiden. Nickname for String Quartet No. 14 in D Minor by Schubert, 1824 (D.810). The work contains a variation set based on Schubert's song *Der Tod und das Mädchen*, on the inevitability of death.

Death and Transfiguration *(Tod und Verklärung)*. Symphonic poem by R. Strauss, 1890, 1st performed in Eisenach. The music depicts the struggle of a sick man with approaching Death, in the lugubrious key of C minor, the tonality of quiet horror and dissolution. But the death motive is transfigured at the end into C major, as the liberated soul departs from the body.

Death in Venice. Opera by Britten, 1973, after the novella of the same name by Thomas Mann; it was 1st performed in Aldeburgh, 1973. An aging German writer, Gustav Aschenbach ("brook of ashes"), goes to Venice in search of emotional experience; there he watches an adolescent Polish boy on a vacation with his family, admiring his Platonic purity and Apollonian beauty. An epidemic of cholera breaks out in Venice; Aschenbach listlessly stays on after the boy's departure and becomes a victim of the dreaded disease. Britten's opera is couched in an austere and yet dramatic manner, monodic in its structure; the part of Aschenbach is set almost entirely in accompanied recitative.

Mann himself visited Venice in 1911 and was impressed by a vacationing Polish boy who became the prototype of his novella. A motion picture has been made of *Death in Venice*, in which the character of Gustav Aschenbach was changed to that of a composer, strongly suggesting Gustav Mahler, and which uses Mahler's music in the soundtrack. Friends of Mahler's family vigorously protested against this unwarranted approximation. It was also discovered that the Polish boy of the novella was still living in Sweden as late as 1970 and remembered having seen Mann in Venice 60 years before.

Death of Klinghoffer, The. Opera by J. Adams, 1991, a postmodern retelling of the murder of the wheelchair-bound American Leon Klinghoffer aboard the kidnapped Italian ship *Achille Lauro* in the Mediterranean, 1985.

Debussy, Claude

Great modern French composer, considered the originator of musical impressionism, whose music created a new poetry of mutating tonalities and became a perfect counterpart of contemporaneous French painting; b. Achille-Claude Debussy, St.-Germain-en-Laye, Aug. 22, 1862; d. Paris, Mar. 25, 1918. Mme. Maute de Fleurville, the mother-in-law of the poet Verlaine, prepared him for the Paris Cons.; he was admitted at the age of 10 and studied piano with Marmontel (2nd prize, 1877) and solfège with Lavignac (3rd medal, 1874; 2nd, 1875; 1st, 1876). He further took courses in harmony with Emile Durand (1877–80) and practiced score reading under Bazille. In 1880 Marmontel recommended him to Mme. Nadezhda von Meck, Tchaikovsky's patroness. She summoned him to Interlaken, and they subsequently visited Rome, Naples, and Fiesole. During the summers of 1881 and 1882, Debussy stayed with Mme. von Meck's family in Moscow, where he became acquainted with the syms. of Tchaikovsky; however, he failed to appreciate Tchaikovsky's music and became more interested in the idiosyncratic compositions of Mussorgsky. Back in France he became friendly with Mme. Vasnier, wife of a Paris architect and an amateur singer.

Debussy made his earliest professional appearance as a composer in Paris (1882), at a concert given by the violinist Maurice Thieberg. In 1880 he had enrolled in the composition class of Guiraud at the Paris Cons. with the ambition of winning the Grand Prix de Rome; after completing his courses, he won the 2nd Prix de Rome in 1883. Finally, in 1884, he succeeded in obtaining the Grand Prix de Rome with his cantata *L'Enfant prodigue*, written in a poetic but conservative manner reflecting the trends of French romanticism. During his stay in Rome he wrote a choral work, *Zuleima* (1885–86), after Heine's *Almanzor*, and began work on another cantata, *Diane au bois*. Neither of these 2 incunabulae was preserved. His choral suite with orch., *Printemps* (1887), failed to win formal recognition. He then set to work on another cantata, *La Damoiselle élue* (1887–89), which gained immediate favor among French musicians.

In 1888 Debussy visited Bayreuth, where he heard *Parsifal* and *Die Meistersinger von Nürnberg* for the 1st time, but Wagner's grandiloquence never gained his full devotion. What thoroughly engaged his interest was the Eastern music, particularly the gamelan, that he heard at the Paris World Exposition in 1889. He was fascinated by the asymmetric rhythms of the thematic content and the new instrumental colors achieved by native players; he also found an inner valence between these oriental modalities and the verses of certain French impressionist and symbolist poets, including Mallarmé, Verlaine, Baudelaire, and Pierre Louÿs. The combined impressions of exotic music and symbolist French verses were rendered in Debussy's vocal works, such as *Cinq poèmes de Baudelaire* (1887–89), *Ariettes oubliées* (1888), *Trois mélodies* (1891), and *Fêtes galantes* (1892). He also wrote *Proses lyriques* (1892–93) to his own texts.

For the piano he composed *Suite bergamasque* (1890–1905), which includes the famous *Clair de lune*. In 1892 he began work on his instrumental *Prélude à l'après-midi d'un faune*, after Mallarmé, which comprises the quintessence of tonal painting with its free modal sequences under a subtle umbrage of oscillating instrumentation. The work was 1st heard in Paris in 1894; a program book cautioned the audience that the text contained sensuous elements that might be distracting to young females. It was about that time that Debussy attended a performance of Maeterlinck's drama *Pelléas et Mélisande*, which inspired him to begin work on an opera on that subject. In 1893 there followed *Trois chansons de Bilitis*, after prose poems by Louÿs, marked by exceptional sensuality of the text in a musical context of free modality; a later work, *Les Chansons de Bilitis* for 2 harps, 2 flutes, and celesta, was heard in Paris in 1901 as incidental music to accompany recited and mimed neo-Grecian poetry of Louÿs. Between 1892 and 1899, Debussy worked on 3 *Nocturnes* for orch.: *Nuages, Fêtes,* and *Sirènes*.

As the 20th century dawned, Debussy found himself in a tangle of domestic relationships. A tempestuous liaison with Gabrielle Dupont (known as Gaby Lhery) led to a break, which so distressed Gaby that she took poison. She survived, but Debussy sought more stable attachments; in 1899 he married Rosalie Texier, with whom he made his 1st attempt to form a legitimate union. But he soon discovered that like Gaby before her, Rosalie failed to satisfy his expectations, and he began to look elsewhere for a true union of souls. This he found in the person of Emma Bardac, the wife of a banker. He bluntly informed Rosalie of his dissatisfaction with their marriage. Like Gaby 7 years before, Rosalie, plunged into despair by Debussy's selfish decision, attempted suicide; she shot herself in the chest but missed her suffering heart. Debussy, now 42 years old, divorced Rosalie in 1905. Bardac and her husband had divorced earlier that year; Debussy married her in early 1908. They had a daughter, Claude-Emma (known as "Chouchou"), born Oct. 15, 1905; she was the inspiration for Debussy's charming piano suite *Children's Corner* (the title was in English, for Chouchou had an English governess). She survived her father by barely a year, dying of diphtheria in 1919.

With his opera *Pélleas et Mélisande*, Debussy assumed a leading place among French composers. It was premiered at the Opéra-Comique in Paris (1902), after many difficulties, including the open opposition of Maeterlinck, who objected to having the role of Mélisande sung by the American soprano Mary Garden, whose accent jarred Maeterlinck's sensibilities; he wanted his mistress, Georgette Leblanc, to be the 1st Mélisande. The production of the opera aroused a violent controversy among French musicians and littérateurs. The press was vicious in the extreme: "Rhythm, melody, tonality, these are 3 things unknown to Monsieur Debussy," wrote the doyen of the Paris music critics, Arthur Pougin. "What a pretty series of false relations! What adorable progressions of triads in parallel motion and 5ths and octaves which result from it! What a collection of dissonances, 7ths and 9ths, ascending with energy! . . . No, decidedly I will never agree with these anarchists of music!" Camille Bellaigue, a classmate of Debussy's at the Paris Cons., conceded that *Pélleas et Mélisande* "makes little noise," but, he remarked, "it is a nasty little noise."

The English and American reports were no less vituperative, pejorative, and deprecatory. "Debussy disowns melody and despises harmony with all its resources," opined the critic of the *Monthly Musical Record* of London. Echoing such judgments, the *Musical Courier* of N.Y. compared Debussy's "disharmony" with the sensation of "an involuntary start when the dentist touches the nerve

Claude Debussy, 1902

COURTESY OF THE NEW YORK PUBLIC LIBRARY

of a sensitive tooth." The American writer James Gibbons Huneker exceeded all limits of permissible literary mores by attacking Debussy's physical appearance. "I met Debussy at the Café Riche the other night," he wrote in the N.Y. *Sun*, "and was struck by the unique ugliness of the man . . . [H]e looks more like a Bohemian, a Croat, a Hun, than a Gaul." These utterances were followed by a suggestion that Debussy's music was fit for a procession of headhunters of Borneo, carrying home "their ghastly spoils of war."

Debussy's next important work was *La Mer*, which he completed during a sojourn to England in 1905; it was 1st performed in Paris. Like his String Quartet (1893) it was conceived monothematically; a single musical idea permeated the entire work, despite a great variety of instrumentation. It consists of 3 symphonic sketches: *De l'aube à midi sur la mer* (From Sunrise to Moon); *Jeux de vagues* (Play of the Waves); and *Dialogue du vent et de la mer* (Dialogue of Wind and the Sea). *La Mer* was attacked by critics with even greater displeasure than *Pélleas et Mélisande*. The American critic Louis Elson went so far as to suggest that the original title was actually *Le Mal de mer*, and that the last movement represented a violent seizure of vomiting. To summarize the judgment on Debussy, a vol. entitled *Le Cas Debussy* was

publ. in Paris (1910). It contained a final assessment of Debussy as a "deformateur musical," suffering from a modern nervous disease that affects one's power of discernment.

Meanwhile, Debussy continued to work. To be mentioned is the remarkable orch. triptych, *Images* (1906–12), comprising *Gigues, Iberia*, and *Rondes de printemps*. In 1908 he conducted a concert of his works in London; he also accepted engagements as conductor in Vienna (1910), Turin (1911), Moscow, and St. Petersburg (1913), and Rome, Amsterdam, and the Hague (1914). Among solo piano works of the period are the *12 Preludes* (2 vols., 1910, 1913) and *12 Études* (2 vols., 1915). *En blanc et noir*, for 2 pianos, dates from 1915. In 1913 Diaghilev produced Debussy's ballet *Jeux* in Paris. In 1917 Debussy played the piano part of his Violin Sonata at its premiere in Paris with violinist Gaston Poulet. But his projected tour of the U.S. with the violinist Arthur Hartmann had to be abandoned when it was discovered that Debussy had irreversible cancer of the colon. Surgery was performed in late 1915, but there was little hope of recovery.

The protracted 1st World War depressed him; his hatred of the Germans became intense as the military threat to Paris increased. He wrote the lyrics and the accompaniment to a song, *Noël des enfants*, in which he begged Santa Claus not to bring presents to German children whose parents were destroying the French children's Christmas. To underline his national sentiments, he emphatically signed his last works "musicien français." Debussy died on the evening in March 1918, as the great German gun, "Big Bertha," made the last attempt to subdue the city of Paris by long-distance (76 miles) bombardment.

Debussy emphatically rejected the term *impressionism* as applied to his music. But it cannot alter the essential truth that like Mallarmé in poetry, he created a style peculiarly sensitive to musical mezzotint, a palette of half-lit delicate colors. He systematically applied the oriental pentatonic scale for exotic evocations, as well as the whole-tone scale (which he did not invent, however; earlier samples of its use are found in works by Glinka and Liszt). His piece for piano solo, *Voiles* (1909), is written in a whole-tone scale, while its middle section is set entirely in the pentatonic scale. In his music Debussy emancipated discords; he also revived the archaic practice of consecutive perfect intervals (particularly 5ths and 4ths). In his formal constructions the themes are shortened and rhythmically sharpened, while in the instrumental treatment the role of individual solo passages is enhanced and the dynamic range made more subtle. Among his many operatic projects, Debussy was only able to complete *Pélleas et Mélisande*: of the begun and unbegun works, 2 exist in sizable fragmentary form: *Rodrigue et Chiméne*, after a Corneille play (1890–92), and *La Chûte de la maison Usher*, after Poe's *The Fall of the House of Usher* (1908–17).

Debussy was very imaginative in his expression marks; here are a few examples:

Ce rhythme doit avoir la valeur sonore d'un fond de paysage triste et glacé. This rhythm must have the sonorous validity of a sad and icy landscape;

Comme un écho de la phrase entendue précédemment. Echoing the phrase previously heard (*La Cathédrale engloutie*);

Comme un tendre et triste regret. Like a tender and sad regret;

Comme une buée irisée. Like a rainbow-colored mist;

Comme une lointaine sonnerie de cors. Like a distant sound of horns;

Comme une plainte lointaine. Like a distant plaint;

Commençer un peu au-dessous du mouvement. Start a little slower than the original tempo (*Préludes*);

Dans le sentiment du debut. In the mood of the opening;

Dans une brume doucement sonore. In a gently resonant mist (*La cathédrale engloutie*);

Frapper les accords sans lourdeur. Strike the chords lightly, without pressing.

début (Fr.). A 1st appearance by a performer or work. *Débutant*, a male performer who makes his debut; *débutante*, a female performer who makes her debut.

decay. The gradual extinction of a sound. See also ENVELOPE.

deceptive cadence. A cadence that instead of resolving to the tonic from the dominant, resolves to the submediant. In major keys the arrival chord is a minor triad a whole step up from the dominant; in minor keys, a major triad a semitone up from the dominant.

déchiffrer (Fr., decipher). Play or sing at sight.

decibel (abbrev. *db*). The minimal increment of sound energy perceptible to the human ear; one-tenth of a bel, the arbitrary unit of sound named for Alexander Graham Bell, the American acoustician and inventor. The range of tolerable loudness of sound varies from 25 decibels to about 100 decibels, corresponding to the sound of a full orch. Rock bands, in their pursuit of deafening noise, reach 120 decibels. Two hundred decibels is the so-called pain threshold, causing physical damage to the eardrum.

decima (Lat.). 1. The interval of a 10th. 2. An organ stop pitched a 10th higher than the 8' stops; TIERCE.

deciso (It.). Decisively, energetically.

declamando (declamato; It.). In declamatory style.

declamation. In vocal music, clear and correct enunciation of the words.

decomposition and reassembly. A freely topological approach to composition. The technique of decomposition and reassembly is suggested by the title of a painting by the futurist artist Umberto Boccioni, *Scomposizione*, in which the normal head of a woman is fragmented and reassembled in a topologically noncongruent shape. The idea is applicable to modern music. A melody can be fractured and its elements redistributed in a different configuration. Variations, tonal and atonal, can be experimentally rearranged, melodically, harmonically, and rhythmically. Decomposition and reassembly may provide interesting and novel combinations of thematic materials and stimulate a disadvantaged composer to explore the laws of musical congruence far beyond his ordinary capabilities.

Decoration Day. Orch.1 sketch by Ives, 1912, 2nd movement of the *Symphony: Holidays*.

decrescendo. DIMINUENDO.

decuplet. A group of 10 equal notes executed in the time proper to 8 notes of like value, or to 4 notes of the next high-

est value, in the established rhythm; marked by a slur and a figure 10:

dedications

Composers since time immemorial have been in the habit of dedicating their works to the high and the mighty. Immortality could be bought for a few florins or ducats. Every music lover knows Mozart's HAFFNER SERENADE; through this piece of sublime music an insignificant Salzburg functionary achieved immortality. Bach's *Goldberg Variations* obliquely glorified Bach's pupil Johann Gottlieb Goldberg, who requested Bach to write these extremely difficult and lengthy keyboard compositions to help Goldberg relieve the insomnia of one of his patrons. Bach was rewarded for his work with a golden goblet and 100 louis d'or, and Goldberg himself received a life stipend, but he died at the age of 29.

Beethoven's *Kreutzer Sonata*, written for the virtuoso violinist Rodolphe Kreutzer, was never actually played by him in public, but his name was not only made glorious through the tremendous eloquence of Beethoven's music but also became a symbol of Tolstoy's antisexual obsession, as expounded in his novella, *The Kreutzer Sonata*. Beethoven dedicated several of his works to titled benefactors and foreign dignitaries, among them the string quartets of op. 59 for the Russian Ambassador in Vienna, Count Rasoumowsky, *Wellington's Victory* inscribed to King George IV of England, and his last trio, the *Archduke*, for Archduke Rudolf. But his most famous dedication was a failed one, the fulsome tribute to Napoleon in the *Eroica Sym.*, which he later retracted.

Dedications were usually written in an extremely flowery and obsequious language, with the exalted status of the royal or aristocratic person to whom the work was dedicated symbolized by large capital letters, and a contrasting self-effacing signature emphasizing the humbleness and insignificance of the author in comparison with the sunlike splendor of the dedicatee. Bach's dedication to the Margrave Brandenburg is striking in this respect:

Since I had a couple of years ago the fortune of having been heard by your Royal Highness at your express command, and since I noticed then that Your Highness took some pleasure at my small talents which Heaven endowed me in music, and since upon taking my departure from your Royal Highness, I was given the honor of receiving from Your Highness a command to write some pieces of my own compositions, I therefore according to these gracious orders, took the liberty of rendering my very humble tasks to your Royal Highness by way of the present concertos which I arranged for several instruments beseeching Your Highness not to make judgment of their imperfection because of the rigor of the fine and delicate taste in music which the whole world knows that Your Highness possesses in the highest degree, but rather to take into benign consideration the profound respect and the most humble obeisance that I have attempted to express by this offering. For the rest, Monsiegneur, I beseech most humbly Your Royal Highness to have the goodness to continue your good graces towards me and to be persuaded that I have nothing as much to my heart than the capacity to be employed in occasions more worthy of Your Highness and in the service of Your Highness, I am, Monsiegneur, with total devotion, a very humble and very obedient servant of Your Royal Highness, Jean Sebastian Bach, Coethen, 24 March 1721.

Schumann dedicated many of his works to his beloved Clara. Beethoven liked to inscribe his piano sonatas to his favorite female pupils. The English composer John Ireland, at the age of 51, dedicated his piano concerto to his 20-year-old pupil, but removed the dedication when she married someone else. Tchaikovsky dedicated his last sym., the *Pathétique*, to his adored nephew Bob, who did not even bother to acknowledge receipt of the score which Tchaikovsky sent him. Finally, a unique negative dedication should be mentioned. Kaikhosru Sorabji dedicated his monumental piano work *Opus Clavicembalisticum* "to the everlasting glory of those few men blessed and sanctified in the curses and execrations of those many whose praise is eternal damnation."

Deep in the Heart of Texas. Song by Don Swander, a Californian who never went to Texas. The song became a hit in numerous Texas-colored movies, beginning with *Heart of the Rio Grande* (1942), where it was sung by Gene Autry.

Deep Purple. Piano piece by Peter De Rose, 1939, regurgitated from disjointed fragments of Rachmaninoff's 2nd Piano Concerto, later provided with lyrics as a treacle-dripping maudlin ballad. Babe Ruth of baseball fame had it performed for him on every birthday before he died. When a new wave of blubbering sentimentality swept over America in 1963, the song became a hit once again. It was later borrowed as the name for a British heavy-metal group.

DeGaetani, Jan(ice), remarkable American mezzo-soprano, specialist in modern music.; b. Massillon, Ohio, July 10, 1933; d. Rochester, N.Y., Sept. 15, 1989. Her father was a lawyer who encouraged her musical talents. She married the conductor Thomas DeGaetani and assumed her conjugal name in her career. However, the marriage was not successful, and they were soon divorced. She subsequently married Philip West, an oboist. She studied at the Juilliard School of Music in N.Y. with Sergius Kagan. Upon graduation she joined the Contemporary Chamber Ensemble, with which she developed a peculiar technique essential for performance of ultramodern vocal works. Since that sort of thing was commercially unrewarding, she uncomplainingly took menial jobs, including baby-sitting and waiting on tables in restaurants. She devoted her free time to a detailed study of the solo part in Schoenberg's *Pierrot lunaire*, which became one of her finest interpretations.

DeGaetani mastered the most challenging techniques of new vocal music, including fractional intervals and even tongue-clicking required in some new works. She also mastered foreign languages so as to be able to perform a wide European repertoire. She became a faithful interpreter of the most demanding works by modern composers, among them Boulez, Crumb, Druckman, Maxwell Davies, Ligeti, Carter, and Davidovsky. She also developed a fine repertoire of Renaissance songs, and soon became a unique phenomenon as a lieder artist, excelling in an analytical capacity to express the most minute vocal modulations of the melodic line while parsing the words with exquisite intellectual penetration of their meaning, so that even experienced critics found themselves at a loss of superlatives to describe her artistry. From 1973 she taught at the Eastman School of Music in Rochester, N.Y. With N. and R. Lloyd, she publ. the useful *The Complete Sightsinger* (1980). She died of irreversible leukemia.

degree. 1. One of the 8 consecutive tones in a major or minor diatonic scale, counted upward from the keynote. 2. A line or space on the staff. 3. A step.

dehnen (Ger.). Prolong.

dehors, en (Fr., outside). With emphasis; bring out.

Deidamia. Opera by Handel, 1741, 1st produced in London, to an Italian libretto. It was Handel's last opera, and its complete failure made him turn toward oratorio, a felicitous development for Handel and for music in general. *Deidamia* was revived in London in English more than 200 years after its original production, with a new appreciation for its musical qualities. The libretto is taken from Homer. Deidamia was a companion of Achilles who bore him a son.

del, dell', della, delle, dello (It.). Of the, than the.

Del Tredici, David (Walter), remarkable American composer; b. Cloverdale, Calif., Mar. 16, 1937. He studied piano, and made his debut as a soloist with the San Francisco Sym. at the age of 16; then enrolled at the Univ. of Calif. in Berkeley, studying composition with Seymour Shifrin, Andrew Imbrie, and Arnold Elston (B.A., 1959). He undertook additional studies at Princeton Univ., where his teachers were Earl Kim and Roger Sessions (M.F.A., 1963). He also continued his pianistic practice, taking private lessons with Robert Helps in N.Y. During the summers of 1964 and 1965 he served as pianist at the Berkshire Music Center in Tanglewood. In 1966 he received a Guggenheim fellowship award; in 1966–67 he was resident composer at the Marlboro Festival in Vermont. From 1966 to 1972 he was assistant prof. of music at Harvard Univ.; in 1973 he joined the music faculty at Boston Univ. In 1984 he began teaching at City College and the Graduate School of the City Univ. of N.Y. While thus retained by pedagogy, he composed avidly.

Fascinated by the creation of new literary forms and the novel language of James Joyce, he wrote the work *I Hear an Army*, based on a Joyce poem, scored for soprano and string quartet, which was performed at Tanglewood on Aug. 12, 1964, and immediately caught the fancy of the cloistered but influential cognoscenti, literati, and illuminati; another significant Joyce poem set by Del Tredici was *Night Conjure—Verse* for soprano, mezzo-soprano, woodwind septet, and string quartet, which he conducted in San Francisco on Mar. 5, 1966. Yet another work inspired by the verbal music of James Joyce was *Syzygy* for soprano, horn, bells, drums, and chamber orch., performed in N.Y. in 1968. For these works he plied a modified dodecaphonic course in a polyrhythmic context, gravid with meaningful pauses without fear of triadic encounters.

But Del Tredici achieved rare fame with a series of brilliant tone pictures after *Alice in Wonderland* by Lewis Carroll, in which he projected, in utter defiance of all modernistic conventions, overt tonal proclamations, fanfares, and pretty tunes that were almost embarrassingly attractive, becoming more melodious and harmonious with each consequent tone portrait of Alice. In a couple of the "Alice pieces" he disarmingly attached a personal signature, the vocal countdown of 13 (i.e., his last name) in Italian. The Alice pieces (all after Carroll) include *An Alice Sym.*, in 5 parts (1. *Speak Gently/Speak Roughly*; 2. *The Lobster Quadrille*; 3. *'Tis the Voice of the Sluggard*; 4. *Who Stole the Tarts?*; 5. *Dream Conclusion*) (1969–76); *Adventures Underground* (1971; premiere, 1975); *Vintage Alice: Fantascene on a Mad Tea Party* for Amplified Soprano, Folk Group, and Orch. (1972); *Final Alice* for Amplified Soprano, Folk Group, and Orch. (1976); *Child Alice*, in 2 parts, for amplified soprano and orch. 1. *In Memory of a Summer Day*, 1980, Pulitzer Prize; 2. *All in the Golden Afternoon*, 1981. In

1984 he was elected a member of the Inst. of the American Academy and Inst. of Arts and Letters. From 1988 to 1990 he was composer-in-residence of the N.Y. Phil.

deliberato (It.). Deliberately.

Delibes, (Clément-Philibert-) Léo, famous French composer; b. St.-Germain-du-Val, Sarthe, Feb. 21, 1836; d. Paris, Jan. 16, 1891. He received his early musical training with his mother and an uncle; then enrolled in the Paris Cons. in 1847 as a student of Tariot; won a *premier prix* in solfège in 1850; also studied organ with Benoist and composition with Adam. In 1853 he became organist of St. Pierre de Chaillot and accompanist at the Théâtre-Lyrique. In 1856 his 1st work for the stage, *Deux sous de charbon*, a 1-act operetta, humorously designated an *asphyxie lyrique*, was produced at the Folies-Nouvelles. Later that year his 2nd work, the operette bouffe *Deux vieilles gardes*, won considerable acclaim at its premiere at the Bouffes-Parisiens. Several more operettas were to follow, as well as his 1st substantial work for the stage, *Le Jardinier et Son Seigneur*, given at the Théâtre-Lyrique in 1863.

In 1864 he became chorus master of the Paris Opéra. With Louis Minkus he collaborated on the ballet score *La Source*, which was heard for the 1st time in 1866 at the Opéra. It was with his next ballet, *Coppélia, ou La Fille aux yeux d'émail*, that Delibes achieved lasting fame after its premiere at the Opéra (1870). Another ballet, *Sylvia, ou La Nymphe de Diane* (1876), was equally successful. He then wrote a grand opera, *Jean de Nivelle* (1880), which was moderately successful; it was followed by his triumphant masterpiece, the opera *Lakmé* (1883), in which he created a most effective lyric evocation of India; the *Bell Song* from *Lakmé* became a perennial favorite in recitals. In 1881 he was appointed prof. of composition at the Paris Cons.; in 1884 was elected a member of the Inst. His last opera, *Kassya*, was completed but not orchestrated at the time of his death; Massenet orchestrated the score, and it was premiered at the Opéra-Comique (1893). Delibes was a master of melodious elegance and harmonious charm; his music possessed an autonomous flow in colorful timbres, and a finality of excellence that seemed effortless while subtly revealing a mastery of the Romantic technique of composition.

delicato (It.). Delicately; in a refined style.

Deliciae Basilenses (Delights of Basel). Sym. No. 4 by Honegger, 1947, using old Swiss tunes.

delirio, con (It.). Deliriously, frenziedly.

Delius, Frederick

~~~ ~~~ ~~~ ~~~ ~~~

Significant English composer of German parentage; b. Fritz Theodor Albert, Bradford, Jan. 29, 1862; d. Grez-sur-Loing, France, June 10, 1934. His father was a successful merchant, owner of a wool company; he naturally hoped to have his son follow a career in industry, but he did not object to Frederick's study of art and music. Delius learned to play the piano and violin. At the age of 22 he went to Solano, Fla., to work on an orange plantation owned by his father; a musical souvenir of his sojourn there was his symphonic suite *Florida*. There he met an American organist, Thomas F. Ward, who gave him a thorough instruction in music theory; this study, which lasted 6 months, gave Delius a foundation for his further progress in music. In 1885 he went to Danville, Va., as a teacher. In 1886 he enrolled at the Leipzig Cons., where he took courses in harmony and counterpoint with Reinecke, Sitt, and Jadassohn. It was there that he met Grieg, becoming his friend and admirer. Indeed, Grieg's music found a deep resonance in his own compositions. An even more powerful influence was Wagner, whose principles of continuous melodic line and thematic development Delius adopted in his own works.

Euphonious serenity reigns on the symphonic surface of his music, diversified by occasional resolvable dissonances. In some works he made congenial use of English folk motifs, often in elaborate variation forms. Particularly successful are his evocative symphonic sketches *On Hearing the 1st Cuckoo in Spring*, *North Country Sketches*, *Brigg Fair*, and *A Song of the High Hills*. His orch.l nocturne *Paris: The Song of a Great City* is a tribute to a city in which he spent many years of his life. Much more ambitious in scope is his choral work *A Mass of Life*, in which he draws on passages from Nietzsche's *Also sprach Zarathustra*.

Delius settled in Paris in 1888; in 1897 he moved to Grez-sur-Loing, near Paris, where he remained for the rest of his life, except for a few short trips abroad. In 1903 he married the painter Jelka Rosen. His music began to win recognition in England and Germany; he became a favorite composer of Beecham's, who gave numerous performances of his music in London. But these successes came too late for Delius; a syphilitic infection which he had contracted early in life eventually grew into an incurable illness accompanied by paralysis and blindness; as Beecham phrased it, "Delius had suffered a heavy blow in the defection of his favorite goddess, Aphrodite Pandemos, who had returned his devotions with an affliction which was to break out many years later."

Still eager to compose, he engaged as his amanuensis the English musician Eric Fenby, who wrote down music at the dictation of Delius, including complete orch.l scores. In 1929 Beecham organized a Delius Festival in London (6 concerts), and the composer was brought from France to hear it. In the same year Delius was made Companion of Honour by King George V and an Hon.Mus.D. by Oxford. A motion picture was made by the British filmmaker Ken Russell on the life and works of Delius. However, he remains a solitary figure in modern music. Affectionately appreciated in England, in America, and to some extent in Germany, his works are rarely performed elsewhere. His operas, virtually forgotten, have received increasing attention: *Irmelin* (1890–92; premiered at Oxford, 1953); *The Magic Foundation*, lyric drama (1893–95; premiere at the BBC, London, 1977); *Koanga*, lyric drama (1895–97; premiere in Elberfeld, 1904); *A Village Romeo and Juliet*, lyric drama (1899–1901; premiere in Berlin, 1907); *Margot la Rouge*, lyric drama (1902; 1st concert perf. BBC, London, 1982; 1st stage perf., St. Louis, 1983); *Fennimore and Gerda*, opera (1908–10; premiere in Frankfurt-am-Main, 1919).

démancher (Fr.). Change finger position on a string instrument to prepare a shift from one register to another.

demiquaver (U.K.). Sixteenth note.

demisemiquaver (U.K.). Thirty-second note.

demi-soupir (Fr., half sigh). Eighth-note rest.

demi-voix (Fr., half voice). SOTTO VOCE.

Demoiselles de la nuit, Les. Ballet by Françaix, 1948, 1st performed in Paris. A youth marries his favorite cat, who is instantly transformed into a human beauty; but she retains her feline habit of prowling around at night. She dies; he dies. They become transfigured in some sort of ailurophiliac heaven and live happy ever after.

demolition. Public destruction of musical instruments, one of the new techniques of the American and British avant-garde came into vogue shortly after the conclusion of World War II, possibly as a sadomasochistic exercise of aggressive tendencies, frustrated by the unconditional surrender of the ex-enemies. Contests in the swiftness of destroying upright pianos have been held in clubs and colleges.

According to the established rules of the game, a piano had to be reduced to comminuted fragments that could be passed through an aperture of specified dimensions (usually a circle 6 inches in diameter). In Stockholm, a young pianist concluded his recital by igniting a dynamite charge previously secreted inside the piano, blowing it up. An exploding splinter wounded him in the leg. The American avant-garde composer La Monte Young set a violin on fire at one of his exhibits. Rock guitarists Pete Townshend and Jimi Hendrix closed their performances with the demolition (Townshend) or setting afire (Hendrix) of their instruments. Bakunin, the scientific anarchist, said, "Die Lust der Zerstörung ist eine schaffende Lust." This "creative impulse of destruction" has received its full vindication in the anti-instrument activities of modern times.

Demon, The. Opera by Anton Rubinstein, 1875, 1st produced in St. Petersburg; the libretto is extracted from a romantic poem by Lermontov. Tamara, a beautiful Caucasian princess, is engaged to a brave nobleman who unfortunately perishes in a mountain ambush. In a dark night vision, she sees a disfranchised demon, who declares his love for her. Horrified, she seeks refuge in a convent, but the demon pursues her even there. He begs her for a kiss, which would redeem his formerly angelic soul. She yields, but his demoniacally virile kiss is lethal, and Tamara dies. The score is saturated with singable tunes. The demon's aria, introducing himself as a "free spirit of the air," continues to be a favorite with old-fashioned Russian singers. The opera itself is never heard outside Russia.

demotic music (from Grk. *dēmotēs*, commoner). A generic category that comprises all genres of popular music: rural, urban, pop, country, folk, western, jazz, Tin Pan Alley, commercial jingles. Modern applications of the sources of demotic music are obtained by diatonic translocation, atonal dismemberment, and rhythmic compression. Hexachordal diatonic melodies may be metamorphosed into complex melorhythmic progressions without losing their demotic morphology. ABECEDARIAN MUSIC for children is a fruitful source of such topological transformation. Not all simple music is necessarily demotic, unless the folk quality is expressed in a composed work with utmost fidelity. Some obscure composers have succeeded in producing tunes that seem to be authentically demotic. The universally popular tune, *Dark Eyes*, regarded by many as an autochthonous Russian Gypsy song, is actually a violin piece entitled *Valse-hommage*, composed by a German band leader active in Russia in the 1880s. The Neapolitan ballad *Funiculi-Funicula*, mistaken by many for a genuine folk tune, was written by an Italian vocal teacher resident in London.

Dempster, Stuart (ROSS), American trombonist and composer; b. Berkeley, Calif., July 7, 1936. He studied at San Francisco State College (B.A. in perf., 1958; M.A. in composition, 1967) and also had private trombone instruction from A. B. Moore, Orlando Giosi, and John Klock. He taught at the San Francisco Cons. of Music (1961–66) and at Calif. State College at Hayward (1963–66); in 1968 he joined the faculty of the Univ. of Wash. in Seattle. He received a Fulbright-Hays Award as a senior scholar in Australia (1973) and a Guggenheim fellowship (1981). His interests also include non-Western instruments, and he has written many pieces for the *didjeridu*. In addition to his own experimental works, Dempster has often collaborated with Pauline Oliveros. He publ. the study *The Modern Trombone: A Definition of Its Idioms* (Berkeley, Calif., 1979).

Demus, Jörg (Wolfgang), noted Austrian pianist; b. St. Polten, Dec. 2, 1928. At the age of 11 he entered the Vienna Academy of Music; also took lessons in conducting with Swarowsky and Krips and in composition with Joseph Marx; continued his piano studies with Gieseking at the Saarbrucken Cons.; then worked with Kempff, Benedetti

Michelangeli, Edwin Fischer, and Yves Nat. He made his debut as a concert pianist at the age of 14 in Vienna; made his London debut in 1950; then toured South America (1951). In 1956 he won the Busoni prize of the International Competition for Pianists. Apart from his solo recitals, he distinguished himself as a lieder accompanist to Dietrich Fischer-Dieskau and other prominent singers. Demus assembled a large collection of historic keyboard instruments; publ. a book of essays, *Abenteuer der Interpretation*, and, with Paul Badura-Skoda, an analysis of Beethoven's piano sonatas. In 1977 he was awarded the Beethoven Ring, and in 1979 the Mozart Medal of Vienna.

Denisov, Edison, remarkable, innovative Russian composer; b. Tomsk, Apr. 6, 1929. He was named after Thomas Alva Edison by his father, an electrical engineer; another aspect in so naming him was that the surname *Denisov* is anagrammatic with *Edison*, leaving out the last letter. He studied mathematics at the Univ. of Moscow, graduating in 1951, and composition at the Moscow Cons. with Shebalin (1951–56). In 1959 he was appointed to the faculty of the Cons. An astute explorer of tonal possibilities, Denisov writes instrumental works of an empirical genre; typical of these is *Crescendo e diminuendo* for Harpsichord and 12 String Instruments, composed in 1965, with the score written partly in graphic notation. The titles of his pieces reveal a lyric character of subtle nuances, often marked by impressionistic colors: *Aquarelle, Silhouettes, Peinture, La Vie en rouge, Signes en blanc, Nuages noires.*

Density 21.5. Work for solo flute by Varèse, 1936, commissioned by the virtuoso flute player Georges Barrère (1876–1944) to mark his acquisition of a flute made of platinum. He gave its premiere in the same year in Carnegie Hall, N.Y. The title designates the atomic weight of platinum; its specific gravity is 21.5 times as dense as water. In the work itself tritones proliferate and the melodic line is angular but strangely affecting; it has been shown that the work is freely adapted from Debussy's *Syrinx.*

Denver, John (born Henry John Deutschendorf, Jr.), popular American singer and songwriter; b. Roswell, N. Mex., Dec. 31, 1942. He played guitar as a youngster; for a time attended Tex. Technical Univ. in Lubbock; then made his way to N.Y., where he played in the Mitchell Trio and wrote the popular song *Leaving on a Jet Plane* (1967). In

1968 he launched a solo career, appearing in concerts all over the U.S.; also made television appearances and recordings. His successful songs included *Rocky Mountain High, Take Me Home, Country Roads,* and *Annie's Song.* He appeared in the movie *Oh, God!* and others.

depress. Lower the pitch (e.g., by a ♭ or ♭♭). *Depression,* chromatic lowering of a note.

derangements. In the pernicious practice of some commercially successful arrangers and antiquated organ soloists in decaying provincial churches, the mutilations practiced upon the dead bodies of works by great composers by means of stuffing the melodic intervals of their tunes with chromatic passing notes, or filling the open harmonies with supernumerary 3rds and 6ths.

derived set. A 12-tone set created by subjecting a smaller subset to the serial transformations of inversion, retrogression, and/or transposition.

Des (Ger.). D-flat.

Des dur (Ger.). D-flat major.

descant. DISCANT.

descant clef (obs.). Soprano clef.

descant recorder. Treble recorder.

descant viol. Treble viol.

descort (Old Fr., disorder). 13th-century chanson genre, cultivated by the French trouvères.

Desert Song, The. Operetta by Rombert, 1926, a comedy of sentimental romance and mistaken identities on the plains of North Africa. Includes the title song, also called *Blue Heaven.*

Déserts. Work by Varèse, 1954, for winds, percussion, and prerecorded electronic tape; it is one of the 1st attempts to combine live players with a recorded electronic score. It was initially performed in Paris.

Deses (Ger.). D double-flat.

Desmond, Paul (born Paul Emile Breitenfeld), American jazz alto saxophonist; b. San Francisco, Nov. 25, 1924; d. N.Y., May 30, 1977. He picked his professional name from a telephone book at random. He gained the rudiments of music from his father, who played the organ for silent movies; Desmond played the clarinet in the high school orch., then at San Francisco State Univ.; eventually concentrated on the alto saxophone. He made rapid strides toward recognition and fame when he joined the Dave Brubeck Quartet (1951), and continued with it until it was disbanded in 1967. He wrote some pieces for the Brubeck Quartet, of which *Take 5*, a jazz composition in 5/4 meter, was adopted as their signature song and became popular.

Desprez (Des Prez), **Josquin,** also known simply as Josquin, masterful Flemish polyphonic composer; b. probably in Hainaut, *c.* 1440; d. Condé-sur-Escaut, near Valenciennes, Aug. 27, 1521. His surname was variously spelled Després, Desprez, Deprés, Depret, Deprez, Desprets, Dupré, and (by the Italians) Del Prato (Latinized as a Prato, a Pratis, Pratensis, etc.); while Josquin (contracted from the Flemish *Jossekin*, little Joseph) appears as Jossé, Jossien, Jusquin, Giosquin, Josquinus, Jacobo, Jodocus, Jodoculus, etc. His epitaph reads *Jossé de Prés*. However, in the motet *Illibata Dei Virgo Nutrix*, of which the text is quite likely of Josquin's authorship, his name appears as an acrostic, thus: I, O, S, Q, V, I, N, D[es], P, R, E, Z; this seems to leave little doubt as to its correct spelling.

Few details of Josquin's early life are known. He may have been a boy chorister of the Collegiate Church at St.-Quentin, later becoming canon and choirmaster there; possibly was a pupil of Ockeghem, whom he greatly admired (in 1497 he wrote *La Déploration sur la mort de Johannes Ockeghem*); from 1459 to 1472 he sang at the Milan Cathedral; by July 1474 he was at the court of Duke Galeazzo Maria Sforza, Milan, as chorister; after the Duke's assassination he entered the service of the Duke's brother, Cardinal Ascanio Sforza; from 1486 to 1494 he was a singer in the papal choir under the Popes Innocent VIII and Alexander VI; he was also active, for various periods, in Florence, where he met the famous theorist Pietro Aron; in Modena; and in Ferrara (where Isaac was also) as maestro di cappella in 1503–1504. Later, Josquin returned to Burgundy, settling in Condé-sur-Escaut (1504), where he became provost of Notre Dame.

As a composer he was considered by contemporary musicians and theorists to be the greatest of his period, and he had a strong influence on all those who came into contact with his music or with him personally, as a teacher; Adriaan Petit Coclicus, who may have been one of Josquin's pupils, publ. a method in 1552 entitled *Compendium musices*, based on Josquin's teaching. He described Josquin as "princeps musicorum." His works were sung everywhere, and universally admired; in them he achieves a complete union between word and tone, thereby fusing the intricate Netherlandish contrapuntal devices into expressive and beautiful art forms. Two contrasting styles are present in his compositions: some are intricately contrapuntal, displaying the technical ingenuity characteristic of the Netherlands style; others, probably as a result of Italian influence, are homophonic. He wrote numerous motets, Masses, and chansons.

Dessau, Paul, German composer; b. Hamburg, Dec. 19, 1894; d. East Berlin, June 27, 1979. He learned to play the violin at an early age and gave a concert when he was 11 years old. In 1910 he enrolled at the Klindworth-Scharwenka Cons. in Berlin, where he studied violin with Florian Zajic and composition with Eduard Behm and Max Loewengard. In 1913 he worked as *répétiteur* at the Hamburg City Theater; in 1914 he was drafted into the German army. After the Armistice in 1918 he became engaged as a composer and conductor in various chamber groups in Hamburg; then served as coach and conductor at the Cologne Opera (1919–23) and in Mainz (1924). In 1925 he was appointed conductor at the Städtische Oper in Berlin, holding this position until 1933; with the usurpation of power by the Nazis, he left Germany; lived in various European cities and visited Palestine.

In 1939 he emigrated to America; lived for some time in N.Y., and in 1944 went to Hollywood, where he worked on the background scores for 14 films as a composer or orchestrator. He returned to Berlin in 1948 and took an active part in German musical life, aligning himself with the political, social, and artistic developments in the German Democratic Republic; he became closely associated with Brecht, and composed music for several of his plays: *Die Verurteilung des Lukullus*, opera (Berlin, 1951); *Furcht und Elend des Dritten Reiches* (1938); *Mutter Courage und ihre Kinder* (1946); *Der gute Mensch von Sezuan* (1947); *Herr Puntila und sein Knecht Matti* (1949); *Mann ist Mann* (1951); and *Der kaukasische Kreidekreis* (1954). Dessau's operas, choral works, songs, and instrumental music are imbued with the progressive ideals of socialist realism; while he believed in the imperative of music for the masses, he made use of modern techniques, including occasional applications of Schoenberg's method of composition with 12 tones.

dessus (Lat., above). In medieval French polyphony, the treble voice.

dessus de viole. Treble viol.

desto (It.). Sprightly.

destra (It.). Right. *Colla destra*, play with the right hand; *destra mano*, play with the right hand (abbrev. *m.d.*).

détaché (Fr., detached). In string instruments, playing successive notes with downbow and upbow in alteration, but not staccato. A broad, even articulation is a component. *Grande détaché*, a full bow-stroke per note.

Dett, R(obert) Nathaniel, distinguished African-American composer, conductor, and anthologist; b. Drummondville (now Niagara Falls), Ontario, Oct. 11, 1882; d. Battle Creek, Mich., Oct. 2, 1943. He came from a musical family; both his parents were amateur pianists and singers. In 1893 the family moved to Niagara Falls, N.Y.; Dett studied piano with local teachers. He earned his living by playing at various clubs and hotels; then enrolled at the Oberlin (Ohio) Cons., where he studied piano with Howard Handel Carter and theory of composition with Arthur E. Heacox and George Carl Hastings, obtaining his B.Mus. in 1908. He also conducted a school choir; eventually choral conducting became his principal profession.

He taught at Lane College in Jackson, Tenn. (1908–11), the Lincoln Inst. in Jefferson, Mo. (1911–13), the Hampton Inst. in Va. (1913–32), and Bennett College in Greensboro, N.C. (1937–42). Concerned about his lack of technical knowledge in music, he continued taking courses. He took lessons with Karl Gehrkens at Oberlin in 1913; attended classes at Columbia Univ., the American Cons. of Music in Chicago, Northwestern Univ., the Univ. of Pa., and, during the academic year 1919–20, Harvard Univ., where he studied composition with Arthur Foote. In the summer of 1929 he went to France to study with Nadia Boulanger at the American Cons. in Fontainebleau; during 1931–32 he attended the Eastman School of Music in Rochester, N.Y., obtaining his M.Mus. in 1932. In the meantime he developed the artistic skills of the Hampton Choir, which toured in Europe in 1930 with excellent success, receiving encomiums in England, France, Belgium, the Netherlands, Germany, and Switzerland. He also periodically led his choir on the radio; in 1943 he became a musical adviser for the USO and worked with the WAC on service duty at Battle Creek, where he died.

His dominating interest was in cultivating Negro music, arranging Negro spirituals, and publishing collections of Negro folk songs. All of his works were inspired by black melos and rhythms; some of his piano pieces in Negro idiom became quite popular, among them the suite *Magnolia* (1912); *In the Bottoms* (1913), which contained the rousing *Juba Dance*; and *Enchantment* (1922). He also wrote a number of choral pieces, mostly on biblical themes, such as his oratorios *The Chariot Jubilee* (1921) and *The Ordering of Moses* (1937). His choruses *Listen to the Lambs*, *I'll Never Turn Back No More*, and *Don't Be Weary, Traveler* became standard pieces of the choral repertoire. He publ. the anthologies *Religious Folk Songs of the Negro* (1926) and *The Dett Collection of Negro Spirituals* (4 vols., 1936).

Dettingen Te Deum. Celebratory religious work by Handel, 1743, commemorating a British military victory.

Deus ex machina (Lat., God from a machine). An archetypal dramaturgical theme in myth, fiction, theater, and epic poetry. In essence, a god would come down from the heavens (or from below) to alter a situation, often at the last moment and usually to the benefit of the main character or characters. When mythical and other stories began to be staged, scenographic technology was developed to permit the descent of actors from above the audience's sight line in the "machine." In opera, an early example can be found in Monteverdi's *Orfeo* (1607); an ironic and multiple use of the device is featured in Glass's *The Voyage* (1992).

deutlich (Ger.). Distinctly articulating the words.

Deutscher Tanz (*Deutscher*, *Teutscher*, etc.; Ger., German dance; Fr. *allemande*; It. *tedesca*). General term for late 18th- and early 19th-century couple dances in triple meter; by the 19th century the genre had branched off into the Ländler (danced with arms interlaced) and the waltz (danced with swift turns and close embraces).

Deutsches Requiem, Ein. The German Requiem by Brahms, 1857–68. It is given this title for no other reason than to indicate that the text is in German, derived from Luther's translation of the Latin text of the Bible. A chronologically erroneous statement proliferated that Brahms wrote the work to glorify the German soldiers who fell in the Franco-Prussian War. His great sorrow over his mother's death (1865) gave a long-gestating work a necessary push. The 1st performance of the final version occurred in Leipzig (1869).

Deutschland, Deutschland über alles. The text of a nationalistic German poem written by a well-meaning German university professor at the time of the political disturbances of 1848, to the tune of Haydn's Austrian national anthem, *Gott erhalte Franz den Kaiser*. The text refers to the German unification movement of the 19th century; in later years, however, the words were misapprehended as "Germany above all," and as sung by the Nazis acquired an ominous meaning; in fact, "über alles" meant "1st of all." After the downfall of the Nazi regime, the song could not be used in this ambiguous form and the words "über alles" were taken out, but the noble tune was kept as the national anthem of West Germany.

deux (Fr.). Two. *Deux temps*, a "2-step" waltz.

development. The working out or evolution (elaboration) of a theme by presenting it in varied melodic, harmonic, or rhythmic treatment.

Devil and Daniel Webster, The. Opera by D. Moore, 1939, in which the American statesman uses his forensic skills to free a poor artisan from a contract to the devil.

Devil and Kate, The. Opera by Dvořák, 1899, 1st produced in Prague. Kate, a middle-aged and garrulous woman, vows to dance with the Devil himself if she cannot find a partner at a country fair. The Devil obligingly materializes and carries her off to Hell. But Kate talks so much that the Devil gets a headache and sends her back to earth.

Devils of Loudon, The. Opera by Penderecki, 1969, based on a novel by Aldous Huxley, 1st produced in Hamburg. The libretto is based on an actual event in Loudon, France, in 1634, when a handsome and radical lay cleric was accused by hysterical nuns of being a sexual incubus, disturbing their dreams. He was eventually burned at the stake. The opera applies the most extreme devices of the avant-garde in its vocal and instrumental parts to portray adequately the *furor uterinus* of the erotic nuns.

Devil's Trill, The. Violin Sonata in G Minor by Tartini, after 1744, 1st publ. posthumously, 1798. Legend has it that, while dreaming, Tartini heard the Prince of Darkness play a violin piece; when he awoke, Tartini wrote down what he could remember and made it the basis for the last movement of this sonata.

Devin du Village, The (The Village Diviner). *Intermède* or comic opera, 1752, by Jean-Jacques Rousseau, who was a composer and theorist as well as a philosopher; 1st produced in Fontainebleau. In Rousseau's libretto a village girl suspects her sweetheart of infidelity; she consults a wise friend, who advises her to pretend she is in love with another. The strategem works, and the couple is reunited. The unpretentious score is important historically because it breaks away from the French tradition of mythological grand opera and presents theatrical music as part of common human experience.

devozione, con (It.). In a devotional style; devoutly.

Dezimett (Ger.). Chamber work for 10 players.

D-flat major. To judge by the music written in D-flat major, this key is descriptive of wide-open spaces, capable of a great variety of expressions. The scale of D-flat major is marvelously pianistic, covering all 5 black keys, making room for 2 white keys at strategic positions. What wealth of resonance in Liszt's *Étude* in D-flat Major, in which the left hand goes over the right hand to maintain the requisite fullness of euphony! On the other side of the spectrum is Debussy's *Clair de lune*, delicate and subtle in its evocation of a moonlit landscape. The celebrated principal theme of the 1st movement of Tchaikovsky's Piano Concerto, nominally described as being in the key of B-flat minor, states its theme in unambiguously triadic D-flat major. A remarkable episode occurs in the 18th variation of Rachmaninoff's *Rhapsody on a Theme of Paganini*, in which he ingeniously inverts the principal A-minor theme to become D-flat major.

Amateur composers who pollute the shelves of American music stores with their creations under such titles as *Deep Purple Hills*, *Red Sunset*, and the like, tend to favor the key of D-flat major. But this key is difficult to handle in orch.l writing, particularly in string instruments. Only one composer, Miaskovsky, has ever written a sym., his 25th, in the acknowledged key of D-flat major.

di (It.). Of, from, to, by, than.

Di Capua, Eduardo, Italian composer of Neapolitan ballads; b. Naples, 1864; d. there, 1917. He earned his living by playing in small theaters and cafés in and around Naples, and later in the cinemas; also gave piano lessons. His most famous song was *O sole mio* (1898); its popularity was immense and never abated. Other celebrated songs were *Maria Mari* (1899); *Torna maggio* (1900); *Canzona bella*, etc. Di Capua sold these songs to publishers outright, and so did not benefit by their popularity. He died in extreme poverty.

di colpo (It.). Suddenly.

di gala (It.). Gaily, merrily.

di molto (It.). Very, extremely. *Allegro di molto*, extremely fast.

di nuovo (It.). Anew; over again.

di posto (It., at the place). Attack a note directly, without PORTAMENTO.

di salto (It.). By leap or jump.

di slancio (It., on impulse). DI POSTO.

Di Tre Re. Subtitle of Arthur Honegger's 5th Sym., 1951, 1st performed by the Boston Sym. Orch. The explanation of the title is that the last note of each of the 3 movements of the work is a *D*, hence the Italian title (*Of 3 D's*).

Diabelli, Anton, Austrian composer and publisher; b. Mattsee, near Salzburg, Sept. 5, 1781; d. Vienna, Apr. 8, 1858. He was a choirboy in the monastery at Michaelbeuren, and at Salzburg Cathedral; studied for the priesthood at the Munich Latin School, but continued his musical work, submitting his compositions to Michael Haydn, who encouraged him. After the secularization of the Bavarian monasteries, Diabelli embraced the career of a musician, went to Vienna (where Joseph Haydn received him kindly), taught piano and guitar for a living, and in 1818 became a partner of Cappi, the music publisher, assuming control of the firm (Diabelli & Co.) in 1824. He publ. much of Schubert's music, but underpaid the composer and complained that he wrote too much. In 1852 he sold his firm to C. A. Spina. A facile composer, Diabelli produced an opera, *Adam in der Klemme* (Vienna, 1809), Masses, cantatas, chamber music, etc., which were consigned to oblivion; his sonatinas are still used for beginners. His name was immortalized through Beethoven's remarkable set of 33 variations (1823, op. 120), on a waltz theme that Diabelli had submitted to numerous European composers for a variation, publ. in an anthology (1824).

Diabelli Variations. A set of *Veränderungen* for piano by Beethoven (op. 120), 1823, based on the waltz that Diabelli had submitted to every Central European composer he could think of (1819), with the goal of publishing an anthology of individual variations.

diabolus in musica (Lat., devil in music). A nickname, laden with theological connotations found in many medieval treatises on music, for the tritone (an interval of 3 whole tones), forbidden because it did not fit into the basic hexachord of ancient musical theory. In Bach's time schoolboys were punished by painful slaps on the knuckles with a ruler for an accidental use of the tritone in musical exercises. It was to be expected that an interval bearing such a satanic designation would be used by composers to characterize sinister forces. Examples are many: the lowered 5th in the violin tune of *Danse macabre* by Saint-Saëns; the leitmotif of the dragon Fafner in act II of Wagner's *Siegfried*, represented by a running Locrian pentachord followed by a staccato interplay between F and B; the motives of the 3 magical winning cards in Tchaikovsky's opera *The Queen of Spades*; the devil's motto in Hanson's opera *Merry Mount*, etc. The Polish composer Lutoslawski used an overlapping series of tritones in an elegy on the death of Bartók.

The diabolus in musica is the formative interval of the diminished-7th chord, a favorite device of romantic operas suggesting mortal danger. In appreciation of this dramatic function, the diminished-7th chord was known in Italian opera circles as the ACCORDE DI STUPEFAZIONE (stupefying chord). Ironically, the diabolus in musica became the cornerstone of the modern techniques of polytonality and atonality; it is also the basic element of the whole tone scale used for coloristic effects in impressionistic works.

Diaghilev, Sergei (Pavlovich), famous Russian impresario; b. Gruzino, Novgorod district, Mar. 31, 1872; d. Venice, Aug. 19, 1929. He was associated with progressive artistic organizations in St. Petersburg, but his main field of activity was in western Europe. He established the Ballets Russes in Paris; he commissioned Stravinsky to write the ballets *The Firebird*, *Petrouchka*, and *The Rite of Spring*; also commissioned Prokofiev, Milhaud, Poulenc, Auric, and other composers of the younger generation. Ravel and de Falla also wrote works for him. The great importance of Diaghilev's choreographic ideas lies in the complete abandonment of the classical tradition; in this respect he was the true originator of the modern dance.

dialectics. Discourse. *Musical dialectics* may be a useful term to describe a kind of meaningful antiphony, an orderly exchange of melodic statements, sufficiently divergent to imply the sense of a debate and yet unified by a general melodic, rhythmic or harmonic idea. Music in a dialectical form ought to be by definition a succession of free associations, not too strict in grammar and syntax, replete with asymmetrical rhythms and unresolved dissonances. The term is large enough to cover many idioms and techniques, from neoclassical structures to serial composition.

Dialogues des carmélites, Les. Opera by Poulenc, 1957, recalling the historical martyrdom of Carmelite nuns during the French Revolution.

Diamond, David (Leo), significant and fantastically prolific American composer; b. Rochester, N.Y., July 9, 1915. His parents were of Eastern European extraction; his father was a cabinetmaker and his mother a dressmaker for the Yiddish theater. To make ends meet, he worked behind the food counter at a N.Y. drugstore. He studied composition with Bernard Rogers at the Eastman School of Music in his hometown (1930–34); then took courses privately with Roger Sessions in N.Y. Seeking a wider application of his growing talents, he went to Paris in 1937, where he took courses with the fabulous French *nourrice* of a generation of composers, Nadia Boulanger, and where he became associated with the most important musicians and writers of the time.

While in France and elsewhere in Europe, he exercised his exceptional linguistic capacity, acquiring fluency in French, Italian, and even Russian by cultivating international acquaintances. Returning to N.Y., he devoted his time exclusively to composition; various grants and awards enabled him to obtain relative financial security. He held the Juilliard Publication Award, 3 Guggenheim fellowships, an American Academy in Rome award, the Paderewski Prize, and a grant from the National Academy of Arts and Letters. He was also lucky in having his music conducted by Hanson, Monteux, Koussevitzky, and Mitropoulos. Other conductors who eventually led his works were Charles Munch, Eugene Ormandy, and Leonard Bernstein.

As a composer Diamond soon succeeded in establishing an original and recognizable style of harmonic and contrapuntal writing with the sense of tonality clearly present; the element of pitch, often inspired by natural folklike patterns, is very strong in all of his music. In his later works he adopted a modified dodecaphonic method, while keeping free of doctrinaire serialism. His instrumental and vocal writing is invariably idiomatic, which makes his music welcome to performers and audiences alike. Some of his works, like *Rounds* for string orch., acquired a flattering popularity in concert performances; this score won the N.Y. Music Critics' Circle Award in 1944.

His strongest power lies in symphonic and chamber music, but he also shows a marked ability for vocal writing, as exemplified by his choral works. In 1989 he was invited to the Soviet Union, where his music was performed to considerable acclaim. He also taught: in 1973 he was appointed to the faculty of the Juilliard School in N.Y. In 1985 he received the William Schuman Award of Columbia Univ.

diapason (Grk.). 1. As applied to Greek music, the interval that runs "through all the tones," that is, the perfect octave. 2. In later centuries, a vocal range; it is used in this sense in French and Russian theory books. 3. (Fr.) Tuning fork; concert pitch. 4. The principal pipe of the organ, usually 8-feet long; the double diapason is a pipe 16 feet in length.

diapason tone. ORGAN TONE.

diapente (Grk.). Medieval term for perfect 5th.

diatessaron (Grk.). Medieval term for perfect 4th.

diatonic (Gr., *dia* + *teinein*, stretch out). Of or relating to the 7 tones of a particular major or minor scale. *Diatonic harmony* or *melody*, that employing the tones of but 1 scale; *diatonic instrument*, one yielding only the tones of that scale of which its fundamental tone is the keynote; *diatonic interval*, one formed by 2 tones of the same scale; *diatonic modulation*, see MODULATION; *diatonic progression*, stepwise progression within 1 scale; *diatonic scale*, see SCALE.

Diddley, Bo (born Ellas Bates McDaniel), African-American rock 'n' roll singer and guitarist; b. Magnolia, Miss., Dec. 30, 1928. He was taken to Chicago in early childhood, where he learned to play the violin and guitar. In 1955 he 1st attracted attention with his recordings of *Bo Diddley* and *I'm a Man*; later that year he appeared on Ed Sullivan's television show and at N.Y.'s Carnegie Hall. His pelvic gyrations and syncopated "Bo Diddley beat" influenced the 1st generation of rock 'n' roll musicians, including Buddy Holly and Elvis Presley. In 1959 he scored great success with his recording of *Say Man*. In 1963 he performed in England and in 1972 at the Montreux Jazz Festival. Later tours included Europe (1986) and Japan (1988).

Diderot, Denis, illustrious French man of letters and philosopher; b. Langres, Oct. 5, 1713; d. Paris, July 30, 1784. He ed. the monumental *Encylopédie* with d'Alembert (1751–65). In his work *Mémoirs sur différents sujets de mathématiques* (The Hague, 1748) are the essays *Principes généraux d'acoustique, Examen d'un principe de mécanique sur la tension des cordes*, and *Projet d'un nouvel orgue*, the latter being an impracticable idea for a new kind of barrel organ.

Dido and Aeneas. Opera by Purcell, 1689, after Virgil's *Aeneid*. It deals with the love of Dido, Queen of Carthage, for the Trojan hero Aeneas, and her self-immolation when he abandons her. It was 1st performed in a school for young gentlewomen in London; there has been recent speculation that the work was performed earlier. About 60 composers of many nations wrote operas on the same subject.

Dies Irae (Lat., day of wrath). Sequence of the Requiem Mass. The most famous Christian doomsday chant, painting the apocalyptic picture of the dissolution of the world into ashes and imploring the Lord not to cast the repentant sinner into outer darkness. The composition of both the words and melody is attributed to the 13th-century musician Thomas of Celano. It is monodic and is not easily classified as to its modality; it is musically more repetitive than most sequences. In the 14th and 15th centuries the Dies Irae became an obligatory part of the Requiem Mass; it was almost always sung as chant until the Council of Trent, which kept it as part of the liturgy (mid-16th century). In numerous polyphonic versions, the Dies Irae is a symbolic invocation of millennial resignation, and appears in many allusions, including the last movement of *Sym. fantastique* of Berlioz, the *Danse macabre* of Saint-Saëns, and *Totentanz* by Liszt. It is also incorporated into the requiems of Mozart, Cherubini, Berlioz, Verdi, and many others.

COURTESY FRANK DRIGGS COLLECTION

Bo Diddley, c. 1960

dièse (*diesis*; Fr., Rus.). Sharp; the sign ♯.

diesis (It.). A semitone in the diatonic Pythagorean scale; later, the quarter-tone in the enharmonic Greek scale. *Greater diesis*, the difference between 4 pure minor 3rds (6/5) and an octave, or 62.6 cents; *lesser diesis*, the difference between an octave and 3 pure major 3rds (5/4), or 41.1 cents.

Dietrich, Albert (Hermann), German conductor and composer; b. Forsthaus Golk, near Meissen, Aug. 28, 1829; d. Berlin, Nov. 19, 1908. He was a pupil of J. Otto in Dresden (1842–47) and of Moscheles and Rietz at Leipzig (1847–51); studied with Schumann at Düsseldorf (1851–54). From 1855 to 1861 he was a concert conductor, and from 1859 municipal music director, at Bonn; from 1861, at Oldenburg; he retired in 1890 and lived in Berlin; was made Royal Prof. in 1899. He wrote *Erinnerungen an Johannes Brahms in Briefen, besonders aus seiner Jugendzeit* (Leipzig, 1898; in Eng., 1899). He is remembered for contributing the 1st movement of the *F–A–E* Violin Sonata (*frei aber einsam*, free but alone); the other movements are by Brahms and Schumann.

Dietz, Howard, American lyricist and film executive; b. N.Y., Sept. 9, 1896; d. there, July 30, 1983. He began writing lyrics for popular songs in 1918; wrote texts for Kern, Gershwin, and Vernon Duke; also wrote songs with Arthur Schwartz. In 1919 he joined the Goldwyn Pictures Corp. as publicity director; when the firm merged into Metro-Goldwyn-Mayer in 1924 he remained with it, becoming its vice president in 1940. He devised its pseudo-Latin logo, *Ars Gratia Artis* (the correct word sequence would be *Ars Artis Gratia*). He invented the 2-handed bridge game which was named after him. He also painted and translated librettos. As a publicity man for Metro-Goldwyn-Mayer he popularized, and possibly made up, Greta Garbo's line "I want to be alone," which became famous.

diferencia (*differencia*; Sp., difference). In Spanish Renaissance music and thereafter, a variation set, one of the earliest types.

difference (differential) tone. A tone produced by the difference of the frequencies of vibration between 2 notes when played loudly on a stringed instrument or on 2 of the same instruments; such a tone lies well beneath the original 2 sounds, and produces a surprising, at times jarring effect; also called TARTINI TONES.

digital. 1. A key on the keyboard of the piano, organ, etc. 2. Recording in which musical tones are translated into binary information, as in a CD. 3. Technology involved in the production of computer-generated sound.

dilapidation of tonality. The disappearance of explicit key signatures from the notation of modern composition was the 1st symptom of the dilapidation of tonality and deterioration of traditional harmony. The key signature has a reason for existence in neoclassical works in which the tonic-dominant relationship is still extant and triadic modulations strong. But the dormant chromaticism erupts all the more viciously against tonal restraints, and the key signature, if it is set down at all, exists only to be denied. The chromaticization of the modern idiom during the last decades of the 19th century resulted in an enormous proliferation of double-sharps and double-flats. As enharmonic modulation reared its multicolored head, the antinomy between the tonality symbolized by the key signature and the florid panchromatic display reached the point of arithmetical incompatibility. Seven notes of the diatonic scale represented by 7 positions on the music staff and 7 letters of the alphabet were to provide notation for the 7 different notes of the chromatic scale. Academic musicians, eager to reserve the fiction of eminent tonality, and being unable to find a common denominator between 7 and 12, erected a fantastic network of accidentals; triple-sharps and triple-flats pullulate in the canons and fugues of Wilhelm Middelschulte. A whole section, acoustically equivalent to C major, masquerades in intervallic enharmonies as B-sharp and D-double-flat major in the piano part of Ravel's Trio. Debussy was similarly involved in exotic structures of double flats and double sharps in a triadic passage of his *Feuilles mortes.*

Even in the 19th century, tonality was often nominal and the key signature an armature without a function. One intermezzo by Brahms (No. 4, op. 76) is ostensibly in B-flat major, but the tonic triad is not reached until the final 2 bars. This type of tonal convention may be described as teleological tonality in which the tonic is the goal rather than the point of departure. The language of atonality arose from the products of the decay of tonal relationships. Genuinely atonal melodies lack the homing instinct; they meander and maunder without the beacon of a tonic in sight. The attraction of the tonic does not exist in atonal writing; the members of an atonal melody are weightless. This atonal assembly deprived of tonal gravity came to be organized by Schoenberg in a mutually gravitating dodecaphonic complex. Key signatures are obviously superfluous in atonal and dodecaphonic music, but not in polytonality, where different key signatures are used simultaneously.

The supremacy of tonality demanded that each composition end in the same key, or in a key related to that in which it began. How strong the prerequisite of this tonal uniformity was felt by composers of the 19th century is illustrated by a whimsical annotation of R. Strauss in his song entitled *Wenn* (publ. 1897). In the orig. version the principal key is D-flat major, but the final 7 measures and the concluding chord are in D major. Strauss supplied an alternative coda in which the transition was made to the original key, with the following footnote: "Vocalists who may perform this song before the end of the 19th century are advised by the composer to transpose the last 7 measures a semitone lower so as to arrive at the end of the song in the same key in which it began."

dilettante (It.). AMATEUR.

diligenza, con (It., with diligence). Carefully.

diluendo (It.). Growing softer, dying away.

diminished interval. A perfect or minor interval contracted by a chromatic semitone. *Diminished chord,* one whose highest and lowest tones form a diminished interval; *diminished subject* or *theme,* one repeated or imitated in diminution; *diminished triad,* a root with minor 3rd and diminished 5th.

diminished-seventh chord. A chord consisting of 3 conjunct minor 3rds, forming the interval of the diminished 7th between the top and bottom notes, e.g., C–E♭–G♭–B♭♭.

diminuendo (It.; abbrev. *dim.*). Decrescendo; diminishing in loudness. The sign is ⊐⊐⊐⊐ .

diminuendo pedal. A pedal-mechanism for gradually pushing in organ stops.

diminution. A Baroque polyphonic device whereby the theme is played twice as fast as its initial appearance, so that quarter notes become converted into 8th notes, 8th notes into 16th notes, etc. The effect is that of a STRETTO, a melodic precipitation in a hurried statement, which heightens the rhythmic tension, usually raising also the dynamic level, anticipating a decisive ending. In its formal and emotional respects, diminution performs the function opposite that of augmentation. Other time relationships (e.g., 3 times as much) can occur.

Dimitrij. Opera by Dvořák, 1882, based on the historical life of the false czar (reigned 1603–1606) who succeeded the Godunovs. Here he has come to believe in his own royalty; his wife Marina reminds him that he is a fugitive monk; he is eventually slain by one of his followers.

Dinah. Song by Harry Akst, 1924, made famous by Ethel Waters. It later became the theme song and 1st name of the popular singer Fanny Rose Shore.

Dinner Engagement, A. Comic opera by L. Berkeley, 1954.

direct. The sign ⁓ set at the end of a staff to show the position of the 1st note on the next staff; also called *custos*.

directional hearing. An ability common to all animals and man to judge the direction and the relative intensity of sound, evolved from the biological necessity of anticipating danger. This faculty plays an important role in stereophonic sound reproduction and also in the newly developed spatial type of music in which the placement of individual performers or performing groups is prescribed by the composer.

direttore del coro (It.). Choral conductor.

direzione (It.). Conducting of an orch. or chorus.

dirge. A funeral song, usually for chorus A CAPPELLA; also, an instrumental composition of a funerary nature. The word is an English contraction of the opening of Matins of the Office of the Dead, "Dirige Domine Deus Meus in conspectu tuo viam meam." In Shakespeare's *Romeo and Juliet*, Capulet reflects on seeing the body of the supposedly deceased Juliet: "Our solemn hymns to sullen dirges change." Stravinsky wrote a dirge *In Memoriam Dylan Thomas*.

Dirigent (Ger.). Conductor.

diritta, alla (It.). In direct motion.

diritto (It.). Direct, straight.

Dis (Ger.). D-sharp.

Dis moll (Ger.). D-sharp minor.

Disappointment, or the Force of Credulity, The. Ballad opera by Andrew Barton, composed in 1767 for the opening of a theater in Philadelphia but canceled by the censors because the text contained satirical references to important colonial officials. The libretto dealt with a group of practical jokers who persuade greedy Philadelphians to dig for buried treasure on the banks of the Delaware River. The tunes were melodies popular in colonial times, including an early version of *Yankee Doodle*. A reconstructed score, with a specially composed overture, 3 instrumental interludes, and Baroque orchestration by Samuel Adler, was produced at the Library of Congress in Washington, D.C., in 1976, as part of the U.S. bicentennial celebration.

disc (or disk). 1. Phonograph record. 2. Compact digital playback record. 3. Video playback record. *Disc jockey* (abbrev. *DJ*), individual responsible for the radio broadcast continuity of music and advertising; as a "jockey," the DJ "rides" the music through commentary between the recordings and commercials. Stations sometimes encourage the development of on-air "personalities" who bring additional listenership. These disc jockeys, who formerly determined the music to be broadcast, were often the willing targets of PAYOLA (bribes) by the record companies to get their product heard. While well-publicized convictions in the 1960s relegated payola to the backrooms and in less traceable forms, DJ personalities continued to promote their stations and themselves. Programming is now usually determined by a station manager or even market studies; in many formats, the DJ has become a nearly anonymous voice.

discant (*descant*; from Lat. *discantus*, singing apart). A term of diverse connotations, the meanings of which have changed throughout history. 1. The 1st attempts at polyphony with contrary motion in the parts (12th century); opposed to the ORGANUM, in which parallel motion was the rule. It was applied to a contrapuntal voice against the CANTUS FIRMUS, as the abbreviation of the Latin *discantus*, a translation of the Greek *diaphonia* (through sound). Discant is generally limited to a counterpoint of the 1st species, note against note, while organum developed eventually as a free counterpoint of the 5th species. The Notre Dame schoolmaster Perotinus was known as an *optimus discantor*. In the late Middle Ages the term became semantically expanded and appeared in the gallicized form of *déchant* or *deschaunt*. 2. Used interchangeably with MOTET and even, unjustifiably so, with FAUXBOURDON. 3. Orig., the upper voice; its use became common again in modern times to denote the highest part in a choral composition.

disco. 1. DISCOTHEQUE. 2. DISCO MUSIC.

Disco Duck. Novelty hit for deejay Rick Dees in 1976 riding on the disco movement.

Disco Inferno. Dance hit for the Trammps in 1978; the height of discomania.

disco music (or disco). A type of lyrically uninhibited, relentlessly rhythmic dance music that evolved from rock and soul music in the 1970s. It is characterized by a heavy accent on strong beats and the consequent weakening of the backbeat (*Turn the Beat Around*). Disco music was extremely popular for a decade and then receded into the background as a substantial influence on other musics, including house and rap.

discord (It. *discordanza*). Generically speaking, DISSO-NANCE. But all definitions are relative: "All discord, harmony not understood" (Alexander Pope); "Medicine, to produce health, has to examine disease; and music, to create harmony, must investigate discord" (Plutarch).

discotheque (Fr., collection of recordings). A gathering place where people dance to the sounds of amplified recordings, 1st evolving in the late 1950s in conjunction with the rise of rock 'n' roll music. These financially advantageous "canned-music" institutions superseded most live-music nightclubs and dance halls, and have continued with the wave of new dance-music styles. See also DISCO.

Discourse. Orch.l sketch by Bliss, 1957, that emulates an argumentative discussion among a group of intellectuals. The work was 1st performed in Louisville.

discrezione, con (It., with discretion). Discreetly, cautiously.

diseuse. A female reciter or narrator. Examples of compositions using a diseuse are Debussy's *The Martyrdom of Saint Sebastian*, Hindemith's *Hérodiade*, and Honegger's *Jeanne d'Arc au bûcher*.

disinvolto (It.). Unrestrained.

disinvoltura, con (It.). With ease, grace; flowingly.

Disis (Ger.). D double-sharp.

disjunct motion. Melodic progression by skips and leaps.

disk. 1. DISC. 2. A computer-data-storage recording; floppy disk.

Diskantschlüssel (Ger.). Treble clef.

dislocation of melodic lines. A special case of modern variation is a linear dislocation of a melodic line. A high note may be pulled upward and a low note may be pulled downward without disrupting the intervallic balance of the melody itself. Virtually any tonal melodic line can be topologically transformed into a dodecaphonic series, with ascending intervals retaining their upward direction and descending intervals conserving their downward motion. Stationary notes in the melody may be pulled upward or downward at will. Examples of intervallic and modulatory translocation can be found in NEO-CLASSICAL compositions. Translocation is also an excellent resource of modern burlesque.

disperato (It.). Desperately. *Disperazione, con*, in a desperate or despairing manner.

dispersed harmony. The positioning of a 4-voice chord so that the 3 upper voices are spread at an interval greater than an octave.

displaced tonality. A modernistic resource in tonal techniques, it has been successfully applied by composers who are reluctant to abandon tonality altogether; a displacement of the tonic by an instant modulation a semitone higher or a semitone lower. Translocation by larger intervals is not effective. Major scales are more suitable for such translocation because of the greater intervallic strength within a major tetrachord, while minor tetrachords are often ambiguous. Transposition of the initial 3 notes of a major scale a semitone higher or lower forms a group of 6 different notes; a similar translocation in a minor key will entail a duplication of only 1 member of the series. Examples of melodic translocation are found in many works of Prokofiev and Shostakovich.

dissonance

A combination of 2 or more tones requiring resolution, i.e., that is not harmonious. A more poetic term for dissonance (from Lat. *dis* + *sonare*, not together + sound) is DISCORD, a disagreement of hearts (Lat. *corda*, hearts). The antonym of dissonance is CONSONANCE (sounding together), of which the synonym is *concord*. In Greek terminology, dissonance is *diaphonia*, while consonance is *symphonia*.

The concept of dissonance has varied greatly through the millennia of musical history. From the standpoint of acoustics the borderline separating dissonances from consonances is as indefinite as the demarcation between 2 neighboring colors of the spectrum. The greater the numbers of the numerator and denominator of a fraction representing the ratio of vibrations between 2 different sounds, the more acute is the resulting dissonance. A minor 2nd is represented by the ratio 16/15 and constitutes a sharper dissonance than a major 2nd whose ratio of vibrations is 9/8. The presence of a single dissonant interval in an otherwise consonant chord converts it into dissonance.

In traditional harmony a dissonant chord imperatively demands a resolution into a consonance. The story is told that Bach, who was a compulsive sleeper, was awakened in the morning by his 2nd wife playing a dominant-7th chord on the harpsichord in the music room. Alarmed by the unresolved dissonance, Bach jumped out of bed still wearing his nightcap, rushed toward the harpsichord, and resolved the dominant-7th chord into the tonic triad. In his song *The Classicist* Mussorgsky ridicules the fear of dissonance by delaying the resolution of a transient dissonance. No composer before 1900 dared to leave a dissonance unresolved. Liszt was perhaps the 1st to break this absolute prohibition when he used a dissonant combination of notes of the so-called GYPSY SCALE in a final cadence.

The concept of inherent dissonance is not arbitrary; there are solid scientific reasons for the traditional division of intervals into consonances and dissonances, depending on the degree of interference of sound waves in a given harmony. The octave sounds harmonious to the ear because 2 waves of the upper note correspond to a single wave of the lower note, when the crests of the waves coincide and mutually reinforce each other. However, in a dissonant interval the sound waves overlap, creating oscillations of dynamic strength. When a minor 2nd is sounded, the higher note produces 16 waves per time unit, against 15 waves of the lower tone. This means that only 1 wave out of 15 or 16 coincides with the other waves, creating an interference that registers as a dissonance in our ears.

That the musical ear can get accustomed to dissonance and treat it as a consonance is proved by the common practice of tonic-7th chords in cadences in jazz music. Actually, the major 7th, when placed in the treble in the tonic-7th chord, forms a consonance with the bass on the tonic, with which it has the vibration ratio 15/1 (15/8). No jazz pianist would think of placing that major 7th in the bass register, where it would create an acute dissonance with the bass, generating a number of beats of interference. Another example of a technical dissonance that is commonly used in contemporary practice is the so-called added 6th. This is a note lying a 2nd above the major triad in the treble, forming a dissonant interval of the major 2nd with the top note of the original major triad. But placed, as it usually is, in the treble, it forms a 27th overtone in relation to the bass note, thus producing the sensation of a consonance, for 27 sound waves emanating from this "added 6th" coincide with a single wave of the bass sound.

The time finally came, early in the 20th century, when composers accepted the art of dissonance as a legitimate idiom, which no longer required the crutch of consonance to lean upon. Inevitably, by the dialectics of the antithesis, dissonances became paramount. The hegemony of consonance gave way to the dictatorship of dissonance.

It was now the turn of consonant combinations to resolve into dissonance. Schoenberg, working contrapuntally in the thematic development of his music, went so far as to exclude all triads from his vocabulary, allowance being made only for an occasional employment of the acceptable concords of the minor 6th and minor 3rd, while perfect octaves were totally banned. Thus Schoenberg reacted with horror when a conductor found an unexpected C-sharp in both the 1st and 2nd trumpet parts in the score of Schoenberg's symphonic piece, *Begleitungsmusik zu einer Lichtspielszene.* "Das ist falsch!" he exclaimed. After a thorough workout of the relevant tone row, it was found that the improperly doubled C-sharp in the higher trumpet should have been C-natur-

al, making the result a proper dissonance. Another example of relativity of consonance: In the score of his grandiose symphonic poem *Arcana,* Varèse introduced a chord consisting of a perfect octave and a perfect 5th. He explained this peculiar consonant intrusion into his integrally dissonant work by his desire to create an effect of contrasting dissonance!

There is a horrifying tale of a young woman whose father, a deranged biologist, fed her on a diet of poisonous herbs to prove his theory of physiological adaptation. When an amorous student fell in love with her and brought her fine tropical fruit, a box of chocolates, and a plate of French pastries, she feasted on them and died, poisoned by their tasty delights. But is there a new light dawning on the world of dissonances? Yes, the danger lies in a renaissance of undiluted triadic harmonies. Several modern composers are celebrating the new deadly bulimia, so far without lethal consequences.

dissonant chord. One containing 1 or more dissonant intervals.

dissonant counterpoint. A term that came into usage in the 1920s as a sort of apologetic declaration by proponents of atonal music. Charles Seeger published a treatise of composition in this style; it emphasized the functional equality of dissonance and consonance in all types of contrapuntal techniques. In fugal writing in particular, a strong tendency was evinced to use the tritone as the interval of entry, instead of the traditional perfect 5th of the tonic-dominant complex. Dissonant counterpoint does not exclude consonances but puts them on probation. However, the perfect octave, as a cadential interval, is generally shunned by the theoreticians of dissonant counterpoint, and is usually replaced by a major 7th.

dissonant interval. Two tones forming a dissonance, i.e., 2nds, 7ths, and all diminished and augmented intervals.

Dissonanzen Quartett (Dissonance Quartet). The nickname for Mozart's String Quartet in C Major, K. 465 (1785), criticized by contemporaries for alleged indulgence in dissonant counterpoint. The closest thing to harsh discord in the work occurs in the introduction to the 1st movement.

distanza (It.). Interval; space, distance. *In distanza,* at a distance; used to mark music to be performed as if far away.

distintamente (*distinto*; It.). Distinctly.

Distler, Hugo, important German composer; b. Nuremberg, June 24, 1908; d. (suicide) Berlin, Nov. 1, 1942. He studied at the Leipzig Cons. with Grabner, Ramin, and Martienssen. In 1931 he became a church organist at Lübeck; joined the faculty of the Cons. there (1933–37); also was a teacher at the School for Church Music in Spandau (1933–37); taught at the Stuttgart Hochschule für Musik (1937–40); from 1940 he was in Berlin.

Distler's early training and his connection with church music determined his style as a composer; his music is marked by a strong sense of polyphony. His greatest legacy is his religious choral music, putting Hindemith's extended tonality in the service of lively and profound interpretations of texts. Among the many works he completed are *Der Jahrkreis,* op. 5 (52 motets, 1932–33); *Choral-Passion,* op. 7 (1933); *Die Weihnachtsgeschichte,* op. 12 (1933); *Geistliche Chormusik,* op. 12 (1934–36, 1941). His secular choral masterpiece is the 3-part collection *Mörike-Chorliederbuch,* op. 19, (1938–39). He wrote some organ music and a Concerto for Harpsichord and String Orch., op. 14 (1935–36); 3 secular cantatas: *An die Natur,* op. 9/2 (1933); *Das Lied von der*

Glocke, op. 9/1 (1933–34); *Lied am Herde*, op. 21/1 (1941). His oratorio *Die Weltalter* (1942) remained unfinished. He also publ. *Funktionelle Harmonielehre* (Kassel and Basel, 1941).

Distratto, Il (The Absent-Minded One). Haydn's Sym. No. 60 in C Major, 1776. The musical material was originally intended to accompany a comedy of the same title produced in Vienna.

dital key. A key which, on pressure by the finger or thumb, raises the pitch of a guitar or lute string by a semitone. *Dital harp*, a guitar-shaped lute with 12 to 18 strings, each having a dital to raise its pitch a semitone; invented by Edward Light in 1819.

dithyramb. An ode to Dionysios (Dionysus), performed by a chorus accompanied by wind instruments and dancers at the Dionysian festivals in ancient Greece; also, a song of this type.

ditonus (Lat., 2 tones). Medieval term for the major 3rd.

diva (It., divine woman). A term introduced by Italian impresarios to describe a female opera singer to whom even the description *prima donna assoluta* (absolutely 1st lady) seems inadequate as falling short of divinity. The term was popular in the 19th century but disappeared from publicity campaigns early in the skeptical 20th century, even as it became part of the vernacular.

divertimento (It., diversion or entertainment; plural, *divertimentos, divertimenti*; Fr. *divertissement*). 1. In Italy beginning in the 17th century, a collection of music for entertainment; such a miscellany contained instrumental or vocal pieces of various genres. 2. In the latter half of the 18th century, an instrumental composition akin to suites or serenades (also *cassation, notturno,* and *partita*). In the 20th century the genre of divertimento was revived; Stravinsky, Bartók, and other modern composers wrote instrumental exemplars.

divertissement (Fr.). 1. DIVERTIMENTO. 2. An ENTR'ACTE in an opera, in the form of a short ballet, etc.

Divertissement. Brilliant orch.l work by Ibert, 1930, replete with familiar quotations, such as Mendelssohn's *Wedding March* and the *Blue Danube Waltz*. It was 1st performed in Paris.

divide. To play DIVISIONS.

divided stop. An ingenious mechanical arrangement in organs made in Spain in the 17th century which allows the use of different registrations, and therefore different timbres, in the treble and the bass. In England divided stops are often called HALF STOPS; in France they are termed REGISTRES COUPÉS.

Divin Poème, Le. Sym. No. 3 by Scriabin, 1904; the 1st of his outwardly mystical pieces, with movements entitled *Grandiose, Luttes, Voluptés,* and *Jeu divin*.

Divina commedia. Unfinished sym. by Liszt, 1867, inspired by Dante's great epic, 1st performed in Dresden. Of the 2 movements, the best music dramatically is in the *Inferno; Purgatorio* is comparatively bland. Liszt was unable to complete the planned 3rd section, *Paradisio*.

Divine Office. See CANONICAL HOURS.

divisi, -e (It., divided; abbrev. *div.*). In works with multiple strings, the indication that 2 parts written on 1 staff are not to be played as double stops, but by the division into 2 bodies of instruments playing from that staff; by implication, the overall division of a string section into subsections.

division. 1. A "dividing up" of a melodic series of tones into a rapid COLORATURA passage; if vocal, the passage is to be sung in 1 breath (now obsolete). *To run a division*, to execute such a passage. 2. In the English Baroque, a free improvisation in rapid figurations against a given ground bass. Manuals for training string, wind, and other performers in this technique were very common in the 17th century.

division mark. The slur or bracket written for duplets, triplets, quadruplets, etc., encompassing a figure 2, 3, 4, etc.

Dixie. This song is associated with the Southern cause in the American Civil War, but it was actually written by a Northerner, Daniel Decatur Emmett of Ohio, and was published a year before the Civil War (1860).

Dixieland. Jazz style, essentially synonymous with NEW ORLEANS STYLE, which represents part of the poorly documented beginnings of jazz in the 1st 2 decades of the 20th century. The term initially referred to white musicians, as is shown by the 1st jazz recordings, made by the all-white Original Dixieland Jazz Band (1917). The distinction was made between the relatively stiff Dixieland style and the more swinging and improvisatory New Orleans style of black musicians. When Dixieland was revived in the 1940s and 1950s, the stylistic gap between it and New Orleans style had closed sufficiently to make the distinction superfluous. Its instruments are typically cornet (or trumpet, trombone), clarinet, piano, banjo (or guitar), tuba (or double bass), and drums; the music developed from the repertoire of the New Orleans marching bands of the turn of the century. At its best, Dixieland is characterized by collective improvisation, dotted rhythms, and syncopation over a ragtimelike accompaniment.

dixtour (Fr.). Chamber work for 10 performers.

DJ. DISC JOCKEY.

Dlugoszewski, Lucia, American composer; b. Detroit, June 16, 1931. She studied piano, and concurrently attended classes in physics at Wayne State Univ. (1946–49). Fascinated with the mathematical aspects of music, she began to study with Edgard Varèse, whose works illuminated this scientific relationship for her. Accordingly, in her own works she emphasizes the sonorific element of music; inspired by the example of Varèse's *Ionisation*, she invented or perfected a number of percussion instruments; 1 of her inventions is the timbre piano, in which she makes use of bows and plectra on the piano strings. She has also composed many dance scores.

Do (It.). 1. The note C. 2. In solmisation, the usual syllable name for the 1st degree of the scale. In the Fixed Do method of teaching, Do is the name for all notes bearing the letter name C, whether keynotes or not; in the Movable Do method, Do is always the keynote, regardless of letter name.

Do I Hear a Waltz? Musical by Rodgers and Sondheim, 1965, about an innocent American female tourist who thinks she hears the Viennese equivalent of bells when she meets a Venetian man-about-town; alas, he is but a married swindler. Includes the title song.

Do That to Me One More Time. Ersatz ballad-hit for the Captain and Tenille in 1980; name changed from *Do It* to garner AM radio play.

docian. An organ stop, sometimes called dulzian, producing a soft, flutelike sound.

Dodds, "Baby" (Warren), African-American jazz drummer, brother of Johnny (John M.) Dodds; b. New Orleans, Dec. 24, 1898; d. Chicago, Feb. 14, 1959. He was the youngest of 6 children, hence his nickname. He studied drums with Dave Perkins, Walter Brundy, and Louis Cottrell, Sr., and, after performing with local jazz musicians, he joined Fate Marable's riverboat band in 1918. He settled in Chicago in 1921, where he played and recorded with King Oliver; he then worked with Louis Armstrong and Jelly Roll Morton and later played with his brother in several combos. He appeared with Jimmie Noone (1941), Bunk Johnson (1944–45), and Art Hodes (1946–47). In 1949–50 he suffered several strokes, and thereafter made infrequent appearances until his retirement in 1957. He was the foremost drummer in the New Orleans style of his era.

Dodds, Johnny (John M.), African-American jazz clarinetist and alto saxophonist, brother of Warren "Baby" Dodds; b. New Orleans, Apr. 12, 1892; d. Chicago, Aug. 8, 1940. He began playing the clarinet when he was 17; although he had lessons with Lorenzo Tio, Jr., he was mainly autodidact. After playing in Kid Ory's band in New Orleans (1912–17; 1919) and in Fate Marable's riverboat band (1917–19), he settled in Chicago; was a member of King Oliver's band and recorded in the mid-1920s with Louis Armstrong's Hot 5 and Hot 7 combos. He led his own band in the 1930s, then joined his brother's quartet in 1940. He was a leading exponent of the NEW ORLEANS STYLE.

Dodecachordon (Grk., 12 modes). Famous theoretical treatise by Glareanus, 1547. Its historical achievement consists in extending the system of authentic and plagal modes (Dorian, Phyrgian, Lydian, Mixolydian) from 8 to 12, by adding the Ionian and Aeolian modes with their plagal derivations. It also contains important analytic descriptions of the works by contemporary masters of polyphony.

dodecaphonic music

In historical perspective dodecaphonic (Grk. *dodeca* + *phone*, 12-sound) music is the product of a luxuriant development of chromatic melody and harmony. A conscious avoidance of all tonal centers led to the abolition of key signatures and a decline of triadic harmony. The type of composition in which all tonal points of reference have been eliminated became known as atonality. It was from this paludous atmosphere of inchoate atonality that the positive and important technical idiom of dodecaphonic composition was gradually evolved and eventually formulated by Schoenberg as the "method of composing with 12 tones related only to one another." Schoenberg's 1st explicit use of his method occurs in his Serenade, op. 24 (1924).

Five fundamental ideas underlie Schoenberg's method: dodecaphonic monothematism, in which the entire work is derived from a 12-tone row (Ger. *Tonreihe*) which comprises 12 different notes of the chromatic scale; the tone-row is utilized in 4 conjugate forms: the original, retrograde, inversion, and retrograde inversion; although the order of the notes in the tone-row is rigidly observed, the individual members of the series can be placed in any octave position, a peculiar feature of dodecaphonic music which results in the wide distribution of the thematic ingredients over the entire vocal or instrumental range of a single part or over sections of different parts; since each of the 4 forms of the basic 12-tone series can be transposed to any starting point of the chromatic scale, the total of all available forms is 48; melody, harmony, and counterpoint are functions of the tone-row, which may appear in all its avatars, horizontally as melody, vertically as harmony, and diagonally as canonic counterpoint. It may also be distributed partly in melodic progressions, partly in harmonic or contrapuntal structures, creating dodecaphonic meloharmony or melocounterpoint.

Because of the providential divisibility of number 12, the 12-tone row can be arranged in 6 groups in 2-part counterpoint, 4 groups in 3-part counterpoint (or harmony), 3 groups in 4-part harmony, or 2 groups in 6-part harmony. In a communication sent to the author in 1939,

Ernst Krenek describes the relationship between atonality and the method of composing with 12 tones as follows: "Atonality is a state of the musical material brought about through a general historical development. The 12-tone technique is a method of writing music within the realm of atonality. The sense of key has been destroyed by atonality. The method of composing with 12 tones was worked out in order to replace the old organization of the material by certain new devices."

Schoenberg was not alone in his dodecaphonic illumination. Several musicians, mostly in Austria and Germany, evolved similar systems of organizing the resources of the chromatic scale in a logical and self-contained system of composition. Jefim Golyscheff, Russian composer and painter who lived in Germany and eventually settled in Brazil, worked on the problem as early as 1914, and in 1924 published a collection called *12 Tondauer Musik*, making use of 12 different tones in thematic structures. At about the same time, Nicolas Obouhov invented a system he called "absolute harmony" that involved the use of all 12 chromatic tones without doubling; he played his piano pieces written in this system at a concert in Petrograd in 1916.

Passages containing 12 different notes in succession, apart from the simple chromatic scale, are found even in classical works. There is a highly chromaticized passage in Mozart's G Minor Sym. derived from 3 mutually exclusive diminished-7th chords, aggregating to 12 different notes. The main subject in the section *Of Science* in the score of *Also sprach Zarathustra* by R. Strauss contains all 12 different notes of the chromatic scale, but they remain uninverted, untergiversated, and otherwise unmetamorphosed, and thus cannot be regarded as a sampler of dodecaphonic writing. Liszt's *Faust Sym.* opens with a theme consisting of 4 successive augmented triads descending by semitones comprising all 12 different tones, but it cannot be meaningfully described as an anticipation of the dodecaphonic method. Ives has a 12-tone series of different chromatic notes in his instrumental piece *Tone Road No. 3*, which he wrote in 1915. This intuitive invention is important not only as an illustration of his prophetic genius, but also as another indication that dodecaphonic ideas appeared in the minds of musicians working in different parts of the world, completely independently of each other.

Among scattered examples of 12-tone composition of the predodecaphonic years is *L'adieu à la vie* for piano by Casella, which ends on a chord of 12 different notes. An amusing example of dodecaphonic prevision is the *Hymn to Futurism* by Cui, written in 1917, when the last surviving member of the Russian "Mighty 5" was 82 years old. Intended as a spoof, the piece contains a passage of 3 mutually exclusive diminished-7th chords in arpeggio adding up to 12 different notes, and another passage comprising 2 mutually exclusive augmented triads with a complementary scale of whole tones passing through the unoccupied 6 spaces, forming another series of 12 different notes. The fact that Cui had 2 dodecaphonic series in his short composition demonstrates that even in a musical satire the thematic use of 12 different notes was a logical outcome of the process of tonal decay, serving as a fertilizer for the germination of dodecaphonic organisms.

Schoenberg was intensely conscious of the imperative need of asserting his priority in the invention of the method of composition with 12 tones. Among contenders for the honor was Fritz Klein, the author of an extremely ingenious composition for orch., *Die Maschine*, subtitled "eine extonale Selbstsatire," published in 1921 under the characteristic pseudonym "Heautontimorumenos" (i.e., self-tormentor). Klein's score contains a remarkable array of inventions: a *Mutterakkord* containing 12 different notes and 11 different intervals, a "Pyramidakkord" (patterns of rhythmically repeated 12 notes), and other procedures, all presaging the future developments of integral serialism. When queried by the author regarding Klein's role in the history of dodecaphonic composition, Schoenberg replied (in English): "Although I saw Klein's 12-tone compositions about 1919, 1920, or 1921, I am not an imitator of him. I wrote the melody for Scherzo composed of 12 tones in 1915. In the 1st edition of my *Harmonielehre* (1911) there is a description of the new harmonies and their application which has probably influenced all these men who now want to become my models."

A much more formidable challenge to Schoenberg's dodecaphonic priority was made by Joseph Matthias Hauer of Vienna, who had experimented with a 12-tone

composition independently from Schoenberg. But his method differed from Schoenberg's in essential aspects. He built 12-tone subjects from 6-tone "tropes" (groupings), and allowed free permutation of each trope, a concept that was entirely alien to Schoenberg's fundamental doctrine of thematic ordering of the tone-row. Still, Schoenberg regarded Hauer's theories as sufficiently close to his own method to take notice of them. Schoenberg described the dodecaphonic situation in Vienna in a retrospective note published in the program book of a concert of his chamber music given in New York in 1950: "In 1921 I showed my former pupil Erwin Stein the means I had invented to provide profoundly for a musical organization granting logic, coherence, and unity. I then asked him to keep this a secret and to consider it as my private method with which to do the best for my artistic purposes." (The arcane character of this report calls to mind a Latin cryptogram in which the astronomer Huygens encoded his discovery of the rings of Saturn to insure the priority of his observations.) "If I were to escape the danger of being his imitator," Schoenberg continued, "I had to unveil my secret. I called a meeting of friends and pupils, to which I also invited Hauer, and gave a lecture on my new method, illustrating it by examples of some finished compositions of mine. Everybody recognized that method was quite different from that of others." Hauer refused to surrender his own claims as the spiritual protagonist of 12-tone music. A man of an irrepressible polemical temper, he even had a rubber stamp made, for his private correspondence, which carried the following legend: "Josef Matthias Hauer, der geistiger Urhaber und trotz vielen schlechten Nachahmern immer noch der einziger Kenner und Könner der Zwölftonmusik."

Although Schoenberg's title to the formulation and practical application of the method of composing with 12 tones was finally recognized, in 1948 he came into an unexpected collision with a fictional claimant, Adrian Leverkühn, the hero of Thomas Mann's novel *Doktor Faustus*, described as the inventor of the 12-tone method of composition. In an indignant letter to the editors of the *Saturday Review of Literature*, Schoenberg protested against this misappropriation of his invention. The idea that Leverkühn might be considered as a fictional portrait of Schoenberg himself infuriated him. "Leverkühn is depicted," Schoenberg wrote, "from beginning to end as a lunatic. I am 74 and I am not yet insane, and I have never acquired the disease from which this insanity stems. I consider this an insult."

The method of composing with 12 tones related only to one another did not remain a rigid dogma. Its greatest protagonists besides Schoenberg himself were his disciples Berg and Webern. Somewhat frivolously, they have been described as the Vienna Trinity, with Schoenberg the Father, Berg the Son, and Webern the Holy Ghost; less frivolously, the 2nd Viennese School. Both Berg and Webern introduced considerable innovations into the Schoenbergian practice. While Schoenberg studiously avoided triadic constructions, Alban Berg used the conjunct series of alternating minor and major triads capped by 3 whole tones as the principal subject of his last work, the Violin Concerto (1935). Schoenberg practically excluded symmetric intervallic constructions and sequences, but Berg inserted, in his opera *Lulu*, a dodecaphonic episode built on 2 mutually exclusive whole-tone scales. Webern dissected the 12-tone series into autonomous sections of 6, 4, or 3 units in a group and related them individually to one another by inversion, retrograde, and inverted retrograde. This fragmentation enabled him to make use of canonic imitation much more freely than would have been possible according to the strict Schoenbergian doctrine.

The commonly used term for dodecaphonic music in German is *Zwölftonmusik*. In American usage it was translated literally as "12-tone music," but English music theorists strenuously object to this terminology, pointing out that a tone is an acoustical phenomenon and that dodecaphony deals with the arrangement of written notes, and that it should be consequently called 12-note music. In Italy the method became known as *dodecafonia* or *musica dodecafonica*. Incidentally, the term *dodecafonia* was 1st used by the Italian music scholar Domenico Alaleona in his article *L'armonia modernissima*, published in *Rivista Musicale* in 1911, but it was applied there in the sense of total chromaticism as an extension of Wagnerian harmony.

The proliferation of dodecaphony in Italy was as potent as it was unexpected, considering the differences between Germanic and Latin cultures, the one introspective and speculative, the other humanistic and practical. Luigi Dallapiccola was one of the earliest adepts, but he liberalized Schoenberg's method and admitted tonal elements. In his opera *Il Prigioniero*, written in 1944, he made use of 4 mutually exclusive triads. The greatest conquest of Schoenberg's method was the totally unexpected conversion of Stravinsky, whose entire esthetic code had seemed to stand in opposition to any predetermined scheme of composition; yet he adopted it when he was already in his 70s.

Many other composers of world renown turned to dodecaphonic devices as a thematic expedient without full utilization of the 4 basic forms of the tone-row. Bartók made use of a 12-tone melody in his 2nd Violin Concerto, but he modified its structure by inner permutations within the 2nd statement of the tone-row. Ernest Bloch, a composer for whom the constrictions of modern techniques had little attraction, made use of 12-tone subjects in his *Sinfonia Breve* and in his last string quartets. English composers who have adopted the technique of 12-tone composition with various degrees of consistency are Tippett, Lennox Berkeley, Benjamin Frankel, Humphrey Searle, and Richard Rodney Bennett. Walton makes use of a 12-tone subject in the fugal finale of his 2nd Sym. Britten joined the dodecaphonic community by way of tonality. In his expressionist opera *The Turn of the Screw* he adopts a motto of alternating perfect 5ths and minor 3rds (or their respective inversions), aggregating to a series of 12 different notes. The Spanish composer Gerhard, who settled in England, wrote in a fairly strict dodecaphonic idiom. In France the leader of the dodecaphonic school is René Leibowitz, who also wrote several books on the theory of 12-tone composition. Wladimir Vogel, a Russian-born composer of German parentage, making his home in Switzerland, has adopted Schoenberg's method in almost all of his works. The Swiss composer Frank Martin has extended the principles of dodecaphonic writing to include a number of tonal and modal ramifications.

In America Schoenberg's method has found a fertile ground, not only among his students but also among composers who had pursued different roads. Babbitt and others extended the method into total serialism. Sessions, Thomson, and Diamond followed Schoenberg's method with varying degrees of fidelity. Copland used the dodecaphonic technique in some of his chamber music works; in the orch.l compositions entitled *Connotations*, commissioned for the opening concert of Lincoln Center, N.Y., in 1962, he applied the totality of dodecaphony to characterize the modern era of music. Piston interpolated a transitional 12-tone passage in his ballet suite *The Incredible Flutist*; he resisted integral dodecaphony until his septuagenarian years, when in his 8th Sym. he adopted Schoenberg's method in all its orthodoxy. Bernstein inserted a 12-tone series in the score of his *Age of Anxiety* to express inner agitation and anguished expectancy of the music. Barber made an excursion into the dodecaphonic field in a movement of his Piano Sonata. Menotti turned dodecaphony into parody in his opera *The Last Savage* to illustrate the decadence of modern civilization into which the hero was unexpectedly catapulted from his primitivistic habitat.

In the USSR, dodecaphony remained officially unacceptable as a "formalistic" device. (In a speech delivered in Moscow in 1963, Nikita Khrushchev, then Prime Minister, observed: "They call it dodecaphony, but we call it cacophony.") Nevertheless, some blithe spirits of the young Soviet generation, among them Andrei Volkonsky, Valentin Silvestrov, and Sergei Slonimsky, have written and published works in the 12-tone idiom.

dodecuplet. A group of 12 equal notes, to be performed in the time of 8 notes of the same kind in the established rhythm.

Dodge, Charles (Malcolm), American composer and teacher; b. Ames, Iowa, June 5, 1942. He studied composition with Richard Hervig and Philip Bezanson at the Univ. of Iowa (B.A., 1964), Darius Milhaud at the Aspen Music School (summer 1961), and Gunther Schuller at the Berkshire Music Center in Tanglewood (summer 1964), where he also attended seminars given by Arthur Berger and Lukas Foss. He then studied composition with Chou Wen-chung and Otto Luening, electronic music with Vladimir Ussachevsky, and music theory with William J. Mitchell at Columbia Univ. (M.A., 1966; D.M.A., 1970). He was a teacher at Columbia Univ. (1967–69; 1970–77) and Princeton Univ. (1969–70); was on the faculty of Brooklyn College of the City Univ. of N.Y. He was president of the American Composers Alliance (1971–75) and the American Music Center (1979–82). In 1972 and 1975 he held Guggenheim fellowships. With T. Jerse, he publ. *Computer Music: Synthesis, Composition, and Performance* (N.Y., 1985, 2nd ed., 1997).

Does Your Chewing Gum Lose Its Flavor (on the Bedpost Over Night)? Annoying 1961 novelty hit for British skiffle star Lonnie Donegan, popular among campers everywhere.

Dohnányi, Christoph von, eminent German conductor of Hungarian descent, grandson of Ernst (Ernö) von Dohnányi; b. Berlin, Sept. 8, 1929. He began to study the piano as a child; his musical training was interrupted by World War II. His father, Hans von Dohnányi, a jurist, and his uncle, Dietrich Bonhoeffer, the Protestant theologian and author, were executed by the Nazis for their involvement in the 1944 attempt on Hitler's life. After the war he studied jurisprudence at the Univ. of Munich; in 1948 he enrolled at the Hochschule für Musik in Munich and won the Richard Strauss Prize for composition and conducting. Making his way to the U.S., he continued his studies with his grandfather at Florida State Univ. at Tallahassee; also attended sessions at the Berkshire Music Center at Tanglewood.

Returning to Germany, he received a job as a coach and conductor at the Frankfurt Opera (1952–57). Progressing rapidly, he served as Generalmusikdirektor in Lübeck (1957–63) and Kassel (1963–66), chief conductor of the Cologne Radio Sym. Orch. (1964–70), and director of the Frankfurt Opera (1968–77). From 1977 to 1984 he was Staatsopernintendant of the Hamburg State Opera. In 1984 he assumed the position of music director of the Cleveland Orch., having been appointed music director-designate in 1982, succeeding Lorin Maazel. In the meantime, he had engagements as guest conductor of the Vienna State Opera, Covent Garden in London, La Scala in Milan, the Metropolitan Opera in N.Y., the Berlin Phil., the Vienna Phil., and the Concertgebouw Orch. in Amsterdam.

Both as sym. and opera conductor, Dohnányi proved himself a master technician and a versatile musician capable of congenial interpretation of all types of music, from Baroque to the avant-garde. He is regarded as a leading exponent of the works of the modern Vienna School, excelling in fine performances of the works of Schoenberg, Berg, and Webern. He is married to the soprano Anja Silja.

Dohnányi, Ernst (Ernö) **von,** eminent Hungarian pianist, composer, conductor, and pedagogue, grandfather of Christoph von Dohnányi; b. Pressburg, July 27, 1877; d. N.Y., Feb. 9, 1960. He began his musical studies with his father, an amateur cellist; then studied piano and music theory with Károly Forstner. In 1894 he entered the Royal Academy of Music in Budapest, where he took courses in piano with Istvan Thomán and in composition with Hans Koessler. In 1896 he received the Hungarian Millennium Prize, established to commemorate the thousand years of existence of Hungary, for his sym. He graduated from the Academy of Music in 1897, then went to Berlin for additional piano studies with Eugen d'Albert. He made his debut in a recital in Berlin (1897); in 1898 he played Beethoven's 4th Piano Concerto in London; then followed a series of successful concerts in the U.S. Returning to Europe, he served as prof. of piano at the Hochschule für Musik in Berlin (1908–15). He then returned to Budapest, where he taught piano at the Royal Academy of Music; served briefly as its director in 1919, when he was appointed chief conductor of the Budapest Phil. Orch. In 1928 he became head of the piano composition classes at the Academy of Music; in 1934 he became its director. In 1931 he assumed the post of music director of Hungarian Radio.

As Hungary became embroiled in war and partisan politics, which invaded even the arts, Dohnányi resigned his directorship in 1941; in 1944 he also resigned his post as chief conductor of the Budapest Phil. Personal tragedy made it impossible for him to continue his work as a musician and teacher: both of his sons lost their lives; one of them, the German jurist Hans von Dohnányi, was executed for his role in the abortive attempt on Hitler's life; the other son was killed in combat. Late in 1944 he moved to Austria. At the war's end rumors were rife that Dohnányi used his influence with the Nazi overlords in Budapest to undermine the position of Bartók and other liberals, and that he acquiesced in anti-Semitic measures. But in 1945 the Allied occupation authorities exonerated him of all blame; even some prominent Jewish-Hungarian musicians testified in his favor. In 1947–48 he made a tour of England as a pianist; determined to emigrate to America, he accepted the position of piano teacher at Tucuman, Argentina; in Sept. 1949 he reached the U.S., where he became composer-in-residence at Florida State Univ. in Tallahassee.

Dohnányi was a true virtuoso of the keyboard, and was greatly esteemed as a teacher; among his pupils were Solti, Anda, and Vázsonyi. His music represented the terminal flowering of European Romanticism, marked by passionate eloquence of expression while keeping within the framework of Classic forms. Brahms praised his early efforts. In retrospect, Dohnányi appears as a noble epigone of the past era, but pianists, particularly Hungarian pianists, often put his brilliant compositions on their programs. His most popular work with an orch. is *Variations on a Nursery Song*; also frequently played is his orch.1 Suite in F-sharp Minor. Dohnanyi himself presented his philosophy of life in a poignant pamphlet under the title *Message to Posterity* (Jacksonville, Fla., 1960).

doigté (Fr.). Fingering.

Doktor Faust. Opera by Busoni, 1925, left incomplete and performed posthumously, with an ending by Busoni's pupil Jarnach, in Dresden. The libretto is derived from the same medieval sources from which Goethe derived his Faust; the eponymous character appears here as a magician and an artist. The opera represents the culmination of the grandiloquent romantic ideal in musical composition, with its complex harmonies and Bach-like counterpoint. Another completion has been proposed by Anthony Beaumount.

Doktor und Apotheker. Opera by Dittersdorf, 1786, wherein 2 lovers are legally united despite the efforts of her pharmacist father to marry her off to an Austrian army captain.

dolce (It.). 1. Sweet, soft, suave, tender, caressingly, sentimental. 2. A sweet-toned organ stop. *Dolcemente*, sweetly, softly.

dolcian (dulcian; Ger. *Dulzian*; It. *dolcino*). 1. A CURTAL, a predecessor of the bassoon. 2. A penetrating, open-flue pipe organ stop, usually 8', sometimes 4'.

dolciato (It.). Softer, calmer.

dolcissimo (It.). Very sweetly, softly; also, a very soft-toned 8' flute stop in the organ.

dolentemente (It.). Dolefully, plaintively.

doloroso (It.). Painfully, full of grief; pathetically, sorrowfully.

Dolphy, Eric (Allan), African-American jazz alto and soprano saxophonist, bass clarinetist, and flutist; b. Los

Angeles, June 20, 1928; d. Berlin, June 29, 1964. He took up the clarinet in early childhood, later studying music at Los Angeles City College. After working with local groups, including Chico Hamilton's quintet (1958–59), he went to N.Y., where he performed with Charles Mingus's quartet (1959–60). He co-led a quintet with Booker Little (1961), then worked with John Coltrane, John Lewis, and again with Mingus. He was a master at improvisation, excelling in both jazz and 3RD STREAM genres. His repertoire included several avant-garde works, including Varèse's *Density 21.5* for solo flute.

dombra. A lutelike Central Asian instrument played with the finger. It differs from the Russian domra by virtue of its long neck and angular body. After 1917 the dombra was successfully introduced into Russian popular string orchs.

dominant. The 5th tone or step in the major or minor scale.

dominant chord. 1. The dominant triad. 2. The dominant chord of the 7th. *Dominant section*, in a particular movement, a section written in the key of the dominant, lying between and contrasting with 2 sections in the tonic key; *dominant triad*, a chord with the dominant as the root.

Dominicus. Mass in C Major by Mozart, 1769 (K. 66).

Domingo, Placido, famous Spanish tenor; b. Madrid, Jan. 21, 1941. His parents were ZARZUELA singers; after a tour of Mexico they settled there and gave performances with their own company. Placido joined his parents in Mexico at the age of 7 and began appearing with them in various productions while still a child; he also studied piano with Manuel Barajas in Mexico City and voice with Carlo Morelli at the National Cons. there (1955–57). He made his operatic debut in the tenor role of Borsa in *Rigoletto* with the National Opera in Mexico City in 1959. His 1st major role was as Alfredo in *La Traviata* in Monterrey in 1961; that same year he made his U.S. debut as Arturo in *Lucia di Lammermoor* with the Dallas Civic Opera; then was a member of the Hebrew National Opera in Tel Aviv (1962–64). He made his 1st appear-

Placido Domingo, c. 1960s

COURTESY FRANK DRIGGS COLLECTION

ance with the N.Y. Opera as Pinkerton (1965). In 1966 he made his Metropolitan Opera debut as Turiddu in a concert performance of *Cavalleria rusticana* at N.Y.'s Lewisohn Stadium; his formal debut on the stage of the Metropolitan followed, in 1968, when he essayed the role of Maurice de Saxe in *Adriana Lecouvreur*, establishing himself as one of its principal members. He also sang regularly at the Vienna State Opera (from 1967), Milan's La Scala (from 1969), and London's Covent Garden (from 1971).

His travels took him to all the major operatic centers of the world, and he also sang for recordings, films, and television. He also pursued conducting. He made his formal debut as an opera conductor with *La Traviata* at the N.Y. Opera in 1973; in 1984 he appeared at the Metropolitan Opera, conducting *La Bohème*. He commissioned Menotti's opera *Goya* and sang the title role at its premiere in Washington, D.C. (1986). In 1987 he had the honor of singing Otello at the 100th anniversary performances at La Scala. On New Year's Eve, 1988, he appeared as a soloist with Zubin Mehta and the N.Y. Phil in a gala concert televised live to millions, during which he also conducted the orch. in the overture to *Die Fledermaus*. One of the best-known lyric tenors of his era, Domingo has gained international renown for his portrayals of such roles as Cavaradossi, Des Grieux, Radames, Don Carlo, Otello, Don Jose, Hoffmann, Canio, and Samson.

Domino, "Fats" (Antoine, Jr.), African-American singer, pianist, and bandleader; b. New Orleans, Feb. 26, 1928. Although he sustained a severe hand injury as a youth, he pursued his career as a pianist; gained fame during the early years of the rock 'n' roll era by mixing blues elements with straight rock; he was successful in nightclubs and movies as a purveyor of popular, jazz, and blues genres.

Domino Noir, Le. Opera by Auber, 1837. A young Spanish novitiate nun, dressed in the eponymous costume, captivates a noble's heart at a masked ball; she is eventually released from her vows and they marry.

domra. A Russian lute, usually played with a plectrum. The domra was very popular in Russia as an instrument of popular entertainment provided by itinerant musicians (Rus. *skomorokhi*). The domra was superseded by the balalaika in the 18th century; but 20th-century musicians revived the instrument in an effort to encourage Russian historical instrumentation. Several domra-and-balalaika orchs. were formed after 1917.

Don Carlos. Opera by Verdi, 1867, 1st produced in Paris. The libretto, modeled after Schiller's drama, is an extravaganza based on the historical relationship between King Philip II of Spain and his son Carlos, whose intended wife, Elisabeth de Valois, became his stepmother. No "incestuous" passion is documented. Carlos was imprisoned in 1567 on the charge of plotting against Philip II, and died (or was murdered) a year later at the age of 23. In the opera, Don Carlos continues his clandestine trysts with his stepmother after her marriage, both appropriately disguised. They are turned in by her lady-in-waiting Princess Eboli (who loves the oblivious Carlos), and the sinister Grand Inquisitor directs Philip to put his son to death. The final confrontation takes place at the tomb of Philip's father, Carlos V, where a monk dressed in the late Emperor's attire (or his ghost?) emerges from behind (within?) the tomb (viz. Mozart's Commendatore), scaring everyone silly. Don Carlos 1) takes advantage of the confusion and flees, or 2) is embraced by Carlos V and taken to a safe haven.

Don Giovanni (Don Juan). Mozart's greatest opera, 1787, described as DRAMMA GIOCOSO (jocular drama), but the subject is not exactly merry. The libretto, in Italian, is by Da Ponte (his 2nd for Mozart). The alternative title was *Il Dissoluto Punito* (The Dissolute One Punished). It was 1st produced in Prague, a city that responded more positively to Mozart's operas than his home city, Vienna. A Vienna production was announced under the title *La Statua parlante* (the speaking statue). Obviously the producers intended to sensationalize the attraction; the speaking statue was that of the Commendatore, whom Giovanni slew in a duel and whose daughter he debauched. There is a great number of masquerades, charades, disguises, and mistaken identities. Giovanni's servant Leporello, in a famous "catalogue aria," ticks off the exact number of Giovanni's conquests in various countries, culminating with *mille e tre* (1,003) seductions

Scene from Don Giovanni

in Spain; he offers this information to one of Giovanni's most recent conquests. In an act of supreme effrontery, Giovanni challenges the statue of the slain Commendatore to have supper with him. With trombones sounding ominously in the orch., the statue accepts Giovanni's defiant invitation and in a deep bass voice speaks his determination to carry him to Hell. The remaining protagonists gather in happy disbelief, promising to pursue their lives much as they did before meeting Giovanni; in that sense, this is a comedy.

Don Juan. Symphonic poem by R. Strauss, 1889, 1st performed in Weimar. This, his 1st important work, was written at the age of 23 and is still one of his most frequently performed compositions. The score was inspired by a poem of Lenau in which Don Juan atones for his sins by death.

Don Pasquale. Comic opera by Donizetti, 1843, in which an elder is duped into marrying his nephew's intended; her shrewish garrulity convinces Pasquale to give her over to the nephew, complete with a considerable dowry.

Don Quichotte. Opera by Massenet, 1910, produced in Monte Carlo.

Don Quixote. Cervantes's pathetic but heroic "knight of the sorrowful countenance," who appears as the principal character of several operas and ballets. In addition to the works with individual entries, there are numerous works named DON CHISCIOTTE by Caldara, Philidor, Piccinni, Salieri, Donizetti, and others.

Don Quixote. Ballet by the Austrian-born Russian dance composer Léon Minkus (1869).

Don Quixote. Symphonic poem by R. Strauss, 1898, for cello, viola, and orch., subtitled *Fantastic Variations on a Theme of Knightly Character*. The 1st performance of this quasi-symphonie concertante took place in Cologne. There are 10 variations depicting various adventures of the hero. The bleating of the sheep, when Don Quixote charges into the herd, is represented by a tremendously cacophonous commotion in muted brass. The cello, like Quixote, dies at the end in a downward glissando toward the tonic D. The viola plays his trusty lieutenant Sacho Panza.

Don Rodrigo. Opera by Ginastera, 1964, 1st produced in Buenos Aires. Don Rodrigo is the Visigoth king in Toledo, Spain, in the 8th century. The governor of Ceuta, whose daughter is raped by Rodrigo in the opening scene of the opera, avenges her honor by invading Spain and defeating Rodrigo's army. But the victim forgives Rodrigo, and he dies in her arms. The score is written in a dodecaphonic system with the application of stereophonic techniques, while the form is built on the classical divisions of an instrumental suite. The idiom is uncompromisingly dissonant, but tonality is not intransigently eschewed.

Donizetti, Gaetano

Famed and prolific Italian composer of operas in the bel canto tradition; b. Bergamo, Nov. 29, 1797; d. there, Apr. 1, 1848. His father was from a poor family of artisans who obtained the position of caretaker in the local pawnshop. At the age of 9 Gaetano entered the Lezioni Caritatevoli di Musica, a charity institution which served as the training school for the choristers of S. Maria Maggiore; he studied singing and harpsichord there; later studied harmony and counterpoint with J. S. Mayr. With the encouragement and assistance of Mayr, he enrolled in the Liceo Filarmonico Comunale in Bologna in 1815, where he studied counterpoint with Pilotti; later studied counterpoint and fugue with Padre Mattei.

His 1st opera, *Il Pigmalione* (1816), appears never to have been performed in his lifetime. He composed 2 more operas in quick succession, but they were not performed. Leaving the Liceo in 1817, he was determined to have an opera produced. His next work, *Enrico di Borgogna*, was performed in Venice in 1818, but it evoked little interest. He finally achieved popular success with his opera buffa *Il Falegname di Livonia, o Pietro il grande, czar delle Russie* (1819). In Dec. 1820 he was exempted from military service when a woman of means paid the sum necessary to secure his uninterrupted work at composition. His opera seria *Zoraide de Granata* (1822) proved a major success. During the next 9 years, Donizetti composed 25 operas, none of which remain in the active repertoire today; however, the great success of his *L'Ajo nell'imbarazzo* (1824) brought him renown at the time. In 1825–26 he served as musical director of the Teatro Carolino in Palermo. From 1829 to 1838 he was musical director of the royal theaters in Naples. With *Anna Bolena* (1830), Donizetti established himself as a master of the Italian operatic theater. Composed for Pasta and Rubini, the opera was an overwhelming success. Within a few years it was produced in several major Italian theaters, and was also heard in London, Paris, Dresden, and other cities. His next enduring work was the charming comic opera *L'elisir d'amore* (1832).

The tragic *Lucrezia Borgia* (1833), although not entirely successful at its premiere, soon found acceptance and made the rounds of the major opera houses. In 1834 Donizetti was appointed prof. of counterpoint and composition at the Cons. di San Pietro a Majella in Naples. His *Maria Stuarda* (1834) was given its 1st performance as *Buondelmonte* in Naples after the Queen objected to details in the libretto. He then went to Paris, where his *Marino Faliero* had a successful premiere at the Théâtre-Italien (1835). Returning to Italy, he produced his tragic masterpiece *Lucia di Lammermoor* (1835). Upon the death of Zingarelli in 1837, Donizetti was named director pro tempore of the Conservatorio in Naples. In 1837, he suffered a grievous loss when his wife died following the 3rd stillbirth of a child, after 9 years of marriage.

Roberto Devereux garnered acclaim at its 1st performance in Naples (1837). In 1838 Donizetti resigned his positions at the Cons. when his post as director was not made a permanent appointment. When the censor's veto prevented the production of *Poliuto* due to its sacred subject (it was written for Nourrit after Corneille's *Polyeucte*), he decided to return to Paris. He produced the highly successful *La Fille du régiment* there (1840). It was followed by *Les Martyrs* (1840), a revision of the censored *Poliuto*, which proved successful. His *La Favorite* (1840) made little impression at its 1st performance, but it soon became one of his most popular operas. He spent 1841–42 in Italy and then went to Vienna. His *Linda di Chamounix* received an enthusiastic reception at its premiere there (1842). The Emperor appointed Donizetti Maestro di Cappella e di Camera e Compositore di Corte.

In 1843 he once more went to Paris, where he brought out his great comic masterpiece *Don Pasquale*. With such famous singers as Grisi, Mario, Tamburini, and Lablache in the cast, its premiere was a triumph (1843). He then returned to Vienna, where he conducted the successful premiere of *Maria di Rohan* (1843). Back again in Paris, he produced *Dom Sebastien* (1843). The audience approved of the work enthusiastically, but the critics were not pleased. Considering the opera to be his masterpiece, Donizetti had to wait until the Vienna premiere (in

German) of 1845 before the work was universally acclaimed. The last opera produced in his lifetime was *Caterina Cornaro* (1844). By this time Donizetti began to age quickly; in 1845 his mental and physical condition progressively deteriorated as the ravages of syphilis reduced him to the state of an insane invalid; in 1846 he was placed in a mental clinic at Ivry, just outside Paris; in 1847 he was released into the care of his nephew and was taken to his birthplace to await his end.

Donizetti was a prolific composer of operas whose fecundity of production was not always equaled by his inspiration or craftsmanship. Many of his operas are hampered by the poor librettos he was forced to use on so many occasions. Nevertheless, his genius is reflected in many of his operas. Indeed, his finest works serve as the major link in the development of Italian opera between the period of Rossini and that of Verdi. Many of his operas continue to hold a place in the repertoire.

Donkey, The. String Quartet in D Minor by Haydn, 1797 (No. 2, op. 76).

Donna del Lago, La. Opera by Rossini, 1819, based on Walter Scott's poem *The Lady of the Lake*, an Arthurian legend in which the king receives his magic sword (Excalibur) from a woman (Morgan le Fay) who lives on an enchanted island (Avalon).

Donna Diana. Comic opera by Reznicek, 1894, taking place during the Catalonian rebellion. The lady of the title is won over by the feigned indifference of her suitor.

Donnermaschine (Ger.). THUNDER MACHINE.

Don't Be Cruel. A 1956 hit for Elvis Presley.

Don't Fence Me In. Cowboy song by C. Porter, 1944, introduced by Roy Rogers in the film *Hollywood Canteen*. It became a hit several times, as sung by Kate Smith, Bing Crosby, and the Andrews Sisters.

Don't Get Around Much Anymore. Song by D. Ellington, 1942.

Doors, The. (Vocal: Jim Morrison, b. Melbourne, Fla., Dec. 8, 1943; d. Paris, France, July 3, 1971; keyboards/vocal:

Ray Manzarek, b. Chicago, Ill., Feb. 12, 1935; guitar: Robbie Krieger, b. Los Angeles, Calif., Jan. 8, 1946; drums: John Densmore, b. Los Angeles, Dec. 1, 1945.) Psychedelic rock group of the 1960s, led by oracular poet Morrison. Originally meeting at UCLA's film school, the band was established at the Los Angeles Whiskey-a-Go-Go club. Signed to Elektra Records in 1966, they scored immediately with Morrison's ode to priapetic power, *Light My Fire*, which was banned by some radio stations because of its sexual lyrics. The group continued to score with their hard-rocking renditions of Morrison's sophomoric verse, including *The End*, *When the Music's Over*, *People Are Strange*, *Love Me 2 Times*, and *Hello, I Love You* (written by Krieger).

In March 1969 the cult of Morrison reached its greatest heights when he supposedly exposed himself while performing on stage in Miami; the brouhaha that ensued helped elevate Morrison to a counterculture god. The band continued to issue recordings, scoring lesser hits through early 1971, when Morrison decided to leave the group to pursue his interest in poetry. However, by July of that year he had died, following years of drug and alcohol abuse; the cause of death, officially a "heart attack," may have been a heroin overdose. The rest of the Doors soldiered on as a trio through 1973.

Despite Morrison's death, the group has remained popular, particularly among adolescent males, to this day, and tales of Morrison's debauchery continue to be cherished by rock fans the world over. Over-the-top director Oliver Stone made a film about the group in 1991. The Doors were ensconced in the Rock and Roll Hall of Fame 2 years later.

dopo (It.). After.

Doppel (*doppelt*, Ger.; It. *doppio*). Double, twice.

Doppelchor (Ger.). Double chorus.

Doppelfuge (Ger.). DOUBLE FUGUE.

Doppelgriff (Ger., double grip). Double stop (bowed string instruments). *Doppelgriffe*, 3rds, 6ths, etc., played with 1 hand (piano).

Doppelkanon. DOUBLE CANON.

Doppelkreuz (Ger.). Double sharp.

Doppelschlag (Ger.; It., gruppetto). An ornamental figure requiring the use of the scale-steps above and below the principal note, e.g., C–D–C–B–C.

Doppelt so langsam (Ger.). Twice as slow.

doppelzunge. Double- or flutter-tonguing on a wind instrument, performed by thrusting the tongue rapidly to produce a fluttering sound.

doppio movimento (It., double movement). Twice as fast.

doppio note (It.). Twice as slow (with the absolute time value of the notes doubled).

doppio pedale (It.). Pedal part in octaves.

doppio trillo (It.). Double trill, i.e., a trill with a turn at the end.

doppio valore (It.). DOPPIO NOTE.

Dorati, Antal, distinguished Hungarian-born American conductor and composer; b. Budapest, Apr. 9, 1906; d. Gerzensee, near Bern, Nov. 13, 1988. He studied with Leo Weiner, both privately and at the Franz Liszt Academy of Music in Budapest, where he also received instruction in com-position from Kodály (1920–24). He was on the staff of the Budapest Opera (1924–28); after conducting at the Dresden State Opera (1928–29), he was Generalmusikdirektor in Munster (1929–32). In 1933 he went to France, where he conducted the Ballets Russes de Monte Carlo, which he took on a tour of Australia (1938).

He made his U.S. debut as guest conductor with the National Sym. Orch. in Washington, D.C., in 1937. In 1940 he settled in the U.S., becoming a naturalized citizen in 1947. He began his American career as music director of the American Ballet Theatre in N.Y. (1941–44); after serving as conductor of the Dallas Sym. Orch. (1945–49), he was music director of the Minneapolis Sym. Orch. (1949–60). From 1963 to 1966 he was chief conductor of the BBC Sym. Orch. in London; then of the Stockholm Phil. (1966–70). He was music director of the National Sym. Orch. in Washington, D.C. (1970–77), and of the Detroit Sym. Orch. (1977–81); was also principal conductor of the Royal Phil. in London (1975–79). He made numerous guest conducting appearances in Europe and North America, earning a well-deserved reputation as an orch. builder. His prolific recording output made him one of the best-known conductors of his time. His recordings of the Haydn syms. and operas were particularly commendable. In 1984 he was made an honorary Knight Commander of the Order of the British Empire. In 1969 he married Ilse von Alpenheim, who often appeared as a soloist under his direction.

Dorian mode. The basic mode of Gregorian chant; originally named *primus tonus* in the system of church modes. The ecclesiastical Dorian mode is not identical with the ancient Greek mode of the same name. If projected onto the diatonic scale represented by the white keys of the piano, the modern Dorian octave would extend from D to D. It is the only authentic mode that is self-invertible, i.e., can be played downward without a change in the order of intervals. The plagal derivation of the Dorian mode is Hypodorian, ranging from A below the tonic D to A an octave above.

Dorian Toccata and Fugue (BWV 538). A great organ work by Bach which has been mistakenly classified as being actually in the Dorian mode; in reality it is simply in the key of D minor. The absence of the key signature is explained by the curious fact that in Bach's time B-flat (B in German nomenclature) was taken for granted and did not have to be inserted in the key signature. All modern editions of the work supply the key signature.

Dorsey, "Georgia Tom" (Thomas Andrew), African-American pianist, blues singer, and gospel songwriter; b. Villa Rica, Ga., 1899. His father was a revivalist preacher; he went to Atlanta in his youth, where he 1st encountered blues pianists. He later took courses at the Chicago College of Composition and Arranging, and then launched his career as a pianist, arranger, and composer, organizing his own Wildcats Jazz Band and making recordings with Ma Rainey as "Georgia Tom." After founding the National Convention of Gospel Choirs and Choruses (with Sallie Martin) and the Thomas A. Dorsey Gospel Songs Music Publishing Co. (1931), he devoted himself entirely to gospel music; wrote the gospel standard *Precious Lord, Take My Hand* (1932).

Dorsey, Jimmy (James), popular American jazz clarinetist, saxophonist, and dance-band leader, brother of Tommy (Thomas) Dorsey; b. Shenandoah, Pa., Feb. 29, 1904; d. N.Y., June 12, 1957. He took up the slide trumpet and cornet when he was 7, then turned to reed instruments when he was 11; led several groups with his brother before working as a freelance musician in N.Y. (1925–34), becoming well known through his recordings. He then was coleader of the Dorsey Brothers Orch. (1934–35); after an argument with his brother, he took sole charge, later rejoining him in the new Dorsey Brothers Orch. (1954–56). He appeared in several films, including the fictionalized *The Fabulous Dorseys* (1947).

Dorsey, Tommy (Thomas), popular American jazz trombonist and dance-band leader, brother of Jimmy (James) Dorsey; b. Shenandoah, Pa., Nov. 19, 1905; d. Greenwich, Conn., Nov. 26, 1956. He studied trumpet with his father before turning to the trombone; led several groups with his brother and then was active in dance bands, pit orchs., and other groups in N.Y. He was coleader of the Dorsey Brothers Orch. (1934–35); following an argument with his brother, he set out on his own as a dance-band leader, becoming a leading figure in the BIG BAND era; his brother rejoined him in the new Dorsey Brothers Orch. (1953–56). He appeared in the fictionalized film *The Fabulous Dorseys* (1947). As an instrumentalist, he developed a virtuoso technique highlighted by his remarkable legato playing.

dot. In music this is much more than a mere punctuation mark. When placed after a note it indicates the increase in its value by one-half (♩. = ♩♪); a dotted quarter note equals the value of a quarter note plus an 8th note (1/4 + 1/8). In the 17th and 18th centuries dotted notes had an indeterminate value, indicating simply that the note with a dot after it had to be prolonged. In order to avoid uncertainty, the double dot (♩.. = ♩♪♪) was introduced late in the 18th century, the value of the 2nd dot being half the value of the 1st. Thus a quarter note with a double dot equaled 7 16th notes (1/4 + 1/8 + 1/16). A triple dot (♩... = ♩♪♪♪) is occasionally encountered; a quarter note with a triple dot equals 15 32nd notes (1/4 + 1/8 + 1/16 + 1/32).

dotara. A Bengal plucked string instrument that usually has 4 strings.

double. 1. A variation. 2. Repetition of words in a song. 3. A prefix indicating a 16' organ stop that matches an 8' stop; as double principal 16', etc. 4. A substitute singer. 5. In change-ringing, changes on 5 bells. 6. Producing a tone an octave lower; as double-bassoon, double-bourdon, etc. 7. Add the higher or lower octave (to any tone or tones of a melody or harmony).

double bar. The 2 vertical lines drawn through the staff at the end of a section, movement, or piece.

double bass. The largest and deepest-toned instrument of the violin family, formerly with either 3 strings (G_1–D–A being the Italian, A_1–D–G the English tuning), now 4 strings (E_1–A_1–D–G). The double bass sounds an octave lower than written. See also VIOLIN.

double bassoon. CONTRABASSOON.

double chorus. A work for 2 choirs, or divided choir, usually in 8 parts; the ensemble itself.

double common meter. See METER.

Double Concerto for Harpsichord, Piano, and 2 Chamber Orchs. Orch. work by E. Carter, 1961, 1st performed in N.Y. The score, ostensibly in a Baroque form, is a formidable attempt to organize musical ingredients in which each instrument and each group of instruments play distinct individual roles in dissonant counterpoint. Stravinsky described it as the 1st true masterpiece by an American composer.

double counterpoint. A type of polyphony in which the upper and the lower voices can be inverted so that the low voice becomes the top voice and vice versa, without breaking contrapuntal rules. See also COUNTERPOINT.

double croche (Fr.). Sixteenth note.

double dièse (Fr.). Double sharp.

double dot. See DOT.

double flat. The sign ♭♭.

double fugue. A fugue with 2 themes (subjects) occurring simultaneously.

double leading-tone cadence. An expansion of the polyphonic LANDINI CADENCE in late medieval music, where the leading-tone-to-submediant motion (7–6) is harmonized by a sustained raised subdominant (♯) (4) and supertonic (2) before resolving into an open 5th and octave:

double note. A breve (𝄺); a note twice the length of a whole note.

double octave. A 15th; interval of 2 octaves.

double open diapason. A 16' open pipe in a large organ, producing a sound an octave below the standard pitch of the manual key or the pedal.

double quartet. Work for pairs of 4 solo voices or instruments, as opposed to a mixed octet. Spohr wrote 4 double string quartets.

double reed. Type of reed used for instruments of the oboe and bassoon families; 2 separate pieces of cane bound together to produce a characteristic vibration.

double repetition mark. The symbol which divides a section of a composition into 2 parts and calls for the repetition of each part.

double sharp. The sign ×.

double stops. The technique of playing 2 notes simultaneously on the violin family instruments. The easiest double stops are in 6ths, but 3rds and octaves are also entirely playable, even in consecutive progressions. True triple and quadruple stops are theoretically ruled out by the curved bridge of the instrument, and the chord must be broken to be played (e.g., the opening of Beethoven's *Kreutzer Sonata*). The alternative is to flatten the bridge, not a practical solution.

douce (*doucement, doux*; It. *dolce*). Softly, sweetly, suavely, gently, tenderly.

douloureux (Fr.). Sorrowfully, dolorously.

Dowland, John, great English composer and famous lutenist; b. probably in London, 1563; d. there (buried), Feb. 20, 1626. In 1580 he went to Paris in the service of Sir Henry Cobham; by 1584 he was back in England, where he eventually married; on July 8, 1588, he was admitted to his Mus.B. from Christ Church, Oxford; in 1592 he played before the Queen. Unsuccessful in his effort to secure a position as one of the Queen's musicians, he set out in 1594 for Germany, where he received the patronage of the Duke of Braunschweig in Wolfenbüttel and the Landgrave of Hesse in Kassel; he then went to Italy and visited Venice, Padua, Genoa, Ferrara, and Florence; in Florence he played before Ferdinando I, the Grand Duke of Tuscany; he then made his way home, returning to England in 1595. In 1598 he was appointed lutenist to King Christian IV of Denmark, remaining in his service until 1606; he then returned to England, where he became lutenist to Lord Howard de Walden. In 1612 he became one of the lutenists to King Charles I.

Dowland was a foremost representative of the English school of lutenist-composers. He was also noted for his songs, in which he made use of novel chromatic developments; he treated the accompanying parts as separate entities, thereby obtaining harmonic effects quite advanced for his time. Most of his vocal music was published as *Bookes of Songes or Ayres of fowre partes with Tableture for the Lute...* (1597, 1600, 1603); *Lachrimae, or 7 Teares Figvred in Seaven Passionate Pauans . . . set forth for the Lute, Viols, or Violons, in fiue parts* (1604); and *A Pilgrimes Solace* (1612). His son Robert Dowland (b. London, *c.* 1591; d. there, Nov. 28, 1641) succeeded his father as lutenist to Charles I (1626). He ed. the anthologies *Varietie of Lute Lessons* (1610) and *A Musicall Banquett* (1610), which included some of his father's songs.

Down in the Valley. Folk opera by Weill, 1948, musically centered on the eponymous American song, and telling the tragic tale of a young man who is hanged for killing a love rival. The work fused American theater with 2 German genres whose evolution Weill participated in: the *Lehrstück* (learning piece) and *Gebrauchsmusik* (music for practical use).

downbeat. 1. The downward stroke of the conductor's hand in beating time, marking the primary or 1st accent in each measure; hence, 2. the accent itself (strong beat, thesis).

down-bow. In playing stringed instruments, the downward stroke of the bow from nut to point. The usual sign is ⊓.

downstroke. DOWN-BOW.

doxology (Grk. *doxa* + *logos*, glorious word). A hymn of praise to God. In church services there are 3 main doxologies: the *greater doxology* represented by the Gloria in excelsis in the Roman Catholic liturgy; the *lesser doxology*, Gloria Patri, used at the end of the psalmody; and metrical doxology, as used in the Anglican liturgy. Of this type the most common is the metrical hymn by the 17th-century divine Thomas Kent:

> Praise God, from whom all blessings flow
> Praise Him all creatures here below
> Praise him above ye heavenly Hosts
> Praise Father, Son, and Holy Ghost.

There are also doxologies for the Jewish liturgy, including the *kaddish* (i.e., mourner's prayer) and the *kedusha* ("Holy, Holy, Holy/Is the Lord of Hosts.")

D'Oyly Carte, Richard. CARTE, RICHARD D'OYLY.

drag. 1. A very slow dance in which the feet are dragged rather than moved on the floor. Scott Joplin wrote a "real slow drag" for his opera *Treemonisha*. 2. A rudimentary drum stroke.

dramatic contralto. See ALTO.

dramatic music. 1. Program music. 2. INCIDENTAL MUSIC.

dramatic soprano. See SOPRANO.

drame lyrique (Fr., lyric drama). French designation for opera, especially in the 19th century. This genre may be lyric or tragic; its designation refers to the use of singing.

dramma giocoso (It., jocular drama). An Italian term current in the 18th century for a comic opera with tragic episodes; literally, "jocular drama." Mozart's *Don Giovanni* is described as a *dramma giocoso* in its subtitle.

dramma lirico (It.). DRAME LYRIQUE.

dramma per musica (It., drama with music). An early term for opera in Italy about 1600. While the Baroque eventually called such works opera seria, Wagner revived the term for his operas (Musikdrama).

drammatico (It.). Dramatically; in a vivid, theatrical style.

drängend (Ger.). Pressing, hastening; STRINGENDO.

Dream, The. String Quartet in F Major by Haydn, 1787 (No. 5, op. 50).

Dream of Gerontius, The. Oratorio by Elgar, 1900, based on the religious poem of Cardinal Newman. Gerontius (from Grk. *geront*, old man) is an archetypal dying man who is conducted through Purgatory by the angel of Death. Elgar was himself a Catholic and to him such a subject was congenial. The work was performed for the 1st time in Birmingham; G. B. Shaw declared it a masterpiece. Its choral writing is expert.

Drehleier (Ger., rotating lyre). A HURDY-GURDY; often confused with DREHORGEL.

Drehorgel (Ger., rotating organ). BARREL-ORGAN; often mistakenly called a HURDY-GURDY, with resulting confusion with the DREHLEIER.

drei (Ger.). Three. *Dreifach*, triple.

Drei Pintos, Die. Unfinished Singspiel by Weber, completed and orchestrated by Mahler, 1888, using materials from Weber's other vocal works; Mahler conducted it for the 1st time in Leipzig. The story deals with romantic adventures in Spain in which 3 pintos, i.e., mottled horses, play a part.

Dreigroschenoper, Die (The Threepenny Opera). Singspiel (ballad opera) by Weill, 1928, 1st produced in Berlin. It is a modern reinterpretation of Gay's *The Beggar's Opera*, with a new text by Brecht denouncing the social hypocrisy of modern life. The score includes quasi-

American fox trots and ragtime. After a happy DEUS EX MACHINA ending, the concluding chorus enjoins the audience to "pursue injustice, but not too much." The production was immensely successful in Germany during the era between the 2 wars. *The Threepenny Opera*, with an English translation by Blitzstein (1954), was equally popular; among the many fine songs the mocking ballad *Mack the Knife* became a perennial favorite in America. Lotte Lenya starred in both the German and American premieres.

Dreiklang (Ger.). Triad.

Dreivierteltakt (Ger.). A 3/4 measure; 3/4 time; waltz time.

dringend (Ger., pressing). Gradually accelerating and becoming animated

drohend (Ger.; It. *tonando*). Menacing; thundering.

droit (*droite*; Fr.). Right. *Main droite*, right hand.

drone. 1. In the bagpipe, a continuously sounding pipe of constant pitch; a drone-pipe. 2. Any sustained tone, in an inner or outer voice, creating the effect of a bagpipe, particularly on an organ. *Drone-bass*, a bass on the tonic, or tonic and dominant, persistent throughout a piece or section.

Druckman, Jacob (Raphael), outstanding American composer; b. Philadelphia, June 26, 1928; d. New Haven, Conn., May 24, 1996. After taking courses in solfège, harmony, and counterpoint with Longy and L. Gesensway in Philadelphia, he studied composition with Copland at the Berkshire Music Center in Tanglewood (summers 1949, 1950), with Mennin, Persichetti, and Wagenaar at the Juilliard School of Music in N.Y. (B.S., 1954; M.S., 1956), and with Aubin at the École Normale de Musique in Paris on a Fulbright fellowship (1954–55). He taught at the Juilliard School of Music in N.Y. (1957–72) and at Bard College (1961–67); was an associate at the Columbia-Princeton Electronic Music Center (1967) and director of the electronic music studio at Yale Univ. (1971–72). After serving as associate prof. of composition at Brooklyn College of the City Univ. of N.Y. (1972–76), he was chairman of the composition dept. and director of the electronic music studio at Yale Univ. (from 1976). From 1982 to 1986 he was composer-in-residence of the N.Y. Phil. He held Guggenheim fellowships in 1957 and 1968. In 1972 he won the Pulitzer Prize in Music for his *Windows* for Orch., and in 1978 he was elected a member of the Inst. of the American Academy and Inst. of Arts and Letters.

In his music he happily combines the strict elements of polyphonic structure, harking back to Palestrina, with modern techniques of dissonant counterpoint, while refusing to adhere to any doctrinaire system of composition. In his orchestrations he makes use of a plethora of percussion instruments, including primitive drums; electronic sonorities have also had increasing importance in his works.

drum machine. Electronic device that performs preprogrammed rhythms and timbres.

drum. In the percussion, an instrument consisting of a cylindrical, hollow body of wood or metal, over 1 or both ends of which a membrane of animal skin or plastic (the head) is stretched tightly by means of a hoop, to which is attached an endless cord tightened by leathern braces, or by rods and screws. Rhythmical drums (side drum, snare drum, bass drum, etc.) do not vary in pitch; musical drums (timpani, tom-tom, etc.) produce musical tones distinct in pitch.

Drumroll Symphony. A nickname for Haydn's Sym. No. 102, 1795, in E-flat Major (Ger. Paukenwirbelsymphonie). The sym. opens with a roll on the timpani. It is the 8th of Haydn's 12 London syms. composed for the Salomon series in London.

duda. A Slavic bagpipe.

Dudelsack (Ger.). Bagpipe.

duduk. A Slavic whistle flute.

due (It.). Two. *A due*, for 2; both together again (after playing DIVISI); *a due voci*, 2 parts or voices.

due corde. CORDA.

Due Foscari, I. Opera by Verdi, 1844, based on Byron's play *The Two Foscari*, 1844. The story recounts a mortal feud between 2 Venetian families. The 2 Foscari of the title, father and son, are innocent of suspected murders, but die from mental anguish and chagrin.

Due Litiganti, I. Opera by Giuseppe Sarti (1729–1802), 1782, produced in Milan. The complete title is *Fra I Due*

Litiganti il Terzo Gode (Between 2 Litigants, a 3rd of the Profits). The opera was extremely popular in its time; Mozart quotes a tune from it in Act II of *Don Giovanni*.

due pedali, con. Both (damper and soft) pedals at once.

due volte. Two times; repeat.

Dueling Banjos. Originally issued in the mid-1950s as *Feudin' Banjos* by Arthur Smith (tenor banjo) and Don Reno (5-string banjo), successfully revived for the film *Deliverance* by Eric Weissberg (5-string banjo) and Steve Mandell (guitar).

Duenna, The. See WEDDING IN A MONASTERY, A.

duet (It. *duetto*). 1. A composition for 2 voices or instruments. In an operatic context, a love scene is often forthcoming, but Schubert and Brahms wrote accompanied duets in the lieder form. 2. A composition for 2 performers on one instrument, as the piano. 3. A composition for the organ, in 2 parts, each to be played on a separate manual.

duettino (It.). A short duet, usually with instrumental accompaniment. Mozart's *Marriage of Figaro* has several.

duetto da camera. A vocal duet, usually of an amorous nature.

Dufay (Du Fay), **Guillaume,** great French composer; b. probably in or near Cambrai, *c.* 1400; d. there, Nov. 27, 1474. His last name is pronounced "du-fah-ee," in 3 syllables, as indicated by the way he set his name to music in *Ave regina caelorum.* He was a choirboy at Cambrai Cathedral, where he came under the influence of Nicolas Malin, its magister puerorum, and his successor, Richard Loqueville. Although there is no evidence that he formally studied with these men, he undoubtedly learned his craft while working under them and other musicians. He remained in Cambrai until at least 1418; shortly thereafter, he entered the service of the Malatesta family in Pesaro, and in 1426 he returned to Cambrai.

Dufay was in Rome as a singer in the papal choir (1428–33), during which period he consolidated his reputation as one of the most significant musicians of his day. His motet *Ecclesie militantis* may have been composed for the consecration of Pope Eugene IV in 1431. He found a patron in Niccolo III, Marquis of Ferrara, in 1433, and made a visit

to his court in 1437; he also found a patron in Louis, Duke of Savoy. He served as maître de chappelle for the marriage of Louis and Anne of Cyprus at the Savoy court (1434). After a visit to Cambrai in that year, he returned to Savoy. He was again a singer in the papal choir (1435–37), which was maintained at this time in Florence until 1436, and then in Bologna. It was about this time that he received a degree in canon law from the Univ. of Turin. In 1436 he was made canon of Cambrai Cathedral. After again serving the Savoy court (1437-–39), he returned to Cambrai in 1440 to assume his duties as canon. In 1446 he was also made canon of Ste. Waudru in Mons. In 1450 he returned to Italy; he visited Turin in the summer of that year and was subsequently active in Savoy from 1451 to 1458, serving once more as maître de chappelle at the court (1455–56). In 1458 he returned to Cambrai, where he lived and worked in comfort for the rest of his life.

He was held in the highest esteem in his lifetime by the church authorities and his fellow musicians; Compère described him as "the moon of all music, and the light of all singers." He was the foremost representative of the Burgundian school of composition. He proved himself a master of both sacred and secular music, producing masses, motets, and chansons of extraordinary beauty and distinction. His contributions to the development of fauxbourdon and the cyclic Mass are particularly noteworthy.

Dukas, Paul, famous French composer and teacher; b. Paris, Oct. 1, 1865; d. there, May 17, 1935. From 1882 to 1888 he was a student at the Paris Cons., studying under G. Mathias (piano), Theodore Dubois (harmony), and E. Guiraud (composition); won 1st prize for counterpoint and fugue in 1886, and the 2nd Prix de Rome with a cantata, *Velléda* (1888); began writing music reviews in 1892; was music critic of the *Revue Hebdomadaire* and *Gazette des Beaux-Arts*; also a contributor to the *Chronique des Arts, Revue Musicale*, etc.; in 1906 was made a Chevalier of the Legion d'honneur; from 1910 to 1913, and again from 1928 to 1935, was prof. of the orch. class at the Cons.; in 1918 was elected Debussy's successor as a member of the Conseil de l'enseignement supérieur there; also taught at the École Normale de Musique; assisted in the revising and editing of Rameau's complete works for Durand of Paris.

Although he was not a prolific composer, he wrote a masterpiece of modern music in his orch.1 scherzo *L'Apprenti sorcier*; his opera *Ariane et Barbe-Bleue* is one of the finest French operas in the impressionist style. Among his other notable works are the Sym. in C Major and the ballet *La Péri*. Shortly before his death he destroyed several MSS of his unfinished compositions.

Duke, Vernon. DUKELSKY, VLADIMIR.

Dukelsky, Vladimir, versatile Russian-American composer of serious and popular music, the latter under the pseudonym Vernon Duke; b. Oct. 10, 1903, in the railroad station of the Russian village of Parfianovka (during his mother's trip to Pskov); d. Santa Monica, Calif., Jan. 16, 1969. He was a pupil at the Kiev Cons. of Glière and Dombrovsky; left Russia in 1920 and went to Turkey, going to the U.S. shortly afterward; later lived in Paris and London; settled in N.Y. in 1929 (naturalized, 1936); was a lieutenant in the Coast Guard (1939–44); went back to France (1947–48) but returned to the U.S. to live in N.Y. and Hollywood.

He began to compose at a very early age; was introduced to Diaghilev, who commissioned him to write a ballet, *Zephyr et Flore*, the production of which put Dukelsky among the successful group of ballet composers. Another important meeting was with Koussevitzky, who championed his music in Paris and in Boston. In the U.S. Dukelsky began writing popular music; many of his songs, such as *April in Paris*, have enjoyed great popularity. At George Gershwin's suggestion he adopted the name Vernon Duke for popular music works; in 1955 he dropped his full name altogether and signed both his serious and light compositions Vernon Duke. He publ. the polemical book *Listen Here! A Critical Essay on Music Depreciation* (N.Y., 1963).

dulcet. A 4' organ stop, producing a soft sound an octave above normal pitch.

dulciana (*dolziana*, It.). 1. An organ stop of 16', 8', or 4', having open metal pipes of a somewhat sharp, thin tone. 2. A CURTAL.

dulcimer (from Lat. *dulcis*, sweet). 1. The hammered dulcimer, a predecessor of the harpsichord and the piano. It has wire strings stretched over a soundboard or resonance-box, usually in trapezoid form resembling the psaltery, or zither; the strings are activated by mallets. The modern

Jean Ritchie, dulcimer player

COURTESY GREENHAYS RECORDS

dulcimer has from 2 to 3 octaves' compass. It was at one time called cembalo. In Hungary it is known as the CIMBALOM. An 18th-century musician named Pantaleon Hebenstreit manufactured an instrument like a dulcimer which became known under his 1st name. 2. The MOUNTAIN DULCIMER, a folk instrument popular in the Appalachian Mountains in the U.S. It consists of an elongated soundbox with a fretted fingerboard and usually has three strings. In contradistinction to the hammered dulcimer and the zither, the strings in the folk instrument are plucked. The mountain dulcimer is frequently used to accompany singers or dancers at country festivals.

dulzian. 1. A CURTAL. 2. An organ stop producing a soft, flutelike sound; also called *dolce*, *dulcian*.

dumb piano. A piano keyboard with no strings attached, used for practicing by aspiring pianists whose crowded lodgings do not permit even a joyful noise of pounding on the keys. G. B. Shaw, writing as Corno di Bassetto (his nom de plume of 1888), reports an inquiry from a correspondent as to whether there is such a thing as a "dumb horn." He claimed that no such contrivance was needed because a French horn is so difficult to play that it remains naturally dumb in the hands of inexpert hornists.

Dumbarton Oaks. Concerto in E-flat Major by Stravinsky, 1938, scored for 14 instruments, commissioned by a rich American music lover who lived on an estate called Dumbarton Oaks, in Germantown, a suburb of Washington, D.C. The work is written in a distinct neo-Baroque style characteristic of Stravinsky's music of the period.

dumka (Pol. *dumać*, ponder). 1. A vocal or instrumental romance, of a melancholy cast; a lament or elegy. Czech composers wrote the best-known exemplars of the dumka: Dvořák named his piano trio (op. 90, 1890–91) the plural form *Dumky*, and wrote other such works. Other composers were Fibich, Janáček, Suk, and Novák. 2. (Ukr., a little thought) Ukrainian lyric narrative ballad, with a meditative, sometimes melancholy character.

Dumky. Piano Trio by Dvořák, 1890–91 (op. 90), in the unusual form of 6 movements in the DUMKA.

dummy pipes. Pipes which do not speak, displayed in the front of the organ.

dump (*dompe, dumpe*). A type of piece, often in ground bass or variation form, for lute or keyboards in the 16th and 17th centuries, harmonized by alternating tonic and dominant chords.

Dunstable (Dunstaple), **John,** great English composer. b. *c.* 1390; d. London, Dec. 24, 1453. Almost nothing is known about his life with any certainty. He may have been the John Dunstaple who was in the service of the Duke of Bedford; if he was the same man he may have accompanied his patron to France. He appears to have been well versed in astronomy and mathematics. The J. Dunstaple buried in the church of St. Stephen, Walbrook (destroyed in the Great Fire of 1666), was undoubtedly the composer. The Old Hall MS (early 15th century) and other MSS reveal the existence of a highly developed art in England in the early 15th century, antedating the full flowering of the Burgundian school of Dufay, Binchois, and other masters.

Dunstable's style appears to be a direct outgrowth of the English school. He was the most important figure in English music in his time. His works were widely known on the Continent as well as in his homeland. Most of his known compositions are preserved in manuscripts on the Continent, although discoveries have recently been made in England. Some works formerly attributed to him are now known to be by Power, Benet, Binchois, and others. Other works remain doubtful. The styles of Dunstable and Power are so comparable that it has not always been possible to separate their works. Dunstable's extant works include Mass movements, motets, and secular songs.

duo (It.). A duet. *Duo* is loosely distinguished from *duet* by applying the 1st term to works for 2 pianos or for voices and/or instruments of different kinds; the 2nd term may be reserved for 2 voices or instruments of the *same* kind (excepting pianos).

duodecima (It.). 1. The interval of the 12th. 2. The 12th, an organ stop.

duodrama. A modern type of dramatic presentation in which only two actors conduct a dialogue, usually reciting

their reciprocal experiences retrospectively without coming to a dramatic clash. It lends itself naturally to chamber opera. The term has been anachronistically applied to 18th-century works.

duolo, con (It.). Dolefully, grievingly.

Duparc (born Fouques-Duparc), **(Marie-Eugène) Henri,** notable French composer of songs; b. Paris, Jan. 21, 1848; d. Mont-de-Marsan, Feb. 12, 1933. He studied with César Franck, who regarded him as his most talented pupil. Duparc suffered from a nervous affliction, which forced him to abandon his composition and seek rest in Switzerland. He destroyed the MS of his Cello Sonata, and several symphonic suites; of his instrumental works only a few MSS have survived, including the symphonic poems *Aux étoiles* (perf. in Paris, Apr. 11, 1874) and *Lénore* (1875) and a suite of 5 piano pieces, *Feuilles volantes* (1869). His songs (1868–82), to words by Baudelaire and other French poets, are distinguished by exquisitely phrased melodies arranged in fluid modal harmonies; among the best are *L'invitation au voyage, Extase, Soupir, Serenade, Chanson triste, La Vague et la cloche, Phidylé, Elégie, Testament, Lamento,* and *La Vie antérieure.*

duple. Double. *Duple rhythm*, rhythm of 2 beats to a measure; *duple time*, see TIME.

duplet. A group of 2 equal notes to be performed in the time of 3 of like value in the established rhythm; written

duplex. Generic term for hybrid brass instruments that combine important features of 2 members of the same instrumental family. The saxophone is probably the most successful example of this phenomenon; another is the double euphonium, which combines a wide euphonium bell along with a narrow trumpet bell activated by a special valve. While duplex is usually associated with the 19th-century madness for invention, such instruments have been a common component of the avant-garde since World War II.

duplum (Lat.). The contrapuntal part against the CANTUS FIRMUS in ORGANUM in ARS ANTIQUA. In ARS NOVA the duplum was also called the *motetus* (from Fr. *mots*, words).

DuPré, Jacqueline, renowned English cellist; b. Oxford, Jan. 26, 1945; d. London, Oct. 19, 1987. She entered the London Cello School at the age of 5; while still a child she began studies with her principal mentor, William Pleeth, making her 1st public appearance on British television when she was 12. She was awarded a gold medal upon graduation from the Guildhall School of Music in London (1960); also studied with Casals in Zermatt, Switzerland, with Tortelier at Dartington Hall and in Paris, and with Rostropovich in Moscow. After winning the Queen's Prize (1960), she made her formal debut in a recital at London's Wigmore Hall (1961). She made her North American debut at N.Y.'s Carnegie Hall as soloist in Elgar's Cello Concerto with Dorati and the BBC Sym. Orch. (1965), an appearance that electrified the audience and elicited rapturous critical reviews.

In 1967 she married in Jerusalem the pianist and conductor Daniel Barenboim, with whom she subsequently performed. In 1973 she was diagnosed as having multiple sclerosis, at which time she abandoned her career. She later gave master classes as her health permitted. In 1976 she was made an Officer of the Order of the British Empire, and in 1979 was awarded an honorary doctorate in music by the Univ. of London. The Jacqueline DuPré Research Fund was founded to assist in the fight against multiple sclerosis.

dur (Ger.). Major, as in C dur (C major), F dur (F major), etc.

duramente (It.). Sternly, harshly.

duration. Length of a sound, rest, movement, or composition.

Durchführung (Ger., going through). 1. The development section in SONATA FORM. 2. The exposition in a FUGUE.

Durchkomponiert (Ger.). THROUGH-COMPOSED.

Durey, Louis (Edmond), French composer; b. Paris, May 27, 1888; d. St. Tropez, July 3, 1979. He studied with Leon Saint-Requier (1910–14); was a member of LES SIX. Durey wrote music fashionable during a wave of anti-Romanticism, proclaiming the need of constructive simplicity in modern dress, with abundant use of titillating discords. Although he was the oldest of Les Six, he wrote the least music. Durey's aesthetic code was radically altered in 1936 when he joined the French Communist Party. During the German occupation of France, he was active in the Resistance, for which he wrote anti-fascist songs. In 1948 he was elected vice president of the Assoc. Française des Musiciens Progressives; in 1950 he became the music critic of the Paris Communist newspaper *L'Humanité*. In 1961 he received the Grand Prix de la Musique Française.

durezza, con (*duro*; It.). Hard, harsh; play with unflinching rhythm and emphatic accentuation. In the 17th century durezza was synonymous with DISSONANCE, in the sense that Frescobaldi named his *Toccata di durezza* after its appoggiaturas.

Düster (Ger.). Gloomy, mournfully, somberly.

Dutilleux, Henri, talented French composer; b. Angers, Jan. 22, 1916. He studied at the Paris Cons. with H. Busser and with Jean and Noel Gallon; won the 1st Grand Prix de Rome in 1938; was director of singing at the Paris Opéra in 1942; subsequently was active on the Paris radio (1943–63). In 1961 he was a prof. at the École Normale de Musique and in 1970 at the Paris Cons. He has developed a modernistic style which incorporates many procedures of IMPRESSIONISM. His chamber music and orch.l works have had numerous performances in France, England, and America.

Dutoit, Charles (Edouard), outstanding Swiss conductor; b. Lausanne, Oct. 7, 1936. His father was Swiss-French; his mother was part German, part English, and, in her remote ancestry, part Brazilian. He learned to play the violin, viola, piano, and drums; studied conducting by watching Ansermet's rehearsals with the Orch. de la Suisse Romande. He studied music theory at the Lausanne Cons. and at the Geneva Cons.; then took courses at the Accademia Musicale in Siena and at the Cons. Benedetto Marcello in Venice; also attended a summer seminar at the Berkshire Music Center in Tanglewood. Returning to Switzerland, he joined the Lausanne Chamber Orch. as a viola player.

He made his conducting debut with the Bern Sym. Orch. in 1963; was engaged as music director there (1967–77). From 1964 to 1971 he was artistic director of the Zurich Radio Orch. For several years he was artistic director of the National Orch. in Mexico City. In 1975 he was appointed conductor of the Goteborg Sym. Orch. in Sweden. In 1977 he was engaged as music director of the Montreal Sym. Orch.; he found the work congenial, since it was centered on French culture; he greatly expanded the orch.'s repertoire; conducted Haydn syms., much music of Mozart and Beethoven, and especially French music, beginning with Berlioz and including Debussy and Ravel. He also promoted new Canadian music. In 1983 he was appointed principal guest conductor of the Minn. Orch. in Minneapolis, and was artistic director and principal conductor of the Philadelphia Orch. summer seasons (1990–91). He made his Metropolitan Opera debut in N.Y., conducting *Les Contes d'Hoffmann*. In 1990 he was named chief conductor of the Orch. National de France in Paris. He was married 3 times; his 2nd wife was the pianist Martha Argerich.

dux (Lat. *leader*). The subject or theme in a fugue; it is followed by the *comes* (Lat., companion), the imitative answer. The terms became fashionable in the 16th century.

dvojnica. South Slavic double flute; the right tube is for melody, the left is a drone.

Dvořák, Antonin

Famous Czech composer; b. Nelahozeves, Kralupy, Sept. 8, 1841; d. Prague, May 1, 1904. His father ran a village inn and butcher shop and intended Antonin (Leopold) to learn his trade. However, when he showed his musical inclinations, his father let him study piano and violin with a local musician. He also received financial help from an uncle. Later, Dvořák went to Prague, where he studied with the director of a church music school, Karel Pitsch, and his successor, Josef Krejci. He also began to compose so assiduously that in a short time he completed 2 syms., 2 operas, and some chamber music.

His 1st public appearance as a composer took place in Prague (1873), with a perf. of his cantata *The Heirs of the White Mountain* (Hymnus). An important event in his career occurred in Prague in 1874, when Smetana conducted his Sym. No. 3 in E-flat Major, op. 10. Dvořák then entered several of his works in a competition for the Austrian State Prize, adjudicated by a distinguished committee that included Herbeck, Hanslick, and Brahms. He won the prize in 1875 and twice in 1877. Brahms, in particular, appreciated Dvořák's talent and recommended him to Simrock for publication of his *Moravian Duets* and the highly popular *Slavonic Dances*. His Stabat Mater (Prague, 1880) and Sym. No. 6 in D Major, op. 60 (Prague, Mar. 25, 1881), followed in close succession, securing for him a leading position among Czech composers.

At the invitation of the Phil. Soc. of London, Dvořák visited England in 1884 and conducted several of his works; then he was commissioned to compose a new sym. for the Phil. Soc.; this was his Sym. No. 7 in D Minor, op. 70, which he conducted in London (1885). His cantata *The Spectre's Bride*, composed for the Birmingham Festival, was accorded an excellent reception when he conducted the English performance there (1885). On his 3rd visit to England he conducted the premiere of his oratorio *St. Ludmila*, at the Leeds Festival (1886). In 1890 he appeared as a conductor of his own works in Russia. That same year he conducted in Prague the 1st performance of his Sym. No. 8 in G Major, op. 88, which became one of his most popular works. In 1891 Dvořák was appointed prof. of composition at the Prague Cons.; he then received honorary degrees from the Charles Univ. in Prague (Ph.D.) and Cambridge Univ. (D.Mus.). There followed his brilliant *Carnival Overture* (1891).

In 1892 Dvořák accepted the position of director of the National Cons. of Music of America in N.Y. He composed his Te Deum for his 1st U.S. appearance as a conductor (N.Y., 1892); he also conducted a concert of his music at the 1892 World Columbian Exposition in Chicago. It was in the U.S. that he composed his most celebrated work, the Sym. No. 9 in E Minor, op. 95 (*From the New World*), which received its premiere performance in late 1893, with Anton Seidl conducting the N.Y. Phil. The melodies seemed to reflect actual Negro and Indian music, but Dvořák insisted upon their absolute originality. Sym. No. 9 is essentially a Czech work from the Old World; nevertheless, by appearing as a proponent of the use of Negro-influenced themes in symphonic music, Dvořák had a significant impact on American musical nationalism. He discussed the idea in an article, "Music in

America" (*Harper's New Monthly Magazine*, Feb. 1895), stating that although Americans had accomplished marvels in most fields of endeavor, in music they were decidedly backward and were content to produce poor imitations of European music; the way to greatness, he suggested, was in the development of a national style based on the melodies of Negroes and Indians. His proposal was greeted with enthusiasm by one segment of America's musical world and roundly rejected by those fearing musical miscegenation. The controversy raged for more than 2 decades.

Dvořák also composed his great Cello Concerto during his American sojourn, and conducted its 1st performance in London (1896). Resigning his N.Y. position in 1895, he returned home to resume his duties at the Prague Cons.; he became its director in 1901. During the last years of his life, Dvořák devoted much of his creative efforts to opera; *Rusalka* (1900) remains best known outside the Czech

Antonin Dvořák

Republic. He made his last appearance as a conductor in 1900, leading a concert of the Czech Phil. in Prague. Dvořák was made a member of the Austrian House of Lords in 1901, the 1st Czech musician to be so honored. Czechs celebrated his 60th birthday with special performances of his music in Prague.

Dvořák's musical style was eclectic. His earliest works reflect the influence of Beethoven and Schubert, then Wagner, culminating in the Classicism of Brahms. After mastering his art he proved himself to be a composer of great versatility and fecundity. A diligent and meticulous craftsman, he brought to his finest works a seemingly inexhaustible and spontaneous melodic invention, rhythmic variety, judicious employment of national folk tunes, and contrapuntal and harmonic skill. His last 5 syms., the Cello Concerto, Stabat Mater, his *Slavonic Dances*, the *Carnival Overture*, and many of his chamber works have become staples of the repertoire.

dyad. A group of 2 pitch classes, usually with reference to a 12-note set.

Dybbuk, The. Ballet by Bernstein, 1974, based on the Shlomo Ansky play depicting the exorcism of a newly bereaved Jewish bride whose body is occupied by the errant soul of her dead bridegroom.

Dylan, Bob (born Robert Allen Zimmerman), American folksinger and songwriter; a beacon of 1960s socially-conscious folk-rock; b. Duluth, Minn., May 24, 1941. He adopted the name Dylan out of admiration for the poet Dylan Thomas. Possessed by wanderlust, he allegedly rode freight trains across the country; played guitar and crooned in the coffeehouses of N.Y. He composed songs that were modeled after blues and ballads, with a wide range of topics from personal to political; the poetic range of his lyrics became his most powerful trait. Dylan's nasalized folk style evolved into electric folk (folk-rock) on the example of the Byrds and other rock groups that performed his songs; despite the alienation of folk purists, his metamorphosis

Bob Dylan, c. 1980

captured the imagination not only of untutored adolescents but also of certified cognoscenti in search of convincing authenticity. A group of militants in the Students for a

Democratic Soc. adopted the name "Weathermen" after a line from Dylan's song *Subterranean Homesick Blues*.

In 1966 Dylan broke his neck in a motorcycle accident, which forced him to interrupt his charismatic career for 2 years. Upon his return to recording in 1968, he had adopted yet another face, that of country-western singer; once again, the Byrds were a major impetus for this. In later years Dylan became a Christian and celebrated his being saved for several albums; he eventually returned to Judaism. While he became increasingly self-parodic in his songwriting and performances, he could still give a sincere and powerful performance in the right circum-stances; a Dylan guest appearance became a rare privilege. His influence on other musicians is incalculable; a 30th-anniversary concert in 1962 featured a great number of important rock, folk, and blues musicians. In 1970 he was awarded an honorary doctorate from Princeton Univ., the 1st such honor given to a popular singer innocent of all academic training.

dynamics. The varying and contrasting degrees of intensity or loudness in musical tones; the notational signs used to designate these degrees (FORTE, PIANO, CRESCENDO, DIMINUENDO, SFORZANDO, etc.).

E. 1. The 5th note of the alphabetical scale and the 3rd note or mediant of the C-major scale. In Italian, Spanish, French, and Russian, E is Mi. 2. (It.) And. When preceding a word beginning with the letter *e*, it should be written *ed*; before other vowels, either *e* or *ed* may be used; before consonants, only *e*.

E dur (Ger.). E major.

E major. E major has 4 sharps in its key signature, difficult to handle in the Classic period, which employed natural brass instruments normally tuned in flat keys. The grandest sym. in E major is the 7th of Bruckner, both in length and in its ambitious concept. In composing this sym., Bruckner's imagination was possessed by Wagner and he said that the 2nd movement (Adagio), in the relative key of C-sharp minor, presaged the death of Wagner. Wagner himself favored the key of E major; he wrote the overture to *Tannhäuser* in that key. To Romantic composers E major was the key of spiritual transfiguration. The 1st Sym. of Scriabin is in the key of E major and it ends with a choral paean to art. E major is found in the final sections of orch.l works nominally in E minor; the most famous example is Mendelssohn's E-minor Violin Concerto.

E minor. This is the tonality of contemplative calm, if we are to judge by the works written in this key. It is not frequently used by the great composers of the Classic period. Mozart neglected it, as did Haydn and Beethoven, but the Romantics loved it. Mendelssohn's Violin Concerto is in E minor. Perhaps the best-known sym. in E minor is the 4th Sym. of Brahms, with its spacious narrative development.

Tchaikovsky couched his 5th Sym. in the key of E minor; the finale, as tradition demanded, is set in the tonic major of the key. Mahler's most serene sym., his 7th, is in E minor. Even though there are lapses into the night's darkness, the finale, in unambiguous C major, reasserts the optimistic aspect of the music, so unusual in Mahler's works. The river Moldau (Vltava) in Smetana's symphonic cycle *Ma vlast* flows poetically in E minor. Dvořák's 9th Sym. (*From the New World*) is in E minor, and the nostalgic quality of this work written during his sojourn in the U.S. fits the key. But perhaps the most congenial use of the key of E minor is found in Rimsky-Korsakov's symphonic suite *Scheherazade*. Although the motto of the work for solo violin is in A minor, the listener's ear registers it as the subdominant of the principal key of E minor.

E moll (Ger.). E minor.

E string. The highest string on the violin; the lowest string on the double bass; the highest and lowest strings on the guitar; not found on the viola or cello.

Eagles, The. (Vocal/guitar: Glenn Frey, b. Detroit, Mich., Nov. 6, 1948; drums/vocal: Don Henley, b. Gilmer, Tex., July 22, 1947; banjo/mandolin/guitar/vocal: Bernie Leadon, b. Minneapolis, Minn., July 19, 1947; bass/vocal: Randy Meisner, b. Scottsbluff, Nebr., Mar. 8, 1946. After 1974, guitar: Don Felder, b. Gainesville, Fla., Sept. 21, 1947; after 1975, guitar: Joe Walsh, b. Wichita, Kans., Nov. 20, 1947, replaced Leadon; after 1977, bass/vocal: Timothy B. Schmit, b. Sacramento, Calif., Oct. 30, 1947, replaced Meisner.) Influential country-rock band of the 1970s. First formed as a backup group for singer Linda Ronstadt, the group recorded soft country-rock, scoring early hits with *Take It Easy*, a mellow, hippie-cowboy anthem, and *Desperado*. They reached their greatest success when they became a more hard-rocking outfit, focusing on social commentary (1977's *Hotel California*; *Life in the Fast Lane*). In 1980 the group disbanded following internal squabbling; 14 years later the group rebanded (with its late-'70s personnel) for a hugely successful "Hell Freezes Over" tour and album. Henley has gone on to the greatest individual success, although Frey also has had solo hits.

ear training. A generic description of educational methods employed to improve the appreciation of intervals and rhythms. Students who happily possess the precious gift of PERFECT PITCH (which cannot be trained artificially) have a tremendous advantage over others not so favored by nature, for perfect pitchers, recognition of intervals, chord formation, melodic structure, counterpoint, etc., presents no more difficulty than for a child to recognize the syllabic values of its native language. A French child who can speak fluent French is not superior to an American child who cannot; a child possessing a sense of perfect pitch is not necessarily superior musically to another who does not. Ear training, therefore, must be highly selective.

Memory is another important branch of ear training; here again, individual gifts may differ greatly. An otherwise unmusical child may possess a natural ability to remember popular tunes he hears in the street, while a virtuoso violinist or pianist may be devoid of such instinctive memorization. The ability to carry a tune is also subject to individual evaluation; some children can pick up tunes and sing or whistle them with extraordinary accuracy, while experienced musicians may be unable to carry a tune. Ravel would have probably failed a test of memory or even pitch recognition; Toscanini sang embarrassingly off pitch when he wanted to instruct the orch. in shaping a musical phrase. Stravinsky had an unusually poor memory even in reconstructing his own works; his ear training by any educational standards was surprisingly deficient. On the other hand, jazz musicians, innocent of strict academic training, often display amazing capacity for picking up and reproducing complex melodies and rhythms.

Earth Angel. A 1954 doo-wop hit for the Crew Cuts, covered by the Penguins and Gloria Mann (1955) and New Edition (1986).

Easter Parade. Song by I. Berlin; the melody originated in 1917; a set of new lyrics was added for the revue *As Thousands Cheer* (1933). The song served as the theme for an eponymous film (1948).

éblouissant (Fr.). Dazzling, resplendent.

ebollimento (It.). A sudden and passionate expression of feeling.

Ebony Concerto. Concerto for clarinet and jazz band by Stravinsky, 1946, written for the clarinetist Woody Herman. The piece was 1st performed by Herman and his band in N.Y., Mar. 25, 1946.

eccitato (It.). Excited.

ecclesiastical modes. The octave scales employed in medieval music; church modes. See also AUTHENTIC MODES; PLAGAL MODES.

echappée (Fr.). Standard abbrev. for *note echappée* (escaped note). This is a fortuitous term to describe a nonharmonic tone which is neither a PASSING NOTE, a CAMBIATA, nor an APPOGGIATURA. It is approached freely, placed a diatonic scale degree above or below the thematic note (forming a strong dissonance with the harmony), and then resolved in the opposite direction from which it was approached. Unlike the NOTA CAMBIATA, the underlying harmony shifts between the starting and ending note:

Bach's works are replete with such usages, which create a pungent aroma of dissonance without disrupting the sense of essential tonality.

echo (It. *eco*). A subdued repetition of a strain or phrase. The natural reflection of sound in mountain landscapes was the inspiration of many composers for the use of canonic imitation. In Greek mythology, the nymph Echo languishes in unrequited love for Narcissus; only her voice remains, as an echo. The legend inspired several opera composers; Gluck wrote *Écho et Narcisse*, in which he made ingenious use of canonic imitation. The device of canonic echoes is employed in many madrigals; in some cases the echo repeats the last syllables of the preceding word, when it makes sense, e.g., *esempio* (example) answered by *empio* (empty). This effect is used poignantly in the last act of Monteverdi's *Orfeo*. The echo is also used in instrumental music. In the last movement of his *Ouvertüre nach französicher Art* (Partita in B Minor, BWV 831), Bach makes use of it; in Mozart's Serenade, K. 286, there is an antiphonal interplay of groups of 4 instruments in a quadruple echo.

echo organ. A separate set of pipes either enclosed in a box within the organ or placed at a distance from the latter to produce the effect of an echo. *Echo stop*, organ stop producing an echolike effect.

echoi. The Greek term for melodic formulas of Byzantine chant, paralleling closely the Gregorian system of 8 modes. Collectively they are known as OKTOECHOS (8 modes). Their emergence has been traced to Syrian chant, which is much older than Gregorian chant; it seems probable that both Byzantine and Gregorian chants were ultimately derived from a Syrian source.

Eckstine, Billy (William Clarence), also known as "Mr. B," African-American jazz singer and bandleader; b. Pittsburgh, July 8, 1914. He worked in nightclubs as a crooner; sang in Hines's big band (1939–43); formed a band of his own (1944–47), proselytizing for bebop; later became successful as a balladeer of "cool" jazz. His place in jazz history is secured by the remarkable list of young musicians he helped establish: Parker, Gillespie, Vaughan, M. Davis, Dameron, Navarro, Gordon, Stitt, and Blakey.

eclecticism (from Grk. *ex* + *leipein*, gather). Compositional or improvisational aesthetic in which the choice of style or period is unlimited. Generally, eclecticism reflects a more pervasive mode of influence than mere QUOTATION.

eco (It.). Echo.

écossaise (Fr., Scottish). Orig., a Scottish round dance in 3/2 or 3/4 time; later, a lively contradanse in 2/4 time. The latter entered continental Europe in the early 19th century; Beethoven, Schubert, von Weber, and Chopin composed them. While known under this and other names (anglaise, française), the écossaise and its relatives probably originated in English country dances. Compare SCHOTTISCHE.

Ecuatorial. Symphonic poem by Varèse, 1934, for bass voice, brass instruments, piano, organ, percussion, and thereminovox, to the texts in Spanish from the sacred book of the Mexican priests. It is one of the earliest works to employ an electronic instrument. The 1st performance took place in N.Y.

edel (Ger.). Noble; refined, chaste.

Edgar. Opera by Puccini, 1889, 1st produced in Milan. Edgar loves 2 women, a wild one appropriately called Tigrana, and a faithful one appropriately named Fidelia. As Edgar vacillates, Tigrana descends on Fidelia and stabs her to death. The opera lacks distinction, and its rare revivals are in the nature of curiosity to see what kind of music Puccini wrote before *La Bohème*.

effeminatamente (It.). In a feminine manner, tenderly.

effetto (It.). Effect, impression.

E-flat major. The natural brass instruments are keyed either in B-flat or E-flat major; thus these are the keys used in festive serenades, military marches, and solemn chorales. Works in E-flat major are suitable for heroic, patriotic, and religious themes. Beethoven's *Eroica Sym.* cannot be imagined in any other key but E-flat major; neither can Beethoven's *Emperor Concerto* (although the title was not Beethoven's invention). One of the greatest Mozart syms., No. 39, is set in the key of E-flat major. Although this key is not particularly violinistic, for the upper 2 strings are not within the scale of E-flat major, Mozart and several other classical composers wrote violin concertos in E-flat major. It is not by accident that Schumann's 3rd Sym. in E-flat Major is surnamed *Rhenish*, for it reflects the nature of life on the river Rhine, with its constant traffic and postilions signaling the departure of stagecoaches in E-flat major. Beethoven's Piano Sonata (which he named *Les Adieux*) begins with an imitation of the postilion's signal in "horn 5ths." Bruckner's *Romantic Sym.*, his 4th, is also in this key, as is Mahler's grandiose 8th, nicknamed the "Sym. of a Thousand."

E-flat major is peculiarly suited to the piano keyboard; its full octave scale runs symmetrically through alternating pairs of white keys and black keys. Piano works in E-flat major number in the thousands. Liszt set his 1st Piano Concerto in E-flat major, but he avoided introducing the key in a triadic exposition; rather he teased the listener with syncopated descent from the tonic into the dominant. This figure generated the abusive words supposedly addressed to the orch.: "Sie sind alle ganz verruckt" (You are all quite off your wits). In his egocentric tone poem *Ein Heldenleben*, R. Strauss wrote a violin solo in the vainglorious key of E-flat major to represent his own self. When von Bülow was asked what his favorite key was, he replied, "E-flat major, for it is the key of the *Eroica Sym.*, and it has 3 B's [B signifies a flat in German] for Bach, Beethoven, and Brahms." This was the origin of the famous grouping the "3 B's of music."

E-flat minor. This is the key of seclusion and aristocratic retreat from the common elements of harmony. With 6 flats in the key signature, it lends itself to brilliant technical devices for a piano virtuoso. But it is utterly unsuitable for orch.l writing. A rare instance of an orch.l work in E-flat minor is Miaskovsky's 6th Sym.

effusione, con (It.). Effusively; with warmth.

Egk (born Mayer), **Werner,** significant German composer; b. Auchsesheim, near Donauwörth, May 17, 1901; d. Inning, near Munich, July 10, 1983. Rumor had it that he took the name Egk as a self-complimentary acronym for "ein grosser [or even 'ein genialer'] Komponist." Egk himself rejected this frivolous suspicion, offering instead an even more fantastic explanation that Egk was a partial acronym of the name of his wife Elisabeth Karl, with the middle guttural added "for euphony." He studied piano with Anna Hirzel-Langenhan and composition with Carl Orff in Munich, where he made his permanent home.

Primarily interested in theater music, he wrote several scores for a Munich puppet theater; was also active on the radio; then wrote ballet music to his own scenarios and a number of successful operas. He was active as opera conductor and music pedagogue. He conducted at the Berlin State Opera from 1938 to 1941 and was head of the German Union of Composers from 1941 to 1945. He was commissioned to write music for the Berlin Olympiad in 1936, for which he received a Gold Medal. He also received a special commission of 10,000 marks from the Nazi Ministry of Propaganda. The apparent favor that Egk enjoyed during the Nazi reign made it necessary for him to stand trial before the Allied Committee for the de-Nazification proceedings in 1947; he was absolved of political taint. From 1950 to 1953 he was director of the Berlin Hochschule für Musik.

As a composer Egk continued the tradition of Wagner and R. Strauss, without excluding, however, the use of acidu-lous harmonies, based on the atonal extension of tonality. The rhythmic investiture of his works is often inventive and bold. He is best known for his dramatic works. He publ. a vol. of essays under the title *Musik, Wort, Bild* (Munich, 1960).

Egmont Overture. The best-known portion of Beethoven's incidental music for Goethe's drama *Egmont*, 1810, which was 1st performed in Vienna. Egmont was a historical figure, a Dutch patriot who organized resistance to the Spanish masters of the Netherlands but was killed in the process.

Egorov, Youri, talented Russian pianist; b. Kazan, May 28, 1954; d. Amsterdam, Apr. 15, 1988. He was a precocious child who learned to play piano at home; at the age of 17 he won a prize at the Long-Thibaud competition in Paris, and at 20 received 3rd prize at the Tchaikovsky Competition in Moscow. In 1978 he made his N.Y. debut, followed by solo performances with various American orchs. He settled in the Netherlands, where his career was cut tragically short by AIDS.

eguale (It.). Equal; even, smooth.

1812 Overture (Overture: 1812). Symphonic poem by Tchaikovsky, 1882, commemorating the 70th anniversary of the defeat of Napoleon's armies in Russia. Tchaikovsky wrote it for the consecration of the Church of Christ the Savior in Moscow, and the performance was given in the open air. The score included such special effects as a contingent of church bells and even cannon shots. The Overture uses musical symbolism with a broad chronological stroke: a Russian religious hymn, the *Marseillaise* representing the French army, a Russian folk song and a prayer, the *Marseillaise* wilting in a minor key, and a triumphant rendition of the Czarist anthem *God Save the Czar.* (Incidentally, the use of this hymn is anachronistic, as it was composed 20 years after Napoleon's invasion of Russia.) While Tchaikovsky found his work "devoid of artistic value," posterity disagreed. After the 1917 Revolution, the *1812 Overture* was not performed in the USSR because of the Czarist anthem; but as patriotic fever rose on the eve of the Nazi attack on Russia, the *1812 Overture* was returned to the Russian concert halls, with the anthem replaced by the melody of the final chorus of Glinka's opera *A Life for the Czar* (whose title had already been changed to *Ivan Susanin*); fortuitously, the substitution worked harmonically.

eighth. 1. An octave. 2. Eighth note.

eilen (Ger.). Hasten, accelerate, go faster. *Eilend*, hastening, stringendo; *eilig*, hasty, hurriedly; rapid, swift.

ein (*eins*; Ger.). One.

Ein klein wenig langsamer, Takt wie vorher zwei (Ger.). A little bit slower, with 1 measure like 2 before (DOPPIO MOVIMENTO).

Eine kleine Nachtmusik (A Little Night Music). String serenade by Mozart, 1787. The work is in 4 movements, in a small-scale symphonic form. Mozart's genius is particularly expressive in this miniature sym.

Eine Nacht in Venedig. Operetta by Johann Strauss, Jr., 1883, full of disguises, extramarital lust, mistaken identities, and 3 women named Barbara (but only 1 of them the *real* Barbara).

Einem, Gottfried von, outstanding Austrian composer; b. Bern, Switzerland (where his father was attached to the Austrian embassy), Jan. 24, 1918; d. Obern, Duvenbach, Austria, July 12, 1996. He went to Germany as a child; studied at Plön, Holstein; then was opera coach at the Berlin State Opera. In 1938 he was arrested by the Gestapo and spent 4 months in prison. After his release he studied composition with Boris Blacher in Berlin (1941–43); was later (1944) in Dresden, where he became resident composer and music adviser at the Dresden State Opera; was then active in Salzburg. In 1953 he visited the U.S.; then settled in Vienna; in 1965 was appointed prof. at the Hochschule für Musik there.

Having absorbed the variegated idioms of advanced techniques, Einem produced a number of successful short operas and ballets; in his music he emphasized the dramatic element by dynamic and rhythmic effects; his harmonic idiom is terse and strident; his vocal line often borders on atonality, but remains singable. His best-known works are the operas: *Dantons Tod* after Büchner (Salzburg, 1947); *Der Prozess* after Kafka (Salzburg, 1953); *Der Zerrissene* after Nestroy (Hamburg, 1964); *Der Besuch der alten Dame*, libretto by Dürrenmatt (Vienna, 1971); *Kabale und Liebe* after Schiller (Vienna, 1976); *Jesu Hochzeit* (Vienna, 1980; caused a scandal for depicting Christ as having taken a wife).

einfach (Ger.). Simple; simply; SEMPLICE.

Eingang (Ger.). Introduction; EINLEITUNG.

Einklang (Ger.). Unison; consonance.

Einlage (Ger.). Interpolation; inserted piece.

Einleitung (Ger.). Introduction; EINGANG.

Einsatz (Ger.). 1. Attack of a note. 2. An entrance of a vocal or instrumental part.

einstimmung (Ger.). Monophonic, 1-voiced.

eis (Ger.). E-sharp.

Eisler, Hanns (Johannes), remarkable German composer of politically oriented works; b. Leipzig, July 6, 1898; d. Berlin, Sept. 6, 1962. He began to study music on his own while still a youth, then studied with Weigl at the New Vienna Cons. and later privately with Schoenberg (1919–23); he also worked with Webern. In 1924 he won the Vienna Arts Prize. He went to Berlin in 1925 and taught at the Klindworth-Scharwenka Cons. In 1926 he joined the German Communist Party; after the Nazis came to power in 1933, he left Germany; made visits to the U.S. and was active in Austria, France, England, and other European countries. He taught at the New School for Social Research in N.Y. (1935–36; 1937 42) and at the Univ. of Calif. in Los Angeles (1942–48); testified before the Committee on Un-American Activities (1947), then left the U.S. under the terms of "voluntary deportation" on account of his Communist sympathies. In 1949 he settled in East Berlin and became a prof. at the Hochschule für Musik and a member of the German Academy of the Arts.

Under Schoenberg's influence Eisler adopted the 12-tone method of composition for most of his symphonic works. However, he demonstrated a notable capacity for writing music in an accessible style. His long association with Bertolt Brecht resulted in several fine scores for the theater; he also worked with Charlie Chaplin in Hollywood (1942–47). His songs and choral works have become popular in East Germany. He composed the music for the East German national anthem, *Auferstanden aus Ruinen*, which was adopted in 1949. His writings include *Composing for the Films* (with T. Adorno; N.Y., 1947), *Reden und Aufsätze* (Berlin, 1959), and *Materialen zu einer Dialektik der Musik* (Berlin, 1973). G. Mayer ed. his *Musik und Politik* (2 vols., Berlin, 1973, and Leipzig, 1982). He never composed his projected opera *Johannes Faustus*, for which he wrote the libretto (1952); there is speculation that he met with resistance from East German cultural officials.

Eitner, Robert, eminent German musicologist; b. Breslau, Oct. 22, 1832; d. Templin, Feb. 2, 1905. He was a pupil of M. Brosig in Breslau; settled (1853) in Berlin as a teacher and gave concerts (1857–59) of his own compositions. He established a piano school in 1863, and publ. *Hilfsbuch beim Klavierunterricht* (1871). He devoted himself chiefly to musical literature and especially to research on works of the 16th and 17th centuries. One of the founders of the Berlin Gesellschaft für Musikforschung, he ed. its *Monatshefte für Musikgeschichte* from 1869 till his death; also the *Publikationen älterer praktischer und theoretischer Musikwerke* (from 1873). His principal work is the great *Biographisch-bibliographisches Quellen-Lexikon der Musiker und Musikgelehrten der Christlichen Zeitrechnung bis zur Mitte des 19. Jahrhunderts* (10 vols., 1899–1904; additions and corrections publ. from 1913 to 1916 in a quarterly, *Miscellanea Musicae Bio-bibliographica*, ed. by H. Springer, M. Schneider, and W. Wolffheim; rev. and enl. ed., 1959–60).

ektara (*ektār*; 1 string). An Indian spike lute; formerly a bamboo stick bearing a single string attached to the center of a small drum; at present the stick is attached to a resonating gourd with a wooden bottom; the string is plucked and produces a drone.

élan, avec (Fr.). With dash, energy; CON SLANCIO.

élargissez (Fr.). ALLARGANDO.

Eldridge, (David) **Roy "Little Jazz,"** outstanding African-American jazz trumpeter; b. Pittsburgh, Jan. 30, 1911; d. Valley Stream, N.Y., Feb. 26, 1989. In 1930 he went to N.Y., where he worked with various musicians, including Teddy Hill, and became a featured member of Fletcher Henderson's orch. (1935–36). With his brother Joe, the saxophonist and arranger, he formed his own band in Chicago in 1936; then took it to N.Y. in 1939, where he gained fame as one of the master instrumentalists of the SWING era. He played with the bands of Gene Krupa (1941–43) and Artie Shaw (1944–45), and also worked with Norman Granz's Jazz at the Philharmonic (from 1948); he later worked with Benny Carter, Johnny Hodges, Ella Fitzgerald, and Coleman Hawkins, and also led his own BIG BAND and combos. Although plagued by ill health after 1980, he made occasional appearances as a singer, drummer, and pianist.

electric guitar. An electronic adaptation of the guitar, with a solid body, metallic strings, and miniature pick-up microphones replacing natural acoustic projection; widely used in modern popular music. Acoustic guitars with added pickup microphones are not considered electric guitars.

electric organ. ELECTRONIC ORGAN.

electric piano. A class of keyboard instruments whose sounds are produced electronically or reproduced electrically. The term applies to instruments ranging from amplified grand pianos to portable keyboards that use metal bars or computer technology to produce pianolike sounds.

electronic instruments. A class of instruments, generally assignable to 1 of 4 categories: 1) original inventions (THEREMIN, ONDES MARTENOT); 2) altered acoustic instruments (ELECTRIC GUITAR, ELECTRONIC ORGAN); 3) acoustic instruments joined to MIDI or other electronic equipment (electronic viola, electronic violin); and 4) ordinary objects joined to electronic equipment, i.e., Trimpin's *Klompen* (wooden shoes).

The earliest surviving electronic instrument, the theremin, was demonstrated as the thereminovox by the Russian inventor, engineer, and cellist Leon Thérémin (Moscow, 1920). The apparatus consisted of a set of cathode tubes, a vertical antenna, and a metal arc; the sound was produced heterodynamically by the movement of the right hand, which changed the electric potential in the area, creating a differential tone which determined the height of pitch. The left hand manipulated the field in the vicinity of the metal arc, regulating the power and the timbre of the sound. In constructing this instrument, Thérémin seemed to carry out Lenin's dictum that "socialism is proletarian dictatorship plus electrification."

Thérémin's invention was followed by a number of electronic instruments. In Germany, Jörg Mager (1880–1939) constructed an electronic organ that he called Spherophon; he later developed the more sophisticated Partiturophon and Kaleidophon. In France, Maurice Martenot invented the *ondes musicales* (musical waves; now called ONDES MARTENOT, 1928), a keyboard electronic instrument for which music is still being written. The wire-based Trautonium (1930) was developed by Friedrich Trautwein (1888–1956); Hindemith wrote music for it. Oscar Sala introduced some innovations to the Trautonium in an electronic organ which he called the Mixturtrautonium.

The most advanced electronic instruments belong to the SYNTHESIZER group, 1st developed in studio settings in the 1950s, commercially available in the 1960s; these are capable of generating any desired pitch, any scale, any rhythm, any tone color, and any degree of loudness. They are the most sophisticated of electronic instruments based on analog principles; the development of personal computers has led to the evolution and refinement of COMPUTER MUSIC synthesis. See also MUSIQUE CONCRÈTE.

electronic music. A general term for compositions created by electronic music. There are categories, listed chronologically: 1) early electrophones based on sound-wave manipulation (see ELECTRONIC INSTRUMENTS); 2) manipulation of phonograph records; 3) MUSIQUE CONCRÈTE, using the tape recorder (invented during World War II); sound is recorded, then manipulated with editing, speed and direction alteration, loops, mixing, or processing; 4) analog synthesis, where sound and manipulation are entirely electronic. Orig. synthesizers required a roomful of equipment; transistors allowed the invention of portable synthesizers, pioneered by Moog and Buchla; 5) live electronics, performing or improvising music on stage; 6) electroacoustic music, in which acoustically produced sound is processed in an interactive relationship with electronic equipment; 7) binary-controlled digital synthesis, using increasingly sophisticated and user-friendly computer equipment.

When required, electronic music notation is nontraditional. One of the earliest attempts at a practical system was made in 1937 by Grainger in his *Free Music* for 4 electronic instruments constructed by Thérémin, indicating pitch and dynamic intensities in a 4-part score on graph paper.

electronic organ. A powerful modern keyboard instrument activated not by pipes but by electronic means and capable of unlimited tone production.

electronic piano. ELECTRIC PIANO.

electrophones. A class of musical instruments that produce their sound by electric or electronic means.

elegant variation. In his *Modern English Usage*, Fowler describes frivolous verbal substitutions as elegant variations. The phrase is suitable, with the application of similar gentle scorn, to some musical procedures. Variations that vary for the sake of variance, with an objective of sophisticated elegance of expression, are as offensive in their tautological and often teratological variety as their counterparts in literary diction. Reger's *Variations on a Theme by Mozart* are typical examples of elegant variation, turgid in reference, redundant in treatment. On the other hand, the 18th variation of Rachmaninoff's *Rhapsody on a Theme of Paganini* is both elegant and varied, for it represents an exact inversion of the minor triadic theme, resulting in a completely transformed yet morphologically congruent melody in which the ascending minor triadic figure of the theme becomes a descending major triadic figure.

elegante (*eleganza, con*; It.). Elegantly; gracefully; in a refined manner.

Elégie. A popular cello solo by Massenet, 1875. It was orig. part of incidental music written for the play *Les Erinnyes* in 1873, to illustrate Electra's libation at the tomb of Agamemnon. It was renamed *Elégie* in 1875.

elegy (Fr. *élégie*; Ger. *Elegie*). A vocal or instrumental composition of a melancholy or nostalgic character, having no fixed form.

Elegy for Young Lovers (Elegie für junge Liebende). Chamber opera by Henze, 1961, 1st produced, in German, in Schwetzingen, Germany. The original English libretto is by W. H. Auden and Chester Kallman; its premiere was in a German translation. The story deals with a poet living in the Swiss Alps who deliberately sends his stepson and his own mistress to the mountains during a raging snowstorm. They die as expected, and their fate gives him the needed inspiration for writing his poem, *Elegy for Young Lovers*. The brutality of the protagonist is expressed by atonal angularities and acrid harmonies in the score.

Elektra. Opera by R. Strauss, 1909, to a libretto after Sophocles's *Libation Bearers* by Hugo von Hoffmannsthal, 1st produced in Dresden. In this work, Strauss reaches greatness; the classical drama of lust and murder, of brother and sister killing their mother to avenge her murder of their father in ancient Greece, is set to a musical score of awesome power, filled with excruciating discords and demanding the utmost exertion of vocal resources.

elevator music. MUZAK.

elevazione, con (It.). In a lofty, elevated style.

Elgar, (Sir) Edward (William)

〰〰 〰〰 〰〰 〰〰 〰〰

Great English composer; b. Broadheath, near Worcester, June 2, 1857; d. Worcester, Feb. 23, 1934. He received his earliest music education from his father, who owned a music shop and was organist for the St. George's Roman Catholic Church in Worcester; he also took violin lessons from a local musician. He rapidly acquired the fundamentals of music theory and served as arranger with the Worcester Glee Club, becoming its conductor at the age of 22; simultaneously he accepted a rather unusual position for a young aspiring musician with the County of Worcester Lunatic Asylum at Powick, where he was for several years in charge of the institution's concert band; he was also engaged in various other musical affairs. In 1885 he succeeded his father as organist at St. George's. He married Caroline Alice Roberts in 1889 and moved to Malvern, where he stayed from 1891 to 1904. During these years he conducted the Worcestershire Phil. (1898–1904); in 1905 he accepted the position of Peyton Prof. of Music at the Univ. of Birmingham, and in 1911–12 served as conductor of the London Sym. Orch. He then settled in Hampstead. His beloved wife died in 1920, at which time he returned to Worcester; his composing virtually ceased.

Elgar's 1st signal success was with the concert overture *Froissart* (Worcester, Sept. 9, 1890). His cantata *The Black Knight* was produced at the Worcester Festival (1893) and was also heard in London at the Crystal Palace (1897); the production of his cantata *Scenes from the Saga of King Olaf* (1896) attracted considerable attention; he gained further recognition with his *Imperial March* (1897), composed for the Diamond Jubilee of Queen Victoria; from then on, Elgar's name became familiar to the musical public. There followed the cantata *Caractacus* (1898) and Elgar's great masterpiece, the oratorio *The Dream of Gerontius* (1900).

He began to give more and more attention to orch. music. On June 19, 1899, Hans Richter presented the 1st performance of Elgar's *Variations on an Original Theme* (generally known as *Enigma Variations*) in London. This work consists of 14 sections, each marked by initials of fancied names of Elgar's friends; in later years Elgar issued cryptic hints as to the identities of these persons, which were finally revealed. He also stated that the theme itself was a counterpoint to a familiar tune, but the concealed subject was never discovered; various guesses were advanced in the musical press from time to time; a contest for the most plausible answer to the riddle was launched in America by the *Saturday Review* (1953), with dubious results.

The success of the *Enigma Variations* was followed (1901–30) by the production of Elgar's *Pomp and Circumstance* marches, the 1st of which became his most famous piece through a setting to words by Arthur Christopher Benson, used by Elgar in the *Coronation Ode* (1902) as *Land of Hope and Glory*; another successful orch. work was the *Cockaigne Overture* (1901). Elgar's 2 syms., written between 1903 and 1910, became staples in the English orch. repertoire. His Violin Concerto, 1st performed by Fritz Kreisler (1910), won notable success; there was also a remarkable Cello Concerto (1919, Felix Salmond soloist, composer conducting).

The emergence of Elgar as a major composer about 1900 was all the more remarkable since he had no formal academic training. Yet he developed a masterly technique of instrumental and vocal writing. His style of composition may be described as functional Romanticism; his harmonic procedures remain firmly within the 19th-century tradition; the formal element is always strong, and the thematic development logical and precise. Elgar had a melodic gift, which asserted itself in his earliest works, such as the popular *Salut d'amour*; his oratorios, particularly *The Apostles*, were the product of his fervent religious faith (he was a Roman Catholic). He avoided archaic usages of Gregorian chant; rather, he presented the sacred subjects in a communicative style of secular drama. His 2 syms. (1907–08, 1909–11) are among the greatest British exemplars of this genre.

Elgar was the recipient of many honors. He was knighted in 1904. He received honorary degrees of Mus.Doc. from Cambridge (1900), Oxford (1905), and Aberdeen (1906); also an LL.D. from Leeds (1904). During his 1st visit to the U.S., in 1905, he received a D.Mus. degree from Yale Univ.; in 1907 he was granted the same degree from the Univ. of Western Pa. (now the Univ. of Pittsburgh). He received the Order of Merit in 1911; was made a Knight Commander of the Royal Victorian Order in 1928 and a baronet in 1931; was appointed Master of the King's Musick in 1924. He was not a proficient conductor, but appeared on various occasions and made recordings with orchs. of his own works; during the 3rd of his 4 visits to the U.S. (1905, 1906, 1907, 1911), he conducted his oratorio *The Apostles* (1907); also led the mass chorus at the opening of the British Empire Exhibition in 1924. His link with America was secured when the hymnlike section from his 1st *Pomp and Circumstance* march became a popular recession march for American high school graduation exercises.

L'Elisir d'amore (The Elixir of Love). Opera by Donizetti, 1832. A tale of an impoverished man's attempts to win the woman of his dreams with an elixir of love, which fails to work until he inherits the wealth of his uncle, a fact that renders the aphrodisiac miraculously potent.

Ellington, "Duke" (Edward Kennedy), famous African-American pianist, bandleader, and composer; b. Washington, D.C., Apr. 29, 1899; d. N.Y., May 24, 1974. He played ragtime as a boy; worked with various jazz bands in Washington, D.C., during the 1910s and early 1920s, and in 1923 went to N.Y., where he organized a big band (orig. 10 pieces) that he was to lead for the next half-century, a band that revolutionized the concept of jazz: no longer was jazz restricted to small combos of 4–6 "unlettered" improvisers; with the Ellington orch., complex arrangements were introduced, requiring both improvising skill and the ability to read scores; eventually these scores were to take on the dimensions and scope of classical compositions while retaining an underlying jazz feeling.

In the early days Ellington's chief collaborator in composition and arrangements was trumpeter James "Bubber" Miley (1903–32); baritone saxophonist Harry Carney (1910–74), another arranger, was with the band from its inception until Ellington's death. Other collaborators were Barney Bigard, Otto Hardwick, Harry James, and Ellington's son Mercer. From 1939 Ellington's main collaborator was pianist-composer Billy Strayhorn (1915–67). Among the many great musicians who played in the Ellington orch. were Greer, Nanton, Carney, Fred Guy, Johnny Hodges, Webster, Jimmy Blanton (the brilliant jazz double bassist who died at age 27 in 1942), Nance, Cat Anderson, Paul Gonsalves, Jimmy Hamilton, and Procope.

Ellington possessed a social elegance and the gift of articulate verbal expression that inspired respect. He was the 1st jazz musician to receive an honorary degree from Columbia Univ. (1973). He was also the recipient of the Presidential Medal of Freedom. He made several European trips under the auspices of the State Dept.; toured Russia in 1970 and also went to Latin America, Japan, and Australia.

Duke Ellington, c. 1945

So highly was he esteemed in Africa that the Republic of Togo issued in 1967 a postage stamp bearing his portrait. After his death his band was led by Mercer (b. Washington, D.C., Mar. 11, 1919; d. Copenhagen, Feb. 8, 1996).

Among his more than 1,000 compositions are *East St. Louis Toodle-Oo* (pronounced "toad-del-lo," 1926); *Black and Tan Fantasy* and *Creole Love Song* (1927); *Mood Indigo* (1930); *Sophisticated Lady* (using a whole-tone scale, 1932); *Diminuendo and Crescendo in Blue* (1937); *Black Brown and Beige* (a tonal panorama of African-American history, 1943); *Liberian Suite* (1948); *My People*, commissioned for the 100th anniversary of the Emancipation Proclamation (1963); *1st Sacred Concert* (San Francisco, 1965); *2nd Sacred Concert* (N.Y., 1968); *The River*, ballet (1970); *Queenie Pie*, musical (completed and performed in Philadelphia, 1986).

Ellis (born Sharpe), **Alexander J(ohn),** English writer on musical science; b. Hoxton (London), June 14, 1814; d. Kensington, Oct. 28, 1890. He studied at Trinity College, Cambridge, graduating in 1837; his subjects were mathematics and philology; he also studied music; was elected Fellow of the Royal Soc. (1864) and was president of the Philological Soc.; publ. valuable papers in the Proceedings of the Royal Society. He was awarded a silver medal for his writings on musical pitch for the *Journal of the Soc. of the Arts*; these were publ. separately (1880–81) and in summary form in the famous appendices to the 2nd ed. (1885) of his trans. of Helmholtz's *Lehre von den Tonempfindungen*, entitled *On the Sensations of Tone, as a Physiological Basis for the Theory of Music*. Ellis's translation and commentary was profoundly influential on 20th-century experimentation with intonation systems.

Elman, Mischa, remarkable Russian-born American violinist; b. Talnoy, Jan. 20, 1891; d. N.Y., Apr. 5, 1967. At the age of 6 he was taken by his father to Odessa, where he became a violin student of Fidelmann and a pupil of Brodsky. His progress was extraordinary, and when Leopold Auer heard him play in 1902, he immediately accepted him in his class at the St. Petersburg Cons. In 1904 he made his debut in St. Petersburg with sensational acclaim; his tour of Germany was equally successful; in 1905 he appeared in England, where he played the Glazunov Violin Concerto. In 1908 he made his American debut in N.Y., and was hailed as one of the greatest virtuosos of the time; he played with every important sym. orch. in the U.S.; with the Boston Sym. alone he was a soloist at 31 concerts. In the following years he played all over the world, and, with Heifetz, became a synonym for violinistic prowess. His playing was the quintessence of Romantic interpretation; his tone was mellifluous but resonant; he excelled particularly in the concertos of Mendelssohn, Tchaikovsky, and Wieniawski; but he could also give impressive performances of Beethoven and Mozart. He publ. several violin arrangements of Classic and Romantic pieces, and he also composed some playable short compositions for his instrument.

Elytres. Chamber ensemble work by Foss, 1964. *Élytre* is French for the exterior wings of certain insects which protect their fragile interior. The scoring exploits the most anxious modalities in the most uncomfortable instrumental registers to portray the creatures with utmost realism. The 1st performance took place in Los Angeles.

embellishment. See GRACE.

embouchure (Fr.). 1. The mouthpiece of a wind instrument. 2. The manipulation of the lips and tongue in playing a wind instrument.

Embryons desséchés. Piano suite by Satie, 1913, in 3 movements, 1913. It purportedly represents musical impressions of desiccated embryos; in the 2nd movement a quotation from Chopin's funeral march identifies it as a mazurka by Schubert. This kind of joke, for the player's eyes only, is found throughout Satie's music.

Emmett, Daniel Decatur, American composer of popular songs; b. Mt. Vernon, Ohio, Oct. 29, 1815; d. there, June 28, 1904. He began his career as a drummer in military bands, then joined the Virginia Minstrels, singing and playing the banjo; later was a member of Bryant's Minstrels. He wrote the lyrics and the music of *Dixie* in 1859, and it was performed for the 1st time in N.Y. that year; upon publication, the popularity of the song spread, and it was adopted as a Southern fighting song during the Civil War (even though Emmett was a Northerner). His other songs, *Old Dan Tucker, The Road to Richmond, Walk Along*, etc., enjoyed great favor for some years but were eclipsed by *Dixie*.

Emperor Concerto. Piano Concerto No. 5 by Beethoven, 1809 (op. 73). The nickname is odd in that the work was dedicated to the Archduke Rudolph of Austria, who never became emperor.

Emperor Jones, The. Opera by L. Gruenberg, 1933, based on O'Neill's play about a former railroad porter who briefly serves as emperor of a West Indian island.

Emperor Quartet. Haydn's string quartet, No. 3, op. 76 (1797). The 2nd movement is a variation set based on his melody for *Gott erhalte Franz den Kaiser*, or *Emperor's Hymn*.

Emperor's Hymn. Former national anthem of the Austrian empire, also called *Gott erhalte Franz den Kaiser* (1797); the melody was derived by Haydn from a Croatian folk song and used as the theme for the variation set in his quartet, No. 3, op. 76. The melody was later used for the German patriotic hymn *Deutschland, Deutschland über alles*.

Empfindsamer Stil (Ger.). An aesthetic movement developed in the middle of the 18th century in Germany. Its adjectival form, *empfindsam*, was launched by the German writer Lessing as the German counterpart of the English word *sentimental*, popularized by Laurence Sterne's unfinished novel *Sentimental Journey*. This "sensitive" or "sentimental" style superseded the Aristotelian striving for compositional unity that characterized the late German Baroque. It had superficial similarities with but stood in opposition to the contemporary French STYLE GALANT and the ROCOCO, which emphasized elegance of form and substance rather than feeling.

Empfindung, mit (Ger.). With emotion; full of feeling.

empirical music. In application to modern techniques of composition, empirical music suggests a pragmatic rather than an inspirational approach. It is, however, less cerebral, less laboratorian than EXPERIMENTAL MUSIC.

emporté (Fr.). Carried away, passionately, emotionally.

en animant (Fr.). Animatedly.

en avant (Fr., advancing). Getting faster.

en cédant (Fr., receding). Slowing down.

en dehors (Fr., outside). Emphasizing or bringing out the melody.

en élargissant (Fr.). ALLARGANDO.

en mesure (Fr.). Misurato.

enchainez (Fr.). Go directly to next section without stopping; ATTACCA.

enclume (Fr.). ANVIL.

encore (Fr., again!). 1. Used in English when recalling an actor or singer for a curtain call; the French cry "Bis!" 2. The piece or performance repeated or added to the scheduled program.

endless melody (*Unendliche Melodie*). A term introduced by Wagner to describe an uninterrupted melodic flow unhampered by sectional cadences. Particularly characteristic is the flow of one leitmotiv into another with a free interchange of voices and instrumental parts. With the decline of the Wagnerian cult in the 20th century, the endless melody lost much of its attraction; modern operas now gravitate toward a Verdian concept of well-adorned operatic numbers.

energia, con (It.; Fr. *avec énergie*; Ger. *energisch*). With energy and decision; energetically. A passage so marked is to be vigorously accented and distinctly phrased.

Enesco, Georges (born George Enescu), famous Rumanian violinist, conductor, teacher, and composer; b. Liveni-Virnav, Aug. 19, 1881; d. Paris, May 4, 1955. He began to play the piano when he was 4, taking lessons with a Gypsy violinist, Nicolas Chioru; began composing when he was 5; then studied with Caudella. On Aug. 5, 1889, he made his formal debut as a violinist in Slanic, Moldavia. In the meantime he had enrolled in the Cons. of the Gesellschaft der Musikfreunde in Vienna (1888), where he studied violin with S. Bachrich, J. Grun, and J. Hellmesberger, Jr.; piano with L. Ernst; harmony, counterpoint, and composition with R. Fuchs; chamber music with J. Hellmesberger, Sr.; and music history with A. Prosnitz, winning 1st prizes in violin and harmony (1892). After his graduation (1894) he entered the Paris Cons., where he studied violin with Marsick and J. White, harmony with Dubois and Thomas, counterpoint with Gedalge, composition with Fauré and Massenet, and early music with Diemer, winning 2nd *accessit* for counterpoint and fugue (1897) and graduating with the *premier prix* for violin (1899). At the same time he also studied cello, organ, and piano, attaining more than ordinary proficiency on each.

In 1897 he presented in Paris a concert of his works, which attracted the attention of Colonne, who brought out the youthful composer's op. 1, *Poème roumain*, the next year. Enesco also launched his conducting career in Bucharest in 1898. In 1902 he 1st appeared as a violinist in Berlin and also organized a piano trio; in 1904 he formed a quartet. In 1903 he conducted the premiere of his *Two Rumanian Rhapsodies* in Bucharest, the 1st of which was to become his most celebrated work. He soon was appointed court violinist to the Queen of Rumania. In 1912 he established an annual prize for Rumanian composers, which was subsequently won by Jora, Enacovici, Golestan, Otescu, and others. In 1917 he founded the George Enescu sym. concerts in Iai.

After World War I he made major tours as a violinist and conductor; he also taught violin in Paris, where his pupils included Menuhin, Grumiaux, Gitlis, and Ferras. He made his U.S. debut in the triple role of conductor, violinist, and composer with the Philadelphia Orch. in N.Y. (1923); he returned to conduct the N.Y. Phil. (1937). He led several of its subsequent concerts with remarkable success; led it in 14 concerts in 1938, and also appeared twice as a violinist; he conducted 2 concerts at the N.Y. World's Fair in 1939. The outbreak of World War II found him in Rumania, where he lived on his farm in Sinaia, near Bucharest. He visited N.Y. again in 1946 as a teacher.

In 1950, during the 60th anniversary season of his debut as a violinist, he gave a farewell concert with the N.Y. Phil. in the multiple capacity of violinist, pianist, conductor, and composer, in a program comprising Bach's Double Concerto (with Menuhin), a violin sonata (playing the piano part with Menuhin), and his *1st Rumanian Rhapsody* (conducting the orch.). He then returned to Paris, where his last years were marked by near poverty and poor health. In July 1954 he suffered a stroke and remained an invalid for his remaining days.

Although Enesco severed relations with his Communist homeland, the Rumanian government paid homage to him for his varied accomplishments. His native village, a street in Bucharest, and the State Phil. of Bucharest were named in his honor. Periodical Enesco festivals and international performing competitions were established in Bucharest in 1958.

Enesco had an extraordinary range of musical interests. His compositions include artistic stylizations of Rumanian folk strains; while his style was neo-Romantic, he made occasional use of experimental devices, such as quartertones in his opera, *Oedipe* (1921–31; premiered Paris Opéra, 1936). He possessed a fabulous memory and was able to perform innumerable works without scores. He not only distinguished himself as a violinist and conductor, but he was also a fine pianist and a gifted teacher. He contributed significantly to the instrumental music of the 20th century.

Enfance du Christ, L'. Oratorio in 3 parts by Berlioz, 1854, tracing the story of Jesus from his birth to the Holy Family's arrival in Egypt.

Enfant et les Sortileges L'. Fantasy opera by Ravel, 1915, to a libretto by Colette, 1st produced in Monte Carlo. In a dream, broken dishes, mutilated toys, and torn books come to haunt the destructive boy who owns them. There is a duet of meowing cats complaining of ill treatment. When the boy awakens from this nightmare of destruction he is totally reformed. The score bristles with ingenious sonorities and subtle rhythms.

enfaticamente (*enfatico*, It.). With emphasis, emphatically.

Engel, Lehman, American composer, conductor, and writer on music; b. Jackson, Miss., Sept. 14, 1910; d. N.Y., Aug. 29, 1982. He began to take piano lessons with local teachers as a child; then studied with Sidney Durst at the Cincinnati College of Music (1927–29) and later with Eduardo Trucco in N.Y.; from 1930 to 1934 he took courses in composition with Rubin Goldmark at the Juilliard School of Music; also took private composition lessons with Roger Sessions (1931–37). While still a student he began to write music for ballet and theatrical plays; in 1934 he wrote incidental music for Sean O'Casey's play *Within the Gates*, which he conducted.

From 1935 to 1939 he led the Madrigal Singers for the Works Progress Administration; later worked with the Mercury Theater as composer and conductor. During World War II Engel enlisted in the U.S. Navy and conducted a military orch. at the Great Lakes Naval Training Station; later was appointed chief composer of the Navy's film division in Washington, D.C. He wrote a great many scores of incidental music for Broadway productions, which he also conducted, among them T. S. Eliot's *Murder in the Cathedral* and Tennessee Williams's *A Streetcar Named Desire*.

As a composer Engel was happiest writing for the theater; he had a special knack for vivid musical illustration of the action on the stage. Of importance are his numerous books on the American music theater. He was also active as a teacher of composition, and he led in N.Y. a seminar on musical lyrics. He conducted the 1st American performance of Kurt Weill's *The Threepenny Opera*; also conducted the productions of *Showboat, Brigadoon, Annie Get Your Gun, Fanny, Guys and Dolls,* and *Carousel*. Engel received 2 Antoinette Perry (Tony) Awards: in 1950 for conducting Menotti's opera *The Consul,* and in 1953 for conducting the operettas of Gilbert and Sullivan. In 1971 he received the honorary degree of D.M. from the Univ. of Cincinnati. He has written extensively on musical theater.

English horn (Fr. *cor anglais*; Ger. *englisches Horn*; It. *corno inglese*). The alto oboe in F, transposing a 5th below the written note. It is not clear why this instrument acquired its name; it certainly did not originate in England. The French name for it may well be the corruption of *cor anglé* (angled horn), but its double-reed mouthpiece is attached to a bent crook rather than placed at an angle. The other distinctive element is the bulb bell. The sound of the English horn suggests a variety of moods, from a pastoral scene to an ominous premonition of unknown danger. Its range is from E below middle C to about C an octave above middle C.

The English horn does not coalesce very well with other instruments in an ensemble and is used mostly for solo parts. It is the English horn that intones the Alpine song after the storm in Rossini's overture to *William Tell,* and it sounds the shepherd's pipe in the 3rd act of Wagner's *Tristan und Isolde*. César Franck shocked the French academicians by including the English horn in the score of his only sym., for the instrument was regarded as unsymphonic. Sibelius assigns to the English horn the role of the mortuary messenger in his symphonic poem *The Swan of Tuonela* (Tuonela is the kingdom of death in Finnish mythology). The English horn has had an increasingly important role in 20th-century orch.1 music, with concertos written for virtuoso specialists.

English Suites. Six keyboard partitas by Bach, BWV 806–11. The source for the name is unknown.

enharmonic ambivalence. The Januslike nature of an enharmonic tone, performing 2 different functions at a modulatory junction, opens the portals of chromatic modulation and establishes a democratic omnivalence of the 12 different tones in dodecaphonic melody and harmony. In this view, chromatic harmony is a functional derivative of enharmonic ambivalence.

enharmonic equivalence (equivalents)

The property of notes that sound the same in the tempered scale but are notated differently. C-sharp and D-flat are enharmonically equal, as are D-sharp and E-flat, or E-sharp and F-natural. Pianists do not have to bother about enharmonic equivalents on the equally tempered keyboard. String instrument players, however, have to grope for their sharps and flats to stay within the tempered scale. String players testify that the descending augmented second, say from E to D-flat, is actually larger than the minor 3rd from E to C-sharp, even though the 2 intervals are enharmonically equivalent; harmonic context is the final determining factor.

In chromatic modulation, proper enharmonic notation is of the essence. A dominant-7th chord can be magically transformed into the chord containing a doubly-augmented 4th and an augmented 6th, which is the signal for the mandatory resolution into the tonic 6/4 chord of the new tonality. Such an enharmonic change occurs, for instance, in the coda of Chopin's Scherzo in B-flat Minor (op. 31), where a chord that the ear perceives as the dominant-7th chord in the key of D is suddenly transformed into its enharmonic equivalent, the augmented-6th chord, leading to the cadential tonic 6/4 chord in the key of D-flat major, with brilliant effect. Robert Browning, who had a keen sense of music, described a modulation from D-sharp minor into D major by enharmonic change in the following lines: "The augmented-6th resolved—from out of the straighter range/of D-sharp minor—leap of disimprisoned thrall/Into thy life and light, D-major natural."

Chromatic harmony thrives on enharmonic chords; of these the most chameleonic is the diminished-7th chord, which can be written in 24 different ways. Depending on the arrangement of sharps and double sharps, flats, and double flats, it can lead into any of the 24 major and minor tonalities. This ambiguity and unpredictability made the diminished-7th chord the darling of the Romantic composers. The equivalence of the augmented 4th, the forbidden DIABOLUS IN MUSICA of the Middle Ages, and the diminished 5th, a perfectly respectable interval, is of fundamental importance in the theory of scales. The leap upward from the subdominant to the leading tone was taboo in strict counterpoint, but the downward skip from the subdominant to the leading tone, with its inevitable resolution to the tonic, is a cliché of Classic music.

Enharmonically equivalent intervals or chords are the musical counterparts of linguistic puns. When the *Pirates of Penzance* are struck by the declaration of the captain of a captive Cunard Liner that he is an orphan (their code of honor prohibiting any offense toward an orphan), the captain replies that he said it only once and not often (*orphan* and *often* are pronounced alike in Penzance). A philological colloquy ensues, the pirates wishing to know whether the captain meant *often*, frequently, or *orphan*, a person without parents. In musical terms, the difference between the 2 words is similar to the difference in notation between the augmented 4th and the diminished 5th.

The doctrine of enharmonic equivalence lost its practical significance in musical notation with the advent of organized atonality as promulgated by Schoenberg in his method of composition with 12 tones related only to one another. Sharps and flats became interchangeable; double flats and double sharps were discarded, and such remote sharps in the cycle of scales as B-sharp or E-sharp and similarly remote flats such as F-flat and C-flat also vanished from modern spelling:

B is a B is a B is a B,
And never C flat will it be.
C is a C is a C is a C,
And never B sharp will it be.
B double-flat is nonsensical
When we know it's just plain old A.
And why be unduly forensical,
Insisting that G double sharp is not A?

enharmonic genus (from Grk. *en* + *harmonia*, in the melody). In Greek theory, a tetrachord that includes 2 consecutive intervals, each approximating a quarter tone: 1/1-28/27-16/15-4/3.

Enigma Variations. Remarkable set of orch. variations by Elgar, 1899. Consists of a theme and 14 variations; each variation bears the initials or nicknames of Elgar and his friends, the 1st being those of Lady Elgar (C.A.E.). Some titles contain sly literary allusions; for instance, the powerful 9th variation is entitled *Nimrod*, the "mighty hunter before the Lord" in Genesis, and represents Elgar's friend A. J. Jaeger, whose name means "hunter" in German. But why is the theme itself described as an enigma? Elgar was asked several times to clarify the mystery, but he invariably parried inquiries by spoofing the inquirers and compounding the confusion with even darker allusions, declaring that the enigma theme might be a hidden counterpoint of a famous classical melody. Many solutions have been offered ("Newsflash: The Enigma Solved!"), but none accepted universally. The work was 1st performed under its complete title, *Variations on an Original Theme, "Enigma,"* in London. The work made Elgar internationally famous; R. Strauss considered it a masterpiece and proof that England, at last, had produced a great composer.

enigmatique (Fr.). Enigmatic, mysterious.

Enjoy Yourself (It's Later Than You Think). Lugubrious song by Carl Sigman, 1948; revived in Woody Allen's *Everyone Says I Love You* (1997) as an ode for dancing shades.

Eno, Brian (Peter George St. John le Baptiste de la Salle), English composer, musician, and producer; b. Woodbridge, Suffolk, May 15, 1948. Although interested in tape recorders and recorded music at an early age, he received no formal music training, studying art at Ipswich and Winchester art schools (1964–69); he then became involved in avant-garde experiments, performing works by

La Monte Young and Cornelius Cardew. He helped found the art-rock band Roxy Music in 1971, leaving it 2 years later for a solo career that resulted in 4 modestly successful progressive-rock albums during the mid-'70s.

In 1975, while confined to bed after being struck by a London taxi, he was also struck by the pleasures of MINIMALISM, shifting his style to what he has termed "ambient," a sort of art-music MUZAK. In addition to his rock-based experimental records he has collaborated with David Bowie, Talking Heads, and U2. In 1979 he became interested in video, subsequently producing "video paintings" and "video sculptures" used as ambient music in galleries, museums, airport terminals, and private homes. His music has influenced both New Wave and New Age genres.

ensemble (Fr., together). 1. Since 1600, a group of instrumental players and/or vocalists performing together. The term is applied to a smaller group of players, larger than a duet but smaller than a chamber orch. 2. Style or quality of a group's performance, especially the accuracy of attack and decay.

Entertainer, The. Ragtime work by Scott Joplin, published in 1902, that became a freak hit in 1973 when it was revived as the theme for the hit film *The Sting*. Its success spurred a revival of interest in Joplin and ragtime in general.

Entführung aus dem Serail, Die. ABDUCTION FROM THE SERAGLIO.

entr'acte (Fr., between acts). A light instrumental composition or short ballet for performance between acts of theater, music, and dance works. The term is often found in Lully's collaborations with Molière.

entrata (It.; Fr. *entrée*). 1. The orch.l prelude to a ballet, following the overture. 2. Music played for the dancers' entrances in the 16th- and 17th-century French ballet. 3. A division in a ballet, like a scene in a play. 4. An old dance like a polonaise, usually in 4/4 time.

entropy. The luxuriant development of chromatic harmony and the concomitant equalization of enharmonic pairs may be described as musical entropy, in which the component thematic particles become evenly distributed in melody and harmony. In physics, entropy signalizes the dissipation of kinetic energy, the neutralization of electric potentials, and an ultimate thermodynamic stability of inertial matter.

The pessimistic cosmology that postulates the eventual end in a total passivity of the universe does not, however, constitute a categorical imperative for composers. Nothing prevents them from reversing the process of entropy and reinstating the primacy of selected modalities. Verdi said: "Torniamo all'antico: sara un progresso."

entrüstet (Ger.). Indignant.

entschieden (*entschlossen*; Ger.). Resolutely, in a determined manner, decisively.

envelope. The shape of a sound's amplitude, changing over time; an important determinant of sound quality.

environ (Fr., in the neighborhood of). Approximately, usually following a metronome marking.

environment. The concept of musical environment embraces the totality of technical resources. Ideally the function of a composer is to establish a favorable environment for these techniques and apply powerful detergents to remove the accumulated tonal impurities. Particularly toxic is chromatic supererogation; conversely, a fine atonal work may suffer from excessive triadic infusion. The environment also includes the parameters of vectorialism; spatial arrangement of instruments on the stage is clearly environmental in its function. In this larger sense the function of environment comprises not only every technical aspect of musical composition, but also the conditions of the performance itself.

epanalepsis. A rhetoric device, often applied to Baroque music, in which the opening of a melody or musical period serves as its closing; SYMPLOCE.

epic opera (epic theater). A highly stylized theatrical form in which a technique called the *alienation effect* (A-effect) attempts to keep the audience aware of theatrical artifice and unable to identify with the characters or experience Aristotelian catharsis. The aesthetic was developed most prominently by Brecht, who collaborated with Weill, Eisler, and Dessau.

epigonism (from Grk. *epi* + *gignesthai*, born after). In Greek mythology and history the word *epigone* was applied to descendants of the 7 heroic warriors who conquered the city of Thebes. A historical phenomenon in the arts, it has been characterized by the emergence of a considerable number of capable artists, writers, or musicians who consciously or unconsciously adopt a mode of formal composition that constitutes a logical continuation of the artistic accomplishments of a master who inspired them. In modern usage epigonism has acquired derogatory connotations; an epigone became regarded as a mediocre follower of a great man.

A perfect example of musical epigonism is the career of Siegfried Wagner, the "little son of a great father." He wrote operas very Wagnerian in their librettos and in their music but totally lacking the greatness that Siegfried's father infused into his music dramas. When von Bülow called R. Strauss "Richard the 2nd," it was not, however, with the purpose of derogation, but rather with the intention of elevating him to the great legacy of Richard the 1st, Wagner. Even though Strauss adopted many Wagnerian dramatic devices, he created works so powerful and so individual that it would be a misnomer to apply the term *epigone* to them. A typical Wagnerian epigone was August Bungert, who wrote 2 operatic cycles built on the model of the RING DES NIBELUNGEN, to librettos drawn from Homer's epics; his elucubrations are pathetic examples of infertile futility.

The adoption of a certain method of composition 1st established by a great master is not necessarily the mark of an epigone. Many contemporary composers have adopted Schoenberg's method of composing with 12 tones, among them such superb musicians as Webern and Berg, and they certainly cannot be described as epigones. Nor does a return to the technique of composers of a much earlier era constitute epigonism. Stravinsky adopted the techniques of the Baroque era, but it would be erroneous to regard his neoclassical works as the products of an epigone. However, the imitators of Stravinsky's emulation of the Baroque are typical epigones, in fact, epigones of the second remove.

In order to justify the introduction of a historical or aesthetic category such as epigonism, it is necessary to establish a direct line of succession from a great master to his less gifted followers. Furthermore, a great master must also be a great innovator in order to generate a line of epigones. Debussy was such a great master, and his epigones are legion. Mere imitators are not epigones in the historical sense of significant succession. Thousands of composers in the 2nd half of the 18th century imitated Handel without creating a distinct movement of epigonism. Millions of composers imitated Mendelssohn in the 2nd half of the 19th century, but they could not be called Mendelssohn's epigones in the aesthetic sense. Boccherini was derisively described as "the wife of Haydn" because of the close kin-

ship of his musical idiom to that of Haydn, but again it would be misleading to call him an epigone of Haydn.

episode. An intermediate or incidental section; in the fugue, a digression from the principal theme interpolated between the statements of the latter.

Epistle sonata. An instrumental work performed in church before the reading of an Epistle from the New Testament.

epithalamium (Grk., at the bedroom). A nuptial ode or festive wedding hymn.

equabile (It.). Equable; even, uniform.

equal temperament. A precise logarithmic division of the octave into a predetermined number of tones. The scale based on 12 equal semitones (called 12-equal temperament) lies at the foundation of Western music since the mid-18th century. It enables the performer to play (or a composer to write) a tune without intervallic distortion in any key, but it inevitably departs from the untempered acoustical purity of all basic intervals except the octave itself. Numerous and sometimes desperate methods were undertaken by practical musicians through the centuries to reconcile these incommensurate intervals. Accordingly, the tuning of keyboard instruments must be made deliberately off pitch for the intervals of the perfect 5th, the perfect 4th, 3rds, and 2nds. The deviations are small, and the musical ear easily accommodates itself to the margin of error, but the impurity of intervals within equal temperament is easily perceived by playing a 5th on the piano and listening to peculiar acoustical "beats," occurring 47 times a minute.

Since violins and other string instruments are tuned in pure 5ths, string players naturally avoid playing double stops on open strings when they play chamber music with piano accompaniment, or else the difference between their untempered intervals and the equally tempered intervals of the piano becomes plainly heard. Some modern theorists and composers propose a return to pure untempered intervals, which many are apt to refer to as Pythagorean. But since the Pythagorean scale is based on the cycle of acoustically pure 5ths, there is an unavoidable residue (see COMMA) at the end of the cycle, since 12 5ths are not equal to 7 octaves.

equal voices. Voices of the same class, i.e., women's and boy's (soprano and alto), or men's (tenor and bass).

equivocal chord. A dissonant chord of uncertain resolution, like the diminished 7th.

Erdödy Quartets. Set of 6 quartets by Haydn, op. 76 (1797); named after its dedicatee.

ergriffen (Ger.). Affected, stirred.

erhaben (Ger.). Lofty, exalted.

Erkel, Franz (Ferenc), distinguished Hungarian pianist, conductor, composer, and pedagogue; b. Gyula, Nov. 7, 1810; d. Budapest, June 15, 1893. He studied in Pozsony (Bratislava) at the Benedictine Gymnasium (1822–25), and with Heinrich Klein; then went to Koloszvar, where he began his career as a pianist and became conductor of the Kaschau opera troupe (1834), with which he traveled to Buda (1835). He became conductor of the German Municipal Theater in Pest in 1836; in 1838 he was made music director of the newly founded National Theater, an influential post he held until 1874; he was conductor at the Opera House from 1884, and also founded the Phil. concerts (1853), which he conducted until 1871. He was the 1st prof. of piano and instrumentation at the Academy of Music, and he was its director from 1875 to 1888. He gave his farewell performance as a pianist in 1890 and as a conductor in 1892.

Erkel was one of the most significant Hungarian musicians of his era. After successfully producing his opera *Báthory Mária* (1840), he gained lasting fame in his homeland with the opera *Hunyady László* (1844), which is recognized as the 1st truly national Hungarian work for the theater. He composed the Hungarian national anthem in 1844. He later achieved extraordinary success with the opera *Bánk Bán* (1861), written in collaboration with his sons Gyula (b. Pest, July 4, 1842; d. Ujpest, Mar. 22, 1909) and Sándor (b. Pest, Jan. 2, 1846; d. Bekescsaba, Oct. 14, 1900). He also collaborated with his other sons, Elek (b. Pest, Nov. 2, 1843; d. Budapest, June 10, 1893) and László (b. Pest, Apr. 9, 1844; d. Pozsony, Dec. 3, 1896), who were successful musicians.

erklingen (Ger.). Resound.

ermattend (*ermattet*; Ger.). Wearily, exhaustedly.

Ernani. Opera by Verdi, 1844, after Hugo's drama *Hernani*, 1st produced in Venice. The libretto is the quintessence of pseudo-historical nonsense. Ernani is a banished scion of the royal house of Aragon; his beloved Elvira is inexorably placed on the apex of a tangled love quadrangle, being loved by Ernani, Silva, her elderly guardian, and the future Emperor Charles V. In the end Ernani stabs himself and dies in her arms. The original production of Hugo's play in Paris in 1830 helped give impetus to the Romantic movement in art. But Hugo himself expressed his dislike of Verdi's opera.

ernst (*ernsthaft*; Ger.). Earnestly, gravely.

Eroica Symphony. 3rd Sym. of Beethoven, 1804. When it was published 2 years later, in 1806, the title page bore the designation in Italian that appears cryptic: "Sinfonia eroica composta per festeggiar il souvenire d'un grand'uomo." But who was the "grand'uomo" whose memory was celebrated by Beethoven in this "heroic sym.?" Even the least knowledgeable music lovers can answer: Napoleon! Indeed, the original title was *Sinfonia grande: Buonaparte*. On the manuscript title page, which is preserved in Vienna, the name *Buonaparte* is still visible, but the rest is carefully crossed out in spiraling chains of the quill pen.

Popular books on Beethoven tell us how, when he was apprised of the fact that Napoleon proclaimed himself Emperor in May 1804, Beethoven flew into a rage, tore up the dedication page, and exclaimed: "Then he is a tyrant like all conquerors!" The story is 1st told in the autobiography of Beethoven's student Friedrich Ries, which he apparently dictated a 3rd of a century after the event, shortly before his own death. Beethoven's official biographer Anton Schindler popularized the scene in which Beethoven denounced Napoleon. How old was Schindler at the time of the *Eroica*? Born in 1795, he was 9 years old; obviously his testimony would not stand the test of even hearsay evidence. Worse still for biographical fantasy: In a letter to his publishers dated August 1804, after Napoleon had already had himself crowned by the Pope, Beethoven still referred to the Sym. as "really named *Buonaparte*." If the *Eroica* was to celebrate Napoleon's victories, why is its 1st movement written in 3/4 time rather than in some kind of *tempo marziale*? And in whose memory was written the funeral march which constitutes the 2nd movement? The ensuing Scherzo, also in 3/4 time, reveals no possible tangibility to the career of Napoleon. As for the finale, Beethoven used thematic materials which he had previously applied to the finale of his ballet score, *The Creatures of Prometheus*, and in his Variations for Piano, op. 35, written prior to the composition of the *Eroica*, but which ex post facto acquired the title *Eroica Variations*.

Any other theory? Perhaps. Beethoven was a friend of the French ambassador in Vienna, and it is possible that a suggestion was made to him to write a sym. about Napoleon, then 1st Consul of the French Republic. When Napoleon became Emperor he was too high to reach even for Beethoven, who must have been annoyed by the apparent inattention and decided to change the dedication from Napoleon to a Vienna music patron, Prince Lobkowitz. At its 1st public performance in Vienna (1805), conducted by Beethoven himself, it was described as "a new grand Symphony in D-sharp." No mention was made in the initial announcement that it was Beethoven's 3rd Sym. and that its opus number was 55. (The listing of the key as D-sharp is incongruous to a modern musician; the key of D-sharp would require 9 sharps, including a couple of double-sharps in its key signature. But such enharmonic usage was not uncommon in Beethoven's time. The key is, of course, that of E-flat major.)

Eroica Variations. Piano variations in E-flat major by Beethoven (op. 35), 1802, on the so-called Prometheus theme that he had used twice previously: the contredanse, No. 7, op. 14, (*c.* 1801), and the finale of the ballet *The Creatures of Prometheus*, op. 43 (1801) (hence the theme's nickname).

eroico, -a (It.). Heroic; strong and dignified.

Erotik (Ger.). A romance or sentimental melody, as in a work by Grieg. Without sexual connotation.

erregt (Ger.). Excitedly.

erschüttert (Ger.). Shaken, agitated.

Erstaufführung (Ger.). Premiere; usually a local performance, as distinguished from URAUFFÜHRUNG, a world premiere.

Erwartung (Expectation). Monodrama by Schoenberg, 1909, 1st produced in Prague, 1924. The score has only 1 singing part, that of a woman who finds the dead body of her lover in a forest and muses over the circumstances that led to his death, after he abandoned her for another woman. The idiom is permeated with atonal anguish; the monologue is performed in SPRECHSTIMME.

Erzählung (Ger.). Story, tale, narration.

es (Ger.). E-flat.

es-Dur (Ger.). E-flat major.

es-moll (Ger.). E-flat minor.

esaltato (*esaltazione, con*; It.). With exaltation; in a lofty, fervent style.

Escales (Ports of Call). Orch.1 suite by Ibert, 1924, portraying cities he visited during his French navy stint: Palermo, Tunis, and Valencia.

escapement (Fr. *échappement*; Ger. *Auslösung*; It. *scappamento*). The part of a piano action that lets the hammer disengage from the striking mechanism and then rebound away from the string while the key remains held down. Except for a few early piano designs, pianos have included escapements since Cristofori (late 17th century).

Eschenbach (born Ringmann), **Christoph,** remarkably talented German pianist and conductor; b. Breslau, Feb. 20, 1940. His mother died in childbirth; his father, the musicologist Heribert Ringmann, lost his life in battle soon thereafter; his grandmother died while attempting to remove him from the advancing Allied armies; placed in a refugee camp, he was rescued by his mother's cousin, who adopted him in 1946. He began studying piano at age 8 with his foster mother; his formal piano training commenced at the same age with Eliza Hansen in Hamburg, and continued with her at the Hochschule für Musik there; he also studied piano with Hans-Otto Schmidt in Cologne, and received instruction in conducting from Wilhelm Brückner-Rüggeberg at the Hamburg Hochschule für Musik. In 1952 he won 1st prize in the Steinway Piano Competition; after winning 2nd prize in the Munich International Competition in 1962, he gained wide recognition by capturing 1st prize in the 1st Clara Haskil Competition in Montreux (1965).

In 1966 he made his London debut; following studies with George Szell (1967–69), the latter invited him to make his debut as soloist in Mozart's Piano Concerto in F Major, K. 459, with the Cleveland Orch. (1969). In subsequent years he made numerous tours as a pianist, appearing in all of the major music centers of the world. He also gave duo concerts with the pianist Justus Frantz. In 1972 he began to make appearances as a conductor; made his debut as an opera conductor in Darmstadt with *La Traviata* in

1978. He pursued a successful career as both a pianist and a conductor, sometimes conducting from the keyboard. After serving as Generalmusikdirektor of the Rheinland-Pfalz State Phil. (1979–81), he was 1st permanent guest conductor of the Zurich Tonhalle Orch. (1981–82); then was its chief conductor (1982–85). In 1988 he became music director of the Houston Sym. Orch. He maintains a varied repertoire, as both a pianist and a conductor; his sympathies range from the standard literature to the cosmopolitan avant-garde.

esclamato (It.). Exclaimed; forcibly declaimed.

esecuzione (It.). Execution, performance.

esercizio (It.; plural *esercizi*). Exercise; D. Scarlatti's sonatas were called *esercizio per gravicembalo*.

es-es (Ger.). E double-flat.

esitando (It.). Hesitatingly.

espandendosi (*espansione, con*; It.). Growing broader and fuller; with growing intensity; expansively.

espirando (It.). Dying away, expiring.

esposizione (It.). EXPOSITION.

espressione, con (*espressivo*; It.). Expressively; with an intimate melodic feeling. *Con molto espressione*, with great expressiveness.

esquisse (Fr.). A sketch.

Estampes (Fr., engravings, prints, etchings). Piano suite by Debussy, 1903, containing 3 picturesque movements: *Pagodes*, *Soirée dans Grenade*, and *Jardins sous la Pluie*.

estampie (Fr.; It. *stampitas*; Prov. *estampida*). A medieval instrumental composition developed by the troubadours in the 13th and 14th centuries. Primarily in ternary meter, the estampie is divided into several sections called *puncta* (melodic units). Different endings are provided for the repetitions of the puncta, similar to the indications of *prima volta* and *seconda volta* in the repeat sections in Classic music. It is most likely that the original estampies were dances; many also had texts.

estinguendo (*estinto*; It.). Extinguishing, dying away; barely audible, enfeebled; very softly; extreme PIANISSIMO.

estompé (Fr.). Softened.

estremamente (It.). Extremely.

estro (It.). Inspiraton. *Estro poetico*, poetic fervor.

Estro armonico, L'. Collection of 12 concertos by Vivaldi, 1712, for various combinations.

Et incarnatus. Portion of the Credo from the Roman Catholic High Mass, often set separately in large-scale works.

Ethiopian songs. Blackface minstrelsy songs written for white performers such as Christy's Minstrels in the 19th century; an example is Stephen Foster's *Old Folks at Home*. The term "Ethiopian" was also applied to songs and musical stage works by African-American composers at the turn of the 20th century.

ethnic resources. National musical cultures have developed from 2 distinct resources: the ethnic legacy, and universally adopted techniques of composition. When Villa-Lobos was asked "What is folklore?" he replied, "I am folklore!" By this declaration he meant to say that in his original melodic inventions he gave expression to the artistic consciousness of the Brazilian people. In his *Bachianas brasileiras*, Bachian counterpoint gives ancillary service to ethnic Brazilianism. Ives created single-handedly a modern American idiom that employs ethnic resources in a perfect syncretism of substance and technique. In the USSR the primacy of ethnic resources was maintained partly by the national spirit of the people and partly by the ideological principles of SOCIALIST REALISM, which prescribed the realistic style of music within the framework of national modalities.

Ethnic musical materials are not necessarily incompatible with modern techniques. It is possible to arrange a popular tune dodecaphonically by applying various intervallic extensions and compressions while retaining the vectorial parameters of the original melody. Perhaps the most congenial modern technique in making use of ethnic resources is EXPRESSIONISM, in which the tonal functions are preserved and enhanced.

ethnomusicology. This is a relatively new term, succeeding COMPARATIVE MUSICOLOGY to describe the rigorous study of traditional music of all peoples. The primary research focus has for many years been on non-European music that would have been labeled "exotic" in previous centuries, such as Asia, Africa, and South America. The initial focus was on recording the music of various groups and then bringing them to university departments for analysis; instruments were gathered for organological purposes or simply the desire to play them. The invention of videotape allowed dance, ceremony, and other visually oriented elements to be recorded for study. In recent years the Eurocentric approach has been severely challenged by more anthropologically and sociologically oriented researchers who try to understand a people's music from its own viewpoint. Additionally, Euro-American "folk music" has been properly renamed traditional music when the element of oral transmission is predominant.

ethos. A doctrine in musical philosophy postulating that each mode corresponds to a particular state of mind. Its classical exposition was given by Plato, who taught that the Dorian mode was noble, elevated, and masculine, the Phyrgian mode passionate, the Lydian mode feminine, plaintive, and seductive, etc. Medieval theorists adapted this system to ecclesiastical modes, not realizing that the ancient Greek modes were scaled in descending order, so that the progression of intervals was reversed. Thus the masculine virtue of the Greek Dorian mode of Plato, representing the descending "white-key" scale E to E, was attributed to the ecclesiastical ascending "white-key" scale D to D.

The doctrine of ethos was applied in Classic music, with great changes. Many composers of the Classic and Romantic periods, impressed by the whiteness of the C-major scale on the piano keyboard, often selected that key to represent immaculate virtue, magnanimity, and strength. F major was associated with pastoral scenes, while minor keys were generally reserved for the themes of melancholy, unrequited love, and world malaise. Tchaikovsky, who was obsessed by the inexorability of Fate, used a disproportionate percentage of minor keys in his music.

étincelant (Fr.). Sparkling.

etiology. The study of causation, or etiology, is of importance not only in medicine and physics, but also in the fine arts. Particularly informing is the etiology of ultramodern music, which is often likened by hostile observers to a symptom of mass dyscrasia. But to its adepts, NEW MUSIC is the revelation of a superior psyche. Dostoyevsky, who suffered from epilepsy, advances the daring notion that during an epileptic grand mal the mind penetrates the ultimate mysteries of life and death. Similarly, the manifestations of the musical AVANT-GARDE, whether in the popular or technically complex field, are to their participants the proleptic vistas of the new universal art. Schoenberg, more than any other composer, endured endless abuse on the part of uncomprehending critics, but he never doubted the correctness of his chosen path. Varèse, who was similarly abused, wrote in a letter in 1931: "I know where I am going, and what will follow. My plan is clearly drawn, its development logical, its result assured." In the perspective of history both Schoenberg and Varèse proved right. The etiology of their genius is a lesson for the future.

Étoile du Nord, L' (The North Star). Opera by Meyerbeer, 1854. Russia's Peter the Great goes to study carpentry abroad incognito, where he woos a village woman, marries her, and makes her his Czarina. The real Peter did study carpentry and shipbuilding incognito in the Netherlands, but the similarity to the opera ends there.

étouffé (Fr.). Stifled, muted. *Étouffoir*, a mute.

étude (study; Fr. *étude*; It. *studio*; Ger. *Studie, Etüde*). An exercise or a study. Orig. the term was applied exclusively to technical exercises. In the 19th century its connotations were enlarged. Études proper, designed for improvement of technique, were called exercises and were usually in the form of simple melodic and rhythmic sequences, scales, trills, arpeggios, and other technical passages. Études evolved into full-fledged compositions, often brilliant displays of instrumental technique in the bravura style. Clementi's *Gradus ad Parnassum* (Steps to Mount Parnassus, the dwelling of the Muses), and Czerny's numerous collections of piano exercises established a higher type of étude in which the purely technical devices were subordinated to the musical conception. Czerny's most famous collection is *Die Schule der Fingerfertigkeit* (School of Finger Readiness, also called The School of Velocity). Études fit for public performance were called concert études, or, in French, ÉTUDES DE CONCERT. Chopin elevated the genre to romantic grandeur in his 2 series of études for piano. Schumann's *Études symphoniques* for piano are neither études nor symphonic compositions, but variations on a theme. Liszt promulgated a superior type of piano étude in his 12 *Études d'execution transcendante*. Scriabin followed Chopin's model in his own group of piano studies, as did Debussy. In all these advanced forms the technical aspect of the étude became merely the means toward the creation of piano works in a bravura manner. Violin virtuosos, above all Paganini, wrote brilliant études for the violin; cellists and other instrumentalists composed études for their own instruments.

Étude de concert (Fr.). An étude designed for public performance.

Étude pour Espace. A fragment by Varèse, 1947, of a projected work, *Espace*, for chorus, pianos, and percussion.

Études d'execution transcendante (Transcendental Studies). Twelve études by Liszt, 1851; their collective title refers to the extremely virtuosic technique required for their execution. Orig. Liszt let the studies speak for themselves as pure music, but he later added programmatic titles, e.g., *Feux follets* (Will o' the Wisps), *Mazeppa, Wilde Jagd* (Wild Hunt), *and Eroica*, (in E-flat major, the key of Beethoven's *Eroica Sym.*). The entire series is dedicated to Liszt's piano teacher Czerny, "in token of gratitude, respect, and friendship."

Études symphoniques. A cycle of piano studies by Schumann (op. 13), 1837; orig. entitled "études of an orch.l character" to emphasize the advanced polyphony employed in the music. The story of their inception is unusual. For one thing, the theme itself is not by Schumann but by the adoptive father of Schumann's 1st fiancée, Ernestine von Fricken. The final title was *Études en forme de Variations (XII Études symphoniques) pour le Pianoforte.* The variations are extremely free, and the last one is based on an aria from the opera *Der Templer und die Jüdin* by Marschner. This unexpected intrusion of a borrowed song has a convoluted explanation: Marschner's opera was based on Walter Scott's novel *Ivanhoe*, and the aria used by Schumann began with the words, "Du stolzes England, freue dich!" (Thou proud England, rejoice!). Since Schumann dedicated his op. 13 to his friend the English composer William Sterndale Bennett, he wished in this manner to gratify Bennett's patriotic feelings. Five more variations which Schumann did not use in the original edition were publ. posthumously and are often added to the original 12 by modern pianists.

Études-Tableaux. Cycles of character pieces for piano by Rachmaninoff (opps. 33 and 39), 1911 and 1917. Any visual implications of the title are secondary to the impressive musical content.

Études transcendentales. ÉTUDES D'EXECUTION TRANSCENDANTE.

etwas (Ger.). Rather, somewhat.

etwas vorwärts gehend (Ger.). POCO PIÙ MOSSO.

Eugene Onegin. Opera by Tchaikovsky, 1879, after Pushkin's poem, 1st produced in Moscow. Two young friends, Onegin and Lensky, are visiting the summer estate of a family with 2 daughters, Tatiana and Olga. Tatiana is fascinated by Onegin and confesses her love to him in a passionate letter aria (in French, the language of Russian high society at the time). The next day he explains that he is not meant for the simple domestic happiness of marriage. At the family ball he pointedly dances with Olga to taunt Lensky, her fiancé. Lensky angrily challenges him to a duel. Onegin kills him and, torn by remorse, departs on a long journey abroad. Returning to Russia many years later, he meets Tatiana, now the wife of a retired general. He is seized with passion for her and begs her to go off with him. She rejects his belated entreaty and he leaves her forever. The music is suffused by lyric melody. *Eugene Onegin* is a perennial favorite in Russia; like Tchaikovsky's *Queen of Spades*, it is regularly if not prolifically heard outside of its native land.

Euler, Leonhard, great Swiss mathematician; b. Basel, Apr. 15, 1707; d. St. Petersburg, Sept. 18, 1783. He was a prof. of mathematics at St. Petersburg (1733) and Berlin (1741); publ. several important works on music theory and acoustics, chief among them being the *Tentamen novae theoriae musicae* (St. Petersburg, 1739). Euler was the 1st to employ logarithms to explain differences in pitch; this would later prove essential to the theory of equal temperament.

Eumenides, Les. Incidental music by Milhaud, 1927, to the final part of the Claudel trilogy drawn from Aeschylus's *Orestia*; the 1st part is *Agamemnon*, the 2nd *Les Choëphores.*

euphonious harmony. Tonal combinations that contain only concords and mild discords and do not contain major 7ths or minor 2nds, acoustically the sharpest dissonances. (The ratio of vibration is 16/15 for a minor 2nd and 15/8 for the major 7th.) Thus all chords consisting of whole tones or their multiples are by this definition euphonious. All 7th chords built on the supertonic, mediant, dominant, submediant, or the leading tone in a major scale are also euphonious; but the tonic 7th and subdominant 7th chords, which have a major 7th from their base, are uneuphonious. All diminished-7th chords are euphonious. The distinction is very important because chromatic harmony, as in, for instance, the introduction to Wagner's *Tristan und Isolde*, uses chords of the augmented-6th, chords containing multiples of whole tones, and dominant-7th chords.

euphonium (Grk., good-sounding). An instrument of the brass family, with a tapered bore of wide scale and a deep cup-shaped mouthpiece. It may have 3 or 4 valves. It is considered the tenor of the tuba family, with the range of a trombone or baritone. It is commonly found in military bands, rarely in classical orchs.

euphony (Grk., good sound). Despite its etymology, euphony is not necessarily synonymous with consonant harmony. A succession of dissonances, if they follow a natural tonal sequence, may sound entirely euphonious to the ear, while a progression of disembodied open 5ths or disemboweled multiple octaves could register as uneuphonious and unsettling. Psychological apperception is the determining factor in this aural impression.

Generally speaking, soft dissonances are tolerated better than loud consonances. Even more decisive is the factor of linear euphony. A single line of an atonal melody impresses an untutored ear as an unacceptable dissonance, even though no simultaneous complex of sounds is involved. If an atonal melody were to be performed at a very slow tempo with long silences between the individual notes, no linear disharmony could then result. But the faster the tempo, the more disruptive to the peace of mind does an atonal melody become. It should be remembered that the word *harmonia* meant "a melody" in ancient Greek music. A rapid succession of tones unconnected by a uniform tonality will appear as a meaningless jumble of notes to an inexperienced listener. On the other hand, a musician trained in the art of listening to serial music will accept atonal melodies as legitimate expressions of a musical sentiment.

The linearity of melody depends exclusively on the instant dampening of a sound in the cochlea without a tinnitus, but the memory of the previous sound persists, much in the manner that the retina of the eye retains the static images of a cinematographic film. It would be interesting to speculate on the possible course of music as an art if the cochlea, too, possessed the ability to retain sounds for a fraction of a second. Suffice it to say that all music, vocal, instrumental, or percussive, would then become polyphonic.

Europe, James Reese, African-American conductor and composer; b. Mobile, Ala., Feb. 22, 1881; d. Boston, May 10, 1919 (stabbed to death by a disgruntled drummer in his band). He studied violin and piano in childhood in Washington, D.C., then went to N.Y., where he was active as a director of musical comedies, founding the Clef Club (1910), a union and contracting agency for black musicians. He also founded the Clef Club sym. orch., which gave performances of works by black composers at Carnegie Hall (1912–14). He was music director and composer for the dancers Irene and Vernon Castle (1914–17) and is credited with composing the 1st fox trot for them. He wrote songs for musicals and composed dances and marches for his orchs. and bands. Although his music predates true jazz, Europe's syncopated rags and dances were the 1st African-American music heard in the Old World, and they caused a sensation.

Europeras. Name of 5 theater works by Cage, written between 1987 and 1991. He wrote, designed, staged, and directed the Europeras, collages comprised of excerpts from extant operas, selected and manipulated by a computer software program, IC (short for the *I Ching*, Cage's favorite means of making choices by chance). Live but self-contained singers interacted with or ignored each other, record players, instruments, settings, and lighting. The Europeras may be seen as a peaceful encounter between tradition and experimentation.

Euryanthe. Opera by Weber, 1823, 1st performed in Vienna. It was announced as a "grand heroic romantic opera," but some critics said that *Euryanthe* should be called "Ennuyanthe" (the annoying one). The libretto is taken from an old French legend in which the enemies of the virtuous wife Euryanthe attempt to charge her with infidelity; she withstands their attacks. The opera failed, but its vivacious overture became a favorite concert piece. Weber himself declared that *Euryanthe* should have for its proper presentation "an allied coalition of all sister arts." This seems to presage Wagner's idea of the GESAMTKUNSTWERK.

eurythmics (eurhythmics; both sp. correct). A system of musical training introduced by Jaques-Dalcroze in 1910 in which pupils were taught to represent and experience complex rhythmic movement with their entire bodies, to the accompaniment of specially composed or improvised music.

evaded cadence. Deceptive cadence. See CADENCE.

Evangelimann, Der (The Evangelist). Opera, 1895, by Wilhelm Kienzl (1857–1941), a Wagnerian composer and writer; this work was by far his greatest success. In *Der Evangelimann*, 2 brothers love the same woman; 1 brother commits arson and blames his brother. The distraught woman commits suicide. The guilty brother belatedly confesses his crimes on his deathbed to his brother.

Evans, Bill (William John), American jazz pianist and composer; b. Plainfield, N.J., Aug. 16, 1929; d. N.Y., Sept. 15, 1980. After taking up the piano, he joined the band of Miles Davis and soon became a leading jazz pianist; after making the classic jazz recording *Kind of Blue* with Davis (1959), he formed his own jazz trio. He received Grammy awards for his recordings *Conversations with Myself* (1963), *Alone* (1970), and *The Bill Evans Album* (1971). Evans played jazz in a cool, sophisticated, and somewhat intellectual manner.

Evans, (Ian Ernest) **Gil(more Green),** Canadian jazz pianist, bandleader, and arranger; b. Toronto, May 13, 1912; d. Cuernavaca, Mexico, Mar. 20, 1988. He went to Calif. in his youth. He was largely self-taught in music; after leading his own band in Stockton (1933–38), he went to N.Y. He made arrangements of popular songs utilizing nonjazz instruments; then became a proponent of cool jazz, and collaborated frequently with Miles Davis (from 1948); he also made arrangements for other groups and recorded his own albums. As he moved toward an increasingly complex modernity, he applied polyharmonic and polyrhythmic procedures to his arrangements. He was, with Ellington, Henderson, Don Sebesky, and a few others, one of the greatest jazz orchestrators.

Evensong (Evening Prayer). In the Anglican church, a daily service to be said or sung at evening; known as Vespers in the Roman Catholic Church.

Everly Brothers. (Vocal/guitar: Don E., b. Brownie, Ky., Feb. 1, 1937; vocal/guitar: Phil E., b. Brownie, Ky., Jan. 19, 1939.) Don appeared at the age of 8 on a radio show managed by their parents at Shenandoah, Iowa. Both Don and Phil then toured with their parents around the country. When they grew up they moved to Nashville, Tenn., and began playing rock 'n' roll, mixing in rhythm and blues, pop, and country-western. Among their many hits were *Bye Bye Love, Wake Up Little Susie, All I Have to Do Is Dream*, and *Cathy's Clown*. Alas, brotherly love did not last forever; they split apart in 1973; their divergent ways led to an impasse, but happily their fraternal records survived and continue to provide joy to a new generation of bobby-soxers and their hippie mates. They finally patched things up and reunited for a concert at London's Royal Albert Hall in 1983. Since then they have broken up and reunited several times, never again achieving the success of their initial years.

evolution and devolution. In a famous definition, Herbert Spencer describes the process of evolution as an integration of matter and concomitant dissipation of motion, during which matter passes from an indefinite, incoherent homogeneity to a definite, coherent heterogeneity. He specifically included music in this process, with reference to the increasing complexity resulting from rhythmic changes and modulatory progressions, its specialization and its gradual differentiation from poetry, drama, and dance. In recent times, however, the evolutionary process has been reversed. Once more, as in antiquity, music has entered into an intimate association with the theater and dance in the modern genre of MIXED MEDIA. ALEATORY procedures have accentuated the devolution of music by increasing the element of homogeneity and the degree of randomness of distribution of constructive elements.

It may be argued that devolution was unavoidable since the integration of music in the Spencerian sense has achieved its maximum of coherence in such techniques as the dodecaphonic method, and that a recoil from the stone wall of determinism reversed the evolutionary process, resulting in an esthetic passivity in which kinetic energy is reduced to zero. In the practice of the AVANT-GARDE the demobilization of technical resources has reached the point of melorhythmic asceticism, with only a few different notes being used in an entire work as though emulating the legendary philosopher Cratylus, who spent his declining years by moving the index finger of his right hand to and fro in front of his nose in the firm belief that this motion was the only demonstrable truth.

Ewing, Maria (Louise), noted American mezzo-soprano and soprano; b. Detroit, Mar. 27, 1950. She commenced vocal training with Marjorie Gordon, continuing her studies with Eleanor Steber at the Cleveland Inst. of Music (1968–70), and later with Jennie Tourel and O. Marzolla. In 1973 she made her professional debut at the Ravinia Festival with the Chicago Sym. Orch., and she subsequently was engaged to appear with various U.S. opera houses and orchs.; she also appeared as a recitalist. In 1976 she made her

Metropolitan Opera debut in N.Y. as Cherubino; she returned there to sing such roles as Rosina, Dorabella, Mélisande, Blanche in *Dialogues des carmélites*, and Carmen. In 1976 she made her 1st appearance at Milan's La Scala as Mélisande; in 1978 she made her Glyndebourne Festival debut as Dorabella; she returned there as a periodic guest. In 1986 she sang Salome in Los Angeles and appeared in *The Merry Widow* in Chicago in 1987. In 1988 she sang Salome at London's Covent Garden, a role she sang to enormous critical acclaim in Chicago that same year; she returned there as Tosca in 1989 and Susanna in 1991. She was married for a time to Sir Peter Hall.

ex abrupto (It.). Abruptly, suddenly, at once.

ex tempore (It.). In an improvisatory style; spontaneously.

Excursions of Mr. Brouček, The. Opera by Janáček, 1920, after Čech's novel. The opera combines 2 short works, written at different times, about a 19th-century Czech burgher of average distinction: *Mr. Brouček's Trip to the Moon*, where he finds life as mundane and stressful as his own; and *Mr. Brouček's Exploits in the 15th Century*, in which he participates in the Hussite nationalist movement.

executed queens. Beheaded queens exercise a morbid attraction on poets, dramatists, and opera composers. Henry VIII, the champion decapitator of his consorts, had to work hard to find legal reasons to have his 2nd wife, Anne Boleyn, axed in the Tower of London in 1536. Her chief insubordination was her failure to give birth to a male child. So Henry charged her with adultery, a capital crime. Anne Boleyn was the mother of Elizabeth I, who herself had her rival queen, Mary Stuart of Scotland, executed. The story of Anne Boleyn was put in an operatic form by the Italian composer Donizetti, under the unnatural Italian spelling *Anna Bolena*; it was 1st performed in Milan in 1830, 6 years short of the tercentenary of her execution. The uxoricidal king had his obsequious Parliament pass a bill of attainder declaring it treason for an unchaste woman to marry the king, and this allowed him to do away with his 5th wife, Catherine Howard, who was proved to be maculate; she was beheaded expeditiously in 1542. Nobody wrote an opera about her. However, Mary Stuart was popular with playwrights and composers. Donizetti wrote 1 of his most enduring operas about her (*Maria Stuarda*, 1835). Thea Musgrave, the Scottish-American composer, composed her *Mary, Queen of Scots* in 1975–77. Even a Soviet composer,

Sergei Slonimsky, wrote on opera on the subject, which had considerable success in Russia and in 1986 was produced in Edinburgh, her former capital.

Perhaps the most sanguinary execution was administered to the mistress of Pedro I of Portugal, Inés de Castro, by order of his tyrannical father Alfonso IV, in 1355. But when her lover ascended the throne he had her body exhumed and crowned as an empress, with her suspected murderers forced to kiss her skeletal hands in solemn procession. At least 2 composers wrote operas about her, Giuseppe Persiani (Naples, 1835) and Thomas Pasatieri (Baltimore, 1976).

execution. 1. Style, manner of performance. 2. Technical ability.

exercise. A short technical study or sequence for training the fingers (or vocal organs) to overcome some special technical difficulty. Also, a short study in composition.

exoticism. A movement in Western art in which coloristic devices are borrowed from native practices as perceived by a visitor; also called orientalism. In transferring exotic samples from a faraway country, the actual scales and rhythms undergo a distorting change, so that Western exoticism becomes a misperceived art, a refracted image not recognizable to those who ostensibly inspired it. The main resource of exoticism in the 18th century was Turkish music, characterized by a simple binary meter. ALLA TURCA is often found in tempo indications in Classic music.

India, China, and Japan provided inspiration for French opera and ballet. Russian composers were fond of exotic subjects; Rimsky-Korsakov's *Scheherazade* is based on a subject of *The Arabian Nights*. The Mongolian invasion of Russia during the Middle Ages gave a historic background for stylized Tatar ballet episodes in Russian operas.

When authentic drummers and other GAMELAN performers from French Indochina appeared at the Paris International Exposition in 1889, young French composers became fascinated by their music. Debussy and Ravel made tasteful impressionistic renditions of these exotic rhythms and melodies in their works. Since ethnic scales are not readily adjustable in terms of traditional diatonic and chromatic intervals, Western musicians created their own exotic tonal progressions in which the augmented 2nd often plays the important part. The aria of the Queen Shemaha in Rimsky-Korsakov's opera *Le Coq d'or* forms an ingenious web of "exotic" arabesques. Less literal and more abstract is the orientalism of Stravinsky's ballet-opera *The Nightingale*.

Orientalism of Chinese and Japanese subjects is pentatonic; examples are found in *Madama Butterfly*, *Mikado*, and various chinoiseries of Ravel and Debussy.

experimental music. Denotative of music which departs from the usual expectations of style, form, and genre as these have developed through history; as distinct from the work of the primarily European avant-garde, its proponents begin with Satie and Ives and move through and beyond the work of Cage, Cowell, and Cardew.

All music is experimental; tradition is merely a congealed experiment. Chromatic harmony was experimental in Wagner's time, and its ultimate dodecaphonic development became the most important type of experimental music of the 20th century. Perhaps the most literally correct application of experimental music is represented by aleatory operations, in which the manipulator merely sets the scene of action and nature supplies an experimental answer. With every turn of the aesthetic wheel, experimental music was decried and deprecated by the adepts of the preceding prevalent style as repugnant to normal senses.

In the 2nd half of the 20th century, experimental music finally moved into its proper enclave, that of the laboratory, where composers and experimenters conducted their research with electronic instruments and computers. There is a danger, however, that an imaginative computer may be hampered in its inventive productions by the limitations of the musical engineer who would program the data so as to adapt them to a preordained order, and in so doing would convert the machine into a mere servant. In one such man-made pseudo-computerized composition, the ending consists of a protracted C-major coda which no computer in its right mental circuit could possibly turn out. The only valid programming of musical composition is that generated by a collection of random numbers ejaculated like so many embryonic seahorses out of their male parent's pouch, to be translated into notes and rhythms according to a predetermined code. In all such experiments caution should be taken to prevent a disgorgement of data from becoming a personal regurgitation of the programmer.

exposition. 1. The opening section of a sonata-form movement, in which the principal themes are presented for the 1st time; the 1st theme is in the tonic, the closing theme usually in the dominant or, in many minor-key works, the relative major. 2. Sections of a fugue which present the subject.

expression mark. Written instructions (sign, word, or phrase) indicating the recommended type of performance. The earliest expression marks appeared in keyboard compositions in the 16th century and were limited to the signs for forte and piano, usually abbrev. to the initials *f* and *p*. A curious expression mark was *E*, for ECHO, found in 17th-century works; it was equivalent to *piano*. The Florentine composers who pioneered the art of opera were in the habit of using elaborate verbal descriptions such as *esclamazione spirituosa* (like a spiritual exclamation) and *quasi favallando* (as if speaking).

In the 20th century verbal expressions achieved extravagant forms, particularly in Scriabin's music, as, for instance, *presque en délire* (almost in a delirium), and in the picturesque descriptions of Debussy, such as *ce rhythme doit avoir la valeur sonore d'un fond de paysage triste et glacé* (this rhythm must have the sonorous validity of a sad and icy landscape). The signs of crescendo and diminuendo did not achieve currency until the late 18th century. The various gradations of *forte* and *piano* were increasingly cultivated by Romantic composers; the ending of the *Pathetique Sym.* by Tchaikovsky is marked with 6 p's in a row—*pppppp*.

expression stop. In the harmonium, a stop which closes the escape-valve of the bellows, so that wind pressure and intensity of tone are partly controlled by the pedals.

expressionism

〜〜 〜〜 〜〜 〜〜 〜〜

A modern aesthetic movement, beginning in music around 1910, giving expression to the inner state of a person's mind and emotion; the term itself originated in painting. Expressionism reflects extreme and anxious moods characteristic of modern life in a musical idiom which frequently uses atonally constructed melodies and spasmodic, restless rhythms; it is quite often covertly autobiographical.

Expressionism stands in a reciprocal relationship to IMPRESSIONISM as its functional and psychological counterpart. Impressionism derives its source of inspiration from external sources, whereas expressionism conjures up its images in the inner world of the human psyche and exteriorizes its states as an intimate subjective report. Impressionism tends to be pictorial and exotic; expressionism is introspective and metaphysical. Impressionistic literature, art, and music are easily projected outside; expressionism is an arcane medium, born in the deepest recesses of the psychic complex, and cannot easily be translated into the common language of the arts. The receiver of colorful images of impressionist art or music has the means of comparing the precise reality with the artist's impressions of it. No such scale of comparison is available to an outside recipient of expressionist art, for it is a product of the artist's dream in which the dreamer experiences shock and surprise despite the fact that he is both the author and the victim of his own dreams. Because of this duality of its process, expressionist art itself suffers from the trauma of illogic; it is characterized by the breakdown of illation and by the disruption of the consequential processes of psychic transmission. The unreality of expressionist drama, poetry, painting, and music is the greatest obstacle for general comprehension. But once the curtain is removed and the secret images of a dreamer reach the observer in the form of poetry, art, or music, expressionism becomes a universal medium of mass communication and a great multiplier of artistic emotion.

It is natural that because of the basic antinomy between the sources of impressionism and expressionism, each should generate a distinctive musical language. Impressionism thrives on equilibrated euphony of harmonious dissonances, while expressionism prefers the harsh syntax of atonality. The coloristic opulence of impressionist music is obtained through the expansion of tonal materials into the spacious structures of resonant harmonies and exotic scales. Expressionism, on the other hand, communicates its deep-seated anxieties through chromatic congestion and atonal dispersion.

Impressionism builds its thematic contents on fluctuating modality, block harmonies, and parallel progressions of triadic formations. Expressionism rejects modality, tonality, and all diatonic textures. Its melodies are constructed parabolically, away from a putative tonic. In its evocation of the classical past, impressionism integrates the diatonic materials into the enhanced edifices of expressionism. The harmonic idiom of expressionism is formed by the superposition of 4ths and 5ths. Progressions of consecutive perfect 4ths or 5ths result in the formation of 12 different notes in a panchromatic complex, preparing the foundation of the method of composing with 12 tones related only to one another, as formulated by Schoenberg.

There are profound differences in the historic, cultural, and geographic factors in the development of impressionism and expressionism. Impressionism is Gallic, expressionism Germanic. The French syllabification of impressionist poetry is a paradigm of euphonious instrumentation, with the vowels acquiring specific weights and distinctive colors. The German texts of expressionist songs offer no sonorous gratification of resonant vocables, but in their guttural strength they seem to deepen the penetration of the philosophical and often mystical notions underlying the words.

Though impressionism in music is a close counterpart of pictorial art, no impressionist composer of any stature has ever tried his hand at painting pictures. Expressionism is basically a psychic development with no esthetic contact with painting, and yet composers of the expressionist school, notably Schoenberg and Berg, possessed a striking talent for painting in the expressionist style. Jefim Golyscheff, the composer of early atonal music, emigrated to Brazil and became an expressionist painter. Carl Ruggles, an American composer who developed a sui generis expressionist style in an atonal idiom, abandoned composition entirely and devoted himself to abstract painting.

expressive organ. The harmonium.

extemporization (from It. *ex tempore*, outside of time). A spontaneous or improvised performance.

extended compass. Tones beyond the usual range of a voice or instrument.

extension pedal. The damper (right) piano pedal.

extravaganza. An elaborate stage show with singing, dancing, dialogue, and little concern for dramaturgical coherence; often marked by exaggerated comic turns and spectacular scenic and lighting effects.

eye music

Composers are often tempted to use a visual representation in their scores to express the mood of a vocal or instrumental composition. From the early Renaissance, illuminated MSS contain examples of such representations; perhaps the most famous early example is the fantastic heart-shaped rondeau *Belle, bonne, sage* by Baude Cordier (*c.* 1400). Madrigal composers of the Renaissance may have used blackened notes to express death, dark of the night, or grief whenever such sentiments were found in the text, disregarding the fact that such blackening affected the time values in mensural notation. Bach used melodic figures that suggested the cross in his *St. Matthew Passion*. The appearance of the score in the storm scene in Beethoven's *Pastoral Sym.* actually suggests vertical rainfall in the wind instruments, swirling streams in the basses, and bolts of lightning in the brief and rapid violin passages.

There is no denying that the visual aspect of a piece of music somehow relates to the auditory impression of it. Brahms used to say that music that looks good will sound good. Some modern composers have advanced the paradoxical argument that music should not be heard at all, but be regarded as a sui generis pictorial art. Experienced score readers claim that they can obtain greater satisfaction and pleasure from reading music and idealizing the sound in an impossible euphony than hearing it. As Keats wrote, "Heard melodies are sweet, but those unheard are sweeter."

Critics sometimes use the term *eye music* (usually in the German form *Augenmusik*) as an opprobrium for works that look orderly and plausible on paper but are unimpressive to the ear. Yet visual symmetry usually corresponds to a fine musical organization. Composers of the avant-garde have adopted the patterns of eye music as points of departure for their musical inspiration. Anestis Logothetis, a Bulgarian-born (1921) Greek composer, exhibited his scores of eye music in Vienna, bearing characteristic geometric titles such as *Cycloid*, *Culmination*, *Interpolation*, *Parallax*, and *Concatenation*. Villa-Lobos experimented with millimetrization by transferring a chart, a curve, or a silhouette onto a piece of graph paper, with the ordinate corresponding to intervals in semitones and the abscissa to the duration of a note.

The American composer George Crumb has utilized eye music for expressive purposes since the mid-1960s. In the *Makrokosmos* piano cycles, scores are written in spiral, square-shaped, and other nontraditional layouts. A single part with multiple images and relationships (e.g., the *Dream Images (Love-Death Music)*, part 11 of *Makrokosmos I*, 1974) separates the bass drone, quasi-Stravinskian treble melody, and "faintly remembered" quotations of Chopin's *Fantasie-Impromptu*. In his chamber music, instruments are indicated only when they are played and are otherwise missing; this can give the performer a stronger sense of ephemerality or surprise. So, Crumb's eye music has it both ways; notation that should affect the audience's response while informing and titillating the performer (although playing some scores seems unnecessarily complicated).

F. The 6th note in the alphabetical scale, and the 4th note of the C major or minor scale. In French, Italian, Spanish, and Russian nomenclature, F is Fa.

f. FORTE.

ff. FORTISSIMO.

fff. FORTISSISSIMO.

F clef. A clef indicating the position on the staff of F, a 5th below middle C. The bass clef (𝄢), with F on the 4th line, is now virtually the only F clef in use. At one time the baritone clef (F on the 3rd line) and sub-bass clef (F on the 5th line) were also used.

F dur (Ger.). F major.

f holes. The 2 *f*-shaped sound-holes in the belly of the violin and other string instruments.

F major. This is predominantly a key of pastoral music, descriptive of gentle landscapes and lyric, often sentimental moods. Beethoven's *Pastoral Sym.* in F Major is a paradigm of the natural affinities of this key. So is the famous *Melody in F* by Anton Rubinstein. The most optimistic of the syms. of Brahms, the 3rd, is in F major. The merriest 2-Part Invention of Bach is in F major. No doubt, examples can be found in which F major suggests an autumnal rather than a vernal mood, but there cannot be too many of these.

F minor. This is a key of lyric reverie touched with melancholy. Composers writing for string instruments or for orch. instinctively shun F minor because it is so unwieldy,

having no open-string representation of the tonic or sub-dominant and only 1 of the dominant (lowest cello string). But F minor is eminently pianistic, and much Romantic music is written in this key. Chopin wrote his 2nd piano concerto in F minor (op. 21); Schubert's most famous *Moment Musical* is in F minor. Only the pansymphonic Miaskovsky ventured to select F minor as a principal key, and not just in 1 sym., but in 2: Nos. 10 and 24.

F moll (Ger.). F minor.

Fa. 1. In solmization, the usual name for the 4th degree of the scale. 2. Name of the tone *F* in Italy, France, Spain, and Russia.

fabordón (Sp.). FALSOBORDONE.

faburden (Old Eng.). In the Renaissance, enhancing a chant melody by parallel 6ths and 4ths below, or with the chant serving as middle voice (i.e., with parallel 3rds below and parallel 4ths above). The result is a progression analogous to consecutive 6/3 chords prior to a tonic-dominant cadence. The technique helped to legitimate the new consonances, which were to replace consecutive open 5ths and 4ths; related to the GYMEL and the FAUXBOURDON.

Façade. An "entertainment" by Walton, 1923, for speaking voice and instruments, to poems by the famous English woman of letters Dame Edith Sitwell. The music is a tossed salad of sentimental and vulgar tunes and quotations from famous operas. The thing was 1st performed in London, when Walton was only 21 years old. A 2nd collection of pieces orig. rejected from this work were collected as *Façade II* and 1st performed in 1979.

Face the Music. Musical by I. Berlin, 1932. The Depression is treated with morbid humor as a crooked cop has to launder stolen money before the law gets to him. His choice of investment: a Broadway show. Includes *Let's Have Another Cup of Coffee.*

Facetter. Sym. No. 3 by Blomdahl, 1951.

facile (It., Fr.). Facile, easy, fluent.

Fackeltanz (Ger.). Torch dance or procession. They were popular at court in 19th-century Prussia, and Spohr and Meyerbeer were among those to supply music for them.

Facsimile. "Choreographic observation" by Bernstein, 1946, where a blasé woman rejects one suitor after the other.

fado. A popular Portuguese song and dance genre.

Fagott (Ger.; It. *fagotto*). 1. BASSOON. 2. An organ reed stop.

Fain (born Feinberg), **Sammy,** American composer of popular music; b. N.Y., June 17, 1902; d. Los Angeles, Dec. 6, 1989. He worked in vaudeville and in the music-publishing business as a song plugger before achieving success as a full-fledged songwriter on Broadway and in Hollywood. In collaboration with the lyricist Irving Kahal, he produced such hits as *Nobody Knows What a Red-Headed Mama Can Do, Let a Smile Be Your Umbrella on a Rainy Day, When I Take My Sugar to Tea, Dear Hearts and Gentle People, That Old Feeling, I Can Dream, Can't I,* and *I'll Be Seeing You;* later, in collaboration with Paul F. Webster, he composed *Secret Love* and *Love Is a Many-Splendored Thing.*

Fairy Tales. Cycles of piano pieces by Medtner, 1905–c. 1932, re-creating the narrative quality of children's stories in classical music forms.

fake. Play without rehearsal from a lead sheet, usually collected in a FAKE BOOK. Also, to do one's best under the circumstances, as in "Fake it!" or "Wing it!"

fake book. A sheet-music collection of standard popular and jazz tunes for instrumentalists in a combo, indicating melodies and chord symbols but no other detail, thereby allowing the players to "fake" or improvise their way around a basic framework. These are also called lead sheets. Chord symbols use capital *M* (or *Maj*) for major and small *m* (or *min*) for minor triads. Numerical figures stand for intervals. A superscript ^{0} indicates diminished and ⁺ denotes augmented; the character *x* is for flat. The FUNDAMENTAL note is given before the indication of the chord symbol. Thus, CM is a C-major triad; CM6 is a C-major triad with an added 6th (i.e., the note A); Cx7 is a C-major triad with a flatted 7th (i.e., dominant-7th chord).

Faktur (Ger., facture). The style and manner of a composition.

Fall River Legend. Ballet by M. Gould, 1st performed in N.Y., Apr. 22, 1947. The subject is derived from the famous murder trial in Fall River, Mass., in which a maiden lady was accused of murdering her stepmother and then her father with an axe. She was acquitted, but the case became part of American folklore, bringing forth the rhyme

> Lizzie Borden took an axe
> and gave her mother 40 whacks.
> When she saw what she had done
> she gave her father 41.

The composer used hymns and ballads of the period to lend local color to the score.

Falla (y Matheu), **Manuel** (Maria) **de,** great Spanish composer; b. Cádiz, Nov. 23, 1876; d. Alta Gracia, Córdoba province, Argentina, Nov. 14, 1946. He studied piano with his mother; after further instruction from Eloisa Galluzo, he studied harmony, counterpoint, and composition with Alejandro Odero and Enrique Broca; then went to Madrid, where he studied piano with José Tragó and composition with Pedrell at the Cons. He wrote several zarzuelas, but only *Los amores de la Inés* was performed in Madrid (1902). His opera *La vida breve* won the prize of the Real Academia de Bellas Artes in Madrid in 1905, but it was not premiered until 8 years later. In 1905 he also won the Ortiz y Cussó Prize for pianists. In 1907 he went to Paris, where he became friendly with Debussy, Dukas, and Ravel, who aided and encouraged him as a composer. Under their influence he adopted the principles of impressionism without, however, giving up his personal and national style. He returned to Spain in 1914 and produced his tremendously effective ballet *El amor brujo* (1915). It was followed by the evocative *Noches en los jardines de España* for piano and orch. (1916). In 1919 he made his home in Granada, where he completed work on his celebrated ballet *El sombrero de tres picos* (1919).

Falla's art was rooted in both the folk songs of Spain and the purest historical traditions of Spanish music. Until 1919 his works were cast chiefly in the Andalusian idiom, and his instrumental technique was often conditioned by effects peculiar to Spain's national instrument, the guitar. In his puppet opera *El retablo de maese Pedro* (1919–22) he turned to the classical tradition of Spanish (especially Castilian) music. The keyboard style of his Harpsichord Concerto (1923–26), written at the suggestion of Wanda Landowska, reveals in the classical lucidity of its writing a certain kinship with Domenico Scarlatti, who lived in Spain for many years. Falla became president of the Instituto de España in 1938. When the Spanish Civil War broke out, and General Franco overcame the Loyalist government with the aid of Hitler and Mussolini, Falla left Spain and went to South America, never to return to his homeland. He went to Buenos Aires, where he conducted concerts of his music. He then withdrew to the small locality of Alta Gracia, where he lived the last years of his life in seclusion, working on his large scenic cantata *Atlántida*. It remained unfinished at his death and was later completed by his former pupil Ernesto Halffter. His writings include *Escritos sobre música y músicos* (Madrid, 1950); *Cartas a Segismondo Romero* (Granada, 1976); *Correspondencia de Manuel de Falla* (Madrid, 1978).

Falling in Love Again. Song by Frederick Hollander, made famous by Marlene Dietrich in the English-language version of the film *The Blue Angel* (1930).

falsa musica (It., false music). A medieval term for accidentals and other alterations not justified by contrapuntal rules.

false relation. CROSS RELATION.

falsetto (It., small false one; Fr. *fausset*; Ger. *Falsett, Fidelstimme*). The practice of voice production by using head tones rather than chest tones, particularly among tenors, thus producing sounds well above the natural range. Falsetto singing was widely practiced in the choirs at the Vatican and Italian cathedrals when the use of female or castrati singers was inappropriate. Falsetto singers were also known under the name of ALTI NATURALI, natural alto singers, to distinguish them from VOCI ARTIFICIALI, the artificial voices of the castrati. Another term for falsetto singers was *tenorini*, little tenors. The word *falsetto* itself is a diminutive of the Italian *falso*, because the singer, although not castrated, applies a "false" way of voice production. Falsetto voices are often used in Baroque operas for comic effects. The part of the Astrologer in Rimsky-Korsakov's *Le Coq d'or* is cast in falsetto to indicate that he is a eunuch. The falsetto is also used in yodeling.

falsobordone (It., false bass; Sp. *fabordón*). A style of chanting or reciting in root-position triads, with all 4 parts (usually 4) written out. The style evolved in the latter 15th century; eventually keyboard works and monodies with BASSO CONTINUO were composed in a similar style throughout the Baroque. This style was revived during the Cecilian movement of the 19th century.

Falstaff. Opera by Verdi, 1893, to a libretto by Boito, traversing the story of Shakespeare's famous fat man, bumbling lover, and cowardly braggart. *Falstaff* was Verdi's last opera and only his 2nd comic opera (it was described by Verdi as "lyric comedy"). The statement found in some reference works that Verdi wrote *Falstaff* when he was 80 is inaccurate: he worked on it from 1890 to 1892 and completed the score when he was barely 79. It was produced at La Scala in Milan, several months short of his 80th birthday. In the opera, Verdi inaugurated a new style, approaching that of music drama; it ends on a magisterial choral fugue with the Shakespearean words "Il mondo e la burla" (All the world's a stage).

Falstaff. Symphonic study by Elgar, 1913. It was 1st performed at the Leeds Festival, with Elgar himself conducting. Elgar was fascinated by the portly figure of the Shakespearean antihero; in this work he outlined, in musical images, Falstaff's life, from his companionship with the future King Henry V to his fall from royal grace and pitiful death. The music is Romantic, with elements of grandeur.

Fanciulla del West, La. GIRL OF THE GOLDEN WEST, THE.

fancy (from It. *fantasia*). 1. A polyphonic vocal composition of 16th-century England. 2. In 16th- and 17th-century England, a freely connected group of tunes, suites, or intabulations in a contrapuntal setting, written for the keyboard or a consort of viols; these were written by Byrd and Purcell, among others. See also FANTASIA.

Fancy Free. Ballet by Bernstein, with choreography by Jerome Robbins, 1944. Three sailors chase competitively after New York women during shore leave. The musical *On the Town* grew out of this idea a few years later.

fandango (Sp.). A lively dance in triple time for 2 dancers, who accompany it with castanets or tambourine.

fanfare. A flourish of trumpets or trumpet-call, traditionally based on the natural overtone series. The fanfare, whether festive or mournful, continues to serve its purely military signal function, but it has become a well-practiced musical device as well; examples include Beethoven's *Fidelio* and Bizet's *Carmen*.

Fanfare for the Common Man. A fanfare by Copland, 1943, for brass and percussion; one of the fanfares commissioned by Eugene Goosens for the Cincinnati Sym. Orch., which he conducted during World War II. It soon became a perennial favorite, and Copland included it in its entirety in the finale of his 3rd Sym.

Fantaisies symphoniques. Sym. No. 6 of Martinů, 1955.

fantasia (It.; Fr. *fantaisie*; Ger. *Fantasie*). 1. An improvisation. 2. A polyphonic instrumental piece in free imitation (17th and 18th centuries). These were compositions for keyboard instruments, lutes, and viols marked by a free thematic development and an abundance of florid cadenzas. This term has a respectable pedigree; Jean-Jacques Rousseau, in his *Dictionnaire de musique*, asserts wittily that a fantasy can never be written down because as soon as it is arranged in notes it ceases to be a fantasy. 3. A composition free in form and more or less fantastic in character. In the 19th century, instrumental fantasies largely abandoned their contrapuntal character and became works in sonata form. When Beethoven described his *Moonlight Sonata* as a "Sonata quasi una fantasia," he apparently intended to convey to it the character of a romantic image, but it is set in strict sonata form. Chopin's *Fantaisie-Impromptu* is organized in a symmetric ternary form. 4. A potpourri or paraphrase.

Fantasia Contrappuntistica. Compositional tour de force by Busoni, 1923, in either 1-piano or 2-piano versions. Several fugues of Bach are woven into an extremely complex contrapuntal fantasy.

Fantasia on a Theme by Thomas Tallis. String orch. work by Vaughan Williams, 1910; this is one of his popular works. Thomas Tallis was one of the greatest English com-

posers of hymns during the reign of Elizabeth I. Vaughan Williams set his solemn melodies in spacious modern modalities. The *Fantasia* was 1st performed in Gloucester.

Fantasia on Greensleeves. Work for harp and string by Vaughan Williams, 1934, based on the tune of *Greensleeves*, one of the most ingratiating English folk ballads. Shakespeare mentions it in *The Merry Wives of Windsor*, where Falstaff says, "Let [the sky] thunder to the tune of *Green Sleeves*" (V/3). Vaughan Williams 1st made use of it in his opera *Sir John in Love* (1929); he then arranged it as the *Fantasia* and conducted its 1st performance in London.

Fantastic Symphony. SYMPHONIE FANTASTIQUE.

Fantasticks, The. Musical by Harvey Schmidt and Tom Jones, 1960 and still running. Like *The Mousetrap* in London, this show has survived all near closings. It is a small-scale fantasy-romance in which girl meets boy, parents test love with remarkable cruelty (thereby unleashing the infamous Rape Ballet), girl leaves boy, boy wins girl back. Includes *Try to Remember*.

fantastico (It.). Fantastic, fanciful.

farandola (It., Fr. *farandole*). Old Provençal and Spanish circle-dance in rapid 6/8 time, accompanied on pipe and tabor. Modern composers have evoked the peasant world in their work; ironically, the most famous example (from Bizet's *L'Arlésienne*) is in duple meter.

Farbenmelodie (Ger., color melody). An aphoristic orchestration technique developed in the 2nd Viennese school, in which changes in timbre and instrumentation become a central element of differentiation. In total serialism, Farbenmelodie is treated in the same manner as pitch and rhythm.

farce. 1. A 1-act opera or operetta. 2. (Lat., stuff) A comic intermezzo in medieval plays with music, making use of songs popular at the time, often of lewd, lascivious, libidinous, ultracomical, or burlesque character. In modern times, a farce still retains the old meaning of a frivolous comedy of manners.

farewell engagements. These are convenient though rarely truthful announcements issued by famous prima donnas of both sexes at the ends of their careers to attract the attention of a long-vanishing public. Long past her prime, Adelina Patti gave an extended series of "farewell" concerts in the U.S.

Farewell Symphony (Ger. *Abschiedssymphonie*). Sym. No. 45 by Haydn, 1772, in the unusual key of F-sharp minor. The work itself is most unusual as well. In it, Haydn instructs one player after another to leave the stage until only the 1st violinist remains. After his last solo, he blows out his candle and makes his departure. Haydn left no clue as to the meaning of this pantomime, but in the course of time an elaborate myth was conjured up: Haydn and his little sym. group, who were employed by the Hungarian Prince Esterházy, desired to leave their stifling place of employment and take a little holiday in merry Vienna. The Prince took the not-so-subtle hint from this performance and let the musicians go on a well-merited vacation. But a much more plausible story is told in a book of memoirs by an obscure friend of Haydn, who relates that it was the Prince who was about to dismiss his resident musicians, which saddened them all, for they enjoyed healthy living and relatively generous emoluments. Haydn arranged this little exhibition to tug at the cockles of the Prince's heart. He fully succeeded, and his group remained in the service of the Prince for many more contented years.

Farinelli (born Carlo Broschi), celebrated Italian castrato soprano; b. Andria, Jan. 24, 1705; d. Bologna, July 15, 1782. His father, Salvatore Broschi, was a musician and most likely Carlo's earliest instructor in music. He later adopted the name Farinelli to honor his benefactor, Farina. He studied with Porpora in Naples, making his 1st public appearance there in his teacher's serenata *Angelica e Medoro* in 1720; subsequent appearances brought him great success, and he soon became famous as *il ragazzo* (the boy). He also sang in Rome, appearing in Porpora's opera *Eumene* at the age of 16. His repeated successes brought him renown throughout Italy and abroad, and led to his 1st appearance in Vienna (1724). He met the celebrated castrato alto Bernacchi in Bologna in 1727; in a singing contest with him, Farinelli acknowledged defeat and persuaded Bernacchi to give him lessons to achieve virtuosity in coloratura. After further visits to Vienna in 1728 and 1731, Porpora called him to London to sing with the Opera of the Nobility; he made his London debut in Hasse's *Artaserse* in 1734, appearing with Senesino and Cuzzoni; he remained with the company until the summer of 1736, when he went to Paris, then returned to it for the 1736–37 season. Having amassed a fortune in

London, Farinelli went to Madrid in 1737. He attained unparalleled success as court singer to King Philip V; his duty was to sing arias every night to cure the King's melancholy, and his influence on the ailing monarch and his Queen was such that Farinelli was able to command considerable funds to engage famous performers for the Madrid court. When his voice began to fail, he served as impresario, decorator, and stage director. He continued to enjoy the court's favor under Philip's successor, Ferdinand VI, who made him a knight of the order of Calatrava in 1750. However, when Carlos III became King in 1759, Farinelli was dismissed. He then returned to Italy in possession of great wealth. He built a palatial villa for himself near Bologna and spent the last years of his life in contentment. His brother Riccardo Broschi (b. Naples, *c.* 1698; d. Madrid, 1756) was a composer who produced several operas in Naples, in which his brother sang. He later settled in Spain with his brother.

Farley, Carole (Ann), talented American soprano; b. Le Mars, Iowa, Nov. 29, 1946. She studied at the Indiana Univ. School of Music (Mus.B., 1968), with Cornelius Reid in N.Y., and on a Fulbright scholarship with Marianne Schech at the Munich Hochschule für Musik (1968–69). In 1969 she made her debut at the Linz Landestheater and also her U.S. debut at N.Y.'s Town Hall; subsequently appeared as a soloist with major orchs. of the U.S. and Europe, and sang with the Welsh National Opera, the Cologne Opera, the Strasbourg Opera, the N.Y. Opera, and the Lyons Opera. She made her Metropolitan Opera debut in N.Y. as Lulu in 1977, and continued to sing there in later seasons; she also sang at the Zurich Opera (1979), the Deutsche Oper am Rhein in Dusseldorf (1980–81; 1984), the Chicago Lyric Opera (1981), and the Florence Maggio Musicale (1985). In addition to her esteemed portrayal of Lulu, which she essayed over 80 times in various operatic centers, she also sang Poppea, Donna Anna, Violetta, Massenet's Manon, Mimi, and various roles in R. Strauss's operas. She married José Serebrier in 1969.

Farwell, Arthur (George), American composer and music educator; b. St. Paul, Minn., Apr. 23, 1872; d. N.Y., Jan. 20, 1952. He studied at the Mass. Inst. of Technology, graduating in 1893; then studied music with Homer Norris in Boston, Humperdinck and Pfitzner in Berlin, and Guilmant in Paris. He was a lecturer on music at Cornell Univ. (1899–1901); from 1909 to 1914 was on the editorial staff of *Musical America*; directed municipal concerts in N.Y.

(1910–13); and was director of the Settlement Music School in N.Y. (1915–18). In 1918 he went to Calif. and lectured on music there; was acting head of the music dept. at the Univ. of Calif., Berkeley (1918–19); in 1919 founded the Santa Barbara Community Chorus, which he conducted until 1921; was the 1st holder of the composers' fellowship of the Music and Art Assoc. of Pasadena (1921–25); taught music theory at Mich. State College in East Lansing (1927–39); eventually settled in N.Y.

Farwell was a pioneer in new American music and tirelessly promoted national ideas in art. He contributed to various ethnological publications. From 1901 to 1911 he operated the Wa-Wan Press (Newton, Mass.), a periodical (quarterly, 1901–1907; monthly, 1907–11) that printed piano and vocal music of "progressive" American composers of the period, the emphasis being on works that utilized indigenous (black, Indian, and cowboy) musical materials (reprinted N.Y., 1970, under the direction of Vera Brodsky Lawrence). Disillusioned about commercial opportunities for American music, including his own, he established at East Lansing, in April 1936, his own lithographic handpress, with which he printed his music, handling the entire process of reproduction, including the cover designs, by himself. He wrote *A Letter to American Composers* (N.Y., 1903) and *Music in America* in *The Art of Music*, IV (with W. Dermot Darby; N.Y., 1915).

Faschingsschwank aus Wien (Carnival Merrymaking in Vienna). Cycle of 5 piano pieces by Schumann (op. 26), 1839–40.

fasciculation. In view of the vagueness of such terms as *section, part, division, subdivision, period, phrase,* etc., it might be useful to introduce into musical nomenclature the term *fascicle* to designate a self-sufficient fragment of a musical work. It is particularly useful in application to serial music. In dodecaphonic exposition, *fascicle I, fascicle II, fascicle III,* and *fascicle IV* would indicate the 4 forms of the basic tone-row. In neoclassical compositions, *fasciculation* may easily replace the conventional Baroque designations of *sequences, modulatory digressions,* and the like. This type of nomenclature may also contribute to the analytical clarity of theoretical discussion.

Fascinating Rhythm. Song by Gershwin, 1924, from the musical *Lady, Be Good!* The rhythm referred to is a polymetric relationship between melody and accompaniment.

Fasola. A singing teaching method which was popular in England and in colonial America. The term specified that only 3 syllables of the GUIDONIAN HAND—Fa, Sol, and La—were to be used to form the major hexachord. By adding the syllable Mi for the 7th degree of the scale, a complete major scale was obtained. In order to facilitate further the immediate recognition of the degrees of the scale, an American musician named William Little notated Fa, Sol, and La in different shapes. This SHAPE NOTE notation, also known as *buckwheat notation,* was for many years used in music classes in America, particularly in the Southern states.

fastosamente (*fastoso*; It.). With pomp; in a stately style; majestically.

fate motive. A nickname given the 4-note theme (3 short, 1 long) that Beethoven used at the beginning of (and throughout) the 5th Sym. (1808). In fact, other Beethoven works of this period (4th Piano Concerto, the *Appassionata,* and the String Quartet, op. 74) use the same motive. There is no biographical proof that the composer thought of this motive in a particular way. But it has cast its spell over the centuries. During World War II the Allied propaganda service broadcast to Nazi-occupied Europe the signal *V* (for Victory) in Morse code, which happens to be 3 dots (short) followed by a dash (long). As the Nazis could not very well censor Beethoven or arrest people who whistled the tune, they tried to steal it from the Allies by equating it with the archaic word *Victoria.* Thus the fight of the fate motive was joined, with both propaganda agencies using it to foretell their respective victories.

Fatum. Symphonic poem by Tchaikovsky, 1869, 1st performed in Moscow. The title shows Tchaikovsky's abiding obsession with the inexorability of fate.

Fauré, Gabriel (-Urbain), great French composer and pedagogue; b. Pamiers, Ariège, May 12, 1845; d. Paris, Nov. 4, 1924. His father was a provincial inspector of primary schools; noticing the musical instinct of his son, he took him to Paris to study with Louis Niedermeyer; after Niedermeyer's death in 1861, Fauré studied with Saint-Saëns, from whom he received thorough training in composition. In 1866 he went to Rennes as organist at the church of St.-Sauveur; returned to Paris on the eve of the Franco-Prussian War in 1870 and volunteered in the light infantry. He was organist at Notre-Dame de Clignancourt (1870), St.-Honoré d'Elyau (1871), and St.-Sulpice (1871–74). He then was named deputy organist (to Saint-Saëns, 1874), choirmaster (1877), and chief organist (1896) at the

Madeleine. In 1896 he was appointed prof. of composition at the Paris Cons. He was an illustrious teacher; among his students were Ravel, Enesco, Koechlin, Roger-Ducasse, F. Schmitt, and N. Boulanger. In 1905 he succeeded Théodore Dubois as director and subsequently served until 1920. Then, quite unexpectedly, he developed ear trouble, resulting in gradual loss of hearing. Distressed, he made an effort to conceal it but was eventually forced to abandon his teaching position. From 1903 to 1921 he wrote occasional music reviews in *Le Figaro* (a selection was publ. as *Opinions musicales*, Paris, 1930). He was elected a member of the Académie des Beaux Arts in 1909, and in 1910 was made a Commander of the Legion d'honneur.

Fauré's stature as a composer is undiminished by the passage of time. He developed a musical idiom all his own; by subtle application of old modes he evoked the aura of eternally fresh art; by using unresolved mild discords and special coloristic effects, he anticipated procedures of IMPRESSIONISM; in his piano works he shunned virtuosity in favor of the classical lucidity of the French masters of the clavecin; the precisely articulated melodic line of his songs is in the finest tradition of French vocal music. His great Requiem and his *Elégie* for cello and piano have entered the general repertoire.

fausse relation (Fr.). CROSS RELATION.

Faust. Grand opera by Gounod, 1859, based on part I of Goethe's dramatic poem, 1st performed in Paris. It is one of the most successful operas of all times. In its melodiousness, harmoniousness, and mellowness, *Faust* has no equal. During the 1st century of its spectacular career, *Faust* had more than 2,000 performances in Paris alone. Its libretto emphasizes the mundane aspects of Goethe's great poem. Faust sells his soul to the canny devil Mephistopheles in exchange for the elixir of youth. No sooner is the deal arranged than Faust is shown an image of the virginal weaver Marguerite. He is conducted to the girl's abode, sings an aria extolling the chastity of her retreat, tempts her anonymously with jewels, which gives her a chance to sing an aria with coloratura trills and frills, and, with worldly advice from the ubiquitous devil, he seduces her. Marguerite's brother Valentin fights Faust in a duel, but is slain; Faust runs off. Marguerite bears Faust's child, but she goes insane and kills her progeny. She is sentenced to die, but a host of cherubim and seraphim carries her to heaven while Faust watches. He goes off with (and to) the devil. The Germans remain so offended by Gounod's earthy treat-ment of Goethe's text that, when the opera is produced in Germany, it is called *Margarete* or *Gretchen*.

Faust Symphony. This work by Liszt (1857) is the only true sym. inspired by Goethe's great epic poem *Faust*. It is subdivided into 3 movements, which are portraits of the main characters: Faust, Gretchen, and Mephistopheles. It was 1st performed in Weimar; the ending is choral. The purely musical distinction of the work is its remarkable opening in 4 arpeggiated augmented triads.

fauxbourdon (Med. Fr., false drone). A term for various contrapuntal techniques that evolved in the 15th century. The term and techniques seem related to the medieval English FABURDEN, which may have been its original source. In actual harmonic usage, fauxbourdon allowed parallel 4ths and 6ths as consonant intervals from the top down, and doubling at the octave where appropriate. The reason for the name "false drone" may be owed to the introduction of the "false bass," not the (usual) tonic of the chord but its mediant. The chant voice was moved to the middle or upper portion of the counterpoint; some of the additional voices were written, others implied. To modern ears the fauxbourdon sound like parallel progressions in 3rds and 6ths. This practice eventually led to the use of consecutive $^6_3$ chords, common in later classical usage. Even a separate fauxbourdon genre of short pieces emerged. Eventually the technique dissolved in the rarefied counterpoint of thelate Renaissance and thereafter; similar passages have appeared on occasion with the return of parallel harmony in the early 20th century, recasting the concept in modern terms (often in the hands of French composers).

Favola d'Orfeo, La. ORFEO, LA FAVOLA D'.

favola per musica (It., fable with music). An early term for an opera libretto based on a mythological story.

Favorite, La (Fr.; It. *La Favorita*). Opera by Donizetti, 1840. The king of Castile allows an unknowing novitiate monk to woo and win the king's favorite mistress as a jest. When the ex-monk discovers the setup, he leaves her to rejoin the monastery. She realizes that she loves him and makes her way to his retreat as a novitiate herself. But she is overcome by moral scruples and dies in his arms.

Fedeltà premiata, La (Fidelity Rewarded). Pastoral opera by Haydn, 1780.

Fedora. Opera by Giordano, 1898; a grim morality tale involving Fedora (a Russian countess-to-be), her assassinated intended, his nihilist killer, Fedora's pursuit of and inadvertent falling for the murderer in Paris, their escape to Switzerland, his (anarchistic?) betrayal of her in Switzerland, and her shock and suicide, dying in his loving arms.

feedback. Loud distortion in amplification equipment caused by the output's being picked up by the input, thus creating a loop of electrically enhanced sound waves. A typical case—an amplifier and an electric guitar attached to it—was the bane of performers until they learned to control the distortion and use it to color the timbre or to serve as the source material for live electroacoustic music (e.g., Jimi Hendrix).

Feen, Die. Opera by Wagner, 1834, 1st produced posthumously in 1888. Based on Gozzi's play *La donna serpente*, it concerns the fate of two lovers, one supernatural, the other natural.

feierlich (Ger.). Ceremonial, solemn, grave.

Feldman, Morton, important American composer of the avant-garde; b. N.Y., Jan. 12, 1926; d. Buffalo, Sept. 3, 1987. He studied piano with Vera Maurina-Press in N.Y. and composition with Wallingford Riegger (1941) and Stefan Wolpe (1944). Profoundly impressed by the abstract expressionism of modern paintings and his friendship with John Cage, he evolved a congenial set of musical concepts based on the seemingly oxymoronic principle of predetermined indeterminacy, as exemplified in his *Projections I–IV* for aleatory instrumental combinations, with only an approximation of the notes in a work performing a musical "action," indicating the instrumental range and the number of notes per specified time unit. In their immarcescible fidelity to the ideals of new music, his works left a profound impression on the theories and practices of the young composers of the waning years of the 20th century, so that even after his early death (of cancer of the pancreas), his works continued to enjoy frequent performances in America and Europe. In his geometric directness and expressive lucidity of technical devices, Feldman is the de Kooning of musical composition.

He received a Guggenheim fellowship (1966); taught at the State Univ. of N.Y. in Buffalo (from 1972), where he held the Edgard Varèse Chair. His groups of works for various instruments include the *Intersections* (1951, 1952, 1953, 1953) and the *Marginal Intersection* for orch. (1951);

Extensions (1951, 1951, 1952, 1953, 1953); *Durations* (1960, 1960, 1961, 1961, 1961); *Vertical Thoughts* for different instrumental combinations (four works, all 1963); *The Viola in My Life* I–IV (1970, 1970, 1970, 1971); *Instruments* I–IV (1974, 1974, 1977, 1978). He also wrote music for string quartet, and many chamber, orch., and vocal works.

Feliciano, Jose, blind Puerto Rican singer, guitarist, and songwriter; b. Lares, Sept. 10, 1945. His family moved to N.Y. when he was 5; he taught himself to play the guitar, then appeared in Greenwich Village clubs; his self-exclamatory record album *Feliciano!* brought him fame (it included his soulful version of the song *Light My Fire*, notable for its sexual and narcotic overtones). His blues rendition of *The Star-Spangled Banner* at the 1968 World Series in Detroit caused a furor, leading many radio stations to boycott him. After a hiatus of several years he was able to renew his career. He toured in the U.S. and in Europe.

Feltsman, Vladimir, prominent Russian pianist; b. Moscow, Jan. 8, 1952. He was born into a musical family; his father, Oskar Feltsman, was a composer of popular music. He began taking piano lessons at the age of 6 from his mother, then enrolled at Moscow's Central Music School, completing his training with Yakov Flier at the Moscow Cons. At 11 he made his debut as a soloist with the Moscow Phil., and later won 1st prize in the Prague Concertino Competition. After capturing joint 1st prize in the Long-Thibaud Competition in Paris in 1971, he pursued a successful career as a soloist with major Soviet and Eastern European orchs.; he made particularly successful appearances in works in the Romantic repertoire—his specialty—in Japan (1977) and France (1978).

His auspicious career was interrupted by the Soviet authorities when in 1979 he applied for a visa to emigrate to Israel with his wife. His application was denied and he subsequently was allowed to give concerts only in remote outposts of the Soviet Union. With the support of the U.S. ambassador he gave several private concerts at the ambassador's official residence in Moscow; in 1984 one of these was surreptitiously recorded and later released by CBS Masterworks. When his plight became a cause célèbre in the West, Feltsman was allowed to give his 1st Moscow recital in almost a decade (1987). That year he was granted permission to emigrate; went to the U.S., where he accepted an appointment at the State Univ. of N.Y. at New Paltz; gave a special concert at the White House for President Reagan, and his 1st N.Y. recital in Carnegie Hall.

feminine ending. An old-fashioned term used by analogy with versification to designate the unaccented syllable at the end of a line. In music many Romantic pieces have such endings, with a stressed dissonant melodic note resolving on a weak melodic beat.

Fenby, Eric (William), English composer; b. Scarborough, Apr. 22, 1906. He studied piano and organ; after a few years as an organist in London he went (1928) to Grez-sur-Loing, France, as amanuensis for Delius, taking down his dictation note by note, until Delius's death in 1934. He publ. his experiences in a book entitled *Delius as I Knew Him* (London, 1936). He was director of music of the North Riding Training School (1948–62); from 1964 was a prof. of composition at the Royal Academy of Music. In 1964 he was made an Officer of the Order of the British Empire. Because of the beneficent work he undertook he neglected his own compositions; however, he wrote some pleasant music for strings.

fermamente (It.). Firmly, decisively.

fermata (It.; Ger. *Fermate*). The sign ⌒ over, or ⌣ under, a note or rest, indicating the prolongation of its time value at the performer's (or conductor's) discretion; doubling the length of the note or rest is a good approximation. A fermata is also called a hold. Placed over a bar, it indicates a slight pause or breathing-spell before attacking what follows; the overall tempo is not affected. A rest for an entire ensemble is called a GRAND PAUSE (abbrev. G.P.).

fermezza, con (It.). In a firm, decided, energetic style.

fermo (It.). Firm, decided; fixed, unchanged. *Canto fermo*, same as CANTUS FIRMUS.

Fern (*Ferne*; Ger.). Distance. *Wie aus der Ferne*, as if from a distance.

Fernand Cortez, ou La Conquête du Mexique. Opera by Spontini, 1809. The story of the conquest of Mexico is liberally interlaced with operatic amours.

Ferne Klang, Der. Opera by Schreker, 1912. A Venetian courtesan is mystically redeemed through her assisting her composer lover reach operatic success. In an updating of Sullivan's *The Lost Chord*, Schreker's composer dies in his lover's arms upon hearing a supernaturally distant harmony.

Ferneyhough, Brian, avant-garde English composer; b. Coventry, Jan. 16, 1943. He studied at the Birmingham School of Music (1961–63); then took courses with Lennox Berkeley and Maurice Miles at the Royal Academy of Music in London (1966–67); furthermore, received instruction in advanced composition with Ton de Leeuw in Amsterdam and Klaus Huber in Basel (1969–73). From 1971 to 1986 he was on the faculty at the Hochschule für Musik in Freiburg im Breisgau; in 1976, 1978, and 1980 lectured at the Darmstadt summer courses. He also taught at the Royal Cons. of the Hague (from 1986) and at the Univ. of Calif. at San Diego (from 1987). The radical qualities of his style involve atypical approaches to dissonant counterpoint and time structure that are totally divorced from the dance-music orientation of most European music; he is probably the least English-sounding of the prominent British composers of the latter 20th century.

feroce (It.). Wild, fierce, vehement, ferociously, savagely.

Ferrier, Kathleen (Mary), remarkable English contralto; b. Higher Walton, Lancashire, Apr. 22, 1912; d. London, Oct. 8, 1953. She grew up in Blackburn, where she studied piano; also began voice lessons there with Thomas Duerden; for a time she was employed as a telephone operator. In 1937 she won 1st prizes for piano and singing at the Carlisle Competition; she then decided on a career as a singer, and subsequently studied voice with J. E. Hutchinson in Newcastle upon Tyne and with Roy Henderson in London. After an engagement as a soloist in *Messiah* at Westminster Abbey in 1943, she began her professional career in full earnest. Britten chose her to create the title role in his *Rape of Lucretia* (Glyndebourne, 1946); she also sang Orfeo in Gluck's *Orfeo ed Euridice* there in 1947 and at Covent Garden in 1953. She made her American debut with the N.Y. Phil. in 1948, singing *Das Lied von der Erde*, with Bruno Walter conducting. She made her American recital debut in N.Y. (1949). Toward the end of her brief career she acquired in England an almost legendary reputation for vocal excellence and impeccable taste, so that her untimely death (from cancer) was greatly mourned. In 1953 she was made a Commander of the Order of the British Empire; she also received the Gold Medal of the Royal Phil. Soc.

fervente (*fervido*; It.). Fervently, ardently, passionately.

Fes (Ger.). F-flat.

Feses (Ger.). F double-flat, theoretically.

Fest (Ger.). 1. Festival. 2. Firm, precise.

festa teatrale (It.). A theatrical festival celebrating a royal anniversary or national victory, and featuring music and dancing.

Feste Romane. ROMAN FESTIVALS.

Festes Zeitmass (Ger.). Precisely in tempo.

Festin de l'araignée, Le. Ballet-pantomime by Roussel, 1913, 1st performed in Paris, 1913. The scenario depicts the feast of a spider with a menu comprising, among other insects, a butterfly and a mayfly. In the end the bloated spider is itself devoured by a praying mantis. The music is impressionistic, with dancing tunes for the entomological scenes.

festivals

This is a generic name for all kinds of festivities, accompanied by singing, playing upon instruments, and dancing. The earliest music festivals were the gatherings of the troubadours in 13th-century France and the Minnesingers in Germany, the latter portrayed in Wagner's operas *Tannhäuser* and *Die Meistersinger*. The oldest regularly produced festival was the Eisteddfod, a bardic gathering held in Wales; after over a century of silence, it was revived as a choral festival in 1880. England was the 1st nation to organize music festivals devoted to performances of classical music. The 1st of these was the 3 Choirs Festival founded in 1724, which took place in the 3 cathedral cities of Gloucester, Hereford, and Worcester in England.

The earliest festival to present the music of a single composer was the Handel Festival, organized in London in the Crystal Palace in 1857. The most grandiose opera festivals devoted to a living composer were the Bayreuth Festivals, begun by Wagner in 1876 with the aid of funds supplied by his fanatical admirer, the young King Ludwig of Bavaria; the opening event presented the complete performance of *Der Ring des Nibelungen*. Music festivals in America in the 19th century tended to emphasize numerical grandeur, as exemplified by the 2 festivals celebrating the end of the Civil War, held in Boston in 1869 and in 1872 under the name Peace Jubilee. It advertised an orch. of 1,000 men and a chorus of 10,000. An important series of music festivals of a high professional order was initiated in Worcester, Mass., in 1858.

In the 20th century several festivals were organized with the express purpose of promoting modern music. Of these the most ambitious in scope were the festivals of the International Soc. for Contemporary Music (founded in 1923), held in the summer or early autumn in various countries of Europe. The Coolidge Chamber Music Festivals were established by Elizabeth Sprague Coolidge, 1st under the name Berkshire Festival of Chamber Music in Pittsfield, Mass. (1918), and then under the auspices of the Library of Congress in Washington, D.C. (1925). In 1930 Howard Hanson inaugurated a series of annual festivals of American music at Rochester, N.Y. In 1940 Koussevitzky and the Boston Sym. Orch. established a series of summer concerts in Tanglewood, Mass., in programs of classical and modern music.

In 1956, Poland opened an annual series of festivals of modern music under the name Warsaw Autumn. The festivals in Donaueschingen, begun in 1921, produced numerous new works, principally by German composers. The International Festival in Edinburgh, founded in 1947, presents programs of opera, sym., and chamber music. The Maggio Musicale Fiorentino (Florentine Musical May) was established in 1933, at 1st on a biennial and then on an annual basis, with varied programs of opera, ballet, and sym. concerts. The biennial Venice Festival has flourished since 1950. In 1958 Menotti organized the Festival of 2 Worlds in the town of Spoleto, Italy, the 2 worlds being Europe and America; in 1977 he opened the American counterpart of the festival in Charleston, N.C. The Israel Festival has been held in principal cities of the country since 1961; its programs emphasize Israeli folk music and works by national composers. In 1957 the millionaire Armenian industrialist Gulbenkian founded annual festivals in Lisbon and other cities of Portugal, known as Festival Gulbenkian de Musica. The Prague Spring Festivals were inaugurated in 1946. Biennial international festivals of contemporary music have been presented in Zagreb. The annual Holland Festival, established in 1948, gives presentations of music in all genres, in Amsterdam and other Dutch cities. In 1948 Britten organized annual summer festivals in Aldenburgh, England. Operas, new and old, are presented during the summer months in Glyndebourne, England.

Regular festival presentations are held in virtually every European city, the most important ones being those in Berlin, Munich, Vienna, Salzburg, Stockholm, and Bergen, Norway. Festivals of the music of Sibelius are given in Helsinki in Dec., commemorating the month of his birth. In the USSR ample musical activities were maintained in Moscow, Leningrad, Kiev, Tbilisi, and other musical centers; festivals of ethnic music, ranging from folk songs to operas and syms., have been given periodically in Moscow. Japan and Australia contribute to the development of festival music.

Jazz festivals of Newport, R.I. (later moved to N.Y.), held during the summer months, provide special interest, as do those in Monterrey, Calif. Concerts and presentations in multimedia are sporadically given by composers of the International Avant-Garde, in N.Y., San Francisco, London, Cologne, and Tokyo.

festivamente (*festivo*; It.; Ger. *Festlich*). Gaily; in a festive mood.

Festschrift (Ger., festive writing; plural *Festschriften*). An offering in honor of an esteemed musical scholar, teacher, or composer on the occasion of an advanced birthday or retirement, in the form of a published volume of collected articles by his or her students and colleagues. The custom generated in Germany, but the German term is retained for non-German publications as well, particularly in the U.S. Festschriften are usually printed on deluxe paper and adorned by a photograph representing the bespectacled visage corrugated by age and scholarly concentration, suggesting that learned pursuits are physiologically deadening.

At their worst the contents of such volumes are grab bags, if not indeed garbage containers, of discarded Ph.D. theses on jejune subjects, fetid paralipomena, and fulsome fecundities, laden with footnotes that frequently retract statements made in the text, and couched in a stupefying pedestrian style that is often grammatically and syntactically indigestible. Such materials are usually intellectual placentas of aborted elucubrations often contributed by students of the person honored; unintentionally, such presentations put in doubt the ability of the master to enlighten or instruct. Until recently, Festschriften seemed to be the exclusive patrimony of men. Exceptions in this wasteland of depressing dullness are Festschriften for composers, such as the ones for Schoenberg which contain valuable articles by his faithful disciples; sometimes, essay collections are organized by subject matter into a worthwhile anthology.

Festspiel (Ger.). German term for a stage play in which music is included. Wagner called *Der Ring des Nibelungen* a Festspiel.

Fétis, François-Joseph, erudite Belgian music theorist, historian, and critic; b. Mons, Mar. 25, 1784; d. Brussels, Mar. 26, 1871. He received primary instruction from his father, an organist at the Mons Cathedral; learned to play the violin, piano, and organ when very young, and in his 9th year wrote a Violin Concerto; as a youth, was organist to the Noble Chapter of Ste.-Waudru. In 1800 he entered the Paris Cons., where he studied harmony with Rey and piano with Boieldieu and Pradher; in 1803 he visited Vienna, there studying counterpoint, fugue, and masterworks of German music. Several of his compositions (a sym., an overture, sonatas, and caprices for piano) were publ. at that time.

In 1806 he began the revision of the plainsong and entire ritual of the Roman Church, a vast undertaking, completed, with many interruptions, after 30 years of patient research. A wealthy marriage in the same year, 1806, enabled him to pursue his studies at ease for a time; but the fortune was lost in 1811, and he retired to the Ardennes, where he occupied himself with composition and philosophical researches into the theory of harmony; in 1813 he was appointed organist for the collegiate church of St.-Pierre at Douai. In 1818 he settled in Paris; in 1821 became a prof. of composition at the Paris Cons.; in 1824 his *Traité du contrepoint et de la fugue* was publ. and accepted as a regular manual at the Cons. In 1827 he became librarian of the Cons., and in the same year founded his unique journal *La Revue Musicale* (to 1835). He also wrote articles on music for *Le National* and *Le Temps*. In 1832 he inaugurated his famous series of historical lectures and concerts. In 1833 he was called to Brussels as maître de chapelle to King Leopold I, and director of the Cons.; during his long tenure in the latter position, nearly 40 years, the Cons. flourished as never before. He also conducted the concerts of the Academy, which elected him a member in 1845.

Fétis was a confirmed believer in the possibility of explaining music history and music theory scientifically; in his scholarly writings he attempted a thorough systematization of all fields of the art; he was opinionated and dogmatic, but it cannot be denied that he was a pioneer in musicology. He publ. the 1st book on music appreciation, *La Musique mise à la portée de tout le monde* (Paris, 1830), and further pedagogical writings. As early as 1806 Fétis began collecting materials for his great *Biographie universelle des musiciens et bibliographie générale de la musique* (8 vols., Paris, 1835–44). This work of musical biography was unprecedented in its scope; entries on composers and performers whom he knew personally still remain prime sources of information. On the negative side are the many fanciful accounts of composers' lives taken from unreliable sources; in this respect Fétis exercised a harmful influence on subsequent lexicographers for a whole century. His *Histoire générale de la musique* goes only as far as the 15th century (5 vols., Paris, 1869–76); this work exhibits Fétis as a profound scholar, but also as a dogmatic philosopher of music propounding opinions without convincing evidence to support them. He was also a composer, although his music has been overshadowed completely by his musicological work. His valuable library of 7,325 vols. was acquired after his death by the Bibliothèque Royale of Brussels; a catalog was publ. in 1877.

fetishes and taboos. In the inexorable course of history and of the arts, yesterday's fetishes become tomorrow's taboos. The following modernistic fetishes of the recent musical past have become taboos: 1. The diminished-7th chord, once favored by It. opera composers, the ACCORDE DI STUPEFAZIONE, used to melodramatize the high points in operatic action. Verdi, who was responsible for some of the most effective applications of this "chord of stupefaction," often in parallel chromatic progressions, in his own operas, issued a stern warning to young composers not to abuse it. No self-respecting composer of today would resort to such unsophisticated practices, except for musical persiflage. 2. Tonal sequences, particularly those rising or descending by degrees, known pejoratively as ROSALIAS, after an old popular Italian ballad, *Rosalia, mia cara.* Indeed, sequences of

any kind have virtually disappeared from 20th-century music. 3. The whole-tone scale, once a fetish of impressionism, has now sunk into noxious desuetude as a cinematic effect used to portray strutting Nazis, mad scientists, or psychotic refugees from plastic surgery. 4. Parallel progressions of major-9th chords and consecutive formations of 2nd inversions of major triads at intervals of minor 3rds, one of the most prized formulas of impressionism. 5. The *Petrouchka chord* (also known as the "Parisian chord"), consisting of 2 major triads at the distance of a tritone. This early instance of bitonality, which became a fetish of modern French music in the 2nd quarter of the 20th century, has been disfranchised and relegated to the category of fraudulent modernism. 6. There are even signs and tokens on the firmament that the sacrosanct fetish of the 20th century, the dodecaphonic method of composition, is on the point of deciduous decay, losing its dodecuple integrity and degenerating into the lipogrammatic hendecaphonic or decaphonic series.

feuerig (Ger.). Fiery, impetuous.

Feuermann, Emanuel, greatly gifted Austrian-born American cellist; b. Kolomea, Galicia, Nov. 22, 1902; d. N.Y., May 25, 1942. As a child he was taken to Vienna, where he 1st studied cello with his father; subsequently studied cello with Friedrich Buxbaum and Anton Walter; made his debut in Vienna in 1913 in a recital. He went to Leipzig in 1917 to continue his studies with Julius Klengel; his progress was so great that he was appointed to the faculty of the Gurzenich Cons. in Cologne by Abendroth at the age of 16; he also was 1st cellist in the Gurzenich Orch. and a member of the Bram Eldering Quartet. In 1929 he was appointed prof. at the Hochschule für Musik in Berlin; as a Jew he was forced to leave Germany after the Nazis took power; he then embarked on a world tour (1934–35). He made his American debut in 1934, with the Chicago Sym. Orch.; then appeared as soloist with many of the leading American orchs.; also played chamber music with Schnabel and Huberman, and later with Rubinstein and Heifetz.

Feuersnot (Fire-Famine). Opera by R. Strauss, 1901, described by him as a *Singgedicht*, a singing poem. The libretto is based on a Flemish legend, *The Extinguished Fires of Audenarde.* A recluse tries to kiss a girl who ridicules him publicly, unaware of the fact that he possesses magical power. In revenge he creates a fire-famine that extinguishes all lights in the village. The girl quickly repents, and he withdraws his ban on fires. The opera was 1st produced in Dresden, with the composer conducting.

Fever. A 1956 Little Willie John hit with a slinky rhythm that has remained a pop favorite; subsequently covered by Peggy Lee (1958), the McCoys (1965), and countless others.

fiacco (It.). Languishing, feeble.

fiasco (It., flask or bottle). An utter failure of a theatrical or other performance. Music history abounds in stories of fiascos of great masterpieces which eventually became parts of the standard repertory. The fiasco of Wagner's *Tannhäuser* in Paris in 1861 is notorious; he withdrew the opera after 3 disastrous performances. The fiasco of the 1st production of *Madama Butterfly* of Puccini in 1904 was a resounding one; Puccini and his librettist notified the publishers that inasmuch as the audience showed its disapproval of the opera, they were withdrawing it from further performances. Melodramatic biographies of Bizet describe his anguish at the fiasco of *Carmen*, which drove him to an early grave. Aside from the fact that nobody, not even composers, ever died of chagrin, *Carmen* was anything but a fiasco. It had a continuous run of 3 months after its initial production, and Bizet died on the night of its 33rd performance. How the Italian word fiasco acquired the meaning of an ignominious failure is not clear.

fiato (It.). Breath. *Stromenti a fiato*, wind instruments.

Fibich, Zdeněk (Zdenko) (Antonín Vaclav), important Czech composer; b. Seboriče, Dec. 21, 1850; d. Prague, Oct. 15, 1900. He studied piano with Moscheles and theory with E. F. Richter at the Leipzig Cons. (1865–66), then composition privately with Jadassohn (1866–67) and in Mannheim with V. Lachner (1869–70). Upon his return to Prague (1871) he was made deputy conductor and chorusmaster at the Provisional Theater (1875–78) and director of the Russian Orthodox Church Choir (1878–81). He wrote a large amount of INCIDENTAL MUSIC and SACRED MUSIC during this period, but most of it has been lost or was destroyed by the composer. With the success of his 3rd opera, *Nevěsta Messinská* (The Bride of Messina, after Schiller, 1882–83), Fibich concentrated more on opera and the once-popular genre of melodrama. His concert works in this genre were for reciter and accompaniment, either piano or orch. The positive reception of these works led to the composition of *Hippodamie* (1888–91), a staged melodrama

trilogy based on tragedies by Sophocles and Euripides, blending speech (without pitch or rhythmic specifications) with a richly orchestrated leitmotivic web. In addition to other operas—most notably *Šárka, Bouře* (The Tempest, after Shakespeare), *Hédy* (after Byron's *Don Juan*); and *Pád Arkuna*), Fibich also completed 3 symphonies, several tone poems and overtures (which influenced both the elder Smetana and the younger Dvořák), 200 songs (in German and Czech), chamber music, and a multitude of works for piano solo and 4 hands.

Fibich was a fine craftsman, a facile melodist, and one of the leading representatives of the Czech nationalist movement in music. Yet his extensive output reveals the pronounced influence of Weber, Schumann, and especially Wagner; it was not until his last works that a Czech sonority was apparent in his orchestration. As his music begins finally to gain an international reputation, it may be the most curious of his works that paves the way: *Nálady, dojmy a upomínky* (Moods, impressions, and reminiscences; 1892–99); a collection of 376 character pieces in the best 19th-century pianistic tradition, with 1 distinctive feature: the subject matter is Fibich's relationship with his mistress, piano student, and librettist Anežka Schulzová (1868–1905). Once the miniatures' coded titles were deciphered in the 1920s, it became clear that the pieces depict specific events, conversations, meetings, expressions of love, journeys, parts of Anežka's body, and her appearance in different sets of clothes. This diary also provided Fibich with a sourcebook for his later works, as well as an opportunity to resuscitate earlier music. The work was published in 4 volumes (the last posthumously); in a strange way, Fibich's collection parallels the late works of Janáček, also inspired by a younger woman, although one who merely tolerated the composer's attentions.

Fibonacci series. A sequence of numbers in which each is the sum of the preceding pair, i.e., 1,2,3,5,8,13,21. Composers such as Bartók used the sequence to predetermine the phrasing and metrical flow of some compositions.

fiddle (from Mid Eng. *fidel*). 1. A violin. 2. Any European bowed string instrument from the Middle Ages onward; usually applied to instruments that do not conform to standardized patterns. 3. A colloquial name for a violin, particularly one of rustic manufacture, or in reference to its use in traditional music. The fiddle is used in many European and American folk musics, and related instruments are found throughout the world. It would be undignified to call the

Fiddler from Harper's Ferry, Virginia

concertmaster of a sym. orch. a fiddler, but it would be incongruous to call the leading fiddle player in a traditional ensemble a concertmaster.

fiddle-bow. Bow.

Fiddler on the Roof. Musical by J. Bock and S. Harnick, 1964, based on stories by Sholom Aleichem. It is 1905 in pogrom-ridden Czarist Russia. Tevye and his wife attempt to marry off their daughters to wealthy Jews; the best they do is a tailor (in one case). One daughter even runs off with a Russian. The solution: emigrate to America. Including *Tradition, Matchmaker Matchmaker, Sunrise Sunset, If I Were A Rich Man*, and *To Life*.

fiddlestick. Bow.

Fidelio, oder Die eheliche Liebe (Conjugal Love). Only opera of Beethoven, 1805, 1st produced in Vienna; it is based on Bouilly's libretto *Léonore*, the title that Beethoven wished for his opera. Florestan is in a dungeon for his opposition to a tyrannical Spanish governor. His faithful wife, Leonore, enters the jail service in a boy's attire, taking the symbolic name Fidelio; she survives the jailer's daughter's crush on her. Political and marital virtue triumph when a new governor, announced by a resonant fanfare from backstage, orders the release of Florestan and the arrest of his tormentor. Beethoven, who revised the work several times, wrote 4 overtures for the opera; the 3 discarded overtures are called *Leonore* No. 1, No. 2, and No. 3. The same story was the basis of operas by Johann Simon Mayr (*L'Amor coniugale*, 1805) and Ferdinando Paer (*Leonora*, 1804).

fidula (Lat.; Mid Eng. *fidel*). Medieval fiddle.

Fiedler, Arthur, highly popular American conductor; b. Boston, Dec. 17, 1894; d. Brookline, Mass., July 10, 1979. Of a musical family, he studied violin with his father, Emanuel Fiedler, a member of the Boston Sym. Orch.; his uncle Benny Fiedler also played violin in the Boston Sym. Orch. In 1909 he was taken by his father to Berlin, where he studied violin with Willy Hess and attended a class on chamber music with Ernst von Dohnányi; he also had some instruction in conducting with Arno Kleffel and Rudolf Krasselt. In 1913 he formed the Fiedler Trio with 2 other Fiedlers.

In 1915, with war raging in Europe, he returned to America and joined the 2nd-violin section of the Boston Sym. Orch. under Karl Muck; later he moved to the viola section; he also doubled on the celesta when required. In 1924 he organized the Arthur Fiedler Sinfonietta, a professional ensemble of members of the Boston Sym. Orch. In 1929 he started a series of free open-air summer concerts at the Esplanade on the banks of the Charles River in Boston, presenting programs of popular American music intermingled with classical numbers. The series became a feature in Boston's musical life, attracting audiences of many thousands each summer. In 1930 Fiedler was engaged as conductor of the Boston Pops, which he led for nearly half a century. Adroitly combining pieces of popular appeal with classical works and occasional modern selections, he built an eager following, eventually elevating the Boston Pops to the status of a national institution. He was seemingly undisturbed by the clinking of beer steins, the pushing of chairs, the shuffling of feet, and other incidental sound effects not provided for in the score but which were an integral part of audience participation at Pops concerts.

Fiedler was a social man, gregarious, fond of extracurricular activities; one of his favorite pastimes was riding on fire engines; this addiction was rewarded by a number of nominations as honorary chief of the fire depts. of several American cities. He became commercially successful and willingly accepted offers to advertise for whiskey or for orange juice; this popularity, however, cost him a degradation to a lower rank of music-makers, so that his cherished ambition to conduct guest engagements in the regular subscription series of the Boston Sym. Orch. never materialized. In 1977 President Ford bestowed upon him the Medal of Freedom. As a mark of appreciation from the city of Boston, a footbridge near the Esplanade was named after him, with the 1st 2 notes of the Prelude to *Tristan und Isolde*, A and F, marking the initials of Arthur Fiedler's name, engraved on the plaque. His death was mourned by Boston music lovers in a genuine outpouring of public grief.

Field, John, remarkable Irish pianist and composer; b. Dublin, July 26, 1782; d. Moscow, Jan. 23, 1837. His father was a violinist; his grandfather, an organist; it was from his grandfather that he received his 1st instruction in music. At the age of 9 he began study with Tommaso Giordani, making his debut in Dublin in 1792. He went to London in 1793 and gave his 1st concert there that same year. He then had lessons with Clementi; was also employed in the salesrooms of Clementi's music establishment. He began his concert career in earnest with a notable series of successful appearances in London in 1800–1801. He then accompanied Clementi on his major tour of the Continent, beginning in 1802. After visiting Paris in 1802, they proceeded to St. Petersburg in 1803; there Field settled as a performer and teacher, giving his debut performance in 1804. He made many concert tours in Russia. Stricken with cancer of the rectum, he returned to London in 1831 for medical treatment. He performed at a Phil. Soc. concert there the following year; later that year he played in Paris, subsequently touring various cities in France, Belgium, Switzerland, and Italy until his health compelled him to abandon his active career. He eventually returned to Moscow, where he died.

Field's historical position as a composer is of importance, even though his music does not reveal a great original talent. He developed the free fantasias and piano recitative while following the basic precepts of Classic music; he was also the originator of keyboard nocturnes, which were models for Chopin. He composed 7 concertos, 4 sonatas, about 30 nocturnes, and polonaises, etc.; also a Quintet for piano and strings (1816) and 2 Divertimentos for piano, strings, and flute (c. 1810–11).

Fierabras. Opera by Schubert, 1823, premiered posthumously in 1897. In the time of King Arthur, Fierabras's sister Clorinde is having a love affair with a soldier.

fieramente (It.). Wildly, boldly.

Fiery Angel, The. Opera by Prokofiev, 1919, premiered posthumously in Venice, 1955. A mystical 16th-century girl becomes possessed by the vision of a former lover whom she identified as her guardian angel. Exorcism is initiated by the Grand Inquisitor, and when it fails, the unfortunate maiden is accused of carnal intercourse with the devil and is burned at the stake. The underlying satirical intent is suggested in the score by acrid harmonies and angular melodies.

fife. 1. An octave cross flute with 6 holes and without keys; compass d^2 to d^4. 2. A piccolo organ-stop.

fifteenth. 1. A double octave. 2. An organ stop of 2' pitch.

fifth. 1. An interval encompassing 5 diatonic degrees (see INTERVAL). 2. The 5th degree of any diatonic scale (the DOMINANT). *False 5th*, a diminished 5th.

Fifth Symphony

〰〰 〰〰 〰〰 〰〰 〰〰

Whenever music lovers speak of "the 5th Symphony," it is tacitly understood that the intended work is Beethoven's 5th, in which "fate knocks at the door." But did Beethoven really say anything like that in relation to the 4 portentous notes of the opening theme?

The story originated with Beethoven's biographer, Anton Schindler, but he was only 12 years old when the 5th Sym. was written. Czerny, who was very close to Beethoven, asserted that the motive was inspired by the call of the oriole or the goldfinch, the 2 birds which Beethoven often heard during his walks in the Vienna woods. And, again, if it were fate, would Beethoven not have orchestrated these notes with a flourish of trumpets or trombones? Yet he did not, preferring to open the sym. with 2 mild clarinets and strings. Furthermore, when we delve into Beethoven's many hesitant sketches for the opening movement of this sym., we find the "fate motive" curiously obfuscated. On the other hand there is the unmistakable evidence that Beethoven was obsessed with the rhythm of 3 short notes and 1 long note during the period when he composed the 5th. The figure occurs, and recurs, in the 4th Piano Concerto, in the *Appassionata* Sonata, and in the String Quartet, op. 74. Remarkably enough, these works are closely related to C minor, the tonality of the 5th Sym. In each case the 3 short notes are 8th notes.

Whatever the origin, the fate of the fate motive is awe-inspiring: During World War II the Allied Propaganda Service broadcast the fate motive to the Nazi-occupied continent of Europe to signal "*V* for Victory" in Morse Code, which happens to be 3 dots and a dash. The 2nd movement of the 5th Sym. is a gentle theme with variations. There follows a scherzo in triple time, and the fate motive makes its appearance once more, scanned persistently in the drums and, after a dynamic transition, explodes in thundering C major in the finale. The 1st performance of the 5th Sym. took place in Vienna (1808). The score is dedicated to Prince von Lobkowitz (the patron of music to whom the *Eroica Sym.* was assigned), and to Count Razumovsky, the Russian ambassador to Vienna.

Mendelssohn's 5th Sym., in D minor and given the surname *Reformation Sym.*, was 1st performed in Berlin, 1832.

As in practically all of Mendelssohn's syms., it is in 4 movements. It is called *Reformation* because the last movement is based on the Lutheran chorale *Ein' feste Burg.*

Tchaikovsky's 5th Sym. is, like his 4th Sym., dominated by the sense of fate. Tchaikovsky referred to this connection in his notebooks. It is remarkable that the opening theme is syncopated similarly to that of the 4th Sym. and that its range is limited to the 1st tetrachord of the minor scale, as is that of its predecessor. The 5th Sym. was 1st performed in St. Petersburg, 1888; together with his 4th and 6th Syms., it has become a standard orch.l work.

Mahler's 5th Sym., in C-sharp minor and sometimes nicknamed *The Giant*, was 1st performed in Cologne in 1904. It is in 5 sections, forming 3 larger movements. The 1st is funereal, passing suddenly to a stormy explosion of sound. The next section is an extended scherzo. It is followed by an adagietto and concludes with a rondo. The work's length inspired its nomination as *The Giant Sym.*, but Mahler specifically disavowed it. Analytically the conceptual structure of the work is remarkable for having sections in every major and minor key (24 in all), specifically marked by corresponding key signatures.

Other significant 5th syms. were composed by Schubert, Bruckner, Dvořák, Nielsen, Shostakovich, and Prokofiev.

figura (Lat.). A note.

figurae musicae (Lat.). Musical figures described by analogy with the rhetorical doctrine of figures; thus melodic turns and ornaments are compared with passages in literature. See also AFFECTS, DOCTRINE OF.

Figuralmusik (Ger.). A contrapuntal part embellished by melodic and harmonic figuration.

figuration. The adorning of melodic phrases and chords by rhythmic figures, arpeggios, passing notes, trills, changing notes, etc.

figure. A group of notes in a melody.

Figure humaine, Le. Cantata by Poulenc, 1945, for double chorus A CAPPELLA, to a symbolic text voicing the irresistible desire for liberty. Poulenc wrote it during the Nazi occupation of Paris; its 1st performance was given in London.

figured bass. BASSO CONTINUO.

filato (It.). Long, drawn out.

filer le son (*filer la voix*; Fr., spin out the sound or voice; It. *filar la voce, filo di voce*). In BEL CANTO vocalization, prolonging a tone with limited crescendo or diminuendo.

Fille du Regiment, La (The Daughter of the Regiment). Opera by Donizetti, 1840, 1st produced in Paris. A girl is brought up by a regiment of soldiers and serves as their army mascot. A crisis occurs when her aunt reclaims her and takes her to her castle. The soldiers lead an assault on her aunt's stronghold and she is reinstated as the "daughter of the regiment."

film music

~~ ~~ ~~ ~~ ~~

During the early years of motion-picture production, theater owners engaged a pianist or an organist to provide appropriate music for the moving images on the screen. The type of accompaniment generally followed the DOCTRINE OF AFFECTS. Romantic scenes called for sentimental salon music; themes of sadness were enhanced by passages in a mournful minor key. Danger and tragedy were depicted by chromatic runs harmonized by the diminished-7th chord, the ACCORDE DI STUPEFAZIONE. Realistic sound effects were provided behind the scene by a homemade rain machine, consisting of a wooden cylinder covered with a piece of rough cloth and rotated by a crank mechanism or a thunder machine, making rolling noise by rubbing corrugated metal plates over a washboard. Most silent-movie pianists were content with playing standard Classic or Romantic pieces within their meager repertory, but there were also truly inspired artists who improvised well-organized compositions, faithfully following the action on the screen. To aid silent-movie pianists and organists, special collections of sheet music were published with a table of contents indicating subject matter: gladness, sadness, madness, married felicity, faithless duplicity, infatuation, assassination, horse races, balloon ascension, et al., all garnished by traditional folk music of many lands.

Apart from such trivialities, respectable composers showed interest in writing scores for movie films, to be played by a movie pianist or to be recorded on the phonograph. One of the earliest cinema scores was composed in 1908 by Saint-Saëns for the French movie *L'Assassinat du Duc de Guise* and is scored for strings, piano, and harmonium. Another early film score, *Napoléon* by Honegger, was issued as an instrumental suite in 1922. The 1st application of a cinematographic scene to the theater was in Satie's ballet *Relâche*, produced in 1924. Other composers who contributed to the art of early film music were Antheil, Auric, Copland, Prokofiev, and Shostakovich. Even R. Strauss condescended to arrange his opera *Der Rosenkavalier* for a film.

With the advent of sound in motion pictures, specially composed background music was provided on the soundtrack. At 1st it consisted of recorded compositions of a popular genre. Quite frequently producers and directors engaged a "ghost" composer to write music according to specifications. Since most movie directors who appear in the list of credits on the screen as composers of musical scores could not read music, they usually engaged a musical amanuensis; their part in such "composition" consisted in whistling snatches of tunes or beating the desired rhythm. Thus Charlie Chaplin availed himself of the services of Eisler and Raksin for several of his films.

The most successful movie composers in Hollywood were not always the most talented or the most imaginative. Of these, the names of Max Steiner and Alfred Newman are outstanding; they enlarged the sonorities of the soundtrack to the dimensions of a full orch. which they conducted themselves; when their imagination flagged, they helped themselves by quotations, literal or garbled, from Wagner, Tchaikovsky, and Rachmaninoff. When Stravinsky came to America, an admirer tried to arrange for him to write a movie score. He submitted the offer to a movie mogul. "Stravinsky?" the mogul granted. "Yes, I've heard of him. How much will he charge?" "Well, $20,000," suggested the go-between. "$20,000?!" exclaimed the magnate. "For 5,000 more I can get Max Steiner!" Stravinsky never wrote a movie score. Before he emigrated to America, Schoenberg composed a score entitled *Accompaniment to a Cinema Scene*; it was subdivided into 3 sections, entitled *Threatening Danger*, *Anxiety*, and *Catastrophe*; Schoenberg, sincerely or derisively, tried to emulate the movie formula, but the score was nevertheless dodecaphonic. As dissonance was not exactly a kettle of fish for movie magnates, the score was never used.

An important contribution to film music was made by Erich Wolfgang Korngold, an erstwhile Viennese wunderkind who spent many years in Hollywood. His scores retain their purely musical significance even when detached from their visual counterpart. Bernard Herrmann successfully combined his theatrical sense with progressive techniques. Ernst Toch excelled in scores for movie mysteries. Raksin wrote numerous remarkable scores for the movies; concert suites from the films *Laura* and *The Bad and the Beautiful* are frequently performed by major sym. orchestras. Among other film composers, the names of Alex North, Virgil Thomson, Miklos Rozsa, and Jerry Goldsmith should be mentioned.

In films of futuristic content, ELECTRONIC MUSIC was supplied by several avant-garde composers, among them Ussachevsky and Ligeti (the latter involuntarily). John T. Williams became highly successful in providing music for films of blatant heroic content, including such science-fiction hits as *Star Wars* and *Close Encounters of the 3rd*

Kind. Henry Mancini specialized in theme songs calculated to appeal to the widest popular tastes. Although individual composers continue to provide entire soundtracks, many films use a selection of songs by various popular artists, hoping that at least one song will be a chart success and thereby increase business.

Composing for films usually requires precise synchronization with the changing images and actions on the screen; a technique was developed in which a click track provides a steady beat for performers, while a sound-editing device measures the exact duration of each scene in a picture. Digital technology has refined this process further.

finale. In instrumental music, the last movement of a composition. In opera or oratorio the finale is a summary of all major musical themes and the resolution of tangled threads of the plot. A *grand finale* is a choral conclusion with the participation of all principal characters. Wagner and his disciples regarded the finale as a musical supererogation, but composers of the non-Wagnerian ilk still find it useful to construct hell-raising finales, if for nothing else than for the sake of an effective catalyst for tumultuous applause.

fine (It.). End; close; indicates either the end of a repetition after a DA CAPO or DAL SEGNO, or the end of a piece.

Fine and Dandy. Musical by Kay Swift, 1930. The life of a fop who courts several women simultaneously and behaves rambunctiously in public. The title song survives.

Fingal's Cave. Concert overture by Mendelssohn, 1832, owing its inspiration to his 1829 visit to the Hebrides in Scotland during a concert tour. He was impressed by the somber dampness and mysterious surroundings of Fingal's Cave, and the result was an expertly fashioned piece in the darksome key of B minor. It was 1st performed in London.

finger cymbals. Miniature cymbals attached to the fingers; used by belly dancers as jingles and in 20th-century revivals of Renaissance ensembles.

fingerboard. The elongated, relatively narrow section on string instruments over which the strings are stretched. On the guitar there are frets spaced along the fingerboard which guide the player's fingers. Violins and other string instru-

ments are not equipped with frets, which is a pity, for such string fretting would spare the nervous fretting of those forced to listen to a young family prodigy practicing on the violin.

fingering (Ger. *Fingersatz,* fingering). 1. The method of applying the fingers to the keys, holes, strings, etc., of musical instruments. The art of fingering musical instruments assumed an educational importance in the 19th century, for contemporaneous editions of classical music, particularly for piano, rarely indicated what fingers to use and when. The task of fingering was left to editors—mostly German—of the classics published in annotated editions of the 19th century. Some established rules of standard piano fingering included not using the thumb on the black keys except in cases of dire necessity, as in F-sharp major arpeggios or in Chopin's "Black Key" Étude. The chromatic scale is fingered by pianists using the thumb and the index finger in alternation, and the middle finger when convenient. The problem of fingering on string instruments is not so complex, since the shifts of positions give the player ample opportunity for technical accommodation. 2. The marks guiding the performer in placing his fingers. *English fingering* (for the piano), where notes taken by the thumb are marked ×, with 1, 2, 3, 4 for the fingers; *German* (or *Continental) fingering*, notes for the thumb marked 1, and the fingers 2, 3, 4, 5.

Finian's Rainbow. Musical by B. Lane and Harburg, 1947. The Irishman Finian settles in the southeastern U.S. and buries a gold nugget. The leprechaun who actually owns it comes to retrieve it, performing a few miracles in the process. Includes *Something Sort of Grandish* and *Old Devil Moon.*

Finlandia. Symphonic poem by Sibelius, 1900, written for his home country before its independence from Russia. When it was premiered, it was called *Suomi*, Finnish for "Finland."

fino (It.). Till; up to; as far as.

Finta Giardiniera, La (The Dissembling Gardener). Opera buffa by Mozart, 1775. An amorous marquise is snubbed by the count she seeks, so she takes on the disguise of a municipal gardener; further intrigues eventually lead to her success.

Fiorello! Musical by Jerry Bock, 1959. A rhapsodic glorification of the former New York mayor Fiorello La Guardia, the "little flower" (1933–45), ending with his 1st election to the post. Includes *Politics and Poker*.

fioretti (It., little flowers). Ornaments.

fioritura (It., floral decoration; plural *fioriture*). An embellishment; an ornamental turn, flourish, or phrase, introduced into a melody. It was a common practice for Italian singers to embellish their arias with arpeggios, gruppetti, and trills, often obscuring the main melodic line by such florid ornamentation. A story is told about Adelina Patti, who as a young girl sang for Rossini one of his own arias. Rossini was voluble in praise of her singing. "But, pray, who is the composer of this aria?" he inquired. In modern times, no prima donna would presume to go beyond the printed text of an aria except in cadenzas. Toscanini was known to explode in flowery Italian invective when a singer added as much as an unauthorized appoggiatura to his or her solo.

fipple flute. Renaissance end-blown vertical flute or recorder; the word is derived from fipple, a plug in the mouthpiece.

Fire and Rain. A 1970 hit for singer/songwriter James Taylor that established his reputation.

Fire Symphony (Ger. *Feuersymphonie*). Sym. No. 59 by Haydn, 1769, in A major. Who gave this name to the work, when, and why are a mystery, but perhaps the music has some connection with the play *The Conflagration* that was presented at Esterház where Haydn was employed.

Firebird, The (Fr. *L'Oiseau de feu*). Stravinsky's 1st ballet, 1910, produced by Diaghilev's Ballets Russes in Paris. Like his predecessors, Stravinsky draws upon Russian folklore for this score. The firebird gives the heroic Ivan Tsarevich a fiery feather as a reward for his letting it go free after capture; the feather is a magic wand that helps Ivan when he himself is captured by the evil magician Kashchey. The infernal dance of the finale is bewitching in its angular rhythms.

In 1937, Warner Bros. made a film entitled *The Firebird*, featuring a profligate roué who plays a phonograph recording of the piece and so impresses a virginal maiden who lives on the floor below that she falls into his arms and is promptly deflowered. Stravinsky sued the film company for defamation of character but the French judge could not understand why Stravinsky became so exercised about it. "Mais c'est le plus grand compliment du monde pour un compositeur quand sa musique peut seduire!" Stravinsky was awarded the token sum of 1 French franc for the "moral damage" he suffered.

Fireworks. Orch. work by Stravinsky, 1908, written on the occasion of the wedding of the daughter of his revered teacher Rimsky-Korsakov. It was 1st performed in St. Petersburg. The score is very much in the tradition of the Russian national school, but its brilliant sparks of rhythmic fire presage the Stravinsky of the future.

Fireworks Music (or *The Musick for the Royal Fireworks*). Orch.1 suite by Handel, 1749, written to celebrate the Peace of Aix-la-Chapelle, ending the protracted and tedious war of the Austrian Succession (also known as King George's War). It was 1st performed at Green Park, London. Peace is portrayed by a modest SICILIANA, followed by a fast march entitled, quite properly, *La Réjouissance*, scored for a huge orch.

first. 1. Of voices and instruments of the same class, the highest, as 1st soprano, 1st violin. 2. On the staff, the lowest, as 1st line, 1st space. 3. The 1st string of an instrument is the highest.

First Time Ever I Saw Your Face. Romantic love ballad by Scottish folksinger Ewan MacColl, became a megahit for soulster Roberta Flack in 1972.

Fis (Ger.). F-sharp.

Fis dur (Ger.). F-sharp major.

Fis moll (Ger.). F-sharp minor.

Fischer, Edwin, eminent Swiss pianist, conductor, and pedagogue; b. Basel, Oct. 6, 1886; d. Zurich, Jan. 24, 1960. He studied with Hans Huber in Basel and Martin Krause in Berlin; then taught at the Stern Cons. in Berlin (1905–14); taught at the Berlin Hochschule für Musik from 1931; between 1926 and 1932 he was also engaged as a conductor in Lübeck, Munich, and Berlin. In 1942 he returned to Switzerland. He was renowned as one of the most intellectual pianists of his time and a distinguished pedagogue. He founded the Edwin-Fischer-Stiftung to assist needy and young musicians. He also publ. several valuable books on music.

Fischer, Johann Caspar Ferdinand, significant German composer; b. *c.* 1665; d. Rastatt, Aug. 27, 1746. He was in the service of the Margrave of Baden (1696–1716), and continued when the court moved to Rastatt in 1716. He adopted Lully's style in his compositions, and thereby influenced other German composers. His *Ariadne musica neo-organoedum* (1702), a collection of 20 organ preludes and fugues in 20 different keys, foreshadowed Bach's *Well-Tempered Clavier.*

Fischer-Dieskau, (Albert) Dietrich, celebrated German baritone; b. Berlin, May 28, 1925. The surname of the family was orig. Fischer; his paternal grandmother's maiden surname of Dieskau was legally conjoined to it in 1937. His father, a philologist and headmaster, was self-taught in music; his mother was an amateur pianist. He began to study piano at 9 and voice at 16; he then studied voice with Hermann Weissenborn at the Berlin Hochschule für Musik (1942–43). In 1943 he was drafted into the German army. He was made a prisoner of war by the Americans while serving in Italy in 1945; upon his release in 1947 he returned to Germany and made his 1st professional appearance as a soloist in the Brahms Requiem in Badenweiler. He continued his vocal training with Weissenborn in Berlin, where he soon was heard on radio broadcasts over the RIAS. In 1948 he made his operatic debut in the bass role of Colas in an RIAS broadcast of Mozart's *Bastien und Bastienne;* later that year he made his stage debut as Rodrigo, Marquis of Posa, in *Don Carlos* at the Berlin Städtische Oper, where he remained an invaluable member for 35 years. He also pursued his operatic career with appearances at leading opera houses and festivals in Europe.

It was as a lieder and concert artist, however, that he became universally known. In 1955 he made his U.S. debut with the Cincinnati Sym. Orch.; his U.S. recital debut followed at N.Y.'s Town Hall (1955). In subsequent years he made tours all over the world to enormous critical acclaim.

His finest operatic roles included Count Almaviva, Don Giovanni, Papageno, Macbeth, Falstaff, Hans Sachs, Mandryka, Mathis der Maler, and Wozzeck. He created the role of Mittenhofer in Henze's *Elegy for Young Lovers* (1961), and the title role in Reimann's *Lear* (1978).

His honors include membership in the Berlin Akademie der Künste (1956), the Mozart Medal of Vienna (1962), Kammersänger of Berlin (1963), the Grand Cross of Merit of the Federal Republic of Germany (1978), honorary doctorates from Oxford Univ. (1978) and the Sorbonne in Paris (1980), and the Gold Medal of the Royal Phil. Soc. of London (1988). He was married to the soprano Julia Varady. Fischer-Dieskau brought the LIED into the modern phonographic age, with his superb recordings of virtually the entire Schubert oeuvre and other important lied composers. He publ. anthologies of song texts and studies of the art of singing.

fischio (It.). A whistle.

fish horn. Colloquial American term for the oboe; common since the middle of the 19th century, to judge by a remarkable order issued by Vice Admiral Porter of the U.S. Naval Academy in Annapolis, Md., dated 1867: "Midshipman Thompson (1st class), who plays so abominably on a fish horn, will oblige me by going outside the limits when he wants to practice or he will find himself coming out of the little end of the horn."

Fisis (Ger.). F double-sharp.

Fistel (*Fistelstimme;* Ger.). FALSETTO.

fistula (Lat., pipe). In the Middle Ages, an organ pipe. *Fistula anglia,* in the Middle Ages, the English flute, i.e., the recorder; *fistula germanica,* in the Middle Ages, the German flute, i.e., the transverse flute.

Fitzgerald, Ella, remarkable African-American jazz singer; b. Newport News, Va., Apr. 25, 1917; d. Beverly Hills, June 17, 1996. She began singing in small clubs in Harlem in the early 1930s; discovered by Chick Webb (one of Harlem's most popular musicians) in 1935, she joined his band; upon his death in 1939, she became its leader; in 1942 she became a freelance singer and subsequently worked with most major jazz musicians and groups. She was particularly adept at scat singing and improvising, frequently creating new melodies over given harmonies, much in the manner of a jazz instrumentalist. Stylistically she was equally at ease in swing and bebop; developing over the years a superlative blend of musicianship, vocal ability, and interpretive insight, she achieved a popularity and respect rarely acquired by jazz singers. In 1987 she was awarded the National Medal of Arts. Her recordings of the "songbooks" of Porter, Ellington, Gershwin, Arlen, Berlin, Kern, Mercer, and Rodgers and Hart are a cornerstone of her legacy.

Five Foot Two, Eyes of Blue. Song by Ray Henderson, 1925. Used in the 1952 film *Has Anybody Seen My Gal?*

Five Orchestral Pieces (Schoenberg). Fünf Orchesterstücke.

Five Pieces for Orchestra. A remarkable set of pieces by Webern, 1911. They are extremely aphoristic; one of them comprises 6 measures, lasts 19 seconds, and is scored for clarinet, trumpet, trombone, mandolin, celesta, harp, drum, violin, and viola, each of these entering alone and thus creating a chain of sounds that may be described as a melody of timbres (Farbenmelodie). Yielding to the temptation of forming symbolic or psychological associations, Webern at 1st attached descriptive titles to each of the pieces: *Urbild, Werwandlung, Rückkehr, Erinnerung, Die Seele* (Initial Idea, Metamorphosis, Return, Recollection, The Soul). Upon sober reflection he rescinded them. Webern conducted its 1st performance in Zurich in 1926.

fixed Do. A system of solmization based on equivalence, e.g., in which the tone C, and all its chromatic derivatives (C♯, C♭, C×, C♭♭) are called Do; D and its derivatives are called Re, etc., no matter what key or harmony in which they may appear. The opposite of movable Do.

fixed-tone instrument. An instrument (e.g., piano, organ) the pitch of whose tones cannot be modified at will while playing; such an instrument is said to have "fixed intonation," unlike the violin and saxophone.

flag. A hook (♪) on the stem of a note: ♪ ♪ ♪ etc.

flageolet (Fr.). 1. A small fipple flute or recorder used in the Renaissance to imitate birdcalls. It was used as a sopranino flute in ensembles until the 19th century. The French flageolet has a compass of 2 octaves and 3 semitones, from g¹ to b³. 2. A small flute stop in the organ, of 1' or 2' pitch.

flageolet-tones. See harmonics.

Flagstad, Kirsten (Malfrid), celebrated Norwegian soprano; b. Hamar, July 12, 1895; d. Oslo, Dec. 7, 1962. She studied voice with her mother and with Ellen Schytte-Jacobsen in Christiania; made her operatic debut there as Nuri in d'Albert's *Tiefland* (Dec. 12, 1913). During the next 2 decades, she sang throughout Scandinavia, appearing in operas and operettas, and in concert. In 1933 she sang a number of minor roles at Bayreuth, then scored her 1st major success there in 1934 when she appeared as Sieglinde. She made an auspicious Metropolitan Opera debut in N.Y. in that same role (1935) and was soon hailed as the foremost Wagnerian soprano of her time. In 1936 she made her 1st appearance at London's Covent Garden, as Isolde. While continuing to sing at the Metropolitan Opera she made guest appearances at the San Francisco Opera (1935–38) and the Chicago Opera (1937), and also gave concerts with major U.S. orchs.

She returned to her Nazi-occupied homeland in 1941 to be with her husband, a decision that alienated many of her admirers. Nevertheless, after World War II she resumed her career with notable success at Covent Garden. In 1951 she returned to the Metropolitan Opera, where she sang Isolde and Leonore; made her farewell appearance there in Gluck's *Alceste* on Apr. 1, 1952. She retired from the operatic stage in 1954 but continued to make recordings; from 1958 to 1960 she was director of the Norwegian Opera in Oslo. Among her other celebrated roles were Brünnhilde, Elisabeth, Elsa, and Kundry.

flamenco. Popular Andalusian art of singing and dancing, accompanied mainly by guitar and castanets, which gradually developed into an important folk art form. Pedrell and Falla played crucial roles in the survival of flamenco through the special festivals they organized. The meters and rhythms are varied and often polymetric and cross-rhythmic. Scales are modal or mixed modal. The lyrics, influenced by Gypsy motives, reflect the nomadic sentiments of love, fortune, sorrow, and death. Principal genres of flamenco singing are known: cante jondo (deep song), with microtonal inflections, and cante chico (small song). The singing is usually introduced by the stimulating exclamations "Ay! Ay!" and accompanied by vigorous heel stamping and passionate gesticulation. When the singing is accompanied by footstamping, the dance is called *zapateado* (shoe dance).

Flanagan, Tommy (Lee), African-American jazz pianist; b. Detroit, Mar. 16, 1930. He commenced clarinet studies at 6 and piano training at 11, working throughout his adolescence in local jazz haunts with various senior musicians, including Milt Jackson, Thad Jones, and Elvin Jones. In 1956 he went to N.Y., where he subsequently was pianist and music director for Ella Fitzgerald; also performed with Oscar Pettiford, J. J. Johnson, Miles Davis, and others.

flat. The character ♭, placed before a note to indicate lowering its pitch by a semitone; the double flat (♭♭) lowers its note by 2 semitones.

flat chord. A chord whose tones are performed simultaneously; a SOLID chord, as opposed to BROKEN.

flat fifth (flat 5). Diminished 5th.

flat pick. A triangle-shaped plectrum, made of tortoise shell or plastic, used for guitar and other instrumental picking in bluegrass and related American music. A heavier-weight pick is used for electric string instruments.

Flatt, Lester (Raymond), American country-music singer and guitarist; b. Overton County, Tenn., June 19, 1914; d. Nashville, May 11, 1979. He joined Bill Monroe's Blue Grass Boys as a singer in 1944; then formed a duo with Earl Scruggs, the banjo player; they organized their own band, the Foggy Mountain Boys, and soon established themselves as leading figures in country music. Flatt became famous for his "Lester Flatt G Run" on the guitar, accompanied by Scruggs's 3-finger banjo style. After their partnership came apart in 1969, Flatt played with the remaining members of the band, which later adopted the name the Nashville Brass. Among the best-known songs of Flatt and Scruggs were *Roll in My Sweet Baby's Arms*, *Old Salty Dog Blues*, *The Ballad of Jed Clampett* (from the inane television comedy series *The Beverly Hillbillies*), and *Foggy Mountain Breakdown* (the theme song of the film *Bonnie and Clyde*).

Flatterzunge (Ger.). Flutter-tonguing.

flautando (It., like a flute). 1. A sound imitating the flute's sonority, especially on the strings. 2. A direction in bowed string music to play near the fingerboard so as to produce this sound; the Italian direction for this effect is *sulla tastiera* (Fr. *sur la touche*; Ger. *am Griffbrett*).

flauto (It.; Ger. *Flöte*). 1. Flute. 2. The name of organ stops, as *Flauto amabile*, etc.

flauto a becco (It.). RECORDER.

flauto di Pane (It.). PANPIPE.

flauto diritto (It.). RECORDER.

flauto dolce (It.). RECORDER.

flauto piccolo or ottavino (It.). PICCOLO.

flauto traverso (It.). TRANSVERSE FLUTE.

Fleadh Cheoil. An annual late-summer music festival in County Kerry, Ireland, featuring singing and indigenous Irish instruments and music.

flebile (It.). Tearful; plaintive, mournful.

Fledermaus, Die (The Bat). Operetta by J. Strauss, Jr., 1874, 1st performed in Vienna. The bat of the title is the costume used by one of the characters at a masked ball. An Austrian baron who is sentenced to prison for a petty offense eludes the police and goes to a masked ball. His wife, suspicious of his conduct, goes to the same ball disguised as a Hungarian countess. Not recognizing her physical attributes, the baron flirts with her. A series of mistaken identities reaches its climax when the baron exchanges clothes with his own lawyer and enters the jail in order to extract a confession from another suspect and clear himself. A happy ending is vouchsafed when all jail sentences are suspended and guests from the masked ball join the principals to drink a toast in praise of champagne, the king of wines. No matter how impenetrable the plot is, particularly to non-Austrians, *Die Fledermaus* enjoys success everywhere.

flehend (Ger.). Pleading, praying.

Fleisher, Leon, distinguished American pianist, conductor, and teacher; b. San Francisco, July 23, 1928, of Jewish-Russian immigrant parents. His father was a tailor; his mother a singing teacher. He received the rudiments of music from his mother, then studied piano with Lev Shorr. He played in public at the age of 6; was sent to Europe for studies with Artur Schnabel at Lake Como, Italy; continued his studies with Schnabel in N.Y. At the age of 14 he appeared as soloist in the Liszt A-major Piano Concerto with the San Francisco Sym. Orch.; at 16 he was soloist with the N.Y. Phil. (1944); in 1952 he became the 1st American to win 1st prize at the Queen Elisabeth of Belgium International Competition in Brussels; this catapulted him into a brilliant career. He made several European tours; also gave highly successful recitals in South America. In 1961–62 he was a soloist with the San Francisco Sym. Orch. to observe its 50th anniversary.

At the peak of his career a pianistic tragedy befell him; in 1964 he was stricken with a mysterious and mystifying neurological ailment that made the fingers of his right hand curl up on themselves, completely incapacitating him as a pianist; this condition was diagnosed as carpal tunnel syndrome. Disabled as he was, Fleisher turned to piano works written for left hand alone commissioned to Ravel, Prokofiev, and others by Paul Wittgenstein, the Austrian pianist who lost his right arm during World War I. Fleisher learned these concertos and performed them successfully. He also began to conduct. He had studied conducting with Pierre Monteux in San Francisco and at the conducting school established by Monteux in Hancock, Maine; he also profited from advice from George Szell. In 1968 he became artistic director of the Theater Chamber Players in Washington, D.C.; in 1970 he became music director of the Annapolis Sym. Orch. as well. From 1973 to 1977 he was associate conductor of the Baltimore Sym. Orch.; then was its resident conductor in 1977–78. He appeared as a guest conductor at the Mostly Mozart Festival in N.Y., and also with the Boston Sym., San Francisco Sym., Cincinnati Sym., and the Los Angeles Chamber Orch.

A treatment with cortisone injections and even acupuncture and the fashionable biofeedback to control the electrophysiological motor system did not help. In 1981 he decided to undergo surgery; it was momentarily successful, and in 1982 he made a spectacular comeback as a bimanual pianist, playing the *Symphonic Variations* by Franck with Sergiu Comissiona and the Baltimore Sym. Orch. In 1985 he became artistic director-designate of the Berkshire Music Center at Tanglewood, and he fully assumed the duties of artistic director in 1986. Fleisher devoted much time to teaching; he joined the faculty of the Peabody Cons. of Music in Baltimore in 1959 and subsequently was named to the Andrew W. Mellon Chair in Piano; he was also a visiting prof. at the Rubin Academy of Music in Jerusalem. Among his brilliant pupils were André Watts and Lorin Hollander.

fleurettes (Fr., little flowers). In contrapuntal parts, rapid notes, sometimes printed in small type.

flexatone (It. *flessatone*). A 20th-century instrument consisting of a metal plate attached to a piece of wood. It produces a twanging, imprecisely pitched sound when the metal plate is plucked. Schoenberg used the instrument in his *Variations for Orch.* and *Moses und Aron*.

flexible notation. A modern type of notation which allows some aspect of a composition to be determined in performance.

Fliegende Holländer, Der. FLYING DUTCHMAN, THE.

fliessend (Ger.). Fluidly, floatingly.

fling. A Scottish dance resembling the reel, in quadruple time.

flores (Lat., flowers; It. *fioretti, fiori*). In the Middle Ages, embellishments in vocal and instrumental music. The insertion of supernumerary notes above and below the melody notes was named *florificatio*. Usually such embellishments were added to the DISCANT, but sometimes even the presumably unalterable CANTUS FIRMUS was adorned by florid ornamentation with *pulchrae ascensiones et descensiones*. Such "pretty ups and downs" were also called *licentiae* (acts of licentiousness) and *elegantiae* (elegancies). All these attractive descriptions have unfortunately become obsolete, ultimately being replaced by generic designations of ornaments.

florid. Embellished with runs, passages, figures, graces, etc.

Flöte (Ger.). 1. A flute. 2. Organ stop with a flute timbre.

Flotow, Friedrich (Adolf Ferdinand) **von,** famous German opera composer; b. Teutendorf, Apr. 27, 1813; d. Darmstadt, Jan. 24, 1883. He was a scion of an old family of nobility; he received his 1st music lessons from his mother; then was a chorister in Gustrow. At the age of 16 he went to Paris, where he entered the Cons. to study piano with J. P. Pixis and composition with Reicha. After the revolution of 1830, he returned home, where he completed his 1st opera, *Pierre et Catherine*, set to a French libretto; it was premiered in a German trans. in Ludwigslust in 1835. Returning to Paris, he collaborated with the Belgian composer Albert Grisar on the operas *Lady Melvil* (1838) and *L'eau merveilleuse* (1839). With the composer Auguste Pilati he composed the opera *Le Naufrage de la Méduse* (Paris, 1839). He scored a decisive acclaim with his romantic opera *Alessandro*

Stradella, based on the legendary accounts of the life of the Italian composer; it was 1st performed in Hamburg (1844) and had numerous subsequent productions in Germany.

He achieved an even greater success with his romantic opera *Martha, oder Der Markt zu Richmond* (1847); in it he demonstrated his ability to combine the German sentimental spirit with Italian lyricism and Parisian elegance. The libretto was based on a ballet, *Lady Henriette, ou La Servante de Greenwich* (1844), for which Flotow had composed the music for act I; the authentic Irish melody *The Last Rose of Summer* was incorporated into the opera by Flotow, lending a certain nostalgic charm to the whole work. Flotow's aristocratic predilections made it difficult for him to remain in Paris after the revolution of 1848; he accepted the post of Intendant at the grand ducal court theater in Schwerin (1855–63); then moved to Austria; he returned to Germany in 1873, settling in Darmstadt in 1880.

flottant (Fr.). Floatingly.

flourish. A trumpet fanfare or call.

Flower Drum Song. Musical by Rodgers and Hammerstein, 1958. A modern male Chinese-American must choose between a San Francisco nightclub performer and an innocent imported from the homeland. After many complications, he chooses the latter. Includes *A Hundred Million Miracles, Chop Suey*, and *I Enjoy Being a Girl*.

Floyd, Carlisle (Sessions, Jr.), American composer; b. Latta, S.C., June 11, 1926. He studied at Syracuse Univ. with Ernst Bacon (Mus.B., 1946; Mus.M., 1949); also took private piano lessons with Rudolf Firkusny and Sidney Foster. In 1947 he joined the staff of the School of Music of Florida State Univ., Tallahassee; in 1976 he became a prof. of music at the Univ. of Houston. His best-known musical drama is *Susannah* (Tallahassee, 1955); it received the N.Y. Music Critics' Circle Award as the best opera of the year. Floyd's other works include several musical plays and operas, a ballet, song cycles, and other vocal and instrumental pieces.

flüchtig (Ger.). Flightily, hastily; lightly, airily.

Flügel (Ger., wing). The grand pianoforte or harpsichord, so-called because of its winged shape.

flügelhorn (Fr. *bugle*; It. *flicorno soprano*). Originally, an unvalved hunting horn in 18th-century Germany; this instrument became known as the BUGLE. In the early 19th century keys were added to the bugle to create the keyed bugle. By the middle of the century the term *flügelhorn* was applied to a similar instrument with cornet range and valves. It is used more in military music and jazz than in classical music.

flüsternd (Ger.). Whispering.

flute

The most ancient wind instrument, spontaneously evolved by populations in all parts of the world, from Mesopotamia to the Andes, from China to Central Africa. Primitive flutes were all vertical pipes, of the type that later came to be called recorders. They were made of baked clay or reeds with perforated holes which would change the pitch when 1 or several of them were covered by a finger. The OCARINA (It. *oca*, goose) is essentially a flute, but it looks like a surrealist sculpture of a goose; hence the name.

Musical mythology is strewn with the appearance of the flute. When the cloven-footed god of the woods, Pan, pursued the nymph Syrinx, she was turned into a reed to escape him. Heartbroken, Pan made a panpipe of reeds to commemorate his beloved. In pre-Columbian South America, Indians made flutes out of bones, samples of which are still extant. There is a legend of a Peruvian Indian whose beloved died young. Disconsolate, he went to her place of burial, exhumed one of her legs, and fashioned a flute out of her tibia bone. He played wistful pentatonic melodies upon it, and this intimate contact with a part of the body of his beloved gave him temporary surcease from his sorrow. The Pied Piper of Hamelin lured away the town children on their fateful journey by playing on his flute. In Mozart's opera *The Magic Flute*, the hero is preserved from disaster by playing a tune on a melodious flute.

In poetry, flutes are forever sweet, soft, and pure. Milton speaks in *Paradise Lost* of "flutes and soft recorders moving in perfect phalanx." Swinburne poetizes about "the pure music of the flutes of Greece." In a grim Grimm tale, a young prince is slain by his brothers in a rivalry for the throne. A shepherd finds one of his whitened bones, makes holes in it, and plays upon it. The bone-flute tells the story of the unbrotherly deed. Mahler set this tale to music in his choral work *Das klagende Lied*.

17th-century flute player

The flute seems to embody the legendary harmony of the spheres, for it is laden with rich overtones; an attentive ear can discern even the nontempered 7th partial tone when playing in its low register. The flute is the heavenly bird of the sym. and opera. Birds of the forest speak to Siegfried in Wagner's *Ring* through the voice of the flutes. Stravinsky's *Firebird* is a flute; so is the helpful bird in Prokofiev's *Peter and the Wolf*. It is the flute that sings the part of the nightingale in Beethoven's *Pastoral Sym.* and in Stravinsky's *Le Chant du rossignol*. The flute is the most agile of wind instruments, capable of skipping from one note to another with the greatest of ease. It mates in perfect harmony with the human voice. When Lucia goes mad in Donizetti's opera, she sings her poignant FIORITURE accompanied by a solo flute.

But with all these advantages the flute did not become a concert instrument until the 18th century. The new flute was the transverse (horizontal, cross) flute, in which the sound is produced by blowing across the side holes. Since it was 1st introduced in Germany, the TRANSVERSE FLUTE became known as the German flute, while the RECORDER, greatly popular in England, acquired the sobriquet of the English flute. The transverse flute came of age when Quantz, the court musician to Frederick the Great (who, incidentally, was the finest flutist among royalty), published

in 1752 his famous treatise on the art of playing the *flute traversière*, as it was known in French. In symphonic works flute parts are frequently used in pairs, like their fellow wind instruments the oboes, clarinets, bassoons, horns, and trumpets. The use of a single flute in a symphonic score, as in Beethoven's 4th Sym., is an exception. Concertos for flute were written by Quantz, Handel, and Mozart.

In the 19th century Theobald Boehm, the great German flute manufacturer, enhanced the technique of flute playing by producing a new system of fingering and rearranging positions of the keys. Boehm's orch.l flute has a tube of cylindrical bore with 14 ventages closed by keys; it is blown through an oval orifice near the upper end. Having been made of wood for centuries, flutes began to be manufactured from alloys of silver; this permitted the flute to compete dynamically with the ever-increasing Western orch. Rich amateurs owned flutes made of gold; the modern French flutist Georges Barrère had a flute made of platinum, and Edgard Varèse wrote a piece for him entitled *Density 21.5*, which is the density of platinum. Brahms assigned a pastoral solo in the finale of his 1st Sym. to the flute. French composers have been particularly fond of the instrument. Debussy wrote a piece for flute solo entitled *Syrinx* in honor of the nymph so persistently pursued by Pan. His *Prélude à l'après-midi d'un faune* opens with a solo flute.

Like all wind instruments, flutes are members of a family. The range of the modern flute (concert flute; Fr. *grande flute*; Ger. *grosse Flöte*; It. *flauto*) extends from middle C through 3 octaves ($c^1–c^4$), but it can be overblown to produce the high C-sharp, D, and even E flat (e^{b4}). In modern flutes a special key is provided to produce the low B (b). The range of the PICCOLO is an octave higher than the regular flute, but it lacks the C and C-sharp in its low register. It can blow through 3 octaves, and its high C (c5) is of the same pitch as the highest note on the piano; no other instrument can rise to such stratospheric heights. Beethoven introduced the piccolo in the finale of his 5th Sym. The ALTO FLUTE is a 4th below the regular concert flute; a transposing instrument, it is also known as flute in G. Ravel's ballet *Daphnis et Chloé* has an important part for the alto flute, which invokes the spirit of Pan. The BASS FLUTE is an elephantine low-voice member, with the range starting an octave below the standard flute (c). It is a long instrument and requires considerable lung power to blow and superlative lip technique to articulate. The Parisian-American composer Betsy Jolas wrote a piece for piccolo and bass flute.

There is also a monster of a flute, the *double-bass flute*, which theoretically ought to produce a sound 2 octaves below the concert flute. But when an American manufacturer of the double-bass flute presented a demonstration of it at a congress of flutists, he blew and blew into it without making even a wheeze. The *flûte d'amour* may also be mentioned; in Italian it is *flauto d'amore*, and in German *Lieblichflöte*; there is no English name for it, which is just as well, since it would be ludicrous to call it a "love flute." It was introduced in the late 18th century, is pitched a minor 3rd below the concert flute, and is more or less obsolete.

Avant-garde composers, annoyed by the sweet sounds of the flute, have tried their best (or their worst) to improve upon it by instructing the players to blow through the flute without producing a recognizable pitch, or to clap the keys without blowing. Double-tonguing and triple-tonguing, known as *Flatterzunge* (flutter-tongue) technique are favorites in modern flute parts; unnatural harmonics have also been coaxed out of it. In the last quarter of the 20th century the flute has been incorporated into rock and jazz groups, which make up for the flute's anatomical weakness by amplifying it electronically.

flute à bec. RECORDER.

flute, direct. RECORDER.

flute stop. A flue stop; formerly a flute, now a string stop.

flutter-tongue (Ger. *Flatterzunge, Zungenschlag*; It. *frullato*; Fr. *coup de langue*). A special effect on the flute and occasionally other wind instruments consisting of the rapid insertion of the tongue in the keyhole, resulting in a staccato: single (performed t-t-t . . .), double (performed t-k/t-k/t-k/. . .), and triple (performed t-k-t/t-k-t/t-k-t/ . . .). Another technique is to roll the tongue as if trying to pronounce the liquid consonants *l* and *r*. It is vulgarly known among wind players as the "French kiss." The technique has been known since the early 18th century but was eschewed in actual playing as being indecent; not until the modern music of 2 centuries later did it come to be widely applied.

Fluxus. New York art coalition (1962–78), loosely run by the architect George Macunias, that gave birth to highly original, mostly theatrical, and often humorous mixed-media stage works frequently involving novel uses of sound; musical scores could be in the form of written instructions or graphs. Among those associated with Fluxus are La Monte Young, Yoko Ono, Dick Higgins, Alison Knowles, Nam June Paik, Jackson Mac Low, Robert Watts, and George Brecht.

Flying Dutchman, The (*Der fliegende Holländer*). Opera by Wagner, 1843, 1st produced in Dresden. The libretto is by Wagner himself after an old legend. Originally Wagner wrote a libretto for an opera, LE VAISSEAU FANTÔME; when another opera of the same name by Louis Dietsch (1808–65) failed, Wagner returned to the legend, rewrote the libretto, and created a minor masterpiece. *The Flying Dutchman* is the name of a ship on which a mariner is doomed to sail until he finds a woman of absolute devotion. Stormy seas drive the ship off course to a Norwegian fjord. The voyager hears a Norwegian girl sing a ballad about the doomed ship; he realizes that she would redeem him. But in her eagerness she leaps toward the ship from a cliff and perishes. Her sacrifice is his redemption, and together they are lifted to the skies.

foco (It.). FUOCO.

Foggy Day in London Town, A. Song by Gershwin, 1937, from the film *A Damsel in Distress*, later resurrected by Frank Sinatra.

foglietto (It., little leaf). 1. First violin part of an orch. 2. Score in which cues for other instruments are written in, helping a player to become oriented within the entire ensemble.

foglio (It., leaf). Page; folio.

Foley, "Red" (Clyde Julian), American country-music singer; b. Blue Lick, Ky., June 17, 1910; d. Fort Wayne, Ind.,

Sept. 19, 1968. He studied briefly at Georgetown (Ky.) College; in 1937 formed the *Renfro Valley Barn Dance* radio program; appeared regularly at the Grand Ole Opry in Nashville. He made popular such country-music classics as *Chattanooga Shoeshine Boy*, *Peace in the Valley*, and *Beyond the Sunset*. In 1967 he was elected to the Country Music Hall of Fame in recognition of his prominent place among modern country-music performers. He died while on tour with the Grand Ole Opry.

Folgend (Ger., following). COLLA PARTE; COLLA VOCE.

folia (Sp.; It. *follia*; Eng. *folly*). A Portuguese dance that originated about 1500, used in popular festivals and theatrical performances, always with singing and accompanied by a rhythmic hand clapping and clacking of castanets. The strange name pointed at an apparently orgiastic type of the dance, particularly in its Spanish form. One Spanish writer of the early 17th century describes the action of the dancers as if "they abandoned all reason." In later theoretical references the folia was usually coupled with sarabandes and chaconnes; 2 related but distinct folias were popular with classical composers from the late 16th century up to Rachmaninoff and beyond. Actually, the folia has very little madness in it; it is a rather stately rhythmic dance in triple time with a long 2nd beat, usually in a minor mode.

folk music. 1. TRADITIONAL MUSIC, passed down through the generations by oral transmission; music indigenous to a people, region, state, or country, often modal and with a variety of rhythmic and metric approaches. 2. In subsequent compositional use, such music in simple arrangement; as material for imitation; and as subject for analysis and reinterpretation. See also FOLK SONG.

folk song. Indigenous song of a people, region, state, or country, passed down through the generations by oral transmissions. In addition to the musical particularities of the style, there is a strong tie to language, and epic and ballad forms are common. See also FOLK MUSIC.

Folksong Symphony. Sym. No. 4 by R. Harris, 1940, the folk songs being of American origin.

Follow Thru. Musical by Ray Henderson, 1929, involving a golf match between 2 women and the male golf champion who falls for 1 of them. Includes *Button Up Your Overcoat*.

follower. CONSEQUENT.

Folsom Prison Blues. A 1968 country hit written and performed by Johnny Cash in his distinctive bass voice.

fondu (Fr., melting down). Dying away.

Fontane di Roma, Le. FOUNTAINS OF ROME, THE.

foot. 1. The common unit measuring the length of a vibrating air column in an organ pipe. In organ playing the standard is an 8' C, corresponding to the pitch of the C 2 lines below the bass staff (C), which agitates an air column about 8' long. By extension, any organ stop producing the normal pitch of the key depressed on the manual or the pedal is called an 8' tone. A 16' tone is 1 octave below this 8' tone, since the air column activated is twice as long (4' stop corresponds to a sound an octave above the note representing an 8' stop). Sometimes this nomenclature is used for other instruments, so that if the cello is said to produce the normal 8' tone, then the double bass can be likened to the organ producing a 16' tone, 1 octave lower than the cello for any given note. 2. A group of syllables having 1 accent, like a simple measure in music. 3. That part of an organ pipe below the mouth.

Foote, Arthur (William), distinguished American composer; b. Salem, Mass., Mar. 5, 1853; d. Boston, Apr. 8, 1937. He studied harmony with Stephen Emery at the New England Cons. of Music in Boston (1867–70) and took courses in counterpoint and fugue with John Knowles Paine at Harvard College (1870–74), where he received the 1st M.A. degree in music granted by an American univ. (1875). He also studied organ and piano with B. J. Lang, and later with Stephen Heller in France (1883). Returning to the U.S., he taught piano, organ, and composition in Boston; was organist at Boston's Church of the Disciples (1876–78) and at the 1st Unitarian Church (1878–1910); frequently appeared as a pianist with the Kneisel Quartet (1890–1910), performing several of his own works; was a founding member and president (1909–12) of the American Guild of Organists. He taught piano at the New England Cons. of Music (1921–37). He was elected a member of the National Inst. of Arts and Letters (1898).

His music, a product of the Romantic tradition, is notable for its fine lyrical élan. His Suite in E Major for strings (op. 63, 1907) enjoyed numerous performances and became a standard of American orch.l music. He publ. several music textbooks. Other compositions include various orch.l, chamber, and piano and organ pieces, as well as many vocal works, including some 100 songs, 52 part-songs, and 35 anthems.

For He's a Jolly Good Fellow. The English version of a satirical French tune, *Malbrouk s'en vat-en guerre.* The surmise that the Malbrouk in the song was the famous Duke of Marlborough, and that the song expressed the French contempt for the great British warrior, is not supported by the evidence.

For Me and My Gal. Song by George Meyer, 1917, popular in vaudeville and later the theme song for a film.

foreign chords or tones. Those that do not belong to a given key or scale.

forlana (It.; Fr. *forlane*). A lively Italian dance in 6/8 or 6/4 that originated in the province of Friuli. It was popular in Venice in the 18th century. Bach has a forlana in his C-major orch.l suite (BWV 1066), and Ravel included a forlane in his *Tombeau de Couperin.*

form. In music, a concept or organization governing the order, character, meter, and key of a composition. The most elementary is BINARY, in which only 2 sections are presented; TERNARY form evolves from binary by the interpolation of a middle section or by the repetition of the 1st section. In a large work, such as a sonata or sym., formal elements often intermingle and are distinguished by their similarities or contrasts.

In matters of organization, musical form is parallel to that found in literature, drama, and the pictorial arts. As in a living organism which comprises separate parts performing disparate functions, all of which are coordinated for the normal operation of the entire body, so in music form assembles all component elements of a musical composition in order to produce the best possible impression of unity. Since only 1 organ, that of hearing, is the object of a musical form, separate sections must contribute to auditory unification. This may be achieved by means of melodic symmetry, organic alternation of melodic sections, successions of tones within the same harmony, combinations of tones within a contrapuntal framework—all these animated by a rhythmic flow following a certain natural pulse of strong and weak accents.

In high developments of the formal elements, a deliberate departure from the basic form of rhythmic or melodic symmetry, harmonic unity, or contrapuntal concordance

results in a new type of form that may impress a rigid musical mind as being formless. The accusation of formlessness was directed at the Wagnerian ENDLESS MELODY, the Lisztian symphonic poem, and impressionistic monothematic compositions. In the course of time such "formless" music becomes itself established as a classical form. Paradoxically, even composers that profess formlessness as their aesthetic aims become inventors of superior forms based on principles of organization far removed from simple symmetry or thematic development. Thus Varèse propounded the principle of ORGANIZED SOUND as the only requirement of formal composition.

formalism. A pejorative term used by USSR authorities to denigrate offending music, i.e., that of Shostakovich, Prokofiev, et al., as "artificial." The term formalism acquired a specific meaning in Soviet aesthetics, as a method inimical to the essence of desirable art. The *Encyclopedic Music Dictionary* (Moscow, 1966) defines formalism as follows:

An artificial separation of form from content, and the attribution to formal elements of self-sufficient primary values to the detriment of musical content. . . . In contemporary aesthetics, formalism becomes a method of art hostile to realism and cultivated especially by the adepts of modernism. Formalism is based on the theory of art for art's sake, counterposing the artist to society and art itself to life, seeking to create an artistic form detached from objective reality. The governing precepts of formalism are the negation of ideological and realistic content of a work of art, a construction of arbitrary new forms, combined with the denial of national cultural heritage. In the final analysis, formalism results in the abolition of artistic imagery and disintegration of formal coherence. In musical practice, formalism rejects the ideational and emotional musical values and denies the capacity of a musical work to reflect reality. Proponents of formalism attempt to justify their fallacious doctrine by pointing out the specific nature of music as an art lacking the external connection with the world of real objects, such as is present in painting or sculpture, and intrinsically incapable of conveying a concrete narrative characteristic of literature. The aesthetic teaching of Marxism refutes formalism by a scientific approach to music as a special form of social ideology. The reactionary theories of formalism are assiduously cultivated in books and articles by the apologists of musical modernism. The struggle for the correct formulation of socialist realism leads to the removal of formalism from its pedestal. One should not confuse formalism, however, with genuine individual originality or with true innovation in the field of musical forms and in the inner substance of a composition, which constitute an unalienable part of authentic realistic art.

formant. In acoustics, the relative strength (amplitude) of partials in the overtone series that determines the timbre of a musical instrument. Stockhausen proposed to specify the term to designate the rhythmic values as functions of the overtone spectrum of a given pitch, so that the 2nd partial tone would represent the rhythmic duration of one-half the metric unit, the 3rd partial (that is, a 5th over an octave) would represent one-third of the rhythmic unit, etc. In ultramodern nomenclature, a formant is the catalytic element that forms, deforms, and transforms a given timbre into another by means of electronic manipulation.

forte (It.). Loud, strong; usually written as *f*.

forte generale (It.). The full organ combination stop.

fortemente (It.). Loudly, forcibly.

forte piano (It.). Accent strongly, then instantly diminishing to piano; written as *fp*.

forte possibile (It.). As loud as possible.

forte tenuto (It.). Loud throughout.

fortepiano (It., loud-soft). A term distinguishing the late-18th-century piano from the earlier HARPSICHORD or the later GRAND PIANO. Cristofori called his early 18th-century invention the *Gravicembalo col piano e forte*.

forte-stop. On the harmonium, a slide opened by a draw-stop or knee-lever, to produce a forte effect.

fortissimo (It.). Very loud; usually written *ff*.

fortississimo (It.). Extremely loud; usually written *fff*.

forza (*con forza*; It.). With force, forcibly.

Forza del destino, La (The Force of Destiny). Opera by Verdi, 1862, 1st produced by an Italian opera company in St. Petersburg. The fate described involves an eager lover who accidentally kills the father of his beloved and flees in horror to a monastery. His intended bride follows him there dressed in men's attire. Her brother, seeking vengeance, tracks him down too, and, not recognizing his sister under her monastic garb, mortally stabs her before dying himself from a wound inflicted by the now completely disoriented monk. But the music is amazingly durable in its uncompromisingly melodramatic lilt.

Forzando (*sforzando*; It.). With force, energy; accent the indicated note or chord strongly; usually written *fz*, *sf*, or *sfz*.

Foss, Lukas

⟿ ⟿ ⟿ ⟿ ⟿

Brilliant German-born American pianist, conductor, and composer; b. Lukas Fuchs, Berlin, Aug. 15, 1922. He was a scion of a cultural family; his father was a prof. of philosophy; his mother, a talented modern painter. He studied piano and music theory with Julius Goldstein-Herford. When the dark shadow of the Nazi dominion descended upon Germany, the family prudently moved to Paris; there Foss studied piano with Lazare Levy, composition with Noël Gallon, and orchestration with Felix Wolfes. He also took flute lessons with Louis Moyse.

In 1937 he went to the U.S. and enrolled at the Curtis Inst. of Music in Philadelphia, where he studied piano with Isabelle Vengerova, composition with Rosario Scalero, and conducting with Fritz Reiner; spent several summers at Tanglewood, Mass., where he studied conducting with Koussevitzky at the Berkshire Music Center; in 1939–40 he took a course in advanced composition with Hindemith at Yale Univ. He became a naturalized American citizen in 1942. Foss began to compose at a very early age; was awarded a Guggenheim fellowship (1945); in 1960 he received his 2nd Guggenheim fellowship. His 1st public career was that of a concert pianist, and he elicited high praise for his appearances as a piano soloist with the N.Y. Phil. and other orchs. He made his conducting debut with the Pittsburgh Sym. Orch. in 1939. From 1944 to 1950 he was pianist of the Boston Sym. Orch.; then traveled to Rome on a Fulbright fellowship (1950–52). From 1953 to 1962 he taught composition at the Univ. of Calif. in Los Angeles, where he also established the Improvisation Chamber Ensemble to perform music of "controlled improvisation."

In 1960 he traveled to Russia under the auspices of the U.S. State Dept. In 1963 he was appointed music director of the Buffalo Phil.; during his tenure he introduced ultramodern works, much to the annoyance of some regular subscribers; he resigned his position in 1970. In 1964–65 he led in N.Y. a series of "Evenings for New Music." In 1965 he served as music director of the American-French Festival at Lincoln Center, N.Y. In 1971 he became principal conductor of the Brooklyn Philharmonia; also established the series "Meet the Moderns" there. From 1972 to 1975 he conducted the Jerusalem Sym. Orch. He became music director of the Milwaukee Sym. Orch. in 1981; relinquished his position in 1986 after a tour of Europe and was made its conductor laureate; continued to hold his Brooklyn post until 1990. He was elected a member of the American Academy and Inst. of Arts and Letters in 1983. Throughout the years he evolved an astounding activity as conductor, composer, and lately college instructor, offering novel ideas in education and performance.

As a composer Foss traversed a protean succession of changing styles, idioms, and techniques. His early compositions were marked by the spirit of Romantic lyricism, adumbrating the musical language of Mahler; some other works reflected the neo-Classical formulas of Hindemith; still others suggested the hedonistic vivacity and sophisticated stylization typical of Stravinsky's productions. But the intrinsic impetus of his music was its "pulse," which evolves the essential thematic content into the substance of original projection. His earliest piano pieces were publ. when he was 15 years old; there followed an uninterrupted flow of compositions in various genres. Foss was fortunate in being a particular protégé of Koussevitzky, who conducted many of his works with the Boston Sym. Orch.; and he had no difficulty in finding other performers. As a virtuoso pianist he often played the piano part in his chamber music, and he conducted a number of his sym. and choral works. Among his other compositions are operas, orch.l works, and chamber works, including 3 string quartets.

Foster, Stephen C(ollins), famous American song composer; b. Lawrenceville, Pa., July 4, 1826; d. N.Y., Jan. 13, 1864. He learned to play the flute as a child but was essentially autodidact as a musician. He publ. his 1st song, *Open Thy Lattice, Love,* when he was 18. While working as a bookkeeper for his brother Dunning Foster in Cincinnati (1846–50), he became interested in songwriting. His song *Old Folks at Home* (1851), sometimes known as *Swanee River,* established him as a truly American composer. It was publ. on Oct. 21, 1851, with the subtitle "Ethiopian Melody as sung by Christy's Minstrels." E. P. Christy, the minstrel troupe leader, was listed as the composer of the song, in consideration of a small payment to Foster, whose name was not attached to it until the expiration of the copyright in 1879. About 40,000 copies of the song were sold during the year after publication.

Foster married Jane McDowell in Pittsburgh in 1850, but the marriage proved unhappy and he left her to live alone in N.Y. (1853–54); he settled there permanently in 1860. His last years were darkened by an addiction to alcohol, and death overtook him as a penniless patient at Bellevue Hospital. Yet his earnings were not small; he received about $15,000 during the last 15 years of his life. Among Foster's most notable songs were *Oh! Susanna* (1848), *Sweetly She Sleeps, My Alice Fair* (1851), *Massa's in de Cold Ground* (1852), *My Old Kentucky Home, Good Night!* (1853), *Jeanie with the Light Brown Hair* (1854), *Camptown Races* (1854), *Gentle Annie* (1856), *Old Black Joe* (1860), and *Beautiful Dreamer* (1864). His other works include hymns, piano pieces, and arrangements of popular melodies in an anthology, *The Social Orch.* (N.Y., 1854).

fougeux (Fr.). Impulsively.

Fountains of Rome, The (*Le Fontane di Roma*). Symphonic poem by Respighi, 1917. Four famous Roman fountains are portrayed in this picturesque scene, forming a fine companion piece for Respighi's *The Pines of Rome*. The 1st performance took place in Rome.

Four Norwegian Moods. Symphonic suite by Stravinsky, 1944, conceived along nonethnological lines and without any quotations from Norwegian folk tunes. He conducted its 1st performance in Cambridge, Mass.

Four Sacred Pieces (Verdi). QUATTRO PEZZI SACRI.

Four Saints in 3 Acts. Opera by V. Thomson, 1934, 1st produced by the Soc. of Friends and Enemies of Modern Music in Hartford, Conn. The libretto is by Gertrude Stein, in accordance with her unpredictable structuralist tenets. Thus there are really 4 acts and a dozen saints, some in duplicate, in the play. Her famous nonsensical line, "Pigeons on the grass, alas," is sung. The music is disarmingly triadic and ostentatiously repetitious, but the opera is mesmerizing to all exposed to it.

Four Temperaments, The. Ballet by Hindemith, 1940, depicting the 4 medieval humors: melancholic, sanguine, phlegmatic, and choleric. Hindemith later converted the work into a theme and variations for piano and orch., 1943.

Four Tops, The. (Vocals: Levi Stubbs, b. L. Stubbles, Detroit, Mich., *c.* 1938; Abdul "Duke" Fakir, b. Detroit, Dec. 26, 1935; Renaldo "Obie" Benson, b. Detroit, *c.* 1937; Lawrence Payton Jr., b. Detroit, *c.* 1936.) Popular Motown group of the 1960s that has continued to perform with its original membership intact over 4 decades. The group's biggest hits came in the mid-'60s, beginning with 1964's *Baby, I Need Your Lovin'* and including *I Can't Help Myself (Sugar Pie, Honeybunch)*, *It's the Same Old Song*, and *Reach Out*, all written by Motown house hitmakers Holland-Dozier-Holland, who groomed the group's sound in the studio. The Tops moved to ABC in the early '70s, where they continued to enjoy hits, most notably *Ain't No Woman (Like the One I Got)*. However, they soon were relegated to the oldies circuit, where they continue to perform and record. They were inducted into the Rock and Roll Hall of Fame in 1990.

four-hand piano. Pieces written for 2 piano players at 1 piano; one player plays the treble parts and the other the bass. Once very popular for piano pupils, 4-hand music has all but disappeared from piano teaching.

fourth. 1. An interval embracing 4 degrees. 2. The 4th degree in the diatonic scale; the SUBDOMINANT.

Fourth of July, The. Orch.1 work by Ives, completed in 1912; the 3rd movement of his *Sym.: Holidays*. As with the other movements, the work is a young boy's impressions of the day.

Fourth Symphony. Work by Mahler, 1901, in G Major. This is the most romantic among Mahler's syms.; Mahler himself conducted the 1st performance in Munich. The sym. is in 4 parts, the last movement having a soprano soloist. The 2 principal themes of the 1st movement are uninhibitedly sentimental, on the threshold of lachrymosity. This quality suggested to the producers of the film *Death in Venice* (1971), after Thomas Mann's novella, to make use of the themes as leading motives. The director Luchino Visconti saw connections between Mahler and the novella's main character, the composer Aschenbach, who falls in platonic love with a young Polish boy in Venice. This interpretation offended homophobic Mahlerites, who protested vehemently; taken a bit less literally, Visconti was probably onto important elements behind Mann's novella. See also DEATH IN VENICE.

Fourth Symphony. Work by Tchaikovsky, 1878, in F minor. This is one of Tchaikovsky's most famous syms., 1st performed in Moscow. Its opening syncopated subject was to Tchaikovsky the call of "Fatum" (fate), although he did not apply this word as a subtitle.

fox-trot. A popular duple-metered ballroom dance that originated in the 1920s; a variety of fox-trot steps evolved. The music derives from ragtime syncopation and was considered a jazz dance when European and other composers borrowed the style for their stage works and instrumental suites.

fp. FORTE PIANO.

Fra Diavolo (Brother Devil). Opera by Auber, 1830, concerning a notorious and nicknamed bandit who unwittingly involves a woman in a robbery. He is traitorously shot, and in his last breaths he exonerates her from all his crimes and urges her to marry her law-abiding suitor.

fraudulent modernism. Commercially successful composers of marketable semiclassical music, eager to gain aesthetic equality with sophisticated musicians, like to inject dissonant notes into their abecedarian and often analphabetic productions; proudly, they exhibit pieces using 12 different notes in a more or less chromatic order to earn membership in socially distinguished dodecaphonic circles. A combination of emaciated melodies in a spurious atonal manner with dietetic harmonies heavily spiced with discordant irrelevancies is the essence of fraudulent modernism. Its adepts often parade in panel discussions, glibly bandying about mispronounced names of the latest celebrities of the avant-garde. Fraudulent modernism fails because of the technical inadequacy of its practitioners and of their naive belief that wrong notes are the credentials of advanced sophistication.

française (Fr.). A dance in triple time, resembling the country dance. See also ÉCOSSAISE.

francamente (It.). Free in delivery; boldly; frankly, ingenuously.

Francesca da Rimini. Symphonic fantasy by Tchaikovsky, 1877, 1st performed in Moscow. The subject was inspired by the tragic episode told in Dante's *Inferno*, in which Francesca and her brother-in-law lover Paolo die at the hands of her jealous husband. Tchaikovsky was very much impressed by the dramatic illustrations of Dante's poem by the popular French painter Gustave Doré. As an epigraph Tchaikovsky selected the lines "Nessun maggior dolore/Che ricordarsi del tempo felice/Nella miseria," which he kept repeating in his letters and conversations as a motto of his own life: there was "no greater sorrow than to recall happy times in the midst of misery." The lyric melody of Francesca is one of the most characteristic effusions of Tchaikovsky's melancholy muse. His depiction of the tempestuous winds in the *Inferno*, with running chromatics, is dramatic.

Francesca da Rimini. Opera by Zandonai, 1914, after a tragedy by D'Annuzio on the same incident as Tchaikovsky's symphonic fantasy. Rachmaninoff wrote an opera on the same subject (1906).

Franck, César (-Auguste-Jean-Guillaume-Hubert)

Great Belgian composer and organist; b. Liège, Dec. 10, 1822; d. Paris, Nov. 8, 1890. He studied 1st at the Royal Cons. of Liège with Daussoigne and others; at the age of 9 he won 1st prize for singing, and at 12 1st prize for piano. As a child prodigy he gave concerts in Belgium. In 1835 his family moved to Paris, where he studied privately with Anton Reicha; in 1837 he entered the Paris Cons., studying with Zimmerman (piano), Benoist (organ), and Leborne (theory). A few months after his entrance examinations he received a special award of "grand prix d'honneur" for playing a fugue a 3rd lower at sight; in 1838 he received the 1st prize for piano; in 1839, a 2nd prize for counterpoint; in 1840, 1st prize for fugue; and in 1841, 2nd prize for organ. In 1842 he was back in Belgium; in 1843 he returned to Paris and settled there for the rest of his life. In that year he presented in Paris a concert of his chamber music; in 1846 his 1st major work, the oratorio Ruth, was given at the Paris Cons. In 1848, in the midst of the Paris revolution, he married; in 1851 he became organist of the church of St.-Jean-St.-François; in 1853, maître de chapelle, and, in 1858, organist at Ste.-Clotilde, which position he held until his death.

In 1872 Franck succeeded his former teacher Benoist as prof. of organ at the Paris Cons. Franck's organ classes became the training school for a whole generation of French composers; among his pupils were d'Indy, Chausson, Bréville, Bordes, Duparc, Ropartz, Pierné, Vidal, Chapuis, Vierne, and a host of others, who eventually formed a school of modern French instrumental music. Until the appearance of Franck in Paris, operatic art dominated the entire musical life of the nation, and the course of instruction at the Paris Cons. was influenced by this tendency. By his emphasis on organ music, based on the contrapuntal art of Bach, Franck swayed the new generation of French musicians toward the ideal of absolute music. The foundation of the famous Schola Cantorum by d'Indy, Bordes, and others in 1894 realized Franck's teachings; indeed, after the death of d'Indy in 1931, several members withdrew from the Schola Cantorum and organized the École César Franck (1938).

Franck was not a prolific composer, but his creative powers rose rather than diminished with advancing age; his only mature sym. (in D minor) was completed when he was 66; his remarkable Violin Sonata was written at the age of 63; his String Quartet was composed in the last year of his life. Lucidity of contrapuntal design and fullness of harmony are the distinguishing traits of Franck's music; in melodic writing he balanced the diatonic and chromatic elements in fine equilibrium. Although he did not pursue innovation for its own sake, he was not averse to using unorthodox procedures. The novelty of introducing an English horn into the score of his Sym. aroused some criticism among academic musicians of the time. Franck was quite alien to the Wagner-Liszt school of composition, which attracted many of his own pupils; the chromatic procedures in Franck's music derive from Bach rather than from Wagner.

Among his works are: Oratorios: *Les Béatitudes* (1869–79); *Rédemption* (1873–75; final version 1875). Orch.: *Les Eolides* (1877); *Le Chasseur maudit* (1883); *Les Djinns* (1885); *Variations symphoniques* for piano and orch. (1886); *Psyché* (1888). Organ: *6 Pièces* (*Fantaisie*; *Grande pièce symphonique*; *Prélude, Fugue, et Variations*; *Pastorale*; *Prière*; *Finale*; 1862); *3 Pièces* (*Fantaisie*; *Cantabile*; *Pièce héroique*, 1878); *3 Chorales* (1890); *L'organiste*, album of 55 pieces (1889–90). Piano: *Prélude, Choral et Fugue* (1884); *Prélude, Aria et Final* (1887); sacred and secular vocal works.

Franklin, Aretha, outstanding African-American soul singer; b. Memphis, Tenn., Mar. 25, 1942. Her father, Rev. C. L. Franklin, was a Baptist preacher; the family settled in Detroit, where he established a pastorate; his church became a hearth of gospel preaching and evangelical group singing. At 18 Aretha went to N.Y., where she quickly attracted attention; her singing at the Newport Jazz Festival in 1963 led to numerous important and lucrative engagements; the sales of her recordings skyrocketed to the million mark. In 1967 she toured Europe; in 1968 she made a sensation with her "soul" version of *The Star-Spangled Banner* at the ill-fated Democratic National Convention in Chicago. Among her outstanding recordings were the albums *I Never Loved a Man the Way I Love You* (1967), *Lady Soul* (1968), *Amazing Grace* (1972), *Young, Gifted and Black* (1972), *Something He Can Feel* (1976), *Jump to It* (1982), and *Who's Zoomin' Who?* (1985). In 1987 she recorded the 2-disc *One Lord, One Faith, One Baptism* in her father's church, which featured Rev. Jesse Jackson delivering a sermon against drug abuse among young black people.

Franklin, Benjamin, great American statesman and amateur polymath; b. Boston, Jan. 17, 1706; d. Philadelphia, Apr. 17, 1790. A musician, he invented (1762) the "armonica," an instrument consisting of a row of glass discs of different sizes set in vibration by light pressure. A string quartet mistakenly attributed to him came to light in Paris in 1945 and was publ. there (1946); the parts are arranged in an ingenious SCORDATURA; only open strings are used, so that the quartet can be played by rank amateurs. Franklin wrote entertainingly on musical subjects; his letters on Scottish music are found in vol. VI of his collected works.

frase large (It., broad phrases). LARGAMENTE.

Frau ohne Schatten, Die (The Woman Without a Shadow). Opera by R. Strauss, 1919, 1st produced in Vienna. An empress, married to an Oriental potentate, is barren because she cannot cast a shadow, a symbol of fertility; also, her husband's life is in danger. The empress is given a tempting offer to buy a poor woman's shadow; she finally desists, not wishing to deprive her of childbearing. For this noble act she is granted the joy of a shadow so that she can become a mother after all, and her husband is saved.

Frauenchor (Ger.). Women's chorus.

freddamente (*freddo*; It.). Coldly; coolly, indifferently.

Frederick II (Frederick the Great), King of Prussia; b. Berlin, Jan. 24, 1712; d. Potsdam, Aug. 17, 1786. He was an enlightened patron of music, a flute player of considerable skill, and an amateur composer. He studied flute with Quantz; in 1740, when he ascended to the throne, he established a court orch. and an opera house; Bach's son Carl Philipp Emanuel was his harpsichordist until 1767. In 1747 J. S. Bach was invited to Potsdam; the fruit of this visit was Bach's *Musical Offering*, written on a theme ostensibly by the King. In addition to composing 121 flute sonatas and 4 flute concertos, Frederick contributed arias to several operas: *Demofoonte* by Graun (1746); *Il Re pastore* (1747; with Quantz and others); *Galatea ed Acide* (1748; with Hasse, Graun, Quantz, and Nichelmann); and *Il trionfo della fedelità* (1753; with Hasse and others).

free canon. Work written with flexibility as to the rules of canonic composition. See also CANON.

free fugue. Fugue written with more or less disregard of strict rules. See also FUGUE.

free jazz. A jazz style of the 1960s and 1970s characterized by collective improvisation without reference to preset harmonic or formal structures.

free part. One added to a canon or fugue to complete the harmony.

free reed. A family of wind instruments in which a series of reeds are securely attached at one end but move freely at the other. The reeds themselves produce the difference in pitch through length and thickness. There are keyboard instruments such as the harmonium, mouth-blown instruments such as the Chinese cheng and Japanese sho, and the hand bellows-driven instruments, such as the accordion and concertina.

free style. In composition, a style in which the rules of strict counterpoint are relaxed.

Freed, Alan, American DJ and passionate popularizer of rock 'n' roll; b. Johnstown, Pa., Dec. 15, 1922; d. Palm Springs, Calif., Jan. 20, 1965. His greatest achievement was to desegregate black music by introducing it into white-sponsored radio stations. He was also credited with originating the term *rock 'n' roll* in 1951, although it had been used long before in a musical about a pleasure-boat cruise. He began broadcasting in Cleveland; then went to N.Y. in 1954 to take command of the radio station WINS, which became one of the most popular purveyors of rock 'n' roll. He also acted in the movie *Rock around the Clock*.

He began having trouble when stabbings and riots occurred at some of his public concerts in 1958; he was even accused of encouraging such shenanigans for the sake of publicity. Then, with a horrifying peripeteia fit for a Greek tragedy, he suffered a monumental downfall in 1963, when he pled guilty to charges of "payola," accepting bribes from commercial record companies for putting their songs on the air. On top of that, he was charged with income-tax evasion. He quit the oppressive city of N.Y. and fled to the more tolerant, laid-back state of Calif., but he soon died, ignored by enemies and friends alike, in the vacuous spa of Palm Springs.

Freeman, "Bud" (Lawrence), American jazz tenor saxophonist; b. Chicago, Apr. 13, 1906; d. there, Mar. 15, 1991. He began his career in Chicago playing with the Austin High School Gang, then went to N.Y., where he worked with Ben Pollack, Red Nichols, Paul Whiteman, Tommy Dorsey, and Benny Goodman. He was active with various combos from 1939, including the World's Greatest Jazz Band (1969–71), and made many recordings; also publ. the books *You Don't Look Like a Musician* (Detroit, 1974) and *If You Know a Better Life, Please Tell Me* (Dublin, 1976).

Frei (Ger.). Free. *Frei im Takt*, metrically free; *frei im Vortrag*, free in style or delivery.

Freie Satz, Der (Free Composition). Theoretical treatise by Schenker, 1935, outlining the basic principles of his analytical method and the concept of "composing out."

Freischütz, Der. Opera by Weber, 1821, premiered in Berlin. An ambitious freeshooter in love with a country girl agrees to trade his soul to the devil for 7 magic bullets that would guarantee a victory in a shooting competition. The last bullet must go where the demonic purchaser directs. The Freischütz hits his 6 preliminary marks but the last is aimed at his bride. She is saved by supernatural intervention; the marksman confesses his deal with the devil but is absolved. *Der Freischütz* is regarded as the 1st truly Romantic opera. The vivacious overture is often performed as a concert piece.

fremente (It.). Furiously.

frémissant (Fr.). Tremblingly.

French horn (horn; Ger. *Horn*; It. *corno*; Sp. *trompa*). A transposing valved brass instrument with a spiral conical tube (ranging from 9 feet to 18 feet in length), tunnel-shaped opening, wide and flaring bell, and small, funnel-shaped mouthpiece. It descends from ancient fingered instruments of animal horn, ivory, or wood; the valveless circular hunting horn (from the 17th century) is the closer antecedent. The modern French horn possesses a rich, sonorous, and mellow tone capable of great expressive power.

The source of the name "French horn" is unclear. The explanation that it is called French horn in order to prevent confusion with the English horn is unconvincing, for in other languages this distinction is not made (see entry heading). It is sometimes called *Waldhorn* (forest horn) in German; the Russians transcribed it as *valtorna*. In its modern construction it is also called *valve horn* to distinguish it from the early valveless horns that could produce only a series of overtones from the horn's fundamental. But even with valves enabling it to play all chromatic tones (the French call it *cor chromatique*), the glory of the French horn remains in the production of the natural overtones.

The horn's range is wider than any other brass instrument, covering nearly 4 octaves, with possible extensions beyond the upper limit. Its tone production is most unusual with its mouthpiece very small and its bell very large. In order to produce high tones, the player must adjust the lips in a precise acrobatic manner. The danger of hitting a wrong note on the horn in the upper registers haunts even the greatest horn virtuosos. One of the most difficult horn solos occurs in *Till Eulenspiegels* by R. Strauss, in which the player reaches high into the empyrean regions. The story goes that the hornist told Strauss before the 1st rehearsal that the passage was unplayable, to which Strauss retorted that he had gotten the idea for this part while listening to the horn player himself practice during the tuning periods.

Prior to the invention of valves and crooks, the natural horn yielded only the harmonics produced by its single FUNDAMENTAL, hence an individual instrument's use was extremely limited. Horn parts were written in classical scores in the key of the composition; from the early 18th century on, when a modulation occurred, the player could insert or remove a piece of tubing, called a *crook*, to obtain the right fundamental. The modern horn, played like a cornet, is much easier to handle. With the advent of the chromatic horn, horn parts came to be written and notated almost invariably in the key of F, and are still notated in an unusual manner: players transpose a 5th down in the treble clef or a 4th up in the bass clef.

Horn players have to empty their instrument periodically to remove the accumulated saliva, which is apt to cause tonal constipation. A violinist who was engaged to play the Horn Trio of Brahms demanded a pair of galoshes before he went on stage.

French overture. A type of overture developed in France in the 17th century consisting of 3 sections: the 1st in slow tempo, the 2nd rather quick, and the 3rd again slow. The French overture usually introduced operas, ballets, or suites; Lully, Purcell, Handel, and Rameau were among the many that used the form. By the late 17th century the overture's structure was often reduced to slow-fast; on the other hand, the SINFONIA of the early 18th century added a closing fast section. A further transformation was the slow introduction to Haydn's fast 1st movements and works by Mozart and the early Romantics. The French overture should not be confused with the OVERTÜRE (Ger.), the equivalent of the Baroque suite.

French sixth. The common name for a chord containing the augmented 6th between the bottom and the top notes, other intervals from the bottom being a major 3rd and an augmented 4th, as in A flat, C, D, and F sharp. The chord resolves to either the tonic major or minor (2nd inversion) or dominant (root position):

Freni (born Fregni), **Mirella,** noted Italian soprano; b. Modena, Feb. 27, 1935. Curiously enough, her mother and the mother of the future celebrated tenor Luciano Pavarotti worked for a living in the same cigarette factory; curiouser still, the future opera stars shared the same wet nurse. Freni studied voice with her uncle, Dante Arcelli, and made her 1st public appearance at the age of 11; her accompanist was a child pianist named Leone Magiera, whom she married in 1955. She later studied voice with Ettore Campogalliani, made her operatic debut in Modena on Feb. 3, 1955, as Micaela in *Carmen*, then sang in provincial Italian opera houses. In 1959 she sang with the Amsterdam Opera Co. at the Holland Festival; then at the Glyndebourne Festival

(1960), Covent Garden in London (1961), and La Scala in Milan (1962).

She gained acclaim as Mimi in the film version of *La Bohème*, produced at La Scala, with von Karajan conducting (1963); when La Scala toured Russia in 1964, Freni joined the company and sang Mimi at the Bolshoi Theater in Moscow. She also chose the role of Mimi for her American debut, with the Metropolitan Opera in N.Y. (1965). She subsequently sang with the Vienna State Opera, the Bavarian State Opera in Munich, the Teatro San Carlo in Naples, and the Rome Opera. In 1976 she traveled with the Paris Opéra during its 1st American tour. In addition to Mimi, she sang the roles of Susanna, Zerlina, Violetta, Amelia in *Simon Boccanegra*, and Manon. She won acclaim for her vivid portrayal of Tatiana in *Eugene Onegin*; she sang this role with many major opera companies, including the Metropolitan Opera in 1989. In 1990 she appeared as Lisa in *Pique Dame* at La Scala. She married Nicolai Ghiaurov in 1981 and subsequently appeared frequently with him in opera performances around the world.

frequency. The rate of vibration of a string or air column; the acoustic-mathematical correlate to the sensation of pitch. The height of pitch is measured by frequency; e.g., in the U.S. (concert tuning), A equals 440 cycles per second (abbrev. cps, Hz). *Frequency modulation*, change made to the frequency of a wave enabling information transfer to electromagnetic wave (FM).

Frère Jacques. French nursery rhyme and canon, 1st published in a *Recueil de Rondes* in 1860. The melody dates to around 1775.

Frescobaldi, Girolamo, great Italian organist and composer; b. Ferrara (baptized), Sept. 9, 1583; d. Rome, Mar. 1, 1643. He studied with Luzzasco Luzzaschi in Ferrara; by the age of 14 was organist at the Accademia della Morte in Ferrara; in early 1607 became organist of S. Maria in Trastevere; then, in June 1607, traveled to Brussels in the retinue of the Papal Nuncio; publ. his 1st work, a collection of 5-part madrigals, in Antwerp in 1608, printed by Phalèse. Returning to Rome in the same year, he was appointed organist at St. Peter's as successor to Ercole Pasquini. He retained this all-important post until his death, with the exception of the years 1628 to 1634, when he was court organist in Florence. A significant indication of Frescobaldi's importance among musicians of his time was that Froberger, who was court

organist in Vienna, came to Rome especially to study with him (1637–41).

Frescobaldi's place in music history is very great; particularly as a keyboard composer, he exercised a decisive influence on the style of the early Baroque; he enlarged the expressive resources of keyboard music so as to include daring chromatic progressions and acrid passing dissonances, *durezze* (harshnesses); in Frescobaldi's terminology, *toccata di durezza* signified a work using dissonances; he used similar procedures in organ variations on chorale themes (*Fiori musicali*, 1635). His ingenious employment of variations greatly influenced the entire development of Baroque music. He publ. 12 books of keyboard music, 1 book of sacred vocal music, 3 books of madrigals, and scattered individual pieces.

fret. A narrow, raised wedge of wood, metal, or ivory crossing the fingerboard of plucked string instruments, e.g., mandolin, guitar, banjo, lute, and balalaika; the strings are "stopped" (pressed by the fingers), guaranteeing proper pitch. The intervals between frets are usually semitones.

fretta, con (*frettando, frettoloso*; It.). Hastily, hurriedly.

Freude (Ger.). Joy. *Freudig* (Ger.), joyfully.

fricassée (Fr.). A musical potpourri; QUODLIBET.

friction drum. A clay pot with a membrane stretched over its top through which a stick or a sturdy string is passed; this stick is rubbed with a wet finger to produce several successive tones. Such drums are prevalent throughout the world, including England (*pasteboard rattle*), Germany (*Reibtrommel; Waldteufel*, forest devil), and France (*cri de la belle-mère*, mother-in-law's cry).

Friedenstag, Der (The Day of Peace). Opera by R. Strauss, 1938, produced in Munich; it deals with the peace that concluded the 30 Years' War which devastated Europe. The opera, written with the customary brilliance that distinguishes works of Strauss, ends with a choral invocation to peace. Its repeated performances on the eve of Hitler's plunge into total war held special meaning to Germans deprived of their freedom of verbal expression; however, revisionist views of Strauss as politically conscious of and antipathetic toward the Nazi menace should be made only with the utmost caution.

Friedhofer, Hugo (William), American composer of film music; b. San Francisco, May 3, 1901; d. Los Angeles, May 17, 1981. He played cello in theater orchs.; studied composition with Domenico Brescia. In 1929 he went to Hollywood, where he worked as an arranger and composer for early sound films. In 1935 he was engaged as an orchestrator for Warner Brothers and received valuable instruction from Erich Wolfgang Korngold and Max Steiner. In Los Angeles he attended Schoenberg's seminars and took additional lessons in composition with Ernst Toch and Kanitz; he also had some instruction with Nadia Boulanger during her sojourn in California. He wrote his 1st complete film score for *The Adventures of Marco Polo* in 1938, and in the following years he composed music for about 70 films. His film music for *The Best Years of Our Lives* won the Academy Award in 1946. His other film scores included *Vera Cruz*, *Violent Saturday*, *The Sun Also Rises*, and *The Young Lions*.

Friedhofer was highly esteemed by the Hollywood theatrical community and by his colleagues in the film studios for his ability to create a congenial musical background, alternatively lyrical and dramatic, for the action on the screen, never sacrificing the purely musical quality for the sake of external effect. He was the only Calif. native of all the famous film composers in Hollywood, the majority of whom were Germans and Austrians. When a Hollywood mogul told Friedhofer to use numerous French horns in a film taking place in France, he acquiesced and, by extension of the dictum, used an English-horn solo to illustrate the approach to the cliffs of Dover of the film characters fleeing the French Revolution.

Friedman, Ignaz, famous Polish pianist; b. Podgorze, near Krakow, Feb. 14, 1882; d. Sydney, Australia, Jan. 26, 1948. He studied music theory with Hugo Riemann in Leipzig and piano with Leschetizky in Vienna. In 1904 he launched an extensive career as a concert pianist; he gave about 2,800 concerts in Europe, America, Australia, Japan, China, and South Africa. In 1941 he settled in Sydney. He was renowned as an interpreter of Chopin, and he prepared an annotated ed. of Chopin's works in 12 vols., publ. by Breitkopf & Härtel; also ed. piano compositions of Schumann and Liszt for Universal Edition in Vienna. Friedman was himself a composer; he wrote 100 or so pieces for piano in an effective salon manner, among them a group of *Fantasiestücke*.

Friedrich II (der Grosse). FREDERICK II (FREDERICK THE GREAT).

Friml (born Frimel), (Charles) **Rudolf,** famous Bohemian-American operetta composer; b. Prague, Dec. 2, 1879; d. Los Angeles, Nov. 12, 1972. He was a pupil at the Prague Cons. of Juranek (piano) and Foerster (theory and composition); toured Austria, England, Germany, and Russia as accompanist to Kubelik, the violinist, going with him to the U.S. in 1900 and again in 1906; remained in the U.S. after the 2nd tour; gave numerous recitals, appeared as soloist with several orchs. (played his Piano Concerto with the N.Y. Sym. Orch.), and composed assiduously; lived in N.Y. and Hollywood, composing for motion pictures. Among his successful operettas were *The Firefly* (1912); *High Jinks* (1913); *Katinka* (1915); *Rose-Marie* (1924; very popular); and *The Vagabond King* (1925; highly successful); other songs and a great number of piano pieces in a light vein. In 1937 MGM made a film of *The Firefly*, the popular *Donkey Serenade* being added to the original score.

frisch (Ger.). Brisk, vigorous; (It.) *brioso*.

friss (*friska*; Hung.). The rapid 2nd section of the Hungarian VERBUNKOS, a type of csárdás.

frog (U.K., nut; Ger. *Frosch*; Fr. *hausse*; It. *tallone*). The lower part of a bow, nearest the player, where the bow-hair is tightened or loosened. Playing "at the frog" produces a hard, vibratoless sound.

froh (*fröhlich*; Ger.). Merrily, joyfully, gaily, gladly.

From Bohemia's Meadows and Groves (*Z českych luhův a hayův*). Fourth symphonic poem of Smetana's cycle *Má vlast*.

From the House of the Dead (*Z mrtvého domu*). Opera by Janáček, 1930, to his own libretto after Dostoyevsky's partly autobiographical novel describing his Siberian exile. It was produced posthumously in Brno.

From the Middle Ages. Orch.1 suite by Glazunov, 1903, built on medieval church modes.

From the New World. Sym. No. 9 of Dvořák, 1893, his most famous, so named because he composed the score during his sojourn in the U.S. It was 1st performed by the N.Y. Phil. The sym. is in E minor; of the 4 movements, the most popular is the 2nd, marked LARGO, which suggests a Negro spiritual. Much speculation was aroused by this approximation, but Dvořák specifically denied having used any specific Negro air and insisted that the melody was simply the expression of the homesickness of an uprooted Czech finding himself in a new land across the ocean. One of Dvořák's American pupils, William Arms Fisher, fit a set of words to the tune to create *Going Home, Going Home*. It is interesting to note that the largo is set in the key of D-flat major, miles away tonally from the tonic E of the sym. The sym. *From the New World* was until recently listed as Dvořák's No. 5, but then 4 earlier unpubl. syms. were discovered and its number had to be changed to No. 9, creating great confusion among cataloguers.

From the Steeples and the Mountains. A remarkable work by Ives, 1905, scored for church bells and brass. Ives wrote in the score: "After the brass stops, the chimes sound on until they die away. . . . From the steeples—the bells! Then the rocks on the mountains begin to shout!" As with most works by Ives, it was not performed until decades after its composition, receiving its 1st public performance in 1965.

Frosch (Ger.). FROG.

Froschquartett. Nickname of Haydn's String Quartet, No. 6, op. 50, in D major, 1787. While expert ranunculogists may have failed to discern froglike croaking in the music, perhaps the publicists heard a frog in the finale's unison *bariolage* effect, where 2 strings, 1 open, 1 stopped, are bowed in succession to produce a quasi-tremolo with constantly changing tone color.

frottola (It.; plural *frottole*). A genre of polyphonic song of the Italian Renaissance period popular in northern Italy between *c.* 1470 and 1530. The term may have been derived from the Italian *frocta*, a conglomeration of random thoughts, in relation to the genre's origins; or *frotta*, a flock, because the frottola was composed of unusual or unconnected melodic ingredients. Many anthologies of frottole were published in the early 16th century by Petrucci; they are arranged in simple harmonies with symmetrical rhythms, with the potential for being accompanied on the lute or viols; often only the treble (soprano) was sung.

Stylistically the frottola is related to the Spanish VILLANCICO and the Italian STRAMBOTTO; it evolved from the reading of poetry to musical accompaniment, widespread in the 15th century. The musical structure was fitted to the metrical and rhyme schemes of the poetry selected. Depiction of the texts, even those by Petrarch, was of little concern to the frottolists; only when the genre evolved into the madrigal did this become important.

frugal ankyloglossia. Art thrives on economy of means, but modernistic frugality must not be allowed to reach the point of tonal ankyloglossia. The criterion is a freedom of expression without cacuminal retroflection.

Frü(h)lingslied (Ger.). Spring song.

Frühlingsstimmen (Voices of Spring). Waltz by J. Strauss, Jr., 1883.

frullato (It.). FLUTTER-TONGUE.

frusta (It.). Whip (percussion instrument).

F-Schlüssel (Ger.). The bass or F clef.

F-sharp major. A tonality which numbers 6 sharps in its key signature; it rarely appears as the principal key of a large work for orch., chorus, or piano. But curiously enough it is favored by children of a tender age on account of its digitally convenient pentatonic disposition on the black keys of the piano. The *Black-Key Étude* of Chopin is in the key of F-sharp major. Scriabin was very fond of this tonality until he abandoned key signatures altogether. The enharmonic tonality of G-flat major has 6 flats in its key signature and enjoys the favor of Romantic composers almost as much as its sharp alter ego.

F-sharp minor. This key, with 3 sharps in its signature, is characterized by a poetic delicacy of sentiment. There are but few syms. in the key of F-sharp minor, but the *Farewell Sym.* of Haydn, in which musicians leave the stage one after another until the conductor is left alone as a mute symbol of unhappiness of parting, is set in F-sharp minor. Miaskovsky, who wrote syms. in practically every major and minor key, assigned F-sharp minor to his 21st sym., entitled, perhaps significantly, *Symphonie-Fantaisie*. It is interesting that 2 Russian piano concertos, the 1st by Rachmaninoff and the only piano concerto by Scriabin, are in the key of F-sharp minor; the romantic essence of these 2 concertos is unmistakably manifested.

Fuchs, Lukas. Foss, LUKAS.

fudging. A rustic form of FUGUING, a type of free hymn singing once cultivated in the Ozark and Appalachian regions of the U.S. and representing a rudimentary canonic form in unison, with traditional homophonic cadences.

fuga (Lat., It.). FUGUE.

fugato (It., like a fugue). A passage or movement consisting of fugal imitations, but not worked out fully, as a true fugue.

Fuge (Ger.). FUGUE.

fughetta (It.). A short fugue; a fugal exposition.

fuging (fuguing) **tune.** An American type of choral psalm vocalization or hymn which became popular in New England in the last half of the 18th century. It is derived from the old English type of psalmody, in which a hymn has a rudimentary canonic section before the concluding cadence. In America the fuging tunes of William Billings became well known; some enthusiastic musicologists describe them as the earliest native American music forms. Cowell and Schuman based works on Billings's tunes.

fugue

The most highly developed form of contrapuntal imitation, based on the principle of the equality of the parts, a theme proposed by one part being taken up successively by all participating parts, thus bringing each in turn into special prominence. The etymological derivation is metaphorically justified, since in the fugue (from It. *fuga*, flight) one voice seems to flee from another. The elements essential to every fugue are: the SUBJECT (DUX, THEME, antecedent, leader); ANSWER (COMES, companion, consequent, follower); *countersubject*; STRETTO. To these are commonly added EPISODES; ORGAN POINT; and a CODA. In a *real fugue* the answer is an exact transposition of the subject; in a *tonal fugue* the subject is modified in the answer in order to lead back to the original key (see below).

With the fugue the art of polyphony reached its supreme achievement. Morphologically the fugue is a successor to the CANON; it is also related to the CACCIA, a musical form of canonic construction (It., chase). But the fugue is far from being a mere development of the canon. The element of imitation is common to both, but while the canon is mechanical in its structure, the fugue introduces an entirely new principle of imitation through modulation from the tonic to the dominant. The classic fugue opens with the statement of the principal subject in a single unaccompanied voice. In the old Latin treatises on fugue this subject is called *dux*, the leader; its imitation, or answer, in the key of the dominant, is *comes*, the companion. When the comes enters in another voice, the part of the dux continues as a suitable counterpoint to the comes; this continuation of the dux is called the *countersubject*. Fugues of only 2 voices are rare, since they inevitably degenerate into a canon with the imitation in the dominant. In a fugue for 3 voices the 3rd voice enters again in the tonic imitating the dux note for note, but in another octave. In the meantime new contrapuntal material is entered in the original part of the dux. If there are 4 voices, the 4th voice comes in again in the dominant, imitating the comes note by note. Fugues of 5 or more voices alternate in the keys of the tonic and the dominant, following the form of the dux and the comes.

What distinguishes this modus operandi from the canon and other types of literal imitation is the peculiar phenomenon of *tonal answer*. In a tonal answer the tonic of the dux is echoed in the comes, even if the subject itself must be altered to accomplish this. This type of imitation constitutes a dislocation of the intervallic structure of the dux. For example, the simple triadic phrase, C–E–G, would normally be literally transposed into the dominant as G–B–D, an exact and therefore *real answer*. But the tonal answer requires that, in the comes, the 3rd note of the subject be altered to match (and thus emphasize) the tonic of the dux; so the 3rd note of the comes is C, not D. Thus C–E–G is answered in the dominant as G–B–C. Still more perplexing is the specification that, once the tonal adjustment is made in the opening of the comes, the transposition of the original subject into the dominant key is resumed as if nothing had happened. Not all fugal subjects can accommodate a tonal answer.

The fugue is not the rigid form its formidable reputation makes it out to be. The entries do not have to follow one another in mechanical succession. Bach, the bellwether of the art of the fugue, never followed the rules that are laid down in pedagogical treatises. His fugues were actually romantic in their flights of fancy, which are revealed in numerous little episodes that are ingeniously inserted between entries. The legend has it that students in the class of the fugue at the Paris Cons. in the 1890s were so studious and ingenious that the professors were forced to adopt the inhuman practice of triage in order to eliminate as many of them as possible. Accordingly, the professors rigged up fugue subjects so tangled in chromaticisms that only students possessing a sort of musical legerdemain could extricate themselves from the maze of possible and impossible combinations.

The formal structure of the fugue consists of 3 sections: exposition, episodic development, and return. The exposition presents the dux and comes in the tonic and the dominant. In the episodic development the subject wanders far away from the initial keys. It is then broken up into fragments gleaned from the intervallic ingredients of both dux and comes, appearing in a variety of keys but usually not far from the principal key along the cycle of scales. Sequential modulatory passages alternate with brief reexpositions of the subject in nontonic keys. These thematic *disjecta membra* are tossed about in free interplay until the saturation point is reached as the dominant of the principal key is sounded, heralding the entrance of the dux. The return is then celebrated in all solemnity, often followed by a coda or codetta, where the dux and the comes are compressed and foreshortened. With the return a stretto (It., narrowing) may make its appearance; in it the entries are telescoped in close canonic succession. If used, the pedal point is embedded deep in the bass on the dominant, preliminary to the eschatological conclusion on the tonic.

Morphological alterations may take place; the dux and comes are stood on their heads by melodic inversion, in which the ascending passages descend and the descending passages ascend. When such things happen the harmony is subjected to the greatest stress. Unimaginable dissonances can be formed in the process, and yet in Bach the teleological drive never falters. To suggest the magnificent symmetry of the main proportions of the fugue and the versatility of its ornaments, Busoni was moved in his monumental edition of Bach's *Well-Tempered Clavier* to give a graphic rendering of the structural elements of the Gothic cathedrals on the title page, which to his mind constituted the architectural counterpart of Bach's grand design. The fugue is indeed a cathedral of polyphony in which the principal lines are never obscured by the gargoyles of florid ornamentation.

full. Whole, complete, all. *Full anthem*, written for chorus without solos; *full band*, a band or orch. having all the customary instruments; *full cadence*, a full authentic perfect CADENCE; *full choir*, draw all organ stops of the choir (great, swell); *full chord*, a chord having one or more of its original 3 or 4 tones doubled in the octave; *full orch.*, compare *full band*; *full organ*, with all stops and couplers drawn; *full to 15th*, draw all stops but mixtures and reeds.

full authentic cadence (full cadence). See CADENCE.

Full Moon and Empty Arms. An antimusical outrage, with words and music by Buddy Kaye and Ted Mossman, perpetrated on the lovely 2nd subject of the defenseless and uncopyrighted body of Rachmaninoff's 2nd Piano Concerto. Crooners galore made capital out of it, as did the original grave-robbers.

full score. Orch.1 score in which all instrumental and vocal parts are written out and aligned vertically.

fundamental (note, tone). 1. The root of a chord. 2. A tone consisting of a HARMONIC SERIES; a generator of HARMONICS; a prime tone. *Fundamental bass* (Fr. *basse fondamentale*), the progression of harmonic roots, as proposed by Rameau (1722); *fundamental chord*, triad, see "Chords," p. xxv; *fundamental position*, any arrangement of chordal tones in which the root remains the lowest; root position.

funèbre (Fr.; It. *funebre*). Funereal, mournful, dirgelike.

funeral march. A march in slow 4/4 time in a minor key, sometimes used as a part of a larger work. The most famous funeral march is the slow movement from Chopin's Piano

Sonata in B-flat Minor (1839, op. 35), often played at the funerals of important persons.

funesto (It.). Somberly, sorrowfully.

Fünf Orchesterstücke. Orch.l suite by Schoenberg (1909, op. 16) in which he introduces new techniques, such as dissonant counterpoint, atonal melodies, and sequences of tone colors. It was 1st performed not in Central Europe, but in London (1912).

Funiculi-Funicula. One of the most popular Neapolitan songs, written by Luigi Denza in 1880 to celebrate the opening of the funicular railway leading to the crater of Mt. Vesuvius. It was commonly believed that it was a folk song and was used as such by Rimsky-Korsakov and R. Strauss in their orch.l works.

funk. 1. An African-American popular music that developed in the 1960s from African polyrhythms and call-and-response textures. Funk songs often use a single chord or a few alternating, sometimes complex harmonies (*vamping*), through which clipped syncopated lines emerge in the electric guitar and bass parts, drums and percussion, keyboards, winds (saxophones, trumpets), and vocal parts. Interjections by different instruments and voices, often recurrent, are another feature, and improvisation falls naturally in place. While many of these elements had existed in earlier popular music styles, the best funk has a highly diverse and often surprisingly thin texture that lends it a unique tension (influencing reggae tremendously). Some of the greatest funk performers have been James Brown, Sly and the Family Stone, Kool and the Gang, Rufus, Ohio Players, War, and Parliament/Funkadelic.

Funk has been able to blend into successive styles. It has always been associated with African-American social protest, and thus found its way into 1980s HIP-HOP, which adapted funk's textures to electronic techniques, editing, and sampling, providing a background for RAP. Reggae musicians (such as Bob Marley and Peter Tosh) drew upon funk, although reggae rhythms quickly became stereotyped. As a dance music funk led quite naturally into the faster, simpler, and less politically threatening disco style; when the group Chic had hits with funk-oriented disco, the latter changed accordingly.

2. HARD BOP.

Funkoper (Ger.). Radio opera.

Funny Face. Musical by Gershwin, 1927. A woman seeks and regains her pearls from her brother with the help of her boyfriend. Includes *'S Wonderful* and *My One and Only*.

Funny Girl. Musical by Styne, 1964. A biography of Fanny Brice, the Ziegfeld Follies star who rose from rags to riches and fell in love with a gangster. The show launched Barbra Streisand as the lead. Includes *Don't Rain on My Parade* and *People*.

Funny Thing Happened on the Way to the Forum, A. Musical by Sondheim, 1962, based on the Roman farces of Plautus. A cunning slave will gain his freedom by supplying his owner with a particular beauty from the bordello next door, but several others covet her too, including the owner's son. Includes *Comedy Tonight, Everybody Ought to Have a Maid*, and *Love, I Hear*.

fuoco, con (*focoso*; It.). With fire; with spirit, impetuously; in a fiery manner.

furiant (*furie*; Cz.). A rapid Bohemian dance written in 3/4 time but with alternating duple and ternary measures and strong cross accents.

furioso (It.). Furiously, wildly.

furlana (It.). FORLANA.

furniture music (Fr. *musique d'ameublement*). A descriptor introduced by Satie to denote purposely unindelible (i.e., background) music. In what some consider his sustained effort to degrade music and reduce it to a menial level, Satie was prompted to inaugurate a demonstration of his musique d'ameublement, which he defined as "new music played during intermission at theatrical events or at a concert, designed to create a certain ambience." At an actual performance at the Paris Art Gallery, Satie placed his musicians in separate groups and urged the public to treat them as functional objects, to speak loudly and not to listen with professional attention. The performers were free to play anything they wished, regardless of the repertoire selected by their confrères.

furore (It.). Fury, passion; rage; mania. *Con furore*, passionately.

Furtwängler, (Gustav Heinrich Ernst Martin) Wilhelm

〰〰 〰〰 〰〰 〰〰 〰〰

Celebrated German conductor; b. Berlin, Jan. 25, 1886; d. Ebersteinburg, Nov. 30, 1954. His father, Adolf Furtwängler, was a noted archeologist. He grew up in Munich, where he received a private education; his musical studies were with Schillings, Rheinberger, and Beer-Walbrunn; he also studied piano with Conrad Ansorge. He later served as *répétiteur* with Mottl in Munich (1908–1909). In 1910 he became 3rd conductor at the Strasbourg Opera; then conducted the sym. concerts in Lübeck (1911–15), and in 1915 was engaged as conductor in Mannheim. From 1919 to 1924 he conducted the Vienna Tonkünstler Orch.; concurrently (from 1921) he served as director of the Gesellschaft der Musikfreunde in Vienna. He led the Berlin Staatskapelle (1920–22); also served as conductor of the Frankfurt Museum concerts. A decisive turn in his career was his appointment in 1922 as chief conductor of the Berlin Phil. as successor to Nikisch; he also assumed Nikisch's post of Kapellmeister of the Leipzig Gewandhaus Orch., which he held until 1928. In 1925 he made his American debut with the N.Y. Phil., which was greeted with general acclaim; he conducted this orch. again in 1926 and 1927. In 1927 he was elected conductor of the Vienna Phil. in succession to Weingartner, holding the post of artistic director until 1930, and continuing as guest conductor later on. Also in 1927 the Univ. of Heidelberg conferred upon him the title of Dr.Phil.; in 1928 the city of Berlin named him Generalmusikdirektor. In 1931 he conducted at the Bayreuth Festival for the 1st time. In 1932 he was awarded the prestigious Goethe Gold Medal. In 1933 he was appointed director of the Berlin State Opera and vice president of the Reichsmusikkammer. He maneuvered adroitly to secure his independence from the increasing encroachment of the Nazi authorities on both his programs and the personnel of the Berlin Phil., and succeeded in retaining several Jewish players. In 1934 he conducted Hindemith's sym. *Mathis der Maler* and was sharply berated by Goebbels, who called Hindemith a "cultural Bolshevist" and "spiritual non-Aryan" (referring to Hindemith's half-Jewish wife). In the face of continued Nazi interference, Furtwängler decided to resign all of his posts in late 1934; however, a few months later he made an uneasy peace with the Nazi authorities and agreed to return as a conductor with the Berlin Phil., giving his 1st concert in the spring of 1935. In 1936 he was offered a contract as permanent conductor of the N.Y. Phil. in succession to Toscanini, but he had to decline the prestigious offer to quiet the rising accusations, on the part of American musicians, of his being a Nazi collaborator. In 1937 he went to London to participate in the musical celebrations in

Wilhelm Furtwängler

COURTESY FRANK DRIGGS COLLECTION

honor of the coronation of King George VI; in 1939 he was made a Commander of the Legion of Honor by the French government. After the outbreak of World War II he confined his activities to Germany and Austria.

Continuing to be loyal to Germany but with ambivalent feelings toward the Nazi government, Furtwängler went to Switzerland in 1945, where he remained during the last months of the war. He returned to Germany in 1946 and faced the Allied Denazification Court, but was absolved from the charges of pro-Nazi activities. In 1947 he conducted the Berlin Phil. for the 1st time since the end of the war, leading an all-Beethoven concert to great acclaim; he also renewed his close association with the Vienna Phil. and the Salzburg Festival. He was tentatively engaged to conduct the Chicago Sym. Orch. in 1949, but the project was canceled when public opinion proved hostile. In western Europe, however, he took both the Vienna and Berlin Phil. orchs. on a number of major tours and was received most enthusiastically; he also became a regular conductor with the Philharmonia Orch. of London. In 1951 he reinaugurated the Bayreuth Festival by conducting Beethoven's 9th Sym.; in 1952 he resumed his post as chief conductor of the Berlin Phil. His last years of life were clouded by increasing deafness, so that his podium had to be wired for sound. He was to conduct the Berlin Phil. on its 1st American tour in the spring of 1955, but death intervened, and von Karajan was elected his successor.

Furtwängler was a perfect embodiment of the great tradition of the German Romantic school of conducting; his interpretations of the music of Beethoven, Schubert, Schumann, Brahms, Bruckner, and Wagner were models of formal purity. He never strove to achieve personal magic with the audience, and never ranked with such charismatic conductors as Stokowski or Koussevitzky in this respect. But to professional musicians he remained a legendary master of orch. sound and symmetry of formal development of sym. music. Furtwängler was also a composer; quite naturally, the style of his works followed the Romantic tradition, with potential exuberance controlled by a severe sense of propriety. Additionally, he wrote several books on music.

fusée (Fr.). A rapid passage.

fusion. See JAZZ-FUNK.

futurism. A literary and musical modern movement that originated in Italy early in the 20th century. It declared a rebellion against traditional art of all kinds, and preached the use of noises in musical composition.

Futurism emerged under the aegis of the Italian poet F. T. Marinetti (1876–1942). Its musical credo was formulated by Francesco Balilla Pratella (1880–1955) in his *Manifesto of Futurist Musicians* (Milan, 1910) and supplemented by a *Technical Manifesto of Futurist Music* (1911). In 1913 Luigi Russolo (1885–1947) published his own Futurist Manifesto (*L'arte dei rumori*, The Art of Noises). In these declarations the Italian futurists proclaimed their complete disassociation from classical, romantic, and impressionist music and announced their aim to build an entirely new music inspired by the reality of life in the new century, with the machine as the source of inspiration. And since modern machines were most conspicuous by the noise they made, Pratella and Russolo created a new art of noises (*arte dei rumori*). Russolo designed special noise instruments and subdivided them into 6 categories. His instruments were rudimentary and crude, with amplification obtained by megaphones, but there is no denying that the Futurists provided a prophetic vision of the electronic future of fifty years later.

It is interesting to note that most Futurist musicians and poets were also painters. Their pictures, notably those of Russolo, emphasized color rather than machinelike abstractions, and generally approximated the manner of abstract expressionism. In the music by Pratella and others we find a profusion of modern devices of their futurist day, with a foremost place given to the whole-tone scale. The futurists gave monody preference over polyphony, and steady rhythm to asymmetry The future of the futurists appears passé, but they opened the gates to the experimenters of the actual chronological future, which none of them lived to witness.

fuyant (Fr.). Fleeing away.

fuzztone. An onomatopoeic term for a distortion effect used primarily on electric guitar in rock. The guitar's electronic path to the amplifier is interrupted by a floor effects box; the fuzztone activating button causes the guitar's signal to overdrive the amplifier, creating a highly controlled FEEDBACK with the desired "dirty" and powerful "fuzz" sound.

G. 1. The 7th degree in the alphabetical scale and the 5th (dominant) of the C-major scale. In France, Italy, Spain, and Russia, G is called Sol, as it appears in the original syllabic hymn of Guido d'Arezzo. SOLMIZATION is the practice of singing scales beginning with Sol, which was the lowest note of the GUIDONIAN HAND. 2. *G.*, *gauche* in *m.g.* (*main gauche*, left hand). 3. *G.* (*G.O.*), *grand orgue* (great organ).

G clef. The treble clef; see "The Clefs" p. xxiii.

G dur (Ger.). G major.

G major. This is a favorite key of Classical and Romantic composers and their public. Its tonic, dominant, and subdominant are strongly represented on the open strings of the violin family. It suggests a cloudless landscape and warm sunshine. Not as identifiably pastoral as the key of F major, G major is wonderfully suitable for solos on the oboe or the flute, occasionally echoed by a muted horn. The number of symphonic works in G major is immense. The *Oxford Sym.* and the *Surprise Sym.* of Haydn are in G major. Mozart made use of G major in his entrancing *Eine kleine Nachtmusik*; Beethoven's 4th Piano Concerto is in G major. One of Dvořák's syms. is in G major, as is Mahler's 4th. Numberless dances for piano are in G major: Paderewski's *Minuet in G* is celebrated.

G minor. This is a key of earnest meditation. Like G major, its tonic and dominant are represented by 2 open strings on every instrument of the string family; as a relative key of B-flat major it provides for natural modulations, especially for woodwind and brass instruments. One of the greatest syms. in G minor is Mozart's Sym. No. 40, in which the key is seldom abandoned in the lively 1st movement, the minuet, and the finale. Among Haydn's syms. the one that bears the name *La poule* (The Hen) is in G minor. There is any number of solo pieces for violin and other instruments in the key of G minor; the Violin Concerto by Max Bruch should be mentioned. The key also lies well for the piano. Among notable examples are the Piano Concerto by Dvořák and the popular 2nd Piano Concerto by Saint-Saëns.

G moll (Ger.). G minor.

G string. The lowest string on the violin. On the viola and cello it is the 2nd string above the lowest string; on the double bass it is the highest string.

Gabrieli, Andrea (called Andrea di Cannaregio), eminent Italian organist and composer, uncle of Giovanni Gabrieli; b. Venice, *c.* 1510; d. there, 1586. He was a pupil of Adrian Willaert at S. Marco and chorister there (1536); was organist at S. Geremia in Cannaregio in 1557–58; was in Frankfurt for the coronation of Maximilian II as court organist of Duke Albrecht V of Bavaria. In 1566 he returned to Venice and was appointed 2nd organist at S. Marco; became 1st organist on Jan. 1, 1585, succeeding Merulo. He enjoyed a great reputation as an organist (his concerts with Merulo, on 2 organs, were featured attractions). Among his pupils were his nephew and Hans Leo Hassler.

A prolific composer, he wrote a large number of works of varied description, many of which were publ. posth., ed. by his nephew. His versatility is attested by the fact that he was equally adept in sacred music of the loftiest spirit and in instrumental music, as well as in madrigals, often of a comic nature. He was one of the 1st composers to mix instrumental and vocal forces in the CORO SPEZZATO style, in motets, masses, psalms, and sacred concertos. His instrumental output includes canzonas *alla francese*, ricercares, organ intonations, toccatas, 3 organ masses, and a battle piece.

Gabrieli, Giovanni, celebrated Italian organist, composer, and teacher, nephew of Andrea Gabrieli; b. Venice, between 1554 and 1557; d. there, Aug. 12, 1612. He lived in Munich from 1575 to 1579. In 1584 he was engaged to substitute for Merulo as 1st organist at S. Marco in Venice; in 1585 he was permanently appointed as 2nd organist (his uncle meanwhile took charge of the 1st organ); retained this post until his death. As a composer he stands at the head of the Venetian school; he was probably the 1st to write vocal works with parts for instrumental groups in various combinations, partly specified, partly left to the conductor, used as accompaniment as well as interspersed instrumental sinfonie (*Sacrae symphoniae*). His role as a composer and teacher is epoch-making; through his innovations and his development of procedures and devices invented by others (free handling of several choirs in the many-voiced vocal works, "concerted" solo parts and duets in the few-voiced vocal works, trio-sonata texture, novel dissonance treatment, speech rhythm, root progressions in 5ths, use of tonal and range levels for structural purposes, coloristic effects) and through his numerous German pupils (particularly Schütz) and other transalpine followers, he gave a new direction to the development of music.

His instrumental music helped to spark the composition of German instrumental ensemble music, which reached its apex in the symphonic and chamber music works of the Classic masters. Of interest also is the fact that one of his ricercari, a 4-part work in the 10th tone (1595), is an early example of the "fugue with episodes." His vocal compositions include sacred concertos, sacred syms., and secular concerted madrigals; his instrumental works include organ intonations, canzonas and sonatas (both for ensemble with basso continuo), toccatas, fantasias, motets and sacred sym. intabulations, and the famous *Sonata pian e forte* (1597). Many of his works also appeared in various collections of the period.

Gabrilowitsch, Ossip (Salomonovich), notable Russian-American pianist and conductor; b. St. Petersburg, Feb. 7, 1878; d. Detroit, Sept. 14, 1936. From 1888 to 1894 he was a pupil at the St. Petersburg Cons., studying piano with A. Rubinstein and composition with Navratil, Liadov, and

Glazunov; graduated as winner of the Rubinstein Prize, then spent 2 years (1894–96) in Vienna studying with Leschetizky; toured Germany, Austria, Russia, France, and England. His 1st American tour (debut Carnegie Hall, N.Y., 1900) was eminently successful, as were his subsequent visits (1901–16).

During the season 1912–13 he gave in Europe a series of 6 historical concerts illustrating the development of the piano concerto from Bach to the present day; on his American tour in 1914–15 he repeated the entire series in several of the larger cities, meeting with an enthusiastic reception. On Oct. 6, 1909, he married the contralto Clara Clemens (daughter of Mark Twain), with whom he frequently appeared in joint recitals. He conducted his 1st N.Y. concert in 1916; was appointed conductor of the Detroit Sym. Orch. in 1918. From 1928 he also conducted the Philadelphia Orch., sharing the baton with Leopold Stokowski, while retaining his Detroit position.

gadulka. Pear-shaped Bulgarian traditional fiddle. Similar to Russian GUDOK.

gagaku. Orch. music of the Japanese court and aristocracy, stately and heterophonic, still performed on appropriate occasions. Gagaku is the oldest extant orch. music in the world. Instruments used include the *nyōteki* (transverse flute), *hichiriki* (shawm), *shō* (mouth organ), and *kakko* (barrel drums).

gai (*gaiement*; Fr.; It.). Gaily, lively, briskly.

gaida. Bagpipe found in Bulgaria, Macedonia, Poland, and Ruthenian regions.

gaillarde (from Fr. *gai*, merry; It. *gagliarda*; Ger. *Gagliarde*). Galliard; a vivacious court couple dance popular in France, Spain, and England during the late 16th century and the early 17th century. At court occasions the gaillarde usually followed the stately pavane. The 2 dances are in fact related melodically, but the gaillarde transforms the symmetric binary meter of the pavane into a lively (but not too rapid) ternary beat. In England the gaillarde was also known under the French name *cinq pas* (five-step), named for its pattern of 4 strong beats ending with an extra rhythmic step. Queen Elizabeth reportedly practiced the gaillarde for her morning exercises.

gaita. Generic Spanish and Portuguese term for pipe; refers to various traditional instruments, including bagpipe, shawm, hornpipe, panpipe, flute, and accordion.

gala (from Fr. *regaler*, amuse, entertain). An advertising term to denote a special event.

gala, di (It.). Gaily, merrily.

galant (Fr., elegant, courtly). GALLANT STYLE.

Galanta Dances. Orch. suite by Kodály, 1933; 5 pieces of a Gypsy character, based on folk tunes from the region of a Hungarian town.

Galanter Stil (Ger.). GALLANT STYLE.

Galanterien (Ger.). In the 18th century, the most fashionable pieces, such as theatrical compositions or dance pieces found in the Baroque suite (minuet, gavotte, bourrée, polonaise, air). As the rococo became passé, the term was used derogatorily.

Galas, Diamanda (Dimitria Angeliki Elena), remarkable American avant-garde composer and vocalist of Greek extraction; b. San Diego, Aug. 29, 1955. She studied biochemistry, psychology, music, and experimental performance at the Univ. of Calif. at San Diego (1974–79); she also took private vocal lessons. In her scientific studies she and a group of medical students began investigating extreme mental states, using themselves as subjects in a series of bizarre mind-altering experiments; her resultant understanding of psychopathology (notably schizophrenia and psychosis) became an underlying subject in most of her work.

After some success as a jazz pianist, she began a vocal career in which her remarkable precision and advanced technique attracted attention. Although she has performed such demanding works as Xenakis's microtonal *N'Shima* (Brooklyn Phil., Jan. 15, 1981) and Globokar's *Misère* (West German Radio Orch., Cologne, 1980), she is best known for her theatrical performances of her own solo vocal works, given at venues ranging from the Donaueschingen Festival to the N.Y. rock club Danceteria. Her compositions, most of which employ live electronics and/or tape, are improvised according to rigorous, complex "navigation(s) through specified mental states." Her performances have stringent requirements for lighting and sound and possess a shattering intensity. Her brother Philip Dimitri Galas, a playwright whose works were as violent as is his sister's music, died of AIDS in the late 1980s; her increasing emotional and political involvement in what she regards as this "modern plague" led to her 4-part work *Masque of the Red Death* (from 1986).

Galilei, Vincenzo, celebrated Italian lutenist, composer, and music theorist, father of the great astronomer Galileo Galilei; b. S. Maria a Monte, near Florence, *c.* 1520; d. Florence (buried), July 2, 1591. A skillful lutenist and violinist, and a student of ancient Greek theory, he was a prominent member of the artistic circle meeting at Count Bardi's house known as the Florentine Camerata; his compositions for solo voice with lute accompaniment may be regarded as the starting point of the monody successfully cultivated by Peri, Caccini, etc., the founders of the OPERA IN MUSICA. A zealous advocate of Grecian simplicity, in contrast with contrapuntal complexity, he publ. several tracts on music advancing his theories, all of considerable historical interest. Galilei placed his music in his *Fronimo* (lute transcriptions and original compositions), 2 books of lute intabulations (1563, 1584), 2 books of 4- and 5-voiced madrigals (1574, 1587), and 2-part CONTRAPUNTI (1584).

gallant style (Fr. *style galant*). This is a contemporaneous advertising term used by composers and aimed at amateurs during the mid–18th century for the "elegant" aesthetic of composition that gradually superseded the strict and purely musical Baroque idiom of Bach and Handel. There is, of course, no particular gallantry in this style; the term denotes music in the salon manner, homophonic rather than polyphonic, serving to entertain rather than to enlighten, evoking sentiment rather than meditation. In this sense it is synonymous with ROCOCO. Paradoxically, the gallant style was given its mark of dignity and even nobility by the sons of the great Bach, Wilhelm Friedemann and Carl Philipp Emanuel, who initiated the EMPFINDSAMER STIL, a pre-Romantic fashion of musical AFFECTS designed to drive music away from austere formalism toward human expressiveness and the "natural" philosophy of Rousseau and the French Encyclopedists. Instrumental pieces composed in the gallant style were sometimes called GALANTERIEN. In this lighter mode, dance movements are the favored forms, brevity the most striking feature; also favored are a symmetry of phraseology, facile melodiousness, and pleasing, charming, humorous, playful, and merry qualities.

galliard. GAILLARDE.

galop (Fr.; Ger. *Galopp*). 1. A lively circle ballroom dance in syncopated 2/4 time from the mid–19th century. Liszt even wrote a *Grand Galop Chromatique.* 2. In many traditional cultures, a group dance featuring rapid movement in imitation of horses.

Galway, James, famous Irish flute virtuoso; b. Belfast, Dec. 8, 1939. His 1st instrument was the violin, but he soon began to study the flute. At the age of 14 he went to work in a piano shop in Belfast; a scholarship enabled him to go to London, where he continued to study flute and took academic courses in music at the Royal College of Music and the Guildhall School of Music and Drama. He then received a grant to go to Paris, where he studied with Gaston Crunelle at the Cons. and privately with Marcel Moyse. His 1st professional job as a flutist was with the wind band at the Royal Shakespeare Theatre in Stratford-upon-Avon. He subsequently played with the Sadler's Wells Opera Co., the Royal Opera House Orch., and the BBC Sym. Orch.; was appointed principal flutist of the London Sym. Orch. and later with the Royal Phil. As his reputation grew, he was engaged in 1969 by Karajan as 1st flutist in the Berlin Phil., a post he held until 1975. Abandoning his role as an orch. flutist, he devoted himself to a career as a concert artist; in a single season, 1975–76, he appeared as a soloist with all 5 major London orchs.; also toured in the U.S., Australia, and the Orient, as well as in Europe. He became successful on television, playing his 18-karat-gold flute; he has commissioned new works for flute and orch. He publ. *Flute* (London, 1982).

gamba (It., knee; from Ger. *Gamben*).   1. A viola da gamba. 2. An organ stop similar in tone. 3. In U.K., the bass viol.

Gambler, The.   Opera by Prokofiev, 1929, after a story by Dostoyevsky; it was 1st performed not in Russia, but in Brussels. The story deals with a Russian general vacationing at a German resort with his very rich grandmother whose fortune he hopes to inherit. But she proceeds to gamble recklessly, and he is in despair. Fortunately, his aide-de-camp manages to break the bank on his own, but this leads to further imbroglios. The imitation of the roulette in centripetal chromatics is highly effective.

game music.   Games of musical compositions, in which cards, each containing a musical phrase, are put together according to special rules, are of considerable antiquity. One such game, "Musikalisches Würfelspiel," was put on the market in London in 1806 and was announced as "Mozart's musical game, enclosed in an elegant box instructing in a system of easy composition by mechanical means of an unlimited number of waltzes, rondos, horn pipes, reels and minuets." The attribution to Mozart is spurious, but the game itself has a certain ingenuity. The players were to throw a pair of dice, and the number indicated the particular card containing a musical phrase. Since the sequence was arranged so that each card was interchangeable with other cards containing melodies in approximately the same range set in similar harmonies, there was obviously no danger of running into difficulties.

A much more modern conceit was suggested by an English musician William Haves in his book entitled *The Art of Composing Music by a Method Entirely New, Suited to the Meanest Capacity*, published in 1751, in which the author, with a rather crude satirical intent, explained the principle of the game: "Take a brush with stiff bristles (like a toothbrush), dip it into an inkwell, and, by scraping the bristles with the finger, spatter with one sweep a whole composition onto the staff paper. You have only to add stems, bar lines, slurs, etc., to make the opus ready for immediate performance. Whole and half-notes are entirely absent, but who cares for sustained tones anyway!" This is indeed a proleptic anticipation of methods of composition used by the avant-garde 200 years after the publication of this lively manual.

An interesting modern game can be devised using several sets of dodecaphonic cards, each set containing all 12 notes of the chromatic scale. The deck is shuffled and distributed among players. One after another, the players put down duplicates in their hands and collect a missing note of the next dodecaphonic series from the cards put down by other players. The winner is the player who 1st assembles all 12 different notes.

The most ambitious musical game of the modern era is *Strategie* by Xenakis, 1st performed at the Venice Festival (1963). In it, 2 conductors lead 2 different orchs. in 2 uncoordinated works. The audience declares the winner, taking into consideration the excellence of each orch. group, marking points on the scoreboard for most striking rhythms, best color effects, and finest instrumental solos.

Modern scores descriptive of games are numerous. Honegger wrote a symphonic movement, *Rugby*; Bliss composed a ballet entitled *Checkmate*; Paul Reif selected *Philidor's Defense* as the title of a work for a chamber orch., inspired by a chess game played in 1858. Stravinsky portrayed a poker game in his *Jeu de Cartes*, a "ballet in 3 deals" in which the joker is defeated by a royal flush in hearts. A more abstract score by Stravinsky, entitled *Agon*, also portrays a competition. Debussy's ballet score *Jeux* depicts an allegorical game of tennis.

gamelan.   A typical Indonesian orch., variously comprised of tuned gongs, chimes, drums, flutes, chordophones,

Gamelan

xylophones, and small cymbals. These ensembles are most strongly associated with but not limited to the islands of Java and Bali. The ensemble is heard on its own accord, or functions as accompaniment to dance and theater performances, some lasting all night. During its height, each royal court had its own set and style of instruments, repertoire, and performers; the end of the monarchical system meant their dispersion; villages have kept the tradition alive.

The repetitive structure of most gamelan music is based on heterophonic and colotomic principles—quasi-monophony in several parts and the signification of meter through a variety of gong strokes. The atmosphere is also leavened by quiet solos and, in Balinese gamelan, spectacularly precise performances of complex rhythmic stops and starts. There are generally 2 tuning systems, the *pelog* (heptatonic) and *slendro* (pentatonic), but there are no absolute guidelines concerning scale interval or actual pitch frequency.

Gamelan music is an example of ethnomusicology at its best. Europe had heard its 1st gamelan at the Paris Exposition of 1889. Interest was great, and recordings circulated. But by the time Western musicologists began serious study in Indonesia, gamelan music was in decline, along with the courts. Western musicologists (and the composer Colin McPhee) studied the instruments; learned, wrote down, and analyzed the music; observed the theater and dance it accompanied; recovered whatever of the older repertoire they could; and, in McPhee's case, helped reinvent a genre (*ketchak*, the monkey dance). Gamelan is one of the most thriving of world musics today. New and historic gamelan orchs. are found throughout the world.

gamut (from Grk. *gamma* + Lat *ut*; It., Rus. *gamma*; Fr. *gamme*). 1. A scale or pitch range; derived from the Guidonian *gamma-ut*, the 1st note of the hexachord. 2. A collection of sounds available to a composer or instrument. 3. Any metaphorical range, e.g., range of expression available to a performer.

Gang (Ger.). Passage. One of Bach's Lydian-mode chorales begins with the text "O schwerer Gang"; the "diffi-

cult passage" comprises 3 successive whole tones, producing the tritone.

gangar. A Norwegian walking dance in 2/4 time.

ganz (Ger.). 1. Whole; *ganze Note*, whole note. 2. Very; *ganz langsam*, very slowly.

Ganztonleiter (Ger.). Whole-tone scale.

garbamente (*garbato*; It.). Gracefully, elegantly; in a refined style.

Garcia, Jerry (Jerome John), American rock musician; b. San Francisco, Aug. 1, 1942; d. Serenity Knolls, Marin County, Calif., Aug. 9, 1995. He was a high school dropout and served in the U.S. Army before associating himself with various rock groups, especially those cultivating the new electric sound. Garcia's most successful creation was a group that became the Grateful Dead. In its original lineup it included keyboard and harmonica player Ron "Pigpen" McKernan (b. San Bruno, Calif., Sept. 8, 1945; d. of complications from drug and alcohol addictions, Corte Madera, Calif., Mar. 8, 1973), classically trained bass guitarist Phil(ip Chapman) Lesh (b. Berkeley, Calif., Mar. 15, 1940); Bob (Robert Hall) Weir (b. San Francisco, Oct. 16, 1947); and drummer Bill Kreutzmann (b. Palo Alto, Calif., June 7, 1946). Later acquisitions included classically trained keyboardist Tom Constanten; percussionist Mickey Hart (b.

N.Y.); vocalist Donna Godchaux (b. San Francisco, Aug. 22, 1947); keyboardist Keith Godchaux (b. San Francisco, July 19, 1948; d. in an auto accident, Ross, Calif., July 23, 1980, a year after he and Donna Godchaux left the group); and keyboardist Brent Mydland (b. 1953; d. July 26, 1990). Garcia and Weir contributed the bulk of the songwriting; all except Lesh, Kreutzmann, Constanten, and Hart provided vocals.

The immediate predecessor of the Grateful Dead was a group named the Warlocks (1965–67), with a strong blues basis provided by McKernan. After some extremely experimental albums, featuring then-new electronics and extended modal solos, the mortuary connotations of the group continued with such albums as *Workingman's Dead*, a turn to a country-rock sound and better-executed vocal harmonies. There were also in its repertoire some antonyms, such as *American Beauty*. Garcia's innovative use of electronic amplification established a state of the art for clean, loud, psychedelic rock sound. The Grateful Dead toured almost endlessly and had a large following known as the Deadheads; yet the group probably played more free concerts than paid ones and started a genuinely charitable foundation. On one notable occasion they made a sensational tour to Egypt to play at the foot of the Pyramids for the benefit of the mummified ungrateful dead once buried there, contributing funds to the Egyptian Dept. of Antiquities.

The Dead were most loved in concert, although many of their recordings feature fine and subtle arrangements and recording techniques. With the significant importance of hallucinogenic and other drugs to group members at different times (Mydland died of an overdose), concerts could range from the mediocre to the sublime; but the community around them seemed to accept whatever they offered. Members of the group made solo albums or albums with other groups of their own devising. Garcia's health became an increasingly difficult issue in the last decade of the Dead's existence; a combination of a heart condition, diabetes, and the effects of years of drug-taking killed him in the summer of 1995; the surviving members of the group soon agreed to disband.

García Lorca, Federico, Spanish poet, playwright, and musician; b. Fuentevaqueros, June 5, 1898; d. murdered during the Spanish Civil War by Franco's Falangists, Granada, July or Aug. 1936. García Lorca was an amateur guitarist and singer who set a number of poems to folk melodies. More important, he was extremely interested in the flamenco genre of CANTE JONDO, and with Falla and others encouraged the revival of the performance of the genre. García Lorca also explored the more profound implications of "deep song" in the Spanish soul and duende. Since his death, many of his poems have been set to music (notably by Crumb, Ohana, and Henze), and his plays are the basis of many operas, including *Blood Wedding* and *Yerma*.

Garden of Fand, The. Symphonic poem by Bax, 1920, depicting the island in Celtic myth occupied by a sorceress who lures sea voyagers to their destruction.

Gardiner, John Eliot, English conductor; b. Springhead, Dorset, Apr. 20, 1943. He was educated at King's College, Cambridge; while still a student there, he founded the Monteverdi Choir (1964); then went to France to study with Nadia Boulanger; upon his return to England, took postgraduate courses with Thurston Dart at King's College, London. He made his 1st major conducting appearance at the Promenade Concerts in London in 1968; also conducted at the Sadler's Wells Opera and at Covent Garden. He continued giving concerts with his Monteverdi Choir; also founded the English Baroque Soloists, a group which played works of the Baroque on original instruments. From 1980 to 1983 he was principal conductor of the CBC Radio Orch. in Vancouver; from 1981 he served as artistic director of the Göttingen Handel Festival, and from 1982 to 1989 of the Orch. de l'Opéra de Lyon. In 1991 he was made chief conductor of the North German Radio Sym. Orch. in Hamburg. He prepared performing eds. of a number of scores by Rameau and others; he is credited with the discovery (in Paris in 1971) of the MS of Rameau's opera *Les Boreades*, which he conducted at Aix-en-Provence in 1982.

Garfunkel, Art, American soft-rock composer and singer; b. N.Y., Nov. 5, 1941. With high school classmate Paul Simon he started a song duo; at the age of 16 they produced a fairly successful record, *Hey, Schoolgirl*, under the group name Tom and Jerry. Their next common effort, as Simon and Garfunkel, *Sounds of Silence*, was a major hit when it was issued as a single in 1965. They demonstrated their versatility by writing the soundtrack for the film *The Graduate*, which featured a song, *Mrs. Robinson*, destined to become very popular. Their album *Bridge Over Troubled Water* was praised in pop circles; then the 2 went their separate ways in 1970. In addition to releasing solo recordings, Garfunkel became interested in acting, and he appeared in *Catch-22, Carnal Knowledge*, and *Bad Timing: A Sensual Obsession*. He also tried his hand at writing poetry. Garfunkel was reunited with Simon in 1982, producing a fine album, *The Concert in Central Park*.

Garland, Judy (born Frances Ethel Gumm), famous American singer of popular music and actress; b. Grand Rapids, Minn., June 10, 1922; d. London, June 22, 1969. Having been reared in a family of vaudeville entertainers, she made her stage debut at the age of 2 and then toured with her sisters before breaking into motion pictures in 1936; subsequently gained wide recognition for her film appearances with Mickey Rooney. She won a special Academy Award as well as film immortality for her portrayal of Dorothy in *The Wizard of Oz* (1939), adopting its *Over the Rainbow* as her theme song. She later appeared in such musical films as *For Me and My Gal* (1942), *Meet Me in St. Louis* (1944), *Easter Parade* (1948), and *In the Good Old Summertime* (1949).

In succeeding years she concentrated mainly on nightclub and concert hall performances; however, she made several more compelling film appearances, most notably in *A Star Is Born* (1954) and *Judgment at Nuremberg* (1961). In spite of many successes, her private life became public when a string of misfortunes, including marital difficulties, drug dependency, and suicide attempts, overwhelmed her. Her fans remained steadfastly loyal until her death at the age of 47. Her daughter Liza Minnelli (b. Los Angeles, Mar. 12, 1946) also became a successful singer and actress but has at times seemed too much like her mother.

Garner, Erroll (Louis), famous African-American jazz pianist and composer; b. Pittsburgh, June 15, 1921; d. Los Angeles, Jan. 2, 1977. Completely untutored and unlettered, he composed tunes extemporaneously, singing and accompanying himself at the piano, with an amanuensis to put down the notes. He also played drums and slap-bass. His nervous rubato style won acclaim from the cognoscenti and jazz aficionados. Incredibly precocious, he played regularly over radio station KDKA in Pittsburgh at the age of 7 with a group called the Candy Kids; as an adolescent he played piano on riverboats cruising the Allegheny River; then was a featured piano player in nightclubs and restaurants. He went to N.Y. in 1944, formed his own trio in 1946. In 1948 he went to Paris, and he made further European tours in 1962, 1964, 1966, and 1969.

His whimsical piano style especially appealed to French jazz critics, who called him "The Picasso of the Piano" and, alluding to his digital dexterity, "The Man with 40 Fingers." In 1971 the Republic of Mali issued a postage stamp in his honor. Among his own songs, the plangent *Misty* became greatly popular; many of his other songs (he composed about 200 of them) reflect similar wistful moods, exemplified by such titles as *Dreamy*, *Solitaire*, and *That's My Kick*.

Garrick Gaieties, The. Revue with 3 editions (1926, 1930, 1936). Includes Rodgers and Hart's *Manhattan* and *Sentimental Me*, and V. Duke's *I Am Only Human After All*.

Gaspard de la nuit. A cycle of 3 piano pieces by Ravel, 1909, entitled *Ondine*, *Le Gibet*, and *Scarbo*. These pieces are fine paradigms of impressionistic writing, portraying a mermaid, a gallows, and a playful sprite. The entire group was performed for the 1st time in Paris.

Gassenhauer (Ger.). Street song; formerly, any authentic folk song or newly composed folk-song-like piece. An eponymous work is probably the best known of the numerous pieces that make up the Orff-Keetmann *Schulwerk*.

gathering note. 1. In chanting, a hold on the last syllable of the recitation. 2. In Anglican churches, the opening note sounded on the organ, a beat before the congregation starts, to give pitch.

gato. A popular country dance of Argentina, in 6/8 and 3/4 time.

gauche (Fr.). Left. *Main gauche*, left hand.

gauche dexterity. Satire and burlesque depend for their effect on a deliberate violation of traditional rules of melodic structure, rhythmic symmetry, and harmonic euphony. A sophisticated imitation of such semiliterate gaucherie often becomes an art in itself. Examples are many: Stravinsky reproduces the heterogeneous harmony of the barrel organ in *Petrouchka*; Milhaud tonalizes the natural cacophony of a barroom in *Le Boeuf sur le toit*. To some, Satie elevated the dexterity of his gaucherie to a high art of musical persiflage; he was helped by his lack of an academic technique of composition; it was easier for him than for formally schooled masters to imitate ineptitude.

Gaudeamus Igitur. A German student song in Latin, suggesting that scholars should enjoy life before it's too late. The song dates back to the 13th century, but the best known use of it is heard in Brahms's ACADEMIC FESTIVAL OVERTURE. The text also figures in a polychoral episode in Berlioz's *La Damnation de Faust*.

gaudioso (It.). Joyous, julibant.

gavotta (It.; Fr. *gavotte*). A Baroque and Classic French dance in alla breve, strongly marked duple time; the upbeat of half a measure slowly became characteristic. The gavotte's formal structure is ternary, the middle section being a MUSETTE (Fr., bagpipe), usually in the dominant key, which often has a pedal point on the tonic and the dominant in the bass, in imitation of the drone of a bagpipe. The derivation of *gavotte* is uncertain; it may be an old local name for the natives of the hill country in Provence. The gavotte has reappeared in isolated cases in Romantic and 20th-century music (e.g., Prokofiev's *Classical Sym.*), but the intent seems more nostalgic than musical.

Gay Divorce, The. Musical by C. Porter, 1932. Mimi, an actress, goes to England to arrange a divorce from a boring husband. Expecting a correspondent, she meets instead a man who has fallen for her. She gets both her divorce and a new spouse. Includes *Night and Day*, *You're in Love*, *I've Got You on My Mind*, and *I Still Love the Red, White, and Blue*.

Gay, John, English poet and dramatist, inventor of the ballad opera and librettist of *The Beggar's Opera*; b. Barnstaple, Devon (baptized), Sept. 16, 1685; d. London, Dec. 4, 1732. *The Beggar's Opera* was premiered in London on Jan. 29, 1728, and was immensely popular for a century, chiefly because of its sharp satire and the English and Scots folk melodies it used. It has had a number of successful revivals. The government disliked it and forbade the performance of its sequel, *Polly*, the score of which was printed in 1729. When *Polly* was finally performed in London on June 19, 1777, it was a FIASCO, because the conditions satirized no longer prevailed.

Gayané. Ballet by Khatchaturian, 1942, 1st performed in the city of Perm by the troupe of the Kirov Theater of Leningrad (which was evacuated to Perm during the war). Gayané is the name of an Armenian farm worker whose husband is a traitor. His attempt to subvert her is foiled; he is apprehended and suffers the supreme penalty, patriotically approved by Gayané. The score contains the celebrated SABRE DANCE. There is also a nostalgic lullaby and other numbers of immediate popular appeal.

Gaye, Marvin (Pentz), gifted African-American soul singer and instrumentalist; b. Washington, D.C., Apr. 2, 1939; d. murdered by his father, a retired Pentecostal preacher, during an argument about money, Los Angeles, Apr. 1, 1984. The family name was Gay, but a mute *e* was added to the end to avoid the slang connotation of the original surname. Marvin sang in the choir of his father's church and also played the drums at school. In 1956 he sang with the group called Rainbows until they split; he joined a separate group, the Marquees, which later became the Moonglows. In 1961 he was recruited by Motown in Detroit; he made duet recordings with Tammi Terrell, including *Ain't No Mountain High Enough* (1967) and *Ain't Nothing Like the Real Thing* (1968). Among his early solo hits was *I Heard It Through the Grapevine* in 1968; among his successful individual albums are *What's Going On* (1970) and *Midnight Love*, including *Sexual Heeling* (1983), on which he also performed almost every instrumental part. His career was broken up by divorces (he was married thrice) and bouts with cocaine and other narcotics. Yet his bringing of the Motown sound into the age of funk was a major and influential accomplishment.

Gazza ladra, La (The Thieving Magpie). Opera semiseria by Rossini, 1817, from a French source, produced at La Scala, Milan. A servant girl is sentenced to hanging on suspicion of stealing a spoon (apparently neither cruel nor unusual punishment early in the 19th century). She is saved from the gallows when the spoon is found in the nest of an errant magpie.

Gebrauchsmusik. Utility music; music for everyday use. This term came into use in Germany after World War I; its earliest mention is found in the German magazine *Signale für die Musikalische Welt* of Dec. 1918. Gebrauchsmusik should ideally be easy to perform by amateurs, and its texture free from the strictures of academic usage. Unresolved dissonances are liberally admitted, while the rhythmic patterns emulate the type of music turned out by untutored composers of popular ballads. Gebrauchsmusik promoted the utilization of new mechanical instruments, the radio, the phonograph, and music for the films.

A variety of Gebrauchsmusik was *Gemeinschaftsmusik* (community music), which cultivated choral singing. The term *Gemeinschaftsmusik* was later changed to *Sing- und Spielmusik*, in the generic category of *Hausmusik*. Probably the 1st work written specially for such groups by a modern composer was *Das neue Werk* by Hindemith. An innovation in Gebrauchsmusik is spoken rhythmic song, a variant of SPRECHSTIMME. In opera the librettos were usually satirical and political, with a radical bent, especially proletarian music. From Germany operatic Gebrauchsmusik was transplanted to America, where economic impoverishment contributed to its popularity. Gebrauchsmusik had little success in Russia, France, or Italy, countries with a rich operatic culture in which there was no necessity of reducing operatic productions to miniature dimensions.

To compensate for the abolition of old educational music, composers of Gebrauchsmusik promulgated a new academic doctrine of giving simple pleasure to beginners. Hausmusik, and Gebrauchsmusik in general, relied on the participation of the audience. Children's music is a natural product of Gebrauchsmusik; the earliest example of such neoacademic Gebrauchsmusik is Hindemith's piece for school children, *Wir bauen eine Stadt*. Orff succeeded in enlarging the academic routine by composing pieces modern in harmony, rhythm, and orchestration and yet demanding little professional skill to perform. Easy humor is an important part of practical Gebrauchsmusik. Toch combined wit with ostensible erudition in his *Geographic Fugue* for speaking chorus, which recites names of exotic places in rhythmic counterpoint. *Mikrokosmos* by Bartók presents Gebrauchsmusik of considerable complexity without losing its musical innocence; modern-minded children enjoy playing it. N. Slonimsky's album of *51 Minitudes* for piano includes varieties of polytonal and atonal music.

gebunden (Ger.). Tied; LEGATO.

gedackt (Ger.). Stopped (organ pipes).

gedämpft (Ger.). Damped; muffled; muted.

gedehnt (Ger.). Sustained, prolonged; slow, stately; LARGAMENTE; STESO.

Gefallen, nach (Ger.). AD LIBITUM.

gefällig (Ger.). Pleasing, graceful.

Gefärte (Ger.). The fugal answer.

Geflüster (Ger.). Whisper, murmur. *Wie ein Geflüster*, like a whisper, murmuring.

Gefühl, mit (Ger.). With feeling, expressively.

Gegensatz (Ger.). The fugal countersubject.

Gegenthema (Ger.). The fugal countersubject.

gehalten (Ger.). Held back, restrained.

gehaucht (Ger., sighed). Very softly and lightly sung (or played).

geheimnisvoll (Ger.). Mysteriously.

gehend (Ger.). ANDANTE.

Geige (Ger.). VIOLIN.

Geigenprinzipal (Ger.). Violin diapason organ stop.

Geisslieder (Ger. *Geissl*, scourge). Chants of the flagellants praying for the cessation of the plague and other calamities during the Middle Ages. These chants became the melodic and rhythmic sources of German folk songs of the Renaissance period.

Geist (Ger.). Spirit, soul; essence.

Geister Trio, Das. GHOST TRIO.

geistliche Musik (Ger.). Sacred music.

gelassen (Ger.). Calm, placid, easy.

geläufig (Ger.). Fluent, easy.

Geläufigkeit (Ger.). Fluency, velocity.

geloso (It.). Jealous.

gemächlich (Ger.). Easily, comfortably, leisurely; COMODO.

gemässigt (Ger.). Measured; moderato.

Gemeinschaftsmusik. A term used by German composers to designate communal singing or playing; although of ancient origin, the practice was popularized as part of the program of HAUSMUSIK, in the generic category of GEBRAUCHSMUSIK.

gemendo (It.). Moaning.

gemessen (Ger.). As measured; MODERATO.

gemischte stimmen (Ger.). Mixed voices.

gemischter Chor (Ger.). Mixed choir, i.e., SATB.

gemshorn (Ger.; Eng. *goat-horn*). 1. A Renaissance obsolete block flute or recorder in the shape of an animal horn. 2. An organ stop making a sweet pastoral sound, suggesting that of a natural horn.

Gemüt(h), mit (Ger.). With feeling; soulfully.

gemüt(h)lich (Ger.). Easily and cheerily; DISINVOLTO; COMODO (in tempo).

Generalbass (Ger.). BASSO CONTINUO.

Generalpause (Ger.). A written silence for an entire orch.

Generalprobe (Ger.). In Europe, an open rehearsal prior to the official 1st night of a production.

generator. 1. A chordal root; harmonic fundamental. 2. A tone which produces a series of harmonics.

generoso (It.). Free, ample.

genius

This word is an unfortunate term when applied to literature, art, or music. It is derived from the name of a tutelary deity, and in Roman usage was applied to a person or his habitation. One does not have to embrace Edison's cynical definition, "Genius is 10% inspiration and 90% perspiration," to warn critics and analysts to use the word with caution. Schumann contributed to the use of the word *genius* when he put it in the mouth of the fictional musician Eusebius, who exclaimed, "Hats off, a genius!" as he began to play Chopin's op. 2, *Variations on a Theme from Mozart's "Don Giovanni."* Another time, as the young Brahms showed to Schumann one of his early works, Schumann noted in his diary: "Johannes Brahms was on a visit. A genius!" When the Vienna music critic Julius Korngold brought his 10-year-old son Erich to Mahler and let him play, Mahler became greatly agitated and kept exclaiming, "A genius! A genius!" Young Korngold eventually became known as the writer of idiomatic film music in Hollywood, while his operas, which had created quite a sensation when they were 1st produced, were forgotten.

Popular mythology prescribes that geniuses must behave erratically, eccentrically, and unpredictably. Beethoven, Berlioz, and Liszt fit this romantic description to some extent. But Beethoven, like Mozart before him, was a craftsman 1st and foremost. Bach upsets the popular picture of a genius. To his contemporaries he appeared as an honest and earnest worker, modestly performing his functions as church composer, organist, and rector of a boys' school. Brahms fit comfortably into the bourgeois framework of the Viennese middle class. Among virtuosos who looked like geniuses was Paganini, whose press agents spared no effort to represent him as being inspired both by God and Satan in his violin playing. The violinist Gidon Kremer virtually sweeps the stage in a concerto performance. Rachmaninoff, who was a great pianist as well as a highly popular composer, presented a visage, as described by a critic, of a provincial banker; another performer described him as the only pianist who did not grimace when playing. Yet a novel has been published under the title *Rachmaninoff's Eyes*, attributing some magical quality thereto.

Ravel seemed to lack all external attributes of a great musician; he had a very poor sense of pitch, his memory was not retentive, he was a mediocre piano player, and he was practically helpless as a conductor. Stravinsky was only marginally better in these external gifts. If one wishes to conjure up the romantic vision of a genius among modern composers, Scriabin would fit the part. His appearance of a distraught visionary, his delicate physique, his inability to cope with the hard realities of life, his messianic complex, his belief that he was called upon to unite all arts in one mystical consummation, all combined to create the impression of a genius incarnate.

But Schoenberg, who came close to reforming music and changing its direction, presented the very opposite to a conventional idea of genius. He was bald and lacked social graces; he was not a good performer on any instrument and only a passable conductor of his own works.

The word *genius* was often applied to symphonic conductors. Toscanini was not extravagant in appearance but he possessed magic as a conductor. Von Bülow was the 1st to establish the outward appearance of a genius of the baton—tall, erect, and imperious. The list of flamboyant conductors, in more or less chronological order, ought to include Artur Nikisch, Serge Koussevitzky, Leopold Stokowski, and Leonard Bernstein. As against these, there is a number of masters of the baton whose outward appearance is unprepossessing. The romantic picture of a genius at work may be accepted only as a literary or artistic device; its definition is vague and its contours inevitably overlap with such concepts as virtuosity, stimulating spirit, ingratiating social qualities, and inability to communicate with people at large.

Genoveva. Opera by Schumann, 1850. Genoveva is left under the protection of a friend of her husband's, who goes off to war. The friend immediately makes advances, which she resists. When the husband returns, the friend accuses her of unfaithfulness. At 1st, the husband orders her put to death, but she proves her innocence. The "friend" flees and judiciously falls off a cliff.

genre. A category of literature, painting, sculpture, and, by extension, a specific form or type of composition. Vocal music genres include opera, oratorio, cantata, or lied; instrumental genres include sym., sonata, concerto, or suite. The term is also applied to specific forms, such as a march, rag, or waltz. However, a genre is not the same as a historic style (Renaissance, Classic, etc.) or an idiom (orch., violin and piano, etc.).

gentilmente (It.). In a graceful, refined style.

Gentlemen Prefer Blondes. Musical by Styne, 1949, based on Anita Loos's novel. The satirical plot demonstrates that a textbook education may not be necessary to succeed when one is irresistibly illiterate, blonde, American, female, and attached to a gray-haired sugar daddy on a European journey. Includes *A Little Girl from Little Rock, Bye Bye Baby,* and *Diamonds Are a Girl's Best Friend.*

Geographical Fugue (Ger. *Fuge aus der Geographie*). A work by Toch, 1930, for spoken chorus, consisting entirely of the rhythmic enumeration of geographical locations. The work is one of the best-known examples of the spoken chorus genre.

geomusic. A relationship existing between soil and soul, between land and life. One of the most remarkable geomusical facts is that an area of some 75,000 square miles (equivalent to about one-third of the size of Tex.) and comprising such focal cultural centers as Bonn, Hamburg, Berlin, Prague, Leipzig, Salzburg, and Vienna, embraces the birthplaces of some of the world's greatest musicians: Bach and Handel, Haydn and Mozart, Beethoven and Schubert, Brahms, Schumann and Mendelssohn, Wagner and Bruckner, Richard Strauss and Johann Strauss, Smetana and Dvořák, Mahler and Schoenberg.

The most accomplished violinists of the 20th century came from Poland, Ukraine, and Lithuania, among them Heifetz, Elman, Isaac Stern, and father and son Oistrakh, all of them Jewish. What is the secret here? What is this peculiar affinity that exists between young Jews of Eastern Europe and the violin? The economic factor proves a dubious explanation.

The small peninsula of Italy generated the finest flowering of opera, a stage form that was born as an art in Florence, which produced through its course of 3 centuries such masters as Monteverdi, Rossini, Verdi, and Puccini, and such great singers as Caruso, Patti, and Pavarotti. It also bore the greatest opera conductor, the uncontrollably temperamental Toscanini. Italians, in fact, were in charge of most opera houses; the Metropolitan Opera of N.Y. was in Italian hands ever since its foundation. The most popular opera composer living in America and writing his own libretti in English is Menotti (who for some reason never applied for American citizenship).

If Italy produces great tenors, Russia is the land of great basses, the grandest among them being Chaliapin. The Russians did not enter the world scene as composers until the 19th century; the names of Glinka, Rimsky-Korsakov, Mussorgsky, and Tchaikovsky testify to the natural gift of Russia in all musical fields. And despite the political upheavals of the Revolution, the Russian achievement continued to be great. Stravinsky, Prokofiev, and Shostakovich remain dominant figures in new Russia; Russian pianists, violinists, and cellists continue to win prizes at international festivals. France contributed to music in a less heroic, less grandiose way; the French of the modern age, Debussy and Ravel among them, provided the music of sensual beauty, leaving the field of sym. and grand opera to the Germans and the Russians.

It is the task of geomusic to account for these selective pursuits within particular nations. And of course, above and behind these nations rise the totally different arts of musical North and South America, Asia, Africa, and Australia. Who could imagine until recently that the 2 greatest American orchs. would be led by Asians, namely Seiji Ozawa and Zubin Mehta? Natural selection plays its irresistible role in art as well as in life.

George M! Musical, 1968, built around the life and songs of George M. Cohan (1878–1942). Includes *Give My Regards to Broadway* (from *Little Johnny Jones*, 1904), *You're a Grand Old Flag*, *Yankee Doodle Dandy*, and *Over There* (1917).

George White's Scandals. A series of N.Y. revues presented between 1919 and 1939. In addition to the female chorus line, songs were composed by George Gershwin (*Somebody Love Me*) and Ray Henderson (*Life is Just a Bowl of Cherries*), and the Blackbottom dance was introduced.

Georgia on My Mind. Hoagy Carmichael composition, with lyrics by Stuart Gurrell, introduced by Mildred Bailey in 1930 and revived in a definitive gospel-tinged version by Ray Charles in 1960. In the 1980s it became the official state song of Georgia, and Charles performed it on the floor of the Ga. State Senate.

gepeitscht, wie (Ger.). As if struck with a whip (Mahler, 6th Sym.).

Gerber, Ernst Ludwig, celebrated German lexicographer; b. Sondershausen, Sept. 29, 1746; d. there, June 30, 1819.

He studied organ and theory with his father; then law and music in Leipzig, becoming a skillful cellist and organist, in which latter capacity he became (1769) his father's assistant, and succeeded him in 1775. He visited Weimar, Kassel, Leipzig, and other cities and gradually gathered together a large collection of musicians' portraits; to these he appended brief biographical notices and finally conceived the plan of writing a biographical dictionary of musicians. Though his resources (in a small town without a public library, and having to rely in great measure on material sent him by his publisher, Breitkopf) were hardly adequate to the task he undertook, his *Historisch-biographisches Lexikon der Tonkünstler* (Leipzig, 2 vols., 1790–92) was so well received, and brought in such a mass of corrections and fresh material from all quarters, that he prepared a supplementary ed. Though the former was intended only as a supplement to Walther's dictionary—and both are, of course, out of date—they contain much material still of value and have been extensively drawn upon by more recent writers. The Viennese Gesellschaft der Musikfreunde purchased his large library.

German dance. DEUTSCHER TANZ.

German flute. The 18th-century name for TRANSVERSE FLUTE or cross flute.

German sixth. A chord of the augmented 6th between the bottom and top notes. Other intervals from the bottom are a major 3rd and doubly augmented 4th, resolving to a tonic 6/4 chord as follows (in C minor):

Gershwin, George

〜〜 〜〜 〜〜 〜〜 〜〜

Immensely gifted American songwriter and composer, brother of Ira Gershwin; b. Jacob Gershvin, N.Y., Sept. 26, 1898; d. Los Angeles, July 11, 1937. His father was an immigrant from Russia whose original name was Gershovitz. Gershwin's extraordinary career began when he was 16, playing the piano in music stores to demonstrate new popular songs. His studies were desultory; he took piano lessons with Ernest Hutcheson and Charles Hambitzer in N.Y.; studied harmony with Edward Kilenyi and Rubin Goldmark; later on, when he was already a famous composer of popular music, he continued to take private lessons; he studied counterpoint with Henry Cowell and Wallingford Riegger; during the last years of his life he applied himself with great earnestness to studying with Joseph Schillinger in an attempt to organize his technique in a scientific manner; some of Schillinger's methods were applied in *Porgy and Bess*. But it was his melodic talent and a genius for

George Gershwin, c. 1920s

rhythmic invention, rather than any studies, that made him a genuinely important American composer.

As far as worldly success was concerned, there was no period of struggle in Gershwin's life; one of his earliest songs, *Swanee*, written at the age of 19, became enormously popular (more than a million copies sold; 2,250,000 phonograph records). He also took time to write a lyrical *Lullaby* for String Quartet (1920). Possessing phenomenal energy, he produced musical comedies in close succession, using fashionable jazz formulas in original and ingenious ways. A milestone in his career was *Rhapsody in Blue* for Piano and Jazz Orch., in which he applied the jazz idiom to an essentially classical form. He played the solo part at a special concert conducted by Paul Whiteman at Aeolian Hall in N.Y. on Feb. 12, 1924. The orchestration was by Ferde Grofé, a circumstance that generated rumors of Gershwin's inability to score for instruments; these rumors, however, were quickly refuted by his production of several orch.l works, scored by himself in a brilliant fashion. He played the piano solo part of his *Concerto in F*, with Walter Damrosch and the N.Y. Sym. Orch. (Dec. 3, 1925); this work had a certain vogue, but its popularity never equaled that of the *Rhapsody in Blue*.

Reverting again to a more popular idiom, Gershwin wrote a symphonic work, *An American in Paris* (N.Y. Phil., Dec. 13, 1928, Damrosch conducting). His *Rhapsody No. 2* was performed by Koussevitzky and the Boston Sym. on Jan. 29, 1932, but was unsuccessful; there followed a *Cuban Overture* (N.Y., Aug. 16, 1932) and Variations for Piano and Orch. on his song *I Got Rhythm* (Boston, Jan. 14, 1934, composer soloist). In the meantime, Gershwin became engaged in his most ambitious undertaking: the composition of *Porgy and Bess*, an American opera in a folk manner, for black singers, after the book by Dubose Heyward. It was 1st staged in Boston on Sept. 30, 1935, and in N.Y. on Oct. 10, 1935. Its reception by the press was not uniformly favorable, but its songs rapidly attained great popularity (*Summertime, I Got Plenty o' Nuthin', It Ain't Neccessarily So, Bess, You Is My Woman Now*); the opera has been successfully revived in N.Y. and elsewhere; it received international recognition when an American company of black singers toured with it in South America and Europe in 1955.

Gershwin's death (of a gliomatous cyst in the right temporal lobe of the brain) at the age of 38 was mourned as a great loss to American music. The 50th anniversary of his death brought forth a number of special tributes in 1987, including a major joint broadcast of his music by the PBS and BBC television networks. His musical comedies include *Our Nell* (1922); *Sweet Little Devil* (1924); *Lady, Be Good!* (1924); *Primrose* (1924); *Tip-Toes* (1925); *Oh Kay!* (1926); *Strike Up the Band* (1927); *Funny Face* (1927); *Rosalie* (1928); *Treasure Girl* (1928); *Show Girl* (1929); *Girl Crazy* (1930); *Of Thee I Sing* (1931; a political satire, the 1st musical to win a Pulitzer Prize); *Pardon My English* (1933); *Let 'em Eat Cake* (1933); for motion pictures: *Shall We Dance, A Damsel in Distress*, and *The Goldwyn Follies* (left unfinished at his death; completed by V. Duke).

Gershwin, Ira (born Israel Gershvin), talented American librettist and lyricist, brother of George Gershwin; b. N.Y., Dec. 6, 1896; d. Beverly Hills, Calif., Aug. 17, 1983. He attended night classes at the College of the City of N.Y., wrote verses and humorous pieces for the school paper, and served as cashier in a Turkish bath of which his father was part-owner. He began writing lyrics for shows in 1918, using the pseudonym Arthur Francis. His 1st full-fledged show as a lyricist was the musical comedy *Be Yourself*, for which he used his own name for the 1st time.

He achieved fame when he wrote the lyrics for his brother's musical comedy, *Lady, Be Good!* (1924). He remained his brother's collaborator until George Gershwin's death in 1937, and his lyrics became an inalienable part of the whole, so that the brothers George and Ira Gershwin became artistic twins, like Gilbert and Sullivan, indissolubly united in some of the greatest productions of the musical theater in America: *Strike Up the Band* (1927), *Of Thee I Sing* (1931), and the culminating product of the brotherly genius, the folk opera *Porgy and Bess* (1935). He also wrote lyrics for other composers, among them V. Duke (*The Ziegfeld Follies of 1936*), Weill (*Lady in the Dark*, 1941, and several motion pictures), Kern (the enormously successful song *Long Ago and Far Away* from the film *Cover Girl*, 1944), Romberg, A. Schwartz, and Arlen.

Ges (Ger.). G flat.

Ges dur (Ger.). G-flat major.

Ges moll (Ger.). G-flat minor.

Gesamtausgabe (Ger.). A complete edition of a composer's works.

Gesamtkunstwerk (Ger.). It was Wagner who promulgated the idea that all arts are interrelated, and that their ultimate synthesis should be the idea of each constituent art: that painting and figurative arts should serve the cause of architecture and stage representations, that poetry should relate to philosophical concepts, and that music should be both the servant and the mistress of its sister arts. In his music dramas Wagner attempted to approximate the ideal of the *Gesamtkunstwerk* (complete art work) by assigning equal importance to the text, orch. music, singing, acting, and scenic design. This operatic reform aimed at the restoration of the unity of the arts of music, literature, and painting, as was believed to have existed in ancient Greek tragedy.

Gesang (Ger.). Singing; a song; melody; vocal part.

Gesang der Jünglinge, Der. Cantata for boy soprano and electronically manipulated children's choir by Stockhausen, 1956, broadcast over 5 groups of loudspeakers surrounding the audience, 1st performed in Cologne. The text is composed of fragments from the Book of Daniel (chapter 3) concerning Shadrach, Meshach, and Abednego and their experience in the Babylonian fiery furnace. This work was among the most successful of the early electronic pieces.

Gesangbuch (Ger.). Songbook, especially a hymn book.

gesangreich (*gesangvoll*; Ger.). Very singingly; CANTABILE.

geschleift (Ger.). Slurred; LEGATO.

geschleppt (Ger.). Dragged out in tempo; SCHLEPPEND.

Geschmackvoll (Ger.). Tastefully.

geschwind (Ger.). Swift, quick, rapid.

Geses (Ger.). G double-flat.

gesprochene Musik (Ger., spoken music). Music consisting entirely of spoken syllables arranged in rhythmic patterns. Very popular in Germany between the 2 World Wars. The best-known example is Toch's *Geographical Fugue*.

gestalt. Gestalt is a psychological term that connotes an ensemble of apperceptions produced by a series of sensory stimuli. Translated as form, figure, configuration, or appearance, gestalt indicates a psychological interaction between the physical nature of a given phenomenon and the inner interpretation of it by a receptive mind. The shape of a white vase against a uniformly black background may be perceived as 2 human figures facing each other if the symmetric sides of the vase are drawn to resemble silhouettes.

In music, gestalt is capable of many interpretations, of which the most literal is enharmonic ambivalence, as for instance the perception of a triad as a dissonance, or the nonrecognition of a scale, in the context of alien harmonies. Another is the expectation built up by a particular harmonic or melodic construct within a given style. The power of a gestalt may lead to performance error, as when a player "corrects" a written chromatic scale with 1 note left out to include the intentionally missing note, or changes an unfamiliar rhythm or meter to a familiar one. The expectation may also cause proofreaders and editors to change what they perceive to be "wrong notes," a problem angrily encountered by Beethoven and Ives, among others.

The grandest application of gestalt is the apprehension of an entire ensemble of musical parameters, comprising form, proportional distribution of consonances and dissonances, diatonic or chromatic tropism, and symmetry or asymmetry of melorhythmic figurations. An analogy may be made to a painter absorbing a landscape so completely that each part of it becomes an integral component of the whole. Schoenberg and others proposed a theory wherein the gestalt of a piece could be found in the opening measures, that is, the whole of the piece "summarized" at its beginning. The idea, like Schenker's URLINIE, has in itself a universality that requires far more and deeper analysis of a piece to support it on an individual basis, lest it become a benignly obstructive substitute for knowledge.

gesteigert (Ger.). Intensified, increasing in dynamics; RINFORZATO.

Gestopft (Ger.). A note stopped by placing a hand in the bell of brass instruments, particularly the French horn.

gestossen (Ger.). 1. STACCATO. 2. DÉTACHÉ.

gestrichen (Ger.). Play with the bow; ARCO.

Get Back. A 1969 hit by the Beatles, in a country vein. Originally slated to be the title track of their last album, which eventually became *Let It Be.*

Get Together. Hippie anthem of the 1960s, written by Jesse Colin Young and recorded by his group, the Youngbloods.

geteilt (Ger.). Divided; DIVISI.

getragen (Ger.). Sustained; SOSTENUTO.

Getz, Stan(ley), famous American jazz tenor saxophonist; b. Philadelphia, Feb. 2, 1927; d. June 6, 1991. While still a teenager he joined Jack Teagarden's group; then played with Stan Kenton, Jimmy Dorsey, and Benny Goodman; after a stint with Woody Herman, he embarked upon a series of recordings with Gerry Mulligan, Dizzy Gillespie, and other noted jazz musicians. He was a major exponent of the SAMBA movement in the 1950s and 1960s; he collaborated with A. C. Jobim and A. Gilberto. He joined the faculty of Stanford Univ. in 1984. He was an impressive exponent of cool jazz.

Gewandhaus (Ger., drapery shop). The building in Leipzig in which the famous Gewandhaus concerts were inaugurated in 1781. The Leipzig Gewandhaus was actually a textile workshop before it was converted into a concert hall.

gewichtig (Ger.). With weight, significantly, ponderously.

gewirbelt (Ger.). 1. Warbled. 2. Execute drumroll rapidly.

gezogen (Ger.). Drawn out, slowing down; LARGAMENTE, SOSTENUTO, STESSO.

ghiribizzoso (It.). Whimsically, capriciously, fancifully.

ghironda (It.). HURDY-GURDY.

Ghost Trio (*Das Geister Trio*). The common German nickname applied to Beethoven's Piano Trio in D Major, No. 1, op. 70. The nickname is attached to the work for no other reason than a mysterious quality to the opening of the 2nd movement.

Gianni Schicchi. Final 3rd of the operatic trilogy *Il Trittico,* 1918, by Puccini, from Dante's *Inferno.* The lawyer Schicchi has a daughter who loves the nephew of a wealthy man who dies at the opera's beginning. The will gives his fortune to the church, but Schicchi devises a plan by which he pretends to be the "not quite dead" old man. The avaricious family comes to collect, but a disguised Schicchi dictates a will that leaves everyone but himself and the young lovers out in the cold.

Giant, The. Nickname for Mahler's 5th Sym.; when written it was the longest instrumental sym. yet composed.

Gibson, (Sir) **Alexander** (Drummond), distinguished Scottish conductor; b. Motherwell, Feb. 11, 1926. He was educated at the Univ. of Glasgow and the Royal College of Music in London; also took courses at the Salzburg Mozarteum and in Siena. He made his debut as conductor at the Sadler's Wells Opera in London in 1952; was subsequently associate conductor of the BBC Scottish Sym. Orch. in Glasgow (1952–54). From 1959 to 1984 he was principal conductor of the Scottish National Orch. in Glasgow. In 1962 he founded that city's Scottish Opera, becoming its 1st music director and serving until 1987. In 1977 Queen Elizabeth II knighted him for his services on behalf of the musical life of his native Scotland and Great Britain. From 1981 to 1983 he was principal guest conductor of the Houston Sym. Orch. He is mainly renowned for his congenial performances of the works of Romantic composers, particularly those of the English school.

Gideon, Miriam, American composer and teacher; b. Greeley, Colo., Oct. 23, 1906. She studied piano with Hans Barth in N.Y. and with Felix Fox in Boston; enrolled at Boston Univ. (B.A., 1926) and took courses in musicology at Columbia Univ. (M.A., 1946); studied composition privately with Lazare Saminsky and Roger Sessions. She served on the music faculty of Brooklyn College (1944–54); in 1955 became a prof. of music at the Jewish Theological Center; in 1967 joined the faculty at the Manhattan School of Music; was a prof. of music at the City Univ. of N.Y. (1971–76); was elected to the American Academy and Inst. of Arts and Letters in 1975, and in 1986 was honored with a special concert in N.Y. on her 80th birthday. She wrote music in all genres, in a style distinguished by its attractive modernism. She has composed many song cycles with various accompaniments.

Gielen, Michael (Andreas), noted German conductor; b. Dresden, July 20, 1927. His father, Josef Gielen, was an opera director who settled in Buenos Aires in 1939; his uncle was the pianist Eduard Steuermann. Gielen studied piano and composition with Erwin Leuchter in Buenos Aires (1942–49); was on the staff of the Teatro Colón there (1947–50), then continued his training with Polnauer in Vienna (1950–53). In 1951 he became a *répétiteur* at the Vienna State Opera, and later was its resident conductor (1954–60). He was principal conductor of the Royal Opera in Stockholm (1960–65), a regular conductor with the Cologne Radio Sym. Orch. (1965–69), and chief conductor of the Orch. National de Belgique in Brussels (1968–73) and the Netherlands Opera in Amsterdam (1973–75). From 1977 to 1987 he was artistic director of the Frankfurt Opera and chief conductor of its Museumgesellschaft concerts; also, was chief guest conductor of the BBC Sym. Orch. in London (1979–82) and music director of the Cincinnati Sym. Orch. (1980–86). In 1986 he became chief conductor of the Southwest Radio Sym. Orch. in Baden–Baden; he was a prof. of conducting at the Salzburg Mozarteum (from

1987). Gielen has acquired a fine reputation as an interpreter of contemporary music; he has also composed music.

Gieseking, Walter (Wilhelm), distinguished German pianist; b. Lyons, France (of German parents), Nov. 5, 1895; d. London, Oct. 26, 1956. He studied with Karl Leimer at the Hannover Cons., graduating in 1916; served in the German army during World War I; began his concert career with extensive tours of Europe; made his American debut at Aeolian Hall, N.Y. (1926), and after that appeared regularly in the U.S. and Europe with orchs. and in solo recitals. He became the center of a political controversy when he arrived in the U.S. in 1949 for a concert tour; he was accused of cultural collaboration with the Nazi regime, and public protests forced the cancellation of his scheduled performances at Carnegie Hall. However, he was later cleared by an Allied court in Germany and was able to resume his career in America. He appeared again at a Carnegie Hall recital (1953), and until his death he continued to give numerous performances in both hemispheres. He was one of the most extraordinary pianists of his time.

A superb musician capable of profound interpretations of both Classic and modern scores, his dual German-French background enabled him to project with the utmost authenticity the masterpieces of both cultures. He particularly excelled in the music of Mozart, Beethoven, Schubert, and Brahms; his playing of Debussy and Ravel was remarkable; he was also an excellent performer of works by Prokofiev and other modernists. He composed some chamber music and made piano transcriptions of songs by R. Strauss.

giga (It.). GIGUE.

gigalira (It.). Xylophone.

Gigi. Film musical by Lerner and Loewe, 1958, based on a Colette novella. A wealthy Parisian gentleman meets Gigi, a beautiful young woman who lacks the appropriate class and financial means to be a suitable match. He offers to make her his mistress; the moral dilemma is resolved when the gentleman sees his hypocrisy and decides to marry Gigi. Includes the title song, *Thank Heaven for Little Girls, Waltz at Maxim's, I Remember It Well, I'm Glad I'm Not Young Anymore,* and *The Night They Invented Champagne.* A 1973 staged version with new songs was not successful.

gigue (from Old Fr. *giguer,* dance; Eng. *jig*). A popular Baroque dance in a rapid tempo, in 6/8 or 12/8 meter, divided into groups of 3 fast notes; more infrequently, in 3/8 or 9/8. The last movement of a Baroque suite was quite frequently a gigue. The It. *giga* tends to be in a livelier tempo than the more stately Fr. gigue. Whether the name derives from the English or Old French is open to question; however, the term appears in English virginal music before Continental sources. See also JIG.

Gigues. The 1st of the 3 orch.l *Images* by Debussy, 1913; the orchestration was completed by André Caplet.

Gilbert, Henry F(ranklin Belknap), remarkable American composer; b. Somerville, Mass., Sept. 26, 1868; d. Cambridge, Mass., May 19, 1928. He studied at the New England Cons. and with E. Mollenhauer; from 1889 to 1892 was a pupil of MacDowell (composition) in Boston. Rather than do routine music work to earn his livelihood (he had previously been a violinist in theaters, etc.), he took jobs of many descriptions, becoming, in turn, a real estate agent, a factory foreman, a collector of butterflies in Florida, etc., and composed when opportunity afforded. In 1893, at the Chicago World's Fair, he met a Russian prince who knew Rimsky-Korsakov and gave Gilbert many details of contemporary Russian composers whose work, as well as that of Bohemian and Scandinavian composers which was based on folk song, influenced Gilbert greatly in his later composition.

In 1894 he made his 1st trip abroad and stayed in Paris, subsequently returning to the U.S.; when he heard of the premiere of Charpentier's *Louise*, he became intensely interested in the work because of its popular character, and, in order to hear it, earned his passage to Paris in 1901 by working on a cattle boat; the opera impressed him so much that he decided to devote his entire time thereafter to composition. In 1902 he became associated with Farwell, whose Wa-Wan Press publ. Gilbert's early compositions. From 1903 he employed Negro tunes and rhythms extensively in his works.

The compositions of his mature period (from 1915) reveal an original style, not founded on any particular native American material but infused with elements from many sources; these are an attempt at "non-European" music, expressing the spirit of America and its national characteristics. His best-known works are the *Comedy Overture on Negro Themes* (1905); *The Dance in Place Congo* (1906); *Negro Rhapsody* (1913); *American Dances* (1915); *Indian Sketches* (1921); *Nocturne*, a "symphonic mood" after Whitman (1928); Suite for Chamber Orch. (1928).

Gilbert, (Sir) **W(illiam) S(chwenck),** English playwright, most famous for his stage collaborations with Sir Arthur Sullivan; b. London, Nov. 18, 1836; d. Harrow Weald, Middlesex, May 29, 1911 (of cardiac arrest following a successful attempt to rescue a young woman swimmer from drowning). He was given an excellent education (at Boulogne and at King's College, London) by his father, who was a novelist. After a routine career as a clerk, Gilbert drifted into journalism, contributing drama criticism and humorous verse to London periodicals. His satirical wit was 1st revealed in a theater piece, *Dulcamara* (1866), in which he ridiculed grand opera. He met Sullivan in 1870, and together they initiated the productions of comic operas, which suited them so perfectly. Some plots borrow ludicrous situations from actual Italian and French operas; Gilbert's librettos, in rhymed verse, were nonetheless unmistakably English. This insularity of wit may explain the enormous popularity of the Gilbert and Sullivan operas in English-speaking countries, while they are practically unknown on the Continent. Despite the fact that the targets of Gilbert's ridicule were usually the upper classes of Great Britain, the operas were often performed at court. He was knighted in 1907. After 20 years of fruitful cooperation with Sullivan, a conflict developed, and the 2 severed their relationship for a time. A reconciliation was effected, but the subsequent productions fell short of their greatest successes. See SULLIVAN's entry for details of the operas.

Gilels, Elizabeta, Russian violinist, sister of Emil (Grigorievich) Gilels; b. Odessa, Sept. 30, 1919. She studied with Stoliarsky at his school for gifted youths in Odessa and later graduated from the Moscow Cons., where she took lessons from A. Yampolsky. She received 3rd place in the Ysaÿe Competition (Brussels, 1937); taught at the Moscow Cons. (from 1967). She played duets with her husband, the violinist Leonid Kogan; their son, Pavel Kogan, was also a talented violinist.

Gilels, Emil (Grigorievich), eminent Russian pianist, brother of Elizabeta Gilels; b. Odessa, Oct. 19, 1916; d. Moscow, Oct. 14, 1985. He entered the Odessa Cons. at the age of 5 to study with Yakov Tkatch, making his 1st public appearance at 9, followed by his formal debut at 13; after further studies with Bertha Ringbald at the Cons., he went to Moscow for advanced studies with Heinrich Neuhaus (1935–38). He won 1st prize at the Moscow Competition in 1933; after taking 2nd prize at the Vienna Competition in 1936, he won 1st prize at the Brussels Competition in 1938;

that same year he became a prof. at the Moscow Cons. Following World War II he embarked upon an esteemed international career. He was the 1st Soviet musician to appear in the U.S. during the Cold War era, making his debut in Tchaikovsky's 1st Piano Concerto with Ormandy and the Philadelphia Orch. (1955). He subsequently made 13 tours of the U.S., the last in 1983. A member of the Communist party from 1942, he received various honors from the Soviet government. Gilels was one of the foremost pianists of his time. He was especially renowned for his performances of Beethoven, Schubert, Schumann, Chopin, Liszt, Tchaikovsky, and Brahms.

Gillespie, "Dizzy" (John Birks), famous African-American jazz trumpeter and bandleader; with Charlie "Bird" Parker, established the bebop style; b. Cheraw, S.C., Oct. 21, 1917; d. Jan. 7, 1993. He picked up the rudiments of music from his father; at the age of 18 he went to Philadelphia, where he joined a local jazz band; in 1939 he became a member of Cab Calloway's orch., and in 1944 he was with Billy Eckstine's band. In 1945 he formed his own band; others followed, none especially long-lived; he led

Dizzy Gillespie, 1948

COURTESY FRANK DRIGGS COLLECTION

different small groups over the years. He met Parker in 1940: the 2 were cofounders of the jazz style variously known as BEBOP, bop, and rebop. Gillespie later experimented with Afro-Cuban jazz (*A Night in Tunisia*). He received the nickname "Dizzy" because of his wild manner of playing, making grimaces and gesticulating during his performances. He was doubtless one of the greatest trumpeters in jazz history and practice, a true virtuoso on his instrument, extending its upper ranges and improvising long passages at breakneck speed. In 1989 he was awarded the National Medal of Arts.

gimmicks. Musical tricks are usually regarded as beneath the dignity of a composer or a performer, but the greatest composers were known to indulge in experimenting with devices that have nothing to do with music as an art. Some highly popular works of great musical significance are based on a fortuitous arrangement of letters of the alphabet translated into musical notes. B–A–C–H (in non-German nomenclature, B♭–A–C–B) was used thematically by the composer and many later musicians; D–S–C–H, from the German spelling of *Shostakovich*, yields D–E♭–C–B (where the *S* becomes *es*, or E-flat).

Schumann often used this technique, most notably in CARNAVAL, based on the hometown of his 1st love. Berg used numbers to represent himself and his paramour, relating their story in the LYRIC SUITE. Castelnuovo-Tedesco programmed names of his friends according to the recurrent series of the English alphabet and wrote variations and fugues for them as birthday greeting cards. The modern American composer Tom Johnson managed to write a whole opera based on only 4 notes. The American composer Ernst Bacon developed a rather curious symmetric technique in his piano works in which both hands play, simultaneously or successively, symmetrically positioned chords or arpeggios, so that E-flat, G, C in the right hand would be accompanied or echoed (counting downwards) by G-sharp, E, B in the left, forming a perfect mirror image of one black key and 2 white keys. A given chord can be imitated by several symmetrical chords, provided the position of black and white keys and the intervals are in precise correspondence.

Visual elements in musical composition are of demonstrable value if for nothing else than the greater understanding of the nature of notation. An 18th century anonymous score exists that, when lying flat on a table, can be played in perfect harmony by 2 violinists sitting across from one another. Naturally the piece is in G major, because the G-major triad in close and open harmony in the treble clef does not change when the page is turned upside down. But subdominant triads become dominant ones. The ingenuity put into the creation of this piece merits total admiration. Another ambitious piano piece of more recent origin is entitled *Vice-Versa*; when it is read from page 1 to page 8, or upside down from page 8 to page 1, it comes out precisely the same. Such devices have been used with some profit for centuries.

The aesthetic and technical value of musical gimmicks lies in the adage that art must be difficult in order to be elevating. Numerous examples of deliberately set limitations in various branches of arts and sciences that lead to interesting discoveries can be cited. A peculiarly absurd example is an American novel written by an eccentric individual who tied down the *e* key on the typewriter and wrote the entire man-uscript without using that most common letter in the English alphabet. Painters who restrict their palette and drawing vocabulary are setting themselves limits. The musical equivalent is the canon and the fugue, in which the composer sets considerable limitations and challenges for both the composing and realization of the works.

gimping. For string instruments, the overspinning of gut strings with fine copper or silver wire, used in the Baroque period mainly on the lower strings, G on the violin, C and G on the viola and cello. To some early music practitioners, excessive gimping precludes an authentic rendering of the true Baroque sound.

Ginastera, Alberto (Evaristo)

Outstanding Argentine composer; b. Buenos Aires, Apr. 11, 1916; d. Geneva, June 25, 1983. His father was of Catalan descent, and Ginastera preferred to pronounce his name with a soft *g*, as in the Catalan language; the standard pronunciation, however, is with a hard *g*. His mother was of Italian origin. He took private lessons in music as a child; then entered the National Cons. of Music in Buenos Aires, where he studied composition with José Gil, Athos Palma, and José André; also took piano lessons with Argenziani.

He began to compose in his early youth; in 1934 won 1st prize of the musical society El Unísono for his *Piezas infantiles* for piano. His next piece of importance was *Impresiónes de la Puna* for flute and string quartet (1942), in which he made use of native Argentine melodies and rhythms; he discarded it, however, as immature; he withdrew a number of other works, some of them of certain value, such as *Concierto argentino* (1935) and the *Sinfonia Portena*, his 1st Sym. (which may be identical in its musical material with *Estancia*; see below). Also withdrawn was his 2nd Sym., the *Sinfonía elegíaca* (1944), even though it was successfully performed. In 1946–47 Ginastera traveled to the U.S. on a Guggenheim fellowship. Returning to Argentina, he was appointed to the faculty of his alma mater, the National Cons. in Buenos Aires, where he taught intermittently from 1948 to 1958; he also served as dean of the faculty of musical arts and sciences at the Argentine Catholic Univ.; also was a prof. at the Univ. of La Plata. In 1968 he left Argentina and lived mostly in Geneva, Switzerland.

From his earliest steps in composition Ginastera had an almost amorous attachment for the melodic and rhythmic resources of Argentine folk music, and he evolved a fine harmonic and contrapuntal setting congenial with native patterns. His 1st significant work in the Argentine national idiom was the ballet *Panambí*, composed in 1935 and performed at the Teatro Colón in Buenos Aires (1940). There followed a group of *Danzas argentinas* for piano, written in 1937; in 1938 he wrote 3 songs; the 1st one, *Canción al árbol del olvido*, is a fine evocation of youthful love; it became quite popular.

In 1941 he was commissioned to write a ballet for the American Ballet Caravan, *Estancia*; the music was inspired by the rustic scenes of the pampas; a suite from the score was performed at the Teatro Colón (1943), and the complete work was brought out there in 1952. A series of works inspired by native scenes and written for various instrumental combinations followed, all infused with Ginastera's poetic imagination and brought to realization with excellent technical skill. Soon, however, he began to search for new methods of musical expression, marked by modern and sometimes strikingly dissonant combinations of sound, fermented by asymmetrical rhythms. Of these works, one of the most remarkable is *Cantata para América mágica*, scored for dramatic soprano and percussion instruments, to apocryphal pre-Columbian texts, freely arranged by Ginastera; it was 1st performed in Washington, D.C. (1961) with excellent success.

An entirely new development in Ginastera's evolution as composer came with his 1st opera, *Don Rodrigo* (1964), produced at the Teatro Colón. In it he followed the general formula of *Wozzeck* in the use of classical instrumental forms, such as rondo, suite, scherzo, and canonic progressions; he also introduced a *Sprechstimme*. In 1964 he wrote the cantata *Bomarzo* on a commission from the Elizabeth Sprague Coolidge Foundation in Washington, D.C. He used the same libretto by Manuel Mujica Láinez in his opera *Bomarzo*, which created a sensation at its production in Washington, D.C. (1967) by its unrestrained spectacle of sexual violence. It was announced for performance at the Teatro Colón later that year but was canceled at the order of the Argentine government because of its alleged immoral nature. The score of *Bomarzo* reveals extraordinary innovations in serial techniques, with thematical employment not only of different chromatic sounds but also of serial progressions of different intervals. His last opera, *Beatrix Cenci*, commissioned by the Opera Soc. of Washington, D.C., and produced there in 1971, concluded his operatic trilogy.

Among instrumental works of Ginastera's last period, the most remarkable was his 2nd Piano Concerto (1972), based on a tone-row derived from the famous dissonant opening of the finale of Beethoven's 9th Sym.; the 2nd movement of the concerto is written for the left hand alone. He was married to the pianist Mercedes de Toro in 1941; they had a son and a daughter. He divorced her in 1995 and married the Argentine cellist Aurora Nátola (1971), for whom he wrote the Cello Sonata, which she played in N.Y. (1979), and his 2nd Cello Concerto, which she performed in Buenos Aires in 1981.

gioco (or It. *giuoco*, etc.), **con** (It. *kohn*). Playfully, sportively, merrily.

Gioconda, La (The Merry Girl). Opera by Ponchielli, 1876, 1st produced in Milan. The action takes place in 17th-century Venice. The jocund street singer is in trouble when her blind mother is denounced as a witch by the Inquisition. The local Inquisitor is willing to release her if the girl submits to his licentious desires. She rebukes him, whereupon he carries out his threat to have her mother put to death. La Gioconda stabs herself and dies. There are also some murky doings around the Venetian palaces involving, among other things, a cuckolded husband who tries unsuccessfully to poison his wife. Incongruously, the score includes the famous ballet *Dance of the Hours*, as rollicking a piece of rhythmic entertainment as was ever produced by an Italian composer.

giocondamente (*giocosamente, giocoso; gioia, con; gioioso; gioja, con; gioviale; giovialità, con;* It.). Playfully, sportively, merrily, jocosely, lively, joyfully, joyously, gaily, jovially, cheerfully.

Gioielli della Madonna, I (The Jewels of the Madonna). Opera by Wolf-Ferrari, 1911. Two rivals for a woman's attention vow to prove their love by an outrageous deed; the winner steals the jewels from a statue of the Holy Virgin and offers them to his beloved. She rejects the blasphemous gift and drowns herself, whereupon the miscreant lays the jewels at the statue's feet and stabs himself to death.

Giordano, Umberto, noted Italian composer; b. Foggia, Aug. 28, 1867; d. Milan, Nov. 12, 1948. He studied with Gaetano Briganti at Foggia, and then with Paolo Serrao at the Naples Cons. (1881–90). His 1st composition performed in public was a symphonic poem, *Delizia* (1886); he then wrote some instrumental music. In 1888 he submitted a short opera, *Marina*, for the competition established by the publisher Sonzogno; Mascagni's *Cavalleria rusticana* received 1st prize, but *Marina* was cited for distinction. Giordano then wrote an opera in 3 acts, *Mala vita*, which was performed in Rome in 1892; it was only partly successful; was revised and presented under the title *Il voto* in Milan (1897). There followed a 2-act opera, *Regina Diaz* (Rome, 1894), which obtained a moderate success. Then he set to work on a grand opera, *Andrea Chenier*, to a libretto by Illica. The production of this opera at La Scala in Milan (1896) was a spectacular success that established Giordano as one of the best composers of Italian opera of the day. The dramatic subject gave Giordano a fine opportunity to display his theatrical talent; but the score also revealed his gift for lyric expression.

Almost as successful was his next opera, *Fedora* (Teatro Lirico, Milan, 1898), but it failed to hold a place in the world repertoire after the initial acclaim; there followed *Siberia*, in 3 acts (La Scala, 1903; rev. 1921; La Scala, 1927). Two short operas, *Marcella* (Milan, 1907) and *Mese Mariano* (Palermo, 1910), were hardly noticed and seemed to mark a decline in Giordano's dramatic gift; however, he recaptured the attention of the public with *Madame Sans-Gêne*, produced at a gala premiere at the Metropolitan Opera in N.Y. (1915), conducted by Toscanini, with Geraldine Farrar singing the title role. With Franchetti he wrote *Giove a Pompei* (Rome, 1921); then he produced *La cena delle beffe* in 4 acts, which was his last signal accomplishment; it was staged at La Scala, 1924. He wrote 1 more opera, *Il Re*, in 1 act (La Scala, 1929). During his lifetime he received many honors, and was elected a member of the Accademia Luigi Cherubini in Florence and of several other institutions. Although not measuring up to Puccini in musical qualities or to Mascagni in dramatic skill, Giordano was a distinguished figure in the Italian opera field for some 4 decades.

Giorno di regno, Un (The Day of Reigning). Opera by Verdi, 1840, 1st performed in Milan. This is Verdi's 1st comic opera, and yet it was written at the most tragic period of his life, when he lost his wife and 2 children in close succession. The opera tells the story of the courageous act of a Polish officer who travels under the guise of King Stanislaw to expose himself in case of regicide so the real King could travel in safety. He is rewarded by a marital union with a young Polish lady.

Giovanna d'Arco. Opera by Verdi, 1845, 1st performed in Milan. In it Joan of Arc falls in love with the Dauphin, goes to battle against the English, is wounded, and dies in the arms of her royal lover, now King Charles VII. This perversion of the historical story of the sainted virgin infuriated the French at the 1st Paris performance of the opera. Still, the score has some nice tunes.

Girl Crazy. Musical by Gershwin, 1930. A rich Arizonan playboy converts a sleepy town into a scene of debauchery; he falls for the prim local postmistress. Includes *I Got Rhythm*, *Embraceable You*, and *But Not for Me*.

Girl Friend, The. Musical by Rodgers and Hart, 1926. A bicycle racer is approached by professional gambler to fix an upcoming race. He refuses, and wins the race, thanks to the help of another racer's daughter; they become an item. Includes the title song and *The Blue Room*.

Girl I Left Behind Me, The. This is an old song, probably of Irish origin, which was popular in the American colonies before the Revolution. At the time of the Civil War a new set of words was adapted to the tune and it became known as the *American Volunteer*. It is used as the graduating class song at the military school in West Point.

Girl of the Golden West, The (*La Fanciulla del West*). Opera by Puccini, 1910, based on Belasco's drama. It was commissioned by and produced at the Metropolitan Opera House in N.Y., with Toscanini conducting and Caruso singing the part of the Western badman, Dick Johnson. He and the sheriff are both in love with Minnie, who owns a saloon. When Dick seeks shelter in her quarters, she challenges the sheriff to a poker game, the stake of which is Dick's freedom. She wins by secreting an extra ace in her petticoat. Together Dick and Minnie ride away into the sunset. The score contains a number of unintentionally hilarious pseudo-Americanisms, and the poker game itself is quite preposterous.

Gis (Ger.). G-sharp.

Gis moll (Ger.). G-sharp minor.

Giselle. Ballet by Adam, 1841; one of the most famous French ballets, produced in Paris, June 28, 1841. Its full title is *Giselle, ou Les Wilis*; Wilis are the disembodied spirits of young girls who die before their announced wedding. The plot concerns the encounter of a young man with his deceased fiancée.

Gisis (Ger.). G double-sharp.

gittern (Fr. *ghisterne*, *guiterne*; Lat. *ghiterna*, *quitarra*). Medieval plucked chordophone, usually with a flat back, fretted neck, and single or double-coursed gut strings; a plectrum was used. The gittern can be traced iconographically to the early 12th century; by 1400 the instrument had given way to the lute. The term *gittern* continued to be used through the 17th century for instruments of the guitar family; not to be confused with the CITTERN.

giubilante (It.). Jubilantly. *Giubilo*, joy, rejoicing, jubilation.

Giuditta. Opera by Lehar, 1934, produced in Vienna. The subject is drawn from the apocryphal Book of Judith, about the Hebrew maiden who skillfully decapitates the sleeping Assyrian army leader and carries his detruncated bearded head back to her city. Finding themselves headless, the Assyrians lift the siege of the Hebrew city. This is the only serious opera Lehar ever wrote; musically it is much inferior to his sparkling operettas.

Giuffre, Jimmy (James Peter), American jazz clarinetist, saxophonist, and composer; b. Dallas, Apr. 26, 1921. He studied at North Texas State Teachers College (B.Mus., 1942), then played in a U.S. Army band; subsequently joined the bands of Jimmy Dorsey, Buddy Rich, and Woody Herman. While he played flute and tenor saxophone, he was primarily known for his cool tone, *sans vibrato*, on the clarinet, especially in its chalumeau register. He wrote an influential score for Woody Herman, *4 Brothers* (1947), which explored the expressive potential of timbre and became known as "the 4 Brothers sound." He was an important figure in avant-garde jazz of the late 1950s and '60s, especially as a proponent of the free-jazz style; he worked in a series of different combos, including those of Jim Hall and Ralph Pena (1956); he also played with Paul Bley and Steve Swallow. He was also active as a teacher, serving on the faculty of the New School for Social Research in N.Y. and the School of Jazz in Lenox, Mass.; he publ. an influential text, *Jazz Phrasing and Interpretation* (N.Y., 1969).

Giulini, Carlo Maria, eminent Italian conductor; b. Barletta, May 9, 1914. He began to study the violin as a boy; at 16 he entered the Conservatorio di Musica di Santa Cecilia in Rome, where he studied violin and viola with Remy Principe, composition with Alessandro Bustini, and conducting with Bernardino Molinari; also received instruction in conducting from Casella at the Accademia Chigiana in Siena; then joined the Augusteo Orch. in Rome in the viola section, under such great conductors as Richard Strauss, Bruno Walter, Mengelberg, and Furtwängler. He was drafted into the Italian army during World War II but went into hiding as a convinced anti-Fascist; after the liberation of Rome by the Allied troops in 1944 he was engaged to conduct the Augusteo Orch. in a special concert celebrating the occasion. He was then engaged as assistant conductor of the RAI Orch. in Rome, and was made its chief conductor in 1946.

In 1950 he helped to organize the RAI Orch. in Milan; in 1952 he conducted at La Scala as an assistant to Victor de Sabata; in 1954 he became principal conductor there; his performance of *La Traviata*, with Maria Callas in the title role, was particularly notable. In 1955 he conducted *Falstaff* at the Edinburgh Festival, earning great praise. On Nov. 3,

1955, he was a guest conductor with the Chicago Sym. Orch. and later was its principal guest conductor (1969–72); during its European tour of 1971, he was joint conductor with Sir Georg Solti. From 1973 to 1976 he was principal conductor of the Vienna Sym. Orch., and in 1975 he took it on a world tour, which included the U.S., Canada, and Japan. In 1975 he led it at a televised concert from the United Nations. In 1978 he succeeded Zubin Mehta as music director of the Los Angeles Phil., and he succeeded in maintaining it at a zenith of orch. brilliance until 1984.

Giulini's conducting style embodies the best traditions of the Italian school as exemplified by Toscanini but is free from explosive displays of temper. He is above all a Romantic conductor who can identify his musical *Weltanschauung* with the musical essence of Beethoven, Verdi, Mahler, and Tchaikovsky; he leads the classics with an almost abstract contemplation. In the music of the 20th century he gives congenial interpretations of works by Debussy, Ravel, and Stravinsky; the expressionist school of composers lies outside of his deeply felt musicality, and he does not actively promote the experimental school of modern music. His behavior on the podium is free from self-assertive theatrics, and he treats the orch. as comrades-in-arms, associates in the cause of music rather than subordinate performers of the task assigned to them. Yet his personal feeling for music is not disguised; often he closes his eyes in fervent self-absorption when conducting without score the great Classical and Romantic works.

Giulio Cesare in Egitto. Opera by Handel, 1724. The opera concentrates on Caesar's encounter with Cleopatra.

giuoco (It.). Joke, game, jest.

giustamente (*giusto*; It.). Exactly, strictly, precisely, appropriately, properly, justly.

Give My Regards to Broadway. Song by G. M. Cohan, from the musical *Little Johnny Jones*, 1904.

Give Peace a Chance. A 1969 peace anthem written by John Lennon during the famous "Bed-In for Peace" held in Toronto with his performance-artist wife, Yoko Ono. The song was recorded live with various participants, including LSD guru Timothy Leary and satirical singer Tommy Smothers. A heavy backbeat had to be added to the single because the singers fell behind the beat halfway through.

Glagolitic Mass. Sacred work by Janáček, 1927, also known as the *Slavonic Mass* or *Festival Mass*, 1st performed in Brno. The text is in old Slavonic, common also to the Russian Orthodox Church. The use of the Slavonic vernacular by Janáček was as much of an innovation as the use of the German language by Brahms in his Requiem.

Glareanus, Henricus, also called Heinrich Glarean (born Heinrich Loris; Lat. Henricus Loritus), Swiss music theorist; b. Mollis, Glarus canton, June 1488; d. Freiburg, Mar. 28, 1563. He studied with Rubellus at Bern, and later with Cochläus at Cologne, where he was crowned poet laureate by Emperor Maximilian I in 1512, as the result of a poem he composed and sang to the Emperor. He 1st taught mathematics at Basel (1514); from 1517 to 1522 he was in Paris, where he taught philosophy; in 1522 returned to Basel, where he stayed till 1529, when he settled in Freiburg. There he was a prof. of poetry, then of theology. His 1st important work, *Isagoge in musicen* (Basel, 1516), dealt with solmization, intervals, modes, and tones. In a still more important vol., the *Dodecachordon* (Basel, 1547), Glareanus advanced the theory that there are 12 church modes, corresponding to the ancient Greek modes, instead of the commonly accepted 8 modes. The 3rd part of the *Dodecachordon* contains many works by 15th- and 16th-century musicians. A copy of the *Dodecachordon*, with corrections in Glareanus's own handwriting, is in the Library of Congress, Washington, D.C.

Glass, Philip

⁓⁓⁓ ⁓⁓⁓ ⁓⁓⁓ ⁓⁓⁓ ⁓⁓⁓

Remarkable American composer; b. Baltimore, Jan. 31, 1937. He entered the Peabody Cons. of Music in Baltimore as a flute student when he was 8; then took courses in piano, mathematics, and philosophy at the Univ. of Chicago (1952–56); subsequently studied composition with Persichetti at the Juilliard School of Music in N.Y. (M.S., 1962). He received a Fulbright fellowship in 1964 and went to Paris to study with Boulanger; much more important to his future development was his meeting with Ravi Shankar, who introduced him to Hindu ragas. During a visit to Morocco, Glass absorbed the modalities of North African melo-rhythms, which taught him the art of melodic repetition. When he returned to N.Y. in 1967, his style of composition became an alternately concave and convex mirror image of Eastern modes, undergoing melodic phases of stationary harmonies in lieu of modulations.

He formed associations with modern painters and sculptors who strove to obtain maximum effects with a minimum of means. He began to practice a similar method in music, which soon acquired the factitious sobriquet of minimalism. Other Americans and some Europeans followed this practice, which was basically Eastern in its catatonic homophony; Steve Reich was a close companion in minimalistic pursuits of maximalistic effects. Glass formed his own phonograph company, Chatham Square, which recorded most of his early works. He also organized an ensemble of electrically amplified instruments, which became the chief medium of his compositions. In 1968 he presented the 1st concert of the Philip Glass Ensemble at Queens College in N.Y., subsequently touring widely with it, making visits abroad as well as traveling throughout the U.S. His productions, both in America and in Europe, became extremely successful among young audiences, who were mesmerized by his mixture of rock realism and alluring mysticism; undeterred by the indeterminability and interminability of his productions, some lasting several hours, these young people accepted him as a true representative of earthly and unearthly art.

The mind-boggling titles of his works added to the tantalizing impenetrability of the subjects that he selected for his inspiration. The high point of his productions was the opera *Einstein on the Beach* (in collaboration with Robert Wilson), which involved a surrealistic comminution of thematic ingredients and hypnotic repetition of harmonic subjects. It was premiered at the Avignon Festival in the summer of 1976 and was subsequently performed throughout Europe. It was given in the autumn of the same year at the Metropolitan Opera in N.Y., where it proved something of a sensation of the season; however, it was not produced as part of the regular subscription series. In Rotterdam (1980) he produced his opera *Satyagraha*, a work based on Gandhi's years in South Africa. "Satyagraha" was Gandhi's slogan, composed of 2 Hindu words: *satya* (truth) and *agraha* (firmness). Another significant production was the 1981 score for the film *Koyaanisqatsi*, a Hopi Indian word meaning "life out of balance." The music represented the ultimate condensation of the basic elements of Glass's compositional style; here the ritualistic repetition of chords arranged in symmetrical sequences becomes hypnotic, particularly since the screen action is devoid of narrative; the effect is enhanced by the deep bass notes of an Indian chant.

His mixed-media piece *The Photographer: Far from the Truth*, based on the life of the photographer Eadweard Muybridge, received its 1st performance in Amsterdam (1983). It was followed by the exotic opera *Akhnaten*, set in ancient Egypt, with a libretto in ancient Akkadian, Egyptian, and Hebrew, with an explanatory narration in English; it was produced in Stuttgart (1984). In collaboration with Robert Moran he produced the opera *Juniper Tree* (Cambridge, Mass., 1985). After bringing out the dance-

theater piece *A Descent into the Maelstrom* (1986) and the dance piece *In the Upper Room* (1986), he wrote a Violin Concerto (1987). His symphonic score *The Light* was 1st performed in Cleveland on Oct. 29, 1987. It was followed by his opera *The Making of the Representative for Planet 8* (to a text by Doris Lessing), which received its premiere in Houston on July 8, 1988. His next opera, *The Fall of the House of Usher*, was 1st performed in Cambridge, Mass., on May 18, 1988. The music-theater piece *1,000 Airplanes on the Roof* was produced in Vienna in 1988. On Nov. 2, 1989, his *Itaipu* for chorus and orch. was premiered in Atlanta.

Among his other works are *Music with Changing Parts* (N.Y., Nov. 10, 1972), *Music in 12 Parts* (N.Y., June 1, 1974), and *North Star* for 2 voices and instruments (1975); *Dance No. 1–5* (1979); *Sinfonia No. 3* for orch. (1986); *Hydrogen Jukebox*, theater piece after Ginsberg (1988); *La Belle et le Bête*, soundtrack opera after Cocteau's film (1994); *The Canyon* for orch. (1988); *Lamento dell'acqua* for orch. (1990); *Low Sym.*, after the album by Bowie and Eno (1992); *Songs from Liquid Days*; *The Screens*, incidental music for Genet's play, collab. with Foday Musa Suso; film soundtracks, including *Thin Blue Line*, *Amina Munda*, *Mishima*, *Powaqqatsi*; *Strung Out* for solo violin (1967) 5 string quartets; piano and organ works.

glass harmonica. In its most primitive form, an instrument consisting of a set of drinking glasses partially filled with water so as to provide a complete diatonic scale. A famous concert of "26 glasses tuned with spring water" was presented by Gluck in London (1746). It is said that Benjamin Franklin attended and subsequently constructed a glass harmonica with mechanical attachments. The ethereal sound is produced by rubbing the rim of the glass with a wet finger. Because of its clarity and purity it was called the *angelic organ*. Glass harmonicas achieved a great popularity in the 18th century under the Italian name *armonica*; even Mozart wrote a piece for it (1791, K.356/617*a*). It fell into desuetude after its romantic attraction was spoiled by a mechanization; R. Strauss used it in his opera *Frau ohne Schatten* for evocative effect. Also called *glasschord* or *musical glasses*.

Glazunov, Alexander (Konstantinovich), eminent Russian composer; b. St. Petersburg, Aug. 10, 1865; d. Neuilly-sur-Seine, Mar. 21, 1936. Of a well-to-do family (his father was a book publisher), he studied at a technical high school in St. Petersburg and also took lessons in music with

N. Elenkovsky. As a boy of 15 he was introduced to Rimsky-Korsakov, who gave him weekly lessons in harmony, counterpoint, and orchestration. He made rapid progress, and at the age of 16 completed his 1st sym., which was conducted by Balakirev in St. Petersburg (1882). So mature was this score that Glazunov was hailed by Stasov, Cui, and others as a rightful heir to the masters of the Russian national school.

The music publisher Belaiev arranged for publication of his works, and took him to Weimar, where he met Liszt. From that time Glazunov composed assiduously in all genres except opera. He was invited to conduct his syms. in Paris (1889) and London (1896–97). Returning to St. Petersburg, he conducted concerts of Russian music. In 1899 he was engaged as an instructor in composition and orchestration at the St. Petersburg Cons. He resigned temporarily during the revolutionary turmoil of 1905 in protest against the dismissal of Rimsky-Korsakov by the government authorities, but returned to the staff after full autonomy was granted to the Cons. by the administration. In 1905 Glazunov was elected director and retained this post until 1928, when he went to Paris. In 1929 he made several appearances as conductor in the U.S. He was the recipient of honorary degrees of Mus.D. from Cambridge and Oxford Univs. (1907).

Although Glazunov wrote no textbook on composition, his pedagogical methods left a lasting impression on Russian musicians through his many students who preserved his traditions. His music is often regarded as academic, yet there is a flow of rhapsodic eloquence that places Glazunov in the Romantic school. He was for a time greatly swayed by Wagnerian harmonies, but he resisted this influence successfully; Lisztian characteristics are more pronounced in his works. Glazunov was one of the greatest masters of counterpoint among Russian composers, but he avoided extreme polyphonic complexity. The national spirit of his music is unmistakable; in many of his descriptive works the programmatic design is explicitly Russian (*Stenka Razin*, *The Kremlin*, etc.). His most popular score is the ballet *Raymonda*. The major portion of his music was written before 1906, when he completed his 8th Sym.; after that he wrote mostly for special occasions. He also completed and orchestrated the overture to Borodin's *Prince Igor* from memory, having heard Borodin play it on the piano.

glee (from Anglo-Sax. *gléo*, entertainment). An English secular composition for 3 or more unaccompanied solo voices, generally for male voices and usually constructed as a series of short movements harmonized homophonically. It reached its flowering in the 18th century. Glee clubs proliferated in England and also found enthusiastic participants in the U.S. Serious glees are written, as well as merry ones.

Gli Scherzi. SCHERZI, GLI.

Glinka, Mikhail (Ivanovich), great Russian composer, called "the father of Russian music" for his pioneering cultivation of Russian folk modalities; b. Novospasskoye, Smolensk district, June 1, 1804; d. Berlin, Feb. 15, 1857. A scion of a fairly rich family of landowners, he was educated at an exclusive school in St. Petersburg (1817–22); he also took private lessons in music; his piano teacher was a resident German musician, Carl Meyer; he also studied violin; when the pianist John Field was in St. Petersburg, Glinka had an opportunity to study with him, but he had only 3 lessons before Field departed.

He began to compose even before acquiring adequate training in theory. As a boy he traveled in the Caucasus, then stayed for a while at his father's estate; at 20 he entered the Ministry of Communications in St. Petersburg, and he remained in government employ until 1828; at the same time he constantly improved his general education by read-

ing; he had friends among the best Russian writers of the time, including the poets Zhukovsky and Pushkin. He also took singing lessons with an Italian teacher, Belloli. In 1830 he went to Italy; he continued irregular studies in Milan (where he spent most of his Italian years); he also visited Naples, Rome, and Venice. He met Donizetti and Bellini.

He became enamored of Italian music, and his early vocal and instrumental compositions are thoroughly Italian in melodic and harmonic structure. In 1833 he went to Berlin, where he took a course in counterpoint and general composition with Dehn; thus he was nearly 30 when he completed his theoretical education. In 1834 his father died and Glinka went back to Russia to take care of the family affairs. In 1835 he was married; the marriage was unhappy, and he soon became separated from his wife, finally divorcing her in 1846.

Glinka's return to his native land led him to consider the composition of a truly national opera on a subject (suggested to him by Zhukovsky) depicting a historical episode in Russian history: the saving of the 1st czar of the Romanov dynasty by a simple peasant, Ivan Susanin. (The Italian composer Cavos wrote an opera on the same subject 20 years previously and conducted it in St. Petersburg.) Glinka's opera was produced in St. Petersburg in 1836, under the title *A Life for the Czar*. The event was hailed by the literary and artistic circles of Russia as a milestone of Russian culture, and indeed the entire development of Russian national music received its decisive creative impulse from Glinka's patriotic opera. It remained in the repertoire of Russian theaters until the Revolution made it unacceptable, but it was revived, under the original title, *Ivan Susanin*, in Moscow (1939), without alterations in the music but with the references to the czar eliminated from the libretto, the idea of saving the country being substituted for that of saving the czar.

Glinka's next opera, *Ruslan and Ludmila*, after Pushkin's fairy tale, was produced in St. Petersburg (1842); this opera, too, became extremely popular in Russia. Glinka introduced into the score many elements of oriental music; 1 episode contains the earliest use of the whole-tone scale in an opera. Both operas retain the traditional Italian form, with arias, choruses, and orch. episodes clearly separated. In 1844 Glinka was in Paris, where he met Berlioz; he also traveled in Spain, where he collected folk songs; the fruits of his Spanish tour were 2 orch. works, *Jota Aragonesa* and *Night in Madrid*. On his way back to Russia he stayed in Warsaw for 3 years; the remaining years of his life he spent in St. Petersburg, Paris, and Berlin.

glissade (*port de voix*; Fr.). PORTAMENTO.

glissando (glissato, glissicando, glissicato; from Fr. *glisser*, slide + It. suffix). A SLIDE; a rapid scale. Some instruments must accommodate the glissando to their graded pitch construction. On the piano it represents an effective ornamental device by sliding quickly over the white keys with the back of the fingernail, observing special care not to bruise the finger painfully; the thumb, or thumb and 1 finger, are used. Glissando on the black keys is possible but rarely used. Piano virtuosos with fingers of steel manage to make glissando in octaves, and even in octaves with an interposed 3rd, using the thumb, the index finger, and the little finger. The glissando effect is natural for the harp, with the hands moving toward and away from the player; it is even possible on a single string, using the pedal.

Other instruments are capable of an uninterrupted slide through a portion of their pitch gamut without a break. Trombone glissandos are applicable for a limited range, as are those on timpani. The clarinet glissando, requiring a special manipulation of the keys, occurs in the opening section of Gershwin's *Rhapsody in Blue*. Players on other wind instruments have improved techniques for sliding on their instruments. All bowed strings offer the true glissando.

Glissando is often mistakenly treated as a synonym for *portamento*. While both indicate an indirect motion from one pitch to another, a true glissando should be even and consistent in its motion; neither departure nor arrival pitch should be unduly emphasized. See PORTAMENTO.

Gloche (Ger.; Fr. *clocke*). A bell.

glockenspiel (Ger., bell playing). 1. CARILLON. 2. A set of steel bars struck by a hammer and producing a bell-like sound. There are 2 types of glockenspiel: the 1st, the mallet glockenspiel, laid out as a keyboard like the xylophone and marimba and fully chromatic; the 2nd, the marching glockenspiel, bars placed in a lyrelike shape held upright, struck with a small hammer, with a gamut smaller than the 2–1/2 octaves of the mallet type. The glockenspiel is included in the score of Mozart's opera *The Magic Flute*, where it is listed simply as *instrumento d'acciacio* (steel instrument). In actual performance it is interchangeable with the CELESTA. 3. An organ stop having bells instead of pipes.

Gloria. The 2nd main division of the Ordinary in the Roman Catholic High Mass. The separate canticles are GLORIA IN EXCELSIS DEO (Glory to God in the Highest), LAUDAMUS TE (We praise you), GRATIAS AGIMUS TIBI (We Give You Thanks), DOMINE DEUS (Lord God), QUI TOLLIS PECCATA MUNDI (Who Bears the Sins of the World), QUI SEDES AD DEXTERAM PATRIS (Who Sits at the Right Hand of the Father), QUONIAM TU SOLUS SANCTUS (For You Alone are Holy), and CUM SANCTO SPIRITU (With the Holy Spirit).

Gloriana. Opera by Britten, 1953, written for the coronation of Queen Elizabeth II and produced at a special gala performance in the Queen's presence at Covent Garden, London. The Gloriana of the title was Queen Elizabeth I; the libretto traverses her romance with the Earl of Essex. There is a masquelike dramaturgy, although the work is otherwise entirely 20th century; Elizabethan tunes are part of the work's melodic material.

glottis. The aperture between the vocal cords, a key element of the development of vocal production.

Gluck, Christoph Willibald, Ritter von

R enowned German composer; b. Erasbach, near Weidenwang, in the Upper Palatinate, July 2, 1714; d. Vienna, Nov. 15, 1787. His father was a forester at Erasbach until his appointment as forester to Prince Lobkowitz of Eisenberg about 1729. Gluck received his elementary instruction in the village schools at Kamnitz and Albersdorf near Komotau, where he also was taught singing and instrumental playing. Some biographers refer to his study at the Jesuit college at Komotau, but there is no documentary evidence to support this contention. In 1732 he went to Prague to complete his education, but it is doubtful that he took any courses at the univ. He earned his living by playing violin and cello at rural dances in the area; also sang at various churches. He met Bohuslav Čzernohorsky, and it is probable that Gluck learned the methods of church music from him. He went to Vienna in 1736 and was chamber musician to young Prince Lobkowitz, son of the patron of Gluck's father. In 1737 he was taken to Milan by Prince Melzi; this Italian sojourn was of the greatest importance to Gluck's musical development. There he became a student of G. B. Sammartini and acquired a solid technique of composition in the Italian style.

Christoph Willibald Gluck

COURTESY OF THE FREE LIBRARY OF PHILADELPHIA

After 4 years of study he brought out his 1st opera, *Artaserse*, to the text of the celebrated Metastasio; it was produced in Milan (1741) with such success that he was immediately commissioned to write more operas. He also contributed separate numbers to several other operas produced in Italy. In 1745 he received an invitation to go to London; on his way he visited Paris and met Rameau. He was commissioned by the Italian Opera of London to write 2 operas for the Haymarket Theatre, as a competitive endeavor to Handel's enterprise. The 1st of these works was *La Caduta dei giganti*, a tribute to the Duke of Cumberland on the defeat of the Pretender; it was produced in 1746; the 2nd was a pasticcio, *Artamene*, in which Gluck used material from his previous operas; it was produced later that year. Ten days later he appeared with Handel at a public concert, despite the current report in London society that Handel had declared that Gluck knew no more counterpoint than his cook (it should be added that a professional musician, Gustavus Waltz, was Handel's cook and valet at the time).

In 1746 Gluck gave a demonstration in London, playing on the glass harmonica. He left London late in 1746 when he received an engagement as conductor with Pietro Mingotti's traveling Italian opera company. He conducted in Hamburg, Leipzig, and Dresden; in 1747

he produced a SERENATA, *Le nozze d'Ercole e d'Ebe*, to celebrate a royal wedding; it was performed at the Saxon court, in Pillnitz. He went to Vienna, where he staged his opera *Semiramide riconosciuta*, after a Metastasio libretto (1748). He then traveled to Copenhagen, where he produced a festive opera, *La Contesa dei Numi* (1749), on the occasion of the birth of Prince Christian.

In 1750 Gluck married Marianna Pergin, daughter of a Viennese merchant; for several years afterward he conducted operatic performances in Vienna. As French influence increased there, he wrote several entertainments to French texts, containing spoken dialogue, in the style of opera comique; of these, the most successful were *Le Cadi dupé* (1761) and *La Rencontre imprévue* (1764; perf. also under the title *Les Pèlerins de la Mecque*, his most popular production in this genre). His greatest work of the Vienna period was *Orfeo ed Euridice*, to a libretto by Calzabigi (with the part of Orfeo sung by the famous castrato Gaetano Guadagni, 1762). Gluck revised it for a Paris performance, produced in French in 1774, with Orfeo sung by a tenor. There followed another masterpiece, *Alceste* (Vienna, 1767), also to Calzabigi's text. In the preface to *Alceste* Gluck formulated his aesthetic credo, which elevated the dramatic meaning of musical stage plays above a mere striving for vocal effects: "I sought to reduce music to its true function, that of seconding poetry in order to strengthen the emotional expression and the impact of the dramatic situations without interrupting the action and without weakening it by superfluous ornaments."

The success of his French operas in Vienna led Gluck to the decision to try his fortunes in Paris, yielding to the persuasion of François du Roullet, an attaché at the French embassy in Vienna who also supplied him with his 1st libretto for a serious French opera, an adaptation of Racine's *Iphigénie en Aulide* (Paris, 1774). He set out for Paris early in 1773, preceded by declarations in the Paris press by du Roullet and Gluck himself explaining in detail his ideas of dramatic music. These statements set off an intellectual battle in the Paris press and among musicians in general between the adherents of traditional Italian opera and Gluck's novel French opera. It reached an unprecedented degree of acrimony when the Italian composer Nicola Piccinni was engaged by the French court to write operas to French texts, in open competition with Gluck; intrigues multiplied, even though Marie Antoinette never wavered in her admiration for Gluck, who taught her singing and harpsichord playing. However, Gluck and Piccinni themselves never participated in the bitter polemics unleashed by their literary and musical partisans.

The sensational successes of the French version of Gluck's *Orfeo* and of *Alceste* were followed by the production of *Armide* (1777), which aroused great admiration. Then followed his masterpiece, *Iphigénie en Tauride* (1779), which established Gluck's superiority to Piccinni, who was commissioned to write an opera on the same subject but failed to complete it in time. Gluck's last

opera, *Echo et Narcisse* (Paris, 1779), did not measure up to the excellence of his previous operas. By that time his health had failed; he had several attacks of apoplexy, which resulted in partial paralysis. In the autumn of 1779 he returned to Vienna, where he lived as an invalid. His last work was a *De profundis* for chorus and orch., written 5 years before his death.

Besides his operas he wrote several ballets, of which *Don Juan* (Vienna, 1761) was the most successful; he also wrote a cycle of 7 songs to words by Klopstock, 7 trio sonatas, several overtures, etc. Wagner made a complete revision of the score of *Iphigénie en Aulide*; this arrangement was so extensively used that a Wagnerized version of Gluck's music became the chief text for performances during the 19th century. A thematic catalogue was publ. by A. Wotquenne (Leipzig, 1904; German trans. with supplement by J. Liebeskind).

Glückliche Hand, Die (The Lucky Hand). Drama with music by Schoenberg, 1913; 1st performed in 1924. A man beset by horrible visions meditates on his search for happiness; a chorus reassures him that his efforts are futile. This expressionist work uses Schoenberg's trademarks: *Sprechstimme*, melodic atonality, and harmonic dissonance.

G.O. (Fr.). *Grand orgue*, great organ.

goat trill (Ger. *Bockstriller*; It. *caprino*, little goat). 1. A curious vocal effect produced when a singer repeats a note very fast and catches a breath after each note; it was introduced by Monteverdi for dramatic purposes. 2. Fanciful 18th-century description of a rasping trill at the interval of a semitone or less. Wagner also used it in *Die Meistersinger*.

God Bless America. Song by I. Berlin, 1918–38. The composer, a Russian-Jewish American immigrant, wrote the song's chorus in 1918 with the intention of using it in a show he staged while he was in the U.S. Army. But the song was withdrawn from the production; it lay dormant until 1938, when the American soprano Kate Smith put it on a patriotic radio program on Armistice Day. In an atmosphere charged with the expectations of an imminent war, the song produced a profound impression. During the war it became an unofficial national anthem, and in 1955 President Eisenhower presented Berlin with a Gold Medal in appreciation of his services to the country for writing *God Bless*

America. Periodically petitions were circulated to have *God Bless America* replace *The Star-Spangled Banner* as the national anthem. Indeed, the tune is much more singable and the words are wider in their patriotic application, devoid of such anachronistic references as "bombs bursting in air." Berlin donated his royalties from *God Bless America* to the Boy and Girl Scouts of America.

God Bless the Child. Bluesy song credited to Billie Holiday, who certainly popularized it through performances and recordings in the 1940s and '50s; revived in 1969 by the rock-jazz band Blood, Sweat, and Tears.

God Save the Czar. Russian Czarist anthem, 1833, composed by the director of the Imperial court chapel Alexis Lvov, and almost immediately adopted as a national anthem, with words set especially by the Russian poet Vassily Zhukovsky. The controversy as to Lvov's authorship of the tune was aroused by the discovery that it was identical with the middle section of a march by a German bandleader, Ferdinand Haas, conductor of the Imperial Russian Preobrazhensky Regiment in St. Petersburg. But Lvov's manuscript, set for chorus and orch., is extant and bears an earlier date than that of Haas's; the consensus of Russian musicologists, therefore, is in favor of its authenticity. The tune, intimately associated with the Czarist regime, became a political landmine after the Russian Revolution. Singing of the tune was abolished, and its quotation in Tchaikovsky's

1812 Overture was replaced synharmonically by the concluding chorus from Glinka's opera *A Life for the Czar*, which itself was renamed *Ivan Susanin*.

God Save the King (*God Save the Queen*). The British national anthem, the tune of which is also used in the U.S. as *My Country, 'Tis of Thee*. It was 1st published in its present form in 1744, but there were adumbrations and approximations in the 17th century. Countless attempts to ascertain its origin have yet to succeed.

Goethe, Johann Wolfgang von, illustrious German poet and dramatist; b. Frankfurt am Main, Aug. 28, 1749; d. Weimar, Mar. 22, 1832. Goethe wrote some of the most famous lyrics set as lieder during the later 18th century and beyond. His novels (*The Sorrows of Young Werther*, the Mignon songs from *Wilhelm Meister's Years of Wandering*) and plays (*Claudine von Villa Bella, Egmont*) served as libretto sources. No work was more influential, magnetic, and overwhelming than *Faust*, parts I (1806) and II (1831); Goethe hoped that Mozart would have set the drama, had death not interceded. He thought Mendelssohn and Schubert too young; so he overcame his resistance to Beethoven and proposed the project to him; the composer considered it, but the work was never written. The only collaboration between Goethe and Beethoven was the incidental music for the drama *Egmont*, performed to Goethe's approval in 1814. He had strong ideas of his own on music (see *Briefwechsel zwischen Goethe und Zelter*, Berlin, 1833; Ferdinand Hiller also shows this in his *Goethes musicalisches Leben*, Cologne, 1883). In recent years Goethe's attitude toward music has been made the subject of investigation by several scholars.

Goldberg, Johann Gottlieb, German organist, harpsichordist, and composer; b. Danzig (baptized), Mar. 14, 1727; d. Dresden, Apr. 13, 1756. As a child he was taken to Dresden by his patron, Count Hermann Karl von Keyserlingk; he is reported to have studied with W. F. Bach and later with J. S. Bach (1742–43); in 1751 he became musician to Count Heinrich Brühl, a post he held until his death. His name is immortalized through the set of 30 variations for keyboard by Bach, the so-called GOLDBERG VARIATIONS, long believed to have been commissioned by Keyserlingk for Goldberg. Although this account is now doubted, it is known that Bach gave Goldberg a copy of the score. Goldberg's own compositions include 2 concertos; polonaises; a sonata with minuet and 12 variations for harpsichord; 6 trios for flute, violin, and bass; a motet; a cantata; etc.

Goldberg Variations. A famous set of variations by Bach, 1741, for harpsichord, on an instrumental "aria." The 30 variations were supposedly written by Bach at the request of his pupil J. G. Goldberg, purportedly as a soporific for Goldberg's employer Count Keyserlingk, who suffered from insomnia; the story seems apocryphal. Yet the work demands considerable attention due to its amazingly skillful contrapuntal devices, and it is a wonder whether it could really put anyone to sleep. The tour de force of the variations is the use of a canon at every 3rd variation, with the interval of the canon expanding arithmetically.

golden section (golden mean, golden ratio; sometimes capitalized). Proportional division of a whole into 2 unequal parts such that the ratio of the smaller to the larger is the same as that of the larger to the whole; the ratio's value is irrational (.618034). Some analysts find evidence of compositional applications by Debussy and Bartók.

Goldsmith, Jerry, American composer; b. Los Angeles, Feb. 10, 1929. He studied piano with Jakob Gimpel and theory and composition with Castelnuovo-Tedesco; then studied music at Los Angeles City College; also sat in on Rosza's sessions on film music at the Univ. of Southern Calif. He wrote music for various CBS radio and television programs (1950–60); then devoted himself mainly to writing music for films. Among his works are the scores for *Freud* (1962); *7 Days in May* (1964); *A Patch of Blue* (1966); *Seconds* (1966); *Planet of the Apes* (1967); *Patton* (1970); *Papillon* (1973); *The Cassandra Crossing* (1976); *Islands in the Stream* (1977); *MacArthur* (1978); *Poltergeist* (1982); *Rambo* (1985); etc. He also wrote chamber music and vocal works.

goliards. Wandering minstrels, usually students or monks, who traveled through Germany during Medieval times. The celebrated collection *Carmina Burana* (Songs of Beuren, a Benedictine monastery where the manuscript was found) consists mainly of goliard songs.

Golitzin, Nikolai (Borisovich), Russian nobleman and patron of music; b. St. Petersburg, Dec. 19, 1794; d. Tambov district, Nov. 3, 1866. He was a talented cello player, but his name is remembered mainly because of his connection with Beethoven, who dedicated the overture *Consecration of the House* (op. 124) and the string quartets opps. 127, 130, and 132 to him. Golitzin was also responsible for the 1st performance of Beethoven's *Missa solemnis* (St. Petersburg Phil. Soc., 1824).

Gondellied (Ger.). BARCAROLE.

Gondoliers, The, or The King of Barataria. Comic opera by Gilbert and Sullivan, 1889. Two Venetian boatmen are revealed to be the heirs to the Baratarian throne. They risk their ascension by unwittingly marrying 2 commoners; but the women turn out to be aristocrats after all, and everyone is happy. This is the most operatic of the Gilbert and Sullivan collaborations.

gong. A suspended circular metal plate, struck with a mallet and producing a sustained reverberation. The gong differs from the TAM-TAM in having a convex circular nub in the plate's middle; the mallet is usually struck on this nub, whose size, along with that of the gong itself, determines the fixed pitch of the instrument.

Good Boy. Musical by Harry Ruby and Herbert Stothart, 1928. A boy from Arkansas tries to make good in N.Y., falls for a chorus girl, and loses her when he fails. Undaunted, he starts a business making dolls for adult tastes. He succeeds, and he gets his girl back. Includes *I Wanna Be Loved by You.*

Good News. Musical by Ray Henderson, 1927; a picture of life on an American college campus where football reigns supreme over academics. Includes *The Best Things in Life are Free.*

Good Vibrations. A 1967 number 1 hit for the Beach Boys, their greatest and most ambitious recording. Features the electronic musical instrument the THEREMIN.

Good-Humored Ladies, The. Ballet by Tommassini, 1917, arranged from keyboard sonatas by Domenico Scarlatti.

Goodman, Benny (Benjamin David), famous American clarinetist and swing bandleader; b. Chicago, May 30, 1909; d. N.Y., June 13, 1986. He acquired a taste for syncopated music as a child by listening to phonograph recordings of ragtime; was playing professionally by the age of 12 (1921), and in 1926 was working with Ben Pollack, one of the leading Chicago jazz musicians of the period. In 1929 he went to N.Y. as a clarinetist in various bands. In 1934 he formed his own band, which became known nationwide from its weekly appearances on the *Let's Dance* radio program. He was among the many important musicians who were guided by the producer John Hammond.

Both as the leader of a large dance band and for his virtuoso performances in various jazz combos, Goodman was the best-known and most successful musician of the swing era; nicknamed the King of Swing, he played with Red Nichols, Ted Lewis, Paul Whiteman, Teddy Wilson, Benny Carter, Fletcher Henderson, Gene Krupa, Lionel Hampton, Harry James, Ziggy Elman, Jess Stacy, and Charlie Christian, who made most of his few recordings with Goodman. He also played clarinet parts in classical works in concert and for records, appearing as soloist in Mozart's Clarinet Concerto with the N.Y. Phil. (1940), and recording works by Copland, Bartók, Stravinsky, Gould, and Bernstein.

Goodnight Irene. Popularized by the folk/blues singer Leadbelly (b. Huddie Ledbetter), this was actually based on a popular turn-of-the-century song. Leadbelly's version was different than the original publication and has become a folk standard. It was a number 1 hit for the folk group the Weavers in 1950, shortly after Leadbelly died.

Goodnight Ladies. Song, published in 1847 as *Farewell, Ladies,* attributed to E. P. Christy (1815–62). The leader of a famous blackface minstrel show, Christy often bought songs outright from their composers (Foster among them) and put his name on them; therefore his authorship is doubtful.

goose. A harsh break in the tone of a clarinet, oboe, or bassoon.

gopak. HOPAK.

Gordon, Dexter (Keith), prominent African-American jazz tenor saxophonist; b. Los Angeles, Feb. 27, 1923; d. Philadelphia, Apr. 25, 1990. He studied clarinet; took up the alto saxophone at the age of 15, then turned to the tenor saxophone and soon began to play in a local band. He worked with Lionel Hampton (1940–43) and Louis Armstrong (1944); then went to N.Y., where he played in Billy Eckstine's band (1944–46); after returning to Los Angeles he appeared with Wardell Gray (1947–52). In 1962 he moved to Copenhagen and continued his career in Europe; then returned to the U.S.; was elected a member of the Jazz Hall of Fame in 1980. He was generally acknowledged as the most influential tenor saxophonist of the bop period. He starred in the film *'Round Midnight* (1986).

Gordy, Berry, Jr., significant African-American record producer, creator of the Motown sound (so named after

Motor Town, that is, Detroit); b. Detroit, Nov. 28, 1929. He trained as a featherweight boxer; then was drafted into the U.S. Army; after discharge he worked on the assembly line for Ford and began writing songs. However, his significance in popular American music was connected not with songwriting but with his recording enterprise. He attracted a number of talented groups, composers, and singers to record for Motown, among them Smokey Robinson and the Miracles, Mary Wells, the Four Tops, Martha and the Vandellas, the Supremes (and Diana Ross), the Temptations, Jr. Walker and the All Stars, Gladys Knight and the Pips, Marvin Gaye, the O'Jays, Stevie Wonder, and the Jackson Five. He contributed to the final desegregation of so-called "race music" and its integration into the mainstream of American popular music, which included rhythm and blues, soul and gospel, and middle-of-the-road pop.

Górecki, Henryk (Mikolaj), significant Polish composer; b. Czernica, Dec. 6, 1933. He studied composition with Boleslaw Szabelski at the Katowice Cons. (1955–60); in 1968 he was appointed to its faculty. In his music he makes use of the entire arsenal of modern techniques while preserving traditional formal design. A radical shift of style toward a mystical and ethereal aesthetic culminated in the 3rd Sym. for Soprano and Orch. (1976); multiple recordings of this work have been immensely successful.

gorgheggiare (It., warble). Sing trills with a guttural voice.

gorgia (It., throat). Guttural mode of speaking or singing.

gospel music

American Negro spirituals, derived from antebellum slave songs. This was the 1st surviving repertoire of African-American music; there were black hymnbooks from the beginning of the 19th century, and important collections of camp-meeting hymns and spirituals, the 1st being the abolitionist *Slave Songs of the U.S.* These postwar gatherings saved an oral tradition for posterity; the music was popularized and made appropriate for the concert hall by the Fisk (Univ.) Jubilee Singers and similar groups associated with black colleges.

2. Twentieth-century African-American Christian songs marked by a directness of appeal or statement of belief. At its most lively the music echoes the popular medium of the day, whether it be the blues, New Orleans, rhythm and blues (the mainstream style), doo-wop (in the gospel quartet), soul, or rap. However, a mainstream style known as gospel hymnody can be found in the hymns of Thomas A. Dorsey and Lucie Campbell; later, Roberta Martin, James Cleveland, and Andrae Crouch. The performance style followed the changes in the musical style; by the 1930s the piano (or organ) had become the primary accompaniment. The call-and-response texture of the old spiritual and the Dixieland gospel style of Bessie Johnson (1920s) were incorporated into the solo-and-chorus texture. Sister Rosetta Tharpe made gospel a best-selling commodity (*Rock Me*, 1938). In the 1950s Mahalia Jackson was the "queen" of gospel music. Later generations provided singers such as Clara Ward, Marion Williams, Inez Andrews, Shirley Caesar (a "singing preacher"), and Edwin and Walter Hawkins. Gospel became a vehicle for inspirational and musical improvisation with Jackson's introduction of *vamping* (recitative over the repetition of a chord progression in free time, a technique borrowed from jazz).

3. A white Protestant church hymn, traditionally sung A CAPPELLA. Although hymnody had existed in the U.S. before the American revolution and was brought forward in the 19th century (particularly the shape-note movement), musicologists tend to limit the definition of "white gospel music" to the popular hymns, camp-meeting spirituals, and other music associated with the revivalist movement. From the beginning this music has had a written basis, although its performance practice was freer in the camp-meeting than the hymnbooks would suggest.

Lowell Mason and George Root were among the earliest composers of gospel hymns; in the next generation Robert Lowry (*Shall We Gather at the River?*) and Elisha Hoffman (*Are You Washed in the Blood of the Lamb?*) were among the important authors.

The last part of the century was the era of Dwight Moody, the preacher, and Ira Sankey, the musician. They held well-attended revival meetings in the U.S. and U.K. in urban settings; they collected hymns into several vols. Similar collaborations between preachers and musicians persisted into the 20th century, up through the triad of preacher Billy Graham and singers Cliff Barrows and George Beverly Shea. In a manner reminiscent of black gospel, old-time, bluegrass, and country musicians have used their talents in the service of gospel music.

Gothic music. A historical analogy with Gothic architecture referring to the austere, even ascetic contrapuntal art of the Middle Ages in northern and western Europe, centered on Notre Dame POLYPHONY. It may be identified with the ARS ANTIQUA, gradually giving way to the ARS NOVA and other late medieval styles.

Gothic Symphony. Sym. No. 1 by H. Brian, 1919–27, 1st performed 1961. A work of Mahlerian proportions, the 4th movement is a Te Deum setting.

Gott erhalte unser Kaiser. Former Austrian national anthem, composed by Haydn, 1797. Haydn was instructed by the Austrian court to compose a hymn melody of a solemn nature that could be used as the anthem. He succeeded triumphantly in this task; he also used this tune as a theme for a set of variations in his String Quartet in C Major (No. 3, op. 76), the EMPEROR QUARTET. The original text for the hymn, written by Lorenz Leopold Haschka, began "Gott erhalte Franz den Kaiser." This hymn had a curious history: a new set of words was written by August Heinrich Hoffmann during a period of revolutionary disturbances in Germany preceding the general European revolution of 1848; its 1st line, "Deutschland, Deutschland über alles," later assumed the significance of German imperialism and fascism; in its original it meant merely "Germany above all (in our hearts)."

Götterdämmerung (The Twilight of the Gods). The final spectacle of Wagner's great tetralogy *Der Ring des Nibelungen* (The Ring of the Nibelung), 1876. It was 1st performed at Wagner's Festival Theater in Bayreuth. Malevolent magic wrought by the Nibelungs makes the hero Siegfried forget his beloved Brünnhilde and fall for another, transforms him into the image of another Nibelung, then restores his memory and his physical shape to him before he is slain. Brünnhilde, who couldn't save his father Siegmund either (in *Die Walküre*), rides into the funeral pyre erected for Siegfried's final rites. The gods, demigods, heroes, the monstrous offspring of the sinister gnome Nibelung, and the Nordic Olympus called Valhalla all perish in the final conflagration. The Rhine River overflows the scene, and the Rhinemaidens regain the accursed Ring; thus the Rhinegold ends where it started off. A labyrinthine network of leitmotifs attempts to guide the listener, trying to trace the principal characters of the music drama. Even such a confirmed Wagnerite as George Bernard Shaw candidly admitted his inability to penetrate the tangled web of the story.

Gottschalk, Louis Moreau

~~~ ~~~ ~~~ ~~~ ~~~

Celebrated American pianist and composer; b. New Orleans, May 8, 1829; d. Tijuca, near Rio de Janeiro, Dec. 18, 1869. His father, an English businessman, emigrated to New Orleans; his mother was of noble Creole descent, the granddaughter of a governor of a Haitian province. His talent for music was developed early: at the age of 4 he began studying violin with Felix Miolan, concertmaster of the opera orch., and piano with François Letellier, organist at the St. Louis Cathedral; at the age of 7 he substituted for Letellier at the organ during High Mass, and the next year he played violin at a benefit for Miolan. In 1841 he was sent to Paris, where he studied piano with Charles Hallé and Camille Stamaty and harmony with Pierre Maleden. He also later studied composition with Berlioz.

In 1845 he gave a concert at the Salle Pleyel that attracted the attention of Chopin. His piano compositions of the period, including *Bamboula*, *Le Bananier*, and *La Savane*, were influenced by Liszt and Chopin but also inspired by childhood recollections of Creole and Negro dances and songs. In 1846–47 he appeared in a series of concerts with Berlioz at the Italian Opera, and in 1850 concertized throughout France and Switzerland, playing his own compositions. In 1851 he appeared in Madrid at the invitation of the Queen and was given the Order of Isabella; during his stay there he developed the "monster concerts," for which he wrote a sym. for 10 pianos, *El sitio de Zaragosa*, later transformed into *Bunker's Hill* by replacing the Spanish tunes with American ones.

Gottschalk returned to give a highly praised concert in N.Y. (1853), followed by many concerts throughout the U.S., Cuba, and Canada during the next 3 years. During the winter of 1855–56 he gave 80 concerts in N.Y. alone. His compositions from this period, including *La Scintilla*, *The Dying Poet*, and *The Last Hope*, written to display his talents, used many novel techniques of the "style pianola." After playing Henselt's Piano Concerto with the N.Y. Phil. (1857), he went to Cuba with the pubescent singer Adelina Patti. He then lived in the West Indies, writing works influenced by its indigenous music. In Havana, on Feb. 17, 1861, he introduced his most famous orch. work, *La Nuit des tropiques* (Sym. No. 1). He also produced several grand "monster concerts" modeled after those of Jullien.

Though he was born in the antebellum South, Gottschalk's sympathies were with the North during the American Civil War; he had manumitted the slaves he inherited after his father's death in 1853. He resumed his U.S. concert career with a performance in N.Y. (1862), and from then until 1865 toured the North and the West with Max Strakosch, playing (by his estimation) over a thousand concerts. His notebooks from this era, posth. publ. as *Notes of a Pianist* (Philadelphia, 1881), perceptively reveal life in Civil War America. After becoming involved in a scandal with a teenage girl in San Francisco, he was forced to flee to South America (1865); he appeared in concert throughout South America, and composed new works based on local melodies and rhythms. During a festival of his music in Rio de Janeiro (1869), he collapsed on stage after playing the appropriately titled *Morte!!*; he died within a month. His remains were exhumed and reburied with great ceremony in Brooklyn in 1870.

Gottschalk was a prolific composer of bravura, pianistic works that enjoyed great popularity for some time even after his death; ultimately they slipped into the ubiquitous centenary oblivion. As a pianist he was one of the most adulated virtuosos of his era. His concerts, featuring his own compositions, emphasized his prodigious technique but were criticized by some as being superficial. A definitive catalog of his works is difficult to assemble, since many of the works referred to in his copious correspondence have not been found; there are revisions of one and the same work using different titles, and several works were publ. using the same op. number. Two catalogs of his music have been published. Gottschalk publ. some of his works using the pseudonyms Steven Octaves, Oscar Litti, A.B.C., and Paul Ernest.

Gould, Glenn (Herbert), remarkable and individualistic Canadian pianist noted for his unorthodox interpretations; b. Toronto, Sept. 25, 1932; d. there, Oct. 4, 1982. His parents were musically gifted and gladly fostered his precocious development; he began to play piano, and even compose, in his single-digit years. At the age of 10 he entered the Royal Cons. of Music in Toronto, where he studied piano with Alberto Guerrero, organ with Frederick C. Silvester, and music theory with Leo Smith; he received his diploma as a graduate at 13, in 1945.

He made his debut in Toronto (1946). As he began practicing with total concentration on the mechanism of the keyboard, he developed mannerisms that were to become his artistic signature. He reduced the use of the pedal to a minimum in order to avoid a harmonic haze; he cultivated "horizontality" in his piano posture, bringing his head down

almost to the level of the keys. He regarded music as a linear art; this naturally led him to an intense examination of Baroque structures; Bach was the subject of his close study rather than Chopin; he also cultivated performances of the early polyphonists Sweelinck, Gibbons, and others. He played Mozart with emphasis on the early pianoforte techniques; he peremptorily omitted the Romantic composers Chopin, Schumann, and Liszt from his repertoire. He found the late sonatas of Beethoven more congenial to his temperament, and, remarkably enough, he played the piano works of the modern Vienna school—Schoenberg, Berg, and Webern—perhaps because of their classical avoidance of purely decorative tonal formations.

Following Gould's U.S. debut in Washington, D.C. (1955), he evoked unequivocal praise at his concerts, but in 1964 he abruptly terminated his stage career and devoted himself exclusively to recording, which he regarded as a superior art to concertizing. This enabled him to select the best portions of the music he played in the studio, forming a mosaic unblemished by accidental mishaps. A great part of the interest he aroused with the public at large was due to mannerisms that marked his behavior on the stage. He used a 14-inch-high chair that placed his eyes almost at the level of the keyboard; he affected informal dress; he had a rug put under the piano and a glass of distilled water within reach. He was in constant fear of bodily injury: he avoided shaking hands with the conductor after playing a concerto, and he sued the Steinway piano company for a large sum of money when an enthusiastic representative shook his hand too vigorously. But what even his most ardent admirers could not palliate was his unshakable habit of singing along with his performance; he even allowed his voice to be audible on his carefully wrought, lapidary phonograph recordings.

Glenn Gould, c. 1950s

Socially, Gould was a recluse; he found a release from his self-imposed isolation in editing a series of radio documentaries for the CBC. He called 3 of them a "solitude tragedy." Symbolically they were devoted to the natural isolation of the Canadian Arctic, the insular life of Newfoundland, and the religious hermetism of the Mennonite sect. He also produced a radio documentary on Schoenberg, treating him as a musical hermit. Other activities included conducting a chamber orch. without an audience. Needless to add, Gould never married.

Gould, Morton, extraordinarily talented and versatile American composer and conductor; b. Richmond Hill, N.Y., Dec. 10, 1913; d. N.Y., Feb. 21, 1996. His father was an Austrian; his mother came from Russia; both fostered his early addiction to music. If the affectionate family memories are to be accepted as facts, Gould composed a piano waltz at the age of 6 (indeed, it was ultimately publ. under the title *Just 6*). Being a prodigy did not harm him. He was bent on learning what music really is. He had piano lessons with Joseph Kardos and Abby Whiteside; later enrolled in the composition class of Vincent Jones at N.Y. Univ.; there, at the age of 16, he presented a concert of his works. To keep body and soul together he played the piano in silent movies and in loud jazz bands, accompanied dancers, and gave demonstrations of musical skill on college circuits. In 1931–32 he served as staff pianist at Radio City Music Hall in N.Y.; from 1934 to 1946 was in charge of the series *Music for Today* on the Mutual Radio network, and in 1943 he became music director of the lucrative *Chrysler Hour* on CBS Radio.

These contacts gave great impetus to Gould's bursting talent for composing singable, playable, and enjoyable light pieces; he was pregnant with the fertile sperm of musical Americana; his *American Symphonette No. 1* (1933) became a popular success; equally accessible to the musical youth of the day was the *Chorale and Fugue in Jazz* for 2 Pianos and Orch. (1934); no less a musical magus than Stokowski put it on the program of the Philadelphia Orch. (1936). Gould then produced 3 more symphonettes (1935, 1938, 1941); No. 3 disgorged the luscious *Pavanne* [*sic*] (the misspelling was a concession to public illiteracy); the piece cloned several arrangements. There followed the *Latin-American Symphonette* (1940), an engaging tetrad of Latin dances (*Rhumba, Tango, Guaracha, Conga*). His *Spirituals* for Strings and Orch. (1941) is Gould's interpretation of the religious aspect of the American people. His other works touch on American history, as exemplified by *A Lincoln Legend* (1941), which Toscanini placed on a program with the NBC Sym. (1942); there followed the rambunctious orch.l *Cowboy Rhapsody* (1943). In 1945 Gould conducted a whole program of his works with the Boston Sym. Orch. He then turned to ballet in his *Fall River Legend* (1947), based on the story of the notorious New England old maid Lizzie Borden, who may or may not have given her mother 40 whacks and "when she saw what she had done she gave her father 41." Gould's *Sym. of Spirituals*, written for the American bicentennial (1976), was a reverential offering; his other bicentennial work, *American Ballads* (1976), is a symphonic florilegium of American songs.

Gould wrote the music for the Broadway show *Billion Dollar Baby* (1945), several scores for Hollywood films, and also background music for the historical television productions *Verdun* (1963), *World War I* (1964–65), and *Holocaust* (1978). But Gould was not so much seduced by public success as not to test his powers in absolute music. He studied ways and means of Baroque techniques, and wrote several concertos: 1 for piano (1937), 1 for violin (1938), 1 for viola (1944); Variations for 2 pianos and orch. (1952); and Inventions for 4 pianos and orch. (1953). On top of these "classical" works he produced a unique shtick, Concerto for Tap Dancer and Orch. (1953). Gould was a conductor of excellent skills; he toured Australia in 1977, Japan in 1979, Mexico in 1980, and Israel in 1981. In 1983 he received the National Arts Award. He was elected a member of the American Academy and Inst. of Arts and Letters in 1986. He was president of ASCAP from 1986 until 1994.

Gounod, Charles (Francois)

〰〰 〰〰 〰〰 〰〰 〰〰

Famous French composer; b. St. Cloud, June 17, 1818; d. Paris, Oct. 18, 1893. His father, Jean François Gounod, was a painter, winner of the 2nd Grand Prix de Rome, who died when Gounod was a small child. His mother, a most accomplished woman, supervised his literary, artistic, and musical education; she taught him piano. He completed his academic studies at the Lycée St. Louis; in 1836 he entered the Paris Cons., studying with Halévy, Le Sueur, and Paer. In 1837 he won the 2nd Prix de Rome with his cantata *Marie Stuart et Rizzio*; in 1839 he won the Grand Prix with his cantata *Fernand*. In Rome he studied church music, particularly the works of Palestrina; composed a Mass for 3 voices and orch., which was performed at the church of San Luigi dei Francesi. In 1842, during a visit to Vienna, he conducted a Requiem of his own; upon his return to Paris he became precentor and organist of the Missions Étrangères; studied theology for 2 years, but decided against taking Holy Orders; yet he was often referred to as "l'Abbé" Gounod; some religious choruses were publ. in 1846 as composed by "Abbé Charles Gounod."

Soon he tried his hand at stage music. In 1851 his 1st opera, *Sapho*, was produced at the Opéra, with only moderate success; he revised it much later, in 1884; but it was unsuccessful. Two more failed operas followed. In the meantime he was active in other musical ways in Paris; he conducted the choral society Orphéon (1852–60) and composed for it several choruses. Gounod's great success came with the production of *Faust*, after Goethe (Théâtre-Lyrique, Mar. 19, 1859; perf. with additional recitatives and ballet at the Opéra, Mar. 3, 1869); Faust remained Gounod's greatest masterpiece, and indeed the most successful French opera of the 19th century, triumphant all over the world without any sign of diminishing effect through a century of changes in musical tastes.

However, it was widely criticized for the melodramatic treatment of Goethe's poem by the librettists Barbier and Carré, and for the somewhat sentimental style of Gounod's music. The succeeding operas were only partially successful, but with *Roméo et Juliette* (Paris, 1867), Gounod recaptured universal acclaim. In 1870, during the Franco-Prussian War, he went to London, where he organized Gounod's Choir, and presented concerts; when Paris fell, he wrote an elegiac cantata, *Gallia*, to words from the Lamentations of Jeremiah, which he conducted in London (1871); it was later performed in Paris. He wrote some incidental music for productions in Paris, without signal success. The last years of his life were devoted mainly to sacred works, of which the most important was *La Rédemption*, a trilogy, 1st performed at the Birmingham Festival in 1882; another sacred trilogy, *Mors et vita*, also written for the Birmingham Festival, followed in 1885.

He continued to write religious works in close succession; a *Requiem* (1893) was left unfinished, and was arranged by Henri Busser after Gounod's death. One of his most popular settings to religious words is *Ave Maria*, adapted to the 1st prelude of Bach's *Well-Tempered Clavier*, but its original version was *Méditation sur le 1er Prélude de Piano de S. Bach* for violin and piano (1853); the words were added later (1859).

Goyescas (Aspects of Goya). Originally, a piano suite by Granados, 1911, revealing his impression of the great Spanish painter's work; Granados later transformed it into an opera, premiered at the Metropolitan Opera, N.Y. (1916).

G.P. Abbrev. for GRAND PAUSE or GENERALPAUSE.

grace note. A vocal or instrumental ornament or embellishment not essential to the melody or harmony. Grace notes are usually written small, usually a scale degree above or below. If the note is crossed by a slant, its rhythmic value is taken from the preceding note; if it is not crossed, it becomes a long note incorporated into the following passage, usually taking half of the value of the note immediately followed. The latter is typical of Classic practice; modern editors usually write these long grace notes out.

gracile (It.). Attenuated; graceful, delicate.

gradatamente (It.). By degrees, gradually.

gradazione (It., gradation). A gradual change of dynamics.

gradevole (It.). Pleasingly, agreeably, pleasantly.

gradual. 1. In the Roman Catholic Mass, a respond (antiphon) sung between the epistle and gospel readings. 2. The main book of the Catholic liturgy containing all the principal sections of the Mass; in this sense it is a comple-ment of the antiphonal (antiphoner, antiphonary), which contains the liturgy of the Divine Office. The word *gradual* is derived from *gradus* (step), because the chants were sung from the steps of the altar.

Gradus ad Parnassum (Lat., steps to Parnassus, the mountain of the muses). 1. Title of the famous Latin treatise on counterpoint by Johann Joseph Fux (1660–1741), published in Vienna in 1725; this was the textbook for composers and theorists for at least a century. 2. Title given by Clementi to his collection of piano studies, issued in 1817.

Graffman, Gary, outstanding American pianist; b. N.Y., Oct. 14, 1928. He won a scholarship to the Curtis Inst. of Music in Philadelphia when he was 8, and studied with Isabelle Vengerova. He was only 10 when he gave a piano recital at Town Hall in N.Y. After graduating in 1946, he was a scholarship student at Columbia Univ. (1946–47). In 1946 he won the 1st regional Rachmaninoff competition, which secured for him his debut with the Philadelphia Orch. in 1947. In 1949 he was honored with the Leventritt Award. Subsequently he received a Fulbright grant to go to Europe (1950–51). Returning to the U.S., he had lessons with Horowitz in N.Y. and Rudolf Serkin in Marlboro, Vt. He was on his way to establishing himself as a pianist of the 1st rank when disaster struck: about 1979 he began to lose the use of his right hand through a rare ailment, designated by some doctors as carpal tunnel syndrome, that attacks instrumentalists. He was appointed to the faculty of the Curtis Inst. of Music in 1980 and was made its artistic director in 1986.

Grainger, (George) Percy (Aldridge)

Celebrated and eccentric Australian-born American pianist and composer; b. Melbourne, July 8, 1882; d. White Plains, N.Y., Feb. 20, 1961. He received his early musical training from his mother; at the age of 10 he appeared as pianist at several public concerts; then had lessons with Louis Pabst; in 1894 went to Germany, where he studied with Kwast in Frankfurt; also took a few lessons with Busoni. From his youngest days Grainger was fascinated by the ideal of the Nordic race, its physical beauty and art. He traveled to Scandinavia and walked many kilometers through the frozen fjords. In 1901 he began his concert career in England, then toured South Africa and Australia. In 1906 he met Grieg, who became enthusiastic about his talent; Grainger's performances of Grieg's Piano Concerto were famous. He later became friendly with Delius in England, whom he revered, and (in Holland) with Röntgen, whom he greatly esteemed.

In 1912 Grainger made a sensational debut, playing his own works (Aeolian Hall, N.Y.); he settled in the U.S. (1914); gave summer sessions at the Chicago Musical College (1919–31); was chairman of the music dept. of N.Y. Univ. (1932–33). A devoted son, he led an intimate exchange of letters in a peculiarly affected baby language with his mother; her suicide (1922) devastated him. But he recovered, and married the Swedish poet and artist Ella Viola Ström (1928) in a spectacular ceremony staged at the Hollywood Bowl, at which he conducted his work *To a Nordic Princess*, written for his bride.

Grainger's philosophy of life and art calls for the widest communion of peoples and opinions; despising urban culture, he dressed in vagabond clothes, and was once refused admission to Carnegie Hall at his own concert until he was properly identified. From composers like Grieg and Delius he gathered the conviction that music must be shaped by native modalities steeped in romantic colors and not be overlong in the individual forms. His profound study of folk music underlies the melodic and rhythmic structure of his own music; he made a determined effort to re-create in art music the free flow of instinctive songs of the people; he experimented with "gliding" intervals within the traditional scales and polyrhythmic combinations with independent strong beats in the component parts.

In a modest way he was a pioneer of electronic music; as early as 1937 he wrote a quartet for Theremin's electronic instruments, notating the pitch by zigzags and curves. He introduced individual forms of notation and orch. scoring, rejecting the common Italian designations of instruments, tempos, and dynamics in favor of plain English descriptions, such as fiddle (violin), middle fiddle (viola), louden lots (molto crescendo), soften (diminuendo), short and sharp (staccato), etc. His list of works, mostly for piano solo or small instrumental or vocal ensembles, is very large. The thematic content is principally based on English and Irish tunes. Of these, *Molly on the Shore* and *Irish Tune from County Derry* are the most popular; they are also arranged for various instrumental combinations.

Athletic by nature, Grainger made unreasonable exertions on his physical body, and let illness encroach on him in his early old age. In 1935 he founded a museum at the Univ. of Melbourne, in which he housed all his MSS and his rich collection of musical souvenirs. In his last will and testament he directed his executors to remove all flesh from his skeleton and to place it in a glass cage in the Grainger Museum for preservation and possible display. But the Univ. refused to abide by his last wishes, and he was buried in an ordinary way.

Grammy. An annual series of awards dispensed by the National Academy of the Recording Arts and Sciences (NARAS) for the most successful recordings in various categories. The award itself is a miniature replica of an old-fashioned Gramophone.

Gramophone (Grk., inscribed sound). 1. A trademark now commonly used in the U.K. for the phonograph. 2. Well-known British classical music magazine.

grande (*grand'*, *gran*; It.). Large, great, full, complete. *Grande* is the regular form, used after nouns; it is abbreviated to *grand'* before vowels, and to *gran* before consonants.

gran cassa (It.). BASS DRUM.

gran tamburo (It.). BASS DRUM.

Granados (y Campina), **Enrique,** outstanding Spanish composer; b. Lerida, July 27, 1867; d. at sea, Mar. 24, 1916 (when the boat he was on, the S.S. *Sussex*, was sunk by a German submarine in the English Channel). He studied piano at the Barcelona Cons. with Jurnet and Pujol, winning 1st prize (1883); then studied composition there with Pedrell (1883–87); in 1887 went to Paris to study with Charles de Bériot; made his recital debut in Barcelona in 1890. He 1st supported himself by playing piano in restaurants and giving private concerts. He attracted attention as a composer with his zarzuela *Maria del Carmen* (1898); in 1900 he conducted a series of concerts in Barcelona; also established a music school, the Academia Granados (1901). He then wrote 4 operas, which were produced in Barcelona with little success.

He undertook the composition of a work that was to be his masterpiece, a series of piano pieces entitled *Goyescas* (1911), inspired by the paintings and etchings of Goya; his fame rests securely on these imaginative and effective pieces, together with his brilliant *Danzas españolas* (1892–1900). Later, Fernando Periquet wrote a libretto based on the scenes from Goya's paintings, and Granados used the music of his piano suite for an opera, *Goyescas* (1916); its premiere took place, in the presence of the composer, at the Metropolitan Opera, N.Y., with excellent success; the score included an orch. *Intermezzo*, one of his most popular compositions. It was during his return voyage to Europe that he lost his life. Granados's music is essentially Romantic, with an admixture of specific Spanish rhythms and rather elaborate ornamentation.

grand. Technical term for GRAND PIANO.

grand(e) (Fr.). Large; great; full; *à grand orchestre*, for full orch.

grand aria. See ARIA DA CAPO.

grand barré. On a lute or guitar, stopping more than 3 strings simultaneously.

Grand Canyon Suite. Orch.1 suite by Grofé, 1931. It depicts chromolithographically 5 scenes of the American desert landscape, from sunrise to sunset. It was 1st performed in Chicago and immediately became a popular concert piece.

grand choeur (*grand jeu*; Fr.). 1. Great organ. 2. Full organ. 3. Harmonium stop.

Grand Ole Opry, The. Since 1925, a durable feast of American country music that was initiated in Nashville, Tenn., and broadcast over radio station WSM (the home station for a life-insurance company whose initials stand for "We Shield Millions"). The original name of the program, which was broadcast on Saturdays, was *Barn Dance*. It received its present name in 1927; the claim of inventing the name was taken by a Nashville reporter. The songs that made up the programs of the Grand Ole Opry were country ballads sung by genuine hillbillies uncontaminated by the preening ways of grand opera. The participants were also fiddlers, banjo players, guitar pickers, double bass pluckers, and performers on the Jew's harp, harmonica, accordion, and other traditional instruments; the country orch. numbered as many as 50 players. There were also such things as "talking blues," comedy routines, and grandiose jamborees, where people gathered on the stage indulging in free comments while performers continued their acts bent over the microphones.

Amazingly enough, the Grand Ole Opry managed to keep its rustic purity more or less intact through the muddy mire of prevailing commercialism; not even the advent of television was able to disrupt its natural folkways. A reactionary tendency set in, especially during the 1960s, but the Grand Ole Opry has learned to accommodate the ever-expanding stylistic panorama of country music.

grand opera. 1. A type of opera, usually in 5 acts, treating a heroic, mythological, or historical subject, sumptuously costumed, and produced in a large opera house; most closely associated with 19th-century French works or works performed in Paris during the same period. 2. In English-speaking countries, any serious work without spoken recitatives.

Grand Opéra. The principal state-supported opera company of Paris, located over the years in various locations.

Grand Pause (abbrev. *G.P.*). A rest for an entire ensemble or orch., often climactic.

grand piano. A generic term for the horizontally strung piano; also, a smaller version of this piano type than the concert grand.

Grande Bande, La. Lully's ensemble, also called the *24 violons du roy.*

grande caisse (Fr.). Bass drum.

Grande Duchesse de Gerolstein, La. Opéra-bouffe by Offenbach, 1867. The head of a mythical European duchy adores men in uniform, but the commoner soldier she promotes to general marries a milkmaid. The downcast duchess plans a conspiracy to slay him, but another soldier who arouses the Duchess appears. He is also of royal blood, making the marriage even simpler. Among the other characters are General Boum and Baron de Vermont-von-bock-bier.

grande-orgue. 1. Full organ. 2. Great organ. 3. Pipe organ.

grandezza, con (It.). With grandeur.

Grandfather's Clock. Ballad by the irrepressible tearjerker H. C. Work, 1876, written for a minstrel show. The image of the grandfather's dying and the clock's stopping simultaneously was irresistible to its audience.

grandioso (*grandisonante*; It.). With grandeur; majestically, pompously, loftily, affectedly, in a grandiose manner; sonorously, resonantly.

granulato (It.). NON LEGATO.

graphic notation

〜〜 〜〜 〜〜 〜〜 〜〜

Symbols of notation other than those traditionally seen in musical scores, often to indicate extremely precise (or intentionally imprecise) pitch, or to stimulate musical behavior or actions in performance.

Ever since 1000 A.D., when Guido d'Arezzo drew a line to mark the arbitrary height of pitch, musical notation has been geometric in its symbolism. The horizontal coordinate of the music staff still represents the temporal succession of melodic notes, and the vertical axis indicates the simultaneous use of 2 or more notes in a chord. Duration values have, through the centuries of evolution, been indicated by the color and shape of notes and stems to which they were attached. The composers of the avant-garde, eager to reestablish the mathematical correlation between the coordinates of the musical axes, have written scores in which the duration was indicated by proportional distance between the notes. Undoubtedly such geometrical precision contributes to the audio-visual clarity of notation, but it is impractical in actual usage. A passage in whole notes or half notes followed by a section in rapid rhythms would be more difficult to read than the imprecise notation inherited from the past. In orch. scores there is an increasing tendency to cut off the inactive instrumental parts in the middle of the page rather than to strew such vacuums with a rash of rests.

New sounds demanded new notational symbols. Cowell, who invented tone clusters, notated them by drawing thick vertical lines attached to a stem. Similar notation was used for similar effects by the Russian composer Vladimir Rebikov. In his book *New Musical Resources* Cowell tackled the problem of nonbinary rhythmic division and outlined a plausible system that would satisfy this need by using square, triangular, and rhomboid shapes of notes. Alois Hába, a pioneer in microtonal music, devised special notation for quarter tones, 3rd tones, and 6th tones. But as long as the elements of pitch, duration, intervallic extension, and polyphonic simultaneity remain in force, the musical staff can accommodate these elements more or less adequately. This was true even when noises were introduced by the Italian futurists into their works. In his compositions the futurist Russolo drew a network of curves, thick lines, and zigzags to represent each particular noise. But still the measure and the proportional lengths of duration retained their validity.

The situation changed dramatically with the introduction of aleatory processes and the notion of indeterminacy of musical elements. The visual appearance of aleatory scores assumes the aspect of ideograms. Cage, in particular, remodeled the old musical notation so as to give improvisatory latitude to the performer. The score of his *Variations I* suggests the track of cosmic rays in a cloud chamber. His *Cartridge Music* looks like an exploding supernova, and his *Fontana Mix* is a projection of irregular curves upon a strip of graph paper. Penderecki uses various graphic symbols to designate such effects as the highest possible sound on a given instrument, free improvisation within a certain limited range of chromatic notes, or icositetraphonic tone clusters.

In music for mixed media, notation ceases to function per se, giving way to pictorial representation of the actions or psychological factors involved. Indeed, the modern Greek composer Jani Christou (1926–70) introduces the Greek letter *psi* to indicate the psychology of the musical action, with geometric ideograms and masks symbolizing changing mental states ranging from complete passivity to panic. The score of *Passion According to Marquis de Sade* by Bussotti looks like a surrealistic painting with musical notes strewn across its path. The British composer Cardew draws black and white circles, triangles, and rectangles to indicate musical action. Xenakis prefers to use numbers and letters indicating the specific tape recordings to be used in his musical structures. Some composers abandon the problem of notation entirely, recording their inspirations on tape.

The chess grandmaster Tarrasch said of a problematical chess move: "If it is ugly, it is bad." *Mutatis mutandis*: the same criterion applies to a composer's musical graph.

Grappelli (Grappelly), **Stephane,** outstanding French jazz violinist; b. Paris, Jan. 26, 1908. He was trained as a classical musician but turned to jazz in the late 1920s; then organized the Quintette du Hot Club de France with the guitarist Django Reinhardt in 1934; subsequently toured widely and made recordings; made his U.S. debut at the Newport (R.I.) Jazz Festival in 1969. He appeared regularly in concert with Yehudi Menuhin from 1973, and later with Nigel Kennedy. In 1974 he made his Carnegie Hall debut in N.Y.; played there for a special 80th-birthday concert in 1988. He was the foremost jazz violinist in the European "Le Jazz hot," a fusion of big band and bebop styles.

Grateful Dead, The. See GARCIA, JERRY.

grave (*gravemente*; It.). 1. Grave or low in pitch. 2. Heavy, slow, ponderous in movement. 3. Serious, gravely, solemnly.

gravicembalo (It.). A 17th-century term for HARPSICHORD. *Gravicembalo col piano e forte*, early Italian name for PIANO; *gravicembalo con pian e forte*, Cristofori's name for his PIANO (early 18th century).

grazia, con (*grazioso*; It.). Gracefully; elegantly.

Great Balls of Fire. The 1958 hit for piano-pounder Jerry Lee Lewis that introduced his gospel-tinged vocals and boogie-woogie piano style to a broad audience. Later the name of a biographical film about the artist featuring actor Dennis Quaid (released in 1989).

Great Friendship, The. Opera, 1947, by Vano (Ilyich) Muradeli (1908–1970), on the Civil War in the Caucasus in 1919. The product of a socialist realist, nationalistic, and (mostly) politically correct Soviet nonentity, the work gained notoriety as the apparent target of a 1948 Communist Central Committee resolution, ostensibly because Muradeli had incorrectly implied that the Chechens had acted in a counter-Bolshevik manner. The attack was a screen for yet another threat to leading Soviet composers (Shostakovich, Prokofiev, and Khachaturian) to respect Party aesthetics.

great octave. Common name for the octave beginning on C, 2 leger lines below the staff of the bass clef. See "The Clefs," p. xxiii.

great organ. The main manual of an organ, and the pipes controlled by it.

Great Waltz, The. Musical derived from the music of the Johann Strausses, Sr. and Jr., 1934. The plot embellishes the careers of the waltz kings, introducing a mythical Russian countess to the tale. *The Blue Danube* flows all over the score.

Greek Passion, The. Opera by Martinů, 1955–59, after Kazantzakis's novel, posthumously produced (1961). Life imitates the Passion Play in a strife-torn Greek village.

Green, Adolph. See COMDEN AND GREEN.

Green, John (Waldo), American pianist, conductor, arranger, and composer; b. N.Y., Oct. 10, 1908; d. Beverly Hills, Calif., May 15, 1989. He studied economics at Harvard Univ. (B.A., 1928), where he also received instruction in music theory from W. R. Spalding; later studied piano with Ignace Hilsberg, orchestration with Adolf Deutsch, and conducting with Frank Tours. Working as an arranger for Guy Lombardo, he produced his 1st hit song, *Coquette* (1928); while working as accompanist to Gertrude Lawrence he wrote the popular *Body and Soul* (1930). He became an arranger for Paramount in Hollywood (1930); made recordings with his own dance band and performed on the radio. He settled in Hollywood as a member of the music staff of MGM (1942), serving as head of its music dept. (1949–58). He prepared award-winning adaptations of the original scores for film versions of *Easter Parade* (1948), *An American in Paris* (1951), *West Side Story* (1961), and *Oliver!* (1968); he also wrote the score for the film *Raintree County* (1957). He was associate conductor of the Los Angeles Phil. (1959–61); also appeared as a guest conductor with several of the major U.S. orchs.

Greensleeves. An old English ballad in minor mode, dated to 1580 but probably older. It is mentioned in Shakespeare's play *The Merry Wives of Windsor*, when Falstaff says, "Let the sky thunder to the tune of 'Green Sleeves'" (V:5).

Gregorian chant

A system of liturgical plainchant in the Christian (Roman Catholic) Church. Its codification is generally attributed to Pope Gregory I, about 600 A.D. Devoid of harmonic connotations, it may appear monotonous to the modern ear, but it compensates for the absence of harmony by the extraordinary melorhythmic richness. The uncertainties of the notation of Gregorian chant led to the proliferation of different renderings of the same manuscripts. Disconcerted by the ambiguity of the chant and its notation, a group of learned Benedictine monks of the village of Solesmes, France, undertook the task of reconciling the different versions of liturgical texts and prepared an edition of early Gregorian chants which was published as the *Editio Vaticana* with the Papal imprimatur.

The text of the Gregorian chant is always in Latin. The syllabic settings are entirely free, so that a syllable may be sung to a single note or to several tied notes. In such climactic passages as the singing of Alleluja, a single syllable may be sung to a group of as many as 20 notes. What makes Gregorian chant both intractable and fascinating is that singers must treat a given chant melodically and rhythmically in a variety of ways, according to its position in the liturgy. In this respect Gregorian chant has a striking resemblance to the practice of Indian ragas, which are to be sung differently according to the time of day. It would be a grave mistake, however, to seek melodic and rhythmic similarities between specific samples of Gregorian chant and Eastern melodies, for there was no historical contact between Roman liturgy and Indian ragas. The improvisatory style of Gregorian melismas is rooted in liturgical prose, as distinct from extemporized instrumental figurations of the Baroque school and the aleatory practices of the 20th century.

On the other hand, similarities between ancient Jewish cantillation in the synagogue and Gregorian chant may indeed have a historical foundation in view of the common heritage of the Judeo-Christian tradition. Equally tenable is the theory of the Greek origin of Gregorian chant; the strongest argument of this theory lies in the modal classification of Gregorian chant and ancient Greek music. Indeed, the names of the modes in Gregorian chant are borrowed from Greece, but medieval theorists responsible for this nomenclature misinterpreted the intervallic structure and direction of the ancient modes (in Greek music, intervals were counted downward, whereas in Medieval church modes, they are scaled upward). The obstinacy and intransigence of the followers of various analysts of the rhythmic and melodic character of Gregorian chant are a marvel to behold. It seems that the deeper the scholarship of these learned men, the more irreconcilable their differences.

A modest practitioner of the practical art of Gregorian chant interprets its rhythmic and melodic values by way of oral tradition, so that the result sounds natural and musically satisfying and more authentic than the profound elucubrations of the various schools of mensuralists, accentualists, or others. Observation of the religious services in the old cathedrals and monasteries in Catholic Europe seems to confirm the conviction that Gregorian chant follows its own intrinsically coherent rules, derived from the reading of religious texts, asymmetrical in musical phraseology, syllabically accentuated according to the dominant spirit and relative textual importance, and gravitating toward changing tonal centers in fluid modality.

Great composers throughout history have made use of Gregorian melodies for their inspired works, adding a new dimension. In such works the generally asymmetrical melodies of Gregorian chant are arranged in the symmetrical measures with harmonic textures. In this aggrandizement and elaboration, Gregorian chant serves as raw material, as does folk music when used for similar purposes. As long as the distinction between the historical art of Gregorian chant and the later art of harmonic and mensural organization is fully understood, the true evaluation and proper interpretation of it will become possible.

Gregory I (the Great); b. Rome, *c.* 540; d. there, Mar. 12, 604. He was Pope from 590 to his death; he is celebrated in music history as the reputed reformer of the musical ritual of the Roman Catholic Church. It is traditionally believed that by his order, and under his supervision, a collection was made in 599 of the music employed in the different churches; that various offertories, antiphons, responses, etc., were revised and regularly and suitably distributed over the entire year in an arrangement which came to be known as Gregorian chant. While for centuries the sole credit for the codification, which certainly took place, had been ascribed to Gregory, investigations by such scholars as Gevaert, Riemann, P. Wagner, Frere, Houdard, Gastoué, Mocquereau, and others have demonstrated that some of Gregory's predecessors had begun this reform and even fixed the order of certain portions of the liturgy, and that the work of reform was definitely completed under some of his immediate successors.

grell (Ger.). Sharply, incisely.

grelots (Fr., pellet bell; Ger. *Schelle*). Vessel rattle.

grido (It.). Cry, shout.

Grieg, Edvard (Hagerup)

Celebrated Norwegian composer; b. Bergen, June 15, 1843; d. there, Sept. 4, 1907. The original form of the name was Greig. His great-grandfather, Alexander Greig, of Scotland, emigrated to Norway about 1765 and changed his name to Grieg. Edvard Grieg received his 1st instruction in music from his mother, an amateur pianist. At the suggestion of the Norwegian violinist Ole Bull, young Grieg was sent to the Leipzig Cons. (1858), where he studied piano with Plaidy and Wenzel and later Moscheles, and theory with E. F. Richter, Robert Papperitz, Moritz Hauptmann, and Reinecke. He became immersed in the atmosphere of German Romanticism, with the aesthetic legacy of Mendelssohn and Schumann; Grieg's early works are permeated with lyric moods related to these influences. In 1863 he went to Copenhagen, where he took a brief course of study with Niels Gade. In Copenhagen he met the young Norwegian composer Rikard Nordraak, with whom he organized the Euterpe Soc. for the promotion of national Scandinavian music, in opposition to the German influences dominating Scandinavian music. The premature death of Nordraak at the age of 23 (1866) left Grieg alone to carry on the project.

After traveling in Italy, he returned to Norway, where he opened a Norwegian Academy of Music (1867) and gave concerts of Norwegian music; he was also engaged as conductor of the Harmonic Soc. in Christiania (now Oslo). In 1867 he married his cousin, the singer Nina Hagerup. At that time he had already composed his 2 violin sonatas and the 1st set of his *Lyric Pieces* for Piano, which used Norwegian motifs. On Apr. 3, 1869, Grieg played the solo part in the world premiere of his Piano Concerto, which took place in Copenhagen. Thus, at the age of 25 he established himself as a major composer of his time. In 1874–75 he wrote incidental music to Ibsen's *Peer Gynt*; the 2 orch. suites arranged from this music became extremely popular. The Norwegian government granted him an annuity of 1,600 crowns, which enabled him to devote most of his time to composition. Performances of his works were given in Germany with increasing frequency; soon his fame spread all over Europe. On May 3, 1888, he gave a concert of his works in London; he also prepared recitals of his songs with his wife.

He revisited England frequently; received the honorary degree of Mus.Doc. from Cambridge (1894) and Oxford (1906). Other honors were membership in the Swedish Academy (1872), the French Academy (1890), etc. Despite his successes, Grieg was of a retiring disposition and spent most of his later years in his house at

Edvard Grieg

PHOTO: ELIOTT & FRY, LONDON, COURTESY OF THE NEW YORK PUBLIC LIBRARY

Troldhaugen, near Bergen, avoiding visitors and shunning public acclaim. However, he continued to compose at a steady rate. His death, of heart disease, was mourned by all Norway; he was given a state funeral and his remains were cremated, at his own request, and sealed in the side of a cliff projecting over the fjord at Troldhaugen.

Grieg's importance as a composer lies in the strongly pronounced nationalism of his music; without resorting to literal quotation from Norwegian folk songs, he succeeded in re-creating their melodic and rhythmic flavor. In his harmony, he remained well within the bounds of tradition; the lyric expressiveness of his best works and the contagious rhythm of his dancelike pieces imparted a charm and individuality which contributed to the lasting success of his art. His unassuming personality made friends for him among his colleagues; he was admired by Brahms and Tchaikovsky.

The combination of lyricism and nationalism in Grieg's music led some critics to describe him as "the Chopin of the North." He excelled in miniatures, in which the perfection of form and the clarity of the musical line are remarkable; the unifying purpose of Grieg's entire creative life is exemplified by his lyric pieces for piano. He composed 10 sets of these pieces in 34 years, between 1867 and 1901. His songs are distinguished by the same blend of Romantic and characteristically national inflections. In orch. composition, Grieg limited himself almost exclusively to symphonic suites and arrangements of his piano pieces; in chamber music, his 3 violin sonatas, a Cello Sonata, and 1 extant String Quartet are examples of fine instrumental writing. He also composed many song cycles and individual songs, and various works for piano.

Grieg, Nina (Hagerup), Norwegian singer; b. near Bergen, Nov. 24, 1845; d. Copenhagen, Dec. 9, 1935. Her father, Herman Hagerup, was a brother of Grieg's mother. Nina Hagerup studied singing with Helsted; she met Edvard Grieg in Copenhagen, and married him on June 11, 1867. Her interpretations of his songs elicited much praise from critics; Delius dedicated 2 sets of songs to her.

Griffbrett (Ger., gripping board). Fingerboard on string instruments. *Griffbrett, am* (Ger., at the fingerboard). To bow near the fingerboard so as to produce a sound imitating the flute's sonority; FLAUTANDO.

Griffelkin. Television opera by Foss, 1955, with a libretto from a German fairy tale; it was broadcast on NBC-TV.

Griffelkin is a young devil who becomes disloyal to hell after a visit on earth. An episode includes an entertaining cacophonous ensemble of pupils practicing their scales.

Griffes, Charles T(omlinson), outstanding American composer; b. Elmira, N.Y., Sept. 17, 1884; d. N.Y., Apr. 8, 1920. He studied piano with a local teacher, Mary S. Broughton; also took organ lessons. In 1903 he went to Berlin, where he was a pupil of Gottfried Galston (piano) and of Rufer and Humperdinck (composition). To eke out his living he gave private lessons; also played his own compositions in public recitals. In 1907 he returned to the U.S. and took a music teacher's job at the Hackley School for Boys at Tarrytown, N.Y.; at the same time he continued to study music by himself; he was fascinated by the exotic art of the French impressionists, and he investigated the potentialities of oriental scales. He also was strongly influenced by the Russian school, particularly Mussorgsky and Scriabin. A combination of natural talent and determination to acquire a high degree of craftsmanship elevated Griffes to the position of a foremost American composer in the impressionist genre; despite changes of taste, his works retain an enduring place in American music, including orch.l, instrumental, and vocal works.

Grofé, Ferde (Ferdinand Rudolph von), American composer, pianist, and arranger; b. N.Y., Mar. 27, 1892; d. Santa Monica, Calif., Apr. 3, 1972. He studied music with Pietro Floridia; then was engaged as viola player in the Los Angeles Phil., at the same time working as pianist and conductor in theaters and cafés; joined Paul Whiteman's band in 1920 as pianist and arranger; it was his scoring of Gershwin's *Rhapsody in Blue* (1924) that won him fame. In his own works Grofé successfully applied jazz rhythms interwoven with simple balladlike tunes; his *Grand Canyon Suite* (Chicago, 1931, Whiteman conducting) became very popular. He also composed other light pieces in a modern vein.

groove. 1. An enjoyable listening experience, especially in jazz and popular music. 2. A steady rhythmic pattern associated with a particular jazz or popular style.

grosse caisse (Fr.). Bass drum.

Grosse Trommel (Ger.). Bass drum.

grosso (It.). Great, grand; full, heavy.

grottesco (It.). Grotesque, comic.

ground bass. An early English form of BASSO OSTINATO, with a continually repeated bass phrase of 4 or 8 measures, even notes; a distinct melodic outline, generally symmetrical in structure, serving as the harmonic foundation of variations in the upper voices, along the lines of a passacaglia or chaconne. The technique was 1st used in the music of the virginalists of the late Renaissance and became prevalent during the English Baroque (e.g., *When I Am Laid in Earth*, Dido's farewell aria in Purcell's *Dido and Aeneas*).

One of the most common patterns in bass parts is the descending figure from the tonic to the dominant; the groups of 16th notes, descending from the tonic to the dominant in the middle section of Chopin's Polonaise in A-flat Major, are expansions of the tonic-dominant descent. Sometimes the bass follows an entire diatonic scale, from the tonic to the lower tonic, in even notes; the 2nd theme in Franck's *Symphonic Variations* for Piano and Orch. is derived in conjunction with the descending BASS LINE. An example of the diatonically descending bass is the accompaniment of Rachmaninoff's song *A Little Island*, with the bass notes in even rhythm while the melody forms counterpoint of several species, including syncopation. Many descending basses are set in chromatic motion, invariably in even notes. In such cases it is the bass line that governs the melody, resulting in a modulatory chromatic sequence. An excellent example is the opening of Grieg's Ballade in G Minor for Piano (op. 24, 1876).

group. 1. A short series of rapid notes, especially when sung to 1 syllable. 2. A section of the orch. (or score) embracing instruments of 1 class, i.e. the strings.

Grove, (Sir) **George,** eminent English musicographer; b. Clapham, South London, Aug. 13, 1820; d. Sydenham, May 28, 1900. He studied civil engineering; graduated in 1839 from the Institution of Civil Engineers and worked in various shops in Glasgow, then in Jamaica and Bermuda. He returned to England in 1846 and became interested in music; without abandoning his engineering profession he entered the Soc. of Arts, of which he was appointed secretary in 1850; this position placed him in contact with the organizers of the 1851 Exhibition; in 1852 he became secretary of the Crystal Palace. He then turned to literary work; was an ed., with William Smith, of the *Dictionary of the Bible*; traveled to Palestine in 1858 and 1861 in connection with his research; in 1865 he became director of the Palestine Exploration Fund. In the meantime he accumulated a private music library; began writing analytical programs for Crystal Palace concerts; these analyses, contributed by Grove during the period 1856–96, established a new standard of excellence in musical exegesis.

His enthusiasm for music led to many important associations; with Arthur Sullivan he went to Vienna in 1867 in search of unknown music by Schubert, and discovered the score of *Rosamunde*. In 1868 he became ed. of *Macmillan's Magazine*; he remained on its staff for 15 years. He received many honors for his literary and musical achievements, among them the DCL., Univ. of Durham (1875), and LL.D., Univ. of Glasgow (1885). In 1883 he was knighted by Queen Victoria. When the Royal College of Music was formed in London (1882), Grove was appointed director, and he retained this post until 1894.

His chief work, which gave him enduring fame, was the monumental *Dictionary of Music and Musicians*, which Macmillan began to publ. in 1879. It was 1st planned in 2 vols., but as the material grew it was expanded to 4 vols. with an appendix, its publication being completed in 1889. Grove contributed voluminous articles on his favorite composers, Beethoven, Schubert, and Mendelssohn; he gathered a distinguished group of specialists to write the assorted entries. The 2nd edition was ed. by Fuller Maitland (5 vols., 1904–10), the 3rd edition (1927–28), by H. C. Colles; an American supplement, 1st publ. in 1920, ed. by W. S. Pratt and C. H. N. Boyd, was expanded and republ. in 1928; the 4th edition, also ed. by H. C. Colles, was publ. in 5 vols., with a supplementary vol. in 1940. E. Blom was entrusted with the preparation of an entirely revised and greatly enlarged 5th ed., which was publ. in 9 vols. in 1954. An entirely new 6th ed. was edited by S. Sadie as *The New Grove Dictionary of Music and Musicians* (20 vols., 1980).

growl. In jazz, altering the natural tone of an instrument by flutter-tonguing, muting, throat vibrato, or a combination.

Gruber, Franz Xaver, Austrian composer, great-great-grandfather of H(einz) K(arl) Gruber; b. Unterweizburg, near Hochburg, Nov. 25, 1787; d. Hallein, near Salzburg, June 7, 1863. He acquired fame as the composer of the Christmas carol *Stille Nacht, Heilige Nacht*. Of a poor family, Gruber had to do manual work as a youth, but he managed to study organ; by dint of perseverance he obtained, at the age of 28, his 1st position, as church organist and schoolmaster at Oberndorf. It was there, on Christmas Eve of 1818, that a young curate, Joseph Mohr, brought him a Christmas poem to be set to music, and Gruber wrote the celebrated song.

Gruber, H(einz) K(arl) (called Nali), Austrian composer, conductor, and double bass player, great-great-grandson of Franz Xaver Gruber; b. Vienna, Jan. 3, 1943. He studied composition with Uhl and Jelinek; also played double bass and horn; took courses in film music at the Hochschule für Musik in Vienna (1957–63); in 1963–64 attended master classes there held by von Einem. He played principal double bass in the Niederösterreiches Tonkünstler-Orch. in Vienna (1961–69); was a cofounder, with Schwertsik and Zukan, of an avant-garde group, MOB art & tone ART (1968). In 1961 he joined the Vienna ensemble Die Reihe as a double bass player; in 1969 was engaged as double bass player in the ORF (Austrian Radio) Sym. Orch. and also performed as an actor.

In his music Gruber maintains a wide amplitude of styles, idioms, and techniques, applying the dodecaphonic method of composition in works of a jazz and pop nature. His "pandemonium" *Frankenstein!!*, which is a megamultimedia affair, with children's verses recited in a bizarre and mock-scary manner, became quite popular.

Gruenberg, Louis, eminent Russian-born American composer; b. near Brest Litovsk, Aug. 3, 1884; d. Los Angeles, June 9, 1964. He was taken to the U.S. as an infant; studied piano with Adele Margulies in N.Y., then went to Berlin, where he studied with Busoni (piano and composition); in 1912 he made his debut as a pianist with the Berlin Phil.; intermittently took courses at the Vienna Cons., where he also was a tutor. In 1919 he returned to the U.S. and devoted himself to composing. He was one of the organizers and active members of the League of Composers (1923); became a champion of modern music, and one of the earliest American composers to incorporate jazz rhythms into works of symphonic dimensions. From 1933 to 1936 he taught composition at the Chicago Music College; then settled in Calif., where he composed several film scores. Of his many operas the most successful was *The Emperor Jones*, after O'Neill's play (Metropolitan Opera, N.Y., 1933; awarded the David Bispham Medal). He finished 4 syms.; violin, viola, and cello concertos; and several cantatas, many influenced by African-American music. He also publ. 4 vols. of Negro spirituals; wrote several violin-and-piano works and string quartet and jazz-inflected music for piano solo.

grunge. See ROCK.

Gruppen. A work of spatial music by Stockhausen, 1959. It is scored for 3 different chamber orchs., with 3 conductors beating 3 different tempi. It was 1st performed in Cologne.

gruppetto (*gruppo*; It., small group). 1. Formerly, a trill. 2. Now, a turn or double appoggiatura; any "group" of grace notes. 3. A melodic ornament, usually indicated by a ~ over the note head, stem, or beam; an alternation of the principal note, 1 scale degree above and 1 below, depending on the direction of the sign. The sign was superseded by a written-out embellishment.

G-sharp minor. This key, relative to B major and armored with 5 sharps in its key signature, is not often encountered as the principal key of a major work. Not even the pansymphonic Miaskovsky ever ventured to write a sym. in G-sharp minor. It has an acrid feeling of bucolic intimacy and is best suited to short piano pieces. Liszt's LA CAMPANELLA for piano is in G-sharp minor.

guajira. Cuban song and dance in a combined 3/4 and 6/8 meter. The name refers to *guajiro*, a colloquialism for the rustic inhabitants of Cuba.

guaracha (Sp.). Lively Spanish dance in binary form; a 2/4 introduction is followed by a rapid movement in a combined 3/4 and 6/8.

guarania. Paraguayan dance in slow 3/4 which became popular in the 20th century. The Guaraní are the indigenous populations of Paraguay, Uruguay, and the maritime provinces of Argentina.

Guarneri family, famous Italian family of violin makers. (The Italian form of the name was derived from the Lat. *Guarnerius*; the instrument labels invariably used the Lat. form.) Andrea Guarneri, head of the family (b. Cremona, *c.* 1625; d. there, Dec. 7, 1698), was a pupil of Nicola Amati; he lived in Amati's house from 1641 to 1646, and again from 1650 to 1654, when, with his wife, he moved to his own house in Cremona and began making his own violins, labeling them as "alumnus" of Amati and, after 1655, "ex alumnis," often with the additional words of "sub titolo Sanctae Theresiae." Andrea's son Pietro Giovanni, "da Mantova" (b. Cremona, Feb. 18, 1655; d. Mantua, Mar. 26, 1720), worked 1st at Cremona, then went to Mantua, where he settled; he also used the device "sub titolo Sanctae Theresiae." Another son of Andrea, Giuseppe Giovanni Battista, "filius Andreae" (b. Cremona, Nov. 25, 1666; d.

there, *c.* 1740), worked in his father's shop, which he eventually inherited; in his own manufactures he departed from his father's model and followed the models of Stradivarius. Giuseppe's son Pietro, "da Venezia" (b. Cremona, Apr. 14, 1695; d. Venice, Apr. 7, 1762), settled in Venice in 1725 and adopted some features of the Venetian masters Montagnana and Serafin. Another son of Giuseppe, (Bartolomeo) Giuseppe Antonio, "Giuseppe del Gesù" (from the initials IHS often appearing on his labels; b. Cremona, Aug. 21, 1698; d. there, Oct. 17, 1744), became the most celebrated member of the family; some of his instruments bear the label "Joseph Guarnerius Andreae Nepos Cremonae," which establishes his lineage as a grandson of Andrea. His violins are greatly prized, rivaling those of Stradivarius in the perfection of instrumental craftsmanship; he experimented with a variety of wood materials, and also made changes in the shapes of his instruments during different periods of his work. Such great virtuoso violinists as Heifetz, Stern, Szeryng, Grumiaux, and Paganini used his instruments.

guasa. Venezuelan song of the CORRIDO type, usually in 6/8 meter.

Gubaidulina, Sofia, remarkable Russian composer of unique individuality; b. Chistopol, Oct. 24, 1931. She was descended of a Tatar father (her grandfather was a mullah) and of a mother who had both Russian and Jewish blood (she once said that she was the place where East and West met). Her sources of inspiration in composition were similarly diverse, extending from mystical Eastern elements to Catholic and Russian Orthodox conformations. She studied at the Kazan Cons. (graduated, 1954); then enrolled at the Moscow Cons. to study composition with Peiko and Shebalin. From her very 1st essays in composition she followed vectorially divergent paths without adhering to any set doctrine of modern techniques. Perhaps her most astounding work is the Concerto for bassoon and low string instruments, in 5 movements (1975); in it, the bassoon is embedded in a net of 4 cellos and 3 double basses, creating a claustrophobic syndrome of congested low sonorities, while the solo instrument is forced to perform acrobatic feats to escape constriction, including such effects as labial glissandos and explosive iterations of a single thematic note.

Her music soon penetrated into the music world far beyond the Soviet frontiers, and her works became solicited by performers in Europe and the U.S. She made several voyages to the U.S. to hear performances of her works, and she was a guest at the Boston Festival of Soviet Music in 1988; but it took a decisive change in official Soviet policy before her music received full recognition in her own country.

gudok. Russian 3-string instrument placed on the knees while playing. Similar to Bulgarian GADULKA.

Guerre des Bouffons (*Querelle des Bouffons*; Fr.). A famous theatrical controversy that erupted in Paris in 1752; that year saw a visit of an Italian opera company (the Bouffons), whose performance of Pergolesi's *La Serva padrona* aroused the admiration of the pro-Italian faction of the Paris intellectuals, including the Encyclopedists; on the other hand, the Italian manner was opposed by the lovers of French opera, fostered by Louis XV. It was followed by a whole series of polemical pamphlets, including Rousseau's historical paper *Lettre sur la musique française*. The controversy subsided when the Bouffons left Paris (1754).

guerriero (It.). Martial, warlike.

guide. 1. A sign at the end of a staff to indicate the location of the 1st note of the next staff. 2. A SUBJECT or ANTECEDENT.

Guido d'Arezzo (Guido Aretinus), famous Italian reformer of musical notation and vocal instruction; b. *c.* 991; d. after 1033. He received his education at the Benedictine abbey at Pomposa, near Ferrara. He left the monastery in 1025, as a result of disagreements with his fellow monks, who were envious of his superiority in vocal teaching; he was then summoned by Bishop Theobald of Arezzo to the cathedral school there; it was because of this association that he became known as Guido d'Arezzo. The assertions that he traveled in France and spent several years at the monastery of Saint-Maur des Fossés, near Paris, are not borne out by documentary evidence. Still more uncertain are the claims of his travels in Germany, and even to England. However it happened, his fame spread and reached the ears of Pope John XIX, who called him to Rome to demonstrate his system of teaching (1028). In his last years he was a prior of the Camaldolite fraternity at Avellano.

Guido's fame rests on his system of SOLMIZATION, by which he established the nomenclature of the major hexachord *Ut, Re, Mi, Fa, Sol, La*, from syllables in the initial lines of the Hymn of St. John:

Ut queant laxis Resonare fibris
Mira gestorum Famuli tuorum,
Solve polluti Labii reatum,
Sancte Joannes.

No less epoch-making was Guido's introduction of the musical staff of 4 lines, retaining the red f-line and the yellow c-line of his predecessors and drawing between them a black a-line, above them a black e-line, and writing the plainsong notes (which he did not invent) in regular order on these lines and in the spaces:

New black line e_____
Old yellow line c_____
New black line a_____
Old red line f_____

He also added new lines above or below these, as occasion required; thus Guido's system did away with all uncertainty of pitch. Another invention credited to Guido is the so-called GUIDONIAN HAND, relating the degrees of the overlapping hexachords to various places on the palm of the left hand, a device helpful in directing a chorus by indicating manually the corresponding positions of the notes. Opinions differ widely as to the attribution to Guido of all these innovations; some scholars maintain that he merely popularized the already-established ideas and that solmization, in particular, was introduced by a German abbot, Poncius Teutonicus, at the abbey of Saint-Maur des Fossés. Guido's most essential treatises are *Micrologus de disciplina artis musicae* (*c.* 1026) and *Epistola de ignoto cantu* (*c.* 1028–29).

Guidonian hand (Lat. *manus guidonis*; named after Guido d'Arezzo, the creator of syllabic solmization). A didactic method of teaching a system of closely related hexachords. The lowest G (the gamut) was represented by the upperside of the thumb of the left hand, the notes progressing scalewise across the palm to the tip of the little finger and continuing along the fingertips to the index finger, then descending and after another turn ending on the top of the middle finger on the E, 2 octaves and a 6th above the initial gamut. In the Middle Ages the choir director indicated the points on the different joints of each finger to dictate the required notes to the singers.

Guillaume de Machaut. MACHAUT, GUILLAUME DE.

Guillaume Tell. WILLIAM TELL.

Martin guitars

güiro (Cub.; Braz. *reco-reco*). A scratcher or a scraper used in Latin American bands. It is made out of a long gourd with notches on its upper side. These notches are scraped with a stick. Although the güiro is usually classified as a percussion instrument, its sound production is actually caused by friction. It is often used in modern scores, most ingeniously at the end of Stravinsky's *Le Sacre du printemps*; in Ravel's *L'enfant et les sortilèges*, it can replace the *rape à fromage*, a cheese grate scraped with a triangle beater.

guitar. Universally popular string instrument, played by plucking or strumming the strings. An instrument of the lute family, the modern Spanish (acoustic) guitar has 6 strings, a compass of 3 octaves, and a 4th, from E to a². The strings are tuned in perfect 4ths, with the exception of the interval between the 2nd and 3rd strings, a major 3rd: E, A, d, g, b, and e¹. The music is written an octave higher than it sounds, in the G clef. The fingerboard is provided with frets to indicate the position of the notes of the scale. By the very nature of the instrument, the guitar is incapable of infinitely sustained harmony but is brilliantly adapted for arpeggiated chords.

The guitar is the proverbial instrument of chivalrous courtship. Scenes of swains serenading their lady loves under their balconies abound in paintings. Etymologically, the word *guitar* can be traced to the Greek KITHARA, but there is no similarity in the structure or sound of the 2 instruments. The guitar in its present form generated in Spain in the 16th century and spread all over the world. It was an inalienable part of equipment for cowboys of the American West and the gauchos on the pampas of South America; it was 2nd only to the horse in the cowboy's affection.

Toward the mid-20th century the guitar was electrically amplified to compensate for its tonal weakness and became a primary instrument of modern rock musicians. In its new role it underwent a change in anatomy. Its folklike outlines were abandoned in favor of a gaudy androgyne shape, thinner in the middle than the classical guitar but sprouting a pair of tinseled shoulders. Despite its popularity, great acoustic guitar players like Segovia maintained the classical instrument and its traditions. Numerous modern composers, among them Castelnuovo-Tedesco and Manuel Ponce, wrote concertos for guitar and orch.

guitar, acoustic. A term for the classical or Spanish instrument, in contrast to the ELECTRIC GUITAR.

guitar, backup. See RHYTHM GUITAR.

guitar, bass. An electrified adaptation of the DOUBLE BASS, built and shaped like the ELECTRIC GUITAR, which it is designed to match in popular music. Some electric models are unfretted, so that the performer can perform the GLISSANDOS and PORTAMENTOS possible on the acoustic instrument; these are mostly used in JAZZ-FUNK (fusion).

guitar, classical. Spanish (acoustic) guitar.

guitar, electric. ELECTRIC GUITAR.

guitar, lead. In rock and other popular groups, the "1st guitarist," performing on an electric guitar and responsible for melodic riffs, fills, and solos. In the orig. ROLLING STONES, Keith Richards generally played lead guitar while Brian Jones played rhythm guitar. A group may have more than one person capable of performing this role, as in the orig. Allman Brothers Band (Duane Allman, Dickie Betts).

guitar, rhythm. In rock and other popular groups, a modern term for the "2nd guitarist," performing on an electric guitar and providing the harmonic and rhythmic support for lead instruments or singers. In the BEATLES, John Lennon generally played rhythm guitar to George Harrison's lead guitar. Also called *backup guitar*.

guitar, Spanish. Acoustic or classical 6-stringed guitar; its predecessors date back to the 13th century, with a varying number of strings. It is made of wood, with a large circular soundhole and a body modeled after the human neck and torso. The neck is attached to a fingerboard supplied with frets to indicate the notes of the chromatic scale. See also GUITARRA ESPAÑOLA.

guitare d'amour (Fr.). ARPEGGIONE.

guitarra española (Sp.). The 5-course guitar of the 16th and 17th centuries.

Guntram. Opera by R. Strauss, 1894. A medieval German duke is murdered by a minstrel named Guntram. The heiress to the throne loves him, so she absolves him; but she refuses to marry him on account of class disparity.

Gurre-Lieder. A secular oratorio by Schoenberg, *c.* 1901–11, 1st performed in Vienna (1913). The work is scored for narrator, solo voices, chorus, and orch. The work was more or less composed by 1901 but not orchestrated until a decade later, by which time Schoenberg's style had changed radically. The text is a German translation of poems by the Danish poet Jacobsen. The events unfold in a Danish castle in Gurre, and the songs tell of the impossible love of the King for a woman not of royal stock. The story is morbid, lugubrious, and impenetrable. The music is glorious, and it absorbs the obscure texts much as Wagner's music dramas overwhelm the obscurities of their plots. In GURRE-LIEDER Schoenberg is still very much of a Wagnerian; the score is indeed meta-Wagnerian.

gusle. 1. One-string fiddle of the South Slavic region, with a long neck and wooden resonator; not the same as the Russian GUSLI. 2. Violin.

gusli. An ancient Russian psaltery, shaped in a trapezoid. The number of strings range from 11 to 36, strung horizontally so that the lowest pitches are furthest from the player. Early gusli types had up to 7 strings, but the number was increased in the 15th century. Glinka has a musical part for a legendary gusli player in *Ruslan and Ludmilla*, but the part

is taken by the orch. harp. 2. An instrument related to the Finnish KANTELE.

gusto (It.). Taste.

gut (Ger.). 1. Good. 2. (Eng.) Abbrev. of CATGUT.

Guthrie, Woody (Woodrow Wilson), legendary American folksinger, guitarist, songwriter, union organizer, and writer; b. Okemah, Okla., July 14, 1912; d. N.Y., Oct. 3, 1967. He left home with his guitar and harmonica when he was 15, riding the rails of freight trains across the U.S. and playing in hobo and migrant camps, bars, and labor meetings during the Great Depression, becoming famous as a champion of disadvantaged Americans and as a supporter of various leftist causes. Among the songs he wrote or arranged were *So Long, It's Been Good to Know Ya*; *This Train Is Bound for Glory*; *Hard Traveling*; *Blowing Down This Old Dusty Road*; and *This Land Is Your Land*. In later years he joined Pete Seeger and others as a member of the Almanac Singers in N.Y. His life and career were gradually destroyed after he was stricken with Huntington's chorea in the early 1950s.

In spite of his freely professed radical convictions, the U.S. government bestowed upon him an award of merit in 1966 as "a poet of the American landscape." He publ. the books *Bound for Glory* (N.Y., 1943) and *American Folksong* (N.Y., 1947; with memoirs). W. Doerflinger ed. his *Seeds of Man: An Experience Lived and Dreamed* (N.Y., 1976). His son, Arlo (Davy) Guthrie (b. N.Y., July 10, 1947), followed in his father's footsteps as a socially conscious folksinger, guitarist, and songwriter; he is most famous for his talking ballad *Alice's Restaurant* (1969); it was the basis for a film in which he starred.

Guys and Dolls. Musical by F. Loesser, 1950, based on stories by Damon Runyon. A playboy engages in a battle of mind and heart with a Salvation Army woman, while a gambler keeps putting off marrying his nightclub dancer girlfriend. Includes the title song, *Fugue for Tinhorns* (actually a 3-part canon), *Sue Me*, *Take Back Your Mink*, *Adelaide's Lament*, and *Luck Be a Lady Tonight*.

Gwendoline. Opera by Chabrier, 1886, concerning a conflict between martial and marital passions during the Viking invasion of England.

gymel (from Lat. *gemellus*, twin). A 2-part counterpoint in 3rds or 6ths, common during the Middle Ages. The historical relationship of this technique to FABURDEN is not clear; the term dates from the 5th century. Same as CANTUS GEMELLUS.

Gymnopédies (from Lat., naked dances). Three piano pieces by Satie, 1888, whose profoundly anti-Romantic nature and anticipation of fin-de-siècle classicism established Satie's notoriety and represent his early style.

gymnosophistical homophony (from Grk. *gymn* + *sophistēs*, naked wise man). The description *gymnosophist* is applied to an Indian sect that flourished about 1000 A.D., who preached abstinence from carnal delights, refused to wear clothes, and limited themselves to the simplest modes of communication.

Archaizing usages and affectation of utmost simplicity in musical composition may well be called gymnosophistical; naked 5ths, in particular, when applied ostentatiously in modern works and creating the impression of luxurious abstemiousness, are gymnosophistical. Satie, in his sophisticated practice of gymnosophistical harmonies in such works as the *Gymnopédies* (1888), provides a perfect example of the style, deliberately bleak in its renunciation of harmonious carnality and yet thoroughly modern in its invocation of secret rites and suggested aberrations. For different reasons Stravinsky adopted gymnosophistical modali-

ties in his neo-Grecian works, as a reaction against the proliferation of colorful sonorities in instrumental music, including his own. Gymnosophistical homophony is a natural medium also for neoecclesiastical composition in quintal or QUARTAL GEMINATION.

Gypsy. Musical by Styne and Sondheim, 1959, based on Gypsy Rose Lee's autobiography. A very romanticized version of the stripper's life, focusing on her struggle with her mother, who gets to sing *Everything's Coming Up Roses*; also includes *Small World, Together Wherever We Go*, and *You'll Never Get Away from Me*.

Gypsy Baron, The (*Der Zigeunerbaron*). Operetta by J. Strauss, 1885. The Ottomans have been routed and forced out of Hungary; Sandor returns to his castle to find it ruined and his fields occupied by Zsupan, a neighbor who is seeking a lost Turkish treasure and whose daughter Arsena Sandor falls for; but she is in love with her governess's son Ottokar. Now a band of Gypsies, led by Czipra, enters the scene; when Sandor, newly anointed as the "Gypsy baron," finds out about Arsena and Ottokar, he falls instead for the gypsy beauty Saffi. After all of this breathless action in the 1st act, 2 more acts and a war against Spain are necessary to straighten everything out happily for all (except for Zsupan, who never finds the treasure; it goes to war funds).

Gypsy music

A nomadic people, Gypsies (properly, the Romany) penetrated many countries in Europe, forming their own communities and so-called tabors, or camps. They elected their "kings" in colorful rituals, but otherwise adapted themselves to the customs of their adoptive land. While the English word for the Romany seems to be a corruption of "Egyptians," Gypsies in all probability came originally out of India, where they were treated as untouchable pariahs. In literature, in painting, in theatrical plays and operas, Gypsies became stereotyped as clever and devious, practicing their arts upon superstitious men and women. They were known as fortune-tellers and thieves, as seducers and international smugglers. They attracted attention by their wearing gaudy apparel and jewelry. They were also described as possessors of magic arts.

The mysteries that make the plot of *Il Trovatore* unintelligible are contrived by the Gypsies; the famous Anvil Chorus in the 2nd act is sung by Gypsy blacksmiths. Bizet's Carmen is a Gypsy who causes Don José to desert the army and join her comrades in a smuggling ring. In Balfe's *The Bohemian Girl*, the heroine is kidnapped by Gypsies as a child. Because many Gypsies came from Bohemia, the nickname Bohemians was attached to rootless artists and wandering adventurers. Paderewski's opera *Manru* glorifies the leader of a Gypsy tribe in the

Carpathian Mountains. Puccini's *La Bohème*, a collective noun meaning "Bohemian life," might well be translated as *The Gypsies*. In numberless literary romances an aristocratic gentleman of wealth is revealed to be a Gypsy, noble of heart if not of pedigree. In Strauss's famous operetta *Der Zigeunerbaron*, a young Hungarian is chosen by the Gypsies to be their leader and is elevated to the rank of a Gypsy baron. But above all, the romanticized Gypsies were passionate and often sinister lovers, such as Aleko, the Gypsy hero of Pushkin's poem *The Gypsies* and the subject for Rachmaninoff's opera. The title of the operetta *Zigeunerliebe* (Gypsy Love) by Lehar is typical for the Gypsy image.

With all their picturesque folkways, the Gypsies failed to develop an autonomous art form. The so-called GYPSY SCALE, containing 2 augmented 2nds, is a misnomer; it might be more properly called a Hungarian scale. But Gypsy music, like proverbial Gypsy love, had a capacity of insinuating itself into the musical modalities of other peoples. In the 19th century, Gypsy music took root in the Balkans, predominately in Rumania. In fact, the Gypsies call themselves "Romany," an allusion to their Rumanian origin. From the Balkans a horde of Gypsy Rumanian musicians invaded Hungary, Austria, and Russia. The most significant incursion of Gypsy music was experienced in Hungary; the national Hungarian form of VERBUNKOS was directly influenced by Rumanian Gypsy musicians. Liszt was an avid listener to Gypsy bands; his *Hungarian Rhapsodies* were mainly derived from these impressions rather than from authentic Magyar folk tunes.

Another curious phenomenon of Gypsy adaptation took place in Russia, where groups of Gypsy singers, guitarists, violinists, and tambourine players—most of them from the annexed Rumanian border state of Bessarabia—established themselves as popular entertainers in restaurants, cafés, circuses, and various places of amusement. "Gypsy romances," or songs, became exceedingly popular in Russia, but their words and music were composed by amateur Russian musicians. "Let us go to the Gypsies" became a byword of dissolute revelers in Russian society. So deeply were these Gypsy romances ingrained in the old regime that after the Revolution Soviet authorities launched a concentrated campaign against these songs. Musicologists were mobilized to supply dialectical arguments to prove that the melodies and harmonies of such songs were not only tasteless but ideologically inadmissible in the new society. Eventually the Soviets yielded to the irrepressible lure of Gypsy music.

Some music historians deny that Gypsy music exists at all as a discernible branch of folk music, asserting that what passes for autochthonous Gypsy modality is really Hungarian music. That might be, but composers for more than a century have used such expressions as *alla gitana* or ALLA ZINGARESE (in a Gypsy manner) as a definite indication of the intended style of performance. Instrumental works with Gypsy titles abound. Among the most famous ones are *Zigeunerweisen* (Gypsy Airs) for violin and piano by Sarasate, and *Tzigane* for violin and orch. by Ravel.

Gypsy scale. An informal name for the minor harmonic scale with a raised subdominant, forming 2 augmented 2nds. This scale is also known as the Hungarian scale.

H. 1. In scores, French horn. 2. In organ music, heel. 3. In keyboard music, hand (r.h., l.h.).

H (Ger.). The note B.

H dur (Ger.). B major.

H moll (Ger.). B minor.

habanera (often misspelled *habañera*). The dance of Havana, in duple meter, at a moderately slow tempo. The origin of the habanera as a folk dance is obscure. The most popular theory, based mainly on its metrical and rhythmical aspects, is that the habanera was an offspring of the English country dance; according to this theory, country dance became *contredanse* in France and *contradanza* in Spain, the name that was abbreviated to *danza* in 1800. In 1825 it appeared in Cuba as *danza habanera*, and later simply as *habanera*. The meter of the habanera is 2/4 and its most characteristic rhythmic formula is a dotted 8th note followed by a 16th note and 2 8th notes.

Perhaps the most famous habanera is the one that Carmen sings in Bizet's opera, but it was not Bizet's own tune. He picked it up from a collection of songs by the Spanish composer Sebastián Yradier, published in 1864, in which it appeared under the title *El Arreglito*, with a French subtitle, *Chanson havanaise*. (Yradier also composed the famous habanera *La Paloma*.) Bizet inserted it shortly before the production of *Carmen* in 1875, yielding to the importunities of the opera management clamoring for a singable song. (But since the action of *Carmen* takes place in southern Spain, what is a ditty from Havana, Cuba, doing in it

anyway?) Among other composers who wrote dances in the rhythm of the habanera are Albéniz, Debussy, Ravel, Chabrier, and de Falla.

Hadjidakis, Manos, Grk. composer; b. Xanthi, Macedonia, Oct. 23, 1925. He wrote piano pieces in an advanced idiom, recalling Prokofiev; then turned to film music. He wrote the theme song for the film released in America under the title *Never on Sunday* (1960). He is well known for his stage works, film scores, and songs.

Haffner Serenade. A work by Mozart, 1776 (K.250). This is a light and charming piece in D major written for the wedding of the daughter of the Bürgomaster of Salzburg named Haffner (Mozart himself had a secret liking for the bride). Thus was immortality acquired by the modest Haffner family. The Serenade has 8 movements and lasts longer than some of Mozart's full-fledged syms.

Haffner Symphony. Sym. No. 35 by Mozart, 1782 (K.385). Haffner strikes twice. This sym. in D major, the same key as the HAFFNER SERENADE, was jotted down by Mozart in a couple of weeks, 8 years after the composition of the *Serenade.* Haffner, the Bürgomaster of Salzburg, endeared himself to Mozart by his many kindnesses to him.

Haggard, Merle (Ronald), American country-western singer, fiddler, and guitarist; b. Bakersfield, Calif., Apr. 6, 1937. His impoverished family moved to Calif., where they lived in an abandoned boxcar near Bakersfield. He started early on a criminal career; escaped 7 times from reform schools, stole cars, and held up a bar, and finally ended up at

San Quentin as prisoner No. 845,200. There he met the notorious "Red-Light Bandit" Caryl Chessman, eventually executed for a series of brutal rapes; Chessman exercised a profound intellectual influence on Haggard, who began improvising songs of destitution, despair, and crime, exemplified by the autobiographical line, "Did you ever steal a quarter when you was 10 years old?" In due time he completed his term, and in 1972 he was pardoned by Ronald Reagan, then governor of Calif. No longer did he have to steal money, for he commanded a fee of $15,000 per concert, sold millions of record albums of his own lyrics and music, and won awards galore in the city of Nashville. He married 3 times and made more successful recordings, gradually reaching the top-notch rank as a country-western singer with such hits as *Okie from Muskogee, Workin' Man Blues, Daddy Frank (the Guitar Man)*, and *Hungry Eyes*. He made the cover of *Time* in 1977.

Hagith. Opera by Szymanowski, 1922, produced in Warsaw. The subject deals with an old king who seeks to regain his youth through the love of a young girl named Hagith. The score is somewhat Wagnerian in facture.

Hahn, Reynaldo, Venezuelan-born French conductor, music critic, and composer; b. Caracas, Aug. 9, 1874; d. Paris, Jan. 28, 1947. His father, a merchant from Hamburg, settled in Venezuela (*c.* 1850); the family moved to Paris when Reynaldo was 5 years old. He studied singing and apparently had an excellent voice; a professional recording he made in 1910 testifies to that. He studied music theory at the Paris Cons. with Dubois and Lavignac and composition with Massenet, who exercised the most important influence on Hahn's own music. He also studied conducting, achieving a high professional standard as an opera conductor. In 1934 he became music critic of *Le Figaro*. He remained in France during the Nazi occupation at a considerable risk to his life, since he was Jewish on his father's side. In 1945 he was named a member of the Inst. de France and in 1945–46 was music director of the Paris Opéra.

Hahn's music is distinguished by a facile, melodious flow and a fine Romantic flair. Socially he was known in Paris for his brilliant wit. He maintained a passionate youthful friendship with Proust, who portrayed him as a poetic genius in his novel *Jean Santeuil*; their intimate correspondence was publ. in 1946. He was a brilliant journalist; his articles were publ. in several collections. Hahn wrote primarily for the stage: operas, operettas, incidental music, and ballets; he also composed concertos for violin, piano, and

cello; a Piano Quintet and a String Quartet; and piano pieces, among them a suite, *Portraits des peintres*, inspired by poems of Proust (1894).

Hail, Columbia. A patriotic song with words by Joseph Hopkinson (1770-1842), to the melody of the *President's March*, attributed to Philip Phile. It was 1st sung as a finale to a play *The Italian Monk*, produced in Philadelphia in 1798. It gradually acquired popularity as a patriotic American anthem.

Hail, Hail, the Gang's All Here. American version (published 1908) of a chorus from Gilbert and Sullivan's *The Pirates of Penzance* (1879). The 2nd line is "What the hell do we care?"

Hail to the Chief. An American marching song of unknown authorship that traditionally accompanies the entrance of the President of the U.S. on state occasions.

Hair. Rock musical by Galt MacDermot, 1967, with book and lyrics by Ragni and Rado. Billed as "the American tribal love-rock musical," it was 1st performed Off-Broadway, then radically rewritten and presented on Broadway (1968). The show represents an anarchistic, dadaistic, and surrealistic subversion of all accepted ideas in the musical theater. To some observers its immorality is total; reflecting the permissive age of pornographic explosion, the songs impudently flaunt a cornucopia of quadriliteral obscenities for the 1st time in any musical on stage. Plotwise *Hair* is a "nonbook musical," but the draft and the Vietnam war lurk behind the seemingly blissful HAPPENINGS (the 1979 film brought these elements to the fore). The hair of the title may be understood as ambiguous.

There are 2 categories of songs: those defiantly challenging of stereotypes (*Sodomy, Colored Spade, White Boys/Black Boys, I'm Black/Ain't Got No*), and those fusing rock with popular song (the title song, *Aquarius, Frank Mills, Where Do I Go?, Easy to Be Hard, Good Morning Starshine, Flesh Failures [Let the Sun Shine In]*). So contagious was the stage show that one N.Y. critic actually undressed himself during *I Got Life* (where most of the cast went naked under dimmed stagelights), to demonstrate his being "with it."

Haitink, Bernard (Johann Herman), eminent Dutch conductor; b. Amsterdam, Mar. 4, 1929. He studied violin at the Amsterdam Cons., then played in the Radio Phil. Orch. in Hilversum. In 1954–55 he attended the conducting course of Ferdinand Leitner, sponsored by the Netherlands Radio; in 1955 he was appointed to the post of 2nd conductor of the Radio Phil. Orch. in Hilversum, becoming its principal conductor in 1957. In 1956 he made his 1st appearance as a guest conductor with the Concertgebouw Orch. of Amsterdam.

He made his U.S. debut with the Los Angeles Phil. Orch. in 1958. In 1959 he conducted the Concertgebouw Orch. in England. In 1961 he became coprincipal conductor of the Concertgebouw Orch., sharing his duties with Eugen Jochum; that same year he led it on a tour of the U.S., followed by one to Japan in 1962. In 1964 he became chief conductor of the Concertgebouw Orch., a position he held with great distinction until 1988. In 1967 he also assumed the post of principal conductor and artistic adviser of the London Phil. Orch., becoming its artistic director in 1969; he resigned from this post in 1978. He made his 1st appearance at the Glyndebourne Festival in 1972, and from 1978 to 1988 was its music director. In 1987 he became music director of the Royal Opera House at London's Covent Garden. He also acted as a guest conductor with the Berlin Phil., Vienna Phil., N.Y. Phil., Chicago Sym., Boston Sym., and Cleveland Orch. In 1982 he led the Concertgebouw Orch. on a transcontinental tour of the U.S.

In his interpretations Haitink avoids personal rhetoric, allowing the music to speak for itself. Yet he achieves eloquent and colorful effect; especially fine are his performances of the syms. of Bruckner and Mahler; equally congenial are his projections of the Classical repertoire. He has received numerous international honors, including the Netherlands' Royal Order of Orange-Nassau (1969), the Medal of Honor of the Bruckner Soc. of America (1970), and the Gustav Mahler Soc. Gold Medal (1971); he was named a Chevalier de l'Ordre des Arts et des Lettres of France (1972). He received the rare distinction of being made an Honorary Knight Commander of the Order of the British Empire by Queen Elizabeth II in 1977.

halb (Ger.). Half.

halbe Note (Ger.). Half note.

Halbkadenz (Ger.). Half cadence.

Halbton (Ger.). Semitone.

Halévy (born Levy), (Jacques-François-) **Fromental (-Elie),** celebrated French composer; b. Paris, May 27, 1799; d. Nice, Mar. 17, 1862. The family changed its name to Halévy in 1807. He entered the Paris Cons. at age 9 as a student of Cazot, then studied with Lambert (piano), Berton (harmony), and Cherubini (counterpoint); he also studied with Méhul, winning the 2nd Prix de Rome in 1816 and 1817 and the Grand Prix de Rome in 1819 with his cantata *Herminie.* He became *chef du chant* at the Théâtre-Italien in 1826. His 1st stage work to be performed was the opéra-comique *L'Artisan* (Opéra-Comique, 1827), which had a modicum of success. He gained further notice with his *Clari,* introduced to Paris by Malibran (Théâtre-Italien, 1828).

His 1st major success came with *Le Dilettante d'Avignon* (Opéra-Comique, 1829). He then was *chef du chant* at the Paris Opera (1829–45); there he scored his greatest triumph with *La Juive* (1835), which established his name and was performed throughout Europe and the U.S. His next opera, *L'éclair* (Opéra-Comique, Dec. 16, 1835), also enjoyed a favorable reception. Among later operas that were retained in the repertoire were *La Reine de Chypre* (1841), *Charles VI* (1843), and *La Magicienne* (1858), all 1st performed at the Opéra. He was also active as a teacher at the Paris Cons., being made a prof. of harmony and accompaniment (1827), of counterpoint and fugue (1833), and of composition (1840). His students included Gounod, Bizet (who became his son-in-law), and Saint-Saëns. He was elected to membership in the Inst. in 1836, and served as its secretary from 1854.

Halévy was an extremely apt composer for the stage; he won the admiration of both Berlioz and Wagner. Yet he could never equal Meyerbeer in popular success; as time went by, only *La Juive* gained a permanent place in the world repertoire. His brother Léon was an important librettist; however, Fromental rarely set his texts, preferring instead those of Scribe and Saint-Georges. He wrote *Leçons de lecture musicale . . . pour les écoles de la ville de Paris* (Paris, 1857).

Haley, Bill (William John Clifton, Jr.), popular American rock 'n' roll singer, guitarist, and bandleader; b. Highland Park, Mich., July 6, 1925; d. Harlingen, Tex., Feb. 9, 1981. He began to play guitar as a youth, and at the age of 15 he embarked on a tour with country-and-western groups; soon formed his own band, the Saddlemen; in 1952 it was renamed the Comets, to impart a more cosmological beat to the music. Haley precipitated the rock 'n' roll era with his rendition of *Crazy Man Crazy* in 1953; there followed his hit version of Joe Turner's *Shake, Rattle and Roll,* which combined the elements of the blues, country music, and urban pop. His fame skyrocketed in 1955 with his strident projection of *Rock Around the Clock*; immortalized in the motion picture *The Blackboard Jungle*, it became the banner of the rising generation of wild, wide-eyed, loose-eared, dance-crazy, rebellious American youth; 22 million albums of this song were sold. But like so many instinctual musicians of the period, Haley gradually sank into a state of oblivious torpor, and his once-agile style gave way to the irresistible ascent of the more sexually explicit art of Elvis Presley.

half note. A note one-half the value of a whole note and represented by a white circle with a stem (♩).

half step. A semitone.

Halffter (Escriche), **Ernesto,** important Sp. composer and conductor; b. Madrid, Jan. 16, 1905; d. there, July 5, 1989. He studied composition with Manuel de Falla and Adolfo Salazar; 1st attracted attention with his *Sinfonietta*, which was included in the program of the Oxford Festival of the ISCM (1931). In his music he continued the tradition of Sp. modern nationalism, following the stylistic and melorhythmic formations of de Falla; he also completed and orchestrated de Falla's unfinished scenic cantata, *Atlántida*, which was 1st performed at La Scala in Milan (1962). Among his works are *Fantaisie portugaise* for orch. (Paris, 1941) and the ballets *Dulcinea* (1940), *Cojo enamorado* (1954), and *Fantasia galaica* (1956; Milan, 1967). He also composed a Guitar Concerto (1968) and several cantatas. His brother Rodolfo Halffter (Escriche) (b. Madrid, Oct. 30, 1900; d. Mexico City, Oct. 14, 1987) and his nephew Cristóbal Halffter (Jiménez) (b. Madrid, Mar. 24, 1930) are also significant composers.

Halka. Opera by Moniuszko, 1846–47, produced in its final form in Warsaw (1858). This is considered the national Polish opera; its popularity has never abated in Poland, but it is rarely if ever performed in Western Europe. The story concerns Halka's eternal love for her seducer; she kills herself when he marries another.

Halle, Adam de la. ADAM DE LA HALLE.

Hallelujah (from Heb. *hallel* + *Jah*, praise Jehovah). Religious exhortation from the Old Testament: "Praise ye the Lord!"

Hallelujah, Baby! Musical by Styne, Comden, and Green, 1967. A commentary on the changing social position of African-Americans in the 20th century, by observers who do not age.

Hallelujah Chorus. There are thousands of Hallelujah arias and choruses, but the most famous of them all is the triumphant incantation, the *Hallelujah Chorus*, at the end of the 2nd part of Handel's *Messiah*. When Handel brought out *Messiah* at its 1st London performance, King George II rose to his feet (for reasons unknown) at the moment the chorus began, at which point the rest of the audience rose to its feet as was required; thus was established a tradition of standing up for the chorus, observed in Great Britain and elsewhere to this day. The chorus was unintentionally debased by the accidental use of its opening notes, in the same rhythm, in the American song popular in the 1920s *Yes, We Have No Bananas.*

Hallelujah meter. A stanza used in a hymn of jubilation, consisting of 6 lines in iambic measure, with the number of syllables usually in the order of 8, 6, 8, 6, 8, 8.

halling. An animated Norwegian dance in 2/4 time, usually accompanied by the HARDINGFELE.

Hamlet. 1. Opera by A. Thomas, 1868, 1st produced in Paris. The libretto faithfully follows Shakespeare's tragedy, and the music overflows with melodious and harmonious arias and ensembles. For some reason the opera failed to achieve the success comparable to Thomas's *Mignon.* 2. A symphonic poem by Liszt, 1858, 1st performed in Sondershausen (1876). 3. An overture-fantasy by Tchaikovsky, 1888, 1st performed in St. Petersburg, in which he followed the principal dramatic points in Shakespeare's tragedy; over Hamlet's main theme he even wrote in English, "To be or not to be."

Hamlisch, Marvin (Frederick), American composer of popular music; b. N.Y., June 2, 1944. His father, an accordionist, trained him in music; he studied piano at the Juilliard School of Music and at Queens College (B.A., 1967). He began writing songs at the age of 15. His 1st signal success came in 1974, when he won 3 Academy Awards for the music scores of the movies *The Way We Were* and *The Sting.* (For the latter the Award was won for a score written mostly by others: the piano music was by Scott Joplin, composed 60–70 years earlier, and the orchestrations were by Gunther Schuller, adapted from 60-year-old stock arrangements.) In 1975 he wrote the score for the musical *A Chorus Line*, which received the Pulitzer Prize for the play and a Tony award for the best musical score; Universal Pictures bought the cinema rights for $5.5 million. The Broadway production opened in 1975, to a chorus line of hosannas from otherwise sobersided critics; an international touring company was started in Toronto the next year, and a national company began its cross-country tour a few days later.

Hammerclavier (*Hammerklavier*, Ger.). Name for the PIANOFORTE in the early 19th century, reflecting technological developments.

Hammerklavier Sonata. This is the title Beethoven gave to his Piano Sonata No. 29 (op. 106). In the spirit of rising nationalism in Central Europe, Beethoven pointedly used a German title rather than the Italian PIANOFORTE. Beethoven's piano sonatas opp. 101, 109, and 110 are also marked "Hammerklavier" by Beethoven, but op. 106 is the one exclusively referred to as the *Hammerklavier Sonata*.

Hammerstein, Oscar, celebrated German-American impresario, grandfather of Oscar (Greeley Clendenning) Hammerstein, II; b. Stettin, May 8, 1846; d. N.Y., Aug. 1, 1919. At the age of 16 he ran away from home; spent some time in England; then went to America, where he worked in a N.Y. cigar factory. Possessing an inventive mind, he patented a machine for shaping tobacco leaves by suction; later ed. a tobacco trade journal. At the same time, he practiced the violin, learned to write music, and dabbled in playwriting; in 1868 he produced in N.Y. a comedy in German; also wrote the libretto and music of an operetta, *The Kohinoor* (N.Y., 1893). His main activity, however, was in management. He built the Harlem Opera House (1888), the Olympia Music Hall (1895), and the Republic Theater (1900), and presented brief seasons of plays and operas in all 3.

In 1906 he announced plans for the Manhattan Opera House in N.Y., his crowning achievement. The enterprise was orig. planned as a theater for opera in English, but it opened with an Italian company in Bellini's *I Puritani* (1906). Hammerstein entered into bold competition with the Metropolitan Opera and engaged celebrated singers, among them Melba, Nordica, Tetrazzini, and Garden; among the spectacular events presented by him were the 1st U.S. performances of 5 operas by Massenet; Charpentier's *Louise*; and Debussy's *Pelléas et Mélisande*. The new venture held its own for 4 seasons, but in the end Hammerstein was compelled to yield; in April 1910 he sold the Manhattan Opera House to the management of the Metropolitan for $1.2 million and agreed not to produce grand opera in N.Y. for 10 years. He also sold to the Metropolitan (for $100,000) his interests in the Philadelphia Opera House, built by him in 1908.

Defeated in his main ambition in the U.S., he transferred his activities to England. There he built the London Opera House, which opened with a lavish production of *Quo Vadis* by Nougues (1911). However, he failed to establish himself in London, and after a season there he returned to N.Y. In contravention of his agreement with the Metropolitan, he announced a season at the newly organized American Opera House in N.Y., but the Metropolitan secured an injunction against him, and he was forced to give up his operatic venture.

Hammerstein, Oscar (Greeley Clendenning), **II,** outstanding American lyricist, most famous for his stage collaborations with Richard Rodgers, grandson of Oscar Hammerstein; b. N.Y., July 12, 1895; d. Highland Farms, Doylestown, Pa., Aug. 23, 1960. He studied law at Columbia Univ., graduating in 1917; then became interested in the theater. He collaborated on the librettos for Friml's *Rose-Marie* (1924), Romberg's *The Desert Song* (1926), and Kern's *Show Boat* (1927; included the celebrated song *Ol' Man River*). In 1943 he joined forces with the composer Richard Rodgers, and together they produced some of the most brilliant and successful musical comedies in the history of the American theater: *Oklahoma!* (1943; Pulitzer Prize); *Carousel* (1945); *Allegro* (1947); *South Pacific* (1949; Pulitzer Prize, 1950); *The King and I* (1951); *Me and Juliet* (1953); *Pipe Dream* (1955); *The Flower Drum Song* (1958); *The Sound of Music* (1959). His lyrics are characterized by a combination of appealing sentiment and sophisticated nostalgia, making them particularly well suited to the modern theater.

Hammond, Laurens, American manufacturer of keyboard instruments; b. Evanston, Ill., Jan. 11, 1895; d. Cornwall, Conn., July 1, 1973. He studied engineering at Cornell Univ.; then went to Detroit to work on the synchronization of electrical motor impulses, a principle which he later applied to the HAMMOND ORGAN (1933), an electronic keyboard instrument resembling a spinet piano which suggests the sound of the pipe organ. Still later he developed a polyphonic electric keyboard which he called the Novachord, designed to simulate the sound of any known or hypothetical musical instrument; he gave the 1st demonstration of the Novachord in the Commerce Dept. auditorium in Washington, D.C. (1939). In 1940 he introduced the Solovox, a monophonic electric keyboard with 3 octaves; it attaches to a regular piano and enables an amateur player to project the melody in organlike tones. A further invention was the CHORD ORGAN, which he introduced in 1950 and which is capable of supplying basic harmonies when a special button is pressed by the performer.

Hammond organ. A keyboard instrument invented by Laurens Hammond (1933). It produces definite tones of the tempered scale by means of electrical generators; a special mechanism can alter the relative strength of overtones of each key, thereby making it possible to produce any desired instrumental timbre. The Hammond organ is usually constructed in the shape of a spinet, but it has 2 manuals and a set of pedals.

Hampson, Thomas, American baritone; b. Elkhart, Ind., June 28, 1955. He studied at Eastern Washington Univ. (B.A., 1977), Fort Wright College (B.F.A., 1979), the Univ. of Southern Calif., and the Music Academy of the West at Santa Barbara, where he won the Lotte Lehmann Award (1978). In 1980 he took 2nd prize at the 's Hertogenbosch International Vocal Competition, and in 1981 1st place in the Metropolitan Opera Auditions. In 1981 he appeared with the Deutsche Oper am Rhein in Düsseldorf, and in 1982 he attracted wide notice as Guglielmo in *Così fan tutte* with the Opera Theatre of St. Louis. In subsequent seasons he appeared with opera companies in Santa Fe, Cologne, Lyons, and Zurich. On Oct. 9, 1986, he made his Metropolitan Opera debut in N.Y. as Almaviva in *Le nozze di Figaro*. He won particular success for roles in operas by Mozart, Rossini, Donizetti, Verdi, and Puccini.

Hampton, Lionel, "Hamp," African-American jazz vibraphonist, drummer, pianist, and bandleader; b. Louisville, Ky., Apr. 12, 1909. He played drums in Chicago nightclubs; then moved to Los Angeles. He was a pioneer in introducing to jazz the vibraphone (vibes), on which he is a virtuoso performer; made the 1st recording of a jazz vibes solo with Louis Armstrong in *Memories of You* (1930). He gained nationwide prominence as a member of the Benny Goodman Quartet (1936–40). From then on he usually led his own bands, most often playing vibes but occasionally performing on other instruments; he is the originator of the "trigger-finger" method of piano playing (2 forefingers drumming upon a single note *prestissimo*). Beginning in 1956 he made several successful European tours. In 1965 he founded a sextet called the Jazz Inner Circle.

Hanacca. A Moravian dance in 3/4 time, like the POLON-AISE, but quicker.

Hancock, Herbie (Herbert Jeffrey), African-American jazz pianist and composer; b. Chicago, Apr. 12, 1940. A pre-

cocious musician, he made an appearance with the Chicago Sym. Orch. at 11; growing to maturity, he studied engineering at Grinnell (Iowa) College (1956–60); then took courses at the Manhattan School of Music and the New School for Social Research in N.Y. While still in school he led his own band; also made appearances with such jazz artists as Coleman Hawkins, Donald Byrd, and Miles Davis, whose quintet of the 1960s made Hancock famous. In 1968 he organized a sextet, which later was reduced to a quartet; with it he appeared in pop concerts. In addition to jazz piano he became adept as a player on an electric piano. In 1972 he went to Los Angeles, and in 1973 converted to a Californian brand of Buddhism.

Hancock's ability to switch between styles has led to success in several fields; his electric jazz-rock (fusion) has produced several hits, including *Watermelon Man*, *Chameleon*, and *Rockit*. Among his most popular albums were *Empyrean Isles* (1964), *Maiden Voyage* (1965), *Speak Like a Child* (1968), *Headhunters* (1973), *V.S.O.P.: The Quintet* (1977), and *Future Shock* (1983). He won an Oscar for his score to the 1986 film *'Round Midnight*.

Lionel Hampton

Handel (Hendel), George Frideric

~~~ ~~~ ~~~ ~~~ ~~~

Outstanding German-born English organist and composer, innovator of the English oratorio and a giant of the late Baroque; b. Georg Friedrich Händel, Halle, Feb. 23, 1685; d. London, Apr. 14, 1759. His father was a barber-surgeon and valet to the Prince of Saxe-Magdeburg; at the age of 61 he took a 2nd wife, Dorothea Taust, daughter of the pastor of Giebichenstein, near Halle; Handel was the 2nd son of this marriage.

As a child he was taken by his father on a visit to Saxe-Weissenfels, where he had a chance to try out the organ of the court chapel. The Duke, Johann Adolf, noticing his interest in music, advised that he be sent to Halle for organ lessons with Friedrich Wilhelm Zachow (1663–1712), the organist of the Liebfrauenkirche there. Zachow gave him instruction in harpsichord and organ playing and also introduced him to the rudiments of composition. Handel proved to be an apt student, and was able to substitute for Zachow as organist whenever necessary; he also composed trio sonatas and motets for church services on Sundays. After the death of his father in 1697 he entered the Univ. of Halle in 1702 and was named probationary organist at the Domkirche there.

In 1703 he went to Hamburg, where he was engaged as "violino di ripieno" by Reinhard Keiser (1674–1739), the famous composer and director of the Hamburg Opera. There he met composer and theorist Johann Mattheson (1681–1764); in 1703 the 2 undertook a journey to Lübeck together, with the intention of applying for the post of organist in succession to Buxtehude, who was chief organist there. It was the custom for an incoming organist to marry a daughter of the incumbent as a condition of appointment; neither Mattheson nor Handel availed themselves of this opportunity. (Bach made the same journey in 1704, and also returned without obtaining the succession.) There was apparently a quarrel between Mattheson and Handel at a performance of Mattheson's opera *Cleopatra*, in which Mattheson asked Handel to yield his place as *maestro al cembalo*; Handel declined, and an altercation ensued, resulting in a duel with swords, which was called off when Mattheson broke his sword on a metal button of Handel's coat. While the episode may be apocryphal, the point is moot, as the 2 apparently reconciled.

Handel's 1st 2 operas, *Almira* and *Nero*, were staged at the Hamburg Opera in 1705. He was then commissioned to write 2 other operas, *Florindo* and *Daphne*, orig. planned as a single opera combining both subjects. In 1706 he undertook a long voyage to Italy, where he visited Florence, Rome, Naples, and Venice. The 1st opera he wrote in Italy was *Rodrigo*, presented in Florence in 1707. Then followed *Agrippina*, produced in Venice in 1709; it obtained an excellent success, being given 27 performances. In Rome he composed the serenata *Il trionfo del Tempo e del Disinganno*, which was performed there in the spring of 1707. Handel's 1st oratorio, *La Resurrezione*, was given in Rome in 1708. Later that year he brought out in Naples his serenata *Aci, Galatea, e Polifemo*; its score was remarkable for a bass solo that required a compass of 2 octaves and a 5th.

During his Italian sojourn he met Alessandro and Domenico Scarlatti. In 1710 he returned to Germany and was named Kapellmeister to the Elector of Hannover, as successor to Agostino Steffani. Later that year he visited England, where he produced his opera *Rinaldo* at the Queen's Theatre in London (1711); it received 15 performances in all. After a brief return to Hannover in the summer of 1711, he made another visit to London, where he produced his operas *Il Pastor fido* (1712) and *Teseo* (1713). He also wrote an ode for Queen Anne's birthday, which was presented at Windsor Palace in 1713; it was soon followed by 2 sacred works, his *Te Deum* and *Jubilate*, to celebrate the Peace of Utrecht; these performances won him royal favor and an annuity of 200 pounds sterling.

An extraordinary concurrence of events persuaded Handel to remain in London, when Queen Anne died in 1714 and Handel's protector, the Elector of Hannover, became King George I of England. The King bestowed many favors upon the composer and augmented his annuity to 400 pounds sterling. Handel became a British subject in 1727, and he Anglicized his name. He continued to produce operas, invariably to Italian librettos, for the London stage. His opera *Silla* was produced in London (1713); it was followed by *Amadigi di Gaula* (1715). In 1716 Handel began to compose *Der für die Sünden der Welt gemarterte und sterbende Jesus*, to the Passion text of the poet Heinrich Brockes.

In 1717 he produced one of his most famous works, written expressly for King George I, the *Water Music*. Its 1st performance occurred during an aquatic fete on the Thames River, held by royal order; the King's boat was followed by a barge on which an orch. of 50 musicians played Handel's score, or at least a major portion of it. The final version of the *Water Music* combines 2 instrumental suites composed at different times: one was written for the barge party; the other is of an earlier provenance. In 1717 Handel also became resident composer to the Duke of Chandos, for whom he wrote the so-called *Chandos Anthems* (1717–18), 11 in number; the secular oratorio *Acis and Galatea* (1718); and the oratorio *Esther* (1718). He also served as music master to the daughters of the Prince of Wales; for Princess Anne he composed his 1st collection of *Suites de pieces pour le clavecin* (1720), also known as *The Lessons*, which includes the famous air with variations nicknamed THE HARMONIOUS BLACKSMITH; the appellation is gratuitous.

In 1719 Handel was made Master of Musick of a new business venture under the name of the Royal Academy of Music, established for the purpose of presenting opera at the King's Theatre. The 1st opera he composed for it was *Radamisto* (1720). In the fall of 1720 the Italian composer Giovanni Bononcini (1670–1747) joined the company. A rivalry soon developed between him and Handel that was made famous by the poet John Byrom:

Some say, compar'd to Bononcini
That Mynheer Handel's but a ninny.
Others aver that he to Handel
Is scarcely fit to hold a candle.
Strange all this difference should be
Twixt tweedledum and tweedledee.

Handel won a Pyrrhic victory when Bononcini had the unfortunate idea of submitting to the London Academy of Music a madrigal which he had appropriated in extenso from a choral piece by the Italian composer Antonio Lotti; Lotti discovered it, and an embarrassing controversy ensued, resulting in Bononcini's disgrace and expulsion from London (he died in obscurity in Vienna, where he sought refuge). The irony of the whole episode is that Handel was no less guilty of plagiarism. An article on Handel in the 1880 ed. of the *Encyclopaedia Britannica* spares no words condemning Handel's conduct: "The system of wholesale plagiarism carried on by Handel is perhaps unprecedented in the history of music. He pilfered not only single melodies but frequently entire movements from the works of other masters, with few or no alterations, and without a word of acknowledgment."

Between 1721 and 1728 he produced the following operas at the King's Theatre: *Florindante, Ottone, Flavio, Giulio Cesare, Tamerlano, Rodelinda Scipione, Alessandro, Admeto, Riccardo Primo, Siroe,* and *Tolomeo*; of these, *Giulio Cesare* and *Rodelinda* became firmly established in the operatic repertoire and had numerous revivals. In 1727 he composed 4 grand anthems for the coronation of King George II and Queen Caroline.

In early 1728 John Gay's *The Beggar's Opera* was premiered in London; this BALLAD OPERA became extraordinarily popular, not the least for its savage parodies of Italian opera. Despite the class differences between audiences of Gay's work and Handel's Italian operas, *The Beggar's Opera* signaled the growing British dissatisfaction with the imported genre. In the spring of 1728 the Royal Academy of Music ceased operations, and Handel became associated with the management of the King's Theatre. The following year he went to Italy to recruit singers for a new Royal Academy of Music. Returning to London, he brought out the operas *Lotario, Partenope, Poro, Ezio, Sosarme,* and *Orlando*; only *Orlando* proved to be a lasting success. In 1732 Handel gave a special performance of a revised version of his oratorio *Esther* at the King's Theatre; it was followed by the revised version of *Acis and Galatea* (1732) and the oratorio *Deborah* (1733). Later that year he produced his oratorio *Athalia* at Oxford, where he also appeared as an organist; he was offered the degree of Mus.Doc. (*honoris causa*), but declined the honor.

Discouraged by the poor reception of his operas at the King's Theatre, Handel decided to open a new season under a different management. But he quarreled with the principal singer, the famous castrato Senesino (Francesco Bernardi, *c.* 1680–*c.* 1759), who was popular with audiences, and thus lost the support of a substantial number of his subscribers, who then formed a rival opera company called Opera of the Nobility. It engaged the famous Italian composer Nicola Porpora (1686–1768) as director, and opened its 1st season at Lincoln's Inn Fields in late 1733. Handel's opera *Arianna in Creta* had its premiere at the King's Theatre (1734), but in July of that year both Handel's company and the rival enterprise were forced to suspend operations.

Handel set up his own opera company at Covent Garden, inaugurating his new season with a revised version of *Il Pastor fido* (1734); this was followed by *Ariodante, Alcina, Atalanta, Arminio, Giustino,* and *Berenice,* all staged between 1735 and 1737; only *Alcina* sustained a success; Handel's other operas met with an indifferent reception. In 1736 he presented his ode *Alexander's Feast* at Covent Garden; in 1737 he brought out a revised version of his oratorio *Il trionfo del Tempo e della Verità.* His fortunes improved when he was confirmed by the Queen as music master to Princesses Amelia and Caroline. He continued to maintain connections with Germany, and traveled to Aachen in 1737.

Upon his return to London he suffered from attacks of gout, an endemic illness of British society at the time, but he managed to resume his work. In 1738 he produced his operas *Faramondo* and *Serse* (an aria from the latter, *Ombra mai fù,* became famous in an anonymous instrumental arrangement under the title *Handel's Celebrated Largo*). There followed a pasticcio, *Giove in Argo* (1739), and *Imeneo* (1740); the following year he produced his last opera, *Deidamia.*

In historical perspective Handel's failure as an operatic entrepreneur was a happy turn of events, for he then directed his energy toward the composition of oratorios, in which he achieved greatness. For inspiration he turned to biblical themes, using English texts. In 1739 he pre-

George Frideric Handel

COURTESY OF THE FREE LIBRARY OF PHILADELPHIA

sented the oratorio *Saul* (including the *Dead March*), followed by *Israel in Egypt,* an *Ode for St. Cecilia's Day,* after Dryden, and his great set of 12 *Concerti grossi,* op. 6. Milton's *L'Allegro and Il Penseroso* inspired him to write *L'Allegro, il Penseroso, ed il Moderato* (1740). In 1741 he was invited to visit Ireland, and there he produced his greatest masterpiece, *Messiah;* working with tremendous concentration of willpower and imagination, he completed part I in 6 days, part II in 9 days, and part III in 6 days. The orchestration took him only a few more days; he signed the score in 1741. The 1st performance of *Messiah* was given in Dublin (1742), and its London premiere the following year. If contemporary reports can be trusted, King George II rose to his feet at the closing chords of the HALLELUJAH CHORUS, and the entire audience followed suit; since then, performances of *Messiah* have moved the listeners to rise during this celebratory chorus.

Handel's oratorio *Samson,* produced in London in 1743, was also successful, but his next oratorio, *Semele* (1744), failed to arouse public admiration. Continuing to work, and alternating between mythological subjects and religious themes, he produced *Joseph and His Brethren* (1744), *Hercules* (1745), and *Belshazzar* (1745). His subsequent works, composed between 1746 and 1752, were the *Occasional Oratorio, Judas Maccabaeus, Joshua, Alexander Balus, Susanna, Solomon, Theodora, The Choice of Hercules,* and *Jephtha.* Of these, *Judas Maccabaeus, Solomon,* and *Jephtha* became favorites with the public.

Besides oratorios, mundane events also occupied his attention. To celebrate the Peace of Aachen he composed the remarkable *Music for the Royal Fireworks,* which was heard for the 1st time in Green Park in London (1749). In 1750 he revisited Germany; but soon he had to limit his activities on account of failing eyesight, which required the removal of cataracts. The operation proved unsuccessful, but he still continued to appear in performances of his music, with the assistance of his pupil John Christopher Smith. Handel's last appearance in public was at a London performance of *Messiah*; 8 days later, on the Saturday between Good Friday and Easter, he died. He was buried at Westminster Abbey; a monument by Roubiliac marks his grave.

A parallel between the 2 great German contemporaries, Bach and Handel, is often drawn. They were born within a few months of each other, Bach in Eisenach, Handel in Halle, a distance of about 130 kilometers apart; but they never met. Bach visited Halle at least twice, but Handel was then away, in London. The difference between their life's destinies was profound. Bach was a master of the Baroque organ who produced religious works for church use, a schoolmaster who regarded his instrumental music as a textbook for study; he never composed for the stage, and traveled but little. By contrast, Handel was a man of the world who dedicated himself mainly to public spectacles, and who became a British subject. Bach's life was that of a German burgher; his genius was inconspicuous; Handel shone in the light of public admiration. Bach was married twice; survivors among his 20 children became important musicians in

their own right. Handel remained celibate, but he was not a recluse. Physically he tended toward healthy corpulence; he enjoyed the company of friends but had a choleric temperament and could not brook adverse argument. Like Bach, he was deeply religious, and there was no ostentation in his service to his God. Handel's music possessed grandeur of design, majestic eloquence, and lusciousness of harmony. Music lovers did not have to study Handel's style to discover its beauty, while the sublime art of Bach could be fully understood only after knowledgeable penetration into the contrapuntal and fugal complexities of its structure.

Handel bequeathed the bulk of his MSS to his amanuensis, John Christopher Smith, whose son presented them in turn to King George III. They eventually became a part of the King's Music Library; they comprise 32 vols. of operas, 21 vols. of oratorios, 7 vols. of odes and serenatas, 12 vols. of sacred music, 11 vols. of cantatas, and 5 vols. of instrumental music. Seven vols. containing sketches for various works are in the Fitzwilliam Collection at Cambridge.

handle organ. BARREL ORGAN.

handle piano. A mechanical PIANOFORTE operating on the same principle as the BARREL ORGAN.

Handlung (Ger.). Act in an opera or ballet.

Handy, W(illiam) C(hristopher), noted African-American pianist, publisher, bandleader, and composer, known as the "father of the blues"; b. Florence, Ala., Nov. 16, 1873; d. N.Y., Mar. 28, 1958. His father and grandfather were ministers. In 1892 he graduated from the Teachers' Agricultural and Mechanical College in Huntsville, Ala.; became a schoolteacher and also worked in iron mills; learned to play the cornet and was a soloist at the Chicago World's Fair (1893); became bandmaster of Mahara's Minstrels. From 1900 to 1902 he taught at the Agricultural and Mechanical College; then conducted his own orch. and toured the South (1903–21). He received the award of the National Assoc. for Negro Music, St. Louis (1937). In 1954 he married his secretary, Irma Louise Logan.

Handy's famous song *Memphis Blues* (publ. 1912; the 2nd piece to be publ. as a "blues," and the 1st blues work to achieve widespread popularity) was orig. written as a campaign song for the mayor of Memphis, E. H. Crump (1909); this song, along with his more celebrated *St. Louis Blues* (1914), opened an era in popular music, turning the theretofore prevalent spirit of ragtime gaiety to balladlike bittersweet nostalgia, with the lowered 3rd, 5th, and 7th degrees ("blue notes") as distinctive melodic traits. He followed these with more blues: *Yellow Dog*, *Beale Street*, *Joe Turner*; the march *Hail to the Spirit of Freedom* (1915); *Ole Miss* for Piano (1916); the songs *Aunt Hagar's Children* (1920), *Loveless Love* (1921), and *Aframerican Hymn* for Band and Chorus (1916). He publ. *Blues: An Anthology* (also publ. as *A Treasury of the Blues*; N.Y.); *Negro Authors and Composers of the U.S.* (N.Y., 1935); *Book of Negro Spirituals* (N.Y., 1938); and *Unsung Americans Sung* (N.Y., 1944); also an autobiography, *Father of the Blues* (N.Y., 1941).

Handy's publ. blues style foreshadowed the urban style that became popular in the 1920s; various claims and counterclaims as to the sources for his music have been made, including his having heard blues sung in the 1890s while he traveled in minstrel troupes; extreme views run from accusing him of heavy borrowing to inventing the blues altogether. No doubt the truth lies in the middle; if Handy was not truly the "father of the blues," he was certainly its greatest early promoter.

Hanna, (Sir) **Roland,** African-American jazz pianist; b. Detroit, Feb. 10, 1932. He began taking piano lessons as a child but soon turned to jazz; commenced his career as a performer in local clubs. During service in the U.S. Army he played in an army band (1950–52); after his discharge he took courses at the Eastman School of Music in Rochester, N.Y., and at the Juilliard School of Music in N.Y. He formed his own trio in 1959, was a leading member of the Thad Jones-Mel Lewis Orch. (1966–74), and then cofounded and played with the N.Y. Jazz Quartet (from 1971). In 1970 he was knighted by the government of Liberia. In his playing, Hanna reveals not only a refined technique, but a profound knowledge of historical jazz piano playing and the ability to integrate wide-ranging ideas into the context at hand.

Hanon, Charles-Louis, French pianist, pedagogue, and composer of keyboard exercises; b. Renescure, near Dunkerque, July 2, 1819; d. Boulogne-sur-Mer, Mar. 19, 1900. Next to Czerny, Hanon was the most illustrious composer of piano exercises, embodied in his chef d'oeuvre, *Le Pianiste-virtuose,* which for over a century has been the vade mecum for many millions of diligent piano students all over the face of the musical globe. He further wrote a collection of 50 instructive piano pieces under the title *Méthode élémentaire de piano*; a useful compilation, *Extraits des chefs-d'oeuvres des grands maîtres*; as well as a selection of 50 ecclesiastical chants, *50 cantiques choisis parmi les plus populaires.* He also attempted to instruct uneducated musicians in the art of accompanying plainchant in a curious didactic publication, *Système nouveau pour apprendre à accompagner tout plainchant sans savoir la musique* (New System for Learning to Accompany All Plainchant Without Knowing the Music).

Hans Heiling. Opera by Heinrich Marschner, 1833, 1st produced in Berlin. Heiling, a hereditary prince of hell, falls in love with a mortal woman; when she discovers his supernatural essence she leaves him for a human lover. He plans to slay his rival, but his subterranean mother persuades him to desist, and he vanishes.

Hänsel und Gretel. Opera by Humperdinck, 1893; it was 1st performed in Weimar and became forthwith a universal favorite. The subject is from a grim Grimm fairy tale: a witch lures the siblings Hansel and Gretel to her gingerbread house, which is built out of baked children. Ingeniously, the 2 intended victims push the witch into the burning oven; she explodes, and the gingerbread children all return to life. The score is Wagnerian to the core.

Hanson, Howard (Harold), important American composer, conductor, and educator; b. Wahoo, Nebr., Oct. 28, 1896; d. Rochester, N.Y., Feb. 26, 1981. His parents emigrated from Sweden to America and made their home in Nebraska, which had a large population of Scandinavian settlers; Hanson's northern ancestry played an important part in his spiritual outlook and his own music. His mother taught him piano; he began to compose very early in life; he also learned to play the cello. He attended the Luther College in Wahoo and played piano and organ in local churches; in 1912 he enrolled in the Univ. of Nebr.; in 1913 he went to N.Y., where he took piano lessons with Friskin and studied composition with Goetschius at the Inst. of Musical Art. In 1915 he enrolled at Northwestern Univ. in Evanston, Ill., where his teachers in composition were Arne Oldberg and P. C. Lutkin; he graduated in 1916 with a B.A. degree.

He progressed rapidly as a composer; his *Symphonic Prelude* was performed by the Chicago Sym. Orch.; he also wrote a Piano Quintet and other works. In 1916, at the age of 20, he received an appointment to teach music at the College of the Pacific in San Jose, Calif.; was named its dean in 1919. In 1921 he became the 1st American to win the prestigious Prix de Rome, which enabled him to spend 3 years at the American Academy there. He composed copiously; the major part of his works reflected his profound sentiment for his ancestral land; his *Scandinavian Suite* for Piano (1919) exemplified this devotion.

He believed in music as a function of the natural environment. During his stay in the West he wrote the score for a *Calif. Forest Play* (1920). The work that gained him admission to Rome was a symphonic poem, *Before the Dawn*; in 1923 he completed a piece for chorus and orch. entitled *North and West*. All these works clearly indicated his future path as a composer; they were permeated with the spirit of the northern country, inspired by both Scandinavia and the American West. There followed his 1st important work, Sym. No. 1, subtitled *Nordic*; he conducted its 1st performance in Rome (1923). In it he expressed, as he himself said, "the solemnity, austerity, and grandeur of the North, of its restless surging and strife, and of its somberness and melancholy." Hanson was often described as an American Sibelius; indeed, he professed profound admiration for the great Finn, with whom he shared an affinity for slowly progressing lyrical modalities and somber harmonies anchored in deep organ points.

In 1924 Hanson conducted the U.S. premiere of his *Nordic Sym.* in Rochester, and met George Eastman, the inventor of Kodak film. Eastman, who knew next to nothing about music, had nonetheless a keen appreciation of ability among artists and composers; in 1924 he offered Hanson the position of director of the Eastman School of Music; Hanson was not quite 28 years old at that time. Eastman's insight was justified; Hanson elevated the Eastman School of Music from a provincial conservatory to one of the most important musical insts. in America. He retained his post as director for 40 years; apart from his teaching, he inaugurated annual festivals of American music in Rochester; as director and conductor of these festivals, he showed an extraordinary measure of liberal choice, programming not only musical compositions that were naturally congenial to him, but also modern works in dissonant harmonies; and he maintained a friendly attitude toward his students even when they veered away into the field of cosmopolitan abstractions. All told, during his tenure in Rochester Hanson presented works by 700 composers and something like 1,500 different compositions; he made numerous recordings with the Eastman School Phil. Orch.

In 1925 Hanson completed one of his most significant works, *The Lament for Beowulf*, for chorus and orch., based on an Anglo-Saxon saga. In 1930 he wrote his 2nd Sym., entitled *Romantic*, on commission from Koussevitzky and the Boston Sym. Orch. on its 50th anniversary; Koussevitzky conducted its 1st performance (1930). Hanson's 3rd Sym. (1936–37) glorified the pioneer spirit of Swedish immigrants; it was presented over the NBC Radio network in 1938, with Hanson himself conducting. In his Sym. No. 4, subtitled *The Requiem*, written in 1943, Hanson paid tribute to the memory of his father; he conducted its 1st performance with the Boston Sym. Orch. in 1943; in 1944 the work received the Pulitzer Prize in music. There followed the 5th Sym., *Sinfonia Sacra*, in a single movement (1954); in it Hanson invoked his deep-rooted Christian faith; it was 1st performed by the Philadelphia Orch. (1955). Hanson wrote his 6th Sym. to commemorate the 125th anniversary of the N.Y. Phil.; Leonard Bernstein conducted it in 1968. Hanson's 7th Sym., *A Sea Sym.*, with chorus, derived from Whitman's poem, was 1st performed in 1977 at the National Music Camp at Interlochen. Whitman's poetry was close to Hanson's creative imagination, and he wrote several other works based on Whitman's poems.

Hanson remained faithful to his musical and philosophical convictions throughout his long career. Like Sibelius, he wrote music of profound personal feeling, set in an idiom which reflected the triumphs and laments of his life and of his double inheritance. In 1933 he composed his opera, *Merry Mount*, based on *The Maypole Lovers of Merry Mount*

by Hawthorne. Hanson dedicated the work to the memory of George Eastman, who had committed suicide 2 years before. It was one of the few operas by an American composer staged at the Metropolitan, and the production was very successful; according to reports, there was a total of 50 curtain calls for Hanson and the singers after its 4 acts. Despite this popular reception and favorable critical reviews, the opera had only 4 performances and was not retained in the repertoire, a fate not unlike that of other American operas produced at the Metropolitan. A symphonic suite drawn from the score enjoyed frequent performances at summer sym. concerts and on the radio.

In the meantime Hanson continued an active career as a conductor. In 1932 he led several concerts of American music in major cities of Europe. During 1961–62 he took the Eastman School Phil. Orch. on a grand European tour, under the auspices of the State Dept.; Hanson received a most gratifying success; he was praised as both a composer and an able conductor; his school orch. also received its share of appreciation. As an educator Hanson enjoyed great prestige; many talented American composers studied under him. He received numerous honorary degrees. In 1935 he was elected a member of the National Inst. of Arts and Letters; in 1938 he became a fellow of the Royal Academy of Music in Sweden. He held, at various times, a presidency of the National Assoc. of Schools of Music; served also as president of the Music Teachers National Assoc. and of the National Music Council. He was awarded 19 honorary doctorates in music. In 1945 he received the Ditson Award, and in 1946 was given the George Foster Peabody Award.

With the radical changes in contemporary composition, Hanson's music seemed to recede into an old-fashioned irrelevance; the number of performances of his music dwindled; only occasionally were his syms. broadcast from old recordings. Hanson never tried to conceal his bitterness at this loss of appreciation in his country for whose artistic progress he labored so mightily. Yet his music cannot in all fairness be judged as unredeemingly obsolete. His array of sonorous harmonies, often in modulations at a tritone's distance of their respective tonics, reaches the borderline of pungent bitonality; his bold asymmetrical rhythms retain their vitality; his orchestration is masterly in its instrumental treatment. True, Hanson never accepted the modern techniques of serialism or a total emancipation of dissonance; yet he maintained a liberal attitude toward these new developments.

Many of his conservative conservatory admirers were surprised by the publication of his book, *Harmonic Materials of Modern Music* (1960), in which he presented an exhaustive inventory of advanced harmonic formulas, tabulating them according to their combinatory potentialities. In recent years the neoromantic tendencies of composition and concert programming have led to a revival of his music.

Happening. A loosely defined type of collective activity or performance among American theater workers, painters, poets, musicians, and participants in the 1950s and 1960s. Allan Kaprow, an art historian, and others staged in a N.Y. art gallery a production under the name *18 Happenings in 6 Parts* (1956). The audience was distributed in 14 groups seated in chairs at random, and its participation in the action was earnestly solicited. The spectacle was synaesthetic, with sound, multicolored lights, and peripheral tactile and olfactory impressions. There were also "visual poems," of the graffiti type randomly lettered in crayon on walls and placards, with such communications as "My Toilet Is Shared by the Man Next Door Who Is Italian." The musical part consisted of aleatory superfetations of loudspeaking musical and antimusical sounds. Kaprow made an ex post facto statement bemoaning his choice of the word *Happening* as unfortunate, but conceded that it helped him to achieve an all-embracing inclusivity in describing the uninhibited exhibits of the AVANT-GARDE.

Cage's 1954 theater piece at Black Mountain College in North Carolina is usually cited as a prototypical Happening; in the 1960s, the Fluxus group and others took up the impulse and pushed it in more extreme directions. In the meantime, *Happening* entered the language, penetrating the common speech so deeply that everyday events are often described as Happenings simply because they have taken place at all. The term became popular in Europe as *Le Happening, El Happening, Il Happening,* or *Das Happening.*

Happy Birthday to You. This famous greeting song, 1893, was 1st published as *Good Morning to All* in *Song Stories for the Kindergarten.* The tune is by Mildred Hill.

Happy Days Are Here Again. Song by Milton Ager, 1930, for the movie musical *Chasing Rainbows.* It accompanies a scene in which the brave doughboys (soldiers) receive news of the Armistice in November 1918. It became the campaign song of Franklin D. Roosevelt in 1932, and of all subsequent Democratic candidates for the Presidency.

happy ending (It., *lieto fine*). In operas and other dramatic works, a morally and emotionally satisfying finale, no matter how improbable or unrealistic, where virtue tri-

umphs, evil is punished or forgiven magnanimously, and lovers unite after overcoming insurmountable odds. It may be said that the PICARDY 3RD cadence is the purely musical equivalent of the happy ending.

harawi (*yaravi*). A slow lyric song of the Incas.

Harawi, chant d'amour et de mort. Song cycle by Messiaen, 1945, for soprano and piano.

Harbach (born Hauerbach), **Otto** (Abels), American lyricist and librettist; b. Salt Lake City, Aug. 18, 1873; d. N.Y., Jan. 24, 1963. He studied at Knox College and Columbia Univ. In 1908 he collaborated with the composer Karl Hoschna on the successful musical *3 Twins*; subsequently wrote more than 40 works for Broadway, often in collaboration with Oscar Hammerstein II; his musical partners included Friml, Youmans, Kern, and Romberg; he also wrote for films. His most popular lyrics included *Rose-Marie* and *Indian Love Call* from Friml's *Rose-Marie* (with Hammerstein; 1924), *The Night Was Made for Love* from Kern's *The Cat and the Fiddle* (1931), and *Smoke Gets In Your Eyes* from Kern's *Roberta* (1932).

Harbison, John (Harris), significant American composer; b. Orange, N.J., Dec. 20, 1938. He grew up in a highly intellectual environment; his father was a prof. of history at Princeton Univ. and his mother was a magazine writer; both were musically endowed. Exceptionally versatile, Harbison studied violin, viola, piano, voice, and tuba at Princeton High School, and also took lessons in music theory. In 1956 he entered Harvard Univ. as a composition student of Piston (B.A., 1960), receiving a Paine Traveling Fellowship for a season of study with Boris Blacher in Berlin. Returning to the U.S., he studied composition privately with Roger Sessions and with Earl Kim at Princeton Univ. (M.F.A., 1963).

From 1963 to 1968 he was a member of the Soc. of Fellows at Harvard, and from 1969 to 1982 taught at the Mass. Inst. of Technology; was composer-in-residence of the Pittsburgh Sym. Orch. (1982–84) and of the Los Angeles Phil. (1985–88). He also made numerous appearances as a conductor; led the Cantata Singers (1969–73; 1980–82). In 1977 he held a Guggenheim fellowship, and in 1987 received the Pulitzer Prize in Music for his vocal work *The Flight into Egypt* (1986).

Equipped with a thorough knowledge of modern compositional technique, Harbison wrote music free from doctrinaire pedestrianism; yet in his melodic structures he adumbrated dodecaphonic procedures. In his Shakespearean opera *The Winter's Tale* he used innovative "dumb shows," acted in pantomime on the stage; in his opera *Full Moon in March* he made use of the PREPARED PIANO, by which the sonorities are altered by manipulating the strings of the piano. He further made use of ready-made recordings for special effects. He is presently at work on an opera based on Fitzgerald's *The Great Gatsby*. Other well-known works include the ballets *Ulysses' Bow* (1983); *Ulysses' Raft* (1983); several concertos and syms.; chamber music, including *Bermuda Triangle* for Tenor Saxophone, Amplified Cello, and Electric Organ (1970); 2 string quartets; and vocal works: *Book of Hours and Seasons* (1975); *The Flower-Fed Buffaloes* for Baritone and Chorus (1976); *Mirabai Songs* for Soprano and Orch. (1982); *The Natural World* for Mezzo-soprano and 5 Instruments (1987).

Harburg, E(dgar) Y(ip) (born Isidore Hochberg), American lyricist; b. N.Y., Apr. 8, 1898; d. Los Angeles (in a car accident), Mar. 5, 1981. He graduated from the City College of N.Y. in 1921; then was coproprietor of an electrical appliance company, which failed during the Depression; he then began to write lyrics for Broadway; with Jay Gorney he produced the famous song *Brother, Can You Spare a Dime*. In 1939 he won an Academy Award for *Over the Rainbow* from *The Wizard of Oz*; his other lyrics include *We're Off to See the Wizard*, *It's Only a Paper Moon*, and *April in Paris*. He was lyricist and coauthor, with Burton Lane and Fred Saidy, of *Finian's Rainbow* (1947). Harburg was probably the most socially outspoken lyricist in the great age of Broadway and film musicals.

hard bop. A jazz style of the 1950s and '60s which returns to the relative simplicities (down-to-earth qualities of bittersweet rhythm and tune) of the blues, resulting in an intensified, more accessible style; a reaction against the complexities and sophistication of BEBOP and COOL jazz.

Hardanger fiddle. HARDINGFELE.

Hardin, Louis Thomas. See MOONDOG.

hardingfele. A traditional Norwegian fiddle with a set of sympathetic strings for resonance, named for the Hardanger region in Norway. It dates to the middle of the 17th century; there are at least 20 SCORDATURA tunings used. The repertoire includes folk songs, dances (SLÅTTER), and bridal marches.

Harfe (Ger.). HARP.

Harlequin (Fr.). The central character in the Harlequinade as presented in COMMEDIA DELL'ARTE. He is in the service of the villainous Pantaloon (Pantalone), and adores Columbine (Columbina), who is the object of Pantaloon's lust. In vulgar Latin, Harlequinus was a benign demon; hence, the Italian form *Arlecchino*. The name may also be connected with the Erlkönig (erl-king), leader of the sprites.

harmonia (Grk.). The artful juxtaposition of contrasting elements; a word of wide significance, conceived by the ancient Greeks and philosophically explained by Plato and Aristotle. Since harmony in the sense of simultaneous combinations of tones did not exist in Greek music, the term does not literally translate to the modern HARMONY.

harmonic. 1. Pertaining to chords (either consonant or dissonant), and to the theory and practice of harmony. 2. HARMONICS.

harmonic curve. The figure described by a vibrating string or other sound source on a SPECTROGRAPH.

harmonic figuration. Broken chords; ARPEGGIO.

harmonic flute. HARMONIC STOP.

harmonic mark (sign, symbol). A degree sign (°) over a note, indicating a HARMONIC.

harmonic minor scale. A natural minor scale with a raised 7th step, producing a LEADING TONE and an AUGMENTED SECOND.

harmonic note. See HARMONICS.

harmonic reed. HARMONIC STOP.

harmonic scale. 1. HARMONIC SERIES. 2. HARMONIC MINOR SCALE.

harmonic series. The natural ascending series of overtones or partials. If the FUNDAMENTAL is set at a given note, then the 2nd member of the series sounds an octave above the fundamental; the 3rd member, a perfect 5th higher than the 2nd member; the 4th member, a perfect 4th higher; the 5th member, a major 3rd higher; the 6th member, a minor 3rd higher, and so forth. The 1st 6 members of the natural harmonic series form the harmony of the major chord, fundamental to all acoustic phenomena. See also HARMONICS.

harmonic stop. Organ stop having pipes double the ordinary length, pierced midway, so that a 16' pipe yields an 8' tone; also called harmonic flute or harmonic reed.

harmonic tone. See HARMONICS.

harmonica. Hand-held free-reed instrument in which a set of graduated metal reeds are mounted in a narrow frame; when blown by the mouth produces different tones on expiration and inspiration. Also called mouth harmonica, mouth organ, or (in U.S. slang) blues harp.

harmonicon. 1. HARMONICA. 2. ORCHESTRION. 3. A keyed harmonica combined with a flue stop or stops.

harmonics (overtones, partials). A series of tones naturally produced by a vibrating string or an air column in a pipe. What we hear as a single tone is actually a complex of tones produced by the vibrations of the string or air column as a whole and also as one-half, one-third, one-quarter, and other subdivisions of the sounding body. If we silently depress a key on the piano keyboard—say a low E—and hold it, and then strike sharply the e an octave higher and let it go, the upper octave will continue to reverberate on the still-open string of the lower E (the FUNDAMENTAL). A weaker but still audible reverberation can be produced by striking a 5th above the octave sound (b), and possibly even e^1, 2 octaves above the open string. Under ideal circumstances on a very well-tuned and resonant piano, even the 5th natural component of the original string, in this case $g\sharp^1$, can be detected, thus forming a full major triad. An acute ear may hear the octave and the 12th (upper e and b on the fundamental E) by striking the fundamental tone very forcibly and letting it vibrate sonorously.

The harmonics are the formative tones determining the timbre of an instrument, depending on their relative strength in the tone complex. The principal harmonics can be produced on a string instrument by lightly touching the string at a chosen point of equal division (node), thus preventing the string to vibrate as a whole. By touching lightly on the node one-third of the length of the open violin string e^2, the upper b^3 an octave and a 5th above will be heard. With some practice one can produce the harmonic series up to its 6th harmonic on the naked strings of the grand piano. Since most bugle calls, trumpet flourishes, and fanfares are derived from

the natural harmonics, an ingenious experimenter can play a variety of common tunes (and even tunes such as the theme of the last movement of Beethoven's Violin Concerto), sliding one's finger over a string. The harmonics of string instruments possess a flutelike quality; this explains the French word for harmonics, *flageolet* (from Old Fr. *flageol*, flute); this is also the term used in German and Russian.

harmonie (Fr.; Ger. *Harmoniemusik*). Wind band; a wind instrument section in a larger ensemble.

Harmonie der Welt, Die. Opera by Hindemith, 1957. "Harmony of the world" refers to the theological, philosophical, and mathematical theories of planetary motion entertained by the astronomer Johannes Kepler (1571–1630). His personal life is brought in as a paradigm to his theories.

Harmonies poétiques et religieuses. A piano cycle by Liszt, 1849, containing 10 pieces; No. 7, *Funérailles*, is frequently performed separately. The cycle is usually assumed to refer to the death of Chopin, Liszt's close friend who died in the 10th month of 1849. An alternative theory is that Liszt was mourning the defeat of the Hungarian Revolution of 1848 and the establishment of Austrian rule over Hungary. *Invocations*, No. 1 of the cycle, 1st publ. in 1834, is audaciously written in constantly changing meters (8/4, 9/4, 10/4, etc.); it bears no key signature and includes such innovations as an emphasis on the tritone and an ending marked *très long silence*. Fifty years later Liszt returned to the exploration of atonality implied in this piece and composed a *Bagatelle ohne Tonart*.

harmonieux (Fr.). Harmonious.

Harmonious Blacksmith, The. A historically unjustified nickname for an air with 5 variations by Handel, 1720, from an E-major harpsichord suite. The origin of the title is told in great detail which, however, is entirely false. It is said that Handel heard this air sung by a blacksmith near London while forging iron, or that he was impressed by the steady beat of the artisan's hammer. To lend essence to this story, the alleged anvil of the fictitious harmonious blacksmith was even exhibited in London. A real blacksmith who practiced his art in the vicinity of London had his tombstone inscribed with the subject of Handel's air (with variations). The earliest ed. of the music under the title of *The Harmonious Blacksmith* was published in England about 1819, 60 years after Handel's death.

harmonique (Fr.). Harmonic (adj.). *Son harmonique*, harmonic, overtone, partial.

harmonisch (Ger.). Harmonic (adj.); harmonious.

harmonium. An organlike portable instrument on which the sound is activated by an airstream, generated by a pair of foot pedals and passing through a set of flexible metal strip reeds. The harmonium became a popular instrument in the 19th century, with a special appeal to amateur performers because it could produce a sustained tone and rudimentary dynamics by pressing the pedal. It became a perfect instrument for the home in the middle-class culture and in small churches as a substitute for the organ. The name REED ORGAN is often applied to the harmonium and the American organ, which uses wind created by suction bellows (vacuum principle) rather than the harmonium's airstream (pressure principle).

harmony

A musical combination of tones or chords, consonant or dissonant; also, the contrapuntal texture of a homophonic piece, as 2-part, 3-part, etc. The Greek word HARMONIA referred to an ideal monophonic music, with an artful coordination between high and low sounds and a balanced rhythmic and melodic arrangement of slow and fast musical phrases. However, for at least a millennium the word *harmony* has meant the simultaneous sounding of several melodies, represented in musical notation by the vertical position, while melody was linear, notated horizontally. Counterpoint partakes of both harmonic and melodic elements insofar as it is a harmonious synchronization of linear melodies.

When harmony 1st emerged as a definite technique, it was entirely consonant, limited to the use of perfect concords, the octave and the 5th. Since a perfect 5th subtracted from an octave formed a perfect 4th, consonant intervals incorporated perfect octaves, 5ths, and 4ths. With the emergence of ORGANUM, contrary motion was added to theretofore exclusively perfect intervals in parallel progressions. At the same time an almost accidental admixture of heterophony introduced dissonant intervals such as 2nds to the available means of harmonic combinations.

The decisive step toward traditional harmony occurred in the late Middle Ages, when 3rds and 6ths were adopted as acceptable noncadential consonant intervals. Triadic harmony made its 1st appearance in naked, sterile forms without the fertilizing mediant. With the accession of FAUXBOURDON, triads received their legitimacy in the form of the 1st inversion. Dissonant passing tones became more and more frequent. Curiously, the cadences of infertile 5ths and octaves in the guise of tonic triads continued to be the rule until the 16th century, when final triads finally acquired the essential mediant. Figured bass appeared as harmonic shorthand that opened the way toward the use of triads and 7th chords on all degrees of the scale.

In the 17th century harmonic composition began to separate itself from contrapuntal techniques. In the next century counterpoint developed into sublime art in the music of Bach, but elsewhere harmony gradually became a vertical group of tones with limited independence of its component parts. Bach's sons embraced harmonic composition governed principally by the laws of chord progressions, with occasional contrapuntal ingredients subordinated to the domination of melody and with the bass as the formative element of harmony in the classical sense of the word. At the conclusion of the Baroque era—about 1750—harmony finally assumed the familiar 4-part setting of the chorale. A relic of 3-part harmony is indicated in the name of the middle section of the minuet, the trio.

Four-part harmony—as it crystallized in Classical and Romantic music—is fundamentally triadic, with the tonic, subdominant, and dominant triads being the main determinants of tonality, for these 3 triads comprise all 7 notes of the diatonic scale. In major keys these triads are major; in minor, the tonic and subdominant are minor but the dominant is made major by raising the 7th degree (creating the LEADING TONE), which is the middle tone of the major dominant triad. As 4-part harmony requires doubling, contrapuntal rules lead to certain tendencies;

essentially the root is the easiest to double; the 5th is next; and the 3rd is almost never doubled.

Four-part harmony makes it possible to achieve complete sets of 7th chords on all degrees of the scale, as well as the diminished-7th chord that occurs functionally upon the leading tone in a harmonic minor key. In strict harmony, triads having a diminished or augmented 5th are not allowed. Consequently a triad built on the 7th degree of either the major or harmonic minor mode cannot be used, nor the supertonic triad in minor keys; however, this rule was less strictly enforced in time.

A perfect 5th or octave moving in the same direction to another perfect 5th or octave, particularly between outer voices is forbidden; parallel movement of different intervals toward 5ths or octaves, known as hidden intervals, is also taboo. A 5th or an octave can be reached only by contrary motion. Any number of examples from Bach's chorales or other sacrosanct sources can be adduced to discredit this stern code of prohibited progressions, but so deeply ingrained are these rules, particularly in 4-part harmony, that a pedantic editor of Liszt's *Liebestraum* deleted one of the inner voices in the coda in order to avoid a pair of consecutive 5ths.

In school exercises the 4 component parts are named after the voices in a vocal quartet: soprano, alto, tenor, bass. The most important consideration in 4-part harmony is voice-leading. Generally speaking, crossing of voices is not admitted—soprano must always be the upper voice, bass must always be the lowest, and alto may not cross under the tenor. Contrary motion is recommended, especially between the soprano and bass. Stepwise motion is preferred. Thirds and 6ths are favored because they can be used in consecutive motion. When 1 voice leaps several scale degrees, the rest of the voices must move stepwise to provide a counterbalance and establish a proper equilibrium. If the soprano has a melodic leap upward, then the bass ought to move stepwise, preferably in the opposite direction; but if in the same direction, it must avoid landing on a perfect 5th or octave which would result in hidden 5ths or octaves.

By and large an ideal exercise in 4-part harmony would present an alternation of 3rds and 6ths between the outer voices, with occasional legitimate parallelisms. The octave is de rigueur in almost every final cadence. The middle voices are less mobile and have less opportunity to move by leaps; often they are stationary, maintaining the common tone between 2 successive chords. Each chord can be arranged in 6 different ways without changing the bass. The distance between soprano and alto or between alto and tenor must not exceed an octave, but the distance between bass and tenor may be as extensive as a 12th. When the 3 upper voices are bunched together within an octave, such an arrangement is called CLOSE HARMONY. When these upper voices are dispersed for a total range of more than an octave, the setting is called OPEN HARMONY.

The notation of 4-part harmony in school exercises retains the numerical indexes of BASSO CONTINUO in Arabic numbers; the degree of the scale is represented by a Roman numeral. These provide 2 necessary and sufficient coordinates to indicate the nature of the chord, although they do not specify the spatial arrangement of the component notes. A triad in root position is marked by the figure $^5/_3$ (which stands for the intervals of a 5th and a 3rd above the given bass note) after the Roman numeral corresponding to the scale degree; a triad in 1st inversion is $^6/_3$, the 2nd inversion, $^6/_4$. The figures for 7th chords and their inversions are $^7/_5/_3$, $^6/_5/_3$, $^6/_4/_3$, and $^6/_4/_2$. When a triad's figures are not notated at all, this indicates a triad in root position.

Similarly, the figure for the 7th chord may be abbreviated to the single number 7, and the last inversion of a 7th chord may be notated simply 2, the other intervals being assumed. Thus, VI signifies the submediant triad, V with the figure $^6/_4/_2$ or simply V_2 denotes the last inversion of the dominant-7th chord, I with the figure $^6/_4$ is the 2nd inversion of the tonic triad, etc. It is taken for granted in traditional harmony that in minor keys the 7th degree is always raised. However, the VII with the figure $^5/_3$ or $^7/_5/_3$ (i.e., 7) indicates the natural flatted 7th; the leading-tone 7th chord has to be indicated with the appropriate accidental before the Roman numeral.

In altered chords, such as the chords of the augmented 6ths, sharps or flats are indicated after the corresponding figures in the superscript. In elementary harmony exercises, however, such alterations that are properly part of figured bass are not indicated. Modulations are notated by equal signs (I = V), meaning that the tonic of the preceding key becomes the dominant of the key into which it modulates; the same event can be indicated in vertical alignment of the preceding and succeeding keys.

Harmony and counterpoint are reciprocal techniques of composition. There are contrapuntal elements in harmony and harmonic elements in counterpoint. Harmony acquires a contrapuntal quality when individual voices carry horizontal segments of a thematic nature. Counterpoint becomes harmonic in structure when the vertical dimension tends to predominate. Counterpoint thrives on mutual imitation of the constituent voices, while harmony, being a vertical compound, does not normally handle imitation. Often, a harmonic or contrapuntal quality of writing is revealed in musical notation rather than in actual sound.

A remarkable example of a purely harmonic structure masquerading as counterpoint occurs in the opening bars of the finale of Tchaikovsky's *Pathétique Sym.* One hears a "pathetic" descending figure in 4-part harmony, but upon examination it appears that the 1st violins constantly cross the part of the 2nd violin, and the violas cross the cellos, so that the melodic line is traced by a zigzag; likewise, the bass line crosses the 2 inner voices. This unusual scoring for the string section of the orch. is explained by Tchaikovsky's reluctance to have a passage in 4-part harmony descending in consecutive motion, even though no patent consecutive octaves or 5ths result from these parallelisms. When the same passage occurs in the recapitulation, Tchaikovsky scores it without the crossing of lines, but this time there is a powerful pedal point in the bass that changes the harmonic denomination and relegates the potentially objectionable parallel motion to the upper voices.

The introduction of chromatic harmony in the works of Liszt, Wagner, and Franck left the tradition of the 4-part setting fundamentally unaltered. Contrary motion is still the preferred modus operandi. Consecutive 3rds and 6ths still determine the flow of the music. The polarity of the upper and lower voices is maintained. Consecutive triadic formations occur exclusively in 1st inversions, which possess the saving grace of 3rds and 6ths. Diminished-7th chords in chromatic motion are often used for dramatic effect, but while they make the basic tonality ambiguous, they are compounds of minor 3rds, eminently suitable for parallel motion. The dominant-9th chord, which was a relative innovation in the age of Wagner and Liszt, is treated as a suspension on the dominant-7th chord and presents no particular problem. Dissonances are still faithfully resolved, and complete tonal cadences happily conclude each important musical section.

A veritable harmonic revolution occurred with an extraordinary suddenness toward the end of the 19th century. In the works of Debussy and his followers the traditional rules of harmony were revised. Naked 5ths and octaves moved in parallel lines as they did a thousand years before in organum. Consecutive triads in close harmony became common, disregarding the fact that such progressions necessarily involve consecutive 5ths. Parallel formations of major triads were rampant, as were consecutive $^6/_4$ chords in major keys. Ravel's String Quartet ends in such a cataract of major $^6/_4$ chords.

Up to about 1900, every dissonant combination had to be resolved into a consonance. The 20th century brought about an emancipation of dissonances. Scriabin built a "mystic chord" of 6 notes that would be regarded in the 19th century as an unresolved suspension to a Wagnerian dominant-9th chord, but Scriabin used it as a metatriadic foundation for his mystical harmony. Seconds and 7ths acquired musical citizenship and were no longer treated as ancillary structures. The whole-tone scale erased the distinction between major and minor and established a neutral mode. Polytonality licensed the use of 2 or more tonal triads simultaneously.

A most remarkable affinity exists between free modulation and a gradually descending tetrachord in the bass, moving diatonically or chromatically from the tonic to the dominant. An example is found in Beethoven's Piano Sonata No. 21, op. 53, the *Waldstein*, where the descending bass C, B, B-flat, A, A-flat, G, in steady motion, gives rise to a progression from C major through G major, B-flat major, F major, F minor, and C minor. A chromatically altered descending bass line determines the modulating plan of sections in the finale of Beethoven's *Moonlight Sonata*. Finally, it must be noted that a pedal point in the bass can sustain a progression of harmonies far removed from the principal key. Examples are numerous; particularly noteworthy is the introduction to the wedding scene in Rimsky-Korsakov's opera *Le Coq d'or* which maintains a steady bass on G, the dominant of C major, while the upper harmonies move freely to A major, E-flat major, and A-flat major.

Diatonic harmony has been enriched by pandiatonicism, which removes prohibitions of unresolved dissonances within a given tonality and cultivates superimposition of different triadic harmonies. Historically, pandiatonicism can be traced to the hypertrophic development of the pedal point on the tonic and dominant over which the subdominant and dominant triads are superimposed.

Particularly effective are the superimpositions of the dominant triadic formations in close harmony in the middle register upon the tonic or subdominant triads in open harmony in the bass register. In fact, the functional role of the tonic, subdominant, and dominant triads fundamental to classical harmony is fully preserved in pandiatonic techniques. Pandiatonicism found its most fruitful application in neo-Baroque music, in which the component notes can be used in quartal harmony. Quartal harmony itself has all but succeeded the tertian harmony of classical music. Quartads such as E–A–D–G, placed upon the pedal tones F–C, is a typical example.

Finally, atonality and its organized development, 12-tone composition or *dodecaphony*, abolished the concept of triadic tonality altogether, replacing it with a new concept of integrated melody and harmony wherein harmony becomes a function of the fundamental dodecaphonic tone-row. Subdivisions of the tempered scale in quartertone music and even smaller microtones prosper modestly as a monophonic art, but experiments have been made in microtonal harmonies as well. Electronic music has freed harmony of all technical impediments and allows the use of precisely calculated, nontempered intervals as well as microtones. As cultivated by the AVANT-GARDE, electronic harmony becomes a structure of fluctuating blobs. The ultimate development of this blob harmony is reached in *white noise*, in which the entire diapason of sounds is employed.

Further harmonic terminology: *chromatic harmony* has chromatic tones and modulations; *compound harmony* has 2 or more essential chord-tones doubled; *dispersed* or *extended harmony*, OPEN HARMONY; *dissonant harmony*, see DISSONANCE; *essential harmony*, fundamental triads of a key; or the harmonic frame of a composition minus all figuration and ornaments; *false harmony*, the inharmonic relation; discord produced by imperfect preparation or resolution; discord produced by wrong notes or chords; *figured harmony* varies the simple chords by figuration of all kinds; *pure harmony*, music performed in pure or just intonation; *spread harmony*, OPEN HARMONY; *strict harmony*, composition according to strict rules for the preparation and resolution of dissonances; *tempered harmony*, music performed in tempered intonation.

harmony of the spheres (music of the spheres, universal harmony). An imaginary concordance of sounds produced by the relative motions of the moon, the sun, and the planets. In early philosophy and theology, the 7 spheres of the geocentric universe produced the diatonic degrees of the scale. In the Middle Ages this system of tonal cosmos was described as *musica mundana*; constellations belonged to the category of *musica celestis*. Subsequent developments of these theological, numerological, and acoustical speculations led to the concept of a concord of angels (*concentus angelorum*) and to *musica angelica*. Kepler, who accepted the heliocentric cosmos, still clung to the philosophical reality of the harmony of the spheres and endeavored to demonstrate its mathematical applicability to the planetary orbits. Hindemith wrote an opera, *Die Harmonie der Welt*, based on Kepler's life. In *Gulliver's Travels*, Jonathan Swift writes: "The officers, having prepared all their musical instruments, played on them for 3 hours without intermission, so that I was quite stunned by the noise. . . . The people of Laputa had their ears adapted to hear the music of the spheres which always played at certain intervals."

Harnasie. Ballet by Szymanowski, 1935, with a scenario based on folktales of the Harnasie peoples in the Carpathian Mountains of Poland.

Harnoncourt, Nikolaus, eminent Austrian cellist, conductor, and musicologist; b. Berlin, Dec. 6, 1929. His father, an engineer, also played the piano and composed; the family settled in Graz. He began to study the cello at the age of 9, later training with Paul Grummer and at the Vienna Academy of Music with Emanuael Brabec. He was a cellist in the Vienna Sym. Orch. (1952–69); founded the Vienna Concentus Musicus (1953), which began giving concerts in 1957, playing on period instruments or modern copies; the group made its 1st tour of England, the U.S., and Canada in 1966. From the mid-1970s he also appeared internationally as a guest conductor, expanding his repertoire to include music of later eras. His writings include *Musik als Klangrede: Wege zu einem neuen Musikverständnis* (Salzburg and Vienna, 1982) and *Der musikalische Dialog: Gedanken zu Monteverdi, Bach und Mozart* (Salzburg, 1984). His wife, Alice Harnoncourt (b. Vienna, Sept. 26, 1930), studied violin with Feist and Moraves in Vienna and with Thibaud in Paris; she became concertmaster of the Vienna Concentus Musicus at its founding.

Harold in Italy. Sym. with viola obbligato by Berlioz, 1834. While the original source of inspiration is disputed, the work was ultimately connected to Byron's *Childe Harold* and his travels; the viola, rarely treated as a concerto soloist, represents Harold. Berlioz was originally commissioned by Paganini, who was disappointed by the solo part's many silences and relative lack of virtuosity. But he let Berlioz keep the fee, and later approved of the piece he never played.

The piece, despite its merits, is the punch line for more than one "viola joke," due to its relatively small role for the soloist. Nonetheless, the work gives Berlioz an opportunity to display his brilliant art of rhythmic fluency and colorful orchestration. It was 1st performed in Paris.

harp

A plucked chordophone with several strings running in a plane perpendicular to a resonator; the modern Western instrument is supported by a frame and pillar. Harps (Lat. *harpa*; It. *arpa*; Fr. *harpe*; Ger. *Harfe*) are often confused with lyres, which have strings attached to a yoke at the same plane as the resonator, and whose construction involves 2 arms and a crossbar.

The harp is an ancient and in many cultures the most glorified musical instrument. Iconographic evidence dates back to Sumeria from the 3rd millennium B.C. on. In the Middle Ages the instrument that David played for Saul was described as a harp, but it must have been the Biblical *kinnor*, a lyre related to the Greek *kithara*. Harps in the modern sense of the word appeared in Ireland and Wales in the 10th century as a bardic instrument, and were soon annexed by the itinerant minstrels. During the Renaissance the harp was domesticated and became the purveyor of melodious and harmonious music in France, Spain, and Italy. Soon its popularity spread all over the civilized world. The harp was portrayed in Renaissance paintings as the instrument of the angels or beautiful young maidens.

The modern orch. harp has a nearly 3-cornered wooden frame, the foot of which is formed by an upright pillar meeting the hollow

Thomas Sully, Lady with a Harp: Eliza Ridgely, *1818*

COURTESY OF THE NATIONAL GALLERY OF ART, WASHINGTON, D.C.

back (the upperside of which bears the soundboard) in the pedestal; the upper ends of pillar and back are united by the curving neck. The gut strings are 46 (or 47) in number; the compass is 6 1/2 octaves, from C_1 to f^4 (or g^4). The range of the modern harp approaches that of the grand piano, and its triangular shape, with a curved neck, is geometrically similar to that of the piano. In fact, if a grand piano were to be dismantled and stood up perpendicularly on the floor, it would make a fairly good simulacrum of a harp, as proven in one of the Marx Brothers' comedies, when the orally abstentious Harpo, a competent harpist in real life, performs a solo on such a harp.

The prototype of the modern harp has only 7 strings per octave; in order to convert it into an instrument capable of chromaticism and modulation, an ingenious "double action" tuning mechanism was patented by the great harp builder Sébastian Érard around 1810 in the form of pedals that could be depressed 1 or 2 notches. Each notch shortens the corresponding string so that it sounds a semitone higher; depressing the pedals 2 notches shortens the string to make it sound another semitone higher. Thus it becomes possible for each of the 7 strings of the octave to be raised a semitone or a whole tone, so the starting scale for the modern harp is tuned in C-flat major.

Since each individual string could be raised a semitone or a whole tone, all major and minor scales become available. But it is still impossible to play a rapid chromatic scale on the harp, for it would necessitate superhuman foot action. A different unusual affect may be achieved by using enharmonic duplication, i.e., setting the pedals to obtain the same pitch on 2 strings, so that the harpist can play a most ingratiating GLISSANDO along the strings as a diminished-7th chord. Glissando, in fact, is one of the truly idiomatic privileges of the harp, an effect that can be produced almost effortlessly.

The harp is plucked with the fingers, never with a plectrum, but modern harp composers have added a whole arsenal of special effects, such as angelic-sounding harmonics, or demoniacal plucking of strings with a nail, or even tapping on the body of the harp. The "key signature" of the harp may strike a nonharpist as the most curious mixture of sharps and flats, but these "accidentals" are simply indications as to the tuning, not signposts of tonality, and are usually placed in the middle of the great staff used in harp music. A chromatic harp was introduced as an experiment in 1845, doing away with the pedals altogether, but like so many simplified devices it has found little favor with harpists.

Although Mozart and Beethoven occasionally wrote for the harp, it never became a Classic orch. instrument. But it reached a luxuriant flowering in the programmatic symphonic poems and operas of the 19th century. The harp was invariably sounded whenever the soul of a female sinner was redeemed in the last act of a Romantic opera. But such celestial implications of harp playing all but disappeared in the less *larmoyant* and antisentimental 20th century, and was metamorphosed into a functional instrument, shunning such time-honored devices as sweeping arpeggios. It is interesting to note that Stravinsky had 3 harps in the original scoring of his early ballet *The Firebird* but eliminated them in a later revision of the score: an eloquent testimony to the obsolescence of the harp as a decorative instrument in modern music. However, harp concertos are far more common than 2 centuries ago.

Harp Quartet. Nickname for Beethoven's String Quartet in E-flat Major, op. 74 (1809). It is, of course, not a quartet of harps, but a string quartet that contains some engaging passages in pizzicato arpeggios which may suggest to some literal-minded musicians the sound of a harp.

harpsichord (Fr. *clavecin*; Ger. *Cembalo, Kielflügel*; It. *cembalo*). A keyboard instrument provided with 1 or 2 manuals and activated by plectrums plucking a set of strings. Italian harpsichords with a single manual and Flemish harpsichords with 2 manuals bore a close resemblance to the modern grand piano. Earlier instruments closely related to the harpsichord included the spinet and virginal; their ranges varied from 3 to 5 octaves, and all were manufactured in a variety of styles and shapes. The harpsichord was eventually superseded by the fortepiano in the early 19th century. It is interesting to note that the black keys of the piano (sharps and flats) were sometimes white on the harpsichord, while the piano's white keys might be colored black or brown on the harpsichord.

The harpsichord was an extremely popular domestic instrument; hundreds of paintings, drawings, and etchings represent women playing on harpsichords. Old harpsichords were often adorned with curved legs and figures of cupids and mermaids. The lids might have carried inspirational legends in Latin such as "Musica dulce laborum levamen" (Music is a sweet solace from labors) or "Laborum dulce lenimen" (Sweet relief from labors).

The harpsichord played an all-important role in Baroque instrument ensembles, serving as the harmonic element of the BASSO CONTINUO; the performer improvised upon the figured bass. Bach and Handel presided over the harpsichord in leading their own works, and even Haydn led his ensemble from

Jan Vermeer, portrait of a 17th-century harpsichord player

the harpsichord during his London visits in the 1790s. The art of playing the harpsichord lapsed in the 19th century with the abandonment of the functional use of basso continuo, but a vigorous revival of the harpsichord, along with a number of other older instruments, took place in the 1st half of the 20th century when dedicated craftsmen, foremost among them Arnold Dolmetsch (1858–1940), began manufacturing excellent replicas. Wanda Landowska, master harpsichordist herself, greatly contributed to this revival by teaching harpsichord playing and commissioning contemporary composers (among them Falla and Poulenc) to write new works for this resurrected Baroque instrument.

Harris, Roy (Leroy Ellsworth), significant American composer; b. Chandler, Okla., Feb. 12, 1898; d. Santa Monica, Calif., Oct. 1, 1979. His parents, of Irish and Scottish descent, settled in Okla.; in 1903 the family moved to Calif., where Harris had private music lessons with Henry Schoenfeld and Arthur Farwell. In 1926 he went to Paris, where he studied composition with Nadia Boulanger; was able to continue his stay in Paris thanks to 2 consecutive Guggenheim fellowship awards (1927, 1928). Upon his return to the U.S. he lived in Calif. and N.Y.; several of his works were performed and attracted favorable attention; Farwell publ. an article in the *Musical Quarterly* (1932) in which he enthusiastically welcomed Harris as an American genius. In his compositions Harris showed a talent of great originality, with a strong melodic and rhythmic speech that is indigenously American. He developed a type of modal symbolism akin to Greek ethos, with each particular mode related to a certain emotional state.

Instrumental music is the genre in which he particularly excelled. He never wrote an opera or an oratorio, but made astute use of choral masses in some of his works. He held many teaching positions over a long and distinguished career, teaching for the longest period of time at the Univ. of Calif., Los Angeles (1961–73). In 1973 he was appointed composer-in-residence at Calif. State Univ., Los Angeles, a post he held until his death. He received honorary D.Mus. degrees from Rutgers Univ. and the Univ. of Rochester in N.Y.; in 1942 he was awarded the Elizabeth Sprague Coolidge Medal "for eminent services to chamber music." In 1936 he married the pianist Johana Harris (born Beula Duffey; b. Ottawa, Ontario, Jan. 1, 1913); she assumed her professional name Johana in honor of J. S. Bach. After Harris's death she married, on Dec. 18, 1982, her 21-year-old piano student John Heggie.

Harris wrote 13 syms, the best-known and most frequently performed being his Symphony No. 3 (Boston, 1939; it was the 1st American sym. to be played in China, during the 1973 tour of the Philadelphia Orch. under the direction of Eugene Ormandy). Among his other symphonies the most played are No. 4, *Folksong Sym.*, with Chorus (Cleveland, 1940); No. 6, *Gettysburg Address* (Boston, 1944); No. 10, *Abraham Lincoln Sym.* for Chorus, Brass, 2 Amplified Pianos, and Percussion (Long Beach, Calif., 1965); and No. 13, *Bicentennial Sym. 1976*, for Chorus and Orch. (1975; premiered as No. 14, Washington, D.C., 1976). He also composed other orch.l, chamber, and choral works.

Harrison, George, English rock singer and guitarist, member of the celebrated group the Beatles; b. Liverpool, Feb. 25, 1943. Like his co-Beatles, he had no formal musical education, and learned to play the guitar by osmosis and acclimatization. Not as extroverted as John Lennon, not as exhibitionistic as Paul McCartney, and not as histrionic as Ringo Starr, he was not as conspicuously projected into public consciousness as his comrades-in-rock. Yet he exercised a distinct influence on the character of the songs that the Beatles sang. He became infatuated with the mystical lore of India; sat at the feet of a hirsute guru; introduced the SITAR into his rock arrangements. He is the author of *Something*, one of the greatest successes of the Beatles.

When the group broke up in 1970, Harrison proved sufficiently talented to impress his individual image in his own music; he also collaborated on songs of social consciousness with Bob Dylan. He brought out the successful albums *All Things Must Pass* (1970) and *The Concert for Bangladesh* (1972). In 1970 he had a big hit with *My Sweet Lord*; however, its similarity to the 1963 Chiffons' hit *He's So Fine* led to a lawsuit; Harrison settled out of court. In 1973 his album *Living in the Material World* (with *Give Me Love*) quickly attained gold status. In 1981 he scored a hit with his single *All Those Years Ago*. His album *Cloud 9* (with *Got My Mind Set On You*, 1987) also proved a success. He was also involved as a producer of films associated with the Monty Python comedy troupe.

Harrison, Lou, inventive American composer and performer, innovator of Western applications of the Indonesian GAMELAN; b. Portland, Oreg., May 14, 1917. He studied with Cowell in San Francisco (1934–35) and with Schoenberg at the Univ. of Calif. at Los Angeles (1941). He taught at Mills College in Oakland, Calif. (1937–40; 1980–85), and various other West Coast colleges. He also was a music critic for the *New York Herald-Tribune* (1945–48). He held 2 Guggenheim fellowships (1952, 1954).

His interests are varied: He invented 2 new principles of clavichord construction; built a Phrygian aulos; developed a process for direct composing on a phonograph disc; in 1938 proposed a theory of interval control, and in 1942 supplemented it by a device for rhythm control; also wrote plays and versified poematically. He was one of the earliest adherents of an initially small group of American musicians who promoted the music of Ives, Ruggles, Varèse, and Cowell; he prepared for publication Ives's 3rd Sym., which he conducted in its 1st performance in 1946. He visited the Orient in 1961, fortifying his immanent belief in the multiform nature of music by studying Japanese and Korean modalities and rhythmic structures.

Seeking new sources of sound production, he organized a percussion ensemble of multitudinous drums and such homely sound makers as coffee cans and flowerpots. He also wrote texts in Esperanto for some of his vocal works. He later composed for the Indonesian gamelan; many of these instruments were constructed by his longtime associate and friend William Colvig (b. Medford, Oreg., Mar. 13, 1917), including psalteries, harps, flutes, monochords, and several complete gamelans; he performed on these instruments in many of Harrison's compositions, as well as on traditional instruments in concerts and lectures. His instruments have been used by the San Francisco Sym. and San Francisco Opera Co., among others; he built the gamelans housed at the Univ. of Calif. at Berkeley and at Mills College in Oakland.

Hart, Lorenz (Milton), outstanding American lyricist, most famous for his stage collaborations with Richard Rodgers; b. N.Y., May 2, 1895; d. there, Nov. 22, 1943. He began as a student of journalism at Columbia Univ. (1914–17); then turned to highly successful theatrical writing. During his 24-year collaboration with Richard Rodgers he wrote the lyrics for 29 musicals, including *Connecticut Yankee* (1927); *On Your Toes* (1936); *Babes in Arms* (1937); *The Boys from Syracuse* (1938); *I Married an Angel* (1938); *Too Many Girls* (1939); *Pal Joey* (1940); *By Jupiter* (1942). Some of their best songs (*Manhattan, Here in My Arms, My Heart Stood Still, Small Hotel, Blue Moon, Where or When, I Married an Angel*) are publ. in the album *Rodgers and Hart Songs* (N.Y., 1951).

Hartmann, Karl Amadeus, outstanding German composer; b. Munich, Aug. 2, 1905; d. there, Dec. 5, 1963. He studied with Joseph Haas at the Music Academy in Munich (1923–27) and later with Scherchen.

He began to compose rather late in life; his 1st major work was a Trumpet Concerto, which was performed in Strasbourg in 1933. During World War II he studied advanced musical composition and analysis with Webern in Vienna (1941–42). After the war he organized in Munich the society Musica Viva. He received a prize from the city of Munich in 1948; in 1952 he was elected a member of the German Academy of Fine Arts, and soon after became president of the German section of the ISCM. Despite his acceptance of a highly chromatic, atonal idiom and his experimentation in the domain of rhythm (patterned after Blacher's "variable meters"), Hartmann retained the orthodox form and structural cohesion of basic classicism. He was excessively critical of his early works and discarded many of them, but some were retrieved and performed after his death. Among his works are the chamber opera, *Des Simplicius Simplicissimus Jugend* (1934–35; Cologne, 1949; a rev. version was retitled *Simplicius Simplicissimus*, 1955); 9 symphonies and other orch.l, chamber, and vocal works.

Háry János. Opera by Kodály, 1926, 1st produced in Budapest. János Háry (in Hungarian the family name is 1st) is in the braggart warrior mold, a fantastic liar who boasts of defeating Napolean all by himself. The opera opens with a deafening orch. sneeze, which is a protestation of either utter disbelief or total integrity in Hungarian conversational custom.

hasosra. An ancient long silver trumpet of Israel, intoned by priests at ritual occasions, producing a fierce and fear-inspiring sound.

Hatikva. The national anthem of Israel, originally a Zionist song. The melody is nearly identical with the main theme of Smetana's symphonic poem *The Moldau*. Recent research suggests that the melody may have originated in Scandinavia. This is one of the rare national anthems in a minor mode.

Hauer, Josef Matthias, influential Austrian composer and music theorist; b. Wiener-Neustadt, near Vienna, Mar. 19, 1883; d. Vienna, Sept. 22, 1959. After attending a college for teachers, he became a public-school instructor; at the same time he studied music. An experimenter by nature, with a penchant for mathematical constructions, he developed a system of composition based on "tropes," or patterns, which aggregated to thematic formations of 12 different notes. As early as 1912 he publ. a piano piece, *Nomos* (Law), which contained the germinal principles of 12-tone music; in his theoretical publications he elaborated on his system.

Hauer vehemently asserted his priority in 12-tone composition; he even used a rubber stamp on his personal stationery proclaiming himself "the true founder of the 12-tone method." This claim was countered, with equal vehemence, but with more justification, by Schoenberg; indeed, the functional basis of 12-tone composition, in which the contrapuntal and harmonic structures are derived from the unifying tone row, did not appear until Schoenberg formulated it and put it into practice in 1924.

Hauer lived his entire life in Vienna, working as a composer, conductor, and teacher. Despite its forbidding character, his music attracted much attention at 1st; after the 1930s, it fell into obscurity. The most visible works are the many pieces included in the *Zwölftonspiele* series.

Haunted Castle, The. Opera by Moniuszko, 1864.

Haupt (Ger., head). Main, chief, principal, as in theme or instrument.

Hauptsatz (Ger.). Principal part of a work; exposition.

Hauptstimme (Ger., main voice). A term 1st used by Schoenberg to indicate the prominent polyphonic voice or tone-row, designated in his scores as H (H⎯), a protracted horizontal line running from the 2nd perpendicular of the letter *H* to the end of the melody at the right.

Hauptzeitmass (Ger.). Principal tempo of a work.

Hausmusik (Ger., home music). After a long period of alienation from the masses, modern composers in Germany came to the conviction that music should cease to be a hermetic art for select audiences and should be returned to its source, the home. Hausmusik was a development parallel to GEBRAUCHSMUSIK. Dissonant harmony and asymmetric rhythms were not excluded, as long as the performance did not present technical difficulties. Usually Hausmusik was written for voices or SPRECHSTIMME, with piano accompaniment and obbligato parts for instruments easy to play, such as recorders, clarinets and violins. See also AMATEUR.

hautbois (Fr.). Oboe.

hautbois d'amour (Fr.). Oboe d'amore.

havanaise (Fr.). A HABANERA.

Hawkins, Coleman (Randolph), **"Bean" or "Hawk,"** outstanding African-American jazz tenor saxophonist; b. St. Joseph, Mo., Nov. 21, 1904; d. N.Y., May 19, 1969. He joined the Kansas City group Jazz Hounds in 1921; from 1923 to 1934 was a member of Fletcher Henderson's band in N.Y.; his full tone and heavy vibrato became the standard for tenor saxophone, and he was considered the foremost performer on the instrument. From 1934 to 1939 he worked in Europe; upon his return to the U.S. in 1939 he made his most influential recording, *Body and Soul*; departing from the usual paraphrase approach of swing improvisation, his extemporized solo became an inspiration to the new generation of jazz musicians and paved the way for the bebop of the 1940s.

Hawkins, (Sir) John, eminent English music historian; b. London, Mar. 29, 1719; d. there, May 21, 1789. He studied law while serving as a clerk, and soon was able to act as an attorney. An ardent devotee of music, he entered the musical society of the time and was on friendly terms with Handel; he also participated in literary clubs, and knew Samuel Johnson, Goldsmith, and others. A wealthy marriage (1753) enabled him to devote his leisure to literature and music. In 1761 he became a magistrate; in 1763, chairman of the Quarter Sessions; he was knighted in 1772. His 1st publication dealing with music was *Memoirs of the Life of Sig. Agostino Steffani* (1758). He then brought out *An Account of the Institution and Progress of the Academy of Ancient Music* (1770).

The culmination of 16 years of labor was his monumental *A General History of the Science and Practice of Music* (5 vols., 1776). The 1st vol. of Burney's *General History of Music* appeared at the same time; thus, Hawkins undoubtedly held priority for the 1st general history of music publ. in England; however, its reception was rather hostile; Burney himself derided Hawkins in an unpubl. poem. Yet the Hawkins work contained much reliable information, particularly dealing with musical life in London in the 18th century. Hawkins died of a paralytic stroke and was buried in Westminster Abbey.

Haydn, Franz Joseph

Illustrious Austrian composer, the 1st master of Viennese Classicism and the "father of the symphony"; brother of (Johann) Michael Haydn; b. Rohrau, Lower Austria, probably Mar. 31, 1732 (baptized, Apr. 1, 1732); d. Vienna, May 31, 1809. He was the 2nd of 12 children born to Mathias Haydn, a wheelwright, who served as village sexton, and Anna Maria Koller, daughter of the market inspector and a former cook in the household of Count Harrach, lord of the village. Their 2nd son, Michael, also became a musician. On Sundays and holidays, music was performed at home, the father accompanying the voices on the harp, which he had learned to play by ear. When Haydn was a small child his paternal cousin Johann Mathias Franck, a choral director, took him to Hainburg, where he gave him instruction in reading, writing, arithmetic, and instrumental playing.

When Haydn was 8 years old, Karl Georg Reutter, Kapellmeister at St. Stephen's Cathedral in Vienna, engaged him as a soprano singer in the chorus. After his voice began to break he moved to the household of Johann Michael Spangler, a music teacher. He obtained a loan of 150 florins from Anton Buchholz, a friend of his father's, and was able to rent an attic room where he could use a harpsichord. In the same house lived the famous Italian poet and opera librettist Pietro Metastasio, who recommended Haydn to a resident Spanish family as a music tutor. He was also engaged as accompanist to students of Nicolo Porpora, for whom he performed various menial tasks in exchange for composition lessons. He made a diligent study of *Gradus ad Parnassum* by J. J. Fux and *Der vollkommene Capellmeister* by Johann Mattheson.

Haydn soon began to compose keyboard music. In 1751 he wrote the singspiel *Der krumme Teufel*. A noblewoman, Countess Thun, engaged him as harpsichordist and singing teacher; he met Karl Joseph von Fürnburg, for whom he wrote his 1st string quartets. In 1759 Haydn was engaged by Count Ferdinand Maximilian von Morzin as Kapellmeister at his estate in Lukaveč. On Nov. 26, 1760, he married Maria Anna Keller, the eldest daughter of his early benefactor, a Viennese wigmaker.

A decided turn in Haydn's life was his meeting with Prince Paul Anton Esterházy. Esterházy had heard one of Haydn's syms. during a visit to Lukaveč, and engaged him to enter his service as 2nd Kapellmeister at his estate in Eisenstadt; Haydn signed his contract with Esterházy on May 1, 1761. Prince Paul Anton died in 1762, and his brother, Prince Nikolaus Esterházy, known as the "Magnificent," succeeded him. He took Haydn to his new palace at Esterháza, where Haydn was to provide 2 weekly operatic performances and 2 formal concerts. Haydn's service at Esterháza was long-lasting, secure, and fruitful; there he composed music of all descriptions, including most of his known string quartets, about 80 of his 104 syms., a number of keyboard works, and nearly all his operas; in 1766 he was elevated to the rank of 1st Kapellmeister.

Prince Nikolaus Esterházy was a cultural patron of the arts, but he was also a stern taskmaster in his relationship to his employees. His contract with Haydn stipulated that each commissioned work had to be performed without delay, and that such a work should not be copied for use by others. Haydn was to present himself in the "antichambre" of the palace each morning and afternoon to receive the Prince's orders, and he was obliged to wear formal clothes, with white hose and a powdered wig with a pigtail or a hairbag; he was to have his meals with the other musicians and house servants. In particular, Haydn was obligated to write pieces that could be performed on the *baryton*, an instrument which the Prince could play; in consequence, Haydn wrote over 100 trios involving the baryton. He also wrote 3 sets of 6 string quartets each (opp. 9, 17, and 20), publ. in 1771–72. His noteworthy syms. include No. 49, in F minor, *La passione*; No. 44, in E minor, known as the *Trauersinfonie*; and No. 45, in F-sharp minor, the famous *Abschiedsinfonie* (FAREWELL SYM.), performed by Haydn at Esterháza in 1772.

In 1780 Haydn was elected a member of the Modena Phil. Soc.; in 1784 Prince Henry of Prussia sent him a gold medal; in 1785 he was commissioned to write a "passione istrumentale," *The 7 Last Words of Christ*, for the

Cathedral of Cadiz; in 1787 King Friedrich Wilhelm II gave him a diamond ring; many other distinctions were conferred upon him. During his visits to Vienna he formed a close friendship with Mozart, who was nearly a quarter of a century younger and for whose genius Haydn had great admiration. If the words of Mozart's father can be taken literally, Haydn told him that Mozart was "the greatest composer known to me either in person or by name." Mozart reciprocated Haydn's regard for him by dedicating to him a set of 6 string quartets.

Prince Nikolaus Esterházy died in 1790, and his son Paul Anton (named after his uncle) inherited the estate. After he disbanded the orch., he granted Haydn an annuity of 1,000 florins; nominally he remained in the service of the new Prince as Kapellmeister, but he took up permanent residence in Vienna.

In 1790 Johann Peter Salomon (1745–1815), the enterprising London impresario, visited Haydn and persuaded him to travel to London for a series of concerts. Haydn accepted the offer, arriving in London on New Year's Day, 1791. On March 11 of that year he appeared in his 1st London concert in the Hanover Square Rooms, presiding at the keyboard. Haydn was greatly feted in London by the nobility; the King himself expressed his admiration for Haydn's art. In 1791 he went to Oxford to receive the honorary degree of Mus.D. For this occasion, he submitted his Sym. No. 92, in G major, which became known as the *Oxford Sym.*; he composed a 3-part canon, *Thy Voice, O Harmony, Is Divine*, as his exercise piece. It was also in England that he wrote his Sym. No. 94, in G major, the *Surprise Sym.* (Ger., known as *Mit Paukenschlag*).

On his journey back to Vienna in the summer of 1792 Haydn stopped in Bonn, where young Beethoven showed him some of his works; Haydn agreed to accept him later as his student in Vienna. In 1794 Haydn went to London once more. His 1st concert, on Feb. 10, 1794, met with great success. His "London" syms., also known as the "Salomon" syms. because Haydn wrote them at Salomon's request, were 12 in number, and they included No. 99, in E-flat major; No. 100, in G major, known as the *Military Sym.*; No. 101, in D major, nicknamed *The Clock* because of its pendulumlike rhythmic accompanying figure; No. 102, in B-flat major; No. 103, in E-flat major, known as the *Drum Roll* Sym., and No. 104, in D major, called the *London* Sym.

Returning to Vienna, Haydn resumed his contact with the Esterházy family. In 1794 Prince Paul Anton died and

was succeeded by his son Nikolaus; the new Prince revived the orch. at Eisenstadt, with Haydn again as Kapellmeister. Conforming to the new requirements of Prince Nikolaus, Haydn turned to works for the church, including 6 masses. His Mass in C major was entitled *Missa in tempore belli* (1796), for it was composed during Napoleon's drive toward Vienna. The 2nd Mass, in B-flat major, the *Heiligmesse*, also dates from 1796. In 1798 he composed the 3rd Mass, in D minor, which is often called the *Nelsonmesse*, with reference to Lord Nelson's defeat of Napoleon's army at the Battle of the Nile. The 4th Mass, in B-flat major (1799), is called the *Theresienmesse*, in honor of the Austrian Empress Maria Theresa. The 5th Mass, in B-flat major, written in 1801, is known as the *Schöpfungsmesse*, for it contains a theme from the oratorio *Die Schöpfung* (The Creation). The 6th Mass, in B-flat major (1802), is referred to as the *Harmoniemesse*, for its extensive use of wind instruments (see HARMONIE).

Between 1796 and 1798 Haydn composed his great oratorio *Die Schöpfung*, which was 1st performed at a private concert for the nobility at the Schwarzenburg Palace in Vienna on Apr. 29, 1798. In 1796 he wrote the Concerto in E-flat Major for trumpet (CLARINO), which became a standard piece for trumpet players. In 1797 Haydn was instructed by the Court to compose a hymn-tune of a solemn nature that could be used as the national Austrian anthem. He succeeded triumphantly in this task (*Gott erhalte unser Kaiser*); he also made use of this tune as a theme of a set of variations in his String Quartet in C Major, No. 3, op. 76, which itself became known as the EMPEROR QUARTET. Between 1799 and 1801 Haydn completed the oratorio *Die Jahreszeiten*; its text was trans. into German from James Thomson's poem *The Seasons*. It was 1st performed at the Schwarzenburg Palace in Vienna on Apr. 24, 1801. In 1802, beset by illness, Haydn resigned as Kapellmeister to Prince Nikolaus.

Despite his gradually increasing debility, Haydn preserved the saving grace of his natural humor; in response to the many salutations of his friends, he sent around a quotation from his old song *Der Alte*, confessing his bodily weakness. Another amusing musical jest was Haydn's reply to a society lady who identified herself at a Vienna party as a person to whom Haydn had dedicated a lively tune ascending on the major scale; she sang it for him, and he replied wistfully that the tune was now more appropriate in an inversion. Haydn made his last public appearance at a concert given in his honor in the Great Hall of the Univ. of Vienna on Mar. 27, 1808, with Salieri conducting *Die Schöpfung*. When Vienna capitulated to Napoleon, he ordered a guard of honor to be placed at Haydn's residence.

Haydn died on May 31, 1809, and was buried at the Hundsturm Cemetery. In consequence of some fantastic events, his skull became separated from his body before his reinterment at Eisenstadt in 1820; it was actually exhibited under glass in the hall of the Gesellschaft der Musikfreunde in Vienna for a number of years, before being reunited with his body in the Bergkirche in Eisenstadt on June 5, 1954, in a solemn official ceremony.

Franz Joseph Haydn

PHOTOGRAPH BY FRITZ HEUSCHKEL, COURTESY OF THE NEW YORK PUBLIC LIBRARY

Haydn was often called "Papa Haydn" by his intimates, in appreciation of his invariable good humor and amiable disposition. Ironically, he never became a papa in the actual sense of the word. His marriage was unsuccessful; his wife was a veritable termagant; indeed, Haydn was separated from her for most of his life. Still, he corresponded with her and sent her money, even though, according to a contemporary report, he never opened her letters.

In schoolbooks Haydn is usually described as "father of the symphony," the creator of the Classic forms of sym. and string quartet. Historically, this absolute formulation cannot be sustained; the symphonic form was established by Stamitz and his associates at the Mannheim School, having evolved from the Italian sinfonia; the string quartet was of an even earlier provenance. But Haydn's music was not limited to formal novelty; its greatness was revealed in the variety of moods, the excellence of variations, and the contrast among the constituent movements of a sym.; string quartets, as conceived by Haydn, were diminutions of the sym.; both were set in the form of a sonata, consisting of 3 contrasting movements—*Allegro, Andante, Allegro* (again, taken from the sinfonia)—with a Minuet interpolated between the last 2 movements.

It is the quality of invention that places Haydn above his contemporaries and makes his music a model of Classic composition. A theory has been put forward that

Haydn's themes were derived from the folk melodies of Croatian origin that he had heard in the rural environment of his childhood, but no such adumbrations or similarities can be convincingly proved. Genius is a gift bestowed on a musician or poet without external urgencies. Haydn also played a historic role in the evolution of functional harmony by adopting 4-part writing as a fundamental principle of composition, particularly in his string quartets.

The intimate *Volkstümlichkeit*, a popular impressiveness of Haydn's music, naturally lent itself to imaginative nicknames of individual compositions. There are among his syms. such appellations as *Der Philosoph* and *Der Schulmeister*; some were titled after animals: *L'Ours* and *La Poule*; others derived their names from the character of the main theme, as in *Die Uhr* (The Clock), the *Paukenschlag* (Surprise), and the *Paukenwirbel* (Drum Roll). Among Haydn's string quartets are *La Chasse*, so named because of the hunting horn fanfares; the *Vogelquartett*, in which one hears an imitation of birdcalls; the *Froschquartett*, which seems to invoke a similarity with frog calls in the finale; and the *Lerchenquartett*, containing a suggestion of a lark call. The famous *Toy Sym.*, scored for an ensemble which includes the rattle, the triangle, and instruments imitating the quail, cuckoo, and nightingale, was long attributed to Haydn; it is actually a movement of a work by Leopold Mozart.

The precise extent of Haydn's vast output will probably never be known. Many works are lost; others, listed in various catalogs, may never have existed or were duplications of extant works; some are of doubtful authenticity, and some are definitely spurious. Haydn kept an *Entwurf-Katalog*, from 1765 on. Several subsequent catalogues were put together, starting in the year after his death. The current definitive catalog was ed. by A. van Hoboken (Mainz, 1957–71).

Haydn's authentic syms. number 104, although Hoboken adds a *Symphonie Concertante* (1792) and 3 early works to the list. In addition to the works mentioned above, nicknamed syms. include: No. 6, in D major, *Le*

Matin (1761); No. 7, in C major, *Le Midi* (1761); No. 8, in G major, *Le Soir* (1761); No. 26, in D minor, *Lamentatione* (1770); No. 30, in C major, *Alleluja* (1765); No. 31, in D major, *Hornsignal* (1765); No. 43, in E-flat major, *Mercury* (1772); No. 48, in C major, *Maria Theresia* (1769); No. 53, in D major, *Imperial* or *Festino* (1778); No. 59, in A major, *Fire* (1769); No. 60, in C major, *Il Distratto* (1774); No. 63, in C major, *La Roxelane* or *Roxolana* (1779); No. 64, in A major, *Tempora mutantur* (1773); No. 69, in C major, *Laudon* or *Loudon* (1776); No. 73, in D major, *La Chasse* (1782); 6 Paris syms. (Nos. 82-87), including: No. 85, in B-flat major, *La Reine* (The Queen) (1785); 12 London or Salomon syms. (Nos. 93-104), including No. 96, in D major, *The Miracle* (1791; London, 1791). Many of the concertos are lost or spurious; surviving are 3 violin concertos; 2 for cello, 1 for hunting horn, 5 for 2 LIRE ORGANIZZATE (HURDY-GURDY), 5 for clavicembalo (i.e., organ or harpsichord), 1 for violin and clavicembalo. Other works include divertimentos, notturnos, sinfonias, overtures, dances, incidental music, and marches.

Although relatively little attention has been paid to them, Haydn wrote numerous operas for the Esterháza theater, some have received revivals in the last quarter-century. *La Canterina*, intermezzo in musica (Bratislava, 1766); *Lo speziale* (The Apothecary), dramma giocoso (Esterháza, 1768); *Le Pescatrici* (The Fisher Women), dramma giocoso (1769; Esterháza, 1770); *L'infedeltà delusa* (Deceit Outwitted), burletta per musica (Esterháza, 1773); *Philemon und Baucis, oder Jupiters Reise auf die Erde*, singspiel/marionette opera (Esterháza, Sept. 2, 1773); *L'incontro improvviso* (The Surprising Encounter), dramma giocoso (Esterháza, Aug. 29, 1775); *Il mondo della luna* (Life on the Moon), dramma giocoso (1777; Esterháza, 1777); *La vera costanza* (True Constancy), dramma giocoso (Esterháza, Apr. 25, 1779; extant music appears only in rev. version, 1785); *L'isola disabitata* (The Desert Island), azione teatrale (Esterháza, 1779; rev. 1802); *La fedeltà premiata* (The Winner Rewarded), dramma pastorale giocoso (1780;

Esterháza, 1781); *Orlando paladino* (Roland the Paladin), dramma eroicomico (1782; Esterháza, Dec. 6, 1782); *Armida*, dramma eroico (1783; Esterháza, Feb. 26, 1784); *L'anima del filosofo, ossia Orfeo ed Euridice* (The Soul of Philosophy, or Orpheus and Euridice), dramma per musica (1791; 1st confirmed perf., Florence, 1951).

Haydn wrote between 10 and 15 masses; several sacred motets (including the 6 *English Psalms, c.* 1794–95); oratorios (including the 2 mentioned above); secular cantatas; Italian orch. arias, mostly for interpolation into others' operas; songs in German and English; nearly 400 British folk song arrangements for voice and trio (1792–1804); vocal duets, trios, and quartets with keyboard accompaniment; and more than 50 canons.

Along with the syms., Haydn's compositional development—and therefore the growth of the Classic style—can best be seen in the several sets of string quartets: op. 1 (6 divertimentos, *c.* 1757–59), including No. 1, in B-flat major, *La Chasse*; op. 2 (4 divertimentos, *c.* 1760–62; 2 are by Roman Hoffstetter); op. 9 (6 divertimentos, 1771); op. 17 (6 divertimentos, 1771), includes No. 5, in G major, *Recitative*; *Sun Quartets*, op. 20 (6 divertimentos, 1772); *Russian Quartets* or *Jungfernquartette*, op. 33 (6, 1781), including No. 2, in E-flat major (*The Joke*); No. 3, in C major, *The Bird*; No. 5, in G major, *How do you do?*; op. 42, in D minor (1785); *Prussian Quartets*, op. 50 (6, 1787), including No. 5, in F major, *Ein Traum*; No. 6, in D major, *The Frog*; *Tost Quartets*, op. 54 (3, 1788); *Tost Quartets*, op. 55 (3, 1788); No. 2, in F minor, *The Razor*; *Tost Quartets*, op. 64 (6, 1790); No. 5, in D major, *The Lark*; *Apponyi Quartets*, op. 71 (3, 1793); *Apponyi Quartets*, op. 74 (3, 1793), including No. 3, in G minor, *The Rider*; *Erdödy Quartets*, op. 76 (1797), including No. 2, in D minor, *Fifths*; No. 3, in C major, *Emperor*; No. 4, in B-flat major, *Sunrise*; *Lobkowitz Quartets*, op. 77 (2, 1799); op. 103, in D minor (1803?; only movements 2 and 3 finished). Other works by Haydn include *c.* 20 string trios; *c.* 30 piano trios; *c.* 40 solo keyboard sonatas, mostly for harpsichord; music for flute-clock.

Haydn, (Johann) **Michael,** distinguished Austrian composer, brother of Franz Joseph Haydn; b. Rohrau, Lower Austria (baptized), Sept. 14, 1737; d. Salzburg, Aug. 10, 1806. He went to Vienna about 1745 and became a chorister at St. Stephen's Cathedral; his voice was remarkable for its wide range, extending 3 octaves. In addition to the acad-

emic and musical training he received as a chorister, he also studied composition on his own by absorbing the theories of Fux as propounded in his treatise on counterpoint, *Gradus ad Parnassum*. He then obtained the post of Kapellmeister to the Bishop of Grosswardein in 1757, and subsequently was named a court musician and

Konzertmeister to Archbishop Sigismund Schrattenbach of Salzburg in 1762.

In 1768 he married Maria Magdalen Lipp (1745–1827), the daughter of the court organist Franz Ignaz Lipp; she was a soprano in the archbishop's service. Haydn also became principal organist of the Dreifatigkeitskirche in 1777 and was Mozart's successor as cathedral organist in 1781. Part of his time he devoted to teaching; Carl Maria von Weber and Anton Diabelli were among his students. When Archbishop Hieronymus Colloredo abdicated in 1800 and the French took control of Salzburg, Haydn lost his positions. Although his last years were made difficult by this change in his fortunes, he turned down the post of vice Kapellmeister to Prince Nikolaus Esterházy, his famous brother's patron.

He was a prolific composer of both sacred and secular music, and particularly esteemed for his mastery of church music. His outstanding Requiem in C minor, *Pro defuncto Archiepiscopo Sigismundo*, was composed in memory of his patron in 1771; it was also performed at Joseph Haydn's funeral. Among his numerous Masses he wrote the fine *Missa sotto il titulo di S. Teresia*, for Maria Theresia (wife of Holy Roman Emperor Franz II), who sang the soprano solos under his direction in Vienna in 1801. He wrote several settings of the Te Deum, Litaniae lauretanae, Salve Regina, Tantum ergo, Regina coeli, and Vespers, as well as nearly 200 sacred motets. His secular output included dramatic works, syms., minuets, marches, concertos, divertimentos, chamber music, etc. His Sym. in G major (1783) was long attributed to Mozart (who composed an introduction to its 1st movement) as K.444/425a.

Hayes, Isaac, African-American singer and songwriter of soul and popular music; b. Covington, Tenn., Aug. 6, 1938. He learned to play saxophone and piano; after singing with local groups, he went to Memphis as a studio saxophonist and pianist. He teamed up with David Porter in 1964 and subsequently penned such successful songs as *Hold On I'm Coming, Soul Man,* and *B-A-B-Y.* After recording his hits *Walk On By* (1969), *By the Time I Get to Phoenix* (1969), and *Never Can Say Goodbye* (1971), he made waves with his music for the film *Shaft* (1972), which garnered him an Academy Award, a Golden Globe, and 2 Grammy Awards; he also won a Grammy for his album *Black Moses* (1972).

head. 1. Point (of bow). 2. In the violin family, the part comprising peg-box and scroll. 3. In the drum, the membrane stretched over 1 or both ends. 4. In notation, the oval (or square) part of a note which determines its place on the staff. *Go to the head*, DA CAPO.

head tone. Note of the vocal upper register. *Head voice*, vocal production of notes in the upper register, giving the illusion of being generated from the top of the head.

health. See MIND AND HEALTH.

hearing

~~~ ~~~ ~~~ ~~~ ~~~

The ancients believed that the exterior ear was the organ of hearing that gathered in the sounds, focusing and amplifying them like a seashell, which it resembles. Expressions such as "perking up one's ear" reflect this belief. Centuries passed before scientists looked inquisitively into the *middle ear* behind the eardrum and discovered there a remarkable recording instrument. A sound wave produces a displacement in the eardrum of less than the diameter of a single hydrogen molecule, but so sensitive is the eardrum that even this submicroscopic distention suffices to produce a distinct sensation of a definite tone.

The transmission mechanism of the middle ear consists of 3 interconnected ossicles (bony structures) that were described by the early anatomists as *hammer, anvil,* and *stirrup* because of their resemblance to those familiar objects. Their miniaturization is astounding; the stirrup is smaller than a grain of rice. The receptive organ for sound waves so transmitted is a snail-like spiral, the *cochlea,* in the inner ear. It was the Italian 19th-century physiologist Alfonso Corti who discovered the transmitting point of sound waves in the follicles attached to the bony ridges inside the spiral of the cochlea, the *organ of Corti.* These tiny appendages are the strings of a microscopic harp that vibrate by resonance with the incoming air waves. The Nobel Prize-winning scientist Georg von Békésy of Budapest found by ingenious experimentation that the organ of Corti converts the sound impulse into electricity which stimulates the auditory nerve. It is at this point that science established the connection between the physical electro-chemical phenomena and the physiological sensation of hearing, generated in the cortex of the brain.

The human ear can discern and discriminate nearly half a million sounds, different as to pitch, tone color, degree of loudness, and the myriad combinations of individual sounds forming additional complexes. It can instantly recognize, analyze, and identify them accurately as the voice of a friend, the meow of a cat, the trill of a bird, or the sound of a trumpet—a feat of classification that even the most modern computers cannot match. The frequencies of vibrations that the human ear can perceive as sounds range from 16 to about 20,000 cycles per second. At levels below this range the tone disintegrates into its component beats.

In his short story *The Modern Accelerator*, H. G. Wells creates the tale of an inventor who distilled a potion that accelerated his vital functions a thousandfold, so that he experienced the consecutive sensation lasting a quarter of an hour for every second of world time. He goes to a concert and watches a cellist play, but hears only heavy beats because the cello tone splits into its components. The summation of such rhythmic beats forms a low tone of about 16 cycles per second. Such a low tone can be heard even without Wells's accelerator. It can be noticed when riding in an old-fashioned streetcar or another electric vehicle on rails. At 1st one hears discrete beats; as the speed increases, they integrate into a distinct tone. Most animals have a sound range similar to humans, but dogs can hear ultrasonic frequencies; the police summon their hounds with a humanly inaudible dog whistle. Still higher ultrasonics are perceived by bats, which emit sounds of very high frequencies and consequently very short wavelengths to detect and catch small flying objects such as insects by bouncing echoes off them.

hebetude and lubricity. A recipe for a musical work providing sensory and intellectual gratification is a judicious mixture of dissonant hebetude and euphonious lubricity. As a product of intellectual elucubration, hebetudinous abstruseness results from indiscriminate use of dodecaphonic, hendecaphonic, pandiatonic or polymodal combinatorialities. Modernistic lubricity, on the other hand, flows from an incontinent evacuation of artificially flavored euphonious fluids sublimated in a feculent plasma. Hebetudinous excogitations by hesychastically minded introverts occasionally reveal serendipitous technicalities of interest, as demonstrated by tonal inventions in *Die Maschine* by Fritz Klein, while lubriciously scabrous effluvia of an abecedarian composer are usually productive of homogeneous sonic matter of glutinous consistency, fetid, infertile, and degenerative.

Hebrides, The. See FINGAL'S CAVE.

heckelphone. A double-reed instrument with a wider conical bore and lower range (A-g²) then the related oboe; it was invented by Wilhelm Heckel (1856–1909) in 1904. It is somewhat misleadingly called the baritone oboe. It is used in some modern scores and gives out a rich, somewhat hollow sound. Strauss used it in *Salome*; Hindemith wrote a sonata for it.

heftig (Ger.). Vehement, impetuous, passionate, tempestuous.

Heifetz, Jascha, celebrated Russian-born American violinist; b. Vilnius, Feb. 2, 1901; d. Los Angeles, Dec. 10, 1987. His father, Ruben Heifetz, an able musician, taught him the rudiments of violin playing at a very early age; he then studied with Ilya Malkin at the Vilnius Music School, and played in public before he was 5 years old; at the age of 6 he played Mendelssohn's Concerto in Kovno. In 1910 he was taken by his father to St. Petersburg, and entered the cons. there in the class of Nalbandian; after a few months he was accepted as a pupil by Leopold Auer.

He gave his 1st public concert in St. Petersburg on Apr. 30, 1911. The following year, with a letter of recommendation from Auer, he went to Berlin; his 1st concert there (1912), in the large hall of the Hochschule für Musik, attracted great attention: Artur Nikisch engaged him to play the Tchaikovsky Concerto with the Berlin Phil. (1912), and Heifetz obtained sensational success as a child prodigy of extraordinary gifts. He then played in Austria and Scandinavia. After the Russian Revolution of 1917, he went to America, by way of Siberia and the Orient. His debut at Carnegie Hall in N.Y. (1917) won for him the highest expression of enthusiasm from the public and in the press. Mischa Elman, a great violinist in his own right, and Leopold Godowsky, a piano virtuoso, attended Heifetz's American debut in 1917. "Hot here," remarked Elman, wiping his brow. "Not for pianists," observed Godowsky.

Veritable triumphs followed during Heifetz's tour of the U.S., and soon his fame spread all over the world. He made his 1st London appearance (1920); toured Australia (1921), the Orient (1923), Palestine (1926), and South America. He revisited Russia in 1934 and was welcomed enthusiastically. He became a naturalized American citizen in 1925, and made his home in Beverly Hills, Calif.; in subsequent years he continued to travel as a concert violinist, visiting virtually every country in the world, but from 1974 he ceased to appear in public as a soloist; he participated in a famous chamber series with Piatigorsky and others, and taught classes of exceptionally talented pupils at the Univ. of Southern Calif., Los Angeles (1962–72).

The quality of his playing was unique in luminous transparency of texture, tonal perfection, and formal equilibrium of phrasing; he never allowed his artistic temperament to superimpose extraneous elements on the music; this inspired tranquillity led some critics to characterize his interpretations as impersonal and detached. Heifetz made numerous arrangements for violin of works by Bach, Vivaldi, and contemporary composers; his most famous transcription is *Hora Staccato* by Grigoras Dinicu, made into a virtuoso piece by adroit ornamentation and rhythmic elaboration. In his desire to promote modern music, he commissioned a number of composers (Walton, Gruenberg, Castelnuovo-Tedesco, and others) to write violin concertos for him, and he performed several of them. When Herbert R. Axelrod authored an "unauthorized pictorial biography" of Heifetz, the violinist filed a lawsuit for $7.5 million against the publisher and compiler, claiming invasion of privacy. Upon sober reflection, the suit was withdrawn.

Heimkehr aus der Fremde, Die (The Return from Abroad). Opera by Mendelssohn, 1829, 1st performed privately; publicly and posthumously in London as *Son and Stranger*, 1851.

Heimlich (Ger., secretly). Mysteriously; misterioso; furtively, stealthily.

Heinrich, Anthony Philip (Anton Philipp), American violinist and composer of German-Bohemian birth; b. Schönbüchel, Mar. 11, 1781; d. N.Y., May 3, 1861. As a boy he acquired proficiency on the piano and violin, but began adult life as a wholesale merchant and banker; in 1810 he emigrated to America, settling in Philadelphia as a merchant and as unpaid music director of the Southwark Theatre. After business reverses in 1817 he moved to the wilds of Ky., 1st to Bardstown and then to nearby Lexington, where he managed to find enough musicians to conduct a performance of a Beethoven sym. Without any knowledge of harmony, he began to compose in 1818; these 1st songs and choral and instrumental pieces he publ. later as op. 1, *The Dawning of Music in Kentucky, or The Pleasures of Harmony in the Solitudes of Nature*, and op. 2, *The Western Minstrel* (both 1820).

He became music director at the Southwark Theatre in Philadelphia; later, in Louisville, Ky. The year 1827 found him in London, playing violin in a small orch.; there he also studied theory, and about 1830 began to write for orch.; returned to the U.S. in 1832. In 1834 he again visited England, as well as Germany and Austria (1835), and had some of his works produced at Dresden, Prague, Budapest, and Graz (his sym. *The Combat of the Condor* was perf. at Graz in 1836; also in France); in Vienna he entered a competition with a sym., but the prize was awarded to Franz Lachner; disappointed, he returned to America and settled in N.Y., where he soon gained immense popularity, becoming known as "Father Heinrich." He was a commanding figure in the musical affairs of the U.S., publishing many of his piano pieces and songs; grand festivals of his works were arranged in N.Y., Philadelphia, and Boston; critics spoke of him as the "Beethoven of America." But a tour of Germany in 1857–58 was a dismal failure; he died in extreme poverty.

The quality of his works is dubious at best; he wrote for an enormous orch., à la Berlioz, and his musical ideas, out of all proportion to the means employed, recall the style of Haydn's imitators; nevertheless, he is historically important as the 1st to employ Native American themes in works of large dimensions and to show decided nationalist aspirations.

In 1917 the Library of Congress acquired Heinrich's memoranda (letters, programs, newspaper clippings, etc.), many publ. works, and almost all the orch. scores, enumerated in a list made by Heinrich himself in 1857. A perusal of the titles is amusing and instructive: *Grand American Chivalrous Sym.*; *The Columbiad, or Migration of American Wild Passenger Pigeons* (1857–58); *The Ornithological Combat of Kings, or The Condor of the Andes and the Eagle of the Cordilleras* (1847); *Pocahontas, the Royal Indian Maid and the Heroine of Virginia, the Pride of the Wilderness* (1837); *The Wild-wood Spirit's Chant or Scintillations of "Yankee Doodle," forming a Grand National Heroic Fantasia scored for a Powerful Orch. in 44 Parts (c. 1842); Manitou Mysteries, or The Voice of the Great Spirit (before 1845); Gran Sinfonia Misteriosa-Indiana* (perf., N.Y., 1975).

heirmos (*hirmos*; Grk., link). A hymnal melody of the Byzantine Church generated in the 7th century; after the introduction of Christianity into old Russia, adapted also in the Russian Orthodox Church. The heirmos usually served as a connection between a Biblical hymn derived from the old Russian and a Christian hymn dedicated to a special saint, and the melody provided a model for such hymns. A collection of such hymns was called a *heirmologion*.

heiter (Ger.). Serene; cheerful; glad; (It.) *gioioso*; merrily, joyfully.

Heldenbariton (Ger.). Heroic baritone, requiring a powerful voice and stamina for difficult operatic parts, particularly Wagner's music dramas.

Heldenleben, Ein (A Hero's Life). Symphonic poem by R. Strauss, 1899, 1st performed in Frankfurt. Upon examination it seems clear that the hero is Strauss himself, for he quotes themes from his earlier tone poems. His critics are depicted by disjointed jabbering of high woodwinds, while the hero reserves for himself an imperturbable violin solo in the noble key of E-flat major.

Heldentenor (Ger.). Heroic tenor, requiring a robust voice and stamina for difficult operatic parts, particularly in Wagner's music dramas.

helicon (Grk., helix, coil). A valved brass instrument, invented in the mid-19th century and used chiefly in military music as a bass; its tube is bent in a circle and it is carried over the shoulder. It is similar in shape to the SOUSAPHONE.

hell (Ger.). Clear, bright.

Hello, Broadway! Revue by G. M. Cohan, with 3 eds. (1914, 1916, 1918). Songs by I. Berlin and others were included; Cohan's title song was the biggest hit.

Hello, Dolly! Musical by J. Herman, 1964, based on Thornton Wilder's *The Matchmaker*. In 1890s New York, Dolly is a widow turned marriage broker. An especially eligible and well-to-do customer comes along and she man-

ages to corral him for herself. The title song was extremely popular; Louis Armstrong had one of his last hits with it, and the 1964 Johnson presidential campaign made it his campaign song as *Hello, Lyndon!* Herman had to endure a plagiarism lawsuit from copyright owners of a forgotten but similar song, *Sunflower* (1948); while the borrowing was undoubtedly unconscious, Herman preferred to settle out of court.

Hellzapoppin'. Revue by Sammy Fain, 1938, on topical subjects.

Helmholtz, Hermann (Ludwig Ferdinand) **von,** celebrated German scientist and acoustician; b. Potsdam, Aug. 31, 1821; d. Berlin, Sept. 8, 1894. He studied medicine at the Friedrich Wilhelm Medical Inst. in Berlin (M.D., 1843); also learned to play the piano. He was an assistant at Berlin's Anatomical Museum, prof. extraordinary at the Academy of Fine Arts (1848–49), assistant prof. and director of Königsberg's Physiological Inst. (1849–55), and prof. of anatomy and physiology at the Univ. of Bonn (1855–58) and the Univ. of Heidelberg (1858–71). He became prof. of physics at the Univ. of Berlin in 1871, and from 1888 served as the 1st director of the Physico-Technical Inst. in Berlin. He was ennobled in 1882.

His most important work for those interested in music was his *Lehre von den Tonempfindungen als physiologische Grundlage für die Theorie der Musik* (Braunschweig, 1863; Eng. trans. by A. Ellis as *On the Sensations of Tone as a Physiological Basis for the Theory of Music*, London, 1875), in which he established a sure physical foundation for the phenomena manifested by musical tones, either single or combined. He supplemented and amplified the theories of Rameau, Tartini, Wheatstone, Corti, and others, furnishing impregnable formulae for all classes of consonant and dissonant tone effects, and proving with scientific precision what Hauptmann and his school sought to establish by laborious dialectic processes. His labors resulted primarily in instituting the laws governing the differences in quality of tone (tone color) in different instruments and voices, covering the whole field of harmonic, differential, and summational tones, and those governing the nature and limits of music perception by the human ear. His influence continued into the 20th century, especially on intonational experimentalists like Partch.

Help, Help, the Globolinks! Satirical opera by Menotti, 1968, to his own libretto; its 1st performance took place in Hamburg. The Globolinks are electronic invaders from outer space bent on converting unwary humans into their own kind. But they are vulnerable to the beautiful sounds of traditional music, and are finally routed by school children led by the exquisite Mme. Euterpova (Euterpe was the Greek musical Muse). The hermaphroditic literature teacher Mr. Lavender-Gas escapes, but the school dean, the unmusical Dr. Stone, becomes a Globolink. The score includes passages of mock-electronic music.

hemidemisemiquaver. A 64th note. *Hemidemisemiquaver rest*, 64th rest.

hemiola (from Grk. *hēmiolios*, the whole and the half; Lat., *sesquialtera*). 1. In mensural notation of the Middle Ages, the use of 3 notes of equal duration in a measure alternating with 2 notes of equal duration, in the same measure length, so that the longer notes equal 1 1/2 shorter ones. In modern notation, the hemiola is represented by a succession of bars in 6/8 and 3/4. Brahms used this device often. 2. The same alternation used in a two-measure form as a precadential rhythmic figure; very common in the Baroque.

Hen, The (Haydn's Symphony No. 83). In the key of G minor (1785); the gallinaceous title is explained by an imagined imitation of a hen's cluck in the 2nd subject of the 1st movement, but it is much less overt than Rameau's outspoken hen in one of his harpsichord pieces. The commonly used French title (*La Poule*) is explained by the fact that this is the 2nd of Haydn's Paris syms.

hendecaphonic serialism. With the gradual relaxation of dodecaphonic strictures in the orthodox Schoenbergian doctrine, serial composers have begun to resort to a lipogrammatic device of omitting a member of a 12-tone subject, reducing the series to a hendecaphonic form, containing only 11 tones. The missing tone, conspicuous by its absence, may be introduced in the coda with a panache suggesting the apparition of an actual tonic.

Henderson, (James) **Fletcher, "Smack,"** African-American jazz pianist, bandleader, and arranger; b. Cuthbert, Ga., Dec. 18, 1897; d. N.Y., Dec. 28, 1952. He studied piano as a child and chemistry as a youth; received a degree in chemistry from Atlanta Univ. College. In 1920 he went to N.Y., where he formed the Fletcher Henderson Band, which rapidly advanced into the front ranks of jazzdom; a number of famous jazz figures played in it, including Russell Procope, Coleman Hawkins, John Kirby, Rex Stewart, J. C. Higginbotham, Lester Young, and Louis Armstrong; the principal arranger was Don Redman. After Redman left in 1927, Henderson became the principal arranger, with some additional arrangements by Benny Carter and others. He was unable to maintain his own band, and by 1939 was working as an arranger for Benny Goodman; from 1941 he led bands and continued to write arrangements. A stroke in 1950 ended his professional career. Although Henderson never attained the popularity of his peers, his arrangements and gifted guidance of so many important jazz musicians made his indirect influence extremely significant.

Henderson (born Brost), **Ray(mond),** American composer of popular songs; b. Buffalo, Dec. 1, 1896; d. Greenwich, Conn., Dec. 31, 1970. He studied music at the Univ. of Southern Calif.; played organ in churches and piano in jazz groups in Buffalo; then went to N.Y. as a song plugger in Tin Pan Alley and soon began writing songs of his own. His 1st success was *Georgette* (1922); this was followed by *Sonny Boy*, which he wrote for Al Jolson's early talkie *The Singing Fool*; subsequent hits were *You're the Cream in My Coffee*, *Button Up Your Overcoat*, *Alabamy Bound*, *Hold Everything*, and *3 Cheers*; some of these songs were written in collaboration with B. G. DeSylva. Unlike most Broadway composers, Henderson could read and write music; he even took private lessons with Britten. His film biography, *The Best Things in Life Are Free*, was made in 1966.

Hendricks, Barbara, greatly admired African-American soprano; b. Stephens, Ark., Nov. 20, 1948. She sang in church and school choirs before majoring in chemistry and mathematics at the Univ. of Nebr. (graduated, 1969); during the summer of 1968 she began vocal training with Jennie Tourel at the Aspen (Colo.) Music School, continuing under her guidance at the Juilliard School in N.Y. (1969–71); she also attended Maria Callas's master class there. In 1971 she won the Geneva International Competition, and in 1972 both the International Concours de Paris and the Kosciuszko Foundation Vocal Competition.

In 1973 she made her debut in Virgil Thomson's *4 Saints in 3 Acts* in the Mini-Metropolitan Opera production presented at the Lincoln Center Forum Theatre in N.Y.; later that year she made her 1st concert tour of Europe. In 1974 she appeared as Erisbe in Cavalli's *Ormindo* at the San Francisco Spring Opera, and in the title role of Cavalli's *La Calisto* at the Glyndebourne Festival. In 1975 she made her formal N.Y. debut as Inez in a concert performance of *La Favorite* at Carnegie Hall. In 1976 she sang Amor in Gluck's

Orfeo ed Euridice with the Netherlands Opera at the Holland Festival; later that year she made her N.Y. recital debut at Town Hall. At the Berlin Deutsche Oper in 1978 she appeared as Mozart's Susanna, a role she quickly made her own. In 1980 she sang Gilda and in 1981 Pamina at the Orange Festival in France; in 1982 she appeared as Gounod's Juliet at both the Paris Opéra and London's Covent Garden. In 1986 she made her Metropolitan Opera debut in N.Y. as Strauss's Sophie. In 1988 she sang at the 70th-birthday celebration for Leonard Bernstein at the Tanglewood Festival, and also starred as Mimi in Luigi Comencini's film version of *La Bohème*. In 1989 she appeared at the Bolshoi Theater in Moscow.

In addition to her operatic career, she has won notable distinction as a recitalist. Her interpretations of the German and French song repertoire, as well as of Negro spirituals, have won accolades. In 1986 she was made a Commandeur des Arts et des Lettres of France. Her unswerving commitment to social justice led the High Commissioner for Refugees at the United Nations to name her a goodwill ambassador of the world body in 1987.

Hendrix, Jimi (James Marshall), African-American rock guitarist, singer, and songwriter; b. Seattle, Nov. 27, 1942; d. as a result of asphyxiation while unconscious after taking an overdose of barbiturates in London, Sept. 18, 1970. Being left-handed, he taught himself to play the guitar upside down; played in a high school band before dropping out of school during his senior year to join the U.S. Army paratroopers. Following his discharge (1961) he worked with groups in Nashville, Vancouver, and Los Angeles. In 1964 he went to N.Y., where he joined the Isley Brothers and found a ready response for his wild attire and erotic body locomotions; after working with Curtis Knight's group (1964–65), he formed his own outfit, Jimmy James and the Blue Flames. He then went to England, where he organized the Jimi Hendrix Experience (1966) with bass guitarist Noel Redding and drummer Mitch Mitchell.

The live Hendrix experience was replete with the most provocative stage manner, which he frequently culminated by setting his guitar on fire. After recording his 1st album, *Are You Experienced?* (1967), he made his immensely successful debut in the U.S. with his group at the Monterey (Calif.) Pop Festival that same year. He then recorded the albums *Axis: Bold as Love* (1968) and *Electric Ladyland* (1968), followed by a knockout appearance at the Woodstock Festival (1969). The last album released during his lifetime was the live *Band of Gypsies*, with Buddy Miles and Billy Cox (1970). Several albums, beginning with *The Cry of Love* (1971), were released posthumously.

Hendrix played comfortably in many styles (soul, rock, blues), and he was beginning to assimilate jazz when he died. He always used his virtuoso technique in the service of musical expression and was the most important figure in the development of the use of feedback in rock. What may ultimately be his most important contribution is the unbridled melodic quality of his playing, no matter what context it was in. The Jimi Hendrix Experience was inducted into the Rock and Roll Hall of fame in 1992.

Hensel, Fanny (Cäcilie) (Mendelssohn-Bartholdy), German pianist and composer, sister of (Jacob Ludwig) Felix Mendelssohn (-Bartholdy); b. Hamburg, Nov. 14, 1805; d. Berlin, May 14, 1847. She began her musical training with her mother, then studied piano with Berger and composition with Zelter; subsequently studied with Marie Bigot in Paris (1816). She later attended Humboldt's lectures on physical geography and Holtei's lectures on experimental physics in Berlin (1825), but music remained her great love. She married the painter W. Hensel on Oct. 3, 1829. From 1843 she oversaw the Sunday morning concerts at Berlin's Elternhaus. Her untimely death was a great shock to Mendelssohn, who died a few months afterward.

She was a talented composer; 6 of her songs were publ. under her brother's name in his opp. 8 and 9 (*Heimweh, Italien, Suleika und Hatem, Sehnsucht, Verlust,* and *Die Nonne*); other works publ. under her own name, some posth.: 4 books of songs, a collection of part-songs entitled *Gärtenlieder* (1829), and an oratorio on biblical themes (1831); String Quartet in E-flat Major (1834), Piano Quartet in A-flat Major (1822), and Piano Trio in D Minor, op. 11; *Das Jahr* (1841) and *Lieder ohne Worte* for Piano.

Henze, Hans Werner, outstanding German composer of the modern school; b. Gütersloh, Westphalia, July 1, 1926. His early studies at the Braunschweig School of Music (1942–44) were interrupted by military service, and for a year he was in the German army on the Russian front. In 1946 he took music courses at the Kirchenmusikalisches Inst. in Heidelberg; at the same time he studied privately with Wolfgang Fortner. He became fascinated with the disciplinary aspects of Schoenberg's method of composition with 12 tones and attended seminars on the subject given by Leibowitz at Darmstadt.

A musician of restless temperament, he joined a radical political group and proclaimed the necessity of writing music without stylistic restrictions in order to serve the masses. In search of natural musical resources, he moved to Italy; lived in Ischia from 1953 to 1956; then stayed in Naples and finally settled in Marino. He successfully integrated musical idioms and mannerisms of seemingly incompatible techniques; in his vocal works he freely adopted such humanoid effects as screaming, bellowing, and snorting; he even specified that long sustained tones were to be sung by inhaling as well as exhaling. Nonetheless, Henze manages to compose music that is feasible for human performance. But political considerations continued to play a decisive role in his career. In 1967 he withdrew from the membership of the Academy of the Arts of West Berlin, in a gesture of protest against its artistic policies. During his stay in Italy he joined the Italian Communist Party. His political stance did not preclude his acceptance in "bourgeois" musical centers, for his works were performed widely in Europe. He held the International Chair of Composition Studies at the Royal Academy of Music in London from 1986. In 1989 he helped found the Munich Biennale. He has written operas, ballets, and chamber works.

hep. An antiquated term for "good" or "cool," as in *hep cat*. Anyone who uses the term *hep* these days is absolutely not hep.

heptachord. A medieval term for an octave containing 7 diatonic scale degrees. *Heptatonic*, containing 7 scale degrees.

Herbert, Victor (August)

Famous Irish-born American composer; b. Dublin, Feb. 1, 1859; d. N.Y., May 26, 1924. He was a grandson of Samuel Lover, the Irish novelist; his father died when he was an infant; his mother married a German physician and settled in Stuttgart (1867), taking the boy with her. He entered the Stuttgart high school but did not graduate; his musical ability was definitely pronounced by then, and he selected the cello as his instrument, taking lessons from Bernhard Cossmann in Baden-Baden. He soon acquired a degree of technical proficiency that enabled him to take a position as cellist in various orchs. in Germany, France, Italy, and Switzerland; in 1880 he became a cellist of the Eduard Strauss waltz band in Vienna; in 1881 he returned to Stuttgart, where he joined the court orch., and studied composition with Max Seifritz at the Cons.

His earliest works were for cello with orch.; he performed his Suite with the Stuttgart orch. in 1883, and his 1st Cello Concerto 2 years later. In 1886 he married the Viennese opera singer Therese Forster (1861–1927); in the same year she received an offer to join the Metropolitan Opera in N.Y., and Herbert was engaged as an orch. cellist there, appearing in N.Y. also as a soloist (played his own Cello Concerto with the N.Y. Phil., 1887).

In his early years in N.Y., Herbert was overshadowed by the celebrity of his wife, but he soon developed energetic activities on his own, forming an entertainment orch. which he conducted in a repertoire of light music; he also participated in chamber music concerts; was a soloist with the Theodore Thomas and Seidl orchs. He was the conductor of the Boston Festival Orch. in 1891; Tchaikovsky conducted this orch. in Philadelphia in a miscellaneous program, and Herbert played a solo. He was associate conductor of the Worcester Festival (1889–91), for which he wrote a dramatic cantata, *The Captive* (1891). In 1893 he became bandmaster of the famous 22nd Regiment Band, succeeding Patrick S. Gilmore. In 1894 he was soloist with the N.Y. Phil. in his 2nd Cello Concerto. In the same year, at the suggestion of William MacDonald, the manager of the Boston Ideal Opera Co., Herbert wrote a light opera, *Prince Ananias*, which was produced with encouraging success in N.Y. (1894). From 1898 to 1904 Herbert was conductor of the Pittsburgh Sym. Orch., presenting some of his own compositions. In 1900 he directed at Madison Square Garden, N.Y., an orch. of 420 performers for the benefit of the sufferers in the Galveston flood. On Apr. 29, 1906, he led a similar monster concert at the Hippodrome for the victims of the San Francisco earthquake. In 1904 he organized the Victor Herbert N.Y. Orch., and gave concerts in N.Y. and neighboring communities.

It is as a composer of light operas that Herbert became chiefly known. In the best of these he unites spontaneous melody, sparkling rhythm, and simple but tasteful harmony; his experience as a symphonic composer and conductor imparted a solidity of texture to his writing that placed him far above the many gifted amateurs in this field. Furthermore, he possessed a natural communicative power in his music, which made his operettas spectacularly successful with the public. Among the more than 40 that he composed, the most successful were *The Serenade* (1897); *The Fortune Teller* (1898); *Cyrano de Bergerac* (1899); *The Singing Girl* (1899); *Babes in Toyland* (1903); *It Happened in Nordland* (1904); *Mlle. Modiste* (1905); *The Red Mill* (1906); *Little Nemo* (1908); *Naughty Marietta* (1910); *Sweethearts* (1913); and *Orange Blossoms* (1922). In the domain of grand opera he was not so fortunate. When the production of his 1st grand opera, *Natoma*, took place in Philadelphia on Feb. 25, 1911, it aroused great expectations; but the opera failed to sustain lasting interest. Still less effective was his 2nd opera, *Madeleine*, staged by the Metropolitan Opera in N.Y. on Jan. 24, 1914. Herbert was one of the founders of ASCAP in 1914, and was vice president from that date until his death. In 1916 he wrote a special score for the motion picture *The Fall of a Nation*, in synchronization with the screenplay.

Herdenglocke (Ger.). Shepherd's bell; an Alpine bell hung over a sheep's neck to help locate the herd. Mozart and Mahler included it in some scores (without the sheep).

heredity. That musical talent is hereditary is unquestionably a fact of statistical analysis. Bach's genealogical tree presents an astonishing proof of the persistence of specific musical endowments. The gift for music usually manifests itself in early infancy. Musicianship can be perfected by solicitous instruction and encouragement, but it cannot be formed without the genetic complex that underlies it. A scientific study of musical heredity is complicated by the impossibility of experimentation, such as breeding musician with musician and observing the results within a generation. Gregor Mendel experimented with peas before he could formulate his laws of heredity; a music historian can only compile statistics and establish a degree of probability in musical genetics. Yet it is entirely possible to formulate a plausible system of musical genetics with its recessive characteristics, mutations, etc., along Mendelian lines.

It takes several generations of competent but undistinguished musicians to arrive, perhaps by random selection, at a summit of genius. Alessandro Scarlatti provided the musical atmosphere for his son Domenico to develop in. Leopold Mozart was a fine and intelligent musician who gave his genius son the benefits of his musical knowledge. Wolfgang Amadeus Mozart himself had sons who became musicians, but their works survive only as curiosities. Beethoven's greatness was an unpredictable mutation, although his father was a court musician at Bonn. Wagner had no ancestors who were musicians, either on the line of his legal parents or of his stepfather, who, according to some Wagnerites, was Wagner's seminal father. Siegfried Wagner, "the little son of a great father," wrote a number of operas that were so many diluted Nibelungs, Lohengrins, and Parsifals.

In modern times, musical heredity often follows the zeitgeist in progressive idioms and techniques of composition. An interesting example of Mendelian natural selection is the family of Tcherepnin. Nicolas Tcherepnin was a nationalist Russian composer of the Rimsky-Korsakov school. His son Alexander developed his own modern technique of composition. Alexander's 2 sons Ivan and Serge plunged headlong into experimental and electronic music composition. Similar progressive trends are sometimes found among performing musicians. Rudolph Serkin is a famed performer of Classic and Romantic piano music; his son Peter turned decisively towards ultramodern works.

In the musical theater the inheritance of talent is even more striking. Sons and daughters of famous performers, particularly singers, often start their careers as children in the theater acts of their parents, learning their skills through imitation. George Bernard Shaw was a firm believer in the inheritance not only of musical talent but even of a technical facility in performance. He asserted in the preface to his play *Back to Methuselah* that "a pianist may be born with specific pianistic aptitude which he can bring out as soon as he can physically control his hands."

Herman, Jerry (Gerald), American composer and lyricist of popular music; b. N.Y., July 10, 1933. He played piano by ear; it was only after becoming a professional musician that he took up the study of theory and harmony; he also studied drama at the Univ. of Miami. He worked as a pianist in nightclubs and wrote for television in N.Y.; composed the revues *I Feel Wonderful* (1954), *Nightcap* (1958), and *Parade* (1960); then won a Tony Award for his Broadway show *Milk and Honey* (1961). After the failure of *Madame Aphrodite* (1961), he came roaring back with the smash hit *Hello, Dolly!* (N.Y., 1964), which garnered 10 Tony Awards. It was followed by another highly successful score, *Mame* (N.Y., 1966), which also won a Tony. Following the relative nonsuccess of *Dear World* (1969), *Mack & Mabel* (1974), and *The Grand Tour* (1979), he again won a Tony with the wonderfully eccentric *La Cage aux folles* (1983).

Herman, Woody (Woodrow Charles), noted American clarinetist, saxophonist, and bandleader; b. Milwaukee, May 16, 1913; d. Los Angeles, Oct. 29, 1987. He studied at Marquette Univ. In 1931 he joined a jazz band as a clarinet player, and in 1937 formed his 1st band; had several thereafter, most called "Herds." In the mid-1940s Herman's was the 1st prominent big band to make the transition from swing to a more advanced, bebop-influenced idiom characterized by "progressive" harmonies; it became known as progressive jazz. In 1946 he presented in Carnegie Hall in N.Y. the 1st performance of Stravinsky's *Ebony Concerto*, written specially for him. He also composed popular songs; the instrumental *The Woodchopper's Ball* was his signature tune.

Hérodiade. Opera by Massenet, 1881, after the Bible, 1st produced in Brussels. The "daughter of Herodias" is Salome, for whom her stepfather Herod, King of Galilee, nurtures an incestuous passion. She rejects him and declares love for the imprisoned John the Baptist. Here the story diverges from Oscar Wilde's *Salome* that served as the libretto for R. Strauss's opera. Here, Salome wants to die with her adored holy man; but he is executed alone; so she stabs herself to death. The opera has several melodious arias.

Hérold, (Louis-Joseph) **Louis,** celebrated French composer; b. Paris, Jan. 28, 1791; d. Thernes, near Paris, Jan. 19, 1833. His father, François-Joseph Hérold (b. Seltz, Bas-Rhin, Mar. 18, 1755; d. Paris, Oct. 1, 1802; pupil of C. P. E. Bach), a piano teacher and composer, did not desire his son to become a musician, and sent him to the Hix School, where his aptitude for music was noticed by Fétis, then assistant teacher there.

After his father's death Hérold began to study music seriously; in 1806 he entered the Paris Cons., taking piano lessons with Louis Adam and winning 1st prize for piano

playing in 1810. He studied harmony under Catel, and (from 1811) composition under Méhul; in 1812 his cantata *Mlle. de la Vallière* won the Prix de Rome. From Rome he went to Naples, where he became pianist to Queen Caroline; he produced his 1st opera, *La gioventu di Enrico Quinto* (1815), which was well received. From Naples he went to Vienna, and after a few months' stay he returned to Paris, where he finished the score of Boieldieu's *Charles de France*, an "opéra d'occasion" (1816), and where all the rest of his operas were produced. The flattering reception of *Charles de France* led to the successful production of *Les Rosières* (1817), *La Clochette* (1817), *Le Premier Venu* (1818), *Les Troqueurs* (1819), and *L'Auteur mort et vivant* (1820); the failure of the last-named opéra caused him to distrust his natural talent and to imitate, in several succeeding stage works, the style then in vogue—that of Rossini.

With the comic opera *Marie* (1826) Hérold returned, however, to his true element, and won instant and brilliant success. Meantime he had obtained the post of chorus master at the Italian Opera (1824); during this period he brought out *Le Muletier* (1823), *Lasthénie* (1823), *Vendôme en Espagne* (1823), *Le Roi René* (1824), and *Le Lapin blanc* (1825). In 1826 he was appointed to the staff of the Opéra, for which he wrote several melodious and elegant ballets, including *La Somnambule* (1827) and *La Fille mal gardée* (1828); *La Somnambule* furnished Bellini with the subject of his popular opera. *Emmeline*, a grand opera (1829), was a failure, but his next opera, *Zampa* (1831), was sensationally successful and placed him in the 1st rank of French composers. He then wrote *L'Auberge d'Aurey* (1830) jointly with Carafa; *La Marquise de Brinvilliers* (1831) in collaboration with Auber, Batton, Berton, Blangini, Boieldieu, Carafa, Cherubini, and Paer; also produced *La Médecine sans médecin* (1832). His last completed work, *Le Pré aux clercs* (1832), had a remarkable vogue.

He died of tuberculosis shortly before his 42nd birthday. His unfinished opera *Ludovic* was completed by Halévy and produced posthumously at the Opéra-Comique (1833). Hérold's piano music (55 opus numbers) consists of sonatas, caprices, rondos, divertissements, fantasies, variations, and potpourris.

Herrmann, Bernard, American conductor and outstanding composer for films; b. N.Y., June 29, 1911; d. Los Angeles, Dec. 24, 1975. He won a composition prize at the age of 13; then enrolled at N.Y. Univ., where he studied with Philip James and Percy Grainger; later took courses with Wagenaar in composition and Albert Stoessel in conducting at the Juilliard Graduate School of Music. In 1934 he was appointed to the staff of CBS as a composer of background music for radio programs and conductor of the CBS Sym. Orch. summer radio series; from 1942 to 1959 he was chief conductor of the CBS Sym. Orch. in boldly progressive programs of modern works, including those by Ives.

He became associated with Orson Welles and wrote several scores for the radio broadcasts of the Mercury Theater. His music for *Citizen Kane* (1940), the 1st of his 61 film scores, is still regarded as a classic of the genre. His use of an electric violin and electric bass in the score for *The Day the Earth Stood Still* (1951) is an example of early application of electronic technology in film music. He subsequently wrote film scores for the thrillers of Alfred Hitchcock, succeeding in capturing the eerie spirit of Hitchcock's peculiar art by the use of atonal devices; of these, the score for *Psycho* (1960), for strings only, was particularly apt.

Among Herrmann's other film scores were *The Devil and Daniel Webster* (1941; also known as *All That Money Can Buy*; received an Academy Award); *Jane Eyre* (1942); *Anna and the King of Siam* (1946); *The Ghost and Mrs. Muir* (1948); *Snows of Kilimanjaro* (1952); *Garden of Evil* (1954); *The Trouble with Harry* (1955); *The Man Who Knew Too Much* (1956); *The Wrong Man* (1957); *Vertigo* (1958); *North by Northwest* (1959); *The Man in the Gray Flannel Suit* (1956); *The 7th Voyage of Sinbad* (1958); *Journey to the Center of the Earth* (1959); *The Birds* (1963); *Fahrenheit 451* (1966); *La Mariée etait en noir* (The Bride Wore Black; 1967); *Sisters* (1973); and *Obsession* (1975).

Herrmann spent the last 10 years of his life in England, but he was in Los Angeles in 1975 to conduct the score for his last film, *Taxi Driver*; he died in his sleep shortly after completing the final recording session.

hervorgehoben (*hervortretend*; Ger., emphasized). Bring the indicated voice or part to the fore, in contrast to the other parts which function as accompaniment.

herzig (Ger.). Hearty, heartily; tenderly.

Heseltine, Philip (Arnold), brilliant English composer and writer who used the pen name Peter Warlock; b. London, Oct. 30, 1894; d. (suicide) there, Dec. 17, 1930. He studied at Eton with Colin Taylor (1908–10), in Germany, and at Oxford; a meeting with Delius in France in 1910 influenced him profoundly in the direction of composition; he adopted a style that was intimately connected with English traditions of the Elizabethan period and yet revealed impressionistic undertones in harmonic writing. Another influence was that of Bernard van Dieren, from whom he absorbed an austerely contrapuntal technique.

He publ. all his musical works under his pen name. He was a conscientious objector during World War I; in 1917–18 he was in Ireland; after the Armistice he returned to London; in 1920 he founded the progressive journal of musical opinion *The Sackbut*; wrote criticism; made transcriptions of early English music; participated in organizing the Delius Festival in 1929. Suffering from depression, he committed suicide by gas in his London flat. He ed. (with P. Wilson) 300 early songs (Elizabethan, Jacobean, and French ayres); was co-ed. of *Oxford Choral Songs* and the *Oxford Orchestral Series*, a collection of early English and Italian dances.

Hesitation Blues. One of the earliest and most popular country blues songs; it plays on verbal innuendo much as the two dances do musically.

hesitation tango. A tango with a sharper syncopation than the standard form. Samuel Barber included a hesitation tango in his set for piano 4-hands, *Souvenirs*.

hesitation waltz. A type of mildly-syncopated waltz, similar to the so called Boston waltz. Its popularity in Europe can be measured by the traffic signs posted in the 1920s in Paris cautioning the pedestrians, "Ne dansez pas la Valse d'hesitation devant les autos." A slow waltz with jazz-like inflections. It emerged as a popular dance in Europe after World War I, but it is practically unknown in America and least of all in Boston.

heterophony (from the Grk. *heteros* + *phōnia*, diversity of sound). A texture in which a melody is played on 2 or more instruments simultaneously, but with variations of various degrees of freedom; prominent in accompanied vocal music of the Near East and Asia, and in Asian court music.

Heure espagnole, L'. Opera by Ravel, 1911, 1st produced in Paris. The action takes place in Toledo, Spain, during the 18th century. The "Spanish hour" of the title is the period of time during which several successive lovers of the wife of a local clockmaker hide themselves in the cabinets of the large clocks in his shop. When he discovers them, they all claim to be bona fide customers, and the greedy clockmaker accepts the explanations, whereupon they all make merry to the sounds of a habanera. The score is one of the finest examples of Ravel's subtle instrumentation and precise rhythms, for the mastery of which he earned the critical sobriquet "the Swiss watchmaker."

Heures séculaires et instantanées (Secular and Instantaneous Hours). A piano cycle by Satie, 1914. Like many Satie piano works, the score is full of private commentary between composer and pianist; but this work includes a famous "warning": "I forbid the text to be read out loud during the performance of the music. Failure to conform with these instructions will cause the transgressor to incur my just indignation."

hexachord. 1. The 6 tones Ut, Re, Mi, Fa, Sol, La in solmization. 2. A set of 6 different pitch classes, usually the 1st (or last) 6 of a 12-note set.

hidden fifths, hidden octaves. Progressions of intervals leading toward an open 5th or octave, from the same direction, forbidden in strict harmony. These are similar to consecutive 5ths and octaves, except that the latter involve 5ths or octaves in the same contrapuntal voice.

Higginbotham, J(ay) C., African-American jazz trombonist; b. Social Circle, Ga., May 11, 1906; d. N.Y., May 26, 1973. He acquired mastery of the trombone in his youth; in 1928 moved to N.Y., where he played with Chick Webb, Fletcher Henderson, and Benny Carter; later worked with Louis Armstrong (1937–40) and Henry "Red" Allen (1940–47); subsequently led his own groups.

Higgins, Dick (Richard Carter), English-born American composer, performer, music publisher, and writer; b. Cambridge, Mar. 15, 1938. He was taken to America as a child; studied piano in Worcester, Mass., and composition with John Cage in N.Y. Eventually he moved to Calif; became active in the mushrooming AVANT-GARDE groups; participated in staging HAPPENINGS across the country; joined the ultramodern group Fluxus in 1961; organized the Something Else Press (1964–73) with the aim of publishing something else; founded Unpublished Editions (1972), which later became Printed Editions (1978). Not averse to academic activities, he taught at the Calif. Inst. of the Arts (1970–71); was a research associate in the visual arts dept. of the State Univ. of N.Y. in Purchase (from 1983).

In his productions he pursues the objective of total involvement, in which music is verbalized in conceptual designs without reification, or expressed in physical action;

the ultimate in this direction is achieved by his work *The Thousand Syms.* (1968), in which the composer shoots machine-gun bullets through MS paper; his *Sym. No. 585,* shot by a sergeant of the army at the composer's behest, was distributed in holographs in No. 6 of the avant-garde magazine *Source* (1969) under the subtitle *The Creative Use of Police Resources.*

high fidelity. An electronic technique of sound reproduction, developed by 1950, making use of highly sensitive devices to integrate the component sound sources, and reflected on the 1st 33 1/3–rpm phonograph record releases. A further improvement was directional stereophonic sound, with 2 separate channels, available commercially by the late '50s. Later developments such as 4-channel quadraphonic sound and "surround" sound did not achieve commercial acceptance.

high hat. In a drum set, a pair of cymbals placed horizontally and facing each other, attached to a floor stand. A foot pedal opens and closes the cymbals, producing a rustling vibration followed by a sharp choke; hence the alternate name *choke cymbals.*

High Mass. See MISSA SOLEMNIS.

highbrow. Outdated colloquialism for individuals professing an interest in subjects and culture of a purportedly profound nature. The term could be used both ways, either as self-definition or as mockery of those who engaged in ostensibly erudite dialogues, commenting glibly and ignorantly on abstruse theories. However, this last view suggests the almost inherent anti-intellectual streak so many Americans maintain.

High-Button Shoes. Musical by Styne, 1947. In 1913, 2 imaginative crooks from N.J. try every possible scam they can. Includes *Get Away for a Day in the Country* and the duet *Papa, Won't You Dance with Me?*

Hildegard von Bingen, remarkable German composer, poet, abbess, and mystic; b. Bemersheim, near Alzey, 1098; d. Rupertsberg, near Bingen, Sept. 17, 1179. Her noble parents, Hildebert and Mechtild, promised to consecrate her to the Church as she was their 10th child; accordingly, she began her novitiate as a child; joined with the reclusive mystic Jutta of Spanheim, who with her followers occupied a cell of the Benedictine monastery of

Disibodenberg. At 15 Hildegard took the veil; she succeeded Jutta as Mother Superior in 1136. Between 1147 and 1150 she founded a monastery on the Rupertsberg (near Bingen) with 18 sisters; around 1165 she founded another house at Eibingen (near Rudesheim). She is called "abbess" in letters drawn up by Frederick Barbarossa in 1163. She was known as the "Sybil of the Rhine," and conducted extensive correspondence with popes, emperors, kings, and archbishops. She was thus greatly involved in politics and diplomacy. Several fruitless attempts were made to canonize her, but her name is included in the Roman Martyrology, and her feast is celebrated on Sept. 17.

Hildegard is musically important through her monophonic chants, several of which were settings of her lyric and dramatic poetry. She collected her poems in the early 1150s under the title *Symphonia armonie celestium revelationum*. This vol. survives in 2 sources, both in early German neumes; it comprises 70-odd liturgical poems (the exact number varies, depending on classification), all with melismatic music. The poetry is rich with imagery, and it shares the apocalyptic language of her visionary writings. The music is not typical of plainchant, but involves a technique unique to Hildegard; it is made of a number of melodic patterns recurring in different modal positions, which operate as open structures allowing for internal variation in different contexts. She also wrote a morality play in dramatic verse, *Ordo virtutum*, which includes 82 melodies which are similarly structured but distinctly more syllabic in style. She pointed out that her music is written in a range congenial to women's voices, contrasting with the formal Gregorian modes. Hildegard was also known for her literary works, which include prophecy, medical and scientific treatises, and hagiographies, as well as letters.

Hill, Bertha "Chippie," African-American blues singer; b. Charleston, S.C., Mar. 15, 1905; d. (struck and killed by an automobile) N.Y., May 7, 1950. She was an offspring of a large family, which included 16 children. She made her way to N.Y., where she 1st appeared as a dancer in Harlem; then toured as a dancer and singer with Ma Rainey; subsequently made tours and recordings with Louis Armstrong and others. She was active in Chicago as a singer in nightclubs; in 1948 she appeared at Carnegie Hall in N.Y.

hillbilly. A once-common description for OLD-TIME, Appalachian folk song and dance music, as cultivated by rustic white musicians in the last century and the 1st 3rd of this one. The most common instruments were the fiddle, guitar, and banjo; double bass and accordion family instruments were also used. Sources include the minstrel show, ballads from the so-called Anglo-Irish tradition, and African-American folk music. The derogatory meanings of *hillbilly* led current practitioners and historians to drop the term, which was often applied to BLUEGRASS as well.

Hiller, Lejaren (Arthur, Jr.), American composer and theorist of computer music; b. N.Y., Feb. 23, 1924; d. Buffalo, N.Y., Jan. 26, 1994. He studied chemistry at Princeton Univ. (Ph.D., 1947) and music at the Univ. of Illinois (M.Mus., 1958); began his career as a chemist; was assistant prof. of chemistry at the Univ. of Illinois (1953–58), and subsequently taught music there, until 1968; then became Frederick B. Slee Prof. of Composition at the State Univ. of N.Y. at Buffalo, and also served as codirector of the Center of the Creative and Performing Arts; was made Birge-Cary Prof. of Music in 1980.

He publ. (with L. Isaacson) a manual, *Experimental Music* (N.Y., 1959), and numerous articles on the application of computers to musical composition. He composed 2 syms. (1953, 1960); Piano Concerto (1949); 7 string quartets (1949, 1951, 1953, 1957, 1962, 1972, 1979); 6 piano sonatas (1946–72), etc. He achieved notoriety with his computer composition *Illiac Suite* for string quartet (in collaboration with L. Isaacson; 1957), the name being an abbreviation of Illinois Accumulator; the result is a programmed, i.e., dictated, production which includes vast stretches of cadential C-major chords. Encouraged by publicity, Hiller wrote a *Computer Cantata* for Soprano, Magnetic Tape, and Chamber Ensemble (1963).

Other works are *Man with the Oboe* (1962); *Machine Music* for Piano, Percussion, and Tape (1964); *An Avalanche* for Pitchmen, Prima Donna, Player Piano, Percussion, and Prerecorded Playback (1968); *HPSCHD* for 1 to 7 harpsichords and 1 to 51 tapes (1968; in collaboration with J. Cage); *A Preview of Coming Attractions* for Orch. (1975); *Midnight Carnival* for a principal tape, an indeterminate number of subsidiary tapes, and other events in an urban environment (1976); *Fast and Slow* for Saxophone Quartet (1984); *The Fox Trots Again* for Chamber Ensemble (1985).

Hin und Zurück (Forth and Back). "A sketch with music" by Hindemith, 1927, 1st performed in the Baden-Baden Festival. The cuckolded husband kills his cheating wife; then the action reverses itself, cinema-wise; the adulteress returns to life, her husband empockets the gun, and the situation is restored to the status quo ante. However, the music is not a precise cancrizans.

hinaufziehen (Ger.). Sliding up; portamento. Mahler uses this expression mark in his 2nd Sym.

Hindemith, Paul

~~~ ~~~ ~~~ ~~~ ~~~

Significant German-born American composer, violist, conductor, pedagogue, and theorist, a leading master of the 20th century and originator of GEBRAUCHSMUSIK; b. Hanau, near Frankfurt am Main, Nov. 16, 1895; d. there, Dec. 28, 1963. He began studying violin at the age of 9; at 14 he entered the Hoch Cons. in Frankfurt, where he studied violin with A. Rebner and composition with Arnold Mendelssohn and Sekles. His father was killed in World War I (in which he also served); Hindemith was compelled to rely on his own resources to make a living. He became concertmaster of the orch. of the Frankfurt Opera (1915–23) and later played the viola in the string quartet of his teacher Rebner; from 1922 to 1929 he was violist in the Amar String Quartet; also appeared as a soloist on the viola and viola d'amore; later was engaged as a conductor, mainly in his own works.

As a composer he joined the MODERN MUSIC movement and was an active participant in the contemporary concerts at Donaueschingen and later in Baden-Baden. In 1927 he was appointed instructor in composition at the Berlin Hochschule für Musik. With the advent of the Hitler regime in 1933, Hindemith began to experience increasing difficulties, both artistically and politically. Although his own ethnic purity was never questioned, he was married to Gertrud Rottenberg, daughter of the Jewish conductor Ludwig Rottenberg, and he stubbornly refused to cease ensemble playing with undeniable Jews. Hitler's propaganda minister, Goebbels, accused Hindemith of cultural Bolshevism, and his music fell into an official desuetude.

Paul Hindemith

Unwilling to compromise with the barbarous regime, Hindemith accepted engagements abroad.

Beginning in 1934 he made 3 visits to Ankara at the invitation of the Turkish government; he helped to organize the music curriculum at the Ankara Cons. He made his 1st American appearance at the Coolidge Festival at the Library of Congress in Washington, D.C., in a performance of his *Unaccompanied Viola Sonata* (Apr. 10, 1937); after a brief sojourn in Switzerland, he emigrated to the U.S.; was instructor at the Berkshire Music Center at Tanglewood in the summer of 1940; from 1940 to 1953 he was a prof. at Yale Univ., where he led an important revivalist COLLEGIUM MUSICUM; he was elected a member of the National Inst. of Arts and Letters, and during the academic year 1950–51 he was Charles Eliot Norton Lecturer at Harvard Univ.

He became an American citizen in 1946. He conducted concerts in the Netherlands, Italy, and England during the summer of 1947; in 1949, revisited Germany for the 1st time since the war, and conducted the Berlin Phil. in a program of his own works (Feb. 14, 1949). In 1953 he went to Switzerland; gave courses at the Univ. of Zurich; also conducted orchs. in Germany and Austria. In 1954 he received the prestigious Sibelius Award of $35,000, offered annually to distinguished composers and scientists by a Finnish shipowner. From 1959 to 1961 he conducted guest appearances in the U.S.; in 1963 he visited America for the last time; then went to Italy, Vienna, and finally Frankfurt, where he died.

Hindemith's early music reflects rebellious opposition to all tradition; this is noted in such works as the opera *Mörder, Hoffnung der Frauen* (op. 12, 1921), and *Suite 1922* for Piano (op. 26); at the same time, he cultivated the techniques of constructivism, evident in his theatrical sketch *Hin und Zurück* (op. 45a, 1927), in which *Krebsgang* (retrograde movement) is applied to the action on the stage, so that events are reversed; in a work of a much later period, *Ludus Tonalis* (1943), the postlude is the upside-down version of the prelude. Along constructive lines is Hindemith's cultivation of so-called GEBRAUCHSMUSIK—that is, music for use; he was also an ardent champion of HAUSMUSIK, to be played or sung by amateurs at home; the score of his *Frau Musica* (as revised in 1944) has an obbligato part for the audience to sing. A neo-Classical trend is shown in a series of works, entitled *Kammermusik*, for various instrumental combinations, polyphonically conceived, and Baroque in style.

Although he made free use of atonal melodies, he was never tempted to adopt an integral 12-tone method, which he opposed on esthetic grounds. Having made a thorough study of early music, he artfully assimilated its polyphony in his works; his masterpiece of this genre was the opera *Mathis der Maler*. An exceptionally prolific composer, Hindemith wrote music of all types for all instrumental combinations, including a series of sonatas for each orch. instrument with piano.

His style may be described as a synthesis of modern, Romantic, Classical, Baroque, and other styles, a combination saved from the stigma of eclecticism only by Hindemith's superlative mastery of technical means. As a theorist and pedagogue he developed a self-consistent method of presentation derived from the acoustical nature of harmonies. Other important works include many operas, ballets, notably *Theme and Variations: The 4 Temperaments* for String Orch. and Piano (N.Y. Ballet, 1946) and *Hérodiade*, with recitation, after Mallarmé (produced as *Mirror before Me*, by the Martha Graham Dance Group, 1944), and orch.1 and chamber works. Hindemith also wrote numerous songs and choruses in German, English, and French; and many song cycles and choral works.

Hines, Earl (Kenneth) **"Fatha,"** remarkable African-American jazz pianist; b. Duquesne, Pa., Dec. 28, 1905; d. Oakland, Calif., Apr. 22, 1983. His father was a professional trumpet player and his mother played piano and organ. He took piano lessons as a child, but became interested mainly in jazz piano. He played with big bands as a young man, and in 1927 joined a quintet led by Louis Armstrong in Chicago. He began recording with Armstrong and under his influence evolved a special type of "trumpet piano style" characterized by sharp accents, octave tremolos in the treble, and insistently repeated melodic notes. In 1928 he organized his own big band in Chicago, and he toured with it in the U.S., including the Southern states; his was one of the 1st black big bands to play in the South; its theme song, *Deep Forest*, became popular. A radio announcer used to introduce him as "Fatha Hines coming through deep forest with his children," and the nickname "Fatha" stuck. After a hiatus of several years Hines reappeared on the jazz horizon as a solo pianist and made a hit wherever he appeared. In 1957 he toured Europe; played in Berlin in 1965 and in Russia in 1966; he also played in Japan. During his last years he made his residence in San Francisco, where he played his last engagement just a week before his death.

hinunterziehen (Ger.). Sliding down; PORTAMENTO on string instruments.

hip-hop. African-American popular dance music of the last 2 decades of the 20th century, which became the underlying musical basis for rap. While inheriting the strong beat of disco, hip-hop reemphasized the backbeat of 1960s popular music, and drew upon house music of the late 1970s. Initially, hip-hop was spartan in texture, especially when accompanying rap; as sampling technology evolved, producers and musicians began including small excerpts, electronically processed and often in repetitive loops, from earlier popular music.

While there have been legal challenges to this practice, most now see it less as plagiarism than as homage to earlier styles and composers, much as the PARODY Mass and motet in the late Renaissance; there is often a sense of irony in the choices. More recent hip-hop developments include reggae hip-hop and an ever more sophisticated and rich musical texture.

Hippodamia. Melodrama trilogy by Fibich, 1891, traversing the tragic saga of murder, cannibalism, and punishment in the mythological house of Tantalus. The 3 components are *Pelops's Courtship*, *The Atonement of Tantalus*, and *Hippodamia's Death*.

Hippolyte et Aricie. Lyric tragedy by Rameau, 1733, based on Racine's *Fèdre* and Euripides's *Hippolyte*. The plot resembles other operas involving Hippolyte, his absent father Theseus, and his amorous stepmother Phaedra; the new element is Alicia, beloved of Hippolyte, who gives a vow of chastity to Phaedra. Theseus returns, hears false rumors, and exiles Hippolyte; Phaedra confesses her guilt and dies; Hippolyte is reunited with Alicia, thus providing a happier ending than usual for this Greek tragedy.

Hirmos. Heirmos.

hirsute chromaticism. A judicious mixture of chromatic and diatonic modes in a serial work is entirely valid as a mode, an idiom, or a style. What cannot be tolerated in a modern composition of any pretensions to self-consistency is the hairy growth of chromatics upon a diatonic or pandiatonic melodic and harmonic surface, with membranous pellicles obscuring the melorhythmic lines without protecting them. When instances of such hirsute chromaticism occur inadvertently, a depilatory agent should be applied in order to restore the basic musical design. At the same time care should be taken not to fall into the extremes of unaesthetic alopecia.

Hirt, Al(ois Maxwell), popular American trumpeter; b. New Orleans, Nov. 7, 1922. He studied with Frank Simon at the Cincinnati Cons. of Music (1940–42); then served in the U.S. Army and played in the 82nd Army Air Force Band; after his discharge in 1946, he played with various bands; in 1956 he formed his own band, and began touring with it in 1960. His 1st major recording, in 1961, was the album *The Greatest Horn in the World*. A versatile musician, he came to espouse the "Nashville sound," being equally at ease in the country-western, jazz, and popular music genres.

Hirtenhorn (Ger.). Shepherd's horn. *Hirtenlied*, shepherd's song.

His (Ger.). B-sharp.

Histoire du soldat, L' (A Soldier's Story). Ballet with narrative by Stravinsky, 1918, 1st performed in Lausanne, Switzerland. The score is for 7 instruments only, and is a tour de force of economy. The story concerns a Russian soldier who sells his soul to the devil. Among the dance numbers are a tango, a waltz, and a ragtime; the use of familiar forms points to Stravinsky's later embracing of neoclassicism.

Histoires naturelles (Natural history). Song cycle by Ravel, 1907, depicting a set of mostly birds (peacock, cricket, swan, kingfisher, guinea hen).

Historische Symphonie. The 6th Sym. by Spohr, 1850. The 4 movements represent the idioms of Bach, Mozart, Beethoven, and himself, respectively.

History of a Soldier, The. Histoire du Soldat, L.

Hit the Deck. Musical by Youmans, 1927. The female owner of a Newport, R.I., coffee shop falls for a sailor customer. She acquires a fortune, but he is not tempted by wealth. Nonetheless, she manages to get pregnant by him, and wills her fortune to the unborn child. Includes *Sometimes I'm Happy* and *Hallelujah!*; the latter was arranged by Sousa and became popular with U.S. Navy bands.

H.M.S. Pinafore, or The Lass Who Loved a Sailor. Comic opera by Gilbert and Sullivan, 1878. A sailor is in love with his captain's daughter. The inequality in rank seems unbridgeable, until a middle-aged baby nurse confesses that she had both the captain and sailor under her care and got them mixed up! This allows the marriage of the 2 lovers to take place. The sharply satirical libretto is matched by the devastating musical parody of Italian opera clichés.

Hoboe (Ger.). Oboe.

Hochzeitlied (Ger.). Wedding song.

hocket (from Lat. *hoquetus*, hiccup; Fr. *hoquet*). A curious contrapuntal device, much in vogue in medieval polyphony, in which one voice stops and another comes in, sometimes in the middle of a word, creating the effect of hiccuping. Sometimes a single contrapuntal line is divided up in this way.

Hodges, Johnny (John Cornelius) **"Rabbit,"** African-American jazz alto and soprano saxophonist; b. Cambridge, Mass., July 25, 1906; d. N.Y., May 11, 1970. After playing drums and piano, he studied the saxophone with Sidney Bechet; then played with Willie "the Lion" Smith, Bechet, and Chick Webb; from 1928 to 1951 he was a member of

Duke Ellington's band; subsequently led his own band and septet for several years; then rejoined Ellington in 1955, remaining with him until his death. He publ. a vol. of his own *Sax Originals* (1945; 2nd ed., 1972). He was one of the most gifted saxophonists of the swing era.

hoedown. Community dancing party, originally in the rural American West, featuring square dances with calling, accompanied by old-time music. The 4th episode of Copland's *Rodeo* ballet suite (1942) is named after and based upon this cultural phenomenon.

Hoffmann, E(rnst) T(heodor) A(madeus), famous German writer, conductor, and composer; b. Königsberg, Jan. 24, 1776; d. Berlin, June 25, 1822. His 3rd Christian name was orig. Wilhelm, but he changed it to Amadeus out of love for Mozart. He studied law at the Univ. of Königsberg; also studied violin with Christian Gladau, piano with Carl Gottlieb Richter, and thoroughbass and counterpoint with Christian Podbielski; after further studies with Gladau he completed his training by taking a course in composition with J. F. Reichardt in Berlin. He served as music director at the theater in Bamberg; then conducted opera performances in Leipzig and Dresden (1813–14). In 1814 he settled in Berlin. He used the pen name of Kapellmeister Johannes Kreisler (subsequently made famous in Schumann's *Kreisleriana*); his series of articles in the *Allgemeine Musikalische Zeitung* under that name were reprinted as *Phantasiestücke in Callots Manier* (1814).

As a writer of fantastic tales he made a profound impression on his period and influenced the entire Romantic school of literature; indirectly, he was also a formative factor in the evolution of the German school of composition. His own compositions are passable from the technical viewpoint, but strangely enough, for a man of his imaginative power, they lack the inventiveness that characterizes his literary productions. His writings on music were ed. by H. von Ende (Cologne, 1896); see also D. Charlton, ed., *E. T. A. Hoffmann's Musical Writings: Kreisleriana, The Poet and the Composer, Music Criticism* (Cambridge, 1989). His best-known musical compositions are the operas *Die Lustige Musikanten* (Warsaw, 1805); *Aurora* (1811); and *Undine* (Berlin, 1816). Of the many adaptations of his novellas and short stories, the most famous are Offenbach's *Tales of Hoffmann*, Delibes's *Coppélia*, Tchaikovsky's *Nutcracker*, Hindemith's *Cardillac*, and Busoni's *Die Brautwahl*.

Hoffnung, Gerard, English caricaturist, producer, and tubist; born Berlin, Mar. 25, 1925; d. London, Sept. 28, 1959. He emigrated with his family to Italy in 1938, then to England a year later with his mother. His lack of interest in school culminated in his expulsion from the Hornsey College of Art (1943); this was compensated for by a precocious drawing ability and a well-developed sense of humor. While teaching in art schools, Hoffnung publ. cartoons and caricatures in magazines, drew advertising posters, and designed program covers; he did illustrations for a version of Colette's *L'enfant et les sortilèges* (the subject of Ravel's opera), but these were never publ. In 1950 he gave the 1st of several radio talks; its success led to his being included on radio panel shows with some of Britain's leading humorists of the day; these broadcasts made him nationally famous. He studied the tuba and became good enough to join the Morley College Orch.

In 1957 he organized the Hoffnung Music Festival Concert at London's Royal Festival Hall, which featured classical music PARODY at a level of grandeur not seen or heard before; its participants included Malcolm Arnold, Dennis Brain (playing hosepipe), Franz Reizenstein, Norman Del Mar, Donald Swann, Humphrey Searle, and Gordon Jacob. Its success led to the 1958 Interplanetary Music Festival, which featured April Cantelo, Lionel Salter, the Dolmetsch Ensemble, Edith Evans, Matyas Seiber, "Bruno Heinz Jaja," P. Racine Fricker, and the immortal *Let's Fake an Opera*. After Hoffnung's death a 3rd and final festival, the Astronautical, took place in 1961, with the assistance of Owen Brannigan, John Amis, Forbes Robinson, William Walton, and Joseph Horovitz, composer of the *Horrotorio* (pace John Cage). Hoffnung's books of musical caricature remain popular.

Hofmann, Peter, outstanding German tenor; b. Marienbad, Aug. 12, 1944. He studied at the Hochschule für Musik in Karlsruhe; made his operatic debut in 1972 in Lübeck as Tamino; in 1973 joined the Württemberg State Theater in Stuttgart. He came to prominence in his performance of the role of Siegmund in the centennial Bayreuth productions of *Der Ring des Nibelungen* (1976); later he appeared as Parsifal at Covent Garden in London. He made his U.S. debut as Siegmund with the San Francisco Opera in 1977; sang Lohengrin with the Metropolitan Opera in N.Y. in 1980. His other roles include Max, Florestan, Alfred in *Die Fledermaus*, Loge, and Bacchus.

Hogwood, Christopher (Jarvis Haley), prominent English harpsichordist, conductor, and musicologist; b.

Nottingham, Sept. 10, 1941. He studied classics as well as music at Pembroke College, Cambridge (B.A., 1964); received instruction in harpsichord from R. Puyana and G. Leonhardt, and also took courses at the Charles Univ. and the Academy of Music in Prague. In 1967 he joined David Munrow in organizing the Early Music Consort, an ensemble devoted to the performance of medieval music. In 1973 he founded the Academy of Ancient Music with the aim of performing music of the Baroque and early Classical periods on original instruments; he toured widely with the ensemble and made many recordings with it, including a complete set of Mozart's syms. utilizing instruments of Mozart's time. He also served as artistic director of the Handel and Haydn Soc. of Boston (from 1986) and music director of the St. Paul (Minn.) Chamber Orch. (from 1988). His guest conducting engagements took him all over Europe and North America. In 1989 he was made a Commander of the Order of the British Empire. He ed. works by J. C. Bach, Purcell, and Croft; was a contributor to *The New Grove Dictionary of Music and Musicians* (1980); and wrote *Music at Court* (London, 1977); *The Trio Sonata* (London, 1979); *Handel* (London, 1984).

höhe Stimmen (Ger.). High voices.

Holberg Suite (*Aus Holberg's Zeit*). String orch. work by Grieg, 1884, to commemorate the bicentennial of the Norwegian poet Ludwig Holberg. The suite is in 5 movements.

hold. See FERMATA.

Hold Everything. Musical by Ray Henderson, 1928. A welterweight prizefighter is torn between a rich socialite and a plebeian but truly loving woman. Being the romantic he is, he chooses the latter. Includes *You're the Cream in My Coffee.*

holding note. A note sustained in one part while the other parts are in motion; ORGAN POINT.

Billie Holiday, c. 1940s

COURTESY SONY/CBS

Holiday, Billie (Eleanora) **"Lady Day,"** outstanding African-American jazz singer; b. Philadelphia, Apr. 7, 1915; d. N.Y., July 17, 1959. She was the illegitimate daughter of Sadie Fagan and the guitarist Clarence Holiday. She began singing in Harlem nightclubs when she was 14; there she was discovered by the impresario John Hammond, who arranged for her to perform and record with Benny Goodman and his band in 1933; she later worked with Teddy Wilson (1935), Fletcher Henderson (1936), Count Basie (1937–38), Artie Shaw, and others before setting out on her own with a lengthy engagement at Café Society, N.Y. (1939). She performed at N.Y.'s Town Hall and appeared in the movie *New Orleans* in 1946. Her otherwise brilliant career was marred by personal tragedies, which included addiction to narcotics and alcohol; she served time for federal narcotics charges in 1946, but made a comeback at N.Y.'s Carnegie Hall in 1948. She subsequently toured throughout the U.S. and also sang in Europe (1954, 1958). Arrested again on a narcotics charge, she died in N.Y.'s Metropolitan Hospital.

She rarely sang classic blues per se; her repertoire consisted of the popular tunes of the day, although her recordings of *Strange Fruit* (1939) and her own *God Bless the Child* (1941) suggest her identification with the social issues of African-Americans. For her, "blues" was a state of mind and means of expression; her unique qualities included her light, subtle, and instrumentlike voice, which she applied with rhythmic and melodic finesse, touching on jazz syncopation and blues intonation.

Holidays: A Symphony. A gathering of 4 symphonic poems by Ives, 1904–13: *Washington's Birthday, Decoration Day, Fourth of July,* and *Thanksgiving (Forefather's Day).*

Holliger, Heinz, outstanding Swiss oboist, pedagogue, and composer; b. Langenthal, May 21, 1939. He commenced playing the recorder at 4 and the piano at 6; later studied oboe with Cassagnaud and composition with Veress at the Bern Cons., then oboe with Pierlot and piano with

Lefebure at the Paris Cons. In 1959 he won 1st prize in the Geneva competition, and then played in the Basel Sym. Orch.; also attended Boulez's master classes in composition in Basel (1961–63). After winning 1st prize in the Munich competition in 1961 he embarked upon a brilliant international career; toured in Europe and the U.S. as soloist with the Lucerne Festival Strings in 1962. He also gave concerts with his wife, the harpist Ursula Hanggi, and his own Holliger Ensemble. In addition to giving master classes, he was a prof. at the Freiburg im Breisgau Hochschule für Musik (from 1965).

He is generally recognized as the foremost oboist of his era, his mastery extending from early music to the commissioned works of such modern composers as Penderecki, Henze, Stockhausen, Krenek, Berio, Jolivet, and Lutoslawski. In his own works he is an uncompromising avant-gardist, having composed untraditional stage works, orch., vocal, and chamber works (including many for solo instruments); many of his pieces include electronic tape.

Holly, Buddy (born Charles Harden Holley), pioneering American rock musician; b. Lubbock, Tex., Sept. 7, 1936; d. in a plane crash in Clear Lake, Iowa, Feb. 2, 1959. He played the fiddle as a small boy, then switched to guitar. He joined a friend playing western and bop music on a local radio station; then teamed with a guitarist, a drummer, and a bass player to form the group the Crickets to record his 1st hit song, *That'll Be the Day*; after Holly's death it was included in an album significantly named *The Great Buddy Holly*. Stylistically, he was distinguished as one of the 1st white performers who used a characteristic "backbeat" of rhythm and blues in country-western music. In 1958 he toured in the U.S. and Australia as a guitarist in a trio with 2 other members of the Crickets. His songs have been reissued in record albums many times since his death and continue to be performed and recorded anew; among the most popular are *Not Fade Away, Peggy Sue, Words of Love* (all 1957); *It's So Easy, Maybe Baby, Rave On, Well Alright* (all 1958).

Holst, Gustav(us Theodore von), significant English composer, father of Imogen (Clare) Holst; b. Cheltenham, Sept. 21, 1874; d. London, May 25, 1934. He was of Swedish descent. He received his primary musical training from his parents. In 1892 he became organist and choirmaster in Wyck Rissington, Gloucestershire; in 1893 he entered the Royal College of Music in London, where he studied composition with Stanford and Rockstro, organ with Hoyte, and piano with Sharpe; he also learned to play

the trombone. After graduating in 1898, he was a trombonist in the orch. of the Carl Rosa Opera Co. (until 1900) and the Scottish Orch. in Glasgow (1900–1903). His interest in Hindu philosophy, religion, and music during this period led to the composition of his settings from the Sanskrit of 4 sets of *Choral Hymns from the Rig Veda* (1908–12). He worked as a music teacher in a Dulwich girls' school (1903-20); was director of music at St. Paul's Girls' School, Hammersmith (1905–34), and of London's Morley College (1907–24). He became a teacher of composition at the Royal College of Music (1919); was also prof. of music at Univ. College, Reading (1919–23).

Plagued by suspicions of German sympathies at the outbreak of World War I in 1914, he removed the German-looking (actually Swedish) nobiliary particle *von* from his surname. He was deemed unfit for military service but served as YMCA musical organizer among the British troops in the Near East in 1918. After the war he visited the U.S. as a lecturer and conductor in 1923 and 1932. However, his deteriorating health limited his activities; his daughter described his mind in the last years of his life as "closed in gray isolation."

Holst's most celebrated work, the large-scale orch.l suite *The Planets* (1914–16), was inspired by the astrological significance of the planets. It consists of 7 movements, each bearing a mythological subtitle: *Mars, the Bringer of War; Venus, the Bringer of Peace; Mercury, the Winged Messenger; Jupiter, the Bringer of Jollity; Saturn, the Bringer of Old Age; Uranus, the Magician; Neptune, the Mystic,* the last with a chorus of female voices singing wordless syllables. It was 1st performed privately in London (1918); the public premiere followed in 1920. The melodic and harmonic style of the work epitomizes Holst's musical convictions, in which lyrical, dramatic, and triumphant motifs are alternately presented in coruscatingly effective orch.l dress; but it is not typical of Holst's musical or philosophical concerns, and its success frightened him. His music in general reflects the influence of English folk songs and the madrigal. He was a master of choral writing; one of his notable works utilizing choral forces was *The Hymn of Jesus* (1917).

Holst's contributions to British music have been overshadowed by his contemporaries; however, he, like Bridge, Britten, Tippett, and others who began composing in the English pastoral tradition, developed a strong personal style with a variety of languages and moods. Holst's vocal music is especially to be prized, whether it be opera (*The Perfect Fool*, 1923; *At the Boar's Head*, 1924; *The Wandering Scholar*, 1930), ballet (*The Lure*, 1921; *The Golden Goose*, 1926; *The*

Morning of the Year, 1927), choral music (*The Hymn of Jesus*, 1917; *Ode to Death*, 1919; *1st Choral Sym.*, 1924; numerous a cappella works), or songs.

Holst, Imogen (Clare), English musician, daughter of Gustav(us Theodore von) Holst; b. Richmond, Surrey, Apr. 12, 1907; d. Aldeburgh, Mar. 9, 1984. She studied at the Royal College of Music in London. She was a faithful keeper of her father's musical materials and writings. From 1952 to 1964 she was musical assistant to Britten; she also conducted the ensemble of the Purcell Singers (1953–67) and served as artistic director of the Aldeburgh Festival (from 1956). In 1975 she was made a Commander of the Order of the British Empire. She wrote several books on her father and his music.

Holzbläser (Ger.). Woodwind players. *Holzblasinstrumente*, woodwind instruments.

Holzblöcke (Ger.). Chinese blocks.

Holzharmonika (Ger.). Old term for Xylophone.

Holztrompete (Ger., wooden trumpet). 1. Alphorn. 2. A hybrid wind instrument built for a solo in the 3rd act of Wagner's *Tristan und Isolde*. However, this solo is usually played by the English horn.

Home on the Range. Legendary American cowboy song with a dubious etiology. The words were 1st published in 1873, and the musical setting was attributed to William Goodwin, under whose name the song was published in 1904 with the title *An Arizona Home*. David Guion made a standard arrangement of the song (1930), and claims were made for him as the sole author. William Goodwin instituted a lawsuit for a million dollars in 1934 demanding official recognition of his authorship, but lost for lack of evidence. Several others managed to put in their claim. In the meantime *Home on the Range* was proclaimed the official song of the state of Kansas. *Home on the Range* joins the honorable company of famous phantom songs, among them *God Save the King*, *Hail to the Chief*, and *Yankee Doodle*, whose authorship is claimed by many but proved by none.

Home, Sweet Home. Popular song of uncertain origin, 1820s. The standard form of this famous song 1st appeared in the opera *Clari, or The Maid of Milan* by Henry Bishop, produced in London, 1823. But—surprise!—the tune 1st popped up in a collection of songs entitled *Melodies of Various Nations* (London, 1821), where it was described as a Sicilian air, and the words were different. After *Home, Sweet Home* became famous, several musical vultures descended upon it and published it as a folk song in numerous arrangements. Bishop's publishers promptly instituted a suit against the trespassers, claiming that the Sicilian air in question was itself composed by Bishop to fill out the album. The contention is at least plausible because no authentic Sicilian or other air has ever been found to match the tune. Yet *Home, Sweet Home* possesses a quasi-Sicilian lilt, particularly if it is arranged in 6/8 time. It appears, therefore, that Bishop plagiarized himself, which is no criminal offense. At any rate, he jealously maintained his claim to the sole and exclusive proprietorship of the tune. He even sued Donizetti when he espied a simulacrum of the piece in Donizetti's opera *Anna Bolena*.

Whatever its origin, the magic of *Home, Sweet Home* has worked well through the years. When a singer performed it at a concert in an American jail in 1885, the inmates were so moved that 7 of them escaped that very night and went directly to their respective homes, where they were apprehended the next day. On the other hand, when an Oklahoma attorney tested its efficacy at a trial in 1935 and sang *Home, Sweet Home* to a jury, pleading for mercy for his client, a bank robber, the jury brought out a verdict of life imprisonment.

homeological variations. Modern variations are often derived from a subject by topological extensions and compressions of the constituent intervals and rhythms, a process known as *homeological*. This term denotes the compatibility of geometric figures which can be topologically altered without disrupting the continuity of their perimeters. Thus a triangle can be stretched or crumpled like rubber and brought into congruity with a square or a circle but not with a torus, which is morphologically noncongruent with triangles, squares, or circles. In Modern Music a diatonic melody may be analogously compressed and extended by intervallic changes, but it cannot be converted into a pointillistic configuration or a Hocket without violating topological laws.

Homerische Welt (The Homeric World). Operatic tetralogy by (Friedrich) August Bungert (b. Mülheim, Ruhr, Mar. 14, 1845; d. Leutesdorf, Oct. 26, 1915). The 4 operas were all premiered in Dresden: *Kirke* (1898); *Nausikaa* (1901); *Odysseus' Heimkehr* (Odysseus's Homecoming; 1896, prior to parts 1 and 2); and *Odysseus' Tod* (Odysseus's Death, 1903). This epigonic tetralogy, desperately imitating Wagner's

Ring, soon sank without a trace into the Hades of stillborn musical fetuses.

hommage (Fr.). A homage, i.e., a dedicatory inscription to a revered personage in the arts, particularly in music. Often such dedicatory compositions are written in the manner of the master who is honored. Copland wrote a piano piece entitled *Hommage à Ives*, approximating Ivesian harmonies. Among the many French works of this type is the *Hommage à S. Pickwick* by Debussy, from his piano *Préludes*, Book II (1913). Debussy always had an ironic sense of devotion to England and thus pays tribute to the famous character from Dickens's *The Pickwick Papers*. In it are disguised quotations from *God Save the King*.

homonymity. In music as in verbal communication, identical sounds often acquire different connotations according to their context. For example, *mental process* in anatomy refers not to the state of mind but to the bony promontory that forms the chin, the key word being derived from the Lat. *mentum* (chin), not *mens* (mind), while the word process comes from proceed in the sense of outgrowth. A C-major chord, if written with an F-flat instead of E, loses its white-key immaculacy and becomes a dissonant suspension over the A-flat major triad. Homonymity plays a particularly significant role in DODECAPHONIC MUSIC. A segment of a 12-tone series may prove to be homonymous with another form of the same series. This fragmentary replication is of great structural importance in the theory and practice of combinatoriality.

homophony (Grk., same sound). 1. A musical texture in which a melody and its accompaniment are clearly hierarchically distinct. In its modern sense, homophony developed in the late 16th century in Florence and was generally adopted in early Baroque operas, as contrasted with the Renaissance's predominantly polyphonic style. In homophonic pieces the component vocal or instrumental parts are subordinated to the melody and form clear chordal harmonies. Parallel formations in 3rds and 6ths, or in 1st-inversion triads, are essentially homophonic procedures since there is no contrast between the voices either contrapuntally or rhythmically.

Some dispute exists concerning the historical validity of the term *homophony*; to some historians it is misleading to describe a Classic, Romantic, or 20th-century work as being homophonic simply because its harmony is subordinated to melody and strict polyphony is absent. However, it may be less confusing to treat the early Baroque monodic style as a form of homophony, since the BASSO CONTINUO accompaniment was by no means reductive nor restricted to block chords. In this sense even some medieval music, notably secular, can be considered homophonic, as well as that of the common practice period and beyond. Homophonic texture, therefore, differs from monophonic, antiphonal, polyphonic, and heterophonic textures.

2. A choral music texture that tends toward homorhythm and a main melodic part, as opposed to the imitative interweavings of polyphonic choral music. An example of homophonic choral music are the catches, glees, and hymns of English-speaking composers of the 18th century; even portions of William Billings's fuguing tunes are homophonic.

Honegger, Arthur (Oscar), remarkable French composer of Swiss heritage; b. Le Havre, Mar. 10, 1892; d. Paris, Nov. 27, 1955. He studied violin in Paris with Lucien Capet; then took courses with L. Kempter and F. Hegar at the Zurich Cons. (1909–11). Returning to France in 1912, he entered the Paris Cons., in the classes of Gedalge and Widor; also took lessons with d'Indy. His name 1st attracted attention when he took part in a concert of Les Nouveaux Jeunes in Paris (1918).

In 1920 the Paris critic Henri Collet publ. an article in *Comoedia* in which he drew a fortuitous parallel between the Russian 5 and a group of young French composers whom he designated as LES SIX. These 6 were Honegger, Milhaud, Poulenc, Auric, Durey, and Tailleferre. The label persisted, even though the 6 composers went their separate ways and rarely gave concerts together. Indeed, only Honegger, Milhaud, and Poulenc became generally known; Auric limited his activities mainly to the theater and the cinema, while Tailleferre produced musical plays, concert pieces, and chamber music; as to Durey, he was known more as a dedicated member of the French Communist Party than as a composer.

In the early years of his career Honegger embraced the fashionable type of urban music, with an emphasis on machinelike rhythms and curt, pert melodies. In 1921 he wrote a sport ballet, *Skating Rink*, and a mock-militaristic ballet, *Sousmarine*. In 1923 he composed the most famous of such machine pieces, *Mouvement symphonique No. 1*, subtitled *Pacific 231*. The score was intended to be a realistic tonal portrayal of a powerful American locomotive bearing the serial number 231. The music progressed in accelerating rhythmic pulses toward a powerful climax, then gradually slackened its pace until the final abrupt stop; there was a simulacrum of a lyrical song in the middle section of the piece. *Pacific 231* enjoyed great popularity and became in the minds of modern-minded listeners a perfect symbol of the machine age.

Honegger's *Mouvement symphonique No. 2*, composed in 1928, was a musical rendering of the popular British sport *Rugby*. His *Mouvement symphonique No. 3* (1933) however, bore no identifying subtitle. This abandonment of allusion to urban life coincided chronologically with Honegger's general trend away from literal representation and toward music in classical forms, often of historical or religious character. Among his most important works in that genre were *Le Roi David* (1921), to a biblical subject, and *Jeanne d'Arc au bûcher* (1935), glorifying the French patriot saint on the semimillennium of her martyrdom.

Honegger's syms. were equally free from contemporary allusions: the 1st 2 lacked descriptive titles; his 3rd was entitled *Liturgique* (1946), with a clear reference to an ecclesiastical ritual; the 4th was named *Deliciae Basilienses* (1946), because it was written to honor the city of Basel; the somewhat mysterious title of the 5th, *Di tre re* (1951), signified nothing more arcane than the fact that each of its movements ended on the thrice-repeated note D.

Honegger spent almost all of his life in France, but he retained his dual Swiss citizenship, a fact that caused some biographers to refer to him as a Swiss composer. In 1926 he married the pianist-composer Andrée Vaurabourg (1894–1980), who often played piano parts in his works. In 1929 he paid a visit to the U.S.; he returned in 1947 to teach summer classes at the Berkshire Music Center at Tanglewood, but soon after his arrival he was stricken with a heart ailment and was unable to complete his term; he returned to Paris and remained there until his death.

honky-tonk. A generic reference to early 20th-century popular piano music, particularly RAGTIME; the term often connotes a loud, raucous, and out-of-tune performance on an upright instrument in a cheap saloon.

hook. 1. FLAG. 2. In popular music, a memorable motive or riff, functioning as an identifying repeated figure in the melody or bass.

hopak (*gopak*). Ukrainian popular dance in rapid, slightly syncopated 2/4 time, corresponding to the anapestic meter (2 8th-notes followed by 1 quarter-note). It is usually danced by men only who employ acrobatic movements, sometimes similar to KOZACHOK. The word *hopak* comes from the Ukrainian imperative *Hop!* (jump). (The identity of meaning with the English *hop* is accidental.) Mussorgsky, Tchaikovsky, and other Russian composers wrote hopaks for their operas.

Hopkins, Sam "Lightnin'," fine African-American blues singer, guitarist, and songwriter; b. Centerville, Tex., Mar. 15, 1912; d. Houston, Jan. 30, 1982. He worked on a farm in Tex.; learned to play the guitar; accompanied his cousin, the singer Texas Alexander, and developed a style of his own, with arpeggiated chords, deep organ points in the bass, and irregular rhythms in the melody. He was a master of extemporized blues, and wrote about 600 songs. He was responsive to world events; composed *Happy Blues* for John Glenn after the astronaut's orbital flight. He was a popular singer at the Village Gate in N.Y. and took part in a hootenanny with Joan Baez and Pete Seeger. He was the subject of the film documentary *Blues Accordin' to Lightnin' Hopkins* (1970).

Hopkinson, Francis, American statesman, writer, and composer; b. Philadelphia, Sept. 21, 1737; d. there, May 9, 1791. By profession a lawyer, he was deeply interested in music; learned to play the harpsichord; studied theory with James Bremner; was a member of an amateur group in Philadelphia who met regularly in their homes to play music and also gave public concerts by subscription. He was the composer of the 1st piece of music written by a native Anglo-American, *Ode to Music* (1754), and of the 1st original Anglo-American song, *My Days Have Been So Wondrous Free* (1759). He makes this claim in the preface to his *7 [8] Songs for the Harpsichord or Forte Piano*, dated Philadelphia, 1788, and dedicated to George Washington: "I cannot, I believe, be refused the Credit of being the 1st Native of the United States who has produced a Musical Composition." Other works: *Ode in Memory of James Bremner* (1780); a contrafactum dramatic cantata, *America Independent, or The Temple of Minerva* (1781); and some songs.

Hopkinson's music was couched in the conventional English style, modeled after pieces by Arne, but he possessed a genuine melodic gift. He also provided Benjamin Franklin's glass harmonica with a keyboard, introduced improvements in the quilling of the harpsichord, and invented the bellarmonic, an instrument consisting of a set of steel bells. He was probably the compiler of *A Collection of Psalm Tunes with a Few Anthems, etc.* (1763). A MS book of songs in Hopkinson's handwriting is in the possession of the Library of Congress. Hopkinson's son, Joseph Hopkinson, wrote the words to *Hail, Columbia*.

hoquet (Fr.). HOCKET.

hora lunga (*doina*; Rum., long song). Traditional Romanian dance or song genre, in 6/8 or 2/4 time, in a leisurely tempo. It may be accompanied by a combination of the shepherd's flute, a leaf held between the lips and used as a reed, a bagpipe, and nonindigenous instruments (violin, panpipes, cimbalom, clarinet, etc.). Bartók's discovery of this increasingly obscure genre in Maramureş, Transylvania, was, in his view, "the most important result of [ethnomusicological] research in recent years" (1935). Particularly unique was the protracted, highly improvised melodies, with a freedom of ornamentation and time, the use of melodic formulas, and the flexibility of the pitch compass. Another remarkable element is the breadth of diffusion that the hora lunga has undergone. With disbelief, then amazement, Bartók studied evidence of or listened to similar music in central Algeria, Ukraine, and Persia; he theorized that one place had to be the common source and chose Persia. Subsequent research has revealed, however, that similar music is found as far west as Albania and Algeria, and as far east as India, Tibet, western China, and Cambodia. Heifetz transcribed for violin a hora by Rumanian composer Grigoras Dinicu and published it under the title *Hora Staccato*.

horn. 1. FRENCH HORN, also called VALVE HORN; distinct from the valveless NATURAL HORN. 2. Any wind instrument in the shape of a horn. 3. In jazz, any wind instrument, particularly the saxophone and trumpet.

horn band. A band of trumpeters. *Russian horn band*, a band of performers on hunting horns, each of which produces but 1 tone.

horn call. Fanfare played on the NATURAL HORN, thus limited to the harmonics of 1 fundamental.

F-B♭ Double Horn by Bach

Horn Call (Ger. *mit dem Hörnersignal*). Sym. No. 31 by Haydn, 1765, in D major. The reason for the nickname becomes evident as one hears a succession of horn signals.

horn fifths. A 2-part harmonic progression of archetypal significance, playable on natural horns or trumpets. The harmonic intervals in the ascending form are a minor 6th, a perfect 5th, and a major 3rd (in C major):

The term *horn 5th* is obviously inaccurate, but it has been traditionally accepted. Examples can be found in innumerable works written during the last 3 centuries, in a variety of rhythmic patterns. The trumpet-calls in Rossini's overture to *William Tell* are examples of rapid horn 5ths. Beethoven's *Les Adieux Sonata* opens with a slow, descending passage of horn 5ths, illustrating the postilion horn announcing the departure of a stage coach. Horn 5ths may be played on any polyphonic instrument or a pair of monophonic ones.

Hornbostel, Erich Moritz von, eminent Austrian musicologist; b. Vienna, Feb. 25, 1877; d. Cambridge, England, Nov. 28, 1935. He studied philosophy in Vienna and Heidelberg; received a Ph.D. in chemistry from the Univ. of Vienna (1900); in 1905–1906 he was the assistant of Stumpf in Berlin; in 1906 he went to the U.S. to record and study Indian music (Pawnee); from 1906 to 1933 he was director of the Phonogramm-Archiv in Berlin, and concurrently a prof. at the Univ. of Berlin (1917–33); then went again to the U.S. In 1934 he went to England. He was a specialist in Asian, African, and other non-European music; also investigated the problems of tone psychology; contributed hundreds of articles to scholarly publications on these subjects. He ed. a collection of records, *Musik des Orients* (1932); from 1922 until his death was coed., with C. Stumpf, of the *Sammelbände für vergleichende Musikwissenschaft*.

Horne, Lena (Calhoun), remarkable African-American singer of popular music; b. N.Y., June 30, 1917. She left school at 16 to help support her ailing mother; began her career as a chorus girl at Harlem's Cotton Club; after singing with Noble Sissle's orch. (1935–36), she appeared with Charlie Barnet's orch. (1940–41) and made a name for herself via such recordings as *Good for Nothing Joe* and

Haunted Town. In 1941 she sang at Carnegie Hall in N.Y.; after finding success as a radio vocalist, she went to Hollywood to star in the all-black musical films *Cabin in the Sky* (1943) and *Stormy Weather* (1943), adopting the title song of the latter as her trademark. In subsequent years she pursued a highly successful career as a vocalist in nightclubs and on television. She scored a triumph in N.Y. with her retrospective appearances in *Lena Horne: The Lady and Her Music* (1981–83), which she took on the road to critical acclaim. Her inimitable renditions of such standards as *Bewitched, Bothered, and Bewildered, Can't Help Lovin' Dat Man, Love Me or Leave Me*, and *Believe in Yourself* placed her in the exalted ranks of the leading vocalists of popular music in her time. In 1947 she married Lennie Hayton.

Horne, Marilyn (Bernice), outstanding American mezzo-soprano; b. Bradford, Pa., Jan. 16, 1934. She studied with William Vennard at the Univ. of Southern Calif. in Los Angeles; also attended Lotte Lehmann's master classes. She then went to Europe, where she made her professional operatic debut as Giulietta at the Gelsenkirchen Opera in 1957; remained on its roster until 1960, appearing in such roles as Mimi, Tatiana, Minnie, Fulvia in *Ezio*, and Marie in *Wozzeck*, the role she repeated in her U.S. debut at the San Francisco Opera (1960). She married the African-American conductor Henry Lewis that same year, and subsequently made a number of appearances under his direction; they were separated in 1976. In 1965 she made her debut at London's Covent Garden, again as Marie. She appeared at Milan's La Scala in 1969, and in 1970 she made her Metropolitan Opera debut in N.Y. as Adalgisa; subsequently became one of the Metropolitan's principal singers. Her notable performances there included Rosina in *Il Barbiere di Siviglia* (1971), Carmen (1972), Fidès in *Le Prophète* (1977), *Rinaldo* (the 1st Handel opera to be staged there, 1984), and Isabella in *L'Italiana in Algeri* (telecast live by PBS, 1986). Acclaimed for her brilliant portrayals in roles by Handel, Rossini, and Meyerbeer, she won equal praise as an outstanding concert artist.

Hörner (Ger.; It. *corni*). Horns.

hornpipe. 1. An old English dance in lively tempo, the earlier ones in 3/2 time, the later in 4/4. 2. British and Irish traditional dance, associated with sailors, that originated in the 16th century, in various meters (3/2, 2/4, 4/4)

Lena Horne, c. 1940s

COURTESY FRANK DRIGGS COLLECTION

and with a characteristic syncopation so that the music approaches that of the jig. Its choreography is less refined than other traditional dances, reflecting the energetic gestures and steps of sailors at play, with hand slapping and floor stomping. Hornpipes—either of folk origin or specially composed dances—have been used frequently in English light operas, as in *H.M.S. Pinafore* by Gilbert and Sullivan. 3. A family of reed instruments, with a simple pipe (of wood, cane, and bone), a reed (of wood and cane), and a cowhorn bell; often 2 pipes are bound together. The earliest type of hornpipe is the aulos, one form of which was iconographically represented in Crete during the 14th century B.C.; subsequent examples are found in Wales, Scotland, the Basque region, Russia, Albania, and Morocco; many other instruments are equipped with bags and fall into another branch of the pipe family.

horo. A Bulgarian round dance, related to the Rumanian hora. There are both fast and slow types; the dance is usually accompanied by flutes, fiddles, and bagpipes. Most remarkable in the horo is the frequency of compound irregular meters such as 5/16, 7/16, and 11/6.

Horowitz, Vladimir

Ukrainian-born American pianist of legendary fame; b. Berdichev, Oct. 1, 1903; d. N.Y., Nov. 5, 1989. Reared in a musically inclined Jewish family, he began playing piano in his early childhood under the direction of his mother, a professional pianist and later an instructor at the Kiev Cons. His other teachers were Sergei Tarnowsky and Felix Blumenfeld. He made his 1st public appearance in a recital in Kiev, 1920, that marked the opening of a fantastically successful career. The revolutionary events in Russia did not prevent him from giving concerts in and around Kiev, until he decided to leave Russia; his 1st official concert abroad took place in Berlin in 1926. Arriving in Paris in 1928, he took brief instruction with Alfred Cortot, and in that same year he made his American debut in Tchaikovsky's 1st Piano Concerto with the N.Y. Phil. under the direction of Sir Thomas Beecham; he subsequently appeared as soloist with several other American orchs., earning the reputation of a piano virtuoso of the highest caliber so that his very name became synonymous with pianistic excellence. He played for President Hoover at the White House in 1931, and in 1933 married Wanda Toscanini, daughter of Arturo Toscanini; he became an American citizen in 1942.

Horowitz seemed to possess every gift of public success; he was universally admired, and his concerts sold out whenever and wherever he chose to appear. His natural affinity was with the Russian repertoire; he formed a sincere friendship with Rachmaninoff, despite the disparity in their ages; Rachmaninoff himself regarded Horowitz as the greatest pianist of the century; Horowitz's performance of Rachmaninoff's 3rd Piano Concerto, which he played numerous times, was his proudest accomplishment. His performances of works by Chopin, Liszt, Schumann, and Tchaikovsky were equally incomparable. Yet amid all these successes, he seemed unable to master his own nervous system. He became subject to irrational fears of failure, and once or twice tried to cancel his engagements at the last minute; it took all the devotion and persuasive powers of his wife for him to overcome his psychological difficulties. Eventually, in 1973, he underwent shock therapy, which appeared to help. In the meantime he underwent an appendectomy, recovering normally.

Horowitz lived for a while in Europe in the hope of a salutary change of environment. During World War II he appeared with Toscanini in numerous patriotic concerts; it was for such a celebration in N.Y.'s Central Park that he made a vertiginous transcription for piano of Sousa's *Stars and Stripes Forever,* a veritable tour de force of pianistic pyrotechnics, which he performed for years as an encore, to the delight of his audiences. In 1949 he gave the world premiere of Samuel Barber's *Piano Sonata in Havana.* In 1953, the 25th anniversary of his American debut, he gave a recital performance in Carnegie Hall. After this recital he withdrew from the stage, not to return for nearly 12 years. However, he enjoyed making recordings when he was free to change his successive versions in the sanctuary of a studio. He also accepted a few private pupils. He then announced a definite date for a concert in Carnegie Hall (1965). Tickets went on sale 2 weeks in advance, and a line formed whose excitement and agitation would equal and surpass that of a queue of fans for a baseball game. Horowitz himself was so touched by this testimony of devotion that he sent hundreds of cups of coffee to the crowd to make the waiting more endurable on a rainy day.

Despite his agonies over solo performances, Horowitz had no difficulty whatsoever appearing as an accompanist to Fischer-Dieskau; he also played trios with Rostropovich and Stern. In 1978 he played at the White House at the invitation of President Carter, a performance that coincided with the 50th anniversary of Horowitz's American debut. In 1982, at the behest of the Prince of Wales, he gave a recital in the Royal Festival Hall in London, marking his 1st appearance in Europe in 31 years. Through his recordings he formed a large following in Japan; to respond to his popularity there, he gave a series of concerts in Tokyo and other Japanese cities (1983). The climax of his career, which became a political event as well, was his decision to accept an invitation to revisit Russia for a series of concerts in 1986. His

Steinway grand piano was tuned and cleaned and placed on a special plane to Moscow. Horowitz was accompanied on this trip by his wife, a piano tuner, and his cook. Special foods consisting of fresh sole and other delicacies were airmailed to Moscow every day. Horowitz made a short introductory speech in Russian before he played. The Russian music-lovers who filled the hall listened almost tearfully to his playing on his return to Russia after 61 years of absence. His program included works by Rachmaninoff, Tchaikovsky, and Scriabin, and also pieces by Scarlatti, Chopin, and Schumann.

The Russian trip seemed to give Horowitz the necessary spiritual uplift. Returning to N.Y., he resumed his concert and recording career. He was awarded the U.S. Medal of Freedom by President Reagan in 1986, and the National Medal of Arts in 1989. He made his last recording on Nov. 1 of that year; 4 days later, in the afternoon, he suddenly collapsed and died of a heart attack. His passing created a universal feeling of loss the world over. His body lay in state in N.Y. and was then flown by his wife to Italy, where it was interred in the Toscanini family plot in Milan.

horse opera. An affectionately derisive name for any television or radio program or film dealing with the fantasy world of the wild West. Like GRAND OPERA, the plots have a tendency toward improbability, melodrama, and sentimentality—except the characters dress differently and ride horses. The music that accompanies horse operas tends to emphasize galloping rhythms and quasi-Western melodies. One of the most famous appropriations of classical music is the use of the final section of the overture to Rossini's *William Tell* as the theme of *The Lone Ranger*.

horse trot. An American ballroom dance popular in the early 20th century—along with other "animal dances"—danced to ragtime music.

Hörspiel. In search of a term that would apply to a great variety of musical works, the practitioners of GEBRAUCHSMUSIK in Germany selected the generic appellation *Hörspiel*. Literally, Hörspiel means a play for hearing: usually it is a short composition for a solo instrument, a small instrumental ensemble, or a choral group. In its idiom, a Hörspiel should not appear strange to untutored ears, but nontoxic dissonances should not be shunned. A Hörspiel is related to the practice of HAUSMUSIK. The term can also apply to radio drama; in a musical form, this is called *Funkoper*.

Horst, Louis, American dance composer and teacher; b. Kansas City, Mo., Jan. 12, 1884; d. N.Y., Jan. 23, 1964. He studied violin and piano in San Francisco, and composition with Richard Stohr in Vienna, as well as with Max Persin and Riegger in N.Y. (1925). From 1915 to 1925 he was music director of the Denishawn Dance Co., and from 1926 to 1948 of Martha Graham's dance company, for which he wrote a number of works that played a crucial role in the development of modern dance. He wrote extensively on the subjects of music and dance; founded and ed. the journal *Dance Observer* (1934); wrote the important *Pre-Classic Dance Forms* (1940) and *Modern Dance Forms* (with C. Russell; 1961). He was also active as a teacher at Bennington (Vt.) College (1934-45), Columbia Univ. Teachers College (1938–41), and the Juilliard School of Music in N.Y. (1958–63).

Hot Chocolates. Revue by Fats Waller, 1929; the cast included Cab Calloway and Louis Armstrong at different times, both of whom sang Waller's *Ain't Misbehavin'* in the show.

Hot Time in the Old Town Tonight, A. Ragtime song by Theodore Metz (1896), a bandleader. There is a story that when he traveled with a minstrel troupe his train stopped in Old Town, La. He noticed several African-American youths trying to put out a fire, and someone remarked, "There'll be a hot time in Old Town tonight," and he fashioned a song out of it. But his detractors claimed that he lifted the song from a saloon entertainer in St. Louis.

Hound Dog. Song by Leiber and Stoller, 1952, in the uptempo rhythm-and-blues style that helped usher in rock 'n' roll. Like many American songs recorded in the segregated era, its 1st recording was by an African-American (Willie Mae "Big Mama" Thornton, 1953) and successful within its black commercial market; it was then covered by a white performer (Elvis Presley, 1956) and became far more successful in a much larger market.

Housatonic at Stockbridge, The. Song by Ives, 1921, to words by Robert Underwood Johnson. The same musical material is used in the last movement of his *3 Places in New*

England. The haunting tune is taken from an anthem, *Missionary Chant*, by Charles Zeuner. One can also perceive a similarity with the theme of Beethoven's 5th Sym., so beloved by Ives.

Houston, Whitney, enormously successful African-American singer of popular music; b. Newark, N.J., Aug. 9, 1963. She joined the choir of the local New Hope Baptist Church when she was 9, later receiving vocal coaching from her mother, the gospel and rhythm-and-blues singer Cissy Houston (b. Newark, N.J., *c.* 1932), with whom she sang in clubs and on recordings. After graduating from high school she attempted to find a niche as a singer, but it was not until the release of the 1983 album *Paul Jabara and Friends*, on which she sang *Eternal Love*, that her career really began. After several television appearances and the release of her single *All at Once*, which proved enormously popular in Europe, she scored a spectacular success with her album *Whitney Houston* (1985). One of its singles, *Saving All My Love for You*, won her a Grammy Award as best female pop vocalist of the year. At one point she broke the Beatles' record for consecutive number 1 hits. Her film career was launched by starring roles in 1993's *The Body Guard* and 1994's *Waiting to Exhale*, although 1996's *The Preacher's Wife* was less successful.

Hovhaness (Hovaness), **Alan** (born Alan Hovhaness Chakmakjian), prolific and proficient American composer of Armenian-Scottish descent; b. Somerville, Mass., Mar. 8, 1911. He took piano lessons with Adelaide Proctor and with Heinrich Gebhard in Boston; his academic studies were at Tufts Univ.; in 1932 he enrolled in the New England Cons. of Music in Boston as a student of Frederick Converse; then was a scholarship student of Martin at the Berkshire Music Center at Tanglewood in 1942. From his earliest attempts at composition he took great interest in the musical roots of his paternal ancestry, studying the folk songs assembled by the Armenian musician Komitas. He gradually came to believe that music must reflect the natural monody embodied in national songs and ancient church hymns.

In his music he adopted modal melodies and triadic harmonies. This parti pris had the dual effect of alienating him from the milieu of modern composers while exercising great attraction for the music consumer at large. By dint of ceaseless repetition of melodic patterns and relentless dynamic tension he succeeded in creating a sui generis type of impressionistic monody, flowing on the shimmering surfaces of euphony, free from the upsetting intrusion of heterogeneous dissonance; an air of mysticism pervades his music, aided by the programmatic titles which he often assigns to his compositions.

After completing his studies he served on the faculty of the New England Cons. of Music (1948–51), then moved to N.Y. He was awarded 2 Guggenheim fellowships (1954 and 1958). In 1959 he received a Fulbright fellowship and traveled to India and Japan, where he collected native folk songs for future use and presented his own works, as pianist and conductor, receiving acclaim. In 1962 he was engaged as composer-in-residence at the Univ. of Hawaii; he then traveled to Korea (he has written several pieces incorporating Korean instruments). Hovhaness eventually settled in Seattle.

A composer of relentless fecundity, he is best known for his over 60 syms.; among them are *Mysterious Mountain* (No. 2, 1955); *St. Vartan* (No. 9, 1950); *All Men Are Brothers* (No. 11, 1960); *Silver Pilgrimage* (No. 15, 1962); *Vishnu* (No. 19, 1966); *Etchmiadzin* (No. 21, 1970). He has also written several operas, quasi-operas, and pseudo-operas, and an enormous amount of choral music. The totality of his output is in excess of 400 op. numbers. In a laudable spirit of self-criticism, he destroyed 7 of his early syms. and began numbering them anew so that his 1st numbered sym. (subtitled *Exile*) was chronologically his 8th. He performed a similar auto-da-fé on other dispensable pieces. Among his more original compositions is a symphonic score *And God Created Great Whales*, in which the voices of humpback whales recorded on tape were used as a solo with the orch.; the work was performed to great effect in the campaign to save the whale from destruction by human (and inhuman) predators.

How Much Is That Doggie in the Window? Song by Bob Merrill, 1953, which became a novelty hit. Among the commercial takeoffs on the song were *How Much Is That Jaguar in the Window?*

How Sweet It Is (To Be Loved by You). Classic Holland-Dozier-Holland Motown sound, 1st a hit for Marvin Gaye in 1965 and subsequently covered by Jr. Walker (1966) and James Taylor (1975).

How to Succeed in Business Without Really Trying. Musical by F. Loesser, 1961. A spoof on climbing the corporate ladder and the "how-to" learning mode popular in postwar America. A humble but ambitious mail clerk uses a manual on success along with his wits, absolute insincerity, and plain dumb luck to rise to the top. Corporate culture, with its indolence, timidity, irresponsibility, unreliability, and lack of integrity, is given full display. Includes *Coffee Break*, *A Secretary Is Not a Toy*, and *I Believe in You*.

H.P. (Horsepower). Ballet by Chávez, 1932, a depiction in dynamic rhythms and powerful dissonances of the modern industrialized world, not without satirical, anticapitalist overtones. Originally called *Caballos de Vapor*.

huapango. A rapid Mexican dance with a polymeter comprising 3/4, 6/8, and 2/4.

Hubbard, Freddie (Frederick De Wayne), African-American jazz trumpeter, pianist, and bandleader; b. Indianapolis, Apr. 7, 1938. After playing with local jazz musicians, including Wes Montgomery, he worked with Blakey, Roach, Hancock, K. Barron, O. Coleman, Coltrane, and others; also played with Friedrich Gulda in Europe. He is a versatile performer in BEBOP, modal, and jazz-rock styles, although he is at his best in the 1st manner. His album *Straight Life* (1970) won a Grammy Award.

Hubička. KISS, THE.

huehuetl. A Mexican vertical drum made from a hollowed-out log, with an animal skin for a head. It is played with sticks or fingers.

Hugh the Drover. Ballad opera by Vaughan Williams, 1924. In the Napoleonic era, an honest and patriotic drover is unjustly accused of being a French spy by his rival in love; all ends well, however.

Huguenots, Les. Grand opera by Giacomo Meyerbeer, 1st produced in Paris, Feb. 29, 1836. One of the most spectacular of 19th-century operas, it embraces history, religious strife, and family tragedy. The climactic scene occurs on the St. Bartholomew's Day massacre of French Protestants, the Huguenots, in 1572. A Catholic nobleman leads an assault on the house in which the Huguenots make their last stand, realizing too late that his own daughter is among them. She perishes with her Huguenot lover and her father is left to bemoan his fate.

huitième de soupir. A 1/32 rest (1/8 X 1/4).

Humes, Helen, African-American jazz and blues singer; b. Louisville, Ky., June 23, 1913; d. Santa Monica,

Calif., Sept. 13, 1981. She 1st gained prominence as a singer with Count Basie's orch. (1938–42). Among her most successful renditions were the songs *If Papa Has Outside Lovin'*, *Do What You Did Last Night*, *Everybody Does It Now*, *Sub-Deb Blues*, and *He May Be Your Man but He Comes to See Me Sometimes*; her greatest hit was *Be-Baba-Leba* (1945).

Humfrey, Pelham, English composer; b. 1647; d. Windsor, July 14, 1674. He was among the 1st children appointed to the restored Chapel Royal in 1660, and (together with fellow-choristers John Blow and William Turner) he wrote the famous Club Anthem. In 1664 King Charles II sent him to study in France and Italy under the Secret Service Funds; that he worked under Lully remains unverified, nor can it be proved that he got to Italy. He returned to England in 1666 as lutenist of the Chapel Royal and was appointed Gentleman of the Chapel Royal on Jan. 24, 1667. An entry in Pepys's diary for Nov. 15, 1667, described him as being "full of form, and confidence, and vanity" and disparaging "everything, and everybody's skill but his own." Humfrey's justification of his self-confidence lay in his undoubted mastery of the Italian declamatory style, greater than anyone had yet achieved in England. On July 14, 1672, he was appointed Master of the Children of the Chapel Royal. Two years later he died, at the early age of 27. One of his wards was the young Henry Purcell, whose style clearly shows Humfrey's influence.

humor. Musical humor can be expressed in a variety of ways, from the grossest form of sonorous assault to the subtlest allusions to some humorous subject by way of quotation. A modern example of limited ethnic humor is the orch. sneeze in *Háry János* by Kodály, which expresses the skepticism of listeners to the boasts of Háry János, a joke that could be understood only by those familiar with this particular Hungarian reaction to a tall tale, in which a sneeze is a sarcastic expression of acceptance and approbation.

Humor by incongruous quotation is illustrated by the insertion of the thematic leitmotiv from *Tristan und Isolde* into Debussy's *Golliwog's Cakewalk* in his piano suite *Children's Corner*, marked "avec une grande emotion" and harmonized impertinently by chromatic passages. The quotation is followed by a brief comment of rhythmic cachinnation. The story goes that Debussy intended to play a joke on the pianist Harold Bauer, a great admirer of Wagner, who gave the very 1st performance of *Children's Corner*. Debussy made a bet with Bauer that he would force him to make fun of Wagner, and he won his bet when Bauer innocently performed the work without ever noticing the quotation in its derisive musical environment.

A purely musical example of humor is represented by Mozart's *Musical Joke*, subtitled *Village Musicians*, in which Mozart ridicules the ineptitude of the rustic players by making the fiddles play a figure in a scale of whole tones and by ending in several different keys. (Of course these devices became acceptable among highly sophisticated nonrustic composers of modern music.) Imitation of animal sounds, such as the bleating of sheep in Don Quixote of Richard Strauss, may produce an otherwise unintended comical effect. Sometimes the title of a piece reveals the humorous intent in the music. Virtually the entire production of Erik Satie depends for its humor on incongruous titles such as *Crepuscule matinal*, *Heures séculaires et instantanées*, etc. Source of PARODY: Anna Russell, Gerard Hoffnung, Spike Jones, P. D. Q. Bach.

humoresque. A light, whimsical instrumental piece, often for piano. The most famous is *Humoresque No. 2* by Dvořák, which is often parodied, including the children's lyrics "Passengers will please refrain from flushing toilet while the train is standing in the station (I love you)." Zez Confrey wrote a jazz adaptation playfully called *Humor-restless*.

Humperdinck, Engelbert, famous German composer and pedagogue; b. Siegburg, near Bonn, Sept. 1, 1854; d. Neustrelitz, Sept. 27, 1921. He began to study piano at 7; commenced composing at 14, then studied at the Cologne Cons. (1872–76). After winning the Mozart Prize (1876), he studied counterpoint and fugue with Rheinberger at Munich's Royal Music School (1877); also studied composition privately there with F. Lachner. In 1879 he won the Mendelssohn Prize of Berlin for his choral work *Die Wallfahrt nach Kevelaar* (1878); then went to Italy, where he met Wagner in Naples (1880); at Wagner's invitation, he worked in Bayreuth (1881–82). In 1881 he won the Meyerbeer Prize of Berlin, which enabled him to visit Paris in 1882. He taught at the Barcelona Cons. (1885–86) and the Cologne Cons. (1887–88); subsequently worked for the Schott publishing firm in Mainz (1888–89). After serving as private teacher to Siegfried Wagner (1889–90), he joined the faculty of the Hoch Cons. in Frankfurt in 1890; was made prof. there in 1896, but resigned in 1897. During this period he also was music critic of the *Frankfurter Zeitung*.

His fame as a composer was assured with the extraordinary success of his opera *Hänsel und Gretel* (1893), written to a libretto by his sister Adelheid Wette. This fairy-tale score,

with its melodies of ingenuous felicity in a Wagnerian idiom, retains its place in the repertoire. Although he continued to write for the stage, his succeeding works left little impression. He was director of a master class in composition at Berlin's Akademische Meisterschule (1900–20); was also a member of the senate of the Berlin Academy of Arts.

Humperdinck, Engelbert (real name Arnold George Dorsey), English popular-music singer; b. Madras, India, May 3, 1936. As a youth, he showed innate aptitude for raucous sentimentality and unmitigated schmaltz; these propensities attracted the attention of a hustler in search of potential rock singers; dissatisfied with the lackluster name of his chosen candidate for lucre and glory, he brazenly picked up the name Engelbert Humperdinck from a music dictionary and conferred it on Dorsey. As luck would have it, the rechristened singer (and his manager) prospered, making a quantum leap from his early beginnings as a hapless entertainer in British pubs to a successful crowd-pleaser in England and America. His voice was bland and colorless, but his stance was sincere, and his records sold prodigiously among British and American music fans.

Hungarian Rhapsodies. Liszt undertook the composition of these works for piano as a "patriotic anthology of the People of Hungary" in 1851. He wrote 15 of them in 3 years, and 5 more during the last few years of his life. Some of these Rhapsodies have specific surnames: No. 3 is the *Héroïde funèbre*, No. 9 is *Carnaval de Pest*, and No. 15 is *Rákóczy March*. The most famous of them all is No. 2, which opens with a typical Hungarian refrain and erupts in a wild dancing rhythm in the finale.

Liszt gleaned the melodic and rhythmic materials for his Hungarian Rhapsodies mainly from Gypsy bands; other tunes were borrowed. This dubious practice brought about an embarrassing contretemps when an obscure German pianist named Heinrich Ehrlich discovered that the thematic material of Liszt's famous 2nd Hungarian Rhapsody was lifted in its entirety from his own work, the manuscript of which he sent to Liszt some years before. Liszt readily acknowledged the borrowing but pointed out that all Hungarian tunes, whether Ehrlich's or anybody else's, derive from the same popular sources. To add to the embarrassment, the manuscript of Ehrlich's score could not be located. Liszt made amends by offering to put the notation in the future editions of his 2nd Rhapsody, "d'après les themes de H. Ehrlich," but somehow this was never done in actual printing.

Hungarian scale. GYPSY SCALE.

Hunnenschlacht. Liszt's symphonic poem inspired by a fresco of the painter Kaulbach representing the battle between the Huns and the Christians; the latter are helped by supernal spirits hovering over the battlefield. The music alternates between scenes of slaughter by parallel diminished-7th chords and angelic hymnody in modal harmonies. It was 1st performed in Weimar, Dec. 29, 1857.

Hunter, Alberta, outstanding African-American blues singer; b. Memphis, Tenn., Apr. 1, 1895; d. N.Y., Oct. 17, 1984. She went to Chicago; began her career there with appearances in nightclubs; subsequently gained fame as an outstanding blues singer; also worked in Europe as a singer and actress. She retired in 1956; after a silence of 21 years, she resumed her career in 1977 and astonished her auditors as one of the last of the great blues singers. She continued to make public appearances in her 89th year.

Hupfeld, Herman, American composer of popular music, singer, pianist, and lyricist; b. Montclair, N.J., Feb. 1, 1894; d. there, June 8, 1951. He served in the U.S. Navy in World War I. While in the service he wrote and performed his songs to his own words. Possessing a natural flair for sentimental melodies and nostalgic lyrics, he contributed successfully to Broadway shows; occasionally employed jazz rhythms, as in his song *When Yuba Plays the Rhumba on the Tuba.* He achieved fame with the theme song for the movie *Casablanca* (with Ingrid Bergman and Humphrey Bogart), *As Time Goes By*, a tune that indelibly impinged on the hearts of millions.

huqin (*hu-ch'in*). A Chinese spike fiddle. A small length of wood is crossed by a handle. The 2 strings, tuned in 5ths, are attached from top to bottom without a fingerboard; the bow is permanently attached between the strings. Also called erhu (*erh-hu*).

hurdy-gurdy. Another name for it is *vièle à roue*, a wheel viol. A once-popular chordophone with a unique playing mechanism involving 2 melody and between 2 and 4 drone strings; a rosined wooden wheel which rotated when operated by a crank and acted as a bow on the strings; and a tangent keyboard that sat on the fingerboard, producing pitches on the unison melody strings when depressed. The bass drone strings, usually tuned in open 5ths, sounded whenever the wheel was rotated.

The 1st form of the instrument occurs in the Middle Ages, where it was known as the organistrum, 1st described by Odo around 900 A.D. Although it began life in the monasteries, the hurdy-gurdy came to be used primarily for secular music accompaniment, eventually finding a place in all social classes. By the 17th century the instrument and its players were viewed negatively in writings and iconography; but by the following century the hurdy-gurdy was used at court, at the Parisian Concert Spirituel, and in the music of the Viennese Classic school and into the early 19th century. Even when the instrument itself wasn't used, references to it could be found—in Schubert's famous song *Der Leiermann* (*Die Winterreise*), with its nostalgic image of a hurdy-gurdy player with the characteristic open 5ths in the bass of the accompaniment to imitate the drone, and in Hindemith's viola concerto *Der Schwanendreher.*

In all cases the hurdy-gurdy is not to be confused with the street organ, which is a piped wind instrument manipulated by a crank.

Hurok, Sol(omon Israelovich), Russian-born American impresario; b. Pogar, Apr. 9, 1888; d. N.Y., Mar. 5, 1974. Fleeing the political iniquities of the Czarist regime in regard to Jews, he emigrated to the U.S. in 1906 and became a naturalized citizen in 1914. In 1913 he inaugurated a series of weekly concerts announced as "Music for the Masses" at the Hippodrome in N.Y.; then became an exclusive manager for famous Russian artists, among them Pavlova, Chaliapin, Artur Rubinstein, Elman, and Piatigorsky, as well as numerous other celebrities in the fields of ballet and opera. He negotiated the difficult arrangements with the Soviet government for American appearances of the Bolshoi Ballet, the Ukrainian dance company, and the Leningrad Kirov Ballet; made frequent trips to Russia, helped by his fluency in the language. Ironically, his N.Y. office became the target of a bomb attack by a militant Jewish organization which objected to Hurok's importation of Soviet artists, even though many of the artists were themselves Jewish.

hurtig (Ger.). Swift, headlong.

Husa, Karel, distinguished Czech-born American composer, conductor, and pedagogue; b. Prague, Aug. 7, 1921. He studied violin and piano in his youth; concurrently took courses in engineering; in 1941 he entered the Prague Cons., studying composition with Jaroslav Řidký; in 1945–46 he attended the Academy of Music; in 1946 was awarded a French government grant to continue his studies in Paris at the École Normale de Musique and the Paris Cons.; his teachers included Arthur Honegger and Nadia Boulanger; he also studied conducting with Jean Fournet and Andre Cluytens. In 1954 he emigrated to the U.S., where he joined the music dept. of Cornell Univ. as teacher of composition and conductor of the student orch. He also taught at Ithaca College (1967–86). He became an American citizen in 1959. He appeared widely as a guest conductor, frequently including his own music in his programs.

In his early works he followed the modern Czech school of composition, making thematic use of folk tunes; later he enlarged his musical resources to include atonal, polytonal, microtonal, and occasional aleatory procedures without following doctrinaire prescriptions to the letter. His music is oxygenated by humanistic Romanticism; as a result, it gains numerous performances. In 1969 Husa received the Pulitzer Prize in music for his 3rd String Quartet. In 1974 he was elected to membership in the Royal Belgian Academy of the Arts and Sciences. In 1986 he received an honorary Doctor of Music degree from Ithaca College.

Hustle, The. A 1975 Van McCoy hit that defined the DISCO era, surviving as the accompaniment to the dance of the same name.

Hutcherson, Bobby (Robert), African-American vibraphone and marimba player and composer; b. Los Angeles, Jan. 27, 1941. Inspired by the example of the great Milt "Bags" Jackson, he took up vibes, soon finding his own voice. In 1962 he went to N.Y., where he worked with Eric Dolphy, Jackie McLean, Archie Shepp, Hank Mobley, Herbie Hancock, and Andrew Hill, all musicians who were beginning to break the boundaries of traditional song forms. He made a series of excellent recordings for Blue Note Records; the album *Medina* (1969), in particular, represents a pure jazz aesthetic. In 1985 he began a series of recordings which incorporated strong Afro-Cuban rhythmic elements; these included *Good Bait* (1985), *Color Scheme* (1986), *In the Vanguard* (1987), *Cruisin' the Bird* (1988), and *Ambos Mandos* (1989).

Hüttenbrenner, Anselm, Austrian composer; b. Graz, Oct. 13, 1794; d. Ober-Andritz, near Graz, June 5, 1868. At the age of 7 he studied with the organist Gell; studied law at the Univ. of Graz; in 1815 he went to Vienna to study with Salieri. Schubert was his fellow student, and it is their friendship that keeps Hüttenbrenner's name alive. Hüttenbrenner also knew Beethoven intimately and was present at his death. He was an excellent pianist and a pro-

lific composer; Schubert praised his works. He wrote 6 operas; an operetta; 8 syms.; many overtures; 10 masses; 4 Requiems; 3 funeral marches; 2 string quartets; a String Quintet; piano sonatas; 24 fugues; other piano pieces; some 300 male quartets; 200 songs. One of his songs, *Erlkönig*, was included in the collection *12 Lieder der deutschen Romantik*, ed. by H. Rosenwald (1929). His reminiscences of Schubert (1854) were publ. by Otto Deutsch in 1906. Hüttenbrenner came into the possession of many Schubert MSS after Schubert's death, among them that of the *Unfinished Sym.*, which he held until 1865. It has been suggested that Hüttenbrenner lost the 3rd and 4th movements of Schubert's work and for that reason was reluctant to part with the incomplete MS, but the extant sketches for the Scherzo make that unlikely.

Hvorostovsky, Dmitri, Russian baritone, distinguished by tremendous vocal splendor; b. Krasnoyarsk, Oct. 16, 1962. He studied piano before receiving vocal instruction from Ekaterina Yofel; subsequently won the Glinka Prize (1987). He then proceeded to Wales, where he won 1st prize in the BBC Cardiff Singer of the World Competition (1989). His European appearances included Amsterdam, London, Dublin, and Nice. In 1990 he appeared in recital in N.Y. and Washington, D.C., obtaining unprecedented acclaim. He enchanted his audiences, particularly with his inspiring renditions of songs by Tchaikovsky and Rachmaninoff. He also seemed to have mastered the standard operatic repertoire, fulfilling engagements at La Scala in Milan and other operatic centers. The press did not spare superlatives, comparing him with the finest masters of song.

Hwang, Byung-Ki, Korean composer, virtuoso kayagum performer, and pedagogue; b. Seoul, May 31, 1936. He studied traditional Korean music and the kayagum (a 12-stringed Korean zither with movable bridges, dating from the turn of the 7th century) at the National Classical Music Inst. in Seoul (1951–58), his principal teachers being Yong-yun Kim, Yun-dok Kim, and Sang-gon Sim. He received 1st prize at the National Competition of Traditional Music (1954, 1956), a National Music Prize (1965), and the Korean Cinema Music Award (1973). From 1974 he was prof. of Korean traditional music at the College of Music, Ewha Women's Univ., in Seoul; in 1985–86 he was a visiting scholar at Harvard Univ. Hwang is noted as the 1st Korean composer to write modern works for the kayagum; he is also a distinguished kayagum player, and has appeared in recital in the U.S., West Germany, France, and Austria. His U.S. debut took place in N.Y.'s Carnegie Hall in 1986, in a program which included a number of his own compositions. His works are translucent and elegant in their structures, and impressionistic in harmonic and melodic design.

hydraulic organ. A small kind of organ invented by Ktesibios of Alexandria (180 B.C.), in which the wind pressure was supplied by a combination of water, gravity, and airflow.

Hykes, David (Bond), distinctive American composer and vocalist; b. Taos, N.Mex., Mar. 2, 1953. He studied filmmaking at Antioch College, in Ohio (1970–74), and arts administration at Columbia Univ. (M.F.A., 1984). He also studied classical Azerbaijani and Armenian music with Zevulon Avshalomov (1975–77) and north Indian raga singing with S. Dahr (1982). In 1975 he founded the Harmonic Choir, whose members employ vocal techniques borrowed from Tibetan and Mongolian music in which strongly resonated upper partials are produced in addition to the fundamental tone. From 1979 the ensemble was in residence at the ideal location of the Cathedral of St. John the Divine in N.Y., and from 1980 it made tours of the U.S. and Europe. In 1981 Hykes traveled to Mongolia under the auspices of the Asian Cultural Council. His compositions for voice use harmonics to produce rich waves of slowly changing sounds over diatonic melodies; the result resembles a sort of modernized chant with an ethereal haze of overtones. Among such compositions are *Hearing Solar Winds* (1977–83), *Current Circulation* (1983–84), and *Harmonic Meetings* (1986); Hykes has recorded solo vocal works; he has also written several film and television scores and a number of instrumental works.

hymn (from Grk. *hymnos*; Fr. *cantique*). 1. Generic name of religious or sacred songs in praise of a deity. In Greek poetry, a hymn was a chant in honor of a god or hero. In Latin, such pre-Christian hymns are usually translated by the word *carmen*. The Christians, however, accepted the Latinized form *hymnus*, in the sense of a poem or a song in praise of the Lord. In established church services a hymn is usually a metrical poem to be sung by a congregation, thus differing in function and form from psalms and canticles.

Hymnody—that is, the doctrine of hymns and the theory of their composition—was generated in the Christian community of Syria about the 4th century. The earliest authenticated Christian hymn, written in Greek notation, was discovered in the town of Oxyrhynchos in Egypt; it is dated approximately 200 A.D. Latin hymns, which are fundamental to the Roman Catholic Church, emerged toward the end of the 4th century in the Christian community of Milan, of which St. Ambrose was the bishop. Hymn tunes of the 1st millennium of our era were almost exclusively monophonic; contrapuntal settings were limited to the intervals of the octave, perfect 5th, and perfect 4th. Polyphonic hymnody was the fruit of the great school of Notre Dame in Paris in the 11th century and achieved its flowering with the advent of the so-called Burgundian and Flemish polyphonic systems of composition.

The Roman Catholic Church retained the Latin form of hymns, but in Germany, even before Luther, a trend developed of writing hymns in the German vernacular, or by combining German verses with the Latin ones. A mixture of German and French vernacular with Latin hymns attained a high degree of poetic expression in the *Carmina Burana*, a collection named after the monastery of Benediktbeuren in Bavaria that contains texts and melodies notated in rudimentary neumes, as they were sung by the goliards, young clerics, and itinerant students who wandered over Germany, much in the manner of the troubadours and trouvères of France.

The Lutheran hymnody absorbed some of the vernacular modalities from popular sources, and the product became the foundation of hymn singing and hymn composing in all Protestant nations. The Anglican Church adopted many Lutheran hymns in the 16th century, among them the most famous hymn believed to have been written by Luther himself, *Ein' feste Burg ist unser Gott* (A Mighty Fortress Is Our God). In England and later in America, the Lutheran hymns assumed a metrical form that almost approaches the secular type of song. English and American hymns are invariably set in a chordal style; occasional canons do not disrupt the prevailing homophonic arrangements. A curious departure from this style is the type of hymn called fuguing tunes, in which the middle section of a homophonic composition contains fugal imitation.

2. In foreign usage, a national song of lofty character, like the French *Marseillaise*.

Hymnen. Electronic work by Stockhausen, 1967, that combines the tune of the national anthems of many lands as a vision of a metaphysical union of all nations. It was 1st performed in Cologne.

Hyperprism. Extraordinary work for wind instruments and percussion by Varèse, 1923; it was 1st performed in N.Y., and was greeted by the critics with expressions of dismay and disgust. Comparisons of the work with a zoo where animals are going berserk were made independently by 2 N.Y. critics. *Hyperprism* has nothing to do with the zoo, however; it is a projection of the 4th-dimensional prism upon the space in 3 dimensions, and the sound may be described as a system of organized sonorous geometry. But the score is dissonant.

hypo-. In the system of church modes, the prefix *hypo-* indicates the starting point of a mode a 4th below its final (tonic); so, if the Dorian mode begins on D, then the Hypodorian mode will begin on A, a 4th below; a similar relationship exists for other modes.

Ii

I (It.; masc. plural). The.

I Am Woman. Helen Reddy's 1972 pop hit that became a theme song for the women's liberation movement.

I Can Get It for You Wholesale. Musical by H. Rome, 1962. Life in the N.Y. garment industry, a thicket of double-crossing and profit-taking. The show introduced Barbara Streisand as the poor befuddled secretary Miss Marmelstein.

(I Can't Get No) Satisfaction. Rolling Stones' hit of 1965, famous for its guitar riff and—for the time—frank lyrics. Covered by Otis Redding in 1966.

I Can't Give You Anything But Love, Baby. Song by Jimmy McHugh, 1928, one of the most enduring hits of the Great Depression, with its protagonist confessing his financial insolvency, leaving love as his only asset.

I Can't Help Myself. Also known as *Sugar Pie, Honey Bunch*. Holland-Dozier-Holland composition made famous by the Four Tops in 1965; their 1st number 1 pop hit.

I Didn't Raise My Boy to Be a Soldier. Song by Plantadosi, 1915, when America was neutral and isolationist. As events began to move national sentiment away from absolute neutrality, the same company published another song, *I Don't Want My Boy to be a Soldier, But I Will Send My Girl to be a Nurse.* Finally, the company published a song reflecting the entry of the U.S. into World War I: *America, Here is My Boy!*

I Fall to Pieces. A 1961 country hit for chanteuse Patsy Cline.

I Got Rhythm. Song by Gershwin, 1930, from the musical *Girl Crazy*. This is an ingeniously intricate and yet disarmingly simple song. Its rhythmical pattern is formed by an 8th-note rest followed by 4 dotted-8ths and another 8th-note rest, all encompassed within a regular 4/4 measure. An earnest modernist addicted to polymetrics would have notated Gershwin's pattern as a bar of 2/16 followed by four bars of 3/16, concluding with another bar of 2/16. With its success, Gershwin arranged it in a brilliant piano solo; he later wrote a variation set on it for piano and orch.

I Got You (I Feel Good). James Brown funk hit of 1965; his biggest pop hit.

I Have a Dream. Cantata by Siegmeister, 1967, based on the famous speech by Martin Luther King, Jr. The work was 1st performed in Long Beach, N.Y.

I Heard It Through the Grapevine. Major Motown hit penned by Holland-Dozier-Holland, unsuccessfully recorded by Gladys Knight and the Pips in 1967 but turned into a smash a year later by Marvin Gaye.

I Left My Heart in San Francisco. 1962 hit and Grammy Award–winner for Tony Bennett that has since become his theme song. Written by Douglass Cross and George Cory.

I Married an Angel. Musical by Rodgers and Hart, 1938. A nobleman of unidentified provenance has so many unhappy experiences with women that he declares he would only marry an angel. Sure enough, a female floats into his room. He is enchanted and marries her. But she proves embarrassing in society because she tells the truth to everyone. It is only when she learns how to deceive, cheat, and be a hypocrite that the hybrid union becomes compatible. Includes the title song and *Spring Is Here*.

I Shot the Sheriff. Bob Marley–penned reggae song popularized by British blues guitarist Eric Clapton in 1974 that helped introduce reggae to English and American pop music.

I Surrender, Dear. Song by Harry Barris, 1930, popularized by Bing Crosby and later Kate Smith.

I Walk the Line. Johnny Cash's 1st pop hit from 1956 that became the model for his lean country sound.

I Wanna Be Loved by You. Song by Stothart and Ruby, 1928; an instant hit in the hands of flapper and "boop-a-doop girl" Helen Kane.

I Want to Be Happy. Song by Youmans, 1924, from his musical *No, No, Nanette*.

I Want to Hold Your Hand. Beatles' 1st U.S. number 1 pop hit, penned by Lennon-McCartney.

I Wonder Who's Kissing Her Now. Song by Howard and Orlob, 1909, from the musical *The Prince of the Night*. Joseph Howard was listed as sole author when the song became a huge hit; therefore it was quite a shock when one Harold Orlob brought a lawsuit against Howard some 40 years later; Orlob claimed to have written the song while working for Howard as an arranger. Remarkably, Orlob did not seek damages, only recognition; Howard conceded his claim, and the song was republished under both of their names.

iamb (iambus). In prosody, a metrical foot of 2 syllables, 1 short and unaccented, followed by 1 long and accented:

Musical phrases following this rhythmic formula may be labeled iambic.

Ibéria. The 2nd movement of the symphonic triptych *Images* by Debussy, 1910. Debussy adored Spain, its rhythms, and the very odor of the streets. The 3 sections of *Ibéria* bear evocative subtitles: *Par les rues et par les cheimins* (In the Streets and Byways); *Les Parfums de la Nuit* (The Fragrances of the Night); and *Le Matin d'un Jour en Fête* (The Morning of a Festival Day). In the last section the violinists are instructed to hold their instruments under the arms and strum them like guitars. Listeners and critics were at 1st bewildered by the sounds of Debussy's imaginary Spain. One of them suggested that *Ibéria* was so foggy that a letter must have been omitted from the title—that the work was more fittingly named *Siberia*. But when a more broadminded music critic was asked who was the best Spanish composer, he replied, "Debussy!"

Ibert, Jacques (François Antoine), distinguished French composer; b. Paris, Aug. 15, 1890; d. there, Feb. 5, 1962. He studied at the Paris Cons. (1911–14); during World War I served in the French navy; returned to the Paris Cons. after the Armistice; received the Prix de Rome in 1919 for his cantata *Le Poète et la fée*; while in Rome he wrote his most successful work, the symphonic suite *Escales* (Ports of Call, 1930), inspired by a Mediterranean cruise he took while serving in the navy. In 1937 he was appointed director of the Académie de France of Rome, and he held this post until 1960; was also administrator of the Réunion des Théâtres Lyriques Nationaux in Paris (1955–56). He was elected a member of the Institut de France (1956).

In his music Ibert combines the most felicitous moods and techniques of IMPRESSIONISM and NEOCLASSICISM; his harmonies are opulent, his instrumentation is coloristic; there is an element of humor in lighter works, such as his popular orch. *Divertissement* and an even more popular piece, *Le Petit âne blanc* (The Little White Donkey) from the piano suite *Histoires* (1922). His craftsmanship is excellent; an experimenter in tested values, he never fails to produce the intended effect. Other works include operas, ballets, and orch.l works.

Ice Cube, rapper, songwriter, and actor; b. Oshea Jackson, Los Angeles, Calif., June 15, 1964. Ice Cube initially gained fame as a member of the group N.W.A. (Niggas with Attitude) and as a solo artist, and then as a film actor. He began rapping in the 9th grade, soon meeting a local deejay named Dr. Dre. The duo produced a parody of the popular rap song *Roxanne, Roxanne* that was a local hit in 1984. They next wrote *Boyz n the Hood*, a song reflecting life in the ghettos of Compton, which was recorded by another friend, Eazy E. The trio then joined with deejay Yella to form N.W.A., but Cube left the group for a while to attend school in Phoenix, not returning until 1988. He recorded with them on 2 albums, the 2nd being 1991's classic *Straight*

Outta Compton, most of which he wrote and which was a megaseller. That same year he released his 1st solo album, *Death Certificate*, and gave a critically well-received performance in John Singleton's 1st feature, *Boyz n the Hood*. His 1992 album, *The Predator*, was the 1st rap album to debut at number 1 on both *Billboard*'s pop and R&B album charts; he followed it a year later with another bestseller, *Lethal Injection*. In 1994 he coproduced, cowrote, and starred in the film *Friday*, a comedy about life in Los Angeles which received mixed reviews.

Icelandic Symphony. Sym. No. 16 by Cowell, 1963, 1st performed in Reykjavík.

Ice-T, rapper and actor, b. Tracy Marrow, Newark, N.J., *c.* 1958. The rap star moved to Los Angeles in the 7th grade to live with his father's sister. In high school, in the Crenshaw area of Los Angeles, he became involved with gangs, and moved out on his own during the 12th grade; he subsequently graduated and joined the Army. In the early 1980s he began rapping, recording *The Coldest Rap* in 1982 for a local label. He then went to N.Y., where he worked with several local rappers; he returned to L.A. by 1986. He was signed to Sire Records in 1987, forming his own Rhyme Syndicate management company and recording label a year later. He appeared in the film *New Jack City* in 1991, and a year later formed the speed metal–rap group Body Count, (in)famous for their song *Cop Killer*, which attracted the attention of neoconservatives across the land who condemned its lyrics. The song led him to be dropped by Time Warner, the megamedia empire that owned Sire, but his recording and acting careers have continued unabated.

ictus (from Lat. *icere*, strike). A separation mark in Gregorian chant before and after an important note in the melody, based on relative prosodic importance.

I'd Rather Be Right. Musical by Rodgers and Hart, 1937. The plot focuses on a boy unable to marry his best girl on account of lack of money; he has a dream in which he meets President Franklin D. Roosevelt and confides his troubles to him. Roosevelt replies that he cannot help the lovers until he balances the national budget. Various hilarious situations ensue before the dreamer awakens and decides to get married, budget or no budget.

Ideale, Die. Symphonic poem by Liszt, 1857, inspired by Schiller's poem by the same name. It was 1st performed in

Weimar for the unveiling of the dual Schiller-Goethe monument. The music fittingly describes the ideals of both Goethe and Schiller.

idée fixe. A term used by Berlioz to describe the recurrent theme of his *Symphonie fantastique*, which occurs in every movement of the work. With it he intended to portray the Shakespearean actress Miss Smithson with whom he was in love. Actually, he made use of the same theme in a piece composed before he ever beheld Miss Smithson on the stage.

idiophones (from Grk. *idios* + *phonos*, one's own sound). The old classification of instruments whose sound is produced by striking or shaking a metallic, wooden, or other surface directly; thus idiophones produce their sound by the substance of the instrument itself (e.g., triangle, chimes, cymbals, xylophone, castanets, rattle, glass harmonica, etc.), unlike the MEMBRANOPHONES.

Idomeneo, Rè di Creta (Idomeneo, King of Crete). Opera by Mozart, 1781, 1st produced in Munich. Returning from the Trojan War, Idomeneo's ship runs into a storm. To placate the sea god Poseidon, Idomeneo promises to sacrifice the 1st person who meets his ship at home; it happens to be his own son. When Idomeneo tries to evade his pledge, the gods send a monster to ravage the island of Crete. At this point comes the proverbial DEUS EX MACHINA who magnanimously arranges a compromise, by forcing Idomeneo's abdication in favor of his son's.

idyl (It. *idillio*; Fr. *idylle*; Ger. *Idylle*). A composition of a pastoral or tenderly romantic nature, without set form.

If I Had a Hammer. A 1948 political-action song by folksingers Pete Seeger and Lee Hays that became a major hit thanks to Peter, Paul and Mary's 1962 recording.

If I Were King (*Si j'étais roi*). Opera by A. Adam, 1852, 1st produced in Paris. The action unfolds in the 16th century in the Indian port of Goa, before its capture by Portugal. A fisherman saves a young girl from drowning, not realizing that she is a royal princess of Goa. When he recognizes her on the beach he tells of his exploits to the King's nephew, who orders him never to mention it again under penalty of death. Aggrieved, the fisherman traces the words "Si j'etais roi" on the sand, and falls asleep. The King, touched by this sight, orders the sleeping man transferred to the royal palace and lets him rule Goa for a day. The fisherman discovers that the King's nephew treacherously conducted negotiations with the Portuguese, preparing to surrender the city. The King expels the traitor, and the Portuguese are repelled. The fisherman marries the princess. The opera is melodious and its overture is often played at popular concerts.

Iglesias (Buga), **Julio,** Spanish singer and songwriter of popular music; b. Madrid, Sept. 23, 1943. He was 20 before he evinced an interest in music, teaching himself to play the guitar. After studying English at Cambridge he entered the Benidorm Song Festival in his native country and carried off all of its prizes (1968); he subsequently pursued a successful international career, turning out some 60 albums in 6 languages which sold over 100 million copies, for which his name was entered in the *Guinness Book of World Records.*

il (It.; masc. singular).   The. *Il più,* the most.

L'isle de Merlin.   Opera by Gluck, 1758, 1st performed in Vienna. Two young Frenchmen find themselves on the island of the magus Merlin and fall in love with his 2 nieces. To gain their objects of matrimony, Merlin insists that they play and win a dice game. The Frenchmen lose, but Merlin helps them win their brides nonetheless. The work is typical of prereform rococo style.

L'isle joyeuse.   Piano piece by Debussy, 1904. One of his most brilliant piano works, it paints in luscious impressionistic harmonies the vision of a "joyous isle."

Illuminations, Les.   Song cycle by Britten, 1940, for voice and string orch.; it was 1st performed in London. The work sets 10 symbolist poems by Rimbaud to music.

Ilya Muromets.   Subtitle of the 3rd Sym., 1912, by Reinhold Glière (b. Kiev, Jan. 11, 1875; d. Moscow, June 23, 1956); it is Glière's most significant work; it was 1st performed in Moscow. In 4 movements, it depicts the deeds of valor performed by the legendary Russian knight Ilya Muromets. The music is eminently romantic with some modernistic touches, such as the employment of whole-tone scales to suggest Ilya's unbounded heroism.

im (Ger.).   In the; *Im tempo,* in the regular tempo; A TEMPO.

Im Weissen Rössl (At the White Horse). Operetta by Ralph Benatzky (b. Moravské-Budejovice, June 5, 1884; d. Zurich, Oct. 16, 1957), 1930, 1st produced in Berlin. It deals with labyrinthine amours in an Austrian hotel, climaxing with the appearance on the scene of Emperor Franz Josef in person. The score abounds in melodious waltzes and includes a tango and a fox-trot.

I'm Always Chasing Rainbows.   A musical mayhem, 1918, perpetrated on the melody of the middle part of Chopin's *Fantaisie-Impromptu* by an unscrupulous Broadway manipulator, with words of ultimate saccharinity; the thing became immensely popular.

I'm Forever Blowing Bubbles.   Song by John William Kellette, 1918. It sold nearly 3 million copies of sheet music. The song's message is optimistic and hedonistic, as were most songs publ. immediatcly after the conclusion of World War I.

I'm in the Mood for Love.   Song by Jimmy McHugh, 1935, a huge and memorable hit featured in several movie musicals.

I'm Just Wild About Harry.   Song by Noble Sissle and Eubie Blake, 1921, introduced in the revue *Shuffle Along.* One of the 1st post-RAGTIME songs to gain wide popularity, it served as Harry Truman's presidential campaign song in 1948.

I'm Looking Over a Four-Leaf Clover.   Song by Harry Woods, 1927, playing on the anomalous plant (clover is usually 3-leaved), which is supposed to bring good luck.

I'm Walkin'.   A 1957 Fats Domino hit covered by Ricky Nelson, his 1st charting hit that same year for the teenyboppers.

Images.   Orch.l suite by Debussy, 1906–12. The 1st movement is entitled *Gigues.* In the 2nd movement, *Ibéria,* Debussy depicts his love of Spain, and in its last section he instructs the violinists to hold their instruments under their arms and strum them like guitars. The 3rd movement, *Rondes de Printemps,* is especially popular; these "dances of spring" are marked by constantly changing rhythms and colorful orch.l timbres. Debussy also wrote 2 piano suites entitled *Images I* (1905) and *Images II* (1907).

Imaginary Landscape.   Generic name for works by Cage. Each one makes use of noises and random combinations of sounds produced by various means, including the chance manipulation of a radio receiver. Cage produced the 1st of these *Landscapes* in 1939.

imbroglio (It., mixture, confusion). 1. The use of rhythmically contrasting and noncoincident sections within a common meter. A simultaneous use of 3/4 and 6/8 in Spanish music is an imbroglio. A similar combination of meters is found in Mozart's opera *Don Giovanni* at the end of the 1st act, and in the street scene in Wagner's *Die Meistersinger*. Much more complex examples of imbroglio are exemplified by the 2nd movement of *3 Places in New England* by Ives, and in the 3rd String Quartet of E. Carter. 2. Literally, "confusion"; a term used to describe scenes in opera where several groups of singers or instrumental ensembles perform together, but each serves a different dramatic purpose.

imitando (It.). Imitating.

imitando il corno (It.). Imitating a horn; an indication found in Paganini's violin *Capricci* and Liszt's transcriptions of them.

imitando il flauto (It.). Imitating a flute; an indication found in Paganini's *Capriccio No. 9* and in Liszt's paraphrase of it (*Études d'exécution transcendante No. 5*).

imitatio per augmentationem. See CANON PER AUGMENTATIONEM.

imitatio per diminutionem. See CANON PER DIMINUTIONEM.

imitatio retrograda. See CANON CANCRIZANS.

imitation. The generic term for the repetition of a motive, phrase, or theme proposed by one part (ANTECEDENT) in another part (CONSEQUENT), with or without modification. It is the most natural and powerful device that lies at the foundation of the CANON and FUGUE and is found in practically all musical forms since the emergence of the Western art of composition from primitive homophony. Progressing from literal repetition of a musical phrase, imitation evolved into a complex polyphonic art in which themes were inverted, taken at half speed (AUGMENTATION) or double speed (DIMINUTION), and further embellished by a variety of ornamental devices. The minimum requirement of all types of imitation is the preservation of its rhythmic pattern, or else it becomes unrecognizable. *Canonic imitation*, strict imitation; *free imitation*, where variants of the antecedent are permitted in the consequent;

strict imitation, where the consequent answers the antecedent note for note and interval for interval.

immer (Ger.). Always; continually. *Immer langsam*, slowly throughout; *immer langsamer*, slower and slower; *immer leise nach und nach*, gradually softening; *immer stärker werdend*, continually growing louder.

Immortal Hour, The. Opera by Rutland Boughton (b. Aylesbury, Jan. 23, 1878; d. London, Jan. 25, 1960), 1914, 1st produced in Glastonbury. A Celtic king plans to marry a girl from the fairyland, but she is lured away by one of her own kind to the land of Heart's Desire. The score is disarmingly harmonious; it enjoyed a spell of success during an arid London season and has been revived recently.

impazientemente (It.). Impatiently.

imperfect cadence. See CADENCE.

imperfect consonance. See CONSONANCE.

imperfect interval. See INTERVAL.

imperfect stop. See STOP.

imperfection (Lat. *imperfectio*). In mensural music, the binary (2-beat) measure, which is "imperfect" (incomplete) without its 3rd beat, which in mensural music made a perfection (PERFECTIO). The Middle Ages connected the ternary perfection to the Holy Trinity.

Imperial Maryinsky Theater. The great opera house founded in St. Petersburg in 1783, which received the name Maryinsky after an Imperial dowager named Marie. Catherine the Great engaged famous Italian and French musicians and choreographers to direct its destinies. The Czars and assorted Grand Dukes used to pick up ballerinas from the ballet troupe of the Imperial Theater for clandestine concubines. The last one, Ksheshinska, who was a favorite of Czar Nicholas II, died in Paris in 1970 at the age of 99. Her name entered history because Lenin made her villa in St. Petersburg his headquarters after the Revolution. At the same time, the name of the Imperial Theater was changed to the State Academy Theater of Opera and Ballet; in 1935 it was renamed Kirov Theater of Leningrad, to commemorate the Soviet leader Kirov, who was assassinated in 1934. The greatest Russian operas and ballets had their

1st performances at the Maryinsky Theater; with the transfer of the Russian capital to Moscow after the Revolution, the 1st place among Russian opera and ballet theaters passed to the Bolshoi Theater in Moscow.

Impériale, L'. Sym. No. 53 in D Major by Haydn, 1779. The 19th-century nickname attests to the majestic sweep of the opening largo MAESTOSO.

imperioso (It.). Imperious, haughty, lofty.

impetuoso (It.). Impetuously, impetuous, vehemently.

imponente (It.). Imposing, impressive.

Impossible Dream, The. Song by Mitch Leigh, 1965, from the musical *Man of La Mancha*. The dreamer of this dream is Don Quixote; the song became a popular representation of idealism, however hopeless. Jack Jones had a pop hit with his version of the song.

impresario (from It. *impresa*, undertaking). The agent or manager of an opera or concert company.

Impresario, The (*Der Schauspieldirektor*). Singspiel by Mozart, 1786, in which a producer has to appease the professional demands of 2 competing prima donnas.

Impressioni Brasiliane. Orch.l suite by Respighi, 1928, which he 1st conducted in São Paulo during a South American tour. The work portrays 3 distinct tropical landscapes.

impressionism. Aesthetic term describing modern French and French-influenced compositions of the early 20th century. By analogy to a late-19th-century artistic movement, subtle impressions rather than emphatic descriptions are conveyed through the use of ethereal modal and nondiatonic harmonies in free modulation and colorful instrumentation. Debussy, considered the 1st impressionist composer, disliked the term, and considered his music closer in spirit to the symbolist literary movement. Perhaps the music of this period synthesizes these 2 elements.

impromptu (Lat. *in promptu*, in readiness). 1. An improvisation. 2. Interludes in theatrical plays in the 17th century, as in Molière's *L'Impromptu de Versailles*. 3. A character piece of varying form and little development, popular in the 19th century. Schubert wrote a number of impromptus for piano; these pieces are built in a symmetric form in which each main section is subdivided into 3 subsections and each subsection is subdivided into 3 subaltern segments, which in turn are split into brief musical phrases in 3-part form. It must be noted, however, that the title *Impromptu* was not original with Schubert but was appended to the music by his publisher. Chopin's impromptus for piano are particularly remarkable in their perfect symmetrical design. Liszt wrote several piano impromptus on themes by other composers; these impromptus come close to a FANTASIA.

Improperia (Lat., reproaches). The Biblical passages chanted during the Roman Catholic Good Friday Mass, representing the plaints of the crucified Jesus to his people, "Popule meus quid feci tibi?" (O my people, what have I done to you?). This is followed by 2 other passages from the Old Testament.

improvisation (from Lat. *improvisus*, unforeseen; *ex improviso*, without preparation). The art of a completely spontaneous performance without a preliminary plan; extemporization. Formerly improvisation was regarded as integral to the craft of composition. Organists in particular were emboldened to improvise freely on a given hymn tune. Among the greatest improvisers on the organ were Frescobaldi and Buxtehude. Bach was a master of organ improvisation in the fugal style. As a child Mozart included improvisations at his performances at the European courts. Beethoven's improvisations for his musical friends left an overwhelming impression. At his recitals Liszt asked musicians in the audience to give him subjects for free improvisations, and he amazed them by the spontaneity of his invention. Organ improvisations continued to be the stock-in-trade of organists in the 20th century, while public improvisations by pianists gradually fell into disfavor.

Doubt persists whether the supposedly spontaneous improvisations were not in fact prepared in advance. Some improvisers prefer to prepare in advance, whether it be in the classical cadenza or the JAZZ solo, particularly in the context of larger ensembles. One group of talented improvisers on the piano and organ were those who accompanied the silent movies early in this century. While they used a book of standard music for certain scenes, these musicians had to be prepared on a moment's notice to change styles, cover gaps, or invent on the spot. Some of them had a real flair for enhancing the visual image on the screen while producing music of considerable validity. Jazz has resurrected the art of improvisation to a new height of brilliance, especially in collective improvisations occurring in jam sessions. Depending on the style involved, jazz improvisation is affected by tonality, accompaniment, or length allotted, from a quick "fill" to an essentially unlimited time space.

improvviso (It.). Suddenly.

In a Little Spanish Town. Song by Mabel Wayne, 1926, emblematic of the popularity of ersatz Spanish rhythms at the time.

In a Summer Garden. Symphonic poem by Delius, 1908, 1st performed in London.

In Memoriam. The 4th Sym. of Malipiero, 1948, reflecting the sadness at the human losses of the 2nd World War. Each of the 4 movements ends in a minor key.

In Nomine. A genre of consort music of the 16th and 17th centuries, with more than 150 examples by many English composers. The name derives from the musical source, the Sarum antiphon *Gloria tibi Trinitas*; the important English religious composer John Taverner (b. South Lincolnshire, *c.* 1490; d. Boston, U.K., Oct. 18, 1545) used it as the CANTUS FIRMUS for a Mass *à* 6. In the Benedictus, the section with the text "in nomine Domini" is reduced to *à* 4. Apparently this section was separated from its source and arranged; by the mid-16th century, instrumental fantasias on In Nomine began to appear. Among the composers who wrote In Nomines are Robert Johnson (I), Tallis, White, the Ferraboscos (I and I), Byrd, Bull, Weelkes, Gibbons, Tomkins, William Lawes, and Purcell. The practice has seen a small revival in the 20th century.

In the Good Old Summertime. Song by George Evans, 1902.

In the Steppes of Central Asia. Symphonic tableau by Borodin, 1880, 1st performed in St. Petersburg. The Russian title is simply *In Central Asia*. It is a poetic evocation of the Oriental atmosphere of Khiva and Bukhara, the Khanates of central Asia absorbed in the middle of the 19th century by the expansionist Russian empire. Moslem chants are imitated in the score, and there are also spacious pentatonic passages to reflect Mongolian modalities.

In the Still of the Nite. A 1956 doo-wop hit by the 5 Satins, later covered by Dion and the Belmonts in 1960. Had to be renamed to avoid confusion with the earlier, 1937 Cole Porter ballad *In the Still of the Night*. Sometimes referred to as *(I Remember) In the Still of the Nite*.

Inbrunst (Ger.). Fervor. *Mit Inbrunst*, fervently.

incalzando (It., pursuing hotly). Growing more vehement, pressing ahead, rushing. *Incalzando e stringendo*, growing more vehement and rapid.

incarnatus, Et. Part of the CREDO.

incaternura (It., concatenation). See QUODLIBET.

incidental music. A set of pieces composed to illustrate selected scenes in a dramatic performance. It is distinguished from an orch.l suite because incidental music is subordinated to the dramatic action; it differs from opera because usually there are no vocal parts. The overture from Beethoven's incidental music to Goethe's *Egmont* is frequently performed as a separate concert piece, as are several numbers from Mendelssohn's score to *A Midsummer Night's Dream*, the *Wedding March* being the most famous. Other examples of incidental music that became popular in concert are *L'Arlésienne* by Bizet and *Peer Gynt* by Grieg. In addition to overtures and marches, interludes, songs, and dances may be provided.

incipit (Lat., it begins). The 1st word or group of words of a Gregorian chant, thereby identifying a particular hymn or a CANTUS FIRMUS. In this sense, REQUIEM, MAGNIFICAT, Kyrie, Gloria, and other parts of the MASS and CANONICAL HOURS are such incipits. In cataloging old MSS, the incipit identifies the beginning of the 1st page; the ending of the manuscript is then indicated by the word *explicit*, meaning "it folds out," that is, it ends.

inciso (It., incisive). Sharply marked or accented. *Incise*, accent the notes sharply.

incollando (It.). Playing all the notes in a chord simultaneously, without arpeggiation.

incomplete stop. A half organ stop.

Incoronazione di Poppea, L' (The Coronation of Poppea). Opera by Monteverdi, 1642, his last; it was 1st performed in Venice. An ambitious Roman matron pressures her lover, the Emperor Nero, to divorce his wife and install her as Empress. He is made to burn so warmly that he agrees, exiles his wife and his lover's husband, and celebrates with Poppea. The score is noteworthy for the enhanced sonorities of its instrumentation; however, there is some question as to the total authenticity of the work.

Incredible Flutist, The. Ballet suite by Piston, 1938, one of the few scores he wrote that was programmatic in its content. The flutist leads a village circus in a series of dances. He is incredible because everyone in the crowd follows his cues. The score ends with an infectious march. It was 1st performed by the Boston Pops Orch.

incrociando (It.). Crossing hands while playing the piano, so that the right hand is below the left hand.

incudine (It.). Anvil, used as a percussion instrument.

indebolente. (It.). Gradually lessening the sound.

indeciso (It.). Irresolute, undecided.

independent chord (harmony, triad). One that is consonant and is, therefore, not obliged to change to another chord by progression or resolution.

Indes Galantes, Les. Opera-ballet by Rameau, 1735, 1st produced in Paris. The "gallant Indies" of the title stretch through Turkey, Persia, and South America. The score includes some interesting samples of tonal painting: a storm is represented by a drum roll. There is also a *danse des sauvages*, in which the actors disport themselves to the rhythm of the French dance CANARY.

indeterminacy. With reference to composition, denotes a conventional score produced by chance; with reference to performance, a score which leaves much to be determined by performers.

Indian Love Call. Song by Friml, 1924, featured in the operetta *Rose-Marie.* The melody is hardly Native American, but the song has a certain charm.

Indian Suite. Orch.1 suite by MacDowell, 1895, in 5 movements, with thematic materials derived from Iroquois, Chippewa, Dakota, and Kiowa melodies; it was 1st performed in N.Y.

Indianische Fantasie. Movement for piano and orch. by Busoni, 1914, which he 1st performed as soloist in Berlin. Original pentatonic Indian themes are used as basic material for the work.

indifferente (It.). Indifferently, carelessly.

indolente (It.). Indolent, freely, unconcernedly. *Con indolenza*, with indolence.

Indonesian music. Politically, Indonesia comprises several thousand islands, great and small, straddling the equator. Musically, the most important of them are Java and Bali; they each developed their own indigenous type of an ensemble, the GAMELAN, which consists of sui generis xylophones and a variety of bells, gongs, and drums. The basic scales of the gamelan are the 5-tone *slendro* system and the 7-tone *pelog* system, with supernumerary tones used as embellishments. However, no 2 gamelan are tuned exactly the same, thus leading to the unique character of each particular ensemble. The intervals of the gamelan cannot be reduced precisely to the Western modes; hence an impression on the Western ear of both the stimulating exotic quality of the sound and the disturbing feeling that the melodies are "out of tune." There are many lesser-known Indonesian musical traditions, involving singing, flutes, and fiddles.

When the gamelan was introduced at the Paris Exposition of 1889, Debussy and other French composers of the modern school were fascinated by it; Debussy tried to imitate its foreign sound in several of his works. The greatest attraction of the gamelan to Western composers is the seeming promiscuity of its modes, so that there is a prevailing sense of enhanced concord even when dissonant combinations are employed; furthermore, rhythmic patterns can be used without regard to a prescribed meter. The duration of the basic time unit never changes in a given dance or song with the accompaniment of the gamelan and repeated uniform beats are common, but the complexity is provided by interlocking polyrhythmic patterns. The music heard on the large islands of Borneo and Sumatra is more "primitive," devoid of the delicacy of the gamelan.

Indy, (Paul-Marie-Théodore) Vincent d'

〜〜 〜〜 〜〜 〜〜 〜〜

Eminent French composer and pedagogue; b. Paris, Mar. 27, 1851; d. there, Dec. 2, 1931. Owing to the death of his mother at his birth, his education was directed entirely by his grandmother, a woman of culture and refinement who had known Grétry and Monsigny and who had shown a remarkable appreciation of the works of Beethoven when that master was still living. From 1862 to 1865 he studied piano with Diemer and Marmontel; in 1865 he studied harmony with Lavignac. In 1869 he made the acquaintance of Henri Duparc, and with him spent much time studying the masterpieces of Bach, Beethoven, Berlioz, and Wagner; at that time he wrote his opp. 1 and 2, and he contemplated an opera on Victor Hugo's *Les Burgraves du Rhin* (1869–72; unfinished).

During the Franco-Prussian War he served in the Garde Mobile, and he wrote of his experiences in *Histoire du 105ème Bataillon de la Garde nationale de Paris en l'année 1870–71* (1872). He then began to study composition with Franck (1872); when the latter was appointed prof. of organ at the Paris Cons. (1873), d'Indy joined the class, winning a 2nd *accessit* in 1874 and the 1st the following year. On his 1st visit to Germany in 1873, he met Liszt and Wagner and was introduced to Brahms; in 1876 he heard the 1st performances of the *Ring* cycle at Bayreuth, and for several years thereafter made regular trips to Munich to hear all the works of Wagner; he also attended the premiere of *Parsifal* in 1882. From 1872 to 1876 he was organist at St. Leu-la-Forêt; from 1873 to 1878, chorus master and timpanist with the Colonne Orch.; for the Paris premiere of *Lohengrin* in 1887 he drilled the chorus and was Lamoureux's assistant. In 1871 he joined the Société Nationale de Musique as a junior member, and he was its secretary and de facto leader from 1876 to 1890, when, after Franck's death, he became president. In 1896 he founded, with Bordes and Guilmant, the famous Schola Cantorum, primarily as a school for plainchant and

the Palestrina style. Gradually the scope of instruction was enlarged to include all musical disciplines, and the inst. became one of the world's foremost music schools.

D'Indy's fame as a composer began with the performance of his dramatic legend *Le Chant de la cloche* at a Lamoureux concert in 1886; the work itself had won the City of Paris Prize in the competition of the preceding year. As early as 1874, Pasdeloup had played the overture *Les Piccolomini* (later embodied as the 2nd part in the *Wallenstein* orch. trilogy), and in 1882 the 1-act opera *Attendez-moi sous l'orme* had been produced at the Opéra-Comique; but the prize work attracted general attention, and d'Indy was recognized as one of the most important of modern French masters.

Although he never held an official position as a conductor, he frequently—and with marked success—appeared in that capacity (chiefly upon invitation to direct his own works); thus he visited Spain in 1897, Russia in 1903 and 1907, and the U.S. in 1905, when he conducted the Boston Sym. Orch. In 1892 he was a member of the commission appointed to revise the curriculum of the Cons. and refused a proffered professorship of composition; but in 1912 he accepted an appointment as prof. of the ensemble class. Besides his other duties he was, from 1899, inspector of musical instruction in Paris; he made his last U.S. visit in 1921. He was made a Chevalier of the Legion of Honor in 1892, an Officer in 1912.

Both as teacher and creative artist, d'Indy continued the traditions of Franck. Although he cultivated almost every form of composition, his special talent was in the field of the larger instrumental forms. Some French critics assign to him a position in French music analogous to that of Brahms in German music. His style rests on Bach and Beethoven; however, his deep study of Gregorian chant and the early contrapuntal style added an element of severity, and not rarely of complexity, that renders his approach somewhat difficult and has prompted the charge that his music is lacking in emotional force. He wrote numerous articles for various journals, which are remarkable for their critical acumen and literary finish; his writings include *Cours de Composition musicale* (Book I, 1903; Book II: Part 1, 1909, Part 2, 1933); *César Franck* (1906); *Beethoven* (1911); and *Wagner et son influence sur l'art musical français* (1930). Other musical works include operas, orch.l works, songs, choral works, and chamber music.

inégales (*notes inégales*; Fr., unequal). In the performance of French Baroque music, the practice of playing a note group of even duration so that the 1st note of each pair takes time away from the 2nd, producing a dotted effect; e.g., 2 8th notes will be played or sung as a dotted 8th and a 16th. But there are subtleties of performance; if the syncopation is meant to be gentle, the note is usually marked *louré*; a more incisive syncopation is marked *pointé* or *piqué*. In addition to the works of French Baroque composers, some editors apply dotting (or even *double-dotting*, which alters 2 8th notes to a doubly-dotted 8th and a 32nd) to some works of Bach and others, inspiring much controversy. Whether justified or not, the rhythmic aberrations in the practice of inégales are a well-coordinated guide to performance.

Inextinguishable, The (*Det uudslukkelige*). Sym. No. 4 by Nielsen, 1916. Nielsen gave the work its moniker without explanation; it may reflect an optimistic view toward humanity's prevailing over war, or a cyclical structural feature in the music.

infernale (It.). Infernal.

infinite canon. See CANON.

infinite melody. One which avoids a cadence; often associated with the melodic meanderings of Wagner in his mature music dramas.

infino (It.). Up to, as far as; until you reach.

infiorare (from It. *fiore*, flower). Ornament with florid melismas.

inganno (It., deception). Deceptive cadence. *Inganno la bella fuga*, in 17th-century Italian music, a modified entry in a fugal passage.

ingenuamente (*ingenuo*; It.). Naturally, ingenuously, artlessly.

inharmonic relation. FALSE RELATION.

iniziale (It.). Initial; the 1st.

inner parts. Parts in harmony or counterpoint lying between the highest (soprano) and lowest (bass).

inner pedal. A pedal point in a middle part (alto, tenor, etc.).

innig (Ger.). Heartfelt, sincere, fervent, intense; INTIMO, *con affetto*.

innigem Ausdruck, mit (Ger.). With heartfelt expression.

inniglich (Ger.). With deep emotion; fervently.

inno (It.). Hymn.

innocente (It.). Innocently, artlessly.

inquieto (It.). Unrestful, uneasy.

insanity and suicide. It is a common belief that musicians are more nervous by nature than other professionals, that a greater percentage of performers and composers end their lives in insane asylums, and that only mathematicians and chess players exceed musicians in this melancholy fate. Statistics fail to support this estimate. Among famous composers, only Schumann, Wolf, and MacDowell became totally insane and had to be committed to asylums. Exaggerated sensitivity to criticism, delusions of grandeur, melancholy, and other aberrations may be typical among artists who are constantly on view before the public, but such neurotic traits do not constitute insanity. Even suicidal impulses are no more frequent among musicians than the law of averages would indicate.

Perhaps the most spectacular premeditated suicide was that of the pianist Alexander Kelberine (1903–40), who arranged his last concert program to consist only of works dealing with death, concluding with Liszt's *Totentanz*, and upon returning home took a lethal overdose of sleeping pills. Rezsö Seress (1899–1968), the composer of *Gloomy Sunday*, a song banned in some European countries because it precipitated a wave of Sunday suicides among young people, jumped out of a window and died shortly thereafter. In 1985 the parents of a teenager who killed himself after listening to a rock song urging suicide sued the performers and their record company for a million dollars, but a judge ruled against the claim.

Inscape. Symphonic poem by Copland, 1967, 1st performed in Ann Arbor. The title is based on an aesthetic-mystical idea of the English 19th-century cleric-poet Gerard Manley Hopkins.

insensible (*insensibilmente*, It.). Insensibly, imperceptible.

inspiration

Musical inspiration differs fundamentally from that of poetry and the visual arts, for it has no external material to draw upon. A poet creates images from a preexisting vocabulary of words and concepts in his or her native language; an artist paints a landscape or portrait from visual impressions or interpretations, or designs abstractions from imagined geometric patterns. But a creative musician depends on a more artificial system of successive or combined tones and rhythms, which have no outward existence except in uncoordinated sounds of nature, bird songs, and bodily rhythms. Musical inspiration is therefore an art of sui generis, comparable to mathematical invention, which also deals with an artificially created system of concepts.

The aesthetic conception of beauty in Eastern music is totally different from that of the West; an exotic melody played on an unfamiliar instrument usually seems meaningless to an outsider. Until ethnomusicology broadened its scope, music history traced mainly the evolution of Western melody, harmony, counterpoint, form, and orchestration; the science of musical aesthetics was therefore also Western. An inspired folk song achieves a perfect balance of melodic and rhythmic elements; in Western music these folk melodies are derived mostly from diatonic modes and symmetric rhythms. If melody and rhythm can be described as available materials for composers, then inspiration must follow their patterns within each national or ethnic unit. But in the last several centuries during which the art of music became formulated as a definite aesthetic code, an individual composer had the task of combining melodic phrases from folk

songs within harmonic and contrapuntal formations in order to make a resulting work meaningful to listeners.

The German word for inspiration is *Einfall* (a falling in, or insight); the state of musical inspiration is indeed such a "falling in," but it comes not from the outside but from the inside of a musician's imagination. Theory always follows practice in formulating the aesthetic code. The grammar and syntax of composition became well established with the advent of classical music. Music teaching made use of works created by acknowledged masters of the art; manuals of melody, harmony, and counterpoint codified the practice. The formal aesthetics became established, and composers, like poets, were enabled to be inspired within a given vocabulary of tonal and harmonic formations.

It is not likely that the electro-chemical process that takes place in the cortex during the *Einfall* will ever be recorded on the electroencephalograph, but some such process must be taking place when a composer figuratively exclaims "Eureka!" and rushes into his or her workroom to put the insight on paper. Most stories about the moment of inspiration are romantic inventions. Beethoven never said, "Thus knocks fate on my door," after he wrote down the famous 4 opening notes of his 5th Sym., for he used the same rhythmic figures in works written around the same time. Immensely complex is the mental formation of a Bach devising a fugal subject that would yield the most interesting contrapuntal developments, a process of musical precognition that even composers less Olympian must follow. The magnitude of Wagner's controlled inspiration in designing his music dramas is extraordinary in that he had to coordinate his own text, the interlacing set of LEITMOTIVS, the limitations imposed by the range of instruments and voices and dynamics in order to create an architecturally stable structure.

The facility of inspiration is not in direct or inverse proportion to the ultimate value of the music. Mozart, Schubert, Rossini, and Mendelssohn possessed an amazing facility of immediate conversion of inspiration into written music. Beethoven labored mightily; his copyist said he would rather copy 20 pages of Rossini than 1 by Beethoven. Improvisation is disciplined inspiration; but great improvisers on the organ or piano were rarely great composers, although great composers were often remarkable improvisers. Inspiration can be stored away, and a musical idea that seems to be irrelevant to a work in progress may suddenly illuminate a different work undertaken at a different time. Musical inspiration, particularly in a work of large dimensions, must be inevitably constrained by the manual labor that goes into the writing of musical notes on several staves. A poet can sketch a sonnet as a result of the lightninglike onset of inspiration, and commit it to paper with the speed of writing. A composer has to deal with an intricate set of notes, lines, and various symbols before recording musical thought in manuscript form.

Mystically inclined composers like to believe that their inspiration came from on high. Scriabin felt that his music was a divine message, and he professed that he was merely a revealer of that message; the atheist Tippett has expressed the same feeling of being a vessel for external (if not necessarily religious) expression. The conviction on the part of the composer that he or she is divinely inspired undoubtedly helps in accomplishing the labor with celerity. Handel could have been justified in believing in such help after he completed the score of his oratorio *Messiah* in 3 and a half weeks. When he heard one of his sacred works recklessly performed by a church choir, he actually whispered apology to God, "Oh Lord! This is not thus that I wrote this music in Thy glory!"

inständig (Ger.; It. *instante*). Urgent, pressing.

instrumental motet. A contrapuntal instrumental composition written on the model of the Renaissance motet, often named with words taken from a specific Latin model, such as the English IN NOMINE.

instrumentation. The theory and practice of composing, arranging, or adapting music for a body of instruments of different kinds. See ORCHESTRATION.

instrumento d'acciaio (It., steel instrument). Mozart's indication in *The Magic Flute* for a glockenspiel.

instruments à cordes (Fr.). String instruments.

instruments à vent (Fr.). Wind instruments.

intabulation (from Lat. *tabula*, table; Ger. *Intabulierung*; It. *intavolatura*). The arrangement of a vocal composition for keyboard or stringed instruments, with added ornamentation to make the original parts more idiomatic. The Italian form of the word also refers to collections of intabulations and TABLATURES.

Intégrales. Chamber work for small orch. and percussion by Varèse, 1925, composed according to his constructivist ideas of organized sound integrated into one self-consistent formal structure. The piece was performed for the 1st time in N.Y. under the auspices of the International Composers Guild with Stokowski conducting. The critics exercised their literary wits and power of animal metaphors to describe the music as suggesting an intoxicated woodpecker, an injured dog's cry of pain, or a cat's yell of midnight rage. By the postwar era *Intégrales* was recognized as a classic of modern music.

intenzione, con (It.). With stress, emphasis.

interference beats. The effect of the simultaneous sounding of 2 different tones; the result, a pulsing change in amplitude, is called *beating*. The theoretical distinction between consonance and dissonance depends on the relative number of beats: The more beats generated by the sounding of 2 or more tones simultaneously, the more dissonant is the resulting combination. The octave, being a perfect consonance, generates no beats. A perfect 5th should also be free of beats, and 2 a cappella voices or violin strings properly tuned will produce this effect; but because the tuning on a piano is tempered, the 5ths are not perfect; on average, the

5th on the piano beats 47 times per minute. See also ACOUSTICS; JUST INTONATION; TEMPERAMENT.

interlude. 1. An Italian INTERMEZZO or French ENTR'ACTE. 2. An instrumental strain or passage connecting the lines or stanzas of a hymn, etc. 3. An organ piece played between choral hymns or psalms of a church service (*interludium*).

intermezzo (It., insertion; Fr. *intermède*; Lat. *intermedium*). 1. A theatrical genre that dates back to the liturgical drama in the 13th century in which they were interpolated between ritual parts of the religious service. Secular intermezzos served to provide diversions at aristocratic weddings, coronations, and other formal functions. Invariably they were of a lighter nature than other parts of the occasion, and they were not necessarily connected with the action in the drama or religious play into which they were interpolated. The genre eventually developed into independent musical presentations, leading ultimately to the formation of OPERA BUFFA.

Since the intermezzos did not have to be connected with the principal spectacle, their authors strove mainly to please the public by whatever means, and often succeeded in attracting more attention than the stage play itself. Thus Pergolesi inserted an intermezzo *La Serva padrona* in a performance of his serious opera *Il Prigioniero superbo*, with the result that the intermezzo became extremely popular; its performances in Paris precipitated the famous GUERRE DES BOUFFONS. Rousseau, who was an ardent partisan of the Italian type of opera, composed an intermezzo, which became quite successful. Richard Strauss wrote an amusing opera of his own in this genre and pointedly entitled it *Intermezzo*. Within operas, intermezzos are instrumental interludes, usually of short duration, between scenes. An intermezzo in Mascagni's *Cavalleria Rusticana* is often performed as an independent concert piece.

2. A character piece of instrumental music in which the title is understood in the sense of a piece written at leisure between times. But it is difficult to justify in this sense the term *intermezzo* that Brahms assigned to his highly elaborate Romantic piano pieces. 3. Incidental music in modern dramas. 4. A short movement connecting the main divisions of a sym.

Intermezzo. Opera by R. Strauss, 1924, to his own libretto. A composer's wife threatens to divorce him when a love letter arrives in his mail by misdirection; fortunately, he proves his total innocence, all to light and harmless music.

intermodulation. Electronic technique of sound manipulation inspired by the interference of 2 signals; used extensively, in principle, by such modern composers as Stockhausen.

Internationale. Proletarian marching hymn written by a wood-carver, Pierre Degeyter, in 1871, shortly after the fall of the Paris Commune. The *Internationale* served as the national anthem of the Soviet Union until 1944.

interrogatio (Lat.). A conventional expressive melodic movement a major or minor 2nd upward at the end of a phrase, used in medieval sacred music as a regular formula, enabling the listener to equate it with a question in punctuation. Baroque composers commonly employed this device, which was also recommended by the theorists of the time.

interruzione, senza (It.). Without interruption.

interval

The distance between 2 notes measured in diatonic degrees. Intervals are regularly measured from the lower tone to the higher. The distance between a note and itself is obviously zero; but in determining an interval, this initial note is treated as a prime or unison and assigned the symbol. The distance between a given note and the next note in the scale is obviously a single unit, but it is called a 2nd, marked with the numerical symbol 2. Thus the names of the intervals indicate not the distance between 2 notes, but the numerical order of their positions proceeding up the scale. The interval of a 3rd contains 2 diatonic units, yet its symbol is 3; and so it goes until the octave (from Lat. *octo*, 8), which contains 7 diatonic units.

The tabulation of intervals, named after the ordinal numbers, is otherwise quite simple: unison, second (2nd), third (3rd), fourth (4th), fifth (5th), sixth (6th), seventh (7th), and octave. Much more solemn and learned are the Latin names of intervals, derived from the Greek; these are *unisonus, tonus, ditonus, diatessaron, diapente, tonus cum diapente, ditonus cum diapente,* and *diapason* (octave). Beyond the octave the intervals are still named by the numerical adjectives in English and in French; they follow Latin forms in German, Italian, Spanish, and Russian.

Intervals are modified by indications of major, minor, augmented, and diminished. It is most unfortunate that the nomenclature of intervals in English borrows the Latin comparative adjectives *major* and *minor* for the size of intervals, and that the same terms are also used to indicate major and minor keys. This brings confusion into the minds of students who are apt to say that the interval E to C is a major 6th, rather than the correct minor 6th, simply because E and C convey to most ears the feeling of a C-major triad, particularly with C in the melody position. The French (*majeur, mineur*), Spanish (*mayor, menor*), and Italian (*maggiore, minore*) follow the Latin pattern. Much more convenient is the German terminology in which the adjectives *grosse* and *kleine* are used for major and minor, so that E to C is unmistakably a *kleine Sexte* (small 6th) and the ambiguity is avoided. The Russians follow the German usage.

The unison, 4th, 5th, and octave are perfect intervals, without a subdivision into major and minor, that is, large and small. Furthermore, all intervals can be augmented or diminished, and some even doubly augmented or doubly diminished. A 4th can be diminished, augmented, and doubly augmented; a 5th can be augmented, diminished, and doubly diminished. All these possibilities are governed by the intrinsic development of the tonalities of which the intervals are diatonic parts.

Several intervallic pairs are enharmonic equivalents, containing identical numbers of semitones. And here we enter a knotted web of anomalies. A minor 3rd is a consonance, but its enharmonic equivalent, an augmented 2nd, which sounds exactly the same, is a dissonance, requiring resolution. This seeming anomaly is accounted for by the fact that it is the musical spelling that determines the belonging of an interval or a chord to a particular tonality, and what is consonant in one tonality may be dissonant in another. An analogy from linguistics may help: The word *four* is a number, but the word *for* is a preposition. *Mother* is the sweetest word in English, dripping in sentimentality, which may well be likened to a perfect consonance, but the same word, *mother*, is defined in *Webster's New Collegiate Dictionary* as "a slimy membrane composed of yeast and bacterial cells that develops on the surface of alcoholic liquids undergoing acetous fermentation and called also a 'mother of vinegar.'"

Augmented interval, wider by a chromatic semitone than major or perfect; *chromatic interval*, augmented or diminished (except augmented 4th, and diminished 5th and 7th); *compound interval*, wider than an octave; *consonant interval*, not requiring resolution; *diatonic interval*, occurring between 2 notes belonging to the same key (except the augmented 2nd and 5th of the harmonic minor scale); *diminished interval*, chromatic semitone narrower than major or perfect; *dissonant interval*, requiring resolution; *enharmonic interval*, see ENHARMONIC EQUIVALENCE; *extended* or *extreme, interval*, augmented; *flat interval*, diminished; *harmonic interval*, both tones sounded together; *imperfect interval*, diminished; *inverted interval*, the higher tone is lowered, or the lower tone raised, by an octave; *major interval*, equal to the standard 2nd, 3rd, 6th, and 7th of the major scale; *melodic interval*, both tones sounded in succession; *minor interval*, a chromatic semitone narrower than major; *parallel* or *consecutive interval* (with an interval preceding), 2-dyad progression in the same direction and at the same interval; *perfect* or *perfect major interval*, equal to the standard unison, 4th, 5th, and octave of the major scale; *redundant interval*, augmented; *simple interval*, not wider than an octave; *standard interval*, measured upward from the keynote; *superfluous interval*, augmented.

intimissimo (It.). Very tenderly, warmly.

intimo (It.). Heartfelt, fervent.

intonarumori (It., noisemakers). Musical instruments invented *c.* 1913 by Italian futurist Luigi Russolo, all of which were destroyed in Paris during World War II.

intonation. 1. The production of tone, either vocal or instrumental, with an emphasis on proper pitch. 2. The method of chanting employed in plainchant. 3. The opening notes leading up to the reciting tone of a chant. *Fixed intonation*, see FIXED-TONE INSTRUMENTS.

intoning. The chanting by the minister, in monotone, of parts of the Anglican Church service.

intrada (It., entry). A short introduction or prelude; an opening piece on a festive occasion, most often arranged for trumpets and horns, and with the character of a fanfare in march time.

intrepidezza, con (It., intrepidly). Boldly, daringly, dashingly.

introduction. 1. An instrumental prelude before an aria in an opera. 2. In a concerto or similar work, an orch.l TUTTI before the entry of the soloist. Such an introduction may be very brief, as for instance the plagal cadential chords in the opening bars of Rachmaninoff's 2nd Piano Concerto, or else it may fill a lengthy section almost qualified to be called an overture, as in the tutti introduction to Beethoven's Violin Concerto. 3. A phrase or division preliminary to and preparatory of a composition or movement. It may be in a parallel minor or major key, as in Beethoven's 4th Sym., which opens in B-flat minor in a long preamble before the transition to the principal key in B-flat major; another example is the opening movement of Haydn's 104th Sym. The 3rd Sym. of Scriabin has a long introduction in D-flat major, the Neapolitan lowered supertonic of the principal key, C minor.

Introduction and Allegro. Chamber piece by Ravel, 1907, for harp, string quartet, flute, and clarinet, 1st performed in Paris. The music exemplifies a modern, impressionistic treatment of the harp.

introduzione (It.). INTRODUCTION.

introit (*introitus*; Lat., entrance). 1. An opening antiphon sung while the priest is approaching the altar to celebrate the Roman Catholic High Mass. It is responsorial in structure, with a soloist alternating with a chorus, or the chorus divided in 2 alternating parts. 2. In the modern Anglican Church, an anthem or psalm sung as the minister approaches the Communion table.

invention (Lat. *inventio*, from *invenire*, find). 1. A musical work that possesses elements of intellectual and artistic discovery. In Renaissance music the word *invention* still preserved its ancient connotation of newness. To the minds of 17th-century musicians, inventions were the product of intuitive observation, both modern in relation to their era and curious with respect to intellectual perception. Musical inventions were born *ex abrupto*. The theory of the musical invention followed the rules of Latin rhetoric going back to Cicero and Quintilian and was retained in the system of schooling in the Baroque era, in a sequence of mental and artistic stages in the following order: *inventio*, *dispositio*, *elaboratorio*, *decoratio*, and *executio*. 2. A short piece in free contrapuntal style developing 1 motive in an impromptu fashion. The high point of this form of invention in music reached its most expressive mark in Bach's 2-part and 3-part keyboard inventions; the 3-part works are also known as sinfonias. In the introductory paragraph to his inventions, Bach states his aims in concordance with the old rhetorical sequence: "A faithful guide, whereby the lovers of the clavier are presented with a plain method of learning not only how to play clearly in 2 parts, but also to progress toward playing 3 obbligato parts well and accurately; at the same time striving not only to obtain fine inventions, but also to develop them appropriately, and above all to secure a cantabile style of playing so as to create a strong foretaste of the art of composition itself."

inversion (from Lat. *vertere*, turn). The transposition of the notes of an interval or chord. 1. *Melodic inversion*, in which the ascending intervals of the original melody are inverted to become descending intervals and vice versa. In some melodies, an inversion becomes identical with retrograde motion, as in a Beethoven contradanza:

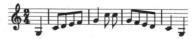

A melodic inversion is said to be *tonal* if it follows the tonality of the melody. The 2nd subject of the G-major Fugue from Book I of Bach's *Well-Tempered Clavier* is such an inversion of the 1st subject. In tonal inversions the intervals are not precise as to the content in semitone units. For instance, the C-major scale when inverted becomes the Phrygian mode, with the initial interval being a semitone rather than a whole tone. A major tetrachord when inverted becomes a minor tetrachord. A broken major triad becomes a broken minor triad when inverted, and vice versa. An interesting example of this reciprocal relationship of major and minor tonalities in inversion is provided by the 18th variation of Rachmaninoff's *Rhapsody on a Theme by Paganini*, in which the original ascending minor tune becomes, in a slower tempo, an emotional romantic theme, descending to the dominant an octave lower. Old contrapuntal composers liked to preface their inversions by tantalizing instructions in Latin, as the Biblical allusion in Jacob Obrecht's *Missa graecorum*: "Qui se exaltat humiliabitur et qui se humiliat exaltabitur;" or simply, "Subverte lineam": invert the (melodic) line.

Inversions of intervals are obtained by placing the low notes an octave above, or the upper note an octave below. When a major interval is inverted it becomes minor; an augmented interval becomes diminished. To obtain the intervallic inversion arithmetically, the original interval must be subtracted from 9. Thus a 2nd inverted becomes a 7th, a 4th becomes a 5th, etc. A perfect interval inverts into another perfect interval, e.g., a perfect 5th inverted becomes a perfect 4th. A consonance inverted becomes another consonance, e.g., 3rds become 6ths; a dissonance inverted becomes a nother dissonance, e.g., a 2nd becomes a 7th. In contrapuntal music, "scientific" inversions of the 9th, 10th, 12th, etc., are often found. In such cases, the inverted interval is complementary not to an octave but to another specified large interval; in the inversions of the 10th, the numerical value of the interval is subtracted from 11. The rules of voice leading become subverted in such types of counterpoint. For instance, in the counterpoint of the 12th, the perfectly legal and desirable consecutive 6ths become, upon inversion, consecutive 7ths inadmissible in traditional harmony.

When Haydn returned, after a long absence, to Vienna, a middle-aged woman rushed to him and exclaimed, "Maestro, do you remember me? You wrote this for me," and she sang:

"Ach! I do remember," Haydn replied. "Unfortunately, now it is this:"

2. *Harmonic inversion*, in which the bass voice is transferred an octave higher and placed on top of the chord. Chord inversions used in traditional harmony are the following: a triad; its 1st inversion known as the 6–3 chord, shortened to 6 chord; and the 2nd inversion or 6–4 chord; the 7th chord and its inversions, the 6–5–3 (or 6–5) chord,

6–4–3 (or 4–3) chord, and 6–4–2 (or 2) chord. (The numbers refer to the interval as counted up from the bass note.) 3. See INVERTIBLE COUNTERPOINT. 4. An organ point found in some other part than the bass. 5. A standard precompositional technique in 12-note composition, wherein all linear intervals of a set are mirrored around a horizontal plane, i.e., reversed in their vertical direction.

inverted mordent (Ger. *Schneller*, fast trill). A short and rapid upper trill that usually begins on the half beat (see MORDENT). The term is highly confusing to modern performers because *mordent* itself was subject to controversy during its heyday. The German Baroque used the picturesque term *Pralltriller* (elastic trill), which might refer to the Schneller or a similar figure which begins after the half beat. The notation of these ornaments is fraught with inconsistencies, but fortunately a healthy decay of stenographic ornamentation has made the correct definition of the inverted mordent of no vital interest to anyone except editors of Baroque MSS, or early-music practitioners who are engaged in ceaseless internecine struggle regarding the meaning of such terms.

invertible counterpoint. A type of polyphonic writing in which contrapuntal parts can be exchanged—say soprano and bass—and remain free of forbidden discord and consecutive motion. While the normal interval of invertibility is the octave, other intervals have been used, such as the 10th or 12th. Among great masters of invertible counterpoint were Brahms, Reger, and Taneyev. Bach nurtured them all in his *Art of the Fugue*, a veritable treasure box of scientific inversions. Also called *double counterpoint*.

Invitation to the Dance (Ger., Aufforderung zum Tanz). Rondo brilliant for piano by Weber, 1819, in D-flat major. A unique composition in its treatment as a concert piece, it became even more famous in the orch.1 arrangement that Berlioz made in 1841.

invocation. Ode or prayer, particularly in ORATORIO or OPERA.

Iolanta. Opera by Tchaikovsky, 1892, 1st performed in St. Petersburg. Iolanta is a blind girl living in 15th-century Provence. A Mauretanian physician promises to cure her if her desire to see is truly passionate; her love for a Burgundian knight provides the necessary passion. The operation is a success; she sees her knight for the 1st time, admires the beauty and symmetry of his facial features, and

463

marries him to much jubilation. The work is not among the composer's masterpieces.

Iolanthe, or The Peer and the Peri. Comic opera by Gilbert and Sullivan, 1882, 1st produced in London. A fairy maiden is banished from her supernatural domain for having loved a mortal; their son, who is "a fairy only down to the waist," is in love with a ward in the Chancery (high government court), but several elderly peers also eye her with obsolescent concupiscence. To gain time, she becomes engaged to 2 earls, one after another. A fairy scandal breaks out when the Lord Chancellor admits that he is Iolanthe's mortal husband. Conscience stricken, he allows his ward to marry his and Iolanthe's son. A final blow to the pride of the House of Lords comes when it turns out that other fairies have also married peers. The Queen of Fairies forgives them all, and the 2 worlds unite in legitimate domestic felicity.

Ionian mode. This mode corresponds to the structure of the major scale. It was added to the 8 traditional ecclesiastical modes by Glareanus in 1547, and placed at the head of the system of church modes as *primus tonus* by Zarlino in 1558. Ironically, the Ionian mode, which has become the starting point for the traditional cycle of scales and the 1st rudiment of musical education, was described in medieval treatises as *modus lascivus*, a lascivious, lewd, or wanton mode.

Ionisation. Percussion ensemble work by Varèse, 1931, with a superadded pair of sirens. The score received its 1st performance in N.Y. (1933). The word *ionisation* is a scientific term which signifies the splitting of atoms into ions. The rhythmic pattern of the score is extremely complex, and the balance of instrumental timbres, such as wood and metal, is maintained with an extraordinary degree of virtuosity. The work, at 1st disdained by musicians at large, has become a classic. It is said that a recording of *Ionisation* was regularly played by scientists working on an atom bomb in 1942.

Iphigénie en Aulide. Opera by Gluck, 1774, after a play by Racine based on Euripides; 1st produced in Paris. The Greek fleet is in doldrums in the port of Aulis and cannot proceed to Troy, for which it is bound, because Agamemnon, King of Crete, had killed a sacred animal in the temple of Artemis, the virgin huntress and moon divinity. A priest warns him that the goddess will not be appeased unless Agamemnon sacrifices his daughter Iphigenia by immolation. He is willing to yield, but her bridegroom

Achilles voices objections and threats; finally, the gods are appeased, and Iphigenia is saved. The overture from the opera is famous as a concert piece.

Iphigénie en Tauride. Opera by Gluck, 1779, after Euripides; 1st produced in Paris. The story is a sequel to the composer's *Iphigénie en Aulide.* The heroine, saved from immolation, travels to Tauris (Greek name for the Crimea), where she joins the local Scythians. When her brother Orestes is seized as an invader, she saves him, rejoins the Greeks, and returns to her native land.

ira, con (It.). With wrath; passionately.

Iris. Opera by Mascagni, 1898, 1st performed in Rome. The action takes place in modern Japan. Iris, pure and innocent, is abducted by a villainous suitor who places her in a bordello. Her blind father curses her, believing her guilty. She throws herself into a sewer, but is lifted by a host of angels to heaven. The music is in the style of verismo; pentatonic progressions are used to suggest Japanese modalities.

Irish reel. A fast variety of the REEL.

Irlandais, -e (Fr.). Hibernian, Irish.

Irma la Douce. Song by Marguerite Monmot, 1956, in French. This ballad was the inspiration for an eponymous American film.

Irmelin. Opera by Delius, 1892, to his own libretto; the work was not performed until 1953. Irmelin is a princess in love with a swineherd who fortuitously turns out to be a prince himself. They meet at a brook, and all ends happily. The music is Wagnerian, diversified by sentimental pastoral episodes.

ironicamente (It.). Ironically.

irregular cadence. See CADENCE.

irresoluto (It.). Irresolute, undecided; vacillating.

Islamey. A popular dance of the Caucasian tribe of the Kabardinians, marked by a drone on the dominant and suggesting the MIXOLYDIAN MODE; it is performed by popular players on the fiddle and the accordion who accompany the dance. The word is derived from *Islam*, i.e., Moslem.

Islamey. Piano fantasy by Balakirev, 1869, long regarded as the most difficult piece ever written for piano.

islancio, con (It.). Vehemently, impetuously; with dash.

Isle of the Dead, The. Symphonic poem by Rachmaninoff, 1909, inspired by the famous mortuary painting by Arnold Böcklin. Rachmaninoff conducted its 1st performance in Moscow. This powerful work is remarkable because of its prevalent meter of 5/8, unusual for Rachmaninoff's symmetrical musical world.

isorhythm (from Grk. *iso* + *rhythmos*, same rhythm). A musicological term to indicate melodies, particularly the cantus firmus of medieval motets that are built on the same rhythmic sequence. The definition was expanded to include a technique popular in the 14th and 15th centuries, where a contrapuntal line uses a repeated pitch pattern (COLOR) and a repeated rhythmic pattern (*talea*). The color and talea do not necessarily coincide, so that the repeated pitches are presented in different rhythms and phrases, eventually returning to the opening pattern.

Israel, Brian M., American composer and pianist; b. N.Y., Feb. 5, 1951; d. Syracuse, N.Y., May 8, 1986. He studied composition with Ulysses Kay at Lehman College in N.Y. (B.A., 1971), and with Robert Palmer, Burrill Phillips, and Karel Husa at Cornell Univ. (M.F.A., 1974; D.M.A., 1975); taught at Cornell (1972–75) and Syracuse Univ. (1975–86). As a performer he advocated contemporary works; his own compositions form an eclectic traversal from Baroque contrapuntal devices to serialism, from ironic humor to profound seriousness. His works include chamber and children's operas, orch.l works, including 6 symphonies, chamber works including 3 string quartets, and works for band, choral works, and songs.

Israel in Egypt. Oratorio by Handel, 1739, after verses from Exodus and the Psalms, to an English text. Handel wrote it when he was a resident of London. Its 1st performance took place in London.

Israel Symphony. Work by Ernest Bloch, 1917; although he was born in Switzerland and lived most of his life in the U.S., Bloch remained faithful to his Jewish heritage. It is in 2 movements, portraying the contemplative religious mood of the Jewish people and the contrasting dramatic outcry of the nation deprived of a home. It was 1st performed in New York, 30 years before the formation of the state of Israel.

Istar Variations. Orch.l variations by d'Indy, 1897, inspired by the Babylonian myth of the goddess Istar, who passes through 7 gates, gradually shedding her vestments until she is nude. Ingeniously, the work begins with the variations and ends with the theme, naked at last. It contains impressionistic elements of tone painting. It was 1st performed in Brussels.

istesso (It.). Same. *L'istesso tempo,* the same tempo or time; signifies either that the tempo of either the measure or basic beat note remains the same after a change of time signature, or that a tempo previously interrupted is to be resumed.

istrumentale (It.). Instrumental.

istrumento (It.; plural *istrumenti*). Instrument.

It Had to Be You. Amorous ballad by Isham Jones, 1924. He made it famous playing it with his band.

It Happened in Nordland. Operetta by Herbert, 1904, 1st performed in N.Y. The American ambassadress to Nordland looks very much like the Nordland queen and is induced to impersonate her when the Queen leaves the country to join her lover; there is a happy ending. The most popular numbers are the march *Commanderess-in-Chief* and the waltz *A Knot of Blue.*

It Was a Very Good Year. Song by Ervin Drake, 1961; according to it, any year at any age before 35 is wonderful. Frank Sinatra put this viewpoint across painlessly.

Italia. Orch.l rhapsody by Casella, 1910, based on Italian melodies and 1st performed in Paris.

Italian Concerto (*Concerto nach italiänischen Gusto*). Solo harpsichord work by Bach, by 1735, requiring a 2-manual instrument. The name is explained by its exploiting the natural antiphony of the 2 manuals, one playing soft and the other loud, in the Italian manner of an instrumental concerto (e.g., Vivaldi).

Italian overture. An overture of the 17th and 18th centuries consisting of 3 sections—quick, slow, quick—as opposed to the French overture, in which the sections are slow, quick, slow. Other overture forms include slow, fast, slow, fast and slow, fast (Purcell, *Dido and Aeneas*).

Italian Serenade. String quartet by Wolf, 1887, in G major; one of the few instrumental works by this composer, and one of his finest.

Italian sixth. An augmented 6th chord type; its 3 notes contain the augmented 6th from bottom to top and a major 3rd from bottom to the middle notes, as in A flat, C, and F sharp; it resolves most often to the 2nd inversion tonic chord, occasionally to a dominant chord (in C major):

Italian Symphony. The 4th Sym. of Mendelssohn, 1833, in A major; it was 1st performed in London. The Italian element is apparent in the finale, which is a rapid saltarello, but Mendelssohn himself never authorized the surname.

Italiana in Algeri, L'. Opera by Rossini, 1813, produced in Venice. The Italian woman in the title seeks her beloved captured by and enslaved by the Bey of Algiers. When after some misadventures she finds him, the wily Bey professes his carnal desire for her. As he relaxes his controls, she frees her lover and escapes with him. The overture is popular as a concert piece.

Ite missa est. This is the valedictory sentence of the Roman Catholic Mass: "Go, you [the congregation] are dismissed." This dismissal is etymologically significant, for the Latin term for the Mass is *Missa*. While considered part of the Ordinary, few polyphonic Masses set this short passage.

It's De-Lovely. Song by Cole Porter, 1936, written for the musical *Red, Hot, and Blue* and built on a scale of superlatives.

It's Not for Me to Say. Song by Robert Allen, 1957, which became a perennial favorite as recorded by Johnny Mathis.

It's Now or Never. A song, 1960, based on the melody of *O Sole Mio* by Eduardo Di Capua; a hit for Elvis Presley.

Itsy Bitsy Teenie Weenie Yellow Polkadot Bikini. A 1960 number 1 novelty hit for Brian Hyland, celebrating the joys of the recently introduced 2-piece bathing suit.

Ivan Susanin. See LIFE FOR THE CZAR, A.

Ivanhoe. Grand opera by Sullivan, 1891, 1st produced in London after he became alienated from his longtime collaborator, Gilbert. Based on the novel by Walter Scott, the opera failed with the public; it was Sullivan's only attempt at a serious opera.

Ives, Charles (Edward)

Outstanding American composer whose music, extraordinarily original and yet deeply national in its sources of inspiration, profoundly changed the direction of American music; b. Danbury, Conn., Oct. 20, 1874; d. N.Y., May 19, 1954. His father, George Ives, was a bandleader of the 1st CT Heavy Artillery during the Civil War, and the early development of Charles Ives was, according to his own testimony, deeply influenced by his father. At the age of 12 he played the drums in the band and also received from his father rudimentary musical training in piano and cornet playing. At the age of 13 he played organ at the Danbury Church; soon he began to improvise freely at the piano, without any dependence on school rules; as a result of his experimentation in melody and harmony, and encouraged by his father, he began to combine several keys, partly as a spoof but eventually as a legitimate alternative to traditional music; at 17 he composed his

Variations on America for organ in a polytonal setting; still earlier he wrote a band piece, *Holiday Quickstep*, which was performed by the Danbury Band in 1888.

He attended Danbury High School; in 1894 he entered Yale Univ., where he took regular academic courses and studied organ with Dudley Buck and composition with Horatio Parker; from Parker he received a fine classical training; while still in college he composed a full-fledged sym., written in an entirely traditional manner demonstrating great skill in formal structure, fluent melodic development, and smooth harmonic modulations. After his graduation in 1898, Ives joined an insurance company; also played organ at the Central Presbyterian Church in N.Y. (1899–1902). In 1907 he formed an insurance partnership with Julian Myrick of N.Y.; he proved himself to be an exceptionally able businessman; the firm of Ives & Myrick prospered, and Ives continued to compose music as an avocation. In 1908 he married Harmony Twichell. In 1918 he suffered a massive heart attack, complicated by a diabetic condition, and was compelled to curtail his work both in business and in music to a minimum because his illness made it difficult to handle a pen. He retired from business in 1930; by that time he had virtually stopped composing.

In 1919 Ives publ. at his own expense his great masterpiece, the *Concord Sonata* for piano, inspired by the writings of Emerson, Hawthorne, the Alcotts, and Thoreau. Although written early in the century, its idiom is so extraordinary, and its technical difficulties so formidable, that the work did not receive a performance in its entirety until John Kirkpatrick played it in N.Y. in 1939. In 1922 Ives brought out, also at his expense, a volume of *114 Songs*, written between 1888 and 1921 and marked by great diversity of style, ranging from lyrical Romanticism to powerful and dissonant modern invocations. Both the *Concord Sonata* and the *114 Songs* were distributed gratis by Ives to anyone wishing to receive copies. His orch. masterpiece, *3 Places in New England*, also had to wait nearly 2 decades before its 1st

Charles Ives

PHOTOGRAPH BY FRANK GERRATANA, COURTESY OF THE NEW YORK PUBLIC LIBRARY

performance; of the monumental 4th Sym., only the 2nd movement was performed in 1927, and a complete performance was given posthumously in 1965. In 1947 Ives received the Pulitzer Prize for his 3rd Sym., written in 1911.

The slow realization of the greatness of Ives and the belated triumphant recognition of his music were phenomena without precedent in music history. Because of his chronic ailment, and also on account of his personal disposition, Ives lived as a recluse, away from the mainstream of American musical life; he almost never went to concerts and did not own a record player or a radio; while he was well versed in the musical classics and studied the scores of Beethoven, Schumann, and Brahms, he took little interest in sanctioned works of modern composers; yet he anticipated many technical innovations, such as polytonality, atonality, and even 12-tone formations, as well as polymetric and polyrhythmic configurations, which were prophetic for his time. In the 2nd movement of the *Concord Sonata* he specified the application of a strip of wood on the white and the black keys of the piano to produce an echolike sonority; in his unfinished *Universe Sym.* he planned an antiphonal representation of the heavens in chordal counterpoint and the earth in contrasting orch.1 groups. He also composed pieces of quarter-tone piano music.

A unique quality of Ives's music was the combination of simple motifs, often derived from American church hymns and popular ballads, with an extremely complex dissonant counterpoint, which formed the supporting network for the melodic lines. A curious idiosyncrasy is the frequent quotation of the "fate motive" of Beethoven's 5th Sym. in many of his works. From the 2nd Sym. onward, QUOTATION and QUODLIBET became a primary compositional technique.

Materials of Ives's instrumental and vocal works often overlap, and the titles are often changed during the process of composition. In his orchestrations he often indicated interchangeable and optional parts, as in the last movement of the *Concord Sonata*, which has a part for flute obbligato; thus he reworked the original score for large orch. of his *3 Places in New England* for a smaller ensemble to fit the requirements of the Chamber Orch. of Boston, conducted by N. Slonimsky, which gave its 1st performance (N.Y., 1931); it was in this version that the work was 1st publ. and widely performed until the restoration of the large score was made in 1974.

In recent years there has been some dissension over the dating of Ives's MSS; he treated some pieces as ongoing works-in-progress, and altered them at different times of his life, e.g., the final dissonant chord of the 2nd Sym., which replaced a major triad in the orig. version. Some interpreted this as an attempt to predate Ives's modernity; others saw it as a valid approach, comparable to other composers who tinkered with their music for years; indeed, in his later years, Ives's standard response to his editors posing questions seems to have been, "Do what you think is best."

Ives possessed an uncommon gift for literary expression; his annotations to his works are both trenchant and humorous; he publ. in 1920 *Essays before a Sonata* as a literary companion vol. to the *Concord Sonata*; his *Memos*, in the form of a diary, reveal an extraordinary power of aphoristic utterance. He was acutely conscious of his civic duties as an American; he once circulated a proposal to have federal laws enacted by popular referendum. His centennial in 1974 was celebrated by a series of conferences at his alma mater, Yale Univ.; in N.Y., Miami, and many other American cities; and in Europe, including Russia.

While during his lifetime he and a small group of devoted friends and admirers had great difficulties in having his works performed, recorded, or publ., a veritable Ives cult emerged after his death; eminent conductors gave repeated performances of his orch. works, and modern pianists were willing to cope with the forbidding difficulties of his works. In terms of the number of orch. performances, Ives stood highest among modern composers on American programs in 1976, and the influence of his music on the new generation of composers reached a high mark, so that the adjective "Ivesian" became common in music criticism to describe certain acoustical and coloristic effects characteristic of his music. America's youth expressed especial enthusiasm for Ives's music, which received its most unusual tribute in the commercial marketing of a T-shirt with Ives's portrait.

All of the Ives MSS and his correspondence were deposited by Mrs. Ives at Yale Univ., forming a basic Ives archive which Kirkpatrick organized and catalogued. The Charles Ives Soc. promotes research and publications. Letters from Ives to the author are reproduced in *Music Since 1900* (N.Y., 5th ed., 1994). A television movie, *A Good Dissonance Like a Man*, produced and directed by Theodor W. Timreck in 1977 with the supervision of Vivian Perlis, depicts the life of Ives with fine dramatic impact. Among his numerous works are the 4 numbered syms. (1896–98; 1897–1902; 1901–1904; 1910–16); fragments of a *Universe Sym.* (1911–16; 1st perf. of a realized version, Los Angeles, 1984); *3 Places in New England*, 1st Orch. Set (1903–14); *Calcium Light Night* for Chamber Orch. (1898–1907); *Central Park in the Dark* (1898–1907); *The Unanswered Question* (1908); *Theater Orchestra Set* (1904–11); *Browning Overture* (1911); *Lincoln, the Great Commoner* for Chorus and Orch. (1912); *A Symphony: Holidays*, in 4 parts; also perf. separately: *Washington's Birthday* (1913), *Decoration Day* (1912), *4th of July* (1913), *Thanksgiving and/or Forefathers' Day* (1904); Orch.1 Set No. 2 (1915); *Tone Roads* for Chamber Orch. (1911–15); Orch.1 Set No. 3 (fragmentary; 1919–27).

His chamber works include String Quartet No. 1, subtitled *A Revival Service* (1896); Trio for violin, clarinet, and piano (1902); *All the Way Around and Back* for piano, violin, flute, bugle, and bells (1907); 4 Violin Sonatas (1908, 1910, 1914, 1915); Trio for Violin, Cello, and Piano (1911); String Quartet No. 2 (1913); Set for String Quartet and Piano (1914). He wrote a large number of vocal works, including Psalm 67 (1898); *The Celestial Country*, cantata (1899); *3 Harvest Home Chorales* for mixed chorus, brass, double bass, and organ (1898–1912); *General William Booth Enters into Heaven* for Chorus with Brass Band (1914); *114 Songs* (1884–1921); and other songs; many Ives songs were arranged for other ensembles by the composer.

Piano works include *3-Page Sonata* (1905); *Some Southpaw Pitching* (1908); *The Anti-Abolitionist Riots* (1908); Sonata No. 1 (1909); 22 (1912); *3 Protests* for Piano (1914); Sonata No. 2 for Piano, subtitled *Concord, Mass., 1840–1860*, (1909–15; requires the application of a strip of wood on the keys to produce tone-clusters); 3 Quartertone Piano Pieces (1903–24).

The *Essays Before a Sonata* (N.Y., 1920), commentaries on the Concord writers who inspired his work and various musical and philosophical matters, were reprinted as *Essays Before a Sonata and Other Writings*, ed. by Howard Boatwright (N.Y., 1961). Most of his other expository writings are publ. as *Memos*, ed. by John Kirkpatrick (N.Y., 1972), composed of autobiography, explanation, and criticism.

Izeÿl. Opera by d'Albert, 1909, from pseudo-Hindu lore. Izeÿl is an Indian princess whose lips are poisonous and who kills her suitors by kissing them until she dies herself when one of the suitors turns out to be immune to her particular brand of poison. Izeÿl was 1st performed in Hamburg.

jack. 1. In the harpsichord and clavichord, an upright slip of wood on the rear end of the key lever, carrying (in the former) a bit of crow-quill or hard leather set at a right angle so as to pluck or twang the string, or (in the latter) a metallic tangent. 2. In the pianoforte, the escapement lever, or hopper.

Jackson, Mahalia, remarkable African-American gospel singer; b. New Orleans, Oct. 26, 1911; d. Evergreen Park, Ill., Jan. 27, 1972. The daughter of a minister, she sang in her father's church at an early age; went when she was 16 to Chicago, where she supported herself by menial labor while singing in the choir of the Greater Salem Baptist Church; began touring with the Johnson Gospel Singers in 1932. She revealed an innate talent for expressive hymn singing, and soon was in demand for conventions and political meetings. She steadfastly refused to appear in nightclubs. Her 1947 recording *Move On Up a Little Higher* brought her renown as the "Gospel Queen." She appeared in a series of concerts at N.Y.'s Carnegie Hall (1950–56); made her 1st European tour in 1952, which was a triumphant success. She sang at President Kennedy's inauguration (1961) and at the civil rights march on Washington, D.C. (1963); made her last tour of Europe in 1971. She publ. an autobiography, *Movin' On Up* (N.Y., 1966).

Jackson, Michael (Joseph), African-American dance-rock superstar; b. Gary, Ind., Aug. 29, 1958. He began his career as a rhythm-and-blues singer, then joined his 4 brothers in a group billed as the Jackson 5, which scored immediate success. But Michael Jackson soon outshone his brothers and was accorded superstar status in the field of popular music with his lycanthropic album *Thriller* (1983), also issued on videocassette, in which Jackson turns into a werewolf, scaring his sweet girlfriend out of her wits. The album sold some 30 million copies universewide, certified in the *Guinness Book of World Records* in 1984 as the largest sale ever of a single album. According to one enthusiast, Jackson could count on an audience of one-quarter of the entire earth's population (*c.* 2 billion).

In 1984 he won a record number of 8 Grammys for his assorted talents. Jackson's androgynous appearance and his penchant for outlandish apparel (he wore a sequined naval commodore's costume at the Grammy show) seem to act like a stream of powerful pheromones on squealing admiring youths of both sexes. Jackson suffered a minor catastrophe when his hair caught fire during the filming of a TV commercial, and he had to be outfitted with an inconspicuous hairpiece to cover the burned spot. In collaboration with Lionel Richie he penned the song *We Are the World* in support of African famine relief; it won a Grammy Award as best song of 1985. In 1987 he brought out the album *Bad* (i.e., good), and then launched a major solo tour of the U.S. in 1988. On Sept. 19, 1986, his *Captain EO* opened at the Disneyland Theme Park in Anaheim, Calif., featuring Jackson as a singing and dancing commander of a motley space crew. His most recent albums, *Dangerous* and *HIStory, Part I*, have done well, although not at the same level as the previous 2. In recent years his career has been subject to personal scandal and disappointment, including a failed marriage to Elvis Presley's daughter.

Jackson, Milt(on), "Bags," African-American jazz vibraphonist; b. Detroit, Jan. 1, 1923. He began his career in 1945 with Dizzy Gillespie; after working with several other musicians, he organized the Milt Jackson Quartet in 1951, with John Lewis, Ray Brown, and Kenny Clarke; in 1952 it was renamed the Modern Jazz Quartet, a group that was crucial in the synthesis of "cool" with "classical" jazz which eventually came to be known as THIRD STREAM. The Quartet disbanded in 1974 but was reformed in the '80s.

Jacquet de la Guerre, Elisabeth, French composer, organist, and clavecinist; b. Paris, 1659; d. there, June 27, 1729. A member of a family of professional musicians and instrument makers, she evinced talent at an exceptionally early age; was favored by the court of Louis XIV, completing her education under the patronage of Mme. de Montespan. She married Marin de La Guerre, organist of several Paris churches. Her works include an opera, a ballet (lost), keyboard suites, trio and violin sonatas, sacred and secular cantatas, and a Te Deum (also lost).

Jacquet, (Jean Baptiste) **Illinois,** African-American tenor saxophonist and bassoonist; b. Broussard, La., Oct. 31, 1922. He was reared in Houston, where he learned to play the soprano and alto saxophones; after working in local jazz circles, he played with Lionel Hampton, Cab Calloway, and Count Basie. He led his own bands from 1946; also played bassoon from 1956, becoming a featured performer at jazz festivals.

Jagd, Die. See CHASSE.

Jagdhorn, Jägerhorn (Ger.). Hunting horn.

Jagdstück (Ger.). Hunting piece.

Jägerchor (Ger.). Hunters' chorus.

Jagger, Mick (Michael Philip). See ROLLING STONES.

Jahreszeiten, Die. SEASONS, THE.

Jakobin, The. Opera by Dvořák, 1889, 1st performed in Prague. The action takes place in a small Bohemian town in 1793. Boguś, a young Bohemian, is denounced by his detractors as a radical "Jacobin," an appellation which bore a particular stigma at the time of the French Revolution, when the Jacobins were regarded as violent radicals. Boguś is forced to leave Bohemia for several years, but virtue triumphs in the end when the villainous calumniators are exposed, the purported radical returns home with his newly acquired French bride, and he inherits a rich patrimony. The name of the dastardly persecutor in the opera is Adolf; the line in the libretto "Wherever brutality reigns, Adolf is there" was loudly applauded at performances during the

Nazi occupation of Czechoslovakia, with an obvious reference to Hitler. The Nazi authorities ordered the name changed to Rudolf, but it did not help because Rudolf was the name of Hitler's henchman, Rudolf Hess. After several incidents the opera was banned by the Nazis and not revived until the liberation of Czechoslovakia.

jaleo (Sp., wild confusion). A Spanish dance for 1 performer, in 3/8 time and moderate tempo.

jaltarang. A set of porcelain cups partially filled with water and tuned according to the intervallic scheme of a specific Indian RAGA; the scale is played with wooden sticks.

jam session (abbrev. of *jamboree*). An informal get-together in which jazz or popular musicians improvise freely, regardless of professional standing. Sometimes the musicians take turns; other times, several performers will "blow" at once, producing an effect not unlike the early New Orleans era of jazz (or the extremes of free jazz).

Jamaican Rumba. Orch.l dance, 1942, by the Australian-British composer Arthur Benjamin (b. Sydney, Sept. 18, 1893; d. London, Apr. 10, 1960), which became his most famous composition. It began life as a 2-piano work (1938); the orch. version was 1st broadcast from N.Y.

jamboree. Noisy gathering of music makers, in an informal assembly, indulging in singing and playing in the country-western music tradition. If the abbrev. *jam* is used, the gathering will most likely be of jazz musicians.

James, Harry (Haag), popular American jazz trumpeter and bandleader; b. Albany, Ga., Mar. 15, 1916; d. Las Vegas, July 5, 1983. His father was a trumpeter and his mother a trapeze artist with the Mighty Haag Circus; he took up the drums at the age of 4 and the trumpet at 8; he became leader of a circus band at 12. He worked as a contortionist until going with his family to Tex., where he played trumpet in local dance bands. After playing with Ben Pollack's band (1935–37), he became a member of Benny Goodman's orch. (1937–39), being featured in such songs as *1 O'Clock Jump*, *Sing, Sing, Sing*, and *Life Goes to a Party*.

His virtuoso technique was striking; he could blow dolce and even dolcissimo, but when needed he blew with deafening fortissimo; he could also perform ultrachromatic glissandos. He struck out on his own as a bandleader in 1939, producing a sensation with his trumpet version of *You Made Me Love You* in 1941; subsequently was a leading figure of the big band era, bringing out many hit recordings and touring extensively; one of his hit songs, *Ciribiribin*, became his theme song. Several of his albums, including the self-proclamatorily titled *Wild About Harry*, sold in the millions, even in wartime, when shellac, from which disks were manufactured, was rationed.

In 1943 he married Betty Grable, the pinup girl of the G.I.s in World War II, famous for the lissome beauty of her nether limbs. She was his 2nd wife, out of a total of 4; they were divorced in 1965. Faithful to the slogan that "the show must go on," James, wracked with the pain of fatal lymphatic cancer, continued to perform; he played his last gig in Los Angeles on June 26, 1983, 9 days before his death. He observed, as he was dying, "Let it just be said that I went up to do a 1-nighter with Archangel Gabriel."

Janáček, Leoš

Greatly significant Czech composer; b. Hukvaldy, Moravia, July 3, 1854; d. Moravská Ostrava, Aug. 12, 1928. He grew up in a musical household; his father was a choirmaster. At the age of 11 he was sent to Brno to serve as a chorister at the Augustinian Queen's Monastery. He then went to the German College in Brno (1869–72); subsequently occupied a teaching post and also served as choirmaster of the men's chorus, Svatopluk (1873–77), taking an opportunity to study organ at the Prague Organ School (1874–75). He conducted the Beseda Choral Soc. in Brno (1876–88), and also pursued studies at the Leipzig Cons., where he took music history courses with Oskar Paul and composition courses with Leo Grill (1879–80).

He continued his composition studies with Franz Krenn at the Vienna Cons.; returning to Brno, he was appointed the 1st director of the new organ school (1881). His social position in Brno was enhanced by his marriage to Zdenka Schulzová, the daughter of the director of the teachers' training college. He also engaged in scholarly activities; from 1884 to 1886 was ed. of the music journal *Hudební Listy* (Music Bulletins); he further became associated with František Bartoš in collecting Moravian folk songs. From 1886 to 1902 he taught music at the Brno Gymnasium. In 1919 he retired from his directorship of the Brno Organ School, and then taught master classes in Brno (1920–25). Throughout all these busy years he worked diligently on his own compositions, showing particular preference for operas.

Janáček's style of composition underwent numerous transformations, from Romantic techniques of estab-lished formulas to bold dissonant combinations. He was greatly influenced by the Russian musical nationalism exemplified by the realistic speech inflections in vocal writing. He visited St. Petersburg and Moscow in 1896 and 1902, and publ. his impressions of the tour in the Brno press. From 1894 to 1903 he worked assiduously on his most important opera, *Její pastorkyňa* (Her Foster Daughter), to a highly dramatic libretto set in Moravia in the mid-19th century involving a jealous contest between 2 brothers for the hand of Jenůfa (the innocent heroine), and infanticide at the hands of a foster mother, with an amazing outcome absolving Jenůfa and her suitors. The opera encountered great difficulty in securing production in Prague because of its grisly subject, but it was eventually produced on various European stages, mostly in the German text and under the title *Jenůfa* (1916).

Another opera by Janáček that attracted attention was *Výlet pana Broučka do XV století* (Mr. Brouček's Excursion to the 15th Century, 1917), depicting the imaginary travel of a Czech patriot to the time of the religious struggle mounted by the followers of the nationalist leader Jan Hus against the established Church. There followed an operatic fairy tale, *Příhody Lišky Bystroušky* (The Adventures of the Vixen Bystrouška, or The Cunning Little Vixen, 1924), and a mystery play, *Věc Makropulos* (The Makropulos Affair, 1926).

Janáček's great interest in Russian literature was reflected in his opera *Kát'a Kabanova* (1921), after the drama *The Storm* by the Russian playwright Ostrovsky, and another after Dostoyevsky, *Z mrtvého domu* (From the House of the Dead, 1930). He further composed a symphonic poem, *Taras Bulba* (the fictional name of a

Ukrainian patriot, after a story by Gogol, 1915–18; Brno, 1921). Like most artists, writers, and composers of Slavic origin in the old Austro-Hungarian Empire, Janáček had a natural interest in the Pan-Slavic movement, with an emphasis on the common origins of Russian, Czech, Slovak, and other kindred cultures; his *Glagolitic Mass* (*Glagolská mše*, 1927), to a Latin text trans. into Old Slavonic, is an example.

Janáček lived to witness the fall of the old Austrian regime and the national rise of the Slavic populations. He showed great interest in the emerging Soviet school of composition, even though he refrained from any attempt to join that movement. Inevitably he followed the striking innovations of the modern school of composition as set forth in the works of Stravinsky and Schoenberg, but he was never tempted to experiment along those revolutionary lines. He remained faithful to his own well-defined style, and it was as the foremost composer of modern Czech music that he secured for himself his unique place in history.

Janizary music. The military music of the Janizary guards of the Turkish sultans. In the wake of the Ottoman invasion of Eastern Europe in the 16th century, this type of music—raucous, loud, and enlivened by a strong rhythmic pulse—exercised the imagination of European writers, painters, and musicians. They were impressed by the physical dimensions of Turkish drums, cymbals, and the Turkish crescent, known popularly as JINGLING JOHNNY, overhung with bells and jingles and crowned with an ornament in the shape of a pavilion. This type of music penetrated into military bands of Poland, Russia, and Austria in the 1st half of the 18th century.

Big drums, triangles, and cymbals *alla turca* served the purpose of providing exotic color in the "oriental" operas of Gluck and Mozart. Haydn stylized the Janizary rhythms in his *Military Sym.*, which includes triangles, cymbals, and a bass drum in the 2nd movement. The famous rondo finale of Mozart's Piano Sonata in A Major, K. 331, is marked "alla turca." Some piano manufacturers made special attachments with bells and cymbals for performances of such "Turkish music," and even supplied clappers to strike at the resonance board in imitation of the bass drum.

Jankó keyboard. A piano keyboard patented by the Hungarian Paul von Jankó (1856–1919) in 1882. It has 6 rows of keys so arranged that any given tone can be struck in 3 different places, that is, on every other row. This permits a smaller stretch of the hand to reach large intervals and complex chords. Despite the opportunity presented, Jankó never thought of this instrument other than one for equally tempered music. Despite a brief flurry of manufacturing at the turn of the century, the Jankó keyboard met the predictable resistance of those who did not want to relearn their fingerings and hand positions for their repertory.

Japanese music

~~~ ~~~ ~~~ ~~~ ~~~

The music of Japan, and in East Asia generally, is derived from ancient pentatonic modes, most commonly of the intervallic type C, D, E, G, A (i.e., a subset of the major scale) or E-flat, G-flat, A-flat, B-flat, D♭-flat (a subset of the minor scale), both free of semitones. But there exists also an authentic Japanese scale of great antiquity that contains semitones, of the type E, F, A, B, C (a subset of the Phrygian mode). Japanese folk music is primarily homophonic without explicit or implicit harmonic connotations of the Western type; but cultured music of Japan includes concepts of consonance and dissonance. Like most oriental music, Japanese music is melodic and rhythmic, with harmonic extension formed by intervallic couplings in 2nds, 4ths, and 5ths. Consecutive progressions, particularly in 3rds or in 6ths, are practically nonexistent; rhythmic patterns possess great variety and in ancient music do not follow any binding meter. Consonances distribute the intervals of the pentatonic scale in open harmony; dissonances are produced when the harmony includes semitones in close formation.

String instruments, wind instruments, and percussion are represented in Japanese music in original forms, most of them metamorphosed from ancient Chinese and Korean instruments imported into Japan in medieval times. The most popular of Japanese string instruments are the *koto*, a long zither with 13 silk strings; the *shamisen* (samisen), a long-necked 3-stringed lute; and the *biwa*, a short-necked pear-bodied lute with 4 strings. Also commonly used are bamboo flutes (e.g., *shakuhachi*), small cymbals, bells, and a great variety of drums, especially of the hourglass type.

The most ancient Japanese music still practiced is *gagaku*, the orch. music of the imperial court originating in the 8th century and still performed on imperial and other official occasions. Gagaku can also accompany a dance style called *bugaku*; both are considered the province of the Japanese upper classes. The most well-attended of the popular theater forms is *kabuki* (from the 17th century), a stylized drama with a large musical ensemble, featuring singing and dancing with male actors, heavily costumed, playing the roles of both males and females. Kabuki was derived from the *noh*, an even more stylized theater (imported from China in the 14th century) with 2 actors and an ensemble of 3 drums and flute.

Like other Japanese theater, the music and songs are subtle and complex in structure, tonality, and rhythm; the action and speech occur at a slow pace. There are the several puppet-theater genres categorized as *bunraku*, with a narrator-singer accompanied by a shamisen. There are also numerous songs of varying provenance, usually for 1 voice and accompaniment on a string instrument. The late-20th-century dance genre *butoh* is radical in its choreography and use of electronic music scores.

Of the purely instrumental genres, there are large solo repertoires for the pitched instruments; the koto and shakuhachi even have many opposing schools of performance and composition. There is also a great deal of chamber music; one combination, the *sankyoku* from the late 19th century, features a trio of shakuhachi, koto, and shamisen. Generally, most Japanese chamber and orch. music has a heterophonic texture of varying degrees; a gagaku piece may appear nearly monophonic, with a liberal use of portamento; a piece for koto duet can approach a modified contrapuntal texture.

The collision of Western and Japanese music has led to several aesthetic approaches. Early 20th-century Japanese composers attempted to learn Western music by imitation; Kosaku Yamada, educated in Europe, was the 1st Japanese composer to adopt European methods of composition in opera, sym., chamber music, and songs. Later composers sought to mesh the 2 worlds, or create a new style based solely on Japanese traditional music; some of the most important Japanese composers later in the century include Yashushi Akutagawa, Kunio Toda, Ikuma Dan, Yoshiřo Irino, Yoritsune Matsudaira, Jōji Yuasa, Toshirō Mayuzumi, Yoshio Mamiya, Yuji Takehashi, Akira Miyoshi, and Tōru Takemitsu. In the U.S. Paul Chihara, an American composer of Japanese descent, employs Japanese modes in an advanced sophisticated manner; others borrow the musical and theatrical elements of Japanese culture (especially Noh).

Operas by modern Japanese composers usually follow European models. Melodramatic operas on Japanese subjects such as Puccini's *Madama Butterfly* are unacceptable in Japan as perversions of national culture; *The Mikado* by Gilbert and Sullivan was banned in Japan until 1945, when it was performed by the American Army of Occupation. (The ban has since returned.) A more effective synthesis of East and West is found in Sondheim's musical *Pacific Overtures*, about the ending of Japanese isolation by the West in the 19th century.

Jaques-Dalcroze, Émile, Swiss music educator and composer, creator of eurhythmics; b. Vienna (of French parents), July 6, 1865; d. Geneva, July 1, 1950. In 1873 his parents moved to Geneva; having completed his courses at the Univ. and at the Cons. there, he went to Vienna for further study under Fuchs and Bruckner; then to Paris, where he studied with Delibes and Fauré; he returned to Geneva as instructor of theory at the Cons. (1892).

Since he laid special stress on rhythm, he insisted that all his pupils beat time with their hands, and this led him, step by step, to devise a series of movements affecting the entire body. Together with the French psychologist Edouard Claparide, he worked out a special terminology and reduced his practice to a regular system, which he called *eurhythmics*. When his application to have his method introduced as a regular course at the Cons. was refused, he resigned, and in

1910 he established his own school at Hellerau, near Dresden. As a result of World War I the school was closed in 1914; he then returned to Geneva and founded the Inst. Jaques-Dalcroze. Interest in his system led to the opening of similar schools in London, Berlin, Vienna, Paris, N.Y., Chicago, and other cities.

Aside from his rhythmical innovations, he also commanded respect as a composer of marked originality and fecundity of invention; many of his works show how thoroughly he was imbued with the spirit of Swiss folk music. His writings include *Le Coeur chante: Impressions d'un musicien* (Geneva, 1900); *Méthode Jaques-Dalcroze* (Paris, 1906–17); *Le rhythme, la musique et l'éducation* (Paris, 1919); *Souvenirs, notes et critiques* (Neuchâtel, 1942); *La Musique et nous: Notes de notre double vie* (Geneva, 1945). Jaques-Dalcroze was also a composer, often in a folk style, other styles for pedagogical purposes; he has many theatrical works to his credit.

jarábe (Sp.). Characteristic Mexican dance in combined 3/4 and 6/8 meter and resembling the rhythm of a MAZURKA in its emphasis on the middle beat.

jarana. A dance song from the Mexican province of Yucatán set in the dual meter of 3/4 and 6/8.

Jarnach, Philipp, German composer and pedagogue of Spanish descent; b. Noisy, France, July 26, 1892; d. Bornsen, near Bergedorf, Dec. 17, 1982. He was a son of a Catalonian sculptor and a Flemish mother. He studied with Risler (piano) and Lavignac (theory) at the Paris Cons. (1912–14). At the outbreak of World War I he went to Zurich, where he met Busoni and taught at the Cons.; this meeting was a decisive influence on his musical development; he became an ardent disciple of Busoni, and after his death completed Busoni's last opera, *Doktor Faust*, premiered in Jarnach's version in Dresden (1925). (Anthony Beaumont has since done a 2nd completion based on additional sketches.) During the years 1922–27 Jarnach wrote music criticism for the *Berliner Börsencourier*. In 1931 he became a German citizen. From 1927 to 1949 he was prof. of composition at the Cologne Cons., and from 1949 to 1970 at the Hamburg Cons.

Jarnach's music is determined by his devotion to Busoni's ideals; it is distinguished by impeccable craftsmanship, but it lacks individuality. He participated in the modern movement in Germany between the 2 world wars, and many of his works were performed at music festivals during that period. He wrote *Prolog zu einem Ritterspiel* for orch. (1917); *Sinfonia brevis* (1923); *Musik mit Mozart* for Orch. (1935);

String Quintet (1920); String Quartet (1924); *Musik zum Gedächtnis des Einsamen* for String Quartet (1952; also for orch.); piano pieces; songs.

Jarre, Maurice, French composer; b. Lyons, Sept. 13, 1924. He studied electrical engineering in Lyons, then attended courses in composition given by Honegger at the Paris Cons. He became best known as a film composer, winning an Academy Award for *Lawrence of Arabia* (1963) and *Lara's Song* from *Dr. Zhivago* (1965); other scores include *The Year of Living Dangerously* (1983); *Witness* (1985); *The Mosquito Coast* (1986); *Gorillas in the Mist* (1988); *Dead Poet's Soc.* (1989); *Almost an Angel* (1990). He also wrote *Armida* for Orch. (1953); *Mouvements en relief* for Orch. (1954); *Polyphonies concertantes* for Piano, Trumpet, Percussion, and Orch.; *Passacaille*, in memory of Honegger, for Orch. (Strasbourg Festival, 1956); *Mobiles* for Violin and Orch. (Strasbourg Festival, 1961).

Jarreau, Al, African-American singer of jazz and popular music; b. Milwaukee, Mar. 12, 1940. He graduated with a psychology degree from the Univ. of Iowa, then went to San Francisco, where he worked as a rehabilitation counselor. He began singing in local clubs, quickly garnering a following with his flexible vocal technique and warm, sometimes even ecstatic performance style; he gained particular attention with his album *We Got By* (1975); he then toured Europe (1976), becoming one of the most popular jazz singers of the day. Other successful albums of this period include *Look to the Rainbow* (1977) and *All Fly Home* (1978). His audience changed substantially in the mid-'80s, when his songs and vocal style became less adventurous, owing to an emphasized and often mundane disco beat. Albums dating from this later period include *High Crime* (1984) and *L Is for Lover* (1986).

Jarrett, Keith, versatile American pianist; b. Allentown, Pa., May 8, 1945. After studying at the Berklee School of Music in Boston, he plunged into the N.Y. jazz scene, coming to prominence as a member of the Charles Lloyd quartet (1966–70); he also worked with Miles Davis (1970–71) and toured with his own trio and as a solo artist. In 1975 he made a sensationally popular recording of solo improvisations, *The Köln Concert*, which established his reputation as a jazz virtuoso. From the early 1980s he made appearances as a classical pianist, specializing in modern works and especially those of Bartók; in 1987 he gave a particularly spirited performance in N.Y. of Lou Harrison's

Piano Concerto, a performance he repeated in Tokyo which served as the basis for the critically acclaimed 1988 recording.

Järvi, Neeme, prominent Estonian conductor; b. Tallinn, June 7, 1937. He graduated with degrees in percussion and choral conducting from the Tallinn Music School, then studied conducting with Mravinsky and Rabinovich at the Leningrad Cons. (1955–60); he pursued postgraduate studies in 1968, and in 1971 he captured 1st prize in the Accademia di Santa Cecilia conducting competition in Rome. He was active in Tallinn as music director of the Estonian State Sym. Orch. (1960–80) and of the Estonian Opera Theater (1964–77). He subsequently served as principal guest conductor of the City of Birmingham Sym. Orch. in England (1981–84). In 1982 he became music director of the Göteborg Sym. Orch. in Sweden; also was principal conductor of the Scottish National Orch. in Glasgow (1984–88). In 1990 he became music director of the Detroit Sym. Orch. His guest conducting engagements have taken him to most of the principal music centers of the world. He has won particular notice in concert settings and on recordings for his efforts in championing such rarely performed composers as Berwald, Gade, Svendsen, Stenhammar, and Tubin.

jazz

A term covering a wide variety of styles of African-American origin, including New Orleans/Dixieland; Chicago; big band/swing; bebop; cool/3rd Stream; free jazz; jazz-rock/jazz-funk; and neotraditionalism. Most are characterized by improvisation and a "swinging" beat composed of a steady, prominent meter and dotted or syncopated rhythms. The word *jazz* appeared for the 1st time in print in the sports column in *The Bulletin of San Francisco* in 1913. Describing the arrival of a baseball team, writer "Scoop" Gleeson reported: "Everybody has come back to the old town, full of the old 'jazz,' and they promise to knock the fans off their feet with their playing." Gleeson then asks himself a rhetorical question: "What is this jazz? Why, it's a little of that 'old life,' the 'gin-i-leer,' the 'pep,' otherwise known as the enthusiasm." Reminiscing about the occasion in an article published in the same San Francisco newspaper in 1938, Gleeson volunteered the information that the expression "jazz" had been picked up by the sports editor during a crap game. According to Gleeson, it was 1st applied to music when one Art Hickman launched his dance band, but there is no evidence of such use in any published source.

The next verified appearance of the word *jazz* was in *Variety* (1916) in a brief communication from Chicago, reporting a concert of jazz music, with the word spelled *jass*. Another item in *Variety* followed in 1917 when it was spelled *Jaz*. An engagement of the Dixie Jass Band of New Orleans in a Chicago cabaret was noted in *Variety* that same year. A week later jazz reached N.Y., and it was spelled *jazz* in yet another report in *Variety*. An item in the *Victor Record Review* (1917) reads: "Spell it Jass, Jas, Jab or jazz—nothing can spoil a Jass band. . . . It has sufficient power and penetration to inject new life into a mummy, and will keep ordinary human dancers on their feet till breakfast time." It was about the same time that the Victor Co. issued the 1st recording bearing the word *Jass—Dixieland Jass 1-Step.*

Some have tried to trace it to American sexual slang or African languages. However, considering the specific, clear, and plausible description of the word when it 1st appeared in print in 1913, there is no reason to doubt that it was a spontaneous colloquialism generated around San Francisco. The entire history of the word *jazz* is thoroughly covered in a pioneering article by Peter Tamony in an ephemeral periodical *Jazz, A Quarterly of American Music*, in its issue of Oct. 1958.

Analytically jazz may be described as a modern development of the counterpoint of the 4th species. Its rhythmic formula is related to the medieval HOCKET, in which the singing line is freely transferred from one voice to another in syncopated singultation. (The word *hocket* itself is an etymological cognate of hiccups.) Another historical antecedent of jazz is the QUODLIBET, orig. a freely improvised interlude within a definite metrical framework. As practiced by untutored performers, jazz produces the collective impact of glossolalia, tonolalia, or rhythmolalia; in the hands of geniuses it becomes a thing of great beauty.

The paradoxical nature of jazz (through the 1950s at least) is its combination of unlimited variety of rhythmic patterns with a metric and modal uniformity: jazz melodies, almost without exception, are set in major keys, in 2/4 or 4/4 time. Within this framework the syncopated melody often departs widely from its harmonic connotations. But the major tonality is modified by the use of BLUE NOTES, the lowered 7th and the lowered 3rd in the melody. Some theorists speculate that the systematic incidence of the blue 7th is an approximation of the 7th overtone and is therefore a natural consonance. The lowered 3rd, however, cannot be explained on acoustical grounds. It may well represent a true case of harmonic equivocation, in which the melodic minor 3rd is projected on the major complex in some sort of polytriadic superfetation. It is significant that this major-minor superfetation is the constant resource of Stravinsky's tonal harmonies.

Historically jazz evolved from RAGTIME, a syncopated type of American music that flourished in the last decade of the 19th century and during the 1st years of the new century. A parallel development is BLUES, a distinctively American ballad form suffused with bittersweetness and redolent of the remembered sufferings of African-Americans, as expressed in Negro spirituals. Semantically the term is connected with the colloquialism "to have the blues." The flattened blue notes received their name in association with this style and remain paramount features. The self-acknowledged creator of the genre was W. C. Handy, whose song *Memphis Blues* (1911) was the 1st to be published. Other early stylistic contributions to jazz were the work songs and field hollers of rural black America; the street cries of peddlers in urban black America; and the most important influence on orchestration, the New Orleans marching band, notable for its use in funeral processions outside of that city (necessary since burial inside that delta city was banned for health reasons).

The *Dixieland jazz* style, with its group improvisations and lack of drums, were never aurally recorded, except for a pale imitation called the Original Dixieland Jazz Band (from 1917). When many New Orleans musicians moved north to Chicago in the 1920s (including Louis Armstrong and Jelly Roll Morton), the ensembles grew smaller and emphasized star improvisers while allowing other band members brief solos in a 12-bar (blues) or 16/32-bar (song) structure. The instrumentation solidified, drawn from cornet (later trumpet), trombone, clarinet, piano, guitar, tuba or double bass, and drums. This style was emotionally "hot," much like its predecessor.

A new era of jazz music dawned in the late 1920s with a riotous explosion of *swing*, which indicated a certain rhythmic manner of performance rather than a definable structural form. The ensemble grew into the *big band*, averaging between 10 and 15 players, and true composition (and orchestration, or arranging) became an element of jazz. Musicians like Ellington, Basie, Henderson, Strayhorn, Redman, Benny Carter, and others created their own recognizable "sounds," mixing their compositional proclivities with the abilities of individual members of their band (Ellington was especially sensitive to this). The big bands of Benny Goodman and Glenn Miller emphasized their role as dance bands, while Ellington and Strayhorn alternated between the "hot" dance music style and the more reflective "cool" style that sought to portray the African-American experience.

Parallel to these developments, *piano jazz* evolved from its RAGTIME beginnings to STRIDE in the 1920s; the oom-pah bass became more aggressive dynamically and harmonically, while the melody lines grew subtly in syncopation. While this style continued to influence piano playing, the 1930s saw the inauguration of BOOGIE-WOOGIE, which turned the bass line into a "walking" ostinato, arpeggiated and often following the 12-bar blues harmonic pattern; the melody lines became more bluesy than modal.

A new jazz form, BEBOP (also rebop or bop), appeared in the 1940s. It is a paradoxical style; the tonal and structural underpinnings seemed to return to those of the 1920s, with the emphasis on simple blues progressions or interpretations of popular standards. But the improvisation reached lightning speeds and, in the hands of Charlie Parker and other good musicians, expanded the harmonic horizons melodically and harmonically with added notes to chords and linear chromaticism; even more important was its unrepressed emotionality, perhaps indicative of the rising black rebellion against Jim Crow segregation, disrespect, and financial desperation. Finally, the sound of the saxophone—with its brassy yet mellow qualities, capable of raucous exuberance or gentle poetry—went to the fore of the melody instruments in jazz; by the 1950s it had virtually replaced the clarinet.

If bebop had a negative result, it was the dividing of jazz's audience into listener-dancers (who wanted to move) and listener-aficionados (who were content to sit down). This divide continued in the next decades. In the 1950s *cool jazz*, spearheaded by Miles Davis, Gil Evans, Gerry Mulligan, Chet Baker, John Lewis, Gunther Schuller (of the THIRD STREAM), and many others, used both small and larger ensembles and returned to swing-era compositional concerns, albeit with music almost devoid of dancing implications and full of the laid-back quality of the "beat generation."

In the 1960s *free jazz* referred both to a highly improvisational style with few if any structural demands, and to the freeing of jazz aesthetics from the need to "belong" to a single style; this had the disadvantage, however, of presenting a divided front to an already smaller audience; many who would have loved the big band era had, in subsequent decades, fallen in instead with dance-oriented African-American rhythm and blues and its Anglo-American outcropping, rock 'n' roll. One set of solutions developed in the 1970s: *jazz-rock* and *jazz-funk*, both of which are examples of the hybrid called *fusion*, which combined the instrumentation and relative accessibility of popular music with the extemporaneous freedom and rhythmic panache of jazz. Often, bass ostinato figures served to support free-wheeling improvisation; in other pieces the metric shifts of art-rock (borrowed from Stravinsky) played with the momentum.

In recent years the work of Wynton Marsalis and others has emphasized the "classic repertoire" approach to jazz, both as a way to explore the accomplishments in this multifaceted category of music, and to regain a larger audience through more traditional jazz styles.

Jazz Concerto. Nickname of the Piano Concerto by Copland, 1927, which does include elements of jazz. It shocked the Boston audience and critics when Copland performed it for the 1st time with the Boston Sym. Orch. under Koussevitzky.

Jazz Pizzicato. Orch. novelty by L. Anderson, 1939, for string orch. This was the 1st of many clever semiclassical works by this composer.

Jazz Singer, The. The 1st "talking picture" film, 1928—actually, only a portion has sound—starring blackface singer Al Jolson, who sings his signature *My Mammy* on bended knee and with outstretched arms.

jazz-funk (jazz-rock). Jazz styles of the late 1960s and 1970s that merge the electric amplification, instrumentation, and directness of rock with some of the more sophisticated improvisatory, rhythmic, and harmonic features of jazz. *Art-rock*, another aberration of the time, contributed shifting meters to the styles; funk and rock provided bass ostinatos.

Jeanie with the Light Brown Hair. Nostalgic ballad by Foster, 1854, in which the protagonist bemoans his unfortunate separation from his beloved. One of his last compositions, and his last major success.

Jeanne d'Arc au bûcher. Dramatic oratorio by Honegger, 1938; it was 1st performed in Basel, in concert form. Honegger described the work as a *mimodrama*, or mimed drama. Joan has a speaking part; various allegorical figures appear, symbolizing sins and virtues. The music represents a deliberate return to the early type of monodic DRAMMA PER MUSICA.

Jeepers, Creepers. Song by Warren and Mercer, 1938, from the movie musical *Going Places*. Louis Armstrong made it the theme song of his band. Its infectiously unsophisticated rhythm and the tantalizingly nonsensical line "Jeepers, creepers/Where did you get them peepers?" made it a perennial favorite.

Jefferson Airplane. (Most successful lineup: Vocals/guitar: Paul Kantner, b. San Francisco, Mar. 12, 1942; vocals: Marty Balin, b. Martyn Jerel Buchwald, Cincinnati, Jan. 30, 1942; vocals: Grace [Wing] Slick, b. Chicago, Oct. 30, 1939; lead guitar: Jorma Kaukonen, b. Washington, D.C., Dec. 23, 1940; bass: Jack Casady, b. Washington, D.C., Apr. 13, 1944; drums: Spencer Dryden, b. N.Y., Apr. 7, 1943.) San Francisco folk-rock band of the mid-1960s that has survived through an amazing number of personnel and name changes through today. The band originally formed around folksinger Marty Balin and guitarists Paul Kantner and Jorma Kaukonen, female vocalist Singe Toly, string-bass player Bob Harvey, and drummer Jerry Pelequin; Alexander "Skip" Spence soon replaced Pelequin. The group gave its 1st performance in San Francisco on Aug. 13, 1965. Their 1st album, under the proud name *Jefferson Airplane Takes Off*, inaugurated the so-called San Francisco sound.

There were inevitable changes in personnel, and the vocalist Grace Slick joined the group in 1966; she had formerly sung in another Bay Area ensemble, the Great Society. Spencer Dryden replaced drummer Spence, who left that same year to form the psychedelic group Moby Grape. Slick brought with her a number of songs, including her composition *White Rabbit*, based on Lewis Carroll's *Alice in Wonderland* and her former husband's ballad *Somebody to Love*, both major hits. The group veered between recording romantic ballads and more politically minded songs, particularly 1969's minor hit *Volunteers* and Kantner's *We Can Be Together*. In 1968 they made a successful European tour, but soon personal discord and political divergencies in their common social radicalism led to a gradual dissolution of the group.

Kaukonen and Casady formed a side group, Hot Tuna, in 1969 to perform traditional blues; they continued to record and perform through much of the '70s. Kantner began showing an interest in science fiction, producing the theme album *Blows Against the Empire* in 1970, featuring members of the group (minus Balin, who was about to leave the band) and many of its peers, including Jerry Garcia, David Crosby, and Graham Nash. The group formed its own vanity label, Grunt, in 1972, releasing various projects, while the band slowly disintegrated.

The group got together again in 1975 under the new name Jefferson Starship, producing the successful album *Red Octopus*—which included Balin's hit *Miracles*—with a returning Marty Balin, but Balin soon was gone again. Another European tour in 1978 was marred by Slick's alcoholism, leading to her leaving the group to dry out until 1981. The group re-formed with lead singer Mickey Thomas in 1979, and Slick came back 2 years later for more hits through 1984. Kantner left that year, suing the group, who were forced to rename themselves Starship, but incredibly the group continued unabated, with major hits including *We Built This City*. Slick was gone again by 1988, and a year later the "original" group of Kantner-Balin-Casady-Slick-Kaukonen regrouped for a modest-selling reunion album. More turmoil followed, with Kantner leading various personnel in a group known as Paul Kantner's Jefferson Starship, with Balin rejoining in 1993 and Slick 2 years later, to little success.

Jefferson, "Blind Lemon," African-American blues singer and guitarist; b. near Wortham, Tex., July 1897; d. Chicago, Dec. 1929. He was afflicted by poor eyesight from childhood; as a youth, he supported himself by singing in the streets of Texas towns and cities. He went to Dallas in 1917, where he formed a blues duo with Huddie Ledbetter (aka Leadbelly; although Leadbelly claimed in later years to be Jefferson's "lead boy" during this period, there is no documentary evidence to support this claim); after touring the South, he settled in Chicago (1925). He made a series of historic blues recordings, many of which highlighted his own songs. His performances represented a Texas blues style akin to that of Leadbelly. His *Matchbox Blues* was later covered by numerous artists, including a revised version by Carl Perkins, which was in turn covered by the Beatles, with Ringo Starr singing.

Jena Symphony. One of those misnomers and misattributions that disturb the musical scene once in a while. The MS was discovered in the town of Jena in 1910 by the German scholar Fritz Stein, with the name of Beethoven scribbled on some of the orch. parts. A great deal of excitement was generated, and the *Jena Sym.* was performed as an early work of Beethoven. The sensation was spurious, as anyone examining the work from either a stylistic or aesthetic standpoint should have known. Eventually the original manuscript was discovered, fully signed with the name of Friedrich Witt (1770–1836), the only begetter of this misnamed work.

Jenkins, Leroy, African-American jazz violinist and composer; b. Chicago, Mar. 11, 1932. He was mainly autodidact in music, playing violin in a local Baptist church and picking up the rudiments of theory while teaching in a ghetto school in Chicago; he became affiliated with the Assoc. for the Advancement of Creative Musicians, and later studied on a scholarship with Bruce Hayden at Florida A&M Univ. He is best known for his atonal improvisations on violin and viola, in a bluesy, romantic style inspired by Charlie Parker. The groups he has led or co-led include the (Paris-based) Creative Construction Co., the Revolutionary Ensemble, the Leroy Jenkins Trio, the Leroy Jenkins Quintet, and Sting. Among his finest recordings, many of which include his own jazz compositions, are *Space Minds, New Worlds, Survival of America*; *The Legend of Al Glatson*; *Solo Concert*; *For Players Only*; *Manhattan Cycles*; and *Leroy Jenkins' Sting: Urban Blues*.

Jenks, Stephen, American composer and tunebook compiler; b. Glocester, R.I., Mar. 17, 1772; d. Thompson,

Ohio, June 5, 1856. He taught in New England and N.Y. singing schools before settling in Ohio (1829), where he engaged in farming. A diligent advocate of American PSALMODY, he publ. 10 vols. of psalmody (1799–1818), which included 127 of his own works; he was the leading composer of FUGUING TUNES of the 19th century.

Jennings, Waylon (Arnold), American country-music singer, guitarist, and songwriter; b. Littlefield, Tex., June 15, 1937. Taking up the guitar in his youth, he dropped out of school at 14, then played bass in Buddy Holly's band (1958–59). He went to Nashville in 1965, where he turned out several albums and starred in the film *Nashville Rebel* (1966). Disdaining the "Nashville sound," he became a leading figure in the promotion of "outlaw" country music, or "redneck rock," with his album *Ladies Love Outlaws* (1972). He subsequently won a wide following with such albums as *Lonesome, On'ry and Mean* (1973), *Honky Tonk Heroes* (1973), *This Time* (1974), *Waylon, the Ramblin' Man* (1974), *Dreamin' My Dreams* (1975), *Wanted: The Outlaws* (1976), and others.

Jenůfa. Opera by Janáček, 1904, 1st produced in Brno under the name *Její pastorkyňa* (Her Foster Daughter); the entry title is the one under which the opera is performed abroad. The subject is grisly, as peasant life in Central Europe often was in the 19th century. Jenůfa is heavy with child by a Moravian farmhand; when the child is born, the moralistic female sexton of the local church drowns it to save Jenůfa from disgrace. The truth is found out, the hideous sexton culprit is taken to prison, and Jenůfa marries a step-brother of her original seducer. The work is one of the most remarkable examples of modern Bohemian music drama. The score underwent several revisions, and not until the performance of the final version in Prague, May 26, 1916, was Janáček recognized as an important international composer.

Jephtha. Oratorio by Handel, 1752. Jephtha, returning from a victorious campaign, makes a reckless promise to Jehovah that he will sacrifice the 1st thing he encounters coming home; like other antiheroes in this position, he meets his own daughter.

Jeremiah Symphony. Sym. No. 1 by Bernstein, 1944, for soprano and orch., on a text from the Bible. It is in 3 sections: *Prophecy*, *Profanation*, and *Lamentation*. Bernstein conducted its 1st performance in Pittsburgh.

Jericho trumpets. In Chapter 6 of the Book of Joshua it is related how the Lord instructed Joshua to destroy the city of Jericho acoustically by having 7 priests blow 7 trumpets made out of ram horn while the people "shouted with a great shout." The noise was such that the walls of Jericho "fell down flat," letting Joshua's people in, whereupon they proceeded to slay "both man and woman, young and old, and ox, and sheep, and ass" (except a local harlot who hid Joshua's spies in her house). Modern acousticians doubt whether a wall could be brought down by sounding trumpets and shouting; even rock musicians using electric amplifiers could never do more than frighten the peaceful bystanders.

Jerusalem, Siegfried, prominent German tenor; b. Oberhausen, Apr. 17, 1940. He began his career as an orch. bassoonist in 1961; was a member of the Stuttgart Radio Sym. Orch. (1972–77). He began vocal study in Stuttgart with Hertha Kalcher in 1972, appearing in minor roles at the Württemberg State Theater from 1975. He sang Lohengrin in Darmstadt and Aachen in 1976, and then at the Hamburg State Opera in 1977; that same year he made his debut at the Bayreuth Festival as Froh, returning in later seasons as Lohengrin, Walther, Parsifal, and Loge in the Solti-Hall mounting of the Ring cycle in 1983. After making his 1st appearance at the Berlin Deutsche Oper as Tamino in 1978, he became a leading member of the company. He made his U.S. debut with the Metropolitan Opera in N.Y. as Lohengrin (1980), his British debut at London's Coliseum as Parsifal (1986), and his Covent Garden debut later that year, singing Erik; he also appeared at the Vienna State Opera, Milan's La Scala, and the Paris Opéra.

Jessonda. This opera by Ludwig Spohr, now a fossil, was once a great favorite, particularly in England. It was 1st performed in Kassel, Germany, where Spohr was court music director, July 28, 1823. Jessonda is the wife of the rajah of Malabar; he dies, and she must immolate herself like the good Brahmin that she is. But lo! Portuguese fanfares are sounded and no less a person than Tristan da Cunha, the explorer for whom a desolate group of islands midway between South America and South Africa was named (1 island of the group is called Inaccessible), enters the scene. He recognizes in Jessonda his ideal woman; she sees in him her ideal man. The chorus of Brahmins urges her on to take her rightful place at her husband's funerary mound, but now she wants to live. When the Portuguese marines land in force, the Brahmins desist in their foul superstition, and the happy ending is assured. The score sounds like any piece of German music of the time; there is no attempt to introduce exotic tunes.

jeté (Fr.). In string playing, throw the upper part of the bow on the string to let it bounce in rapid even notes down to the end of the bow. Virtuoso violinists can fit 8 quick notes in 1 jeté.

jeu (Fr.). 1. Style of playing. 2. A stop of an organ. *Grand jeu* or *plein jeu*, full organ or power; *demi-jeu*, half power.

Jeu de cartes (The Card Game). Ballet "in 3 deals" by Stravinsky, 1937, 1st performed in N.Y. with the composer conducting. Stravinsky, a devotee of poker, portrays in this score a poker game, with the joker constantly intruding to confuse the players. The sequence of dances follows the classical tradition.

Jeu de Robin et de Marion. Medieval play with music by Adam de la Halle, *c.* 1280; an amorous pastorale with dialogue and songs; the 1st extant secular musical drama.

jeu de timbres (Fr.). GLOCKENSPIEL.

Jeunehomme Concerto. Nickname for the Piano Concerto No. 9 in E-flat Major, K. 271 (1777), that Mozart wrote for a French pianist, Mlle. Jeunehomme, who played it in Salzburg.

Jeux d'eau. Piano piece by Ravel, 1902, in which he anticipated Debussy by introducing a remarkable new type of piano sonority, spreading across the entire keyboard and emphasizing tertian chords formed by cumulative 3rds. At one point in *Jeux d'eau* Ravel replaced the required low G-sharp below the range of the keyboard with the lowest available note, A, which coalesced with the intended harmony. The piece was 1st performed in Paris.

Jeux d'enfants (Children's Games). Suite by Bizet, 1871, for piano duet, with the 12 pieces describing the carousel, doll, spinning top, and other appropriate objects. Bizet orchestrated 5 of the pieces as the *Petite suite* (1872).

Jeux vénitiens. (Venetian Games). Work for chamber orch. by Lutosławski, 1961, 1st performed in Venice. It is arranged in 5 panels that are performed either simultaneously or canonically, according to optional procedures.

Jew's harp. A small instrument with rigid iron frame having a thin vibratile metal tongue; the frame is held between the teeth and the metallic tongue is plucked with the finger (*Jew's harp* may be a corruption of *jaw's harp*). Various pitches are attained by changing the shape of the mouth. The instrument has been included in folk ensembles throughout the world, from China to Borneo, from northern Europe to Appalachia.

jig (from Fr. *giguer*, move rapidly to and fro). A lively English dance, similar to the sailor's dance known as the hornpipe. The jig is a country dance, with many modifications of step and gesture, in compound quadruple time, and rapid tempo. The jig was very popular in the 17th century among lower classes; one writer described it as "only fit for Fantastical, and Easie-Light-Headed People." However, jigs penetrated the English court and apparently became favorites with the English aristocracy. The *Fitzwilliam Virginal Book* includes a jig with the provocative title *Nobodyes Gigge.* In the courts the jig died out at the end of the Elizabethan era and was replaced by the more courtly and dignified French GIGUE; but the jig continued as a traditional dance and music, and persists to this day in Anglo-Irish-Scottish culture.

Jim Crack Corn (Blue Tail Fly). Popular minstrel show song by D. Emmett, 1846; it was a particular favorite of President Lincoln's.

Jim Crow. Blackface minstrel song and dance, *c.* 1829, by Thomas Dartmouth "Daddy" Rice (1808–60); it marked the beginning of the American blackface minstrel show. The final lines, "Ev'ry time I wheel about/I jump Jim Crow," gave birth to the expression "Jim Crow," synonymous with racial segregation.

Jingle Bells. American Christmas song by James Pierpont, *c.* 1850, written for a Sunday school entertainment.

Jingling Johnny (Johnnie) (Turkish crescent, Chinese pavilion, Chinese hat; Ger. *Schellenbaum*, ringing tree). An ornate Eastern percussion instrument. It consists of a stick with crossbars in the shape of crescents topped over by a hatlike decoration and with bells and jingles. It was popular in Europe during the 18th century.

jitterbug. 1. An American jazz dance of the 1930s and 1940s, notable for its attempt to match the "heat" of the music with appropriate physical gestures and floor movements; among its components are slow dig steps, quicksteps, and sidesteps (shuffles). The dance was exported to Europe with the American armed forces in World War II. 2. Someone who dances the jitterbug.

jive. 1. A collective noun that describes the action of jazz. A *jive session* is a display of coordinated glossolalia or tonolalia, spontaneous and self-conscious in their manifestation. A JAM SESSION is conducted in the language of jive. The semantic distinctions and confluences of these terms are illustrated by the jazzy glossolalia in a song recorded in 1940: "Romp it, stomp it, ride it too./Jam it, jump it, jive it through." 2. The dance steps of the JITTERBUG.

Job. A masque for dancing by Vaughan Williams, 1930, with a scenario inspired by Blake's *Illustrations of the Book of Job*. It was 1st performed as a concert piece in Norwich.

jodel. YODEL.

Joel, Billy (William Martin), top-seeded American pianist, singer, and songwriter of popular music; b. N.Y., May 9, 1949. Prematurely sophisticated, he joined the rock band the Echoes, which later metamorphosed into a more belligerent group called the Hassles. When the group disintegrated after internecine hassles, Joel teamed up with drummer Jon Small to form a duo named Attila. They recorded an album, which did not sell. Joel then organized a band of his own and recorded his 1st solo album, *Cold Spring Harbor* (1972), for the Family Productions label. It did not sell either, and after a family feud with the label, Joel went over to Columbia Records, moved to Los Angeles, and thereafter marched on the gold-paved road to neon-lighted success.

He composed a ballad called, autobiographically, *Piano Man* (1973), which made a hit. He soon progressed on the periodic table of elements from gold to platinum, receiving a certified platinum award for his song *Just the Way You Are* from the album *The Stranger* in 1978. Other smash albums followed, including *52nd Street*, which captured a Grammy Award for best album of 1979; it also made him the Grammy Award male pop vocalist of the year. Other hit singles are numerous, including *My Life*, *Big Shot*, and *Honesty*; also *Say Goodbye to Hollywood* and *You May Be Right*. He signified his gratitude to his generating force in the top hit *It's Still Rock 'n' Roll to Me*. By 1984 he could demand, and get, million-dollar advances from royalty distributors. In the 1980s he was prolific; particularly notable albums of this decade include *The Nylon Curtain*, *An Innocent Man*, *The Bridge*, and *Kohupt*, a 2-record set of live concerts in Moscow and Leningrad in 1987. In the early '90s he issued *River of Dreams*, which yielded some minor hits.

Johansen, Gunnar, remarkable Danish-American pianist, composer, and teacher; b. Copenhagen, Jan. 21, 1906; d. Blue Mounds, Wis., May 25, 1991. He made his public debut at the age of 12 in Copenhagen, where he studied with V. Schioler; went to Berlin when he was 14, becoming a member of the Busoni circle; after further piano studies with F. Lamond and E. Fischer, he completed his training with E. Petri at the Hochschule für Musik (1922–24). He toured Europe (1924–29) and then settled in the U.S., where he pursued an active concert career, gaining particular distinction for his series of 12 historical piano recitals encompassing works from Frescobaldi to Stravinsky, which he presented in San Francisco, Chicago, and N.Y. in the late 1930s; he held the specially created position of artist-in-residence at the Univ. of Wisconsin at Madison (1939–76).

He produced a sensation when he substituted on short notice for a colleague as soloist in the piano version of Beethoven's Violin Concerto with Ormandy and the Philadelphia Orch. in N.Y. (1969). He excelled in works of transcendental difficulty; he played and recorded the complete solo piano works of Liszt and Busoni, including the latter's Bach transcriptions, as well as the complete solo clavier works of Bach. He was a composer of fantastic fecundity; among his compositions are 3 piano concertos (1930, 1970, 1981), 31 piano sonatas (1941–51), and 515 piano sonatas improvised directly on the keyboard and recorded on tape (1952–82).

John, Elton (born Reginald Kenneth Dwight), phenomenally successful English rock pianist, singer, and songwriter; b. Pinner, Middlesex, Mar. 25, 1947. He took up the piano in early childhood, then won a fellowship to the Royal Academy of Music in London at age 11; after dropping out of school when he was 17 he earned his keep as a jazz pianist in various London clubs and pubs; then joined a rock group bearing the pretentious appellation Bluesology, adopting the name Elton John by borrowing Elton from the sax player Elton Dean, of whom he was inordinately fond, and John from the 1st name of the leader of the band, John Baldry.

For all his aspirations, John is capable of forming lines of communication with kindred souls on a comparable level of intelligence among his audiences. He affects bizarre behavior, wearing multicolored attires and psychedelic eyeglasses of which he has collected several hundred. In 1971 he flew across the ocean and captivated American rock audiences with his strangulated voice and uninhibited conduct; during the 1970s he was the most popular rock artist in the U.S. He wrote most of his earlier songs with lyricist Bernie Taupin. In May 1979 he gave 4 concerts in Leningrad and 4 in Moscow before thousands of young Soviet fans screaming with delight; as the 1st Western rock star to play in Moscow, his appearance was documented in the film *From Elton with Love*. Among his most successful albums are *Madman across the Water, Honky Chateau, Don't Shoot Me I'm Only the Piano Player, Goodbye Yellow Brick Road, Blue Moves, Ice On Fire, Single Man*, and *Too Low for Zero*.

Johnny Johnson. Musical fable by Weill, 1936, 1st produced in N.Y. Weill's 1st American work concerns the fate of an idealistic soldier, Johnny Johnson, who fights Germany in World War I, which he truly believes is the war to end all wars. He tries to immunize the military by channeling a laughing gas into them, but in the process of securing world peace he loses his girl and is put into an insane asylum. Being an ideological play, it failed at the box office.

Johnson, "Bunk" (William Geary), African-American jazz trumpeter; b. New Orleans, Dec. 27, 1889?; d. New Iberia, La., July 7, 1949. As a youth he played trumpet with Dixieland bands; toured with minstrel shows, circus troupes, and numerous jazz aggregations. He lost all his teeth due to the ravages of pyorrhea and had to stop playing. After many years of musical inactivity he was "rediscovered" in 1937 by "hot jazz" aficionados, working in sugarcane fields; fitted with dentures, he resumed his career and enjoyed belated fame in a revival of Dixieland music. He made his 1st recording in 1942 and subsequently performed in N.Y., Boston, and Chicago.

Johnson, Edward, distinguished Canadian-born American tenor and operatic administrator; b. Guelph, Ontario, Aug. 22, 1878; d. there, Apr. 20, 1959. He sang in concert and oratorio performances before going to N.Y. in 1899 to study with Mme. von Feilitsch; after appearing in the U.S. premiere of Oscar Straus's *A Waltz Dream* in 1907, he continued his studies with Richard Barthelemy in Paris (1908) and Vincenzo Lombardi in Florence (1909); made his oper-atic debut as Andrea Chenier at the Teatro Verdi in Padua on Jan. 10, 1912, using the stage name of Edoardo Di Giovanni; he subsequently appeared in Milan at La Scala, where he sang as Parsifal at its 1st complete stage production in Italy (1914).

He made his U.S. debut as Loris in *Fedora* at the Chicago Grand Opera on Nov. 20, 1919, remaining on its roster until 1922; then made his Metropolitan Opera debut in N.Y. as Avito in *L'amore dei tre Re* on Nov. 16, 1922, continuing to sing there until 1935, when he became its general manager, guiding its fortunes through the difficult years of World War II and the postwar era; he retired in 1950. Although he became an American citizen in 1922, he maintained a close connection with Canada; he returned there after his retirement. He was particularly esteemed for such roles as Romeo, Tannhäuser, Don Jose, Siegfried, Canio, and Pelléas; he also created leading roles in Deems Taylor's *The King's Henchman* (1927) and *Peter Ibbetson* (1931) at the Metropolitan.

Johnson, Frank (Francis), black bandmaster and composer; b. probably on the island of Martinique, 1792; d. Philadelphia, Apr. 6, 1844. He settled in Philadelphia (*c.* 1809), where he organized his own band and dance orch. After touring England with his band in 1837, he led promenade concerts with his band throughout the U.S., highlighting his own works; in Philadelphia, his concerts were often graced by the presence of prominent white artists, an unheard-of practice in his era.

Johnson, James P(rice), African-American jazz pianist and composer; b. Brunswick, N.J., Feb. 1, 1891; d. N.Y., Nov. 17, 1955. He studied piano with his mother; began his career as a pianist in N.Y. and Atlantic City nightclubs; later led his own bands and appeared as soloist. He was the leading Harlem STRIDE pianist of his day; he also was a gifted composer. Among his best known piano pieces are *Caprice Rag* (1914); *Harlem Strut* (1917); *Carolina Shout* (1925); *Snowy Morning Blues* (1927); *You've Got to Be Modernistic* (1930); and *Fascination* (1939).

Johnson, "J. J." (James Louis), outstanding African-American jazz trombonist and accomplished composer; b. Indianapolis, Jan. 22, 1924. He began to play the piano at the age of 9 and the trombone at 14; toured with Clarence Love and Isaac "Snookum" Russell (1941–42) before attracting attention as a member of Benny Carter's orch. (1942–45). After working with Count Basie in N.Y. (1945–46), he did stints with various artists there; also made a tour of Korea, Japan, and the South Pacific with a group led by Oscar Pettiford for the USO (1951). After a hiatus from the jazz scene he resumed his career, touring with Kai Winding in a trombone duo known as Jay and Kai; then formed his own quintet (1956–60), with which he toured Europe. After working with Miles Davis (1961–62), he led his own quartet and sextet; gave increasing attention to composition, moving to Los Angeles as a composer for film and television in 1970; he returned to Indianapolis in 1988, at which time he was awarded an honorary doctorate by Indiana Univ. Johnson is acknowledged as one of the pioneer figures of the bop era. Among his works are *Poem* for Brass (1956), *Sketch* for Trombone and Band (1959), *El camino real* (1964), *In Walked Horace* (1966), and *Concepts in Blue* (1980).

Johnson, Robert, influential African-American blues musician; b. Hazlehurt, Miss., *c.* 1912; d. Greenwood, Miss., Aug. 16, 1938. Relatively little about his life is known; he played at dance parties, worked with other musicians, and made recordings in Texas during the last 2 years of his life. He was apparently poisoned by a jealous husband after flirting with the man's wife. Johnson played guitar and sang within the Delta blues tradition, having been influenced by Son House, Charley Patton, and the jazz guitarist Lonnie Johnson (no relation), and borrowed extant songs in the manner of oral tradition. But Johnson added other elements to create a unique and powerful style, including a taut and penetrating vocal style, a strong rhythmic sense on the guitar, an agitated slide technique, the use of a walking bass, and personal themes of fatalistic torment. His versatile guitar playing created as full a sound as had yet been heard on an acoustic guitar; it is said that Johnson was very interested in the newly developed electric guitar, but no record exists of his having played one.

After his death Chicago blues musicians kept his music and name alive; but the widespread modern revival of his work began in the 1960s, when white blues and rock musicians introduced their audiences to Johnson's legacy, including *Crossroads*, *Hellhound on My Trail*, *Dust My Broom*, *Kind Hearted Woman*, *Terraplane Blues*, *Love in Vain*, *Ramblin' on My Mind*, and *If I Had Possession Over Judgment Day*.

Johnston, Ben(jamin Burwell), American composer and pedagogue; b. Macon, Ga., Mar. 15, 1926. He studied at the College of William and Mary in Williamsburg, Va. (A.B., 1949), the Cincinnati Cons. of Music (M.Mus., 1950), and Mills College in Oakland, Calif. (M.A., 1953); held a Guggenheim fellowship (1959–60). He taught at the Univ. of Illinois in Urbana (1951–83). He worked with Harry Partch in 1949–50; the experience confirmed his instinctive interest in just intonation; he composed in equal

temperament during the 1950s, but began moving toward just intonation in the 1960s. He has developed a different, less restrictive intonation system than Partch's; he has also written for traditional instruments (most successfully for strings and retuned piano), not being inclined to build instruments, as Partch did. In addition to the many fine chamber and vocal works, Johnson's flair for the dramatic and ironic is seen to good advantage in his theater works, which include operas, orch.l and chamber works, a cantata, *Night* (1955), and other choral music, songs, and piano pieces.

Jolie Fille de Perth, La (The Pretty Girl of Perth). Opera by Bizet, 1867, based on a novel by Walter Scott. Like so many operas, the plot involves a betrothed couple, a lecherous Duke, a young Gypsy woman with her own agenda, and an apprentice who can't hold his drink. The whole mess almost ends with a fatal duel, but the Gypsy saves the day and the couple is reunited in the nick of time.

Jolson, Al (Asa Yoelson), popular Lithuanian-born American singer and actor; b. Srednike, Lithuania, May 26, 1886; d. San Francisco, Oct. 23, 1950. His family emigrated about 1894 to the U.S., where he began his professional career as a performer in vaudeville, burlesque, and minstrel shows. He 1st attracted wide notice in N.Y. as a member of Lew Dockstader's Minstrels (1909); subsequently was engaged as a leading performer at the Winter Garden (1911), introducing his famous blackface character of Gus in *Whirl of Society* (1912); he continued to appear in popular shows there. He starred in the 1st feature sound film, *The Jazz Singer* (1927), winning immortality with his rendition in blackface of the song *My Mammy*; he appeared in several other films, and also

COURTESY FRANK DRIGGS COLLECTION *Al Jolson, 1930s*

returned to Broadway in *The Wonder Bar* (1931) and *Hold On to Your Hats* (1940).

During the last few years of his life he appeared on radio and television; his voice was also used on the soundtracks for the films *The Jolson Story* (1946) and *Jolson Sings Again* (1949). He popularized many songs, including *Swanee*; *California, Here I Come*; *Toot, Toot, Tootsie!*; *April Showers*; *Rockaby Your Baby with a Dixie Melody*; *Let Me Sing and I'm Happy*; *There's a Rainbow 'Round My Shoulder*; and *Sonny Boy*. He was married to Ruby Keeler (1928–39).

Jones, Booker T., African-American organist, founder of Booker T. and the MGs (Memphis Group), noted for its "Memphis sound"; b. Memphis, Sept. 12, 1944. The group lit the rock firmament in 1962 with their smash hit *Green Onions*; their primary role was as the backing band for artists recording at the Stax record label until its demise. In 1965 Jones authored a blues song with the pseudo-astrological title *Born Under a Bad Sign*. Seized by a peculiar yen for musical culture, he received a degree in applied music from Indiana Univ. Fortunately this academic distinction did not kill off his natural gift for pleasing the public. His records sold well; among his greatest hits were *Soul Limbo* (1968) and *Time Is Tight* (1969).

Jones, Elvin (Ray), drummer; b. Pontiac, Mich., Sept. 9, 1927. He performed with local groups in Pontiac and Detroit before playing in military bands during his service in the U.S. Army (1946–49); he performed in Michigan, then went to N.Y. (1956), where he played with J. J. Johnson's quintet and Donald Byrd's quintet, as well as with Bud Powell, Sonny Rollins, and Stan Getz. He then performed with John Coltrane's group (1960–66), acquiring renown for his imaginative drumming; subsequently led his own groups, touring widely in the U.S., Europe, South America, and the Orient.

Jones, George, American country-western singer; b. Saratoga, Tex., Sept. 12, 1931. He began to play the guitar when he was 9; made some appearances locally before serving in the Korean War; then worked as a house painter. In 1955 he recorded his 1st hit song, *Why, Baby, Why*; subsequently gained fame with such songs as *Window Up Above* (1961), *She Thinks I Still Care* (1962), and *We Must Have Been Out of Our Minds* (1963). Jones is comfortable in both the honky-tonk and sentimental ballad styles; he has survived periods of being subjected to the worst excesses of the "Nashville sound." He was married to the country-music star Tammy Wynette (1969–75); after their divorce they continued to record; eventually he returned to bolstering his image as heartbroken heavy drinker with *If Drinking Don't Kill Me (Her Memory Will)*. He continues to surprise with good recordings, such as *I Don't Need Your Rockin' Chair*. Elvis Costello paid him tribute with an album of country-western covers, *Almost Blue* (1981).

Jones, Hank (Henry), pianist; b. Vicksburg, Miss., July 31, 1918. He was taken in early childhood to Pontiac, Mich., where he began his piano training; as a teenager, he performed with groups in Michigan and Ohio, then went to N.Y. (1944), where he worked with "Hot Lips" Page; had stints with various jazz artists, including Coleman Hawkins and Billy Eckstine. He was an accompanist for Ella Fitzgerald (1948–53) and also worked with Charlie Parker; then was a staff musician with CBS (1959–76), during which period he also toured; later was a pianist and conductor for the Broadway musical *Ain't Misbehavin'*, based on the music of Fats Waller. He made innumerable recordings.

Jones, Jo(nathan), African-American jazz drummer, also known as Kansas City Jo Jones and Papa Jo Jones; b. Chicago, Oct. 7, 1911; d. N.Y., Sept. 3, 1985. He was reared in Alabama; studied saxophone, trumpet, and piano before mastering the drums; joined Count Basie's band in 1934 and remained with his group, off and on, until 1948, establishing his own distinctive rhythmic style stressing all 4 beats of the bar and diversifying it with a wire-brush technique on the high hat cymbal. In 1957 he traveled to Europe with Ella Fitzgerald and Oscar Peterson; then led his own groups. He appeared in several films, including *Jammin' the Blues* (1944), *Born to Swing* (1973), and *Last of the Blue Devils* (1979).

Jones, "Philly Joe" (Joseph Rudolph), American jazz drummer; b. Philadelphia, July 15, 1923; d. there, Aug. 30, 1985. He studied piano with his mother, saxophone with Jimmy Oliver, and drums with James Harris; then played with local groups. Making his way to N.Y., he played with Zoot Sims, Lee Konitz, and Miles Davis. In 1967 he went to Europe, remaining there until 1972; eventually formed the jazz-rock group Le Gran Prix (1975), with which he toured the U.S.; appeared at N.Y.'s Carnegie Hall (1980).

Jones, Quincy (Delight, Jr.), versatile African-American pianist, trumpeter, bandleader, recording executive, composer, and film producer; b. Chicago, Mar. 14, 1933. Moved to Seattle at the age of 10, took up the trumpet at 14; later studied with Clark Terry (1950). He played in Lionel Hampton's band (1951–53), then was a performer-arranger in Dizzy Gillespie's touring band in the Near East (1956–57); subsequently worked in Europe (1957–60), where he toured with his own big band. After returning to the U.S. he was an artist and repertoire man for Mercury Records, becoming vice president (1964); later founded his own record company. He composed such works as *Stockholm Sweetnin'* (1956), *Evening in Paris* (1956), *The Quintessence* (1961), *Walking in Space* (1969), *Soundpiece* for String Quartet and Contralto, and *Soundpiece* for Jazz Orch. He won a number of Grammy Awards, being honored in 1985 as producer of the recording and video productions of *We Are the World*, which helped raise millions of dollars for famine-relief efforts in Africa. He also composed the score for and was coproducer of the film *The Color Purple* (1985).

Jones, Sissieretta (born Matilda Sissieretta Joyner), noted African-American soprano, known as the "Black Patti" (with reference to Adelina Patti); b. Portsmouth, Va., Jan. 5, 1868; d. Providence, R.I., June 24, 1933. She studied at the New England Cons. of Music in Boston; also with Louise Capianni and Mme. Scongia in London. She made her debut at a concert at N.Y.'s Steinway Hall (1888), then began to tour from 1890, giving concerts in the West Indies, North America, and Europe. She gained prominence as a result of her appearances at the Grand Negro Jubilee at N.Y.'s Madison Square Garden and at the White House in a command performance for President Harrison (1892); then sang at the Pittsburgh Exposition and the Chicago World's Columbian Exposition (1893). N.Y.'s Metropolitan Opera considered her for African roles in *Aida* and *L'Africaine*, but racial attitudes and conservative management policies precluded such appearances. She was the principal soprano of the vaudeville troupe known as Black Patti's Troubadours (1896–1915), with which she toured throughout the world; she starred in its operatic "kaleidoscope," in which she sang a medley of arias from operas in staged scenes; she also sang art songs and popular ballads.

Jones, "Spike" (Lindley Armstrong), American bandleader and musical satirist; b. Long Beach, Calif., Dec. 14, 1911; d. Los Angeles, May 1, 1965. He played drums as a boy; then led a school band. In 1942 he made a recording of a satirical song, *Der Führer's Face*, featuring a Bronx-cheer razzer; then toured the U.S. with his multitalented band the City Slickers, which included a washboard, a Smith and Wesson pistol, antibug flit guns in E-flat, doorbells, anvils, hammers to break glass, and a live goat trained to bleat rhythmically. Climactically he introduced the Latrinophone (a toilet seat strung with catgut). With this ensemble he launched a Musical Depreciation Revue. He retired in 1963, when the wave of extravaganza that had carried him to the crest of commercial success subsided. In his heyday he was known as the "King of Corn"; any piece of music was fair game for his slapstick approach; for every Jonesian *William Tell Overture* there was a *Cocktails for 2* in his own image.

Jones, Thad(deus Joseph), trumpeter, cornetist, flügelhornist, bandleader, arranger, and composer; b. Pontiac, Mich., Mar. 28, 1923; d. Copenhagen, Aug. 20, 1986. He taught himself to play trumpet when he was about 13; subsequently appeared professionally with his brother Hank at age 16, and also with Sonny Stitt; after working with various dance and show bands, he joined his brother Elvin as a member of Billy Mitchell's quintet in Detroit (1950–53). He worked with Charles Mingus (1954–55) and was a featured soloist and arranger with Count Basie's orch. (1954–63); also appeared with Thelonious Monk and Gerry Mulligan. With Mel Lewis, in 1965 he formed his own band, which subsequently gained fame through its tours of the U.S. and Europe, including a smashing visit to the Soviet Union in 1972. He left the band in 1979 and settled in Denmark, where he organized his own big band, the Thad Jones Eclipse; he was also active as an arranger and composer with Danish Radio. He returned to the U.S. to briefly take charge of Count Basie's orch. (1985). His best-known composition was *A Child Is Born*, which gained the status of a jazz classic.

Jones, Tom (real name, Thomas Jones Woodward), Welsh singer and drummer; b. Pontypridd, June 7, 1940. He sang, as most Welshmen do, with a natural feeling for melody; dropped out of school at 16 and began to play the drums and sing in British pubs; his big chance at success came when he was heard by Gordon Mills, a Welshman himself, who decided to propel him into fame; but 1st he had to abbreviate his name. His greatest asset was lung power; he could outscream anyone in the rock field; he wore extremely tight "sexy" pants, whose protuberances excited middle-aged women; with these assets he successfully invaded the U.S. By the late 1980s his fame had largely dissipated, his performances relegated to the nostalgia circuit.

jongleur (Fr.; from Lat. *joculator*, maker of jokes; Sp. *juglares*). A medieval entertainer employed by royalty and aristocracy to provide amusement, including songs and jests; the word itself corresponds to the English *juggler*, suggesting that the jongleur also performed acrobatic acts. By the 12th century the jongleurs had become known as *ménestriers*, those who administered to traveling troubadours and trouvères; the term further evolved to *ménestrels* (Eng. *minstrels*). English minstrels were also known as *gleemen*.

Jongleur de Notre Dame, Le. Opera by Massenet, 1902, 1st produced in Monte Carlo. The action takes place in France in the 14th century, focusing on a street juggler who performs for and then collapses in front of a statue of the Holy Virgin. Before he dies, the Virgin silently blesses him with her marmoreal hand, and he becomes, in legend and tradition, "the juggler of Our Lady." This is one of the few operas ever written which has no human female roles.

Jonny spielt auf (Johnny Strikes Up). Opera by Krenek, 1927, to his own text, 1st produced in Leipzig. It became sensationally successful as the 1st opera making use of the jazz idiom. Jonny (without an *h* in his name and pronounced "Yonny") is a Negro musician who becomes a famous jazz-band leader, captivating audiences around the globe. The fox-trot and the Charleston rhythms animate the score, but there are also lyric episodes. The work was translated into 18 languages, and even a brand of Austrian cigarettes was named after it. When the opera was 1st produced by the Metropolitan Opera in N.Y. (1929), the role of Jonny was changed into that of a blackface musician in order not to offend the segregationist sensitivities of some of the patrons, particularly in scenes when Jonny consorts with white chambermaids.

Joplin, Janis (Lyn), plaintive American rock and blues singer; b. Port Arthur, Tex., 1943; d. of an overdose of heroin, Los Angeles, Oct. 4, 1970. She spent an unhappy childhood; ran away from home and delved into the bohemian life of San Francisco. After a brief stint in college, she joined the rock group Big Brother and the Holding Company as lead vocalist in 1966, winning acclaim for her rendition of *Ball and Chain* when she appeared with the group at the Monterey International Pop Festival in 1967. Her passionate wailing in a raspy voice immediately established her as an uninhibited representative of the younger generation.

After recording the album *Cheap Thrills* (1967) she left Big Brother and struck out on her own: she formed her own backup group, the Kozmic Blues Band, in 1968, and then appeared in such esoteric emporia as the Psychedelic Supermarket in Boston, Kinetic Playground in Chicago, Whisky A-Go-Go in Los Angeles, and Fillmore East in N.Y. She produced the albums *I Got Dem Ol' Kozmic Blues Again Mama* and *Pearl* before her early demise. She was arrested in Tampa, Fla., in 1969 for having hurled porcine epithets at a policeman, which further endeared her to her public. On the more positive side, the Southern Comfort Distillery Co. presented her with a fur coat in recognition of the publicity she gave the firm by her habitual consumption of a quart of Southern Comfort at each of her appearances; she injected religious passion into a commercial theme in one of her own songs, *Mercedes Benz*. Her biggest hit was the posthumously released *Me and Bobby McGee*.

Joplin, Scott

〰〰 〰〰 〰〰 〰〰 〰〰

Remarkable African-American pianist and composer, best known for his piano rags; b. probably near Marshall, Tex., Nov. 24, 1868; d. N.Y., Apr. 1, 1917. He learned to play the piano at home in Texarkana and later studied music seriously with a local German musician. He left home at 17 and went to St. Louis, earning his living by playing piano in local emporia. In 1893 he moved to Chicago (drawn by the prospect of music-making and other gaiety of the World's Fair), and in 1896 went to Sedalia, Mo., where he took music courses at George Smith College, a segregated school for blacks. His 1st music publications were in 1895, of genteel, maudlin songs and marches, typical of the period. His success as a ragtime composer came with the *Maple Leaf Rag* (1899; the most famous of all piano rags), which he named after a local dance hall, the Maple Leaf Club. The sheet-music edition sold so well that Joplin was able to settle in St. Louis and devote himself exclusively to composition; he even tried to write a ragtime ballet (*The Ragtime Dance*, 1902) and a ragtime opera, *A Guest of Honor* (the music is lost; newspaper notices indicate it was probably perf. by the Scott Joplin Opera Co. in 1903).

In 1907 he went to N.Y., where he continued his career as a composer and teacher. Still intent on ambitious plans, he wrote an opera, *Treemonisha*, to his own libretto (the title deals with a black baby girl found under a tree by a woman named Monisha); he completed the score in 1911 and produced it in concert form in 1915 without success. Interest in the opera was revived almost 60 years later; T. J. Anderson orchestrated it from the piano score, and it received its 1st complete performance in Atlanta on Jan. 28, 1972.

Despite Joplin's ambitious attempts to make ragtime "respectable" by applying its principles to European forms, it was with the small, indigenous dance form of the piano rag that he achieved his greatest artistic success. As a noted historian phrased it, these pieces are "the precise

Scott Joplin, c. 1910

COURTESY OF THE NEW YORK PUBLIC LIBRARY

American equivalent, in terms of a native dance music, of minuets by Mozart, mazurkas by Chopin, or waltzes by Brahms."

Altogether he wrote about 50 piano rags, in addition to the 2 operas, and a few songs, waltzes, and marches. The titles of some of these rags reflect his desire to transcend the trivial and create music on a more serious plane: *Sycamore*, "A Concert Rag" (1904); *Chrysanthemum*, "An Afro-American Intermezzo" (1904); *Sugar Cane*, "A Ragtime Classic 2-Step" (1908); *Fig Leaf Rag*, "A High Class Rag" (1908); *Reflection Rag*, "Syncopated Musings" (1917). In his last years he lamented at having failed to achieve the recognition he felt his music merited. Suffering from syphilis, he became insane and died shortly afterward in a state hospital. More than 50 years later, an extraordinary sequence of events—new recordings of his music and its use in an award-winning film, *The Sting* (1974)—brought Joplin unprecedented popularity and acclaim: among pop recordings, *The Entertainer* (1902) was one of the best-selling disks for 1974; among classical recordings, Joplin albums represented 74 percent of the best-sellers of the year. In 1976 he was awarded exceptional posthumous recognition by the Pulitzer Prize Committee.

Jordan, Louis, African-American jazz alto saxophonist and singer; b. Brinkley, Ark., July 8, 1908; d. Los Angeles, Feb. 4, 1975. He took up the clarinet and the alto saxophone; from 1929 he played with various bands, including Chick Webb; formed his own "jump" (JIVE) band in N.Y., the Tympany 5 (1939). As a soloist he recorded with Louis Armstrong, Ella Fitzgerald, and other jazz luminaries; in later years he toured with his own combo, visiting England (1962) and Asia (1967 and 1968). Among his biggest hits are *Is You Is Or Is You Ain't My Baby?* (1944); *Choo Choo Ch'boogie* (1946); *Ain't Nobody Here But Us Chickens*; *Open the Door Richard* (1947); and *Baby It's Cold Outside* (with Ella Fitzgerald, 1949).

joropo. Characteristic dance of Venezuela, in 3/4 time, with a strongly syncopated melody against a steady bass.

Josquin Desprez (Des Prez). DESPREZ (DES PREZ), JOSQUIN.

jota (Sp.). A national dance song of northern Spain, dating to the 17th century, in rapid triple time, somewhat like a fast waltz. It is usually played by the guitar, mandolin, and castanets. Composers such as Glinka (see *Jota aragonese*), Rimsky-Korsakov (*Capriccio Espagnole*), and Liszt (*Rhapsodie espagnole, c.* 1863) included jotas in their music.

Jota aragonese. Symphonic dance by Glinka, 1845, based on the authentic Spanish motives he collected during his travels in Spain. The work was 1st performed in St. Petersburg, 1850.

Jour d'été à la montagne. Rhapsody by d'Indy, 1906, for piano and orch., in 3 sections (Dawn, Day, and Night). One of his most effective works, it was 1st performed in Paris.

juba. Syncopated dance step, generated in the Caribbean in the 18th century and popular among African-Americans in the South. A rapid rhythmic beat accentuated by slapping hands and legs is known as patting juba.

Jubilee. Musical by C. Porter and M. Hart, 1935. The royal family in an unspecified exotic country is bored stiff by the protocol. Taking advantage of a brief student rebellion, they leave the palace and, dropping all their inhibitions, mingle with the common people incognito. Includes *Just 1 of Those Things* and the celebrated *Begin the Beguine*.

jubilus. In Roman Catholic liturgical chant, the often lengthy group of ornaments sung on the last syllable of the word *alleluia*, suggesting the intended jubilation in a manner approaching glossolalia.

Judith. Opera by Serov, 1863, 1st performed in St. Petersburg. The libretto is drawn from the Apocrypha. Judith, a patriotic Jewess, decides to risk her virtue in penetrating the tent of the Assyrian chieftain Holofernes, whose army besieges her city. She plies him with wine and, as he sinks into a drunken torpor, she cuts off his head, packs it in a sack, and returns to the city. She holds aloft the richly bearded head of the enemy king at an assembly and the Jewish people explode in jubilation. The score contains elements of a monumental oratorio style in the manner of Handel. It once enjoyed great popularity in Russia.

Judith. Opera by Honegger, 1926, on the same subject as Serov's work; 1st performed in Monte Carlo. It was originally intended as a biblical drama in 13 scenes and was eventually made into a full opera.

Judith. Choreographic poem by Schuman, 1950, a "concerto for dancers and orch."; it was 1st performed in Louisville, Ky. The subject is the same as the above 2 works.

jug. An earthen pitcher used in African-American traditional music; blowing into it produces a low, hollow tone.

jug band. A 20th-century African-American traditional ensemble featuring found objects such as jugs, bones, and washboards, along with strings, harmonica, kazoo, and winds in various combinations. It is associated with medicine shows and other rural settings.

Juive, La. Grand opera by Halévy, 1835. Underneath the highly melodramatic plot and heavily Romantic music, there is a study of anti-Semitism and its ill effects on all involved. Before the opera begins in Constance, a Jew (Éléazar) has rescued the daughter of a magistrate (now Cardinal Brogni), who thought her lost in a war; Éléazar has raised her as Rachel, a Jewess. Cardinal Brogni has been persecuting the Jews of the city for years. Rachel has a lover, Prince Léopold, who pretends to be a Jew named Samuel and, unknown to her, is already married. Eventually he has to reveal his true status; the shattered and betrayed Rachel denounces him to the court; both are condemned to death, along with Éléazar. Rachel changes her story to save Léopold's life; but Éléazar refuses to save his and her lives by converting. The Jew hints to the Cardinal of the survival of his long-lost daughter, but the 2 are still burned at the stake. As the flames rise, Brogni asks 1 more time if his daughter is alive; when Éléazar says yes, the Cardinal pleads to know where she is. "There!" says Éléazar, pointing to Rachel; the 2 die as the curtain falls.

Julien. Opera by G. Charpentier, 1913, as a failed sequel to the highly successful *Louise* (1900). Julien, a painter who figured in the earlier opera, is visited by the deceased Louise's spirit in a vision to encourage him to continue working on his art. Eventually he follows her to the land of death.

Julius Caesar. See GIULIO CESARE IN EGITTO.

Jullien, Louis (George Maurice Adolphe Roch Albert Abel Antonio Alexandre Noé Jean Lucien Daniel Eugène Joseph-le-brun Joseph-Barême Thomas Thomas Thomas-Thomas Pierre Arbon Pierre-Maurel Barthélemi Artus Alphonse Bertrand Dieudonné Emanuel Josué Vincent Luc Michel Jules-de-la-plane Jules-Bazin Julio César), famous eccentric French conductor and composer; b. Sisteron, Apr. 23, 1812; d. Paris, Mar. 14, 1860. The son of a bandmaster, he went to Paris in 1833 and studied composition with Le Carpentier and Halévy, but could not maintain the discipline of learning music, and began to compose light dances instead; of these, the waltz *Rosita* attained enormous, though transitory, popularity in Paris. He left the Cons. in 1836 without taking a degree, and became engaged as conductor of dance music at the Jardin Turc. He also attempted to launch a musical journal, but an accumulation of carelessly contracted debts compelled him to leave France (1838). He went to London, where he conducted summer concerts at the Drury Lane Theatre (1840) and winter concerts with an enlarged ensemble of instrumentalists and singers (1841). He then opened a series of "society concerts," at which he presented large choral works, such as Rossini's *Stabat Mater*, as well as movements from Beethoven's syms.

In 1847 he engaged Berlioz to conduct at the Drury Lane Theatre, which he had leased. He became insolvent in 1848, but attempted to recoup his fortune by organizing a "concert monstre" with 400 players, 3 choruses, and 3 military bands. He succeeded in giving 3 such concerts in London in 1849. He then essayed the composition of an opera, *Pietro il Grande*, which he produced at his own expense at Covent Garden (1852). He used the pseudonym Roch Albert for his spectacular pieces, such as *Destruction of Pompeii*; publ. some dance music (*Royal Irish Quadrille*, etc.) under his own name. In 1853 he was engaged by P. T. Barnum for a series of concerts in the U.S. For his exhibition at the Crystal Palace in N.Y. (1854), attended by a great crowd, he staged a simulated conflagration for his *Fireman's Quadrille*.

Despite his eccentricities, however, Jullien possessed a true interest in musical progress. At his American concerts he made a point of including several works by American composers: *Santa Claus Sym.* by William Henry Fry and some chamber music by George Frederick Bristow. In 1854 he returned to London; his managerial ventures resulted in another failure. In 1859 he went to Paris, but he was promptly arrested for debt and spent several weeks in prison. He died a few months later in an insane asylum to which he had been confined.

Jumbo. Musical by Rodgers and Hart, 1935. Two circus managers are locked in fierce business rivalry. The daughter of one is in love with the son of the other. The financial rivalry is settled, somewhat unethically and even illegally, when the press agent of the girl's father arranges a piece of arson and collects a large amount of money in insurance; the couple can then get married. Includes *My Romance, Little Girl Blue*, and *The Most Beautiful Girl in the World*.

Junge Lord, Der. Opera by Henze, 1965, 1st performed in Berlin. In a typical Henze musical diatribe against the bourgeoisie, a well-dressed ape arrives with his master in a small German town. The snobbish residents take the ape's simian grunts as the laconic utterances of a British lord. Naturally, the locals get their comeuppance.

Jupiter Symphony. Mozart wrote many syms. in the key of C major, but the greatest of them all is his last one, no. 41, K.551, known under the name "Jupiter." Who assigned the Olympian attribute to this work is unknown, but it became indissolubly connected with the music. The finale is a paragon of fugal construction with the main subject based on the simple progression of 4 notes: C–D–F–E.

just intonation. A system of tuning relying on the precise relationships between string lengths, expressed in ratios. Unaccompanied voices or open strings will usually follow just (or pure) intonation; other instruments can either be refingered, retuned, adapted, or newly built to play just relationships. Like other intonations, just intonation affects both the horizontal (melodic) and vertical (harmonic) elements of pitch; it has its unique qualities (e.g., true consonance and the expansion of consonance beyond the triad) and limitations (finding instruments to play the unlimited possibility of ratios, thereby permitting modulation). Ancient Greek theory operated in just intonation, and it seems possible that this approach persisted into the 2nd millennium A.D. There were a few attempts to accommodate just intonation (or sufficiently expanded EQUAL TEMPERAMENT, e.g., 31-equal temperament) over the centuries; but only in the 20th century did musicians appear who were willing to challenge the established equally tempered chromatic scale by building or adapting instruments and then devising the theory and notation to compose in just tuning (Partch, Johnston, Lou Harrison, and many West Coast composers). See also ACOUSTICS.

Kk

Kabalevsky, Dmitri (Borisovich), noted Russian composer; b. St. Petersburg, Dec. 30, 1904; d. Moscow, Feb. 14, 1987. When he was 14 years old his family moved to Moscow; he received his primary musical education at the Scriabin Music School (1919–25); also studied music theory privately with Gregory Catoire; in 1925 he entered the Moscow Cons. as a student of Miaskovsky in composition and Goldenweiser in piano; in 1932 he was appointed instructor in composition there; in 1939 he became a full prof. As a pedagogue he developed effective methods of musical education; in 1962 he was elected head of the Commission of Musical Aesthetic Education of Children; in 1969 became president of the Scientific Council of Educational Aesthetics in the Academy of Pedagogical Sciences of the USSR; in 1972 he received the honorary degree of president of the International Soc. of Musical Education.

As a pianist, composer, and conductor he made guest appearances in Europe and the U.S. Kabalevsky's music represents a paradigm of the Russian school of composition in its Soviet period; his melodic writing is marked by broad diatonic lines invigorated by an energetic rhythmic pulse; while adhering to basic tonality, his harmony is apt to be rich in euphonious dissonances. A prolific composer, he wrote in all musical genres; in his operas he successfully reflected both the lyrical and the dramatic aspects of the librettos, several of which are based on Soviet subjects faithful to the tenets of socialist realism. His instrumental writing was functional, taking into consideration the idiomatic capacities of the instruments. His compositions include operas; orch.l works including 4 symphonies (1932, 1934, 1934, 1956: *The Comedians*); concerti; 2 string quartets (1928, 1945); piano works, including 24 Preludes (1943); children's pieces; vocal works, including numerous school songs and choruses; requiem for voices and orch. (Moscow, 1963); an oratorio, *A Letter to the 30th Century* (1970); incidental music for plays; and film scores.

kachampa. Peruvian war dance in rapid 2/4 time, marked by vigorous accents.

Kaddish. Sym. No. 3 by Bernstein, 1963, for female speaker, mixed chorus, soprano solo, a choir of boys, and orch. The Kaddish is a Hebrew lamentation for the dead; Bernstein dedicated his score to the memory of President Kennedy. The text is partly in Hebrew and partly in Aramaic, the language spoken by Jesus Christ. The 1st performance of the work took place in Tel Aviv with Bernstein conducting.

Kadenz (Ger.). 1. CADENCE. 2. CADENZA.

Kagel, Mauricio (Maurizio Raúl), remarkable Argentine composer; b. Buenos Aires, Dec. 24, 1931. He studied in Buenos Aires with Juan Carlos Paz and Alfredo Schiuma; also attended courses in philosophy and literature at the Univ. of Buenos Aires. In 1949 he became associated with the Agrupación Nueva Musica. From 1949 to 1956 he was choral director at the Teatro Colón. In 1957 he obtained a stipend from the Academic Cultural Exchange with West Germany and went to Cologne, where he made his permanent home. From 1960 to 1966 he was a guest lecturer at the International Festival Courses for New Music in Darmstadt; in 1961 and 1963 he gave lectures and demonstrations of modern music in the U.S., and in 1964–65 was

Slee Prof. of composition at the State Univ. of N.Y. at Buffalo. In 1969 he became director of the Inst. of New Music at the Rheinische Musikschule in Cologne. In 1974 he was made prof. at the Cologne Hochschule für Musik.

As a composer Kagel evolved an extremely complex system in which a fantastically intricate and yet wholly rational serial organization of notes, intervals, and durations is supplemented by aleatory techniques; some of these techniques are derived from linguistic permutations, random patterns of lights and shadows on exposed photographic film, and other seemingly arcane processes. In his hyperserial constructions he endeavors to unite all elements of human expression, ultimately aiming at the creation of a universe of theatrical arts in their visual, aural, and societal aspects.

Kaiserquartett. Emperor Quartet.

kaleidophonia. By analogy with kaleidoscopic images, a musical composition derived from multiple mirrorlike reflections of a central subject. By selecting a code of parameters determining intervals and durations, a kaleidophonic structure can be designed as a harmonic complex composed of contrapuntal lines in quaquaversal rhythmic dispersion. Joseph Schillinger published in 1940 a volume of musical patterns which he entitled *Kaleidophone*.

Kalevala. The great national epic of Finland, compiled by the Finnish scholar Elias Lönnrot (1802–84). The source material, medieval epic songs, had survived primarily in oral tradition. Its verses contain numerous references to therapeutic properties of music; in several passages the wounds of heroes are healed by chanting the history of its infliction. Sibelius and other Finnish composers have drawn widely on the *Kalevala* for the subjects of their symphonic and other works.

kalimba. See LAMELLAPHONES.

Kalinnikov, Vasili (Sergeievich), Russian composer; b. Voin, near Mtzensk, Jan. 13, 1866; d. Yalta, Jan. 11, 1901. He studied in Orel; in 1884 he enrolled at the Moscow Cons., but he had to leave it a year later because of inability to pay; he then studied the bassoon at the Music School of the Moscow Phil. Soc., which provided free tuition. He earned his living by playing bassoon in theater orchs.; also studied composition with A. Ilyinsky and Blaramberg.

While still a student he composed his 1st work, the symphonic poem *The Nymphs* (Moscow, 1889); later wrote another symphonic poem, *The Cedar and the Palm* (1897–98), the incidental music for A. K. Tolstoy's *Czar Boris* (Moscow, 1899), and the prelude to the unfinished opera *In the Year 1812* (1899–1900). In 1895 he completed his most successful work, the Sym. in G Minor (1897); a 2nd sym., in A major (1898), was not as successful; he also wrote a cantata, *John of Damascus* (1890; not extant), songs, and piano pieces.

Kálmán, Emmerich (Imre), Hungarian-born American composer; b. Siofok, Oct. 24, 1882; d. Paris, Oct. 30, 1953. He studied with Koessler at the Royal Academy of Music in Budapest; wrote music criticism, won the Franz Josef Prize (1907), then became a successful composer of operettas and cabaret songs in Vienna. He went to Paris in 1939, then to the U.S. in 1940, becoming an American citizen in 1942; he returned to Europe in 1949. His most successful operettas were *Die Csárdásfürstin* (Vienna, 1915); *Gräfin Mariza* (Vienna, 1924); and *Die Zirkusprinzessin* (Vienna, 1926).

Kalomiris, Manolis, distinguished Greek composer and pedagogue; b. Smyrna, Dec. 26, 1883; d. Athens, Apr. 3, 1962. He studied piano with Bauch and Sturm, composition with Grädener, and music history with Mandyczewski at the Cons. of the Gesellschaft der Musikfreunde in Vienna (1901–1906); then went to Russia, where he taught piano at a private school in Kharkov. He settled in Athens, where he taught at the Cons. (1911–19); was founder-director of the Hellenic Cons. (1919–26) and of the National Cons. (1926–48). He was greatly esteemed as a teacher; publ. several textbooks on harmony, counterpoint, and orchestration; wrote music criticism. Kalomiris was the protagonist of Greek nationalism in music; almost all his works are based on Greek folk-song patterns, and many are inspired by Hellenic subjects. In his harmonies and instrumentation he followed the Russian school of composition, with a considerable influx of lush Wagnerian sonorities. His compositions include operas, orch.l works, chamber music, piano music, choruses, and songs.

kamānja (from Pers. *kamān*, bow; Arab. *kamānja*). Persian spike fiddle, dating from the end of the 1st millennium A.D., with a round- or heart-shaped body, long neck and long spike, and 2 or 4 strings tuned (singly or in pairs) a perfect 4th apart.

kamarinskaya. Russian peasant dance, usually performed by men only, set in quick 3/4 time; the words are often of a humorous character.

Kamarinskaya. Symphonic fantasy by Glinka, 1850, based on 2 Russian songs, a wedding march, and an eponymous dance (see above entry). Tchaikovsky considered the entire Russian symphonic school to be enveloped in this work, as an oak is in an acorn.

Kammer (Ger.). Chamber; court. *Kammermusik,* chamber music; *Kammermusiker,* court musician; *Kammerkantate,* chamber cantata; *Kammerton* (Ger., chamber tone), tuning fork.

Kammersymphonie (Chamber Sym.). Work by Schoenberg, 1906, 1st performed in Vienna (1913). In Schoenberg's stylistic evolution this is a transitional work in which harmonies are built on 4ths rather than 3rds and the use of the whole-tone scale points toward a departure from tonality. The 1-movement *Kammersymphonie* is a structural fusion of sonata form and symphonic structure. One bemused German critic suggested that the title of the work should be changed to *Grauskammersymphonie* (Chamber-of-Horrors Sym.).

Kancheli, Giya (Alexandrovich), Russian composer; b. Tbilisi, Aug. 10, 1935. He studied composition at the Tbilisi Cons. (1959–63); in 1970 he was appointed to its faculty. His sources of inspiration are nourished by Caucasian melos, with its quasi-oriental fiorituras and deflected chromatics which impart a peculiar aura of lyric introspection to the music; but his treatment of these materials is covertly modernistic and overtly optimistic, especially in sonoristic effects. Among his works are 2 stage works—*The Pranks of Hanum,* musical comedy (1973); *Music for the Living,* opera (Moscow, 1984)—symphonies (1968, 1970, 1973, 1975 [In Memoriam], 1978, 1980); other orch.l works; and film scores.

Kander, John (Harold), American composer of popular music; b. Kansas City, Mo., Mar. 18, 1927. He studied piano with Wiktor Labunski, then took courses with Beeson, Luening, and Douglas Moore at Columbia Univ. He tried his hand at a Broadway musical, *The Family Affair* (1962) but was unsuccessful; also in 1962 he teamed up with the lyricist Fred Ebb (b. N.Y., Apr. 8, 1932), with whom he produced the hit songs *My Coloring Book* and *I Don't Care Much.* Encouraged by their success, they wrote the musical *Flora, the Red Menace* (1965) as a vehicle for Liza Minnelli; it was followed by their smash hit *Cabaret* (1966), which won the Tony and Drama Critics Awards and later was made into a film (1972). Among their subsequent shows were *The Happy Time* (1968), *Zorba* (1968), *Chicago* (1975), *The Act* (1977), *Woman of the Year* (1981), and *The Rink* (1984).

Kantate (Ger.). CANTATA.

kantele. A PSALTERY dating from at least the 11th century; the national instrument of Finland, mentioned in the KALEVALA. The instrument has a trapezoidal shape; originally the 4 horsehair strings were tuned to the scale (G–A–B♭–C–D); now the instrument comes with a variable number of metal strings. The kantele is held in the lap and played with bare fingers. There are numerous related instruments in Eastern Europe, such as the Russian GUSLI, Estonian *kannel,* Latvian *kokle,* and Lithuanian *kanklės.*

Kantner, Paul. See JEFFERSON AIRPLANE.

Kapelle (Ger., chapel; from Lat. *cappella*). 1. A private band or choir, especially in Central European courts. 2. An orch.

Kapellmeister (Ger., chapel master; Fr. *maître de chapelle*). Conductor of an orch. or a choir, especially at Central European courts. The Kapellmeister was, in effect, in charge of all music at a court (e.g., Haydn), although some employers divided the role into sacred and secular masters.

Kapellmeistermusik (Ger., conductor's music). Derisive term applied to orch.l compositions by professional conductors pedantically respectable but devoid of any spark of musical life. Hans von Bülow and Furtwängler wrote works of Kapellmeistermusik, and attempts have been made to revivify them. Mahler was known during his lifetime primarily as a conductor; his syms. were dismissed by music critics as Kapellmeister musik; posterity ruled otherwise. (No doubt Bruckner's works would have been called *Organistmusik* by its detractors.)

493

Karajan, Herbert von

〜〜 〜〜 〜〜 〜〜 〜〜

Preeminent Austrian conductor in the grand Germanic tradition; b. Salzburg, Apr. 5, 1908; d. Anif, near Salzburg, July 16, 1989. He was a scion of a cultured family of Greek-Macedonian extraction whose original name was Karajannis. His father was a medical officer who played the clarinet and his brother was a professional organist. Karajan himself began his musical training as a pianist; he took lessons with Franz Ledwinka at the Salzburg Mozarteum. He further attended the conducting classes of the Mozarteum's director, Bernhard Paumgartner. Eventually he went to Vienna, where he pursued academic training at a technical college and took piano lessons from one J. Hofmann; then entered the Vienna Academy of Music as a conducting student in the classes of Clemens Krauss and Alexander Wunderer.

In 1928 he made his conducting debut with a student orch. at the Vienna Academy of Music; shortly afterward, in early 1929, he made his professional conducting debut with the Salzburg Orch. He then received an engagement as conductor of the Ulm Stadttheater (1929–34). From Ulm he went to Aachen, where he was made conductor of the Stadttheater; he subsequently served as the Generalmusikdirektor there (1935–42). In 1938 he conducted his 1st performance with the Berlin Phil., the orch. that became the chosen medium of his art. Later that year he conducted *Fidelio* at his debut with the Berlin Staatsoper. After his performance of *Tristan und Isolde* soon thereafter, he was hailed by the *Berliner Tageblatt* as "das Wunder Karajan."

His capacity of absorbing and interpreting the music at hand and transmitting its essence to the audience became his most signal characteristic; he also conducted all of his scores from memory, including the entire *Ring des Nibelungen*. His burgeoning fame as a master of both opera and sym. led to engagements elsewhere in Europe. In 1938 he conducted opera at La Scala in Milan and also made guest appearances in Belgium, the Netherlands, and Scandinavia. In 1939 he became conductor of the sym. concerts of the Berlin Staatsoper Orch.

There was a dark side to Karajan's character, revealing his lack of human sensitivity and even a failure to act in his own interests. He became fascinated by the ruthless organizing solidity of the National Socialist party; in 1933 he registered in the Salzburg office of the Austrian Nazi party, where his party number was 1 607 525; barely a month later he joined the German Nazi party in Ulm, as No. 3 430 914. He lived to regret these actions after the collapse of the Nazi empire, but he managed to obtain various posts; however, in 1947 he was officially denazified by the Allied army of occupation. His personal affairs also began to interfere with his career. He married the operetta singer Elmy Holgerloef in 1938, but divorced her in 1942 to marry Anita Gütermann. Trouble came when the suspicious Nazi genealogists discovered that she was one-quarter Jewish and suggested that he divorce her. But World War II was soon to end, and so was Nazi hegemony. He finally divorced Gütermann in 1958 to marry the French fashion model Eliette Mouret.

The irony of Karajan's racial pretensions was the physical inadequacy of his own stature. He stood only 5'8" tall, but he made up for his modest height by cultivating his rich chevelure of graying hair, which harmonized with his romantic podium manner. Greatly successful with the commercial world, he made about 800 sound and video recordings, which sold millions of copies. Karajan was also an avid skier and mountain-climbing enthusiast; he piloted his own plane and drove a fleet of flamboyant and expensive sports cars. He acquired considerable wealth, and kept homes in Switzerland and on the French Riviera.

Supplementing his devotion to modern technology, Karajan was also a devotee of assorted physical and spiritual fads. He practiced yoga and aerobics, and for a while embraced Zen Buddhism. Moreover, he was known to believe in the transmigration of souls, and he expressed a hope of being reborn as an eagle soaring above the Alps, his favorite mountain range. As an alternative he investigated the technique of cryogenics, hoping that his body could be thawed a century or so later to enable him to enjoy yet another physical incarnation. None of these endeavors prevented him from being overcome by a sudden heart attack in his home at Anif in the Austrian Alps. A helicopter with a medical staff was quickly summoned to fly him to a hospital, but it arrived too late.

Karajan was characteristically self-assertive and unflinching in his personal relationships and in his numerous conflicts with managers and players. Although he began a close relationship with the Vienna Sym. Orch. in 1948, he left it in 1958. His association as conductor of the Philharmonia Orch. of London from 1948 to 1954 did more than anything to reestablish his career after World War II, but in later years he disdained his relationship with that ensemble. When Wilhelm Furtwängler, the longtime conductor of the Berlin Phil., died in 1954, Karajan was chosen to lead the orch. on its 1st tour of the U.S. However, he insisted that he would lead the tour only on the condition that he be duly elected Furtwängler's successor. Protesters were in evidence for his appearance at N.Y.'s Carnegie Hall with the orch. in 1955, but his Nazi past did not prevent the musicians of the orch. from electing him their conductor during their visit to Pittsburgh on March 3. After their return to Germany, the West Berlin Senate ratified the musicians' vote on Apr. 5, 1955.

Karajan soon came to dominate the musical life of Europe as no other conductor had ever done. In addition to his prestigious Berlin post, he served as artistic director of the Vienna Staatsoper from 1956 until he resigned in a bitter dispute with its general manager in 1964. He concurrently was artistic director of the Salzburg Festival (1957–60) and thereafter remained closely associated with it. From 1969 to 1971 he held the title of artistic adviser of the Orch. de Paris. In the meantime he consolidated his positions in Berlin and Salzburg. In 1963 he conducted the Berlin Phil. in a performance of Beethoven's 9th Sym. at the gala concert inaugurating the orch.'s magnificent new concert hall, the Philharmonie. In 1967 he organized his own Salzburg Easter Festival, which became one of the world's leading musical events. In 1967 he renegotiated his contract and was named conductor-for-life of the Berlin Phil. He made a belated Metropolitan Opera debut in N.Y. in 1967, conducting *Die Walküre*. He went on frequent tours of Europe and Japan with the Berlin Phil., and also took the orch. to the Soviet Union (1969) and China (1979).

In 1982 Karajan personally selected the 23-year-old clarinetist Sabine Meyer as a member of the Berlin Phil. (any romantic reasons for his insistence were not apparent). The musicians of the orch. rejected her because of their standing rule to exclude women, but also because the majority of the musicians had less appreciation of Fraulein Meyer as an artist than Karajan himself did. A compromise was reached, however, and in 1983 she was allowed to join the orch. on probation. She resigned in 1984 after a year of uneasy coexistence.

In 1985 Karajan celebrated his 30th anniversary as conductor of the Berlin Phil., and in 1988 his 60th anniversary as a conductor. In 1987 he conducted the New Year's Day concert of the Vienna Phil., which was televised to millions on both sides of the Atlantic. In early 1989 he made his last appearance in the U.S., conducting the Vienna Phil. at N.Y.'s Carnegie Hall; soon thereafter he announced his retirement from his Berlin post, citing failing health. Shortly before his death, he dictated an autobiographical book to Franz Endler; it was publ. in an English trans. in 1989.

karatāli. Indian circular wooden clappers with short handles; each clapper is held in 1 hand and clicked together. The instrument is known throughout many different Indian cultures and language groups (Sanskrit, Hindustani, Bengali, Marathi, Punjabi).

Kashchei, the Immortal. Opera by Rimsky-Korsakov, 1902, 1st performed in Moscow, 1902. Like her father, Kashchei's daughter is sinister. By means of a magic potion, she induces Prince Ivan to forget his beloved bride; this done, she sharpens a sword with which she plans to kill Ivan, but at the crucial moment a tempest clears the air and awakens the Prince. He returns to his beloved and Kashchei's evil domain is blown away. The opera is rarely performed, even in Russia, but it is an important work that influenced a whole generation of Russian composers. Stravinsky's symphonic poem *The Firebird* (which features a dance of Kashchei's pagan hordes) makes ample use of harmonic and rhythmic innovations introduced by Rimsky-Korsakov in this opera.

Káta Kabanová. Opera by Janáček, 1921, 1st produced in Brno. The libretto is based on the tragedy *The Storm* by the Russian playwright Alexander Ostrovsky (1823–86).

Káta carries on clandestinely with a friend of her husband's. Internal guilt and external condemnation drive her to suicide during a storm, which she accomplishes by diving into the Volga.

katabasis (Grk., retreat, descent). In the DOCTRINE OF AFFECTS, descending melodic passages illustrating states of mind such as depression and humiliation. The settings of texts relating to falls from grace and descents into hell are examples of katabasis.

Katerina Izmailova. LADY MACBETH OF THE MTZENSK DISTRICT.

Kavafian, Ani, gifted Turkish-born American violinist of Armenian descent, sister of Ida Kavafian; b. Istanbul, May 10, 1948. In 1956 she went with her family to the U.S., where she took violin lessons with Ara Zerounian (1957–62) and Mischakoff (1962–66) in Detroit; then entered the Juilliard School of Music in N.Y., where she received instruction in violin from Galamian and in chamber music performance from Galimir and members of the Juilliard Quartet (M.A., 1972). In 1969 she made her debut at Carnegie Recital Hall in N.Y.; her European debut followed in Paris in 1973. She appeared as soloist with the leading orchs.; also played chamber music concerts, serving as an artist-member of the Chamber Music Soc. of Lincoln Center (from 1980); likewise gave duo performances with her sister. She taught at the Mannes College of Music (from 1982), and at the Manhattan School of Music and Queens College of the City Univ. of N.Y. (from 1983).

Kavafian, Ida, talented Turkish-born American violinist of Armenian descent, sister of Ani Kavafian; b. Istanbul, Oct. 29, 1952. She went with her family to the U.S. (1956), where she took up violin studies with Ara Zerounian in Detroit at the age of 6; she later received instruction from Mischakoff there; entered the Juilliard School in N.Y. (1969), where she continued her training with Shumsky and Galamian (M.A., 1975); she won the Vianna da Motta International Violin Competition in Lisbon (1973) and the silver medal at the International Violin Competition of Indianapolis (1982). She helped to found the chamber group Tashi (1973), and subsequently toured with it; made her N.Y. recital debut (1978) and her European debut in London (1982); played in duo concerts with her sister.

Kavatine (Ger.). CAVATINA.

Kay, Hershy, American composer, arranger, and orchestrator; b. Philadelphia, Nov. 17, 1919; d. Danbury, Conn., Dec. 2, 1981. He studied cello with Felix Salmond and orchestration with Randall Thompson at the Curtis Inst. of Music in Philadelphia (1936–40); then went to N.Y. and began a fruitful career as an arranger of Broadway musicals and ballets. He orchestrated a number of Leonard Bernstein's theater works: *On the Town* (1944), *Peter Pan* (incidental music; 1951), *Candide* (1956; revival 1973), *Mass* (1971), and the Bicentennial pageant *1600 Pennsylvania Avenue* (1976). His last arrangement for Bernstein was *Olympic Hymn* (Baden-Baden, Sept. 23, 1981). His other orchestrations for Broadway include *A Flag Is Born* (1947), *The Golden Apple* (1954), *Once upon a Mattress* (1958), *Juno* (1958), *Sand Hog* (1958), *Livin' the Life* (1958), *Milk and Honey* (1961), *The Happiest Girl in the World* (1961), *110 in the Shade* (1963), *Coco* (1969), *A Chorus Line* (1975), *American Musical Jubilee* (1976), *Music Is* (1976), *On the 20th Century* (1977), *Evita* (1979), *Carmelina* (1979), and *Barnum* (1980).

He made numerous arrangements for the N.Y. Ballet, among them *Cakewalk* (1951, after Gottschalk), *Western Sym.* (1954, after cowboy songs and fiddle tunes), *The Concert* (1956, after Chopin), *Stars and Stripes* (1958, after Sousa), *Who Cares?* (1970, after Gershwin), and *Union Jack* (1976, after popular British music). His ballet arrangements for other companies include *The Thief Who Loved a Ghost* (1950, after Weber), *L'Inconnue* (1965), *The Clowns* (1968; a rare 12-tone arrangement), *Meadowlark and Cortège Burlesque* (1969), *Grand Tour* (1971, after Noël Coward), and *Winter's Court* (1972). He also orchestrated a Gottschalk piano piece, *Grand Tarantella*, for piano and orch. (1957), and completed the orchestration of Robert Kurka's opera *The Good Soldier Schweik* (N.Y., Apr. 23, 1958).

Kay, Ulysses Simpson, eminent African-American composer; b. Tucson, Ariz., Jan. 7, 1917; d. Englewood, N.J., May 20, 1995. He received his early music training at home; on the advice of his uncle King Oliver, he studied piano. In 1934 he enrolled at the Univ. of Arizona at Tucson (Mus.B., 1938); he then went to study at the Eastman School of Music in Rochester, N.Y., where he was a student of Bernard Rogers and Howard Hanson (M.M., 1940); later attended the classes of Paul Hindemith at the Berkshire Music Center in Tanglewood (1941–42).

He served in the U.S. Navy (1942–45); then studied composition with Otto Luening at Columbia Univ. (1946–49); went to Rome as winner of the American Rome

Prize, and was attached there to the American Academy (1949–52). From 1953 to 1968 he was employed as a consultant by Broadcast Music Inc. in N.Y.; was on the faculty of Boston Univ. (1965) and of the Univ. of Calif., Los Angeles (1966–67); in 1968 he was appointed prof. of music at the Herbert H. Lehman College in N.Y.; was made Distinguished Prof. there in 1972; retired in 1988.

He received honorary doctorates from several American univs. His music follows a distinctly American idiom, particularly in its rhythmic intensity, while avoiding ostentatious ethnic elements; in harmony and counterpoint he pursues a moderately advanced idiom, marked by prudentially euphonious dissonances; his instrumentation is masterly. His compositions include operas, a ballet score, orch.l works, chamber and solo works, band music, choral pieces, songs, and film scores, including *The Quiet One* (1948).

Kaye, Sammy, American bandleader; b. Lakewood, Ohio, Mar. 13, 1910; d. Ridgewood, N.J., June 2, 1987. He graduated from Ohio Univ.; having learned to play the clarinet and alto saxophone, he organized his own band, which gained notice in a coast-to-coast radio broadcast in 1935. He scored his 1st hit with a recording of the title song from the film *Rosalie* (1937); after appearing in N.Y. (1938), he became one of the most popular bandleaders of the swing era, as millions were enticed to "Swing and Sway with Sammy Kaye." He was host of the *Sunday Serenade* radio show, and later made appearances on television. During a career of some 50 years he made more than 100 recordings; among the most popular were *The Old Lamp-Lighter*, *Harbor Lights*, *Remember Pearl Harbor*, *I Left My Heart at the Stage Door Canteen*, and *Walkin' to Missouri*.

kazachok (from Turk. *kasak*, Cossack). Popular Caucasian and Ukrainian dance. This couple dance, in lively 2/4 time, was also popular as a ballroom dance in the 19th century.

kazoo. A toy instrument consisting of a short tube with membranes at each end, into which the player hums, producing a curiously nasal tone. It is also known as a MIRLITON; in the 17th century, a *flûte-eunuque* (eunuch flute).

keck; mit Keckheit (Ger.). Boldly, confidently.

Kempff, Wilhelm (Walter Friedrich), distinguished German pianist; b. Juterbog, Nov. 25, 1895; d. Positano, Italy, May 23, 1991. He studied piano with his father, also named Wilhelm Kempff; at the age of 9 he entered the Berlin Hochschule für Musik, where he studied composition with Robert Kahn and piano with Heinrich Barth; also attended the Univ. of Berlin. He began his concert career in 1916; in 1918 he made the 1st of many appearances with the Berlin Phil.; from that time he toured throughout Europe, South America, and Japan, featuring improvisation as part of his programs. From 1924 to 1929 he was director of the Stuttgart Hochschule für Musik; from 1957 he gave annual courses in Positano, Italy. He made his London debut in 1951 and his American debut in N.Y. in 1964. He continued to appear in concerts well past his octogenarian milestone; in 1979 he was a soloist with the Berlin Phil., after having had an association with it for more than 60 years. Kempff epitomized the Classic tradition of German pianism; he eschewed flamboyance in his performances of Mozart, Beethoven, Schubert, and other masters.

Kennedy, Nigel (Paul), versatile English violinist; b. Brighton, Dec. 28, 1956. He was born into a family of cellists; in 1972 he became a student of Dorothy DeLay at the Juilliard School in N.Y. In 1977 he made his London debut as soloist with the Philharmonia Orch., and subsequently performed throughout his homeland and on the Continent; in 1985 he made his 1st tour of the U.S. His interests range over the field of serious jazz, rock, and pop music; he has been closely associated with jazz notable Stephane Grappelli and has led his own rock group. Kennedy's repertoire extends from Bach to Ellingon; he also played the Walton Viola Concerto.

Kepler, Johannes, illustrious German astronomer; b. Weil der Stadt, Württemberg, Dec. 27, 1571; d. Regensburg, Nov. 15, 1630. He explored Pythagorean concepts of harmony and relationships among music, mathematics, and physics in books 3 and 5 of his *Harmonices mundi* (Linz, 1619).

Keppard, Freddie, African-American jazz cornetist; b. New Orleans, Feb. 15, 1889; d. Chicago, July 15, 1933. He learned to play the mandolin, violin, and accordion before mastering the cornet; organized his own group, the Olympia Orch. (1906); later became coleader of the Original Creole Orch. (1912), playing with it in Los Angeles, Chicago, and N.Y.; after moving to Chicago, he played with King Oliver, Jimmie Noone, and others. Although forgotten in the last years of his life, he was one of the pioneer jazz figures; he had few equals as a cornetist in his time.

Kern, Jerome (David), famous American composer for stage and screen; b. N.Y., Jan. 27, 1885; d. there, Nov. 11, 1945. He was educated in N.Y. public schools; studied music with his mother, then with Paolo Gallico and Alexander Lambert (piano) and Austin Pearce and Albert von Doenhoff (theory) at the N.Y. College of Music (1902–1903); subsequently studied theory and composition in Heidelberg (1903–1904). He then returned to N.Y., where he became a pianist and salesman for a publishing firm in 1905; publ. his 1st song, *How'd You Like to Spoon with Me?*, which became famous; in 1906 he was in London, where he was connected with a theatrical production.

He obtained his 1st success as a composer for the stage with his musical comedy *The Red Petticoat* (Nov. 13, 1912). After that he produced musical comedies in rapid succession, bringing out more than 40 works; also wrote several film scores. Kern's greatest success was *Show Boat* (Washington, D.C., Nov. 15, 1927); a most remarkable score, and one of the finest of its kind in the genre, it contains the famous song *Ol' Man River*. In 1985 Kern was immortalized in the 1st 22-cent American postage stamp, designed by James Sharpe of Westport, Conn.

Kern's 40 stage musicals (all perf. in N.Y. unless otherwise indicated) include: *Very Good, Eddie* (1915); *Oh Boy!* (1917); *Miss 1917* (revue, collab. with V. Herbert; 1917); *Night Boat* (1920); *Sally* (ballet music by V. Herbert, 1920; film, 1929); *Good Morning, Dearie* (1921); *Sunny* (1925; films, 1930 and 1941); *Show Boat* (Washington, D.C., 1927; films, 1929, 1936, and 1951); *Sweet Adeline* (musical romance; 1929; film, 1935); *The Cat and the Fiddle* (1931; film, 1933); *Music in the Air* (1932; film, 1934); *Roberta* (1933; films, 1935 and 1952); *Very Warm for May* (1939). Among the films he scored were *Swing Time* (1936); *High, Wide and Handsome* (1937); *Joy of Living* (1938); *You Were Never Lovelier* (1942); *Can't Help Singing* (1944); *Cover Girl* (1944); *Centennial Summer* (1946).

He also wrote songs interpolated into other musicals and films; among the most popular were *They Didn't Believe Me* for *The Girl from Utah* (1914) and *The Last Time I Saw Paris* for *Lady Be Good* (1941). Among the lyricists he worked with were Oscar Hammerstein II, Dorothy Fields, Johnny Mercer, and Ira Gershwin. Kern's concert works include *Scenario* for Orch. (based on themes from *Show Boat*; 1941) and Mark Twain Suite for Orch. (Cincinnati, 1942).

kettledrum. See TIMPANI.

key. 1. (Fr. *tonalité*; Ger. *Tonalität, Tonart*; It. *tonalità*; Sp. *tonalidad*) The series of tones forming any given major or minor scale, considered with reference to their harmonic relations, particularly the relation of the other tones to the tonic or keynote. *Attendant key*, see ATTENDANT KEY; *chromatic key*, one having sharps or flats in the signature; *extreme key*, a remote key; *major key*, one having a major 3rd and 6th; *minor key*, one having a minor 3rd and 6th; *natural key*, one with neither sharps nor flats in the key signature; *parallel key*, either a minor key with the same keynote as a given major key, or vice versa; or a RELATIVE KEY; *remote key*, an indirectly related key. 2. (Lat. *clavis*; Fr. *touche*, touched one; Ger. *Taste*; It., *tasto*; Sp. *tecla*; Rus. *klavisha*) A digital or finger lever in the keyboard of a piano or organ, traditionally covered with ivory; also, a pedal or foot key in the organ or pedal piano. 3. (Fr. *clef*; Ger. *Klappe*; It. *chiave*; Sp. *llave*). A flat padded disk attached to a lever worked by the finger or thumb, closing the sound-holes of various wind instruments. 4. A wrest, or tuning wrench.

key action. In the keyboard of a piano or organ, the keys and the entire mechanism connected with and set in action by those keys.

key bugle. See BUGLE.

key chord. The tonic triad.

key harp (keyed harp; It. *clavi-arpa*). A frame harp controlled by a keyboard; the strings are plucked by the piano-like mechanism. The instrument was 1st reported in the 17th century.

key signature. The accidentals at the beginning of a composition (and each succeeding staff) which indicates the prevalent tonality of the piece (or of the piece at that moment). Discounting the enharmonically equal keys, there are 12 different major keys and 12 minor, identified by the number of sharps or flats in the key signature. Key signatures of 7 sharps are not infrequent; a famous example is the 3rd fugue in C-sharp major in the 1st book of Bach's *Well-Tempered Clavier*. An example of 7 flats in a key signature is the opening of Stravinsky's *The Firebird*.

Changes of key signature in the course of a composition are common, but they are not made frivolously for each passing modulation. Even the extensive exposition of the 2nd subject in a sonata form movement, usually in the dominant key, never carries a change of the key signature. In works not bound by a strict key relationship, in which tonalities range far and wide, composers often prefer to signalize a modulation by changing the key signature. The score of Mahler's 6th Sym. includes episodes in every single major and minor key, each carrying an appropriate key signature.

Relative major and minor keys are those having the same key signature; the customary raised 7th (leading tone) in a minor key is marked by an accidental, as a G-sharp in the key of A minor, or an F-double-sharp in the key of G-sharp minor. In key signatures loaded with flats, the raised 7th in a minor key is the cancellation of the corresponding flat, becoming a natural, e.g., D natural in E-flat minor. Attempts have been made by modern composers, among them Bartók, to add accidentals in the key signature; a piece in G minor would then carry the mandatory 2 flats but also the extracurricular F-sharp. In 20th-century music, however, the vexing problem of frequent changes of key signatures in a rapidly modulating musical piece has become as irrelevant as the antimacassar on the back of Victorian armchairs in modern times.

Key signatures began to disappear from the scores of modern composers at the end of the 1st quarter of the 20th century, as they became needless armatures in an atonal ocean. A flickering restoration of the key signature in the works of pragmatic antimodernists made its unexpected epiphany at the *fin de 20ème siècle*.

key stop. A key attached to the fingerboard of a violin so as to replace the fingers in stopping the strings; the instrument is called a key-stop (keyed-stop) violin.

key trumpet (keyed trumpet). A natural trumpet provided with keys that function much as woodwind instrument keys do; the usual number of keys was 5. The instrument was 1st made in Germany in the late 18th century; it had a softer tone than its predecessor and thus never became popular as a solo instrument. By the mid-19th century it had been superseded by the valve trumpet.

keyboard

A set of depressible keys or levers, usually laid out in horizontal manuals, that actuates the sound-inducing mechanism on pianos, organs, harpsichords, and other instruments of similar construction. A large organ may have as many as 5 manuals, a harpsichord either 1 or 2. A special feature on the organ is the pedal keyboard, arranged in rows of large white and black keys, that are operated by the feet. (Pedal pianos and pedal harpsichords have also been built.)

Through the centuries the arrangement of the 12 chromatic notes within the octave has been formed with 7 white keys on the lower level of the keyboard (Ger. *Klaviatur, Tastatur, Klavier*; Fr. *clavier*; It. *tastiera, tastatura*) and 5 shorter black keys on the slightly elevated level. The row of white keys forms a diatonic scale; the row of black keys represents the pentatonic scale. The opposition of the white and the black keys is standard on all piano keyboards, but the harpsichord, clavichord, and spinet may possess a different contrast in the coloring of the diatonic and the pentatonic rows.

There are antique harpsichords in which the color scheme is reversed, the diatonic keys being black and the pentatonic keys white; there are also specimens using red keys in either of the rows, much as in some chess games with chess pieces being red and white instead of the standard black and white. The dimensions of the keys on all keyboard instruments are adjusted to the normal relaxed position of the 5 fingers of a human player resting on the 5 consecutive white keys.

In his book *Travels into Several Remote Nations of the World*, Jonathan Swift describes a Brobdingnagian spinet in vivid practical detail: "The spinet was near sixty foot long, each key being almost a foot wide, so that, with my arms extended, I could not reach to above five keys, and to press them down required a good smart stroke with my fist. . . . Yet I could not strike above sixteen keys, nor consequently play the bass and treble together, as other artists do; which was a great disadvantage to my performance." Actually, one did not have to go to Brobdingnag to find a gigantic keyboard. The keys of early organs were so wide that the monks who manipulated them had to play their church hymns with clenched fists, and even elbows, in order to depress the keys sufficiently to activate the pipes.

Numerous attempts have been made to make the keyboard more handy, to adapt it for playing scales without a constant change of fingering. It is most interesting to speculate what a hexadactylous pianist (there have been such in existence) could do with scale playing using 6 fingers on each hand. But pending the growth of an extra finger, one might consider the JANKÓ KEYBOARD, comprising a keyboard of 6 different but aligned rows of keys, one slightly above the other, with a system of levers making it possible to play the chromatic scale with the greatest of ease by letting the fingers walk from one row to another. The narrower Jankó keys made it possible for a pianist to reach the interval of a 14th with 1 hand, a great convenience for players who want to execute properly some unbridgeable intervals such as found in Schumann's *Symphonic Études*.

Alas! Poor Jankó died, and the Jankó keyboard died with him. Then there was the Clutsam keyboard, in the form of a fan arc, with the radius that of an arm's length. A pianist playing it must presumably be placed in the center of the circle, using outstretched arms at all times. The Clutsam keyboard also went the way of all impractical ivory toys. Finally, the Fokker organ with 31-equal tuning uses 3 colors and 4 sequential keyboards at a diagonal to allow the performance of the extra notes-per-octave.

keynote. The 1st note of a key or scale; TONIC.

Khachaturian, Aram (Ilich), brilliant Russian composer of Armenian descent, uncle of Karen (Surenovich) Khachaturian; b. Tiflis, June 6, 1903; d. Moscow, May 1, 1978. His father was a bookbinder. Khachaturian played tuba in the school band and also studied biology. He then went to Moscow and entered the Gnessin Music School (1922–25); later studied composition with Gnessin (1925–29). In 1929 he became a student at the Moscow Cons., graduating in 1934 in the class of Miaskovsky; finished his postgraduate studies there (1937).

He commenced composing at the age of 21, and soon progressed to the 1st rank of Soviet composers of his generation. His music was in the tradition of Russian orientalism; he applied the characteristic scale progressions of Caucasian melos, without quoting actual folk songs. His *Sabre Dance* from his ballet *Gayane* became popular all over the world. In 1948 he was severely criticized by the Central Committee of the Communist party, along with Prokofiev, Shostakovich, and others, for modernistic tendencies; although he admitted his deviations in this respect, he continued to compose essentially in his typical manner, not shunning highly dissonant harmonic combinations. He was made a People's Artist of the USSR in 1954. He appeared as a conductor of his own works in Reykjavík in 1951; conducted in Bulgaria in 1952, in Finland in 1955, in London in 1955 and again in 1977, in Japan in 1963, and in Greece in 1965.

He made his American debut in Washington, D.C., in 1968, conducting the National Sym. Orch. in a program of his works; later that year he conducted in N.Y. to a rousing audience reception. In 1933 he married the composer Nina Makarova. His nephew Karen (Surenovich) Khachaturian (b. Moscow, Sept. 19, 1920) is a composer and pedagogue. His works include ballets *Shchastye* (Happiness; Erevan, 1939); *Gayane*, including the *Sabre Dance* (Perm, 1942; rev. 1952 and 1957); orch.l and other vocal works, mostly in praise of Soviet leaders and ideology; film music; marches for band; chamber music; and piano music.

Khan, (Ustad) **Ali Akbar,** Indian sarod player, composer, and, with Ravi Shankar, one of the leading exponents of bringing Indian music to an international audience; b. Shibpur, Bengal (now Bangladesh), Apr. 14, 1922. The son of the master musician and teacher (Ustad) Alauddin Khan (b. Bengal, *c.* 1865; d. Bengal, Sept. 6, 1972), who was his teacher (as well as Shankar's). His 1st performances took place in 1936; he later became a court musician in Jodhpur. His 1st U.S. performance took place in N.Y. (1955); the interest aroused led to many return visits. In 1956 he founded a college of music in Calcutta, and in 1967 a similar institution in Marin County, Calif. Khan's instrumental skill and improvisational virtuosity have kept his reputation secure in his homeland, unlike Shankar, who has been accused (perhaps unfairly) of compromising the purity of Indian classic music. He is presently recording the secret repertoire of his father's, traditionally passed down through the generations; he has chosen to do this because he has not found a disciple capable of holding this great responsibility.

khorovod (Rus. *khor* + *vod*, leading chorus). Russian round dance of ancient origin; a scene featuring an adaptation of it is included in Stravinsky's *Firebird*.

Khovanshchina. Music drama by Mussorgsky, 1886, posthumously produced in St. Petersburg. The title means "Khovanskyism," a contemptuous reference by young Peter the Great to the rebellious activity of the followers of Prince Khovansky, the leader of the "Old Believers." Surrounded by Peter's loyal troops, they immolate themselves in fiery death. The score, left unfinished and unorchestrated by Mussorgsky, was completed by Rimsky-Korsakov, who smoothed down Mussorgsky's harmonic asperities and straightened up some awkward melodic progressions.

Khrennikov, Tikhon (Nikolaievich), Russian music administrator and composer; b. Elets, June 10, 1913. He was the 10th child in the family of a provincial clerk; his parents, brothers, and sisters were musical, played the Russian guitar and the mandolin, and sang peasant songs. He took piano lessons with a local musician; in 1927 he went to Moscow, where he was introduced to Gnessin, who accepted him as a student in his newly founded musical Technicum; there he studied counterpoint with Litinsky and piano with Ephraim Hellman.

After graduation he entered the Moscow Cons., where he studied composition with Shebalin and piano with Neuhaus (1932–36); later continued postgraduate work with Shebalin. He developed a mildly modernistic and technically idiomatic type of composition which remained his recognizable style throughout his career as a composer. In 1961 he joined the faculty of the Moscow Cons., and he was named a prof. in 1966. In the meantime he became engaged in the political life of the country. He was attached to the music corps of the Red Army and accompanied it during the last months of World War II; in 1947 he joined the Communist party and also became a deputy of the Supreme Soviet. In 1948 he was named personally by Stalin as secretary-general of the Union of Soviet Composers, and in 1949 became president of the music section of the All-Union Soc. for Cultural Exchange with Europe and America. He further served as head of the organizing committee for the International Festivals and the Tchaikovsky Competitions in Moscow.

He received numerous honors: was a member of the Soviet delegation to the U.S. in 1959; was named a Hero of Socialist Labor in 1973; and in 1974 received the Lenin Prize. Amid all this work he never slackened the tempo of his main preoccupation, that of composition. He wrote operas, ballets, syms., and concertos, and appeared as a piano soloist. During his entire career he was a stout spokesman for Soviet musical policy along the lines of socialist realism. He compromised himself, however, by his vehement con-

demnation of "formalist" directions in modern music, specifically attacking Stravinsky, Prokofiev, Shostakovich, and, later, Schnittke and Gubaidulina.

But as Soviet aesthetical directions underwent a liberal change, Khrennikov himself became the target of sharp criticism. He defended himself by claiming that he had protected a number of young musicians from attacks by entrenched functionaries of the Soviet musical establishment, and he succeeded in retaining his position as secretary-general of the Union of Soviet Composers for several years. His compositions express forcefully the desirable qualities of Soviet music, a flowing melody suggesting the broad modalities of Russian folk songs, a vibrant and expressive lyricism, and effective instrumental formation.

Kid Boots. Musical by Harry Tierney, 1923. A crooked golf caddie with a heart of gold fixes games by using a loaded ball, but he also straightens out fractured love affairs. The memorable song of the show was the interpolated *Dinah*, written by Harry Akst and made famous by Eddie Cantor.

Kikimora. Symphonic scherzo by Liadov, 1909. Kikimora is a Russian infant girl who did not live long enough to be baptized. She becomes a mischievous spirit suspended between heaven and hell. The music is alternately tender and boisterous. Kikimora's demoniacal side is depicted by the frequent use of the tritone, the DIABOLUS IN MUSICA of the Middle Ages.

Killing Me Softly with His Song. A 1973 number 1 pop hit written by Charles Fox and Norman Gimbel, popularized by Roberta Flack, purportedly written about Don Maclean. Revived by the HIP-HOP/pop group the Fugees in 1996.

Kinder der Heide, Die (Children of the Plains). Opera by A. Rubinstein, 1861, 1st performed in Vienna. A band of Ukrainian Gypsies plans an attack on and robbery of the caretaker of a large estate. But the owner is warned by a shepherd who is in love with his daughter; she in turn is loved by a neighboring count. The shepherd slays the count and flees with the Gypsies, led by a young woman (not the caretaker's daughter) who herself loves the ubiquitous shepherd. Finally, soldiers surround the gypsy camp and seize the murderer, at which point the Gypsy woman stabs herself to death. The magnitude of slaughter sets something of a record, even for Romantic operas.

Kindertotenlieder (Songs on the Death of Children). Song cycle by Mahler, 1905, based on poems by Rückert.

This powerful quartet of tragic songs was prophetic of personal loss when his eldest daughter died of scarlet fever in 1907.

kindlich (Ger.). Childlike, artless.

kinetic energy. When applied to music, kinetic energy during a given interval of time connects the velocity (number of notes per time unit), amplitude (degree of loudness in decibels), and the height of pitch expressed in semitones counting from the lowest note in the audible range. Kinetic energy is the product of all these parameters. From this it follows that the auditory impact is directly proportional to velocity, loudness, and frequency of vibrations per second. There is also a psychological factor that affects the subjective measurement of kinetic energy. The off-beat chord in Haydn's *Surprise Sym.*, though in itself possessing a modest impact, carries a relatively greater charge of psycho-kinetic energy because it is unexpected. Generally speaking, a greater impression is produced by detonations of sonic quanta in asymmetrical rhythms than much stronger discharges occurring at regular intervals of time.

King and I, The. Musical by Rodgers and Hammerstein, 1951; the plot is based on historical events. When a Victorian widow is engaged by the Siamese King as a governess to his multiple offspring, their association and the clash of 2 widely different cultures provide an exotic panoply for dramatic action. Rodgers virtually avoided writing any "oriental" music; this renunciation of artificial flavor only contributes to the validity of the score. The show contains many hits, including *Getting to Know You*, *We Kiss in the Shadow*, *I Have Dreamed*, *I Whistle a Happy Tune*, *Hello Young Lovers*, and *Shall We Dance*.

King, "B. B." (Riley B.), important African-American blues singer and guitarist; b. Itta Bena, Miss., Sept. 16, 1925. While working on a farm he learned to play the guitar; then worked as a disc jockey for a Memphis radio station under the name "Blues Boy," which became "B. B." In 1950 he scored his 1st hit with his recording of *Three O'Clock Blues*; in the late 1960s he assumed a prominent place among the great blues singers and guitarists; in 1968 he made his 1st tour of Europe, then headed an all-blues concert at Carnegie Hall in N.Y. in 1970. He won a Grammy Award in 1981 for his album *There Must Be a Better World Somewhere*. Utilizing an electric guitar (named Lucille), he is regarded as one of the most innovative blues artists of his era, with an aphoristic and emotional direct style. Other well-known King performances include *Rock Me Baby*, *Paying the Cost to Be Boss*, *Confessin' the Blues*, *The Thrill Is Gone*, *Ask Me No Questions*, and *Hummingbird*.

King, James, American tenor; b. Dodge City, Kans., May 22, 1925. He studied at the Univ. of Kansas City; also received vocal training from Martial Singher and Max Lorenz. He then went to Europe and made his professional debut as Cavaradossi in Florence (1961); subsequently sang at the San Francisco Opera, the Berlin Deutsche Oper, the Salzburg Festival, the Bayreuth Festival, the Metropolitan Opera in N.Y. (debut as Florestan, 1966), London's Covent Garden, and Milan's La Scala. He taught voice at the Indiana Univ. School of Music in Bloomington (from 1984). Among his prominent roles were Lohengrin, Walther von Stolzing, Parsifal, and Verdi's Otello.

King, Carole (born Carol Klein), American pop singer and songwriter; b. N.Y., Feb. 9, 1941. She took piano lessons as a child; an intellectually precocious teenager, she started a female vocal ensemble in school under a trigonometrical name, the Co-Sines. At 17 she met the songwriter Gerry Goffin, whom she soon married. They produced a hit song, *Will You Love Me Tomorrow*. Several other hits followed, among them *Some Kind of Wonderful*, *When My Little Girl Is Smiling*, *One Fine Day*, *I'm Into Something Good*, *Up on the Roof*, *Take Good Care of My Baby*, *Do the Loco-Motion*, and *Goin' Back*. On her own she produced the smash hits *It Might As Well Rain Until September*, *You've Got a Friend*, *It's Too Late*, and *I Feel the Earth Move*, all of which had a direct appeal to folk-rockers of all ages. After 2 divorces, she married the songwriter Rick Evers; he died of a cocaine overdose in Los Angeles in 1978. King recently appeared in N.Y. as the female lead in the British musical *Blood Brothers*.

King Lear. Concert overture by Berlioz, 1834. Berlioz was extremely fond of Shakespeare, although he could not read the Bard in English; this orch.l work is a typical act of homage to the playwright. Berlioz conducted its 1st performance in Paris.

King of the Road. A 1965 Roger Miller country smash that also ranked high on the pop charts. One of the 1st odes to the life of the trucker, it inspired numerous parodies, including *Queen of the Road*.

King Priam. Opera by Tippett, 1962, to his own libretto based on the *Iliad*; it was premiered in Coventry. Paris, son of Priam of Troy, abducts Helen (wife of the Greek King Menelaus), thereby precipitating the Trojan War. The opera focuses on Priam and the Greek hero Achilles. Priam's son Hector kills Patroclus, who has fought in disguise instead of the brooding Achilles. Achilles is roused from his tent and kills Hector in revenge. Priam comes to gather the body of his son in Achilles's tent; the old King and the young hero find a moment of understanding among enemies. By the end, Achilles is dead, and his son kills Priam as he kneels in prayer while Troy falls.

King Roger (*Król Roger*). Opera by Szymanowski, 1926, premiered in Warsaw. The plot concerns the conversion of the medieval Sicilian King to the mystical creed of an Indian holy man; the work concludes with a pagan bacchanale.

King's Henchman, The. Opera by D. Taylor, 1st performed at the Metropolitan Opera in N.Y., Feb. 17, 1927, one of the few American operas given by that institution. It had 14 performances and then sank into harmless desuetude. The libretto was not American. Its hero was the messenger of the King of England who was sent to fetch the royal bride from overseas. Instead he appropriates her himself and commits suicide when his treachery is revealed. The score is distinctly Wagnerian, as is the subject.

Kipnis, Alexander, eminent Russian-born American bass, father of Igor Kipnis; b. Zhitomir, Feb. 13, 1891; d. Westport, Conn., May 14, 1978. He studied conducting at the Warsaw Cons. (graduated 1912); later took voice lessons with Ernst Grenzebach at Berlin's Klindworth-Scharwenka Cons. In 1913 he sang at Monti's Operetten Theater and in 1914 at the Filmzauber operetta theater. At the outbreak of World War I he was interned as an enemy alien, but he was soon released and made his operatic debut as the hermit in *Der Freischütz* at the Hamburg Opera in 1915; sang there until 1917, then was a member of the Wiesbaden Opera (1917–22). He made his U.S. debut as Pogner in *Die Meistersinger von Nürnberg* with the visiting German Opera Co. in Baltimore in 1923; he then was a member of the Chicago Civic Opera (1923–32). He also sang regularly at the Berlin Städtische Oper (1922–30), the Berlin State Opera (1932–35), and the Vienna State Opera (1935–38).

He became an American citizen in 1931. During these years he made guest appearances at the Bayreuth, Salzburg, and Glyndebourne festivals, as well as at Covent Garden in London and the Teatro Colón in Buenos Aires. In 1940 he made his belated Metropolitan Opera debut in N.Y. as Gurnemanz in *Parsifal*, and he continued to sing there until 1946; he then devoted himself mainly to teaching. Through the years he appeared as a soloist with R. Strauss, Siegfried Wagner, and Toscanini.

Kipnis, Igor, distinguished American harpsichordist and fortepianist, son of Alexander Kipnis; b. Berlin, Sept. 27, 1930. In 1938 the family moved to the U.S., where he took piano lessons with his maternal grandfather, Heniot Levy; after attending the Westport (Conn.) School of Music, he studied with Randall Thompson and Thurston Dart at Harvard Univ. (B.A., 1952). He also took harpsichord lessons with Fernando Valenti. After graduation Kipnis served abroad in the Signal Corps of the U.S. Army. Returning to the U.S., he eked out his living as a bookstore salesman in N.Y.; later was employed as an editorial adviser to Westminster Records Co.

He made his concert debut as a harpsichordist in a N.Y. radio broadcast in 1959; his formal concert debut followed there in 1962. He taught at the Berkshire Music Center in Tanglewood (summers 1964–67); in 1967 he made his 1st European tour, and subsequently toured throughout the world. He served as an associate prof. of fine arts (1971–75) and artist-in-residence (1975–77) at Fairfield Univ. in Conn.; also taught and played at the Festival Music Soc. concerts in Indianapolis and taught at its Early Music Inst. In 1981 he made his debut as a fortepianist in Indianapolis; he did much to revive that instrument. He also promoted interest in modern music. Several contemporary composers, among them Ned Rorem, George Rochberg, Richard Rodney Bennett, Barbara Kolb, and John McCabe, have written works for him.

Kirchenmusik (Ger.). Church music.

Kirchner, Leon, significant American composer; b. N.Y., Jan. 24, 1919. In 1928 the family went to Los Angeles, where he studied piano with Richard Buhlig; in 1938 he entered the Univ. of Calif., Berkeley, where he took courses in theory with Albert Elkus and Edward Strickland (B.A., 1940; M.M., 1949); he also took lessons with Ernest Bloch in San Francisco. In 1942 he returned to N.Y., where he had fruitful private lessons with Sessions; in 1943 he entered military service in the U.S. Army; after demobilization in 1946, he was appointed to the faculty of the San Francisco Cons., concurrently teaching at the Univ. of Calif., Berkeley;

in 1948 he received a Guggenheim fellowship; from 1950 to 1954 he served as associate prof. at the Univ. of Southern Calif., Los Angeles; subsequently taught at Mills College in Oakland, Calif. (1954–61), and in 1961 was named prof. of music at Harvard Univ. He was elected a member of the National Inst. of Arts and Letters and the American Academy of Arts and Sciences in 1962; in 1967 he was awarded the Pulitzer Prize in Music for his 3rd String Quartet.

In his music Kirchner takes the prudential median course, cultivating a distinct modern idiom without espousing any particular modernistic technique, but making ample and effective use of euphonious dissonance; the contrapuntal fabric in his works is tense but invariably coherent. Through his natural inclinations toward Classical order he prefers formal types of composition, often following the established Baroque style.

Kirk, Andy (Andrew Dewey). See WILLIAMS, MARY LOU.

Kirk, (Rahsaan) **Roland,** African-American jazz instrumentalist, composer, and activist; b. Columbus, Ohio, Aug. 7, 1936; d. Bloomington, Ind., Dec. 5, 1977. He lost his sight in infancy and was brought up at the Ohio State School for the Blind; learned to play trumpet, tenor saxophone, flute, clarinet, manzello, strich (both saxophone hybrids), and nose flute; he also invented several hybrids of his own, and he was one of the 1st jazz musicians to exploit circular breathing. He had an uncanny ability to play 2 or 3 wind instruments simultaneously; he could still play with 1 hand after a 1975 stroke. In 1963 he organized his own band, with which he toured Europe, Australia, and New Zealand. He composed many songs of the pop variety; typical titles are *Serenade to a Cuckoo*; *Here Comes the Whistleman*; *I Talk with the Spirits*; *Rip, Rig and Panic*; and *Funk Underneath*. In the 1970s Kirk led the Jazz and People's Movement, which protested the lack of African-American music and musicians in U.S. mainstream broadcast culture.

Kirkby, Emma, English soprano; b. Camberley, Feb. 26, 1949. She studied classics at Oxford; made her debut in London in 1974; specialized in early music; was a member of the Academy of Ancient Music, the London Baroque, and the Consort of Musicke. In 1978 she toured the U.S.; then gave concerts in the Middle East with the lutenist Anthony Rooley. Her repertoire ranges from the Italian quattrocento to arias by Handel, Mozart, and Haydn. The careful attention she pays to the purity of intonation free from intrusive vibrato has been praised.

Kirnberger, Johann Philipp, noted German music theorist and pedagogue; b. Saalfeld (baptized), Apr. 24, 1721; d. Berlin, July 26 or 27, 1783. He studied violin and harpsichord at home, then took organ lessons with J. P. Kellner in Grafenroda and H. N. Gerber in Sondershausen; also studied violin with Meil there; completed his studies with Bach in Leipzig (1739–41). He then traveled in Poland (1741–51) as a tutor in various noble Polish families; from 1751 to 1754 he was violinist to Frederick the Great in Berlin, and from 1754 to 1758 to Prince Heinrich of Prussia; from 1758 to 1783 he was Kapellmeister to Princess Anna Amalie.

He was greatly renowned as a teacher; among his pupils were J. A. P. Schulz, C. P. E. Bach, the Graun brothers, and J. F. Agricola. As a theoretical writer he was regarded as one of the greatest authorities of his time, even though his presentations were often disorganized to such an extent that he had to call upon others to edit or even rewrite his publications. In his compositions he displayed an amazing contrapuntal technique, and he seriously strove to establish a scientific method of writing according to basic rules of combination and permutation; his *Der allezeit fertige Polonoisen- und Menuetten-componist* (1757) expounded the automatic method of composition.

Kismet. A musical extravaganza, 1953, thrown together by a couple of Broadway hacks, using materials from the works of the defenseless and uncopyrighted Borodin. The mephitic plot parades the ambitious wife of the Baghdad chief of police who drowns her husband in a fountain in order to marry the young Caliph. The slow section from Borodin's *Polovtzian Dances (Prince Igor)* is perverted into a loathsome mess of fulsome treacle, *Stranger in Paradise*, wherein the Mongol Polovtzi are transformed into spurious Arabs. Another hit, *This Is My Beloved*, is purloined from a Borodin string quartet. The stench that this iniquitous travesty raised in the nostrils of decent music lovers moved them to an outcry of protest, which must have made the perpetrators smile while counting the shekels at the box office; but *Kismet* was merely the latest in a long tradition of texting instrumental pieces. The Turkish word *kismet* (*quismah* in Arabic) means "fate."

Kiss Me, Kate. Musical by C. Porter, 1948. The plot concerns a group of actors performing Shakespeare's *The Taming of the Shrew* in Baltimore. Because the 2 lead players are in a similar situation in life as Petruchio and Kate are in the play, the roles become confused, with Porter's lyrics superimposed on Elizabethan language. There is the inevitable happy ending in both play and life. Includes *Always True to You in My Fashion*, *Brush Up Your Shakespeare*, *Another Op'nin' Another Show*, *So in Love*, and *Wunderbar*.

Kiss, The (*Hubička*). Opera by Smetana, 1876. A widower is engaged to a young woman in his village, but she won't seal their betrothal with the traditional kiss for fear of arousing his dead wife's jealousy. Angered, the widower brings a girl from out of the tavern and kisses her. The bride-to-be is outraged and runs into the ever-dangerous woods. He finally tracks her down and forces a kiss.

Kissin, Evgeny, amazingly precocious Russian pianist possessing interpretive capacity remarkable even for his proverbial wunderkindland; b. Moscow, Oct. 10, 1971. He enrolled at the Gnessin Music School for Gifted Children in Moscow at the incredible (but verified) age of 6 as a student of Anna Kantor, who remained his only teacher even after he began his rise toward the musical stratosphere. At the age of 12 he gave performances of both Chopin piano concertos with the Moscow Phil. International reputation came to him when he was engaged in 1987 to perform Tchaikovsky's 1st Piano Concerto with Karajan and the Berlin Phil. In 1990 he made his U.S. debut playing Chopin's 1st Piano Concerto with the N.Y. Phil., conducted by Zubin Mehta. Ten days later there followed his appearance at Carnegie Hall, which astonished audience and critics alike by a digital velocity and propulsive dexterity sensational enough to capture the imagination of the most seasoned and experienced listeners. Predictions are often false, but Kissin's concert successes, multiplied by the issuance of many recordings, make his accession to pianistic stardom a matter of certainty.

kit. The small violin used by dancing masters, about 16 inches long, and tuned c^1–g^1–d^2.

kithara (*cithara*; Grk.). National instrument of ancient Greece, a member of the lyre family. It consists of a square soundbox made of wood, with between 3 and 11 strings stretched from one side to the other, connected by a crossbar. The tuning was fundamentally pentatonic, but smaller intervals could be introduced by appropriate tuning. Iconographical evidence shows that similar instruments existed in Mesopotamia; the 1st Greek examples are depicted on vases from the 7th century B.C.

Kitt, Eartha, African-American singer of popular music and actress; b. North, S.C., Jan. 26, 1928. She was taken to N.Y. as a child; there she sang in church, received piano training, and studied dance at the High School for Performing Arts; won a scholarship to study dance with Katherine Dunham (1944), and then traveled with her troupe in South America and Europe until 1950; subsequently concentrated her career upon singing and acting, appearing in nightclubs, theaters, and films, and on recordings, radio, and television. She excelled particularly in earthy, passion-laden songs delivered in a low-key monotone; she appeared in George Kleinsinger's musical *Shinbone Alley* (1954).

K-K-K-Katy. Stammering love song by Geoffrey O'Hara, popular during World War I.

klagend (*im klagenden Ton*; Ger.). Mournfully, plaintively.

Klagende Lied, Das (The Song of Lament). Cantata by Mahler, 1880, on a text by the composer. The original version consisted of 3 parts: *Waldmärchen*, *Der Spielmann*, and *Hochzeitsstück*; in a subsequent revision the 1st part was separated from the cantata.

Klang (Ger.). 1. A sound; sonority. 2. A composite musical tone (a fundamental tone with its harmonics); CLANG. 3. A chord, as in *Dreiklang* (triad).

Klangfarbe (Ger.). Tone color. In the last century *Klangfarbe* has come to refer to a special dimension of the musical sound. "It must be possible," Schoenberg states in his *Harmonielehre* (1911), "to form a succession of Klangfarben possessing a mutual relationship of a logical type equivalent to that of the melody formed by a succession of different tones." This melody of tone colors is exemplified in the movement originally entitled *The Changing Chord* in his *Fünf Orchesterstücke*, op. 16 (1909). Webern developed the idea in the direction of serialism of Klangfarben, almost reaching the ultimate dodecaphonic order, in which the fundamental Klangfarbe series is formed by the successive sounding of 12 different notes by 12 different instruments.

Klangfarbenmelodie (Ger.). A melody of tone colors. This description was 1st used by Schoenberg in his book on harmony in 1911; he proposed to regard the change of instrumental color as a melodic change. Thus a tone color melody can be created by playing the same note successively on different instruments. Schoenberg himself really never carried out the idea literally; his disciples Alban Berg and Anton von Webern developed it more fully. It received its complete fruition in their avant-garde followers, in serial and electronic music.

Klangfolge (Ger.). Progression of sounds or chords, applied particularly to sonorous complexes of different tone colors, according to Schoenberg's concept of KLANGFAR-BENMELODIE.

Klappe (Ger.). KEY.

Klappenhorn (Ger.). KEY BUGLE.

Klarinette (Ger.). CLARINET.

Klaviatur (Ger.). KEYBOARD.

Klavier (Ger.). 1. KEYBOARD. 2. A keyboard stringed instrument; in the 18th century, a clavichord or harpsichord; now a pianoforte of any kind.

Klavierauszug (Ger.). Piano arrangement, particularly a reduction from a full score; vocal score.

klaviermässig (Ger.). Suitable for the piano; in piano style.

Klavierstück (Ger.). Piano piece, usually brief.

Klaviertrio (Ger.). Chamber work for piano, violin, and cello. *Klavierquartett*, work for (usually) piano, violin, viola, and cello; *Klavierquintett*, work for (usually) piano and string quartet.

Kleiber, Carlos, outstanding German-born Austrian conductor, son of Erich Kleiber; b. Berlin, July 3, 1930. He left Nazi Germany with his parents in 1935, eventually settling in South America in 1940. He evinced an early interest in music, but his father opposed it as a career; after studying chemistry in Zurich (1949–50), he turned decisively to music and completed his training in Buenos Aires. In 1952 he became a *répétiteur* and stage assistant at the Theater am Gärtnerplatz in Munich, making his conduct-

ing debut in 1954 with Millöcker's *Gasparone* in Potsdam, where he was active until becoming a *répétiteur* (1956) and conductor (1958) at the Deutsche Oper am Rhein in Düsseldorf. After conducting at the Zurich Opera (1964–66) he served as 1st conductor at the Württemberg State Theater in Stuttgart (1966–68).

From 1968 to 1978 he conducted at the Bavarian State Opera in Munich. In 1966 he made his British debut conducting *Wozzeck* at the Edinburgh Festival; he led performances of *Tristan und Isolde* for his 1st appearances at the Vienna State Opera in 1973 and at the Bayreuth Festival in 1974, the year in which he made his 1st appearances at London's Covent Garden and Milan's La Scala with Der Rosenkavalier. In 1977 he made his U.S. debut conducting *Otello* at the San Francisco Opera. His 1st appearance with a U.S. orch. came in 1978, when he led the Chicago Sym. Orch. In 1979 he conducted the Vienna Phil. and in 1982 the Berlin Phil. In 1988 he made his Metropolitan Opera debut in N.Y. conducting *La Bohème*, and in 1989 he conducted the New Year's Day Concert of the Vienna Phil. He became a naturalized Austrian citizen in 1980.

Kleiber has been accorded accolades from critics, audiences, and his fellow musicians. His brilliant performances reflect his unreserved commitment to the score at hand, his authority, and his mastery of technique. His infrequent appearances combined with his passion for perfection have made him a legendary figure among the world's contemporary podium celebrities.

Kleiber, Erich, eminent Austrian conductor, father of Carlos Kleiber; b. Vienna, Aug. 5, 1890; d. Zurich, Jan. 27, 1956. He studied at the Prague Cons. and the Univ. of Prague; made his debut at the Prague National Theater in 1911; then conducted opera in Darmstadt (1912–19), Barmen-Elberfeld (1919–21), Düsseldorf (1921–22), and Mannheim (1922–23). In 1923 he was appointed Generalmusikdirektor of the Berlin State Opera. His tenure was outstanding, both for the brilliant performances of the standard repertoire and for the exciting programming of contemporary works. He conducted the world premiere of *Wozzeck* (Dec. 14, 1925). In 1934, in protest against the German National Socialist government, he resigned his post and emigrated to South America. He conducted regularly at the Teatro Colón in Buenos Aires from 1936 to 1949.

Having 1st conducted at London's Covent Garden in 1937, he returned there from 1950 to 1953. He then was appointed Generalmusikdirektor once more of the Berlin

State Opera in 1954, but resigned in March 1955, before the opening of the season, because of difficulties with the Communist regime. He was renowned for his performances of the music of Mozart and Beethoven. He also composed; among his works are a Violin Concerto, a Piano Concerto, orch. variations, *Capriccio* for Orch., and numerous chamber music works, piano pieces, and songs.

kleine Flöte (Ger.). PICCOLO.

kleine Trommel (Ger.). SIDE DRUM.

Kleinmeister (Ger., little masters). Disparaging appellation for an undifferentiated mass of journeymen (or women) of music who flourished in the 18th century. These individuals wrote the euterpian equivalent of the Romantic "well-made play"; everything in its right place, obeying all the rules, following all the formulas, and devoid of genius or even real talent.

Klemperer, Otto

Celebrated German conductor; b. Breslau, May 14, 1885; d. Zurich, July 6, 1973. After early musical training from his mother he entered the Hoch Cons. in Frankfurt (1901), where he studied piano with Kwast and theory with Knorr; he later received instruction in composition and conducting from Pfitzner in Berlin. He made his debut conducting Max Reinhardt's production of *Orpheus in the Underworld* in Berlin in 1906; on Mahler's recommendation he then was appointed chorus master and subsequently conductor of the German Theater in Prague; he assisted Mahler in the latter's preparations for the Munich premiere of his 8th Sym. in 1910. He became a conductor at the Hamburg Opera in 1910 but was obliged to leave in 1912 as the result of a scandalous liaison with the recently married soprano Elisabeth Schumann.

After minor appointments at Barmen (1913–14) and Strasbourg (1914–17), where he was Pfitzner's deputy, he was appointed music director of the Cologne Opera in 1917. While in Cologne he conducted the German premiere of *Káta Kabanová*. In 1924 he was named music director of the Wiesbaden Opera. He made his U.S. debut as guest conductor with the N.Y. Sym. Orch. in 1926. In 1927 he became music director of Berlin's Kroll Opera, where he was given a mandate to perform new works and present repertoire pieces in an enlightened manner. He conducted the world premiere of Hindemith's *Neues vom Tage* (1929) as well as the 1st Berlin performances of Hindemith's *Cardillac*, Stravinsky's *Oedipus Rex*, and

Schoenberg's *Die glückliche Hand*; he also conducted the premiere performance of Schoenberg's *Begleitungsmusik* as part of the Kroll concerts.

When political and economic pressures forced the Kroll Opera to close in 1931, Klemperer became a conductor at the Berlin State Opera; when the Nazis came to power in 1933, he was compelled to emigrate to the U.S. That same year he became music director of the Los Angeles Phil.; he also appeared as a guest conductor in N.Y., Philadelphia, and Pittsburgh. His career was disrupted in 1939 when he underwent an operation for a brain tumor. In 1947 he was engaged as conductor at the Budapest State Opera, where he remained until 1950. He made his 1st appearance as a guest conductor with the Philharmonia Orch. of London in 1951; was appointed its principal conductor in 1959, and retained that position when the orch.'s manager, Walter Legge, unsuccessfully attempted to disband it in 1964.

Klemperer was accident-prone and a manic depressive all his life; the 2 sides of his nature were reflected in his conducting styles on either side of World War II. He had earlier been noted for his energetic and hard-driven interpretations, but during his late London years he won great renown for his measured performances of the Viennese classics. He particularly distinguished himself by conducting a memorable series of the Beethoven syms. at the Royal Festival Hall. In the early 1960s he conducted new productions of *Fidelio*, *Die Zauberflöte*, and *Lohengrin* at Covent Garden. His serious and unsentimental readings of Mahler's syms. were largely responsible for the modern critical and popular interest shown in that composer's music. In 1970 he conducted in Jerusalem and accepted Israeli citizenship. He retired in 1972.

He was also a composer; he studied with Schoenberg during the latter's American sojourn, but his compositional style had more in common with that of Pfitzner. He wrote an opera, *Das Ziel* (1915; rev. 1970), a Missa sacra (1916), 6 syms. (from 1960), 17 pieces for voice and orch. (1967–70), 9 string quartets (1968–70), and about 100 songs. He publ. *Meine Erinnerungen an Gustav Mahler* (Zurich, 1960).

Kluge, Die (The Wise One). Opera by Orff, 1943, 1st performed in Frankfurt, based on a Grimm fable. A king marries a peasant woman who is far superior to him in intelligence; this annoys him so much that he decides to divorce her, but he gives her unqualified permission to take from the palace a thing she values above all else. Thereupon the wise woman gives the king a soporific and carries him to her modest little house. When he awakes he realizes that, for her, he himself is the most precious object in the palace. He restores her to royal status and they live happily ever after.

Knabenchor (Ger.). Boys' choir.

Knabenstimme (Ger.). A boy's voice.

knee stop. A knee lever under the manual of the reed organ. There are 3: 1 to control the wind supply, a 2nd to open and shut the swell-box, and a 3rd to draw all the stops.

Knickerbocker Holiday. Musical by Weill and M. Anderson, 1938, based on Washington Irving's *Father Knickerbocker's History of New York.* The scene is set in 17th-century N.Y., when it was Dutch and named New Amsterdam. Governor Peter Stuyvesant (a historical figure) is represented as a protofascist; the antifascist spirit is represented by a young Dutchman who is also the governor's rival in love. The show was a relative failure, but it includes *September Song*, which has become a perennial favorite.

Kniegeige (Ger., knee violin). VIOLA DA GAMBA.

Knight, Gladys, American R&B singer/group leader, b. Atlanta, Ga., May 28, 1944. Gladys Knight has performed for over 40 years as the leader of the family-based group the Pips, and as a solo artist. A child prodigy, she began singing with a gospel group at age 4; 3 years later she was a winner on TV's *Ted Mack's Original Amateur Hour.* She began singing with her brother Merald "Bubba" (b. Sept. 4, 1942) and cousin William Guest (b. June 2, 1941), among other family members, when she was 8 years old; by the time she was 13 the group was on the road opening for Jackie Wilson and Sam Cooke.

Initial recordings for Brunswick and other small labels were less than successful, until 1961 when they had a major R&B hit with *Every Beat of My Heart* on Vee Jay. After recording for other small labels, the group finally hooked up with Berry Gordy's Soul label (a subsidiary of his Motown empire) in 1965, beginning 8 years of major R&B and pop hit-making. By this time the group lineup had settled around the 2 Knights, their cousin Guest, and Edward Patten (b. Aug. 2, 1939), another cousin. Major hits included *The End of the Road, Friendship Train, If I Were Your Woman, Neither One of Us (Wants to Be the First to Say Goodbye)*, and *Daddy Could Swear, I Declare.*

The Pips left Motown in 1973 to join Buddah, where they had one of their biggest hits with *Midnight Train to Georgia.* In 1978 Gladys signed a solo deal with Columbia, and the Pips began recording on their own, but neither had much success. By the mid-'80s they were back together, scoring a smash hit in 1987 with *Love Overboard.* Today, Knight performs as a solo artist and on occasion with the Pips. The group was inducted into the Rock and Roll Hall of Fame in 1996.

Knot Garden, The. Opera by Tippett, 1970, 1st produced at Covent Garden in London. Tippett's libretto (based symbolically on Shakespeare's *The Tempest*) depicts a knotty psychological involvement in which a white musician and a black poet have a homosexual relationship, a feminist revolutionary confronts her hidden lesbianism, and a nubile maiden tries to escape the clutches of a married voluptuary, whose wife has retreated into a perfumed garden of desperate eroticism.

Knoxville: Summer of 1915. Work by Barber, 1948, for soprano and orch., inspired by a passage in *A Death in the Family* by James Agee, reminiscing of the time he was a child in Tennessee. It was 1st performed in Boston.

Knussen, (Stuart) **Oliver,** English composer; b. Glasgow, June 12, 1952. Remarkably precocious, he began playing piano as a small boy and showed unusual diligence also in his studies of music theory, mostly with John Lambert (1963–69) while attending the Central Tutorial School for Young Musicians (1964–67). In 1968 he made musical headlines when, at the age of 15, he conducted the London Sym. Orch. in the premiere performance of his own 1st Sym., written in an eclectic, but astoundingly effective, modern style. He was awarded fellowships for advanced study with Schuller at the Berkshire Music Center in Tanglewood (1970–73). He served as an artistic director of the Aldeburgh Festivals (from 1983) and as coordinator of contemporary music activities at Tanglewood (from 1986).

Koanga. Opera by Delius, 1904, 1st performed in Elberfeld, Germany. A beautiful young mulatto woman on a Mississippi plantation loves the handsome African prince Koanga; but the slave owner lusts after her himself. The lovers organize a vodun ritual to exorcise their white foes. Eventually Koanga dies, and his beloved stabs herself with his spear. The score contains some authentic African chants.

kocalho. Chocalho.

Kodály, Zoltan

Renowned Hungarian composer, ethnomusicologist, and music educator; b. Kecskemét, Dec. 16, 1882; d. Budapest, Mar. 6, 1967. He was brought up in a musical family; received general education at the Archiepiscopal Grammar School in Nagyszombat; at the same time, he took lessons in piano, violin, viola, and cello. He soon began to compose, producing an overture when he was 15; it was performed in Nagyszombat in 1898. He then went to Budapest (1900), where he entered the univ. as a student of Hungarian and German; also studied composition with Koessler at the Royal Academy of Music (diplomas in composition, 1904, and teaching, 1905; Ph.D., 1906, with a diss. on the stanzaic structure of Hungarian folk song). He became associated with Bartók, collecting, organizing, and editing the vast wealth of national folk songs; he made use of these melodies in his own compositions.

In 1906 he went to Berlin, and in 1907 proceeded to Paris, where he took some lessons with Widor; but it was the music of Debussy which most profoundly influenced him in his subsequent development as a composer. He was appointed a prof. at the Royal Academy of Music in Budapest in 1907. In collaboration with Bartók he prepared the detailed paper *Az uj egyetemes nepdalgyujtemeny tervezete* (A Project for a New Universal Collection of Folk Songs) in 1913. They continued their collecting expeditions until World War I intervened.

Kodály wrote music criticism for several newspapers in Budapest (1917–19); in 1919 he was appointed deputy director of the Budapest Academy of Music, but lost his position that same year for political reasons; however, he resumed his teaching there in 1922. In 1923 he was commissioned to write a commemorative work in celebration of the half-century anniversary of the union of Buda, Pest, and Obuda into Budapest. The resulting work, the oratorio *Psalmus hungaricus* (1923), brought him wide recognition. The initial performance in Budapest was followed by numerous productions all over Europe, and also in America.

Another major success was his opera *Háry János* (1926); an orch.l suite from this work became highly popular in Hungary and throughout the world. His orch.l works *Marosszéki táncok* (Dances of Marosszek; 1930, based on a piano work) and *Galántai táncok* (Dances of Galánt; for the 80th anniversary of the Budapest Phil. Soc., 1933) were also very successful. His reputation as one of the most significant national composers was firmly established with the repeated performances of these works. Among his most important subsequent works were the orch.l pieces *Variations on a Hungarian Folk Song "Felszállott a páva"* (Peacock Variations; for the 50th anniversary of the Amsterdam Concertgebouw Orch., 1939), and the Concerto for Orch. (for the 50th anniversary of the Chicago Sym. Orch., 1941).

His great interest in music education is reflected in his numerous choral works, which he wrote for both adults and children during the last 30 years of his life. He also pursued his ethnomusicological studies; from 1940 he was associated with the Hungarian Academy of Sciences, serving as its president (1946–49). He continued to teach at the Academy of Music until 1940, then gave instruction in Hungarian folk music until 1942; even after his retirement, he taught the latter course there. He toured as a conductor of his own music in England, the U.S., and the Soviet Union (1946–47); then throughout Western Europe. In succeeding years he held a foremost place in the musical life of his country, receiving many honors; was awarded 3 Kossuth Prizes (1948, 1952, 1957). He also received foreign honors, being made an honorary member of the Moscow Cons. (1963) and the American Academy of Arts and Sciences (1963); was also awarded the Gold Medal of the Royal Phil. Soc. of London (1967). An International Kodály Soc. was organized in Budapest in 1975.

As a composer Kodály's musical style was not as radical as that of Bartók; he never departed from basic tonality, nor did his experiments in rhythm reach the primitivistic power of Bartók's percussive idiom. He preferred a Romantic treatment of his melodic and harmonic materials, with an infusion of impressionistic elements. All the same, he succeeded in producing a substantial body of music of notable distinction. He was married twice; his 1st wife, Emma, whom he married in 1910, died in 1958; the following year he married Sárolta Peczély, a student (b. 1940).

Koechlin, Charles (Louis Eugène), noted French composer, pedagogue, and writer on music; b. Paris, Nov. 27, 1867; d. Le Canadel, Var, Dec. 31, 1950. He studied for a military career but was compelled to change his plans when stricken with tuberculosis; while recuperating in Algeria, he took up serious music studies; then entered the Paris Cons. (1890), where he studied with Gedalge, Massenet, and Fauré, graduating in 1897. He lived mostly in Paris, where he was active as a composer, teacher, and lecturer; with Ravel and Schmitt he organized the Societé Musicale Indépendante (1909) to advance the cause of contemporary music; with Satie, Roussel, Milhaud, and others, he was a member of the group Les Nouveaux Jeunes (1918–20), a precursor to Les Six.

Although Koechlin composed prolifically in all genres, he became best known as a writer on music and as a lecturer. He made 3 lecture tours of the U.S. (1918, 1928, 1937). He became president of the Fédération Musicale Populaire (1937). His pro-Communist leanings caused him to promote music for the proletariat during the 1930s; wrote a number of works "for the people" and also film scores. In spite of the fact that such works as his *Sym. d'hymnes* (Prix Cressent, 1936) and Sym. No. 1 (Prix Halphan, 1937) won honors, his music made no real impact.

Taking Fauré as his model, he strove to preserve the best elements in the French classical tradition. A skillful craftsman, he produced works of clarity and taste, marked by advanced harmonic and polyphonic attributes. A prolific writer, he wrote treatises on counterpoint, harmony, fugue, and orchestration; he also wrote monographs on Debussy, Fauré, choir school, Pierre Maurice (a Swiss composer who, like Koechlin, synthesized German and French elements), and wind instruments.

Koechlin was a prolific composer; the core of his output are the works based on Kipling: *3 poèmes du "Livre de la Jungle"* for SATB soloists, SAT chorus, and orch. (1899–1910); *La Course de printemps*, after Kipling (1908–25); *La Méditation de Purun Bhagat*, after Kipling (1936); *La Loi de la jungle*, after Kipling (1939); *Les Bandar-log*, after Kipling (1939); his other sym. poems include *La Forêt* in 2 parts: *Le Jour* (1897–1904) and *La Nuit* (1896–1907); *En mer, la nuit*, after Heine (1899–1904); *L'automne* (1896–1906); *Nuit de walpurgis classique (Ronde nocturne)*, after Verlaine (1901–1907); *Soleil et danses dans la forêt* and *Vers la plage lointaine* (1898–1909); *Le Printemps* and *L'Hiver* (1908–16: *L'Été* in 2 parts: *Nuit de juin* and *Midi en août* (1908–11), *Sur les flots lointaines* (1933); *Hymne à la jeunesse* after Gide (1934); *La Cité nouvelle, rêve d'avenir*, after Wells (1938); *Le Buisson ardent*, after Rolland (1938); *Le Docteur Fabricius*, after C. Dollfus (1941–44).

Among Koechlin's other orch. works are the 7-movement Ballade for Piano and Orch. (1911–15); Sym. No. 1 (1911–16); *Choral fugué du style modal* for Organ and Orch. (1933); *7 Stars Sym.*, sketches of 7 Hollywood stars (1933) *Sym. d'hymnes* (1936); *Offrande musical sur le nom de BACH* (1942); Partita for Chamber Orch. (1945); *Introduction et 4 interludes de style atonal-seriel* (1947). There are also many works for piano, including *Paysages et marines* (12 pieces; 1915–16); *Les Heures persanes* (16 pieces; 1916–19); *L'Ancienne Maison de campagne* (12 pieces; 1932–33);

chamber music; choral works; band music; film-inspired scores; organ music; songs.

Kogan, Leonid (Borisovich), outstanding Russian violinist, married to Elizabeta Gilels; b. Dnepropetrovsk, Nov. 14, 1924; d. on the train at the Mytishcha railroad station, Dec. 17, 1982. His father was a photographer who played the violin; when Kogan was 10 years old the family moved to Moscow, where he became a pupil of Abram Yampolsky, 1st at the Central Music School and later at the Cons. (1943–48). He was obviously a wunderkind, but was prudently spared harmful exploitation. In 1947 he was a cowinner of the 1st prize at the World Festival of Democratic Youth in Prague; then won 1st prize in the Queen Elisabeth of Belgium Competition in 1951. His career was instantly assured; he played recitals in Europe to unanimous acclaim.

He made an auspicious American debut, playing the Brahms Violin Concerto with Monteux and the Boston Sym. Orch. in 1958. In 1952 he joined the faculty of the Moscow Cons.; was named prof. in 1963 and head of the violin dept. in 1969; in 1965 he received the Lenin Prize. His playing exemplified the finest qualities of the Russian School: an emotionally romantic élan and melodious filigree of technical detail. In addition to the standard repertoire, in which he excelled, he also played modern violin works, particularly those by Soviet composers.

He was married to the violinist Elizabeta Gilels. Following the violinistic genetic code, their 2 children were also musical: a girl played the piano, and a boy, Pavel Kogan (b. Moscow, June 6, 1952), was so good on the violin that in 1970 he won the Sibelius contest in Finland. In 1975 Pavel was soloist with the Philadelphia Orch. Pavel later was active as a conductor at Moscow's Bolshoi Theater (from 1988), the Zagreb Phil. (from 1988), and the Moscow Sym. Orch. (from 1989). The family shunned politics, and Leonid resolutely declined to participate in any protests, domestic or foreign, against the presumed anti-Semitism in Russian politics, even though he himself was patently Jewish.

Kokkonen, Joonas, prominent Finnish composer; b. Iisalmi, Nov. 13, 1921; d. Jarvenpaa, Oct. 4, 1966. He studied with Palmgren, Ranta, and Hannikainen at the Sibelius Academy in Helsinki (diploma, 1949); also studied musicology with Krohn at the Univ. of Helsinki (M.A., 1948). He taught at the Sibelius Academy (from 1950); was prof. of composition (1959–63) and chairman of the dept. (1965–70). In 1963 he was elected to membership in the Finnish Academy; in 1973 he was awarded the Sibelius Prize.

Like all composers of his generation in Finland he experienced the inevitable influence of Sibelius, but he soon abandoned the characteristic diatonic modalities of Finnish folk music and formed an individual style of composition marked by a curiously anfractuous chromaticism and involuted counterpoint, freely dissonant but hewing to clearly identifiable tonal centers. For a period he dabbled in dodecaphonic writing, but he found its doctrinaire discipline uncongenial. He derives his techniques from the contrapuntal procedures of Bach and, among the moderns, from Bartók. Thematically he adopts an objective method of formal structure, in which a free succession of formative motifs determines the content. His international fame received its greatest boost with the opera *Viimeiset Kiusaukset* (The Last Temptations), concerning the life of a 19th-century Finnish evangelist (Helsinki, 1975).

Kol Nidrei (Hebr., all the vowels). A very old Jewish religious song, sung on the eve of Yom Kippur, the Day of Atonement, set in an expressive minor mode and marked by a profound religious sentiment. *Kol Nidrei* for Cello and Orch. by Bruch; it is his most popular work; he wrote it in 1880 for the Jewish community of Liverpool, although he himself was Protestant.

kolo (Serb., wheel). Round dance of the southern Slavic region, with a constantly repeated refrain; there are slow and fast types of the kolo. The dance is related to the Rumanian *lora* and Bulgarian HORO.

Kolorierung (Ger., coloration). Keyboard ornamentation in the Baroque century, tastefully applied; while frowned upon by "purists" of succeeding centuries, these convenient clichés assured that performances of Baroque music would not be jejune.

Komponist (Ger.). COMPOSER.

kondak. KONTAKION.

König Hirsch (The Stag King). Opera by Henze, 1956, 1st produced in Berlin; it was subsequently revised and restaged, 1963, under the original name of Gozzi's fable *Il Re cervo*. As the title suggests, the King is transformed into a stag. Eventually he sheds his horns, regains his human figure, and returns to his native town. The musical idiom is dodecaphonic and dissonant, but the score follows the classical Italian tradition in its formal set arias and ensemble numbers.

Königskinder (The Royal Children). Opera by Humperdinck, 1910, 1st produced in N.Y. The libretto reverses the course of events of Humperdinck's famous children's opera, *Hänsel und Gretel*. Here the malevolent witch feeds poisonous candy to the young prince and the girl whom he loves, and they both die. The opera is an expanded version of his incidental music for a play *Königskinder*, produced in 1897, notable for its use of SPRECHSTIMME long before Schoenberg; similar to other Humperdinck works in its Wagnerian ethos.

Kontakion (Rus., kondak). A portion of the Byzantine liturgical Hours, sung as an ode in the kanñ. Legend has it being given to a 6th-century Byzantine poet known as Roman the Melodious (Melode Romanous) by the Blessed Virgin. It is a morality poem, containing a narrative recited by a soloist, followed by a choral refrain. The kontakion was eventually limited to the Orthodox Matins; but it remained a major influence on ecclesiastical poetry and music. The kontakion was eventually superseded by the Byzantine canon. After the conversion of Russia to Christianity in the 10th century, the kontakion was used in Russian church singing.

Kontakte. Work by Stockhausen, 1960, for piano, percussion, and electronic sounds, 1st performed in Cologne. The "contacts" of the title signify the coexistence of electronic and traditional acoustic instruments. It is one of the most significant, if not the earliest, experiments in organized electronic music.

Kontarsky, Alfons, German pianist, brother of Aloys and Bernhard Kontarsky; b. Iserlohn, Westphalia, Oct. 9, 1932. He studied piano with Else Schmitz-Gohr and Maurits Frank at the Cologne Hochschule für Musik (1953–55) and with Eduard Erdmann in Hamburg (1955–57); with his brother Aloys, won 1st prize for duo-piano playing in the Bavarian Radio Competition in Munich (1955); they subsequently toured throughout the world, giving performances of many modern scores; they have recorded works by Boulez, Stockhausen, Bartók, Stravinsky, B.A. Zimmermann, and Ravel. He taught at the Cologne Hochschule für Musik (from 1967). He publ. *Pro musica nova: Studien zum Spielen neuer Musik für Klavier* (Cologne, 1973).

Kontarsky, Aloys, German pianist, brother of Alfons and Bernhard Kontarsky; b. Iserlohn, Westphalia, May 14, 1931. He studied piano with Else Schmitz-Gohr and Maurits Frank at the Cologne Hochschule für Musik (1952–55) and with Eduard Erdmann in Hamburg (1955–57); with his brother Alfons, won 1st prize for duo-piano playing at the Bavarian Radio Competition in Munich (1955); thereafter they made tours throughout the world, specializing in contemporary music; they have recorded works by Boulez, Stockhausen, Bartók, Stravinsky, B.A. Zimmermann, and Ravel. He taught master classes at the Cologne Hochschule für Musik (from 1969).

Kontarsky, Bernhard, German pianist and conductor, brother of Alfons and Aloys Kontarsky; b. Iserlohn, Westphalia, Apr. 26, 1937. He studied at the Cologne Hochschule für Musik and at the Univ. of Cologne. In 1964 he received the Mendelssohn Prize in Chamber Music. He was a conductor at the Württemberg State Theater in Stuttgart; also appeared as a pianist, both as a soloist and in ensemble with his brothers.

Konzert (Ger.). 1. CONCERTO. 2. CONCERT.

Konzertmeister (Ger.). CONCERTMASTER.

Konzertsaal (Ger.). Concert hall.

Konzertstück (Ger.; It. *concertino*). 1. A concert piece. 2. A short concerto with orch. in one movement and free form. Examples include works by Weber (piano); Chopin (*Allegro de concert*); Mendelssohn (*Capriccio brillant*); Schumann (*Concertstück* for 4 Horns); and an unfinished Stravinsky work for piano that was incorporated into *Petrouchka*.

Koopman, Ton, remarkable Dutch organist, harpsichordist, and conductor; b. Zwolle, Oct. 12, 1944. He studied organ with Simon Jansen and harpsichord with Gustav Leonhardt in Amsterdam, and also took courses in musicology; obtained doctorates in all 3 (1968–70), then won the Prix d'excellence for organ (1972) and harpsichord (1974). After serving as director of Musica Antiqua and as a teacher at the Sweelinck Cons. in Amsterdam, he founded the Amsterdam Baroque Orch. (1979). He toured widely in subsequent years as a conductor, organist, and harpsichordist, excelling in early music performances. He has recorded works by Bach, Frescobaldi, Telemann, Stanley, and Buxtehude.

Kopfstimme (Ger., head voice). FALSETTO.

Koppel (Ger.). Coupler (organ). *Koppel ab*, take coupler off; *Koppel an*, draw coupler; couple.

kora. A plucked harp-lute of West Africa, associated with the Mandinka and Maninka peoples. The standard instrument has 21 nylon (formerly leather) strings, attached with tuning collars at the top of a long wooden neck, which passes through a large gourd resonator. The strings are attached at bottom by an iron anchor ring. The professional performer (*jali*), who sits on the ground, faces the head of the resonator, called the *soundboard* and made with antelope skin or cowhide; the player holds the instrument with attached wooden handles. The strings are divided into two ranks running perpendicular to the soundboard; they pass over a single bridge with notches in either side to help tune the 21 strings.

The range of the kora covers 3 octaves; there are numerous tunings, each of which is usually applicable to only a few pieces. The *jali*'s repertory is comprised of praise songs, honoring a family or clan, and songs in an Islamic vein. The complex accompaniment blends linear and vertical elements in a mostly steady rhythm; there are several playing techniques, including flicking a nail against the instrument to fill in a rhythmic interruption. The sonority is sometimes heightened by a jingle attached to the bridge with wire loops. The 1st Western report of the instrument dates from 1799. The family of koralike instruments include the *ekorro*, *seron*, *bolon*, *mvet*, *fan harp*, etc.

Korean temple blocks. Rounded and hollowed woodblocks, struck with a drumstick. The pitch is approximate, but definite enough to create a pentatonic effect when the appropriate blocks are combined.

Kornett (Ger.). CORNET À PISTONS; CORNET.

Korngold, Erich Wolfgang, remarkable Austrian-born American composer; b. Brunn (Brno), May 29, 1897; d. Los Angeles, Nov. 29, 1957. He received his earliest musical education from his father, the noted Viennese music critic Julius Korngold (b. Brunn [Brno], Dec. 24, 1860; d. Los Angeles, Sept. 25, 1945), then studied with Fuchs, Zemlinsky, and Gradener in Vienna. His progress was astounding; at the age of 12 he composed a Piano Trio, which was soon publ., revealing a competent technique and an ability to write in a style strongly influenced by R. Strauss. About the same time he wrote (in piano score) a

pantomime, *Der Schneemann*; it was orchestrated by Zemlinsky and performed at the Vienna Court Opera (1910), creating a sensation. In 1911 Nikisch conducted Korngold's *Schauspiel-Ouvertüre* with the Leipzig Gewandhaus Orch.; that same year the youthful composer gave a concert of his works in Berlin, appearing also as a pianist; his *Sinfonietta* was conducted by Weingartner and the Vienna Phil. in 1913.

Korngold was not quite 19 when his 2 short operas, *Der Ring des Polykrates* and *Violanta*, were produced in Munich. His 1st lasting success came with the simultaneous premiere in Hamburg and Cologne of his opera *Die tote Stadt* (1920). In 1929 he began a fruitful collaboration with the director Max Reinhardt; in 1934 he went to Hollywood to arrange Mendelssohn's music for Reinhardt's film version of *A Midsummer Night's Dream*. He taught at the Vienna Academy of Music (1930–34) before settling in Hollywood, where he wrote some of the best Romantic film scores of the era. He became a naturalized U.S. citizen in 1943.

Korngold's music represents the last breath of the Romantic spirit of Vienna; it is marvelously consistent with the melodic, rhythmic, and harmonic style of the judicious modernity of the nascent 20th century. When Mahler heard him play some of his music as a young boy, he kept repeating, "Ein Genie! Ein Genie!" Korngold never altered his established idiom of composition and was never tempted to borrow modernistic devices, except for some transitory passages in major 2nds or an occasional whole-tone scale.

After the early outbursts of incautious enthusiasm on the part of some otherwise circumspect critics nominating Korngold as a new Mozart, his star, his erupting nova, began to sink rapidly, until it became a melancholy consensus to dismiss his operas at their tardy revivals as derivative products of an era that had itself little to exhibit that was worthwhile. Ironically, his film scores, in the form of orchestrated suites, experienced long after his death a spontaneous renascence, particularly on records, and especially among the unprejudiced and unopinionated American musical youth, who found in Korngold's music the stuff of their own new dreams.

Korrepetitor, -in (Ger., choral coach; Fr. *répétiteur, -euse*). Assistant conductor or pianist who leads preliminary rehearsals with singers and dancers in opera and ballet.

Kortholt (Ger.). Obsolete double-reed windcap instrument, with a cylindrical double-channel bore. The instrument is similar to the curtal, except for the latter's conical bore; also, the *bass sordone*, except for the latter's lack of a windcap.

koto. National Japanese instrument of the long zither type, with a rectangular body made of strong wood planks that is laid on the floor. It has 7 to 13 silk strings that are plucked with fingers, fingernails, or a plectrum; some modern kotos may have as many as 17 strings. The koto is commonly used to accompany the Japanese GAGAKU, the music of the medieval Japanese court. In subsequent centuries, schools of solo performance emerged, and music was written down (including the timeless *Variations on Rokudan*). In the 20th century the koto evolved into a virtuoso instrument. Several Japanese composers have written music for the instrument, making use of modern techniques, including dodecaphony. Henry Cowell, among other American composers, wrote 2 concertos for koto and orch.

Koussevitzky (Kussevitsky), Serge (Alexandrovich)

~~~ ~~~ ~~~ ~~~ ~~~

Celebrated Russian-born American conductor and double-bass virtuoso; b. Vishny-Volochok, July 26, 1874; d. Boston, June 4, 1951. His father and his 3 brothers were all amateur musicians. Koussevitzky learned to play the trumpet and took part, with his brothers, in a small wind ensemble, numbering 8 members in all; they earned their living by playing at balls and weddings and occasionally at village fairs. At the age of 14 he went to Moscow; since Jews were not allowed to live there, he was baptized. He then received a fellowship with free tuition at the Musico-Dramatic Inst. of the Moscow Phil. Soc., where he studied double bass with Rambousek; he also studied music theory with Blaramberg and Kruglikov.

In 1894 he joined the orch. of the Bolshoi Theater, succeeding Rambousek as principal double-bass player in 1901, retaining that post until 1905. In the meantime he became known as a soloist of the 1st magnitude; he made his public debut in Moscow in 1901. He garnered great attention with a double-bass recital in Berlin (1903). To supplement the meager repertoire for his instrument, he arranged various works; he also wrote several pieces. With some aid from Glière, he wrote a double-bass concerto, which he performed for the 1st time in Moscow (1905). Later that year he married Natalie Ushkov, daughter of a wealthy tea-merchant family. He soon resigned from the orch. of the Bolshoi Theater; in an open letter to the Russian publication *Musical Gazette* he explained the reason for his resignation as the economic and artistic difficulties in the orch. He then went to Germany, where he continued to give double-bass recitals; played the 1st Cello Concerto by Saint-Saëns on the double bass.

In 1907 he conducted a student orch. at the Berlin Hochschule für Musik; his 1st public appearance as a conductor took place in 1908, with the Berlin Phil. In 1909 he established a publishing house, Editions Russes de Musique; in 1915 he purchased the catalog of the Gutheil Co.; among composers with whom he signed contracts were Scriabin, Stravinsky, Prokofiev, Medtner, and Rachmaninoff; the association with Scriabin was particularly fruitful, and in subsequent years Koussevitzky became the greatest champion of Scriabin's music. In 1909 he organized his own sym. orch. in Moscow, featuring works by Russian composers, but also including classical masterpieces; played many Russian works for the 1st time, among them Scriabin's *Promethée*. In the summer of 1910 he took his orch. to the towns along the Volga River in a specially chartered steamboat. He repeated the Volga tour in 1912 and 1914.

The outbreak of World War I in 1914 made it necessary to curtail his activities; however, he continued to give his concerts in Moscow; in 1915 he presented a memorial Scriabin program. After the Revolution of 1917 he was offered the directorship of the State Sym. Orch. (former Court Orch.) in Petrograd; he conducted it until 1920; also presented concerts in Moscow, despite the hardships of the revolutionary times. In 1920 he left Russia; went 1st to Berlin, then to Rome, and finally to Paris, where he organized the Concerts Koussevitzky with a specially assembled orch.; presented many new scores by French and Russian composers, among them Ravel's orchestration of Mussorgsky's *Pictures at an Exhibition*, Honegger's *Pacific 231*, and several works by Prokofiev and Stravinsky.

In 1924 Koussevitzky was appointed the conductor of the Boston Sym. Orch., a position he held with great eminence until 1949. Just as in Russia he championed Russian composers, in France the French, so in the U.S. he encouraged American composers to write works for him. Symphonic compositions by Copland, Harris, Piston, Barber, Hanson, Schuman, and others were performed by Koussevitzky for the 1st time. For the 50th anniversary of the Boston Sym. Orch. (1931), he commissioned works from Stravinsky (*Sym. of Psalms*), Hindemith, Honegger, Prokofiev, Roussel, Ravel (Piano Concerto), Copland, Gershwin, and others.

A highly important development in Koussevitzky's American career was the establishment of the Berkshire Music Center at Tanglewood, Mass. This was an outgrowth of the Berkshire Sym. Festival, organized in 1934 by Henry Hadley; Koussevitzky and the Boston Sym. Orch. presented summer concerts at the Berkshire Festival in 1935 for the 1st time; since then the concerts have become an annual institution. The Berkshire Music Center was opened on July 8, 1940, with Koussevitzky as director and Copland as assistant director; among the distinguished guest instructors were Hindemith, Honegger, and Messiaen; Koussevitzky himself taught conducting; he was succeeded after his death by his former student Leonard Bernstein.

Koussevitzky held many honorary degrees: Mus.Doc. from Brown Univ. (1926), Rutgers Univ. (1937), Yale Univ. (1938), Univ. of Rochester (1940), Williams College (1943), and Boston Univ. (1945); LL.D. from Harvard Univ. (1929) and Princeton Univ. (1947). He was a member of the French Legion of Honor and held the Cross of Commander of the Finnish Order of the White Rose. He became a naturalized American citizen on Apr. 16, 1941. His wife died in 1942; he established the Koussevitzky Foundation as a memorial to her, the funds to be used for commissioning works by composers of all nationalities. He married Olga Naoumoff (1901–78), a niece of Natalie Koussevitzky, on Aug. 15, 1947.

As a conductor Koussevitzky possessed an extraordinary emotional power; in Russian music, and particularly in Tchaikovsky's syms., he was unexcelled; he was capable of achieving the subtlest nuances in the works of the French school; his interpretations of Debussy were notable. As a champion of modern music he had few equals in his time; his ardor in projecting unfamiliar music before new audiences in different countries served to carry conviction among the listeners and the professional music critics. He was often criticized for the liberties he allowed himself in the treatment of classical masterpieces, undoubtedly his performances of Bach, Beethoven, Brahms, and Schubert were untraditional; but they were nonetheless musicianly in the sincere artistry that animated his interpretations.

Koven, Reginald de. De Koven, Reginald.

koza (Pol., goat). Polish bellows-blown bagpipe, with a goatskin bag and a chanter with around 8 fingerholes and a drone bent at a 90° angle. Both the chanter and drone end in an upturned bell of horn or metal.

kräftig (Ger.). Forza.

krakowiak (Pol.; Fr. *cracovienne*; Ger. *Krakauer Tanz*). Fast syncopated Polish dance in 2/4 time, developed in the region of Kraków; examples date back to tablatures and songbooks of the 16th century, where it was called *chorea polonica* or *volta polonica*. It is sometimes considered the Polish national dance, although the polonaise predates it. The krakowiak became an important component of the musical stage; Chopin wrote a *Krakowiak* rondo for piano

and orch., op. 14 (1828), and another for the finale of the 1st Piano Concerto, op. 11 (1830).

Kraus (Trujillo), **Alfredo,** distinguished Spanish tenor of Austrian descent; b. Las Palmas, Canary Islands, Sept. 24, 1927. He had vocal training with Gali Markoff in Barcelona and Francisco Andres in Valencia, then completed his studies with Mercedes Llopart in Milan (1955). In 1956 he won 1st prize in the Geneva Competition and made his operatic debut as the Duke of Mantua in Cairo; he also made his European debut in Venice as Alfredo Germont, a role he repeated for his British debut at London's Stoll Theatre in 1957. After he scored a remarkable success in the same role at Lisbon's Teatro São Carlo on Mar. 27, 1958, an international career beckoned. In 1959 he appeared at London's Covent Garden for the 1st time, as Edgardo in *Lucia di Lammermoor*. His U.S. debut followed at the Chicago Lyric

Opera, as Nemorino in *L'elisir d'amore* (1962). He made his Metropolitan Opera debut in N.Y. as the Duke of Mantua (1966). A consummate artist with a voice of remarkable beauty, he was particularly noted for his portrayals of Rossini's Count Almaviva, Don Ottavio, Ernesto in *Don Pasquale*, Des Grieux in *Manon*, Nadir in *Les Pêcheurs de perles*, and Werther.

Krebsgang (Ger., crab walk). RETROGRADE.

Krebskanon (Ger., crab canon). See CANON.

Kreisler, Fritz (Friedrich), great Austrian-born American violinist; b. Vienna, Feb. 2, 1875; d. N.Y., Jan. 29, 1962. His extraordinary talent manifested itself when he was only 4, and it was carefully fostered by his father, under whose instruction he made such progress that at age 6 he was accepted as a pupil of Jacob Dont; he also studied with Jacques Auber until, at 7, he entered the Vienna Cons., where his principal teachers were Hellmesberger, Jr. (violin), and Bruckner (theory); he gave his 1st performance there when he was 9 and was awarded its gold medal at 10. He subsequently studied with Massart (violin) and Delibes (composition) at the Paris Cons., sharing the premier prix in violin with 4 other students (1887). He made his U.S. debut in Boston (1888); then toured the country during the 1889–90 season with the pianist Moriz Rosenthal, but he had only moderate success.

Returning to Europe, he abandoned music to study medicine in Vienna and art in Rome and Paris; then served as an officer in the Austrian army (1895–96). Resuming his concert career, he appeared as a soloist with H. Richter and the Vienna Phil. (1898). His subsequent appearance as a soloist with Nikisch and the Berlin Phil. (1899) launched his international career. Not only had he regained his virtuosity during his respite, but he had also developed into a master interpreter. On his 2nd tour of the U.S. (1900–1901), both as a soloist and as a recitalist with Hofmann and Gerardy, he carried his audiences by storm. In 1902 he made his London debut as a soloist with Richter and the Phil. Soc. orch.; was awarded its Gold Medal in 1904. Elgar composed his Violin Concerto for him, and Kreisler gave its premiere under the composer's direction in London (1910).

At the outbreak of World War I in 1914, Kreisler joined his former regiment, but upon being quickly wounded he was discharged. He then returned to the U.S. to pursue his career; after the U.S. entered the war in 1917, he withdrew from public appearances. With the war over, he once again performed in N.Y. (1919) and once again resumed his tours. From 1924 to 1934 he made his home in Berlin, but in 1938 he went to France and became a naturalized citizen. In 1939 he settled in the U.S., becoming a naturalized citizen (1943). In 1941 he suffered a near-fatal accident when he was struck by a truck in N.Y.; however, he recovered and continued to give concerts until 1950.

Kreisler was one of the greatest masters of the violin. His brilliant technique was ably matched by his remarkable tone, both of which he always placed in the service of the composer. He was the owner of the great Guarneri "del Gesu" violin of 1733 and of instruments by other masters. He gathered a rich collection of invaluable MSS; in 1949 he donated the original scores of Brahms's Violin Concerto and Chausson's *Poème* for violin and orch. to the Library of Congress. He wrote some of the most popular violin pieces in the world, among them *Caprice viennois*, *Tambourin chinois*, *Schön Rosmarin*, and *Liebesfreud*.

He also publ. a number of pieces in the classical vein, which he ascribed to various composers (Vivaldi, Pugnani, Couperin, Padre Martini, Dittersdorf, Francoeur, Stamitz, and others). In 1935 he reluctantly admitted that these pieces were his own, with the exception of the 1st 8 bars from the "Couperin" *Chanson Louis XIII*, taken from a traditional melody; he explained his motive in doing so as the necessity of building up well-rounded programs for his concerts that would contain virtuoso pieces by established composers, rather than a series of compositions under his own, as yet unknown name. He also wrote the operettas *Apple Blossoms* (N.Y., Oct. 7, 1919) and *Sissy* (Vienna, Dec. 23, 1932), publ. numerous arrangements of early and modern music (Corelli's *La Folia*, Tartini's *The Devil's Trill*, Dvořák's *Slavonic Dances*, a *Danza española* by Granados, Tango by Albeniz, etc.), and prepared cadenzas for the Beethoven and Brahms violin concertos.

Kremer, Gidon, brilliant Latvian violinist; b. Riga, Feb. 27, 1947. His parents were violinists in the Riga Sym. Orch. He obtained the elements of violin study from his father and grandfather, then continued professional studies with David Oistrakh at the Moscow Cons. He took part in several competitions, culminating in 1st prizes at the Paganini Competition in Genoa in 1968 and the Tchaikovsky Competition in Moscow in 1970. He made an auspicious N.Y. debut at Avery Fisher Hall (1977). In subsequent years he appeared as a soloist with many of the major orchs. of the world, gave recitals, and performed in chamber music settings. He has won special commendation for his efforts to broaden the repertoire for his instrument; his great contribution to modern music has been the consistent presentation of new violin works, particularly those of Soviet composers, among them Alfred Schnittke and Sofia Gubaidulina. He has also given notable performances of the works of the Estonian composer Arvo Pärt.

Krenek, Ernst

Remarkable Austrian-born American composer, whose intellect responds equally to his musical philosophy and his imaginative technique of composition; b. Ernst Křenek, Vienna, Aug. 23, 1900; d. Palm Springs, Calif., Dec. 23, 1991. He studied with Franz Schreker in Vienna (from 1916), and at the Berlin Academy of Music (1920–23). He then was a conductor and composer at the operas in Kassel and Wiesbaden (1925–27). He returned to Vienna in 1928; was a writer for the Frankfurter Zeitung (1930–33); also traveled widely in Europe as a lecturer and an accompanist in programs of his own songs.

With the *Anschluss* of 1938 he settled in the U.S.; became a naturalized American citizen in 1945 and altered the spelling of his name. He was a prof. of music at Vassar College (1939–42); then head of the music dept. at Hamline Univ. in St. Paul, Minn. (1942–47). He subsequently made his home in Calif. He married Gustav Mahler's daughter, Anna, in 1923; they were divorced in 1925, and he married Berta Hermann; later married Gladys Nordenstrom (1950).

Krenek's evolution as a composer mirrors the development of modern music in general. The tradition of Mahler, strengthened by the domestic ties of Krenek's 1st marriage, was the dominant influence of his early life in music; he then became associated with the modern groups in Vienna, particularly Schoenberg, Berg, and Webern. In Germany he was associated with Hindemith as a creator of modern opera in a satiric manner. He achieved a masterly technique of composition in his earliest works, and developed his melodic and harmonic idiom in the direction of atonality and polytonality.

His 1st international success came to him at the age of 26, with the production of his opera *Jonny spielt auf* (Leipzig, 1927). Although it is described as a "jazz opera," no such designation appears in the score. It deals with a jazz fiddler whose fame sweeps the world; in the apotheosis, Jonny sits atop a gigantic globe; it was staged at the Metropolitan Opera in N.Y. (1929) with the hero as a black-faced musician rather than a black as in the original. In 1933 Krenek adopted an integral 12-tone method of composition; his historical opera *Karl V* was written in this idiom. In his treatment of 12-tone composition, however, he introduced numerous textual and textural indulgences, such as division of the basic 12-tone theme into fractional groups, permutation of thematic elements, and shifting the initial notes of the basic dodecaphonic system.

The accession of the Nazi governments in Germany and Austria forced the exclusion of performances of Krenek's works from Europe where the Hitlerites held sway; the scheduled production of *Karl V* in Vienna was canceled after Austria was occupied by the Nazis. Even though Krenek was of unimpeachable Aryan origin, his music was banned from performance by the Nazi authorities because of his adherence to an advanced musical idiom which was proscribed by the Nazis. His viciously retouched photograph was featured, along with those of Mahler, Schoenberg, and others, in the infamous collection of Entartete Musik (Degenerate Music). Deprived of all means of subsistence, he went to the U.S.; friends and admirers secured for him a modest engagement as teacher of composition at the Malkin Cons. in Boston, and a few performances of his works by American orchs. followed. Still, his modernistic idiom upset some American musiclovers; a Boston Sym. Orch. dowager was heard to say after a performance of Krenek's Piano Concerto, "Conditions must be terrible in Europe!"

Strangely enough, there have been fewer performances of Krenek's works in the U.S., where he made his home, than in Europe. Stravinsky, who admired him as an intellectual and as a composer, predicted in 1963 that Krenek will one day be honored in both America and Europe. Krenek himself wrote, in his 1950 autobiography, *Selbstdarstellung*: "It is quite possible that the unusual variety of my output has baffled observers accustomed to more homogeneous phenomena. It is my impression that this confusion has surrounded my work with an unusual obscurity—almost anonymity."

Stravinsky's prediction came at least partially true when the liberated Austrian government awarded Krenek the Grand State Prize of 1963. A number of festivals and other celebrations, timed for Krenek's 90th birthday in 1990, included the world premiere of his oratorio *Opus sine nomine* (op. 238; Vienna, May 8, 1990); 3 short operas, *Der Diktator*, *Das geheime Königreich*, and *Schwergewicht, oder Die Ehre der Nation* (Vienna, June 4–6, 1990); the Salzburg Festival presenting Krenek's orch. music (Aug. 22, 1990); a revival of *Jonny spielt auf* at the Leipzig Opera (Sept. 30, 1990); and concluded with the Stuttgart Krenek Festival (Nov. 16–23, 1990). Krenek's autobiography, completed in 1950 and deposited at the Library of Congress, is not to be opened until 15 years after his death.

Kreutzer Sonata. The common name for Beethoven's most famous Violin Sonata, op. 47. Although it bears the name of his contemporary Rodolphe Kreutzer, the famous French violinist, pedagogue, and composer (b. Versailles, Nov. 16, 1766; d. Geneva, Jan. 6, 1831), the violinist never performed it. The 1st performance was given on May 24, 1803, in Vienna, with Beethoven himself playing the piano part and George Polgreen Bridgetower (c. 1779–1860), the orig. dedicatee, on the violin. Tolstoy took it as the title of his famous moralistic novella, *The Kreutzer Sonata*, in which a middle-class Russian woman rehearses the sonata with a dashing violinist and eventually succumbs to his advances. Technically the novel is flawed because the difficulties of Beethoven's work would deter any music amateur from tackling it and continuous attempts to perform it would have so frustrated the players that they would have probably ended up hating each other.

Kreuz (Ger., cross). Sharp (♯).

Krone (Ger., crown). Tubing inserted in natural horns or trumpets to change the fundamental tuning. The invention of valve horns eliminated the need for this device.

Krummhorn (Ger., crooked horn). Crumhorn.

Krupa, Gene, successful American jazz drummer; b. Chicago, Jan. 15, 1909; d. Yonkers, N.Y., Oct. 16, 1973. He joined a jazz band when still in his adolescence; studied percussion with Al Silverman, Ed Straight, and Roy Knapp (1925); worked with local musicians. He then went to N.Y. (1929), where he performed in bands led by Red Nichols and Irving Aaronson; after working with others (1932–34), he became a featured member of Benny Goodman's band (1934), winning acclaim for his brilliant playing in the recording of *Sing, Sing, Sing*. He left Goodman in 1938, forming his own band (featuring singer Anita O'Day); he toured Europe and the Orient and became internationally famous. He was again a member of Goodman's band (1943), and then of Tommy Dorsey's band (1943–44). He subsequently led his own band (until 1951); later toured with Jazz at the Phil., and with his own trios and quartets.

He and Cozy Cole cofounded a school of percussion in N.Y. Possessed with a phenomenal technique and despite a penchant for exhibitionism, Krupa "popularized" the drums with extended, virtuosic solos. He recorded the soundtrack for the largely fictional film *The Gene Krupa Story* (1959).

Krútňava (The Whirlpool). Opera by Suchoň, 1949, 1st performed in Bratislava. The whirlpool of the title is the moral dilemma in which a young village girl finds herself when her lover is killed by an unknown assailant. Suspicion is directed against another villager who succeeds in persuading the bereaved woman to marry him, but when a child is born to her it becomes clear that the child's father was her slain lover. The killer is tortured by his memories and goes back to the scene of the crime to retrieve a gun he buried there. He is apprehended and brought to justice. *Krútňava* is considered one of the most successful Czech operas in the post-Janáček era.

Kubelík, Jan, famous Czech-born Hungarian violinist, father of (Jeronym) Rafael Kubelík; b. Michle, near Prague, July 5, 1880; d. Prague, Dec. 5, 1940. He began violin training with his father, then studied with Sevcik (violin) and Foerster (composition) at the Prague Cons. (1892–98); continued his studies in Vienna, where he performed for the 1st time on Nov. 26, 1898. In 1900 he made his London debut, and thereafter made a series of triumphant tours of Europe and the U.S. He was awarded the Gold Medal of the Phil. Soc. of London in 1902. In 1903 he married a Hungarian countess and became a naturalized Hungarian citizen. He continued his active career for over 4 decades, giving a series of farewell concerts in 1939–40. In 1940, he gave his last concert in Prague, after his beloved homeland had been dismembered by the Nazis.

Kubelik was one of the foremost virtuosos of his day. He also composed; wrote 6 violin concertos, as well as a Sym. and some chamber music; likewise, he prepared cadenzas for the Beethoven, Brahms, and Tchaikovsky violin concertos.

Kubelík, (Jeronym) **Rafael,** eminent Czech-born Swiss conductor, son of Jan Kubelík; b. Býchory, near Kolín, June 29, 1914; d. Lucerne, Aug. 11, 1996. He studied violin with his father, and then continued his musical training at the Prague Cons.; he made his conducting debut with the Czech Phil. in Prague on Jan. 24, 1934, then was conductor at the National Theater in Brno (1939–41). He was chief conductor of the Czech Phil. from 1942 to 1948, one of the most difficult periods in the history of the orch. and the Czech nation. He refused to collaborate with the Nazi occupation authorities; when the Communists took control of the government in 1948, he left the country for the West, vowing not to return until the political situation changed.

He appeared as a guest conductor in England and Western Europe, then made his U.S. debut with the Chicago Sym. Orch. (1949); his success led to his appointment as the orch.'s music director in 1950; however, his inclusion of many contemporary works in his programs and his insistence on painstaking rehearsals antagonized some of his auditors, including members of the Chicago press, causing him to resign his post in 1953. He subsequently was music director at the Royal Opera House at Covent Garden in London (1955–58); his tenure was notable for important productions of *Les Troyens, Boris Godunov* (in the orig. version), and *Jenůfa.* He then was chief conductor of the Bavarian Radio Sym. Orch. in Munich (1961–79).

He made his Metropolitan Opera debut in N.Y. as its 1st music director in 1973, conducting *Les Troyens*; however, he again became an epicenter of controversy, and soon submitted his resignation. In spite of the contretemps, his artistic integrity remained intact; he continued to appear widely as a guest conductor in Western Europe and the U.S. In light of his controversial tenure in Chicago it was ironic that he became an honored guest

conductor with that orch. in later years. He retired in 1985, although he returned to Czechoslovakia in 1990 after an absence of 42 years to conduct the Czech Phil. in 2 performances of Smetana's symphonic cycle *Ma Vlast* during the opening of the Prague Spring Festival, despite his increasingly ill health.

Kubelík was the foremost Czech conductor of his generation; in addition to his idiomatic and authoritative performances of the music of his native country, he was greatly esteemed for his distinguished interpretations of the standard repertoire, which were marked by a pristine musicianship, unfettered by self-indulgence. Kubelík became a Swiss citizen in 1966. His 2nd wife was the Australian soprano Elsie Morison. He also composed several operas, including *Veronika* (Brno, 1947) and *Cornelia Faroli* (Augsburg, 1972); a number of orch.l and choral works; 6 string quartets and other chamber music works; and songs.

Kuhglocke (*Kuhhorn, Kuhreigen*; Ger.). RANZ DES VACHES.

kujawiak. A Polish dance from the Kujawiak region in the rhythm of a MAZURKA, but at a faster tempo.

kulintang. Gong-chime of the Phillippines, consisting of between 8 and 12 bossed gongs placed open-face down in 2 rows suspended and isolated by taut strings; played with a pair of padded sticks. Similar instruments are found in Malaysia and many parts of Indonesia; it is a constituent of the GAMELAN.

kultrún (*cultrún*). Rattle drum of the Araucano people of Chile, with a wooden platter or calabash body, attached to a horseskin head, holding pebbles, and played by a drumstick.

Kulturboschewismus. Cultural bolshevism; a term used by Nazi officials to condemn music, particularly that of the 2nd Viennese school, Stravinsky, and Jewish composers, as artistically radical and thus socially and politically suspect. Another, more general ideological Nazi term for the music was *entartete Musik* (degenerate music).

Kunc, Božidar. See MILANOV, ZINKA.

kurz (Ger.). Short. *Kurz und bestimmt,* short and with determination.

Kussevitsky, Serge (Alexandrovich). KOUSSEVITZKY, SERGE (ALEXANDROVICH).

kymbala (Grk.). Ancient cymbals, either plate-like or bulbous in shape; when struck together they produce a dull percussive sound. Greek writers compared their sound with galloping horse hooves. Not the same as *antique cymbals* (CROTALES).

Kyrie (Grk., Lord). The 1st section of the Ordinary in the Roman Catholic Mass; it is sung after the introit. The brief text is divided into three sentences, with repetitions: *Kyrie eleison* (Lord, have mercy), *Christe eleison* (Christ, have mercy), and *Kyrie eleison.*

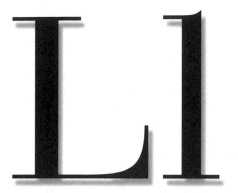

L

L. (Ger., *links*). Left, as in *l.h.*, left hand.

La. 1. The 6th note of Guido d'Arezzo's hexachord, corresponding to the last line of the Hymn to St. John, "Labii reatum." *La* is still used to designate the 6th diatonic degree of the scale in Romance languages and in Russian; it is also used in the system of MOVABLE DO, where it is also called *Lah.* 2. (It., Fr., singular) The.

La Bamba. Latin American folk song popularized by Richie Valens in 1959 and again in the biopic made about his life in 1987 (performed by the Mexican-American band Los Lobos).

La Barbara, Joan (Linda Lotz), American composer and outstanding experimental vocalist; b. Philadelphia, June 8, 1947. She learned piano from her grandfather; later sang in church and school choirs and joined a folk music group. She studied voice with Helen Boatwright at the Syracuse Univ. School of Music (1965–68) and music education at N.Y. Univ. (B.S., 1970); also studied voice with Phyllis Curtin at the Berkshire Music Center at Tanglewood (1967–68) and with Marion Szekely-Freschl at the Juilliard School in N.Y. In 1971 she made her debut as a vocalist at N.Y.'s Town Hall with Steve Reich and Musicians, with whom she continued to perform until 1974; also worked with Philip Glass (1973–76). She toured in the U.S. and Europe; in 1979 she was composer-in-residence in West Berlin under the aegis of the Deutscher Akademischer Austauschdienst; taught voice and composition at the Calif. Inst. of the Arts in Valencia (from 1981). In 1979 she married the composer Morton Subotnick. A champion of contemporary music, she developed her performing talents to a high degree; her vocal techniques include multiphonics and circular breathing, with unique throat clicks and a high flutter to match. Her compositions effectively exploit her vocal abilities.

La cadenza sia corta (It.). Let the cadenza be short.

La Guerre, Élisabeth Jacquet de. Jacquet de La Guerre, Elisabeth.

La-La-Lucille. Musical by Gershwin, 1919. A puritanical matron wills her considerable fortune to her nephew on the condition that he divorce his wife, a chorus girl. He decides to comply with the terms, divorce his wife, get the legacy, and then remarry her. A Philadelphia hotel employee named Lucille arranges for him to be surprised in the company of a woman not his wife, a mandatory contrivance to obtain a divorce on grounds of adultery. He registers at the hotel as John Smith, only to discover that there are 38 other John Smiths registered in the hotel, providing the mistaken identities necessary for some visceral laughs. The 1st musical entirely composed by Gershwin, it features the song *Nobody But You.*

Labèque, Katia (b. Hendaye, Mar. 3, 1950), **and Marielle Labèque** (b. Hendaye, Mar. 6, 1952), French duo-pianists. The sisters began to study piano in early childhood with their mother, a pupil of the great French pianist Marguerite Long (1874–1966), making their formal debut in Bayonne in 1961. After completing their studies with Jean-Bernard Pommier at the Paris Cons., they were awarded 1st prize at their graduation in 1968. They subsequently embarked upon a remarkable career as duo-pianists, touring widely in Europe, North America, the Middle East, and the Far East. In addition to giving numerous recitals, they also appeared with the leading orchs. of the world. Their repertoire is catholic, ranging from the masterworks of the past to contemporary scores by Messiaen, Boulez, Berio, and others; they play popular works as well, from Scott Joplin to Gershwin; they championed the latter's duo-piano versions of *Rhapsody in Blue*, *Concerto in F*, and *An American in Paris*.

Lacrimosa (Lat.). A part of the Requiem Mass. *Lacrimoso*, tearfully.

Lady, Be Good! Musical by Gershwin, 1924. A brother-and-sister dance team (orig. played by Adele and Fred Astaire) encounter an heiress who falls in love with the brother; he feels he cannot return her affection. After several imbroglios, the dénoument is optimistic. One of Gershwin's best-known songs, *The Man I Love*, was dropped from the show just before its N.Y. opening (it resurfaced in *Strike Up the Band*, 1927). The song *Fascinating Rhythm*, which survived the cuts, remains a rare example of polymeter in American popular song: the accompaniment presents a steady 4/4, while the vocal line shifts between 4/4 and 3/4, giving the impression of an upbeat to an upbeat.

Lady in the Dark. Musical by Weill and I. Gershwin, 1941. The eponymous character is the editor of a woman's magazine who undergoes a strenuous program of psychoanalysis; this gives a clue to 3 extended dream episodes as she recounts them to the analyst. The dreams plainly indicate that she should marry the magazine's managing editor, and so she does. Includes *Tchaikowsky*, a tongue-twisting tour de force for the comedian Danny Kaye, who must recite the names of 50 Russian composers, *prestissimo*.

Lady Is a Tramp, The. Song by Rodgers and Hart, 1937, from the musical *Babes in Arms*; later interpolated in the 1957 film of their musical, *Pal Joey*.

Lady Macbeth of the Mtzensk District (Katerina Izmailova). Opera by Shostakovich, 1934, 1st performed in Leningrad. The story depicts adultery and murder in Russia in the middle of the 19th century. The title is hardly justified, since the protagonist conspires with her lover to murder her husband, not her husband's potential rival as in Shakespeare's tragedy. The culprits are convicted and sent to Siberia. When he takes another mistress there, she kills her rival and then commits suicide. The music attains a maximum of realism, including a suggestive sliding trombone passage illustrating the act of adultery itself. Unexpectedly, *Pravda*, the official organ of the Soviet Communist Party,

attacked the opera as a product of bourgeois decadence and damned it for its cacophonous modernity. Shostakovich apologized abjectly for his musical sins and stopped writing operas for a number of years. The opera was eventually revived in a sanitized version under the title *Katerina Izmailova*, 1963, after the name of the heroine.

Lage (Ger.). 1. Position (of a chord). 2. Left-hand playing position on violin family instruments, moving up and down on the fingerboard. *Enge Lage*, close position or harmony. *Weite Lage*, open position or harmony.

lagrimoso (It., tearfully). Plaintively, like a lament.

Lah. In TONIC SOL-FA, the equivalent of La.

lai (Fr., lay). Chansons of the French trouvères and late medieval composers. Like most French song forms of the period, the texts are strophic; in the case of the lai there are nearly as many poetic (and thus musical) forms as there are examples. The lai could also be a poem without music; Machaut wrote several of both types. The term *lai* may refer to 1 of several related genres: *descort*, *Leich*, *estampie*, *ductia*, *ensalada*, and even the liturgical SEQUENCE (and related portions).

Lakmé. Opera by Delibes, 1883, 1st performed in Paris. Lakmé, the daughter of a priest of Brahma, is loved by a British officer. He inadvertently profanes the Buddhist temple by entering it with his shoes on, and is denounced by the priest. In the end Lakmé realizes the futility of her love, plucks a poisonous flower, and dies. The score is permeated with attractive pseudo-oriental melodies and rhythms. Lakmé's *Bell Song* is a perennial favorite with COLORATURA sopranos.

Lalo, Édouard (-Victoire-Antoine), distinguished French composer of Spanish descent, father of Pierre Lalo; b. Lille, Jan. 27, 1823; d. Paris, Apr. 22, 1892. He studied violin and cello at the Lille Cons.; after his father objected to his pursuing a career as a professional musician, he left home at age 16 to study violin with Habeneck at the Paris Cons.; he also studied composition privately with Schulhoff and Crevecoeur. He then made a precarious living as a violinist and teacher; also began to compose, producing some songs and chamber music between 1848 and 1860. In the meantime he became a founding member of the Armingaud Quartet (1855), serving 1st as a violist and subsequently as 2nd violinist. Since his own works met with indifference, he was discouraged to the point of abandoning composition after 1860. However, his 1865 marriage to the contralto Bernier de Maligny, who sang many of his songs, prompted him to resume composition.

He wrote an opera, *Fiesque*, and sent it to a competition sponsored by the Théâtre-Lyrique in Paris in 1867. It was refused a production, a rebuke that left him deeply embittered. He was so convinced of the intrinsic worth of the score that he subsequently reworked parts of it into various other works, including the 1st *Aubade* for Small Orch., the *Divertissement*, and the Sym. in G Minor. Indeed, the *Divertissement* proved a remarkable success when it was introduced at the Concert Populaire (1872). Sarasate then gave the premiere performance of his Violin Concerto (1874), and subsequently of his *Symphonie espagnole* for Violin and Orch. (1875). The latter work, a brilliant virtuoso piece with vibrant Spanish rhythms, brought Lalo international fame. It remains his best-known composition outside his native country.

While continuing to produce orch.l works, he had not given up his intention to write for the stage. In 1875 he began work on the opera *Le Roi d'Ys*. The major portion of the score was finished by 1881, which allowed extracts to be performed in concerts. However, no theater was interested in mounting a production. While pursuing his work on several orch.l pieces, he accepted a commission from the Opéra to write a ballet. Although the resulting work, *Namouna* (1882), failed to make an impression, he drew a series of orch.l suites from it that became quite popular. He finally succeeded in persuading the Paris Opéra-Comique to produce *Le Roi d'Ys*. Its premiere in 1888 was an enormous success. Lalo was rewarded by being made an Officer of the Legion of Honor (1888).

While *Le Roi d'Ys* is considered his masterpiece by his countrymen, his instrumental music is of particular importance in assessing his achievement as a composer. His craftsmanship, combined with his originality, places him among the most important French composers of his time.

Lamb, Joseph F(rancis), remarkable American ragtime pianist and composer; b. Montclair, N.J., Dec. 6, 1887; d. N.Y., Sept. 3, 1960. Although he had no formal musical training and spent most of his life in the textile import business, he was one of the most important composers of piano rags during the heyday of ragtime; also wrote a number of songs for Tin Pan Alley. After almost 30 years he was rediscovered in 1949 and began composing rags again; also appeared as a ragtime pianist. His most notable piano rags

were *Sensation* (1908), *Ethiopia Rag* (1909), *Excelsior Rag* (1909), *Champagne Rag* (1910), *American Beauty Rag* (1913), *Cleopatra Rag* (1915), *Contentment Rag* (1915), *The Ragtime Nightingale* (1915), *Reindeer* (1915), *Patricia Rag* (1916), *Top Liner Rag* (1916), and *Bohemia Rag* (1919). An anthology of his works appeared in N.Y. in 1964.

Lambert, (Leonard) **Constant,** remarkable English conductor, composer, and writer on music; b. London, Aug. 23, 1905; d. there, Aug. 21, 1951. He won a scholarship to the Royal College of Music in London, where he studied with R. O. Morris and Vaughan Williams (1915–22). His 1st major score, the ballet *Romeo and Juliet* (Monte Carlo, May 4, 1926), was commissioned by Diaghilev. This early association with the dance proved decisive, for he spent most of his life as a conductor and composer of ballets. His interest in jazz resulted in such fine scores as *Elegiac Blues* for Orch. (1927), *The Rio Grande* for Piano, Chorus, and Orch. (1927; to a text by S. Sitwell), and the Concerto for Piano and 9 Performers (1930–31). Of his many ballets, the most striking in craftsmanship was his *Horoscope* (1937). In the meantime he became conductor of the Camargo Soc. for the presentation of ballet productions (1930).

He was made music director of the Vic-Wells Ballet (1931), and remained in that capacity after it became the Sadler's Wells Ballet and the Royal Ballet, until resigning in 1947; he then was made 1 of its artistic directors (1948), and subsequently conducted it on its 1st visit to the U.S. (1949). He also appeared at London's Covent Garden (1937; 1939; 1946–47); was associate conductor of the London Promenade Concerts (1945–46), and frequently conducted broadcast performances over the BBC. He contributed articles on music to *The Nation* and *Athenaeum* (from 1930) and to the *Sunday Referee* (from 1931). He also penned the provocative book *Music Ho! A Study of Music in Decline* (1934). Lambert was one of the most gifted musicians of his generation. However, his demanding work as a conductor and his excessive consumption of alcohol prevented him from fully asserting himself as a composer in his later years.

Lambert, Michel. See LULLY, JEAN-BAPTISTE.

lamellaphones. A class of handheld musical instruments indigenous to sub-Saharan Africa whose sound is produced by the vibration of thin tongues of metal or wood plucked by the thumbs; the tongues are attached to a rectangular wooden or metal resonator. Among the best known lamellaphones are the sanza (sansa), mbira, likembe, and kalimba; also called thumb pianos.

lament. This is a generic term for dirges chanted upon the death of an important person or a beloved friend. Extant specimens of such laments date back to the death of Charlemagne in 814. In France the laments bore the names of *déploration*, *plainte*, and TOMBEAU. Thus Ockeghem wrote a lament on the death of Binchois and was in turn musically lamented by Josquin, who was upon his own death eulogized by Gombert. Couperin le Grand wrote an apotheosis for Lully, but he himself had to wait for nearly 2 centuries to be musically commemorated with comparable grandeur by Ravel in his *Le Tombeau de Couperin*. Other types of laments are the DIRGE, ELEGY, and THRENODY.

Apart from composed laments, there exists a culture of ethnic cries, sobs, wails, and outcries among the rural populations in Slavic countries. Professional women lamenters were engaged who actually shed copious tears at funerals, at military conscriptions bemoaning a young man's mobilization, and at peasant weddings when the fate of a youthful bride was deplored with great ululations. A remarkable example of such a wedding *déploration* is found in Stravinsky's wedding cantata *Les Noces*, with its agonized anticipation of the bride's loss of virginity, contrasted with an antiphonal exchange of gross comments among the male guests as to how much they would pay in rubles, individually and collectively, to "swell the belly" of the innocent bride.

lamento (It., lamentation, complaint). A common regular type of aria in Italian opera in which a character expresses unquenchable sorrow and complains about his or her misery. *Lamento d'Arianna*, the only surviving segment from Monteverdi's opera *Arianna*, written in 1608, is an outstanding example of such an aria. In it, Ariadne laments her painful abandonment by the treacherous Theseus.

lamentoso (It.). Lamentingly, plaintively, mournfully.

Landini cadence (Burgundian cadence). A cadence in which the melodic leading tone is diverted to the submediant before resolving to the tonic (7–6–8). It is said to be named after Francesco Landini, whose extensive use of it made it characteristic of the later Middle Ages. Its survival into the 15th century (Dufay, Binchois) led to more melismatic treatment of the resolution. In works *à* 2, the lower voice held the supertonic while the upper voice sounded the 7–6, then resolved downward to form an octave. Works *à* 3

added a middle resolution of the subdominant upward to the dominant. The most characteristic (and controversial) form of this resolution is the DOUBLE LEADING-TONE CADENCE. Some hear a momentary impression of a PLAGAL CADENCE with the Landini type.

Landini, Francesco (Franciscus Landino, Magister Franciscus de Florentia, Francesco degli orghany, Magister Franciscus Cecus Horghanista de Florentia, Cechus de Florentia), important Italian composer; b. probably in Florence, *c.* 1325; d. there, Sept. 2, 1397. His father was the painter Jacopo Del Casentino (d. 1349), cofounder of Florence's guild of painters (1339). After being blinded by smallpox as a child, Francesco turned to music; he learned to play the organ and other instruments and also sang. He became well known as an organist, organ builder, organ tuner, and instrument maker; was also active as a poet. He was organist at the monastery of S. Trinita (1361); was *cappellanus* at the church of S. Lorenzo from 1365 until his death. His output is particularly significant, for it represents about a quarter of extant Italian 14th-century music. Some 154 works have been identified as his; these include 90 *ballate* for 2 voices, 42 for 3 voices, and 8 in both 2- and 3-part versions; 9 *madrigali* (of the Trecento, not Renaissance type) for 2 or 3 voices; 1 French virelai; and 1 caccia; many of the works set to his own texts, although the extent of this practice is unknown.

Ländler (Ger.; Fr. *Tyrolienne*). A slow folk dance of the German-speaking areas of Europe in 3/4 or 6/4 time, a precursor of the more urbane 19th-century waltz. The Ländler dates from the 17th century and has been known under numerous names, including the German dances (DEUTSCHER TANZ) written by Haydn and Mozart and intended for courtly dancers; in its orig. form it was an outdoor dance, with hopping, stamping, and passing under while the couple holds each other by the waist; songs associated with this music might include yodeling. The Ländler survived into the 19th century, but it evolved into a faster, more refined, and lighter dance. By the early 20th century the music of the Ländler held great nostalgic value for Austrian composers such as Mahler and Berg.

Landowska, Wanda (Alexandra), celebrated Polish-born French harpsichordist, pianist, and pedagogue.; b. Warsaw, July 5, 1879; d. Lakeville, Conn., Aug. 16, 1959. She studied piano at the Warsaw Cons. with Michalowski and in Berlin with Moszkowski. In 1900 she went to Paris, where she married Henry Lew, a writer. She traveled widely in Europe as a pianist, and as a harpsichordist from 1903; in 1909 she made a tour of Russia, and played for Tolstoy, who showed great interest in her ideas on classical music. Subsequently she devoted her efforts principally to reviving the art of playing upon the harpsichord. In 1912 she commissioned the Pleyel firm of Paris to construct a harpsichord for her; this was the 1st of the many keyboard instruments built for her in subsequent years. In 1913 she was invited by Kretzschmar to give a special course in harpsichord playing at the Berlin Hochschule für Musik.

The outbreak of World War I in 1914 found her in Germany, and she was interned there until the Armistice; in 1918 her husband was killed in an automobile accident in Berlin. In 1919 she gave master classes in harpsichord playing at the Basel Cons.; then returned to Paris. In 1925 she bought a villa in St.-Leu-la-Forêt, near Paris, and established there a school for the study of early music. A concert hall was built there in 1927; she presented regular concerts of early music, and gave lessons on the subject; also assembled a large collection of harpsichords. Her school attracted students from all over the world; she also taught at the Fontainebleau Cons., and frequently appeared at concerts in Paris, as both a pianist and as a harpsichordist. She commissioned de Falla to compose a chamber concerto, and she played the solo part in its 1st performance in Barcelona (1926); another commission was Poulenc's *Concert champêtre* for Harpsichord and Small Orch. (1929). She appeared for the 1st time in America as soloist with the Philadelphia Orch., under Stokowski (1923); then returned to France. When the Germans invaded France in 1940, Landowska fled to Switzerland, abandoning her villa, her library, and her instruments. In 1941 she reached N.Y.; she presented a concert of harpsichord music there in 1942, then devoted herself mainly to teaching; also made recordings; settled in her new home at Lakeville, Conn.

She was acknowledged as one of the greatest performers on the harpsichord; her interpretations of Baroque music were notable in their balance between Classical precision and freedom from rigidity, particularly in the treatment of ornamentation. If there is a consistent criticism against her, it is directed at the instruments Pleyel built

Wanda Landowska

COURTESY FRANK DRIGGS COLLECTION

for her, beginning in 1912; designed to counter criticism that harpsichord tone was "feeble," these instruments had pianolike dimensions and heavy 2-manual registrations; this naturally affected the timbral aspect of her playing. She wrote several books on music, along with cadenzas for Mozart's concertos.

Lane, Burton (born Morris Hyman Kushner), American composer of popular music; b. N.Y., Feb. 2, 1912. He studied with Simon Bucharoff; after writing for revues, he began to compose Broadway musicals: *Hold On to Your Hats* (1940); *Laffing Room Only* (1944); *Finian's Rainbow* (including *Something Sort of Grandish, Old Devil Moon, How Are Things in Glocca Morra?*); *On a Clear Day You Can See Forever* (1965); and *Carmelina* (1979). He has written for some 40 films, including *St. Louis Blues, Babes on Broadway* (including *How About You?*), *Ship Ahoy*, and *Royal Wedding* (including *Too Late Now*). Among the lyricists who worked with him were Ira Gershwin, Frank Loesser, E. Y. Harburg, and Alan Jay Lerner.

Langridge, Philip (Gordon), esteemed English tenor; b. Hawkhurst, Kent, Dec. 16, 1939. He studied violin at the Royal Academy of Music in London; took voice lessons with Bruce Boyce and Celia Bizony; was active as a violinist but also began to make appearances as a singer from 1962. He 1st sang at the Glyndebourne Festival in 1964, and made regular appearances there from 1977; also sang at the Edinburgh Festivals from 1970. He appeared at Milan's La Scala in 1979; then sang for the 1st time at London's Covent Garden as the Fisherman in Stravinsky's *The Nightingale* in 1983. He made his Metropolitan Opera debut in N.Y. as Ferrando in *Così fan tutte* on Jan. 5, 1985. He was chosen to create the role of Orpheus in Birtwistle's opera *The Mask of Orpheus* at London's English National Opera (1986). Admired as both an operatic and a concert singer, he maintains an extensive repertoire ranging from the Baroque masters to contemporary works. He is married to the singer Ann Murray.

langsam (Ger.). Slow. *Langsamer,* slower.

languendo (*con languore*; It.). Languishing, plaintively, languid.

Lanner, Joseph (Franz Karl), historically significant Austrian violinist, conductor, and composer, father of August (Joseph) Lanner; b. Vienna, Apr. 12, 1801; d. Oberdöbling, near Vienna, Apr. 14, 1843. A self-taught violinist and composer, he joined Pamer's dance orch. when he was 12. In 1818 he formed a trio; Johann Strauss, Sr., joined it in 1819, making it a quartet. The group grew in size, and by 1824 it was a full-sized classical orch. that became famous and performed in coffeehouses, taverns, at balls, etc. The orch. was subsequently divided into 2 ensembles, with Lanner leading one and Strauss the other. Strauss went his own way in 1825. With Strauss, Lanner is acknowledged as the creator of the 19th-century Viennese waltz. Lanner's output totals 209 popular pieces, including 112 waltzes, 25 Ländler, 10 quadrilles, 3 polkas, 28 galops, and 6 marches; overture to the fairy tale *Der Preis einer Lebensstunde*; *Banquet-Polonaise*; *Tarantella*; and *Bolero*. His son August (Joseph) Lanner (b. Vienna, Jan. 23, 1834; d. there, Sept. 27, 1855) was a talented violinist, dance composer, and conductor; he died in his 22nd year.

Lanza, Mario (born Alfredo Arnold Cocozza), American tenor and actor; b. Philadelphia, Jan. 31, 1921; d. Rome, Oct. 7, 1959. He studied singing with Enrico Rosati; appeared in recitals and opera. In 1951 he starred in the title role of a highly successful film, *The Great Caruso*; also appeared in 6 other films, including *The Toast of New Orleans*, in which he sang his most popular song, *Be My Love*. His career quickly unraveled shortly thereafter as obesity overtook him, which led to his early death.

larga (*maxima*; Lat., large). In mensural notation, the longest durational symbol, exceeding even the LONGA. Its symbol is a very long rectangular bar with a downward flag attached to its right side. The larga is either twice or thrice the length of a longa, depending on the mensural context (binary or ternary).

largamente (It., broadly). With a vigorous and sustained tone and general breadth of style, without change of tempo.

largando (It., growing broader). Get slower and more marked; generally a CRESCENDO is implied.

larghetto (It.). Diminutive of LARGO, demanding a more rapid tempo, nearly ANDANTINO.

largo (It., broad). A very slow and stately tempo, with ample breadth of style. *Largo assai, largo di molto, molto largo,*

Mario Lanza, 1951

larghissimo, very slowly and broadly; *poco largo*, with some breadth; may occur even during an ALLEGRO.

Lark Ascending, The. Work for violin and orch. by Vaughan Williams, 1921, 1st performed in London; inspired by the George Meredith poem.

Lark Quartet (Hornpipe Quartet; Ger. *Lerchenquartett*). String Quartet, No. 5, op. 64, in D major by Haydn (1790–92). The opening tune in the high violin can be construed as imitative of a lark song.

larmoyant (Fr.; It. *lacrimoso*). Tearfully.

Larrocha (y de la Calle), **Alicia de,** brilliant Spanish pianist; b. Barcelona, May 23, 1923. She studied piano with Frank Marshall and theory with Ricardo Lamote de Grignon. She made her 1st public appearance at the age of 5; was soloist with the Orquesta Sinfónica of Madrid at the age of 11. In 1940 she launched her career in earnest; she began making major tours of Europe in 1947; made her 1st visit to the U.S.

in 1955 and thereafter toured throughout the world to great acclaim. She served as director of the Marshall Academy in Barcelona from 1959. Her interpretations of Spanish music have evoked universal admiration for their authentic quality, but she has also been exuberantly praised by sober-minded critics for her impeccable taste and exquisitely polished technique in classical works, particularly Mozart.

lascivious mode. IONIAN MODE.

Lasso, Orlando di, great Franco-Flemish composer, known in Latin as Orlandus Lassus and in French as Roland de Lassus; b. Mons, 1532; d. Munich, June 14, 1594. He entered the service of Ferrante Gonzaga when he was about 12 years old and subsequently traveled with him; was placed in the service of Constantino Castrioto of Naples at the age of 18. He later proceeded to Rome and entered the service of Antonio Altoviti, the Archbishop of Florence; then was maestro di cappella at St. John Lateran (1553–54). He went to Antwerp (1555), where he enjoyed a fine reputation both socially and artistically; his 1st works were publ. that year in Venice, containing 22 madrigals set to poems of Petrarch; also that year he brought out a collection of madrigals and motets set to texts in Italian, French, and Latin in Antwerp.

In 1556 he became a singer at the Munich court chapel of Duke Albrecht of Bavaria. He took Regina Wechinger (Wackinger), an aristocratic woman, in marriage in 1558. In 1563 he was made maestro di cappella of the Munich court chapel, a position he held with great eminence until his death. He made occasional trips, including to Flanders to recruit singers (1560), to Frankfurt for the coronation of Emperor Maximilian II (1562), to Italy (1567), to the French court (1571; 1573–74), again to Italy (1574–79), and to Regensburg (1593). In 1570 he received from the Emperor Maximilian a hereditary rank of nobility.

Lasso represents the culmination of the great era of Franco-Flemish polyphony; his superlative mastery in sacred as well as secular music renders him one of the most versatile composers of his time; he was equally capable of writing in the most elevated style and in the popular idiom; his art was supranational; he wrote Italian madrigals, German lieder, French chansons, and Latin motets. Musicians of his time described him variously as the "Belgian Orpheus" and the "Prince of Music."

The sheer scope of his production is amazing: more than 2,000 works in various genres. The *Patrocinium Musices* (12 vols., Munich, 1573–98) contains 7 vols. of Lasso's works: I,

21 motets; II, 5 Masses; III, Offices; IV, a Passion, vigils, etc.; V–VI, 23 Magnificats; 13 Magnificats; VII, 6 Masses. There are far more examples of these genres in his output. Other important collections publ. during his lifetime include books of: madrigals; part chansons; deutscher Lieder; *sacrae cantiones*; *Psalms of David* (1584); after his death, collections publ. include the *Lagrime di S Pietro* (1595) and *Prophetiae Sibyllarum* (1600). Lasso's sons publ. 516 of his motets under the title *Magnum opus musicum* (1604). Eitner publ. *Chronologisches Verzeichnis der Druckwerke des Orlando di Lassus* (Berlin, 1874). W. Boetticher publ. a complete catalogue of his works (Berlin, 1956).

lassú (Hung.). The opening slow section of the CSÁRDÁS or VERBUNKOS.

Last Savage, The (*Le dernier sauvage*). Opera buffa by Menotti, 1963, to his own libretto; orig. in Italian, it was 1st performed in French at the Paris Opéra-Comique. It is plotted along familiar Menotti lines. An eccentric Chicago millionairess goes to India in quest of the Abominable Snowman. Scheming individuals produce a tall human whom they declare to be the Snowman. Delighted, the heiress imports him to America, but he is appalled by modern life and abominates the snows of Chicago. When he hears a concert of dodecaphonic music, he decides to quit, and goes back to the Himalayas.

Last Time I Saw Paris, The. Ballad by Kern, 1940, a lament on the fate of the city under Nazi occupation; it was sung by Kate Smith. The song was interpolated in the film *Lady Be Good* (1941).

Latin American Symphonette. Orch.l suite by M. Gould, 1941; each of its 4 movements are inspired by Latin American dances.

lauda (It.; plural *laude, laudi*). Hymn of praise. These hymns were particularly popular with itinerant monastic orders, the penitents as well as the flagellants. Because of the peripatetic character of these orders, laude became overgrown with unrelated dance forms, such as the frottola and ballata, without however losing its basic religious characteristics. The laude influenced the development of the oratorio in the early 17th century.

Laudamus te (Lat., We praise Thee). Part of the Gloria of the Mass.

laudi spirituali (Lat.). Medieval songs of devotion.

Lauds (Lat. *laudes*, thanksgiving). Orig., the 2nd Canonical Hour (at dawn, after Matins); it is now the 1st of the Roman Catholic daily prayers. It usually comprises the psalms *Laudate Dominum*, *Cantate Domino Canticum novum*, and *Laudate Dominum in sanctis ejus.*

Lauf (Ger., run). Rapid passage in running scales.

launeddas. Sardinian triple pipe, each with a single reed and constructed divergently. The 2 melodic pipes are on the outside, the drone in the center; the right pipe is shorter than the left; all 3 are mouthed. The instrument may be of Phoenician origin.

launig (Ger.). 1. With light, gay humor. 2. With facile, characteristic expression.

Laura. Song by D. Raksin, 1944, originally wordless; it served as the theme song for an eponymous film. The emotional inspiration for Raksin was a farewell letter from a woman (not named Laura). Johnny Mercer's words were added later; in this form it sold millions of disks. The song is special in having been liked by 2 great songwriters, Porter and Berlin, who rarely liked anything by anyone but themselves. *Laura*'s melody is unusual in that it traverses chromatic steps suggesting a consanguinity with Wagner's *Tristan* motif.

Laute (Ger.). Lute.

Lavignac, (Alexandre Jean) **Albert,** eminent French musicologist and pedagogue; b. Paris, Jan. 21, 1846; d. there, May 28, 1916. He studied at the Paris Cons. with Marmontel (piano), Bazin and Benoist (harmony), and A. Thomas (composition); won several prizes (1857–65); was appointed assistant prof. of solfège (1871), prof. of solfège (1875), and then prof. of harmony (1891) there. His *Cours complet théorique et pratique de dictée musicale* (6 vols., Paris and Brussels, 1882) attracted considerable attention and led to the introduction of musical dictation as a regular subject in all the important European cons.; it was followed by several educational texts. His magnum opus was the famous *Encyclopédie de la musique et Dictionnaire du Conservatoire* (Paris, 3 vols., 1920–31), which he ed. from 1913 until his death. He also wrote *La Musique et les musiciens* (Paris, 1895); *Le Voyage artistique à Bayreuth* (Paris, 1897); *Les*

Gaités du Conservatoire (Paris, 1900); and *Notions scolaires de musique* (Paris and Brussels, 1905).

lavolta. Volta.

Law, Andrew, American singing teacher and composer; b. Milford, Conn., Mar. 21, 1749; d. Cheshire, Conn., July 13, 1821. He graduated from Rhode Island College, receiving his M.A. in 1778; then studied theology and was ordained in Hartford (1787); subsequently he was active as a preacher in Philadelphia and Baltimore, later as a pioneer singing teacher in New England. He invented a new system of notation, patented in 1802, which employed 4 (later increased to 7) different shapes of notes without the staff; it was not successful and was used in only a few of his own books. A 2nd innovation (at least as far as American usages were concerned) was his setting of the melody in the soprano instead of in the tenor. In 1786 he received an honorary M.A. degree from Yale Univ.; in 1821, an LL.D. from Allegheny College in Meadville, Pa. He compiled and/or wrote several collections of hymns and instructional books on music. Only 1 of his hymn tunes, *Archdale*, acquired some popularity; but his teaching books, quaintly but clearly written, contributed considerably to early music education in America.

Laws, Hubert, African-American flutist; b. Houston, Nov. 10, 1939. He learned to play saxophone, piano, and guitar as well as flute; played saxophone with the Jazz Crusaders (1954–60) while pursuing classical music studies; played with the N.Y. Jazz Sextet (from 1967); was a member of other groups before joining the Metropolitan Opera Orch. in N.Y. as a flutist. He also appeared as a soloist with the N.Y. Phil.; continued to appear in jazz settings. Among his recordings are *Crying Song* (1969), *Afro-Classic* (1971), *At Carnegie Hall* (1973), *How to Beat the High Cost of Living* (1980), and *Storm Then the Calm* (1994). His brother Ronnie Laws (b. Houston, Oct. 3, 1950) is a tenor saxophonist and leader. After 1971, he performed with Quincy Jones, Hugh Masekela, Kenny Burrell, Ramsey Lewis, the band Earth, Wind and Fire, and his brother. As a bandleader he is best known for *Pressure Sensitive* (1984).

le (It., Fr.). The.

Le Caine, Hugh, Canadian, physicist, acoustician, and innovative creator of prototypical electronic musical instruments; b. Port Arthur, Ontario, May 27, 1914; d. Ottawa, July 3, 1977, of a stroke suffered 364 days after a motorcycle accident en route to Montreal. Although his childhood training combined music and science, he chose to emphasize science in his formal studies; he received a B.S. degree from Queen's Univ. in Kingston, Ontario, in 1938 and an M.S. in 1939, and obtained his Ph.D. in nuclear physics from the Univ. of Birmingham in 1952; he also studied piano briefly at the Royal Cons. of Music of Toronto and privately with Viggo Kihl.

His childhood dream was to one day apply scientific techniques to the development and invention of new musical instruments, and he went on to develop groundbreaking electronic musical instruments which ultimately formed the basis of pioneering electronic music studios at the Univ. of Toronto (1959) and McGill Univ. in Montreal (1964). He exhibited electronic-music instruments at Expo '67 in Montreal and contributed numerous articles on his findings in various scholarly journals.

While he saw himself as a designer of instruments that assisted others in creative work, he himself realized a number of striking electronic compositions in the course of his development, among them the now-classic *Dripsody* (1959), which used only the sound of a single drop of water falling; other compositions were *Alchemy* (1964) and *Perpetual Motion for Data Systems Computer* (1970). His instruments revolutionized musical composition; his Sackbut synthesizer (1945–48; 1954–60; 1969–73) is today recognized as the 1st voltage-controlled synthesizer; among his other instruments are the Spectrogram (1959–62; designed to facilitate the use of complex sine tones in composition), the Alleatone (*c.* 1962; "a controlled chance device selecting one of 16 channels with weighted probabilities"), Sonde (1968–70; which can generate 200 sine waves simultaneously), and Polyphone (1970; a polyphonic synthesizer operated by a keyboard with touch-sensitive keys).

lead. 1. The giving-out or proposition of a theme by one part. 2. A cue.

lead guitar. GUITAR, LEAD.

lead sheet. A modern form of tablature that includes the melody (on a staff) and its harmony marked in shorthand (e.g., C_7 or G min) above or below the melody. The 1st verse of the text may be placed below the melody line, the additional verses at the bottom of the page.

Leadbelly (Lead Belly; born Huddie Ledbetter), influential African-American folksinger, guitarist, and songwriter; b. Mooringsport, La., Jan. 21, 1885; d. N.Y., Dec. 6, 1949. He never had an education in music but possessed a genuine talent for folk-song singing. After mastering the 12-string guitar, he claimed to work as accompanist to Blind Lemon Jefferson in Dallas; however, there is evidence to suggest that the 2 may never have met. In any case, while in Texas he was jailed for murder (1918–25); served another term for attempted homicide at the La. State Penitentiary (1930–34), where he was discovered by folk researchers John and Alan Lomax, who recorded him in prison and helped obtain his release. He then settled in N.Y., where he made a series of historically significant recordings for the Library of Congress (1935–40). He served another term for assault (1939–40). He spent his last years playing in nightclubs.

A cult arose around his name after his death; the "hootenanny" movement was much influenced by his style. He adapted a turn-of-the-century popular song, *Goodnight, Irene*, into a unique personal version, but it did not become popular until after his death. Other songs associated with Leadbelly are Jefferson's *Match Box Blues*, *If It Wasn't for Dicky*, *Honey I'm All Out and Down*, *Becky Deem*, *Good Morning Blues*, *On a Monday*, *I Ain't Goin' Down to the Well No More*, and *Rock Island Line*. His career was made the subject of the film *Leadbelly* (1975). A biography of the singer by Charles Wolfe and Kip Lornell was published in 1992.

Leadbelly, 1949

leader. 1. Conductor, director. 2. (U.K.) In the orch., the 1st violin; in a band, the 1st cornet; in a mixed chorus, the 1st soprano. 3. An antecedent (DUX).

leading. 1. (*noun*) The melodic progression or conduct of any part. 2. (*adj.*) Principal, chief; guiding, directing. *Leading chord*, the dominant 7th chord; *leading melody*, principal melody or theme; *leading motive*, see LEITMOTIV; *leading note*, *leading tone*, the 7th degree of the major and harmonic minor scales.

leading tone (Ger. *Leitton*; Fr. *note sensible*; It. *nota sensibile*; Lat. *subsemitonium*). The 7th degree of the diatonic scale that—to the tonally oriented ear—urges the resolution into the tonic, a semitone upward. In minor keys the 7th degree in the natural scale is raised to provide the necessary leading tone (producing the HARMONIC MINOR SCALE). In modal writing, however, increasingly in vogue in neoclassical music, the leading tone has lost its absolute imperative.

leaning note. APPOGGIATURA.

leap. 1. In piano playing, a spring from one note or chord to another. 2. In harmony, a skip.

Lear. Opera, 1978, by Aribert Reimann (1936–), 1st performed in Munich, based on Shakespeare's *King Lear*. The lead role was created by Fischer-Dieskau; the musical style is highly atonal and expressionist.

Leave It to Me. Musical by C. Porter, 1938. A woebegone Kansas industrialist contributes a lot of money to the campaign fund of a political party in exchange for an attractive ambassadorial post, but his expectations are cruelly frustrated when he is appointed ambassador to the drab and unexciting USSR. Once in Moscow, he does everything in his power to compromise himself and be recalled, but whatever he does turns out to be politically expedient, even when he shoots a Soviet delegate to the party plenum (the victim turns out to be a pernicious Trotskyite). He finally succeeds in attaining his goal. While the political satire of the show failed, the score included a bit of whimsy, a pleasingly scabrous song *My Heart Belongs to Daddy*, which was a big hit and launched the musical-comedy career of Mary Martin.

Leben des Orest, Das. Opera by Krenek, 1930, 1st produced in Leipzig. The composer's libretto departs from the mythological story; after Elektra incites her brother to kill their adulterous mother, she is slain by an outraged mob. The musical idiom is atonal.

lebhaft (Ger.). Lively, animated. *Lebhaft, aber nicht zu sehr*, lively, but not too much.

lebhaftesten Zeitmasse, im (Ger.). In the liveliest possible tempo.

Lebhaftigkeit (Ger.). Animation. *Mit Lebhaftigkeit und durchaus mit Empfindung und Ausdruck*, with animation, and with feeling and expression throughout.

lectionary (from Lat. *legere*, read). A calendar of liturgical readings for the church year; in a secular sense, a collection of readings (from *lectio*, the act of reading) as opposed to a collection of speakings (from *dictio*, the act of speaking); hence the author's use of *lectionary* rather than *dictionary* in a 1989 publication.

Ledbetter, Hudie (Leadbelly). LEADBELLY.

ledger lines (leger lines). Extra horizontal lines placed above or below the regular staff to accommodate the notes either too high or too low in a given range. In early music, composers made use of a great number of clefs for this purpose, thus avoiding the cluttered look of too many ledger lines. In modern notation only 2 clefs, the treble and the bass, are used in piano music. When the notes rise to stratospheric altitudes, then the sign 8va⎯⎯⎯, meaning to be played an octave higher, is placed above them to reduce the number of ledger lines; when the notes sink too deeply into the infernal region below the bass staff, the sign 8ba⎯⎯⎯ or the words OCTAVE BASSA are used. For very high notes the symbol 15va⎯⎯⎯, meaning 2 octaves higher, is occasionally employed. *Ledger space*, a space bounded on either side or both sides by a ledger line.

Led Zeppelin. (Vocal: Robert Plant, b. West Bromwich, U.K., Aug. 20, 1948; guitar: Jimmy Page, b. London, Jan. 9, 1944; bass/keyboards: John Paul Jones [John Baldwin], b. Sidcup, U.K., Jan. 3, 1946; drums: John Bonham, b. Birmingham, U.K., May 31, 1947; d. Windsor, U.K., Sept. 25, 1980.) Exceptional heavy-metal group of the 1970s. Born out of the ashes of the blues-rock band the Yardbirds, the band was a massive success from their 1st album, in 1968. This was followed by an immensely successful U.S. tour, and the band's heavy-metal sound soon spread far and wide. The band enjoyed their greatest success in 1971 with the FM-radio hit *Stairway to Heaven*, still a rock favorite. The band continued to record and tour through the '70s, with a mid-decade break from fall 1975 for over a year while lead singer Plant recovered from an automobile accident. The group was already winding down when drummer Bonham died in classic rock 'n' roll style from inhaling his own vomit following heavy debauchery; this quickly led to the group's formal dissolution. The group reunited twice in the '80s for the mega Live Aid concert and again for Atlantic Records' 40th anniversary party; in 1995 Page and Plant reunited for an *MTV Unledded* show, which lead to a follow-up tour. A year later the group was inducted into the Rock and Roll Hall of Fame.

Lee, Peggy (born Norma Dolores Egstrom), popular American singer, songwriter, and actress; b. Jamestown, N.Dak., May 26, 1920. After graduating from high school she sang on a radio station in Fargo; in 1941 Benny Goodman chose her as vocalist with his band; her 1st success was *Why Don't You Do Right?* She soon launched a solo career; with her 1st husband, Dave Barbour, she collaborated on writing such hits as *Mañana, Golden Earrings,* and *I Don't Know Enough About You,* which she interpreted with great acumen; she was equally successful with her sophisticated renditions of *Lover, Fever,* and particularly *Is That All There Is?,* which became her theme song. With the composer Paul Horner and the playwright William Luce she wrote the autobiographical musical *Peg* (1983).

left-hand music. The Austrian pianist Paul Wittgenstein (1887–1961) lost his right arm fighting on the Eastern Front during the preposterous war of 1914–18, was taken prisoner by the Russians, spent a year in Omsk, Siberia, and was repatriated to Austria in 1915 as representing no danger to Imperial Russia. Being of a philosophical bent of mind (his brother was the analytical logician Ludwig Wittgenstein), he developed a startling virtuosity with his left hand and, taking advantage of his family wealth, commissioned a number of important, and some unimportant, composers—among them Ravel, R. Strauss, Prokofiev, Korngold, Britten, and F. Schmidt—to write for him concertos for piano lefthand and orch. The American pianist Gary Graffman, a victim of a rare carpal tunnel syndrome affecting the fingers of his right hand, made a specialty of playing most of these left-handed concertos.

When the Hungarian nobleman and amateur musician Count Zichy lost his right arm in a hunting accident, he decided to compose piano pieces for the left hand which he performed at social occasions in Budapest. He also made arrangements for 3 hands and even played the arrangement of a patriotic Hungarian march with Liszt, supplying the bass line with his extant left hand. Scriabin was so eager to become a piano virtuoso in a grand style that he strained his right hand while a conservatory student in Moscow, trying to compete with his classmate Josef Lhévinne; Lhévinne was physically robust, while Scriabin was rather frail and could never rival him on the concert platform. So he bandaged his ailing right hand and as a consolation prize wrote a charming group of piano pieces for left hand alone. Even pianists with both hands in perfect order like to play these pieces in public.

legando (It., binding). 1. LEGATO. 2. An expression mark calling for the smooth execution of 2 or more consecutive tones by a single stroke of the glottis (voice), in 1 bow (violin, etc.), a single stroke of the tongue (wind instruments), or LEGATISSIMO (organ or piano).

legatissimo (It., very connected). Very smoothly and evenly, without a break between the notes in the melody. On the piano, an indication that each finger is to hold its note as long as possible.

legato (legate; It., connected). Slurred; a direction to perform the passage in a smooth and connected manner, with no break between the tones; also indicated by the legato mark, a curving line under or over notes to be so executed. The opposite is STACCATO, detached.

legend (Lat. *legenda,* item to be read; Ger. *Legende;* Fr. *légende*). A vocal or instrumental composition depicting the course of a short tale of legendary character; a narrative romantic ballad.

Legend of the Invisible City of Kitezh and the Maiden Fevronia, The. Mystical opera by Rimsky-Korsakov, 1907, 1st produced in St. Petersburg. Because of its sustained devotional character and the hymnlike character of its theme, it was often described as "the Russian *Parsifal.*" The action takes place in the year 6751 after Creation, at the time of the Tartar invasion of Russia. Fevronia, the bride of the Prince of Kitezh, prays that the city of Kitezh be made invisible so as to be saved from the invaders. Her prayer is answered. As the city vanishes, only the pealing of the church bells reveals its existence. A symphonic interlude depicting the battle between the Russians and the Tartars is based on a scale of alternating whole tones and semitones, which in Russia is known as the Rimsky-Korsakov scale and elsewhere as the octatonic scale.

Legende von der heiligen Elisabeth, Die. Oratorio by Liszt, 1857; he conducted its 1st performance in Budapest, 1865. The subject was suggested to Liszt by the frescoes of Moritz Schwind in Wartburg. St. Elisabeth was the Hungarian wife of a German crusader who perished during the wars. She was expelled by her German mother-in-law, took refuge in a nearby cave, and became a saint.

Legendenton, im (Ger.). In the manner of a legend.

leger lines. LEDGER LINES.

Legge, Walter. See SCHWARZKOPF, (OLGA MARIA) ELIZABETH (FRIEDERIKE).

leggeramente (*leggero, leggiero*; It.). Lightly, briskly.

leggiadramente (It.). Neatly, elegantly, gracefully.

Leginska (born Liggins), **Ethel,** English-born American pianist, teacher, and composer; b. Hull, Apr. 13, 1886; d. Los Angeles, Feb. 26, 1970. She showed a natural talent for music at an early age; the pseudonym Leginska was given to her by Lady Maud Warrender, under the illusion that a Polish-looking name might help her artistic career. She studied piano at the Hoch Cons. in Frankfurt, and later in Vienna with Leschetizky. After making her London debut (1907) she toured Europe; in 1913 she appeared for the 1st time in America, at a recital in N.Y.

Her playing was described as having masculine vigor, dashing brilliance, and great variety of tonal color; however, criticism was voiced against an individualistic treatment of classical works. In the midst of her career as a pianist she developed a great interest in conducting; she organized the Boston Phil. Orch. (100 players), later the Women's Sym. Orch. of Boston; appeared as a guest conductor with various orchs. in America and in Europe. In this field of activity she also elicited interest, leading to a discussion in the press of a woman's capability of conducting an orch. While in the U.S. she took courses in composition with Rubin Goldmark and Ernest Bloch; wrote music in various genres, distinguished by rhythmic display and a certain measure of modernism. She married the composer Emerson Whithorne (born Whittern, 1884–1958) in 1907 (divorced

in 1916). In 1939 she settled in Los Angeles as a piano teacher. She also composed 2 operas, various works for orch., piano pieces, and songs.

legno, col (It., with the wood). Strike the strings with the wooden part of the bow.

Legrand, Michel, French composer of popular music; b. Paris, Feb. 24, 1932. He entered the Paris Cons. at the age of 11; while still a student, he began making professional jazz arrangements; wrote for radio, television, and the cinema. His inventive score for the motion picture *Les Parapluies de Cherbourg* (1965), in which the characters sang throughout, received merited praise. Among his other soundtracks are *The Picasso Summer, Summer of '42, Brian's Song, Best Friends,* and *The Thomas Crown Affair.*

Lehár, Franz (Ferenc), celebrated Austrian operetta composer of Hungarian descent; b. Komorn, Hungary, Apr. 30, 1870; d. Bad Ischl, Oct. 24, 1948. He began his music training with his father, Franz Lehár (1838–98), a military bandmaster. He then entered the Prague Cons. at 12 and studied violin with A. Bennewitz and theory with J. Foerster. In 1885 he was brought to the attention of Fibich, who gave him lessons in composition independently from his studies at the Cons. In 1887 Lehár submitted 2 piano sonatas to Dvořák, who encouraged him in his musical career. In 1888 he became a violinist in a theater orch. in Elberfeld; in 1889 he entered his father's band (50th Infantry) in Vienna and assisted him as conductor. From 1890 to 1902 Lehár led military bands in Pola, Trieste, Budapest, and Vienna.

Although his early stage works were unsuccessful, he gained some success with his marches and waltzes. With *Der Rastelbinder* (Vienna, 1902) he established himself as a composer for the theater. His most celebrated operetta, *Die lustige Witwe,* was 1st performed in Vienna on 1905; it subsequently received innumerable performances throughout the world. From then on Vienna played host to most of his finest scores, including *Der Graf von Luxemburg* (1909), *Zigeunerliebe* (1910), and *Paganini* (1925). For Berlin he wrote *Der Zarewitsch* (1927), *Friederike* (1928), and *Das Land des Lächelns* (1929; rev. version of *Die gelbe Jacke,* 1923). Lehár's last years were made difficult by his marriage to a Jewish woman, which made him suspect to the Nazis. Ironically, *Die lustige Witwe* was one of Hitler's favorite stage works. After World War II Lehár went to Zurich (1946); then returned to Bad Ischl shortly before his death.

Lehár's music exemplifies the spirit of gaiety and frivolity that was the mark of Vienna early in the 20th century; his superlative gift for facile melody and infectious rhythms is combined with genuine wit and irony; a blend of nostalgia and sophisticated humor, undiminished by the upheavals of wars and revolutions, made a lasting appeal to audiences. In addition to his stage works, Lehár also wrote a number of orch.l pieces, including several symphonic poems; 2 violin concertos; about 65 waltzes, the most famous being his *Gold und Silber* (1899); more than 50 marches; various works for piano, including sonatas; over 90 songs; etc. S. Rourke ed. a thematic index of his works (London, 1985).

Lehmann, Lotte, celebrated German-born American soprano; b. Perleberg, Feb. 27, 1888; d. Santa Barbara, Calif., Aug. 26, 1976. She studied in Berlin with Erna Tiedka, Eva Reinhold, and Mathilde Mallinger. She made her debut in 1910, as the 2nd Boy in *Die Zauberflöte* at the Hamburg Opera, but soon was given important parts in Wagner's operas, establishing herself as one of the finest Wagnerian singers. In 1914 she made her 1st appearance in London, as Sophie at Drury Lane. In 1916 she was engaged at the Vienna Opera. Richard Strauss selected her to sing the Composer in the revised version of *Ariadne auf Naxos* when it was 1st performed in Vienna (1916); then she appeared as Octavian, and later as the Marschallin, which became one of her most famous roles. In 1922 she toured in South America. In 1924 she made her 1st appearance at London's Covent Garden as the Marschallin, and she continued to sing there regularly with great success until 1935; appeared there again in 1938.

In 1930 she made her U.S. debut as Sieglinde with the Chicago Opera, and in 1934 she sang the same role at her Metropolitan Opera debut in N.Y. She continued to appear at the Metropolitan, with mounting success, in the roles of Elisabeth in *Tannhäuser*, Tosca, and the Marschallin, until her farewell performance as the Marschallin (1945). In 1946 she appeared as the Marschallin for the last time in San Francisco. In 1945 she became a naturalized American citizen; gave her last recital in Santa Barbara, Calif. (1951), and thereafter devoted herself to teaching.

Lehmann was universally recognized as one of the greatest singers of the century. The beauty of her voice, combined with her rare musicianship, made her a compelling artist of the highest order. In addition to her unforgettable Strauss roles, she excelled as Mozart's Countess and Donna Elvira, Beethoven's Leonore, and Wagner's Elisabeth, Elsa, and Eva, among others. She publ. a novel, *Orplid, mein Land* (1937), and several books on music.

Lehrstück. A teaching piece, cultivated in Germany after World War I, designed as an exercise for amateur performers which would raise political and/or artistic consciousness. The problems of writing music in a modern idiom adaptable for educational purposes among workers and young people preoccupied a number of German composers in the 1920s. The idea of a Lehrstück for accompanied chorus with the liberal application of inflected voice, SPRECHSTIMME, arose in Germany about that time. Brecht was especially interested in the ideological aspect of the Lehrstück, and applied his dramatic theories in order to reach audiences. He collaborated with Weill, Hindemith, Eisler, Toch, and others. A typical example is a play by Brecht with music by Weill entitled *Der Jasager* (1930), based on a Chinese story and prefaced by the following declaration of intent by Brecht: "The pedagogical practice of this music is to let the student bypass specialized study by concentrating intensively on a definite idea presented graphically through the medium of music, an idea that penetrates the student's mind much more strongly than formal learning."

leicht (*leichtlich*; Ger.). Lightly, briskly; easily, with facility. *Leicht bewegt*, lightly and swiftly; with slight agitation.

leichtfertig (Ger.). Frivolously; expression mark used by R. Strauss in *Till Eulenspiegels*.

leidenschaftlich (Ger.). With passion; passionately, ardently.

leidvoll (Ger.). Sorrowful, mournful.

Leigh, Mitch (real name, Irwin Mitchnick), American composer, arranger, and conductor of popular music; b. N.Y., Jan. 30, 1928. He studied with Hindemith at Yale Univ.; upon graduation he entered the field of commercial music productions; founded Music Makers, Inc. His most successful work was the musical *Man of La Mancha* (1965), which included the title song and the hit song *The Impossible Dream*.

Leinsdorf (real name, Landauer), **Erich,** eminent Austrian-born American conductor; b. Vienna, Feb. 4, 1912; d. Zurich, Sept. 11, 1993. He entered a local music school when he was 5; began piano studies with the wife of Paul Pisk at age 8; then continued his piano studies with Paul Emerich (1923–28), and subsequently studied theory and composition with Pisk. In 1930 he took a master class in conducting at the Mozarteum in Salzburg, and then studied for a short time in the music dept. of the Univ. of Vienna; from 1931 to 1933 he took courses at the Vienna Academy of Music, making his debut as a conductor at the Musikvereinsaal upon his graduation. In 1933 he served as assistant conductor of the Workers' Chorus in Vienna; in 1934 he went to Salzburg, where he had a successful audition with Bruno Walter and Toscanini at the Salzburg Festivals and was appointed their assistant.

In 1937 he was engaged as a conductor of the Metropolitan Opera in N.Y.; he made his American debut there, conducting *Die Walküre* on Jan. 21, 1938, with notable success; he then conducted other Wagnerian operas, ultimately succeeding Bodanzky as head of the German repertoire there in 1939. In 1942 he became an American citizen. In 1943 he was appointed music director of the Cleveland Orch.; however, his induction into the U.S. Army in Dec. 1943 interrupted his term there. After his discharge in 1944 he once again conducted at the Metropolitan in 1944–45; also conducted several concerts with the Cleveland Orch. in 1945 and 1946, and made appearances in Europe. From 1947 to 1955 he was music director of the Rochester (N.Y.) Phil. Orch. In the fall of 1956 he was briefly music director of the N.Y. City Opera; then returned to the Metropolitan as a conductor and musical consultant in 1957. He also appeared as a guest conductor in the U.S. and Europe. In 1962 he received the prestigious appointment of music director of the Boston Sym. Orch., a post he retained until 1969; then he conducted opera and sym. concerts in many of the major music centers of America and in Europe; from 1978 to 1980 he held the post of principal conductor of the (West) Berlin Radio Sym. Orch. He publ. *The Composer's Advocate: A Radical Orthodoxy for Musicians* (1981).

leise (Ger.). Low, soft; PIANO.

leiser (Ger.). Softer. *Immer leiser*, softer and softer.

Leiter (Ger., ladder). Scale.

leitmotiv

Any striking musical motive (theme, phrase) associated with or accompanying one of the characters in a musical drama; also, some particular idea, emotion, or situation therein. The concept of the leitmotiv (Eng.; from Ger. *leiten*, to lead) is commonly associated with Wagner's music dramas, but the term was 1st used in an annotated catalogue of works by Weber, published in 1871, in which it was described as a "strong delineation of each individual character in an opera." The leitmotiv was aesthetically defined and analyzed by the Wagnerian theorist Wolzogen in 1876. Wagner himself never used the term, but described the identifying motives in his operas as "melodic moments," "thematic motives," "fundamental themes," "idea motives," or "remembrance motives."

The main purpose in Wagner's application of leading motives in his operas was to identify each character and each important idea. By employing them in contrapuntal combinations, and by varying the rhythm and sometimes the intervallic structure of these motives, Wagner intended to establish "a new form of dramatic music, which possesses the unity of a symphonic movement." This unity can be achieved, Wagner averred, "in a network of basic themes permeating the entire work, analogously to the themes in a sym. They are contrasted with each other, supplement each other, assume new shapes, separate and coalesce . . . according to dramatic action." Thomas Mann describes the leitmotiv as a "magic formula valid in both the past and the future developments." But Wagner's use of leading motives is not limited to the characters on the stage. He carefully tabulates the motives of material objects, such as the ring and the sword in DER RING DES NIBELUNGEN, and abstract concepts such as the Covenant, Conflict, Transformation, Love, and many others.

Wagner was, of course, not the 1st to introduce identifying themes in opera. Papageno's appearances in Mozart's *Zauberflöte* are announced by a scale on his magic bell; there are definite leading motives in Weber's

Der Freischütz. Verdi used leading motives in several of his operas. Tchaikovsky can hardly be called a Wagnerian, but the presence of identifying motives in his operas is discerned without difficulty. Before Wagner, Berlioz used the IDÉE FIXE, a device related to the leitmotiv, in his *Symphonie fantastique*. The true innovation in Wagner's operas is the conscious, philosophical affirmation of unity through plurality, the GESAMTKUNSTWERK, an artistic synthesis, which was Wagner's grand ideal. One of the most fascinating aspects of Wagnerian leading motives is the unexpected musical similarity of the dramatically contrasting characters or ideas. Thus, by a "topological" alteration, the theme of love-death in *Tristan und Isolde* can be converted into the leading motive of the Holy Grail in *Parsifal*.

Wagner's influence in the use of leading motives was enormous. Hardly a single opera written since Wagner escaped this unifying concept. Faithful Wagnerians compiled catalogues of leading motives in his music dramas, including melodic fragments that were merely transitional passages. Wagner societies were formed in many countries, even in France, which had just been defeated by Wagner's compatriots in the Franco-Prussian War. Among composers who have absorbed the Wagnerian gospel was R. Strauss, who introduced the leading motives into his symphonic works as well as his operas. Humperdinck, Janáček, and to some extent even Debussy all experienced Wagnerian influences. Berg consciously outlined the significance of leading motives in his opera *Wozzeck*, a doctrine which enables the composer "by means of leading motives, to achieve the connections and relationships and thereby attain again a unity." Schoenberg's 12-tone themes as applied in his operas, particularly in the score of *Moses und Aron*, are logical developments of the leading motive. A more obvious and vulgar exploitation of identifying motives is represented by commercial jingles in advertising; a cleverly selected tune is designed to form a lasting association with the advertised product and promote its sales. Also *leitmotif*.

Leitton (Ger.). LEADING TONE.

lenezza, con (It.). Faintly, gently, quietly.

Leningrad Symphony. The commonly accepted name of the 7th Sym. of Shostakovich, 1942, which he dedicated to the heroes of the siege of Leningrad in 1941. It was 1st performed in the town of Kuibyshev (formerly Samara). The finale prophesies the victorious end of the "great patriotic war," as the anti-Nazi war was known in Russia. It reaffirmed Shostakovich's status in the Soviet Union and made him sufficiently famous to appear on the cover of *Time*.

Lennon, John (Winston; later changed to Ono), English rock singer, guitarist, songwriter, and poet; member of the fantastically popular rock group the Beatles; b. Liverpool, Oct. 9, 1940, during a German air raid on the city; d. N.Y., Dec. 8, 1980, gunned down by a wacko in front of his apartment building. See the entry on the Beatles for Lennon's early life and career.

In 1968, as the Beatles were coming apart, Lennon began performing on his own, often accompanied by his paramour (and then wife), Yoko Ono. The 2 made 2 albums of "electronic" music, really MUSIQUE CONCRÈTE or tape collages: *Two Virgins* (1968), with its famous cover photo where they appeared fully nude, and *Life with the Lions* (1969). *Wedding Album* (also 1969) documented their marriage and associated brouhaha. Holding several "bed-ins for peace" to celebrate their nuptials, the pair recorded in a Montreal hotel room the song *Give Peace a Chance*, credited to "the Plastic Ono Band" and featuring the assembled reporters and friends on the chorus (including LSD guru Timothy Leary and satirist Tommy Smothers).

Lennon's 1st true "solo" album was the self-titled *John Lennon/Plastic Ono Band* (1970). An extremely sparse recording, the songs were influenced by Lennon's and Ono's participation in primal scream therapy under the guidance of a Calif. therapist named Dr. Janov. The album had several powerful songs, including *Mother* and *God*. More successful was its follow-up, *Imagine* (1971), with the hit title cut. Lennon and Ono then embarked on a political partnership with N.Y.C.-based radicals including Abbie Hoffman; the result was an album of wretched topical songs, *Some Time in New York* (1972).

Lennon returned to singer/songwriter material on his next 2 albums, producing minor hits with *#9 Dream* and a number 1 hit with *Whatever Gets You Through the Night*. An ill-conceived album of oldies followed, and then Lennon went into self-imposed retirement, becoming a "house husband" to care for his newly born son, Sean. He came out of retirement in 1980 with the album *Double Fantasy*, featuring tracks by both him and Ono. The album produced several hits, including the 1950s-style opening track, *(Just Like) Starting Over*. Sadly, Lennon was gunned down by a crazed assailant, Mark David Chapman, on his way home from a recording session in December 1980. Subsequently, several unfinished tracks were issued on various albums. In 1996 the Beatles regrouped to finish 2 of Lennon's last songs, *Free as a Bird* and *Real Love*.

leno (It.). Faint, gentle, quiet.

lentamente (It.). Slowly. *Lentando*, growing slower.

lentezza (It.). Slowness. *Con lentezza*, slowly.

lento (It.). Slow; calls for a tempo between ANDANTE and LARGO. Also, a movement in that tempo. *Adagio non lento*, slowly, but not dragging.

Lenya, Lotte (born Karoline Wilhelmine Blamauer), sultry Austrian-American singer and actress, wife of Kurt Weill; b. Vienna, Oct. 18, 1898; d. N.Y., Nov. 27, 1981. She began her stage career as a dancer in Zurich, where she went at the outbreak of World War I in 1914; in 1920 she went to Berlin. There she met Kurt Weill, whom she married in 1926; in 1927 she made her debut as a singer in the Brecht-Weill scenic cantata *Kleine Mahagonny* in Baden-Baden; in 1928 she created the role of Jenny in the premiere of the Brecht-Weill *Die Dreigroschenoper* in Berlin (1928); she created the role of the singing Anna in *The 7 Deadly Sins* (1933). She and Weill fled Nazified Berlin in 1933, and after a couple of years in Paris and London went to America. Although not a singer of a profes-

Lotte Lenya, c. 1950s, in The Threepenny Opera

sional caliber, Lenya adapted herself to the peculiar type of half-spoken, half-sung roles in Weill's works with total dedication. She created the roles of Miriam in his *The Eternal Road* (1937) and the Duchess in his *The Firebrand of Florence* (1945). After his death in 1950, she devoted herself to reviving his works for the American stage, especially the work that came to be known as *The Threepenny Opera* (1954). She also performed in other music theater works, notably Kander and Ebb's *Cabaret*.

Leoncavallo, Ruggero

〰〰 〰〰 〰〰 〰〰 〰〰

Noted Italian opera composer; b. Naples, Apr. 23, 1857; d. Montecatini, Aug. 9, 1919. He attended the Naples Cons. (1866–76), where his teachers were B. Cesi (piano) and M. Ruta and L. Rossi (composition), and at 16 made a pianistic tour. His 1st opera, *Tommaso Chatterton*, was about to be produced in Bologna (1878) when the manager disappeared, and the production was called off. Leoncavallo earned his living as a young man by playing piano in cafés; this life he continued for many years, traveling through Egypt, Greece, Turkey, Germany, Belgium, and the Netherlands before settling in Paris. There he found congenial company; composed chansonettes and other popular songs; wrote an opera, *Songe d'une nuit d'été* (after Shakespeare's *Midsummer Night's Dream*), which was privately sung in a salon.

He began to study Wagner's scores, and he became an ardent Wagnerian; he resolved to emulate the master by producing a trilogy, *Crepusculum*, depicting in epical traits the Italian Renaissance; the separate parts were to be *I Medici*, *Girolamo Savonarola*, and *Cesare Borgia*. He spent 6 years on the basic historical research; having completed the 1st part, and with the scenario of the entire trilogy sketched, he returned in 1887 to Italy, where the publisher Ricordi became interested in the project but kept delaying the publication and production of the work. Annoyed, Leoncavallo turned to Sonzogno, the publisher of Mascagni, whose opera *Cavalleria rusticana* had just obtained a tremendous vogue. Leoncavallo submitted a short opera in a similarly realistic vein; he wrote his own libretto based on a factual story of passion and murder in a Calabrian village and named it *Pagliacci*. The opera was given with sensational success at the Teatro dal Verme in Milan under the direction of Toscanini (May 21, 1892), and rapidly took possession of operatic stages throughout the world; it is often played on the same evening with Mascagni's opera, both works being of brief duration. Historically, these 2 operas signalized the important development of Italian operatic verismo, which influenced composers of other countries as well.

The enormous success of *Pagliacci* did not deter Leoncavallo from carrying on his more ambitious projects. The 1st part of his unfinished trilogy, *I Medici*, was finally brought out at the Teatro dal Verme in Milan on Nov. 9, 1893, but the reception was so indifferent that he turned to other subjects; the same fate befell his youthful *Tommaso Chatterton* at its production in Rome (Mar. 10, 1896). His next opera, *La Bohème* (1897), won consider-able success, but it had the ill fortune of coming a year after Puccini's masterpiece on the same story and was dwarfed by comparison. There followed a light opera, *Zazà* (1900), which was fairly successful, and was produced repeatedly on world stages. In 1894 he was commissioned by the German Emperor Wilhelm II to write an opera for Berlin; this was *Der Roland von Berlin*, on a German historic theme; it was produced in Berlin in late 1904, but despite the high patronage it proved a fiasco.

In 1906 Leoncavallo made a tour of the U.S. and Canada, conducting his *Pagliacci* and a new operetta, *La Jeunesse de Figaro*, specially written for his American tour; it was so unsuccessful that he never attempted to stage it in Europe. Back in Italy he resumed his industrious production; the opera *Maia* (1910) and the operetta *Malbrouck* (1910) were produced within the same week; another operetta, *La Reginetta delle rose*, was staged simultaneously in Rome and in Naples (1912). In the autumn of that year Leoncavallo visited London, where he presented the premiere of his *Gli Zingari* (1912); a year later he revisited the U.S., conducting in San Francisco. He wrote several more operettas but they made no impression; 3 of them were produced during his lifetime: *La Candidata* (1915), *Goffredo Mameli* (1916), and *Prestami tua moglie* (1916); posthumous premieres were accorded the operetta *A chi la giarettiera?* (1919), the opera *Edipo re* (1920), and the operetta *Il primo bacio* (1923). Another score, *Tormenta*, remained unfinished. Salvatore Allegra collected various sketches by Leoncavallo and arranged from them a 3-act operetta, *La maschera nuda*, which was produced in Naples on June 26, 1925. Of Leoncavallo's many songs, he is most famous for *Mattinata* (1904).

Leoninus (Leonin, Magister Leoninus, Magister Leonini, Magister Leo, Magister Leonis), celebrated French composer and poet, master of the Notre Dame School of Paris.; b. Paris, *c.* 1135; d. there, *c.* 1201. He most likely received his initial education at the Notre Dame Cathedral schools in Paris; was active at the collegiate church of St. Benoit in Paris by the mid-1150s, eventually serving as a canon there for some 20 years. He was also a member of the clergy of Notre Dame by reason of his position at St. Benoit. He had earned the academic degree of master by 1179, probably in Paris; later became a canon at Notre Dame, where he was a priest by 1192; was also a member of the congregation of St. Victor by 1187. His great achievement was the creation of ORGANUM to augment the divine service; this has come down to us as the *Magnus liber organi de graduali et antiphonario pro servitio divino multiplicando*. It is also possible that he prepared many of the revisions and variant versions of the organa, preceding the work of revision by Perotin. The original form of the work is not extant, but there are 3 extant later versions dating from the 13th and 14th centuries. As a poet he wrote the extensive *Hystorie sacre gestas ab origine mundi*.

Léonore, ou L'Amour conjugal. Opera, 1798, by Pierre Gaveaux (1760–1825), based on the same libretto as

Beethoven's FIDELIO; also an opera, 1804, by Ferdinando Paer (1771–1839), based on the same subject as *Fidelio*.

Leonore Overtures. Beethoven wrote 4 overtures for his opera FIDELIO; the 1st 3 are each called *Leonore Overture*, after the heroine of the opera. The 4th overture is the *Fidelio Overture* proper; it was 1st used for the 1814 revival of the opera. *Leonore No. 3* is the one most often performed as a concert piece, and it is sometimes played before the dungeon scene.

Lerner, Alan Jay, distinguished American lyricist and playwright, most famous for his collaborations with Frederick Loewe; b. N.Y., Aug. 31, 1918; d. there, June 14, 1986. He was educated at Harvard Univ. (graduated, 1940); also attended the Juilliard School of Music in N.Y. (summers 1936, 1937). He met the composer Frederick Loewe in 1942, resulting in their collaboration on the musical *What's Up?* (1943). It proved a failure, but they had better luck with their next work, *The Day Before Spring* (1945). Their collaborative efforts paid off when they produced the outstanding score of *Brigadoon* (1947). Following the popular *Paint Your Wagon* (1951), they wrote the smashing success *My Fair Lady* (1956), after George Bernard Shaw's play *Pygmalion*. There followed their film score *Gigi* (1958; after Colette's story), which garnered 9 Academy Awards. They returned to the Broadway stage with the enormously successful musical *Camelot* (1960). After Loewe's retirement Lerner continued to write musicals, but he failed to equal his previous successes. His most popular work was *On a Clear Day You Can See Forever* (1966), written in collaboration with Burton Lane; a film version appeared in 1970. Lerner and Loewe collaborated on 1 more film score, *The Little Prince* (1974).

lesni roh (Czech., forest horn; Ger., Waldhorn). Formerly, natural horn; now, French horn.

lesson (Fr. *leçon*; Ger. *Übung*). English and (less commonly) French instrumental pieces of the Baroque, composed mostly for the harpsichord or organ. The term's early pedagogical implications were quickly expanded to cover almost any piece. Lessons 1st

Lerner & Loewe. L to r: Frederick Loewe and Alan Jay Lerner

appeared in mid-16th-century lute collections; Morley publ. his *1st Booke of Consort Lessons* in 1599; Byrd included 1 *Lesson or Voluntarie* in his MS *My Ladye Nevells Booke* (1591). Thereafter, Matthew Locke, William Babell, Krieger, Handel, Rameau, and Bach wrote or publ. lessons or similar works; sometimes the term has alternative meanings, e.g., Couperin's *Leçons de ténèbres*, where it refers to the liturgical reading. The ambiguous "lesson" eventually evolved into the less ambiguous "study" (ÉTUDE).

lesto (It.). Gay, lively, brisk.

Let 'Em Eat Cake. Musical by Gershwin, 1933. The show is a sequel to the Pulitzer Prize–winning *Of Thee I Sing*. President Wintergreen is defeated but refuses to concede and starts a revolution. A radical trade union group proclaims a dictatorship of the proletariat and sentences Wintergreen to die on a guillotine especially imported from France. But the proletarian rule is overthrown, and Wintergreen is reinstated in the White House. The choral number *Union Square* is the least forgotten piece of the show, which failed dramatically; it was the last musical Gershwin wrote for Broadway.

Let Me Call You Sweetheart. Ballad by Leo Friedman, 1910; immensely successful.

Let's Face It. Musical by C. Porter, 1941. Three American women get even with their philandering husbands by picking up a trio of gigolos for themselves, recruited from a nearby military camp. Includes *Ace in the Hole* and an interpolated Sylvia Fine number, the patter song *Melody in Four F*, sung by her husband, Danny Kaye.

Let's Make an Opera. "An entertainment for young people" by Britten, 1949, with optional audience participation; 1st produced at the Aldeburgh Festival, England. The organizers of the opera discuss on stage the music, the production, and the story. Then the opera, ostensibly planned in front of an audience, is actually produced; it is entitled *The Little Sweep*. The story recounts the inhumane practice of sweeping the chimneys in Victorian

England by lowering children from the roof into the fireplace to clean the soot with their little bodies.

Levine, James (Lawrence), brilliant American pianist and conductor; b. Cincinnati, June 23, 1943. His maternal grandfather was a cantor in a synagogue; his father was a violinist who led a dance band; his mother was an actress. He absorbed music by osmosis and began playing the piano as a small child. At the age of 10 he was soloist in Mendelssohn's 2nd Piano Concerto at a youth concert of the Cincinnati Sym. Orch.; he then studied music theory with Walter Levin, 1st violinist in the La Salle Quartet; in 1956 he took piano lessons with Rudolf Serkin at the Marlboro School of Music; in 1957 he began piano studies with Rosina Lhevinne at the Aspen Music School. In 1961 he entered the Juilliard School of Music in N.Y. and took courses in conducting with Jean Morel; he also had conducting sessions with Wolfgang Vacano in Aspen.

In 1964 he graduated from the Juilliard School and joined the American Conductors Project, connected with the Baltimore Sym. Orch., where he had occasion to practice conducting with Alfred Wallenstein, Max Rudolf, and Fausto Cleva. In 1964–65 he served as an apprentice to George Szell with the Cleveland Orch.; then became a regular assistant conductor with it (1965–70). In 1966 he organized the Univ. Circle orch. of the Cleveland Inst. of Music; also led the student orch. of the summer music inst. of Oakland Univ. in Meadow Brook, Mich. (1967–69). In 1970 he made a successful appearance as guest conductor with the Philadelphia Orch. at its summer home at Robin Hood Dell; subsequently appeared with other American orchs. In 1970 he also conducted the Welsh National Opera and the San Francisco Opera. He made his Metropolitan Opera debut in N.Y. in 1971, in a festival performance of *Tosca*; his success led to further appearances and to his appointment as its principal conductor in 1973; he then was its music director from 1975 until becoming its artistic director in 1986. In 1973 he also became music director of the Ravinia Festival, the summer home of the Chicago Sym. Orch., and served in that capacity with the Cincinnati May Festival (1974–78). In 1975 he began to conduct at the Salzburg Festivals; in 1982 he conducted at the Bayreuth Festival for the 1st time.

He continued to make appearances as a pianist, playing chamber music with impeccable technical precision. But it is as a conductor and an indefatigable planner of the seasons at the Metropolitan Opera that he inspired respect. Unconcerned with egotistical projections of his own personality, he presided over the singers and the orch. with concentrated efficiency. He has made some inroads on the unadventurous "musical museum" programming of the Metropolitan, with works by Janáček, Schoenberg, Corigliano, and important revivals joining the ranks of the predictable.

Lewis, Jerry Lee, rollicking American rock 'n' roll and country-music pianist and singer; b. Ferriday, La., Sept. 29, 1935. He assaulted the piano keys with unusual ferocity, as if seeking the rock bottom of the sound, and whenever he had a chance he also vocalized in a frenetic seizure of the larynx. He tried every style, including rock, folk, western, and rhythm and blues, always hitting hard on mental torment. He never wrote his own songs, but he sure could metamorphosize and transmogrify ready-made tunes such as *Great Balls of Fire* (1957). His rendition of *Whole Lotta Shakin' Going On* (1957) became a rock 'n' roll classic. His career came to a halt in 1958 during his English tour after it was revealed in lurid headlines that he was traveling with a 13-year-old girl, who he said was his 1st cousin and child wife. Even his records were put on the shelf at radio stations, and he was reduced to playing at village fairs and roadhouses. It was not until 1968 that he was able to return to public favor, with records such as *Another Place, Another Time* and *What's Made Milwaukee Famous (Has Made a Loser Out of Me)*. In 1977 he recorded an autobiographical single, *Middle-Age Crazy*. With his sister Linda Gail Lewis he brought out the album *Together* (1969); his later albums include *The Session* (1973), *Southern Roots* (1973), *Jerry Lee Lewis Keeps Rockin'* (1978), and *Killer Country* (1980).

Lewis, John (Aaron), esteemed African-American jazz pianist and composer; b. La Grange, Ill., May 3, 1920. He studied anthropology and music at the Univ. of New Mexico; completed his studies at the Manhattan School of Music (M.A., 1953). In 1952 he founded the Modern Jazz Quartet (piano, vibraphone, drums, double bass), a group that for 22 years was one of the focal points of both "cool" jazz and "classical" jazz, a merger known as 3rd Stream. To this end he composed and arranged works that, while leaving room for jazz improvisation, also included such formal devices as fugal counterpoint; he composed extended compositions requiring the additional forces of string quartet or orch., several movie scores (*Odds Against Tomorrow, No Sun in Venice, A Milanese Story*), and a ballet, *Original Sin* (San Francisco Ballet, March 1961). Significantly, the Modern Jazz Quartet (known as MJQ) abandoned the usual nightclub habitat of jazz in favor of formal, tuxedoed performances in concert halls. The Modern Jazz Quartet disbanded in 1974, but in later years its members reunited for occasional tours; Lewis also led his own sextet.

Lewis, Meade (Anderson) **"Lux,"** African-American jazz pianist; b. Chicago, Sept. 4, 1905; d. in an automobile accident in Minneapolis, June 7, 1964. He was nicknamed "The Duke of Luxembourg" as a child, hence the contraction "Lux." He studied violin and piano; played in nightclubs and bars in Chicago; then went to N.Y., where he played with Pete Johnson and Albert Ammons; then appeared as a soloist in N.Y. and Calif. nightclubs. He was a leading exponent of the boogie-woogie style; his recording of *Honky Tonk Train Blues* (1927) was a landmark of the era.

lexicography (from Grk. *lexis*, word, speech). The editing or creating of a dictionary or lexicon; also, the principles behind these processes. This kind of research concentrates on vocabulary, not grammar or construction.

Lhévinne, Josef, celebrated Russian pianist and pedagogue; b. Orel, Dec. 13, 1874; d. N.Y., Dec. 2, 1944. After some preliminary study in his native town, he was taken to Moscow and entered Safonov's piano class at the Cons. (1885); at the age of 15 he played the *Emperor Concerto*, with Anton Rubinstein conducting; he graduated in 1891 and won the Rubinstein Prize in 1895. In 1900 he traveled to the Caucasus; taught piano at the Tiflis Cons.; from 1902 to 1906 he taught at the Moscow Cons. In 1906 he went to the U.S.; made his American debut in N.Y. with the Russian Sym. Orch., conducted by Safonov (1906); afterward he made numerous concert tours in America. He lived mostly in Berlin from 1907 to 1919; he was interned during World War I but was able to continue his professional activities. In 1919 he returned to the U.S.; appeared in recitals, and with major American orchs.; also in duo recitals with his wife, Rosina Bessie, whom he married in 1898. They established a music studio, where they taught numerous pupils; also taught at the Juilliard Graduate School in N.Y. (from 1922). He publ. *Basic Principles in Pianoforte Playing* (1924).

Lhévinne's playing was distinguished not only by its virtuoso quality but by an intimate understanding of the music, impeccable phrasing, and fine gradations of singing tone. He was at his best in the works of the Romantic school; his performances of the concertos of Chopin and Tchaikovsky were particularly notable. His wife Rosina (Bessie) Lhévinne (b. Kiev, Mar. 28, 1880; d. Glendale, Calif., Nov. 9, 1976) was also a distinguished pianist and pedagogue; she graduated from the Moscow Cons. in 1898, winning the gold medal; that same year she married Josef. She appeared as a soloist in Vienna (1910), St. Petersburg (1911), and Berlin (1912); remained in Berlin with her husband through World War I; in 1919 they went to the U.S., where they opened a music studio; also taught at the Juilliard Graduate School in N.Y. (from 1922); later taught privately. Among her famous students were Van Cliburn, Mischa Dichter, John Browning, and Garrick Ohlsson.

Liberace (born Wladziu Valentino Liberace), flamboyant American pianist and showman; b. West Allis, Wis., May 16, 1919; d. Palm Springs, Calif., Feb. 4, 1987. He received musical training from his father, a horn player; then studied piano, exhibiting so natural a talent that no less a master than Paderewski encouraged him to try for a concert career. However, he was sidetracked from serious music by jobs at silent-movie houses and nightclubs, where he was billed as Walter Busterkeys. In 1940 he moved to N.Y. and soon evolved a facile repertoire of semiclassical works, such as a synthetic arrangement of the 1st movement of Beethoven's *Moonlight Sonata* and

Liberace, c. 1960s

Rachmaninoff's Prelude in C-sharp Minor, taking advantage of the fact that both works are in the same key. He prospered and made lucrative inroads into television (1951–55; 1958–59); also made numerous recordings and toured extensively overseas.

He built himself a house in Calif. complete with a piano-shaped swimming pool. Inspired by a popular movie on Chopin, he placed a candelabrum on the piano at his public appearances; this decorative object identified him as a Romantic musician, an impression enhanced by his dress suit of white silk mohair and a wardrobe of glittering cloaks, which he removed with theatrical flair before performing. In 1959 he won a lawsuit for defamation of character against the *London Daily Mirror* and its columnist Cassandra (William Neil Connor) for suggesting in print that he was a practitioner of the inverted mode of love. But then in 1982 his former chauffeur-bodyguard-companion sued him for $380 million for "services rendered in an exclusive nonmarital relationship." In 1984 most of the suit was quashed, and in 1986 Liberace settled out of court for $95,000. When he died of AIDS in 1987, his multimillion-dollar estate containing valuable curiosa was sold at auction. A large percentage of the sale price was bequeathed to charities, for Liberace was a generous man. In spite of his critics, he once said, he cried all the way to the bank.

liberamente (It.). Freely, boldly.

librettist. Author of the libretto, i.e., the play to be set to music as an opera, operetta, etc.

libretto

The book containing the text or play of an opera; also, the text or play itself. Such librettos (It., little book; plural *librettos*, *libretti*) were distributed to the audience to acquaint them with the subject of the opera. In the 19th century it was common to supply a translation into the language of the country in which the opera was performed. Italian librettos usually carried an *argomento* (not an argument, but a summary), listing the acts and scenes, the cast of characters, and sometimes a *protesta* (a protestation by the author of the libretto that his use of names of pagan deities should not be understood as a lack of Christian faith). A paragon of the art was Metastasio, whose librettos were set to music by some 50 composers, accounting for over 1,000 different Italian operas.

Some librettos have independent literary value, such as Boito's rendering of Shakespeare for Verdi, or Hofmannsthal's thoughtful texts for R. Strauss. Then there were Gilbert and Sullivan, in whose comic operas the merit is distributed equally for literature and music. (The "heavenly twins" eventually quarreled, mainly because of Sullivan's ambition to write grand opera and his dissatisfaction at being stereotyped as a composer of operettas.) In a class by itself is the composer-librettist, of whom Wagner was supreme. In modern times Menotti has written the librettos for his own operas, as well as 2 for Barber.

The plots of most operas before the 20th century are based on standard formulas. Many, especially in the Baroque, were drawn from Greek mythology and drama. In other plots, mistaken identities abound. Rigoletto hires assassins to kill the seducer of his daughter; in the darkness of the night they kill the daughter instead and deliver her body to her father in a sack. A most unlikely story, but plausibility is not a virtue among most librettists. A very common theme may be described as *seduta e abbandonata*. Seduction followed by desertion is at the root of *Faust*, *La Bohème*, *La Traviata*, and, on a lighter note, *Ariadne auf Naxos*. Suicides are common, with female self-destruction outnumbering male. Examples are the seduced granddaughter of *The Queen of Spades*, the murderess in *Lady Macbeth of Mtzensk*, and the eponymous heroine of *Lakmé*. Lodoletta in Mascagni's opera of that name does not commit suicide but dies in the snow outside her lover's Paris house.

Infanticide is the central element in *Jenůfa*. Transvesticism is another common device in opera plots. The faithful Leonora dresses as a boy, assumes the symbolic name Fidelio, and penetrates the prison in which her beloved is unjustly held; in *Le Nozze di Figaro*, Cherubino, a young lad played by a woman, disguises him/herself as a maid to avoid the infantry. The motive of rescue is so ubiquitous that "rescue opera" has entered the dictionaries of musical terms. Religious fanaticism, particularly in the Inquisition, is a convenient dramatic feature in many operas. Thus in *La Juive* the fanatical cardinal has a girl burned at the stake moments before he finds out that she is his natural daughter. Superstition plays a helpful role in libretti of all kinds, as in *Il Trovatore*. Operatic murders, particularly by stabbing, are too numerous to tabulate. Insanity should not be overlooked. Mad scenes in opera are most effective recourses. Fortunately, most of the victims, a majority of them female, recover their sanity as soon as the dramatic situation is favorable for such a development; then again, there is Boris Godunov.

It is very easy to ridicule opera; the difficulty is to suggest the rational and sensible substitute for operatic librettos. Of course, it is ludicrous for Verdi to have the King of Ethiopia overhear Radames as he relates military secrets to the King's daughter Aida. The hidden King even offers comments in recitative from behind a potted palm. Here Coleridge's injunction regarding the poetic approach as being a "willing suspension of disbelief" is particularly helpful. An operagoer must leave his skepticism with his hat in the vestiary. But Tolstoy, great writer as he was, felt insulted when he attended a rehearsal of the opera *Feramors* by Anton Rubinstein, by the nonsense depicted on the stage. His humorless account of that occasion in his extraordinary tract *What Is Art* (in which he also demolishes music, ballet, painting, and Shakespeare) is worth quoting:

> The procession began with a recitative of a person dressed up in Turkish costume who with a mouth open at an unnatural angle sings: "I accompany the bri-i-i-i-de." After singing this, he waves his arm, naked of course, under his mantle. The procession opens, but here the French horn accompanying the recitative does something wrong, and the conductor, suddenly startled as if a disaster had happened, taps on the music stand with his stick, and the whole thing starts all over again. The libretto

of the opera is one of the greatest absurdities imaginable. An Indian king wants to marry; a bride is presented to him, and he changes his attire to that of a minstrel. The bride falls in love with the supposed minstrel, and becomes desperate at this development. Fortunately, she soon finds out that the minstrel is the King, and everyone is well content. That such Indians never existed, that the personages in the opera do not resemble any Indians or indeed any people, except those in other operas, can be no doubt whatsoever; that nobody talks in recitative, that no group of four people place themselves at measured distances from one another to perform a quartet, constantly waving their arms to express their emotions; that nobody, except on the stage, walks in pairs carrying halberds made of foil and wearing slippers instead of shoes; that no one ever becomes angry or tender as in the theater, no one laughs or cries like that, and that no one can possibly be moved by such a spectacle, is obvious. And all this repellent nonsense is being put together not in the spirit of social entertainment and fun, but with malice and bestial brutality.

A historical footnote: The rehearsal in question was conducted by the famous Russian musician Wasily Safonov, and the participants were students of the Moscow Conservatory, of which he was director. It was Tolstoy himself who asked Safonov's permission to be present at the rehearsal; his account of it did not endear him to Safonov, who never treated the orch. or the singers with "bestial brutality" of which Tolstoy accused him.

Sometimes stories of operas are changed for political or social reasons. Glinka's opera *A Life for the Czar* could not very well be staged in Russia after the Revolution, and the Soviet authorities changed the title to *Ivan Susanin*, the self-sacrificial peasant hero of the opera, and instead of saving the Czar he is made to save a patriotic Russian officer. Attempts were made in Soviet Russia to rewrite other librettos in order to make them revolutionary. Thus *Tosca* became *The Commune*, and *The Huguenots* was changed to *The Decembrists* (the revolutionary Russian group of December 1825 who rebelled against Czar Nicholas I).

Some operas cannot be performed in certain countries. *The Mikado* is forbidden in Japan because the Japanese Emperor is portrayed in an undignified manner. Gounod's *Faust* was renamed *Gretchen* in Germany because the sentimental treatment of Goethe's great poem in the libretto was an affront to German literature. The libretto of Verdi's *Un Ballo in maschera* was based on the historical event, the assassination of the King of Sweden. The opera was forbidden for performance in Italy because of the rash of attempted regicides in Europe at the time. Accordingly, the libretto was changed, and the mythical "Governor of Boston" was substituted for the Swedish King.

Sometimes religious restrictions make it impossible to have an opera performed under any circumstances. For instance, *Samson and Delilah* by Saint-Saëns could not be performed for nearly a century on the British stage because of a regulation whereby biblical personages could not be represented in the theater; the restriction, however, did not apply to oratorios or cantatas. In Czarist Russia there was a rule against the representation of a member of the reigning dynasty on the stage. So, when Catherine the Great was to make her entrance in Tchaikovsky's *The Queen of Spades*, the Imperial March announcing her presence was played, but the Empress herself did not appear. No restrictions were applied to the Russian Czars before the Romanov dynasty. In Mussorgsky's opera *Boris Godunov*, Czar Boris is a child murderer. Ivan the Terrible is treated by Rimsky-Korsakov in his opera *The Maid of Pskov* as the brute that he was. Ironically, Stalin decreed rehabilitation of the historic Ivan, perhaps because he felt an affinity with his remote precursor. Prokofiev had trouble in his scenic oratorio *Ivan the Terrible*, trying to conform with the new official attitude. The Imperial censors demanded some minor changes to Pushkin's verses as used by Rimsky-Korsakov in his opera Le Coq d'or, to avoid embarrassing similarities between the bumbling Czar of the opera and the last Czar, Nicholas II, who was not very bright; the composer refused, and it was not until after his death that the work was performed.

A sui generis hazard requires adjustments of the texts of some operas when performed in a different country. The name of Pinkerton in *Madama Butterfly* had to be changed in German productions to Linkerton because *pinkeln* means to urinate in colloquial German. When *Boris Godunov* was performed in Lisbon in 1921, the dying Czar's injunction to his son containing the imperative *karai* had to be changed to another Russian word because *karai* means the male sexual organ in Portuguese. The declaration of the young man in *Iolanthe* of Gilbert and Sullivan that he is "a fairy only down to the waist" makes semisophisticated audiences of the 20th century giggle. The opening phrase of Dido's lament in Purcell's opera, "When I am laid, am laid, in earth," evokes similar subdued sophomoric merriment when it is sung at contemporary concerts.

Libuše. Opera by Smetana, 1881, produced at the inauguration of the National Theater in Prague. The eponymous Queen of Bohemia searches for a consort worthy of her and able to contribute his masculine strength to governance. She finds a satisfactory candidate and marries him; he becomes king.

licenza (It.). Freedom, license. *Con alcuna licenza*, with a certain (degree of) freedom. The meanings are manifold: freedom to insert a cadenza, or rhythmic freedom, or just about any liberty taken by a performer.

lick. In jazz and popular music, a brief improvised or stereotypical solo passage, or a portion of a longer passage; a "hot lick" is a particularly intriguing and stimulating exemplar. The implication is that the lick is set off from its surroundings by register or rest. Similar but not identical to the RIFF.

Lidice Memorial. Symphonic elegy by Martinů, 1943, commemorating the Nazi obliteration of the Czech community of Lidice in June 1942. Its 1st performance took place in N.Y.

lié (Fr.). Tied; either one note to the next note of identical pitch (TIED NOTES), or in the sense of LEGATO.

Liebe der Danae, Die. Opera by Strauss, 1944, orig. scheduled for production in 1944 but canceled the day before its premiere by the Nazis, who closed all theaters in light of the deteriorating war situation. The work was finally performed in Salzburg (1952). In a newly invented episode the mortal Danae is in a quandary; she must choose between Jupiter (Zeus, the shower of gold) and Midas (of the dubious power to create gold by touch) for a lover. She chooses Midas and does not yield, even when Jupiter assumes the shape of Midas to deceive her. Jupiter accepts defeat magnanimously.

liebeglühend (Ger.). Glowing with love; an expression mark found in scores by R. Strauss.

Liebesflöte (Ger., love flute). FLAUTO D'AMORE.

Liebesfuss (Ger., love foot; Fr. *pavillon d'amour*). The bulbous opening at the end of the English horn, which has the effect of dampening the sound. The same type of extension was characteristic of the manufacture of a clarinetto d'amore, flauto d'amore, oboe d'amore, and other "amorous" instruments, now largely obsolete. In French this bulbous extension is called PAVILLON D'AMOUR.

Liebesgeige (Ger.). VIOLA D'AMORE.

Liebeshoboe (Ger.). OBOE D'AMORE.

Liebesklarinette (Ger.). CLARINETTO D'AMORE.

Liebesträum. Characteristic piano genre by Liszt, 1850; the title usually remains untranslated, to avoid the relatively pedestrian *Dream of Love* or *Love's Dream*. Liszt wrote 3 *Liebesträume* in 1850, originally for voice and piano; No. 3 in A-flat Major for Piano is particularly favored. Each bore a subtitle *Notturno*, and each was provided with an epigraph from German poetry. The 1st praised exalted love, the 2nd was a meditation on saintly death, and the 3rd sang of earthly love.

Liebesverbot, Das (The Ban on Love). Opera by Wagner, 1836, 1st performed in Magdeburg, after Shakespeare's *Measure for Measure*. Unmarried love being a capital crime, an incautious youth is sentenced to death for fornication. But his liberal-minded sister arouses the populace against the brutality of the law, and her brother is saved. The score is imitative of von Weber.

lieblich (Ger.). Lovely, sweet, charming.

lied (Ger. *Lied*; Eng. *song*; plural, *Lieder*). An art (Classical) song in German for voice and piano; a "composed" song as distinguished from a "spontaneous" song of folk origin. The standard form of the lied is for a single voice with piano accompaniment. The structure is most often strophic, requiring only a single musical setting for each stanza of the poem. German poems most suitable to be set to music in this form are rhymed verses containing the same number of syllables in each line; this symmetry of design in the poem corresponds to the symmetry of the musical setting.

Music historians ascribe the creation of the lied to Schubert, who, in 1814, when he was only 16 years old, wrote his 1st lied, *Gretchen am Spinnrade* (Gretchen at the Spinning Wheel), an act of inspiration that compares favorably to the descent of the fiery tongues on the apostles at Pentecost. Schubert did have predecessors, notably Zelter and Reichardt, but also C. P. E. Bach and Beethoven. All 4 wrote songs to German texts in a manner distinguished by a fluid singing line, poignant lyricism of expression, and a symmetry of rhythmical design. Besides the great Schubert, other 19th-century composers of lieder were Mendelssohn, Schumann, Liszt, Brahms, Wagner, Loewe, and Wolf. Wolf expanded the piano accompaniment into an integral part of the lied as an art form; he furthermore introduced a chromatic harmony that earned him the sobriquet "the Wagner of the lied." Mahler, R. Strauss, and M. Reger, although not primarily composers of lieder, have contributed to the art.

Toward the end of the 19th century the German lied went into decline, at least in its structural aspect. Most songs of this period were *durchkomponiert* (through-composed), with each stanza written anew. Schoenberg created a novel type of lied in his 15 settings of poems by Stefan George, *Das Buch der hängenden Garten*, by introducing a songful narrative, SPRECHSTIMME, in which the text is recited in rising and lowering inflections. While the Romantic German lied cultivated poems of love, sorrow, and death, the modern German lied annexed topical elements, often of a political import, as in the songs of Eisler and Weill.

Going back in time we find a proliferation of the so-called *Generalbasslied*; that is, songs provided with BASSO CONTINUO, which indicated the intervallic content of the harmonies. To the same category belong the homophonic arias of the early opera and oratorio, closely related to Italian forms of accompanied song. Somewhere in the interstices of time we find the *volkstümliche Lied*, song in the folk manner, also known as *Lieder im Volkston*. German composers have always possessed a knack of assimilating the elements of popular songs so completely as to be able to regurgitate their rhythmic and melodic elements in new patterns. Anthologies of German popular songs are replete with samples of lieder whose composers are perfectly identifiable. What can be more *volkstümlich* than *Lorelei*, to words by Heine? Yet, it is not a folk song; it was written by a lesser lied composer named Silcher.

Lied von der Erde, Das (Song of the Earth). Sym. by Mahler, 1911, in 6 parts, for tenor, contralto, and orch.; the text is a group of Chinese poems in German trans. The work was 1st performed posthumously in Munich. Mahler superstitiously chose not to number the work (it would have been No. 9) because of earlier composers who didn't write more than 9 syms. (primarily Beethoven and Bruckner); he did write a No. 9, but died before he could finish No. 10. Despite the derivation of the text, the music has nothing of the Orient in it; rather, it is a series of profoundly Romantic impressions.

Lieder ohne Worte. Characteristic piano pieces by Mendelssohn, 1829–45, publ. in 8 sets. These "songs without words" are aptly named, for they present their moods and pictures in a characteristic lied manner. A few other composers have followed in Mendelssohn's generic footsteps.

Liederabend (Ger.). An informal or formal evening in which Classic and Romantic lieder are performed.

Liederspiel (Ger., play of songs). A dramatic format alternating set arias with spoken dialogue.

Liedertafel (Ger., song table). A male choral society organized in Berlin in 1809. Numerous branches of the soc. sprang up in many other cities of Germany and among German musical groups in America. The original Liedertafel was organized in imitation of the legendary King Arthur's Round Table, and the singers, like the knights of yore, were expected to be loyal to their group in serving the cause of music.

lieto (It.). Merrily, joyfully.

lieto fine (It.). HAPPY ENDING.

Lieutenant Kijé. Symphonic suite by Prokofiev, 1934, for an unfinished film of the same name. The suite was 1st performed in Paris, with Prokofiev himself conducting (1937). The name Kijé is a Russian misprint resulting from an accidental joining of a suffix with an expletive. The compound is inadvertently mistaken for a name, and stupid military bureaucrats of Nicholas I promote the suffix plus expletive to a higher rank. Since the Czar has already appended his signature to the promotion, Lieutenant Kijé becomes an official person; he "lives" a concocted glorious life and heroically tragic death. The music is appropriately grinning, full of vibrant rhythms and mock-sentimental romances; it has been borrowed for films by Alec Guinness and Woody Allen, among others.

lieve (It.). Lightly.

Life for the Czar, A. Opera by Glinka, 1936, 1st produced in St. Petersburg. The Czar of the opera is young Michael Romanov, elected in 1612 to rule Russia after a long period of social unrest. The Poles, intermittently warring with Russia, send a group of soldiers to kill Michael. Losing their way, they ask the peasant Ivan Susanin to guide them to the Czar's house, but he instead leads them into an impenetrable forest. The invaders kill him, but the Czar is saved. The opera is regarded as the 1st theatrical work in a national Russian style, even though its facture is largely Italian. It includes genuine Russian folk songs and a remarkable chorus in 5/4 time. Obviously the opera could not be performed after the Revolution under its original title; accordingly, the libretto was renamed after the heroic peasant: *Ivan Susanin.* The words in the finale chorus, which contain the glorification of the Czar, were altered to extol the greatness of Russia itself.

Life Is Just a Bowl of Cherries. Song by Ray Henderson, 1931, popularized by Bing Crosby and Ethel Merman. It provided solace to victims of the Great Depression by its optimistic reassurance.

ligature (from Lat. *ligare*, bind, tie). In mensural notation, a fusion of 2 or more melodic notes into one notational symbol. The component parts of a ligature indicate not only the relative pitch, but also the rhythmic values, following an elaborate but sometimes self-contradictory set of rules. Depending on the number of notes in a ligature, they were classified as *binary, ternary, quaternary,* etc. At the next level of classification the terminology of various ligatures was standardized with the establishment of square-note notation. The most common binary and ternary ligatures correspond to accents and other diacritical signs of the alphabet: *pes* (foot) corresponds to the acute accent, indicating a rise of a degree; *clivis* (incline) corresponds to the grave accent, indicating a descent of one degree; *torculus* (twisted) corresponds to the circumflex accent, thus denoting a rise and a fall of one degree, etc. 2. A tie of 2 or more notes, sometimes resulting in a syncopation. 3. A group or series of notes to be executed in 1 breath, to 1 syllable, or as a legato phrase.

Ligeti, György (Sándor), eminent Hungarian-born Austrian composer and pedagogue; b. Dicsöszentmárton, Transylvania, May 28, 1923. The original surname of the family was Auer; his great-uncle was Leopold Auer. He studied composition with Ferenc Farkas at the Kolozsvar Cons. (1941–43) and privately with Pal Kadosa in Budapest (1942–43); then continued his training with Sandor Veress, Pal Járdányi, Farkas, and Lajos Bardos at the Budapest Academy of Music (1945–49), where he subsequently was a prof. of harmony, counterpoint, and analysis (from 1950). After the Hungarian revolution was crushed by the Soviet Union in 1956, he fled his homeland for the West; in 1967 he became a naturalized Austrian citizen.

He worked at the electronic music studio of the West German Radio in Cologne (1957–58); from 1959 to 1972 he lectured at the Darmstadt summer courses in new music; from 1961 to 1971 he also was a visiting prof. at the Royal Stockholm Academy of Music. In 1972 he served as composer-in-residence at Stanford Univ., and in 1973 he taught at the Berkshire Music Center at Tanglewood. In 1973 he became a prof. of composition at the Hamburg Hochschule für Musik. He has received numerous honors and awards. In 1964 he was made a member of the Royal Swedish Academy in Stockholm, in 1968 a member of the Akademie der Künste in Berlin, and in 1984 an honorary member of the American Academy and Inst. of Arts and Letters; in 1986 he received the Grawemeyer Award of the Univ. of Louisville; in 1988 he was made a Commandeur in the Ordre National des Arts et Lettres in Paris.

In his bold and imaginative experimentation with musical materials and parameters, Ligeti endeavors to bring together all aural and visual elements in a synthetic entity, making use of all conceivable effects and alternating tremendous sonorous upheavals with static chordal masses and shifting dynamic colors. He describes his orch.l style as *micropolyphony*. The Kyrie from his Requiem for Soprano, Mezzo-Soprano, 2 Choruses, and Orch. (1965) was "borrowed" for the film score to *2001: A Space Odyssey*. Other works include *Le Grand Macabre*, a musical theater piece (1974–78), and various orch.l, chamber, and vocal works. Early in his career, Ligeti also wrote works for electronic instruments.

Light My Fire. A 1967 number 1 hit for the Doors that introduced sartorial lead singer Jim Morrison to a large audience. It was then covered a year later successfully by blind guitarist José Feliciano.

light opera. OPERETTA.

Like a Rolling Stone. A number 3 smash for Bob Dylan in 1965; his 1st "electric" number, with rambling, poetic lyrics. The title comes from Muddy Waters, not Mick Jagger.

Like a Virgin. The Material Girl's 1st number 1 song, in which Madonna plays off her image as a good/bad girl.

Lilburn, Douglas (Gordon), New Zealand composer; b. Wanganui, Nov. 2, 1915. He studied with J. C. Bradshaw at Canterbury Univ. College (1934–36), then won the Grainger Competition with his tone poem *Forest* (1936); subsequently studied with Edward Mitchell (piano) and Vaughan Williams (composition) at the Royal College of Music in London (1937–40), where he received the Cobbett Prize for his *Phantasy* for String Quartet (1939). He began teaching at Victoria Univ. in Wellington (1947); was made prof. and director of the electronic music studio (1970), positions he held until his retirement in 1979. He composed 3 syms. (1951; 1951, rev. 1974; 1961, and other orch.l, chamber, piano, and vocal works, as well as works for tape.

limpido (It.). Clearly, distinctly.

Lin, Cho-Liang, outstanding Chinese-born American violinist; b. Hsin-Chu, Taiwan, Jan. 29, 1960. He began to study the violin as a child and won the Taiwan National Youth Violin Competition at the age of 10; when he was 12 he became a pupil of Robert Pikler at the New South Wales State Conservatorium of Music in Sydney; at 15 he went to the U.S., where he enrolled at the Juilliard School in N.Y. as a scholarship student of Dorothy DeLay (graduated, 1981). He won wide notice when he was chosen to play at the inaugural concert for President Jimmy Carter in 1977; that same year he won 1st prize in the Queen Sofia International Competition in Madrid. In subsequent years he pursued a highly rewarding career as a virtuoso, touring throughout the world; he appeared as a soloist with virtually every major orch., and also was active as a recitalist and chamber music player. In 1988 he became a naturalized U.S. citizen. His extensive repertoire ranges from the standard literature to specially commissioned works. In his performances he combines effortless technique with a beguiling luminosity of tone. He has recorded works by Arensky, Brahms, Bruch, Mozart, Nielsen, Sibelius, Tchaikovsky, Haydn, Saint-Saëns, Prokofiev, Stravinsky, Mendelssohn, and Vieuxtemps.

Lincoln Portrait. Ode for narrator and orch. by Copland, 1942; it became one of his most celebrated works. The text is selected from Lincoln's own speeches, and there are modified quotations from ballads of the time. It was 1st performed in Cincinnati, with the poet Carl Sandberg narrating and André Kostelanetz conducting.

Lincoln, the Great Commoner. Song by Ives, 1912–13, to a poem by Edward Markham; there are 2 versions: for voice and piano, and for unison voices and orch.

Lind, Jenny (Johanna Maria), celebrated Swedish soprano, nicknamed the "Swedish Nightingale"; b. Stockholm, Oct. 6, 1820; d. Wynds Point, Herefordshire, Nov. 2, 1887. She made her 1st stage appearance in Stockholm at the age of 10 (1830); that same year she entered the Royal Opera School there, where she studied with C. Craelius and I. Berg; during this period she also sang in many comedies and melodramas; continued her studies with A. Lindblad and J. Josephson at the school, and then made her formal operatic debut as Agathe in *Der Freischütz* at the Royal Opera in Stockholm (Mar. 7, 1838); later that year appeared as Pamina and Euryanthe there, and then as Donna Anna (1839) and Norina (1841). In 1840 she was appointed a regular member of the Royal Swedish Academy of Music, and she was also given the rank of court singer. However, she felt the need to improve weaknesses in her voice, and went to Paris to study with Manuel Garcia (1841–42).

Upon her return to Stockholm she sang Norma (1842); later appeared there as the Countess, Anna in *La Sonnambula*, Valentine in *Les Huguenots*, and Anna Bolena. Although Meyerbeer wrote the role of Vielka in his opera *Ein Feldlager in Schlesien* for her, the role was 1st sung by Tuczec in Berlin (1844); Lind 1st essayed it there the following year. She also sang in Hannover, Hamburg, Cologne, Koblenz, Frankfurt, Darmstadt, and Copenhagen. She appeared at the Leipzig Gewandhaus (1845) and made her Vienna debut as Norma at the Theater an der Wien (1846); subsequently sang throughout Germany, returning to Vienna as Marie in 1847 and creating a sensation. Later that year Lind made a phenomenally successful London debut as Alice in *Robert le Diable* at Her Majesty's Theatre in London; her appearances in *La Sonnambula* and *La Fille du régiment* were acclaimed; she then created the role of Amalia in Verdi's *I Masnadieri* there (1847).

After touring the English provinces Lind decided to retire from the operatic stage, making her farewell appearance as Norma in Stockholm (1848) and as Alice at London's Her Majesty's Theatre (1849). If her success in Europe was great, her U.S. concert tour exceeded all expectations in public agitation and monetary reward. Sponsored by P. T. Barnum, she was seen as a natural phenomenon rather than an artist; nonetheless, her outstanding musicality made a deep impression upon the musical public. She made her N.Y. debut in 1850, subsequently giving 93 concerts in all, her final one in Philadelphia (1851). In 1852 she married her accompanist, Otto Goldschmidt, in Boston; they returned to Europe, settling permanently in England in 1858. She continued to appear in concert and oratorio performances until her retirement in 1883, when she became prof. of singing at London's Royal College of Music. She also devoted much time to charitable causes.

Lind possessed an extraordinary coloratura voice, with a compass reaching high G (g^3), although her middle register remained veiled from overuse in her early career. Despite this, she was, without question, one of the greatest vocal artists of her era.

Linda di Chamounix. Opera by Donizetti, 1842, 1st produced in Vienna. The eponymous heroine loves an artist who for some reason has concealed his noble parentage. She goes insane when he goes away; but when he returns, he sings an old love song for her, she regains her wits, thus assuring a LIETO FINE.

Lindy hop. An exuberant American jazz dance, 1927, in syncopated 2/4 time; named after Charles Linbergh's aeronautical solo hop to Paris. The dances take 2 slow steps, then 2 quicksteps, with occasional sidesteps (shuffles) and other variants.

linear counterpoint. A modern term describing a type of contrapuntal writing in which individual lines are the main considerations in the ensemble.

lining out. The common usage in American rural churches for the preliminary reading by a congregation member of a line from a hymn just before the entire congregation sings it; a similar practice was called DEACONING.

Linus. A mythological Greek hero who tried to teach music to Hercules and was slain by his pupil with his own LYRE when he tried to correct an error Hercules made during a lesson. A *Song of Linus* was sung each year at harvest time in Homer's day to commemorate his tragic death.

Linz Symphony. Sym. No. 36 by Mozart in C Major, 1783 (K. 425). It was written to honor a patron of music in the Austrian city of Linz.

Lion Sleeps Tonight, The. Adaptation of the traditional South African folk song *Wimoweh*, which became a number 1 hit for the Tokens in 1961. Revived in the popular Disney film *The Lion King* (1995).

lion's roar. A membranophone of the frictional type, consisting of a bucket covered with a membrane through which a rosined cord is passed. When the cord is pulled vigorously, a sound resembling the roar of a lion is produced. Its generic English name is friction drum; it is found in various forms throughout the Americas, Europe, India, and Japan. Varèse wrote a part for it in his *Ionisation*.

lip. 1. In a flue pipe, the flat surfaces above (upper) and below (lower) the mouth. 2. Lipping; that is, the art of so adjusting the lips to the mouthpiece of a wind instrument as to get a good tone.

Lipatti, Dinu (actually Constantin), outstanding Romanian pianist and composer; b. Bucharest, Apr. 1, 1917; d. Chêne-Bourg, near Geneva, Dec. 2, 1950. His father was a violinist who had studied with Sarasate, and his mother was a pianist; his godfather was Enesco. He received his early training from his parents; then studied with Florica Musicescu at the Bucharest Cons. (1928–32). He received a 2nd prize at the International Competition at Vienna in 1934, a judgment which prompted Cortot to quit the jury in protest; Lipatti then studied piano with Cortot, conducting with Munch, and composition with Dukas and Boulanger in Paris (1934–39). He gave concerts in Germany and Italy, returning to Rumania at the outbreak of World War II. After escaping from Rumania in 1943, he settled in Geneva as a teacher of piano at the Cons. After the war he resumed his career; played in England 4 times (1946–48).

His remarkable career was tragically cut short by lymphogranulomatosis. He was generally regarded as one of the most sensitive interpreters of Chopin, and was also praised for his deep understanding of the Baroque masters; he was a fine composer. Lipatti was married to the pianist and teacher Madeleine Cantacuzene. His compositions include works for solo piano (a sonata, nocturnes, a fantasy, a sonatina for left hand, a concertino with orch., dances); piano duo (a suite, dances, a symphonie concertante with orch.); piano trio (a fantasy, an improvisation); a violin sonatina; the *Aubade* for Wind Quartet; the symphonic poem *Satrarii*; songs.

lira (Grk. *lyra*). 1. Bowed string instrument of modern Greece, Bulgaria, and Dalmatia. It has a pear-shaped wooden body, a peg disc to hold the lateral pegs for 3, occasionally 4 strings. The neck is indistinct; the strings are fingered laterally, obviating the need for a fingerboard. Earliest references to the lira are found in the late 1st millennium A.D.; it should not be confused with the LYRE.

lira da braccio (It., lyre of the arm). A bowed chordophone, probably an outgrowth of the medieval FIDDLE but held against the player's body. There were 2 sizes, the smaller held against the shoulder, the larger (sometimes known as the *lirone da gambe*) was held lower. The instrument normally had 5 playing strings and 2 drones; most sources indicate that the fingerboard was fretted. Its popularity dates from the late 1400s to the early Baroque.

lira da gamba (It., lyre of the knee). LIRONE.

lira organizzata ("organized" lyre; Fr. *vielle organisée*; Ger. *Orgelleier*). A HURDY-GURDY in which the sound is enhanced by organ pipeworks and bellows, produced by a rotating wheel; thus the term *organized* refers to the instrument, not the way someone keeps her or his business files. The instrument is usually built in a guitarlike shape.

lira rustica (It.), **lira tedesca** (Ger.). HURDY-GURDY.

lirone (*archi viola*; It. *large lira*). *Lira da gamba*, a VIOLA DA GAMBA–like bowed chordophone with a wide fretted neck, with 2 drone strings and 9–14 melody strings, held between the knees. Its popularity was brief: from the mid-16th to the mid-17th centuries.

liscio (It.). Smoothly, flowing.

Listen to the Mockingbird. Song by Septimus Winner, 1855, described on the publ. edition's cover as "a sentimental Ethiopian ballad." This was one of the most successful songs of this type, selling 20 million copies of sheet music.

l'istesso, lo stesso (It.). The same. *L'istesso tempo*, the same tempo.

Liszt, Franz

Greatly celebrated Hungarian pianist and composer, creator of the modern form of the symphonic poem, and innovating genius of modern piano technique; b. Ferenc Liszt (baptized Franciscus), Raiding, near Odenburg, Oct. 22, 1811; d. Bayreuth, July 31, 1886. His father was an amateur musician who devoted his energies to the education of his son; at the age of 9, young Liszt was able to play a difficult piano concerto by Ries.

A group of Hungarian music-lovers provided sufficient funds to finance Liszt's musical education. In 1822 the family traveled to Vienna. Beethoven was still living, and Liszt's father made every effort to persuade Beethoven to come to young Liszt's Vienna concert (1823). Legend has it that Beethoven did come and was so impressed that he ascended the podium and kissed the boy on the brow. There is even in existence a lithograph that portrays the scene, but it was made many years after the event by an unknown lithographer, and its documentary value is dubious. Liszt himself perpetuated the legend, and he often showed the spot on his forehead where Beethoven was supposed to have implanted the famous kiss. However that might be, Liszt's appearance in Vienna created a sensation; he was hailed by the press as "child Hercules." The link with Beethoven was maintained through Liszt's own teachers: Czerny, who was Beethoven's student and friend and with whom Liszt took piano lessons, and the great Salieri, who was Beethoven's early teacher and who at the end of his life became Liszt's teacher in composition.

In 1823 Liszt gave a concert in Pest. The announcement of the concert was made in the florid manner characteristic of the period: "Esteemed Gentlemen! Highborn nobility, valorous army officers, dear audience! I am a Hungarian, and before traveling to France and England, I am happy now to present to my dear Fatherland the 1st fruits of my training and education." Salieri appealed to Prince Esterházy for financial help so as to enable Liszt to move to Vienna, where Salieri made his residence. "I recently heard a young boy, Francesco Liszt, improvise on the piano," Salieri wrote, "and it produced such a profound impression on me that I thought it was a dream."

Apparently Esterházy was sufficiently impressed with Salieri's plea to contribute support.

Under the guidance of his ambitious father (a parallel with Mozart's childhood suggests itself), Liszt applied for an entrance examination at the Paris Cons., but its powerful director, Cherubini, declined to accept him, ostensibly because he was a foreigner (Cherubini himself was a foreigner, but was naturalized). Liszt then settled for private lessons in counterpoint from Antoine Reicha, a Parisianized Czech musician who instilled in Liszt the importance of folklore. Liszt's father died in 1837; Liszt remained in Paris, where he soon joined the brilliant company of men and women of the arts. Paganini's spectacular performances of the violin in particular inspired Liszt to emulate him in creating a piano technique of transcendental difficulty and brilliance, utilizing all possible sonorities of the instrument. To emphasize the narrative Romantic quality of his musical ideas, he accepted the suggestion of his London manager, Frederick Beale, to use the word *recital* to describe his concerts, and in time the term was widely accepted by other pianists.

In his own compositions Liszt was a convinced propagandist of program music. He liked to attach descriptive titles to his works, such as *Fantasy, Reminiscence,* and *Illustration*. The rhapsody was also made popular by Liszt, but he was not its originator; it was used for the 1st time in piano pieces by Tomaschek. A true Romantic, Liszt conceived himself as an actor playing the part of his own life, in which he was a child of the Muses. Traveling in Switzerland, he signed his hotel register as follows: "Place of birth—Parnasse. Arriving from—Dante. Proceeding to—Truth. Profession—Musician-philosopher." He was fascinated by Étienne Pivert de Senancour's popular novel *Obermann* (1804) that depicted an eponymous fictional traveler; Liszt wrote a suite of piano compositions under the general title *Années de pèlerinage*, in which he followed in music the imaginary progressions of Obermann.

Handsome, artistic, a brilliant conversationalist, Liszt was sought after in society. His 1st lasting attachment was with an aristocratic married woman, the Comtesse Marie d'Agoult (1805–76); they had 3 daughters, 1 of whom, Cosima, married Liszt's friend von Bülow before abandoning him for Wagner. D'Agoult was fluent in several European languages and had considerable literary talents, which she exercised under the nom de plume of Daniel Stern. Liszt was 22 when he entered his concubinage with her; she was 28. She confided her impressions of Liszt in her diary: "He was tall and rather slender with a pale visage and green eyes, the color of seawater, which suddenly came to life with sparks of excitement. He talked very fast, exposing his ideas with a strange passion. The spark of his looks, his gesticulation, his conversational manner, his smile, all these traits were full of depth and infinite tenderness."

The growing intimacy between Liszt and d'Agoult soon became the gossip of Paris. Berlioz warned Liszt not to let himself become too deeply involved with her. "She possesses a calculated attraction," he told Liszt. "She has a lively spirit, but she lacks true friendship." D'Agoult rapidly established herself as a salon hostess in Paris; she was a constant intermediary between Liszt and his friend Chopin. Indeed, the Chopin biography publ. under Liszt's name just after the Polish composer's death was largely written by d'Agoult, whose literary French was much superior to Liszt's. His 2nd and final lasting attachment was with another married woman, Princess Carolyne von Sayn-Wittgenstein, who was separated from her husband. Her devotion to Liszt exceeded all limits, even in a Romantic age. "I am at your feet, beloved," she wrote him. "I prostrate myself under your footprints." Liszt tried to marry Sayn-Wittgenstein, but he encountered resistance from the Roman Catholic Church, to which they both belonged; an attempt at an annulment was refused, and, after the husband's death, the prohibition against marriage to a divorced woman militated against it. After more than 15 years of trying, Liszt gave up, and he set up a separate residence from the Princess's. Thus, Liszt, the great lover of women, never married.

Liszt became known informally as "Abbé," thanks to 4 minor orders (ostuary, lector, exorcist, and acolyte) conferred upon him by Pope Pius IX (1865), but his religious affiliations were not limited to the Catholic church. He was also a member of the order of Freemasons and served as a tertiary of the Order of St. Francis. In 1879 he received the tonsure and an honorary canonry. But he was never ordained a priest, and thus was free to marry an appropriate woman if he so wished. When he met an attractive woman in Rome, he said to her, "Under this priestly cloak there beats the passionate heart of a man."

Liszt's romantic infatuations did not interfere with his brilliant virtuoso career. One of his greatest successes was his triumphant tour in Russia in 1842. Russian musicians and music critics exhausted their flowery vocabulary to praise Liszt as the miracle of the age. "How fortunate we are that we live in the year 1842 and so are able to witness the living appearance in our own country of such a great genius!" wrote the music critic Stasov. His Majesty Czar Nicholas I himself attended a concert given by Liszt in St. Petersburg, and expressed his appreciation by sending him a pair of trained Russian bears. Liszt acknowledged the imperial honor but did not venture to take the animals with him on his European tour; they remained in Russia.

Liszt was a consummate showman. In Russia, as elsewhere, he had 2 grand pianos installed on the stage at right angles, so that the keyboards were visible from the right and the left respectively and he could alternate his playing on both. He appeared on the stage wearing a long cloak and white gloves, discarding both with a spectacular gesture. Normally he needed eyeglasses, but he was too vain to wear them in public.

It is not clear why, after all his triumphs in Russia and elsewhere in Europe, Liszt decided to abandon his career as a piano virtuoso and devote his entire efforts to composition. He became associated with Wagner, his son-in-law, as a prophet of "music of the future." Indeed, Liszt anticipated Wagner's chromatic harmony in his works. A remarkable instance of such anticipation is illustrated in his song *Ich möchte hingehen* (1845, rev. 1860), which prefigures, note for note, the theme from the prelude to *Tristan und Isolde*. Inevitably Liszt and Wagner became objects of derision on the part of conservative music critics. A pictorial example of such an attack was an extraordinary caricature entitled "Music of the Future," distributed in N.Y. (1867). It represented Liszt with arms and legs flailing symmetrically over a huge orch. that comprised not only human players but also goats, donkeys, and a cat placed in a cage with an operator pulling its tail. At Liszt's feet there was placed a score marked "Wagner, not to be played much till 1995."

In 1848 Liszt accepted the position of Court Kapellmeister in Weimar. When Wagner was exiled from Saxony, Liszt arranged for the production of *Lohengrin* in

Weimar on Aug. 28, 1850; he was also instrumental in supervising performances in Weimar of *Der fliegende Holländer* and *Tannhäuser*, as well as music by Berlioz and a number of operas by other composers. Liszt also established a teaching series at his home. A vivid description of these classes was compiled by one of his students, August Göllerich. Liszt was invariably kind to his students; occasionally he would doze off, but he would always wake up when a student completed his or her playing and say "Schön." When one of his American students called to his attention that the date was July 4, Liszt asked if someone would play variations on *Yankee Doodle* for him, for, as he said, "Today we are all Americans." Apparently Liszt gave instruction gratis. He was also generous to colleagues and often lent them money; Wagner, who constantly had financial difficulties, often asked Liszt for loans (which were seldom, if ever, returned), and Liszt invariably obliged. He was also hospitable to his colleagues; during his Weimar years, for instance, young Brahms stayed in his home for 3 weeks.

Liszt was very much interested in the progress of Russian music. In Weimar he received young Glazunov, who brought with him his 1st sym. He played host to Borodin and Cui, who came to Weimar to pay their respects, and was lavish in his appreciation of their works; he also expressed admiration for Rimsky-Korsakov and Mussorgsky, although they never came to see him personally. When Rimsky-Korsakov asked him to contribute a variation to a Russian collection based on *Chopsticks* (then a waltz), Liszt obliged with his own contribution, adding, "There is nothing wittier than your variations. Here you have at last a condensed manual of harmony and counterpoint. I would gladly recommend this album to conservatory professors as an aid to teaching composition."

In his Weimar years Liszt aged rapidly. Gone were the Classical features that had so fascinated his contemporaries, especially women, during his virtuoso career. Photographs taken in Weimar show him with snow-white hair descending upon his shoulders. He walked with difficulty, dragging his feet. He suffered attacks of phlebitis in his legs and had constant intestinal difficulties. He neglected his physical state, and finally developed double pneumonia and died during a sojourn in Bayreuth at the age of 74.

In his secular works Liszt was deeply conscious of his Hungarian heritage, but he gathered his material mainly from Gypsy dance bands that played in Budapest. In a strange show of negligence, he borrowed a theme for one of the most famous of his *Hungarian Rhapsodies* from an unpubl. work by an obscure Austrian musician named Heinrich Ehrlich, who had sent him a MS for possible inclusion in one of Liszt's recitals. He explained this faux pas as an oversight. While Liszt is usually thought of as a great Hungarian composer, he was actually brought up in the atmosphere of German culture. He spoke German at home, with French as a 2nd language. His women companions conversed with him in French, and most of Liszt's own correspondence was in that language. It was not until his middle age that he decided to take lessons in Hungarian, but he never acquired fluency. He used to refer to himself jocularly as "half Gypsy and half Franciscan monk." This self-identification haunted him through his life, and beyond; when the question was raised after his death in Bayreuth regarding the transfer of his body to Budapest, the prime minister of Hungary voiced objection, since Liszt never regarded himself as a purely Hungarian musician.

As a composer Liszt made every effort to expand the technical possibilities of piano technique; in his 2 piano concertos, and particularly in his *Études d'exécution transcendante*, he made use of the grand piano, which expanded the keyboard in both the bass and the extreme treble. He also extended the field of piano literature with his brilliant transcriptions of operatic excerpts, from works by Mozart, Verdi, Wagner, Donizetti, Gounod, Rossini, and Beethoven. These transcriptions were particularly useful at the time, when the piano was the basic musical instrument at home (and the phonograph still a dream of the future).

Liszt was a great musical technician. He organized his compositions with deliberate intent to create music that was essentially new. Thus he abandoned the traditional succession of 2 principal themes in sonata form. In his symphonic poem *Les Préludes* the governing melody dominates the entire work. In his popular 3rd *Liebestraum* for Piano the passionate melody modulates by 3rds rather than by Classically anointed 5ths and 4ths. The great *Faust Sym.* is more of a literary essay on Goethe's great poem than a didactic composition. His 2 piano concertos are free from the dialectical contrasts of the established Classical school. The chromatic opening of the 1st Concerto led von Bülow to improvise an insulting line to accompany the theme, "Sie sind alle ganz verrückt!"

(They are all quite mad!), and the introduction of the triangle solo aroused derisive whoops from the press. Liszt was indifferent to such outbursts. He was the master of his musical fate in the ocean of sounds.

Liszt was an eager correspondent; his letters, written in longhand, in French, and in German, passed upon his death into the possession of Sayn-Wittgenstein; after her death in 1887, they were inherited by her daughter, Marie Hohenlohe-Schillingsfürst. She, in turn, left these materials to the Weimar court; eventually they became part of the Liszt Museum in Weimar.

Liszt's numerous works fall into nearly every genre, and a selective list must be well short of comprehensiveness. Many of his orch. works were orchestrated by Raff or Conradi (although Liszt often redid the orchestrations later); these will be marked with an asterisk. Among the pieces that he is best remembered for are 2 syms.: *Eine Faust-Symphonie in drei Charakterbildern* for Tenor, Men's Voices, and Orch. (1854–57; Weimar, 1857); *Eine Symphonie zu Dantes Divina commedia* (1855–56; only 2 movements completed; Dresden, 1857); 13 symphonic poems; 4 piano concertos; *Piano Concerto in the Hungarian Style* (1885); *Malédiction* for Piano and Strings (1833); *Totentanz* for Piano and Orch. (1849; rev. 1853 and 1859; The Hague, 1865); *2 Episodes from Lenau's Faust* (No. 1, 1860–61; No. 2, Weimar, 1861); *Rákóczy March* (1865; rev. 1867; Budapest, 1875); *2nd Mephisto Waltz* (Budapest, 1881). Additional piano works include *Étude en douze exercices* (1826); *Grandes études de Paganini* (1831); *Harmonies poétiques et religieuses* (1833; rev. 1835); *Apparitions* (1834); *Vingt-quatre grandes études* (1837);

Album d'un voyageur (3 vols., 1835–38); *Études d'exécution transcendante d'après Paganini* (1838–39); *Venezia e Napoli* (c. 1840; rev. 1859); *Tre sonetti del Petrarca* (1844–45); *19 Hungarian Rhapsodies*, 1846–1885, including No. 15 in A Minor, *Rákóczy March* (1851; rev. 1871); *6 Consolations* (1844–48); *Trois études de concert* (c. 1848); *Années de pèlerinage: Deuxième année, Italie* (1837–49); *Études d'exécution transcendante* (1851); *Harmonies poétiques et religieuses* (1840–52); Sonata in B Minor (in 1 movement, perhaps his most influential and groundbreaking work; 1851–53); *Années de pèlerinage: Première année, Suisse* (1848–52); *Weinen, Klagen, Sorgen, Zagen, Präludium* (1859); *Variationen über das Motiv von Bach* (1862); 2 Konzertetuden: No. 1, *Waldersrauschen*, and No. 2, *Gnomenreigen* (1862–63); *Années de pèlerinage, troisième année* (1867–77); *Wiegenlied—Chant du berceau* (1880); *Nuages gris* (1881); *La lugubre gondola* (1882; rev. 1885); *R.W.—Venezia* (1883); *Am Grabe Richard Wagners* (1883); *Schlaflos, Frage und Antwort* (1883); *En rêve* (1885); *Ruhig* (1883–86); *Recueillement* (1887); numerous arrangements and transcriptions.

He also wrote many vocal works, including sacred and choral music and numerous solo songs (in several languages). Lizst's canon also includes organ and chamber music. Liszt published 2 thematic catalogues of his works (1855; 1877). A complete thematic catalogue is found in L. Friwitzer, "Chronologisch-systematisches Verzeichnis sämtlicher Tonwerke Franz Liszts," *Musikalische Chronik* V (Vienna, 1887); the corresponence was catalogued in C. Suttoni, "Franz Liszt's Published Correspondence: An Annotated Bibliography," *Fontes Artis Musicae* XXVI (1979).

litany. A song of supplication imploring God, the Blessed Virgin, and assorted saints with a promise to repent in exchange for divine intercession. A litany is chanted by the priest in an oscillating monotone with the choir or congregation responding. The most auspicious time for a litany is the period of Rogation Days (from Lat. *rogare*, to beg). The unrelenting repetitiousness of a litany is of the essence for cumulative impact on the more compassionate saints. Litanies of the Anglican Church are less impressive, and the words often have a somewhat colloquial inflection (e.g., "Spare us, Good Lord").

Little Drummer Boy, The. Annoying Christmas perennial written by Harry Simeone and Henry Onorati, and a chart hit (every Christmas, natch) for Simeone in 1958, 1959, 1960, 1961, and 1962.

Little Nemo. See WHIFFENPOOF SONG, THE.

Little Night Music, A. Musical by Sondheim, 1973, based on the Ingmar Bergman film *Smiles of a Summer Night*. Its most memorable song is *Send in the Clowns*, winner of a Grammy Award in Judy Collins's rendition (1976); other numbers include *Now-Later-Soon*, *Every Day a Little Death*, *It Would Have Been Wonderful*, and *Liaisons*.

Little Russian Symphony. Tchaikovsky's 2nd Sym., 1873, in C minor, 1st performed in Moscow. The title, as it commonly appears in English, is misleading: it is not an infantile sym., but a sym. of Little Russia, a condescendingly imperialistic designation in Czarist Russia for Ukraine. Indeed, Ukrainian songs are used thematically in the work.

Little Sweep, The. See LET'S MAKE AN OPERA.

liturgical drama. Medieval plays in Latin containing action, dialogue, and occasional singing episodes. While liturgical drama makes use of biblical subjects, it never became part of the Roman Catholic liturgy itself, but remained a TROPE. One of the most popular types of liturgical drama is the genre of miracle plays, reciting stories of saints, of whom St. Nicholas was a favorite. During the Renaissance liturgical drama developed into mystery plays (a misconstrued title actually meaning ministerial plays, from the Latin word *ministerium*, a service). Gradually such plays assumed a secular theatrical role while adhering to biblical subjects. Incidental music such as dances, trumpet flourishes, processions—even folk songs—was used. In Italy these dramas with music became known as *sacre rappresentazioni*, and as *autos* (acts) in Spain and Portugal. These festivals were true predecessors of scenic oratorios and, by ramification, Wagnerian music dramas.

Liturgical Symphony (*Symphonie liturgique*). The 3rd sym. by Honegger, 1946, 1st performed in Zurich. The 3 movements are labeled *Dies Irae*, *De Profundis*, and *Dona nobis pacem*.

liturgy (Old Grk. *leōs* + *ergon*, people work). The most comprehensive term for the official service of the established Christian Church. In the Byzantine ritual, the liturgy is synonymous with the Mass.

lituus (Lat.). 1. A hooked bronze trumpet, originally Etruscan, taken up by the ancient Romans. 2. CORNETT. 3. Instrument called for by Bach in his motet *O Jesu Christ, mein's Lebens Licht* (BWV 118); musicological opinion is that Bach intended the cornet or trumpet.

liuto (It.). LUTE.

live electronic music. Music which requires ELECTRONIC MUSIC in its performance beyond simple tape playback or amplification of sound. When a singer or acoustic instrumentalist performs through electronic or computer equipment so that the final sound has been processed, the output is called *electroacoustic music.*

livret (Fr.). LIBRETTO

llamada (Sp., fanfare). Generic term for works of a proclamatory nature.

Lloyd Webber, Andrew, tremendously successful English composer, brother of Julian Lloyd Webber; b. London, Mar. 22, 1948. His father, William Southcombe Lloyd Webber (1914–82), was a composer and the director of the London College of Music; his mother was a piano teacher; inspired and conditioned by such an environment, Lloyd Webber learned to play piano, violin, and horn, and soon began to improvise music, mostly in the style of American musicals. He attended Westminster School in London, then went to Magdalen College, Oxford, the Guildhall School of Music, and the Royal College of Music in London. In college he wrote his 1st musical, *The Likes of Us*, dealing with a philanthropist. In 1967 he composed the theatrical show *Joseph and the Amazing Technicolor Dreamcoat*, which was performed at St. Paul's Junior School in London in 1968; it was later expanded to a full-scale production and achieved considerable success for its amalgam of a biblical subject with rock music, French chansonnettes, and country-western songs. In 1970 it was produced in America, and in 1972 was shown on television.

He achieved his 1st commercial success with *Jesus Christ Superstar*, an audacious treatment of the religious theme in terms of jazz and rock. It premiered in London in 1972 and ran for 3,357 performances; it was as successful in America. Interestingly enough, this "rock opera" was 1st released as a record album, which eventually sold 3 million copies. *Jesus Christ Superstar* opened on Broadway in 1971, even before the London production. There were protests by religious groups against the irreverent treatment of a sacred subject; particularly offensive was the suggestion in the play of a carnal relationship between Jesus and Mary Magdalen; Jewish organizations, on the other hand, protested against the implied portrayal of the Jews as guilty of the death of Christ. The musical closed on Broadway on June 30, 1973, after 720 performances; it received 7 Tony Awards. In 1981 the recording of *Jesus Christ Superstar* was given the Grammy Award for best cast show album of the year. The great hullabaloo about the musical made a certainty of his further successes.

His early musical *Joseph and the Amazing Technicolor Dreamcoat* was revived at the off-Broadway Entermedia Theater in N.Y.'s East Village (1981), and from there moved to the Royale Theater on Broadway. In the meantime, he produced a musical with a totally different chief character, *Evita*, a semifictional account of the career of the 1st wife of Argentine dictator Juan Perón; it was staged in London on June 21, 1978; a N.Y. performance soon followed, with splendid success. But perhaps his most spectacular production was *Cats*, inspired by T. S. Eliot's *Old Possum's Book of Practical Cats*; it was produced in London (1981) and was brought out in N.Y. in 1982 with fantastic success; *Evita* and *Joseph and the Amazing Technicolor Dreamcoat* were still playing on Broadway, so that Lloyd Webber had the satisfaction of having 3 of his shows running at the same time. Subsequent successful productions were his *Song and Dance* (1983) and *Starlight Express* (London, 1984).

His series of commercial successes reached a lucrative apex with the production of *The Phantom of the Opera* (London, 1986; N.Y., 1988), a gothically oriented melodramatic tale of contrived suspense. In 1989 his musical *Aspects of Love* opened in London. He then adapted the famous film *Sunset Boulevard* for the stage, premiering in London in 1993 and a year later on Broadway. Apart from popular shows, Lloyd Webber wrote a mini-opera, *Tell Me on a Sunday*, about an English girl living in N.Y., which was produced by BBC Television in 1980. Quite different in style and intent were the *Variations* for Cello and Jazz Ensemble (1978), written for his brother; and *Requiem* (N.Y., 1985).

Lloyd Webber, Julian, talented English cellist, brother of Andrew Lloyd Webber; b. London, Apr. 14, 1951. He studied with Douglas Cameron (1964–67) and then at the Royal College of Music in London (1967–71); he also studied with Pierre Fournier in Geneva. He made his concert debut at London's Queen Elizabeth Hall in 1972; subsequently played many engagements as a soloist with English orchs. He made his American debut in N.Y. in 1980. In 1978 he became prof. of cello at the Guildhall School of Music in London. He ed. *Song of the Birds: Sayings, Stories and Impressions of Pablo Casals* (London, 1985).

lo (It.). The.

lo stesso (It.). The same. *Lo stesso tempo*, the same tempo; *lo stesso tempo e animando sempre più*, the same rate of speed, with ever increasing animation (of expression).

Lobgesang (Ger.). Song of praise.

loco (It., from Lat. *locus*, place). Play in the normal (written) register, following an *8va* or similar passage (up or down).

Locrian mode. Modern term for a theoretical church mode, corresponding to the scale from B to B on the white keys of the piano keyboard. Since its dominant F stands to its tonic B in the relation of a "forbidden" diminished 5th (the DIABOLUS IN MUSICA), the Locrian mode was not used in Gregorian chant. Glareanus called this mode *hyperaeolian* (above the AEOLIAN).

Lodoïska. Opera by Cherubini, 1791, successfully produced in Paris. The eponymous heroine loved a political prisoner held by a medieval Polish warlord who covets her himself. When his castle is besieged by the invading Tartar army, Lodoïska escapes with her lover. The plot must have pleased the French revolutionaries; Cherubini himself was able to weather the numerous changes in French leadership until his death in 1842.

Loeffler, Charles Martin (born Martin Karl Löffler), outstanding German-born American composer, violinist, and violist; b. Berlin, Jan. 30, 1861; d. Medfield, Mass., May 19, 1935. His father was a writer who moved the family to Russia, where he was engaged in government work in the Kiev district; later they lived in Debrecen and Switzerland. In 1875 Martin Karl began taking violin lessons in Berlin with Rappoldi, who prepared him for study with Joachim; he studied theory with Kiel; also took lessons with Bargiel at the Berlin Hochschule für Musik (1874–77). Sometime between 1875 and 1878 his father was arrested on political grounds; he died in 1884 after suffering a stroke. This was the pivotal event of his son's life; he developed such an antipathy toward the German empire that he changed his name (jettisoning the umlaut), made himself an Alsatian by birth, and adopted the French soul for his own. (His wife and sister were the only people he told the story to until his death.)

Loeffler then went to Paris, where he continued his musical education with Massart (violin) and Guiraud (counterpoint and composition). He was engaged briefly as a violinist in the Pasdeloup orch.; then was a member of the private orch. of the Russian Baron Paul von Derwies at his sumptuous residences near Lugano and in Nice (1879–81). When Derwies died in 1881, Loeffler went to the U.S., with letters of recommendation from Joachim; he became a naturalized citizen in 1887. He played in the orch. of Leopold Damrosch in N.Y. in 1881–82. In 1882 he became 2nd concertmaster of the newly organized Boston Sym. Orch., but was able to accept other engagements during late spring and summer months; in the spring of 1883 he traveled with the Thomas Orch. on a transcontinental tour; the summers of

1883 and 1884 he spent in Paris, where he took violin lessons with Hubert Leonard. He resigned from the Boston Sym. Orch. in 1903, and devoted himself to composition and farming in Medfield. He was married to Elise Burnett Fay (1910). After his death she donated to the Library of Congress in Washington, D.C., all of his MSS, correspondence, etc.; by his will, he left the material assets of his not inconsiderable estate to the French Academy and the Paris Cons. He was an officer of the French Academy (1906); a Chevalier in the French Legion of Honor (1919); a member of the American Academy of Arts and Letters; Mus.Doc. (honoris causa), Yale Univ. (1926).

Loeffler's position in American music is unique, brought up as he was under many different national influences: French, German, Russian, and Ukrainian. One of his most vivid scores, *Memories of My Childhood* (Evanston, Ill., 1924), reflects the modal feeling of Russian and Ukrainian folk songs. But his aesthetic code was entirely French, with definite leanings toward impressionism; the archaic constructions that he sometimes affected, and the stylized evocations of ARS ANTIQUA, was also in keeping with the French manner. His most enduring work, *A Pagan Poem* (Boston, 1907), is cast in such a neoarchaic vein. He was a master of colorful orchestration; his harmonies are opulent without saturation; his rhapsodic forms are peculiarly suited to the evocative moods of his music. His only excursion into the American idiom was the employment of jazz rhythms in a few of his lesser pieces. He is best known for his instrumental music, especially those involving the viola and viola d'amore.

Loesser, Arthur, esteemed American pianist, teacher, and writer on music, half-brother of Frank (Henry) Loesser; b. N.Y., Aug. 26, 1894; d. Cleveland, Jan. 4, 1969. He studied with Stojowski and Goetschius at the Inst. of Musical Art in N.Y.; made his debut in Berlin (1913). He 1st played in N.Y. in 1916; after touring the Orient and Australia (1920–21), he appeared widely in the U.S. In 1926 he was appointed a prof. of piano at the Cleveland Inst. of Music. In 1943 he was commissioned in the U.S. Army as an officer in the Japanese intelligence dept.; mastered the language and, after the war, gave lectures in Japanese in Tokyo; was the 1st American musician in uniform to play for a Japanese audience (1946). He publ. *Humor in American Song* (N.Y., 1943) and an entertaining vol., *Men, Women and Pianos: A Social History* (N.Y., 1954).

Loesser, Frank (Henry), talented American composer and lyricist, half-brother of Arthur Loesser; b. N.Y., June 29, 1910; d. there, July 28, 1969. He was educated at City College in N.Y., where he began writing songs for college activities; he subsequently was active as a reporter, singer, and vaudeville performer. In 1931 he settled in Hollywood and devoted himself mainly to writing musical comedies. During World War II he was in the U.S. Army and wrote several Army songs, including *Praise the Lord and Pass the Ammunition* (1942) and *Roger Young* (1945). Although he continued to compose successful songs, he found his greatest reward in producing shows for Broadway; these included *Where's Charley?* (1948), *Guys and Dolls* (1950), *The Most Happy Fella* (1956), and *How to Succeed in Business Without Really Trying* (1961), which won a Pulitzer Prize and ran for 1,416 performances. His last musical was *Pleasures and Palaces* (Detroit, 1965).

Loewe, Frederick, remarkable Austrian-American composer of popular music; b. Vienna, June 10, 1901; d. Palm Springs, Calif., Feb. 14, 1988. He studied piano in Berlin with Busoni and d'Albert and composition with Reznicek; emigrated to the U.S. in 1924, and after a period as a concert pianist, devoted himself to composing popular music. Adapting adroitly to the American idiom, he became one of the most successful writers of musical comedies. His 1st musical comedies were *Salute to Spring* (St. Louis, June 12, 1937), *Great Lady* (N.Y., Dec. 1, 1938), and *The Life of the Party* (Detroit, Oct. 8, 1942). He met the lyricist and playwright Alan Jay Lerner in 1942, which led to their collaboration on the unsuccessful musical *What's Up?* (N.Y., Nov. 11, 1943). Their next effort, *The Day Before Spring* (N.Y., Nov. 22, 1945), received a respectable hearing, but it was with *Brigadoon* (N.Y., Mar. 13, 1947) that they achieved success. After *Paint Your Wagon* (N.Y., Nov. 12, 1951), they took Broadway by storm with *My Fair Lady* (N.Y., Mar. 15, 1956; with 2,717 subsequent perfs.), based on George Bernard Shaw's *Pygmalion*. They then brought out the film score *Gigi* (1958), after a story by Colette, which won 9 Academy Awards. Their final Broadway collaboration was the highly acclaimed musical *Camelot* (N.Y., Dec. 3, 1960). Loewe came out of retirement in 1974 to collaborate with Lerner on the score to the film *The Little Prince*. See A. Sirmay, ed., *The Lerner and Loewe Songbook* (N.Y., 1962).

Loewe, (Johann) **Carl** (Gottfried), outstanding German composer of lieder; b. Lobejun, near Halle, Nov. 30, 1796; d. Kiel, Apr. 20, 1869. His father, a schoolmaster and cantor, taught him the rudiments of music; when he was 12 he was sent to the Francke Inst. in Halle, where his attractive manner, excellent high voice, and early ability to improvise brought him to the attention of Jerome Bonaparte, who granted him a stipend of 300 thalers annually until 1813. His teacher was Türk, the head of the Francke Inst.; after Türk's death in 1813, Loewe joined the Singakademie founded by Naue. He also studied theology at the Univ. of Halle, but soon devoted himself entirely to music.

He had begun to compose as a boy; under the influence of Zelter, he wrote German ballades, and developed an individual style of great dramatic force and lyrical inspiration; he perfected the genre, and was regarded by many musicians as the greatest song composer after Schubert and before Brahms. His setting of Goethe's poem *Erlkönig* (1818), which came just after Schubert wrote his great setting to the same poem, is one of Loewe's finest creations; other songs that rank among his best are *Edward, Der Wirthin Töchterlein, Der Nock, Archibald Douglas, Tom der Reimer, Heinrich der Vogler, Oluf,* and *Die verfallene Mühle.* Loewe was personally acquainted with Goethe, and also met Weber. In 1820 he became a schoolmaster at Stettin, and in 1821 music director there and organist at St. Jacobus Cathedral. He lived in Stettin, except for frequent travels, until 1866, when he settled in Kiel. He visited Vienna (1844), London (1847), Sweden and Norway (1851), and Paris (1857), among other places.

Loewe was an excellent vocalist and was able to perform his ballades in public. He publ. the pedagogic works *Gesang-Lehre, theoretisch und practisch* (Stettin, 1826); *Musikalischer Gottesdienst: Methodische Anweisung zum Kirchengesang und Orgelspiel* (Stettin, 1851); *Klavier- und Generalbass-Schule* (Stettin, 2nd ed., 1851). In addition to his 368 ballades, Loewe wrote 6 operas, oratorios, cantatas, syms., piano concertos, string quartets, piano sonatas, and a piano trio.

Lohengrin. Opera by Wagner, 1850, to his own libretto, 1st performed in Weimar. Liszt conducted it in Wagner's absence, who was in exile in Switzerland as a fugitive from Saxony, being sought by authorities for his rather nominal involvement in the 1848 Revolution. In *Lohengrin,* as always, Wagner shows his fascination with Nordic legends. Elsa of Brabant has a mystic dream of a noble knight who would defend her from a monstrous accusation of fratricide. Her dream knight arrives in a boat drawn by a swan. She marries him to the strains of the famous bridal chorus (which has sanctified millions of ordinary marriages in Europe and America). Although he adjures her never to ask his name and origin, she breaks the injunction. He then reveals that he is Lohengrin, the Knight of the Holy Grail,

son of Parsifal; his swan is Elsa's brother, believed to be dead. The swan's human shape is restored, but Lohengrin must leave now that his identity is known. Swanless, he summons a dove to draw the boat away. The opera is Wagner's 1st great masterpiece, but as the critical mass usually gets the point late (if at all), it is possible to understand why *The Musical World* of London opined so disparagingly of it in 1855: "*Lohengrin* is an incoherent mass of rubbish. Being a Communist, Herr Wagner affirms that national melody is unhealthy. . . . The true basis of harmony is cast away for a reckless, wild, extravagant and demagogic cacophony, the symbol of profligate libertinage."

lointain (Fr.). Distant, far away; sounding faintly.

Lomax, Alan, important American ethnomusicologist, b. Austin, Tex., Jan. 31, 1915. He acquired his metier from his father, John Avery Lomax (b. Goodman, Miss., Sept. 23, 1867; d. Greenville, Miss., Jan. 26, 1948); then studied at the Univ. of Tex. in Austin (B.A., 1936) and at Columbia Univ. (1939). He joined his father as a researcher in 1933; collected folk songs in the Southwestern and Midwestern regions of the U.S.; they supervised field recordings of rural and prison songs, discovering Leadbelly; they rediscovered Jelly Roll Morton and recorded interviews with him at the Library of Congress in Washington, D.C. (1938). He also collected folk songs in Europe. In 1963 he was made director of the Bureau of Applied Social Research and, at Columbia Univ., the project on *cantometrics,* a theory of cultural identification through a measurement of musical and other elements. He has written numerous books, both alone and with his father, drawing on his collecting activities.

Lombardi alla prima Crociata, I (The Lombards at the 1st Crusade). Opera by Verdi, 1843, dealing with 2 crusading brothers from Lombardy who are rivals in love. The more ambitious one plans to kill the other but slays their father by mistake. To expiate his sin he goes to Jerusalem and becomes a hermit. His niece is captured by the infidels but falls in love with her captor's son. Her lover is wounded but is baptized by the hermit just in time to save his expiring heathen soul. As the battle rages the brothers are reunited; the parricide hermit is forgiven by his brother and dies in peace. The opera was 1st performed in Milan; it was then staged in London in 1846 and in N.Y. in 1847; in France, Germany, Poland, and Russia it played under the title *Jerusalem,* and returned to La Scala as *Gerusalemme.*

London Bridge Is Falling Down. A nursery rhyme that became popular in England and the U.S. during the last quarter of the 19th century.

London Symphonies. A group of 12 syms. by Haydn, beginning with No. 93 and ending with his last sym., No. 104. He wrote these syms. for the London violinist and impresario Salomon, who arranged for his London tours in 1791–92 and again in 1794–95. (It took Haydn 17 days to reach London from Vienna by stagecoach and sailboat.)

London Symphony, A. Vaughan Williams's Sym. No. 2, 1914, one of his most popular; it was 1st performed in London. Within its 4 movements there are realistic musical allusions to the noises of London streets, while the chimes of Big Ben are heard through it all. Vaughan Williams exhorted the listeners to treat this sym. as a piece of ABSOLUTE MUSIC, taking in the street cries and other London scenes as incidental.

Londonderry Aire (Air). A famous Irish melody, apparently an authentic folk song, which was 1st published in 1855. Since genuine Irish tunes are pentatonic, it is probable that the leading tone that opens the melody in the common version of the tune is an adjustment, and that the submediant was probably the original tone; this emendation destroyed the pentatonic character of the melody. In 1913 Frederick Weatherly wrote a set of lyrics to the tune, entitled *Danny Boy*.

Long Christmas Dinner, The. Opera by Hindemith, 1961, to an English libretto by him and Thornton Wilder, based on the latter's play; it was 1st performed in Mannheim (in German). The dinner is indeed long, lasting a century, with one generation following another for a meal; the work consists of consecutive interdependent scenes.

Long Tall Sally. Little Richard's 1st major crossover hit, from June 1956; 2 months later it was shamelessly covered by white-bread teen throb Pat Boone; 7 years later, covered by the Beatles.

longa (Lat., long). In mensural notation, a note equal to 2 or 3 breves, depending on context. It is indicated by a square with a downward stem to its right.

longevity

Cursory reading of actuarial tables seems to indicate that musicians as a class of people live on the average about 12 years longer than nonmusicians under similar social and geographical conditions. When an aging sym. conductor showed a desperate reluctance to quit, an unfeeling music critic remarked: "Conductors rarely die and never resign." The greatest conductor of modern times, Arturo Toscanini, continued to lead an orch. well into his 80s and resigned only after he suffered an embarrassing lapse of memory at a concert. Leopold Stokowski conducted concerts and made recordings after he turned 91. Pierre Monteux had already arranged a program he expected to conduct with the Boston Sym. Orch. on his 90th birthday, but unfortunately predeceased the date by a few months.

Organists are apt to live longer than sym. conductors. The celebrated French organist Charles-Marie Widor lived to be 93. There are several cases on record when church organists died at the console. Among them was the blind French organist Louis Vierne, who died while playing one of his new compositions at the organ of Notre Dame de Paris (1937); he was only 66. The record of longevity for pianists is not as impressive as that of organists. The American pianist Henry Holden Huss, who was also a composer of sorts, made a point of playing a program of his works on his 90th birthday. Artur Rubinstein continued to give concerts even after he became blind; he died at the age of 95. Violinists and cellists usually stop playing in public after 70, but the greatest cellist of the 20th century, Pablo Casals, continued to play publicly until shortly before his death at 97. Among singers, Manuel Garcia lived to be 101, but he abandoned his professional singing career long before, and became active mainly as a teacher.

Marie Olénine d'Alheim (1869–1970) terminated her career as a concert singer in her middle age to enter radical politics; she joined the French Communist party and went to Moscow, where she died at the round age of 100.

One has to cite less universally known names to find nonagenarians and centenarians among composers. Havergal Brian reached the age of 96. Henri Büsser died at the age of 101, but he was little known outside of France. Carl Ruggles lived to be 95, and he was fortunate in acquiring a solid reputation before he died. Eubie Blake, the American black ragtime virtuoso, appeared on television in his late 90s; he died a few days after reaching his 100th anniversary. The most spectacular case of a composer's longevity is that of the American composer Margaret Ruthven Lang, who reached the age of 104 before she finally died. Descending further into the depths of obscurity we find the name of Victor Kuzdo, a Hungarian-American violinist and composer whose vital enzymes sustained him in Glendale, Calif., until his death at the age of 106, an all-time record in the annals of musical biography.

Statistically, mediocre musicians live much longer than men of genius. Among truly great composers only Verdi lived well into his 80s. Wagner did not even reach the biblically sanctified age of 3-score and 10. Beethoven, Debussy, Ravel, and Tchaikovsky died before their 60th birthdays. And Chopin, Schubert, Schumann, and Mendelssohn, not to mention Mozart, died in their 30s or 40s, at the height of their genius. Is it that angels are eager to carry away the best musicians for heavenly concerts?

longhair. A derogatory characterization of a person interested in classical music; synonymous with HIGHBROW. It derives from the conventional portraiture of older musicians sporting a luxuriant head of long hair; Liszt in his last photograph appears thus uncropped.

long-playing records (recordings). Phonograph discs intended to rotate at 33 1/3 revolutions per minute (rpm), introduced by Columbia Records in 1947. This makes it possible to place 25 minutes (more or less) on a single side of a disc, as opposed 4 1/2 minutes on a side of the 78-rpm disc. This result was accomplished by having more circular grooves in combination with a slower speed of recording. Long-playing records inaugurated a new era in phonograph recordings enabling the phonograph companies to record a whole act of an opera or a whole sym. on a single disc. Long-playing records are often called LPs for short.

lontana (It.). Far away. *Da lontana*, from a distance.

lontano (It.). LOINTAIN. *Tuono lontano*, distant thunder (Verdi: *Otello*).

Look for the Silver Lining. Song by Kern, 1920, included in the musical *Sally*. It provided the sentimental leitmotiv in the biopic on Kern, *Till the Clouds Roll By*; it has been revived by Garrison Keillor on his *Prairie Home Companion* broadcasts.

Loriod, Yvonne, distinguished French pianist and teacher; b. Houilles, Seine-et-Oise, Jan. 20, 1924. She studied at the Paris Cons., winning no less than 7 *premiers prix*; among her mentors were L. Lévy, I. Philipp, Marcel Ciampi, Messiaen, and Milhaud for composition. She began collaborating with Messiaen on the premiere of *Visions de l'Amen* for 2 Pianos (1943); she would later play the 1st performances of all of his piano parts. After World War II she toured extensively; made her U.S. debut in the premiere of Messiaen's *Turangalila-Symphonie* with the Boston Sym. Orch. (1949). She taught at the Paris Cons. A foremost champion of the music of Messiaen, she married him in 1961. She also excelled in performances of the music of Bartók, Schoenberg, Barraqué, and Boulez.

Lortzing, (Gustav) **Albert,** celebrated German opera composer; b. Berlin, Oct. 23, 1801; d. there, Jan. 21, 1851. His parents were actors, and the wandering life led by the family did not allow him to pursue a methodical course of study. He learned acting from his father, and music from his mother at an early age. After some lessons in piano with Griebel and in theory with Rungenhagen in Berlin, he continued his own studies, and soon began to compose. In 1823 he married the actress Rosina Regina Ahles in Cologne; they had 11 children. In 1824 he wrote his stage work, the singspiel *Ali Pascha von Janina, oder Die Französen in Albanien*, which, however, was not produced until 4 years later (Munster, 1828). He then brought out the liederspiel *Der Pole und sein Kind, oder Der Feldwebel vom IV. Regiment*

(1832) and the singspiel *Szenen aus Mozarts Leben* (Osnabruck, 1832), which were well received on several German stages.

From 1833 to 1844 he was engaged at the Municipal Theater of Leipzig as a tenor; there he launched a light opera, *Die beiden Schützen* (1837), which became instantly popular; on the same stage he produced his undoubted masterpiece, *Zar und Zimmermann, oder Die zwei Peter* (1837). It was performed with enormous success in Berlin (1839), and then in other European music centers. His next opera, *Caramo, oder Das Fischerstechen* (Leipzig, 1839), was a failure; there followed *Hans Sachs* (Leipzig, 1840) and *Casanova* (Leipzig, 1841), which passed without much notice; subsequent comparisons showed some similarities between *Hans Sachs* and *Die Meistersinger von Nürnberg*, not only in subject matter, which was derived from the same source, but also in some melodic patterns; however, no one seriously suggested that Wagner was influenced by Lortzing's inferior work.

There followed a comic opera, *Der Wildschütz, oder Die Stimme der Natur* (Leipzig, 1842), which was in many respects the best that Lortzing wrote, but its success, although impressive, never equaled that of *Zar und Zimmermann*. At about the same time Lortzing attempted still another career, that of opera impresario, but it was short-lived; his brief conductorship at the Leipzig Opera (1844 45) was similarly ephemeral. Composing remained his chief occupation; he produced *Undine* in Magdeburg (1845) and *Der Waffenschmied* in Vienna (1846). He then went to Vienna as conductor at the Theater an der Wien, but soon returned to Leipzig, where he produced the light opera *Zum Grossadmiral* (1847).

The revolutionary events of 1848 seriously affected his position in both Leipzig and Vienna; after the political situation became settled, he produced in Leipzig an opera of a Romantic nature, *Rolands Knappen, oder Das ersehnte Gluck* (1849). Although at least 4 of his operas were played at various German theaters, Lortzing received no honorarium, owing to a flaw in the regulations protecting the rights of composers. He was compelled to travel again as an actor, but he could not earn enough money to support his large family, left behind in Vienna. In the spring of 1850 he obtained the post of conductor at Berlin's nondescript Friedrich-Wilhelmstadt Theater. His last score, the comic opera *Die Opernprobe, oder Die vornehmen Dilettanten*, was produced in Frankfurt am Main while he was on his deathbed in Berlin; he died the next day. His opera *Regina*, written in 1848, was ed. by Richard Kleinmichel, with the composer's libretto

revised by Adolf L'Arronge, and performed in Berlin as *Regina, oder Die Marodeure* (1899); his singspiel *Der Weihnachtsabend* was produced in Münster (1832). Lortzing also wrote an oratorio, *Die Himmelfahrt Jesu Christi* (Münster, 1828); some incidental music to various plays; choral works; and songs.

It is as a composer of characteristically German Romantic operas that Lortzing holds a distinguished, if minor, place in the history of dramatic music. He was a follower of Weber, without Weber's imaginative projection; in his lighter works he approached the type of French operetta; in his best creations he exhibited a fine sense of facile melody, and infectious rhythm; his harmonies, though unassuming, were always proper and pleasing; his orchestration, competent and effective.

Lost Chord, The. Organ piece by A. Sullivan, 1877, composed during the eventually fatal illness of his beloved brother Fred. The "lost chord" is the 2nd inversion of the dominant 7th chord, mounted upon a pedal point, and forming an acerbic dissonance.

Lost in the Stars. Musical tragedy by Weill, 1949; the plot is based on Alan Paton's novel *Cry, the Beloved Country*. A young black South African takes part in a robbery and kills a white man. He is caught and sentenced to hang. The father of the slain white man goes to see the murderer's father; the 2 find a way to reconcile their racial differences in mutual sorrow. The score approaches a type of scenic oratorio; arias and choruses bear a religious character. Outstanding among them are the lament *Cry, the Beloved Country* and *Lost in the Stars*.

Lott, Felicity (Ann), English soprano; b. Cheltenham, May 8, 1947. She studied in London at Royal Holloway College, Univ. of London, and at the Royal Academy of Music; in 1976 she sang at Covent Garden in the world premiere of Henze's *We Come to the River*; she also appeared there as Anne Trulove in *The Rake's Progress*, Octavian, and other roles. She appeared in Paris for the 1st time in 1976; made her Vienna debut in 1982 singing the *4 letze Lieder* of R. Strauss; in 1984 was engaged as soloist with the Chicago Sym. Orch. In 1986 she sang at the wedding of the Duke and the Duchess of York at Westminster Abbey. In 1990 she was made a Commander of the Order of the British Empire; also in 1990 she made her Metropolitan Opera debut in N.Y. as the Marschallin.

Among her other fine roles are Pamina, Countess Almaviva, Donna Elvira, and Arabella.

loud pedal. The far-right pedal of the piano; when depressed, it releases (lifts) all dampers normally resting on the strings, allowing the strings that have been struck to continue vibrating (i.e., sound). This makes it necessary to change the pedaling quickly when the harmony changes to avoid unwelcome cacophony. The handling (or more accurately, the footing) of the loud pedal must therefore be considered with great care on general musical grounds rather than narrowly pianistic grounds. One of the natural safety impulses among pianists unsure of their technique is to step on the right pedal to create a universal resonance in which the annoying wrong notes may be conveniently drowned out. When a composer writes for piano orchestrally, requiring sustained tones in changing harmonies, a compromise must be sought using the skill of subtle half-pedaling. An outstanding example is a variation in Schumann's *Études symphoniques*, in which the theme occurs in the bass while the harmony changes above, making it extremely difficult to achieve both the legato in the left hand and the changing harmonies in the right hand.

Louie Louie. Richard Berry's ode to a Caribbean sailor and his lost love, which became popular in the Northwest, where it was covered by Paul Revere and the Raiders (unsuccessfully) and the Kingsmen. The later version shot up the charts in 1963 and inspired an FBI probe into the supposedly "obscene" lyrics. Since then, a favorite of garage bands everywhere and a rock classic! Subject of a book by Dave Marsh (1993).

Louise. "Roman musical" by G. Charpentier, 1900, to his own libretto; the work was an immediate success, with nearly 1,000 performances during the 1st half of the century. The opera is a counterpart of the Italian VERISMO and even includes imitated cries of vegetable vendors on Parisian streets. Louise is a poor seamstress who yields to the passion of Julien, a young Paris artist. Her fate is uncertain at the end of the opera, but in its sequel, *Julien*, she is spoken of as dead.

Louisiana Story. Film score by Thomson, 1948, composed for a eponymous documentary film, for which he won the Pulitzer Prize. Thomson drew a suite from the score, which he called *Acadian Songs and Dances*; it was premiered in Philadelphia (1951).

lourdement (Fr.). Heavily.

loure (Fr., bagpipe). A dance in 6/4 or 3/2 time and slow tempo, the downbeat strongly marked, with syncopation. The loure is often included in the Baroque instrumental suite as well as the French ballets and overtures of the rococo period.

louré (Fr., bagpipe; It. *portato*). Slurred, legato, nonstaccato. The origin of the word itself is from *lura* (bagpipe, implying a dronelike sound), which also generated the term *louré* as a kind of bowing technique on string instruments in which several notes are played in one bow stroke but in a detached manner. The most common marking is a slur encompassing dotted notes.

Love for Three Oranges, The. Opera by Prokofiev, 1921, 1st produced in Chicago, with the composer conducting. The composer's libretto is based on a Gozzi COMMEDIA DELL'ARTE play. "Spectators" observe the goings-on from a gallery and participate in the action. A witch (Fata Morgana) decrees that the young Prince of Clubs, who laughed when she suffered an embarrassing fall, would be doomed to wander in search of 3 oranges. In the desert, the Prince meets Tchelio, the court magician, who warns them not to open the oranges unless they are near water. The Prince steals the large oranges from a castle cook; he and his companion Truffaldino rest in the desert with the oranges. While the Prince sleeps the thirsty Truffaldino slices open an orange; a princess steps out, begs for water, and dies. Truffaldino repeats his tragic mistake, and runs away. The Prince awakens and opens the last orange; Princessa Ninetta steps out and is saved from death by the Spectators, who rush in with a bucket of water. The Princess is then changed into a rat; she and the Prince undergo more trials but are eventually victorious; the rat returns to human form, and, as Fata Morgana is led away to prison, the royal couple celebrates. The suite from the opera is popular, especially the March.

Love Life. Musical by Weill, 1948. An American couple married in 1791 are still together a century and a half later. Although there are no signs that death will soon do them part, they neither love nor cherish each other anymore, mainly because of divergent desires for individual prosperity. Their longevity provides a stencil for a musical history of the U.S., from glee singers to crooners. Includes *Green-Up Time* and *Mr. Right*.

Love Makes the World Go 'Round. Song by Bob Merrill, 1961, featured in the musical *Carnival*.

Love Me Tender. Theme from Elvis's 1st film, and a number 1 hit. It was adapted from the traditional folk song *Aura Lee.*

luce (It., light). A proposed *color organ* marked by Scriabin in the score of his last symphonic work, *Prométhée;* according to Scriabin's unfulfilled hopes, the luce would have bathed the concert hall in shimmering hues that changed along with the harmonies.

lucernarium (Lat. *lucerna,* lamp). Former term for the canonical hour of Vespers; it refers to the necessary lighting of candles for an evening service.

Lucia di Lammermoor. Opera by Donizetti, 1835, 1st produced in Naples. The libretto is based on Walter Scott's novel *The Bride of Lammermoor.* Edgar loves Lucia, but her ambitious brother wants her to marry a British Lord. When Edgar goes to the wars, Lucia is told that he was unfaithful to her; when Edgar returns he finds her engaged to be married to the Lord. He pronounces a curse on the whole family, after taking part in a famous sextet, the other 5 singers being Lucia, her brother, Lucia's husband-to-be, his chaplain, and Lucia's lady-in-waiting. On her wedding night Lucia murders the Lord and goes insane. In this celebrated "mad scene" she imagines being married to Edgar; she then swoons and dies. Vowing to join her in eternity, Edgar stabs himself to death. For all its hyperventilating narrative, *Lucia di Lammermoor* is one of the most mellifluous products of the Italian art of BEL CANTO.

Lucier, Alvin (Augustus, Jr.), important American composer of the experimental school; b. Nashua, N.H., May 14, 1931. He studied with Howard Boatwright, Richard Donovan, David Kraehenbuhl, and Quincy Porter at Yale Univ. (1950–54); continued his training with A. Berger, I. Fine, and H. Shapero at Brandeis Univ. (1958–60); also studied with Lukas Foss (composition) and Copland (orchestration) at the Berkshire Music Center in Tanglewood (1958, 1959); then went to Rome on a Fulbright scholarship (1960–62). He was on the faculty of Brandeis Univ. (1962–70), where he served as choral director. With Robert Ashley, David Behrman, and Gordon Mumma, he founded the Sonic Arts Union (1966), an electronic-music performing group with which he toured the U.S. and Europe. He joined the faculty of Wesleyan Univ. (1970); was music director of the Viola Farber Dance Co. (1972–77). He contributed many articles to music journals

and other publications; with D. Simon, he publ. *Chambers* (Middletown, Conn., 1980). In 1990 he was in Berlin on a Deutscher Akademischer Austauschdienst fellowship.

His works exploit virtually all known musical and nonmusical resources available to the creative artist, and redefine the term *music* in radical terms. Devices used by Lucier include amplified brain waves, vocoder, moving large and small resonant environments, acoustic orientation by means of echolocation, electromagnetic tape, responsive surfaces, strewn material, closed-circuit television system, unattended percussion, microphones, loudspeakers, sound-producing object, audio oscillators, electronic monochord, sound-sensitive lights, electronic music system powered and controlled by sunlight, pure-wave oscillators, acoustic pendulums, sound installation, amplified clock, galvanic skin response sensor, digital delay system, open umbrella, and glass oven dish. Many of these tools have been incorporated into SOUND INSTALLATIONS.

Lucio Silla. Opera by Mozart, 1772, 1st performed in Milan, Dec. 26, 1772. Silla was the Roman general who reached the highest power after he was elected consul in 81 B.C. and then proclaimed himself dictator of Rome. In Mozart's opera he renounces his power and returns it to the people. Mozart was only 16 when he wrote this opera.

Lucrezia Borgia. Opera by Donizetti, 1833, 1st produced in Milan. Lucrezia, the most infamous of the historical Borgia family in 16th-century Italy, shelters her illegitimate son in the Borgia castle and helps him to elude arrest by her husband's henchmen. While handing cups of poisoned wine to some of them, she unwittingly passes poison to her son. Ostensibly the libretto was drawn from a tragedy by Victor Hugo, but he was outraged when the opera was produced, and demanded a total revision. This was done; Lucrezia turned Turkish, and the title was changed to *La Rinnegata* (The Renegade).

ludi spirituales (Lat., spiritual plays). Medieval sacred mystery plays on biblical subjects.

Ludus Tonalis. Piano cycle by Hindemith, 1944, which he subtitled *Studies on Counterpoint, Tonal Organization, and Piano Playing.* Among the several contrapuntal devices used here, the introductory praeludium is converted into the final postludium by turning the page upside down and therefore reading the music backward, with some liberal dispensation for accidentals. The body of the work consists of 12 fugues with intervening interludes. The work was 1st performed in Chicago.

Ludwig, Christa, remarkable German soprano; b. Berlin, Mar. 16, 1924. She was reared in a musical family; her parents both sang. Ludwig studied at the Hochschule für Musik in Frankfurt; in 1946 she made her operatic debut in Frankfurt in the role of Orlofsky in *Die Fledermaus*, singing there until 1952. In 1954 she sang the roles of Cherubino and Octavian at the Salzburg Festival; in 1955 she was engaged by the Vienna State Opera; made her Metropolitan Opera debut in N.Y. as Cherubino (1959). In subsequent years she made considerable impact as a Wagnerian singer, being equally successful in such disparate roles as Kundry, Fricka, Venus, and Magdalene in *Die Meistersinger von Nürnberg*. She also obtained brilliant success as the Marschallin and other roles in operas by R. Strauss; she also sang the female leads in the 2 Berg operas.

In the Italian repertoire she gave fine interpretations of the roles of Amneris, Rosina, and Lady Macbeth.

Her career took her to opera theaters all over the world; she sang at La Scala in Milan, Covent Garden in London, the Teatro Colón in Buenos Aires, and the Nissei Theater in Tokyo. Sober-minded, skeptical music critics in Europe and America exerted their vocabularies to extol Ludwig as a superb singer not only in opera but also in the art of German lieder; some even praised her physical attributes. In 1962 she was named a Kammersängerin of Austria, and in 1969 she received the Cross of Merit, 1st Class, of the Republic of Austria. In 1980 she received the Golden Ring, and in 1981 was made an honorary member of the Vienna State Opera; in 1980 she was awarded the Silver Rose of the Vienna Phil. In 1957 she married Walter Berry, the Austrian baritone; they frequently appeared together in the same opera; they separated and in 1970 were divorced; in 1972 she married the French actor Paul Deiber.

Luening, Otto (Clarence)

Multifaceted American composer, teacher, flutist, and conductor; b. Milwaukee, June 15, 1900; d. N.Y., Sept. 2, 1996. He was of deeply rooted German ancestry, traceable to one Manfried von Luninck, who flourished in 1350; one of Luening's maternal ancestors was said to be a descendant of Martin Luther's sister. Luening's great-grandfather emigrated to the U.S. in 1839 and settled in Wisconsin; he made the 1st barley beer in Milwaukee. Luening's paternal grandfather was American-born; he became active in bilingual culture in Wis. and was an organizer of the German-English Academy. Luening's father was an educated musician who received his training at the Leipzig Cons.; he had met Wagner and sung in performances of Beethoven's 9th Sym., with Wagner conducting; returning to Milwaukee, he became active in German-American music; he kept his cultural associations with Germany, and in 1912 took his family to Munich. There Luening enrolled in the Akademie der Tonkunst, where he studied flute with Alois Schellhorn, piano with Josif Becht, and composition with A. Beer-Walbrunn. He gave his 1st concert as a flutist in Munich (1916).

When America entered World War I in 1917, Luening went to Switzerland, where he studied with Philip Jarnach and Volkmar Andreae at the Zurich Cons. (until 1920); he also had an opportunity to take private lessons with Busoni; pursuing his scientific interests, he attended a seminar in abnormal psychology at the Univ. of Zurich, and also appeared as an actor in the English Players Co. in Switzerland. It was during this period that he began to compose; his 1st violin sonata and a sextet were performed at the Zurich Cons. Luening returned to the U.S. in 1920; he earned a living as a flutist and conductor in theater orchs. In 1925 he moved to Rochester, N.Y., where he served as coach and executive director of the opera dept. at the Eastman School of Music; in 1928 he went to Cologne; from 1932 to 1934 he was on the faculty of the Univ. of Arizona in Tucson. In 1934 he became chairman of the music dept. at Bennington College in Vermont, keeping this position until 1944. After teaching at Barnard College in N.Y. (1944–47), he was on the music faculty at Columbia Univ. (1949–68), where he also was codirector of the Columbia-Princeton Electronic Music Center (1959–80) and music chairman of the School of the Arts (1966–70); likewise taught composition at the Juilliard School (1971–73).

An important development in Luening's career as a composer took place in 1952, when he began to experiment with the resources of the magnetic tape; he composed a strikingly novel piece, *Fantasy in Space*, in which he played the flute with its accompaniment electronically transmuted on tape; Stokowski featured it on his program in N.Y. on Oct. 28, 1952, along with Luening's 2 other electronic pieces, *Low Speed* and *Invention*. He found a partner in Vladimir Ussachevsky, who was also interested in musical electronics. Together they produced the 1st work that combined real sounds superinduced on an electronic background, *Rhapsodic Variations* for Tape Recorder and Orch., performed by the Louisville Orch. on Mar. 20, 1954; its performance anticipated by a few months the production of Varèse's similarly constructed work, *Déserts*. Another electronic work by Luening and Ussachevsky, *A Poem in Cycles and Bells* for Tape Recorder and Orch., was played by the Los Angeles Phil. on Nov. 18, 1954.

Bernstein conducted the 1st performance of still another collaborative composition by Luening and Ussachevsky, *Concerted Piece* for Tape Recorder and Orch., with the N.Y. Phil. on Mar. 31, 1960. Thenceforth, Luening devoted a major part of his creative effort to an integration of electronic sound into the fabric of a traditional orch., without abandoning the fundamental scales and intervals; most, but not all, of these works were in collaboration with Ussachevsky. Unaided, he produced *Synthesis* for Electronic Tape and Orch. (1960) and *Sonority Canon* (1962). He also wrote straightforward pieces without electronics; of these the most important is *A Wisconsin Sym.*, a sort of musical memoir of a Wis.-born composer; it was performed in Milwaukee, Luening's birthplace, on Jan. 3, 1976. His native state reciprocated proudly, awarding Luening an honorary doctorate from the Univ. of Wis. in Madison, a medal from the Wis. Academy of Sciences, Arts, and Letters, and a citation from the Wis. State Assembly. In addition to many other honors, he also held Guggenheim fellowships in 1930–31 and 1974–75.

luftig (Ger.). Airy, light.

Luftpause (Ger., breathing rest). A break between melody notes, and particularly at the end of a phrase. It is often used and abused by pseudo-Romantic performers, particularly violinists, who either cannot sustain a passage in legato or feel that a melody without a soulful luftpause would lack expressive power.

lugubre (It.). Mournful.

Lugubre Gondole, Le. Piano piece by Liszt, 1883, composed in Venice a few weeks before Wagner died there. Mystically inclined admirers of Wagner saw in this "lugubrious gondola" a premonition of death; but Liszt wrote *Pensée des Morts* as a youth nearly 50 years earlier and no death among his close friends followed its composition. Liszt did write a memorial piece upon learning of Wagner's death in Venice entitled *Richard Wagner: Venezia*. Contrary to expectations, there are no quotations from Wagner's own music, except for the ostentatious use of augmented triads, vaguely reminiscent of *The Ride of the Valkyries*.

Luisa Miller. Opera by Verdi, 1849, 1st produced in Naples. The gruesome libretto is derived from Schiller's tragedy *Kabale und Liebe*. Luisa loves Rodolfo, whose father wants him to marry a duchess and forces Luisa to write him a letter renouncing her love. Rodolfo poisons her and himself, but Luisa has just enough singing breath in her to tell him that she has been coerced. With his dying strength he kills the coercer, a henchman of his father's.

Lullaby of Broadway. Song by Harry Warren, from the musical *Gold Diggers of 1935*.

Lully, Jean-Baptiste

Celebrated Italian-born French composer; b. Giovanni Battista Lulli, Florence, Nov. 28, 1632; d. Paris, Mar. 22, 1687. The son of a poor Florentine miller, he learned to play the guitar at an early age. His talent for singing brought him to the attention of Roger de Lorraine, Chevalier de Guise, and he was taken to Paris in 1646 as a page to Mlle. de Montpensier, a young cousin of Louis XIV. He quickly adapted to the manner of the French court; although he mastered the language, he never lost his Italian accent. There is no truth in the report that he worked in the kitchens, but he did keep company with the domestic servants, and it was while he was serving in Mlle. de Montpensier's court in the Tuileries that he perfected his violin technique. He also had the opportunity to hear the 24 VIOLONS DU ROI (GRANDE BANDE) and was present at performances of Luigi Rossi's *Orfeo* at the Louvre in 1647.

When Mlle. de Montpensier suffered political disgrace in 1652 and was forced to leave Paris, Lully was released from her service, and early in 1653 he danced with the young Louis XIV in the ballet *La Nuit*. Shortly thereafter he was made *compositeur de la musique instrumentale du Roi*, with joint responsibility for the instrumental music in court ballets. At some time before 1656 he became conductor of Les Petits Violons du Roi, a smaller offshoot of the grand bande. This ensemble was heard for the 1st time in 1656 in *La Galanterie du temps*. Thanks to Lully's strict discipline with regard to organization and interpretation, Les Petits Violons soon came to rival the parent ensemble. The 2 groups were combined in 1664.

Lully became a naturalized French citizen in 1661, the same year in which he was appointed *surintendant de la musique et compositeur de la musique de la chambre*; he also became *maître de la musique de la famille royale* in 1662. His father-in-law was Michel Lambert, the eminent French composer (b. Champigny-sur-Veude, near Chinon, Indre-et-Loire, 1610; d. Paris, June 29, 1696). His association with Molière commenced in 1664; he provided Molière with the music for a series of COMÉDIES-BALLETS, culminating with *Le Bourgeois gentil-homme* in 1670. Lully acquired the sole right to form an Académie Royale de Musique in 1672, and thus gained the power to forbid performances of stage works by any other composer. From then until his death he produced a series of TRAGÉDIES LYRIQUES, most of which were composed to texts by the librettist Philippe Quinault. The subject matter for several of these works was suggested by the King, who was extravagantly praised and idealized in their prologues. Lully took great pains in perfecting these texts, but he was often content to leave the writing of the inner voices of the music to his pupils.

His monopoly of French musical life created much enmity. In 1674 Henri Guichard attempted to establish an Académie Royale des Spectacles, and their ensuing rivalry resulted in Lully accusing Guichard of trying to murder him by mixing arsenic with his snuff. Lully won the court case that followed, but the decision was reversed on appeal. A further setback occurred when Quinault was thought to have slandered the King's mistress in his text of *Isis* (1677) and was compelled to end his partnership with Lully in disgrace for some time. The King continued to support Lully, however, in spite of the fact that the composer's homosexuality had become a public scandal (homosexuality at the time was a capital offense). Lully's acquisition of titles culminated in 1681, when noble rank was conferred upon him with the title Secretaire du Roi. In his last years he turned increasingly to sacred music. It was while he was conducting his *Te Deum* in 1687 that he suffered a symbolic accident, striking his foot with a pointed cane used to pound out the beat. Gangrene set in, and he died of blood poisoning 2 months later.

Lully's historical importance rests primarily upon his music for the theater. He developed what became known as the French OVERTURE, with its 3 contrasting slow-fast-slow movements. He further replaced the Italian recitativo secco style with accompanied French recitative. Thus through the Italian-born Lully, French opera came of age. Some of his best-known stage works include *Cadmus et Hermione* (1673); *Alceste, ou Le Triomphe d'Alcide* (1674); and *Acis et Galatée, pastorale héroïque* (1686). He also scored numerous ballets and theatrical work. His sacred and choral works include *Te Deum* (1677); *De profundis* (1683); *Motets à deux pour la chapelle du Roi* (Paris, 1684); 6 grands motets for 2 choirs and orch. (1685); and 14 petits motets. Lully also wrote a variety of instrumental pieces, including overtures, suites, dances, and organ pieces. A complete catalog of his works was ed. by H. Schneider (Tutzing, 1981).

Lulu. Opera by Berg, 1928–35, produced posthumously in Zurich, 1937. Berg, a slow worker, was only able to complete 2 of 3 acts; one section of the 3rd act was included in the *Lulu Suite* that was premiered in 1934. The libretto is drawn from 2 dramas of Wedekind (*Pandora's Box* and *Earth Spirit*). Lulu, a prodigiously magnetic if promiscuous woman, spares neither young nor old, neither man nor woman; directly or otherwise, she leads many of them to death. She meets her own doom when, reduced to prostitution, she is disemboweled by Jack the Ripper in London. The score is a tour de force of Berg's elastic use of 12-tone composition; it preserves the structure of a classical suite while creating a dramatic arch (many of the characters of act I return transformed in act III), and relies on a Wagnerian use of LEITMOTIVS. In a true tale of mystic mania and musical mystery, Berg in fact had virtually finished a short score of the 3rd act, and a vocal score had been drawn up; but Berg's widow banned its publication. Unknown to her, the Austrian composer Friedrich Cerha was surreptitiously orchestrating the 3rd act under the auspices of Berg's publisher. After years of work, Cerha completed the 3rd act (1962–74); after Berg's widow's death (1976), the premiere of the complete version took place at the Paris Opéra (1979).

lumineux (Fr.). Luminuous, bright. *Luminosità* (It.), luminosity.

lunga, -o (It., long). Sustained, prolonged. Written over or under a fermata (⌢, ⌣), indicates that the pause is to be decidedly prolonged; often written *lunga pausa* or *pausa lunga*.

luogo (It.). Loco.

Lupu, Radu, outstanding Romanian pianist; b. Galai, Nov. 30, 1945. He began his piano studies at the age of 6, making his recital debut when he was 12; then studied with Florica Muzicescu and on scholarship at the Moscow Cons. (1963), where he studied with Heinrich and Stanislau Neuhaus until 1969. In quick succession he won 1st prize in the Van Cliburn (1966), Enesco (1967), and Leeds (1969) competitions. In 1972 he made his American debut as soloist with the Cleveland Orch., and subsequently played with the Chicago, Los Angeles, N.Y., and Boston orchs. In Europe he made successful appearances in Berlin, Paris, Amsterdam, London, Vienna, and other cities in varied programs ranging from Classic to modern works.

lur (Dan.). A late Nordic Bronze Age brass instrument of Scandinavia, comprised of a conical tube, 3 to 6 feet in length, twisted into a loose *S*; a cupped, lip-vibrated mouthpiece; and a disc ornamented with geometric figures instead of a bell. The lur is one of the most common finds in archeological digs in the region.

lusingando (It., coaxing, ingratiating). A particularly sentimental type of violin phrasing, with exaggerated vibrato and PORTAMENTO.

lusinghiero (It.). Coaxingly, caressingly, flatteringly, seductively.

lustig (Ger.). Gaily, merrily.

Lustige Witwe, Die. MERRY WIDOW, THE.

lute (It. *lauto*; Fr. *luth*, Ger. *Laute*). A generic name for a variety of plucked string instruments, most popular from the 16th through 18th centuries, iconographically familiar from innumerable Renaissance paintings. The body of the lute is shaped like a half of a pear; its neck is turned back at the right angle. The fingerboard has embossed frets indicating the positions of the notes of the scale. The lute usually has five sets of double strings, plus a single string for the highest sound, and they are plucked with the fingers. The tuning is in perfect 4ths, with a 3rd in the middle, the lowest string being G or A, and with a range of 2 octaves. The lute was the favorite instrument of the aristocracy during its golden age in the 16th and 17th centuries. About the middle of the 18th century it inexplicably lost its lure and joined the honorable company of obsolete instruments; it has become a major component of the early music revival.

Lutelike instruments existed in Mesopotamia in great antiquity, but they had only 2 or 3 strings, and there is no evidence that the familiar lute of the Renaissance actually descended by way of imitation or import of these precursors. Long-necked lutes existed in Persia and Arabia in the Middle Ages; their European variety was called *colascione*; it usually had 5 strings. A small variety of the Arabian lute was called *'ud*; another lutelike instrument of Arabian provenance was the *tanbur*. The Russian *domra* was popular at the same time as the European lute; when it went out of fashion, it was superseded by the *balalaika*. The MANDOLIN is of the lute family, and it managed to retain its popularity through the 20th century. Other types of lutes are the MANDORA, a large variety of the mandolin, and PANDORA. Two very large lutes are the THEORBO and CHITARRONE. None of these instruments, however, have the unique characteristic of a turned neck.

A whole musical literature was created for the lute at the time of its greatest popularity; a large number of collections of music written specially for the lute was published in the 16th and 17th centuries. It is from these books that music historians are able to trace the formal development of European dances, instrumental works, and vocal compositions. Most early lute music was written in tablature, in which the player was given a diagram of the strings and the posi-

Andrew Rooley of the Consort of Musicke playing a lute

COURTESY BYERS, SCHWALBE & ASSOCIATES, INC.

tion on which the fingers should be placed to secure the required notes or harmonies.

Lutenists enjoyed great renown in the Renaissance period, particularly in England. The English-born lutenist John Dowland, who was a contemporary of Shakespeare, commanded salaries equaling those of high officials. The Italian court lutenist Rizzio, who was brought to Scotland by Mary Stuart, assumed such power at the Scottish court that Mary's antagonists arranged for his assassination. Portraits of lutenists, both men and women, were favorites with the great painters of the Renaissance. There are numerous references to lute players in English literature beginning with Chaucer.

lutheal. A mechanical attachment invented in 1919 by the Belgian piano manufacturer Georges Cloetens, to be placed on the metal framework inside the grand piano, imparting to it the sound of a clavecin. Ravel was quite fascinated by the potentialities of the lutheal, and made use of it in the piano part of his violin piece *Tzigane*, 1st performed in Paris, Oct. 15, 1924. But the lutheal failed to prove attractive to the public or the music critics; accordingly, Ravel made another version of *Tzigane* for violin and piano, and still another version for violin with orch. accompaniment. Ravel further made use of the lutheal in the original setting of *L'Enfant et les sortilèges*, but in the final version he decided to reproduce the effects of the lutheal by various orch.l timbres.

Luther, Martin, great German religious reformer; b. Eisleben, Nov. 10, 1483; d. there, Feb. 18, 1546. As part of the changes that led to Protestantism and the Reformation, Luther wrote tracts on a new German liturgy; the 1st German Mass was sung in Wittenberg in 1524. Johann Walter (1696–1770), who aided Luther in organizing the music for the Mass, transcribed melodies that Luther played on the flute, and together they created new hymns in the vernacular. Many hymns are attributed to Luther; but it seems that while some are fully his, others were German translations or adaptations of Latin hymns.

luthier (Fr.). A maker of lutes; applied to makers of any stringed instrument.

Lutoslawski, Witold, outstanding Polish composer; b. Warsaw, Jan. 25, 1913; d. there, Feb. 7, 1994. He learned to play the piano as a child; then studied violin with Lidia Kmitowa (1926–32) and theory and composition with Witold Maliszewski (from 1927); also studied mathematics at the Univ. of Warsaw (1931–33). He entered the Warsaw Cons. (1932), where he continued composition studies with Maliszewski and also studied piano with Jerzy Lefeld (graduated as a pianist, 1936, and as a composer, 1937). He served in the Polish Army (1937–38); was mobilized in the summer of 1939 and was taken prisoner of war by the invading Nazi armies at the outbreak of World War II; he managed to escape to Warsaw, where he earned a living by playing piano in cafés (1939–44); participated in clandestine concerts in private homes. After the war, he worked briefly for the Polish Radio (1945), then devoted himself to composition; when his *renommée* reached the outside world, he obtained prestigious engagements as a lecturer and instructor in England, West Germany, Denmark, and Sweden; he also appeared as a conductor of his own works from 1963.

As his reputation grew he received numerous awards. He was made an honorary member of Hamburg's Freie Akademie der Künste (1966), extraordinary member of West Berlin's Akademie der Künste (1968), honorary member of the ISCM (1969), corresponding member of East Berlin's Deutsche Akademie der Künste (1970), corresponding member of the American Academy of Arts and Letters (1975), honorary member of London's Royal Academy of Music (1976), etc. He also received honorary D.Mus. degrees. His early works are marked by a neoclassical tendency, with an influx of national Polish motifs; gradually he turned to a more structural type of composition in which melodic and rhythmic elements are organized into a strong unifying network, with occasional incursions of dodecaphonic and aleatory practices.

He was also extraordinarily open-minded; he was attracted by the music of John Cage, finding useful applications in operations of chance. The influence of Bartók is felt in the constantly changing colors, angular intervallic progressions, and asymmetrical rhythms. In this respect Lutoslawski's *Musique funèbre* for String Orch., dedicated to the memory of Bartók—thematically built on a concatenation of upward tritones and downward semitones—is stylistically significant. He freely applied sonorism in building orch. colors. Although possessing a masterful technique of composition, he allowed himself plenty of time for revisions; willing to make any number of successive changes to attain his goal, it took him fully 10 years to achieve the desired balance of structural contents to complete his 3rd Sym. His list of

works is therefore not exceptionally large, but each composition, whatever its length, is an accomplished masterpiece.

luttuosamente (*luttuoso*; It.). Mournfully, plaintively.

Lydian mode. The ecclesiastical mode that corresponds to the scale from *F* to *F* on the white keys of the piano (F–G–A–B–C–D–E–F). Although the name is inherited from Greece, the Lydian mode is not identical with the ancient Greek mode of the same name. Its arresting characteristic is the presence of the tritone between the tonic and the subdominant, the forbidding (and forbidden) DIABOLUS IN MUSICA. Beethoven emphatically indicates the presence of the Lydian mode in the slow movement of his last string quartet, op. 132. Chopin made the Lydian mode sound peculiarly expressive in some of his Slavic-scented mazurkas.

Lydische Quarte (Ger.). Lydian 4th, i.e., augmented 4th characteristic of this mode.

Lynn, Loretta (Webb), American country-music singer, guitarist, and songwriter; b. Butcher Hollow, Ky., Apr. 14, 1932. A coal miner's daughter, she taught herself the rudiments of guitar playing; making her way to Nashville, Tenn., she joined the GRAND OLE OPRY; later organized her own group, the Blue Kentuckians, with which she toured widely. Unable to read music, she nevertheless scored enormous success with such songs as *Don't Come Home A-Drinkin' (with Lovin' on Your Mind)*, *The Pill*, *You Ain't Woman Enough (to Take My Man)*, and *Coal Miner's Daughter*.

lyra viol (U.K.). VIOLA BASTARDA.

lyre. 1. An ancient Greek stringed instrument, the body made of wood or tortoise shell, from which rose 2 curving arms joined above by a crossbar; the strings, from 3 to 10 in number, were stretched from this crossbar to or over a bridge set on the soundboard and were plucked with a plectrum. It is related to the KITHARA; both were associated with Apollo, and they are often reproduced in sculptures and drawings of the Greek god of beauty. 2. In military bands, a mallet instrument consisting of loosely suspended steel bars tuned to the scale and struck with a hammer.

lyric (lyrical; It., *lirico*). Literally, pertaining to or proper for the lyre, or for accompaniment by the lyre; by extension, that which is appropriate for singing or for expression in song. The lyric mode is opposed to epic (narrative) and dramatic (scenic, accompanied by action). *Lyric drama* (Fr. *drame lyrique*), opera; *lyric opera*, one in which the lyric mode predominates; *lyric stage*, the operatic stage.

Lyric Suite (*Lyrische Suite*). Work for string quartet by Berg, 1927, 1st performed in Vienna. It is in 6 movements, set in the technique of 12-tone composition. Its lyric sentiment is emphatically expressed by a quotation from the prelude to *Tristan und Isolde*. Fifty years later, it was discovered that the melodic line of the finale was a setting of a hitherto secret text, celebrating Berg's love for Hanna Fuchs-Robettin. The work was 1st performed in this version in N.Y., 1979.

lyricist. The author of verses for popular songs, including show tunes.

lyrics (lyric). The text of a popular song, including show tunes.

Mm

M. Abbrev. for It. MANO; Fr. MAIN; MANUAL (organ); METRONOME MARKING (usually *M.M.*).

m.d. Abbrev. for Fr. MAIN DROITE; It. MANO DESTRA.

m.g. Abbrev. for Fr. MAIN GAUCHE.

m.s. Abbrev. for It. MANO SINISTRA.

ma (It.). But. *Allegro ma non troppo*, rapidly, but not too fast.

Ma Mère L'Oye (Mother Goose). Suite of 5 children's pieces by Ravel, 1910, for piano 4-hands, which he later orchestrated. The subjects are taken from the famous book of fairy tales by Charles Perrault. Ravel composed these pieces for 2 Parisian girls, one 10 years old, the other only 6; they gave the work its 1st performance at a concert in Paris.

Má vlast (My Country). Symphonic cycle by Smetana, 1874–79. There ere 6 movements: *Vyšehrad* (the old citadel of Prague); *Moldau* (Vltava, the river on which Prague was built); *Šárka* (a legendary warrior woman); *Z českých luhův a hájuv* (From Bohemia's Meadows and Groves); *Tábor* (an ancient city; it includes the Hussite war song); and *Blaník* (a Bohemian hill on which the Hussites congregated).

Ma, Yo-Yo, brilliant Chinese cellist; b. Paris, Oct. 7, 1955. He was born into a musical family active in Paris; his father was a violinist, his mother a mezzo-soprano. He began to study violin as a small child, then graduated to the viola and finally the cello; was taken to N.Y. when he was 7, and enrolled at the Juilliard School of Music when he was 9; his principal teachers were Leonard Rose and Janos Scholz; he subsequently received additional musical training at Harvard Univ. He quickly established a formidable reputation as a master of the cello in his appearances with the great orchs. of the world, as a recitalist, and as a chamber music player, being deservedly acclaimed for his unostentatious musicianship, his superlative technical resources, and the remarkable tone of his melodious lyricism. In order to extend his repertoire he made a number of effective transcriptions for his instrument. He was awarded the Avery Fisher Prize in 1978.

Maazel, Lorin (Varencove)

Brilliant American conductor; b. Neuilly, France (of American parents), Mar. 6, 1930. His parents took him to Los Angeles when he was an infant. At a very early age he showed innate musical ability; he had perfect pitch and could assimilate music osmotically; he began to study violin at age 5 with Karl Moldrem, and then piano at age 7 with Fanchon Armitage. Fascinated by the art of conducting, he went to sym. concerts and soon began to take lessons in conducting with Vladimir Bakaleinikov, who was an associate conductor of the Los Angeles Phil.; in 1938 he conducted a performance of Schubert's *Unfinished Sym.* with the visiting Univ. of Idaho orch.

In 1938 Bakaleinikov was appointed assistant conductor of the Pittsburgh Sym. orch., and the Maazel family followed him to Pittsburgh. From Bakaleinikov, Maazel quickly learned to speak Russian. In 1939 he made a sensational appearance in N.Y. conducting the National Music Camp Orch. of Interlochen at the World's Fair, eliciting the inevitable jocular comments (he was compared to a trained seal). Maazel was only 11 when he conducted the NBC Sym. Orch. (1941) and 12 when he led an entire program with the N.Y. Phil. (1942). He survived these traumatic exhibitions, and took academic courses at the Univ. of Pittsburgh; in 1948 he joined the Pittsburgh Sym. Orch. as a violinist, and at the same time was appointed its apprentice conductor.

In 1951 he received a Fulbright fellowship for travel in Italy, where he undertook a serious study of Baroque music; he also made his adult debut as a conductor in Catania (1953). In 1955 he conducted at the Florence May Festival, in 1957 at the Vienna Festival, and in 1958 at the Edinburgh Festival. In 1960 he became the 1st American to conduct at the Bayreuth Festival, where he led performances of *Lohengrin*. In 1962 he toured the U.S. with the Orch. National de France; that year he made his Metropolitan Opera debut in N.Y., conducting *Don Giovanni*. In the summer of 1963 he made a tour of Russia, conducting concerts in Moscow and Leningrad. From 1965 to 1971 he was artistic director of the Deutsche Oper in West Berlin; from 1965 to 1975 also served as chief conductor of the (West) Berlin Radio Sym. Orch.

He was associate principal conductor of the New Philharmonia Orch. of London from 1970 to 1972, and its principal guest conductor from 1976 to 1980. In 1972 he became music director of the Cleveland Orch., a position he held with great distinction until 1982; was then made conductor emeritus. He led the Cleveland Orch. on 10 major tours abroad, including Australia and New Zealand (1973), Japan (1974), twice in Latin America, and twice in Europe, and maintained its stature as one of the world's foremost orchs. He was also chief conductor of the Orch. National de France from 1977 to 1982; then was its principal guest conductor until 1988, and then its music director until 1991. In 1980 he became conductor of the famous Vienna Phil. New Year's Day Concerts, a position he retained until 1986. In 1982 he assumed the positions of artistic director and general manager of the Vienna State Opera, the 1st American to be so honored; however, he resigned these positions in the middle of his 4-year contract in 1984 after a conflict over artistic policies with the Ministry of Culture. He then served as music consultant to the Pittsburgh Sym. Orch. (1984–86); was its music adviser and principal guest conductor in 1986, becoming its music director that same year.

Maazel is equally adept as an interpreter of operatic and symphonic scores; he is blessed with a phenomenal memory, and possesses an extraordinary baton technique. He also maintains an avid interest in nonmusical pursuits; a polyglot, he is fluent in French, German, Italian, Spanish, Portuguese, and Russian. He was married twice; 1st in 1952, to the Brazilian-American pianist Miriam Sandbank, and, after their divorce in 1969, to the Israeli pianist Israela Margalit (also later divorced). Maazel was the recipient of many awards; he received an honorary doctorate from the Univ. of Pittsburgh in 1965, the Sibelius Prize in Finland, the Commander's Cross of the Order of Merit from West Germany, and, for his numerous recordings, the Grand Prix de Disque in Paris and the Edison Prize in the Netherlands.

Mac Low, Jackson, American poet, composer, painter, and multimedia performance artist; b. Chicago, Sept. 12, 1922. He studied piano, violin, and harmony at Chicago Musical College (1927–32) and Northwestern Univ. Music School (1932–36); then took courses in philosophy, poetics, and English at the Univ. of Chicago (1941); also studied Greek at Brooklyn College of the City Univ. of N.Y. (1958); had piano lessons with Shirley Gablis (1943–44), Grete Sultan (1953–55), and Franz Kamin (1976–79), composition with Erich Katz (1948–49), recorder with Tui St. George Tucker (1948–53), experimental music with Cage at the New School for Social Research in N.Y. (1957–60), and voice with Pandit Pran Nath (1975–76). He taught at N.Y. Univ. (1966–73), the Mannes College of Music in N.Y.

(1966), the State Univ. of N.Y. at Albany (1984), Binghamton (1989), and Buffalo (1990), and Temple Univ. (1989); in 1990 was Regents Lecturer at the Univ. of Calif. at San Diego.

Among his 25 books, many—*Stanzas for Iris Lezak* (1972), *21 Matched Asymmetries* (1978), *Asymmetries 1–260* (1980), *"Is That Wool Hat My Hat?"* (1982), *Bloomsday* (1984), *Representative Works: 1938–1985* (1986), and *Words nd Ends from Ez* (1989)—comprise or include works realizable as musical-verbal performances. He wrote several chance-generated plays, including *The Marrying Maiden* (1958; unpubl.), *Verdurous Sanguinaria* (1961; publ. in anthology, 1980), and *The Twin Plays: Port-au-Prince and Adams County Illinois* (1963, 1966). *The Pronouns* (1964, 1971, 1979) are both poems and dance instructions, realized in the U.S., England, and Australia; he also wrote, directed, and performed in several Hörspiel.

Mac Low adopted chance operations, indeterminacy, and related methods in 1954. His many "simultaneities" include musical, verbal, and visual elements; these and other compositions are for live voices, instruments (often variable), and/or tape multitracking, and usually involve guided improvisation and indeterminacy. He has performed extensively throughout North America, Western Europe, and New Zealand, often with the painter, multimedia performance artist, composer, and writer Anne Tardos. An 8-hour retrospective concert on the occasion of his 60th birthday was given at Washington Square Church in N.Y. (1982). His awards include fellowships from N.Y. State's Creative Artists Public Service Program (1973–74; 1976–77), the NEA (1979), the Guggenheim Memorial Foundation (1985), and the N.Y. Foundation for the Arts (1988); he also received a Fulbright grant for travel in New Zealand and a composer's grant from New Zealand's Queen Elizabeth II Art Council (both 1986).

Macbeth. 1. Opera by Verdi, 1847, 1st performed in Florence. The Italian libretto follows faithfully the main events of Shakespeare's play, but the opera itself is not one of Verdi's best. 2. Opera by Ernest Bloch, 1910, 1st performed in Paris. The score bristles with unorthodox harmonies and asymmetric rhythms and was judged severely by conservative Paris critics. 3. Symphonic poem by R. Strauss, 1890, after Shakespeare; the 1st of 7 remarkable works in this genre, each based on an explicit story or a literary work. It was 1st performed in Weimar.

MacDowell, Edward (Alexander)

~~~ ~~~ ~~~ ~~~ ~~~

Greatly significant American composer; b. N.Y., Dec. 18, 1860; d. there, Jan. 23, 1908. His father was a Scotch-Irish tradesman; his mother, an artistically inclined woman who encouraged his musical studies. He took piano lessons with Juan Buitrago and Paul Desvernine; also had supplementary sessions with Teresa Carreño, who later championed his works. In 1876, after traveling in Europe with his mother, MacDowell enrolled as an auditor in Savard's elementary class at the Paris Cons.; in 1877 he was admitted as a regular student; he also studied piano with A.-F. Marmontel and solfège with Marmontel's son Antonin. Somewhat disappointed with his progress, he withdrew from the Cons. in 1878 and went to Wiesbaden for further study with Louis Ehlert; in 1879 he enrolled at the newly founded but already prestigious Hoch Cons. in Frankfurt as a student of Carl Heymann in piano, of Raff (the Cons. director) in composition, and of Franz Böhme in counterpoint and fugue. During MacDowell's stay there, Raff's class had a visit from Liszt, and MacDowell performed the piano part in Schumann's Quintet, op. 44, in Liszt's presence. At another visit MacDowell played Liszt's *Hungarian Rhapsody No. 14* for him; 2 years later he visited Liszt in Weimar, and played his own 1st Piano

Concerto for him, accompanied by d'Albert at the 2nd piano. Encouraged by Liszt's interest, MacDowell sent him the MS of his *Modern Suite*, op. 10, for piano solo; Liszt recommended the piece for performance at the meeting of the Allgemeiner Deutscher Musikverein (Zurich, 1882); he also recommended MacDowell to the publishers Breitkopf & Härtel, who subsequently brought out the 1st works of MacDowell to appear in print, the *Modern Suites* for Piano, opp. 10 and 14.

Despite his youth, MacDowell was given a teaching position at the Darmstadt Cons.; he also accepted private pupils, among them Marian Nevins of Conn.; they were secretly married on July 9, 1884, in N.Y., followed by a public ceremony in Waterford, Conn., on July 21. During the early years of their marriage the MacDowells made their 2nd home in Wiesbaden, where MacDowell composed industriously; his works were performed in neighboring communities; Carreño put several of his piano pieces on her concert programs. There were also performances in America. However, the MacDowells were beset by financial difficulties; his mother proposed that he and his wife live on the family property, but MacDowell declined. He also declined an offer to teach at the National Cons. in N.Y. at the munificent fee of $5 an hour. Similarly he rejected an offer to take a clerical position at the American Consulate in Krefeld, Germany.

In 1888 he finally returned to the U.S., where he was welcomed in artistic circles as a famous composer and pianist; musical America at the time was virtually a German colony, and MacDowell's German training was a certificate of his worth. The Boston Sym. Orch. conductors Gericke, Nikisch, and Paur, all Austro-Germans, played his works. In late 1888 MacDowell made his American debut as a composer and pianist at a Boston concert of the Kneisel String Quartet, featuring his *Modern Suite*, op. 10. In 1889 he was the soloist in the premiere performance of his 2nd Piano Concerto with the N.Y. Phil., under the direction of Theodore Thomas. Frank van der Stücken invited MacDowell to play his concerto at the spectacular Paris Exposition (1889). MacDowell had no difficulty having his works publ., although for some reason he preferred that his early piano pieces, opp. 1–7, be printed under the pseudonym Edgar Thorn.

In 1896 Columbia Univ. invited MacDowell to become its 1st prof. of music, "to elevate the standard of musical instruction in the U.S., and to afford the most favorable opportunity for acquiring instruction of the highest order." MacDowell interpreted this statement to its fullest; by 1899 2 assistants had been employed, Leonard McWhood and Gustav Hinrichs, but students received no credit for his courses. At the same time he continued to compose and to teach piano privately; he also conducted the Mendelssohn Glee Club (1896–98) and served as president of the Soc. of American Musicians and Composers (1899–1900). In the academic year 1902–1903 he took a sabbatical; played concerts throughout the U.S. and in Europe; played his 2nd Piano Concerto in London (1903). During his sabbatical, Columbia Univ. replaced its president, Seth Low, with Nicholas Murray Butler, whose ideas about the role of music in the univ. were diametrically opposed to the ideals of MacDowell. MacDowell resigned in 1904 and subsequently became a cause célèbre, resulting in much acrimony on both sides. It was not until some time later that the Robert Center Chair that MacDowell had held at Columbia Univ. was renamed the Edward MacDowell Chair of Music to honor its 1st recipient.

Through the combination of the trauma resulting from this episode, an accident with a hansom, and the development of what appears to have been tertiary syphilis, MacDowell rapidly deteriorated mentally; he showed signs of depression, extreme irritability, and a gradual loss of vital functions; he eventually lapsed into total insanity, and spent the last 2 years of his life in a childlike state, unaware of his surroundings. In 1906 a public appeal was launched to raise funds for his care; among the signers were Horatio Parker, Victor Herbert, Arthur Foote, George Chadwick, Frederick Converse, Andrew Carnegie, J. Pierpont Morgan, and former President Grover Cleveland.

MacDowell was only 47 years old when he died. The sum of $50,000 was raised for the organization of the MacDowell Memorial Assoc. Marian MacDowell, who outlived her husband by nearly half a century (she died in Los Angeles at the age of 98, in 1956), deeded to the Assoc. her husband's summer residence at Peterborough, N.H. This property became a pastoral retreat, under the name of the MacDowell Colony, for American composers and writers, who could spend summers working undisturbed in separate cottages, paying a minimum rent for lodging and food. During the summer of 1910 Mrs. MacDowell arranged an elaborate pageant with music from MacDowell's works; the success of this project led to the establishment of a series of MacDowell Festivals at Peterborough.

MacDowell received several awards during his lifetime, including 2 honorary doctorates (Princeton Univ., 1896; Univ. of Pa., 1902) and election into the American Academy of Arts and Letters (1904); in 1940 a 5-cent U.S. postage stamp with his likeness was issued; in 1960 he was the 2nd composer elected to the Hall of Fame at N.Y. Univ., where, in 1964, a bust was unveiled.

Among American composers, MacDowell occupies a historically important place as the 1st American whose works were accepted as comparable in quality and technique with those of the average German composers of his time. His music adhered to the prevalent representative Romantic art. Virtually all of his works bear titles borrowed from mythical history, literature, or painting; even his piano sonatas, set in classical forms, carry descriptive titles, indicative of the mood of melodic resources, or as an ethnic reference.

Since he lived in Germany during his formative years, German musical culture was decisive in shaping his musical development; even the American rhythms and melodies in his music seem to be European reflections of an exotic art. A parallel with Grieg is plausible, for Grieg was also a regional composer trained in Germany. But Grieg possessed a much more vigorous personality, and

he succeeded in communicating the true spirit of Norwegian song modalities in his works. Lack of musical strength and originality accounts for MacDowell's gradual decline in the estimation of succeeding generations; his romanticism was apt to lapse into salon sentimentality. The frequency of performance of his works in concert (he never wrote for the stage) declined in the decades following his death, and his influence on succeeding generations of American composers receded to a faint recognition of an evanescent artistic period.

Among his works are several symphonic poems; 2 orch.l suites (1891–94; 1896, the "Indian" Suite); 2 piano concertos (1885–88; 1889); choruses, mostly male; several sets of songs; piano music, his principal oeuvre, including *Forgotten Fairy Tales*, op. 4 (1898); *1st Modern Suite*, op. 10 (1880); *2nd Modern Suite*, op. 14 (1881); *Forest Idyls*, op. 19 (1884); *6 Idyls After Goethe*, op. 28 (1887); *6 Poems After Heine*, op. 31 (1887); *12 Studies*, books I and II, op. 39 (1890); Sonata No. 1, *Tragica*, op. 45 (1893); *12 Virtuoso Studies*, op. 46 (1894); Sonata No. 2, *Eroica*, op. 50 (1895); *Woodland Sketches*, his best-known piano cycle, op. 51 (1896); *Sea Pieces*, op. 55 (1898); Sonata No. 3, *Norse*, op. 57 (1900); Sonata No. 4, *Keltic*, op. 59 (1901); *Fireside Tales*, op. 61 (1902); and *New England Idyls*, op. 62 (1902). MacDowell's writings were collected by W. Baltzell and publ. as *Critical and Historical Essays* (N.Y., 1912).

Machaut (Machault, Machau, Mauchault), **Guillaume de** (Guillelmus de Mascaudio), important French composer and poet; b. probably in Machaut, Champagne, *c.* 1300; d. probably in Rheims, Apr. 13[?], 1377. He entered the service of John of Luxembourg, King of Bohemia, about 1323; was his secretary until the King's death (1346). He was granted a canonry in Verdun (1330), another in Arras (1332), and yet another in Rheims (1333), retaining the 1st 2 until 1335. He settled in Rheims permanently about 1340; from 1346 he was in the service of the French nobility, including the future King Charles V. His renown is testified to by the number of surviving presentation MSS dedicated solely to his music. His *Messe de Nostre Dame* for 4 Voices is the 1st polyphonic setting of the Mass attributable to one composer. He also wrote 42 ballades, 33 virelais, 23 motets, 22 rondeaux, 19 lais, a double hocket (*Hoquetus David*), a complainte, and a chanson royal; some of the lais and virelais are conservatively monophonic. His poem *Remede de*

Fortune, considered an early work, contains songs in almost every genre in which he composed. Other poems without music are *La louanges des dames* and *Le livre du Voir dit*, a work of the 1360s that contains autobiographical information concerning Machaut's love for a 19-year-old woman, Péronne d'Armentières.

machine music. The modern machine became an object of artistic inspiration early in the 20th century. The Italian futurists made a cult of automobiles and airplanes. Antheil's *Ballet mécanique* shocked concert audiences by its bruitism. Max Brand (1896–1980) produced the 1st machine opera in *Machinist Hopkins* (1929). Honegger made a declaration of love for powerful American locomotives in his symphonic movement *Pacific 231*. Frederick Converse (1871–1940) glorified the Ford car in his automobilistic musicorama *Flivver 10,000,000* (1927). But locomotives, automobiles, and airplanes soon lost their glamour and became public nuisances.

By mid-century the machine as an affirmative artistic object became obsolete. It is ironic that no composer was moved to extol in lofty tones the greatest machine adventure of all ages, the landing on the moon.

Machover, Tod, American cellist, conductor, and composer; b. N.Y., Nov. 24, 1953. He studied composition at the Univ. of Calif. at Santa Cruz (1971–73), Columbia Univ. (1973–74), and the Juilliard School in N.Y. (B.M., 1975; M.M., 1977); among his mentors were Dallapiccola (1973), Sessions (1973–75), and Carter (1975–78); also studied computer music at the Mass. Inst. of Technology and at Stanford Univ. He was 1st cellist in the orch. of the National Opera of Canada in Toronto (1975–76), guest composer (1978–79) and director of musical research (1980–84) at the Inst. de Recherche et de Coordination Acoustique/Musique (IRCAM) in Paris, and a teacher at the Mass. Inst. of Technology (from 1985). Among his honors were the Koussevitzky Prize (1984) and the Friedheim Award (1987). While he has written for purely acoustic media, Machover is primarily associated with electroacoustical experiments and live interactive installations. His best-known work is the opera *Valis*, based on a Philip K. Dick novel (Paris, 1987). He has also written several orch. works, solo acoustic works, and piano pieces, and many pieces for electronic instruments and recording tape.

mächtig, machtvoll (Ger.). Powerfully, mightily.

Mack the Knife, The Ballad of (*Die Moritat von Mackie Messer*). Song by Weill and Brecht, 1928, from the ballad opera *Die Dreigroschenoper* (The Threepenny Opera). The German name translates as "The Murderous Deeds of Mackie Messer"; "Mackie Messer" is the nickname of Macheath, the notorious gangster at the center of the plot. When he translated *Die Dreigroschenoper* for its American premiere (1954), Marc Blitzstein translated Macheath's nickname literally. *The Ballad of Mack the Knife* is, not surprisingly, ironic in the extreme.

macrotime. A term proposed by Stockhausen (1955) to designate the duration of each rhythmic pulse, as quantitatively contrasted with MICROTIME, the number of vibrations of a given note.

macumba. A ritual festival of Afro-Brazilians, marked by a display of animal power and indeed related to primitive animalism. The festival includes elements of African and Indian folklore combined with Christian symbols, accompanied by music and dance believed to possess magical powers.

Madama Butterfly. Opera by Puccini, 1904, after the Belasco play, 1st produced in Milan. Pinkerton, a lieutenant in the U.S. Navy on a visit to Nagasaki, becomes enraptured with a local 15-year-old Japanese girl nicknamed Cio-Cio (butterfly); she is also formally referred to as Cio-Cio-San, the last word corresponding to Madame. She and Pinkerton go through a Japanese marriage ceremony, which he knows is not legally binding. He then sails to the U.S., leaving her barefoot and pregnant. But she has faith in him, expressing her feelings in an aria (*Un bel dì vedremo*), based on a pentatonic theme, which has become a favorite of the soprano repertoire. A son is born to Cio-Cio-San. When Pinkerton returns, he brings with him his American wife. Cio-Cio-San yields to the American Mrs. Pinkerton's entreaties to let her have the child. After the Pinkertons leave, she then commits a ritual hara-kiri.

The score is remarkable in its bold innovations, making use of consecutive triads, unresolved discords, and percussive orch.l effects. The strains of *The Star-Spangled Banner* are heard in the background; there is also a fair amount of pseudo-Japanese melodies. After a opening-night fiasco, Puccini revised the work for a 2nd premiere, this time successful. Recent excavations of the original version have divided the critics as to the relative merits of the 2.

Mademoiselle Fifi. Opera by Cui, 1903, 1st performed in Moscow, based on a Maupassant short story. During the Franco-Prussian War of 1870, a Prussian officer, nicknamed Mlle. Fifi by the French for his effeminacy, is stabbed to death by a French *fille de joie* when he insults France. The opera was moderately successful; Glière wrote an opera on the same story named *Rachel*, the name of the patriotic murderess. This work was never performed on the stage.

Mademoiselle Modiste. Comic opera by Herbert, 1905, 1st performed in N.Y. A modest modiste in a Paris hat shop is loved simultaneously by a French nobleman (whose snobbish family rejects her) and an American millionaire. As a preliminary step to conquest, the American sponsors her career as a singer; she becomes a prima donna under an Italian stage name. When she sings at a charity bazaar at her French suitor's castle, the 2 recognize that the old flame has been rekindled; this time his family is only too happy to sanction the match. The score contains one of Herbert's most famous tunes, *Kiss Me Again*.

Maderna, Bruno, outstanding Italian-born German conductor and composer; b. Venice, Apr. 21, 1920; d. Darmstadt, Nov. 13, 1973. He commenced musical studies at 4, and soon took violin lessons; began touring as a violinist and conductor when he was only 7, appearing under the name Brunetto in Italy and abroad. He studied at the Verdi Cons. in Milan, with Bustini at the Rome Cons. (diploma in composition, 1940), and with Malipiero at the Venice Cons.; also took a conducting course with Guarnieri at the Accademia Chigiana in Siena (1941). He then served in the Italian army during World War II, eventually joining the partisan forces against the Fascists. After the war he studied conducting with Scherchen in Darmstadt; taught composition at the Venice Cons. (1947–50); then made his formal conducting debut in Munich (1950).

He subsequently became a great champion of the avant-garde; with Berio he helped to form the Studio di Fonologia in Milan (1954); also with Berio he was conductor of the RAI's *Incontri Musicali* (1956–60). He taught conducting and composition in various venues, including Darmstadt (from 1954), the Salzburg Mozarteum (1967–70), the Rotterdam Cons. (from 1967), and the Berkshire Music Center in Tanglewood (1971–72). He was chief conductor of the RAI in Milan from 1971. In 1963 he became a naturalized German citizen. Stricken with cancer, he continued to conduct concerts as long as it was physically possible. He was held in great esteem by composers of the international avant-garde, several of whom wrote special works for him. Maderna's compositions follow the trends of new European music of the period, including the overlayering of 2 or more separate works to create a new one; after a period of neglect, his music has undergone a revival in recent years. His works include operatic and stage works, orch.l and chamber works, vocal works, and many electronic pieces.

Madonna (born Madonna Louise Veronica Ciccone), fabulously popular and audacious American rock singer and actress; b. Bay City, Mich., Aug. 16, 1958. She took up acting and dancing while attending junior high school in Pontiac, Mich.; after private dance lessons with Christopher Flynn (1972–76), she studied on a scholarship at the Univ. of Michigan (1976–78). Making her way to N.Y., she eked out a living by modeling and acting in an underground soft-core film; aboveground she worked with Alvin Ailey's dance group and studied choreography with Pearl Lang; then studied drums and guitar with Dan Gilroy. After working with the disco star Patrick Hernandez in Paris, she returned to N.Y., appearing as a drummer and singer with the Gilroy's Breakfast Club rock group. In 1982 she organized her own band, and in 1983 brought out her 1st album, *Madonna*; with her album *Like a Virgin* (1984) she captured the imagination of America's youth, which led to her 1st coast-to-coast tour.

In 1985 Madonna pursued her thespian bent by appearing in the critically acclaimed film *Desperately Seeking Susan*; also acted in *Who's That Girl?* (1987). The popular movie *Dick Tracy* (1990) featured Madonna as a slinky, sequined, torch-singer gun moll. Her album *True Blue* (1986) proved a popular success. In 1987 she made a smashingly successful tour of Europe. In 1989, the year of her album *Like a Prayer*, she was listed among *People* magazine's "20 Who Defined the Decade"; she also was awarded *Musician* magazine's highest editorial distinction, "Artist of the Decade."

Her trendsetting fashions created a legion of young female fans known as "Madonna wannabes." Her athletic "Blond Ambition" tour of 1990 was criticized for its use of more than 50% canned music; however, it was hardly the 1st tour of its kind. That same year she brought out the sizzling video *Justify My Love*. After a few years out of the limelight and the top of the charts, Madonna bore a child, at first refusing to name its father; she also played the eponymous lead role in a film of *Evita*, from the Lloyd Webber musical; despite its mixed critical response, it attracted many ticket buyers and CD purchasers, and it revived the "wannabe" syndrome.

Madras Symphony. Sym. No. 13 by Cowell, 1959, based on Indian motives.

madrigal. A secular (less often liturgical) polyphonic composition of Italian extraction that achieved its flowering during the Renaissance and survived in other forms in the Baroque period, though it lapsed into obsolescence in the 19th century. The etymology of the word is uncertain.

There are really 2 types of Italian *madrigale*, although the poetic form for both arose in the 14th century and was marked by a fairly definite scheme in iambic pentameter. The 1st type, composed by Landini and his Trecento contemporaries, is written for 2 or 3 texted voices, with the lower part commonly doubled instrumentally; such madrigals were usually pastoral in nature. The madrigal reinvented itself during the Renaissance; subservient during the 15th century to the lighter genres (FROTTOLA, CANZONA, *canzonetta, barzelletta, capitolo, strambotto*), the madrigal was revived in the 16th century, when the strict formality of the verses and tunes were abandoned in favor of a more relaxed, more imaginative, and more individual type. These polyphonic settings increased to 4, 5, and 6 parts; instrumental doubling was rare.

By the beginning of the 17th century the role of the melodic line became more and more pronounced; concomitantly, the polyphonic style gave way to homophony, forming a natural bridge to opera; a dramatic genre of madrigal cycle developed into the MADRIGAL COMEDY. Early examples of monody were still called madrigals (e.g., Monteverdi's *Madrigali guerrieri e amorosi*, 1638), but the term soon disappeared; its form survived in the lightweight glees of Baroque and Classic England and America.

Among great (and not necessarily Italian) madrigal composers are Arcadelt, de Rore, Andrea Gabrieli, Lasso, Marenzio, Gesualdo, and Monteverdi. Palestrina was the greatest writer of spiritual madrigals, as opposed to the more common secular type cultivated by most madrigalists. Elizabethan composers in England, among them William Byrd, eagerly followed the Italian model. A great impetus to the development of the English madrigal school was the publication in England of a collection of Italian madrigals in translation, *Musica Transalpina* (1588).

madrigal comedy (madrigal opera). A chain of madrigals united in content and forming a dramatic sequence; a contemporary of the early DRAMMA PER MUSICA, i.e., opera. The best-known composers of madrigal comedy are Vecchi and Banchieri. A distant relative of the COMMEDIA DELL'ARTE, its origins may be found in Renaissance madrigal collections with a common theme, often found in courtly weddings.

Madrigali guerrieri e amorosi. A famous book of madrigals by Claudio Monteverdi, published in 1638. These "madrigals of war and love" for voices and instruments are written in the STILE CONCITATO ("excited style"), in this instance combining love with "warlike expression."

Maelzel, Joahnnes Nepomuk, German inventor; b. Regensburg, Aug. 15, 1772; d. on board the brig *Otis* in the harbor of La Guiara, Venezuela, en route to Philadelphia, July 21, 1838. He studied music with his father, an organ manufacturer. In 1792 he went to Vienna, where he began constructing mechanical instruments, which attracted great attention there and subsequently in other European cities; of these, the Panharmonicon, a bellows-driven instrument with cylindrical pins, was particularly effective. He then purchased the "automatic chess player," which he claimed was his invention; in fact it was designed and built by

Wolfgang von Kempelen. He was able to impress the public by his "scientific" miracle, but it was soon exposed by skeptical observers, among them Edgar Allan Poe, as an ingenious mechanical contrivance concealing a diminutive chess master behind its gears. He subsequently invented the automatic trumpeter, displaying it and a new version of the Panharmonicon in his Kunstkabinett in 1812.

In 1816 he constructed the METRONOME, the idea for which he obtained from Winkel of Amsterdam, who had exhibited similar instruments but without the scale divisions indicating the number of beats per minute. Maelzel put the metronome on the market, despite a lawsuit brought by Winkel. Beethoven wrote a piece for the Panharmonicon, which he subsequently orchestrated and publ. as *Wellington's Victory*. After Maelzel declared that the composition was his property, Beethoven sued him in the Viennese courts, but nothing ever came from his legal action. After obtaining a metronome, Beethoven apparently placed tempo markings on his syms.; these have been a contentious issue for later interpreters, as their relatively fast markings have seemed unplayable to most, and therefore the machine he used has been blamed. Recent performances by Roger Norrington and John Eliot Gardiner have challenged the so-called impossibility of the tempos.

maestoso (It.). Majestic, dignified; in a style characterized by lofty breadth.

maestro (It., master). An honorary appellation accorded, often without merit, to composers, conductors, teachers, and even to lower species of musical eminences. In Italian the word conveys little more than a common term for a teacher, but when used by Englishmen, Americans, or Russians in addressing a musical celebrity, it sounds lofty and deferential. *Maestro al cembalo*, a Baroque harpsichordist who functions as ensemble leader and sets the tempo; *maestro di cappella*, orig., the director of a court chapel; now, a choirmaster or conductor.

Magaloff, Nikita. See SZIGETI, JOSEPH.

maggiore (It.). MAJOR.

maggot. A pleasing whim or notion, not the modern meaning of a repellent legless larva that infests putrefying bodies. The word was often attached to pieces of pleasurable content, often with a lady's name, as in *My Lady Winwood's Maggot.*

magic

～～ ～～ ～～ ～～ ～～

The magic rites of ancient times or of so-called primitive peoples in our time have always been accompanied by some musical performance, no matter how inchoate, no matter how artless. The myth of Orpheus, the godlike singer who could move people—particularly women—and even inanimate objects by his songs, is a classical invocation of artistic magic. Amphion was a magical player on the lyre; such was his skill that the stones used in the construction of the walls of Thebes were drawn into their proper places by his playing. The famous lines of William Congreve testify to the belief of this power: "Music has charms to soothe a savage breast/To soften rocks, or bend a knotted oak."

Musical magic is inherent in religious incantations, which are products of man's primitive impulse to vociferate in joy or lament in sorrow. Certain rhythms assume a magical significance in the society in which they originate. The relentlessly repetitive drum beats of the jungle portend warnings of danger. In the 1920s the Cuban government forbade the manufacture and use of Afro-Cuban drums (e.g., conga) because they affected the villagers so as to create serious disturbances and even revolts. To Jews in southern Russia the very opening notes of the Russian Czarist hymn suggested the beginning of a pogrom organized by groups of extreme anti-Semitic monarchists and condoned by the police. The cantillation of the rabbis in a synagogue, the high-pitched songs of the Moslem criers from the perches of the minarets, the monotonous recitations of the Latin Catholic rosary, even the familiar strains of a lullaby—all draw upon musical magic.

Epic literature of all nations and cultures is replete with instances of magical healing, effected simply by intoning melorhythmic phrases which through constant use became associated with curative faculties. In the Finnish epic *Kalevala* the musical magician recites a spell related to the origin of a wound, whether inflicted by an animal or by a sword, and by revealing its nature he exorcises the wound. The Siberian shamans accompany their healing rites by ululations and savage beating upon primitive tambourines or metal plates. The vodun priests of Haiti make noise 1st and begin their curative exercise after the subject has become completely relaxed and submissive to incantation. For the opposite of healing, the most ominous of all forms of magic—the sticking of pins into an effigy of a person to be ruined—is never performed in silence. Sinister cries accompany the imposition of taboo in primitive societies, and such cries inevitably assume the form of a musical incantation. Through constant repetition the musical accompaniment of the ritual of taboo becomes a magical symbol of the act itself, so it is no longer necessary to utter any words or symbolic verbal sounds to impose a taboo on a house, a mountain, a river, or a person; the music itself suffices.

Priests, witch doctors, and military leaders alike apply magic by ruthless repetition of slogans, often in singsong fashion. This type of crude magic is also successfully plied by commercial advertisers on the radio and television. An idiotically repetitive and musically repulsive jingle may drive the captive listener to distraction, but the commercial purpose is attained—that of involuntary and irrevocable mental insinuation. Religious proselytism impressed magic on would-be converts during missionary work by endless repetition of Latin phrases that meant nothing to the possessors of the souls to be saved. The power of magical repetition is recognized in the endless incantations of *Ave Maria* in the Roman Catholic prayers or religious radio broadcasts. The musical exhibition in N.Y.C. in 1963 that featured the complete performance of a brief and vacuous piece by Satie, *Vexations*, involving 840 repetitions, was a case of magic by cumulative stultification.

Several composers in times past believed that their works were of magical origin and that they could transfer this magic onto the audiences. Scriabin planned the composition of a *Mysterium* whose magical power would be such that its 1st performance would actually precipitate the end of the world, in which he himself and all participants in its performance would be consumed in an act of universal ecstasy. Whatever vestigal magic, musical and verbal, may still survive in its virgin state in such regions as the upper Amazon or in Polynesia, however, has prob-

ably been polluted and denatured by a potent flow of Western commercial musical "culture" by radio and other instantaneous means of communication.

Magic Flute, The (Die Zauberflöte). Singspiel by Mozart, 1791, his penultimate stage work, produced in Vienna less than 10 weeks before his death. The German libretto is by Emanuel Schikaneder, an impresario and actor; its labyrinthine entanglements are prodigious. The gorgeous music absorbs the listener entirely, letting the plot to proceed on its irrational course. An earnest youth (Tamino) falls in love with the portrait of the daughter of the Queen of the Night. He is given a magic flute to enable him to penetrate the fortress in which she is held in captivity somewhere in Egypt. His companion is a comical birdcatcher (Papageno) who owns a set of magic bells (in the score, an *instrumento d'acciacio*), capable of paralyzing any foe. After a series of

perilous adventures and tests, the youth and the Queen's daughter (Pamina) are united under the guidance of Sarastro, the father of Pamina, who serves as the light to the Queen's darkness. The Queen and her forces are defeated, and Tamino and Pamina sing a hymn to the sun symbolizing the conquest of love and art over the powers of darkness; even Papagena finds himself a wife.

The Magic Flute is not only the favorite opera of many Mozart aficionados, but also perhaps the most complex, both musically and dramatically. A partial clue to the story may lie in its heavy pseudo-oriental symbolism, such as was cultivated in the Masonic Order, of which both Mozart and his librettist were members. At the beginning Tamino is pursued by a serpent, which is killed by the female messengers of the protective Queen of the Night; the multiheaded serpent was a well-known Masonic symbol. The lovers undergo an initiation similar to that of the Masonic Order and give a vow of silence, commonly administered in the French Order of Masons in the 18th century. Various theatrical scenes are modeled after the rituals of Masonic lodges. The Egyptian pyramid, which is the locale of 1 of the scenes, is a famous Masonic symbol (reproduced on the reverse side of the Great Seal of the U.S. and on the $1 bill). The similarity between the symbols used in the libretto and the Masonic ritual may have angered the members of Mozart and Schikaneder's lodge; but the tale that the Masons resolved to put Mozart to death for the revelation of Masonic secrets is pure fantasy.

Scene from The Magic Flute

magic square. An arrangement of numbers placed in such a way that each of its horizontal or vertical rows equals the same sum, e.g.,

$$
\begin{array}{ccc}
1 & 2 & 3 \\
2 & 3 & 1 \\
3 & 1 & 2
\end{array}
$$

This arrangement provides a model for the disposition of the dodecaphonic system.

Magnard, (Lucien-Denis-Gabriel-) **Albéric,** distinguished French composer; b. Paris, June 9, 1865; d. (killed by German soldiers at his home) Baron, Oise, Sept. 3, 1914. He was reared in an intellectual family of means; his father was ed. of *Le Figaro*. He studied with Dubois and Massenet at the Paris Cons. (1886–88; *premier prix* in harmony, 1888) and with d'Indy (1888–92); subsequently taught counterpoint at the Schola Cantorum. He was killed while defending his property during the early days of World War I. He was a composer of high attainments; his mastery of orchestration is incontestable, and the rhapsodic sweep of his 3rd and 4th syms. is impressive. Despite these qualities, none of his music found a permanent place in the repertoire. Among his works are operas, orch.1 and chamber works, and songs.

Magnificat (Lat.). The most important hymn of the Vespers service in the Roman Catholic liturgy, namely the canticle of the Blessed Virgin Mary; its opening words are "Magnificat anima mea Dominum." The text is taken from Luke 1:46–55. Many pious composers wrote Magnificats as separate choral works. In the Anglican Church service the Magnificat is a part of Evensong, using the English words, "My soul doth magnify the Lord."

Magyar cadence. GYPSY CADENCE.

Magyar scale. GYPSY SCALE.

Mahler, Gustav

Outstanding Austrian composer and conductor in the late Romantic tradition; b. Kalischt, Bohemia, July 7, 1860; d. Vienna, May 18, 1911. He attended school in Iglau; in 1875 entered the Vienna Cons., where he studied piano with Julius Epstein, harmony with Robert Fuchs, and composition with Franz Krenn. He also took academic courses in history and philosophy at the Univ. of Vienna (1877–80). In the summer of 1880 he received his 1st engagement as a conductor, at the operetta theater in the town of Hall in Upper Austria; subsequently he held posts as theater conductor at Ljubljana (1881), Olmütz (1882), Vienna (1883), and Kassel (1883–85). In 1885 he served as 2nd Kapellmeister to Anton Seidl at the Prague Opera, where he gave several performances of Wagner's operas. From 1886 to 1888 he was assistant to Arthur Nikisch in Leipzig; in 1888 he received the important appointment of music director of the Royal Opera in Budapest.

In 1891 he was engaged as conductor at the Hamburg Opera; during his tenure there he developed a consummate technique for conducting. In 1897 he received a tentative offer as music director of the Vienna Court Opera, but there was an obstacle to overcome: Mahler was Jewish, and although there was no overt anti-Semitism in the Austrian government, an imperial appointment could not be given to a Jew. Mahler was never orthodox in his religion, and had no difficulty in converting to Catholicism, the prevailing faith in Austria. He held this position at the Vienna Court Opera for 10 years; under his guidance, it reached the highest standards of artistic excellence. In 1898 Mahler was engaged to succeed Hans Richter as conductor of the Vienna Phil. Here, as in his direction of opera, he proved a great interpreter, but he also allowed himself considerable freedom in rearranging the orchestration of classical scores when he felt it would redound to greater effect. He also aroused antagonism among the players by his autocratic behavior toward them. He resigned from the Vienna Phil. in 1901; in 1907 he also resigned from the Vienna Court Opera.

In the meantime he became immersed in strenuous work as a composer; he confined himself exclusively to composition of symphonic music, sometimes with vocal parts; because of his busy schedule as conductor, he could compose only in the summer months, in a villa on the Worthersee in Carinthia. In 1902 he married Alma Schindler (see Werfel, Alma Mahler); she had studied music with Zemlinsky, Schoenberg's brother-in-law, but was forced to give up composition after her marriage by her autocratic husband. They had 2 daughters; the younger, Anna, was briefly married to Ernst Krenek; the elder, Maria, died of scarlet fever, in 1907. While in mourning Mahler found out about his own heart condition, which he understood would eventually kill him.

Having exhausted his opportunities in Vienna, Mahler accepted the post of principal conductor of the Metropolitan Opera in N.Y. in 1907. He made his American debut there on Jan. 1, 1908, conducting *Tristan und Isolde*. In 1909 he was appointed conductor of the N.Y. Phil. His performances both at the Metropolitan and with the N.Y. Phil. were enormously successful with the audiences and the N.Y. music critics, but inevitably he had conflicts with the board of trustees in both organizations, which were mostly commanded by rich women. The N.Y. newspapers publ. lurid accounts of his struggle for artistic command with the 2 governing committees. Alma Mahler was quoted as saying that although in Vienna even the Emperor did not dare to order Mahler about, in N.Y. he had to submit to the whims of 10 ignorant women. He resigned from the Metropolitan Opera; on Feb. 21, 1911, he conducted his last concert with the N.Y. Phil. and then returned to Vienna; he died of a heart attack brought on by a bacterial infection, at age 50. The newspaper editorials mourned Mahler's death but sadly noted that his N.Y. tenure had been a failure.

As to Mahler's own compositions, the *N.Y. Tribune* said bluntly, "We cannot see how any of his music can long survive him." His syms. were sharply condemned in the press as being too long, too loud, and too discordant. It was not until the 2nd half of the 20th century that Mahler became fully recognized as a composer, the last great Romantic symphonist. Mahler's syms. were drawn on the grandest scale, and the technical means employed for the realization of his ideas were correspondingly elaborate. The sources of his inspiration were twofold: the lofty concepts of universal art, akin to those of Bruckner, and ultimately stemming from Wagner; and the simple folk melos of the Austrian countryside, in pastoral moods recalling the intimate episodes in Beethoven's syms.

True to his Romantic nature, Mahler at 1st attached descriptive titles to his syms.: the 1st was named the *Titan* (after Jean Paul); the 2nd, *Resurrection*; the 3rd, *Ein Sommermorgentraum*; and the 5th, *The Giant*. The great 8th became known as the *Sym. of a Thousand* because it required about 1,000 instrumentalists, vocalists, and soloists for performance; however, this sobriquet was the inspiration of Mahler's agent, not of Mahler himself. Later in life Mahler tried to disassociate his works from their programmatic titles; he even claimed that he never used them in the 1st place, contradicting the evidence of the

MSS, in which the titles appear in Mahler's own handwriting. Mahler was not an innovator in his harmonic writing; rather, he brought the Romantic era to a culmination by virtue of the expansiveness of his emotional expression and the grandiose design of his musical structures.

Morbid by nature, Mahler brooded upon the inevitability of death; one of his most poignant compositions was the Rückert cycle for voice and orch. *Kindertotenlieder*; he wrote it in 1901–1904, a few years before his daughter Maria's death, and he blamed himself superstitiously for this anticipation of his personal tragedy (Alma may have contributed to this feeling). In 1910 he consulted Sigmund Freud in Leiden, Holland, but the treatment was brief and apparently did not help Mahler to resolve his psychological problems completely. In the 3rd movement of his unfinished 10th Sym., significantly titled *Purgatorio*, he wrote on the margin, "Madness seizes me, annihilates me," and appealed to the devil to take possession of his soul. But his neuroses never pushed him over the edge; he gained understanding about his negative contributions to a troubled marriage, and indicated regret at having stifled Alma's musical creativity.

Mahler's importance to the evolution of modern music is very great; the early works of Schoenberg and Berg show the influence of Mahler's concepts. A society was formed in the U.S. in 1941 "to develop in the public an appreciation of the music of Bruckner, Mahler, and other moderns." An International Gustav Mahler Soc. was formed in Vienna in 1955, with Bruno Walter as honorary president. On Mahler's centennial, the government of Austria issued a memorial postage stamp of 1–1/2 shillings, with Mahler's portrait.

Mahler destroyed the MSS of several of his early works, among them a Piano Quartet (perf. in Vienna, 1878, with the composer at the piano; 1 movement survives) and 3 projected or unfinished operas: *Herzog Ernst von Schwaben*, to a drama by Uhland; *Die Argonauten*, from a trilogy by Grillparzer; and *Rübezahl*, after Grimm's fairy tales. He also made an arrangement of Weber's unfinished *Die drei Pintos* (Leipzig, 1888, Mahler conducting), *Euryanthe*, and *Oberon*; also transcribed Bruckner's 3rd Sym. for 2 Pianos (1878). Mahler made controversial performing editions or arrangements of syms. by Bach, Mozart, Beethoven, Schubert, Schumann, and Bruckner, and a version for string orch. of Beethoven's String Quartet in C-sharp Minor, op. 131.

Maid of Orleans, The. Opera by Tchaikovsky, 1881, 1st performed in St. Petersburg, loosely based on Schiller's romantic play. Joan of Arc, the maid of Orleans, hears mysterious voices urging her to save France from the English, who approach the City of Orleans. Joan helps the pusillanimous French King Charles VII to win the battle, but she is accused of consorting with the Devil and turned over to the authorities who sentence her to be burned at the stake as an incorrigible heretic. The libretto follows history a little more closely than Verdi's *Giovanni d'Arco*, but like the Verdi, unwarranted amorous episodes are included. In reality Joan was condemned for—among other things—cutting her hair short and wearing masculine attire, not for heterosexual behavior. Tchaikovsky's heroine does get to sing a beautiful aria bidding farewell to the fields and hills of her native farmland.

Maid of Pskov, The. Opera by Rimsky-Korsakov, 1873, 1st produced in St. Petersburg. The action takes place in Pskos, 1570, where Ivan the Terrible, accompanied by his dreaded henchmen, enters the city to subdue an incipient rebellion. He discovers that a girl betrothed to a rebel is his natural daughter Olga, born to Vera Sheloga. As his soldiers are about to lay Pskov waste, Ivan orders them to desist to spare Olga; but she runs out into the streets and is slain. In 1898 Rimsky-Korsakov wrote a 1-act opera called *Boyarina Vera Sheloga*, depicting the original affair between Vera and Ivan.

main (Fr.). Hand. *Main droite* (*gauche*), right (left) hand; often written *m.d.* (*m.g.*).

Mairzy Doats. Nonsense song by Milton Drake, Al Hoffman, and Jerry Livingston, 1943, which caught the imagination of the nation in wartime, in need of some inspired gibberish. The story is that the incomprehensible words were actually imitations of a small person talking very rapidly and seeming to make sense with words that made none.

maître (Fr.). Master. *Maitre de chapelle*, choirmaster; conductor.

Maître-chanteur (Fr.). MASTERSINGER.

majestätisch (Ger.). MAESTOSO.

majeur (Fr.). MAJOR.

major (Lat.). Greater; opposed to minor (lesser; see INTERVAL). *Major cadence*, one ending with a major triad; *major chord* or *triad*, one having a major 3rd and perfect 5th upward from the root (lowest note); *major interval*, in any major scale, the distances between the 1st degree (tonic) and its 2nd, 3rd, 6th, and 7th degrees; *major scale*, standard pitch ordering consisting, from 1st degree (tonic) upward, of 2 consecutive whole tones (major 2nds), followed by 1 semitone (minor 2nd), 3 whole tones, and 1 semitone.

major-minor syndrome. In Baroque music most minor-key works end on a major triad; such a major 3rd acquired the name PICARDY THIRD (*tierce de Picardie*), a term introduced by Rousseau in his dictionary; the etymology is unknown. The preference for the major over minor 3rds in final chords may be explained by its privileged position as the 5th overtone of the harmonic series, whereas a minor 3rd above the fundamental tone does not occur in a lower-numbered (i.e., more consonant) partial. In the practice of modern composers a major 3rd is often superimposed on a minor 3rd. Scriabin employed such a major-minor syndrome in his last opus numbers, but he spread the harmony widely, so that the frictional dissonance of a semitone was avoided. It was Stravinsky who cultivated a true major-minor syndrome in placing both the minor and the major 3rd within a triad. He made use of it as a motto in his choral work *Le Roi des étoiles* (1912); it occurs also in *Le Sacre du Printemps*. Most importantly, Stravinsky uses it as a melodic palimpsest, breaking up the combined chord, with both the major and the minor 3rd assuming a thematic significance.

Majority. Song by Ives, 1915, for unison voices and orch.; the alternative title is *The Masses*. A version for voice and piano appeared in *114 Songs* (1921); in it there are tone clusters in the piano part to be played by pressing a strip of wood over the keys.

Makeba, Miriam, black South African singer; b. Prospect, near Johannesburg, Mar. 4, 1932. She sang in a mission choir in Pretoria; then joined an itinerant minstrel show. She 1st attracted attention when she sang the leading part in the African opera *King Kong* (Johannesburg, 1959). In 1959 she went to the U.S.; appeared in N.Y. nightclubs and on television; had several hit records, including *Pata Pata*; testified at the United Nations on the racist policies of South Africa; made a successful tour of Europe; also traveled to Ethiopia and Kenya as a representative of black art. She was married to the African-American activist Stokely Carmichael from 1968 to 1978.

Makropoulos Affair, The. Opera by Janáček, 1926, 1st performed in Brno, based on the Karel Čapek play. A singer made immortal by her alchemist father in the 17th century is living in Prague under the name Emilia Marty, bewitching all around her while desperately searching for the cabalistic formula that her father wrote down before she turns 300 and dies. An accusation of forgery on an old document forces her to reveal her identity as the nearly 300-year-old Elena Makropoulos to a shocked coterie. She regains the formula, but, weary of life and unable to give it away, burns the paper and dies with its destruction.

Malagueña (Sp.). An old Spanish dance folk music originating in the provinces of Málaga and Murcia, in rapid triple time. Its main harmonic characteristic is a PHRYGIAN cadence from the tonic down to the dominant, harmonized by consecutive triads—a tonic minor, a major triad based on the natural 7th degree, and descending through the submediant triad to the major dominant.

Malédiction. Sketch for piano and orch. by Liszt, *c.* 1840. The name refers solely to the 1st theme of the work, and was so labeled by Liszt.

Malheurs d'Orphée, Les. Opera by Milhaud, 1926, 1st produced in Brussels. In this persiflage of the Greek myth, Orpheus is a pharmacist who befriends Eurydice. They go to the country, where she dies; he tries in vain to resuscitate her with modern drugs.

Malibran, Maria (Felicità Garcia), famous Spanish mezzo-soprano, b. Paris, Mar. 24, 1808; d. Manchester, Sept. 23, 1836. She was the daughter of Manuel (del Popolo Vicente Rodríguez) Garcia (b. Seville, Jan 21, 1775; d. Paris, June 9, 1832), one of the great tenors and singing teachers of his era. Maria was taken to Naples, where she sang a child's part in Paer's *Agnese* (1814); studied voice with her father from the age of 15; also studied solfeggio with Panseron. She made her debut as Rosina at the King's Theatre in London (June 7, 1825); then went to N.Y., where she sang in the same opera in her family's season at the Park Theatre, which commenced on Nov. 29, 1825. She became a popular favorite, singing in *Otello, Tancredi, La Cenerentola, Don Giovanni*, and the 2 operas written for her by her father, *L'amante astuto* and *La figlia dell'aria*. She married the French merchant François Malibran, but he soon became bankrupt and she returned to Europe without him in 1827.

Malibran made her Paris debut as Semiramide at the Théâtre-Italien (1828); then alternated her appearances in Paris and London during the 1829–32 seasons. She subsequently went to Italy, singing in Bologna (1832) and Naples (1833); made her debut at Milan's La Scala as Norma (1836). She met the violinist Charles de Bériot in 1829; they lived together until her marriage to Malibran was annulled in 1836, and then were married that same year. Malibran suffered serious injuries when thrown from her horse in 1836; since she was pregnant, complications developed and she lost her life. Her voice was of extraordinary compass, but the medium register had several "dead" tones. She was also a good pianist, and composed numerous nocturnes, romances, and chansonnettes, publ. in album form as *Dernières pensées*.

malinconia (It.). Melancholy.

malinconicamente, malinconico, malinconia (col), malinconioso, or malinconoso (It.). With melancholy expression, melancholy; dejectedly.

Malipiero, Francesco, Italian composer, grandfather of Gian Francesco Malipiero; b. Rovigio, Jan. 9, 1824; d. Venice, May 12, 1887. He studied with Melchiore Balbi at the Liceo Musicale in Venice. At the age of 18 he wrote an opera, *Giovanna di Napoli*, which was produced with signal success; Rossini praised it. Other operas were *Attila* (1845; renamed *Ildegonda di Borgogna*); *Alberigo da Romano* (1846; his best); and *Fernando Cortez* (1851).

Malipiero, Gian Francesco, eminent Italian composer and conductor; b. Venice, Mar. 18, 1882; d. Treviso, near Venice, Aug. 1, 1973. His grandfather, Francesco, was an opera composer; his father, Luigi Malipiero, was a pianist and conductor. In 1898 Gian Francesco enrolled at the Vienna Cons. as a violin student; in 1899 he returned to Venice, where he studied at the Liceo Musicale Benedetto Marcello with Marco Bossi, whom he followed to Bologna in 1904, and took a diploma in composition at the Liceo Musicale G. B. Martini that same year; subsequently worked as amanuensis to Smareglia, gaining valuable experience in orchestration. He studied briefly with Bruch in Berlin (1908). In 1912–13 he committed an act of notoriety by submitting 5 works to a Roman competition, each under a different pseudonym, and winning 4 of 5 prizes. Malipiero went to Paris (1913), where he absorbed the techniques of musical impressionism, cultivating parallel chord formations and amplified tonal harmonies with characteristic added 6ths, 9ths, and 11ths.

However, his own style of composition was determined by the polyphonic practices of the Italian Baroque.

In 1921 Malipiero returned to Italy; was a prof. of composition at the Parma Cons. (1921–23); afterward lived mostly in Asolo, near Venice. He was made prof. of composition at the Liceo Musicale Benedetto Marcello in Venice (1932), continuing there when it became the Cons. (1940); was its director (1939–52). He ed. a complete edition of the works of Monteverdi (16 vols., Bologna and Vienna, 1926–42) and many works by Vivaldi, as well as works by other Italian composers. He was made a member of the National Inst. of Arts and Letters in N.Y. in 1949, the Royal Flemish Academy in Brussels in 1952, the Institut de France in 1954, and the Akademie der Künste in West Berlin in 1967.

Malipiero's work reflects many of the styles of his century—impressionism, expressionism, symbolism, futurism, eclecticism, archaism, improvisatory rather than symphonic composition, chromaticism. An extremely prolific composer (35 operas, 6 ballets, 18 works for voice/s and orch., 17 sinfonias, 11 concertos, many other orch.l works, and numerous vocal pieces, chamber and instrumental works, piano music), Malipiero's work is notably uneven in quality; but he is considered one of the best 20th-century Italian composers, comparable to Dallapiccola and Casella; his breadth of subject matter is typically wide. His works in series provide an overview of his contributions, among them the Dialoghi: No. 1, *con M. de Falla*, for orch.; No. 2 for 2 pianos; No. 3, *con Jacopone da Todi*, for Voice and 2 Pianos; No. 4 for Wind Quintet; No. 5 for Viola and Orch.; No. 6 for Harpsichord and Orch.; No. 7 for 2 Pianos and Orch.; No. 8, *La morte di Socrate*, for Baritone and Small Orch. (all 1956–57). He also composed a series of sinfonias, both numbered and unnumbered; 6 piano concertos; and other orch.l works.

Malipiero was an active writer, in addition to his editing work. He wrote many scholarly works and textbooks on music between 1920 and 1969. His nephew Riccardo Malipiero (b. Milan, July 24, 1914) is also a composer; he studied with his uncle at the Liceo Musicale Benedetto Marcello in Venice (1937–39).

mambo. A ballroom dance derived from the rumba. It appeared in Cuba during the 1940s and was made popular in the U.S. particularly by Perez Prado and his band; the mambo had spread to non-Hispanic audiences by the 1950s. This couple dance, in 4/4, uses forward and backward steps, beginning on the upbeat, to a percussive polyrhythmic accompaniment. The mambo was a major influence on the CHA-CHA.

Mame. Musical by Jerry Herman, 1966. Mame is a totally uninhibited woman who lives it up in N.Y. and at the same time is entrusted with the fate of her young orphaned nephew. He is shocked by the scandalous behavior of his "Auntie Mame," but manages to retain his sanity through it all, marries a nice woman, and has a son. At the end of the comedy, Mame takes her great-nephew on a trip around the world, determined to educate him by her own rule: "Life is a banquet; most poor sons-of-bitches are starving to death." The title song became a hit, particularly as sung by Louis Armstrong.

Mamelles de Tirésias, Les (The Breasts of Tirésias). Opera buffa by Poulenc, 1947, 1st produced in Paris. The libretto deals with transsexual transformation. Tirésias is weary of being a woman; she ignites her bulging breasts, which rise and pop like balloons. Her husband, on the other hand, wants to be a woman. He succeeds brilliantly and gives birth to 40,000 children. In the end they return to their original genders and appeal to the audience to breed energetically in order to repopulate the French countryside devastated by war. The score is glorified slapstick, recalling the world of Les 6.

Man I Love, The. Song by Gershwin, 1924, orig. intended for the musical *Lady, Be Good!* but was cut just before its Broadway opening; it was eventually included in *Strike Up the Band* (1927). A haunting song, with a blue note enhanced by a descending chromatic lead in the middle voice.

Man of La Mancha. Musical by Mitch Leigh, 1965, 1st performed in N.Y., based on Cervantes's parody epic *Don Quixote.* The libretto identifies Cervantes with his creation, the valorous knight of the woeful countenance, and the action shifts from the Seville prison cell in which he was confined to the scenes of Quixote's exploits. The major characters in the musical are a common serving woman whom he idolizes as Dulcinea, the windmill which he believes is a monster, the mule drivers whom he fights, and his faithful henchman Sancho Panza. Includes the title song and the immensely popular *Impossible Dream.*

Man on the Flying Trapeze, The. A vaudeville waltz-song of unknown origin, 1st popular in the 1870s. Its 2nd line was used by William Saroyan as the title of his novel *The Daring Young Man on the Flying Trapeze.*

mancando (It.). Decreasing in loudness, dying away.

Mancini, Henry, highly successful American composer, arranger, pianist, and conductor of popular music. b. Cleveland, Apr. 16, 1924; d. Los Angeles, June 14, 1994. He studied flute and piano in childhood; later received training from Max Adkins in Pittsburgh and attended the Juilliard Graduate School in N.Y. (1942). He worked as a pianist and arranger with Tex Beneke's orch. (1945–47); also studied composition with M. Castelnuovo-Tedesco, E. Krenek, and A. Sendrey in Los Angeles. He then was on the music staff of Universal-International film studios (1952–58), for which he wrote many scores. He also wrote for television, gaining success with his music for the *Peter Gunn* series (1958).

His scores for the films *Breakfast at Tiffany's* (1961)—which included the hit song *Moon River*—and *Days of Wine and Roses* (1962) both won him Academy and Grammy Awards; other scores included *Touch of Evil*, *Experiment in Terror*, *Hatari*, *Charade*, *The Pink Panther*, *2 for the Road*, *The Molly Maguires*, *Sometimes a Great Notion*, *The Silver Streak*, *Victor/Victoria*, and television soundtracks such as *Mr. Lucky* and *The Thorn Birds*. In later years he appeared widely as a guest conductor in concerts of popular fare with American orchs. He publ. *Sounds and Scores* (1962), a guide to orchestration.

mandocello (It.). Bass MANDOLIN.

mandola (It.). 1. Alto MANDOLIN. 2. MANDORA.

mandolin (U.K., Fr. *mandoline*; Ger. *Mandoline*; It. *mandolino*). A smaller member of the lute family which originated in Italy in the 17th century. The name itself is the diminutive of *mandola*. It is shaped like a pear half and has a fretted fingerboard with 4 pairs of strings tuned like those of the violin (G, D, A, E). It is played with a plectrum type called the *mediator*. Progressively larger sizes of the mandolin are the mandola, the mandoloncello, and the mandolone or mandocello. An ensemble consisting of mandolins, combined with guitars, is popularly known as

Gibson F–4 mandolin, c. 1921

PHOTOGRAPH COURTESY OF GEORGE GRUHN, GRUHN GUITARS, NASHVILLE, TENN.

a Neapolitan orch. Although the mandolin is generally regarded as a popular or traditional instrument, Mozart and Beethoven wrote for it. The mandolin is also included in Mahler's 7th Sym., in Schoenberg's *Serenade*, op. 24, and in Webern's *Fünf Stücke für Orchester*.

Among folk and traditional performers, Bill Monroe is most closely associated with the mandolin. He developed a rapid style of playing, emphasizing sharp, rhythmic chords and breathtakingly fast melodic runs, which became the basis for the bluegrass style. Monroe's influence has been great, and his disciples have expanded the instrument's repertoire into jazz music. David Grissman is the most prominent contemporary performer, who plays both in traditional bluegrass style and his own compositions with a quartet including 2 mandolins in a jazz-swing style.

mandolinata (It.). 1. A mandolin piece of quiet character, like a serenade. 2. In piano playing, play with a mandolin effect.

mandolino (It.). A smaller MANDOLIN.

mandoloncello (It.). Bass MANDOLIN.

mandolone (It.). Bass MANDOLIN.

mandora or mandore. A large instrument similar to a MANDOLIN; also called *mandola*.

maneria (Lat.). A medieval theoretical term for ecclesiastical modes of both authentic and plagal types; the modes were labeled by Latinized Greek ordinal numbers: *protus*, *deuterus*, *tritus*, and *tetradus*.

Manfred Symphony. Orch. work by Tchaikovsky, 1886, 1st performed in Moscow. The program of the work is inspired by Byron's famous poem depicting Manfred wandering in the Alps in search of oblivion. The score is in 4 movements and is often listed by literal-minded musicologists as Tchaikovsky's 7th Sym. Although brilliant and dramatic, *Manfred* is musically inferior to Tchaikovsky's full-fledged symphonies.

Manhattan. Song by Rodgers and Hart, 1925, included in the revue *Garrick Gaieties* and subsequently interpolated in several movie musicals.

maniera (It.). Manner, style, method. *Con dolce maniera*, in a suave, delicate style.

mannerism. A generic term descriptive of a certain preciosity of artistic execution. In painting, *mannerism* refers to the 16th- and early 17th-century Italian painting that used exaggeration of dimension and color contrast to impart a heightened reality, symbolic or otherwise; Parmigianino and Caravaggio are among the Mannerists. Applying this term to music has proven controversial; for different critics it has meant late Baroque and rococo schools, whose music is marked by curvilinear designs and ornamental arabesques; the Mannheim school, for its *recherché* style of composition and performance; or the madrigal and motet composers of the late Renaissance, embodied in the highly chromatic music of Gesualdo.

Mannheim school. A group of musicians active at the court of the German city of Mannheim in the middle of the 18th century; they developed a method of composition and performance that marked a radical departure from the monolithic style of the Baroque period. Their animator and mentor was the Bohemian master Johann Stamitz, who inaugurated in his orch.l works the principle of melodic guidance and symmetrical formal structure. Harmony, too, underwent a decided change in the works of the Mannheim school, away from the rigid dependence on BASSO CONTINUO. In performance the Mannheim group introduced novel dynamic usages, the most important of which was the effect of continuous crescendo and corresponding diminuendo, in contrast with the antiphonal structure of mutually responsive sections of forte and piano in Baroque music. Among other innovations were arpeggiated chords (in ascending melodic form, known as the "rocket theme"), extensive tremolos, abrupt general pauses, pyrotechnical accents, simulated sighs, and various emotional devices almost Romantic in nature.

With regard to the orch., the Mannheim musicians cultivated greater independence of the wind instruments. In respect to form there was a pronounced articulation of subsections in the minuet and the expansion of protosonata form to symphonic dimensions. The achievements of the Mannheim school soon became known in Paris and London and exercised considerable influence on the evolution of symphonic and chamber music. On the other hand there was a great deal of opposition on the part of traditional and academic musicians who dubbed the innovations of the Mannheim school mannerist; the circumstance that most of the Mannheim musicians came from Bohemia rather than from the main centers of German musical culture gave occasion for narrow nationalistic disdain. In a letter to Mozart, his father referred to the "overmannered Mannheim taste." But there was no gainsaying the power of the Mannheim dynamic characteristics. A musician who heard the Mannheimers play reports that "their crescendo makes the listeners rise involuntarily from their seats, and gradually sink back out of breath with the corresponding diminuendo."

Manning, Jane (Marian), English soprano; b. Norwich, Sept. 20, 1938. She studied at the Royal Academy of Music in London; in 1964 she made her debut in London in a program of contemporary music, and subsequently established herself as a leading interpreter of modern music in England. She married the composer Anthony Payne in 1966. She publ. the vol. *New Vocal Repertory: An Introduction* (1986). In 1990 she was made a member of the Order of the British Empire.

mano (It.). Hand. *Mano destra* (*sinistra*), right (left) hand.

Manon. Opera by Massenet, 1884, 1st produced in Paris. Manon, an emotionally perturbed 18th-century French girl, intends to become a nun but is diverted from her purpose by a dashing cavalier who carries her off to Paris. His father urges him to renounce the ways of the world and join the priesthood. Manon is arrested on suspicion of moral turpitude. Although her lover secures her freedom by bribing the authorities, she has no more strength to live, and dies of inanition. In *Manon* Massenet is at his sentimental best; its libretto differs from that of Puccini's opera *Manon Lescaut*, but both are drawn from Prévost's novel *Manon Lescaut*.

Manon Lescaut. Opera by Puccini, 1893, 1st produced in Turin. A beautiful French girl intends to enter a convent, but a traveling companion induces her to join him in Paris. She becomes debauched by city life but agrees to take a ship to America with her lover. They make the voyage safely, but despite his solicitude, she dies in New Orleans. The libretto differs from that of Massenet's opera *Manon*, but both are drawn from Prévost's novel *Manon Lescaut*.

Manru. Opera by Paderewski, 1901, 1st produced in Dresden. Manru is a dissolute Gypsy; his wife, unable to bear his constant infidelities, kills herself. Manru is eventually destroyed by a man whose bride he abducted to his camp. The opera is written in a conventional Romantic manner. Despite Paderewski's fame as a virtuoso pianist, his only opera was rarely produced, even in his lifetime.

manual. An organ keyboard; opposed to *pedal*.

manualiter (Lat.). On the manual(s) alone.

maqām (Arab.; Turk. *makam*; Azeri. *mugam*; Central Asia *makom*). 1. General term for the modal systems of Western Asia, based on a microtonal pitch gamut (usually treated as quarter tones). Each system has several modal scales, with a set group of pitches, upon which both melodies and improvisations are built; the performers must incorporate and develop motivic figures associated with each scale. Modalities are not necessarily transposable by the octave, as the pitches may differ in a higher octave. 2. A vocal or instrumental composition in cyclic form.

maracas. Latin American rattles; usually a pair of gourds filled with dry seeds and shaken vigorously rhythmically to accompany traditional and popular dances. In the 20th century maracas began to be used as percussion instruments in modern scores, quite independently from their ethnic content. Thus Prokofiev uses a pair in his patriotic oratorio *Alexander Nevsky*; Varèse has a part for maracas in his "atomic" work, *Ionisation*.

Marais, Marin, great French viola da gambist and composer; b. Paris, May 31, 1656; d. there, Aug. 15, 1728. He studied bass viol with Sainte-Colombe and composition with Lully (whom he addresses as teacher in a letter publ. in his 1st book of pieces for his instrument); became a member of the royal orch. (1676); was made Ordinaire de la chambre du Roi (1679); retired (1725). Marais possessed matchless skill as a virtuoso on the viola da gamba and set a new standard of excellence by enhancing the sonority of the instrument. He also established a new method of fingering, which had a decisive influence on the technique of performance.

As a composer he was an outstanding master of bass viol music, producing 5 extensive collections between 1686 and 1725, numbering some 550 works in all. In his dramatic music he followed Lully's French manner; his recitatives comport with the rhythm of French verse and the inflection of the rhyme. The purely instrumental parts in his operas were quite extensive; in *Alcione* (1706) he introduced a "tempeste," which is one of the earliest attempts at stage realism in operatic music. His other operas are *Alcide* (Paris, 1693), *Ariane et Bacchus* (Paris, 1696), and *Sémélé* (Paris, 1709). He also publ. 5 books of pieces for viola da gamba (1686–1725); trios (or syms.) for violin, flute, and viola da gamba (1692); a book of trios for violin, viola da gamba, and harpsichord under the title *La Gamme* (1723). He was married in 1676 and had 19 children; his son Roland Marais was also a talented viola da gambist who publ. 2 books of pieces for his instrument with basso continuo (Paris, 1735, 1738) and a *Nouvelle méthode de musique pour servir d'introduction aux acteurs modernes* (Paris, 1711; not extant).

marcato, -a (It.). With distinctness and emphasis. *Marcatissimo*, with very marked emphasis.

march

~~ ~~ ~~ ~~ ~~

A composition of strongly marked rhythm, suitable for timing the steps of a body of persons proceeding at a walking pace. The march (from Lat. *marcare*, mark; Sp. *marcha*; Fr. *marche*; It. *marcia*; Ger. *Marsch*) is a universal step corresponding to the natural alternation of the right and left foot in walking. (If there were a race of 3-footed humans, they would march in waltz time.) Since uniform steps are essential in military practice, the march has become the chosen rhythm of armies all over the world. While the time signature for a march is commonly 4/4, or ALLA BREVE, there are marches in 6/8 or 12/8, a type known as *Reiter-Marsch* (rider march), for binary time with rapid subdivisions in triplets suggesting a galloping horse. Schubert's song *Erlkönig* is a rider march, descriptive of the desperate ride of the father with a dying son in his arms.

The most immediate function of the march is military; indeed, a military march, or, in French, MARCHE MILITAIRE, is a distinctive musical form. A perfect example of a military march is the one in *Faust*. But march time can be adopted to a variety of functions: a solemn religious march as exemplified by the *March of the Priests* in *Aida*; a wedding march in Mendelssohn's music for *A Midsummer Night's Dream* and in *Lohengrin*; a children's march in *Carmen*. Patriotic marches abound; of these the grandest is *La Marseillaise*. A category by itself is the funeral march. The slow movement in Beethoven's *Eroica Symphony* is a funeral march. The march from Chopin's Piano Sonata in B-flat Minor is the one customarily performed at funerals; some frivolous American set this march to the words "Pray for the Dead, and the Dead will pray for you." There are also funeral marches with an ironic intent, such as Gounod's *Marche funèbre d'une marionette* and Alkan's *Marche funèbre sulla morte d'un papagallo*. An example of a funeral march gone berserk is a set of *3 Funeral Marches* by Lord Berners: *For a Statesman*, *For a Canary*, and *For a Rich Aunt*, the last naturally full of gaiety in anticipation of a lucrative inheritance.

While most national hymns are in *march time*, there are numerous exceptions. *The Star-Spangled Banner* is in slow waltz time, as is the British national anthem, *God Save the Queen*. Elgar wrote 5 military marches under the general title *Pomp and Circumstance*, of which number 1 is celebrated; its slow section, set to the words "Land of Hope and Glory," is widely used as a commencement march in American schools. Sousa, the American "March King," composed more than 100 military marches, of which *Stars and Stripes Forever* is one of the most rousing. Incidentally, the usual tempo of a marching tune in England and America is 80 steps per minute, which corresponds to the normal pulse beat. *Alla marcia*, in march style; *March form*, a structure found in American and British marches with an introduction; 1 or 2 sections in the tonic key in 16- or 32-bar phrases; a trio section in the dominant or subdominant key and often the implied lighter texture; and a concluding section in the tonic, either a repetition of the previous tonic sections or a new section. All but the last section have internal repeats.

marche funèbre (Fr.).   Funeral march.

Marche funèbre d'une marionette.   Orch.l piece by Gounod, 1873, humorously intended. The melody acquired popularity in the 1950s when Alfred Hitchcock, British director of lugubriously morbid horror films, selected it as his television program's signature tune.

marche militaire (Fr.).   Military march. Schubert wrote several piano pieces and duets with this redundant title; they are popular with students and teachers alike.

marche redoublée (Fr.).   A march in a more rapid tempo than usual.

Marche Slave.   Orch.l work by Tchaikovsky, 1876, to celebrate the liberation of Serbia from the Ottoman Empire. Its thematic materials combine Serbian and Russian elements, with the Russian Czarist anthem emerging victorious. Although Tchaikovsky regarded it as a patriotic gesture of no musical significance, *Marche Slave* became a regular repertory piece in Russia and elsewhere. It had its 1st performance in Moscow.

marche triomphale (Fr.).   Triumphant or victory march; popular in operatic crowd scenes.

Marching Through Georgia.   Song by Henry Clay Work, 1865, written to celebrate General William Tecumsah Sherman's scorched-earth campaign against the Confederates toward the end of the Civil War, especially the 1864 march "from Atlanta to the sea." This song has the schizophrenic distinction of having been one of the South's most hated; yet its tune became a standard among traditional musicians there.

Mari à la Porte, Un (A Husband at the Door). Operetta by Offenbach, 1859, premiered in Paris. The composer of an unperformed opera called *The Midnight Corpse* invades the flat of a newly married Parisian housewife. When her husband appears at the door, the intruding composer escapes through the window. What, no prospect of adultery? Apparently none.

Maria di Rudenz. Opera by Donizetti, 1838, 1st performed in Venice. A fortune hunter seeks to marry an heiress of the Count di Rudenz. The Count's daughter Maria suddenly returns to Rudenz and asserts her rights to inheritance. Complications set in when she herself falls in love with the dashing fortune hunter; in order to eliminate competition, she stabs her rival and pretends to inflict a lethal wound on herself. But she miscalculates and begins to die in earnest. The man who caused all these calamities and who in the meantime has murdered his own brother, loses his chances at a fortune with either of the 2 heiresses, 1 dying, 1 dead.

Maria Golovin. Opera by Menotti, 1958, premiered in Brussels, to the composer's libretto. Maria's husband is a prisoner of war; in his absence she has a strange liaison with a blind man. When the war ends and Maria's husband returns, her lover is inflamed with fury. Guided by the sound of her voice, he fires a pistol in her direction. She falls silent, pretending to be dead; he departs, satisfied with his blind vengeance. The opera was no more successful than the would-be murderer.

Maria Padilla. Opera by Donizetti, 1841, 1st performed in Milan. The eponymous heroine, mistress of King Pedro the Cruel of Castille, threatens suicide unless he marries her. For reasons of state he weds a Bourbon princess. Maria invades the palace and snatches the crown from her rival's head, then kills herself. (In a censored version, she dies overwrought by emotion.)

Maria Stuarda. Opera by Donizetti, 1835, concerning the ill-fated Queen of Scotland. The popularity of this work is a typical result of the post–World War II BEL CANTO revival.

Maria Theresia. Haydn's Sym. No. 48 (1769), in the sunny key of C major. It was so nicknamed because the Austrian empress Maria Theresia paid a visit at Esterházy's country estate where Haydn was employed and liked the sym. that Haydn played for her.

mariachi. An ensemble music of Mexico, featured in festivities and café and nightclub entertainment. Mariachi bands consist of violins, *guitarrón* (large guitar), guitar, trumpets, and Mexican percussion instruments, particularly the marimba. The songs are typically sung in parallel 3rds and use the subject matter of the Mexican CANCIÓN or *corrida*. The origin of the word itself is obscure, but it is suggested that it represents a corruption of the French word *mariage*, and that it was 1st used at the time of the Emperor Maximilian (19th century). Copland made use of typical mariachi tunes in his symphonic work *El Salón Mexico*, named after a once popular nightclub in Mexico City.

Mariage aux Lanternes, Le. Opera by Offenbach, 1857, produced in Paris. A farmer loves his cousin Denise, and asks their common uncle for advice. He replies mystifyingly that his nephew would find his greatest treasure in the garden. He digs and realizes that it was Denise who is his greatest treasure. They get married by the light of lanterns. The opera is short and pleasing.

Marienleben, Das (The Life of Mary). Song cycle by Hindemith, 1923, to 15 poems by Rilke, depicting the life of the Virgin Mary. It was 1st performed at the Donaueschingen Festival. Hindemith revised the cycle in 1941, with the purpose of bringing out the voice part as the dominant factor in the contrapuntal structure.

marimba. Family of African and Latin American xylophones with tuned resonators placed underneath the wooden bars to produce a richer sound. In the traditional instruments, gourds are used as resonators. The marimba is of ancient origin, but its modern form was created in Guatemala early in the 20th century. From there it spread to the U.S. and later to Europe. Its range, at 1st limited, has been gradually expanded to 6 octaves.

marimbaphone. Trade name of the American MARIMBA, patented in Chicago, 1915; the resonators are wooden blocks carefully tuned to their bars for full but unflawed resonance. In some modern versions of the instrument, electric amplification is used to reinforce its sound.

marinera (Sp.). Peruvian song-dance, with strophically set quatrains and 6/8 SEGUIDILLA refrains. The texts often include historical narrative and sociopolitical commentary. The genre has mostly disappeared from urban areas; in the Andes it often functions as a courtship dance. The marinera is related to the *chilena* and *cueca*.

Marines' Hymn, The. A march song usually known by its opening line, "From the halls of Montezuma to the shores of Tripoli." The references are to the entry of American Marines in Mexico City in 1847 and the Marine landing in North Africa in the war against the Barbary pirates in 1805. The tune is taken from an operetta by

Offenbach, *Geneviève de Brabant*, published in 1868, but it seems that Offenbach himself picked it up from some less dignified source. The uncopyrighted sheet music edition of the U.S. Marine Corps Publicity Bureau in 1918 attributed the text to an unidentified Marine officer during the Mexican War. How the words came to be latched to an Offenbach air is a puzzle.

Maritana. Opera, 1845, by William Vincent Wallace (1812–65), 1st performed in London with considerable success; but its romantic appeal was exhausted and the opera fell into desuetude. The libretto concerns the life and loves of a Gypsy woman.

markiert (Ger.). Accented, marked.

Marley, Bob (Robert Nesta), Jamaican reggae singer and composer; b. Rhoden Hall, Feb. 6, 1945; d. Miami, May 11, 1981. He was taken to Kingston as a child and worked as an electrical welder. He picked up popular tunes in the streets and from the radio, opened a small recording shop of his own, and then began making records of some of his own tunes, a mixture of calypso and soul music. He helped found a group, the Wailers, which became the most popular purveyor of REGGAE; Marley later went solo and produced highly successful records that reached an international audience and influenced rock musicians profoundly from the 1970s; another result was the intriguing mixture known as hip-hop reggae.

Marley joined the Rastafarian religious group, followers of Haile Selassie of Ethiopia (whose original name was Ras Tafari). In 1976 he became embroiled in politics, supporting the Jamaican People's National Party; as he was preparing to sing at a band concert in late 1976, he was shot and wounded. After that episode he went to Europe, scoring an unusual popular success, particularly in England, Sweden, the Netherlands, and West Germany. In 1977 he made a tour of the U.S., where his fame had preceded him via his record albums.

His songs, in Jamaican dialect, preached revolution; typical of them were *Rebel Music*, *Everywhere Be War*, and *Death to the Downpressors*. But his 1974 album, *Natty Dread* (a pun on the Rasta hair style), mixes sociopolitics (*Them Belly Full*, *Revolution*), religion (*So Jah Seh*), self-image (*Lively Up Yourself*), and relationships (*No Woman No Cry*) with subtle arrangement and rhythmic counterpoint to reach an apogee that Marley and other reggae artists were unable to sustain, as reggae fell into stereotyped syncopations.

Marosszék Dances. Orch.l suite by Kodály, 1930, based on dance tunes that he collected while traveling in the environs of Marosszék, Hungary.

Mârouf, Savetier du Caire (Marouf, Shoemaker of Cairo). Opera, 1914, by Henri (Benjamin) Rabaud (1873–1949), 1st performed in Paris. The story is drawn from *The Arabian Nights*. Shipwrecked, Mârouf makes his way to the Sultan's palace, pretending to be a wealthy merchant. The Sultan gives his daughter in marriage to him. Mârouf robs the palace and flees with his still faithful and credulous wife. He redeems himself by securing a magic ring with which he conjures up a palace of his own. This is Rabaud's most successful opera; the score contains some effective evocations of Arabic songs and rhythms.

Marriage of Figaro, The (*Le Nozze di Figaro*). Comic opera by Mozart, 1786, 1st produced in Vienna; the libretto is the 1st that Da Ponte wrote for Mozart and is based on Beaumarchais's sequel to his *The Barber of Seville*. Count Almaviva is now married to Rosina; Figaro, formerly a cunning barber, is now the Count's valet; he wants to marry the Countess's maid Susannah, but the Count himself covets her; particularly insidious is the Count's refusal to give up a traditional "right of way" to his female servants just prior to their marriage. The Countess laments her husband's flighty ways (*Dove sono*), and Figaro stages complex stratagems to arouse the Count's jealousy, in order to bring him closer to his wife. The youthful page Cherubino is used by Figaro to play the suitor of the Countess; as the Count enters the house, the page puts on a maid's dress to hide his sex. (Since the part of Cherubino is entrusted to a soprano, the donning of female dress either restores the performer's true gender or gives new meaning to transvestism.) The complications increase exponentially, and the plot reaches the apex of its absurdity when an elderly female housekeeper whom Figaro has promised to marry is revealed as his own mother. But the more absurd the situations are, the more beautiful the music.

Marriner, (Sir) **Neville,** outstanding English conductor; b. Lincoln, Apr. 15, 1924. He studied violin with his father, and then with Frederick Mountney; subsequently entered the Royal College of Music in London when he was 13, but his studies were interrupted by military service during World War II; after resuming his training at the Royal College of Music, he completed his violin studies in Paris with René Benedetti and took courses at the Cons. He was active as a violinist in chamber music ensembles; was a prof. of violin at the Royal College of Music (1949–59); joined the Philharmonia Orch. of London as a violinist (1952); was principal 2nd violinist of the London Sym. Orch. (1956–58). His interest in conducting was encouraged by Pierre Monteux, who gave him lessons at his summer school in Hancock, Maine (1959).

In 1958 he founded the Academy of St.-Martin-in-the-Fields; served as its director until 1978, establishing an international reputation through recordings and tours. From 1968 to 1978 he also served as music director of the Los Angeles Chamber Orch.; then was music director of the Minnesota Orch. in Minneapolis (1978–86). In 1981 he became principal guest conductor of the Stuttgart Radio Sym. Orch.; was its chief conductor from 1983 to 1989. He appeared as a guest conductor with many of the world's leading orchs. In 1979 he was made a Commander of the Order of the British Empire. He was knighted in 1985.

Marriner has proved himself one of the most remarkable conductors of his day. His extensive activities as a chamber music player, orch. musician, and chamber orch. violinist-conductor served as an invaluable foundation for his career as a sym. conductor of the 1st rank. His enormous repertoire encompasses works from the Baroque era to the great masterworks of the 20th century. In all of his performances he demonstrates authority, mastery of detail, and impeccable taste.

Marsalis, Wynton,

outstanding African-American trumpet virtuoso; b. New Orleans, Oct. 18, 1961. He was born into a cultured musical family; his father, Ellis Marsalis, was a modern bop pianist who insisted that his sons receive professional training. Wynton's younger brother Delfeayo is a trombonist; his older brother Branford (b. Breaux Bridge, La., 1960) is a saxophonist of considerable talent who has played with Clark Terry, Miles Davis, Blakey, Gillespie, and the English rock musician Sting; he has also had his own groups. In 1974 Ellis Marsalis founded the jazz program for the nascent New Orleans Center for the Creative Arts, which nurtured important new talent. Wynton took up the trumpet at age 6; later studied with John Longo, and also received instruction at his father's school. He appeared as soloist in the Haydn Trumpet Concerto with the New Orleans Phil. when he was 14; also performed with local groups in classical, jazz, and rock settings. He won the Harvey Shapiro Award as the most gifted brass player at the Berkshire Music Center at Tanglewood at age 17; then attended the Juilliard School in N.Y. (1979–81).

He joined Art Blakey's Jazz Messengers (1980–81); played with them at the jazz festival at Montreux, Switzerland (1980); then toured with his own quintet, which included his brother Branford, a fine saxophonist; he also worked with Miles Davis. In 1984 he achieved unprecedented success when he won Grammy awards in both the jazz and classical categories for his recordings. As of 1990 he had released 12 jazz and 5 classical recordings, for which he garnered a grand total of 8 Grammy Awards. He is credited with leading a jazz revival which has brought forward many young musicians of great talent.

In 1990 Marsalis hosted a benefit concert for Graham-Windham (a private child-care agency), the Autism Soc. of America, and the Immunohematology Research Foundation at Alice Tully Hall in N.Y.; featured were musical members of his family: patriarch Ellis on piano, youngest brother Jason, making his debut on drums, Branford on saxophone, and Wynton on trumpet. The Marsalis clan was joined by the members of Wynton's jazz septet in an evening of critically acclaimed hard-bop. Wynton has narrated a television series on the history of jazz, part of his attempt to enlarge jazz's audience; he is a versatile performer stylistically, although some colleagues find his work lacking in depth.

Marschner, Heinrich

(August), important German opera composer; b. Zittau, Saxony, Aug. 16, 1795; d. Hannover, Dec. 14, 1861. He sang in the school choir at the Zittau Gymnasium, and also studied music with Karl Hering. In 1813 he went to Leipzig, where he studied jurisprudence at the Univ.; encouraged by the cantor of the Thomasschule, J. C. Schicht, he turned to music as his main vocation. In 1816 he became a music tutor in Count Zichy's household in Pressburg, and also served as Kapellmeister to Prince Krasatkowitz. In his leisure hours he began to compose light operas; his 1st opera, *Titus* (1816), did not achieve a performance, but soon he had 2 more operas and a singspiel produced in Dresden.

His 1st signal success was the historical opera *Heinrich IV und d'Aubigné*, which was accepted by Weber, who was then music director at the Dresden Court Opera, and was produced there on July 19, 1820. In 1817 he was in Vienna, where he was fortunate enough to meet Beethoven. In 1821 Marschner moved to Dresden and had his singspiel *Der Holzdieb* staged at the Court Opera (1825). He expected to succeed Weber as music director at the Court Opera after Weber died in London, but he failed to obtain the post. He went to Leipzig, where he became Kapellmeister of the Stadttheater and wrote for it 2 Romantic operas, in the manner of Weber: *Der Vampyr* (1828) and *Der Templer und die Jüdin*, after the famous novel *Ivanhoe* by Walter Scott (1829). In 1830 he received the position of Kapellmeister of the Hannover Hoftheater.

His most successful opera, *Hans Heiling* (Berlin, 1833), exhibited the most attractive Romantic traits of his music: a flowing melody, sonorous harmony, and nervous rhythmic pulse; the opera formed a natural transition to the exotic melodrama of Meyerbeer's great stage epics and to Wagner's early lyrical MUSIC DRAMAS. Historically important was his bold projection of a continuous dramatic development, without the conventional type of distinct arias separated by recitative. In this respect he was the heir of Weber and a precursor of Wagner. His later operas were not successful.

Marseillaise, La. The French national anthem, one of the most beautiful of all anthems, both in the patriotic text and the rousing melody. It was composed, or rather improvised on the spur of the moment, by Rouget de Lisle, a French Army officer in Strasbourg, on the night of Apr. 24–25, 1792, and it was published almost immediately under the title *Chant de guerre pour l'Armée du Rhin*. It was then widely sung as a patriotic song during the war with Austria. The title *La Marseillaise* was adopted later by a revolutionary volunteer group from Marseilles during the final phase of the French Revolution.

Marteau sans Maître, Le (The Hammer Without a Master). Work by Boulez, 1955, for soprano and chamber ensemble, on surrealist poems by René Char. It was 1st performed in Baden-Baden.

martellato (It., hammered; Fr. *martelé*). In violin playing, play the notes with a sharp, decided stroke (♪); on the piano, strike the keys with a heavy, inelastic plunge of the finger, or (in octave playing) with the arm staccato.

martellement (Fr.). In older Baroque music, the MORDENT.

Martenot, Maurice (Louis Eugène), French inventor of an electronic instrument dubbed the Ondes musicales, better known as the ONDES MARTENOT. b. Paris, Oct. 14, 1898; d. there, Oct. 10, 1980, as a result of a velocipede accident. He studied composition at the Paris Cons. with Gedalge; began to work on the construction of an electronic musical instrument with a keyboard, which he called the Ondes musicales. He gave its 1st demonstration in Paris in

the spring of 1928, and, later that year, the 1st musical work for the instrument, *Poème symphonique pour solo d'Ondes musicales et orchestre*, by Dimitri Levidis (*c.* 1885–1951), was presented in Paris. Martenot publ. *Méthode pour l'enseignement des Ondes musicales* (Paris, 1931).

The instrument became popular, especially among French composers: it is included in the score of Honegger's *Jeanne d'Arc au bûcher* (1935); Koechlin's *Le Buisson ardent*, part 1 (1938); Martinon's 2nd Sym., *Hymne à la vie* (1944); and Messiaen's *Turangalila-Symphonie* (1946–48). It was used as a solo instrument in Koechlin's *Hymne* (1929), Jolivet's Concerto (1947), Landowski's Concerto (1954), Bondon's *Kaleidoscope* (1957), and Jacques Charpentier's *Concertino alla francese* (1961). Many other composers were attracted to it as well. Of all the early electronic instruments—Ondes Martenot, Trautonium, and Theremin—only Martenot's has proved a viable musical instrument. When Varèse's *Ecuatorial*, written in 1934 for a brass ensemble and including a Theremin, was publ. in 1961, the score substituted an Ondes Martenot for the obsolescent Theremin. Martenot's sister, Ginette Martenot, became the chief exponent of the Ondes Martenot in concert performances in Europe and the U.S.

Martha. Opera by Flotow, 1847, produced in Vienna. Queen Anne is ruling England as the action takes place in Richmond, England. The Queen's maid of honor decides to go to the town marketplace dressed as a country girl named Martha. She hires herself as a servant maid to a young farmer, not realizing that the indenture she signed is a legal contract; her maid signs a similar obligation. Martha sings *The Last Rose of Summer*; at night both girls return to the palace. As Lady Harriet, "Martha" refuses to recognize the farmer to whom she was indentured, but he is now hopelessly in love with her. As operatic luck would have it, he is revealed to be a hereditary earl; but it is now his turn to rebuke Lady Harriet when she begins to feel the pangs of love. To bring him back she reproduces the marketplace in her garden, puts on her rustic clothes, and waits for her lover to return, which he does not fail to do. There is a doubly happy ending, since Lady Harriet's maid marries the Earl's foster brother. The music rolls without hindrance; the overture is popular at summer concerts, but the opera itself is rarely heard.

Martin, Frank, greatly renowned Swiss composer. b. Geneva, Sept. 15, 1890; d. Naarden, the Netherlands, Nov. 21, 1974. He was the last of 10 children of a Calvinist minister, a descendant of the Huguenots. He studied privately with Joseph Lauber in Geneva (1906–14), who instructed him in the basics of the conservative idiom of Swiss music of the fin de siècle; then had lessons with Hans Huber and Frederic Klose, who continued to emphasize the conservative foundations of the religious and cultural traditions of the Swiss establishment. However, Martin soon removed himself from the strict confines of Swiss scholasticism, encouraged in this development by Ernest Ansermet, then conductor of the Orch. de la Suisse Romande in Geneva.

In 1918 Martin went to Zurich and, in 1921, to Rome; finally settled in Paris in 1923, then the center of modern music. He returned to Geneva in 1926 as a pianist and harpsichordist; taught at the Inst. Jaques-Dalcroze (1927–38), was founder and director of the Technicum Moderne de Musique (1933–39), and served as president of the Assoc. of Swiss Musicians (1942–46). He moved to the Netherlands in 1946; also taught composition at the Cologne Hochschule für Musik (1950–57).

Martin is one of Switzerland's few international figures in composition; he is also an excellent representative. His early music showed the influence of Franck and French impressionists, but soon he succeeded in creating a distinctive style supported by a consummate mastery of contrapuntal and harmonic writing and a profound feeling for emotional consistency and continuity. Still later he became fascinated by the logic and self-consistency of Schoenberg's method of composition with 12 tones, and adopted it in a modified form in several of his works. He also demonstrated an ability to stylize folk-song materials in modern techniques.

In his music Martin followed the religious and moral precepts of his faith in selecting several subjects of his compositions. In 1944 the director of Radio Geneva asked him to compose an oratorio to be broadcast immediately upon the conclusion of World War II. He responded with *In terra pax* for 5 Soli, Double Chorus, and Orch., which was given its broadcast premiere from Geneva at the end of the war in Europe, May 7, 1945; a public performance followed in Geneva 24 days later. He publ. *Responsabilité du compositeur* (Geneva, 1966); M. Martin ed. his *Un compositeur médite sur son art* (Neuchâtel, 1977). Among his many fine works are 2 operas, *Der Sturm* (The Tempest), after Shakespeare (1952–54); and *Monsieur de Pourceaugnac*, after Molière (1960–62); many orch.l and vocal works, including oratorios and requia, and incidental music for the stage.

Martin, Mary (Virginia), American singer, dancer, and actress; b. Weatherford, Tex., Dec. 1, 1913; d. Rancho Mirage, Calif., Nov. 3, 1990. The daughter of a lawyer and a violinist, she 1st established a dance school in Weatherford. She studied at the Ward-Belmont School in Nashville, Tenn.; then went to N.Y., where, although totally unknown to the general public, she stopped the show with her rendition of the song *My Heart Belongs to Daddy* in Cole Porter's musical comedy *Leave It to Me* (1938). Her N.Y. success brought her a film contract with Paramount studios in Hollywood, which was short-lived, as she preferred the theater.

On the stage she scored a series of hits, beginning with a starring role in the Rodgers and Hammerstein musical *South Pacific* (1949) and later in *The Sound of Music* (1959), 2 of the longest-running musicals in Broadway history. She became best known for her 1954 creation of the lead character in the musical *Peter Pan*, in which she seemed to fly through the air; her career was once interrupted when she suffered an accident during levitation. In 1969 she retired to Brazil with her husband; after his death, she resumed her career (1979). In 1989 Martin was honored by the Kennedy Center of the Performing Arts in Washington, D.C., for her achievements in the theater. Her son, Larry Hagman, is a veteran television actor whose fame was assured when he was cast as the villainous J. R. Ewing in the nighttime soap series *Dallas*.

Martinů, Bohuslav (Jan), remarkable Czech composer; b. Policka, Dec. 8, 1890; d. Liestal, near Basel, Aug. 28, 1959. He was born in the bell tower of a church in the village where his father was a watchman. He studied violin with the local tailor when he was 7; from 1906 to 1909 he was enrolled at the Prague Cons.; then entered the Prague Organ School (1909), where he studied organ and theory, but was expelled in 1910 for lack of application; played in the 2nd violin section in the Czech Phil. in Prague (1913–14), returning to Policka (1914–18) to avoid service in the Austrian army; after World War I he reentered the Prague Cons. as a pupil of Suk, but again failed to graduate; also played again in the Czech Phil. (1918–23).

In 1923 he went to Paris and participated in progressive musical circles; took private lessons with Roussel. In a relatively short time his name became known in Europe through increasingly frequent performances of his chamber works, ballets, and symphonic pieces; several of his works were performed at the festivals of the ISCM. In 1932 his String Sextet won the Elizabeth Sprague Coolidge Award. He remained in Paris until June 1940, when he fled the German invasion and went to Portugal; finally reached the U.S. in 1941 and settled in N.Y.; personal difficulties prevented him from accepting an offer to teach at the Prague Cons. after the liberation of Czechoslovakia in 1945; later was a visiting prof. of music at Princeton Univ. (1948–51).

Although Martinů spent most of his life away from his homeland, he remained spiritually and musically faithful to his native country. He composed a poignant tribute to the martyred village of Lidice when, in 1943, the Nazi authorities ordered the execution of all men and boys over the age of 16 to avenge the assassination of the local Gauleiter. Martinů immortalized the victims in a heartfelt lyric work entitled *Memorial to Lidice*. In 1953 he returned to Europe, spending the last 2 years of his life in Switzerland. On Aug. 27, 1979, his remains were taken from Schonenberg, Switzerland, to Policka, Czechoslovakia, where they were placed in the family mausoleum. Martinů's centennial was celebrated in 1990 all over Czechoslovakia.

As a musician and stylist he belonged to the European tradition of musical nationalism. He avoided literal exploitation of Czech or Slovak musical materials, but his music is nonetheless characterized by a strong feeling for Bohemian MELORHYTHMS; his stylizations of Czech dances are set in a modern idiom without losing their authenticity or simplicity. In his large works he followed the neoclassical trend, with some impressionistic undertones; his mastery of modern counterpoint was extraordinary. In his music for the stage his predilections were for chamber forms; his sense of operatic comedy was very strong, but he was also capable of sensitive lyricism.

Martirano, Salvatore, American composer of the modern school; b. Yonkers, N.Y., Jan. 12, 1927; d. Urbana, Ill., Nov. 17, 1995. He studied piano and composition at the Oberlin Cons. of Music (1951); then composition at the Eastman School of Music in Rochester, N.Y., with Bernard Rogers (1952); later went to Italy, where he took courses with Luigi Dallapiccola at the Cherubini Cons. in Florence (1952–54). He served in the U.S. Marine Corps; played clarinet and cornet with the Parris Island Marine Band; from 1956 to '59 he held a fellowship to the American Academy in Rome, and in 1960 he received a Guggenheim fellowship and the American Academy of Arts and Letters Award. In 1963 he joined the faculty of the Univ. of Ill. at Urbana.

He writes in a progressive AVANT-GARDE idiom, applying the quaquaversal techniques of unmitigated radical modernism, free from any inhibitions and fond of multimedia and electronic means. His works include *The Magic Stones*, chamber opera after the *Decameron* (1952); *O, O, O, O, That Shakespeherian Rag* for Mixed Chorus and Instrumental Ensemble (1958); *Cocktail Music* for Piano (1962); *Underworld* for 4 Actors, 4 Percussion Instruments, 2 Double Basses, Tenor Saxophone, and Tape (1965; video version, 1982); *Ballad* for Amplified Nightclub Singer and Instrumental Ensemble (1966); *L's.G.A.* for a Gas-Masked Politico, Helium Bomb, 3 16mm Movie Projectors, and Tape (1968); *Action Analysis* for 12 People, Bunny, and Controller (1968); *Sal-Mar Construction I–VII* for tape (1971–75); *Look at the Back of My Head for Awhile*, video piece (1984); *Sampler: Everything Goes When the Whistle Blows* for Violin and Synthetic Orch. (1985; rev. 1988); *Phleu* for Amplified Flute and Synthetic Orch. (1988); and *LON/dons* for Chamber Orch. (1989).

Marton, Eva, outstanding Hungarian soprano; b. Budapest, June 18, 1943. She studied with Endre Rösler and Jenöd Sipos at the Franz Liszt Academy of Music in Budapest; made her formal operatic debut as the Queen of Shemakha in *Le Coq d'or* at the Hungarian State Opera there in 1968, remaining on its roster until joining the Frankfurt Opera in 1971; then became a member of the Hamburg State Opera in 1977. In 1975 she made her U.S. debut in N.Y. as a soloist in the world premiere of Hovhaness's folk oratorio *The Way of Jesus*; then made her 1st appearance at the Metropolitan Opera there as Eva in *Die Meistersinger von Nurnberg* on Nov. 3, 1976. After singing at the Bayreuth Festivals (1977–78) and at Milan's La Scala (1978), she scored a notable success as the Empress in *Die Frau ohne Schatten* at the Metropolitan Opera in 1981; thereafter she was one of its most important artists, appearing as Elisabeth in *Tannhäuser* (1982), Leonore in *Fidelio* (1983), Ortrud in *Lohengrin* (1984), Tosca (1986), and Lady Macbeth (1988). She 1st sang Turandot at the Vienna State Opera in 1983; appeared as Elektra there in 1989. Her appearances as an oratorio and lieder artist were also well received.

Martyrs, Les. French version of *Poliuto* by Donizetti, 1840.

Mary Had a Little Lamb. A nursery rhyme whose tune is identical with the 2nd section of the song *Good Night Ladies*, to the words "Merrily we roll along," composed by the American bandmaster E. P. Christy in 1847. According to tradition, the story of little Mary who took her lamb to school is factual.

Maryland, My Maryland. Contrafactum based on the German Christmas tune *O Tannenbaum*; the words, written in 1861, were fitted to the German melody. The State of Maryland adopted it as its state song in 1939; it is also played at the horse races at Pimlico.

marziale (It.). Martial, warlike.

Masaniello. See MUETTE DE PORTICI, LA.

Mascagni, Pietro

∿∿ ∿∿ ∿∿ ∿∿ ∿∿

Famous Italian opera composer. b. Livorno, Dec. 7, 1863; d. Rome, Aug. 2, 1945. His father was a baker who wished him to continue in that trade, but he yielded to his son's determination to study music. He took lessons with Alfredo Soffredini in his native town until he was enabled, by the aid of an uncle, to attend the Milan Cons., where he studied with Ponchielli and Saladino (1882). However, he became impatient with school discipline and was dismissed from the Cons. in 1884. He then conducted operetta troupes and taught music in Cerignola.

He composed industriously; in 1888 he sent the MS of his 1-act opera *Cavalleria rusticana* to the music publisher Sonzogno for a competition and won 1st prize. The opera was performed at the Teatro Costanzi in Rome on May 17, 1890, with sensational success; the dramatic story of village passion, and Mascagni's emotional score, laden with luscious music, combined to produce an extraordinary appeal to opera lovers. The short opera made the tour of the world stages with amazing rapidity, productions being staged all over Europe and America with never-failing success; the opera was usually presented in 2 parts, separated by an "intermezzo sinfonico" (which became a popular orch. number performed separately). *Cavalleria rusticana* marked the advent of the operatic style known as VERISMO, in which stark realism was the chief aim and the dramatic development was condensed to enhance the impressions.

When, 2 years later, another "veristic" opera, Leoncavallo's *Pagliacci*, was taken by Sonzogno, the 2 operas became twin attractions on a single bill. Ironically, Mascagni could never duplicate or even remotely approach the success of his 1st production, although he continued to compose industriously and opera houses all over the world were only too eager to stage his successive operas. Thus his opera *Le maschere* was produced in 1901, at 6 of the most important Italian opera houses simultaneously (Rome, Milan, Turin, Genoa, Venice, Verona); it was produced 2 days later in Naples. Mascagni himself conducted the premiere in Rome. But the opera failed to fire the imagination of the public; it was produced in a revised form in Turin 15 years later (June 7, 1916), but was not established in the repertoire even in Italy.

In 1902 he made a tour of the U.S., conducting his *Cavalleria rusticana* and other operas, but, owing to mismanagement, the visit proved a fiasco; a South American tour in 1911 was more successful. He also appeared frequently as a conductor of sym. concerts. In 1890 he was made a Knight of the Crown of Italy; in 1929 he was elected a member of the Academy. At various times he also was engaged in teaching; from 1895 to 1902 he was director of the Rossini Cons. in Pesaro. His last years were darkened by the inglorious role that he had played as an ardent supporter of the Fascist regime, so that he was rejected by many of his old friends. It was only after his death that his errors of moral judgment were forgiven; his centennial was widely celebrated in Italy in 1963. The following operas have been revived recently: *Guglielmo Ratcliff* (c. 1885); *L'amico Fritz* (1891); *Silvano* (1895); *Zanetto* (1896); *Iris* (1898; rev. 1899); *Isabeau* (1911); *Parisina* (1913); *Lodoletta* (1917); *Scampolo* (1921); *Il piccolo Marat* (1921); and *Nerone* (1935).

Maschere, Le (The Masks). Opera by Mascagni, 1901, with the familiar characters of the COMMEDIA DELL'ARTE engaged in traditional encounters. So great were the auguries of success for *Le maschere* that the opera was premiered on the same day in 6 Italian cities: Milan (conducted by Toscanini), Venice, Turin, Verona, Genoa, and Rome (where Mascagni himself conducted). Only half facetiously Mascagni dedicated the opera "to my distinguished self." But this simultaneous exhibition was a humiliating debacle; in Genoa the audience hissed and booed so vehemently that the management had to lower the curtain without completing the performance.

Maskarade. Comic opera by Nielsen, 1906, 1st performed in Copenhagen. The parents of a young man and a young woman in 18th-century Denmark make arrangements for them to marry each other; the young couple resists this impersonal pairing. But as luck would have it they meet at a masked ball and spontaneously become enamored with each other. Happiness is vouchsafed to both the parents and the young lovers when their identities are revealed.

Masnadieri, I (The Robbers). Opera by Verdi, 1847, 1st produced in London, based on Schiller's drama. Two brothers dispute an inheritance; when one loses out in court, he organizes a band of robbers to fight injustice, but eventually surrenders to the authorities. The opera was not successful.

Mason, Daniel Gregory, eminent American composer and educator, grandson of Lowell Mason, nephew of William Mason; b. Brookline, Mass., Nov. 20, 1873; d. Greenwich, Conn., Dec. 4, 1953. He was a scion of a famous family of American musicians; his father, Henry Mason, was a cofounder of the piano manufacturing firm Mason & Hamlin. He entered Harvard Univ., where he studied with J. K. Paine (B.A., 1895); after graduation he continued his studies with Arthur Whiting (piano), Goetschius (theory), and Chadwick (orchestration). Still feeling the necessity for improvement of his technique as a composer, he went to Paris, where he took courses with d'Indy. Returning to America, he became active as a teacher and composer. In 1905 he became a member of the faculty of Columbia Univ.; in 1929 he was appointed MacDowell Professor of Music; he was chairman of the music dept. until 1940 and continued to teach there until 1942, when he retired.

As a teacher he developed a high degree of technical ability in his students; as a composer he represented a conservative trend in American music; while an adherent to the idea of an American national style, his conception was racially suspect and regionally narrow, accepting only the music of Anglo-Saxon New England and the "old South"; he was an outspoken opponent of the "corrupting" and "foreign" influences of 20th-century African-American and Jewish-

American music. His ideals were those of the German masters of the Romantic school; but there is an admixture of impressionistic colors in his orchestration; his harmonies are full and opulent, his melodic writing expressive and songful. The lack of strong individuality, however, has resulted in the virtual disappearance of his music from the active repertoire, with the exception of the festival overture *Chanticleer* (1928) and the Clarinet Sonata (1912–15). He also composed 3 syms., chamber works, and vocal works. Most of his writings are pedagogical; 3 exceptions are *Music as a Humanity, and Other Essays* (1921); *Artistic Ideals* (1925); and *The Dilemma of American Music* (1928).

Mason, Lowell, distinguished American organist, conductor, music educator, and composer, grandfather of Daniel Gregory and father of William Mason; b. Medfield, Mass., Jan. 8, 1792; d. Orange, N.J., Aug. 11, 1872. As a youth he studied singing with Amos Albee and Oliver Shaw; at 16 he directed the church choir at Medfield; in 1812 he went to Savannah, Ga.; studied harmony and composition with Frederick Abel; taught singing in schools (1813–24) and became principal of the singers (1815) and organist (1820) of the Independent Presbyterian Church. In 1827 he went to Boston and was president of the Handel and Haydn Soc. (until 1832); established classes on Pestalozzi's system, teaching it privately from 1829 and in the public schools from 1837. He founded the Boston Academy of Music in 1833 with George J. Webb; was superintendent of music in the Boston public schools (1837–45), remaining active as a teacher until 1851; made 2 sojourns in Europe to study pedagogic methods (1837; 1851–53).

In 1854 he settled in Orange, N.J. He received an honorary doctorate in music from N.Y. Univ. (1855), only the 2nd such conferring of that degree in the U.S. He publ. *Musical Letters from Abroad* (N.Y., 1853). M. Broyles ed. *A Yankee Musician in Europe: The 1837 Journals of Lowell Mason* (Ann Arbor, 1990). Mason became wealthy through the sale of his many collections of music, including *Handel and Haydn Society's Collection of Church Music* (1822; 16 later eds.); *Lyra Sacra* (1832); *Boston Academy Collection of Church Music* (1836); *The Psaltery* (1845); *Cantica Laudis* (1850); *New Carmina Sacra* (1852); *Song Garden* (3 parts; 1864–65); etc. Many of his own hymn tunes, including *Missionary Hymn (From Greenland's Icy Mountains)*, *Olivet, Boylston, Bethany, Hebron*, and *Olmutz*, are still found in hymnals. His valuable library, including 830 MSS and 700 vols. of hymnology, was given to Yale College after his death.

Mason, Luther Whiting, American music educator; b. Turner, Maine, Apr. 3, 1828; d. Buckfield, Maine, July 4, 1896. He studied with Lowell Mason at the Boston Academy of Music, and may have been a distant relative; in 1853 he became a music teacher in Louisville schools, then in 1856 in Cincinnati, where he invented the National System of music charts and books, which had instant success and made him famous. He settled in Boston in 1864, and reformed music instruction in the primary schools; in 1880 he was invited by the Japanese government to supervise music in the schools of Japan, where he labored 3 years with notable results (school music in Japan was termed "Mason-song"). He spent some time in Germany perfecting his principal work, *The National Music-Course.*

Mason, William, esteemed American pianist, pedagogue, and composer, son of Lowell Mason, uncle of Daniel Gregory; b. Boston, Jan. 24, 1829; d. N.Y., July 14, 1908. He studied with Moscheles, M. Hauptmann, E. F. Richter, Dreyschock, and Liszt (1853–54); his *Memories of a Musical Life* provide an anecdotal overview of his travels. A fine pianist, he preferred teaching, and became a leading N.Y. teacher; he also established a chamber music series with Theodore Thomas which introduced new Romantic music to audiences (1855–68). He wrote many piano pieces.

masque. An English spectacle or a social assembly during the 16th and 17th centuries that featured a variety of artistic presentations, including poetry, drama, dance, and music. The subjects of such masques were usually taken from Greek mythology. Members of the aristocracy were themselves often engaged to perform the parts of shepherds and shepherdesses, benevolent gods and goddesses, etc. Among poets whose masques were produced at the English court were Ben Jonson and Milton. A curious byproduct of the masque was the 17th-century introduction of an *antimasque*, a comic or grotesque interlude between the allegorical scenes, analogous to the *kyōgen* interludes of the medieval Japanese *noh* drama. When opera was introduced into England, the masques became integrated with it and disappeared as an independent form.

Masquerade. Incidental music by Khatchaturian, 1941, for Lermontov's play, 1st produced with this music in Moscow. Its melodiousness and harmoniousness made the score very attractive to Russians and non-Russians alike.

Masques et bergamasques. Orch.l suite by Fauré, 1919, 1st performed in Monte Carlo as incidental music. The title is taken from Verlaine's poem *Clair de Lune*. A bergamasque is a Renaissance dance that originated in the northern Italian town of Bergamo.

Mass

The primary and the most solemn service of the Roman Catholic Church, which includes recitation of the sacred texts, singing, and playing on the organ. The Mass (Lat. *Missa*, dismissed) is the most significant manifestation of religious music; its theory and practice through the centuries determined the development of polyphonic music in all parts of Europe before the Reformation; virtually every composer in the musically productive countries—Italy, Germany, France, and Spain—wrote Masses. As a distinct musical form the Mass reached its greatest flowering during the Renaissance period when great masters of the Netherlands and Italy applied themselves to the composition of large religious works.

The most eloquent and devout Mass is the *Missa solemnis*, the High Mass, also known as *Missa cantata*, that is, "sung Mass." A lesser Mass is *Missa lecta*, the "read Mass," or Low Mass, which has no purely musical parts. The ORDINARY of the Mass (*ordinarium Missae*), contains chants that are included in every service and therefore in most Masses written by composers through the centuries that are performed not only in church but in concert. These divisions are KYRIE, GLORIA, CREDO (the Nicene Creed, also known as *Symbolum apostolicum*), SANCTUS, AGNUS DEI, and ITE, MISSA EST (or the *Benedicamus Domino*). The Kyrie is the only division of the Mass that is in the Greek language; the rest is in Latin.

Besides the Ordinary of the Mass there exists a group of divisions with texts to be sung on particular days; the totality of these items is known as the PROPER of the Mass (*proprium Missae*). They consist of the INTROIT (*psalmus ad introitum*), which precedes the Kyrie; next are the GRADUAL, the ALLELUIA (or TRACT, on solemn occasions), and SEQUENCE, which are sung between the Gloria and Credo; the Credo is followed by the OFFERTORY. The conclusion of the Proper of the Mass is the *Communion* (*psalmus ad communionem*), after which the congregation is dismissed. Both the Ordinary and Proper are interwoven with recitations and readings: in the Ordinary, the *Canon*; in the Proper, the *Collect, Epistle, Gospel, Secret, Preface*, and *Post-Communion*. Although the Latin texts of the Mass are traditional, the melodies are not. There are hundreds of different settings of individual numbers of the Mass. An extremely important and musically fruitful extension of the Mass is the REQUIEM (or MISSA PRO DEFUNCTIS), so named because it opens with the Introit *Requiem aeternam dona eis Domine* (Peace Eternal give them, Lord).

Although the Mass is the most solemn religious service, it could not separate itself entirely from the world outside the church. As a result the songs of the common people began to intrude on the holy precincts of the Mass. This alien incursion, repellent as it must have seemed to the devout, produced some extremely original musical forms, among them the CANTUS FIRMUS Mass and, later in the Renaissance, the PARODY Mass and paraphrase Mass. The cantus firmus Mass involves a use of fragments of Gregorian plainchant, usually in a hidden middle voice. The parody Mass type does not imply the modern meaning of parody (imitative caricature), but preserves its original Greek meaning of *para-ode* (near-song). The parody Mass reached its peak during the Renaissance, its principal feature being a use of religious polyphony, secular madrigals, and even folk songs; sometimes an entire motet or other choral composition is incorporated. The paraphrase Mass is the free use of material, chant, or polyphony.

Of such interpolations the most famous was the medieval popular song *L'Homme armé* (The Armed Man), which glorified the soldier. In this respect a Mass using preexisting material is a compound or synthetic work. It is not to be derogated for that; most great composers wrote Masses based on nonecclesiastical melodies. Even the great Palestrina wrote a parody Mass based on *L'Homme armé*. The practice so shocked the orthodox that a council of the Roman Church, held at Trent in the middle of the 16th century, issued a prohibition against using secular melodies as the cantus firmus in the Mass. By the Baroque period, Masses were generally freely written. In the late Baroque, Bach wrote his great B-minor Mass, and nearly another century later Beethoven composed his glorious *Missa Solemnis*. Schubert, Weber, Liszt, Franck, Gounod, and Bruckner wrote Masses marked by a grandeur of design that befits the subject.

While the great Masses from Palestrina to Beethoven are polyphonic in structure, homophonic Masses were produced in the less devout 19th century. The Lutheran church retains most of the divisions of the Mass, as does the Anglican church. But such Masses are designed not for the great Gothic cathedrals but for the humble surroundings of a parochial chapel. Sometimes separate items of the Mass, particularly the Gloria, attract a modern composer with the aim of stylization rather than reconstruction of the ancient model. Requiem Masses which contain the dramatic section Dies Irae somehow respond to the state of mind of the Romantic composer. Mozart, Berlioz, Verdi, and Brahms wrote Requiem Masses, and Britten contributed a moving *War Requiem*, interweaving settings of the soldier-poet Wilfred Owen with the Latin liturgy. Bernstein wrote *Mass*, which he described as a theater piece to the texts of the Roman liturgy and a libretto by Stephen Schwartz (*Godspell*). The Latin version of the Mass became liturgical history in the 1950s, when the Roman Catholic church instructed that the Mass be sung and spoken in the vernacular language of each country. *High Mass*, one celebrated at church festivals, with music and incense; *Low Mass*, one with limited or no music.

Mass in a Time of War (*Missa in tempore belli*). Mass in C Major by Haydn, 1796; the score is nicknamed *Paukenmesse* (timpani mass), because of the prominence given those instruments in the work.

Mass of a Life, A. Cantata by Delius, 1909, inspired by Nietzsche's *Also sprach Zarathustra*; it was 1st performed in London.

Massa's in the Cold Ground. Song by Foster, 1852, falling into the "Ethiopian" category designed for blackface minstrelsy. This suspension of disbelief concerns a slave's mourning the death of a humane owner.

Massenet, Jules (-Émile-Frédéric), illustrious French composer. b. Montaud, near St.-Etienne, Loire, May 12, 1842; d. Paris, Aug. 13, 1912. At the age of 9 he was admitted to the Paris Cons.; studied with Laurent (piano), Reber (harmony), and Savard and Thomas (composition); after taking 1st prize for piano (1859), he carried off the Grand Prix de Rome with the cantata *David Rizzio* (1863). In 1878 he was appointed prof. of composition at the Cons., and at the same time was elected a member of the Académie des Beaux-Arts; he continued to teach at the Paris Cons. until 1896; among his students were Alfred Bruneau, Gabriel Piérne, and Gustave Charpentier. As a pedagogue he exercised a profound influence on French opera.

After Gounod, Massenet was the most popular French opera composer; he possessed a natural sense of graceful melody in a distinctive French style; his best operas, *Manon*, *Werther*, and *Thaïs*, enjoy tremendous popularity in France; the celebrated *Méditation* for Violin and Orch. from *Thaïs* was a regular repertoire number among violinists. Among his many operas are *Le Roi de Lahore* (1877); *Hérodiade* (1881); *Manon* (1884); *Le Cid* (1885); *Esclarmonde* (1889); *Werther* (1892); *Thaïs* (1894); *La Navarraise* (1894); *Sapho* (1897; rev. 1909); *Cendrillon* (1899); *Grisélidis* (1901); *Le Jongleur de Notre Dame* (1902); *Chérubin* (1905); *Thérèse* (1907); *Don Quichotte* (1910); and *Cléopâtre* (1914). He also composed incidental music; oratorios, secular works, and cantatas; 200 songs; orch.l works; and piano works, both for 2 and 4 hands. He completed and orchestrated Delibes's opera *Kassya* (1893).

mässig (Ger.). Measured; moderately. *Mässig geschwind*, *mässig schnell*, moderately fast; *mässig langsam*, moderately slow.

Mastersinger (Ger. *Meistersinger*; Fr. *maître-chanteur*). In Germany, the artisan successors to the aristocratic MINNESINGER. The Guild of Mastersingers emerged in Germany after the end of the Crusades and the concurrent decline of the Minnesingers. Socially they differed from the Minnesingers, who were mainly knights; the Mastersingers were men of the people who plied common trades, such as shoemaking and carpentry, and at the same time were devoted to music, organized communal singing, and culti-

vated folk arts. The founder of the Mastersingers is reputed to be one Frauenlob (praise of women), who was also regarded as the last of the Minnesingers. If this link is to be accepted, then the birth of the Mastersingers can be dated to the early decades of the 14th century.

The Mastersingers proved to be a very durable society, which was carried well into the 19th century before finally dissolving under the pressure of modern professionalism. Wagner's opera *Die Meistersinger von Nürnberg* (1868) reflects the atmosphere of the social and professional activities in the German townships of the 16th century with remarkable fidelity. Most of the characters in Wagner's music drama are historical, and Wagner makes use of actual melodies of the Guild.

Masur, Kurt, eminent German conductor; b. Brieg, Silesia, July 18, 1927. He received training in piano and cello at the Breslau Music School (1942–44); then studied conducting with H. Bongartz and took courses in piano and composition at the Leipzig Hochschule für Musik (1946–48). In 1948 he commenced his career with appointments as *répétiteur* and conductor at the Halle Landestheater; held the title of 1st conductor at the Erfurt City Theater (1951–53) and at the Leipzig City Theater (1953–55). He was conductor of the Dresden Phil. (1955–58), Generalmusikdirektor of the Mecklenburg State Theater in Schwerin (1958–60), and senior director of music at the Komische Oper in East Berlin (1960–64). In 1967 he returned to the Dresden Phil. as its music director, a position he retained until 1972.

In 1970 he assumed the time-honored position of Gewandhauskapellmeister of Leipzig, where he served as music director of the Gewandhaus Orch. with notable distinction. He also made extensive tours with his orch. in Europe and abroad. In 1973 he made his British debut as a guest conductor with the New Philharmonia Orch. of London; his U.S. debut followed in 1974 as a guest conductor with the Cleveland Orch. In 1981 he conducted Beethoven's 9th Sym. at the gala opening of the new Gewandhaus in Leipzig. In 1988 he was named principal guest conductor of the London Phil. In the autumn of 1989, during the period of political upheaval in East Germany, Masur played a major role as peacemaker in Leipzig. In 1990 he was appointed music director of the N.Y. Phil., to commence with the 1991–92 season. While he has earned a reputation as a faithful guardian of the hallowed Austro-German repertoire, he frequently programs contemporary scores as well.

Matchiche, La (Braz. *maxixe*). Song, 1903, by Charles Borel-Clerc (1879–1959); an extremely popular vaudeville song published under various titles. This is a French version of the name of the Brazilian dance *maxixe*, which dates to the 1870s and is related to the polka. Gershwin quoted it as a typical Parisian song in his orch.l sketch, *An American in Paris*. A bit of doggerel was made up to be sung to the tune: "My ma gave me a nickel, to buy a pickle; I didn't buy a pickle, I bought some chewing-gum."

Matelots, Les (The Sailors). Ballet by Auric, 1925, 1st performed in Paris. A sailor is engaged to a woman of Marseilles. To test her loyalty, he, in the company of 2 of his friends, assumes a disguise. When she resists the advances of the other sailors, he is satisfied that she is faithful. The ballet is a typical product of post–World War I French culture.

Materna. Hymn tune by Samuel Augustus Ward, 1888, orig. for the text *O Mother Dear Jerusalem*. It was later adapted to the words *America the Beautiful* by Katherine Lee Bates.

Mathis der Maler (Mathis the Painter). Opera by Hindemith, 1938, to his own libretto inspired by the Colmar triptych of the painter known as Matthias Grünewald (*fl.* 1st half of the 16th century). In the opera the artistic career of Mathis is interrupted by a peasant uprising of 1542; essentially apolitical and beholden to religious authorities, he hides 2 fleeing rebels and gradually comes to espouse the rebel cause. But realizing that injustice is done in either camp, he withdraws from the materialistic world and dedicates himself to art. The score is permeated with the spirit of the German Renaissance in its choral-like structure; the savant polyphony is transparent; the idiom is modern but tonal. Despite the originality of the score and its ideological acceptability to the Nazis, Hitler's ministry put obstacles in the way of the production. Not only was Hindemith a relatively AVANT-GARDE composer and modern music festival organizer, although he was a pure Aryan, but he was married to a woman who was partly Jewish. Before the opera's premiere, Hindemith assembled a sym. from 3 extended orch. excerpts, which retains a place in the classical repertoire (1934). The 1st performance of *Mathis der Maler* took place in Zurich, Switzerland (1938); shortly afterward, Hindemith emigrated to the U.S.

Mathis, Johnny (John Royce), African-American singer of popular music; b. San Francisco, Sept. 30, 1935. He received classical vocal training before deciding upon a singing career as a popular vocalist; appeared as a nightclub singer; subsequently made tours of the U.S., Europe, Africa, and the Far East. He was particularly adept in renditions of pseudo-romantic ballads such as *Misty, Chances Are, The 12th of Never*, and *Wonderful, Wonderful*.

Matin, Le. Haydn's Sym. No. 6 (1761), in the key of D major. Some sense of the mists of early morning is conveyed by the adagio opening.

matins. The music sung at morning prayer; the 1st of the Canonical Hours.

Matrimonio segreto, Il. Opera by Cimarosa, 1792, based on Colman and Garrick's comedy *The Clandestine Marriage*; it was 1st performed in Vienna and was so successful that Emperor Leopold II ordered an immediate encore of the entire opera. A rich man of Bologna tries to arrange a marriage of his older daughter to a titled Britisher, incongruously named Count Robinson. But Robinson likes the proffered bride's younger sister better; however, she is already married secretly to a young lawyer. They plan to run away to escape the complications, aggravated further by the bride's aunt's infatuation with the Count. Identities become intentionally falsified; assorted lovers experience unintended encounters in bedchambers; but in the end the situation is clarified, and the "matrimonio segreto" is finally revealed not to be a secret after all.

Matthews, Artie, African-American ragtime composer; b. Braidwood, Ill., Nov. 15, 1888; d. Cincinnati, Oct. 25, 1958. He spent his formative years in Springfield, Ill.; learned ragtime from the pianists Banty Morgan and Art Dillingham. After working in the tenderloin district of St. Louis (*c.* 1908), he took lessons in piano, organ, and theory; was active as a composer and arranger for local theaters. In 1915 he went to Chicago as a church organist, and after World War I settled in Cincinnati; obtained a degree from the Metropolitan College of Music and Dramatic Arts (1918). Together with his wife, Anna Matthews, he founded the Cosmopolitan School of Music for classical training of black musicians in 1921. He was an outstanding composer of piano rags, producing 5 *Pastime Rags* (1913, 1913, 1916, 1918, 1920); also wrote a jazz classic for piano, *Weary Blues* (1915), and several songs.

mattinata (It.). Morning song.

Mauceri, John (Francis), American conductor; b. N.Y., Sept. 12, 1945. He studied with Gustav Meier at Yale Univ.

(B.A., 1967; M.Phil., 1972) and with Maderna, Colin Davis, Ozawa, and Bernstein at the Berkshire Music Center at Tanglewood (1971). He conducted the Yale Univ. Sym. Orch. (1968–74); subsequently appeared widely as a guest conductor of opera, musical theater, and sym. orchs. He was music director of the Washington (D.C.) Opera (1980–82), the American Sym. Orch. in N.Y. (1984–87), the Scottish Opera in Glasgow (from 1987), and the Hollywood Bowl Orch. (from 1990).

Mavra. Opera by Stravinsky, 1922, after Pushkin's *The Little House at Kolomna.*

maxima (Lat.). LARGA.

Maximilien. Opera by Milhaud, 1932, 1st performed in Paris. The libretto follows the historical account of the unfortunate Austrian archduke who was set up as Emperor of Mexico in 1864 and was executed by Mexican rebels. Milhaud makes use of Mexican folk tunes and rhythms in a highly stylized, modern manner.

Maxwell Davies, Peter. DAVIES, PETER MAXWELL.

May Night. Opera by Rimsky-Korsakov, 1880, premiered in St. Petersburg, based on a Gogol short story. In a small Ukrainian town, a young man in love tries to persuade his father to let him marry his beloved. Help from an unexpected source: the water sprites, who suspect that there is a malevolent witch among them. The youth finds her, thus freeing the water sprites from a curse. In return he receives a magic letter addressed to his father urging him not to stand in the way of his son's love. There is a happy ending.

May Wine. Musical by Romberg and Hammerstein, 1935. A Viennese psychiatrist marries a baroness but seems to nurture a secret passion for an impoverished Viennese nobleman. The psychiatrist takes to drink, and in his hallucinations shoots a stuffed figure that he mistakes for his wife. (Oliver Sacks, where are you?) He recovers his senses and his marriage is saved. Includes *I Built a Dream* and *Somebody Ought to be Told.*

Mayall, John, English blues singer; b. Manchester, Nov. 29, 1933. An ardent promoter of African-American blues, he formed a group called the Bluesbreakers, which served as a laboratory for instrumentalists, including Eric Clapton, Peter Green, John McVie, Mick Taylor, Aynsley Dunbar,

and Mick Fleetwood. The Bluesbreakers released a number of successful albums, among them *A Hard Road* and *The Turning Point* (with no drummer), and the 1st classic of British blues, under the title *Bluesbreakers with Eric Clapton.* Another album, *U.S. Union*, produced a workable amalgam of jazz and blues. Eventually Mayall emigrated to America.

Maytime. Operetta by Romberg, 1917, 1st produced in N.Y. The story takes place over 3 generations. A couple in love, doomed to separation in the mid-19th century, bury the deed to the family home in N.Y. in the hope that their descendants would discover it and make a fortune. The suitor's grandson falls in love with granddaughter of the girl his grandfather once loved, and they discover the valuable document; the money realized from it helps to rebuild and redecorate her dress shop. Among memorable songs in the score is the waltz *Will You Remember?*

Mayuzumi, Toshirō, eminent Japanese composer; b. Yokohama, Feb. 20, 1929. He studied with T. Ikenouchi and A. Ifukube at the National Univ. of Fine Arts and Music in Tokyo (1945–51); then took courses at the Paris Cons. with Aubin (1951–52). Returning to Japan, he organized the modern group Ars Nova Japonica and also worked at the electronic music studio in Tokyo. His style of composition embodies sonorous elements from traditional Japanese music, serial techniques, and electronic sounds, all amalgamated in a remarkably effective manner; he is also a successful composer of film scores, including that for *The Bible.* His best known works include *Sphenogramme* for Voice and Instruments (1951); *Ectoplasme* for Electronic Instruments, Percussion, and Strings (1956); *Mikrokosmos* for 7 Instruments (1957); *Phonologie symphonique* (1957); *Nirvana Symphony* (1958); *U-So-Ri*, oratorio (1959); *Mandala-Symphonie* (1960); *Music with Sculpture* for Winds (1961); *Samsara*, symphonic poem (1962); *Texture* for Band (1962); *Essay in Sonorities* (1963); BUGAKU, ballet (1963); *Fireworks* for Band (1963); *Pratidesana*, Buddhist cantata (1963); *The Ritual Overture* for Band (1964); *The Birth of Music*, symphonic poem (1964); *Showa Tempyo Raku* (Old and Present Music), symphonic poem (1970); *Kinkakuji* (The Temple of the Golden Pavilion), opera (1976); *The Kabuki*, ballet (1985).

Mazeppa. 1. The 4th of the *12 Transcendental Études* by Liszt, 1851, after the eponymous poem by Hugo; portrays in pianistic bravura the adventurous life of the Cossack chieftain who defied Peter the Great and lost. The galloping horses are represented by the harmonies of the diminished-

7th chords, while the martial mood is portrayed by triadic leaps and bounds; lyrical digressions find their place in candid melodies richly accompanied by harmonious arpeggios. 2. An orchestration by Raff of the work above and 1st performed in Weimar.

mazurka (Polish). A moderately lively Polish national dance in triple time that, as the name indicates, originated from the Mazur district in northern Poland. Its main characteristic is an off-beat accent and a syncopated 1st beat. Its popularity as an art form is owed mainly to Chopin, who adorned the basic rhythmic design of mazurkas with ingenious chromatic pianistic embellishments. KUJAWIAK and OBEREK are distinctive varieties of the mazurka.

mazza (It.). Mallet.

mazzo di legno (It.). Large wooden mallet, used to strike pieces of wood.

mbira. See LAMELLAPHONES.

McCartney, Sir (John) **Paul,** English rock singer, songwriter, and guitarist; member of the fantastically popular rock group the Beatles. b. Liverpool, June 18, 1942. He picked out chords on a family piano (his father was an amateur ragtime player), and at puberty began playing a left-handed guitar. He was the only Beatle who attended college, studying English literature. Fascinated by Elvis Presley, he tried to emulate the spirit of American rock 'n' roll (and rhythm and blues) *à l'anglaise*. With fellow Liverpudlians John Lennon, George Harrison, and Stuart Sutcliffe, he formed the group known as the Silver Beatles, which later took the name the Beatles (see BEATLES entry for the remainder of the group's history).

In 1970 McCartney went to court to end the Beatles' Apple Corps partnership and asked for an accounting of assets and income. He subsequently was active as a solo act and with his own group, Wings. As his post-Beatle work made clear, and as the Lennon-McCartney songwriting team proved to involve many separate songs by Lennon and McCartney, it became clear that McCartney, beginning with *Yesterday*, had a closer connection to the popular music of the past and present. McCartney is a better melodist than lyricist; for those who mourned the end of the Beatles, it gives evidence of the remarkable influence that McCartney and Lennon had on each other, whether literally collaborating or not.

McFerrin, Bobby (Robert)

~~~ ~~~ ~~~ ~~~ ~~~

Gifted African-American popular vocalist and conductor; b. N.Y., Mar. 11, 1950. His father, Robert Ferrin (b. Marianna, Ariz., Mar. 19, 1921), was a significant baritone who, in 1949, appeared in the 1st productions of Weill's *Lost in the Stars* and Still's *Troubled Island.* He won the Metropolitan Auditions of the Air in 1953; became the 1st black male to join the company, making his debut in 1955, as Amonasro in *Aida.* He sang the role of Porgy (played by Sidney Poitier) in the film version of *Porgy and Bess* (1959); also sang on the recording. He toured internationally, giving recitals of arias, art songs, and spirituals.

Bobby studied music theory from the age of 6 and played piano in high school, forming a quartet that copied the styles of Henry Mancini and Sergio Mendes. In 1970 he heard Miles Davis's fusion album *Bitches Brew* and completely changed his musical direction. He studied music at Sacramento State Univ. and at Cerritos College; then played piano professionally until 1977, when he began to develop his voice; toured in 1980 with jazz vocalist Jon Hendricks, and debuted a solo act in 1982.

His recordings include *Bobby McFerrin* (1982), *The Voice* (1984), *Spontaneous Improvisation* (1986), *Simple Pleasures* (1988; arranged as overdubbed a cappella; includes the song *Don't Worry, Be Happy,* which made him a household name), and *Medicine Music* (1991); also made several music videos and sang with Herbie

Hancock, Yo-Yo Ma, Manhattan Transfer, and others. In 1989 he established the 11-voice ensemble voicestra, with which he created the soundtrack for *Common Threads*, a 1989 documentary on the AIDS quilt; the group's 1st concert tour, in 1990, received critical acclaim. McFerrin began studying conducting in 1989, making his debut with a performance of Beethoven's Sym. No. 7 with the San Francisco Sym. (1990); he has also toured with Chick Corea in this capacity.

McFerrin is a virtuoso, using a remarkable range of voices with sophisticated control and accompanying them with body percussion, breath, and other self-generated sounds. Aesthetically he fuses a number of musical styles, including jazz, rock, gospel, and New Age, in a brilliant palette; his solo and ensemble shows are based on various improvisatory structures through which he produces highly polished, expertly burnished works.

McGhee, Brownie (Walter), African-American blues guitarist, singer, and songwriter; b. Knoxville, Tenn., Nov. 30, 1915. He was known for his deft guitar playing and mellifluous singing in partnership with Sonny Terry, the blues harmonica player; Terry wailed vocally and instrumentally and McGhee melded this into a smooth, closely integrated blend. During their 40-year association (1939–79) they appeared in concert and at blues and folk music festivals throughout the U.S., Europe, New Zealand, and Australia. They also recorded some 30 record albums, many of which featured McGhee's songs: *Life Is a Gamble*, *Tell Me Why*, *Blues Had a Baby (And They Called It Rock and Roll)*, *Walk On*, *Hole in the Wall*, *I Couldn't Believe My Eyes*, *My Father's Words*, *Watch Your Close Friend*, and *Rainy Day*.

McPartland, Jimmy (James), American jazz trumpeter and bandleader; b. Chicago, Mar. 15, 1907; d. Port Washington, N.Y., Mar. 13, 1991. He studied violin, then took up the cornet; at the age of 16 he organized a band with his brother; subsequently played with Bix Beiderbecke, Ben Pollack, and Jack Teagarden. After military service in World War II he resumed his career by organizing his own quartet in Chicago; later led his own band on tours. He married Marian McPartland in 1945.

McPartland, Marian (Margaret Turner), English-born American jazz pianist and composer; b. Windsor, Mar. 20, 1918. She 1st played violin; then won a scholarship to the Guildhall School of Music in London, where she studied piano. She began her career as a jazz pianist in joint appearances with the jazz pianist Billy Mayerl; in 1945 she married Jimmy McPartland; in 1946 she went to America and played in a combo with her husband; in 1951 she organized her own trio. She wrote a number of songs in the popular vein, including the successful *There'll Be Other*

Times. A vol. of her collected articles appeared as *All in Good Time* (N.Y., 1987).

McPhee, Colin (Carhart), outstanding American composer and ethnomusicologist; b. Montreal, Canada, Mar. 15, 1900; d. Los Angeles, Jan. 7, 1964. He studied piano and composition with Harold Randolph and Gustav Strube at the Peabody Cons. in Baltimore (graduated, 1921), then took piano lessons with Arthur Friedheim in Toronto (1921–24); continued his studies with Paul Le Flem (composition) and Isidor Philipp (piano) in Paris (1924–26). Returning to the U.S. (1926), he joined the modern movement in N.Y. and was briefly a student of Varèse; wrote scores for the experimental films *H20* and *Mechanical Principles* in 1931. He became infatuated with the gamelan music of Java and Bali; moved to Indonesia in 1931 and, except for brief interruptions, remained there until 1939. He then returned to the U.S. and was a consultant to the Office of War Information during World War II; later was active with the Inst. of Ethnomusicology at the Univ. of Calif. at Los Angeles (1958–64).

His *Tabuh-Tabuhan* for 2 Pianos, Orch., and Exotic Percussion, composed and premiered during an interlude in Mexico City (1936), is the quintessential work in his Bali-influenced style. He wrote the books *A House in Bali* (N.Y., 1946), *A Club of Small Men* (N.Y., 1948), and *Music in Bali* (New Haven, 1966). Among his other works are 3 syms.; *Transitions* for Orch. (1954); *Nocturne* for Chamber Orch. (1958); Concerto for Wind Orch. (1960); Concerto for Piano and Wind Octet (1928); and piano works, including *4 Piano Sketches* (1916); *Kinesis* (1930); and *Balinese Ceremonial Music* for 2 Pianos (1934–38).

McRae, Carmen, African-American jazz vocalist and pianist; b. N.Y., Apr. 8, 1922; d. Beverly Hills, Calif., Nov. 10, 1994. She joined Benny Carter's band in 1944; subsequently sang with the bands of Count Basie, Mercer Ellington, and others; made tours in Europe and Japan. She was married to the drummer Kenny ("Klook") Clarke (b. Pittsburgh, Jan. 9, 1914; d. Montreuil-sous-Bois, Paris, Jan. 26, 1985), and recorded several songs as Carmen Clarke. In 1980 she was a featured performer at N.Y.'s Carnegie Hall.

McShann, Jay "Hootie," African-American jazz pianist, blues singer, and bandleader; b. Muskogee, Okla., Jan. 12, 1909. He took up the piano at an early age; led his own group during the big-band era in Kansas City. Among his hits were *Hootie Blues* (a title from which he got his nickname), *Confessin' the Blues*, and *Swingmatism*. The legendary jazz figure Charlie Parker was a member of McShann's band. After a stint in the U.S. Army (1943–45), he resumed his career, working mainly in California. He continued to be active well into old age; in 1974 he toured Europe with the show *The Musical Life of Charlie Parker*; in 1975 he took part in the Montreux Jazz Festival; in 1979 he played at the Alexandra Palace Jazz Festival in London. He publ. *Boogie Woogie and Blues Piano Solos*. He also appeared in the film *The Last of the Blue Devils*.

Me. In TONIC SOL-FA, stands for MI.

Me and Juliet. Musical by Rodgers and Hammerstein, 1953. A theatrical love triangle involves an assistant manager, the chorus girl he loves, and the electrician who covets her so violently that he's willing to kill them both. Fortunately, love triumphs in the end. Although *Me and Juliet* fell far short of the successes had by *Oklahoma!* and *South Pacific*, the score has its merits. One of the best numbers, *No Other Love*, was used by Rodgers in his score for the television documentary *Victory at Sea*.

Me and My Shadow. Song by Rose and Jolson, 1927.

meantone temperament. See TEMPERAMENT.

measurable music. Mensurable music.

measure. The notes and rests contained within 2 vertical lines; the metrical unit in composition, with regular accentuation, familiarly called a bar. *Measure note*, a note shown by the time signature to be an even divisor of a measure; thus 3/4 shows that each measure has 3 quarter notes, and the measure note is then a quarter note; *measure rest*, see REST.

mechanical instruments. Those whose sound is generated neither by acoustic (human) nor electronic means, e.g., pianola or music box.

mechanism (Fr. *mécanisme*). Technical ability or skill; mechanical dexterity or training.

Meck, Nadezhda von. See TCHAIKOVSKY, PETER ILICH.

Medea. Italian version of Cherubini's *Medée*. Although the return of this version after World War I was part of the bel canto revival, the French version is the original.

Medea's Meditation and Dance of Vengeance. Symphonic scene by Barber, 1956. This piece is the 4th incarnation of a ballet that began life as *The Serpent Heart*, choreographed by Martha Graham (1946); it was revised and performed the following year as *Cave of the Winds*. That same year Barber created a ballet suite, using the title *Medea* for the 1st time.

Médecin malgré lui, Le (The Doctor in Spite of Himself). Opera by Gounod, 1858, 1st produced in Paris, based on a Molière play. A maltreated wife intends to get even with her husband by spreading the rumor that he is a miracle worker in medicine. When he fails to cure the daughter of a wealthy citizen, he is manhandled by the servants. But she is not sick at all, and feigns illness to elope with her lover. Eventually the lovers inherit a fortune; the girl's father is reconciled to her marriage, and the maltreated wife of the hapless "doctor" forgives him. The opera is melodious and harmonious.

Medée. 1. Tragédie lyrique by M.-A. Charpentier, 1693, 1st produced in Paris. The libretto is derived from the ancient Greek myth of Medea, wife of Jason, who is enraged by his plan to take a younger wife; she wreaks vengeance by arranging the bride-to-be's death and by murdering their two sons. 2. Opera by Cherubini, 1797, based on the same myth as the above work. It is considered his masterpiece, but it fell into relative obscurity. A century and a half later the postwar BEL CANTO revival led to the revival of this opera in its Italian form (*Medea*) by Callas and others. The early music movement has led to recent performances in its original French version.

medesimo (It.). The same. *Medesimo tempo*, the same tempo.

mediant. The 3rd degree of the scale.

mediator. Plectrum used for special effects in harp and mandolin playing. The mediator is used in the harp part of Mahler's *Das Lied von der Erde*.

medicinale (Ger., Mid. Fr., from Lat. *Medius* + *canon*, half psaltery). Medieval name for a small PSALTERY.

meditation (Lat. *meditari*). An elegy. *Méditation* for solo violin in the opera *Thaïs* by Massenet is a favorite concert number. The coaxingly viscid *Ave Maria* by Gounod, superimposed on the 1st Prelude in C Major of Bach's 1st book of the *Well-Tempered Clavier*, is subtitled *Méditation*.

Medium, The. Tragedy by Menotti, 1946, to his own English libretto. It was 1st produced in New York on Broadway (the 1st of his "Broadway operas"). The medium Madame Flora arranges for ghosts to speak to bereaved relatives through a hidden microphone. So realistic are the voices, produced by her daughter, that the medium begins to believe in their reality. In a panic, she shoots and kills her deaf-mute helper whom she finds in the closet. *The Medium* is one of the composer's most successful works; its dramatic impact is considerable.

medley. See POTPOURRI.

Medtner, Nicolai (Nikolai Karlovich), notable Russian pianist and composer of German descent; b. Moscow, Jan. 5, 1880; d. London, Nov. 13, 1951. He 1st studied piano with his mother, and then with his uncle, Theodore Goedicke; in 1892 he entered the Moscow Cons., where he took courses with Sapelnikov and Safonov (piano) and Arensky and Taneyev (composition); graduated in 1900, winning the gold medal; that same year he won the Rubinstein prize in Vienna; for the next 2 years he appeared with much success as a pianist in the European capitals; returning to Russia, he taught at the Moscow Cons. (1902–3; 1909–10; 1914–21); then lived in Berlin and Paris; eventually settled in London (1935). He made tours of the U.S. (1924–25; 1929–30) and the Soviet Union (1927). He publ. a collection of essays as *Muza i moda* (The Muse and Fashion; Paris, 1935).

In Russian music he was a solitary figure; he never followed the nationalist trend, but endeavored to create a new type of composition, rooted in both the Classic and the Romantic traditions; his sets of fairy tales in sonata form are unique examples of his favorite genre. He wrote his best compositions before he left Russia; although he continued to compose during his residence abroad, his late music lacks the verve and Romantic sincerity that distinguish his earlier works. He wrote almost exclusively for the piano and for the voice. A revival of his music was begun in Russia after his death, and a complete ed. of his works appeared in Moscow (12 vols., 1959–63). His works include 3 piano concertos, a piano quintet, and numerous pieces; 3 violin sonatas; and 107 songs.

Meeresstille und glückliche Fahrt (Calm Sea and Happy Voyage). Concert overture by Mendelssohn, 1828. Despite its reassuring title, the music becomes quite turbulent, but the voyage ends happily. It was 1st performed in Berlin, and may be regarded as a companion piece to his *Fingal's Cave*, written about the same time.

Meet Me in St. Louis, Louis. Song by Kerry Mills, 1904, written for the St. Louis World's Exposition. Despite the silly repeated name and trivial tune, the song became and remained popular over the decades.

Mefistofélé. Opera by Boito, 1868, 1st produced in Milan. Boito's libretto drew from both parts of Goethe's great philosophical poem *Faust*, unlike Gounod's opera, which ends with the death of Marguerite. Boito adds the encounter with Helen of Troy, and ends with the redemption of Faust. The role of the eponymous devil is one of the great operatic bass roles. *Mefistofélé* has excellent musical and literary qualities, but it has never attained the success vouchsafed to Gounod's *Faust*.

Mehta, Mehli, Indian violinist and conductor, father of Zubin Mehta; b. Bombay, Sept. 25, 1908. He studied at the Univ. of Bombay and at Trinity College of Music in London (licentiate, 1929). He founded the Bombay Sym. Orch. in 1935; was its concertmaster (until 1945) and then its conductor (until 1955); subsequently was assistant concertmaster of the Halle Orch. in Manchester (1955–59). He then settled in the U.S., where he played in the Curtis String Quartet in Philadelphia (1959–64); subsequently went to Los Angeles, where he founded the American Youth Sym. Orch. (1964); also taught at the Univ. of Calif. there (1964–76), serving as conductor of its sym. and chamber orchs.

Mehta, Zubin

E xuberant, effulgent, and eloquent Indian conductor; b. Bombay, Apr. 29, 1936. The family belonged to the historic tribe of Parsi nobles, the fire-worshipping followers of Zarathustra who fled en masse from the turbulence of Persia 13 centuries before Zubin Mehta's birth. He was tutored in music by his father Mehli Mehta.

Zubin learned to play violin and piano; when he was 16 he successfully conducted a rehearsal of the Bombay Sym. Orch. Before deciding on a musical career, he took a course in medicine at St. Xavier College in Bombay; but he turned away from the unaesthetic training in dissection and instead went to Vienna, where he practiced to play the double bass at the Academy of Music and took conducting lessons with Hans Swarowsky. During the summers of 1956 and 1957 he attended conducting classes at the Accademia Chigiana in Siena with Carlo Zecchi and Alceo Galliera. In 1957 he graduated from the Vienna Academy of Music; he had made his professional debut conducting the Tonkünstler Orch. in the Musikverein. In 1958 he married the Canadian singer Carmen Lasky; they had 2 children but were divorced in 1964; she married Zubin Mehta's brother Zarin in 1966, thus making Zubin an uncle by marriage of his own children. In 1969 he married the actress Nancy Kovack in a dual ceremony, Methodist and Zoroastrian.

In the meantime his career progressed by great strides; he won the competition of the Royal Liverpool Phil. in 1958, and conducted it for a season as an assistant; later he obtained guest engagements in Austria and Yugoslavia. In 1959 he competed in a conducting test in Tanglewood and won 2nd prize. In 1960 he received a bona fide engagement to conduct the Vienna Sym. Orch.; that same year he also made a highly successful appearance as a guest conductor with the Philadelphia Orch.; later in 1960 he conducted 2 concerts of the Montreal Sym. Orch. and produced such a fine impression that he was appointed its music director. In 1962 Mehta took the Montreal Sym. Orch. to Russia, where he gave 8 concerts; then conducted 2 concerts with it in Paris and 1 in Vienna, where he took 14 bows in response to a vociferous ovation. In the meantime he received a contract to conduct the Los Angeles Phil., becoming its associate conductor in 1961 and its music director in 1962; he was thus the holder of 2 major conducting jobs, a feat he was able to accomplish by commuting on newfangled jet airplanes; he was also the youngest conductor to function in this dual capacity. His career was now assuming the allure of a gallop, aided by his ability—rare among conductors—to maintain his self-control under trying circumstances. He has the reputation of a bon vivant; his joy of life is limitless.

Professionally he maintains an almost infallible reliability; he conducts all of his scores, even the most mind-boggling modern scores, and operas as well, from memory. He is also a polyglot; not only is he eloquent in English and Hindi, but he is fluent in German, French, and Spanish; he even speaks understandable Russian. He made his debut at the Metropolitan Opera in N.Y. (1965), conducting *Aida*. His performances of *Carmen* and *Turandot* were highly praised. In 1967 he resigned his post in Montreal; in 1968 he was named music adviser of the Israel Phil.; in 1977 he became its music director. In

Zubin Mehta

1978 he left the Los Angeles Phil. after he received an offer he could not refuse, the musical directorship of the N.Y. Phil.; in 1980 he toured with it in Europe. In 1991 he left his post with the N.Y. Phil. His association with the Israel Phil. was particularly affectionate; he conduct-ed it during the 6-Day War and at the 25th anniversary of Israel's independence; in 1974 he was given an honorary Ph.D. by Tel Aviv Univ. No Jew could be more Israeli than the Parsi Mehta. *Time* glorified him with a cover story (1968).

Meistersinger (Ger.). MASTERSINGER.

Meistersinger von Nürnberg, Die *(The Mastersingers of Nuremberg).* Opera by Wagner, 1868, his 1st to include elements of comedy intentionally. It was produced in Munich, 1868, von Bülow conducting. As in all Wagner's opera, the text is his own. The action takes place in Nuremberg in the 16th century. A singing contest is organized by the Guild of Master singers under the guidance of the cobbler Hans Sachs (a historical figure who played an important role in organizing singing societies in Germany in the 16th century). The 1st prize is the hand of Eva, daughter of the local goldsmith. Walter von Stolzing, in love with Eva, sings a supremely beautiful song, but the pedantic clerk Beckmesser faults him for violation of rules. (Beckmesser was modeled by Wagner after the famous Viennese music critic Eduard Hanslick, persistent opponent of Wagner; in the early sketches of *Die Meistersinger* Wagner used the name Hans Lick for Beckmesser.) After the prize is given to Walter, Hans Sachs explains the prin-ciples underlying the art of German song. The opera is interesting for its many realistic details. For instance, Eva, Beckmesser, and others call on the cobbler-master singer to have their shoes repaired. The contrapuntal texture of the music is glorious; unhampered by the LEITMOTIVS, the music flows with rhapsodic freedom.

mejorana. Panamanian dance song, consisting of a rhymed quatrain, each line of which is then developed separately. The descending melodies, featuring falsetto and melisma, are set in 2/4 or 6/8 time, with the accompaniment in 3/4 providing hemiola effects throughout.

mejoranera. Small short-necked guitar of Panama. It is made of cedar and uses nylon strings; it is most closely associated with the MEJORANA.

melancolia (It.). Melancholy.

mélange (*méslange*; Fr.). A POTPOURRI.

Melba, (Dame) Nellie

Famous Australian soprano; b. Helen Porter Mitchell Armstrong, Burnley, near Richmond, May 19, 1861; d. Sydney, Feb. 23, 1931. Her father, who had decided objections to anything connect-ed with the stage, was nevertheless fond of music and proud of his daughter's talent. When she was only 6 years old he allowed her to sing at a concert in the Melbourne Town Hall, but he would not consent to her having singing lessons; instead she was taught piano, violin, and harp, and even had instruction in harmony and composition. As she grew older she frequently played the organ in a local church, and she was known among her friends as an excellent pianist, while all the time her chief desire was to study singing. Not until after her marriage in 1882 to Captain Charles Armstrong was she able to gratify her ambition, when she began to study with a local teacher, Cecchi; her 1st public appearance as a singer was in 1884, in a benefit concert in Melbourne. The next year her father received a government appointment in London, and she accompanied him, determined to begin an operatic career. She studied with Mathilde Marchesi in Paris.

Melba gave her 1st concert in London (1886). Her debut as Gilda at the Théâtre Royal de la Monnaie in Brussels (1887) created a veritable sensation; the famous impresario Augustus Harris immediately engaged her for the spring season at London's Covent Garden, where she appeared in 1888, as Lucia, to only a half-full house. However, she scored a major success at the Paris Opera as Ophelia in Thomas's *Hamlet* (1889); then sang with great success in St. Petersburg (1891), Milan (1893; immense triumph over a carefully planned opposition), Stockholm and Copenhagen (1893), N.Y. (Metropolitan Opera, as Lucia, 1893), and Melbourne (1902). From her 1st appearance at Covent Garden she sang there off and on until 1914; besides being one of the most brilliant stars of several seasons at the Metropolitan Opera in N.Y., she also sang with Damrosch's Opera Co. (1898) and at Hammerstein's Manhattan Opera (1906–1907 and 1908–1909), and made several transcontinental concert tours of the U.S. In 1915 she began teaching at the Albert Street Cons. in Melbourne; returned to Covent Garden for appearances in 1919, 1923, and a farewell performance (1926). Then she returned to Australia and retired from the stage.

Melba was by nature gifted with a voice of extraordinary beauty and bell-like purity; through her art she made this fine instrument perfectly even throughout its entire compass (B flat–f³) and wonderfully flexible, so that she executed the most difficult fioriture without the least effort. As an actress she did not rise above the conventional, and for this reason she was at her best in parts demanding brilliant COLORATURA (Gilda, Lucia, Violetta, Rosina, Lakme, etc.). On a single occasion she attempted the dramatic role of Brünnhilde in *Siegfried* (Metropolitan Opera, N.Y., 1896) and met with disaster. In 1918 she was created a Dame Commander of the Order of the British Empire. She was a typical representative of the golden era of opera; a prima donna assoluta, she exercised her powers over the public with perfect self-assurance and a fine command of her singing voice. Among her other distinguished roles were Mimi, Else, Nedda, Aida, Desdemona, and Marguerita.

As a measure of Melba's universal popularity it may be mentioned that her name was attached to a delicious dessert (Peach Melba) and also to Melba Toast, patented in 1929 by Bert Weil. A motion picture based on her life was produced in 1953 with Patrice Munsel as Melba.

Melchior, Lauritz (born Lebrecht Hommel), celebrated Danish-born American tenor; b. Copenhagen, Mar. 20, 1890; d. Santa Monica, Calif., Mar. 18, 1973. He studied with Paul Bang at the Royal Opera School in Copenhagen, making his operatic debut in the baritone role of Silvio at the Royal Theater there (1913); continued on its roster while studying further with Vilhelm Herold, and then made his tenor debut as Tannhäuser (1918). In 1921 he went to London to continue his training with Beigel, and then studied with Grenzebach in Berlin and Bahr-Mildenburg in Munich. In 1924 he made his Covent Garden debut in London as Siegmund, returning there regularly from 1926 to 1939. He was in Bayreuth in 1924 to study with Kittel; made his 1st appearance at the Festspielhaus there as Siegfried in 1924 and continued to make appearances there until 1931. In 1926 he made his Metropolitan Opera debut in N.Y. as Tannhäuser, and he quickly established himself as one of its principal artists; with the exception of the 1927–28 season, he sang there regularly until his farewell performance as Lohengrin in 1950. In 1947 he became a naturalized U.S. citizen. After the close of his operatic career Melchior appeared on Broadway and in films; also contin-

ued to give concerts. He was accorded a preeminent place among the Wagnerian Heldentenors of his era.

melisma. A melodic ornament or grace; coloratura. *Melismatic*, ornamented, embellished; *melismatic song*, one in which more than one tone is sung to a syllable; opposed to syllabic song.

melodeon. 1. REED ORGAN. 2. Button accordion.

melodia (It.). Melody. *Marcata la melodia*, emphasize the melody.

melodic. 1. In the style of a melody; progressing by single tones. 2. Vocal, singable; as a melodic interval.

melodic minor scale. A minor scale which eliminates the interval of an augmented 2nd between the 6th and 7th degrees of the harmonic minor scale, thereby providing a smoother melodic progression. When ascending, the 6th and 7th degrees are raised (C–D–E♭–F–G–A♮–B♮–C); when descending, these notes are unaltered (C–B♭–A♭–G–F–E♭–D–C).

melodion. Friction-bar keyboard instrument; steel bars are pressed against a revolving cylinder in place of strings; invented by J. C. Dietz in the early 19th century.

melodioso (It.). Melodious, singing.

melodium. 1. American portable HARMONIUM of the mid-19th century. 2. Monophonic electrophone, invented in Germany during World War II.

mélodrame (Fr.). In opera, orch.l interlude between scenes.

melodrama

Originally, any musical drama. 2. A form of declamation with musical accompaniment, ranging from piano to full orch. 3. A romantic and sensational drama in which music plays a subordinate part.

During the last century the term *melodrama* has acquired the meaning of a theatrical production calculated to excite the sensations of an audience by piling up suspense upon suspense, with natural disasters adding to human conflict and individual misfortunes. The adjective *melodramatic* conveys the derogatory meaning of a cheap exhibition masquerading as a real drama. The text of a typical melodrama corresponds in spirit to Gothic novels. Dramatic peripeteia, sudden reversals of fortune, mysterious portents and premonitions, often with supernatural overtones, suitably illustrated by chromatic runs or tremolos on the diminished-7th chord, are potent melodramatic devices. Theatrical melodramas were highly successful in the 19th century, and not only among socially disfranchised artistic groups. But in stage presentations, the 1st half of the word *melodrama* was fortuitous, for there was no *melos*—no singing, no music—in these productions.

But melodrama in the etymological sense of the word had a long and respectable history. In 17th-century Italy it was synonymous with DRAMMA PER MUSICA; that is, opera. The 1st melodrama, so named specifically by its composer, was *Il Tito* by Antonio Cesti, produced in 1666. In the early years of opera the terms *melodramma*, TRAGEDIA LIRICA, and DRAMMA LIRICO were used interchangeably for a true opera; this practice continued through the 19th century in France, with operas often described as DRAME LYRIQUE or TRAGÉDIE LYRIQUE.

In the meantime the term *melodrama* imperceptibly acquired the meaning of a recitation or theatrical performance in which lines were spoken with musical accompaniment, which can range from a piano to a full orch.; many melodramas are staged. The 1st melodrama of this last type was probably *Ariadne auf Naxos* by Georg Anton Benda (1722–95), produced in 1775, which greatly impressed Mozart, who heard it 3 years later. Zdeněk Fibich wrote a trilogy of melodramas, entitled *Hippodamia*, that enjoyed numerous performances in Prague. Humperdinck enhanced the genre with his opera *Königskinder*, produced in 1897, by indicating the inflection of the spoken voice in written notes, marking the approximate level of pitch in each syllable. Schoenberg elevated melodrama to high art in his *Pierrot Lunaire*, which is specifically described as a melodrama in the score. In it Schoenberg introduced SPRECHSTIMME—inflected speech-voice—midway between speaking and singing.

Parallel to these developments there emerged a more mundane and by the same token more popular type of melodrama, incorporating the simultaneous use of recitation and music, as distinguished from SINGSPIEL and OPÉRA COMIQUE, in which the spoken dialogue and singing alternate. Schumann and Liszt wrote these kinds of melodramas. Prokofiev in *Peter and the Wolf* and Walton in *Façade* made use of this technique. The genre was particularly popular in Russia, where it became known under the more proper title *melodeclamation*.

melody

~~~ ~~~ ~~~ ~~~ ~~~

The rational progression of single tones; contrast-ed with HARMONY, the rational simultaneity of several tones. 2. The leading part (usually the soprano). 3. An air or tune.

Melody (from Grk. *melos* + *aeidein*, sung music; Fr. *mélodie*; It., Lat. *melodia*; Ger. *Melodie*) involves successive tones possessing a self-governing sense of logical progres-sion. In modern usage melody is a tonal line vivified by rhythmic beat. To the Greeks such a rhythmed melody was defined by another musical word, HARMONIA. In Western melos a melody has harmonic implications, but the word *harmony* connotes a simultaneous sounding of several melodies. Aesthetically an ideally beautiful melody has a perfect balance between the high and low registers and a symmetric alternation of ascending and descending tonal groups.

The main body of the melody resides in the middle register, its center of gravity. If melodies are analyzed with reference to these contrasts, it will usually be found that the number of high notes multiplied by the duration of each note equals the number of notes below the center of gravity multiplied by the duration of each of these coun-terbalancing notes. The frequency of incidence increases toward the middle register, finally converging upon the melodic center of gravity.

Much theorizing has been done about the force of gravity in melodic structures, which manifests itself in the musical necessity of reversing the melodic motion after the melody has reached its apogee or perigee, as the case may be. This does not mean, of course, that the melody must, like the King of France in the nursery rhyme, march up the hill with 40,000 men and then come back down again. But the metaphor of gravity is applicable to the melodic rule that demands that after a wide leap the melody should come down at least one diatonic degree, and vice-versa. Rhythmic values must be also taken into consideration in such an equation, so that in an ideal melody a long high note would be coun-terbalanced by a long low note, or by a succession of short low notes.

Most memorable melodies move within the range of an octave between 2 dominants (5ths) in a major key, with the important points on the tonic (root), the mediant (major 3rd), and the upper dominant. This octave is out-lined by the 3rd (lower dominant), 4th (tonic) 5th (medi-ant), and 6th (upper dominant), partials in the naturally occurring harmonic series; it is therefore reasonable to conjecture that Western melodic lines are functions of this harmonic series, with preference given to the notes of the major triad. This is supported by the fact that these notes are naturally produced by the bugle, horns without valves, and other wind instruments. There are many con-vincing tunes that are limited to these notes, resulting in a variety of bugle calls. Cohan's World War I song *Over There* is based primarily on these open bugle notes. The 1st and the last movements of Mozart's *Eine kleine Nachtmusik* are derived from a subject contained between the two dominants of the key of G major. The finale of Haydn's *Military Sym.* (no. 100) is also based on the sem-inal progression of the harmonic series from the 3rd to the 6th partials.

The interpolated supertonic (2nd) and subdominant (4th) complete a major pentachord, with the dominant duplicated below the tonic. The number of melodies so constructed tallies in the thousands, if not millions; all are in a major key, and many of them beginning with an ascending leap from the dominant to the tonic. Among famous examples are *La Marseillaise*, the last movement of Beethoven's Violin Concerto, the overture to Rossini's *William Tell*, the *"Waltz of the Flowers"* from Tchaikovsky's *Nutcracker* Suite, and the *Wedding March* from Wagner's *Lohengrin*. Melodies of this formation are not as numerous in minor keys as in major, but they still comprise a respectable inventory; examples are the theme of the 2nd movement of Tchaikovsky's violin concerto and that of *Moldau* from Smetana's orch.1 suite *Má vlast*. Numerous examples can be found by consulting the the-matic catalogues of Classical sonatas and symphonies.

Many consider the derivation of so many melodies from the harmonic series to be one of the most reliably persistent and logically substantiated phenomena in melodic construction, and therefore in all music. Harmonic implications of Classical melodies, and of a great majority of folk tunes of Western nations, are very much in evidence. The pendulumlike swing between the tonic and the dominant is the most frequent harmonic characteristic. However, the inapplicability of these principles in many musical cultures has caused others to put forth the roles of sociological, cultural, and compositional influences on melodic construction.

While most melodies are contained within the octave from the dominant to the dominant, continuous melodic lines extending over an octave are not rare. A remarkable example is the auxiliary theme in the last movement of Beethoven's *Choral Sym.*, which begins on the tonic, rises to the 6th in the octave above, and ends on the tonic in that higher octave, with all melodic notes of equal rhythmic value. But while such an enlarged range is acceptable for instrumental passages, it becomes almost intractable for the human voice. The range of *The Star-Spangled Banner* is an octave and a 5th, which makes it difficult for most to sing; futile attempts have been made to arrange it so that the 2nd half could be transposed to a lower key. Wagner introduced the notion of *unendliche Melodie* (infinite or endless melody), a Romantically exaggerated description of a melody that naturally flows into the beginning of the next motive with an avoidance of perfect cadences, analogous to a circle or any other closed curve.

Another resource of basic importance in traditional Western music is the sequence within the key, a melodic pattern repeated on an ever-changing set of scale degrees. Beethoven's 5th Sym. opens with such a sequence, that of a falling 3rd from the dominant to the minor mediant followed by a falling 3rd from the subdominant to the supertonic. Typically these kinds of sequences imply the familiar harmonic swing from the tonic to the dominant. A longer sequence occurs toward the end of the overture to Tchaikovsky's opera *Eugene Onegin*, having 8 chain-links and descending fully 2 octaves; even more extreme is the seemingly endless chain of 4 descending steps in his *1812 Overture*, prior to the final apotheosis.

Atonal melodies follow the structural plans of melodic lines entirely different from those of tonal melodies. Atonality excludes all triadic conformations and has no link with the harmonic series. The organized atonal systems, particularly the dodecaphonic techniques, follow their own rules of aesthetic structures, with the ideal of beauty derived from special considerations of intervallic motion. But even in dodecaphonic melodies, the center of gravity is present as the arithmetical mean of high and low notes.

It should be noted that the principles underlying the melodic structure of much non-Western music differ widely from those of Western melos. There are few harmonic implications in much of this music; the scales themselves are formed from sets of intervals not necessarily contained within an octave. The study of non-Western melodies, therefore, must take place within a special discipline in ethnomusicology, acoustics, or theory.

melograph. Mechanical devices for recording the music played on a piano.

meloharmony. In a triadically constructed melody, the harmonic arrangement is clearly outlined. In such instances it is proper to speak of meloharmony as a 2-dimensional entity. In DODECAPHONIC MUSIC, meloharmony acquires a particular significance, because the fundamental series can be distributed horizontally (i.e., melodically), and vertically (harmonically), and still preserve its continuity. It is also possible to speak of melocontrapuntal structures, arranged vertically, horizontally, or diagonally. A cognate term is *melorhythm*, in which melody and rhythm are combined into a dual entity.

melopée, melopoeia (Grk. *melos* + *poein*, create song). Ancient Greek term denoting all types of musical composition and performance. In Plato's *Symposion*, melopeia is described as the art of musical forms, while Aristotle defines it as the science of melody. The Aristotelian meaning was revived in the Renaissance in the theories of the HARMONY OF THE SPHERES. A rather tautological definition of the term is given by Mersenne: "Melopoeia nil aliud est quam ars melodiae" (Melopeia is nothing but the art of melody).

melophone. A portable keyboard accordion, shaped like a cello, harp, or guitar; resting on the lap, the melophone's sound is produced by bellows operated by a right-hand handle, capable of vibrato or trumpet effects; the left hand works the varying number of keys. Conceptually the instrument suggests a bizarre hurdy-gurdy; it is not surprising that within 3 years of its invention (1837) the HARMONIUM was being developed to replace it.

melorhythm. The term *meloritmo*—frequently used by Spanish and Latin American writers on music and signifying a synthetic 2-dimensional entity possessing both melodic and rhythmic attributes—is sufficiently useful to be adopted in other languages. It is also a convenient substitute for the definition of a musical phrase, which must necessarily have the dual melorhythmic consistency. In serial music, melorhythms may be regarded as the integrals of the melodic and rhythmic differential series.

melos (Grk., song). The name bestowed by Wagner on the style of recitative employed in his later MUSIC DRAMAS.

melosomatic effect. The neologism *melosomatic* suggests an interaction between *melos* (song) and the physical *soma* (body). It may be traumatic when loud music is played without relief. But a more insidious psychological lesion is produced by personal associations. In his short story *The Black Monk*, Chekhov, who was a professional physician, describes the deadly effect produced on a young intellectual by the playing of *Angel's Serenade* by Gaetano Braga, resulting in a fatal cerebral hemorrhage when the piece is played again after a long interval of time. Autosuggestion may have been responsible for the death of the Hungarian composer Rezső Seress, author of the pessimistic popular song *Gloomy Sunday* (it was banned in various localities after numerous suicides were purportedly engendered by it). By a delayed reaction 40 years after writing this song, the composer himself jumped out of a window. The Russian pianist Alexander Kelberine (1903–40) took a lethal dose of barbiturates after his last concert in Town Hall in N.Y., for which he arranged a funeral program, consisting entirely of works in minor keys, the last number being Liszt's *Totentanz*.

Sexual stimulation is highly melosomatic, as amply demonstrated by the reactions of the young to concerts of popular music, particularly ROCK 'N' ROLL. Leo Tolstoy, who turned against sex after a lifetime of indulgence and 16 illegitimate children, presented a philosophical study of musical sexuality in his novel *The Kreutzer Sonata*, wherein he tells how the last movement of Beethoven's work, with its propulsive syncopation, overwhelms the natural restraints of the performers, a middle-class married Russian woman pianist and a male violinist, hurling them into a frenzy of illicit pas-

sion. It may be questioned that amateurs could ever master the technical difficulties of that diabolically intricate last movement, let alone create enough excitement to carry them away. There is a famous painting illustrating the climactic scene of the novel, showing the mustachioed violinist implanting a passionate kiss on the lips of a lady pianist while holding both the violin and the bow in his left hand, suggesting that he had the presence of mind to switch the bow from the right hand to the left, but leaving it unexplained as to why he did not deposit the instrument on the lid of the piano in that crucial moment. The painting was widely used as an advertisement for a brand of perfume with a sexy name.

Melosomatic associations were responsible for the extraordinary vogue of the piano piece *A Maiden's Prayer* by a Polish composer named Thekla Badarzewska, a wishfulfilling favorite of several generations of unmarried females. In 1937 Stravinsky instituted in Paris a suit against Warner Bros. for the production of a film entitled *The Firebird*, in which a submissive young girl is so unnerved by the phonograph playing of *Katschei's Infernal Dance* from Stravinsky's *Firebird* that she wanders into the flat of a professional seducer, who had the piece played continually with malice aforethought, and yields to his infamous desires. The judge failed to appreciate Stravinsky's attitude, since the seductive power of music is supposed to be the composer's greatest pride, and adjudicated the case by granting Stravinsky a token sum of 1 French franc in compensation for the offense.

membi. Indigenous vertical flute found in Paraguay and southern Brazil.

membranophones. In the Hornbostel-Sachs classification system, drums whose playing area is made of stretched animal skin (membrane). At present many of these instruments (especially in the Western classical orch.) use plastic instead of skin.

même (Fr.). Same. *À la même,* TEMPO PRIMO.

Memphis Blues, The. Song by W. C. Handy, 1912, which launched the blues as a national genre. Handy originally wrote the tune as a campaign song for a candidate for mayor of Memphis, Tenn. He published the song in 1912 as a piano solo; the lyrics were added in 1913. *The Memphis Blues* is considered the 1st publ. blues; but its most important effect was to combine popular music and country blues (which predates the 20th century) to invent the more sophisticated urban blues. Handy, a black composer and trumpet player, lived long enough to enjoy its merited fame. In 1941 a movie musical, *The Birth of the Blues*, added to his glory, and after his death a postage stamp showing him playing the trumpet was issued by the U.S. Post Office.

Men and Mountains. Orch.l suite by Ruggles, 1924, 1st performed in N.Y., inspired by Blake's line "Great things are done when men and mountains meet." The score is set in dissonant counterpoint, but it maintains a curiously lyric musical ambience.

Mendelssohn (-Bartholdy), (Jacob Ludwig) Felix

Famous German composer, pianist, and conductor; b. Hamburg, Feb. 3, 1809; d. Leipzig, Nov. 4, 1847. He was a grandson of the philosopher Moses Mendelssohn and the son of the banker Abraham Mendelssohn; his mother was Lea Salomon; the family was Jewish, but upon its settlement in Berlin the father decided to become a Protestant and added Bartholdy to his surname. Mendelssohn received his 1st piano lessons from his mother; subsequently studied piano with Ludwig Berger and violin with Carl Wilhelm Henning and Eduard Rietz; he also had regular lessons in foreign languages and in painting (he showed considerable talent in drawing with pastels); he also had piano lessons with Marie Bigot in Paris, where he went with his father for a brief stay in 1816.

His most important teacher in his early youth was Carl Friedrich Zelter, who understood the magnitude of Mendelssohn's talent; in 1821 Zelter took him to Weimar and introduced him to Goethe, who took considerable interest in the boy after hearing him play. Zelter arranged for Mendelssohn to become a member of the Singakademie in Berlin in 1819 as an alto singer; in that year his 19th Psalm was performed by the Akademie. In 1825 Mendelssohn's father took him again to Paris to consult Cherubini on Mendelssohn's prospects in music; however, he returned to Berlin, where he had better opportunities for development.

Mendelssohn was not only a precocious musician, both in performing and in composition; what is perhaps without a parallel in music history is the extraordinary perfection of his works written during adolescence. He played in public for the 1st time at the age of 9 in Berlin (1818), performing the piano part of a trio by Wölffl. He wrote a remarkable octet at the age of 16; at 17 he composed the overture for the incidental music to Shakespeare's *A Midsummer Night's Dream*, an extraordinary manifestation of his artistic maturity, showing a mastery of form equal to that of the remaining numbers of the work, which were composed 15 years later.

He proved his great musicianship when he conducted Bach's *St. Matthew Passion* in the Berlin Singakademie in 1829, an event that gave an impulse to the revival of Bach's vocal music. In that spring Mendelssohn made his 1st journey to England, where he conducted his Sym. No. 1 in C minor (seated, after the fashion of the time, at the keyboard); later he performed in London the solo part in Beethoven's *Emperor Concerto*; he then traveled through Scotland, where he found inspiration for the composition of his overture *Fingal's Cave* (*Hebrides*), which he conducted for the 1st time during his 2nd visit to London (1832); 10 days later he played in London the solo part of his G-minor Concerto and his *Capriccio brillante*. He became a favorite of the English public; Queen Victoria was one of his most fervent admirers; altogether he made 10 trips to England as a pianist, conductor, and composer.

From 1830 to 1832 Mendelssohn traveled in Germany, Austria, Italy, and Switzerland, and also went to Paris. In May 1833 he led the Lower-Rhine Music Festival in Düsseldorf; then conducted at Cologne in June 1835. He was still a very young man when, in 1835, he was offered the conductorship of the celebrated Gewandhaus Orch. in Leipzig; the Univ. of Leipzig bestowed upon him an honorary degree of Ph.D. Mendelssohn's leadership of the Gewandhaus Orch. was of the greatest significance for the development of German musical culture; he engaged the violin virtuoso Ferdinand David (1810–73) as concertmaster of the orch., which soon became the most prestigious symphonic organization in Germany. In 1837 he married Cecile Charlotte Sophie Jeanrenaud of Frankfurt, the daughter of a French Protestant clergyman. Five children (Carl, Marie, Paul, Felix, and Elisabeth) were born to them, and their marriage was exceptionally happy.

Felix Mendelssohn

COURTESY FRANK DRIGGS COLLECTION

At the invitation of King Friedrich Wilhelm IV, Mendelssohn went in 1841 to Berlin to take charge of the music of the court and in the cathedral; he received the title of Royal Generalmusikdirektor, but residence in Berlin was not required. Returning to Leipzig in 1842, he organized the famous Cons. Its splendid faculty comprised, besides Mendelssohn (who taught piano, ensemble playing, and later composition), Schumann, who taught classes in piano and composition; Hauptmann, in music theory; David, in violin; Becker, in organ; and Plaidy and Wenzel, in piano. The Cons. was officially opened on April 1843. The financial nucleus of the foundation was a bequest from Blumner of 20,000 *thaler*, left at the disposal of the King of Saxony for the promotion of the fine arts. Mendelssohn made a special journey to Dresden to petition the King on behalf of the Leipzig Cons. During his frequent absences the Gewandhaus Concerts were conducted by Hiller (1843–44) and Gade (1844–45).

In the summer of 1844 Mendelssohn conducted the Phil. Concerts in London; this was his 8th visit to England; during his 9th visit he conducted the 1st performance of his oratorio *Elijah* in Birmingham (1846). It was in England that the *Wedding March* from Mendelssohn's music to *A Midsummer Night's Dream* began to be used to accompany the bridal procession; the performance of the work was for the marriage of Tom Daniel and Dorothy Carew at St. Peter's Church, Tiverton (1847); the organist was Samuel Reay; it became particularly fashionable, however, when it was played at the wedding of the Princess Royal in 1858. He made his 10th and last visit to England in the spring of 1847; this was a profoundly painful period of his life, for his favorite sister, Fanny Mendelssohn Hensel, died in May 1847. Mendelssohn's own health began almost immediately to deteriorate, and he died at the age of 38. The exact cause of his early death is not determined; he suffered from severe migraines and chills before he died, but no evidence could be produced by the resident physicians for either a stroke or heart failure. The effect of Fanny's death on her brother has been the subject of much armchair speculation.

The news of Mendelssohn's death produced a profound shock in the world of music; not only in Germany and England, where he was personally known and beloved, but in distant America and Russia as well, there was genuine sorrow among musicians. Mendelssohn societies were formed all over the world; in America the Mendelssohn Quintette Club was founded in 1849. A Mendelssohn Scholarship was established in England in 1856; its 1st recipient was Arthur Sullivan.

The innate gift of music is an instinct, akin to the natural gift of language. Mythology may be closer to truth than musicology in that some men, women, and children are endowed with a divine spark of tonal imagination. Of all musicians known to history, Mendelssohn possessed the instinct of music in its purest form. Not even Mozart as a child had his genius developed to a perfection found in Mendelssohn's earliest works. A number of his string syms., written during his adolescent years, later came to light, revealing an extraordinary mastery of musical technique. This is not to say that the quality of Mendelssohn's music is comparable to Mozart's; rather, his art was an example of perfection that appears to be attained without gradual learning.

Mendelssohn's muse personified his Romantic spirit. There were no tempestuous outbursts of drama or tragedy in his syms., chamber music, piano compositions, or songs. His works could serve as a manual of proper composition of his time; his modulations were wonderfully predictable in their tonal fusion. His melodies were born on the wings of song; his counterpoint was never obtrusive; his orchestration was euphonious in its colorful harmony. Yet the very perfection of Mendelssohn's musical canon was the cause of the gradual decline of his popularity among musicians of the succeeding sesquicentennial. His music became associated with the spirit of Biedermeyer, too facile, too fulsome in its *Gemütlichkeit*.

Mendelssohn did not create disciples of his imitators; he could only attract epigones. But in performance by orchs. and instrumentalists his music is ever alive; his syms., notably the *Scottish* and *Italian*, maintain their smiling flow; his *Songs Without Words* are favorites of amateur and professional pianists alike. The popularity of his Violin Concerto remains undiminished among students and virtuosos. His trios and other chamber music are radiant in their communal cohesion. In sum, Mendelssohn was the musical personification of German Romanticism. But he was also a Jew by birth, and was thus anathema to the 3rd Reich; his very name was removed from music history books and encyclopedias publ. in Germany during that time, and the barbarians of the Nazi reign tore down his statue before the Gewandhaus in Leipzig; it was lovingly restored after Germany returned to civilization.

Prolific throughout his career, Mendelssohn left the following works, among others: Stage: *Die Hochzeit des Camacho*, op. 10, opera (1825; Berlin, 1827; dialogue not extant); *Die Heimkehr aus der Fremde*, op. 89, Liederspiel (written for the silver wedding anniversary of Mendelssohn's parents, perf. at their home, Berlin, 1829); *Ruy Blas*, incidental music to Hugo's play (1839); *A Midsummer Night's Dream*, op. 61, incidental music to Shakespeare's play (Potsdam, 1843). Oratorios: *St. Paul*, op. 36 (1834–36; Düsseldorf, 1836, composer conducting); *Elijah*, op. 70 (Birmingham, 1846, composer conducting); other sacred music, including psalms, hymns, cantatas, motets, Mass movements, anthems. Secular cantatas and choral songs, including *Die erste Walpurgisnacht* for Chorus and Orch., after Goethe, op. 60 (Berlin, Jan. 1833).

Solo songs: several of these were composed by his sister Fanny and publ. under his name (marked with *): 12 songs, op. 8 (1828): *Minnelied, Das Heimweh*, Italien*,*

Erntelied, Pilgerspruch, Frühlingslied, Maienlied, Andres Maienlied (Hexenlied), Abendlied, Romanze, Im Grünen, Suleika und Hatem*; 12 songs, op. 9 (1829–30): *Frage, Geständnis, Wartend, Im Frühling, Im Herbst, Scheidend, Sehnsucht*, Frühlingsglaube, Ferne, Verlust*, Entsagung, Die Nonne**; 6 songs, op. 19a (1830–34): *Frühlingslied, Das erste Veilchen, Winterlied, Neue Liebe, Gruss, Reiselied*; 6 songs, op. 34 (1834–36): *Minnelied, Auf Flügeln des Gesanges, Frühlingslied, Suleika, Sonntagslied, Reiselied*; 6 songs, op. 47 (1832–39): *Minnelied, Morgengruss, Frühlingslied, Volkslied, Der Blumenstrauss, Bei der Wiege*; 6 songs, op. 57 (1839–43): *Altdeutsches Lied, Hirtenlied, Suleika, O Jugend, Venetianisches Gondellied, Wanderlied*; 6 songs, op. 71 (1842–47): *Trostung, Frühlingslied, An die Entfernte, Schilflied, Auf der Wanderschaft, Nachtlied*; 6 songs, op. 86 (1831–51): *Es lauschte des Laub, Morgenlied, Die Liebende schreibt, Allnächtlich im Träume, Der Mond, Altdeutsches Frühlingslied*; 6 songs, op. 99: *Erster Verlust, Die Sterne schau'n, Lieblingsplätzchen, Das Schifflein, Wenn sich zwei Herzen scheiden, Es weiss und rat es doch keiner*; vocal duets.

Orch.: 13 string syms. (sinfonias; 1821–23); 5 orch. syms.: No. 1, in C minor, op. 11 (1824); No. 2, in B-flat major, a sym.-cantata for solo voices, chorus, and orch., *Lobgesang* or Hymn of Praise, op. 52 (Leipzig, 1840, composer conducting); No. 3, in A minor, *Scottish*, op. 56 (1830–42; Leipzig, 1842, composer conducting); No. 4, in A major, *Italian*, op. 90 (London, 1833, composer conducting); No. 5, in D major, *Reformation*, op. 107 (1830–32; Berlin, 1832, composer conducting). Concertos: violin, D minor, with strings (1822; Yehudi Menuhin gave its 1st perf. from the MS, N.Y., 1952); piano, A minor, with strings (1822); violin and piano, D minor, with strings (1823); 2 pianos, E major (1823; Berlin, 1824); 2 pianos, A-flat major (1824; Stettin, 1827); *Capriccio brillant*, piano, in B minor, op. 22 (1825–26; London, 1832); piano No. 1, G minor, op. 25 (Munich, 1831, composer soloist); *Rondo brillant*, piano, E-flat major., op. 29 (1834); piano No. 2, D minor, op. 40 (Birmingham, Sept. 1837, composer soloist); Serenade and Allegro giocoso, piano, B minor, op. 43 (1838); violin, E minor, op. 64 (1844; Leipzig, 1845; Ferdinand David, soloist; composer conducting).

Other orch.: *Ein Sommernachtstraum*, overture for Shakespeare's *A Midsummer Night's Dream*, op. 21 (1826; Stettin, 1827); *Meeresstille und glückliche Fahrt* (Calm Sea and Prosperous Voyage), overture after Goethe, op. 27

(Berlin, 1828); *Die Hebriden oder Fingals Höhle* (The Hebrides or Fingal's Cave), overture, op. 26 (1830; London, 1832); *Die schöne Melusine* (The Fair Melusina), overture after Grillparzer, op. 32 (1833; London, 1834); *Ruy Blas*, overture after Hugo, op. 95 (Leipzig, March 1839). Chamber: several works for: piano trio; piano quartet; violin and piano; string quartet; string quintet; string sextet; clarinet and piano; string octet; cello and piano; harp and piano; clarinet, basset horn, and piano. Piano works, including sonatas, variations (such as *Variations sérieuses* in D minor, op. 54, 1841); preludes and fugues; characteristic pieces, including the *Lieder ohne Worte* (Songs without Words), 8 books: opp. 19 (1829–30), 30 (1833–34), 38 (1836–37), 53 (1839–41), 62 (1842–44), 67 (1843–45), 85 (1834–45), 102 (1842–45); organ music. Breitkopf & Härtel publ. a *Thematisches Verzeichnis im Druck erschienener Compositionen* (Leipzig, 1846; 2nd ed., 1853; 3rd ed., 1882).

ménestrel, ménéstrier (Fr.). Minstrel.

Mengelberg, (Josef) **Willem,** celebrated Dutch conductor; b. Utrecht, Mar. 28, 1871; d. Chur, Switzerland, Mar. 21, 1951. He studied at the Utrecht Cons., and later at the Cologne Cons. with Seiss, Jensen, and Wullner. He was appointed municipal music director in Lucerne in 1891, and his work there attracted so much attention that in 1895 he was placed at the head of the Concertgebouw Orch. in Amsterdam, holding this post for 50 years (resigning in 1945), a record tenure for any conductor; during his directorship he elevated that orch. to a lofty position in the world of music; was also director of the Museumgesellschaft concerts in Frankfurt from 1908 to 1921. In addition, he became conductor of the Toonkunst choral society in Amsterdam (1898); appeared frequently as guest conductor in all the European countries; in England he was an annual visitor from 1913 until World War II.

He 1st appeared with the N.Y. Phil. in 1905; then conducted it regularly from 1922 to 1930, with Toscanini serving as associate conductor in 1929–30. In 1928 he received the degree of Mus.Doc. at Columbia Univ. (honoris causa); in 1933 he was appointed prof. of music at Utrecht Univ. During the occupation of the Netherlands by the Germans, Mengelberg openly expressed his sympathies with the Nazi cause, and lost the high respect and admiration that his compatriots had felt for him; after the country's liberation (1945), he was barred from professional activities there, the ban to be continued until 1951, but he died in that year in exile in Switzerland.

Mengelberg was an outstanding representative of the Romantic tradition in symphonic conducting. His performances of the Beethoven syms. were notable for their dramatic sweep and power, if not for their adherence to stylistic proprieties. He was a great champion of many of the major composers of his era, including Mahler and Strauss; both men appeared as guest conductors of the Concertgebouw Orch., and became Mengelberg's friends. Mahler dedicated his 5th and 8th syms. to Mengelberg and the Concertgebouw Orch., and Strauss dedicated his *Ein Heldenleben* to the same forces. Mengelberg was the 1st to lead a major cycle of Mahler's works, in Amsterdam in 1920. His nephew Karel (Willem Joseph) Mengelberg (b. Utrecht, July 18, 1902; d. Amsterdam, July 11, 1984) was a composer and conductor. Another nephew, Kurt Rudolf Mengelberg (b. Krefeld, Feb. 1, 1892; d. Beausoleil, near Monte Carlo, Oct. 13, 1959), was a musicologist and composer. A great-nephew, Misha Mengelberg (b. Kiev, June 5, 1935), is a composer.

Mennin (born Mennini), **Peter,** eminent American composer and music educator, brother of Louis Mennini. b. Erie, Pa., May 17, 1923; d. N.Y., June 17, 1983. His family stemmed from Italy; his brother did not cut off the last letter of his name as Peter did. His early environment was infused with music, mostly from phonograph recordings; he studied piano with Tito Spampani. In 1940 he enrolled in the Oberlin Cons. in Ohio, where he took courses in harmony with Normand Lockwood. He quickly learned the basics of composition, and at the age of 18 wrote a sym. and a string quartet. In 1942 he enlisted in the U.S. Army Air Force; was discharged in 1943, and resumed his musical studies at the Eastman School of Music in Rochester, N.Y., where his teachers were Howard Hanson and Bernard Rogers.

He worked productively; wrote another sym. in 1944; a movement from it, entitled *Symphonic Allegro*, was performed by the N.Y. Phil., Leonard Bernstein conducting (1945). His 3rd Sym. was performed by Walter Hendl with the N.Y. Phil. (1947). Mennin progressed academically as well; he obtained his Ph.D. from the Eastman School of Music in 1947. He received a Guggenheim fellowship grant in 1948; a 2nd Guggenheim grant followed in 1956. From

1947 to 1958 he taught composition at the Juilliard School of Music in N.Y.; in 1958 he assumed the post of director of the Peabody Cons. in Baltimore. In 1962 he received his most prestigious appointment, that of president of the Juilliard School of Music, serving in that capacity until his death.

Despite his academic preoccupations, he never slackened the tempo of his activities as a composer; he diversified his syms. by adding descriptive titles; thus his 4th Sym. (1949) was subtitled *The Cycle* and was scored for chorus and orch.; his 7th Sym. (1964) was called *Variation Sym.*; the 4 movements of his 8th Sym. (1974) bore biblical titles. Increasingly also, he began attaching descriptive titles to his other works; his Concertato for Orch. was named *Moby Dick* (1952); there followed a *Canto* for Orch. (1963), a

Cantata de Virtute (1969), *Reflections of Emily*, to texts by Emily Dickinson (1976), and *Voices* (1976).

Mennin's musical mind was directed toward pure structural forms; his music is characterized by an integrity of purpose and teleological development of thematic materials, all this despite the bold infusion of dissonant sonorities in contrapuntal passages. He held honorary doctorates from the Univ. of Chicago, the Univ. of Wisconsin, Temple Univ., and the Univ. of Heidelberg in Germany. His brother Louis (Alfred) Mennini (b. Erie, Pa., Nov. 18, 1920) was a composer and music educator.

meno (It.). Less; not so. *Meno allegro*, not so fast; *meno mosso*, not so fast (usually shortened to simply *meno*).

Menotti, Gian Carlo

~~~ ~~~ ~~~ ~~~ ~~~

Prolific Italian composer and librettist. b. Cadegliano, July 7, 1911. He was the 6th of 10 children. He learned the rudiments of music from his mother, and began to compose as a child, making his 1st attempt at an opera, entitled *The Death of Pierrot*, at the age of 10. He studied at the Milan Cons. (1924–27); then went to the U.S., and entered the Curtis Inst. of Music in Philadelphia (1927–33), where he studied with Rosario Scalero; subsequently taught composition there; traveled often to Europe; made his home in Mt. Kisco, N.Y. Although Menotti associated himself with the cause of American music, and spent much of his time in the U.S., he retained his Italian citizenship.

As a composer he is unique on the American scene, being the 1st to create American opera possessing such an appeal to audiences as to become established in the permanent repertoire. Inheriting the natural Italian gift for operatic drama and an expressive singing line, he adapted these qualities to the peculiar requirements of the American stage and to the changing fashions of the period; his serious operas have a strong dramatic content in the realistic style stemming from the Italian verismo. He

wrote his own librettos, marked by an extraordinary flair for drama and for the communicative power of the English language; with this is combined a fine, though subdued, sense of musical humor. Menotti made no pretensions at extreme modernism, and did not fear to approximate the successful formulas developed by Verdi and Puccini; the influence of Mussorgsky's realistic prosody is also in evidence, particularly in recitative. When dramatic tension required a greater impact, Menotti resorted to atonal and polytonal writing, leading to climaxes accompanied by massive dissonances.

His 1st successful stage work was *Amelia Goes to the Ball*, an opera buffa in 1 act (originally to an Italian libretto by the composer, as *Amelia al ballo*), staged at the Academy of Music, Philadelphia (1937). This was followed by another comic opera, *The Old Maid and the Thief*, commissioned by NBC, 1st performed on the radio, 1939, and on the stage, by the Philadelphia Opera Co. (1941). Menotti's next operatic work was *The Island God*, produced by the Metropolitan Opera, N.Y. (1942), with indifferent success; but with the production of *The Medium* (N.Y., 1946), Menotti established himself as the foremost composer-librettist of modern opera. The imaginative libretto, dealing with a fraudulent spiritualist who falls victim to her own practices when she imagines that ghostly voices are real, suited Menotti's musical talent to perfection; the opera had a long and successful run in N.Y., an unprecedented occurrence in the history of the American lyric theater.

A short humorous opera, *The Telephone*, was 1st produced by the N.Y. Ballet Soc., 1947, on the same bill with *The Medium*; these 2 contrasting works were subsequently staged all over the U.S. and in Europe, often on the same evening. Menotti then produced *The Consul* (Philadelphia, 1950), his best tragic work, describing the plight of political fugitives vainly trying to escape from an unnamed country but failing to obtain the necessary visa from the consul of an anonymous power; very ingeniously, the author does not include the title character in the cast, since the consul never appears on the stage but remains a shadowy presence. *The Consul* exceeded Menotti's previous operas in popular success; it had a long run in N.Y., and received the Pulitzer Prize. On Christmas Eve, 1951, NBC presented Menotti's television opera *Amahl and the Night Visitors*, a Christmas story of undeniable poetry and appeal; it became an annual television production every Christmas in subsequent years.

His next opera was *The Saint of Bleecker Street*, set in a N.Y. locale (N.Y., 1954); it won the Drama Critics' Circle Award for the best musical play of 1954, and the Pulitzer Prize for 1955. A madrigal ballet, *The Unicorn, the Gorgon and the Manticore*, commissioned by the Elizabeth Sprague Coolidge Foundation, was 1st presented at the Library of Congress, Washington, D.C., 1956. His opera *Maria Golovin*, written expressly for the International Exposition in Brussels, was staged there (1958).

In 1958 he organized the Festival of 2 Worlds in Spoleto, Italy, staging old and new works; in 1977 he inaugurated an American counterpart of the festival in Charleston, S.C. In many of the festival productions Menotti acted also as stage director. In the meantime he continued to compose; he produced in quick succession *Labyrinth*, a television opera to his own libretto (N.Y., 1963); *Death of the Bishop of Brindisi*, dramatic cantata with the text by the composer (Cincinnati, 1963); *The Last Savage*, opera buffa, orig. with an Italian libretto by Menotti, produced at the Opéra-Comique in Paris in a French trans. (1963; produced in Eng. at the Metropolitan Opera, N.Y., 1964); *Martin's Lie*, chamber opera to Menotti's text (Bath, England, 1964); *Help, Help, the Globolinks!*, "an opera in 1 act for children and those who like children" to words by Menotti, with electronic effects (Hamburg, 1968); *The Most Important Man*, opera to his own libretto (N.Y., 1971); *The Hero*, comic opera (Philadelphia, 1976); *The Egg*, a church opera to Menotti's own libretto (Washington Cathedral, 1976); *The Trial of the Gypsy* for treble voices and piano (N.Y., 1978); *Miracles* for Boys' Choir (Fort Worth, 1979); *La Loca*, opera to Menotti's own libretto dealing with a mad daughter of Ferdinand and Isabella (San Diego, 1979); *A Bride from Pluto*, opera (Washington, DC, 1982).

Among Menotti's nonoperatic works are the ballets *Sebastian* (1944) and *Errand into the Maze* (N.Y., 1947); Piano Concerto No. 1 (Boston, 1945); *Apocalypse*, symphonic poem (Pittsburgh, 1951); Violin Concerto (Philadelphia, 1952, Zimbalist soloist); Triplo Concerto a tre, in 3 movements (N.Y., 1970); *Landscapes and Remembrances*, cantata to his own autobiographical words (Milwaukee, 1976); 1st Sym., subtitled *The Halcyon* (Philadelphia, 1976); Piano Concerto No. 2 (Miami, 1982). Menotti is the author of the librettos for Samuel Barber's operas *Vanessa* (Metropolitan Opera, N.Y., 1958), *A Hand of Bridge* (1959), and the rev. *Antony and Cleopatra* (N.Y., 1975); he wrote a play without music, *The Leper* (Tallahassee, 1970).

mensural notation, mensuration. A type of rhythmic notation and system, in use from the 13th to the 17th centuries, based on a system of ligatures that determine duration according to succession and context, rather than metrically.

menuet (Fr.; Ger. *Menuett*). A minuet.

Menuhin, Hephzibah, American pianist, sister of Yehudi Menuhin; b. San Francisco, May 20, 1920; d. London, Jan. 1, 1981. Like her brother, she appeared in public at a very early age in San Francisco (1928); studied there and later with Ciampi in Paris; toured widely as a recitalist with her brother in the U.S. and Europe.

Menuhin, (Sir) Yehudi

Celebrated American violinist. brother of Hephzibah Menuhin; b. N.Y., Apr. 22, 1916. He was born of Russian-Jewish parents (the family surname was originally Mnuhin). As a child he was taken to San Francisco, where he began to study violin with Sigmund Anker; in 1923 he began taking lessons with Louis Persinger, who was then concertmaster of the San Francisco Sym. Orch. In 1924 he made his public debut in Oakland playing Bériot's *Scéne de ballet* with Persinger as accompanist; Menuhin was only 7 at the time. On Jan. 17, 1926, when he was 9 years old, he played a recital in N.Y. He made his European debut in Paris (1927), with Paul Paray and the Lamoureux Orch. In Paris he began to study with Georges Enesco, who became his most influential teacher, and who guided his future career.

Returning to America, Menuhin played the Beethoven Concerto with Fritz Busch and the N.Y. Sym. Orch. (1927), winning unanimous acclaim from the public and the press. He subsequently made tours throughout America and Europe; in 1929, he appeared with Bruno Walter and the Berlin Phil., playing concertos by Bach, Beethoven, and Brahms on the same program; later that year, he made his London debut. He continued to pursue his studies with Enesco, and also received additional instruction from Adolf Busch. On the sesquicentennial of the 1st concert given at the Gewandhaus in Leipzig, he appeared as soloist with the Gewandhaus Orch. in the Mendelssohn Concerto (1931). In 1935 he completed his 1st world tour, giving concerts in 73 cities in 13 countries, including Australia.

He also became active in organizing music festivals; in 1956 he established the Gstaad Festival in Switzerland. In 1959 he made his home in London, and founded the Bath Festival, which he directed

Yehudi Menuhin

COURTESY FRANK DRIGGS COLLECTION

until 1968; he also founded the Windsor Festival and directed it from 1969 to 1972. He toured as soloist with his own chamber orch.; later he devoted much time to conducting and musical education. He toured Japan in 1951 and Russia in 1956. In 1963 he founded his own boarding school for musically gifted children at Stoke d'Abernon, Surrey. In 1965 he received an honorary knighthood from Queen Elizabeth II. In 1970 he received honorary citizenship from the community of Saanen, Switzerland, and assumed Swiss national allegiance while preserving his American citizenship.

In 1971 he succeeded Barbirolli as president of Trinity College of Music in London. In 1976 he was awarded an honorary doctorate by the Sorbonne of Paris, the 1st musician to be so honored during its entire history. In Sept. 1981 he celebrated the 50th anniversary of his 1st appearance in Leipzig by performing the Brahms Concerto with Kurt Masur and the Gewandhaus Orch. In 1985 he was granted honorary British citizenship, and thereby formally became Sir Yehudi. In 1986 President Mitterand made him a Grand Officer of the Légion d'Honneur of France. In 1987 he was made a member of the Order of Merit.

Apart from Menuhin's musical activities, he became deeply interested in art, politics, and above all, psychology and philosophy. He embraced the cause of oriental religions, practiced yoga exercises, and even lectured on these abstruse subjects. In 1963 he appeared on the BBC in London in a discussion entitled *Yehudi Menuhin and His Guru*. He also adopted a health diet, eschewing carbohydrates and some other foods. In his political utterances he antagonized many factions in many lands. He was enthusiastically received in Israel during his tours in 1950, 1951, 1952, and 1953, but aroused Israeli animosity when he gave benefit concerts for Palestinian refugees. He embarrassed the Russians at a music congress in Moscow in 1971 when in his speech, which he read in understandable Russian, he appealed to them on behalf of human rights; he was never invited to Russia again.

In the meantime his artistry suffered somewhat; critics began to notice a certain unsteadiness in his intonation and technique; as a conductor he performed not more than satisfactorily. Still, he never slackened his energetic activities, musical or nonmusical. He publ. a collection of essays under the title *Theme and Variations* (London, 1972); with Curtis W. Davis, *The Music of Man* (London, 1980), based on the television series of the same title; and *Life Class* (London, 1986).

Mephisto Waltz. Four piano pieces by Liszt, publ. individually; the 1st, 1859, is the most famous. Its initial cumulative chord, formed by a series of perfect 5ths separated by a minor 6th, was a great innovation at the time, and Liszt was berated by stern academic critics for taking such harmonic liberties. Liszt's Mephisto is not Goethe's philosophic Beelzebub, but a demonic spirit from *Faust* by the German poet Lenau. Originally Liszt wrote his 1st *Mephisto Waltz* for orch. as the 2nd movement, entitled *Der Tanz in der Dorfschenke* (The Dance in the Village Tavern), to his score *2 Episodes from Lenau's "Faust."* The 2nd *Mephisto Waltz* was written in 1881, originally for orch. and later transcribed for piano. The 3rd waltz was a piano piece Liszt wrote in 1883; the 4th, for piano (1885), was not published until many years after his death.

Mer, La. Symphonic suite by Debussy, 1905, 1st performed in Paris. Although the piece is a song of the sea, Debussy was not too fond of sea travels, and even his infrequent trips to England were trying for him. The 3 sketches of this sea poem are impressions in instrumental colors of 3 aspects or events: *De l'aube à midi sur la mer* (From the Dawn to Noon on the Sea), *Jeux de vagues* (Play of the Waves), and *Dialogue du vent et de la mer* (Dialogue of the Wind and the Sea). The character of the music seems to justify the label of impressionism attached to *La Mer*, although Debussy himself deprecated this cliché borrowed from painting. From a purely analytical standpoint the work is remarkable. The primary theme is pentatonic in structure; there are anamorphic variations that expand it into a whole tone scale. Traditionally minded critics damned the work as formless (but isn't the sea itself without a stable form?); one American critic even drew his own program for it, in which a sea traveler gets sea-sick and vomits in the last movement. When Satie was asked which movement of *La Mer* he liked best, he said the 1st, *From Dawn to Noon*, and more specifically, "about a quarter of 11."

Mercer, Johnny (John Herndon), American lyricist and composer of popular music; b. Savannah, Ga., Nov. 18, 1909; d. Los Angeles, June 25, 1976. He went to N.Y. as a youth, and attracted the attention of Paul Whiteman; subsequently wrote songs for him, Benny Goodman, and Bob Crosby. In 1940 he went to Hollywood, where he founded Capitol Records. His 1st success as a lyric writer was *Lazybones*, with music by Hoagy Carmichael; another great success was *Ac-cent-tchu-ate the Positive*, which he wrote for his psychoanalyst, as was *Moon River*, for the film *Breakfast at Tiffany's*. He wrote both words and music for *Something's Gotta Give* and other hits. He received 4 Academy Awards for his lyrics.

Mercer, Mabel, English-born American songstress; b. Burton upon Trent, Staffordshire, Feb. 3, 1900; d. Pittsfield, Mass., Apr. 20, 1984. Her father, an African-American, died before she was born; her mother was a white British vaudeville singer. She became a stage performer in her early adolescence; was a dancer in a music hall in London; after World War I she went to Paris, where she made a success as a nightclub singer; became a *vedette* at Bricktop's. In 1938 she went to America and settled in N.Y. She continued her career as a nightclub singer, but also gave regular recitals of popular songs. In 1983 she received the Medal of Freedom from President Reagan. She was briefly married to jazz musician Kelsey Pharr.

Mercury Symphony. Sym. No. 43 in E-flat Major by Haydn (1772). The reason for this nomenclature is obscure, and who decided to name it *Mercury* remains unknown. It is, however, clear that the Mercury referred to here is the winged messenger of the gods, not the smallest planet of the solar system or the liquid metal.

Mère coupable, La (The Guilty Mother). Opera by Milhaud, 1966, 1st performed in Geneva. The libretto is drawn from Beaumarchais's *The Barber of Seville*, but Milhaud's treatment, modern, satirical, and somewhat surrealistic, differs completely from Rossini's famous opera on the same subject.

Merengue, meringue. Characteristic Afro-Cubanesque song dance of Venezuela, Haiti, and the Dominican Republic. It uses quatrain and refrain verse forms and is concerned with regional subject manner. Responsorial singing, POLYRHYTHMS, and 5/8 effects are layered over the basic 2/4 beat.

Merman, Ethel (born Ethel Agnes Zimmerman), popular American singer and Broadway star, famous American singer of popular music; b. N.Y., Jan. 16, 1908; d. there, Feb. 14, 1984. She was of German-Scottish extraction. She took a commercial course in high school and held several jobs as a secretary while trying to satisfy her desire to be a singing actress. She never took vocal lessons but developed her booming powerful voice naturally. She obtained some bookings at Long Island night spots, and soon attracted the attention of Broadway managers. She auditioned for George Gershwin, who hired her to sing in his musical *Girl Crazy* in 1930; she brought the house down with the hit song *I Got Rhythm,* holding a high C for 16 bars in the coda against the orch. playing the melodic line.

Among the musicals in which she starred were Cole Porter's *Anything Goes* (1934), Irving Berlin's *Annie Get Your Gun* (1946) and *Call Me Madam* (1950), and Jule Styne's *Gypsy* (1959). She also sang in 14 movie musicals, among them *There's No Business Like Show Business* and *It's a Mad, Mad, Mad, Mad World.* In 1970 she made her last appearance on Broadway; her last public appearance was in 1982, when she took part in a Carnegie Hall benefit concert. Merman had unbounded confidence in her stardom; she could also act in an uninhibited manner, which suited most of the roles she sang on Broadway.

She was arrogant and foul-mouthed in her dealings with agents, managers, directors, and even composers, but she knew how to put the music across; her ability to make the most of each song, and her sense of perfect intonation, made her the darling of Broadway. Indeed, she was dubbed the "queen of Broadway." "Broadway has been very good for me," she once said, "but I've been very good for Broadway." Her private life was tempestuous; she married and divorced 4 times; her daughter from the 2nd marriage committed suicide. In 1983 she underwent surgery to remove a brain tumor. When the

Ethel Merman, 1960

COURTESY FRANK DRIGGS COLLECTION

news of her death was announced, Broadway theaters observed a minute of silence to honor her memory.

Merry Mount. Opera by Hanson, 1934, 1st produced in N.Y., based on Hawthorne's *The Maypole of Merry Mount.* The action takes place in New England in 1625, where Satan is a living presence in the troubled minds of the inhabitants. A Puritan cleric, a victim of unfulfilled desires, is induced by a woman of free morals to take part in pagan games on Merry Mount. When he becomes horrified by his consorting with evil forces, he enters a church set aflame by Indians, and perishes in the inferno together with his seductress.

Merry Widow, The (*Die lüstige Witwe*). Operetta by Lehár, 1905, 1st produced in Vienna. A rich Austrian widow is the object of courtship on the part of a Slavic fortune-seeker, who finally corrals her in Paris. *The Merry Widow* is probably the most popular Viennese operetta of the century. The recitative glorifying Maxim's restaurant in Paris was inserted by Lehár as a token of gratitude to the chef of that establishment who allowed him to have free meals there during his impecunious days.

Merry Wives of Windsor, The. Opera by Nicolai, 1849, 1st produced in Berlin. The libretto follows Shakespeare faithfully, with Falstaff remaining the principal, pathetically comic character. The opera became tremendously popular in Germany; its sprightly overture remains a standard piece at summer concerts.

Mersenne, Marin, eminent French mathematician, philosopher, and music theorist; b. La Soultière, near Oizéî, Sept. 8, 1588; d. Paris, Sept. 1, 1648. He studied at the college of Le Mans; then at the Jesuit school at La Fléche (from 1604); then at the College Royal and the Sorbonne in Paris from 1609. He began his novitiate at the Nigeon monastery, near Paris (1611), completing it at St. Pierre de Fublaines, near Meaux, where he took holy orders (1612); then served the Minim monastery at the Paris Place Royale, becoming a deacon and a priest. He taught philosophy (1615–17) and theology (1618) at the Nevers monastery, and then was made correcter there. In

1619 he returned to Paris as conventual of the order. He made 3 trips to Italy between 1640 and 1645. He maintained a correspondence with the leading philosophers and scientists of his time.

His writings provide source material of fundamental importance for the history of 17th-century music, particularly in the areas of national performance styles, pedagogy, notation, ornamentation, organology, and acoustics. His correspondence, ed. by C. de Waard and B. Rochot, began publication in Paris in 1932. His writings (all publ. in Paris) include: *Quaestiones celeberrimae in Genesim* (1623); *Traité de l'harmonie universelle* (1627); *Questions harmoniques* (1634); *Les préludes de l'harmonie universelle* (1634); *Harmonicorum libri, in quibus agitur de sonorum natura* (1635–36); *Harmonicorum instrumentorum libri IV* (1636).

mescolanza (It.). POTPOURRI.

messa (It.; Fr. *messe*; Ger. *Messe*). MASS.

messa da requiem (It.). REQUIEM.

Messe de requiem. Sacred work by Fauré, 1887, one of the most beautiful choral works. Its peculiarity is the omission of the DIES IRAE; Fauré preferred to express faith, charity, and hope in his music rather than the vengeful drama of Judgment Day.

messe des morts (Fr.). REQUIEM.

messa di voce (It.). The attack of a sustained vocal tone *pianissimo*, with a swell to *fortissimo*, and slow decrease to *pianissimo* again:

Messiaen, Olivier (Eugène Prosper Charles)

Outstanding French composer and pedagogue; b. Avignon, Dec. 10, 1908; d. Paris, Apr. 28, 1992. A scion of an intellectual family (his father was a translator of English literature; his mother, Cécile Sauvage, a poet), he absorbed the atmosphere of culture and art as a child. A mystical quality was imparted by his mother's book of verses *L'Âme en bourgeon*, dedicated to her as-yet-unborn child. He learned to play piano; at the age of 8 composed a song, *La Dame de Shalott*, to a poem by Tennyson. At the age of 11 he entered the Paris Cons., where he attended the classes of Jean and Noël Gallon, Marcel Dupré, Maurice Emmanuel, and Paul Dukas, specializing in organ, improvisation, and composition; he carried 1st prizes in all these depts.

After graduation in 1930 he became organist at the Trinity Church in Paris. He taught at the École Normale de Musique and at the Schola Cantorum (1936–39). He also organized, with André Jolivet, Ives Baudrier, and Daniel-Lesur, the group La Jeune France, with the aim of promoting modern French music. He was in the French army at the outbreak of World War II in 1939; was taken prisoner; spent 2 years in a German prison camp in Görlitz, Silesia; he composed there his *Quatuor pour la fin du temps*; was repatriated in 1941 and resumed his post as organist at the Trinity Church in Paris. He was prof. of harmony and analysis at the Paris Cons. (from 1948). He also taught at the Berkshire Music Center in Tanglewood (1948) and in Darmstadt (1950–53).

Young composers seeking instruction in new music became his eager pupils; among them were Boulez, Stockhausen, Xenakis, and others who were to become important composers in their own right. He received numerous honors; was made a Grand Officier de la Légion d'Honneur; was elected a member of the Inst. de

France, the Bavarian Academy of the Fine Arts, the Accademia di Santa Cecilia in Rome, the American Academy of Arts and Letters, and other organizations. He married the pianist Yvonne Loriod in 1961.

Messiaen was one of the most original of modern composers; in his music he made use of a wide range of resources, from Gregorian chant to oriental rhythms (he called himself a "rhythmic mathematician"). A mystic by nature and Roman Catholic by religion, he strove to find a relationship between progressions of musical sounds and religious concepts; in his theoretical writing he tried to postulate an interdependence of modes, rhythms, and harmonic structures. Ever in quest of new musical resources, he employed in his scores the ONDES MARTENOT and exotic percussion instruments; a synthesis of these disparate tonal elements finds its culmination in his grandiose orch. work *Turangalîla-Symphonie*.

One of the most fascinating aspects of Messiaen's innovative musical vocabulary is the phonetic emulation of bird song in several of his works; in order to attain ornithological fidelity, he made a detailed study notating the rhythms and pitches of singing birds in many regions of several countries. The municipal council of Parowan, Utah, where Messiaen wrote his work *Des canyons aux étoiles*, glorifying the natural beauties of the state of Utah, resolved to name a local mountain Mt. Messiaen (1978). In 1983 his only opera, *St. François d'Assise*, was premiered, to international acclaim, at the Paris Opéra. In addition to this masterpiece, Messiaen's oeuvre includes orch.l, chamber, and vocal works, and compositions for organ. Messiaen discussed his theories of rhythm and mode in *Technique de mon langage musical* (2 vols., 1944); also publ. individual articles on musical ornithology and other subjects.

Messiah. Religious oratorio by Handel, 1742, which he wrote in an astonishingly brief period of 3 and a half weeks, when he was living in Dublin, Ireland; it was 1st performed there, with Handel himself conducting at the organ. A Dublin paper reported: "Words are wanting to express the exquisite Delight it afforded to the admiring crowded Audience. The Sublime, the Grand, and the Tender, adapted to the most elevated, majestic and moving words, conspired to transport and charm the ravished Heart and Ear." Although *Messiah* was a Lenten oratorio, it eventually became a standard choral work to be performed at Christmas time as well. The score of *Messiah* lends itself to unlimited amplification of means employed; some London performances numbered more than 3,000 singers, and as many as 27 bassoons and other instruments in proportion. The English libretto is selected from the King James Bible, detailing the world's response to Jesus, before, during, and after His presence. Although Handel never learned to speak English grammatically and his German accent was prodigious, he revealed an extraordinary sensitivity to the prosody of the English text.

Word of caution: The title is simply *Messiah*, not *The Messiah*, as persistently misapplied in thousands of performances. Handel's working score of *Messiah* was published in facsimile in 1974; it shows graphically the many changes Handel made in subsequent years, with some sections practically composed anew, others radically revised or reassigned to other voices. Of the many famous numbers in the score, the *Hallelujah Chorus* is the most familiar.

mestamente, mesto (It.). Plaintively, grievingly, pensively, sadly, with melancholy.

mesuré (Fr.). 1. Measured, moderate. 2. In exact time.

metabolé (Grk., modification). In rhetorics, a permutation of different words within a sentence; in music, the changed order of notes within a leitmotiv, as well as changes in tempo, rhythm, tonality, or interval structure within a musical period. In its ultimate development, metabole is a variation on a theme.

Metamorphosen. Threnody, mournful piece by R. Strauss, scored for 23 string instruments. He wrote it at the end of the war that destroyed Germany in 1945 and concluded his manuscript with the words "In Memoriam." The work contains quotations from the funeral march from Beethoven's *Eroica Sym.* It was performed for the 1st time in Zurich the following year.

metamorphosis. Radical variations on a theme. The borderline between the classical type of variation and a metamorphosis necessarily lies in a penumbra. In a metamorphosis the key, rhythm, and intervallic structure of a theme may be changed, with only the basic line discernible. The IDÉE FIXE in Berlioz's *Sym. fantastique* undergoes a radical metamorphosis in the course of the work. Hindemith composed a *Symphonic Metamorphosis on Themes of Carl Maria von Weber*.

metamusic. Metaphysical visions have obsessed composers through the ages. They dreamed of a metamusical sym. in which all mankind would participate as a responsive reverberating assembly of congenial souls. Shortly before he died, Scriabin wrote an outline of a metamusical *Mysterium* that would embrace all senses in a pantheistic mystical action. Much more earthbound—but musically fascinating—was the project of a *Universe Sym.* by Charles Ives, a work that he hoped to see performed by several orchs. stationed on hilltops overlooking a valley; there have been realizations of this project in recent years. The Russian mystical composer Nicolas Obouhov envisioned a metamusical union of all religions. He completed a major part of this work, which bore the title *Le Livre de vie.* He kept the manuscript on a self-made altar under an icon, in a corner of his small room in Paris. Since this was to be the book of his own life, body and soul, he made all annotations in the original scores in his own blood. He tried to interest American music lovers to have this work produced in a specially built temple in Hollywood, but died with his dream unfulfilled.

Composers of the AVANT-GARDE have at their disposal the means of producing metamusical scores with the aid of electronic synthesizers. They may even plan to hitch their metamusical chariot if not to the stars then at least to the planets. There is nothing mystical in the term metamusic. It simply means an art transcending traditional music, by analogy with Aristotle's metaphysics, which indicates the position of a chapter dealing with philosophy, directly after a discussion of physics in his *Organon.*

metaphors. A great number of metaphorical expressions and similes are taken from musical practice: soft pedal, face the music, blow your own horn, play it by ear, 2nd fiddle, jazz it up, conduct yourself properly, muted applause, etc.

Metastasio, Pietro (born Antonio Domenico Bonaventura Trapassi), famous Italian poet and opera librettist b. Rome, Jan. 3, 1698; d. Vienna, Apr. 12, 1782. He was the son of a papal soldier named Trapassi, but in his professional career assumed the Greek trans. of the name, both Trapassi (or Trapassamento) and Metastasio meaning transition. He was a learned classicist; began to write plays as a young boy; studied music with Porpora; he achieved great fame in Italy as a playwright; in 1729 was appointed court poet in Vienna by Emperor Charles VI. He wrote 27 opera texts, which were set to music by Handel, Gluck, Mozart, Hasse, Porpora, Jommelli, and many other celebrated composers; some of them were set to music 60 or more times.

His librettos were remarkable for their melodious verse, which naturally suggested musical associations; the libretto to the opera by Niccolo Conforto, *Nitteti* (1754; Madrid, 1756), was on the same subject as *Aida,* anticipating the latter by more than a century. For a catalogue, see A. Wotquenne, *Alphabetisches Verzeichnis der Stücke in Versen von Zeno, Metastasio und Goldoni* (Leipzig, 1905).

metempsychosis. A recurrence of a theme in an altered melorhythmic shape, suggesting the effect of *déjà entendu* without literal resemblance, may be called musical metempsychosis. The IDÉE FIXE in the *Sym. fantastique* of Berlioz does not fall into this category because here it was deliberately implanted and reproduced in a clearly recognizable form. The discovery of melorhythmic revenants may give a clue to the composer's inner impulses, and it is particularly fruitful in serial compositions, where metempsychosis may appear subliminally, despite the composer's efforts to guard against unintentional thematic references.

meter (U.K., metre). 1. The placing of musical rhythms into beats, and then beats into symmetrical or asymmetrical, regular or irregular groupings. 2. In verse, the division into symmetrical lines. The meter of English hymns is classified into three types, according to the kind of feet used (the figures show the number of syllables in each line):

Iambic meters: *Common meter* (C.M.), 8 6 8 6; *long meter* (L.M.), 8 8 8 8; *short meter* (S.M.), 6 6 8 6. These have regularly 4 lines to each stanza; when doubled to 8 lines they are called *common meter double* (C.M.D.), *long meter double* (L.M.D.), and *short meter double* (S.M.D.). They may also have 6 lines in each stanza and are then named *common particular meter* (C.P.M.), 8 6 8 8 6; *long particular meter* (L.P.M.) or *long meter six lines,* 8 8 8 8 8 8; and *short particular meter* (S.P.M.), 6 6 8 6 6 8. Besides the above, there are *sevens and sixes,* 7 6 7 6; *tens,* 10 10 10 10; *hallelujah meter,* 6 6 6 6 8 8 (or 6 6 6 6 4 4 4 4), etc.

Trochaic meter: *Sixes,* 6 6 6 6; *sixes and fives,* 6 5 6 5; *sevens,* 7 7 7 7; *eights and sevens,* 8 7 8 7, etc.

Dactylic meter: *Elevens,* 11 11 11 11; *elevens and tens,* 11 10 11 10, etc.

These are most of the meters in general use; hymnbooks use the system as a means of cross-reference and allow the possibility of putting a different text to a melody, or vice versa.

Metopes. Three poems for piano by Szymanowski, 1915, inspired by Homer's epic poetry. The title refers to ornamentation on Doric columns.

metric modulation. In the broadest sense, a change of time signature. In modern usage, proleptically applied by Charles Ives and systematically cultivated by Elliott Carter (who coined the term), a technique in which a rhythmic pattern is superimposed on another, heterometrically, and then supersedes it and becomes the basic meter. Usually, such time signatures are mutually prime, e.g., 4/4 and 3/8, and so have no common divisors. Thus the change of the basic meter decisively alters the numerical content of the beat, but the minimal denominator (1/8 when 4/4 changes to 3/8; 1/16 when, e.g., 5/8 changes to 7/16, etc.) remains constant in duration.

metronome (Gr. *metro* + *nomos*, law of measurement). A mechanical device that beats time, indicating the tempo of a composition. It consists of a graduated pendulum that is adjusted by sliding a small weight up or down its length. The design most commonly used was invented by J. N. Maelzel about 1816; the 1st metronome was developed a few years earlier by an obscure Amsterdam mechanic named Winkel, whose invention lacked the gradations. It is rumored, however, that Maelzel, who was something of a charlatan (he 1st acquired notoriety by exhibiting an "automatic" chess player, which concealed a dwarf chessmaster underneath the chessboard who moved the pieces by magnets). However that might be, the initials MM (Maelzel metronome, or metronome marking)

Electrical (l) and mechanical (r) metronomes

have for a century and a half adorned most student editions of classical works. The marking MM ♩ = 120 indicates that there are 120 quarter-notes per minute; by setting the weight on the pendulum at 120, the proper beat is obtained whereby each tick of the pendulum counts for 1 quarter note (as it happens, a half-second).

Beethoven, who believed in the power of modern inventions (he patronized quacks to alleviate his deafness), seized upon Maelzel's metronome as the perfect instrument to perpetuate the correct tempos of his works. It is the traditional view that either he trusted Maelzel too well (unlikely after their contretemps over *Wellington's Victory*); the machine that he had at his disposal was defective (the usual interpretation); or else (perish the thought!) Beethoven's own sense of tempo had betrayed him, for he assigned metronome marks that would accelerate the logical tempi beyond rational limits, in one instance converting an Allegretto into Prestissimo. As a consequence, performers of Beethoven's late works are apt to ignore his metronome marks. It should be noted that some conductors have begun to follow the markings which, with a smaller orch., seem at least possible.

Until lately the metronome was a familiar pyramidal accoutrement perched on the piano in the drawing room of every teacher and student; but with the advance of technology it was replaced by an unsightly cube that emitted electronic bleeps regulated by a dial. Some modern composers discovered that the metronome clicks make legitimate percussive effects. Ligeti, one of the most imaginative of the musical AVANT-GARDE, wrote a piece for 100 metronomes beating different tempi; visually, the spectacle is extraordinary.

Mexican Hayride. Musical by Porter, 1944. The plot involves an American female bullfighter in Mexico and the charge d'affaires of the U.S. embassy in Mexico City. He is enraptured by the matadora, but is upset when she appears to throw the defeated bull's ear at an American fugitive from justice. Not only does she prove to the diplomat that this was a mistake, but she takes part in a successful hunt after the outlaw. Includes *I Love You* and *Count Your Blessings*.

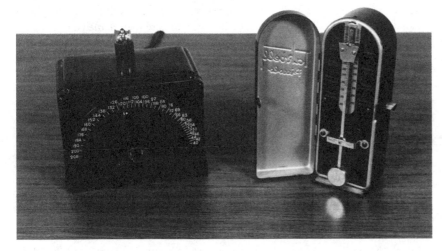

Meyerbeer, Giacomo

Famous German composer. b. Jakob Liebmann Beer, Vogelsdorf, near Berlin, Sept. 5, 1791; d. Paris, May 2, 1864. He was a scion of a prosperous Jewish family of merchants named Beer. He added the name Meyer to his surname, and later changed his 1st name for professional purposes. He began piano studies with Franz Lauska, and also received some instruction from Clementi; made his public debut in Berlin when he was 11. He then studied composition with Zelter (1805–7), and subsequently with B. A. Weber. It was as Weber's pupil that he composed his 1st stage work, the ballet-pantomime *Der Fischer und das Milchmädchen*, which was produced at the Berlin Royal Theater (1810). He then went to Darmstadt to continue his studies with Abbé Vogler until late 1811; one of his fellow pupils was Carl Maria von Weber.

While under Vogler's tutelage he composed the oratorio *Gott und die Natur* (1811) and also the operas *Der Admiral* (1811; not perf.) and *Jephthas Gelübde* (1812). His next opera, *Wirth und Gast, oder Aus Scherz Ernst* (1813), was not a success; revised as *Die beyden Kalifen* for Vienna, it likewise failed there (1814). However, he did find success in Vienna as a pianist in private musical settings. In Nov. 1814 he proceeded to Paris, and in Dec. 1815 to London. He went to Italy early in 1816 and there turned his attention fully to dramatic composition. His Italian operas—*Romilda e Costanza* (1817), *Semiramide riconosciuta* (1819), *Emma di Resburgo* (1819), *Margherita d'Angiu* (1820), *L'Esule di Granata* (1821), and *Il Crociato in Egitto* (1824)—brought him fame there, placing him on a par with the celebrated Rossini in public esteem. The immense success of *Il Crociato in Egitto* in particular led to a successful staging at London's King's Theatre (1825), followed by a triumphant Paris production (also 1825), which made Meyerbeer famous throughout Europe. To secure his Paris position he revamped *Margherita d'Angiu* for the French stage as *Margherita d'Anjou* (1826). He began a long and distinguished association with the dramatist and librettist Eugène Scribe in 1827 as work commenced on the opera *Robert le diable*. It was produced at the Paris Opéra in 1831, with extraordinary success.

Numerous honors were subsequently bestowed upon Meyerbeer; he was made a Chevalier of the Legion d'Honneur and a Prussian Hofkapellmeister in 1832, a member of the senate of the Prussian Academy of Arts in 1833, and a member of the Inst. de France in 1834. He began work on what was to become the opera *Les Huguenots* in 1832; set to a libretto mainly by Scribe, it was accorded a spectacular premiere at the Opéra (1836). Late in 1836 he and Scribe began work on a new opera, *Le Prophète*. He also commenced work on the opera *L'Africaine* in 1837, again utilizing a libretto by Scribe; it was initially written for the famous soprano Marie-Cornelie Falcon; however, after the loss of her voice, Meyerbeer set the score aside; it was destined to occupy him on and off for the rest of his life. In 1839 Wagner sought out Meyerbeer in Boulogne. Impressed with Wagner, Meyerbeer extended him financial assistance and gave him professional recommendations. However, Wagner soon became disenchanted with his prospects and berated Meyerbeer in private, so much so that Meyerbeer was compelled to disassociate himself from Wagner. The ungrateful Wagner retaliated by giving vent to his anti-Semitic rhetoric.

Meyerbeer began work on *Le Prophète* in earnest in 1838, completing it by 1840. However, its premiere was indefinitely delayed as the composer attempted to find capable singers. In 1842, *Les Huguenots* was performed in Berlin. On June 11, 1842, Meyerbeer was formally installed as Prussian Generalmusikdirektor. From the onset of his tenure, disagreement with the Intendant of the Royal Opera, Karl Theodor von Küstner, made his position difficult. Finally, in late 1848, Meyerbeer was dismissed from his post, although he retained his position as director of music for the royal court; in this capacity he composed a number of works for state occasions, including the opera *Ein Feldlager in Schlesien*, which reopened the opera house in 1844, following its destruction by fire. The leading role was sung by Jenny Lind, one of Meyerbeer's discoveries. It had a modicum of success after its 1st performance in Vienna under the title *Vielka* in 1847, although it never equaled the success of his Paris operas.

In 1849 he again took up the score of *Le Prophéte*. As he could find no tenor to meet its demands, he completely revised the score for the celebrated soprano Pauline Viardot-Garcia. With Viardot-Garcia as Fidès and the tenor Gustave Roger as John of Leyden, it received a brilliant premiere at the Opéra (1849), a success that led to Meyerbeer's being made the 1st German Commandeur of the Legion d'Honneur. His next opera was *L'Étoile du nord*, which utilized music from *Ein Feldlager in Schlesien*; its 1st performance at the Opéra-Comique (1854) proved an outstanding success. Equally successful was his opera *Le Pardon de Ploërmel* (Opéra-Comique, 1859). In 1862 he composed a special work for the London World Exhibition, the *Fest-Ouverture im Marschstyl*, and made a visit to England during the festivities.

In the meantime, work on *L'Africaine* had occupied him fitfully for years; given Scribe's death in 1861 and Meyerbeer's own failing health, he was compelled to finally complete it. In April 1864 he put the finishing touches on the score and rehearsals began under his supervision. However, he died on the night of May 2, 1864, before the work was premiered. His body was taken to Berlin, where it was laid to rest in official ceremonies attended by the Prussian court, prominent figures in the arts, and the public at large. Fétis was subsequently charged with making the final preparations for the premiere of *L'Africaine*, which was given at the Paris Opéra to notable acclaim (1865).

Meyerbeer established himself as the leading composer of French grand opera in 1831 with *Robert le diable*, a position he retained with distinction throughout his career. Indeed, he became one of the most celebrated musicians of his era. Although the grandiose conceptions and stagings of his operas proved immediately appealing to audiences, his dramatic works were more than mere theatrical spectacles. His vocal writing was truly effective, for he often composed and tailored his operas with specific singers in mind. Likewise, his gift for original orchestration and his penchant for instrumental experimentation placed his works on a high level. Nevertheless, his stature as a composer was eclipsed after his death by Richard Wagner. As a consequence his operas disappeared from the active repertoire, although revivals and several recordings saved them from total oblivion in the modern era.

mezzo, -a (It.). 1. Half. Written alone, as an expression mark, it refers to either an *f* or a *p* that follows. *Mezzo forte (mf)*, half loud; *mezzo legato*, half legato; in piano playing, use a light touch with less pressure than in legato; *mezzo piano (mp)*, half soft (less loud than *mezzo forte*); *mezzo voce*, with half the power of the voice.

mezzo-soprano (*mezzo*; It.). The female voice between soprano and alto, partaking of the quality of both, and usually of small compass (a-f^2, or a-g^2), but very full toned in the medium register.

mezzo-soprano clef. See "The Clefs," p. xxiii.

mezzo-staccato. Play in a manner between DETACHÉ and staccato; indicated by a slur over dotted notes.

Mi. The 3rd Aretinian syllable; name of the note *E* in France, Italy, etc.

Miaskovsky, Nikolai (Yakovlevich), eminent Russian composer and teacher; b. Novogeorgievsk, near Warsaw, Apr. 20, 1881; d. Moscow, Aug. 8, 1950. His father was an officer of the dept. of military fortification; the family lived in Orenburg (1888–89) and in Kazan (1889–93). In 1893 he was sent to a military school in Nizhny-Novgorod; in 1895 he went to a military school in St. Petersburg, graduating in 1899. At that time he developed an interest in music and tried to compose; took lessons with Kazanli; his 1st influences were Chopin and Tchaikovsky. In 1902–1903 he was in Moscow, where he studied harmony with Glière. Returning to St. Petersburg in 1903, he took lessons with Kryzhanovsky, from whom he acquired a taste for modernistic composition in the impressionist style. In 1906, at the age of 25, he entered the St. Petersburg Cons. as a pupil of Liadov and Rimsky-Korsakov, graduating in 1911.

At the outbreak of World War I in 1914, Miaskovsky was called into active service in the Russian army; in 1916 he was removed to Reval to work on military fortifications; he remained in the army after the Bolshevik Revolution of 1917; in 1918 he became a functionary in the Maritime Headquarters in Moscow; was finally demobilized in 1921. In that year he became prof. of composition at the Moscow Cons., remaining at that post to the end of his life. A composer of extraordinary ability, a master of his craft, Miaskovsky wrote 27 syms., much chamber music, piano pieces, and songs; his music is marked by structural strength and emotional élan; he never embraced extreme forms of modernism, but adopted workable devices of tonal expansion short of polytonality, and freely modulating melody short of atonality. His style was cosmopolitan; only in a few works did he inject folkloric elements. S. Shlifstein ed. a vol. of articles, letters, and reminiscences (1959) and a vol. of articles, notes, and reviews (1960).

Michelangeli, Arturo Benedetti, celebrated Italian pianist and pedagogue; b. Brescia, Jan. 5, 1920; d. Lugano, June 12, 1995. He received his formal music training at the Venturi Inst. in Brescia, where he took violin lessons with Paolo Chiuieri; at the age of 10 he entered the Milan Cons. as a piano pupil of Giuseppe Anfossi, obtaining his diploma at the age of 13. In 1939 he won the Concours International de Piano in Geneva; later joined the piano faculty at the Martini Cons. in Bologna. He was a lieutenant in the Italian air force; after the German occupation and the formal surrender of Italy to the Allies, he was active in the country's anti-Fascist underground; he was taken prisoner by the Germans but escaped after a few months. Despite these peripeteias, he somehow managed to practice, acquiring a formidable virtuoso technique. However, he also developed idiosyncrasies, often canceling scheduled performances, and engaged in such distracting (and dangerous) activities as automobile racing, skiing, and mountain climbing. Both his virtuosity and his eccentricities contributed to his legend, and his rare concerts were invariably public successes.

He toured the U.S. in 1950 and in 1966; played in the Soviet Union in 1964; also gave concerts in South America. Eventually he returned to Italy and dedicated himself mainly to teaching; organized an International Academy for pianists in a rented palazzo in Brescia with a multitude of pianos in soundproof studios; among his pupils were Jörg Demus, Walter Klien, Maurizio Pollini, and Martha Argerich.

microtime. Term invented by Stockhausen (1955) to designate the number of vibrations corresponding to individual pitch, as contrasted with MACROTIME, which he applies to the duration of each rhythmic pulse.

microtonality

〜〜 〜〜 〜〜 〜〜 〜〜

Division of the octave into intervals smaller than the half tone, the smallest interval used within the 12-semitone equal-tempered scale (i.e., Fokker's 31-note organ, Partch's 43-note percussion instruments, etc.). Intervals smaller than semitones were used in ancient Greece but were abandoned in Western music with the establishment of the ecclesiastical modes. When greater sensitivity toward tonal elements developed in modern times, composers and theorists began investigating the acoustical, coloristic, and affective aspects of intervals smaller than a semitone, particularly quarter tones.

The Mexican composer Julian Carrillo (1875–1965) experimented with microtonal intervals as early as 1895, when he published his *Sonido 13* (13th Sound); the title referred to the tonal resources beyond the 12 notes of the chromatic scale. Later he organized an international soc. for the exploration of microtonality under the grandiose name Cruzada Intercontinental Sonido 13. He devised special instruments for performance of microtonal intervals and proposed a numerical notation of 96 divisions of the octave, which enabled him to designate precise intervallic values for half tones, quarter tones, 6th tones, 8th tones, and 16th tones. As an exercise in microtonality he arranged Beethoven's 5th Sym. in quarter tones by dividing each interval into 2, so that the octave became a tritone, and the entire range of the work shrank to about 3 octaves, like some monstrous simulacrum of a physical universe in which the sensorium of auditory frequencies undergoes an extraction of the square root.

The English musician John Foulds (1880–1939) experimented with quarter tones in 1898. He writes in his book *From Music Today* (1934):

In the year 1898 I had tentatively experimented in a string quartet with smaller divisions than usual of the intervals of our scale, quarter tones. Having proved in performance their practicability and their capability of expressing certain psychological states in a manner incommunicable by any other means known to musicians, I definitely adopted them as an item in my composing technique. . . . Facetious friends may assert roundly that they have heard quarter tones all their lives, from the fiddle strings and larynxes of their mutual friends, who produced them without any difficulty.

The most systematic investigation of the theory and practice of quarter tones was undertaken by Alois Hába in Czechoslovakia. "As a boy of 12," he writes,

I played with my 3 older brothers in my father's village band. We were poor; there were 10 children in the family, and I had to contribute to household expenses. When we played for village festivals it often happened that folk singers used intervals different from the tempered scale, and they were annoyed that we could not accompany them properly. This gave me the idea to practice at home playing nontempered scales on my violin in intervals smaller than a semitone. This was my 1st "conservatory" for music in quarter tones and in 6th notes.

Probably the 1st entirely self-consistent work in quarter tones was the String Quartet written by Hába in 1919. He also compiled the 1st manual containing detailed instructions on composing in quarter tones, 3rd tones, and 6th tones, which he published under the fitting title *Neue Harmonielehre* in 1928. Under Hába's supervision the August Foerster piano manufacturing company of Czechoslovakia constructed the 1st model of a quarter-tone piano, which was patented on Mar. 18, 1924. At the same time Hába established the 1st seminars of microtonal music, at the Prague Cons. He and his students publ. a number of works in quarter tones, in Hába's special notation containing symbols for half a sharp, a sharp and a half, half a flat, and a flat and a half.

A quarter-tone upright piano was constructed by Willi Möllendorf even before Foerster's, but it was only an ordinary piano tuned in quarter tones and not a specially built instrument. It now sits in the Deutsches Museum in Munich as a historic relic. The same museum also possesses a quarter-tone harmonium built by Foerster and a harmonium of 19 divisions of the octave designed by Melchior Sachs.

In 1917 the Russian composer Ivan Wyschnegradsky (1893–1980) devised a system of quarter tones with a motto inspired by Heraclitus, "Everything flows." In 1924, then living in Paris, he formulated the concept of *pansonority*, which in his nomenclature meant a discrete continuum of quarter tones. To produce fairly accurate quarter tones he used 2 pianos or 2 pairs of pianos tuned a quarter tone apart. In November 1945 he conducted in Paris an entire program of his works, including a symphonic poem for 4 pianos entitled *Cosmos*. In Russia itself quarter-tone music had a brief period of success in the early 1920s, cultivated by the Quarter-Tone Soc. of Leningrad, founded by Rimsky-Korsakov's grandson Georg. Charles Ives, whose universal genius touched on many aspects of modern composition, contributed some pieces written in quarter tones. He claims that he became aware of the new resources of microtonal music when his father, a bandleader in the Union Army during the Civil War, experimented in tuning band instruments a quarter tone apart.

Probably the earliest publ. composition containing quarter tones was a group of 2 pieces for cello and piano by Richard H. Stein, composed in 1906, but quarter-tone passages in them were used only as occasional ultrachromatic interludes. Ernest Bloch inserted quarter tones in his 1st piano quintet, mainly for their affective value in coloristic appoggiaturas. American composers David Zeikel and William Harold Halberstadt investigated the potentialities of quarter tones in the 1940s, and they wrote special works, mostly for the violin, in quarter tones. For the sake of completeness:

The 1st quarter-tone piano manufactured in the U.S. was patented by Hans Barth on July 21, 1931. His instrument had 2 keyboards of 88 notes each. The upper keyboard was tuned at the regular international pitch and had the usual 5 black keys and 7 white keys. The lower keyboard was tuned a quarter tone down, and its keys were blue and red. James Paul White, a Boston musician, constructed in 1883 a microtonal keyboard which he called the *harmon,* and used a notation in which deviations from regular pitch were indicated by plus and minus signs. He theorized that 612 equal divisions of an octave would provide the most practical approximation to pure intonation. His instrument is preserved at the New England Conservatory of Music.

Quarter tones were used by composers to suggest the Greek enharmonic mode through the centuries. Halévy incorporated a few quarter tones into his symphonic poem *Prométhée enchaîné,* and Berlioz wrote an interesting account of its 1st performance in *Revue et Gazette Musicale de Paris* (Mar. 1849): "The employment of quarter tones in Halévy's work is episodic and very short, and produces a species of groaning sound in the strings, but its strangeness seems perfectly justified here and enhances considerably the wistful prosody of the music."

It may be mentioned that the author composed an overture for strings, trumpet, and percussion in the PHRYGIAN MODE, using as his theme an extant version of an ancient Greek tune from the accompaniment to the tragedy *Orestes,* produced in Athens in 400 B.C.; he conducted this arrangement at the Hollywood Bowl (1933). In order to produce the needed 2 quarter tones, the open strings of the violins, violas, and cellos were tuned a quarter tone up, with the rest of the string instruments preserving the ordinary pitch. The Romanian composer Georges Enesco inserted a transitional passage in quarter tones in his opera *Oedipe,* produced in Paris in 1936. In this case, too, the composer's intention was to evoke the effect of the ancient Greek enharmonic scale.

Other equal temperaments have been proposed. Perhaps the most complete research in this direction was done by Joseph Yasser in his book *A Theory of Evolving Tonality* (N.Y., 1932), in which he proposed a system of "supra-tonality," with accidentals designated by special symbols for supra-sharp, supra-flat, and supra-natural of the synthetic scale. He believed that 19-equal temperament was the most logical step after the present system. Krenek experimented with 13-equal temperament; Stockhausen used temperaments for which the basic interval was something other than the octave. There is also the concept of *macrotonality,* in which there are fewer than 12 equally tempered notes per octave.

The return to ancient Greek theory also inspired composers to revive the just intonation system, where intervallic relationships were determined rationally, not logarithmically. Perhaps the most ambitious project in justly tuned music was undertaken by the American composer Harry Partch, who devised an asymmetrical scale of 43 unequal intervals in an octave, and adapted or constructed a number of special instruments, among them a microtonal viola, a reed organ, marimbas (including one in diamond shape), plucked dulcimers, and modern versions of the Greek kithara. His work has influenced many subsequent composers, instrument makers, and theorists.

It must be said that in actual performance on instruments manipulated by humans, quarter tones and other microtonal divisions are only rough approximations of their true acoustical value. With the advent of electronic instruments and computer music, it became possible to reproduce microtonal intervals with absolute precision. But despite the extraordinary new resources, composers of the avant-garde have remained singularly indifferent to the thorough exploration of microtones; the Polish modernist Krzysztof Penderecki has used quarter tones in massive multioctave tone clusters, creating powerful sonorous complexes in icositetraphonic harmony, but intervallic and harmonic relationships involving microtones are not an issue.

A curious disquisition on quarter tones and other fractional intervals as a logical extension of Chopin's sensitive use of chromatic harmony is contained in a pamphlet by Johanna Kinkel, *Acht Briefe an eine Freundin über Clavier-Unterricht* (Stuttgart, 1852):

> As we wonder what it is that grips us and fills us with foreboding and delight in Chopin's music, we are apt to find a solution that might appear to many as pure fantasy, namely that Chopin's intention was to release upon us a cloud of quarter tones, which now appear only as phantom doppelgänger in the shadowy realm within the intervals produced by enharmonic change.
>
> Once the quarter tones are emancipated, an entirely new world of tones will open to us. But since we have been accustomed to the long-established divisions into semitones, these new sounds will seem weird, suggest-

ing a splash of discordant waves. Yet the children of the next generation, or the one after next, will suck in these strange sounds with mother's milk, and may find in them a more stimulating and doubly rich art. Chopin seems to push at these mysterious portals; his melodies stream in colliding currents through the semitones as if groping for finer and more spiritual nuances than those that were available for his purposes. And when this door is finally sprung open, we will stand a step nearer to the eternal domain of natural sounds. As it is we can only give a weak imitation of the Aeolian harp, of the rustle of the forest, of the magical ripple of the waters, unable to render them in their true impressions, because our so-called scales made up of whole tones and semitones are too coarse and have too many gaps, while Nature possesses not only quarter-tones and eighth-tones but an infinite scale of split atoms of sound!

middle C. The C (actually, c¹) in the middle of the piano keyboard:

MIDI (Music Instrument Digital Interface). Computer language used to connect computers, synthesizers, sequencers, and other electronic musical instruments so that they may "communicate with" (send data to) each other; also, the device carrying this information. This simplifies live electroacoustic processing and output. *MIDI compatible*, able to read MIDI data; *MIDI jack*, *MIDI port*, the connecting device on electronic musical instruments intended for the MIDI.

Midi, Le. Haydn's Sym. No. 7 (1761), a sequel to his Sym. No. 6, *Le Matin*. The music of *Le Midi* is in the bright key of C major, to suggest the warm sun at midday.

Midler, Bette, lovable American singer, actress, and comedienne; b. Paterson, N.J., Dec. 1, 1945. She studied drama in Honolulu, then settled in N.Y., where she sang in a variety of gay venues, including bathhouses and clubs, and on Broadway (*Fiddler on the Roof* and *Tommy*); subsequently engaged Barry Manilow as her music director and a backup trio known as the Harlettes and developed a raucous cabaret routine through which she generated a loyal following, becoming known as "The Divine Miss M"; her 1972 album of that name won a gold record; subsequent albums of note include *Bette Midler* (1973), *Songs for the New Depression* (1976), *Live at Last* (1977), and *Broken Blossom* (1977). She starred in the film *The Rose* (1979), based on the life of Janis Joplin, for which she received an Academy Award nomination; her soundtrack LP sold in the millions; other successful films were *Down and Out in Beverly Hills* (1986), *Ruthless People* (1986), *Outrageous Fortune* (1987), and *Beaches* (1989), for which she sang the Grammy Award–winning title song, *Wind beneath My Wings*. Her covers of songs by artists as varied as Bruce Springsteen, Kurt Weill, Hoagy Carmichael, and Tom Waits evidence her great stylistic diversity. Her comedic gifts—an integral aspect of her live performances—are captured on the recording *Mud Will Be Flung Tonight* (1985), in which she revitalizes the spicy, sometimes lewd anecdotes of the late Sophie Tucker. She authored the comic memoirs *A View from a Broad* (1980) and a children's book, *The Saga of Baby Divine* (1983).

Midori (born Goto Mi Dori), prodigiously gifted Japanese wunderkind of the violin; b. Osaka, Oct. 25, 1971. She studied with her mother, Setsu Goto; in 1981 she went to the U.S., where she took violin lessons with Dorothy DeLay at the Aspen Music School and continued her training with that mentor at N.Y.'s Juilliard School. She attracted the attention of Zubin Mehta when she was 10 years old; he subsequently engaged her as a soloist with the N.Y. Phil., with which she traveled on an extensive Asian tour that included Hong Kong, Singapore, Korea, Thailand, and her native Japan. There followed concerts with the Berlin Phil., the Boston Sym. Orch., the Chicago Sym. Orch., the Cleveland and Philadelphia Orchs., the Los Angeles Phil., the London Sym. Orch., and other European and American orchs., in programs that included not only classical concertos but also modern works, under the direction of such renowned conductors—besides Mehta—as Bernstein, Previn, Maazel, C. von Dohnányi, Leppard, and Barenboim. She also attracted the attention of popular television programs, and appeared as a guest of President and Mrs. Reagan at the White House during the NBC television special

Christmas in Washington (1983). Most important, she won the admiration of orch. members for her remarkable artistic dependability. On one occasion, when a string broke on the concertmaster's violin during an orch. introduction, she demonstrated her sangfroid; since she had a few minutes to spare before her entrance as a soloist, she handed her own violin to the player and coolly changed the broken string in time to continue the performance without pause. In 1990 she made her N.Y. recital debut at Carnegie Hall

Midsommarvaka (Midsummer Vigil). First of 3 Swedish Rhapsodies for orch. by Alfvén, 1904; his most celebrated piece, performed for the 1st time in Stockholm. It was produced as a ballet under the title *La Nuit de Saint-Jean* in Paris (1920), and received over 25 performances in 4 years.

Midsummer Marriage, The. Opera by Tippett, 1955, 1st produced in London, to his own libretto. This romantically lyric but neoclassical work essays archetypal symbolism in a quasi-realistic setting. A young couple quarrel on their wedding day. They reconcile their differences by going through a series of initiations in which a clairvoyant takes part. The bride and groom achieve the needed catharsis and are spiritually united in marriage. The influence of *The Magic Flute* is made even more palpable by other characters with analogues to the Mozart opera.

Midsummer Night's Dream, A. 1. Incidental music by Mendelssohn to Shakespeare's play. The overture, op. 21, was composed in 1826, when he was 17. He later composed songs and additional instrumental music for the play (1842), including the *Wedding March*, once a staple of the marital ceremony. The music was 1st performed in its entirety in Potsdam (1843). 2. Opera by Britten, 1960, based on Shakespeare, 1st performed in Aldeburgh, England. The score is subdivided into set pieces; the idiom is deliberately eclectic, with elements of impressionism applied to the magical creatures, and the realistic scene depicted in a folklike manner.

Mi-fa. In medieval treatises, theoretical shorthand for a warning not to connect the mediant of one hexachord with the subdominant of a related hexachord without 1st making sure that imperfect intervals do not result from such a promiscuous crossbreeding. The original Latin prohibition reads, "Mi contra fa est diabolus in musica."

Mignon. Opera by A. Thomas, 1866, 1st performed in Paris. The opera is based on Goethe's novel *Wilhelm Meister's Years of Apprenticeship*. The Gypsy girl Mignon, maltreated by her people, is rescued by Meister, who indentures her as his maidservant. They are joined by a wandering minstrel who is searching for his daughter kidnapped by Gypsies. The purple threads of the romantic narrative are not nicely intertwined, for Mignon is the kidnapped girl.

migratory tonics. When tonalities are in a state of constant flux, the laws of probability will still lead to the accidental formation of *tonal centers*, notes that occur more frequently than others, much in the line of the well-known paradox that if only 3 dozen individuals are assembled at a party, the odds are even that 2 of them will have the same day and month for a birthday. Such statistically established keynotes in an otherwise free modulatory environment may be called *migratory tonics*, a term particularly suitable for works in which tonality is not renounced unequivocally.

Mikado, The, or The Town of Titipu. Comic opera by Gilbert and Sullivan, 1885, 1st produced in London. Yum-Yum is a delicious Japanese maiden whose guardian hopes to marry her. The heir to the Japanese throne, disguised as a minstrel, also loves her. Since in Japan flirting is punishable by death, beheadings are frequently scheduled. However, the Lord High Executioner has an innate aversion to killing any living thing. When the Mikado's son reveals his identity, the Emperor is elated, cancels all executions, and lets his son marry Yum-Yum. *The Mikado* is banned in Japan, as it makes fun of the Emperor.

Miki, Minoru, Japanese composer; b. Tokushima, Mar. 16, 1930. He studied with Ifukube and Ikenouchi at the National Univ. of Fine Arts and Music in Tokyo (1951–55); was a founder of the Nihon Ongaku Shudan (Pro Musica Nipponia; 1964), an ensemble dedicated to performing new music for traditional Japanese instruments; later served as its artistic director. He lectured at the Tokyo College of Music; was founder-director of Utayomi-za (1986), a musical-opera theater. His works include operas; syms.; Western and Japanese orch. music; concertos for koto, marimba, Japanese classical trio, and percussion; solo and chamber works, most involving Japanese instruments; and vocal and choral works.

Mikrokosmos. Set of 6 books of progressive piano pieces by Bartók, 1926–39. The remarkable innovation of this collection is its introduction of modal scales and asymmetric rhythmic patterns. Many pieces bear picturesque titles, such as *From the Diary of a Fly*; others indicate the technical substratum, as in *Imitation Reflected, Accents*, etc. The concluding *6 Dances in Bulgarian Rhythm* are not only excellent valedictory pieces, they also give an informative glance at the rhythmic and harmonic structures that the composer discovered during his many years of ethnomusicological research.

Milanov, Zinka (Kunc), famous Croatian-American soprano; b. Zagreb, May 17, 1906; d. N.Y., May 30, 1989. She studied at the Zagreb Academy of Music, then with Milka Ternina, Maria Kostrencic, and Fernando Carpi; made her debut as Leonora in *Il Trovatore* in Ljubljana (1927); subsequently was principal soprano of the Zagreb Opera (1928–35), where she sang in over 300 performances in Croatian. After appearing at Prague's German Theater (1936), she was invited by Toscanini to sing in his perfor-

mance of the Verdi Requiem at the Salzburg Festival (1937). She then made her Metropolitan Opera debut in N.Y. as Leonora (1937), and was one of the outstanding members on its roster (1937–41; 1942–47; 1950–66); gave her farewell performance there as Maddalena in *Andrea Chénier* (April 1966). In addition to appearing in San Francisco and Chicago, she also sang at Buenos Aires's Teatro Colón (1940–42), Milan's La Scala (1950), and London's Covent Garden (1966–67). She married Predrag Milanov in 1937, but they were divorced in 1946; she then married Ljubomir Ilic in 1947. Blessed with a voice of translucent beauty, she became celebrated for her outstanding performances of roles in operas by Verdi and Puccini. Her brother was the pianist and composer Božidar Kunc (b. Zagreb, July 18, 1903; d. Detroit, Apr. 1, 1964).

Milhaud, Darius

≈≈≈ ≈≈≈ ≈≈≈ ≈≈≈ ≈≈≈

Eminent French composer; b. Aix-en-Provence, Sept. 4, 1892; d. Geneva, June 22, 1974. He was the descendant of an old Jewish family, settled in Provence for many centuries. His father was a merchant of almonds; there was a piano in the house, and Milhaud improvised melodies as a child; he then began to take violin lessons. He entered the Paris Cons. in 1909, almost at the age limit for enrollment; studied with Berthelier (violin), Lefèvre (ensemble), Leroux (harmony), Gédalge (counterpoint), Widor (composition and fugue), and d'Indy (conducting); he played violin in the student orch. under Dukas. He received 1st "accessit" in violin and counterpoint, and 2nd in fugue; won the Prix Lepaulle for composition. While still a student he wrote music in a bold, modernistic manner; became associated with Satie, Cocteau, and Claudel. When Claudel was appointed French minister to Brazil, he engaged Milhaud as his secretary; they sailed for Rio de Janeiro early in 1917; returned to Paris (via the West Indies and N.Y.) shortly after the armistice of Nov. 1918.

Milhaud's name became known to a larger public as a result of a newspaper article by Henri Collet in *Comoedia* (Jan. 16, 1920), grouping him with 5 other French composers of modern tendencies (Auric, Durey, Honegger, Poulenc, and Tailleferre) under the sobriquet "Les 6," even though the association was stylistically fortuitous. In 1922 he visited the U.S.; lectured at Harvard Univ., Princeton Univ., and Columbia Univ.; appeared as pianist

Darius Milhaud with Leslie Caron and Gene Kelly, c. 1950s

COURTESY FRANK DRIGGS COLLECTION

and composer in his own works; in 1925 he traveled in Italy, Germany, Austria, and Russia; returning to France, he devoted himself mainly to composition and teaching. At the outbreak of World War II he was in Aix-en-Provence; in July 1940 he went to the U.S.; taught at Mills College in Oakland, Calif. In 1947 he returned to France; was appointed prof. at the Paris Cons., but continued to visit the U.S. as conductor and teacher almost annually, despite arthritis, which compelled him to conduct while seated; he retained his post at Mills College until 1971; then settled in Geneva.

Exceptionally prolific from his student days, he wrote a great number of works in every genre; introduced a modernistic type of music drama, "opera à la minute," and also the "miniature sym." He experimented with new stage techniques, incorporating cinematic interludes; also successfully revived the Greek type of tragedy with vocal accompaniment. He composed works for electronic instruments, and demonstrated his contrapuntal skill in such compositions as his 2 string quartets (No. 14 and No. 15), which can be played together as a string octet. He was the 1st to exploit polytonality in a consistent and deliberate manner; he applied the exotic rhythms of Latin America and the West Indies in many of his lighter works; of these, his *Saudades do Brasil* are particularly popular; Brazilian movements are also found in his *Scaramouche* and *Le Boeuf sur le toit*; in some of his works he drew upon the resources of jazz. His ballet *La Création du monde* (1923), portraying the Creation in terms of Negro cosmology, constitutes the earliest example of the use of the blues and jazz in a symphonic score, anticipating Gershwin in this respect.

Despite this variety of means and versatility of forms, Milhaud succeeded in establishing a style that was distinctly and identifiably his own; his melodies are nostalgically lyrical or vivaciously rhythmical, according to mood; his instrumental writing is of great complexity and difficulty and yet entirely within the capacities of modern virtuoso technique; he arranged many of his works in several versions. For an extremely prolific and facile composer, Milhaud's music is remarkably consistent in quality. Among his works are operas, incidental music, orch.l works, numerous sets of songs, many set to the poems of Paul Claudel, several psalms and other religious works, and works for piano. His essays were 1st collected in *Études* (1926).

militarmente (It.). In military (march) style. *Alla militare*, in the style of a march.

military band. BAND, MILITARY.

Military Polonaise. Chopin's Polonaise in A Major, No. 1, op. 40 (1838).

Military Symphony. Haydn's Sym. No. 100 in G Major, 1794, the 8th of his 12 symphonies written for performance in London during his tours there. The composer's nickname refers to the orchestration of the 2nd movement, which includes not only the standard timpani but a triangle, cymbals, and the bass drum, practically an entire setup for JANIZARY MUSIC of the pseudo-Turkish type. This and the *Surprise Sym.* are among the most popular of Haydn's syms.

Milk and Honey. Musical by J. Herman, 1961. The plot deals with love and heartaches among American tourists in Israel. A celebration of the 4th of July in Jerusalem gives an occasion for an exciting dance, *Independence Day Hora*; also includes *Shalom*.

Miller, (Alton) **Glenn,** famous American trombonist and bandleader; b. Clarinda, Iowa, Mar. 1, 1904; d. in an airplane accident flying from London to Paris, Dec. 15, 1944. He spent his formative years in Fort Morgan, Colo., where he began his musical training; played with the local Boyd Senter Orch. (1921) and took courses at the Univ. of Colorado; after performing with Ben Pollack's band on the West Coast (1924–28), he followed Pollack to N.Y. and then became active as a freelance musician; helped to found an orch. for Ray Noble (1934), and subsequently studied orchestration with Joseph Schillinger; began experimenting with special effects, combining clarinets with saxophones in the same register.

He organized his 1st band in 1937, but it failed to find an audience and dissolved in 1938; that same year he organized another band, which caught on only in 1939 through its radio broadcasts and recordings. It subsequently became one of the most successful aggregations of the day, producing such popular recordings as *Moonlight Serenade* (1939), *In the Mood* (1939), *Tuxedo Junction* (1940), *Chattanooga Choo Choo* (1941), and *A String of Pearls* (1941); it also appeared in the films *Sun Valley Serenade* (1941) and *Orchestra Wives* (1942).

Miller joined the U.S. Army Air Force as a captain in 1942 and put together a band for entertaining the troops; it was based in England from 1944. A film, *The Glenn Miller Story*, was produced in 1953.

millimetrization. Term introduced by Villa-Lobos to describe the transfer of mathematical curves or outlines of photographs onto graph paper, precise to a millimeter. His best-known piece arranged according to millimetrization is *The New York Skyline* (1940).

Millöcker, Carl, Austrian conductor and composer; b. Vienna, Apr. 29, 1842; d. Baden, near Vienna, Dec. 31, 1899. His father was a jeweler, and Millöcker was destined for that trade but showed irrepressible musical inclinations and learned music as a child; played the flute in a theater orch. at 16; later took courses at the Cons. of the Gesellschaft der Musikfreunde in Vienna. Upon the recommendation of Franz von Suppé, he received a post as theater conductor in Graz (1864). In 1866 he returned to Vienna; from 1869 to 1883 he was 2nd conductor of the Theater an der Wien. He suffered a stroke in 1894, which left him partially paralyzed. As a composer, Millöcker possessed a natural gift for melodious music; although his popularity was never as great as that of Johann Strauss, Jr., or Lehár, his operettas, e.g., *Der Bettelstudent* (1882), captured the spirit of Viennese life.

Milnes, Sherrill (Eustace), distinguished American baritone; b. Downers Grove, Ill., Jan. 10, 1935. He learned to play piano and violin at home, then played tuba in a school band; after a period as a medical student at North Central College in Naperville, Ill., he turned to music; subsequently studied voice with Andrew White at Drake Univ. in Des Moines and with Hermanus Baer at Northwestern Univ. He sang in choral performances under Margaret Hillis in Chicago; then was a member of the chorus at the Santa Fe Opera, where he received his 1st opportunity to sing minor operatic roles. In 1960 he joined Boris Goldovsky's Boston-based opera company and toured widely with it. He met Rosa Ponselle in Baltimore in 1961, and she coached him in several roles; he 1st appeared with the Baltimore Civic Opera as Gerard in *Andrea Chénier* in 1961.

He made his European debut as Figaro in *Il Barbiere di Siviglia* at the Teatro Nuovo in Milan (1964); later that year he made his 1st appearance at the N.Y. City Opera, singing the role of Valentin in *Faust*. His Metropolitan Opera debut in N.Y. followed (1965), in the same role. He rose to a stel-

lar position at the Metropolitan, being acclaimed for both vocal and dramatic abilities; also sang with other opera houses in the U.S. and Europe. His notable roles include Don Giovanni, Escamillo, the Count di Luna, Tonio, Iago, Barnaba, Rigoletto, and Scarpia.

milonga. South American dance song, popular in the southern part of the continent. Its characteristics include a polyrhythm of 2/4 against 6/8, improvised vocal duels, lighthearted texts, standard verse structures, and refrains in parallel 3rds.

Milstein, Nathan (Mironovich), celebrated Russianborn American violinist; b. Odessa, Dec. 31, 1903. His father was a well-to-do merchant in woolen goods; his mother was an amateur violinist who gave him his 1st lessons. He then began to study with Piotr Stoliarsky in Odessa, remaining under his tutelage until 1914; then went to St. Petersburg, where he entered the class of Leopold Auer at the St. Petersburg Cons. (1915–17). He began his concert career in 1919, with his sister as piano accompanist. In Kiev he met Vladimir Horowitz, and they began giving duo recitals in 1921; later they were joined by Gregor Piatigorsky and organized a trio. Russia was just emerging from a devastating civil war, and communications with Western Europe were not established until much later.

In 1925 Milstein was able to leave Russia; he went to Berlin and then to Brussels, where he met Eugène Ysaÿe, who encouraged him in his career. He gave several recitals in Paris, then proceeded to South America. On Oct. 28, 1929, he made his American debut with the Philadelphia Orch. conducted by Stokowski. In 1942 he became an American citizen. He celebrated the 50th anniversary of his American debut in 1979 by giving a number of solo recitals and appearing as soloist with American orchs. As an avocation he began painting and drawing, arts in which he achieved a certain degree of self-satisfaction. He also engaged in teaching; held master classes at the Juilliard School of Music in N.Y., and also in Zurich. Milstein was renowned for his technical virtuosity and musical integrity. He composed a number of violin pieces, including *Paganiniana* (1954); prepared cadenzas for the violin concertos of Beethoven and Brahms.

mimesis (Grk., imitation). In 18th-century rhetorical theory, the imitation of a phrase in one voice by a similar phrase in another; mimesis is now obsolete in musical nomenclature.

mimodrama. A dramatic or musical spectacle in which the performers convey the dramatic action by gestures and choreography, without speaking; same as PANTOMIME (1).

minaccioso (It.). In a menacing or threatening manner.

Mingus, Charles, remarkable African-American jazz double-bass player, pianist, bandleader, and composer; b. Nogales, Ariz., Apr. 22, 1922; d. Cuernavaca, Mexico, Jan. 5, 1979. He was reared in Los Angeles; during his high school years he studied double bass with Red Callender and Herman Rheinschagen and composition with Lloyd Reese; after working with Barney Bigard (1942), Louis Armstrong (1943), and Lionel Hampton (1947–48), he led his own groups as "Baron Mingus" before attracting notice as a member of Red Norvo's trio (1950–51); then settled in N.Y., where he worked with Billy Taylor, Duke Ellington, Stan Getz, Art Tatum, and Bud Powell. He was head of his own recording company, Debut Records (1952–55); also became active as a composer; worked with various musicians in small combos and eventually developed a close association with Eric Dolphy.

A highly explosive individual, Mingus became known as the "angry man of jazz" for his opposition to the white commercial taint of his art form. After his 2nd recording company (Charles Mingus label, 1964–65) failed, and his financial situation became desperate, he retired from the public scene (1966–69). He resumed his career and was awarded a Guggenheim fellowship (1971) and subsequently devoted much time to composing; also led his own groups until being stricken with amyotrophic lateral scle-

Charlie Mingus, c. 1950s

rosis, which sidelined him in 1978. Mingus was a master instrumentalist and a versatile composer, producing both conventionally notated works and dictated pieces. In his unique series of works *Fables and Meditations* he achieved a style that effectively erased the lines between jazz improvisation and notated composition.

His influence is likely incalculable. His most important work, the 2-hour *Epitaph* for 30 Instruments, which was discovered by his wife several years after his death, received its premiere performance posthumously in N.Y. on June 3, 1989. Among his best recordings are *The Black Lady and the Sinner, The Town Hall Concert, Goodbye Pork Pie Hat, Jazz Composers Workshop, Mingus Dynasty, 3 or 4 Shades of Blue, Reincarnation of a Lovebird, Pithecanthropus Erectus, Nostalgia in Times Square, Mingus Moves, Meditations on Integration,* and *Mingus in Wonderland.*

miniature score. An orch.l score reproduced in a small size so that it can be easily used for study purposes. Full scores of symphonic works, chamber music, and even complete operas began publication in Germany in the 19th century. In pocket size, they were convenient to carry around for study purposes, or for reading while listening to the actual music played. The most active music publisher of miniature scores was Eulenberg of Leipzig.

minim (U.K.). A half note. *Minim rest,* a half rest.

minima. In medieval mensural music, a note value, indicated by a black diamond with a stem; depending on the context, 2 or 3 minimas equal 1 SEMIBREVE.

minimalism

A neologism for a school of composition, influenced by Cage and contemporaneous painting of the 1950s, in which a pointillistic musical texture prevails, with a generous use of silence and the evolution of graphic and verbal scores. 2. More recently, a conceptual term denoting works based on the repetition and gradual alteration of short rhythmic and/or melodic figures; also referred to as *process music*.

Music history has progressed for millennia in a parallel evolution of animals species, from simple cellules of unaccompanied voice to grandiose edifices of sounds consisting of voices with a variety of manufactured instruments, ultimately including electronically produced tones. Then, like an enormous dinosaur whose very bulk made it impossible for him to find sufficient food to survive, the symphonic and operatic forms developed in the 19th century could no longer sustain their acoustical size. As early as 1918, Stravinsky declared his belief that music had reached its maximum of possible dimensions, and he urged composers to write in limited forms. The direction from Lilliputian to Brobdingnagian works had to be reversed once again, initiating musical NEOCLASSICISM. But this was not enough; composers had to cope with the untempered growth of dissonant counterpoint and concomitant loss of the sense of harmony and tonality.

Accordingly, composers of the last quarter of the 20th century restored triadic harmony. Modulations were reduced to phases; a single note would change in an arpeggio signalizing the formation of a new inversion and remain there for a number of bars. Dissonances occurred now and then, but a consonant *quietus* would become the rule. A novel term emerged to describe the unexpected turn of events, *minimalism*, a musical synecdoche, *a pars pro toto*. It came to life in the form of a fossilized renewal, mainly in America. Parallel to the purification of tonal masses there was a gradual abandonment of rhythmic complexity. Repetitions of established patterns became the norm. Other influences came from the Pacific Rim, from India and Indonesia, with their hypnotic drone effect and repetitive interlocking musical patterns that had been a part of Western musical culture since the late 19th century.

Among American pioneers of the 2nd school of minimalism were La Monte Young, Terry Riley, Steve Reich, and Philip Glass. Young professed to revive the Pythagorean modes, using retuned pianos and playing with the dampers lifted throughout. In Riley's 1964 piece *In C* for any instruments, musicians play in the key of C major until the last few measures, where he allows the passing entry of an F-sharp. Reich reinforced his technique by a study of African drumming, utilizing shifting phase and other repetitive techniques in works for similar and mixed ensembles. Glass enriched the uniformity of repetitive music by writing music for surrealistically imagined stage plays of sometimes inordinate length and heterogeneous content, such as *Einstein on the Beach* (collab. with Robert Wilson, 1976). Less extreme is the minimalist idiom of John Adams, whose music embraces in its points of inspiration such contrasting methods as in *Harmonium* for Chorus and Orch. (1981) and the sensational opera *Nixon in China* (1987). There seem to be no pure followers in Europe, though there are exponents elsewhere, such as the Dutch composer Louis Andriessen.

Minkus, Léon (Aloisius Ludwig), Austrian violinist and composer; b. Vienna, Mar. 23, 1826; d. there, Dec. 7, 1917. He went to Russia in his youth and was engaged by Prince Yusupov as concertmaster of his serf orch. in St. Petersburg (1853–56). From 1862 to 1872 he was concertmaster of the Bolshoi Theater in Moscow. In 1869 the Bolshoi Theater produced his ballet *Don Quixote* to the choreography of the famous Russian ballet master Petipa; its success was extraordinary, and its appeal to the Russian audiences was so durable that the work retained its place in the repertoire of Russian ballet companies for more than a century, showing no signs of diminishing popularity. Equally popular was his ballet *La Bayadère*, produced by Petipa in St. Petersburg in 1877; another successful ballet was his *La Fiametta, or The Triumph of Love*, originally produced in Paris in 1864.

From 1872 to 1885 Minkus held the post of court composer of ballet music for the Imperial theaters in St. Petersburg; he remained in Russia until 1891, then returned to Vienna, where he lived in semiretirement until his death at the age of 91. The ballets of Minkus never took root outside Russia, but their cursive melodies and bland rhythmic formulas suit old-fashioned Russian choreography to the airiest *entrechat*.

Minnelli, Liza (May), successful American singer of popular music and actress; b. Los Angeles, Mar. 12, 1946. She was the daughter of the legendary songstress Judy Garland by her 2nd husband, the film director Vincente Minnelli. She dropped out of high school to devote herself exclusively to singing; made her professional debut as a singer in the 1963 off-Broadway revival of *Best Foot Forward*

(1941). In 1965 she appeared in the Broadway musical *Flora, the Red Menace*, for which she won a Tony Award. She established herself as a film actress in *The Sterile Cuckoo* (1969); also starred in the highly acclaimed film *Cabaret* (1972), for which she won an Academy Award. She further won Tony Awards for her 1-woman show *Liza* (1974) and for her appearance in the Broadway musical *The Act* (1977); she appeared opposite Dudley Moore in the romantic film comedy *Arthur* (1981) and its sequel, *Arthur on the Rocks* (1988). After starring in the musical *The Rink* (1983–84), she underwent treatment for drug and alcohol dependency in 1984. Following rehabilitation, she made extensive tours in the U.S. and abroad. In 1997 she briefly took over the lead from Julie Andrews in *Victor, Victoria*.

Minnesinger (Ger.). The German aristocratic poet-musicians of the 12th to 14th centuries, predecessors to the MEISTERSINGER. Minnesingers traveled through central Europe singing lyric songs in royal German courts, ducal castles, and villages. Like their Frankish counterparts, the TROUVÈRES and TROUBADOURS, they were mostly of noble birth and regarded their profession as an expression of knightly valor and idealistic dedication to the real or imaginary ladies of their hearts (*Minne* is Old German for "love"). With the end of the Crusades, and with a certain stabilization of the German states, the role of the Minnesingers declined, and the cultivation of lyric or heroic songs gradually was transferred to the town guilds and local craftsmen represented by them (*Meistersinger*).

minor (from Lat., small; It. *minore*; Fr. *mineur*; Ger. *moll*). 1. Intervals within a natural minor scale between the tonic (1st degree) and the 2nd, 3rd, 6th, and 7th scale degrees. 2. A type of scale (e.g., A-minor scale), key (A minor), or triad (A-minor chord, with a minor 3rd and perfect 5th above the root). In each case the 3rd degree of the scale forms an interval of a minor 3rd with the root.

minstrel. In the Middle Ages, professional musicians who sang or declaimed poems, often of their own composition, to a simple instrumental accompaniment. They were employed by royalty and feudal lords in Europe. They served as entertainers, players upon the lute or the flute, jesters, and sometimes as participants in domestic and political intrigues. The term *minstrel* 1st appeared in the 14th century and was derived from the French appellation *ménéstrier* (minister). With the decay of feudal society, the profession of minstrels disappeared, but it was revived in America as Negro min-

strelsy. Toward the middle of the 19th century, white minstrel groups were organized to perform in blackface in a repertoire of genuine Negro songs and newly minted numbers known as "Ethiopian songs." Stephen Foster was the greatest composer of such songs, even though he never lived in the South and was not personally familiar with the conditions of Negro life or slavery. The American minstrel show became standardized about 1830 with the introduction of a theatrical type of performance called JIM CROW.

minuet (Fr. *menuet*; It. *minuetto*; Ger. *Menuett*). The most popular court dance in triple time danced by couples, distinguished by the stately grace of its choreography and the symmetry of its musical structure. The standard minuet consisted of 3 sections, of which the 1st and 3rd were identical; the middle section, set in the dominant, subdominant, or relative key, was called the trio because it was written usually for 3 instruments, whereas the minuet proper was usually arranged for a fuller ensemble.

It is generally surmised that the minuet derived from a provincial French dance tune, but as a mature form it was introduced at the court of Louis XIV. Lully, his court musician, wrote a number of minuets for royal balls; it is said that the King himself often ventured to dance to Lully's music, although his mature corpulent figure was ill-adapted for choreographic exercise. The vogue of minuet dancing spread to all the courts of Europe; it was tremendously popular in Russia, Spain, and Italy, but less so in England or Germany. Eventually the minuet became an integral part of the Baroque instrumental suite, and in Classic sonatas and symphonies. In the 19th century the minuet yielded its place in sonatas and syms. to the more whirlwind mood of the SCHERZO, which usually conserved the 3/4 time signature as well as the characteristic interpolation of the trio.

Minute Waltz. A nickname for Chopin's Waltz in D-flat Major, op. 64, which is supposedly possible to negotiate in about 1 minute. Omitting the repeats, the time can be cut to 48 seconds. But a digitally controlled synthesizer can reduce the time to a few seconds.

miracle plays. Sacred dramas, often with music, which were popular in England in the Middle Ages; the stories were usually on biblical subjects or parables; later examples of this genre were called *moralities*.

Miraculous Mandarin, The. Pantomime by Bartók, 1926. The subject is sordid; it relates the story of a mandarin's lust for a prostitute who is set on robbing him, but the mandarin is so sturdy that he survives all attempts to kill him by her accomplices. Both on account of the subject and its dissonant music, the work had a difficult time obtaining performances. After its production in Cologne (1926) it was taken off the repertoire by order of Mayor Konrad Adenauer, the future chancellor of West Germany.

Miranda, Carmen (born Maria do Carmo Miranda da Cunha), charismatic Portuguese-American singer of popular music and actress; b. Marco de Canaveses, near Lisbon, Feb. 9, 1909; d. Beverly Hills, Calif., Aug. 5, 1955. She spent her formative years in Rio de Janeiro; after performing throughout South America she made her 1st appearance on Broadway in 1939 in the revue *The Streets of Paris*; she was dubbed the "Brazilian Bombshell." She went on to gain an extensive following via many film appearances, recordings, nightclub engagements, and television appearances. She is particularly remembered for her spiky high-heeled shoes and fantastic headdresses made of fruit; in the movie musical *The Gang's All Here* (1943), with lavish choreography by Busby Berkeley, she comically careened her way through the number *The Lady in the Tutti Frutti Hat*.

Mireille. Opera by Gounod, 1864, 1st produced in Paris. There are 2 versions; in one, Mireille, daughter of a wealthy farmer, dies at the end of a story involving her love for a poor basket weaver, the attempts of her father to impose another man as her husband, the resurrection of the murdered basket weaver by a sorceress from the Valley of Hell, and the Church of Saint Mary-by-the-Sea, where Mireille collapses after running through the fields on a hot sunny day without a hat. The 2nd version provides a happy ending with yet another resurrection, this time of Mireille, by the saints.

mirliton (Fr.). Small tubular musical instrument, the sound of which is produced by a membrane set vibrating by the human voice; same as the KAZOO.

Miroirs. Piano suite by Ravel, 1906; its 5 movements are entitled *Noctuelles, Oiseaux tristes, Un Barque sur l'océan, Alborada del gracioso,* and *La Vallée des cloches.* They are among the finest specimens of impressionist piano writing. The mirrors of the title reflect nocturnal moths, wistful birds, a lonesome boat on the ocean, the morning serenade of a jester, and the valley of bells. The suite was 1st performed in Paris.

mirror canon. CANON CANCRIZANS.

Carmen Miranda, 1939

Miserere. The opening Latin word of the 50th Psalm, in the Roman Catholic (Vulgate) numbering; thereby, musical settings of the Psalm. The imploration "Have mercy" is a part of the Holy Week Service known as TENEBRAE (darkness). There is a credible story that Mozart as a small boy attended the performance of a Miserere by Gregorio Allegri (1582–1652) in the Vatican, memorized the entire setting for 9 voices, and wrote it down shortly afterward. Allegri's Miserere was an exclusive property of the Papal choir, and Mozart's feat of memory must have caused considerable discomfiture, but the piece was eventually publ. and became famous.

Miserly Knight, The. Opera by Rachmaninoff, 1906, after a play of Pushkin, 1st performed in Moscow. The old miser has accumulated a treasure trove of gold, but he refuses to let anyone, even his own son, share in his fortune. In desperation the youth goes to the duke of the land for help.

His father publicly accuses him of planning his murder. But as he utters the monstrous charge, he is seized with mortal pain and dies with the words, "Where are the keys to my treasure?" The score was composed when Rachmaninoff was only 22 years old; it has the charm of unpretentious Romantic flair.

Miss Julie. Opera by Rorem, 1965, after the drama by Strindberg, 1st produced in N.Y. The play is typical of Strindberg's preoccupations with social contradictions. Miss Julie is of noble birth; strangely, she falls under the spell of the family majordomo, who dominates her so fully that at his behest she robs her own father. Distressed and repentant, she commits suicide. The music is appropriately melodramatic, set in a moderately modernistic manner.

Miss Liberty. Musical by I. Berlin, 1949. In 1885 New York City, 2 famous newspaper editors (James Bordon Bennett and Joseph Pulitzer) are waging a publicity war for the coverage of the recently arrived Statue of Liberty, presented by France to N.Y. Their representatives are trying to locate the Paris model for the statue; this search involves a romance between a putative model and the reporter who brings her to N.Y. She is accused of fraudulent misrepresentation, but Pulitzer proves her innocence. In the finale she sings a song to the text engraved at the base of the statue, "Give me your tired, your poor."

missa (Lat.). MASS. *Missa brevis*, short Mass; *Missa cantata*, sung (High) Mass; *Missa lecta*, spoken (Low) Mass; *Missa pro defun[c]tis*, REQUIEM; *Missa solemnis*, High Mass.

Missa Luba. Choral work by David Fanshawe (1942–), an adaptation of the ORDINARY to southern African choral singing and percussion accompaniment.

Missa Papae Marcelli. Mass by Palestrina, publ. 1567, bearing the name of Pope Marcellus II, whose reign lasted 3 weeks in 1555. It is set in a homophonic style quite different from his earlier polyphonic works. It was supposed that Palestrina wrote this Mass at the behest of Marcellus in response to the papal criticism of the lack of clarity in the text of polyphonic religious works. While this story may be legendary, it is not inconceivable that Palestrina chose to honor a deceased pope in this way, as the Council of Trent was fighting over musical matters vigorously, and the Mass was without a CANTUS FIRMUS or PARODY model.

Missouri Waltz. Popular piece, 1914, by Frederick Knight Logan (1871–1928), who was reluctant to admit its authorship because of a lamentable lack of musical quality in it. He 1st published it as a piano solo, with his name on the cover as arranger. But when the words were added in 1916, the sheet music sold a million copies and was adopted by the State of Missouri as its official song. President Harry Truman loved to play the piano, and the *Missouri Waltz* became associated, for better or worse, with his image and period.

Mr. Brouček's Excursion to the Moon **and** *Mr. Brouček's Excursion into the 15th Century.* Two fantasy operas by Janáček, 1908–17, premiered in Prague, 1920. A tipsy burgher imagines himself traveling to the moon (49 years before the actual landing) and then back in time into the 15th century with the Hussites.

Mister President. Musical by I. Berlin, his last, 1962. The President of the U.S. makes an informal trip to Moscow, where he engages in friendly talk, not with Soviet officials but with simple workers. But his unusual method of diplomacy arouses an uproar in the U.S., and he is defeated at the next election. A romance between the President's daughter and a secret service man provides love interest. Includes *Empty Pockets Full of Love* and *Meat and Potatoes.*

Mr. Sandman. Song by Pat Ballard, 1954; someone wrote a Christmas parody on it with the name *Mr. Santa.*

Mr. Tambourine Man. Folk-rock ballad by Bob Dylan that was the Byrds' 1st number 1 hit in 1965.

Mrs. Robinson. Theme song from the 1968 film *The Graduate,* written by Paul Simon and a number 1 hit for him with his crooning partner, Art Garfunkel.

misterioso (It.). Mysteriously; suggestive of hidden meaning.

Misty. Song by Erroll Garner, 1955; a sentimental ballad that became extremely popular in Johnny Mathis's rendition.

misurato (It.). With the measure; in exact time.

mit (Ger.). With. For phrases beginning with this preposition, see noun or adjective following.

Mitchell, Joni (born Roberta Joan Anderson), Canadian singer and songwriter of popular music; b. McLeod, near

Lethbridge, Alberta, Nov. 7, 1943. She was reared in Saskatoon and took piano lessons in childhood; later learned to play guitar; attended the Alberta College of Art in Calgary for a year and sang in a local coffeehouse; then performed in Toronto, where she met and married the folksinger Chuck Mitchell; she kept his last name after their divorce. She wrote the hit song *Both Sides Now* (1968), made famous in Judy Collins's recording; Mitchell included it in her album *Clouds* (1969), which captured a Grammy Award for best folk recording in 1970. Her album *Ladies of the Canyon* (1970) attained gold status; the album *Court and Spark* (1974) also proved highly popular. In her interpretations, she closely followed the folk-song style, with an admixture of jazzy syncopation and unusual guitar tunings. For a while she collaborated with Mingus; after his death in 1979, she wrote a moving song in his memory, somewhat sacrilegiously entitled *God Must Be a Boogie Man*. Other interesting albums include *Hejira* (1976), *Don Juan's Reckless Daughter* (1978), *Dog Eat Dog* (1986), and *Chalk Mark in a Rain Storm* (1988).

Mitridate, Re di Ponto. Opera by Mozart, 1770, 1st performed in Milan. Mozart was only 14 when he wrote this work. The libretto after Racine deals with the dramatic story of Mithridates, King of Pontus, who loves a young Greek girl who is loved also by his 2 sons. All kinds of involvements ensue. Mithridates is fatally wounded in battle and urges his 2nd son to marry the girl they all love.

Mitropoulus, Dimitri, celebrated Greek-born American conductor and composer; b. Athens, Mar. 1, 1896; d. after suffering a heart attack while rehearsing Mahler's 3rd Sym. with the orch. of the Teatro alla Scala, Milan, Nov. 2, 1960. He studied piano with Wassenhoven and harmony with A. Marsick at the Odeon Cons. in Athens; wrote an opera after Maeterlinck, *Soeur Beatrice* (1918), performed at the Odeon Cons. (May 20, 1919); in 1920, after graduation from the Cons., he went to Brussels, where he studied composition with Paul Gilson; in 1921 he went to Berlin, where he took piano lessons with Busoni at the Hochschule für Musik (until 1924); concurrently was *répétiteur* at the Berlin State Opera.

He became a conductor of the Odeon Cons. orch. in Athens (1924); was its coconductor (1927–29) and principal conductor (from 1929); was also prof. of composition there (from 1930). In 1930 he was invited to conduct a concert of the Berlin Phil.; when the soloist Egon Petri became suddenly indisposed, Mitropoulos substituted for him as soloist in Prokofiev's Piano Concerto No. 3, conducting from the keyboard (1930). He played the same concerto in Paris in 1932 as a pianist-conductor, and later in the U.S. His Paris debut as a conductor (1932) obtained a spontaneous success; he conducted the most difficult works from memory, which was a novelty at the time; also led rehearsals without a score.

He made his American debut with the Boston Sym. Orch. on Jan. 24, 1936, with immediate acclaim; that same year he was engaged as music director of the Minneapolis Sym. Orch.; there he frequently performed MODERN MUSIC, including works by Schoenberg, Berg, and other representatives of the atonal school; the opposition that naturally arose was not sufficient to offset his hold on the public as a conductor of great emotional power. He resigned from the Minneapolis Sym. Orch. in 1949 to accept the post of conductor of the N.Y. Phil.; shared the podium with Stokowski for a few weeks, and in 1950 became music director. In 1956 Leonard Bernstein was engaged as associate conductor with Mitropoulos, and in 1958 succeeded him as music director. With the N.Y. Phil., Mitropoulos continued his policy of bringing out important works by European and American modernists; he also programmed modern operas (*Elektra, Wozzeck*) in concert form.

A musician of astounding technical ability, Mitropoulos became very successful with the general public as well as with the musical vanguard whose cause he so boldly espoused. While his time was engaged mainly in the U.S., Mitropoulos continued to appear as guest conductor in Europe; he also appeared on numerous occasions as conductor at the Metropolitan Opera in N.Y. (debut conducting *Salome*, 1954) and at various European opera theaters. He became an American citizen in 1946. As a composer Mitropoulos was one of the earliest among Greek composers to write in a distinctly modern idiom.

Mittelsatz (Ger.). Middle section of a movement or piece.

mixed cadence. A form of authentic cadence in which chords other than the tonic and dominant are involved, e.g., V–VI–II^6–V^7–I.

mixed chorus. A chorus comprised of both male and female voices, traditionally with all 4 basic voice types represented (soprano, alto, tenor, bass), with or without divisions.

mixed media. Works in which musical, dramatic, verbal, literary, etc. elements are conjoined in a single composition, usually in novel ways. Musicians of the AVANT-GARDE are increasingly laboring toward the coordination and unification of modern musical productions with those of other arts—painting, sculpture, phonograph recording, theater, radio, television, electronics. The practice represents in fact a return to the ancient ideal of unity of liberal arts, with music occupying the honorable position as *ancilla artis*. This tendency has generated a number of novel developments of catalytic artistic powers.

Mixolydian mode. A mode corresponding to the progression from G up to G on the white keys of the piano (G–A–B–C–D–E–F–G). Although the word is Greek, the Mixolydian mode is not identical with the ancient Greek mode of the same name. To the modern ear it sounds like a major scale with a lowered 7th degree, thus devoid of a LEADING TONE; it therefore lends itself naturally to attractive plagal cadences. Bartók among others made effective use of the peculiarities of this mode; it is strongly associated with Irish-British traditional music and its American counterparts.

mixture. A compound auxiliary flue stop with from 3 to 6 ranks of pipes, sounding as many harmonics of any note played. The effect produced corresponds to RIPIENO (replenished sound), resulting in what is known as FULL organ.

Mlada. Opera by Rimsky-Korsakov, 1892; premiered in St. Petersburg. Although the action takes place in the Slavic settlement on the Baltic shore in the 10th century, the cast of characters is mostly preternatural. Mlada herself is a dead princess who visits her fiancé in his dreams. Slavic apparitions tell him that Mlada was murdered by the girl he now plans to marry. He swears vengeance and kills the accused murderess. He dies too, and rejoins Mlada in heaven.

M.M. 1. Trademark of Maelzel's METRONOME, invented 1816. 2. More commonly, an abbrev. for "metronome marking."

mobile (from Lat. *movēre*, to move; It.). 1. Readily responsive to emotion or impulse. 2. In modern sculpture, a delicately balanced construction of metal or wood, easily swayed by gentle flow of air. Modern composers have adopted this term to describe a similarly flexible melorhythmic structure, usually scored for a small number of instruments and characterized by a fine intervallic equilibrium, most often maintained by serial arrangements.

mobile form. A term used, with obvious debt to the sculptor Alexander Calder, to describe works composed in

such a way that sections may be arranged variously in time without disturbing structural integrity; also referred to as *open form*. Stockhausen and Roman Haubenstock-Ramati (1919–93) were among the exponents of mobile form.

modal harmony. The harmonic possibilities derived from church, exotic, mixed, or invented modes, apart from tonal harmony, which concerns the common major and minor keys. Modal harmony may or may not operate on the tonic-dominant principle; some modes are free from tonal resolution altogether.

modality. A 20th-century term applied to a revival of diatonic modes other than major and minor. A systematic avoidance of authentic cadences with a raised 7th degree in minor keys is the most important manifestation of modern modality. A favored cadence in modern modal music is the progression of the subdominant major triad to the tonic minor in the Dorian mode, thus mixing both major and minor scale elements. Modulations into other keys are accomplished by direct landing on the intended tonic triad from any convenient point of the scale. While flatted-7th chords are freely used in modal works, the dominant-7th chord, with its mandatory resolution into the tonic, is studiously avoided.

Chromatic harmony is incompatible with the spirit of modality, but a chromatic melody may be harmonized in spacious triads, which preserves the feeling of modality. A corollary of modality is the use of harmonic progressions in triads rather than their inversions, often giving an impression of exotic origin. Debussy used triadic harmonies in modal writing to allude to Greek melos; Ravel used modality to conjure up the aura of times long past. The masters of the Russian national school, particularly Mussorgsky, resorted to modal progressions to evoke the spirit of the Russian soul. Most curious is the application of broad modalities used by Stravinsky in *Le Sacre du printemps*, where, despite the prevalence of acrid dissonant harmonies, the inner triadic structures are always in evidence. While most modal compositions follow the basic rules of tonal connections in contrary motion, some modern composers adopt the practice of moving triadic formations in parallel lines. Vaughan Williams, Prokofiev, Villa-Lobos, Casella, Copland, and others project the sense of modality by shifting triadic masses in parallel sequences. In many modal writings, pedal points supply a sonorous foundation, indicating the eventual tonic of the work.

mode. 1. A generic term applied to ancient Greek melodic progressions and to church scales established in the

Middle Ages and codified in the system of Gregorian chant. The intervals of the Greek modes were counted downward, and those of the medieval modes were counted upward, so the intervallic contents were different between the Greek and the church systems. However, the church modes retained the Greek names of the modes. If played on the white keys of the piano, the church modes are: from C to C, Ionian; from D to D, Dorian; from E to E, Phrygian; from F to F, Lydian; from G to G, Mixolydian; from A to A, Aeolian; and from B to B, Locrian (theoretical). The modes continued to underlie all Western music through the 17th century, then gradually gave way to the tonal major and minor keys. 2. The distinction between a major key (mode) and minor key (mode). 3. Any scalar pattern of intervals, either indigenous to a culture (Indian, Japanese, Indonesian, etc.) or invented. 4. A system of rhythmic notation used in the 13th century (MENSURAL NOTATION).

moderato (It.; Fr. *modéré*). At a moderate tempo or rate of speed. *Allegro moderato*, moderately fast.

moderazione, con (It.). Moderate in tempo or emotion.

modern music. American colloquialism for contemporary dance music and popular songs. In the card catalogue of the British Museum, works written after 1800 are included in a section marked "Modern Music." Medieval MSS dealing with musical theory often open with the phrase "Brevitate gaudent moderni." The moderns that relished brevity were, in the opinion of the anonymous authors of these treatises, the adherents of ARS NOVA. In present classical usage *modern music* refers to that written since 1900. Variants may include 20th-century Music, New Music, Music of Our Time, Music of Today, and Contemporary Music.

modernism. Musical composition as it developed early in the 20th century, in which modulation from one key to another reached complete freedom of diatonic and chromatic progressions, and dissonances acquired equal rights with traditional chords; several keys could be combined in a technique called POLYTONALITY, and the melody was allowed to veer away from its tonal foundations, becoming sometimes completely atonal. This sensibility of progress and "the new" that emerged *c.* 1910 was expressed in the paintings of Picasso and Kandinsky, the novels of Joyce and Proust, and the music of Schoenberg and Stravinsky; later supplanted by *postmodernism*, which refers to a relaxation of concern with matters of time, history, and progression.

moderno, -a (It.). Modern. *Alla moderna*, in modern style.

modes of limited transposition. For Messiaen, modes which contain repeating intervallic units and thus can only be transposed a limited number of times before the identical set is repeated; discussed in *Technique de mon langage musical* (2 vols., Paris, 1944).

modinha. Brazilian and Portuguese art song of the 18th and 19th centuries. Sentimental in tone, the modinha was usually accompanied by guitar; its originally simple qualities changed with the influence of operatic aria, leading to elaborate melodies and some ornamentation. In its latter Brazilian stage, the modinha became truly lyrical and folk song–like.

modo narrativo, in (*narrante*; It., in a narrating mode). Sing or speak with distinct declamation.

modulate. To pass from one key or mode into another.

modulation

Transition from one key or mode to another within a single composition. The idea of a modulation dates back to the system of hexachords of Guido d'Arezzo, in which a modulation from one hexachord to another can be achieved by renaming a syllabic degree in the initial hexachord by a syllabic degree of the terminal hexachord. For example, if *La* in the hexachord Ut–Re–Mi–Fa–Sol–La is renamed *Mi*, then a modulation is effected into the hexachord Fa–Sol–La, etc., in which *La* is the 3rd note. In polyphonic writing of the

Middle Ages and the Renaissance, modulation was effected by a similar "Guidonian" substitution of a degree of the scale. Such modulations produce a strange impression on the modern ear, leading some enthusiastic scholiasts to proclaim the "modernity" of medieval composers.

The cardinal principle operating in such modulations has nothing to do with the rules of tonal harmony that were formulated over a century later; rather, such "sudden" medieval modulations were justified by the acoustical primacy of the major chord, so that if in the course of the composition the melody wandered into an alien field guarded by a sharp or flat, the harmony adjusted itself to the new situation, forming a major triad in the fundamental position. A remnant of this practice is found in the familiar PICARDY 3RD, the major cadence of a piece in a minor key.

As modality fell into desuetude, and major and minor keys became established as dual counterparts of tonality, the rules of modulation were drawn according to the principle of kinship of keys having the same number of sharps or flats in the key signature, or of neighboring keys having 1 more or 1 less sharp or flat relative to the initial key. This relationship was incorporated in a scientific-looking CIRCLE OF 5THS in the image of the face of a clock in which the sharps move clockwise and flats move counterclockwise. Any composer desiring to modulate from one key to another that was not adjacent in the circle of 5ths had to make his way through the intermediate stopovers, step by step.

Departing from C major (virginally clear of accidentals), with a goal of A major, (which has 3 sharps), one has to traverse successively the stops that have 1 and 2 sharps in the key signature. This could be done by moving, for variety's sake, 1st to a minor key having 1 sharp (E minor), then to a major key having 2 sharps (D major), and from there landing in A major via a regular cadence. But what if a modulating traveler had to go to a key 4 or 5 sharps away from the starting point? Surely movement by steps across the clock of the circle of 5ths would be tedious. Providentially, each minor key has a major dominant, which enables the modulating composer to jump 4 stops in the direction of sharps, clockwise. For instance, the dominant of A harmonic minor is E major, a key which has 4 sharps in its key signature. Emulating Guido

d'Arezzo, we hit the dominant and then declare it, by Guidonian fiat, the tonic of a new key, E major. Starting from C major we can detour to its relative minor key (A minor), and from there make a direct transition to E major. We append a nice cadence, and the job is done.

The circle of 5ths is not the only itinerary for modulation. There is a powerful chromatic resource in *enharmonic modulation*, in which neo-Guidonian substitution is effected by enharmonic change. Let us take a common, ordinary dominant-7th chord in the key of C, G–B–D–F. Change F enharmonically to E sharp, a note identical with F in sound but not in meaning; E sharp functions as the top note of an augmented 6th chord whose bottom note is the former dominant G. Thus the E sharp has an irresistible instinct to rise to F sharp, while the bottom note G has a hardly more resistible instinct to sink to the lower F sharp. When both notes, following their instincts, land on an F-sharp octave, we find ourselves in the locus of the tonic $^6_4$ chord of B minor. The rest is just a cadential matter.

In *chromatic modulation*, chords can be protean. Consider the diminished-7th chord. Depending on 1 of its 24 musically possible spellings, it can instantly modulate to any of the 24 major or minor keys. No wonder it was called by Italian opera composers *accorde di stupefazione*, for it stupefied the listener into catatonic suspense, particularly when played tremolo in the strings. Since the diminished-7th chord consists of minor 3rds which are free to move in parallel motion, dramatic chromatic rises and falls are most effective. Romantic operas, even by respectable composers, are full of such crawling chords. But even nonoperatic composers are not averse to taking advantage of this facility. In the coda of his B-flat minor Scherzo for Piano (op. 20), Chopin uses a series of ornamented diminished-7th chords with nerve-tingling appoggiaturas in the middle voices that finally resolve into the long-anticipated key of D-flat major. Mendelssohn portrays a storm with diminished-7ths in his *Fingal's Cave* overture.

Other types of modulations: *diatonic modulation*, one effected by use of diatonic intervals; *final modulation*, one in which the new key is retained or still another follows; *passing, transient, transitory modulation*, one in which the original key is speedily regained.

modulation convergente (Fr.). A modulation that eventually leads to (converges on) the initial (home, tonic) key.

modulation divergente (Fr.). A modulation that diverges from (wanders away from) the initial (home, tonic) key.

modus (Lat., mode). In mensural notation, the ratio of note values between the MAXIMA and LONGA, and between the longa and BREVIS. The former ratio is called *modus major*, the latter, *modus minor*. Like other mensural note values, these ratios can either be *perfect* (a PERFECTION) containing 3 units of the lesser note values, or *imperfect* (an IMPERFECTION) containing only 2 units of the lesser note values. Thus *modus major imperfectus* is a measure containing 2 longas; *modus minor imperfectus* contains 2 breves.

möglich (Ger.). Possible. *So rasch wie möglich*, as fast as possible.

Moldau. The 2nd and most famous movement of Smetana's symphonic cycle *Má vlast*, 1874; the Czech title is *Vltava*. The work is a tribute to the river on which the city of Prague is situated. The main theme, in E minor, is ingratiatingly Romantic. Whether by actual borrowing or through an extraordinary coincidence, this melody was adopted for the Zionist anthem at the 1st International Zionist Conference in Basel (1897); it eventually evolved into the Israeli national anthem, *Hatikvah* (Hope). Investigators found that the melody of *Moldau* was remarkably similar to a Swedish song written in 1822, and the melody has also been traced to folk songs of Dutch and Polish origin.

moll (Ger.). Minor. *Molltonart*, minor key.

molto, -a (It.). Very, much. *Molto adagio*, very slowly; *molto allegro*, very fast; *con molta passione*, with great passion; *di molto* or *molto molto*, exceedingly, extremely; *crescendo molto molto*, growing very much louder.

moment form. A short-lived structural concept developed by Stockhausen describing works which, in theory, rely less for their auditory coherence on relationships between movements than on the experience of "the moment."

moment musical (Fr.). Romantic character piece, usually for piano. Schubert wrote 6 pieces of this title, publ. under the incorrect French title *Moments musicals*.

Momente. Work by Stockhausen, 1962, scored for soprano, 4 choruses (who sing, speak, scream, and clap), 13 instruments, and percussion; 1st performed in Cologne. In the score, Stockhausen introduced the term *Moment-Groups* to designate the premeditated or unpremeditated simultaneity of occurrence of certain sounds produced by voices and instruments.

Mompou, Federico, significant Catalan composer; b. Barcelona, Apr. 16, 1893; d. there, June 30, 1987. After preliminary studies at the Barcelona Cons., he went to Paris, where he studied piano with Philipp and composition with Rousseau. He returned to Barcelona during World War I; then was again in Paris from 1921 to 1941, when he once more went back to Spain. His music is inspired by Spanish and Catalan melos, but its harmonic and instrumental treatment is entirely modern. He wrote mostly for piano: *Impressions intimes* (1911–14); *Scènes d'enfants* (1915); *Suburbis* (1916–17); *3 pessebres* (1918); *Cants magics* (1919); *Festes Llunyanes* (1920); *Charmes* (1921); 3 variations (1921); *Dialogues* (1923); a series, *Canción y Danza* (1918–62); 10 preludes (1927–51); *Paisajes* (1942, 1947, 1960); *Música callada* (Silent Music; 4 albums, 1959–67); *Suite compostelana* for guitar (1963); choral works and songs.

Mona. Opera by H. Parker, 1912, 1st staged at the Metropolitan Opera in New York as the winner of a prize of $10,000 for an all-American opera. Despite the emphasis on Americanism (the librettist and the entire cast, with the exception of 1 minor part, were all Americans), the libretto itself was taken from an old British legend. Mona is the last defender of the Celtic Queen Boadicea, who fought against Roman rule. The opera had only 4 performances; attempts at revivals foundered. Yet the music is not all bad. An interesting innovation is the assignment of certain keys to different characters; Mona is identified by the key of E-flat major.

Mona Lisa. Opera, 1915, by Max von Schillings (b. Düren, Apr. 19, 1868; d. Berlin, July 24, 1933), 1st performed in Stuttgart. The whimsical libretto relates a visit by a married couple in Florence. A local monk tells them the story of Mona Lisa, her husband Giocondo, and the love she nurtured for a Florentine youth, Giovanni. The smile on the lips of the woman tourist seems strangely familiar, and no wonder, for she is Mona Lisa *rediviva*, traveling with her husband, and the monastic teller of the story is Giovanni. The score is couched in an unreservedly Wagnerian idiom.

Mond, Der (The Moon). Opera by Orff, 1939, to his own text after a fairy tale by Grimm; 1st produced in Munich. The story tells of 4 boys who steal the moon and use it as a bedside lamp. When they die, they arrange to take the moon with them to their graves. The sudden illumination arouses the dead. St. Peter comes down to restore order, and puts the moon up in the sky where it belongs. As are most of Orff's operas, *Der Mond* is a theatrical spectacle, containing spoken dialogue, a pantomime, and several symphonic interludes in which a plethora of percussion instruments make interesting noises.

Mondo della luna, Il (The World of the Moon). Opera buffa by Haydn, 1777, 1st performed at the estate of Prince Esterházy where Haydn was music director. An astronomer, fittingly named Dr. Ecclittico (ecliptic), drugs a rich Venetian and convinces him that he is on the moon and that the lunar authorities have ordered him to let his daughter marry her impecunious suitor. The music is spirited and ingratiating to the ears of inhabitants of any celestial body.

money and music

Musicians do not manufacture material goods and therefore, like poets, must subsist parasitically. In times of catastrophic social disturbances—wars, famine, plagues—music stops. In times of prosperity, musicians attach themselves to the dominant powers, to the church, to the royal court, to educational institutions (which themselves must depend on the powers of the state), or to wealthy merchants. In the church, and particularly in the most organized historical church of Rome, musicians performed the essential duties of writing for sacred services. When great royal courts emerged in the Middle Ages, kings, emperors, dukes, and other secular potentates employed musicians to lend decorum to their mundane preoccupations. With the emergence of industrial civilization, money kings took pleasure in sponsoring musical activities. Singers found easy employment in the church; instrumentalists were less in demand; composers had the least opportunity, unless they acted also as performers, conductors of military bands, or instructors in universities. In public demand of their services, a similar order exists; popular singers can make a fortune, but artists specializing in classical music rarely attract large audiences.

A curious inverse ratio exists in relation to a singer's musical education or professional excellence and commercial success. Some of the most successful jazz and rock 'n' roll performers could never learn to read music. Even the most celebrated opera tenor, Caruso, sang by ear, even though he was already an international star. Instrumentalists come 2nd in popular acclaim; among them, pianists enjoy the greatest opportunity of monetary success, followed by violinists and cellists. Symphonic conductors may be described as instrumentalists of the baton. Sometimes they have rivaled performing artists in public education, but since symphonic music is the food for the sophisticate and the connoisseur, and since they cannot pursue their profession with a maximum of proficiency without an orch. of great excellence, they may remain philosophers of music, even when they become idols of the audience. Infinitely more successful financially are the leaders of dance bands, from the "Waltz King," Johann Strauss, Jr., and the "March King," John Philip Sousa, to the leaders of some big bands.

In terms of both popular success and financial reward, composers find themselves on the lowest rung of the ladder. Some composers of semiclassical music and popular songs have achieved a certain prosperity, but authors of large symphonic works or chamber music have little hope of attaining even a moderate income. The history of musical biography is a study in inauspicious beginnings and unhappy endings. Mozart wrote pathetic letters to a friendly banker asking for petty loans. (One of these letters sold some 200 years later to an autograph collector for a sum a thousand times as large as the loan requested by Mozart.) Beethoven flaunted his poverty with proud assertion of his status as a "brain owner." Tchaikovsky had a rich admirer in the person of Mme. von Meck, who gave him an annual grant. Wagner was put in a debtor's prison in Paris when he was already a well-known composer. Bartók complained bitterly during his last years of life in America that he could not even find piano pupils to provide pocket money; a friendly Hungarian émigré arranged for him to make a recording of his piano music, but sales were so poor that his friend decided to doctor his royalty account to make it appear more respectable. (A picture postcard with Bartók's handwriting sold after his death for $165.) Schoenberg applied to the Guggenheim Foundation for a grant to enable him to complete his opera *Moses und Aron*, but he was turned down. (A few pages of Schoenberg's orchestration of a Viennese operetta which he did as a young man was priced at several thousand dollars at an auction sale after Schoenberg's death.) Scriabin suffered desperate financial difficulties after the death of his Maecenas, the publisher Belaieff; sometimes, living in Switzerland, he even lacked enough money for a postage stamp.

The situation of composers has improved considerably in the 20th century; in Europe, by the creation of government grants, prizes, and other awards to composers of serious music; in America, by the formation of ASCAP and BMI, which protect their royalty interests. Furthermore, "prestige" payments are often made by publishers to composers, the sale of whose works is not profitable commercially.

monism. A philosophical doctrine postulating the existence of a basic element that is the prime constituent of all material objects. In music, monism denotes an analogous primacy of a concept or a function. The DODECAPHONIC series is a monistic factor which determines the development of an entire work. A set of variations is intrinsically monistic since it is derived from a primary source, but it is pluralistic if the variations are regarded as mutually independent entities.

Moniuszko, Stanislaw, famous Polish composer; b. Ubiel, Minsk province, Russia, May 5, 1819; d. Warsaw, June 4, 1872. In 1827 his family went to Warsaw, where he studied piano and music with August Freyer; continued his training with Dominick Stefanowica in Minsk and with Rungenhagen in Berlin (1837). He went to Vilnius in 1840; there he served as organist at St. John's; he gained attention as a composer when he publ. vol. I of his *Spiewnik domowy* (Songbook for Home Use; 1843); gained the support of various Polish figures in the arts, and also won the admiration of Glinka, Dargomizhsky, and Cui in Russia. In 1848 a concert performance of the 2-act version of his opera *Halka* was given for the 1st time in Vilnius; after he expanded it to 4 acts, it was staged in Warsaw (1858), scoring a great success. He then settled in Warsaw (1859), becoming conductor of opera at the Grand Theater; he continued to compose for the stage, and also taught at the Music Inst. (from 1864); publ. *Pamiętnik do nauki harmonii* (Textbook on Harmony; 1871).

Moniuszko holds a revered place in Polish music history as the outstanding composer of opera in his era; he also excelled as a composer of songs. His other works include operas and operettas, incidental music to 14 plays, and ballets. He also composed orch.l and chamber music, and religious and secular choral works.

Monk, Meredith (Jane), noted American composer, singer, and filmmaker; b. Lima, Peru (of American parents), Nov. 20, 1942. She studied *eurythmics*, the educational method that relates music to movement, from an early age; was educated at Sarah Lawrence College (B.A., 1964), then was a pupil in voice of Vicki Starr, John Devers, and Jeanette Lovetri, in composition of Ruth Lloyd, Richard Averee, and Glenn Mack, and in piano of Gershon Konikow. She pursued an active career as a singer, filmmaker, director, choreographer, recording artist, and composer. In 1968 she organized the House in N.Y., a company devoted to interdisciplinary approaches to the arts; in 1978 she founded there her own vocal chamber ensemble, with which she toured widely in the U.S. and abroad. In 1972 and 1982 she held Guggenheim fellowships; received various ASCAP awards and many commissions. Her powerful soprano vocalizations employ a wide range of ethnic and AVANT-GARDE influences.

As one of the 1st and most natural of performance artists, she developed a flexible, imaginative theatrical style influenced by dream narrative and physical movement. Among her works are *Candy Bullets and Moon* for Voice, Electric Organ, Electric Bass, and Drums (1967; in collaboration with D. Preston); *Blueprint: Overload/Blueprint 2* for Voice, Echoplex, and Tape (1967); *Juice*, theater cantata for 85 Voices, Jew's Harp, and 2 Violins (1969); *A Raw Recital* for Voice and Electric Organ (1970); *Key*, album of invisible theater for Voice, Electric Organ, Vocal Quartet, Percussion, and Jew's Harp (1970–71); *Vessel*, opera epic for 75 Voices, Electric Organ, Dulcimer, and Accordion (1971); *Education of the Girlchild*, opera for 6 Voices, Electric Organ, and Piano (1972–73); *Our Lady of Late* for Voice and Wine Glass (1972–73); *Quarry*, opera for 38 Voices, 2 Pump Organs, 2 Soprano Recorders, and Tape (1976); *Songs from the Hill* for Voice (1976–77); *Tablet* for 4 Voices, Piano 4-Hand, and 2

Soprano Recorders (1977); *Dolmen Music* for 6 Voices, Cello, and Percussion (1979); *Recent Ruins* for 14 Voices, Tape, and Cello (1979); *Turtle Dreams (Waltz)* for 4 Voices and 2 Electric Organs (1980–81); *Specimen Days* for 14 Voices, Piano, and 2 Electric Organs (1981); *Ellis Island* for 2 Pianos (1982); *The Games* for 16 Voices, Synthesizer, Keyboards, Flemish Bagpipes, Bagpipes, Chinese Horn, and Rauschpfeife (1983); *Panda Chant I* for 4 Voices and *II* for 8 Voices (1984); *Book of Days* for 25 Voices, Synthesizer, and Piano (1985); *Scared Song* for Voice, Synthesizer, and Piano (1986); *Window in 7's* (for Nurit) for Piano (1986); *The Ringing Place* for 9 Voices (1987); *Do You Be* for 10 Voices, 2 Pianos, Synthesizer, Violin, and Bagpipes (1987); *Book of Days*, film score for 10 Voices, Cello, Shawm, Synthesizer, Hammered Dulcimer, Bagpipes, and Hurdy-gurdy (1988); *Fayum Music* for Voice, Hammered Dulcimer, and Double Ocarina (1988); *Atlas*, opera (1991).

Monk, Thelonious (Sphere), noted African-American jazz pianist and composer; b. Rocky Mount, N.C., Oct. 10, 1917; d. Englewood, N.J., Feb. 17, 1982. He spent most of his professional life in Harlem, where he played in nightclubs; gradually surfaced as a practitioner of BEBOP, set in angular rhythms within asymmetrical bar sequences. His eccentric behavior was signalized by his external appearance; he wore skullcaps and dark sunglasses; time and again he would rise from the keyboard and perform a rhythmic dance. Although not educated in the formal sense, he experimented with discordant harmonies, searching for new combinations of sounds. Paradoxically, he elevated his seeming limitations to a weirdly cogent modern idiom, so that even deep-thinking jazz critics could not decide whether he was simply inept or prophetically innovative. Monk's own tunes, on the other hand, seemed surprisingly sophisticated, and he gave them impressionistic titles, such as *Crepuscule with Nellie* (Nellie was the name of his wife) and *Epistrophy*, or else ethnically suggestive ones, as in *Rhythm-a-ning*.

A profoundly introspective neurotic, he would drop out of the music scene for years, withdrawing into his inner self. During the period between 1973 and 1976 he stayed with an admirer, the Baroness Pannonica de Koenigswarter, in her apartment in Weehawken, N.J., but was visited daily by his wife, Nellie. He made his last public appearance at the Newport Jazz Festival in 1976, but seemed a faint shadow, a weak echo of his former exuberant personality. His song *Criss-Cross* (1951) was used by Gunther Schuller for his *Variations on a Theme of Thelonious Monk*. Other important tunes by Monk include *'Round Midnight, Misterioso, Ruby My Dear, Blue Monk, Pannonica, Well You Needn't, Little Rootie Tootie, Brilliant Corners, Jackie-ing, Bemsha Swing, I Mean You, Hackensack*, and *Straight, No Chaser.*

Monkees, The. (Guitar/vocal: Michael Nesmith, b. Houston, Tex., Dec. 30, 1942; vocal/tambourine: Davy Jones, b. Manchester, England, Dec. 30, 1945; bass/vocal: Peter Tork, b. P. Torkelson, Washington, D.C., Feb. 13, 1944; drums/vocal: Michael "Micky" Dolenz, b. Tarzana, Calif., Mar. 8, 1945.) Known as the "Pre-Fab Four," the Monkees were a group created to cash in on the popularity of the Beatles and their films for the TV/teenage market. They achieved great popularity from 1966, when their TV show premiered, until 1969, when the group disintegrated. Auditioned for their looks as much as their musical talents (or lack thereof), they scored hits primarily with songs written by pop tunesmiths such as Goffin-King, Neil Diamond, and, particularly, Tommy Boyce and Bobby Hart. Hits include Boyce and Hart's *Last Train to Clarksville* and *Valleri*, Leiber and Stoller's *D. W. Washburn*, John Stewart's *Daydream Believer*, and Goffin-King's *Pleasant Valley Sunday*. Aspiring to transcend their teenybopper roots, the group made the impressionistic film *Head* (1968), working with director Bob Rafaelson and Jack Nicholson; it perplexed their younger fans while failing to win over the sophisticated crowd, although today it is considered something of a cult classic. That same year, they toured the country to prove that they could indeed play their own instruments; as an opening act, they enlisted a then little-known guitarist named Jimi Hendrix, but their teenage fans were dismayed by his pyrotechnics and he was quickly dropped from the tour.

After the group disbanded, Nesmith formed a country-rock band known as the 1st National Band, and enjoyed some success as a songwriter (his *Different Drum* was a hit for Linda Ronstandt and the Stone Ponys in 1969). In the 1970s Nesmith became involved in the nascent field of music video, developing a prototype for what would become MTV and producing various films. In 1986, with the rerelease of Monkee recordings again selling briskly, Jones, Tork, and Dolenz reunited for a comeback album and tour, although Nesmith resisted the temptation to join the mass cash-in until the mid-'90s, when he too took to the road with his old ape-mates.

monochord. An ancient chordophone. As the name indicates, it had a single string, which was stretched over a soundbox, and a shifting bridge that allowed the string to be adjusted to different pitches. It was and is used to test acoustic theories.

monodrama. A stage work in which only one actor, speaker, or singer acts, recites, or sings. Schoenberg introduced a type of singing recitation, SPRECHSTIMME, in which the actor enunciates his lines in an inflected manner following the melorhythmic design of the music, a technique that came to its full fruition in his *Pierrot Lunaire*. The classic example of a staged monodrama is his *Erwartung*. The Russian composer Vladimir Rebikov evolved a novel type of monodrama which he described as *psychodrama*; in it an actor recites his state of mind with a musical accompaniment. In Schoenberg's *Die glückliche Hand*, the central character sings and mimes the story, and a chorus comments on the action in Sprechstimme.

monody (from Lat., single song). Usually, the recitative-like BASSO CONTINUO song style of early-17th-century Italy.

monophonic. 1. Texture of unaccompanied melody. 2. Instrument capable of producing but 1 tone at a time.

monothematic. A composition with a single subject.

monothematism and polythematism. In the 19th and 20th centuries, composers turned to monothematism, in which a single subject might govern an entire composition. Monothematism, an extension of *organicism* ("growing" a piece from one melody or even motif) and related to thematic transformation, is basic to the structure of a theme with variations; but if variations depart too widely from the theme, the result may be polythematic. Rigid monothematism carries an intrinsic danger of monotony; on the other hand, extreme polythematism courts the opposite danger of discontinuity. In monothematism, the single theme must recur a sufficient number of times to produce an impression of uniformity; in polythematic constructions, similarities among successive themes must be avoided, at least overtly.

monotone. 1. A single unaccompanied and unvaried tone. 2. Recitation (intoning, chanting) on such a tone.

Monroe, Bill (William Smith), American country-music singer, mandolin player, and songwriter; b. near Rosine, Ky., Sept. 13, 1911; d. Springfield, Tenn., Sept. 9, 1996. He studied with his uncle, Pendleton Vandiver, a fiddler; then played fiddle in a band formed by his brothers Birch and Charlie; Charlie and Bill performed as the Monroe Brothers for a few years. In 1938 Bill organized his own band, the Blue Grass Boys, which gained fame through appearances on the *Grand Ole Opry* radio program in Nashville. His innovations in string-band music led to the development of the bluegrass style, notable for its syncopated rhythm and complex but invariably tonal harmonies. His most famous band included Lester Flatt and Earl Scruggs, who introduced bluegrass-style banjo (fingerpicking melodies using 3 fingers equipped with metallic picks). This group lasted from about 1946 to 1949.

Monroe composed many bluegrass standards, including the waltz *Blue Moon of Kentucky* (covered by Elvis Presley in 1956 and changed into a rollicking rock 'n' roll tune), *Uncle Pen*, in honor of his fiddling relative, and many other vocal works, and dozens of classic instrumentals, including *Rawhide*, *Wheelhoss*, and *Scotland*. Many of the most notable bluegrass and newgrass musicians played in Monroe's band, including Stringbean (Dave Akeman), Jimmie Martin, Sonny Osborne, Vassar Clements, Buddy Spicher, Kenny Baker, Ralph Rinzler, Richard Greene, Bill Keith, and Peter Rowan. In 1970 he was elected a member of the Country Music Hall of Fame.

Monsieur de Bourceaugnac. Opera by F. Martin, 1963, based on a Molière comedy. A rich French landowner is intent on marrying a young woman who loves another. The object of his attention calls for help, and a bevy of feigned doctors and false lawyers persuade Monsieur de Bourceaugnac that such a marriage would be hazardous to his health, not to mention illegal. He finally desists.

Montemezzi, Italo, eminent Italian opera composer; b. Vigasio, near Verona, Aug. 4, 1875; d. there, May 15, 1952. He was a pupil of Saladino and Ferroni at the Milan Cons., and graduated in 1900; his graduation piece, conducted by Toscanini, was *Cantico dei Cantici*, for Chorus and Orch. He then devoted himself almost exclusively to opera. In 1939 he went to the U.S.; lived mostly in Calif.; in 1949 he returned to Italy. Montemezzi's chief accomplishment was the maintenance of the best traditions of Italian dramatic music, without striving for realism or overelaboration of technical means. His masterpiece in this genre was the opera *L'amore dei tre re* (Milan, Apr. 10, 1913), which became a standard work in the repertoire of opera houses all over the world.

Monteux, Pierre, celebrated French-born American conductor; b. Paris, Apr. 4, 1875; d. Hancock, Maine, July 1, 1964. He studied at the Paris Cons. with Berthelier (violin), Lavignac (harmony), and Lenepveu (composition); received 1st prize for violin (1896); then was a viola player in the Colonne Orch., and later chorus master there; also played viola in the orch. of the Opéra-Comique. He then organized his own series, the Concerts Berlioz, at the Casino de Paris (1911); that same year he also became conductor for Diaghilev's Ballets Russes; his performances of modern ballet scores established him as one of the finest technicians of the baton. He led the world premieres of Stravinsky's *Petrouchka, Le Sacre du printemps,* and *Le Rossignol*; Ravel's *Daphnis et Chloé*; and Debussy's *Jeux*; conducted at the Paris Opéra (1913–14); founded the Soc. des Concerts Populaires in Paris (1914); appeared as guest conductor in London, Berlin, Vienna, Budapest, etc.

In 1916–17 he toured the U.S. with the Ballets Russes; in 1917 he conducted the Civic Orch. Soc., N.Y.; from 1917 to 1919, at the Metropolitan Opera there. In 1919 he was engaged as conductor of the Boston Sym. Orch., and he held this post until 1924; from 1924 to 1934 he was associate conductor of the Concertgebouw Orch. in Amsterdam; from 1929 to 1938 he was principal conductor of the newly founded Orch. Symphonique de Paris. From 1936 until 1952 he was conductor of the reorganized San Francisco Sym. Orch. He became a naturalized U.S. citizen in 1942. He appeared as a guest conductor with the Boston Sym. Orch. from 1951, and also accompanied it on its 1st European tour in 1952, and then again in 1956; likewise was again on the roster of the Metropolitan Opera (1953–56). In 1961 (at the age of 86) he became principal conductor of the London Sym. Orch., retaining this post until his death. He was married in 1927 to Doris Hodgkins (b. Salisbury, Maine, 1895; d. Hancock, Maine, Mar. 13, 1984), an American singer who cofounded in 1941 the Domaine School for Conductors and Orchestral Players in Hancock, Maine, of which Monteux was director. After Monteux's death, she established the Pierre Monteux Memorial Foundation.

As an interpreter, Monteux endeavored to bring out the inherent essence of the music, without imposing his own artistic personality; unemotional and restrained in his podium manner, he nonetheless succeeded in producing brilliant performances in an extensive repertoire ranging from the classics to the 20th century.

Monteverdi (Monteverde), Claudio (Giovanni Antonio)

Outstanding Italian composer who established the foundations of modern opera; b. Cremona (baptized), May 15, 1567; d. Venice, Nov. 29, 1643. His surname is also rendered as Monteverde. He was the son of a chemist who practiced medicine as a barber-surgeon; studied singing and theory with Marc' Antonio Ingegneri, maestro di cappella at the Cathedral of Cremona; he also learned to play the organ. He acquired the mastery of composition at a very early age; he was only 15 when a collection of his 3-part motets was publ. in Venice; there followed several sacred madrigals (1583) and canzonettas (1584). In 1589 he visited Milan, and he made an appearance at the court of the Duke of Mantua; by 1592 he had obtained a position at the court in the service of Vincenzo I as "suonatore" on the viol (viola da gamba) and violin (viola da braccio). He came into contact with the Flemish composer Giaches de Wert, maestro di cappella at the Mantuan court, whose contrapuntal art greatly influenced Monteverdi.

In 1592 Monteverdi publ. his 3rd book of madrigals, a collection marked by a considerable extension of harmonic dissonance. In 1595 he accompanied the retinue of the Duke of Mantua on forays against the Turks in Austria and Hungary, and also went with him to Flanders in 1599. He married Claudia de Cattaneis, one of the Mantuan court singers, in 1599; they had 2 sons; a daughter died in infancy. In 1601 he was appointed maestro di cappella in Mantua following the death of Pallavicino. The publication of 2 books of madrigals in 1603 and 1605 further confirmed his mastery of the genre.

Having already composed some music for the stage, he now turned to the new form of the opera. *L'Orfeo*, his 1st opera, was given before the Accademia degli Invaghiti in Mantua in Feb. 1607. In this pastoral he effectively moved beyond the Florentine model of recitative-dominated drama by creating a more flexible means of expression; the score is an amalgam of MONODY, MADRIGAL, and instrumental music of diverse kinds. In 1607 Monteverdi was made a member of the Accademia degli Animori of Cremona. He suffered a grievous loss in the death of his wife in Cremona (Sept. 1607). Although greatly depressed, he accepted a commission to compose an opera to celebrate the marriage of the heir apparent to the court of Mantua, Francesco Gonzaga, to Margaret of Savoy. The result was *L'Arianna*, to a text by Rinuccini, presented in Mantua (1608). Although the complete MS has been lost, the extant versions of the *Lamento d'Arianna* from the score testify to Monteverdi's genius in expressing human emotion in moving melodies.

In 1614 he prepared a 5-part arrangement of his 6th book of madrigals, also publ. separately (Venice, 1623). He further wrote 2 more works for wedding celebrations, the prologue to the pastoral play *L'Idropica* (not extant) and the French-style ballet *Il ballo delle ingrate*. His patron, Duke Vincenzo of Mantua, died in 1612; and his successor, Francesco, did not retain Monteverdi's services. However, Monteverdi had the good fortune of being called to Venice in 1613 to occupy the vacant post of maestro di cappella at San Marco, at a salary of 300 ducats, which was raised to 400 ducats in 1616. His post at San Marco proved to be the most auspicious of his career, and he retained it for the rest of his life. He composed mostly church music, but he did not neglect the secular madrigal forms. He accepted important commis-

COURTESY MUSICAL HERITAGE SOCIETY

Claudio Monteverdi

sions from Duke Ferdinando of Mantua. His ballet *Tirsi e Clori* was given in Mantua in 1616.

In 1619 he publ. his 7th book of madrigals, significant in its bold harmonic innovations. In 1624 his dramatic cantata, *Il combattimento di Tancredi e Clorinda*, after Tasso's *Gerusalemme liberata*, was performed at the home of Girolamo Mocenigo, a Venetian nobleman. The score is noteworthy for the effective role played by the string orch. Other works comprised intermedi for the Farnese court in Parma. A great inconvenience was caused to Monteverdi in 1627 when his son Massimiliano, a medical student, was arrested by the Inquisition for consulting books on the Index Librorum Prohibitorum; he was acquitted. In 1630 Monteverdi composed the opera *Proserpina rapita* for Venice; of it only 1 trio has survived.

Following the plague of 1630–31 he wrote a Mass of thanksgiving for performance at San Marco (the Gloria is extant); in 1632 he took holy orders. His *Scherzi musicali* for 1 and 2 voices was publ. in 1632. Then followed his *Madrigali guerrieri et amorosi*, an extensive retrospective collection covering some 30 years (1638). In 1637 the 1st public opera houses were opened in Venice, and Monteverdi found a new outlet there for his productions. His operas *Il ritorno d'Ulisse in patria* (1640), *Le nozze d'Enea con Lavinia* (1641; not extant), and *L'incoronazione di Poppea* (1642) were all given in Venice. (Research by Alan Curtis suggests that the latter opera owes its final form to Francesco Sacrati.) The extant operas may be considered the 1st truly modern operas in terms of dramatic viability. Monteverdi died at the age of 76 and was accorded burial in the church of the Frari in Venice. A commemorative plaque was erected in his honor, and a copy remains in the church to this day.

Monteverdi's place in the history of music is of great magnitude. He established the foundations of modern opera conceived as a drama in music. For greater dynamic expression, he enlarged the orch., in which he selected and skillfully combined the instruments accompanying the voices. He was one of the earliest, if not the 1st, to employ such coloristic effects as string TREMOLO and PIZZICATO; his recitative assumes dramatic power, at times approaching the dimensions of an arioso. In harmonic usage he introduced audacious innovations, such as the use of the dominant 7th-chord and other dissonant chords without preparation. He is widely regarded as having popularized the terms *prima prattica* and *secunda prat-* *tica* to differentiate the polyphonic style of the 16th century from the largely monodic style of the 17th century, corresponding also to the distinction between *stile antico* and *stile moderno*. For this he was severely criticized by the Bologna theorist Giovanni Maria Artusi, who publ. in 1600 a vitriolic pamphlet against Monteverdi, attacking the *musica moderna* which allowed chromatic usages in order to achieve a more adequate expression.

Montezuma. Opera by Sessions, 1964. The libretto recounts the Spanish conquest of Mexico led by Cortés and the death of the Aztec emperor Montezuma II (1520).

Mood Indigo. Piece, later hit song by Ellington, 1930, popularized by his orch.; it generated a whole series of imitations, depicting colorful moods from the deepest blue to the most cheerful red.

Moody Blues, The. (Best-known lineup: Guitar/vocal/keyboard/sitar: Justin Hayward, b. Swindon, Wiltshire, Oct. 29, 1944; keyboards/guitar: Mike Pinder, b. Birmingham, Dec. 27, 1941; bass/vocals: John Lodge, b. Birmingham, July 20, 1945; bass: Ray Thomas, b. Stourport-on-Severn, Dec. 29, 1942; drums: Graeme Edge, b. Rochester, Kent, Mar. 30, 1944.) Pretentious British art-rock group best-remembered for their symphonic/rock fusions, which greatly influenced future groups including Genesis, Emerson, Lake, and Palmer, Yes, and ELO. Originally centering on singer/songwriter Denny Laine, the group 1st scored a popish hit with the song *Go Now* in 1965; however, Laine left a year later, and the group radically changed directions. With new hands Hayward and Lodge, they released the concept album, *Days of Future Passed*, in 1968, featuring the London Sym. Orchestra. It produced the hit *Tuesday Afternoon* and also included *Nights in White Satin*, which, 4 years later, became another chartbuster. The original band soldiered on through 1973, continuing to produce richly textured thematic albums, featuring many orch.l and electronic instruments, including the mellotron. The group disbanded in 1973 and has since reunited from time to time, achieving a hit in 1981 with *The Voice*, and their biggest recent hit, *Wildest Dreams*, in 1986. They continue to tour and perform with various lineups.

Moog, Robert (Arthur), American designer of electronic musical instruments; b. Flushing, N.Y., May 23, 1934. He studied at Queens College (B.S. in physics, 1957), Columbia Univ. (B.S. in electrical engineering, 1957), and Cornell Univ. (Ph.D. in engineering physics, 1965). He founded the R. A. Moog Co. in 1954 for the purpose of designing electronic musical instruments; in 1964 he introduced the 1st synthesizer modules; his company was incorporated in 1968, with its headquarters at Trumansburg, N.Y. In 1970 he brought out the Minimoog, a portable monophonic instrument; in 1971 the company became Moog Music and went to Buffalo, N.Y.; in 1973 it became a division of Norlin Industries, with which Moog was associated until 1977. He founded another firm, Big Briar, in Leicester, N.C., which manufactured devices for precision control of analog and digital synthesizers. He was associated with Kurzweil Music Systems of Boston (1984–89). His synthesizers and other electronic devices were used by both classical and rock musicians.

Moon River. Song by Mancini and Mercer, 1961; the theme song for the film *Breakfast at Tiffany's*. A hit that year for both Mancini in his instrumental version and as a song for Jerry Butler.

Moonlight Sonata. Popular nickname for Beethoven's piano sonata *Quasi una fantasia*, No. 2, op. 27 (1801). An imaginative and sentimental German writer opined in print that the slowly rolling arpeggios of the opening movement reminded him of moonlight on the quiet surface of Lake Lucerne in Switzerland. The work is in C-sharp minor, in 3 movements. In the finale, the wind whips up quite a little storm on the lake, and the moonlight is refracted violently.

Moore, Douglas (Stuart), distinguished American composer and music educator; b. Cutchogue, N.Y., Aug. 10, 1893; d. Greenport, N.Y., July 25, 1969. He studied at Yale Univ. with D. S. Smith and Horatio Parker; wrote several univ. songs, among them the football song *Good Night,*

Harvard, which became popular among Yale students; after obtaining his B.A. (1915) and Mus.Bac. (1917), he joined the U.S. Navy; following the Armistice of 1918, he attended classes of d'Indy at the Schola Cantorum in Paris and also took lessons in organ with Tournemire and in composition with Boulanger, and with Bloch in Cleveland. Returning to the U.S., he served as organist at the Cleveland Museum of Art (1921–23) and at Adelbert College, Western Reserve Univ. (1923–25); in 1925 he received a Pulitzer traveling scholarship in music and spent a year in Europe. In 1926 he was appointed to the faculty of Columbia Univ.; in 1940 he became head of the music dept. there; many American composers were his students. He retired in 1962.

A fine craftsman, Moore applied his technical mastery to American subjects in his operas and symphonic works. He achieved popular success with his "folk opera" *The Ballad of Baby Doe*, dealing with the true story of a historical figure during the era of intensive silver mining; the opera was staged in 1956, at Central City, Colo., where its action took place; the opera had numerous revivals in America, and also in Europe. He publ. the books *Listening to Music* (1932) and *From Madrigal to Modern Music: A Guide to Musical Styles* (1942). He is best known for his operas, including *The Devil and Daniel Webster* (N.Y., 1939); *Giants in the Earth* (1949; 1951; awarded the Pulitzer Prize in music); *The Ballad of Baby Doe*, folk opera (1956); *The Wings of the Dove* (1961); *Carry Nation*, to the story of the notorious temperance fighter (Kans., 1966). He also scored a ballet, *Greek Games*, and wrote incidental music and film scores. His orch.l works include *The Pageant of P. T. Barnum*, suite (1924); *Moby Dick*, symphonic poem (1927); *A Sym. of Autumn* (1930); *Overture on an American Tune* (1932); *In Memoriam*, symphonic poem (1944); Sym. No. 2 in A Major (1946); *Farm Journal*, suite for Chamber Orch. (1948); *Cotillion*, Suite for Strings (1952). He also wrote chamber works, piano pieces, organ music, choral works, and songs.

Moore, Gerald, renowned English piano accompanist. b. Watford, July 30, 1899; d. Penn, Buckinghamshire, Mar. 13, 1987. He 1st studied with Wallis Bandey at the local music school; after the family went to Canada in 1913, he continued his studies with Michael Hambourg; then he made appearances as a solo recitalist and accompanist; following his return to England (1919), he completed his training with Mark Hambourg. He began recording in 1921 and 1st gained distinction as accompanist to John Coates in 1925; he subsequently achieved well-nigh legendary fame as

the preeminent accompanist of the day, appearing with such celebrated singers as Ferrier, Fischer-Dieskau, Schwarzkopf, Baker, and others. He retired from the concert platform in 1967 but continued to make recordings. He was made a Commander of the Order of the British Empire (1954); was made an honorary D.Litt. by the Univ. of Sussex (1968) and Mus.D. by Cambridge Univ. (1973). Of a purely didactic nature are his books *Singer and Accompanist: The Performance of 50 Songs* (1953), *The Schubert Song Cycles* (1975), and *"Poet's Lore" and Other Schumann Cycles and Songs* (1984).

Moorman, (Madeline) **Charlotte,** avant-garde American cellist, b. Little Rock, Ark., Nov. 18, 1933; d. N.Y., Nov. 8, 1991. She took a B.A. degree in music at Centenary College in Shreveport, La., before studying cello with Horace Britt at the Univ. of Tex. in Austin and then completed her training in the late 1950s at the Juilliard School. A fascination with the avant-garde led her to found the N.Y. Avant-Garde Art Festival in 1963, with which she remained active until 1982. She 1st attracted attention in 1965 when she performed the *Cello Sonata No. 2 for Adults Only*. In 1967 she became something of a sensation when she performed Nam June Paik's *Opéra Sextronique* in accordance with the composer's instructions; i.e., nude from the waist up. Her performance was halted by her arrest; although she was tried and convicted for unseemly exposure, her sentence was eventually suspended and she resumed her championship of the avant-garde unhindered. Among her other notable performances were *TV Bra for Living Sculpture* (1969), which called for a bra made of 2 small televisions, and Paik's *The TV Cello* (1971), in which she played a cello made out of 3 television sets. Varèse was so taken with Moorman that he dubbed her the "Jeanne d'Arc of New Music." Ironically, she succumbed to breast cancer, a relatively forgotten figure, in 1991.

moralities. A later form of the MIRACLE PLAYS.

Moran, Robert (Leonard), important American composer of the avant-garde; b. Denver, Jan. 8, 1937. He studied piano; went to Vienna in 1957 and took lessons in 12-tone composition with Hans Erich Apostel. Returning to America, he enrolled at Mills College in Oakland, Calif., where he attended seminars of Luciano Berio and Darius Milhaud (M.A., 1963); completed his training with Roman Haubenstock-Ramati in Vienna (1963); also painted in the manner of Abstract Expressionism. He was active in AVANT-GARDE music circles; with Howard Hersh he was founder and codirector of the San Francisco Cons.'s New Music Ensemble; was composer-in-residence at Portland (Oreg.) State Univ. (1972–74) and at Northwestern Univ. (1977–78), where he led its New Music Ensemble; also appeared extensively as a pianist in the U.S. and Europe in programs of contemporary music. In his compositions he combines the "found art" style with aleatory techniques; some of his works are in graphic notation animated by a surrealistic imagination; others play off the gestalt of an earlier piece, place, or era. Moran has composed mixed media works of the environmental type, more common in Europe than in the U.S., but predicted in Ives's unrealized *Universe Sym.*

Among his works are the operas *Let's Build a Nut House*, chamber opera in memory of Paul Hindemith (who wrote *Wir bauen eine Stadt*; 1969); *Divertissement No. 3: A Lunchbag Opera* for paper bags and instruments (1971); *Metamenagerie*, department-store-window opera (1974); *Hitler: Geschichten aus der Zukunft* (1981); *The Juniper Tree*, children's opera (in collab. with Glass; 1985); *Arias and Inventions from Desert of Roses* (1992); and *The Dracula Diary*, opera macabre; and ballet scores and other stage works. His orch.1 compositions include *L'Après-midi du Dracoula* for any group of instruments capable of producing any kind of sound (1966); *Elegant Journey with Stopping Points of Interest* for any ensemble (1967); *Jewel-Encrusted Butterfly Wing Explosions* (1968); *Silver and the Circle of Messages* for Chamber Orch. (1970); *Angels of Silence* for Viola and Chamber Orch. (1975); and *Pachelbel Promenade* for Guitar Ensemble, Folk Instruments, String Ensemble, and Jazz Ensemble (1975). Chamber works include *Eclectic Boogies* for 13 Percussionists (1965); *Within the Momentary Illumination* for 2 Harps, Electric Guitar, Timpani, and Brass (1965); *The Last Station of the Albatross* for 1 to 8 Instruments (1978); *BASHA* for 4 Amplified Clavichords (1983); *Chorale Variations: 10 Miles High over Albania* for Harp (1983); *Survivor from Darmstadt* for Bass Oboes (1984); *Rocky Road to Kansas* for Percussion; *Open Veins* for Ensemble; *3 Dances* for Piano Ensemble; *Cryptograms for Derek Jarman* for Ensemble; *Music from the Towers of the Moon* for String Quartet.

Perhaps most unusual are his MIXED-MEDIA compositions, including *Smell Piece for Mills College* for Frying Pans and Foods (Mills College, 1967; originally intended to produce a conflagration sufficiently thermal to burn down the college); *39 Minutes for 39 Autos* for 30 Skyscrapers, 39 Auto Horns, Moog Synthesizer, and Players, employing 100,000 persons, directed from atop Twin Peaks in San Francisco,

and making use of autos, airplanes, searchlights, and local radio and television stations (San Francisco, Aug. 20, 1969, the night of the moon landing); *Titus* for Amplified Automobile and Players (1969); *Hallelujah*, "a joyous phenomenon with fanfares" for Marching Bands, Drum and Bugle Corps, Church Choirs, Organs, Carillons, Rock 'n' Roll Bands, Television Stations, Automobile Horns, and any other sounding implements, commissioned by Lehigh Univ. for the city of Bethlehem, Pa., with the participation of its entire population of 72,320 inhabitants (Bethlehem, Apr. 23, 1971); *From the Market to Asylum* for Performers (1982). He has also composed vocal works.

morbidezza (It.). Gentleness, softness. *Con morbidezza*, softly, delicately; *morbido*, soft, tender.

morceau (Fr.). A piece, composition. *Morceau de genre*, characteristic piece; *morceau de musique*, a piece of music.

morceaux choisis (Fr., selected pieces). An anthology of popular piano pieces appropriate to the diligent student, provincial teacher, or sincere amateur.

mordent (also Ger.; Fr. *mordant*). A grace consisting of the single rapid alternation of a principal note with an auxiliary a minor 2nd below:

Inverted mordent, the alternation of the principal note with the higher auxiliary:

morendo (It.). Dying away.

moresca (It.; Sp. *morisca*). A Moorish dance. It achieved popularity in Spain during the final phase of the struggle against Moorish power in southern Spain. It often contained a representation of a sword fight. Apparently the English MORRIS DANCE is a late derivation of the moresca. Interludes of Moorish dances in exotic costumes were often included in French ballets of the period.

Moreschi, Alessandro. See CASTRATO.

Morganfield, McKinley. See WATERS, MUDDY.

Morgenlied (*Morgenständchen*; Ger.). Morning serenade; AUBADE.

Morley, Thomas, famous English composer; b. Norwich, 1557 or 1558; d. London, Oct. 1602. He studied with William Byrd. From 1583 to 1587 he was organist and master of the choristers at Norwich Cathedral. In 1588 he received his B.Mus. from Oxford. About this time he became organist at St. Paul's Cathedral. By 1591 he had turned spy for the government of Queen Elizabeth I. In 1592 he was sworn in as a Gentleman of the Chapel Royal and was made Epistler and then Gospeller. He was also active as a printer, holding a monopoly on all music publ. under a patent granted to him by the government in 1598. In addition to publishing his own works (which he called canzonets, madrigals, ballets, and aires), he acted as editor, arranger, translator, and publisher of music by other composers. Notable among his eds. was *The Triumphes of Oriana* (1601), a collection of madrigals by 23 composers, all dedicated to Queen Elizabeth I. He gained distinction as a music theorist; his *A Plaine and Easie Introduction to Practicall Musicke* (1597) became famous as an exposition of British musical schooling of his time.

mormorando (*mormoroso*; *come un mormorio*; It.). Murmuring, murmurous; in a very gentle, subdued tone. *Mormorio*, murmur.

morphology. The emergence of a great variety of new forms of composition makes it difficult to classify them according to traditional categories. It may be desirable therefore to substitute the 20th-century term *morphology* for formal analysis, with the nomenclature of botany replacing that of traditional historic terminology. The geometrical rubrics of botanical classification would add imaginative metaphors suitable to modern musical usages. It would be possible, for instance, to speak of radial symmetry in neoclassical music, of a chromatic inflorescence in an atonal melody, or even of agamogenetic axes in dodecaphonic cross-pollination. The advantage of such botanical similes lies in precision and specificity of the terms and in their easy applicability to intervallic structures.

Morris dance. A characteristic and highly structured English dance for men only adorned in exotic costumes or wearing animal masks, apparently borrowing several features of the Spanish MORESCA yet without losing its essentially English rhythmic verse. The tempo is moderate and can be played by 1 or more traditional instrumentalists. The use of swords in a noncombatant manner suggests the presence of symbolic character play. The Morris dance went into hibernation before its conscious revival by British ethnomusicologists early in the 20th century.

Morris, James (Peppler), outstanding American bass-baritone; b. Baltimore, Jan. 10, 1947. After studies with a local teacher, he won a scholarship to the Univ. of Md.; concurrently received invaluable instruction from Rosa Ponselle; then continued his studies with Frank Valentino at the Peabody Cons. of Music in Baltimore (1966–68); made his debut as Crespel in *The Tales of Hoffmann* with the Baltimore Civic Opera (1967). After further training with Nicola Moscona at the Philadelphia Academy of Vocal Arts (1968–70), he made his Metropolitan Opera debut in N.Y. as Amonasro in *Aida* in 1971; appeared with the Opera Orch. of N.Y. and sang widely in Europe. In 1975 he scored a notable success as Don Giovanni at the Metropolitan. Although closely associated with the Italian and French repertoires, he appeared as Wotan in *Die Walküre* at the Baltimore Civic Opera in 1984; subsequently sang that role in the San Francisco Opera's *Ring* cycle in 1985, eliciting extraordinary critical acclaim. His other esteemed roles include Count Almaviva, Philip II, the Dutchman, the 4 villains in *The Tales of Hoffmann*, Timur in *Le Roi de Lahore*, Scarpia, and Claggart in *Billy Budd*.

Morrison, Jim (James). See DOORS, THE.

Morrison, Van (real name George Ivan), Irish-American rock singer, guitarist, saxophonist, and songwriter; b. Belfast, Aug. 13, 1945. He taught himself to sing and play the guitar, harmonica, and saxophone; after dropping out of high school when he was 16, he set off with his rhythm-and-blues outfit, the Monarchs, for Germany; returning to Belfast, he put together the group called Them (1963), with which he began his recording career. After Them folded (1966), he went to the U.S.; he produced the hit song *Brown-Eyed Girl* (1967), and that same year brought out his 1st solo album, *Blowin' Your Mind* (with the powerful *T. B. Sheets*). The album *Astral Weeks* (1968) established his expanded consciousness and galactic dreams; went on to record such successful albums as *Moondance* (1970), *Wavelength* (1978), *Into the Music* (1979), and *The Inarticulate Speech of the Heart* (1983). While his recorded output suffers from repetitiousness, in concert on a good night Morrison is as good a blue-eyed soul singer as has ever performed.

COURTESY BMG MUSIC GROUP

Jelly Roll Morton and His Red Hot Peppers, c. 1925

Morton, "Jelly Roll" (Ferdinand Joseph Lemott, LaMothe, La Menthe), pioneer Creole-American composer and pianist of ragtime, blues, and jazz; b. New Orleans, Oct. 20, 1890; d. Los Angeles, July 10, 1941. Born into a French-speaking family that proudly recalled its former days of wealth and position, Morton grew up surrounded by musical instruments and frequently attended performances at the New Orleans French Opera House. He took up piano when he was 10 and began working in the bordellos of Storyville when he was 12; by the time he was 14 he was traveling throughout La., Miss., Ala., and Fla. while making New Orleans his main haunt; he was a colorful and flamboyant figure, given to extravagant boasting and flashy living; in addition to his being a musician, he was a professional gambler (cards and billiards), nightclub owner, and producer; he made and lost several fortunes. As a result of his travels he assimilated various black, white, and Hispanic musical idioms to produce a form of music akin to jazz.

After performing in Los Angeles (1917–22), he went to Chicago, where he made his 1st solo recordings in 1923 of his own *New Orleans Blues* (1902), *Jelly Roll Blues* (1905), and *King Porter Stomp* (1906), and, with a sextet of his own, *Big Foot Ham* (1923); with his own New Orleans–style band, the Red Hot Peppers, he recorded *Grandpa's Spells* (1911), *The Pearls* (1919), and *Black Bottom Stomp* (1925). He went to N.Y. in 1928 but found himself outside the mainstream of jazz developments; later ran a jazz club in Washington, D.C., where he made infrequent appearances as a pianist; in 1938 Alan Lomax, the folklorist, recorded him for the Library of Congress, capturing him on disc playing piano, singing, relating anecdotes, and preserving his view of the history of jazz; the disc was issued in 1948.

Mosè in Egitto (Moses in Egypt). Opera by Rossini, 1818, 1st produced in Naples. The libretto follows the biblical narrative of the escape of the Hebrews across the miraculously distended Red Sea, and the destruction of the pursuing Egyptian army when the waters converge on them. The opera was selected by Mussolini to be performed at the gala reception of Hitler in Rome in 1935, oblivious to the fact that his anti-Semitic partner could have hardly enjoyed watching Jews escape.

Moses und Aron. Opera by Schoenberg, 1930–32, to his own text; acts I and II completed; act III, probably never started, libretto extant; produced posthumously in Hamburg (1954). The score is in the 12-tone idiom, with many episodes written in SPRECHSTIMME. The religious conflict between spirituality and materialism, personified by Moses and his brother Aaron, underlies the text. Schoenberg gives indications in the score that an orgy staged around the idol of the Golden Calf should include the immolation of 4 naked virgins and other scenes of ancient depravity; a realistic production along these lines was attempted in London in 1965, but the alleged virgins wore loincloths; subsequent productions have left the loinclothes in the dressing room.

The omission of the 2nd *a* in the German title was due to Schoenberg's triskaidekaphobia; if *Aaron* were spelled with 2 *a*'s, the sum of the letters in the complete title would have been 13. Many theories abound as to why Schoenberg could not compose the final, relatively brief act over nearly 2 decades time; the most interesting involves the identification of the somewhat messianic Schoenberg with his characters.

mosh pit. A recently devised area on a popular dance floor where patrons are permitted to practice such sports as slam dancing, pogoing, and lifting individuals above the floor involuntarily. Enough damage has been done to bones and flesh that clubs now warn that patrons who enter the pit do so at their own risk.

Mosolov, Alexander (Vasilievich), Russian composer; b. Kiev, Aug. 11, 1900; d. Moscow, July 12, 1973. He fought in the Civil War in Russia (1918–20); was wounded and decorated twice with the Order of the Red Banner for heroism. After the war he studied composition with Glière in Kiev; then studied harmony and counterpoint with Glière, composition with Miaskovsky, and piano with Prokofiev and Igumnov at the Moscow Cons. (1922–25). He played his 1st Piano Concerto in Leningrad (1928). In his earliest works he adopted modernistic devices; wrote songs to texts of newspaper advertisements. His ballet *Zavod* (Iron Foundry; Moscow, 1927) attracted attention because of the attempt to imitate the sound of a factory at work by shaking a large sheet of metal. However, Mosolov's attempt to produce "proletarian" music by such means elicited a sharp rebuke from the official arbiters of Soviet music.

In 1936 he was expelled from the Union of Soviet Composers for staging drunken brawls and behaving rudely to waiters in restaurants. He was sent to Turkestan to collect folk songs as a move toward his rehabilitation. After settling in Moscow in 1939 he continued to make excursions to collect folk songs in various regions of Russia until just before his death. He wrote 5 syms., 2 piano concertos, 1 concerto apiece for harp and cello, 4 operas, oratorios, choral and solo vocal works, 5 piano sonatas, 2 string quartets, and other music.

mosso (It., moved). Standing alone as a tempo mark, it is the same as CON MOTO. In the phrases *meno mosso* (less rapid), *più mosso* (more rapid), and *poco mosso* (somewhat rapid), it means "rapid." *Allegretto poco mosso*, a rather lively allegretto, almost allegro; *mosso agitato*, a fast and agitated movement; *assai mosso e agitato*, very rapid and agitated.

Most Happy Fella, The. Musical by F. Loesser, 1956. The story centers on a middle-aged Italian California grape grower in love with a young waitress in a San Francisco restaurant. He courts her by mail; when she asks for his picture, she gets a photo of one of his workers. When she finally arrives at his ranch vineyard, she is shocked at the discovery that her fiancé is old, but consoles herself by a lightning and impregnating affair with the young man in the photograph; meanwhile, the grape grower breaks his leg. Eventually she returns to her aging suitor in search of emotional and financial security. The score, composed as an almost continuous stream of music, has many fine songs, among them *Young People, How Beautiful the Days, Big "D," Somebody Somewhere, Standing on the Corner,* and *Abbondanza.*

motet (from Mid. Fr. *mot,* word; Ger. *Motette;* It. *mottetto*). A sacred vocal composition in contrapuntal style, without accompaniment until the Baroque period (where one might be called an ANTHEM). This modest term embraces half a millennium of the most fruitful developments of polyphonic music, stretching from the Middle Ages to the Renaissance and continuing through the period of the Baroque. The motet was cultivated in the church, both of the Roman Catholic and the Protestant rites, as well as in multilingual secular practices. In Middle French, *mot* signified a verse, strophe, or stanza; this is seemingly corroborated by the fact that the contrapuntal voice above the tenor, originally called *duplum,* acquired in the 13th century the name motet and carried a text. Franco of Cologne, writing in the 13th century, describes the motet as "discantus cum diversis litteris" (contrapuntal part with different texts). In the course of 2 centuries the motet was supplemented by more contrapuntal parts, some of them in the French vernacular.

During the Renaissance the confusion of bilingual texts and diverse rhythms led to the segregation of the Latin motet from the secular motet, which absorbed numerous colloquial elements. Further developments, both unified and heterogeneous, are found in the great polyphonic works of the masters of the Flemish school—Ockeghem, Obrecht, and Josquin des Pres. Later, Palestrina in Italy, Victoria in Spain, Tallis in England, Hassler in Germany, and Goudimel in France contributed to the newly burnished art of the motet. In England the motet assumed homophonic forms, leading to the formation of a specific British type of anthem. In Germany, Schütz and, nearly a century later, the great Bach (whose greatest work in the motet style was written for double chorus and 8 solo voices) created the specific form of the German motet. The motet suffered an irreversible decline in the 19th century; the few composers who stubbornly cultivated it, particularly in Germany, did so more out of reverence to its Gothic past than out of inner imperative. In the 20th century the motet suffered its final rigor mortis.

Mother, The. Opera by Hába, 1927–29, to his own libretto; 1st performed (in German) in Munich, 1931. The story concerns the enmity between the children of the 1st and 2nd marriages in a Czech family. The work is of historic significance because it includes quarter tones in the score, to be played by specifically constructed instruments. The singers received special training to be able to sing the minute intervals accurately.

Mother of Us All, The. Opera by Thomson, 1947, to a libretto by Gertrude Stein; 1st produced in N.Y. The universal mother of the title is Susan B. Anthony, the American suffragette who fought for the right to vote for women. The cast of characters are 2 modestly abbrev. names, Virgil T. and Gertrude S. The music is disarmingly triadic but greatly sophisticated in its seeming simplicity.

Mothers of Invention, The. See ZAPPA, FRANK.

motif (Fr.). MOTIVE.

motion. 1. The progression or conduct of a single part or melody; it is *conjunct* when progressing by steps, *disjunct* when progressing by skips. 2. The movement of one part in relation to that of another; in *contrary* or *opposite* motion, one part ascends while the other descends; in *oblique* motion, one part retains its tone while the other moves; in *parallel* motion, both parts move up or down by the same interval; in *similar* motion, both move up or down together by dissimilar intervals; in *mixed* motion, 2 or more of the above varieties occur at once between several parts.

motive (Ger. *Motiv*; Fr. *motif*). 1. A short phrase or figure used in development or imitation. 2. A leading motive. *Measure motive*, one whose accent coincides with that of the measure's downbeat.

moto (It.). Motion; speed; movement, tempo. *Con moto*, with animated and energetic movement; *moto perpetuo*, describing short pieces in very fast tempo in rondo form; also, the title of such pieces; *moto precedente*, at the previous tempo.

motteggiando (It.). In a bantering, facetious style.

motus (Lat.). MOTION; in music, contrapuntal motion, e.g., *motus contrarius*, contrary motion; *motus obliccus*, oblique motion; *motus rectus*, parallel motion.

Mountain Greenery. Song by Rodgers and Hart, 1926, from that year's edition of *The Garrick Gaieties*. The song resurfaced in the cinematic biography on these songwriters, *Words and Music* (1948).

mountain music. See OLD-TIME MUSIC.

Mourning Becomes Electra. Opera, 1967, by Martin David Levy (b. Passaic, N.J., Aug. 2, 1932), 1st performed in N.Y.; based on O'Neill's play. The ancient Aeschylus drama is here transmuted into a tragedy of conflicting emotions in the wake of the American Civil War. The wife of a returning soldier poisons him in order to continue her liaison with another. Her son, an Orestes *redivivus*, kills his mother's lover; the mother then kills herself. Horrified by his part in the tragedy, he also commits suicide, and the daughter is doomed to live alone in mourning. The score is written in an acridly atonal idiom, but occasional harmonious arias are vouchsafed to the singers.

Mourning Symphony. Haydn's Sym. No. 44 in E Minor (1772). The somewhat somber mood of the work must have suggested this nickname. The German title is *Trauersinfonie*.

mounted cornet. Organ stop mounted on a separate soundboard to render its tone louder.

mouth organ. Colloquialism for HARMONICA.

mouthpiece. That part of a wind instrument which a player places upon or between his lips.

mouvement (Fr.). Movement; tempo.

mouvementé (Fr.). In a lively tempo.

movable Do[h]. A SOLFÈGE (solfeggio) method used primarily to teach sight-singing, in which the major diatonic scale is sung to the original syllables of the method of Guido d'Arrezo (Doh, Rey, Me, Fah, Soh, Lah), with the leading tone designated by the syllable *Te*. For minor scales and chromatic progressions, the vowels are changed to *e* for sharp and *a* (pronounced "aw") for flat. The distinction of movable Doh is that the tonic note is also called Doh, whatever the key. This system, widely accepted in English-speaking countries, has the unfortunate consequence of divorcing the absolute sound from its adopted name; the British call this system TONIC SOL-FA. In all Latin countries and in Russia, the FIXED Do method is in use; Doh is immovable, is spelled Do, and designates the sound of pitch class C.

movement. 1. Tempo. 2. A principal division or section of a composition.

movendo il tempo (It.). Growing faster.

movimento (It.). Movement.

moyenne difficulté (Fr.). Of moderate difficulty; a term found on French eds. of instrumental works to alleviate the fear of potential buyers frightened by the sight of multiple pitch-black ligatures and fast-tempo marks.

Mozart, Franz Xaver Wolfgang, Austrian pianist and composer, grandson of (Johann Georg) Leopold Mozart, nephew of Maria Anna "Nannerl" Mozart Berchthold zu Sonnenburg, son of Wolfgang Amadeus Mozart and often called by his father's name; b. Vienna, July 26, 1791; d.

Carlsbad, July 29, 1844. He studied piano with F. Niemetschek in Prague while living with the Dusek family; continued his training with S. Neukomm, Andreas Steicher, Hummel, Salieri, G. Vogler, and Albrechtsberger in Vienna. After a period as a teacher in Lemberg and environs (1807–19), he embarked upon a major tour of Europe as a pianist (1819–21); then returned to Lemberg as a teacher (1822), receiving additional instruction in counterpoint from Johann Mederitsch or Gallus (1826); that same year he organized the Lemberg Cäcilien-Chor. He settled in Vienna (1838); was named honorary Kapellmeister of the Dom-Musik-Verein and the Mozarteum in Salzburg (1841); was made maestro compositore onorario of Rome's Congregazione ed Accademica Santa Cecilia (1842).

As a composer he revealed a gift for pianistic writing; among his works are 2 piano concertos; *Konzertvariationen* for Piano and Orch. (1820); Sinfonia in D Major; Piano Quintet, op. 1; 2 violin sonatas; *Grande Sonate* in E Major for Violin or Cello and Piano, op. 19 (1820); Rondo (Sonate) for Flute and Piano; Piano Sonata, op. 10 (1808); 3 sets of polonaises, and 11 sets of variations. Vocal: 4 cantatas, including 1 for Haydn's birthday (1805; not extant); unaccompanied choral pieces; songs.

Mozart, (Johann Georg) **Leopold,** German-born Austrian composer, violinist, and music theorist, father of Wolfgang Amadeus Mozart and Maria Anna "Nannerl" Mozart Berchthold zu Sonnenburg, and grandfather of Franz Xaver Wolfgang Mozart; b. Augsburg, Nov. 14, 1719; d. Salzburg, May 28, 1787. A bookbinder's son, he studied at the Augsburg Gymnasium (1727–35); continued his studies at the Lyceum attached to the Jesuit school of St. Salvator (1735–36). In 1737 he went to Salzburg, where he studied philosophy and law at the Benedictine Univ.; he received his bachelor of philosophy degree in 1738. Subsequently he entered the service of Johann Baptist, Count of Thurn-Valsassina and Taxis, the Salzburg canon and president of the consistory, as both valet and musician. In 1743 he became 4th violinist in the Prince-Archbishop's Court Orch.; also taught violin and keyboard to the choirboys of the Cathedral oratory. In 1757 he became composer to the court and chamber; in 1758 he was promoted to 2nd violinist in the Court Orch.; in 1762 he was appointed Vice-Kapellmeister. He married Anna Maria Pertl of Salzburg (1747); of their 7 children, only Maria Anna and Wolfgang survived infancy. He dedicated himself to the musical education of his children, but his methods of presentation of their concerts at times approached frank exploitation, and his advertisements of their appearances were in poor taste. However, there is no denying his great role in fostering his son's career.

Leopold was a thoroughly competent composer; the mutual influence between father and son was such that works long attributed to his son proved to be his. He was also important as a music theorist. He produced an influential violin method in his *Versuch einer gründlichen Violinschule* (Augsburg, 1756). His *Nannerl-Notenbuch* is a model of a child's music album; it was publ. in 1759. His vocal works include sacred cantatas, masses, litanies, school dramas, and secular lieder. He composed syms.; the famous *Kindersinfonie*, long attributed to Haydn, was in all probability a work by Leopold. Other orch.1 works include several concertos, among them *Die musikalische Schlittenfahrt* (1755); dances; etc. He also composed chamber music and works for the keyboard.

Mozart, Wolfgang Amadeus

~~~ ~~~ ~~~ ~~~ ~~~

Supreme and prodigious Austrian composer whose works in every genre are unsurpassed in lyric beauty, rhythmic variety, and effortless melodic invention, son of (Johann Georg) Leopold Mozart, father of Franz Xaver Wolfgang Mozart, and brother of Maria Anna "Nannerl" Mozart Berchthold zu Sonnenburg; b. Salzburg, Jan. 27, 1756; d. Vienna, Dec. 5, 1791. Wolfgang and his sister were the only 2 among the 7 children of Anna Maria and Leopold Mozart to survive infancy. Mozart's sister was 4 1/2 years older; she took harpsichord lessons from her father, and Mozart as a very young child eagerly absorbed the sounds of music. He soon began playing the harpsichord himself, and later studied the violin.

Leopold was an excellent musician, but he also appreciated the theatrical validity of the performances that Wolfgang and Nannerl began giving in Salzburg. In Jan. 1762 he took them to Munich, where they performed before the Elector of Bavaria. In Sept. 1762 they played for Emperor Francis I at his palace in Vienna. The family returned to Salzburg in Jan. 1763, and in June 1763 the children were taken to Frankfurt, where Wolfgang showed his skill in improvising at the keyboard. In Nov. 1763 they arrived in Paris, where they played before Louis XV; it was in Paris that Wolfgang's 1st compositions were printed (4 sonatas for harpsichord, with violin ad libitum). In Apr. 1764 they proceeded to London; there Wolfgang played for King George III.

In London he was befriended by Bach's son Johann Christian Bach, who gave exhibitions improvising 4-hands at the piano with the child Mozart. By that time Mozart had tried his ability in composing serious works; he wrote 2 syms. for a London performance, and the MS of another very early sym., purportedly written by him in London, was discovered in 1980. Leopold wrote home with undisguised pride: "Our great and mighty Wolfgang seems to know everything at the age of 7 that a man acquires at the age of 40." Knowing the power of publicity, he diminished Wolfgang's age, for at the time the child was fully 9 years old. In July 1765 they journeyed to the Netherlands, then set out for Salzburg, visiting Dijon, Lyons, Geneva, Bern, Zurich, Donaueschingen, and Munich on the way.

Arriving in Salzburg in Nov. 1766, Wolfgang applied himself to serious study of counterpoint under the tutelage of his father. In Sept. 1767 the family proceeded to Vienna, where Wolfgang began work on an opera, *La finta semplice*; his 2nd theater work was a singspiel, *Bastien und Bastienne*, which was produced in Vienna at the home of Dr. Franz Mesmer, the protagonist of the famous method of therapy by "animal magnetism," later known as Mesmerism. In Dec. 1768 Mozart led a performance of his *Missa solemnis* in C Minor before the royal family and court at the consecration of the Waisenhauskirche.

Upon Mozart's return to Salzburg in Jan. 1769, Archbishop Sigismund von Schrattenbach named him his Konzertmeister; however, the position was without remuneration. Still determined to broaden Mozart's artistic contacts, his father took him on an Italian tour. The announcement for a concert in Mantua on Jan. 1770, just a few days before Mozart's 14th birthday, was typical of the artistic mores of the time:

> A Sym. of his own composition; a harpsichord Concerto, which will be handed to him and which he will immediately play *prima vista*; a Sonata handed him in like manner, which he will provide with variations and afterwards repeat in another key; an Aria, the words for which will be handed to him and which he will immediately set to music and sing himself, accompanying himself on the harpsichord; a Sonata for harpsichord on a subject given him by the leader of the violins; a Strict Fugue on a theme to be selected, which he will improvise on the harpsichord; a Trio in which he will execute a violin part *all' improvviso*; and, finally, the latest sym. by himself.

Legends of Mozart's extraordinary musical ability grew; it was reported, for instance, that he wrote out the entire score of the Miserere by Allegri, which he had heard in the Sistine Chapel at the Vatican only twice. Young Mozart was subjected to numerous tests by famous Italian musicians, among them Giovanni Sammartini, Piccini, and Padre Martini; he was given a diploma as an elected member of the Accademia Filarmonica in Bologna after he had passed examinations in harmony and counterpoint. In Oct. 1770 the Pope made him a Knight of the Golden Spur. He was commissioned to compose an opera; the result was *Mitridate, re di Ponto*, which was performed in Milan on Dec. 1770; Mozart himself conducted 3 performances of this opera from the harpsichord; after a short stay in Salzburg he returned to Milan in 1771, where he composed the serenata *Ascanio in Alba* for the wedding festivities of Archduke Ferdinand (Oct. 1771). He returned to Salzburg late in 1771; his patron, Archbishop Schrattenbach, died about that time, and his successor, Archbishop Hieronymus Colloredo, seemed to be indifferent to Mozart as a musician.

Once more Mozart went to Italy, where his newest opera, *Lucio Silla*, was performed in Milan (Dec. 1772). He returned to Salzburg in Mar. 1773, but in July of that year he went to Vienna, where he became acquainted with the music of Haydn, who greatly influenced his instrumental style. Returning to Salzburg once more, he supervised the production of his opera *Il re pastore*, which was performed on Apr. 23, 1775.

In Mar. 1778 Mozart visited Paris again for a performance of his *Paris Sym.* (No. 31) at a Concert Spirituel. His mother died in Paris on July 3, 1778. Returning to Salzburg in Jan. 1779, he resumed his duties as Konzertmeister and also obtained the position of court organist at a salary of 450 gulden. In 1780 the Elector of Bavaria commissioned from him an opera seria, *Idomeneo*, which was successfully produced in Munich (Jan. 1781). In May 1781 Mozart lost his position with the Archbishop in Salzburg and decided to move to Vienna, which became his permanent home. There he produced the operatic masterpiece *Die Entführung aus dem Serail*, staged at the Burgtheater (July 1782), with excellent success. In Aug. 1782 he married Constanze Weber, the sister of Aloysia Weber, with whom he had previously been infatuated.

Two of his finest syms.—No. 35 in D Major, the *Haffner*, written for the Haffner family of Salzburg, and No. 36 in C Major, the *Linz*—date from 1782 and 1783, respectively. From this point forward Mozart's productivity reached extraordinary dimensions; but despite the abundance of commissions and concert appearances, he was unable to earn enough to sustain his growing family. Still, melodramatic stories of Mozart's abject poverty are gross exaggerations. He apparently felt no scruples in asking prosperous friends for financial assistance. Periodically he wrote to Michael Puchberg, a banker and a brother Freemason (Mozart joined the Masonic Order in 1784), with requests for loans (which he never repaid); invariably Puchberg obliged, but usually granting smaller amounts than Mozart requested. (The market price of Mozart autographs has grown exponentially; a begging letter to Puchberg would fetch, some 2 centuries after it was written, a hundred times the sum requested.)

In 1785 Mozart completed a set of 6 string quartets which he dedicated to Haydn; unquestionably the structure of these quartets owed much to Haydn's contrapuntal art. Haydn himself paid a tribute to Mozart's genius; Mozart's father quoted him as saying, "Before God and as an honest man I tell you that your son is the greatest composer known to me either in person or by name." In May 1786 Mozart's great opera buffa *Le nozze di Figaro* was produced in Vienna, obtaining a triumph with the audience; it was performed in Prague early in 1787 with Mozart in attendance. It was during that visit that Mozart wrote his 38th Sym. in D Major, known as the *Prague Sym.*; it was in Prague, also, that his operatic masterpiece *Don Giovanni* was produced, in Oct. 1787. It is interesting to note that at its Vienna performance the opera was staged under the title *Die sprechende Statue*, unquestionably with the intention of sensationalizing the story; the dramatic appearance of the statue of the Commendatore, introduced by the ominous sound of trombones, was a shuddering climax to the work. During the banquet scene leading up to the final confrontation between Giovanni and the Commendatore, Mozart quotes a melody from a then popular opera, *Un cosa rara* by (Atanasio Martín Ignacio) Vicente (Tadeo Francisco Pellegrin) Martín y Soler (1754–1806); even more intriguingly, Da Ponte was the librettist on that opera as well.

In Nov. 1787 Mozart was appointed Kammermusicus in Vienna as a successor to Gluck, albeit at a smaller salary: he received 800 gulden per annum as against Gluck's salary of 2,000 gulden. The year 1788 was a glorious one for Mozart and for music history; it was the year when he composed his last 3 syms.: No. 39 in E-flat Major; No. 40 in G Minor; and No. 41 in C Major, known under the name *Jupiter* (the Jovian designation was apparently attached to the work for the 1st time in British concert programs; its earliest use was in the program of the Edinburgh Festival in Oct. 1819). In the spring of 1789 Mozart went to Berlin; on the way he appeared as soloist in 1 of his piano concertos before the Elector of Saxony in Dresden, and also played the organ at the Thomaskirche in Leipzig. His visits in Potsdam and Berlin were marked by his private concerts at the court of Friedrich Wilhelm II; the King commissioned from him a set of 6 string quartets and a set of 6 piano sonatas, but Mozart died before completing these commissions.

Returning to Vienna, he began work on his opera buffa *Così fan tutte*; the opera was 1st performed in Vienna (Jan. 1790). In Oct. 1790 Mozart went to Frankfurt for the coronation of Emperor Leopold II. Returning to Vienna, he saw Haydn, who was about to depart for London. In 1791, his last year of life, he completed the score of *Die Zauberflöte*, with a German libretto by Emanuel Schikaneder. It was performed for the 1st time on Sept. 30, 1791, in Vienna. There followed a mysterious episode in Mozart's life; a stranger called on him with a request to compose a Requiem; the caller was an employee of Count Franz von Walsegg, who intended to have the work performed as his own in memory of his wife. Mozart was unable to finish the score, which was completed by his pupil Süssmayr, and by Eybler.

The immediate cause of Mozart's death at the age of 35 has been the subject of much speculation. Almost immediately after the sad event, myths and fantasies appeared in the press; the most persistent of them all was that Mozart had been poisoned by Salieri out of professional jealousy; this particularly morbid piece of invention gained circulation in European journals; the story was further elaborated upon by a report that Salieri confessed his unspeakable crime on his deathbed in 1825. Pushkin used the tale in his drama *Mozart and Salieri* (1830), which Rimsky-Korsakov set to music in his opera of the same title (1898); a fanciful dramatization of the Mozart-Salieri rivalry was made into a successful play, *Amadeus*, by Peter Shaffer, which was produced in London in 1979 and in N.Y. in 1980; it subsequently gained wider currency through its award-winning film version of 1984. The notion of Mozart's murder also appealed to the Nazis; in the ingenious version propagated by some German writers of the Hitlerian persuasion, Mozart was a victim of a double conspiracy of Masons and Jews who were determined to suppress the flowering of racial Germanic greatness; the Masons, in this interpretation, were outraged by his revealing of their secret rites in *Die Zauberflöte*, and allied themselves with plutocratic Jews to prevent further spread of his dangerous revelations.

Another myth related to Mozart's death that found its way into the majority of Mozart biographies and even into respectable reference works was that a blizzard raged during his funeral and that none of his friends could follow his body to the cemetery; this story is easily refuted by the records of the Vienna weather bureau for the day. It is also untrue that Mozart was buried in a pauper's grave; his body was removed from its original individual location because the family neglected to pay the mandatory dues.

The universal recognition of Mozart's genius during the 2 centuries since his death has never wavered among professional musicians, amateurs, and the general public, although those who preferred the larger-than-life qualities of Beethoven would fail to hear the proto-Romantic element amidst the Classic aesthetic in Mozart. In his music, smiling simplicity was combined with somber drama; lofty inspiration was contrasted with playful

diversion; profound meditation alternated with capricious moodiness; religious concentration was permeated with human tenderness.

Wolfgang Amadeus Mozart with his father and sister

Devoted as Mozart was to his art and respectful as he was of the rules of composition, he was also capable of mocking the professional establishment. A delightful example of this persiflage is his little piece *Ein musikalischer Spass* (1787), subtitled *Dorfmusikanten*, a "musical joke" at the expense of "village musicians," in which Mozart all but anticipated developments of MODERN MUSIC—using forbidden consecutive 5ths, allowing the violin to escape upward in a whole-tone scale, ending the entire work in a welter of polytonal triads.

Mozart is also probably the only great composer to have a town named after him—the town of Mozart, in the province of Saskatchewan, Canada, lying between Synyard and Elfros on a CPR main line that skirts the south end of Big Quill Lake. It consists of 2 elevators, a covered curling rink, a Centennial hall, a co-op store, and a handful of well-kept homes. A local recounts that the town was named in the early 1900s by one Mrs. Lunch, the wife of the stationmaster, who was reportedly a talented musician and very well thought of in the community. She not only named the town Mozart but also brought about the naming of the streets after other, equally famous musicians: Chopin, Wagner, and Liszt.

The variety of technical development in Mozart's works is all the more remarkable considering the limitations of instrumental means in his time; the topmost note on his keyboard was F above the 3rd ledger line, so that in the recapitulation in the 1st movement of his famous C-major piano sonata, the subject had to be dropped an octave lower to accommodate the modulation. The vocal technique displayed in his operas is amazing in its perfection; to be sure, the human voice has not changed since Mozart's time, but he knew how to exploit vocal resources to the utmost. This adaptability of his genius to all available means of sound production is the secret of the eternal validity of his music, and the explanation of the present popularity of minifestivals, such as the N.Y. concert series advertised as "Mostly Mozart."

The standard system of identification was established by L. von Köchel in his *Chronologisch-thematisches Verzeichnis sämtlicher Tonwerke Wolfgang Amadé Mozarts* (Leipzig, 1862; 6th ed., rev. by F. Giegling, A. Weinmann, and G. Sievers, Wiesbaden, 1964). The catalogue numbers of the original catalogue are known as *K.*; the rev. numbers of the 6th ed., which follow, are often referred to as K^6. Mozart also kept a catalogue during the latter part of his life, known as *Mozarts Werkverzeichnis 1784–1791*. Among the multiplicity of his music one may find the following operas: *La finta giardiniera*, K. 196, opera buffa (Munich, 1775); *Il re pastore*, K. 208, dramma per musica (Archbishop's palace, Salzburg, 1775); *Zaïde*, K. 344, 336b, singspiel (unfinished; dialogue rewritten and finished; overture and finale added by Anton André, Frankfurt, 1866); *Lo sposo deluso*, K. 430, 424a, opera buffa (unfinished); *Der Schauspieldirektor*, K. 486, singspiel (Schonbrunn Palace, Heitzing, 1786); *La clemenza di Tito*, K. 621, opera seria (National Theater, Prague, 1791). Ballet: *Les Petits Riens*, K. Anh. 10, 299b (Opéra, Paris, 1778); arias, duets, ensembles, and scenes for voice and orch.; canons; songs for voice and keyboard. Religious vocal: *Die Schuldigkeit des ersten Gebots*, K. 35, sacred drama (part 1 by Mozart, Salzburg, 1767); Missa Solemnis in C Minor, K. 139, 47a, *Waisenhausmesse* (Vienna, 1768); Missa brevis in D Minor, K. 65, 61a (Collegiate Church, Salzburg, 1769); Missa in C Major, K. 66, *Dominicus* (St. Peter's, Salzburg, 1769); *La Betulia liberata*, K. 118, 74c, oratorio (1771); Missa in C Major,

K. 167, *In honorem Ssmae Trinitatis* (1773); Missa brevis in F Major, K. 192, 186f (1774); Missa brevis in D Major, K. 194, 186h (1774); Missa brevis in C Major, K. 220; 196b, *Spatzenmesse* (1775–76); Missa in C Major, K. 262, 246a (1775); Missa in C Major, K. 257, *Credo* (1776); Missa brevis in C Major, K. 258, *Spaur* (1776); Missa brevis in C Major, K. 259, *Organ Solo* (1776); Missa brevis in B-flat Major, K. 275, 272b (St. Peter's, Salzburg, 1777); Missa in C Major, K. 317, *Coronation* (1779); Missa Solemnis in C Major, K. 337 (1780); *Die Maurerfreude*, K. 471, cantata ("Zur gekronten Hoffnung" Lodge, Vienna, 1785); *Eine kleine Freimaurer-Kantate*, K. 623 (1791; "Zur neugekronten Hoffnung" Lodge, Vienna, 1791); Requiem in D Minor, K. 626 (1791; unfinished; completed by Süssmayr, Eybler); motets; liturgical pieces.

Although the traditional count is 41 syms., present estimates list more than 50 such works, although a few early works remain in dispute. The problem is Mozart's using the normal way of learning music in his day—writing it down—so that works found in his handwriting were mistaken for his compositions; this occurs in early syms. and piano concertos. While it is impossible to describe the stylistic development in the syms. here, it can be posited that No. 25 in G Minor, K. 183, 173dB (late 1773) is the 1st of the "mature" syms. it forecasts the haunting effect of the later G-minor sym. (No. 40). Among the subsequent works in this genre are: No. 28 in C Major, K. 200, 189k (1774); No. 29 in A Major, K. 201, 186a (1774); No. 30 in D Major, K. 202, 186b (1774); No. 31 in D Major, K. 297, 300a, *Paris* (1778: with 2 slow movements); No. 33 in B-flat Major, K. 319 (1779); No. 34 in C Major, K. 338 (1780); No. 35 in D Major, K. 385, *Haffner* (1782); No. 36 in C Major, K. 425, *Linz* (1783); No. 38 in D Major, K. 504, *Prague* (1786); No. 39 in E-flat Major, K. 543 (1788); No. 40 in G Minor, K. 550 (1788); No. 41 in C Major, K. 551, *Jupiter* (1788). Piano concertos: Included in the traditional count of 27 are 4 pastiches of other composers' pieces, done as exercises; No. 7 in F Major for 3 Pianos, K. 242 (1776); and No. 10 in E-flat Major for 2 Pianos, K. 365, 316a (1779).

For Mozart the piano concerto was the best way to show off his talents as keyboard player, composer, leader, and provider of the newest musical novelties. Fashion and faddism were as much a part of the Classic music scene as of today's popular music, a fact that Mozart struggled with for most of his career. His piano concertos from the Vienna period include: No. 12 in A Major, K. 414, 385p (1782); No. 11 in F Major, K. 413, 387a (1782–83); No. 13 in C Major, K. 415, 387b (1782–83); No. 14 in E-flat Major, K. 449 (1784); No. 15 in B-flat Major, K. 450 (1784); No. 16 in D Major, K. 451 (1784); No. 17 in G Major, K. 453 (1784); No. 18 in B-flat Major, K. 456 (1784); No. 19 in F Major, K. 459 (1784); No. 20 in D Minor, K. 466 (1785); No. 21 in C Major, K. 467 (its middle movement was used in an otherwise forgettable film, *Elvira Madigan*; the piece became famous as a result; 1785); No. 22 in E-flat Major, K. 482 (1785); No. 23 in A Major, K. 488 (1786); No. 24 in C Minor, K. 491 (1786); No. 25 in C Major, K. 503 (1786); No. 26 in D Major, K. 537, *Coronation* (1788); No. 27 in B-flat Major, K. 595 (1788?–91); also 2 rondos for piano and orch.; 5 authentic violin concertos; other works with orch.: *Concertone* in C Major for 2 Violins, K. 90, 186e (1774); Rondo in B-flat Major for Violin, K. 269, 261a (1776); Sinfonia concertante in E-flat Major for Violin and Viola, K. 364, 320d (1779); Rondo in C Major for Violin, K. 373 (1781). Wind instruments: Concerto for Bassoon in B-flat Major, K. 191, 186e (1774); Concerto for Flute in G Major, K. 313, 285c (1778); Concerto for Oboe or Flute in C/D Major, K. 314, 285d (1778); Andante for Flute in C Major, K. 315, 285e (1779–80); Concerto for Flute and Harp in C Major, K. 299, 297c (1778); Rondo for Horn in E-flat Major, K. 371 (1781; unfinished); 4 concertos for horn (1783–1791); Concerto for Clarinet in A Major, K. 622 (1791).

Numerous functional and occasional works, including: Serenata notturna in D Major, K. 239 (1776); Serenade in D Major, K. 250, 248b, *Haffner* (1776); Divertimento in D Major, K. 251 (1776); Serenade in D Major, K. 320, *Posthorn* (1779); *Maurerische Trauermusik* in C Minor, K.

477, 479a (1785); *Ein musikalischer Spass* in F Major, K. 522 (1787; *Eine kleine Nachtmusik* in G major, K. 525 (1787); divertimentos for wind ensemble; marches (2 not extant); over 100 German dances, ländler, and contredanses.

The chamber music includes 23 string quartets, including the 6 quartets dedicated to Haydn: G Major, K. 387 (1782); D Minor, K. 421, 417b (1783); E-flat Major, K. 428, 421b (1783); B-flat Major, K. 458, *Jagd* (1784); A Major, K. 464 (1785); C Major, K. 465, *Dissonanz* (1785); 6 string quintets (2 violins, 2 violas, and cello), the finest examples of this genre ever written; 4 quartets for flute, violin, viola, and cello (1777–87); Quartet in F Major for Oboe, Violin, Viola, and Cello, K. 370, 368b (1781); Quintet in E-flat Major for Horn, Violin, 2 Violas, and Cello, K. 407, 386c (1782); Quintet in A Major for Clarinet, 2 Violins, Viola, and Cello, K. 581 (1789); various string chamber works, including Duo in G Major for Violin and Viola, K. 423 (1783); Duo in B-flat Major for Violin and Viola, K. 424 (1783); Trio (Divertimento) in E-flat Major for Violin, Viola, and Cello, K. 563 (1788). Keyboard and other instruments: 7 trios (including 1 divertimento, 1776–88); Quintet in E-flat Major for Piano, Oboe, Clarinet, Bassoon, and Horn, K. 452 (1784); 2 quartets for piano, violin, viola, and cello; Adagio and Rondo in C Minor for Glass Harmonica, Flute, Oboe, Viola, and Cello, K. 617 (1791); over 30 keyboard and violin sonatas, many unfinished (1762–88); 17 solo keyboard sonatas (1775–89); 5 sonatas for keyboard duet; Sonata in D Major for 2 Keyboards, K. 448, 375a (1781); 16 variations for keyboard solo and 1 for keyboard duet; many miscellaneous pieces, including 17 sonatas for organ, most with 2 violins and bassoon.

Mozart Berchthold zu Sonnenburg, Maria Anna "Nannerl," Austrian pianist and teacher, (Johann Georg) Leopold Mozart, aunt of Franz Xaver Wolfgang Mozart, and sister of Wolfgang Amadeus Mozart; b. Salzburg, July 30, 1751; d. there, Oct. 29, 1829. She was taught music by her father from her earliest childhood, and appeared in public as a pianist with her brother; after their travels together in Europe she returned to Salzburg and eventually devoted herself mainly to teaching. In 1784 she married Baron von Berchthold zu Sonnenburg, who died in 1801. She went blind in 1825. Although nearly 5 years older than Wolfgang, she survived him by 38 years.

Mozart i Salieri. Opera by Rimsky-Korsakov, 1898, to a libretto after Pushkin's poem; 1st produced in Moscow. Pushkin's text gives literary sanction to a legend that spread shortly after Mozart's death, accusing the eminently respectable Italian composer Salieri (who was for a time a teacher of Beethoven) of poisoning Mozart. In Pushkin's poem and in the opera, Salieri declares that were Mozart allowed to live on, other composers—honest, industrious, but not blessed by genius—would be condemned to futility. Rimsky-Korsakov used authentic excerpts from Mozart's compositions as well as musical allusions to Salieri's opera *Tarare*, which Mozart prized highly.

Mozartiana. The 4th orch.l suite by Tchaikovsky, 1887, arranged from various instrumental and choral works by Mozart. It was 1st performed in Moscow.

mp. Mezzo-piano.

mṛidaṅgam. Classical drum of southern India, in an elongated barrel shape with 2 heads of different diameters. It is made of wood, although its name refers to clay. The heads, as in many other wooden MEMBRANOPHONES, are attached to hoops and tightened by leather thongs; tuning is accomplished by tension wedges and a paste, different for each head. The 2 heads are tuned an octave apart.

muance (Fr.). In medieval solmization, mutation from one hexachord to another.

mudanza (Sp.). A stanza in a VILLANCICO of the Renaissance period.

Muddy Waters. WATERS, MUDDY.

Muette de Portici, La (The Mute Girl of Portici; also called *Masaniello*). Opera by Auber, 1828, 1st performed in Paris. The Neopolitan fisherman Masaniello, the brother of the mute girl of Portici (a small fishing village near Naples), leads a rebellion against the Spanish rule; he is mysteriously murdered just as he achieves his goal of overthrowing the Spanish viceroy in Naples. His deaf-mute sister throws herself into the crater of Mt. Vesuvius during an eruption. The story has a historical foundation: an actual Masaniello led a successful uprising in 1647; he did get murdered, but Mt. Vesuvius erupted 16 years before it did in the finale of *La Muette de Portici*. When the opera was performed in Brussels in 1830, the people in the audience became so excited by this operatic cry for freedom that they spilled out into the streets demanding independence for Belgium; a year or so later they achieved it. *Post hoc ergo propter hoc?*

mugam (Azeri.). MAQĀM.

Mulligan, Gerry (Gerald Joseph), outstanding American jazz baritone saxophonist and arranger; b. N.Y., June 4, 1927; d. Darien, Conn., Jan. 19, 1996. His formative years were spent in Philadelphia, where he learned to play piano; played reed instruments and worked professionally as an arranger while still in his teens; then went to N.Y. (1946), where he played reed instruments and wrote arrangements for Gene Krupa's big band; after performing with Miles Davis (1948–50), he acquired a reputation as one of the finest baritone saxophonists of his era. In 1952 he formed the 1st of several "pianoless" quartets, with which he toured extensively and made recordings; led his own big band on a tour of Europe in 1960 and of Japan in 1964; also made appearances with various jazz notables, and began playing the soprano saxophone. He was an important figure in the development of "cool" jazz, remaining a protean figure in jazz circles for decades.

multiphonics. A modern method of wind sound production that through overblowing and special fingerings results in 2 or more sounds simultaneously by a single performer on a monophonic instrument.

Munch (born Münch), **Charles,** eminent Alsatian conductor; b. Strasbourg, Sept. 26, 1891; d. Richmond, Va., Nov. 6, 1968. His father, Ernst Münch (b. Niederbronn, Dec. 31, 1859; d. Strasbourg, Apr. 1, 1928), was an organist and choral conductor. Charles studied violin at the Strasbourg Cons. and with Lucien Capet in Paris; at the outbreak of World War I (1914) he enlisted in the German army; made a sergeant of artillery, he was gassed at Peronne and wounded at Verdun; after the end of the war (1918) and his return to Alsace-Lorraine (1919), he became a French citizen. Having received further violin training from Carl Flesch in Berlin, he pursued a career as a soloist; was also prof. of violin at the Leipzig Cons. and concertmaster of the Gewandhaus Orch. there. In 1932 he made his professional conducting debut in Paris with the Straram Orch.; studied conducting with Alfred Szendrei there (1933–40).

He quickly rose to prominence; was conductor of Paris's Orch. de la Soc. Philharmonique (1935–38) and became a prof. at the École Normale de Musique (1936). In 1938 he became music director of the Soc. des Concerts du Conservatoire de Paris, remaining in that post during the years of the German occupation during World War II; refusing to collaborate with the Nazis, he gave his support to the Resistance and was awarded the Légion d'Honneur in 1945. He made his U.S. debut as a guest conductor of the Boston Sym. Orch. (1946); a transcontinental tour of the U.S. with the French National Radio Orch. followed in 1948. In 1949 he was appointed music director of the Boston Sym. Orch., which he and Monteux took on its 1st European tour in 1952; they took it again to Europe in 1956, also touring in the Soviet Union, making it the 1st U.S. orch. to do so.

After retiring from his Boston post in 1962, Munch made appearances as a guest conductor; also helped to launch the Orch. de Paris in 1967. Munch acquired an outstanding reputation as an interpreter of the French repertoire, his performances being marked by spontaneity, color, and elegance. French music of the 20th century also occupied a prominent place on his programs; he introduced new works by Roussel, Milhaud, Honegger, and others. He wrote *Je suis chef d'orchestre* (Paris, 1954).

Mundstück (Ger.). A mouthpiece for wind instruments.

Munrow, David (John), gifted English recorder player; b. Birmingham, Aug. 12, 1942; d. (suicide) Chesham Bois, Buckinghamshire, May 15, 1976. He studied English at Pembroke College, Cambridge; during this period (1961–64) he founded an ensemble for the furtherance of early English music and organized a recorder consort. In 1967 he formed the Early Music Consort of London, with which he gave many successful concerts of medieval and Renaissance music; also was active with his own BBC radio program. He lectured on the history of early music at the Univ. of Leicester (from 1967) and was prof. of recorder at London's Royal Academy of Music (from 1969); publ. the vol. *Instruments of the Middle Ages and Renaissance* (London, 1976). He killed himself for obscure reasons in his early maturity.

munter (Ger.). Lively, gay, animated.

Muradeli, Vano (Ilyich). See GREAT FRIENDSHIP, THE.

murky bass. A curious term of puzzling origin applied to rudimentary accompaniment in broken octaves in the bass, much in use in rococo music. Some philologists suggest that *murky* is taken from the English word that means exactly what it says: unclear and obfuscating.

Musealer Klangmaterialismus (Ger.). A neologism coined by a German musicologist meaning approximately "museumesque materialism of timbre," i.e., the attempt of instrument makers, performers, and arrangers to replicate the precise sound of an obsolete instrument.

musette (Fr.). 1. A small oboe. 2. A reed stop on the organ. 3. A small French bagpipe, very popular in the Baroque era. It was much more ornate in appearance than the Scottish bagpipe and was used in ballets given at the French court. Music was written for the instrument by Hotteterre, Boismortier, Rameau, and Montéclair. 4. A pastoral dance of the French ballet, characterized by a protracted drone and 12/8 meter; the music reflects its fragile character, totally opposed to the gigue in character. Musettes are found in many Baroque instrumental suites by French composers, and also in the English Suite No. 3 of Bach; as late as 1925, Schoenberg included one in his op. 25 piano suite. The middle section of the Gavotte is often called *Musette* when it has a sustained drone on the tonic and dominant. An older name for the musette is *cornemuse*.

Musgrave, Thea, remarkable Scottish composer; b. Barnton, Midlothian, May 27, 1928. She pursued preliminary medical studies at the Univ. of Edinburgh, and concurrently studied with Mary Grierson (musical analysis) and Hans Gál (composition and counterpoint), receiving her B.Mus. (1950) and winning the Donald Tovey Prize; then studied privately and at the Paris Cons. with Boulanger (1952–54); later was a scholarship student of Copland at the Berkshire Music Center in Tanglewood (1959). She taught at the Univ. of London (1958–65), then was a visiting prof. of composition at the Univ. of Calif. at Santa Barbara (1970); also lectured at various other U.S. and English univs.; likewise made appearances as a conductor on both sides of the Atlantic. She held 2 Guggenheim fellowships (1974–75; 1982). In 1971 she married the American violinist Peter Mark, who later served as conductor of the Virginia Opera Assoc. in Norfolk. She was named Distinguished Prof. of Music at Queens College in N.Y. in 1987.

At the outset of her career she followed the acceptable modern style of composition, but soon the diatonic lyricism of the initial period of her creative evolution gave way to increasingly chromatic constructions, eventually systematized into serial organization. She described her theatrical works as "dramatic abstracts" in form, because even in the absence of a programmatic design they revealed some individual dramatic traits. Appreciated by critics and audiences alike, her compositions, in a variety of styles but invariably effective and technically accomplished, enjoyed numerous performances in Europe and America. She is best known for her vocal works; these include the operas *Abbott of Drimock*, chamber opera (1955); *The Decision* (1964–65; London, 1967); *The Voice of Ariadne* (1972–73); *Mary, Queen of Scots* (1976); *A Christmas Carol* (1979); *An Occurrence at Owl Creek Bridge*, radio opera (1981); *Harriet, the Woman Called Moses* (1985). She has also composed music for ballets, and orch.l and chamber works.

music

〰〰 〰〰 〰〰 〰〰 〰〰

The word *music* (It. *musica*; Ger. *Musik*; Fr. *musique*) is derived from the Greek *mousikē*, an art of the Muses (sing. *mousa*). Euterpe, the Muse of Tragedy and flute playing, and Polyhymnia, the Muse of singing, are regarded as the inspiring deities of music—Euterpe because in ancient Greece music was closely connected with tragedy and theatrical spectacles were invariably accompanied by the playing on the flute, and Polyhymnia because the beginning of music was marked by a multiplicity of songs.

In present terms *music* may be defined as a meaningful succession of perceptible sounds in temporal motion. These sounds may be single sonorous units (as in melody) or combinations of several such units (as in harmony and counterpoint). The temporal motion may consist of sounds of equal duration (simple chant) or of unequal duration (rhythmed melody, or MELORHYTHM). Melorhythms may be patterned symmetrically, in well-demarcated periods (corresponding to unchanged meter in versification), or in asymmetrical fragments. The perfection of a melorhythmic figure is determined by the balance between melody and rhythm. When melodic elements (tones) vary greatly in pitch, the rhythm may be allowed to remain quiescent; when the melody is confined to a few notes, and in extreme cases to a single note, then rhythm must show variety. This interdependence of melody and rhythm in a melorhythm may be expressed by the formula $R \times M = C$, where R stands for rhythm, M stands for melody, and C stands for an empirical constant. The validity of this formula may be verified by examining some folk songs or great melodies by famous composers. When the melodic range is narrow, the rhythm usually exhibits variety; when melodic tones are constantly in flux, the rhythm may adhere to symmetric or uniform patterns. The essence of melorhythm depends on the proper balance between melody and rhythm.

Music is written down by means of symbols or notes. A medieval monk, St. Isidore of Seville, opined in the 7th century that music is an art that can be preserved by oral tradition only because tones can never be notated (*scribi non possunt*). The history of musical notation has indeed been arduous, but for the last 4 centuries it has assumed a fairly uniform aspect. The height of a musical tone is measured by the relative position on a staff of 5 lines, with clefs indicating the selected pitch of a specific note, usually G, C, or F, placed on any of the 5 lines on the staff; the rest of the notes are calculated from the clef note, with each space and each line reckoning for 1 diatonic degree.

The concept of music does not necessarily signify beauty or attractiveness; indeed, music of primitive peoples, which is beautiful to them, may appear chaotic and ugly to an outsider. Within the memory of many musicians, compositions by modern masters were condemned by critics as cacophonous. In his famous treatise on aesthetics, *Vom Musikalisch-Schönen*, Hanslick defines music as "a tonally moving form." This definition begs the question, for the key word *tonally* embraces the "moving forms" of Liszt, Wagner, and other representatives of the "music of the future," which was anathema to Hanslick. Kant described music as "an artistic arrangement of sensations of hearing," which is logically acceptable, for it includes any subjectively artistic succession of musical elements. Hegel declared that the aim of music is "to render in sounds the innermost self which moves in itself according to the subjective feeling for one's ideal soul," a statement that is so involved that it may signify any sound, or any combination of sounds, that expresses an emotion.

The most extreme manifestations of the modern avant-garde would find their place in the definition of music by the most rigid and most obfuscating of German philosophers, Schopenhauer, to whom the human will was the source of all action. He asserted that music is a "reflection of the will itself, revealing its very essence, whereas other arts treat but the shadows of the will." The Romantic poet Jean Paul describes music as "a reflected sound from a remote world." Inspired by the medieval concept of the HARMONY OF THE SPHERES, Schelling senses in music "the perceived rhythm and harmony of the observable universe itself." Musical theorists seeking to delimit music from other arts emphasize its unique capacity to convey emotions and meaning, to express spiritual and sensory phenomena in terms which use no language and no pictorial representation. Hegel himself admitted that music is "sufficient unto itself and therefore self-explanatory."

Great poets extolled music as a catalyst of passion and a motive force for bravery. Shakespeare expressed this quality in the ringing lines, "The man that hath no music in himself/nor is not moved with concord of sweet sounds/. . . let no such man be trusted." In his *Ode on a Grecian Urn*, Keats said that music should be perceived in silence: "Heard melodies are sweet, but those unheard are sweeter." Longfellow followed the philosophers in saying that "music is the universal language of mankind." Scientists seem to agree, to judge by the suggestion of an astronomer that a diagram of a Bach fugue should be included in a rocket sent outside the solar system on the chance that it will be intercepted and decoded by the hypothetical beings in distant galaxies.

In the Middle Ages music was part of mathematics, included in the quadrivium of the universities. In poetic language, the word *numbers* means music. "Will no one tell me what she sings?" Wordsworth questioned, and surmised: "Perhaps the plaintive numbers flow/For old, unhappy, far-off things." Leibniz said: "Music is a kind of counting performed by the mind without knowing that it is counting." This definition comes remarkably close to Bertrand Russell's description of mathematics as "the subject in which we never know what we are talking about, nor whether what we are saying is true."

music(al) box. Mechanical musical instruments that were perfected shortly after the invention of clockwork, about the year 1200. The 1st mechanical music instrument was the BARREL ORGAN, manufactured for the Archbishop of Salzburg in 1502. It had 350 pipes into which music was channeled from a barrel with flexible pins. This was followed by mechanical carillons, the best of which were made in Flanders and Holland in the 17th century. Chiming watches that played tunes appeared in France in the 18th century.

The Swiss music box has steel tongues with a definite pitch which are plucked by pins on a rotating metal cylinder or barrel, turned by clockwork. The 1st models were made by Antoine Favre of Geneva in 1796. The music box industry reached its greatest development about 1870; it declined with the appearance of the phonograph, a rival too mighty for the tinkling pins and tongues. Apart from chiming watches, music boxes were manufactured in the form of snuff boxes and sewing boxes. Musical dolls are music boxes which survive into the present time.

Music Box Revue, The. An annual series of revues, 1921–24, with songs composed by I. Berlin; the shows took place at the eponymous theater that he co-owned. Among the songs written for or interpolated in the revues are *Say It with Music, Lady of the Evening, What'll I Do?,* and *All Alone.*

music drama. The original description of opera as it evolved in Florence early in the 17th century (*dramma per musica*); Wagner adopted this term in order to emphasize the dramatic element in his spectacles (*Musikdrama*).

Music for Strings, Percussion, and Celesta. A multi-movement work by Bartók, 1937, in which percussion instruments play a major part. The 4-part structure can be viewed as the slow-fast *verbunkos* form (twice), or perhaps the late Baroque sinfonia; the opening string fugue is as powerful as any since Beethoven's late quartets. The piece was 1st performed in Basel.

Music for the Theater. Suite for chamber orch. by Copland, 1925, in 5 contrasting movements. It was premiered by the Boston Sym. Orch. under Koussevitzky.

music hall. A place and type of light entertainment popular in British cities in the Victorian and Edwardian eras; it was modeled after the Paris CAFÉ CHANTANT. Music halls usually featured songs and dances spiced by an infinitesimal display of sensuality, sufficient to make moral guardians shudder with horror at the depravity of the thing. A further degradation was afforded by the adjacent *cabinets particuliers*, where a peer or a lord might entertain a lady of a lower class away from the common herd. As the 20th century proceeded, music hall performers entered the traveling vaudeville circuits, which persisted in Britain until World War II.

Music in the Air. Musical by Kern and Hammerstein, 1932. The story describes a love affair between a schoolteacher and the daughter of the leader of a local choral society in Bavaria. The 2 collaborate on a song and try to get it published in Munich; there the young schoolteacher is attracted to a prima donna and the girl flirts with an opera librettist. Not achieving professional success and tired of extracurricular romances, the couple return to their

mountain town. Includes *I've Told Ev'ry Little Star* and *The Song Is You.*

music journals

〰〰 〰〰 〰〰 〰〰 〰〰

Before the advent of mass publications of general newspapers which included a special department devoted to the review of concerts, music criticism existed only in the form of theoretical discussions in specially printed pamphlets. Heated polemical exchanges accompanied the progress of the GUERRE DES BOUFFONS and the famous Gluck-Piccini controversy in the 18th century. Germany was a pioneer in musical journalism; essays on technical subjects were published in connection with public performances. The 1st musical periodical that published critical evaluations of musical works was the *Allgemeine musikalische Zeitung*, founded in 1798 and published, with an occasional hiatus, until 1881. It was for this journal that Schumann wrote, at the age of 19, his unsigned article saluting Chopin as a genius.

In 1834 Schumann founded his own publication, *Neue Zeitschrift für Musik*, dedicated to the propaganda of "new music" of a Romantic mold; after many interruptions it was reincarnated after World War I. The German music weekly, *Signale für die musikalische Welt*, founded in 1841, lasted almost a century until World War II finally killed it off. The informative weekly *Allgemeine Musikzeitung* was also the victim of World War II after 70 years of a relatively prosperous existence. With the exception of Schumann's journal, these publications adopted a conservative, not to say reactionary, attitude toward the novel musical tendencies of each successive period. In France, *La Revue Musicale* continued its uncertain existence from 1827 to 1880, was reincarnated under the same title in 1920, only to falter and die of inanition. *Le Ménestrel* lasted more than 100 years after its founding in 1833, with the inevitable collapse during the Paris Commune and the 1st World War; the 2nd World War put a finish to it. Its critical attitudes during the 1st century of its existence were definitely reactionary; it damned Wagner and Debussy with equal fervor. In England, the most durable monthly is *The Musical Times*, founded in 1844 and still

going strong after nearly 150 years. In the U.S., musical journals of opinion had a relatively brief life. In the 19th century, *Dwight's Journal of Music* enjoyed respect; it was dull, and it damned Wagner.

In the meantime, artists of varying degrees of excellence; German, Italian, and Russian music teachers; and minor musicians of all calibers became commodities of European import and commanded a great deal of advertising. In America these demands were met in a multiplicity of commercial music periodicals, of which *The Musical Courier* and *Musical America* were particularly prominent. They published weekly issues that featured dispatches by specially assigned European correspondents, and reproduced excellent photographs of the current celebrities who bought advertising space. For a modest fee even for those times, these publications carried cover portraits of mustachioed tenors and amplebosomed prima donne, and occasionally even an American face. The ads informed on the activities of music teachers ("Mr. X has returned from Europe and will accept a limited number of exceptionally talented pupils"), voice teachers with Italian surnames ("Guarantee bel canto within 6 months by inhaling bottled compressed air from Naples"), "Miss Y triumphs in Muleshoe, Texas," etc.

As the careers of these musical worthies became less and less profitable and interest in the artistic and amorous goings-on in the musical world waned, the journals themselves began to languish and finally expired. *Musical America* survived as a shriveled appendix to *High Fidelity*; it, too, has disappeared. *The Etude* appealed mainly to music lovers and amateurs; it published sentimental biographies of contemporary musicians, as well as simplified selections of their more digestible compositions, but it, too, succumbed to the disenchantment of the times. In place of these publications there arose a crop of commercialized periodicals devoted to recordings, radio, and television, with only a sprinkling of informative material on their pages. Musicological journals carried on a subsidized existence.

In America, *The Musical Quarterly* is the most important publication in the scholarly field; in England, *Music and Letters* and *Music Review* purvey selective information. There are also music journals of some value in Italy. In Russia, the monthly *Sovietskaya Musica* furnishes information on Soviet music. In Latin America, only the

Revista Musical Chilena appears with some regularity. The international AVANT-GARDE puts out sporadic issues of great interest to their particular audiences. The most extreme of them was *Source*, published in Calif., without visible financial support, printing the most fantastic samples of ultramodern productions lavishly illustrated in a variety of colors; it carried a feverish existence for several years before collapsing.

Music Man, The. Musical by M. Willson, 1957. An affable flim-flam man cons officials in small towns in the Midwest by getting them to form school bands, collecting money for instruments, and then moving on to the next town to trick other victims. But his would-be victims are so inspired by his rhetoric, and he so influenced by a librarian named Marian, that he decides to see the thing through, resulting in a splendid marching band. Many songs have endured, including *76 Trombones*, *Trouble*,

Goodnight My Someone, My White Knight, Till There Was You, and *Gary, Indiana*.

music of the spheres. See HARMONY OF THE SPHERES.

music theater (U.K. *theatre*). Any small to moderate musical stage work involving a dramatic element in its performance; frequently distinguished from opera by its scale and scope.

music therapy

≈≈ ≈≈ ≈≈ ≈≈ ≈≈

The study and use of musical stimuli and activity in the evaluation, remediation, or maintenance of health; it developed into a bona fide profession at about the time of World War II in the U.S., with univ. curricula following within the decade.

In earlier times, anecdote served the role that research does now. A Sicilian youth suspected that his beloved was faithless. His suspicions were further inflamed by the sounds of flute music in the Phrygian mode. Seized by madness, he rushed into her house; Pythagoras, taking temporary leave of his mathematical calculations, took notice of the young man's condition and ordered the flute player to change from the Phrygian to the Dorian mode; this modulation had an immediate soothing effect on the youth, who became philosophically calm. The ancient Greek PHRYGIAN mode (which, it should be noted, corresponds to the IONIAN mode in Gregorian chant, identical with C major), was regarded by the Greeks as most apt to cause hyperventilation in a human being.

At the time when tempers were short and modes were untempered, Alexander the Great was so sensitive that when a musician played a Phrygian air on the lyre he unsheathed his sword and slew one of his guests. The musician precluded further slaughter by switching to a less-exciting mode. Aristotle tells of alleviating the pain of slaves by causing flute music to be played while they were being punished by flogging. Terpander pacified a menacing crowd of rebellious citizens by singing in beneficial modalities, accompanying himself on a 7-string lyre of his invention. So impressed were his listeners that they burst into tears and rushed to kiss the feet of their tyrant. Tyrtacus, the Athenian, was sent to Sparta on a mission to undermine the indomitable Spartan spirit by playing an elegy, *Eunomia* (good law), to them, but when he inadvertently changed to the martial DORIAN mode, the Spartans rose in wrath and marched belligerently on Athens.

Plato declared that civil obedience can be achieved by means of music. Indeed, public decrees were often recited in ancient Greece to the melodious accompaniment on the lyre. Damon of Athens succeeded in quieting down drunken youths by playing spondaic measures on the flute. Maecenas, the legendary patron of Roman poetry, cured his chronic insomnia by listening to distant sounds of music. The Phrygian mode was recommended by Theophrastus, favorite disciple of Aristotle, for cure of sciatica, with the vertical flute to be held close to the affected nerve ganglion. Many victims of melancholy regained their self-confidence when Phrygian tunes were played for them, Theophrastus reports. Flute playing in the Phrygian mode was also proposed by Caelius Aurelianus for temporary relief from lumbago and arthritis; at the sound of the flute, the ailing person would begin to tremble, thus stimulating the nerves affected and curing the disease.

Belief in the beneficial and curative properties of music persisted even when the model dichotomy of the Phrygian and Dorian modes were replaced by "scientific" reasoning and experimentation. Peter Lichtenthal, in a remarkable volume, *The Musical Doctor*, published in 1811, suggests musical remedies for a variety of human ills; his list includes incidence of stupidity among school children, particularly girls. Quoting a contemporary French physician, he reports that a young girl, affected by irresistible nymphomania, became morally restrained when she was forced to listen to sweet music 3 times a day.

"Music has charm to soothe the savage breast," William Congreve wrote, but the statement is not always true. If the chroniclers can be trusted, Eric the Good, King of Denmark, ordered all weapons removed from his reach before the court lutenist began to play for fear that he might be moved to violence by the sounds of music. So strong was this impulse, it is said, that the moment the lutenist began to play, the King rushed out, seized a sword, and slew 4 men. On the other side of the ledger, King Philip the 2nd of Spain engaged the famous castrato Farinelli to sing for him every night to allay his chronic melancholy; Farinelli sang the same 4 songs for the King every night for 25 years, until the royal sufferer finally gave up the ghost.

One of the most bizarre chronicles of musical therapy concerns *tarantism*, an uncontrollable compulsion to dance, which erupted in Taranto, Italy, in the 15th century. This morbid choreographic condition was caused by the bite of the tarantula spider, and according to contemporary reports could be cured by playing the Italian tarantella, a rapid dance in 6/8 time. The legend even found its way into some reputable music encyclopedias. A plausible claim can be made, however, for the psychiatric benefit of music for retarded or autistic children. Playing rhythmic dance music—particularly in binary meter (which corresponds to the natural alternation of steps, inspirations, and expirations, and the diastolic and systolic heartbeats)—may well have a soothing effect on disturbed individuals; the most beneficial tempo is 80 beats a minute, which corresponds to the normal pulse rate.

What kind of music should be played for medicinal purposes? As long ago as 1852, the German physiologist Lotze wrote in his book *Medizinische Psychologie*: "A careful study of melodies shows that we are completely ignorant of the circumstances under which the change from one type of nerve excitation to another corresponds to the physical substratum of the aesthetic sensations generated by the music." Some music-loving physicians assert that music can directly affect the seat of emotion in the cerebral cortex. Numerous experiments have been conducted on mental patients to establish what particular type of music is best for them, with no conclusive results. Musical statistics have been compiled by psychologists to prove that the piano music of Chopin and Rachmaninoff was good for unbalanced persons, while Stravinsky and Schoenberg upset their mental equilibrium.

There is no denying that music can move masses of people to frenzy; the annals of political history are full of instances in which a revolutionary song inflamed the masses and led them to victory. The Institute of Musical Therapy, organized in Poland in 1974, suggested the following musical program to be played prior to open-heart surgery for the beneficial effect on the patient as well as the surgeon: Gavotte in A Major by Gluck, *Clair de lune* by Debussy, Siciliana by Bach, and Adagio by pseudo-Albinoni.

musica (Lat.). Music. As a medieval term, it is incorporated in several expressions of the period: *musica artificialis*, composed music; *musica chordae*, string music; *musica da camera*, chamber music; *musica da chiesa*, church music; *musica divina*, sacred music; *musica harmonica*, vocal music; *musica humana*, harmony of body and soul; *musica instrumentalis*, music as performed and heard; *musica mundana*, music of the universe; *musica organica*, organ or wind music; *musica pulsus*, percussive music; *musica rhythmica*, music produced by finger striking; *musica sacra*, sacred music; *musica ventus*, wind music; *musica vocalis*, vocal music; *musica vulgaris*, secular music (not vulgar music).

Musica enchiriadis. Important anonymous Latin treatise, dating from *c.* 900, which includes discussion of the tetrachord, parallel organum, and notation.

musica ficta (Lat.). In music from the 10th through the 16th centuries, theoretically ambiguous chromatic alterations supposedly made in performance. The term, which means "manufactured music," originated in the 14th century to replace the misleading derogatory term *musica falsa*. Both terms described the perfectly innocent and in fact necessary practice of attaching accidentals, mainly sharps, to newly formed hexachords during the process of modulation. The expression *musica conjuncta* used by some writers is preferable because it alludes to the functional conjunction made between the hexachords by accidentals. Compilers of medieval Latin treatises fully realized how inadequate these terms were. In one of them an anonymous author speaks of the new type of modulation as "non tamen falsa musica, sed inusitata" (not so much false music, but useless music). But another anonymous author terms this "useless" music as "causa necessitatis et causa pulchritudinis cantus per se" (for the reason of necessity and beauty, an independent melody). Still another writer claims that "falsa musica non est inutilis immo necessaria" (false music is not useless, but quite necessary); this opinion is echoed by the positive pronouncement of Philippe de Vitry to the effect that "musica ficta sive falsa est musica vera et necessaria" (musica ficta or musica falsa is true and necessary music).

The practical consequences of musica ficta, whatever the term itself might connote, were far-reaching. Medieval music theorists had followed the GUIDONIAN HAND with slavish obsequiousness. Their cautious modulations had to be *in manu* (in the hand), but musica ficta led music to the regions *extra manum* (outside the hand), venturing into the territory that required remote sharps and flats, at 1st only F-sharp and B-flat but later C-sharp and other accidentals. It should be remembered that B-flat, or *B rotundum* (round B) was very much *in manu*, the flatting of B being necessary to avoid the nefarious tritone, the DIABOLUS IN MUSICA.

So much was the presence of B-flat in musical notation taken for granted that it often was omitted from the key signature altogether. The MS of Bach's Organ Toccata and Fugue in D Minor has no B-flat in the key signature and was therefore mistakenly dubbed the *Dorian Toccata* because it looked like the Dorian mode on paper. In compositions requiring several flats in the key signature, B-flat was customarily omitted as self-evident, and this abnormal condition prevailed well into the 18th century.

In the meantime musica ficta generated subsidiary terms such as *vox ficta*, a contrapuntal part containing extra sharps or flats, and *cantus fictus*, a theme written in an alien key. Not until the reluctant admission on the part of music theorists that all keys are intervallically alike and that notation was the *anicilla musicae* (maidservant of music) were musica ficta and musica falsa exonerated from the suspicion of falsity.

musica figurata (Lat.). Music arranged in contrasting contrapuntal figurations.

musica reservata (Lat.). A 16th-century term applied to a particularly sophisticated type of contrapuntal music, related to musica ficta and "reserved" for masters of the craft.

Musica transalpina. A collection of Italian madrigals with English translations, 1588. This anthology gave a great impetus to the development of the English madrigal school.

musical. American or English MUSICAL COMEDY or REVUE.

musical bow. Generic name for the monochord, consisting of a flexible rod curved by a string and played with a stick. A resonator may be attached, or the mouth used as one. The instrument is found almost universally at one time or another. Despite earlier theories, many cultures that play a musical bow do not hunt with bow and arrow.

musical comedy. A generic term applied to a play with music or opera with a comic or at least nontragic libretto. At its broadest the term can be applied to works beginning in the 16th century; however, the word *comedy* derives from the Italian *commedia*, which simply means "story" or "play" and does not guarantee the presence of humor; similarly, the French OPÉRA COMIQUE may not necessarily leave them laughing, e.g., *Carmen*.

In the last century this term has been shortened to *musical*, and refers generally to a work with dialogue and songs; works that present songs only are descendants of VAUDEVILLE and are considered examples of the REVUE. Either type is known colloquially as a *show*. The American musical began developing in the post–Civil War era; the genre was influenced by French dancing chorus lines, Viennese operettas, and British musical comedy (Gilbert and Sullivan) and music hall. Early musicals were closer in essence to revues, as in the notorious *The Black Crook* (1866).

At the turn of the century Victor Herbert brought the operetta to Broadway; others in this group were Friml and Romberg. At the same time George Cohan developed a more American genre, full of vibrancy, with songs, choruses, dance numbers, and the thinnest of plots. After World War I many musicals reflected the political and social issues of the day, however flippantly; Jerome Kern's great *Showboat* (1928) was a profound exception, with its close study of racism. The Gershwins, Rodgers and Hart, Cole Porter, and Irving Berlin were the most known of many who contributed prolifically to the genre; the best songs were stunning exemplars of the popular song, lyrically and musically; the librettos remained mostly flimsy, using familiar comic opera devices such as mistaken identity, disguise, and satire. Gershwin's most serious work, *Porgy and Bess*, was called and written as an opera.

With the 1943 *Oklahoma!*, Rodgers and Hammerstein reintroduced the "serious musical comedy" on a steadier basis; whether the subject matter (*West Side Story*) or the source (*Kiss Me, Kate, My Fair* Lady) was the strength behind the show, the postwar musical was a more total work of art than any of its predecessors. In the last decades of the 20th century this kind of musical has survived and expanded in the hands of Stephen Sondheim; the other major development, musicals based on independently popular music such as rock and soul, has produced mixed results.

musical saw. A special quasi-musical instrument producing a twanging sound when stroked.

musicale. A musical presentation or a concert given as part of a social gathering for the rich, or affluent music lovers; an abbrev. of *soirée musicale* (musical evenings).

musico (It.). MUSICIAN.

musicology. The science of music; the concept includes all branches of music, i.e., theory, history, aesthetics, lexicography, bibliography, etc. The term originated in France early in the 19th century (*musicologie*) and was later adopted by German music theorists (*Musikwissenschaft*) and domesticated in England and America as musicology. The province of musicology was at 1st limited to the gnostic division of musical knowledge, with an emphasis on abstruse historical and semantic subjects. Musicological dissertations were apt to be extremely circumscribed in their statements, e.g., "certain conjectural elements in the quattrocento French motet" or "the possible urban Iberian origin of the Passacaglia."

But as the teaching of musicology expanded and embraced general historiography of music and even biography, Ph.D. degrees were awarded by leading universities for dissertations with such titles as "Plausible Deciphering of Beethoven's Notes to His Housekeeper Instructing Her to Buy Candles and Yellow Soap" (the specification *gelbe* for the color of the soap was credited by the author to an eminent Beethovenologist), "New Data Establishing Schumann's Syphyllitic Infection," etc. Analysis of works, bibliographical studies of all kinds, and newfangled theories dealing with melody, harmony, or counterpoint all gradually fell in the category of musicology until it truly became a science of history, music theory, and musical biography. The only requirement to qualify, so it seemed, was a profusion of learned footnotes, some of which actually contradicted the author's postulates, e.g., "But cf. A. M. Dzegelenok, op. cit., who cogently refutes the above." Several musicological journals give space for the publication of such esoteric subjects which, it must be admitted, occasionally furnish useful information.

musicus (Lat.; Ger. *Musikant*). Medieval designation of a learned musician profoundly versed in the mathematical theory (and theology) of materials of which music is made, as contrasted with a mere CANTOR, who could sing or play music without understanding what it was.

Musikalien (Ger.). Printed musical compositions.

Musikdirektor (Ger.). Music director of an opera company, sym. orch., school, or other educational institution.

Musikdruck (Ger.). Music printing or publishing.

Musikfest (Ger.). Music festival.

Musikforschung (Ger.). Music research.

Musikgeschichte (Ger.). Music history.

Musikgesellschaft (Ger.). Music society.

Musikschule (Ger.). Music school.

Musikverein (Ger.). Music association.

Musikwissenschaft (Ger., musical science). MUSICOLOGY.

Musikzeitung (Ger.). Music periodical.

musique concrète (Fr., concrete music). Composition on tape using recorded natural sounds and editing and processing them to produce a piece. Musique concrète was discovered and named in April 1948 in Paris by Pierre Schaeffer, a French radio engineer. Experimenting with the newly invented magnetic tape, he found that a heterogeneous collection of songs, noises, conversations, radio commercials, etc. recorded on tape presented a realistic phonomontage which may serve for actual composition by superimposing fragments of tape recordings in a polyphony of random sounds, splicing the tape in various ways, running it at different speeds, or backward, etc.

The raw materials of musique concrète are susceptible to all kinds of treatment and are therefore capable of unlimited transformations. The technique of double and triple recording on the same length of tape makes it possible to create a polyphonic musique concrète of great complexity. In fact it is possible to recompose a classical sym. from a recording of a single note, which can subsequently be changed in pitch and arranged in the requisite rhythmic order, superimposed on other tones derived from the original note, altered in tone color by additional electronic manipulation, until a whole work is reconstructed from these constituent tonal dynamic and instrumental elements. In the U.S., Luening, Ussachevsky, and Varèse were the most important early exponents of musique concrète.

musique d'ameublement (Fr., furniture music). Background music; a concept invented by Satie.

musique de chambre (Fr.). Chamber music.

musique d'écurie. (Fr., music of the stable). Field music; that is, music played in unison by trumpets and signal horns.

musique de scène (Fr.). Incidental music.

musique funèbre (Fr.). Funeral music.

Musique funèbre. Threnody for string orch. by Lutoslawski, 1958, written in memory of Bartók, 1st performed in Katowice, Poland. Its introduction is based on a symmetrical tune consisting of an ascending tritone and a descending semitone.

musique mesurée (Fr.). Late 16th-century settings of *vers mesurés*, French poetry that utilizes classical Greek and Latin versifying principles. This concept was retained in various forms in French Baroque opera.

musique populaire (Fr.). Folk music (not popular music).

musique sacrée (Fr.). Sacred music.

Mussorgsky, Modest (Petrovich)

~~~ ~~~ ~~~ ~~~ ~~~

Great Russian composer, the greatest of the "Mighty 5"; b. Karevo, Pskov district, Mar. 21, 1839; d. St. Petersburg, Mar. 28, 1881. He received his 1st instruction on the piano from his mother; at the age of 10 he was taken to St. Petersburg, where he had piano lessons with Anton Herke, remaining his pupil until 1854. In 1852 he entered the cadet school of the Imperial Guard; composed a piano piece entitled *Porte-enseigne Polka*, which was publ. (1852); after graduation (1856) he joined the regiment of the Guard. In 1857 he met Dargomyzhsky, who introduced him to Cui and Balakirev; he also became friendly with the critic and chief champion of Russian national music, Vladimir Stasov. These associations prompted his decision to become a professional composer. He played and analyzed piano arrangements of works by Beethoven and Schumann; Balakirev helped him to acquire a knowledge of form; he tried to write music in Classical style, but without success; his inner drive was directed toward "new shores," as Mussorgsky expressed it.

The liquidation of the family estate made it imperative for him to take a paying job; he became a clerk in the Ministry of Communications (1863), being dismissed 4 years later. During this time he continued to compose, but his lack of technique compelled him time and again to leave his various pieces unfinished. He eagerly sought professional advice from his friends Stasov (for general aesthetics) and Rimsky-Korsakov (for problems of harmony); to the very end of his life he regarded himself as being only half-educated in music, and he constantly acknowledged his inferiority as a craftsman. But he yielded to no one in his firm faith in the future of national Russian music. When a group of composers from Bohemia visited St. Petersburg in 1867, Stasov publ. an article in which he for the 1st time referred to the "mighty handful of Russian musicians" (i.e., the "Mighty 5") pursuing the ideal of national art. The expression was picked up derisively by some journalists, but it was accepted as a challenge by Mussorgsky and his comrades-in-arms Balakirev, Borodin, Cui, and Rimsky-Korsakov. In 1869 he once more entered government service, this time in the forestry dept. He became addicted to drink and had epileptic fits; he died a week after his 42nd birthday.

The significance of Mussorgsky's genius did not become apparent until some years after his death. Most of his works were prepared for publication by Rimsky-Korsakov, who corrected some of his harmonic crudities and reorchestrated the symphonic works. Original versions of his music were preserved in MS and eventually publ. But despite the availability of the authentic scores, his works continue to be performed in Rimsky-Korsakov's eds., made familiar to the whole musical world. In his dramatic works and in his songs, Mussorgsky draws a boldly realistic vocal line in which inflections of speech are translated into a natural melody. His 1st attempt in this genre was an unfinished opera, *The Marriage*, to Gogol's comedy; here he also demonstrated his penetrating sense of musical humor. His ability to depict tragic moods is revealed in his cycle *Songs and Dances of Death*; his understanding of intimate poetry is shown in his children's songs.

His greatest work is the opera *Boris Godunov* (to Pushkin's tragedy), which has no equal in its stirring portrayal of personal destiny against a background of social upheaval. In it Mussorgsky created a true national music drama without a trace of the Italian conventions that had theretofore dominated the operatic works by Russian composers. He wrote no chamber music, perhaps because he lacked the requisite training in contrapuntal technique. Of his piano music, the set of pieces *Pictures at an Exhibition* (somewhat after the manner of Schumann's *Carnaval*) is remarkable for its vivid representation of varied scenes (it was written to commemorate his friend, the painter Victor Hartmann, whose pictures were the subjects of the music); the work became famous in the brilliant orchestration of Ravel.

Although Mussorgsky was a Russian national composer, his music influenced many composers outside Russia and he came to be regarded as the most potent talent of the Russian national school. The paintings of Victor Hartmann that inspired PICTURES AT AN EXHIBITION were reproduced by Alfred Frankenstein in his article on the subject in the *Musical Quarterly* (July 1939); he also brought out an illustrated ed. of the work (1951). Mussorgsky composed many powerful if rough-edged works, including several operas, most notably *Boris Godunov*, after Pushkin (1st version, with 7 scenes, 1868–69; Leningrad, 1928; 2nd version, with prologue and 4 acts, 1871–72, rev. 1873; St. Petersburg, 1874). His orch.l works include *Ivanova noch'na Lisoy gore* (St. John's Night on Bald Mountain; 1860–67; reorchestrated by Rimsky-Korsakov; 1886); and *Vyzatiye Karsa* (The Capture of Kars, Mar. 1880). He also composed choral works and songs, and piano works.

muta (It.). Change either the instrument or (in prevalve brass instruments) the crook.

mutation. 1. Change of voice. 2. Change of position, shifting (violin). 3. In medieval solmization, movement from one hexachord to another.

mutations. In search for synonyms or paronyms to replace the ambiguous nomenclature of academic musicology, some modern composers have begun using the scientific-sounding words *variants* or *mutations* for *variations*. Mutations may be beneficial, musically speaking, when the mutant genes add to the brilliance of thematic adornment, as in some variations in the diaphanous music of Ravel; or they may be detrimental to the biomusical organism, as in the cluttered polyphony of Max Reger. Recessive mutations such as Stravinsky's neo-Baroque ornamentation may become dominant characteristics, with uncertain benefits.

In human terms, mutations are found in large musical families in which the embryo develops fully conditioned by the genetic complex of his parents. A striking example is that of Siegfried Wagner, a musical mutant who fully absorbed the musical genes of his father but acquired mutations that made him sterile. Some mutations are products of defective genes of the theme itself, a condition that may lead to melodic dyscrasia, harmonic dyslogia, and contrapuntal dyskinesia. There is no relief in such cases but to destroy the theme *in statu nascendi* in order to eliminate mutagenic elements and build afresh an untainted homunculus.

mute. 1. A piece of metal fitted to the bridge of a violin, et al., designed to deaden the sound when put into position. The direction for putting on the mutes is *con sordini*; for taking them off, *senza sordini*. 2. A leather-covered pad, pasteboard cone, or wooden cylinder inserted in the bell of brass instruments to modify the tone.

mut(h)ig (Ger.). Spiritedly, boldly.

Muti, Riccardo, greatly talented Italian conductor; b. Naples, July 28, 1941. After receiving instruction in violin and piano from his father, a physician who possessed a natural Neapolitan tenor voice, Riccardo studied composition with Jacopo Napoli and Nino Rota at the Conservatorio di Musica San Pietro a Majella in Naples, taking a diploma in piano; he then studied conducting with Antonino Votto and composition with Bruno Bettinelli at the Verdi Cons. in Milan; he also attended a seminar in conducting with Franco Ferrara in Venice (1965).

After winning the Guido Cantelli Competition in 1967, he made his formal debut with the RAI in 1968; then conducted in several of the major Italian music centers. His success led to his appointment as principal conductor of the Teatro Comunale in Florence in 1970; also conducted at the Maggio Musicale Fiorentino, becoming its artistic director in 1977. In

the meantime he began his advancement to international fame with guest conducting appearances at the Salzburg Festival in 1971 and with the Berlin Phil. in 1972. He made his U.S. debut with the Philadelphia Orch. (1972). In 1973 he conducted at the Vienna State Opera, and that same year became principal conductor of the New Philharmonia Orch. in London (it resumed its original name of Philharmonia Orch. in 1977). In 1974 he conducted the Vienna Phil., and in 1977 he appeared at London's Covent Garden.

His successful appearances with the Philadelphia Orch. led to his appointment as its principal guest conductor in 1977. In 1979 he was also named music director of the Philharmonia Orch. In 1980 he succeeded Eugene Ormandy as music director of the Philadelphia Orch., and he subsequently relinquished his posts in London and Florence in 1982. In 1986 he became music director of Milan's La Scala but retained his Philadelphia position. Muti announced his resignation as music director of the Philadelphia Orch. in 1990 but agreed to serve as its laureate conductor from 1992. His brilliance as a symphonic conductor enabled him to maintain, and even enhance, the illustrious reputation of the Philadelphia Orch. established by Stokowski and carried forward by Ormandy. Unlike his famous predecessors, he excels in both the concert hall and the opera pit.

Mutter, Anne-Sophie, talented German violinist; b. Rheinfeldin, June 29, 1963. At the age of 6 she won 1st Prize with Special Distinction at the "Jungen Musiziert" National Competition, the youngest winner in its annals. In 1976 she came to the notice of Karajan during her appearance at the Lucerne Festival; in 1977 he invited her to be a soloist with him and the Berlin Phil. at the Salzburg Easter Festival; this was the beginning of an auspicious career. She subsequently appeared regularly with Karajan and the Berlin Phil., and also recorded standard violin concertos with him; likewise she appeared as soloist with many other leading conductors and orchs. on both sides of the Atlantic. She held the 1st International Chair of Violin Studies at London's Royal Academy of Music (from 1986). In 1988 she made her N.Y. recital debut.

Mutter, Die. MOTHER, THE.

Muzak. Trademark of the 1st U.S. company to have license to produce, distribute, and transmit background music for public consumption. Known colloquially as "canned music" or "elevator music," Muzak may also be supplied to restaurants, stores, mall plazas, doctors' offices, terminals, and waiting rooms. The kinds of music purveyed by Muzak consist of glutinous ballads and saccharine instrumental arrangements of popular or semiclassical songs.

Muzak was the brainchild of an Army general who was bemused by the commercial possibilities of "wired radio" as an entertainment medium. When the company was founded in 1934, it was in fact named "Wired Radio, Inc." Later it was suggested to combine the popular brand name in photography, Kodak, with music, and the result was Muzak. Soon there were over 300 Muzak franchises around the world. Muzak executives liked to describe themselves as "Specialists in the Physiological and Psychological Applications of Music," and their product as "a nonverbal symbolism for the common stuff of everyday living in the global village, promoting the sharing of meaning because it massifies symbolism in which not few but all can participate." However, not all share joyfully. Driven to desperation, N.Y. commuters brought out a class-action suit to show cause why this tonal pollution at the Grand Central terminal in N.Y. should not be declared a public nuisance. Surprisingly, they won.

My Blue Heaven. Song by Walter Donaldson, which he wrote in 1924. It became a tremendous hit in 1927 on the radio, and its recordings sold millions of copies. It was also incorporated in several movie musicals.

My country 'tis of thee. The 1st line of the patriotic hymn *America*.

My Fair Lady. Musical by Lerner and Loewe, 1956, based on G. B. Shaw's play *Pygmalion*. The orig. plot is based on the myth of the sculptor Pygmalion, who fell in love with one of his feminine creations. In the Shavian and musical version, one Prof. Henry Higgins is fascinated by the speech of a Cockney flower girl and takes her on as a challenge, aiming to improve her diction and demeanor. He succeeds, but romance rears its head, not without difficulties. It is a tribute to Lerner and Loewe that they succeeded in making a musical out of a play about linguistics; that they could turn such a British-seeming play into a Broadway hit; and that Shaw gave his blessing to this attempt shortly before his death. The great British music hall performer Stanley Holloway was a cast member. The excellent score includes *The Rain in Spain, I Could Have Danced All Night, On the Street Where You Live, Get Me to the Church on Time,* and *I've Grown Accustomed to Her Face.*

My Gal Sal. Popular ballad by Paul Dresser, 1905; it was his last song, and he died before it became a tremendous hit.

My Girl. A 1965 number 1 pop and R&B hit for the Motown group the Temptations, penned by the famous Holland-Dozier-Holland trio.

My Heart Belongs to Daddy. Song by C. Porter, 1938, written for the musical *Leave It to Me*. In the original, Mary Martin sang the lubricious lines with a disarmingly titillating air of babylike innocence. The daddy referred to is not a relative.

My Heart Stood Still. Song by Rodgers and Hart, 1927, from the musical *A Connecticut Yankee*. A hit in London, its popularity was helped by the future Duke of Windsor (then Prince of Wales), who liked to sing it himself.

My Melancholy Baby. Song by Ernie Burnett, 1912. The lyrics were by his wife, but he divorced her and had his publisher rearrange the words. She promptly sued him; the courts awarded her the damages. This was not the end of Burnett's tribulations. In 1965 the son of a nightclub pianist named Ben Light claimed that the song was actually his father's and that Burnett had lifted it from him. But by that time everyone concerned with the song's origin was deceased, so that the loyal son of the putative composer had to drop his claim.

My Old Kentucky Home. Song by Foster, 1853, of the Ethiopian ballad type. He was inspired by a visit to a cousin in Kentucky, where he observed a group of black children playing games. The state song of Kentucky, it is also the anthem of the Kentucky Derby.

My Sweet Lord. George Harrison's 1970 paean to Krishna later got him into secular hot water when Ronald Mack, the songwriter of *He's So Fine*, realized that Harrison had unintentionally borrowed his tune for the hit.

My Way. Adapted in 1969 from the French song *Mon Habitude* by Paul Anka, with music by Claude François and Jacques Revaux; became Frank Sinatra's unofficial theme song in the '70s.

My Wild Irish Rose. Song by Chauncey Olcott, 1899, made popular by him in vaudeville; it became one of the most successful sentimental Irish ballads.

mysteries. Medieval Bible plays, often with vocal and instrumental music. In the form called MORALITIES, abstract ideas were personified on the stage (e.g., *Jedermann*). Modern versions of the mysteries have been successfully revived in Britain.

Mysterious Mountain. Sym. No. 2 by Hovhaness, 1955, inspired by the mystic vision of a phantom peak somewhere in the Himalayas. The score is written in an impressionistic manner emphasizing colorful instrumental contrasts. It was 1st performed in Houston, Tex., with Stokowski conducting. Several ordinarily sober music critics admitted that they were fascinated by the static homophony of the work.

Mysterium. An unfinished, in fact virtually unbegun, crowning work of Scriabin that was to embody the synthesis of all arts and of all human senses: visual, auditory, tactile, gustatory, and olfactory. With his erotic obsession, Scriabin called the tactile sense a "caress." He envisioned the *Mysterium* as a final sacrament, with himself as the high priest of the production. The work was to terminate in a universal ecstasy that would consume humanity in a mystical act marking the end of the *manvantara*, the theosophic era borrowed from Hindu cosmogony. The nearest approximation to *Mysterium* was Scriabin's *Poem of Ecstasy*. He planned an intermediate link between it and *Mysterium*, a work for all media that he called a Preliminary Act. An attempt was made by a group of Russian musicians to orchestrate several of Scriabin's piano pieces of his last period and arrange them in a suite approximating the idea of *Mysterium*, but the project was totally unsuccessful.

Mystic Chord. The theosophic name that Scriabin attached to a chord consisting of six notes—C–F-sharp–B-flat–E–A–D—which lies at the foundation of his last symphonic work, *Promethée*. It is also known as the Prometheus chord. The chord was adumbrated in several of Scriabin's previous compositions in which it usually resolved into the dominant-9th chord by moving A to B-flat and F-sharp to G, thus resolving the 2 suspensions. Scriabin arrived at the formation of this chord intuitively, but later rationalized its construction as consisting of higher overtones forming a 6-tone scale from the 8th to the 14th overtones (C, D, E, F-sharp, A, B-flat). No one after Scriabin made use of the Mystic Chord, and it remains a solitary mausoleum.

Nn

Nabucco. Opera by Verdi, 1842, 1st performed in Milan; based on the biblical story of the Hebrews and Nebuchadnezzar (Daniel 1–4), the Babylonian king who defeated them and held them in "Babylonian captivity." The king eventually goes mad but saves himself by converting to the Judaic religion. While not a masterpiece, *Nabucco* has had several revivals in the 20th century.

nach (Ger.). After; according to.

nach Belieben (Ger.). At will; A PIACERE.

nach gefallen (Ger.). AD LIBITUM.

nach und nach (Ger.). Little by little, gradually. *Nach und nach schneller*, gradually faster.

Nachahmung (Ger.). Imitation.

nachdrücklich (Ger.). With emphasis, marked. *Mit vielem Nachdrück*, with great emphasis.

nachgebend (Ger., yielding). Ever slower; RALLENTANDO.

nachgelassenes Werk (Ger.). Posthumous work.

nachgiebiger (Ger.). Still slower.

nachlässig (Ger.). Carelessly.

Nachschlag (Ger.). The end notes of a trill.

Nachspiel (Ger., afterplay). Epilogue; postlude.

Nachthorn (Ger.). A covered stop in the organ, having covered pipes of 2', 4', or 8' pitch.

Nachtmusik (Ger., night music). A SERENADE.

Nachtschall (Ger.). See NACHTHORN.

Nachtschwalbe, Die (The Night Swallow). "Dramatic nocturne" by Blacher, 1948, dealing with the life of a prostitute in a small German town who turns out to be an illegitimate daughter of the head of the vice squad. Its 1st performance (in Leipzig) provoked quite a scandal because of its frankness in staging.

Nachtstück (Ger., night piece). A NOCTURNE.

Nachtwacht, De. Opera by Badings, 1950, inspired by the famous Rembrandt painting *The Night Watch*; it was 1st performed in Antwerp.

Nagano, Kent (George), American conductor; b. Morro Bay, Calif. (of Japanese-American parents), Nov. 22, 1951. He studied at Oxford Univ. (1969), with Grosvenor Cooper at the Univ. of Calif. in Santa Cruz (B.A., 1974), at San Francisco State Univ. (M.M., 1976), and at the Univ. of Toronto; also had instruction in conducting from Laszlo Varga in San Francisco. He was associated with Sarah Caldwell's Opera Co. of Boston (1977–79); was made music director of the Berkeley (Calif.) Sym. Orch. (1978) and of the Ojai (Calif.) Music Festival (1984). While working as an assistant conductor with the Boston Sym. Orch., he was called upon to substitute for Ozawa at the last moment and led a notably successful performance of Mahler's 9th Sym. without benefit of rehearsal (Nov.

30, 1984). In 1985 he was the 1st corecipient (with Hugh Wolff) of the Affiliate Artist's Seaver Conducting Award. He subsequently appeared as a guest conductor with various orchs. on both sides of the Atlantic. In 1989 he became chief conductor of the Opéra de Lyon.

nail fiddle. A primitive instrument in use for a time in the 18th century. It consisted of a wooden board with nails of different sizes affixed in a semicircle; it was played with an ordinary violin bow on the nails.

Naissance de la lyre, La. Opera by Roussel, 1925, to an libretto after Sophocles, relating the birth of the Greek lyre; 1st performed in Paris.

naked fifth. A harmonic perfect 5th (dyad) without a 3rd; open 5th.

naker (Mid. Eng.; Arab. *naqqāra*; Fr. *nacaire*; It. *nacchera*). A small kettledrum of the Middle East, played in pairs; subsequently spread to India and Europe, where it was briefly in vogue; Walter Scott revived the term in the novel *Ivanhoe* (1819).

Nancarrow, Conlon, remarkable American-born Mexican composer, innovator in the technique of recording notes on a player-piano roll; b. Texarkana, Ark., Oct. 27, 1912. He played the trumpet in jazz orchs., then took courses at the Cincinnati College–Cons. of Music (1929–32); subsequently traveled to Boston, where he became a private student of Nicolas Slonimsky, Walter Piston, and Roger Sessions. In 1937 he joined the Abraham Lincoln Brigade and went to Spain to fight in the ranks of the Republican Loyalists against the brutal assault of General Franco's armies. Classified as a premature anti-Fascist after the Republican defeat in Spain, he was refused a U.S. passport and moved to Mexico City, where he remained for 40 years, eventually obtaining Mexican citizenship (1956).

In 1981, with political pressures defused in the U.S., Nancarrow was able to revisit his native land and to participate in the New American Music Festival in San Francisco. In 1982 he was a composer-in-residence at the Cabrillo Music Festival in Aptos, Calif.; also traveled to Europe, where he participated at festivals in Austria, Germany, and France. An extraordinary event occurred in his life in 1982, when he was awarded the "genius grant" of $300,000 by the MacArthur Foundation of Chicago, enabling him to continue his work without any concerns about finances.

The unique quality of most of Nancarrow's compositions is that they can be notated only by perforating player-piano rolls to mark the notes and rhythms, and can be performed only by activating such piano rolls. This method of composition gives him total freedom in conjuring up the most complex contrapuntal, harmonic, and rhythmic combinations that no human pianist or number of human pianists could possibly perform. The method itself is extremely laborious; a bar containing a few dozen notes might require an hour to stamp out on the piano roll. Some of his studies were publ. in normal notation in Cowell's *New Music Quarterly.* Copland, Ligeti, and other contemporary composers expressed their appreciation of Nancarrow's originality in high terms of praise.

In 1984 Nancarrow gave a concert of his works in Los Angeles, in a program including his *Prelude and Blues* for acoustic piano and several of his studies. A number of Nancarrow's studies for player piano that could be adequately notated were publ. in *Soundings* 4 (1977), accompanied with critical commentaries by Gordon Mumma, Charles Amirkhanian, John Cage, Roger Reynolds, and James Tenney. In 1988 his 3rd String Quartet was given its premiere performance in Cologne by the London-based Arditti Quartet, one of the very few ensembles in the world capable of realizing Nancarrow's exceedingly complex scores.

napolitana (It.). An old type of Italian madrigal, revived in modern times in the form of a popular song.

napura (Sans., Beng. *nūpura*). Indian vessel rattle in the form of a hollow copper ring filled with pebbles; worn on the ankles by dancers.

narcolepsy. Sym. concerts are notoriously conducive to narcolepsy, and their attendance is sometimes recommended by psychologists as an effective cure for insomnia. Statistical surveys indicate that the narcogenic factors are mainly the pendulumlike rhythmic beats in classical music, particularly when there is no change in dynamics. An unexpected sforzando will wake up even the most inveterate narcoleptic, as illustrated by the story of Haydn's *Surprise Sym.* with its famous chord in the slow movement that was supposed to arouse the somnolent London concertgoers from their middle-aged slumber. On the other hand, modern works rarely put people to sleep because of the constant changes in rhythm and dynamics.

Narcolepsy is also an inevitable outcome of lectures on musicology; according to observations conducted by a trained psychologist at a session of the International Musicological Congress in N.Y., a deep coma overtook practically the entire audience during the 1st 20 seconds of a reading from manuscript of a paper by an eminent Dutch musicologist. At the same occasion, attention was suddenly increased by the appearance on the podium of the inventor of a double-bass flute and an ultrasonic piccolo. He could never succeed in blowing through the long tube of the big flute, which met with sympathy in the audience. The hyper-piccolo could not be heard by humans, but a terrier dog who strayed into the hall showed agitation at the ultrasonics that canines can hear easily. Both the dog and the inventor were rewarded by hearty applause.

narrante (It.). Narrating; as if telling a story; declaim distinctly.

narrator. A speaking part in Baroque oratorios, corresponding to the Italian TESTO, designed to promote the continuity of the plot. In the 20th century, the narrator plays an important part in Stravinsky's *Oedipus Rex* and *Histoire du soldat*, and, in a lighter vein, Prokofiev's *Peter and the Wolf*.

nasard (Fr.; Ger. *Nasat*). The 12th (organ stop) of 2 2/3–foot pitch (large sizes 10 2/3 and 5 1/3, smaller size 1 1/3).

national anthems. Songs that by accident or intention assume the status of a patriotic hymn; most of them are anonymous. Few transcend their functional role and possess genuine musical beauty; only one, the former Austro-Hungarian anthem *Gott erhalte unsern Kaiser*, was written by a major composer (Haydn); the same melody has been used as Germany's anthem with different texts during the 20th century.

nationalism. A late-19th-century movement, prominent in Russia, Bohemia, etc., wherein composers consciously strived to embody and reveal aspects of national identity in their music.

Natoma. Opera by V. Herbert, 1911, 1st produced in Philadelphia; his only attempt to write in a grand operatic manner. The action takes place in Calif. under Spanish rule. Natoma is an Indian girl in love with a U.S. Navy lieutenant, but she yields him to her rival, a white woman from Santa Barbara, and finds solace in her loveless life in the invocation to her ancestral Great Spirit.

natural. 1. The sign ♮, canceling a sharp or flat. 2. A white key on the keyboard. *Natural harmonics*, those produced on an open string; *natural horn*, a horn without valves; *natural interval*, one found between any 2 tones of a diatonic major scale; *natural key*, C major; *natural pitch*, that of any wind instrument when not overblown; *natural scale*, one having neither sharps nor flats, i.e., C major; *natural tone*, any tone obtained on a wind instrument with cupped mouthpiece, without using keys, valves, or the slide.

natural minor scale. The basic minor scale, without chromatic alterations, and therefore lacking the leading tone. The scale uses the sharps or flats indicated in the key signature shared by its relative major scale, whose tonic is a minor 3rd above the minor tonic.

natural tone series. See HARMONICS.

naturalism. In musical usage, naturalism appears as an extreme case of VERISMO. Naturalistic opera emphasizes the negative phenomena of life without the redeeming quality of romance. In Soviet parlance, naturalism has acquired a pejorative meaning; the word was used as a verbal missile in the attacks on Shostakovich's opera LADY MACBETH OF THE DISTRICT OF MTZENSK, particularly with reference to the scene of adultery illustrated in an orch.l interlude by sliding trombones.

naturalmente (It.). In a natural, unaffected style.

Nature Boy. Song by Eden Ahbez, 1946, which skyrocketed in popularity in the post–World War II years, when the ideas of living according to nature, eating organic food, and doing yoga were in the air, particularly in Calif.

Naturhorn (Ger.). FRENCH HORN without valves or pistons.

Naturlaut (Ger.). Natural sound. *Wie ein Naturlaut*, like a sound of nature (Mahler's 1st Sym.).

Naughty Marietta. Operetta by V. Herbert, 1910, 1st performed in N.Y. The action takes place in 18th-century New Orleans. Marietta is an Italian girl from Naples who travels to Louisiana in search of a convenient marriage. She has a peculiar dream in which she hears an enchanting melody, which remains unfinished as she wakes up. Anxious to complete it, she promises her hand to a man who can find a satisfactory ending to the tune. A dashing army captain offers a reasonable ending, and she marries him. The dream tune is *Ah, Sweet Mystery of Life*, one of the greatest songs Herbert ever wrote.

Nausicaa. Opera by Glanville-Hicks, 1961; 1st performed in Athens, after Homer's *Odyssey*.

Navarraise, La (The Woman of Navarra). Opera by Massenet, 1894; 1st produced in London. The heroine becomes involved with a royal officer during the dynastic strife of 16th-century Spain. When he is killed, she goes insane. The score makes use of techniques associated with Italian verismo.

Navarro, "Fats" (Theodore), American jazz trumpeter; b. Key West, Fla., Sept. 24, 1923; d. N.Y., July 7, 1950. He 1st took up the tenor saxophone, then mastered the trumpet; subsequently played with several groups, including those of Andy Kirk (1943–44) and Billy Eckstine (1945–46); he later worked in N.Y. as a leading exponent of the bop style.

Nazareth (Nazare), **Ernesto** (Julio de), Brazilian pianist and composer; b. Rio de Janeiro, Mar. 20, 1863; d. there, Feb. 4, 1934. He was a pioneer in fostering a national Brazilian type of composition, writing pieces in European forms with Brazilian melorhythmic inflections; among the genres he invented were *fado brasileiro, tango brasileiro, valsa brasileira, marcha brasileira*, etc.; he also composed original dances in the rhythms of the samba and chôro. In his declining years he became totally deaf.

Neapolitan cadence. A cadence in which the customary subdominant triad is replaced by the lowered supertonic triad in the 1st inversion, known as the NEAPOLITAN SIXTH. The bass of the Neapolitan 6th (or Neapolitan chord) is the same as that of the subdominant chord; thus the substitution is logical. As in the regular cadence, the Neapolitan chord is followed by the dominant, often with an interpolation of the tonic $^6_4$ chord, ending on the tonic. The Neapolitan cadence, like the Neapolitan chord, received its name from its frequent use by composers of the Neapolitan school, particularly in the 18th century. A remarkable example of an instrumental composition that starts with the Neapolitan chord is the 1st Ballade in G Minor by Chopin, which opens with a lengthy and elaborate cadenza based on the 1st inversion of the lowered supertonic of the key of G minor.

Scriabin's 3rd Sym., *Le Poème divin*, is nominally in C minor, but it begins with a Neapolitan cadence on D-flat.

Neapolitan sixth. The 1st inversion of a flatted supertonic chord ($^♭$II^6); in C major, the notes F-A$^♭$-D$^♭$. The Neapolitan 6th is used as a functional substitute for the subdominant in a cadence. While the composers of the Baroque Neapolitan school did not invent the chord, they used it so often as to become associated with it.

Near, Holly, American popular vocalist, songwriter, and actress; b. Ukiah, Calif., June 6, 1949. She sang in public from childhood; worked in film and television and had a leading role on Broadway in the rock musical *Hair*. She took a commercially and artistically independent stance with her music, forming the Redwood label to record *Hang In There* (1973), *Live Album* (1974), *You Can Know All I Am* (1976), and *Imagine My Surprise* (1979), all of which became known largely by word of mouth. Her later recordings include *Fire in the Rain* (1981), *Speed of Light* (1982), *Journeys* (1983), *Watch Out!* (1984), *Sing to Me the Dream* (1984), *Harp* (1985, with Arlo Guthrie and Pete Seeger), *Singing with You* (1986), *Don't Hold Back* (1987), *Sky Dances* (1989), and *Singer in the Storm* (1990). While preferring smaller venues for her performances, she appeared at Carnegie Hall in N.Y. and the Royal Albert Hall in London; also made film and television appearances, participated in benefit concerts, and engaged in philanthropic work. With Meg Christiansen and Cris Williamson, she is one of the most important and influential musicians in the feminist and lesbian communities; her excellent voice, flexible acting skills, and fiery personality have won her a large and general audience.

Nearer My God to Thee. Protestant hymn by Lowell Mason, *c.* 1850; it became a standard song in Christian churches of the world. Ives quotes the tune in his 4th Sym. and other works to evoke the devotional atmosphere of old America.

Nebensatz (Ger., adjacent part). The 2nd expository theme in a sonata-form movement.

Nebenstimme (Ger., adjacent voice). A term invented by Schoenberg to denote the 2nd polyphonic voice, abbrev. in his scores as N⎤. See HAUPTSTIMME.

neck. On some chordophones, the section of the body by which they are held; also called the *handle*.

negative music. Negative music is synonymous with ANTIMUSIC, but there is a scintilla of a difference between the 2 terms. Antimusic stresses its opposition to any musical actions, whereas negative music operates on the supposition that there may exist negative frequencies as mathematical abstractions, related to audible music as a negative to the positive in photography. Negative music would reverse dynamic values; a vocal text containing tender sentiments would be harmonized by loud dissonant noises; conversely, a symphonic poem on the subject of nuclear war would be depicted by the minutest distillation of monodically concentrated tones. The field for experimentation in negative music is limitless, precisely because it is impossible to speculate about its nature.

negli (It.). In the.

negligente (It.). In a style expressive of negligence; carelessly.

nei, nel, nell', nella, nelle, nello (It.). In the.

nella parte di sopra (It.). In the higher or highest part.

Nelly Bly. Song by Foster, 1848.

Nelson, Judith (Anne Manes), American soprano; b. Chicago, Sept. 10, 1939. She studied at St. Olaf College in Northfield, Minn., then sang with music groups of the Univ. of Chicago and the Univ. of Calif., Berkeley; she made her operatic debut as Drusilla in Monteverdi's *L'incoronazione di Poppea* in Brussels in 1979. She appeared widely as a soloist and recitalist. Although she is particularly noted for her performances of Baroque music, she also introduced compositions by American and English composers.

Nelson Mass. A nickname for Haydn's Mass in D Minor, written in 1798, in which a trumpet flourish in the Benedictus was supposed to suggest Nelson's victory at Abukir (Egypt). It is also called the Imperial Mass.

Nelson, Prince Roger. PRINCE.

Nelson, Willie (Hugh), American country-music singer, guitarist, and songwriter; b. Abbott, Tex., Apr. 30, 1933. For a short time he attended Baylor Univ. in Waco, Tex.; he then made appearances in local honky-tonk bars; also began to write songs, which included *Hello Walls,*

Willie Nelson, c. 1980

Crazy, and *Night Life,* made famous by leading singers of the day. He then went to Nashville, Tenn., where he played bass in the band of Ray Price and gained renown with such songs as *The Party's Over* and *Little Things* in his many appearances with the Grand Ole Opry. He eventually returned to Tex. and became instrumental in the development of the Austin sound, also called outlaw country or redneck rock. With the album *Red-headed Stranger* (1975) he gained success and went on to produce a number of others, including *Stardust* (1978), *Willie and Family Live* (1978), *Honeysuckle Rose* (1980), *Always on My Mind* (1982), and *Angel Eyes* (1984). He also became a competent actor, making appearances in the films *Electric Horseman* (1979) and *Honeysuckle Rose* (1980).

neoclassicism. A revival—in 20th-century compositions—of 18th-century (or earlier) musical precepts, exemplified by many of the post–World War I works of both Stravinsky and Schoenberg but anticipated by French composers at the turn of the century. When the luxuriance of IMPRESSIONISM reached its point of saturation, it became clear to many composers that further amplification of coloristic devices was no longer stimulating or novel. The Weber-Fechner Law postulates that the force of physical impact must be increased exponentially in order to produce an arithmetical increase in the sensory impression, so that a hundredfold magnification of sound is needed to provide a tenfold increase in the physiological effect. It was to be expected that composers and audiences alike would rebound from such sonic inundation. This reaction coincided with the economic collapse following World War I, so that it became financially impossible to engage large orchs. or grandiose operatic companies.

The cry went all over Europe: "Back to Bach!" To this was added the slogan of NEW SIMPLICITY. Since it was no longer feasible to move forward, musical tastes, with the aid of intellectual rationalization, made a 180° turn toward the past. But the past could not be recaptured in its literal form, and the new retrograde movement was launched under the name of neoclassicism. It was characterized by the following traits: (1) Rehabilitation of diatonicism as the dominant idiom, using enhanced pandiatonic constructions, in which all 7 degrees of the diatonic scale are functionally equal; (2) elimination of all programmatic and Romantic associations, either in the titles or the tonal content of individual works; (3) a demonstrative revival of the Baroque forms of sonata, serenade, scherzo, passacaglia, toccata, and the florid type of variation; (4) demotion of chromatic elements of the scale to their traditional role as passing notes; (5) restrained use of massive sonorities and renunciation of all external and purely decorative effects, such as nonthematic melismas and nonessential harmonic figurations; (6) cultivation of compact forms, such as syms. and sonatas in 1 movement and operas without a chorus and with a reduced orch. contingent (usually containing 13 instruments), with an important piano part performing the function of the cembalo in Baroque music; (7) reconstruction of old Baroque instruments, particularly the harpsichord, and their employment in modernized classical techniques; (8) exploration of canonic and fugal writing without adherence to strict rules of classical polyphony; (9) radical curtailment of the development section in Baroque forms with a purely nominal recapitulation, and a concise coda free from redundant repetition of final tonic chords.

neomedievalism. New classicism, anticipated by the writings of Busoni and French music at the turn of the 20th century, resuscitated Baroque music in a new guise of pandiatonic harmonies and asymmetrical rhythms. Retreating still further into the past, some modern composers discovered a world of surprisingly modernistic devices such as HOCKETUS, HETEROPHONY, and QUODLIBET, and the techniques of inversion and retrograde composition, which are basic to SERIAL MUSIC. Modernization of these resources resulted in the stylized idiom of neomedievalism, which adopted not only the old musical modalities but the verbal usages of ecclesiastical Latin for texts. The most remarkable example of this trend is Stravinsky's oratorio *Oedipus Rex*, with a specially written text in medieval Latin. Orff produced a number of successful works in a neomedieval style, notably *Carmina Burana*, to texts in Latin and German dialects. A significant trait of these works is their imaginative repetitive technique. The liberating power of literal repetition has a particular attraction for composers of the AVANT-GARDE who follow Eastern religious practices, exemplified by the interminable turning of the Tibetan prayer wheel.

neomodality. The system of modes—so potent for centuries—nearly lost all its binding power under the impact of ATONALITY and DODECAPHONY. Dormant strains have achieved a new renaissance in the ethnically deep-rooted works of Bartók. A surprising revival of modality was its adoption by the purveyors of rock 'n' roll. Roy Harris has built a sui generis ethos of modes by assigning specific emotions to each, according to the intervallic magnitude of the opening tetrachord, ranging from the most spacious, LYDIAN MODE, expressing optimism, to the least spacious, LOCRIAN MODE, expressing pessimism. Avenir H. Monfred has developed a practical method of modern modal composition, *diatonic neomodality*, in which a modal change is effected by altering the key signature. Thus the Dorian mode on D can be transformed, either during the process of composition or by spontaneous improvisation, into any other mode by adding sharps or flats to the key signature; it would be transmuted into D major by placing 2 sharps in the key signature into the PHRYGIAN MODE by 2 flats, etc.

neomysticism. The words *Laus Deo*, which Haydn used to append to every manuscript upon its completion, were simply the expression of his piety and did not imply a claim of direct communication with the Deity. Mystical composers of the 20th century, on the other hand, believed that they were oracles of higher powers. Mahler thought he was possessed by Beelzebub. He scrawled appeals to Satan in the manuscript of his unfinished 10th Sym.; he believed in the mystical magic of all of his music. But it was left to Scriabin to formalize his mystical consciousness in musical terms. His sym. *Prometheus* is based on a 6-note chord that he called the MYSTIC CHORD. Shortly before his death he sketched out the text for a *Mysterium*, which he envisioned as a synaesthetic action which would comprise all human senses as receiving organs. A large ensemble of bells was an instrumental feature of this eschatological creation, to be performed high over the Himalayan Mountains.

neophobia. A neurotic fear of radical innovations. Professional music critics are particularly prone to suffer from it, a condition that they attempt to disguise as profound devotion to the immutable laws of music. Like mental patients, they regard themselves as the only rational human beings in a mad world. The more enlightened among them often correct their former misapprehensions. At the 1st American performance of *Don Juan* by R. Strauss, Philip Hale described it as "a good deal of a bore." Eleven years later he called it a work of "fascinating, irresistible insolence and glowing passion." Heinrich Strobel, who became the great panjandrum of the avant-garde, had contributed some choice invectives against the American moderns in his report of a concert in Berlin in 1932:

> For 2 hours Nicolas Slonimsky bore down on the musicians of the Berlin Philharmonic, until finally they could no longer refrain from openly showing their disgust. For an hour and three-quarters the public tolerated the noise, but by the cacophonous melee of *Arcana* by Varèse the audience lost their patience. A scandal broke loose. It was understandable. No ear can endure this sort of noise for any length of time. It has nothing to do with music. It does not shock and it does not amuse. It is simply senseless.

neoprimitivism. An art saturated with culture is invariably tempted to return to its simple origins, chronologically to the cave paintings of primitive man and to the haunting drum rhythms of *Homo protomusicus*, and biologically to INFANTILOQUY. Supreme mastery of design is used by abstract expressionist painters to emulate prehistoric color drawings, and a sophisticated instrumental technique is utilized by modern composers for children's pieces in asymmetrical rhythms. From these dual resources, intuitively developed by primitive man and by a human child, grew the language of neoprimitivism. Discarding the civilized garments of Romantic images and impressionistic colors, it seeks to attain the crude power of massively arrayed sonorities, asymmetrical rhythms, and percussive instrumentation.

In neoprimitivism, melodies are brief refrains, often limited to the range of a major tetrachord. Reiteration of single notes in unchanged speed is cultivated to the point of stupefaction. Vacuous progressions of naked 5ths and 4ths are used to form an impression of inarticulate eloquence. *Heterophony*, in which a mobile voice elaborates on the principal subject while ignoring the niceties of counterpoint, is

encountered in numerous scores of neoprimitivist music, as a curious recessive characteristic.

Neoprimitivism is almost invariably nationalistic in character. The greatest masterpiece of neoprimitivism, Stravinsky's *Le Sacre du Printemps*, bears the subtitle *Scenes of Pagan Russia*. Bartók's music evokes the neoprimitivist landscape of immortal Pannonia. Villa-Lobos recreates the inchoate sound of the Brazilian jungle in his syms. Neoprimitivism is nurtured on the essential character of the race, but the composer himself need not be an archeologist; he derives his inspiration from the art of his own time. The French painter Henri Rousseau copied the subjects and color patterns of his exotic paintings from illustrations in a French children's book. Gauguin painted his Tahitian women from photographs, preferring them to living models. Nonetheless, both created a genuinely novel type of pictorial neoprimitivism. In music, however, neoprimitivist representation cannot be effected without a complete mastery of modern techniques of composition. The theory that an analphabetic musician can write primitivistically authentic works by simply disregarding the civilized rules of harmony and counterpoint is false.

neoromanticism. A term for a 20th-century revival of works embodying 19th-century musical precepts; one such revival occurred in the years before and during World War II, a 2nd in the last quarter of the century (in the U.S.; see NEW ROMANTICISM). Neoromanticism represents a secondary phase of the modern stylistic upheaval, following the repudiation of programmatic music as a valid medium. The frustrations of World War I sharpened a general disenchantment among poets, artists, and musicians, but the purely negative intellectual movements, such as dadaism, soon exhausted their shock power and gave way to a mitigated type of Romantic music in the form of neoromanticism. Coloristic elements, so ingratiatingly used in the syms. of Sibelius, in the tone poems of R. Strauss, and in the early ballet scores of Stravinsky were applied with apprehensive circumspection by neoromantic composers. Representational onomatopoeia and literal reproduction of natural sounds replaced the subjective effusions of modern pictorialism. Britten's seagulls in the interludes of his opera *Peter Grimes*, Messiaen's bird songs in his score *Chronochromie*, and the phonograph record of the song of a real nightingale in Respighi's *The Pines of Rome* are modern instances of neoromanticism.

nera (It., black one). Quarter note.

Nero. Opera by Rubinstein, 1879, 1st performed in Hamburg. In it Rubinstein tried to emulate the genre of French grand opera. In the last act Nero plays the anachronistic fiddle while Rome burns.

Nerone. Opera by Boito, left unfinished after decades of work. It was finished by Toscanini and others, and premiered posthumously in Milan, 1924. The opera dramatizes the contrast between the pagan world of the Roman emperor Nero and the emerging Christianity. In the finale Rome has its famous conflagration.

nervoso (It.). In a forcible, agitated style.

Nesterenko, Evgeni (Evgenievich), distinguished Russian bass; b. Moscow, Jan. 8, 1938. He 1st studied architectural engineering; graduated from the Leningrad Structural Inst. in 1961, then enrolled in the Leningrad Cons., where he studied voice with Lukanin. He began his opera career at the Maly Theater in Leningrad (1963–67); then was a member of the Kirov Opera and Ballet Theater there (1967–71). In 1970 he won 1st prize at the Tchaikovsky Competition in Moscow; in 1971 he joined the Bolshoi Theater. He then embarked on a European concert tour; also sang in the U.S. In 1975 he was appointed chairman of the voice dept. at the Moscow Cons. He excelled in such roles as Boris Godunov and Méphistophélès. In 1982 he was awarded the Lenin Prize.

nettamente (It.). In a neat, clear, and distinct style.

Neue Sachlichkeit (Ger.). A movement launched in Germany after World War I to describe the "new objectivity" in drama, art, and music as a reaction against the hyperromantic tendencies of 19th-century culture. In music it cultivated functional modus operandi, pursuing well-defined objectives in clearly outlined forms. The economic necessity of cutting down the cost of production of musical presentations resulted in the creation of new modern types of chamber opera, without a chorus, and a partial return to the Classical type of orch. composition. In many respects the movement coincided with the aims of GEBRAUCHSMUSIK.

Neues vom Tage (Daily News). Opera by Hindemith, 1929, 1st produced in Berlin. The events of the libretto begin with a marital separation; another couple also becomes entangled in divorce proceedings. The libretto includes a bathtub aria which scandalized the critics.

Another novelty was a chorus of stenographers at their percussive typewriters.

neumes. MENSURAL NOTATION signs used in the later Middle Ages to represent pitch and rhythm.

Never on Sunday. Song by Hadjidakis, 1960, for the film of the same name, featuring Melina Mercouri as a pious Greek prostitute who refuses to ply her trade on the Sabbath.

Nevěsta Messinská (The Bride of Messina). Opera by Fibich, 1884, 1st produced in Prague, after Schiller's tragedy.

New England Triptych. Orch.l work by Schuman, 1956, using themes from hymns and other tunes by the 18th-century composer Billings; it was 1st performed in Miami.

New Moon, The. Musical by Romberg, 1928. The story deals with an 18th-century Frenchman indentured to a rich man in New Orleans, then under French rule. He is sought by the French royalist police on the suspicion of political intrigue, and a ship called the *The New Moon* is sent to New Orleans to bring him back to France to trial. But there is a mutiny on board and *The New Moon* alights on a small Caribbean island. In the meantime the news arrives of the French Revolution; the fugitive now becomes a hero. He takes possession of the island in the name of the French revolutionary government. He summons the girl he loves in New Orleans and marries her. The popular score includes *Softly as in a Morning Sunrise, One Kiss,* and the chorus *Stout-Hearted Men.*

new music. A term for music of the 20th century that is intended to distinguish it from music of the past and in advance of its own time. Newness is a recurring motive in musical nomenclature. The emergence of rhythmic modalities in the 14th century became historically known as ARS NOVA. A collection of monodic compositions by the Florentine operatic initiator G. Caccini was published under the name *Nuove musiche.* In painting, *art nouveau* was the description given the French art that flourished in the 1890s. The term *new music* became current about 1920; it denoted a type of modern music marked by a dissonant counterpoint, atonality, and brevity of expression. Later, new music became synonymous with ULTRAMODERN MUSIC.

New Romanticism. A U.S. movement, begun in the 1970s, wherein composers returned to the gestures, forms, genres, and harmonies of the 19th century.

New Simplicity. 1. During the neoclassical flowering of the 1920s the slogan "New Simplicity" was raised among composers eager to divest themselves of an enforced sophistication of the period. In practice, New Simplicity meant a return to elementary and sometimes abecedarian melodic and harmonic practices, barely covered with a patina of NONTOXIC DISSONANCES. 2. A 1970s movement, especially among central European, Scandinavian, and Dutch composers, toward a simplified style of composition highly influenced by the American minimalists.

New Wave. See ROCK.

New World Symphony. See FROM THE NEW WORLD.

New York Skyline, The. A graphic score by Villa-Lobos, 1940, composed with his system of musical MILLIMETRIZATION, by which he transferred the outline of a painting or a photograph to music paper, allowing a semitone for every millimeter of the graph. The musical result was broadcast from Rio de Janeiro to N.Y. for the opening of the Brazilian Pavillion at the N.Y. World's Fair.

Newman, Alfred, American film composer and conductor, uncle of Randy Newman; b. New Haven, Conn., Mar. 17, 1900; d. Los Angeles, Feb. 17, 1970. He studied piano with Sigismund Stojowski and composition with Rubin Goldmark; also had private lessons with Schoenberg in Los Angeles. He began his career in vaudeville shows billed as "The Marvelous Boy Pianist"; later, when he led theater orchs. on Broadway, he was hailed as "The Boy Conductor" and "The Youngest Conductor in the U.S.A." In 1930 he went to Hollywood and devoted himself entirely to writing film music; he wrote about 230 film scores; of these, 45 were nominated for awards of the Motion Picture Academy, and 9 were winners. Among his most successful scores were *The Prisoner of Zenda* (1937), *The Hunchback of Notre Dame* (1939), *Wuthering Heights* (1939), *Captain from Castille* (1947), The *Robe* (1953), and *The Egyptian* (1954; partly written by the original assignee, Bernard Herrmann). Stylistically he followed an eclectic type of theatrical Romanticism, often mimicking, almost literally, the most popular works of Tchaikovsky, Rachmaninoff, Wagner, and Liszt, and amalgamating these elements in colorful free fantasia; in doing so he created a category of composition that was to become known, with some disdain, as "movie music."

Newman, Randy, American societal singer, pianist, and songwriter, nephew of Alfred Newman; b. Los Angeles, Nov. 28, 1943. He spent his childhood in southern Calif., where he took regular music lessons. His songs often veered toward the unacceptable, unthinkable, and inconceivable in terms of targets and the means by which he hit at them: *Davy the Fat Boy* from *Randy Newman*; *Yellow Man* from *12 Songs*; *Political Science* and *Sail Away* from *Sail Away*; and the entire 1974 album *Good Old Boys*. In 1977 he released *Little Criminals*, which once again assailed bigotry, but one number, *Short People*, was misconstrued as an attack on vertically challenged persons; it was neither the 1st nor last time that Newman overestimated the ability of many to perceive irony. What gets lost in such controversy is the breadth of Newman's songwriting: an almost Ivesian capacity for nostalgia (*Dayton Ohio—1903*); considerable insight into the fear of sex and other hedonisms (*You Can Leave Your Hat On, Lucinda*); a fine sense of humor (*Burn On, Mama Told Me Not to Come*); and an ability to write beautifully painful songs (*I Think It's Gonna Rain Today, Guilty*). He followed with the album *Born Again* (with *It's Money That I Love*, 1979); then brought out the albums *Ragtime* (soundtrack, 1981) and *Trouble in Paradise* (1983). More recently, Newman has released his quasi-biographical *Land of Dreams* and a musical, *Faust* (1995). He has written several film scores.

Nichols, "Red" (Ernest Loring), American jazz cornetist and bandleader; b. Ogden, Utah, May 8, 1905; d. Las Vegas, June 28, 1965. His father taught him cornet, and he played in his father's brass band from the age of 12. He then cut a swath in the world of popular music with his own band, advertised as Red Nichols and His 5 Pennies (actually, the number of "Pennies" was 10); among its members were such future celebrities as Jimmy Dorsey, Benny Goodman, and Glenn Miller. A maudlin motion picture, *The 5 Pennies*, was manufactured in 1959 and catapulted Nichols into the stratosphere of jazzdom. Heuristic exegetes of European hermeneutics bemoaned the commercialization of his style, giving preference to his earlier, immaculate, jazzification.

nicht (Ger.). Not. *Nicht zu langsam*, not too slow.

Nicolai, (Carl) **Otto** (Ehrenfried), famous German composer and conductor; b. Königsberg, June 9, 1810; d. Berlin, May 11, 1849. He studied piano at home; in 1827 he went to Berlin, where he took lessons in theory with Zelter; he also took courses with Bernhard Klein at the Royal Inst. for Church Music. In 1833 he made his concert debut in Berlin as a pianist, singer, and composer. He then was engaged as organist to the embassy chapel in Rome by the Prussian ambassador, Bunsen. While in Italy he also studied counterpoint with Giuseppe Baini.

In 1837 he proceeded to Vienna, where he became a singing teacher and Kapellmeister at the Kärnthnertortheater. In 1838 he returned to Italy; in 1839 he presented in Trieste his 1st opera, *Rosmonda d'Inghilterra*, given under its new title as *Enrico II*. His 2nd opera, *Il Templario*, was staged in Turin (1840). In 1841 he moved to Vienna, where he was appointed court Kapellmeister in succession to Kreutzer. Nicolai was instrumental in establishing sym. concerts utilizing the musicians of the orch. of the Imperial Court Opera Theater; in 1842 he conducted this ensemble featuring Beethoven's 7th Sym.; this became the inaugural concert of the celebrated

Vienna Phil. In 1848 he was appointed Kapellmeister of the Royal Opera in Berlin. In 1849 his famous opera *Die lustigen Weiber von Windsor*, after Shakespeare, was given at the Berlin Royal Opera; it was to become his only enduring creation. Nicolai died 2 months after its production.

In 1887 Hans Richter, then conductor of the Vienna Phil., inaugurated an annual "Nicolai-Konzert" in his memory, and it became a standard occasion. It was conducted by Gustav Mahler (1899–1901); by Felix Weingartner (1909–27); by Wilhelm Furtwängler (1928–31, 1933–44, and 1948–54); by Karl Böhm (1955–57 and 1964–80); and by Claudio Abbado in 1980 and 1983. Nicolai also composed sacred choral music, secular vocal music for vocal ensemble and piano, 2 syms. (1831; 1835), overtures, chamber music, and solo songs.

Nielsen, Carl (August)

Greatly significant Danish composer; b. Sortelung, near Nørre-Lyndelse, June 9, 1865; d. Copenhagen, Oct. 3, 1931. He received violin lessons in childhood from his father and the local schoolteacher; played 2nd violin in the village band and later in its amateur orch. After studying cornet with his father he played in the Odense military orch. (1879–83), serving as its signal horn and alto trombone player; also taught himself to play piano. While in Odense he began to compose, producing several chamber pieces; then received financial assistance to continue his training at the Royal Cons. in Copenhagen, where he studied violin with V. Tofte, theory with J. P. E. Hartmann and Orla Rosenhoff, and music history with N. Gade and P. Matthison-Hansen (1884–86).

He was a violinist in Copenhagen's Royal Chapel Orch. (1889–1905); in the interim he achieved his 1st success as a composer with his *Little Suite* for Strings (1888); then continued private studies with Rosenhoff for a number of years. In 1901 he was granted an annual pension; he was conductor of the Royal Theater (1908–14) and the Musikforeningen (1915–27) in Copenhagen; also appeared as a guest conductor in Germany, the Netherlands, Sweden, and Finland; taught theory and

composition at the Royal Cons. (1916–19) and was appointed its director a few months before his death.

The early style of Nielsen's music, Romantic in essence, was determined by the combined influences of Gade, Grieg, Brahms, and Liszt, but later on he experienced the powerful impact of MODERN MUSIC, particularly in HARMONY, which in his works grew more and more chromatic and dissonant; yet he reserved the simple diatonic progressions, often in a folk-song manner, for his major climaxes; in his orchestration he applied opulent sonorities and colorful instrumental counterpoint; there are instances of bold experimentation in some of his works, as, for example, the insertion of a snare-drum solo in his 5th Sym., playing independently of the rest of the orch.

Nielsen is sometimes described as the Sibelius of Denmark, despite obvious dissimilarities in idiom and sources of inspiration; while the music of Sibelius is deeply rooted in national folklore, both in subject matter and melodic derivation, Nielsen seldom drew on Danish popular modalities; Sibelius remained true to the traditional style of composition, while Nielsen sought new ways of modern expression. It was only after his death that Nielsen's major works entered the world repertoire;

festivals of his music were organized on his centennial in 1965, and his syms. in particular were played and recorded in England and America, bringing him belated recognition as one of the most important composers of his time.

In 1988 Queen Margrethe II dedicated the Carl Nielsen Museum in Odense. His writings include *Living Music* (Copenhagen, 1925) and *My Childhood in Funen* (Copenhagen, 1927). His son-in-law was the Hungarian Emil Telmanyi, a violinist, conductor, and teacher (b. Arad, June 22, 1892; d. June 12, 1988). He studied with Hubay at the Royal Academy of Music in Budapest. In 1911 he began an active career as a violinist; in 1918 he married Ann Marie, Carl Nielsen's daughter. Telmanyi supervised the devising of a curved bow for the playing of Bach's violin works, which became known as the Vega bow (1954).

Virtually all premieres of Nielsen's music occurred in Copenhagen. His best-known works are the 6 syms.: No. 1, op. 7 (1890–92; 1894); No. 2, op. 16, *Die fire temperamenter* (The 4 Temperaments; 1902); No. 3, op. 27, *Sinfonia espansiva*, with 2 solo singers (1912); No. 4, op. 29, *Det uudslukkelige* (The Inextinguishable; 1916); No. 5, op. 50 (1922); and No. 6, *Sinfonia semplice* (an oddly sarcastic work, 1925). He composed 2 great Danish operas; the tragedy *Saul og David* (1902); and the comedy *Maskarade* (1906); also a melodramma, *Snefrid* (1894); incidental music for many plays. He wrote many other orch.l, chamber, solo, and vocal works.

niente (It.). Nothing. *Quasi niente*, barely audible.

Nietzsche, Friedrich (Wilhelm), celebrated German philosopher; b. Röcken, near Lützen, Oct. 15, 1844; d. Weimar, Aug. 25, 1900. He was prof. of classical philology at the Univ. of Basel (1869–79); was at 1st a warm partisan of Wagner, whom he championed in *Die Geburt der Tragödie aus dem Geiste der Musik* (1872; 2nd ed., 1874) and *Richard Wagner in Bayreuth* (1876). In *Der Fall Wagner* and *Nietzsche contra Wagner* (both 1888) and in *Götzendämmerung* (1889) he turned against his former idol and became a partisan of Bizet. Nietzsche tried his hand at composition, producing both sacred and secular choral works, songs, and piano pieces.

Night and Day. Song by C. Porter, 1932; its effect lies with the constant chromatic shifts of harmony, while the tune itself remains mesmerisingly monotonous.

Night Flight. 1. Opera by Dallapiccola (*Volo di notte*), 1940, based on the novel *Vol de nuit* by Antoine de Saint-Exupéry, 1st produced in Florence. The story deals with a dramatic night flight over the Andes in a single-engine monoplane. Dallapiccola set it to music in a dynamic atonal idiom verging on dodecaphony. The score includes spoken dialogue and a wordless passage of a disembodied voice warning the pilot of dangers facing him. 2. Symphonic poem, 1944, by Gardner Read (b. Evanston, Ill., Jan. 2, 1913), inspired by the Saint-Exupéry novel described above. It was 1st performed in Rochester, N.Y.

Night on Bald Mountain, A. Symphonic poem by Mussorgsky, 1867; the orig. Russian name translates as "St. John's Night on the Bare Mountain." Russian composers have often been partial to devilry; Mussorgsky's contribution pictures broom-riding witches who celebrate a Black Mass, but the church bells at midnight scare them away. Mussorgsky, who was diffident about his orchestration, left the score half finished. Rimsky-Korsakov completed it in his usual well-meaning fashion and conducted its 1st performance, 5 years after Mussorgsky's death, in St. Petersburg, 1886.

Night Piece, A. Work for flute and strings by A. Foote, 1919; one of his finest instrumental pieces.

Nightingale, The (*Le Rossignol*). Opera by Stravinsky, 1914, 1st produced in Paris. The Chinese Emperor is dying, and his life is supported by the singing of a nightingale. But when the Japanese Ambassador thoughtlessly presents the Emperor with a mechanical nightingale, the real bird flies away, and the Emperor's health declines dangerously. As a discordant funeral march is played, the real nightingale is brought in, and the Emperor regains his strength. The moral seems to be that human ills ought to be left to natural cure. The compositional history of the work reveals that the 1st 2 acts were composed before the groundbreaking ballets *Petrouchka* and *The Rite of Spring*; the last act was composed afterward, and Stravinsky struggled to maintain consistency (as Wagner had to do in *Siegfried*). The score mixes Russian melos, Debussy-like tone color, and the occasional harsh dissonance with harmonies built on the tritone and the major 7th.

Nights in the Gardens of Spain. Symphonic impression for piano and orch. by de Falla, 1916, 1st performed in Madrid. The 3-movement work describes the sounds of music and dancers in Andalusia.

Nilsson, (Märta) **Birgit,** greatly renowned Swedish soprano; b. Västra Karups, May 17, 1918. She studied with Joseph Hislop at the Royal Academy of Music in Stockholm; made her debut as Agathe in *Der Freischütz* at the Royal Theater in Stockholm (1946), gaining her 1st success as Verdi's Lady Macbeth (1947); then sang major roles in operas by Wagner, Puccini, and Strauss with increasing success. She 1st appeared as Brünnhilde in *Götterdammerung* in Stockholm during the 1954–55 season and sang this role in the Ring cycle for the 1st time in Munich during the same season; likewise appeared at the Vienna State Opera (1954) and at the Bayreuth Festival (1954), to which she returned regularly from 1959 to 1970.

In 1956 she made her U.S. debut at the Hollywood Bowl; then sang Brünnhilde in *Die Walküre* at the San Francisco Opera (1956); subsequently made her 1st appearance at London's Covent Garden (1957). She made her long-awaited Metropolitan Opera debut in N.Y. as Isolde (1959). She was universally acclaimed as one of the greatest Wagnerian dramatic sopranos of all time. After an absence of 5 years she returned to the Metropolitan Opera for a gala concert in 1979. She then rejoined the company., appearing as Elektra in 1980. She retired from the operatic stage in 1982. In addition to her brilliant Wagnerian roles, she excelled as Beethoven's Leonore, Turandot, and Salome.

Nine. Musical, 1982, by Maury Yeston (b. Jersey City, N.J., Oct. 23, 1945); until *9* opened, Yeston was known as a theorist of classical music. Based on Fellini's movie *8 1/2*, it includes opulent recollections of Baroque and Romantic styles, continuing the operatic trend in musical theater established by Loesser, Sondheim, and Lloyd Webber.

ninth. The interval of an octave plus a major or minor 2nd.

ninth chord. Although 9th chords are defined as chords consisting of a series of 4 superimposed 3rds on any degree of the scale, their use is confined in practice to dominant 9th chords. These chords were cultivated systematically by Wagner, Liszt, and Bruckner, always within a given tonality. The 9th chord requires 5-part harmony for its totality; in 4-part harmony the 5th above the root is left out. The necessity of the resolution into the dominant 7th chord is felt very strongly in cadential formations, as, for instance, toward the end of the overture of *Die Meistersinger*. The dramatic attraction of the 9th chord led Scriabin to the formation of his so-called MYSTIC CHORD, which eliminates the 5th but includes an upper and lower appoggiatura to it. Debussy emancipated the tonal implications of the dominant 9th chord by moving it in parallel formation, either chromatically or by minor 3rds, without resolving.

Numerous composers of the 20th century used this device to create a feeling of vague harmonic uncertainty. The fascination of the 9th chord ceased abruptly with the decline of musical impressionism in the 2nd quarter of the 20th century, and parallel 9th chords, once the darlings of modernism, were relegated to a type of "mood music." Ninth chords built on degrees of the scale other than the dominant lack the proper euphony to provide much interest to composers of modern music, and examples of such use are rare.

Ninth Symphonies. Many composers have reached number 9 in their symphonic production, among them Mahler and Bruckner, but when musicians speak simply of "The 9th," it is understood that the great *Choral Sym.* of Beethoven is meant.

Ninth Symphony. Sym. by Mahler, 1908–1909. The work is in 4 movements; it's one of his longest syms. Its musical idiom is overladen by constant chromatic deviations; even the tonal plan exhibits this, as a work in D major ends in D-flat major. Psychologically motivated analysts perceive Mahler's premonition of death in the music.

Nirvana. (Guitar/vocal: Kurt Cobain, b. Hoquiam, Wash., Feb. 20, 1967; d. Seattle, Wash., Apr. 5, 1994; bass: Krist Novoselic, b. Los Angeles, May 16, 1965; drums: David Grohl, b. Warren, Ohio, Jan. 14, 1969.) Archetypical grunge-rock outfit. Cobain and Novoselic were childhood friends in Aberdeen, Wash.; they formed Nirvana together in 1987. Playing locally with various supporting members, they were signed to the small Sub Pop label, recording their 1st album, which featured the single *Love Buzz* backed with *Negative Creep*, both hits among the nascent grunge community. Grohl joined the lineup in time for their major-label debut, *Nevermind*, released on DGC Records in 1990. The song *Smells Like Teen Spirit* made the album an immediate chart-busting hit and established the group as the voice of their (plaid-clad) generation.

The band produced a 2nd album, *In Utero*, banned by Wal-Mart and other chain stores but still happily consumed by teens everywhere. An appearance on *MTV Unplugged* helped listeners actually understand the group's lyrics—previously nearly obliterated by their ear-crunching sound—and some were surprised by Cobain's sensitivity, others by his disturbing sentiments. In 1992 Cobain wed Courtney Love, the big-lunged vocalist and songwriter with the group Hole, and the couple's escapades were soon making tabloid headlines. Cobain himself had trouble adjusting to adulation and fame, attempting suicide in Mar. 1994 and, 1 month later, shooting himself in the head at his home. An outpouring of grief-stricken grungers held a vigil outside of his home. Following Cobain's death, Grohl formed the Foo Fighters. Love continued to record and perform and also costarred in the film *The People vs. Larry Flynt* (1996).

Nixon in China. Opera by J. Adams, 1987, depicting in fancifully realistic scenes President Richard Nixon's historical trip to China in 1972, with Nixon's role assigned to a baritone, Mao Zedung as a Wagnerian Heldentenor, and his wife as a mindless ingenue. The world premiere was given, of all places, in Houston, Tex.; quite a few people made the trip from N.Y. and other populated centers. The production was directed by Peter Sellars, the libretto by Alice Goodman. Two orch.l excerpts from the work, *Short Ride in a Fast Machine* and *The Chairman Dances*, are frequently programmed.

Nixon, Marni (born Margaret Nixon McEathron), American soprano; b. Altadena, Calif., Feb. 22, 1930. She studied with Carl Ebert at the Univ. of Southern Calif. in Los Angeles, Jan Popper at Stanford Univ., and Boris Goldovsky and Sarah Caldwell at the Berkshire Music Center at Tanglewood. She pursued a multifaceted career: sang on the soundtracks of the films *The King and I*, *West Side Story*, and *My Fair Lady*; starred in her own children's program on television; appeared in musical comedy and opera; was a soloist with major orchs. in the U.S. and abroad. She taught at the Calif. Inst. of the Arts (1969–71) and the Music Academy of the West in Santa Barbara (from 1980).

No Admission. 1. An indication that a theater is closed or that there is no performance that day. 2. An indication that tickets are free of charge. See also RÉLACHE.

No, No, Nanette. Musical by V. Youmans, 1924, extremely popular; 1st performed in Detroit, Chicago, and London before its N.Y. debut (1925). The plot centers on a publisher of Bibles with a penchant for nubile young women. He obtains 3 of them but has to contend with a narrow-mind-

ed wife; in the end he straightens out his difficulties. The best-known song is the beloved *Tea for 2*; others include the title song and *I Want to Be Happy*.

No Strings. Musical by Rodgers, 1962. An American writer in Paris falls in love with a black model. He wants to take her back to the U.S., but she recoils at the thought of the reaction to their interracial romance. Still, he feels that only in America can he write his projected novel; they part wistfully. Includes the title song and *The Sweetest Sounds*.

Nobilissima Visione. Ballet suite by Hindemith, 1938, 1st performed in Venice. In 3 movements it portrays the virtues of St. Francis: poverty, obedience, and chastity. The musical material was drawn from the eponymous "dance legend" of the same year.

nobilmente (It.). In a refined, chaste, and lofty style; Elgar uses this term in the 1st movement of his cello concerto.

Nobody Knows the Trouble I've Seen. African-American spiritual collected in Charleston, S.C., before the American Civil War; 1st published in the collection *Slave Songs of the United States*, 1867. The melody possess a type of syncopation similar to that of ragtime and jazz.

Nobody Knows You When You're Down and Out. A 1923 song by James Cox that became a blues hit for Bessie Smith, among others, and a favorite in the Depression era.

Noces, Les (The Wedding). Choreographic scenes by Stravinsky, 1923, and 1st produced by Diaghilev's Ballets Russes in Paris. It is scored for chorus, soloists, 4 pianos, and 17 percussion instruments; generically it might be called a staged cantata. The music is rooted in Russian folk song, but the harmonic and contrapuntal realization is propulsive and acrid while always keeping within a diatonic framework. The libretto consists of 4 scenes tracing the rituals of a peasant betrothal and wedding. The Russian title is *Svadebka* (Little Wedding).

noch (Ger.). Still; yet. *Noch rascher*, still faster.

Noches en los jardines de España. NIGHTS IN THE GARDENS OF SPAIN.

Nocturnal. Work by Varèse based on Anaïs Nin's novel *The House of Incest*; never completed, but edited by his student Chou Wen-Chung (1973). A portion of the work was premiered in N.Y. in 1961. *Nocturnal* is scored for soprano, bass chorus, small orch., piano, and percussion. Varèse planned another work, *Nocturnal II*, even as *Nocturnal* lay unfinished; this 2nd work never got beyond sketches.

nocturne (Fr., night piece; It. *notturno*). A piece of dreamily Romantic or sentimental character, set in euphonious melody and harmony, and without fixed form. The nocturne emerged as a distinct genre of Romantic piano pieces early in the 19th century, primarily through the poetic creations of Chopin. The pioneer of piano nocturnes was the Irish composer John Field, but his pieces fall far below those of Chopin in quality. Even though nocturnes are creatures of the night, Chopin often includes dramatic turbulence in the middle sections. Schumann also wrote nocturnes, but, in conformity with the prevalent nationalistic sentiment of the time, he assigned to them a German name, *Nachtstück*.

Nocturnes. Orch.l suite by Debussy, 1901, in 3 movements entitled *Nuages*, *Fêtes*, and *Sirènes*; it was 1st performed in its entirety in Paris. The 1st movement (Clouds) is a musical monochrome: the clouds are simply white and gray. The 2nd movement (Festivals) is full of rhythmic sounds and light. The 3rd movement, which includes a female chorus, depicts the laughing sirens singing their mysterious songs.

Nocturns. A portion of the Matins service of the Roman Catholic daily Hours, held during the night.

nodal figures. The calculations corresponding to the "nodal lines" of a vibrating plate of wood, glass, etc.; rendered visible by strewing fine dry sand on the plate, this sand being tossed by the vibrating portions of the plate to the nodal lines, which are points of perfect or comparative rest. *Nodal point*, see NODE.

node (nodal point). A point or line in a vibrating body (such as a string, soundboard, trumpet, bell) which remains at rest during the vibration of the other parts of the body.

noël (Fr.; from Lat. *natalis*, birthday). A Christmas carol or hymn with sacred or secular texts, including drinking songs.

noire (Fr.). Quarter note.

noise. Scientifically speaking, sound with indefinite pitch used as a compositional element in many 20th-century com-

positions; a collection of tonally unrelated simultaneous sounds of different frequencies and intensities, meaningless to musical or even unmusical ears. *White noise* is an integral assembly of sounds of numerous frequencies but more or less equal intensities. In radio transmission, noise is called static, and a similar electromagnetic disturbance in television is called snow. Metaphorically, old-fashioned music critics often describe unfamiliar music as noise.

nola (It.). An abbrev. for *campanola*, the Italian diminutive of CAMPANA (bell). See also TINTINNABULUM.

Nola. Popular instrumental by Felix Arndt, 1915, written in tribute to a girlfriend. Its most remarkable feature is the pentatonic structure of the melody in ragtime rhythm (playable on the black keys of the piano).

non (It.). Not.

Non nobis Domine. A famous vocal CANON of the latter 16th century; its composition is usually attributed to the great Elizabethan madrigalist William Byrd. Since the canon is not written out it must be classified as a *riddle canon*, and indeed it can be sung in several different formations, all of them quite harmonious. It is set in 3 parts; the treble enters 1st, the middle voice then comes in a perfect 4th below, and the bass enters a 5th below the middle voice. One of the voices may even be inverted without disastrous consequences to the harmony. In England this canon was often sung as a grace before meals.

non vibrato (It.). A emphatic negative exhortation often marked as a warning against the natural tendency of string players and singers to play VIBRATO and thus produce what the Baroque considered an *affect* and what became a standard performance technique of Romantic (and other) music. Other considerations for the use of non vibrato are the period of music being performed (e.g., EARLY MUSIC MOVEMENT) and the performance of untempered pitch (just intonation).

None. A daily service, part of the Roman Catholic Divine Office, celebrated at 3 P.M., the time when Jesus died on the cross (counted as the 9th hour from sunrise, hence the name). This service is one of the 4 so-called Little Hours.

nonet. A composition for 9 voices or instruments. Usually the instrumentation involves more than 1 instrumental family; but Copland wrote a nonet for violin, viola, and cello, 3 apiece (1961).

Nonnengeige (Ger., nun violin). A whimsical appellation common in the 14th century for the TROMBA MARINA, which itself is a curious name for a monochord, a box with 1 string. German nuns supposedly favored this instrument.

Nono, Luigi, remarkable Italian composer who earned a unique place in the history of modern music through his consistent devotion to social problems; b. Venice, Jan. 29, 1924; d. there, May 8, 1990. He became a student at the Venice Cons. (1941), where he received instruction in composition with Malipiero (1943–45); also studied law at the Univ. of Padua (graduated, 1946); later had advanced harmony and counterpoint lessons with Maderna and Scherchen. A man of extraordinary courage, he joined the Italian Communist Party while the country was still under the dictatorship of Mussolini, and he was an active participant in the Italian Resistance Movement against the Nazis. In 1975 he was elected to the Central Committee of the Communist Party, and he remained a member until his death.

Although Nono's works are extremely difficult to perform and practically all of them are devoted to leftist propaganda, he found support among a number of liberal composers and performers. At the end of his life he acquired an enormous reputation as a highly original composer in a novel technical idiom as well as a fearless political agitator. In his technique of composition he followed the precepts of Schoenberg without adhering to the literal scheme of DODECAPHONIC composition. As a resolutely engaged artist Nono mitigated the antinomy between the modern idiom of his music and the conservative Soviet ideology of Socialist Realism by his militant political attitude and his emphasis on revolutionary subjects in his works, so that even extreme dissonances may be dialectically justified as representing the horrors of fascism. He made several visits to the Soviet Union, the last in 1988, but his works are rarely performed there because of the intransigence of his idiom.

Nono made use of a variety of techniques: serialism, sonorism (employing sonorities for their own sake, à la *Klangfarbenmelodie*), ALEATORY and CONCRETE MUSIC, and electronics. Perhaps his most militant composition, both politically and musically, is his opera *Intolleranza 1960*, utilizing texts by Brecht, Eluard, Sartre, and Mayakovsky; the work is a powerful protest against imperialist policies and

social inequities. At its production in Venice (1961) a group of neofascists showered the audience with leaflets denouncing Nono for his alleged contamination of Italian music by alien doctrines, even making a facetious allusion to his name as representing a double negative. Nono married Schoenberg's daughter, Nuria, in 1955; they separated on friendly terms after several years; they had 2 daughters. Nuria settled in her father's last residence in Los Angeles, while Nono traveled widely in Europe. He died of a liver ailment at the age of 66.

nonretrogradable rhythm. For Messiaen, denotative of symmetrical patterns which, by nature, exhibit no change upon inversion: ♩ ♪♩ ♪♪ .

nontoxic dissonances. Dissonances can be said to be nontoxic or noncorrosive if they are embanked within a tonal sequence, or if their cadential illation corresponds to traditional modalities. It is the harmonic context that determines the toxicity of a dissonance for an untutored ear. Among the most corrosive dissonances are atonal combinations in which intervals of a high degree of discordance—such as major 7ths, minor 2nds, and the tritone—are combined with acoustically euphonious intervals of a perfect 5th and a perfect 4th. The absence of 3rds, whether major or minor, is the distinctive feature of corrosive harmony, but toxic sonic effects result also from the simultaneous use of 2 homonymous major and minor triads on account of the interference between the major and minor 3rds. Changes in biochemical balance and nervous reactions to the impact of toxic dissonances can be measured on a neurograph, providing a scientific clue to the apperception of modern music.

noodling. Mindless preludizing and arpeggiating on an instrument, as if warming up for real playing; thus, a negative critique of an improvisation.

Nordic Symphony. The 1st sym. by Hanson, 1923, containing elements of Scandinavian folk rhythms.

Norfolk Rhapsody No. 1. Symphonic picture by Vaughan Williams, 1906, 1st performed in London. The melodic materials are taken from authentic English songs. The composer wrote 2 more rhapsodies but decided not to include them in his catalogue.

Norma. Opera by Bellini, 1831, 1st produced in Milan. Norma is the High Priestess of the Druid Temple in ancient Gaul during its occupation by the Romans. As behooves all operas, natural enemies fall in love. Here, not only Norma herself becomes involved with a Roman Proconsul and bears him a couple of clandestine children, but a virgin of the Temple also loves him, in violation of her vow of chastity. The Proconsul is caught desecrating the Temple of the Druids, but Norma cannot bring herself to put him to death as she ought to do in her capacity as High Priestess. She confesses her own unchastity and ascends the punitive pyre with the Proconsul for ritual incineration. *Norma* is Bellini's most melodious and most harmonious opera, a perennial favorite of the public of all races and geographical locations. The aria *Casta diva*, in which Norma appeals to the goddess of the moon, is a paragon of melodic beauty. Even Wagner professed his admiration for *Norma*.

Norman, Jessye, exceptionally gifted African-American soprano; b. Augusta, Ga., Sept. 15, 1945. She received a scholarship to study at Howard Univ. in Washington, D.C. (1961), where she had vocal lessons from Carolyn Grant; continued her training at the Peabody Cons. of Music in Baltimore and at the Univ. of Michigan, where her principal teachers were Pierre Bernac and Elizabeth Mannion. She won the Munich Competition (1968), then made her operatic debut as Elisabeth in *Tannhäuser* at the Berlin Deutsche Oper (1969); she appeared in the title role of *L'Africaine* at Florence's Maggio Musicale (1971), and the following year sang Aida at Milan's La Scala and Cassandra in *Les Troyens* at London's Covent Garden; subsequently made major recital debuts in London and N.Y. (1973).

After an extensive concert tour of North America (1976–77) she made her U.S. stage debut, as Jocasta in *Oedipus rex* and as Purcell's Dido on a double bill with the Opera Co. of Philadelphia (1982). She made her Metropolitan Opera debut in N.Y. as Cassandra (1983). In 1986 she appeared as soloist in Strauss's *Vier letzte Lieder* with the Berlin Phil. during its tour of the U.S. In 1989 she was the featured soloist with Zubin Mehta and the N.Y. Phil. in its opening concert of its 148th season, which was telecast live to the nation by PBS. Her extraordinary repertoire ranges from Purcell to Richard Rodgers; she commended herself in Mussorgsky's songs, which she performed in Moscow in Russian; in her recitals she gave performances of the classical German repertoire as well as contemporary masterpieces, such as Schoenberg's *Gurrelieder* and *Erwartung*, and the French moderns, which she invariably performed in the original tongue. This combination of scholarship and artistry contributed to her consistently successful career as one of the most versatile concert and operatic singers of her time.

Norrington, Roger (Arthur Carver), scholarly English conductor; b. Oxford, Mar. 16, 1934. He was educated at Clare College, Cambridge, and the Royal College of Music in London; was active as a tenor. In 1962 he founded the Schütz Choir in London, with which he 1st gained notice as a conductor. From 1966 to 1984 he was principal conductor of the Kent Opera, where he produced scores by Monteverdi utilizing his own performing eds.; served as music director of the London Baroque Players (from 1975) and the London Classical Players (from 1978); also was principal conductor of the Bournemouth Sinfonietta (1985–89). In 1989 he made an auspicious N.Y. debut at Carnegie Hall conducting Beethoven's 8th and 9th syms. In 1990 he became music director of the orch. of St. Luke's in N.Y. In 1980 he was made an Officer of the Order of the British Empire; in 1990, a Commander of the Order of the British Empire.

Norrington entered controversy by insisting that the classical tempo is basic for all interpretation. He also insisted that Beethoven's metronome markings, not usually accepted by performers, are in fact accurate reflections of Beethoven's inner thoughts about his own music. He obtained numerous defenders of his ideas (as one critic put it, "inspired literalism") for the interpretation of classical music, which aroused sharp interest as well as caustic rejection. However that might be, his performances, especially in the U.S., received a great deal of attention, and he was particularly praised for the accuracy and precision of his interpretations. In 1985 he began an annual series of musical "experiences": weekends devoted to in-depth exploration of some major classical work, comprising lectures, open rehearsals, research exhibits, and performances of other works by the same composer (which have included Haydn and Berlioz as well as the inevitable Beethoven) and his contemporaries, selected to explicate the musical centerpiece.

North, Alex

〰〰 〰〰 〰〰 〰〰 〰〰

Gloriously gifted American composer and conductor with a predilection for uniquely colored film music; b. Chester, Pa., Dec. 4, 1910; d. Pacific Palisades, Calif., Sept. 8, 1991. His father, a blacksmith, was an early immigrant from Russia. North studied piano and music theory at the Curtis Inst. of Music in Philadelphia; later received a scholarship to study at the Juilliard School of Music in N.Y., where he took courses in composition (1929–32). A decisive change in his life came with his decision to go to Russia as a technology specialist at a time when Russia was eager to engage American technicians. He became fascinated with new Russian music and received a scholarship to attend the Moscow Cons., where he studied composition with Anton Weprik and Victor Bielyi (1933–35). He also was music director of the propaganda group of German Socialists called "Kolonne Links" (Column to the Left).

He mastered the Russian language and acquired a fine reputation in Russia as a true friend of Soviet music. Returning to the U.S., he took additional courses in composition with Aaron Copland (1936–38) and Ernst Toch (1938–39). In 1939 he conducted 26 concerts in Mexico as music director of the Anna Sokolow Dance Troupe; during his stay in Mexico City, he had some instruction from Silvestre Revueltas. In 1942 North entered the U.S. Army; promoted to captain, he became responsible for entertainment programs in mental hospitals. He worked closely with the psychiatrist Karl Menninger in developing a theatrical genre called psychodrama, which later became an accepted mode of psychological therapy.

During his Army years North also worked with the Office of War Information, composing scores for over 25 documentary films. During all these peregrinations he developed a distinct flair for theater music while continuing to produce estimable works in absolute forms. His concerto, *Revue* for Clarinet and Orch., was performed by Benny Goodman in N.Y. under the baton of Leonard Bernstein (1946). He further expanded his creative talents to write a number of modern ballets. The result of these multifarious excursions into musical forms was the formation of a style peculiarly recognizable as the specific art of North.

His concentrated efforts, however, became directed mainly toward the art of FILM MUSIC, a field in which he triumphed. John Huston stated in 1986 that "it is the genius of Alex North to convey an emotion to the audience"; other directors praised North's cinemusical abilities in similar terms. Among the writers with whom he worked were Tennessee Williams, John Steinbeck, and Arthur Miller. But no success is without disheartening frustration. North was commissioned to write the score for *2001: A Space Odyssey*, on which he worked enthusiastically. But much to his dismay the director, Stanley Kubrick, decided to replace it by a pasticcio that included such commonplaces as *The Blue Danube Waltz*. North refused to be downhearted by this discomfiture and used the discarded material for his 3rd Sym. He was nominated 15 times for an Academy Award for best film music, but it was not until 1986 that the Academy of Motion Picture Arts and Sciences finally awarded him an Oscar for lifetime achievement.

Among his outstanding scores are *A Streetcar Named Desire* (1951), *Death of a Salesman* (1951), *Viva Zapata!* (1952), *The Rose Tattoo* (1955), *The Bad Seed* (1956), *The Rainmaker* (1956), *Spartacus* (1960), *The Misfits* (1961), *Cleopatra* (1963), *The Agony and the Ecstasy* (1965), *Who's Afraid of Virginia Woolf?* (1966), *Under the Volcano* (1984), *Prizzi's Honor* (1985), *The Dead* (1987), and *Good Morning, Vietnam* (1988). His song *Unchained Melody* (1955) became a popular hit. North has also composed ballets, children's theater, orch.l music, choral music, and chamber music.

Norvo, Red (born Kenneth Norville), American jazz xylophonist, vibraphonist, and bandleader; b. Beardstown, Ill., Mar. 31, 1908. He played piano and xylophone while attending classes in mining engineering at the Univ. of Missouri (1926–27); later joined Paul Whiteman's orch. In 1935 he organized his own band in N.Y.; also worked with Benny Goodman (1944–45) and Woody Herman (1945–46). He was temporarily married to the blues singer Mildred Bailey.

Nose, The. Opera by Shostakovich, 1930, after the fantastic tale by Gogol; it was produced in Leningrad. The story deals with the nose of a government functionary that mysteriously disappears from his face during shaving and goes off as an independent individual. All sorts of absurdities occur, interspersed with satirical darts at Czarist bureaucracy. In the end the nose resumes its rightful place, above the mouth and under the eyes, much to the owner's relief. The score is a brilliant exercise in grotesquerie. It includes an octet of janitors in dissonant counterpoint, gigantic orch.l sneezes, and other effects. The production was greeted with great exhilaration by Soviet musicians but received a chilly reception by the Kremlin bureaucracy, and Shostakovich was charged with imitating the decadent Western models. Many years elapsed before *The Nose* was revived on the Soviet stage.

nose flutes. Family of wind instruments blown with nasal rather than oral breath; some can be blown in both ways. The materials used and form (e.g., transverse, end-blown) vary widely. Examples of the nose flute can be found on all continents, notably in Melanesia and Polynesia, rarely in Europe.

nóta (Hung.). An urban song, such as *Rákóczi-nóta*, a song about Rákóczi.

nota cambiata (It., changing note). An extra note inserted 1 diagonal degree above the principal note before descending to the next (as in the melody C–D–B, where the D has interrupted the downward motion C–B).

nota cattiva (It., bad note). An unaccented note.

nota sensibile (It.). Leading tone.

notation

The art of representing musical tones, and their modifications, by means of written characters; the craft of writing symbols that represent sounds. It took a millennium to develop a musical notation capable of even an approximate rendition of the pitch and duration of each individual note. The Spanish theologian Isidore of Seville, who flourished in the 7th century, asserted that musical sounds could be transmitted from one generation to another only by oral tradition because they could not be properly notated (*scribi non possunt*). The old monk's pessimistic declaration seems to be prophetically fulfilled in many modern scores of the 2nd half of the 20th century, which abandon all attempts at precise notation of pitch or duration, and resort instead to such approximations as *najwyszy dzwiek instrumentu* (the highest possible sounds of the instrument), a Polish direction in the works of Penderecki; instructions in a work by Stockhausen for the performer to strike any note on the piano and hold it indefinitely; a similarly stupefying exhortation by Cage: "This is a composition indeterminate of its performance, and the performance is of actions which are often indeterminate of themselves"; the declaration of Cornelius Cardew, the inventor of "scratch music," in which "the notation may be accomplished using any means, verbal, graphic, musical, or by collage."

Music of ancient Greece was notated by letters, some of them turned backward or put upside down apparently to indicate a certain type of interval. Toward the end of the 1st millennium A.D. an early system of notation appeared in the form of *neumes*, a Greek word for a nod, a sign, or a signal, indicating single notes or groups of notes (ligatures). Such neumes were placed directly in the text above the lines and indicated the rise or fall of the vocal inflection, graphically derived from the acute, grave, and circumflex accents. An acute accent represented by a slant to the right denoted the rise of a 2nd, a 3rd, or another small interval. With the establishment of square notation, the intervallic norms became more definite. Rhythmic values were determined according to an elaborate set of rules that varied from century to century and from country to country, so that the transcription of medieval chants becomes a matter of editorial discretion.

In the course of time, embryonic neumes developed into groups of notational cells that were embodied in graphic shapes and assumed expressive Latin names, such as *punctum* (point), *virga* (comma), *pes* (foot), *clivis* (declivity), *scandicus* (ascent), *climacus* (climaxing), *torculus* (torque), and *porrectus* (erect). These gave rise to symbols for ornaments in Baroque music; thus *pes* became the lower appoggiatura, and *clivis* an upper appoggiatura. *Scandicus* became an ascending double appoggiatura, and *climacus* a descending double appoggiatura. *Torculus* was the ancestor of the inverted mordent, and the *porrectus* that of the mordent.

Mensural notation, or notation that can be measured, emerged in the middle of the 13th century, and its invention, or at least its codification, is usually ascribed to Franco of Cologne. In the early centuries of mensural notation, white notes of different shapes were used; black notes appeared in the course of time when a necessity arose of writing rapid passages. The standard notation of note lengths was the following: *maxima, longa, brevis* (or *breve*), *semibrevis* (or *semibreve*), *minima, semiminima, fusa,* and *semifusa.* Each of these equaled 2 or 3 notes of the next smaller durations; thus *maxima* had 2 or 3 *longas*, a *longa* had 2 or 3 *breves*, a *breve* had 2 *semibreves*, etc. As if *maxima* was not long enough, a *larga* was introduced, which had the value of 2 or 3 *maximas*.

It is ironic that the *semibreve* (half-brief) note of the mensural notation became in the course of time the longest note of modern notation, designated as a whole note, which occupied an entire bar in 4/4 time. It appears that in the Middle Ages time was running at a slower tempo. The shapes of these notes were either oblongs or rhomboids, with or without stems attached. *Semiminima* was notated either as a black rhomboid with a stem stuck into it from above like a toothpick in an olive, or else as a white rhomboid with a flag. As time went on, and as musicians became more and more agitated in their rhythmical mores, additional flags were attached to the stems of small notes, and theorists ran out of such qualifying prefixes as *demi-, semi-, hemi-*, etc., in order to designate these very fast notes.

Arithmetically, in modern notation a whole note equals 2 half notes, a half note equals 2 quarter notes, etc. But in mensural notation a note could equal either 2 or 3 of the next smaller note. In modern notation a dotted half-note equals 3 quarter notes, etc., but in mensural

notation the operation had to be indicated verbally or by a system of ligatures that are most misleading in view of the absence of barlines and other auxiliary symbols. The verbal clues were contained in the adjectives (in Latin, of course) *perfectum* or *imperfectum*. These words did not mean "perfection" or "imperfection" in the moral or physical sense, but in the etymological Latin sense of completion and incompletion. *Perfectio* was the subdivision of a note into 3 smaller note values, subdivisions into 2 being examples of *imperfectio*.

Furthermore, there were special terms for the mutual relationships between each pair of adjacent note values. The relationship between *brevis* and *semibrevis* was called *tempus*; the relationship between a *semibrevis* and *minima* was *prolatio* (prolation). If both *tempus* and *prolatio* were perfect, the result was a bar of 9 whole notes subdivided into 3 groups; if the *tempus* were perfect and the *prolatio* imperfect, this denoted 3 groups, each of which had 2 beats. If the *tempus* were imperfect but the *prolatio* perfect, then there were 2 divisions of 3 beats each. The perfection was symbolized by a perfect circle in the time signature; the imperfection was indicated by a semicircle; we inherited the sign of imperfection in the 4/4 time signature that looks like the capital letter *C*. (Hence, a frequent error in interpreting the imperfection signature—medieval binary time—as modern common time, quadruple time.) Some theologically minded music theorists of the Middle Ages suggested that triple time is perfect, because it stands for the Trinity.

Painful complications ensue as we plunge more deeply into ligatures—groups of notes glued together or hanging to one another precariously by the corner of an oblong or to the side of a rhombus. Musicologists who are willing to devote their lives to the inscrutable mysteries of mensural notation come figuratively to blows in their internecine polemics. As a result, transcriptions of medieval MSS in mensural notation are rarely in agreement.

In modern usage, fractional names designate musical notes: whole note, half note, quarter note, 8th note, 16th note, 32nd note, 64th note, etc. Individual 8th notes have flags attached to them; groups of 8th notes are united by black beams; 16th notes have 2 flags; their groups are united by double beams; 32nd notes have 3 flags and are united by triple beams, and so forth. Identical graphic symbols are used in all Western music, but the names may differ. Thus in British usage quarter notes are called crotchets, 8th notes are quavers, 16th notes are semiquavers, 32nd notes are demisemiquavers, 64th notes are hemidemisemiquavers, and 128th notes are called semi-hemidemisemiquavers. A dot next to the note head adds 50% to the value of the note. Thus a half note has 2 quarter notes and a dotted half note has 3. In British usage, a minima has 2 crochets and a dotted minima has 3; a crochet has 2 quavers, a dotted crochet has 3; a quaver has 2 semiquavers, a dotted quaver has 3, and so on. The same augmentations by 50% are effected by dots placed after rests.

With the virtual disappearance of special signs indicating ornamentation (mordents, inverted mordents, etc.) in the 19th century, the present system of notation became an entirely workable method of writing down notes corresponding precisely to the intended pitch and duration of each note; the invention of the metronome made it possible to measure metrical units in fractions of a second. Interpretation remained a personal matter, but liberties could be taken only in dynamics, variations in tempo, etc. True, the written notes did not always reflect the composer's ideal, and some great masters allowed themselves to write passages that could not be performed adequately or even approximately. Beethoven wrote sustained chords in some of his piano sonatas that could not be held by pedal without muddying up the harmony, or by the fingers which were occupied elsewhere. Schumann has a melody in his *Études symphoniques* for Piano that is to be played legato in the bass but cannot be carried on without interruption. The addition of the barline in the notational system is a great metric support, but the persistent habit of stressing the 1st beat has resulted in a brutalization of the basic rhythmic design.

There are numerous examples in great masterpieces in which the composer seems to be following a different beat in his rhythmic design than appears in the metric arrangement. A musical person listening to the rapid finale of Schumann's piano concerto will hear an unmistakable rhythm of a slow Viennese waltz, but the conductor must engage in a trick of legerdemain to square the apparent *contretemps* with the soloist. The trouble here is that Schumann notated this passage in rapid 3/4 with stresses on the 1st and 3rd beats of the 1st bar and on the 2nd beat of the 2nd bar, the 2 bars forming a metric unit. A most extraordinary incongruence between the visual notation and auditory perception occurs in the 1st movement of the 1st Sym. of Brahms, where a rhythmic period of 3 eighth-notes enters on the 2nd beat of 6/8, with the accented notes overlapping the barlines. A modern composer would probably write a bar of 1/8 and then resume 6/8 time until the notated rhythm and meter coincide. Quite often the ear groups several bars into 1 unit in a fast tempo. When Beethoven indicates that the scherzo of his 9th Sym. is to be perceived in *ritmo di tre battute* (rhythm of 3 bars), he reveals the inadequacy of notation and its incommensurability with auditory perception.

A system that pursued a totally different track from the universally accepted notation was TABLATURE, which indicated graphically the position of each note on the lute, guitar, ukulele, and keyboard instruments. Tablatures were widely used by lute players beginning in the 15th century and went out of use in the 18th century, together with the lute itself. After 3 centuries of almost total extinction, the tablature was revived in published editions for the guitar to enable popular performers who could not read music to pick out the necessary chords. The notation for the ukulele, a Hawaiian instrument of the guitar family that became popular in the U.S. in the 1st quarter of the 20th century, was always in the form of a tablature, resembling that of the lute but having no historic connection with it. A modern keyboard tablature, Klavarskribo (clavier notation in Esperanto), which indicates the positions of notes on a diagram of the piano keyboard, was launched in Holland.

Ultramodern composers of the 2nd half of the 20th century tried to remedy the ills of musical notation with the aid of science, at least as far as meter and rhythm were concerned. Instead of the uncertainties of tempo marks, time signatures, and rhythmical units in metrical frames, some ultramodern notation specifies the duration of each note in time units, usually in seconds or fractions of seconds. Visually, too, a whole note occupies all the room of a bar of 4/4 time, a half note takes up exactly one-half of such a bar, and passages in smaller notes are notated proportionately to the time they consume. In dynamics the newest notation blithely specifies differences between pianissimo (*pp*) and pianississimo (*ppp*), fortissimo (*ff*) and fortississimo (*fff*), and so forth, up and down the dynamics range. The trouble of course is that human performers cannot execute such scientific niceties with any degree of precision or with the requisite aplomb. Electronic instruments have come to the rescue.

Such is the perversity of human nature that just as musical notation seemed to achieve a scientific precision, composers of the AVANT-GARDE developed a yen for indeterminacy. Of course, indeterminacy is itself a respectable scientific doctrine, and the theory of probabilities, which is closely related to it, possesses a mathematical aura that is quite idiosyncratic in its application. But a human being is also a tangle of probabilities; it is logical, therefore, that ultramodern notation should have absorbed the human element.

Xenakis, Stockhausen, Earle Brown, Bussotti, Cage, and many others in Europe, America, Japan, and Greece have adopted a graphic notation that not only deals in probabilistic elements but resorts to pictorial representations of human faces experiencing prescribed emotions, from saintly tranquillity to raging madness. When an occasional music staff is inserted in such scores, it may be covered with blobs of black ink or surrealistic geometrical curves. Verbalization of the basic elements of notation expands enormously here, and the performer is often urged to play or sing anything at all. Some modern musicians are possessed by a desire to represent new music by visual images; others have returned to older notational and stylistic modes.

note. One of the signs used to express the relative time value of tones. *Note against note*, counterpoint in equal notes.

note row. See SET.

Notendruck (Ger.). Music printing.

Notenstich (Ger.). Music engraving.

notes inégales (Fr.). INÉGALES.

Notierung (Ger.). NOTATION.

Notre Dame school. A religious compositional school that flourished in Paris in the 12th and 13th centuries. Its greatest masters were Leoninus and Perotinus. But whether they were actually attached to the present cathedral of Notre Dame itself is a matter of conjecture, because the cornerstone of the famous church was not laid until the middle of the 12th century, and the construction was not completed for 2 more centuries.

notturno (It., night piece). 1. A NOCTURNE. 2. An instrumental genre of the 18th century, akin to the DIVERTIMENTO, SERENADE, and CASSATION. Haydn and Mozart were among the many composers of notturnos.

Novachord. See HAMMOND, LAURENS.

Novellette (Ger.). Character piece, usually for piano solo, introduced by Schumann; free in form, bold in harmony, Romantic in character, and of considerable length. It is characterized by a number of melodically unrelated themes that are united by a common rhythmic lift. The term does not mean "a little novel" as may be imagined; Schumann invented it (op. 21, 1838) to express his admiration for the English singer Clara (Anastasia) Novello (1818–1908). This was not the 1st time that Schumann engaged in such verbal trickery; he also wrote pieces that he described as "Wiecketten," after the maiden name of his beloved wife Clara. But novelette seemed such a beguiling name that many composers have knowingly adopted Schumann's playful title, using the term precisely in the sense of little novels or stories. Did Balakirev, Liadov, and other composers of novelettes ever realize that they were unwittingly paying homage to Clara Novello?

novelty. Popular instrumental piece or song not easily classified, such as nonsense songs, kiddie rhymes, pieces with unusual orchestration (e.g., typewriter, clock, toy balloons, tinkling bells), exotica, etc. Leroy Anderson specialized in orch.l novelties, such as *The Syncopated Clock*.

Noye's Fludde. Opera by Britten, 1958, 1st performed in Oxford; based on the medieval Chester miracle play. Except for Noye (Noah), the roles are to be filled by children.

Nozze di Figaro, Le. MARRIAGE OF FIGARO, THE.

nuane (Fr., nuance). Shading; change in musical expression, either in the tone color, tempo, or degree of force.

number. 1. A subdivision of an opera or oratorio. 2. A smaller, and more or less complete, portion of a large work, such as a song, aria, interlude, etc. 3. Any single piece on a program. 4. An opus number.

number opera (Ger. *Nummernoper*). An opera in which the principal ingredients—arias, vocal ensembles, instrumental interludes, etc.—are clearly separated from each other, or are connected by recitative or spoken dialogue. Virtually all operas before Wagner were number operas, but an argument can be advanced that transitions between separate numbers create a continuity characteristic of "music drama" of the Wagnerian type. Wagner's theories virtually determined the operatic practice of the 2nd half of the 19th century, but a return to the more formal type of number opera was marked in the 20th century. Modern composers, especially Stravinsky, successfully revived the seemingly extinct genre and even took delight in emphasizing its archaic traits.

number pieces. A designation for the late works by the American composer John Cage bearing numbers as titles (*74*, *13*, *1⁵*, etc.). The numbers refer to the number of players called for in the score; superscript numbers are used to differentiate multiple compositions with the same number of players, and thus the same number title (e.g., *2⁴*, the 4th work composed for 2 players).

numbers. The Latin word *numeri* had a 2nd meaning, music, which was governed by the law of proportions between 2 different sounds. In Shakespearean English, numbers refer to musical composition. St. Augustine drew a distinction between *numeri sonantes*, the actual musical tone perceived by the senses, and *numeri recordabiles*, music that is remembered. In St. Augustine's concept a melody was formed by a single sound instantaneously perceived and memorably associated with several preceding sounds. Long before St. Augustine, Aristoxenus likened the musical tones of a melody to letters in a language. So intimate was the connection felt between numbers and music that in medieval univs. music was taught as part of the quadrivium of exact sciences, along with arithmetic, geometry, and astronomy. This association with numbers was lost in Classical and Romantic music. Not until the 20th century did the numerical element in music regain its status.

Mathematical parameters lie at the foundation of serial music. The calculus of sets is an important tool in rhythmic serialization. Some composers have applied the Fibonacci numbers, in which each term is the sum of its 2 predecessors, to metrical, rhythmic, and intervallic parameters. Simple arithmetical progressions also yield material for rhythmic arrangements. The application of numbers to composition is limitless; the difficulty is to select numerical sets that would provide material for purely musical structures. Numbers also served as a poetic synonym for music, often used in the sense of a song by Shakespeare, Milton, and other writers.

numerology. Several composers, superstitiously credulous regarding the importance of some numbers in their lives, reflected these beliefs in their musical compositions. There are indications that Bach favored mystic numbers derived from the position of the letters of his last name in the alphabet. B–A–C–H would then equal $2 + 1 + 3 + 8 = 14$; according to the same ordering, the numerical value of J–S–B–A–C–H equals 41. One of Bach's late portraits has 14 buttons on the breast. In his last completed composition, *Vor deinen Thron*, the initial staff has 14 notes, the entire melody 41 notes.

The curious, and quite serious, case of triskaidekaphobia that preoccupied Rossini and Schoenberg had an apparent bearing on the date of their deaths; Rossini died on Friday the 13th (like many Italians, he was superstitiously fearful of such a combination), and Schoenberg, who regarded the number 13 as ominous because he was born on the 13th of the month, went so far as to remove the 2nd *A* in the title of his unfinished work *Moses und Aron* (i.e., Aaron) because the sum of the letters in the title added up to 13. He died on the 13th of the month, at the age of 76, the digits of which add up to 13.

Nummernoper (Ger.). NUMBER OPERA.

Nun's fiddle (Ger. *Nonnengeige*). TROMBA MARINA.

nuovamente (It.). Again, anew.

nuove musiche (It., new musics). Originally the title of a selection of monodies by Giulio Caccini (1601), it became a slogan of the Camerata, a group of erudite poets, philosophers, and musicians who successfully reversed the musical trend of ever-increasing complexity of polyphonic music in favor of a simple homophonic style of solo arias and madrigals with simple harmonic accompaniments. So potent was the desire on the part of music lovers to return to the original sources of vocal music uncomplicated by artful devices that soon the entire period of the early 17th century was designated as the period of nuove musiche; its monodic style gave birth to opera, oratorio, and cantata and inaugurated the era of the Baroque.

The creators of nuove musiche also established the historically important principle that the text should be the determining factor of musical expression rather than be subordinated to the prearranged melodic structure. The extreme development of Baroque polyphony reversed the stream once more toward greater complexity, but the predominance of the text over polyphony was once more proclaimed a century and a half later by Gluck and basically subscribed to by Wagner and Debussy.

Nurock, Kirk, innovative American composer and originator of "natural sound"; b. Camden, N.J., Feb. 28, 1948. He held scholarships for study at the Juilliard School in N.Y. and at the Eastman School of Music in Rochester, N.Y. His teachers in composition were Persichetti, Sessions, and Berio. He was awarded the Elizabeth Sprague Coolidge Prize in chamber music in 1970. From his earliest essays in composition, he adhered to extraordinary and unusual sound production; became active as a conductor of idiosyncratic theater productions, among them the temporarily objectionable musical *Hair*, which aroused indignant protests on the part of tender-minded listeners. He further developed a natural ability to perform advanced keyboard jazz music. In 1971 he developed an experimental vocal technique which he called "natural sound," founded on the assumption that every person's vocal cords, as well as other parts of their bodies, are capable of producing variegated sound.

In several works he annexed animal noises; the most challenging of them being Sonata for Piano and Dog (N.Y., 1983) and *Gorilla, Gorilla* for Solo Piano (N.Y., 1988). Audience participation is welcomed as an integral part of natural sound productions. Several of Nurock's works are specifically scored for untrained, improvisatory participants. Interestingly enough, many newspaper reviews of his presentations seem to revive the alarmed outcries of shocked innocence that greeted 1st performances of the now-recognized works of Prokofiev, Stravinsky, Schoenberg, and Varèse.

nut. 1. The ridge over which the strings pass at the end of the fingerboard next to the head of a violin, etc. 2. The sliding projection at the lower end of the violin bow, by means of which the hair is tightened or slackened; also called FROG. 3. The "lower nut" on the violin is the ridge between the tailpiece and tailpin (or button).

Nutcracker, The. Ballet by Tchaikovsky, 1892, 1st performed in St. Petersburg. That Tchaikovsky could write this sunlit music in the same year as his mournful *Pathétique Sym.* proves (if proof is needed) that musical inspiration and accomplishment have nothing to do with the psychological states of a composer. The subject of the ballet is taken from the fairy tale *Casse-Noisette* by Alexander Dumas *père*, itself borrowed from a tale by E. T. A. Hoffmann. A girl dreams of a fight between a nutcracker and mice. She helps the nutcracker, who then is transformed into a beautiful prince and takes her into the magic land of sweets and candies. *The Nutcracker* is a full-length ballet; an instrumental suite drawn from the score contains an overture, a march, and 6 dances: *Dance of the Sugar Plum-Fairies*, in which Tchaikovsky includes the celesta for the 1st time in any orch. work; *Ukrainian Dance*, *Trepak*; *Arabian Dance* (coffee); *Chinese Dance* (tea); *Pastorale*; and *Waltz of the Flowers*.

N.W.A., Popular rap group of the early 1990s. (Vocals: Ice Cube; b. O'Shea Jackson, Los Angeles, Calif., June 15, c. 1969; Dr. Dre, b. Andre Young, Los Angeles, Feb. 18, 1965; Eazy-E, b. Eric Wright, Los Angeles, Sept. 7, 1963; d. there, Mar. 26, 1995; MC Ren, b. Lorenzo Patterson, Los Angeles, June 16, year unknown; DJ Yella, b. Antoine Carraby, Los Angeles, Dec. 11, year unknown.) The group coalesced around the performer/record company owner Wright (aka Eazy-E), and composers Jackson (Ice Cube) and Young (Dr. Dre). Eazy-E had a hit with Cube and Dre's *Boyz-n-the-Hood*, inspiring them to join forces in the group, N.W.A. (Niggaz Wit Attitude). Their debut album, 1989's *Straight Outta Compton*, featured early antisocial rap attitudes, including *F—k the Police* and *Dopeman*. Despite its success, Cube felt he was shortchanged by the group, and left it soon after. He has since enjoyed a successful solo recording and acting career.

The group's second album, *Efil4zaggin* ("Niggaz 4 life" spelled backwards), was another smash hit. On it they spouted more misogynist lyrics while attacking ex-member Ice Cube (establishing the dissing wars so favored by rap acts). However, the group soon splintered into individual activities. Eazy-E gained notoriety on his own as a producer/performer, as did Dr. Dre. Easy-E died of AIDS in Mar. 1995, brought on by his promiscuous lifestyle.

nyckelharpa (Swed.). Keyed folk fiddle, dating from the Renaissance and still played. Like the hurdy-gurdy, the strings are stopped by keys; unlike it, the nyckelharpa strings rest on a flat bridge and are bowed. The number of strings has remained flexible: between 1 and 2 melody strings, and between 2 and 3 drones; in post-18th-century instruments, up to 11 sympathetic strings were added.

o. 1. When placed over G, D, A, or E in a violin part (or the equivalent for other string instruments), the lowercase *o* stands for the word *open* and indicates that the notes so marked must be played on an OPEN STRING, i.e., without depressing the strings with the fingers. 2. It appears sometimes in the BASSO CONTINUO part as a sign that only the bass note or its octave should be used in the accompaniment to a given passage without filling in the harmony. 3. Placed above a note, usually in string parts, it signifies the use of HARMONICS. 4. In chord tablature, used in sheet music, a diminished 5th or chord. 5. (It.) Or; written before either vowels or consonants; *od* is an unusual form.

O sole mio! One of the most famous Neapolitan ballads, composed in 1899 by Eduardo Di Capua (1864–1917).

obbligato (It., obligatory; Ger. *obligato*). Orig., an instrumental part that was essential in the performance, such as the many sonatas for piano and another instrument obbligato. The meaning expanded to any instrumental or vocal part that is a concerted (and therefore essential) part. Through some paradoxical inversion of meaning, *obbligato* began to be used, particularly in popular arrangements, to indicate an optional part; for example, a song with *cello obbligato* would mean that such a part would be a desirable addition to the accompaniment, but not essential.

oberek (from Pol. *obrót*, turn around). A lively Polish dance in rapid 3/8 meter and off-beat accents similar to the MAZURKA; it is also known as the *obertas*.

Oberon. Opera by Weber, 1826, 1st produced in London, with the composer conducting on his London tour; the plot is vaguely reminiscent of Shakespeare's *A Midsummer Night's Dream*. Oberon is King of the Elves; Titania is his Queen. There are numerous exotic characters springing up here and there. Oberon's appointed task in life is to find a pair of lovers undeterred by any misadventure. He succeeds with the help of his magic horn. There is a grand reunion at the end, at the court of Charlemagne. The libretto (in English, because the work was commissioned by Covent Garden, London) is magnificent in its absurdity. The glorious overture survives on the concert podium, but the opera is never (well, hardly ever) performed in its entirety.

Oberto, Conte di San Bonifacio. Opera by Verdi, 1839, produced in Milan; the 1st of his operas to be performed. Oberto is killed by his daughter's lover in a duel. The murderous seducer leaves Italy never to return, and the abandoned girl is left to her futile lamentations. The opera was successful and still maintains a spark of life at its infrequent revivals on the Italian stages.

Oberton (Ger.). OVERTONE.

objets trouvés (Fr.). A term rather defiantly introduced by AVANT-GARDE painters and sculptors, meaning quite literally "found objects." Marcel Duchamp was probably the 1st to exhibit an objet trouvé, a urinal from a men's lavatory. Man Ray exhibited a sewing machine wrapped up in a piece of canvas, and Andy Warhol managed to create a sensation by selling a Brobdingnagian representation of a Campbell's soup can for a reputed sum of $70,000. A plate with remnants of an unfinished dinner was exhibited as an objet trouvé, as was "bagel jewelry," being an actual bagel set in a jewelry box. Found or ready-made objects are also incorporated by modern artists as part of a sculpture or a montage.

Ultramodern composers sometimes insert passages from works by other composers as a token of homage and partly as an experiment in construction. Such objets trouvés need not harmonize with their environment, which may be completely alien to the nature of the implant. An early example is the sudden appearance of the tune *Ach, du lieber Augustin* in Schoenberg's 2nd String Quartet. Others make use of musical objets trouvés by the simple device of playing another composer's music. An example of an embroidered and incrustated objet trouvé is Luciano Berio's *Sinfonia*, incorporating whole chunks of music from Mahler, Ravel, and others.

oblique motion. A type of 2-part counterpoint in which one voice moves and the other remains stationary.

oboe (Fr. *hautbois*, high wood; Ger. *Oboe*; It. *oboe*). 1. An orch.l instrument with conical wooden tube, 9 to 14 keys, and a double reed; its present compass is 2 octaves and a 7th, from b^0 to a^3. The oboe 1st made its appearance toward the middle of the 17th century in France. The tone is very reedy and penetrating, although not harsh. Only 2 kinds are in ordinary use, the treble oboe (just described), and the ENGLISH HORN (alto oboe) of lower pitch. The oboe is rather limited in its agility, in contrast to the lambent flute or the peripatetic clarinet. But the oboe compensates for these real or imaginary deficiencies by the precision of its intonation and by the strength of its sound; indeed, it can pierce through the entire orch.l fabric as easily as the trumpet. In orch.l writing oboes are commonly used in pairs, like flutes, clarinets, and bassoons. As a solo instrument the oboe is not as popular as the flute, clarinet, or even bassoon, but Handel wrote several concertos for it; it *Oboe players* is difficult to imagine a solo recital even

PHOTOGRAPH BY JIM STEERE, COURTESY OF THE CHICAGO SYMPHONY ORCHESTRA

by a great oboe virtuoso, but such concerts have been given. As the intonational mainstay of the orch., the oboe stands unchallenged, as it gives the introductory A to tune up the orch. 2. In the organ, an 8' reed stop with conical pipes surmounted by a bell and cap.

oboe da caccia (It., hunting oboe). An instrument tuned a 5th below the oboe. It was in use during the Renaissance period but was eventually replaced by the ENGLISH HORN.

oboe d'amore (It., love oboe; Fr. *hautbois d'amour*; Ger. *Liebeshoboe*, love oboe). An oboe pitched in A, a minor 3rd below the standard instrument, with either a standard oboe or bulbous bell. It was the most popular of the woodwind d'amore instruments, but like the others it is essentially obsolete.

Obrecht (Obreht, Hobrecht, Obertus, Hobertus), **Jacob,** famous Netherlandish composer; b. probably in Bergen-op-Zoom, Nov. 22, 1450 or 1451; d. Ferrara, 1505. He is 1st mentioned as *zangmeester* in Utrecht (*c.* 1476–78); then became choirmaster for the Corp. of Notre Dame at St. Gertrude in Bergen-op-Zoom (1479); took holy orders, and said his 1st Mass as an ordained priest (1480). He was made *maitre des enfants* at Cambrai (1484), but was dismissed for his neglect of the choirboys as well as financial irregularities (1485); then was made succentor at St. Donatian in Bruges (1486). At the invitation of the Duke of Ferrara he obtained a leave of absence to travel to Italy; arrived in Ferrara in late 1487, returning to Bruges in 1488; was made *maitre de chapelle* there in 1490; obtained remission from his position (1491). By 1494 he was at Notre Dame in Antwerp, serving as Capellanie magister in 1495; he returned to St. Gertrude in Bergen-op-Zoom in 1496–97, and then received a benefice connected to the altar of St. Josse in Notre Dame at Antwerp in 1498. He was again at St. Donatian in Bruges from 1499 until his retirement in 1500; then lived in Bergen-op-Zoom and made visits to Antwerp; in 1504 he returned to the ducal court in Ferrara, where he died of the plague. Obrecht was one of the leading composers of his era, his Masses and motets being of particular importance. He also wrote chansons, many to Dutch texts.

ocarina (It., little goose). A bulbous flute in the shape of a bird. Ocarinas are usually manufactured from terra-cotta, with finger holes and a whistle mouthpiece; they are often used as whistles. Rimsky-Korsakov includes an ocarina tuned in an alternating scale of whole tones and semitones in the score of his opera-ballet *Mlada*.

Ocean Symphony. Anton Rubinstein's 2nd Sym., 1854, in C major. He wrote it when he was only 24 years old, and it became his most popular symphonic work. It was 1st performed in Leipzig. The *Ocean Sym.* was criticized as having "too much water and too little ocean," but it endured for half a century, as long as its kind of expansive Germanic Romanticism held sway. It was a sort of ritual for the N.Y. Phil. to open its seasons with the *Ocean Sym.* Then suddenly something snapped; the work became unacceptable to aesthetically minded music lovers, and it simply vanished from the repertory. *Sic transit Oceanus!*

Ochs, Phil, American social-protest singer/songwriter; b. El Paso, Tex., Dec. 19, 1940; d. Far Rockaway, N.Y., Apr. 19, 1976. A contemporary of Bob Dylan's in the early 1960s—to whose work his was often compared—Ochs was a more polished performer and wrote a variety of satirical songs on issues of the day. Although born in Tex., he 1st performed while a college student in Cleveland, as half of a duo who became known as the Sundowners. In 1961 he relocated to Greenwich Village, where he became a solo act. His work was quickly championed by *Broadside* magazine, a folk publication specializing in topical songs. He was signed to the folk label Elektra, where he recorded his 1st album, *All the News That's Fit to Sing*. Early hits included *I Ain't a Marchin' Anymore* and *There but for Fortune* (covered in 1965 by Joan Baez).

In 1967 Ochs relocated to California and began writing in a more personal, confessional style. Taking yet another odd turn in his career, he returned to N.Y. to perform at Carnegie Hall in 1971, oddly dressed in a gold lamé suit—garb he had originally worn on his ironically titled *Greatest Hits* album, which in fact did not contain any hits at all but was entirely made up of new material; the audience, stunned by his personality shift, was not pleased. Ochs traveled in the early '70s to Africa and England, and then returned to the N.Y. area by 1974, taking up new causes, including organizing a concert against the dictatorial government of Chile. Depressed by his lack of success, he took his own life by hanging himself while visiting his sister in 1976.

Ochsenmenuette. OX MINUET.

Ockeghem (Okeghem, Okengheim, Ockenheim, etc.), **Johannes** (Jean, Jehan de), great Flemish composer; b. *c.* 1410; d. probably in Tours, Feb. 6, 1497. He may have been a pupil of Binchois. He is 1st listed among the *vicaires-chanteurs* at Notre Dame in Antwerp in 1443; he served there until 1444; by 1446 he was in the service of Charles I, Duke of Bourbon, in Moulins, remaining there until at least 1448. By 1452 he was in the service of Charles VII of France as 1st among the singer-chaplains who were nonpriests; by 1454 he was *premier chapelain*. He subsequently served Louis XI and Charles VIII; in 1459 the latter made him treasurer of the church of St. Martin-de-Tours. Under Louis XI he was a canon at Notre Dame in Paris from 1463 to 1470. He likewise was a chaplain at St. Benoit. In Jan. 1470 he traveled to Spain at the King's expense. In 1484 he journeyed to Bruges and Dammes. Upon his death, Guillaume Cretin wrote a poetic *Déploration*, and Josquin Des Prez and Lupi composed musical epitaphs.

With his contemporaries Dufay and Josquin, Ockeghem ranks among the foremost masters of the Franco-Flemish style of composition in the 2nd half of the 15th century. Among his settings of the Mass is the earliest extant polyphonic Requiem. The inventiveness displayed in his Masses is only excelled in his superb motets. His achievements in the art of imitative counterpoint unquestionably make his music a milestone on the way to the a cappella style of the coming generations.

Octandre. Work by Varèse, 1924, for 7 wind instruments and a double bass; premiered in N.Y. The title refers to a flower with 8 stamens. Like all of Varèse's works at 1st performances, it aroused shrieks of indignation and dismay from the otherwise sober-minded critics.

octave (Eng., Fr.; from Lat. *octava*, 8th; It. *ottava*; Ger. *Oktave*). 1. A series of 8 consecutive diatonic tones. 2. The interval between the 1st and 8th tones of such a series. The octave is the only interval in the tempered system which is acoustically pure; it represents the ratio of vibrations of 2:1. The octave sound is the 1st harmonic above the fundamental and is therefore an integral part of any musical tone. The octave ingredient can be perceived quite clearly by a sensitive ear, even when a single tone is played, and it can be picked out with a surprising effect by silently holding down a piano key and then forcefully striking a key an octave below; the depressed key will respond with an octave sound, loud and clear.

Different octaves bear special names, more or less acceptable in international nomenclature (see "The Scales," p. xxiv). The earliest type of "polyphonic" singing was at the interval of an octave, with boys singing an octave higher than men. A curious explanation as to why the octave is the most perfect interval is given in an anonymous medieval music treatise—because *Octavo die Abraha circumcisus erat* (because it was "on the 8th day that Abraham was circumcised"). *Concealed, covered,* or *hidden octaves* (or 5ths), parallel octaves (or 5ths) suggested by the progression of 2 parts in similar motion to the interval of an octave (or 5th); *parallel octaves,* CONSECUTIVE OCTAVES; *rule of the octave,* a series of harmonies written over the diatonic scale as a bass; *short octave,* the lowest octave of some old organ manuals, in which some keys (and pipes) are omitted.

3. In the organ, a stop whose pipes sound tones an octave higher than the keys touched, e.g., the principal.

octave coupler. One uniting the 8' tones of one keyboard with those an octave higher on another.

octave flute. 1. The piccolo. 2. An organ stop of 4' pitch.

octave sign. See OTTAVA.

octave stop. See OCTAVE (3).

octet (Fr. *octour*; It. *ottetto*; Ger. *Oktett*). A composition for 8 voices or instruments.

octobasse. Oversized double bass patented by Jean-Baptiste Vuillaume in 1849. Its 3 strings were stopped by levers worked by pedals, and the bow was supported by oarlocks. It was 12 feet high and was pitched 1 octave below the cello.

ode. 1. A chorus in ancient Greek plays. 2. A musical work of praise.

Ode. Orch.1 work by Stravinsky, 1943, in 3 parts—*Eulogy, Eclogue,* and *Epitaph*—written in memory of Mrs. Serge Koussevitzky. The *Eclogue* was originally intended as incidental music to a motion picture, *Jane Eyre,* but the film was never produced and Stravinsky made use of the hunting episode from it for the *Ode.* The work was 1st performed by the Boston Sym. Orch., with Koussevitzky conducting.

Ode to Billy Joe. Bobby Gentry's self-penned country and pop smash hit of 1967. The song was considered scandalous for its time, particularly for a country number,

because of the implication that the protagonist threw her baby off of the Tallahatchie Bridge. Later inspired a tepid feature film.

Ode to Joy. The accepted English title of the choral finale of Beethoven's 9th Sym., to the words of Schiller's poem *An die Freude,* inviting the multitudes to embrace each other and expressing faith in the ultimate brotherhood of men.

Ode to Napoleon. Melodrama by Schoenberg, 1942, for speaking voices, piano, and strings; 1st performed in N.Y. As a protest against the Nazis, Schoenberg chose Byron's poem, in which he voices his wrath against Napoleon. In his score Schoenberg makes use of a modified 12-tone technique, ending in a clear major chord.

oder (Ger.). Or; or else.

Odhecaton. The 1st printed collection of polyphonic music, publ. by Petrucci, 1501; the title means "100 Songs" (*ode + hecaton*). Actually there are only 96 songs in the collection, but its historical value would have been great no matter what the number of songs. Only 9 of them are furnished with a text, but at the time the *Odhecaton* was published, instrumental tunes were commonly sung, and songs were often played on instruments.

odoroso (It.). Fragrant; a rare expression mark, found in one of Medtner's *Fairy Tales* for piano. There is no record of a composer using the antonym *malodoroso,* even though some should consider it.

Oedipe. Opera by Enesco, 1936, 1st performed in Paris. The subject is drawn from the tragedies of Aeschylus and Sophocles; the basic events of Greek mythology are preserved. Oedipus inadvertently kills his father and mistakenly marries his mother, but he is vindicated at the tragic end as a victim of fate. The peculiarity of the score is that Enesco does not resort to stylization, but internationalizes the theme, even to the point of making use of Romanian melorhythms. He briefly makes use of quarter tones.

Oedipus der Tyrann. Opera by Orff, 1959, after Sophocles' tragedy. The score is animated by a persistent rhythmic pulse, enchanced by a battery of percussion instruments. Some portions are spoken; the singing episodes often consist of repeated (reciting) notes.

Oedipus Rex. Opera-oratorio by Stravinsky, 1927, 1st performed in concert form in Paris; the stage premiere took place in Vienna (1928). In order to make the legend of Oedipus more timeless, Stravinsky arranged to have Jean Cocteau's libretto translated into Latin. The music follows this impulse; it is majestically static, like a row of marble Doric columns. Significant musical phrases are relentlessly reiterated to drive their meaning into the mind of the listener; but Italian opera provides models for Stravinsky (e.g., Jocasta's aria). A somewhat arch narrator recites the events in between the musical numbers.

oeuvre (Fr.). A work. *Oeuvres choisies*, selected works; *oeuvres complètes*, complete works; *oeuvres inédites*, unpublished works; *oeuvres posthumes*, posthumous works.

Of Mice and Men. Opera by C. Floyd, 1970, based on John Steinbeck's novel. Two brothers working on a farm dream of buying a ranch of their own. One of them, a simpleminded boy, commits murder; his normal brother shoots him dead to save him from execution. The title is taken from Robert Burns's famous line, "The best laid schemes of mice and men."

Of Thee I Sing. Musical by Gershwin, 1931. The work is a savage thrust at the American Presidential campaign conducted on the platform of love. The candidate, Wintergreen, wins, but instead of marrying the winner of the contest for Miss White House he elects a plainer girl who can make corn muffins for the White House functions. An impeachment process is avoided when Vice President Throttlebottom marries the beauty contest winner. The lyrics, by Gershwin's brother Ira, are incisive. The leading songs are the title song, *Love Is Sweeping the Country*, and *Who Cares?* The critic Brooks Atkinson found the work "funnier than the government, and not nearly so dangerous." It was the 1st musical to win the Pulitzer Prize.

off. In organ music, a direction to push in a stop or couplet. *Off pitch*, false in pitch or intonation.

off-beat. A peculiar feature of ragtime and jazz in which the metrically unaccented parts of the melody are played with a strong rhythmic stress.

Offenbach, Jacques (Jacob), famous French composer of German descent; b. Cologne, June 20, 1819; d. Paris, Oct. 5, 1880. He was the son of a Jewish cantor, whose original surname was Eberst; Offenbach was the town where his father lived. He studied violin before taking up the cello when he was 9; after training with Joseph Alexander and Bernhard Breuer in Cologne, he settled in Paris (1833); following cello studies with Vaslin at the Cons. (1833–34) he played in the orch. of the Opéra-Comique; also received further instruction from Louis Norblin and Halévy; then pursued a career as a soloist and chamber-music artist (from 1838); subsequently was a conductor at the Théâtre-Français (1850–55). His *Chanson de Fortunio* for Musset's *Chandelier* (1850) proved tremendously popular.

In 1855 he ventured to open his own theater, the Bouffes-Parisiens, at the Salle Marigny; late that year it moved to the Salle Choiseul, where he scored his 1st great success with the operetta *Orphée aux enfers* (1858). His *La Belle Hélène* (Variétés, 1864) proved to be one of his most celebrated works, soon taken up by theatrical enterprises all over the world. Having abandoned the management of the Bouffes-Parisiens in 1866, he nevertheless continued to write for the stage. His *La Vie parisienne* (1866), *La Grande-Duchesse de Gérolstein* (1867), and *La Périchole* (1868) were notably successful. In 1873 he took over the management of the Théâtre de la Gaîté, where he brought out his rev. version of *Orphée aux enfers* as an *opéra-féerique* (1874). In 1876 he undertook a tour of the U.S., describing his impressions in *Notes d'un musicien en voyage* (1877) and *Offenbach en Amerique* (Paris, 1877). His only grand opera, the masterpiece *Les Contes d'Hoffmann*, remained unfinished at his death; recitatives were added by E. Guiraud, along with the famous barcarolle from Offenbach's *Die Rheinnixen* (1864), in which the tune was used for a ghost song; the completed score was premiered at the Opéra-Comique in Paris (1881) with instantaneous success, and it subsequently was performed on both sides of the Atlantic.

Offenbach is a master of the operetta; his music is characterized by an abundance of flowing, rollicking melodies seasoned with ironic humor, suitable to the extravagant burlesque of the situations. His irreverent treatment of mythological characters gave Paris society a salutary shock; his art mirrored the atmosphere of precarious gaiety during the 2nd Empire. In addition to his more than 60 operettas and operas-comiques, Offenbach wrote several pieces for the cello, including 6 works with orch., several pieces for cello and piano, solo works, and pedagogical works.

Offertory (Fr. *offertoire*; It. *offertorio*; Lat. *offertorium*). In the Roman Catholic Mass, the verses or anthem following the CREDO and sung by the choir while the priest is placing the consecrated elements on the altar, during which the offerings of the congregation are collected.

This is the 4th division of the PROPRIUM of the Mass; its original name was Antiphona ad offerendum. The earliest musical procedure of the Offertory contained the reading of psalms followed by a responsorial chant or some other antiphonal singing. Many organ pieces bear the title *Offertory*, but most works of the Offertory type are religious motets in a polyphonic setting.

Officium Divinum (Lat.). Divine Office. See CANONICAL HOURS.

Offrandes. Work by Varèse, 1922, for soprano and chamber orch., 1st performed in N.Y.

Offrandes oubliées, Les. Symphonic meditation by Messiaen, 1931; a devotional invocation to Jesus; 1st performed in Paris.

Oh, Bury Me Not on the Lone Prairie. A famous American song the origin of which appeared to be lost in the stagnant pools of ambiguous historicity. It was 1st published as an "authentic folk song" in 1907 by cowboy folklorist John Lomax and was included in his 1910 collection *Cowboy Songs* under the title *The Dying Cowboy*. However, Lomax didn't realize that the song was in fact based on a sentimental poem written by E. H. Chapin in 1839 called *The Ocean Burial*, where the injunction was not against a prairie burial but rather a watery one; it was set to music by George N. Allen a decade later, and subsequently the lyrics were transmuted into a classic of cowboy expression.

Oh! Dear, What Can the Matter Be? An English song published in London as long ago as 1792 and possibly earlier. It has retained its popularity as a nursery song.

Oh, How I Hate to Get Up in the Morning. Song by I. Berlin, 1918, ruefully lamenting the annoying sound of the reveille during his stint as an American soldier in World War I.

Oh, Kay! Musical by Gershwin, 1926. Kay is a sister of an English duke; they use their family yacht for liquor smuggling during Prohibition. Amorous sentiment is injected when an American playboy falls in love with Kay. There are several fine songs in the score, including *Do, Do, Do, Clap Yo' Hands,* and *Someone to Watch Over Me.*

Oh, Pretty Woman. Roy Orbison's number 1 1964 hit, with his famous growled interjection, has remained a pop favorite. Covered by heavy-metalists Van Halen in 1982.

Oh, Promise Me! This lyric promissory note was a last-minute insertion in the operetta *Robin Hood* by R. De Koven, produced in Chicago in 1890. The song became a nuptial hit, 2nd in popularity only to Wagner's *Here Comes the Bride.*

Oh, Susanna. Song by Foster, 1848; it became a favorite during the Calif. Gold Rush of 1849. The rapid polka time fits the words perfectly and the banjo accompaniment is equally congenial. The song remains a popular component of children's singing.

Oh, What a Beautiful Mornin'. An outburst of melodious matutinal euphoria by Rodgers and Hammerstein, 1943, from the musical *Oklahoma!*

Oh Where, Oh Where Has My Little Dog Gone? A German song, 1847, in which the protagonist laments a lost sock, not a lost dog. In 1864 the popular songwriter Septimus Winner (1827–1902) set English lyrics to the melody; he called it *Der Deitcher's Dog* and it was a dialect song.

Oh, You Beautiful Doll. Song by Nat Ayer, 1911, subsequently featured in several screen musicals.

Ohana, Maurice, French composer and pianist; b. Casablanca (of Spanish parents), June 12, 1914; d. Paris, Nov. 13, 1992. He studied piano with Frank Marshall in Barcelona and with Lazare Lévy at the Paris Cons.; also had lessons in counterpoint with Daniel-Lesur at the Schola Cantorum (1937–40). Following service in the British Army during World War II, he completed his training with Alfredo Casella at Rome's Accademia di Santa Cecilia (1944–46), then settled in Paris. In 1981 he was made a Commandeur des Arts et Lettres. He won the Prix National de Musique (1975) and the Honegger (1982) and Ravel (1985) prizes. Ohana's music combines elements of his Spanish background and the world of *The Rite of Spring* and *Les Noces* with a keen ear for percussion and timbre; he was resolutely against the avant-garde world of Boulez. He also composed operas, orch.1 and chamber works, keyboard music, including 24 Preludes (1972–73) for Piano, and group and solo vocal works.

Ohio. Ballad by L. Bernstein, 1953, from the musical *Wonderful Town.*

ohne (Ger.). Without. *Ohne Ausdruck*, expressionless; *ohne Verschiebung*, without fluctuation.

Oiseaux exotiques. Work by Messiaen, 1956, for piano, wind instruments, and percussion, in which instrumental approximations of bird songs from exotic lands are incorporated. It was 1st performed in Paris.

Oistrakh, David (Fyodorovich), great Russian violinist; b. Odessa, Sept. 30, 1908; d. Amsterdam, Oct. 24, 1974. He studied violin as a child with Stoliarsky in Odessa; made his debut there at the age of 6; continued his studies with Stoliarsky at the Odessa Cons. (1923–26); then appeared as soloist in Glazunov's Violin Concerto under the composer's direction in Kiev in 1927. In 1928 he went to Moscow; in 1934 he was appointed to the faculty of the Moscow Cons. His name attracted universal attention in 1937 when he won 1st prize at the Ysaÿe Competition in Brussels, in which 68 violinists from 21 countries took part. He played in Paris and London in 1953 with extraordinary success; made his 1st American appearances in 1955, as soloist with major American orchs., and in recitals, winning enthusiastic acclaim; also made appearances as a conductor from 1962. He died while on a visit to Amsterdam as a guest conductor with the Concertgebouw Orch.

Oistrakh's playing was marked—apart from a phenomenal technique—by stylistic fidelity to works by different composers of different historical periods. Soviet composers profited by his advice as to technical problems of violin playing; he collaborated with Prokofiev in making an arrangement for violin and piano of his Flute Sonata. (He also played a chess match with Prokofiev.) A whole generation of Soviet violinists numbered among his pupils, 1st and foremost his son Igor Oistrakh (b. Odessa, Apr. 27, 1931), who has had a spectacular career in his own right; he won 1st prize at the International Festival of Democratic Youth in Budapest (1949) and the Wieniawski Competition in Poznan (1952); some critics regarded him as equal to his father in virtuosity.

Okeghem, Johannes. OCKEGHEM, JOHANNES.

Oklahoma! Musical by Rodgers and Hammerstein, 1943; the 1st collaboration between one of the great Broadway teams. The action takes place in the old Indian Territory. A love triangle results in a fight between 2 suitors in which one of them, Jud (the real aggressor), is accidentally killed by Curly; after being absolved of all blame by a judge on the

Oklahoma! *original cast photograph*

spot, he and his bride go off to the land grab in the future state of Oklahoma. The musical was tremendously successful and became a classic of the modern musical theater in America. Among the many imperishable tunes in the score are the title song, *Oh, What a Beautiful Mornin', People Will Say We're in Love*, and *The Surrey with the Fringe on Top*.

oktoechos. A system of 8 ECHOI as practiced in Byzantine chant. The doctrine and practice of oktoechos probably originated in Syria early in the 6th century, possibly by analogy with the ancient Greek modes.

Ol' Man River. Song by Kern and Hammerstein II, 1927, from the musical *Show Boat*. Next to Foster's *Swanee River*, it is the greatest American river song, glorifying the mighty Mississippi that "just keeps rollin' along"; Winston Churchill quoted it as a song symbolizing the greatness of America. Implicit in the song, however, is the difficult life of the black population of the Delta.

Old Black Joe. Song by Foster, 1860. According to an accepted legend, Joe was a black servant in the house of Foster's fiancée.

Old Folks at Home. Song by Foster, 1851; one of his most famous; he sold it for a pittance to the famous minstrel performer and manager E. P. Christy, who published it as his own. Only after Christy's copyright expired was the injustice righted and Foster's name given as composer in the new edition, but by that time he was dead. The song is commonly known under the title *Swanee River*. Actually the name comes from the Suwanee River in Florida, the name of which Foster, who never lived in the South, picked up from a map.

Old Gray Mare, The. An anonymous American song, 1858; the original melody was also called *Down in Alabam'*. The words have gone through several metamorphoses.

Old Hundred. A tune originally set to the words of the 100th Psalm (*Make a Joyful Noise Unto the Lord, All Ye Lands*); it is also known as a hymn of praise, *All People that on Earth Do Dwell*. The hymn *Old Hundred* was 1st printed in the English Psalter (1563); it appears in the 1st Bay Psalm Book (1640); Ives quotes the tune in his music.

Old MacDonald Had a Farm. An old nursery rhyme with imitations of animal sounds. The lyrics have been traced back to an English song by Thomas d'Urfey which appeared in print as early as 1706, while the 1st-known American publication of the melody appeared under the title *Litoria! Litoria!* in 1859. In 1917 the 1st appearance of words and music as we know them today came under the title *Ohio*, although the farmer was called "MacDougal." Surprisingly enough, today's version was not published until 1920, when it was included in a Boy Scout book, which helped regularize the name of the farmer and the cast of animal characters.

Old Maid and the Thief, The. Opera by Menotti, 1939, written for radio and the 1st such work broadcast over the NBC network; it was not performed on stage until 1949, in Philadelphia. An old maid takes a transient into her home. She grows dependent on him, and yielding to his increasing demands, she engages in theft. When the thefts are discovered, everyone suspects the stranger. Irritated by this injustice, he robs her of all her possessions and disappears.

Olé! Spanish exclamation used as a refrain in various song genres.

olio (Sp., pot, stew). A specialty act or a medley at a burlesque show, featuring a variety of vocal and instrumental numbers, comic dialogues, and "exotic" dances.

oliphant (Old Fr. *olifant*, elephant). Abbrev. for *cor d'olifant*, a Byzantine signal trumpet, sometimes made of elephant's tusk, imported from the Orient and employed for ceremonial occasions. The instrument penetrated Europe during the Middle Ages. An alternate philological theory is that oliphant is a verbal corruption of "eloquent."

Oliver, "King" (Joseph), outstanding African-American jazz cornetist and bandleader, uncle of Ulysses (Simpson) Kay; b. on a plantation near Abend, La., May 11, 1885; d. Savannah, Ga., Apr. 8, 1938. In 1907 he was working in Storyville (the red-light district of New Orleans) with the Melrose Brass Band; in subsequent years he was with a number of other brass bands there, and in 1915 he formed his own group, eventually known as the Creole Jazz Band; by 1917 he had acquired the nickname "King," traditionally reserved for the leading jazz musicians. However, it was also in 1917 that the city government closed the bordellos in Storyville, putting most of the musicians out of work. The following year Oliver moved his band to Chicago, leading a migration of jazz musicians to the city that was largely responsible for the dispersion of the black New Orleans jazz style throughout the country. In 1922 Louis Armstrong, whom he had known in New Orleans, joined the band, helping to make it the most polished exponent of New Orleans collectively improvised jazz; the group's 1923 recordings were the most influential early jazz recordings ever made; they have been reissued by the Smithsonian Inst. Subsequent bands formed by Oliver remained a potent force in jazz until around 1928.

Oliveros, Pauline

American composer; b. Houston, May 30, 1932. Her mother and grandmother, both piano teachers, taught her the rudiments of music; she received instruction in violin from William Sydler, accordion from Marjorie Harrigan, and horn from J. M. Brandsetter; studied composition with Paul Koepke and accordion with William Palmer at the Univ. of Houston (1949–52); continued her studies at San Francisco State

College (B.A., 1957) and privately with Robert Erickson (1954–60). She was codirector of the San Francisco Tape Music Center (1961–65); after it became the Mills Tape Music Center, she was its director (1966–67); she then taught at the Univ. of Calif. at San Diego (1967–81), and held a Guggenheim fellowship (1973–74). She publ. *Pauline's Proverbs* (1976) and *Software for People: Collected Writings 1963–80* (1984).

Initiated by Robert Erickson into modern harmony, the art of asymmetrical rhythms, group improvisation, and acoustical sonorism, she gradually expanded her receptivity into the range of subliminal sounds derived from the overtone series, differential tones, and sonic abstractions. In 1960 she composed a Piano Sextet which explored a variety of such elusive tonal elements; it received the Pacifica Foundation National Prize. Advancing further into the domain of new sonorities, she wrote a choral work, *Sound Patterns*, to wordless voices (1962), which received a prize in the Netherlands. While in San Diego she was able to develop her ideas still further. Taking advantage of her skill as a gardener, she arrayed garden hoses and lawn sprinklers as part of a musical ensemble accompanied by the sounds of alarm clocks and various domestic utensils. Occasionally a musician was instructed to bark. To this enriched artistic vocabulary was soon added a physical and psychosomatic element; performers acted the parts of

PHOTOGRAPH BY BECKY COHEN, 1981. USED BY PERMISSION.

Pauline Oliveros

a magician, a juggler, and a fortune-teller. Page turners, piano movers, and floor sweepers were listed as performing artists.

In her later works she reduced such kinetic activities and gradually began to compose ceremonial works of sonic meditation, sotto voce murmuration, lingual lallation, and joyful ululation, with the purpose of inducing an altered state of consciousness; sometimes an exotic but usually digestible meal was served at leisurely intervals. She often presided over such sessions, singing and playing her faithful accordion; sometimes this music was left to be unheard by ordinary ears, but it could be perceived mystically.

In 1977 she obtained 1st prize from the city of Bonn for a work commemorating the sesquicentennial of Beethoven's death; the piece was verbally notated with the intention to subvert perception of the entire city so that it would become a perceptual theater. As she moved higher into the realm of cosmic consciousness, she introduced the psychic element into her works; in 1970 she drew an equation for an indefinite integral of the differential psi (for psychic unit), to create the state of Oneness. Her most controversial work was *To Valerie Solanis and Marilyn Monroe, in Recognition of Their Desperation*, a verbally notated score (1970) as a tribute to Solanis, the founder of SCUM (Society to Cut Up Men), who shot the pop artist Andy Warhol; and to Monroe, who committed suicide.

olla podrida (olio; Sp., rotten pot). The term is sometimes applied in the same meaning as the French *potpourri*: a miscellany or medley of musical or comic dialogues and "exotic" dances at a burlesque show.

Olympians, The. Opera by Bliss, 1949, 1st produced in London. The libretto, by J. B. Priestly, depicts the pathetic destiny of once-powerful Greek gods who are reduced to the status of itinerant actors and are allowed to return to Mt. Olympus for a vacation only once a year.

ombra scene (It.). A shadow scene; a dramatic operatic episode taking place in the nether regions, in a cemetery, or in a place where ghosts congregate. It is usually cast in the monodic manner of an accompanied recitative in triadic harmonies; for some reason the key of E-flat major was de rigueur in such scenes. Ombra scenes abound in general pauses, tremolos, exclamations, and other emotional outbursts; the clarinet, French horn, and trombone are favorite instruments for shadow scenes in Baroque operas. Mozart introduces the ghostly statue of the Commendatore in *Don Giovanni* with an ominous trombone passage.

omnitonality. In search of terms signifying various degrees of modulatory freedom, modern musicologists have chanced upon omnitonality to indicate a totality of tonalities entailing frequent collisions of different keys. Omnitonality enjoyed a certain vogue as a compromise definition for modern techniques that retained the basic sense of tonality but expanded it to the entire cycle of major and minor scales. It is almost synonymous with PANTONALITY.

omnitonic. Having or producing all tones; chromatic (as in an instrument).

Omphale. Opera, 1700, by André Cardinal Destouches (b. Paris, Apr. 6, 1672; d. there, Feb. 7, 1749); 1st performed in Paris. Its premiere passed without particular notice, but it became a cause célèbre in 1752 when the Alsatian diplomat Friedrich Melchior Grimm publ. a *Lettre sur Omphale*, precipitating the notorious GUERRE DES BOUFFONS. He was an advocate of Rameau and a critic of earlier French opera; he included *Omphale* in the latter group, although he was not totally critical of this opera. The libretto of *Omphale* took the subject from Greek mythology, as was the ingrained habit of French Baroque opera makers; but the formidable Omphale, who captures Hercules and makes him spin the yarn in her spindle while she struts in a lion's skin, in a light rather than heroic manner, and therefore anticipated the development of French LIGHT OPERA.

On a Clear Day You Can See Forever. Musical by Lerner and B. Lane, 1965. The whimsical plot deals with a girl who is not only clairvoyant, but who can also see back in time. Her skeptical psychiatrist is astounded by her ability to locate misplaced objects, to anticipate the exact moment when the phone will ring, and to make flowers grow unnaturally fast. When in a trance she identifies herself with an 18th-century English lady and research proves that there was such a person, the psychiatrist falls in love with both her antecedent in time and her present self. Includes the title song, *Come Back to Me*, and *What Did I Have That I Don't Have Now?*

On a Slow Boat to China. An imaginative love song by F. Loesser, 1948; it became a hit, selling more than a million records.

On Hearing the First Cuckoo in Spring. Symphonic poem by Delius, 1913; one of his most popular orch.l works. Its style is Romantic, with impressionistic touches. It was 1st performed in Leipzig on Oct. 2, 1913.

On the Banks of the Wabash, Far Away. Ballad by Paul Dresser, 1897, describing the place he grew up in. It swept the country and was ground out on every barrel organ in the streets of N.Y. In 1913 it was adopted as the state song of Indiana.

On the Good Ship Lollipop. Song by Richard Whiting, 1934; made famous by 6-year-old Shirley Temple in the movie *Bright Eyes*.

On the Road to Mandalay. Song, 1907, by Oley Speaks (b. Canal Winchester, Ohio, June 28, 1874; d. N.Y., Aug. 27, 1948). Based on Kipling's poem, the song became a great favorite of overweight baritones. Mandalay is in Burma.

On the Sunny Side of the Street. Song by Jimmy McHugh with lyrics by Dorothy Fields, 1930, featured in the *International Revue*. It was subsequently used in several movies as a sentimental declaration of an optimistic philosophy of life.

On the Town. Musical by L. Bernstein, 1944, his 1st; premiered in Boston. The score is an adaptation of his ballet *Fancy Free*; it deals with the amorous frolics of 3 sailors on leave in N.Y. The famous opening episode pictures the city of *New York, New York*.

On Top of Old Smokey. A mountain folk song popularized in 1951 by Pete Seeger, originally known as *Little Mohee*. Satirized by Tom Glazer as *On Top of Spaghetti* (". . . all covered with cheese/I lost my poor meatball/When somebody sneezed") to become a number 14 hit in 1963.

On Wenlock Edge. An extended song by Vaughan Williams, 1909, for tenor, piano, and string quartet, to a text from *A Shropshire Lad* by A. E. Housman. The music is full of spacious modalities and English refrains. It was 1st performed in London.

On Your Toes. Musical by Rodgers and Hart, 1936. A lowly vaudeville hoofer decides to get class through classical ballet, but fails utterly at it. At the advice of a Russian ballerina he stages a modern-dance show under the topical title *Slaughter on 10th Avenue*, which scores an immediate hit. The music itself, a symphonic jazz poem, remains popular; the song *There's a Small Hotel* has also remained a favorite.

Once Upon a Mattress. Musical by Mary Rodgers (b. N.Y., Jan. 11 1931; daughter of R. Rodgers), 1959. The story is taken from the classical fairy tale by the Brothers Grimm, *The Princess and the Pea*. A queen wishes to make sure that her son marries a real princess. When a bedraggled girl arrives at the palace after a journey from her own land, the prince is charmed by her. The wily queen subjects her to an unfailing test of her lineage by placing a pea under 20 mattresses in the bed she is to sleep on; only a real princess would be sensitive to this encumbrance and be unable to sleep; the girl passes. Only after her engagement to the prince is announced is the horrible truth discovered: the sympathetic court jester filled the mattresses with all kinds of sharp metal objects. But by now the prince loves her too much to give her up.

ondeggiamento (*ondeggiante*; It.; Fr. *ondulé*). Undulating, billowy; rocking (as by waves). A tremolo on a single note, or an arpeggiolike figure; the effect is achieved by varying intensity in applying the bow.

Ondes Martenot. An electronic keyboard instrument named after its French inventor Maurice Martenot; he orig. named it the ONDES MUSICALES. As in the Thereminovox and other early electronic instruments, the sound is produced heterodynamically, as a differential of 2 frequencies. It was 1st exhibited in Paris (1928). Several composers have written works for the Ondes Martenot; André Jolivet even composed a full-fledged concerto for it.

Ondes musicales. The orig. name for the electronic musical instrument invented by Martenot; now called ONDES MARTENOT.

one-step. An American ballroom dance of the 1910s and 1920s in 2/4 time.

One Touch of Venus. Musical by Weill, 1943. A romantic New Yorker puts the engagement ring he has bought for his best girl on the little finger of a statue of Venus in an art museum. The love goddess becomes imbued with a vital spark and makes a tour of the city with her bemused companion. In the end he returns to his fiancée-to-be and Venus is restored to her rightful place in the art gallery. Includes *Speak Low* and *I'm a Stranger Here Myself*.

ongarese (It.). Hungarian.

Only You. The Platters's DOO-WOP classic, originally recorded in 1955 and quickly covered by the white-bread Hilltoppers. The Platters sang it in the Bill Haley teen flick *Rock Around the Clock*.

Ono, Yoko, Japanese-born American vocalist, songwriter, and performance artist; b. Tokyo, Feb. 18, 1933. She was born to a wealthy banking family; in 1947 she moved to N.Y., where she entered Sarah Lawrence College (1953). She became active in Manhattan conceptual-art circles, notably the Fluxus group; in 1966 she met John Lennon of the Beatles; they became companions and collaborators, marrying in 1969. Under her influence Lennon became interested in AVANT-GARDE ideas that drew him away from rock, contributing to the breakup of the Beatles in 1970. After Lennon's death in 1980 Ono produced several posthumous collaborations.

Her solo recordings include *Yoko Ono/Plastic Ono Band* (1970), *Fly* (1971), *Approximately Infinite Universe* (1973), *Feeling the Space* (1973), *Seasons of Glass* (1981), *It's Alright* (1982), and *Every Man Has a Woman* (1984). Her recordings with Lennon include *Unfinished Music No. 1: 2 Virgins* (1968), *Unfinished Music No. 2: Life with the Lions* (1969), *Wedding Album* (1969), *Live Peace in Toronto 1969* (1970), *Double Fantasy* (1980), *Milk and Honey* (1982), and *Heart Play: Unfinished Dialogue* (1983). Ono's work is often bizarre, her shrill tremolo voice moving over a fluid, arrhythmic background reflecting Asian influences; some of her recordings, notably those between 1980 and 1984, are popular in style.

onomatopoeia. Imitation of sounds of nature, or industry, abound in Classic, Romantic, and modern music. Familiar examples are the thunderstorms of Beethoven's *Pastoral Sym.* and in the overture to Rossini's *William Tell*. Birdcalls are natural resources for musical imagination. Sounds of industry were reproduced with varying degrees of verisimilitude in numerous works of modern music. In his *Pacific 231* Honegger created a stimulating impression of an American locomotive gathering speed by the simple device of increasing the number of accented beats in each successive bar. The whirring of an early airplane propeller is realistically imitated in a piece entitled *The Aeroplane* by the American composer Emerson Whithorne. The Italian Futurists attempted to emulate the noises of 20th century city life by the use of megaphones. The stroke of midnight is sounded by the chimes in the score of Mussorgsky's *Night on Bald*

Mountain. The clatter of steel-making is realistically illustrated by the shaking of a sheet of metal in the ballet *Iron Foundry* by the Soviet composer Alexander Mosolov.

Amusing attempts to illustrate a sneeze are found in *The Nose* by Shostakovich and *Háry János* by Kodály. In the latter the sneeze expresses the Hungarian reaction of extreme skepticism about adventures recited by a boastful storyteller. A realistic piece of grim onomatopoeia occurs in *Robespierre's Overture* by Henry Charles Litolff, in which the fall of Robespierre's head after his execution on the guillotine is rendered by a thud of the bass drum.

oompah (-pah). An onomatopoeic vocable to denote the alternating bass between the tonic and the dominant in the tuba, ophicleide, serpent, and other deep bass instruments, particularly in marches and galops, placed by military bands, and borrowed by Romantic Italian opera composers.

open diapason. See ORGAN.

open form. See MOBILE FORM.

open form composition. Works based on controlled improvisation in which materials are selected from available resources have a venerable ancestry; classical composers supplied alternative versions for transitions and endings as a matter of course. In its modern avatar, open form composition often delegates the ordering of component parts to the performer. Chronological priority in developing such techniques belongs to the American composer Earle Brown, whose *Folio*, written in 1952, affords great latitude in the arranging of given materials. Stockhausen further developed this technique in his *Klavierstücke*, consisting of separate sections which can be performed in any order.

open harmony. In 4-part harmony, an arrangement of voices such that the 3 upper voices have a total range of more than an octave (as in C–G, E, C); most suitable for choral writing, as opposed to CLOSE HARMONY, easier for keyboard harmony.

open pedal. The loud (damper) piano pedal.

open pipe. Organ pipes with open tops; these sound 1 octave above closed pipes otherwise identical in dimensions.

open string. On any chordophone with a fingerboard, a string in its natural, unstopped state; similarly, it is played without being stopped by the finger. When an open string is to be played, a small circle is placed above the note. Because the sounds of open strings are so distinctive from stopped notes, they are avoided in melodic passages; they become increasingly essential in double-, triple-, and quadruple-stops. Some works exploit open strings for reasons of euphony or symbolism. Saint-Saëns builds his *Danse macabre* on the open strings of the solo violin, suggesting a witch tuning her fiddle; Berg insists on open strings in passages of his Violin Concerto. A string quartet erroneously attributed to Benjamin Franklin, the MS of which was discovered in 1945, is written entirely for open strings so that the rankest amateurs could play it; but the string are tuned in an ingenious SCORDATURA, so that unexpected and even dissonant harmonics can be formed.

opera. A form of drama, of Italian origin, in which vocal and instrumental music are essential and predominant. The several acts, usually preceded by instrumental introductions, consist of vocal scenes, recitatives, songs, arias, duets, trios, choruses, etc., accompanied by the orch. This is the *grand* or *heroic* opera; a *comic* opera is a versified comedy set to music; an OPERETTA or SINGSPIEL has spoken interludes.

opera buffa (It.; Fr. *opéra bouffe*). Comic opera, as opposed to OPERA SERIA. In a typical cast of an opera buffa there are standard comic characters, some of which are borrowed from the commedia dell'arte. It thrives on schemes and stratagems found in comedies of Shakespeare, Molière, and other classics of dramatic literature. Such plays are replete with mistaken identities, disguises, deceptions, and intrigues; but virtue triumphs in the end; the dupes forgive their tormentors, young couples are united, and the spirit of entertainment overcomes all the stumbling blocks of blatant absurdities.

opéra-comique (Fr.). French opera with spoken dialogue instead of recitative; it is not necessarily humorous in nature. When it became a regular art form in the 18th century, the word *comic* had dignified connotations, on par with Dante's *Divina Commedia*, which, of course, is anything but a comedy. The music of such operas was of a light dramatic texture, often introducing concepts of morality and proper social behavior. In the 19th century in France opéra-comique denoted an opera with spoken dialogue. The Paris Opéra-Comique was originally the theater intended for the production of French dramatic works that contained musical numbers and spoken dialogues in about equal measure. But this opera house also saw productions, such as Bizet's *Carmen*, which could hardly be called comical.

opera in musica (It., musical work; usually abbrev. to *opera*). A dramatic presentation for singers and instruments performing in costume on the stage. Spoken dialogue may alternate with musical sections.

opera seria (It.). Serious (grand, heroic, tragic) opera. It is virtually identical with the concept of grand opera; it denotes an eloquent music drama replete with emotional upheavals, tragic conflicts, scenes of triumph and disaster, with insanity, murders, and suicides filling the action. By tradition, an opera seria ought to have at least 3 acts, but may well extend into 5 acts. It can also include ballet. The opposite of opera seria is OPERA BUFFA.

operetta (It.; Fr. *opérette*). A "little opera" in which the libretto is in a comic, mock-pathetic, parodistic, or anything-but-serious vein; the music is light and lively and often interrupted by dialogue.

ophicleide (from Grk. *ophis* + *kleidos*, serpent with keys; Fr. *ophicléide*; Ger. *Ophikleide*; It. *oficleide*). 1. A large, deep-toned keyed bugle with U-shaped conical tube with slightly flared bell and cup mouthpiece, built by Halary, *c.* 1817. George Bernard Shaw volunteers the information that his uncle played it and then "perished by his own hand." The ophicleide itself became extinct shortly after Shaw's uncle's suicide and was replaced by the tuba. 2. Large-scale cylindrical reed organ stop, 8' or 16'.

oppure (It.; abbrev. *opp.*). OSSIA.

opus (Lat.). Work; abbrev. *Op.* or *op. Opus number*, the number assigned for chronological identification of a work or group of works by a particular composer. Unfortunately, composers and their publishers seldom were entirely accurate in coordinating the chronology with the opus numbers. For instance, Chopin's Piano Concerto in F Minor, bearing the opus number 21, was actually composed a year earlier than his Piano Concerto in E Minor, which bears the opus number 11. Sometimes competing publishers would have their own sets of opus numbers for a particular composer, thus creating more than 1 op. 1, op. 2, etc. The use of opus numbers became an established practice in the 19th century, but it fell off

among many modern composers. Mozart's works are identified not by opus numbers but by K. numbers, after Köchel, the 1st Mozart cataloguer.

oratorio (It.). An extended, more or less dramatic composition for vocal solos and chorus, with accompaniment by orch. and/or organ, sung without stage play or scenery. The genre, known also as *historia*, developed in 17th-century Italy as a way for operatic composers to keep busy during Lent, when theaters were closed.

Orbison, Roy (Kelton), American rock singer, guitarist, and songwriter; b. Wink, Tex., Apr. 23, 1936; d. Hendersonville, Tenn., Dec. 6, 1988. He studied geology at North Tex. State College; after performing with local rockabilly bands he began a recording career in 1956; also was active as a songwriter in Nashville, Tenn. He possessed an excellent lyric tenor voice, so unusual among the common breed of rockers that he won a distinctive niche uncontested by others in the field of popular music. Among his hit songs were *Crying, Many Moods,* and *Regeneration.* His song *Oh, Pretty Woman* became his signature tune. Among his anthologies were *Orbisongs* and *There Is Only 1 Roy Orbison.* Shortly before his death in 1988 he joined George Harrison, Bob Dylan, and others to produce the album *The Traveling Wilburys,* on which he added prominent vocals to the songs *Not Alone Anymore, End of the Line,* and *Handle with Care.* He also recorded a final solo album with Jeff Lynne producing, which produced a minor hit with *You Got It,* revived in 1995 by Bonnie Raitt.

orchestra (Ger. *Orchester*; Fr. *orchestre*). A company of musicians performing on the instruments usually employed in opera, oratorio, concerto, or sym.; hence also the instruments taken together.

orchestral. Pertaining to or resembling the orch. *Orchestral piano playing,* the style of Liszt and his disciples, who tried to compose orch.l effects on the piano.

Orchestral Variations. Work by Copland, 1958; an orch. version of his *Piano Variations* (1930); it was premiered in Louisville, Ky.

orchestration. The art of writing music for performance by an orch.; the science of combining, in an effective manner, the instruments constituting the orch.

orchestrion. A large stationary barrel organ, generally played by clockwork.

order. The arrangement of the chord tones above a given bass, *open order* and *close order* being the same as OPEN HARMONY and CLOSE HARMONY.

Ordinary (Lat. *ordinarium*). In the Roman Catholic High Mass, the sung sections with fixed texts: KYRIE, GLORIA, CREDO, SANCTUS, AGNUS DEI (and the closing *Ite, missa est* or *Benedicamus Domino*). These sections are interwoven with the PROPRIUM, with changing texts according to the Church calendar.

ordre. A term used by Couperin and other French clavecinists for a group of keyboard pieces in the manner of the instrumental SUITE. The ordre usually contains, in addition to the traditional movements of the suite (allemande, courante, sarabande), pieces with whimsical descriptive titles, designed to appeal to the amateurs who played them, such as *Les Petits moulins à vent, Les Barricades mystérieuses,* etc.

Oresteia. Operatic trilogy by Taneyev, 1895, 1st performed in St. Petersburg. The libretto follows Aeschylus; the 3 parts are *Agamemnon, Choëphorai* (Libation Bearers), and *Eumenides* (Furies). After the murder of Agamemnon by his wife, Clytemnestra, their son swears vengeance and kills her and her lover. The Furies pursue him but he finds refuge in the temple of Apollo. The music is written in the austere style of modal counterpoint.

Orfeo ed Euridice. "Azione teatrale per musica" by Gluck, 1762, 1st produced in Vienna in Italian with the part of Orfeo sung by the famous castrato Gaetano Guadagni. The work acquired its greatest historical significance after its performance with a French libretto in Paris (1774). The opera demonstrates Gluck's doctrine of subordinating music to the text so as to achieve the maximum degree of dramatic verity. The story follows the Greek myth of the singer Orpheus trying to recover his beloved Euridice from the land of death and losing her when he fails to obey the injunction not to look back at Hell's entrance; unlike the myth, a LIETO FINE is provided. The customary ballet required of all works at the Paris Opéra is fulfilled by the famous *Dance of the Blessed Spirits.*

Orfeo, L'. "Fable in music" by Monteverdi, 1607, 1st performed privately in Mantua. The libretto follows the familiar legend of Orpheus trying to recover his beloved Euridice from the Kingdom of the Dead. For aesthetic reasons, Monteverdi omitted the original ending, the dismembering of Orpheus by a mob of crazed Corybants. Instead, Orpheus is taken to Elysium by Apollo as the DEUS EX MACHINA. The historical significance of *L'Orfeo* lies in its skillful alternation of monody and more old-fashioned textures, providing the 1st balanced approach to early opera. Also of interest is its orchestration, which includes clavicembalos, harps, trombones, cornets, a clarino (a high trumpet), recorders, organs, and a large contingent of string instruments.

Orff, Carl, outstanding German composer; b. Munich, July 10, 1895; d. there, Mar. 29, 1982. He took courses with Beer-Walbrunn and Zilcher at the Munich Academy of Music (graduated 1914); later had additional instruction from Heinrich Kaminski in Munich. He was a conductor at the Munich Kammerspiele (1915–17); after military service during World War I (1917–18), he conducted at the Mannheim National Theater and the Darmstadt Landestheater (1918–19); later was conductor of Munich's Bach Society (1930–33).

Orff initiated a highly important method of musical education, which was adopted not only in Germany but in England, America, and Russia; it stemmed from the Günther School for gymnastics, dance, and music which Orff founded in 1924 with Dorothee Günther in Munich, with the aim of promoting instrumental playing and understanding of rhythm among children; he commissioned the piano manufacturer Karl Maendler to construct special percussion instruments that would be extremely easy to play; the "Orff instruments" became widely adopted in American schools. Orff's ideas of rhythmic training owe much to the eurhythmics of Jaques-Dalcroze, but he simplified them to reach the elementary level; as a manual, he compiled a set of musical exercises, *Schulwerk* (1930–35, rev. 1950–54). He also taught composition at the Munich Staatliche Hochschule für Musik (1950–55).

As a composer Orff sought to revive the early monodic forms and to adapt them to modern tastes by means of dissonant counterpoint, with lively rhythm in asymmetrical patterns, producing a form of "total theater." His most famous score is the scenic oratorio *Carmina Burana* (1937); the words (in Latin and middle German) are from 13th-century student poems found in the Benediktbeuren monastery in Bavaria. His other works were primarily for the stage, including operas, musical plays, and vocal works. He also wrote 3 stage works after Monteverdi in 1925: *Klage der Ariadne; Orpheus;* and *Tanz der Spröden;* all 3 were rev. in 1940.

organ

The pipe organ (Ger. *Orgel*; Fr. *orgue*; It. *organa*) is the largest of the keyboard instruments. Its very appearance is most imposing, with its several rows of vertical pipes usually arranged in a tasteful symmetrical position. The pipes, of which there are 2 main divisions—flue pipes and reed pipes—are made to speak by wind admitted from the bellows upon pressing the keys. The organ has 2 or more manuals or keyboards and a complex system of *stops* or registers that govern the tone color. It also has a pedal keyboard; a master organist must therefore be a virtuoso with his feet as well as with his hands. His musicianship must be of such a high caliber as to enable him to coordinate the multiple devices of his instrument in order to produce optimum results. The organ is thus a simulacrum of a full orch.

A strict hierarchy is maintained in the planning of the manual, but each manual, whatever its order of importance, can given an adequate rendition of the music. The most prominent manual bears the proud name of the Great Organ, which is supplied with the loudest stops. The 2nd manual is the Swell Organ, which enables the organist to produce a tremendous crescendo. The 3rd manual is called Choir Organ; it is used for the purpose of accompaniment.

The Solo Organ is designed to bring out a special instrumental tone color. In large modern organs there is a 5th manual, the Echo Organ, which can produce the effect of a distant sound. The manuals are arranged in staircase-like steps, so that the Great Organ is the nearest to the player, and the Echo Organ the highest up. The order of the lower manuals may differ depending on the manufacturer. In any case the organist's torso must be constantly exercised in reaching out for the var-

Organ, Warner Concert Hall, Oberlin College

ious manuals. Considering that his feet must be very agile, the organist is obliged to perform physical work in excess of all other instrumentalists. Fortunately there is a plethora of ingenious helping devices for the organist "at the console."

The pedal organ sounds an octave below the manuals. The stops of the pedal are so fixed that the sound may be lowered 2 and even 3 octaves. The stops are named according to the sizes of the sets of pipes they activate. The normal pitch of the manual commands an 8-foot stop, called the *open diapason* stop, which opens a pipe approximately 8 feet long. Other pipes—4 feet long and 2 feet long—sound respectively an octave or 2 higher. In the low range there is a 16-foot pipe and a 32-foot pipe, and even a 64-foot pipe, which will produce sounds 2, 3, and 4 octaves lower than the given note. Both the manuals and the pedals possess special stops that can bring into play upper or lower octaves, or indeed all of them together, producing a gigantic unison that lends the particular magnificence to a cathedral organ

And that is not all. There are *couplers* by which 2 manuals can be connected, so that the organist can amplify the sound by playing on only 1 of these coupled manuals.

And it is also possible to double the sound an octave above or below by these couplers. Furthermore, the organist can prepare the *registration*, the system of stops, in advance so that he could start playing in octaves or double octaves—both in the manuals and in the pedals—and in desired tone colors. Special registers or stops can be interconnected selectively or for the entire organ. Hence the expression "pulling out all the stops" to describe an organ in full glory, sound, and fury. (The metaphor obviously has sarcastic connotations when applied to a salesman or a politician.)

The names of the organ stops provide a whole inventory of acoustical terms. The king of the stops is the *diapason* stop, which implies a totality of tones (*diapason* means "through all" in Greek). Metaphorically, the word can be used in the same sense as *gamut*, meaning the entire compass of audible sounds from the lowest to the highest. Other stops are named after the instruments they attempt to duplicate (flute, oboe, clarinet, bassoon, strings, etc.). Two registrations have poetic names—VOX ANGELICA and VOX HUMANA. Obviously the 1st is supposed to convey the impressions of an angel singing solo, and the 2nd the voice of a human. Much sarcasm has been poured on the bland, effeminate tone of the angelic registration, and the human stop suggested to the celebrated 18th-century British historian Dr. Burney, "the cracked voice of an old woman of 90." But perhaps he had the bad luck to listen to poor organists playing on a poor organ.

The spirit of competition in building larger and larger organs is particularly strong in the U.S. The organ in one Chicago stadium has 6 manuals and 828 different stops. One of the most elaborate electronic organs ever built was constructed for Carnegie Hall, N.Y., in 1974. It has 192 speakers in 29 cabinets, and 5 manuals with a frequency range from 16 cycles to 20,000 cycles. But, according to reports, Convention Hall in Atlantic City boasts of a Brobdingnagian organ with 7 manuals and 1,200 stops.

organ point. See PEDAL POINT.

organ tone. The tone of the 8-foot open diapason on the Great Organ manual. Also called *diapason tone*.

organetto (It.). 1. A portative organ, used in the Middle Ages and Renaissance, placed on the left knee and played as a melody instrument with the right hand while the left hand operates the bellows. 2. Street or BARREL ORGAN.

organista (Lat.). 1. Organ player. 2. Composer of ORGANUM; Leoninus was praised as *optimus organista*.

organistrum. Medieval HURDY-GURDY in a fiddle shape with 3 strings.

organized sound. Sound is an acoustical phenomenon, which all by itself does not make it music. Composition begins at the point when 2 sounds are connected in linear succession or vertical superposition. But the nature of these links is not circumscribed by any rules of melody or harmony. With the emancipation of dissonances in the 20th century, the vertical combinations became free from restraints imposed on them by tradition. Linear progressions, once bound within the framework of modes and scales, are developed in atonal designs. Schoenberg replaced diatonic melody and consonant harmony by the new dodecaphonic discipline. To avoid the associations with the word *music*, Varèse advanced the concept of organized sound, as a complex of successive acoustical phenomena unrelated to one another except by considerations of sonic equilibrium.

Dissonant combinations are preferred because they constitute a probabilistic majority and therefore are entitled to greater representation in organized sound. For the same statistical reasons, successions of melodic notes are apt to generate atonal configurations. The form of works written according to the doctrine of organized sound is athematic, and the rhythms are usually asymmetric. The valence between successive units, in melody, harmony, and rhythm, under such conditions is an *idempotent*.

organo (It.). Organ. *Organo pleno*, full organ.

organum (Lat.). 1. An organ. 2. The earliest attempts at harmonic or polyphonic music. This practice 1st developed between 900 and 1200 A.D. Its earliest forms consisted of a tenor part, with the addition of 1, 2, or at most 3 contrapuntal parts. The only intervals used were octaves and 5ths, but perfect 4ths resulted when the 5th note was inserted between 2 octave points. To the modern ear such *parallel organum* sounds extremely arid—no more polyphonic than a mechanical duplication. This view is erroneous, for the actual practice of the masters of organum was much more free than the naked definitions implied. Indeed, contrary and oblique motion between the tenor and the contrapuntal voices were introduced as soon as the practice spread in general church usage. It became possible, then, to move from an octave to a 5th in contrary motion, and vice versa, and even use dissonant passing tones from one "legitimate" interval to another.

Another century saw the development of *melismatic organum,* in which contrapuntal parts were assigned florid passages while the principal voice continued to hold the original tone; hence the term TENOR for that voice, i.e., a "tenant," or "one who holds." With the advent of mensural counterpoint and notation, the art of organum became a complex discipline of polyphonic writing. The most notable achievements in this highly developed organum were reached by the 2 great masters of the Notre Dame school in Paris, Leoninus and Perotinus. The peak of the organum era of composition was achieved with the impressive *organum quadruplum,* in which the principal voice was accompanied by 3 intricate contrapuntal voices.

Orgel (Ger.). Organ.

Orgelleier (Ger.). Organized HURDY-GURDY.

orgue (Fr.). Organ. *Orgue de barbarie,* a street organ operated by a crank and producing a "barbarous" crackling sound while playing a tune.

orientalism. See EXOTICISM.

Ormandy, Eugene (born Jenő Blau), outstanding Hungarian-born American conductor; b. Budapest, Nov. 18, 1899; d. Philadelphia, Mar. 12, 1985. He studied violin with his father; entered the Royal Academy of Music in Budapest at the age of 5; began studying with Hubay at 9 and received an artist's diploma at 13; received a teacher's certificate in 1917; then was concertmaster of the Blüthner Orch. in Germany; also gave recitals and played with orchs. as a soloist.

In 1921 he went to the U.S.; became an American citizen in 1927; obtained the position of concertmaster of the Capitol Theater Orch., N.Y., and remained there for 2 1/2 years; made his debut as conductor with that orch. in 1924; in 1926 he became its associate music director; in 1929 he conducted the N.Y. Phil. at Lewisohn Stadium; in 1930 he became guest conductor with the Robin Hood Dell Orch., Philadelphia; in 1931 he conducted the Philadelphia Orch. In 1931 he was appointed music director of the Minneapolis

Sym. Orch.; in 1936 he was engaged as associate conductor of the Philadelphia Orch. (with Stokowski); became its music director (1938); traveled with it on transcontinental tours (1937, 1946, 1948, 1957, 1962, 1964, 1971, 1974, and 1977); made an extended tour in England (1949); in the spring of 1955 he presented concerts with it in 10 European countries; in the summer of 1958 he led it on another European tour (including Russia).

He appeared on numerous occasions as guest conductor with European orchs.; in Australia (summer of 1944); South America (summer of 1946); Latin America (1966); the Far East (1967, 1978); and Japan (1972). In 1970 he received the Presidential Medal of Freedom. In 1973 he took the Philadelphia Orch. to China and led it in several cities there; this was the 1st appearance of an American sym. orch. in the People's Republic of China. Ormandy was made an officer of the French Legion of Honor (1952; was promoted to Commander in 1958); was made a Knight of the Order of the White Rose of Finland (1955); became a holder of the medal of the Bruckner Society (1936); received an honorary Mus.D. from the Univ. of Pa. In 1976 he was named an honorary Knight Commander of the Order of the British Empire by Queen Elizabeth II in honor of the American Bicentennial; altogether he received 26 awards and 23 honorary doctorates.

In his interpretations Ormandy revealed himself as a Romanticist; he excelled in the works of Beethoven, Schumann, and R. Strauss, conducting all scores from memory. After 42 seasons as music director of the Philadelphia Orch., he retired at the close of the 1979–80 season and was named Conductor Laureate.

Ormindo. Opera by Cavalli, 1644, premiered in Venice at Carnival time. Two young army men are in love with the Queen of the land. The King discovers the intrigue but forgives the youthful adventurers. *Ormindo* is one of the earliest extant MONODIC operas.

ornament. A grace, embellishment.

Ornamente. Piano piece by Blacher, 1950, in which he introduced VARIABLE METERS. Blacher later used this technique in the 1953 *Orchester Ornament,* a suite in 3 movements, 1st performed in Venice.

Orontea. Opera by Cesti, 1659; premiered in Innsbruck in Italian. The story deals with a seriocomic confusion between princely characters and their lowly servants, one of which,

Orontea, turns out to be a princess in her own right who was registered in the wrong column in the church birth records. The style is MONODIC, the dialogue mostly in RECITATIVE; there is no chorus.

Orphée aux enfers (Orpheus in Hell). Operetta by Offenbach, 1858, 1st produced in Paris; his 1st major success. The gods of Olympus are here exposed as bumbling creatures intent on having their pleasure on earth rather than in heaven. Orpheus is in love with a shepherdess, and Jupiter is attracted by Euridice, the wife of Orpheus, abducted by Hades; eventually she becomes a Bacchante. The score includes a can-can, which shocked the sensibilities of some proper Parisians. Incidentally, Saint-Saëns makes a seemingly incongruous use of the can-can from *Orphée aux enfers* in the section called *Tortoise* in his *Carnival of the Animals*; the connection here is that Orpheus made his lute out of a tortoise shell.

Orphéon. A choral society in France in the 19th century with a membership recruited mainly among amateurs. It was named, of course, after the mythical singer Orpheus, whose art could enchant humans and animals alike and move inanimate objects. The Orphéon became an important branch of musical education in France; several periodicals were publ. devoted to its activities, among them *La France Orphéonique* and *L'Echo des Orphéons*. In Barcelona the Orfeo Catalan was organized with the purpose of performances of choral and other music. In Brazil Villa-Lobos founded an "Orpheonic concentration," in which thousands of school children participated. The repertoire of the original French Orphéon was enlarged by works specially written by Berlioz, Gounod, and others. In England an Orpheonic Choral Festival was staged in 1860, with the participation of thousands. Toward the end of the 19th century the extent of activities of the Orphéon abated, and in the 20th century the movement went into decline.

Orpheus. Ballet by Stravinsky, 1948, 1st performed in N.Y. The choreography recreates the classical French ballet; the music uses NEOCLASSICAL means to match it.

Ory, "Kid" (Edward), African-American jazz trombonist and bandleader; b. La Place, La., Dec. 25, 1886; d. Honolulu, Jan. 23, 1973. He played the banjo as a child; then took up trombone; later joined bands led by Louis Armstrong and King Oliver. After a hiatus from performing (1933–42) he organized his own band and toured with it in Europe (1956–59). He was known for his "tailgate" style of trombone playing. He was the composer of the well-known *Muskrat Ramble*.

oscillator. An electronic device used to produce a wave form.

osservato (It.). Carefully observed. *Stile osservato*, strict style.

ossia (It.). Or; or else; *oppure, ovvero*. *Ossia* may indicate an alternative (or facilitated) reading or fingering of a passage; an alternate title to an opera; a choice of instrument or voice; optional parts in a score; optional edits in a score.

ostinato

〰〰 〰〰 〰〰 〰〰 〰〰

This term came into musical usage about 1700 in the sense of *basso continuo obbligato*, an obligatory bass figure. The earliest dictionary definition, in Walther's *Musikalisches Lexikon*, was "that figure which once begun is continued, and never deviated from." A more modern and definitive description was given by Riemann: "Ostinato is the continued recurrence of a theme accompanied by constantly changing contrapuntal parts." Thus the practice of ostinato (It. *obstinate*) involves dual elements of constancy: a constancy of the theme, and the constant variations in contrapuntal voices. The ostinato is therefore both the binding and the versifying substance of a musical composition.

Long before the term became part of musical terminology, the practice of repetition of the thematic phrase became common in motets and canons. Secular motives in medieval polyphonic compositions are particularly notable when regarded as early occurrences of ostinato figures. The vendor's cry "fresh strawberries, wild blackberries" occurs in a French medieval motet. But it must be observed that such incidental uses of melodic and rhythmic repetition of a musical phrase are natural manifestations of folk songs and vocal compositions and therefore cannot be regarded as a conscious and technical application of the ostinato technique.

While it is most tempting to seek the sources of ostinato in Asian music, particularly in the Indian RAGAS, or in modern jazz techniques, such as boogie-woogie, riff, stomp, etc., such citations are misleading. Equally misleading is the notion of explaining composition in 12 tones as a manifestation of the ostinato technique. The true ostinato is the brainchild of the Baroque, and the forms in which ostinato is applied properly and consistently are the PASSACAGLIA, CHACONNE, GROUND BASS, and their related forms; in these genres the ostinato appears invariably in the bass and therefore becomes a true BASSO OSTINATO. The majestic creations of Bach in these forms are justly compared with the greatest achievements of Gothic architecture or epic poems in literature.

With the decline of the Baroque in the middle of the 18th century, the use of the basso ostinato gradually declined. In Classic music, melody was the queen and the bass was the faithful servant. Obviously, such a base servant could not be obstinate. Indeed, Mozart and Haydn found the use of the governing basso ostinato artificial and "unnatural." Samples of *ritmo ostinato* (persistent rhythm) in the bass part are found in Mozart's sacred music, but even in such works a certain variation of rhythmic figures is easily discernible.

Interest in the artificial devices of the ostinato technique revived toward the end of the 19th century. The finale of the 4th Sym. of Brahms is a passacaglia. Reger, a Baroque revenant, wrote passacaglias like a Bach incarnate. The 1st opus number by Anton von Webern bears the title *Passacaglia*. In his opera *Lulu*, written in the 12-tone idiom, Berg includes a passacaglia movement. Implicit formations peculiar to the ostinato technique can be found in piano works of Bartók and Hindemith. And, naturally, composers of neoclassical music find the ostinato formula most congenial.

Finally, in the last century, the ostinato technique has shifted in some cases from the bass to the middle and even melodic voices, as a structural unifying device. In Nielsen's 5th Sym. the violas play a tremolo of a minor 3rd for the 1st several minutes of the work; Stravinsky's *Petrouchka* and Janáček's Sinfonietta feature ostinatolike melodies; and *The Rite of Spring* is a cornucopia of ostinato figures.

Otello. Opera by Verdi, 1887; 1st produced in Milan. The masterly libretto by Boito is generally faithful to Shakespeare's play, from which it is derived, and the Italian text is exemplary. (The spelling "Otello," without an *h*, is proper in Italian.) Otello is a Moor who leads the Venetian army to victories over the Turks. Provoked by Iago, his malicious aide-de-camp, he suspects his wife Desdemona of infidelity and strangles her. When he finds out his monstrous error he stabs himself to death. The opera, which Verdi completed at the age of 73, is remarkable for its departure from the style and idiom of his previous operas, toward the direction of the modern concept of music drama.

Otello, ossia Il Moro di Venezia. Opera by Rossini, 1816, after Shakespeare; 1st produced in Naples. While revivals have occurred on occasion, it cannot match the musical and popular success of Verdi's opera on the same source (see entry above).

ottava (It.). Octave. *All' ottava* (written 8va———— or 8————), "at the octave," an octave higher; *coll' ottava*, "with the octave," that is, in octaves; *ottava alta*, the higher octave; *ottava bassa* (8va *bassa*), the lower octave, an octave below.

ottavino (It.). A piccolo.

Otter, Anne Sofie von, Swedish mezzo-soprano; b. Stockholm, May 9, 1955. She began her training at the Stockholm Musikhogskölan; then studied with Erik Werba in Vienna and Geoffrey Parsons in London, and later with Vera Rozsa. In 1982 she joined the Basel Opera; in 1984 she sang at the Aix-en-Provence Festival. She made her 1st appearance at London's Covent Garden in 1985 as Cherubino; that same year she made her U.S. debut as soloist in Mozart's C-minor Mass with the Chicago Sym. Orch. In 1987 she sang at La Scala in Milan and at the Bavarian State Opera in Munich. In

1988 she appeared as Cherubino at the Metropolitan Opera in N.Y. She sang widely as a soloist with major orchs. and as a recitalist. Her other operatic roles include Gluck's Orfeo, Mozart's Idamantes and Dorabella, Tchaikovsky's Olga, and Octavian.

ottetto (It.). An octet.

ottoni (It.). Brass instruments.

ou (Fr.). Or; or else. See also OSSIA.

oud. 'ŪD.

ouvert (Fr.). Open sound. *Accord à l'ouvert*, a chord played on open strings.

Over There. Celebrated patriotic song by George M. Cohan, 1917, written shortly after the U.S. entered the war against Germany. It sold over 2 million copies of sheet music and over a million phonograph records. Caruso sang it for the American troops. Cohan received the Congressional Medal of Honor for the song and it was featured in Cohan's movie biography, *Yankee Doodle Dandy*, in 1942.

overblowing. With wind instruments, forcing the wind through the tube in such a way as to cause any harmonic to sound, in order to play the upper registers.

overstring. To arrange the strings of a piano in 2 sets, one lying over and diagonally crossing the other; a piano so strung is called an *overstrung* piano, in contradistinction to *vertical*.

Overton, Hall (Franklin), American composer; b. Bangor, Mich., Feb. 23, 1920; d. N.Y., Nov. 24, 1972. He studied piano at the Chicago Musical College; served in the U.S. Army overseas (1942–45). After World War II he studied composition with Persichetti at the Juilliard School of Music, N.Y., graduating in 1951; also took private lessons with Wallingford Riegger and Darius Milhaud. At the same time he filled professional engagements as a jazz pianist and contributed to the magazine *Jazz Today*. He was awarded 2 Guggenheim fellowships (1955, 1957); also taught at Juilliard (1960–71), the New School for Social Research in N.Y. (1962–66), and at the Yale Univ. School of Music (1970–71). His works include 3 operas; 2 syms. (1955, 1962); 3 string quartets (1950, 1954, 1967); viola, cello, and piano sonatas; other orch. and chamber works; piano music; songs.

overtones (overtone series). See HARMONICS.

overture

〰〰 〰〰 〰〰 〰〰 〰〰

Alternate name for the Baroque instrumental SUITE. 2. Orig., a musical introduction to a play, opera, or ballet; in the 19th century the overture (from Fr. *ouverture,* opening; Ger. *Ouvertüre*) also became an independent concert piece, the CONCERT OVERTURE.

An overture to an opera served often as a thematic table of contents, with the tunes of the most important arias, choruses, and instrumental interludes passing in review and preparing the listener for the melodic joys during the course of the work itself. As a musical form the overture made its 1st appearance in France in the 17th century, and the practice particularly by Lully gave rise to a special form of the FRENCH OVERTURE, which consisted of 2 contrasting sections, the 1st being in a slow tempo marked by dotted rhythms and concluding on the dominant of the principal key, and the 2nd part in a faster tempo, often culminating in a fugal development. This binary form later expanded into a ternary structure by the simple expedient of returning to the initial slow part, varied at will. The French overture was also much in use in instrumental suites.

In the 18th century the French overture went into decline and was replaced by the more vivacious ITALIAN

OVERTURE. The slow movement was placed in the middle between 2 fast sections; such a formation was obviously more exhilarating to the listener than the French genre in which the overture began and ended in slow motion. In early Italian operas the overture was called *sinfonia*—that is, an instrumental section without singing—and, in more recent times, *preludio*. The type of "summary overture" that incorporates materials from the opera itself is exemplified by Mozart's overtures to *Don Giovanni* and *The Magic Flute*, Beethoven's 3 *Leonore Overtures*, Weber's *Der Freischütz* overture, any overture by Meyerbeer, and virtually all overtures by Russian composers of the 19th century.

Wagner's overtures to his early operas and *Die Meistersinger* belonged to the category of summary overtures, but in his music dramas of the later period, and particularly in *Der Ring des Nibelungen*, he abandoned the idea of using material from the opera itself and returned to the type of prelude, usually of short duration, to introduce the opera. R. Strauss followed the Wagnerian type of introduction in his own operas, and so did a great majority of modern opera composers, including Puccini and composers of the verismo school. Only the Russians of the Soviet period remained faithful to the Italian type of summary overture.

Overtures form an integral part of scores of incidental music for dramatic performances. In numerous cases operas, even by famous composers, drop out of the repertoire while their overtures continue their independent lives on the concert stage. Performances of Beethoven's *Fidelio* are relatively rare, but his *Leonore Overtures* are played constantly. Rossini's opera *William Tell* has virtually disappeared from the repertory, but its overture is one of the most popular pieces of the concert repertoire. A special case is the *Roman Carnival Overture* by Berlioz, a summary overture based on a previously written opera (*Benvenuto Cellini*).

In the realm of incidental music there is Beethoven's *Egmont*, part of his music to Goethe's *Egmont*; and Mendelssohn's overture to Shakespeare's *A Midsummer Night's Dream* was written long before the other pieces that he wrote for the play. Finally there is the concert overture not connected and not intended for any opera. Among the most famous are *Fingal's Cave* by Mendelssohn, the *Faust Overture* by Wagner, and 2 by Brahms, *Academic Festival Overture* and *Tragic Overture*. Among overtures in a lighter vein, the concert overture *Poet and Peasant* by von Suppé achieved a tremendous popularity that showed no signs of abating for well over a century.

Overture: 1812. 1812 OVERTURE.

Overture to the School of Scandal. Concert overture by Barber, 1933, after Sheridan's comedy, 1st performed in Philadelphia.

ovvero (It.). OSSIA.

Owens, Buck (Alvis Edgar, Jr.), American country-music singer, guitarist, and songwriter; b. Sherman, Tex., Aug. 12, 1929. He took up the piano in his youth, and then the electric guitar; he began playing in honky-tonks when he was 16, and later established himself as one of the most successful country-music entertainers, performing in what was called the Bakersfield (Calif.) style; made many appearances on radio, television, and on tours. He was cohost (with Roy Clark) of the inane but highly successful *Hee Haw* television program (1969–86).

Ox Minuet (Ger. *Ochsenmenuette*). A piece misattributed to Haydn but actually composed by Seyfried as part of his light opera of the same name (1823). In an unsubstantiated anecdote, Haydn composed a minuet for his favorite butcher; the butcher asked the name of it; Haydn facetiously replied, "Ox Minuet"; the butcher sent him an ox as a token of gratitude. While the tune of the minuet was by the ridiculous Seyfried, the rest of the opera was arranged from various authentic tunes by Haydn. Fortunately for the latter, he was long dead when the *Ox Minuet* was produced.

Oxford Symphony. Sym. No. 92 by Haydn (1789), in the key of G major. The title is misleading, because Haydn did not compose it especially for the university town of Oxford, England, but had it performed there during his trip to England. He was rewarded for it by an honorary degree of Doctor of Music.

Ozark Set. Orch.1 suite by Siegmeister, 1944, descriptive of the folkways of the Ozark mountain people; it was 1st performed in Minneapolis.

Ozawa, Seiji

Brilliant Japanese conductor; b. Fenytien, China (of Japanese parents), Sept. 1, 1935. His father was a Buddhist, his mother a Christian. The family went back to Japan in 1944 at the end of the Japanese occupation of Manchuria. Ozawa began to study piano; at 16 he enrolled at the Toho School of Music in Tokyo, where he studied composition and conducting; one of his teachers, Hideo Saito, profoundly influenced his development as a musician; he graduated in 1959 with 1st prizes in composition and conducting. By that time he had already conducted concerts with the NHK (Japan Broadcasting Corp.) Sym. Orch. and the Japan Phil.; upon Saito's advice he went to Europe; to defray his expenses he became a motor-scooter salesman for a Japanese firm, and promoted the product in Italy and France.

In 1959 he won 1st prize at the international competition for conductors in Besançon and was befriended by Munch and Eugène Bigot; he then studied conducting with Bigot in Paris. Munch arranged for Ozawa to go to the U.S. and to study conducting at the Berkshire Music Center in Tanglewood; in 1960 he won its Koussevitzky Prize and was awarded a scholarship to work with von Karajan and the Berlin Phil. Bernstein heard him in Berlin and engaged him as an assistant conductor of the N.Y. Phil. In 1961 he made his 1st appearance with the orch. at Carnegie Hall; later that year he accompanied Bernstein and the orch. on its tour of Japan. In 1962 he was invited to return as a guest conductor of the NHK Sym. Orch., but difficulties arose between him and the players, who objected to being commanded in an imperious manner by one of their own countrymen; still, he succeeded in obtaining engagements with other Japanese orchs., which he conducted on his periodic visits to his homeland.

After serving as sole assistant conductor of the N.Y. Phil. (1964–65), Ozawa's career advanced significantly;

from 1964 to 1968 he was music director of the Ravinia Festival, the summer home of the Chicago Sym. Orch.; in 1969 he served as its principal guest conductor; from 1965 to 1969 he also was music director of the Toronto Sym. Orch., which he took to England in 1965. From 1970 to 1976 he was music director of the San Francisco Sym. Orch., and then its music adviser (1976–77); took it on an extensive tour of Europe, garnering exceptional critical acclaim. Even before completing his tenure in San Francisco, he had begun a close association with the Boston Sym. Orch.; with Gunther Schuller he became coartistic director of its Berkshire Music Center in 1970; in 1972 he assumed the post of music adviser of the Boston Sym. Orch., and in 1973 he became its music director and sole artistic director of the Berkshire Music Center, an astonishing event in American music annals, marking the 1st time an Asian musician was chosen solely by his merit to head the Boston Sym. Orch., which since its foundation had been the exclusive preserve of German (and later French and Russian) conductors.

In 1976 Ozawa took the Boston Sym. Orch. on a tour of Europe; in 1978 he escorted it to Japan, where those among Japanese musicians who had been skeptical about his abilities greeted his spectacular ascendance with national pride. Another unprecedented event took place in the spring of 1979, when Ozawa traveled with the Boston Sym. Orch. to the People's Republic of China on an official cultural visit; later that year Ozawa and the orch. went on a tour of European music festivals. The centennial of the Boston Sym. Orch. in 1981 was marked by a series of concerts under Ozawa's direction that included appearances in 14 American cities and a tour of Japan, France, Germany, Austria, and England.

With dormant racial prejudices finally abandoned in American society, Ozawa's reputation rose to universal recognition of his remarkable talent. He proved himself a consummate master of orch. playing, equally penetrating in the Classical repertoire as in the works of modern times; his performances of such demanding scores as Mahler's 8th Sym. and Schoenberg's *Gurrelieder* constituted proofs of his commanding technical skill, affirmed a fortiori by his assured presentation of the rhythmically and contrapuntally intricate 4th Sym. of Charles Ives. All these challenging scores Ozawa consuetudinarily conducted from memory—an astonishing feat in itself. He was married twice: 1st to the Japanese pianist Kyoko Edo, and then to a Eurasian, Vera Ilyan. He received an honorary doctorate in music from the Univ. of San Francisco in 1971, and one from the New England Cons. of Music in 1982. His remarkable career was the subject of the documentary film *Ozawa*, telecast by PBS in 1987.

P. Abbrev. for pedal (*P*; *Ped.*); pianoforte (*Pf.*). Dynamics: start softly, then suddenly loud (*pf*); soft (*p*); softer (*pp*); even softer (*ppp*); loud, then suddenly soft (*fp*); somewhat soft (*mp*); somewhat loud (*mf*).

pacato (It.). Peacefully, calmly.

pachanga, la. A Cuban dance step and song, originally performed by Havana bands playing drums, flutes, piano, and strings. The music resembles a merengue with a refrain; it emerged in the 1960s and superseded the MAMBO and CHA-CHA in popularity. The name means a wild party in Caribbean slang.

Pachelbel, Johann, celebrated German organist, pedagogue, and composer; b. Nuremberg (baptized), Sept. 1, 1653; d. there (buried), Mar. 9, 1706. He studied music in Nuremberg with Heinrich Schwemmer; received instruction in composition and instrumental performance from G. C. Wecker; pursued his academic studies at the local St. Lorenz school; also attended the lectures at the Auditorium Aegidianum. He then took courses briefly at the Univ. of Altdorf (1669–70), and served as organist at the Lorenzkirche there. He subsequently was accepted as a scholarship student at the Gymnasium Poeticum in Regensburg and took private music lessons with Kaspar Prentz. In 1673 he went to Vienna as deputy organist at St. Stephen's Cathedral. In 1677 he assumed the position of court organist in Eisenach. In 1678 he became organist at the Protestant Predigerkirche in Erfurt.

It was in Erfurt that he established his reputation as a master organist, composer, and teacher. He was a friend of the Bach family, and was the teacher of Johann Christoph

Bach, who in turn taught Johann Sebastian Bach. In 1681 Pachelbel married Barbara Gabler; she and their infant son died during the plague of 1683. He then married Judith Drommer in 1684; they had 5 sons and 2 daughters. In 1690 he accepted an appointment as Württemberg court musician and organist in Stuttgart. However, with the French invasion in the fall of 1692 he fled to Nuremberg; in Nov. of that year he became town organist in Gotha. In 1695 he succeeded Wecker as organist at St. Sebald in Nuremberg, a position he held until his death.

Pachelbel was one of the most significant predecessors of Bach. His liturgical organ music was of the highest order, particularly his splendid organ chorales. His nonliturgical keyboard music was likewise noteworthy, especially his fugues and variations; of the latter, his *Hexachordum Apollinis* of 1699 is extraordinary. He was equally gifted as a composer of vocal music. His motets, sacred concertos, and concertato settings of the Magnificat are fine examples of German church music.

He was a pioneer in notational symbolism of intervals, scales, and pitch levels arranged to correspond to the meaning of the words. Thus his setting of the motet *Durch Adams Fall* is accomplished by a falling figure in the bass; exaltation is expressed by a rising series of arpeggios in a major key; steadfast faith is conveyed by a repeated note; satanic evil is translated into an ominous figuration of a broken diminished-7th chord. Generally speaking, joyful moods are portrayed by major keys, mournful states of soul by minor keys, a practice which became a standard mode of expression through the centuries.

His organ works include numerous chorales; 95 Magnificat fugues; 26 nonliturgical fugues, 16 toccatas, 7 preludes, 6 fantasias, 6 ciacconas, 3 ricercars; the set of arias with variations called *Hexachordum Apollinis, sex arias exhibens . . . quam singulis suae sunt subjectae variationes* (1699); 17 suites, and chorale variations. Pachelbel is responsible for the (in)famous Canon and Gigue in D Major for 3 Violins and Basso Continuo, which remains extremely popular with modern audiences and has been publ. and republ. in numerous arrangements for various instruments; he also composed 7 string and basso continuo partitas. His vocal works include several German motets for 2 4-part choruses; 2 Latin motets: sacred German concertos; arias with basso continuo; music for Vespers: Magnificat settings; and 2 Masses.

Pacific 231. Symphonic movement by Honegger, 1924, 1st performed in Paris. The designation 231 indicates the number of wheels (2-3-1) on the American locomotive of the Pacific type. Honegger explained that he was as passionately infatuated with locomotives as other men are with horses or women. The score represents a highly effective if rudimentary representation of accelerated motion, beginning with 1 note to a bar, and progressing through 2, 3, 4, 5, 6, picking up the tempo as a locomotive gains speed. There is a lyric middle section before *Pacific 231* slows down to a stop.

Paderewski, Ignacy (Jan)

Celebrated Polish pianist and composer; b. Kurylowka, Podolia (Russian Poland), Nov. 18, 1860; d. N.Y., June 29, 1941. His father was an administrator of country estates; his mother died soon after his birth. From early childhood Paderewski was attracted to piano music; he received some musical instruction from Peter Sowinski, who taught him 4-hand arrangements of operas. His 1st public appearance was in a charity concert at the age of 11, when he played piano with his sister. His playing aroused interest among wealthy patrons, who took him to Kiev. He was then sent to Warsaw, where he entered the Cons., learned to play trombone, and joined the school band. He also continued serious studies of piano playing; his teachers at the Warsaw Cons. were Schlozer, Strobl, and Janotha.

In 1875 and 1877 he toured in provincial Russian towns with the Polish violinist Cielewicz; in the interim periods he took courses in composition at the Warsaw Cons., and upon graduation in 1878 he was engaged as a member of the piano faculty there. In 1880 he married a young music student named Antonina Korsak, but she died 9 days after giving birth to a child later that year. In 1882 he went to Berlin to study composition with Kiel; there he met Anton Rubinstein, who gave him encouraging advice and urged him to compose piano music. He resigned from his teaching job at the Warsaw Cons. and began to study orchestration in Berlin with Heinrich Urban.

While on a vacation in the Tatra Mountains (which inspired his *Tatra Album* for piano) he met the celebrated Polish actress Modjeska, who proposed to finance his further piano studies with Leschetizky in Vienna. Paderewski followed this advice and spent several years as a Leschetizky student. He continued his career as a concert pianist. In 1888 he gave his 1st Paris recital; later that year he played a concert in Vienna, both with excellent success. He also began receiving recognition as a composer. Anna Essipoff (who was married to Leschetizky) played his piano concerto in Vienna under the direction of Hans Richter. Paderewski made his London debut in 1890.

In 1891 he played for the 1st time in N.Y. and was acclaimed with an adulation rare for pianists; by some counts he gave 107 concerts in 117 days in N.Y. and other American cities and attended 86 dinner parties; his wit, already fully developed, made him a social lion in wealthy American salons. At one party it was reported that the hostess confused him with a famous polo player who was also expected to be a guest, and greeted him effusively. "No," Paderewski is supposed to have replied, "He is a rich soul who plays polo, and I am a poor Pole who plays solo." American spinsters beseeched him for a lock of his luxurious mane of hair; he invariably obliged, and when his valet observed that at this rate he would soon be bald, he said, "Not I, my dog." There is even a story related by a gullible biographer that Paderewski could charm beasts by his art and that a spider used to come down from the ceiling in Paderewski's lodgings in Vienna and sit at the piano every time Paderewski played a certain Chopin étude. Paderewski eclipsed even Caruso as an idol of the masses.

In 1890 he made a concert tour in Germany; he also toured South America, South Africa, and Australia. In 1898 he purchased a beautiful home, the Villa Riond-Bosson on Lake Geneva, Switzerland; in 1899 he married Helena Gorska, Baroness von Rosen. In 1900, by a deed of trust, Paderewski established a fund of $10,000 (the original trustees were William Steinway, H. L. Higginson, and William Mason), the interest from which was to be used for triennial prizes given "to composers of American birth without distinction as to age or religion" for works in the following categories: syms., concertos, and chamber music. In 1910, on the occasion of the centennial of Chopin's birth, Paderewski donated $60,000 for the construction of the Chopin Memorial Hall in Warsaw; in the same year he contributed $100,000 for the erection of the statue of King Jagiello in Warsaw, on the quinquecentennial of his victory over the Teutonic Knights in 1410. In 1913 he purchased a ranch in Paso Robles in Calif.

Although cosmopolitan in his culture, Paderewski remained a great Polish patriot. During the 1st World War he donated the entire proceeds from his concerts to a fund for the Polish people caught in the war between Russia and Germany. After the establishment of the independent Polish state, Paderewski served as its representative in Washington; in 1919 he was named prime minister of the Polish Republic, the 1st musician to occupy such a post in any country at any period. He took part in the Versailles Treaty conference; it was then that Prime Minister Clemenceau of France welcomed Paderewski with the famous, if possibly apocryphal, remark: "You, a famous pianist, a prime minister! What a comedown!" Paderewski resigned his post in late 1919.

He reentered politics in 1920 in the wake of the Russian invasion of Poland that year, when he became a delegate to the League of Nations; he resigned in 1921 and resumed his musical career. In 1922 he gave his 1st concert after a hiatus of many years at Carnegie Hall in N.Y. In 1939 he made his last American tour. Once more during his lifetime Poland was invaded, this time by both Germany and Russia; once more Paderewski was driven to political action. He joined the Polish government-in-exile in France and was named president of its parliament in early 1940. He returned to the U.S. later that year, a few months before his death. At the order of President Roosevelt, his body was given state burial in Arlington National Cemetery, pending the return of his remains to Free Poland.

Paderewski received many honors. He was awarded many degrees and also the Grand Cross of the French Legion of Honor (1922). A postage stamp with his picture was issued in Poland in 1919, and 2 postage stamps honoring him in the series "Men of Liberty" were issued in the U.S. in 1960.

As an artist Paderewski was a faithful follower of the Romantic school, which allowed free, well-nigh improvisatory declensions from the written notes, tempos, and dynamics; judged by 20th-century standards of precise rendering of the text, Paderewski's interpretations appear surprisingly free, but this very personal freedom of performance moved contemporary audiences to ecstasies of admiration. Also, Paderewski's virtuoso technique, which astonished his listeners, has been easily matched by any number of pianists of succeeding generations. Yet his position in the world of the performing arts remains undiminished by the later achievements of younger men and women pianists.

As a composer Paderewski also belongs to the Romantic school. At least one of his piano pieces, the *Menuet in G* (which is a movement of his set of *6 Humoresques* for piano), achieved enormous popularity. His other compositions, however, never sustained a power of renewal and were eventually relegated to the archives of unperformed music. His opera *Manru* (1897–1900), dealing with folk life in the Tatra Mountains, was produced in Dresden (1901) and was also performed by the Metropolitan Opera in N.Y. (1902). Another major work, the B-minor Sym., was 1st performed by the Boston Sym. Orch. in 1909. His other works included a Piano Concerto in A Minor (1888); *Fantaisie polonaise* for Piano and Orch. (1893); Violin Sonata (1880); songs; and solo piano works.

padiglione cinese (It., Chinese pavilion). JINGLING JOHNNY.

Padmâvatî. Opera-ballet by Roussel, 1923; premiered in Paris. The eponymous heroine is the wife of the king of

Ichitor in 13th-century India; it is specified in the cast of characters that she must possess "une grande beauté physique." The Mongol Khan, warring on Ichitor, is willing to conclude peace provided the King turns Padmâvatî over to him. To save her husband from a painful dilemma, she stabs him to death and, as behooves any traditional Hindu widow, dies with him on his funeral pyre. The score makes no attempt to imitate Indian rāga or introduce Indian instruments into the orch.; the idiom is modernist without being avant-garde.

padovana (It.). A fast dance whose name was used interchangeably with PAVANE, although the latter was a more stately dance.

paean. Song of praise or thanksgiving; often used to invoke the spirit of ancient Greece. The term is derived from the Greek *Paian*, a reverential epithet found in the Hymn to Apollo.

Paër, Ferdinando. See LEONORA.

Pagan Poem, A. Symphonic poem by Loeffler, 1907, for piano and orch., inspired by an eclogue of Virgil in which the central character is a sorceress; it was 1st performed in Boston. Its free mixture of archaic counterpoint and impressionistic colors pleased the public and the critics, until this type of synthetic paganism went out of fashion.

Paganini, Niccolo (Nicoló)

L egendary Italian violinist; b. Genoa, Oct. 27, 1782; d. Nice, May 27, 1840. His father, a poor dockworker, gave him his 1st lessons on the mandolin and violin; he then studied with Giovanni Servetto, a violinist in the theater orch. By this time the young Paganini was already composing; he also began to study harmony with Francesco Gnecco, and subsequently studied violin with Giacomo Costa, who arranged for him to play in local churches. His 1st documented public appearance took place at the church of S. Filippo Neri in 1794. It was about this time that he was indelibly impressed by the Franco-Polish violin virtuoso Auguste Frédéric Durand (later billed as Duranowski), who was a brilliant showman.

Having made phenomenal progress in his studies, he was sent to Parma in 1795 to study with Alessandro Rolla. Upon his arrival in Parma, Rolla is reported to have told him that there was nothing left to teach him and suggested that he study composition with Paër instead. Paër in turn sent him to his own teacher, Gasparo Ghiretti. After study with both Ghiretti and Paër, Paganini returned to Genoa (1796), appearing as a violinist in private performances. With Napoleon's invasion of Italy the family moved to Ramairone; by 1800 he was with his father in Livorno, where he gave concerts; he also appeared in Modena. They returned to Genoa in 1801; that same year, in the company of his older brother Carlo, who was also a violinist, he went to Lucca to play at the Festival of Santa Croce. His appearance there was a brilliant success. He settled there, becoming concertmaster of the national orch.

As a soloist Paganini captivated his auditors by his pyrotechnics. During an engagement in Livorno he so impressed a wealthy French merchant that he was rewarded with a valuable violin. With the arrival of Princess Elisa Baciocchi, the sister of Napoleon, as ruler of Lucca (1805), musical life there was reorganized. The 2 major orchs. were dissolved and replaced by a chamber orch. Paganini was retained as 2nd violinist, then made solo court violinist (1807). After the chamber orch. itself was dissolved (1808), he played in the court string quartet and also served as violin teacher to Prince Felix Baciocchi. Dissatisfied with his position, he broke with the court in Dec. 1809 and pursued a career as a virtuoso.

He came to national prominence in 1813 with a series of sensationally successful concerts in Milan. He subsequently toured throughout Italy, his renown growing from year to year and his vast technical resources maturing and augmenting such that he easily displaced the would-be rivals Lafont in Milan (1816) and Lipinski in Piacenza (1818). In 1824 he met the singer Antonia Bianchi, who became his mistress; she bore him a son, Achilles, in 1825, whom Paganini had legitimized in 1837. In 1827 he was made a Knight of the Golden Spur by Pope Leo XII. When he left Italy for his 1st tour abroad in 1828, he immediately gained a triumph with his opening concert in Vienna. He gave 14 concerts during his stay in Vienna, and was accorded the honorary title of chamber virtuoso by the Emperor and presented with the city's medal of St. Salvator. He made his 1st appearance in Berlin in 1829. He also played in Frankfurt, Darmstadt, Mannheim, and Leipzig. In 1831 he made his Paris and London debuts. He subsequently gave concerts throughout Great Britain (1831–33).

Paganini's artistic fortunes began to decline in 1834; his long-precarious health was ruined, but he managed to retain his fame and considerable wealth. He continued to give sporadic concerts in subsequent years, but he spent most of his time at his villa in Parma, making occasional visits to Paris. A critical illness in Oct. 1838 led to the loss of his voice; in Nov. 1839 he went to Nice for his health, and he died there the following spring.

Paganini's stupendous technique, power, and control, as well as his romantic passion and intense energy, made him the marvel of his time. He also was not above employing certain tricks of virtuosity, such as tuning up the A string of his violin by a semitone or playing the *Witches' Dance* on 1 string after severing the other 3 on stage, in sight of his audience, with a pair of scissors. He was also a highly effective composer for the violin, and gave regular performances of his works at his concerts with great success. Outstanding among his compositions are the violin works: the 24 solo caprices (1805); 6 concertos, *Moto perpetuo*, and other works with orch. Chamber: 3 string quartets (1800–1805); 21 quartets for various combinations of instruments (1806–20); and sonatas.

Page, Patti (born Clara Ann Fowler), American popular singer; b. Claremore, Okla., Nov. 8, 1927. She sang in a church choir in Tulsa; then appeared on a local radio program, adopting her stage name. She subsequently became a recording artist, her 1st hit being *Confess* (1948); gained fame with her recording of *Tennessee Waltz* in 1950, which became the official state song of Tenn.; in later years she made guest appearances in pop concerts with U.S. orchs.

page turner. A page turner is a necessary adjunct to the pianist in a chamber music ensemble, and to a piano accompanist in song recitals. He or she sits on the left hand side of the player and turns the music page, holding the right tip of the page delicately between the fingers. Under no circumstances should the page turner put his arm across the pianist's field of vision; any facial expression of aesthetic delight or, still worse, a grimace of disgust are impermissible; any attempt at humming, rhythmic breathing, or similar musical or unmusical sounds are criminal offenses. An ideal page turner must be unobtrusive, respectful, and helpful. The American composer Pauline Oliveros raised the social function of a page turner to the status of a full-fledged participant in a piece she wrote explicitly titled *Trio for Violin, Piano, and Page Turner*.

Pageant of P. T. Barnum, The. Orch. suite by D. Moore, 1926, 1st performed in Cleveland, glorifying the greatest showman/huckster of all time.

Pagliacci. Opera by Leoncavallo, 1892, 1st performed in Milan. Here, Leoncavallo made a deliberate effort to emulate the success of Mascagni's *Cavalleria Rusticana*, produced about 2 years before *Pagliacci*. He succeeded beyond all expectations; *Pagliacci* attained greater popularity than its model. Since the 2 operas are short, they are invariably paired like symmetric twins on operatic playbills and are commonly referred to as *Cav* and *Pag*. With these 2 works Leoncavallo and Mascagni inaugurated a realistic movement in opera that came to be known as *verismo*. The correct title of Leoncavallo's opera is *Pagliacci*, not *I pagliacci*, as is often listed; this is shown on the orig. MS score in the Library of Congress in Washington, D.C.

The story of *Pagliacci* is derived from an actual event, when an actor killed his unfaithful wife after a theatrical performance in which they both took part. (Leoncavallo's father was the judge at the murder trial.) The opera is set as a play within a play; a group of traveling actors performs in a booth in the center of the stage. The cast of characters is that of the COMMEDIA DELL'ARTE. Just before the curtain rises in the booth, the *pagliaccio* (clown) learns that his wife, who plays

Columbina in the play within the play, has a lover. He sings his famous aria, *Vesti la giubba* (with which Caruso moved a generation of operagoers to tears), lamenting the necessity of putting on a clown's garb when his heart is breaking. As the play progresses he begins to identify himself with the character of the drama. He demands to know the name of his wife's lover. Horrified at the reality of his actions, she refuses, and he stabs her to death. Her lover rushes in from the stage audience and is killed in turn. The clown then announces to the shocked spectators, "La commedia e finita" (the play is over).

Paik, Nam June, Korean-American avant-garde composer and experimenter in the visual arts; b. Seoul, July 20, 1932. He studied 1st at the Univ. of Tokyo, then took courses in music theory with Thrasybulos Georgiades in Munich and with Wolfgang Fortner in Freiburg im Breisgau. Turning toward electronics, he did experimental work at the Electronic Music Studio in Cologne (1958–60) and attended the summer seminars for new music at Darmstadt (1957–61). In his showings he pursues the objective of total art as the sum of integrated synesthetic experiences, involving all sorts of actions: walking, talking, dressing, undressing, drinking, smoking, moving furniture, engaging in quaquaversal commotion intended to demonstrate that any human or inhuman action becomes an artistic event through the power of volitional concentration of an ontological imperative.

Paik attracted attention at his duo recitals with the topless cellist (Madeline) Charlotte Moorman, at which he acted as a surrogate cello, with his denuded spinal column serving as the fingerboard for Moorman's cello bow, while his bare skin provided an area for intermittent pizzicati. About 1963 Paik began experimenting with videotape as a medium for sounds and images; his initial experiment in this field was *Global Groove*, a high-velocity collage of intermingled television bits, which included instantaneous commercials, fragments from news telecasts, and subliminal extracts from regular programs, subjected to topological alterations. He was also associated with the FLUXUS group.

Paik's list of works (some of them consisting solely of categorical imperatives) includes *Ommaggio a Cage* for piano demolition, breakage of raw eggs, spray painting of hands in jet black, etc. (1959); *Symphony for 20 Rooms* (1961); *Variations on a Theme of Saint-Saëns* for cello and piano, with the pianist playing *The Swan* while the cellist dives into an oil drum filled with water (1965); *Performable Music*, wherein the performer is ordered to make with a razor an incision of no less than 10 centimeters on his left forearm (1965);

Opera sextronique (1967); *Opera electronique* (1968); *Creep into the Vagina of a Whale* (c. 1969); *Young Penis Symphony*, a protrusion of 10 erectile phalluses through a paper curtain (c. 1970; 1st perf. at La Mamelle, San Francisco, 1975, under the direction of Ken Friedman, who also acted as 1 of the 10 performers). Of uncertain attribution is Sym. No. 3, which Paik delegated to Friedman, who worked on it in Saugus, Calif., the epicenter of the earthquake of Feb. 9, 1971, and of which the earthquake itself constituted the finale.

Paine, John Knowles, prominent American composer and pedagogue; b. Portland, Maine, Jan. 9, 1839; d. Cambridge, Mass., Apr. 25, 1906. His father ran a music store and conducted the band in Portland. He studied organ, piano, harmony, and counterpoint with Hermann Krotzschmar, then took courses with K. Haupt (organ), W. Wieprecht (orchestration and composition), and others in Berlin (1858–61); concurrently appeared as an organist and pianist in Germany and England. He settled in Boston, becoming organist of the West Church (1861); joined the faculty of Harvard Univ. (1862), where he also was organist at its Appleton Chapel; was prof. of music at Harvard (1875–1906), the 1st to hold such a position at a U.S. univ.; was made a member of the National Inst. of Arts and Letters (1898), and was awarded the honorary degrees of M.A. from Harvard (1869) and Mus.D. from Yale (1890).

He greatly distinguished himself as a teacher, serving as mentor to J. A. Carpenter, F. S. Converse, A. Foote, E. B. Hill, D. G. Mason, W. Spalding, and many others. He publ. *The History of Music to the Death of Schubert* (Boston, 1907). His compositions include 2 syms.: No. 1 (Boston, 1876); No. 2, *In the Spring* (Cambridge, 1880); *As You Like It*, overture (c. 1876); 2 symphonic poems: *The Tempest* (c. 1876) and *An Island Fantasy* (c. 1888); and Duo Concertante for Violin, Cello, and Orch. (c. 1877). He also composed chamber and choral works; songs; and piano and organ works.

Paint Your Wagon. Musical by Lerner and Loewe, 1951. The action takes place during the gold rush in Northern Calif., in a mid-19th-century mining camp. A prospector discovers gold, but suffers from loneliness and purchases 1 of the wives of a traveling Mormon at an auction. The gold is soon depleted, the town falls into decay, and she falls in love with another. The sentimental ballad *I Talk to the Trees* has musical vitality, as has the torch song *All for Him*.

paired notes. Two parallel series of notes played on the piano with 1 hand.

Paisiello, Giovanni. See BARBER OF SEVILLE, THE.

Pajama Game, The. Musical by Adler and Ross, 1954. The story rhapsodizes the efforts of workers at the Sleep-Tite Pajama Factory for a pay raise of 7 1/2 cents an hour. The score includes a memorable song in tango time called *Hernando's Hideaway* as well as *Hey There.*

Pal Joey. Musical by Rodgers and Hart, 1940. Pal Joey is a sleazy character employed as a dancer in a Chicago nightclub, but he is liked by the ladies. One of them, an affluent matron, sets him up in an apartment of his own, and he is willing to abandon his loving girlfriend for a life of luxury. Eventually both women give him up and he is left alone and penniless. Includes *Bewitched, Bothered, and Bewildered.*

Palestrina. Opera by Pfitzner, 1917, to his own libretto, 1st performed in Munich. It is subtitled *Musikalische Legende*, to account for its notion that Palestrina wrote his famous *Missa Pape Marcelli* at the behest of the angels in order to convince the skeptical members of the Council of Trent that POLYPHONY is, and ought to be, an integral part of church music. The score of *Palestrina* has its moments of academic grandeur.

Palestrina, Giovanni Pierluigi da

Great Italian composer; b. probably in Palestrina, near Rome, 1525 or 1526; d. Rome, Feb. 2, 1594. In his letters he customarily signed his name as Giovanni Petraloysio. He is 1st listed as a choirboy at S. Maria Maggiore in 1537; it is likely that he studied with each of the maestros of the period, Robin Mallapert, one Robert, and Firmin Lebel. In 1544 he was appointed organist of the cathedral of S. Agapit in Palestrina, where his duties also included teaching music to the canons and choirboys.

On June 12, 1547, he married Lucrezia Gori; they had 3 sons, Rodolfo (1549–72), Angelo (1551–75), and Iginio (1558–1610). In 1550 the bishop of Palestrina, Cardinal Giovanni Maria Ciocchi del Monte, was elected pope, taking the name of Julius III. On Sept. 1, 1551, he appointed Palestrina maestro of the Cappella Giulia in succession to Mallapert; Palestrina dedicated his 1st book of masses to him in 1554. In 1555 the pope rewarded him by making him a member of the Cappella Sistina even though he was a married man; he was admitted without taking the entrance examination and without receiving the approval of the other singers.

In Sept. 1555 Pope Paul IV dismissed Palestrina and 2 other singers after invoking the celibacy rule of the chapel, although he granted each of them a small pension; a month later Palestrina became maestro di cappella of the great church of St. John Lateran, where his son Rodolfo joined him as a chorister. Palestrina's tenure was made difficult by inadequate funds for the musical establishment, and he resigned his post in July 1560. From 1561 to 1566 he was maestro di cappella of S. Maria Maggiore. In 1562–63 the Council of Trent took up the matter of sacred music. Out of its discussions arose a movement to advance the cause of intelligibility of sacred texts when set to music. Palestrina's role with this Council remains a matter of dispute among historians, but his *Missa Pape Marcelli* is an outstanding example of a number of its reforms.

From 1564 he was also in charge of the music at the summer estate of Cardinal Ippolito II d'Este in Tivoli, near Rome. He apparently took up a full-time position in the Cardinal's service from 1567 to 1571. From 1566 to 1571 he likewise taught at the Seminario Romano, where his sons Rodolfo and Angelo were students. In 1568 the court of Emperor Maximilian II offered him the position of imperial choirmaster in Vienna, but Palestrina demanded so high a salary that the offer was tacitly withdrawn. In Apr. 1571, upon the death of Giovanni Animuccia, he resumed his post as maestro of the Cappella Giulia. In

1575 his salary was increased to forestall his move to S. Maria Maggiore. In 1577, at the request of Pope Gregory XIII, Palestrina and Annibale Zoilo began the revision of the plainsong of the Roman Gradual and Antiphoner. Palestrina never completed his work on this project; the revision was eventually completed by others and publ. as *Editio Medicaea* in 1614.

In 1580, having lost his eldest sons and his wife to the plague, Palestrina made a decision to enter the priesthood; he soon changed his mind, however, and instead married Virginia Dormoli, the widow of a wealthy furrier, in 1581. In succeeding years he devoted much time to managing her fortune while continuing his work as a musician. In 1583 he was tendered an offer to become maestro at the court of the

COURTESY OF THE NEW YORK PUBLIC LIBRARY

Giovanni Palestrina

Duke of Mantua, but again his terms were rejected as too high. In 1584 he publ. his settings of the Song of Solomon. In 1593 he began plans to return to Palestrina as choirmaster of the cathedral, but he was overtaken by death early the next year. He was buried in the Cappella Nuova of old St. Peter's Church.

With his great contemporaries Byrd and Lassus, Palestrina stands as one of the foremost composers of his age. He mastered the polyphonic style of the Franco-Flemish school, creating works of unsurpassing beauty and technical adroitness. His sacred music remains his most glorious achievement. Highly prolific, he composed 104 masses, over 375 motets, 68 offertories, over 65 hymns, 35 Magnificats, over 140 madrigals (both sacred and secular), Lamentations, litanies, and Psalms.

palimpsest. In musical semantics the term *palimpsest* may be used as a substitution for an intentionally erased composition. This erasure may be complete or partial, with some elements of the original idea left under the sonic surface. The hidden design may be discovered by intervallic analysis, comparable to the use of ultraviolet rays in detecting the old text in a parchment covered by a newer piece of writing.

palindrome. Palindromic words and sentences do not change when they are read backward. Reger, whose last name is a palindrome, replied wittily to an admirer who complained that he could see only his back while he conducted a concert: "I am no different front or back." Musical palindromes are synonymous with retrograde movements. In a palindromic section in Berg's opera *Lulu*, the music revolves backward to depict the story of Lulu's incarceration and escape. Samplers of palindromic canons are found in the author's *Thesaurus of Scales and Melodic Patterns*.

palingenesis. The meaning of the word *palingenesis* is "rebirth," and it is parasynonymous with METEMPSYCHOSIS. In modern musical usage palingenesis corresponds to a reprise, with the important difference that the original material is not recapitulated literally but appears metempsy-

chotically in a form as dissimilar from its progenitor as a reincarnated cat is from its former human avatar. Palingenesis is a particularly convenient term to designate an electronically altered sonic substance, or a topologically metamorphosed thematic idea.

palmas (Sp.). Clapping of hands, as found in Latin American and other dances.

palpitant (Fr.). Trembling, palpitating.

Pampeanas. A series of works by Ginastera, inspired by the pampas, the Argentinian prairie; the 1st of these works is for violin and piano (1947), the 2nd for cello and piano (1950), and the 3rd for orch., under the specific title *Pastoral Sym.* (1954).

Panama Hattie. Musical by C. Porter, 1940. The eponymous heroine is a top canary at a low-grade cabaret in the Panama Canal Zone who is in love with a Philadelphia blue-blooded official. She makes the grade when she thwarts a plot to blow up the canal locks. She also acquires manners and eventually marries her Philadelphia friend. Among the best tunes are *I've Still Got My Health, Let's Be*

Buddies, Make It Another Old-Fashioned, Please, and *I'm Throwing a Ball Tonight.*

Panambi. Ballet by Ginastera, 1940, 1st performed in Buenos Aires; an orch.l suite from it was performed in Buenos Aires 3 years earlier. The ballet depicts the folkways of the Indians of Argentina; the suite ends with the effective *Dance of the Warriors.*

pandeiro (Port.; Sp. *pandero*). TAMBOURINE.

pandiatessaron. This is a vertical column consisting of perfect 4ths (from the Greek *diatessaron*, the interval of a 4th). The pandiatessaron contains all 12 notes of the tempered scale and represents a dodecaphonic integration of quartal melodies.

pandiatonicism. A system of diatonic harmony making use of all 7 degrees of the scale in dissonant combinations; the functional importance of the primary triads, however, remains undiminished in pandiatonic harmony. The term was coined by the author in 1937. Pandiatonicism possesses both tonal and modal aspects, with the distinct preference for major keys. The earliest pandiatonic extension was the added major 6th over the tonic major triad. A cadential chord of the tonic major 7th is also of frequent occurrence.

Independently from the development of pandiatonicism in serious music, American jazz musicians adopted it as a practical device. Concluding chords in piano improvisations in jazz are usually pandiatonic, containing the tonic, dominant, mediant, submediant and supertonic, with the triad in open harmony in the bass topped by a series of perfect 4ths. In C major such chords would be, from the bass up, C–G–E–A–D–G. It is significant that all the components of this pandiatonic complex are members of the natural harmonic series. With C as the fundamental generator, G is the 3rd partial, E the 5th partial, D the 9th, B the 15th and A the 27th. The perfect 4th is excluded both theoretically and practically, for it is not a member of the harmonic series— an interesting concordance of actual practice and acoustical considerations.

With the dominant in the bass, a complete succession of 4ths, one of them an augmented 4th, can be built: G–C–F–B–E–A–D–G, producing a satisfying pandiatonic complex. When the subdominant is in the bass, the most euphonious result is obtained by a major triad in open position, F–C–A, in the low register, and E–B–D–G in the upper register. Polytriadic combinations are natural resources of pandiatonicism, with the dominant combined with the tonic, e.g., C–G–E–D–G–B, making allowance for a common tone; dominant over the subdominant, as in the complex F–C–A–D–G–B, etc.

True polytonality cannot be used in pandiatonicism, since all the notes are in the same mode. Pedal points are particularly congenial to the spirit of pandiatonicism, always following the natural spacing of the component notes, using large intervals in the bass register and smaller intervals in the treble. The aesthetic function of pandiatonicism is to enhance the resources of triadic harmony; that is the reason why the superposition of triads, including those in minor, are always productive of a resonant diatonic bitonality. Although pandiatonicism has evolved from tertian foundations, it lends itself to quartal and quintal constructions with satisfactory results. Pandiatonicism is a logical medium for the techniques of neoclassicism. Many sonorous usages of pandiatonicism can be found in the works of Debussy, Ravel, Stravinsky, Casella, Malipiero, Vaughan Williams, Copland, and R. Harris.

pandora. A plucked chordophone akin to a bass cittern, with fixed frets and 6 double courses; it is reported in the period between 1560 and 1670; commonly used in BASSO CONTINUO. The name was also applied to the theorbo-lute.

pandura (Sp.). BANDOLA.

pandurria (Sp.). BANDURRIA.

panpentatonicism. By analogy with pandiatonicism, which denotes a free use of the 7 diatonic degrees, panpentatonicism grants a similar dispensation to the 5 notes of the pentatonic scale. Consecutive 4ths and 5ths are frequent contrapuntal resources. Since the leading tone is missing in the pentatonic scale, plagal cadences are the only available endings. Panpentatonic tone clusters are more euphonious than the pandiatonic ones; when projected against a perfect 5th in the bass, they create an attractive sonority of a modernistic panpentatonic chinoiserie.

panpipes. The most ancient of wind instruments, consisting of several reeds of different sizes that are bound together; its name is explained by the legend that the god Pan invented it. The panpipes is the prototype of the mouth organ, with reeds arranged to produce a continuous diatonic scale. The panpipes exist in all primitive cultures. In South American countries they are known under various names:

antara in Peru, *rondador* in Ecuador, *capador* in Colombia, and *sico* in Bolivia. In China primitive panpipes are arranged in 2 mutually exclusive whole-tone scales, one of which is regarded as a masculine symbol and the other as feminine.

pantaleon. Large cimbalom (hammered dulcimer) invented by the great performer Pantaleon Hebenstreit (1667–1750); it was given its name by Louis XIV in 1705. The instrument was appreciated for its breadth of dynamic variation; it was eventually superseded by the new fortepiano, although it lent its name to the new instrument for a brief time.

pantomime (Grk., all-imitating). 1. A balletlike performance without speech or singing, in which the action is suggested by gestures and choreography. 2. In the U.K., a pageant holiday play with songs, slapstick; an outgrowth of MUSIC HALL; often shortened to *panto*.

pantonality. Schoenberg's preferred synonym for ATONALITY, denoting the possibility of all tonalities or the conscious absence of a single, preeminent tonality. Pantonality is almost synonymous with OMNITONALITY, the only difference being that pantonality includes atonal melodic progressions and uninhibited dissonant textures, while omnitonality tends to enhance the basic sense of tonality.

pantoum. A Malaysian word describing a particular form of a poem popular in Indochina. In his search for exotic descriptions, Ravel attached it to the scherzo in his Piano Trio; he himself borrowed it from a poem by Victor Hugo.

Panufnik, Andrzej, eminent Polish-born English conductor and composer; b. Warsaw, Sept. 24, 1914; d. London, Oct. 27, 1991. His father was a Polish manufacturer of string instruments, his mother an Englishwoman who studied violin in Warsaw. He began his musical training with his mother; after studying composition with Sikorski at the Warsaw Cons. (diploma 1936) he took conducting lessons with Weingartner at the Vienna Academy of Music (1937–38); he subsequently completed his training with Gaubert in Paris, and studied in London (1938–39). He returned to Warsaw in 1939, remaining there during the Nazi occupation, playing piano in the underground; after the liberation he conducted the Krakow Phil. (1945–46) and the Warsaw Phil. (1946–47); he then left his homeland in protest of the Communist regime (1954), settling in England, where he became a natu-

ralized British citizen (1961). After serving as music director of the City of Birmingham Sym. Orch. (1957–59), he devoted himself to composition. His wife, Scarlett Panufnik, publ. *Out of the City of Fear* (London, 1956), recounting his flight from Poland. In 1988 he appeared as a guest conductor of his own works with the N.Y. Chamber Sym. and in 1990 with the Chicago Sym. Orch.

In his early years he belonged to the vanguard group of Polish composers. He made use of advanced techniques, including quarter tones, and made certain innovations in notation; in several of his orch. works he left blank spaces in the place of rests to indicate inactive instrumental parts. In his later music he adopted a more circumspect idiom—expressive, direct, and communicative. His compositions to 1944 were destroyed during the Warsaw uprising. He composed 10 symphonies and other orch.l works, 4 string quartets, other chamber and piano works, as well as choral works.

Papillons. Piano suite of 12 pieces by Schumann, 1831, publ. as op. 2; they are descriptive of fleeting butterflies in feminine disguises. Schumann was inspired by the Romantic novel *Flegeljahre* (Years of Indiscretion) by Jean-Paul Richter. The lambent motive might well reflect Schumann's own indiscretion, for it is based on the notes A, E-flat, C, and B, spelling, in German nomenclature (where E-flat is Es, i.e., S; and B is H), the name of the town of Asch where he experienced his 1st infatuation. He used the same theme in his later piano work *Carnaval*.

parable aria. A type of aria, much in vogue in the 18th century, in which the singer expresses his emotions by way of a parable or metaphor. A famous example is the protestation of 1 of the ladies in Mozart's *Così fan tutte* that she would remain as firm as a rock in resisting temptation; the rock is the crux of the metaphor in the parable.

Parables. Orch.l work by Martinů, 1959, premiered by the Boston Sym. Orch. The 3 movements reflect the parables of sculpture, a garden, and a labyrinth.

Parade. "Realistic ballet" by Satie, 1917; premiered in Paris. It was in the form of a vaudeville show, a series of disconnected scenes with imitations of early jazz. With the collaboration of Cocteau and Picasso (whose designs are decidedly cubist), Satie created a model for dadaist art while inspiring almost as much of an uproar as Stravinsky's *The Rite of Spring* had in 1913.

paradiddle. A rhythmic drumroll consisting of 4 rapid, even notes struck with the right and left hands alternately. *Paradiddle flam-flam*, a paradiddle followed by 2 notes of twice the value, e.g., 4 16th notes followed by 2 8th notes.

parallel harmony. Parallel motion of chords, as in medieval fauxbourdon and 20th-century impressionism. Traditional harmony prohibited the use of consecutive octaves and 5ths, and parallel chord formations, even when no such forbidden intervals were consecutively used (e.g., the 2nd and 3rd inversion of the dominant 7th chord).

parallel intervals. See CONSECUTIVE INTERVALS.

parallel motion. Voice-leading in harmony or counterpoint in which intervals move in the same direction. In traditional harmony, parallel 3rds and 6ths are recommended, while parallel 5ths and octaves are forbidden; parallel 4ths are acceptable only in certain eras and under specific conditions.

parameter. A term denoting any one of the 4 principal aspects of musical sound, i.e., pitch, duration, dynamic level, and timbre.

paraphrases and transcriptions. An adaptation or rearrangement of a vocal or instrumental piece for a different medium, sometimes with variations. When music became a democratic art in the 19th century, not only the aristocracy but the middle class had pianos or harmoniums in their drawing rooms, and professional musicians found a new outlet for their wares. Music was brought to the people; opera and sym. had to be reduced to manageable proportions to be made accessible to the masses. Popular arias, marches, and ballet numbers from favorite operas were arranged by highly capable musicians for the piano. Amateur adults and young children were offered arrangements of classical masterpieces that were not only musically adequate but also provided a social means of musical communication and entertainment. German publishers put out reams of musical literature for piano 4-hands or for piano solo.

Some great pianists, themselves composers of stature, were not averse to participate in this democratization of music. Liszt made piano transcriptions of opera and symphonic compositions (includes the complete Beethoven syms.), and of songs of Schubert and Schumann; he also wrote fantasies on the motives of current opera favorites. Liszt's teacher, and Beethoven's pupil, Carl Czerny, took time off from writing his myriad piano exercises to publish

arrangements of operatic airs. Such arrangements pursued an eminently practical aim, namely to acquaint music lovers with the operatic and symphonic music of the day.

Liszt introduced semantic distinctions among various categories of transcriptions. The most literal arrangement was, in his terminology, an *Übertragung* (transference); a more idiomatic transference was the *Bearbeitung* (reworking). The next more liberal arrangement was a *transcription*; then followed a FANTASIA, sometimes further expanded as a *free fantasia* or *romantic fantasia*. An even more unrestricted type of free fantasia Liszt liked to call *reminiscences*, things remembered from listening to the music of this or that opera or sym. As an auxiliary category Liszt introduced the term *illustrations* for recurring thematic allusion. Finally, paraphrases united all characteristics of an arrangement, transcription, fantasy, or romantic fantasy, illustration, or reminiscence. To indicate the publishing category of a given transcription, Liszt sometimes used the word *Klavierpartitur* (piano score).

pardessus de viole (Fr.). Treble VIOLA D'AMORE.

Pardon de Ploërmel, Le. Opera by Meyerbeer, 1859, 1st performed in Paris. As a young shepherd takes his bride to their wedding, a local warlock tells him that he can find a buried treasure if he lives a year in total solitude. His bride, shaken by his sudden disappearance, finds refuge in that wonderful operatic convenience, madness. After a year has passed the shepherd has discovered no treasure. He meets his beloved at the dam just as a bolt of lightning destroys it and threatens her. He leaps to rescue her, and she immediately recovers her reason. He realizes that the treasure he sought was she; they finally repair to Ploërmel for their delayed wedding; thus he is pardoned for his sin of avarice. Despite the libretto, absurd even by operatic standards, the opera enjoyed considerable success for a time, thanks mainly to the effective coloratura part for the heroine, vouchsafing her a lot of trills and thrills.

Parerga and Paralipomena. Like Schopenhauer, who published fragments of his philosophical writings under the high-sounding name *Parerga and Paralipomena*, R. Strauss gathered some residual materials from his *Symphonia domestica* and incorporated them in a work commissioned by the amputated pianist Paul Wittgenstein, denominated *Parergon zur Symphonia domestica* and scored for piano left-hand and orch. While such creative thrift is justified when Schopenhauer or Strauss practice it, collections and arrangements of *disjecta membra* put together by composers of lesser endowment, and particularly those whose technical progress was arrested at the abecedarian or analphabetic *niveau*, are clearly objectionable.

Parergon zur Symphonia domestica. Work for piano left-hand and orch. by R. Strauss, 1925, premiered in Dresden. *Parergon* means leftovers. See PARERGA AND PARALIPOMENA.

Paride ed Elena. Opera by Gluck, 1770, 1st performed in Vienna. The libretto is based on the classical tale of Paris of Troy who kidnaps Helen, the beautiful wife of the King of Sparta. The legend has been set to music by a number of composers. This is the 3rd opera by Gluck, after *Orfeo ed Euridice* and *Alceste*, in which he formulated his basic principle that music should be the handmaid of the text rather than its mistress.

Paris Symphonies. This is the traditional classification for Haydn's syms. Nos. 82, 83, 84, 85, 86, and 87, written especially for performances in Paris in 1786.

Parisina. Opera by Donizetti, 1833, premiered in Florence; the libretto is based on Byron's poem. In this tragic romance, Parisina loves her stepson. The young lovers try to flee but the enraged cuckold intercepts them and has his son executed. Parisina dies when she sees the lifeless body of her beloved.

Parker, Charlie (Charles Christopher, Jr.), noted African-American jazz alto saxophonist, also called Bird or Yardbird; b. Kansas City, Kans., Aug. 29, 1920; d. N.Y., Mar. 12, 1955. He was self-taught, on an alto saxophone given to him at age 13 by his mother; at 15 he left school and became a professional musician. He was a member of Jay McShann's band (1937–44), with which he toured and made his 1st recordings (1941); after performing in Earl Hines's band (1942–44), which included Dizzy Gillespie and other young jazz artists, he played in Billy Eckstine's band (1944–45); after work they would meet in a club called Minton's, and there gradually evolved the new style of BEBOP. Parker became the acknowledged leader of this style as he developed an improvising technique characterized by virtuosic speed, intense tone, complex harmonies, and florid melodies

Charlie Parker

COURTESY OF OTTO F. HESS COLLECTION, THE NEW YORK PUBLIC LIBRARY

having irregular rhythmic patterns and asymmetric phrase lengths.

After the mid-1940s he usually worked in small combos led either by himself or by 1 of the other members of the small, close-knit circle of boppers; occasionally he also worked with larger ensembles (including a string orch. for which he wrote the arrangements). As a composer he usually worked with the 12-bar blues patterns (but always in an unstereotyped manner; he made 175 blues recordings, all markedly different) or with chord progressions of well-known standards: his *Ornithology*, for instance, is based on the progressions of *How High the Moon.*

He achieved a prominence that made him a living legend (a leading N.Y. club, Birdland, was named after him); his life, though, in addition to being tragically short, was plagued by the consequences of narcotics addiction (acquired when he was in his mid-teens) and alcoholism. He had a nervous breakdown in 1946 and was confined at Camarillo State Hospital in Calif. for 6 months; because of suspected narcotics possession, the N.Y. City police rescinded his cabaret license in 1951, thereby denying him the right to work in N.Y. clubs; he attempted suicide twice in 1954, and subsequently entered Bellevue Hospital in N.Y. He died in the N.Y. apartment of a fervent admirer, the Baroness Pannonica de Koenigswarter, the sister of Lord Rothschild. Despite the difficulties of his personal life, Parker's music has survived and become part of the essential jazz canon; it has also been interpreted as rebellious commentary on the place of the African-American during latter-day U.S. segregation. His life was the subject of the 1988 film *Bird.*

Parker, Horatio (William), eminent American composer and pedagogue; b. Auburndale, Mass., Sept. 15, 1863; d. Cedarhurst, N.Y., Dec. 18, 1919. He studied piano with John Orth, theory with Emery, and composition with Chadwick in Boston; subsequently went to Germany, where he took courses in organ and composition with Rheinberger in Munich (1882–85); under his tutelage he wrote a cantata, *King Trojan* (1885). Returning to the U.S., he settled in N.Y. and taught at the cathedral schools of St. Paul and St. Mary (1886–90), at the General Theological Seminary (1892), and at the National Cons. of Music (1892–93); was organist and choirmaster at St. Luke's (1885–87), St.

Andrew's (1887–88), and the Church of the Holy Trinity (1888–93); in 1893 he went to Boston as organist and choirmaster at Trinity Church, remaining there until 1902. He attracted attention with the 1st performance of his oratorio *Hora novissima* (N.Y., 1893), in which he demonstrated his mastery of choral writing, while his harmonic and contrapuntal style remained securely tied to German practices. In 1894 he was engaged as a prof. of theory at Yale Univ.; in 1904 he became dean of its School of Music, and remained there until his death.

Many American composers received the benefit of his excellent instruction; among them was Ives, who kept his sincere appreciation of Parker's teaching long after he renounced Parker's conservative traditions. In 1895 he founded the New Haven Sym. Orch., which he conducted until 1918. Parker conducted performances of his works in England in 1900 and 1902; received an honorary degree of Mus.Doc. at Cambridge Univ. in 1902. Returning to the U.S., he served as organist and choirmaster at the collegiate church of St. Nicholas in Boston from 1902 to 1910. He continued to compose industriously, without making any concessions to the emerging modern schools of composition; his choral works are particularly notable.

In 1911 his opera *Mona* won the $10,000 prize offered by the Metropolitan Opera in N.Y., and was produced there in 1912; he also won a prize offered by the National Federation of Women's Clubs for his 2nd opera, *Fairyland*, which was produced in Los Angeles (1915). Neither of the operas possessed enough power to survive in the repertoire. Other important works include orch. works, including *Regulus*, overture heroïque (1884), Sym. in C major (Munich, 1885), *A Northern Ballad*, symphonic poem (Boston, 1899), and the Organ Concerto (Boston, 1902); chamber music, including a string quartet (1885), suite (trio) for piano, violin, and cello (1893), string quintet (1894), and suite for piano and violin (1894); secular and religious choral music; songs; and many organ works, including the E-flat sonata (op. 65).

parlando (or parlante) (It.). "Speaking"; singing with clear and marked enunciation. In piano playing, *parlante* calls for a clear, crisp *non legato*.

parody. 1. A parasitic literary or musical genre that emerged in the 18th century and flourished in the 19th, particularly in opera; it usually followed on the heels of a successful or at least notorious theatrical production. Weber's opera *Der Freischütz* was lampooned in England as "a new muse-sick-all and see-nick performance from the new German uproar, by the celebrated Bunny-bear." Wagner's *Tannhäuser*, which suffered a notorious debacle at its 1st Paris production, engendered a number of French parodies, among them 1 entitled *Ya-Meine Herr, Cacophonie de l'Avenir*. Occasionally a parody anticipates the main event. One such parody, *Tristanderl und Süssholde*, was produced in Munich before *Tristan und Isolde* itself. These anti-Wagner parodies were the last of the species.

2. (from Grk. *para + aidein*, side-song) A type of Mass or motet composition, common in the Renaissance, in which composers borrowed whole pieces or parts of pieces (usually motets) and built new pieces around them. As used in old music theory, this term meant "like something else" and was quite devoid of the contemporary sense of travesty. This method is distinct from the cantus firmus and paraphrase types, which borrow one melodic line.

Parsifal. "Sacred festival drama" by Wagner, 1882, produced in Bayreuth less than a year before his death. The libretto, by Wagner himself, is drawn from the legend of the Holy Grail, the chalice from which Jesus drank at the Last Supper. The religious symbolism of *Parsifal* requires some explanation. Before the opera begins, Amfortas, the King of the Grail, allows himself to be seduced by the sorceress Kundry in the service of Klingsor, the magician, who inflicts a grievous wound on the King. The wound can be healed only by the touch of the sacred spear, and only one pure of heart who has acquired wisdom through pity can take the spear away from Klingsor, who has it in his possession.

Young Parsifal satisfies these requirements; he is sent by the Knights of the Holy Grail to Klingsor's domain. Realizing the danger, Klingsor mobilizes a gardenful of flower maidens to lure and confuse Parsifal, and as a further inducement to him Kundry kisses him on the lips. This elicits from Parsifal the most unexpected response in all operatic literature, "Amfortas! The spear wound!" Whatever hematological connection may exist between Kundry's lips and the King's wound, she instantly grasps its significance and suddenly changes from a sorceress into a humble supplicant for salvation, having been cursed for laughing at Jesus on his way to Golgotha. Parsifal seizes the spear which Klingsor hurls at him and makes the sign of the cross with it; the power of the Christian symbol utterly destroys Klingsor's kingdom. Parsifal makes his way to the Temple of the Holy Grail, where Kundry precedes him. He is named King of the Grail. Amfortas bares his wound and Parsifal heals it with the touch of the sacred spear. Parsifal then raises the Holy

Grail in the air; at the sight of it Kundry collapses and dies, free of her curse at last.

In *Parsifal* Wagner preserves his system of leading motives, but because of the religious content of the work, he also makes use of chorales and other sacred melodies. The harmonic and contrapuntal structure is purer and simpler than in Wagner's *Ring* tetralogy and his other music dramas.

Parsons, Gram (born Cecil Connor), American country-rock singer, guitarist, and songwriter; b. Winter Haven, Fla., Sept. 5, 1946; d. Joshua Tree National Monument, Calif., Sept. 19, 1973. He twanged the guitar in Georgia bands and somehow managed to take time out to study theology at Harvard; it was in those patrician surroundings that he organized a country-rock group that he called the International Submarine Band. He also contributed to the Byrds in their famous album *Sweetheart of the Rodeo*, with his songs *Hickory Wind* and *100 Years from Now*. In 1968 he formed the Flying Burrito Brothers, which recorded his greatest success, *The Gilded Palace of Sin*. There followed *Burrito Deluxe* and *The Last of the Red Hot Burritos*. Just before dying of immoderate drug use he composed his last song, ironically titled *Grievous Angel*.

part. 1. The series of tones written for and executed by a voice or instrument, either as a solo or together with other voices or instruments. 2. A division of a homophonic movement devoted to the exposition of 1 melody or musical idea; like the 2-part and 3-part song forms.

Pärt, Arvo, remarkably inventive Estonian composer; b. Paide, Sept. 11, 1935. He studied composition with Heino Eller at the Tallinn Cons., graduating in 1963; from 1958 to 1967 he was attached to the music division of Estonian Radio. In 1980 he emigrated to the West, settling in West Berlin (1982). He began to compose in a traditional manner, writing instrumental pieces in a neo-Baroque idiom, strict to form, freely dissonant in harmony; under the influence of Western musical modernism he gradually levitated toward the empyreal emporium of empiric sonorism without renouncing, however, the historic foundation of tonality. The spectrum of his musical vocabulary extends from abecedarian minimalism to quaquaversal polytonality, from impressionistic pointillism to austere serialism. One of his specialties is a technique he calls "tintinnabula," in which he applies shifting phases of a given chord.

Pärt was the 1st Estonian composer to use the authentic Schoenbergian method of composition with 12 different tones related only to one another to form melodic and harmonic dodecaphonic structures. He applied it in his arresting *Nekrolog*, dedicated to the victims of the Holocaust. Extending the concept of integral dodecaphony, he makes use of pandiatonic and panpentatonic tone clusters, culminating in the formation of a Brobdingnagian blob of white noise. He occasionally resorts to aleatory proceedings; also harks upon occasion back to historic antecedents in applying the austere precepts of ARS ANTIQUA. In this, Pärt commends himself as a true *Homo ludens*, a musician playing a diversified game. His orch.l works include *Nekrolog*, dedicated to the victims of fascism (1960), and 3 symphonies: No. 1, *Polyphonic* (1963); No. 2 (1966); No. 3 (1971). He also composed for other orch.l and chamber ensembles; vocal works; and works for solo piano.

part music. Concerted or harmonized vocal music.

part singing. The singing of PART MUSIC, usually without instrumental accompaniment.

part song. A homophonic composition for at least 3 voices in harmony, without accompaniment, and for equal or mixed voices; a melody with choral harmony with any reasonable number of voices to each part.

partbooks. Separate parts for singers or instrumentalists, in common use in the 16th century. Singers were seated around a table, each with an individual partbook, coordinating by subtle signals, anticipation of breath, etc., without using a general score. The practice of PART SINGING from partbooks has been recently revived by various English singing groups.

Partch, Harry, innovative American composer, performer, and instrument maker; b. Oakland, Calif., June 24, 1901; d. San Diego, Sept. 3, 1974. Largely autodidact, he began experimenting with instruments capable of producing fractional intervals, which led him to the formulation of a 43-tone scale; he expounded his findings in his book *Genesis of a Music* (1949; 2nd ed., rev. and augmented, 1974). He built or adapted instruments to fit his theories and to compose with; among these are a viola with elongated neck, a chromelodeon (reed organ), kitharas with 72 strings, harmonic canons with 44 strings, boos (made of giant Philippine bamboo reeds), cloud-chamber bowls, blow-boys (a pair of bellows with an attached automobile horn), etc. As more instruments were added to his ensemble, Partch revised earlier works to avail himself of new possibilities while adjusting to the changes in or elimination of an instrument.

Seeking intimate contact with American life, he wandered across the country, collecting indigenous expressions of folkways, inscriptions on public walls, recording speech-song, etc., for texts in his 1930s and 1940s works; some of these travels were described in *Bitter Music* (1935–36). Partch's later theatrical pieces were based on Greek tragedy and other mythological sources. Partch wrote a wide variety of compositions, mostly for ensembles of instruments of his own design, based on his own microtonal scale.

parte (It.). Part. *Colla parte*, a direction to accompanists to follow yieldingly and discreetly the solo part or voice.

parterre (Fr., parquet). The last rows in a concert hall.

Parthenia in-violata. An English collection of pieces for virginals and bass viol, 1614; the title is based on that of the 1st printed collection of virginals music, publ. a year earlier (works by William Byrd, John Bull, and Orlando Gibbons). The only complete copy of *Parthenia in-violata* is in the N.Y. Public Library.

partial stop. A half stop.

partials (partial tones). See HARMONICS.

particella (It., particle). A reduced score. Some composers prefer writing down symphonic scores or even operas in arrangements for 2 or 3 staves: 1 for woodwinds, 1 for brass, 1 or 2 for strings, with the vocal part, if any, in small printing on top. A vocal score of a choral work such as an oratorio is usually published in the form of particella, with the orch.l part arranged for piano. Schubert and Wagner wrote some of their works 1st in particella form. Prokofiev systematically adopted this abridged form of orch.l writing and engaged a knowledgeable assistant to convert such a particella into a full orch. score according to indications of instrumentation given by him. A major part of the musical legacy of Ives consists of piano arrangements with instrumental cues written in. Stravinsky composed *The Rite of Spring* 1st for piano 4-hands, which is essentially a particella. Many publishers now issue abridged scores for conductors, often with optional instrumental parts written in.

partie (Fr.). Instrumental or vocal part.

partimento (It., division). The 17th- and 18th-century practice of improvising melodies over a given bass, which necessarily determined the harmonic progressions of the exercise. The practice of partimento had didactic uses, but it waned at the end of the Baroque when the BASSO CONTINUO gave way to entirely written-out scores.

partita (*parthia*; It.). Originally, a VARIATION; by the Baroque era, a SUITE.

partitino (It., little score). Supplementary parts, printed separately, for a work with instruments or vocal part that do not appear often in the score. Examples include the "Turkish" percussion in Mozart's *The Abduction from the Seraglio*; the trombone and the chorus in his *Don Giovanni*; and the children's chorus in Puccini's *La Bohème*. The partitino saves time and paper that would otherwise be wasted on vacuous rests and pauses.

partition (Fr.; Ger. *Partitur*, It. *Partitura*). A score.

Parton, Dolly (Rebecca), successful American singer, guitarist, and songwriter of country and popular music; b. Locust Ridge, near Sevierville, Tenn., Jan. 19, 1946. Born into a poverty-stricken family, she began to sing as a child; after graduating from high school she went to Nashville, Tenn., to seek her fortune; in 1967 she became a member of Porter Wagoner's band. She quickly assumed a leading place among country-music stars; in 1976 she moved into the pop-rock field and toured widely with her own group, Gypsy Fever. She composed such popular songs as *Coat of Many Colors*, *Tennessee Mountain Home*, *Joshua*, *Jolene*, and *Love Is Like a Butterfly*; she was particularly successful with the country album *Here You Come Again* and the pop-rock album *Heartbreaker*. To top it all, she made herself famous by appearing as 1 of the 3 rather odd secretaries in the comedy film *9 to 5* (1980), for which she wrote and recorded the theme song.

Pas d'acier, Le. Ballet by Prokofiev, 1927, 1st performed by Diaghilev's Ballets Russes in Paris. The title means "the leap of steel" and features characters purported to represent the new industrial class of Soviet Russia. The score is appropriately discordant, and it created something of an inverse sensation among the anti-Soviet Russian émigrés in Paris who were shocked by this exhibition of "Bolshevik" music, since Prokofiev himself was, technically speaking, an émigré in their midst. The Soviet critics, on the other hand, felt that

Prokofiev used the very serious business of industrial construction in new Russia as an improper means to entertain the bourgeoisie with musical pap.

pas de patineurs (Fr.). A ballroom dance, symbolic of the movement of a skater in fast march tempo.

pas de quatre (Fr.). A ballroom dance for 4 participants, usually in 4/4 or 12/4 meter in moderate tempo.

Pas des Écharpes (Scarf Dance). A *pièce de musique de salon*, 1888, by Cécile Chaminade (1857–1944); once a favorite among amateur pianists.

pas d'Espagne (Fr.). Generic name for a dance in a Spanish vein, usually of the stately bolero type.

Pasatieri, Thomas, talented American opera composer; b. N.Y., Oct. 20, 1945. He began to play the piano by spontaneous generation, and picked up elements of composition, particularly vocal, by a similar subliminal process; between the ages of 14 and 18 he wrote some 400 songs. He persuaded Nadia Boulanger to take him as a student by correspondence between Paris and N.Y. when he was 15; at 16 he entered the Juilliard School of Music, where he became a student of Vittorio Giannini and Vincent Persichetti; he also took a course with Darius Milhaud in Aspen, Colo., where his 1st opera, *The Women*, to his own libretto, was performed when he was only 19 (1965).

It became clear to him that opera was his natural medium, and that the way to achieve the best results was by following the evolutionary line of Italian operatic productions characterized by the felicity of BEL CANTO, facility of harmonic writing, and euphonious fidelity to the lyric and dramatic content of the subject. In striving to attain these objectives, Pasatieri ran the tide of mandatory inharmoniousness; while his productions were applauded by audiences, they shocked music critics and other composers. This attitude is akin to that taken by some toward Vittorio Giannini and Gian Carlo Menotti. From 1967 to 1969 Pasatieri taught at the Juilliard School; he then was engaged at the Manhattan School of Music (1969–71); from 1980 to 1983 he was Distinguished Visiting Prof. at the Univ. of Cincinnati College–Cons. of Music. In addition to many operas, he also wrote works for vocal groups and instrumental accompaniment.

paseo (Sp., promenade). South American dance in moderate waltz time.

pasillo (Sp.). Latin American dance of Spanish origin in waltz time, sometimes combined with 6/8 to produce characteristic cross rhythms. In Colombia it is called *vals del pais* (country waltz).

paso doble (Sp.). Latin American social dance, in a marchlike step, usually in 6/8 meter.

paspy (U.K.). PASSEPIED.

passacaglia (It.; from Sp. *pasar una calle*, pass along a street; Fr. *passacaille*). Orig., a procession of a chorus playing and singing in march time, probably derived from the Spanish *pasacalle*. In the 17th century the passacaglia acquired the characteristics of sui generis variation form in triple meter. Its salient feature is an ostinato bass progression with melodic and harmonic variations in the upper voices. In the Baroque period the passacaglia became 1 of the most important instrumental forms for keyboard. Bach, Handel, Couperin, and Rameau all contributed to the perfection of the genre. In the 18th century it coalesced with the CHACONNE; while the distinction between the 2 forms is not always clear, 1 set of criteria states that the passacaglia is polyphonically constructed in a precise and rigorous style, while the chaconne is often chordal and homophonic.

passage. 1. A portion or section of a piece, usually short, not necessarily developmental in nature. 2. A rapid repeated figure, either ascending or descending, especially in piano writing. A scale passage is generally called a run.

passaggio (It.). 1. Renaissance term for ornamental passages in instrumental works. 2. Technical passage work, especially in piano writing.

passamezzo (It., step and a half). An old Italian dance in duple time, like the PAVANE but faster. It is usually symmetrical in form.

passepied (Fr., pass the foot; U.K. *paspy*). A 17th-century French dance in 3/8 or 6/8 time with 3 or 4 reprises; like the minuet in movement but quicker.

passing notes or tones. Notes or tones foreign to the chords they accompany and passing by a step from one chord to another. They differ from suspensions in not being prepared and in entering (usually) on an unaccented beat.

passion, passion music. A musical setting of a text descriptive of Christ's sufferings and death on the cross (passion); it retains its original Latin meaning of suffering. The great Bach passions are in the vernacular, and the characters, including Jesus and the apostles, speak and sing in German, while the chorus supplies the narrative. There is a great deal of conventional melorhythmic symbolism: the passion—that is, the actual pain experienced by Jesus—is rendered in chromatics; the resurrection is set in clear major arpeggios; while the powers of the dark are expressed in the falling basses in broken diminished-7th chords.

Passion of Jonathan Wade, The. Opera by C. Floyd, 1962, 1st performed in N.Y. The composer's libretto depicts life during Reconstruction in the American South, when the hero falls victim to the bigotry and vindictiveness of the Ku Klux Klan.

passione, con (It.). Passionately, in an impassioned style, fervently.

Passione, La. Haydn's Sym. No. 49 in F Minor (1768). The temperature of the passion in this sym. is moderate.

passo a sei (It., 6-step). Swiss folk dance.

pasteboard rattle (U.K.). See FRICTION DRUM.

pastiche (Fr.; It. *pasticcio*, pie). A musical medley of extracts from different works, pieced together and provided with new words so as to form a "new" composition. The word is often used disdainfully to designate a motley medley of unrelated tunes by unrelated composers, arranged in a sequence with artificial connective tissue between numbers.

Historically, *pasticcio* performed a useful function in acquainting music lovers with popular opera arias, dance movements, and concert pieces, presented as an appetizing plate of musical dessert. Unfortunately, the musical semantics of *pasticcio* departed from its original meaning and began to be applied indiscriminately to sets of variations by several composers, musical nosegays offered to friends, etc. The Viennese publisher Diabelli caused the publication of such a *pasticcio* by commissioning 51 composers to write variations on a waltz tune of his own; Liszt, as a child of 11, also contributed a variation. Beethoven obliged with 33 variations which made Diabelli's name immortal. Several Russian composers (Borodin, Rimsky-Korsakov, Cui, and Liadov) got together to perpetrate variations on *Chopsticks*;

Liszt later added a variation of his own to their collection. Then there is the *Hexameron* for Piano on the march theme from Bellini's opera *I Puritani*, written in 1837 by 6 composers, including Chopin and Liszt. The Italian AVANT-GARDE composer Luciano Berio concocted a bouillabaisse with chunks of Bach, Debussy, Ravel, and Mahler, and called the result *Sinfonia*. See also POTPOURRI.

Pastor Fido, Il. Opera by Handel, 1712, produced in London. This simple pastorale, about the archetypal faithful shepherd, was one of the composer's 1st works for the English stage.

pastoral (Fr., It. *pastorale*). 1. A scenic cantata representing pastoral life; a pastoral opera. 2. An instrumental piece imitating in style and instrumentation rural and idyllic scenes.

Pastoral Symphony (It. *Sinfonia Pastorale*). The 6th Sym. by Beethoven, 1808 (op. 68), 1st performed in Vienna. The sym. is set in the key of F major, often associated with pastoral moods; it is the only work of Beethoven having a program. It is in 5 movements, and the descriptions by Beethoven himself are very specific: 1. *Revival of Pleasant Feelings upon Arriving in the Country Scene*; 2. *By the Brook*; 3. *Merry Gathering of Country Folk*; 4. *Thunderstorm*; 5. *Shepherd's Song of Joyful Gratitude After the Storm*. Like many composers who 1st sketch out a descriptive program for their compositions and then soberly retract the original tonal painting, Beethoven added a word of caution: "It is rather an expression of feeling than pictorial representation." However, the literalness of bird songs in the score cannot be denied—the trill of the nightingale, the syncopated rhythm of the quail, and the familiar falling 3rd of the cuckoo. And what could be more pictorial than a thunderstorm? It even looks like lightning bolts and heavy rainfall graphically in the score itself. And the serene conclusion gives the listener the feeling of the Austrian landscape after an invigorating rainfall. Another feature of the 6th Sym. is the lack of pauses between the last 3 movements, expanding a structural concept Beethoven introduced in the 5th Sym.

Pastoral Symphony, A. The 3rd Sym. of Vaughan Williams, 1922, 1st performed in London. As was the case with Beethoven, who emphasized that the title of his *Pastoral Sym.* should be understood only as an expression and a sentiment rather than as a literal tone painting, so Vaughan Williams insisted that his *Pastoral Sym.* should be judged as pure music. The work, in 4 traditional movements, is typical of the contemplative nature of Vaughan Williams as a composer, for the music seems to bear an unspoken message. The finale contains a vocal part without words.

pastourelle (Fr.). Pastoral song in the repertoire of the troubadours and trouvères; also, a song in the spirit of this medieval genre.

patetico, -a (It.). Pathetic.

pathétique (Fr.; from Grk. *pathētikos*, capable of feeling). A French adjective found in titles of musical compositions to describe their being greatly emotional; it is not synonymous with the English *pathetic*, meaning pitiful.

Pathétique Sonata. Beethoven's Piano Sonata in C Minor, 1797–98 (op. 13). The "pathetic"—that is, emotional—quality is dramatically expressed in the extreme contrast between its slow introduction and subsequent allegro. The complete title is *Grande Sonate pathétique*, written down in French by Beethoven himself, as was the fashion of the day. (He composed it during the last year of the 1700s, the "French century.") The 2nd movement in A-flat major is a set of variations on one of Beethoven's most engaging ROCOCO themes.

Pathétique Symphony. Tchaikovsky's 6th Sym., 1893; Tchaikovsky conducted its 1st performance in St. Petersburg, 9 days before he died of cholera. It has 4 movements and is set in the somber key of B minor. The title was suggested to Tchaikovsky by his brother Modest after the work was already completed. The music epitomizes Tchaikovsky's obsession with Fate; the *Pathétique* possesses some extraordinary moments, such as a quotation from the Russian Mass for the Dead in the trombones. An exceptional feature is a "waltz in 5/4 time," as it came to be known, in the 2nd movement.

Tchaikovsky dedicated the *Pathétique* to his favorite nephew, Bob. He confessed that he loved the *Pathétique* more than any of his works, and that he actually wept while composing the music. He suffered when Bob failed to acknowledge the receipt of the score, which he sent to him. Although the work represented the utmost in human pessimism, it retains an unchallenged position in the Soviet Union, where optimism is mandatory. Some extreme scholiasts of the official doctrine of Socialist Realism suggested an ingenious explanation of Tchaikovsky's general popularity: his music, with its constant minor modalities and melancholy melodic inflections, represents a solemn lamentation on the coffin of the ruling class of the Russian bourgeoisie, and, therefore, gives a proletarian audience a natural satisfaction to know that the enemy class had such a definite send-off.

Patience, or Bunthorne's Bride. Comic opera by Gilbert and Sullivan, 1881, 1st performed in London. The poet Bunthorne (Bunyan + Hawthorne?) is admired by aesthetically inclined young women, but he spurns them in favor of Patience, a milkmaid. He loses her to a dragoon, who dons a motley dress and puts on aesthetic airs. The opera is a transparent satire on Oscar Wilde, whose postures were then amusing and irritating Victorian society.

patimento (It.). Suffering; grief. *Con espressione di patimento*, with mournful or plaintive expression.

Patineurs, Les (The Skaters). A famous waltz by Waldteufel (1882).

patter song. A rapid, syllabic humorous song. Patter songs are particularly effective in comic dialogues. The tessitura is in the middle register, and the singing approximates the PARLANDO style. Mozart and Rossini excelled in Italian patter song. The greatest master of patter song in English was Sullivan in setting Gilbert's witty lines in their comic operas.

Pauken (Ger.). TIMPANI.

Paukenmesse. See MASS IN A TIME OF WAR.

Paul Bunyan. An operetta by Britten, 1941, to a libretto by W. H. Auden; it was 1st performed at Columbia University, N.Y., when both Britten and Auden were in America. The story recounts the exploits of the legendary American frontiersman Paul Bunyan in a series of tuneful episodes. After being laid aside for 35 years, the opera was revived at the 29th Musical Festival at Aldeburgh, England, in 1976, as a bicentennial tribute to America.

pauroso (It.). Fearful, timid.

pausa (It.). A rest; a pause. *Pausa lunga*, long pause; *pausa generale*, a pause for all performers.

pause. 1. A full stop. 2. A rest. 3. A fermata (⌒).

Pause del silenzio. Sym. suite by Malipiero, 1918, expressing the sevenfold spirit of serenity, crudity, melancholy, gaiety, mystery, war, and savagery, leading to a pause of silence. It was 1st performed in Rome. Malipiero later wrote a sequel to this work containing 5 "symphonic expressions," which was performed for the 1st time by the Philadelphia Orchestra (1927).

Pauvre Matelot, Le (The Poor Sailor). Opera by Milhaud, 1927, 1st performed in Paris. A faithful wife waits for her sailor husband's return; she unwittingly murders him when she fails to recognize him in his disguise.

pavane (It. *pavana*). A stately court dance in deliberate 4/4 time. The supposed derivation of the word comes from the Latin word *pavo* (peacock) and was conjectured at one time because of the imagined similarity of the dance with the strutting step of the bird. Actually, the pavane originat-ed in the 16th century in Padua, Italy; *Pava* is a dialect name for Padua. Because of its dignified choreography, the pavane became a favorite court dance in Europe and particularly in England during the Elizabethan times. The tempo indication *Alla pavana* is also found. Many modern composers stylized the pavane in various novel ways. A common misspelling, *pavanne*, has taken root in some American samples of the pavane style.

Pavane. Orch.l work with choral *ad libitum* by Fauré, 1887. It is couched in a style evoking the old French court dance.

Pavane pour une infante défunte (Pavane for a Dead Princess). A piano piece by Ravel, 1899, 1st performed in Paris, 1902. It is a fine stylization of the slow courtly dance, whose French title provided a verbal assonance equivalent to the music for Ravel.

Pavarotti, Luciano

Greatly renowned Italian tenor; b. Modena, Oct. 12, 1935. His father, a baker by trade, sang in the local church choir; Luciano learned to read music and began singing with the boy altos; later joined his father in the choir and also sang in the chorus of the local Teatro Comunale and the amateur Chorale Gioacchino Rossini. To prepare himself for a career as a schoolteacher, he attended the local Scuola Magistrale; then taught in an elementary school, augmenting his income by selling insurance. In the meantime he began vocal studies with Arrigo Polo in Modena (1955), then went to Mantua, where he continued his training with Ettore Campogalliani (1960). He made his operatic debut as Rodolfo in La Bohéme at the Teatro Municipale in Reggio Emilia (1961).

He obtained his 1st major engagement when he appeared as the Duke of Mantua at the Teatro Massimo in Palermo (1962). His 1st important appearance outside his homeland was as Edgardo with the Netherlands Opera in Amsterdam (1963). That same year he made his Vienna State Opera debut as Rodolfo, a role he also sang for his 1st appearance at London's Covent Garden (1963). In 1965 he made his U.S. debut as Edgardo opposite Joan Sutherland's Lucia with the Greater Miami Opera. After his 1st appearance at Milan's La Scala as Alfredo (1965), he made a summer tour of Australia with the Sutherland Williamson International Grand Opera Co., a venture featuring the celebrated diva. He subsequently scored his 1st triumph on the operatic stage when he essayed the role of Tonio in *La Fille du régiment* at Covent Garden (1966); with insouciant aplomb he tossed off the aria *Pour mon âme*, replete with 9 successive high C's, winning an ovation. He was dubbed the "King of the High C's," and a brilliant international career beckoned.

He made his debut at the San Francisco Opera as Rodolfo (1967), a role he chose for his 1st appearance at the Metropolitan Opera in N.Y. (1968). In subsequent seasons he became a mainstay at both houses, and he also appeared regularly with other opera houses on both sides of the Atlantic. He made frequent appearances in solo recitals and concerts with orchs. In 1977 he starred as Rodolfo in the 1st *Live from the Met* telecast by PBS. In

1978 he made an acclaimed solo recital debut at the Metropolitan Opera, which was also telecast by PBS. In 1980 he founded the Opera Co. of Philadelphia/Luciano Pavarotti International Voice Competition. In 1983 he was 1 of the featured artists at the Metropolitan Opera Centennial Gala. In 1984 he gave a concert before 20,000 admirers at N.Y.'s Madison Square Garden, which was also seen by millions on PBS. He celebrated the 25th anniversary of his operatic debut by singing his beloved Rodolfo at the Teatro Comunale in Modena (1986). In 1988 he sang Nemorino at the Berlin Deutsche Oper, eliciting thunderous applause and no less than 15 curtain calls. In 1989 he appeared in concert with the N.Y. City Opera Orch. in a special program at Avery Fischer Hall at N.Y.'s Lincoln Center for the Performing Arts, televised live by PBS. In 1990 he appeared at the Bolshoi Theater in Moscow.

The most idolized tenor since Caruso, Pavarotti made such roles as Nemorino in *L'elisir d'amore*, Riccardo in *Un ballo in maschera*, Fernando in *La Favorite*, Manrico in *Il Trovatore*, Cavaradossi in *Tosca*, and Radames in *Aida*, as well as the ubiquitous Rodolfo, virtually his own. Indeed, through recordings and television appearances, he won an adoring global following. Always of a jocular rotundity, he announced in 1988 that he had succeeded in dropping 85 pounds from his original body weight.

COURTESY FRANK DRIGGS COLLECTION

Luciano Pavarotti

paventoso (It.). Fearfully, timidly.

pavillon (Fr.). The bell of the brass instrument family. *Pavillon en l'air*, hold the bell up for greater sonority.

pavillon d'amour (Fr., love bell; Ger. *Liebesfuss*, love foot). A bulbous opening at the end of the English horn that has the effect of dampening the sound. The same type of extension was characteristic of the manufacture of a clarinetto d'amore, fagotto d'amore, oboe d'amore, and other "amorous" instruments, now largely obsolete.

payola. American slang for bribes to disc jockeys for "plugging" (promoting) particular records of popular music on radio.

peabody. A fast American ballroom dance in open position.

Peacock Variations. Name sometimes used for the orch.l *Variations on a Hungarian Folksong* by Kodály, 1939; it was 1st performed in Amsterdam. The work is based on an authentic Hungarian folk tune, *Fly, Peacock, Fly*.

Peanut Vendor, The. An arrangement of the Latin American tune *El Mansiero*; it was popularized by several orchs. and interpolated in the 2nd version of the film *A Star Is Born* (1954).

Pearl Jam. (Lead vocal: Eddie Vedder, b. Chicago, Dec. 23, 1964; guitar: Mike McCready, b. Seattle, Apr. 5, 1965; rhythm guitar: Steve "Stone" Gossard, b. Seattle, July 20, 1966; bass: Jeff Ament, b. Big Sandy, Mont., Mar. 10, 1963; drums: Dave Krusen, replaced by Dave Abbruzzese in 1992 and Jack Irons in 1995.) Seattle grunge-rock band who along with Nirvana launched thousands of plaid-shirted rockers. They are famous also for waging battle with Ticketmaster, refusing to play in venues that use the popular ticketing agency, who they claim overcharges for its services.

The group formed in 1990 and signed quickly to Epic Records, scoring an immediate success with their 1991 LP,

10, which produced the hits *Even Flow, Jeremy, Alive,* and *Release.* They joined the alternative-rock tour Lollapalooza in 1992 on its 2nd outing, cementing their reputation among the grunge crowd. The year 1993 brought a second album, *Vs.*, and an appearance on the popular *MTV Unplugged* program. They also toured Europe with Neil Young, leading to a long association with the grandfather of all things grungy (they would back Young on his album *Mirror Ball* in 1995). *Vitalogy* came in 1994, which they released 1st on vinyl only and then, 2 weeks later, on CD and cassette; band fans ended up buying both, lining the denim pockets of the group's members. Their 1995 summer tour was plagued by their ongoing fight with Ticketmaster.

Pearly (Fr. *perlé*; Ger. *perlend*). A style of piano touch producing a clear, round, smooth effect of tone, especially in scale passages.

Pears, (Sir) **Peter** (Neville Luard), renowned English tenor; b. Farnham, June 22, 1910; d. Aldeburgh, Apr. 3, 1986. He began his career as temporary organist at Hertford College, Oxford (1928–29), then was director of music at the Grange School, Crowborough (1930–34). He was a scholarship student at the Royal College of Music in London (1933–34); concurrently sang in the BBC chorus and then was a member of the BBC Singers (1934–38) and the New English Singers (1936–38). During this period he received vocal instruction from Elena Gerhardt and Dawson Freer.

In 1936 he met Benjamin Britten; they gave their 1st joint recital in 1937 and thereafter remained lifelong personal and professional companions. After singing in the Glyndebourne chorus (1938), he accompanied Britten to the U.S. (1939); continued his vocal training with Therese Behr and Clytie Hine-Mundy. In 1942 he returned to England with Britten, making his stage debut that same year in the title role of *Les Contes d'Hoffmann* at London's Strand Theatre. In 1943 he joined the Sadler's Wells Opera Co., gaining fame when he created the title role in Britten's *Peter Grimes* (1945). In 1946 he became a member of the English Opera Group, and thereafter greatly distinguished himself in operas by Britten; among the roles he created were Albert Herring, the Male Chorus in *The Rape of Lucretia*, Captain Vere in *Billy Budd*, Essex in *Gloriana*, Quint in *The Turn of the Screw*, Flute in *A Midsummer Night's Dream* (was colibrettist with the composer), the Madwoman in *Curlew River*, Sir Philip Wingrave in *Owen Wingrave*, and Aschenbach in *Death in Venice*. It was in the last role that he made his Metropolitan Opera debut in N.Y. (1974). He was 1 of the founders of the Aldeburgh Festival (1948), serving as a director and as a teacher of master classes until his death.

Pears sang in several 1st performances of Britten's non-operatic works, including the *Serenade* for tenor, horn, and strings, the *Michelangelo Sonnets*, and the *War Requiem*. He also excelled in the works of other English composers, among them Elgar, Holst, Vaughan Williams, and Walton, as well as those by Schütz, Bach, Mozart, Schubert, and Schumann. He was made a Commander of the Order of the British Empire in 1957, and was knighted in 1978.

Pêcheurs de Perles, Les. Opera by Bizet, 1863, premiered in Paris. Two fishermen in Ceylon are rivals in love, but their object of adoration is a priestess bound to chastity. One of the suitors is elected a tribal chief and promises her a priceless pearl if she remains chaste; she spurns the pearl and flees the island with the other fisherman. A melodious duet in the score is a paradigm of musical poetry.

ped. Stands for PEDAL; signifies that the right (loud) piano pedal is to be pressed, or (in organ music) that notes so marked are to be played on the pedals.

pedal. 1. A foot key on the organ or pedal piano. 2. A foot lever; as the piano pedals, or the organ swell-pedal. 3. A treadle, like those used for blowing the reed organ. 4. A stop knob or lever worked by the foot (organ). 5. A contraction for pedal point.

pedal note or tone. A sustained or continuously repeated note (tone).

pedal organ. The set of stops controlled by the organ pedals.

pedal piano. A PIANOFORTE provided with a PEDALIER.

pedal point (organ point; Fr. *point d'orgue*; Ger. *Orgelpunkt*; Sp. *bajo de organo*, organ bass). A tone sustained in one part to harmonies executed in the other parts, usually a bass tone, tonic, and/or dominant. Pedal point is a sustained note, usually in the bass (in French, *pedale inférieure*) and usually on the dominant or on the tonic, or on both simultaneously. It is called pedal point because on the organ—an instrument on which the pedal point is particularly effective—it is played on a pedal by the foot. A protracted organ point on the dominant usually heralds the authentic cadence on the tonic. So great is the bond, so strong is the harmonic hold of the pedal point on the dominant, that it can support chords on all degrees of the diatonic scale as well as modulations into the lowered supertonic or the lowered submediant in a major key. Among examples of this holding power of the dominant pedal point are the conclusion of the church scene in Gounod's opera *Faust*, the relevant passages in the overture to Wagner's *Die Meistersinger*, and in the wedding procession in Rimsky-Korsakov's opera *Le Coq d'or*, which contains modulations into several unrelated keys before finally resolving into the tonic. Scriabin maintains a pedal point on the tonic in the finale of his *Poem of Ecstasy* for about 5 minutes.

Cadenzas in piano concertos are based on a prolonged pedal point on the dominant in the bass. Cadences in fugal compositions are often reinforced by the pedal point in the bass, as for instance in the 2nd fugue of the 1st book of Bach's *Well-Tempered Clavier*. Pedal points in the bass can be sustained on the modern piano by the use of the middle, or sustaining, pedal. Pedal point in the middle voices (*pedale intérieure* in French) are relatively rare, but there are examples to be found of pedal points in the high treble. Rimsky-Korsakov's *Scheherazade* concludes on such a high pedal point. Remarkably enough, some composers writing in an atonal idiom or employing dodecaphonic techniques occasionally allow themselves the use of pedal points to establish the binding element missing in a system of composition that theoretically disenfranchises both the tonic and the dominant.

pédale (Fr.). PEDAL POINT.

pedale doppio (It.). Pedal-part in octaves.

pedale ogni battuta (It.). Take the pedal with each measure.

pedalier. A set of pedals, either (1) so adjusted as to play the low octaves of the piano, after the manner of organ pedals, or (2) provided with separate strings and action, to be placed underneath the piano.

pedanteria, con (It.; Ger. *pedantisch*). Pedantically; in an even, unemotional style.

pedes muscarum (Lat., flies' feet). A curious term applied by some medieval musicians to cursive NEUMES that remotely resembled the eponymous appendages.

Pedrell, Felipe, eminent Spanish musicologist and composer; b. Tortosa, Feb. 19, 1841; d. Barcelona, Aug. 19, 1922. He became a chorister at Tortosa Cathedral when he was about 7, receiving instruction from Juan Antonio Nin y Serra. In 1873 he went to Barcelona as deputy director of the Light Opera Co., where he produced his 1st opera, *L'ultimo Abenzeraggio* (1874). After a visit to Italy (1876–77) and a sojourn in Paris, he settled in Barcelona (1881), where he devoted himself mainly to musicological pursuits. In 1882 he founded the journals *Salterio Sacro-Hispano* and *Notas Musicales y Literarias*, both of which ceased publication in 1883. He then was founder-ed. of the important journal *La Illustración Musical Hispano-Americana* (1888–96). During this period he worked on his operatic masterpiece, the trilogy *Los Pirineos/Els Pirineus* (1890–91), and also publ. the book *Por nuestra música* (1891), which served as its introduction and as a plea for the creation of a national lyric drama based on Spanish folk song. In 1894 he went to Madrid, where he was named prof. of choral singing at the Cons. and prof. of advanced studies at the Ateneo; was also elected a member of the Royal Academy of Fine Arts. Upon his return to Barcelona (1904) he devoted himself to writing, teaching, and composing. Among his outstanding pupils were Albéniz, Falla, Granados, and Gerhard.

Although Pedrell was admired as a composer by his contemporaries, his music has not obtained recognition outside his homeland. His lasting achievement rests upon his distinguished work as a musicologist, in which he did much to restore interest in both historical and contemporary Spanish sacred music. He contributed studies of Spanish, Catalan, Latin American, and Portuguese music, theoretical works, bibliographies, early and new music studies, dictionaries, studies of Spanish liturgy and religious festivals, composer monographs, organological works, and examinations of opera and Spanish song. He ed. several collections of religious and secular works.

Peer Gynt. 1. Incidental music by Grieg, 1876, for Ibsen's eponymous drama; premiered in Christiania (now Oslo). Two orch.1 suites were drawn from it: the 1st is particularly celebrated; it contains the poetic pastorale *In the Morning*, followed by the mournful dirge *Ase's Death*, a mazurkalike *Anitra's Dance*, and the sinister rollicking piece *In the Hall of the Mountain King*. The 2nd suite, performed separately in

Christiania, Nov. 14, 1891, includes *Ingrid's Lament*, *Arabian Dance*, *Stormy Evening on the Seashore*, and *Solveig's Song*. 2. Opera by Egk, 1938, 1st produced in Berlin. The libretto, drawn from Ibsen's great philosophical drama, traverses Peer Gynt's travels in search of adventure and pleasure. He visits Algiers, where Anitra dances for him; he courts the daughter of the King of the Trolls in his mountain palace. In the end he returns to his everfaithful Solvieg and dies in her arms. Egk's opera was unexpectedly praised by Hitler, who attended its 1st performance; this assured its success for a few brief years. However, Egk survived Hitler and his deadly accolade; his *Peer Gynt* resurfaced with its reputation for solidity and vitality intact.

Peerce, Jan (born Jacob Pincus Perelmuth), noted American tenor; b. N.Y., June 3, 1904; d. there, Dec. 15, 1984. He played the violin in dance bands and sang at various entertainment places in N.Y. In 1932 he was engaged as a singer at Radio City Music Hall; made his operatic debut in Philadelphia as the Duke of Mantua (1938) and gave his 1st solo recital in N.Y. (1939). His lyrical voice attracted attention, and he was engaged by the Metropolitan Opera in N.Y.; made his debut there as Alfredo (1941); sang also the parts of Cavaradossi, Rodolfo, and Gounod's Faust; remained on the staff of the Metropolitan until 1966, appearing again in 1967–68; retired in 1982. He was the brother-in-law of Richard Tucker.

Peggy-Ann. Musical by Rodgers and Hart, 1926. A girl in a small town in N.Y. tries to escape her uninteresting environment and an impending marriage to an unglamorous local man in a world of fantasy. In her dreams she is an adventuress in the city, where she is a guest on a yacht and a bride of a rich playboy. Eventually she abandons her fantasies and returns to the bittersweet reality of the only existence granted her by fate. Includes *A Tree in the Park* and *Maybe It's Me*.

Peggy Sue. Buddy Holly's 1957 number 3 hit, his biggest U.S. hit during his lifetime. Inspired the follow-up *Peggy Sue Got Married*.

Peitsche (Ger.). The WHIP, used as a percussion instrument.

Pelléas et Mélisande (1). Lyric drama by Debussy (1893–1902), to a libretto drawn from Maeterlinck's tragedy of the same name. It was 1st performed in Paris (1902), a premiere of historical significance; Debussy's operatic masterpiece changed the face of the musical theater and inaugurated a new genre of music drama.

Golaud finds Mélisande wandering in a forest. He marries her, but soon an affectionate though innocent alliance develops between Mélisande and Golaud's half-brother, Pelléas. When she lets her long hair fall from her window, Pelléas caresses it. Golaud's jealousy is aroused; he becomes violent. In a famous scene he drags Mélisande on the floor by her hair. In a triumph of understatement she whispers, "I am not happy today." When Golaud finds her with Pelléas at the fountain in the park, he kills Pelléas. Mélisande is about to bear Golaud's child; dying in childbirth, she forgives her husband for his crime.

So unusual is the music, so dramatic is its departure from the traditional type of French opera, that Paris music critics were bewildered. When R. Strauss attended a performance of *Pelléas et Mélisande* in Paris, he turned to a friend during the 1st act and asked: "Is it going to go on and on like this?" To an uninitiated listener Debussy's music appears static and monotonous. A Paris critic whose physiological aversion to Debussy's music was irrepressible admitted by way of a compliment, "True, this music makes little noise, but it is a nasty little noise." Debussy's free use of unresolved dissonances, the frequent progressions of dominant-9th chords, the unstable tonality, all contributed to critical incomprehension. It took many years for *Pelléas et Mélisande* to take its rightful place among operatic masterpieces.

Pelléas et Mélisande (2). 1. An orch.l suite by Fauré, 1898, written as part of his sentimental incidental music for Maeterlinck's play, described in the previous entry; it was 1st performed in London. There are 4 movements; the most popular is the 3rd, *Sicilienne*, arranged from a cello piece. 2. Symphonic poem by Schoenberg, 1905, based on the same play as described above; he conducted its 1st performance in Vienna. The work is in the late hyper-Romantic style.

pelog. One of 2 principal scale categories in gamelan music; a pentatonic group in various tunings; a common example resembles the tempered scale E–F–G–B–C, i.e., with 2 semitones and a large gap between C and E.

Penderecki, Krzysztof

Celebrated Polish composer; b. Debica, Nov. 23, 1933. He was educated in Krakow, where he took courses at the Jagellonian Univ.; after private composition studies with F. Skolyszewski, he received instruction in theory from A. Malawski and S. Wiechowicz at the State Higher School of Music (1955–58); was a lecturer in composition there (1958–66), remaining with it when it became the Academy of Music as rector (1972–87) and as prof. (from 1972); also was prof. of composition at the Essen Folkwang Hochschule für Musik (1966–68) and at Yale Univ. (from 1973). He rapidly acquired a reputation as one of the most original composers of his time, receiving numerous honors: received honorary memberships in the Royal Academy of Music in London (1975), the Akademie der Künste of the German Democratic Republic (1975), the Royal Academy of Music in Stockholm (1975), etc.; was awarded the Herder Prize of the Federal Republic of Germany (1977), the Grand Medal of Paris (1982), the Sibelius Prize of Finland (1983), the Premio Lorenzo il Magnifico of Italy (1985), etc.; received honorary doctorates from several univs.

After a few works of an academic nature, he developed a hypermodern technique of composition in a highly individual style, in which no demarcation line is drawn between consonances and dissonances, tonal or atonal melody, traditional or innovative instrumentation; an egalitarian attitude prevails toward all available resources of sound. While his idiom is naturally complex, he does not disdain tonality, even in its overt triadic forms. In his creative evolution he has bypassed orthodox serial procedures; his music follows an athematic course, in constantly varying metrical and rhythmic patterns. He utilizes an entire spectrum of modern sonorities, expanding the domain of tone to unpitched elements, making use of such effects as shouting, hissing, and verbal ejaculations in vocal parts, at times reaching a climax of aleatory glossolalia; tapping, rubbing, or snapping the fingers against the body of an instrument; striking the piano strings by mallets, etc. For this he designed an optical notation, with symbolic ideograms indicating the desired sound; thus a black isosceles triangle denotes the highest possible pitch; an inverted isosceles triangle, the lowest possible pitch; a black rectangle for a sonic complex of white noise within a given interval; vertical lines tied over by an arc for arpeggios below the bridge of a string instrument; wavy lines of varying amplitudes for extensive vibrato; curvilinear figures for aleatory passages; dots and dashes for repetitions of a pattern; sinusoidal oscillations for quaquaversal glissandos; etc. He applies these modern devices to religious music, including Masses in the orthodox Roman Catholic ritual.

Penderecki's most impressive and most frequently perf. work is his *Tren pamieci ofiarom Hiroszimy* (Threnody in Memory of Victims of Hiroshima) for 52 String Instruments (1959–60), rich in dynamic contrasts and ending on a tone cluster of 2 octavefuls of icositetraphonic harmony.

Pénélope. Lyric drama by Fauré, 1913, 1st performed in Monte Carlo. The libretto is drawn from Homer's *Odyssey*, dealing with the faithful wife of Ulysses. She kept weaving during his long sea voyages, although she suffered the importunities of her many suitors. Pénélope is represented in the score by strings, Ulysses mostly by wind instruments. The music is modal in its structure.

penitential sounds. Musical settings for psalms expressing penitence and imploring mercy, particularly *De profundis* and *Miserere*.

Pennies from Heaven. Sentimental song by Arthur Johnston, 1936, introduced by Bing Crosby in a movie musical of the same name. In the verses, heavenly bliss is equated to a pecuniary solvency, an ideal state for all true believers.

Penniman, Richard Wayne (called Little Richard), pioneering African-American rock 'n' roll singer and songwriter, extolled by his followers as the "King of Rock 'n' Roll"; b. Macon, Ga., Dec. 5, 1932. Possessed by religious fervor, he sang in local church choirs, then switched to a traveling medicine show. He won a talent contest in Atlanta at the age of 19, recorded "demo" (demonstration) records, and hit the proverbial jackpot with *Tutti Frutti* (1954). Some of his hits were focused on girls, some with 1st-name titles: *Lucille, Jenny Jenny*, and *The Girl Can't Help It* (which was the title song of a film he appeared in). Other smash hits were *Keep a-Knockin', Good Golly Miss Molly, Long Tall Sally*, and *Slippin' and Slidin'*. He was the harbinger of the unrestrained but puissant manner of American music that produced such individuals as Mick Jagger, Jerry Lee Lewis, James Brown, and Jimi Hendrix. Then, in the midst of his popular and commercial successes, he suddenly hit the religion trail, went to college in Alabama to study theology, embraced the ministry, toured the gospel circuit, and denounced rock 'n' roll as the tool of the devil. Still, he put out an autobiographical album entitled *The King of Rock and Roll* before abandoning the sinful world for God. His personal hosannas survived in his early albums, *Here's Little Richard, Fabulous Little Richard*, and (more to the point) *Wild and Frantic Little Richard*.

penorcon. Bass cittern with 9 pairs of strings, according to Praetorious.

pensiero (It.). A thought. *Pensiero del(la)* . . ., souvenir of . . . , recollections of . . . .

pensoso (It.). Pensive, thoughtful.

pentachord. The 1st 5 degrees of the scale.

pentagramma (It.). The musical staff of 5 lines.

pentatonic scale. A 5-tone scale, usually avoiding semitonic steps by skipping the 4th and 7th degrees in major, and the 2nd and 6th in natural minor. Pentatonic melodies were found in the ancient songs of geographically distant lands, in Scotland and Tibet, in China and pre-Columbian America, in Iceland and Australia. Is the pentatonic scale then some pangeographic pananthropic root of natural inventions? Not so. The intervals between component degrees are different in Asian, African, or European scale formations. Western composers equate pentatonic scales to tonal progressions that can be played on the black keys of the piano keyboard. Such Westernized scales can be classified as major and minor, major pentatonic being simulated by a scale starting on F-sharp of the "black key scale," and the minor pentatonic by one starting on E-flat. Consecutive 5ths and consecutive 4ths are the formative intervals of pentatonic scales, and the

harmonization usually tends to be based on pedal points on the presumed tonic and dominant. This type of music sounds alluringly exotic, but the resulting effect is hardly anything more genuine than an artificial chinoiserie.

The best examples of modern pentatonic music are found in the works of Debussy and Ravel; Debussy uses the pentatonic scale in the middle section of his piano piece *Voiles*, and Ravel, in the 3rd piece of his suite *Ma Mère L'Oye*, entitled *The Empress of the Pagodas*. The Chinese themselves would never recognize such Gallic pagodas as their own. Among modern operas containing materials from the pentatonic structures of the Orient are Puccini's *Madama Butterfly*, which employs Japanese melodic patterns, and *Turandot*, presenting examples of pseudo-Chinese melodies. Actually, the most common Japanese mode, although pentatonic, contains a semitone and so cannot be reduced to a "black key" scale. On the other side of the world, Irish and Scottish melodies contain pentatonic scales that in their structural aspects are quite different from Oriental exemplars. Unfortunately, some of the best-known Irish melodies have apparently been inaccurately transcribed. There seems to be considerable evidence that the initial leading tone in the *Londonderry Aire* should be a minor 3rd, not a 2nd.

People Will Say We're In Love. Song by Rodgers and Hammerstein, 1943, from the musical *Oklahoma!*

Pepper, Art(hur Edward, Jr.), American jazz alto saxophonist; b. Gardena, Calif., Sept. 1, 1925; d. Los Angeles, June 15, 1982. His father was of German origin; his mother was Italian. He played jazz clarinet and alto saxophone in school bands; got married at 17; was drafted into the U.S. Army; after discharge, he joined Stan Kenton's band (1946–52). His darkly emotional temperament led him to develop a passionate manner of shaping music which became known as the "West Coast Style." He began making records, sometimes under the punning pseudonym Art Salt, but his highly promising career was ruined by his demonic addiction to heroin and other narcotic drugs. He squandered his earnings and, besotted by need of expensive drugs, descended into thievery and brawls. He was busted in 1952 on narcotics charges and served time in the Los Angeles County jail; was paroled to the U.S. Public Health Service Hospital at Fort Worth (1953–54), but got in trouble again and was sentenced to jail in Los Angeles, where he served from 1954 to 1956 and again in 1960–61. Unable to control his habits, he was arrested as a recidivist and sent to San Quentin, where he served from 1961 to 1964 and, after another transgression, in 1965–66. Finally freed, he played with Buddy Rich's Big Band (1968–69). In 1977 and 1978 he completed 2 highly successful tours of Japan. A film documentary on Pepper's life was presented at the Berlin Film Festival in 1982.

per (It.). For, by, from, in, through. *Per l'organo*, for the organ; *per il flauto solo*, for solo flute.

per arsin et thesin. ARSIN ET THESIN, PER.

Perahia, Murray, outstanding American pianist of Spanish-Jewish descent; b. N.Y., Apr. 19, 1947. He studied piano with J. Haien (1953–64); then entered the Mannes College of Music, where he studied conducting and composition (B.S., 1969); he also continued his piano studies with Artur Balsam and Mieczyslaw Horszowski. In 1968 he made his Carnegie Hall debut in N.Y.; in 1972 he became the 1st American to win (by a unanimous vote of the jury) the Leeds International Pianoforte Competition; in 1975 he was awarded the 1st Avery Fisher Prize, sharing it with the cellist Lynn Harrell. He appeared as soloist with the leading orchs. of the U.S. and Europe; also gave many recitals in the U.S. and abroad. In 1982 he was appointed coartistic director of the Aldeburgh Festival. He excels in Classical music; mastered all of Mozart's concertos, often conducting from the keyboard; he is praised also for his congenial interpretation of the standard concert repertoire.

percussion

The striking or sounding of a dissonance. 2. The striking or beating of one body against another. Instruments of percussion (from Lat. *percutere*, strike, beat) are the drums, tambourine, cymbals, bells, triangle, etc., as well as the dulcimer and pianoforte. Not all instruments now classified in the percussion group really "percuss" (*percussus* is the past participle of *percutere*). There are in the battery (from Fr. *batterie*, fight) of *percuss*ion instruments of concussion (from Lat. *concutere*, to shake violently), shaken instruments such as the popular Latin American maracas; and instruments of friction, such as the guiro; the castanets that are clapped together rather than struck also do not fit easily into the rubric of percussion.

Since most percussion instruments perform a rhythmic function, perhaps the term *rhythm instruments*, which has been gaining increasing acceptance not only in jazz playing but also in classical music, should be considered as an alternative for *percussion*. There is a tendency to include keyboard instruments among percussion instruments, but this would be historically and functionally wrong, for although the piano and its predecessor, the harpsichord, are indeed percussed, their function is not rhythmical par excellence; perhaps the concept should be limited to some orch.l and ensemble pieces of the 20th century. On the other hand the celesta (which looks like an small spinet piano), the marimba, the vibraphone, and the xylophone, which possesses a keyboard, are customarily included in the percussion section.

The German terms *Schlaginstrumente* (striking instruments) and *Schlagzeug* (striking battery) also fail to include the rhythmic effects produced by concussion and friction instruments. In the orch.l scores of the Baroque and Classical periods, percussion was relegated to a subordinate position and often notated on a supplementary line. Those instruments of indefinite pitch—bass drum, cymbals, triangles—were exotic imports described as *Janizary music*, because they were included in the military bands of Turkey, led by the court musicians of the Sultan; the use of ethnic percussion continues into the following centuries. Other special sounds, such as the whip, were added as needed.

The 1st percussion instruments of definite pitch in the 18th-century orch., the TIMPANI, were usually found in pairs and tuned to the tonic and the dominant, performing the function of reinforcing the bass; their parts were often placed below the bass line in the score. Among percussion instruments of a definite pitch, the largest group is the KEYBOARDS, all of them playing in the treble. The GLOCKENSPIEL has a penetrating bell-like sound and is often used whenever an exotic color is invoked; it is the magic "instrument of steel" in the score of Mozart's opera *Die Zauberflöte*. Tchaikovsky makes effective use of the glockenspiel in the *Chinese Dance* of his *Nutcracker Suite*. Its keyboard equivalent, the CELESTA, is a relatively recent invention. The 1st composer to use it was Tchaikovsky, in his *Dance of the Sugar-Plum Fairies* in *The Nutcracker*. Another type of celesta manufactured in the 20th century is called *dulcitone*; its "dulcet" tone is obtained through the substitution of steel bars by clear and overtone-free tuning forks.

The XYLOPHONE (from Grk., wood sound) is a newcomer in Western orch.l literature, although it was known under the name of *Holzharmonika* (Ger., wood harmonica) in the 16th century. Saint-Saëns used it most effectively in his *Danse macabre* to imitate the clatter of skeleton bones. It is quite frequently used in modern scores because of its clear and articulate timbre. The MARIMBA, a Latin American import, is a keyboard instrument with resonators attached underneath; the vibraphone is made with steel bars and is electrically amplified; both are recent entries in popular and serious modern music. Milhaud wrote a concerto for the marimba, and many composers have included the VIBRAPHONE in their scores.

Russian opera composers often use church BELLS in their scores; Tchaikovsky in his *1812 Overture*, Rimsky-Korsakov in his opera *The Legend of the Invisible City of Kitezh*, Mussorgsky in the conclusion of his witch-riddled score of *Night on Bald Mountain* (actually added by Rimsky-Korsakov in his revision of the work). Khatchaturian used a lot of bells in his 2nd Sym. to glorify the Russian resistance to the Nazi invasion in World War II; in fact, this sym. has been called *Sym. with a Bell*. The tubular bells, also called the orch. chimes, are often used to represent church bells or as a substitute for them, such as the *Witches' Sabbath* in Berlioz's *Sym. fantastique*. Bell-like sounds are produced by other instruments made of metal: the cymbals, a pair of which is struck together; the large GONGS (pitched) and TAM-TAMS (unpitched); the triangle; and a variety of shaken jingles, such as sleigh bells. The TAMBOURINE has a drum head with little cymbals attached.

Drums, big and small, have furnished realistic effects in a number of scores in which military references are made, or to portray an execution, as in *Till Eulenspiegels* by R. Strauss or the *Robespierre Overture* by Litolff. In his 5th Sym. Nielsen has a long passage for a SNARE (side) DRUM in which the player is instructed to keep drumming as if determined to interrupt the progress of the music itself. The BASS DRUM looks and sounds impressive enough to suggest ominous events. CHINESE BLOCKS have a percussive sound almost as clear and penetrating as the xylophone, except that their pitch is indefinite. Among other percussion instruments, CLAVES are an integral part of Latin American popular bands, but the instrument has also been adopted in many modern scores. Its sound is produced by striking together 2 pieces of resonant hardwood.

A tremendous expansion of the role of the percussion section in modern orch.l scores has put drummers in a privileged position in the orch. Some percussion parts demand real virtuosity, as for instance in Stravinsky's score *L'Histoire du soldat*, in which a single performer must be able to handle several instruments in a truly acrobatic fashion. Orff elevated the rhythm instruments to a commanding position in elementary music education. Percussion ensembles specializing in music expressly written for percussion have proliferated in Europe and America; especially notable in this category is *Music for 18 Musicians* by Steve Reich. And there is at least 1 masterpiece of percussion literature, *Ionisation* of Edgard Varèse, scored for 42 percussion instruments and 2 sirens.

percussion stop. A reed organ stop, which strikes the reed a smart blow when sounding it to render its vibration prompter and stronger.

percussive. Sounded by striking.

perdendosi (It.). Dying away. MORENDO or DIMINUENDO, together (in modern music) with a slight RALLENTANDO.

Perfect Day, A. Song, 1910, by Carrie Jacobs Bond (1862–1946), the tune of which was filched none too discreetly from Anton Rubinstein's *Melody in F*. The song fits into any kind of social function, from a private club's entertainment to nondenominational funerals, even for singing drunkenly in pubs. Five million copies of sheet music were sold, and the pursuit of happiness of millions of American spinsters was encouraged by this song.

Perfect Fool, The. Comic opera by Holst, 1923, to his own libretto, 1st produced in London. In it Holst ridicules, by means of stylistic allusions, both the German and the Italian types of conventional opera.

perfect pitch. Ability to name instantly and without fail any note struck on the piano keyboard or played on an instrument; also called absolute pitch. This is an innate faculty that appears in a musical child at a very early age, distinct from relative pitch, common among all musicians, in which an interval is named in relation to a previously played note. Absolute pitch is rare, even among professional musicians and is not a sure indication of great musical talent. Wagner, Berlioz, Tchaikovsky, Ravel, and Stravinsky lacked it, but many obscure musicians possess it to an astonishing degree, being able to name the most complicated dissonant chords. Some musicians, particularly singers, can simulate the sense of perfect pitch by assaying the stress on the vocal cords required to reproduce the note in question. Despite repeated claims by educationists, perfect pitch cannot be attained by ear training.

The acuteness of perfect pitch varies widely when chord recognition is tested. Some musicians can name a highly complex conglomerate of sounds without hesitation. Especially difficult are chords containing tritones and major 7ths separated by perfect 5ths (e.g., in ascending order, D–A–A♭–E♭). Since the frequency (cycles per second) of the standard A has risen during the last century, older Europeans might hear contemporary orchs. as playing a semitone higher than written; the perfectly pitched are driven to the edge when they hear transpositions of familiar works, especially with the scores before them.

Physiologically, perfect pitch is analogous to absolute discrimination of colors in the visual spectrum; in both cases the criterion is the ability to name the frequency of vibration in the corresponding spectrum. Is the lack of perfect pitch a kind of "tone deafness" by analogy with color blindness? It is possible that prehistoric individuals possessed perfect pitch and used it in communication; even today there are isolated peoples who have retained perfect pitch without the intellectualizing of its properties. Finally, did ancient Greek scales exist outside of fixed pitch, as many speculate, or is the key to the Greek musical ethos and spirit the fixed pitches themselves?

perfection (Lat. *perfectio*). In mensural notation, a LONGA having the value of 3 units; theologically, ternary time represented the Holy Trinity.

Pergolesi, Giovanni Battista, remarkable Italian composer; b. Jesi, near Ancona, Jan. 4, 1710; d. Pozzuoli, near Naples, Mar. 16, 1736. The orig. family name was Draghi; the name Pergolesi was derived from the town of Pergola, where Pergolesi's ancestors lived. He was the only surviving child of his parents, 3 others having died in infancy. His childhood seems to have been plagued by ill health; a later caricature depicts him as having a deformed leg. He 1st studied music with Francesco Santi, the maestro di cappella of the Jesi Cathedral; he also studied violin with Francesco Mondini. He then was given a stipend by the Marchese Cardolo Maria Pianetti, which enabled him to enter the Conservatorio dei Poveri di Gesù Cristo in Naples; he studied violin there with Domenico de Matteis, and composition with Gaetano Greco, its maestro di cappella, Leonardo Vinci, and Francesco Durante. He became highly proficient as a violinist, playing at the Cons. and throughout Naples.

His 1st work to be performed was the *dramma sacro Li Prodigi della divina grazia nella conversione di S. Guglielmo Duca d'Aquitania,* which was given by the Conservatorio at the monastery of S. Agnello Maggiore in 1731. He graduated shortly thereafter and received a commission for his 1st opera, *La Salustia* (Naples, Jan. 1732). He then became maestro di cappella to Prince Ferdinando Colonna Stigliano, equerry to the Viceroy of Naples, in 1732. His *Lo Frate 'nnamorato* (Naples, Sept. 27, 1732) proved highly successful. In Dec. 1732 he composed several sacred works for performance at the church of S. Maria della Stella as a votive offering following a series of severe earthquakes in Naples. He was next commissioned to write an opera seria to celebrate the birthday of the empress on Aug. 28, 1733; however, the premiere of the resulting *Il Prigionier superbo* was delayed until Sept. 5, 1733; it contained the 2-act intermezzo *La Serva padrona,* which became his most celebrated stage work. He was named deputy to the maestro di cappella of Naples in 1734. During a brief sojourn in Rome, his Mass in F Major was performed at the church of S. Lorenzo in Lucina.

After returning to Naples, Pergolesi became maestro di cappella to Marzio Domenico IV Carafa, the Duke of Maddaloni. For the birthday of the king's mother, he was commissioned to write the opera *Adriano in Siria;* it was premiered, without success, in Naples on Oct. 25, 1734, with the intermezzo *La Contadina astuta* (subsequently staged under various titles). He then was commissioned to write an opera for Rome's Teatro Tordinona, resulting in his unsuccessful opera seria *L'Olimpiade* (Jan. 8 or 9, 1735). His last popular success for the stage was the *commedia musicale Il Flaminio* (1735). By 1735 his health had seriously declined, most likely from tuberculosis. Early in 1736 he went to the Franciscan monastery in Pozzuoli, where he soon died at the age of 26. He was buried in the common grave adjacent to the Cathedral.

Following his death his fame spread rapidly through performances of *La Serva padrona* and several other stage works. The Paris revival of the work in 1752 precipitated the QUERELLE DES BOUFFONS between the partisans of the Italian and French factions. His fame was further increased by performances of the *Salve regina* in C Minor and the *Stabat Mater* in F Minor. The chaotic entanglement of spurious, doubtful, and authentic works attributed to Pergolesi was unraveled in M. Paymer's *G.B.P.: A Thematic Catalogue of the Opera Omnia with an Appendix Listing Omitted Compositions* (N.Y., 1976).

Peri, Jacopo, significant Italian composer, called "Il Zazzerino" for his abundant head of hair; b. Rome, Aug. 20, 1561; d. Florence, Aug. 12, 1633. He was descended from a noble Florentine family. At an early age he went to Florence, where he entered the convent of Ss. Annunziata in 1573 and became a singer; also studied music with Cristofano Malvezzi. He was organist at the Badia (1579–1605) and a singer at S. Giovanni Battista (by 1586); entered the service of the Medici court of Grand Duke Ferdinando I (1588); was also in the service of the Mantuan court (from the early 1600s). The Florentine Camerata met at the home of Count Giovanni de' Bardi in the 1580s, and it is likely that Peri participated in its activities.

As early as 1583 he collaborated with other composers in writing music for the intermedi to Giovanni Fedini's dramatic comedy *Le due Persilie*. In the 1590s the home of Jacopo Corsi became the meeting place for many Florentine musicians, poets, and philosophers, and Peri undoubtedly attended, for Corsi collaborated with him in setting Ottavio Rinuccini's pastoral *Dafne* to music. The 1st known performance of this work was a private one in Florence in 1598. Later versions were given in 1599, 1600, and 1605. *Dafne* is generally recognized as the 1st opera in monodic style (i.e., vocal solos supported by instruments), which was termed *stile rappresentativo.*

Peri's next opera was *Euridice*, again to a text by Rinuccini; some of the music was rewritten by Caccini for the 1st performance, which was given for the wedding of Maria de' Medici and Henri IV of France at the Palazzo Pitti in Florence (1600). He composed the opera *Tetide* (libretto by Cini) for Mantua in 1608, but it was not performed. His next opera, *Adone* (libretto by Cicognini), was

finished by 1611; a performance scheduled for Mantua in 1620 never took place. Another work of the period, *La liberazione di Tirreno e d'Arnea* (1617), may be by Peri; it is also possible that he collaborated with da Gagliano on the score, or it may be totally the work of Gagliano. Peri collaborated with Gagliano on the opera *Lo sposalizio di Medoro e Angelica.* It was given in honor of the election of Emperor Ferdinand III at the Palazzo Pitti, Florence (1619). He also composed the role of Clori for the opera *La Flora*, the remainder of the music being by Gagliano. It was 1st performed in honor of the wedding of Margherita de' Medici and Duke Odoardo Farnese of Parma at the Palazzo Pitti (Florence, 1628). Peri also collaborated with Gagliano on 3 oratorios, *La benedittione di Jacob* (Florence, 1622), *Il gran natale di Christo salvator nostro* (Florence, 1622), and *La celeste guida, o vero L'Arcangelo Raffaello* (Florence, 1624), but these works are not extant. In addition to individual songs publ. in various collections of the time, he also brought out *La varie musiche* (for 1 to 3 voices) *con alcune spirituali in ultimo, per cantare, harpsichord, chitarrone, ancora la maggior parte di esse per sonare semplicemente, organ* (Florence, 1609).

Péri, La. Choreographic poem by Dukas, 1912, 1st performed in Paris. The oriental story centers on a flowerlike sleeping beauty who vanishes into the air when she is approached by an eager youth in search of immortality. The piece is often performed as a purely orch.l work; its style is ingratiatingly impressionist.

Périchole, La. Operetta by Offenbach, 1868, 1st performed in Paris. The eponymous heroine is a Peruvian street singer in the 18th century, when the country was under Spanish rule. She loves her singing partner, but the Spanish viceroy hires her as a staff member at his court. She undergoes all kinds of temptations but in the end returns to her lover. This is one of Offenbach's most famous works; several tunes from it remain exceedingly popular.

pericón (Sp.). Argentine dance in 3/8 time.

périgourdine (Fr.; It. *perigordino*). An old Flemish dance.

period. A complete musical thought of 8, 12, or 16 measures ending with an authentic cadence. A typical structure is that of the question-answer (antecedent-consequent) type, where the 1st half of the period ends in the dominant, the 2nd half with an authentic cadence in the tonic.

periodicity. A category of musical time, with formants indicating temporal recurrence at equal or unequal distances. An example appears in Stockhausen's *Klavierstück IX*.

periodique (Fr., periodic). A publisher's catalogue, as produced in London and Paris in the 18th century, sometimes focusing on a single work. These publications facilitated the purchase of published music by concert socs. and individual musicians. Gradually, literary annotations and short analyses of the work(s) offered for sale were added to the periodique, eventually giving rise to the publication of music magazines.

Perkins, Carl, noted rockabilly guitarist and songwriter; b. near Tiptonville, Tenn., Apr. 9, 1932. He grew up in rural Tenn., where he learned the guitar from an early age. He formed a family band with his brothers Jay and Clayton and local drummer W. S. Holland by his teen years, playing for local dances and events. By Perkins's early 20s the band was successful enough to earn a recording contract with the tiny Flip label; in 1955 they signed with Memphis-based Sun Records, hot off its success with another Southern crooner, Elvis Presley. Perkins's second release, *Blue Suede Shoes*, topped the country, pop, and R&B charts, selling over 2 million copies. Booked to appear on national television, the band was involved in a serious automobile accident en route to the performance; brother Jay died and Carl was seriously injured. Although Perkins had other hits, his career never regained its momentum.

Perkins signed with Columbia Records in 1958, but by the early 1960s he was more popular in England than at home. One of his British fans, guitarist George Harrison of the Beatles, did much to popularize Perkins's songs, recording with the mop-topped group versions of *Honey, Don't, Everybody's Trying to Be My Baby*, and *Matchbox* (itself a remake of Blind Lemon Jefferson's classic 1920s blues song). Perkins became part of Johnny Cash's roadshow in the sixties, touring with the deep-voiced country singer through the mid-seventies. Although he has staged various "comebacks" over the past decades, Perkins has never really broken out of the nostalgia circuit. He was inducted into the Rock and Roll Hall of Fame in 1987.

Perlman, Itzhak, brilliant Israeli-American violinist; b. Tel Aviv, Aug. 31, 1945. He was stricken with polio when he was 4, which left his legs paralyzed; for the rest of his life he had to walk on crutches. Despite this ghastly handicap, he began to play the violin and gave regular recitals at Tel Aviv.

In 1958 he was discovered in Israel by Ed Sullivan, the TV producer, and appeared on his show in N.Y. (1959). Perlman's courage and good humor endeared him to the public at once. He remained in N.Y., where his parents soon joined him, and he was accepted as a scholarship student in the classes of Ivan Galamian and Dorothy DeLay at the Juilliard School of Music. He made his professional American debut in 1963, playing with the National Orch. Assoc. in N.Y. In 1964 he won 1st prize in the Leventritt Competition, which carried, besides the modest purse of $1,000, a significant bonus—an appearance with the N.Y. Phil. It also brought about a lasting friendship with Isaac Stern, who promoted him with all the enthusiasm of a sincere admirer. Perlman's career was no longer a problem: he toured the U.S. from coast to coast in 1965–66 and toured Europe in 1966–67. He also began to teach and in 1975 was appointed to the faculty of Brooklyn College.

Perlman seemed to be overflowing with a genuine love of life; he played not only classical music but also Tin Pan Alley song arrangements, ragtime, and jazz; with Isaac Stern and Pinchas Zukerman he indulged in public charivari on television to which he furnished enjoyable commentaries like a professional comedian. He became quite a habitué of the White House, being particularly popular with President Reagan, who savored Perlman's showbiz savvy; his being handicapped only added to the public appreciation of his TV appearances in the center of American power. In 1986 he was awarded the U.S. Medal of Freedom.

permeability. A factor that determines the degree of interpenetrability of thematic, nonthematic, and bruitistic elements, reinforcing the structure of a given tonal complex, and occasionally coming to a mutually annihilating collision, in which the resulting gestalt becomes a terraced and tessellated ziggurat. The term *permeability* is also used to describe the process of mutual osmosis among parameters of ORGANIZED SOUND.

permutation. In serial music, a theoretical term for the changing of the order of individual notes in the basic series, either through the three basic operations (retrograde, inversion, retrograde inversion), cell operations (exchanging 3- or 4-note row fragments with the same intervallic content), arithmetic processes (taking every other pitch, etc.), or rotation (transposing the row according to its own constituents).

pernicious interference. The law of contrasts is basic to every piece of modern music, but supererogatory expansion and ornamental promiscuity of melodic and harmonic elements constitute pernicious interference. Taste and technical skill are the sole means to avoid this danger.

Perotin (called Perotinus Magnus and Magister Perotinus), celebrated composer who flourished in the 12th century. His very identity, as well as a general outline of his life, remains open to speculation. Research by H. Tischler indicates that he was born between 1155 and 1160, may have studied with Leonin, carried out his major work on the revision of the *Magnus liber* between 1180 and 1190, was involved in the early development of the MOTET between 1190 and 1200, wrote his works for 4 voices at the close of the century, and died between 1200 and 1205. Another chronology has been propounded by Reckow, Rokseth, and Sanders, who maintain that he wrote the works for 4 voices in the 1190s, which were the early years of his career, worked on the *Magnus liber* during the 1st years of the new century, wrote elaborate clausulas about 1210, was instrumental in creating Latin motets between 1210 and 1220, and died about 1225.

perpetual canon. A canon in which the final cadence leads back into the opening measures; a ROUND.

perpetuum mobile (Lat., perpetual motion). MOTO PERPETUO; a type of short and rapid composition, usually for a solo instrument.

Perséphone. Ballet by Stravinsky, 1934, with singing and narration; it was premiered in Paris. The plot involves the mythical tale of Persephone's descent into Hades and her return to this earth.

Persichetti, Vincent (Ludwig)

≈≈ ≈≈ ≈≈ ≈≈ ≈≈

Remarkable American composer whose finely amalgamated instrumental and symphonic music created an image of classical modernity; b. Philadelphia, June 6, 1915; d. there, Aug. 13, 1987. His father was a native of Abruzzi, Italy, who emigrated to the U.S. in 1894. His mother was of German extraction, hailing from Bonn. Persichetti's middle name was given to him not to honor Beethoven but to commemorate his maternal grandfather, who owned a saloon in Camden, N.J. Vincent studied piano, organ, double bass, tuba, theory, and composition as a youth; began his career as a professional musician when he was only 11 years old; became a church organist at 15. He took courses in composition with Russell King Miller at the Combs Cons. (MusB., 1936); then served as head of the theory and composition dept. there; concurrently studied conducting with Fritz Reiner at the Curtis Inst. of Music (diploma, 1938) and piano with Olga Samaroff and composition with Nordoff at the Philadelphia Cons. (M.Mus, 1941; D.Mus, 1945); also studied composition with Roy Harris at Colorado College. From 1941 to 1947 he was head of the theory and composition dept. of the Philadelphia Cons.; in 1947 he joined the faculty of the Juilliard School of Music in N.Y.; in 1963 he was named chairman of the composition dept. there. In 1952 he became director of music publishing of Elkan-Vogel, Inc. With F. Schreiber he wrote a biography of William Schuman (N.Y., 1954); publ. a valuable manual, *20th Century Harmony: Creative Aspects and Practice* (N.Y., 1961).

Persichetti's music is remarkable for its polyphonic skill in fusing the ostensibly incompatible idioms of Classicism, Romanticism, and stark modernism while the melodic lines maintain an almost Italianate diatonicism in a lyrical manner. The skillful concatenation of ostensibly mutually exclusive elements created a style that was characteristically Persichetti's. He was not interested in program music or in any kind of descriptive tonal works (except a piece of background music written for the Radio City Music Hall organs, performed in 1969). His significance for American music, therefore, is comprised in his 9 syms. and, most particularly, in his 12 piano sonatas and 6 piano sonatinas.

Although he stood far from the turmoil of musical politics, he unexpectedly found himself in the center of a controversy when he was commissioned by the 1973 Presidential Inauguration Committee to write a work for narrator and orch. for a performance at President Richard Nixon's inauguration. Persichetti selected the text of Abraham Lincoln's 2nd inaugural address, but, surprisingly, objections were raised by certain groups to the passionate denunciation of war in the narrative, at a time when the Vietnam War was very much in the news. The scheduled performance by the Philadelphia Orch. was hurriedly canceled, and the work's premiere was deferred to a performance by the St. Louis Sym. Orch. in Jan. 1973. In 1987 Persichetti contracted cancer of the lungs, but even when racked by disease he continued to work on his last opus, *Hymns and Responses for the Church Year*, vol.

II. He requested that his body be donated to medical science. His devoted wife suffered a stroke and died on Thanksgiving Day in the same year.

Persichetti's works include the opera *Parable XX: The Sibyl* (1976; 1985); 9 symphonies (1942; 1942; 1946; 1951; Sym. for Strings, 1953; Sym. for Band, 1956; *Liturgical*, 1958; 1967; *Sinfonia: Janiculum*, 1970); and other orch.1 works; chamber compositions including 4 string quartets (1939; 1944; 1959; 1972); keyboard compositions, including 12 piano sonatas (1939–80); 6 piano sonatinas (1950–54); 8 harpsichord sonatas (1951–84); choral works; and a number of songs, including the major cycle for soprano and piano entitled *Harmonium*, after poems of Wallace Stevens (N.Y., 1952).

pes (Lat.). Harmonic support or accompaniment to a round.

pesante (It.; Fr. *pesamment*). Heavily, ponderously; firmly, vigorously.

Peter and the Wolf. Symphonic fairy tale by Prokofiev, 1936, for narrator and orch. He wrote it for the Moscow Children's Theater in a couple of weeks, to his own text. Peter is a Russian lad who takes care of his pet animals, including a bird, a duck, and a cat. When a wolf invades his outdoor menagerie, Peter organizes a hunt, rounds up the predator, and saves his beloved creatures. The score pursues a didactic purpose, each animal being represented by a different instrument(s) and theme. It was 1st performed in Moscow, and became enormously popular all over the world.

Peter Grimes. Opera by Britten, 1945, his most popular, 1st produced in London. The libretto is taken from G. Crabbe's 19th-century poem *The Borough*. The music is alternately lyric and tragic; the symphonic interludes, descriptive of the sea, and particularly one imitating the cries of the gulls, are very fine. Peter Grimes is a fisherman whose apprentice is lost at sea. Everyone suspects Grimes of murder, and he is enjoined at the inquest not to hire other apprentices. He disobeys the order and hires a new helper, who falls off a cliff to his death. A sympathetic sea captain advises the by now demented Grimes to sail off and "sink the boat" so that he perishes at sea.

Peter Ibbetson. Opera by D. Taylor, 1931, 1st performed at the Metropolitan Opera, N.Y. The plot, based on a novel

by Du Maurier, involves Peter and his childhood sweetheart Mary; they live separate lives but have vivid dreams of each other. Peter is sentenced to life imprisonment for murder; Mary marries, is widowed, and dies. Either in dreams, or in anticipated reality, the lovers are reunited. The music has its merits, and the opera was acclaimed at its performances; but after a few seasons it evaporated like the dream stuff its story was made of.

Peter Pan. Symphonic poem by Toch, 1956, performed in Seattle, based on the J. M. Barrie tale.

Peter, Paul and Mary. (Guitar/vocal: Peter Yarrow, b. N.Y., May 31, 1938; guitar/vocal: Noel Paul Stookey, b. Baltimore, Md., Nov. 30, 1937; vocal: Mary Travers, b. Louisville, Ky., Nov. 7, 1937.) Famed folk trio of the 1960s who introduced the songs of Bob Dylan to a mass audience. Formed by canny promoter Albert Grossman, the group 1st hit it big with their interpretations of traditional folk songs like *900 Miles* and modern folk-styled compositions, including Pete Seeger's *Where Have All the Flowers Gone*. They had a major hit with Bob Dylan's *Blowin' in the Wind* in 1963, followed by his *Don't Think Twice It's All Right*, and subsequently recorded songs by other young singer/songwriters, including Tom Paxton, John Denver, and Gordon Lightfoot. The group had their greatest success in 1967 with Denver's *Leaving on a Jet Plane*, along with Yarrow's composition *The Song Is Love*. A children's album, playfully titled *Peter, Paul and Mommy*, produced a major hit with *Day Is Done* and helped revive their 1962 hit, *Puff, the Magic Dragon*. They broke up in 1970 to pursue solo careers with varying degrees of success; they reunited in 1978, continuing to record and perform to today.

Peterson, Oscar (Emmanuel), noted Canadian jazz pianist; b. Montreal, Aug. 15, 1925. He studied piano; made appearances on Canadian radio; also played with the orch. of Johnny Holmes (1944–47). In 1949 he went to N.Y. and soon established himself as one of the finest jazz pianists of the day. He made numerous tours, often appearing with a guitarist and bass player as fellow musicians (he later replaced the guitar with drums); he also was successful as a guest artist with American orchs. He was made an Officer of the Order of Canada (1973). In 1991 he was named chancellor of York Univ. in Toronto.

petit, -e (Fr.). Small, little.

petite flûte (Fr.). PICCOLO.

Petite Suite. Work for piano 4-hands by Debussy, 1888. The movements are *En bateau, Cortège, Menuet,* and *Ballet;* the music is nicely romantic. Henri Büsser later arranged it for orch.

Petite Symphonie Concertante. Chamber orch. work by F. Martin, 1946, scored for harp, harpsichord, piano, and strings; 1st performed in Basel. This successful neoclassicist work is one of the 1st in which Martin employs DODECA-PHONIC procedures.

Petri, Egon, eminent German pianist and pedagogue of Dutch descent; b. Hannover, Mar. 23, 1881; d. Berkeley, Calif., May 27, 1962. His father, Henri Wilhelm Petri (1856–1914), was a Dutch violinist who served as concertmaster in Hannover and of the Leipzig Gewandhaus orch.; his mother was a singer. He studied violin and organ as well as piano from an early age; began piano lessons with Carreno, later studying with Buchmayer, Draeseke, and Busoni; also received composition lessons from Kretzchmar. Having pursued a career as an orch. violinist and as a member of his father's string quartet, he launched his career as a piano virtuoso in 1902; subsequently toured extensively in Europe; was also active as a teacher, serving on the faculties of the Royal Manchester College of Music (1905–11) and the Berlin Hochschule für Musik (1921–26); then taught in Zakopane. In 1932 he made his U.S. debut in N.Y., then performed on both sides of the Atlantic until the outbreak of World War II; also taught at Boston's Malkin Cons. (1934–35).

After World War II he resumed his extensive tours; having taught at Cornell Univ. (1940–46), he then settled in Calif. to teach at Mills College (1947–57) and the San Francisco Cons. (1952–62). He made his farewell concert appearance in a recital in 1960. As Busoni's foremost student he followed in his mentor's grand manner of piano virtuosity. His performances of Bach and Liszt were formidable; he also championed the works of Alkan and Medtner as well as Busoni.

Petri, Michala, gifted Danish recorder player; b. Copenhagen, July 7, 1958. She began to play at the incredible age of 3 and appeared on Danish radio when she was 5; made her concert debut as a soloist in Copenhagen in 1969. She formed a trio with her mother, a harpsichordist, and her cellist brother, and toured widely with it. She studied with Ferdinand Conrad at the Hannover Staatliche Hochschule für Musik (1970–76). In addition to chamber music performances, she toured extensively as a soloist; made her U.S. debut with N.Y.'s 92nd St. Y Chamber Orch. in 1982, and 1st played in Japan in 1984. Her repertoire ranges from the early Baroque era to contemporary music; she has commissioned a number of composers to write works for her.

Petrouchka (*Pétrouchka, Petrushka*). Stravinsky wrote this most strikingly Russian work while away from Russia, completing it in Switzerland when he was only 28 years old (1911). The famous bitonal combination in the score, which became known as the Petrouchka chord, is a superposition of C-major and F-sharp major triads, white keys against black keys on the piano keyboard, falling easily under the fingers of both hands. Stravinsky played sketches of a piano and orch. work for the famous Russian impresario Diaghilev, who thought the music would make an excellent ballet; the piano work was reconceived as a dance work (although there remains a large piano part in *Petrouchka*). The scenario represented the Russian spring carnival, featuring a puppet show that evolves into the ballet itself. One puppet is named Petrouchka, an affectionate peasant form of Peter. He woos a beautiful ballerina puppet but is thwarted by a rich Moor puppet who throws poor Petrouchka out of her quarters. There is a pathetic interlude, with Petrouchka's motive derived from the broken bitonal chord. Eventually the Moor murders Petrouchka; his ghost appears at the ballet's end to haunt the puppeteer.

For his basic materials Stravinsky made ample use of popular street songs of old Russia, but he also borrowed some Austrian waltzes and even French chansonettes. There is an imitation of the barrel organ with its seductive disharmonies. *Petrouchka* was performed in the Diaghilev series of Russian ballets in Paris; it was an immediate success. Debussy was greatly impressed by it. In a private letter he described Stravinsky as a young savage who swept away all the musical rules and conquered the listeners. Strangely enough, *Petrouchka* was criticized by some Russian critics who said that Stravinsky betrayed his national heritage by a vulgar and distorted treatment of native songs to please the decadent Parisian tastes. Some American critics found the score unfit for a concert performance because it smacked of circus and vaudeville. But all such fault-finding was soon forgotten. The score of *Petrouchka* still stands, after 75 years, as a remarkable specimen of true musical MODERNISM.

Pettersson, Gustaf Allan, remarkable sui generis Swedish composer; b. Vastra Ryd, Sept. 19, 1911; d. Stockholm, June 20, 1980. His father was a blacksmith; his mother was a devout woman who could sing; the family moved to Stockholm and lived in dire poverty. Pettersson sold Christmas cards and bought a violin from his meager returns. He also practiced keyboard playing on a church organ. In 1930 he entered the Stockholm Cons., studying violin and viola with J. Ruthstrom and music theory with H. M. Melchers. From 1940 to 1951 he played viola in the Stockholm Concert Soc. Orch., and also studied composition with Otto Olsson, Tor Mann, and Blomdahl. In his leisure hours he wrote poetry; he set 24 of his poems to music. In 1951 he went to Paris to study with Honegger and Leibowitz. Returning to Sweden, he devoted himself to composition in large forms.

His music is permeated with dark moods, and he supplied deeply pessimistic annotations to his syms. and other works. In 1963 he began suffering from painful rheumatoid arthritis; he stubbornly continued to compose while compulsively proclaiming his misfortunes in private and in public print. He described himself as "a voice crying out, drowned in the noise of the times." The Stockholm Phil. played several of his syms., but when his 7th Sym., originally scheduled for its American tour in 1968, was taken off the program, Pettersson, wrathful at this callous defection, forbade performance of any of his music in Sweden.

Stylistically Pettersson's music is related to Mahler's symphonic manner, in the grandiosity of design and in the passionate, exclamatory dynamism of utterance. Most of his syms. are cast in single movements, with diversity achieved by frequent changes of mood, tempo, meter, and rhythm. Characteristically, all 16 of them except No. 10 are set in minor keys. His Sym. No. 1, composed in 1950–51, was

withdrawn with instructions to perform it only posthumously! He also composed other orch.1 works, including 3 concertos for string orch. (1949–50; 1956; 1956–57); and chamber and vocal works, notably *24 Barfotasånger* (24 Barefoot Songs) for Voice and Piano (1943–45); *Vox humana*, 18 songs for soprano, alto, tenor, baritone, mixed chorus, and string orch., to texts by Native Americans (1974; Stockholm, 1976).

Petty, Tom, noted American rock 'n' roll singer and songwriter, leader of the group the Heartbreakers, b. Gainesville, Fla., Oct. 20, 1953. The nasal-voiced singer/songwriter has enjoyed a long career, both as the leader of the Heartbreakers and as a solo artist. Petty is greatly influenced by his 1960s predecessors, including the Byrds, Bob Dylan (with whom he has performed), and Neil Young, creating music that sounds eerily reminiscent of their earlier hits. He began performing during high school in Gainesville, joining the band Mudcrutch on his graduation along with local guitarist Mike Campbell and pianist Benmont Tench. By the early 1970s they were in Los Angeles, where they gained a recording contract with Shelter Records. Now known as Tom Petty and the Heartbreakers, they recorded two albums for the label, producing some local hits. But when the label was sold to MCA, they entered a protracted legal battle that led to a hiatus in recording.

On their own Backstreets label, Petty and the group produced their 1st major hit in 1979 with *Refugee*. Two years later a duet with popular Calif. chanteuse Stevie Nicks on *Stop Draggin' My Heart Around* elevated Petty's stature greatly among pop fans. The band took a break to pursue individual projects from 1983 to 1985, then returned to the charts with *Don't Come Around Here No More*. In 1986 they toured and recorded with Bob Dylan, giving audiences a chance to hear 2 treble-toned singers on the same bill! Two years later, joining with Dylan, George Harrison, Roy Orbison, and producer Jeff Lynne, Petty became a member of the mock-band the Travellin' Willburys, who scored a series of surprise hits. He produced a successful solo album with several hits, including *I Won't Back Down* and *Free Fallin'*, in collaboration with Lynne. The Heartbreakers returned to recording and touring with Petty in 1991. Petty has since continued to record with the band, even for "solo" projects like 1994's *Wildflowers*. He scored the film *She's the One* in 1995, which produced the hit *Heart So Big*.

peu à peu (Fr.). Little by little; POCO A POCO. *Un peu*, a little.

pezzi (It.). Pieces. *Pezzi concertati*, concerted pieces; *pezzi staccati*, any numbers separated from an opera, etc.

pezzo (It.). A piece; a number (of an opera, etc.).

pf. Abbrev. for *pianoforte*; start softly, then get louder suddenly.

Pfeife (Ger.). Fife.

Pfitzner, Hans (Erich), eminent German composer and conductor; b. Moscow (of German parents), May 5, 1869; d. Salzburg, May 22, 1949. He studied piano with James Kwast and composition with Iwan Knorr at the Hoch Cons. in Frankfurt; in 1899 he eloped with Kwast's daughter and took her to England, where he married her. In 1892–93 he taught piano and theory at the Cons. of Koblenz; then served as assistant conductor of the Municipal Theater in Mainz (1894–96); from 1897 to 1907 he was on the faculty of the Stern Cons. in Berlin; concurrently he conducted at the Theater Westens (1903–1906). During the 1907–1908 season he led the renowned Kaim Concerts in Munich. From 1908 to 1918 he was in Strasbourg as municipal music director and also served as dean at the Strasbourg Cons.; from 1910 to 1916 he conducted at the Strasbourg Opera. During the 1919–20 season he was music director of the Munich Konzertverein; from 1920 to 1929 he led a master class at the Berlin Academy of Arts; from 1929 to 1934 he taught composition at the Akademie der Tonkunst in Munich.

Being of certified German stock, though born in Russia, he was favored by the Nazi authorities and became an ardent supporter of the 3rd Reich; he reached the nadir of his moral degradation in dedicating an overture, *Krakauer Begrüssung*, to Hans Frank, the murderous Gauleiter of occupied Poland in 1944. After the collapse of Hitler's brief millennium, Pfitzner had to face the denazification court in Munich in 1948; owing to his miserable condition in body and soul, he was exonerated. He was taken to a home for the aged in Munich and later was transferred to Salzburg, where he died in misery. Eventually his body was honorably laid to rest in a Vienna cemetery.

In his better days Pfitzner was hailed in Germany as a great national composer. He presented a concert of his works in Berlin in 1893, with excellent auguries. After the premiere of his opera *Der arme Heinrich* in Mainz (1895), the critics, among them the prestigious Humperdinck, praised the work in extravagant terms. Even more success-

ful was his opera *Palestrina*, making use of Palestrina's themes, written to his own libretto, which was conducted by Bruno Walter at its 1st performance in Munich (1917). The Pfitzner Soc. was formed in Munich as early as 1904, and a Hans Pfitzner Assoc. was established in Berlin in 1938, with Furtwängler as president. Although Pfitzner's music is traditional in style and conservative in harmony, he was regarded as a follower of the modern school, a comrade-in-arms of his close contemporary R. Strauss. Very soon, however, his fame began to dwindle; there were fewer performances of his operas and still fewer hearings of his instrumental works; he himself bitterly complained of this lack of appreciation of his art. It was a miserable end for a once important and capable musician.

Phantasie (Ger.). 1. A FANTASIA. 2. Fancy, imagination.

Phantasiestück (Ger.). A FANTASIA; in modern music, a short piece of a romantic and intensely subjective cast with no set form.

phase composition. A type of minimalism, developed in the 1960s by Steve Reich, in which shared melodic lines are gradually shifted from one another by the addition or subtraction of 1 time unit; this approach could also be applied to ELECTRONIC MUSIC, whether through tape loops or the use of *gating*, programmed phase shifting.

phases. A term invented by Stockhausen to designate the time interval between 2 successive tones that results from the probabilistic or intentional distribution of the basic rhythmic unit into equal or unequal time value.

Philharmonic Concerto. Variations for orch. by Hindemith, 1932, for the 50th anniversary of the Berlin Phil., which gave its 1st performance. There are 6 variations played with changing emphasis on one or another orch.l group.

Philidor, André Danican (l'aîné), father of François-André Danican Philidor; b. Versailles, *c.* 1647; d. Dreux, Aug. 11, 1730. He was the son of Jean Danican (*c.* 1620–1679), a composer and royal musician. In 1659 André entered the *grande écurie*, succeeding Michel Danican (*c.* 1600–59), a family member; in it he played the cromorne, trompette marine, and drums. He subsequently played the oboe, bassoon, and bass cromorne in the royal chapel and *chambre du roi*. In 1684 King Louis XIV appointed him royal music librarian, a position he held until his death. During his long tenure he acquired operas, ballets, sacred music, partbooks, etc. from various periods of French history for the collection. A large portion of this collection eventually passed to St. Michael's College, Tenbury. It is now part of the collections at the Bibliothèque Nationale in Paris and the Bibliothèque Municipale in Versailles. Philidor continued to serve as a musician in the royal chapel until 1722 and in the royal service until 1729. By his 1st wife he had 16 children, and by his 2nd, 5; his most famous son was François-André Danican Philidor.

André's best-known works are his *opéras-ballets*: *Le Canal de Versailles* (Versailles, 1687); *Le Mariage de la couture avec la grosse Cathos* (Versailles, 1687?); *La Princesse de Crète* (Marly, 1700?); *La Mascarade du roi de la Chine* (Marly, 1700); *La Mascarade du vaisseau marchand* (Marly, 1700); *La Mascarade de la noce village* (Marly, 1700); also instrumental works, including dances, marches, etc.

Philidor, François-André Danican, the greatest in the line of musicians in the Philidor family, the youngest son of André Danican Philidor (l'aîné); b. Dreux, Sept. 7, 1726; d. London, Aug. 31, 1795. He was a page boy in the royal chapel in Versailles, where he studied music with the maître de chapelle, André Campra. It was also at that time that he learned to play chess. A motet by him was performed in the royal chapel when he was 12. In 1740 he went to Paris, where he supported himself by copying and teaching. His interest in chess continued; he gained distinction as an outstanding player by defeating a number of celebrated chess masters of the day. He publ. a fundamental treatise on chess, *L'Analyze des échecs* (1749). As a member of the St. James Chess Club in London he gave lectures and demonstrations as a master; a famous chess opening was named after him. In the meantime he began a successful career as a composer for the theater. His 1st success was *Le Maréchal ferrant* (1761), which was accorded numerous performances. His *Le Sorcier* (1764) was also a triumph. Although *Tom Jones* (1765) was an initial failure, it enjoyed great popularity after its libretto was revised by Sedaine and performed in 1766. The same fate attended his *Ernelinde, princesse de Vorvège* when it was 1st given at the Paris Opéra in 1767. It was subsequently revised by Sedaine and performed most successfully as *Ernelinde* in Versailles in 1773. Philidor continued to compose for the stage until his death, but he allowed his love for chess to take more and more of his time. He made frequent trips to London after 1775 to play at the St. James Chess Club.

Philidor was one of the finest early composers of OPÉRA-COMIQUE. Although his scores are often hampered by poor librettos, his orch. writing is effective. He was an inventive composer, and introduced the novelty of a vocal quartet a cappella (in *Tom Jones*). He wrote sacred music as well. His choral work, the *Carmen saeculare*, after Horace, proved most successful at its premiere in London in 1779. Other vocal works include *12 ariettes périodiques*.

Philippe de Vitry. VITRY, PHILIPPE DE.

Philosoph, Der. Sym. No. 22 by Haydn, 1764, in E-flat major. As in most of Haydn's nicknamed symphonies, the title was invented by person or persons unknown for reasons unfathomable.

phonograph

The idea of preserving the sound of speech or music occupied the minds of poets and scientists for centuries. In the domain of fable, sound was captured in lead pipes. When the nature of sound was proved to be airwaves that could be recorded by attaching a stylus to a tuning fork and traced as a series of sinusoidal zigzags on a rotating blackened cylinder, the problem seemed to be near solution. All that had to be done was to play back the grooves on the cylinder with a sharp point and the original sound produced by the tuning fork would be returned. In 1877 Thomas Alva Edison attached a sensitive membrane to a stylus that impressed grooves on a wax cylinder. By retracing the grooves with the same stylus, the membrane was set in reciprocal motion and Edison heard the sound of his own voice reciting *Mary Had a Little Lamb*. Edison named this new invention the phonograph (Grk., sound writing; U.K. *gramophone*).

Most epoch-making inventions appear simultaneously, and indeed Edison had a close rival in the person of the Paris inventor Charles Cros, who developed a talking machine that he named the *parlephone* (speaking sound). Edison exhibited his phonograph at fairs and scientific expositions, but for many years it was regarded merely as an amusing toy. The rendition of the voice was squeaky and scratchy, but progress was rapid. A horn was attached to the recording membrane above the cylinder that amplified the sound so it could be heard at a distance.

Edison visited Russia in 1890 and showed his instrument to eminent musicians who were tremendously impressed. Rimsky-Korsakov signed an endorsement: "I heard the phonograph and I marveled at this invention of genius. Being a musician I can foresee the possibility of wide application of this device in the domain of musical art. A precise reproduction of talented interpretations of musical compositions, of outstanding singing voices, recording of folk songs, and improvisations by the means of the phonograph can be of incalculable importance to music. The phonograph also possesses the amazing capacity of accelerating and slowing down the tempo and to transpose [*sic*]. Glory be to great Edison!" Rimsky-Korsakov's vision proved to be correct; in 1894 the Russian collector of folk songs Mme. Lineva undertook a series of trips in the Volga region with a specially constructed phonograph and published her authentic findings.

A decisive step in transforming an entertaining toy into an important musical instrument was the invention by Emile Berliner of a phonograph disc in 1888. Despite the obvious advantages of a phonograph disc, Edison continued to manufacture cylinders introducing some improvements, finally yielding the field to the disc in 1929. In the meantime the phonograph became a major industry, particularly in America. In 1900 the Victor Talking Machine Co. adopted as its advertising symbol a picture of a dog listening to "His Master's voice" on a disc phonograph. So famous did the dog (named Nipper) and the slogan become that the phonograph itself became generally known after the name of this company, Victrola. The standard speed was established as 78 revolutions per minute (rpm).

The great drawback of the early phonograph was its limited length and the bulk of its discs. Each side of the disc could play only 4 minutes and 30 seconds, and when records were made of syms. and operas, individual movements had to be split into several sections. Just as the invention of the phonograph itself was a natural development of known scientific facts, so the method of increasing the duration of the music on a single disc was substantially enlarged by a seemingly obvious improvement in the late 1940s. By increasing the number of grooves on the disc and simultaneously slowing down the number of rpms from 78 to 33 1/3 or 45 rpms, it became possible to produce the 12-inch (diameter) long-playing record ("LP"), with each 33 1/3 disc accommodating nearly half an hour of music. (The "45" disc is a 7-inch disc that accommodates up to about 7 or 8 minutes.) Furthermore, manufacturers began making records out of an unbreakable plastic material that was lighter than the shellac of the fragile 78s. An opera recorded on a "78" required many discs that weighed several pounds, whereas on the new 33 1/3 LPs the same opera could be recorded on 2 or 3 discs.

At the same time, progress was made in simulating natural hearing by placing microphones at strategic positions when recording an orch. or an opera. Soon the 1st step toward a more realistic sound was made with the introduction of binaural recording, in which 2 separate monophonic channels were combined; by 1958 the technique was expanded to stereophonic recording ("stereo"), from the Greek word *stereos* (solid), in which sound could be distributed freely between the 2 channels through "mixing" of the recorded sound. Recording through 4 channels, giving a vivid impression of being "surrounded" by sound, was introduced in 1970 under the name *quadraphonic*; it was a commercial failure.

Finally in the 1980s a remarkable and theoretically imperishable improvement was made with the invention of *compact discs*, or *CDs* for short. The stylus and analog recording are dispensed with; instead sound is registered as a series of numbers (i.e., digitally) and transferred onto the metal-coated disc by laser. Old recordings were not scrapped, however. Using ingenious methods of salvaging and amplifying early recordings, the voices of Caruso, Adelina Patti, and others were resurrected. At the same time, successful recordings were made of the playing of famous composers, among them Debussy, Paderewski, and Scriabin, from well-preserved paper rolls of the pianola.

By the last quarter of the 20th century the phonograph industry became a multibillion-dollar business. Its prosperity is nourished by untold millions of albums recorded by the great stars of rock 'n' roll, country-western music, and a wide variety of popular artists. The slang expression "in the groove" testifies to the popularity of the recording industry. Some small recording companies specialize in novelties, resurrecting the forgotten masterpieces of the past or giving a chance to modern composers to record their works. As a result of these activities, large record libraries have in their catalogues records covering the entire course of music history and providing invaluable educational material for students and music lovers.

Phorion. Orch. work by Foss, 1967, with organ, electric piano, and electric guitar added. The piece was premiered by the N.Y. Phil. The title derives from a Greek word meaning "something stolen"; what has been purloined is a portion from the prelude of Bach's E-major partita for solo violin.

phorminx. An ancient Greek CHORDOPHONE, either a 4-string plucked lyre or an early kithara, mentioned by Homer.

phrase. Half of an 8-measure period. Also, any short figure or passage complete in itself and unbroken in continuity.

phrase mark. A curved line connecting the notes of a phrase.

phrasing. 1. The bringing out into proper relief of the phrases (whether motives, figures, subjects, or passages). 2. The signs of notation devised to further this end.

Phrygian mode. A church mode corresponding to the scale from E up to E on the white keys of the piano (E–F–G–A–B–C–D–E). Although the name is inherited from Greece, the Phrygian mode is not identical with the ancient Greek mode of the same name, which corresponds to the Ionian ecclesiastical mode. The plagal mode corresponding to the Phrygian mode is Hypophrygian, with the ambitus extending from the dominant B of the Phrygian mode to the next dominant and thus becoming identical in construction, although not in function, with the theoretical Locrian mode.

physharmonica. Small free-reed organ, invented by Anton Häckl of Vienna (1818), designed to be placed under a piano keyboard to play the melody simultaneously in order to sustain it. This and similar instruments were the precursors of the HARMONIUM.

piacere, a (It.). At pleasure; freely, without precise regard of notation.

piacevole (It.). Pleasant, agreeable; use a smooth, suave delivery free from strong accents.

Piaf, Edith (born Giovanna Gassion), noted French chanteuse; b. Paris, Dec. 19, 1915; d. there, Oct. 11, 1963. Her childhood was tragic; she was abandoned by her mother, an Italian café singer and prostitute; traveled with her father, a circus contortionist, taking part in his act as a shill for his street-corner acrobatics. She then became a street singer in Paris, earning the nickname "la môme Piaf" (the waif sparrow, in Parisian argot) on account of her ragged and emaciated appearance. She was befriended by a cabaret owner; when he was murdered, she was held by the French police as a material witness. During World War II and the German occupation she entertained French prisoners in Germany; as a result she was accused of collaboration, but she was exonerated. She made her 1st tour of the U.S. in 1947; sang widely in subsequent years, making appearances in films and on television.

Although untutored, Piaf developed a type of ballad singing that was infused with profound sentiment and expressive artistry, eliciting an enthusiastic response from nightclub audiences and sophisticated music critics alike. Not a songwriter, she made many chansonettes internationally famous, including *La Vie en Rose, What Can I Do?, I'll Remember Today, Hymne à l'Amour,* and *Les Trois Cloches.*

piangevole (It.). Tearfully; in a mournful, plaintive style.

pianino (It.). An upright PIANOFORTE.

pianissimo (It.). Very soft; abbreviated *pp*.

pianississimo (It.). Extremely soft; abbreviated *ppp*.

piano

Soft, softly (sign *p*). *Piano pedal*, the soft (or left) spedal of the PIANOFORTE. 2. Standard abbrev. for *pianoforte* used in this dictionary. The piano (It.) is a keyboard stringed instrument whose tones are produced by hammers striking the strings. The principal parts are the *frame*, the *soundboard*, the *strings*, the *action*, and the *pedals*. The most popular musical instrument in the home and on the concert stage, the piano was invented in the 1st decade of the 18th century by Bartolommeo Cristofori, who called it a "gravicembalo col piano e forte" (large keyboard with soft and loud). This rather clumsy description was soon abbreviated to pianoforte or (particularly in Russia) fortepiano. Subsequently it became known under its present name, a rather inadequate and illogical name for an instrument that was invented in order to achieve both soft and loud sonorities.

The most important innovation of the piano, as distinguished from its keyboard predecessors, the harpsichord and clavichord, was in its mechanism of sound production. In the clavichord the tone was produced by metal tangents striking the string; on the harpsichord the strings were plucked. In the piano's *hammer action* the sound is produced by hammers striking the strings from below. Although the mechanism activating the hammers seems simple, the technical construction of the pianoforte required a great deal of ingenuity and inventive skill. The hammers had to fall back to their original position after striking the strings without accidentally rebounding, and then a soft damper that is lifted when the key is struck must quickly fall back on the string to avoid its continued reverberation. But if rapid repetition of the same note is needed, a special device had to be provided to make the hammer drop to an intermediate height between the original position and the strings, so that it could strike the string again in an instant. All of these requirements were met by the mechanical conglomeration called *escapement*.

In order to produce a sound an octave deeper, a string must be doubled in length. If all piano strings were of the same thickness, then the string for the lowest C in the bass, 7 octaves below the highest C on the keyboard, would have to be 128 times as long as the string for the high C, an obvious manufacturing impossibility. An examination of the soundboard under the lid of the GRAND PIANO will show that the bass strings are much thicker than the treble strings, and it is through a combination of increased thickness and increased length that the bass strings can be accommodated within the winglike shape of the piano. (The German word for the grand piano is *Flügel*, wing.) Curiously enough, Beethoven adopted the German name *Hammerklavier* for the sonatas of his last period; the word simply means "hammer keyboard."

The piano strings in the bass range are single for each tone; in the middle range they are paired, to give more resonance, and in the extreme treble there are 3 strings to each tone to enhance the resonance still more. Dampers are absent in the extreme upper register of the piano because the thin strings do not sustain enough resonance to require dampening. A pianist may find it rewarding and intriguing to play rapid and loud passages in the uppermost octave on the keyboard and listen to the curious effect of an acoustic cloud or white noise that lingers for a fraction of a second.

Modern pianos have 3 pedals; the right-hand

Square piano, 19th century

(damper, loud) pedal releases all the dampers and gives out a resonant harmony that includes the sounds of all the keys played while the pedal is held down. It is therefore properly applied only in passages of a predominantly chordal consistency. Unfortunately, many amateur pianists become addicted to the loud pedal even when the harmony is not uniform, thus producing a chaos of unrelated sounds but at the same time covering up possible wrong notes that become drowned in the tonal mass. The left-hand (soft) pedal shifts the entire keyboard slightly to the right, with the result that the hammers strike the bass strings obliquely, thus diminishing their volume, and strike only 2 out of 3 strings for each tone in the middle and upper registers. That is why the application of this pedal is often marked in classical scores as *una corda* (1 string), or, more rarely, *due corde* (2 strings), depending on the extent of the shift. When the left pedal is taken off, the action is indicated by the words *tre corde*. Grand pianos and most modern pianos contain a middle pedal, the *sostenuto* (sustaining), which releases the dampers off of any notes that are being held down by the fingers when this pedal is applied; like the damper pedal, these notes are kept sounding until the sostenuto pedal is released. Debussy, Ravel, Bartók, Crumb, and others have used this pedal to good effect.

The range of the early pianoforte was about the same as that of the contemporary harpsichord, about 4 1/2 octaves, the upper limit being F above the staff of the treble clef (f^3). Because of the lack of higher notes, 18th-century composers for piano often had to transpose the recapitulation section in sonata form an octave lower in the middle of a sequence, as in Mozart's famous C-major piano sonata, K. 545. Similar sudden transpositions occur in Beethoven's early sonatas. The range of the piano keyboard was extended rapidly in the 19th century and soon stabilized in its present standard keyboard of 7 octaves and a minor 3rd, from A_2 to c^5. The Austrian firm of Bösendorfer manufactured early in the 20th century a piano that extended to C_2 (an added 6th below the standard low A), but it remains a curiosity and seldom if ever is used in concert. In the 19th century the French manufacturer Pleyel invented the *pédalier*, a pedalboard akin to that of an organ, designed to be attached to the piano and played with the feet. Alkan wrote music for pianos thus equipped.

Editors of classic piano music have been preoccupied with the problem of adapting these works, written for a limited range, so as to make use of the normal keyboard of modern pianos. Such a revision raises the speculative question whether Mozart would have taken advantage of the newly available higher notes in the recapitulation of his C-major Sonata K. 545 to avoid the awkward shift of register. As for Beethoven, he actually had a chance to revise his earlier sonatas for publication when the range of the keyboard was considerably extended within his own lifetime, but he failed to do so, possibly because he felt disinclined to spend time on such a revision, more likely because he felt no need to. But it certainly would be worthwhile to change the low A_2 to $G\sharp_2$ in the octave cascade in Ravel's *Jeux d'eau*, whenever this piece is performed on a piano with the extra notes in the bass.

piano à queue (Fr., piano with a tail). GRAND PIANO.

piano quartet. Composition for piano, violin, viola, and cello.

piano quintet. Composition for piano and string quartet.

piano score. An arrangement or reduction of an orch.l work for piano.

piano trio. Composition for piano, violin, and cello.

pianoforte (It., loud-soft). See PIANO.

Pianola. Trade name for a mechanical (player) piano; in classical music, it had some popularity in the late 1910s (compositions by Stravinsky); later revitalized in a highly original body of works for the instrument by Nancarrow.

Piatigorsky, Gregor, great Russian-born American cellist and pedagogue; b. Ekaterinoslav, Apr. 17, 1903; d. Los Angeles, Aug. 6, 1976. He received his 1st music lessons from his father, a violinist; then took cello lessons with Alfred von Glehn at the Moscow Cons.; played in various orchs. in Moscow. In 1921 he left Russia; took cello lessons with Julius Klengel in Leipzig; after serving as 1st cellist of the Berlin Phil. (1924–28), he devoted himself to a solo career. He played the solo part in *Don Quixote* by R. Strauss under the composer's direction many times in Europe, and was probably unexcelled in this part; Strauss himself called him "mein Don Quixote." He went to America in 1929, and made his American debut in Oberlin, Ohio, in 1929; later that year he played the Dvořák Concerto with the N.Y. Phil., eliciting great praise.

Piatigorsky was regarded as the world's finest cellist after Casals; continued giving solo recitals and appearing with major European and American orchs. for many years; gave 1st performances of several cello works commissioned by him from Hindemith, Dukelsky, Castelnuovo-Tedesco, and others. He became a naturalized U.S. citizen in 1942; taught at the Curtis Inst. of Music in Philadelphia (1942–51) and at the Berkshire Music Center in Tanglewood; was a prof. at the Univ. of Southern Calif., Los Angeles (1962–76); presented a series of trio concerts with Heifetz and Pennario. He was the recipient of honorary D.Mus degrees from many universities.

piatti (It.). Cymbals.

pibcorn (Welsh). A hornpipe dating from the Middle Ages to the 18th century, recently revived. It consists of a single or double cylindrical tube with a single beating reed, protected by a cowhorn mouth bell, terminating in a cowhorn bell. The tube, made of bone, wood, or cane, generally had 6 fingerholes and 1 rear fingerhole.

pibroch (Gael.). Genre in variation form for the Scottish Highland bagpipe.

Picardy Third. The frequent practice in Baroque music of ending a minor-key piece with a major tonic chord; the Picardy 3rd in this case is the major 3rd from the tonic. The French philosopher Jean-Jacques Rousseau, who was also a professional composer and music scholar, described this practice as *tierce de Picardie*, the reason being that the usage was particularly strong in the French region of Picardy, where there were numerous cathedrals and organs. Acoustic reasons suggest the preference of ending with a major 3rd, an interval within the overtone series, whereas the tonic minor 3rd is not. Examples can be found literally by the millions, in the cadences of chorales, in the coda of each of Bach's fugues in minor keys, etc. The principle of the *tierce de Picardie* is also extended into whole sonatas and symphonies in minor keys, in which a work in a minor key ends in major; the most resplendent illustration of this usage is Beethoven's 5th Sym. in C Minor, which ends in resounding C major.

piccanteria, con (It.). With piquant, sprightly expression.

picchiettato (It.). Detached, staccato; PIQUÉ.

Piccinni, (Vito) **Niccolò** (Nicola) (Marcello Antonio Giacomo), significant Italian composer; b. Bari, Jan. 16, 1728; d. Passy, near Paris, May 7, 1800. His father was a violinist at Bari's Basilica di San Nicola, and his maternal uncle was the composer Gaetano Latilla. His precocity manifested itself at an early age; thanks to Muzio Gaeta, archbishop of Bari, he was able at 14 to enter Naples's Cons. di S. Onofrio, where he studied with Leo and Durante; upon graduation (1754) he commenced his career as a composer for the stage with his comic opera *Le Donne dispettose* (Naples, 1754).

His theatrical instinct led him to select librettos rich in dramatic content; his melodic invention was fresh, and his arias were written in a pleasing style eminently suited to the voice; he elaborated the conventional climactic scenes so that dramatic interest was sustained to the end; he varied the tempos and the harmonies in the ensembles, which further contributed to the general effect. His *Zenobia* (Naples, 1756) was his 1st attempt at a serious opera. After several other operas for Naples, he received a commission to write an opera for Rome, *Alessandro nelle Indie* (1758); it was followed by his comic opera *La Cecchina, ossia La Buona figliuola* (Rome, 1760), which proved a great success at home and abroad. In subsequent years he wrote prolifically for the stage, producing well over 100 operas for the major Italian theaters.

Making his home in Naples, he served as 2nd maestro di cappella at the Cathedral, was active as an organist in convents, and taught singing. Piccinni's fortunes in Rome declined with the rise of Anfossi, his former pupil and protégé, in 1773. However, he still found success in Naples with a 2nd *Alessandro nelle Indie* (1774) and *I Viaggiatori* (1775). In 1776 he was called to Paris by the French court, where his presence precipitated the "querelle célèbre" between the "Gluckists" and "Piccinnists."

Piccinni's 1st French opera, *Roland* (1778), won considerable success. He then served as director of an Italian troupe in Paris (1778–79). Although he was promised by the Paris Opera that his *Iphigénie en Tauride* would be produced before Gluck's masterpiece on the same subject, it was not given until 1781, some 2 years after the Gluck premiere. While it was fairly successful, he gained his only major success with the opera *Didon* (1783), the same year in which he finally was granted a pension by the French court. In 1784 he was appointed maître de chant at the École Royale de

Chant et de Déclamation Lyrique in Paris. In spite of their rivalry, Piccinni held the highest regard for Gluck; indeed he suggested that an annual memorial concert be given in Gluck's memory, but financial support was not forthcoming. Upon the death of another rival, Sacchini, Piccinni spoke in homage at his funeral.

With the coming of the French Revolution Piccinni lost his post as maître de chant, and his pension. In 1791 he returned to Naples; upon his daughter's marriage to a French Jacobite, he was placed under house arrest in 1794; he finally gained freedom in 1798 and returned to Paris, where he obtained a partial restoration of his pension; his appointment as 6th inspector at the Cons. came when he was too ill to pursue an active life. Piccinni demonstrated a remarkable facility in writing both comic and serious operas. His historical importance rests upon his establishment of the Italian operatic style as the model for his French and German successors.

Piccinni's son Luigi (Lodovico) Piccinni (b. 1764; d. Passy, July 31, 1827) was also a composer; he studied with his father and then wrote operas for Paris and several Italian cities; was Kapellmeister to the Swedish court in Stockholm (1796–1801); then taught singing. Piccinni had another son, who in turn sired an illegitimate son, Louis Alexandre (Luigi Alessandro; Lodovico Alessandro) Piccinni (b. Paris, Sept 10, 1779; d. there, Apr. 24, 1850), who also became a composer; studied piano with Haussmann and composition with Le Sueur; also received some instruction from his grandfather; was active as an accompanist and rehearsal pianist in several Parisian theaters, and was also active as a conductor; taught in various French cities, serving as director of the Toulouse music school (1840–44); wrote numerous works for the theater.

piccolo. The octave flute, a small flute pitched an octave higher than the orch.l flute. Although its English name ("small") is Italian in origin, Italians call it *flauto piccolo*, or *ottavino*.

Piccolo Marat, Il. Opera by Mascagni, 1921, produced in Rome. At the time of the French Revolution a young aristocrat earns the sobriquet "the little Marat" for his revolutionary eloquence, worthy of the great Marat assassinated in his bath by Charlotte Corday. But his political extremism is only a cover for his passion for the niece of the president of the dreaded Comité de Salut Publique. He finally flees France with his beloved. The opera had a few lukewarm performances and then sank into innocuous desuetude.

pick. Pluck or twang the strings of a guitar, mandolin, etc.; also, a plectrum to do this with.

Picture That Is Turned Toward the Wall, The. A hand-wringing and heart-rending song by Charles Graham, executed by him in 1921. It became a hit with the Salvation Army, the Women's Christian Temperance Union, and other devout organizations that allow no leeway for sin. The picture that was turned toward the wall was that of a farmer's daughter who went off with a (horrors!) man. Chromolithographs in gaudy colors, showing the farmer in the process of turning his daughter's picture toward the wall, enjoyed great popularity in the 19th century.

Pictures at an Exhibition. When his friend, an otherwise mediocre Russian painter named Victor Hartmann, died, Mussorgsky was disconsolate. After going to a posthumous exhibition of Hartmann's pictures, he wrote in 1874 a suite of short piano pieces, each descriptive of 1 of the paintings. That Hartmann's name is remembered at all is owed to Mussorgsky's genius of musical pictorialism. Among the more striking musical portraits are *An Old Castle*, *Ballet of Unhatched Chickens in Their Eggshells*, *The Hut of Baba Yaga*, and the triumphant *Great Gate of Kiev*. Music lovers know *Pictures at an Exhibition* mainly in the brilliant orchestration made by Ravel in 1922 (many others have orchestrated this public-domain work).

piece. 1. A musical composition. 2. An instrument, taken as a member of an orch. or band.

pièce (Fr.). A piece. *Suite de pièces*, set of pieces.

pieno (It.). 1. Full. 2. A mixture stop.

Pierrot Lunaire. A song cycle for speaking voice, piano, flute/piccolo, clarinet/bass clarinet, violin/viola, and cello by Schoenberg, 1912, 1st performed in Berlin. As in his *Gurre-Lieder*, which used poems by a non-German translated into German, so the text of *Pierrot Lunaire* (Moonstruck Pierrot) is taken from 21 poems by a Belgian poet, Albert Giraud, rendered into German. The music is a tour de force of fascinating contrapuntal artifices, with instrumental timbres and the speaking voice forming an absorbing network of aural impressions. It is a genuine atonal masterpiece.

pietoso (It., pitiful, moving). Demands a sympathetic and expressive delivery.

piffero (It.). A fife; also, a primitive kind of oboe or shawm.

Pijper, Willem, renowned Dutch composer and pedagogue; b. Zeist, Sept. 8, 1894; d. Leidschendam, Mar. 18, 1947. He received a rudimentary education from his father, an amateur violinist; then went to the Toonkunst School of Music in Utrecht, where he studied composition with Johan Wagenaar and piano with Mme. H. J. van Lunteren-Hansen (1911–16); from 1918 to 1923 he was music critic of *Utrecht Dagblad*, and from 1926 to 1929 coeditor of the monthly *De Muziek*. He taught theory at the Amsterdam Cons. (from 1918) and was a prof. of composition there from 1925 to 1930; served as director of the Rotterdam Cons. from 1930 until his death.

In his music Pijper continued the Romantic tradition of Mahler, and he also adopted the harmonic procedures of the modern French School. He postulated a "germ-cell theory," in which an opening chord or motif is the source of all succeeding harmonic and melodic development (akin to Schoenberg's gestalt theory); he also cultivated the octatonic scale of alternating whole tones and semitones, regarding it as his own, not realizing that it was used abundantly by Rimsky-Korsakov (in Russian reference works it is termed the Rimsky-Korsakov scale); the "Pijper scale," as it became known in the Netherlands, was also used by Anton von der Horst and others. During the German bombardment of Rotterdam in May 1940, nearly all of Pijper's MSS were destroyed by fire, including the unpubl. reduced scoring of his large 2nd Sym. (restored in 1961 by Pijper's student Karel Mengelberg); also destroyed was the unpubl. Divertimento for piano and string orch.

Pilgrim's Progress, The. Morality play by Vaughan Williams, 1951, 1st performed in London. Based on Bunyan's classic allegory, the score contains several scenes passed by the Pilgrim on his journey: the City of Destruction, Valley of Humiliation, Vanity Fair, and the Delectable Mountains.

pincé (Fr.). 1. Plucked; as the strings of a harp. 2. Pizzicato (in violin playing).

Pines of Rome, The (*I Pini de roma*). Symphonic poem by Respighi, 1924, 1st performed in Rome. The music describes, by deft allusion, 4 pine groves in and around Rome. The score introduces an innovation, the playing of a recording of a nightingale. The piece has become a perennial favorite at sym. concerts.

Pink Floyd, overwrought British rock group. (Guitar/vocal: Roger "Syd" Barrett, b. Cambridge, England, Jan. 6, 1946; keyboard/vocal: Rick Wright, b. London, July 28, 1945; bass/piano/vocal: Roger Waters, b. Great Bookham, England, Sept. 6, 1944; drums: Nick Mason, b. Birmingham, England, Jan. 27, 1945; Barrett was replaced by David Gilmour, b. Cambridge, England, Mar. 6, 1944, in 1968; band dissolved in 1983; regrouped in 1987 without Waters.) Originally a leader in psychedelic rock, then one of the originators of progressive rock, the band is best remembered for 1973's concept opus *The Dark Side of the Moon*, still a best-seller nearly 25 years later.

The various members came together in London in the mid-1960s while attending art and architecture schools. Taking their name from two American blues singers (Pink Anderson and Floyd Collins), they became a favorite at trendy clubs like London's Marquee and UFO. Originally led by guitarist/songwriter Syd Barrett, the group produced a major hit with their second release, *See Emily Play*, a single so complex that it could not be reproduced onstage. Their 1st album, *The Piper at the Gates of Dawn*, continued the psychedelic trend, with moody arrangements complementing Barrett's often dense lyrics. However, Barrett soon began displaying disturbing behavior, and by early 1968 was ousted from the group to be replaced by David Gilmour; although Barrett made a few more recordings, he disappeared from public view, becoming a cult figure.

With Barrett gone, Waters came to the foreground as the main creative force in the band. A series of albums and elaborate tours followed, culminating in Waters's masterpiece, *Dark Side of the Moon*, which featured the group's 1st chart-busting U.S. hit, *Money*. The album remained on the U.S. charts for over 14 years, a major achievement. Further recordings and mammoth tours followed, with the group's massive sound equipment complemented by equally massive set pieces (the famed flying pig being one of their better efforts). Another megahit concept album came in 1979 with *The Wall*, which produced a hit theme song, a spectacular tour unparalleled in the annals of rock excess, and a 1982 film. However, this proved to be something of a swansong, as by 1983 the group had disbanded.

In 1987 the group reunited sans Waters, who complained bitterly that the other bandmembers were treading on his creative toes. Now Gilmour took control of the group, writing the material for their *A Momentary Lapse of Reason* album, which was another steady seller for the band. Waters retaliated with several solo efforts, as well as a mammoth production of *The Wall* in 1990 staged at (where else?) the

Berlin Wall. Although continuing to record without Waters into the '90s, the band has failed to achieve recent success. However, for their long record of achievement they gained a place in the Rock and Roll Hall of Fame in 1996.

pinky (Lat. *minimus*). American slang for the little finger; used by country guitar-pickers to designate the delicately subdued sound achieved by that finger.

Pinocchio. Concert overture by Toch, 1936; premiered in Los Angeles. This "merry overture" depicts the classic tale of the puppet come to life whose nose grows longer with each lie he tells.

Pins and Needles. Political revue by H. Rome, 1937. This was intended as a proletarian show and was produced by the International Ladies' Garment Workers' Union; it dealt with the labor problems of the 1930s. The opening song, *Sing Me a Song of Social Significance*, epitomizes the character of the production; others include *1 Big Union for 2* and *It's Better With a Union Man*.

Pinza, Ezio (baptized Fortunio), celebrated Italian bass; b. Rome, May 18, 1892; d. Stamford, Conn., May 9, 1957. The family moved to Ravenna when he was an infant; he studied engineering; also was active in sports. He began to study voice at the age of 18 with Ruzza and Vizzani at the Bologna Cons.; made his opera debut as Oroveso in Norma in Soncino (1914); after military service in World War I, he resumed his career, making his 1st important appearance as Comte Des Grieux in Rome (1920); then sang at La Scala in Milan (1922–24); was selected by Toscanini for the leading part in the world premiere of Boito's *Nerone* (May 1, 1924). He made his American debut at the Metropolitan Opera in N.Y. as Pontifex Maximus in Spontini's *La Vestale* (Nov. 1, 1926) and remained on its staff until 1947; appeared also in San Francisco, Chicago, etc.; sang in Europe and in South America; his most celebrated roles were Mephistopheles in Gounod's *Faust*, Don Giovanni, and Boris Godunov. In 1949 he appeared as a musical comedy star in *South Pacific* and immediately became successful in this new career; also appeared in films.

Ezio Pinza, 1949

COURTESY FRANK DRIGGS COLLECTION

pipa (Chin.). Short-necked wooden lute used since antiquity. The body is pear-shaped, with a wooden soundboard, crescent soundholes, a fingerboard with 4 frets (the other 6 to 13 are on the belly), and 4 silk strings. It is the predecessor of the Japanese biwa. Much of the pipa repertoire stresses military depictions, in part due to the relative fast decay time; variations for the instrument have been written and published.

pipe. 1. A rude flageolet or oboe. 2. An organ pipe. In *flue pipes* the tone is produced by the vibration of a column of air within a tube or body; they are either *open* or *covered* (stopped, plugged), a stopped pipe yielding a tone an octave lower than an open pipe of like length. In *reed pipes*, the tone is produced by a reed.

Pipe Dream. Musical by Rodgers and Hammerstein, 1955, based on Steinbeck's novel *Sweet Thursday*. The central character is a timid marine biologist who paradoxically romances a young female hitchhiker. Includes *The Man I Used to Be*.

piqué (Fr.). In violin family playing, the mezzo-staccato called for by a slur with staccato dots; notes so marked to be played in 1 bow (PICCHIETTATO).

Pirata, Il. Opera by Bellini, 1827, produced in Milan. The heroine of the opera is deserted by her lover who, *en passant*, murders her husband. The adulterous slayer is caught and sentenced to hang; the poor woman goes insane. But who is the pirate?

Pirates of Penzance, The, **or** *The Slaves of Duty.* Comic opera by Gilbert and Sullivan, 1879, 1st produced in London. The hero of the opera is apprenticed to be a pirate on his 21st birthday, but as he was born on Leap Day, he would not reach majority until 1940, at the time a very remote date indeed. The pirate's strict code prevents them from doing any real damage and, after many verbal confusions, they abandon their dismal calling and proclaim their undivided loyalty to Queen Victoria. Includes the chorus that eventually became known as *Hail, Hail, the Gang's All Here*.

Pistol Packin' Mama. Song by Al Dexter, 1943, made famous by Bing Crosby and the Andrew Sisters.

piston. See VALVE.

Piston, Walter (Hamor, Jr.), outstanding American composer and pedagogue; b. Rockland, Maine, Jan. 20, 1894; d. Belmont, Mass., Nov. 12, 1976. The family name was originally Pistone; his paternal grandfather was Italian. He received his primary education in Boston; took courses in architectural drawing at the Mass. Normal Art School, graduating in 1916; then took piano lessons with Harris Shaw and studied violin with Fiumara, Theodorowicz, and Winternitz; played in restaurants and places of public entertainment as a youth. During World War I he was in the U.S. Navy; after the Armistice he entered Harvard Univ., graduating in musical subjects summa cum laude in 1924; while at Harvard, he conducted concerts of the univ. orch., the Pierian Sodality. For a time he was employed as a draftsman for Boston Elevated Railway. In 1924 he went to Paris on a John Knowles Paine Traveling Fellowship and became a student of Nadia Boulanger; also took courses with Paul Dukas at the École Normale de Musique (1925); returning to the U.S. in 1926, he was appointed to the faculty of Harvard Univ.; in 1944 he became a prof. of music; was named prof. emeritus in 1960.

As a teacher Piston was greatly esteemed, not only because of his consummate knowledge of music and pedagogical ability, but also because of his immanent humanity in instructing students whose aesthetics differed from his own; among his grateful disciples was Leonard Bernstein. As a composer Piston followed a cosmopolitan course, adhering to classical forms while extending his harmonic structures toward a maximum of tonal saturation; he was particularly expert in contrapuntal writing. Beginning about 1965 Piston adopted a modified system of 12-tone composition, particularly in initial thematic statements; his Sym. No. 8 and Variations for Cello and Orch. are explicitly dodecaphonic. Piston rejected the narrow notion of ethnic Americanism in his music; he stated once that an artist could be as American working in the Library of the Boston Atheneum as roaming the Western prairie, yet he employed upon occasion the syncopated rhythms of jazz.

Piston received Pulitzer Prizes for his Sym. No. 3 and Sym. No. 7, and N.Y. Music Critics' Circle Awards for his Sym. No. 2, Viola Concerto, and String Quartet No. 5. He held the degree of D.Mus *honoris causa* from Harvard Univ.; he was elected a member of the National Inst. of Arts and Letters (1938), the American Academy of Arts and Letters (1955), and the American Academy of Arts and Sciences (1940). He traveled little and declined invitations to go to South America and to Russia under the auspices of the State Dept., preferring to live in his house in suburban Belmont, near Boston. His working habits were remarkably methodical; he rarely altered or revised his music once it was put on paper, and his handwriting was calligraphic. With 2 exceptions, he never wrote for voices.

His best-known work is *The Incredible Flutist*, a ballet (Boston, 1938; suite, Pittsburgh, 1940). He wrote many orch.l works, including 8 syms. (1938; 1944, N.Y. Music Critics' Circle Award; 1948, Pulitzer Prize in music; 1951; 1954; 1955; 1961, Pulitzer Prize in Music; 1965). His chamber works include 5 string quartets (1933, 1935, 1947, 1951, 1962; the last received the N.Y. Music Critics' Circle Award). He also composed vocal and keyboard works. He wrote widely used textbooks: *Principles of Harmonic Analysis* (Boston, 1933); *Harmony* (N.Y., 1944; 5th ed., rev. and enlarged by M. DeVoto, 1987); *Counterpoint* (N.Y., 1947); *Orchestration* (N.Y., 1955).

pitch. The position of a tone in the musical scale. Pitch is relative, or absolute. The *relative* pitch of a tone is its position (higher or lower) as compared with some other tone. (See INTERVAL.). Its *absolute* pitch is its fixed position in the entire range of musical tones. To indicate absolute pitch, the musical scale is divided into a fixed series of octaves, named and lettered as in "The Clefs," p. xxiii. The number of vibrations made by a tone establishes its absolute pitch; the standard *French pitch* (also called *international* or *low* pitch) gives the tone a^1 = 435 cycles (complete vibrations) per second (cps; Hz). The standard of pitch in the U.S. is a^1 = 440 cps; some orchs. are known to tune up to a^1 = 450 cps:

Acoustically, pitch is determined by the frequency of vibrations of a given tone. The smaller the sound producing instrument, the higher the pitch; a whistle is small, thus its pitch is high; the bass tuba is large, so its pitch is very low. On string instruments and on the piano, the shorter and thinner the string, the higher the pitch. A relatively small minority of musicians possess the faculty of PERFECT PITCH, which enables them to name without fail any note within the audible range. Perfect (or absolute) pitch is innate, and persons who were not born to it cannot be trained to acquire it, any more than a color-blind person can be trained to tell red from green. Relative pitch, however, enables a person to name the interval between 2 pitches; this ability can be acquired. To those who are particularly obtuse in recognizing even relative pitch, a remedial course may be taught by identifying intervals through their similarity with the patterns of well-known songs.

The present standard pitch for A in the middle octave is 440 vibrations per second; in the orch., the oboe gives out the standard A to which all the other instruments tune because it is an instrument little affected by changes of temperature and humidity. However, this standard pitch has been fluctuating widely through the centuries. In the 19th century the middle A was considerably lower than that of the later standard pitch. If Mozart listened to a 20th-century rendition of his *Jupiter Sym.*, he would think that it had been transposed to C-sharp major instead of the written key of C major.

pitch class. A term denoting a set of all pitches with the same name; i.e., pitch class A, inclusive of all possible A's, regardless of register.

pitch pipe. A small wooden or metal reed pipe which sounds 1 or more tones of fixed pitch, to give the tone for tuning an instrument, or for a choir.

pittoresco (It.). Picturesque.

più (It.). More. When *più* stands alone, as a TEMPO MARK, MOSSO is implied; as an EXPRESSION MARK it refers to the next preceding *f* or *p*. *Più andante*, orig. more lively; by the Classic period, more slowly; *più largo*, more slowly; *più marcato del principio*, a little more emphasized than at the beginning; *più mosso, più moto*, faster; *più mosso ancora*, still faster; *più sostenuto*, a little more sustained; *più vicino*, a little nearer (as if getting closer and louder); *con un poco più di moto*, with a little more movement, somewhat faster.

piuttosto (It.). Somewhat; rather. *Piuttosto lento*, somewhat slowly.

pivot chord. In MODULATION, a chord pivotal to both the old key and the new key, that is, belonging to both keys. Particularly in chromatic modulation, the diminished-7th chord functions as such a *passe-partout* device.

pizzicato (It., pinched). Plucked with the finger; a direction, in music, to violinists, etc., to play the notes by plucking the strings with the bowing hand; abbrev. *pizz. Left-hand pizzicato*, plucking the string (usually open) with the fingering hand; this device was favored by 19th-century virtuosos, starting with Paganini (*Caprice No. 24*). *Snap pizzicato*, pull the string and release with sufficient force that the string snaps against the fingerboard; also known as the *Bartók pizzicato*, because of that composer's characteristic use of it.

placidamente (*placido*; It.). Placidly, tranquilly, smoothly.

plagal cadence (from Grk. *plagios*, oblique). A cadence in which the tonic is preceded by the subdominant rather than by the dominant, the authentic cadence. The authentic cadence displaced the plagal cadence almost completely after 1500, which retained its hold only on the conclusion of the hymn with the word *Amen*, but it returned with a vengeance in the 20th century when many composers felt an impulse to return to early modality.

plagal mode. In Gregorian chant, plagal modes were formed by placing the outer notes a 4th below and a 5th above that of the corresponding authentic mode. This derivation is denoted by adding the prefix *hypo* (below) to the authentic modes. The final, however, remains the same as in the corresponding authentic mode. On the white keys of the piano keyboard, the DORIAN MODE extends from D to D, and the HYPODORIAN MODE would extend from A (a 4th below D) to A (a 5th above D); both share the final D. In the 16th century the plagal modes were incorporated into the general system of 12 modes. See also AUTHENTIC MODE.

plagiarism

〜〜 〜〜 〜〜 〜〜 〜〜

The stealing of intellectual property. It was used for the 1st time in this sense of a fraudulent appropriation of another writer's work by the Roman poet Martial and eventually became a universal term in all languages. The essential element of plagiarism (from Lat. *plagiarius*, plunderer) is deliberate intent. Remembered folk sayings, reminiscences of proverbial expressions, or verses from classical works of literature do not constitute plagiarism. As for musical plagiarism it must be realized that the most naturally attractive melodies in classical music are derived from the diatonic scale, and that rhythmic arrangements of such melodies are limited to certain symmetric formulas within a binary or a ternary meter. This makes accidental coincidences almost inevitable. John Stuart Mill wrote sententiously: "I was seriously tormented by the thought of the exhaustibility of musical combinations. The octave consists only of 5 tones and 2 semitones, which can be put together in only a limited number of ways of which but a small proportion is beautiful; most of these, it seemed to me, must have been already discovered." To his credit, Mill adds: "This sort of anxiety may, perhaps, be thought to resemble that of the philosophers of Laputa, who feared lest the sun be burnt out."

Still, eager plagiarism hunters devote considerable time and effort to prove that there is nothing new under the musical sun, and they exult in pointing out that the great opening theme of Beethoven's *Eroica* is identical with that of an early Mozart overture, thus brilliantly demonstrating that the 3 notes of the major triad can be arranged in a variety of ways in 3/4 time. The theme of the finale of Mozart's *Jupiter Sym.* in C Major is identical in its structure and rhythm with the main theme of the finale of Haydn's Sym. No. 13 in D Major, written many years before Mozart's time. In the middle of the 18th century the German writer and composer Friedrich Wilhelm Zacharias proposed to compile a source dictionary of such unintentional as well as intentional borrowings.

In 1731 an otherwise respectable Italian composer, Giovanni Bononcini, who was a serious rival of Handel for royal and aristocratic favors in London (a famous rhyme ran, "Some say, com par'd to Bononcini/that Mynheer Handel's but a ninny," etc.), made the grievous error of submitting to the Academy of Ancient Music in London a madrigal by the contemporary Italian composer Lotti as his own. When this reckless act of patent plagiarism was discovered, Bononcini was disgraced and had to leave England. But Handel himself was not averse to frank borrowings of whole arias from other composers for his use in his operas. Fortunately for him, this practice was either

obscure or tolerated enough in his time, so that he was buried in Westminster Abbey with great solemnity. In fact, an early edition of the *Encyclopedia Britannica* referred to Handel as "a common thief and shameless borrower."

A most interesting coincidence is found between an early song by Liszt and the principal phrase in the introduction to Wagner's opera *Tristan und Isolde*; the notes are exactly the same without transposition. Since Wagner was very close to Liszt, there may have been a subconscious reminiscence of chromatic procedures that was not realized by either Wagner or Liszt. Still, musical petty larceny was regarded with benign tolerance throughout the 18th and 19th centuries, forgivable because the financial profit was negligible.

The situation changed in the 20th century when popular music became big business. The copyright laws protected the composer only partially; if the plagiarist disguised his handiwork sufficiently, the intent to defraud could not be proven in a court of law. Indeed, fraudulent claims of plagiarism against successful publishers and composers of popular tunes launched by the writers of songs bearing only a superficial similarity to the money making pieces became so common in the U.S. that publishers often bought off such claimants to avoid costly defense procedures. In a learned handwritten decision, Learned Hand, United States Judge of N.Y., ruling in a case involving the composer of the popular song *I Didn't Raise My Boy to Be a Soldier*, put a plague on both parties by declaring, "The defendant is a casual composer of melodies, though he has small knowledge of musical notation and small skill in playing. I am aware that in such simple and trivial themes as these it is dangerous to go too far upon suggestions of similarity. For instance, the whole of the leading theme of the song is repeated literally from a chorus of *Pinafore*, though there is not the slightest reason to suppose that the plaintiff ever heard of the opera. It is said that such similarities are of constant occurrence in music and that little inference is permissible." But when Stravinsky used the tune of *Happy Birthday to You* in a symphonic dedication (*Greeting Prelude*) to Monteux on his 80th birthday (1955), he ran afoul of the copyright and had some trouble having it performed.

plainchant, plainsong. The unison vocal music of the Christian church, probably dating from the 1st centuries of the Christian era, the style being still obligatory in the Roman Catholic ritual, although now in the vernacular rather than church Latin.

planarianism. A musical composition which can be dissected into 2 or more parts, with each growing out into a separate independent body may be called planarian, by analogy with the flatworm of that name that possesses a trifid intestine and is capable of regenerating each of its severed parts into new flatworms. The structure of a work in the style of planarianism may reach great complexity. Stockhausen has written autogenetic works that can be cut up, with each musical planarian becoming a self sufficient sonic organism. This process of vermiculation and its concomitant divisibility has been further advanced by John Cage; at his hands each musical platyhelminth becomes a unique and irreproducible species.

Planets, The. Orch.l suite by Holst, 1914–16, 1st performed publicly in its entirety in London, 1920. There are 7 movements, corresponding to the 7 planets known before the discovery of Pluto, and the designations of these movements are mythological: *Mars, the Bringer of War*; *Venus, the Bringer of Peace*; *Mercury, the Winged Messenger*; *Jupiter, the Bringer of Jollity*; *Saturn, the Bringer of Old Age*; *Uranus, the Magician*; and *Neptune, the Mystic* (with a wordless female chorus). The work is by far the most celebrated of Holst's productions, and oft quoted; the Jovian joviality of the Jupiter movement is particularly striking. Yet *The Planets* is atypical of Holst's music; he never understood its popularity.

Planquette, (Jean-) **Robert.** See Cloches de Corneville, Les.

plantation songs. A broad category of secular music associated with the work songs and ballads of black slaves in the antebellum South and its imitations in the "Ethiopian" music of Foster and blackface minstrelsy.

plants and music. In a wacky book, *The Secret Life of Plants*, a claim is made in all seriousness that plants are "tuned to the Music of the Spheres" and react sensitively to music. An Indian authority has testified that by playing ragas to an appreciative audience of asters, petunias, onions, sesame, radishes, sweet potatoes, and tapioca he proved "beyond any shadow of a doubt that harmonic soundwaves

Leaf of plainsong from a 15th-century choir book

affect the growth, flowering, fruiting, and seed-yields of plants." An American horticulturist piped some music into greenhouses, claiming it caused his plants to germinate quicker and bloom more abundantly and more colorfully. A Canadian botanist played a recording of Bach's violin sonatas in his garden, with the result that despite the poor quality of soil, wheat grew better than in the richest earth, demonstrating conclusively that "Bach's musical genius was as good or better than material nutrients." Inspired by these experiments, a botanist in Illinois played a recording of Gershwin's *Rhapsody in Blue* for different plants; they "sprouted earlier than those given the silent treatment, and their stems were thicker, tougher, and greener."

The acme of scientific experimentation with the harmonic life of plants was achieved by a mezzo-soprano who was a regular soloist at Denver's Beach Supper Club. She played the taped musical notes C and D on the piano every second, alternating with periods of silence; as a result the African violets, drooping at 1st, began to flower joyously. No lover of rock 'n' roll, she successfully proved that squashes hated ROCK MUSIC so much that they actually grew away from the transistor radio broadcasting it, and even, in their desperation, tried to climb the slippery walls of the greenhouse. On the other hand, the cucurbits curled around the radio speaker broadcasting Beethoven and Brahms. When she exposed corn and zinnias to rock music, they grew in abnormal shapes and finally withered and died. But plants subjected to the sounds of "intellectual, mathematically sophisticated music" of the East reacted with such enthusiasm that they bent toward the source of the music at angles of more than 60 degrees, some of them entwining the loudspeaker.

Well, Victor Hugo heard a tree sing when bathed in light—"L'Arbre, tout pénétré de lumière, chantait"—but then he was a poet.

planus (Lat.). Full. *Planus corus*, full chorus.

plastic, elastic, and spastic variations. Plasticity of texture is essential in modern variations, securing a malleability of tonal materials. Tonal elasticity adds intervallic flexibility to a plastic theme. A rhythmic effect can be achieved by spastic convulsions of the melodic line, producing implosions which impart a stimulating sense of disquiet to the music.

Plato, great Greek philosopher; b. probably in Athens, *c.* 428 B.C.; d. there, 347/348 B.C. In his *Timaeus* he formulated a system of music in which he likened the movements of music to those of the soul, whose development may therefore be influenced by the art of music.

platter. Slang for phonograph record, especially in 1950s.

player piano. A mechanical device that combines the principles of airstream propulsion and percussive hammer action for automatic reproduction of a performance on the piano. A roll of very strong paper is rotated on a cylinder and is perforated in such a way that the holes made on it correspond in pitch and duration to the notes originally played on the piano. The pitches are represented by the horizontal parameter, and the duration, including rest, by the vertical. Since the cylinder rotates, a rapid scale would register visually as a terraced pattern. To reproduce the original performance a stream of air is passed through the perforations and activates the corresponding hammers, which then strike the piano strings and simultaneously depress the keys of the piano keyboard. The visual impression of such automatic piano playing is that of a magical performance by the invisible fingers of a phantom pianist.

The player piano, under various trademarks such as the Pianola, the Welte-Mignon, etc., became highly popular after its introduction late in the 19th century, and its popularity did not diminish until the advent of the modern phonograph. Several composers, among them Stravinsky and Hindemith, composed and recorded pieces for the player piano. The defect of the pianola and similar reproductive mechanical instruments, however, was a lack of dynamic nuance, but the discovery in 1957 of piano rolls made by Welte-Mignon early in the century, which made use of columns of incompressible mercury to register precise pressure on the piano keys, made it possible to have faithful renditions of performances played by famous pianists of the time. These performances were then rerecorded on the phonograph, restoring with a remarkable fidelity the manner of playing by Paderewski and other famous musicians of yore.

The player piano possesses the unique capacity of enabling a composer to make perforations directly on the roll guided by desired measurements, and modern composers have availed themselves of this facility. Most remarkable results were achieved in this technique by the American composer domiciled in Mexico, Conlon Nancarrow, who constructed a number of etudes and other pieces by direct perforation on the roll, resulting in melodic, harmonic, and rhythmic patterns of extreme complexity and utmost precision that could not be played by any human pianist or even any number of pianists.

Please Mr. Postman. Early Motown number 1 pop hit for the Marvelettes in 1961; covered in 1964 by the Beatles and in 1975 by the Carpenters.

Please Please Me. The Beatles' 1st British number 1 (although it only made number 3 in the U.S.). John Lennon said the punning title was inspired by a Bing Crosby song in which the crooner asked his loved one to "please listen to my pleas."

Pleasure Dome of Kubla Khan, The. Symphonic poem by Griffes, 1919, inspired by Coleridge's incomplete poem. The music is typically impressionist, with some orientalist nuances.

plectrum. A pick; a small piece of ivory, tortoise shell, metal, or plastic, held between the forefinger and thumb, or fitted to the thumb by a ring, and used to pluck or twang the strings of the mandolin, zither, guitar, Asian zithers and lutes, etc.

plein (Fr.). Full.

plein-jeu (Fr.). 1. A stop or combination of stops bringing out the full power of the organ, harmonium, etc. 2. FOURNITURE.

plena (Sp.). Puerto Rican ballad similar to the calypso songs of Trinidad.

Pleyel, Ignace Joseph (Ignaz Josef), eminent Austrian-French pianist, piano manufacturer, music publisher, and composer, father of (Joseph Stephen) Camille Pleyel; b. Ruppertsthal, near Vienna, June 18, 1757; d. on his estate near Paris, Nov. 14, 1831. He was the 24th of 38 children in the impoverished family of a schoolteacher; however, he received sufficient education, including music lessons, to qualify for admittance to the class of Wanhal; thanks to the generosity of Count Ladislaus Erdödy, he became Haydn's pupil and lodger in Eisenstadt (*c.* 1772–77), and then was enabled to go to Rome. In 1783 he became 2nd Kapellmeister at the Strasbourg Cathedral; was advanced to the rank of 1st Kapellmeister in 1789 but lost his position during the turbulent times of the French Revolution. He conducted the Professional Concerts in London during the 1791–92 season and honored his teacher Haydn by playing a work of his at the opening concert (1792). After several years he returned to Strasbourg to liquidate his estate; in 1795 he went to Paris, where he opened a music store which was in business until 1834, and in 1807 founded a piano factory, which manufactured famous French pianos; the firm eventually became known as Pleyel et Cie., and it continued to prosper for over a century and a half.

The name Pleyel is mainly known through his piano manufacture, but Ignace was a prolific and an extremely competent composer. His productions are so close in style to those of Haydn that specialists are still inclined to attribute certain works in Haydn's catalogues to Pleyel. He composed about 45 syms., 6 symphonies concertantes, 2 violin concertos, 5 cello concertos, other concertos, 16 string quintets, a septet, a sextet, more than 70 string quartets, many trios and duos, and some vocal music, including 2 operas, *Die Fee Urgele* for puppet theater (Eszterház, Nov.

1776) and *Ifigenia in Aulide* (Naples, May 30, 1785), and some songs. His son (Joseph Stephen) Camille Pleyel (b. Strasbourg, Dec. 18, 1788; d. Paris, May 4, 1855) was pianist, piano manufacturer, and composer; his wife was Marie-Félicité-Denise Moke Pleyel (b. Paris, Sept. 4, 1811; d. St.-Josse-ten-Noode, near Brussels, Mar. 30, 1875), was a fine pianist, teacher, and composer. Berlioz fell in love with her (1830), but she married the younger Pleyel that same year, while Berlioz was in Rome; she separated from Pleyel in 1835.

plica. A NEUME introduced in the Notre Dame school MSS, indicating a pitch and its ornamentation. The direction and length of the ligature or its stem represented the type to be used—what would now be called the MORDENT or APPOGGIATURA. In mensural notation the term *plica* was followed by an indication of the type, such as *plica descendens*.

Plow That Broke the Plains, The. Orch.l suite by V. Thomson, 1936, arranged from score to a documentary film depicting the joys and miseries of American farming.

plugging. American slang for the promotion, by means fair or foul, of books, films, records, videos, etc. See also PAYOLA.

pluralism. As in collage, the use of different styles within a single composition, sometimes simultaneously.

pluralistic structures. An epistemological concept connoting a multiplicity of causes and events. Developments of modern music support the pluralistic view in such styles as neoclassicism, impressionism, or expressionism, in which the factors of melody, rhythm, and intervallic values are of different formulation. But the same type of structure becomes monistic if it is derived from a uniform set, as for instance in variations. Pluralism and monism are mutually specular, but they are reconciled in SERIAL MUSIC. Analogies with the visible spectrum invite themselves. White light is monistic in its sensory perception but pluralistic when it is analyzed into the prismatic constituents of the rainbow. White sound is a monistic aggregation of sonic particles, which can be separated into a pluralistic collection of its tonal components.

plus (Fr.). More. *Plus à l'aise,* more relaxed; *plus lent,* slower.

po' (It.; contraction of *poco*). Little. *Con un po' d'espansione,* with a certain display of emotion; *alzando un po' la* *voce*, raising the voice a little; *ritenendo un po'*, becoming a trifle slower.

pochette (Fr., little pocket). A very small violin that could be carried in the pocket of a dancing master, used to accompany his pupils in rehearsal. See also KIT.

pochissimo (It.). Very little.

poco (It.). Little. *A poco a poco*, little by little, gradually; *poco allegro*, rather fast; *poco largo*, rather slow; *poco meno*, when standing alone as a tempo mark, *mosso* is implied, i.e., *poco meno mosso*, a little less fast (a little slower); *poco più*, standing alone, also implies *mosso* (a little faster); *poco più lento della prima volta*, somewhat slower than the 1st time.

Poème ailé. Piano piece by Scriabin, 1906. This "winged poem" is characteristic of the composer's mystical leaning.

Poème de l'extase, Le (Poem of Ecstasy). Symphonic poem by Scriabin, 1905–1908; it had its 1st performance in N.Y. by the Russian Sym. Soc., conducted by Modest Altschuler (1908). The work justified its title; Scriabin provided a multitude of sectional subtitles, in French, detailing the intermediate states leading to ecstasy, which is represented by 53 consecutive bars in resonant C major in its final musical orgasm.

Poème divin, Le (Divine Poem). Sym. No. 3 by Scriabin, 1902–1904, 1st performed in Paris, 1905. It is Scriabin's 1st work of mystic inspiration; the titles of its 4 movements (all in the original French) are indicative of this: *Grandiose, Luttes, Voluptes*, and *Jeu divin*. The work is in C minor, with an ending in resonant C major, "avec une joie éclatante."

Poème électronique. Environmental musical work by Varèse, 1958, for sounds entirely electronically produced and recorded on tape. It was commissioned for the Philips Pavilion at the Brussels World Exposition in 1958, with the sound projected stereophonically from 400 loudspeakers distributed throughout the building.

Poéème satanique. Piano piece by Scriabin, 1903. Curiously enough, this devilish piece is written in the celestial key of C major. The satanism of the music is symbolic and is defeated, musically, by heavenly forces. Despite the prevalent cultivation of the devil in Russia early in the 20th century, Scriabin was decidedly on the side of the angels.

Pohjola's Daughter. Symphonic poem by Sibelius, 1906, 1st performed in St. Petersburg. Pohjola is the northern land, protected by Louhi; her daughter makes her home sitting on a rainbow. Her enticing beauty lures Väinämöinen, the hero of the *Kalevala*, but he cannot create the talisman she demands of him; he engages a smith, who succeeds; but the daughter prefers the smith to the hero, and ends up marrying him.

poi (It.). Then; thereafter.

point. A musicomathematical term used to enhance the impression of profundity by AVANT-GARDE composers in the last 3rd of the decaying 20th century. When attentively examined in context, it means a convergence of autonomous sounds resulting either in optimum WHITE NOISE comprising all pitches, or the geometrical zero in absolute silence; such points can be arrived at by various acoustical encounters.

point d'orgue (Fr., organ point). 1. PEDAL POINT. 2. Pause. 3. Cadenza.

pointe (Fr.). 1. Point or head of a bow. 2. In ballet, the toe (abbrev. *p.*).

pointe d'archet (Fr.). Tremolo with the point of the bow.

pointillism. In the nomenclature of modern art, pointillism is a method of applying colored dots to the canvas, forming a cumulative design. In modern music the term is descriptive of atonal and athematic idioms, in which separate notes are distributed individually rather than as parts of an integral melorhythmic curve. The maximal dispersion of members of a dodecaphonic series in different octave positions is an example of serial pointillism. This emphasis upon single notes in a serially organized process was brought to fruition by Webern.

points of sound. Determined conglomerations of different sounds synchronized by a controlled simultaneity of individual sounds; the opposite of *groups of sound* (or noises), occurring by chance of an unpremeditated simultaneity of several sound groups resulting from autonomous individual sound actions.

Poisoned Kiss, The. Romantic extravaganza by Vaughan Williams, 1936, 1st performed in Cambridge, U.K. A sorcerer's daughter thrives on a diet of assorted poisons; not realizing that her lips are venomous, an unlucky few meet their end. She manages to detoxify her lips when she meets a man she loves; there is a happy ending.

polacca (*pollacca, polonese*; It.). Polonaise. *Alla polacca*, in the style of a polonaise.

polemics

Music theorists are not fighters, and their polemical exchanges are rarely spiced with invectives commonly encountered in political campaigns. Still, there are a few famous battles in music history. One Giovanni Spataro inveighed mightily against the renowned lexicographer Gafurio, calling him a "master of errors." The entire title is worth reproducing: *Dilucide et probatissime demonstratione de Maestro Zoanne Spatario musico bolognese contra certe frivole et vane excusatione da Franchino Gafurio (Maestro de li errori) in luce aducte, Bolgone, 1521* (Lucid and most probative demonstration of Maestro Zoanne Spatario [the name varies], a Bologna musician, against certain frivolous and vain accusations of Franchino Gafurio—master of errors—brought to light). Few scholars could wade through this vast tirade full of superlative degrees of comparison and exclamatory punctuation, but the book remains a characteristic document. Four hundred years after its issuance it was translated and publ. in German.

Of more interest are attacks leveled at Monteverdi by an obscure contemporary, Giovanni Maria Artusi, under the self-asserting title *L'Artusi, ovvero delle imperfettioni della moderna musica*, published in Venice in 1600. Not content to attack Monteverdi, Artusi also shot a fuse against his own teacher, Zarlino, and against Vincenzo Galilei (father of the famous astronomer). Galilei, too, attacked Zarlino for his theory that major and minor triads are mutual mirror reflections of their component major and minor 3rds. Monteverdi dismissed Artusi's attacks in a brief paper entitled *Ottuso accademico* (Obtuse Academician), but apparently was sufficiently nettled to take a glancing blow at his detractors in a preface to one of his books of madrigals.

The famous GUERRE DES BOUFFONS that rent asunder the French musical community in the middle of the 18th century lacked personal attacks and concentrated on the dispute between the adherents of the Italian buffi (that is, comedians) and the proponents of French national opera. King Louis XV and his powerful mistress Madame de Pompadour sided with the French national school, while Rousseau and the encyclopedists, supported by the Queen, favored the melodious and harmonious ways of Italian operas. While Rousseau fulminated against writers of opera in French, a language that he regarded as inferior for singing, he failed to attack the personalities; as a result the whole guerre des bouffons remained a war of abstractions. Eventually the French national school created its own style of opera buffa known as *comédie melée d'ariettes*. A few decades later the Parisians were taking sides on the Gluck vs. Piccinni controversy; but neither composer took sides.

In subsequent centuries 2 types of controversies occurred: those in which the listening public and critics perpetrated, and those between composers. Sometimes the composer battles were indirect: Wagner's greatest critic was a critic, Hanslick, not another composer; Wolf criticized Brahms (after 1st having supported him) on behalf of Wagner, or, more accurately, Wagnerianism, as that composer was deceased. Pfitzner threw diatribes at every composer he could think of who didn't write in his conservative style; Schoenberg and Stravinsky wouldn't speak to one another; Boulez celebrated the death of Schoenberg (metaphorically, one hopes); academic serialists condemned neoromanticists, and vice versa; and for many years virtually everyone else denied that minimalist composers were writing music.

Police, The. Hit-making British new wave band. (Lead vocal/bass: Gordon Sumner, aka "Sting," b. Wallsend, England, Oct. 2, 1951; guitar: Andrew Summers, b. Poulton-le-Fylde, England, Dec. 31, 1942; drums/vocals: Stewart Copeland, b. Alexandria, Va., July 16, 1952.) The group formed originally in the mid-1970s out of the remains of various minor progressive-rock bands. Schoolteacher and semiprofessional musician Gordon Sumner (known in his youth as "Sting" because he favored a black-and-yellow striped soccer jersey), originally from the Newcastle area, and London-based drummer Stewart Copeland were joined by guitarist Henry Padovani for the group's 1st single in 1976; however, Padovani was soon replaced by American-born, British-raised guitarist Andy Summers, who had previously worked with Soft Machine and the Animals.

Signed to the American A&M label, the group toured the U.S. at their own expense in 1978, achieving their 1st chart recognition here with Sting's song *Roxanne* in early 1979. Their 2nd album sold steadily for 2 years on the American charts, although it produced only a minor hit here, *Message in a Bottle*. However, in 1980 the group broke through big time with *Don't Stand So Close to Me*, followed a year later by *Every Little Thing She Does Is Magic*, both Sting-penned, rollicking pop songs. The group produced the classic album *Synchronicity* in 1983, showing a diversity of influences from world rhythms to jazz and rock. Critically acclaimed, it proved to be their last effort; Sting pursued a successful acting and solo career, scoring many major hits through the 1980s and 1990s, while Copeland became a successful soundtrack composer and Summers sessioned and recorded on his own.

political tonalities. Major keys are optimistic. Minor keys are pessimistic. This dichotomy dates since the Renaissance, and it was restated with all the power of government by the 1st Commissar of Education of the Soviet Union, Anatoly Lunacharsky, who declared in his introductory speech at a Moscow concert of Dec. 10, 1919:

> Major keys possess the characteristics of lifting a sound a semitone. By their exultant sense of joy such sounds elevate the mood; they cheer you up. By contrast, minor keys droop; they lead to a compromise, to a surrender of social positions. Allow me, as an old Bolshevik, to formulate this observation: Major tonalities are Bolshevik music, whereas minor keys are deeply rooted in Menshevik mentality.

Still, Bolsheviks loved the music of Tchaikovsky, even though 85% of his works are set in minor keys. The resolution of this anomaly has been proposed by the learned theorists of the Society of Proletarian Musicians: Workers and peasants enjoy the music of Tchaikovsky because it eloquently celebrates the funeral of the enemy class, the bourgeoisie. Q.E.D.

Poliuto. Opera by Donizetti, 1840, 1st produced in Paris. The libretto is based on Corneille's tragedy *Polyeucte*, an Armenian Christian whose ambition is to become a martyr. He magnanimously yields his wife to her previous lover, a pagan, but is sentenced to death by his father-in-law, the Roman governor of Armenia. After his execution she joins him in martyrdom; the Governor eventually becomes a Christian.

polka (Bohem. *pulka*; It. *polca*). A lively round dance in 2/4 time, originating about 1830 as a peasant dance in Bohemia, despite a name suggesting Polish origin (polka means a Polish girl). It generated suddenly in Prague in 1847 and almost immediately spread all over Europe. In this process it lost its specific Bohemian characteristics and became a popular salon dance. Johann Strauss wrote a famous *Pizzicato Polka* and many other composers followed suit. Stravinsky wrote a *Circus Polka* for a dance of elephants in an American circus.

polka mazurka. A form of mazurka accommodated to the steps of the polka.

polka schnell. A fast polka; a designation used by J. Strauss, Jr. (e.g., *Vergnügungszug*, pleasure train) and others.

Pollini, Maurizio, famous Italian pianist and conductor; b. Milan, Jan. 5, 1942. A precocious child, he began piano studies at an early age with Lonati; made his debut at age 9, then studied with Vidusso at the Milan Cons. After sharing 2nd prize in the Geneva Competition in 1958, he took his diploma in piano at the Milan Cons. (1959); also studied with Michelangeli. After capturing 1st prize in the Chopin Competition in Warsaw (1960), he launched an acclaimed career as a virtuoso; appeared throughout Europe as a soloist with the leading orchs. and as a recitalist; made his U.S. debut at N.Y.'s Carnegie Hall (1968). In later years he made appearances as a conductor, leading concerts from the keyboard and also mounting the podium and taking charge in the opera pit. Pollini is a foremost master of the keyboard; he has won deserved renown for making his phenomenal technical resources a means of exploring a vast repertoire, ranging from Bach to the cosmopolitan avant-garde. In 1987 he was awarded the Ehrenring of the Vienna Phil.

pollution. Harmonic pollution is characterized by indiscriminate disposal of chromatic refuse in a diatonic landscape. The process is vividly illustrated by a fetid organ arrangement of Chopin's Nocturne in E-flat Major, in which the initial ascending interval of a major 6th, from B-flat to G, is infested by noxious chromatic runs. A polluted version of Prokofiev's *Peter and the Wolf* has been published in America in the absence of a copyright agreement with the Soviet Union; it is characterized by vulgar insertion of auxiliary material in every available melodic or harmonic vacancy.

Orch.l pollution manifests itself in a general sonic flatulence and an infarction of supernumerary 3rds and 6ths. The rhythmic line, too, is an easy victim of pollution. In the remarkable compound rhythmic design in Gershwin's song *I Got Rhythm*, the original asymmetric line is often grossly mutilated, reducing it to abecedarian syncopation. Erudite arrangements of works of Bach and other classics, made by musicians of intelligence and taste, cannot be cited as examples of musical pollution. Even hyperchromatic pullulation found in some transcriptions by Max Reger possesses validity, though they should be labeled "artificially flavored with chromatic additives."

Some morphological transformations and homeological modifications are legitimate means of modernization. Examples of such artistic enhancement are *Symphonic Metamorphoses on Themes of Carl Maria von Weber* by Hindemith and the ballet *Le Baiser de la Fée* by Stravinsky, imaginatively deformed from themes of Tchaikovsky.

polo (Sp.). A syncopated Spanish dance in triple time, from Andalusia.

polonaise (Fr.; It. *polonese*). A dance of Polish origin, in 3/4 time and moderate tempo; formerly in animated processional style, but now merely a slow promenade opening a ball:

RHYTHM:

LAST MEASURE:

Examples of polonaises are found in instrumental works of Bach, Beethoven, and Schubert, but it was Chopin who elevated the polonaise to the heights of artistry in his piano music.

polska. Paradoxically this dance form, the name of which is the feminine adjective of Poland in the Polish language, corresponding to the French form *polonaise*, is not a Polish but a Swedish dance. The polska must have originated shortly before the 30 Years' War in the 17th century in which Sweden was actively involved. In its domesticated Swedish rhythms the polska resembles the MAZURKA.

polychoral style (It. *coro spezzato*, broken chorus). Compositional texture in which a chorus is divided into 2, 3, or 4 sections, sung alternately or antiphonally, combined their forces in the finale.

polymeter. The simultaneous use of several different meters. Polymeter dates back to the Renaissance, exemplified in the double time signature of Spanish dance music, 3/4 against 6/8. In operatic usage polymeter is encountered in scenes descriptive of simultaneous uncoordinated action, known under the name IMBROGLIO (It., entanglement). Stravinsky used the technique in *Petrouchka*. Elliott Carter employs METRIC MODULATION by changing meter and tempo in polyphonic writing; at the points of modulation, some players would be thinking in the present meter and tempo, while others would be viewing their music in terms of the next meter and tempo. Ben Johnston's *Knocking Piece* for 2 Percussionists and Piano Lid is a tour de force of reinterpreting time and measure virtually measure by measure.

Perhaps the most remarkable instance of contrapuntal polymeter is found in the 2nd movement of *3 Places in New England* by Ives, illustrating the meeting of 2 marching bands, with similar marching tunes played simultaneously at different tempi, in the ratio 4/3, so that 4 bars of the faster march equal 3 bars of the slower tempo. In his original MS Ives coordinated these different tempos within the uniform measures in 4/4 time, marking cross-accents wherever they occurred. At the suggestion of the author Ives agreed to incorporate in the published score an alternative arrangement with noncoincidental barlines in clear polymetric notation. In his performances of the work the author conducted 3 bars in 4/4 time with his right hand and 4 bars in ALLA BREVE time with his left hand. Those in the orch. who had parts with the faster march were to follow the conductor's left hand and the rest his right hand.

(A critic remarked that Slonimsky's performance was evangelical, for his right hand knew not what his left hand was doing.)

Among examples of implicit polymetry not marked as such by time signatures is the coda of Schumann's Piano Concerto, where the systematic syncopation in the piano part in 3/4 time results in a polymetric combination of 3/2 in the piano part versus 2 bars of 3/4 in the orch. In Gershwin's *I Got Rhythm*, the implicit polymetry consists of one bar in 2/16 time, 4 bars of 3/16 time, and 1 bar of 2/16 time, adding up to 16/16, that is, 4/4, which is the notated time signature. Sometimes the term *polymetry* is applied, inaccurately, to a succession of different times signatures. The proper term for such usages is changing meters.

polymodality. Polymodality is a special case of POLYTONALITY in which the principal melodic lines are modal rather than explicitly major or minor. Polymodal harmonies are disposed with the best effect by the use of a triple pedal point in open harmony in a minor key, suggesting Dorian, Phrygian or Aeolian constructions.

polyphonic. 1. See POLYPHONY. 2. Describing an instrument normally capable of producing 2 or more tones simultaneously, like the piano, harp, or organ.

polyphony

The combination in harmonious progression of 2 or more independent melodies; the independent treatment of the parts; counterpoint, in the widest sense. This is a musical term so pregnant with historical and structural signification that it becomes dissolved in its own universality. In the ancient Greek the word bore a derogatory meaning of multivoiced chatter. In a medieval treatise polyphony (from Grk. *poly* + *phone*, many sounds) is described as "modus canendi a pluribus diversam observantibus melodiam" (a method of singing a diverse melody from many components). In the musical lexicon published by J. G. Walther in 1732, polyphony is defined simply as "a many-voiced composition."

In the 19th century polyphony was identified with counterpoint in which each voice has a destiny of its own, as contrasted with HOMOPHONY, in which the melody is a dominating part with the rest of the musical fabric subordinated to it harmonically. The dichotomy of polyphony and harmony has been described in geometric terms as horizontal and vertical coordinates of musical composition. The term *linear counterpoint* gained some acceptance in the 20th century to emphasize the prevalent horizontality of polyphonic ingredients. In a polyphonic composition, the individual parts are interdependent and mutually accommodating in forming a euphonious ensemble. Contrapuntal IMITATION is a polyphonic system par excellence, the FUGUE being the summit of a polyphonic technique.

The difficulties of writing a double fugue with a 2nd subject being the melodic inversion of the principal theme, or DUX, as exemplified in the A-minor fugue of the 1st book of Bach's *Well-Tempered Clavier*, are enormous; that this particular fugue came out with such architectonic splendor is no less an achievement than a mathematical formula that unites the symbols of the base of natural logarithms, an imaginary number and the transcendental number π. Polyphonic trickery, such as revealed in an anonymous 18th-century piece that can be played in perfect harmony by 2 violinists, one reading it right side up and the other upside down, is as legitimate and as consequential a pursuit as a clever mathematical puzzle.

Polyphony attained its culmination with the great works of Bach and went on a decline almost immediately after his death; indeed, the rush toward homophony was led by Bach's sons. In place of "diversity in unity"—the essence of polyphonic composition—the masters of Classic music of the 2nd half of the 18th century and the succeeding 4 generations of Romantic composers made melody paramount and harmony its ancillary coordinate. An artistic development of polyphonic technique was hampered by rigid rules of contrapuntal practice; thus 2nd inversions of triads were forbidden because of the presence of the objectionable perfect 4th between the bass and upper voices; melodic progressions of the augmented 4th, or *tritones*, were deprecated. In Bach's time music students were physically punished by a painful strike of the instructor's cane on the knuckles of the fisted hand for using the tritone. Theorists went to inordinate lengths to account for apparent violations of the rules of strict polyphony by postulating the existence of a putative missing voice. Thus one eminent scholar, confronted with the use of the supertonic 7th chord in a Classic work (not allowed, according to the defenders of the faith), explained it as a dominant-11th chord with a missing bass and 3rd.

In the 20th century Reger revived the art of polyphony with extraordinary success; his teacher, Riemann, told him in all seriousness that he could become a 2nd Bach if he so desired. Reger failed to become a 2nd Bach, but he did produce a large amount of respectable polyphony. The technique of composition with 12 tones related only to one another, as promulgated by Schoenberg, is an avatar of strict polyphony. In this system polyphonic voices are all derived from a single basic theme; both the horizontal and vertical lines—melody and harmony—are coalesced in the governing series of 12 tones. Strict polyphony, in its purely structural aspects, which includes canonic imitation, fugue, and the devices of inversion (retrograde, augmentation, and diminution), is a doctrine scientifically conceived and precisely executed. Polyphony may be an obsolescent art, but in the hands of its greatest practitioners it remains a Gothic wonder of human genius.

polyrhythm. The simultaneous occurrence of several different rhythms. Polyrhythm differs from POLYMETER in that the former indicates a combination of 2 rhythmic groups, usually consisting of mutually prime numbers of notes or irregular groups of noncoincident patterns (i.e., cross rhythms), while the latter merely indicates the superposition, or a palimpsest, of 2 different meters usually having the same note values as their common denominator. Polyrhythm denotes the simultaneous occurrence of several fundamentally different rhythms, each clearly recognizable through idiosyncratic accents. All polyphonic music entails the use of different rhythms at the same time, but to qualify as polyrhythm such rhythms must be maintained for a considerable number of bars in each individual part. In this sense polyrhythm is the product of new music developed mainly in the 20th century.

The notational aspects of polyrhythmic usage is marked by different rhythmic groups overlapping the barlines. When notated in 8th notes, 16th notes, and smaller divisions, the ligatures cross the barlines. The familiar practice of imbroglio in opera, in which different rhythms are used in different vocal and instrumental parts, does not constitute polyrhythmic usage per se, because the metric units remain independent from one another. Nor does the simultaneous use of 3/4 time and 6/8 time, as is common in Hispanic songs and dances, fit the definition of polyrhythm. It may be argued that the use of triplets, quintuplets, and other odd rhythmical figures against binary rhythms is intrinsically polyrhythmic. One of the most remarkable examples is found in Chopin's *Fantaisie-Impromptu* for Piano, where groups of 4 16th notes in the right hand are accompanied by triplets in the left hand.

polystylistic music. ECLECTICISM in composition; a term invented by Alfred Schnittke in 1971. Either term may apply either to composers who use different historical or current styles in different works, or to a single piece that exhibits a variety of aesthetics.

polytetrachord. A term introduced by the author in his *Thesaurus of Scales and Melodic Patterns*, the polytetrachord is omnitonal. A major polytetrachord consists of 12 conjunct major tetrachords, traversing all 12 keys of the cycle of major scales. A minor polytetrachord consists of 12 keys of the cycle of minor scales. A partial use of the polytetrachord affords a rapid linear modulation into any major or minor key.

polytonality. Polytonality is the simultaneous use of several keys. In actual practice it is difficult to sustain the acoustical separation of more than 2 different keys, thus reducing polytonality to bitonality. Four mutually exclusive triads are workable in linear arpeggios (e.g., C major, F-sharp major, D minor, and G-sharp minor distributed in ascending quadritonal passages), but the same 4 keys in columnar superposition could be made effective only by careful differentiation of instrumental groups (e.g., C major in the strings, F-sharp major in muted horns, D minor in clarinets and oboes, and G-sharp minor in flutes and piccolos, with optional support of the strings by the bassoons and contrabassoons).

Approximations of polytonality, or rather bitonality, can be found in the fairly frequent instances of near synchronization of the lowered supertonic 1st inversion chord (♭II⁶) with the dominant triad in a Neapolitan cadence. In this coupling 2 triadic harmonies, having their tonics at the distance of a tritone, collide with a curiously euphonious effect. Stravinsky formalized this polytonal usage in the score of his ballet *Petrouchka*, in which the triads of C major and F-sharp major coagulate in close proximity. More explicitly, Milhaud used the same combination in the score of his ballet *Le Boeuf sur le toit*. Strictly speaking, however, this bitonal usage does not constitute integral polytonality, which demands the use of simultaneous combinations of 4 different triads, aggregating to all available notes of the tempered scale. It is entirely possible, of course, to arrange an integral panchromatic chord containing all 12 notes of the tempered scale in groups that would spell out all 24 major and minor triads and assign such triads to different instrumental groups so as to make them stand out individually, but the separation of the triadic groupings may be acoustically difficult.

An amusing example of polytonality is Mozart's *Ein musikalischer Spass*, where he makes the horns play in different keys from the rest of the orch. But Mozart's professed intention in this "musical joke" was to ridicule the ignorance of village musicians. He could not have anticipated the time when such musical jokes would become a new technique.

polytriads. Polytriadic harmony may be regarded as a special case of polytonality, with mobile parts containing complete triads. If the triads move along a single scale or a mode, the resulting technique is POLYMODALITY. Homonymous triads, major and minor, encased within the compass of a perfect 5th (e.g., C, E♭, E♮, G), are often found in modern works. Such polytriads are *e duobus unum*, giving rise to modes possessing the characteristics of both major and minor keys.

Pommer (Ger.). Bass SHAWM, now obsolete.

Pomo d'Oro, Il (The Golden Apple). "Festa teatrale" by Cesti, 1667, performed in Vienna during Carnival. The work comprised a prologue and 5 acts, broken down into 66 "scenes"; the production involved 24 set changes and lasted 8 or more hours; as one can imagine, the expense was immense. The plot is based on the mythological choice of Paris between 3 goddesses for their beauty; choosing Aphrodite, he gets Helen, whom he kidnaps to Troy, whence the war described in Homer's *Iliad*. The music that has survived reveals a skillful use of monody; the work was never revived, unsurprisingly; as it is, *Il Pomo d'Oro* could have literally been the opera to end all operas.

Pomp and Circumstance. Five orch. marches by Elgar (1902–1907, 1930). The expression "pomp and circumstance" comes from Shakespeare's *Othello*. The most famous of these marches is the 1st; its middle section has been set to the words *Land of Hope and Glory*, and it is used by almost every American school as a processional at graduation ceremonies. The 1st 2 marches were introduced in Liverpool, England, 1901.

Pomp, mit (Ger.). Solemnly.

pompe (Fr.). 1. Trombone slide. 2. Additional tubing inserted in natural brass instruments.

pomposo (It.). Pompously, loftily; in a majestic, dignified style.

Ponce, Manuel (Maria), distinguished Mexican composer; b. Fresnillo, Dec. 8, 1882; d. Mexico City, Apr. 24, 1948. He studied piano with his older sister; in 1904 he went to Europe, where he took lessons in composition with Enrico Bossi at Bologna and in piano with Martin Krause in Berlin. Upon his return to Mexico he taught piano at the Mexico City Cons. (1909–15). He gave a concert of his compositions in Mexico City in 1912, which included a piano concerto. During World War I he lived in N.Y. and in Havana; then went to Paris for additional study and took lessons with Paul Dukas. His contact with French music wrought a radical change in his style of composition; his later works are more polyphonic in structure and more economical in form.

He possessed a great gift of melody; one of his songs, *Estrellita* (1914), became a universal favorite and was often mistaken for a folk song. In 1941 he made a tour in South America, conducting his own works. He was the 1st Mexican composer of the 20th century to employ an identifiably modern musical language; his contributions to the guitar and orch. repertoire are substantial; his place in the history of Mexican music is a very important one. His works are often performed in Mexico; a concert hall was named after him in the Inst. de Bellas Artes.

Ponchielli, Amilcare, celebrated Italian composer; b. Paderno Fasolaro, near Cremona, Aug. 31, 1834; d. Milan, Jan. 15, 1886. He studied with his father, a shopkeeper and organist at the village church; entered the Milan Cons. as a nonpaying student when he was 9; his mentors included Pietro Ray (theory), Arturo Angeleri (piano), Felice Frasi (composition), and Alberto Mazzucato (music history, esthetics, and composition); while a student there he collaborated on the operetta *Il sindaco babbeo* (Milan Cons., Mar. 1851); also wrote the sym. *Scena campestre* (1852). After his graduation (1854) he went to Cremona as a church organist; he was named assistant to Ruggero Manna, director of Cremona's Teatro Concordia (1855), where he brought out his opera *I promessi sposi* (Aug. 30, 1856). He was conductor of the municipal bands in Piacenza (1861–64) and Cremona (from 1864), where he also conducted opera; he continued to pursue his interest in composing for the theater. He finally achieved notable success with the revised version of his *I promessi sposi* (Milan, Dec. 4, 1872), which was subsequently performed throughout Italy; his *La Gioconda* (Milan, Apr. 8, 1876) secured his reputation.

Ponchielli was prof. of composition at the Milan Cons. in 1880 and again from 1881; he also served as maestro di cappella at Bergamo's S. Maria Maggiore (1881–86). He married the soprano Teresina Brambilla in 1874. His birthplace was renamed Paderno Ponchielli in his honor. *La Gioconda* remains his only work to have acquired repertoire status; it includes the famous ballet number *Dance of the Hours*. In addition to his numerous stage works, he composed many band pieces, vocal chamber music, chamber works, and piano pieces.

ponderoso (It.). Ponderous; in a vigorous, impressive style.

ponticello (It.). Bridge. *Sul ponticello*, near the bridge.

Pop! Goes the Weasel. A famous Anglo-American nursery rhyme in gig time. In the British version the word *weasel* had nothing to do with the rodent but was the name of a household utensil, like a flatiron. *Pop* was the colloquial word for the pawnshop, so that the lines "that's the way the money went, pop goes the weasel" described a predicament of a poor Englishman who had to hock his flatiron. In the American version the weasel is definitely an animal.

pop(ular) music. A general term to denote a wide variety of musical styles, generally characterized by their easy accessibility to wide audiences; usually of modest length, with prominent and memorable melodies and a simple, unassuming harmonic language. Definitions and sources for popular music are broad and plentiful, from Tin Pan Alley to musicals, Anglo-Irish traditional to country-western,

blues to soul, classical to environmental urban sound; in the last quarter of the 20th century, influences from around the world have become primary. The term *popular music* can only be interpreted as music with a commercial aspect, unlike authentic indigenous music; in this sense it holds a social position similar to most classical music, which has also had a monetary goal in most cases, as opposed to folk music. To a classical audience, "popular" may seem vulgar, downgraded, repellant, lethal, and socially divisive; but that suggests an inability or unwillingness to hear the multitude of difference in the many kinds of popular music; it is perfectly analogous to those who would listen to classical music and declare that it all sounds the same.

Porgy and Bess. Opera by George Gershwin, 1935, to a libretto by his brother Ira, based on a contemporary American play by DuBose and Dorothy Heyward; it was 1st performed in Boston. The startling innovation of the opera was its selection of a subject from Negro life; the cast of characters consisted almost exclusively of African-Americans. Porgy is a cripple; Bess is his girl. He kills her former convict lover and is arrested, but he is released for lack of evidence. In the meantime Bess is spirited away to N.Y. by a worldly gent with an engaging nickname, Sportin' Life. At the end of the opera Porgy is still looking for Bess. Several songs from the opera have become classics of American music, including *Summertime*, *A Woman Is a Sometime Thing*, *My Man's Gone Now*, *I Got Plenty o' Nuthin'*, *Bess, You Is My Woman Now*, and *It Ain't Necessarily So*, which irreverently casts doubt on the most cherished stories of the Bible. The musical idiom of *Porgy and Bess* is an artistic recreation of Negro spirituals, jazz, and blues.

pornographic music. It was Hanslick who said that the last movement of Tchaikovsky's Violin Concerto suggested to him the hideous notion that music can actually stink to the ear. The literal depiction of an episode in *Symphonia domestica* by R. Strauss, which illustrates his retirement to the bed chamber with Frau Strauss, to the suggestive accompaniment of 2 conjugated trumpets, impressed some listeners at its 1st performance as indecent. In a symphonic interlude in Shostakovich's opera *Lady Macbeth of the District of Mtzensk*, with the marital bed occupying the center of the stage, the trombone glissandi seem to give an onomatopoeic representation of sexual intercourse. Graphic notation offers excellent opportunities for suggestive pictorial pornography. The tetraphallic score *Mooga Pook* by the American composer Charles Amirkhanian is a fine example.

portale la voce (It., carry the voice; Fr. *port de voix*). Sing PORTAMENTO.

portamento (It.). A smooth gliding from one tone to another, differing from the legato in its more deliberate execution and in the actual (though very rapid and slurring) sounding of the intermediate tones.

portando (It., carrying). Play PORTAMENTO. *Portando la voce*, vocal PORTAMENTO.

portative. A small portable organ which could be used in religious processions.

portato (It., carried; Fr. *louré*). An articulation on bowed chordophones lying between legato and staccato; component notes are separated while preserving the feeling of continuity.

Porter, Cole (Albert), remarkable American composer of popular music; b. Peru, Ind., June 9, 1891; d. Santa Monica, Calif., Oct. 15, 1964. He was educated at Yale Univ. (B.A., 1913); then took academic courses at Harvard Law School and later at the Harvard School of Music (1915–16); also received instruction in counterpoint, composition, orchestration, and harmony from d'Indy at the Paris Schola Cantorum (1919). While at Yale he wrote football songs (*Yale Bull Dog Song, Bingo Eli Yale*, etc.); also composed music for college functions. He 1st gained success as a composer for the stage with his *Wake Up and Dream* (London, 1929); his 1st production in N.Y. was *See America First* (1916). There followed a cascade of musical comedies for which he wrote both the lyrics and the music, which placed him in the front rank of the American musical theater. His greatest success came with his musical comedy *Kiss Me, Kate*, after Shakespeare's *The Taming of the Shrew* (N.Y., 1948). A motion picture musical biography of Porter, starring Cary Grant, was produced by Warner Bros. in 1946 as *Night and Day*.

Porter was a master of subtle expression without sentimentality, a kinetic dash without vulgarity, and a natural blend of word poetry with the finest of harmonious melodies. Among his other musicals are (all are musicals 1st perf. in N.Y.): *Fifty Million Frenchmen* (1929); *Gay Divorce* (1932); *Anything Goes* (1934); *Jubilee* (1935); *Red Hot and Blue* (1936); *Du Barry was a Lady* (1939); *Panama Hattie* (1940); *Something for the Boys* (1943); *Mexican Hayride* (1944); *Kiss Me, Kate* (1948); *Out of This World* (1950); *Can-Can* (1953); *Silk Stockings* (1955); etc. Of his many songs at least half a dozen became great favorites: *Begin the Beguine; It's De-Lovely; Night and Day; My Heart Belongs to Daddy; Don't Fence Me In; Wunderbar.* He also composed numerous film scores, including *Rosalie* (1937), *You'll Never Get Rich* (1941), *Les Girls* (1957), and *Aladdin* (1958).

Portsmouth Point. Concert overture by Walton, 1926, premiered at the ISCM Festival in Zurich. It was inspired by an 18th-century English print of the eponymous British naval arsenal. The music portrays the commotion of sailors bustling to and fro in syncopated rhythms.

Portuguese Hymn. Obsolete nickname of *Adeste Fidelis* (O, Come All Ye Faithful); it was regularly performed in the Portuguese chapel in London during the early 1800s.

posato (It.). Sedate, dignified.

Posaune (Ger.). Trombone. Also, a reed stop in the organ, of 8' (manuals) or 16' (pedal) pitch.

pose de la voix (Fr.). Attack the vocal tone with precise articulation.

positif (Fr.). Choir organ.

position. 1. The place of the left hand on the fingerboard of the violin, etc. In the 1st position the forefinger stops the tone (or semitone) above the open string; by shifting up, so that the 1st finger takes the place previously occupied by the 2nd, the 2nd position is reached, and so on. In the half position the 2nd, 3rd, and 4th fingers occupy the places taken in the 1st position by the 1st, 2nd, and 3rd fingers. 2. The arrangement of notes in a chord, with reference to the lowest part; in the 1st, or fundamental position, the lowest

Cole Porter, 1930s

782

part takes the root; in the 2nd it takes the 3rd, etc. 3. Close (open) position, see HARMONY, *close* and *open*.

positive organ (Ger. *Positiv*). Medieval portable organ with a single manual and no pedal. To operate the bellows that pumped air into the pipes, an assistant was required. It was often used at the homes of pious church musicians and parishioners.

possibile (It.). Possible. *Pianissimo possibile*, as soft as possible; *il più presto possibile*, as rapid as possible.

post horn. A horn without valves or keys, used on post coaches. The sound of the post horn was associated with departure, sorrowful or joyful; Beethoven used such an association in his *Les Adieux* piano sonata, where the opening post horn call is sounded in the descending cadence known as HORN FIFTHS.

posthumous works. The expression is barbaric, for how can a work occur after the death of its author? The dictionaries give a 2nd definition as "published after death." Other definitions of posthumous works are those that have been discovered after the composer's death. But what about a work that has been played numerous times during the composer's lifetime but was published only after his death?

This distinction is so important that it led to numerous debates about the nature of the federal copyright law, and at least to 1 serious lawsuit, brought by Peter Bartók, son of Béla Bartók, against the composer's publishers Boosey and Hawkes in 1973, concerning the renewal of the copyright of Bartók's *Concerto for Orchestra*. As a rule a copyrighted work must be renewed after 28 years. Both Peter Bartók and the publishers applied for the renewal of the copyright. The U.S. Copyright Office declined to decide who had the right to have the copyright renewed. Since the *Concerto for Orchestra* was published after the composer's death in 1945, the publishers claimed the right to renew the copyright, but Peter Bartók asserted his right as the lawful heir to his father's estate and declared that the work in question was performed several times during his father's life and therefore could not be regarded as posthumous. The judge ruled in favor of the publishers, basing his findings on the specific meaning that the word posthumous conveys in regard to works published after the composer's death, and cited the usage of the word accepted since the middle of the 19th century, with a specific reference to many "posthumous" works by Chopin, referring to a Chopin work that was published as a posthumous

opus in 1855, 6 years after his death, although it had been written in 1828 and 1st performed in 1830. He ruled, therefore, that since the definition of the word in the field of music applied for more than a century to any composition published after the death of its composer, Boosey and Hawkes had the right to renew the copyright.

Postillon de Longjumeau, Le. Opera by A. Adam, 1836, premiered in Paris. The coachman of a *carosse de diligence* develops a fine tenor voice in the course of announcing schedules and designations. He rides to Paris and fame. There he courts by proxy a rich Parisian woman. In one of those coincidences that happen only in opera, the object of his attention turns out to be his lawful wedded wife, whom he abandoned in Longjumeau. There are no recriminations between the 2, since both made good in a new life, and their marriage is happily reaffirmed. The opera continues to play to French opera audiences.

postlude. 1. A closing voluntary on the organ. 2. A refrain.

postmodernism. See MODERNISM.

potpourri (*mélange, méslange*; Fr., rotten pot; It. *mescolanza*). A musical medley exhibiting a motley variety of unrelated refrains and fragments connected in an arbitrary manner. In an enlarged sense *potpourri* was used by music publishers—particularly in Germany—for any collection of favorite arias or instrumental pieces; the word did not acquire its somewhat derogatory meaning until much later. But modern composers of the NEOCLASSICAL persuasion revived the genre of potpourri in a nostalgically attractive manner, as a series of disconnected musical sketches.

Poule, La. HEN, THE.

Poulenc, Francis (Jean Marcel), brilliant French composer; b. Paris, Jan. 7, 1899; d. there, Jan. 30, 1963. He was born into a wealthy family of pharmaceutical manufacturers; his mother taught him music in his childhood; at 16 he began taking formal piano lessons with Ricardo Viñes. A decisive turn in his development as a composer occurred when he attracted the attention of Satie, the *arbiter elegantiarum* of the arts and social amenities in Paris. Deeply impressed by Satie's fruitful eccentricities in the then-shocking manner of DADAISM, Poulenc joined an ostentatiously self-descriptive musical group called the Nouveaux Jeunes. In a gratuitous parallel with the Russian 5, the French critic Henri Collet renamed the "New Youths" *Le Groupe de 6*, and the label stuck under the designation LES SIX. The 6 musicians included, besides Poulenc, were Auric, Durey, Honegger, Milhaud, and Tailleferre. Although quite different in their styles of composition and artistic inclinations, they continued collective participation in various musical events. Poulenc served in the French army (1918–21) and then began taking lessons in composition with Koechlin (1921–24). An excellent pianist, Poulenc became in 1935 an accompanist to the French baritone Pierre Bernac, for whom he wrote numerous songs.

Compared with his fortuitous comrades-in-6, Poulenc appears a classicist. He never experimented with the popular devices of "machine music," asymmetrical rhythms, and polyharmonies as cultivated by Honegger and Milhaud. Futuristic projections had little interest for him; he was content to follow the gentle neoclassical formation of Ravel's piano music and songs. Among his other important artistic contacts was the ballet impresario Diaghilev, who commissioned him to write music for his Ballets Russes. Apart from his fine songs and piano pieces, Poulenc revealed himself as an inspired composer of religious music, of which his choral works *Stabat Mater* and *Gloria* are notable. He also wrote remarkable music for the organ, including a concerto that became a minor masterpiece. A master of artificial simplicity he pleases even sophisticated listeners by his bland triadic tonalities spiced with quickly passing diaphanous discords.

Pound, Ezra (Loomis), greatly significant American man of letters and amateur composer; b. Hailey, Idaho, Oct. 30, 1885; d. Venice, Nov. 1, 1972. He was educated at Hamilton College (Ph.B., 1905) and the Univ. of Pa. (M.A., 1906). He went to England, where he established himself as a leading experimental poet and influential critic. He also pursued a great interest in early music, especially that of the troubadours, which led him to try his hand at composing. With the assistance of George Antheil he composed the opera *Le Testament*, after poems by François Villon (1923; Paris, 1926); it was followed by a 2nd opera, *Calvacanti* (1932), and a 3rd, left unfinished, based on the poetry of Catullus. In 1924 he settled in Rapallo. Although married to Dorothy Shakespear, daughter of one of Yeats's friends, he became intimate with the American violinist Olga Rudge; Rudge bore him a daughter in 1925 and his wife bore him a son in 1926. Through the influence of Rudge, his interest in music continued and he became a fervent champion of Vivaldi; he also worked as a music reviewer and ran a concert series with Rudge, "Inverno Musicale."

A growing interest in economic history and an inordinate admiration for the Fascist dictator Benito Mussolini led Pound down the road of political obscurantism. During World War II he made many broadcasts over Rome Radio on topics ranging from literature to politics. His condemnation of Jewish banking circles in America and the American effort to defeat Fascism led to his arrest by the Allies after the collapse of Il Duce's regime. In 1945 he was sent to a prison camp in Pisa. In 1946 he was sent to the U.S. to stand trial for treason, but he was declared insane and confined to St. Elizabeth's Hospital in Washington, D.C. Finally in 1958 he was released and allowed to return to Italy, where he died.

Among his writings on music is his *Antheil and the Treatise on Harmony* (1924). He also composed several works for solo violin for Rudge, including *Fiddle Music* (1924) and *Al poco giorno* (Berkeley, 1983); he also arranged Gaucelm Faidit's *Plainte pour la mort du roi Richart Coeur de Lion*. The uncatalogued collection of Pound's musical MSS at Yale Univ. includes various musical experiments, including rhythmic and melodic realizations of his poem *Sestina: Altaforte*. Among the composers who have set his poems to music are Copland, Luytens, and Berio.

poussé (Fr.). Up-bow.

Pousseur, Henri (Léon Marie Thérèse), Belgian composer of the ULTRAMODERN school; b. Malmédy, June 23, 1929. He studied at the Liège Cons. (1947–52) and the Brussels Cons. (1952–53); had private lessons in composition from André Souris and Pierre Boulez; until 1959, worked in the Cologne and Milan electronic music studios, where he came in contact with Stockhausen and Berio; was a member of the AVANT-GARDE group of composers "Variation" in Liège. He taught music in various Belgian schools (1950–59); was founder (1958) and director of the Studio de Musique Électronique APELAC in Brussels, from 1970 a part of the Centre de Recherches Musicales in Liège; gave lectures at the summer courses of NEW MUSIC in Darmstadt (1957–67), Cologne (1966–68), Basel (1963–64), the State Univ. of N.Y. in Buffalo (1966–69), and the Liège Cons. (from 1970), where he became director in 1975.

In his music he tries to synthesize all the expressive powers of which man, as a biological species *Homo sapiens*, is capable in the domain of art (or nonart); the technological resources of the subspecies *Homo habilis* (magnetic tape, electronics/synthesizers, aleatory extensions, the principle of indeterminacy, glossolalia, self-induced schizophasia) all form part of his rich musical (or nonmusical) vocabulary for multimedia (or nullimedia) representations. The influence of his methods (or nonmethods) of composition (or noncomposition) is pervasive.

Powell, "Bud" (Earl), African-American jazz pianist; b. N.Y., Sept. 27, 1924; d. there, Aug. 1, 1966. After dropping out of school at the age of 15 he began playing with local groups in N.Y. Following the zeitgeist, he adopted the bop style, and in 1943 he joined Cootie Williams and his band; he also played concerts with Dizzy Gillespie, Sid Catlett, and John Kirby, achieving recognition as a fine bop pianist. He was a frequent participant in the formative jazz sessions at Minton's Playhouse. He gradually discarded the prevalent "stride" piano style, with its regular beat, and emancipated the left-hand rhythm by introducing a contrapuntal line with asymmetrical punctuation. His brief career was periodically interrupted by mental eclipses caused by immoderate use of hallucinogenic drugs.

pp. Pianissimo.

ppp. Pianississimo.

prächtig (Ger.). Grandly, majestically.

Praeconium paschale (Lat., Paschal sermon). Roman Catholic Easter hymn sung on Holy Saturday.

præludium (*praeambulum*; Lat.; Fr. *préambule*). Prelude.

Praetorius, Michael, great German composer, organist, and music theorist; b. Creuzburg an der Werra, Thuringia, Feb. 15, 1571; d. Wolfenbüttel, Feb. 15, 1621. The surname of the family was Schultheiss (sometimes rendered as Schultze), which he Latinized as Praetorius. He was the son of a Lutheran pastor. He studied with Michael Voigt, the cantor of the Torgau Lateinschule; in 1582 he entered the Univ. of Frankfurt an der Oder; in 1584 he continued his studies at the Lateinschule in Zerbst, Anhalt. From 1587 to 1590 he was organist of St. Marien in Frankfurt. In 1595 he entered the service of Duke Heinrich Julius of Braunschweig-Wolfenbüttel as an organist; in 1604 he also assumed the duties of court Kapellmeister. Upon the death of his patron in 1613, the Elector Johann Georg of Saxony obtained his services as deputy Kapellmeister at the Dresden court. He retained his Dresden post until 1616 and then resumed his duties in Wolfenbüttel.

Praetorius devoted only a part of his time to Wolfenbüttel, for he had been named Kapellmeister to the administrator of the Magdeburg bishopric and prior of the monastery at Ringelheim in 1614. He also traveled a great deal, visiting various German cities. These factors, coupled with a general decline in his health, led to the decision not to reappoint him to his Wolfenbüttel post in 1620. He died the following year a wealthy man. Deeply religious, he directed that the greater portion of his fortune go to organizing a foundation for the poor.

Praetorius was one of the most important and prolific German composers of his era. His *Musae Sioniae*, a significant collection of over 1,200 settings of Lutheran chorales, is a particularly valuable source for hymnology. He also published collections of motets, psalms, sacred songs, madrigals, bicinia and tricinia, litanies, works with bass continuo, and a collection of French instrumental dances under the title *Terpsichore, musarum aoniarum quinta a 4–6* (1612).

Praetorius is even better known for his *Syntagma musicum*, publ. in 3 vols. as follows: *Syntagmatis musici tomus primus* (Wittenberg and Wolfenbüttel, 1614–15), a historical and descriptive treatise in Latin on ancient and ecclesiastical music and ancient secular instruments; *Syntagmatis musici tomus secundus* (Wolfenbüttel, 1618; with an appendix, *Theatrum instrumentorum*, Wolfenbüttel, 1620), in German, a most important source of information on musical instruments of the period, describing their form, compass, tone quality, etc.; the organ is treated at great length, and the appendix contains 42 woodcuts of the principal instruments enumerated; *Syntagmatis musici tomus tertius* (Wolfenbüttel, 1618), is a valuable and interesting account of secular composition of the period, with a treatise on solmisation, notation, etc.

Prague Symphony. Mozart's Sym. No. 38 in D Major, performed for the 1st time in Prague in 1787, bringing Mozart expressions of admiration in the public and in the press, the like of which he rarely tasted in Vienna. Mozart was always fond of Prague.

Prairie, The. Cantata by Foss, 1944, to texts by Carl Sandburg, premiered in N.Y. Although American in essence, the score does not quote actual folk songs.

Praise the Lord and Pass the Ammunition. Song by F. Loesser, written shortly after the Japanese attack on Pearl Harbor (1941). This somewhat unchristian entreaty is attributed to a U.S. Navy chaplain.

Pralltriller (Ger.). Upper MORDENT, repeated multiple times.

Pratella, Francesco Balilla. See FUTURISM.

Prayers of Kierkegaard. Work for soprano solo, chorus, and orch. by Barber, 1954, inspired by the writings of the Danish mystic philosopher Kierkegaard. The music is appropriately ascetic, but its contrapuntal fabric is acrid. The work was 1st performed in Boston.

präzis (Ger.). Precise.

Pré aux Clercs, Le (The Meadow of the Scholars). Opera by Hérold, 1832, premiered in Paris. The libretto is based on a historical episode during the time of the French king Charles IX and tells of a romance between the maid-of-honor of the Queen of Navarre and a young nobleman.

precedente (It.). Preceding. *Moto precedente*, in the preceding tempo.

precentor. A director and manager of a choir, and of musical services in general; in the Anglican Church, 2nd in rank to the deacon.

precipitando (*precipitoso*; It.). With precipitation, impetuosity, dash.

preciso (It.). With precision.

precocity. Music is a gift that is revealed at a very early age; virtually all professional musicians were child prodigies. Among those who achieved greatness was Mozart, whose father even exhibited him at the courts of Europe as a wonder child (and slyly diminished his age by a year in his public announcements of young Mozart's presentations). Saint-Saëns amazed the French public by performing concerts at the age of 10. A younger contemporary of Saint-Saëns, Emile Paladilhe, also showed an astonishing talent as a very young Paris conservatory pupil, but in the course of time he settled into the easy chair of oblivion. On the other side of the coin, many great composers did not shine brilliantly at the beginnings of their careers, most of them because they did not play an instrument with any degree of virtuosity. The names of Wagner, Verdi, Berlioz, Schumann, Tchaikovsky, Rimsky-Korsakov, Stravinsky, Debussy, and Ravel belong in this category. None of them were ever *wunderkinder*.

Singers are never child prodigies simply because they have to reach physical maturity before they can perform in public. The most precocious conductor was Willy Ferrero, who led concerts at the age of 8, arousing amazement wherever he gave his exhibitions. He ended his career as a conductor of a provincial Italian opera house. The American conductor Lorin Maazel, who appeared at the N.Y. World's Fair in 1939 at the age of 9, aroused guarded skepticism (1 orch. musician wondered whether the next guest conductor would be a trained seal), but he overcame his extraordinary precocity and eventually became a successful sym. conductor.

pregando (It.). Imploring, beseeching.

preghiera (It.). Prayer.

prelude (from Lat. *praeludium*, preplay; Fr. *prélude*; It. *preludio*; Ger. *Vorspiel*). A musical introduction to a large work or fugue; also, an independent composition. The earliest instrumental preludes correspond to the etymological signification of the term; they consisted usually of introductory chords and arpeggios and a brief melody with a homophonic accompaniment. During the Baroque period preludes served as introductions to an instrumental suite, usually for piano or organ. The most famous introductory preludes are those paired with fugues in Bach's *Well-Tempered Clavier*, each in the key of the fugue that follows. In the 19th century, however, the prelude emancipated itself and became an independent form. Chopin's *Preludes* for piano are not preambles to anything, but self-sufficient compositions.

Debussy, Rachmaninoff, and Scriabin followed Chopin in fashioning their own piano preludes. The opening *Promenade* in Mussorgsky's piano suite *Pictures at an Exhibition* is of the nature of a prelude; similar "promenades" are interposed between numbers in the rest of this suite, where they assume the role of interludes. The antonym of the prelude is the postlude. In Hindemith's piano suite *Ludus Tonalis*, the postlude is the physical inversion of the prelude, obtained by playing the pages of the prelude upside-down and adjusting the accidentals.

Prélude à l'Après-midi d'un faune (Prelude to the Afternoon of a Faun). Symphonic poem by Debussy, 1894, 1st performed in Paris. This is probably the most poetic creation of Debussy's impressionistic genius, scored for a small orch. in which the woodwinds, horns, harps, and a pair of antique cymbals form an exquisite image; the work was the opening salvo in the rejection of late Romanticism. The *Prélude* is inspired by a poem by the French symbolist Mallarmé, and it depicts the silent contemplation by a sensuous faun of nymphs and other creatures of the woods on a sunny afternoon. For a performance subsequent to the premiere, a note was inserted explaining that the complete text of the poem could not be printed because young girls attended the concerts. An American music publ. house issued an arrangement of the work with a picture of a fawn on the cover; the publisher did not know the difference between the Greek demigod faun and a young animal of the deer family.

Préludes. Piano cycles by Debussy; book I was composed in 1909–10; book II was composed in 1910–13, although earlier pieces may have been included.

Préludes, Les. Symphonic poem by Liszt, 1854, 1st performed in Weimar with Liszt conducting. The title is taken from a poem by Lamartine in which the poet asks the rhetorical question, What is life but a series of preludes? The music is successively dramatic, lyrical, and solemn; it is a good example of thematic transformation.

premiere (from Fr. *première audition*, 1st hearing). The 1st performance of a musical (or other) work. In Europe the premiere of a large work is often preceded by a RÉPÉTITION GÉNÉRALE (dress rehearsal) to which press and dignitaries are invited.

preparation. 1. The preparation of a dissonance consists in the presence, in the preceding chord and same part, of the tone forming the dissonance. 2. The insertion of screws, nuts, bolts, etc., under the strings of a grand piano, in accord with instructions contained in the score and in advance of the performance of a work for PREPARED PIANO.

prepared piano. An instrument whose timbre is altered by placing such objects as screws, bolts, nuts, metal paperclips, coins, safety pins, clothespins, cardboard, rubber wedges, wires, pencil erasers, metal strips, and virtually anything that can be attached or placed between, on top of, or below the strings of a grand piano. The idea may be traced to the old schoolboy trick of putting a piece of paper on the piano strings to produce a tinkling, harpsichordlike sound. Cage invented the term in the early 1940s; the results produce buzzing effects, muting, and resonance. Cage's *Sonatas and Interludes* (1946–48), a major work for prepared piano, was performed in 1949 in Carnegie Hall; the work earned

him awards from both the Guggenheim Foundation and the National Institute of Arts and Letters, for "having thus extended the boundaries of musical art."

prepense music. This is music aforethought; it is the antonym of UNPREMEDITATED MUSIC.

Present Arms. Musical by Rodgers and Hart, 1928. The action takes place in Hawaii, with an English lord's daughter being pursued by a sailor from Brooklyn and a German baron. The sailor wins the lady after performing feats of heroism in a shipwreck. Musical ersatz Hawaiiana enlivens the score.

Presley, Elvis (Aron), fantastically popular American rock 'n' roll singer and balladeer; b. Tupelo, Miss., Jan. 8, 1935; d. Memphis, Tenn., Aug. 16, 1977. He was employed as a mechanic and furniture repairman in his early youth; picked up guitar playing in his leisure hours; sang cowboy ballads at social gatherings. With the advent of rock 'n' roll he revealed himself as the supreme genius of the genre; almost effortlessly he captivated multitudes of adolescents by the hallucinogenic consistency of his vocal delivery, enhanced by rhythmic pelvic gyrations (hence the invidious appellation "Elvis the Pelvis"); made recordings that sold

Elvis Presley, 1956

COURTESY FRANK DRIGGS COLLECTION

millions of albums. He made America conscious of the seductive quality of rock 'n' roll tunes; he aroused primitive urges among his multitudinous admirers with his renditions of such songs, among them *Don't Be Cruel, Hound Dog, Love Me Tender, All Shook Up, Jailhouse Rock, Heartbreak Hotel, Rock around the Clock, It's Now or Never*; his audience responded by improvising songs about him: *My Boy Elvis, I Wanna Spend Christmas with Elvis*, and *Elvis for President*. He also appeared as an actor in sentimental motion pictures, and served in the U.S. Army in Germany.

His art was an important inspiration for the famous Liverpudlian quartet the Beatles. An International Elvis Presley Appreciation Society was organized by 1970. Presley was indeed the King of Kings of rock. His death (of cardiac arrhythmia aggravated by an immoderate use of tranquilizers and other drugs) precipitated the most extraordinary outpouring of public grief over an entertainment figure since the death of Rudolph Valentino. His entombment in the family mausoleum in Memphis was the scene of mob hysteria, during which 2 people were run over and killed by an automobile; 2 men were arrested for an alleged plot to spirit away his body and hold it for ransom. In the early '90s the U.S. post office held an informal contest to determine whether their customers preferred the young or old Elvis to grace a postage stamp; youthful Elvis beat out the bloated Vegas denizen hands down. The stamp proved to be one of the all-time best sellers in postal history.

pressando (It.; Fr. *pressez*). Pressing onward, accelerating.

Pressler, Menahem, German-born American pianist and teacher; b. Magdeburg, Dec. 16, 1923. He was taken to Palestine by his family after the Hitlerization of Germany; he studied piano with Eliah Rudiakow and Leo Kestenberg; then played with the Palestine Sym. Orch. In 1946 he won the Debussy Prize at the piano competition in San Francisco. In 1955 he became a member of the School of Music at Indiana Univ.; that year he became pianist in the Beaux Arts Trio, with which he made numerous tours; he also continued his career as a soloist.

prestamente (It.). Rapidly.

prestissimo (It.). Very rapidly.

presto (It.). Fast, rapid; faster than *allegro. Presto assai*, extremely rapid; *presto parlante*, a direction in recitatives meaning to "speak" rapidly.

Pretty Girl Is Like a Melody, A. Song by I. Berlin, 1919, written for the Ziegfeld Follies of that year. It became a permanent fixture and was interpolated in several movie musicals.

Preussisches Märchen. Opera by Blacher, 1952, 1st produced in Berlin and based on a true incident from 1900. In this Prussian fairy tale an enterprising young man puts on a military uniform and makes himself a captain. The story became famous for its portrayal of obsequiousness and mindless obedience to superiors. The score is terse, lively, and dissonant.

Previn, André (George) (born Andreas Ludwig Priwin), brilliant German-born American pianist, conductor, and composer; b. Berlin, Apr. 6, 1929. He was of Russian-Jewish descent. He showed an unmistakable musical gift as a child; his father, a lawyer, was an amateur musician who gave him his early training; they played piano, 4-hands, together at home. At the age of 6 he was accepted as a pupil at the Berlin Hochschule für Musik, where he studied piano with Prof. Breithaupt; as a Jew, however, he was compelled to leave school in 1938. The family then went to Paris; he continued his studies at the Paris Cons., Marcel Dupré being one of his teachers.

In 1939 the family emigrated to America, settling in Los Angeles, where his father's cousin, Charles Previn, was music director at Universal Studios in Hollywood. He took lessons in composition with Joseph Achron, Ernst Toch, and Mario Castelnuovo-Tedesco. He became an American citizen in 1943. Even before graduating from high school he obtained employment at MGM; he became an orchestrator there and later one of its music directors; he also became a fine jazz pianist. He served in the U.S. Army (1950–52); stationed in San Francisco, he took lessons in conducting with Pierre Monteux, who was music director of the San Francisco Sym. Orch. at the time. During these years he wrote much music for films; he received Academy Awards for his arrangements of *Gigi* (1958), *Porgy and Bess* (1959), *Irma la Douce* (1963), and *My Fair Lady* (1964). Throughout this period he continued to appear as a concert pianist. In 1962 he made his formal conducting debut with the St. Louis Sym. Orch.; conducting soon became his principal vocation.

From 1967 to 1969 he was conductor-in-chief of the Houston Sym. Orch. In 1968 he assumed the post of principal conductor of the London Sym. Orch., retaining it with distinction until 1979; then was made its conductor emeritus. In 1976 he became music director of the Pittsburgh Sym. Orch., a position he held with similar distinction until a dispute with the management led to his resignation in 1984. He had already been engaged as music director of the Royal Phil. Orch. of London in 1982, a position he held from 1985 to 1987; he then served as its principal conductor. Previn also accepted appointment as music director of the Los Angeles Phil. Orch. after resigning his Pittsburgh position; he formally assumed his duties in Los Angeles in 1985 but gave up this position in 1990 after disagreements with the management over administrative procedures.

During his years as a conductor of the London Sym. Orch. he took it on a number of tours to the U.S., as well as to Russia, Japan, South Korea, and Hong Kong. He also took the Pittsburgh Sym. Orch. on acclaimed tours of Europe in 1978 and 1982. He continued to compose popular music, including the scores for the musicals *Coco* (1969) and *The Good Companions* (1974); with words by Tom Stoppard, he composed *Every Good Boy Deserves Favour* (1977), a work for actors and orch. He also wrote orch. works, piano pieces, and songs. He ed. the book *Orchestra* (1979); also publ. *Andre Previn's Guide to Music* (1983). He was married 4 times (and divorced thrice): to the jazz singer Betty Bennett, to the jazz poet Dory Langdon (who made a career of her own as composer and singer of pop songs), to the actress Mia Farrow, and in 1982 to Heather Hales.

Prey, Hermann, outstanding German baritone; b. Berlin, July 11, 1929. He studied with Günther Baum and Harry Gottschalk at the Berlin Hochschule für Musik; won 1st prize in a vocal competition organized by the U.S. Army in 1952, and that same year made his operatic debut as the 2nd prisoner in Fidelio in Wiesbaden. After appearing in the U.S. he joined the Hamburg State Opera (1953); also sang in Vienna (from 1956), Berlin (from 1956), and in Salzburg (from 1959). In 1959 he became a principal member of the Bavarian State Opera in Munich; made his Metropolitan Opera debut in N.Y. as Wolfram (1960); appeared for the 1st time in England at the Edinburgh Festival (1965), and later sang regularly at London's Covent Garden (from 1973). He also appeared as a soloist with the major orchs. and as a recitalist; likewise starred in his own Munich television show. In 1982 he became a prof. at the Hamburg Hochschule für Musik. Among his finest operatic roles are Count Almaviva, Papageno, Guglielmo, and Rossini's Figaro; he also sang a number of contemporary roles. As a lieder artist he distinguished himself in works by Schubert, Schumann, and Brahms.

Prez, Josquin des. DESPREZ (DES PREZ), JOSQUIN.

pribautki (Rus.). A quick-rhymed refrain or couplet. Stravinsky set 4 of them for voice and a few instruments in 1914.

Price, (Mary Violet) **Leontyne,** remarkably endowed African-American soprano; b. Laurel, Miss., Feb. 10, 1927. She was taught piano by a local woman and also learned to sing. She went to Oak Park High School, graduating in music in 1944; she then enrolled in the College of Education and Industrial Arts in Wilberforce, Ohio, where she studied voice with Catherine Van Buren; received her B.A. degree in 1948, then was awarded a scholarship at the Juilliard School of Music in N.Y.; there she took vocal training from Florence Page Kimball and joined the Opera Workshop under the direction of Frederic Cohen. Virgil Thomson heard her perform the role of Mistress Ford in Verdi's *Falstaff* and invited her to sing in the revival of his opera *4 Saints in 3 Acts* in 1952. She subsequently performed the role of Bess on a tour of the U.S. (1952–54) and in Europe (1955).

In 1954 she made a highly acclaimed debut as a concert singer in N.Y.; later that year she sang at the 1st performance of Barber's *Prayers of Kierkegaard* with the Boston Sym. Orch., conducted by Munch. In 1955 she performed Tosca on television, creating a sensation both as an artist and as an African-American taking up the role of an Italian diva. Her career was soon assured without any reservations. In 1957 she appeared with the San Francisco Opera; later that year she sang Aida, a role congenial to her passionate artistry. In 1958 she sang Aida with the Vienna State Opera under the direction of Karajan; on July 2, 1958, she sang this role at Covent Garden in London; and again as Aida she appeared at La Scala in Milan in 1959, the 1st black woman to sing with that most prestigious and most fastidious opera company.

In 1961 she made her 1st appearance with the Metropolitan Opera in N.Y. in the role of Leonora in *Il Trovatore*. A series of highly successful performances at the Metropolitan followed: Aida, Madama Butterfly, Donna Anna (all 1961); Tosca (1962); Pamina (1964). She created the role of Cleopatra in the premiere of Barber's *Antony and Cleopatra* at the opening of the new Metropolitan Opera House at Lincoln Center in N.Y. (1966). In 1973 she sang Madama Butterfly at the Metropolitan once more. In 1975 she appeared there in the title role of Manon Lescaut; and she sang Aida, a role she repeated for her farewell operatic performance in a televised production broadcast live from the Metropolitan Opera by PBS (1985). She then continued her concert career, appearing with notable success in the major music centers.

She was married in 1952 to the baritone William Warfield (who sang Porgy at her performances of *Porgy and Bess*) but separated from him in 1959; they were divorced in 1973. She received many honors during her remarkable career; in 1964 President Johnson bestowed upon her the Medal of Freedom, and in 1985 President Reagan presented her with the National Medal of Arts.

Pride, Charley, African-American country-music singer and guitarist; b. on a cotton farm near Sledge, Miss., Mar. 18, 1938. He learned to play the guitar, but, bent on a career in baseball, he played in the minor leagues (1954–64); also tried his luck as a singer. He subsequently appeared with the Grand Ole Opry in Nashville, becoming the 1st black country-music singer to gain admission to this shrine of populist entertainment.

Prière d'une Vièrge (The Maiden's Prayer). A salon masterpiece for piano by Thekla Badarzewska, 1851. This is undoubtedly the most celebrated piano piece ever written. Serious musicians deprecated it as a deplorable piece of sentimental salon music, but young ladies all over the world continued to play it in their stuffy drawing rooms. More than 100 separate editions of *Prière d'une Vièrge* were published. The composer, a 17-year-old Polish girl, died a few years after the publication of the thing and probably never knew what a poisoned gift she had bestowed on the musical world. One heartless critic wrote in her obituary that her early death saved humanity from drowning in a flood of sentimental treacle.

Prigioniero, Il. Opera by Dallapiccola, 1950, 1st performed in Florence. A prisoner is deliberately allowed to escape into the garden, but his freedom is a fraud perpetrated by the grand inquisitor, who tortures prisoners by hope only to crush it. The score is dodecaphonic, but Dallapiccola introduces triadic progressions in the thematic series.

Příhody Lišky Bystroušky. CUNNING LITTLE VIXEN, THE.

prima (It.). See PRIMO.

prima donna (It., 1st lady). The leading soprano in opera, be it in a particular role or as a public figure to be worshipped. *Prima donna assoluta* is an absolute prima donna superior to the *seconda donna* or *prima donna altra*. The cult of the prima donna reached its height in the 19th century. A typical prima donna was an amply bosomed Italian or German soprano possessing great lung power. The chronicles of opera are replete with tales about temperamental prima donnas engaging in fistfights and flights of invective with other prima donnas over the size of lettering in their names on theatrical posters, the space allocated in their private rooms at the opera house, the extent of publicity, the efficiency of the hired claque, etc. More than 1 prima donna have lost their engagements over such seemingly minor matters.

Prima la Musica e Poi le Parole. Opera by Salieri, 1786, commissioned by Emperor Joseph II and premiered at the Schönbrunn Palace, Vienna, on the same bill with Mozart's *Der Schauspieldirektor*. The comic plot tackles the age-old conflict between composers and librettists: Which is more important, the music or the words?

prima prattica (It., 1st practice). A term used in early 17th-century Italian theoretical treatises to denote the dense polyphonic style of the previous century, synonymous with *stile antico*. This was distinct from the SECONDA PRATTICA, the homophonic, monodic style cultivated by the early opera composers such as Monteverdi; also called the *stile moderno*.

primary accent. The downbeat, or thesis; the accent beginning the measure, directly following the bar.

primary triad. One of the 3 fundamental triads of a key (those on the 1st, 5th, and 4th degrees).

prime. The 1st note of a scale.

prime tone. See FUNDAMENTAL.

primitivism. As *primitive music*, a term generally applied to songs created spontaneously by untutored musicians of a culture other than one's own, with the implication of artlessness in a positive sense and lack of artfulness in a negative sense. The term also carries a suggestion of a certain condescension on the part of educated musicians; conversely, musicians surfeited by an abundance of art music seek fresh inspiration in primitive folk songs and dances as a source of new techniques. At this point the term *primitivism* applies. Thus a Picasso was inspired by the artless productions of primitive cultures in creating his own super-primitive art; similarly, Stravinsky sought new resources in the asymmetrical melodies and rhythms of ancient Russian songs. A lack of musical education thus becomes an advantage in the eyes and ears of a modern artist who has reached an impasse at the end of uncontrolled amplification of available resources. What Ives had to say about primitive village musicians who are artistically "right" even when they play wrong notes strikes at the core of this antinomy.

primo, -a (It.). First; a 1st or leading part, as in a duet. *Prima buffa*, leading lady in comic opera; *prima donna*, leading lady in opera; *prima vista*, at 1st sight; *prima volta*, the 1st time (written *Ima volta*, or simply *I*, or *1*), indicates that the measure(s) under its brackets are to be played the 1st time, before the repeat, whereas, on repeating, those marked *seconda volta* (or *IIda volta*, or *II*, or *2*) are to be performed instead.

primo rivolto (It.). Chord of the 1st inversion; the $^6/_3$, or 6 chord.

primo uomo (It., 1st man). The male equivalent of the PRIMA DONNA; not widely used.

Primrose, William, eminent Scottish-born American violist and pedagogue; b. Glasgow, Aug. 23, 1903; d. Provo, Utah, May 1, 1982. He studied violin in Glasgow with Camillo Ritter, at London's Guildhall School of Music, and in Belgium (1925–27) with Ysaÿe, who advised him to take up viola so as to avoid the congested violin field. He became the violist in the London String Quartet (1930–35), with which he made several tours. In 1937 he settled in the U.S. and was engaged as the principal violist player in the NBC Sym. Orch. in N.Y. under Toscanini, holding this post until 1942. In 1939 he established his own string quartet. In 1953 he was named a Commander of the Order of the British Empire; he became a naturalized U.S. citizen in 1955. From 1954 to 1962 he was the violist in the Festival Quartet. He also became active as a teacher: was on the faculty of the Univ. of Southern Calif. in Los Angeles (1962) and at the School of Music of Indiana Univ. in Bloomington (1965–72); in 1972 he inaugurated a master class at the Tokyo Univ. of Fine Arts and Music; returning to the U.S., he taught at Brigham Young Univ. in Provo, Utah (1979–82).

Primrose was greatly esteemed as a viola virtuoso; he gave 1st performances of viola concertos by several modern composers. He commissioned a viola concerto from Bartók, but the work was left unfinished at the time of Bartók's death, and the task of reconstructing the score from Bartók's sketches remained to be accomplished by Bartók's friend and associate Tibor Serly; Primrose gave its 1st performance with the Minneapolis Sym. Orch. on Dec. 2, 1949. He publ.

A Method for Violin and Viola Players (London, 1960) and *Technique in Memory* (1963); also ed. various works for viola and made transcriptions for the instrument.

Prince (born Prince Roger Nelson), provocative African-American rock singer, instrumentalist, and songwriter; b. Minneapolis, June 7, 1958. His father led a jazz group called the Prince Roger Trio, and his mother sang with it. He took up piano, guitar, and drums in his youth; before graduating from high school he formed a soul-rock band and soon learned to play a whole regiment of instruments and to write songs. When his group, renamed Champagne, proved less than a bubbling success, he made the trek to Los Angeles to conquer the recording industry. After producing the albums *For You* (1978) and *Prince* (1979), he found a lucrative and successful métier with his sexually explicit *Dirty Mind* (1980). This sizzling tour de force featured such songs as *Head*, a joyful tribute to oral sex, and *Sister*, a hymn to incest. His next album, *Controversy* (1981), faithfully lived up to its title by including the song *Private Joy*, a glorification of masturbation.

Proclaiming himself His Royal Badness, he proceeded to attain ever-higher orgasmic plateaus. His hit album *1999* (1982) was followed by the sensationally acclaimed film and soundtrack album *Purple Rain* (1984), which won an Oscar for best original song score in 1985. One of its songs, *Darling Niki*, incited the formation of the P.M.R.C. (Parents' Music Resource Center) and its efforts to regulate album labeling. After producing the album *Parade* (1986), he starred in the films *Sign o' the Times* (1987) and *Graffiti Bridge* (1990). His album *Lovesexy* (1988), which says it all, comes with a nude photo. He also changed his stage name into an unpronounceable symbol, forcing the media to refer to him as The Artist Formerly Known as Prince. In 1995 he embarked on a protracted battle with his record company, Warner Bros., claiming they were refusing to issue his music the way he wished it to be produced; he finally freed himself of his contract, entering into a new distribution deal in 1996 with EMI.

Prince Igor. Opera by Borodin, 1890, produced posthumously in St. Petersburg. Borodin, a professor of chemistry, neglected his musical compositions and failed to complete many scores, among them *Prince Igor*; this task devolved on Rimsky-Korsakov and Glazunov. The libretto is based on a Russian 12th-century chronicle recounting the story of the heroic Russian warrior Prince Igor. He is about to lead his army against the Mongol invaders, the Polovtzi, when an unpredicted eclipse of the sun throws his superstitious soldiers into disarray. (*Prince Igor* is the only opera which has a solar eclipse.) The celestial phenomenon is of sinister import; Igor suffers defeat and is captured. The Polovtzian Khan treats him royally in captivity, however, and is willing to let him go free provided he promises not to go to war against him again; the Khan also offers him a choice of beautiful slave girls who stage the famous Polovtzian dances. Igor rejects all these allurements; he eventually escapes and rejoins his loving wife. The music is the most gorgeous panoply of Russian orientalism.

Prince of the Pagodas, The. Ballet by Britten, 1957, 1st performed in London. It follows the same plot as the fairy tale *The Beauty and the Beast*, in which a beautiful maiden is willing to give her love to a monster who is really a charm-

ing prince made a victim of sorcery. Britten sets the atmosphere not with orientalism (e.g., pentatonic scales), but with gamelanism.

principal chords. The basic chords of a key, i.e. the triads built on the tonic, dominant, and subdominant, with the dominant-7th chord.

principal diapason. An open diapason organ pipe sounding an octave higher than the normal (i.e., closed) pipe.

principio (It.). Beginning, 1st time. *In principio*, at the beginning; *più marcato del principio*, more marked than the 1st time.

printing and publishing of music

A lmost immediately after the appearance of Gutenberg's Bible set from moveable type, experiments began to set musical notes in type. The 1st book with printed musical examples was *Psalterium*, set in type in 1457 in Gutenberg's workshop. An important development in music printing was the use of woodblocks in which complete musical examples, notes, and lines were carved out and inked. This method was particularly handy for books on music theory in which the text alternated with musical examples. These early specimens were usually printed in very large notes and widely separated lines. A significant advance toward modern printing was made by the Venetian printer Petrucci, who began printing vocal music books in the 1st year of the 16th century; he may well be considered the Gutenberg of music printing. He also printed the 1st tabulatures for the lute.

In early printed music a double process was involved. The lines of the staff were printed 1st, usually colored in red, and black notes were superimposed on the staff. Toward the end of the 16th century metal plates began to

be used, with both the lines and notes engraved by hand. In the 18th century music engraving reached the point of a graphic art, particularly when punches and hammers were applied. Professional craftsmen sometimes accepted work in music engraving; Paul Revere, who was a silversmith by trade, became the 1st American to engrave music. The 18th-century French violinist and composer Jean-Marie Leclair (l'aîné) entrusted the engraving of his music to his wife, who was a trained toolmaker. (Leclair was stabbed to death in his home; evidence strongly pointed to his wife as the killer, for the wounds were inflicted by metal punches such as used in music engraving.)

A decisive progress in music printing was made in applying *lithography*, that is, printing from a stone surface with a viscous ink, a process developed by the German printer Senefelder in 1796. Weber apprenticed himself to Senefelder and introduced some improvements of his own in lithography. *Type printing*, in which musical symbols had to be placed on the staff separately by hand, a method too laborious for music printing but which yielded artistic results, was perfected in the 2nd half of the 18th century. This method was used concurrently with copper-plating and lithography for special purposes, such as the reproduction of musical examples in theory books. The greatest era of music printing from copper plates was reached in the middle of the 19th century. Beautiful editions of instrumental music, orch.l scores, and complete operas were published by the German publishers Schott, Peters, and particularly Breitkopf & Härtel. Excellent editions of works by Russian composers, financed by the wealthy Russian merchant Belaieff, were printed on the German presses in Leipzig.

The 18th century was dominated in England by the publishing house of Walsh, which began publishing Handel's operas and also reprinted many works by continental composers. Several important publishing enterprises emerged in Great Britain in the 19th century and prospered unflaggingly into the last part of the 20th; they are Chappell, founded in 1810, and Boosey, founded in 1816. Boosey's competitor was Queen Victoria's trumpet player, Hawkes, who formed an independent printing shop specializing, like Boosey, in orch.l and chamber music. In 1930 the inheritors of Boosey and Hawkes joined in a highly successful publishing house, Boosey & Hawkes. Another important British publishing house was Novello, established in 1829 and concentrating on choral music; also to be mentioned are the firms of Curwen, Augener, and Chester, who became active in the middle of the 19th century.

The U.S., even after its independence, continued to rely on England for its music, which was mostly imported from the former mother country. Among the earliest American publishers, or rather importers, of music was Benjamin Carr, who emigrated to America after the Revolution and set up the 1st American music store, Carr's Musical Depository, in Philadelphia. The 1st important American-born publisher of music was Oliver Ditson, who established a business as a music seller in Boston in 1835 and continued in business for about a decade. The American dependence on Great Britain for music publishing continued until the middle of the 19th century, when the predominant influence on all branches of music in the U.S. was asserted by German immigrants. The year 1861 marked the foundation of the most important music publishing firm in America, established by Gustav Schirmer. Another German-born music publisher, Carl Fischer, settled in N.Y. and established an important publishing organization in 1872. Among American-born music

publishers, Theodore Presser established his own firm in 1883. An important source of income for American music publishers was the representation of European publishers who held the rights on lucrative operas, popular orch.l pieces, and pedagogical literature.

Italy occupies an important position in music publishing, thanks to the almost exclusive rights on famous Italian operas. The firm of Ricordi, formed in 1808, holds the richest grants of Italian operatic literature. The entire stock of plates and publications was wantonly destroyed in a barbarous air attack on Milan, the site of the Ricordi publishing house, in 1943, but like a musical phoenix it emerged from the ashes and resumed its important position in the world of music. In Austria, Hungary, and the Scandinavian countries, local publishers maintain a close cooperation with the large German or English publishing houses. Among French publishers the firm of Durand, founded in 1870, became the most important as well as prosperous. Éditions Salabert, organized in 1896, proliferated into the lucrative field of popular arrangements of theater music.

Before the Revolution Russia had several important publishers that supplied the Russians with European music literature, but it also published works by Russian composers. Among them Jurgenson, Tchaikovsky's publisher, played a significant role in championing Russian music; Belaieff generously sponsored the publication of music by composers of the Russian national school. Koussevitzky and his very rich wife founded his own firm with the specific purpose of publishing works by modern Russian composers, among them Scriabin, Stravinsky, and Prokofiev. After the Revolution the Soviet government nationalized all Russian publishing houses and established a Central State Publishing House. Since the Soviet government was the sole publisher, problems of expenses were solved within the general budget of the State. It therefore became possible for Russia to publish music extensively, almost extravagantly. For instance, all 27 symphonies of Miaskovsky were published from engraved plates, including the orch.l parts.

Collected works of Russian classical composers were systematically issued. But even composers less known in Russia and quite unknown abroad had their works published as a matter of routine. Similar policies in publishing music existed in Communist Poland, Yugoslavia, Czechoslovakia, Rumania, and Bulgaria. With the end of Communism in Eastern Europe, these countries will have to follow the examples of their Western capitalist counterparts.

Prinz von Homburg, Der. Opera by Henze, 1960, premiered in Hamburg, after the play by Kleist. The prince dallies with an alien princess instead of attending to his military duties; for his dereliction of duty he is sentenced to death by the relentlessly militant King. He is eventually reprieved and leads his army to victory, as he had done before. The eclectic score combines Italian verismo with German expressionism.

Prinzessin auf der Erbse, Die (The Princess upon the Pea). Opera by Toch, 1926, premiered in Baden-Baden, after the same fable of Hans Christian Andersen used in Mary Rodgers's musical *The Princess and the Pea*.

probability. The probability of incidence of certain intervals, notes, and rhythms in a given piece of music depends on its predetermined melorhythmic idiom. The probability of occurrence of an unresolved major 7th in a composition written before 1900 is virtually nil, while the probability of such incidence in dodecaphonic music is very high. Similarly, the probability of a concluding chord being a dissonance is zero for the 19th century, but it increases exponentially after 1900. The commanding importance of the tritone in atonal and dodecaphonic music makes its appearance a probable event in compositions in which the key signature is absent. The probability of incidence of all 12 different notes and 12 different intervals in relation to the starting tone in a full chromatic scale is obviously 100%.

Probe (Ger.). Rehearsal. *Generalprobe*, final dress rehearsal, sometimes open to press and dignitaries; *Hauptprobe*, principal (full) rehearsal; *Sitzprobe*, 1st rehearsal for all participants, but without staging; *Schwimmprobe*, swimming rehearsal for the Rhine maidens in Wagner's *Der Ring des Nibelungen*.

procelloso (It.). Stormy.

Procesión del Rocio, La. Symphonic poem by Turina, 1913, premiered in Seville. The piece portrays the religious "procession of the dew" in that city.

process music. See MINIMALISM.

processional. A hymn sung in church during the entrance of choir and clergy.

Prodigal Son, The. Church parable by Britten, 1968, 1st performed at the Aldeburgh Festival. The text is based on the biblical parable of a wandering son who is welcomed home by his lenient father, to the dismay of the prodigal's brothers.

Professor Longhair. BYRD, HENRY ROELAND.

profondo (It.). Deep. *Basso profondo*, deep bass.

program music

A class of instrumental compositions intended to represent distinct moods or phases of emotion, or to depict actual scenes of events; as opposed to ABSOLUTE MUSIC. Perhaps *descriptive music* would be a more adequate definition, but the terms above have established themselves solidly in English-speaking countries. In the 19th century the preferable description of program music (programmatic music; Ger. *Programmusik*; Fr. *musique à programme*) was *tone painting*. A pioneer in program music was Liszt. His ideas were eagerly accepted and developed by many German composers of the 2nd half of the 19th century, culminating in the symphonic poems of R. Strauss. Abstract mathematical terms became the ultimate development of program music in the works of Varèse.

The romantic notion that music can express something was attacked on philosophical and aesthetic grounds in the famous tract *Vom Musikalisch-Schönen* by the greatest musical reactionary who ever lived, Hanslick. He wielded his caustic pen as an influential critic in

Vienna. With casuistic cunning, Hanslick quoted an array of German writers on music who seemed to have been Lisztians long before Liszt. Johann Mattheson, a contemporary of Bach and Handel, is quoted as saying, "In writing a melody, the main purpose should be to express a certain emotion." Another famous 18th-century theorist, Friedrich Wilhelm Malpurg, wrote: "It is the composer's task to copy nature, to express the vital stirrings of the soul and the innermost feelings of the heart."

The music historian Johann Nikolaus Forkel equated music to rhetoric. Hanslick then quotes several weighty German dictionaries that define music as "the art of expressing sensations and states of mind by means of pleasing sounds," and "Music is the art of producing sounds capable of expressing, exciting, and sustaining feelings and passions." A professor of aesthetics is quoted with an obvious distaste by Hanslick as stating that "each feeling and each state of mind has its own inherent sound and rhythm." No wonder Hanslick as a critic became an inveterate opponent of Liszt and Wagner and an exuberant admirer of Brahms, a composer who never demeaned himself by painting a landscape in music. But what about Beethoven's *Pastoral Sym.*? Did Hanslick condemn it also? No, for Hanslick had a perfect rebuttal of this in Beethoven's own words written on the score: "Mehr Ausdruck der Empfindung als Mahlerey" (More of an expression of feeling rather than painting).

Sounds in nature, particularly the singing of birds, are obvious sources of literal program music and are found in a number of compositions centuries before the movement of Romantic program music became pronounced. Among famous examples are *La poule* by Rameau, imitating the cackling of hens, *Les abeilles*, with its murmurations of innumerable bees by Couperin, *The Cuckoo* by Daquin, and the 3 birds in Beethoven's *Pastoral Sym.* In the domain of literary musical narratives, the earliest examples are a set of biblical stories written for harpsichord by Johann Kuhnau; the *4 Seasons* concertos by Vivaldi; and Karl Ditters von Dittersdorf's 12 syms. illustrating Ovid's *Metamorphoses.*

Probably the most explicit piece of symphonic program music is the *Sym. fantastique* of Berlioz, written by him to express his love for the Shakespearean actress Miss Smithson. Among Liszt's symphonic poems, the ones that bear direct literary connections are *Les Préludes* and the *Faust Symphony.* Litolff composed an overture *Robespierre,*

in which the falling of the severed head of Robespierre into the basket is rendered as a thud on the bass drum.

The 19th century saw the greatest flowering of program music; the infatuation with the idea that music must mean some thing recognizable to the listener led to the regrettable practice of affixing imaginative but more often trite nicknames to musical compositions whose composers never intended to write programmatic music. It is ironic that most of the familiar titles attached to Mendelssohn's *Songs Without Words* are the products of the publisher's eagerness to attract Romantically inclined players; for example, the title *Spring Song* does not appear in Mendelssohn's MS. Haydn's syms. and string quartets received popular nicknames that represent the general eagerness to seek familiar images in the sounds of music. But even so, it is as difficult to trace the rationale of some of these titles as it is to conjure up the animal figures in the constellations of the zodiac seen by ancient stargazers.

Among Haydn's syms. we have *The Philosopher, The Schoolmaster,* and *The Absent-Minded Man.* Only the *Surprise Sym.,* which in German has a more concrete description, *Paukenschlag* (Drumstroke), has a musical meaning behind the title, because in the 2nd movement there is a sudden loud chord at the end of the theme, inserted there supposedly by Haydn to wake the somnolent ladies in the audience. Among some puzzling titles of Haydn's string quartets are the *Razor Quartets.* But the *Emperor Quartet* has a perfect explanation: it contains the tune that became the national anthem of Austria, unfortunately to be degraded by the text attached to it in Imperial Germany ("Deutschland, Deutschland, über alles"). There is no explanation why Mozart's great C-major Sym. should be called the *Jupiter Sym.* Nor is there any reason to call Beethoven's E-flat piano Concerto the *Emperor Concerto.* Both nicknames were apparently invented in England. The *Moonlight Sonata* of Beethoven received its programmatic name thanks to a critic who said that its opening movement suggested to him moonlight on Lake Lucerne. Although the *Sonata Appassionata* seems appropriate to describe Beethoven's impassionate music, the title was invented by a publisher.

Even when the composer himself specifically denies any programmatic significance, descriptive nicknames are excised with difficulty. The so-called *Raindrop Prelude* of Chopin is supposed to have been inspired by his listening to raindrops fall on the roof of his house on the Island of

Mallorca, but he expressly denied this. More to the point is the title *Revolutionary Étude*, since it is marked by rebellious upward passages in the left hand, and it was composed by Chopin at the time Warsaw was captured by the Russians, leading to the partition of his beloved fatherland. The nickname for Chopin's *Minute Waltz* seems obvious, but no human pianist can play it in 60 seconds flat with all the repeats.

Personal references and all kinds of musical asides are found galore in music literature. Certainly Schumann's *Carnaval*, built on the 4 notes spelling the name of the Bohemian town of Asch in the German musical alphabet, is a piece of program music with autobiographical allusions, for it was in Asch that Schumann met a once-beloved lady (not Clara). Another famous autobiographical piece of program music was *Symphonia domestica* by Richard Strauss, in which the composer portrayed in music the nightly bath of his infant son; the exact time, 7 o'clock, is represented by the chimes striking 7. Tchaikovsky's *Pathétique Sym.* is a piece of program music after the fact, since the descriptive title was attached to it after the score was completed. What is interesting is that it contains a passage in the trombones from the Russian Mass for the Dead, as if Tchaikovsky had a premonition of his death a few days after the 1st performance of the work.

It must be stated that there is no objective way of determining whether a composition "means" something from just listening to it. Tchaikovsky expatiated at great length in his letter to patroness Mme. von Meck that his 4th Sym., dedicated to her, represented the inexorability of Fate. Schoenberg, to whom music was a pure art *an und für sich*, yielded to the request of his publisher to attach titles to his 5 Orchestral Pieces. And years later he was even willing to change the title of the 3rd piece, originally called *The Changing Chord*, to *Summer Morning by the Lake*. In his *Kinderszenen* for piano, Schumann depicted a child's moods, of which *Träumerei* is the most moving. In his *Pictures at an Exhibition*, Mussorgsky presented a series of pictures come to life.

Any composition, no matter how abstract or classically sober, can be interpreted as an image. Modern ballet composers often use movements from symphonic works for choreographical spectacles of a romantic nature with suitable titles attached to them. Some pieces of program music would lose their attraction if they were deprived of their titles. The witty interlude *Pianists* in *The Carnival of the Animals* of Saint-Saëns would be pointless were it not for the inclusion of pianists among the animals of the title. In some pieces of program music the title becomes more important than the music itself. This is particularly true about the humorous creations of Satie, whose music would hardly be the same without those fantastically oxymoronic titles, such as *Heures séculaires et instantanées* (Century-Long Instantaneous Hours).

Sometimes composers yield to the temptation of attaching programmatic titles to their works only to cancel them later. Mahler bestowed programmatic titles to several of his syms.—*Titan* for the 1st, *Summer Morning's Dream* for the 3rd, *The Giant* for the 5th—but subsequently withdrew all these titles and insisted that he never authorized anyone to use them for identification. Stravinsky's *Scherzo fantastique* was originally published with a long quotation from Maeterlinck's *Life of the Bees*; he even added specific subtitles, such as *Queen Bee's Nuptial Flight*, to parts of his score, but later denied that the music was inspired by any insects whatsoever.

The principle of absolute beauty in music so eloquently proclaimed by Hanslick is opposite to the doctrine of Socialist Realism, as propounded by the theoreticians of the Soviet Union, who insist that all music has a specific meaning. The musical philosophy of the People's Republic of China goes even farther in espousing the primacy of programmatic music. In January of 1974 the official organ of the Communist Party of the Chinese Republic published a leading article entitled *Works of Music Without Titles Do Not Reflect the Class Spirit*, and specifically condemned Piano Sonata No. 17 by "the German capitalist musician, Beethoven" and the Sym. in B Minor by the "Romantic Austrian capitalist musician, Schubert."

Ives was certainly a composer of program music, with America as his program. In his symphonic *4th of July*, he assembled a heterogeneous orch. with a wildly dissonant climax representing the explosion of multicolored fireworks. In his memo on the work he wrote: "It is pure program music—it is also pure abstract music," and he added a quotation from Mark Twain's *Huckleberry Finn*, "You pays yer money, and you takes yer choice." Antheil insisted that his *Ballet mécanique*, scored for several player pianos, 2 airplane propellers, door bells, and a plethora of drums, was not program music of a mechanical world but "the most abstract of the abstract."

progression. The advance from one tone to another, or from one chord to another; the former is *melodic*, the later *harmonic* progression.

progressive composition. In songwriting, the setting of each strophe to different music, following the changing mood more closely than in the ballad or folk song, where melody and harmony are generally the same for each verse; also called through-composed songwriting.

progressive jazz. In the 1st half of the century jazz was often a spontaneous product of mass or single improvisation, with self-taught instrumentalists achieving fantastic virtuosity simply because they were not told by any teacher that the technical tricks they performed were unplayable. In 1950 a natural desire arose among a later generation of jazz players to acquire gloss, polish, and even theoretical knowledge. They studied with eminent European composers resident in the U.S. and listened to records of modern music. They became conversant with such terms as *atonality* and *poly-tonality* and even *dodecaphony*. In some cases they annexed a full complement of strings in their orchs. With full credentials, a movement was launched grandly described as progressive jazz, incorporating both *cool* and *3rd stream* styles. Technical resources kept pace with the dignity of the orch.l presentation. The whole-tone scale was rediscovered as a sonority and played in unison by the violins. Two different keys were used simultaneously in a display of polytonality. The square time was diversified occasionally by asymmetric rhythms; sometimes compound meters were inserted. But despite these adornments and borrowings from respectable sources, progressive jazz could never attain distinction and soon gave way to a less European but more appropriate style of jazzification.

progressive rock. See ROCK.

progressive tonality. A term used to denote symphonic works that end in keys other than those in which they began.

Prokofiev (Prokofieff), Sergei (Sergeievich)

Great Russian composer of modern times, creator of new and original formulas of rhythmic, melodic, and harmonic combinations that became the recognized style of his music; b. Sontsovka, near Ekaterinoslav, Apr. 27, 1891; d. Moscow, Mar. 5, 1953. His mother was born a serf in 1859, 2 years before the emancipation of Russian serfdom, and she assumed (as was the custom) the name of the estate where she was born, Sontsov. Prokofiev was born on that estate on Apr. 27, 1891, although he himself erroneously believed that the date was Apr. 23; the correct date was established with the discovery of his birth certificate. He received his 1st piano lessons from his mother, who was an amateur pianist; he improvised several pieces and then composed a children's opera, *The Giant* (1900), which was performed in a domestic version. Following his bent for the theater, he put together 2 other operas, *On Desert Islands* (1902) and *Ondine* (1904–7); fantastic subjects obviously possessed his childish imagination.

He was 11 years old when he met the great Russian master Taneyev, who arranged for him to take systematic private lessons with Reinhold Glière, who became his tutor at Sontsovka during the summers of 1903 and 1904, and by correspondence during the intervening winter. Under Glière's knowledgeable guidance in theory and harmony, Prokofiev composed a sym. in piano version and still another opera, *Plague*, based upon a poem by Pushkin. Finally, in 1904, at the age of 13, he enrolled in the St. Petersburg Cons., where he studied composition with Liadov and piano with Alexander Winkler; later he was accepted by no less a master than Rimsky-Korsakov, who instructed him in orchestration. He also studied conducting with Nikolai Tcherepnin and form with Wihtol. Further, he entered the piano class of Anna Essipova. During the summers he returned to Sontsovka or traveled in the Caucasus and continued to compose, already in quite an advanced style; the Moscow publisher Jurgenson accepted his 1st work, a piano sonata, for publication; it was premiered in Moscow on Mar. 6, 1910. It was then that Prokofiev made his 1st visit to Paris, London, and Switzerland (1913); in 1914 he graduated from the St. Petersburg Cons., receiving the Anton Rubinstein Prize (a grand piano) as a pianist-composer with his Piano Concerto No. 1, which he performed publicly at the graduation concert.

Because of audacious innovations in his piano music (he wrote one piece in which the right and left hands played in different keys), Prokofiev was described in the press as a "futurist," and because of his addiction to dissonant and powerful harmonic combinations, some critics dismissed his works as "football music." This idiom was explicitly demonstrated in his *Sarcasms* and *Visions fugitives* for Piano—percussive and sharp yet not lacking in lyric charm. Grotesquerie and irony animated his early works; he also developed a strong attraction toward subjects of primitive character. His important orch. work, the *Scythian Suite* (arr. from music written for a ballet, *Ala and Lolly*, 1915), draws upon a legend of ancient Russian sun-worship rituals. While a parallel with Stravinsky's *The Rite of Spring* may exist, there is no similarity between the styles of the 2 works.

The original performance of the *Scythian Suite*, scheduled at a Koussevitzky concert in Moscow, was canceled on account of the disruption caused by war, which did not prevent the otherwise intelligent Russian music critic Sabaneyev, blissfully unaware that the announced premiere had been canceled, from delivering a blast of the work as a farrago of atrocious noises. (Sabaneyev was forced to resign his position after this episode.) Another Prokofiev score, primitivistic in its inspiration, was the cantata 7, *They Are 7*, based upon incantations from an old Sumerian religious ritual. During the same period Prokofiev wrote his famous *Classical Sym.* (1916–17), in which he adopted with remarkable acuity the formal style of Haydn's music. While the structure of the work was indeed classical, the sudden modulatory shifts and subtle elements of grotesquerie revealed decisively a new modern art.

After conducting the premiere of his *Classical Sym.* in Petrograd (1918), Prokofiev left Russia by way of Siberia and Japan for the U.S. (the continuing war in Europe prevented him from traveling westward). He gave concerts of his music in Japan and later in the U.S., playing his 1st solo concert in N.Y. Some American critics greeted his appearance as the reflection of the chaotic events of Russia in revolution, and Prokofiev himself was described as a "ribald and Bolshevist innovator and musical agitator." "Every rule in the realm of traditional music writing was broken by Prokofiev," one N.Y. writer complained. "Dissonance followed dissonance in a fashion inconceivable to ears accustomed to melody and harmonic laws." Prokofiev's genteel *Classical Sym.* struck some critics as "an orgy of dissonant sound, an exposition of the unhappy state of chaos from which Russia suffers." Another N.Y. critic indulged in the following: "Crashing Siberians, volcano hell, Krakatoa, sea-bottom crawlers. Incomprehensible? So is Prokofiev." But another critic issued a word of caution, suggesting that "Prokofiev might be the legitimate successor of Borodin, Mussorgsky, and Rimsky-Korsakov." The critic was unintentionally right; Prokofiev is firmly enthroned in the pantheon of Russian music.

In 1920 Prokofiev settled in Paris, where he established an association with Diaghilev's Ballets Russes, which produced his ballets *Chout* (a French transliteration of the Russian word for buffoon), *Le Pas d'acier* (descriptive of the industrial development in Soviet Russia), and *L'Enfant prodigue*. In 1921 Prokofiev again visited the U.S. for the production of the opera commissioned by the Chicago Opera Co., *The Love for 3 Oranges*. In 1927 he was invited to be the pianist for a series of his own works in Russia. He gave a number of concerts in Russia again in 1929 and eventually decided to remain there. In Russia he wrote some of his most popular works, including the symphonic fairy tale *Peter and the Wolf* (1936), staged by a children's theater in Moscow; the historical cantata *Alexander Nevsky* (1939; based on the soundtrack to the eponymous film by Eisenstein); the ballet *Romeo and Juliet* (1935–36); and the opera *War and Peace* (1941–52), which went through numerous revisions.

Unexpectedly, Prokofiev became the target of the so-called proletarian group of Soviet musicians who accused him of decadence, a major sin in Soviet Russia at the time. His name was included in the official denunciation of modern Soviet composers issued by reactionary Soviet politicians. He meekly confessed that he had been occasionally interested in atonal and polytonal devices during his stay in Paris, but insisted that he had never abandoned the ideals of classical Russian music. Indeed, when he composed his 7th Sym. he described it specifically as a youth sym., reflecting the energy and ideals of new Russia.

There were also significant changes in his personal life. He separated from his Spanish-born wife, the singer Lina Llubera, the mother of his 2 sons, and established a companionship with Myra Mendelson, a member of the Young Communist League. She was a writer and assisted him on the libretto of *War and Peace*. He made one final attempt to gain favor with the Soviet establishment by writing an opera, *A Tale about a Real Man* (1947–48), based on a heroic exploit of a Soviet pilot during the war against the Nazis. But this, too, was damned by the servile Communist press as lacking in true patriotic spirit, and the opera was quickly removed from the repertory. After a decade of illness Prokofiev died suddenly of heart failure on Mar. 5, 1953, a few hours before the death of Stalin. Curiously enough, the anniversary of Prokofiev's death is duly commemorated, while that of his once powerful nemesis is officially allowed to be forgotten.

Among other works by Prokofiev are operas: *Maddalena* (1912–13, piano score only; orchestrated by Edward Downes; BBC Radio, 1979); *The Gambler*, after Dostoyevsky (1915–16; Brussels, 1929); *The Fiery Angel* (1919; Paris, 1954); *Semyon Kotko* (Moscow, 1940); *Betrothal in a Convent*, after Sheridan's *Duenna* (1940; Leningrad, 1946). Ballets: *Sur le Borysthène* (1930; Paris, 1932); *Cinderella* (1940–44; Moscow, 1945); *A Tale of the Stone Flower* (1948–50; Moscow, 1954); incidental music; film music, including *Lt. Kije* (1933; film lost or never completed); *Ivan the Terrible* (1942–45, directed by Eisenstein; 2 of 3 parts completed); choral music, most of which represents Prokofiev's attempts to please Stalin and his cronies. Orch.: 7 syms., of which the *Classical* (No. 1) and No. 5 are the most popular; 5 piano concertos, with No. 4 written for the left hand alone; Sinfonietta (1915); Violin Concerto No. 1 (1923); Divertissement (1929); Violin Concerto No. 2 (1935); Cello Concerto (1938; evolved into the *Sinfonia Concertante*, premiered by Rostropovich, 1954); suites from the operas, ballets, and film scores. Chamber music: 2 string quartets; sonatas for violin (2), violin solo, violin duo, cello, flute. Piano: 9 sonatas (1909–1947; No. 10, 1953, unfinished); *Toccata* (1912); *Tales of an Old Grandmother* (1918); 2 sonatinas (1931–32); *Pensées* (1933–34); songs, including *The Ugly Duckling*, after Andersen (1914).

prolatio (Lat., prolation). Smallest division in mensural notation. It represents the division of the TEMPUS into 2 or 3 values of prolatio, which in turn can either be a PERFECTION (divided into 3 units) or an IMPERFECTION (into 2 units). Ockeghem wrote a *Missa prolationum* that contains all 4 possible divisions of the tempus into prolatio units in mensural notation; in modern notation these prolations correspond to the time signatures of 2/4, 3/4, 6/8, and 9/8, respectively.

prolepsis. Schlegel wrote, "Der Historiker ist ein rückwärts gekehrter Prophet." The notion that a historian might be a prophet of the past is most provocative. The modern cultivation of some of the recessive traits of the musical past represents such a prophecy turned backward. Consecutive 5ths were the rule before the advent of tertian counterpoint; they were strictly forbidden in classical music but returned early in the 20th century in the guise of neoarchaic usages and were further reinforced in the practice of consecutive triadic harmonies. The dissonant heterophony of ancient modalities was incorporated as a novelty in neoprimitivism. Satie drew a table of anticommandments in his *Catéchisme du Conservatoire* in which he ridiculed the elevation of once forbidden practices to the status of harmonic laws:

> Avec grand soin tu violeras
> Des régles du vieux rudiment.
> Quintes de suite tu feras
> Et octaves pareillement.
> Au grand jamais ne résoudras
> De dissonance aucunement.
> Aucun morceau ne finiras
> Jamais par accord consonnant.

The exclusion of major triads in the Schoenbergian table of commandments is the most striking instance of prolepsis. Indeed, every determined violation of the academic rules becomes a case for prolepsis if such a violation becomes itself a rule.

proletarian music

~~~ ~~~ ~~~ ~~~ ~~~

The ideological upheaval that accompanied the Soviet revolution of 1917 posed an immediate problem of creating arts that would be consonant with the aims and ideals of socialist society. Since the political structure of the Soviet government was that of the dictatorship of the proletariat, it was imperative to postulate a special type of literature, drama, art, and music that would be proletarian in substance and therefore accessible to the popular masses. Some Soviet theoreticians proposed to wipe off the slate of the arts the entire cultural structure that preceded the revolution and to create a tabula rasa on which to build a new proletarian edifice. Among suggestions seriously offered by some musicians in the early days of the Soviet revolution was the confiscation of all musical instruments in order to abolish the tempered scale, and to construct new instruments based on the acoustically pure intervals. A more appropriate suggestion was made to compose music which included sounds familiar to a proletarian worker. A sym. of the factory was actually staged in an experimental demonstration, with singers and players placed on rooftops. Shostakovich included a factory whistle in the score of his *May 1st Sym.* Alexander Mossolov wrote a ballet called *Iron Foundry* in which a large sheet of steel was shaken to imitate the sound of the forge.

Unsuccessful attempts were made to proletarianize the librettos of old operas. In one production Puccini's *Tosca* was advanced from the Napoleonic times to those of the Paris Commune. Tosca kills not the chief of the Roman police but the anti-Communard general Gallifet, disregarding the fact that the actual general Gallifet died in bed long after the fall of the Commune. Meyerbeer's opera *The Huguenots* was renamed *The Decembrists* and the action transferred to Dec. 1825 to celebrate the rebellion of a group of progressive-minded aristocrats against the accession to the throne of the Czar Nicholas I. The notorious Russian Association of Proletarian Musicians (RAPM) was founded in 1924 to pass judgment on the fitness and unfitness of all music for proletarian consumption. It stipulated an arbitrary code of desirable musical attributes, among them unrelenting optimism, militant socialism, proletarian class consciousness, representational programmaticism, and the preferential use of major keys. Beethoven was commended by the RAPM for his rebellious spirit; among Russian composers, Mussorgsky was singled out as a creator of realistic art.

A difficult problem was posed by Tchaikovsky. His profound pessimism and fatalism, his reactionary political views, and particularly his homosexuality seemed an insurmountable barrier for the RAPM theoreticians to overcome. However, Tchaikovsky was a favorite composer not only of the popular masses but also of the entire Presidium of the Soviet of People's Commissars. Even from the purely musical standpoint, Tchaikovsky was theoretically unacceptable. His preference for minor keys and for melancholy moods in his operas and syms. were the very antinomy of all that the new society of Soviet Russia stood for. In their attempt to rationalize the popularity of the *Pathétique Sym.*, the RAPM reached the acme of casuistry. In this work, so the argument went, Tchaikovsky delivered a magnificent funeral oration on the tomb of the bourgeoisie, and the superb artistic quality of this lamentation could not fail to please proletarian listeners. But soon the dialectical self-contradictions became evident even to the most obdurate members of the RAPM, and factional strife pulled their ideology apart.

There were also signs of repugnance against the vicious attacks led by the RAPM against the surviving composers of the prerevolutionary times, greatly esteemed Conservatory professors and any others who dared to oppose its untenable ideology. The entire controversy was suddenly resolved when the Soviet government summarily disbanded the RAPM. As one composer expressed the nearly unanimous satisfaction at this action, "We could once again dare to write music in 3/4 time," alluding to the RAPM's ridiculous insistence that proletarian music ought to be written in march time.

The valid residue of proletarian music found its way to Germany and to America, assuming special national idioms. Simplicity of form, utilization of popular dance rhythms, and, in theatrical music, a selection of subjects from Revolutionary history or class warfare were the main characteristics of music for the proletariat. In America proletarian opera flourished briefly in the 1930s, with Marc Blitzstein as its chief proponent. In Germany Kurt Weill, working in close collaboration with the dramatist Bertolt Brecht, created a type of music drama that in its social consciousness had a strong affinity with proletarian music. In Russia itself, after the disbandment of the RAPM, viable ideas of proletarian music were absorbed in the doctrine of SOCIALIST REALISM.

prolixity. Brevity is not necessarily an ideal; prolixity is not always a fault. In classical music, prolixity was ingrained in the forms of sonata and court dances, with the required repetitions of complete sections. Only the impatience of modern performers impels them to disregard such redundancies. ("Brevitate gaudent moderni," to quote a recurring incipit of medieval musical treatises.) Beethoven's *Eroica Sym.* concludes with the tonic chord repeated 28 times. By contrast, Prokofiev's *March* from *Love for 3 Oranges* ends abruptly on a single C-major triad. The natural aversion of modern musicians to restatement and overstatement extends also to tonal sequences with their predictable turns. This homologophobia led finally to the collapse of the tonal system itself and inspired Schoenberg to promulgate the principle of nonrepetition of thematic notes and the formulation of his method of composition with 12 tones related only to one another.

prologue. An introductory part of an opera. Wagner described his music drama *Das Rheingold* as the *Vorabend* (literally, the evening before) to the main trilogy of *Der Ring des Nibelungen*. A typical short prologue is that sung before the beginning of Leoncavallo's *Pagliacci*; here it is used in a Shakespearean sense, signifying a person who addresses the audience to explain the meaning of the play. The prologue is usually short, usually sung or narrated, and prepares the audience verbally; the overture is instrumental and, in most cases, a musical table of contents of the opera to follow.

Promenade. See PRELUDE.

Prométhée. Symphonic work by Scriabin, 1911, subtitled *Le Poème du feu* (The Poem of Fire), a reference to Prometheus, who stole fire from Heaven. The score calls for an important piano part, organ, choruses, full orch., and a "color organ" that Scriabin called in French *clavier à lumières* and, in Italian, *luce*. This instrument was supposed to produce colors that would inundate the concert hall along with the hanging harmonies. The score is musically built on the so-called MYSTIC CHORD, which Scriabin regarded as a concord of a higher order. *Prométhée* was 1st performed by Koussevitzky in Moscow, 1911, with Scriabin playing the piano part; no attempt was made to introduce the color organ.

Prometheus. Symphonic poem by Liszt, 1850, premiered in Weimar, after Shelley's *Prometheus Unbound*. The work portrays the god Prometheus's release from his enchainment to a rock (Aeschylus's play on the subject is lost); his freedom is symbolized by a fugato.

Prometheus. Opera by Orff, 1968, 1st performed in Stuttgart. The libretto is the original Greek text of Aeschylus's *Prometheus Bound*. The work is scored for a large orch., including some 75 percussion instruments.

Promises, Promises. Musical by Bacharach and David, 1968, based on Neil Simon's screenplay *The Apartment*. A mild-mannered insurance clerk lends his apartment to executives in his company for illicit assignations. He suffers a heartache when he discovers that his favorite restaurant waitress has been to his pad with the personnel director. Includes the title song, *I'll Never Fall in Love Again*, and *Whoever You Are*.

prompter. A rather important person in opera, seated in the proscenium with the score in front of him (or her), who gives cues to singers. The "invisible" place where the prompter stands is called the *box*. Such a prompter is introduced to the audience in the whimsical opera *Capriccio* by R. Strauss. In the last act of *Tristan und Isolde* a prompter is sometimes ensconced under the dying Tristan's couch. In France, Germany, and Russia the prompter is called *souffleur* (one who breathes); in Italy he is known as *Maestro suggeritore* (a master suggester). Depending on the acoustics of the hall, the prompter's voice may unexpectedly carry to some parts of the orch. seats. Incautious prompters have been known to hum the tune. One such suggester, named Adriano Petronio, cued the singers at a performance at the Metropolitan Opera House in N.Y. in the famous sextet from *Lucia di*

Lammermoor so loudly that the ensemble was facetiously referred to by the *habitués* as the "septet from *Lucia*."

Proms, The. Affectionate abbrev. for the Promenade Concerts of London, which began in 1837 in imitation of Paris popular concerts launched by Philippe Musard in 1833. The programs consisted usually of ballroom dances, overtures, and occasionally short pieces of choral music. In London, Promenade Concerts were given in the summer in Drury Lane Theater, which was turned into an "agreeable promenade in hot weather." The name *Promenade* was firmly established by 1840. The eccentric French conductor Julien was the 1st *animator* of these concerts; he was followed by the German August Manns in 1859; in 1875 the Italian Luigi Arditi conducted Promenade Concerts at Covent Garden. In 1893 Henry Wood took over the series, and his name became forever associated with the most brilliant period of the Promenade Concerts, which by then had become known as the Proms. On the night of May 10, 1941, the Queen's Hall was hit by Nazi aerial bombardment, but the Proms did not expire. The concerts moved to the Royal Albert Hall.

In 1944 the Proms were officially named the Henry Wood Promenade Concerts, as homage to the conductor, who died that year. Among his successors were Adrian Boult, Malcom Sargent, John Barbirolli, and Colin Davis. A great deal of avant-garde music was eventually included in the Proms programs, such as *The Whale* by John Tavener (1969), Tim Souster's *Triple Music II* and *The Soft Machine*, a rock piece offering such tunes as *Esther's Nose Job* and *Out-Bloody-Rageous* (1970), and Stockhausen's *Carré* for 4 orchs.

pronto (It.). Promptly, swiftly.

pronunziato (It.). Pronounced, marked. *Ben pronunziato*, well, clearly enunciated.

proper. See PROPRIUM.

Prophète, Le. Opera by Meyerbeer, 1849, 1st performed in Paris. The prophet here is based on the historical John of Leyden, the leader of the Anabaptist sect in the 16th century. In order to maintain his self-proclaimed divine status, he denies his identity and repudiates his mother. When his beloved Bertha realizes what he has become, she stabs herself to death. The army of the Holy Roman Emperor advances on Leyden; they set John's palace afire, and he per-

ishes in the cataclysm, along with his forgiving mother. The coronation march accompanying the prophet's entry into the cathedral is famous.

proportion. A term of medieval music theory relating to the proportionate duration of the notes of the melody, and also the ratio of vibrations of these notes.

proportional notation. A system of notation developed by Earle Brown in which durations of notes are shown proportionally, relative only to one another and independent of any strict metric system. Also called time-space notation.

proportional representation. Among thousands of conflicting musical theories, each claiming superiority over the others, no attempt has yet been made to conduct a statistical survey of the frequency of occurrence of every note of the scale in a given composition. Yet such a computation might well provide illuminating insight into proportional representation of diatonic and chromatic notes and the role of tonal centers. In serial composition in particular, a statistical analysis can measure the strength of the gravitational force that attracts atonal and serial groups to a putative keynote. The duration of each note will have to be considered as a multiplying factor. Thus if the least common denominator is an 8th note, then a half note would carry the same specific weight as 4 8th notes. It would also be possible to evaluate the relative hierarchy of the members of a tone row.

A serial composer may plan in advance a proportional representation of specific notes, intervals, and durations. If desired, an artificial tonic can be posited by assigning to it the greatest frequency of incidence. This technique is applicable to all serial sets, even those containing only 3 or 4 notes. Rhythmic sets can be similarly arranged according to a predetermined formula of proportional representation. The method is particularly fruitful in building melodies and rhythms of a primitivist type, in which the repetition is of the essence.

proposta (Lat., proposal). Fugal subject; DUX.

Proprietas (Lat., propriety). In mensural notation, a property of a ligature where the 1st of the 2 notes is a breve; such a ligature is marked by a descending tail left of the 1st note when descending, and no tail in ascending. *Opposita proprietas*, a property of ligatures that are semibreves, marked with an ascending left tail; *cum proprietate*, a property of ligatures that are breves; *sine proprietate*, a property of ligatures that are semibreves.

proprium (Lat.). The Roman Catholic Mass Proper; the portions of the liturgy that regularly occur, but with changing text, depending on the feast day and readings for that service. The proper pertinent to one or more saints is called *proprium sanctorum*. The musical sections of the Proper are interwoven with the sections of the Ordinary as follows (Ordinary in italics): Introit, *Kyrie*, *Gloria*, Gradual, Alleluia (or Tract), Sequence, *Credo*, Offertory, *Sanctus*, *Agnus Dei*, Communion, *Ite missa est* (or *Benedicamus Domino*).

Protagonist, Der. Opera by Weill, 1926, premiered in Dresden. In a play within a play set in Elizabethan England, the leading actor kills the leading actress out of jealousy while the spectators admire the realism of their acting.

Proud Mary (Rollin' on the River). John Forgerty–penned song that was a big hit for his group, Creedence Clearwater Revival, in 1967, although it is now more closely associated with the energetic version by Ike and Tina Turner released in 1969.

prova (It.; Ger. *Probe*). A rehearsal, particularly in opera.

Prozess, Der (The Trial). Opera by von Einem, 1953, to a libretto drawn from the morbid novel by Kafka, 1st performed in Salzburg. The opera comments on the fate of the victim of a monstrous bureaucracy tried on unnamed charges. A recurrent rhythmic pulse serves as a sinister leitmotiv.

psalette (Fr.). Ecclesiastical choir school; *maîtrise*.

psalm (from Grk. *psallein*, pluck; Fr. *psaume*; It. *salmo*; Ger. *Psalm*). A hymn; a sacred song. The psalm is one of the most important categories of prayerful biblical poems to be sung with instrumental accompaniment. Innumerable works, beginning with the simplest type of plainchant, have been set to the texts from the Book of Psalms. Biblical tradition holds that King David wrote most of the Psalms and sang them, and he is therefore known as the Psalmist.

psalm tones. In Gregorian chant, the recitation formulas to be used by a soloist for intoning complete psalms. Each of the original 8 church modes has its own psalm tone; each psalm tone begins with an ascent to a reciting tone (tenor, holding tone, sustaining tone) a 5th above the mode's tonic degree; when the end of the verse is reached, the melody descends to the tonic. There is an additional psalm tone called the *tonus peregrinus* (wandering tone) that can be used with any of the 8 modes by changing the *tenor*.

psalmodicon. Swedish bowed zither, invented in 1829 by Johann Dillner. In its orig. form it resembled the 1-stringed TROMBA MARINA with additional metal drone strings. It was used as a substitute for the organ in churches and schools and evolved a cellolike body, but the invention of the HARMONIUM ended its usefulness in accompanying singing.

psalmody. Music sung in Protestant churches in England and the U.S. from the 17th century to the early 19th century.

Psalmus Hungaricus. Oratorio by Kodály, 1923, premiered in Budapest; the work is scored for tenor, chorus, children's chorus *ad libitum*, organ, and orch.

Psalter. Collection of psalms in the vernacular. Numerous national Psalters have been translated by various hands. Some Psalters are known by their place of publication, such as the Calvinist *Geneva Psalter*, published with polyphonic settings from 1546, and the *Bay Psalm Book*, the 1st book published in America; 13 musical settings were added to it in 1698.

psaltery. An ancient instrument in use to the 17th century; known to the Hebrews as the *Kinnor*, to the Germans as the *Rotta*. A kind of harp-zither with a varying number of strings plucked by the fingers or with a plectrum.

pseudoexoticism. To an imaginative composer, the attraction of exotic lands is in inverse ratio to available information about such lands and in direct ratio to the square of the distance from the nonbeholder. "Turkish" music, which had nothing in common with real Turkish modalities, enjoyed a great vogue in the 18th century and was used as a pseudoexotic resource by Mozart and others. When dancers from Indochina came to perform at the Paris Exposition of 1889, French musicians were fascinated by the unfamiliar sounds of resonant bells and muffled drums in the percussion group that accompanied the dancers. The emergence of impressionism in France owes much to this dance music from the Orient as refracted through the ears of a European.

The legends of the East provided poetic materials for song texts and operatic librettos. These tenuous impressions were transmuted into a *musique nouvelle*, vibrant with voluptuous *frissons*. Eastern scales were represented in the works of Debussy, Ravel, and their imitators by the pentatonic scale, which could be conveniently played on the black keys of the piano keyboard. Great composers were able to create a new art derived, however inaccurately, from Eastern sonorities; in fact, several composers—natives of Asia—who studied music in Paris began to mold their own authentic modes in the impressionistic manner.

When the novelty began to fade, the pentatonic scale, the tinkling bells, and other paraphernalia of pseudoexotica found their way into the commercial factories of vulgar musicians plying their trade with much profit in the semi-classical division of "modern" music, in Broadway shows, and on the soundtrack of exotic movie spectaculars. The proliferation of this pseudoexoticism resulted in the contamination of the genuine product, so that genuine Eastern music was threatened with extinction.

pseudonyms. Pseudonyms in literature are common; historically, women novelists have often assumed masculine names to facilitate publication of their works. In music, pseudonyms are relatively rare, except in cases in which a dignified composer writes undignified music. MacDowell, in the beginning of his career, published a number of short pieces under various pseudonyms. Among pseudonymous writers of light music is Albert William Ketelbey, whose real name was William Aston. Professional composers of popular songs often wrote under pseudonyms. Vladimir Dukelsky, a serious symphonic composer, adopted the nom de plume of Vernon Duke in writing popular songs.

More widespread is pseudonymity among singers, both in opera and on the popular stage. Since Italians have become proverbially associated with excellence in opera, many non-Italians, anxious to make an opera career, have assumed Italian names; thus the American soprano Lillian Norton became Nordica. At the turn of the century the belief was that a musician bearing an Anglo-Saxon name could not write successful songs, and that a surname ending in *-ski* (to imitate a Polish suffix) or *-ska* for women was essential. Thus the British pianist Ethel Liggins became Ethel Leginska, but it did not help her much in her American career. A flight from obviously Jewish names was pronounced among musical performers until recently. In the beginning of his spectacular career, Leonard Bernstein was strongly advised to change his name, but he indignantly refused and did rather well under his real name.

psychology. Like all artists, professional musicians possess an exaggerated *amour-propre*. Composers, representing as they do the intelligentsia of the musical profession, are the least prone to self-aggrandizement, but even they are apt

to be intransigent about the uniqueness of their talent. Schoenberg regarded musical composition derived from folk materials as devoid of aesthetic value, and he defended this philosophy with considerable vehemence. On a less dignified plane are the vanities of performing musicians in their desire to climb the ladder of fame and fortune. Anecdotes abound. The pianist Vladimir de Pachman would applaud himself at a public concert. In order to enhance his social status, the pianist Sigismond Thalberg supported the rumor that he was the illegitimate son of a minor German duke. It is said that the American musician and composer Silas Gamaliel Pratt said to Wagner, to whom he was introduced, "You are the Silas Gamaliel Pratt of Germany."

Symphonic conductors of the recent past were notorious for their conviction of being incomparable. Their megalomania sometimes reached extraordinary proportions. Hans von Bülow was particularly famous for his contemptuous treatment of his musicians. Toscanini was brought to court in Milan after he broke the violin bow on the head of his concertmaster; his defense lawyer pleaded that a musician can be regarded as legally insane when he creates music. During the last rehearsal that Toscanini conducted before his death, he shouted at the orch., "Imbecili!" The orch. forgave him this outburst in deference to his greatness and age.

The musical psychology of singers, at least in times past, was motivated by the lowest of animal instincts. Operatic PRIMA DONNAS would tear each others' hair out for the honor of being classified as *prima donna assoluta*, with larger-sized posters or a more sumptuous carriage. The institution of the CLAQUE was peculiar only to opera singers and flourished until well into the 20th century.

In popular credence musicians were often regarded as eternal adolescents not responsible for their actions. Even the fundamentalist sect of Jehovah's Witnesses finds attenuating circumstances for King David's sins of adultery and murder: "As an outstanding musician he most likely was an emotional man."

Public Enemy, landmark socially conscious rap group. (Members: Chuck D, b. Carlton Ridenhauer, N.Y., Aug. 1, 1960; MC Flavor Flav, b. William Drayton, N.Y., Mar. 16, 1959; Professor Griff, b. Richard Griffin; Terminator X, b. Norman Lee Rogers, N.Y., Aug. 25, 1966. Griffin left the group in 1989.) Formed originally at N.Y.'s Adelphi University in 1982, the group scored massive hits in the mid-'80s with their commentaries on contemporary black life. Songs like *Prophets of Rage, Bring the Noise*, and *Party for Your Right to Fight* made them immediately successful.

However, the group was shrouded in controversy; when group "Minister of Information" Professor Griff made some anti-Semitic statements, he was ousted from its membership in 1989. The group quickly bounced back with 1990's *Fear of a Black Planet*, featuring the hit *Fight the Power* (which became the theme for Spike Lee's film *Do the Right Thing*, in which they performed). Not shying away from controversy, the group released *By the Time I Get to Arizona* in 1991, denouncing that state's refusal to honor Martin Luther King Jr. However, by the early '90s their activities slowed. In 1994 they were producing more mainstream pop material, scoring a hit with *Give It Up*.

Puccini, Giacomo (Antonio Domenico Michele Secondo Maria)

Celebrated operatic composer; b. Lucca, Dec. 22, 1858; d. Brussels, Nov. 29, 1924. He was the 5th of 7 children of Michele Puccini, who died when Giacomo was only 5; his musical training was thus entrusted to his uncle, Fortunato Magi, a pupil of his father; however, Giacomo showed neither inclination nor talent for music. His mother, determined to continue the family tradition, sent him to the local Istituto Musicale Pacini, where the director, Carlo Angeloni—who had also studied with Michele Puccini—became his teacher. After Angeloni's untiring patience had aroused interest and then enthusiasm in his pupil, progress was rapid and he soon became a proficient pianist and organist.

He began serving as a church organist in Lucca and environs when he was 14, and began composing when he was 17. After hearing *Aida* in Pisa in 1876, he resolved to win laurels as a dramatic composer. Having written mainly sacred music, it was self-evident that he needed further training after graduating from the Istituto (1880). With financial support from his granduncle, Dr. Nicolao Ceru, and a stipend from Queen Margherita, he pursued his studies with Antonio Bazzini and Amilcare Ponchielli at the Milan Cons. (1880–83). For his graduation he wrote a *Capriccio sinfonico*, which was conducted by Faccio at a Cons. concert, eliciting unstinting praise from the critics.

In the same year, Ponchielli introduced Puccini to the librettist Fontana, who furnished him the text of a 1-act opera; in a few weeks the score was finished and sent to the Sonzongo competition. It did not win the prize, but in 1884 *Le villi* was produced at the Teatro dal Verme in Milan, with gratifying success. Ricordi, who was present, considered the work sufficiently meritorious to commission the young composer to write a new opera for him; but 5 years elapsed before this work, *Edgar* (3 acts; text by Fontana), was produced at La Scala in Milan (1889), scoring only a moderate success. By this time Puccini had become convinced that in order to write a really effective opera, he needed a better libretto than Fontana had provided. Accordingly, he commissioned Domenico Oliva to write the text of *Manon Lescaut*; during the composition, however, Puccini and Ricordi practically rewrote the entire book, and in the publ. score Oliva's name is not mentioned. With *Manon Lescaut* (4 acts), 1st produced at the Teatro Regio in Turin (1893), Puccini won a veritable triumph; this was surpassed by his next work, *La Bohème* (4 acts; text by Illica and Giacosa), produced at the same theater in 1896. These 2 works not only carried their composer's name throughout the world, but also have found and maintained their place in the repertoire of every opera house.

With fame came wealth, and in 1900 Puccini built a magnificent villa at Torre del Lago, where he had been living since 1891. His next opera, Tosca (3 acts; text by Illica and Giacosa), produced at the Teatro Costanzi in Rome (1900), is Puccini's most dramatic work; it has become a fixture of the standard repertoire and contains some of his best-known arias. At its premiere at La Scala (1904), *Madama Butterfly* (2 acts; text by Illica and Giacosa) was hissed. Puccini thereupon withdrew the score and made some slight changes (division into 3 acts, and addition of the tenor aria in the last scene). This revised version was greeted with frenzied applause in Brescia later that same year. Puccini was now the acknowledged ruler of the Italian operatic stage, his works rivaling those of Verdi in the number of performances.

The 1st performance of *Madama Butterfly* at the Metropolitan Opera in N.Y. (1907) took place in the presence of the composer, whom the management had invited especially for the occasion. It was then suggested

Giacomo Puccini

COURTESY OF THE NEW YORK PUBLIC LIBRARY

that he write an opera on an American subject, the premiere to take place at the Metropolitan. He found his subject when he witnessed a performance of Belasco's *The Girl of the Golden West*; he commissioned C. Zangarini and G. Civinini to write the libretto, and in the presence of the composer the world premiere of *La Fanciulla del West* occurred, amid much enthusiasm, at the Metropolitan (1910); while it never equaled the success of his *Tosca* or *Madama Butterfly*, it returned to favor in the 1970s as a period piece. Puccini then brought out the operettalike *La Rondine* (3 acts; Monte Carlo, 1917) and the 3 1-act operas *Il Tabarro* (after Didier Gold's *La Houppelande*), *Suor Angelica*, and *Gianni Schicchi* (performed as *Il Trittico* at the Metropolitan Opera, 1918). His last opera, *Turandot* (after Gozzi), was left unfinished; the final scene was completed by Franco Alfano and performed at La Scala with Toscanini conducting (1926).

Puff, The Magic Dragon. The 1962 megahit children's song by the group Peter, Paul and Mary; not about drugs, despite the rumors otherwise.

pugno, col (It.). Strike the keys with the fist.

puk (Korean). Drum.

Pulcinella. Ballet with song by Stravinsky, 1920, consisting of a number of Italian songs and dances based on works once attributed to Pergolesi. (It is clear that none of the source works are Pergolesi's; most remain anonymous.) The ballet score, composed for Diaghilev, was 1st performed by the Ballets Russes in Paris. Stravinsky arranged a concert suite from the score, 1st performed by the Boston Sym. Orch. (1922). He also transcribed some of the movements of the suite for cello and piano, and for violin and piano, under the title *Suite italienne*. Despite the feminine ending, Pulcinella is a male character that appeared in the Italian COMMEDIA DELL'ARTE in the 17th century, depicted as a deceitful scoundrel and a rogue.

pulkatants (Est.). Estonian male dance in syncopated 2/4 time; like the English MORRIS DANCE, the dancers use sticks.

pulse. A beat or accent.

Pult (Ger.; from Lat. *pupitum*, pulpit). Music stand.

punctus (Lat.). 1. A dot that serves as a bar of separation between rhythmic groups in mensural notation; *punctus divisionis*. 2. A dot that adds half of the duration of the note so dotted; *punctus additionis*.

punitive music. Relentless playing of a trivial tune arranged in repellent harmonies may well be used, and possibly has been used by dictatorial regimes, to extract confessions from suspected music lovers. A similar practice is pursued in the form of a musical massage in democratic countries by means of juke boxes or other instruments of torture—in public restaurants, in jet planes waiting for a chance to make a scheduled departure, at bus terminals and railroad stations—with the ultimate intention of weakening sales resistance to a commercial product among captive listeners. For an entirely different purpose Satie—who detested audiences—directed to have his piano piece, pointedly titled *Vexations*, to be performed 840 times in succession. His punitive design, however, was circumvented by a group of sadomasochists who carried Satie's instructions to the letter; in 1963 a complete performance of *Vexations* occurred in N.Y., played without interruption by a relay of willing pianists who obtained thereby not only a measure of secret gratification but also a great deal of publicity.

punta (It.). Point (of the bow). *Colla punta dell'arco*, at the point of the bow.

punto (Sp.). A Cuban song combining 3/4 and 6/8 meters, with occasional injections of 2/4. Although clearly of Spanish origin, the Caribbean punto developed its own style, marked by percussive syncopation.

pupitre (Fr.). Music stand.

Purcell, Henry, great English composer; b. London, 1659; d. Dean's Yard, Westminster, Nov. 21, 1695. His parentage remains a matter of dispute, since documentary evidence is lacking. His father may have been Henry Purcell (d. Westminster, Aug. 11, 1664), a singer, Master of the Choristers at Westminster Abbey, and a Gentleman of the Chapel Royal. It is also possible that his father was Thomas Purcell (d. Westminster, July 31, 1682), a singer and composer, most likely the brother of the elder Henry Purcell, a Gentleman of the Chapel Royal, composer for the violins (with Pelham Humfrey), marshal of the Corp. of Music, and a musician-in-ordinary in the King's Private Musick.

Whatever the case, the young Henry Purcell became a chorister of the Chapel Royal under Cooke and Humfrey (1669) and also received instruction from Blow; when his voice broke (1673), he was appointed Assistant Keeper of the Instruments; he was named composer-in-ordinary for the violins (1677). He became Blow's successor as organist of Westminster Abbey (1679) and 1 of the 3 organists of the Chapel Royal (1682); was named organ maker and keeper of the king's instruments (1683). His 1st printed work was a song in Playford's *Choice Ayres* (vol. I, 1675); vol. II (1679) contains other songs and an elegy on the death of Matthew Locke. In 1680 he publ. some of his finest instrumental works, the *Fantasias* for Strings; in that same year he began writing odes and welcome songs; although their texts are almost invariably insipid or bombastic, he succeeded in clothing them in some of his finest music; his incidental music for the stage also dates from that year.

He wrote the anthem *My Heart is Inditing* for the coronation of King James II (1685). With *Dido and Aeneas* he produced the 1st great English opera. In the remaining years of his life he devoted much time to composition for the theater; he also wrote some outstanding sacred music: the Te Deum and Jubilate in D; for the funeral of Queen Mary he wrote the anthem *Thou knowest, Lord, the Secrets of our Hearts* (1695); it was performed, along with his 4 canzonas for brass and 2 elegies, at his own funeral later that year.

Purcell lies in the north aisle of Westminster Abbey, and his burial tablet well expresses contemporary estimation of his worth: "Here lyes Henry Purcell, Esq.; who left this life, and is gone to that blessed place where only his harmony can be exceeded." His church music shows him to be an original melodist and a master of form, harmony, and all contrapuntal devices; his music for the stage is equally rich in invention, dramatic instinct, and power of characterization; his chamber works surpass those of his predecessors and contemporaries. Among his many works are the opera *Dido and Aeneas* (libretto by Tate; London, 1689; evidence shows that the work may date from the mid-1680s). Semioperas (plays with varying degrees of music): *The Prophetess, or The History of Dioclesian* (1690); *King Arthur, or The British Worthy* (1691); *The Fairy Queen* (1692); *The Indian Queen* (1695; final masque by D. Purcell); *The Tempest, or The Enchanted Island* (c. 1695). Incidental music to numerous plays, including several by D'Urfey, Tate, Dryden, Crowne, Southerne, Shadwell, Lee, Congreve, D'Avenant.

Purcell also composed numerous anthems and services (c. 1677–c. 1693), a Magnificat and Nunc dimitiis (n.d.), Morning and Evening Service (1682), and Te Deum and Jubilate (1694), as well as other sacred works. His other vocal works include 24 odes and welcome songs, numerous songs for solo voice and basso continuo, songs for 2 or more voices and basso continuo, and catches. His instrumental works include various pieces for winds and strings, including 14 fantasias, 3 overtures, 5 pavans, 24 sonatas, etc.; also many harpsichord pieces. His brother Daniel Purcell (b. London, c. 1660; d. there, Nov. 26, 1717) was an organist and composer; Daniel completed 1 or more of his brother's pieces after Henry's demise.

Puritani di Scozia, I (The Puritans of Scotland). Opera by Bellini, 1835, 1st performed in Paris a few months before Bellini's untimely death. The libretto is derived, after several translations and retranslations from French and Italian, from Walter Scott's novel *Old Mortality*. The Puritans are the Roundheads, fanatical followers of Oliver Cromwell. The action takes place in 1649 after the execution of the Stuart King Charles I of England. A noble cavalier faithful to the King's cause is engaged to the daughter of a Puritan but fails to appear at the altar in order to get the widowed queen out of Cromwell's murderous clutches. His bride is bewildered by his unexplained defection and goes insane. Her mad scene rivals in effectiveness that of Donizetti's *Lucia di Lammermoor*, which is also derived from Walter Scott. Having saved the Queen, the faithful bridegroom returns to his beloved, causing her to regain her mental faculties. But, oh horror! Cromwell's soldiers surprise them and carry the hapless youth to the execution block; once more his bride-to-be lapses into madness. But lo! A trumpet fanfare announces a new victory for Cromwell and his magnanimous decision to grant amnesty to his foes. Once more the situation is saved. As if on cue, the bride regains her senses and a happy chorus congratulates them.

The popularity of *I Puritani* in the 19th century was enormous. The famous male duet of 2 Roundheads was performed at the premiere by 2 of the loudest singers in Europe; as Rossini quipped, they must have been heard as far as Mt. Vesuvius. The same duet was the subject of the *Grandes variations de bravoure sur la marche des Puritans* for Piano by Liszt.

Purlie. Musical by Gary Geld, 1970. Purlie is a black preacher in the cotton region of Georgia. He is dedicated to the goal of building a black church, but is opposed in this by a villainous old white overseer on the plantation. The old man dies when he discovers that his own son, an easygoing guitar picker, works with Purlie. The score contains elements of Negro gospel songs, folk ballads, and rhythm and blues; the final number, *Walk Him Up the Stairs*, has an authentic flavor of old hymnody.

puzzle canon. A riddle canon; a canon presented as a single melodic line and playful, intentionally obscure instructions as to its solution. An example is the phrase "cancer eat plenis et redeat medius" (let the crab go forth entire and return in half); deciphered, this instructs that the melody should be performed in retrograde, and then in normal (forward) sequence, but with note values halved, i.e., twice as fast. See also CANON.

pyramidon. An organ stop with short stopped pipes, giving out the lowest notes of the organ's range. Its name stems from the fact that it is covered by short pyramidal pipes more than 4 times as wide on top as at their base.

Qq

qin (Ch'in). An early Chinese zither, the most honored of all Chinese musical instruments. The qin is associated with the Confucian ruling class, which played meditatively upon its strings while pondering life as they knew it.

quadrille. A French ballroom square dance, the name of which is derived from the Spanish *quadrilla*, that is, 4 dancing pairs. Its main figures are 5: *le Pantalon, l'Été, la Poule, la Pastourelle (la Trenise)*, and *la Finale*. The time alternates between 3/8 (6/8) and 2/4. The quadrille attained its greatest popularity in the early 19th century, in Europe (including Russia) and America.

quadrivium. A faculty of 4 sciences in medieval universities, of which music was 1, regarded as the doctrine dealing with the physical part of sound perception; the other 3 sciences were arithmetic, geometry, and astronomy.

quadruple counterpoint. See COUNTERPOINT.

quadruple croche (Fr.). A 64th note.

quadruple meter or time. That characterized by 4 beats to the measure.

quadruplet. A group of 4 equal notes, to be executed in the time of 3 or 6 of the same kind in the established rhythm, written

quality of tone. That characteristic peculiarity of any vocal or instrumental tone that distinguishes it from the tone of any other class of voices or instruments. Also called *tone color, timbre.*

Quantz, Johann Joachim, famous German flutist, writer on music, and composer; b. Oberscheden, Hannover, Jan. 30, 1697; d. Potsdam, July 12, 1773. His father was a village blacksmith; young Johann revealed a natural gift for music and played the double bass at village festivals at age 8; his father died when he was 10, and he was apprenticed to his uncle, Justus Quantz, a "Stadtmusikus" in Merseburg, in 1708, and later to J. A. Fleischhack; he received instruction on string and wind instruments, becoming particularly adept on the violin, oboe, and trumpet; he also studied harpsichord with J. F. Kiesewetter. He completed his apprenticeship in 1713, but remained a journeyman under Fleischhack until 1716; then became a member of the Dresden municipal band; during a 3-month leave of absence (1717) he studied counterpoint with J. D. Zelenka in Vienna; subsequently became oboist at the Polish chapel of Augustus II (1718), being active in Dresden and Warsaw, but soon turned to the transverse flute, receiving some lessons from P. G. Buffardin.

In 1724 he went to Italy in the entourage of the Polish ambassador and sought out F. Gasparini in Rome for further counterpoint training; after a sojourn in Paris (1726–27) he visited England (1727) before returning to Dresden as a flutist in the court Kapelle (also 1727). He made his 1st visit to Berlin in the entourage of Augustus II (1728), where he was engaged as teacher to Crown Prince Friedrich; he continued to visit Berlin regularly to instruct the Crown Prince while carrying out his duties in Dresden, which included the making of flutes from 1739. Friedrich ascended the throne as King of Prussia in 1740 and the next year called Quantz to Berlin, where it was his special province to oversee the King's private evening concerts; he was granted an annual salary of 2,000 thalers, plus an honorarium for each new composition and flute he produced. Quantz was held in such high esteem by his patron that he was the only individual granted the right to criticize Friedrich's performances as a musician.

His extensive output included some 300 concertos for flute, strings, and basso continuo; 7 concertos for 2 flutes, strings, and basso continuo; 2 concertos for horn, strings, and basso continuo (1 may not be by Quantz); 2 concertos for oboe, strings, and basso continuo; Concerto for Oboe d'Amore, Strings, and Basso Continuo (not extant); about 200 sonatas for flute and basso continuo; some 60 trio sonatas; 12 duets for 2 flutes or other instruments; 12 capriccios for flute; 8 fantasias for flute; 22 hymns; 6 songs; etc. On the whole these works reveal Quantz as a transitional figure in the movement from the Baroque to the Classic style. He publ. the invaluable treatise *Versuch einer Anweisung die Flöte traversiere zu spielen* (Berlin, 1752).

quaquaversal dispersion. Macropolysyllables are not necessarily frivolous when they define a phenomenon in a memorable or picturesque phrase. Quaquaversal dispersion is a convenient macropolysyllable to describe a radial expansion of the central cumulus of sonic matter, similar to the process of gradual sliding of geological layers, to which the term *quaquaversal* (literally, turning in different directions) is applied in science.

quart de soupir (Fr., quarter of a sigh). A 16th-note rest.

quarta (It.; Ger. *Quarte*). Perfect 4th.

quartal harmony. A system of harmonic structure based on the superposition of the intervals of the 4ths rather than the traditional 3rds. Such harmonic structures became increasingly attractive to 20th-century composers seeking to break the chains of triadic tonality.

quartegeige (Ger.). A quarter-violin, smaller than and tuned a 4th higher than the standard violin, now obsolete.

quarter note. A CROTCHET (♩), equal to 1 beat in any time signature with a denominator of 4.

quarter rest. A rest equal in time value to a quarter note: ♿ or ♩.

quarter tone. Half a semitone; a logarithmic interval which is used by some modern composers; also used in some non-Western music. Quarter tones are not modern inventions; they are found in the ancient Greek enharmonic scale. Many romantic composers of the 19th century thought of reviving quarter tones as a unit of an icositetraphonic scale. George Ives, father of Charles Ives, who was an Army band leader during the Civil War, experimented with tuning his instruments a quarter tone apart.

The attraction of quarter tones for modern composers is explained by the desire to develop a finer and more subtle means of musical expression. A pioneer of the modern revival of quarter tones was Julián Carrillo of Mexico, who published a treatise on *Sonido 13* in 1895, the number 13 referring to the tonal resources beyond the chromatic scale. Alois Hába of Czechoslovakia codified the usages of quarter tones in his *Neue Harmonielehre*, published in 1928.

The 1st quarter-tone piano (with 2 keyboards tuned a quarter tone apart) was built in 1924. Rimsky-Korsakov's grand son Georg founded a quarter-tone society in Leningrad in the 1920s. The Russian composer Ivan Wyschnegradsky, who made his home in Paris, wrote much music for 2 pianos tuned a quarter tone apart. Charles Ives wrote a chorale for strings in quarter tones as early as 1914. Several systems of notation for quarter tones have been proposed, the most logical of which is the one by Hába using slashed signs for flats and sharps. Ernest Bloch used quarter tones in his Piano Quintet, notated simply as flatted or sharped notes. See also MICROTONALITY.

quartet (*quartette*; Fr. *quatuor*; It. *quartetto*; Ger. *Quartett*). 1. A concerted instrumental composition for 4 performers, such as the string quartet, for 2 violins, viola, and cello. 2. A composition, movement, or number, either vocal or instrumental, in 4 parts; a vocal quartet might involve one each of the 4 standard voices, labeled SATB. 3. A particular ensemble designed to perform these genres.

Quartet for the End of Time (*Quatuor pour la fin du temps*). A work for violin, clarinet, cello, and piano by Messiaen, 1941, in 8 movements; a devotional meditation on the end of time. He wrote it while a prisoner of war in Germany and had it performed in the prisoner's camp Stalag 8A, Görlitz, Silesia.

quartettino (It.). A small quartet.

Quartsextakkord (Ger.). The 2nd inversion triad; the $^6_4$ or 6–4 chord.

quasi (It.). As if; as it were; nearly; approaching. *Andante quasi allegretto*, andante approaching allegretto. *Quasi niente*, almost nothing; *quasi trombi*, like trumpets; used by Liszt in his piano music; *quasi una fantasia*, like a fantasia, as in the op. 27 piano sonatas of Beethoven; *quasi zimbalo*, like a cimbalom, used by Liszt in his Hungarian Rhapsodies and other works in the Hungarian manner; he primarily imitated the rhythmic quality of this hammered dulcimer's music.

quasihemidemisemiquaver (U.K.). A 128th note.

quatre (It. *quattro*). Four.

quatricinium (Lat.). A 4-voice composition, or a wind quartet for German STADTPFEIFER. The term 1st appeared in the 17th century.

quattro (It.). Four. *A quattro mani*, for 4 hands.

Quattro pezzi sacri (4 Sacred Pieces). Choral works by Verdi, 1896, written in his very old age when he turned toward religious music after the composition of his last opera, *Falstaff*. They are *Ave Maria, Laudi alla Vergine Maria, Stabat Mater,* and *Te Deum.* In the *Ave Maria,* Verdi uses a curious scale that he found in a musical journal, where it was called SCALA ENIGMATICA. Just what was especially enigmatic in this scale is difficult to fathom. It is simply an altered major scale with the lower supertonic and raised subdominant, dominant, and submediant, but it does create the feeling of a whole tone scale in the middle section.

Quattro rusteghi, I (The 4 Rascals). Opera by Wolf-Ferrari, 1906; in Munich known as *Die vier Grobiane.* Four gross and arrogant married men try to rule their households like feudal lords. They are outwitted by their wives and daughters, who arrange the marriage of the daughter of one of the most intransigent of them against his will.

quatuor à cordes (Fr.). String quartet.

quaver (U.K.). An 8th note.

Que Sera, Sera. Song by Jay Livingston and Ray Evans, 1956, flaunting the fatalism of love and death. It was sung by Doris Day in the film *The Man Who Knew Too Much* (version no. 2) by Alfred Hitchcock.

Queen. British exponents of glitter rock. (Vocal/keyboards: Freddie Mercury, b. Frederick Bulsana, Zanzibar, Africa, Sept. 5, 1946; d. Kensington, England, Nov. 24, 1991; lead guitar: Brian May, b. Twickenham, England, July 19 1947; bass: John Deacon, b. Leicester England, Aug. 19, 1951; drums: Roger Taylor, b. Kings Lynn, England, July 26, 1949.) Lead by flamboyant vocalist Freddie Mercury, Queen was one of the most critically reviled but commercially successful outfits in rock from the mid-1970s to the early 1980s; their career enjoyed another bump in popularity in the early '90s when their music was featured in the film *Wayne's World.*

The group was formed out of the remnants of other bands in early 1971. Slaving away, they produced a series of albums through the mid-'70s, finally breaking through to pop stardom with 1975's *Bohemian Rhapsody,* promoted through one of the 1st rock videos. It was followed by more chart-toppers expressing characteristic bombastic sentiments, including 1976's *We Will Rock You* and 1980's *Another One Bites the Dust.* Their macho posing and grandiose tours thrilled adolescent boys everywhere. The group's popularity waned in the early '80s, however, and they broke up by 1986. Mercury, long rumored to be homosexual, announced he had contracted AIDS just a day before his death in Nov. 1991. This led to an overblown tribute concert and renewed Queenmania. *Bohemian Rhapsody* was affectionately revived in the film *Wayne's World,* and the video and song enjoyed another run of success.

Queen, The. Sym. No. 85 in B-flat Major (1785) by Haydn. This is the 4th in a series of 6 symphonies that Haydn wrote for Paris performances; the title, usually listed in French (*La Reine*), is explained by the fact that Marie Antoinette heard it 7 years before she died on the guillotine.

Queen of Sheba, The. Opera, 1875, by Karl Goldmark (b. Keszthely, May 18, 1830; d. Vienna, Jan. 2, 1915), 1st performed in Vienna. The libretto tells the story of King Solomon and the eponymous Queen, with an added episode involving her involvement with a commoner. There is a sandstorm in the desert in the finale. The music follows the stereotype of Romantic opera.

Queen of Spades. Opera in 3 acts by Tchaikovsky, after Pushkin's tale; 1st produced in St. Petersburg, Dec. 19, 1890. A Russian army officer tries to elicit the secret of 3 winning cards from an old woman who had received them from the magician Cagliostro. His strange demand frightens the old woman, and she dies, but her ghost appears to him in a lifelike hallucination and gives him the 3 winning cards: 3, 7, and ace. He gambles on these cards, and wins on the 1st 2. But instead of picking up the winning ace, he draws the Queen of Spades for the last card and loses all. The card face of the Queen grimaces at him and he recognizes the old woman in it. He goes out and kills himself. The score is highly dramatic and is in constant repertory in Russia, although not too frequently staged elsewhere.

quena (quechua). Generic term for a vertical flute made of bamboo or baked clay, popular among the Guaraní Indians in Argentina, Bolivia, Peru, and the Amazon basin.

Querelle des Bouffons. Guerre des Bouffons.

Querflöte (Ger.). Transverse flute.

Querpfeife (Ger.). Transverse fife.

quickstep. 1. A march, usually in 6/8 time. 2. A rapid American fox-trot that evolved *c.* 1920.

quijada (*qui jada del burro*; Sp., jawbone of an ass). An Afro-Cuban instrument as described in its name, with its teeth left in. The quijada can be used as a scraper, a rattle, or a percussive instrument (hit with the fist). It dates to at least the 18th century.

quilisma. An ornament indicating an ascending semitone in neumatic notation.

quindecima (It.). A 15th (either the interval or the organ stop). *Alla quindecima* (written simply *15ma*), 2 octaves higher (or lower).

quint. 1. The interval of a 5th. 2. A 5 1/3' organ stop, sounding a 5th higher than the normal 8' pitch. 3. The E string of the violin.

quinte (*quinte de violon*; Fr.). Obsolete name for the viola.

Quintenquartett. This is the string quartet No. 2, op. 76 (1797), by Haydn, in the key of D minor. Its nickname refers to the interplay of 5ths in the 1st movement. The quartet is also known as *The Bell* or *The Donkey.* Furthermore, the minuet in it became known as the *Witch Minuet* because of its supposedly bewitching quality.

Quintenzirkel (Ger.). Cycle (circle) of 5ths.

Quinterne (Ger.). Gittern.

quintet (Fr. *quintette, quintour*; It. *quintetto*; Ger. *Quintett*). 1. A concerted instrumental composition for 5 performers. 2. A composition, movement, or number, vocal or instrumental, in 5 parts. 3. Also the performers as a group.

quintina (It.). Quintuplet.

quinton (Fr.). A 17th-century term for the treble viola d'amore.

Quintsextakkord (Ger.). The 1st inversion dominant-7th chord; the $\frac{6}{5}$, 6–5, or 6–5–3 chord.

quintuple rhythm or time. Grouping of 5 beats to the measure.

quintuplets (It. *quintina*; Ger. *Quintole*; Fr. *quintolet*). A group of 5 notes of equal duration played against a normal grouping of 4 or 3 notes. An interesting example of a whole section of quintuplets in 8th notes against a waltz rhythm of 3/4 is found in the *Dance of the Mermaids* in Rimsky-Korsakov's opera *Sadko*.

quitter (Fr.). To quit, leave. *Sans quitter la corde*, without quitting the string.

quodlibet (from Lat., as you like it). As cultivated by medieval students in Central Europe, a free medley of popular melodies, religious hymns, and cosmopolitan madrigals. No wonder the French name for the quodlibet was *fricassée* (stewed meat). The secret of attraction of such fricassees was the joy of recognition of familiar tunes in an otherwise solemn context. Even Bach himself succumbed to the lure of the quodlibet by combining 2 popular melodies in the last movement of his *Goldberg*

Variations. In modern times a quodlibet formed by the superposition of the Russian song *Dark Eyes* and Chopin's F-minor étude was popular among Russian conservatory students. Another popular modern quodlibet is a combination of the tunes *La Matchiche* and *Petite Tonkinoise.* See also POTPOURRI.

quotation. In music, the inclusion of musical materials in a composition that allude to other compositions or musics. Folk songs, contrapuntal elaborations on a given cantus firmus, and the doom-laden chant DIES IRAE have been for centuries a favorite resource of quotations. R. Strauss inserted the theme of the funeral march from Beethoven's *Eroica Sym.* in the score of his *Metamorphosen,* a dirge on the death of Germany written during the last weeks of World War II. Berg quoted Bach's chorale *Es ist genug* at the conclusion of his Violin Concerto as a memorial for Manon Gropius, the young daughter of Mahler's widow by another marriage.

Quotations from a composer's own scores are not rare; a notorious modern example is the egocentric series of quotations used by Strauss in the score of his symphonic poem *Ein Heldenleben.* But perhaps the most extraordinary assembly of assorted thematic memos, memories, and mementos is found in *Sinfonia* by Berio, in which he quotes metamorphosed fragments from works of Mahler, Debussy, Ravel and others. The situation is different, of course, when a quotation of a famous song is deliberately made for purposes of characterization or as a historical reference, as for instance the *Marseillaise* in Tchaikovsky's *1812 Overture* and in Giordano's opera *Andrea Chenier,* or *The Star-Spangled Banner* in Puccini's *Madama Butterfly.*

Rr

R. Stands for *right* (Ger. *rechte*); *r.h.*, right hand (*rechte Hand*). In French organ music *R* stands for *clavier de récit* (swell manual).

Ra (Fr.). Onomatopoeic syllable indicating the drum figure with 2 sticks, alternating rapidly between right and left hands. *Ra de quatre*, drum figure in 4 beats; *Ra de trois*, drum figure in 3 beats; *Ra et sauté*, drum figure in 2 beats with a break in between.

rabāb (Arab.). Middle Eastern bowed spiked fiddle, 1st recorded in the 10th century, and based on a Persian plucked lute. The rabāb has a pear-shaped body, sickle-shaped peg-box, and between 3 and 5 strings. Related forms of it are played in southern Asia and Indonesia, the latter as a gamelan instrument called *rebab*; it was introduced there in the 16th century as a result of the Arab invasions. By the 11th century the rabāb had reached Europe; it evolved into the REBEC, which survived into the 18th century.

rabbia, con (It.). With passion, frenzy; furiously.

raccoglimento, con (It.). Collectedly, coolly; meditatively.

raccontando (It.). Narrating, as if telling a story.

Rachmaninoff, Sergei (Vassilievich)

Greatly renowned Russian-born American pianist, conductor, and composer; b. Semyonovo, Apr. 1, 1873; d. Beverly Hills, Mar. 28, 1943. He was of a musical family; his grandfather was an amateur pianist, a pupil of John Field; his father also played the piano; Rachmaninoff's Polka was written on a theme improvised by his father; his mother likewise played piano, and it was from her that he received his initial training at their estate, Oneg, near Novgorod. After financial setbacks the family estate was sold and he was taken to St. Petersburg, where he studied piano with Vladimir Demiansky and harmony with Alexander Rubets at the Cons. (1882–85); acting on the advice of his cousin, Alexander Siloti, he enrolled as a piano student of Nikolai Zverev at the Moscow Cons. (1885); then entered Siloti's piano class and commenced the study of counterpoint with Taneyev and harmony with Arensky (1888).

He met Tchaikovsky, who appreciated his talent and gave him friendly advice. He graduated as a pianist (1891) and as a composer (1892), winning the gold medal with his opera *Aleko*, after Pushkin. Then followed his Prelude in C-sharp Minor (from the *Morceaux de fantaisie*, No. 2, op. 3); publ. in 1892, it quickly became one of the most celebrated piano pieces in the world. His 1st Sym., given in Moscow (1897), proved a failure, however. Discouraged, Rachmaninoff destroyed the MS, but the orch. parts were preserved; after his death the score was restored and performed in Moscow (1945).

In the meantime Rachmaninoff launched a career as a piano virtuoso; also took up a career as a conductor, joining the Moscow Private Russian Orch. (1897). He made his London debut in the triple capacity of pianist, conductor, and composer with the Phil. Soc. (1899). Although he attempted to compose after the failure of his 1st Sym., nothing significant came from his pen. Plagued by depression, he underwent treatment by hypnosis with Nikolai Dahl, and then began work on his 2nd Piano Concerto. He played the 1st complete performance of the score with Siloti conducting in Moscow (1901); this concerto became the most celebrated work of its genre written in the 20th century, and its singular charm has never abated since; it is no exaggeration to say that it became a model for piano concertos by a majority of modern Russian composers and also of semipopular virtuoso pieces for piano and orch. written in America.

In 1902 Rachmaninoff married his cousin Natalie Satina; they spent some months in Switzerland, then returned to Moscow. After conducting at Moscow's Bolshoi Theater (1904–1906) he decided to spend most of his time in Dresden, where he composed his 2nd Sym., one of his most popular works. Having composed another major work, his 3rd Piano Concerto, he took it on his 1st tour of the U.S. in 1909. His fame was so great that he was offered the conductorship of the Boston Sym. Orch., but he declined; the offer was repeated in 1918, but once again he declined.

Rachmaninoff lived in Russia from 1910 until after the Bolshevik Revolution of Oct. 1917, at which time he left Russia with his family, never to return. From 1918 until 1939 he made annual tours of Europe as a pianist, and also of the U.S. (from 1918 until his death), where he spent much of his time; he owned a villa in Lucerne (1931–39), and it was there that he composed one of his most enduring scores, the *Rhapsody on a Theme of Paganini* (1934). In 1932 he was awarded the Gold Medal of the Royal Phil. Soc. of London. After the outbreak of World War II (1939) he spent his remaining years in the U.S. He became a naturalized U.S. citizen a few weeks before his death, having made his last appearance as a pianist in Knoxville, Tenn.

Among Russian composers Rachmaninoff occupies a very important place. The sources of his inspiration lie in the Romantic tradition of 19th-century Russian music; the link with Tchaikovsky's lyrical art is very strong; melancholy moods prevail and minor keys predominate in his compositions, as in Tchaikovsky's; but there is an unmistakable stamp of Rachmaninoff's individuality in the broad, rhapsodic sweep of the melodic line, and particularly in the fully expanded sonorities and fine resonant harmonies of his piano writing; its technical resourcefulness is unexcelled by any composer since Liszt.

Despite the fact that Rachmaninoff was an émigré and stood in avowed opposition to the Soviet regime (until the German attack on Russia in 1941 impelled him to modify his stand), his popularity never wavered in Russia; after his death Russian musicians paid spontaneous tribute to him. Rachmaninoff's music is much less popular in Germany, France, and Italy; on the other hand, in England and America it constitutes a potent factor on the concert stage.

Rachmaninoff worked on several operatic projects, but only completed A*leko*, *The Miserly Knight*, op. 24, after Pushkin (1903–1905; Moscow, 1906), and *Francesca da Rimini*, op. 25, after Dante's *Inferno* (1900–1905; Moscow, 1906). For orch. he wrote 3 syms., 4 piano concertos, the Paganini Rhapsody, and several symphonic poems, including *Prince Rostislav* (1891); *The Rock* (1893; Moscow, 1896); *The Isle of the Dead*, op. 29, after Böcklin's painting—like the waltz movement of Tchaikovsky's *Pathétique Sym.*, 5/4 meter is prominent (Moscow, 1909); also the *Symphonic Dances*, op. 45 (Philadelphia, 1941). His best-known chamber work is the Cello Sonata in G Minor, op. 19 (1901). His Russian orthodox choral music is among his finest creations: *Liturgy of St. John Chrysostom*, op. 31 (Moscow, 1910); *All-Night Vigil*, op. 37 (1915); he also composed *The Bells*, choral sym. for soprano, baritone, chorus, and orch., op. 35, after Poe (St. Petersburg, 1913).

As a virtuoso pianist Rachmaninoff followed the 19th-century tradition of composing music to show off his abilities; unlike most of his predecessors he wrote some excellent music in this vein, including the *Fantaisie-tableaux*: Suite No. 1 for 2 Pianos, op. 5 (1893); 6 *Moments musicaux*, op. 16 (1896); Suite No. 2 for 2 Pianos, op. 17 (1900–1901); *Variations on a Theme of Chopin*, op. 22 (1902–1903); 10 Preludes, op. 23 (1901–1903); Sonata No. 1, op. 28 (1907); 13 Preludes, op. 32 (1910); *Études-tableaux*, op. 33 (1911); Sonata No. 2, op. 36 (1913; rev. 1931); *Études-tableaux*, op. 39 (1916–17); *Variations on a Theme of Corelli*, op. 42 (1931); also 82 songs (1890–1916).

racket (Ger. *Rachett, Rankett*; Fr. *Cervelas, cervelat*; It. *rocchetta, cortalo*). Obsolete wind instrument of the 16th and 17th centuries; its double reed is partly covered by its mouthpiece, a *pirouette*. The body, made of ivory or wood, is shaped like a small tree stump; the tube consists of a connected series of narrow channels bored up and down the body. Fingerholes are bored obliquely into the channels, thus requiring a player to use the tip and middle joints of a finger to cover a hole. The racket also has ventholes and a water escape. As a closed pipe it sounds an octave lower than its length; but it cannot be overblown, so that the ranges on the 3 types of racket are only an octave and a perfect 5th; the lowest racket (great bass) has a range C_1–G_0; the highest (soprano), G_0–d^1. The racket has had an occasional role in the early music revival of the 20th century.

raddolcente (It.). Growing calmer and gentler.

raddoppiato (It.). Double the tempo.

Radel (Ger.). Vocal canon.

radial distribution. Radial distribution of a linear series is a maximum dispersion of the constituent tones, such as occurs in a technique commonly described by a term borrowed from art, pointillism. The visual impression from an actual score is a picture of tonal particles appearing and disappearing in the outer registers of orch.l instruments, or extreme octaves on the piano keyboard. The geometry of this image is particularly striking in the appearance of the instrumental works by Webern.

radical cadence. A close—either partial or complete—formed with 2 fundamental chords.

radio opera. When radio was in its infancy, the musical community became worked up with the idea of channeling opera into homes. The utopian dream seemed to be the *renou-* *veau* of the prospect described in the novel *Look Backward: 2000–1887*, by the American writer Edward Bellamy, who was so impressed by the miracle of the telephone that he boldly prophesied that in 2000 A.D. looking backward to the year 1887, the year the novel was written, people would be able to listen to music on the telephone, with special programs transmitted from a central station each day from 5 to 7 o'clock in the evening. Radio opera did not need telephone wires, but essentially the idea was the same as Bellamy's.

Listeners still had to use earphones when excerpts from *Pagliacci* were broadcast from the Metropolitan Opera in N.Y. in 1910. The 1st complete broadcast of an opera was that of *Hänsel und Gretel*, transmitted from Covent Garden in London (1923). In 1924 *Aida* was broadcast from the Metropolitan Opera. In 1930 *Fidelio* was broadcast from Dresden by transatlantic radio. Apparently the 1st opera ever written specifically for broadcasting was Charles Wakefield Cadman's *The Willow Tree*, transmitted from N.Y., 1933.

The greatest flowering of radio opera came by way of the phonograph. With the development of long-playing records, it was possible in the 1950s to put on the air entire operas, even obscure ones, because of the fortunate arrangement whereby no royalties had to be paid for broadcasting phonograph records; this has since changed. It might seem that television would bring about a real revolution in expanding the walls of an opera house to embrace the entire world. This was not to be, however, because of the cost of television productions. The most successful opera written specially for television was *Amahl and the Night Visitors* by Menotti, commissioned by NBC in 1951 for a Christmas show and repeated annually (with few omissions) at Christmastime.

Raff, (Joseph) **Joachim,** greatly renowned Swiss pedagogue and composer; b. Lachen, near Zurich, May 27, 1822; d. Frankfurt am Main, June 24, 1882. He was educated at the Jesuit Gymnasium in Schwyz; was a schoolteacher in Rapperswill (1840–44) but pursued an interest in music; sent some of his piano pieces to Mendelssohn (1843), who recommended them for publication; having met Liszt in Basel (1845), he received his encouragement and assistance in finding employment; later was Liszt's assistant in Weimar (1850–56), where he became an ardent propagandist of the new German school of composition; then went to Wiesbaden as a piano teacher and composer; there he married the actress Doris Genast; subsequently was director of the Hoch Cons. in Frankfurt (1877–82), where he also taught composition; students flocked from many countries to study with him; these included MacDowell.

Raff was a composer of prodigious fecundity, a master of all technical aspects of composition. He wrote 214 opus numbers that were publ., and many more that remained in MS. In spite of his fame, his music fell into lamentable desuetude after his death. He publ. *Die Wagnerfrage: Wagners letzte kunstlerische Kundgebung im Lohengrin* (Braunschweig, 1854).

Raff is best known for his 11 syms., among them No. 1, *An das Vaterland* (1859–61); No. 3, *Im Walde* (1869); No. 5, *Leonore* (his most famous work; 1872); No. 7, *In den Alpen* (1875); No. 8, *Frühlingsklänge* (1876); No. 9, *Im Sommer* (1878); No. 10, *Zur Herbstzeit* (1879); No. 11, *Der Winter* (1876; unfinished; completed by M. Erdmannsdörfer); also several concert overtures; 2 violin concertos (1870–71; 1877); Piano Concerto (1873); 2 cello concertos (1874, 1876); 4 orch. suites (1863, 1871, 1874, 1877). His vocal music consists of 6 operas, various choral works with orch., and many unaccompanied choral works. He was also an active composer of chamber works, piano pieces, and arrangements. For a thematic catalogue, see A. Schafer, *Chronologisch-systematisches Verzeichnis der Werke Joachim Raffs* (Wiesbaden, 1888).

raffranando (It.). Holding back.

raga

〰〰 〰〰 〰〰 〰〰 〰〰

A system of modes used in the classical music of northern India, representing not only a succession of certain intervals (not necessarily corresponding to the tempered scale) but a meaningful relationship to spiritual values. For listeners attuned to the infinite gradations of the semantics of the ragas (Sanskrit, colors; sing. *rāg*), the correspondences exist not only with human moods, such as joy or sorrow, loneliness and waiting, love and revulsion, but also with a definite time of the day or season of the year. The playing of the ragas by native musicians assumed therefore a mystical and magical quality of meditation and communication.

The subtlety of moods and modes of the raga may well elude a Western listener; a long improvisation played on indigenous Indian string instruments (VIÑA, SITĀR, SARŌD, SĀRANGĪ, etc.), bamboo flutes, voice, and (more recently) violin, accompanied by a variety of membranophones, usually in pairs (TABLĀ or and a symbolic drone, TAMBURĀ), may be difficult to absorb because of classical Indian music's apparent lack of harmonic combinations; but such impressions are superficial. Another problem is the paradoxical combination that comprises the Indian musical aesthetic: a highly theorized system at least 1,500 and perhaps as much as 2,500 years old vs. a tradition taught orally by apprenticeship; and the desire to educate non-Indians vs. the near-impossibility of applying Western notational principles because of the improvisatory nature of the performances.

The modes of the ragas are usually pentatonic in their primary structure; supplementary tones may be added, increasing the gamut to that of 7 degrees. A rāg may exceed a range of an octave by a few pitches; many ragas differ in pitch, going up from going down, as does the Western melodic minor scale. The hierarchy of the primary and secondary tones of the ragas is strictly observed, and transitions from one rāg to another, corresponding to Western modulations, cannot be made within the same performance. The goal of improvisation is the expression of the intended meaning of a rāg; the means involve the emphasis on each note, with the appropriate ornamentation, and moving appropriately within the rāg.

The melodic improvisation requires the support of and challenge by the tablā player, who also has a system to work within, the TĀLA. The rhythmic structure of the tala is additive and cumulative; it is additive in the sense that divisions containing different numbers of beats in each are added to form a fixed rhythmic unit of considerable complexity, often making an arithmetic progression (e.g., 4 + 5; 2 + 3 + 4 + 5; 3 + 5 + 7); it is cumulative (cyclical) because such rhythmic units are repeated to form larger units. To an uninitiated listener it appears magical that a group of native performers, playing without scores and without a visible signal by a principal player, could strike several drums or sound several instruments together after a long interval of time. This ability is explained by the fact that professional musicians can conceive such units, usually up to a 16-beat (*tīn-tāl*) cycle but potentially larger. To this capacity must be added the constant rhythmic varia-

tions that are skillfully but instinctively fitted into the main metrical divisions.

The standard form of the classical Indian improvisation is as follows: 1) The opening *ālāpa*, for the melodic and drone instruments. After a musical tuning check the rāg is introduced in its basic form and improvised upon in a slow, arhythmic, meditative manner; 2) the *joḍ*(*jhālā*) or *tānam*, an improvisation with a regular pulse produced on the drone strings with repeated motives or sung with repetitive nonsense syllables; 3) the *gat* adds the tablā and tāl to the melodic instrument; the drone continues but is virtually inaudible. This final section alternates between a brief precomposed piece and free improvisation, with a friendly rivalry between melodic instrumentalist and drummer. The work concludes with a cadential formula repeated 3 times, assuring a smooth ending.

ragtime

A syncopated, primarily African-American music, popular from about 1896 to 1918. During this period the term included vocal and instrumental music and dance styles associated with the music. As an instrumental genre it existed as both a popular ballroom style and as a highly significant contribution to early jazz. In today's usage the ragtime genre refers almost exclusively to piano works.

The usual explanation for the term *ragtime* (1st used in 1896 by the black performer Ernest Hogan) is a derivation from "ragged time," i.e., syncopation. Syncopation was a prevalent component of American popular music in the 19th century, especially with the dance music and song of the black slaves and ex-slaves and its adaptation into blackface minstrelsy, notably in the music of Foster, D. D. Emmett, and others. After the Civil War black performers reasserted their musical birthright by moving into the world of minstrelsy, creating and performing vaudevillelike revues featuring the cakewalk, buck-and-wing, and walk-around dances.

As African-American minstrelsy moved into the theater in the late 19th century, songs and later instrumental pieces in syncopated quadruple or duple time became popular. The other major influence came from the march, a truly popular genre in the U.S. after the Civil War in the hands of Sousa, P. S. Gilmore, E. W. Goldman, D. W. Reeves, A. Pryor, and others. The march's emphasis on the quadruple beats and the practical use of the genre left relatively little opportunity for syncopation; but in the cakewalk, walk-around, and related black popular genres, the ragtime piano's left-hand accompaniment in the bass—the lowest single note on the downbeat, a single note on the 3rd beat, triads in higher registers on the offbeats—became standard. The melody, in 8th notes, became more syncopated, using among others the rhythms below:

Ragtime was the 1st African-American genre to attain wide popularity in the U.S. without the strongly racist overtones of blackface minstrelsy. It 1st emerged in piano playing for American saloons, barrooms, bordellos, and burlesque houses; in the vernacular such pianists were referred to as "perfessors" (professors). Later, in the compositional hands of Scott Joplin (author of *Maple Leaf Rag* and *The Entertainer*), T. Turpin, J. Scott, J. Lamb, L. Chauvin, A. Matthews, M. F. Aufderheide, and many others, ragtime could acquire a "classic" quality of elegance in moderate tempo (cf. Joplin's warning that "ragtime should never be played too fast") or a lively and even humorous quality more suitable for dancing. The rapid motion and cross-accents of ragtime proved irresistible to classical composers. Henry F. Gilbert and Ives cultivated ragtime rhythms early in the century. Ragtime became very popular in Europe as well; Debussy made use of ragtime rhythms in his *Golliwog's Cake Walk* (from *Children's Corner*); Stravinsky and others wrote pieces closely modeled on ragtime.

The proliferation of ragtime must have been pervasive, considering the outcries of shock and indignation in the music periodicals in the dying days of the 19th century. An editorial writer fulminated in an article entitled *Degenerate Music*, published in *The Musical Courier* (1899):

> A wave of vulgar, filthy, and suggestive music has inundated the land. The pabulum of theater and summer hotel orchs. is 'coon music' [heinous 19th-century epithet for black persons]. Nothing but ragtime prevails, and the cake-walk with its obscene posturings, its lewd gestures.... One reads with amazement and disgust of the historical and aristocratic name joining in this sex dance. Our children, our young men and women, are continually exposed to the contiguity, to the monotonous attrition of this vulgarizing music. It is artis-

tically and morally depressing, and should be suppressed by press and pulpit.

The monthly *Journal of the International Music Society* (1905) described ragtime in the following words: "It suggests the gait of a hurried mule among anthills; there is a cross-rhythm, with a kind of halting contrapuntal ornamentation in the accompaniment which sometimes brings a stress onto the 4th beat of the bar. The phrases, being no longer presented with regular and recurrent pulsations, give rise to a sense of disorder, which, combined with the emotional expression of the music, suggests an irresponsibility and a sense of careless jollity agreeable to the tired or vacuous brain." As late as 1916, ragtime was still a phenomenon to be abhorred, to judge by a letter to the editor publ. in the *New York Evening Sun*: "The rhythm of ragtime suggests the odor of the saloon, the smell of backyards and subways. Its style is decadent. It is music meant for tired and materially bored minds. It is essentially obvious, vulgar, and yet shockingly strong for the reason that it ends fortissimo."

But there were also some philosophically analytic voices in the press. Rupert Hughes wrote soberly in the *Musical Record of Boston* (1899): "If ragtime were called *tempo di raga* or *rague temps*, it might win honors more speedily. If the word could be allied to the harmonic rage of the East Indians, it would be more acceptable. The Negroes call their clog-dancing 'ragging' and the dance a 'rag.' There is a Spanish verb *raer* (scrape), and a French naval term, *ragué* (scraped), both doubtless from the Latin *rado*. Ragtime will find its way gradually into the works of some great genius and will thereafter be canonized, and the day will come when the decadents of the next, the 20th century, will revolt against it and will call it 'a hidebound, sapless, scholastic form, dead as its contemporaries, canon and fugue.' Meanwhile, it is young and unhackneyed, and throbbing with life. And it is racial [used positively]."

Rag-Time. Ensemble piece by Stravinsky, 1918, in which he included the cimbalom.

Raimondi, Ruggero, Italian bass; b. Bologna, Oct. 3, 1941. He was educated at the Accademia di Santa Cecilia in Rome; made his debut as Colline in Spoleto in 1964; from 1967, sang at Milan's La Scala. In 1970 he made his Metropolitan Opera debut in N.Y. as Silva in *Ernani*. His

other signal appearances were at the Paris Opéra, the Bavarian State Opera in Munich, and the Deutsche Oper in Berlin. He was distinguished in the roles of Don Giovanni and Mozart's Figaro; he was also praised for his dramatic rendition of Boris Godunov.

Raindrop Prelude. Common and unsubstantiated nickname for Chopin's Prelude in D-flat Major (No. 15, op. 28).

Legend states that Chopin composed the Prelude while waiting for George Sand and her children to return from a shopping trip on the island of Majorca, where they were living. A slow steady rain was falling, stimulating Chopin's ostinato on the dominant A flat of the tonic key; the A flat changes enharmonically to G sharp in the piece's middle section. Chopin specifically denied this story, which was circulating already during his lifetime, but picturesque sentimental tales are notoriously hard to kill.

Rainey, Ma (born Gertrude Pridgett), prominent African-American blues, jazz, and vaudeville singer; b. Columbus, Ga., Apr. 26, 1886; d. Rome, Ga., Dec. 22, 1939. She made her 1st appearance in public in Columbus when she was 12; after touring with the Rabbit Foot Minstrels and Tolliver's Circus, she organized her own Georgia Jazz Band; made numerous recordings before retiring to Columbus in 1935. Her style of blues singing influenced Bessie Smith.

Rainy Day Women #12 & #35. Bob Dylan's biggest pop hit ever, with its anthemic refrain: "Everybody must get stoned."

Raitt, Bonnie, American popular music singer and guitarist; b. Los Angeles, Nov. 8, 1949. Her father was John (Emmet) Raitt (b. Santa Ana, Calif., Jan. 29, 1917), a versatile popular singer best known for his Broadway appearances in *Oklahoma!, Carousel, Pajama Game,* and *Annie Get Your Gun.* Bonnie took up the guitar when she was 12; after attending Radcliffe College (1967–69) she departed the academic scene to pursue a career as a recording artist, mixing blues, rock, and ballads. She made a number of fine albums, including *Give It Up* (1972) and *Sweet Forgiveness* (1977). She never attained the commercial heights expected of her; her career was derailed for a time by alcoholism, but she fought her way back to sobriety and success. In 1990 she captured 4 Grammy Awards, including best album of the year for *Nick of Time* (1989). She has since released *Luck of the Draw* (1991) and *Longing in Their Hearts* (1994).

Rake's Progress, The. Opera by Stravinsky, 1951, 1st performed in Venice. The libretto, in English, was written by W. H. Auden and Chester Kallman; the title is taken from a series of satirical lithographs by the 18th-century artist Hogarth. The story is a parable; the rake of the title is led into a series of adventures. He marries a bearded lady of the circus and invests a fortune in a device that grinds stones into flour and makes bread. He gambles for his soul with the devil, and though the devil loses, the rake loses his mind. The moral, pronounced in the epilogue, is very much in the manner of 18th-century fabulists: "For idle hearts and hands and minds, the devil finds work to do."

The music is set in a neo-Baroque manner, with an ostentatious cultivation of formal arias, recitatives, choral intermezzos, and other settecento accoutrements. But the rhythmic scheme is alive with angularities and asymmetries in the characteristic Stravinskyian vein. The counterpoint is acrid and dissonant, the texture pandiatonic, the orchestration economical, with the harpsichord (with a written-out part) serving as the connective tissue of the musical organism.

Rákóczy March. A celebrated Hungarian piece with great patriotic associations. Francis II Rákóczy (1676–1735) was the leader of the 1703 Hungarian rebellion against the Austrians, but the tune bearing his name did not appear until a century later. János Bihari, a Hungarian Gypsy violinist attached to a Hungarian regiment during the Napoleonic wars, is credited with the composition of the march. It was 1st printed in 1820 in a collection of popular Army marches and quickly became a favorite. Liszt played it as a piano solo during his tour of Hungary in 1838, and later incorporated it in his *Hungarian Rhapsody* No. 15. Berlioz arranged the *Rákóczy March* for orch. in 1846 under the title *Marche Hongroise*; he also included it as a separate number in his dramatic legend *The Damnation of Faust*.

Raksin, David, American composer for films; b. Philadelphia, Aug. 4, 1912. He studied piano in his childhood and also learned to play woodwind instruments from his father, a performer and conductor; when barely past puberty he organized his own jazz band. In 1931 he entered the Univ. of Pa.; also studied composition privately with Isadore Freed (1934–35). In 1935 he went to Hollywood to assist Charlie Chaplin with the music for his film *Modern Times* (which he later orchestrated with Edward Powell); this provided Raksin a wonderful companionship with the great comedian. Raksin wrote a delectable piece of reminiscences, *Life with Charlie* (*Quarterly Journal of the Library of Congress*, 1983). When Chaplin was forced into exile by the Red-baiters of the U.S. Congress for his alleged radical activities, Raksin struck out on his own, including private studies with Schoenberg.

He composed more than 100 film scores, some of which attained great popularity; his greatest success was the theme song for *Laura*—ingratiatingly melodious in its sinuous and convoluted pattern, it generated more than 300 different versions. Apart from his activities as a composer and conductor, he appeared as an actor and commentator in television programs. Using material from his film music, he composed several symphonic suites, among them *Forever Amber* and *The Bad and the Beautiful*. Other scores were *Force of Evil*, *Carrie*, *The Redeemer*, and *Separate Tables*. He also wrote incidental music, symphonic pieces, and vocal works, including *Oedipus memneitai* (Oedipus Remembers) for Bass-baritone Narrator/Soloist, 6-Part Mixed Chorus, and Chamber Ensemble (1986). At the request of Stravinsky, he made the original band instrumentation of *Circus Polka* for Balanchine's production with the Barnum and Bailey Circus. He taught at the Univ. of Southern Calif.; also taught film and television composition at the Univ. of Calif., Los Angeles, and was on the faculty of the Univ. of Southern Calif. School of Public Administration (1968–89).

rallentando (*ralenti*; It.; abbrev. rall.). Gradually becoming LENTO. A distinction is sometimes made between rallentando and RITENUTO; the former is a gradual process lasting several measures, while the latter requires a more or less sudden slackening of the tempo.

rallentare (It.). Grow slower. *Senza rallentare*, without slackening the pace.

Rameau, Jean-Philippe

Great French composer, organist, and music theorist; b. Dijon (baptized), Sept. 25, 1683; d. Paris, Sept. 12, 1764. His father was organist of St. Étienne in Dijon. He learned to play the harpsichord as a small child; from age 10 to 14 he attended the Jesuit Collège des Godrans in Dijon, where he took up singing and composing instead of concentrating on his academic studies; at 18 his father sent him to Milan, where he stayed for only a brief time before joining the orch. of a traveling French opera troupe as a violinist. In 1702 he received a temporary appointment as organist at Avignon Cathedral; later that year he became organist at Clermont Cathedral. By 1706 he was in Paris, where he publ. his 1st *Livre de pièces de clavecin*; was active there as a church organist until 1708.

He succeeded his father as organist at Notre Dame Cathedral in Avignon in 1709; became organist to the Jacobins in Lyons in 1713; then was organist at Clermont Cathedral (1715–23); there he wrote his famous *Traité de l'harmonie* (Paris, 1722). This epoch-making work, though little understood at the time, attracted considerable attention and roused opposition, so that when he settled definitely in Paris (1723) he was by no means unknown. The fact that he failed in 1727 in a competition for the position of organist at St.-Vincent-de-Paul did not injure his reputation, for it was generally known that Marchand (probably out of jealousy) had exerted his powerful influence in favor of Daquin, who was in every respect inferior to Rameau.

In 1732 Rameau became organist at Ste.-Croix-de-la-Bretonnerie and soon was recognized as the foremost organist in France. In 1726 appeared his *Nouveau système de musique théorique*, an introduction to the *Traité*. The leading ideas of his system of harmony are: chord-building by 3rds; classification of a chord and all its inversions as one and the same, thus reducing the multiplicity of consonant and dissonant combinations to a fixed and limited number of root chords; and his invention of a fundamental bass (*basse fondamentale*), an imaginary series of root tones forming the real basis of the varied chord progressions employed in a composition. The stir these novel theories occasioned, and his reputation as the foremost French organist, by no means satisfied Rameau's ambition; his ardent desire was to bring out a dramatic work at the Opéra.

He had made a modest beginning with incidental music to Alexis Piron's comedy *L'Endriague* in 1723.

After contributing further incidental music to Piron's comedies *L'Enrôlement d'Arlequin* (1726) and *La Robe de dissension, ou Le Faux Prodigue* (1726), he became music master to the wife of the "fermier-général" La Pouplinière; the latter obtained from Voltaire a libretto for *Samson*, which Rameau set to music; but it was rejected on account of its biblical subject and is now lost. A 2nd libretto, by Abbé Pellegrin, was accepted, and *Hippolyte et Aricie* was produced at the Opéra in 1733; its reception was cool, despite undeniable superiority over the operas of Lully and his following.

Rameau considered abandoning composing any further works for the theater, but the persuasions of his friends, who also influenced public opinion in his favor, were effective; in 1735 he brought out the successful opera-ballet *Les Indes galantes*, and in 1737 his masterpiece, *Castor et Pollux*, a work that for years held its own beside the operas of Gluck. A career of uninterrupted prosperity commenced; he was recognized as the leading theorist of the time, and his instruction was eagerly sought; for the next 30 years his operas dominated the French stage; he was named Compositeur du cabinet du roy in 1745, and was ennobled 4 months before his death.

From the beginning of his dramatic career Rameau roused opposition and at the same time found ardent admirers. The 1st war of words was waged between the "Lullistes" and the "Ramistes." This had scarcely been ended by a triumphant revival of *Pygmalion* (1748) in 1751 when the production of Pergolesi's *La Serva padrona* (1752) caused a more prolonged and bitter controversy between the adherents of Rameau and the "Encyclopedistes," a struggle known as the GUERRE DES BOUFFONS in which Rameau participated by writing numerous essays defending his position. Practically the same charges were made against him as would be made a century later against Wagner: unintelligible harmony, lack of melody, preponderance of discords, noisy instrumentation, etc. But when 25 years later the war between Gluckists and Piccinnists was raging, Rameau's works were praised as models of beauty and perfection.

It is a matter for regret that Rameau was indifferent to the quality of his librettos; he relied so much upon his musical inspiration that he never could be brought to a realization of the importance of a good text; hence the inequality of his operas. Nevertheless, his operas mark a decided advance over Lully's in musical characterization, expressive melody, richness of harmony, variety of modulation, and expert and original instrumentation.

Rameau wrote other important theoretical treatises, including *Génération harmonique ou Traité de musique théorique et pratique* (1737); *Prospectus, où l'on propose au public, par voye de souscription, un code de musique pratique, composé de sept méthodes* (1757); *Réponse de M. Rameau à MM. les éditeurs de l'Encyclopédie* (1757); *Lettre à M. d'Alembert sur ses opinions en musique* (1760).

Rameau wrote 30 sung dramas, premiered in Paris or Versailles, in various genres (tragédie en musique, opéra-ballet, comédie-ballet, ballet-héroïque, divertissment, acte de ballet, pastorale, pastorale-héroïque, opéra comique en vaudevilles, tragédie lyrique, ballets, intermède en musique). He also contributed incidental music for several comedies by A. Piron. Rameau wrote a relatively small amount of secular and sacred vocal music. His best-known instrumental pieces are the harpsichord works, many with amusing descriptive titles: *Premier livre de pièces de clavecin* (1706); *Pièces de clavecin avec une méthode sur la mécanique des doigts* (1724; rev. 1731 as *Pièces de clavecin avec une table pour les agréments*); *Nouvelles suites de pièces de clavecin* (1728?); *Cinq pièces pour clavecin seul, extraites des Pièces de clavecin en concerts* (1741). Chamber music: *Pièces de clavecin en concerts* for Harpsichord, Violin or Flute, and Viol or Violin (1741).

Ramey, Samuel (Edward), outstanding American bass; b. Colby, Kans., Mar. 28, 1942. He attended Kansas State Univ., then studied voice with Arthur Newman at Wichita State Univ. (B.Mus., 1968); after singing with the Grass Roots Opera Co. in Raleigh, N.C. (1968–69), he continued his studies with Armen Boyajian in N.Y. He made his professional operatic debut as Zuniga in Carmen at the N.Y. City Opera (1973), and within a few seasons established himself as its principal bass; also made guest appearances at the Glyndebourne Festival (1976), the Netherlands Opera in Amsterdam (1978), the Hamburg State Opera (1978), Milan's La Scala (1981), and the Vienna State Opera (1981). In 1984 he made a brilliant debut at the Metropolitan Opera in N.Y. as Argante in Handel's *Rinaldo*. He subsequently appeared with leading opera houses around the world, and was engaged as a soloist with the major orchs. Among his notable roles are Leporello, Don Giovanni, Figaro, Gounod's Mephistopheles, the 4 villains in *Les Contes d'Hoffmann*,

Attila, and Boito's Mefistofele; he sang the role of Figaro for the soundtrack recording of the award-winning film *Amadeus* (1984).

Rampal, Jean-Pierre (Louis), celebrated French flutist, conductor, and teacher; b. Marseilles, Jan. 7, 1922. He studied flute as a child with his father, 1st flutist in the Marseilles orch. and a prof. at the Cons.; then studied medicine until being drafted for military service by the German occupation authorities in 1943; when he learned that he was to be sent to Germany as a forced laborer, he went AWOL; subsequently attended flute classes at the Paris Cons., winning the *premier prix* in 5 months. He played solo flute in the orch. of the Vichy Opera (1946–50);

Jean-Pierre Rampal

COURTESY FRANK DRIGGS COLLECTION

concurrently began to tour, often in duo recitals with the pianist and harpsichordist Robert Veyron-Lacroix. He was solo flutist in the orch. of the Paris Opéra from 1956 to 1962, and also became a popular artist on the Paris Radio. He subsequently toured throughout the world with phenomenal success as a virtuoso, appearing as soloist with all the major orchs. and in innumerable recitals. In later years he also appeared as a guest conductor. He taught at the Paris Cons., and gave master classes worldwide.

His repertoire is vast, ranging from the Baroque masters to jazz, from the music of Japan to that of India, from arrangements to specially commissioned works. Of the last, such composers as Poulenc and Jolivet wrote pieces for him. Through his countless concerts and recordings he did more than any other flutist of his time to bring his instrument into the mainstream of musical life. He was made a Chevalier of the Legion d'Honneur in 1966 and an Officier des Arts et Lettres in 1971.

ranchera (Sp.). Argentine rural dance in 3/4 time associated with the pampas (prairie) region.

rank. A row of organ pipes. A mixture stop is said to have 2, 3, or more ranks, according to the number of pipes sounded by each key.

rant. An old country dance, or a REEL. It was used in instrumental suites by 17th-century English composers.

ranz des vaches (Fr.; Ger. *Kuhreigen*). One of the airs sung, or played on the alpine horn, in the Swiss Alps as a call to the cattle. The tune itself is marked by an asymmetrical rhythm; it appears to lean toward the Lydian mode, with the characteristic augmented 4th as the formative melodic interval. A version of the ranz des vaches appears in print in the 16th century. It is also supposed to have magic and curative qualities and is often combined with religious motives.

rap. A style of urban black popular music that emerged in the mid-1970s characterized by (often) improvised rhymes performed to a rhythmic accompaniment; frequently performed a cappella, with sexual, socially relevant, or political lyrics. The music itself became known as HIP-HOP.

Rape of Lucretia, The. Opera by Britten, 1946, 1st performed at the Glyndebourne Festival. This is Britten's 1st chamber opera, with a small orch. and small number of roles (the "chorus" is represented by 2 soloists, male and female). Based on an ancient legend, the opera glorifies the "Christian" virtue of Lucretia, who, awaiting her husband returning from war, is confronted by Tarquinius, the Roman Commander. Imperiously he demands that she submit to him; when she refuses, he rapes her. Later, when her husband returns, she recounts her tragedy and shame to him before sinking a dagger into her breast. The musical idiom of the score is philosophically restrained, quite in opposition to the melodramatic Italian style of treating similar subjects.

rapido (It.). Rapidly.

Rappresentazione di anima e di corpo, La. Rappresentazione sacra by Emilio de' Cavalieri (b. *c.* 1550; d. Rome, Mar. 11, 1602). This monodic work represents the 1st theatrical application of the SECONDA PRATTICA to religious themes. The title reflects the content, a dramatic parable of the soul and body, in which metaphysical and abstract entities such as Virtue and Valor take part, much like a medieval mystery play.

rappresentazione sacra (It., sacred performance). A religious spectacle; a distinct theatrical genre in Florence beginning in the 15th century. Musically it contained a succession of polyphonic canzonas. The 1st monodic exemplar of the genre was *La Rappresentazione di anima e di corpo*, 1600, by Cavalieri; this work was a predecessor to the Italian *historia* and ORATORIO as well as the Viennese *sepolochro*.

rapsodie (Fr.). A RHAPSODY.

Rapsodie Espagnole. Orch. suite by Ravel, 1908, premiered in Paris. The 4 movements reflect Ravel's fascination with Spanish dance rhythms and modalities.

Rapsodie Nègre. Work for baritone and ensemble by Poulenc, 1917, marked by inventive and fresh exoticism. It was premiered in Paris.

rasch (Ger.). Fast; ALLEGRO. *Noch rascher*, still faster; *so rasch wie möglich*, as fast as possible.

rasgueado (Sp., ripping). A rapid strum across the guitar strings, downward or upward, using certain fingers; the strums are often grouped and usually stopped rather than allowed to sound after the last (or only) strum.

Rasoumowsky Quartets (*Razumovsky Quartets*). The name given to Beethoven's 3 String Quartets, op. 59. Count Rasoumowsky was the Russian ambassador to Vienna who liked to play the violin. The result demonstrates how immortality could be bought by commissioning a great composer to dedicate a piece to an important official or a wealthy man. Beethoven used in the 1st 2 quartets of this group a Russian popular song which he picked up from a German collection. For this reason the *Rasoumowsky Quartets* are also known as the *Russian Quartets*.

raspa. Cuban ballroom dance, usually in 6/8 time and rapid tempo.

Rassel (Ger.). Rattle; a shaken idiophone.

rastral (from Lat. *rastrum*, rake; Ger. *Raster*). Tool for drawing the 5-line music staff in one sweep.

ratamacue. A drumming rudiment, in the rhythm

rataplan. A drumming rudiment, in the rhythm

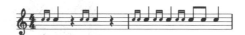

ratchet (Ger. *Ratsche*). An idiophone that consists of a wooden tablet; scraped by a cogwheel, it produces a grating trill. R. Strauss uses it in his *Till Eulenspiegels* and *Don Quixote*.

Rätselkanon (Ger.). PUZZLE CANON.

Ratsmusiker (Ger.). Town musicians, engaged by German municipalities to blow fanfares from the platform of the city hall.

Rattle, Simon (Denis), brilliant English conductor; b. Liverpool, Jan. 19, 1955. He began playing piano and percussion as a child; appeared as a percussionist with the Royal Liverpool Phil. when he was 11 and was a percussionist in the National Youth Orch.; also took up conducting in his youth and was founder-conductor of the Liverpool Sinfonia (1970–72); concurrently studied at the Royal Academy of Music in London (1971–74). After winning 1st prize in the John Player International Conductors' Competition (1974), he was assistant conductor of the Bournemouth Sym. Orch. and Sinfonietta (1974–76); made his 1st tour of the U.S. conducting the London Schools Sym. Orch. (1976). In 1977 he conducted at the Glyndebourne Festival; then was assistant conductor of the Royal Liverpool Phil. (1977–80) and the BBC Scottish Sym. Orch. in Glasgow (1977–80). He made his 1st appearance as a guest conductor of a U.S. orch. with the Los Angeles Phil. in 1979; was its principal guest conductor (from 1981); also appeared as a guest conductor with other U.S. orchs., as well as with those in Europe. In 1980 he became principal conductor of the City of Birmingham Sym. Orch.; led it on its 1st tour of the U.S. in 1988. In 1987 he was made a Commander of the Order of the British Empire.

Rauscher (Ger.). Rapidly repeated notes; a term used in the 18th century.

Rauschpfeife (Ger.). Renaissance German reed-cap SHAWM family with a nonflaring bell. They were held like recorders and played by RATSMUSIKER and others on festive occasions.

Ravel, (Joseph) Maurice

Great French composer; b. Ciboure, Basses-Pyrénées, Mar. 7, 1875; d. Paris, Dec. 28, 1937. His father was a Swiss engineer and his mother was of Basque origin. The family moved to Paris when he was an infant. He began to study piano at the age of 7 with Henri Ghis and harmony at 12 with Charles-René. After further piano studies with Emile Descombes, he entered the Paris Cons. as a pupil of Eugène Anthiome in 1889; won 1st medal (1891) and passed to the advanced class of Charles de Bériot; also studied harmony with Emile Pessard. He left the Cons. in 1895 and that same year completed work on his song *Un Grand Sommeil noir*, the *Menuet antique* for Piano, and the *Habanera* for 2 Pianos (later orchestrated for the *Rapsodie espagnole*); these pieces, written at the age of 20, already reveal great originality in the treatment of old modes and of Spanish motifs; however, he continued to study; in 1897 he returned to the Cons. to study with Fauré (composition) and Gédalge (counterpoint and orchestration); his well-known *Pavane pour une infante défunte* for piano was written during that time (1899).

In 1899 he conducted the premiere of his overture *Shéhérazade* in Paris; some elements of this work were incorporated in his song cycle of the same name (1903). In 1901 he won the 2nd Prix de Rome with the cantata *Myrrha*; ensuing attempts to win the Grand Prix de Rome were unsuccessful; at his last try (1905) he was eliminated in the preliminaries and so was not allowed to compete; the age limit then set an end to his further effort to enter. Since 6 prizes all went to pupils of Lenepveu, suspicion of discrimination was aroused; Jean Marnold publ. an article, "Le Scandale du Prix de Rome," in the *Mercure de France* (1905) in which he brought the controversy into the open; this precipitated a crisis at the Cons.; its director, Theodore Dubois, resigned, and Fauré took his place. By that time Ravel had written a number of his most famous compositions and was regarded by most French critics as a talented disciple of Debussy.

No doubt Ravel's method of poetic association of musical ideas paralleled that of Debussy; his employment of unresolved dissonances and the enhancement of the diatonic style into pandiatonicism were techniques common to Debussy and his followers; some of Ravel's expression marks were in the spirit of the period, e.g., *en demi-teinte et d'un rythme las* (half-tinted and in a weary rhythm). But there were important differences: whereas Debussy adopted the scale of whole tones as an integral part of his musical vocabulary, Ravel resorted to it only occasionally; similarly, augmented triads appear much less frequently in Ravel's music than in Debussy's; in his writing for piano Ravel actually anticipated some of Debussy's usages; in a letter addressed to Pierre Lalo and publ. in *Le Temps* (1907), Ravel pointed out that at the time of the publication of his piano piece *Jeux d'eau* (1902) Debussy had brought out only his suite *Pour le piano*, which had contained little that was novel.

In Paris, elsewhere in France, and soon in England and other European countries, Ravel's name became well known, but for many years he was still regarded as an ultramodernist. A curious test of audience appreciation was a "Concert des Auteurs Anonymes" presented by the Soc. Indépendante de Musique in 1911; the program included Ravel's *Valses nobles et sentimentales*, a set of piano pieces in the manner of Schubert; yet Ravel was recognized as the author. Inspired evocation of the past was but one aspect of Ravel's creative genius; in this style are his *Pavane pour une infante defunte*, *Le Tombeau de Couperin*, and *La Valse*; luxuriance of exotic colors marks his ballet *Daphnis et Chloé*, his opera *L'Heure espagnole*, the song cycles *Shéhérazade* and *Chansons madécasses*, and his virtuoso pieces for piano *Miroirs* and *Gaspard de la nuit*; other works are deliberately austere, even ascetic, in their pointed classicism: the piano concertos, the piano Sonatine, and some of his songs with piano accompaniment.

His association with Diaghilev's Ballets Russes was most fruitful; for Diaghilev he wrote one of his masterpieces, *Daphnis et Chloé*; another ballet, *Boléro*, commissioned by Ida Rubinstein and performed at her dance recital at the Paris Opéra (1928), became Ravel's most spectacular success as an orch. piece; its relentless ostinato-driven crescendo was irresistible to all but the composer, who complained bitterly of its musical limitations, all the way to *la banque*. Ravel was also an original orchestrator who developed textures both sensuous and transparent; in addition to orchestrating 8 of his own piano works, some songs, and *Tzigane*, he arranged works by Rimsky-Korsakov, Satie, Schumann, Chabrier, and Mussorgsky, most notably the *Pictures at an Exhibition* (orig. for piano; 1922).

Ravel never married, was for the most part extremely shy, and lived a life of semiretirement, devoting most of his time to composition; he accepted virtually no pupils, although he gave friendly advice to Vaughan Williams, Gershwin, and others; he was never on the faculty of any school. As a performer he was not brilliant; he appeared as a pianist only in his own works, and often accompanied singers in programs of his songs; although he accepted engagements as a conductor, his technique was barely sufficient to secure a perfunctory performance of his music. When World War I broke out in 1914, he was rejected for military service because of his frail physique, but he was anxious to serve; his application for air service was denied but he was received in the ambulance corps at the front; his health gave way, and in the autumn of 1916 he was compelled to enter a hospital for recuperation.

In 1922 he visited Amsterdam and Venice, conducting his music; in 1923 he appeared in London; in 1926 he went to Sweden, England, and Scotland; in 1928 he made an American tour as a conductor and pianist; in the same

year he received the degree of D.Mus. honoris causa at Oxford Univ. In 1929 he was honored by his native town by

Maurice Ravel

the inauguration of the Quai Maurice Ravel. In 1932 he was apparently uninjured in an automobile accident, but the event seemed to contribute to his final illness: difficulties in muscular coordination, attacks of aphasia, and headaches; at the time he thought he had "cerebral anemia," but the illness is now believed to have been Pick's disease. His last new work, *Don Quichotte à Dulcinée* for Baritone and Orch. (1932–33), was followed by several abortive projects. He declined steadily; he underwent brain surgery in Dec. 1937 but it was not successful; he died 9 days later.

Among Ravel's other notable works are *L'Enfant et les sortilèges* (fantaisie lyrique, 1920–25); 2 violin sonatas (1897; 1923–27); *Introduction et Allegro* for Harp, Flute, Clarinet, and String Quartet (1907); Piano Trio (1914), Sonata for Violin and Cello (1920–22); *Trois poèmes de Stéphane Mallarmé* for Voice and Ensemble (1914). Voice and piano: *5 Popular Greek Songs* (1904–1906), *Histoires naturelles* (1907); *2 Hebrew Songs* (1914).

---

ravvivando (It.). Reviving. *Ravvivando il tempo*, accelerate the tempo.

Ray. Stands for *Re* in TONIC SOL-FA.

Razor Quartet (Ger. *Rasiermesserquartett*). String quartet by Haydn, late 1780s, in F minor (op. 55, no. 2). The nickname has an apocryphal story behind it: Haydn was so dis-

turbed by the bluntness of his straight razor that he exclaimed, "I will give my best string quartet for a new razor." A London publisher named John Bland overheard him, offered, and later made the exchange. That Haydn would choose to give him a minor-key work is open to interpretation.

Razumovsky, Count (later Prince) **Andrei.** See BEETHOVEN, LUDWIG VAN; *Rasoumowsky Quartets*.

Re (It.; Fr. Ré). The 2nd of the Aretinian syllables and the name of the note *D* in France, Italy, etc.

Re Pastore, Il. Opera by Mozart, 1775, premiered in Salzburg. The setting follows the conventional pastoral drama in which true love is tested by the obstacles before him. Not a major work of Mozart's, it has some fine set numbers.

Read, Daniel, important American tunebook compiler and composer; b. Attleboro, Mass., Nov. 16, 1757; d. New Haven, Conn., Dec. 4, 1836. He worked on a farm as a youth; studied mechanics, and was employed as a surveyor at 18; began to compose at 17. He served in the Continental Army as a private; at 21 he settled at New Stratford; later went to New Haven. In 1782–83 he maintained a singing school on the North River. He also was a comb maker. At his death, he left a collection of some 400 tunes by him and other composers. He publ. *The American Singing Book, or a New and Easy Guide to the Art of Psalmody, Devised for the Use of Singing Schools in America* (New Haven, 1785; 5th ed., 1795); the *American Musical Magazine* (containing New England church music; compiled with Amos Doolittle; New Haven, 12 numbers, 1786–87); Supplement to *The American Singing Book* (New Haven, 1787); *The Columbian Harmonist* (3 vols., 1793–95); *The New Haven Collection of Sacred Music* (New Haven, 1818).

realism. A musical aesthetic adopted by 19th-century composers determined to bring music closer to humanity. It differs from simple imitation of sounds in character pieces such as *The Music Box, The Nightingale, The Brook,* and *The Cuckoo*; it rather attempts to reflect in musical terms the reality of existence. Realism finds its most logical application in vocal music, particularly in opera. The emergence of DRAMMA PER MUSICA was prompted by the desire to express the inflections of common speech in music. Among early opera composers Caccini stated his aim as creating a melody "by means of which it would be possible to speak in musical tones." His contemporary Peri spoke of applying in opera "the accents which we unintentionally employ at moments of profound emotion." Gluck and Berlioz declared similar beliefs decades later; Wagner sought to intensify the power of ordinary speech, but his use of leitmotivs precluded true realism. It was left to the Russian composers of the National School, particularly Dargomyzhsky and Mussorgsky, to declare their determination to articulate in popular Russian accents the arias and particularly the recitatives in their operas; in this they opposed the Italian and the German ideals of music for music's sake.

The Italian operatic realism found its application in the school of VERISMO. A specific type of realism motivated by a political purpose arose in the Soviet Union under the somewhat specious genre of SOCIALIST REALISM. A modern excrescence of musical realism is vocal surrealism, in which accents of common speech are intentionally displaced. Stravinsky subjected the natural inflections of Russian speech in the vocal parts of his *Les Noces* to surrealistic distortions. In the score of his opera *The Rake's Progress* he departs completely from the natural prose of the English libretto, shifting the accents toward the weak syllables in order to produce the effect of forceful angularity.

realization. 1. A written-out basso continuo part, designed for those inexperienced in performing with figured bass. 2. An edited arrangement of an old work; an adaptation for a specific purpose. This term came into use in the 20th century, favored particularly by English composers and arrangers. An arrangement requires complete fidelity to at least the melody, rhythm, and harmony of the original, whereas a realization has a greater degree of freedom in transcribing the original work. 3. The creation of a whole, playable composition from an unfinished score or sketches. 4. The modern practice, responsive to indeterminate compositional procedures, of carrying out instructions, either explicitly or implicitly indicated in a given score, to perform a composition.

rebab. RABĀB.

rebec. A precursor of the violin that originated in Islamic nations in Asia. It found its way to Spain and into France, where it remained popular until the violin displaced it. It had only 3 strings and was pear-shaped and long-necked. This instrument was also know by the Arabic name, RABĀB.

recapitulation. A return of the initial section (EXPOSITION) of a movement in sonata form.

recessional. A hymn sung in church during the departure of choir and clergy after a service.

recht (Ger.). Right. *Recht Hand*, right hand.

recital. A concert at which either (*a*) all pieces are executed by one soloist (or solo performer with accompanist), or (*b*) all pieces are by 1 composer. The word was invented by the manager of Liszt's concert appearances in London to convey a suggestion of a narrative and so to please romantically inclined music lovers. The term is not applied to a concert by a trio, quartet, etc.

recitando (It.). In declamatory style.

recitative (Fr. *récitatif*, Ger. *Recitativ*, It. *recitativo*). 1. A musical narrative, as contrasted with arias and other formal parts in an opera or oratorio, which carries the action from one aria to another. In early opera *recitativo secco* (dry) was the common practice, with singers reciting a musical phrase following the accents and inflections of the spoken language accompanied by and alternating with a bare minimum of chords played on the harpsichord. In Classic opera Mozart and others experimented with *recitativo accompagnato* (accompanied), where the vocal line was supported by an economical use of the full orch. In the 19th century the demarcation between the accompanied recitative and the aria began to blur, until in Wagner's music dramas they coalesced into one continuous song, the "endless melody." *Recitativo instrumentato*, a recitative-like effect in instrumental music, either by an instrument playing solo in an ensemble piece or, in piano playing, a crisp delivery of the melody, free in tempo and rhythm.

reciting note. In plainchant, the tonus on which most of each verse (psalm or canticle) is continuously recited; usually the dominant above the tonus.

record album. 1. Orig., the bound holder for 78-rpm discs, whether for a single work or a collection. 2. A long-playing 33 1/3-rpm disc, containing 1 or more works performed by the same artist or group, in the same genre, from a soundtrack, etc.

record player. PHONOGRAPH.

recorder (Fr. *flûte à bec*; Ger. *Blockflöte*; It. *flauto dritto*). An end-blown vertical flute with a whistle mouthpiece popular during the Baroque period; later superseded by the transverse flute. Recorders of all compasses, from bass to treble, were used as solo instruments in chamber ensembles, under such names as sopranino, sopranino recorder, descant, treble recorder, and *flauto d'Eco*, which is included in Bach's *4th Brandenburg Concerto*. After being dormant for over a century, a spectacular revival of recorders took place in the 20th century, fostered by archeophiliac performers and instrument makers; at 1st the movement was primarily pedagogical in nature (e.g., the works by Hindemith and colleagues), but it later involved the reincarnation of early music in an "authentic" form. This rebirth also engendered the composition of many new works for the instrument.

records. See PHONOGRAPH.

reco-reco. Afro-Brazilian guiro; a scraper made of a hollowed-out gourd with carved notches or ridges on its surface; the sound is produced by a rubbing stick. Like many similar instruments throughout the world, it is used for sharp rhythmic effects in indigenous and popular music.

recte et retro (Lat., forth and back). A RETROGRADE canon in which the subject is combined simultaneously with its own retrograde. It is a most ingenious species of the type of mirror canon in which 2 players read the same page from opposite sides, or else turn the page upside down and have one performer read it in the mirror as the other reads the original, with the same results.

rectus modus (Lat., straight motion). The forward-moving version of a melody or other patterns, as opposed to its RETROGRADE.

recueilli (Fr., collected). Meditative.

Red Mass. A solemn Roman Catholic votive Mass, in which the celebrants wear red vestments. Such a Mass is celebrated at the openings of congresses, courts, and councils, as well as for some martyred saints.

Red Mill, The. Operetta by V. Herbert, 1906. Two American tourists are stranded without funds at the hostelry "The Sign of the Red Mill." A young Dutch woman is being held a virtual prisoner there by her imperious suitor who is governor of the province, whereas she wants to marry a youth of her own choosing. The Americans help her escape by placing her on the arm of a rotating windmill. Her chosen suitor turns out to be an heir to a fortune and is able to win his bride through social pressure. One of the score's most popular songs is *The Isle of Our Dreams*.

Red Pony, The. Soundtrack by Copland, 1948, for the film based on John Steinbeck's story about a young boy on a ranch and his pet horse. A suite drawn from the soundtrack was 1st performed in Houston.

Red Poppy, The. Ballet by Glière, 1927, 1st performed in Moscow. The title symbolizes the blossoming of the revolutionary sentiment among downtrodden Chinese. The score includes a *Sailor's Dance*, based on a popular Soviet song; there are also snatches of the *Internationale*. In the apotheosis the visiting Soviet sailors and Chinese proletarians swear an eternal friendship.

Redding, Otis, popular African-American rhythm-and-blues and soul singer and songwriter; b. Dawson, Ga., Sept. 9, 1941; d. in an airplane crash near Madison, Wis., Dec. 10, 1967. He sang in church, took part in revival meetings, and adopted the "shouting" manner of projection. His early record *Shout Bamalama* is a fair example of this technique. He then progressed toward a more refined type of gospel and soul singing, and in 1966 issued an album called *Dictionary of Soul*. His 1967 performance at the Monterey Pop Festival was recorded on film and remains a powerful sampling of his art; his loss at 26 was widely mourned and commemorated. Redding's most successful hits, sung in a powerful baritone voice, include *Respect, (Sittin' on) The Dock of the Bay, Try a Little Tenderness, Shake, Mr. Pitiful, I've Been Loving You Too Long,* and *Tramp* (with Carla Thomas).

Redman, Don(ald Matthew), African-American jazz instrumentalist, composer-arranger, and bandleader; b. Piedmont, W.Va., July 29, 1900; d. N.Y., Nov. 30, 1964. He began his studies on trumpet as a child; eventually mastered all the wind instruments. He was an arranger for Fletcher Henderson's band (1924–27), then directed McKinney's Cotton Pickers; worked with the Dorsey Brothers, Jack Teagarden, Coleman Hawkins, Fats Waller; also arranged for Paul Whiteman, Ellington, Ben Pollack, and others. He toured Europe with his own band (1946–47); then appeared on television and served as music director for Pearl Bailey. His arrangement of *Deep Purple* for Jimmy Dorsey became a major hit. He personally taught or indirectly influenced many important arrangers.

redoublé (Fr. doubled). Play twice as fast. *Marche redoublée*, a rapid march.

redowa. A Bohemian dance, like the mazurka, though less strongly accented, in 3/4 or 3/8 time and lively tempo. It was popular in 19th-century Europe.

reduce. In organ music, a direction to decrease the volume of tone by retiring the louder stops.

reduction. Rearrangement of a composition for a smaller number of instruments while preserving its form as far as possible; the term is used more in French, as *réduction pour la piano.*

redundancy. In electronics guidance systems, redundancy is a safety factor in the proper functioning of the machine. If a part fails, its redundant replacement immediately goes into action; and if that one fails, still another part is activated to perform the same function. In music, redundancy is represented by an ostentatious repetition of a thematic motive. It has its application in serial complexes of intervallic, rhythmic, and coloristic parameters. By assigning a certain interval for a redundant use by an instrument, an associative equation is established, so that the interval becomes the identifying motto of the instrument itself. Some serial composers assign a single note to an instrument, so that the instrument and the note become inalienably bound. This evokes the memories and practices of serf orchs. in Czarist Russia, consisting of wind instruments, of which each could produce but a single note, so that each serf playing that instrument often became known under the nickname of E-flat, F-sharp, etc. (When several serfs escaped from the estate of a music-loving Russian landlord, he put out an official notice asking the police to be on the lookout for the fugitives, giving their musical names as identification.)

reed. A flexible thin strip of cane, wood, or metal attached to the open end of a woodwind instrument so that the opening is almost completely closed; this aperture is set by an air current in vibration, which it communicates to an enclosed column (organ, etc.), long pipe with a series of holes that can be covered to obtain different notes (clarinet, oboe, etc.), or directly to the free air, thus producing a musical tone. (In playing a brass instrument, the lips perform the function of the reeds.) Reed instruments are commonly divided into two categories, single reeds (clarinet, saxophone, modern tárogató) and double reeds (oboe, bassoon, crumhorn, shawm, racket). In a double reed the 2 reeds vibrate against each other. Reeds made of a hard metal which produce only 1 pitch are used in the harmonium, accordion, regal, and organ reed stops. A *free reed* vibrates within the aperture without striking the edges; a *beating reed* strikes on the edges.

reed instrument. One whose tone is produced by the vibration of a reed (sometimes 2 reeds) in its mouthpiece or at one end of its air supply chamber.

Reed, Lou(is Alan). See VELVET UNDERGROUND.

reed organ. A keyboard instrument whose tones are produced by free reeds: the HARMONIUM (invented 1843 by A. Debain of Paris), the bellows forcing compressed air outward through the reeds; and the AMERICAN ORGAN, in which a suction bellows draws the air in through them. Either style has a variety of stops of different quality.

reed pipe. See PIPE.

reed section. In jazz bands, the clarinet and saxophone players.

reel. A lively dance of Britain and Ireland, usually in 4/4 time, with little or no syncopation and reprises of 8-measure sections; danced in a 4-couple set.

Reformation Symphony. Mendelssohn's 5th Sym., 1832, in D minor, 1st performed in Berlin. Its name comes from the final movement, which is based on the Lutheran chorale, *Ein' feste Burg.*

refrain (Lat. *refractum*, fragmented; It. *ritornello*; Old Eng., *burden*). A recurring melody and text of a song, usually at the end of a stanza. It is often called the chorus, either in popular music, or because the main stanza or verse is performed solo and the following chorus is by an ensemble. A refrain often repeats the last line or 2 of the verse with the same text and melody, particularly if it summarizes the moral of the verse. A religious refrain may be a single word, *Amen*, intoned by the congregation in response to the minister or cantor. In Spain a common refrain is OLE!, expressing enthusiasm by a crowd.

regal. A portable organ with regal pipes (reed pipes without resonator) used between the 15th and 18th centuries, particularly in smaller churches.

regens chori (Lat.). Choir director.

regent. Leader of a Russian Orthodox church choir.

Reger, (Johann Baptist Joseph) **Max(imilian),** celebrated German composer; b. Brand, Upper Palatinate, Bavaria, Mar. 19, 1873; d. Leipzig, May 11, 1916. His father, a schoolteacher and amateur musician, gave him instruction on the piano, organ, and various string instru-

ments. In 1874 the family moved to Weiden, where he studied organ and theory with Adalbert Lindner; he then attended the teacher-training college; after visiting the Bayreuth Festival in 1888, he decided on a career in music. He went to Sondershausen to study with Riemann in 1890 and continued as his pupil in Wiesbaden (1890–93); was also active as a teacher of piano, organ, and theory (1890–96). Following military service he returned to Weiden in 1898 and wrote a number of his finest works for organ.

He went to Munich in 1901, 1st gaining general recognition as a pianist, and later as a composer; was prof. of counterpoint at the Königliche Akademie der Tonkunst (1905–1906). Prominent compositions from this period included the Piano Quintet, op. 64 (1901–1902), the Violin Sonata, op. 72 (1903), the String Quartet, op. 74 (1903–1904), the *Variationen und Füge über ein Thema von J. S. Bach* for Piano, op. 81 (1904), and the Sinfonietta, op. 90 (1904–1905). He went to Leipzig as music director of the Univ. (1907–1908) and as prof. of composition at the Cons. (from 1907). His fame as a composer was enhanced by his successful tours as a soloist and conductor in Germany and throughout Europe.

While he continued to produce major chamber works and organ pieces, he also wrote such important orch.l compositions as the *Variationen und Füge über ein lustiges Thema von J. A. Hiller*, op. 100 (1907), the Violin Concerto, op. 101 (1907–1908), the *Symphonischer Prolog zu einer Tragödie*, op. 108 (1908), the Piano Concerto, op. 114 (1910), *Eine Lustspielouvertüre*, op. 120 (1911); *Konzert im alten Stil*, op. 123 (1912); *Eine romantische Suite*, op. 125 (1912); *Vier Tondichtungen nach Arnold Böcklin*, op. 128 (Essen, 1913); *Eine Ballettsuite, op. 130* (1913); and the *Variationen und Füge über ein Thema von Mozart*, op. 132 (1914).

As a result of having been awarded an honorary Ph.D. from the Univ. of Jena in 1908, he composed his most distinguished sacred work, the Psalm 100, op. 106 (1908–1909). He was called to Meiningen as conductor of the Court Orch. in 1911, assuming the title of Hofkapellmeister; was also Generalmusikdirektor (1913–14). He settled in Jena in 1915.

Reger was an extraordinarily gifted musician, widely respected as a composer, pianist, organist, conductor, and teacher. A master of polyphonic and harmonic writing, he carried on the hallowed Classic and Romantic schools of composition. Although he wrote major works in nearly every genre (particularly choral and chamber music), his music has not found a place of permanence in the repertoire. Given his compositional propensities for highly chromatic, restless tonal plans, it is not surprising that he should have publ. *Beiträge zur Modulationslehre* (Leipzig, 1903; 24th ed., 1952). A thematic catalogue was published as F. Stein, ed., *Thematisches Verzeichnis der im Druck erschienenen Werke von Max Reger einschliesslich seiner Bearbeitungen und Ausgaben* (Leipzig, 1953).

reggae. Jamaican popular music marked by insistent square rhythms counterpointed by strong off-beat syncopation, similar to but more irregularly than in rock 'n' roll. Reggae emerged in the shantytowns of Kingston in the mid-1960s, combining elements of African-American soul, the steady-state rhythms of calypso and other Caribbean dance music, the polyrhythmic elements of African music, and a Jamaican skifflelike genre called ska. Particularly in the hands of Bob Marley, Peter Tosh, Black Uhuru, and others, reggae became an important medium of social protest and religious belief. In the 1980s it merged with HIP-HOP to form a type of accompaniment for RAP.

Regina. Opera by Blitzstein, 1949, based on Lillian Hellman's play *The Little Foxes*, 1st performed in Boston. The play recounts the mutual deceptions and self-destructive hatreds among members of a family in the South at the turn of the century. Much of the score is couched in dramatic recitative.

register. 1. A set of pipes or reeds controlled by one drawstop; a stop (organ stop). 2. A portion of the vocal compass; as *high* or *low* register; *chest-* or *head-*register. 3. A portion—in the range of certain instruments—differing in quality from the other portions.

registration. 1. The art of effectively employing and combining the various stops of the organ. 2. The combination of stops employed for any given composition.

registres coupés (Fr.). DIVIDED STOP.

rehearsal (Fr. *répétition*; It. *prova*; Ger. *Probe*, a tryout). Literally, rehearing; a practice session for a chamber music ensemble, a song recital, a symphonic work, an opera, a jazz band, a rock group, etc. A prerequisite for a fruitful rehearsal is a willingness to achieve a mutual accommodation among the participants so as to achieve proper balance in harmony, fluctuations of tempo, and dynamic equilibration. Basic elements can, of course, be agreed upon in advance, but the subtler nuances have to be felt intuitively. A tale is told about a rehearsal of a cello sonata when the cellist asked the pianist to play softer. "I can't hear myself," he complained. "You're lucky," the pianist replied. "Unfortunately, I can."

The collision of vanities at rehearsals is a constant hazard. When the violinist Henryk Wieniawski toured the United States with Anton Rubinstein in the 1870s, the 2 were not on speaking terms, but according to reports their mutual animosity did not affect the excellence of their performances. More recently Heifetz and Piatigorsky reached the point of such mutual irritability during a rehearsal for trio concerts that they had to communicate through the pianist Pennario for matters of tempos, bowing, etc. An abominable practice of deputy players existed in France at orch.l rehearsals, so that often the personnel of the orch. that plays the actual concert is quite different from that at the rehearsal. When an orch.l player told Toscanini at a Paris rehearsal that he would send a deputy to play the concert, Toscanini said, "Then I will send a deputy to conduct the concert," and walked off the podium.

reibtrommel (Ger., rubbing drum). FRICTION DRUM.

Reich, Steve (Stephen Michael)

American composer; b. N.Y., Oct. 3, 1936. He had a normal childhood; took piano lessons and also studied drumming with Roland Koloff, timpanist of the N.Y. Phil.; synchronously he became infatuated with jazz and Bach by way of Stravinsky's stylizations. He studied philosophy at Cornell Univ. (B.A.,

1957), where he became fascinated with the irrationally powerful theories of Ludwig Wittgenstein, who enunciated the famous tautological formula "Whereof one cannot speak, thereof one must be silent." (Reich in his music would confute this dictum by speaking loudly of tonalities and modalities which had remained in limbo for a millennium.) In N.Y. he took private composition lessons with Hall Overton and earned his living by driving a taxicab. From 1958 to 1961 he took courses with William Bergsma and Vincent Persichetti at the Juilliard School of Music; later went to California, where he entered Mills College in Oakland in the classes of Darius Milhaud and Luciano Berio (M.A., 1963); during this period he became interested in electronic composition and African music.

He launched his career as a composer with scores for the underground films *The Plastic Haircut* and *Oh Dem Watermelons* in 1963, utilizing tape sounds. His subsequent works for tape included *It's Gonna Rain* (1965) and *Come Out* (1966); he wrote in the electroacoustic vein in *Violin Phase* for Violin Solo and Interactive Electronics. He also made the acquaintance of other pioneers in what would become known as minimalist music. Reich returned to N.Y. and in 1966 organized his own ensemble, Steve Reich and Musicians, which began as a trio with Arthur Murphy and Jon Gibson and eventually expanded into an ensemble. With the recording of his *4 Organs* for 4 Electric Organs and Maracas (1970), he 1st made an impact outside his small circle of friends.

In the summer of 1970 Reich traveled to Accra, Ghana, where he practiced under the tutelage of indigenous drummers; this experience bore fruit with the composition *Drumming* (1971), which became quite popular. In 1973 he studied the Balinese gamelan with a native teacher at the American Soc. for Eastern Arts Summer Program at the Univ. of Washington in Seattle. Becoming conscious of his ethnic heredity, he went to Jerusalem in 1976 to study the traditional forms of Hebrew cantillation. In 1974 he received grants from the NEA and from the N.Y. State Council on the Arts; was also invited to Berlin as an artist-in-residence. He subsequently received grants from the Martha Baird Rockefeller Foundation (1975, 1979, 1980, and 1981) and a 2nd grant from the NEA (1976). In 1978

he was awarded a Guggenheim fellowship. He publ. a book, *Writings about Music* (N.Y., 1974).

Slowly but surely Reich rose to fame; his group was invited to perform at the Holland Festival and at the radio stations of Frankfurt and Stuttgart. His increasing success led to a sold-out house when he presented a concert of his works at N.Y.'s Carnegie Hall (1980). In 1986 he took his ensemble on a world tour. His music was astoundingly audacious; rather than continue in the wake of obsolescent modernism, inexorably increasing in complexity, he deliberately reduced his harmonic and contrapuntal vocabulary and defiantly explored the fascinating potentialities of repetitive patterns. He was mainly a constructivist of infinitesimal quantities which he integrated in his most successful works: *Music for Mallet Instruments Voices and Organ*, *Music for 18 Musicians*, *Music for a Large Ensemble*, *Tehillim*, *The Desert Music*, and *Sextet* for Percussion, Piano, and Synthesizers.

Reich's techniques have been variously described as minimalist (for it was derived from a minimum of chordal combinations), phase music (because it shifted from one chord to another, a note at a time), modular (because it was built on symmetric modules), and pulse music (because it derived from a series of measured rhythmic units). Another term is process music, suggesting tonal progressions in flux. This system of composition is akin to serialism in its application of recurrent melodic progressions and periodic silences. Despite his apparent disregard for musical convention, or indeed for public taste, Reich likes to trace his musical ancestry to the sweetly hollow homophonic music of the ARS ANTIQUA, with particular reference to the opaque works of the great master of the Notre Dame school of Paris, Perotin.

For many years he deliberately avoided programmatic references in his work titles, preferring to define them by names of instruments, or numbers of musical parts; recent works such as *The 4 Sections* for Orch. and *Electric Counterpoint* for Guitar and Tape continue this pattern. But other recent works suggest his interest in programmatic and historical connections, as in *Different Trains*, concerning the Holocaust, for string quartet and tape, partly MUSIQUE CONCRÈTE; and the multimedia *The Cave*.

Reichardt, Johann Friedrich. See GOETHE, JOHANN WOLFGANG VON.

Reihe (Ger.). Tone row, series.

reihengebundene Musik (Ger., music bound by a series). DODECAPHONIC MUSIC.

Reine de Saba, La. Opera by Gounod, 1862, 1st produced in Paris. The Queen of Sheba falls in love with a wandering minstrel and decides to leave King Solomon and follow her lover. But as she rejoins him, he is slain by one of his own followers. The score is melodious and harmonious, but it is not a major work of Gounod's.

Reiner, Fritz, eminent Hungarian-born American conductor; b. Budapest, Dec. 19, 1888; d. N.Y., Nov. 15, 1963. He studied piano with Thoman and composition with Koessler at the Royal Academy of Music in Budapest; concurrently took courses in jurisprudence. He was conductor of the Volksoper in Budapest (1911–14) and of the Court (later State) Opera in Dresden (1914–21); also conducted in Hamburg, Berlin, Vienna, Rome, and Barcelona. In 1922 he was engaged as music director of the Cincinnati Sym. Orch.; was naturalized as a U.S. citizen in 1928. In 1931 he became a prof. of conducting at the Curtis Inst. of Music in Philadelphia; among his students were Leonard Bernstein and Lukas Foss.

In 1936–37 he made guest appearances at London's Covent Garden; between 1935 and 1938, was guest conductor at the San Francisco Opera; from 1938 to 1948 he was music director of the Pittsburgh Sym. Orch.; then was a conductor at the Metropolitan Opera in N.Y. until 1953. He achieved the peak of his success as a conductor with the Chicago Sym. Orch., which he served as music director from 1953 to 1962 and which he brought up to the point of impeccably fine performance in both classical and modern music. His striving for perfection created for him the reputation of a ruthless master of the orch.; he was given to explosions of temper, but musicians and critics agreed that it was because of his uncompromising drive toward the optimum of orch. playing that the Chicago Sym. Orch. achieved a very high rank among American symphonic organizations.

Reinhardt, Django (Jean Baptiste), Belgian jazz guitarist; b. Liberchies, Jan. 23, 1910; d. Fontainebleau, May 16,

Django Reinhardt, 1947

1953. He began his career in Paris in 1922; gained recognition through his recordings with the singer Jean Sablon and the violinist Stephane Grappelli; in 1934 he formed the Quintette du Hot Club de France with Grappelli. After World War II he toured the U.S.; appeared with Duke Ellington in N.Y. He was an innovative figure in the early jazz movement in Europe; in later years he utilized electrical amplification in his performances.

rejdowak. Bohemian ballroom dance in ternary time; later popular in Europe as the REDOWA.

relâche (Fr., release). 1. Indication that a theater is closed; in theatrical jargon, dark, or no performance. 2. Indication that a performance is canceled.

Relâche. "Instantaneous ballet" by Satie, 1924, 1st produced in Paris. At the premiere the curtain bore the inscription in huge letters: "Erik Satie est le plus grand musicien du monde," adding that those who disagreed with this estimate were invited to leave the hall.

related keys. Those keys with the 1st degree of relationship with the main key; their triads are contained within the available diatonic degrees of the main key. Thus E minor is related to C major, D major, G major, and B minor; E minor appears in these keys as the mediant, supertonic, submediant, and subdominant, respectively. See also RELATIVE KEY.

relation(ship). The degree of affinity between keys, chords, and tones.

relative key. A natural minor key is relative to that major key, the tonic of which lies a minor 3rd above its own; a major key is relative to that natural minor key, the tonic of which lies a minor 3rd below its own. As a result, the 2 keys share key signatures; e.g., G major is the relative of E minor, sharing a signature of 1 sharp (F[sharp-sign]). Chopin's Preludes, op. 28, are ordered by the cycle of 5ths, further arranged by alternating a major key with its relative minor (C major, A minor, G major, E minor, etc.).

relative pitch. Ability to name an interval, or the exact 2nd note, after hearing an interval and being given the identity of the 1st note. This ability can be learned, unlike PERFECT PITCH, the ability to name a pitch without a reference point; this is considered an innate talent.

religiosity. Religious symbolism left many traces in musical notation. Perfect time consisting of 3 beats is defined in the medieval treatises as being an attribute of the Christian Trinity. But even in secular works, composers paid tribute to piety. Haydn signed most of his syms. with the devotional phrase "Deo soli gloria." Bruckner dedicated his 9th Sym. "An meinem lieben Gott." Stravinsky's inscription on the title page of his *Sym. of Psalms* reads: "Composed for the glory of God and dedicated to the Boston Sym. Orchestra." When the English composer Arnold Bax was asked to contribute a program note for one of his symphonies, he declined, explaining that the music was dictated to him by God.

Performing musicians, not many of whom are naturally religious, have been known to rely on divine help for the quality of their performances. But some are apt to renounce God when they fail. When it rained on the day of the American debut of the Russian bass Sibiriakov, he shook his fists at the skies and cried out: "If God has such weather for Sibiriakov's concert, then God is a bastard!" The adulation of symphonic conductors leads some of them to accept the projected God-like image. "I know who you are," gushed a Boston dowager entering the reception room of Serge Koussevitzky. "You are God!" "I know my responsibilities," Koussevitzky replied imperturbably. When the mercurial Artur Rodzinski took over the New York Philharmonic, he decided to dismiss 14 players. But, he assured the manager, he would 1st seek divine counsel. The next morning he declared: "God spoke to me, and he said 'Fire the bastards!'"

religioso (It.). In a devotional style.

R.E.M. Popular American alternative rock band. (Vocals: [John] Michael Stipe, b. Decatur, Ga., Jan. 4, 1960; guitar/mandolin: Peter [Lawrence] Buck, b. Berkeley, Calif., Dec. 6, 1956; bass/keyboards/vocals: Michael [Edward] Mills, b. Orange, Calif., Dec. 17, 1958; drums/vocals: Bill Berry, b. William Thomas Berry, Duluth, Minn., July 31, 1958.) The group takes its name from *rapid eye movement*, a stage of sleep. They were formed in Athens, Ga., in 1980 by 4 Univ. of Georgia students; a year later they released independently the single *Radio Free Europe*, gaining them a contract with I.R.S. Records. An EP and then an LP followed in rapid succession.

The group toured Europe in 1983 and continued to record, building a reputation among critics and alternative music listeners. They became known for their dense sound, featuring vocals mixed far in the background (and Stipe's sometimes incoherent muttering style) so that it was difficult if not impossible to understand exactly what each song was about. They scored a minor hit in 1986 with the song *Fall On Me* but did not break through big-time until a year later, with the hit songs *The One I Love* and *It's the End of the World as We Know It (And I Feel Fine)* from the album *Document*. This led to their signing with heavy-hitting label Warner Bros.

Their 1st major pop hit came in 1991 with *Losing My Religion* from their 2nd Warners' album, *Out of Time*, on which the band took a more acoustic, softened approach to their work. They continued to enjoy hits with 1992's *Everybody Hurts* and *Man on the Moon* in a similar style, but then came back to a harder-edged sound with 1994's *Monster*, featuring the hit *What's the Frequency, Kenneth?* A world tour followed in 1995, during which they recorded their next album, *New Adventures in Hi-Fi*, which failed to yield any hits.

remedio. Argentine song in 3/8 time; intended as a remedy for unrequited love.

remote key. An unrelated key.

Renaissance. In music history, the period 1400 to 1600.

Renard. Chamber opera by Stravinsky, 1922, 1st produced in Paris. Subtitled *A Fable About a Fox, a Rooster, a Cat, and a Ram, a Merry Spectacle with Singing and Music after Popular Russian Fairy Tales*, it tells of a fox outfoxed by other, less sophisticated animals. The score demonstrates Stravinsky's dexterity in a modernistic distillation of folk-song materials.

renversement (Fr.). 1. Inversion of an interval. 2. Inversion of a chord.

repeat. 1. The sign or or , signifying *a* that the music between the double-dotted bars is to be repeated; *b* and *c*, that the preceding and also the following division is to be repeated. 2. A section or division of music to be repeated. Repeats are usually indicated in Classic sonatas, or works in sonata form (quartet, sym.), but such repeats are very often disregarded by the performer, particularly if the exposition section is very long. Repeats are de rigueur in dance forms; a particularly important set of obligatory repeats occurs in minuets and gavottes, when the 1st section is repeated after the contrasting 2nd section (ternary form).

repercussio (Lat.). In Gregorian chant, the repetition of a melodic pattern that characterizes a particular modality. Certain neumes, particularly those signifying a rapid repeat, are classified in this character.

repercussion. 1. Repetition of a tone or chord. 2. In a fugue, the regular reentrance of subject and answer after the episodes immediately following the exposition.

repetend. A musical phrase that is constantly repeated for many bars, such as the protracted ending of the initial theme in the 1st movement of Beethoven's *Pastoral Sym.*, in which the violin figure is repeated 10 times. Concluding chords in a Classic coda are typical conventional repetends. Modern composers tend to do away with repetends; Prokofiev ends the March in his opera *Love for 3 Oranges* with a single C-major chord, where his Classic and Romantic predecessors might have had 16 or 32 chords.

répétiteur, -euse (Fr.). A choral or opera rehearsal assistant; one who conducts rehearsals as opposed to the actual performances; sometimes called an opera coach. The répétiteur, humblest of functionaries in the realm of grand opera, often has the tedious duty to train inept singers to keep time. But these musical menials acquire valuable practice and sometimes rise to conductorship. The remarkable Greek conductor Dimitri Mitropoulos served as répétiteur at the Berlin Opera in the beginning of his career.

répétition (Fr.). A rehearsal.

répétition générale (Fr.). A dress rehearsal for an opera, ballet, etc., open to the press and dignitaries before the official premiere.

replica (It.). A repeat or reprise. *Da capo senza replica*, play from the beginning without observing the repeats.

replication. In their search for effective and direct musical formulas, modern composers have increasingly turned back to the primitivist pattern of simple repetition, a sort of biomusical replication of a subject keeping its identity as unalterable as the design on an ancient Peruvian poncho. The most celebrated instance of such replication is Ravel's *Boléro*, in which the variations are limited to changes from one instrumental color to another. A less literal type of replication is monothematicism, of which Debussy's String Quartet is a perfect example. Still another variant is the thematic replication of a musical monogram, which spells out a name of a common word in letter-notes, usually in German notation. A modern example is the 8th String Quartet by Shostakovich, which is built on his initials in German spelling (D–S–C–H, with the letter *S* representing *Es*, i.e., E-flat, and H representing B natural). Shostakovich uses the same personal monogram in his 10th Sym., as did other composers in homage to him. Some members of the avant-garde have carried the principle of replication to the ultimate limit of a single note recorded on tape without any change in dynamics and without a rhythmic interruption.

reprenez le mouvement (Fr.). Take up the tempo again; same as A TEMPO.

reprise (from Fr., retaking; It. *ripresa*; Ger. *Reprise*). 1. The total and unaltered repeat of a section of a musical composition; usually is marked by 2 symmetric repeat signs, 1 in the beginning with 2 dots on the right of the double bar and 1 at the end of the repeat section with 2 dots to the left of the double bar. 2. In some French Baroque harpsichord music, a mark of repetition indicating the section to be repeated in a rondo-like piece; or the repetition of the last few measures as a form of coda. 3. In present usage reprise is virtually synonymous with RECAPITULATION, wherein the EXPOSITION is "retaken," with necessary modifications in the modulatory plan.

requiem (from Lat. *requies*, rest). The 1st word in the Mass for the dead; hence the title of the musical setting of that Mass. Its divisions are (1) Requiem, Kyrie; (2) Dies iræ,

Requiem; (3) Domine Jesu Christe; (4) Sanctus, Benedictus; and (5) Agnus Dei, Lux æterna.

Requiem Canticles. Work by Stravinsky, 1966, for voices and orch., 1st performed in Princeton; this was the composer's last major work.

res facta (Lat.). In early music, a description of a composition that is fully written out, as opposed to counterpoint figured out mentally and improvised from the cantus firmus at sight. It is sometimes equated by music theorists of the 16th century with *musica figurativa*—music with all auxiliary ornaments written out. This identification is the *Institution musicale*, published in Paris in 1556, where res facta is translated literally as *chose faite*. Res facta is sometimes used interchangeably with *cantus fractus* (broken song) or *musique rompue* (broken music).

rescue and escape terms. Many new musicological terms ambiguously descriptive of a modern style, idiom, or technique are rescue and escape terms, words and phrases used as nebulous definitions of uncertain musical events. The term OMNITONALITY belongs to this category; others may be found by industrious perusal of music magazines beginning in 1910.

rescue opera. A fanciful term to describe an opera in which the central character is rescued from mortal peril by extraordinary means. A perfect example is Beethoven's *Fidelio*, in which the prisoner's faithful wife enters prison service in a man's attire to rescue him; she succeeds. In Puccini's *Tosca* the rescue of the prisoner seems assured at the risk of the heroine's virtue but a twist of fate turns hope into despair and death. The rescue opera usually involves human activity rather than the work of a DEUS EX MACHINA.

reservata, musica. This term is a philosopher's stone of musical historiography, for its meaning is arcane, its origin recondite, its connotations cryptic, and its function enigmatic. Musica reservata 1st appeared in print in *Compendium Musices* by Adrian Coclico (1552). On etymological grounds, one is tempted to translate the word reservata as "reserved" in the sense of being exclusive, connoting a style of composition appreciated only by expert musicians. An alternative explanation of the term is that the element of "reservation" indicated a restricted use of ornamentation.

résolu (Fr.). Resolutely, decisively.

resolution. The progression of a dissonance, whether a simple interval or a chord, to a consonance. Generally semitone motion is a controlling factor, whether moving from leading tone to tonic or from subdominant to mediant (in the dominant 7th chord). Augmented intervals tend to resolve by expansion; diminished intervals resolve by contracting. *Direct resolution*, immediate progression from the dissonance to the consonance; *indirect* (or *delayed, deferred, retarded*) *resolution*, one passing through some intermediate dissonance(s) before reaching the final restful consonance.

resonance. The resounding of upper harmonics over the fundamental.

resonance box. A hollow resonant body like that of the violin or zither. See also RESONATOR.

Resonancias. Orch.l work by Chávez, 1964, 1st conducted by the composer in Mexico City. Thematic elements are reflected by resonance, forming new melodic patterns.

resonator. Any object that amplifies sound. The soundboard of the grand piano is a resonator of the strings; the hollow bodies of chordophones serve the same purpose; caverns are natural resonators. The elimination of unwelcome resonance is the most vexing and least predictable part of a proper architectural plan in constructing a concert hall. Vibrating surfaces on musical instruments can create an embarrassing QUODLIBET during an orch.l performance. Orch.l players usually dampen their instruments to preclude "sympathetic vibrations," in which a particular pitch played on an instrument produces a sudden increase in loudness out of keeping with the rest of the gamut. Is this the real meaning of that hoary cliché "Beware of bad vibes"?

Respect. The 1965 composition and recording by Otis Redding that became a major hit when it was covered 2 years later by Aretha Franklin, who turned it into a women's liberation anthem. Refrain "Sock it to me" became a catchphrase for the TV show *Laugh-In*.

Respighi, Ottorino, eminent Italian composer; b. Bologna, July 9, 1879; d. Rome, Apr. 18, 1936. He studied violin with F. Sarti and composition with L. Torchi and G. Martucci at Bologna's Liceo Musicale (1891–1900). In 1900 he went to Russia and played 1st viola in the orch. of the Imperial Opera in St. Petersburg; there he took lessons with Rimsky-Korsakov, which proved a decisive influence in

Respighi's coloristic orchestration. From 1903 to 1908 he was active as a concert violinist; also played the viola in the Mugellini Quartet of Bologna. In 1913 he was engaged as a prof. of composition at Rome's Liceo (later Cons.) di Santa Cecilia; in 1924 he was appointed its director, but he resigned in 1926, retaining only a class in advanced composition; subsequently devoted himself to composing and conducting. He was elected a member of the Italian Royal Academy in 1932. In 1925–26 and again in 1932 he made tours of the U.S. as a pianist and a conductor.

Resphigi's style of composition is a highly successful blend of songful melodies with full and rich harmonies; he was one of the best masters of modern Italian music in orchestration. His power of evocation of the Italian scene and his ability to sustain interest without prolixity is incontestable. Although he wrote several operas, he achieved his greatest success with 2 symphonic poems, *Le fontane di Roma* and *I pini di Roma*, each consisting of 4 tone paintings of the Roman landscape; a great innovation for the time was the insertion of a phonograph recording of a nightingale into the score of *I pini di Roma*.

Resphigi's orch.l works remain his best known; others include the *Ballata delle Gnomidi* (1918–20); *Adagio con variazioni* with Cello (1920); *Concerto gregoriano* with Violin (1921); *Vetrate di chiesa* (1925); *Poema autunnula* with Violin (1925); *Trittico botticelliano* (1927); *Impressioni brasiliane* (1928); *Feste romane* (1928); *Toccata* with Piano (1928). He also wrote arrangements, including *Antiche arie e danze per liuto* (1917, 1923, 1931), and musical syntheses of other composers' work. He was prolific as a composer of vocal music: he wrote 9 operas, several songs and song cycles, and chamber music, including the Violin Sonata in B Minor (1917); *Quartetto dorico* for String Quartet (1924). His wife, Elsa Olivieri Sangiacomo Respighi (b. Rome, Mar. 24, 1894; d. 1996), was his pupil; she wrote a fairy opera, *Fior di neve*, the symphonic poem *Serenata di maschere*, and numerous songs; she was also a concert singer; she finished her husband's opera *Lucrezia* (1937).

respiro (It.). Pause; rest.

response (respond; Fr. *réponse*). 1. RESPONSORY. 2. An answer, in call-and-response texture. 3. The musical reply, by the choir or congregation, to what is said or sung by the priest or officiant.

responsory (Lat. *reponsorium*; Fr. *répons*). 1. That psalm, or part of one, sung in alternation between soloist and congregation after the reading of lessons; the practice dates to at least the 11th century. The great responsories are found in the Matins and monastic Vespers. Polyphonic settings were mostly in the form of motets and continued to be composed up until the 18th century. 2. The GRADUAL. 3. A *respond*; that is, the 1st part of a responsory psalm, sung by the congregation.

rest. A pause or interval of silence between 2 tones; hence the sign indicating such a pause. See "Notes and Rests," p. xxiii.

restez (Fr., remain). In music for stringed instruments, means play on the same string or remain in the same position, i.e., do not shift.

Retablo de Maese Pedro, El (Master Peter's Puppet Show). Puppet opera by de Falla, 1923, based on Cervantes's *Don Quixote*; it was 1st performed in Seville. The Knight of the Woeful Countenance watches a puppet show in which a young damsel keeps being throttled by disasters left and right; finally Quixote can no longer bear it and he attacks the puppet theater and demolishes it. The score demonstrates de Falla's skill at investing Spanish folk song material with sophisticated harmony.

retard. RITARDANDO.

retardation. The device of retardation—melodic, harmonic, or contrapuntal—consists of holding over a certain note or a harmonic complex while other parts of the musical fabric are shifted. In modern music, retardation is not developed in accord with the moving elements but continues indefinitely in order to create a sustained discord. In pandiatonic techniques this procedure results in a chain of superpositions of the principal triadic harmonies.

retarded progression. A suspension resolving upward.

retenir (Fr.). Hold back. *Retenu*, RITENUTO.

retirada (Sp.). Recession, as opposed to INTRADA. Such introductory and recessional movements were common in suites.

retrograde. 1. Performing a melody backward; a pedantic melodic device often encountered in polyphonic works, much beloved by composers of puzzle canons, and usually prefaced by them with fanciful phrases such as *Vade retro Satanas* (Get Thee behind me, Satan; Mark 8:33), *Ubi alpha ibi omega* (Where alpha is, omega is too), *Canite more Hebraeorum* (Sing in the Hebrew manner, i.e., from right to left), and (the most famous designation) CANCRIZANS (literally, walking like a crab).

In the Minuet of his Sym. No. 47 Haydn explicitly marked AL ROVESCIO, meaning it could be played backward without any change of the original music. Bach's *Das musikalisches Opfer* has a 2-part canon in which the original subject is sounded simultaneously with its retrograde form. Beethoven has a crab motion in the final fugue of his *Hammerklavier Sonata*. A remarkable example of a very melodious and harmonious piece representing a combination of the original and its retrograde form is exemplified by an anonymous canon, erroneously attributed to Mozart, playable by 2 violinists reading a page across the table from one another, so that the player opposite performs the tune beginning with the last note and ending with the 1st note of his vis-à-vis partner. The wonder of it is that the result is in perfect harmony, and that a sharp applies to 2 different notes in the opposite parts without creating an unresolved dissonance.

2. One of 3 standard precompositional techniques in 12-note composition, wherein all notes of a set are played in reverse order. After a century of neglect the technique of retrograde motion staged a revival in the music of the 20th-century Vienna School. Schoenberg has a retrograde canon in No. 18 of *Pierrot lunaire*, and so does Berg in the middle section of his opera *Lulu*. Retrograde motion is of fundamental importance in 12-tone music, in which 2 of the 4 principal melodic forms of the tone row include retrograde and inverted retrograde.

retrograde canon. CANON CANCRIZANS.

retrograde inversion. A standard technique in 12-note composition wherein all notes of a set are played in a reverse succession, which also mirrors (inverts) the original set.

Reuben, Reuben. Song by Percy Gaunt, 1893, a hit in the vaudeville show *A Trip to Chinatown*.

reveille (Fr. *réveil*). The military signal for (1) getting up in the morning and (2) the 1st military formation of the day; based on the 2nd, 3rd, and 4th notes of the harmonic series playable on a bugle.

revenez (Fr.). Return. *Revenez peu à peu au premier mouvement*, return gradually to the original tempo.

reverie (Fr.). Dreamy meditation; title of many Romantic pieces.

reverse motion. RETROGRADE.

reversion. RETROGRADE imitation.

revidierte Ausgabe (Ger.). Revised edition.

Revisor, Der. Comic opera by Egk, 1956, based on Gogol's comedy *The Inspector General*, 1st performed in Schwetzingen. The story describes the confusion created in a small Russian town by the arrival of a supposed secret investigator sent by the Czar. When the deception is exposed, a real investigator makes his appearance, plunging the various functionaries into even greater consternation. The score makes use of Russian songs and dances to lend authenticity to the music.

Revolution. A 1968 Beatles song, 1st released as a hard-rocking single, then as a more subdued album track on the famous *White Album*. John Lennon can't decide whether you should count him out or in when it comes to violent revolutionary activities, so he sings it both ways!

Revolutionary Étude. The popular name of Chopin's Piano Étude in C Minor, No. 12, op. 10, supposedly composed when Chopin heard the sad news of the occupation of Warsaw by the Russians. The stormy surging scales in the left hand lent credibility to this story.

revue. A generic term for theatrical spectacles in which singing, speaking, dancing, and entertainment of all types are combined into a package that has no pretense for inner cohesion or a unified plot. Each sketch in a revue is self-sufficient; the genres vary from sentimental ballads and duets to satire on topical subjects, from classical dances to popular marches. Revues originated in France under the reign of the "bourgeois" King Louis Philippe in 1830; a "Revue de fin d'année" was actually a review of events during the year past. In the 2nd half of the 19th century such revues were called *variétés*.

The most brilliant and the most daring revue of the 1st quarter of the 20th century was the theater named Folies-Bergère (follies of the district of Bergère) in Paris. In the 19th century the boldest exhibition of the female body was the high-kicking *can-can*, which titillated tourists and provided purists with subjects for sermons on the decay of public morality; but in the middle of the 20th century, nudity in revues was de rigueur. German revues, especially those in Berlin, imitated Parisian examples. The British had 2 types: the revues, which emphasized political satire, and MUSIC HALL, focusing on social humor and sentimentality. After a century of oppressive censorship by the Society for the Prevention of Vice in N.Y., uninhibited gaiety exploded in American musicals, as musical comedies came to be known. Variety shows continued to thrive in burlesque theaters.

Revueltas, Silvestre, remarkable Mexican composer; b. Santiago Papasquiaro, Dec. 31, 1899; d. Mexico City, Oct. 5, 1940. He began violin studies when he was 8 in Colima; then entered the Juérez Inst. in Durango at age 12; after studies with Tello (composition) and Rocabruna (violin) in Mexico City (1913–16), he took courses at St. Edward College in Austin, Tex. (1916–18) and with Sametini (violin) and Borowski (composition) at the Chicago Musical College (1918–20); he returned to Chicago to study violin with Kochanski and Sevcik (1922–26).

He was active as a violinist and conductor in Texas and Alabama (1926–28); was assistant conductor of the Orquesta Sinfónica de Mexico (1929–35); only then did he begin to compose. In 1937 he went to Spain, where he was active in the cultural affairs of the Loyalist government during the Civil War. His health was ruined by exertions and an irregular lifestyle, and he died of pneumonia. His remains were deposited in the Rotonda de los Hombres Ilustres in Mexico City on Mar. 23, 1976, to the music of his *Redes* and the funeral march from Beethoven's *Eroica Sym.* He possessed an extraordinary natural talent and an intimate understanding of Mexican music; he succeeded in creating works of great originality, melodic charm, and rhythmic vitality.

r.h. Right hand.

rhapsody (from Grk. *rapto + ode*, woven song; Fr. *rapsodie*). In Homeric times, itinerant singers, called *rhapsodes* (song weavers), recited their odes at festivals and at political events. The rhapsodic concept was revived toward the end of the 18th century, when Christian F. D. Schubart published a collection of songs entitled *Musicalische Rhapsodien*. By the 19th century the reincarnated rhapsody was an instrumental improvisation on folk songs or on motives taken from indigenous music. Later the meaning of rhapsody was expanded to include instrumental compositions without

source material. Liszt wrote a series of piano works (later orchestrated) called HUNGARIAN RHAPSODIES; Brahms composed several untitled piano rhapsodies. Among other composers who wrote rhapsodies were Dvořák, Glazunov, Ravel, Bartók, and Enesco.

Rhapsody in Blue. Sym. piece for piano and orch. by Gershwin, 1924, 1st performed by him in N.Y. This was one of the 1st symphonic pieces that used the idiom of the blues; it was said that Gershwin "made an honest woman out of jazz." The piece is both lyrical and dramatic; its expansive melody and pleasingly modernistic harmonies made *Rhapsody in Blue* a landmark in American music.

Rhapsody in Rivets. Rhapsody No. 2 for Piano and Orch. by Gershwin, 1932, which he wrote for Koussevitzky and the Boston Sym. Orch. Gershwin was the piano soloist in the Boston premiere. *Rivets* in the title (later discarded) refers to the rhythmic sound of the riveting being done by construction workers throughout the streets of N.Y.; besides jazzy rhythms there is also a RUMBA.

Rheingold, Das. Music drama by Wagner (1851–54), designated as the *Vorabend* (fore-evening) to the great tetralogy *Der Ring des Nibelungen*, to his own loftily poetical text strewn with evocative Germanic neologisms; it was premiered in Munich (1869).

The maidens of the river Rhine guard a horde of gold, which in this case is not just a precious yellow metallic element of atomic number 79, but a magical substance. Whoever forges a ring out of the Rhine gold will be master of the world. The Nordic gods who mill around their castle in their abode of Valhalla are no less quarrelsome than the gods of Mt. Olympus, and are beset as much as the Greeks by trouble with disobedient underlings. The dwarf Alberich of the Nibelung clan renounces his love in order to obtain the gold; from it he forges the baneful ring of the Nibelung. Wotan, the Nordic Jupiter, succeeds in abstracting the ring from the incautious Alberich, who then pronounces a curse upon it. But Wotan has to contend with an annoying couple of giants, Fasolt and Fafner, who demand payment for their work in building Valhalla. Although Wotan offers them the goddess of youth, Freia, in partial payment, they demand the gold as well. Having obtained it, the giants quarrel among themselves and the more vicious of them, Fafner, slays the other.

Realizing that Valhalla must be protected against the foes, Wotan procreates 9 Valkyries, the stallion-riding warrior maidens generously endowed with brass-plated bosoms.

Their main tasks are to take the bodies of slain heroes to Valhalla, where they could be restored to life, and to protect the stronghold. Wotan also begets human children, Siegmund and Sieglinde, who in time will beget Siegfried. Wotan's hope is that Siegfried, the ideal of a Nordic hero, would track down the giant Fafner, recapture the ring, and return it to the Rhine maidens. A whole encyclopedia of leitmotivs is unfolded in *Das Rheingold* and stored away for future use in the remaining tetralogy. Not only the gods, giants, and dwarfs are characterized by these leitmotivs, but also objects or ideas involved in the action: the ring itself, the

curse imposed upon it, the magic helmet that can transform a person into any human or animal shape, and the sword Nothung, the Nordic equivalent of King Arthur's Excalibur.

Rhenish Symphony. Schumann's 3rd Sym., 1851, in E-flat major. Exceptionally, it is in 5 movements, but the penultimate movement, descriptive of the Cologne Cathedral, may be regarded as an intermezzo. The composer's title is justified because in this work Schumann intended to reflect life in the Rhine countryside. It was 1st performed, appropriately, in the Rhenish town of Düsseldorf.

rhythm

The measured movement of similar tone-groups; that is, the effect produced by the systematic grouping of tones with reference to regularity both in their accentuation and in their succession as equal or unequal in time value. A rhythm (It. *ritmo*; Fr. *rythme*; Ger. *Rhythmus*) is, therefore, a tone-group serving as a pattern for succeeding identical groups; traditionally it follows the prosody of verse. Rhythm is the animating element of all music and constitutes the essential formative factor in melody; a melody divested of rhythm loses its recognizable meaning, while rhythm without melodic content may possess an independent existence. The interdependence of melody and rhythm is expressed in the term MELORHYTHM. Rhythm must be distinguished from METER, which is an expedient grouping of rhythmical units upon which the rhythm is superimposed. A metrical group can itself constitute a rhythm, but a rhythmic figure cannot form a metrical entity; St. Augustine already makes this distinction in his treatise *De musica* (5th century A.D.): "Omne metrum rhythmus, non monis rhythmus etiam metrum est" (Every meter is rhythm, but not every rhythm is also meter).

The simplest rhythm beyond the monotonous repetition of the same note value is an alternation of a long and a short note, corresponding to the trochee in poetry. The metrical arrangement of such a rhythmic figure may be 3/16, 3/8, or any multiples of these fractions. The ear can-

not distinguish 1 bar of 6/8 from 2 bars of 3/8, except by applying the extraneous considerations of known forms, or by depending on the tempo. The famous *Barcarolle* from Offenbach's opera *The Tales of Hoffmann* can be perceived aurally as a waltz unless one knows that a barcarolle must be in 6/8 time.

One of the most remarkable instances of a complete divorce between meter and rhythm occurs in the finale of Schumann's Piano Concerto, in which the ear registers a leisurely waltz time while the conductor fights against the aural rhythm by giving the downbeat on a rest every other bar. One of the most common cross-rhythms is having 3/4 superimposed on 6/8 in Spanish popular dances. The so-called COMPOUND METERS of 5, 7, 11 beats et al. in a measure usually represent 2 rhythmic groups. The "waltz" in Tchaikovsky's 6th Sym. is in 5/4 time, with the rhythmic figures easily separated into 2 sections of 2 and 3 beats each, but in Rimsky-Korsakov's *Dance of the Mermaids* from the opera *Sadko*, the quintuple rhythms are not subdivided into groups. In Russian and Bulgarian music the metrical units of 8 beats are sometimes split into rhythmic groups of 3 + 3 + 2.

In the 20th century there is a marked tendency among modern composers to write music without barlines, thus abolishing metrical groupings all together. More durable was the attempt to equate rhythm with meter at all times and change the time signature when the rhythmic figure was altered. The *Danse sacrale* in Stravinsky's score *The Rite of Spring* is an example of such subordination of meter to rhythm. An intriguing case of incommensurability between meter and rhythm is found in Gershwin's song *I Got Rhythm*, in which the square measure of 4/4 is in effect subdivided into 1 bar of 1/8, 4 bars of 3/8, and 1 bar of 1/8. Blacher introduced the method of VARIABLE METERS, with time signatures in which the numerator increases by 1 in each successive bar until a bar of 5 beats is reached, whereupon the metrical numerator decreases by 1 beat in each measure.

Elliott Carter made use in his works of what he called METRICAL MODULATION, wherein a subordinate rhythm in a given metrical set becomes the primary meter, and the former primary meter is reduced to a subordinate position. Rhythmical figures without a common denominator relative to the principal metrical set are found in numerous modern works in which groups of notes, usually in prime numbers—such as 5, 7, 11, 13, 17, or 19—are bracketed against an approximate number of beats within the principal meter. In the compositions of the avant-garde both meter and rhythm are often replaced by durations given in seconds or fractions of a second. In his book *New Musical Resources* Cowell proposed new shapes of musical note values making subdivisions into any kind of rhythmic groupings possible.

rhythm and blues (R&B; race music; jump blues). A type of black urban popular music blending strong repetitive rhythms, 4/4 or 6/8 meter, blues-related melodies and harmonic patterns (often based on a boogie-woogie bass), gospel music, swing, and electric blues instrumentation (electric guitar/s, acoustic double bass, keyboards, a small big band–like section, and drums). The solo vocalist was often accompanied by a few backup singers. Sometimes the singing was closer to the *a cappella* gospel quartets of the pre–World War II era; this slower, sentimental rhythm-and-blues style was the predecessor of 1950s *doo-wop*.

In the 1940s, rhythm and blues was considered strictly black music by the majority, and segregated by record companies into divisions they called "race records" (for Columbia, the label was Okeh; for Victor, Bluebird; other labels simply reserved specific series numbers). In the segregated world of the U.S., rhythm and blues was, in the conservative view, a crucial part of the "devil's formula" for destroying the morals of white teenagers. But white audiences began to purchase these recordings to listen or dance to, despite their parents. Gradually white musicians such as Bill Haley and (later) Elvis Presley recorded many of the black musicians' material and were thus able to crack the color barrier musically if not literally. Not all the white artists were appropriate for this task; many of these so-called cover versions are as limp as the originals are gut-wrenching, and it is a historical truism that many rhythm-and-blues artists of the 1940s and early 1950s were kept from the success they deserved by segregation.

Slight changes in style led to the white equivalent of rhythm and blues, ROCK 'N' ROLL; this new variant not only brought the influence of country-western (Carl Perkins, Jerry Lee Lewis, and Buddy Holly), but black musicians reinvented rhythm and blues to please all audiences (Chuck Berry, Little Richard, Fats Domino).

rhythm guitar. GUITAR, RHYTHM.

rhythm section. Percussion section in a jazz band consisting of piano, bass, and drums, supplying the main beat; if a guitar is used it will function within this section at times.

ribattuta (It., back stroke). 1. BEAT. 2. A device for beginning a trill by dwelling longer on the principal tone than on the auxiliary.

ribs. The curved sides of the violin, connecting belly and back.

ricercar (It. *ricercare*, *ricercata*, research, inquire). Instrumental composition of the 16th and 17th centuries generally characterized by imitative treatment of the theme or themes. Ricercar is one of the most vaguely defined forms, encompassing elements of canon, fugue, fantasy, and early sonata. Early in the 16th century ricercar retained a more or less literal meaning of "trying out," as in tuning the lute and playing improvisatory arpeggios and melodic fiorituras as a sort of preamble in the tonality of the intended principal section of the work. An Italian 16th-century theorist describes the ricercar as a sequence of *suoni licenziosi*, not in the sense of "licentious sounds" but of sounds arranged with a certain degree of license, to be played *senza arte* (without artifice, artlessly). Vincenzo Galilei wrote about a musician who played "una bella ricercata con le dita" (a fine ricercar with his fingers) and then began to sing.

Orig. the ricercar was a prelude to a song, to a keyboard composition, or to a dance tune played on a lute, but within a century it assumed an independent significance comparable to a fugue and a sonata, in a contrapuntal style far removed from its pristine "artlessness." It tended toward short themes closely imitated, resulting in a very strict manner in comparison with the later "free fugue." When Bach presented his *Musical Offering* to Frederick the Great of Prussia, he chose the ricercar as the center of his work and devised an acrostic in Latin, *Regis Iussu Cantio Et Reliqua Canonica Arte Resoluta* (By the King's command the theme and additions resolved in canonic style). The Baroque ricercar lapsed into innocuous desuetude in the 19th century but was revived in the 20th century by several composers, among them Stravinsky, Martinů, and Malipiero, when the slogan "Back to Bach" became fashionable.

Rich, Buddy (Bernard), remarkable American jazz drummer and bandleader; b. N.Y., June 30, 1917; d. Los Angeles, Apr. 2, 1987. His parents were vaudeville performers who made him a part of their act before he was 2; he was only 4 when he appeared as a drummer and tap dancer on Broadway; made his 1st tour of the U.S. and Australia at the age of 6; led his own stage band by the time he was 11. In 1937 he joined the band of Joe Marsala; after working with Bunny Berigan, Harry James, Artie Shaw, and Benny Carter, he performed with Tommy Dorsey (1939–42; 1944–45); then led his own band until 1951. He again performed with James (1953–54; 1955–57; 1961–66) and Dorsey (1954–55), and also led his own combo (1957–61); in 1966 he founded his own big band, with which he toured throughout the world until it folded in 1974. In subsequent years he made appearances at his own N.Y. club, Buddy's Place, leading a small combo; during the last years of his life he also toured with his own jazz-rock big band. Rich was one of the outstanding swing drummers of his time.

Richard Cœur-de-Lion. Opera by Grétry, 1784, 1st performed in Paris. Richard I of England led the 3rd Crusade into the Holy Land; while returning he was captured and held for several years in Austria. The opera focuses on the exploits of the King's jester, who successfully plots his deliverance. Beethoven wrote a set of piano variations on the aria *Une Fièvre brûlante* from this opera.

Richard Wagner: Venezia. A homage for piano by Liszt, 1883, written when he learned of his son-in-law Wagner's death in Venice. Contrary to expectations, there are no quotations of Wagner's music, except for the ostentatious use of augmented triads, vaguely reminiscent of the *Ride of the Valkyries*.

Richards (Richard), **Keith.** See ROLLING STONES, THE.

Richter, Sviatoslav (Teofilovich), outstanding Russian pianist; b. Zhitomir, Mar. 20, 1915. Both his parents were pianists; the family moved to Odessa when he was a child. He was engaged as a piano accompanist at the Odessa Opera and developed exceptional skill in playing orch.l scores at sight. He made his formal debut as a concert artist at the Odessa House of Engineers in 1934; entered the Moscow Cons. in 1937 as a student of Heinrich Neuhaus, graduating in 1947. He acquired a notable following even during his student years; in 1945 he made a stunning appearance at the All-Union Contest of Performances and was awarded its highest prize; received the Stalin Prize in 1949. In subsequent years he played throughout the Soviet Union and Eastern Europe. During the Russian tour of the Philadelphia Orch. in 1958, Richter was soloist, playing Prokofiev's 5th Piano Concerto in Leningrad; he made several international concert tours, including visits to China (1957) and the U.S. (1960).

Both in Russia and abroad he has earned a reputation as a piano virtuoso of formidable attainments; is especially praised for his impeccable sense of style, with every detail of the music rendered with lapidary perfection. His performances of the Romantic repertoire have brought him great renown, and he has made notable excursions into the works of Debussy, Ravel, and Prokofiev as well; gave the 1st performances of Prokofiev's 6th, 7th, and 9th sonatas.

ricochet. A special down-bow stroke on the violin, achieved by throwing the upper 3rd of the bow on the same string, resulting in a bouncing series of rapid notes in one stroke. See SPRINGING BOW.

ricordanza (It.). Reminiscence; sometimes used in titles of Romantic compositions.

riddle canon. A canon that is not written out; the performer must decipher when the imitating voices must come in, and at what interval; PUZZLE CANON.

Rider Quartet. RITTERQUARTETT.

Riders to the Sea. Opera by Vaughan Williams, 1937, based on the 1904 play by J. M. Synge; it was 1st performed in London. The drama is a lament on the fate of an Irishwoman who has lost all her sons at sea. Vaughan Williams enhances the depressing monotony of the story in his monodic setting, occasionally relieved by acrid dissonances.

Riemann, (Karl Wilhelm Julius) **Hugo,** eminent German musicologist; b. Gross-Mehlra, near Sondershausen, July 18, 1849; d. Leipzig, July 10, 1919. He began his training with his father, a landowner and civil servant who was an amateur musician; then continued his study of theory in Sondershausen with Heinrich Frankenberger, August Bartel, and Theodor Ratzenberger; also took courses at the Sondershausen and Arnstadt Gymnasiums. After studying classical languages and literature at the Rossleben Klosterschule (1865–68) he took courses in law and German philology and history at the Univ. of Berlin and in philosophy at the Univ. of Tübingen. He studied harmony with Jadassohn and piano and composition with Reinecke in Leipzig (1871–72); then received his Ph.D. in 1873 from the Univ. of Göttingen with the dissertation *Über das musikalische Hören* (Leipzig, 1874). He taught at Bielefeld (1876–78); after qualifying as a lecturer at the Univ. of Leipzig (1878) he taught in Bromberg (1880–81); then taught piano and theoretical courses at the Hamburg Cons. (1881–90); after a brief stay in Sondershausen (1890) he taught at the Wiesbaden Cons. (1890–95). In 1895 he resumed his lectures at the Univ. of Leipzig; was made prof. in 1905, and also director of the Collegium Musicum in 1908 and of the Forschungsinst. für Musikwissenschaft in 1914. He was honored with a Mus.Doc. from the Univ. of Edinburgh (1899) and with a Festschrift on his 60th birthday.

The mere bulk of Riemann's writings, covering every branch of musical science, constitutes a monument of indefatigable industry, and is proof of enormous concentration and capacity for work. When one takes into consideration that much of this work is the result of painstaking research and of original, often revolutionary, thinking, one must share the great respect and admiration in which Riemann was held by his contemporaries. Although many of his ideas are now seen in a different light, his works on harmony were considered to constitute the foundation of modern music theory. His researches in the field of music history have solved a number of vexing problems and thrown light on others. And finally, in formulating the new science of musicology the labors of Riemann were of great significance. His name is indelibly linked to the MUSIK-LEXIKON that bears his cognomen. He contributed innumerable articles to various journals and also wrote numerous pedagogical and other works.

Rienzi (*Cola Rienzi, der letzte der Tribünen*). Opera by Wagner, 1842, produced in Dresden. The composer's libretto is based on the historical novel by Bulwer-Lytton (who also authored the line "It was a dark and stormy night"). Rienzi is a member of a powerful Roman family in the 14th century; he is trying to restore Roman self-government but is caught up in the framework of the internecine struggle between his and other leading families. In the opera—as in the novel and actual history—Rienzi, his sister, and a handful of his adherents perish in a fire at the Capitol. This is one of Wagner's early Italianate operas; its overture with its stirring trumpet calls is performed in concert, but the opera is rarely performed in its entirety.

riff. 1. An antiphonal refrain in jazz consisting of sharply rhythmed brief turns often given out by wind and percussion instruments as an interlude after a solo. Such riffs produce the effect of stopping for a few beats, simulating exhaustion and a deceptive sudden ending. 2. As per (1) but, in popular music, played on whatever instrument is chosen (keyboards and electric guitar are common), and often contained within a solo improvisation. 3. HOOK.

rifiorimento (It., reflowering). Using melodic and rhythmic ornamentation.

rigadoon (Fr. *rigaudon*; It. *rigodone*). A lively dance originating in the 17th century in southern France. Set in ALLA BREVE time, it usually opens on a quarter-note upbeat and contains a trio section and a number of reprises. The rigadoon was often part of the instrumental suites of the 17th and 18th centuries. Ravel included a rigadoon in his piano suite *Le Tombeau de Couperin.*

Rigoletto. Opera by Verdi, 1851, to a libretto based on Hugo's play *Le Roi s'amuse*, 1st performed in Venice. Rigoletto, a hunchbacked court jester, mocks an aggrieved father whose daughter was seduced by the libidinous Duke of Mantua, and is cursed by the victim of his insensitive raillery. The curse is prophetic, for his own daughter is debauched in turn by the despicable rake. Incensed, Rigoletto hires an assassin with the task of killing the Duke and delivering his body in a sack at the door of a tavern. But when he arrives there at midnight he hears the ineffable Duke repeat his immortal and immoral misogynist aria, *La Donna è mobile*. Horrified, he opens the sack and finds his dying daughter, who had been stabbed when she disguises herself and voluntarily takes the knife intended for the Duke, whom she still loves. "Maledizione!" he cries out, recalling the curse. The opera is a perennial favorite; the Duke's aria is sung by a myriad of tenors; there is also a magnificent vocal quartet. Liszt wrote a paraphrase for piano on the themes from *Rigoletto*.

rigor(e) (It.). Rigor, strictness. *Al* (or *con*) *rigore di tempo*, *a rigor di tempo*, in strict time.

rigoroso (It.). In strict time.

rilasciando (It.). Rallentando.

Riley, Terry (Mitchell), American composer and performer of West Coast experimental tendencies; b. Colfax, Calif., June 24, 1935. He studied piano with Duane Hampton at San Francisco State College (1955–57) and composition with Seymour Shifrin and William Denny at the Univ. of Calif. at Berkeley (M.A., 1961). Riley's *In C* (1965) is in mobile form, played by members of an ensemble who proceed freely from one segment to another (total of 53), along with an unrelenting high C octave; this piece launched the 2nd wave of MINIMALISM. Later in the 1960s Riley went to Europe and played piano and saxophone in cabarets in Paris and in Scandinavia. In 1970 he was initiated in San Francisco as a disciple of Pandit Pran Nath, the North Indian singer, and followed him to India. He was a creative associate at the Center for Creative and Performing Arts at the State Univ. of N.Y. at Buffalo (1967); from 1971 to 1980 he was associate prof. at Mills College in Oakland, Calif. In 1979 he held a Guggenheim fellowship.

In his music Riley explores the extremes of complexity and gymnosophistical simplicity, applying the notion of varied repetition to a highly programmatic minimalist aesthetic; he anticipates the work of John Adams but without the latter's symphonic/operatic leanings. Riley's titles suggest connections with the Beat Generation, non-Western religion, and a new age sensibility in its primordial, less vacuous stage. Among his many works are: Tape and Instrumental: *I Can't Stop No*, *Mescalin Mix*, and *She Moves* for Tape (1962–63); *In C* for variable ensemble, notated in fragments to be played any number of times at will in the spirit of aleatory latitudinarianism, all within the key of C major, with an occasional F-sharp providing a *trompe l'oreille* effect (San Francisco, 1965); *Descending Moonshine Dervishes* for Electronic Organ (1975); *Shri Camel* for Electric Organ with Tape Delay (1976); *The Harp of New Albion* for Justly Tuned Piano (1984); *Cadenza on the Night Plain* for String Quartet (1984); *Salome Dances* for String Quartet (1989); *Mexico City Blues* for Orch.

Pieces with synthesizer: *Poppy Nogood and the Phantom Band* (1966); *A Rainbow in Curved Air* (1968); *Chorale of the Blessed Day* for Voice and 2 Synthesizers or Piano and Sitar (1980); *Eastern Man* for Voice and 2 Synthesizers (1980); *Embroidery* for Voice and 2 Synthesizers or Piano, Synthesizer, Sitar, Tabla, and Alto Saxophone (1980; last 3 works combined into *Songs for the 10 Voices*, 1982); *Song from the Old Country* for Voice, Piano, Sitar, Tabla, String Quartet, and Synthesizer (1980); *G–Song* for Voice, String Quartet, and Synthesizer (1981); *Remember This Oh Mind* for Voice and Synthesizer (1981); *Sunrise of the Planetary Dream Collector* for Voice, Synthesizer, and String Quartet (1981); *The Ethereal Time Shadow* for Voice and 2 Synthesizers (1982); *Offering to Chief Crazy Horse* for Voice and 2 Synthesizers (1982); *The Medicine Wheel* for Voice, Piano, Sitar, Tabla, String Quartet, and Synthesizer (1983); *Song of the Emerald Runner* for Voice, Piano, String Quartet, Sitar, Tabla, and Synthesizer (1983). Film scores: *Les Yeux Fermés* (1973); *Le Secret de la Vie* (1975); improvisational pieces.

rimettendo (It.). Resume a preceding tempo, whether after accelerating or retarding.

Rimsky-Korsakov, Nikolai (Andreievich)

~~~ ~~~ ~~~ ~~~ ~~~

Great Russian composer and master of orchestration, member of the "Mighty 5"; b. Tikhvin, near Novgorod, Mar. 18, 1844; d. Liubensk, near St. Petersburg, June 21, 1908. He remained in the country until he was 12 years old; in 1856 he entered the Naval School in St. Petersburg, graduating in 1862. He took piano lessons as a child with provincial teachers, and later with a professional musician, Theodore Canille, who introduced him to Balakirev; he also met Cui and Borodin. In 1862 he was sent on the clipper Almaz on a voyage that lasted 2 1/2 years; returning to Russia in the summer of 1865, he settled in St. Petersburg, where he remained most of his life. During his travels he maintained contact with Balakirev and continued to report to him the progress of his musical composition. He completed his 1st Sym. (which was also the earliest significant work in this form by a Russian composer), and it was performed under Balakirev's direction at a concert of the Free Music School in St. Petersburg (1865). In 1871 Rimsky-Korsakov was engaged as a prof. of composition and orchestration at the St. Petersburg Cons., even though he was aware of the inadequacy of his own technique. He would remain on the faculty until his death, with the exception of a few months in 1905 when he was relieved of his duties as prof. for his public support of the rebellious students during the revolution of that year.

In 1873 Rimsky-Korsakov abandoned his naval career, but he was appointed to the post of inspector of the military orchs. of the Russian navy, until it was abolished in 1884. From 1883 to 1894 he was also assistant director of the Court Chapel and led the chorus and the orch. there. Although he was not a gifted conductor, he gave many performances of his own orch. works; made his debut at a charity concert for the victims of the Volga famine, in St. Petersburg (1874); the program included the 1st performance of his 3rd Sym. From 1886 until 1900 he conducted the annual Russian Sym. concerts organized by the publisher Belaieff; in June 1889 he conducted 2 concerts of Russian music at the World Exposition in Paris; in 1890 he conducted a concert of Russian music in Brussels; led a similar concert there in 1900. His last appearance abroad was in the spring of 1907, when he conducted in Paris 2 Russian historic concerts arranged by Diaghilev; in the same year he was elected corresponding member of the French Academy, to succeed Grieg.

These activities, however, did not distract Rimsky-Korsakov from his central purpose as a national Russian composer. His name was grouped with those of Cui, Borodin, Balakirev, and Mussorgsky as the "Mighty 5," and he maintained an intimate friendship with most of them; at Mussorgsky's death he collected his MSS and prepared them for publication; he also revised Mussorgsky's opera *Boris Godunov*; it was in Rimsky-Korsakov's version that the opera became famous. Later some criticism was voiced against Rimsky-Korsakov's reduction of Mussorgsky's original harmonies and melodic lines to an academically acceptable standard. He had decisive influence in the affairs of the Belaieff publishing firm and helped publish a great number of works by Russian composers of the St. Petersburg group; only a small part of these sumptuously printed scores represents the best in Russian music, but culturally Rimsky-Korsakov's solicitude was of great importance.

Although he was far from being a revolutionary, he freely expressed his disgust at the bungling administration of Czarist Russia; he was particularly indignant about the attempts of the authorities to alter Pushkin's lines in his own last opera, *The Golden Cockerel* (1906–1907; Moscow, 1909), and he refused to compromise; he died, of angina pectoris, with the situation still unresolved; the opera was produced posthumously, with the censor's changes; the original text was not restored until the revolution of 1917.

Rimsky-Korsakov was one of the greatest masters of Russian music. His source of inspiration was Glinka's operatic style; he made use of both the purely Russian idiom and coloristic oriental melodic patterns; such works as his symphonic suite *Scheherazade* (symphonic suite, op. 35; St. Petersburg, 1888) and *The Golden Cockerel* represent Russian orientalism at its best; in the purely Russian style the opera *Snow Maiden* (1880–81; St. Petersburg, 1882) and the *Russian Easter Overture* (op. 36, 1888) are outstanding examples. The influence of Wagner and Liszt in his music was small; only in his opera *The Legend of the Invisible City of Kitezh* (1903–1905; St. Petersburg, 1907) are there perceptible echoes from *Parsifal*.

In the art of orchestration Rimsky-Korsakov had few equals; his treatment of instruments in solo passages and in ensemble was invariably idiomatic. In his treatise on orchestration he selected only passages from his own works to demonstrate the principles of practical and effective application of registers and tone colors (unlike Berlioz, who included the work of others in his groundbreaking treatise). Although an academician in his general aesthetics, he experimented boldly with melodic progressions and ingenious harmonies that pointed toward modern usages. He especially favored the major scale with the lowered submediant and the octatonic scale of alternating whole tones and semitones (which Russian reference works called "Rimsky-Korsakov's scale"); in the score of his opera-ballet *Mlada* (opera-ballet, 1889–90; St. Petersburg, 1892) there is an ocarina part tuned in this scale; in *The Golden Cockerel* and *Kashchei the Immortal* (Moscow, 1902) he applied dissonant harmonies in unusual superpositions; but he set for himself a definite limit in innovation, and severely criticized R. Strauss, Debussy, and d'Indy for their modernistic practices.

As a music educator Rimsky-Korsakov was of the greatest importance to the development and maintenance of the traditions of the Russian national school; among his students were Glazunov, Liadov, Arensky, Ippolitov-Ivanov, Gretchaninov, Nikolai Tcherepnin, Maximilian Steinberg, Gnessin, and Miaskovsky. Stravinsky studied privately with him from 1903 on. In addition to the works previously mentioned, Rimsky-Korsakov wrote many operas, orch.l works, including Overture on 3 Russian Themes, op. 28 (1st version, 1866; 2nd version, 1879–80); Fantasia on Serbian Themes, op. 6 (1st version, 1867; 2nd

version, 1886–87); Sym. No. 2, op. 9, Antar (1st version, 1868; 2nd version, 1875; 3rd version, 1897); Sym. No. 3, op. 32 (1st version, 1866–73; St. Petersburg, Mar. 2, 1874; 2nd version, 1886); and Piano Concerto in C-sharp Minor, op. 30 (1882–83); and chamber works for string quartet (1875–99) and other instrumental combinations.

He wrote many choral works with orch.l accompaniment, as well as a cappella choruses. His piano works include many character pieces, including variations. He was also a prolific arranger and editor, including of his edition of 100 Russian folk songs, op. 24 (1876). He orchestrated Dargomyzhsky's posthumous opera Kamennyi gost (The Stone Guest) and Borodin's Prince Igor. His greatest task of musical reorganization was the preparation for publication and performance of Mussorgsky's works; he reharmonized the cycle *Songs and Dances of Death* and the symphonic picture *St. John's Night on Bald Mountain*; orchestrated the opera *Khovanshchina*; revised *Boris Godunov* (melody, harmony, and orchestration).

Among his pedagogical works the book on harmony (1884) is widely used in Russian music schools. Two of Rimsky-Korsakov's relations were important Russian musicians. Andrei (Nikolaievich) Rimsky-Korsakov (b. St. Petersburg, Oct. 17, 1878; d. Leningrad, May 23, 1940) studied philology. He devoted his energies to Russian music history. In 1915 he began the publication of an important magazine, *Musikalny Sovremennik* (The Musical Contemporary), but the revolutionary events of 1917 forced suspension of its publication. He ed. books on his father, and Mussorgsky; compiled the catalog, *Musical Treasures of the MS Department of the Leningrad Public Library* (1938). He was married to the composer Julia Weissberg. Nikolai's grandson (and Andrei's nephew) Georgi (Mikhailovich) Rimsky-Korsakov (b. St. Petersburg, Dec. 26, 1901; d. Leningrad, Oct. 10, 1965) in 1923, founded a society for the cultivation of quarter-tone music (1923) and composed some works in that system; also studied Scriabin's intentions for the "luce" part in *Prometheus*. He later became active in work on electronic musical instruments; was co-inventor of the *Emeriton* (1930), capable of producing a complete series of tones at any pitch and of any chosen or synthetic tone color; wrote for it.

Rinaldo. Opera by Handel, 1711, premiered in London, based on an incident, in Tasso's epic poem *Gerusalemme lib-* *erata*, often used by composers. Rinaldo is a Crusader engaged to Almira, daughter of the leader of the Crusaders, who are besieging Islamic Jerusalem. The enchantress Armida is determined to seduce Rinaldo and kill Almira. With the aid of a benign magus the crusaders destroy Armida's magic garden, so that Rinaldo can now marry Almira without obstacles placed by evil forces.

rinforzando (*rinforzato*; It.). With special emphasis; indicates a sudden increase in loudness, either for a tone or chord, or throughout a phrase of short passage; SFORZANDO.

rinforzare, senza (It.). Without growing louder.

Ring des Nibelungen, Der (The Ring of the Nibelung). Operatic tetralogy by Wagner, 1876, described by him as "a stage festival play for 3 days and a preliminary evening." The entire cycle was produced for the 1st time at the 1st Bayreuth Festspiele over 4 evenings. The individual titles are *Das Rheingold, Die Walküre, Siegfried*, and *Götterdämmerung*. The cycle is musically united by a whole encyclopedia of leitmotivs identifying not only the personages involved but also objects and ideas. Wagnerian statisticians have counted as many as 90 leading motives in the cycle, and special manuals have been published to guide the listener through the Wagnerian jungle. See also individual operas.

ring modulator. An electronic device that produces, from 2 inputs of frequencies (x, y), 2 new modulated frequencies (x + y and x − y).

Ringeltanz (Ger.). Ring or round dance performed by pairs holding hands in a circle.

rip. In big band jazz, a determined leap to the initial note of a tune starting with an upbeat a 4th or 5th below.

ripetizione (repetizione; It.). Repetition.

ripieno (It., filling up, supplementary). 1. Any orch.l part that reinforces leading orch.l parts by doubling them or by filling in the harmony. 2. In scores, a direction calling for the entrance of the full string band (in military music, the clarinets, oboes, etc.). In Baroque music the term refers to the full instrumental complement (the TUTTI) in a concerted (concertante) work, where ripieno sections alternate with sections written for the solo group, CONCERTINO (also called *senza ripieno*, without reinforcement). 3. A combination stop drawing all registers of any given manual.

ripigliare (It.). Resume.

riposo, con (It.). In a calm, tranquil manner; reposefully.

riposta, -o (Lat., companion). Answer to the subject in a fugue or canon; COMES.

riprendendo (It.). Resuming. *Riprendendo poco a poco il tempo*, gradually regaining the preceding rate of speed.

ripresa (It., repetition). 1. REPRISE. 2. In Italian madrigals, the refrain.

Rise and Fall of the City of Mahagonny, The. AUFSTIEG UND FALL DER STADT MAHAGONNY.

Rise 'n' Shine. Song by Youmans, 1932, taken from the musical *Take a Chance*. The song was written in the style of a Negro spiritual; the title became a colloquialism for waking up reluctant sleepers.

risoluto (It.). In a resolute, vigorous, decided style.

Rispetti e Strambotti. String Quartet by Malipiero, 1920, commissioned by the Elizabeth Sprague Coolidge Foundation and 1st performed in Pittsburgh, Pa. *Rispetti* (respects) are stanzaic poetic forms set in frottolas and madrigals; *strambotti* are similar, with an emphasis on rural subjects and set in early monody as well. The contrast between the aristocratic and the rustic forms constitutes the musical content of Malipiero's work.

risposta (It.). 1. The answer or COMES in the FUGUE. 2. In the Italian madrigal, a section acting as a response.

risvegliato (It.). Lively, animated.

ritardando (It., retard; abbrev. *ritard., rit.*). Growing slower and slower. This term should be distinguished from RITENUTO, which means holding back and thus establishes a slower tempo at once. Propensity toward unauthorized and musically unjustified ritardando is an abiding sin of many performers who cover up technical deficiency and inability to play difficult passages in proper tempo. One American singer, when told by the exasperated accompanist that ritardandos could not be tolerated in Figaro's rapid aria from Rossini's *The Barber of Seville*, retorted, "I didn't make any ritardando, I just slowed down a little."

ritardare, senza (It.). Without slackening the pace.

ritardato (It.). At a slower pace.

Rite of Spring, The (*Le Sacre du Printemps*). Ballet by Stravinsky, 1913, with choreography by Nijinsky; 1st performed by Diaghilev's Ballets Russes in Paris. This is the most celebrated score of the 20th century; its premiere created a public scandal that reverberated mightily through music history. The ballet is subtitled *Scenes of Pagan Russia* and portrays in jagged, ponderous sequences the ancient rites as perceived by a highly sophisticated and imaginative modern musical mind. The basic melodic material is reduced to the diatonic tetrachord but the harmonic dressing is harshly polytonal and the orchestration is arranged in huge blocks and globes of sound; the angular rhythms are set in constantly changing meters. The difficulties created for conductors and instrumentalists were enormous and decades elapsed before the work could be handled by ordinary performers. The impact of the score was incalculable; hardly a single composer anywhere in the world escaped its powerful influence. It is no exaggeration to state that, with *The Rite of Spring*, the Romantic period ended and the modern musical era began.

ritenendo (It.). RALLENTANDO. *Ritenendo un po'*, slow down slightly.

ritenuto (It.; Fr. *retenue*, held back). Play at a slower rate of speed; not identical with RITARDANDO, which involves a gradual slowing down.

ritmico (It.). Rhythmically; precisely in tempo; MISURATO.

ritmo di quattro battute (It., rhythm of 4 measures). Count each measure as one beat, so that 4 measures equals 4 beats (i.e., 1 hypermeasure). *Ritmo di tre battute*, count each measure as one beat, so that 3 measures equals 3 beats (1 hypermeasure). Beethoven uses both indications in the scherzo of the *Choral Sym.*

ritornello (stornello; It.; Fr. *ritornelle*). 1. The burden of a song. 2. A repeat or modified repeat. 3. In accompanied vocal works, an instrumental prelude, interlude, or postlude (refrain), sometimes with modifications. 4. In a concerto, the orch.l refrain, sometimes with modifications.

Ritorno d'Ulisse in Patria, Il. Opera by Monteverdi, 1641, 1st performed in Venice. The libretto traces the return of Ulysses (Odysseus) home after his 10-year journey returning from the Trojan War. It is written in monodic style, but Monteverdi's orchestration is remarkably advanced.

Ritterquartett. Quartet in G Minor by Haydn, 1793 (No. 3, op. 74). The *Rider Quartet* receives its nickname from the opening movement with its galloping rhythm.

riversa, alla (riverso; It.). 1. Melodic inversion. 2. RETROGRADE motion.

Roach, Max(well Lemuel), remarkable African-American jazz drummer and composer; b. Elizabeth City, N.C., Jan. 10, 1924. He was taken to N.Y. as a child; after playing in a church drum-and-bugle corps he was a drummer in his high school band; also sat in on jam sessions in various jazz haunts around the city. He began his professional career as a member of Dizzy Gillespie's quintet, becoming immersed in the bebop movement; after a stint with Benny Carter's band (1944–45) he joined Charlie Parker's quintet (1947) and became widely recognized as one of the most innovative drummers of his era. He also studied composition with John Lewis at the Manhattan School of Music. He then led his own groups (from 1949), perfecting his hard bop style. With the trumpeter Clifford Brown, he was co-leader of an outstanding quintet (1953–56). In subsequent years he led various groups, including M'Boom Re, a percussion ensemble (from 1970).

With his own quartet he played throughout the U.S., Europe, and Japan (1976–77). He became a prof. of music at the Univ. of Mass. in Amherst (1972), where he instituted a jazz studies program. As a composer he became best known for his *Freedom Now Suite* (1960), an expression of his solidarity with the U.S. civil rights movement. He also wrote and recorded the avant-garde scores *Force* (1976; dedicated to Mao Zedong) and *1 in 2—2 in 1*

Max Roach, 1947

(1978). He was awarded an honorary Mus.D. degree from the New England Cons. of Music in Boston in 1982.

Robert Browning Overture. Symphonic poem by Ives, 1911, based on Browning's *Paracelsus*; Ives used some of the same music in a song entitled *Paracelsus*.

Robert le diable. Opera by Meyerbeer, 1831, premiered in Paris. Robert, a medieval duke in Palermo, is actually half-devil, half-human. When Robert falls in love with a young Sicilian woman, his father, the devil-in-chief, keeps him from winning a crucial tournament, the prize of which is her hand. But he is aided by his virtuous half-sister (who is all human), and wins his bride after all. The opera was tremendously successful in the 19th century, and has had sporadic performances in the 20th.

Roberta. Musical by Kern, 1933. An American football player suffering from unrequited love goes to Paris to his aunt, who owns a *salon de mode*; although her name is Minnie, everyone knows her as Roberta. The nephew joins the establishment in company with a shop designer who is revealed to be a genuine Russian princess. The score includes the classic ballad *Smoke Gets in Your Eyes*; other songs are *The Touch of Your Hand*, *Something's Got to Happen*, and *Yesterdays*.

Roberto d'Evereux, Conte di Essex. Opera by Donizetti, 1837, 1st produced in Naples. The melodramatic plot concerns the fateful infatuation of Queen Elizabeth I of England with Robert Devereux, the married 2nd Earl of Essex who, after many brilliant victories over Spain, is accused of treason and executed. The opera, also known as *Elizabeth and Essex*, is melodious, harmonious, and has flashes of genuine musical drama.

Robeson, Paul (Bustill), great African-American bass and actor; b. Princeton, N.J., Apr. 9, 1898; d. Philadelphia, Jan. 23, 1976. He 1st studied law (B.A., 1919, Rutgers Univ.; LL.B, 1923, Columbia Univ.); when his talent for singing and acting was discovered he appeared in plays in the U.S. and England; acted the eponymous lead in Eugene O'Neill's play *The Emperor Jones* and Louis Gruenberg's operatic version of it; he also performed Crown in *Porgy*, the folk play by DuBose and Dorothy Heyward that was later the subject of Gershwin's opera. In 1925 Robeson gave his 1st Negro spiritual recital in N.Y.; then toured in Europe. In 1928 he scored an enormous success in the musical *Show Boat* in London, becoming deservedly famous for his rendition of *Ol' Man River*. In 1930 he appeared in the title role of Shakespeare's *Othello* in London. Returning to the U.S. he continued to give recitals, but his outspoken admiration for the Soviet regime from the 1940s on interfered with the success of his career; he was blacklisted. In 1952 he was awarded the International Stalin Peace Prize ($25,000). During the summer of 1958 he made an extensive European tour. He continued to sing abroad until he was stricken with ill health and returned to the U.S. in 1963.

Robin Hood. Operetta by De Koven, 1890, premiered in Chicago. Its libretto is based on the exploits of the legendary English highwayman who robbed the rich to enrich the poor. Its most famous song, *O Promise Me!*, was inserted a year after the premiere in a London performance.

Robinson, Smokey, African-American singer, songwriter, and recording executive, b. William Robinson, Detroit, MI, Feb. 19, 1940. Robinson was singing, performing, and writing songs before he entered high school; in his teen years he formed the vocal group the Matadors, who became, in 1957, the Miracles. They signed with the local End label a year later and then, in 1959, joined with Berry Gordy Jr.'s fledgling Motown operation. In 1960 they scored their 1st national hit, *Shop Around*, written by Robinson and Gordy.

Through the mid-'60s Smokey and the Miracles continued to produce hits, many written by Robinson, including 1963's *You've Really Got a Hold on Me*, *Ooo Baby, Baby*, *My Girl*, and *The Tracks of My Tears* from 1965, and 1968's *I Second That Emotion*. At the same time, Robinson wrote for other Motown acts and produced many hits, beginning with the Temptations's *The Way You Do the Things You Do* in 1964. The original Miracles ceased recording in 1972; since then Robinson has pursued a sporadic solo career while also working as an executive at Motown; he left the label in 1988 but continues to record and perform on occasion.

robusto (It.). Firmly and boldly.

Rochberg, George, significant American composer; b. Paterson, N.J., July 5, 1918. He took courses in counterpoint and composition with Hans Weisse, George Szell, and Leopold Mannes at the Mannes College of Music in N.Y. (1939–42); after military service during World War II he took courses in theory and composition with Rosario Scalero and Gian Carlo Menotti at the Curtis Inst. of Music in Philadelphia (B.Mus., 1947); also studied at the Univ. of

Pa. (M.A., 1948). He taught at the Curtis Inst. (1948–54); was in Rome on Fulbright and American Academy fellowships (1950). In 1951 he became music ed. of the Theodore Presser Co. in Philadelphia, and soon after was made its director of publications; in 1960 he joined the faculty of the Univ. of Pa. as chairman of the music dept., a position he held until 1968; then continued on its faculty as a prof. of music, serving as Annenberg Prof. of the Humanities from 1979 until his retirement in 1983. He held 2 Guggenheim fellowships (1956–57; 1966–67); was elected to membership in the American Academy and Inst. of Arts and Letters (1985) and was made a fellow of the American Academy of Arts and Sciences (1986); was awarded honorary doctorates from the Univ. of Pa. (1985) and the Curtis Inst. of Music (1988).

He publ. the study *The Hexachord and Its Relation to the 12-Tone Row* (Bryn Mawr, Pa., 1955). A collection of his writings was ed. by W. Bolcom as *The Aesthetics of Survival: A Composer's View of 20th-Century Music* (Ann Arbor, 1984). In his style he pursues the ideal of tonal order and logically justifiable musical structures; the most profound influence he experienced was that of Schoenberg and Webern; many of his early works follow the organization in 12 different notes; more recently, he does not deny himself the treasures of the sanctified past, and even resorts to overt quotations in his works of recognizable fragments from music by composers as mutually unrelated as Schütz, Bach, Mahler, and Ives, treated by analogy with the "objets trouvés" in modern painting and sculpture. He has at times tried to synthesize his pre–20th century influences, at other times practiced collage or assemblage, or set one style against another within one work (e.g., String Quartet No. 3, in which different movements feature either strong atonality, Bartokian rhythm, or a Brahmsian variation set).

Other works by Rochberg include the opera *The Confidence Man*, opera, after Melville (1982) and the monodrama *Phaedra* for Mezzo-soprano and Orch. (1974–75). His orch.l works include 6 syms: No. 1 (1948–57); No. 2 (1955–56); No. 3 for Solo Voices, Chamber Chorus, Double Chorus, and Orch. (1966–69); No. 4 (Seattle, 1976); No. 5 (1984); and No. 6 (1987), among other works. He wrote seven string quartets, 2 piano trios (1963, 1985), and other chamber works; piano works; and vocal works, both accompanied and unaccompanied.

rock

A term that covers a variety of popular American styles dating from the 1960s, each an outgrowth of the rock 'n' roll of the 1950s, itself a descendant of primary black and white musical influences. American rock 'n' roll evolved from the dual resources of urban and rural folk songs and their derivatives. Urban popular music found its initial inspiration in the unique modalities of the Negro spirituals, with their lowered 3rds and 7ths, which constitute the foundation of the blues, ragtime, jazz, swing, and such lateral developments as bebop and boogie-woogie, all preserving the character of city music. Quite different was the type of popular music cultivated in the rural regions of the country, which represented mostly the tradition of European—and particularly English—folk songs. This country music was marked by a leisurely pace devoid of the nervous excitement and syncopated beat peculiar to the popular productions of city life.

With the advent of the electronic age the barriers between urban and rural music were brought down. In the ensuing implosion and fusion of both genres a new art was born that found its fullest expression in the phenomenon of rock 'n' roll. By the early 1960s the most popular genres were late examples of rhythm 'n' blues (both fast and slow), sentimental rock 'n' roll ballads, novelty songs, and, most significant, the "girl-group" trios with richly orchestrated accompaniment but a wide range of emotion from the lachrymose to the lusty. Elvis Presley was coming to the end of his rock 'n' roll star period and was evolving into a Las Vegas showman.

Then came the Beatles of Liverpool, England, whose members had been listening to American popular music since the mid-1950s. Their early songs and covers represented a turn to textures dominated by electric guitars with percussive rhythmic support. Over the years the Beatle songwriters (especially Lennon and McCartney) found various syntheses of the elements that had gone into rock 'n' roll, adding others along the way (notably harmonic and structural), and moving rock instrumentation into new territory. On the other end of the spectrum were the Rolling Stones, whose influences went further into rhythm-and-blues style harsher than what the Beatles had drawn from. This choice, plus the sexualized stance taken by Jagger and Richards in their songs, made the Beatles seem tame by comparison in term of raw energy. Both groups contributed to a major change in popular music: where rock 'n' roll was strongly rooted in dance, rock grew increasingly into a listening and even concert music.

The U.S. also contributed its influences on rock. One such style predated the "English invasion" of the 1960s, namely the surfing music of the West Coast (Beach Boys, Jan and Dean) that combined doo-wop and rock 'n' roll successfully. Another was an African-American development known as Motown or soul, depending on whether the music was centered on Detroit or Memphis, respectively. Both drew on gospel music and rhythm and blues; Motown also borrowed the girl-group sound for most of their artists; the Memphis sound brought more of the older blues singing style to its recordings, most done by solo artists or duets.

The term ROCK, seemingly an abbrev. for *rock 'n' roll*, gradually replaced the older appellation as the music moved into nonblues harmonic patterns and made the electric guitar the primary lead melody instrument, replacing the saxophone. Soon musical styles and pseudo-styles were given geographic names as a marketing ploy; the most legitimate of these were the San Francisco and Los Angeles sounds. The former was associated with the hippie movement, drug experimentation, and antiwar protest; the latter was less specific in nature and primarily reactive to its northern neighbor. Musicians of both cities borrowed from many styles, regardless of origin; these musicians also brought the expanded improvised solo to rock.

From there rock has flourished for 30 years plus, often challenged commercially and artistically: by disco in the 1970s and other dance music thereafter; by hip-hop and rap in the 1980s; by soul in its balladic forms, etc. But rock has shown a great capacity for reinventing itself when the creative juices are about to run dry; e.g., when the overblown art rock of the 1970s seemed destined to make rock a dinosaur, the new wave and punk movements came out of England, reinventing both the Beatles' and the Rolling Stones' contributions to early rock. This survival instinct seems to back an idea familiar to musical Darwinists: When a style can no longer absorb influences, it dies (e.g., the *Ars subtilior* of the late 14th century; ragtime); at best it can be absorbed into another style (as ragtime contributed to jazz).

Among the numerous endless subgenres that have grown out of 1960s rock, several are seemingly self-explanatory: *Acid rock*, reputedly influenced by drug-taking, using a penetrating, "buzzing" tone on the lead guitar equipped with a sustaining pedal; associated with the San Francisco sound; *art rock*, an odd mixture of rock instrumentation (with a strong emphasis on keyboards) and classical orch. or imitations thereof (e.g., the *mellotron*); the music can be original, in the style of a classical piece, or "borrowed" from actual works; *blues rock*, an especially British genre, taking both rural and urban blues into a rock context, with a strong dose of guitar (also keyboard and harmonica) improvisation; *folk rock*, putting folk songs or neotraditional songs into a rock context, much as the Byrds and then Bob Dylan did with Dylan songs; aurally less threatening than other rock of its time; extremely influential on European musicians aiming for a national character; *hard rock*, similar to acid rock but with a higher dynamic level, thicker texture, and an unmistakable hook; this is the predecessor to *heavy metal* (also called *metal*), which pushes the envelope further by even greater concentration on the rhythm guitar, the lead guitar becoming buried in the thick texture and adding a theatrical element; *jazz rock* (also known as *fusion*), a mixture of the harmonic and melodic elements of jazz with the rhythm and instrumentation of rock; represented jazz's attempt to overcome commercial failure during the 1960s and rock's desire for fresh materials and respect; *mellow rock* (*soft rock*), rock's contribution to MOR (middle of the road), easy listening, and Muzak; it grew out of folk rock's merging with late rock 'n' roll balladry, with Carole King at the head of the pack; *new wave*, a late 1970s English revival of the lean sound of 1960s rock (in reaction to art rock and disco) with a postmodernist sensibility; *punk rock* (*punk*), historically synchronous with new wave but influential by the "garage bands" of the

1960s and hard rock; originally had connection to British youth's social rage but eventually became a fashion statement; the punk spirit survived into the 1990s with *grunge*, an Americanized variant with more depression than alienation. Along the way rock has at times borrowed from other styles (classical, disco, reggae, hip-hop) without losing its essence. And musicians like Frank Zappa have been able to play most rock styles and parody them with great skill.

The greatest mass demonstration of rock and perhaps the greatest manifestation of the attractive power of music in all history was the Woodstock Festival in Bethel, N.Y. (Aug. 1969). Tens of thousands of young people converged on a farmer's field, disdaining the hardships of travel, feeding, sleeping, and mud in order to be amongst their rock idols. The happening had a profound sociological significance as well, for the audience, consisting of youthful nonconformists popularly known as hippies, seemed to be infused with the spirit of mutual accommodation, altruism, and love of peace. At least on that occasion, rock proved that it has indeed the power to soothe a savage breast.

The Canadian underground newspaper grandly named *Logos* gave in 1969 this description of rock as a social force: "Rock is mysticism, revolution, communion, salvation, poetry, catharsis, eroticism, satori, total communication, the most vibrant art form in the world today. Rock is a global link, as young people everywhere plug into it and add to the form. What this new music suggested was raising your level of consciousness away from the fragmented, intellectual, goal-oriented time and material world to a unified sensual direction in a timeless spiritual environment."

Guardians of public morals and even medical doctors became concerned with spiritual and physiological effects of rock on young people. Examinations of the auditory capacities of habitual rock players and their customers revealed the loss of hearing in the upper ranges. But the moral perils of rock hung heaviest among those who were born old. In 1975 the pastor of a Baptist Church in Florida cited statistical records to the effect that 984 out of 1,000 teenage girls who became pregnant out of wedlock committed fornication while rock music was being played. Even plants seem to react adversely to the sound of rock. In a book entitled *Noise: The New Menace* the author claims that all plants exposed to rock leaned away from the sound as if trying to escape, and would not bloom. In the meantime the rock recording industry reached gross sales totaling in the billions of dollars.

rock ’n’ roll

~~~ ~~~ ~~~ ~~~ ~~~

A popular American style of the 1950s that emerged from the African-American popular style of rhythm and blues. The origin of the term itself dates back to the motion picture *Transatlantic Merry-Go-Round*, produced in 1934, which featured a song, *Rock and Roll*, by Whiting and Clare; there is no inkling in the rhythmic and harmonic characteristics of this song of the type of rock ’n’ roll that would develop into an overwhelmingly potent musical machine some two decades later. The term is probably related to various songs using double entendre, especially a slang expression for sex.

As opposed to the prevailing ballad style of the time, which featured singers with smooth orch.l background, rock ’n’ roll featured a percussively heavy reinforcement of the meter (beat) played by combos consisting, minimally, of piano, bass, drums, and guitars, often with a single saxophonist or small wind section. Blues harmonic structures were common but without the corresponding mood.

Rock owes its popularity to small radio stations that pioneered in broadcasting rock records promoted commercially by a special class of music agents known as disc jockeys (DJ's; riders on record discs). One of the earliest specimens of mature rock ’n’ roll was the song *Crazy,*

Man, Crazy, recorded in 1953 by Bill Haley and the Comets. A Cleveland DJ named Alan Freed is generally credited with popularizing these songs under the generic term rock 'n' roll. In 1956 the landscape of rock 'n' roll was brightened by the rise of Elvis Presley. Dressed in outlandish attire and sporting 3-inch sideburns, he sang accompanying himself on an ear-splitting electric guitar; he developed a pelvic technique of rhythmic swing, gyrating suggestively around his lower axis—a body language that earned him the moniker Elvis the Pelvis.

Rock 'n' roll suffered temporary eclipse when it was discovered that DJ's accepted bribes from recording companies for pushing their rock records, a practice that became known as *payola*. (An even greater scandal erupted in the 1970s when executives of a major recording corporation admitted that they pampered their best-selling rock artists into signing exclusive contracts through the influence of wine, women, and drugs.) But no scandal could stop the inexorable march of rock 'n' roll. In 1960 Chubby Checkers and his innovative dance, the Twist, added a new beat to rock 'n' roll, operating in the new-fangled discotheques, successors to nightclubs, which used long-playing records amplified to the threshold of pain.

In rock 'n' roll the pendulumlike rhythmic motion produces a tremendous accumulation of kinetic energy, leading to a state of catatonic stupefaction among the listeners and the players themselves. The effect of this constant rhythmic drive is similar to that of the sinusoid wave with a steadily increasing amplitude created by the march of a regiment of soldiers across a suspension bridge, which can break the strongest steel. Thanks to the electronic amplification, rock 'n' roll became the loudest music to date. Otologists have warned that its addicts may lose the sensitivity to the higher harmonics of the human voice and become partially deaf. Ralph Nader, the American Cassandra of urban civilization, has cautioned the public against the danger of sonic pollution by rock 'n' roll in a letter addressed to a member of the Congress of the United States.

A more remarkable and less threatening feature of rock 'n' roll is the revival of archaic modality with its characteristic plagal cadences, the Dorian mode being a favorite. In harmony the submediant is lowered in major keys and becomes the minor 3rd of the minor subdominant triad. Parallel triadic progressions, adopted by rock 'n' roll, also impart an archaic modal quality to the music. It may well be that the fusion of old modes and modern rhythms will create a new type of syncretism of musical folkways.

Time magazine described rock 'n' roll in June 1956: "An unrelenting, socking syncopation that sounds like a bull whip; a choleric saxophone honking mating-call sounds; an electric guitar turned up so loud that its sound shatters and splits; a vocal group that shudders and exercises violently to the beat while roughly chanting either a near-nonsense phrase or a moronic lyric in hillbilly idiom." In other words an honest, poetic, out-of-touch critic in the centuries-old tradition of those who were not yet ready, or would never be ready, to "get it."

(We're Gonna) Rock Around the Clock. Rock 'n' roll song by Freedman and De Knight, 1953, made famous by Bill Haley and his Comets in 1954 and even more so when it was used in the 1955 film *Blackboard Jungle*.

Rock of Ages. An 18th-century English hymn by Hastings and Toplady with continuing popularity.

Rock-a-Bye Baby. Lullaby by a 15-year-old Effie Crockett, 1872; other than the 1st line of text the song is entirely her creation.

Rocked in the Cradle of the Deep. Sea ballad by Willard and Knight, 1839, introduced in N.Y.; the vocal part is best performed by a *basso lugubrioso*.

rococo (from Fr. *roc*, shell). An architectural term applied to a transitional era of composition current from about 1725 to 1775; some musicologists use the terms GALANT STYLE or "early Classic." In part, rococo served to lighten, even eliminate the "Gothic" contrapuntal textures of composers like Bach, who was increasingly considered old-fashioned; it reemphasized monodic homophony while maintaining the pervasive ornamentation, character pieces, dance forms, and tonality of the Baroque. But it was a period of intense experimentation; at the formal level, as Haydn and others developed what was later called sonata form; at the rhetorical level, as C. P. E. Bach and others found that the meditative aside and sudden pause could have great expressive effect; on other levels such as dynamics (the crescendos in the Mannheim school) and orchestration (the determination of the modern orch., incorporating winds, even in concerted pieces). One result, the question-and-answer phrase based on tonic-dominant-tonic harmonic motion, became the essence of Classic music; the transition from rococo to Classic can be seen in the difference in the music of Mozart the wunderkind from that of Mozart the composer in his twenties.

Rodelinda. Opera by Handel, 1725, 1st produced in London, based on an apparently historical incident. Rodelinda is the dethroned Queen of the Lombards, coveted by the usurper king who threatens to murder her child if she does not yield to his desires. But the lawful ruler returns and Rodelinda's virtue and bravery are rewarded. The quasi-historic libretto has elements of a RESCUE OPERA; the score is regarded as one of Handel's best.

Rodeo. Ballet by Copland, 1942, premiered in N.Y. with choreography by Agnes de Mille. The scenario concerns the adventures of a cowgirl at a ranch, following the archetypal plot of the strong woman who loses her independence in order to attract a man. Copland drew a 4-part orch. suite from the score, emphasizing his emulations of traditional American western music.

Rodgers, Jimmie (James Charles), pioneering American country-music singer, guitarist, and songwriter; b. Meridian, Miss., Sept. 8, 1897; d. N.Y., May 26, 1933. He worked on the railroad until his retirement in 1925. He made his 1st recordings in 1927 and became known as the "Singing Brakeman" and "America's Blue Yodeler," meshing the old-time style with rural blues. His short-lived career was dogged by tuberculosis and an inability to control his spendthrift lifestyle. In 1961 his name was the 1st to be placed in the Country Music Hall of Fame in Nashville, and in 1977 a U.S. postage stamp was issued to commemorate the 80th anniversary of his birth. He is duly recognized as the father of modern country music.

Rodgers, Richard (Charles), celebrated American composer of popular music; b. Hammels Station, Long Island, N.Y., June 28, 1902; d. N.Y., Dec. 30, 1979. He began piano lessons when he was 6; studied at Columbia Univ. (1919–21) and at the Inst. of Musical Art in N.Y. (1921–23), receiving instruction in the latter from Krehbiel and Goetschius. He collaborated with the lyricist Lorenz Hart in a series of inspired and highly popular musical comedies: *The Girl Friend* (1926); *A Connecticut Yankee*

(1927); *On Your Toes* (1936); *Babes in Arms* (1937); *I Married an Angel* (1938); *The Boys from Syracuse* (1942). After Hart's death in 1943 Rodgers became associated with Oscar Hammerstein II. Together they wrote the greatly acclaimed musical *Oklahoma!* (1943; Pulitzer Prize, 1944), followed by a number of no less successful productions: *Carousel* (1945); *State Fair* (film, 1945); *Allegro* (1947); *South Pacific* (1949; Pulitzer Prize, 1950); *The King and I* (1951); *Me and Juliet* (1953); *Pipe Dream* (1955); *The Flower Drum Song* (1958); *The Sound of Music* (1959). After Hammerstein's death in 1960 Rodgers wrote his own lyrics for his next musical, *No Strings* (1962); then followed *Do I Hear a Waltz?* (1965) to the lyrics of Stephen Sondheim. He also composed the soundtrack to the television series *Victory at Sea* (1952).

Rogers, Ginger. See ASTAIRE, FRED.

Röhrenglocken (Ger.). TUBULAR CHIMES.

Roi Carotte, Le (King Carrot). Bouffe-féerie by Offenbach, 1872, premiered in Paris, based on the play by Victorien Sardou. This is a satire of the recently defunct Second Empire of Napoléon III. Prince Fridolin XXIV of Krokodyne is overthrown by the revolutionary vegetable Carotte. Monkeys, bees, and ants attack Fridolin, but the lovely Rosée-du-Soir rescues him, while the usurper Carotte is eaten by a monkey.

Roi David, Le. Dramatic psalm by Honegger, 1921, 1st performed in Mézières, Switzerland. Honegger's 1st theatrical work, it is scored for narrator, singer, chorus, and small

Rodgers and Hammerstein, c. 1950

orch. The libretto concentrates on the story of David's struggles against the Philistines.

Roi de Lahore, Le. Opera by Massenet, 1877, 1st performed in Paris; the libretto is drawn from the Indian epic *Mahabharata.* The King of Lahore is murdered by an official coveting his favorite wife, but the king returns to earth reincarnated as a beggar. His beloved recognizes him under his rags and kills herself in the hope of joining him in the world beyond. The score is melodious, harmonious, and exotically perfumed.

Roi d'Ys, Le. Opera by Lalo, 1888, premiered in Paris. Two daughters of the King of Ys (a town in Brittany) are in love with the same handsome youth. The one who loses out in the contest opens the floodgates and lets the sea inundate the town. Horrified by her deed, she kills herself. The opera is seldom performed but the overture is popular on concert programs.

Roi l'a dit, Le (The King Has Spoken). Opera by Delibes, 1873, 1st performed in Paris. A marquis of the court of Louis XVI boasts falsely of the valor of his male heir, when in fact he has only daughters. When the King commands him to bring his son to the palace the marquis brings in a peasant boy whom he dresses up to play the role of his son. But the benighted rustic makes one faux pas after another, and the marquis marries him off to a conveniently available young damsel. The opera is harmonious but falls below the excellence of Delibes's ballet scores.

Roi malgré lui, Le (The King in Spite of Himself). Opera by Chabrier, 1887, premiered in Paris. The labyrinthine 16th-century plot involves a conspiracy against Henri de Valois, a reluctant candidate for the throne of France. To find out what the plotters have against him, he joins the conspiracy in disguise. In the end the plotters are foiled and willy-nilly Henri becomes King Henri II. The score contains some attractive ballet numbers.

Roland. Tragédie lyrique by Lully, 1685, premiered in Paris. The libretto is drawn from the well-known Italian epic *Orlando furioso* by Ariosto; the subject was suggested by King Louis XIV himself. The central episode concerns the passion of Orlando, Knight of Charlemagne, for a young woman who rejects his love. He finds consolation in his victorious battles. This story is the subject of many other operas, including one by Haydn (*Orlando paladino*, 1782).

Roldán, Amadeo, Cuban violinist, conductor, and composer; b. Paris (of Cuban parents), July 12, 1900; d. Havana, Mar. 2, 1939. He studied violin at the Madrid Cons. with Fernandez Bordas, graduating in 1916; won the Sarasate Violin Prize; subsequently studied composition with Conrado del Campo in Madrid and with Pedro Sanjuan. In 1921 he settled in Havana; in 1924 he became concertmaster of the Orquesta Filarmonica; in 1925, assistant conductor; in 1932, conductor. In the late 1920s and early 1930s he kept company with the members of Grupo de Avance, who sought to modernize Cuban artistic culture; he later became prof. of composition at the Cons. (from 1935). In his works he employed the melorhythms of Afro-Cuban popular music, particularly indigenous mestizo folk music (and folklore); his percussion ensemble works anticipate Varèse's *Ionisation.*

roll. 1. A tremolo or trill on the drum. The sign in notation is

Long roll, the prolonged and reiterated drum signal to troops, for attack or rally. 2. In organ playing, a rapid arpeggio. 3. On the tambourine, the rapid and reiterated hither- and thither-stroke with the knuckles.

Rolling Stones, The

Also called the Stones, long-lived English rock group, with the Beatles the prime movers of the transition from rock 'n' roll to rock in the 1960s. (Vocals/harmonica/guitar: Mick [Michael Philip] Jagger, b. Dartford, Kent, July 26, 1944; lead guitar/vocal: Keith Richards [Richard], b. Dartford, Kent, Dec. 18, 1943;

guitar/vocal: Brian Jones [born Lewis Brian Hopkins-Jones] b. Cheltenham, Feb. 28, 1942; d. London, July 3, 1969; Bass: Bill Wyman [born William Perks], b. Penge, SE London, Oct. 23, 1936; drums: Charlie Watts, b. Neasden, N. London, June 2, 1941; piano: Ian Stewart, b. 1938; d. London, Dec. 12, 1985. Jones was replaced in 1969 by Michael "Mick" Taylor, b. Welwyn Garden City, England, Jan. 17, 1948, and then Taylor was replaced in 1974 by Ron Wood, b. Hillingdon, England, June 1, 1947; Bill Wyman was replaced in 1992 by Darryl Jones.) The group played the rhythm-and-blues circuit in England until Andrew Loog Oldham (b. 1944) saw them and, like Brian Epstein with the Beatles, made the Stones ready for more general consumption, the scruffy answer to the sweet-faced Liverpudlians. Oldham demoted Ian Stewart from full membership because of his overall appearance (much as Epstein had replaced Pete Best with Ringo Starr); the pianist played with the group on recordings and on tours, functioned as tour manager, and became their trusted confidant.

With a recording contract the Stones combined their rhythm-and-blues covers (*Not Fade Away, It's All Over Now*) with rock balladry (*Tell Me, Time Is on My Side*). By 1965 Jagger and Richards were collaborating on most of their material, which found its stylistic niche in sexually oriented rock (*The Last Time, Satisfaction*); While the Beatles continued to focus on love and relationships, the Stones' songs turned to sometimes bitter social commentary (*Get Off of My Cloud, 19th Nervous Breakdown, Mother's Little Helper, Have You Seen Your Mother Baby*) even as more usual commentary continued (*Paint It Black, Let's Spend the Night Together*). The bizarre album *Their Satanic Majesties Request* (late 1967) failed to separate psychedelia from pretension (not to mention parody), but it helped to reinforce the Stones' differences from the Beatles, who were no longer touring, losing their stylistic cohesion as Lennon and McCartney wrote separate songs under their paired name

and sounding at a remove even when dealing with difficult issues.   Jagger and Richards solidified their outlaw image with the hard rock classic *Jumpin' Jack Flash* the following year. *Satanic Majesties* also taught the Stones the usefulness of vaguely conceptual albums; this was seen in the brilliant 1968 album *Beggars Banquet*, which included *Sympathy for the Devil, Street Fighting Man, Salt of the Earth, No Expectations*, and others. This was Brian Jones's last album; his positive musical contributions were now outweighed by his drug addictions, alcoholism, overall bad health, and unreliability; he was gently forced out of the group and was dead 2 months later, drowned in his own swimming pool. He was replaced by Mick Taylor, slide guitarist, formerly of John Mayall's Bluesbreakers; he stayed with the group until 1975, when he was replaced by Ron Wood, who had played with Jeff Beck and the Faces.

After another hit single (*Honky Tonk Woman*), another brilliant album followed: *Let It Bleed*, including *Gimme Shelter*, one of the Stones' most successful arrangements, but which came to represent the dark side, with its association with the Charles Manson cult murders and the free Altamont concert (1969) with security provided by Hell's Angels and the death of an 18-year-old black audience member. For a few more years Stones albums were generally of high quality; but by 1973's *Goat's Head Soup* the Stones were out of the innovatory loop; they have continued to tour and make recordings with other influences than rock (the discofied *Miss You*) as well as characteristic hard rock (*Start Me Up*). All five members released solo projects, none as successful as the group efforts but at least one highly distinctive: Watts's ventures into big band, in concert and on record. In the late 1980s and early 1990s the Stones were mostly silent, due to a feud between Jagger and Richards; they eventually reunited and, while they are not as active as they were, the Rolling Stones have survived, with only one subsequent change: the retirement of Wyman.

Rollins, "Sonny" (Theodore Walter), outstanding African-American jazz tenor saxophonist; b. N.Y., Sept. 7, 1929. He 1st worked with Babs Gonzales, Bud Powell, and Fats Navarro; then went to Chicago, where he studied with Ike Day. After making recordings with Miles Davis, he made appearances with Charlie Parker, Thelonious Monk, and other leading jazz musicians; also served as a member of the Modern Jazz Quartet. At the height of his

career, he ranked among the foremost masters of the tenor saxophone.

Roman Carnival, The (Le carnaval romain). Concert overture by Berlioz, 1844; 1st performed in Paris with the composer conducting. This is the most successful overture that Berlioz wrote. It is an arrangement of 2 episodes from his underrated but unsuccessful opera *Benvenuto Cellini*

(1838). Since Cellini was a notorious profligate, the overture is full of sensual joy.

Roman Festivals (Feste Romane). Symphonic poem by Respighi, 1929, 1st performed in N.Y.

Roman numerals. This system of enumeration is used for the designation of instrumental parts (Flute I, Flute II, etc.); analysis of harmonic progression in the vertical plane, based on scale steps (I = tonic, V = dominant, etc.); and as a method of enumerating works according to the composer's whim (i.e., Berio's *Sequenza* series, Stockhausen's *Klavierstücke*).

romance. 1. Orig. a type of Spanish poetic narrative, a ballad or popular tale in verse; later, Romance lyrical songs. The French and Russian romance is a short art song or a lied composed of several stanzas. 2. (Ger. *Romanze*) Short instrumental pieces of sentimental or romantic cast, without specific form. *Romances sans paroles*, songs without words.

romancero (Sp.). Collections of ballads or romances (heroic tales), sung or recited by *juglares* (minstrels).

romanesca. A type of court dance that originated in the Roman countryside in Italy in the 16th century. It is structurally related to the FOLIA, with its persistent bass formation (tonic, dominant, submediant, mediant) upon which there are embroidered melodies, either written out or improvised by singers.

Romantic. In music history, the period from about 1815 to 1915, overlapping with late Classic on one end and impressionism, expressionism, and primitivism on the other.

Romantic Suite. Orch.l work by Reger, 1912, in 3 movements; 1st performed in Dresden.

Romantic Symphony (1). Sym. No. 4 by Bruckner, 1874, in E-flat minor; the name is Bruckner's. The work is one of Bruckner's shortest syms.; the themes are spacious, and the development rich and resonant. Like many Bruckner syms., there were major revisions of the work; it was 1st performed in its final form in Vienna, 1888.

Romantic Symphony (2). Sym. No. 2 by Hanson, 1930, premiered in Boston; the name is Hanson's.

Romany music. See GYPSY MUSIC.

romanza (It.). A short romantic song or a solo instrumental piece.

Romeo and Juliet (1). Ballet by Prokofiev, 1938, after Shakespeare, 1st produced in Brno. It is the most engaging ballet by Prokofiev; he drew two orch.l suites from it.

Romeo and Juliet (2). Overture-fantasy by Tchaikovsky, 1870, after Shakespeare, 1st performed in Moscow. This is Tchaikovsky's 1st important orch.l work. It opens with a chorale, which is followed by a series of spasmodic syncopated passages illustrative of the strife between the 2 warring houses in Shakespeare's drama. The highest point of the overture is the songful lyric theme of love, which has charmed audiences all over the world for more than a century.

Roméo et Juliette (3). Sym. romantique by Berlioz, 1839, after Shakespeare, 1st performed in Paris. Scored for voices, chorus, and orch., Berlioz created a type of Romantic oratorio, with musical episodes taken from Shakespeare, of which the scherzo *Queen Mab* is a prodigious display of orch. coruscation.

Roméo et Juliette (4). Opera by Gounod, 1867, after Shakespeare, premiered in Paris. Like other works by this composer, the music possesses a peculiar quality of sweetness that delights Gounod's admirers and repels his detractors. *Roméo et Juliette* was tremendously successful from the outset and almost equaled his *Faust* in popularity.

Romeo und Julia auf dem Dorfe. VILLAGE ROMEO AND JULIET, A.

Romero, family of famous Spanish-born American guitarists constituting a quartet known as Los Romeros: Celedonio (b. Málaga, Mar. 2, 1918) pursued a career as a soloist in Spain; he served as mentor to each of his 3 sons, Celin (b. Málaga, Nov. 23, 1940), Pepe (b. Málaga, Mar. 8, 1944), and Angel (b. Málaga, Aug. 17, 1946); they eventually appeared together as a guitar quartet, playing engagements throughout Spain. The family emigrated to the U.S. in 1958 and made their 1st tour of the country in 1961; billed as "the royal family of the guitar," they toured with great success worldwide. In addition to making their own arrangements and transcriptions, they commissioned works from various composers, including Rodrigo and Federico Moreno Torroba.

ronde (Fr.). 1. Whole note. 2. Round dance.

rondeau (Fr.). 1. A medieval French song of the fixed form type, with a musical refrain and verse repeating in a nonalternating manner, comprising one stanza of 8 lines. 2. Baroque instrumental form, alternating a refrain (*grand couplet*) with various episodes (couplets); the etymological and musical predecessor of the RONDO.

rondel, rondelet (Fr.). Early names for the RONDEAU.

rondellus (Lat.). The 13th-century British vocal genre, in 3 voices, in which the technique of VOICE EXCHANGE is employed, either in the upper 2 voices (with a repetitive TENOR or PES) or all 3.

rondena. Spanish round dance similar to a FANDANGO.

Rondine, La (The Swallow). Opera by Puccini, 1917, premiered in Monte Carlo. A loving and lovable young woman of the 2nd Empire becomes the mistress of a banker, but she finds time to dally with a youthful admirer. Eventually, like a swallow, she returns to her older, safe, and reliable protector. The music's quality falls far below the dramatic excellence of Puccini's other operas.

rondo (Fr. *rondeau*). An instrumental piece in which the opening thematic section or refrain (A) is repeated in the tonic, alternating with contrasting sections in related keys (with the common exception of the penultimate section, also in the tonic). In general there are 5- and 7-part rondo forms; a typical pattern—with letters representing thematic sections—might be A-B-A-C-A-B-A. Sometimes these episodes are expanded so as to create secondary thematic sources; variations are widely applied, and there is usually a coda to conclude the work. The rondo is often used as the finale of Classic syms., concertos, and sonatas.

rondo-sonata form. SONATA-RONDO FORM.

Rooley, Anthony. See KIRKBY, EMMA.

root. The lowest note of a chord in actual pitch. *Root position*, arrangement of a chord where the lowest pitch (usually the bass) is the root of the chord.

Rorem, Ned, brilliant American composer, pianist, and writer; b. Richmond, Ind., Oct. 23, 1923. His parents were distinguished in various fields; his father was a medical economist and a founder of Blue Cross; his mother was active in various peace movements. At a very young age he was inculcated with piano music, which was taught to him at home by 3 consecutive female instructors. The family moved to Chicago, where Rorem began his formal study of theory and harmony with Leo Sowerby at the American Cons. (1938–39). He then entered Northwestern Univ., where he took composition courses with Alfred Nolte (1940–42). In 1943 he received a scholarship to study at the Curtis Inst. of Music in Philadelphia; there he studied counterpoint and harmony with Rosario Scalero; he also had beneficial instruction in dramatic and vocal music with Gian Carlo Menotti. In 1944 Rorem moved to N.Y. and entered the Juilliard School of Music, where he studied composition with Bernard Wagenaar (B.S., 1946; M.S., 1948); he also took private lessons in orchestration with Virgil Thomson (1944); in the summers of 1946 and 1947 he studied modern harmony with Aaron Copland at the Berkshire Music Center at Tanglewood, in Lenox, Mass.

He was fortunate in obtaining the Gershwin Memorial Award, which enabled him to travel to France. There he rapidly absorbed the musical arts of the period and also mastered the French language. From 1949 to 1951 he sojourned in Morocco. Returning to Paris, he obtained the patronage of a famous friend of the arts, the Vicomtesse Noailles, and entered the circle of modern Parisian composers. The French influence remains the most pronounced characteristic of his music, particularly in his songs. Upon his return to the U.S. in 1958 he was appointed composer-in-residence at the State Univ. of N.Y. at Buffalo (1959–60); also taught at the Univ. of Utah (1966–67) and the Curtis Inst. of Music (1980–86).

Rorem developed as a composer of substance and originality, proclaiming that music must sing, even if it is written for instruments. Between times he almost unexpectedly discovered an astonishing talent as a writer. An elegant stylist in both French and English, he publ. a succession of personal journals, recounting with gracious insouciance his encounters in Paris and N.Y. He continued to obtain commissions from such prestigious institutions as the Ford Foundation and the Elizabeth Sprague Coolidge Foundation, as well as from a number of prominent performing groups. He received 2 Guggenheim fellowships (1956–57; 1978–79), and in 1976 was the recipient of the Pulitzer Prize in music for his *Air Music*. He proudly declared that he wrote music for an audience and that he did not wish to indulge in writing songs and symphonic poems for an indefinite, abstract group. Rorem is regarded as one of the finest song composers in America; a born linguist, he has a natural feeling for vocal line and for prosody of text.

Rosalia. A term of opprobrium for a modulating sequence to a key a major 2nd higher; the term comes from a once popular Italian song, *Rosalia, mia cara*. The Germans called this type of modulating sequence *Cousin Michel*, after an old German song of that name, or (contemptuously) *Schusterfleck* (shoemaker's patch). But Beethoven, Schubert, Liszt, and Bruckner used the Rosalia type of sequence most admirably for dramatic effect; it was popular in semiclassical pieces of the 19th century; 20th-century popular music often uses a modulation of a minor 2nd higher as a clichéd climactic effect.

Rosamunde. Incidental music by Schubert, 1823, to the play *Rosamunde, Princess of Cyprus* by Helmina von Chézy (who wrote the underwhelming libretto to Weber's *Euryanthe*). The popular overture still performed as that of *Rosamunde* belonged originally to the music for *Die Zauberharfe* (1820); to confuse the situation further, the overture originally performed in the 1823 production of *Rosamunde* was taken from the opera *Alfonso und Estrella* (1822).

Rose-Marie. Operetta by Friml, 1924. The story concerns Rose-Marie La Flamme, a young French-Canadian woman who is adored by a multitude of competing males; her true love is a Royal Canadian Mountie, who is falsely accused of murder. He is cleared, and Rose-Marie's faith in him is vindicated. Includes the famous duet *Indian Love Call*.

Rosenberg, Hilding (Constantin), important Swedish composer and teacher; b. Bosjökloster, Ringsjon, Skåne, June 21, 1892; d. Stockholm, May 19, 1985. He studied piano and organ in his youth, then was active as an organist. He went to Stockholm in 1914 to study piano with Andersson; then studied composition with Ellberg at the Stockholm Cons. (1915–16), and later took a conducting course there. He made trips abroad from 1920; then studied composition with Stenhammer and conducting with Scherchen. He was a *répétiteur* and assistant conductor at the Royal Opera in Stockholm (1932–34); also appeared as a guest conductor in Scandinavia and later in the U.S. (1948), leading performances of his own works; likewise was active as a teacher, numbering Bäck, Blomdahl, and Lidholm among his students.

Rosenberg was the foremost Swedish composer of his era. He greatly influenced Swedish music by his experimentation and stylistic diversity, which led to a masterful style marked by originality, superb craftsmanship, and refinement. His works include 9 operas; 4 ballets; a pantomime; 2 melodramas; 5 oratorios; 4 cantats; 8 numbered syms. (1917; *Sinfonia grave*, 1928–35; *The 4 Ages of Man*, 1952; *The Revelation of St. John*, with baritone and chorus, 1940; *The Keeper of the Garden*, with alto and chorus; *Sinfonia semplice*, 1951; 1968; *In candidum*, with chorus, 1971); *Sinfonia da chiesa* No. 1 (1923; Stockholm, 1925) and No. 2 (1924; Stockholm, 1926); Sym. for wind and percussion (1966; Goteborg, 1972); concertos for violin (1924; 1951), trumpet (1928), viola (1942), cello (1939; 1953), strings or orch. (1946; 1949; *Louisville*, 1955; 1966); piano (1950); other orch. works (1915–64); incidental music to almost 50 plays; film scores.

Chamber: 12 string quartets (1920; 1924; *Quartetto pastorale*, 1926; 1939; 1949; 1954; 1956; 1956; 1956; 1956; *Quartetto riepilogo*, 1956); Trio for flute, violin, and viola (1921); Sonata No. 1 for Violin and Piano (1926); Trio for Oboe, Clarinet, and Bassoon (1927); *Taffelmusik* for Piano Trio or Chamber Orch. (1939); Sonata No. 2 for Violin and Piano (1940); Wind Quintet (1959); 3 sonatas for solo violin (1921; 1953; 1963); Sonata for Solo Flute (1959); Sonata for Solo Clarinet (1960); numerous piano works; also choral pieces; songs.

Rosenkavalier, Der. Opera by R. Strauss, 1911, to a libretto by his most imaginative collaborator, Hofmannsthal, 1st produced in Dresden. The intricacy of the plot, with its manifold entanglements, amatory cross-currents, transvestism, and contrived mistaken identities, is in the most extravagant manner of 18th-century farce. The action takes place in Vienna in Mozart's time. The personages embroiled in the comedy are the *Feldmarschallin* (the wife of the field-marshal), a young count (Octavian) whom she takes as a sporadic lover, an aging baron (Ochs), and an innocent young woman (Sophie) whom the ineffable baron proposes to marry.

According to the quaint custom of the time, the prospective bridegroom must send to his betrothed a young messenger carrying a rose; the Feldmarschallin selects her young lover for this role. Naturally the Rose Cavalier and the young lady fall in love. The scene becomes further confused when the Feldmarschallin orders the young cavalier to put on a servant girl's dress to conceal his presence in her bedroom. Dressed as a girl, he attracts the attention of the foraging baron, and to save the situation, agrees to a tryst with him. As if this were not enough, the part of the Rosenkavalier is entrusted to a mezzo-soprano, so that when he/she changes his/her dress, the actress singing the role actually engages in double transvestitude (as does the actress playing Cherubino in *The Marriage of Figaro*). The finale unravels the knotted strands of the plot. The music is almost Mozartean in its melodious involvement; the Viennese waltzes enliven the score. After the morbid and somber scores of his earlier operas *Salome* and *Elektra*, Strauss proved that he could combine BEL CANTO with musical invention.

Rosenthal, Moriz, famous Austrian pianist; b. Lemberg, Dec. 17, 1862; d. N.Y., Sept. 3, 1946. He studied piano at the Lemberg Cons. with Karol Mikuli, who was a pupil of Chopin; in 1872, when he was 10 years old, he played Chopin's Rondo in C for 2 Pianos with his teacher in Lemberg. The family moved to Vienna in 1875, and Rosenthal became the pupil of Joseffy, who inculcated in him a passion for virtuoso piano playing, which he taught according to Tausig's method. Liszt accepted Rosenthal as a student during his stay in Weimar and Rome (1876–78). After a hiatus of some years, during which Rosenthal studied philosophy at the Univ. of Vienna, he returned to his concert career in 1884, and established for himself a reputation as one of the world's greatest virtuosos; was nicknamed (because of his small stature and great pianistic power) "little giant of the piano." Beginning in 1888 he made 12 tours of the U.S., where he became a permanent resident in 1938. He publ. (with L. Schytte) a *Schule des höheren Klavierspiels* (Berlin, 1892). His wife, Hedwig Kanner-Rosenthal, was a distinguished piano teacher.

Roses of Picardy. Song by Haydn Wood, 1916, very popular during World War I.

Roslavetz, Nikolai (Andreievich), remarkable Russian composer; b. Suray, near Chernigov, Jan. 5, 1881; d. Moscow, Aug. 23, 1944. He studied violin with his uncle and theory with A. M. Abaza in Kursk; then studied violin with Jan Hrimaly, and composition with Ilyinsky and Vassilenko, at the Moscow Cons., graduating in 1912; won the Silver Medal for his cantata *Heaven and Earth*, after Byron. A composer of advanced tendencies, he publ. in 1913 an atonal Violin Sonata, the 1st of its kind by a Russian composer; his 3rd String Quartet exhibits 12-tone properties. He ed. a short-lived journal, *Muzykalnaya Kultura*, in 1924, and became a leading figure in the modern movement in Russia.

With a change of Soviet cultural policy toward socialist realism and nationalism, Roslavetz was subjected to severe criticism in the press for persevering in his aberrant ways. To conciliate the authorities, he tried to write operettas; then was given an opportunity to redeem himself by going to Tashkent to write ballets based on Uzbek folk songs; he failed in all these pursuits. But interest in his music became pronounced abroad, and posthumous performances were arranged in West Germany. He composed a sym. (1922); symphonic poems (*Man and the Sea*, after Baudelaire (1921) and *End of the World*, after Paul Lafargue (1922); Cello Sonata (1921); Violin Concerto (1925); a cantata, *October* (1927); Nocturne for Harp, oboe, 2 violas, and cello (1913); 3 String Quartets (1913, 1916, 1920); 3 piano trios; 4 violin sonatas; 3 Dances for Violin and Piano (1921); Cello Sonata (1921); 5 piano sonatas.

Ross, Diana, African-American pop and soul singer; b. Detroit, Mar. 26, 1944. She sang for social events in Detroit; then organized a female trio whose other members were her close contemporaries Florence Ballard and Mary Wilson, assuming the grandiose name of the Supremes, under which name the trio became the most successful of the 1960s Motown "stable" of artists. Florence Ballard dropped out in 1967 and was replaced by Cindy Birdsong, and the group thenceforth was called Diana Ross and the Supremes. Their hits included *Come See About Me, Stop! In the Name of Love, Baby Love, You Can't Hurry Love, I Hear a Symphony*, ad infinitum. The Supremes, and Ross as their top singer, broke the curse of drugs and alcohol besetting so many pop singers by campaigning for virtue and love *sans* narcotics.

In 1969 Ross left the Supremes and started on a highly successful career as a solo singer, in cabarets, in nightclubs, on the radio, on television, in Las Vegas, on Broadway, and in the movies, where she starred in a film biography of Billie Holiday, *Lady Sings the Blues* (1970), which produced a number 1 soundtrack album; her next film, *Mahogany* (1972), was less successful. As a soloist she hit the top of the charts with an antidrug number, *Reach Out and Touch*, and her signature song *Ain't No Mountain High Enough*; she recorded the eponymous album *Diana! An Evening with Diana Ross*, a duet album with Marvin Gaye, the generic song *Why Do Fools Fall in Love*, and a duet with Lionel Richie, *Endless Love*. Other solo hits include *Touch Me in the Morning, Do You Know Where You're Going* (from *Mahogany*), *Love Hangover, Upside Down, I'm Coming Out, Muscles,* and *Missing You*.

Rossignol, Le. NIGHTINGALE, THE.

Rossini, Gioachino (Antonio)

Great Italian opera composer possessing an equal genius for shattering melodrama in tragedy and for devastating humor in comedy; b. Pesaro, Feb. 29, 1792; d. Paris, Nov. 13, 1868. He came from a musical family; his father served as town trumpeter in Lugo and Pesaro and played brass instruments in provincial theaters; his mother sang opera as *seconda donna*. When his parents traveled he was usually boarded in Bologna. After the family moved to Lugo his father taught him to play the horn; he also had a chance to study singing with a local canon. Later the family moved to Bologna, where he studied singing, harpsichord, and music theory with Padre Tesei; also learned to play the violin and viola. Soon he acquired enough technical ability to serve as maestro al cembalo in local churches and at occasional opera productions. He studied voice with the tenor Matteo Babbini.

In 1806 he was accepted as a student at the Liceo Musicale in Bologna; there he studied singing and solfeggio with Gibelli, cello with Cavedagna, piano with Zanotti, and counterpoint with Padre Mattei. He also began composing. On Aug. 11, 1808, his cantata *Il pianto d'Armonia sulla morte d'Orfeo* was performed at the Liceo Musicale in Bologna and received a prize. About the same time he wrote his 1st opera, *Demetrio e Polibio*; in 1810 he was commissioned to write a work for the Teatro San Moise in Venice; he submitted his opera *La cambiale di matrimonio*, which won considerable acclaim. His next production was *L'equivoco stravagante*, produced in Bologna in 1811. There followed a number of other operas: *L'inganno felice* (Venice, 1812), *Ciro in Babilonia* (Ferrara, 1812), and *La scala di seta* (Venice, 1812). In 1812 he obtained a commission from La Scala of Milan; the resulting work, *La pietra del paragone*, was a fine success.

In 1813 he produced 3 operas for Venice: *Il Signor Bruschino*, *Tancredi*, and *L'Italiana in Algeri*; the last became a perennial favorite. The next 3 operas, *Aureliano in Palmira* (Milan, 1813), *Il Turco in Italia* (Milan, 1814), and *Sigismondo* (Venice, 1814), were unsuccessful. By that time Rossini, still a very young man, had been approached by the famous impresario Barbaja, the manager of the Teatro San Carlo and the Teatro Fondo in Naples, with an offer for an exclusive contract, under the terms of which Rossini was to supply 2 operas annually for Barbaja. The 1st opera Rossini wrote for him was *Elisabetta, regina d'Inghilterra*, produced at the Teatro San Carlo in Naples in 1815; the title role was entrusted to the famous Spanish soprano Isabella Colbran, who was Barbaja's favorite mistress. An important innovation in the score was Rossini's use of *recitativo stromentato* in place of the usual *recitativo secco*.

His next opera, *Torvaldo e Dorliska*, produced in Rome in 1815, was an unfortunate failure. Rossini now determined to try his skill in composing a full-scaled opera buffa, *Il Barbiere di Siviglia*, based on the famous play by Beaumarchais; it was an audacious decision on Rossini's part, since an Italian opera on the same subject by Giovanni Paisiello (1740–1816), also called *Il Barbiere di Siviglia* (1782), was still playing with undiminished success. To avoid confusion, Rossini's opera on this subject was performed at the Teatro Argentina in Rome under a different title, *Almaviva, ossia L'inutile precauzione*. Rossini was only 23 years old when he completed the score, which proved to be his greatest accomplishment and a standard opera buffa in the repertoire of theaters all over the world. Rossini conducted its 1st performance in Rome (1816), but if contemporary reports and gossip can be trusted, the occasion was marred by various stage accidents that moved the unruly Italian audience to interrupt the spectacle with vociferous outcries of derision; however, the next performance scored a brilliant success. For later productions he used the title *Il Barbiere di Siviglia*.

Strangely enough, the operas he wrote immediately afterward were not uniformly successful: *La Gazzetta*, produced in Naples in 1816, passed unnoticed; the next opera, *Otello*, also produced in Naples in 1816, had some initial success but was not retained in the repertoire after a few sporadic performances. There followed *La Cenerentola* and *La gazza ladra*, both from 1817, which fared much better. But the following 7 operas—*Armida, Mosè in Egitto, Ricciardo e Zoraide, Ermione, La Donna del lago*, *Maometto II*, and *Zelmira*—produced in Naples between 1817 and 1822, were soon forgotten; only the famous Prayer in *Mosé in Egitto* saved the opera from oblivion. The *prima donna assoluta* in all these operas was Isabella Colbran; after a long association with Barbaja she went to live with Rossini, who finally married her in 1822. This event, however, did not result in a break between the impresario and the composer; Barbaja even made arrangements for a festival of Rossini's works in Vienna at the Kärnthnertortheater, of which he became a director. In Vienna Rossini met Beethoven. Returning to Italy, he produced a fairly successful mythological opera, *Semiramide* (Venice, 1823), with Colbran in the title role. Rossini then signed a contract for a season in London with Giovanni Benelli, director of the Italian opera at the King's Theatre.

Rossini arrived in London late in 1823 and was received by King George IV. He conducted several of his operas and was a guest at the homes of the British nobility, where he played piano as an accompanist to singers, at very large fees. In 1824 he settled in Paris, where he became director of the Théâtre-Italien. For the coronation of King Charles X he composed *Il viaggio a Reims*, which was performed in Paris under his direction (1825). He used parts of this *piece d'occasion* in his opera *Le Comte Ory*. In Paris he met Meyerbeer, with whom he established an excellent relationship. After the expiration of his contract with the Théâtre-Italien, he was given the nominal titles of Premier Compositeur du Roi and Inspecteur General du Chant en France at an annual salary of 25,000 francs. He was now free to compose for the Paris Opéra; there, in 1826, he produced *Le Siege de Corinthe*, a revised French version of *Maometto II*. Later he also revised the score of *Mosé in Egitto* and produced it at the Paris Opéra in French as *Moïse et Pharaon* (1827). There followed *Le Comte Ory* (1828).

In 1829 Rossini was able to obtain an agreement with the government of King Charles X guaranteeing him a lifetime annuity of 6,000 francs. In return he promised to write more works for the Paris Opéra. Later that year his *Guillaume Tell* was given its premiere at the Opéra; it became immensely popular. And then, at the age of 37, Rossini stopped writing operas. The French revolution of July 1830, which dethroned King Charles X, invalidated his contract with the French government. Rossini sued the government of King Louis Philippe, the successor to the throne of Charles X, for the continuation of his annuity; the incipient litigation was settled in his favor (1835).

In 1832 Rossini met Olympe Pélissier, who became his mistress; in 1837 Rossini legally separated from Colbran. She died in 1845, and in 1846 Rossini married Pélissier. From 1836 to 1848 they lived in Bologna, where Rossini served as consultant to the Liceo Musicale. In 1848 they moved to Florence; in 1855 he decided to return to Paris, where he was to remain for the rest of his life. His home in the suburb of Passy became the magnet of the artistic world. Rossini was a charming, affable, and gregarious host; he entertained lavishly; he was a great gourmet, and he invented recipes for Italian food that were enthusiastically adopted by French chefs. His wit was fabulous, and his sayings were eagerly reported in the French journals.

He did not abandon composition entirely during his last years of life, despite illness and depression; in 1867 he wrote a Petite messe solennelle; as a token of gratitude to the government of the 2nd Empire he composed a "hymn to Napoleon III and his valiant people," *Dieu tout puissant*. Of great interest are the numerous piano pieces, songs, and instrumental works that he called *Péchés de vieillesse* (Sins of Old Age, 1857–68), a collection containing over 150 pieces.

What were the reasons for Rossini's decision to stop writing operas? Rumors flew around Paris that he was unhappy about the cavalier treatment he received from the management of the Paris Opéra, and that he had spoken disdainfully of yielding the operatic field to "the Jews" (Meyerbeer and Halévy), whose operas captivated the Paris audiences. The report does not bear the stamp of truth, for Rossini was friendly with Meyerbeer until Meyerbeer's death in 1864. Besides, he was not in the habit of complaining; he enjoyed life too well. It seems more plausible that he was deeply affected by his mother's death in 1827; that, well-to-do and confident of continuing governmental financial support, he wanted to rest from what had been a hectic career; or, that increasing illnesses led him into a deep depression that did not correct itself until the mid-1850s, when he returned to composing with remarkable energy.

Rossini was called "Le Cygne de Pesaro" (The Swan of Pesaro). The story went that a delegation arrived from Pesaro with a project of building a monument to Rossini; the town authorities had enough money to pay for the pedestal, but not for the statue itself. Would Rossini contribute 10,000 francs for the completion of the project? "For

10,000 francs," Rossini was supposed to have replied, "I would stand on the pedestal myself." He had a healthy sense of self-appreciation, but he invariably put it in a comic context. While his mother was still living he addressed his letters to her as "Mother of the Great Maestro."

The circumstance that Rossini was born on a leap-year day was the cause of many a bon mot on his part. On Feb. 29, 1868, he decided to celebrate his 19th birthday, for indeed, there had been then only 19 leap years since his birth. He was superstitious; like many Italians, he stood in fear of Friday the 13th. He died on Nov. 13, 1868, which was a Friday. In 1887 his remains were taken to Florence for entombment in the Church of Santa Croce.

Rossini was the consummate composer of Italian opera buffa between Mozart and Donizetti. Many individual arias are well-known, although relatively few operas are revived, as the librettos do not present many opportunities for genuine dramatic tension. Certainly it is by his overtures that Rossini remains most popular; their light-hearted essence embodies the old Italian sinfonia in late Classic form. Surprisingly, he has also become known for a few works of sacred music: Messa di gloria (1820), Stabat Mater (1842), and the Petite messe solennelle (1864).

Rossini's melodies have been used by many composers as themes for various works: Respighi utilized Rossini's *Quelques riens* in his ballet *La Boutique fantasque*, and other themes in his orch. suite *Rossiniana*. An opera entitled *Rossini in Neapel* was written by Bernhard Paumgartner. Britten made use of Rossini's music in his orch. suites *Soirées musicales* and *Matinées musicales*. The most famous arrangement of any of Rossini's compositions is the Prayer from *Mosé in Egitto*, transcribed for violin by Paganini.

Rostropovich, Mstislav (Leopoldovich)

~~~ ~~~ ~~~ ~~~ ~~~

Famous Russian cellist and conductor; b. Baku, Mar. 27, 1927. A precocious child, he began cello studies with his father Leopold Rostropovich (b. Voronezh, Mar. 9, 1892; d. Orenburg, July 31, 1942); also had piano lessons from his mother. In 1931 the family moved to Moscow, where he made his debut when he was 8; continued his training at the Central Music School (1939–41); then studied cello with Kozolupov and composition with Shebalin and Shostakovich at the Moscow Cons. (1943–48); subsequently studied privately with Prokofiev. He won the International Competition for Cellists in Prague in 1950, and the next year made his 1st appearance in the West in Florence. A phenomenally successful career ensued.

He made his U.S. debut at N.Y.'s Carnegie Hall in 1956, winning extraordinary critical acclaim. He became a teacher (1953) and a prof. (1956) at the Moscow Cons., and also a prof. at the Leningrad Cons. (1961). A talented pianist, he frequently appeared as accompanist to his wife, the soprano Galina Vishnevskaya (see below), whom he married in 1955. In 1961 he made his 1st appearance as a conductor. As his fame increased he received various honors, including the Lenin Prize in 1963 and the Gold Medal of the Royal Phil. Soc. of London in 1970.

In spite of his eminence and official honors, Rostropovich encountered difficulties with the Soviet authorities, owing chiefly to his spirit of uncompromising independence. He let the dissident author Aleksandr Solzhenitsyn stay at his dacha near Moscow, protesting the Soviet government's treatment of the Nobel Prize winner for literature in a letter to *Pravda* in 1969.

Although the letter went unpubl. in his homeland, it was widely disseminated in the West. As a result, Rostropovich found himself increasingly hampered in his career by the Soviet Ministry of Culture. His concerts were canceled without explanation, as were his wife's engagements at the Bolshoi Theater. Foreign tours were forbidden, as were appearances on radio, television, and recordings.

In 1974 he and his wife obtained permission to go abroad accompanied by their 2 daughters. He made a brilliant debut as a guest conductor with the National Sym. Orch. in Washington, D.C. (1975); his success led to his appointment as its music director in 1977. Free from the bureaucratic annoyances of the USSR, he and his wife publicized stories of their previous difficulties at home in Russia. Annoyed by such independent activities, the Moscow authorities finally stripped them both of their Soviet citizenship as "ideological renegades." The Soviet establishment even went so far as to remove the dedication to Rostropovich of Shostakovich's 2nd Cello Concerto. The whole disgraceful episode ended when the Soviet government, chastened by perestroika, restored Rostropovich's citizenship in 1990 and invited him to take the National Sym. Orch. to the USSR. Besides conducting the American orch. there, Rostropovich appeared as soloist in Dvořák's Cello Concerto. His return to Russia was welcomed by the populace as a vindication of his principles of liberty.

Rostropovich, known simply as "Slava" (glory), is duly recognized as one of the greatest cellists of the century, a master interpreter of both the standard and the contemporary literature. To enhance the repertoire for his instrument, he commissioned and premiered numerous scores, including works by Prokofiev, Shostakovich, Britten, Piston, and Foss. As a conductor he proved himself an impassioned and authoritative interpreter of the music of the Russian national and Soviet schools of composition. He organized the 1st Rostropovich International Cello Competition in Paris in 1981 and the Rostropovich Festival in Snape, England, in 1983. He was made an Officer of the French Legion d'honneur in 1982 and received an honorary knighthood from Queen Elizabeth II of England in 1987. Rostropovich's wife and musical partner, Galina (Pavlovna) Vishnevskaya (b. Leningrad, Oct. 25, 1926) was one of Russia's most prominent sopranos. In 1952 she joined the operatic staff of the Bolshoi Theater in Moscow; her roles there were Violetta, Tosca, Madama Butterfly, and an entire repertoire of soprano parts in Russian operas. She made her debut at the Metropolitan Opera in N.Y. in 1961 as Aida. Britten wrote the solo soprano part in his *War Requiem* for her.

rota (Lat., wheel). 1. A somewhat obscure term for the English ROUND; *Sumer is icumen in* is the only work in MS so labeled. 2. Latinization of *rote* (Mid. Eng., CRUIT). Compare with ROTTA.

Rota (born Rinaldi), **Nino,** brilliant Italian composer; b. Milan, Dec. 3, 1911; d. Rome, Apr. 10, 1979. He was a precocious musician; at the age of 11 he wrote an oratorio which had a public performance, and at 13 composed a lyric comedy in 3 acts, *Il Principe porcaro*, after Hans Christian Andersen. He entered the Milan Cons. in 1923 and took courses with Delachi, Orefici, and Bas; after private studies with Pizzetti (1925–26), he studied composition with Casella at the Accademia di Santa Cecilia in Rome, graduating in 1930; later went to the U.S. and enrolled in the Curtis Inst. of Music in Philadelphia, studying composition with Rosario Scalero and conducting with Fritz Reiner. Returning to Italy, he entered the Univ. of Milan to study literature, gaining a degree in 1937. He taught at the Taranto music school (1937–38); then was a teacher (from 1939) and director (1950–78) at the Bari Liceo Musicale.

Rota's musical style demonstrates a great facility, and even felicity, with occasional daring excursions into the forbidding territory of dodecaphony. However, his most durable compositions are related to his music for the cinema; he composed the soundtracks of a great number of films of the Italian director Federico Fellini covering the period from 1950 to 1979, including *Lo sceicco bianco* (The White Sheik; 1950); *La strada* (1954); *Notti di Cabiria* (1957); *La dolce vita* (1959); *Otto de mezza* (8 1/2 ; 1963); *Giulietta degli spiriti* (Juliet of the Spirits; 1965); *Satyricon* (1969); *The Clowns* (1971); *Fellini Roma* (1972); *Amarcord* (1974); *Casanova* (1977); *Orchestra Rehearsal* (1979). He also wrote scores for other directors, notably for Francis Ford Coppola's *The Godfather I* (1972) and *II* (1974) and Wertmuller's *Love and Anarchy* (1974). Other works include: 11 operas, most notably *Il cappello di paglia di Firenzi* (Florentine Straw Hat; 1946); 3 ballets, 3 syms. (1936–39; 1938–43; 1957); and other orch.l works. Vocal: 5

oratorios; 3 masses (1960–62); songs. Chamber: Various works, for 1 to 11 players; keyboard music.

rotation. In post-Schoenbergian developments of dodecaphony the 12-tone series is often modified by rotation. As the term implies, the series is shifted a space, so that at its next occurrence it begins with the 2nd note and ends with the 1st; in the subsequent incidence it starts on the 3rd note and ends on the 2nd, etc. Rotation in its various further developments is a fertile device of DODECAPHONIC techniques particularly favored by Stravinsky.

rotondo (It.). Round, full.

roto-toms. Mounted TOM-TOM-like percussion used in jazz and occasionally modern classical music. The plastic drumhead is not supported by a resonating body; instead it rotates on a stand that permits the tuning of definite pitches. While flexible in the manner of the timpani, the sound is not comparable to a true membranophone.

rotrouenge. Type of troubadour and trouvère song with a refrain and a rhyme scheme; its identity remains obscure, as there are few surviving examples; the name disappears around 1200.

rotta. Medieval triangular psaltery, found throughout Europe. The instrument is also called the *cruit* (Irish Gael.), which is used for a medieval triangular harp. Compare with ROTA.

rotulus. A roll of parchment sheets sewn together, the usual form of books in ancient times up to the 4th century, but remained in use for another millennium for musical MSS. Several medieval motets owe their preservation to the sturdiness of such *rotuli*.

Rouget de l'Isle (Lisle), **Claude-Joseph.** MARSEILLAISE, LA.

roulade (Fr.). A grace consisting of a run or ARPEGGIO from one principal melody tone to another; a vocal or instrumental flourish.

roulante (Fr., rolling). *Caisse roulante*, a tenor drum.

round. A perpetual canon, usually in 3 parts, sometimes with a harmonic support or accompaniment (*pes*). The entrances of the voices are rhythmically equidistant; the melody itself, usually in a major key, is built on the tonic triad, so that the counterpoint is in 3rds and a complete triadic harmony is achieved when all the voices come in. *Frère Jacques* is a famous example of a round.

round dance. Ballroom dance performed by couples in a circular motion, such as a waltz.

roundelay. A song or lai with continued reiteration or refrain.

Rounds. String orch.1 piece by Diamond, 1944, 1st performed in Minneapolis under the direction of Mitropoulos. This popular work is in 3 movements with a fugal finale.

Rousseau, Jean-Jacques, great Swiss-born French philosopher and author; b. Geneva, June 28, 1712; d. Ermenonville, near Paris, July 2, 1778. Without other musical training besides desultory self-instruction, Rousseau made his debut as a music scholar at the age of 29, reading a paper before the Académie in Paris (1724), which was received and publ. as a *Dissertation sur la musique moderne* (1743). His opera *Les Muses galantes* had only 1 private representation, at the house of La Pouplinière in 1745; his revision of the intermezzo *La Reine de Navarre* (by Voltaire and Rameau) was a failure in Paris; but his opera *Le Devin du village* (Fontainebleau, 1752; Paris Opéra, 1753) was very successful and remained in the repertoire for 75 years.

In the meantime his musical articles for the *Encyclopédie* had evoked scathing criticism from Rameau and others; improved by revision and augmentation, they were republ. as his *Dictionnaire de musique* (Geneva, 1767?; 1st known ed., Paris, 1768). In 1752 commenced the dispute, known as the GUERRE DES BOUFFONS, between the partisans of French and Italian opera; Rousseau sided with the latter, publ. a *Lettre a M. Grimm au sujet des remarques ajoutées à sa lettre sur Omphale* (1752), followed by the caustic *Lettre sur la musique française* (1753; to which the members of the Opéra responded by burning him in effigy and excluding him from the theater) and *Lettre d'un symphoniste de l'Académie royale de musique à ses camarades* (1753). He wrote 2 numbers for the melodrama *Pygmalion* (1770; Paris, 1775). Publ. posthumously were 6 new arias for *Le Devin du village* and a collection of about 100 romances and duets, *Les Consolations des misères de ma vie* (1781), and fragments of an opera, *Daphnis et Chloé* (1780). His writings on music are included in the *Oeuvres complètes de Jean-Jacques Rousseau* (4 vols., 1959–69);

for his letters see R. Leigh, ed., *Correspondance complète Jean-Jacques Rousseau* (18 vols., 1965–73).

Roussel, Albert (Charles Paul Marie), outstanding French composer; b. Tourcoing, Département du Nord, Apr. 5, 1869; d. Royan, Aug. 23, 1937. Orphaned as a child, he was educated by his grandfather, mayor of his native town, and after the grandfather's death by his aunt. He studied academic subjects at the Collège Stanislas in Paris; music with the organist Stoltz; then studied mathematics in preparation for entering the Naval Academy; at the age of 18 he began his training in the navy; from 1889 to Aug. 1890 he was a member of the crew of the frigate *Iphigénie*, sailing to Indochina. This voyage was of great importance to Roussel, since it opened for him a world of oriental culture and art, which became one of the chief sources of his musical inspiration. He later sailed on the cruiser Devastation; received a leave of absence for reasons of health, and spent some time in Tunis; was then stationed in Cherbourg, and began to compose there. In 1893 he was sent once more to Indochina. He resigned from the navy in 1894 and went to Paris, where he began to study music seriously with Eugène Gigout. In 1898 he entered the Schola Cantorum in Paris as a pupil of Vincent d'Indy; continued this study until 1907, when he was already 38 years old, but at the same time he was entrusted with a class in counterpoint, which he conducted at the Schola Cantorum from 1902 to 1914; among his students were Erik Satie, Stan Golestan, Paul Le Flem, Roland-Manuel, Guy de Lioncourt, and Varèse.

In 1909 Roussel and his wife, Blanche Preisach-Roussel, undertook a voyage to India, where he became acquainted with the legend of the queen Padmavati, which he selected as a subject for his famous opera-ballet. His choral sym. *Les Evocations* (1912) was also inspired by this tour. At the outbreak of World War I in 1914 Roussel applied for active service in the navy but was rejected, and volunteered as an ambulance driver. After the Armistice of 1918 he settled in Normandy and devoted himself to composition. In the autumn of 1930 he visited the U.S.

Roussel began his work under the influence of French Impressionism, with its dependence on exotic moods and poetic association. However, the sense of formal design asserted itself in his symphonic works; his *Suite en fa* (1927) signalizes a transition toward neoclassicism; the thematic development is vigorous, and the rhythms are clearly delineated, despite some asymmetrical progressions; the orchestration, too, is in the Classic tradition. Roussel possessed a keen sense of the theater; he was capable of fine characteri-

zation of exotic or mythological subjects, but also knew how to depict humorous situations in lighter works. An experiment in a frankly modernistic manner is exemplified by his *Jazz dans la nuit* for Voice and Piano (1928).

rovesciamento (It.). In double counterpoint, the inversion of voices.

rovescio (It., reverse). 1. Melodic inversion. A famous example is *Contrapuntus VI* in Bach's *Die Kunst der Fuge*. The eighteenth variation in Rachmaninoff's *Rhapsody on a Theme of Paganini* is a precise melodic inversion of the theme; since the theme is encompassed by a minor triad, its inversion becomes a melody in major. 2. Among some Baroque composers the term *rovescio* (along with its cognates *riverso* and *rivolto*) refers to RETROGRADE (cancrizans) motion. The postlude of Hindemith's *Ludus Tonalis* represents both an inversion and a retrograde movement (allowance being made for shifting accidentals).

Row, Row, Row Your Boat. American round of uncertain authorship, 1st published in 1852.

Roxelane, La. Haydn's Sym. No. 63, 1779, in C major. The feminine title may be explained by the fact that the allegretto from this sym. is a variant of the French song *Roxelane*; however, the similarity is less than it seems.

Rozsa, Miklos, brilliant Hungarian-American composer; b. Budapest, Apr. 18, 1907; d. Los Angeles, July 27, 1995. He studied piano and composition in Leipzig with Hermann Grabner; musicology with Theodor Kroyer. In 1931 he settled in Paris, where he became successful as a composer; his works were often performed in European music centers. In 1935 he went to London; composed there for the films; in 1940 he emigrated to the U.S. and settled in Hollywood; was on the staff of MGM (1948–62); also taught at the Univ. of Southern Calif. in Los Angeles (1945–65). His orch. and chamber music is cast in the advanced modern idiom in vogue in Europe between the 2 world wars; neoclassical in general content, it is strong in polyphony and incisive rhythm; for his film music he employs a more Romantic and diffuse style, relying on a Wagnerian type of grandiloquence. He won Oscars for his film scores to *Spellbound* (1945), *A Double Life* (1947), and *Ben-Hur* (1959). Rózsa was more successful than most in balancing concert and film music careers, and both types of works continue to be performed.

rubando (It.). Performing in a *rubato* style. *Affretando e rubando il tempo*, perform with increasing speed, and dwell on accented tones.

rubato, tempo (rubato; It., stolen time). Play with a free treatment of the melody; specifically, dwell on and (often almost insensibly) prolong prominent melody tones or chords. This requires an equivalent subsequent acceleration of less prominent tones, which are thus "robbed" of a portion of their time value. The measure remains constant, and the accompaniment is not disrupted. Tempo rubato is the musical equivalent of the saying, "robbing Peter to pay Paul." A different kind of total rubato, affecting an entire musical section, occurs in the performing practice of the Romantic era.

Rubinstein, Anton (Grigorievich), renowned Russian pianist, conductor, composer, and pedagogue, brother of Nikolai (Grigorievich) Rubinstein; b. Vykhvatinetz, Podolia, Nov. 28, 1829; d. Peterhof, near St. Petersburg, Nov. 20, 1894. He was of a family of Jewish merchants who became baptized in Berdichev in July 1831. His mother gave him his 1st lessons in piano; the family moved to Moscow, where his father opened a small pencil factory. A well-known Moscow piano teacher, Alexandre Villoing, was entrusted with Rubinstein's musical education, and was in fact his only piano teacher. In 1839 Villoing took him to Paris, where Rubinstein played before Chopin and Liszt; remained there until 1841; then made a concert tour in the Netherlands, Germany, Austria, England, Norway, and Sweden, returning to Russia in 1843.

Since Anton's brother Nikolai evinced a talent for composition, the brothers were taken in 1844 to Berlin, where, on Meyerbeer's recommendation, Anton studied composition, with Dehn; subsequently made a tour through Hungary with the flutist Heindl. He returned to Russia in 1848 and settled in St. Petersburg. There he enjoyed the enlightened patronage of the Grand Duchess Helen, and wrote 3 Russian operas: *Dmitri Donskoy* (1852), *The Siberian Hunters* (1853), and *Thomas the Fool* (1853). In 1854, with the assistance of the Grand Duchess, Rubinstein undertook another tour in western Europe. He found publishers in Berlin, and gave concerts of his own works in London and Paris, exciting admiration as both composer and pianist; on his return in 1858 he was appointed court pianist and conductor of the court concerts.

He assumed the direction of the Russian Musical Soc. in 1859; in 1862 he founded the Imperial Cons. in St. Petersburg, remaining its director until 1867. For 20 years thereafter he held no official position; from 1867 until 1870 he gave concerts in Europe, winning fame as a pianist 2nd only to Liszt. During the season of 1872–73 he made a triumphant American tour, playing in 215 concerts, for which he was paid lavishly; appeared as a soloist and jointly with the violinist Wieniawski (with whom he was apparently not speaking at the time). He produced a sensation by playing without the score, a novel procedure at the time. Returning to Europe, he elaborated a cycle of historical concerts, in programs ranging from Bach to Chopin; he usually devoted the last concert of a cycle to Russian composers. In 1887 he resumed the directorship of the St. Petersburg Cons., resigning again in 1891, when he went to Dresden. He returned to Russia the year of his death. In 1890 he established the Rubinstein Prize, an international competition open to young men between 20 and 26 years of age. Two prizes of 5,000 francs each were offered, 1 for composition, the other for piano. Quinquennial competitions were held in St. Petersburg, Berlin, Vienna, and Paris.

Rubinstein's role in Russian musical culture was of the greatest importance. He introduced European methods into education and established high standards of artistic performance. He was the 1st Russian musician who was equally prominent as composer and interpreter. According to contemporary reports his playing possessed extraordinary power (his octave passages were famous) and insight, revealed particularly in his performance of Beethoven's sonatas. His renown as a composer was scarcely less. His *Ocean Sym.* was one of the most frequently performed orch. works in Europe and America; his piano concertos were part of the standard repertoire; his pieces for piano solo, *Melody in F*, *Romance*, and *Kamennoi Ostrow*, became perennial favorites.

After his death his orch.l works all but vanished from concert programs, as did his operas (with the exception of *The Demon*, which is still perf. in Russia); his Piano Concerto No. 4 in D Minor is occasionally heard. Among his compositions are: 28 operas, including *Die Kinder der Heide* (Vienna, 1861); *Feramors* (1863); *The Demon* (1871); *Nero* (1875–76); *The Merchant Kalashnikov* (1877–79); *Sulamith* (1882–83); *Moses* (1885–91); and 1 ballet. He composed 6 syms.: No. 1, op. 40 (1850); No. 2, op. 42, *Ocean* (4-movement version, 1851; 7-movement vers., 1880); No. 3, op. 56 (1854–55; orig. No. 4); No. 4, op. 95, *Dramatic* (1874); No. 5, op. 107 (1880); No. 6, op. 111 (1886); 7 piano concertos: 2 unnumbered (1847; 1849); No. 1, op. 25 (1850); No. 2, op. 35 (1851); No. 3, op. 45 (1853–54); No. 4, op. 70 (1864); No. 5, op. 94 (1874); other orch.l works; and concert and programmatic overtures, including *Faust*, op. 68 (1864); *Ivan the Terrible*, op. 79 (1869); *Russia* (1882); *Fantasia eroica*, op. 110 (1884); *Antony and Cleopatra*, op. 116 (1890). His chamber works include: 3 violin sonatas (1851; 1855; 1876); 5 piano trios, 3 unnumbered: No. 1, op. 15 (1851); No. 2, op. 15 (1851); op. 52 (1857), op. 85 (1870), and op. 108 (1883); 10 string quartets (1852–80); and works for other instruments. He also wrote numerous piano pieces; choral works; songs.

His brother Nikolai (Grigorievich) Rubinstein (b. Moscow, June 14, 1835; d. Paris, Mar. 23, 1881), was a prominent pianist, conductor, teacher, and composer. In 1859 Nikolai became head of the Moscow branch of the Russian Musical Soc.; this soc. opened the Moscow Cons., which he directed until his death. Among his pupils were Taneyev, Alexander Siloti, and Emil Sauer.

Rubinstein, Arthur (Artur), celebrated Polish-born American pianist; b. Lodz, Jan. 28, 1887; d. Geneva, Dec. 20, 1982. He was a product of a merchant family with many children, of whom he alone exhibited musical propensities. He became emotionally attached to the piano as soon as he saw and heard the instrument; at the age of 7, on Dec. 14, 1894, he played pieces by Mozart, Schubert, and Mendelssohn at a charity concert in Lodz. His 1st regular piano teacher was one Adolf Prechner. He was later taken to Warsaw, where he had piano lessons with Alexander Roycki; then went to Berlin in 1897 to study with Heinrich Barth; also received instruction in theory from Robert Kahn and Max Bruch. In 1900 he appeared as soloist in Mozart's A-major Concerto, K.488, in Potsdam; he repeated his success that same year when he played the work again in Berlin under Joachim's direction; then toured in Germany and Poland.

After further studies with Paderewski in Switzerland (1903) he went to Paris, where he played with the Lamoureux Orch. and met Ravel, Dukas, and Thibaud. He also played the G-minor Piano Concerto by Saint-Saëns in the presence of the composer, who commended him. The ultimate plum of artistic success came when Rubinstein received an American contract. He made his debut at Carnegie Hall in N.Y. in 1906, as soloist with the Philadelphia Orch. in his favorite Saint-Saëns concerto. His American tour was not altogether successful, and he returned to Europe for further study. In 1915 he appeared as soloist with the London Sym. Orch. During the season 1916–17, he gave numerous recitals in Spain, a country in which he was to become extremely successful; from Spain he went to South America, where he also became a great favorite; he

developed a flair for Spanish and Latin American music, and his renditions of the piano works of Albéniz and de Falla were models of authentic Hispanic modality.

Villa-Lobos dedicated to Rubinstein his *Rudepoema*, regarded as one of the most difficult piano pieces ever written. Symbolic of his cosmopolitan career was the fact that he maintained apartments in N.Y., Beverly Hills, Paris, and Geneva. He was married to Aniela Mlynarska in 1932. Of his 4 children, 1 was born in Buenos Aires, 1 in Warsaw, and 2 in the U.S. In 1946 he became an American citizen. In 1958 Rubinstein gave his 1st postwar concert in Poland; in 1964 he played in Moscow, Leningrad, and Kiev. In Poland and in Russia he was received with tremendous emotional acclaim. But he forswore any appearances in Germany as a result of the Nazi extermination of the members of his family during World War II. In 1976, at the age of 89, he gave his farewell recital in London.

Rubinstein was one of the finest interpreters of Chopin's music, to which his fiery temperament and poetic lyricism were particularly congenial. His style of playing tended toward bravura in Classic compositions, but he rarely indulged in mannerisms; his performances of Mozart, Beethoven, Schumann, and Brahms were particularly inspiring. In his characteristic spirit of robust humor he made jokes about the multitude of notes he claimed to have dropped, but asserted that a worse transgression against music would be pedantic inflexibility in tempo and dynamics. He was a *bon vivant*, an indefatigable host at parties, and a fluent though not always grammatical speaker in most European languages, including Russian and his native Polish.

In Hollywood he played on the sound tracks for the motion pictures *I've Always Loved You* (1946), *Song of Love* (1947), and *Night Song* (1947). He also appeared as a pianist, representing himself, in the films *Carnegie Hall* (1947) and *Of Men and Music* (1951). A film documentary entitled *Artur Rubinstein, Love of Life* was produced in 1975; a 90-minute television special, *Rubinstein at 90*, was broadcast to mark his entry into that nonagenarian age in 1977; he spoke philosophically about the inevitability of dying. He was the recipient of numerous international honors: a membership in the French Académie des Beaux Arts and the Legion d'Honneur, and the Order of Polonia Restituta of Poland; he held the Gold Medal of the Royal Phil. Soc. of London and several honorary doctorates from American institutions of learning. He was a passionate supporter of Israel, which he visited several times. In 1974 an international piano competition bearing his name was inaugurated in Jerusalem.

In 1976, he received the U.S. Medal of Freedom, presented by President Ford. During the last years of his life he was afflicted with retinitis pigmentosa, which led to his total blindness; but even then he never lost his joie de vivre. He once said that the slogan "wine, women, and song" as applied to him was 80% women and only 20% wine and song. He slid gently into death in his Geneva apartment, as in a pianissimo ending of a Chopin nocturne, ritardando, morendo . . . Rubinstein had expressed a wish to be buried in Israel; his body was cremated in Switzerland; the ashes were flown to Jerusalem to be interred in a separate emplacement at the cemetery, since the Jewish law does not permit cremation.

Ruddigore, or The Witch's Curse. Comic opera by Gilbert and Sullivan, 1887, 1st produced in London. The house of Ruddigore is doomed by an ancient curse to commit a crime a day, but their young scion decides to rescind this protocol; he flees the ancestral castle and falls in love with a village belle. To renounce a daily crime is to court suicide, itself a criminal act; but the youth obtains a release from the curse by the ghost of his uncle and is free to marry his love. The libretto is set to music in an engaging Italianate manner.

Rudepoema. Piano piece by Villa-Lobos (1921–26), written for the pianist Artur Rubinstein. The title literally means "rude poem," in the sense of unrestrained savagery; it is technically so difficult that for many years only the greatest virtuosos could tackle it. Villa-Lobos subsequently orchestrated the piece, and conducted its 1st performance in Rio de Janeiro, 1942.

Rudhyar, Dane

French-American mystical visionary, painter, poet, and composer; b. Daniel Chennevière, Paris, Mar. 23, 1895; d. San Francisco, Sept. 13, 1985. He changed his name in 1917 to Rudhyar, derived from an old Sanskrit root conveying the sense of dynamic action and the color red, astrologically related to the zodiacal sign of his birth and the planet Mars. He studied philosophy at the Sorbonne in Paris (baccalaureat, 1911) and took music courses at the Paris Cons. In composition he was largely self-taught; he also achieved a certain degree of proficiency as a pianist; developed a technique which he called "orchestral pianism." In Paris he studied at the Cons. and attended the famous premiere of Stravinsky's *The Rite of Spring* (1913). At the same time he joined the modern artistic circles in Paris.

In 1916 he went to America; became a naturalized American citizen in 1926. His "dance poems" for orch., *Poèmes ironiques* and *Vision vegetale*, were performed at the Metropolitan Opera in N.Y. (1917). In 1918 he visited Canada; in Montreal he met the pianist Alfred Laliberté, who was closely associated with Scriabin, and through him Rudhyar became acquainted with Scriabin's theosophic ideas. He also publ. a collection of French poems, *Rapsodies* (Toronto, 1918).

In 1920 Rudhyar went to Hollywood to write scenic music for *Pilgrimage Play, The Life of Christ*, and also acted the part of Christ in the prologue of the silent film version of *The Ten Commandments* produced by Cecil B. DeMille. In Hollywood he initiated the project of "Introfilms," depicting inner psychological states on the screen through a series of images, but it failed to receive support and was abandoned. Between 1922 and 1930 he lived in Hollywood and N.Y.; was one of the founding members of the International Composers Guild in N.Y. His symphonic poem *Soul Fire* won the $1,000 prize of the Los Angeles Phil. (1922); in 1928 his book *The Rebirth of Hindu Music* was publ. in Madras.

After 1930 Rudhyar devoted most of his time to astrology. His 1st book on the subject, *The Astrology of Personality* (1936), became a standard text in the field; it was described by Paul Clancy, the pioneer in the publication of popular astrological magazines, as "the greatest step forward in astrology since the time of Ptolemy." A new development in Rudhyar's creative activities took place in 1938 when he began to paint, along nonrepresentational symbolistic lines; the titles of his paintings (*Mystic Tiara, Cosmic Seeds, Soul and Ego, Avatar*, etc.) reflect theosophic themes. His preoccupation with astrology left him little time for music; but in the 1960s he undertook a radical revision of some early compositions, and wrote several new ones; was also active as a lecturer. He published, in English, some poetry and a number of books on psychospiritual formulation of astrology; he was awarded a doctorate from the Calif. Institute of Transpersonal Psychology.

The natural medium for Rudhyar's musical expression was the piano; his few symphonic works were mostly orchestrations of original piano compositions. In his writing for piano he built sonorous chordal formations supported by resonant pedal points, occasionally verging on polytonality; a kinship with Scriabin's piano music was clearly felt, but Rudhyar's harmonic idiom was free from Scriabin's Wagnerian antecedents. Despite his study of oriental religions and music, Rudhyar did not attempt to make use of Eastern modalities; he called his creations "syntonic," built mostly on dissonant but euphonious harmony He lived his last years in Palo Alto, Calif., and kept active connections with the world of theosophy. Before his death, when his wife asked him whom he expected to meet beyond the mortal frame, he replied, "Myself."

Rudolph, Archduke of Austria.
See BEETHOVEN, LUDWIG VAN.

Rudolph the Red-Nosed Reindeer.
Christmas ballad by J. Marks, 1949. The immediate appeal of the song lead to its selling 4 million copies of sheet music and over 6 million disks as sung by Gene Autry.

ruffle. A roll of rapidly vibrating metered drumbeats; sometimes called *ruff.*

ruffle and flourish. A vibrating drumbeat accompanied by a fanfare on a ceremonial occasion.

Rugby. *Mouvement symphonique No.*
2 by Honegger, 1928, that describes in kinetic rhythms of a rugby game. It was 1st performed in Paris and was subsequently performed, during the intermission of an international rugby match between France and England, in Paris later that year.

ruggiero. A BASSO OSTINATO figure upon which instrumentalists improvised counterpoints. The bass melody, in a mixture of Ionian and Mixolydian modes, duple time, and 4 phrases, is 1st found in mid-16th century MSS without name; it acquired its name later in that century and was most popular in the 1st half of the 17th century. In the early monodic era, vocal music began to be written on this bass; later, it was used for dance music. It virtually disappeared after 1650.

COURTESY FRANK DRIGGS COLLECTION

Carl Ruggles

Ruggles, Carl (Charles Sprague), remarkable American composer; b. Marion, Mass., Mar. 11, 1876; d. Bennington, Vt., Oct. 24, 1971. He learned to play violin as a child; then went to Boston, where he took violin lessons with Felix Winternitz and theory with Josef Claus; later enrolled as a special student at Harvard Univ., where he attended composition classes of John Knowles Paine. Impressed with the widely assumed supremacy of the German school of composition (of which Paine was a notable representative), Ruggles Germanized his given name from Charles to Carl. In 1907 he went to Minnesota, where he organized and conducted the Winona Sym. Orch. (1908–12). In 1917 he went to N.Y., where he became active in the promotion of modern music; was a member of the International Composers Guild and of the Pan American Assoc. of Composers; taught composition at the Univ. of Miami (1938–43).

Ruggles wrote relatively few works, which he constantly revised and rearranged, and they were mostly in small forms. He did not follow any particular modern method of composition but instinctively avoided needless repetition of thematic notes, which made his melodic progressions atonal; his use of dissonances, at times quite strident, derived from the linear proceedings of chromatically inflected counterpoint. A certain similarity with the 12-tone method of composition of Schoenberg resulted from this process, but Ruggles never adopted it explicitly. In his sources of inspiration he reached for spiritual exaltation with mystic connotations, scaling the heights and plumbing the depths of musical expression. Such music could not attract large groups of listeners and repelled some critics; one of them remarked that the title of Ruggles's *Sun-Treader* ought to be changed to "Latrine-Treader."

Unable and unwilling to withstand the prevailing musical mores, Ruggles removed himself from the musical scene; he went to live on his farm in Arlington, Vt., and devoted himself mainly to his avocation, painting; his pictures, mostly in the manner of abstract Expressionism, were occasionally exhibited in N.Y. galleries. In 1966 he moved to a nursing home in Bennington, where he died at the age of 95. A striking revival of interest in his music took place during the last years of his life, and his name began to appear with increasing frequency on the programs of American orchs. and chamber music groups. His MSS were recovered and publ.; virtually all of his compositions have been recorded.

ruhig (Ger.). Calmly, tranquilly.

Rührtrommel (Ger., touch drum). Tenor drum; other German synonyms are *Rolltrommel*, *Wirbeltrommel*, and *Land-sknechtstrommel*.

Rührung (Ger.). Emotion.

Rule Britannia. Patriotic British song by Arne, 1740, publ. with the subtitle *celebrated ode in honour of Great Britain*. Wagner remarked, somewhat caustically, that the melody epitomizes in its initial 8 notes the entire English character as a nation.

rullando (It.). Rapid drum trill.

Rumanian Rhapsodies. Set of 2 orch.l pieces by Enesco, 1903; it was 1st performed in Bucharest with the composer conducting. The 1st of these is especially popular.

rumba (rhumba). A syncopated Cuban dance in quadruple time, popular in the U.S. in the 1930s–'50s, having acquired elements of SWING.

run. 1. A rapid scale passage; in vocal music, usually such a passage sung to one syllable. *Run a division*, perform such a passage, i.e., a dividing up of a melodic phrase into a rapid coloratura passage. 2. A leak of air in the organ windchest.

Rundfunk (Ger.). Radio broadcasting service.

Ruralia Hungarica. Orch.l suite by E. von Dohnányi, 1924, based on piano music inspired by rural Hungarian folk music. The 1st performance in Budapest was conducted by the composer.

Rusalka (The Nixie) (1). Opera by Dargomyzhsky, 1856, based on Pushkin's dramatic poem, 1st performed in St. Petersburg. A miller's daughter is seduced and impregnated by a local prince who marries a lady of his own station. The wronged girl throws herself into the river Dnieper, thus becoming a Rusalka (nixie, a female water sprite). In her submarine existence she continues to exercise a profound emotional influence on the prince, who often comes to the river bank to evoke memories of his tragic love. The Rusalka sends her daughter, who was born in the Dnieper, to the prince, asking him to visit her mother, who is now queen of the waters. The prince follows his daughter and rejoins her in the river. The opera is important for its use of natural inflections of Russian speech. It is a classic in Russia (and was extremely influential on the Mighty 5); but it almost never receives performances outside its home country.

Rusalka (The Nixie) (2). Opera by Dvořák, 1901, 1st performed in Prague. A nixie (see above entry) leaves her watery realm and falls in love with a normal prince; but because of the disparity of their ranks, a marriage is impossible. She returns to her lake, but the prince realize he really loves her. He follows her to the watery deep and expires in her arms. The opera is very popular in the Czech lands; it is probably the most performed Dvořák opera in the non-Slavic world.

Ruslan and Ludmila. Opera by Glinka, 1842, 1st produced in St. Petersburg. The libretto follows Pushkin's fairy-tale of that name. Ludmila, daughter of the Grand Duke of Kiev, is betrothed to the valiant Russian knight Ruslan, but during the wedding feast she mysteriously vanishes as the scene is darkened and lightning and thunder rend the skies. The Grand Duke promises her hand to anyone who will find her. Two suitors besides Ruslan take part in the hunt, but Ruslan is helped by a benign magician. He discovers that Ludmila was abducted by the sinister magus Chernomor (the name means "Black Mortifier"), who might reside in his long beard; this presents an obvious clue to the resolution of the problem. Ruslan is confronted with horrendous obstacles, most spectacularly a huge severed head guarding Chernomor (the part of the head is sung by a vocal quartet), but of course he regains his beloved in the end. The score contains interesting harmonic innovations such as whole-tone scales and is profoundly imbued with Russian folk song inflections.

Russell, George (Allan), African-American jazz pianist, music theorist, teacher, and composer; b. Cincinnati, June 23, 1923. He took up the drums in his youth; then turned to composition, composing for Benny Carter, Gillespie, Hines, and others; his interest in a contemporary music combining bop and 20th-century classical is spelled out in one of his early hits, *A Bird in Igor's Yard* (1949). He developed a modal technique called the Lydian Chromatic Concept of Tonal Organization (1945–46); subsequently studied composition with Stefan Wolpe. After teaching at the Lenox (Mass.) School of Jazz (1959–60), he became active as a pianist in his own sextet (1960–61); later taught at the New England Cons. of Music in Boston (from 1969). He publ. *The Lydian Chromatic Concept of Tonal Organization* (1953); has composed for his own groups for several decades.

Russian bassoon (bassoon serpent). A serpent built with an upright brass bell, somewhat similar in appearance to a bassoon, including a mouthpiece on a crook; invented in the late 18th century, used in the 19th, especially in Russian military bands.

Russolo, Luigi. See FUTURISM.

rustico (It.). Rural, pastoral.

Rute (Ger.). A light brush used in jazz and some modern scores to produce a soft glissando on the snare drum head and other effects; the American slang is *brushes*; jazz drummers usually play with a pair.

Ruth. Opera by L. Berkeley, 1956, based on the biblical heroine, 1st performed in London.

ruvido (It.). In a rough, harsh style.

Ruy Blas. Concert overture by Mendelssohn, 1939, 1st performed in Leipzig under the composer's direction. The program, based on V. Hugo's eponymous play, involves an eponymous servant who is placed in the service of the Spanish queen by a disgruntled courtier, with the object of compromising her. When Ruy Blas realizes what he is expected to do, he kills the conspiring grandee and poisons himself.

Rysanek, Leonie, distinguished Austrian soprano; b. Vienna, Nov. 14, 1926. She studied at the Vienna Cons. with Rudolf Grossmann, whom she later married. She made her debut as Agathe in *Der Freischütz* in Innsbruck in 1949; then sang at Saarbrücken (1950–52). She 1st attracted notice when she appeared as Sieglinde at the Bayreuth Festival in 1951; became a member of the Bavarian State Opera in Munich in 1952 and went with it to London's Covent Garden in 1953, where she sang Danae; in 1954 she joined the Vienna State Opera; also sang in various other major European opera houses. On Sept. 18, 1956, she made her U.S. debut as Senta at the San Francisco Opera; later made a spectacular appearance at the Metropolitan Opera in N.Y. in 1959, when she replaced Maria Callas in the role of Lady Macbeth on short notice; she remained on its staff until 1973 and sang there again in 1975–76 and subsequent seasons. She received the Lotte Lehmann Ring from the Vienna State Opera in 1979. Her younger sister Lotte Rysanek (b. Vienna, Mar. 18, 1928) attained a fine reputation in Vienna as a lyric soprano.

rythmé (Fr.). Measured. *Bien rythmé*, well-balanced and elegant in rhythmical effect; *rythme brisé*, uneven or broken rhythm.

Rzewski, Frederic (Anthony), American pianist, teacher, and avant-garde composer of Polish descent; b. Westfield, Mass., Apr. 13, 1938. He studied counterpoint with Thompson and orchestration with Piston at Harvard Univ. (B.A., 1958) and continued his studies with Sessions and Babbitt at Princeton Univ. (M.F.A., 1960); then received instruction from Dallapiccola in Florence on a Fulbright scholarship (1960–61) and from Carter in Berlin on a Ford Foundation grant (1963–65). With Curran and Teitelbaum—other similarly futuroscopic musicians—he founded the M.E.V. (Musica Elettronica Viva) in Rome in 1966; was active as a pianist in various avant-garde settings; played concerts with the topless cellist (Madeline) Charlotte Moorman; also devoted much time to teaching. In 1977 he became prof. of composition at the Liège Cons.

As a composer he pursues the shimmering distant vision of optimistic, positivistic antimusic. He is furthermore a granitically overpowering piano technician, capable of depositing huge boulders of sonoristic material across the keyboard without actually wrecking the instrument.

Ss

s. Abbrev. for *segno* in *al segno, dal segno*; for *subito* in the phrase *Volti subito* (V.s.); and for *senza, sinistra, solo, soprano*, and *sordino/-i*.

Sabre Dance. Excerpt from *Gayané* by Khachaturian, 1942. The most famous number from the ballet, its quasi-Oriental melody depicts a Caucasian military dance full of animal energy.

Sachs, Hans, famous German poet and Meistersinger; b. Nuremberg, Nov. 5, 1494; d. there, Jan. 19, 1576. He was educated at the Nuremberg grammar school (1501–1509); after serving his apprenticeship (1511–16) he returned to Nuremberg as a master shoemaker in 1520; joined the Meistersinger guild about 1509, where he received instruction from Linhard Nunnenbeck. Under Sachs, the Meistergesang was an active force in the Reformation movement from 1520. He wrote over 6,000 poetical works, ranging from Meisterlieder to dramatic pieces; he also wrote 13 *Meistertöne* (melodies to which texts can be later fitted). Sachs is the central figure in Wagner's opera *Die Meistersinger von Nürnberg*.

sackbut (Fr. *saqueboute*). 1. Early form of trombone, dating back to 1000 A.D. 2. In the Bible, the translation of *sabbek*, a harplike instrument.

Sackpfeife (Ger.). BAGPIPE.

Sacre du printemps, Le. RITE OF SPRING, THE.

sacred concerto (Ger. *geistliche Konzert*; It. *sacra symphonia*). An early Baroque religious genre, a predecessor to the cantata; composers such as the Gabrielis and Schütz sought to incorporate the new *concertato* (concerted) style, with divided choruses and instrumental groups, into sacred contexts. Schütz was especially successful and prolific with the sacred concerto, and many other German Baroque composers contributed to the genre; eventually the development of set pieces (aria, recitative, chorus) led to the cantata of Buxtehude and Bach.

Sadko. Opera by Rimsky-Korsakov, 1898, 1st produced in Moscow. The libretto is based on an ancient Russian epic. Sadko is a popular minstrel in Novgorod, the 1st capital of Russia. He has mercantile dreams of selling wares abroad, a dream that is fanatically realized when a flock of swans on Lake Ilmen, in reality the feathered daughters of the King of the Ocean, take him to their abode on the bottom of the lake. He catches magic goldfish that turn out to be made of real gold. He returns to Novgorod a rich man. *Sadko* is a paradigm of the Russian fairy-tale opera. The *Song of India*, sung by a Hindu merchant visiting Novgorod, is a perennial favorite on the concert platform. The score of *Sadko* abounds in bold innovations. A chorus in 11/4 meter was regarded so difficult to perform that Russian opera choristers devised a line of 11 syllables as a mnemonic aid: "Rimsky-Kor-sa-kov-is-al-to-ge-ther-mad!"

Sadra, I Wayan, significant Indonesian composer, performer, and writer on music; b. Denpasar, Bali, Aug. 1, 1953. He attended Konservatori Karawitan (KOKAR; graduated 1972), where he specialized in traditional Balinese music, particularly *gender wayang* (music for the Balinese shadow play). In 1973–74 he worked with the well-known experimental Indonesian choreographer Sardono W. Kusumo; after touring with his group in Europe and the Middle East, Sadra settled in Jakarta, where he studied painting and taught Balinese gamelan at Inst. Kesenian Jakarta (IKJ, Jakarta Fine Arts Inst.; 1975–78); also taught Balinese music at the Indonesian Univ. (1978–80) and experimental composition, Balinese gamelan, and music criticism at Sekolah Tinggi Seni Indonesia Surakarta (STSI, National College of the Arts; from 1983), where he earned a degree in composition (1988); concurrently wrote NEW MUSIC criticism for various Indonesian newspapers, including *Suara Karya* and *Bali Post*.

He appeared widely as a performer with traditional Indonesian ensembles; performed throughout Indonesia and Europe, and in Singapore, Japan, Hong Kong, Australia, and Seoul. In 1988 he was keynote speaker at the national Pekan Komponis (Composers' Festival) in Jakarta; in 1989 he appeared in Calif. at the Pacific Rim Festival; in 1990 was a featured participant at Composer-to-Composer in Telluride, Colo. Concurrent with the development of Indonesia's national identity has come an increase of national new-music festivals, increased interaction among artists from different regions, and a greater degree of individual freedom to create autonomous music; all have contributed to the emergence of a distinct Indonesian aesthetic and a contemporary art music.

Sadra is one of the outstanding young composers to emerge from this period, and his works have contributed much to the development of *musik kontemporer, komposisi,* and *kreasi baru* (new creations). He is also concerned with the social context of performance, considering audience development as important as the development of new works. His compositions are often scored for unusual combinations of instruments. In an experimental piece performed at the Telluride Inst., raw eggs were thrown at a heated black panel; as the eggs cooked and sizzled they provided both a visual and sonic element for the closing of the piece. He also proposed to the mayor of Solo, Central Java, a new work entitled *Sebuah Kota Yang Bermain Musik* (A City That Plays Music), wherein the entire population of the city would make sounds together for a specified 5 minutes; the proposal was not accepted, but Sadra hopes for its realization in the future.

Saga, En. Symphonic poem by Sibelius, 1893, 1st performed in Helsinki conducted by Sibelius himself. With this work Sibelius established his individual musical style; it is based on a motive in a minor mode that reflects the millennial Scandinavian spirit—introspective, strong, persevering. The work is indeed a saga of Finland.

Sagittarius, Henricus. SCHÜTZ, HEINRICH.

Sailor's Hornpipe. Traditional English dance tune, 1st printed in America as early as 1796.

sainete (Sp., small farce). Spanish musical comedy popular in the 18th century; eventually displaced by the ZARZUELA.

St. Francis. Ballet by Hindemith, 1938, subtitled *Nobilissima visione*, premiered in London; at about or near the same time Hindemith arranged an orch. suite.

St. François d'Assise. Opera by Messiaen, 1983, produced at the Paris Opéra. Messiaen's only opera, to his own libretto, is based on the mystical life of St. Francis, whose devotion was not limited to humans alone but embraced the adoration of birds and all other God's creatures. Messiaen himself was a religious birdman who collected songs of the flying species and used them with melodic twits, twirls, and trills of his own.

St. François d'Assise prédicant aux oiseaux. The 1st of 2 *Legends* by Lizst, 1866, descriptive of the saint's sermon to the birds.

St. François de Paule marchant sur les flots. The 2nd of 2 *Legends* by Lizst, 1866, descriptive of the saint's walking on the water during a storm.

St. Louis Blues. Song by Handy, 1914; it stabilized the form of urban blues anticipated in his previous success, *The Memphis Blues*. The sheet music sales and recordings of *St. Louis Blues* leaped into millions.

Saint of Bleecker Street, The. Music drama by Menotti, 1954, to his own libretto, 1st produced in N.Y. The action takes place in an Italian section of Greenwich Village in N.Y.; Bleecker Street is the actual name of the street there. An Italian girl believes she has the sacred stigmata, but her agnostic brother derides her. He himself is ridiculed by his girlfriend for his devotion to his sister, and in an argument he accidentally kills her. He flees, returning to Bleecker Street as his sister enters the convent. She becomes overwrought emotionally and dies as she pledges her vow.

Saint-Saëns, (Charles-) Camille

〜〜 〜〜 〜〜 〜〜 〜〜

elebrated French composer; b. Paris, Oct. 9, 1835; d. Algiers, Dec. 16, 1921. His widowed mother sent him to his great-aunt, Charlotte Masson, who taught him to play piano. He proved exceptionally gifted, and gave a performance in a Paris salon before he was 5; at 6 he began to compose; at 7 he became a private pupil of Stamaty; so rapid was his progress that he made his pianistic debut at the Salle Pleyel in 1846, playing a Mozart concerto and a movement from Beethoven's C-minor concerto, with orch.

After studying harmony with Pierre Maleden, he entered the Paris Cons., where his teachers were Benoist (organ) and Halévy (composition). He won the 2nd prize for organ in 1849, and the 1st prize in 1851. In 1852 he competed unsuccessfully for the Grand Prix de Rome, and failed again in a 2nd attempt in 1864 when he was already a composer of some stature. His *Ode à Sainte Cécile* for voice and orch. was awarded the 1st prize of the Soc. Sainte-Cécile (1852). On Dec. 11, 1853, his 1st numbered sym. was performed; Gounod wrote him a letter of praise, containing a prophetic phrase regarding the "obligation de devenir un grand maître." From 1853 to 1857 Saint-Saëns was organist at the church of Saint-Merry in Paris; in 1857 he succeeded Lefébure-Wély as organist at the Madeleine. This important position he filled with distinction, and he soon acquired a great reputation as virtuoso on the organ and a master of improvisation. He resigned in 1876 and devoted himself mainly to composition and conducting; also continued to appear as a pianist and organist.

From 1861 to 1865 he taught piano at the École Niedermeyer; among his pupils were André Messager and Gabriel Fauré. Saint-Saëns was one of the founders of the Soc. Nationale de Musique (1871), established for the encouragement of French composers, but he withdrew in 1886 when d'Indy proposed to include works by foreign composers in its program. In 1875 he married Marie Truffot; their 2 sons died in infancy; they separated in 1881 but were never legally divorced; Madame Saint-Saëns died in Bordeaux in 1950 at the age of 95. In 1891 Saint-Saëns established a museum in Dieppe (his father's birthplace), to which he gave his MSS and his collection of paintings and other art objects. In 1907 he witnessed the unveiling of his own statue (by Marqueste) in the court foyer of the opera house in Dieppe.

He received many honors: in 1868 he was made a Chevalier of the Legion of Honor; in 1884, Officer; in 1900, Grand-Officer; in 1913, Grand-Croix (the highest rank). In 1881 he was elected to the Inst. de France; he was also a member of many foreign organizations; received an honorary Mus.D. degree at Cambridge Univ. He visited the U.S. for the 1st time in 1906; was a representative of the French government at the Panama-Pacific Exposition in 1915 and conducted his choral work *Hail California*, written for the occasion, in San Francisco. In 1916, at the age of 81, he made his 1st tour of South America; continued to appear in public as conductor of his own works almost to the time of his death. He took part as conductor and pianist in a festival of his works in Athens in May 1920. He played a program of his piano pieces at the Saint-Saëns museum in Dieppe (1921). For the winter he went to Algiers, where he died.

The position of Saint-Saëns in French music is very important. His abilities as a performer were extraordinary; he aroused the admiration of Wagner during the latter's stay in Paris (1860–61) by playing at sight the entire scores of Wagner's operas; curiously, Saint-Saëns achieved greater recognition in Germany than in France during the initial stages of his career. His most famous opera, *Samson et Dalila*, was produced in Weimar (1877) under the direction of Eduard Lassen, to whom the work was suggested by Liszt; it was not performed in France until nearly 13 years later, in Rouen. He played his 1st and 3rd piano concertos for the 1st time at the Gewandhaus in Leipzig.

Solidity of contrapuntal fabric, instrumental elaboration, fullness of sonority in orchestration, and a certain harmonic saturation are the chief characteristics of his music, qualities that were not yet fully exploited by French composers at the time, the French public preferring the lighter type of music. However, Saint-Saëns overcame this initial opposition, and toward the end of his life was regarded as an embodiment of French traditionalism. The shock of the German invasion of France in World War I made him abandon his former predilection for German music, and he wrote virulent articles against German art. He was unalterably opposed to modern music, and looked askance at Debussy; he regarded later manifestations of musical modernism as outrages, and was outspoken in his opinions.

That Saint-Saëns possessed a fine sense of musical characterization, and true Gallic wit, is demonstrated by his ingenious suite *Carnival of the Animals*, his most famous and favorite work, which he wrote in 1886 but did not allow to be publ. during his lifetime; it includes representation of human animals, a few choice musical parodies, and the beloved *The Swan*, famous as a cello piece and a dance. The work has been orchestrated (posthumously), and the American poet Ogden Nash composed some verses which are often performed with the work. He also publ. a book of elegant verse (1890).

Among Saint-Saëns's compositions are 13 operas, of which only 2 (*Samson et Dalila*; *Henry VIII*, Paris, 1883) are still performed; 1 ballet; incidental music to 5 plays; and a pioneering film score, *L'Assassinat du Duc de Guise* (1908). Saint-Saëns's current reputation rests primarily on his orch. music, including 5 syms.: A major (*c.* 1850); No. 1 (Paris, 1853); *Urbs Roma* (Paris, 1857); No. 2 (Leipzig, 1859); No. 3, *Organ* (with an obbligato organ part; one of Saint-Saëns's most performed works; London, 1886); 5 piano concertos (all 1st perf. with Saint-Saëns as soloist): No. 1 (1858; Leipzig, 1865); No. 2 (Paris, 1868); No. 3 (Leipzig, 1869); No. 4 (Paris, 1875); No. 5, *Egyptian* (Paris, 1896); 3 violin concertos: No. 1 (1859; Paris, 1867); No. 2 (1858; Paris, 1880); No. 3 (Paris, 1881); *Introduction and Rondo capriccioso* for Violin and Orch. (1863); Tarantelle for Flute, Clarinet, and Orch. (1857); 2 cello concertos: No. 1 (Paris, 1873); No. 2 (1902; Paris, 1905); Romance for Flute or Violin and Orch. (1871); Romance for Horn or Cello and Orch. (1874); Romance for Violin and Orch. (1874); Morceau de concert for Violin and Orch. (1880); *Wedding Cake* (Caprice-Valse) for Piano and Orch. (1885); *Havanaise* for Violin and Orch. (1887); Morceau de concert for Horn and Orch. (1887); *Africa* for Piano and Orch. (Paris, 1891); *Caprice andalous* for Violin and Orch. (1904); *Odelette* for Flute and Orch. (1920); symphonic poems, including: *Le Rouet d'Omphale* (Paris, 1872); *Phaéton* (Paris, 1873); *Danse macabre* (Paris, 1875); *La Jeunesse d'Hercule* (Paris, 1877); *Trois tableaux symphoniques d'aprés La foi* (1908); orch. suites, overtures, dances, rhapsodies, marches; band music.

He also composed chamber music for various ensembles; numerous piano pieces; sacred vocal works; secular choral works; song cycles; about 100 solo songs; also cadenzas to Mozart's piano concertos K.482 and K.491, and to Beethoven's 4th Piano Concerto and Violin Concerto; and made various transcriptions and arrangements. For a complete list of his works see the Durand *Catalogue général et thématique des oeuvres de Saint-Saëns* (Paris, 1897; rev. ed., 1909).

Saite (Ger.). A string.

Saiteninstrumente (Ger.). String instruments.

Salammbô. Unfinished opera by Mussorgsky, 1863–66, after Flaubert's novel, orchestrated by Z. Peskó and premiered at RAI, Milan, 1980. The plot resembles that of Bellini's *Norma*; here it is Mathô, the Libyan, falling for Salammbô, priestess of the goddess Tanit; the locale is Carthage; the result is death for both. Mussorgsky wrote about half the opera, although crucial events (i.e., the love scenes) were never set. When asked why he didn't finish a work that was going well, Mussorgsky burst out laughing and then, becoming serious, said, "We have already had enough of the Orient with [Alexander] Serov's *Judith*. Art is not a pastime; time is precious."

salicional stop. Narrow, open cylindrical stop producing a string-like tone; usually 4′ or 8′.

Salieri, Antonio

Famous Italian composer and teacher; b. Legnago, near Verona, Aug. 18, 1750; d. Vienna, May 7, 1825. He studied violin and harpsichord with his brother, Francesco, then continued violin studies with the local organist, Giuseppe Simoni. He was orphaned in 1765; subsequently was taken to Venice, where he studied thoroughbass with Giovanni Pescetti, deputy maestro di cappella of San Marco, and singing with Ferdinando Pacini, a tenor there. Florian Gassmann took Salieri to Vienna in 1766 and provided for his musical training and a thorough education in the liberal arts; there he came into contact with Metastasio and Gluck, the latter becoming his patron and friend. His 1st known opera, *La Vestale* (not extant), was premiered in Vienna in 1768. His comic opera, *Le Donne letterate*, was successfully performed at the Burgtheater in 1770. The influence of Gluck is revealed in his 1st major production for the stage, *Armida* (1771).

Upon the death of Gassmann in 1774, Salieri was appointed his successor as court composer and conductor of the Italian Opera. After Gluck was unable to fulfill the commission for an opera to open the Teatro alla Scala in Milan, the authorities turned to Salieri; his *L'Europa riconosciuta* inaugurated the great opera house (1778). While in Italy he also composed operas for Venice and Rome. He then returned to Vienna, where he brought out his Lustspiel, *Der Rauchfangkehrer* (1781). With Gluck's encouragement Salieri set his sights on Paris. In an effort to provide him with a respectful hearing, Gluck and the directors of the Paris Opéra advertised Salieri's *Les Danaïdes* (1784) as a work from Gluck's pen; following a number of performances, it was finally acknowledged as Salieri's creation.

Returning to Vienna, he composed 3 more stage works, including the successful *La grotta di Trofonio* (1785). His French opera *Les Horaces* (Paris, 1786) proved a failure. However, his next French opera, *Tarare* (Paris Opéra, 1787), was a triumphant success. After Da Ponte rev. and trans. Beaumarchais's French libretto into Italian and Salieri thoroughly recomposed the score, it was given as *Axur, re d'Ormus* (Vienna, 1788); it was then performed throughout Europe to great acclaim. Salieri was appointed court Kapellmeister in Vienna in 1788; he held that position until 1824; however, he did not conduct operatic performances after 1790. He continued to compose for the stage until 1804, his last major success being *Palmira, regina di Persia* (1795).

Salieri's influence on the musical life of Vienna was considerable. From 1788 to 1795 he was president of the Tonkünstler-Sozietät, the benevolent society for musicians founded by Gassmann in 1771; he was its vice president from 1795; he was also a founder of the Gesellschaft der Musikfreunde. He was widely celebrated as a pedagogue, his pupils including Beethoven, Hummel, Schubert, Czerny, and Liszt. He was the recipient of numerous honors, including the Gold Medallion and Chain of the City of Vienna; he was also a Chevalier of the Légion d'Honneur and a member of the French Inst. Salieri's eminence and positions in Vienna earned him a reputation for intrigue; many unfounded stories circulated about him, culminating in the fantastic tale that he poisoned Mozart; this tale prompted Pushkin to write his drama *Mozart and Salieri*, which subsequently was set to music by Rimsky-Korsakov; a contemporary interpretation of the Mozart-Salieri rivalry, Peter Shaffer's *Amadeus*, was successfully produced in London in 1979 and in N.Y. in 1980; it later obtained even wider circulation through the award-winning film version of 1984.

Salieri was a worthy representative of the traditional Italian school of operatic composition. He was a master of harmony and orchestration. His many operas are noteworthy for their expressive melodic writing and sensitive vocal treatment. All the same, few held the stage for long, and all have disappeared from the active repertoire. He also composed numerous sacred works; secular works, including cantatas, choruses, and songs; and instrumental pieces.

Sally. Musical by Kern, 1920. Sally is a dishwasher, clever enough to pose as a Russian ballerina at the mansion of a millionaire on Long Island. By an unfathomable quirk of fate she becomes a real dancer, is a hit on Broadway, and marries a rich American. Includes the title song, *Whip-Poor-Will, Wild Rose,* and the best-known song, *Look for the Silver Lining.*

salmo (It.). PSALM.

Salome. Opera by R. Strauss, 1905, based on a German trans. from the orig. French play by Oscar Wilde; it was 1st performed in Dresden. The story, obliquely connected with the biblical narrative, is centered on Salome, stepdaughter of Herod, tetrarch of Judea. John the Baptist, imprisoned by Herod, is brought out to the palace at Salome's request. She is fascinated by him; even though he curses her, she brazenly cries, "I want to kiss your mouth!" Herod, who lusts after Salome, asks her to dance for him. She agrees on condition that he will fulfill her unspoken wish, and performs the provocative *Dance of the 7 Veils.* The reward she demands is the severed head of John the Baptist. Herod tries to dissuade her from her monstrous intention, but he yields in the end. When the head is brought out on a platter, Salome mocks it: "You wouldn't let me kiss your mouth!" she cries, and kisses it passionately on the lips. Provoked beyond endurance by this act of depravity, Herod commands the guards to kill her.

The score is a masterpiece of stark realism, set to music of overwhelming power, ranging from exotic melodiousness to crashing dissonance. The opera aroused unusually vehement opposition when it was staged at the Metropolitan Opera in N.Y. (1907); the moralistic uproar in the public and press was such that the management was compelled to cancel further performances. It took 2 decades for the American public to mature sufficiently to absorb the opera. Strauss also wrote a French version (*Salomé*).

Salomon, Johann Peter. See HAYDN, FRANZ JOSEPH.

Salón México, El. Orch. piece by Copland, 1937, inspired by Mexican tunes. The title refers to a dance hall in Mexico City in which Copland heard a local group play Mexican popular music; the 1st performance of the work was given there, with Chávez conducting; it became one of the most popular works of Copland.

salon music. The music that flourished in Paris and Vienna in the 18th and 19th centuries, a salon being the drawing-room in aristocratic mansions, and salon music therefore satisfying the need for light entertainment. Liszt complained of the "atmosphere lourde et mephitique des salons" (dull and noxious atmosphere of the salons). During his Paris sojourn the German poet Heine voiced his despair at the universal proliferation of piano music "that one hears in every house, day and night," adding that "at the very moment of the writing of this report a couple of young ladies in the neighboring house are playing a morceau for 2 left hands." The word *salon* gradually became synonymous with BIEDERMEIER culture.

Chopin was not averse to writing piano music designed for salon performances, and Schumann described him as the "vornehmste Salonkomponist" (most elegant salon composer), and his famous Waltz in A-flat Major as a "Salonstück der nobelsten Art, aristokratisch durch und durch" (salon piece of the noblest art, aristocratic through and through). Lesser composers frankly entitled their works *Études de Salon, Petites Fleurs de Salon,* etc. Perhaps the most "mephitic" piece was *Prière d'une Vièrge* by a young Polish girl named Thekla Badarzewska, which spread through Europe and America with an irresistible force of distilled sentimentality.

Although salon music largely disappeared with the cataclysmic outbreak of World War I, social salons continued to be maintained by wealthy hostesses in Paris and other music capitals. Countess de Polignac, the daughter of the American sewing machine manufacturer Singer, married a French aristocrat, began a series of musical matinees, and commissioned works by Stravinsky, de Falla, and others for performance at the salon.

salon orchestra. Salon orchs. were organized for performances of light music in cafés, cabarets, and the houses of the rich. The minimal ensemble was the piano trio. The so-called Vienna type of salon orch. consisted of a seated violinist, a standing violinist, and cello, flute, and percussion. The Berlin salon ensemble added the clarinet, cornet, trombone, viola, and double bass; the Paris salon orch. usually employed piano, violin, cello, flute, cornet, and drums. Special editions were published for these orchs. to enable them to play light overtures or dance suites in so-called theater arrangements, in which cues were inserted in the piano parts to replace the missing instruments. Although salon music was deprecated for its low taste, the salon orch. performed a positive educational role, providing classical and semiclassical music in workable arrangements.

Salonen, Esa-Pekka, Finnish conductor and composer; b. Helsinki, June 30, 1958. He entered the Sibelius Academy in Helsinki as a horn pupil of Holgar Fransman in 1973, taking his diploma in 1977; then studied composition with Rautavaara and conducting with Panula; subsequently studied with Donatoni in Siena, attended the Darmstadt summer course, and finally received instruction from N. Castiglioni in Milan (1980–81). After appearances as a horn soloist, he took up conducting; was a guest conductor throughout Scandinavia, and later extended his activities to include Europe. In 1984 he made his U.S. debut as a guest conductor with the Los Angeles Phil. He became principal conductor of the Swedish Radio Sym. Orch. in Stockholm in 1984; led it on a tour of the U.S. in 1987; also served as principal guest conductor of the Oslo Phil. (from 1984) and the Philharmonia Orch. in London (from 1985). In 1989 he was appointed music director of the Los Angeles Phil., his tenure to begin in 1992.

In his music he tends toward pragmatic aural accessibility, employing fairly modern techniques while preserving the formal centrality of traditional tonality. He has composed orch. works (mostly with solo instrument/s) and chamber music, including a cello sonata, wind quintet, and a series of solo works called *YTA*.

salpinx. Straight conical trumpet with a narrow bore and slightly flared bell. It is mentioned in Homer's *Illiad*; a surviving instrument is made of ivory with a brass bell.

salsa (Sp., sauce). Modern Latin American dance in a raucous rhythmic manner. It originated in the Caribbean islands, most notably Cuba, with traceable African roots; it emigrated to the U.S. with those fleeing Castro's 1959 revolution. Salsa may have received its name because of its hot, peppery, and pervasive rhythm over a hypnotically repetitive melodic line. Its meter is invariably 4/4, with quarter notes alternating with 8th notes in syncopated beats.

saltarella, -o (It.). 1. A 2nd division in many 16th-century dance tunes, in triple time, the skipping step marked in the rhythm

2. An Italian dance in 3/4 or 6/8 time.

saltato (It.). A rapid spiccato, played with a bouncing bow. See RICHOCHET; SPRINGING BOW.

salto (It.). Leap; skip. *Di salto*, by a leap or leaps.

Salzedo (Salzédo), (León) **Carlos,** eminent French-born American harpist, pedagogue, and composer; b. Arcachon, France, Apr. 6, 1885; d. Waterville, Maine, Aug. 17, 1961. He studied at the Bordeaux Cons. (1891–94), winning 1st prize in piano; then entered the Paris Cons., where his father, Gaston Salzédo, was a prof. of singing; studied with Charles de Bériot (piano), gaining 1st prize in 1901, and with Hasselmans (harp), also receiving 1st prize. He began his career as a concert harpist upon graduation; traveled all over Europe (1901–1905); was solo harpist of the Assoc. des Premiers Prix de Paris in Monte Carlo (1905–1909); in 1909 he settled in N.Y.; was 1st harpist in the orch. of the Metropolitan Opera (1909–13). In 1913 he formed the Trio de Lutèce (from Lutetia, the ancient name for Paris), with Georges Barrère (flute) and Paul Kéfer (cello).

In 1921 he was cofounder, with Edgard Varèse, of the International Composers' Guild in N.Y., with the aim of promoting modern music; this organization presented many important contemporary works; in the same year he founded a modern music magazine, *Eolian Review*, later renamed *Eolus* (discontinued in 1933). He became an American citizen in 1923; was elected president of the National Assoc. of Harpists; held teaching positions at the Inst. of Musical Art in N.Y., and the Juilliard Graduate School of Music; organized and headed the harp dept. at the Curtis Inst. of Music in Philadelphia. In 1931 he established the Salzedo Harp Colony at Camden, Maine, for teaching and performing during the summer months. Salzedo introduced a number of special effects and publ. special studies for his new techniques; designed a "Salzedo Model" harp, capable of rendering novel sonorities (Eolian flux, Eolian chords, gushing chords, percussion, etc.).

His own compositions are rhythmically intricate and contrapuntally elaborate and require a virtuoso technique. He publ. *Modern Study of the Harp* (N.Y., 1921), *Method for the Harp* (N.Y., 1929), and *The Art of Modulating* (with L. Lawrence; N.Y., 1950). Like any composer-virtuoso, Salzedo composed for his instrument: numerous solo pieces and transcriptions, harp ensembles, chamber works with and without voice, and a few concerto and concertolike works.

samba. Characteristic Brazilian dance marked by a rolling rhythm in 2/4 time and vigorous syncopation. Samba has also become a generic description of any Brazilian dance in a fast tempo.

sambuca (Lat.; from Grk. *sambykē*). Greco-Roman angular harp, with a horizontal pegboard and vertical soundboard.

sambuca lincea (Lat.). An enharmonic harpsichord, so named by its inventor Fabio Colonna, also known as Linceo. It was designed around 1618, with 8 separate keyboards; it was tuned according to a complicated scheme combining Pythagorean intervals with various tempered adjustments; the resulting octave had 17 unequal microtones, and the instrument had a total of 50 strings (possibly bichordally strung).

sambuca rotata (Lat.). HURDY-GURDY.

sampler. Electronic digital recorder capable of recording a sound and then storing it in the form of digital information, which then may be converted into an "instrument" for performance or compositional use. *Sampling*, a modern studio technique in which small bits of earlier recordings are stored and then interwoven into a new work to varying degrees; a technique fully developed in RAP.

Samson et Dalila. Opera by Saint-Saëns, 1877, 1st performed in Weimar to a German libretto. It tells the biblical story of Delilah, the priestess of the Philistine temple, who entices the Hebrew warrior Samson and during his sleep cuts his hair, which is the source of his physical power. He is then blinded, chained, and taken to the Philistine temple in Gaza. There, summoning his remaining strength, he breaks the pillars supporting the roof, bringing the temple down on himself and on the miscreant worshippers. On account of the restrictions with respect to theatrical representation of biblical characters, the opera was not performed on the stage in France until 1892, and not in England until 1909.

sämtliche Werke (Ger.). Collected works.

sānāyī (*shannāi*; Sansk.; Pers. *surnā*). A conical SHAWM of North India, made of wood, with finger holes and a wide bore; sometimes the bell is metallic.

Sanctus. A section of the Mass ORDINARY; it comprises the *Sanctus, Benedictus,* and the *Osanna* (Hosanna).

sanft (Ger.). Softly, quietly.

sanglot (Fr., tearful sigh). In rococo arias, an emotional appoggiatura, commonly set with interjections such as "Oh!," "Ah!," or "Helas!" An effective Romantic sanglot can be achieved by a closing of the vocal box. Such a COUP DE GLOTTE was a great specialty of Caruso, in his rendition of such arias as Canio's *Vesti la giubba* in *Pagliacci.*

sanjuanito. National dance of Ecuador, dedicated to St. John, in 2/4 time.

Sankey, Ira D(avid), noted American evangelistic singer, gospel hymn composer, and hymnbook compiler; b. Edinburgh, Pa., Aug. 28, 1840; d. N.Y., Aug. 13, 1908. As a youth of 17 he became choir leader in the Methodist Church of New Castle, Pa.; served for a year with the N.Y. 12th Infantry Regiment at the time of the Civil War. In 1870 he was a delegate to the YMCA convention at Indianapolis, where his forceful singing attracted the attention of the evangelist preacher Dwight L. Moody. He joined Moody as music director and remained at this post for some 30 years, until approaching blindness forced his retirement in 1903. Of his many gospel tunes the most popular has proved to be *The 90 and 9* (1874), which he improvised at a moment's notice during a service in Edinburgh, Scotland. His chief publs. were *Sacred Songs and Solos* (London, 1873) and 6 vols. of *Gospel Hymns and Sacred Songs* (1875–91). As president of the publ. firm of Biglow & Main (1895–1903) he brought out numerous works, including many of his own. He is not to be confused with another gospel song writer, Ira Allan Sankey, a lesser light than Ira D(avid) Sankey.

sans (Fr.). Without. *Sans presser*, without hurrying; *sans quitter la corde*, without leaving the string; *sans ralentir*, without slowing down.

Santa Lucia. Neapolitan ballad by Teodor Cottrau, publ. 1850; like many others of its kind, its popularity has never abated.

Santūr (Turk.; Arab., Pers. *santir*; Mod. Grk. *santouri*). Trapezoidal hammered dulcimer, with 14 courses of 4 metal strings apiece and curved blade-shaped beaters. The instrument dates from the 15th century and may be the ancestor of the Chinese *yangqin.*

Sapho (1). Opera by Gounod, 1851, 1st produced in Paris. The libretto describes in melodramatic terms the life of the Greek poetess who flourished on the island of Lesbos. This was Gounod's 1st opera, and the score anticipates the gift of melody that became second nature for him.

Sapho (2). Opera by Massenet, 1897, based on a story by Alphonse Daudet; 1st produced in Paris. The heroine poses as an artist's model in this role. A young man from the country falls in love with her, but their differences are such that they eventually separate and go their separate ways. The score is not one of Massenet's best, but it is invariably pleasing in its melodious lilt and harmonious tilt.

saraband (sarabande; It. *sarabanda*; Fr. *sarabande*; Ger. *Sarabande*). A dance of Spanish or Middle Eastern origin, at 1st a dance song in 16th-century Hispanic countries. The origin of the word is conjectural; its etymology has been variously traced to Arabia via Moorish Spain, to Mexico, or to Panama. Ironically, one of the earliest mentions of the word *saraband* occurs in the ruling of the Spanish Inquisition in 1583, which forbade the performing of the saraband on penalty of a fine and imprisonment, apparently due to its immoral and suggestive nature. Half a century after its proscription in Spain, the saraband quietly slithered into France and even Elizabethan England, becoming a stately dance in TRIPLE TIME; it remained popular in the 17th and 18th centuries; fast and slow types developed. The saraband became an integral part of the Baroque instrumental suite, found in works by Bach, Handel, and other masters. The instrumental form usually has 2 8-measure reprises, in slow tempo and triple time; its place in the suite, as the slowest movement, is before the GIGUE.

sarambo. Popular dance of the Dominican Republic in rapid 6/8 time, accompanied by indigenous percussion instruments and accordion.

sāraṅgī (Sans.). Indian bowed chordophone, with 3 or 4 playing strings and a number of sympathetic strings below them. The instrument is played between the knees of a seated performer; its bow is thick and short; formerly a folk instrument, it now participates in the classical music of India.

Sarasate (y Navascuez), **Pablo** (Martín Melitón) **de,** celebrated Spanish violinist and composer; b. Pamplona, Mar. 10, 1844; d. Biarritz, Sept. 20, 1908. He commenced playing the violin when he was 5; after making his public debut at age 8 he was granted a private scholarship to study with M. Saez in Madrid; with the assistance of Queen Isabella he pursued his studies with Alard at the Paris Cons. (from 1856), where he took *premiers prix* in violin and solfège (1857), and in harmony (1859). He launched his career as a virtuoso with a major concert tour when he was 15. In 1866 he acquired a Stradivarius violin. His playing was noted for its extraordinary beauty of tone, impeccable purity of intonation, perfection of technique, and grace of manner.

In the early years of his career his repertoire consisted almost exclusively of fantasies on operatic airs, most of which he arranged himself. He later turned to the masterpieces of the violin literature. His tours, extending through all of Europe, North and South America, South Africa, and the Orient, were an uninterrupted succession of triumphs. He bequeathed to his native city the gifts that had been showered upon him by admirers throughout the world; the collection was placed in a special museum. Among the works written for him were Bruch's 2nd Concerto and *Scottish Fantasy*, Lalo's Concerto and *Sym. espagnole*, Saint-Saëns's 1st and 3rd concertos and *Introduction et Rondo capriccioso*, and Wieniawski's 2nd Concerto. Sarasate's compositions, pleasing and effective, include his *Zigeunerweisen* (1878), *Spanische Tänze* (4 books, 1878–82), and the *Carmen Fantasy* in 4 movements (1883).

sardana. Catalonian round dance in 6/8 time, alternating rapid and slow sections. Casals wrote an orch. *Sardana* that stylizes the authentic rhythm and melody.

Šárka (1). Opera by Fibich, 1897, premiered in Prague. After the death of the legendary Queen of Bohemia, Libuše, the power passes to her husband, much to the chagrin of the women warriors of the land. When the king refuses to restore their civil rights, they declare war on all men. Šárka challenges a masculine knight to a duel, but he scornfully rejects her proposal. She then resorts to a ruse; her companions tie her to a tree. When he enters the forest he finds her and hears her false story about the maltreatment she has suffered at their hands. Fascinated by her muscular charms, he releases her. But now she herself is fascinated by him and warns him that her companions lie in ambush. Boldly he defies the women but is captured. Desperate to save him from imminent execution, Šárka goes to the king for help. His soldiers arrive, kill most of the women, and liberate Šárka's beloved. He wants to take her to his castle, but she is tormented by her treason and hurls herself from a cliff to her death. This was Fibich's penultimate opera; he would soon turn to composing melodramas.

Šárka (2). Symphonic poem by Smetana, 1877, premiered in Prague. Šárka is the leader of a fierce women's group in Bohemia, engaged in a constant fight with the local knights. In order to overcome them, she lets herself be tied to a tree in the forest. One of the knights finds her and carries her off as a prize. As the knights celebrate her capture, they fall into a drunken stupor in their castle. Šárka then signals her female warriors to descend upon the castle and slaughter every one of the knights. This bloody event is set to music *con brio*, with a romantic duet for clarinet—representing Šárka—and cello, representing the knight who captured her. *Šárka* was incorporated into Smetana's orch. cycle *Má vlast* (as No. 3).

sarōd. An unfretted, plucked, pear-shaped classical Indian lute. It has 6 metal playing strings (2 of which may be paired) and 12 or more sympathetic strings below them. Like the larger SITĀR, it uses bulbous gourds for resonance, and was once a bowed chordophone (although that use is rare now). Both instruments are played in a sitting position, but the sarōd is played like a Western lute or guitar, while the sitār is held nearly upright.

sarrusophone. A brass wind instrument with a double reed, invented (1863) by and named after the bandmaster Sarrus of Paris. Although a family of sarrusophones was manufactured, the bass alone survives, as a contrabass instrument in military bands.

Satie, Erik (Alfred-Leslie)

Celebrated French composer, originator of the intentionally unindelible *furniture music* who elevated his eccentricities and verbal virtuosity to the plane of high art; b. Honfleur, May 17, 1866; d. Paris, July 1, 1925. He received his early musical training from a local organist, Vinot, who was a pupil of Niedermeyer; at 13 he went to Paris, where his father was a music publisher, and received instruction in harmony from Taudou and in piano from Mathias; however, his attendance at the Cons. was only sporadic between 1879 and 1886. He played in various cabarets in Montmartre; in 1884 he publ. a piano piece which he numbered, with malice aforethought, op. 62.

His whimsical ways and Bohemian manner of life attracted many artists and musicians; he met Debussy in 1891; joined the Rosicrucian Society in Paris in 1892 and began to produce short piano pieces with eccentric titles intended to ridicule modernistic fancies and classical pedantries alike. Debussy thought highly enough of him to orchestrate 2 numbers from his piano suite *Trois Gymnopédies* (1888). In 1898 he moved to Arcueil, a suburb of Paris; there he held court for poets, singers, dancers, and musicians, among whom he had ardent admirers. Satie was almost 40 when he decided to pursue serious studies at the Paris Schola Cantorum, taking courses in counterpoint, fugue, and orchestration with d'Indy and Roussel (1905–8). Milhaud, Sauguet, and Desormière organized a group, which they called only half-facetiously École d'Arcueil, in honor of Satie as master and leader.

But Satie's eccentricities were not merely those of a Parisian poseur; rather, they were adjuncts to his aesthetic creed, which he enunciated with boldness and a total disregard for professional amenities (he was once brought to court for sending an insulting letter to a music critic). Interestingly enough, he attacked modernistic aberrations just as assiduously as reactionary pedantry, publishing manifestos in prose and poetry. Although he was dismissed by most serious musicians as an uneducated person who tried to conceal his ignorance of music with persiflage, he exercised a profound influence on the young French composers of the 1st quarter of the 20th century; moreover, his stature as an innovator in the modern idiom grew after his death, so that the avant-garde musicians of the later day accepted him as inspiration for their own experiments; thus environmental or SPACE MUSIC could be traced back to Satie's *Musique d'ameublement* (Furniture Music, 1920; collaborated with Milhaud), in which players were stationed at different parts of a hall playing different pieces in different tempos.

The instruction in his piano piece *Vexations*, to play it 840 times in succession, was carried out literally in N.Y.

in 1963, by a group of 5 pianists working in relays overnight, thus setting a world's record for duration of any musical composition (to that time). When critics accused Satie of having no idea of form, he publ. *Trois Morceaux en forme de poire* (for piano 4-hands, 1903), the eponymous fruit being reproduced in color on the cover; other pieces bore self-contradictory titles, such as *Heures séculaires et instantanées* and *Crépuscule matinal de midi*; other titles were *Pièces froides, Embryons desséchés, Prélude en tapisserie, Trois véritables préludes flasques (pour un chien), Descriptions automatiques*, etc.

In his ballet *Parade* (ballet realiste, 1917; collaborated with Cocteau, Picasso, Massine) he introduced jazz for the 1st time in Paris; at the performance of his ballet *Relâche*, with "entr'acte cinematographique" (*ballet instananée*, 1924; collaborated with Picabia, Borlin, Clair), the curtain bore the legend "Erik Satie is the greatest musician in the world; whoever disagrees with this notion will please leave the hall." While the composer may have designed this slogan with his tongue in both cheeks, the late 20th-century listener may well enjoy the absurd humor and commentary, rebellious attitude, strong harmonic sense, virtually total lack of romanticism, and popular origins of "le maître d'Arcueil." Satie publ. a facetious autobiographical notice as *Mémoires d'un amnésique* (1912); N. Wilkins trans. and ed. *The Writings of Erik Satie* (1980).

Satz (Ger.). A movement in a wholly or primarily instrumental work, such as a sonata, quintet, or sym.

Satzlehre (Ger.). Theory of polyphonic composition; literally, the study of contrapuntal composition (or rules); perhaps a more complete term is *Tonsatzlehre*, the study of tonal settings. It is distinguished from other theories of composition in that it does not preoccupy itself with the acoustical, harmonic, or intervallic elements of chords and contrapuntal combinations, but is concerned mainly with the larger considerations of structure and style.

saudade (Port.). A Brazilian dance characterized by nostalgia or longing.

Saudades do Brasil. Orch. suite by Milhaud, 1921, premiered in Paris. Like the dance (see entry above), the title refers to nostalgia or longing; for Milhaud it means recalling Brazilian dance rhythms.

sauteuse (Fr., woman who jumps). French waltz in 6/8 time, usually allegretto, popular in the early 19th century.

sautillé (Fr.; It. *saltando*). See RICOCHET; SPRINGING BOW.

Sāvitri. Opera by Holst, 1916, to a libretto drawn from the Hindu epic *Mahabharata*; 1st performed in London. Death calls on the eponymous heroine's husband, but she succeeds in staving off the fateful visitor by ingratiating wiles. In this opera Holst attempted to use classical Indian melos in a Western contrapuntal context.

Savoyards. Members of the D'Oyly Carte Opera Company that produced the Gilbert and Sullivan operas at the Savoy Theatre in London (hence the term *Savoy opera*, not limited to Gilbert and Sullivan). The company continued producing into the middle of the 20th century.

Sawallisch, Wolfgang, eminent German conductor; b. Munich, Aug. 26, 1923. He began piano study when he was 5; later pursued private musical training with Ruoff, Haas, and Sachse in Munich before entering military service during World War II (1942); then completed his musical studies at the Munich Hochschule für Musik. In 1947 he became *répétiteur* at the Augsburg Opera, making his conducting debut there in 1950; then was Generalmusikdirektor of the opera houses in Aachen (1953–58), Wiesbaden (1958–60), and Cologne (1960–63); also conducted at the Bayreuth Festivals (1957–61). From 1960 to 1970 he was chief conductor of the Vienna Sym. Orch.; made his 1st appearance in the U.S. with that ensemble in 1964; also was Generalmusikdirektor of the Hamburg State Phil. (1961–73). From 1970 to 1980 he was chief conductor of the Orch. de la Suisse Romande in Geneva; from 1971 also served as Generalmusikdirektor of the Bavarian State Opera in Munich, where he was named Staatsoperndirektor in 1982.

In 1990 he was named music director of the Philadelphia Orch., effective with the 1993–94 season. He appeared as a guest conductor with a number of the world's major orchs. and opera houses. A distinguished representative of the revered Austro-German tradition, he has earned great respect for his unostentatious performances; he has also made appearances as a sensitive piano accompanist to leading singers of the day.

Sax, Adolphe (Antoine-Joseph), Belgian inventor of the saxophone, son of Charles-Joseph Sax; b. Dinant, Nov. 6, 1814; d. Paris, Feb. 4, 1894. He acquired great skill in manipulating instruments from his early youth; his practical and imaginative ideas led him to undertake improvements of the clarinet and other wind instruments. He studied the flute and clarinet at the Brussels Cons.; in 1842 he went to Paris with a wind instrument of his invention, which he called the "saxophone," made of metal, with a single-reed mouthpiece and conical bore. He exhibited brass and woodwind instruments at the Paris Exposition of 1844, winning a silver medal; his father Charles-Joseph Sax (1791–1865) joined him in Paris, and together they continued the manufacture of new instruments; evolved the saxhorn (improved over the bugle-horn and ophicleide by replacing the keys with a valve mechanism) and the saxotromba, a hybrid instrument producing a tone midway between the bugle and the trumpet.

Conservative critics and rival instrument makers ridiculed Sax's innovations, but Berlioz and others warmly supported him; he also won praise from Rossini. His instruments were gradually adopted by French military bands. Sax won a gold medal at the Paris Industrial Exposition of 1849. Financially, however, he was unsuccessful, and he was compelled to go into bankruptcy in 1856 and again in 1873. He taught the saxophone at the Paris Cons. from 1858 to 1871, and also publ. a method for his instrument. He exhibited his instruments in London (1862) and received the Grand Prix in Paris (1867) for his improved instruments. Although Wieprecht, Červeny, and others disputed the originality and priority of his inventions, legal decisions gave the rights to Sax; the saxophone became a standard instrument; many serious composers made use of it in their scores.

The instrument fell into desuetude after Sax's death, but about 1918 a spectacular revival of the saxophone took place, when it was adopted in jazz bands; its popularity became worldwide; numerous methods were publ. and special schools established; and there appeared saxophone virtuosos for whom many composers wrote concertos.

saxhorn. A brass wind-instrument family, patented 1845 by Adolphe Sax, the inventor of the saxophone. It is essentially an improved key bugle or ophicleide, having from 3 to 5 valves instead of keys. The instruments, whose nomenclature is exceedingly confused, are still found in bands.

saxophone (sax; It. *sassofono*). A metal wind-instrument family, patented 1846 by Adolphe Sax (see above), having a clarinet mouthpiece with single reed, the key mechanism

A. C. Reed with saxophone

and fingering also resembling those of the clarinet. It has a mellow, penetrating tone of veiled quality. In the latter part of the 19th century the saxophone became a standard instrument; many serious composers made use of it in their scores. The instrument fell into desuetude after Sax's death (1894), but about 1918 a spectacular revival of the saxophone took place, when it was adopted in jazz bands; its popularity became worldwide; numerous methods were publ. and special schools established; and there appeared saxophone virtuosos for whom many composers wrote concertos. It remains a popular band instrument, an essential part of most jazz ensembles, and a relatively infrequent but timbrally significant contributor to classical music.

saxtromba. A saxhorn with a trumpetlike bell, patented by Adolphe Sax (1845).

Say It with Music. Song by I. Berlin, from the *Music Box Revue*, 1921.

sbalzato (It.). Dashingly, impetuously.

scabellum (Lat.; Grk. *kroupalon, kroupezion*). Wooden foot clapper, attached like a sandal, used to keep time for music, dancing, or public games.

Scala, La. Teatro alla Scala, the most famous Italian opera house; it was founded in 1778 in Milan. Although it is popularly imagined that the theater owes its name to its spectacular ladder leading to its portals (scala being Italian for ladder), the theater was actually named after Regina della Scala, the wife of the Duke Visconti of Milan. A whole galaxy of Italian composers—Rossini, Donizetti, Bellini, Verdi, and Puccini—had their operas premiered at La Scala, and great conductors, including Toscanini, presided over these performances. In 1943 La Scala was almost entirely destroyed by an Allied air attack on the city. It was piously rebuilt in 1946 with the financial assistance of musicians and music lovers from all over the civilized world, and was reopened in May 1946, with Toscanini conducting. The restoration was remarkably faithful.

The Teatro alla Scala has 6 tiers, 4 of which are taken over by 146 boxes lined with elegant multicolored fabrics, with the lighting provided by a sumptuous chandelier. In 1955 the Teatro all Scala gave birth, in a splendid parturition, to an offspring called La Piccola Scala, suitable for performances of chamber opera and modern ballet.

Scala di Seta, La (The Silken Ladder). Opera by Rossini, 1812, 1st produced in Venice. A youthful couple are united in a *matrimonio segreto*, and the bridegroom is compelled to use a ladder every time he goes to her room upstairs in her father's house.

scala enigmatica. A scale that the elderly Verdi found in an Italian music journal and which he used in his *Ave Maria* from his *Quattro pezzi sacri*. The journal called the scale *scala enigmatica*, but the name is hardly justified, for the scale (C–D♭–E–F♯–G♯–A♯–B–C) is nothing more than a slightly ornamented whole-tone scale.

scales (It. *scala*, ladder). 1. In the tubes of wind instruments (especially organ pipes), the ratio between width of bore and length. 2. The compass of a voice or instrument; also, the series of tones producible on a wind instrument. 3. A series of tones which form (a) any major or minor key (*diatonic* scale); (b) the *chromatic* scale of successive semitonic steps; or (c) any predetermined series of tones within a modal or tonal system.

The American pedagogue Percy Goetschius used to play the C major scale for his students and ask them a rhetorical question, "Who invented this scale?" and answer it himself, "God!" Then he would play the whole-tone scale and ask again, "Who invented this scale?" And he would announce disdainfully, "Monsieur Debussy!" Debussy did not invent the whole-tone scale, but he made ample use of it, as did many other composers of his time. Other scales, built on quaquaversal intervallic progressions, engaged the attention of composers: the Gypsy scale, the pentatonic scale suitable for quasi-Eastern melismas, and the octatonic scale of alternating whole tones and semitones, used by Rimsky-Korsakov, Pijper, Liszt, Tchaikovsky, Stravinsky, and many other composers.

Scriabin derived a scale of 6 notes from his mystic chord, composed of 3 whole tones, a minor 3rd, a semitone, and a whole tone. Alexander Tcherepnin devised a scale of 9 notes: a whole tone, a semitone, a semitone, a whole tone, a semitone, a semitone, a whole tone, a semitone, a semitone. The Spanish composer Oscar Esplá wrote music based on the scale of the following intervals: semitone, whole tone, semitone, semitone, semitone, whole tone, whole tone, whole tone. Verdi was impressed by a "scala enigmatica" that he found in an Italian music journal, consisting of a semitone, an augmented 2nd, 3 consecutive whole tones, and 2 consecutive semitones.

Busoni experimented with possible scales of 7 notes and stated that he had invented 113 different scales of various intervallic structures. The 1st theorist to examine and classify scales based on the symmetrical division of the octave was Alois Hába in his book *Neue Harmonielehre*. Joseph Schillinger undertook a thorough codification of all possible scales having any number of notes from 2 to 12, working on the problem mathematically. In his *Thesaurus of Scales and Melodic Patterns* the author tabulated some 2 thousand scales within the multiple octave range, including such progressions as the polytetrachord, bitonal scales of 8 notes, and scales of 3 disjunct major or minor pentachords aggregating to 2 octaves.

Progressions of large intervals (3rds, 4ths, 5ths, etc.) cannot be properly described as scales without contradicting the etymology of the word (which implies step-wise motion). But helix-like constructions, involving spiraling chromatics, may well be called scales. Quarter-tone scales and other microtonal progressions also belong in this category.

Scapino. Comedy overture by Walton, 1941, premiered in Chicago. Scapino is a traditional commedia dell'arte character, a mischievous gallant who causes trouble in amorous and other affairs.

Scaramouche. Suite by Milhaud, 1937, for 2 pianos, 1st performed in Paris. Scaramouche is a standard character of Italian commedia dell'arte (Scamarella), a clownish braggart.

Scarf Dance. See PAS DES ECHARPES.

Scarlatti, (Giuseppe) **Domenico,** famous Italian composer, harpsichordist, and teacher, son of (Pietro) Alessandro (Gaspare) Scarlatti; b. Naples, Oct. 26, 1685; d. Madrid, July 23, 1757. Nothing is known about his musical training. In 1701 he was appointed organist and composer at the Royal Chapel in Naples, where his father was maestro di cappella. The 2 were granted a leave of absence in June 1702, and they went to Florence; later that year Domenico returned to Naples without his father and resumed his duties. His 1st opera, *Ottavia ristituita al trono*, was performed in Naples in 1703. He was sent to Venice by his father in 1705, but nothing is known of his activities there.

In 1708 he went to Rome, where he entered the service of Queen Maria Casimira of Poland; he remained in her service until 1714 and composed a number of operas and several other works for her private palace theater. He became assistant to Bai, the maestro di cappella at the Vatican, in 1713; upon Bai's death the next year, he was appointed his successor; he also became maestro di cappella to the Portuguese ambassador to the Holy See in 1714. During his years in Rome he met such eminent musicians as Corelli and Handel. An unconfirmed story tells that Scarlatti and Handel engaged in a friendly contest, Scarlatti being judged the superior on the harpsichord and Handel on the organ. .

Scarlatti resigned his positions in 1719; by 1724 he was in Lisbon, where he took up the post of mestre at the patriarchal chapel. His duties included teaching the Infanta Maria Barbara, daughter of King John V, and the King's younger brother, Don Antonio. In 1728 Maria Barbara married the Spanish Crown Prince Fernando and moved to Madrid. Scarlatti accompanied her, remaining in Madrid for the rest of his life. In 1724 he visited Rome, where he met Quantz; in 1725 he saw his father for the last time in Naples; in 1728 he was in Rome, where he married his 1st wife, Maria Caterina Gentili. In 1738 he was made a Knight of the Order of Santiago. When Maria Barbara became queen in 1746, he was appointed her maestro de camera. His last years were spent quietly in Madrid; from 1752 until 1756 Antonio Soler studied with him. So closely did he become associated with Spain that his name eventually appeared as Domingo Escarlatti.

Scarlatti composed over 500 single-movement sonatas for solo keyboard. Although these works were long believed to have been written for the harpsichord, the fact that Maria Barbara used pianos in her residences suggests that some of these works were written for that instrument as well; at least 3 were written for the organ. It is clear by the key pairings and shared motivic material that many of the sonatas are meant to be performed in pairs. His sonatas reveal his gifts as one of the foremost composers in the "free style" (a homophonic style with graceful ornamentation, in contrast to the formal contrapuntal style). He also obtained striking effects by the frequent crossing of hands, tones repeated by rapidly changing fingers, etc.

During his lifetime 3 collections of his keyboard works were publ. (London, 1738; London, 1739; Paris, 1742–46); the sonatas were variously called "essercizi per gravicembalo," "suites de pièces pour le clavecin," and "pieces pour le clavecin." Alessandro Longo, Ralph Kirkpatrick, and Giorgio Pestelli prepared chronological catalogues of his sonatas; none can be proven definitive. Scarlatti also composed 17 orch. sinfonias; 15 operas, some with collaborators; 1 oratorio, 9 secular cantatas and serenatas, numerous arias, and sacred vocal music. Domenico Scarlatti's nephew, Giuseppe Scarlatti (b. Naples, *c.* 1718; d. Vienna, Aug. 17, 1777), was an operatic composer.

Scarlatti, (Pietro) **Alessandro** (Gaspare), important Italian composer, father of (Giuseppe) Domenico Scarlatti; b. Palermo, May 2, 1660; d. Naples, Oct. 22, 1725. Nothing is known concerning his musical training. When he was 12 he went with his 2 sisters to Rome, where he found patrons who enabled him to pursue a career in music. His 1st known opera, *Gli equivoci nel sembiante*, was performed there in 1679. By 1680 he was maestro di cappella to Queen Christina of Sweden, whose palace in Rome served as an important center for the arts. He also found patrons in 2 cardinals, Benedetto Pamphili and Pietro Ottoboni, and served as maestro di cappella at S. Gerolamo della Carità.

From 1684 to 1702 he was maestro di cappella to the Viceroy at Naples. During these years he composed prolifically, bringing out numerous operas; he also composed serenatas, oratorios, and cantatas. In addition, he served as director of the Teatro San Bartolomeo, where he conducted many of his works. His fame as a composer for the theater soon spread, and many of his works were performed in the leading music centers of Italy; one of his most popular operas, *Il Pirro e Demetrio* (1694), was even performed in London. His only confirmed teaching position dates from this period, when he served for 2 months in the spring of 1689 as a faculty member of the Conservatorio di Santa Maria di Loreto.

Tiring of his exhaustive labors, he was granted a leave of absence and set out for Florence in June 1702; Prince Ferdinando de' Medici had been one of his patrons for some years in Florence, and Scarlatti hoped he could find permanent employment there. When this did not materialize he settled in Rome and became assistant maestro di cappella at S. Maria Maggiore in 1703; he was promoted to maestro di cappella in 1707. One of his finest operas, *Il Mitridate Eupatore*, was performed in Venice in 1707. Since the Roman theaters had been closed from 1700, he devoted much of his time to composing serenatas, cantatas, and oratorios. In late 1708 he was again appointed maestro di cappella to the Viceroy at Naples. His most celebrated opera from these years, *Il Tigrane*, was given in Naples in 1715.

His only full-fledged comic opera, *Il trionfo dell'onore*, was performed in Naples (1718). Scarlatti's interest in purely instrumental music dates from this period, and he composed a number of conservative orch. and chamber music pieces. Having again obtained a leave of absence from his duties, he went to Rome to oversee the premiere of his opera *Telemaco* (1718). His last known opera, *La Griselda*, was given there in 1721. From 1722 until his death he lived in retirement in Naples, producing only a handful of works.

Scarlatti was the foremost Neapolitan composer of the late Baroque era in Italy. He composed 58 operas (1679–1721); 27 serenatas (*c.* 1680–1723); 36 oratorios, passions, and other sacred pieces (1679–1720); over 600 secular cantatas; masses and mass movements; motets; madrigals. His instrumental music includes 12 *sinfonie di concerto grosso*, keyboard toccatas; trio sonatas; suites, etc. Scarlatti also produced some pedagogical manuals.

scat (singing). A style of jazz performance in which a singer improvises nonsense syllables, often quite rapidly but always with a strong rhythmic impulse; occasionally the singer imitates the sounds produced by instruments. The technique originated in the 1920s, with Louis Armstrong as its major proponent; later, Ella Fitzgerald made the technique her trademark, and many other singers in the bebop and subsequent traditions scatted to their heart's content.

Scelsi, Giacinto (born Conte Giacinto Scelsi di Valva), remarkable Italian composer; b. La Spezia, Jan. 8, 1905; d. Rome, Aug. 9, 1988. He was descended from a family of the nobility. He received some guidance in harmony from Giacinto Sallustio; after studies with Egon Koehler in Geneva, he completed his formal training with Walter Klein in Vienna (1935–36), where he became interested in the Schoenbergian method of writing music outside the bounds of traditional tonality; at the same time he became deeply immersed in the study of the musical philosophy of the East, in which the scales and rhythms are perceived as functional elements of the human psyche. As a result of these multifarious absorptions of ostensibly incompatible ingredients, Scelsi formulated a style of composition that is synthetic in its sources and pragmatic in its artistic materialization.

His works began to have a considerable number of performances in Italy and elsewhere, most particularly in the U.S. A curious polemical development arose after his death, when an Italian musician named Vieri Tosatti publ. a sensational article in the *Giornale della Musica*, declaring "I was Giacinto Scelsi." He claimed that Scelsi used to send him thematic sections of unfinished compositions, usually in the 12-tone system, for development and completion, using him as a ghostwriter. Scelsi sent so many such "improvisations" to Tosatti that the latter had 2 other musicians to serve as secondary "ghosts," who in turn confirmed their participation in this peculiar transaction. The matter finally got to the court of public opinion, where it was decided that the works were genuine compositions by Scelsi, who improvised them on his electric piano, and that they were merely ed. for better effect by secondary arrangers.

scemando (It.). DIMINUENDO.

scena (from Grk., stage). In opera, an accompanied dramatic solo consisting of arioso and recitative passages, bearing the character of explanatory narrative, and often ending with an aria.

scenario. A concise script outlining the contents of a play, opera, ballet, or other performance work, with an indication of the participating characters/performers.

scene (Fr. *tableau*). Usually, a part of an act; e.g., an opera may contain 3 acts and 7 scenes that are distributed among the 3 acts. Sometimes a composer subdivides an opera in scenes without specifying the number of acts, e.g., Prokofiev's *War and Peace* and Mussorgsky's *Boris Godunov*.

Schaeffer, Pierre, French acoustician, composer, and novelist; b. Nancy, Aug. 14, 1910. Working in a radio studio in Paris, he conceived the idea of arranging a musical montage of random sounds, including outside noises. In 1948 he formulated the theory of musique concrète, which was to define such random assemblages of sounds. When the magnetic tape was perfected, Schaeffer made use of it by rhythmic acceleration and deceleration, changing the pitch and dynamics and modifying the nature of the instrumental timbre. He made several collages of elements of "concrete music," among them *Concert de bruits* (1948) and (with

Pierre Henry) *Sym. pour un homme seul* (1950); also created an experimental opera, *Orphée 53* (1953). He incorporated his findings and ideas in the publ. *A la recherche d'une musique concrète* (Paris, 1952) and in *Traité des objets sonores* (Paris, 1966). Eventually he abandoned his acoustical experimentations and turned to literature. He publ. both fictional and quasi-scientific novels, among them *Le Gardien de volcan* (1969); *Excusez-moi si je meurs* (1981); *Prélude, Chorale et Fugue* (1983).

Schafer, R(aymond) Murray, Canadian composer; b. Sarnia, Ontario, July 18, 1933. He studied at the Royal Cons. of Music of Toronto with John Weinzweig (1952–55); went to Vienna in 1956 and then on to England, where he was active with the BBC (1956–61). Returning to Canada in 1961, he served as artist-in-residence at Memorial Univ. (1963–65) and taught at Simon Fraser Univ. (1965–75); held a Guggenheim fellowship in 1974. He was active with the World Soundscape project from 1972. In 1987 he received the Glenn Gould Award. He developed a sui generis system of topological transmutation, exemplified by his satire/tribute for orch. and tape, *The Son of Heldenleben* (Montreal, 1968), in which he systematically distorted the thematic materials of *Ein Heldenleben* by Richard Strauss, retaining the essential motivic substance of the original score. Schafer is best known for his experimental use of language and performance environments; he is an active and innovative educator and author.

Schäferlied (Ger.). Shepherd's song; pastorale.

schalkhaft (Ger.). Roguish, sportive, wanton, mischievous; expression mark in Schumann's *Album für die Jugend.*

Schall (Ger.). Audible sound.

Schallplatte (Ger., sound platter). Phonograph record.

Schallwandler (Ger., sound changer). A transformer that turns electrical impulses into sound.

Schallwellen (Ger.). Sound waves.

Schalmei (Ger.). SHAWM.

Schandeflöte (Ger., flute of shame). A heavy vertical flute made of iron that was hung on a tight ring around the neck of a town fifer in medieval Germany, as punishment for the crime of playing too many wrong notes in the performance of his duties. A sign was placed on his jacket spelling out the extent of his inharmonious conduct so that he could receive the full brunt of public disgrace. Theories that this symbol replaced the wearing of a red-lettered *S* (for *Schande*) around the fifer's neck cannot be verified.

scharf (Ger.). Sharply; throw off sharply; expression mark in Mahler's 1st Sym.

schattenhaft (Ger.). Somberly, as if in shadow; expression mark in R. Strauss's *Till Eulenspiegels.*

schauernd (Ger.). Shudderingly; expression mark found in Mahler's *Das Lied von der Erde.*

schaurig (Ger.). In a style expressive of (or calculated to inspire) mortal dread; weirdly.

Schauspieldirektor, Der. IMPRESARIO, THE.

Schauspielmusik (Ger.). Theater music.

Scheherazade. Symphonic suite by Rimsky-Korsakov, 1888, based on *1,001 Nights*; it was 1st performed in St. Petersburg. The connecting link within the suite is a brief violin solo representing the narrative of the Sultan's most resourceful wife, who saves herself from the Sultan's customary execution of each of his wives after the wedding night by telling him exciting tales. The score is a paradigm of orch.l brilliance; its synthetic Orientalism even influenced Arab composers. The work has often been choreographed as a ballet.

schelmisch (Ger.). Joking, roguish.

Schelomo. "Hebrew rhapsody" by Ernest Bloch, 1917, for cello and orch., 1st performed in N.Y. *Schelomo* is the original Hebrew word for Solomon; the solo cello portrays the eloquent voice of the wise King of the Hebrews.

Schenker, Heinrich, outstanding Austrian music theorist; b. Wisniowczyki, Galicia, June 19, 1868; d. Vienna, Jan. 13, 1935. He studied jurisprudence at the Univ. of Vienna (Dr.Jur., 1890); concurrently took courses with Bruckner at the Vienna Cons. He composed some songs and piano pieces; Brahms liked them sufficiently to recommend

Schenker to his publisher, Simrock. For a while Schenker served as accompanist of the baritone Johannes Messchaert; then returned to Vienna and devoted himself entirely to the development of his theoretical research; gathered around himself a group of enthusiastic disciples who accepted his novel theories, among them Otto Vrieslander, Hermann Roth, Hans Weisse, Anthony van Hoboken, Oswald Jonas, Felix Salzer, and John Petrie Dunn.

He endeavored to derive the basic laws of musical composition from a thoroughgoing analysis of the standard masterworks. The eventual result was the contention that each composition represents a horizontal integration—through various stages—of differential triadic units derived from the overtone series. By a dialectical manipulation of the thematic elements and linear progressions of a given work, Schenker succeeded in preparing a formidable system in which the melody is the *Urlinie* (basic line), the bass is *Grundbrechung* (broken ground), and the ultimate formation is the *Ursatz* (background). The result seems as self-consistent as the Ptolemaic planetary theory of epicycles. Arbitrary as the Schenker system is, it proved remarkably durable in academia; some theorists have even attempted to apply it to modern works lacking in the triadic content essential to Schenker's theories. Schenker wrote many articles and books outlining his theories. See also SCHENKER SYSTEM.

Schenker system (Schenkerianism).

A theory of musical analysis evolved over several decades by Heinrich Schenker. It derives its principle from the natural series of overtones. The continuum of these overtones is defined as *Klang* (clang), that is, a cumulative sound. The linear distribution of this Klang is the *Urlinie*, the fundamental line, governing the melodic design. The bass line is named *Grundbrechung* (fundamental arpeggio). The process of analysis is in several stages. The actual composition is defined as foreground (*Vorgrund*); its partial reduction is middle-ground (*Mittelgrund*); its final schematization, the background (*Hintergrund*), constitutes the *Ursatz*, the ultimate irreducible structure, representing the summation of the Urlinie and the Grundbrechung. These successive stages are obtained by a series of *Züge* (motions). Since the harmonic series is the basic source of the Ursatz, the Schenker system postulates the absolute preponderance of the tonic major triad, with the subdominant and dominant triads as its derivatives and with minor triads accounted for by procrustean adjustments.

In his original historical exposition Schenker covers the common practice period from Bach to Brahms (Wagner is omitted). Analysis of chromatic harmony is made by even further adjustments. Following this modus operandi it is possible to analyze even modern works (Schenker once analyzed a piece of Stravinsky to point out the composer's "errors"), but the limitations of the Schenker system become increasingly evident with every successive step toward ATONALITY.

Scherz (Ger.). Joke.

scherzando (It.; Ger. *scherzhaft*). Like a scherzo, i.e., in a sportive, toying manner; playfully, lightly, jestingly.

Scherzi, Gli. One of several nicknames for the Haydn quartets op. 33 (Nos. 37–42, 1781). The minuets in them are marked either *scherzo* or *scherzando*, indicating that they were to be played faster than the usual minuet tempo. The same group of quartets is known as *Jungfernquartette* (Maiden Quartets) because the title page of the 1st edition represented a luscious Teutonic female; they are also known as the *Russian Quartets* because they were dedicated to a Russian grandduke.

scherzo (It., joke; Ger. *Scherz*). 1. A vivacious movement in the late Classic and Romantic sym., with strongly marked rhythms and sharp, unexpected contrasts in both rhythm and harmony. In the 2nd half of the 18th century the term *scherzo* was standardized as an instrumental composition in 3/4 or 3/8 time in a rapid tempo. (Occasionally duple-meter scherzos were composed.) Structurally scherzo was a modification of the ternary Classic minuet; in the 19th century it usually replaced the Classic minuet in sonatas, chamber music, and syms. Like the minuet, the scherzo contains a contrasting middle part, the TRIO (because these were 1st written for 3 instruments only). While in most late Classic syms. the scherzo was placed in the position formerly occupied by the minuet (i.e., the 3rd movement), Beethoven shifted it to the 2nd movement in his 9th Sym. 2. In the Romantic era, an instrumental piece of a light, piquant, humorous character. Chopin elevated it to a form of prime importance; his 4 piano scherzos are extended, virtuosic compositions while retaining their ternary form. Paul Dukas called his symphonic poem *The Sorcerer's Apprentice* a scherzo; Stravinsky wrote an orch. work entitled *Scherzo fantastique*, inspired by Maeterlinck's essay *Les Abeilles* (The Bees). 3. In the 16th century, a vocal composition in a lighter manner, although titles such as *Scherzi sacri* (sacred scherzos) are also found.

Scherzo à la russe. Orch. work by Stravinsky, 1944, for jazz big band; he conducted an orch. arrangement in San Francisco, 1946. The piece is a sophisticated potpourri of Russian folklike motives.

Scherzo fantastique. Orch. work by Stravinsky, 1909, premiered in St. Petersburg. The composition was inspired by Maeterlinck's half-literary, half-scientific essay *Les Abeilles* (The Bees). Each section of the score corresponds to a beehive event: birth of the queen, nuptial flight, swarming, etc. The publs. quoted from the book in the score, and Maeterlinck, a hot-tempered poet, promptly sued Stravinsky for infringement of copyright. Fifty years later in one of his conversation books with Robert Craft, Stravinsky denied ever intending to use the Maeterlinck book as a programmatic source; but his own 1907 letter to Rimsky-Korsakov plainly contradicts this.

Schickele, Peter, American composer and musical humorist; b. Ames, Iowa, July 17, 1935. He was educated at Swarthmore College (B.A., 1957); studied composition with Roy Harris in Pittsburgh (1954), Milhaud at the Aspen School of Music (1959), and Persichetti and Bergsma at the Juilliard School of Music in N.Y. (M.S., 1960). After serving as composer-in-residence to the Los Angeles public schools (1960–61), he taught at Swarthmore College (1961–62) and at the Juilliard School of Music (from 1962). He rocketed to fame at N.Y.'s Town Hall in 1965, in the rollicking role of the roly-poly character P. D. Q. Bach, the mythical composer of such outrageous travesties as *The Civilian Barber* (a suite from an unrediscovered opera), *Gross Concerto for Divers Flutes* (featuring a nose flute and a Wiener Whistle to be eaten during the perf.), *Concerto for Piano vs. Orchestra, Iphigenia in Brooklyn, The Seasonings, Pervertimento for Bagpipes, Bicycles & Balloons, No-No Nonette, Schleptet, Fuga Meshuga, Missa Hilarious, Sanka Cantata, Fantasie-Shtick,* and the opera *The Abduction of Figaro* (Minneapolis, 1984). He publ. *The Definitive Biography of P. D. Q. Bach (1807–1742?)* (N.Y., 1976). In 1967 he organized a chamber-rock-jazz trio known as Open Window, which frequently presented his own compositions, including orch. works, vocal pieces (including rounds), film and television scores, and chamber music. He hosted a weekly radio show, *Schickele Mix,* which redefined music appreciation.

schietto (It.). Simply, quietly; neatly, deftly; unaffectedly.

Schifrin, Lalo (Boris), Argentine-American pianist, conductor, and composer; b. Buenos Aires, June 21, 1932. He studied music at home with his father, the concertmaster of the Teatro Colón orch.; subsequently studied harmony with Juan Carlos Paz; won a scholarship to the Paris Cons. in 1950, where he received guidance from Koechlin and took courses with Messiaen. He became interested in jazz, and represented Argentina at the International Jazz Festival in Paris in 1955; returning to Buenos Aires, he formed his own jazz band, adopting the bebop style. In 1958 he went to N.Y. as arranger for Xavier Cugat; then was pianist with Dizzy Gillespie's band (1960–62); composed for it several exotic pieces, such as *Manteca, Con Alma,* and *Tunisian Fantasy,* based on Gillespie's *Night in Tunisia.* In 1963 he wrote a ballet, *Jazz Faust.*

In 1964 he went to Hollywood, where he rapidly found his métier as composer for films and television; among his scores are *The Liquidator* (1966), *Cool Hand Luke* (1967), *The Fox* (1967), *The 4 Musketeers* (1973), *Voyage of the Damned* (1975), *The Amityville Horror* (1978), *The Sting II* (1983), and *Bad Medicine* (1985). He also experimented with applying the jazz idiom to religious texts, as, for instance, in his *Jazz Suite on Mass Texts* (1965). He achieved his greatest popular success with the theme for the television series *Mission: Impossible* (1966–73), in 5/4 time, for which he received 2 Grammy Awards.

His adaptation of modern techniques into mass media placed him in the enviable position of being praised by professional musicians. His oratorio *The Rise and Fall of the 3rd Reich,* featuring realistic excerpts and incorporating an actual recording of Hitler's speech in electronic amplification, was premiered at the Hollywood Bowl in 1967. His other works include *The Ritual of Sound* for 15 Instruments (1962); *Rock Requiem* (1970); *Pulsations* for Electronic Keyboard, Jazz Band, and Orch. (Los Angeles, 1971); *Madrigals for the Space Age,* in 10 parts, for Narrator and Chorus (Los Angeles, 1976); *Tropicos,* chamber orch. (1983); *Cantos Aztecas* for Vocal Soloists, Chorus, and Orch. (1988); *La Nouvelle Orleans* for Wind Quintet; concertos and concerto-like works; and chamber works. He served as music director of the newly organized Paris Phil. from 1988.

Schikaneder, Emanuel (Johannes Joseph). See MAGIC FLUTE, THE.

Schiller, (Johann Christian) **Friedrich von,** great German man of letters; b. Marbach, Nov. 10, 1759; d. Weimar, May 9, 1805. Many of his works were set in one form or another: *Die Räuber, Kabale und Liebe, Don Carlos,* the *Wallenstein* trilogy, *Maria Stuart, Die Jungfrau von Orleans, Die Braut von Messini, Wilhelm Tell;* and the ode *An die Freude.*

Schindler, Anton Felix. See BEETHOVEN, LUDWIG VAN.

schizzo (It.). Sketch.

Schlag (Ger.). A beat or stroke. *Schlagen*, beat time or hit.

Schlager (Ger.). Popular song or hit.

Schlaginstrumente (Ger.). Percussion instruments.

Schlagzeug (Ger.). Percussion.

schleichend (Ger., lingering). Dragging, slowing up the tempo.

Schleifer (Ger., slur; Eng. *slide, elevation, double blackfall*; Fr. *coulé*). A Baroque ornamental figure in which (1) a primary note is approached by 2 conjunct secondary notes, encompassing a 3rd, and starting on the beat; or (2) (Fr. *tierce coulée*) a dyad of a 3rd that, when indicated, adds a passing tone to become a run of 3 conjunct notes.

schleppen (Ger.). Drag, retard. *Nicht schleppen*, do not drag.

schlicht (Ger.). Simple, unaffected.

Schlitztrommel (Ger.). SLIT DRUM.

Schlummerlied (Ger., slumber song). Berceuse, lullaby.

Schluss (Ger.). End; close cadence.

Schluss (Ger., conclusion). The signification of the final section (subsection, phrase) of a composition. The last movement of a large work is sometimes referred to in German as *Schluss-Satz* (concluding part). The Schluss in a simple chant may be limited to 2 notes, the *penultima vox* (next-to-last voice) and *ultima vox* (last voice), to use the terminology of medieval Latin treatises. An ideal Schluss in Classic music is provided by Mozart's Sym. No. 39 in E-flat Major, which concludes with a simple restatement of the principal theme, suggesting a signature in Gothic characters. One of the most prolix Schluss is that of the 2nd Sym. of Sibelius, consisting of a seemingly interminable succession of ascending scales, which, upon reaching the 6th degree of the key, retreat to the leading tone in the lower octave, only to resume their Sisyphus-like ascension. The most abrupt Schluss occurs with the C-major chord at the end of Prokofiev's *March* from the opera *Love for 3 Oranges*. The most numbing C-major Schluss is found in the finale of the 1st Piano Concerto by Shostakovich.

By definition the Schluss must be a unison or a concord, but Chopin and Schumann sometimes end an individual piece of a cycle on an unresolved dominant-7th chord. The final chord in Mahler's grand sym. *Das Lied von der Erde* is a discord. In atonal writing a dissonant ending is de rigueur, unless it happens to be a single tone lost in mid-air, pianissimo. Toward the middle of the 20th century several composers, among them Stockhausen, Earle Brown, and Cage, developed a concept of works without an ascertainable Schluss, wherein any moment of a composition may be either a beginning or an end.

Schlüssel (Ger.). Clef.

schmachtend (Ger.). Languishing(ly); longing(ly).

schmaltz (Yidd., grease, fat). Inordinately sentimental playing of semipopular music, exaggerating every permissible expression to an intolerable limit, either through a natural lack of aesthetic taste, or with satirical intent.

schmeichelnd (Ger.). Flatteringly; in a coaxing, caressing manner.

schmelzend (Ger., melting). Lyrical.

schmerzlich (Ger.). Painfully, sorrowfully, plaintively.

Schmetternd (Ger.). For brass instruments, play with a blared or brassy tone.

Schmidt, Franz, important Austrian composer and pedagogue; b. Pressburg, Dec. 22, 1874; d. Perchtoldsdorf, near Vienna, Feb. 11, 1939. He began his musical training with the Pressburg Cathedral organist, Maher; in 1888 his family settled in Vienna, where he had piano lessons from Leschetizky and also studied composition with Bruckner, theory with Fuchs, and cello with Hellmesberger at the Cons. (from 1890). He was a cellist in the orch. of the Vienna Hofoper (1896–1911); also taught cello at the Cons. of the Gesellschaft der Musikfreunde (1901–8) and was prof. of piano (1914–22) and of counterpoint and composition (from 1922) at the Vienna Staatsakademie; also served as director (1925–27); subsequently was director of the Vienna Hochschule für Musik (1927–31). In 1934 he was awarded an honorary doctorate from the Univ. of Vienna. After his retirement in 1937, Schmidt received the Beethoven Prize of the Prussian Academy in Berlin. His 2nd wife, Margarethe Schmidt, founded the Franz Schmidt–Gemeinde in 1951.

Schmidt's music is steeped in Viennese Romanticism; the works of Bruckner and Reger were particularly influential in his development, but he found an original voice in his harmonic writing. Although he is regarded in Austria as a very important symphonic composer, his music is almost totally unknown elsewhere. Outside his homeland he remains best known for his orch. suite *Zwischenspiel aus einer unvollstandigen romantischen Oper* (1903), taken from his opera *Notre Dame* (1902–1904; Vienna, 1914). Among his other significant works are 4 syms.: No. 1 (1896–99; Vienna, 1902); No. 2 (1911–13; Vienna, 1913); No. 3 (Vienna, 1928); No. 4 (1932–33; Vienna, 1934); Piano Concerto for Left Hand and Orch., for Paul Wittgenstein (1923; Vienna, 1924); and the oratorio *Das Buch mit Sieben Siegeln* (1935–37; Vienna, 1938). He also composed 2 String Quartets (1925, 1929) and other chamber works, 2 piano sonatas, and organ music.

Schnabel, Artur, celebrated Austrian-born American pianist and pedagogue, father of Karl Ulrich Schnabel; b. Lipnik, Apr. 17, 1882; d. Axenstein, Switzerland, Aug. 15, 1951. He 1st studied with Hans Schmitt and made his debut at 8; then studied with Leschetizky in Vienna (1891–97). He went to Berlin in 1900; there he married the contralto Therese Behr (1905), with whom he frequently appeared in recitals; he also played in recitals with leading musicians of the day, including Flesch, Casals, Feuermann, Huberman, Primrose, and Szigeti; likewise gave solo recitals in Europe and the U.S., presenting acclaimed cycles of the Beethoven sonatas; taught at the Berlin Hochschule für Musik (from 1925). After the advent of the Nazi regime in 1933 he left Germany and settled in Switzerland; taught master classes at Lake Como and recorded the 1st complete set of the Beethoven sonatas. With the outbreak of World War II in 1939 he went to the U.S.; became a naturalized citizen in 1944; taught at the Univ. of Michigan (1940–45); then returned to Switzerland.

Schnabel was one of the greatest pianists and pedagogues in the history of keyboard playing; eschewing the role of the virtuoso, he concentrated upon the masterworks of the Austro-German repertoire with an intellectual penetration

and interpretive discernment of the highest order; he was renowned for his performances of Beethoven and Schubert; prepared an ed. of the Beethoven piano sonatas. He was also a composer; in his works he pursued an uncompromisingly modernistic idiom, thriving on dissonance and tracing melodic patterns along atonal lines; among these works are 3 syms. (1938–40; 1941–42; 1948); Piano Concerto (1901); Rhapsody (Cleveland, 1948); Duodecimet (inc.; comp. and orch. by R. Leibowitz). Chamber: 5 string quartets; Notturno for Voice and Piano (1914); Piano Quintet (1916); Sonata for Solo Violin (1919); Sonata for Solo Cello (1931); Violin Sonata (1935); solo piano pieces; songs. His writings include *Reflections on Music* (1933) and *Music and the Line of Most Resistance* (1942).

Schnaderhüpfel (Ger., dialect). Song of the Bavarian Alps in 3/4 time, usually consisting of symmetric stanzas with a harmonic scheme of alternating tonic and dominant harmonies.

Schnarre (Ger.). Rattle.

Schnarrtrommel (Ger., rattle drum). Snare drum.

schnell (Ger.). Fast, quick, rapid. *Schneller,* faster; *nach und nach schneller,* gradually faster.

Schneller (from Ger. *schnellen,* jerk). Inverted mordent; short trill on the beat using the upper auxiliary (neighbor) note.

Schnittke, Alfred (Garrievich), prominent Russian composer of German descent; b. Engels, near Saratov, Nov. 24, 1934. He studied piano in Vienna (1946–48), where his father was a correspondent of a German-language Soviet newspaper; then took courses in composition with Golubev and in instrumentation with Rakov at the Moscow Cons. (1953–58); after serving on its faculty (1962–72) he devoted himself fully to composition. He pursued many trips abroad, and in 1981 was a guest lecturer at the Vienna Hochschule für Musik and Darstellende Kunst. In 1981 he was elected a member of the West German Akademie der Kunste. In 1985 he survived a serious heart attack. After writing in a conventional manner, he became acutely interested in the new Western techniques, particularly in serialism and *sonorism,* in which dynamic gradations assume thematic significance; soon he became known as one of the boldest experimenters in contemporary composition in Russia; he also developed an international reputation. Schnittke has also written many pieces that take a postmodern look at neoclassicism and neo-Baroque music.

Schoeck, Othmar, eminent Swiss pianist, conductor, and composer; b. Brunnen, Sept. 1, 1886; d. Zurich, Mar. 8, 1957. He was the son of the painter Alfred Schoeck; went to Zurich, where he took courses at the Industrial College before pursuing musical training with Attenhofer, Freund, Hegar, and Kempter at the Cons. (from 1905); after further studies with Reger in Leipzig (1907–1908), he returned to Zurich and conducted the Aussersihl Men's Chorus (1909–15), the Harmonie Men's Chorus (1910–11), and the Teachers' Chorus (1911–17); then was conductor of the St. Gallen sym. concerts (1917–44). Schoeck was one of the most significant Swiss composers of his era; he won his greatest renown as a masterful composer of songs, of which he wrote about 400. He was also highly regarded as a piano accompanist and conductor. Among his many honors were an honorary doctorate from the Univ. of Zurich (1928), the 1st composer's prize of the Schweizerische Tonkünstlerverein (1945), and the Grand Cross of Merit and Order of Merit of the Federal Republic of Germany (1956). In 1959 the Othmar Schoeck Gesellschaft was founded to promote the performance of his works.

Schoenberg (Schönberg), Arnold (Franz Walter)

Outstanding Austrian-born American composer and theorist whose new method of musical organization in 12 different tones related only to one another profoundly influenced the entire development of modern techniques of composition; b. Vienna, Sept. 13, 1874; d. Los Angeles, July 13, 1951. He studied at the Realschule in Vienna; learned to play the cello, and also became proficient on the violin. His father died when Schoenberg was 16; he took a job as a bank clerk to earn a living; an additional source of income was arranging popular songs and orchestrating operetta scores.

Schoenberg's 1st original work was a group of 3 piano pieces, which he wrote in 1894; it was also about that time that he began to take lessons in counterpoint from Alexander Zemlinsky, whose sister Mathilde he married in 1901. He also played cello in Zemlinsky's instrumental group, Polyhymnia. In 1897 Schoenberg wrote his unnumbered string quartet, in D major, which achieved public performance in Vienna (1898). About the same time he wrote 2 songs with piano accompaniment which he designated as op. 1.

In 1899 he wrote his 1st true masterpiece, *Verklärte Nacht*, set for string sextet, which was 1st performed in Vienna by the Rosé Quartet and members of the Vienna Phil. (1902). It is a fine work, deeply imbued with the spirit of Romantic poetry, with its harmonic idiom stemming from Wagner's modulatory procedures; it remains Schoenberg's most frequently performed composition, known principally through its arrangement for string orch.

About 1900 he was engaged as conductor of several amateur choral groups in Vienna and its suburbs; this increased his interest in vocal music. He then began work on a choral composition, *Gurre-Lieder*, of monumental proportions, to the translated text of a poem by the Danish writer Jens Peter Jacobsen. For grandeur and opulence of orch. sonority it surpassed even the most formidable creations of Gustav Mahler or Richard Strauss; it calls for 5 solo voices, a speaker, 3 male choruses, an 8-part mixed chorus, and a very large orch. Special music paper of 48 staves had to be ordered for the MS. He completed the 1st 2 parts of *Gurre-Lieder* in the spring of 1901, but the composition of the remaining section was delayed by 10 years; it was not until 1913 that Franz Schreker was able to arrange its complete performance with the Vienna Phil. and its choral forces.

In 1901 Schoenberg moved to Berlin, where he joined E. von Wolzogen, F. Wedekind, and O. Bierbaum in launching an artistic cabaret, which they called Überbrettl. He composed a theme song for it with trumpet obbligato, and conducted several shows. He met Strauss, who helped him to obtain the Liszt Stipendium and a position as a teacher at the Stern Cons. He returned to Vienna in 1903 and formed friendly relations with Mahler, who became a sincere supporter of his activities; Mahler's power in Vienna was then at its height, and he was able to help him in his career as a composer.

In 1904 Schoenberg organized with Alexander Zemlinsky the Vereinigung Schaffender Tonkünstler for the purpose of encouraging performances of new music. Under its auspices he conducted the 1st performance of his symphonic poem *Pelleas und Melisande* (1905); in this score occurs the 1st use of a trombone glissando. There followed a performance in 1907, of Schoenberg's *Kammersymphonie*, op. 9, with the participation of the Rosé Quartet and the wind instrumentalists of the Vienna Phil.; the work produced much consternation in the audience and among critics because of its departure from traditional tonal harmony, with chords built on 4ths and nominal dissonances used without immediate resolution. About the same time he turned to painting, which became his principal avocation.

In his art, as in his music, he adopted the tenets of EXPRESSIONISM; that is, freedom of personal expression within a self-defined program. Schoenberg's reputation as an independent musical thinker attracted to him such progressive-minded young musicians as Alban Berg, Anton von Webern, and Egon Wellesz, who followed Schoenberg in their own development. His 2nd String Quartet, composed in 1908, which included a soprano solo, was his last work that carried a definite key signature, if exception is made for his Suite for Strings (1934), ostentatiously marked as in G major, which he wrote for school use in America in 1934.

In 1909 Schoenberg completed his piano piece No. 1, op. 11, which became the 1st musical composition to dispense with all reference to tonality. In 1910 he was appointed to the faculty of the Vienna Academy of Music; in 1911 he completed his important theory book *Harmonielehre*, dedicated to the memory of Mahler; it comprises a traditional exposition of chords and progressions but also offers illuminating indications of possible new musical develop-

ments, including fractional tones and melodies formed by the change of timbre on the same note. In 1911 he went again to Berlin, where he became an instructor at the Stern Cons. and taught composition privately.

In 1912 he brought out a work that attracted a great deal of attention: *5 Orchesterstücke*, which was performed for the 1st time not in Germany nor in Austria, but in London, under the direction of Sir Henry Wood (1912); the critical reception was that of incomprehension, with a considerable measure of curiosity. The score was indeed revolutionary in nature, each movement representing an experiment in musical organization. In the same year Schoenberg produced another innovative work, a cycle of 21 songs with instrumental accompaniment, entitled *Pierrot Lunaire*, op. 21, and consisting of 21 "melodramas," to German texts translated from verses by the Belgian poet Albert Giraud. Here Schoenberg made systematic use of SPRECHSTIMME, with a gliding speech-song replacing precise pitch (not an entire innovation, for Engelbert Humperdinck had applied it in his incidental music to Rosmer's play *Königskinder* in 1897). The work was given, after some 40 rehearsals, in Berlin (1912), and the reaction was startling, the purblind critics drawing upon the strongest invective in their vocabulary to condemn the music.

Meanwhile Schoenberg made appearances as conductor of his works in various European cities (Amsterdam, 1911; St. Petersburg, 1912; London, 1914). During World War I he was sporadically enlisted in military service; after the Armistice, he settled in Mödling, near Vienna. Discouraged by his inability to secure performances for himself and his associates in the NEW MUSIC movement, he organized in Vienna, in 1918, the Verein für Musikalische Privataufführungen (Soc. for Private Musical Performances), from which critics were demonstratively excluded, which ruled out any vocal expression of approval or disapproval. The organization disbanded in 1922.

In 1924 Schoenberg's creative evolution reached the all-important point at which he found it necessary to establish a new governing principle of tonal relationship, which he called the "method of composing with 12 different notes related entirely to one another." This method was adumbrated in his music as early as 1914, and is used partially in his *5 Klavierstücke*, op. 23, and in his Serenade, op. 24; it was employed for the 1st time in its integral form in the Piano Suite, op. 25 (1924); in it the thematic material is based on a group of 12 different notes arrayed in a certain prearranged order; such a tone row was henceforth Schoenberg's mainspring of thematic invention; development was provided by the devices of inversion, retrograde, and retrograde inversion of the basic series; allowing for transposition, 48 forms were obtainable in all, with counterpoint and harmony, as well as melody, derived from the basic tone row. Immediate repetition of thematic notes was admitted; the realm of rhythm remained free.

As with most historic innovations, the 12-tone technique was not the immaculate conception of Schoenberg's alone, but was rather a logical development of many currents of musical thought. Josef Matthias Hauer rather unconvincingly claimed priority in laying the foundations of the 12-tone method (his method did not involve a row in any case); among others who had elaborated similar ideas at about the same time with Schoenberg was Jef Golyscheff, a Russian émigré who expounded his theory in a publication entitled *12 Tondauer–Musik*. Instances of themes consisting of 12 different notes are found in the *Faust Sym.* of Liszt and in the symphonic poem *Also sprach Zarathustra* of R. Strauss in the section on science.

In 1925 he was appointed prof. of a master class at the Prussian Academy of Arts in Berlin. With the advent of the beastly Nazi regime, the German Ministry of Education dismissed him from his post as a Jew. As a matter of record, Schoenberg had abandoned his Jewish faith in Vienna in 1898, and in a spirit of political accommodation converted to Lutheranism; 35 years later, horrified by the hideous persecution of Jews at the hands of the Nazis, he was moved to return to his ancestral faith and was reconverted to Judaism in Paris (1933). With the rebirth of his hereditary consciousness, he turned to specific Jewish themes in works such as *A Survivor from Warsaw* (op. 46, 1947); and *Moses und Aron* (acts I–II, 1930–32; act III not composed).

Although Schoenberg was well known in the musical world, he had difficulty obtaining a teaching position; he

Arnold Schoenberg

finally accepted the invitation of Joseph Malkin, founder of the Malkin Cons. of Boston, to join its faculty. He arrived in the U.S. in the fall of 1933. After teaching in Boston for a season, he moved to Hollywood. In 1935 he became a prof. of music at the Univ. of Southern Calif., and in 1936 he accepted a similar position at the Univ. of Calif. in Los Angeles, where he taught until 1944, when he reached the mandatory retirement age of 70. In 1941 he became a naturalized American citizen. In 1947 he received the Award of Merit for Distinguished Achievements from the National Inst. of Arts and Letters. In the U.S. he changed the spelling of his name from Schönberg to Schoenberg.

Schoenberg's great achievement was the establishment of the basic 12-tone row and its changing forms as foundations of a new musical language; using this idiom, he was able to write music of great expressive power. The tonal composition of the basic row is devoid of tonality; an analysis of Schoenberg's works shows that he avoided using major triads in any of their inversions, and allowed the use of only the 2nd inversion of a minor triad. He deprecated the term *atonality* that was commonly applied to his music. He suggested, only half in jest, the term *atonicality*, i.e., absence of the dominating tonic. The most explicit work of Schoenberg couched in the 12-tone idiom was his *Klavierstück*, op. 33a, written in 1928–29, which exemplifies the clearest use of the tone row in chordal combinations. Other works that present a classical use of dodecaphony are *Begleitungsmusik zu einer Lichtspielszene*, op. 34 (1929–30); Violin Concerto (1934–36); and Piano Concerto (1942).

Schoenberg's disciples Berg and Webern followed his 12-tone method in general outlines but with some personal deviations; thus, Berg accepted the occasional use of triadic harmonies, and Webern built tone rows in symmetric groups. Other composers who made systematic use of the 12-tone method were Wellesz, Ernst Krenek, René Leibowitz, Roberto Gerhard, Humphrey Searle, and Luigi Dallapiccola.

As time went on, dodecaphony became a lingua franca of universal currency; even in Russia, where Schoenberg's theories were for many years unacceptable on ideological grounds, several composers, including Shostakovich in his last works, made use of 12-tone themes, albeit without integral development. Ernest Bloch used 12-tone subjects in his last string quartets, but he refrained from applying inversions and retrograde forms of his tone rows. Stravinsky, in his old age, turned to the 12-tone method of composition in its total form, with retrograde, inversion, and retrograde inversion; his conversion would have been the greatest artistic vindication for Schoenberg, who regarded Stravinsky as his most powerful antagonist, but Schoenberg was dead when Stravinsky saw the light of dodecaphony.

Schoenberg's personality was both heroic and egocentric; he made great sacrifices to sustain his artistic convictions, but he was also capable of engaging in bitter polemics when he felt that his integrity was under attack. He strongly opposed the claims of Hauer and others for the priority of the 12-tone method of composition, and he vehemently criticized in the public press the implication he saw in Thomas Mann's novel *Doktor Faustus*, in which the protagonist was described as the inventor of the 12-tone method of composition; future historians, Schoenberg argued, might confuse fiction with facts, and credit the figment of Mann's imagination with Schoenberg's own discovery.

He was also subject to superstition in the form of triskaidekaphobia, the fear of the number 13; he seriously believed that there was something fateful in the circumstance of his birth on the 13th of the month. Noticing that the title of his work *Moses und Aaron* contained 13 letters, he crossed out the 2nd *a* in *Aaron* to make it 12. When he turned 76 and someone remarked facetiously that the sum of the digits of his age was 13, he seemed genuinely upset, and during his last illness in July 1951 he expressed his fear of not surviving July 13; indeed, he died late in the evening of that date. Schoenberg placed his MSS in the Music Division of the Library of Congress in Washington, D.C.; the remaining materials were deposited after his death at the Schoenberg Inst. at the Univ. of Southern Calif. in Los Angeles. Schoenberg's centennial in 1974 was commemorated worldwide. A *Journal of the Schoenberg Institute* began publ. in 1976, under the editorship of Leonard Stein.

Schoenberg's personality, which combined elements of decisive affirmation and profound self-negation, still awaits a thorough analysis. When he was drafted into the Austrian armed forces during World War I (he never served in action, however) and was asked by the examiner whether he was the "notorious" modernist composer, he answered "someone had to be, and I was the one." He could not understand why his works were not widely performed. He asked a former secretary to Serge Koussevitzky why the Boston Sym. Orch. programs never included any of his advanced works; when the secretary said that Koussevitzky simply could not understand them, Schoenberg was genuinely perplexed. "Aber, er spielt doch Brahms!" he said. To Schoenberg his works were the natural continuation of German classical music.

Schoenberg lived in Los Angeles for several years during the period when Stravinsky was also there, but the two never made artistic contact. Indeed, they met only once, in a downtown food market, where they greeted each other, in English, with a formal handshake. Schoenberg wrote a satirical choral canon, *The New Classicism* (No. 3, op. 28), with a reference to "Herr Modernsky" (i.e., Stravinsky), whose neoclassical works ("ganz wie Papa Bach") Schoenberg lampooned. But once Schoenberg was dead, Stravinsky forgave him in appreciation of his expertise in canonic writing.

In his private life Schoenberg had many interests; he was a fairly good tennis player, and he also liked to play chess. In his early years in Vienna he launched several theoretical inventions to augment his income, but none of them ever went into practice; he also designed a set of playing cards. The MSS of arrangements of Viennese operettas and waltzes he had made in Vienna to augment his meager income were eventually sold for large sums of money after his death.

That Schoenberg needed money but was not offered any by an official musical benefactor was a shame. After Schoenberg relocated to Los Angeles, which was to be his final destination, he obtained successful appointments as a prof. at the Univ. of Southern Calif. and eventually at the Univ. of Calif., Los Angeles. His pension from the Univ. of Calif., Los Angeles, amounted to $38 a month. His difficulty in supporting a family with growing children became acute and eventually reached the press. He applied for a grant from the munificent Guggenheim Foundation, pointing out that since several of his own students had received such awards, he was now applying for similar consideration, but the rule of age limitation defeated him there as well. It was only after the Schoenberg case and its repercussions in the music world that the Guggenheim Foundation canceled its offensive rule. Schoenberg managed to square his finances with the aid of his publ. income, however, and in the meantime his children grew up. His son Ronald (an anagram of *Arnold*) eventually became a city judge, an extraordinary development for a Schoenberg!

Schola cantorum (Lat.). A school for singers. The term dates to the 7th century, when a schola cantorum was established in Rome for the purpose of teaching the proper type of Gregorian chant. Pope Pius X decreed in 1903 that the establishment of similar singing schools should be undertaken in all Catholic churches. The name was also used by academic organizations not connected with the Church, notably the Schola cantorum in Paris, which was founded in 1894.

Schöne Melusine, Die. Concert overture by Mendelssohn, 1834, premiered in London. Melusine is a mermaid who marries an earth creature on condition that he never ask her where she comes from. When he does, she, like Lohengrin, returns to her (in this case watery) domain.

School Days. Song by Gus Edwards, 1907, introduced by him in a vaudeville act. It proliferated spontaneously and achieved the status of a standard for American grade schools, encouraging school children to study reading, 'riting, and 'rithmetic, with a caveat that in the contrary case they might be exposed to the application of the hickory stick.

Schoolmaster, The (*Der Schulmeister*). Haydn's Sym. No. 55, 1774, in E-flat major. There is a somewhat didactic presentation of musical material in its 2nd movement, hence the title. Who decided to attach the pedagogical name to the work is unknown.

Schöpfung, Die. CREATION, THE.

Schottische (Ger.). German round dance in leisurely 2/4 time, a variety of the POLKA. The schottische attained tremendous popularity in Europe and the U.S. in the mid-19th century. The name is sometimes used interchangeably with the rapid polka-like ECOSSAISE; despite that name, it has nothing to do with Scotland.

Schubert, Franz (Peter)

〰〰 〰〰 〰〰 〰〰 〰〰

Great Austrian composer, a supreme melodist and an inspired master of lieder, brother of Ferdinand (Lukas) Schubert; b. Himmelpfortgrund (then a suburb of Vienna and now a part of that city), Jan. 31, 1797; d. Vienna, Nov. 19, 1828. He studied violin with his father, a schoolmaster, and received instruction on the piano from his brother Ignaz; in addition he took lessons in piano, organ, singing, and theory with Holzer, the choirmaster. In 1808 he became a member of the Vienna Imperial Court chapel choir, and also entered the Stadtkonvict, a training school for court singers, where he studied music with the Imperial Court organist Wenzel Ruzicka and with the famous court composer Salieri. He played violin in the school orch. and conducted it whenever an occasion called for it.

He began composing in school; wrote a fantasia for piano 4-hands, several chamber music works, orch. overtures, and the unfinished singspiel *Der Spiegelritter*. His 1st song, *Hagars Klage*, comes from the spring of 1811. In 1813 he left the Stadtkonvict, but Salieri, evidently impressed by his talent, continued to give him instruction. He further attended a training college for teachers in Vienna, and then became an instructor at his father's school. Although very young, he began writing works in large forms; between 1813 and 1816 he composed 5 syms., 4 masses, several string quartets, and some stage music. He also wrote his 1st opera, *Des Teufels Lustschloss*. It was then that he started writing some of his most famous lieder.

He was only 17 when he wrote *Gretchen am Spinnrade*, and 18 when he composed the overpowering dramatic song *Erlkönig*. The prodigious facility that Schubert displayed is without equal; during the year 1815 he composed about 140 songs; on a single day he wrote 8 lieder. From his sketches it is possible to follow his method of composition; he would write the melody 1st, indicate the harmony, and then write out the song in full; often he subjected the finished work to several revisions. He became friendly with the poets Johann Mayrhofer and Franz von Schober, and set a number of their poems to music.

In 1817 he lodged with Schober and his widowed mother, arranging to pay for his keep from his meager resources. It was then that he met the noted baritone Johann Michael Vogl, who put many of Schubert's songs on his concert programs. Outstanding lieder from this period include the *3 Harfenspieler, Der Wanderer, Der Tod und das Mädchen, Ganymed, An die Musik*, and *Die Forelle*. During the summer of 1818 he served as music tutor to the family of Count Esterházy at Zelesz in Hungary. In 1818 his Overture in C major, "in the Italian style," became his 1st orch. work to be accorded a public performance in Vienna. In 1820 his singspiel *Die Zwillingsbrüder* was performed at the Kärnthnertortheater in Vienna; later that year his incidental music for the play *Die Zauberharfe* was heard at the Theater an der Wien; this score's overture later became popular as the overture to *Rosamunde*, although it was not composed for the score to the play *Rosamunde, Fürstin von Zypern*, produced at the Theater an der Wien more than 3 years later, in late 1823.

Although Schubert still had difficulties in earning a living, he formed a circle of influential friends in Vienna and appeared as a pianist at private gatherings; sometimes he sang his songs, accompanying himself at the keyboard; he was also able to publ. some of his songs. A mystery is attached to his most famous work, begun in 1822, the Sym. in B Binor, known popularly as the *Unfinished Sym.* Only 2 movements are known to exist; portions of the 3rd movement, a scherzo, remain in sketches. What prevented him from finishing it? Speculations are as rife as they are worthless, particular-

ly since he was usually careful in completing a work before embarking on another composition.

In 1823 Schubert completed his masterly song cycle *Die schöne Müllerin*; in 1824 he once again spent the summer as a private tutor in Count Esterházy's employ in Zelesz. In 1827 he wrote another remarkable song cycle, *Die Winterreise*. In the spring of 1828 he presented in Vienna a public concert of his works. In that year, which proved to be his last, Schubert wrote such masterpieces as the piano sonatas in C minor, A major, and B-flat major; the String Quintet in C Major; and the 2 books of songs posthumously named the *Schwanengesang*. He took a counterpoint lesson with the noted theorist Simon Sechter (1788–1867); he doubtlessly would have continued his studies. His health was frail, and he moved to the lodgings of his brother Ferdinand. On the afternoon of Nov. 19, 1828, Schubert died, at the age of 31. There is no incontrovertible evidence that Schubert died of syphilis; from all accounts of his daily life, he was never promiscuous and was not known to engage in unseemly liaisons.

Schubert is often described as the creator of the genre of strophic lieder; this summary description is chronologically untenable; Zelter and Reichhardt wrote strophic lieder a generation before him. Goethe, whose poems were set to music by Zelter, Beethoven, and Schubert, favored Zelter's settings. What Schubert truly created was an incomparably beautiful florilegium of lieder typifying the era of German Romantic sentiment and conveying deeply felt emotions, ranging from peaceful joy to enlightened melancholy, from philosophic meditation to throbbing drama; the poems he selected for his settings were expressive of such passing moods. He set to music 72 poems by Goethe, 47 by Mayrhofer, 46 by Schiller, 44 by Wilhelm Müller (who wrote the poetry for the 2 song cycles), 28 by Matthison, 23 by Hölty, 22 by Kosegarten, 13 by Körner, 13 by Klopstock, 12 by Schober, 11 by Claudius, and 6 by Heine.

In a sense, Schubert's *Moments musicaux*, impromptus, and other piano works are songs without texts; on several occasions he used musical material from his songs for instrumental works, as in the great *Wanderer Fantasia* for Piano, based on his song *Der Wanderer*, and the *Trout Quintet* for Piano and Strings, in which the penultimate movement is a set of variations on the song *Die Forelle*. His String Quartet in D Minor includes a set of variations on his song *Der Tod und das Mädchen* in its 2nd movement. But Schubert was not given to large theater works and oratorios; his operas were unsuccessful or unperformed; wrote 7 masses, including a *Deutsche Messe*, but most of his religious music was single movements and composed before 1821.

Even his extended works in sonata form are not conceived on a grand scale but instead are constructed according to the symmetry of recapitulations; his music captivates the listeners not by recurring variety but by the recalled felicities; time and again in his MSS he simply indicates the repetition of a group of bars by number. Therein lies the immense difference between Schubert and Schumann, both Romantic poets of music: where Schubert was satisfied with reminding the listener of a passage already heard, Schumann variegates. Schubert was indeed the most symmetrical composer in the era of free-flowing musical prose and musical poetry.

Much confusion exists in the numbering of Schubert's syms., the last being listed in most catalogues as No. 9; the missing uncounted sym. is No. 7, which exists as a full draft, in 4 movements, of which the 1st 110 bars are fully scored; several completions exist, the most recent constructed with artful imitation of Schubert's ways and means by Brian Newbould, in 1977. The *Unfinished Sym.* is then No. 8. There remains the "Gmunden" or "Gastein" Sym., so named because Schubert was supposed to have written it in Gastein, in the Tirol, in 1825. It was long regarded as irretrievably lost, but was eventually identified with Sym. No. 9, the "Great" (D. 944, 1825). Incredibly, as late as 1978 there came to light in a somehow overlooked pile of music in the archives of the Vienna Stadtsbibliothek a sketch of still another Schubert sym., composed during the last months of his life; this insubstantial but magically tempting waft of Schubert's genius was completed by Newbould; it is numbered as his 10th.

The recognition of Schubert's greatness was astonishingly slow. Fully 40 years elapsed before the discovery of the MS of the "Unfinished" Sym. Posthumous performances were the rule for his sym. premieres, and the publication of his syms. was exceedingly tardy. Schumann, ever sensitive to great talent, was eager to salute the kindred genius in Schubert's syms., about whose "heavenly length" he so admiringly complained. But it took half a century for Schubert to become firmly established in music history as one of the great "Sch's" (with Chopin and Shostakovich phonetically counted in).

Among the great number of compositions left by Schubert are: Stage: 18 works, including operas, Singspiele, incidental music, and melodrama, many unfinished or in sketch form; among them, *Des Teufels Lustschloss*, D. 84, opera (1813–15; 2 versions; Vienna, Dec. 12, 1879); *Der vierjahrige Posten*, D. 190, singspiel (1815; Dresden, Sept. 23, 1896); *Fernando*, D. 220, singspiel (1815; Vienna, Apr. 13, 1907); *Die Freunde von Salamanka*, D. 326, singspiel (1815; Halle, May 6, 1928); *Alfonso und Estrella*, D. 732, opera (1821–22; Weimar, June 24, 1854); *Die Verschworenen* (*Der hausliche Krieg*), D. 787, singspiel (1823; Vienna, Mar. 1, 1861); *Fierabras*, D. 796, opera (1823; Karlsruhe, Feb. 9, 1897). Church: 7 Masses: F major, 1814; G major, 1815; B-flat major, 1815; C major, 1816; A-flat major, 1819–22; *Deutsche Messe*, 1827; E-flat major, 1828; shorter religious pieces; secular choruses, almost entirely for men's voices and in German.

Songs: Of the hundreds of lieder Schubert composed, the following is a small selection: *Der Taucher*, D. 77 (1813–15); *Gretchen am Spinnrade*, D. 118 (1814); *Szene aus Goethes Faust*, D. 126, with 4 voices (1814); *Die Liebe* (Klärchens Lied), D. 210 (1815); *Heidenröslein*, D. 257 (1815); *Erlkönig*, D. 328 (1815); *An mein Klavier*, D. 342 (1816?); *Der König in Thule*, D. 367 (1816); *Fragment aus dem Aeschylus*, D. 450 (1816); *Orpheus, als er in die Hölle ging*, D. 474 (1816); *Harfenspieler I–III* (Gesänge des Harfners), D. 478–80 (1816–22); *Der Wanderer*, D. 489 (1816); *Der Jüngling an der Quelle*, D. 300 (1817?); *Der Tod und das Mädchen*, D. 531 (1817); *Ganymed*, D. 544 (1817); *Der Jüngling und der Tod*, D. 545 (1817); *An die Musik*, D. 547 (1817); *Die Forelle*, D. 550 (1817?–21); *Gruppe aus dem Tartarus*, D. 583 (1817); *An den Frühling*, D. 587 (1817); *Einsamkeit*, D. 620 (1818); Petrach Sonnets I–III (1818); Novalis Hymns I–IV (1819); *Nachtstück*, D. 672 (1819); *Suleika*, D. 720 (1821); *Schwanengesang*, D. 744 (1822); *Am See*, D. 746 (1822?); *Der Müsensohn*, D. 764 (1822); *Am Flüsse*, D. 766 (1822); *Wandrers Nachtlied*, D. 768 (1824); *Du bist die Ruh*, D. 776 (1823); *Viola*, D. 786 (1823); *Die schöne Müllerin*, song cycle, D. 795 (1823); *Dithyrambe*, D. 801 (1826); *Nacht und Träume*, D. 827 (Collin; 1823); *Die junge Nonne*, D. 828 (1825); *Im Walde*, D. 834 (1825); *4 Mignon-Gesänge aus Wilhelm Meister*, D. 877 (1826); *Gesang* (*An Sylvia*; Who Is Sylvia?), D. 891 (1826); *Die Winterreise*, song cycle, D. 911 (1827); *Auf dem Strom*, D. 943, with horn or cello obbligato (1828); *Schwanengesang*, D. 957 (1828; includes *In der Ferne; Der*

Atlas; *Ihr Bild*; *Die Stadt*; *Am Meer*; *Der Doppelgänger*, *Die Taubenpost*); *Der Hirt auf dem Felsen*, D. 965, with clarinet obbligato (1828).

Orch.: 9 syms. (1813–28), of which 7 are complete (Nos. 1–6, and 9, the "Great," 1825–26), one is No. 7, in E minor/major, D. 729 (1821; sketched in score; several performing versions), and one is No. 8, the "Unfinished" (2 movements and a scherzo fragment, 1822); 8 concert and theatrical overtures (1812?–19), including 2 "in Italian style"; 3 short pieces for violin and orch. (1816–1817).

Piano: 18 sonatas, many of which are unfinished to varying degrees (1815–28); 3 fantasies, including the *Grazer Fantasie* (D. 605a, 1818?) and the *Wanderfantasie* (D. 760, 1822); impromptus, including 6 *Momens musicals* [*sic*] (D. 780, 1823–28), 4 Impromptus (D. 899, 1827); 4 Impromptus (D. 935, 1827); 3 Klavierstücke (D. 946, 1828); 3 fugues; 2 variations; other shorter works. Piano 4-hands (of which Schubert was the greatest exponent): 4 fantasies, including the *Grande sonate* (D. 48, 1813); 3 sonatas, including the *Grand duo* (D. 812, 1824; formerly a candidate for the missing "Gastein" sym., and orch. as

such); 19 marches, including the famous *Marches militaires* (D. 733, 1818); 10 polonaises; other works. Dances for piano: waltzes, minuets with trios, Deutsche, Ländler, ecossaises, galops, and a cotillon.

Chamber: 16 string quartets, including *Der Tod und das Mädchen* (D. 810, 1824); 4 piano trios; violin and piano works, including sonatas, duos, *Rondo Brillant* (D. 895, 1826), and Fantasy (D. 934, 1827); Piano Quintet (with Double Bass), *The Trout*, D. 667 (1819?); String Quintet, D. 956 (1828); other ensemble and solo works.

The standard Schubert catalogue is O. Deutsch (with D. Wakeling), *Schubert: Thematic Catalogue of All His Works in Chronological Order* (London, 1951). "D. numbers" are used to group Schubert's works, just as "K. numbers" are used for Mozart. Franz Schubert's brother Ferdinand (Lukas) Schubert (b. Lichtenthal, near Vienna, Oct. 18, 1794; d. Vienna, Feb. 26, 1859) was a composer and teacher. He was devoted to his brother and took charge of his MSS after his death. He wrote 2 singspiels and much sacred music, including 4 masses and a Requiem.

schüchternd (Ger.). Timidly.

Schule der Fingerfertigkeit, Die (Ger., finger readiness). A set of piano studies by Czerny, op. 740.

Schule der Geläufigkeit, Die (Ger., velocity). A set of piano studies by Czerny, op. 299.

Schuller, Gunther (Alexander), significant American composer, conductor, and music educator; b. N.Y., Nov. 22, 1925. He was of a musical family; his paternal grandfather was a bandmaster in Germany before emigrating to America; his father was a violinist with the N.Y. Phil. He was sent to Germany as a child for a thorough academic training; returning to N.Y., he studied at the St. Thomas Choir School (1938–44); also received private instruction in theory, flute, and horn. He played in the N.Y. City Ballet orch. (1943); then was 1st horn in the Cincinnati Sym. orch. (1943–45) and the Metropolitan Opera orch. in N.Y. (1945–49). At the same time he became fascinated with jazz; he played the horn in a combo conducted by Miles Davis; also began to compose jazz pieces.

He taught at the Manhattan School of Music in N.Y. (1950–63), the Yale Univ. School of Music (1964–67), and

the New England Cons. of Music in Boston, where he greatly distinguished himself as president (1967–77). He was also active at the Berkshire Music Center at Tanglewood as a teacher of composition (1963–84), head of contemporary-music activities (1965–84), artistic codirector (1969–74), and director (1974–84). In 1984–85 he was interim music director of the Spokane (Wash.) Sym. Orch.; then was director of its Sandpoint (Idaho) Festival. In 1986 he founded the Boston Composers' Orch. In 1988 he was awarded the 1st Elise L. Stoeger Composer's Chair of the Chamber Music Soc. of Lincoln Center in N.Y. In 1975 he organized Margun Music to make available unpubl. American music.

He founded GunMar Music in 1979; in 1980 he organized GM Recordings. He publ. the manual *Horn Technique* (N.Y., 1962) and the very valuable study *Early Jazz: Its Roots and Musical Development* (N.Y., 1968). A vol. of his writings appeared as *Musings* (N.Y., 1985). In his multiple activities he tried to form a link between serious music and jazz; he popularized the style of cool jazz. In 1957 he launched the slogan "3rd stream" to designate the combination of classical forms with improvisatory elements of jazz as a synthesis of disparate but not necessarily incompatible entities, and wrote fanciful pieces in this synthetic style; in many of these he worked in close cooperation with John Lewis of the Modern Jazz Quartet.

As part of his investigation of the roots of jazz he became interested in early ragtime and formed, in 1972, the New England Cons. Ragtime Ensemble; its recordings of Scott Joplin's piano rags in the original small band arrangements (*The Red Back Book*) were instrumental in bringing about the "ragtime revival." In his own works he freely applied serial methods, even when his general style was dominated by jazz. He received honorary doctorates in music from Northwestern Univ. (1967), the Univ. of Illinois (1968), Williams College (1975), the New England Cons. of Music (1978), and Rutgers Univ. (1980). In 1967 he was elected to membership in the National Inst. of Arts and Letters, and in 1980 to the American Academy and Inst. of Arts and Letters. In 1989 he received the William Schuman Award of Columbia Univ. In 1991 he was awarded a MacArthur Foundation grant.

Schuman, William (Howard), eminent American composer, music educator, and administrator; b. N.Y., Aug. 4, 1910; d. Feb. 15, 1992. He began composing at 16, turning out a number of popular songs; also played in jazz groups. He took courses at N.Y. Univ.'s School of Commerce (1928–30) before turning decisively to music and taking private lessons in harmony with Max Persin and in counterpoint with Charles Haubiel (1931) in N.Y. After attending summer courses with Bernard Wagenaar and Adolf Schmid at N.Y.'s Juilliard School (1932–33), he pursued his education at Teacher's College of Columbia Univ. (B.S., 1935; M.A., 1937); also studied conducting at the Salzburg Mozarteum (summer 1935) and composition with Roy Harris, both at the Juilliard School (summer 1936) and privately (1936–38).

He came to the attention of Koussevitzky, who conducted the premieres of his *American Festival Overture* (1939), 3rd Sym. (1941; received the 1st N.Y. Music Critics' Circle Award), *A Free Song* (1943; received the 1st Pulitzer Prize in music), and the *Sym. for Strings* (1943); Rodzinski conducted the premiere of his 4th Sym. (1942). After teaching at Sarah Lawrence College (1935–45) he served as director of publications of G. Schirmer, Inc. (1945–52), and as president of the Juilliard School of Music (1945–62), where he acquired a notable reputation as a music educator; he subsequently was president of Lincoln Center for the Performing Arts in N.Y. (1962–69).

He was chairman of the MacDowell Colony (from 1973) and the 1st chairman of the Norlin Foundation (1975–85). The recipient of numerous honors, he held 2 Guggenheim fellowships (1939–41); was elected a member of the National Inst. of Arts and Letters (1946) and the American Academy of Arts and Letters (1973); was awarded the gold medal of the American Academy and Inst. of Arts and Letters (1982); won a 2nd, special Pulitzer Prize (1985); and received the National Medal of Arts (1987). Columbia Univ. established the William Schuman Award in 1981, a prize of $50,000 given to a composer for lifetime achievement; fittingly, Schuman was its 1st recipient.

His music is characterized by great emotional tension, which is maintained by powerful asymmetric rhythms; the contrapuntal structures in his works reach a great degree of complexity and are saturated with dissonance without, however, losing the essential tonal references. In several of his works he employs American melorhythms, but his general style of composition is cosmopolitan, exploring all viable techniques of modern composition.

Among Schuman's important works are: the opera *The Mighty Casey* (1951–53); several ballet scores; 10 syms.: No. 1 for 18 Instruments (N.Y., 1936; withdrawn); No. 2 (N.Y., 1938; withdrawn); No. 3 (Boston, 1941); No. 4 (Cleveland, 1942); No. 5, *Sym. for Strings* (Boston, 1943); No. 6 (Dallas, 1949); No. 7 (Boston, 1960); No. 8 (N.Y., 1962); No. 9, *Le fosse ardeatine* (Philadelphia, 1969); No. 10, *American Muse* (Washington, D.C., 1976); a piano concerto (1938; N.Y., 1943); *American Festival Overture* (Boston, 1939); various other orch.1 works; vocal works with various accompaniments; 5 string quartets: No. 1 (N.Y., 1936; withdrawn); No. 2 (1937); No. 3 (1939; N.Y., 1940); No. 4 (Washington, D.C., 1950); No. 5 (N.Y., 1988); other chamber works; and piano works.

Schumann, Clara (Josephine) **Wieck,** famous German pianist, teacher, and composer, wife of Robert (Alexander) Schumann; b. Leipzig, Sept. 13, 1819; d. Frankfurt am Main, May 20, 1896. She was only 5 when she began musical training with her father, (Johann Gottlob) Friedrich Wieck (1785–1873), a leading pedagogue; made her debut at the Leipzig Gewandhaus in 1828, where she gave her 1st complete recital in 1830; her father then took her on her 1st major concert tour in 1831–32, which included a visit to Paris. Upon her return to Leipzig she pursued additional piano training as well as studies in voice, violin, instrumentation, score reading, counterpoint, and composition; she also publ. several works for piano. In 1838 she was named kk. Kammervirtuosin to the Austrian court.

Schumann entered Clara's life in 1830 when he became a lodger in the Wieck home; in 1837 he asked her to marry him, a request which set off a contentious battle between the couple and Clara's father; the issue was only settled after the couple went to court, and they were finally married in 1840. They went to Dresden, and then to Düsseldorf (1850). In spite of her responsibilities in rearing a large family, she continued to pursue a concert career. She also became active as a teacher, serving on the faculty of the Leipzig Cons. and teaching privately. After her husband's death in 1856, she went to Berlin in 1857; after a sojourn in Baden-Baden (1863–73) she lived intermittently in Berlin (1873–78). Throughout these years she toured widely as a pianist; made regular appearances in England from 1856; toured Russia in 1864. In 1878 she settled in Frankfurt as a teacher at the Hoch Cons., a position she retained with distinction until 1892. She made her last public appearance as a pianist in 1891.

As a pianist she was a masterly and authoritative interpreter of Schumann's compositions; later she became an equally admirable interpreter of Brahms, her lifelong friend. She was completely free of all mannerisms, and impressed her audiences chiefly by the earnestness of her regard for the music she played. A remarkable teacher, she attracted students from many countries. As a composer she revealed a genuine talent especially in her numerous character pieces for piano. She wrote a piano concerto (1836), a piano trio (1847), a piano concertino (1847), 3 romances for violin and piano (1853), and some songs. Robert Schumann made use of Clara's melodies in several of his works. She wrote cadenzas to Beethoven's concertos in C minor and G major; ed. the Breitkopf & Härtel edition of Schumann's works, and some of his early correspondence; also ed. finger exercises from Czerny's piano method.

Schumann, Robert (Alexander)

Great German composer of surpassing imaginative power whose music expressed the deepest spirit of the Romantic era, husband of Clara (Josephine) Wieck Schumann; b. Zwickau, June 8, 1810; d. Endenich, near Bonn, July 29, 1856. He was the 5th and youngest child of a Saxon bookseller, who encouraged his musical inclinations. At the age of 10 he began taking piano lessons from J. G. Kuntzsch, organist at the Zwickau Marienkirche. In 1828 he enrolled at the Univ. of Leipzig as *studiosus juris*, although he gave more attention to philosophical lectures than to law. In Leipzig he became a piano student of Friedrich Wieck, his future father-in-law. In 1829 he went to Heidelberg, where he applied himself seriously to music; in 1830 he returned to Leipzig and lodged in Wieck's home; he also took a course in composition with Heinrich Dorn.

His family life was unhappy; his father died at the age of 53 of a nervous disease not distinctly diagnosed; his sister Emily committed suicide at the age of 19. Of his 3 brothers, only 1 reached late middle age. Schumann became absorbed in the Romantic malaise of Weltschmerz; his idols, the writers and poets Novalis, Kleist, Byron, Lenau, and Hölderlin, all died young and in tragic circumstances. He hoped to start his music study with Carl Maria von Weber, who also died unexpectedly. Schumann wrote plays and poems in the Romantic tradition and at the same time practiced his piano playing in the hope of becoming a virtuoso pianist. He never succeeded in this ambition; ironically it was his beloved bride, Clara, who became a famous concert pianist, and Schumann himself was often introduced to the public at large as merely her husband.

His own piano study was halted when he developed an ailment in the index and middle fingers of his right hand. He tried all the fashionable remedies of the period, allopathy, homeopathy, and electrophysical therapy; in addition, he used a mechanical device to lift the middle finger of his right hand, but it only caused him harm. His damaged fingers exempted him from military service; the medical certificate issued in 1842 stated that the index and middle fingers of his right hand were affected so that he was unable to pull the trigger of a rifle.

Schumann had a handsome appearance; he liked the company of young ladies and enjoyed beer, wine, and strong cigars; this was in sharp contrast with his inner disquiet; as a youth he confided to his diary a fear of madness. He had auditory hallucinations which caused insomnia; he also suffered from acrophobia. When he was 23 years old he noted sudden onsets of inexpressible angst, momentary loss of consciousness, and difficulty in breathing. He called his sickness a pervasive melancholy, a popular malaise of the time. He thought of killing himself. What maintained his spirits then was his great love for Clara Wieck, 9 years his junior; he did not hesitate to confess his psychological perturbations to her. Her father must have surmised the unstable character of Schumann, and resisted any thought of allowing Clara to become engaged to him; the young couple had to go to court to overcome Wieck's objections and were finally married in 1840, the day before Clara turned 21. In 1843, when Schumann and Clara already had 2 daughters, Wieck approached him with an offer of reconciliation. Schumann gladly accepted the offer, but the relationship remained only formal.

Whatever inner torment disturbed Schumann's mind, it did not affect the flowering of his genius as a composer; some psychologists have even expressed the belief that madness is a necessary attribute of genius, and that poetry, art, and music are but external aspects of a delusion. However that might be, as a young man he wrote music full of natural beauty, harmonious and melodious in its flow; his compositions are remarkably free from the somber and dramatic qualities that characterize the music of Beethoven and his Romantic followers.

The life and music of Schumann represent the flowering of German Romanticism, with its drama, its ecstasies, and its ultimate tragedy. The great difference between the musical Classic and Romantic lies in the fusion of personal events with musical production. Haydn wrote innumerable syms. and countless string quartets, but his life was free of perturbations and dreamlike visions; it was like a plain with scant vegetation. Schumann's works, on the other hand, were rich and varied in musical flora; each of his pieces was an expression of his passing mood; his life

followed the catalogue of his works. He lived in musical fantasies, until his mental world became a fantasy itself.

One of the most extraordinary features of Schumann's artistic imagination was his fanciful way of personifying his friends and intimates through musical acronyms. His platonic love for Ernestine von Fricken, of the little town of Asch in Bohemia, inspired him to use the notes A–E♭ (Es)–C–B♮ (H); or A♭ (As)–C–B (H). Both spelled Asch and were used as themes for his most famous piano pieces, *Papillons* and *Carnaval*. The latter piece features sections named *Chiarina* (Schumann's nickname for Clara) and *Chopin* (see below). Incidentally it was Ernestine's adoptive father, an amateur flutist, who gave him the theme for his remarkable set of variations for piano titled *Études symphoniques*. His op. 1 was a set of variations on the notes A–B–E–G–G, which spelled the name of Countess Meta von Abegg, to whom he was also poetically attached.

As Schumann's talent for music grew and he became recognized as an important composer, he continued his literary activities. In 1834 he cofounded a progressive journal, *Neue Zeitschrift für Musik*, in which he militated against the vapid mannerisms of fashionable salon music and other aspects of musical stagnation. He wrote essays, signing them with the imaginary names of Florestan, Eusebius, or Meister Raro. Eusebius was the name of 3 Christian saints; etymologically, it is a Greek compound, *eu + sebiai*, good worship; Florestan is "one in a state of flowering"; Raro, which means "rare," could be formed from the juxtaposition of his and Clara's names: Cla*raro*bert.

As early as 1831 Schumann, in the guise of Eusebius, hailed the genius of Chopin in an article containing the famous invocation "Hut ab, ihr Herren, ein Genie!" The article appeared in the *Allgemeine Musikalische Zeitung*; it was signed only by his initials; in an editorial note, he was identified merely as a young student of Prof. Wieck; but the winged phrase became a favorite quotation of biographers of both Chopin and Schumann, cited as Schumann's discovery of Chopin's talent. Actually Chopin was a few months older than Schumann and had already started on a brilliant concert career, while Schumann was an unknown. Another fanciful invention of Schumann was the formation of an intimate company of friends, which he named *Davidsbündler* to describe the sodality of David, dedicated to the mortal struggle against Philistines in art and to the passionate support of all that was new and imaginative. He immortalized this society in his brilliant piano work *Davidsbündlertänze*.

Another characteristically Romantic trait was Schumann's attachment to nocturnal moods, nature scenes, and fantasies; the titles of his piano pieces are typical: *Nachtstücke, Waldszenen*, and *Fantasiestücke*, the last including the poetic *Warum?* and the explosive *Aufschwung*. A child at heart himself, he created in his piano set of exquisite miniatures, *Kinderszenen*, a marvelous musical nursery which included the beautifully sentimental dream piece *Träumerei*. Parallel with his piano works, Schumann produced some of his finest lieder, including the song cycles to poems by Heine (op. 24) and Eichendorff (op. 39), *Frauenliebe und -Leben* (op. 42), and *Dichterliebe*, to Heine's words (op. 48). In 1841, in only 4 days, he sketched out his 1st Sym., in B-flat major, born, as he himself said, in a single "fiery hour." He named it the *Spring Sym*. It was followed in rapid succession by 3 string quartets (op. 41), the Piano Quintet (op. 44), and the Piano Quartet (op. 47). To the same period belongs also his impassioned choral work *Das Paradies und die Peri*. Three more syms. followed the *Spring Sym*. within the next decade, and also a piano concerto, a masterpiece of a coalition between the percussive gaiety of the solo part and songful paragraphs in the orch.; an arresting HOCKET occurs in the finale, in which duple meters come into a striking conflict with the triple rhythm of the solo part.

In 1843 Schumann was asked by Mendelssohn to join him as a teacher of piano, composition, and score reading at the newly founded Cons. in Leipzig. In 1844 he and Clara undertook a concert tour to Russia; in the autumn of 1844 they moved to Dresden, remaining there until 1850. To this period belong his great C-major Sym. (1846), the Piano Trio (1847), and the opera *Genoveva* (1848). In 1847 he assumed the conducting post of the Liedertafel, and in 1848 organized the Chorgesang-Verein in Dresden. In 1850 he became town music director in Düsseldorf, but his disturbed condition began to manifest itself in such alarming ways that he had to resign the post, though he continued to compose. In 1853 he completed a violin concerto. Joachim, in whose care Schumann left the work, thought it not worthy of his genius, and ruled that it should not be performed until the centennial of Schumann's death.

In the 1930s an eccentric Hungarian violinist, Jelly d'Aranyi, declared that Schumann's ghost had appeared before her at a seance, revealed to her the place where the MS was kept (which was no secret, anyway), and urged her to perform it. She was cheated out of the prize, however, and the concerto was 1st performed by another violinist in Berlin, in late 1937. Aranyi had to be satisfied with giving its 1st British performance.

Schumann's condition continued to deteriorate. In Feb. 1854 he threw himself into the Rhine, but was rescued; a month later he was placed, at his own request, in a sanatorium at Endenich, near Bonn, remaining there until the end of his life. Strangely enough he did not want to see Clara, and there were months when he did not even inquire about her and the children. But Brahms was a welcome visitor, and Schumann enjoyed his company during his not infrequent periods of lucidity; in Feb. 1855 Brahms played piano, 4-hands, with him. Schumann made a notation in his diary, "Visit from Brahms. A genius." The common assumption that Schumann's illness was syphilitic in origin remains moot, but cumulative symptomology and clearly observed cyclothymic sudden changes of moods point to tertiary syphilis and final general paresis. Among other symptoms he suffered from tinnitus, hearing a painful single tone ringing in his ears. (The syphilitic Smetana also suffered this symptom, and incorporated it into a string quartet.) The doctor who treated Schumann was inclined to diagnose his condition as the result of a sclerosis of the brain; other physicians described it as *dementia praecox*. Schumann had 7 children; 3 daughters lived to a very old age, but one son suffered from mental disease. Schumann left works in most genres; he is best known for his vocal and piano music.

Schuppanzigh, Ignaz. See BEETHOVEN, LUDWIG VAN.

Schusterfleck (Ger.). See ROSALIA.

Schütz, Heinrich (Henrich), **also called Henricus Sagittarius,** great German composer; b. Köstritz, Oct. 8, 1585; d. Dresden, Nov. 6, 1672. He was born into a prosperous family of innkeepers; in 1590 the family settled in Weissenfels, where his father became burgomaster. He was trained in music by Heinrich Colander, the town organist. In 1599 he became a choirboy in the court chapel of Landgrave Moritz of Hessen-Kassel; in Kassel he pursued his academic studies with Georg Otto, the court Kapellmeister. On Sept. 27, 1608, he entered the Univ. of Marburg to study law; an opportunity to continue his musical education came in 1609 when Landgrave Moritz offered to send him to Venice to take lessons with the renowned master Giovanni Gabrieli. Under Gabrieli's tutelage he received a thorough training in composition, and he also learned to play the organ. In 1611 he brought out a book of 5-voice madrigals, which he dedicated to his benefactor, Landgrave Moritz. After Gabrieli's death in 1612 Schütz returned to Kassel, serving as 2nd organist at the court chapel.

In 1615 the Elector invited him to Dresden as Saxon Kapellmeister; Praetorius was also active at the Dresden court for special occasions at this time. In 1616 Landgrave Moritz asked the Elector to allow Schütz to return to Kassel, but the Elector declined; in 1617 Schütz assumed fully his duties as Saxon Kapellmeister, being granted an annual salary of 400 florins from 1618. In addition to providing music for court occasions, he was responsible for overseeing the functions of the court chapel. In 1619 he publ. his 1st collection of sacred music, the *Psalmen Davids sampt etlichen Moteten und Concerten*. On June 1, 1619, he married Magdalena Wildeck, the daughter of a court official in Dresden. They had 2 daughters. His wife died on Sept. 6, 1625, and Schütz remained a widower for the rest of his life.

During a court visit to Torgau, Schütz produced the 1st German opera, *Dafne*, set to Opitz's translation and adaptation of Rinuccini's libretto for Peri's opera; it was presented at Hartenfels Castle on Apr. 13, 1627, to celebrate the wedding of the Princess Sophia Eleonora of Saxony to Landgrave Georg II of Hesse-Darmstadt. In 1628 he was granted a leave of absence, and he went to Italy. There he had an occasion to study the new operatic style of Monteverdi; he adopted this new style in his *Sym. sacrae* (publ. in Venice, 1629). He returned to his post in Dresden in 1629. When Saxony entered the 30 Years' War in 1631, conditions at the Dresden court chapel became difficult. In 1633 Schütz accepted an invitation to go to Copenhagen, where he obtained the post of Kapellmeister to King Christian IV. In June 1634 he returned to Dresden. His *Musicalische Exequien*, composed for the interment of Prince Heinrich Posthumus, appeared in 1636. He also publ. 2 vols. of *Kleine geistliche Concerte* (1636 and 1639).

He composed the music for the opera-ballet *Orpheus und Euridice*, which was performed in Dresden on Nov. 20, 1638, to celebrate the marriage of Prince Johann Georg of Saxony and Princess Magdalena Sybilla of Brandenburg. In late 1639 Schütz obtained another leave of absence to serve as Kapellmeister to Georg of Calenberg, who resided in Hildesheim. After a year's stay in Dresden, in 1641–42, he set out once more for Copenhagen, where he again served as Kapellmeister, until Apr. 1644. Returning to Germany, he lived mostly in Braunschweig (1644–45) and was active at the court of nearby Wolfenbüttel. In 1645 he returned to Dresden; the Elector declined his request for retirement but did allow him to live a part of each year in Weissenfels. Schütz continued to compose industriously during these years. The 2nd book of his *Sym. sacrae* appeared in 1647, followed by his *Geistliche Chor-Music* in 1648.

In succeeding years Schütz repeatedly asked to be pensioned, but his requests were ignored. Finally, when Johann Georg II became Elector in 1657, Schütz was allowed to retire on a pension with the title of Chief Kapellmeister. His Passions on St. Luke, St. John, and St. Matthew all date from these last years, as does his *Christmas Oratorio*. About 1670 he returned to Dresden to settle his affairs and await his end, which came peacefully in 1672, in his 87th year.

The importance of Schütz in music history resides in his astute adaptation of the new Italian styles to German music; his work was the inspiration for most German Baroque composers, directly or indirectly. He was extraordinarily productive, but not all of his works survived; the majority of his extant compositions are vocal works of a sacred nature. The most important collection of Schütz's MSS is housed in the Hessische Landesbibliothek in Kassel. A catalogue of his works, ed. by W. Bittinger, is found in his Schütz-Werke-Verzeichnis (SWV): Kleine Ausgabe (Kassel, 1960).

schwach (Ger.). Weakly. *Schwächer*, softer, fainter.

Schwanda the Bagpiper (*Švanda dudák; Schwanda der Dudelsackpfeifer*). Opera, 1927, by Jaromir Weinberger (b. Prague, Jan. 8, 1896; d. St. Petersburg, Fla., Aug. 8, 1967), 1st performed in Prague. It subsequently proved to be one of the most successful 20th-century operas. Schwanda's expertise on the bagpipe is such that he wins the affection of the frosty Queen, nicknamed Ice Heart; when she finds out that he has a wife, she sentences him to death. He flees from her wrath, but because of a thoughtless blasphemy he commits, he is sent to hell. A friendly magician wins his soul in a rather dishonest card game with the devil, and Schwanda is freed. Eventually he returns to his patient and loyal wife. The *Polka* and *Fugue* from *Schwanda* are perennially popular summer symphonic concerts.

Schwanendreher, Der (The Organ Grinder). Concerto for viola and small orch. by Hindemith, 1935; he played the solo part at its premiere in Amsterdam. The organ grinder of the title is a minstrel who plays folk tunes from the Middle Ages and Renaissance that he had heard during his travels; the score includes melodic and rhythmic materials derived from medieval folk songs. The title literally means "the swan turner," referring to a swan revolving on top of the organ grinder's instrument.

Schwanengesang (Swansong). A posthumous collection of lieder by Schubert, 1828, publ. in Vienna. Most of the settings are of poems by Rellstab and Heine; however, there is no evidence that Schubert intended to compose a cycle on this basis; he often set one poet's work for a certain period before moving on.

schwankend (Ger.). Hesitantly.

Schwantner, Joseph, American composer; b. Chicago, Mar. 22, 1943. As a youth he studied classical guitar and wrote jazz compositions. He enrolled in the Chicago American Cons. and studied composition with Bernard Dieter (B.M., 1964); then went to Northwestern Univ., where he worked with Anthony Donato and Alan Stout (M.M., 1966; D.M., 1968), garnering 3 B.M.I. Student Composer awards. In 1970 he joined the faculty of the Eastman School of Music in Rochester, N.Y., and became prof. of composition in 1980; from 1982 to 1985 he was composer-in-residence of the St. Louis Sym. Orch. The recipient of various awards and numerous commissions, Schwantner won the Pulitzer Prize in music in 1979 for his orch. score *Aftertones of Infinity*. His early works followed the dictates of serialism, but he eventually developed an eclectic style, incorporating tonal materials into harmonically complex works. Interested in new devices of color, texture, and timbre, he often employs tonalities produced by unusual and sometimes unorthodox musical instruments.

schwärmend (Ger.). Dreamily.

schwärmer (Ger.). A Baroque ornament consisting of rapid repetitions on a single note, akin to a tremolo. This figure was well-suited to the clavichord (BEBUNG).

Schwartz, Arthur, American composer of popular music; b. N.Y., Nov. 25, 1900; d. Kintnersville, Pa., Sept. 3, 1984. He studied English at N.Y. Univ. (B.A., 1920) and literature at Columbia Univ. (M.A., 1921), where he subsequently took a degree in law (1924). He taught himself to play the piano and began writing songs while still in college; after practicing law (1924–28) he turned to music. With the lyricist Howard Dietz he began a successful collaboration on works for the N.Y. musical stage, such as the revues *3's a Crowd* (1930; includes *Something to Remember You By*), *The Band Wagon* (includes *Dancing in the Dark*; the film version of 1953 includes *That's Entertainment*), and *Flying Colors* (1932; includes *Louisiana Hayride*) and the musicals *Revenge with Music* (1934; includes the songs *If There Is Someone Lovelier Than You* and *You and the Night and the Music*) and *Between the Devil* (1937; includes *I See Your Face Before Me*). With Dorothy Fields, he wrote the musicals *Stars in Your Eyes* (1939), *A Tree Grows in Brooklyn* (1951), and *By the Beautiful Sea* (1954). Again with Dietz, he produced the revue *Inside USA* (1948) and the musicals *The Gay Life* (1961) and *Jennie* (1963). He also wrote for films (1936–55).

Schwartz, Stephen. See GODSPELL.

Schwarzkopf, (Olga Maria) **Elisabeth** (Friederike), celebrated German soprano; b. Jarotschin, near Posen, Dec. 9, 1915. She studied with Lula Mysz-Gmeiner at the Berlin Hochschule für Musik; made her operatic debut as a Flower Maiden in *Parsifal* at the Berlin Städtische Oper (1938); then studied with Maria Ivogün while continuing on its roster, appearing in more important roles from 1941. In 1942 she made her debut as a lieder artist in Vienna, and also sang for the 1st time at the State Opera there as Zerbinetta, remaining on its roster until the Nazis closed the theater in 1944. Having registered as a member of the German Nazi Party in 1940, Schwarzkopf had to be de-Nazified by the Allies after the end of World War II.

In 1946 she rejoined the Vienna State Opera and appeared as Donna Elvira during its visit to London's Covent Garden in 1947; subsequently sang at Covent Garden regularly until 1951. In 1947 she made her 1st appearance at the Salzburg Festival as Susanna; also sang regularly at Milan's La Scala (1948–63). Furtwängler invited her to sing in his performance of the Beethoven 9th Sym. at the reopening celebrations of the Bayreuth Festival in 1951. She then created the role of Anne Trulove in *The Rake's Progress* in Venice in 1951. In 1953, she gave her 1st recital at N.Y.'s Carnegie Hall; made her U.S. operatic debut as the Marschallin with the San Francisco Opera (1955). In 1964 she made her belated Metropolitan Opera debut in

N.Y. in the same role, continuing on its roster until 1966. In 1975 she made a farewell tour of the U.S. as a concert singer. In 1953, she married Walter Legge (b. London, June 1, 1906; d. St. Jean, Cap Ferrat, Mar. 22, 1979), an influential English recording executive, orch.l manager, and writer on music. In addition to her acclaimed Mozart and Strauss roles, she was also admired in Viennese operetta. As an interpreter of lieder she was incomparable.

schwebend (Ger.). Floating, soaring; buoyant(ly); in a lofty, elevated style.

Schwegelpfeife (Ger.). Obsolete name for a fife, whether vertical or transverse.

Schweigsame Frau, Die (The Silent Woman). Opera by R. Strauss, 1935, 1st produced in Dresden. The plot follows the outline of Ben Jonson's play *Epicoene* (c. 1605). A cantankerous old man, appropriately named Morosus, is looking for a wife who would keep silent. His nephew turns up with a theatrical group that includes his own wife, whom he introduces to his uncle as "the silent woman." A fraudulent marriage contract is drawn between her and the old man, but as soon as she moves into his house she begins to behave like a garrulous shrew. The old man is distraught by this transformation and is only too glad to restore her to her lawful husband, his nephew, and even give him money. The score represents the humorous strain in the music of Strauss, in the manner of *Der Rosenkavalier*.

Schweitzer, Albert, famous Alsatian theologian, philosopher, medical missionary, organist, and music scholar; b. Kaysersberg, Jan. 14, 1875; d. Lambarene, Gabon, Sept. 4, 1965. He studied piano as a child with his father, a Lutheran pastor; then began organ studies at 8, his principal mentors being Eugen Munch in Mulhouse, Ernst Munch in Strasbourg, and Widor in Paris. He pursued training in philosophy (Ph.D., 1899) and theology (Ph.D., 1900) at the Univ. of Strasbourg; also received instruction in music theory from Jacobsthal in Strasbourg and in piano from Philipp and M. Jaell in Paris. In 1896 he became organist of the Bach Concerts in Strasbourg; also joined the faculty of the Univ. there in 1902, where he also completed his full medical course (M.D., 1912); concurrently was organist of the Bach Society in Paris (1905–13).

In 1913 he went to Lambarene in the Gabon province of French Equatorial Africa and set up a jungle hospital, which subsequently occupied most of his time and energy.

However, he continued to pursue his interest in music, theology, and philosophy, making occasional concert tours as an organist in Europe to raise funds for his hospital work among the African natives. In 1952 he was awarded the Nobel Peace Prize, the only professional musician to hold this prestigious award. His philosophical and theological writings had established his reputation as one of the foremost thinkers of his time. In the field of music he distinguished himself as the author of one of the most important books on Bach, greatly influencing the interpretation of Bach's music, and contributing to the understanding of Bach's symbolic treatment of various musical devices. He ed. *J. S. Bach: Complete Organ Works: A Critico-practical Edition* (N.Y.; vols. I–V, 1912–14, with C. Widor; vols. VI–VIII, 1954–67, with E. Nies-Berger). He also wrote *J. S. Bach, le musicien-poète* (Paris, 1905); *Deutsche und französische Orgelbaukunst und Orgelkunst* (Leipzig, 1906); also various theological and philosophical books. A complete German ed. of his writings was ed. by R. Grabs (5 vols., Munich, 1974).

schwellen (Ger.). To swell, as in an organ.

Schwellwerk (Ger.). Swell organ.

schwer (Ger.). Heavy, ponderous; difficult.

schwermüt(h)ig (Ger.). Sad, melancholy.

Schwertsik, Kurt, Austrian composer of the avant-garde, horn player, and teacher; b. Vienna, June 25, 1935. He studied composition with Marx and Schiske, and horn with Freiberg at the Vienna Academy of Music (1949–57); then continued his composition studies with Stockhausen in Cologne and Darmstadt (1959–62), where he also worked with Kagel and Cage in 1962 and later was associated with Cardew; pursued the study of analysis with Polnauer in 1964–65. With Friedrich Cerha he founded the contemporary music ensemble "Die Reihe" in Vienna in 1958. He also played horn in the Niederösterreichisches Tonkünstler-Orch. (1955–59; 1962–68) and with the Vienna Sym. Orch. from 1968. In 1966 he was a visiting prof. of composition at the Univ. of Calif. at Riverside, where he took further instruction in modern analysis from Oswald Jonas. He taught composition at the Vienna Cons. from 1979.

An all-Schwertsik concert was given by Cerha and "Die Reihe" in Vienna in honor of his 50th birthday in 1985. Although he wore a scholarly beard, he repeatedly militated against rebarbative neoclassicism. Indeed, his works reject the "false beards" of scholasticism, seeking a fruitful symbiosis of serialism and post-serialism with a flexibly handled, rich tonality. A skillful and imaginative composer, he explores in his works many new paths in synthesizing the experimental with the traditional, even writing vocal music in the Austrian dialect. Collaborations with his wife Christa Schwertsik, a singer, have been especially successful.

schwindend (Ger.). Dying away, *morendo*.

Schwingung (Ger.). Vibration.

schwungvoll (Ger.). Swingingly; buoyantly; with sweep and passion.

scintillante (It.). Sparkling, brilliant.

scioltamente (sciolto; It.). Freely, unrestrainedly, fluently, nimbly; without pedantic observation of melorhythmic precision.

scivolando (It.). In piano playing, GLISSANDO.

scoop. Vocal tones arrived at by a rough and imprecise *portamento* from a lower tone, instead of a firm and just attack.

scop (Old Eng.). Ancient English *bard* or poet-musician.

scordatura (from It. *discordatura*, mistuning). Retuning an instrument for greater ease of playing certain notes or for achieving a timbral effect. The practice arose in the 16th century to facilitate the playing of the lute in different keys. Scordatura received its highest development in early Baroque music, with composers ingeniously changing the tuning of string instruments to enable them to play easily in keys of several sharps or flats. A pioneer of scordatura was Heinrich von Biber, whose *Mystery Sonatas* for violin are systematically arranged in scordatura so that the violin becomes in effect a transposing instrument, with each string having its own transposition; under such conditions not only the notes themselves but the intervals between them become altered. Vivaldi also applied scordatura in his concertos.

The visual appearance of the music, notated in traditional clefs, can suggest modernistic cacophony. An anonymous string quartet misattributed to Benjamin Franklin uses different scordaturas for different instruments in different movements; thus a quartet of absolute amateurs, playing on open strings only, can produce a fairly intricate contrapuntal work.

With the progress of instrumental techniques and construction, scordatura lost its raison d'etre, but modern composers occasionally apply it to secure a fundamental harmony in a minor key by tuning down a semitone the 2 lower strings of a violin, viola, or cello. In the coda of Tchaikovsky's *Pathétique Sym.* the melodic line descends to F-sharp but the violins playing the passage have to stop at their lowest note, G, and the final F-sharp has to be taken over by other instruments. To avoid this frustrating sense of incompleteness Stokowski instructed the violinists to tune down the open G string to F-sharp, a procedure that can be classified as scordatura.

score. A systematic notation of music for several instruments or voices in which the individual parts are placed one below another; exact vertical alignment of all parts symbolizes simultaneity, so that the music can be read in its totality. A *full* or *orchestral score* lists all instruments, with the woodwinds on top, brass instruments in the middle, and the strings in the lowest section. Percussion and keyboard (excerpt basso continuo) are placed between the brass and the strings. In concertos the solo parts are placed immediately above the string section, as are the vocal parts and choruses in operas, oratorios, and other vocal works.

The 1st page of a full score must list all instruments as a sort of inventory, with instruments in the high range placed above those of the lower range (within each instrumental family); thus, the bottom line of a score is occupied by the double-bass part. In order to save space the staves of instruments that have rests on a particular page in the score are omitted and only the active parts are printed. As a rule, 1st and 2nd flutes and other paired instruments share the same staff in the orch. score, although it is often necessary to split individual string sections into several staves when they play *divisi*. The task of an orch.l or operatic conductor, in surveying these musical masses under his or her command, is further complicated by the fact that clarinets, the English horn, saxophones, French horns, and most trumpets are transposing instruments. Some 20th-century composers, notably Prokofiev, wrote the parts of transposing instruments in the key of C, so that the conductor does not have to be confounded by the polytonal look of the score, gazing at a clarinet part with 1 sharp in the key signature while the strings have 1 flat.

In chamber music with piano participation, the piano part is placed invariably below the other instruments, which in turn are disposed according to their relative pitch. Thus in a string quartet the 1st violin is placed on top, then the 2nd violin, the viola, and at the bottom, the cello. Other kinds of scores include: *Close* or *compressed score*, short score; *open score*, orch. score; *organ score*, like a piano score, with a 3rd staff for pedal bass; *piano score*, piano arrangement of an orch. score, the words of any leading vocal parts being inserted above the music, often without their notes; *short score*, any abridged arrangement or skeleton transcript; also a 4-part vocal score on 2 staves; *supplementary score*, one appended to the body of the score when all parts cannot be written on one page; *vocal score*, that of an a cappella composition, or one in which the vocal parts are written out in full, usually on separate staves, the piano accompaniment, arranged or compressed from the full score, on 2 staves below.

scoring. INSTRUMENTATION; ORCHESTRATION.

scorrendo (scorrevole; It.). Fluently, smoothly, flowing.

Scotch Bagpipe Melody. Traditional Scottish melody in 6/8 time, 1st published in 1609 with the text of *Have I Ridden Upon My Gray Nag*.

Scotch snap or catch. The rhythmic motive ♫ · found in many Scottish airs. This "inverted dotting" on the beat is also characteristic of STRATHSPEY and other Scottish dances.

Scotch Symphony. Mendelssohn's 3rd Sym., 1842, op. 56, in A minor; it was 1st performed in Leipzig. As in most of Mendelssohn's syms., the *Scotch Sym.* is in 4 movements. The most Scottish of these movements is the 2nd (Vivace), which seems to be impressed with Scottish modalities. Mendelssohn dedicated the work to Queen Victoria.

scotophilia. In biology, the receptive phase of circadian rhythm in which the chief activity is performed in the dark; vampire bats, usually nocturnal, are outstanding examples of scotophiliac animals. As applied to musical composition, scotophilia is the love of dark and somber sonorities marked by a statistically certifiable prevalence of low registers and slow tempos, as in the syms. of Sibelius. Interestingly enough, avant-garde composers, whose chosen self-appellation connotes a rapid movement forward, betray a curious addiction to static, somber, and darksome moods and compositorial habits; such composers may well be called scotophiliacs.

Scotto, Renata, famous Italian soprano; b. Savona, Feb. 24, 1933. She commenced music study in Savona at age 14; when she was 16 she went to Milan for vocal training with Emilio Ghirardini, then with Merlini, and finally with Mercedes Llopart; made her debut as Violetta in Savona in 1952. After winning a national vocal competition in 1953, she made her formal debut as Violetta at Milan's Teatro Nuovo; then joined Milan's La Scala, where she sang secondary roles until being called upon to replace Maria Callas as Amina during the company's visit to the Edinburgh Festival in 1957. She made her U.S. debut at the Chicago Lyric Opera in 1960, as Mimi, a role she also chose for her Metropolitan Opera debut in N.Y. (1965). She scored a brilliant success with her portrayal of Mimi in the Metropolitan Opera production of *La Bohème* in the *Live from Lincoln Center* telecast on PBS (1977); thereafter she was a stellar figure in the U.S. opera scene; also toured widely as a recitalist. Among her other fine roles were Lucia, Gilda, Elena in *I Vespri Siciliani*, Norma, Manon Lescaut, Luisa Miller, Francesca da Rimini, and Elizabeth of Valois.

scozzese, alla (It.). In Scottish style.

Scratch Orchestra. An organization founded in 1969 by the British avant-garde composer Cornelius Cardew, an outgrowth of his Scratch Music concept. He defined the orch. as "a large number of enthusiasts pooling their resources (not primarily musical) and assembling for action." He further declared that "the word *music* and its derivatives are not understood to refer exclusively to sound. Each member of the orch. is provided with a notebook (or a scratchbook) in which he notates a number of accompaniments performable continuously for indefinite periods. . . . Scratch Music can be entitled Scratch Overture, Scratch Interlude, or Scratch Finale, depending on its position in the concert." Cardew pursued a strictly revolutionary Communist outlook, to the point of self-excoriation as an unregenerate bourgeois mind, an attitude projected onto the entire Orch. during a "Discontent Meeting," when members were urged to develop along true Marxist dialectical lines. The highlight of the Scratch Orch. history was the 1972 performance of Cardew's *The Great Learning* (after Confucius, in Pound's trans.). He later repudiated the work, saying that "a revolution is not a dinner party, but an insurrection, an act of violence by which one class overthrows another."

Scriabin, Alexander (Nikolaievich)

Remarkable Russian composer whose solitary genius had no predecessors and left no disciples; b. Moscow, Jan. 6, 1872 (Russian Orthodox Christmas); d. there, Apr. 27, 1915. His father was a lawyer; his mother, Lyubov Petrovna (nee Shchetinina), was a talented pianist who had studied with Leschetizky at the St. Petersburg Cons.; his mother died of tuberculosis when he was an infant, and his father remarried and spent the rest of his life in the diplomatic service abroad. Scriabin was reared by an aunt, who gave him initial instruction in music, including piano; at 11 he began regular piano lessons with Georgi Conus, and at 16 became a pupil of Zverev; in 1885 he commenced the study of theory with Taneyev. When he entered the Moscow Cons. in 1888 he continued his studies with Taneyev; he also received instruction in piano with Safonov. He practiced assiduously, but never became a virtuoso pianist; at his piano recitals he performed mostly his own works.

Graduating with a gold medal from Safonov's class, Scriabin remained at the Moscow Cons. to study fugue with Arensky, but he failed to pass the required test and never received a diploma for composition. Upon leaving the Cons. in 1892 he launched a career as a concert pianist. By that time he had already written several piano pieces in the manner of Chopin; the publisher Jurgenson brought out his opp. 1, 2, 3, 5, and 7 in 1893. In 1894 Belaieff became his publisher and champion, financing his 1st European tour in 1895; in 1896 Scriabin gave a concert of his own music in Paris. Returning to Russia, he completed his 1st major work, a piano concerto, and was soloist in its 1st performance in Odessa (1897). In the same year he married the pianist Vera Isakovich. They spent some time abroad; in early 1898 they gave a joint recital in Paris in a program of Scriabin's works.

From 1898 to 1903 Scriabin taught piano at the Moscow Cons. His 1st orch. work, *Reverie*, was conducted in Moscow by Safonov (1899); he also conducted the 1st performance of Scriabin's 1st Sym. (1901). Scriabin's 2nd Sym. was brought out by Liadov in St. Petersburg (1902). After the death of Belaieff in 1904, Scriabin received an annual grant of 2,400 rubles from the wealthy Moscow merchant Morosov; he went to Switzerland, where he began work on his 3rd Sym., *Le Poème divin*; it had its 1st performance in Paris in 1905, under the direction of Arthur Nikisch. At that time Scriabin separated from Vera Isakovich and established a household with Tatiana Schloezer, sister of the music critic Boris de Schloezer, who subsequently became Scriabin's close friend and biographer.

In late 1906 he appeared as a soloist with Modest Altschuler and the Russian Sym. Society in N.Y.; also gave recitals of his works there and in other U.S. music centers. Tatiana Schloezer joined him in N.Y. in Jan. 1907, but they were warned by friends familiar with American mores of the time that charges of moral turpitude might be brought against them, since Scriabin had never obtained a legal divorce from Isakovich, and Schloezer would have been considered his common-law wife. There was no evidence that such charges were actually contemplated, but to safeguard themselves against such a contretemps, they went to Paris in Mar. 1907. Altschuler continued to champion Scriabin's music, and in 1908 he gave the world premiere with his Russian Sym. Orch. of Scriabin's great work *Le poème de l'extase*; the 1st Russian performance followed in St. Petersburg (1909).

In the spring of 1908 Scriabin met Serge Koussevitzky, who became one of his most ardent supporters, both as a conductor and as a publisher. He gave Scriabin a 5-year contract with his newly established publishing firm Éditions Russes, with a generous guarantee of 5,000 rubles annually. In the summer of 1910 Koussevitzky engaged Scriabin as soloist on a tour in a chartered steamer down the Volga River, with stopovers and concerts at all cities and towns of any size along the route. Scriabin wrote for Koussevitzky his most ambitious work, *Promethée*, the *Poème du feu*, with an important piano part, which featured the composer as soloist at its premiere in Moscow (1911). The score also included a color keyboard (*clavier à lumière* or, in Italian, *luce*) intended to project changing colors according to the scale of the spectrum, which Scriabin devised (for at that time he was deeply immersed in the speculation about parallelism of all arts in their visual and auditory aspects). The construction of such a color organ was, however, entirely unfeasible at the time, and the premiere of the work was given without *luce*. A performance with colored lights thrown on a screen was attempted by Altschuler at Carnegie Hall in N.Y. in 1915, but it was a total failure. (Subsequent attempts have ranged from utter failures to near approximations.)

The unique collaboration between Scriabin and Koussevitzky came to an unfortunate end soon after the production of *Promethée*; Scriabin regarded Koussevitzky as the chief apostle of his messianic epiphany, while Koussevitzky believed that it was due principally to his promotion that Scriabin reached the heights in musical celebrity; to this collision of 2 mighty egos was added a trivial disagreement about financial matters. Scriabin left Koussevitzky's publishing firm and in 1912 signed a contract with Jurgenson, who guaranteed him 6,000 rubles annually. In 1914 Scriabin visited London and was soloist in his piano concerto and *Promethée* at a concert led by Sir Henry Wood; he also gave a recital of his own works there. His last public appearance was in a recital in Petrograd in Apr. 1915; upon his return to Moscow, an abscess developed in his lip, leading to blood poisoning; he died after a few days' illness.

In his time Scriabin was the Russian composer who most separated himself from the realm of national music; he created works of great originality derived from his inner tonal world. Scriabin was a genuine innovator in harmony. At 1st his music was redolent of strongly felt influences (Chopin, Liszt, and Wagner) and especially the cumulative use of dominant-9th chords; but he adorned these chords with unresolved suspensions so that they became independent formations. Scriabin gradually evolved in his own melodic and harmonic style, marked by extreme chromaticism; in his piano piece *Désir*, op. 57 (1908), the threshold of polytonality and atonality is reached; the key signature is dispensed with in his subsequent works; chromatic alterations and compound appoggiaturas create a harmonic web of such complexity that all distinction between consonance and dissonance vanishes.

Building chords by 4ths rather than by 3rds, Scriabin constructed his MYSTIC CHORD of 6 notes (C–F♯–B♭–E–A–D), the harmonic foundation of *Promethée*. In his Piano Sonata No. 7 (1913) Scriabin introduces a chordal structure of 25 notes (D♭–F♭–G–A–C, repeated in 5 octaves), which was dubbed "a 5-story chord." These harmonic extensions were associated in Scriabin's mind with theosophic doctrines; he aspired to a universal art in which the impressions of the senses projecting all human senses, tactile, olfactory, gustatory, as well as aural and visual. The titles of most of Scriabin's later works were the expressions of his mystic strivings: *Le Poème divin, Le Poème de l'extase, Vers la flamme*. His 11 piano sonatas (including the Sonata-Fantasy, op. 19, 1892–97; the *Messe blanche*, op. 64, 1911; and the *Messe noire*, op. 68, 1913) revealed a similar state of constant yearning, with tempestuous melodic lines in rising and falling waves of richly compounded harmonies.

He made plans for the writing of a *Mysterium* to accomplish such a synthesis, but only the text of a preliminary poem (*L'Acte préalable*) was completed at his death. Scriabin dreamed of having the *Mysterium* performed as a sacred action in the Himalayas, and actually made plans for going to India; the outbreak of World War I in 1914 put an end to such a project. Scriabin's fragmentary sketches for *L'Acte préalable* were arranged in 1973 by the Russian musician Alexander Nemtin, who supplemented this material with excerpts from Scriabin's 8th Piano Sonata, *Guirlandes*, and the Preludes, op. 74; the resulting synthetic score was performed in Moscow (1973) under the title *Universe*; a species of color keyboard was used at the performance, projecting colors according to Scriabin's musical spectrum.

In addition to the works mentioned above, Scriabin wrote many other piano works in Chopinesque genres, including mazurkas, nocturnes, impromptus, études, and preludes. Scriabin also composed several "poems"—piano character pieces with unstated lyrical associations—much as the later symphonic works: *2 poèmes*, op. 32 (1903); *Poème tragique*, op. 34 (1903); *Poème satanique*, op. 36 (1903); *Poème*, op. 41 (1903); *2 poèmes*, op. 44 (1905); *Poème-nocturne*, op. 61 (1911); *2 poèmes*, op. 63 (1911); *2 poèmes*, op. 69 (1913); *2 poèmes*, op. 71 (1914); *Vers la flamme*, op. 72 (1914).

Scriabin was the most poetic (not to say extravagant) composer in the use of expression marks; his marks attempt to communicate to the performer what Scriabin felt about the music at hand; this in turn would inspire the performer to experience and therefore inspire similar feelings in the listener. Unlike Satie's satirical comments on the score, Scriabin's are absolutely serious; in his choice of French markings he allies himself with Chopin, impressionism, and beyond. Among his many unique markings are the following:

Avec entraînement et ivresse. With impetuosity and inebriated abandon (*Divine Poem*).

Avec un intense désir. With an intense desire (*Prometheus*).

Avec une ardeur profonde et voilée. With a profound but veiled ardore (10th Piano Sonata).

Avec une chaleur contenue. With contained passion (6th Piano Sonata).

Avec une douce ivresse. With tender inebriation (10th Piano Sonata).

Avec une douce langueur de plus en plus éteinte. With sweet languor gradually fading away (10th Piano Sonata).

Avec une douceur de plus en plus caressante et empoisonnée. With a tenderness ever more caressing and venomous (9th Piano Sonata).

Avec une ivresse debordante. With overflowing inebriation (3rd Piano Sonata).

Avec une joie débordante. With an overflowing joy (7th Piano Sonata).

Avec une joie éteinte. With an extinguished joy (*Prometheus*).

Avec une passion naissante. With a nascent passion (*Poème-nocturne*, op. 61, 1911).

Brumeux. Misty; an indistinct, unspoken quality.

Comme des éclairs. Like lightning flashes (7th Piano Sonata).

Comme en un rêve. Like a dream (*Poème-nocturne*).

Comme un cri. Like a cry (Preludes).

Comme un murmure confus. Like an indistinct murmur (*Poème-nocturne*).

Comme une ombre mouvante. Like a moving shadow (*Poème-nocturne*).

Con luminosité. With luminosity (5th Piano Sonata).

Con una ebbrezza fantastica. With a fantastic sense of inebriation (5th Piano Sonata).

Dans un vertige. Vertiginously; in a state of dizziness (*Prometheus*).

De plus en plus lumineux et flamboyant. Ever more luminously and flamboyantly.

Désordonnée. Disordered (*Flambes sombres*, No. 2, op. 73, 1914).

Ecroulement formidable. A terrible catastrophe (*Divine Poem*).

Effondrement subit. A sudden collapse (Sixth Piano Sonata).

Épanouissement des forces mystérieuses. Flowering of mysterious forces.

Épouvante surgit, L', elle se mêle à la danse délirante. Terror rises and joins in the delirious dance.

Flot lumineux. Luminous stream (*Prometheus*).

Haletant. Out of breath (10th Piano Sonata).

Pâmé. Faintly, as if in a fainting spell (*Divine Poem*).

Presque en délire. Almost delirious.

Rêve prend forme, Le. The dream takes shape (6th Piano Sonata).

Riso ironico (It.). Ironic laughter (*Poème satanique*).

Tout devient charme et douceur. All becomes enchantment and fragrance.

Scriabin's 3 children with Tatiana Schloezer were legitimized at his death. His son Julian, an exceptionally gifted boy, drowned accidentally at age 11 in the Dnieper River at Kiev (1919); Julian's 2 piano preludes, written in the style of the last works of his father, were publ. in a Scriabin memorial vol. (Moscow, 1940). His daughter Marina Scriabine (b. Moscow, Jan. 30, 1911) was a music aesthetician scholar and composer; in 1927 she settled in Paris. She studied music theory with René Leibowitz; in 1950 she joined the Radiodiffusion Française and worked in electronic techniques; composed a *Suite radiophonique* (1951); also a ballet, *Bayalett* (1952), and some chamber music. She publ. *Problèmes de la musique moderne* (collaborated with her uncle, Boris de Schloezer; Paris, 1959); *Le Langage musical* (Paris, 1963); *Le Miroir du temps* (Paris, 1973). She has also written biographically about her father.

Scribe, (Augustin) **Eugène,** famous French dramatist and librettist; b. Paris, Dec. 24, 1791; d. there, Feb. 20, 1861.

He was a scholarship student at the Collège Ste.-Barbe in Paris; after training in the law he turned to the theater; was made a member of the Académie Française (1836). He was closely associated as a librettist with Meyerbeer, but also wrote librettos for Auber, Bellini, Donizetti, Gounod, Halévy, Offenbach, Verdi, and others. His complete writings cover 76 vols.

Scruggs, Earl (Eugene), American country-music singer and banjo player; b. Flint Hill, N.C., Jan. 6, 1924. He took up the banjo as a child and developed such a mastery of the instrument that he made a hit as a member of Bill Monroe's Blue Grass Boys; he then teamed up with Lester Flatt, the guitarist, and they organized their own band, The Foggy Mountain Boys, which quickly assumed a prominent place in country-music circles. Scruggs's 3-finger banjo style was artistically complemented by Flatt's accomplished guitar playing. After they dissolved their partnership in 1969, Scruggs formed his own group, the Earl Scruggs Revue; with it he cultivated the country-rock genre. He starred in the movie *Banjo Man* in 1975. The Flatt-Scruggs partnership resulted in such successful songs as *Roll in My Sweet Baby's Arms, Old Salty Dog Blues, The Ballad of Jed Clampett* (from the stereotype-ridden television comedy series *The Beverly Hillbillies*), and *Foggy Mountain Breakdown* (the theme song of the film *Bonnie and Clyde*). He publ. the book *Earl Scruggs and the 5-String Banjo* (N.Y., 1968).

Sculthorpe, Peter (Joshua), eminent Australian composer; b. Launceston, Tasmania, Apr. 29, 1929. He studied at the Univ. of Melbourne Conservatorium of Music (B.Mus., 1951); then took courses from Egon Wellesz and Edmund Rubbra at Wadham College, Oxford (1958–60); returning to Australia, he became a lecturer in music at the Univ. of Sydney in 1963; was made a reader there in 1969. He also was composer-in-residence at Yale Univ. while on a Harkness Fellowship (1965–67) and a visiting prof. of music at the Univ. of Sussex (1971–72). In 1977 he was made an Officer of the Order of the British Empire. In 1980 he received the honorary degree of Doctor of Letters from the Univ. of Tasmania; later received an honorary D.Litt. degree from the Univ. of Sussex and an honorary D.Mus. degree from the Univ. of Melbourne (both 1989).

In his music Sculthorpe rejects European techniques such as serialism in favor of a typically Australian approach to music. He has looked to Asia, in particular Japan, Indonesia, and Tibet, for both literary and musical inspiration. As a result, his music is often a battleground for European expressionism and indigenous spiritual rituality. He has also been influenced by the physical environment of Australia, as in *Sun Music* I–IV for orch. (1965–1967), and in his utilization of birdcalls and insect sounds.

Scythian Suite. Orch. work by Prokofiev, 1916, 1st performed in Petrograd with the composer conducting. This, the 1st important orch. score by Prokofiev, has the subtitle of *Ala and Lolli*, the names of Scythian gods. The finale describes the sunrise in sonorous displays of B-flat major. Prokofiev was very conscious of the importance of the sun, and he even circulated a questionnaire among his friends, inquiring simply, "What is your opinion of the sun?"

sdegnoso (It.). Scornfully, wrathfully, angrily, disdainfully, indignantly.

sdrucciolando (It.). Sliding across the piano keys; *glissando*.

se (It.). If. *Se bisogna*, if necessary; *se piace*, if you please.

sea chanty. See SHANTY.

Sea Drift. Cantata by Delius, 1906, for baritone, chorus, and orch., after Whitman's poem of that name; it was 1st performed in Essen, Germany. The work is pervaded by the spirit of German Romanticism.

Sea Symphony, A. The 1st Sym. of Vaughan Williams, 1910, for vocal soloists, chorus, and orch., to texts from Walt Whitman. Its 4 movements are entitled *A Song for All Seas All Ships, On the Beach at Night Alone, The Waves*, and *The Explorers*. Vaughan Williams conducted its 1st performance at the Leeds Festival.

Seasons, The (*Die Jahreszeiten*). Secular oratorio by Haydn, 1801, to a libretto by van Swieten. The work is based on an English poem by J. Thomson; it was then trans. into German and premiered at the Schwarzenburg Palace, Vienna.

secco (It.; Fr. *sec*). Dry, staccato; simple, not dwelt upon. *Recitativo secco*, half-spoken, one with a simple figured-bass accompaniment, usually on harpsichord.

sécheresse, avec (Fr.). Dryly; without dwelling on or embellishing.

Sechter, Simon. See SCHUBERT, FRANZ (PETER).

Sechzehntel (Ger.). Sixteenth notes.

second. 1. The interval between 2 conjunct degrees. 2. The alto part or voice. 3. Performing a part lower in pitch than the 1st, as 2nd bass, 2nd violins. 4. Lower in pitch, as 2nd string. 5. Higher; as 2nd line of staff.

second dessus (Fr.). Second soprano.

Second Hurricane, The. Children's opera by Copland, 1937, 1st performed in N.Y. The work was written for performance by nonprofessional young musicians. The libretto bears the imprint of a newspaper story. A group of children organize aid to victims of a flood in the Ohio Valley after a hurricane. They charter a plane and fly there with food and medicine. But the hurricane strikes for the 2nd time in the same location, and the rescuers themselves have to be rescued. The music is rhythmic, lyrical, and energetic.

seconda prattica (It., second practice). A concept promulgated by Monteverdi in his *Scherzi musicali* (1607), also called *stile moderno*; as distinguished from PRIMA PRATTICA (*stile antico*), the older manner of contrapuntal music defended by Artusi. The seconda prattica is characterized by monodic settings, in which the emphasis is placed on the clear articulation of the text and simplicity of harmonic accompaniment. This principle is enunciated in the succinct axiom, "The words must be the master of music, and not its servant." In many ways, seconda prattica anticipates the reforms of Gluck and later composers.

seconda volta (It., second turn). A 2nd ending in a repeated section of a composition.

secondary chords. Subordinate chords.

secondary set. In set theory, a 12-note set formed from the 2nd half of a set and the 1st half of a different form of the same set.

secondo, -a (It.). 1. Second. 2. A 2nd part or performer in a duet; in a piece for piano 4-hands, the bass part.

secondo partito (It.). The 2nd voice.

secondo rivolto (It.). The 2nd inversion of a chord; for a triad, the $^6_4$ chord; for a dominant-7th chord, the $^6_4{}_3$ or $^6_3$ chord.

Secret of Susanna, The. SEGRETO DI SUSANNA, IL.

Secret, The (*Tajemstvi*). Opera by Smetana, 1878, premiered in Prague. The secret is the tunnel through which 2 lovers can communicate without attracting attention. It is a minor work by Smetana, seldom performed even in the Czech lands.

section. A short division (1 or more periods) of a composition, having distinct rhythmic and harmonic boundaries; specifically, half a phrase.

section. In jazz big bands the division into musically determined family: the *melody* (clarinets, saxophones, trumpets, trombones) and *rhythm* sections (piano, guitar, double bass, percussion). Sometimes the last group is subdivided into *harmony* (piano and other keyboards, guitar, etc.) and *rhythm* sections (double bass, percussion).

secular music. Music other than that intended for worship and devotional purposes.

secundal and septimal harmonies. A distinct shift in harmonic structures occurred early in the 20th century as the tertian harmonies of triadic derivation began to give way to the more acute progressions in secundal harmonies and their septimal inversions. Debussy wrote special studies in consecutive major 2nds, treating them as concords requiring no resolution. Secundal harmonies are also represented in impressionistic works in the form of consecutive last inversions of 7th chords. Septimal harmonies are the familiar devices in early jazz cadences, in which the 7th was a BLUE NOTE. Composers of the later generation used tonic major 7ths as cadential chords. Secundal and septimal harmonies are commonly used in pandiatonic structures.

See You Later, Alligator. Song by Bobby Guidry, made popular by Bill Haley and the Comets in the 1955 film musical *Rock Around the Clock*.

Seeger, Charles (Louis), eminent American musicologist, ethnomusicologist, teacher, and composer; b. Mexico City (of American parents), Dec. 14, 1886; d. Bridgewater, Conn., Feb. 7, 1979. He was educated at Harvard Univ. (graduated, 1908); after conducting at the Cologne Opera (1910–11), he returned to the U.S. as chairman of the music dept. of the Univ. of Calif. at Berkeley (1912–19), where he gave the 1st classes in musicology in the U.S. (1916); then taught at N.Y.'s Inst. of

Musical Art (1921–33) and the New School for Social Research (1931–35); at the latter he gave the 1st classes (with Henry Cowell) in ethnomusicology in the U.S. (1932); was also active in contemporary music circles, as a composer and a music critic. He served as a technical adviser on music to the Resettlement Administration (1935–38), as deputy director of the Federal Music Project of the Works Progress Administration (1938–41), and as chief of the music division of the Pan-American Union (1941–53) in Washington, D.C.; was also a visiting prof. at Yale Univ. (1949–50). He subsequently was a research musicologist at the Inst. of Ethnomusicology at the Univ. of Calif. in Los Angeles (1960–70), and then taught at Harvard Univ. (from 1972).

He was a founder and chairman (1930–34) of the N.Y. Musicological Soc., which he helped to reorganize as the American Musicological Soc. in 1934; was its president (1945–46) and also president of the American Soc. for Comparative Musicology (1935) and the Soc. for Ethnomusicology (1960–61; honorary president from 1972). Seeger also was instrumental (with Cowell and Joseph Schafer) in the formation of the N.Y. Composers' Collective (1932); since he was profoundly interested in proletarian music throughout the 1930s, he wrote on the need for a revolutionary spirit in music for such publications as the *Daily Worker*; he also contributed songs under the name Carl Sands to *The Workers Song Books* (1934, 1935).

Two of his essays are of especial historical interest: *On Proletarian Music* (*Modern Music*, XI/3, 1934), which lamented the dearth of folk songs in the work of professional musicians, and *Grassroots for American Composers* (*Modern Music*, XVI, 1938–40), which, by shedding earlier Marxist rhetoric, had wide influence on the folk movement in the 1950s. Since many of his compositions were destroyed by fire at Berkeley in 1926, his extraordinary contribution to American music rests upon his work as a scholar whose uniquely universalist vision for the unification of the field of musicology as a whole continues to challenge the various, sometimes contentious contributing factions: musicology, ethnomusicology, and comparative musicology.

Charles Seeger was also a noted teacher; one of his most gifted students, Ruth (Porter) Crawford, became his 2nd wife. In addition to his son Pete(r) Seeger, 2 other of his children became musicians: Mike (Michael) Seeger (b. N.Y., Aug. 15, 1933) is a folksinger and instrumentalist; after learning to play various folk instruments on his own, he became active in promoting the cause of authentic folk music of the American Southeast; became widely known for his expertise as a banjo player; with John Cohen and Tom

Paley, he organized the New Lost City Ramblers in 1958; then founded the Strange Creek Singers in 1968. Peggy (Margaret) Seeger (b. N.Y., June 17, 1935) is a folksinger, songwriter, and song collector; studied both classical and folk music; after further training at Radcliffe College, she became active as a performer; settled in England in 1956, becoming a naturalized subject in 1959; became a leading figure in the folk-music revival. She collaborated with and married composer, performer, and ethnomusicologist Ewan MacColl (1915–1989).

Seeger, Pete(r), noted American folksinger, songwriter, and political activist, son of Charles (Louis) Seeger; b. Patterson, N.Y., May 3, 1919. He studied sociology at Harvard Univ. before turning to folk music; taking up the banjo, he became active as a traveling musician; with Lee Hays and Millard Lampell, he organized the Almanac Singers in 1941, and subsequently appeared before union and political audiences; then joined the Weavers in 1949, with which he became well known via Leadbelly's *Goodnight Irene*. His political activism was targeted by the House Committee on Un-American Activities, which cited him for contempt of Congress in 1956; in spite of his being blacklisted, he pursued his career and his commitment to various causes. A leading figure in the folk-song revival of the late 1950s, he won notable success with his songs *Where Have All the Flowers Gone?* and *If I Had a Hammer*. In all, he wrote over 100 songs, many of which became popular via his many tours through the U.S. and abroad. He wrote manuals for the 5-string banjo (1948) and the 12-string guitar (collaborated with J. Lester; 1965). J. Schwartz ed. a collection of his essays as *The Incompleat Folksinger* (1972). He has ed. several song collections, beginning with *The People's Songbook* (collaborated with W. Guthrie; N.Y., 1948).

Seeger, Ruth Crawford. See CRAWFORD (SEEGER), RUTH PORTER.

seelenvoll (Ger.). Soulfully.

segno (It.). A sign. *Al segno*, to the sign; *dal segno* (D.S., from the sign), directions to the performer to turn back and repeat from the place marked by the sign (𝄋) to the word *Fine*, or to a double-bar with fermata (𝄐); *segno di silenzio*, silence; a pause.

Segovia, Andrés, Marquis of Salobreia, great Spanish guitarist and teacher; b. Linares, near Jaén, Feb. 21,

1893; d. Madrid, June 2, 1987. He took up the guitar at a very early age; his parents opposed his choice of instrument and saw to it that he received lessons in piano and cello instead, all to no avail; while taking courses at the Granada Inst. of Music, he sought out a guitar teacher; finding none, he taught himself the instrument; later studied briefly with Miguel Llobet. He made his formal debut in Granada at the age of 16; then played in Madrid in 1912, at the Paris Cons. in 1915, and in Barcelona in 1916; toured South America in 1919. He made his formal Paris debut in 1924; his program included a work written especially for him by Roussel, entitled simply *Segovia*.

Andrés Segovia

COURTESY FRANK DRIGGS COLLECTION

He made his U.S. debut at N.Y.'s Town Hall (1928); subsequently toured all over the world, arousing admiration for his celebrated artistry wherever he went. He did much to reinstate the guitar as a concert instrument capable of a variety of expression; made many transcriptions for the guitar, including one of Bach's Chaconne from the Partita No. 2 for Violin. He also commissioned several composers to write works for him, including Ponce, Turina, Castelnuovo-Tedesco, Moreno-Torroba, Villa-Lobos, and Tansman. He continued to give concerts at an advanced age; made appearances in 1984 in celebration of the 75th anniversary of his professional debut. He received many honors during his long career; a commemorative plaque was affixed in 1969 to the house where he was born, honoring him as the "hijo predilecto de la ciudad." In 1981 King Juan Carlos of Spain made him Marquis of Salobreia; that same year the Segovia International Guitar Competition was founded in his honor. In 1985 he was awarded the Gold Medal of the Royal Phil. Society of London.

Segreto di Susanna, Il (The Secret of Susanna). Opera by Wolf-Ferrari, 1909, 1st performed (in German) in Munich. The momentous secret is the presence of cigarette butts in Susanna's room; this makes her husband suspect that during her absence she was receiving a male visitor. He is both relieved and shocked when he discovers that Susanna herself indulges in tobacco, a horrendous breach of feminine mores at the turn of the 20th century. But their marriage is saved. The brief opera enjoyed tremendous success, and still receives occasional performances; its lively overture gets played regularly.

segue (It., follow). 1. A copyist's indication at a page bottom of a player's part that the player is to continue through to the next page, without stopping. *Segue l'aria*, the aria follows. 2. SIMILE.

seguendo (It.). Following. *Seguendo il canto*, COL CANTO, COLLA VOCE.

seguidilla (Sp.). A Spanish song and dance in triple meter, some types being leisurely, others lively. The genre is usually in a minor key, accompanied by guitar, voice, and at times castanets; the structure often alternates between guitar solos and ensemble. The famous *Seguidilla* in Bizet's *Carmen* is a stylization of the folk dance. See also MARINERA.

Sehnsucht (Ger.). Yearning, longing. *Sehnsüchtig*, longingly; in a yearning manner.

sehr (Ger.). Very, greatly, highly. *Sehr schnell*, very fast.

Seine at Night, The. Symphonic poem by Thomson, 1948, a musical offering to his beloved city of Paris, 1st performed in Kansas City.

seis. Song and dance genre of the Dominican Republic and Puerto Rico, in alternating 6/8 and 3/4 time.

seises (Sp., six). Groups of 6 choirboys installed in Spanish churches in the 15th century. Spanish composers of the time wrote works especially for the seises.

seitenbewegung (Ger., side motion). Oblique motion in voice leading.

seitensatz (Ger., side section). the 2nd section (theme group) in the exposition of sonata form, as contrasted with HAUPTSATZ, the 1st (main) section.

self-quotations. Composers are apt to amuse themselves by quoting appropriate passages from their own works. In the score of *Don Giovanni*, Mozart takes pleasure in quoting the admonition to Cherubino from *The Marriage of Figaro, Non più andrai.* Wagner quotes *Tristan und Isolde* in the score of *Die Meistersinger.* R. Strauss rather brazenly quoted themes from his previous tone poems in the score of *Das Heldenleben,* in which he himself is the hero unafraid of the petty assaults of critics.

Sellars, Peter, provocative American theater producer; b. Pittsburgh, Sept. 27, 1957. His fascination with the stage began at age 10, when he began working with a puppet theater; he then attended Harvard Univ., where his bold theatrical experiments resulted in his expulsion from student theater groups. He gained wide notice when he produced Gogol's *The Inspector General* for the American Repertory Theater in Cambridge, Mass., in 1980. During the 1981–82 season he staged a highly controversial mounting of Handel's *Orlando,* in which the protagonist is depicted as an astronaut. In 1983 he became director of the Boston Shakespeare Co. and in 1984 of the American National Theater Co. at the Kennedy Center in Washington, D.C. In 1987, at the Houston Grand Opera, he produced John Adam's opera *Nixon in China,* which he then mounted in other U.S. cities and at the Holland Festival in 1988; that same year he jolted the Glyndebourne Festival with his staging of Nigel Osborne's *Electrification of the Soviet Union.* He directed the 3 Mozart-Da Ponte operas for television. He oversaw the Los Angeles Festival in 1990.

Semele. Secular oratorio by Handel, 1744, 1st performed in London. Semele is loved by Jupiter. After failing to get rid of her rival, Juno, Jupiter's imperious consort urges Semele to ask Jupiter to reveal himself in the full splendor of his divine presence, aware that no mortal could survive the radiance of such a manifestation. Semele requests it; Jupiter tries to avoid doing it; Semele insists upon it; Jupiter reveals himself; Semele is destroyed. The tenor aria *Wheree'er You Walk* is a recital favorite.

semibiscroma (It.). Sixty-fourth note.

semibreve. A whole note; like other U.K. terms based on Latin mensural notation, it is relatively faster than the original.

semibrevis (Lat., half short). In mensural notation, a duration lasting half of a BREVIS or a quarter of a LONGA. The notation is a black rhombus.

semicroma (It.). Sixteenth note.

semidiapente (It.). Medieval term for the diminished 5th.

semiditonus (It.). Medieval term for the minor 3rd.

semiminima (Lat., half of the smallest). A duration of half a minima; in mensural notation it is written as a black rhombus with an upward stem and a flag, resembling the modern 8th note.

semiquaver (U.K). Sixteenth note.

Semiramide. Opera by Rossini, 1823, 1st produced in Venice. Semiramide is the Queen of Babylon. She conspires with her lover to kill the king. This done, she takes another lover, a young barbarian, but to her horror she discovers that he is her own son by a previous union. When her 1st lover attacks her son, she intercepts his dagger and dies; thereupon her son slays her 1st lover and by hereditary rights becomes king. The opera is seldom performed but the overture is a concert favorite. A number of other composers wrote operas on this subject, among them Porpora, Gluck, Salieri, Cimarosa, Meyerbeer, and, in the 20th century, Respighi. None of these is still performed.

semiseria (It.). Baroque and Classic OPERA SERIA with a happy ending, sometimes including comic and parodic elements.

semitone (Lat. *semitonus*). A half tone or step, the smallest division in the equally tempered scale, roughly corresponding to the justly tuned interval 16/15. The major scale contains 2 semitones: between the 3rd and 4th steps and the 7th and 8th (tonic) steps. The chromatic scale of 1 octave contains 12 semitones. *Diatonic semitone,* one in which the 2 components are a minor 2nd apart, as B–C, F–G♭, A♯–B; *enharmonic semitone,* one in which the 2 components are an augmented unison apart, i.e., share pitch names, as E♭–E, D–D♯, A♭–A♮.

Semper Fidelis. March by Sousa, 1886, dedicated to the U.S. Marine Corps.

Semper Paratus. Song by Francis Saltus von Boskerck, 1928. A captain of the U.S. Coast Guard, he published it, and it has become the official march of the Coast Guard.

semplice (It.; Fr. *simplement*). In a simple, natural, unaffected style.

sempre (It.). Always, continually, throughout; used in expressions as *sempre crescendo, sempre forte, sempre in tempo, sempre legato, sempre piano, sempre staccato*, etc.

Semyon Kotko. Opera by Prokofiev, 1940, 1st performed in Moscow. Kotko was a revolutionary soldier demobilized in 1918 after the conclusion of an armistice between the Soviet government and Germany. The opera is written in an energetic manner, typical of Prokofiev, and contains fine lyrical episodes. There is also a characteristically operatic mad scene, enacted by the young bride of a Bolshevik sailor slain by the counterrevolutionary Ukrainian nationalists. Despite its commendable qualities of socialist realism, *Semyon Kotko* is rarely performed.

Send in the Clowns. Song by Sondheim, 1973, from the musical *A Little Night Music*. The song, a philosophical look at youth and aging, is the composer's best-known song; a recording of it won a Grammy Award in 1976.

Sensemayá. Work by Revueltas, orig. for voice and orch.; 1st performed in a rev. version for large orch. without voice in Mexico City, 1938. It is described as an "indigenous incantation to kill a snake," with the words by the Afro-Cuban poet Guillen, representing a vodun ritual.

sensibile (It.). Audible; sensitive. *Con sensibilità*, with feeling; *nota sensibile*, LEADING TONE.

sensible, note (Fr.). LEADING TONE.

sensory impact. The musical effect on a listener, often reaching the threshold of physical pain. Incessant playing of modern dance music, electronically amplified beyond the endurance of an average person, may well produce a positive conditioned reflex among the young. Professional music critics have for a century complained about the loudness of modern music, beginning with that of Wagner, but in their case the sensory impact is measured not so much by the overwhelming volume of sound as by the unfamiliarity of the idiom. Epithets such as *barbaric* were applied with a fine impartiality to the works of Wagner, Tchaikovsky, Berlioz, and Prokofiev, while Debussy, Strauss, and Mahler were often described as "cacophonous."

It is the relative modernity that makes the sensory impact intolerable to a music critic. "This elaborate work is as difficult for popular comprehension as the name of the composer," wrote the *Boston Evening Transcript* in its review of Tchaikovsky's 1st Piano Concerto. An index of vituperative, pejorative, and deprecatory words and phrases, the "Invecticon" appended to the author's *Lexicon of Musical Invective* demonstrates the extraordinary consistency of the critical reaction to unfamiliar music. Even the gentle Chopin did not escape contumely; he was described in a daily London newspaper as a purveyor of "ranting hyperbole and excruciating cacophony."

sentence. A passage of symmetrical rhythmic form, generally not over 16 measures long, and usually ending with a full tonic cadence.

sentimentale (It.). Feelingly.

sentito (It.). With feeling, expression, special emphasis.

senza (It.; abbrev. *s.*). Without. *Senza abbandonare la corda*, without leaving the string; *senza affretare*, without getting faster; *senza allagare, senza di slentare*, without slowing down; *senza interruzione*, without interruption; *senza misura* (without measure), not in strict time, freely; *senza passione* (without passion), quietly; *senza piatti* (without cymbals), have one performer play cymbals and bass drum; *senza rallentare*, without slowing down; *senza rinforzare*, without getting louder; *senza ritardare*, without getting slower; *senza sordini*, see SORDINO; *senza stringere*, without getting faster; *senza suono* (without tone), spoken; *senza tempo*, same as *senza misura*, used by Liszt.

sept. The interval of a 7th.

sept chord (Ger. *Septakkord*). Seventh chord.

September Song. Ballad by Weill, 1938, from the musical *Knickerbocker Holiday*. As rendered by Walter Huston, it became a hit.

septet (Ger. *Septett*; Fr. *septuor*; It. *settimino*). A concerted composition for 7 voices or instruments; in the latter case, wind and string instruments are usually mixed in with a piano part (Beethoven, Stravinsky). Ravel's *Introduction and Allegro* has the unusual scoring of harp, flute, clarinet, and string quartet.

septième (Fr.; Ger. *Septime*; It. *settimo*). Interval of a 7th.

septimole (It.; Ger. *Septole*; Fr. *septolet*). Septuplet; a group of 7 equal notes to be performed in the time or 4 or 6 of the same kind in the established rhythm.

sequence (1) (from Lat. *sequentia*). In Gregorian chant, a freely composed, wide-ranging chant category (also called prose) with syllabic texts, popular for about 3 centuries starting in *c*. 850 A.D. A couplet form was common, with 2 lines of text per melodic line, followed by a different couplet melody. Gradually the texts rhymed and scanned and grew increasingly strophic. For many centuries sequences were composed to the needs of the liturgical calendar and were incorporated into the PROPRIUM. But the 16th-century Council of Trent eliminated all but 5 sequences from the chant books (*Victimae Paschali, Lauda Sion, Veni sancte spiritus, Stabat Mater, Dies irae*). Many of the surviving texts were set by later composers.

sequence (2). The repetition, at different pitch levels and at least twice in succession, of a melodic motive. This is an extremely fruitful technical device that achieved a near universality in Baroque music. In a sequence a thematic phrase is imitated in the same voice a degree higher or lower, without altering its rhythmic pattern. In its simplest form a sequence contains 2 segments, connoting the tonic and the dominant harmonies effectively. Examples of such sequences are found by the thousands in classical works. The theme of Mozart's A-major piano sonata (K. 331) is typical; the opening notes of Beethoven's 5th Sym. and the subsequent phrase also constitute such a tonic-dominant sequence.

As with fugal answers, sequences are considered *tonal* if they move along a given key; they are *real* if they are true as to the precise interval and thus represent a modulation. The longest tonal sequence occurs toward the end of Tchaikovsky's overture to the opera *Eugene Onegin*, which contains 8 segments and descends fully 2 octaves by consecutive degrees. Real sequences are effective when they modulate through major and minor keys in the direction of flats in the cycle of 5ths, making use of dominant-7th chords; for instance, the 1st inversion of the dominant-7th chord of F major (C^6_5) would be followed, after its resolution into the tonic F minor, by the 1st inversion of the dominant-7th chord of D minor (A^6_5), resolving into the tonic D minor, etc. Also effective are modulating sequences generated by the descending chromatic bass, as for instance the 3rd inversion of the dominant-7th chord in G (D_2) resolving into the 1st inversion of G major (G^6), followed by the 3rd inversion of the dominant-7th chord in F (C_2) resolving into the 1st

inversion of F major (F^6), producing the bass line C–B–B♭–A, etc. It is particularly effective when the leading tone is in the melody.

A curious revulsion against the employment of sequences arose in the 20th century. Some modern composers completely renounce all sequential formulas, regarding them as automatic devices impeding the flow of free invention. However, composers of the neoclassical persuasion ostentatiously revived the use of sequences, particularly tonal sequences, often with the purpose of emphatic stylization; others (Bartók, Hindemith) used them to control their use of extended tonality.

sequencer. An electronic device that supplies a sequence of predetermined voltages in sound synthesis or processing; repetitious patterns akin to tape loops can be produced with the sequencer.

serenade (from It. *serenata*, evening song). 1. From the 16th century a song, traditionally performed by a lover before the beloved's window; it was habitually accompanied on the lute or guitar and delivered at day's end. A serenade is a favorite device in opera; an example of a mock serenade is that of Mephistopheles in Gounod's *Faust*. Eventually any song or instrumental piece in this amorous style could be considered a serenade. See also AUBADE. 2. From the mid-18th century, a multimovement piece of instrumental entertainment music, practically synonymous with a DIVERTIMENTO. An instrumental serenade is usually scored for a small ensemble, designed for an open-air performance or at a festival occasion. Mozart wrote his *Haffner Serenade* for a wedding in the family of the Burgomaster of Salzburg. In the 19th century the title *Serenade* was often attached to a multimovement instrumental work (e.g., Brahms).

Sérénade d'Arlequin. Excerpt, 1900, by Riccardo Drigo (1846–1930), from the ballet *Les Millions d'Arlequin* (Arlekinada); a cello solo much loved by its performers.

Serenade for String Orchestra. Multimovement work by Tchaikovsky, 1882, 1st performed in Moscow, a work of symphonic proportions. Tchaikovsky said that in it he paid his debt to Mozart and deliberately imitated Mozart's manner. But the music has more of the spirit of the Baroque, and its finale makes use of the Russian song *Under the Green Apple Tree*. When Tchaikovsky thought he imitated somebody, he invariably composed most like himself.

Sérénade mélancolique. Concert piece by Tchaikovsky, 1876, for violin and orch., 1st performed in Moscow. It is a short lyric elegy in the melancholy key of B-flat minor, in the manner of a nocturne. It is a favorite with violinists all over the world.

Serenade to Music. Choral work by Vaughan Williams, 1938, to a text from Shakespeare's *The Merchant of Venice*, for 16 solo voices and orch. The work was premiered in London.

serenata (It.; from Lat. *serenus*, serene). 1. A species of dramatic cantata in vogue during the 18th century. 2. An instrumental composition midway between a suite and a sym. but freer in form than either, having 5, 6, or more movements, and in chamber music style. 3. See SERENADE.

serendipity. In music, a chance combination of 2 unrelated tunes, so that a harmonious setting results when played simultaneously; an example is the perfect blending of the Russian popular song *Dark Eyes* with Chopin's étude in F minor. Etymologically, the general term was coined by Horace Walpole in 1754, derived from the Arabian tale of the princes of Serendip who made important discoveries and found fortune by opportune accident and sagacious surmise. In composition, serendipity is almost equivalent to intuition or inspiration, but it is applicable particularly to the realization of melodic, harmonic, and intervallic relationships seemingly unconnected with the primary aim of a composer or theorist.

sereno (It.). In a serene, tranquil style.

serialism

Serialism is a method of composition in which thematic units are arranged in an ordered set. Tonal serialism was promulgated by Schoenberg in 1924, as the culmination of a long period of experiments with atonal chromatic patterns; in retrospect Schoenberg's method may be regarded as a special case of integral serialism, much as the special theory of relativity is a subset of general relativity. Schoenberg's method deals with the 12 different notes of the chromatic scale; integral serialism organizes different intervals, different rhythmic values, dynamics, etc. in autonomous sets.

Fritz Klein expanded the serial concept of dodecaphonic sets to different rhythmic and intervallic values. In his score *Die Maschine*, publ. in 1921, he employs sets of 12 identical notes in irregular rhythms, "pyramid chords" comprising intervals arranged in a decreasing arithmetical progression of semitones, and a harmonic complex consisting of 12 different notes and 11 different intervals, the *Mutterakkord.* The mathematical term *set*, for a tone row, was introduced by the American composer Milton Babbitt in 1946. He experimented with techniques of tonal, rhythmic, and intervallic sets. George Perle proposed the term *set complex* to designate 48 different forms generated by a fundamental dodecaphonic series. In all these sets the magic number 12 plays a preponderant role. In the general concept of serialism, sets may contain any number of pitches, in any scale, including nontempered intervals.

A summary of serial parameters comprises the following: (1) 12 different pitches as developed by using the method of composition with 12 tones, including apocopated sets, hendecaphonic, decaphonic, enneaphonic, octophonic, heptaphonic, hexaphonic, pentaphonic, tetraphonic, triphonic, diphonic, monophonic, and zerophonic; (2) organization of melody containing 12 different intervals, from a semitone to the octave and the concomitant chords containing 12 different notes and 11 different intervals; (3) 12 different rhythmic values that may contain a simple additive set of consecutive integers, a geometrical progression, a set of Fibonacci numbers, etc.; (4) 12 different *Klangfarben*, in which a melody consists of a succession of disparate notes played by 12 different instruments either in succession, in contrapuntal conjugation, or harmonic coagulation; (5) spatial serialism, in which 12 different instruments are placed in quaquaversal positions with no instruments in close proximity; (6) vectorial serialism, in which the sound generators are distributed at 12 different points of the compass, according to 12 hour marks on the face of a clock, or else arranged spatially on the ceiling, on the floor, in the corners of the auditorium; (7) dynamic serialism, with 12 different dynamic values ranging from pianississississimo to fortississississimo, including the intermediate shadings of *mp* and *mf*; (8) ambulatory serialism, in which 12 musicians make their entrances and exits one by one, in contrapuntal groups, in stretto, or in the fugue, the latter being understood in the literal sense of running; (9) expressionistic serialism, in which actors and singers assume definite facial expressions marking their psychological identity; (10) serialism of 12 different sound generators, including steamrollers, motor lawn mowers, steam pipes, radiators, ambulance sirens, etc.; (11) serialism of 12 visually different mobiles, each producing a distinctive noise; (12) serialism of 12 teratological borborygmuses and sonic simulacra of venous physiological functions. See also DODECAPHONY.

series. 1. An ordering of pitch classes or other elements as a precompositional stage. 2. See SET.

serietà, con (It.). Seriously.

serio, -a (It.). Serious. *Opera seria*, grand or tragic opera; *tenore serio*, dramatic tenor.

serioso (It.). In a serious, grave, impressive style.

serious music. In publ., a common if outdated designation of printed music by classical and modern composers, as distinguished from popular music and jazz.

Serkin, Peter (Adolf), outstanding American pianist, son of Rudolf Serkin; b. N.Y., July 24, 1947. At age 11 he enrolled at the Curtis Inst. of Music in Philadelphia, where he studied with M. Horszowski, L. Luvisi, and his father (graduated, 1964); made his debut as a soloist with A. Schneider and a chamber orch. at the Marlboro (Vt.) Music Festival (1958); later studied there with the flutist M. Moyse and received additional piano training from Karl Ulrich Schnabel. He made his N.Y. debut as a soloist with Schneider and his chamber orch. (1959); his N.Y. recital debut followed (1965). In 1973 he formed the group Tashi ("good fortune" in Tibetan) with clarinetist Richard Stoltzman, violinist Ida Kavafian, and cellist Fred Sherry; the group toured extensively, giving performances of contemporary music in particular. After leaving the group in 1980 Serkin renewed his appearances as a soloist and recitalist. While he championed modern music, he acquired a distinguished reputation as an interpreter of both traditional and contemporary scores. He excels in works by Mozart, Beethoven, Schubert, Brahms, Stravinsky, Schoenberg, Messiaen, Takemitsu, Peter Lieberson, and others. He also made appearances as a fortepianist. In 1983 he was awarded the Premio of the Accademia Musicale Chigiana in Siena.

Serkin, Rudolf, eminent Austrian-born American pianist and pedagogue of Russian descent, father of Peter (Adolf) Serkin; b. Eger, Mar. 28, 1903; d. Guilford, Vt., May 8, 1991. He studied piano with Richard Robert and composition with Joseph Marx and Arnold Schoenberg in Vienna; made his debut as a soloist with Oskar Nedbal and the Vienna Sym. Orch. at age 12; his career began in earnest with his Berlin appearance with the Busch chamber orch. in 1920; thereafter he performed frequently in joint recitals with Adolf Busch, whose daughter he married in 1935. He made his U.S. debut in a recital with Busch at the Coolidge Festival in Washington, D.C., in 1933; then made a critically acclaimed appearance as a soloist with Toscanini and the N.Y. Phil. (1936).

In 1939 he became a naturalized U.S. citizen. After World War II he pursued an international career; appeared as a soloist with all the major orchs. of the world, gave recitals in the leading music centers, and played in numerous chamber music settings. In 1939 he was appointed head of the piano dept. at the Curtis Inst. of Music in Philadelphia; was its director from 1968 to 1976. In 1950 he helped to establish the Marlboro (Vt.) Music Festival and school, and subsequently

Rudolf Serkin

served as its artistic director. In 1985 he celebrated his 70th anniversary as a concert artist. He received the Presidential Medal of Freedom in 1963; in 1988 he was awarded the National Medal of Arts. The authority and faithfulness of his interpretations of the Viennese classics placed him among the masters of the 20th century.

Sermon, a Narrative and a Prayer, A. Cantata by Stravinsky, 1962, based on the New Testament; 1st performed in Basel, the work is scored for alto, tenor, chorus, and orch.

serpent. 1. A bass wind instrument invented by Canon Edme Guillaume of Auxerre in 1590. It was indeed constructed in the shape of a snake, consisting of several pieces of wood bound together by a leather covering; keys were added later. Its original use was to double ecclesiastical chanting; despite its ungainly appearance and a considerable difficulty in handling, by the 18th century the serpent had come to provide the deep bass in military bands, in support of the bassoon. The serpent was also known as a Russian bassoon because it was regularly used in Russian military bands. It was still in use as a band instrument in the 1st half of the 19th century, but Berlioz derided it as a laughable monstrosity in his orchestration treatise. This damnation was the serpent's last hiss; by the 20th century it was found only in a few village churches. The serpent has played a small role in the early music revival. 2. In the organ, a reed stop.

serrando (It.). Speeding up.

serrant (*serré*; Fr., pressed, tightened). Playing faster and with more excitement.

Serse **(Xerxes).** Opera by Handel, 1738, 1st produced in London. Two brothers in ancient Persia are in love with the same woman, but Xerxes loses out despite his royal stature. The opera rates very low among Handel's creations, but it opens with the celebrated aria *Ombra mai fù*, known to the musical multitudes simply as "Handel's Largo." Its text, *The Shade Never Was*, is unintentionally (or intentionally?) sarcastic, because Xerxes, standing in the desert before a single tree, comments upon its cooling shade.

Serva Padrona, La **(The Maid as Mistress).** Opera buffa by Pergolesi, 1733, as an intermezzo to his opera *Il Prigionier superbo* (The Proud Prisoner), 1st performed in Naples. The opera itself is forgotten but the intermezzo

became a *cause célèbre* in the thundering polemical exchange between the advocates of Italian and French opera after a performance of it in Paris, 1752. Amazingly enough, Rousseau sided with the Italian concept of operatic universalism cultivating bel canto; he later reversed his position. The plot, a typical 18th-century farce, involves a scheming servant girl ("la serva") who sets her sights on her middle-aged master; to prove to him that she is desirable to men of higher rank, she induces his valet to don the uniform of an army captain and pretend to be in love with her. The master is impressed and decides to marry her; thus she becomes "la padrona," the mistress of the house.

servetta (It.). See SOUBRETTE.

service. A generic name to describe the totality of religious hymns, canticles, psalms, etc. In most Christian churches the services are named after the time of day; e.g., in the Church of England (Anglican), the morning service contains canticles bearing the incipits in Latin, even though such services are sung in English (Te Deum, Benedictus, Jubilate). The evening service (evensong) usually includes the Magnificat and Nunc Dimittis.

sesquialtera (It.). 1. In the organ, either a mutation stop a 5th above the fundamental tone, or (usually) a compound stop of from 2 to 5 ranks. 2. (Lat.; Grk. *hemiole*) The ratio of 3/2, denoting a perfect 5th between the 2nd and 3rd partials. 3. In mensural notion, the diminution of a note value by one-third, so that 3 notes were played in the time usually allotted to 2 notes, resulting in triplets.

sesquipedalian macropolysyllabification. Quaquaversal lucubration about pervicacious torosity and diverticular prosiliency in diatonic formication and chromatic papulation, engendering carotic carmination and decubital nyctalopia, causing borborygmic susurration, teratological urticulation, macroptic dysmimia, bregmatic obstipation, crassamental quisquiliousness, hircinous olophonia and unflexanimous luxation, often produce volmerine cacumination and mitotic ramuliferousness leading to operculate onagerosity and testaceous favillousness, as well as faucal obsonation, parallelepipedal psellismus, pigritudinous mysophia, cimicidal conspurcation, mollitious deglutition and cephalotripsical stultitiousness, resulting despite Hesychastic omphaloskepsis, in epenetic opisthography, boustrophedonic malacology, lampadodromic evagination, chartulary cadastration, merognostic heautotimerousness, favaginous moliminosity, fatiscent operosity, temulencious libration and otological oscininity, aggravated by tardigrade inturgescence, nucamentacious oliguria, emunctory sternutation, veneficial pediculation, fremescent dyskinesia, hispidinous cynanthropy, torminal opitulation, crapulous vellication, hippuric rhinodynia, dyspneic nimiety and favillous erethism, and culminating in opisthographic inconcinnity, scotophiliac lipothymia, banausic rhinorrhea, dehiscent fasciculation, oncological vomiturition, nevoid paludality, exomphalic invultuation, mysophiliac excrementatiousness, flagitious dysphoria, lipogrammatic bradygraphy, orectic aprosexia, parataxic parorexia, lucubicidal notation, permutational paranomasia, rhonchial fremitus, specular subsaltation, crapulous crepitation, ithyphallic acervation, procephalic dyscrasia, volitional volitation, piscine dermatology, proleptic pistology, verrucous alopecia, hendecaphonic combinatoriality, microaerophilic pandiculation and quasihemidemisemibreviate illation.

sesquitone scales. Scale based on the sesquitonus (Lat.), an interval of 3 semitones. The sesquitone scale is a progression of minor 3rds, or augmented 2nds, depending on notation, and is identical with the arpeggiated diminished-7th chord. Attractive ornamental effects can be obtained by infrapolation, interpolation, and ultrapolation, or a combination of these processes. An infra-inter-ultrapolation of the sesquitone scale produces a chromatically inflected melodic pattern of an orientalist type. The interpolation of a single note between the successive degrees of the sesquitone scale forms a scale of alternating whole tones and semitones, the octatonic scale, widely used by many composers, beginning with Liszt, Tchaikovsky, and Rimsky-Korsakov.

Sessions, Roger (Huntington), eminent American composer and teacher; b. Brooklyn, Dec. 28, 1896; d. Princeton, N.J., Mar. 16, 1985. He studied music at Harvard Univ. (B.A., 1915); took a course in composition with Horatio Parker at the Yale School of Music (B.M., 1917); then took private lessons with Ernest Bloch in Cleveland and N.Y.; this association was of great importance for Sessions; his early works were strongly influenced by Bloch's rhapsodic style and rich harmonic idiom verging on polytonality. He taught music theory at Smith College (1917–21); then was appointed to the faculty of the Cleveland Inst. of Music, 1st as assistant to Bloch, then as head of the dept. (1921–25). He lived mostly in Europe from 1926 to 1933, supporting himself on 2 Guggenheim fellowships (1926, 1927), an American

Academy in Rome fellowship (1928), and a Carnegie Foundation grant (1931); also was active with Copland in presenting the Copland-Sessions Concerts of contemporary music in N.Y. (1928–31), which played an important cultural role at that time.

His subsequent teaching posts included Boston Univ. (1933–35), the New Jersey College for Women (1935–37), Princeton Univ. (1935–44), and the Univ. of Calif. at Berkeley (1944–53); returned to Princeton as Conant Professor of Music in 1953 and as codirector of the Columbia-Princeton Electronic Music Center in N.Y. in 1959; subsequently taught at the Juilliard School of Music in N.Y. (1965–85); also was Bloch Prof. at Berkeley (1966–67) and Norton Prof. at Harvard Univ. (1968–69). In 1974 he received a special citation of the Pulitzer Award Committee "for his life's work as a distinguished American composer." In 1982 he was awarded a 2nd Pulitzer Prize for his Concerto for Orch.

In his compositions Sessions evolved a remarkably compact polyphonic idiom, rich in unresolvable dissonances and textural density and yet permeated with true lyricism. In his later works he adopted a sui generis method of serial composition. The music of Sessions is decidedly in advance of his time; the difficulty of his idiom, for both performers and listeners, creates a paradoxical situation in which he is recognized as one of the most important composers of the century, while actual performances of his works are exasperatingly infrequent.

set. A term adopted from mathematical set theory to denote a grouping of pitch classes or other musical elements; normally refers to a 12-note set containing all pitch classes within the equal tempered system but may also refer to elements indicating duration, time points, and/or dynamic levels; also called a *series*.

Set for Theater Orchestra. Suite for small orch. by Ives, 1906, containing *In the Cage*, *In the Inn*, and *In the Night*.

set piece. In music, a separate movement or readily identifiable portion of an opera, etc., formal in structure and cohesive in idiom (as a finale).

settima (It.). Interval of a 7th.

seul (*seulement*; Fr.). Alone; single, only one; solely, merely.

Seven Deadly Sins, The (*Die sieben Todsünden*). Ballet in song by Weill, 1933, for soprano, dancer, male vocal quartet, and orch., with text by Brecht, premiered in Paris. Both soprano and dancer play the character Anna, who comments on 20th-century interpretations of the classic components of reprobatology, while the quartet offers an extra dose of irony. Although *The 7 Deadly Sins* has much of the character of earlier Brecht-Weill collaborations, it masterfully distills them into their most salient musical and textual features; it was also the last theatrical collaboration between the 2.

Seven Rituals of Music. The 11th Sym. by Cowell, 1954, premiered in Louisville, Ky. The 7 rituals are not unlike Shakespeare's 7 stages of man, from birth to death. The score contains 7 recognizable sections, beginning with an andantino, mounting to a presto, and then subsiding to an andante.

Seven Studies on Themes of Paul Klee. Orch. suite by Schuller, 1959, 1st performed in Minneapolis. Each study refers to a different painting by the great abstract expressionist Swiss artist (1879–1940); the musical style is eclectic, with THIRD STREAM among the parties. Schuller later wrote a related work, *American Triptych: Studies in Texture Work*, tonally illustrating paintings by 3 abstract expressionists: Calder, Pollock, and Stuart Davis (1965).

1776. Musical by Sherman Edwards, 1969. This is one of the few historical musicals that have succeeded in the theater despite their lofty content. The play traverses the spring and summer of 1776 in Philadelphia, with a grand climax on July 4. J. Adams, B. Franklin, G. Washington, and T. Jefferson duly appear onstage. The historical details are remarkably free of facile fictionalizing; there is even a discussion of the details of the text of the Declaration of Independence. Among the songs are *Cool, Cool, Considerate Men, Sit Down, John, Piddle, Twiddle and Resolve*, and *Molasses to Rum*.

seventeenth. 1. Interval of 2 octaves plus a 3rd. 2. Same as TIERCE (organ stop).

seventh chord. A chord of the 7th, composed of a root with its 3rd, 5th, and 7th.

Seventh Symphony. Sym. by Mahler, 1908, in 5 movements, premiered in Prague with the composer conducting. Longer than his 5th Sym. (*The Giant*), the 7th has both pessimistic and optimistic passages, and is as bipolar a work as any Mahler composed.

Seventy-Six Trombones. Marching song by M. Willson, 1957, from the musical *The Music Man*; it became a tremendous hit.

severo (It.). Strictly, with rigid observance of tempo and expression marks.

Sext. 1. The interval of a 6th. 2. One of the *Little Hours* of the Office of the Roman Catholic liturgy; originally, the 5th hour in the daily cycle; since the 1972 liturgical reform, the 3rd (after Lauds and Terce); in either case, it is the service associated with noontime. 3. A compound organ stop of 2 ranks (a 12th and a 17th) a 6th apart.

Sextakkord (Ger.). Sixth or $^6_4$ chord.

Sexte (Ger.). Interval of a 6th.

sextet (It. *sestet, sestetto*; Ger. *Sextett*; Fr. *sextuor*). A concerted composition for 6 Voices or Instruments. Most works for string sextet call for pairs of violins, violas, and cellos (Boccherini, Brahms, Dvořák, Schoenberg); Beethoven wrote a mixed sextet and a wind sextet. The most famous vocal sextet is in Donizetti's *Lucia di Lammermoor*.

sextuplet (It. *sestole, sestolet*; Ger. *Sextole*; Fr. *sextolet*). A group of 6 equal notes to be performed in the time of 4 of the same kind in the established rhythm. In the *true* sextuplet the 1st, 3rd, and 5th notes are accented; the *false* sextuplet is simply a double triplet.

sfogato (It., exhaled). Sing lightly and in a relaxed manner. *Soprano sfogato*, a high soprano voice.

sfoggiando (It.). Brilliantly.

sforzando, sforzato (It., forced). Play with a sudden sharp accent, with special stress, or marked and sudden emphasis; written *sfz, sf*; Beethoven uses the expression mark *sfp*, sforzando followed by piano. *Sforzatissimo*, even more SFORZANDO; marked *sffz*.

sfrenatamente (It.). Unbridled; impetuously.

sfuggevole (It.). Fleetingly.

sfumate, sfumato (It.). Very lightly, like a vanishing smoke ring. *Sfumatura*, a nuance.

shading. 1. In the interpretation of a composition, the combination and alternation of any or all the varying degrees of tone power between fortissimo and pianissimo, for obtaining artistic effect. 2. The placing of anything so near the top of an organ pipe as to affect the vibrating column of air within.

shake. An obsolete term for TRILL. *Shaked graces*, the shaked beat, backfall, cadent, and elevation, and the double relish (all obsolete).

shakuhachi. A Japanese end-blown notched flute that came from China at the end of the 1st millennium A.D.; it has not survived in its home country. It is made of lacquered bamboo. It has been associated with Japanese priests since the 16th century; its pieces are typically programmatic and contemplative in character.

shamisen (samisen). A Japanese long-necked plucked lute, held upright in a seated position. It has 3 strings running over a slender neck, running from a reverse pegbox to an ivory or wood (now plastic) bridge; there are 3 standard tunings and variants, allowing the playing of as many open pitches as possible, depending on the function of the shamisen in the musical context; it is played with a large plectrum. The original form of this chordophone, the *jamisen*, came from China *c.* 1400.

shank. The crook in wind instruments; an extra length of tubing to be inserted in a trumpet, cornet, or horn. The practice of using shanks was essential in the 18th and early 19th centuries but was superseded by the invention of chromatic brass instruments (valve or piston).

Shankar, Ravi, famous Indian sitarist and composer; b. Benares, Apr. 7, 1920. He was trained by his brother, Uday Shankar (b. Udaipur, Rajasthan, Dec. 8, 1900; d. Calcutta, Sep. 29, 1977), a dancer and choreographer of international renown. Ravi began his career as a musician and a dancer, often touring with his brother's troupe; then engaged in a serious study of the Indian classical instrument, the sitar; in time became a great virtuoso on it. As a consequence of the growing infatuation with oriental arts in Western countries in the 1960s, he suddenly became popular, and his concerts were greeted with reverential awe by youthful multitudes. This popularity increased a thousandfold when the Beatles went to him to receive the revelation of Eastern musical wisdom, thus placing him on the pedestal usually reserved for untutored guitar strummers.

As a composer he distinguished himself by several film scores, including the famous *Pather Panchali* trilogy; he also wrote the film scores for *Kabulliwallah* and *Anuradha*. For the Tagore centenary he wrote a ballet, *Samanya Kshati*, based on Tagore's poem of the same name; it was produced in New Delhi (1961). Shankar wrote 2 concertos for sitar and orch. (1970, 1976) and has collaborated with Y. Menuhin and Glass, among others. His efforts to introduce Indian music to the world have often met with disapproval by those Indians who believe that the tradition of apprenticeship and oral learning should not be disturbed.

Shannāi. SĀNĀYĪ.

shanty (*chantey, chanty;* from Fr. *chanter*, sing). A characteristic song of the English working class in centuries past; most commonly, the *sea shanty*, a sailor's work song designed to facilitate the difficult gang labor aboard ship.

Shapey, Ralph, American conductor, teacher, and composer; b. Philadelphia, Mar. 12, 1921. He studied violin with Emanuel Zeitlin and composition with Stefan Wolpe; served as assistant conductor of the Philadelphia National Youth Administration Sym. Orch. (1938–47). In 1954 he founded and became music director of the Contemporary Chamber Players of the Univ. of Chicago, with which he presented new works; in 1963–64 he taught at the Univ. of Pa., and then was made prof. of music at the Univ. of Chicago in 1964; after serving as Distinguished Prof. of Music at the Aaron Copland School of Music at Queens College of the City Univ. of N.Y. (1985–86) he resumed his duties at the Univ. of Chicago. Disappointed by repeated rejections of his works by performers and publishers, Shapey announced in 1969 that he would no longer submit his works to anyone for performance or publ. However, in 1976 he had a change of heart and once more gave his blessing to the performance and publication of his works. In 1982 he became a MacArthur Fellow and in 1989 was elected a member of the American Academy and Inst. of Arts and Letters. His music employs serialistic but uncongested procedures in acrid counterpoint while formally adhering to neoclassical paradigms.

sharmanka (Rus.; Pol. *katarinka*). HURDY-GURDY, introduced into Russia from France in the early 19th century.

sharp (adjective). 1. (of tones or instruments) Too high in pitch. 2. (of intervals) Major or augmented. 3. (of keys)

Having a sharp or sharps in the signature. 4. (of organ stops) Shrill. 5. (of digitals) The black keys, or any white key a semitone above another white key (i.e., F and C).

sharp (noun). The character ♯, which raises the pitch of the note immediately following it by a semitone; the double sharp, ✕, raises the note by 2 semitones.

Sharp, Cecil (James), English folk music collector and ed.; b. London, Nov. 22, 1859; d. there, June 23, 1924. He studied mathematics and music at Uppingham and Clare College, Cambridge; in 1882 he went to Australia, settling in Adelaide, where he worked in a bank and practiced law, becoming associate to the Chief Justice of Southern Australia; in 1889 he resigned from the legal profession and took up a musical career; was assistant organist of the Adelaide Cathedral, and codirector of the Adelaide College of Music. In 1892 he returned to England; was music instructor of Ludgrove School (1893–1910) and principal of the Hampstead Cons. (1896–1905). At the same time he became deeply interested in English folk songs; publ. a *Book of British Songs for Home and School* (1902); then proceeded to make a systematic survey of English villages with the aim of collecting authentic specimens of English songs. In 1911 he established the English Folk Dance Society; also was director of the School of Folk Song and Dance at Stratford-upon-Avon. During World War I he was in the U.S., collecting folk music in the Appalachian Mountains, with a view to establishing their English origin. In 1923 he received the degree of M.M. *honoris causa* from the Univ. of Cambridge. In 1930 the Cecil Sharp House was opened in London as headquarters of the English Folk Dance Society (amalgamated with the Folk Song Society as the EFDSS in 1932). Much of his pioneering work resulted from a collaboration with Maud Karpeles (1885–1976), who met Sharp in 1909 and worked with him until his death, including on the Appalachian collecting trip. Sharp's writings include (all publ. in London): *English Folk-song: Some Conclusions* (1907); *Folk-singing in Schools* (1912); *Folk-dancing in Elementary and Secondary Schools* (1912); *The Dance: An Historical Survey of Dancing in Europe* (with A. Oppe; 1924); he ed. more than 10 anthologies of folk songs.

Shave and a Haircut. Words sung to a musical refrain so well known that it can be recognized simply by tapping out its rhythm. There are many forms of this piece of doggerel, e.g., "Bum di-de-de-dum bum, that's it," "Shave and a haircut, bay rum," and "Shave and a haircut, 2 bits" (in old American slang, 2 bits equaled a quarter, not that any U.S. coinage of a "bit" existed).

Shaw, Artie (born Arthur Jacob Arshawsky), outstanding American jazz clarinetist, bandleader, composer, and arranger; b. N.Y., May 23, 1910. He was brought up in New Haven, Conn., where he became an alto saxophonist in Johnny Cavallaro's dance band when he was 15; took up the clarinet at 16 and then worked as music director and arranger for the Austin Wylie Orch. in Cleveland until 1929; subsequently toured as a tenor saxophonist with Irving Aaronson's band, going with it to N.Y., where he played in Harlem and found a mentor in Willie "the Lion" Smith. After a stint as a freelance studio musician (1931–35), he formed a sophisticated band that stirred excitement with its rendition of his *Interlude in B-flat* in N.Y. in 1936; in 1937 he organized a swing band that won enormous success with the hit recording of Cole Porter's *Begin the Beguine* in 1938.

In 1940 he went to Hollywood, where he produced the hit recording *Frenesi*; toured again with his own big band, from which he drew members of the Gramercy 5, a group with which he was active off and on from 1940 until its last recording session in 1954. In the interim he led several big bands, winning his greatest acclaim with his recording of *Little Jazz* (1945). His interest in the classical repertoire for his instrument led him to appear as a soloist with various orchs.; also performed at N.Y.'s Carnegie Hall. In 1983 he came out of retirement to lead still another big band. Shaw is a remarkable clarinetist; his superb playing is perhaps best revealed in his recording *Concerto for Clarinet* (1940). He was married 8 times, numbering among his wives the film stars Lana Turner and Ava Gardner. He publ. a quasi-autobiographical novel, *The Trouble with Cinderella: An Outline of Identity* (N.Y., 1952), and the novel *I Love You, I Hate You, Drop Dead!* (1965).

Shaw, George Bernard, famous Irish dramatist; b. Dublin, July 26, 1856; d. Ayot St. Lawrence, England, Nov. 2, 1950. Before winning fame as a playwright he was active as a music critic in London, writing for the *Star* under the name of "Corno di Bassetto" (1888–89) and for the *World* (1890–94). In 1899 he publ. *The Perfect Wagnerite*, a highly individual socialist interpretation of the *Ring of the Nibelung*. His criticisms from the *World* were reprinted as *Music in London* (3 vols., 1932); those from the *Star* as *London Music* in 1888–89 (London and N.Y., 1937); selected criticisms were ed. by E. Bentley (N.Y., 1954). Shaw's play *Arms and the Man* was made into an operetta, *The Chocolate*

Soldier, by Oscar Straus (1908); his *Pygmalion* was converted into a highly successful musical comedy under the title *My Fair Lady*, with a musical score by Frederick Loewe (1956).

shawm (Fr. *chalemie*; Ger. *Schalmei*; It. *piffaro*; bass shawm: Fr. *bombarde*; Ger. *Pommern*). An early form of oboe; brought into Europe in the 12th century, it remained popular until the 17th century, when the oboe superseded it. The shawm's shape was like that of a bassoon; it was made of a long piece of wood with a curved metal bell. From the 16th century there were open-reed and reed-capped types. At the height of its popularity there were shawms of all sizes, providing a range from bass to high soprano. When George Bernard Shaw, in his days as a music critic, received a letter addressed to G. B. Shawm, he thought it was a spelling error until someone told him that it was an obsolete wind instrument producing a forced nasal sound.

She Loves Me. Musical by J. Bock, 1963. In the year before Hitler was to take over Germany, a young man and woman experience romantic love and intermittent quarrels. Includes the title song, *Dear Friend, You and Me*, and *Ice Cream*.

Shéhérazade. Song cycle by Ravel, 1904, for voice and orch., premiered in Paris, to a text by Tristan Klingsor. The music is permeated with an impressionistic quasi-oriental flavor.

sheng (Chin.). A Chinese free-reed mouth organ; the earliest known example of this instrument type (mentioned in *c.* 1100 B.C.). The traditional shape is described as a phoenix; it involves a mouthpiece, wind chest, and around 17 bamboo pipes pointing upward; 4 of these are dummy pipes, to provide symmetry. Each pipe has a small finger hole which must be closed in order to sound; like the harmonica, different pitches are created by inhaling and exhaling.

shepherd's bell. HERDENGLOCKE.

shepherd's horn. A generic name for a lip-vibrated wind instrument of ancient origin, originally made of animal horn or tusk. The instrument was used functionally to communicate, call animals, or to perform magical or religious rituals.

Shifrin, Seymour, American composer and teacher; b. N.Y., Feb. 28, 1926; d. Boston, Sept. 26, 1979. After studies at N.Y.'s High School of Music and Art, he received private instruction from Schuman (1942–45); continued his training at Columbia Univ. (B.A., 1947), where he completed his graduate study in composition with Luening (M.A., 1949); then pursued additional training with Milhaud in Paris on a Fulbright scholarship (1951–52). He held 2 Guggenheim fellowships (1956, 1960); taught at Columbia Univ. (1949–50), City College of the City Univ. of N.Y. (1950–51), the Univ. of Calif. at Berkeley (1952–66), and at Brandeis Univ. (1966–79).

He wrote music of high chromatic consistency, with finely delineated contrapuntal lines often resulting in sharp dissonance. He wrote orch. works; chamber music, including 5 string quartets (1949; 1962; 1965–66; 1966–67; 1971–72); *In eius memoriam* for Flute, Clarinet, Violin, Cello, and Piano (1967–68); Duo for Violin and Piano (1969); Piano Trio (1974); *The Nick of Time* for Flute, Clarinet, Percussion, Piano Trio, and Double Bass (1978); piano works, including *4 Cantos* (1948), *The Modern Temper* for Piano 4-Hands (1959), Fantasy (1961), *Responses* (1973); vocal works, including *Cantata to Sophoclean Choruses* for Chorus and Orch. (1957–58; Boston, 1984); *Odes of Chang* for Chorus, Piano, and Percussion (1963); *Satires of Circumstance* for Mezzo-soprano, Flute, Clarinet, Violin, Cello, Double Bass, and Piano (1964; his best-known work); *Chronicles* for 3 Male Soloists, Chorus, and Orch. (1970; Boston, 1976); 5 Last Songs for Soprano and Piano (1979).

shift. In playing the violin, etc., a change by the left hand from the 1st position; the 2nd position is called the *half-shift*, the 3rd the *whole shift*, and the 4th the *double shift*. When out of the 1st position, the player is *on the shift*, and *shifting up* or *down*, as the case may be.

shimmy. An African-American fox-trot of the 1920s, emphasizing movement of the upper torso, in quick ragtime rhythm.

shō. A Japanese free-reed mouth organ, with continuous sound production possible through both inhalation and exhalation; closely related to the SHENG.

shofar. An ancient Jewish ritual trumpet, made from a ram's horn, and blown only at the beginning of the Jewish new year.

Shore, "Dinah" (Frances Rose). DINAH.

Short, Bobby (Robert Waltrip), African-American singer and pianist of popular music; b. Danville, Ill., Sept.

15, 1926. He was self-taught in music; appeared in vaude-ville as a child; later went to N.Y., where he began his career as a highly successful nightclub entertainer; also appeared in Los Angeles, London, and Paris with equal success. He ultimately garnered a reputation as the leading café singer of his time; he has kept a regular engagement at the Café Carlyle in N.Y. for many years.

short octave. A deficient lowest octave in early keyboard instruments that omitted the chromatic tones and used black keys to sound the notes usually assigned to the white keys, with only B-flat keeping its proper position. The short octave had only 5 white keys and 3 black keys. The white keys were tuned for E, F, G, A, B, and the black keys for the sounds of C, D, and B-flat. (An alternative was C, F, G, A, B, for white keys, and D, E, B-flat for the black). The rationale for the omission of chromatic tones except for B-flat was that chromatics were used very seldom in the deep bass register in keyboard compositions of the Baroque period. There were also advantages. Thanks to the short octave, organists or harpsichordists could play chords in widely spread positions because the stretch of the short octave was only 5 white keys. In his E-minor Toccata for harpsichord, Bach has a difficult interval of the 10th in the bass; but in the short octave it would require the stretch of only 1 octave. The retention of the B-flat in the short octave is explained by the great frequency of that note in scales, dating back to the Middle Ages.

Shostakovich, Dmitri (Dmitrievich)

Preeminent Russian composer of the Soviet generation whose style and idiom of composition largely defined the nature of new Russian music; b. St. Petersburg, Sept. 25, 1906; d. Moscow, Aug. 9, 1975. He was a member of a cultured Russian family; his father was an engineer employed in the government office of weights and measures; his mother was a professional pianist. Shostakovich grew up during the most difficult period of Russian revolutionary history, when famine and disease decimated the population of Petrograd. Of frail physique, he suffered from malnutrition; Glazunov, the director of the Petrograd Cons., appealed personally to the Commissar of Education, Lunacharsky, to grant an increased food ration for Shostakovich, essential for his physical survival.

At the age of 9 he commenced piano lessons with his mother; in 1919 he entered the Petrograd Cons., where he studied piano with Nikolayev and composition with Steinberg; graduated in piano in 1923, and in composition in 1925. As a graduation piece he submitted his 1st Sym., written at the age of 18; it was 1st performed by the Leningrad Phil. in 1926, under the direction of Malko, and subsequently became one of Shostakovich's most popular works. He pursued postgraduate work in composition until 1930.

His 2nd Sym., composed for the 10th anniversary of the Soviet Revolution in 1927, bearing the subtitle *Dedication to October* and ending with a rousing choral finale, was less successful despite its revolutionary sentiment. He then wrote a satirical opera, *The Nose*, after Gogol's whimsical story about the sudden disappearance of the nose from the face of a government functionary; here Shostakovich revealed his flair for musical satire; the score featured a variety of modernistic devices and included an interlude written for percussion instruments only. *The Nose* was produced in Leningrad (1930), with considerable popular acclaim, but was attacked by officious theater critics as a product of "bourgeois decadence" and quickly withdrawn from the stage.

Somewhat in the same satirical style was his ballet *The Golden Age* (1930), which included a celebrated dissonant polka, satirizing the current disarmament conference in Geneva. There followed the 3rd Sym., subtitled *May 1st* (Leningrad, 1930), with a choral finale saluting the

International Workers' Day. Despite its explicit revolutionary content, it failed to earn the approbation of Soviet spokesmen, who dismissed the work as nothing more than a formal gesture of proletarian solidarity.

Shostakovich's next work was to precipitate a crisis in his career, as well as in Soviet music in general; it was an opera to the libretto drawn from a short story by the 19th-century Russian writer Leskov, entitled *Lady Macbeth of the District of Mtzensk*, and depicting adultery, murder, and suicide in a merchant home under the Czars. It was produced in Leningrad (1934) and was hailed by most Soviet musicians as a significant work comparable to the best productions of Western modern opera. But both the staging and the music ran counter to growing Soviet puritanism; a symphonic interlude portraying a scene of adultery behind the bedroom curtain, orchestrated with suggestive passages on the slide trombones, shocked the Soviet officials present at the performance by its bold naturalism. After the Moscow production of the opera, *Pravda*, the official organ of the Communist party, publ. an unsigned (and therefore all the more authoritative) article accusing Shostakovich of creating a "bedlam of noise." The brutality of this assault dismayed Shostakovich; he readily admitted his faults in both content and treatment of the subject, and he declared his solemn determination to write music according to the then-emerging formula of "socialist realism."

His next stage production was a ballet, *The Limpid Brook*, portraying the pastoral scenes on a Soviet collective farm. In this work he tempered his dissonant idiom, and the subject seemed eminently fitting for the Soviet theater; but it, too, was condemned in *Pravda*, this time for an insufficiently dignified treatment of Soviet life. Having been rebuked twice for 2 radically different theater works, Shostakovich abandoned all attempts to write for the stage and returned to purely instrumental composition. But as though pursued by vengeful fate, he again suffered a painful reverse. His 4th Sym. (1935–36) was placed in rehearsal by the Leningrad Phil. but withdrawn before the performance when representatives of the musical officialdom and even the orch. musicians themselves sharply criticized the piece.

Shostakovich's rehabilitation finally came with the production of his 5th Sym. (Leningrad, 1937), a work of rhapsodic grandeur, culminating in a powerful climax; it was hailed, as though by spontaneous consensus, as a model of true Soviet art, classical in formal design, lucid in its harmonic idiom, and optimistic in its philosophical connotations.

The height of his rise to recognition was achieved in his 7th Sym. He began its composition during the siege of Leningrad by the Nazis in the autumn of 1941; he served in the fire brigade during the air raids; then flew from Leningrad to the temporary Soviet capital in Kuibishev, on the Volga, where he completed the score, which was performed there in 1942. Its symphonic development is realistic in the extreme, with the theme of the Nazis, in mechanical march time, rising to monstrous loudness, only to be overcome and reduced to a pathetic drum dribble by a victorious Russian song. The work became a musical symbol of the Russian struggle against the overwhelmingly superior Nazi war machine; it was given the subtitle *Leningrad Sym.* and was performed during the war by virtually every orch. in the Allied countries.

After the tremendous emotional appeal of the *Leningrad Sym.*, the 8th Sym., written in 1943, had a lesser impact; the 9th, 10th, and 11th syms. followed (1945, 1953, 1957) without attracting much comment; the 12th Sym. (1960–61), dedicated to the memory of Lenin, aroused a little more interest. But it was left for his 13th Sym. (Leningrad, 1962) to create a controversy which seemed to be Shostakovich's peculiar destiny; its vocal 1st movement for solo bass and male chorus, to words by the Soviet poet Evtushenko, expressing the horror of the massacre of Jews by the Nazis during their occupation of the city of Kiev and containing a warning against residual anti-Semitism in Soviet Russia, met with unexpected criticism by the chairman of the Communist party, Nikita Khrushchev, who complained about the exclusive attention in Evtushenko's poem to Jewish victims, and his failure to mention the Ukrainians and other nationals who were also slaughtered. The text of the poem was altered to meet these objections, but the 13th Sym. never gained wide acceptance.

There followed the remarkable 14th Sym. (1969), in 11 sections, scored for voices and orch., to words by García Lorca, Apollinaire, Rilke, and the Russian poet Küchelbecker. Shostakovich's 15th Sym., his last (perf. in Moscow under the direction of his son Maxim, 1972), demonstrated his undying spirit of innovation; the score is set in the key of C major, but it contains a dodecaphonic passage and literal allusions to motives from

Rossini's overture to *Wilhelm Tell* and the FATE MOTIVE from Wagner's *Die Walküre*. Shostakovich's adoption, however limited, of themes built on 12 different notes—a procedure that he had himself condemned as anti-musical—is interesting from both psychological and sociological standpoints; he experimented with these techniques in several other works; his 1st explicit use of a 12-tone subject occurred in his 12th string quartet (1968).

Equally illuminating is his use in some of his scores of a personal monogram, D–S–C–H (for D, Es, C, H in German notation, i.e., D, E-flat, C, B). One by one his early works, originally condemned as unacceptable to Soviet reality, were returned to the stage and the concert hall; the objectionable 4th and 13th syms. were publ. and recorded; the operas *The Nose* and *Lady Macbeth of the District of Mtzensk* (rev. and renamed *Katerina Izmailova*, after the name of the heroine) had several successful revivals.

Shostakovich excelled in instrumental music. Besides the 15 syms., he wrote 15 string quartets, a string octet, piano quintet, 2 piano trios, cello sonata, violin sonata, viola sonata, 2 violin concertos, 2 piano concertos, 2 cello concertos, 24 Preludes for Piano (op. 34, 1932–33), 24 Preludes and Fugues for Piano (op. 87, 1950–51), 2 piano sonatas, and several short piano pieces; also choral works and song cycles.

What is remarkable about Shostakovich is the unfailing consistency of his style of composition. His entire oeuvre, from his 1st work to the last (147 opus numbers in all), proclaims a personal article of faith. His idiom is unmistakably of the 20th century, making free use of dissonant harmonies and intricate contrapuntal designs yet never abandoning inherent tonality; his music is teleological, leading invariably to a tonal climax, often in a triumphal triadic declaration. Most of his works carry key signatures; his metrical structure is governed by a unifying rhythmic pulse.

Dmitri Shostakovich

COURTESY FRANK DRIGGS COLLECTION

Shostakovich is equally eloquent in dramatic and lyric utterance; he has no fear of prolonging his slow movements in relentless dynamic rise and fall; the cumulative power of his kinetic drive in rapid movements is overwhelming. While the syms. have given Shostakovich great visibility in the concert hall, the string quartets are more personal and more indicative of his compositional moods. Yet through all the peripeties of his career he never changed his musical language in its fundamental modalities. When the flow of his music met obstacles, whether technical or external, he obviated them without changing the main direction.

Shostakovich's continual worries about the unpredictable Stalin and his henchmen have made the composer a textbook study of survival under the worst of political circumstances; at one period of his life (the years between 1945 and Stalin's death in 1953) he wrote compositions that he simply put away until the dust cleared. In a special announcement issued after Shostakovich's death, the government of the USSR summarized his work as a "remarkable example of fidelity to the traditions of musical classicism, and above all, to the Russian traditions, finding his inspiration in the reality of Soviet life, reasserting and developing in his creative innovations the art of socialist realism, and in so doing, contributing to universal progressive musical culture."

His honors, both domestic and foreign, were many: The Order of Lenin (1946, 1956, 1966), People's Artist of the USSR (1954), Hero of Socialist Labor (1966), Order of the October Revolution (1971), honorary membership in the American Inst. of the Arts (1943), honorary Doctor of Oxford Univ. (1958), Laureate of the International Sibelius Prize (1958), and Doctor of Fine Arts from Northwestern Univ. (1973). He visited the U.S. as a delegate to the World Peace Conference in 1949, as a member of a group of Soviet musicians in 1959, and to receive the degree of D.F.A. from Northwestern Univ. in 1973.

shout. 1. An African-American audience response involving foot-stamping, hand-clapping, singing drones, and interjecting shrill vocal commentary between phrases of gospel music. Such spontaneous performances could be musically organized, as was done by Gershwin in *Porgy and Bess* (he had heard the shouting ritual during a stay on Folly Island off the S.C. coast). 2. A genre of stride piano piece, 1st composed in the 1920s; the most famous example is James P. Johnsons's *Carolina Shout* (1925).

Show Boat. Musical by Kern and Hammerstein, 1927, based on the novel by Edna Ferber. The story concerns a Miss. show boat that carries a versatile assortment of passengers. The captain's daughter falls in love with a gambler and marries him. Distressed by his dishonest ways, she leaves him and joins a Chicago nightclub as a singer. Her father eventually takes her back to the show boat, where her gambler husband is waiting for her; she decides to give him another chance. This work took its genre to new heights of topicality (race relationships) and musical integrity, producing a truly unified work, immediately hailed by critics as a classic of American musical theater. Paul Robeson established his national reputation with his performance of *Ol' Man River*; other songs include *Can't Help Lovin' Dat Man, Make Believe, Why Do I Love You?, Bill*, and *You Are Love*.

Show Girl. Musical by Gershwin, 1929. The story traces the rise to fame and fortune of a young woman named Dixie who becomes the star of the Ziegfield Follies. Includes *Liza (All the Clouds'll Roll Away)*.

shtick (Yidd., piece). Slang for a vaudevillian or post-vaudevillian routine; also called a *bit*.

shuffle. A syncopated dance with a dragging, sliding step, meant to appear somewhat random and confused.

Shuffle Along. Musical by E. Blake and N. Sissle, 1921. After the wartime hiatus on black musical theater in N.Y., this revue-like work burst on the scene. The insubstantial plot deals with a mayoral election in a small town. Its considerable success was due in no small part to songs such as *Everything Reminds Me of You, If You've Never Been Vamped, I'm Just Wild About Harry*, and *Love Will Find a Way*.

Shuffle Off to Buffalo. Song by Harry Warren, 1933, which became a hit in the movie musical *42nd Street*.

Si (It.). 1. The 7th solmization syllable. 2. You are to; one must. *Si leva il sordino*, take off the mute; *si levano i sordini*, take off the mutes; *si piace, si libet*, at pleasure; *si replica*, repeat; *si segue*, proceed; *si tace*, be silent; *si volta*, turn the page; *si ha s'immaginar la battuta di 6/8*, imagine the time to be 6/8.

si bisogna da copa al segno (It.). Repeat from the beginning to the sign.

Sibelius, Jean

Great Finnish composer whose music, infused with the deeply felt modalities of national folk songs, opened a modern era of Northern musical art; b. Johan Julius Christian, Hämeenlinna, Dec. 8, 1865; d. Järvenpää, Sept. 20, 1957. The family name stems from a Finnish peasant named Sibbe, traced back to the late 17th century; the Latin noun ending was commonly added among educated classes in Scandinavia. Sibelius was the son of an army surgeon; from early childhood he showed a natural affinity for music. At the age of 9 he began to study piano; then took violin lessons with Gustaf Levander, a local bandmaster. He learned to play violin well enough to take part in amateur performances of chamber music. In 1885 he enrolled at the Univ. of Helsingfors (Helsinki) to study law, but abandoned it after the 1st semester. In the fall of 1885 he entered the Helsingfors Cons., where he studied violin with Vasiliev and Csillag; he also took courses in composition with Wegelius.

In 1889 a string quartet (his 2nd) was performed in public and produced a sufficiently favorable impression to obtain for him a government stipend for further study in Berlin, where he took lessons in counterpoint and fugue with Albert Becker. Later he proceeded to Vienna for additional musical training and became a student of Robert Fuchs and Karl Goldmark (1890–91). In 1892 he married Aino Järnefelt. From then on his destiny as a national Finnish composer was determined; the music he wrote was inspired by native legends, with the great Finnish epic *Kalevala* as a prime source of inspiration. Later that year his symphonic poem *Kullervo*, scored for soloists, chorus, and orch., was 1st performed in Helsingfors. There followed one of his most remarkable works, the symphonic poem entitled simply *En Saga*; in it he displayed to the full his genius for variation forms, based on a cumulative growth of a basic theme adorned but never encumbered with effective contrapuntal embellishments.

From 1892 to 1900 he taught theory of composition at the Helsingfors Cons. In 1897 the Finnish Senate granted him an annual stipend of 3,000 marks. In 1899 he conducted in Helsingfors the premiere of his 1st Sym. He subsequently conducted the 1st performances of all of his syms., the 5th excepted. In 1900 the Helsingfors Phil. gave the 1st performance of his most celebrated and most profoundly moving patriotic work, *Finlandia*. Its melody soon became identified among Finnish patriots with the aspiration for national independence, so that the Czarist government went to the extreme of forbidding its performances during periods of political unrest. In 1901 Sibelius was invited to conduct his works at the annual festival of the Allgemeiner Deutscher Tonkünstlerverein at Heidelberg. In 1904 he settled in his country home at Järvenpää, where he remained for the rest of his life; he traveled rarely.

In 1913 he accepted a commission for an orch. work from the American music patron Carl Stoeckel, to be performed at the 28th annual Festival at Norfolk, Conn. For it he contributed a symphonic legend, *Aalotaret* (Nymphs of the Ocean; it was later rev. as *The Oceanides*). He took his only sea voyage to America to conduct its premiere (1914); on that occasion he received the honorary degree of Mus.D. from Yale Univ. Returning to Finland just before the outbreak of World War I, Sibelius withdrew into seclusion but continued to work. He made his last public appearance in Stockholm, conducting the premiere of his 7th Sym. in 1924. He wrote a few more works thereafter, including a score for Shakespeare's *The Tempest* and a symphonic poem, *Tapiola*; he practically ceased to compose after 1927.

Jean Sibelius

At various times rumors were circulated that he had completed his 8th Sym., but nothing was forthcoming from Järvenpää. One persistent story was that Sibelius himself decided to burn his incomplete works. Although willing to receive journalists and reporters, he avoided answering questions about his music. He lived out his very long life as a retired person, absorbed in family interests; in some modest ways he was even a bon vivant; he liked his cigars and his beer, and he showed no diminution in his mental alertness. Only once was his peaceful life gravely disrupted; this was when the Russian army invaded Finland in 1940; Sibelius sent an anguished appeal to America to save his country, which by the perverse fate of world politics became allied with Nazi Germany. But after World War II Sibelius cordially received a delegation of Soviet composers who made a reverential pilgrimage to his rural retreat.

Honors were showered upon him; festivals of his music became annual events in Helsinki; in 1939 the Helsinki Cons. was renamed the Sibelius Academy in his honor; a postage stamp bearing his likeness was issued by the Finnish government on his 80th birthday; special publications—biographical, bibliographical, and photographic—were publ. in Finland. Artistically, too, Sibelius attained the status of greatness rarely vouchsafed to a living musician; several important contemporary composers paid him homage by acknowledging their debt of inspiration to him, Vaughan Williams among them. Sibelius was the last representative of 19th-century nationalistic Romanticism. He stayed aloof from modern developments, but he was not uninterested in reading scores and listening to performances on the radio of works of such men as Schoenberg, Prokofiev, Bartók, and Shostakovich.

The music of Sibelius also marked a culmination of the growth of national Finnish art, in which Pacius was the protagonist and Wegelius a worthy cultivator. Like his predecessors, he was schooled in the Germanic tradition, and his early works reflect German lyricism and dramatic thought. He opened a new era in Finnish music when he abandoned formal conventions and began to write music that seemed inchoate and diffuse but followed a powerful line of development by variation and repetition; a parallel with Beethoven's late works has frequently been drawn. The thematic material employed by Sibelius is not modeled directly on known Finnish folk songs; rather he recreated the characteristic melodic patterns of folk music. The prevailing mood is somber, even tragic, with a certain elemental sweep and grandeur.

His instrumentation is highly individual, with long songful solo passages and protracted transitions that are treated as integral parts of the music. His genius found its most eloquent expression in his syms. and symphonic poems; he wrote only a moderate amount of chamber music, much of it in his earlier years. His only opera, *The Maid in the Tower* (1896), to a text in Swedish, was never publ. He wrote some incidental music for the stage; the celebrated *Valse triste* was written in 1903 for *Kuolema*, a play by Arvid Järnefelt, brother-in-law of Sibelius.

In addition to the pieces mentioned above, Sibelius's works included incidental music for the theater; 7 syms. (1899; 1902; 1904–1907; 1911; 1915; 1923; 1924); symphonic poems and other orch.l works; chamber works, including string quartets (1885; 1889; 1890; 1909, *Voces intimae*; other works) and various other combinations; works for piano: over 25 works composed between 1893 and 1929, including the Sonata in F Major, op. 12 (1893); organ pieces; numerous choral works; and 95 songs composed between 1891 and 1917.

Sibila. A verse preceding Christmas Mass as celebrated on the islands of Majorca and Sardinia, which consist of the prophecies of the Apocalypse and is usually sung in Catalan ("Jesucrist, Rei universal . . .").

sich Zeit lassen (Ger.). Play unhurriedly (Mahler, 4th Sym.).

Sicilian Vespers, The (*I Vespri Siciliani*). Opera by Verdi, 1855, 1st produced in Paris at the Grande Exposition under the French title *Les Vêpres siciliennes*. The subject was not the most politic choice for a French audience, as it dealt with the expulsion of the French from Sicily in the 13th century. The Vespers of the title are the church bells rung by a patriotic Sicilian noblewoman as a signal for the expected uprising. The opera ends in a massacre of the French. Not a major Verdi opera, it is surprisingly tenacious in the world's opera houses.

siciliana, -o (It.; Fr. *sicilienne*). A pastoral dance in moderate tempo and 6/8 or 12/8 time, frequently in a minor key; it somewhat resembles a BARCAROLLE. The characteristic rhythm is dotted 6–8; in its classical form it is often orchestrated with flutes and oboes and included in the Baroque suite. Its origins are not clearly understood. *Alla siciliana*, arias in this style, with frequent use of the Neapolitan 6th chord.

side drum (U.K.). SNARE DRUM.

sidemen. Members of a jazz or popular group accompanying a soloist.

Sidewalks of New York, The. Song by Black and Lawlor, 1894; originally performed in vaudeville, it became the unofficial N.Y. anthem, lustily intoned by the hoarse voices of candidates for political office. Alfred Smith adopted it for his presidential campaign (1928), and N.Y.'s colorful if corrupt mayor James Walker loved it. The song is also known by the 1st line of its chorus, *East Side West Side*.

Siège de Corinthe, Le. Opera by Rossini, 1826, 1st performed in Paris. The story deals with a daughter of the governor of Corinth who refuses to submit to the commander of the Turkish army besieging Corinth as the price of its relief; she dies with her father in the city ruins. Since the 1st production of the opera happened to take place during the uprising against the Ottoman rulers by Greek nationalists, to whom the French were highly sympathetic, it won a particularly warm reception. Actually the score was a revision of an opera on a similar subject that was 1st produced in Naples, 1820, under the title *Maometto II*.

Siegfried. Music drama by Wagner, the 3rd part of the tetralogy *Der Ring des Nibelungen*, 1st produced in 1876 as part of the inaugural Bayreuth Festival. Siegfried is child of the incestuous Siegmund and Sieglinde, children of Wotan. He is guarded by the Nibelung dwarf Mime. Wotan predicts that a hero will emerge who will make the mighty sword with which to kill the murderous giant Fafner, magically transformed into a dragon. Siegfried fulfills Wotan's prophecy, forges the sword, and slays Fafner. Inadvertently he touches the hot gore of the slain dragon; putting his finger to his lips, he suddenly becomes aware that he can understand the language of the birds. Siegfried also reads the mind of Mime and realizes that he plots his death. He kills the malevolent dwarf and goes forth to his next adventure, to rescue Brünnhilde, the disobedient Valkyrie who was punished by Wotan and placed on a rock surrounded by a ring of fire. He reaches her as she lies in deep sleep, and puts the fateful ring of the Nibelung, now in his possession, on her finger. He awakens her with a kiss. The score contains some of the most gorgeous episodes in Wagner's tetralogy; the scene with the birds is both poetic and onomatopoeic.

Siegfried Idyll. Work by Wagner, 1870, for small orch. This piece was composed and conducted by Wagner in his home on Lake Lucerne as a surprise for the birthday of his wife, Cosima, on Christmas Day, celebrating the birth of their son Siegfried. In the MS the work is titled simply *Symphonie*. In its score Wagner made use of several leading motives from his opera *Siegfried*.

Sierra, Roberto, Puerto Rican composer; b. Vega Baja, Oct. 9, 1953. He began musical training at the Puerto Rico Cons. of Music and at the Univ. of Puerto Rico (graduated, 1976); then pursued studies in London at the Royal College of Music and the Univ. (1976–78), at the Inst. of Sonology in Utrecht (1978), and with György Ligeti at the Hamburg Hochschule für Musik (1979–82). He was assistant director (1983–85) and director (1985–86) of the cultural activities dept. at the Univ. of Puerto Rico, then dean of studies (1986–87) and chancellor (from 1987) at the Puerto Rico Cons. of Music. In 1989 he became composer-in-residence of the Milwaukee Sym. Orch.

sight reading. An ability to read unfamiliar music with ease. In singing it is synonymous with SOLFÈGE. Before the system of notation was firmly established, sight reading included perforce a great deal of improvisation within the given meter and key. Choirboys were trained to sing mensural music by sight in churches and chapels. Contemporary chronicles report the case of a 14-year old chorister known as Frater Georgius from Pisa who could sing at sight from the most intricate parts of polyphonic music. But the real challenge to professional musicians came in the 19th century, when to read at sight a difficult piece of piano music required a superior ability to coordinate melody, harmony, and rhythm.

All professional instrumentalists and vocalists must be able to read at sight as a matter of routine, but there are some extraordinary musicians who can play complicated works with great precision and fluency at sight. Piano accompanists to singers and instrumentalists are routinely expected to play their parts and follow the soloist without rehearsal, so that playing *a prima vista* or À LIVRE OUVERT (Fr., at the open book) became a necessity in a practical concert career when little time is available for rehearsal. In popular music the question of instant transposition can come into play; accompanists at auditions should know the standard repertoire well enough to play in any key requested.

A particularly difficult task is to reduce a full orch.l score at sight on the piano; it would involve instantaneous transposition of transposing instruments, coordinating string and wind groups at a glance, and reducing all this, with the agility of a computer, to a pianistically feasible arrangement without losing the tempo and component contrapuntal rhythms. To be sure, it can be managed with a traditional score, in which harmonies can be assumed to be compatible in different instrumental groups, but in a modern score, where atonality is a tonal hurdle and polytonality is a common hazard, such an instantaneous piano reduction of an orch.l score is practically impossible.

signa externa (Lat.). In mensural notation, symbols indicating the number of beats in each unit; the opposite is *signa intrinseca*, with specific rhythmic figures.

signal horn. A bugle.

signature, key. In modern notation, the accidentals (sharps or flats) that predetermine the tonality (tonalities) to be used.

signature, time. In modern notation, a numerical indication of the numbers of beats in a measure.

signature tune. A brief musical phrase that becomes associated with a popular band on the radio, played at the beginning and/or at the end of a program or performance.

Signor Bruschino, Il. Opera by Rossini, 1813, premiered in Venice. A young 18th-century Italian woman is urged by her guardian to marry his son, but the son loves another. Her lover then impersonates her guardian's son and, as can happen only in an opera, inveigles the old man into sanctioning their union. The overture is occasionally performed as a separate number at concerts.

signum intensionis (Lat., sign of intensity). Sharp sign.

signum remissionis (Lat., sign of lowering). Flat sign.

signum restitutionis. (Lat., sign of restoration). Natural sign.

Silbermann, Gottfried, organ and piano builder, who built the 1st German pianofortes; b. Klein-Bobritzsch, Jan. 14, 1683; d. Dresden, Aug. 4, 1753. Apprenticed to a bookbinder, he ran away and joined his brother Andreas (see below) in Strasbourg about 1702 as his helper; during his brother's sojourn in Paris (1704–1706) he ran the family business; upon his brother's return to Strasbourg they worked as partners. After working on his own there and in other cities, he went to Freiberg in 1711. His finest organ was the instrument built for the Katholische Hofkirche in Dresden (3 manuals, 44 stops), begun in 1750 and completed after his death by his pupil Zacharias Hildebrandt. He owes his fame, however, mainly to the manufacture of pianos in Germany, in which field he was a pioneer; the hammer action in his instruments was practically identical with that of Cristofori, the piano inventor. Silbermann also invented the *cimbal d'amour,* a clavichord with strings of double length, struck in the middle by the tangents, thus yielding the equivalent pitch of the normal string length.

He supplied 3 pianos to Frederick the Great for Potsdam, and Bach played on them during his visit there in 1747, preferring them to the Silbermann pianos he had examined in the 1730s. Gottfried's brother Andreas Silbermann, (b. Klein-Bobritzsch, Saxony, May 16, 1678; d. Strasbourg, Mar. 16, 1734) worked with the organ builder Friedrich Ring in Alsace before going to Strasbourg in 1702; was in Paris, 1704–1706, then returned to Strasbourg; built the Munster organ there (1713–16) and 33 others.

silence. Literally, the absence of sound; in the 20th century, introduced as a viable element of music. Poets often speak of the eloquent and the harmonious quality of silence. The lines in Félicien David's *Symphonic Ode* are appropriate:

> Ineffables accords de l'éternel silence!
> Chaque grain de sable
> à sa voix
> Dans l'ether onduleux le
> concert se balance:
> Je le sens, je le vois!

The longest silence explicitly written out is the 5-bar rest in the score of *The Sorcerer's Apprentice* by Dukas. Ligeti composed a work consisting of a quarter-note rest. The most ambitious composition utilizing the effect of total silence is *4'33"* by Cage, scored for any combination of instruments, tacet, and subdivided into 3 movements during which no intentional sounds are produced. It was unheard for the 1st time at Woodstock, N.Y., in 1952, with David Tudor at the silent piano.

Silent Night (*Stille Nacht, heilige Nacht*). Christmas song by Franz Gruber, composed on Christmas Eve, 1818. It is the most popular Christmas song in Germany, England, and the U.S.

silenzio (It.). Silence. *Lurgo silenzio,* a long pause.

Silk Stockings. Musical by C. Porter, 1955, based on the film *Ninotchka.* The heroine is a thoroughly indoctrinated young Soviet woman who is sent to Paris on a cultural mission but becomes involved in the bourgeois ways of life and love. She is spirited back to Russia by 3 grim Soviet commissars, but her American lover eventually brings her back to Paris. The anti-Soviet jokes involve a USSR agent who, when told that Prokofiev has died, is puzzled: "I didn't even know he was arrested." The agent carries with him the book *Who's Still Who.* The best anti-Soviet song is *Siberia;* the songs also include *All of You.*

Sills, Beverly (born Belle Miriam Silverman), celebrated American soprano and operatic administrator; b. N.Y., May 25, 1929. Her father was an insurance salesman from Romania and her mother a rather musical person from Odessa. At the age of 3 she appeared on the radio under the cute nickname "Bubbles" and won a prize at a Brooklyn contest as the most beautiful baby of 1932. From this auspicious beginning she performed in television, radio, film, and commercials. She began formal vocal studies with Estelle Liebling when she was 7; also studied piano with Paolo Gallico. In 1947 she made her operatic debut as Frasquita in *Carmen* with the Philadelphia Civic Opera; then toured with several opera companies and sang with the San Francisco Opera (1953) and the N.Y. City Opera (1955), quickly establishing herself at the latter as one of its most valuable members.

She extended her repertoire to embrace modern American operas, including the title role of Moore's *The Ballad of Baby Doe*; she also sang in the American premiere of Nono's avant-garde opera *Intolleranza 1960*. She was a guest singer at the Vienna State Opera and in Buenos Aires in 1967, at La Scala in Milan in 1969, and at Covent Garden in London and the Deutsche Oper in Berlin in 1970. She made her 1st appearance with the Metropolitan Opera as Donna Anna in a concert production of Don Giovanni on July 8, 1966, at the Lewisohn Stadium in N.Y.; her formal debut with the Metropolitan took place at Lincoln Center in N.Y. as Pamira in *Le Siège de Corinthe* (1975).

At the height of her career she received well-nigh universal praise, not only for the excellence of her voice and her virtuosity in bel canto coloratura parts, but also for her intelligence and erudition, rare among the common run of operatic divas. She became general director of the N.Y. City Opera in 1979 and made her farewell performance as a singer in 1980. She showed administrative talent; during her tenure with the N.Y. City Opera she promoted American musicians and broadened the operatic repertoire; retired in 1988; also produced television shows dealing with opera and concert singing. In her personal life she suffered a double tragedy; 1 of her 2 children was born deaf and the other was mentally retarded. (In 1972 she accepted the national chairmanship of the Mothers' March on Birth Defects.)

Beverly Sills, c. 1960s

COURTESY FRANK DRIGGS COLLECTION

She received honorary doctorates from Harvard Univ., N.Y. Univ., and the Calif. Inst. of the Arts. In 1971 she was the subject of a cover story in *Time*. In 1980 she was awarded the U.S. Presidential Medal of Freedom. Her most notable roles included Cleopatra in Handel's *Giulio Cesare*, Lucia, Elisabeth in *Roberto Devereux*, Anna Bolena, Elvira in *I puritani*, and Maria Stuarda.

silofono (It.). XYLOPHONE.

silorimba (It.). XYLORIMBA.

similar motion. Motion of voices in the same direction (not necessarily parallel), as distinguished from CONTRARY MOTION.

simile (It.). Similarly; a direction to perform the following measures or passages in the same style as the preceding. *Simile mark*, ⫽ or ⫽, means that a measure or group of notes must be repeated.

Simon, Paul, popular American singer, guitarist, and songwriter; b. Newark, N.J., Oct. 13, 1941. While in high school in N.Y. he got together with Art Garfunkel; as Tom and Jerry they recorded the rock 'n' roll song *Hey, Schoolgirl* in 1957, and appeared on Dick Clark's *American Bandstand* television show. He then studied English literature at Queens College at the City Univ. of N.Y.; also was active as a promoter and songwriter for various N.Y. music publishers. After appearing in N.Y. clubs he teamed up with Garfunkel again and—as Simon and Garfunkel—brought out the album *Wednesday Morning 3 A.M.* (1964), which included the song *The Sound of Silence*, rerecorded and issued as a hit single in 1965. In 1966 they brought out an album entitled *Sound of Silence*, which secured their reputation. Among their subsequent albums were *The Graduate* (1968; from the film of the same title; includes the hit song *Mrs. Robinson*), *Bookends* (1968), and *Bridge over Troubled Water* (1970).

Simon and Garfunkel became a hyphenated entity as far as the public was concerned, but the difference between them was great. Simon was an introspective intellectual who wrote poetry of surprising excellence, while Garfunkel was adept in practical endeavors, composing little but singing and acting in films. Simon's solo albums included *Paul*

Simon (1972), *There Goes Rhymin' Simon* (1973), *Still Crazy After All These Years* (1975), *1-Trick Pony* (1980; from his own film of the same title), *Hearts and Bones* (1983), the controversial, Grammy Award–winning *Graceland* (1986), and *The Rhythm of the Saints* (1990).

Simone, Nina (born Eunice Kathleen Waymon), African-American jazz singer, keyboardist, and composer; b. Tryon, N.C., Feb. 21, 1933. After completing her high school training, her hometown residents raised the money to send her to the Juilliard School of Music in N.Y., where she studied piano and theory with Carl Friedberg; then continued her studies with Vladimir Sokoloff at the Curtis Inst. of Music in Philadelphia. In 1954 she began singing at an Atlantic City, N.J., nightclub, and subsequently devoted herself to popular music genres, appearing as a jazz, pop, and soul artist. She also composed instrumental music and over 50 songs.

Simone Boccanegra. Opera by Verdi, 1857, premiered in Venice. Boccanegra ("black mouth") was a historical Doge of Genoa in the 14th century. He lives with the memory of a daughter he had by a Genoese noblewoman; the mistress is now deceased and the child has disappeared. Many years elapse before the opera takes place; as it turns out, his daughter has been raised by his grandfather. Her romance with a young patrician is temporarily thwarted by a jealous rival. The true identities and relationships between grandfather, father, and granddaughter are disclosed in the last act; before his natural death, Boccanegra proclaims his daughter's lover as the new Doge. The opera, although less significant than Verdi's masterpieces, nevertheless retains a hold on the major opera houses.

simple. 1. Tones or intervals that are not compound, i.e., less than an octave. 2. Counterpoint, imitation, rhythm, and other elements that are neither complex, overly developed, or varied.

Simple Simon. Musical by Rodgers and Hart, 1930. Simple Simon tends a newspaper staff but is a dreamer of storybook fantasies. The show has at least one classic of the depression era, *10 Cents a Dance*, a sorrowful narrative of a young woman in a dancehall working as a taxi dancer.

simplement (Fr.). Simply, SEMPLICE.

simultaneity. Refers to the simultaneous sounding of multiple tones, as in a chord, but without reference to diatonic or harmonic function.

Sinatra, Frank (Francis Albert), phenomenally popular American singer and actor. b. Hoboken, N.J., Dec. 12, 1915, of immigrant Italian parents. He had no training as a singer and could not read music; after singing in a school glee club and on amateur radio shows, he appeared on N.Y. radio shows. In 1939 he became a singer with Harry James, and then gained fame as a vocalist with Tommy Dorsey (1940–42). Inspired by the tone production of Dorsey's trombone playing, he evolved, by convex inhalation from a corner of the mouth, a sui generis "mal canto" in SOTTO VOCE delivery, employing a Caruso-like COUP-DE-GLOTTE at climactic points. This mode of singing, combined with an engagingly slender physique, stirred the young females of the World War II era to fainting frenzy at his performances. Sinatra's press agents were quick to exploit the phenomenon, dubbing him "Swoonlight Sinatra." He eventually overcame his anesthetic appeal and became a successful baritone crooner.

In 1952 he revealed an unexpected dramatic talent as a movie actor, eliciting praise from astonished cinema critics and an Academy Award for his appearance in *From Here to Eternity*. Other successful films followed (*Guys and Dolls, The Manchurian Candidate*), and his singing career gained momentum as he toured throughout the globe. He also made numerous recordings and television appearances. A fixture on the nightclub circuit, the Univ. of Nevada at Las Vegas conferred on him the honorary degree of Literarum Humanitarum Doctor, in appreciation of his many highly successful appearances in the hotels and gambling casinos of Las Vegas (1976). President Reagan was moved to present him with the U.S. Presidential Medal of Freedom in 1985.

sine tone (wave). The sound (and its visual correlate) of 1 pure frequency. The flute is the acoustic instrument closest to producing this kind of sound wave.

sinfonia (It.). 1. A sym., especially in the 18th century. 2. Within larger vocal works, an overture.

Sinfonia antartica. The 7th Sym. by Vaughan Williams, 1953, scored for soprano, female chorus, and orch.; it was 1st performed in Manchester, England. In this work Vaughan Williams adapted the background music he wrote for the film *Scott of the Antarctic* (1948), about the polar explorer who perished in 1912. The music abounds in special effects while preserving its balance between drama and contemplation of eternity. The text is taken from Shelley, Coleridge, and John Donne, ending with quotations from the notebook of Scott.

sinfonia concertante (It.). SYMPHONIE CONCERTANTE.

Sinfonia da requiem. Orch. work by Britten, 1941, composed during the composer's sojourn in the U.S., premiered in N.Y.

Sinfonía de antígona. Sym. No. 1 by Chávez, 1933, with thematic material extracted from incidental music for a production of Sophocles's *Antigone*; the composer conducted the premiere in Mexico City.

Sinfonia espansiva. Sym. No. 3 by Nielsen, 1912, premiered in Copenhagen. The expansiveness suggested in the subtitle denotes a subjective, all-encompassing flight of fantasy. The 2nd movement contains 2 vocalise parts.

Sinfonía india. Sym. No. 2 by Chávez, 1936, in 1 movement making use of 3 authentic indigenous Mexican themes and a great number of native Mexican percussion instruments. The composer conducted the premiere in N.Y.

Sinfonía proletaria (Llamadas) (Calls). Choral sym. by Chávez, 1934, premiered by the composer in Mexico City. The work glorifies in majestic tones the call to action of the international proletariat.

Sinfonía romántica. Sym. No. 4 by Chávez, 1953, in 3 economical and not particularly extravagant movements; the composer conducted the premiere in Louisville, Ky.

Sinfonia sacra. Sym. No. 5 by Hanson, 1955. The source of inspiration is the 1st Easter; the ecclesiastical theme is treated dramatically. The premiere was given in Philadelphia.

Sinfonia semplice. Sym. No. 6 by Nielsen, 1925, premiered in Copenhagen with the composer conducting. Not even the composer could explain the subtitle convincingly; the sym. (his last) ranges from Romantic rumination to antimodernist sarcasm; one is left with an insecure, almost schizoid afterglow.

Sinfonia sevillana. Orch. work by Turina, 1920, portraying the festive and amorous life near Seville in Spain. It was 1st performed in San Sebastian.

Sinfonia visionaria. Sym. No. 9 by Atterberg, 1956, premiered in Helsinki.

Sinfonie (Ger.). SYMPHONY.

sinfonietta (It., little sym.). A smaller-scaled sym., sometimes for a chamber orch.

Sinfonietta. Orch. work by Janáček, 1926, an outgrowth of a school fanfare composed 2 years earlier (which functions here as the opening and closing sections). The work exudes Janáček's love of tunes built of short ostinatos, transformed Czech modality, an almost cubist approach to meter, and economical orchestration.

Singakademie. A historically important musical institution organized in Berlin in 1791 to present concerts of vocal music. In 1829 Mendelssohn conducted in the Berlin Singakademie a performance of Bach's *St. Matthew Passion* that greatly contributed to the renewed appreciation of Bach's music.

singbar (*singend*; Ger.). Singable; melodiously; CANTABILE. *Sehr singbar vorzutragen*, perform in a very singing style.

singhiozzando (It., catching breath). Sobbing; with extreme emotion.

singing

~~~ ~~~ ~~~ ~~~ ~~~

The repetitive emission of sound energy in a sequence of melodious tones. It is the most natural vocal action of humans, birds, and some marine animals such as whales. When the witty Austrian tenor Leo Slezak was asked how early he began studying voice, he replied, "I vocalized the chromatic scale when I was 6 months of age." The organ that produces the melodious sounds within a definite range is the voice box in the larynx. The impulse to sing (or to speak) is generated in the muscles of the diaphragm, which pushes air upward into the lungs, and from there into the larynx and the vocal cords, which are set in periodical vibrations.

The ability of a trained singer to produce sounds of tonal purity and definite pitch constitutes the art of singing. Since a singer has no instrument outside his or her own body to practice upon, voice training requires nothing more than the control of the vocal cords and the propulsion of air from the lungs; however, it is a task easier said than done (and even more difficult to maintain). The range of the singing voice is usually not more than 30 tones, but these tones can be modulated in an extraordinary versatility of inflections and dynamic nuances; a professional singer is able to project the voice with great subtlety in degrees of power ranging from the faintest pianissimo to the thundering fortissimo.

Because the Roman Catholic Church frowned on women opening their mouths in church or any other public arena, prepubescent boys and specially trained male singers were required to perform the higher vocal parts. The barbarous practice of creating CASTRATO singers kept adult male voices artificially high for a lifetime, permitting the singing of male soprano and alto roles in opera and church. Fortunately the practice began to disappear as women gained the right to act in public, so that even by Mozart's day the castrato was a rarity; the practice did continue in the Roman Catholic Church until the mid-19th century, with the last castrato dying in the early 20th century.

During the so-called Golden Age of opera, the concept of proper singing was limited to the bel canto of Italian singing; even the gondoliers of Venice knew how to sing *O Sole Mio* with the inflections of a Caruso. Italians and non-Italians strove for perfection in opera companies all over the world, from Italy to Russia, England, the U.S., and South America. But as late Romantic vocal writing made new demands of range and endurance on singers, the bel canto ideal fell by the wayside, not to be revived until after the 2nd World War.

There are exceptional cases of men and women extending their voices by training. The American composer Henry Cowell was able to sing covering practically the entire audible range, from the lowest notes of the bass to the highest treble. Hans Werner Henze wrote a work for voice and orch. that demands such a fantastic vocal range, and there are singers who train themselves to satisfy this requirement. In works by avant-garde composers, singers are given parts requiring the production of all kinds of physiological sounds, such as howling, shrieking, hissing, grunting, moaning, buzzing, gurgling, chuckling, and coughing. There are even individuals who can sing upon both inhaling and exhaling (circular breathing), so that it becomes possible to sustain a note indefinitely. Finally there are those who can sing through the nose. A widely used special technique is SPRECHSTIMME, which preserves the inflection upward or downward but does not require tonal singing.

With all the avant-garde demands on vocal production, the novelty of singing approaches to 20th-century nonclassical music seem mild by comparison. Jazz singing tends to maintain the ideals of bel canto, but without the heavy vibrato long standard in operatic performance; the same is true of sentimental and soul balladry. On the other hand, blues singing has long capitalized on a husky, penetrating quality for expressive purposes; this was taken over later in rhythm and blues, rock 'n' roll, rock, soul (e.g., Otis Redding, who could sing in both uptempo and slow styles with success), and the subsequent evolution of popular music from the 1970s on, culminating in hip-hop and RAP on the one hand, and metal, punk, and GRUNGE on the other.

Singin' in the Rain. Song by N. H. Brown and A. Freed, 1929. It 1st appeared in the screen musical *Hollywood Revue*; then Judy Garland revived it successfully in another film musical, *Little Nellie Kelly* (1940); then, in yet another cinemusical, *Singin' in the Rain* (which included many earlier Brown and Freed songs), Gene Kelly and his umbrella did their unforgettable dance to the song.

single reed. A thin piece of wood, cane, or other material that is attached securely to an aperture at one end of a single-reed woodwind instrument; it provides the necessary vibration to start the flow of air through the instrument, provided by the player through the resulting mouthpiece. The pitch heard is determined by the fingering used.

single relish. An ornament in English lute music of the 17th century, corresponding to a very fast MORDENT.

Singspiel (Ger.). From a literary viewpoint, a theatrical piece, usually lighthearted, with interpolated musical numbers. The German Singspiel developed and was particularly popular in the 18th century (Mozart wrote 2 of them and half of a 3rd). From a musical viewpoint the difference between the Singspiel and a full-fledged opera lies in the use of spoken dialogue (as opposed to RECITATIVE), but this distinction became less pronounced when purely operatic works began admitting dialogue as part of the action. Many features of the Singspiel were adopted in German Romantic opera.

Singstimme (Ger.). The singing voice.

singultation. The modern practice of onomatopoeic singultation is derived from the medieval HOCKET, in which the singing line is interrupted by a syncopated translocation of thematic components, producing hocket or a singultus (both words mean hiccups). Brief detonations of kinetic energy in modern works are forms of singultation.

sinistra (It.). Left. *Mano sinistra* (*m. sinistra*), left hand; *colla sinistra*, with the left hand.

sino (It.). To, up to, as far as, until. *Sino* (or *sin'*) *al fine*, continue to the end.

Sir John in Love. Opera by Vaughan Williams, 1929, 1st produced in London. The story deals mainly with Falstaff; the text is selected from Shakespeare's comedy, *The Merry Wives of Windsor*. An arrangement of the English folk song *Greensleeves*, which was to become famous, occurs in this opera.

Sissle, Noble (Lee), African-American singer, bandleader, lyricist, and composer; b. Indianapolis, July 10, 1889; d. Tampa, Dec. 17, 1975. He became a singer in Edward Thomas's Male Quartet (1908) and then in Hann's Jubilee Singers (1912); subsequently attended DePauw Univ. and Butler Univ. After conducting a hotel orch. in Indianapolis, he sang with Bob Young's band in Baltimore (1915), where he met Eubie Blake; the two then worked with James Reese Europe's Soc. Orch. in N.Y. Following service as a drum major in the 369th Regimental Infantry Band in France during World War I,

Sissle returned to the U.S. and teamed up with Blake as a vaudeville duo (1919).

After success with their musicals *Shuffle Along* (1921) and *Chocolate Dandies* (1924), they performed in Europe. Sissle remained in Europe to work with his own band and as a solo performer from 1927 until returning to the U.S. to resume his association with Blake in 1933; they then produced the show *Shuffle Along*. He was subsequently active with his own bands, making regular appearances at Billy Rose's Diamond Horseshoe in N.Y. (1938–50); later operated his own nightclub, dubbed Noble's.

sistrum. An ancient Egyptian idiophone used in religious ritual, composed of a semicircular metal frame with crossbars overhung with tinkling rings.

Sisyfos. Choreographic orch. suite by Blomdahl, 1954, symbolizing the hopeless struggle of Sisyphus, who is condemned to push a large stone uphill only to have it roll down again from the summit; the music is appropriately pessimistic. It was 1st performed in Stockholm.

sitār. A classical South Asian stringed instrument with a bowl-shaped body and metal frets, plucked with a plectrum. Like the smaller SAROD, it uses bulbous gourds for resonance and was once a bowed chordophone (although that use is rare now). Both instruments are played in a sitting position, but the sarōd is played like a Western lute or guitar, while the sitār is held nearly upright.

Sitkovetsky, Dmitry. See DAVIDOVICH, BELLA.

Sri Lankan sitarist, 1989

(Sittin' On) The Dock of the Bay. Posthumous number 1 pop hit for soul singer Otis Redding, coauthored with session guitarist Steve Cropper. Redding tragically died, along with his backup band, The Bar-Kays, in an airplane crash shortly before the song hit the charts.

Six epigraphes antiques. Pieces for piano 4-hands by Debussy, 1917; the composer and Roger-Ducasse premiered the work in Paris; the *Epigraphes* were later orchestrated by Ernest Ansermet. Debussy always felt an affinity with ancient Greek prosody, and these pieces are instances of his Grecian moods.

Six, Les. A group of younger French composers, 1st called Les Nouveaux Jeunes, who formed a loose concert-giving alliance in the years just after World War I. Although dissimilar in musical personality and aesthetic, the composers (Auric, Durey, Honegger, Milhaud, Poulenc, and Tailleferre) shared an anti-Romantic attitude typical of the era. Les 6 was sustained, at least in the public eye, by its connections to Satie and Jean Cocteau, who as the apostles of this age of disenchantment preached the new values of urban culture, with modern America as a model. Satie urged young composers to produce "auditory pleasure without demanding disproportionate attention from the listener," while Cocteau elevated artistic ugliness to an aesthetic ideal. Most of Les 6 practiced a neoclassical strategy and had resolutely unmonumental artistic goals; but Durey, an avowed Communist, was the 1st to reject this lack of "seriousness." The 5 remaining members stayed around long enough to contribute incidental music to Cocteau's play *Les Mariés de la Tour Eiffel* (1921), but the group soon faded from the scene as the individuals pursued their own destinies.

six–five chord. The 1st inversion of the 7th chord ($^6_5$), especially the supertonic and dominant chords.

six–four chord. The 2nd inversion of the triad ($^6_4$), especially the tonic chord.

Sixteen Tons. Merle Haggard song that became a number 1, finger-snappin' hit for Tennessee Ernie Ford in 1955; satirized by Mickey Katz in the immortal *16 Tons (of Kosher Salami)*.

sixteenth note. Half of the value of an 8th note.

sixth. Interval comprising 6 diatonic degrees (when the 1st degree is counted as 1).

sixth chord. The 1st inversion of a triad (^{6} or $^6_3$).

sixty-fourth note. Half the value of a 32nd note.

skald. Ancient Scandinavian poet-musician; a MINSTREL or BARD.

Skalkottas, Nikos (Nikolaos), greatly talented Greek composer; b. Chalkis, island of Euboea, Mar. 8, 1904; d. Athens, Sept. 19, 1949. He studied violin with his father, with his uncle, and with a nonrelated violinist at the Athens Cons. (1914–20). In 1921 he went to Berlin, where he continued his violin studies at the Hochschule für Musik (until 1923); then took lessons in music theory with Philipp Jarnach (1925–27). But the greatest influence on his creative life was Schoenberg, with whom he studied in Berlin (1927–31); Schoenberg, in his book *Style and Idea*, refers to Skalkottas as one of his most gifted disciples. Skalkottas eagerly absorbed Schoenberg's instruction in the method of composition with 12 tones related only to one another, but in his own music applied it in a very individual manner, without trying to imitate Schoenberg's style. In Berlin, Skalkottas also received some suggestions in free composition from Kurt Weill (1928–29).

He returned to Athens and earned his living by playing violin in local orchs., but continued to compose diligently, until his early death from a strangulated hernia. His music written between 1928 and 1938 reflects Schoenberg's idiom; later works are tonally conceived, and several of them are in the clearly ethnic Greek modalities, set in the typical asymmetric meters of Balkan folk music. After his death a Skalkottas Soc. was formed in Athens to promote performances and publications of his works; about 110 scores of various genres are kept in the Skalkottas Archives in Athens; many of his works were premiered only after his death.

skiffle. A British popular music style, popular in the 1950s, in which percussion included washboard (hence the onomatopoeic name); the harmonica and kazoo were part of the ensemble, and the goal was a more acoustic, less electrified sound. Many of the performers were jazz musicians and future rock 'n' rollers; others became the leaders of the 1960s British Invasion, such as the Beatles.

skip. Melodic progression by an interval wider than a second; *disjunct* progression.

Skizze (Ger.). Sketch.

skomorokhis (Rus.). Minstrels who provided entertainment for the Russian court and aristocracy up to the 18th century; they cultivated versatile talents as singers, actors, and acrobats.

Skriabin, Alexander (Nikolaievich). Scriabin, Alexander (Nikolaievich).

Skyscrapers. Ballet by J. A. Carpenter, 1926, 1st performed in N.Y. This was the 1st theatrical work inspired exclusively by the American urban landscape. Elements of jazz are much in evidence.

slanciante (It., thrown off). Played lightly and deftly, or with force and vehemence.

slancio, con (*con islancio*; It.). With dash, vehemence; impetuously.

slancio, di (It.). The direct and hammerlike attack on a higher or lower tone, contrasted with the slide or "carry" of the portamento; also called *di posto*.

slap-bass. The manner of playing on the double bass by slapping the strings with the palm of the right hand for rhythmic effect; associated almost exclusively with jazz.

slargando (*slentando*; It.). Growing slower.

Slatkin, Leonard (Edward), prominent American conductor; b. Los Angeles, Sept. 1, 1944. His father was Felix Slatkin (b. St. Louis, Dec. 22, 1915; d. Los Angeles, Feb. 8, 1963), a violinist and conductor who played with the St. Louis Sym. Orch. (1931–37) and founded the Hollywood String Quartet (1947–61); he also was active as a conductor. Slatkin received musical training in his youth, studying violin, viola, piano, and conducting; after attending Indiana Univ. (1962) and Los Angeles City College (1963) he received valuable advice from Susskind at the Aspen Music School (1964); then studied conducting with Morel at the Juilliard School of Music in N.Y. (Mus.B., 1968). In 1968 he joined the St. Louis Sym. Orch. as assistant conductor to Susskind and was successively named associate conductor (1971), associate principal conductor (1974), and principal guest conductor (1975). He made his European debut in London as a guest conductor with the Royal Phil. in 1974.

He was music adviser of the New Orleans Phil. (1977–80); also music director of the Minnesota Orch. sum-

mer concerts (from 1979). In 1979 he became music director of the St. Louis Sym. Orch.; took it on a major European tour in 1985. In 1990 he also became music director of the Great Woods Performing Arts Center in Mansfield, Mass., the summer home of the Pittsburgh Sym. Orch., and in 1991 of the Blossom Music Center, the summer home of the Cleveland orch. He appeared widely as a guest conductor of major orchs., both in North America and Europe, demonstrating particular affinity for works of the 19th and 20th centuries. In 1996 he became music director of the National Sym. Orch. in Washington, D.C.

Slavonic Dances. Two sets of orch. dances by Dvořák, 1878 and 1886 (opp. 46 and 72). These dances are not mere transcriptions or inventions based on authentic Slavonic tunes, but original creations of Dvořák in the manner of Slavic folk songs; the melodies employ Ukrainian, Serbian, Polish, and of course Czech rhythms. Dvořák also arranged them for 2 pianos.

Sleeping Beauty, The. Ballet by Tchaikovsky, 1890, 1st performed in St. Petersburg. The scenario is taken from a classical tale. An evil fairy, scorned at the royal court, dooms a young princess to die when she comes of age. But a good fairy transforms the seeming death into a deep sleep, from which she awakens when a prince charming, providentially named Desire, kisses her. The score represents one of Tchaikovsky's most poetic creations. Particularly popular is the *Waltz*. A suite of 5 numbers has been drawn from the score.

Sleigh Ride. Rollicking orch. novelty by L. Anderson, 1950, which attained great success.

sleighbells. Small round bells traditionally attached to the harness of a horse drawing a sleigh; now a similarly constructed idiophone (horse and sleigh not required). Some modern scores use the sleighbells, including Varèse's *Ionisation* and Mahler's 4th Sym.

slendro. One of 2 gamelan scale types (the other is PELOG). Slendro is the family of pentatonic scales used, some approximating the "black-key pentatonic," others quite different; in any case the concept of a universal tuning standard does not have much consequence, only as long as an individual set of gamelan instruments are tuned properly to one another.

slide. 1. The movable U-shaped tube that fits inside the stationary tubing of the trombone; by extending or shortening the composite tube, one lowers or raises the pitch. 2. In the organ, a slider. 3. Three or 4 swiftly ascending or descending scale tones. 4. On a violin bow, that part of the nut which slides along the stick. 5. Obs. term for TRILL.

slide horn, trombone, or trumpet. A brass instrument that uses a slide instead of keys or valves. In return there is the *valve trombone* used in bands, where the trombone slide is replaced by valves.

sliphorn. Slang for trombone.

slit drum (Ger. *Schlitztrommel*; Fr. *tambour de bois*). A wooden tube of varying size used for centuries among the peoples of central Africa and Australia; it is mistakenly called a drum or gong. The earliest examples were huge hollowed-out tree trunks placed over pits and stamped on. In later manifestations the trunk was hollowed out through a longitudinal slit, struck by beaters, and sometimes placed on a stand; it is similar to the *teponaztli* of South America. Instruments have gradually grown smaller, even portable; the number of slits has been increased to provide more pitches; commercial versions for children's use are now commonplace. In some areas the slit drum has served as a method of communication; simple messages can be trans-

Slit drums, Melanesia

PHOTOGRAPH COURTESY OF THE SMITHSONIAN INSTITUTION, NATIONAL ANTHROPOLOGICAL ARCHIVES

mitted through rhythmic beats carrying the tidings of danger, joy, death, or war. Some modern composers, among them Orff and Stockhausen, make use of the slit drum.

Slonimsky, Nicolas

Legendary Russian-born American musicologist of manifold endeavors, author of this dictionary; b. Nikolai Leonidovich, St. Petersburg, Apr. 27, 1894; d. Los Angeles, Dec. 25, 1995. A self-described failed wunderkind, he was given his 1st piano lesson in 1900 by his illustrious maternal aunt Isabelle Vengerova (b. Minsk, Mar. 1, 1877; d. N.Y., Feb. 7, 1956). Possessed by inordinate ambition, aggravated by the endemic intellectuality of his family of both maternal and paternal branches (novelists, revolutionary poets, literary critics, university professors, translators, chessmasters, economists, mathematicians, inventors of useless artificial languages, Hebrew scholars, speculative philosophers), he became determined to excel beyond common decency in all these doctrines; as an adolescent he wrote out his future biography accordingly, setting down his death date as 1967 (he survived that date).

He enrolled in the St. Petersburg Cons. and studied harmony and orchestration with 2 pupils of Rimsky-Korsakov, Kalafati and Maximilian Steinberg; also tried unsuccessfully to engage in Russian journalism. After the Revolution he made his way south; was a rehearsal pianist at the Kiev Opera, where he took some composition lessons with Glière (1919); then was in Yalta (1920), where he earned his living as a piano accompanist to displaced Russian singers, and as an instructor at a dilapi-

943

dated Yalta Cons.; then proceeded to Turkey, Bulgaria, and Paris, where he became secretary and piano-pounder to Serge Koussevitzky. In 1923 he went to the U.S.; became coach in the opera dept. of the Eastman School of Music in Rochester, N.Y., where he took an opportunity to study some more composition with the visiting prof. Selim Palmgren, and conducting with Albert Coates; in 1925 he was again with Koussevitzky in Paris and Boston, but was fired for insubordination in 1927.

He learned to speak polysyllabic English and began writing music articles for the *Boston Evening Transcript* and the *Christian Science Monitor*; he ran a monthly column of musical anecdotes of questionable authenticity in the *Étude*; taught theory at the Malkin Cons. in Boston and at the Boston Cons.; conducted the Pierian Sodality at Harvard Univ. (1927–29) and the Apollo Chorus (1928–30). In 1927 he organized the Chamber Orch. of Boston with the purpose of presenting modern works; with it he gave 1st performances of works by Charles Ives, Edgard Varèse, Henry Cowell, and others. He became a naturalized U.S. citizen in 1931. In 1931–32 he conducted special concerts of modern American, Cuban, and Mexican music in Paris, Berlin, and Budapest under the auspices of the Pan-American Assoc. of Composers, producing a ripple of excitement; he repeated these programs at his engagements with the Los Angeles Phil. (1932) and at the Hollywood Bowl (1933), which created such consternation that his conducting career came to a jarring halt.

From 1945 to 1947 he was by happenstance a lecturer in Slavonic languages and literatures at Harvard Univ. (the head of the dept. had died of a heart attack). In 1962–63 he traveled in Russia, Poland, Yugoslavia, Bulgaria, Rumania, Greece, and Israel under the auspices of the Office of Cultural Exchange at the U.S. State Dept., as a lecturer in native Russian, ersatz Polish, synthetic Serbo-Croatian, Russianized Bulgarian, Latinized Rumanian, archaic Greek, passable French, and tolerable German. Returning from his multinational travels, he taught variegated musical subjects at the Univ. of Calif., Los Angeles; was irretrievably retired after a triennial service (1964–67), ostensibly owing to irreversible obsolescence and recessive infantiloquy; but disdaining the inexorable statistics of the actuarial tables, he continued to agitate and even gave long-winded lecture-recitals in institutions of dubious learning.

As a composer he cultivated miniature forms, usually with a gimmick, e.g., *Studies in Black and White* for Piano (1928) in "mutually exclusive consonant counterpoint"; a song cycle, *Gravestones*, to texts from tombstones in an old cemetery in Hancock, N.H. (1945); and *Minitudes*, a collection of 50 quaquaversal piano pieces (1971–77). His only decent orch. work is *My Toy Balloon* (1942), a set of variations on a Brazilian song, which includes in the score 100 colored balloons to be exploded *fff* at the climax. He also conjured up a *Möbius Strip-Tease*, a perpetual vocal canon notated on a Möbius band to be revolved around the singer's head; it had its 1st and last performance at the Arriere-Garde Coffee Concert at UCLA, with the composer officiating at the piano non-obbligato (1965).

A priority must be conceded to him for writing the earliest singing commercials to authentic texts from *Saturday Evening Post* advertisements, among them *Make This a Day of Pepsodent, No More Shiny Nose*, and *Children Cry for Castoria* (1925). More scholarly though no less defiant of academic conventions is his *Thesaurus of Scales and Melodic Patterns* (1947), an inventory of all conceivable and inconceivable tonal combinations, culminating in a mind-boggling "Grandmother chord" containing 12 different tones and 11 different intervals. Beset by a chronic itch for novelty, he coined the term *pandiatonicism* (1937), which, *mirabile dictu*, took root and even got into reputable reference works, including the 15th ed. of the *Encyclopaedia Britannica*.

In his quest for trivial but not readily accessible information, he blundered into the muddy field of musical lexicography; publ. *Music Since 1900*, a chronology of musical events, which actually contains some beguiling serendipities (N.Y., 1937; 5th ed., 1994); took over the vacated editorship (because of the predecessor's sudden death during sleep) of *Thompson's International Cyclopedia of Music and Musicians* (4th to 8th eds., 1946–58) and accepted the editorship of the 5th, 6th, 7th, and 8th eds. of the prestigious *Baker's Biographical Dictionary of Musicians* (N.Y., 1958, 1978, 1984, 1991). He also abridged this venerable vol. into *The Concise Baker's Biographical Dictionary of Musicians* (N.Y., 1988).

Despite a publ. comment disparaging the idea, he mobilized his powers of retrospection in 1978 by preparing an autobiography, *Failed Wunderkind*, subtitled *Rueful Autopsy* (in the sense of self-observation, not dissection of the body); the publishers, deeming these titles too lugubrious, renamed it *Perfect Pitch* (N.Y., 1988). He also translated Boris de Schloezer's biography of Scriabin from the original Russian (Berkeley and Los Angeles, 1987), which was followed by his *Lectionary of Music*, a compendium of short articles on music (1988).

His other writings include *Music of Latin America* (1945); *The Road to Music*, ostensibly for children (1947); *A Thing or Two About Music* (1948; inconsequential; also lacking an index); *Lexicon of Musical Invective*, a random

collection of pejorative reviews of musical masterpieces (1952); numerous articles for encyclopedias; also a learned paper, *Sex and the Music Librarian*, valuable for its painstaking research; the paper was delivered by proxy, to tumultuous cachinnations, at a symposium of the Music Library Assoc., at Chapel Hill, N.C., (1988); it was subsequently publ. in the *Newsletter of the Inst. for Studies in American Music* (Brooklyn). His nephew, Sergei (Mikhailovich) Slonimsky (b. Leningrad, Aug. 12, 1932), is a greatly talented composer.

slow bounce. In jazz drumming, putting a DRAG stroke on every beat.

slur. A curved line under or over 2 or more notes, signifying that they are to be played LEGATO. In bowed string music the slur signifies a group to be played on one bow; in vocal music the slur unites notes to be sung in one breath; the notes so sung are also called a slur. In piano writing, a slur can indicate the extension of a musical phrase, often suggesting a slight crescendo followed by a corresponding diminuendo. See also TIE.

slurred melody. One in which 2 or more tones are sung to 1 syllable; opposed to *syllabic* melody.

Sly. Opera by Wolf-Ferrari, 1927, 1st performed in Milan, based on Shakespeare's *The Taming of the Shrew*. Christopher Sly is found in a drunken stupor by the lord of the mansion, who decides to play a trick on him by ordering his servants to treat him like an honored guest before returning him to reality. All kinds of Shakespearean imbroglios result from this situation; the score is vivacious.

small octave. See "The Clefs," p. xxiii.

smaniante (It.). In an impetuous, passionate style.

smanioso (It.). Frantically.

Smetana, Bedřich

Great Bohemian composer; b. Leitomischl, Mar. 2, 1824; d. Prague, May 12, 1884. His talent manifested itself very early, and although his father had misgivings about music as a profession, he taught his son violin; Bedřich also had piano lessons with a local teacher, making his 1st public appearance at the age of 6 (1830). After the family moved to Jindřichův Hradec in 1831, he studied with the organist František Ikavec; continued his academic studies in Jihlava and Německý Brod, then entered the Classical Grammar School in Prague in 1839; also had piano lessons with Jan

Batka, and led a string quartet for which he composed several works.

His lack of application to his academic studies led his father to send him to the gymnasium in Plzeň, but he soon devoted himself to giving concerts and composing. He met a friend of his school days there, Kateřina Kolářová, whom he followed to Prague in 1843; he was accepted as a theory pupil of Kolářová's piano teacher, Josef Proksch, at the Music Inst. To pay for his lessons Bedřich Kittl, director of the Prague Cons., recommended Smetana for the position of music teacher to the family of Count

Leopold Thun. He took up his position in Jan. 1844, and for 3 1/2 years worked earnestly in the count's service; also continued to study theory and to compose.

Bent on making a name for himself as a concert pianist, Smetana left the count's service in the summer of 1847 and planned a tour of Bohemia; however, his only concert in Plzeň proved a financial disaster, and he abandoned his tour and returned to Prague, where he eked out a meager existence. He wrote to Liszt, asking him to find a publisher for his op. 1, the *6 Characteristic Pieces* for Piano; Liszt was impressed with the score, accepted Smetana's dedication, and found a publisher. In 1848 Smetana established a successful piano school, and on Aug. 27, 1849, he married Kolářová. In 1850 he became court pianist to the abdicated Emperor Ferdinand.

His reputation as a pianist, especially as an interpreter of Chopin, grew, but his compositions made little impression. The death of his children and the poor health of his wife (who had tuberculosis) affected him deeply; he set out for Sweden in 1856; gave a number of successful piano recitals in Göteborg, where he remained. He soon opened his own school and became active as a choral conductor. His wife joined him in 1857, but the cold climate exacerbated her condition; when her health declined, they decided to return to Prague (1859), but she died en route, in Dresden, on Apr. 19, 1859. Stricken with grief, Smetana returned to Göteborg. Before his wife's death, he had composed the symphonic poems *Richard III* and *Valdštýnv tabor* (Wallenstein's Camp); he now began work on a 3rd, *Hakan Jarl.*

On July 10, 1860, he married Betty Ferdinandi, which proved an unhappy union. During Smetana's sojourn in Sweden, Austria granted political autonomy to Bohemia (1860) and musicians and poets of the rising generation sought to establish an authentic Bohemian voice in the arts. Agitation for the erection of a national theater in Prague arose; although earlier attempts to write operas in a Bohemian vein had been made by such composers as František Škroup and Jiří Macourek, their works were undistinguished.

Smetana believed the time was ripe for him to make his mark in Prague, and he returned there in May 1861. However, when the Provisional Theater opened on Nov. 18, 1862, its administration proved sadly unimaginative, and Smetana contented himself with the conductorship of the Hlahol Choral Soc., teaching, and writing music

criticism. In his articles he condemned the poor musical standards prevailing at the Provisional Theater. In 1862–63 he composed his 1st opera, *Braniboři v Čechách* (The Brandenburgers in Bohemia), conducting its successful premiere at the Provisional Theater on Jan. 5, 1866. His next opera, *Prodaná nevěsta* (The Bartered Bride), proved a failure at its premiere in Prague under his direction on May 30, 1866, but eventually it was accorded a niche in the operatic repertoire at home and abroad.

Smetana became conductor of the Provisional Theater in 1866. He immediately set out to reform its administration and to raise its musical standards. For the cornerstone laying of the National Theater on May 16, 1868, he conducted the 1st performance of his tragic opera *Dalibor*, which was criticized as an attempt to Wagnerize the Bohemian national opera. In 1871, when there was talk of crowning Emperor Franz Josef as King of Bohemia, Smetana considered producing his opera *Libuše* for the festivities; however, no coronation took place and the work was withheld.

Hoping for a popular success, he composed the comic opera *Dvě vdovy* (The 2 Widows), which proved to be just that at its premiere under his direction on Mar. 27, 1874. Smetana's success, however, was short-lived. By the autumn of 1874 he was deaf and had to resign as conductor of the Provisional Theater. In spite of the bitter years to follow, marked by increasingly poor health, family problems, and financial hardship, he continued to compose. Between 1874 and 1879 he produced his 6 orch. masterpieces collectively known as *Má vlast* (My Country): *Vyšehrad* (referring to a rock over the river Vltava, near Prague, the traditional seat of the ancient kings of Bohemia), *Vltava* (Moldau), *Šárka* (a wild valley, near Prague, depicting the legendary story of the warrior woman Šárka), *Z Českych luhů a hájů* (From Bohemia's Woods and Fields), *Tabor* (the medieval town in southern Bohemia, the seat of the Hussites, and thus the traditional symbol of freedom and religion; the work is based on the chorale Ye Who Are God's Warriors), and *Blaník* (the mountain that served as a place of refuge for the Hussites; the previously mentioned chorale serves as the foundation of the work).

From 1876 dates his famous String Quartet in E Minor, subtitled *Z mého života* (From My Life), which he described as a "remembrance of my life and the catastrophe of complete deafness." His opera *Hubička* (The Kiss) was successfully premiered in Prague on Nov. 7, 1876. It was followed by the opera *Tajemství* (The Secret), which was heard for the 1st time on Sept. 18, 1878. For the opening of the new National Theater in Prague on June 11, 1881, his opera *Libuše* was finally given its premiere performance. The ailing Smetana attended the opening night and was accorded sustained applause. His last opera, *Čertova stěna* (The Devil's Wall), was a failure at its 1st hearing in Prague on Oct. 29, 1882.

By this time Smetana's health had been completely undermined by the ravages of syphilis, the cause of his deafness. His mind eventually gave way and he was confined to an asylum. At his death in 1884 the nation was plunged into a state of mourning. The funeral cortège passed the National Theater as Smetana was carried to his final resting place in the Vyšehrad cemetery.

Smetana was the founder of the Czech national school of composition, and it was through his efforts that Czech national opera came of age. Although the national element is predominant in much of his music, a highly personal style of expression is found in his String Quartet No. 1 and in many of his piano pieces. Outside his homeland he remains best known for *The Bartered Bride*, *Má vlast*, and the aforementioned string quartet. The centenary of his death in 1984 was marked by numerous performances of his music in Czechoslovakia and a reaffirmation of his revered place in the history of his nation. In addition to the operatic and orch. works discussed above, Smetana contributed many works, mostly secular, to the well-established Czech choral tradition. He also composed a 2nd string quartet (1882–83), a piano trio (1855), and numerous smaller-scaled piano pieces.

Smiles. Song by Lee Robert, 1917, to cheer up American soldiers in military camps. It sold over 3 million copies of sheet music and was interpolated in numerous movie musicals as a theme song.

sminuendo (It.). DIMINUENDO.

sminuito (It.). More softly.

Smith, Bessie (Elizabeth), beloved African-American blues, jazz, and vaudeville singer, frequently and accurately billed as the "Empress of the Blues"; b. Chattanooga, Tenn., Apr. 15, 1894; d. Clarksville, Miss., Sept. 26, 1937 (from injuries sustained in an automobile accident near Coahana, Miss., and not attended to quickly enough for racist reasons). Born to a wretchedly poor family, she joined Rainey's Rabbit Foot Minstrels (blues pioneer Ma Rainey was her teacher) in 1912 and developed a style of singing that rapidly brought her fame. Her 1st record, *Down Hearted Blues*, sold 800,000 copies in 1923; in all, she made over 200 recordings; also appeared in the film *St. Louis Blues* (1929). Her last years were marred by alcoholism. She was a large, impressive woman—5'9" and weighing over 200 pounds—and had a powerful voice to match; the excellence of her

Bessie Smith, c. 1928

COURTESY SONY RECORDS

vocal equipment, along with her natural expressive qualities and improvisatory abilities, combined to make her the consummate blues singer of her time.

Smith, Gregg, American conductor and composer; b. Chicago, Aug. 21, 1931. He studied composition with Leonard Stein, Lukas Foss, and Ray Moreman and conducting with Fritz Zweig at the Univ. of Calif. at Los Angeles (M.A., 1956). In 1955 in Los Angeles he founded the Gregg Smith Singers, a chamber choir, with which he toured and recorded extensively; from 1970 he was active with it in N.Y. He also taught at Ithaca College, the State Univ. of N.Y. at Stony Brook, the Peabody Cons. of Music in Baltimore, Barnard College, and the Manhattan School of Music in N.Y. His repertoire extends from early music to works by contemporary American composers. He ed. the Gregg Smith Choral Series; wrote much vocal music, including 2 operas, choral works, songs, and pieces for chamber orch.

Smith, John Stafford. See STAR-SPANGLED BANNER, THE.

Smith, Kate (Kathryn Elizabeth), famous American singer of popular music; b. Greenville, Va., May 1, 1907; d.

Raleigh, N.C., June 17, 1986. As a child she sang in church socials and later for the troops in Army camps in the Washington, D.C., area during World War I. Although she had no formal training in music, she landed a part in the musical Honeymoon Lane in Atlantic City, N.J., in 1926, and then appeared in it on Broadway; subsequently sang in the Broadway musicals *Hit the Deck* (1927) and *Flying High* (1930). She began singing on her own radio show in 1931, opening her 1st broadcast with *When the Moon Comes over the Mountain*, which thereafter served as her theme song. In 1938 she introduced Irving Berlin's *God Bless America*, which she immortalized in innumerable subsequent performances; when the original MS for the song was discovered in Las Vegas in 1990, the Kate Smith God Bless America Foundation of N.Y. put it up for sale for $295,000.

Thanks to her enormous popularity, she raised more money for U.S. War Bonds during World War II than any other artist. She starred in her own television show (1950–55; 1960), and continued to make guest appearances until 1975. President Reagan awarded her the U.S. Medal of Freedom in 1982. Smith was one of the most successful singers of popular music in her time. During her lengthy career she made over 15,000 radio broadcasts, introducing over 1,000 songs; also recorded nearly 3,000 songs.

Smith, Willie "the Lion" (William Henry Joseph Bonaparte Bertholoff), remarkable African-American jazz pianist and composer; b. Goshen, N.Y., Nov. 24, 1897; d. N.Y., Apr. 18, 1973. He attended Howard Univ. in Washington, D.C., and studied music privately with Hans Steinke. After serving in the U.S. Army in World War I, he settled in Harlem, where he established himself as one of the great "stride" pianists. He toured Europe several times, and toured in Africa in 1949–50. His own compositions (*Fingerbuster, Echoes of Spring, Portrait of the Duke*) had an authenticity that described perfectly the atmosphere of Harlem jazz piano between the 2 World Wars. Duke Ellington dedicated his *Portrait of a Lion* to him.

Smoke Gets in Your Eyes. Song by Kern, 1933, from the musical *Roberta*. It was tremendously successful and was incorporated in the film biography of Kern, *Till the Clouds Roll By* (1946).

smorendo (It.). Dying away.

smorfioso (It.). With affected expression, coquettishly.

smorzando (It.). Dying away, DIMINUENDO, MORENDO.

Smyth, (Dame) **Ethel** (Mary), eminent English composer; b. London, Apr. 22, 1858; d. Woking, Surrey, May 8, 1944. She became a pupil of Reinecke and Jadassohn at the Leipzig Cons. in 1877 but soon turned to Heinrich von Herzogenberg for her principal training, following him to Berlin; her String Quintet was performed in Leipzig in 1884. She returned to London in 1888; presented her orch. Serenade and an overture, *Antony and Cleopatra* (both 1890).

Her prestige as a serious composer rose considerably with the presentation of her Mass for solo voices, chorus, and orch. at the Albert Hall (1893). After that she devoted her energies to the theater. Her 1st opera, *Fantasio*, to her own libretto in German, after Alfred de Musset's play, was produced in Weimar (1898); this was followed by *Der Wald* (Berlin, 1902), also to her own German libretto; it was produced in London in the same year, and in N.Y. by the Metropolitan Opera (1903). Her next opera, *The Wreckers*, was her most successful work; written originally to a French libretto, *Les Naufrageurs*, it was 1st produced in a German version as *Strandrecht* (Leipzig, 1906); the composer herself trans. it into English, and it was staged in London in 1909; the score was revised some years later and produced at Sadler's Wells, London (1939). She further wrote a comic opera, *The Boatswain's Mate* (London, 1916); a 1-act opera, described as a "dance-dream," *Fête galante* (Birmingham, 1923); and the opera *Entente cordiale* (Bristol, 1926).

Other works are a Concerto for Violin, Horn, and Orch. (London, 1927); *The Prison* for Soprano, Bass Chorus, and Orch. (London, 1931); 2 String Quartets (1884; 1902–12); Sonata for Cello and Piano (1887); Sonata for Violin and Piano (1887); 2 Trios for Violin, Oboe, and Piano (1927); choral pieces, including *Hey Nonny No* for Chorus and Orch. (1911), and *Sleepless Dreams* for Chorus and Orch. (1912); songs; etc.

Her music never relinquished strong German characteristics, in the general idiom as well as in the treatment of dramatic situations on the stage. At the same time she was a believer in English national music and its potentialities. She was a militant leader for women's suffrage in England, for which cause she wrote *The March of the Women* (1911), the battle song of the WSPU. After suffrage was granted, her role in the movement was officially acknowledged; in 1922 she was made a Dame Commander of the Order of the British Empire. She publ. a number of books in London, mostly autobiographical in nature; also some humorous essays and reminiscences: *A 3-Legged Tour in Greece* (1927); *A*

Final Burning of Boats (1928); *Female Pipings in Eden* (1934); *Beecham and Pharaoh* (1935); *Inordinate (?) Affection* (1936).

snare drum (U.K., side drum; Ger. *Trommel*; Fr. *tambour*; It. *tamburo*). A smaller cylindrical drum of wood or metal, across the lower head of which are stretched several gut strings or strands of metal wire (snares), whose rattling against the head reinforces and alters the tone. The upper head is struck alternately or simultaneously with 2 drumsticks. This is the most commonly used drum in symphonic bands and scores.

Snow Maiden, The (*Snegurotchka*). Opera by Rimsky-Korsakov, 1882, 1st produced in St. Petersburg. The Snow Maiden is the delicate offspring of incompatible parents, Frost and Spring. At the peril of her life she must not let warmth, physical or emotional, enter her heart. A young villager is captivated by her icy beauty and follows her wherever she goes. Her mother warns her to keep away from the destructive rays of the sun as summer approaches. She ignores her warnings, and melts away like spring snow. The opera is one of the most poetic productions of the Russian operatic stage, but it is rarely, if ever, staged outside Russia.

so rasch wie möglich (Ger.). As fast as possible.

soap opera. Radio and (later) television serials of continuous episodes from the life of an American family or, more recently, the lives of good-looking, well-dressed, and melodramatic individuals in various states of singlehood or marriage, separation or divorce, pregnancy or abortion, drug addiction or criminality, sexual certainty or ambiguity, economic feast or famine, and physical illness or psychological disorder. The term "opera" in nonmusical genres is found in Westerns (horse opera); the term *soap opera* derives from the fact that soap manufacturers sponsored most of these serials in early years. At one time organ music accompanied every moment of menace with chromatic runs, diminished and augmented chords, and whole-tone scales; parodies often emphasize this element. At present music is used environmentally, such as in nightclub, dancing, and bar scenes.

soave (It., suavely). Gently, sweetly, softly, flowingly.

Sobre las Olas (Over the Waves). Mexican waltz by Juventino Rosas, 1888. It became a perennial favorite all over the world.

socialist realism

~~~ ~~~ ~~~ ~~~ ~~~

The official USSR aesthetic espoused in 1932, addressing the artist's responsibility to emphasize a real world inclined toward a socialist future. The former Soviet Union was the 1st modern state that attempted to regulate its art, literature, drama, and music according to explicitly defined ideological principles. Since the structure of the Soviet government was derived from the doctrine of the dictatorship of the proletariat, a Russian Association of Proletarian Musicians (RAPM) arrogated to itself the right to dictate the proper musical forms suitable for the consumption of proletarian masses. It was disbanded by the Soviet government in 1932 after its failure to help in the creative formulation of mass music became evident.

With the rise of the national consciousness in the component republics of the Soviet Union, it was realized by Soviet authorities that proletarian internationalism was no longer sufficient to serve as an enduring ideology. Surviving masters of old Russian music had to be accepted as representatives of the Russian masses; their classical precursors were glorified as exponents of progressive ideals consonant with the new Socialist reality of the Soviet era. Soviet composers were urged to create an art national in form and socialist in content, a method which eventually became known as socialist realism.

Stylistically socialist realism requires the retention of the tonal system of composition, broadly based on the folk modalities of Russian songs and the native chants of the other republics. The doctrine of socialist realism concentrates on the national development of operas and secular oratorios, in which revolutionary ideals can be expressed verbally as well as musically. The Aristotelian formula of catharsis through pity and terror underlies the librettos of most Soviet operas and the scenarios of most Soviet ballets. Patriotic subjects are particularly recommended; they lend themselves readily to the tripartite formula that opens with a scene of happiness, goes through a period of sudden horror, and concludes in a victory over adverse circumstances. The *Leningrad Sym.* of Shostakovich is a remarkable example of this Aristotelian construction, particularly so because it was written during continued retreats of the Soviet armies before the Nazis, and yet its finale predicts victory. The classical tradition of the TIERCE DE PICARDIE, with its major cadence, suits perfectly the Soviet preference for major keys. Anatoly Lunacharsky, 1st Commissar of Education of the USSR, explained the political advantage of major keys by comparing them with the convictions of the Bolshevik party, while minor keys were reflecting the introvert pessimism of the Mensheviks.

The doctrine of socialist realism does not preclude lyrical expression or individual allusions. Shostakovich uses the monogram D-S-C-H, corresponding in German notation to the notes D, E-flat, C, and B as the main subject of his 10th Sym. However, many among Soviet composers—even as eminent as Miaskovsky—were often criticized by the exponents of socialist realism for their musical morbidity, anxiety, and solipsistic introspection. In the domain of rhythm, marching time is a natural medium for the optimistic attributes of socialist realism, but it is reserved for its proper position in the finale of a sym. or the final chorus of an opera. In this respect socialist realism merely continues the old tradition of Russian music. Even such melancholy composers as Tchaikovsky and Rachmaninoff excelled in triumphant march-time movements.

In authoritative Soviet declarations, socialist realism is opposed to *formalism*, which is described as an artificial separation of form from content and the excessive cultivation of purely external technical devices, particularly atonality, polytonality, and dodecaphony. The statutes of the Union of Soviet Composers provide a specific guidance to Soviet composers for their ideological concepts:

> The greatest attention of Soviet composers must be given to the victorious progressive foundations of reality, to the heroic and luminous beauty that distinguishes the spiritual world of Soviet man, which must be incarnated in musical images full of life-asserting force. Socialist realism demands an implacable opposition against antisocial modernistic movements, expressive of the decadence and corruption of contemporary bourgeois art, against genuflection and slavish obsequiousness before the culture of the bourgeoisie.

With the Soviet vision of socialist realism a not-too-distant memory, one may look to the People's Republic of China for a communist country's attempts to deal politically with musical culture. In Red China's relatively short history (founded in 1949) there have been dramatic shifts of official policy, most notably the Cultural Revolution of the 1960s, which denounced Western and traditional Chinese music equally; this may be compared with attempts to assimilate Western classical music, most famously the *Yellow River Concerto* for Piano and Orch., officially written by a committee; or one may look at the adaptations of Peking opera with proletariat-appropriate titles as *The Red Detachment of Women* and *Taking Tiger Mountain by Strategy*.

Socrate. Symphonic drama by Satie, 1920, for high solo voices and instruments, premiered in Paris. The texts are French translations of excerpts from Plato's dialogues concerning his great teacher, including the description of his forced suicide.

soffocato (*suffocato*; It.). Muffled, damped; choked.

soft pedal. The left pedal on the piano, which reduces and changes the sound by shifting the keyboard so that (1) only 2 of the 3 strings for each note (i.e., *course*) in the middle piano register are struck by the hammers, and (2) only 1 of the 2 strings of each course in the bass register are struck. In the 19th century the soft pedal could shift in 2 stages, with the corresponding results; Beethoven refers to this as *due corde* and *una corda*, with the full release of the pedal indicated by *tre corde*.

soggetto (It.). A subject or theme, as in contrapuntal and fugal writing.

soggetto cavato (It., excavated subject). A curious form in which the subject is derived from the letters, syllables, or vowels in a name or other source; B–A–C–H is a typical modern example. A case where only vowels have been "excavated" is the hymn *Ut queant laxis*, which forms the syllables of hexachord of Guido d'Arezzo (Ut, Re, Mi, Fa, Sol, La). Josquin Des Prez wrote the *Missa Hercules Dux Ferrarie* for a patron. The vowels in the dedication here are *e, u, e, u, e, a, i, e*, which correspond to the solmization syllables Re, Ut, Re, Ut, Re, Fa, Mi, and Re (i.e., D–C–D–C–D–F–E–D). Derived subjects have been used by several modern composers applying equalizations to the complete alphabet. Castelnuovo-Tedesco devised birthday greeting cards in which the name of the recipient was derived by arranging several successive alphabets in English corresponding to the chromatic scale. This method generates melodic patterns at angular intervals.

sognando (It.). Dreamily.

Soh. Stands for Sol, in TONIC SOL-FA.

Soir, Le. Haydn's Sym. No. 8 in G Major (1761), a sequel to *Le Midi*, his Sym. No. 7. Sometimes called *La Tempesta*; the music is not too tempestuous, however, and the evening mood is unperturbed.

Sol. The 5th degree of the scale of Guido d'Arezzo, corresponding to the dominant of the diatonic scale.

solenne (It.). Solemnly, in a lofty style.

Soler (Ramos), **Antonio** (Francisco Javier José), important Catalan composer and organist; b. Olot, Gerona (baptized), Dec. 3, 1729; d. El Escorial, near Madrid, Dec. 20, 1783. He entered the Montserrat monastery choir school in 1736, where his mentors were the maestro Benito Esteve and the organist Benito Valls. About 1750 he was made maestro de capilla in Lérida; in 1752, was ordained a subdeacon and also became a member of the Jeronymite monks in El Escorial, taking the habit, and then being professed in 1753; was made maestro de capilla in 1757. He also pursued studies with José de Nebra and Domenico Scarlatti.

Soler was a prolific composer of both sacred and secular vocal music, as well as instrumental music. Among his works are 9 Masses, 5 Requiems, 60 psalms, 13 Magnificats, 14 litanies, 28 Lamentations, 5 motets, and other sacred works; 132 villancicos (1752–78); 120 keyboard sonatas; 6 quintets for string quartet and organ (1776); *6 conciertos de dos organos obligados*; liturgical organ pieces. His writings include *Llave de la modulación, y antigüedades de la müsica en que se trata del fundamento necessario para saber modular: Theórica, y prática para el más claro conocimiento de qualquier especie de figuras, desde el tiempo de Juan de Muris, hasta hoy, con albunos cánones enigmáticos, y sus resoluciones* (Madrid, 1762), *Satisfacción a los reparos precisos hechos por D. Antonio Roel del Rio, a la Llave de la modulación* (Madrid, 1765), *Carta escrita a un amigo en que le da parte de un diálogo ultimamente publicado contra su Llave de la modulación* (Madrid, 1766), and *Combinación de Monedas y Cálculo manifiesto contra el Libro anónimo inititulado: Correspondencia de la Moneda de Cataluña a la de Castilla* (Barcelona, 1771).

Soler, Vicente Martin y. See MARRIAGE OF FIGARO, THE.

sol-fa. 1. TONIC SOL-FA. 2. Solmization, and the syllables sung in it.

solfège (Fr.; It. *solfeggio*). A vocal exercise either on 1 vowel, on the solmization syllables (SOL-FA), or to words. The term has expanded to include pedagogy in ear training, vocalization, and a study of clefs, meters, and rhythms.

solito (It.). Accustomed, habitual. *Al solito*, as usual.

solmization. A method of teaching the scales and intervals by syllables, the invention of which is ascribed to Guido d'Arezzo. It was based on the hexachord, or 6-tone scale; the 1st 6 tones of the major scale (c, d, e, f, g, a) were named *Ut, Re, Mi, Fa, Sol, La*. The 7th syllable *Si*, for the leading tone, was added during the 17th century; about the same time, the name *Ut* for *C* was changed to *Do*, except in France.

solo (It., alone). A piece or passage for a single voice or instrument, or one in which 1 voice or instrument predominates. In orch.l scores it marks a passage where 1 instrument takes a leading part. In a 2-hand arrangement of a piano concerto, *solo* marks the entrances of the solo piano. *Violino solo*, violin alone; 1st violin (accompanied).

solo pitch. SCORDATURA.

solo quartet. 1. A quartet consisting of 4 singers (4 solo voices). 2. A piece or passage in 4 parts for 4 singers. 3. A nonconcerted piece for 4 instruments, 1 of which has a leading part.

Solovox. See HAMMOND, LAURENS.

Solti, (Sir) **George** (György), eminent Hungarian-born English conductor; b. Budapest, Oct. 21, 1912. He began to study the piano when he was 6, making his 1st public appearance in Budapest when he was 12; at 13 he enrolled there at the Franz Liszt Academy of Music, studying piano with Dohnányi and, briefly, with Bartók; took composition courses with Kodály. He graduated at the age of 18 and was engaged by the Budapest Opera as a *répétiteur*; also served as an assistant to Bruno Walter (1935) and Toscanini (1936, 1937) at the Salzburg Festivals.

In 1938 he made a brilliant conducting debut at the Budapest Opera with *Le nozze di Figaro*; but the wave of anti-Semitism in Hungary under the reactionary military rule forced him to leave Budapest (he was Jewish). In 1939 he went to Switzerland, where he was active mainly as a concert pianist; in 1942 he won the Concours International de Piano in Geneva; finally, in 1944, he was engaged to conduct concerts with the orch. of the Swiss Radio. In 1946 the American occupation authorities in Munich invited him to conduct *Fidelio* at the Bavarian State Opera; his success led to his appointment as its Generalmusikdirektor, a position he held from 1946 to 1952. In 1952 he became Generalmusikdirektor in Frankfurt, serving as director of the Opera and conductor of the Museumgesellschaft Concerts.

He made his U.S. debut with the San Francisco Opera, conducting *Elektra* (1953); later conducted the Chicago Sym. Orch., the N.Y. Phil., and at the Metropolitan Opera in N.Y., where he made his 1st appearance in late 1960, with *Tannhäuser*. He was then engaged as music director of the Los Angeles Phil., but the appointment collapsed when the board of trustees refused to grant him full powers in musical and administrative policy. In 1960–61 he was music director of the Dallas Sym. Orch. In the meantime he made his Covent Garden debut in London in 1959; in 1961 he assumed the post of music director of the Royal Opera House there, retaining it with great distinction until 1971. In 1969 he became music director of the Chicago Sym. Orch., and it was in that capacity that he achieved a triumph as an interpreter and orch. builder, so that the "Chicago sound" became a synonym for excellence.

Under his direction the Chicago Sym. Orch. became one of the most celebrated orchs. in the world. He took it to Europe for the 1st time in 1971, eliciting glowing praise from critics and audiences; subsequently led it on a number of acclaimed tours there; also took it to N.Y. for regular appearances at Carnegie Hall. He held the additional posts of music adviser of the Paris Opéra (1971–73) and music director of the Orch. de Paris (1972–75), which he took on

a tour of China in 1974; he served as principal conductor and artistic director of the London Phil. from 1979 to 1983; was then accorded the title of conductor emeritus. During all these years he retained his post with the Chicago Sym. Orch. while continuing his appearances as a guest conductor with European orchs.

In 1983 he conducted the *Ring* cycle at the Bayreuth Festival, in commemoration of the 100th anniversary of the death of Richard Wagner. Solti retained his prestigious position with the Chicago Sym. Orch. until the close of the 100th anniversary season in 1990–91, and subsequently held the title of Laureate Conductor. In 1992–93 he assumed the post of artistic director at the Salzburg Music Festival. In 1968 he was made an honorary Commander of the Order of the British Empire; in 1971 he was named an honorary Knight Commander of the Order of the British Empire. In 1972 he became a British subject and was knighted.

Solti is generally acknowledged as a superlative interpreter of the symphonic and operatic repertoire. He is renowned for his performances of Wagner, Verdi, Mahler, R. Strauss, and other Romantic masters; he also conducts notable performances of Bartók, Stravinsky, Schoenberg, and other composers of the 20th century. He showed himself an enlightened disciplinarian and a master of orch. psychology, so that he could gain and hold the confidence of the players while demanding from them the utmost in professional performance. His recordings received innumerable awards; his international reputation was secured through his complete stereo recording of Wagner's *Ring*, the 1st.

sombre (Fr.). Dark, veiled, obscure.

Sombrero de tres picos, El (The 3-Cornered Hat). Ballet by de Falla, 1919, 1st performed in London by the Diaghilev Ballet. The confusing picaresque story centers on the governor of a Spanish province who tries to seduce the comely wife of a local miller and carelessly leaves the emblem of his authority, a Napoleonic 3-cornered hat, on the premises. All kinds of nonsensical peripeteia ensue. The music sparkles with Spanish rhythms.

Some Enchanted Evening. Song by Rodgers and Hammerstein, 1949, from their musical *South Pacific*.

Somebody Loves Me. An engaging song by Gershwin, 1924, written for that season's ed. of the revue called *George White's Scandals*, named for its producer. The same 3 magic words were used as an incipit in an 1892 song by Hattie Starr, the 1st woman composer on Tin Pan Alley.

Some Day I'll Find You. Song by N. Coward, 1930. It served as the theme song of his play *Private Lives*.

Something for the Boys. Musical by C. Porter, 1943. Three cousins (2 female, 1 boy) inherit a huge Texas ranch. One of the young women takes a liking to one of the airmen at a nearby military base. She discovers that she can intercept radio messages in the Carborundum filling in her tooth. This inspires the commanding officer to install similar receiving sets in the teeth of his men. Among the funny songs in the score is *When We're Home on the Range*.

Sometime. Operetta by Friml, 1918. The sentimental plot deals with a quarrel between lovers caused by jealousy. There is a happy ending. Among the best songs in the score are *Keep on Smiling* and *The Tune You Can't Forget*.

Somewhere Over the Rainbow. Song by Arlen and Harburg, 1939, made extraordinarily popular by Judy Garland in the film *The Wizard of Oz*.

sommesso, -a (It.). Subdued.

sommo, -a (It.). Utmost, highest, greatest, extreme. *Con sommo espressione*, with intensest feeling; used by Liszt.

son (Fr.). Sound; tone.

son (Sp., sound). Generic name of indigenous songs of Cuba and neighboring islands, reflecting the influence of African rhythms, and set usually in a strongly accented 2/4 time. This ZAPATEADO dance type allows great freedom with contrapuntal embellishments; it includes texts in couplet form on the subject of beauty and guitar accompaniment with RASGUEADO strumming.

son bouché (Fr., stopped note; Ger. *gestopft*; It. *chiuso*). Placing the hand tightly inside the horn bell so that the expected pitch is transposed a semitone higher and the tone is altered; the symbol + is placed over such pitches; similar to CUIVRÉ.

son concomitant (Fr., attendant sound). Overtone.

son d'echo (Fr.). On the horn, an echolike sound.

son et lumière. A spectacle involving sound and light, originating in France about 1950 and therefore usually known under the French name. The idea is credited to Robert Houdin, grandson of the magician Houdini, while he was curator of the chateau at Chambourg, France. The text of a typical son-et-lumière spectacle relates to the history of the monument around which it is enacted. Whenever possible the producers try to record realistic sounds such as cannon fire from an actual piece of artillery from the time of Louis XIV, the shouts of a crowd, etc. A special score, often of electronic sounds, enhances the spectacle. Because of the authenticity of the narrative and careful research, the spectacles also have educational value. Since 1960 such productions have been staged at the Tower of London, with its grim background of imprisonment and execution, Schonbrünn Palace in Vienna, the jubilee celebrations in Persepolis in Iran, the Acropolis in Athens, Napoleon's tomb in Paris, and Independence Hall in Philadelphia.

son étouffé (Fr., stewed sound). On wind instruments, a stifled sound.

son harmonique (Fr.). Harmonic.

sonabile (It.). Sounding, resounding, sonorous, resonant.

sonagli (It.). Harness bell-rattle (Prokofiev, *Lieutenant Kijé*).

sonare (*suonare*; It.). Play; sound.

sonare a libro aperto (It., play from an open book). Play at sight.

sonare alla mente (It., play from the mind). Play at sight.

sonata (It.). An instrumental composition in 3 or 4 extended movements contrasted in theme, tempo, and mood; usually for a solo instrument with accompaniment or chamber ensemble.

sonata a tre (It.). Trio sonata.

sonata da camera (It.). Chamber sonata, for 1 or more solo instruments and basso continuo, with several dance movements in the manner of a Baroque SUITE, often with a prefatory movement. In the later Baroque the term replaced SONATA DA CHIESA and became less specific in structure.

sonata da chiesa (It.). Church sonata, not necessarily religious in connotation; it is a 4-part work in alternating slow and fast movements. It is different from the SONATA DA CAMERA (see above entry). The sonata da chiesa was a favorite form of early Baroque composers, but it gradually vanished as a separate type of composition in the 18th century.

sonata form. A structure or procedure usually used for 1st movements of Classic and Romantic syms., sonatas, and chamber works; it may be used for other movements as well. The sonata form fuses binary and ternary forms; from binary, sonata form took the division at the piece's halfway point, with its repeat signs; the 2nd half's beginning in the dominant or a key other than the tonic; and the return to the tonic by piece's end; from the ternary it took the tripartite form of the ABA structure and renamed the 3 parts EXPOSITION, DEVELOPMENT, and RECAPITULATION. The essential difference between the exposition and recapitulation is that while the exposition ends in a nontonic key, the recapitulation "repeats" the exposition but adjusts it harmonically so that it will end in the tonic key. Sonata form is also known as *sonata allegro form* and *1st movement form*.

sonata-concerto form. A combination of sonata form with the RITORNELLO procedure.

sonata-rondo form. A rondo-form movement in at least 7 sections, where the central episode (e.g., *C* in ABA-CABA) functions as a DEVELOPMENT section; and, while the initial B section emphasizes a key other than the tonic, the repeat of B is adjusted or simply transposed into the tonic.

sonatille (*sonatille galante*; Fr.). Brief instrumental piece for musette and bass.

sonatina (Fr. *sonatine*; Ger. *Sonatine*). A short sonata in 2 or 3 (rarely 4) movements, the 1st in an abbreviated SONATA FORM.

Sondheim, Stephen (Joshua), brilliant American composer and lyricist; b. N.Y., Mar. 22, 1930. Of an affluent family, he received his academic education in private

Stephen Sondheim, c. 1960

COURTESY FRANK DRIGGS COLLECTION

schools; composed a school musical at the age of 15. He then studied music at Williams College, where he wrote the book, lyrics, and music for a couple of college shows; graduated magna cum laude in 1950. In quest of higher musical learning, he went to Princeton Univ., where he took lessons in modernistic complexities with Milton Babbitt and acquired sophisticated techniques of composition.

He made his mark on Broadway when he wrote the lyrics for Bernstein's *West Side Story* (1957). His 1st success as a lyricist-composer came with the Broadway musical *A Funny Thing Happened on the Way to the Forum* (1962), which received a Tony award. His next musical, *Anyone Can Whistle* (1964), proved an interesting failure, but *Company* (1970), for which he wrote both lyrics and music, established him as a major and innovative composer and lyricist on Broadway. There followed *Follies* (1971), for which he wrote 22 pastiche songs; it was named best musical by the N.Y. Drama Critics Circle. His next production, *A Little Night Music*, with the nostalgic score harking back to the turn of the century, received a Tony, and its leading song, *Send in the Clowns*, was awarded a Grammy in 1976. This score established Sondheim's characteristic manner of treating musicals; it is almost operatic in conception, and boldly introduces dissonant counterpoint *à la moderne*.

In 1976 he produced *Pacific Overtures*, based on the story of the Western penetration into Japan in the 19th century, and composed in a stylized Japanese manner, modeled after the Kabuki theater; he also wrote the score to the musical *Sunday in the Park with George* (1982; N.Y., 1984), inspired by the painting by Georges Seurat entitled *Sunday Afternoon on the Island of La Grande Jatte*, which received the Pulitzer Prize for drama in 1985. In 1987 his musical *Into the Woods*, based on 5 Grimm fairy tales, scored a popular success on Broadway. It was followed by the disturbing musical *Assassins* (1990) and the 1994 operatic musical *Passion*.

Soneria di campana (It.). Set of bells.

Sonetti del Petrarca. Piano pieces by Liszt, 1844–45, inspired by specific sonnets of Petrarch (nos. 47, 104, 123); included in the 2nd volume of the *Années de pèlerinage*. Their execution requires the utmost capacity in varying subtle nuances, particularly in pianissimo.

sonevole (It.). Sonorous, resounding.

song. A short poem with a musical setting characterized by a structure in simple periods. There are *folk songs* (indigenous or traditional) and *art songs* (classical). The latter may be either in SONG FORM (ABA, ternary), STROPHIC FORM (successive stanzas sung to the same music, with a change if any in the final stanza), or *progressively composed* or THROUGH-COMPOSED (where the music changes to suit the text).

Singing is the most natural faculty of the human condition, which must have emerged at the dawn of civilization, even before articulate speech. A song may be limited to a single burst of pitched sound, a manifestation of sexual attraction, or a savage war cry; it may be a succession of sounds, in monotone or in varying pitch levels. Rhythm is an integral part of a song even at the most primitive stage; this intrinsic union is expressed in the Spanish language by the term MELORHYTHM, in which melos (melody) carries a definite rhythmic line. The simplest melorhythm is illustrated by the series of sounds produced by a Native American slapping himself on the mouth in rhythmic succession. Oddly enough, composers of the avant-garde who have discovered the fascination of the primitive, in music as well as in painting and poetry, are apt to cultivate elementary melorhythms as a relief from the complexity of the modern arts. It is tempting to summarize the history of human song as a progression from the primeval monotone to the explosive monumental discord of modern times and back again to the primordial molecule of song.

In a modern lexicographical sense, a song is a relatively short composition, either spontaneously generated by an anonymous mass of people or consciously devised by a musically trained person. It is a paradox of music history that the popularity of an individual song stands in an inverse ratio to the eminence of its composer. When the identity of the putative composer reaches zero, as in most popular songs, we then witness the formation of a spontaneous folk song. The wealth within such a song resides in its very brevity and its limited tonal compass. The seminal melodies in Stravinsky's *The Rite of Spring* evoke the Russian folk melorhythms; most of the melodic themes are limited to 4 or 5 successive diatonic degrees, and their rhythm is similarly restrictive. And yet this score is a landmark of modern music, thanks mainly to the polytonal harmonization of the melodic material.

Less experienced listeners often misuse the term *song* to mean any kind of musical composition, be it sym., piano piece, or opera; given the overwhelming presence of songs in popular mass media, this is not surprising, but it is an error worth correcting.

song-and-dance man. Colloquial term for a vaudeville performer who can sing and dance; several great Broadway stars began their careers in this lowly capacity.

song form. A form of composition, either vocal or instrumental, which has 3 sections and 2 themes, the 2nd (contrasting) theme occupying the 2nd section.

Song of Norway. Operetta pastiche, based on the music of Grieg. The plot is a distorted biography of Grieg in which he tries to persuade the parents of Nina Hagerup that his music has the seeds of commercial success. This he achieves by composing and playing excerpts from his piano concerto and instantaneously achieves fame and fortune. He also has personal squabbles with Nina; eventually he marries her as the real Grieg did in real life. Apart from the piano concerto, several of his piano pieces, the Peer Gynt suite, and some songs are ignominiously lacerated, macerated, and mutilated. There is also a ballet extravaganza, called *Song of Norway*. Protests of American and European music critics against the outrage availed nothing—and the show actually enjoyed a period of fetid prosperity.

Song of Orpheus, A. Work by Schuman, 1962, for cello and orch.; it was premiered in Indianapolis.

Song of Summer, A. Orch.l piece by Delius, 1932, one of his final works; it was dictated by him to his musical amanuensis, Eric Fenby, note by note, when he was struck with blindness and paralysis. It was 1st performed in London.

Song of the Night. The 3rd Sym. by Szymanowski, 1917, scored for tenor/soprano, chorus, and orch., with a text trans. from the Persian poetry of Rùmi; it was 1st performed in St. Petersburg.

Songs My Mother Taught Me. A set of lieder by Dvořák, 1880, composed to German texts.

Songs Without Words (*Lieder ohne Worte*). Cycles of piano pieces by Mendelssohn, 1829–45, in 8 books. However, most of the individual titles of these pieces, such as *Spring Song*, with its centrifugal rapid passages, and the *Bee's Wedding*, with its buzzing chromatics, are the inventions of publishers. There are only 3 authentic titles given by Mendelssohn himself: *Gondola Song*, *Duetto*, and *Folksong*.

songspiel. A hybrid English-German designation of a modern satirical opera, cabaret, or vaudeville show; it emerged in Germany between the 2 world wars. The English "song" had a narrowed meaning of "cabaret song" in German. Weill's opera *Aufsteig und Fall der Stadt Mahagonny* bears the designation *Songspiel*, which is authentic, and not a misprint for SINGSPIEL.

sonic exuviation. The effectiveness of a modernistic climax depends on an astute interplay of contrasts. One of the most effective dynamic devices is sonic exuviation, the shedding of old skin of instrumental sonority, a return to a state of primordial nakedness and a new dressing-up of musical materials and a gradual building of another climax, a cut-off of sonic matter, leaving a soft exposed bodily shape. Such a dramatic exuviation occurs at the end of the last movement of *3 Places in New England* by Charles Ives, where a tremendously powerful heterogeneous complex of sound suddenly crumbles, and a residual gentle chord is heard in the quiet air.

sonic organization. Varèse defines music as "organized sound." It is logical to describe any musical composition, especially of the modern constructivist type, as a sonic organism that follows biomusical laws. It is autogenetic, capable of natural replication induced by contrapuntal interpenetration of contrasting melorhythmic entities. Sonic organization presupposes an engineering plan, which takes into consideration an appropriate cross-pollination of musical themes.

Sonnambula, La (The Sleepwalker). Opera by Bellini, 1831, 1st produced in Milan, 1831. The libretto is by Scribe, who had a genius for turning out librettos marked by total implausibility. The somnambulist of the title is a young orphaned woman betrothed to a villager in Switzerland early in the 19th century. The marriage is nearly wrecked when she wanders in her sleep into the bedroom of a visiting nobleman who is there to court the proprietess of the local tavern. Nobody believes that she wandered into the visitor's room in her sleep. But as they argue pro and con, she appears on the ledge of the house singing a sad aria. Her bridegroom is reassured of her fidelity. The score is full of beautiful melodies, as befits the composer's name.

Sonnenquartette. Haydn's 6 string quartets, 1772, op. 20. The sunny title has nothing to do with the music, but refers to the engraving of a rising sun on the cover of an early edition of the quartets.

sonnerie (Fr.). 1. An arrangement of bells in a tower; also, the signal played on those bells. 2. A trumpet or bugle signal for military or hunting purposes.

sonnette (Fr.). Formerly a pellet bell, often attached to clothing or birds' legs; now, a handbell.

sono (It.). Sound; tone.

sonology. In the late 20th century, the study of the sound as a structural unit in composition and the laws governing both the acoustical nature of sound and its artistic application to music in the theater and concert hall.

sonorism. In the 2nd half of the 20th century, the analysis and application of sonority in the broadest sense, including noise.

sonority (from Lat. *sonus*, sound; Fr. *sonorité*). Resonance.

sonoro, -a (It.; Fr. *sonore*). Sonorously, resoundingly, resonantly, ringingly.

sonus (Lat.). General term for sound, however produced. *Sonus* denotes the physical aspect of sound, while *vox* describes a particular tonal quality.

Sophisticated Lady. Song by Ellington, 1933, 1st composed as an instrumental piece; it was later given lyrics and became one of Ellington's biggest hits.

sopila (*sopella*, *sopelo*; Croat.; It. *tororo*). An indigenous SHAWM of Croatia, with a short wide double reed; usually played in pairs of different-sized instruments, either in parallel 3rds or 6ths, occasionally heterophonic. It is unusual in that, in order to tighten the sopila's 3 joints, water is poured into the tube through the bell.

sopilka (*sopjelka*; Ukr.). End-flown flute with finger holes but no mouthpiece.

sopra (It.). On, upon; above, over; higher. In piano music, *sopra* written in the part for either hand means that the hand is to play (reach) *over* the other. *Sopra una corda*, on 1 string; *come sopra*, as above; *nella parte di sopra*, in the higher (or highest) part.

sopranino (It., little soprano). A very high (or highest) member of a particular instrument family, e.g., sopranino saxophone, sopranino clarinet, and sopranino recorder (with a range similar to that of the piccolo).

soprano (It.; from Lat. *superanus*, standing over; Ger. *Sopran*). 1. The highest class of the human voice; the *treble* voice. The normal compass of the soprano voice ranges from c^1 to a^2; solo voices often reach above c^3, some as high as c^4. Some vocal parts call for a boy soprano, meaning a natural voice of an preadolescent boy. *Coloratura soprano*, a singer with an unusually high range and a strong affinity with bel canto; *dramatic soprano, soprano drammatico, soprano giusto*, a singer capable of dynamic, dramatic, and tragic qualities; the expectation of a strong upper register is matched by an evenness of power throughout the range; many Verdi roles call for a dramatic soprano; *lyric soprano*, a singer distinguished by a poetic quality of phrasing in bel canto; many Puccini roles call for a lyric soprano; *soprano leggiero*, a light soprano; *soprano sfogato*, a high soprano. 2. A high member of a particular instrument family, e.g., soprano saxophone, soprano recorder, soprano trumpet.

soprano clef. The C clef on the 1st line.

soprano string. The E string on the violin.

Sorcerer's Apprentice, The (*L'Apprenti sorcier*). Symphonic scherzo by Dukas, 1897, premiered in Paris, with a story made famous in America by its inclusion in the Disney animated feature *Fantasia* (1940). An apprentice to a sorcerer tries to make his cleaning chores easier while his master is away, by using magic spells; he succeeds in getting them going (in the film, the water-carrying brooms), but he doesn't know how to stop them, and everything goes haywire until the sorcerer returns, repairs the damage (magically, of course), and gives his young apprentice a verbal lashing he won't soon forget. This is by far Dukas's best-known work, with its rather classicist approach to impressionist harmonies, perhaps best considered symbolist in the Debussyan sense. Whatever its analysis, the work was to Dukas what *Boléro* would be to Ravel: a great success and a bane to its composer.

sordamente (It.). With a veiled, muffled tone.

sordina (It.). 1. A string instrument mute. *Con sordini*, with the mutes; *senza sordini*, without the mutes; *si levano i sordini*, take off the mutes. 2. Damper (of the piano). *Senza sordini*, with damper pedal; so used by Beethoven, who wrote *con sordini* to express the release (raising) of the damper pedal, instead of ❋.

sordino (It.). This rare masculine form refers to the trumpet mute, as opposed to SORDINA (see above entry).

sortita (It.). 1. A closing voluntary. 2. The 1st number sung by any leading character in an opera. An *aria di sortita* is, however, also an air at the conclusion of which the singer makes his or her exit.

Sosarma, Re di Media. Opera by Handel, 1732, 1st performed in London.

sospirando (*sospiroso*; It.). Sighing, sobbing; catching the breath; plaintively, mournfully.

sostenuto (It.). Sustained, prolonged. Standing alone, as a tempo mark, it is much the same as *andante cantabile*; it may also imply *a tenuto*, or a uniform rate of decreased speed. *Più sostenuto* is much the same as *meno mosso*.

sostenuto pedal. The middle piano pedal, invented in the 1860s and now commonplace on grand pianos, which sustains (keeps lifted) dampers already raised by depressed keys, thus prolonging the tones of strings affected; the effect is not unlike a pedal point or points.

sotto (It., below, under). In piano music, a direction for either hand to play (reach) under the other. *Sottovoce* (*sotto voce*), in an undertone, as an aside, under the breath; dramatic lowering of the normal vocal or instrumental tone; not necessarily *pp*.

sotto-dominante (It.). The subdominant.

soubrette (Fr., little kitten; from Prov. *soubret*, coy; It. *servetta*). In comic opera and operetta, a maidservant or lady's maid or an ingenue of intriguing and coquettish character; also applied to light roles of similar type. Susanna in *Le nozze di Figaro* and Papagena in *The Magic Flute* are typical soubrette roles. The coloratura soubrette is exemplified in Rosina from *The Barber of Seville* and by Zerbinetta in *Ariadne auf Naxos*. Curiously, the term *soubrette* is used mostly in Germany; the French prefer a term in honor of a famous French singer, Louise Dugazon (1755–1821), who sang such roles: *jeune Dugazon.*

soudain (Fr.). Suddenly.

souillante (It.). Resonantly.

soul. A style of African-American rhythm and blues, 1st associated with the South, from the 1960s on. There are 2 basic strains: upbeat, funky music associated with the Stax and Atlantic labels, whose studio bands (e.g., Booker T. and the MGs) established the model; and the sentimental ballads, an outgrowth of the Motown sound, often accompanied by strings; these became popular from the 1970s on, once the backlash against doo-wop had subsided. In either case a passionate, embellished singing style is typical.

sound. A generic name for all audible sensations, produced by sound waves ranging from about 16 to 25,000 cycles per second (cps). The low tones generate long sound waves; high tones generate short sound waves. Dogs can hear ultrasonic *frequencies* of vibrations far higher than the human range, and bats hear frequencies still higher. A pure tone unencumbered by overtones, such as is produced by the tuning fork, generates a sinusoidal sound wave that can be schematically represented as a semicircle above a horizontal line followed by a similar semicircle below this line. Two such semicircles form 1 cycle of the sound wave. The total number of cps is also called the frequency of vibrations (Hz) of the sound waves.

The *pitch* of a sound is measured by the frequency of vibrations per second. Low sounds or pitches have a low frequency; high pitches have high frequencies. When a frequency is tripled, we hear an octave and a 5th above. When a frequency is quadrupled, we hear a pitch 2 octaves and a major 3rd above the original sound. This order of frequencies is called a series of overtones, or HARMONICS, and the system of traditional harmony is usually said to be based on it. The ratios of vibrations can be arithmetically derived from it: the octave ratio is 2:1, a 5th 3:2, a 4th 4:3, and a major 3rd 5:4.

The relative strength of the overtones produced by the sound of a musical instrument determines its *timbre* or tone color. Middle C on the piano, on the violin, or on the flute has the same frequency of vibrations per second, but they all differ in their timbre, a difference immediately recognizable by a musical ear. Sound waves created by each instrument are compounded with the sound waves of the overtones involved, and the resulting curve is no longer sinusoidal, but complex, having several peaks. When many instruments play together sounding different pitches, the resulting sound wave requires a complex geometric study to reconstruct its components. But a musical ear, particularly in a person who has the sense of perfect pitch, can make this analysis instantly and name all the pitches and all the tone colors constituting the resulting sound.

The loudness of a tone depends on the *amplitude*, or the swing, produced by the vibrations of a sounding body. The amplitude can be observed visually by plucking a string and letting it vibrate, producing a blur. *Noise* is a sound without a definite pitch. When the entire spectrum of tones and noises is produced together, the effect is called white noise, by analogy with the mixture of all the colors of the rainbow making up the color white.

sound bow. The thick rim of a bell, against which the clapper strikes.

sound effects. The onomatopoeic simulations of natural or industrial sounds employed in radio, television, and motion-picture productions. These may include such devices as a thunder machine (R. Strauss, *Alpine Sym.*), imitation of falling rain, galloping horses, the whirring of airplane propellers, etc. Some professional technicians have developed an extraordinary ability to imitate animal cries and industrial noises by means of appropriate amplification of ordinary sounds. The sound engineers working for the Walt Disney studios in Hollywood have in their repertoire almost 1,000 different "instruments." Thus hoofbeats can be produced by clapping 2 coconut half-shells together. Among other imitations is the sound of the arrow hitting the mark, produced by plucking a Jew's harp over a microphone. Various gurgling noises are usually produced orally. One Disney technician has evolved a method of imitating the sound of a swarm of bees by blowing through a rubber condom stretched over a wooden spool. With the invention of the sampler and MIDI, the possibility of both imitation and creation of new effects has grown exponentially.

sound figures. The autonomous and unpredictable formations of sounds once the performer has produced and released them.

sound hole. A hole cut in the belly of a stringed instrument.

sound installation. A form of mixed media in which the visual (usually sculpture) and aural (sound of any kind) are combined. Two basic categories exist: the noninteractive installation, where all elements are controlled by the creators or by random factors not under human control; and the interactive installation, where the spectator affects the sound by tactile contact with the sculptural element or by interfering with electronic devices (such as breaking an invisible beam, adjusting controls, etc.).

Sound of Music, The. Musical by Rodgers and Hammerstein, 1959. Inspired by the true story of the Trapp family of singers who escaped from Hitlerized Austria and achieved international fame as an ensemble. A postulant in an Austrian nunnery accepts the position as a governess to the 7 children of a highborn widower. She teaches them music; the didactic song *Do Re Mi* has become a classic for young children. Inevitably the governess falls in love with the widower and they are married; the entire family then escapes during one of their performances and reach safety. *The Sound of Music* has become one of the most durable and admired American musicals; the score also includes the title song, *Maria, My Favorite Things, Climb Ev'ry Mountain, Edelweiss,* and *16 Going on 17.*

soundboard. Thin plate of wood placed below or behind the strings of various instruments to reinforce and prolong their tones; in the organ, the cover of the windchest.

soundpost. In the violin, etc., the small cylindrical wooden prop set inside the body, between belly and back, just behind (nearly beneath) the treble foot of the bridge.

soupir (Fr., sigh). Quarter rest.

sourd et en s'eloignant (Fr.). Muted, as if receding (Debussy, *Masques*).

sourdine (Fr.). 1. A harmonium stop that partially cuts off the wind supply, so full chords can be played softly. 2. Mute. *Avec sourdines,* put on mutes; *sans sourdines,* take off mutes.

sous-dominante (Fr.). Subdominant.

Sousa, John Philip, famous American bandmaster and composer; b. Washington, D.C., Nov. 6, 1854; d. Reading, Pa., Mar. 6, 1932. He was the son of a Portuguese father and a German mother. He studied violin and orchestration with John Esputa, Jr., and violin and harmony with George Felix Benkert in Washington, D.C.; also acquired considerable proficiency on wind instruments. After playing in the Marine Band (1868–75) he was active in theater orchs.; in 1876 he was a violinist in the special orch. in Philadelphia conducted by Offenbach during his U.S. tour. In 1880 he was appointed director of the Marine Band, which he led with distinction until 1892. He then organized his own band and led it in its 1st concert in Plainfield, N.J., in 1892. In subsequent years he gave successful concerts throughout the U.S. and Canada; played at the Chicago World's Fair in 1893 and at the Paris Exposition in 1900; made 4 European tours (1900, 1901, 1903, and 1905), with increasing acclaim, and finally a tour around the world, in 1910–11.

His flair for writing band music was extraordinary; the infectious rhythms of his military marches and the brilliance of his band arrangements earned him the sobriquet "The March King"; particularly celebrated is his march *The Stars and Stripes Forever,* which became famous all over the world; in 1987 a bill was passed in the U.S. Congress and duly signed by President Ronald Reagan making it the official march of the U.S. During World War I, Sousa served as a lieutenant in the Naval Reserve. He continued his annual tours almost to the time of his death. He was instrumental in the development of the sousaphone, a bass tuba with upright bell, which has been used in bands since the 1890s.

Sousa composed 10 operettas, the most famous being *El Capitan* (1895; Boston, 1896). Among the cornucopia of Sousa marches are (alphabetically listed): *America 1st* (1916); *Anchor and Star* (1918); *The Aviators* (1931); *The Belle of Chicago* (1892); *Ben Bolt* (1888); *The Black Horse Troop* (1924); *El Capitan* (1896); *Columbia's Pride* (1914); *Congress Hall* (1882); *The Crusader* (1888); *Daughters of Texas* (1929); *The Diplomat* (1904); *Esprit de*

John Philip Sousa, c. 1915

Corps (1878); *The Fairest of the Fair* (1908); *The Federal* (1910); *From Maine to Oregon* (1913); *The Gallant Seventh* (1922); *The Gladiator* (1886; the 1st work to sell a million copies); *Globe and Eagle* (1879); *Golden Jubilee* (1928); *The Golden Star* (1919); *Hands Across the Sea* (1899); *The High School Cadets* (1890); *The Honored Dead* (1876); *The Invincible Eagle* (1901); *Jack Tar* (1903); *King Cotton* (1895); *The Legionnaires* (1930); *The Liberty Bell* (1893); *The Loyal Legion* (1890); *Magna Carta* (1927); *Manhattan Beach* (1893); *The National Game* (1925; for the 50th anniversary of the National League of baseball); *The Naval Reserve* (1917); *The Northern Pines* (1931); *Old Ironsides* (1926); *On Parade* (1892); *The Phoenix March* (1875); *The Picador* (1889); *Powhatan's Daughter* (1907); *The Pride of the Wolverines* (1926); *Review* (1873; his 1st publ. march); *Riders for the Flag* (1927); *The Royal Welch Fusiliers* (No. 1, 1929; No. 2, 1930); *Sable and Spurs* (1918); *The Salvation Army* (1930); *Semper Fidelis* (1888); *Sesquicentennial Exposition March* (1926); *Solid Men to the Front* (1918); *Sound Off* (1885); *The Stars and Stripes Forever* (1896; made the official march of the U.S. by act of Congress, 1987); *The Thunderer* (1889); *Triumph of Time* (1885); *The Volunteers* (1918); *The Washington Post* (1889); *The White Rose* (1917); also, band suites; overtures; descriptive pieces; instrumental solos; orch. works; about 76 songs, ballads, hymns; many arrangements and transcriptions. He wrote *The Trumpet and Drum* (1886), *National Patriotic and Typical Airs of All Lands* (1890), and 3 novels: *The 5th String* (1902), *Pipetown Sandy* (1905), and *The Transit of Venus* (1919).

sousaphone. A spiral type of bass tuba (helicon), coiled around the player, with a large bell turned forwards. The sousaphone is named after J. P. Sousa, who used it in his bands.

soutenu (Fr.). Held or sustained.

South America, Take It Away. Song by Rome, 1946, from the revue *Call Me Mister*. The song is a cry of despair at the inundation of the world by Latin American rhythms.

South Pacific. Musical by Rodgers and Hammerstein, 1949. The plot is based on James Michener's *Tales of the South Pacific*. The central character is a French-American plantation owner on a South Pacific island. After the Japanese attack on Pearl Harbor he enlists in an American intelligence unit and falls in love with an American girl serving in the U.S. Navy. There is a happy ending for him and his new love, who was at 1st repelled by his former unsanctified union with a Polynesian woman. *South Pacific* was one of the greatest Broadway successes, 2nd only to *Oklahoma!* It received the Pulitzer Prize. The love ballad *Some Enchanted Evening* became a classic of the American musical theater; the memorable score also includes *Bali Ha'i, I'm Gonna Wash That Man Right Outa My Hair, There Is Nothin' Like a Dame, A Wonderful Guy, Younger Than Springtime,* and *Happy Talk.*

space. In the staff, the interval between 2 lines or ledger lines.

space (or spatial) **music.** A modern development of performance in which the placement of musicians and singers is considered as essential to the composition itself; in some modern works the players are positioned at far distances from one another.

spagnoletta. Italian dance of the 16th century, similar to the pavane; it is in triple meter, played in moderate tempo, and of Spanish origin.

spagnuolo, alla (It.). In a Spanish manner.

Spanish guitar. See GUITAR, SPANISH.

Spannung (Ger.). Tension.

spartire (It.). Assemble a score from separate parts; especially important for most pre-Baroque vocal music.

spartito (spartitura, partitura; It.). Score.

Spasshaft (Ger.). SCHERZANDO.

spatial distribution. The placement of musicians on the stage, long a matter of tradition, has assumed an unexpected significance in modern times in the guise of musical vectorialism. Elliott Carter specifies the exact position of the players in his string quartets. Lukas Foss, in his *Elytres* for 12 Instruments, places the musicians at maximum distances available on the stage. The use of directional loudspeakers in performances of ultramodern works is an electronic counterpart of spatial distribution. In German broadcasting studios experiments have been made in distributing a 12-tone row in serial works among 12 electronic amplifiers placed in a clocklike circle, with each amplifier being assigned an individual note of the series. Empirical applications of the principle of spatial distribution have been made by various composers early in the century, notably by Erik Satie in his *Musique d'ameublement*.

spatial music. See SPACE MUSIC.

spectrum. By analogy with the prismatic spectrum of primary colors, a totality of Klangfarben can be described as a tonal spectrum. Before the era of electronic music the colors of the auditory spectrum were limited to the available instruments of actual manufacture. With the aid of electronic generators it is possible to build a spectrum possessing an infinite capacity for instrumental colors, and the style and idiom of an entire work can be programmed by the proportional strength for such instrumental colors. The metaphor of a musical spectrum is therefore justified by the actuality of its realization.

specular reflection. The mirror image in Baroque counterpoint is applied to mutually conjugated melodic inversions in which the ascending intervals are reflected by descending intervals, and vice versa. It is theoretically possible to construct an infinite specular reflection, in which the intervallic distance between the 2 mirrors recedes, so that intervals are inverted in the outer regions of the instrumental range, extending even into the inaudible spectrum of ultrasonic and infrasonic sounds. In some modern works written specially for dog audiences, ultrasonics can achieve considerable effectiveness. Beyond the canine auditory range, a gap occurs until the frequency of light waves is reached. Mystically inclined composers may find pantheistic inspiration in these notions of passing from men through dogs to infinity.

speculative music. Obsolete English term for scientific music theory, as opposed to *practical music* (now called applied music). The difference is explained by Thomas Morley in his *Plaine and Easie Introduction* (1597): "Musicke is either speculative or practicall. Speculative is that kinde of musicke which, by mathematicall helpes, seeketh out the causes, properties, and natures of soundes. Practicall is that which teacheth all that may be knowne in songs."

speditamente (It.). Expeditiously; quickly.

spesso (It.). Frequently; densely.

Speziale, Lo (The Apothecary). Comic opera by Haydn, 1768, 1st performed in Esterház. A ward of an apothecary is loved by a rich old man and a youth; naturally her guardian prefers the rich man. Both are outwitted when the young suitor dons the cloak of a notary and writes out a marriage contract with his own name as the bridegroom. As a counteraction the rich contender appears dressed in Turkish disguise and offers the post of an ambassador in Turkey to the bewildered apothecary. When the other rejects the scheme the exasperated suitor wrecks his shop. After that the apothecary is only too glad to yield his ward to her beloved.

spianato, -a (from It. *piano*, softly). Softly, tranquilly, without affectation.

spiccato (It.). In string playing, separate the notes very distinctly; in a very rapid tempo, spiccato results in saltando, played with a bouncing bow. In Baroque string playing, spiccato is akin to detaché.

Spiel (Ger.). Play; performance; game. *Spielen*, play (as verb).

Spielmann (Ger.). Itinerant musician of the Middle Ages.

spigliatezza (It.). Agility, dexterity. *Spigliato*, pertly, with agility.

spinet. A keyboard instrument of the harpsichord family, closely related to the virginal. The shape of the spinet is more like that of the modern grand piano than the virginal, which is rectangular. The spinet was popular during the 18th century and then abruptly disappeared from the musical scene. The modern instrument that took up the name *spinet* has little in common with the venerable Baroque instrument—it is simply a small upright piano.

Spinnenlied (Ger.). A spinning song; orig. a traditional work song; in classical music the spinning-wheel is often represented by a circulating ostinato around a pedal point. Goethe's *Gretchen am Spinnrade* (from *Faust*, part I) is a lyric that invites this kind of approach; Schubert's setting (1814) is the apotheosis of the spinning song.

spinto (It., compelled, intense). A high operatic soprano or tenor role of a dramatic yet passive type (Madama Butterfly, Desdemona); as opposed to dramatic and lyric roles.

spirito, con (It.). Spiritedly; with spirit, animation, energy.

spiritual. A term related to the European spiritual song, composed in many languages and for many different forces. The shortened term was then applied to religious songs cultivated by black slaves in the antebellum South. In reality this African-American music is a form of the American gospel hymn, a term usually reserved for the music of white churches. Whatever the case, the Negro spiritual went in 2 directions: it froze as a musical style, as the spiritual, and continued to be performed in concerts by choirs or solo singers; or it evolved along various paths to subsequent forms of gospel music, following the developmental paths of African-American popular music. For a fuller description, see GOSPEL.

Spirituals for Orchestra. Suite by M. Gould, 1941, in 5 movements, 1st performed in N.Y. The melodic materials are original, but the basic inspiration comes from the religious songs of the American South, both Anglo-American and African-American.

spitze (Ger.). 1. Point (of the bow). 2. Toe (in organ playing).

Spitzharfe (Ger.). ARPANETTA.

spitzig (Ger.). Sharp, pointed.

Spohr, Louis (Ludewig, Ludwig)

Celebrated German violinist, composer, and conductor; b. Braunschweig, Apr. 5, 1784; d. Kassel, Oct. 22, 1859. His name is entered in the church registry as Ludewig, but he used the French equivalent, Louis. The family moved to Seesen in 1786; his father, a physician, played the flute, and his mother was an amateur singer and pianist. Spohr began violin lessons at the age of 5 with J. A. Riemenschneider and Dufour, a French émigré. In 1791 he returned to Braunschweig, where he studied with the organist Carl August Hartung and the violinist Charles Louis Maucourt; also composed several violin pieces.

Duke Carl Wilhelm Ferdinand admitted him to the ducal orch. and arranged for his further study with the violinist Franz Eck. In 1802 Eck took him on a tour to Russia, where he met Clementi and Field; returned to Braunschweig in 1803 and resumed his post in the ducal orch. The violin technique and compositional traits of Pierre Rode, whom Spohr met on his return, were major influences on both his compositions and his violin technique. In 1804 Spohr made his 1st official tour as a violinist to Hamburg (his 1st actual tour to Hamburg in 1799 proved a failure, and a 2nd, early in 1804, was abort-

ed when his Guarnerius violin was stolen); gave concerts in Berlin, Leipzig, and Dresden. In 1805 he became concertmaster in the ducal orch. at Gotha.

In 1806 Spohr married the harpist Dorette (Dorothea) Scheidler (1787–1834); he wrote many works for violin and harp for them to perform together, and he toured with her in Germany (1807). His reputation as a virtuoso established, he began writing compositions in every genre, all of which obtained excellent success. In 1812 he gave a series of concerts in Vienna and was acclaimed both as a composer and as a violinist; was concertmaster in the orch. of the Theater an der Wien until 1815. He then made a grand tour of Germany and Italy, where Paganini heard him in Venice. In 1816 Spohr's opera *Faust*, skillfully employing many devices that foreshadowed developments in later German operas, was performed by Weber in Prague.

After a visit to Holland in 1817 he became Kapellmeister of the Frankfurt Opera, where he produced one of his most popular operas, *Zemire und Azor*. In 1820 he and his wife visited England and appeared at several concerts of the London Phil. Soc.; this was the 1st of his 6 visits to England, where he acquired an immense reputation as a violinist, composer, and conductor; his works continued to be performed there long after his death. On his return trip to Germany he presented concerts in Paris; his reception there, however, failed to match his London successes, and he proceeded to Dresden, where Weber recommended him for the Kapellmeistership at the court in Kassel; attracted by the lifetime contract, Spohr accepted the post and settled there in 1822, producing his operatic masterpiece, *Jessonda*, which remained popular throughout the rest of the 19th century, in 1823. Following this success were performances of his oratorio *Die letzten Dinge* (1826) and his 4th Sym., *Die Weihe der Töne* (1832), both of which elicited great praise. The *Violinschule*, a set of 66 studies covering every aspect of his violin style, was publ. in 1831.

Spohr's wife died in 1834; in 1836 he married the pianist Marianne Pfeiffer, the sister of his friend Carl Pfeiffer, librettist of *Der Alchymist* (1830). In 1837 Spohr began having difficulties with the Electoral Prince of Kassel, who caused the cancellation of a festival in Kassel and forbade Spohr from making a trip to Prague, which the composer made nevertheless to conduct *Der Berggeist* (1825); on his return he visited Mozart's widow and birthplace in Salzburg. He traveled to England in 1839 for the Norwich Festival but could not obtain permission from the Prince to return for the performance of his *Fall of Babylon* in 1842. In 1841, returning from the Lucerne Festival, he took the suggestion from his wife to use 2 orchs. for his 7th Sym. in 3 parts, portraying the mundane and divine elements in life. In 1843, in England, his success was so great that a special concert was given by royal command; it was the 1st time a reigning English monarch attended a Phil. Concert.

In 1844 he received the silver medal from the Soc. des Concerts in Paris, and a festival honoring him was held in Braunschweig. Spohr never visited the U.S., in spite of the fact that his daughter lived in N.Y. and an invitation to hold a festival in his honor was issued. In 1845 he received a golden wreath from the Berlin Royal Opera. In 1847 he visited England for the 3rd time,

then went to Frankfurt for the German National Assembly. In 1853 he appeared at the New Phil. Concerts in London. Returning to Kassel, he found himself in an increasingly difficult position because of his dissident political views; the Elector of Hesse refused him further leaves of absence; Spohr ignored the ban, however, traveling to Switzerland and Italy. In the litigation that followed with the Kassel court, Spohr was ordered to forfeit part of his yearly income. He was retired from Kassel in 1857, on a pension despite his lifetime contract. Although he fractured his left arm in a fall in late 1857, he conducted *Jessonda* in Prague in July 1858; he conducted his last performance in Meiningen later that year.

Spohr's compositional style was characteristic of the transition period between the Classic and Romantic. He was technically a master; while some of his works demonstrate a spirit of bold experimentation (*The Historical Sym.*, No. 6; the abovementioned Sym. No. 7 for 2 orchs.; the Concerto for string quartet and orch.; the Nonet), in his aesthetics he was an intransigent conservative. He admired Beethoven's early works but confessed a total inability to understand those of his last period; he also failed to appreciate Weber. It is remarkable, therefore, that he was an early champion of Wagner; in Kassel he produced *Der fliegende Holländer* (1843) and *Tannhäuser* (1853), despite strenuous opposition from the court. He was a highly esteemed teacher; among his students were Ferdinand David and Moritz Hauptmann.

The Spohr Soc. was founded in Kassel in 1908, disbanded in 1934, and revived in 1952. A *Thematisch-bibliographisches Verzeichnis der Werke von Louis Spohr*, compiled by F. Göthel, was publ. in Tutzing in 1981. In addition to the operas and oratorios mentioned above, Spohr wrote 10 syms.; 18 violin concertos (*c.* 1799–1844); 4 clarinet concertos; 2 "concertantes" for 2 violins; 2 concertante for harp and violin; and 6 concert overtures. His chamber works include 34 string quartets, 7 string quintets, 4 "double quartets" for strings; 14 violin duets; 5 piano trios; and 3 sonatas for harp and violin.

Spontini, Gasparo (Luigi Pacifico), significant Italian opera composer; b. Majolati, Ancona, Nov. 14, 1774; d. there, Jan. 24, 1851. His father, a modest farmer, intended him for the church and gave him into the charge of an uncle, a priest at Jesi, who attempted to stifle his musical aspira-

tions. Spontini sought refuge at Monte San Vito with another relative, who not only found a competent music teacher for him, but effected a reconciliation so that, after a year, he was able to return to Jesi. In 1793 he entered the Cons. della Pietà de' Turchini in Naples, where his teachers were Tritto (singing) and Sala (composition). When he failed to obtain the position of maestrino there in 1795, he quit the Cons. without permission.

He rapidly mastered the conventional Italian style of his time; some of his church music performed in Naples came to the attention of a director of the Teatro della Pallacorda in Rome, who commissioned him to write an opera. This was *Li puntigli delle donne*, produced during Carnival in 1796. He served as maestro di cappella at Naples's Teatro del Fondo during Carnival in 1800, and that same year went to Palermo to produce 3 operas. Returning to the mainland in 1801, he produced operas for Rome and Venice before going to Paris in 1803.

After eking out an existence as a singing teacher, Spontini found a patron in the Empress Joséphine. He 1st gained success as a composer in Paris with a revised version of his *La finta filosofa* (1804); it was followed by *La Petite Maison* (also 1804), which proved unsuccessful. All the same the poet Étienne de Jouy now approached Spontini to write the music to his libretto *La Vestale*, a task previously turned down by Boieldieu, Cherubini, and Méhul. In the meantime Spontini brought out 2 more operas without much success: *Milton* (1804) and *Julie, ou Le Pot de fleurs* (1805). However, he won appointment as composer of Joséphine's private music in 1805; for her he wrote several occasional pieces, including the cantata *L'eccelsa gara* (1806), celebrating the battle of Austerlitz.

Thanks to Joséphine's patronage, *La Vestale* won a triumphant success at its premiere (1807), in spite of virulent opposition. Spontini's next opera, Fernand Cortez (1809), failed to equal his previous success, although the 2nd version (1817) won it a place in the repertoire. In 1810 he was awarded the *prix decennal* for having composed the finest grand opera of the preceding decade; that same year he married Céleste Erard, daughter of Jean-Baptiste Erard, and accepted the post of director of the Théâtre-Italien. Although his artistic policies were successful, his personality clashed with those of his superiors and he was dismissed in 1812. In 1814 his opera *Pélage, ou Le Roi et la paix*, celebrating the Restoration, was successfully produced. The following month he was named director of Louis XVIII's private music and of the Théâtre-Italien, although soon after he sold his privilege to the latter to Catalani.

Having become a favorite of the Bourbons, he was made a French citizen by the king in 1817 and was granted a pension in 1818. In spite of his favored position, his grand opera *Olimpie* proved a dismal failure at its premiere (1819). The next year he went to Berlin as Generalmusikdirektor, scoring an initial success with the revised version of *Olimpie* (1821). However, his position of eminence quickly waned. He had been placed on an equality with the Intendant of the Royal Theater, and there were frequent misunderstandings and sharp clashes of authority, not mitigated by Spontini's jealousies and dislikes, his overweening self-conceit, and his despotic temper. Partly through intrigue, partly by reason of his own lack of self-control, he was formally charged in criminal court with lèse-majesté in Jan. 1841.

In Apr. 1841, during a performance of *Don Giovanni* which he was conducting, a riot ensued and Spontini was compelled to leave the hall in disgrace. In July 1841 he was sentenced to 9 months in prison, and soon thereafter he was dismissed as Generalmusikdirektor by the King, although he was allowed to retain his title and salary. In 1842 his sentence was upheld by an appeals court, but the king pardoned him that same month. He then went to Paris, where illness and growing deafness overtook him. In 1844 he was raised to the papal nobility as the Conte di San Andrea. In 1850 he retired to his birthplace to die.

Spontini's importance to the lyric theater rests upon his effective blending of Italian and French elements in his serious operas, most notably in *La Vestale* and *Fernand Cortez*. His influence on Berlioz was particularly notable. He also composed songs, choral music, and instrumental pieces.

Spottlied (Ger.). Song of mockery.

Sprechstimme (*Sprechgesang*; Ger., speech song). A type of inflected vocal delivery, with pitches indicated approximately on the music staff. The singer follows the pitch contour without actually voicing any notes; the effect is exaggerated speech. It was popularized by its expressive use by Schoenberg in *Pierrot Lunaire* and later works. The method was used systematically for the 1st time in 1897 in the operatic melodrama *Königskinder* by Engelbert Humperdinck. This technique is often used in contemporary opera and song cycles; variants such as Partch's "intoning voice" are also found.

sprezzatura (*esprezzatura*; It.). Expressivity, particularly by the judicious use of rubato.

Spring Sonata. Beethoven's sonata in F major for violin and piano, 1800–1801, op. 24. The key of F major is often associated with a revival of nature and love.

Spring Symphony (1). The 1st Sym. by Schumann, 1841, in B-flat major (op. 38), premiered in Leipzig. Schumann, who gave this title to the work, composed it during the winter months, at the happiest time of his life; he had just married his beloved Clara.

Spring Symphony (2). Work for voices and orch. by Britten, 1949, premiered during the Holland Music Festival in Amsterdam. Unpretentiously arranged to words from English poems glorifying springtime, the work ends with an allusion to the medieval English round, *Sumer is icumen in.*

springar. Traditional couple dance of Norway, in triple meter, usually accompanied by the HARDINGFELE.

Springsteen, Bruce, seeded American rock singer, guitarist, and songwriter; b. Freehold, N.J., Sept. 23, 1949. He sang and played guitar in honky-tonks in Newark and in Greenwich Village in N.Y. He began recording songs of personal discontent and societal alienation with such titles as *It's Hard to Be a Saint in the City.* He recruited several similarly dissident rock musicians to form the E-Street Band, and in 1975 produced the album *Born to Run,* which struck a sympathetic chord with disillusioned youth and soon made Springsteen a cult figure. The title song received a certified gold award. His next release was *Darkness on the Edge of Town* (1978), further exploiting the general malaise of American youth. In 1980 he produced his greatest hit, *The River,* an album that glorified, with bitter irony, the automobile as a symbol of the age, with titles such as *Stolen Car, Drive All Night,* and *Wreck on the Highway.*

In 1981 he made an extraordinarily successful tour of Europe. He won a Grammy Award as best male vocalist in 1984. After bringing out the hit album *Born in the USA* (1984), he made a triumphant world tour. He subsequently brought out the albums *Bruce Springsteen & the E-Street Band Live/1975–1985* (1985) and *Tunnel of Love* (1987), the latter winning him a Grammy Award in 1987. In 1988 he was active with the Amnesty International "Human Rights Now!" tour; in 1990 he ended his 16-year affiliation with the E-Street Band; he has continued to record solo albums.

square dance. A parlor or country dance, such as a quadrille, performed by several couples in a square formation.

square time. A popular term for 4/4 time; march time.

squillante (It.). Ringing, tinkling; piercing.

SRO. STANDING ROOM ONLY.

Stabat Mater (dolorosa) (Lat.). A Latin sequence on the Crucifixion sung in the Roman Catholic liturgy, commemorating the 7 sorrows of the Virgin, used in several Divine Offices. With its emotional appeal and liturgical acceptability by the 16th-century Council of Trent, this sequence has been set to music by composers such as Des Prez, Palestrina, Pergolesi, Haydn, Rossini, Schubert, Verdi, and Dvořák.

stabile (It.). Steady, firm.

staccato (It., detached). Play as a series of separate, disconnected notes, the opposite of LEGATO. On a string instrument, the bow does not leave the string, unlike SAUTILLÉ. The effect is successful on most instruments. Played forte, the effect is MARTELLATO; in pianissimo and rapid tempo it is sometimes described as *virtuoso staccato.*

staccato mark. A dot (◌) or wedge-shaped stroke (◌) over a note, the former indicating a less abrupt STACCATO than the latter. The MEZZO-STACCATO is indicated by dotted notes under or over a slur.

Stade, Frederica von. VON STADE, FREDERICA.

Stadler Quintet. Clarinet quintet by Mozart, 1789, K. 581, who wrote it for the virtuoso clarinet player Anton (Paul) Stadler (b. Bruck an der Leitha, June 28, 1753; d. Vienna, June 15, 1812).

staff (stave). The 5 parallel lines used in modern pitch notation; plainchant used at most 4 lines. For the plural, *staves* is preferred to *staffs. Staff notation,* the staff and all musical signs connected with it; *grand* or *great staff,* one of 11 lines, middle C occupying the (middle) 6th.

stagione (It., season). Scheduled performances for an operatic or concert music organization over a specific time period up to 1 calendar year.

stalls (U.K.). In a theater, the front rows of the orch. (seating) section; otherwise identical.

Stammakkord (Ger.). A chord in the fundamental (root) position.

stampitas (It.). ESTAMPIE.

stanchezza, con (stanco; It.). Wearily, draggingly.

Stand By Me. Ben E. King classic that was a pop hit for him both in 1961 and again in 1984; cover versions that charted were cut by Spyder Turner (1967), John Lennon (1975), and Mickey Gilley (1980).

Stand By Your Man. Tammy Wynette country megahit of 1969 that set women's liberation back about a thousand years. Also became the title of her autobiography.

Ständchen (Ger.). Serenade.

standing ovation. Unanimous and tumultuous applause at the end of a particularly exciting musical performance, when the audience is so transported by admiration for the artist, conductor, singer, pianist, violinist, other soloist, or ensemble that through body chemistry the listeners are impelled by simultaneous and massive production of adrenaline to rise from their seats and clap their hands mightily and sometimes even rhythmically, joyously abandoning themselves to unrestrained vociferation and, in extreme cases, animalistic ululation. The spontaneity of such manifestations, however, is often suspect (as are similar outbursts of collective enthusiasm for politicians; see CLAQUE).

Standing Room Only (SRO). An indication in some theaters that all seats for a particular performance are sold out, but that a few places remain where a hardy individual can enter and watch the performance standing up behind the last row of seats.

stanghetta (It.). Barline.

stanza. A symmetric unit of a song text, of 4 or more lines; a unified section in and a component of a lied or other song type.

Star Dust. Love ballad by H. Carmichael, 1929. The tune was written while Carmichael was reminiscing about a young woman he knew at the Univ. of Ind.; the lyrics were added later. The extraordinary popularity of this song is attested to by the great number of arrangements, for every conceivable combination, that it has been subjected to.

stark (Ger.). Loudly, forcibly; FORTE.

stärker (Ger.). Louder, more forcibly; PIÙ FORTE.

Starker, János, renowned Hungarian-born American cellist and pedagogue; b. Budapest, July 5, 1924. He made his 1st public appearance when he was only 6, and at 7 studied cello with Adolf Cziffer at the Budapest Academy of Music; made his solo debut there at the age of 11. After graduating he served as 1st cellist of the Budapest Opera Orch. (1945–46), but he decided to leave Hungary; he emigrated to the U.S. in 1948; became a naturalized citizen in 1954; held the positions of 1st cellist in the Dallas Sym. Orch. (1948–49), the Metropolitan Opera Orch. (1949–53), and the Chicago Sym. Orch. (1953–58); subsequently he embarked upon a solo career.

In 1958 he was appointed a prof. of music at the Indiana Univ. School of Music in Bloomington, where he was named Distinguished Prof. of Music in 1965. As a soloist he achieved renown in performances of Bach's unaccompanied cello suites; also devoted much attention to modern music; promoted cello works of Kodály and gave 1st performances of works by Messiaen, Peter Mennin, Miklos Rózsa, and others. He publ. *An Organized Method of String Playing* (1961).

starr (Ger.). Insistently.

Starr, Ringo (born Richard Starkey), English rock 'n' roll drummer and singer, member of the celebrated Liverpudlian group the Beatles; b. Liverpool, July 7, 1940 (delivered by forceps on account of his enormous puerperal bulk). His nickname originated from his ostentatious habit of wearing several rings on each of his fingers. As an adolescent he performed menial jobs as a messenger boy for British railways, a barman on a boat, etc. A sickly boy, he spent several years in hospitals to cure an effusion on the lung, but he played drums in ward bands. He spontaneously evolved a rhythmic technique of an overwhelming animal vitality. In 1962 he accepted an invitation to join the Beatles; his association with them continued until the dissolution of the group in 1970. His histrionic ability in handling the drums became the most striking visual feature in the Beatlophonic ritual, contributing much to the mass frenzy that attended their shows wherever the band went. After the Beatles disbanded, Starr had an often successful career as a performer and actor; he also had the distinction of being the only 1 of the Beatles to work with the other 3 after 1970.

Stars and Stripes Forever. March by Sousa, 1897, that became his best-known work, with its rousing patriotism. While Sousa added words later, the most familiar are anonymous, meant to begin the trio section: "Be kind to your web-footed friends./A duck may be somebody's mother."

Star-Spangled Banner, The. The official U.S. national anthem since 1931. The tune is that of *To Anacreon in Heaven*, 1st published in London about 1780. Its composition is ascribed to John Stafford Smith (b. Gloucester [baptized], Mar. 30, 1750; d. London, Sept. 21, 1836), a scholar, organist, and composer; as a member of the Anacreontic Soc., London, he wrote the song as a whimsical glorification of the Greek poet Anacreon, famous for his odes to love and wine. The words are by Francis Scott Key (b. Carroll County, Md., Aug. 1, 1779; d. Baltimore, Jan. 11, 1843), a lawyer who wrote part of the text aboard a British ship (where he was taken as a civilian emissary to intercede for release of a Maryland physician) on the morning of Sept. 14, 1814, inspired by the sight of the American flag still waving at Fort McHenry near Baltimore during the British bombardment of it on the previous night; Key later wrote additional verses, none of which are ever sung. The poem was printed in a broadside under the title *Defence of Fort McHenry*, to the Smith tune. Although *The Star-Spangled Banner* was a de facto national anthem in the 19th century, and was used as such by the U.S. Army and Navy, it did not become the official American anthem until President Hoover signed the Senate bill to that effect.

Because of the awkward range of the tune, extending to an octave and a 5th, several attempts have been made—all abortive—to transpose the 2nd part of the song to a lower key. The anthem has been used to symbolize America in numerous compositions, including Puccini's opera *Madama Butterfly*. A law exists in some American state statutes against the mutilation or disfigurement of the melody or harmony of the anthem, and it was invoked by the Boston police to preclude a performance of Stravinsky's arrangement of the anthem at a Boston Sym. Orch. concert in 1942.

static music. Although the general trend of music since 1900 has been toward greater complexity of texture and greater variety of dynamics, an opposite movement has manifested itself in some circles of the avant-garde, aimed at total tonal immobility and static means of expression. Static music finds its logical culmination in works that are limited to a single note in unchanging dynamics, usually in pianissimo. The melosomatic impact of such a production may be considerable if the listener is forced to hear a single note played by an instrumentalist for a long time. The expectation of some change, constantly deceived, may cause an emotional perturbation of great psychological interest.

stave. Staff; for the plural, *staves* is preferred to *staffs*.

Stayin' Alive. Disco hit of 1978 from the popular *Saturday Night Fever* flick, performed in falsetto glory by the Bee Gees.

steam organ. The CALLIOPE.

steel band (drum). A type of ensemble developed spontaneously in Trinidad, with the instrumentation provided by steel oil barrels discarded by local oil companies. The players, called panmen, select drum tops that are dented in such a way that each dent produces a different tone. By further manipulating these drum tops, a whole diatonic scale can be produced. The natives, who have absorbed the sounds of American and British popular music, have learned to form whole orchs. of steel drum tops, performing in 4-part harmony. The highest pitch is called ping-pong, and the bass is called boom. The steel band is usually supplemented by several pairs of maracas and guiros. The songs are of the CALYPSO type, with the text commenting on topical events.

Steg (Ger.). The bridge on stringed instruments. *Am Steg*, bowing near the bridge.

Steiner, Max(imilian Raoul Walter), Austrian-born American composer; b. Vienna, May 10, 1888; d. Los Angeles, Dec. 28, 1971. He studied at the Vienna Cons. with Fuchs and Gradener, and also had some advice from Mahler. At the age of 14 he wrote an operetta. In 1904 he went to England; in 1911 he proceeded to Paris. In 1914 he settled in the U.S.; after conducting musical shows in N.Y. he moved in 1929 to Hollywood, where he became one of the most successful film composers. His music offers a fulsome blend of lush harmonies artfully derived from both Tchaikovsky and Wagner, arranged in a manner marvelously suitable for the portrayal of psychological drama on the screen. Among his film scores, of which he wrote more than 200, are *King Kong* (1933), *The Charge of the Light Brigade* (1936), *Gone with the Wind* (1939), and *The Treasure of the Sierra Madre* (1948).

Steinway & Sons. Celebrated family of German-American piano manufacturers. The founder of the firm was Heinrich Engelhard Steinweg (b. Wolfshagen, Germany,

Feb. 15, 1797; d. N.Y., Feb. 7, 1871; in 1864 he Anglicized his name to Henry E. Steinway). He learned cabinetmaking and organ building at Goslar, and in 1818 entered the shop of an organ maker in Seesen, also becoming church organist there. From about 1820 he became interested in piano making and worked hard to establish a business of his own. He built his 1st piano in 1836. In 1839 he exhibited one grand and 2 square pianos at the Braunschweig State Fair, winning the gold medal. The Revolution of 1848 caused him to emigrate to America with his wife, 2 daughters, and 4 of his 5 sons: Charles (actually, Christian Karl Gottlieb; b. Seesen, Jan. 4, 1829; d. there, Mar. 31, 1865); Henry (actually, Johann Heinrich Engelhard; b. Seesen, Oct. 29, 1830; d. N.Y., Mar. 11, 1865); William (actually, Johann Heinrich Wilhelm; b. Seesen, Mar. 5, 1835; d. N.Y., Nov. 30, 1896); and (Georg August) Albert (b. Seesen, June 10, 1840; d. N.Y., May 14, 1877). The management of the German business at Seesen was left in charge of the eldest son, (Christian Friedrich) Theodore (b. Seesen, Nov. 6, 1825; d. Braunschweig, Mar. 26, 1889).

The family arrived in N.Y. on June 29, 1850, and for about 2 years father and sons worked in various piano factories there. On Mar. 5, 1853, they established a factory of their own under the above firm name, with premises on Varick St. In 1854 they won a gold medal for a square piano at the Metropolitan Fair in Washington, D.C. Their remarkable prosperity dates from 1855, when they took 1st prize for a square overstrung piano with cast-iron frame (an innovation then) at the N.Y. Industrial Exhibition. In 1856 they made their 1st grand, and in 1862 their 1st upright. Among the numerous honors subsequently received may be mentioned 1st prize at London, 1862; 1st grand gold medal of honor for all styles at Paris, 1867 (by unanimous verdict); diplomas for "highest degree of excellence in all styles" at Philadelphia, 1876.

In 1854 the family name (Steinweg) was legally changed to Steinway. In 1865, upon the death of his brothers Charles and Henry, Theodore gave up the Braunschweig business and became a full partner in the N.Y. firm; he built Steinway Hall on 14th St., which, in addition to the offices and retail warerooms, housed a concert hall that became a leading center of N.Y. musical life. In 1925 headquarters were established in the Steinway Building on 57th St. Theodore was especially interested in the scientific aspects of piano construction, and he made a study of the acoustical theories of Helmholtz and Tyndall, which enabled him to introduce important improvements. He returned to Germany in 1870.

On May 17, 1876, the firm was incorporated and William was elected president; he opened a London branch in 1876, and established a European factory at Hamburg in 1880. In the latter year he also bought 400 acres of land on Long Island Sound and established there the village of Steinway (now part of Long Island City), where since 1910 the entire manufacturing plant has been located. Control and active management of the business, now the largest of its kind in the world, has remained in the hands of the founder's descendants. Theodore E. Steinway (d. N.Y., Apr. 8, 1957), grandson of Henry E. Steinway, was president from 1927; also a stamp collector, he was honored by Liechtenstein with his portrait on a postage stamp (1972); in 1955 he was succeeded by his son, Henry Steinway.

The firm was sold to CBS in 1972, although the Steinway family continued to be closely associated with the business. In 1988 Steinway & Sons celebrated its 135th anniversary with a special concert in N.Y. and the unveiling of its 500,000th piano.

stem. The vertical line attached to a note head.

stendando (*stentato*; It.). Delaying, retarding, dragging, heavily.

stentorphone. An extremely loud open diapason pipe in a large organ, named after the legendary Greek hero Stentor in the Trojan War, who could outshout 50 enemies.

step. A melodic progression of a second; also, a degree. *Chromatic step*, progression of a chromatic second; *diatonic step*, progression between neighboring tones of any diatonic scale; *half step*, step of a semitone; *whole step*, step of a whole tone.

Stepping Stones. Musical by Kern, 1923. The title alludes to the fact that Kern wrote the show for 3 members of Fred Stone's family. The story modernizes *Little Red Riding-Hood* with a wolf named Otto de Wolfe; Red Riding-Hood is rescued by a plumber named Peter Plug. Includes *Once in a Blue Moon* and *Raggedy Ann*.

sterbend (Ger.). Dying; MORENDO.

stereophonic (Grk., solid sound). A recording technique developed in the 1950s, using several microphone channels to produce an impression of listening to an actual concert performance by having the sounds come from 2 directions (i.e., speakers).

Stern, Isaac, outstanding Russian-born American violinist; b. Kremenetz, July 21, 1920. He was taken to the U.S. as an infant and was trained in music by his mother, who was a professional singer. He studied the violin at the San Francisco Cons. (1928–31), then with Louis Persinger; also studied with Naoum Blinder (1932–37). In 1936 he made his orch. debut as soloist in Saint-Saëns's 3rd Violin Concerto with the San Francisco Sym. Orch.; his N.Y. debut followed in 1937. After further training in San Francisco, he returned to N.Y. and gave a notably successful concert (1939); his Carnegie Hall debut there was a triumph (1943). In 1947 he toured Australia; made his European debut at the Lucerne Festival in 1948; subsequently appeared regularly with American and European orchs.; in 1956 he made a spectacularly successful tour of Russia. In 1961 he organized a trio with the pianist Eugene Istomin and the cellist Leonard Rose, which toured widely until Rose's death. In 1986 he celebrated the 50th anniversary of his orch. debut.

He received various honors; in 1979 he was made an Officer of the Legion d'honneur of France, in 1984 he received the Kennedy Center Honors Award, and in 1987 was given the Wolf Prize of Israel. Stern belongs to the galaxy of virtuoso performers to whom fame is a natural adjunct to talent and industry; he is also active in general cultural undertakings, and is an energetic worker for the cause of human rights.

stesso (It.). The same. *Lo stesso* (or *l'istesso*) *movimento*, the same movement.

Steuermann, Edward (Eduard), eminent Polish-American pianist, pedagogue, and composer; b. Sambor, near Lemberg, June 18, 1892; d. N.Y., Nov. 11, 1964. He studied piano with Ferruccio Busoni in Berlin (1911–12), and theory with Schoenberg (1912–14); also took some composition lessons with Engelbert Humperdinck. Returning to Poland, he taught at the Paderewski School in Lwow, and concurrently at the Jewish Cons. in Krakow (1932–36). In 1936 he emigrated to the U.S.; taught piano at the Juilliard School of Music in N.Y. (1952–64); also was on the faculty of the Philadelphia Cons. (1948–63); gave summer classes at the Mozarteum in Salzburg (1953–63) and Darmstadt (1954, 1957, 1958, 1960).

As a concert pianist and soloist with major orchs., Steuermann was an ardent champion of NEW MUSIC, particularly of Schoenberg; gave the 1st performance of Schoenberg's Piano Concerto (1944); made excellent arrangements for piano of Schoenberg's operatic and symphonic works, among them *Erwartung, Die glückliche Hand,* Kammersymphonie No. 1, and the Piano Concerto; received the Schoenberg Medal from the ISCM in 1952. Although he did not follow Schoenberg's method of composition with 12 tones with any degree of consistency, his music possesses an expressionistic tension that is characteristic of the 2nd Viennese School. His nephew, Michael (Andreas) Gielen (b. Dresden, July 20, 1927) is a noted conductor who specializes in Schoenberg.

Stiffelio. Opera by Verdi, 1850, 1st produced in Trieste. It failed miserably, and no wonder—the libretto was uncharacteristically static. Stiffelio, an evangelical minister, faces a problem: his wife allowed herself to be seduced by a local reprobate. As a Christian, should he forgive her? As a man, should he throw her out? The Italian censors stepped in and their intervention gave the opera its coup de grace. Still, there was music to salvage, and Verdi tried to graft it to another opera called *Aroldo,* but it failed under the new name, too.

stil (Ger.; It. *stile*). Style. *Stile osservato,* strict style, especially of pure vocal music; *stile rappresentativo,* dramatic monodic song with instrumental accompaniment in chords; the kind of operatic recitative originating towards the close of the 16th century.

Still, William Grant, eminent African-American composer; b. Woodville, Miss., May 11, 1895; d. Los Angeles, Dec. 3, 1978. His father was bandmaster in Woodville; after his death when Still was in infancy, his mother moved the family to Little Rock, Ark., where she became a high school teacher. He grew up in a home with cultured, middle-class values, and his stepfather encouraged his interest in music by taking him to see operettas and buying him operatic recordings; he was also given violin lessons. He attended Wilberforce College in preparation for a medical career but became active in musical activities on campus; after dropping out of college he worked with various groups, including that of W. C. Handy (1916); then attended the Oberlin College Cons.

During World War I he played violin in the U.S. Army; afterward he returned to work with Handy, and became oboist in the Shuffle Along Orch. (1921); then studied composition with Varèse, and at the New England Cons. of Music in Boston with Chadwick; held a Guggenheim fellowship in 1934–35; was awarded honorary doctorates by Howard Univ. (1941), Oberlin College (1947), and Bates College (1954). Determined to develop a symphonic type of

Negro music, he wrote the *Afro-American Sym.* (1930). In his music he occasionally made use of actual Negro folk songs, but mostly he invented his thematic materials. His 2nd wife was the writer Verna Arvey, who collaborated with him as librettist in his stage works.

Still's well-written music is not well enough known. It includes operas; ballets; incidental music. He composed 5 syms.: No. 1, *Afro-American Sym.* (1930; Rochester, N.Y., 1931); No. 2 in G Minor, *Song of a New Race* (Philadelphia, 1937); No. 3 (1945; discarded; new No. 3, *The Sunday Sym.*; 1958); No. 4, *Autochthonous* (1947; Oklahoma City, 1951); No. 5, *Western Hemisphere* (revision of discarded No. 3, 1945; Oberlin, Ohio, 1970); as well as other orch.l and chamber works; choral works; songs, including *Songs of Separation* (1949); *From the Hearts of Women* (1961); piano pieces; works for band; and arrangements of spirituals.

Stillgedackt (Ger.). A soft-toned stopped organ register.

Stimme (Ger.). 1. Voice. 2. Vocal or instrumental part; *mit der Stimme*, COLLA PARTE. 3. Organ stop. 4. Soundpost. *Mit zartem Stimmen*, with soft-toned organ stops.

Stimmung (Ger.). Tuning, pitch, *accordatura*; mood, frame of mind. *Stimmung halten*, to keep in tune; *Stimmungsbild*, a mood picture, i.e., a short character piece.

stinguendo (It.). Dying away.

stiracchiando (It.). Slowly; receding in speed.

stirato (It.). Dragging, delaying.

stiriana (It.). STYRIENNE.

stochastic (from Grk. *stochos*, target). A term, borrowed from probability theory, denoting a modern compositional process which is governed by rules of probability. The term was introduced into music by the Greek engineer and composer Iannis Xenakis, to designate an aleatory projection in which the sonic trajectory is circumscribed by the structural parameters of the initial thematic statement. Stochastic procedures are in actual practice equivalent to controlled improvisation.

Stockflöte (Ger., cane flute). Vertical flute or recorder inserted in the upper part of a walking stick. It was manufactured in the 1st half of the 19th century in Austria and

attained popularity among poetically inclined *Spaziergänger* in the Vienna woods, hills, and environs.

Stockhausen, Karlheinz, outstanding German composer; b. Mödrath, near Cologne, Aug. 22, 1928. He was orphaned during World War II and was compelled to hold various jobs to keep body and soul together; all the same, he learned to play the piano, violin, and oboe; then studied piano with Hans Otto Schmidt-Neuhaus (1947–50), form with H. Schroder (1948), and composition with Frank Martin (1950) at the Cologne Staatliche Hochschule für Musik; also took courses in German philology, philosophy, and musicology at the Univ. of Cologne; after studies in Darmstadt (1951), he received instruction in composition from Messiaen in Paris (1952); subsequently studied communications theory and phonetics with Werner Meyer-Eppler at the Univ. of Bonn (1954–56).

He was active at the electronic music studio of the West German Radio in Cologne (from 1953); also was a lecturer at the Internationalen Ferienkürse für Musik in Darmstadt (until 1974) and was founder/artistic director of the Cologne Kürse für Neue Musik (1963–68); likewise served as prof. of composition at the Cologne Hochschule für Musik (1971–77). He was made a member of the Swedish Royal Academy (1970), the Berlin Academy of Arts (1973), and the American Academy and Inst. of Arts and Letters (1979); also was made a Commandeur dans l'Ordre des Arts et des Lettres of France (1985) and an honorary member of the Royal Academy of Music in London (1987).

Stockhausen investigated the potentialities of MUSIQUE CONCRÈTE and partly incorporated its techniques into his own empiric method of composition, which from the very 1st included highly complex contrapuntal conglomerates with uninhibited applications of noneuphonious dissonance as well as recourse to the primal procedures of obdurate iteration of single tones; all this set in the freest of rhythmic patterns and diversified by constantly changing instrumental colors with obsessive percussive effects. He further perfected a system of constructivist composition in which the subjective choice of the performer determines the succession of given thematic ingredients and their polyphonic simultaneities, ultimately leading to a totality of aleatory procedures in which the ostensible application of a composer's commanding function is paradoxically reasserted by the inclusion of prerecorded materials and by recombinant uses of electronically altered thematic ingredients.

Stockhausen evolved energetic missionary activities in behalf of new music as a lecturer and master of ceremonies at avant-garde meetings all over the world; having mastered the intricacies of the English language, he made a lecture tour of Canadian and American univs. in 1958; in 1965 he was a visiting prof. of composition at the Univ. of Pa.; was a visiting prof. at the Univ. of Calif. at Davis in 1966–67; in 1969 he gave highly successful public lectures in England that were attended by hordes of musical and unmusical novitiates; publ. numerous misleading guidelines for the benefit of a growing contingent of his apostles, disciples, and acolytes.

Stockhausen is a pioneer of "time-space" music, marked by a controlled improvisation and adding the vectorial (i.e., directional) parameter to the 4 traditional aspects of serial music (pitch, duration, timbre, and dynamics), with performers and electronic apparatuses placed in different parts of the concert hall; such performances, directed by himself, are often accompanied by screen projections and audience participation; he also specifies the architectural aspects of the auditoriums in which he gives his demonstrations; thus at the world's fair in Osaka, Japan, in 1970, he supervised the construction of a circular auditorium in the German pavilion; these demonstrations continued for 183 days, with 20 soloists and 5 lantern projections in live performances of his own works, each session lasting 5 1/2 hours; the estimated live, radio, and television audience was 1,000,000 listeners.

His annotations to his own works were publ. in the series entitled *Texte* (6 vols., Cologne, 1963–88). See also R. Maconie, ed., *Stockhausen on Music: Lectures and Interviews* (1989). Several of the composer's children play instruments and participate in his more recent performances.

Stokowski, Leopold (Anthony)

Celebrated, spectacularly endowed, and magically communicative English-born American conductor; b. London (of a Polish father and an Irish mother), Apr. 18, 1882; d. Nether Wallop, Hampshire, Sept. 13, 1977. He attended Queen's College, Oxford, and the Royal College of Music in London, where he studied organ with Stevenson Hoyte, music theory with Walford Davies, and composition with Charles Stanford. At the age of 18 he obtained the post of organist at St. James, Piccadilly. In 1905 he went to America and served as organist and choirmaster at St. Bartholomew's in N.Y.; became a U.S. citizen in 1915. In 1909 he was engaged to conduct the Cincinnati Sym. Orch.; although his contract was for 5 years, he obtained a release in 1912 in order to accept an offer from the Philadelphia Orch. This was the beginning of a long and spectacular career as a sym. conductor; he led the Philadelphia Orch. for 24 years as its sole conductor, bringing it to a degree of brilliance that rivaled the greatest orchs. in the world.

In 1931 he was officially designated by the board of directors of the Philadelphia Orch. as music director, which gave him control over the choice of guest conductors and soloists. He conducted most of the repertoire by heart, an impressive accomplishment at the time; he changed the seating of the orch., placing violins to the left and cellos to the right. After some years of leading the orch. with a baton, he finally dispensed with it and shaped the music with the 10 fingers of his hands. He emphasized the colorful elements in the music; he was the creator of the famous "Philadelphia sound" in the strings, achieving a well-nigh bel canto quality.

Tall and slender, with an aureole of blond hair, his figure presented a striking contrast with his stocky, mustachioed German predecessors; he was the 1st conductor to attain the status of a star comparable to that of a motion picture actor. Abandoning the proverbial ivory tower in which most conductors dwelt, he actually made an appearance as a movie actor in the film *100 Men and a Girl*. In 1940 he agreed to participate in the production of Walt Disney's celebrated film *Fantasia*, which featured both live performers and animated characters; Stokowski conducted the music and in one sequence engaged in a bantering colloquy with Mickey Mouse. He was lionized by the Philadelphians; in 1922 he received the Edward Bok Award of $10,000 as "the person who has done the most for Philadelphia."

Stokowski was praised in superlative terms in the press, but not all music critics approved of his cavalier treatment of sacrosanct masterpieces, for he allowed himself to alter the orchestration; he doubled some solo passages in the brass, and occasionally introduced percussion instruments not provided in the score; he even cut out individual bars that seemed to him devoid of musical action. Furthermore, Stokowski's own orch. arrangements of Bach raised the pedantic eyebrows of professional musicologists; yet there is no denying the effectiveness of the sonority and the subtlety of color that he succeeded in creating by such means. Many great musicians hailed Stokowski's new orch.l sound; Rachmaninoff regarded the Philadelphia Orch. under Stokowski, and later under Ormandy, as the greatest with which he had performed.

Stokowski boldly risked his popularity with the Philadelphia audiences by introducing modern works. He conducted Schoenberg's music, culminating in the introduction of his formidable score *Gurrelieder* in 1932. An even greater gesture of defiance of popular tastes was his world premiere of *Amériques* by Varèse (1926), a score that opens with a siren and thrives on dissonance. Stokowski made history by joining the forces of the Philadelphia Orch. with the Philadelphia Grand Opera Co. in the 1st American performance of Berg's masterpiece *Wozzeck* (Mar. 31, 1931). The opposition of some listeners was now vocal; when audible commotion in the audience erupted during his performance of Webern's Sym., he abruptly stopped conducting, walked off the stage, then returned only to begin the work all over again.

From his earliest years with the Philadelphia Orch., Stokowski adopted the habit of addressing the audience, to caution them to keep their peace during the performance of a modernistic score, or reprimanding them for their lack of progressive views; once he even took to task the prim Philadelphia ladies for bringing their knitting to the concert. In 1933 the board of directors took an unusual step in announcing that there would be no more "debatable music" performed by the orch.; Stokowski refused to heed this proclamation. Another eruption of discontent ensued when he programmed some Soviet music at a youth concert and trained the children to sing the *Internationale*.

Stokowski was always interested in new electronic sound; he was the 1st to make use of the THEREMIN in the orch. in order to enhance the sonorities of the bass section. He was instrumental in introducing electrical recordings.

In 1936 Stokowski resigned as music director of the Philadelphia Orch.; he was succeeded by Eugene Ormandy but continued to conduct concerts as coconductor of the orch. until 1938. From 1940 to 1942 he took a newly organized All-American Youth Orch. on a tour in the U.S. and in South America. During the season 1942–43 he was associate conductor, with Toscanini, of the NBC Sym. Orch.; he shared the season of 1949–50 with Mitropoulos as conductor of the N.Y. Phil.; from 1955 to 1960 he conducted the Houston Sym. Orch. In 1962 he organized in N.Y. the American Sym. Orch. and led it until 1972; on Apr. 26, 1965, at the age of 83, he conducted the orch. in the 1st complete performance of the 4th Sym. of Charles Ives. In 1973 he went to London, where he continued to make recordings and conduct occasional concerts; he also appeared in television interviews. He died in his sleep at the age of 95; rumor had it that he had a contract signed for a gala performance on his 100th birthday in 1982.

Stokowski was married 3 times: his 1st wife was the pianist Olga Samaroff, whom he married in 1911; they were divorced in 1923; his 2nd wife was Evangeline Brewster Johnson, heiress to the Johnson and Johnson drug fortune; they were married in 1926 and divorced in 1937; his 3rd marriage, to Gloria Vanderbilt, produced a ripple of prurient newspaper publicity because of the disparity in their ages; he was 63, she was 21; they were married in 1945 and divorced in 1955. Stokowski publ. *Music for All of Us* (N.Y., 1943), which was translated into the Russian, Italian, and Czech languages.

Stoltzman, Richard (Leslie), outstanding American clarinetist; b. Omaha, July 12, 1942. He began clarinet lessons when he was 8 and gained experience playing in local jazz settings with his father, an alto saxophonist. He then studied mathematics and music at Ohio State Univ. (B.Mus., 1964); also studied clarinet with Robert Marcellus; after studies at Yale Univ. (M.Mus., 1967), he completed his clarinet training with Harold Wright at the Marlboro Music

School and with Kalman Opperman in N.Y.; pursued postgraduate studies at Columbia Univ.'s Teachers College (1967–70). He played in many concerts at Marlboro; cofounded the group Tashi ("good fortune" in Tibetan) with pianist Peter Serkin, violinist Ida Kavafian, and cellist Fred Sherry in 1973, and toured widely with the group; likewise taught at the Calif. Inst. of the Arts (1970–75).

He made his N.Y. solo recital debut in 1974; after being awarded the Avery Fisher Prize in 1977, he pursued an international career as a virtuoso; appeared as soloist with many of the major orchs., as a chamber music artist, and as a solo recitalist. In 1982 he became the 1st clarinetist ever to give a solo recital at N.Y.'s Carnegie Hall. In 1986 he received the Avery Fisher Artist Award. He maintains an extensive repertoire, ranging from the classics to the avant-garde and including popular music genres; he has also commissioned works and made his own transcriptions.

stomp. A generic term for a beat pattern in AFRICAN MUSIC, in which a foot stomping on the ground is integral to the rhythm, often engendering a correspondingly obstinate melodic lilt.

stonatura (It.). Production of a tone intentionally different from that prescribed in the score; playing or singing deliberately off pitch; not the same as SCORDATURA.

Stone Guest, The (*Kamennyi gost*). Opera by Dargomyzhsky, 1872, after Pushkin's poem of the same name. The score was left unfinished at Dargomyzhsky's death, and was completed by Rimsky-Korsakov and Cui; the 1st performance took place posthumously in St. Petersburg. Pushkin's story is based on the same story as Da Ponte's *Don Giovanni* libretto for Mozart. The Stone Guest of the title is the statue of the Commendatore slain by Don Juan. Not only does Juan try to seduce his widow, but he also invites the statue to supper. The marble handshake of the Stone Guest crushes Don Juan, and he falls dead. The opera is of importance because of Dargomyzhsky's fruitful attempt to treat the inflections of Russian speech realistically rather than in a conventional operatic style.

Stookey, (Noël) **Paul.** See YARROW, PETER.

stop (1). One of numerous devices on the organ console, each in the form of a knob. The player draws (pulls) a stop according to the desirable tone color or instrumental quality which is marked on each knob. That part of the mechanism in turn admits and stops (directs) the flow of wind to the grooves beneath the chosen pipe. Several stops can be drawn simultaneously to produce a stronger or more complex sound (hence the expression "pull out all the stops").

Rows of organ pipes of like character are arranged in graduated succession. These are called *speaking* or *sounding* stops, classified as *flue* (having flue pipes) and *reed* (having reed pipes) work. The flue work has 3 subclasses: (a) *principal work*, having cylindrical flue pipes of diapason quality; (b) *gedackt work*, having stopped pipes; and (c) *flute work*, including all flue stops of a scale too broad or too narrow to produce diapason tone, together with such stopped pipes as have chimneys, and all 3- or 4-sided wooden pipes.

Auxiliary stop, one to be drawn with some other stop(s), to reinforce the tone of the latter; *complete stop*, one having at least 1 pipe for each key of the manual to which it belongs; *compound stop*, MIXTURE STOP; *divided stop*, one the lower half of whose register is controlled by a different stop-knob from the upper and bears a different name; *flue stop*, one composed of flue pipes; *foundation stop*, one of normal 8' pitch; *half, incomplete*, or *imperfect stop*, one producing (about) half the tones of the full scale of its manual; *mechanical stop*, one not having a set of pipes, but governing some mechanical device; *mixture stop*, one with 2 or more ranks of pipes, thus producing 2 or more tones for each key; *mutation stop*, one producing tones a major 3rd or perfect 5th (or a higher octave of either) above the 8' stops; *partial stop*, a HALF STOP; *pedal stop*, a stop on the pedal; *reed stop*, one composed of reed pipes; *solo stop*, one adapted for the production of characteristic melodic effects, whether on the solo organ or not; *sounding* or *speaking stop*, one having pipes and producing musical tones.

stop (2). 1. On the violin, etc., the pressure of a finger on a string to vary the latter's pitch; a *double stop* is when 2 or more strings are so pressed and sounded simultaneously. 2. On wind instruments with finger holes, the closing of a hole by finger or key to alter the pitch. 3. On instruments of the horn family, the partial or total closing of the bell by inserting the hand.

stop time. A rhythmic device in jazz in which the group suddenly stops playing while 1 or more members play a solo or cadenza; then the ensemble resumes as before. In older jazz, stop times were worked out in advance; in later jazz the soloist could improvise more freely and thus direct the return of the group, or the individual members might return gradually rather than all at once. The most effective use of stop time is in uptempo music; but the cadenza for the soloist before the piece ends is standard in all tempos.

stopped diapason. Organ flue pipe, closed at the top with a removable plug.

stopped note. Tone obtained with a STOP (2); opposed to OPEN.

stopped pipe. Organ pipes closed (plugged or covered) at the top; opposed to OPEN.

Stormy Weather. Ballad by H. Arlen, 1933, originally part of the *Cotton Club Parade* of 1933. Its melancholy, hypnotic power later found a platform in the eponymous film of 1943, as sung by Lena Horne.

straccicalando (It.). Babbling, prattling.

Stradella, Alessandro. ALESSANDRO STRADELLA.

Stradivari (Latinized as Stradivarius), **Antonio,** celebrated Italian violin maker; b. probably in Cremona, 1644; d. probably there, Dec. 18, 1737. He was a pupil of Niccolò Amati in the early 1660s; his earliest known violin dates from 1666; he may have worked for Amati and others from 1666 before purchasing the house that contained his workshop from 1680. His finest instruments were made in the period from 1700 to 1725, but he still worked up to the year of his death; he made his last instrument at the age of 92. His label reads: "Antonius Stradivarius Cremonensis. Fecit Anno . . . (A x S)." His cellos command even higher prices than the violins, and violas the highest of all, for he made very few of them. Stradivari had 11 children; of them Francesco (1671–1743) and Omobono (1679–1742) were his coworkers. Stradivari also made viols of early types, guitars, lutes, mandolins, etc.

strain. In general, a song, tune, air melody; also, some well-defined passage in, or part of, a piece. Technically, a period, sentence, or short division of a composition; a motive or theme.

strambotto (It., rustic song). A 16th-century vocal genre akin to the madrigal and frottola, set to poetry with specific stanza and rhyme schemes; a form favored by Lord Byron. The strambotto is distinguished by simplicity, symmetry of phrase, and accessible harmony.

Strange Fruit. Although often attributed to Billie Holiday, who performed the song as part of her nightclub act and made it famous, it was actually written by Lewis Allen. The song tells the story of a lynching in the South; an early statement in support of Civil Rights, it took considerable bravery on Holiday's part to perform it.

Stranger in Paradise. A *contrafactum à la Broadway* in which the slow section of the *Polovtsian Dances* from Borodin's *Prince Igor* is transmogrified into a hit song; from the musical *Kismet*, 1953, a show whose score is entirely made up of Borodin's unprotected music. Who gets the royalties? Not the real composer, of course.

Strangers in the Night. *Doobie-doobie-doo,* as Frank Sinatra croons in the chorus. A rare number 1 pop hit for Ol' Blue Eyes in the '60s, the 1966 Kaempfert-Snyder-Singleton ditty was featured in the film *A Man Could Get Killed* and netted Frank a Grammy.

Straniera, La. Opera by Bellini, 1829, premiered in Milan. The stranger of the title is Agnès, the 1st wife of King Philippe of France, who has banished her; she lives in a château in self-inflicted solitude until a romantic lord seeks her out and wins her love. The king is then deposed, and Agnès is proclaimed queen, putting her out of nuptial reach of the mere lord. Thwarted, he stabs himself to death, and she prays for death herself.

stranka (strančica). Transverse wooden flute of Croatia and Slavonia, with a cylindrical bore and 5 or 6 finger holes; it is associated with shepherds.

strappando (It.). Abruptly, explosively.

strappare (It., pluck off). In piano playing, throw off a note or chord by a rapid, light turn of the wrist.

strascinando (It.). Dragging, drawling. *Strascinando l'arco,* drawing the bow so as to bind the notes.

strascinare la voce (It.). Sing a PORTAMENTO with exaggerated dragging or drawling.

Straszny Dwóri. HAUNTED CASTLE, THE.

Stratas, Teresa (real name, Anastasia Stratakis), outstanding Canadian soprano of Greek extraction; b. Toronto,

May 26, 1938. Her father owned a restaurant in a town near Toronto, and she was allowed from her earliest childhood to sing for customers. She also sang in concert with her brother, a violinist, and her sister, a pianist. In 1954 she entered the Royal Cons. of Music of Toronto, where she studied voice with Irene Jessner; she graduated with an Artist Diploma in 1959. She made her professional operatic debut with the Toronto Opera Festival as Mimi on Oct. 13, 1958. In 1959 she was a cowinner of the Metropolitan Opera Auditions, which led to her formal debut with the company in N.Y. in 1959, as Poussette in *Manon*. She soon established herself as a singer of great versatility.

She sang virtually all the standard soprano parts, and demonstrated her particular mettle and fettle in the complete version of Berg's *Lulu*, which was given for the 1st time in Paris in 1979; in N.Y. she created the role of Marie Antoinette in Corigliano's *The Ghosts of Versailles* (1986). She won international acclaim for her dramatic portrayal of Violetta in Zeffirelli's film version of *La Traviata* (1983). In 1972 she was made an Officer of the Order of Canada. A film portrait of Stratas was made by Harry Rasky as *StrataSphere*.

strategy and tactics. Modern composers are forever seeking metaphors from other fields to enrich the rapidly obsolescent musical nomenclature derived from vague Italian words indicating form, speed, dynamic force, or expression. Among such new metaphors are strategy and tactics. The general scheme of a modern sym. or a sonata is strategic, while variations, cadenzas, and contrapuntal elaborations are tactical devices. Iannis Xenakis, the originator of the STO-CHASTIC method of composition, extended the concept of strategy and tactics into an actual tournament between 2 orchs. and 2 conductors, exemplified in his antiphonal sym. entitled *Stratégie*. According to the composer's specifications, 2 orchs. perform simultaneously 2 different compositions, following the uncoordinated pair of conductors and stopping at climactic points to survey the mutual gains and losses. At the end of the maneuver the audience votes to nominate the winner of this instrumental encounter.

strathspey (Scot., valley of the Spey River). A lively Scottish dance, somewhat slower than the reel, also in 4/4 time, progressing rhythmically as 1 16th note followed by a dotted 8th note (SCOTCH SNAP).

Strauss. Family of celebrated Austrian waltz composers and musicians:

(1) **Johann** (Baptist) **Strauss** (I), violinist, conductor, and composer, known as "The Father of the Waltz"; b. Vienna, Mar. 14, 1804; d. there, Sept. 25, 1849. He was born into a humble Jewish family of Hungarian descent; called "black Schani," he made a concerted effort to conceal his Jewish origins (when the ancestry of the family was realized by the chagrined Nazis a century later, they falsified the parish register at St. Stephen's Cathedral in 1939 to make the family racially pure). His father was an innkeeper who apprenticed him to a bookbinder, but his musical talent revealed itself at an early age; after Strauss ran away, his parents consented to his becoming a musician. He studied the violin under Polyschansky and harmony under Seyfried; at 15 he became a violist in Michael Pamer's dance orch., where he found a friend in Josef Lanner; in 1819 he became a member of the latter's small band, and later served as 2nd conductor of Lanner's orch. (1824–25).

In 1825 he organized his own orch., which quickly became popular in Viennese inns; composed his 1st waltz, *Täuberln-Walzer*, in 1826; his reputation was secured with his appearances at the Sperl, where Pamer served as music director. His renown spread, and his orch. increased rapidly in size and efficiency; from 1833 he undertook concert tours in Austria, and in 1834 was appointed bandmaster of the 1st Vienna militia regiment. His tours extended to Berlin in 1834, and to the Netherlands and Belgium in 1836; in 1837–38 he invaded Paris with a picked corps of 28 and had immense success both there and in London. In 1846 he was named k.k. (i.e., *kaiserlich und königlich*, imperial and royal) Hofballmusikdirektor.

After catching scarlet fever from one of his children, he died at the age of 45. Among his publ. waltzes, the *Lorelei-, Gabrielen-, Taglioni-, Cäcilien-, Victoria-, Kettenbrucken-,* and *Bajaderen-Walzer* are prime favorites; also popular are his *Elektrische Funken, Mephistos Höllenrufe,* and the *Donau-Lieder*. He also wrote 33 galops; 14 polkas; 33 quadrilles; cotillions and contredances; 23 marches (including the *Radetzky-Marsch,* 1848); and 9 potpourris. He had 3 sons who carried on the family musical tradition:

(2) **Johann** (Baptist) **Strauss** (II), greatly renowned violinist, conductor, and composer, known as "The Waltz King"; b. Vienna, Oct. 25, 1825; d. there, June 3, 1899. His father intended him for a business career, but his musical talent manifested itself when he was a mere child; at 6 he wrote the 1st 36 bars of waltz music that later was publ. as *Erster Gedanke*. While he was still a child, his mother arranged for him to study secretly with Franz Amon, his father's concertmaster; after his father left the family in 1842, he was able to

pursue violin training with Anton Kohlmann; also studied theory with Joseph Drechsler until 1844.

He made his 1st public appearance as conductor of his own ensemble at Dommayer's Casino at Hietzing (1844). His success was instantaneous, and his new waltzes won wide popularity. Despite his father's objections to this rivalry in the family, Johann continued his concerts with increasing success; after his father's death in 1849, he united his father's band with his own; subsequently made regular tours of Europe (1856–86). From 1863 to 1871 he was k.k. Hofballmusikdirektor in Vienna. In 1872 he accepted an invitation to visit the U.S., and he directed 14 "monster concerts" in Boston and 4 in N.Y. He then turned to the theater.

His finest operetta is *Die Fledermaus*, an epitome of the Viennese spirit that continues to hold the stage as one of the masterpieces of its genre. It was 1st staged at the Theater an der Wien (1874), and within a few months was given in N.Y.; productions followed all over the world. It was performed in Paris with a new libretto as *La Tzigane* (1877); the original version was finally presented there as *La Chauve-souris* in 1904. Also very successful was the operetta *Der Zigeunerbaron* (Vienna, 1885). All his operettas were 1st produced in Vienna, with the exception of *Eine Nacht in Venedig* (Berlin, 1883).

Although Strauss composed extensively for the theater, his supreme achievement remains his dance music. He wrote almost 500 pieces of it (498 op. numbers); of his waltzes the greatest popularity was achieved by *On the Beautiful Blue Danube* (1867), whose main tune became one of the best known in all music. Brahms wrote on a lady's fan the opening measures of it, and underneath: "Leider nicht von Brahms" (Alas, not by Brahms); Wagner, too, voiced his appreciation of the music of Strauss. Other fine waltzes by Johann II include *Acceration* (1860), *Morgenblätter* (1864), *Artist's Life* (1867), *Tales of the Vienna Woods* (1868), *Wine, Women, and Song* (1869), *Wiener Blut* (1873), *Where the Citrons Bloom* (1874), *Roses from the South* (1880), *Voices of Spring* (1883), and *Emperor* (1889).

He contracted 3 marriages: to the singer Henriette Treffz, the actress Angelika Dittrich, and Adele Strauss, the widow of the banker Anton Strauss, who was no relation to Johann's family. Strauss also composed numerous quadrilles, polkas, polka-mazurkas, marches, galops, etc.; also several pieces in collaboration with his brothers.

(3) **Josef Strauss,** conductor and composer; b. Vienna, Aug. 22, 1827; d. there, July 21, 1870. He studied theory with Franz Dolleschal and violin with Franz Anton. He was versatile and gifted; despite lifelong illnesses, he wrote poetry, painted, and patented inventions. He 1st appeared in public conducting in Vienna a set of his waltzes (1853); later regularly appeared as a conductor with his brother Johann's orch. (1856–62); their younger brother Eduard joined them in 1862, but Johann left the orch. in 1863 and Josef and Eduard continued to conduct the family orch. He wrote 283 op. numbers, many of which reveal a composer of remarkable talent. Among his outstanding waltzes are *Perlen der Liebe* (1857), *5 Kleebald'ln* (1857), *Wiener Kinder* (1858), *Schwert und Leier* (1860), *Friedenspalmen* (1867), and *Aquarellen* (1869); he also wrote polkas, quadrilles, marches, and other works.

(4) **Eduard Strauss,** conductor and composer; b. Vienna, Mar. 15, 1835; d. there, Dec. 28, 1916. He studied theory and composition with Gottfried Preyer and Simon Sechter, violin with Amon, and harp with Parish-Alvars and Zamara. After playing harp in his brother Johann's orch., he made his debut as a conductor and composer with it at the Wintergarten of the Dianabad-Saal (1862); after Johann left the orch. in 1863, Eduard and his brother Josef shared the conductorship of the orch. until the latter's death in 1870. From 1870 to 1878 he was k.k. Hofballmusikdirektor; subsequently made annual tours of Europe as a guest conductor, and also with his own orch.; in 1890 and 1900–1901 he toured throughout the U.S. In 1901 he retired. He wrote some 300 works, but they failed to rival the superior works of his brothers.

Strauss, Richard (Georg)

〜〜 〜〜 〜〜 〜〜 〜〜

Great German composer and distinguished conductor, one of the most inventive music masters of the modern age; b. Munich, June 11, 1864; d. Garmisch-Partenkirchen, Sept. 8, 1949. His father was Franz (Joseph) Strauss (b. Parkstein, Feb. 26, 1822; d. Munich, May 31, 1905), a horn player and composer who, although a violent opponent of Wagner, was valued highly by the master, who entrusted to him the solo horn passages at the premieres of *Tristan und Isolde*, *Die Meistersinger von Nürnberg*, and *Parsifal*. Growing up in a musical environment, Richard studied piano as a child with August Tombo, harpist in the Court Orch.; then took violin lessons from Benno Walter, its concertmaster, and later received instruction from the court conductor, Friedrich Wilhelm Meyer.

According to his own account, he began to improvise songs and piano pieces at a very early age; among such incunabula was the song *Weihnachtslied*, followed by a piano dance, *Schneiderpolka*. In 1881 his 1st orch. work, the Sym. in D Minor, was premiered in Munich under Hermann Levi. This was followed by the Sym. in F Minor, premiered by the N.Y. Phil. under Theodore Thomas (1884). Strauss also made progress as a performing musician; when he was 20 years old Hans von Bülow engaged him as assistant conductor of his Meiningen Orch. About that time Strauss became associated with the poet and musician Alexander Ritter, who introduced him to the "music of the future," as it was commonly called, represented by orch. works of Liszt and operas by Wagner.

In 1886 Strauss received an appointment as the 3rd conductor of the Court Opera in Munich. In 1887 he conducted in Munich the 1st performance of his symphonic fantasy *Aus Italien*. This was followed by the composition of his 1st true masterpiece, the symphonic poem *Don Juan*, in which he applied the thematic ideas of Liszt; he conducted its premiere in Weimar (1889); it became the 1st of a series of his symphonic poems, all of them based on literary subjects.

His next symphonic poem of great significance in music history was *Tod und Verklärung*; Strauss conducted it for the 1st time in Eisenach, on the same program with the premiere of his brilliant *Burleske* for Piano and Orch., featuring Eugen d'Albert as soloist (1890). There followed the 1st performance of the symphonic poem *Macbeth*, which Strauss conducted in Weimar (also 1890). In these works Strauss established himself as a master of program music and the most important representative of the nascent era of musical modernism; as such, he was praised extravagantly by earnest believers in musical progress and damned savagely by entrenched traditionalists in the press. He effectively adapted Wagner's system of leitmotivs to the domain of symphonic music. His symphonic poems were interwoven with motives, each representing a relevant programmatic element. Explanatory brochures listing these leading motives were publ. like musical Baedekers to guide the listeners. Bülow, ever a phrasemaker, dubbed Strauss "Richard the 2nd," recognizing him as the rightful heir of "Richard the 1st," Wagner.

Turning to stage music, Strauss wrote his 1st opera, *Guntram*, for which he also composed the text; he conducted its premiere in Weimar on May 10, 1894, with the leading soprano role performed by Pauline de Ahna; she was married to Strauss on Sept. 10, 1894, and remained with him all his life; she died on May 13, 1950, a few months after Strauss himself. While engaged in active work as a composer, Strauss did not neglect his conducting career. In 1894 he succeeded Bülow as conductor of the Berlin Phil., leading it for a season. Also in 1894 he became assistant conductor of the Munich Court Opera; he became chief conductor in 1896. In 1896–97 he filled engagements as a guest conductor in European music centers. His works of the period included the sparkling *Till Eulenspiegels lustige Streiche* (Cologne, Nov. 5, 1895), *Also sprach Zarathustra*, a philosophical symphonic poem after Nietzsche (Frankfurt am Main, Nov. 27, 1896, Strauss conducting), and *Don Quixote*, variations with a cello solo, after Cervantes (Cologne, Mar. 8, 1898).

In 1898 Strauss became a conductor at the Berlin Royal Opera; in 1908 he was made its Generalmusikdirektor, a position he held until 1918. He conducted the 1st performance of his extraordinary autobiographical symphonic poem *Ein Heldenleben* in Frankfurt am Main on Mar. 3, 1899; the hero of the title was Strauss himself, while his critics were represented in the score by a cacophonous charivari; for this exhibition of musical self-aggrandizement, he was severely chastised in the press. There followed his 1st successful opera, *Feuersnot* (Dresden, Nov. 21, 1901).

In June 1903 Strauss was the guest of honor of the Strauss Festival in London. It was also in 1903 that the Univ. of Heidelberg made him Dr.Phil., honoris causa. For his 1st visit to the U.S. he presented to the public the premiere performance of his *Symphonia domestica* at Carnegie Hall in N.Y. on Mar. 21, 1904. The score represented a day in the Strauss household, containing an interlude describing, quite literally, the feeding of the newly born baby. The reviews in the press reflected aversion to such a musical self-exposure. There followed his opera *Salome*, to the German trans. of Oscar Wilde's play.

Schuch led its premiere in Dresden on Dec. 9, 1905. *Salome* had its American premiere at the Metropolitan Opera in N.Y. on Jan. 22, 1907; the ghastly subject, involving intended incest, 7-fold nudity, and decapitation followed by a labial necrophilia, administered such a shock to the public and the press that the Metropolitan Opera took it off the repertoire after only 2 performances.

Scarcely less forceful was Strauss's next opera, *Elektra*, to a libretto by the Austrian poet and dramatist Hugo von Hofmannsthal, in which the horrors of matricide were depicted with extraordinary force in unabashedly dissonant harmonies. Schuch conducted its premiere in Dresden on Jan. 25, 1909. Strauss then decided to prove to his admirers that he was quite able to write melodious operas to charm the musical ear; this he accomplished in his next production, also to a text of Hofmannsthal, *Der Rosenkavalier*, a delightful opera-bouffe in an endearing popular manner; Schuch conducted its premiere in Dresden on Jan. 26, 1911. Turning once more to Greek mythology, Strauss wrote, with Hofmannsthal again as librettist, a short opera, *Ariadne auf Naxos*, which he conducted for the 1st time in Stuttgart on Oct. 25, 1912; he later expanded it into a full-length work.

In June 1914 Strauss was awarded an honorary D.Mus. degree from Oxford Univ. His next work was the formidable and quite realistic score *Eine Alpensinfonie*, depicting an ascent of the Alps and employing a wind machine and a thunder machine in the orch. to illustrate an alpine storm. Strauss conducted its 1st performance with the Dresden Court Orch. in Berlin on Oct. 28, 1915. Then, again with Hofmannsthal as librettist, he wrote the opera *Die Frau ohne Schatten* (Vienna, Oct. 10, 1919), using a complex plot, heavily endowed with symbolism.

In 1917 Strauss helped to organize the Salzburg Festival and appeared there in subsequent years as conductor. In 1919 he assumed the post of codirector with Franz Schalk of the Vienna State Opera, a position he held until 1924. In 1920 he took the Vienna Phil. on a tour of South America; in 1921 he appeared as a guest conductor in the U.S. For his next opera, *Intermezzo* (Dresden, Nov. 4, 1924), Strauss wrote his own libretto; then, with Hofmannsthal once more, he wrote *Die ägyptische Helena* (Dresden, June 6, 1928). Their last collaboration was *Arabella* (Dresden, July 1, 1933).

When Hitler came to power in 1933, the Nazis were eager to persuade Strauss to join the official policies of the 3rd Reich. Hitler even sent him a signed picture of himself with a flattering inscription, "To the great composer Richard Strauss, with sincere admiration." Strauss kept clear of formal association with the Führer and his cohorts, however. He agreed to serve as president of the newly organized Reichsmusikkammer on Nov. 15, 1933, but resigned from it on July 13, 1935, ostensibly for reasons of poor health. He entered into open conflict with the Nazis by asking Stefan Zweig, an Austrian Jew, to provide the libretto for his opera *Die schweigsame Frau*; it was duly produced in Dresden on June 24, 1935, but then taken off the boards after a few performances. His political difficulties grew even more disturbing when the Nazis found out that his daughter-in-law was Jewish. Zweig himself managed to escape Nazi horrors, and emigrated to Brazil, but he was so afflicted by the inhumanity of the world that he and his wife together committed suicide.

Strauss valiantly went through his tasks; he agreed to write the *Olympische Hymne* for the Berlin Olympic Games in 1936. On Nov. 5, 1936, he was honored with the Gold Medal of the Royal Phil. Soc. in London; the next day he conducted the visiting Dresden State Opera in a performance of his *Ariadne auf Naxos* at Covent Garden. For his next opera he chose Joseph Gregor as his librettist; with him Strauss produced *Daphne* (Dresden, Oct. 15, 1938), which was once more a revival of his debt to Greek mythology. For their last collaboration Strauss and Gregor produced the opera *Die Liebe der Danae*, also on a Greek theme. Its public dress rehearsal was given in Salzburg on Aug. 16, 1944, but by that time World War II was rapidly encroaching on devastated Germany, so that the opera did not receive its official premiere until after Strauss's death. The last opera by Strauss performed during his lifetime was *Capriccio*. Its libretto was prepared by the conductor Clemens Krauss, who conducted its premiere in Munich on Oct. 28, 1942. Another interesting work of this period was Strauss's Horn Concerto No. 2, 1st performed in Salzburg on Aug. 11, 1943.

During the last weeks of the war Strauss devoted himself to the composition of *Metamorphosen*, a work for string orch. mourning the disintegration of Germany; it contained a symbolic quotation from the funeral march from Beethoven's *Eroica Sym.* He then completed another fine score, the Oboe Concerto. In 1945 he went to Switzerland; 2 years later he visited London for the Strauss Festival and also appeared as a conductor of his own works. Although official suspicion continued to linger regarding his relationship with the Nazi regime, he was officially exonerated of all taint on June 8, 1948. A last flame of creative inspiration brought forth the deeply moving *Vier letzte Lieder* (1948) for Soprano and Orch., inspired by poems of Herman Hesse and Eichendorff. With this farewell, Strauss left Switzerland in 1949 and returned to his home in Germany, where he died at the age of 85.

Undeniably one of the finest master composers of modern times, Strauss never espoused extreme chromatic techniques, remaining a Romanticist at heart. His genius is unquestioned as regards such early symphonic poems as *Don Juan* and *Also sprach Zarathustra*; many of his operas have attained a permanent place in the repertoire, while his *Vier letzte Lieder* stand as a noble achievement of his Romantic inspiration.

stravagante (It.). Extravagant, fantastic, whimsical; applied to practitioners of the SECONDA PRATTICA (such as Monteverdi) as a criticism of their treatment of harmonic progression and resolution.

Stravinsky, Igor (Feodorovich)

Great Russian-born French, later American, composer, one of the supreme masters of 20th-century music, whose works exercised the most profound influence on the evolution of music through the emancipation of rhythm, melody, and harmony; b. Oranienbaum, near St. Petersburg, June 17, 1882; d. N.Y., Apr. 6, 1971 (his body was flown to Venice and buried in the Russian corner of the cemetery island of San Michele). His father was Feodor (Ignatievich) Stravinsky (b. Noviy Dvor, near Rechitza, June 20, 1843; d. St. Petersburg, Dec. 4, 1902), one of the greatest Russian basses before Chaliapin, distinguished not only for the power of his voice, but also for his dramatic talent on the stage; he made 1,235 appearances in 64 operatic roles.

Igor was brought up in an artistic atmosphere; he often went to opera rehearsals when his father sang, and acquired an early love for the musical theater. He took piano lessons with Alexandra Snetkova, and later with Leokadia Kashperova, who was a pupil of Anton Rubinstein; but it was not until much later that he began to study music theory, 1st with Akimenko and then with Kalafati (1900–1903). His progress in composition was remarkably slow; he never entered a music school or a cons., and never earned an academic degree in music. In 1901 he enrolled in the faculty of jurisprudence at St. Petersburg Univ.; he took courses there for 8 semesters, without graduating; a fellow student was Vladimir Rimsky-Korsakov, a son of the composer.

In the summer of 1902 Stravinsky traveled in Germany, where he met another son of Rimsky-Korsakov, Andrei, who was a student at the Univ. of Heidelberg; Stravinsky became his friend. He was introduced to Rimsky-Korsakov and became a regular guest at the latter's periodic gatherings in St. Petersburg. In 1903–1904 he wrote a piano sonata for the Russian pianist Nicolai Richter, who performed it at Rimsky-Korsakov's home. In 1905 he began taking regular lessons in orchestration with Rimsky-Korsakov, who taught him free of charge; under his tutelage Stravinsky composed a Sym. in E-flat Major; the 2nd and 3rd movements from it were performed in 1907, by the Court Orch. in St. Petersburg, and a complete performance of it was given by the same orch. (1908). The work, dedicated to Rimsky-Korsakov, had some singularities and angularities that showed a deficiency of technique; there was little in this work that presaged Stravinsky's ultimate development as a master of form and orchestration. At the same concert his *Le Faune et la bergère* for Voice and Orch. had its 1st performance; this score revealed a certain influence of French impressionism.

To celebrate the marriage of Rimsky-Korsakov's daughter Nadezhda to the composer Maximilian Steinberg (1908), Stravinsky wrote an orch. fantasy entitled *Fireworks*. Rimsky-Korsakov died a few days after the wedding; Stravinsky deeply mourned his beloved teacher and wrote a *Chant funèbre* for Wind Instruments in his memory; it was 1st performed in St. Petersburg (1909). There followed a *Scherzo fantastique* for Orch., inspired by Maeterlinck's book *La Vie des abeilles*. Stravinsky had at 1st planned a literal program of composition, illustrating events in the life of a beehive; some years later, however, he gratuitously denied all connection between his piece and Maeterlinck's book.

A signal change in Stravinsky's fortunes came when the famous impresario Diaghilev commissioned him to write a work for the Paris season of his company, the Ballets Russes. The result was the production of his 1st ballet masterpiece, *The Firebird*, staged by Diaghilev in Paris (1910). Here he created music of extraordinary brilliance, steeped in the colors of Russian fairy tales. There are numerous striking effects in the score, such as a glissando of harmonics in the string instruments; the rhythmic drive is exhilarating, and the use of asymmetrical time signatures is extremely effective; the harmonies are opulent; the orchestration is coruscating. He drew 2 orch. suites from the work; in 1919 he reorchestrated the music to conform to his new beliefs in musical economy; in effect he plucked the luminous feathers off the magical firebird, but the original scoring remained a favorite with conductors and orchs.

Stravinsky's association with Diaghilev demanded his presence in Paris, which he made his home beginning in 1911, with frequent travels to Switzerland. His 2nd ballet for Diaghilev was *Petrouchka*, produced in Paris in that year, with triumphant success. Not only was the ballet remarkably effective on the stage, but the score itself, arranged in 2 orch. suites, was so new and original that it marked a turning point in 20th-century music; the spasmodically explosive rhythms, the novel instrumental sonorities—with the use of the piano as an integral part of the orch.—the bold harmonic innovations in employ-

ing 2 different keys simultaneously (C major and F-sharp major, the *Petrouchka chord*) became a potent influence on modern European composers. Debussy voiced his enchantment with the score, and young Stravinsky, still in his 20s, became a Paris celebrity.

Two years later he brought out a work of even greater revolutionary import, the ballet *The Rite of Spring* (*Le Sacre du printemps*; the Russian title is *Vesna sviashchennaya*, the sacred spring); its subtitle was *Scenes of Pagan Russia*. It was produced by Diaghilev with his Ballets Russes in Paris in 1913, with choreography by Nijinsky. The score marked a departure from all conventions of musical composition; while in *Petrouchka* the harmonies, though innovative and dissonant, could still be placed in the context of modern music, the score of *The Rite of Spring* contained such corrosive dissonances as scales played at the intervals of major 7ths and superpositions of minor upon major triads with the common tonic, chords treated as unified blocks of sound, and rapid metrical changes that seemingly defied performance. The score still stands as one of the most daring creations of the modern musical mind; its impact was tremendous; to some of the audience at its 1st performance in Paris, Stravinsky's "barbaric" music was beyond endurance; the Paris critics exercised their verbal ingenuity in indignant vituperation; one of them proposed that *Le sacre du printemps* would be better titled *Le massacre du printemps*. In a few years the work had become a popular concert piece.

In 1914 Diaghilev produced Stravinsky's lyric fairy tale *Le Rossignol*, after Hans Christian Andersen. Stravinsky had started composing the opera before *Petrouchka* and *The Rite of Spring*; the corrosive discords are not yet present, and other elements seem closer to *The Firebird* and the orientalisms of his teacher Rimsky-Korsakov's music; this would be appropriate to what is an exotic Eastern fantasy. From 1914 to 1918 Stravinsky worked on his ballet *Les Noces* (Nuptials; Russian title *Svadebka*, little wedding), evoking Russian peasant folk modalities; it was scored for an unusual ensemble of chorus, soloists, 4 pianos, and 17 percussion instruments.

The devastation of World War I led Stravinsky to conclude that the era of grandiose Romantic music had become obsolete, that a new spirit of musical economy was imperative in an impoverished world. As an illustration of such economy he wrote the musical stage play *L'Histoire du soldat*, scored for only 7 players, with a narrator (Lausanne, 1918); About the same time he wrote a work for 11 instruments entitled *Ragtime*, inspired by the new American dance music. He continued his association with Diaghilev's Ballets Russes in writing the ballet *Pulcinella*, based on themes once attributed to Pergolesi but now known to be by other 18th-century Italian composers, with 3 vocal soloists (Paris Opéra, 1920). He also wrote for Diaghilev 2 short operas: *Renard*, to a Russian fairy tale (Paris, 1922), and *Mavra*, after Pushkin (Paris, 1922). These 2 works were the last in which he used Russian subjects, with the sole exception of the orch.l *Scherzo à la russe* (1944).

Stravinsky had now entered a stylistic period usually designated as neoclassical. The most significant works of this stage of his development were his Octet for wind instruments (Paris, 1923), and the Piano Concerto (with wind instruments, double basses, and percussion; Paris, 1924), commissioned by Koussevitzky. In these works he abandoned the luxuriant instrumentation of his ballets and their aggressively dissonant harmonies; instead he used pandiatonic structures, firmly tonal but starkly dissonant in their superposition of tonalities within the same principal key. His reversion to old forms, however, was not an act of ascetic renunciation, but rather a grand experiment in reviving Baroque practices that had fallen into desuetude. The Piano Concerto provided him with an opportunity to appear as soloist; Stravinsky was never a virtuoso pianist, but he was able to acquit himself satisfactorily in such works as the Piano Concerto; he played it with Koussevitzky in Paris and during his 1st American tour with the Boston Sym. Orch. (1925).

The Elizabeth Sprague Coolidge Foundation commissioned him to write a pantomime for string orch.; the result was *Apollon Musagète*, given at the Library of Congress in Washington, D.C. (1928). This score, serene and emotionally restrained, evokes the manner of Lully's court ballets. He continued to explore the resources of neo-Baroque writing in his Capriccio for Piano and Orch., which he performed as soloist, with Ansermet conducting, in Paris (1929); this score is impressed by a spirit of hedonistic entertainment, harking back to the style galant of the 18th century; yet it is unmistakably modern in its polyrhythmic collisions of pandiatonic harmonies. Stravinsky's growing disillusionment with the external brilliance of modern music led him to seek eternal verities of music in ancient modalities.

His well-nigh monastic renunciation of the grandiose edifice of glorious sound to which he himself had so abundantly contributed found expression in his opera-oratorio *Oedipus Rex*; in order to emphasize its detachment from temporal aspects, he commissioned a Latin trans. for the libretto, even though the original play was in Greek; its music is deliberately hollow and its dramatic points are emphasized by ominous repetitive passages. Yet this very austerity of idiom makes *Oedipus Rex* a profoundly moving play. It had its 1st performance in 1927; its stage premiere took place in Vienna the following year.

A turn to religious writing found its utterance in Stravinsky's *Sym. of Psalms*, written for the 50th anniversary of the Boston Sym. Orch. and dedicated "to the glory of God" (Brussels, 1930). The work is scored for chorus and orch., omitting the violins and violas, thus emphasizing the lower instrumental registers and creating an austere sonority suitable to its solemn subject. In 1931 he wrote a violin concerto commissioned by Samuel Dushkin and performed by him in Berlin. On a commission from the ballerina Ida Rubinstein he composed the ballet *Perséphone* (Paris Opéra, 1934); here again he exercised his mastery of simplicity in formal design, melodic patterns, and contrapuntal structure.

For his American tour he wrote *Jeu de cartes*, a "ballet in 3 deals" to his own scenario depicting an imaginary game of poker (of which he was a devotee); he conducted its 1st performance at the Metropolitan Opera in N.Y. (1937). His concerto for 16 instruments, *Dumbarton Oaks* (named after the Washington, D.C., estate of Mr. and Mrs. Robert Woods Bliss, who commissioned the work), was 1st performed in Washington (1938); in Europe it was played under the noncommittal title Concerto in E-flat; its style is hermetically neo-Baroque. It is germane to note that in his neoclassical works Stravinsky began to indicate the key in the title, e.g., Concerto in D for Violin and Orch. (1931), Sym. in C (1938), Concerto in D for String Orch. (1946), and Serenade in A for Piano (1925).

With World War II engulfing Europe, Stravinsky decided to seek permanent residence in America. He had acquired French citizenship in 1934; in 1939 he applied for American citizenship; he and Vera became American citizens in late 1945. To celebrate this event he made an arrangement of *The Star-Spangled Banner*, which contained a curious modulation into the subdominant in the coda. He conducted it with the Boston Sym. Orch. in

1944, but because of legal injunctions existing in the state of Massachusetts against intentional alteration or any mutilation of the national anthem, he was advised not to conduct his version at the 2nd pair of concerts, and the standard version was substituted. In 1939–40 Stravinsky was named Charles Eliot Norton lecturer at Harvard Univ.; about the same time he accepted several private students, a pedagogical role he had never exercised before.

His American years form a curious panoply of subjects and manners of composition. He accepted a commission from the Ringling Bros. to write a *Circus Polka* "for a young elephant" (1942; arr. by Stravinsky for sym. orch. and conducted by him with the Boston Sym. Orch., Cambridge, Mass., 1944). In 1946 he wrote *Ebony Concerto* for Woody Herman's swing band. In 1951 he completed his opera *The Rake's Progress*, inspired by Hogarth's famous series of engravings, to a libretto by W. H. Auden and C. Kallman. He conducted its world premiere in Venice that year, as part of the International Festival of Contemporary Music there. The opera is a striking example of Stravinsky's protean capacity for adopting different styles and idioms of composition to serve his artistic purposes; *The Rake's Progress* is an ingenious conglomeration of disparate elements, ranging from 18th-century British ballads to cosmopolitan burlesque.

But whatever transmutations his music underwent during his long and productive career, he remained a man of the theater at heart. In America he became associated with the brilliant Russian choreographer Balanchine, who produced a number of ballets to Stravinsky's music, among them his *Apollon Musagète*, Violin Concerto, *Sym. in 3 Movements* (1942–45; N.Y., 1946), *Scherzo à la russe, Pulcinella*, and *Agon*, a ballet for 12 Dancers (1954–57; Los Angeles, 1957). It was in *Agon* that he 1st essayed the dodecaphonic method of composition as promulgated by Schoenberg; *Agon* (Greek for competition) bears the subtitle *Ballet for 12 Tones*, no doubt an allusion to this fact. Yet the 12-tone method had been the very antithesis of his previous tenets; in fact, an irreconcilable polarity existed between Stravinsky

Igor Stravinsky

and Schoenberg even in personal relations. Although both resided in Los Angeles for several years, they never met socially; Schoenberg once wrote a canon in which he ridiculed Stravinsky as "Herr Modernsky," who put on a wig to look like "Papa Bach" (*Satires*, no. 2, op. 28).

After Schoenberg's death Stravinsky felt free to examine the essence of the 12-tone method, which was introduced to him by his faithful musical factotum Robert Craft; Stravinsky adopted dodecaphonic writing in its aspect of canonic counterpoint as developed by Webern. In this manner he wrote his *Canticum sacrum ad honorem Sancti Marci nominis*, which he conducted at San Marco in Venice (1956). Other works of the period were also written in a modified 12-tone technique, among them *The Flood* (for narrator, mime, singers, and dancers), presented in a CBS-TV broadcast in N.Y. in 1962.

Stravinsky was married twice; his 1st wife, Catherine Nosenko, whom he married in 1906, and who bore him 3 children, died in 1939; the following year Stravinsky married his longtime mistress, the dancer Vera de Bosset (b. St. Petersburg, Dec. 25, 1888; d. N.Y., Sept. 17, 1982), who was formerly married to the Russian painter Serge Sudeikin. An ugly litigation for the rights to the Stravinsky estate continued for several years between his children and their stepmother; after Vera Stravinsky's death it was finally settled in a compromise, according to which 2/9 of the estate went to each of his 3 children and a grandchild and 1/9 to Robert Craft.

The value of the Stravinsky legacy was spectacularly demonstrated in 1982, when his working draft of *The Rite of Spring* was sold at an auction in London for the fantastic sum of $548,000, higher than any MS by any composer. The purchaser was Paul Sacher, the Swiss conductor, philanthropist, and archival collector. Even more fantastic was the subsequent sale of the entire Stravinsky archive, consisting of 116 boxes of personal letters and 225 drawers containing MSS, some of them unpubl. Enormous bids were made for it by the N.Y. Public Library and the Morgan Library, but they were all outbid by Sacher, who offered the winning purse of $5,250,000. The materials are being assembled in a specially constructed 7-story Sacher Foundation building in Basel, to be eventually opened to scholars for study.

In tribute to Stravinsky as a naturalized American citizen, the U.S. Postal Service issued a 2-cent stamp bearing his image to mark his centennial in 1982, an honor theretofore never granted to a foreign-born composer (a possible exception being Victor Herbert, whose entire career was made in America).

Few composers have escaped the powerful impact of Stravinsky's music; ironically it was his own country that had rejected him, partly because of the opposition of Soviet ideologues to modern music in general, and partly because of Stravinsky's open criticism of Soviet ways in art. But in 1962 he returned to Russia for a visit and was welcomed as a prodigal son; as if by magic his works began to appear on Russian concert programs, and Soviet music critics issued a number of laudatory studies of his works. Yet it is Stravinsky's early masterpieces, set in an

attractive colorful style, that continue to enjoy favor with audiences and performers, while his more abstract and recursive scores are appreciated mainly by specialists.

A sharp debate raged, at times to the point of vitriolic polemical exchange, among Stravinsky's associates as to the degree of credibility of Craft's reports in his dialogues, or even of the factual accounts of events during Stravinsky's last years of life. Stravinsky was never a master of the English language; yet Craft quotes him at length as delivering literary paragraphs of impeccable English prose. Craft admitted that he enhanced Stravinsky's actual words and sentences (which were never recorded on tape), articulating the inner—and at times subliminal—sense of his utterances. Craft's role was made clear beyond dispute by Stravinsky himself, who in a 1958 letter to his publishing agent urged that the title of the book be changed to *Conversations with Igor Stravinsky by Robert Craft*; he emphatically asserted that the text was in Craft's language, and that in effect Craft had "created" him.

Strayhorn, Billy (William Thomas), African-American jazz pianist, composer, and arranger; b. Dayton, Ohio, Nov. 29, 1915; d. N.Y., May 31, 1967. He studied music in Pittsburgh; joined Duke Ellington's band as lyricist and arranger in 1939. Many songs credited to Ellington (*Chelsea Bridge, Perfume Suite, Such Sweet Thunder, A Drum Is a Woman*) are in fact products of a mutually beneficial musical symbiosis, with Ellington suggesting the initial idea, mood, and character and Strayhorn doing the actual writing, often using Ellington's quasi-impressionistic techniques (modal harmonies, whole-tone scales, etc.). Strayhorn's own acknowledged songs such as *Lush Life* and *Take the A Train* are jazz standards.

straziante (It.). Anxiously.

street cries. Street vendors used to peddle their wares in melodious jingles before the age of commercialized trade; each product had its own recognizable tune. Such street cries were common in France as early as the 13th century, and they were often incorporated in contemporary motets. Street cries were also used by English composers of the early Renaissance period; notable are those for fresh oysters and hot mutton pieces. Newsboys often sold their papers in 19th century London with a pleasant

modal lift. (A 20th-century rendition of newsboys' calls can be heard in Partch's *San Francisco*.) Charpentier's opera *Louise* includes a quodlibet of peddlers of carrots and other vegetables. Even Bach deigned to include the popular tune *Cabbage and Turnips* at the end of his great *Goldberg Variations*.

In the present century Luciano Berio's *Cries of London* is unusual; it is scored for 8 voices, to authentic vending tunes; the tune urging customers to buy garlic is amusing. In Cuba, Brazil, and Argentina, knife sharpeners and shoeshine boys open up a whole sym. of vendors' tunes at early tropical sunrise. Street organs with reed pipes used to be a ubiquitous sight and sound in Italy, with a monkey passing a hat for donations. A story is told that Giuseppe Verdi, annoyed by street organs playing the tune *La donna e mobile* from his *Rigoletto* before his window, paid off the street musicians to stop playing or change their song. Modern singing commercials are the radio and television successors to the old vending cries.

Street Scene. Opera by Weill, 1947, based on a play by Elmer Rice, with lyrics by Langston Hughes, premiered in N.Y. The somber story involves the residents of a typically multiethnic N.Y. walkup apartment building. In one family a frustrated housewife has been following the path of least resistance with a milkman, as her husband has become hardened and angered by life. One day, while she and her lover are dallying in her apartment, he comes home, surprises them in flagrante delicto and shoots them both dead. Of their 2 children the daughter is the more affected; although she has grown fond of a student who would give up his religion for her, she realizes that her life is too full of burdens and uncertainties to make any commitment, and she leaves N.Y. alone for a happier place and a new start. The work is probably the most ambitious attempt of Weill's to recreate his Berlin-Brecht style, integrating popular music with more classical (but very much tonal) sonorities. In a very seamless show, a last-minute addition to the score, *Moon-Faced, Starry-Eyed*, is the best-known number.

Streichinstrumente (Ger.). String instruments.

Streichorchester (Ger.). String orch.

Streichquartett (Ger.). String quartet.

Streisand, Barbra (Barbara Joan), popular American singer and actress; b. N.Y., Apr. 24, 1942. She studied acting for a short time in N.Y.; also learned to sing in Greenwich Village. In 1962 she made her Broadway debut in *I Can Get It for You Wholesale*; then made a hit in *Funny Girl* in 1964, a musical she filmed in 1968 and for which she received an Academy Award. Her other films include *On a Clear Day You Can See Forever* (1970), *A Star Is Born* (1976), and *Yentl* (1983). As a recording artist she received gold-record awards for her albums *People* (1965), *My Name Is Barbra* (1965), *Color Me Barbra* (1966), *Stoney End* (1971), *Barbra Joan Streisand* (1972), *The Way We Were* (1974), *A Star Is Born* (1976), *Superman* (1977), and others.

streng (Ger.). Severely, strictly.

streng im Takt (Ger.). Strictly in time.

streng im Tempo (Ger.). Strictly in tempo.

streng wie ein Kondukt (Ger.). Severely, as if in a funeral procession (Mahler, 5th Sym.).

streng Zeitmass (Ger.). Strictly in tempo.

strenger Satz (Ger.). Strict style of composition.

strepitoso (It.). In a noisy, boisterous, impetuous style.

Strepponi, Giuseppina (Clelia Maria Josepha). VERDI, GIUSEPPE (FORTUNINO FRANCESCO).

stretch. On a keyboard instrument, a wide interval or spread chord whose tones are to be taken simultaneously by the fingers of 1 hand.

stretto, -a (It., straitened, narrowed; Fr. *strette*). A musical climax that usually occurs at the point when thematic and rhythmic elements have reached the point of saturation. A classic example is the finale of the 2nd act in Mozart's *Le nozze di Figaro*, in prestissimo tempo. A stretto at the end of an impassioned aria or a dramatic duet is virtually synonymous with a CABALETTA. Particularly effective is a stretto in a fugue, in which the "narrowing" process is achieved by piling up the subject, the answer, and their fractional particles in close succession and overlap, producing the effect of accelerated canonic imitation; this is particularly effective in the final fugal exposition.

It should be noted that whereas in a homophonic style a stretto can be achieved by a purely dynamic process, a stretto in a fugue is a profound polyphonic exercise that has to be foreordained by the configuration of the theme and the answer at the inception of the fugue. *Andante stretto*, ANDANTE AGITATO; *stretto pedale*, in piano playing, a quick, deft shifting of the damper pedal, in a strongly marked chord passage, so that the harmonies may be at once forcible and distinct.

Strich (Ger.). A stroke of the bow. *Strich für Strich*, use separate bow strokes; DÉTACHÉ.

strict style. A style of composition in which (most) dissonances are regularly prepared and resolved.

stride piano. Jazz piano style of the 1920s and 1930s that retained elements of ragtime and in which the highly syncopated and elaborate melody is accompanied by the left hand's "strides" between single bass notes on the strong beat of the measure and middle-register chords on the weak beat in a regular oompah rhythm. One great performer was Fats Waller, in songs such as *I Would Do Anything for You*.

stridendo (*stridente*; It.). Stridently; sharply, piercingly; MARTELLATO.

Strike Up the Band. Musical by Gershwin, 1929. There is an American-Swiss war over the tariff on Swiss chocolate. The U.S. wins after discovering the Swiss yodeling code. The title song is very popular; another famous song, *The Man I Love*, was cut after the out-of-town tryouts; then again it was used to this treatment, having already been cut from *Lady, Be Good!* (1924); it was felt that the song held the action up.

string. A tone-producing cord. *First string*, the highest of a set; *open string*, one not stopped or shortened; *silver string*, one covered with silver wire; *soprano string*, the E string of the violin; *the strings*, the string group in the orch.

string bass. Double bass.

string drum. An instrument more familiarly known as a "lion's roar" (Ger. *Löwenebrull*; It. *rugghio di leone*; Fr. *tambour à cordes*); a friction drum with a cylindrical-shaped bucket through which a length of cord or gut string is pulled to produce a distinct "roaring" sound; favored among modern composers.

string(ed) instruments. All instruments whose tones are produced by strings, whether struck, plucked, or bowed. A wise tradition reserves the term *string instruments* for members of the violin and related families in which the strings are brought into vibration primarily by bowing. String instruments manipulated by plucking, such as the lute, guitar, balalaika, mandolin, banjo, and many Eastern instruments, are usually included in a category of their own. Another important distinction between these 2 categories of instruments is that on traditional string instruments, which include the violin, viola, cello, and double bass, the player must find the notes with 4 fingers of the left hand by groping, whereas the guitar, lute, etc. have frets or marking points indicating the position of the 12 notes of the chromatic scale.

It is noticeable visually that the distances between frets diminish for each successive chromatic interval. The violin string measuring 13 1/2 inches sounds an octave higher when it is stopped in the middle point, that is, at the distance of 6 3/4 inches from the peg and the bridge. But the next octave takes only a quarter of the string to span, and the next octave only 1/8 of the string. Thus even a mediocre violinist must develop an extraordinary capacity of judging small distances by touch. String instruments lend themselves to organization in any combination; even a duet for violin and double bass has been written. But the most common combinations, in addition to an unaccompanied string instrument, are string quartet, string quintet, string sextet (often including the double bass), or a string orch.

string piano. A traditional piano that is sounded by acting directly upon the strings, i.e. strumming, plucking, hammering, etc.

string quartet. Historically the most significant type of chamber music. A string quartet consists of 2 violins, viola, and cello. Such an ensemble provides a rich 4-part harmony and an articulate interplay of contrapuntal forms, especially canon and fugue. Opportunities for expressive and effective solo parts are many, with the solo instrument accompanied by the other 3 instruments; episodic duos and trios furnish another resource. The traditional structure of a string quartet is that of the sonata, consisting of 4 movements and usually including a minuet or a scherzo.

Goethe compared the playing of a string quartet with "a conversation of 4 educated people." The 1st violin is a natural leader. The 2nd violin is the leader's faithful partner; the somewhat derogatory expression "playing 2nd fiddle" suggests its subordinate function. The viola fills the harmony and emerges as an important member of the quartet, usually in canonic passages. The cello holds the important duty of the bass voice, determining the harmony; its sonorous arpeggios lend an almost orch.l quality to the ensemble. The employment of special effects such as pizzicato and the availability of double stops contribute further to the harmonic richness of string quartets.

Claims for the priority of composing string quartets have been made for several composers of the 17th century, but the 1st composer of stature to establish the string quartet as a distinctive musical form was Haydn, who wrote 83 string quartets. (This is not, however, the maximum; Boccherini wrote 102.) Mozart's string quartets brought the art of the string quartet to its highest flowering for the 18th century; his so-called *Dissonanzenquartett* aroused a heat of controversy because of its innovative use of dissonant harmonic combinations. Beethoven's last quartets caused contemporary critics to opine that they were the products of the composer's loss of hearing; as usual, he heard far better than the critics were ready to.

The taste and attraction of string quartets suffered a sharp decline in the modern era. Debussy, Ravel, and Stravinsky wrote only a single string quartet each. Schoenberg and Bartók revived the string quartet with considerable departures from tradition; Schoenberg even used a vocal solo in one of his. Russian composers continued to cultivate string quartets assiduously. Shostakovich wrote 15 of them.

string quintet. 1. A chamber music ensemble with 5 string instruments, usually 2 violins, 2 violas, and cello. 2. A composition, usually multimovement, for this combination (or a close variant). The most prolific composer of string quintets was Boccherini (12); Mozart wrote 6; Beethoven wrote 3; Mendelssohn wrote 2, as did Brahms. Schubert's great C-major quintet is scored for 2 violins, viola, and 2 cellos. 3. The string component of the orch., normally written in 5 parts (2 violins, viola, cello, and double bass).

string trio. 1. An ensemble for 3 string instruments, often consisting of violin, viola, and cello. 2. A composition, usually multimovement, for this combination (or a close variant). Historically the string trio is an offshoot of the TRIO SONATA. Haydn wrote as many as 20 trios for 2 violins and cello; Mozart and Beethoven also contributed to the form. Schoenberg's string trio is set in the 12-tone idiom.

stringendo (It.). Hastening; accelerating the movement, usually suddenly and rapidly, with a CRESCENDO.

stringere (It.). To hasten. *Senza stringere*, without hastening.

stringy. Having the quality of tone—string tone—peculiar to bowed instruments.

strisciando (It.). Gliding, smooth, GLISSANDO.

Strohfiedel (Ger., straw fiddle). Obsolete term for older type of xylophone in which the slabs were separated by straw.

stromenti a fiato (It.). Wind instruments.

strophe (Grk., turning). A rhythmic system composed of a repeated unit of 2 or more lines (refrain); it provides a break in the continuity of a stanzaic song, leading to a new section but preserving the unity of rhythm and musical setting. The strophe is often confused with the STANZA.

strophic bass. Repeated bass in a song accompaniment, to which the melody varies freely.

strophic composition (song). See SONG.

Strouse, Charles (Louis), American composer; b. N.Y., June 7, 1928. He studied at the Eastman School of Music in Rochester, N.Y., and later took private lessons in composition with Aaron Copland and Nadia Boulanger, under whose guidance he wrote some ambitious instrumental music. He was mainly active as a composer for Broadway and films; with the lyricist Lee Adams (b. Mansfield, Ohio, Aug. 14, 1924) he wrote the musicals *Bye Bye Birdie* (1960) and *Applause* (1970), both of which won Tony Awards. His other musicals include *Golden Boy* (1964), after a play by Clifford Odets, and *Annie* (1977). He also composed a piano concerto and other orch. pieces, and a string quartet.

structure. In the 20th century, an analyzable system within the totality of musical parameters, denoting the methods and mechanisms applied and contributing to the ultimate structural integrity of a work. While *structure* is often used as a synonym for *form* (in the sense of design), it can refer to elements such as harmony, counterpoint, melody, and rhythm; it can refer to a specific idiom, such as dodecaphonic, stochastic, linear, tonal, motivic, and symmetrical structures; or, in its adjectival form it can identify structural conceptions, such as layering, variants, accentuation, groupings, symbolism, gestalt, and perception. The present usage of the term indicates a composer's concern for rational control and structural meaning.

strumentatura (It.). Instrumentation.

strumento (*stromento*; It.). Instrument. *Strumenti a corda*, string instruments; *strumenti a fiato*, wind instruments; *strumenti da tasto*, keyboard instruments.

Stück (Ger.). A piece; a number. *Klavierstück*, a piece for piano. See also SHTICK.

Student Prince (in Heidelberg), The. Operetta by Romberg, 1924, premiered in N.Y. A royal prince enrolls in the Univ. of Heidelberg. He engages in a romance with a lovely German waitress, strictly incognito. When the news comes of his father's death in whatever small principality he comes from, the prince becomes a king and is forced to abandon his waitress to marry a prim princess. The score is full of sentimental songs and duets; a choral drinking song has become a favorite.

Studer, Cheryl, American soprano; b. Midland, Mich., Oct. 24, 1955. After training in Ohio and at the Univ. of

Tenn., she studied voice with Hans Hotter at the Vienna Hochschule für Musik. She appeared in concerts in the U.S. before singing at the Bavarian State Opera in Munich in 1980; then was a member of the Darmstadt Opera (1983–85). In 1984 she made her U.S. operatic debut as Micaela at the Chicago Lyric Opera. In 1985 she joined the Deutsche Oper in West Berlin. She also sang at the Bayreuth Festivals (from 1985), at the Paris Opéra (from 1986), and at La Scala in Milan (from 1987). Among her prominent roles are Pamina, Donna Anna, Elsa, Eva, Sieglinde, and Chrysothemis.

study. An étude; teaching piece.

Study in Sonority. A work for 10 violins by Riegger, 1929, in which the G strings of the violins are tuned down to E. (The work can also be performed with multiples of 10 violins). The piece is set in dissonant counterpoint with megachords containing from 8 to 12 different notes. It was performed for the 1st time in Philadelphia by Stokowski, using 40 violins.

Sturm und Drang (Ger., storm and stress). German literary term borrowed to describe a highly emotional minor-key style that emerged during the early Classic period, particularly the 1770s and 1780s. The literary movement arose in the last part of the 18th century, eventually taking its name from the title of a popular play by Friedrich Klinger (1776). It became eponymous with a growing sentiment among the youth of the time that a rebellion against the conservatism in social politics and in art was necessary; it also brought to the fore the extreme emotions that Goethe portrayed in *The Sorrows of Young Werther* (1774). In music it gave a glimpse of the extreme, non-Classic contrasts that would be a stylistic trademark of the Romantic style of composition. But the movement retreated into the aesthetic wilderness until younger writers such as Jean Paul, E. T. A. Hoffman, the brothers Grimm, and the British gothic school redefined the meaning of aesthetics and composers like Beethoven (and to a lesser extent Weber) composed from the soul as well as the ear. In this sense Schumann's struggle against musical Philistinism, and the programmatic concepts of many of his works, are indirect descendants of Sturm und Drang.

Stürmisch (Ger.). Tempestuously, passionately, impetuously.

style brisé (Fr., broken style). In French music of the 17th century, a form of chordal arpeggiation in which the bass note sounded 1st, then the melody, and with the middle voices in a similarly free manner. Many of Louis Couperin's harpsichord preludes provide examples of this manner in notation.

style élégant (Fr.). GALANTERIEN.

style galant (Fr.). GALLANT STYLE.

Styne, Jule (born Julius Kerwin Stein), English-born American composer of popular music; b. London, Dec. 31, 1905; d. Sept. 20, 1994. He was taught piano by his parents; was taken to the U.S. at the age of 8; appeared with the Chicago Sym. Orch. as a child pianist but did not pursue a concert career; won a scholarship to the Chicago College of Music at 13; after playing piano in jazz groups and dance bands he went to Hollywood (1940) and rapidly established himself as a successful song composer for films; also was notably successful as a composer of Broadway musicals, which included *High Button Shoes* (1947), *Gentlemen Prefer Blondes* (1949), *Bells Are Ringing* (1956), *Gypsy*, based on the life of striptease artist Gypsy Rose Lee (1959), *Do Re Mi* (1960; no relation to *The Sound of Music*), *Funny Girl*, scenes from the life of the singer-comedienne Fanny Brice (1964), *Hallelujah, Baby!* (1967), and *Sugar* (1972).

styrienne (Fr.; It. *stiriana*). An air in slow movement and 2/4 time, often in a minor key, with a *Jodler* (yodel) after each verse; for vocal or instrumental solo.

su (It.). Above, on, upon, by, near. *Arco in su*, up-bow.

suave (It.). SOAVE.

subbass, subbourdon. An organ stop of 16' or 32' pitch, generally on the pedal, and stopped.

subdominant. The tone below the dominant in a diatonic scale; the 4th degree.

subito (It.). Immediately; suddenly; without pause. *Volti subito*, turn over (the page) quickly; *subito piano* or *p subito*, an abrupt change to *piano*, without gradation.

subject. A melodic motive or phrase on which a composition or movement is founded; a theme. In a fugue, the antecedent or DUX.

submediant. The 3rd scale tone below the tonic; the 6th degree.

suboctave. 1. The octave below a given note. 2. The double contra-octave.

subordinate chords. Chords not fundamental or principal; the triads on the 2nd, 3rd, 6th, and 7th degrees, and all 7th chords but the dominant 7th.

Subotnick, Morton, American composer and teacher; b. Los Angeles, Apr. 14, 1933. He studied at the Univ. of Denver (B.A., 1958) and with Milhaud and Kirchner at Mills College in Oakland, Calif. (M.A., 1960); then was a fellow of the Inst. for Advanced Musical Studies at Princeton Univ. (1959–60). He taught at Mills College (1959–66), N.Y. Univ. (1966–69), and the Calif. Inst. of the Arts (from 1969); also held various visiting professorships and composer-in-residence positions. In 1979 he married Joan La Barbara. His compositions run the gamut of AVANT-GARDE techniques, often with innovative use of electronics and electroacoustic devices known as *ghost electronics.*

His works include: *Lamination* for Orch. and Tape (1968); *Axolotl* for Cello, Chamber Orch., and Electronics (1982); *Liquid Strata* for Piano, Orch., and Electronics (1982); *The Key to Songs* for Chamber Orch. and Synthesizer (1985); *Mr. and Mrs. Discobolos* for Clarinet, Violin, Cello, Narrator-Mime, and Tape (1958); *Play! No. 1* for Wind Quintet, Tape, and Film (1963); *4 Butterflies* for Tape and 3 Films (1973); *The Double Life of Amphibians,* theater piece (1984); *Jacob's Room* for Voice and String Quartet (1984; San Francisco, Jan. 11, 1985); incidental music; *The Tarot* for Chamber Ensemble (1965); *The Fluttering of Wings* for String Quartet (1982); *Passages of the Beast* for Clarinet and Electronics (1978); *Ascent into Air* for 10 Instruments and Electronics (1981); *Silver Apples of the Moon* (1967); *The Wild Bull* (1968); *Touch* (1969); *Sidewinder* (1971); *Until Spring* (1975); *A Sky of Cloudless Sulphur* (1978).

subprincipal. A subbass pedal stop of 32' pitch.

subsemitonium modi (Lat., lower semitone of the mode). LEADING TONE.

substitution. 1. In contrapuntal progression, the resolution or preparation of a dissonance by substituting, for the regular tone of resolution or preparation, its higher or lower octave in some other part. 2. The use of alternate harmonies to fill a chord in a standard progression, e.g., the 1st inversion of the supertonic 7th chord instead of the subdominant.

subtonic. The leading tone (rarely used).

subtonium. An additional tone placed below a church mode, in time coming to mean a whole tone below the final of the mode. As the modes gradually gave way to modern tonality, the subtonium was replaced by the SUBSEMITONIUM, the modern leading tone.

succentor. A member of the Anglican church clergy, assistant to the precentor in musical and other matters.

suffocato (It.). SOFFOCATO.

sugli, sui (It.). On the; near the.

suite. An instrumental genre designating a succession of movements not necessarily related to one another and unified only by the homonymous key. The most important of this category is the *Baroque suite,* composed primarily of dance forms. The standard selection and ordering of the movements is allemande, courante, sarabande, and gigue. Several optional movements, mostly derived from popular dances, are interpolated between the sarabande and gigue, notably a minuet or gavotte; some suites end with a BOURRÉE. Bach expanded the length and content of his instrumental suites, but the meaning of the adjectives *English* and *French,* applied to 6 keyboard suites apiece, is conjectural. Bach also wrote suites bearing the designation PARTITA.

Baroque harpsichord composers, who were still contending with the problems of tuning in meantone temperament, realized that it was best to construct suites in only 1 key so that a substantial work could be performed without constant retuning between pieces. The French composers F. Couperin and Rameau (who called their suites *ordres*) began to name their suite movements with fanciful programmatic titles; many of these pieces were far removed from the usual dance models.

The character of the suite was changed radically in the 19th century. While Bach, Handel, and other composers of the Baroque period followed the contrapuntal style of composition, composers of the later centuries regarded the suite mainly as an assemblage of variegated movements, often arranged from operas, ballets, and theater music. Sometimes such suites became the only viable remnants of a score of incidental music, as for instance in the suites *L'Arlésienne* of Bizet, or *Peer Gynt* of Grieg. Tchaikovsky's *Nutcracker Suite* is one of the most popular examples of the genre. The suite from *Lulu* was the only music Berg ever heard from his 2nd opera.

Neoclassical composers of the 2nd quarter of the 20th century, notably Stravinsky and Hindemith, made a serious effort to revive the Baroque suite, with a titillating titivation of the ancient forms by means of dissonant treatment; other composers have used the term *suite* in its loosest sense—a collection of pieces or movements, often but not necessarily of a lighter character, for 1 instrument or ensemble, to be played consecutively.

Suite bergamasque. A set of 4 piano pieces by Debussy, 1889–1905, in a hybrid form of the suite. Its 3rd movement is the famous *Clair de lune*. Debussy took the title *Suite bergamasque* from the alliterative lines in Verlaine's poem entitled *Clair de lune*, "masques et bergamasques." The name bergamasque is derived from a dance of Bergamo, Italy.

Suite Provençale. Orch. suite by Milhaud, 1937, based on dance melodies of Provence; it was 1st performed in Venice.

suivez (Fr.). 1. Same as COLLA PARTE. 2. Continue, go on.

sul, sull', sulla, sulle (It.). (Play) on the, near the. *Sulla corda La*, play on the A string; *Sulla tastiera*, play near or above the fingerboard, FLAUTANDO; *sul ponticello*, play near the bridge; *sul tasto*, on the keyboard.

suling. Family of bamboo flutes in Indonesia and surrounding areas. They can be transverse, nose, whistle, or ring (end-blown) flutes; are of various sizes; have anywhere from 3 to 7 finger holes; are known by various names; and are used either as a solo instrument or in gamelan and more modern ensembles. The relationship between the suling and the human voice is spiritual and musical.

Sullivan, (Sir) Arthur (Seymour)

Famous English composer and conductor; famous for his collaborations with the celebrated humorist (Sir) William S(chwenck) Gilbert; b. London, May 13, 1842; d. there, Nov. 22, 1900. His father, Thomas Sullivan, was bandmaster at the Royal Military College, Sandhurst, and later prof. of brass instruments at the Royal Military School of Music, Kneller Hall; his musical inclinations were encouraged by his father, and in 1854 he became a chorister in the Chapel Royal, remaining there until 1858 and studying with the Rev. Thomas Helmore; in 1855 his sacred song *O Israel* was publ.

In 1856 he received the 1st Mendelssohn Scholarship to the Royal Academy of Music in London, where he studied with Sterndale Bennett, Arthur O'Leary, and John Goss; then continued his training at the Leipzig Cons. (1858–61), where he received instruction in counterpoint and fugue from Moritz Hauptmann, in composition from Julius Rietz, in piano from Ignaz Moscheles and Louis Plaidy, and in conducting from Ferdinand David. He conducted his overture *Rosenfest* in Leipzig (1860) and wrote a string quartet and music to *The Tempest* (Leipzig, 1861). His cantata *Kenilworth* (Birmingham Festival, 1864) stamped him as a composer of high rank. In 1864 he visited Ireland and composed his *Irish Sym.* (London, 1866).

In 1866 he was appointed prof. of composition at the Royal Academy of Music in London. About this time he formed a lifelong friendship with Sir George Grove, whom he accompanied in 1867 on a memorable journey to Vienna in search of Schubert MSS, leading to the discovery of the score of *Rosamunde*. The year 1867 was also notable for the production of the 1st of those comic operas upon which Sullivan's fame chiefly rests. This was *Cox and Box* (libretto by F. C. Burnand), composed in 2 weeks and performed in 1867, in London. Less successful were *The Contrabandista* (London, 1867) and *Thespis*

(London, 1871; music lost); but the latter is significant as inaugurating Sullivan's collaboration with Gilbert, the celebrated humorist, who became the librettist of all Sullivan's most successful comic operas, beginning with *Trial by Jury* (1875). This was produced by Richard D'Oyly Carte, who in 1876 formed a company expressly for the production of the Gilbert and Sullivan operas.

The 1st big success obtained by the famous team was *H.M.S. Pinafore* (1878), which had 700 consecutive performances in London and enjoyed an enormous vogue in "pirated" productions throughout the U.S. In an endeavor to protect their interests, Gilbert and Sullivan went to N.Y. in 1879 to give an authorized performance of *Pinafore*; while there they also produced *The Pirates of Penzance*. In 1881 came *Patience*, a satire on exaggerated aesthetic poses exemplified by Oscar Wilde, whose American lecture tour was conceived as a "publicity stunt" for this work. In 1882 *Iolanthe* began a run that lasted more than a year. This was followed by the comparatively unsuccessful *Princess Ida* (1884), but then came the universal favorite of all the Gilbert and Sullivan operas, *The Mikado* (1885). The list of these popular works is completed by *Ruddigore* (1887), *The Yeomen of the Guard* (1888), and *The Gondoliers* (1889).

After a quarrel and a reconciliation, the pair collaborated in 2 further works, of less popularity: *Utopia Limited* (1893) and *The Grand Duke* (1896). Sullivan's melodic inspiration and technical resourcefulness, united with the delicious humor of Gilbert's verses, raised the light opera to a new height of artistic achievement, and his works in this field continue to delight countless hearers.

Sullivan was also active in other branches of musical life. He conducted numerous series of concerts, most notably those of the London Phil. Soc. (1885–87) and the Leeds Festivals (1880–98). He was principal of, and a prof. of composition at, the National Training School for Music from 1876 to 1881. He received the degree of Mus.Doc. *honoris causa* from Cambridge (1876) and Oxford (1879); was named Chevalier of the Legion of Honor (1878); was grand organist to the Freemasons (1887); etc. He was knighted by Queen Victoria in 1883.

Parallel with his comic creations he composed many "serious" works, including the grand opera *Ivanhoe* (1891), which enjoyed a momentary vogue. Among his cantatas the most successful was *The Golden Legend*, after Longfellow (Leeds Festival, 1886); he also wrote the famous hymn *Onward, Christian Soldiers*, to words by Rev. Sabine Baring-Gould (1871). His songs were highly popular in their day, and *The Lost Chord*, to words by Adelaide A. Proctor (1877), is still a favorite. Among his oratorios *The Light of the World* (Birmingham Festival, 1873) may be mentioned. Other stage works (all 1st perf. in London) include *The Zoo* (1875); *The Sorcerer* (Gilbert; 1877); *Haddon Hall* (1892); *The Beauty Stone* (1898); the romantic opera *The Rose of Persia* (1899); and *The Emerald Isle* (completed by E. German; 1901).

sum (summation) **tone.** A tone resulting from the addition of the frequencies of 2 or more original tones forming a consonant interval; a sum tone is much weaker than its opposite, the difference tone formed by the difference of the same original frequencies; therefore the sum tone is usually less disturbing to the player or listener.

Sumer is icumen in (Summer Is Coming In). The incipit of the earliest known canon, written for 4 voices, with the harmony formed by a double PEDAL POINT, or pedal (which is actually designated as *pes* [foot] in the original MS). The canon is of English origin, and the MS on parchment is preserved in the British Museum. The title above the music is *Rota* (round). A controversy exists as to the date of its composition; the estimate varies between 1250 and 1320. The text of the canon is as follows:

Sumer is icumen in
Lhude sing cuccu!
Groweth sed and bloweth med,
And springth the wude nu
Sing cuccu!

Ezra Pound, in one of his sardonic moods, wrote a parody that begins, "Winter is icumen in/Lhude sing goddamm!"

Summer Morning's Dream (*Ein Sommermorgentraum*). The original subtitle of Mahler's 3rd Sym., 1896, as given in the original MS. The work is in D minor (although the MS also indicates its being in the relative key of F major). The 3rd Sym. is in 6 movements, each with a romantically descriptive communication: "The summer arrives," "What the flowers tell me," "What the animals tell me," "What humanity tells me," "What the angels tell me" (accompanied by voices), and "What love tells me." Mahler conducted the 1st complete performance in Krefeld, 1902.

Summer Night on the River. Symphonic sketch by Delius, 1913, set in a characteristically Romantic manner. It was 1st performed as a companion piece to another work of his, *On Hearing the 1st Cuckoo in Spring*, in Leipzig.

Summertime. The opening aria (after the Jasbo Brown Blues prologue) of Gershwin's Porgy and Bess, 1935; a woman sings a lullaby to her infant. In a work with many memorable moments, *Summertime* stands out as perhaps the most famous, and certainly the most covered by later artists.

Sun Ra (born Herman Blount), innovative African-American jazz pianist, electric keyboardist, bandleader, composer, and self-proclaimed extraterrestrial; b. Birmingham, Ala., May 1914; d. there May 30, 1993, of a stroke. He learned to play the piano and 1st gained notice as a member of Fletcher Henderson's orch. (1946–47); then went to Chicago, where he became a prominent figure in the avant-garde jazz scene; in 1956 founded his own band, which was variously known as Solar Arkestra, Intergalactic Myth-Science Arkestra, Space Arkestra, etc.; later was active in N.Y. and Philadelphia; also toured throughout the U.S. and Europe; was a featured artist on the *Saturday Night Live* television show (1976). Compositionally he developed an abrasive and complex style in which avant-garde techniques are combined with electronic resources.

Sunny. Musical by Kern, 1925. Sunny is an equestrienne in England, and she is serenaded by American soldiers during World War I. She falls in love with one of the GI's and stows away aboard his ship sailing for the U.S. Besides the title song, there is an attractive duet, *Who?*

Sunny Boy. Sentimental ballad by Ray Henderson, 1925, made instantly famous in Al Jolson's interpretation in the musical *The Singing Fool*.

Sun-Treader. Symphonic poem by Ruggles, 1926–31, inspired by a line from a poem by Robert Browning, "Sun-treader, light and life be thine forever." The work is set in a powerful dissonant idiom, in which contrapuntal layers are constantly lifted and lowered in a titanic harmonic struggle. Like most of Ruggles's works, the composer continued to revise it after its premiere in Paris, 1932.

suonare (It.). Obsolete form of SONARE.

suonata (It.). Alternate spelling of SONATA.

suono (It.). Sound. *Suono alto*, high sound; *suono grave*, low sound; *suono harmonico*, harmonic.

Suor Angelica. Opera by Puccini, 1918, 1st produced by the Metropolitan Opera in N.Y., as the 2nd part of his operatic triptych *Il Trittico*; the 1st part was *Il Tabarro* and the 3rd *Gianni Schicchi*. Sister Angelica, who abandoned her own child, enters the convent to redeem her sin. When she learns that the child is dead, she takes poison. Because of the sincerity of her repentance, the Madonna appears to her holding Angelica's transfigured child in her arms; Angelica receives her absolution. Puccini's own sister was a nun; when he finished the vocal score, he played it for her at her convent.

šupeljka. Macedonian and Bulgarian end-blown shepherd's flute, with cylindrical bore, 6 finger holes, and no mouthpiece.

superbamente (It.). Proudly, loftily.

superdominant. The 6th degree of a diatonic scale; the SUBMEDIANT.

superfetation. When several viable musical ideas occur simultaneously and are contrapuntally conjugated without a preliminary statement, a melorhythmic superfetation is the result. The thematic embryos may then be separated to pursue their different courses; or else the nonidentical geminal subjects may remain unified like Siamese twins, treated collectively as bipartite entities that subsequently may enter into a secondary superfetation. Given a complete freedom of dissonant counterpoint, superfetation can be extended to thematic triplets, quadruplets, quintuplets, sextuplets, septuplets, octuplets, etc., interpenetrating and disengaging themselves in a multiplicity of instrumental or vocal lines.

superfluous. Augmented, as in chord or interval.

superoctave. 1. An organ stop of 2' pitch. 2. A coupler bringing into action keys an octave above those struck, either on the same manual or another. 3. The octave above a given tone.

supertonic. The 2nd degree of a diatonic scale. In a major key the supertonic triad is minor; in a minor key the supertonic triad is diminished, traditionally proscribed harmonically. However, the 1st inversion of the supertonic triad, whether in major or minor, serves as a dignified surrogate (substitute) for the subdominant triad in a cadence, as they have the same bass note. In the Neapolitan cadence the 1st inversion of the lowered supertonic (e.g., in C major or minor, F–A♭–D♭) is a treasured cadential chord ever since its introduction in the 17th century, its advantage being that it provides a resonant major tonal harmony in place of a weak minor modal harmony.

Suppé, Franz (von) (born Francesco Ezechiele Ermenegildo, Cavaliere Suppé-Demelli), famous Austrian composer; b. Spalato, Dalmatia (of Belgian descent), Apr. 18, 1819; d. Vienna, May 21, 1895. At the age of 11 he played the flute, and at 13 he wrote a Mass. He was then sent by his father to study law at Padua; on his father's death he went with his mother to Vienna in 1835; he continued serious study at the Cons. with Sechter and Seyfried. He conducted at theaters in Pressburg and Baden; then at Vienna's Theater an der Wien (1845–62), Kaitheater (1862–65), and Carltheater (1865–82). All the while he wrote light operas and other theater music of all degrees of levity, obtaining increasing success rivaling that of Offenbach.

His music possesses the charm and gaiety of the Viennese genre, but also contains elements of more vigorous popular rhythms. His most celebrated single work is the overture to *Dichter und Bauer* (Poet and Peasant; 1846), which still retains a firm place in the light repertoire. His total output comprises about 30 comic operas and operettas and 180 other stage pieces, most of which were brought out in Vienna; of these the following obtained considerable success: *Paragraph 3* (1858); *Die Kartenaufschlägerin* (Queen of Spades; 1862); *Zehn Mädchen und kein Mann* (1862); *Die flötten Burschen* (1863); *Die schöne Galatea*

(Berlin, 1865); *Die leichte Kavallerie* (1866); *Banditenstreiche* (1867); *Die Frau Meisterin* (1868); *Tantalusqualen* (1868); *Isabella* (1869); *Fatinitza* (1876; extremely popular); *Boccaccio* (1879; very popular); *Donna Juanita* (1880); *Die Afrikareise* (1883); *Das Modell* (1895). Other works include syms., concert overtures, a Requiem, 3 Masses, and other sacred works, choruses, dances, string quartets, and songs.

supplicando (It.). In a style expressive of supplication, entreaty, pleading.

sur la touche (Fr., at the fingerboard; It. *sulla tastiera*; Ger. *am Griffbrett*). Bow near the fingerboard so as to produce a sound imitating the flute's sonority; hence the Italian synonym FLAUTANDO.

Sur le Pont d'Avignon. French children's song, 1845, 1st published in a Parisian collection of nursery rhymes. The 1st line reads, "On the bridge of Avignon, they dance, they dance."

Surfin' Safari. First chart hit in 1962 for the Beach Boys, penned by group leaders Brian Wilson and Mike Love; it led the way to *Surfin' USA* (largely borrowed from Chuck Berry) and *Surfer Girl*.

Surprise Symphony. Sym. No. 94 by Haydn, 1792, in G major. This is the 3rd of 12 so-called *London Syms.*, which he wrote for performance at the concerts conducted by the German violinist Salomon in London. The surprise is furnished by the sudden loud chord in the middle of the quiet opening theme of the slow 2nd movement, a variation set. The anecdote is often told that Haydn put the loud chord in to wake up the somnolent English ladies who went to concerts for a nice refreshing nap, but when it was 1st performed the papers failed to note such effect. One critic said that the loud chord suggested to him the discharge of a musket on a pastoral scene when a shepherdess lulled herself to sleep contemplating nature and a distant waterfall. (No historical evidence of the presence of shepherdesses at the London premiere of this sym. has been discovered.) As if to disabuse people of such stories, German catalogues list the *Surprise Sym.* simply as *Paukenschlag*, that is, the *Drumstroke*.

surrealism

~~~ ~~~ ~~~ ~~~ ~~~

A word coined in 1903 by the French poet Guillaume Apollinaire in his fantastic play *Les Mamelles de Tirésias*, concerning the problem of a transsexual transplantation of breasts and gender roles, which he subtitled *drame surréaliste*. The etymology of the word implies a higher degree of realism, penetrating into the subliminal human psyche. Surrealism became a fashionable movement when André Breton published a surrealist manifesto in 1924. In it he described surrealism as "psychic automatism," antirationalistic in essence and completely spontaneous in its creative process.

Fantasy and free association were the normative factors of surrealistic literature and art. Apollinaire described surrealism as the rational technique of the improbable. Jean Cocteau equated it with the essence of poetry; in his film *Le Sang d'un poète* he proposed to give a "realistic account of unreal phenomena." The famous French handbook, Nouveau Petit Larousse, defines *surrealism* tersely as "tendance d'une école à négliger toute préoccupation logique." Surrealism is oxymoronic in essence, thriving on the incompatibility of the opposites, exemplified by such images as cold flame, thunderous silence, painstaking idleness, and quiet desperation.

Surrealist artists are fascinated by musical subjects. As early as the Renaissance, paintings representing Biblical scenes in which musicians perform on the lute and the theorbo are both anachronistic and surrealistic in their effect. Salvador Dali humanized musical instruments. In one of his paintings a faceless cellist plays on the spinal column of a human cello mounted on a pin. On its buttocks there are the familiar resonators in the forms of symmetric gothic *F*'s. Another musical painting by Dali, bearing the surrealistic title *6 Apparitions of Lenin on a Piano*, represents several heads of Lenin crowned with aureoles strewn across the keyboard. The Belgian surrealist René Magritte painted a burning bass tuba. In the art work *Object for Destruction* by the American surrealist Man Ray, a print of a human eye was attached to the pendulum of a metronome. Real metronomes are the instruments in a score by the Hungarian modernist György

Ligeti, containing 100 metronomes all ticking at different speeds. In his vision of socialist music of the future the Soviet poet Vladimir Mayakovsky conjured up a sym. with rain conduits for flutes. The American band leader Spike Jones introduced a latrinophone, a surrealistic lyre made of a toilet seat strung with violin strings.

Apollinaire urged artists, poets, and musicians to cultivate "the insane verities of art." No one has followed his advice more ardently than Erik Satie; he incarnated the spirit of inversion. He entitled his utterly surrealistic score *Parade* "ballet réaliste." Jean Cocteau wrote: "Satie's *Parade* removes the sauce. The result is a completely naked object which scandalizes by its very nakedness. In the theater everything must be false in order to appear true." Satie was very much in earnest when he wrote, "J'emmerde l'art c'est un métier de con." The titles of his piano pieces are typical of surrealistic self-contradiction: such as *Heures séculaires et instantanées* or *Trois morceaux en forme de poire*.

Surrealism in art is the superposition of extraneous elements on reality. If tonality is accepted as musical reality, then polytonality could be described as musical surrealism, with the surrealistic effect supplied by the addition of unrelated tonalities. Numeral surrealism is employed by Virgil Thomson in his opera *4 Saints in 3 Acts*, which really has about 2 dozen saints and is set in 4, not 3, acts. Surrealist music is also inherently futuristic. Operatic surrealism is exemplified by *The Nose* by Shostakovich, after Gogol's tale, in which the nose escapes from the face of a government functionary and assumes an independent existence, including even sneezes. In the "jazz opera" *Jonny spielt auf* by Ernst Krenek, a jazz player surrealistically surmounts the terrestrial globe. In Hindemith's *Hin und Zurück* the action is a palindrome, whereby the opera ends at its starting point.

Stravinsky's ballet *Petrouchka*, in which puppets are more real than their manipulators, is surrealistic; in this work Stravinsky exploits the tonal polarity of C major and F-sharp major as an example of harmonic surrealism. The same type of bitonality is used by Darius Milhaud in his ballet *Le Boeuf sur le toit*, which depicts incongruous events in an American saloon. In the ballet *The Miraculous Mandarin* by Bartók, the fantastic surrealism of the action (in which the Mandarin is impervious to mortal wounds as long as lust attaches him to a prosti-tute) is illustrated by a discordant musical score. Henri Bergson describes music itself as a surrealist phenomenon, for it imposes the tonal language upon the world in which the primary means of communication is through verbal expression.

Survivor from Warsaw, A. Cantata by Schoenberg, 1948, scored for speaker, male chorus, and orch.; it was 1st performed in Albuquerque, N.Mex. The words are by Schoenberg himself, in English; the text narrates the story of a Jew who survived the Nazi horrors in Warsaw. The Nazi commands are uttered in German, and the work concludes with the singing of the most important Jewish prayer, *Hear O Israel* (in Hebrew). The score is written in a 12-tone idiom, which adds to the tension by its acrid tonality.

Susannah. Opera by C. Floyd, 1955, to his own libretto; premiered in Tallahassee, Fla. A pious minister succumbs to the charms of a pretty sinner. When her brother surprises him with Susannah, he kills the minister. A menacing mob forms near Susannah's, but she takes a resolute stand at the porch with a shotgun and the villagers disperse. The music is tonal and folklike.

Susato, Tylman, German music publisher and composer; b. *c.* 1500; d. probably in Antwerp, *c.* 1562. He may have been born in Antwerp, where he pursued his career; was a calligrapher at the Cathedral (1529–30), becoming a trumpeter there in 1531; then was a town musician (1532–49). After serving as a partner in a printing venture (1541–43), he set up his own press in 1543 and remained active until at least 1561. His press produced 25 books of chansons, 3 books of Masses, 19 books of motets, and 11 *Musyck boexken*. He was a fine composer of cantus firmus chansons for 2 or 3 voices (1544; *c.* 1552).

suspension. A dissonance caused by suspending (holding over) a tone or tones of a chord while the other tones progress to a new harmony, thus creating a discord demanding immediate resolution. Downward diatonic suspensions are by far more frequent than upward ones. While the resolutions of downward suspension follow the degrees of the diatonic scale, upward suspensions are, by instinctive feeling, almost invariably semitones. Suspensions and appoggiaturas are analogous in producing a dissonant harmony on the strong beat of the measure; the difference is that while a sus-pension is a prepared dissonant combination, the appoggiatura is an ornament placed on the harmony note without preparation. The resolution of a suspended note may be detoured by a NOTA CAMBIATA, ECHAPPÉE, or a combination of nonharmonic tones, but this must not delay the resolution for too long.

suspirium (Lat., breath). In mensural notation, a brief pause.

süss (Ger.). Sweetly.

Süssmayr, Franz Xaver. See MOZART, WOLFGANG AMADEUS.

sussurando (It.). In a whisper.

sustain. To hold during the full time value (of notes); also, to perform in SOSTENUTO or LEGATO style.

sustaining pedal. A misnomer for the SOSTENUTO PEDAL.

susurrante (It.). In a whispering, murmurous tone.

Sutherland, (Dame) **Joan,** celebrated Australian soprano; b. Sydney, Nov. 7, 1926. She 1st studied piano and voice with her mother; at age 19 she commenced vocal training with John and Aida Dickens in Sydney, making her debut there as Dido in a concert performance of *Dido and Aeneas* in 1947; then made her stage debut there in the title role of Judith in 1951; subsequently continued her vocal studies with Clive Carey at the Royal College of Music in London; also studied at the Opera School there. She made her Covent Garden debut in London as the 1st Lady in *Die Zauberflöte* in 1952; attracted attention there when she created the role of Jenifer in *The Midsummer Marriage* (1955) and as Gilda (1957); also appeared in the title role of Alcina in the Handel Opera Soc. production (1957). In the meantime she married Richard Bonynge (1954), who coached her in the bel canto operatic repertoire.

After making her North American debut as Donna Anna in Vancouver (1958), she scored a triumph as Lucia at Covent Garden (1959). From then on she pursued a brilliant international career. She made her U.S. debut as Alcina in Dallas in 1960. Her Metropolitan Opera debut in N.Y. as Lucia (1961) was greeted by extraordinary acclaim. She continued to sing at the Metropolitan and other major opera houses on both sides of the Atlantic; also took her own company to Australia in 1965 and 1974; during her husband's music directorship with the Australian Opera in Sydney (1976–86) she made stellar appearances with the company. In 1990 she made her operatic farewell in *Les Huguenots* in Sydney.

Sutherland was universally acknowledged as one of the foremost interpreters of the bel canto repertoire of her time. She particularly excelled in roles from operas by Rossini, Bellini, and Donizetti; she was also a fine Handelian. In 1961 she was made a Commander of the Order of the British Empire, and in 1979 was named a Dame Commander of the Order of the British Empire.

Suzuki, Shin'ichi, influential Japanese music educator and violin teacher; b. Nagoya, Oct. 18, 1898. He was the son of Masakichi Suzuki (1859–1944), a maker of string instruments and the founder of the Suzuki Violin Seizo Co. He studied violin with Ko Ando in Tokyo and with Karl Klinger in Berlin (1921–28); upon his return to Japan he formed the Suzuki Quartet with 3 of his brothers; also made appearances as a conductor with his own Tokyo String Orch. He became president of the Teikoku Music School in 1930; subsequently devoted most of his time to education, especially the teaching of children. He maintained that any child, given the right stimuli under proper conditions in a group environment, could achieve a high level of competence as a performer.

In 1950 he organized the Saino Kyoiku Kenkyu-kai in Matsumoto, where he taught his method most successfully. In subsequent years his method was adopted for instruction on other instruments as well. He made many tours of the U.S. and Europe, where he lectured and demonstrated his method. See K. Selden, trans., *Where Love Is Deep: The Writings of Shin-ichi Suzuki* (1982).

Suzuki Method. A process of musical education based upon the repetition of (and adaptation to) external stimuli; founded by Shin'ichi Suzuki. Although the program ranges through adolescence, it seems to be most successful with very young children, especially those between the ages of 4 and 8, who are taught to play the violin by imitating the physical movements and the visual placement of the fingers on the strings.

Švanda dudák. SCHWANDA THE BAGPIPER.

svanirando (*svaporando*; It., evaporating). Vanishing; fainter and fainter; reducing the dynamic level to the threshold of audibility.

Svätopluk. Opera, 1960, by Eugen Suchoň (b. Pezinok, Slovakia, Sept. 25, 1908; d. Bratislava, Aug. 5, 1993), premiered in Bratislava. In 9th-century Moravia, Svätopluk is an ambitious prince who takes part in a conspiracy against his father the King. His plot is foiled, but the King, shaken by this treachery, dies. Svätopluk's younger brother ascends to the throne. Ancient Slavic motives are utilized in the score; the musical realization is in the tradition of Smetana and Mussorgsky.

svegliato (It.). Lively, animatedly, briskly, alertly. *Svelto*, light, nimble; *sveltezza*, alertness.

svirala (*sviralina*; Serb.). Generic term for indigenous flute family instruments, also found in Croatia and Slavonia (*jedina*).

svolazzando (It.). Soaring; used by Liszt.

svolgimento (It.). Development section.

Swan Lake. Ballet by Tchaikovsky, 1st performed in Moscow, Mar. 4, 1877. The scenario is the quintessence of Romanticism. A young girl loved by a prince is changed into a swan by witchcraft. She can be saved only if he identifies her in the swan lake. But he fails, selecting the wrong swan. His beloved perishes, and he jumps from the cliff into the water to his death. The score contains some of Tchaikovsky's most romantic music; an instrumental suite has been drawn from the ballet.

Swan of Tuonela, The. The 3rd movement of the symphonic cycle *Lemminkäinen* by Sibelius, 1893, based on the Finnish epic *Kalevala*. Tuonela is the Kingdom of Death, surrounded by a winding stream; the swan guards the entrance; its melody is given to the English horn.

swan song. The legend that swans sing beautifully at the approach of death is of ancient origin. Plato states that dying swans sing so sweetly because they know that they are about to return to the divine presence of Apollo, to whom they are sacred. Another Greek writer reports that flocks of swans regularly descend on Apollo's temple during festive days and join the choir. But Lucian, skeptical as ever, made a journey to the swan breeding grounds in Italy and inquired among the local peasants whether they ever heard a swan sing. He was told that swans only croak, cackle, and grunt in a most disagreeable manner. So-called mute swans maintained on royal preservations in Britain are not voiceless; they growl, hiss, and even trill. Despite these unpleasant characteristics, the swan—with its graceful long neck (18 vertebrae, as compared with the giraffe's 7)—remains a symbol of beauty and poetry.

Rossini was called the Swan of Pesaro, his birthplace. Although he possessed a self-deprecating sense of humor, it never occurred to him how ambiguous this compliment really was. In his *Carnival of the Animals* Saint-Saëns assigns his beautiful cello solo to the swan, and it inspired Anna Pavlova's famous dance creation *The Dying Swan*. Sibelius wrote a symphonic poem entitled *The Swan of Tuonela*, with a mellifluously nasal English horn solo representing the dying swan song. A group of Schubert's posthumous songs was given the title *Schwanengesang* by the publs. Yet no composer has dared to reproduce the true sound of the swan's song; not even the bassoon in its lowest register is ugly enough to render justice to a dying swan's croaking. In Hans Christian Andersen's tale *The Ugly Duckling*, a swan egg is deposited in a nest of ducks; after it is hatched, the young gray swan is an ugly duckling compared to its anserine siblings, until one fine day it is a beautiful white. Prokofiev wrote a poetic ballad for voice and piano based on this tale.

Swanee. Song by Gershwin, 1919, included in *The Capitol Revue*. It was his 1st hit song, and the biggest commercial success he ever had. Some 2 million records and a million copies of sheet music were sold within a year of release.

Swanee River. Common name for Foster's *Old Folks at Home*.

Sweelinck (born Swybbertszoon), **Jan Pieterszoon,** great Dutch organist, pedagogue, and composer; b. Deventer, May[?] 1562; d. Amsterdam, Oct. 16, 1621. He was born into a musical family; his father, paternal grandfather, and uncle were all organists. He went as a youth to Amsterdam, which was to be the center of his activities for

the rest of his life. Jacob Buyck, pastor of the Oude Kerk, supervised his academic education; he most likely commenced his musical training under his father, then studied with Jan Willemszoon Lossy. He is believed to have begun his career as an organist in 1577, although 1st mention of him is in 1580, as organist of the Oude Kerk, a position his father held until his death in 1573.

Sweelinck became a celebrated master of the keyboard, so excelling in the art of improvisation that he was called the "Orpheus of Amsterdam." He was also greatly renowned as a teacher, numbering among his pupils most of the founders of the so-called north German organ school. His most famous pupils were Jacob Praetorius, Heinrich Scheidemann, Samuel and Gottfried Scheidt, and Paul Siefert. The output of Sweelinck as a composer is now seen as the culmination of the great Dutch school of his time. Among his extant works are about 250 vocal pieces (33 chansons, 19 madrigals, 39 motets, and 153 Psalms) and some 70 keyboard works.

Sweelinck was the 1st to employ the pedal in a real fugal part; he originated the organ fugue built up on 1 theme with the gradual addition of counterthemes leading to a highly involved and ingenious finale—a form perfected by Bach. In rhythmic and melodic freedom his vocal compositions show an advance over the earlier polyphonic style, though they are replete with intricate contrapuntal devices. His son and pupil, Dirck Janszoon Sweelinck (b. Amsterdam [baptized], May 26, 1591; d. there, Sept. 16, 1652), was an organist, music ed., and composer; he was his father's successor as organist at the Oude Kerk (from 1621), where he acquired a notable reputation as an improviser.

Sweet Adeline (1). Song by H. W. Armstrong, 1903, an American musician who named it in honor of the famous Italian prima donna Adelina Patti, who was having one of her recurrent farewell concert tours in America at the time. It was once a staple of barbershop quartets; when sung in characteristic close harmony with chromatic intercalations, *Sweet Adeline* eventually acquired a peculiar odor of an amiable state of male inebriation.

Sweet Adeline (2). Musical by Kern, 1929. The story relates the career of a songstress who falls in love with a sailor; when he goes off to fight the Spanish-American War, she joins a musical comedy troupe and becomes involved with the sponsor of the show. The score is redolent of the aroma of the Gay '90s; among the best songs is the waltz-time ballad *The Sun About to Rise*.

Sweet and Low. Song by Joseph Barnby, 1863, to words by Tennyson, published in London and extremely popular thereafter.

Sweet Charity. Musical by Cy Coleman, 1966. The central character is a hostess in a dance hall whose name is actually Charity. She is disappointed in men because one character stole her purse and threw her into the Central Park lake; another put her in the bedroom closet while he was making love to his regular date; the 3rd and last is a guy who got stuck with her in a stalled elevator and again in a parachute-jump ride at a carnival. Includes *If My Friends Could See Me Now*, *Baby, Dream Your Dream*, and *Big Spender*.

sweet potato. American slang for OCARINA.

Sweet Psalmist of Israel, The. Work for soprano and orch., 1956, by Paul Ben-Haim (b. Munich, July 5, 1897; d. Tel Aviv, Jan. 14, 1984), on the subject of King David.

Sweet Rosie O'Grady. Song by Maude Nugent, 1896, published in N.Y. It is a typical Irish waltz, steadily successful through the years. There has been some controversy as to whether her husband, the songwriter William Jerome, was the actual composer.

Sweethearts. Operetta by V. Herbert, 1913. The plot is based on the romantic adventures of the daughter of the king of Naples in the 15th century, but the time is changed to the 19th century. The young woman is the crown princess of Zilania who was kidnapped as a child and brought up by a laundress. A prince courts her, but she is reluctant to marry out of her own class. It is only later that her royal blood is proved, and she happily weds her prince. Includes the popular waltz *Sweethearts*.

swell. 1. In the organ, a set of pipes enclosed in a box with movable shutters which may be opened and closed by a pedal, affecting the dynamic level. 2. The swell organ: the chest, the pipes enclosed, and their keyboard. 3. A crescendo (◁▭▷), or crescendo and diminuendo (◁▭▷▭▷).

swing. A smooth, sophisticated style of jazz playing, popular in the 1930s and early 1940s. Its distinctive characteristic was a trend away from small jazz groups, who improvised by musical instinct, toward a well-organized ensemble of professional instrumentalists. The main outline of melody and harmony was established during rehearsals, but jam sessions were freely interpolated, with extended solos. The new style of performance required a larger band, so that the "swing era" became synonymous with the BIG BAND era.

Among the many ephemeral terms descriptive of varieties of jazz, swing has gained a permanent historical position. It is not a new expression. The word *swing* appears in the titles of old American dance tunes: Society Swing of 1908, Foxtrot Swing of 1923, Charleston Swing of 1925. In 1932 Duke Ellington wrote a song with the incipit *It Don't Mean a Thing If It Ain't Got That Swing*. Swing music achieved its 1st great boom in 1935, largely through the agency of the jazz clarinet player Benny Goodman, advertised as the King of Swing. The American magazine *Downbeat* described swing in its issue of January 1935 as "a musician's term for perfect rhythm." The Nov. 1935 issue of the magazine carried a glossary of "Swing terms that cats use," in which swing was defined as "laying it in the groove." This metaphor, borrowed from the phonograph industry, gave rise to the once popular adjective *groovy*, in the sense of "cool," "bad," "outtasight," or simply musically well executed.

Swing music is a natural product of the jazz era that created a demand for larger bands and a great volume of sound. The advent of swing music coincided with the development of the radio industry when, about 1930, millions could hear concerts broadcasting into homes. As the name seems to indicate, swing symbolized an uninhibited celebration of the youthful spirit of the age. Big bands of the swing era were usually catapulted into syncopated action by a clarinetist, a trumpet soloist, or a saxophone player. The instrumentation of a big swing band derived from its jazz predecessor, with clarinet, saxophone, trumpet, trombone, percussion, and piano as its mainstays.

If the media is to be believed, swing music must have exercised a hypnotic effect on the youth of the 1930s. *The New York Times* (May 30, 1938) ran the banner headline "Swing Band Puts 23,400 in Frenzy . . . Jitterbugs Cavort as 25 Orchestras Blare in Carnival." Self-appointed guardians of public morals lamented the new craze, as another *New York Times* headline showed: "Pastor Scores Swing as Debasing Youth, Declares it Shows an Obvious Degeneracy in our Culture and Frothiness of Age." Loud swing music late at night so upset the sensitive burghers in the once-peaceful boroughs of Greater N.Y. that they went to court to muzzle the swingers. They lost, as *The New York Times* reported (June 30, 1898): "2 A.M. Swing Music Upheld by Court. Residents Lose Pleas to Curb 15-Piece Band. Can't Sleep, They Assert. But Magistrate Rules That Lively

Strains Do Not Disturb the Peace." Revenants from another century added literary denunciations of swing as "music which squawked and shrieked and roared and bellowed in syncopated savagery." Eventually, even swing music was found not loud enough, and in the course of time it yielded to the still louder sound of rock 'n' roll.

Visitors from Europe were more kind to swing. Stravinsky, then a recent arrival to America, endorsed big band. *Time* quoted him as saying in Jan. 1941: "I love swings. It is to the Harlem I go. It is so sympathetic to watch the Negro boys and girls dancing and to watch them eating the long, what is it you call them, frankfurters, no—hot dogs—in the long rolls. It is so sympathetic. I love all kinds of swings." In 1945 Stravinsky further demonstrated his faith in swing by composing his *Ebony Concerto* for "ebony stick" (swing term for the clarinet) and band.

Swing Low, Sweet Chariot. A Negro spiritual, 1st published in 1872; one of the most famous and poetic gospel spirituals, with a pentatonic melody; it has often been arranged and reinterpreted.

syllabic melody. One melody, each TONE of which is sung to a separate syllable.

syllable name. A syllable taken as the name of a note or tone; as Do for C.

symbolic analysis. An overwhelming compulsion on the part of many modern composers to return the art of music to its source, mathematics, is behind many manifestations of the avant-garde. Yet no attempt has been made to apply symbolic logic to the stylistic and technical analysis of modern music. A simple statistical survey can determine the ratio between unresolved dissonances and consonant structures in modern works as compared to those of the past. Such an analysis would indicate in mathematical terms the process of the emancipation of dissonances. The next step would be to tabulate certain characteristics of a given modern school of composition and note their presence in another category, which would help to measure the extent of its influence.

The whole-tone scale, for instance, was cultivated particularly by the French impressionists, but it can be found in works of composers who do not subscribe to impressionist aesthetics. Progressions of 2nd inversions of major triads in parallel formation, moving by sesquitones, are typical of IMPRESSIONISM. But the same formations can be encountered in the music of nonimpressionists. Ravel concludes his string

quartet with such a triadic progression, and so does Gustav Holst in his suite *The Planets*, but they are never found in the works of Hindemith, a paragon of neoclassicism, or in those of Prokofiev. The index of tonality is very strong, amidst dissonances, in Stravinsky, but is totally absent in Schoenberg.

All these styles, idioms, and techniques can be designated by a system of symbols; intervals would be numbered in semitones; upward motion would he symbolized by the plus sign, downward motion by the minus sign. In this scheme the whole-tone scale would be shown by the formula 6 (2), denoting 6 degrees of 2 semitones each, with a plus or minus sign indicating the direction of the movement. A bitonal chord such as formed by C major and F-sharp major can be indicated by the symbol *MT* for major triad and the number 6 for the tritone. The synchronization of these triads can be indicated by brackets: (MT) (MT + 6). More importantly, symbolic formulas can describe a style.

The music of Hindemith, which lacks the impressionist element entirely, can be formulated as 50% NC (for neoclassical) + 50% NR (neoromantic), with dissonant content and strength of tonal centers indicated by additional symbols or subscripts. Stravinsky's early music could be circumscribed by the symbol *ED* for ethnic dissonance. The dodecaphonic method could be indicated by the coefficient 12. Other symbols would denominate metric and rhythmic symmetry or asymmetry. In the symbolic analysis of an eclectic composer such as Delius, with basic romanticism modified by a considerable influx of impressionistic harmonies and colors, the following formula would be satisfactory, with *R* for Romanticism, *C* for Classicism, *E* for ethnic quality, and *I* for impressionism: 40% R + 20% C + 30% E + 10% I.

A table of styles, idioms, and techniques may be drawn in the manner of the periodical table of elements. Just as vacant spaces in Mendeleyev's schematic representation indicated unknown elements that were actually discovered at a later time, so new techniques of modern composition may well come into being by searching application of symbolic analysis.

symbolism. Denoting compositions of the late 19th and early 20th centuries which, like their counterparts in the poetic and visual arts, are characterized by epigrammatic, sometimes oblique representations of emotions, topical themes, and events.

sympathetic strings. Strings stretched below or above the principal strings of lute and gamba family instruments to provide sympathetic resonance and thus amplify the sounds of the melodic strings; these strings are generally not played upon. They are still found on chordophones such as the HARDINGFELE of Norway and many of the classical Indian instruments. Some piano manufacturers add sympathetic strings above the strings in the treble to add resonance to the tinny sound of the upper range; these are called ALIQUOT STRINGS.

symphonia. In the Middle Ages, *consonance*, in contrast to *diaphonia*, dissonance. In Baroque music the term was used indiscriminately for all genres of ensemble music, but eventually a sym. became crystallized as a specific form of orch.l composition. R. Strauss used the old meaning of the term in his *Sym. domestica*, for a work that is not a real sym.

Symphonia Serena. Work by Hindemith, 1947, premiered in Dallas.

symphonic. Resembling, or relating or pertaining to, a sym. *Symphonic ode*, a symphonic composition combining chorus and orch.; *symphonic poem*, an extended orch.l composition that follows in its development the thread of a story or the ideas of a poem, repeating and interweaving its themes appropriately; it has no fixed form, nor has it set divisions like those of a sym.

symphonic band. BAND, SYMPHONIC.

Symphonic Dances. Orch.l suite by Hindemith, 1937, in 4 movements, 1st performed in London. The score was originally designed for presentation as a ballet based on the life of St. Francis of Assisi; Hindemith later decided to write a different score for that purpose, entitled *St. Francis*, with the subtitle *Nobilissima Visione*.

Symphonic Dances. Suite by Rachmaninoff, 1941, his last major work, premiered in Philadelphia.

Symphonic Metamorphosis on a Theme by Carl Maria von Weber. Orch.l suite by Hindemith, 1944, that makes an anamorphic use of various themes of Weber's 4-hand piano music and theater scores. The work was 1st performed in N.Y.

Symphonie cévenole. SYMPHONY ON A FRENCH MOUNTAIN THEME.

symphonie concertante (Fr.; It. *sinfonia concertante*). An orch.l work that combines the formal elements of a sym. and a concerto, by the use of soloists. Mozart made good use of this form, as testified by his works for violin and viola (K. 364, 1779), 2 flutes, 2 oboes, and 2 bassoons (K. 320, 1779), and other unfinished works. In a sense this genre is the Classic equivalent of the CONCERTO GROSSO.

Symphonie domestica. An autobiographical sym. cum symphonic poem by R. Strauss, 1904, for which he conducted the premiere in N.Y. The work describes a day in the family of Richard Strauss. When the clock strikes 7:00 A.M. the new baby is given a bath. Admiring relatives exclaim "Just like Papa!" or "Just like Mama!," depending on whether they are paternal or maternal relatives. A domestic argument is introduced by a double fugue.

Symphonie fantastique. Program sym. by Berlioz, 1830, premiered in Paris; the 1st of its kind. Of all the compositions of the Romantic age, the "Fantastic Sym." by Berlioz is the most literal and also the most literary. Consider its inception: Berlioz attends in Paris a performance of Hamlet given by the Shakespearean Company of London, with Henrietta Smithson as Ophelia. He instantly becomes infatuated with her. He walks the streets of Paris in a state of fantastic obsession. He decides to express his passion/obsession in the language he knows best—music. In the work Miss Smithson is identified by a recurrent theme which Berlioz calls the IDÉE FIXE (a predecessor to the LEITMOTIV). The sym. is premiered; but Miss Smithson does not attend the concert. Eventually they meet. They marry. He speaks no English. She speaks no French. They are unhappy. Berlioz leaves her. Miss Smithson dies, victim of precocious senility. Worse still, it turns out that Berlioz wrote the *March to the Gallows* long before he beheld the Shakespearean Miss Smithson, and incorporated it in a composed overture, and that the idée fixe was an earlier idea of the *Sym. fantastique* ex post facto.

Incongruously, the printed score is dedicated not to his beloved, but to the Czar of All the Russias, Nicolas I. Why? Berlioz, romantic soul that he was, also had proper regard for earthly necessities. During his concert tour to Russia in 1847 he was advised to seek the imperial favor in the hope of obtaining a pecuniary reward. So he put the name of the Emperor on the opening page of his sym. But there is no record of his receiving any emolument; the Czar was notoriously insensitive to art.

Rather than follow the formal subdivisions of a sym., Berlioz decided to integrate the music with the idée fixe, appearing in various guises through the movements of the *Sym. fantastique*. To point out the personal nature of the work he subtitled it *Épisode de la vie d'un artiste*, namely its composer. The 5 movements of the score are: I. *Reveries, Passions* (sonata form with slow introduction); II. *A Ball* (fast waltz); III. *Scene in the Fields* (spacious pastorale); IV. *March to the Scaffold* (scherzo in duple meter); V. *Dream of a Witches' Sabbath* (hybrid finale, in which thematic transformation comes into full glory, including quotations of the Dies Irae). As a 5-movement sym. the work bears comparison with Beethoven's 6th Sym., although the *Sym. fantastique* veers into satire long before the end.

Berlioz supplied a literary program to the music: a "young musician of morbid sensibilities" takes opium to find surcease from amorous madness. Berlioz himself, be it noted, never smoked opium, but this hallucinogenic substance was in vogue at the time and was the subject of several mystic novels and pseudo-scientific essays.

Symphonie pathétique. French name for Tchaikovsky's 6th Sym.

symphony

n orch. genre with distinct movements or divisions, each with its own theme or themes (in the 19th and 20th centuries, sometimes shared); the totality of a sym. (from Grk. *syn* + *phōnē*, sounding together; Fr. *symphonie*; Ger. *Sinfonie*; It. *sinfonia*) is made coherent by tonality and planning of contrasting mood. A typical plan in the Classic period might be a 4-movement work, organized as: *Allegro* in the tonic key (sonata form, often with a slow introduction); *Adagio* in a related key (choice of ternary, variation, "sonata without development" forms); *Minuet* or *Scherzo* in the tonic key (in triple meter, with trio); and *Allegro* or *Presto* in the tonic key (choice of sonata form, rondo, sonata-rondo, variation forms).

This is the most significant and most complex form of musical composition, which, in its Classic form, represents the supreme achievement of Western music. In the 17th century the term *symphonia* was divested of its general meaning as a musical composition and was applied exclusively to an instrumental ensemble without voices; it was used for instrumental overtures or interludes in early operas.

In the 1st half of the 18th century the instrumental SINFONIA was formally stabilized as a composition in 3 symmetric movements: Allegro, Andante, Allegro. The opening Allegro was of the greatest evolutionary importance, for it followed the germinal SONATA FORM, with clearly demarcated sections that became defined by theorists as exposition, development, and recapitulation. Haydn is commonly regarded as the "father of the sym.," but in fact several composers before Haydn's time wrote

orch.l works that already comprised the formal elements of symphonic style. Particularly important among these predecessors were the musicians of the Mannheim School, who in their performances emphasized contrasts of style, tempo, and instrumental combinations. Furthermore, they introduced the dynamic elements of crescendo and diminuendo while preserving the chiaroscuro contrasts of forte and piano.

The era of the Classic sym. began in the 2nd half of the 18th century. Its most illustrious representatives were Mozart and Haydn; a legion of opaque luminaries labored in obscurity in Central Europe and in Italy throughout the Classic period. Most Classic syms. comprised a supernumerary dance movement, usually a Minuet. Despite the vaunted versatility of the symphonic form, its structure was essentially uniform.

A revolutionary change in the history of the symphonic form occurred in the 19th century. The form of a sym. became individualized; like opera, it was no longer manufactured in large quantities, according to a prescribed formula. Syms. acquired individual physiognomies; the *Eroica Sym.* of Beethoven is a famous example. In his 9th Sym. Beethoven added a chorus, an extraordinary innovation at the time. Schubert failed to complete one of his most famous syms., which became forever known as the *Unfinished Sym.*

Although the numbering of composition of Schumann's syms. is chronologically inaccurate, they are individually marked creations. Bruckner discarded his 1st sym., which he chose to describe as Sym. No. 0 (zero; in fact there were at least 2 other pre–Sym. No. 1's by Bruckner). Four syms. by Dvořák remained unpublished in his lifetime, creating havoc in their numbering. As a result, his most famous sym., *From the New World*, which was originally catalogued as No. 5, has been renumbered as No. 9. Several early syms. by Mendelssohn have been added to his catalogue by later editors.

Often syms. of the Romantic period were autobiographical. Berlioz wrote a grandly programmatic orch. work that he entitled *Sym. fantastique*, as a musical confession of his love for an English Shakespearean actress. The 10 syms. of Mahler are Romantic revelations of the most intense character. Liszt selected 2 literary epics, Dante's *Divina Commedia* and Goethe's *Faust*, for his syms.

Several composers who proclaimed themselves as fervent nationalists wrote syms. in a traditional Romantic style. Among the greatest was Sibelius, who assigned national Finnish subjects for his symphonic poems but whose 7 syms. bear no programmatic subtitles. Saint-Saëns was a grandiloquent symphonist. Bizet's youthful sym., which he discarded, was rediscovered more than half a century after his death and became a favorite. For some reason Debussy and Ravel were never tempted to write syms.; it is only in the 20th century that modern French composers, particularly Milhaud and Honegger, contributed to the genre. The Russians remain faithful to the traditional form of the sym. Tchaikovsky wrote 6 syms.; Glazunov wrote 8, Scriabin and Rachmaninoff composed 3 each, Shostakovich produced 15, several of which include vocal soloists and chorus. The champion symphonist in Russia was Miaskovsky, who wrote 27 syms.

Virtually every Russian composer of the Soviet period has written syms. in idioms varying from neoclassical to moderately modernistic. Strangely enough, Germany and Austria, the countries that created and maintained the art of symphonic composition, showed a decline of symphonic production in the 20th century. Perhaps the fact that Wagner, the most potent influence in post-Classic Germany, devoted his energies totally to the musical theater (his youthful sym. was not published until many years after his death) drew the German composers of the post-Wagnerian generation away from symphonic composition. R. Strauss wrote 2 syms., *Sym. domestica* and the *Alpine Sym.*, but they are panoramic, symphonic in name only. Hindemith was not a Wagnerian but rather a mod-

ern follower of Reger, but neither he nor Reger wrote syms. in the traditional formal manner.

The 3 great composers of the modern Vienna school, Schoenberg, Berg, and Webern, abstained from composing works of truly symphonic dimensions. Stravinsky, who began his career as a follower of Rimsky-Korsakov's pictorial symphonism, wrote several syms., but they were closer to the pre-Classic type of sinfonia than to the traditional type of Classic or Romantic sym. Ever since Haydn's symphonic journeys to London, England was a willing receptacle of German musical style. In the 20th century Elgar wrote 2 grand syms. and Vaughan Williams wrote 9, some of them highly modern in idiom. Arnold Bax composed 7 syms.; the until recently obscure Havergal Brian wrote 32. Of the younger generation, William Walton wrote 2. Benjamin Britten, generally regarded as the most remarkable English composer of the 20th century, never felt the symphonic urge; his works in symphonic form approach the manner of orch.l suites. The Danish composer Carl Nielsen wrote 6 syms., with somewhat programmatic content expressed in such subtitles as *Expansive* and *Inextinguishable*. The most prolific Italian composer of syms. was Malipiero, who wrote at least 10, several of which he equipped with suggestive subtitles.

In the U.S., among composers who pursued the symphonic career steadfastly through the years are Roy Harris, who wrote 14, and Walter Piston, William Schuman, David Diamond, Peter Mennin, and Vincent Persichetti, who wrote 8 syms. each. Howard Hanson, who proclaimed his faith in Romantic music, wrote 6 syms. Of Aaron Copland's symphonic works the most significant is his 3rd Sym., which incidentally includes his famous *Fanfare for the Common Man*, quoted *in extenso*. A unique American sym. is the 4th Sym. of Charles Ives, which consists of 4 movements written at different times and in widely divergent idioms. His 1st Sym. is entirely academic; his 2nd Sym. is a Romantic populist work; his 3rd Sym.'s essence is the world of the revivalist camp meeting.

The main structure of a sym. during the 2 centuries of its formulation has not radically changed. The lively scherzo replaced the mannered minuet. The 4 traditional movements were often compressed into 1. The general tendency early in the 20th century was to reduce the orch. to the bare bones of the Baroque sinfonia. In his *Sym. of Psalms* Stravinsky eliminates the violins altogether in order to conjure up the desired aura of austerity. The piano—not a symphonic instrument per se and not used in the syms. of Schumann, Mendelssohn, Tchaikovsky, Brahms, or any other composer of the Romantic century regardless of their individual styles—became a welcome guest in the syms. of the 20th century, with an obvious intent to provide sharp articulation and precise rhythm. Shostakovich wrote an important piano part in his 1st Sym. Mahler used sleighbells in his syms., but he did so in order to recreate the atmosphere of the countryside, serving as dainty embellishments rather than modernistic decorations.

Symphony Fantasia. Sym. No. 21 by Miaskovsky, 1940.

Symphony for Organ and Orchestra. Sym. work by Copland, 1925, 1st performed in N.Y. with Copland's teacher Nadia Boulanger playing the solo part. Walter Damrosch conducted; he gratuitously declared to the audience after the performance that a youth who could write such music at the age of 24 would be capable of murder a few years later.

Symphony: Holidays. HOLIDAYS: A SYMPHONY.

Symphony in Three Movements. Orch. work by Stravinsky, 1946, 1st premiered in N.Y. with the composer conducting. The work demonstrates the possibilities of continually evolving organic symphonic form.

Symphony of a Thousand. An unsanctioned name for the 8th Sym. by Mahler, 1906–1907, in the key of E-flat major. The title is justifiable by the work's requiring a huge ensemble with vocal soloists, 2 mixed choruses, and a boys' chorus, as well as a battery of percussion instruments. It was 1st performed in Munich, 1910, the last sym. of his that he heard. While Mahler never sanctioned the nickname, he wrote extravagantly about the significance of the work: "In this symphony the whole universe begins to sound in musical tones; it is no longer human voices, but planets and suns that are in motion here." The *Sym. of a Thousand* is in effect an oratorio. It consists of 2 lengthy choral sections, the 1st based on the medieval Pentecostal hymn, *Veni, Creator Spiritus*, and the 2nd a rendition of a philosophical part of Goethe's *Faust*.

Symphony of Psalms (*Sym. des Psaumes*). Work by Stravinsky, 1930, for Chorus and Orch., dedicated "to the glory of God on the occasion of the 50th anniversary of the Boston Sym. Orch." Because of a postponement of the Boston performance, the actual world premiere of the *Sym. of Psalms* was given in Brussels; the Boston Sym. Orch. performance followed 1 week later. The text is in Latin, as it was in Stravinsky's opera-oratorio *Oedipus Rex* (1927); by using an ancient language Stravinsky again intended to emphasize the timeless character of the subject; unlike the opera, the psalms are set to perhaps the most serene music the composer ever wrote.

Symphony on a French Mountain Theme. Sym. No. 1 by d'Indy, 1887, with Piano Obbligato, premiered in Paris. The work is also called the *Sym. cévenole*, named after Cévennes, a mountain region in southern France.

Symphony on a Hymn Tune. Work by Thomson, 1928, premiered in N.Y., 1945.

symploche. A rhetorical musical device in which the beginning of a musical phrase serves also as its ending. A highly artistic example is the initial phrase of the ending to Mozart's Sym. No. 39 in E-flat Major, K. 543.

synaesthesia

〰〰 〰〰 〰〰 〰〰 〰〰

Color associations with certain sounds or tonalities are common subjective phenomena. It is said that Newton chose to divide the visible spectrum into 7 distinct colors by analogy with the 7 degrees of the diatonic scale. Individual musicians differed greatly in associating a sound with a certain color.

The most common association between tonality and color is that of C major and whiteness. It is particularly strong for pianists for the obvious reason that the C-major scale is played on white keys. However, Scriabin—who had a very strong feeling for color associations—correlated C major with red. By all conjecture F-sharp major should be associated with black, for it comprises all 5 different black keys of the piano keyboard, but Scriabin associated it with bright blue and Rimsky-Korsakov with dull green.

Any attempt to objectivize color associations is doomed to failure if for no other reason than the arbitrary assignment of a certain frequency to a given note. The height of pitch rose nearly a semitone in the last century, so that the color of C would now be associated with C-sharp in relation to the old standards.

The most ambitious attempt to incorporate light into a musical composition was the inclusion of a projected color organ in Scriabin's score *Prometheus*, in which the changes of instrumental coloration were to be accompanied by changing lighting in the concert hall. Composers in mixed media, anxious to embrace an entire universe of senses, are seeking ultimate synaesthesia by intuitive approximation, subjective objectivization, and mystical adumbrations. Schoenberg was extremely sensitive to the correspondences between light and sound. In the score of his monodrama *Die glückliche Hand* he indicates a "crescendo of illumination" with the dark violet light in 1 of the 2 grottos quickly turning to brownish red, to blue green, and then to orange yellow.

Some composers dreamed of a total synaesthesia in which not only audio-visual but tactile, gustatory, and olfactory associations would be brought into a sensual synthesis. Baudelaire said: "Les parfums, les couleurs et les sons se répondent." J. K. Huysmans conjured up an organ of liqueurs. He describes it in chapter IV of his book *A Rebours*:

Interior symphonies were played as one drank a drop of this or that liqueur creating the sensations in the throat analogous to those that music pours into the ear. In this organ of liqueurs, Curaçao sec corresponded to the clarinet with its somewhat astringent but velvety sound; Kummel suggested the oboe with its nasal quality; menthe and anisette were like the flute, with its combination of sugar and pepper, petulance and sweetness; kirsch recalled the fury of the trumpet; gin and whiskey struck the palate with the strident explosions of cornets and trombones; vodka fulminated with deafening noise of tubas, while raki and mastic hurled thunderclaps of the cymbal and of the bass drum with full force.

Huysmans continued by suggesting a string ensemble functioning in the mouth cavity, with the violin representing vodka, the viola tasting like rum, the cello caressing the gustatory rods with exotic liqueurs, and the double bass contributing its share of bitters.

synapse. In the Greek melodic system, the conjunction of 2 tetrachords by which the last (highest) note of the lower tetrachord also serves as the 1st (lowest) note of the higher tetrachord.

synchrony. Metric or rhythmic synchrony is an inclusive term, of which polymeter and polyrhythm are specific instances. Synchronization demands absolutely precise simultaneity of sets of mutually primary numbers of notes within a given unit of time, e.g., 3:2, 5:3, 11:4, etc. Triplets and quintuplets are of course common in free cadenzas since Chopin's time. (There is a consistent use of 4 beats against 3 in Chopin's *Fantaisie-Impromptu*.) But arithmetical precision in synchronizing larger mutually primary numbers of notes cannot be obtained by a human performer no matter how skillful, or by several performers playing different rhythms at once.

Such synchrony becomes feasible with the aid of electronic machines. In 1931 Henry Cowell, working in collaboration with the Russian electric engineer Leon Theremin, constructed a device, in the form of concentric wheels, which he called the Rhythmicon. By manipulating a rheostat with a rudimentary crank, the performer automatically produced precise synchronization of the harmonic series, the number of beats per time unit being equal to the position in the series, so that the fundamental tone had 1 beat per second, or any other time unit, the 2nd partial note had 2 beats, the 3rd, 3 beats, etc. up to 32 beats produced by the rim of the Rhythmicon. The result was an arithmetically accurate synchrony score of 32 different time pulses. Since only the mutually nonprimary numbers of beats coincided in the process, the collateral effect of rotating the machine was the production of an eerie scale of upper overtones, slower in its initial notes, faster as the position of the overtone was higher. The speed of rotation of the Rhythmicon wheel could be regulated at will, so as to create any desired alteration in tempo or pitch. The initial chord of each main division contains, necessarily so, the entire spectrum of overtones, and their simultaneous impact is of tremendous power, a perfect concord of multitonal consistency in non-tempered intonation.

An entirely novel idea of producing synchrony with mathematical precision was initiated by Conlon Nancarrow, an American composer living in Mexico City. He worked with a player-piano roll, punching holes at distances proportional to the desired rhythms. He wrote a series of études and canons, which could be performed only on the player piano and which achieved the synchronization of different tempos that could not be attained by living instrumentalists. In his works he was free to select numbers with a fairly low common denominator, in which case there were occasional coincidences between the constituent parts. But the majority of his chosen proportions of the pulse tempos are such that the common denominator was not attained until the end of the piece, if at all. He also wrote a composition in which the relationship of the tempos was 2 to the square root of 2, and since the latter is an irrational number (which Nancarrow approximated to 3 decimal points), the contrapuntal parts could, at least theoretically, never meet.

Synchrony. Orch. work by Cowell, 1931, 1st performed in Paris. As the title suggests, this is an essay in orch. synchronization; the technique of tone clusters invented by Cowell is prominently used.

synclavier. Digital synthesizer, developed in 1976.

syncopate. Efface or shift the accent of a tone or chord falling on a naturally strong beat, by emphasizing a weak or in-between note, or by tying over from the preceding weak beat to the strong beat. See also SYNCOPATION.

Syncopated Clock, The. Orch.1 novelty by L. Anderson, 1950, in which an old-fashioned clock seems to get rhythmically out of kilter.

syncopated pedal. The release of the damper pedal on striking a chord, followed by immediate depression of the pedal.

syncopation (from Grk. *syncope*, clash between disparate elements; missed heartbeat). One of the most powerful sources of rhythmic diversification. In music, syncopation typically takes 3 forms: an ACCENT on a normally unaccented beat or part of a beat; a continuation of a note "over the bar" so as to avoid striking a note on a normally accented beat; and the conflict of unequal rhythms in 2 or more parts.

In MENSURAL NOTATION, syncopation was used to make changes in the main stress. The consequence of such rhythmic displacement was the generation of a discordant tonal combination that had to be resolved into a consonance. In contrapuntal theory, syncopation is classified as the 4th SPECIES of counterpoint. Syncopated notes were initially marked as auxiliary ornaments and were often written in small notes placed before the principal note. SUSPENSIONS and APPOGGIATURAS furnish the characteristic elements of dissonant syncopation. In the works of the Romantic era, syncopation served to enhance the emotional stress in the melorhythmic continuum.

Syncopation is the spice of music in dance forms. In triple meter, Viennese waltzes create an effect of syncopation by stressing the 3rd beat of the measure, while the mazurka tends to accent the 2nd beat. In quadruple meter, marches emphasize the main beat, but they supply syncopation in smaller rhythmic divisions against a regular beat. Ragtime developed the march form into a highly syncopated melodic style; jazz gradually eliminated the need for emphasis of the regular beat, thus elevating syncopation into a texture. Popular music in the U.S. since World War II has oscillated between a return to uniform rhythms with an accent on the strong beats of the measure (rock 'n' roll, Motown, disco) and various degrees of syncopation, sometimes quite subtle (rock, funk, new wave), sometimes less so (reggae, grunge).

syncretism. In history and theology syncretism denotes the coalescence of incompatible elements or concepts. Etymologically, the word is derived from the union of ancient Greece with Crete. *Syncretism* is a useful term in music as well, applied to describe the affinity between autogenetic ethnic melodies and cultivated triadic harmonies. A typical example of syncretism is the arrangement of pentatonic tunes in tonal harmonies, often resulting in the alteration of the intervallic content, as for instance in *Londonderry Air*, a pentatonic melody that has been altered by its arranger by changing the opening interval of a minor 3rd to a semitone in order to provide the leading tone and to convert the modality of the song into a familiar major key. In modern music, syncretism assumes a polytechnical character through the application of widely incompatible techniques in a single work. An example is Alban Berg's *Lulu*, a serial work, which contains also triadic progressions as well as harmonic figurations and tonal sequences.

synergy. *Synergy* is defined by the American architect Buckminster Fuller, the discoverer of new principles of spherical stability in designing structures, as the "behavior of a whole system unpredicted by the behavior of any of its separate parts, or the subassemblies of its parts." Synergy in music is a technique whereby the last note of a segment of several thematic notes is the 1st note of the 2nd segment. These segments can be separated, in which case the conjunctive note is repeated. The method is of considerable value in building serial chains, in which the concatenations of adjacent links may be freely dissolved. With this separation of links the function of the connecting tone becomes ambiguous, serving as the imaginary tonic of the 1st segment or an imaginary dominant of the 2nd segment. The specification "imaginary" is important because of the aesthetic differences created by such a split of the chain.

synthesizer. A class of electronic devices that make possible the creation of any sound via electronic synthesis. Like the personal computer, modern synthesizers are self-contained units that can be operated with a minimum of accessories, as opposed to the 1st electronic music synthesizers, composed of several modules that could take up an entire wall or even room in the early years. Unlimited musical horizons opened to ELECTRONIC MUSIC with the introduction of synthesizers capable of producing any frequency with the utmost precision and distributing the relative strength of the overtones so as to create any desired instrumental timbre. While synthesizers through the 1960s were driven analogically (i.e., with dials approximating the desired parameters), the addition of computers to the process permitted digital synthesis using the powerful mathematical capabilities of computers to control all sonic parameters. With an ever-increasing availability of programs, calculations that would have been nearly inconceivable at one time (divisions of the octave, stochastic control, pitch alteration) are now commonplace.

Syrian chant. A Christian hymnody in use in the early Christian communities in Syria, derived originally from the churches of Antioch, traditionally considered the oldest Christian churches. There are Orthodox, non-Orthodox, and reunified rites (the latter with the Roman Catholic Church), with similar rites influenced by Gypsy, Arab, and other non-Western music. Among related liturgies are the Assyrian and Maronite.

syrinx. Ancient Greek pan pipes made of a set of reeds (usually 7) of varying sizes and therefore pitches. According to myth, Syrinx was a nymph beloved by the Greek god Pan; she was changed into a reed to escape his pursuit.

Syrinx. Piece for solo flute by Debussy, 1913, named after the nymph described in the previous entry. Theorists have discovered that this work was the model for Varèse's own solo flute work, *Density 21.5.*

system. Generally referring to compositional practices based on the systematic treatment of some organizing aspect(s) of music.

Székely fonó (The Transylvanian Workshop). Lyrical play by Kodály, 1932, 1st performed in Budapest. A landlady's fiancé is forced to flee the country because of an unjust accusation of a crime, but he is arrested and brought back in chains. Fortunately, an old woman at the workshop recognizes the real criminal among those present; the landlady's beloved is freed, and a happy ending is celebrated by all with dances and songs colored by Hungarian rhythms.

Szell, George (actually, György), greatly distinguished Hungarian-born American conductor; b. Budapest, June 7, 1897; d. Cleveland, July 30, 1970. His family moved to Vienna when he was a small child. He studied piano with Richard Robert and composition with Mandyczewski; also composition in Prague with J. B. Foerster. He played a Mozart piano concerto with the Vienna Sym. Orch. when he was 10 years old, and the orch. also performed an overture of his composition. At the age of 17 he led the Berlin Phil. in an ambitious program that included a symphonic work of his own. In 1915 he was engaged as an assistant conductor at the Royal Opera of Berlin; then conducted opera in Strasbourg (1917–18), Prague (1919–21), Darmstadt (1921–22), and Düsseldorf (1922–24).

He held the position of 1st conductor at the Berlin State Opera (1924–29); then conducted in Prague and Vienna. He made his U.S. debut as guest conductor of the St. Louis Sym. Orch. in 1930. In 1937 he was appointed conductor of the Scottish Orch. in Glasgow; he was also a regular conductor with the Residentie Orkest in the Hague (1937–39). He then conducted in Australia. At the outbreak of war in Europe in 1939 he was in America, which was to become his adoptive country by naturalization in 1946. His American conducting engagements included appearances with the Los Angeles Phil., NBC Sym., Chicago Sym., Detroit Sym., and Boston Sym. In 1942 he was appointed a conductor of the Metropolitan Opera in N.Y., where he received high praise for his interpretation of Wagner's music dramas; remained on its roster until 1946. He also conducted performances with the N.Y. Phil. in 1944–45. In 1946 he was appointed conductor of the Cleveland Orch., a post which he held for 24 years; he was also music adviser and senior guest conductor of the N.Y. Phil. from 1969 until his death.

He was a stern disciplinarian, demanding the utmost exertions from his musicians to achieve tonal perfection, but he was also willing to labor tirelessly at his task. Under his guidance the Cleveland Orch. rose to the heights of symphonic excellence, taking its place in the foremost rank of world orchs. Szell was particularly renowned for his authoritative and exemplary performances of the Viennese classics, but he also was capable of outstanding interpretations of 20th-century masterworks.

Szeryng, Henryk, celebrated Polish-born Mexican violinist and pedagogue; b. Zelazowa Wola, Sept. 22, 1918; d. Kassel, Mar. 3, 1988. He commenced piano and harmony training with his mother when he was 5; at age 7 he turned to the violin, receiving instruction from Maurice Frenkel; after further studies with Carl Flesch in Berlin (1929–32) he went to Paris to continue his training with Jacques Thibaud at the Cons., graduating with a *premier prix* in 1937. In 1933 he made his formal debut as soloist in the Brahms Concerto with the Warsaw Phil. With the outbreak of World War II in 1939 he became official translator of the Polish prime minister Wladyslaw Sikorski's government-in-exile in London; later was made personal government liaison officer. In 1941 he accompanied the prime minister to Latin America to find a home for some 4,000 Polish refugees; the refugees were taken in by Mexico; Szeryng, in gratitude, settled there himself, becoming a naturalized citizen in 1946.

Throughout World War II he appeared in some 300 concerts for the Allies. After the war he pursued a brilliant international career; was also active as a teacher. In 1970 he was made Mexico's special adviser to UNESCO in Paris. He celebrated the 50th anniversary of his debut with a grand tour of Europe and the U.S. in 1983. A cosmopolitan fluent in 7 languages, a humanitarian, and a violinist of extraordinary gifts, Szeryng became renowned as a musician's musician by combining a virtuoso technique with a probing discernment of the highest order.

Szigeti, Joseph, eminent Hungarian-born American violinist; b. Budapest, Sept. 5, 1892; d. Lucerne, Feb. 19, 1973. He began his studies at a local music school; while still a child he was placed in the advanced class of Hubay at the Budapest Academy of Music; then made his debut in Berlin at age 13. He made his 1st appearance in London when he was 15; subsequently toured England in concerts with Busoni; then settled in Switzerland in 1913; was a prof. at the Geneva Cons. (1917–25). He made an auspicious U.S. debut, playing the Beethoven Concerto with Stokowski and the Philadelphia Orch. at N.Y.'s Carnegie Hall (1925); thereafter he toured the U.S. regularly while continuing to appear in Europe. With the outbreak of World War II he went to the U.S. (1940), becoming a naturalized citizen in 1951. After the end of the war he resumed his international career; settled again in Switzerland in 1960, and gave master classes.

Szigeti was an artist of rare intellect and integrity; he eschewed the role of the virtuoso, placing himself totally at the service of the music. In addition to the standard repertoire, he championed the music of many 20th-century composers, including Stravinsky, Bartók, Ravel, Prokofiev, Honegger, Bloch, and Martin. He wrote the books *With Strings Attached* (N.Y., 1947), *A Violinist's Notebook* (London, 1965), and *Szigeti on the Violin: Improvisations on a Violinist's Themes* (N.Y., 1969). His son-in-law, Nikita Magaloff (b. St. Petersburg, Feb. 21, 1912), is a pianist noted for his lyrico-dramatic interpretations of Chopin and his lapidary attention to detail.

Szymanowski, Karol (Maciej), outstanding eminent Polish composer; b. Timoshovka, Ukraine, Oct. 6, 1882; d. Lausanne, Mar. 28, 1937. The son of a cultured landowner, he grew up in a musical environment. He began to play the piano and compose very early in life. His 1st teacher was Gustav Neuhaus in Elizavetgrad; in 1901 he went to Warsaw, where he studied harmony with Zawirski and counterpoint and composition with Noskowski until 1904. With Fitelberg, Rózycki, and Szeluto he founded the Young Polish Composer's Publishing Co. in Berlin, which was patronized by Prince Wladyslaw Lubomirski; the composers also became known as Young Poland in Music, publishing new works and sponsoring performances for some 6 years. Among the works the group publ. was Szymanowski's op. 1, 9 Piano Preludes (1906).

He was greatly influenced by German Romanticism, and his 1st major orch. works reveal the impact of Wagner and Strauss. His 1st Sym. was premiered in Warsaw on Mar. 26, 1909; however, he was dissatisfied with the score, and withdrew it from further performance. In 1911 he completed his 2nd Sym., which demonstrated a stylistic change from German dominance to Russian influences, paralleling the harmonic evolution of Scriabin; it was played for the 1st time in Warsaw on Apr. 7, 1911.

After a Viennese sojourn (1911–12) and a trip to North Africa (1914) he lived from 1914 to 1917 in Timoshovka, where he wrote his 3rd Sym.; he appeared in concert with the violinist Paul Kochanski in Moscow and St. Petersburg, giving 1st performances of his violin works; it was for Kochański that he composed his violin triptych, *Mythes* (*La Fontaine d'Aréthuse* in this cycle is one of his best-known compositions). About this time his music underwent a new change in style, veering toward French impressionism. During the Russian Revolution of 1917 the family estate at Timoshovka was ruined, and Szymanowski lost most of his possessions.

From 1917 to 1919 he lived in Elizavetgrad, where he continued to compose industriously, despite the turmoil of the Civil War. After a brief stay in Bydgoszcz he went to Warsaw in 1920. In 1920–21 he toured the U.S. in concerts with Kochański and Rubinstein. Returning to Warsaw, he gradually established himself as one of Poland's most impor-tant composers. His international renown also was considerable; his works were often performed in Europe and figured at festivals of the ISCM. He was director of the Warsaw Cons. (1927–29) and reorganized the system of teaching along more liberal lines; was rector of its successor, the Warsaw Academy of Music (1930–32).

His Stabat Mater (1925–26) produced a profound impression, and his ballet-pantomime *Harnasie* (1923–31), based on the life and music of the Tatra mountain dwellers, demonstrated his ability to treat national subjects in an original and highly effective manner. In 1932 he appeared as soloist in the 1st performance of his 4th Sym., *Sym. concertante* for Piano and Orch., at Poznan, and repeated his performances in Paris, London, and Brussels. In Apr. 1936, greatly weakened in health by chronic tuberculosis, he attended a performance of his *Harnasie* at the Paris Opéra. He spent his last days in a sanatorium in Lausanne. Szymanowski developed into a national composer whose music acquired universal significance.

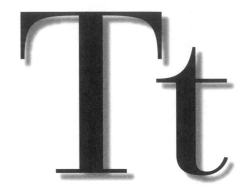

t. Abbrev. for TASTO; TEMPO; TENOR; *toe* (in organ music); TRE (*T.C.*, TRE CORDE); TUTTI.

Tabarro, Il (The Cloak). Opera by Puccini, 1918, produced as the 1st part of *Il Trittico* (Triptych) by the Metropolitan Opera in N.Y. The story deals with a love triangle along the Seine River. A barge owner suspects his helper of conducting an affair with his wife. He kills him, covers the body with his wife's cloak, and then kills her, too.

tablā. One of a pair of single-headed South Asian drums (the other, smaller drum is the *bāmyā*) featured in North Indian classical music. The body, made of clay, wood, or metal, is roughly hourglass-shaped; the head and body are laced with zigzagging thongs, on which rest the wooden dowels to tighten the head (and thus change tuning, as timpani do). Tuning and timbre are also affected by special black tuning paste placed on the head of the 2 drums; the formula is personal to each performer. The drum pair is played while sitting; during the performance of a rāg, after an improvised solo by the melody instrument, the drummer enters with a TALA, which gives the rest of the performance a rhythmic structure within which the melody instrument and drummer may improvise.

tablature (from Lat. *tabula*, board; It. *intavolatura*; Ger. *Tablatur*). 1. Visual musical notation, in which the notes are indicated by their positions on the keyboard, fingerboard, or other playing areas. Letters, numbers, or other signs are used instead of staff notation. Tablature was used for keyboard music (14th to 17th centuries); lute music (16th to mid-17th centuries); guitar music (mid-16th to mid-18th; a simplified system is still used in popular sheet music and for other plucked string instruments); recorder music (16th century); and vocal music, the most successful being TONIC SOL-FA. As percussion music has evolved from occasional timpani strokes to a panoply of timbral cornucopia, composers have used the conventional staff, single lines, or other means to indicate which instrument is to be played (when pitch is not concerned). Partch, who built his own instruments in nontraditional tunings and shapes, created tablatures suitable to individual instruments and therefore incompatible with each other. 2. The rules and regulations for the poetry and song of the Meistersinger.

tableau (Fr.). SCENE, in the theatrical sense.

tabor. A small shallow drum of the border region between France and Spain, held with a strap over the shoulder and played with only 1 hand, enabling the playing of a fife or pipe simultaneously; 1st reported in the 12th century.

Tablā

Tábor. A 5th sym. poem from the cycle *Má vlast* by Smetana, 1880, about an old Hussite stronghold; it is based on the 15th-century Hussite chorale *Those Who Are God's Warriors*.

Tabourot, Jehan. See ARBEAU, THOINOT.

tacet (Lat., it is silent). In orch. parts, a mark indicating a movement in which the instrument in question is not used.

tactus (Lat., beat, stroke). In medieval theory, a standard beat, including downbeat and upbeat (Lat. *positio* and *elevatio*; Grk. *thesis* and *arsis*). The duration of a complete tactus was almost uniformly one second.

Tafelklavier (Ger., table keyboard). The square piano, constructed similarly to the clavichord and specifically adapted for hammer action, as distinct from the harpsichord in which the strings are impinged. The French square piano (*piano carré*) was 1st manufactured in 1742. It became very popular in England and in the U.S. before yielding to the upright piano.

Tafelmusik (Ger., table music; Fr. *musique de table*). Musical entertainment provided for banquets and similar festive occasions. Respectable composers contributed to the genre, a typical example are Telemann's instrumental suites. There is a witty spoof on Tafelmusik in the finale of the 2nd act of Mozart's opera *Don Giovanni*, where a band plays selections from various operas, including Mozart's own. The French composer Michele-Richard Delalande published in 1703 a collection of "syms. qui se jouent ordinairement au souper du Roy." While this sort of music, "ordinarily played at the King's supper," was disdained in the 19th century, the hedonistic composers of the 20th century revived it gleefully; in its more extreme manifestations it functions as background music to other activities, in the form of live musicians, recordings, or Muzak.

Tagelied (Ger., day song). A poem of farewell made popular by the Minnesingers. They are usually songs of partings between lovers, sung at sunrise. Wagner has such a Tagelied in the 2nd act of *Tristan und Isolde*, in the form of a warning against imminent danger. In France and other Latin countries, the Tagelied is known as *alba* or *aubade*, a "morning" or "dawn" song.

taiko (*daiko*; Jap.). Generic term for Japanese barrel drums, played with sticks.

tail. The stem; a vertical line attached to the note head.

tailgate. Hot jazz style featuring sliding trombone effects; derives from New Orleans parade jazz bands, carried by horse wagons, where the trombonist sat in the open tailgate so that the slide tubing could be extended when needed.

taille (Fr., edge). Obsolete term for a voice or instrument performing a part between the low and the high registers, such as tenor, viola, or English horn. *Taille de viola*, tenor VIOLA DA GAMBA; *taille de violon*, tenor violin; also, obsolete term for viola, used occasionally by Bach.

Tailleferre (born Taillefesse), (Marcelle) **Germaine,** significant French composer, a female member of LES SIX. b. Parc-St.-Maur, near Paris, Apr. 19, 1892; d. Paris, Nov. 7, 1983. She altered her name to dispel an unwanted anatomical association in the 2nd syllable. She studied harmony and solfège with H. Dallier (*premier prix*, 1913), counterpoint with G. Caussade (*premier prix*, 1914), and accompaniment with Estyle at the Paris Cons.; also had some informal lessons with Ravel. She received recognition as the only female member of the group of French composers known as Les 6 (the others were Honegger, Milhaud, Poulenc, Auric, and Durey).

Her style of composition was neoclassic; Jean Cocteau invoked a comparison with a young French woman painter, Marie Laurencin, saying that Tailleferre's music was to the ear what the painter's pastels were to the eye. Indeed, most of her works possess a fragile charm of unaffected *joie de jouer la musique*. She was married to an American author, Ralph Barton, in 1926, but soon divorced him and married a French lawyer, Jean Lageat. She visited the U.S. in 1927 and again in 1942. She composed 6 operas, an operetta, and a ballet; concertos for piano, duo pianos, harp, and other orch.l works; chamber music, including *Image* for Piano, Flute, Clarinet, String Quartet, and Celesta (1918); sonatas and other works for violin, clarinet, and flute; solo sonatas for clarinet and harp; a string quartet (1917–19); piano trio (1978); piano works; and much distinguished vocal music, including *Chansons françaises* for Voice and Instruments (1930); *Cantate du Narcisse* for Voice and Orch. (1937); *Concerto des vaines paroles* for Baritone and Orch. (1956).

Take a Chance. Musical by V. Youmans, 1932. The plot deals with the passing joys and lasting miseries in producing a musical show. One song, *Rise 'n' Shine*, redeemed the entire production and remained a perennial favorite.

Take Me Along. Musical by Bob Merrill, 1959, based on Eugene O'Neill's comedy *Ah, Wilderness!* The action occurs in a New England town during the puritanical 1st decades of the 20th century; the dramatis personae includes a newspaper ed. who reeks with rectitude, but whose brother-in-law drinks heavily (delaying his marriage to a decent woman) and whose son writes decadent poetry that horrifies the father of his girlfriend. However, things get straightened out for a happy denouement. The title song became a hit.

Take Me Out to the Ball Game. Song by Albert von Tilzer, 1908, introduced by him in vaudeville; it became the unofficial anthem of American baseball. The composer himself never went to a ball game until some 20 years after he wrote the song.

Take the A Train. Jazz piece by B. Strayhorn, 1941, written for Duke Ellington, who adopted it as his signature tune. The A train is a West Side N.Y. Subway line that runs express to 125th Street, the center of Harlem's cultural life.

Takemitsu, Tōru, prominent Japanese composer. b. Tokyo, Oct. 8, 1930; d. there Feb. 20, 1996. He studied composition privately with Yasuji Kiyose. In 1951, jointly with Yuasa and others, he organized in Tokyo the Jikken Kobo (Experimental Workshop), with the aim of creating new music that would combine traditional Japanese modalities with modernistic procedures. In 1970 he designed the Space Theater for Expo '70 in Osaka, Japan. In 1975 he was a visiting prof. at Yale Univ. In 1981 he served as regent lecturer at the Univ. of Calif. at San Diego. He lectured at Harvard Univ., Boston Univ., and Yale Univ. in 1983, and also was composer-in-residence of the Colorado Music Festival that same year. In 1984 he was composer-in-residence at the Aldeburgh Festival. He received numerous honors; in 1979 he was made an honorary member of the Akademie der Künste of the German Democratic Republic, in 1984 he was elected an honorary member of the American Academy and Inst. of Arts and Letters, and in 1985 he received the Ordre des Arts et des Lettres of the French government.

His music belies Kipling's famous asseveration that "East is East and West is West, and never the twain shall meet," for Takemitsu performs through music just this kind of interpenetration; in an Eastern way it is often formed from short motives played out as floating dramas, subtle and exotic, through which Takemitsu seeks "to achieve a sound as intense as silence"; and on the Western side he employs every conceivable technique developed by the European and American modernists. He composed orch.1 works, string quartets, keyboards, and vocal works. Many of his works employ traditional Japanese instruments incorporated into a Western ensemble.

Taking a Chance on Love. Song by V. Duke, 1940, featured in the all-black musical *Cabin in the Sky*; still a perennial favorite.

Takt (Ger.). 1. A beat. 2. A measure, bar. 3. Time, tempo. *Ein Takt wie vorher zwei* (1 measure like 2 before), twice as fast, DOPPIO MOVIMENTO; *streng im Takt*, strictly in time.

Taktart (Ger.). Meter.

taktmässig (Ger.). In strict meter.

Taktmesser (Ger., measure knife). Metronome.

Taktstock (Ger., time stick). Conductor's baton.

Taktstrich (Ger.). Barline.

Taktzeichen (Ger.). TIME SIGNATURE.

Tal, Josef (born Joseph Gruenthal), prominent German-born Israeli composer, pianist, and pedagogue; b. Pinne, near Posen, Sept. 18, 1910. He took courses with Tiessen, Hindemith, Sachs, Trapp, and others at the Berlin Staatliche Hochschule für Musik (1928–30). In 1934 he emigrated to Palestine, settling in Jerusalem as a teacher of piano and composition at the Cons. in 1936; when it became the Israel Academy of Music in 1948, he served as its director (until 1952); also lectured at the Hebrew Univ. (from 1950), where he was head of the musicology dept. (1965–70) and a prof. (from 1971); likewise was director of the Israel Center of Electronic Music (from 1961). He appeared as a pianist and conductor with the Israel Phil. and with orchs. in Europe. In 1971 he was awarded the State of Israel Prize and was made an honorary member of the West Berlin Academy of Arts; in 1975 he received the Arts Prize of the City of Berlin, and in 1982 he became a fellow of its Inst. for Advanced Studies.

A true musical intellectual, he applies in his music a variety of techniques, being free of doctrinal introversion and open to novel potentialities without fear of public revulsion. Patriotic Hebrew themes often appear in his productions.

He composed 10 operas and dramatic scenes, among them *Ashmedai*, which includes electronics (1968; Hamburg, 1971); orch.l works, including 3 piano concertos (1944; 1953; with tenor, 1956); 4 syms. (1953; 1960; 1978; Hayovel [Jubilee], 1985); concertos for viola, cello, violin and cello, flute, duo piano, and clarinet; chamber music, including sonatas for violin, oboe, and viola; 3 string quartets (1959; 1964; 1976); a woodwind quintet, piano trio, and piano quartet; works for solo instruments; piano pieces; organ works; vocal and choral works. Tal is an active electronic composer, often composing entire works or accompaniments on tape, including 5 dance pieces, piano concertos No. 4–6 (1962; 1964; 1970), a harpsichord concerto (1964), harp concerto (1971), and *Frequencies 440–462: Hommage à Boris Blacher* (1972).

tala. In Indian classical music, the system of cyclical rhythmic organization maintained by the pair of drums known collectively as TABLĀ. The concept of tala is similar to Western meter but differs in that the number of beats in 1 complete cycle (*tal*) can be 16 or more, and the cycle can last far longer than a measure. The tala system is taught by mnemonic syllables and hand gestures that can be incorporated into the performance itself; the TABLĀ player may improvise then within the cycle and its subdivisions (*āvarta*).

Tale About a Real Man, A. Opera by Prokofiev, 1948, 1st produced unofficially in Leningrad. The libretto was based on an actual episode in World War II in which a Soviet flyer lost both feet in combat but was patriotically determined to continue in active duty even though he had to wear prosthesis; he succeeded brilliantly in aerial combat. Prokofiev hoped to vindicate himself with this opera against official Soviet critics who accused him of pursuing decadent Western ways: a false hope, for the opera was attacked by Soviet spokesmen as failing to achieve the correct line of socialist realism. The opera was revived in Moscow in a posthumous gesture of rehabilitation (1960); the hero glorified in the opera attended the performance in person.

Tale of Czar Saltan, The. Opera by Rimsky-Korsakov, 1900, after a fairy tale by Pushkin, 1st produced in Moscow. The mythical Czar Saltan is searching for a bride; 3 sisters compete; he selects and marries the youngest; she bears him a son. But her envious sisters tell the Czar that the child is a monster; horrified, he orders both mother and child put in a barrel to sail the ocean on their own. The prince grows up quickly; the barrel lands on an island; he saves a swan from a

hawk. The swan turns out to be a magic princess; she endows him with the power to transform himself into any living creature. He turns himself into a bumblebee, flies back to his hometown, and, spotting his treacherous aunts in the garden, stings them viciously. (The orch.l representation of the *Flight of the Bumblebee* is very famous.) The denouement is happy: the heir to the throne marries the magic princess, his mother is reinstated, and even her evil sisters are forgiven.

talea (Lat.). See ISORHYTHM.

Tales of Hoffmann The. Opera by Offenbach, 1881, based on stories of the German fabulist E. T. A. Hoffmann, premiered in Paris. Hoffmann himself is the focus of the opera, telling the stories of his 3 great loves: with a lithe mechanical puppet, a blithe Venetian courtesan, and a tubercular German maiden. In an ideal production not only does Hoffman appear in all 3 acts (plus prologue and epilogue), but the characters representing the force of evil, the servant, and in some productions the beloveds are each acted by 1 singer. Offenbach died before completing the score, which was finished by Guiraud for its posthumous premiere in Paris. The 2nd act contains the famous *Barcarolle*.

Tales of Our Countryside. Suite for Piano and Orch. by Cowell, 1941, in 4 movements of Irish inspiration. It was 1st performed in Atlantic City, N.J.

Talking Heads. See BYRNE, DAVID.

talon (*hausse*; Fr., heel; Ger. *Frosch*; It. *tallone*). The NUT of the string bow.

tamborito (Sp., little drum). A lively accompanied dance song of Panama, usually in a major key and duple meter.

tambour (Fr.). Drum. *Tambour à friction*, friction drum. *Tambour de basque*, a tambourine (not used by the Basques).

tambour militaire (Fr.). A small side drum used in military bands. It has no definite pitch, but produces a dry, well-articulated sound in the general tenor register. As a rhythmic instrument it is used in sym., opera, and even chamber music. Nielsen gives the tambour militaire an important part in his 5th Sym., instructing the player to beat the drum following its own rhythm "as if trying to stop the rest of the orchestra." A solo on the military drum introduces the execution by hanging of *Till Eulenspiegels* in the eponymous work by R. Strauss. Varèse gives the military drum the leading "tenor" part in his *Ionisation*.

tambourin (Fr., small drum). 1. A cylindrical drum covered with skin on both ends; it is possibly of Arab origin. 2. An old dance in southern France accompanied by a pipe and a tambourin. Rameau wrote a piece for clavecin entitled *Tambourin*, with rhythmic imitations of the characteristic beat of the instrument.

tambourine (Fr. *tambour de basque*; It. *tamburino*; Ger. *Schellentrommel*). A popular instrument of Spanish origin, consisting of a single drumhead bordered by a shallow wooden ring with a number of metallic jingles. The tambourine can be played in a variety of ways: shaking, thumping, plunking, clicking, striking against the knee or against the opposing hand. The sound produced is dry and short, with no resonance or reverberation. The tambourine is regularly used to accompany Spanish dances, notably flamenco. Bizet makes use of it in his opera *Carmen*, Rimsky-Korsakov in his orch.l score *Capriccio Espagnol*, Debussy in *Ibéria*, and Ravel in *Rapsodie espagnole*. A tambourine of Biblical times, the *timbrel*, was furnished with several pairs of bronze jingles, which Biblical women shook to attract male attention. One extant specimen, unearthed in Babylon and dating back to about 2700 B.C., has ten pairs of bronze jingles and is beautifully ornamented with precious stones. In the Bible Miriam, sister of Moses, used a timbrel during the Exodus from Egypt.

tamburā (tamboura, tampura). A long-necked Indian lute, played while seated and held vertically, with a gourd resonator and 4 strings tuned to the pitch of the instruments or voice that it accompanies as a drone. The tamburā's strings are gently plucked in a slow ostinato unrelated to the melody and percussion players' tempo, by which it represents a Hindu conception of universal harmony and therefore a perfection that the soloists can never hope to attain. Even the tamburā's special role has been lost to the modern era, in this case via the HARMONIUM (which is also blamed for the loss of pitch subtleties in Indian music).

tamburo basco (It., Basque drum). Tambourine.

tamburo di legno (It., wooden drum). Generic term for a resonant wooden box used as an IDIOPHONE.

tamburo grosso (It.). Bass drum.

tamburo rullante (It., rolling drum). Tenor drum, slightly larger than the snare drum.

tamburo scordato (It., drum without strings). Small drum without snares.

tamburone (It.). Obsolete for BASS DRUM.

Tamerlano. Opera by Handel, 1724, 1st performed in London. The central character is Tamerlane (Tamburlaine), the powerful Mongol conqueror, who is preparing to be married but who meanwhile falls in love with a captive Turkish woman; however, she is in love with a Greek prince. Multilateral jealousies complicate the action, but in the end the conqueror returns to his betrothed and yields the Turkish woman to her prince.

Taming of the Shrew, The. Play by Shakespeare, *c.* 1596, a comedy along the politically incorrect lines of a man subjugating an unwilling woman to his will. There are at least 3 important operas by lesser-known composers based on this work, with the same title: Hermann Goetz (1840–1876; a composer whom G. B. Shaw found superior to Brahms), 1874; Vittorio Giannini (1903–66), 1953; and Vissarion Shebalin (1902–63; Shostakovich's friend and fellow victim of Soviet bullying), 1955.

Tammany. Political song by Gus Edwards, 1905. Set in a pseudo-Indian style, it satirizes the powerful N.Y. Tammany Hall, stronghold of the Democratic party. Despite the song's satirical content, Tammany Hall itself adopted it as its official song.

tampon (Fr.). Drum stick.

tam-tam. 1. A large Eastern unpitched gong, suspended from a stand and struck with a felt-covered stick. The instrument spread through Europe in the 18th century; Gossec used the tam-tam for the funeral march in *Mirabeau* (1791). Tchaikovsky used it in the *Pathétique sym.* to express the inexorability of fate; R. Strauss includes it for similar funereal effect in his *Death and Transfiguration*. There are 2 common misconceptions concerning the tam-tam: 1) that it can only represent tragic situations (and J. Arthur Rank movies); it functioned in courts, temples, and elsewhere to give signals; and 2) that it is identical to a true gong, such as is found in GAMELAN. Such gongs have raised hubs in the middle, upon which the instrument is struck and dampened by stick and that are factors in tuning, along with the gong sizes; the tam-tam has a white-noise sound, no particular place to be struck, and a much slower, more unpredictable decay. 2. The Hindoo drum.

tanbūr (Pers., Turk.). Long-necked Near Eastern lute with a small pear-shaped body, fretted neck, and a variable number of metal strings.

Tancredi. Opera by Rossini, 1813, premiered in Venice. The story deals with Tancred, a crusader who took part in the siege of Jerusalem. He is emotionally torn between 2 loves: a devoted Syrian girl and a Persian woman warrior, Clorinda, whom he loves profoundly. But as he encounters her wearing full armor, he mistakes her for a masculine enemy and fatally wounds her. This tragic episode is also the subject of Monteverdi's dramatic madrigal, *Il combattimento di Tancredi e Clorinda* (1624).

tändelnd (Ger.). In a toying, bantering style.

Taneyev, Sergei (Ivanovich), greatly significant Russian composer and pedagogue; b. Vladimir district, Nov. 25, 1856; d. Dyudkovo, Zvenigorodsk district, June 19, 1915. He began taking piano lessons at the age of 5; was only 9 when he entered the Moscow Cons.; after academic training for a year, he reentered the Cons. in 1869 as a piano pupil of Eduard Langer; also received instruction in theory from Nikolai Hubert and in composition from Tchaikovsky, who became his lifelong friend; in 1871 Nikolai Rubinstein became his piano mentor. In 1875 he made his formal debut as a pianist as soloist in the Brahms D-minor Concerto in Moscow; later that year he was soloist in the Moscow premiere of the Tchaikovsky 1st Concerto, and subsequently he was soloist in all of Tchaikovsky's works for piano and orch.

He graduated from the Cons. in 1875 as the 1st student to win the gold medal in both performance and composition. In 1876 he toured his homeland with Leopold Auer. In 1878 he succeeded Tchaikovsky as prof. of harmony and orchestration at the Moscow Cons.; after the death of Rubinstein in 1881 he took over the latter's piano classes there; in 1883 he succeeded Hubert as prof. of composition; after serving as its director (1885–89) he taught counterpoint (1889–1905).

Taneyev was a 1st-class pianist; Tchaikovsky regarded him as one of the finest interpreters of his music. His position as a composer is anomalous: he is one of the most respected figures of Russian music history, and there is a growing literature about him; his correspondence and all documents, however trivial, concerning his life are treasured as part of the Russian cultural heritage; yet outside Russia his works are rarely heard.

He wrote a respected treatise on counterpoint, *Podvizhnoi kontrapunkt strogavo pisma* (1909). The style of his compositions presents a compromise between Russian melos and Germanic contrapuntal writing; the mastery revealed in his syms. and quartets is unquestionable. His most ambitious work was the operatic trilogy *Oresteia*, after Aeschylus, in 3 divisions: *Agamemnon*, *Choëphorai*, and *Eumenides*, 1st performed in St. Petersburg (1895). After his death an almost-completed treatise *Ucheniye o kanone* (The Study of Canon) was found and publ. (Moscow, 1929). His other compositions include 4 syms. (1873–74; 1877–78; 1884; 1896–97); a piano concerto (1876); 5 unnumbered string quartets (1874–76; 1880; 1882–83; 1883; 1911); 5 numbered string quartets (1890; 1895; 1886; 1899; 1903); 2 string trios (1879–80; n.d.); 2 string quintets (1901; 1904); a piano quartet (1906); a trio for violin, viola, and tenor viola (1910); a piano quintet (1911); a violin sonata (1911); piano pieces; choral works; and songs.

tangent. A brass blade attached to the back of a key on the clavichord, which strikes the intended string when the key is pushed down.

tango. The most celebrated dance of Argentina, danced by a couple, characterized by strongly marked syncopation. Although attempts have been made by some respectable lexicographers to derive the word from the Latin *tangere* (touch), all evidence points toward an indigenous onomatopoeic derivation, perhaps imitative of the drumbeat. Musically the tango has the characteristics of the HABANERA; both are in 2/4 time with a dotted rhythmical figure in the accompaniment, and the 1st section is set in a minor key, and the 2nd in major. In the accompanying ensemble the guitar and the bandonion are the primary melodic and harmonic instruments, with others including piano, double bass, saxophone, and percussion. A vocal part is sometimes added.

The tango developed as entertainment in the red-light districts of Buenos Aires in the last decades of the 19th century. It quickly became popular in the ballrooms of the U.S. and Europe in the years immediately preceding World War I. Its frank sexuality shocked the guardians of morality, and protests against it were voiced by the clergy and government authorities, so that the Argentine ambassador to France found it necessary to state that the tango was the product of bordellos and was never tolerated in decent society. Fortunately for tango lovers, the concept of "decent society" has evolved a great deal, to the point that this once indecent dance has been performed on the legitimate stage, and the music of Astor Piazzolla (1921–92), who did for tango what Chopin did for the waltz, is valued by classical and popular music audiences alike.

tango-milonga. A dance song fusing the older rural MILONGA with the modern urban TANGO.

Tannhäuser. Opera by Wagner, 1845, to his own libretto, 1st produced in Dresden. Wagner described the score as a *Handlung* (action). The complete title is *Tannhäuser und der Sangerkrieg auf dem Wartburg.* Tannhäuser was a historical figure, a German Minnesinger who led a wandering life in the 13th century and participated in a crusade.

In Wagner's opera Tannhäuser succumbs to the pleasures of the flesh in the Venusberg, a mountain in central Germany in whose caves, according to medieval legends, the Goddess Venus herself holds court. But he yearns to return to his own world and to his beloved Elisabeth. He joins a group of pilgrims in the valley of the Wartburg, which includes his friend Wolfram (who was also a historical figure). A singing contest is held in the Wartburg castle. Tannhäuser shocks the assembly by singing a song in praise of Venus. He is expelled from the Wartburg and joins the pilgrims on their way to Rome where he hopes to obtain absolution from the Pope. Wolfram sings a song appealing to the evening star (that is, Venus) for protection of Elisabeth. Having failed to obtain forgiveness in Rome, Tannhäuser returns home, and encounters a funeral procession; it is that of Elisabeth. He collapses before her coffin and dies. He achieves redemption when the papal staff, brought back from Rome by the pilgrims, sprouts leaves. The opera marks a turning point in music history as an artistic affirmation of the Romantic ideal.

Tannhäuser, Der, German Minnesinger; b. *c.* 1205; d. *c.* 1270. He was of noble lineage; was active in the 5th Crusade to the Holy Land (1228–33) and the Cypriot war; later was at the court of Friedrich II "der Streitfare" in Vienna and at the court of Otto II of Bavaria in Landshut, among others. His name became legendary through the tale of the Venusberg, pagan intimacy with Venus, penitence, pilgrimage to Rome, and the miracle of the flowering of his pilgrim's staff. Wagner's *Tannhäuser* is based on this legend, which has nothing to do with the life of the real Tannhäuser.

Tansman, Alexandre, Polish-born French pianist, conductor, and composer; b. Lodz, June 12, 1897; d. Paris, Nov. 15, 1986. He studied at the Lodz Cons. (1902–14); then pursued training in law and philosophy at the Univ. of Warsaw; also received instruction in counterpoint, form, and composition from Rytel in Warsaw. In 1919 he went to Paris, where he appeared as a soloist in his own works (1920). In 1927 he appeared as a soloist with the Boston Sym. Orch.; he then played throughout Europe, Canada, and Palestine. He later took up conducting; made a tour of the Far East (1932–33). After the occupation of Paris by the Germans in 1940, he made his way to the U.S.; lived in Hollywood, where he wrote music for films; returned to Paris in 1946.

His music is distinguished by a considerable melodic gift and a vivacious rhythm; his harmony is often bitonal; there are some impressionistic traits that reflect his Parisian tastes. He composed 6 operas, 6 ballets, 7 syms. (1925; 1926; 1931, Sym. concertante; 1939; 1942; 1943, In Memoriam; 1944), as well as other orch.1 works. His compositions for piano include 20 *pieces faciles polonaises* (1924); 5 sonatas; mazurkas and other Polish dances; *Sonatine transatlantique* (1930); and *Pour les enfants,* 4 albums. He also wrote the monograph *Stravinsky* (Paris, 1948).

tanto (It.). As much, so much, too (much). *Allegro non tanto,* not too fast; *a tanto possibile,* as much as possible.

tantric chants. Ritual singing of Hindu or Buddhist sects, designed to attain purification of soul and body, combined with body exercises such as yoga. The text of the tantric chants is fashioned from the mystic syllables of the sacred mantras; the symbols are inspired by the diagrams of the ritual mandalas. Some Tibetan Buddhist chants last for over 7 hours.

Tanz (Ger.). A dance.

Tanzhalle (Ger.). A dance hall; a place of entertainment that flourished in Berlin and elsewhere in Germany in the 1st third of the 20th century in which physical contact was facilitated between customers.

Tanzlied (Ger.). Song in the rhythm of a dance, often accompanying a dance.

tanzmässig (Ger.). In a dancelike character.

tap dance. A type of American dance in which distinct rhythmic patterns are produced by the tapping of the performer's feet on the floor. Typical tap shoes have metal plates on the soles to enhance the sound. Tap dancing in wooden shoes was called buck-and-wing dancing, while in "soft-shoe" dancing the performer applied sliding and shuffling on the floor. Dancing pairs would trade rhythmically complex riffs with one another in a call-and-response manner; the best dancers could also work with timbral contrasts. Tap dance was popular in vaudeville, revues and musicals, and film; it entered the concert hall when Morton Gould wrote a 4-movement Concerto for tap dancer and orch. (1952).

tape recording. A method involving a lacquered, extremely thin, magnetized plastic tape onto which processed sound signals are entered in electronic form (through a *recording head*), to be reproduced on a tape recorder or player with the appropriate pickup (*playback head*).

The concept of recording without going directly to disc had been pondered since the beginning of the 20th century; the direct predecessor to tape was *wire recording*, which became an instrument of peace and war for Nazi Germany. A great number of musical performances were recorded, with the theoretically unlimited length of wire permitting far longer uninterrupted recordings than 78-rpm disc recording could make; it was also used for secret military communication. The fragility of the wire led Nazi engineers to seek another medium for recording, and they began to develop what would later be called recording tape, or *reel-to-reel*. When the Allies stormed Germany in 1945, they found some early versions of the new tape-recording machine and brought them back to the U.S. for further development. (The story goes that Varèse was sent such a machine in the late 1940s and realized immediately its compositional potential.)

As a home medium reel-to-reel began to give way to the long-playing record in the 1950s, although prerecorded tapes continued to be made into the early 1960s. Other tape media evolved: the *8-track*, on which the narrow tape is wound as a loop and runs continuously, except for switching from one "program" to the next (4 programs, each in stereo, hence 8-track). Its period of popularity was brief, as the *cassette* was developed in the 1970s. This tape involves even narrower tape in a miniature reel-to-reel format, on which both sides are recorded in stereo (hence its early name *4-track*); it can play for longer than the 8-track, is more convenient to store, can be used for home recording (unlike the 8-track), and has developed sound comparable to most long-playing records.

As a studio medium the reel-to-reel tape recorder was the principal means of recording all kinds of music from the late 1940s to the 1980s. Reel-to-reel tape could range from 1/4" to 1" in width (and larger), and record several simultaneous tracks (channels) with different instruments, voices, effects, etc.; this allowed each to be recorded with relatively little acoustic interference and then *mixed* and *equalized* (combined and balanced) to produce a final product. *Editing* allows for correcting errors by cutting and splicing desirable passages; one can also record over undesirable passages on individual channels while saving others. Multitrack recording also allows for the *overdubbing technique*, where 1 performer can add layers onto a single recording, to the point where a single person is the sole or nearly sole performer on a richly textured album (e.g., Stevie Wonder, Paul McCartney, Steve Winwood, Roy Wood, Richard Thompson). Reel-to-reel is still widely used, but it is being replaced by *digital recording*, in which computer technology records music as a constant numerical sampling of information, stored on a drive or database and capable of extremely precise editing and imaginative processing.

tapeur (from Fr. *taper*, pound). A rather unkind description of a pianist accompanying dance rehearsals.

Tapiola. Sym. poem by Sibelius, 1926, performed for the 1st time in N.Y. as a commissioned work. Tapiola is the god of Finnish forests, and the music is appropriately somber and majestic.

täppisch (Ger.). Clumsily (Mahler, 9th Sym.).

tār (Pers.). Long-necked Persian lute, also played in Central Asia. It is generally made from one piece of hollowed-out wood, with membrane belly, movable frets, and between 2 and 5 strings, played with a plectrum. Cowell makes use of the tār in his chamber work *Persian Set*.

tarantella (It.; Ger. *Tarantelle*). A southern Italian dance in 6/8 time, with the rate of speed gradually increasing and the mode alternating between major and minor; also an instrumental piece in 3/8 or 6/8 time, in a very rapid tempo and bold and brilliant style. The tarantella, named after the city of Taranto, was especially popular in the 19th century. According to legend, the playing of the tarantella cured tarantism, an uncontrollable impulse to dance, supposedly caused by the bite of the tarantula spider. However, medical investigations of persons bitten by the tarantula have revealed no such choreographic symptoms.

Ta-Ra-Ra-Boom-De-Re. Nonsense march song of uncertain authorship, 1891; the downbeat is on "boom." In addition to its own popularity the song is well-suited to lyrical parody.

Tarare. Opera by Salieri, 1787, 1st produced in Paris. The libretto, written specially for Salieri by Beaumarchais, deals with a soldier of fortune named Tarare who is involved in a mortal combat with the King of the fabled town of Ormuz (Hormuz) in the Persian Gulf. Tarare wins the battle and becomes King. The opera was immensely successful in its 1st production in Paris and later in an Italian version under the title *Azur, Re d'Ormus*, in Vienna. *Tarare* was one of the earliest operas to introduce an element of pseudo-oriental mysticism. Mozart liked *Tarare* very much; his own opera *The Magic Flute* (1791) had a libretto similar to that of *Tarare*.

Taras Bulba. Orch.l rhapsody for orch. by Janáček, 1915–18, after Gogol's novel; it was 1st performed in Brno, 1921. The 3 movements depict the struggle of the Cossacks against Polish domination in the 15th century, involving Bulba and his 2 sons. The younger son, who betrays his land for the sake of a Polish girl, is taken prisoner by Bulba, who despite his anguish executes him; the elder son is caught by the Polish army and executed; and Bulba, also captured and executed, is transformed to a state of greater glory at the end.

tardamente (It.). Slowly, lingeringly. *Tardando*, delaying, lingering; *tardato*, delayed, slower; *tardo*, slow, lingering.

tárogató. Traditional Hungarian wind instrument made of wood with a conical bore. First mentioned in the 13th century, it apparently was brought by Arabs to southeastern Europe in the trading process; at the time it was shawmlike, with the reeds covered by a pirouette and without fingerholes. By the 19th century the double reed was reduced to a single one, the mouthpiece became clarinetlike (although still partly covered), and the fingering was altered to resemble a saxophone's. The instrument's cultural importance is testified to by its role as a "national Hungarian instrument"

Giuseppe Tartini

since the Rákóczy rebellion in the 18th century.

Tartini, Giuseppe, famous Italian violinist, teacher, music theorist, and composer; b. Pirano, Istria, Apr. 8, 1692; d. Padua, Feb. 26, 1770. His parents prepared him for a monastic life by entrusting his education to clerics in Pirano and Capodistria, where he received some violin instruction. In 1708 he renounced the cloister but remained a nominal candidate for the priesthood. In 1709 he enrolled at the Univ. of Padua as a law student, and at the age of 19 contracted a secret marriage to the 21-year-old Elisabetta Premazore, a protégée of the powerful Cardinal Cornaro, who vengefully brought a charge of abduction against him.

Tartini had to take refuge from prosecution at the monastery of the Friars Minor Conventual in Assisi, where he joined the opera orch. He was pardoned by the Paduan authorities in 1715; then lived in Venice and Padua, being made *primo violino e capo di concerto* at the basilica of S. Antonio in Padua in 1721. He also was allowed to travel as a virtuoso, and he soon acquired a distinguished reputation. From 1723 to 1726 he served as chamber musician to Count Kinsky in Prague; then resumed his residence in Padua, where he organized a music school in 1728; among his students there were Nardini and Pugnani.

He subsequently developed a brilliant career as a violinist, making numerous concert tours in Italy. He retained his post at S. Antonio until 1765, and also remained active at his school until at least 1767. In 1768 he suffered a mild stroke which effectively ended his career. His style of playing, and in particular his bowing, became a model for other concert violinists.

Among Tartini's compositions, the most famous is the violin sonata in G minor known under the sobriquet *The Devil's Trill* (Trillo del diavolo; after 1744), supposedly inspired by Tartini's dream in which the devil played it for him; the trill appears in the last movement of the sonata. Tartini was a prolific composer of violin music, including *c.* 135 concertos, *c.* 135 sonatas with basso continuo, 30 sonatas for solo violin or with basso continuo ad libitum; 18 sonatas for 2 violins and bass continuo. Other works include concertos for other instruments; 40 trio sonatas; 4 sonatas a quattro; and religious music. Many of these works were published in collections during his lifetime.

Although Tartini lacked scientific training, he made several acoustical discoveries, the most important of which were the sum (summation) and difference (differential) tones; Tartini observed these effects in 1714 and summarized his findings in his *Trattato di musica secondo la vera scienza dell'armonia* (Padua, 1754) and other treatises; the difference tone became known also as a Tartini tone, or TERZO SUONO. This phenomenon was actually described in an earlier German publ., *Vorgemach der musicalischen Composition* by Georg Sorge (1745–47). These tones were also known, rather misleadingly, as "beat tones"; they are in fact produced by the interference of frequencies of higher overtones. The WOLF tone of string instruments is different in origin, being produced by vibrations of the body of the instrument. Violinists are usually aware of interferences from difference tones and the less audible sum tones resulting from added frequencies; they correct them empirically by a slight alteration of tuning.

Tartini tones. DIFFERENCE TONES produced by playing double-stops in perfect nontempered tuning. They were 1st discovered and described by Giuseppe Tartini in 1754, as TERZO SUONO (3rd tones).

Tartiniana. Sym. fantasia for violin and orch. by Dallapiccola, 1952, premiered in Bern, Switzerland. As the title suggests, it is based on melodies by Giuseppe Tartini.

Taschengeige (Ger.). Pocket violin; POCHETTE.

Tasso, Lamento e Trionfe. Sym. poem by Liszt, 1854, recounting the life, suffering, and eventual triumph of the great Italian poet Torquato Tasso. Liszt's 1st version of the work was 1st performed in 1849; both this and the subsequent version were premiered in Weimar.

tastatura (It.). Keyboard; fingerboard.

Taste (Ger.). A key on a keyboard.

Tasteninstrument (Ger.). Keyboard instrument.

tastiera (It.). Keyboard; fingerboard. *Sulla tastiera* (Fr. *sur la touche*; Ger. *am Griffbrett*); on (near) the fingerboard; FLAUTANDO.

tastiera per luce (It., light keyboard). The color organ envisioned by Scriabin and included in his sym. poem *Promethée*.

tasto (It.). Key; fret; touch; fingerboard. *Sul tasto*, on (near) the fingerboard; *tasto solo*, in BASSO CONTINUO, play the bass line, either as written or in octaves, without chords.

Tate, Jeffrey, talented English conductor; b. Salisbury, Apr. 28, 1943. Although a victim of spina bifida, he pursued studies at Cambridge Univ. and at St. Thomas's Medical School; then attended the London Opera Centre (1970–71). He was subsequently a member of the music staff at the Royal Opera, Covent Garden (1971–77); and served as an assistant conductor at the Bayreuth Festivals (1976–80). In 1978 he made his formal conducting debut with *Carmen* at the Göteborg Opera; in 1980 he made his 1st appearance at the Metropolitan Opera in N.Y., conducting *Lulu*; his debut at Covent Garden followed, with *La Clemenza di Tito* (1982). He has performed as a guest conductor at numerous major opera companies around the world. In 1983 he made his 1st appearance with the English Chamber Orch., being named its principal conductor in 1985; led it on tours abroad, including one to the U.S. in 1988. In 1986 he also became principal conductor at Covent Garden. In 1990 he was made a Commander of the Order of the British Empire. He became chief conductor of the Rotterdam Phil. in 1991. His extensive operatic and concert repertoire encompasses works from the Classic to the contemporary eras.

tattoo (It.; from Lat. *tactus*). 1. Beat. 2. Military signals in a rapid articulate rhythm used to summon soldiers back to the barracks. A stylized tattoo occurs in *Carmen*: the infatuated Don José refuses to heed his, with dramatic consequences for his fate.

Tatum, Art(hur), noted African-American jazz pianist; b. Toledo, Ohio, Oct. 13, 1910; d. Los Angeles, Nov. 5, 1956. He was blind in one eye and had limited vision in the other; he attended a school for the blind in Columbus, Ohio, and learned to read Braille music notation; at the age of 16 he began to play in nightclubs. In 1932 he went to N.Y. and became successful on the radio. In 1938 he made a spectacular tour of England; then pursued his career in N.Y. and Los Angeles; organized his own trio in 1943. In 1947 he appeared in the film *The Fabulous Dorseys*. His art as a jazz improviser was captured on more than 600 recordings. He brought "stride" piano playing to a point of perfection, achieving small miracles with ornamental figurations in the melody while throwing effortless cascades of notes across the keyboard and imagination as fast as his fingers; he also had a knack of improvising variations on popular classical pieces.

Tauber, Richard, eminent Austrian-born English tenor; b. Linz, May 16, 1891; d. London, Jan. 8, 1948. He was the illegitimate son of the actor Richard Anton Tauber; his mother was a soubrette singer. He was christened Richard Denemy after his mother's maiden name, but he sometimes used the last name Seiffert, his mother's married name. He took courses at the Hoch Cons. in Frankfurt am Main and studied voice with Carl Beines in Freiburg; made his debut at Chemnitz as Tamino (1913) with such success that he was engaged in the same year at the Dresden Court Opera; made his 1st appearance at the Berlin Royal Opera as Strauss's Bacchus in 1915, and later won particular success in Munich and Salzburg for his roles in Mozart's operas. About 1925 he turned to lighter roles, and won remarkable success in the operettas of Lehar. He made his U.S. debut in a 1931 N.Y. recital. In 1938 he settled in England, where he appeared as Tamino and Belmonte at London's Covent Garden. In 1940 he became a British subject. He wrote an operetta, *Old Chelsea*, taking the leading role at its premiere (London, 1943). He made his last American appearance at Carnegie Hall in N.Y. in 1947.

Tavener, John (Kenneth), English organist, pedagogue, and mystic religious composer; b. London, Jan. 28, 1944. He studied with Lennox Berkeley at the Royal Academy of Music in London (1961–65) and privately with David Lumsdaine (1965–67); was organist at St. John's, Kensington (from 1960); taught composition at Trinity College of Music in London (from 1969). Among the formative influences of his creative evolution were medieval hymnology and Indian transcendentalism; his technical equipment is, by contrast, ultramodern, including combinatorial serialism and electronic generation of sound.

His early works were free collages of styles and full of the contrasts found in other works of the 1960s, e.g., *The Cappemakers*, dramatic cantata (1964); *Cain and Abel*, dramatic cantata for soloists and chamber orch. (1966); and *The Whale*, his best known early work, a dramatic cantata for narrator, soloists, chorus, and orch. (1966). His conversion to Eastern Orthodox Christianity affected both his materials and styles as a true believer.

Taylor, Cecil (Percival), African-American jazz pianist and composer; b. N.Y., Mar. 15, 1933. He began piano lessons at age 5; was improvising and composing by the age of 8; later studied percussion. He studied harmony and composition at the N.Y. College of Music; subsequently studied composition at the New England Cons. of Music in Boston; also immersed himself in the Boston jazz scene. He then worked with his own combos in N.Y.; 1st appeared at the Newport Jazz Festival (1957); gained a name for himself as a performer in the off-Broadway production of Jack Gelber's *The Connection* (1959).

He made his 1st tour of Europe in 1962, and then played in many jazz centers on both sides of the Atlantic; performed at N.Y.'s Carnegie Hall in 1977. He made a number of remarkable recordings, including the albums *Into the Hot* (1961), *Unit Structures* (1966), *Silent Tongues* (1975), *The Cecil Taylor Unit (1978)*, and *3 Phasis* (1978). His digitally agile piano style and penchant for extended atonal improvisation made him an important figure in avant-garde jazz circles in his time.

Taylor, James, sweet-voiced singer/songwriter, b. Boston, Mass., Mar. 12, 1948. Taylor was raised in Chapel Hill, N.C., the son of a college professor. He attended boarding school outside of Boston, where he suffered a nervous breakdown; by summer 1966 he was discharged from the mental hospital and living in N.Y., where he formed a rock band with guitarist Danny "Kootch" Kortchmar called the Flying Machine. The band played local clubs and made some recordings that went unissued until Taylor achieved fame on his own; they disbanded in late 1967.

The year 1968 found Taylor in London, where a demo tape ended up in the hands of Paul McCartney and producer Peter Asher, then in the process of scouting for talent for the Beatles's new Apple label. Taylor recorded 1 album for the label, but with the Beatles's empire crumbling amidst inter-group strife, the recording went nowhere. He returned to the U.S. in 1969 and signed with Warner Bros. Records. Still working with Asher, he produced the landmark *Sweet Baby James* album, which included the hits *Fire and Rain*, *Country Roads*, and the title cut. Taylor's soft folk-rock sound gained him an immediate following, and he continued to enjoy success through most of the '70s with his own material and covers of earlier hits.

The '80s and '90s have seen him become primarily a touring artist. His recordings continue to chart on occasion, but he has become more popular on the road than on the radio. Taylor's brothers and sister have also recorded, including Livingston (b. 1950, Chapel Hill, N.C.), who has recorded in a more soft-pop vein than his brother.

Tchaikovsky, Piotr Ilyich

Greatly popular Russian composer; b. Votkinsk, Viatka district, May 7, 1840; d. St. Petersburg, Nov. 6, 1893. The son of a mining inspector at a plant in the Urals, he was given a good education; had a French governess and a music teacher. When he was 10 the family moved to St. Petersburg and he was sent to a school of jurisprudence, from which he graduated at 19, becoming a government clerk; while at school he studied music with Lomakin, but he did not display conspicuous talent as either a pianist or composer. At the age of 21 he was accepted in a musical inst., newly established by Anton Rubinstein, which was to become the St. Petersburg Cons. He studied with Zaremba (harmony and counterpoint) and Rubinstein (composition); graduated in 1865, winning a silver medal for his cantata to Schiller's *Hymn to Joy*. In 1866 he became prof. of harmony at the Moscow Cons.

As if to compensate for a late beginning in his profession, he began to compose with great application. His early works (a programmatic sym. subtitled *Winter Dreams*, some overtures and small pieces for string quartet) reveal little individuality. With his sym. poem *Fatum* (1868) came the 1st formulation of his style, highly subjective, preferring minor modes permeated with nostalgic longing and alive with keen rhythms. In 1869 he undertook the composition of his overture-fantasy *Romeo and Juliet*; not content with what he had written, he profited by the advice of Balakirev, whom he met in St. Petersburg; he revised the work in 1870; but this version proved equally unsatisfactory; Tchaikovsky laid the composition aside, and did not complete it until 1880; in its final form it became one of his most successful works.

The Belgian soprano Desirée Artot, a member of an opera troupe visiting St. Petersburg in 1868, took great interest in Tchaikovsky, and he was moved by her attentions; for a few months he seriously contemplated marrying her, and so notified his father (his mother had died of cholera when he was 14 years old). But this proved to be a passing infatuation on her part, for soon she married the Spanish singer Padilla; Tchaikovsky reacted to this event

with a casual philosophical remark about the inconstancy of human attachments.

Throughout his career Tchaikovsky never allowed his psychological turmoil to interfere with his work. Besides teaching and composing, he contributed music criticism to Moscow newspapers for several years (1868–74), made altogether 26 trips abroad (to Paris, Berlin, Vienna, N.Y.), and visited the 1st Bayreuth Festival in 1876, reporting his impressions for the Moscow daily *Russkyie Vedomosti*. His closest friends were members of his own family, his brothers—particularly Modest (b. Alapaevsk, Perm district, May 13, 1850; d. Moscow, Jan. 15, 1916), a playwright, librettist for 2 of his brother's operas, and his future biographer—and his married sister Alexandra Davidov, at whose estate, Kamenka, he spent most of his summers.

The correspondence with them, all of which was preserved and eventually publ., throws a true light on Tchaikovsky's character and his life. His other close friends were his publisher, Jurgenson, Nikolai Rubinstein, and several other musicians. The most extraordinary of his friendships was the epistolary association with Nadezhda von Meck (b. Znamenskoye, near Smolensk, Feb. 10, 1831; d. Wiesbaden, Jan. 13, 1894), a wealthy widow whom he never met but who was to play an important role in his life. Through the violinist Kotek she learned about Tchaikovsky's financial difficulties; she commissioned him to write some compositions, at large fees; then arranged to pay him an annuity of 6,000 rubles. For more than 13 years they corresponded voluminously, even when they lived in the same city (Moscow, Florence); on several occasions she hinted that she would not be averse to a personal meeting, but Tchaikovsky invariably declined such a suggestion, under the pretext that one should not see one's guardian angel in the flesh. On Tchaikovsky's part this correspondence had to remain within the circumscribed domain of art, personal philosophy, and reporting of daily events, without touching on the basic problems of his existence.

In 1877 Tchaikovsky contracted marriage with a conservatory student, Antonina Milyukova, who had declared her love for him. This was an act of defiance of his own nature; Tchaikovsky was a homosexual, and made no secret of it in the correspondence with his brother Modest, who was also a homosexual. He thought that by flaunting a wife he could prevent the already rife rumors about his sexual preference from spreading further. But when she tried to sit on his lap on their wedding night, the result was disastrous, and Tchaikovsky fled from his wife in horror. He attempted suicide by walking into the Moskva River in order to catch pneumonia, but he suffered nothing more severe than simple discomfort. He then went to St. Petersburg to seek the advice of his brother Anatol, a lawyer, who made suitable arrangements with Tchaikovsky's wife for a separation. (They were never divorced; she died in an insane asylum in 1917.) Von Meck, to whom Tchaikovsky wrote candidly of the hopeless failure of his marriage (without revealing the true cause of that failure), made at once an offer of further financial assistance, which he gratefully accepted.

He spent several months during 1877–78 in Italy, Switzerland, Paris, and Vienna. During these months he completed one of his greatest works, the 4th Sym., dedicated to von Meck. It was performed for the 1st time in Moscow in 1878, but Tchaikovsky did not cut short his sojourn abroad to attend the performance. He resigned from the Moscow Cons. in the autumn of 1878, and from that time dedicated himself entirely to composition. The continued subsidy from von Meck allowed him to forget money matters. Early in 1878 he completed his most successful opera, *Evgeny Onegin* ("lyric scenes" after Pushkin); it was 1st produced in Moscow by a cons. ensemble in 1879 and gained success only gradually; the 1st performance at the Imperial Opera in St. Petersburg did not take place until 1884.

Tchaikovsky's natural state of mind was still morbid depression, but every new work sustained his faith in his destiny as a composer, despite many disheartening reversals. His Piano Concerto No. 1, rejected by Nikolai Rubinstein as unplayable, was given its world premiere (somewhat incongruously) in Boston in 1875—played by Hans von Bülow—and afterward was performed all over the world by famous pianists, including Nikolai Rubinstein. The Violin Concerto, criticized by Leopold Auer (to whom the score was originally dedicated) and attacked by Hanslick with sarcasm and virulence at its

world premiere by Brodsky in Vienna (1881), survived all its detractors to become one of the most celebrated pieces in the violin repertoire. The 5th Sym. (1888) was successful from the very 1st.

Early in 1890 Tchaikovsky wrote his 2nd important opera, *The Queen of Spades* (also based on Pushkin), which was produced at the Imperial Opera in St. Petersburg in that year. His ballets *Swan Lake* (1876) and *The Sleeping Beauty* (1889) became famous on Russian stages. But at the peak of his career Tchaikovsky suffered a severe psychological blow; von Meck notified him of the discontinuance of her subsidy, and with this announcement she abruptly terminated their correspondence. He could now well afford the loss of the money, but his pride was deeply hurt by the manner in which von Meck had acted. A plausible explanation is that her grown children had found out the truth about Tchaikovsky's peculiarity (which in those times was a crime as well as a sin) and that she was shocked by his duplicity in misrepresenting his reluctance to meet her.

It is indicative of Tchaikovsky's inner strength that even this desertion of one whom he regarded as his staunchest friend did not affect his ability to work. In 1891 he undertook his only voyage to America. He was received with honors as a celebrated composer; he led 4 concerts of his works in N.Y. and 1 each in Baltimore and Philadelphia. He did not linger in the U.S., however, and returned to St. Petersburg in a few weeks. Early in 1892 he made a concert tour as a conductor in Russia, then proceeded to Warsaw and Germany. In the meantime he had purchased a house in the town of Klin, not far from Moscow, where he wrote his last sym., the *Pathétique*.

Despite the perfection of his technique, he did not arrive at the desired form and substance of this work at once, and discarded his original sketch. The title *Pathétique* was suggested to him by his brother Modest; the score was dedicated to his nephew, Vladimir Davidov. Its music is the final testament of Tchaikovsky's life, and an epitome of his philosophy of fatalism. In the 1st movement the trombones are given the theme of the Russian service for the dead. Remarkably, the score of one of his most lighthearted works, the ballet *The Nutcracker* (1891–92), was composed simultaneously with the early sketches for the *Pathétique*.

Tchaikovsky was in good spirits when he went to St. Petersburg to conduct the premiere of the *Pathétique* in 1893 (which was but moderately successful). A cholera epidemic was then raging in St. Petersburg, and the population was specifically warned against drinking unboiled water, but apparently he carelessly did exactly that. He showed the symptoms of cholera soon afterward, and nothing could be done to save him. The melodramatic hypothesis that the fatal drink of water was a defiance of death, in perfect knowledge of the danger, since he must have remembered his mother's death of the same dread infection, is untenable in the light of publ. private letters between the attendant physician and Modest Tchaikovsky at the time. Tchaikovsky's fatalism alone would amply account for his lack of precaution.

Piotr Ilyich Tchaikovsky, c. 1890s

COURTESY FRANK DRIGGS COLLECTION

Almost immediately after his death, a rumor spread that he had committed suicide, and reports to that effect were publ. in respectable European newspapers (but not in Russian publications), and repeated even in some biographical dictionaries (particularly in Britain). Many years later an émigré Russian musicologist publ. a story of a homosexual scandal involving a Russian nobleman's nephew, which led to a private tribunal that offered Tchaikovsky a choice between honorable suicide or disgrace and possible exile to Siberia; having chosen the former solution, Tchaikovsky was supplied with arsenic; a conspiracy of silence involving his family doctor and Tchaikovsky's own brothers, assured that the truth would remain buried. This fabrication was accepted as historical fact by some biographers, and even found its way into the pages of *The New Grove Dictionary of Music and Musicians* (1980). In Russia the truth of Tchaikovsky's homosexuality was totally suppressed, and any references to it in his diary and letters were expunged.

As a composer Tchaikovsky stands apart from the militant national movement of the MIGHTY FIVE. The Russian element is, of course, very strong in his music, and upon occasion he made use of Russian folk songs in his works, but this national spirit is instinctive rather than consciously cultivated. His personal relationship with the St. Petersburg group of nationalists was friendly without being close; his correspondence with Rimsky-Korsakov,

Balakirev, and others was mostly concerned with professional matters. Tchaikovsky's music was frankly sentimental; his supreme gift of melody, which none of his Russian contemporaries could match, secured for him a lasting popularity among performers and audiences.

His influence was profound on the Moscow group of musicians, of whom Arensky and Rachmaninoff were the most talented. He wrote in every genre and was successful in each; besides his stage works, syms., chamber music, and piano compositions, he composed a great number of lyric songs that are the most poignant creations of his genius. By a historical paradox, Tchaikovsky became the most popular Russian composer under the Soviet regime. His subjectivism, his fatalism, his emphasis on melancholy moods, even his reactionary political views (including a brand of amateurish anti-Semitism), failed to detract from his stature in the new society. In fact, official spokesmen of Soviet Russia repeatedly urged Soviet composers to follow in the path of Tchaikovsky's aesthetics. His popularity is also very strong in Anglo-Saxon countries, particularly in America; much less so in France and Italy; in Germany his influence is insignificant.

He composed 11 operas, the 3 ballets mentioned above (and their suites); and 6 numbered syms.: No. 1, op. 13, *Winter Dreams* (1866–1874) No. 2, op. 17, *Little Russian* or *Ukrainian* (1872–80) No. 3, op. 29, *Polish* (1875); No. 4, op. 36 (1877–78); No. 5, op. 64 (1888); No. 6, op. 74, *Pathétique* (1893). Other works include the *Manfred Sym.*, op. 58 (Moscow, 1886) *Burya* (The Tempest), sym. fantasia, op. 18 (Moscow, 1873); Piano Concerto No. 1, op. 23 (Boston, 1875); *Sérénade mélancolique* for violin with orch., op. 26 (Moscow, 1876); *Francesca da Rimini*, sym. fantasia, op. 32, after Dante (Moscow, 1877); *Variations on a Rococo Theme* for Cello and Orch., op. 33 (Moscow, 1877); Violin Concerto, op. 35 (1878; Vienna, 1881); Suite No. 1, op. 43 (Moscow, 1879); Piano Concerto No. 2, op. 44 (1879–80; N.Y., 1881); *Italian Capriccio*, op. 45 (Moscow, 1880); Serenade for strings, op. 48 (St. Petersburg, 1881); Suite No. 2, op. 53 (Moscow, 1884); Suite No. 3, op. 55 (St. Petersburg, 1885);

Suite No. 4, op. 61, *Mozartiana* (Moscow, 1887); *Hamlet*, fantasy overture, op. 67 (St. Petersburg, 1888); *Voyevoda*, sym. ballad, op. 78 (Moscow, 1891).

Chamber: 3 string quartets (1871; 1874; 1876); Piano Trio, op. 50 (Moscow, 1882); *Souvenir de Florence* for string sextet, op. 70 (1890–92; St. Petersburg, 1892). Piano: Sonata, op. 80 (1865); *Les Quatre Saisons*, 12 characteristic pieces for each month of the year (1875–76); Sonata, op. 37 (1878); *Dumka: Russian Rustic Scene*, op. 59 (1886). Vocal: Choral: *Liturgy of St. John Chrysostom* for unaccompanied chorus, op. 41 (1878); *Vesper Service* for unaccompanied chorus, op. 52 (1881–82); about 100 songs. Writings: Tchaikovsky's diaries for the years 1873–91 were publ. in Moscow and Petrograd (1923). He wrote a treatise which was publ. in an Eng. trans. as *Guide to the Practical Study of Harmony* (Leipzig, 1900). A complete ed. of his literary works and correspondence commenced publ. in Moscow in 1953.

Te. 1. In TONIC SOL-FA, the leading tone in major scales or the supertonic in minor scales. 2. In French, Italian, Spanish, and Russian pitch nomenclature, the leading tone in C major (B in English, H in German).

Te Deum. A song of praise in the Roman Catholic liturgy, sung in Matins on Sunday and feast days. It is generally referred to as an Ambrosian hymn, although it has been shown that St. Ambrose was not the author; text analysis has shown that it dates to before the 4th century. In chant it sets 30 verses strophically, with a reciting formula centering around A for the body of the text and later an alternatim performance style, choral polyphony with chant or organ versets. The Te Deum is essentially a hymn of thanksgiving, salutation, or commemoration, and thus one of the most popular religious texts for polyphonic setting, with organum examples dating to the 10th century. Composers include Binchois, Taverner, John Sheppard, Lassus, Lully, Purcell (in English), Handel (2, in English) and both Haydns. Handel wrote a *Te Deum for the Peace of Utrecht*, and Berlioz contributed one for the Paris Exposition (1855). Later famous works to set this text are by Bruckner (1885), Dvořák (1896), Verdi (1898), Vaughan Williams (1928), Britten (1935), Kodály (celebrating 25 years of Hungarian independence, 1936), and Walton (in English, 1953).

Te Deum Symphony. Bruckner's 9th Sym., whose finale he never completed. Before his death he suggested that his Te Deum might be used instead; it was 1st performed in this version in Vienna (1903) but is usually played as a 3-movement work. There have been recent attempts to compose an appropriate finale from the sketches Bruckner left behind.

Te Kanawa, (Dame) **Kiri,** brilliant New Zealand soprano; b. Gisborne, Mar. 6, 1944. Her father was an indigenous Maori who traced his ancestry to the legendary warrior Te Kanawa; her mother was Irish. She attended Catholic schools in Auckland, and was coached in singing by a nun. She was sent to Melbourne to compete in a radio show; won 1st prize in a *Melbourne Sun* contest. In 1966 she received a grant for study in London with Vera Rozsa. She made her operatic debut at the Camden Festival in 1969, in Rossini's *La Donna del Lago*; 1st appeared at London's Covent Garden in a minor role that same year, then as the Countess in *The Marriage of Figaro* in 1971. She made her U.S. debut in the same role with the Santa Fe Opera in 1971; it became one of her most remarkable interpretations. She sang it again with the San Francisco Opera in 1972.

A proverbial *coup de théâtre* in her career came in 1974, when she was called upon to substitute at a few hours' notice for the ailing Teresa Stratas in the role of Desdemona at the Metropolitan Opera in N.Y.; it was a triumphant achievement, winning for her unanimous praise. She also sang in a film version of *The Marriage of Figaro*. In 1977 she appeared as Pamina at the Paris Opéra; later that year she took the role of Rosalinde in a Covent Garden production of *Die Fledermaus*, which was televised to the U.S. She excelled equally as a subtle and artistic interpreter of lyric roles in Mozart's operas and in dramatic representations of Verdi's operas. Among her other distinguished roles were the Marschallin and Arabella. She also won renown as a concert artist.

In later years she expanded her repertoire to include popular fare, including songs by Cole Porter and Leonard Bernstein's *West Side Story*. Hailed as a PRIMA DONNA ASSOLUTA, she pursued one of the most successful international operatic and concert careers of her day. In 1973 she was made an Officer of the Order of the British Empire; in 1982 she was named a Dame Commander of the Order of the British Empire.

Tea for Two. Song by Youmans and Caesar, 1924, from the extremely popular musical *No, No, Nanette*. It was included in the list of all-time hit-parade songs issued by ASCAP (1963). In 1958 an imitation-Latin cha-cha version rekin-dled its popularity; before that Shostakovich made a salon orch. arrangement of it as the *Tahiti Trot* (1927).

teaching

George Bernard Shaw put an unfair kibosh on teachers when he delivered his dictum, "Those who can, do; those who cannot, teach." True, many retired virtuosos turn to teaching when they can no longer perform; true also that to some of them the teaching profession is merely a vehicle to exercise their misanthropical disappointment at the failure of becoming great artists. The ancient Greek legend has it that Hercules slew his music teacher Linus with his own lyre when he reprimanded Hercules for playing a wrong note.

Still, music teaching is an honorable profession. From times immemorial music traditions were carried from one generation to another by devoted elders. Instruction in singing and playing was essential in ancient cultures, primarily in religious rituals. Music was also an integral part of Greek tragedy, in the synthetic art that included poetry and dancing. The musical tradition was preserved in the early centuries of Christianity by monks who taught the traditional rules of plainchant to apprentices and novitiates.

In the 11th century Guido d'Arezzo promulgated the 1st systematic method of music theory by arranging a system of hexachords represented by the positions on the palm of the left hand. The GUIDONIAN HAND could also be used for conducting a choir, with the singers following the indicated position on the hand. So firmly established was the hand method of teaching and conducting that medieval music instructors or theorists allowed only such progressions and keys that could be found *in manu*, (in the hand); *non est in manu* was a dictum sufficient to condemn certain melodic progressions in ecclesiastical chant.

Secular teaching of music was part of the QUADRIVIUM in medieval universities, in which music theory was included among the 4 mathematical arts, the other 3 being arithmetic, geometry, and astronomy. Music as taught in the Middle Ages was mostly concerned with mathematical relationships between the length of a string or air column and the pitch, as well as the numerical proportion of pitches producing a certain interval. The metaphor of music of the spheres expanded musical learning to philosophical arenas. Theology also played a great role in medieval music science. Triple time was called *tempus perfectum*, a term explained by the theological doctrine of the perfect Trinity.

At the time of the Renaissance the teaching profession was mainly in the hands of church organists. Music aspirants flocked from all over Europe to study with Girolamo Frescobaldi at the Vatican, where he was organist early in the 17th century. Bach and Handel undertook an arduous journey to Lübeck to hear the great Buxtehude play the organ, hoping to succeed him at his post after his death. But since the stipulation for succession was marriage to the incumbent's eldest daughter, both Bach and Handel demurred. Music history gained much from this misadventure; while Handel, having gone to London, did not teach music professionally, Bach became the music master of the St. Thomas School in Leipzig, where he had many students, including his own sons.

Royal houses habitually engaged a music master to teach the princesses the art of playing the lute, harp, and singing. Mary Stuart engaged an Italian lutenist, David Rizzio, who was suspected of being her lover; he was eventually murdered by the Scottish court clique. A singing master was often a comic character in opera; an example is Don Basilio in *The Barber of Seville*.

Institutional music-teaching originated in Italy in the 16th century. Such music schools were known as CONSERVATORIES, in the literal sense of the word, for they were founded to "conserve" (protect) orphaned or ailing girls; in fact, these conservatories were called *ospedali* (hospitals). A French musician, visiting one of these hospitals in Venice early in the 18th century, reported his enchantment with the singing girls: "They sing like angels. There can be nothing more ravishing than to watch a young girl in a white frock with a spray of pomegranate flowers over her ear perform for her audience."

Soon conservatories and other music schools spread all over the world. Italian musicians established a virtual monopoly on the teaching of singing, while the Germans specialized in teaching composition and theory. In the 20th century the Russians invaded musically underdeveloped countries mainly as piano teachers. Other Slavic countries, particularly Bohemia and Poland, sent the surplus of their music educators abroad. A geographical map of this historic migration of music teachers from Central and Eastern Europe is edifying, for it seems to prove that the musical Garden of Eden was located in a relatively small area of Central Europe. On the other hand, travel to Germany in quest of musical education became universal in the 19th century; a great number of British, American, and Russian composers participated in this pilgrimage, and simultaneously German musicians traveled to Great Britain, Russia, and America in search of employment and fortune.

Not until the middle of the 19th century did the French music teachers acquire a world reputation. In the 20th century, one French teacher in particular, Nadia Boulanger, was without equal in her influence upon the dozens of composers who traveled from far corners to study with her. Her weekly salons, instituted in 1921, were affectionately called *Boulangerie*; her American composers-students included Copland, Piston, Thomson, Glass, R. Thompson, and R. Harris. British and American music teachers finally asserted themselves in the 20th century.

The genealogy of private musical teaching gives us a vivid panorama of music history: Haydn taught Beethoven, Beethoven taught Czerny, Czerny taught Liszt, Liszt taught Siloti, Siloti taught Rachmaninoff, who then gave advice to Vladimir Horowitz, who in turn occasionally gave lessons to younger pianists. In his last years in Weimar Liszt used to receive young pianists, mostly female, who played for him. Too often Liszt dozed off while listening to a student play, but as soon as she stopped he would wake up and murmur, "Schön."

Great national schools of composition often arose as a result of mutual teaching, in or out of a conservatory. The "Mighty 5" of Russia had Balakirev as their chief mentor. Rimsky-Korsakov received his early instruction from Balakirev. Subsequently Rimsky-Korsakov himself became the teacher of 2 generations of Russian composers, including Stravinsky. Among celebrated composers who were active as teachers of composition and directors of national conservatories were Vincent d'Indy and Gabriel Fauré in France, Max Reger in Germany, and Dvořák in Bohemia. Legendary fame distinguished many teachers of performing arts. In the violin field, no one was greater than Leopold Auer, from whose fiddle nursery in St. Petersburg came Jascha Heifetz, Mischa Elman, and hundreds of other violinists. (Gershwin even wrote a song: "When we were 6 our tone was sour/until a man, professor Auer/came right along and taught us all/how to pack 'em in Carnegie Hall!")

Among great piano teachers was Theodor Leschetizky, who taught Paderewski; several of Leschetizky's consecutive wives, the most resplendent among them being Anna Essipoff, became distinguished teachers themselves. Tobias Matthay taught 3 pianistic generations in London; the Matthay System, as his teaching method was known, became a passport to educational competence in England and America. Isidor Philip established himself in Paris and taught many pianists who made fine careers. David Popper taught quite a few good cellists and wrote pleasing pieces for the cello.

As for singing, Manual García was the 1st true professional teacher; his daughter, the fabulous Malibran, was one of his pupils. He was also the inventor of the laryngoscope, used to probe the voice box in the larynx. To enumerate former opera stars who became great teachers is tantamount to compiling an inventory of singers. But among the greatest opera singers, Chaliapin and Caruso never descended from their pedestals to teach.

teatro (It.). Theater. *Teatro lirico*, opera house.

Tebaldi, Renata, celebrated Italian soprano; b. Pesaro, Feb. 1, 1922. Her mother, a nurse, took her to Langhirano after the breakup of her marriage to a philandering cellist. Renata was stricken with poliomyelitis when she was 3 but survived; after initial vocal training from Giuseppina Passani, she studied with Ettore Campogaliani at the Parma Cons. (1937–40) and Carmen Melis at the Pesaro Cons. (1940–43). She made her operatic debut in Rovigo as Elena in Boito's *Mefistofele* in 1944. In 1946 Toscanini chose her as one of his artists for the reopening concert at

La Scala in Milan, and she subsequently became one of its leading sopranos.

She made her 1st appearance in England in 1950 with the visiting La Scala company at London's Covent Garden as Desdemona; also in 1950 she sang Aida with the San Francisco Opera. In 1955 she made her Metropolitan Opera debut in N.Y. as Desdemona; she continued to appear regularly there until 1973. She toured Russia in 1975 and 1976. Her repertoire was almost exclusively Italian; she excelled in both lyric and dramatic roles; was particularly successful as Violetta, Tosca, Mimi, and Madame Butterfly. She also sang the role of Eva in *Die Meistersinger von Nürnberg*. In 1958 she was the subject of a cover story in *Time* magazine.

technic, technique. All that relates to the purely mechanical part of an instrumental or vocal performance; mechanical training, skill, dexterity.

tecla (Sp.). Key on a keyboard.

tedesco, -a (It.). German. *Alla tedesca*, in the German style, e.g. in waltz rhythms, with changing tempo; DEUTSCHER TANZ.

Teen Angel. Number 1 hit for Mark Dinning in 1960, composed by Jean and Red Surrey. A syrupy ballad.

Teenager in Love. Dion and the Belmonts scored big in 1959 with this Pomus-Shuman confection out of N.Y.'s Brill Building.

Teil (Ger.). A part or section; a movement.

Telemann, Georg Philipp, significant German composer; b. Magdeburg, Mar. 14, 1681; d. Hamburg, June 25, 1767. He received his academic training at a local school; also learned to play keyboard instruments and the violin; he acquired knowledge of music theory from the cantor Benedikt Christiani. He subsequently attended the Gymnasium Andreanum in Hildesheim, where he became active in student performances of German cantatas. In 1701 he entered the Univ. of Leipzig as a student of jurisprudence; in 1702 he organized a collegium musicum there; later was appointed music director of the Leipzig Opera, where he used the services of his student singers and instrumentalists. In 1705 he went to Sorau as Kapellmeister to the court of Count Erdmann II of Promnitz. In 1708 he was

appointed Konzertmeister to the court orch. in Eisenach; later he was named Kapellmeister there.

In 1709 he married Louise Eberlin, a musician's daughter, but she died in 1711 in childbirth. In 1712 Telemann was appointed music director of the city of Frankfurt; there he wrote a quantity of sacred music as well as secular works for the public concerts given by the Frauenstein Soc., of which he served as director. In 1714 he married Maria Katharina Textor, the daughter of a local town clerk. They had 8 sons and 2 daughters, of whom only a few survived infancy. His wife later abandoned him for a Swedish army officer. In 1721 he received the post of music director of 5 churches in Hamburg, which became the center of his important activities as composer and music administrator. In 1722 Telemann was appointed music director of the Hamburg Opera, a post he held until 1738. During his tenure he wrote a number of operas for production there, and also staged several works by Handel and Keiser. In 1737–38 he visited France. His eyesight began to fail as he grew older; his great contemporaries Bach and Handel suffered from the same infirmity.

An extraordinarily prolific composer, Telemann mastered both the German and the Italian styles of composition prevalent in his day. While he never approached the greatness of genius of Bach and Handel, he nevertheless became an exemplar of the German Baroque at its grandest development; more than his 2 great contemporaries, Telemann bridged the gap into the rococo and early Classic styles. His works include 35 operas, many of them German intermezzos, including *Der gedültige Socrates* (Hamburg, 1721) and *Pimpinone, oder Die ungleiche Heyrath*, intermezzo (Hamburg, 1725); 7 oratorios, the best known being *Der Tag des Gerichts* (1762); over 1,250 cantatas, including 4 major sacred collections; 46 Passions; Masses; psalms; motets.

In the instrumental realm Telemann's greatest collection was the *Musique de table* (Hamburg, 1733), containing 3 orch. suites, 3 concertos, 3 quartets, 3 trios, and 3 sonatas. His prodigious orch.l output comprised numerous overtures, concertos, sonatas, quartets, quintets, etc. His grandson Georg Michael Telemann (b. Plön, Apr. 20, 1748; d. Riga, Mar. 4, 1831) was a composer and writer on music, reared and trained in music by his grandfather in Hamburg; he served as Kantor and teacher at the cathedral school in Riga (1773–1828), where he oversaw performances of many of his grandfather's works in his own eds.

Telephone, The. Opera by Menotti, 1947, to his own libretto, 1st produced on Broadway in N.Y. Menotti describes the opera as "l'amour à trois," the 3rd member being the telephone itself; it is constantly in use because its female owner is a compulsive talker. After many attempts to get her full attention, her desperate suitor leaves her apartment and calls her on the phone from the corner drugstore to propose marriage. The story is trifling but *The Telephone* has become a popular success, no doubt due to its accessible postverismo manner.

telephone broadcasting. A fanciful method of musical broadcast discussed in Edward Bellamy's novel *Looking Backward: 2000 Back to 1887* (1888), about a man who falls asleep for over a century and awakes to find a brave new world. The telephone of Alexander Graham Bell has been technically expanded so that performances can be transmitted far away from their places of origin, to be heard by anyone picking up their telephone and requesting the operator for the appropriate connection. This was a 24-hour service requiring mostly live performance (as Bellamy did not foresee long-playing records or tapes). According to Bellamy, the N.Y. press was generally approving of this "scientific wonder"; today it could be considered the forerunner of the "1-900" telephone number.

teller (Ger.). Cymbals.

Telmányi, Emil. See Nielsen, Carl (August).

tema (It.). Theme. *Tema con variazioni*, theme and variations.

temperament. A calculated alteration of the acoustical values of musical intervals to make possible the division of the perfect octave into 12 equal semitones. Purely tuned tones of very nearly the same pitch, like C-sharp and D-flat, are made to sound enharmonically identical by slightly altering or tempering them (i.e., slightly raising or lowering the pitch). When applied to all the tones of an instrument (as the piano), this system is called EQUAL TEMPERAMENT; when only the keys most used are so tuned (as was done formerly), the system is UNEQUAL TEMPERAMENT or *meantone tuning*.

Theorists and performing musicians struggled for centuries to find a practical way of reconciling the perfect octave with the pure perfect 5th (the interval between the 2nd and 3rd partials of the harmonic series), perfect 4th, and major 3rd. The *Pythagorean tuning* system, developed in ancient Greece and perhaps earlier, uses multiples of the perfect fifth to create its gamut. It is arithmetically impossible, however, to equate any multiple of 3:2, the ratio of frequencies (cps, Hz) for the pure untempered 5th, with any multiple of 2:1, which is the ratio of frequencies for a perfect octave.

It is but visual self-deception that the circle of 12 5ths on a piano keyboard equals the circle of 7 octaves, with their common terminal on the highest C of the keyboard; for in fact the final acoustic perfect 5th would be the hypothetical B-sharp, around 24 cents (an 8th-tone) higher than the C of the last octave. The situation became more complicated with the advent of tonality in the Baroque era; now the major and minor 3rds had to be tuned accurately to support triadic harmony and modulation.

The 1st set of solutions involved trying to tune as many of the 5ths and/or 3rds in a 12-note scale so that as many keys as possible were usable without having to retune (which would be impossible on wind instruments, in any case). The various approaches that proliferated were classed as meantone tunings, including *well temperament*, the system used by Bach for his 2 volumes of *The Well-Tempered Clavier*, each containing 24 preludes and fugues in every key in chromatic order. The difference between this and equal temperament is crucial; while equal temperament seeks a total tuning compromise, unequal temperaments allowed certain keys a special timbre or color that composers responded to.

Other theorists, wanting to avoid the potential chaos of unequal division, decided to contract a pure 5th (702 cents) to an imperfect, tempered 5th (700 cents), which was slightly less than its theoretical 3:2 ratio. The same imperfect 5th was transposed logarithmically to the other 11 steps of the circle of 5ths; as a result the acoustical purity of other intervals was affected, to a greater degree than the perfect 5th (or its inversion, the perfect 4th). By sacrificing the acoustical purity of the pure intervals of the generative harmonic series, however, it became possible to play a tune beginning on any key at all and modulate freely from one key to another, getting the same scalar intervals; it also permitted a piece in one key to be transposed to another key without seeming "out of tune."

Tempest, The. Opera by F. Martin, 1956, after Shakespeare, premiered in German in Vienna.

tempestoso (*tempestosamente*; It.). Stormily, passionately, impetuously.

temple blocks. CHINESE BLOCKS.

Templer und die Jüdin, Der (The Templar and the Jewess). Opera by Marschner, 1829, 1st produced in Leipzig. The libretto is based on Walter Scott's novel *Ivanhoe*, with a specific concentration on Ivanhoe's abortive love for a Jewess. The opera was very popular in its time; Schumann used an aria from it, *Du stolzes England, freue dich!* (Proud England, rejoice!) in the 12th variation of his *Études symphoniques*; he dedicated the work to his English friend the composer William Sterndale Bennett, hoping in this manner to gratify Bennett's patriotic feelings.

tempo (It.; Fr. *temps*). Rate of speed, movement; time, measure. Two systems of tempo indications (marks) have developed since the Baroque period. The earlier type, still very much in use, indicates tempo verbally; the most common indications are in Italian: largo, adagio, moderato, andante, allegro, allegretto, presto, and prestissimo. These terms are often qualified by additional words of caution such as *ma non troppo* or *poco*. The 1st attempt to put some precise meaning into these vague Italian modifiers was made by J. J. Quantz, who defined the natural speed measure as the human heartbeat, at 80 beats per minute. Taking 4/4 as the basic meter, he assigned the exact duration of the pulse-beat to a half note in allegro, to a quarter note in allegretto, and to an 8th note in adagio.

The second system came with the invention in the early 19th century of the metronome, a mathematical measurement of the tempo; theoretically this would standardize tempo terminology. Beethoven, the 1st great composer to make systematic use of the metronome, set down the "scientific" tempo for several of his works, even marking early works retrospectively. However, most modern interpreters found Beethoven's instructions untenable, blaming a "faulty" metronome. Beethoven set the metronome mark for the *Funeral March* from his *Eroica Sym.* at 80 8th notes per minute, but most conductors prefer a slower tempo: actual timing of Toscanini's performance (1935) scored only 52 8th notes a minute, 35 percent slower than what Beethoven apparently intended. Many modern composers, particularly Stravinsky, abandoned the traditional Italian tempo marks entirely and replaced them by the precise metronome number. Since Stravinsky insisted on precision in the performance of his works and abhorred Romantic aberrations, his metronome marks were "final."

The rediscovery of recordings of great artists of the past disclosed a shocking departure from tempo markings indicated by the composer. The sentimental leanings among German musicians and theorists of the 2nd half of the 18th century,

epitomized in the word *Empfindung* (affect, feeling), and their desire to achieve a perfect human expression in performance led to constant shifts of tempo and dynamics—an astonishing practice contradicting the modern idea of the precise and ordered execution of classical works. Even Leopold Mozart commented favorably on the device of "stolen time," an anticipation of the Romantic RUBATO so despised by modern interpreters. The tendency in the mid-20th century as regards tempo was generally in the direction of precision, away from unauthorized ritardandos (so commonly resorted to in difficult technical passages), and LUFTPAUSEN.

But toward the last 3rd of the 20th century a curious counterreaction set in. Music critics and the general public began to complain about the metronomic monotony of modern performers. An unscientific nostalgia spread through the music world. Once again, as in the preceding century, "personality" was hailed as superior to the fidelity to the printed music. Even composers themselves welcomed flexible tempos affected by celebrated interpreters to vitalize the spirit of the music. Some compromise between musical permissiveness and pedantry seemed inevitable. Perhaps the dictum of Wanda Landowska can serve as a guide: "One must approach classical music as a well-mannered guest. One need not be too obsequious or reverential to the hostess, but one must not put one's feet on the table at meals."

A tempo, return to the preceding pace; *in tempo*, same as A TEMPO; *in tempo misurato*, in strict time (after a passage marked TEMPO A PIACERE); *l'istesso tempo*, or *lo stesso tempo*, the same tempo, despite a rhythmic change; *sempre in tempo*, always at the same pace; *senza tempo*, same as TEMPO A PIACERE; *tempo a piacere*, play at will in terms of pace; *tempo ad libitum*, metrically free; *tempo com(m)odo*, at a comfortable, convenient pace; *tempo di Ballo, Minuetto, Valse* etc., in the movement of a ballet, minuet, waltz, etc.; *tempo giusto*, at a proper, appropriate pace; *tempo primo*, at the original pace; *tempo rubato*, see RUBATO.

tempo mark. A word or phrase indicating the rate of speed at which a piece should be performed. Thus, "Adagio (M.M. = 56)" signifies a tranquil movement in which a quarter note has the time value of one beat of the metronome set at 56 (i.e., 56 beats per minute).

temporal parameter. The conjectural duration of a musical composition is a factor of importance per se, a temporal parameter that has a decisive bearing on the cohesion and relative stability of the constituent parts of the entire work. The 20th century cultivated a type of Brobdingnagian grandiosity that seemed to equate quantity with quality. Among relatively well-known sym. works, the *Alpine Sym.* by R. Strauss once held the record for absolute length, but it was eclipsed by the *Gothic Sym.* of the English composer Havergal Brian, containing 529 pages of full score. The longest piano work of the century is *Opus Clavicembalisticum* by the English-born composer Kaikhosru Sorabji, which he personally played for the 1st and last time in Glasgow in 1930. The work consists of 12 movements in the form of a theme with 44 variations and a passacaglia with 81 variations. Characteristically it is dedicated "to the everlasting glory of those few men blessed and sanctified in the curses and execrations of those many whose praise is eternal damnation."

While some composers kept expanding the duration of their individual works, their contemporaries followed the opposite trend toward extreme brevity of musical utterance. The pioneer of this modern concision was Anton Webern; one of his pieces, written in 1911 for several instruments, lasts only 19 seconds. The Hungarian composer György Ligeti wrote a movement consisting of a single quarter-tone rest. The ultimate in the infinitesimally small musical forms was achieved by John Cage in his *0' 00"*, "to be performed in any way by anyone," and 1st presented in this ambiguous form in Tokyo in 1962.

temps faible (Fr.). Weak beat in a measure.

temps fort (Fr.). Strong beat in a measure.

Temptation. Song by N. H. Brown, 1933, sung by Bing Crosby in the screen musical *Going Hollywood*; it became tremendously popular.

Temptations, The. Popular Motown group of the 1960s. (Core group: Eddie Kendricks, b. Birmingham, Ala., Dec. 17, 1939; d. there, Oct. 5, 1992; David Ruffin, b. Meridian, Miss., Jan. 18, 1941, d. Philadelphia, Pa., June 1, 1991; Otis Williams, b. Otis Miles, Texarkana, Tex., Oct. 30, 1941; Melvin Franklin, b. David English, Montgomery Ala., Oct. 12, 1942; d. Los Angeles, Calif., Feb. 23, 1995; Paul Williams, b. Birmingham, Ala., July 2, 1939; d. Detroit, Mich., Aug. 17, 1973.) One of the best of the Motown groups, the Temptations were noted for their fleet-footed choreography and double-lead vocals, provided by Kendricks and Ruffin. The group was formed out of two Detroit ensembles of the late '50s, the Primes and the Distants. Signed to Motown in 1960 when they were known as the Elgins, they changed their name a year later to

the Temptations scoring their 1st hit in 1962 with *Dream Come Home*. Ruffin joined the group in 1963 and the classic lineup was in place.

Joining with producer/songwriter Smokey Robinson, the group started 1964 with a major hit with *The Way You Do the Things You Do*. The classic *My Girl* followed, along with a number of other hits. In 1968 Ruffin left the group; new producer Norman Whitfield changed the group's orientation to reflect the popularity of "psychedelic" music. They scored with several more hits, including *Psychedelic Shack* and the funky *Papa Was a Rolling Stone*. However, Kendricks left the group in 1971, ending the classic period for the group. He enjoyed a modest solo career, while the group itself continued to score minor hits. Over the next 2 decades the group continued to perform with various members, with Kendricks and Ruffin occasionally rejoining them. They also paired with white soulsters Daryl Hall and John Oates for a 1985 concert and album to celebrate the newly refurbished Apollo Theater in New York. However, in 1991 Ruffin died of a drug overdose, and a year later Kendricks succumbed to lung cancer.

tempus (Lat.). In medieval theory, the shortest duration in which a sung note can be clearly perceived, lasting less than a second but more than a half second. Later *tempus* represented a time value divisible into either 2 (*tempus imperfectum*) or 3 (*tempus perfectum*) semibreves.

Ten Cents a Dance. Song by Rodgers and Hart, 1930, from the musical *Simple Simon*. This Depression-era classic is the sorrowful narrative of a young woman working as a "taxi dancer."

Tender Land, The. Opera by Copland, 1954, 1st performed in N.Y. The tender land of the title is the American Midwest. A young harvest worker has a summer romance with a farm girl, but he is indecisive about elopement and marriage. Eventually he leaves the farm. Her love is more profound, and she sets forth in search of him. The score represents Copland's modern lyricism at its best.

tenebrae (Lat., darkness). Roman Catholic liturgy for Holy Week, specifically the Matins and Lauds of Holy Thursday, Good Friday, and Holy Saturday. The name derives from the ritual of blowing out a candle after each psalm until all are extinguished. The text includes excerpts from the Lamentations of Jeremiah. Settings of this liturgy include works by Gesualdo, Lassus, Palestrina, Victoria, Couperin, and Stravinsky.

tenebroso (It.). Somberly.

teneramente (It.). Tenderly.

tenero (It.). Tenderly, with tender emotion; delicately, softly.

Tennessee Waltz. Song by Redd Stewart and Pee Wee King, 1948, which captured the essence of the state of Tennessee well enough that the assembly there voted it the official state song in 1965.

Tenney, James (Carl), highly influential American pianist, conductor, teacher, and composer; b. Silver City, N.Mex., Aug. 10, 1934. He studied engineering at the Univ. of Denver (1952–54) before devoting himself to music; received instruction in piano from Steuermann at the Juilliard School of Music in N.Y. (1954–55), took courses in piano and composition at Bennington (Vt.) College (B.A., 1958) and worked with Gaburo, Hiller, and Partch at the Univ. of Illinois (M.Mus., 1961); was also associated with Chou Wen-chung, Ruggles, and Varèse (1955–65). He was active as a performer with the Steve Reich and Philip Glass ensembles; concurrently conducted research at the Bell Laboratories (with Max Mathews; 1961–64), Yale Univ. (1964–66), and the Polytechnic Inst. of Brooklyn (1966–70). He taught at the Calif. Inst. of the Arts (1970–75), the Univ. of Calif. at Santa Cruz (1975–76), and York Univ. in Toronto (from 1976).

As both a performer and a scholar, he is a prominent advocate and theorist of contemporary music; is also a notable authority on Ives and Nancarrow. His compositions include *Quiet Fan for Erik Satie* (1970) and *Clang* (1972) for Orch; *Quintext* for String Quartet and Double Bass (1972); *In the Aeolian Mode* for Prepared Piano and Variable Ensemble (1973); *Harmonia I–VI* for Various Ensembles (1976–81); *Saxony* for Saxophone and Tape Delay (1978); *3 Indigenous Songs* for 2 Piccolos, Alto Flute, Bassoon, and Percussion (1979); *Glissade* for Viola, Cello, Double Bass, and Tape Delay (1982); *Koan* for String Quartet (1984); works for solo instruments, including *Spectral Canon for Conlon Nancarrow* for Player Piano (1974); pioneering works on tape or for computer, including *Collage No. 1: Blue Suede* (1961); *Stochastic Quartet: String Quartet* for Computer or Strings (1963); *Fabric for Che* (1967); *For Ann (rising)* (1969); vocal and theater works. Tenney publ. an influential essay on compositional aesthetics and morphology, *Meta + Hodos* (New Orleans, 1964); other writings are *META Meta +*

Hodos (1977); *A History of "Consonance" and "Dissonance"* (N.Y., 1988).

tenor (from Lat. *tenere*, hold; It. *tenore*). 1. The highest and most expressive male voice. The etymological derivation derives from the fact that the cantus firmus in early vocal polyphony was given to a voice called the tenor, whose function was to "hold" the melody while other voices moved contrapuntally in relation to it. The voice part gradually became independent of its original function and came to refer simply to the voice range. From the beginning of operatic history, tenors enjoyed great social and financial success as well as adulation. But tenors were also traditionally regarded as being mentally deficient; an Italian joke lists the degrees of comparison, "stupido, stupidissimo, tenore." Although Enrico Caruso never learned to read music, he could hardly be called "stupido"; he was also talented in drawing pencil caricatures. Another nonstupid tenor was Leo Slezak (1873–1946), who possessed a Viennese kind of *Witz*, often at the expense of his fellow singers.

The ordinary range of the tenor voice is two octaves, from the C below middle C to the C above it ($c^0 - c^2$). The tenor part is usually notated in the treble clef (from middle C), sounding an octave lower. Some singers in the bel canto era could go higher in falsetto; Giovanni Battista Rubini (1794–1854) regularly hit f^2. In some opera scores the tenor part is indicated by a combined tenor and treble clef. The mark of distinction for great tenors is their ability to hold high C for a long time, often ignoring the musical and harmonic necessity to let go. Old film prints of opera arias show tenors running up to the footlights of the stage during a highly dramatic duet to project a high C into the audience and then retreating to join an awaiting soprano. Even more bizarre, in a 1950s film of *Don Giovanni* is a duet during which the soprano is singing a passage alone; the camera shifts to the tenor in anticipation of his entrance and finds a singer completely ignoring his partner and instead shrugging at the camera, then going back immediately into character in time for his sound blast.

Categories include the *dramatic tenor* (It. *tenore di forza*), with a full and powerful quality and a range from c to b^1 (Rodolpho in *La bohème*, Manrico in *Il trovatore*); the *heroic tenor* (Ger. *Heldentenor*), with a strong sonority throughout their range, including Siegfried in the *Ring* and Otello; and the *lyric tenor* (It. *tenore di grazia*), sweeter and less powerful and a range from d to c^2 (or $c\sharp^2$; Gounod's Faust and Almaviva in *The Barber of Seville*).

2. A prefix to the names of instruments with a similar relationship to other members of the same family, as *tenor trombone, tenor tuba, tenor violin.*

tenor C. Small c:

tenor clef. The C clef on the 4th line, sometimes used in cello, bassoon, or tenor trombone parts.

tenor drum. Side drum, without snares, larger and therefore deeper sounding than a military drum, also of indefinite pitch.

tenor saxophone. Saxophone in B-flat, transposing down a whole tone; its range is $B\flat_0 - f^2$. The tenor saxophone is commonly found in jazz ensembles; a nontransposing "melody" tenor saxophone in C is still used in marching and wind bands.

tenor violin (Fr. *taille de violon*; Ger. *Tenorgeige*). A generic term for large violas, 1st made in the 16th century, with the bottom string G_0 an octave below the violin g^0; it resembles the bass VIOLA DA BRACCIO; also called *tenor-viola, violon-ténor, viola tenore, Oktavgeige,* and *controviolino.*

tenorini (It.). Tenor singing in falsetto.

tenorino (It.). High tenor voice of a sweetly adolescent quality.

Tenorposaune (Ger.). Tenor trombone.

Tenorschlüssel (Ger.). TENOR CLEF.

tenth (Lat. *decima*). The diatonic interval of an octave plus 2 degrees.

Tenth Symphony. Unfinished work by Mahler, 1910–11. Two movements are more or less complete, the Adagio and the Purgatorio; they were 1st performed posthumously in Vienna, 1924. In them, Mahler's idiom reaches the ultimate of complexity for his time, making use of extremely dissonant combinations of tones. The hand-written inscriptions in the manuscript point toward serious mental turbulence: "Madness possesses me! Devil, come and seize me, the cursed one!" The British musician Deryck Cooke (1919–76) completed the sym., making use of some of Mahler's sketches and fragments; his 1st of 3 performing versions received the approbation of Alma Mahler Werfel, the composer's widow, and was given its premiere in London, 1964.

tenuto (It., held; abbrev. *ten.*). 1. Sustain a tone for its full time-value. 2. Use an emphatic and attentive legato. *Forte tenuto* (*f ten.*), *forte* throughout; *tenuto mark*, a short stroke over or under a notehead.

tepidamente (It.). Lukewarmly; in an even, dispassionate style.

teponaxtl. South American slit drum, traditionally made out of a hollowed-out tree trunk; played with sticks. See also SLIT DRUM.

Tequila. Funky instrumental hit for the Champs in 1958.

teratological borborygmus. Modern works of the 1st quarter of the 20th century systematically increased the amount of massive sonorities as though their intention was to induce orological acousma or some other tonitruous Brobdingnagian teratological borborygmus, a huge and monstrous intestinal rumbling issuing from the mouthpieces of brass instruments coupled with shrill flageolets of the piccolos and high harmonics in the strings. It was inevitable that a reaction against this loss of all moderation should have set in among composers of the avant-garde. This reaction was made necessary because of the catastrophe of World War I, when it was no longer feasible to place huge orch.l apparatus at the service of composers of macrosonic works. The era of teratological borborygmus seemed to end without a hope of recurrence, but the emergence of new audio technology in general and electrically amplified popular music in specific generated an electronic circus that promised to eclipse the deafening potentialities of the past.

terce. In both the old and revised Roman Catholic liturgy, the daily Canonical Hour celebrated at 9 a.m.

ternary. Composed of, or progressing by, 3s. *Ternary form,* ABA form, such as the minuet and trio; DA CAPO form; *ternary measure,* simple triple time.

terraced dynamics (Ger. *Terrasendynamik*). The primarily Baroque style of dynamic changes by a direct transition from one degree of loudness to another as from piano to mezzoforte, from mezzopiano to fortissimo, etc., without an intervening crescendo or decrescendo. The term was introduced by Busoni. Terraced dynamics were in common usage in the Baroque era perhaps owing to the inability of the cembalo to graduate the sound with a distinct change from piano to forte or vice-versa. In the Elizabethan period explicit indications such as *lowd, lowder, softer*, etc. were in use. Beethoven favored the terraced dynamics in the form of a *subito piano* after a forte. During his neoclassical period Stravinsky began to cultivate terraced dynamics almost exclusively, to signify his return to Baroque usage.

Terry, Clark, African-American jazz trumpet and flügelhorn player and scat singer; b. St. Louis, Dec. 14, 1920. He worked with Charlie Barnet (1947) and Count Basie (1948–51); in 1951, joined Duke Ellington's band and enjoyed a richly rewarding 8-year association. During his collaborations with Oscar Peterson, Terry evolved his trademark "mumbles" style of scat singing, which he described as sounding like an old man storytelling while drifting into incoherence; he also evolved a style of musical monologue made up of wittily juggled fragments of musical thought. He played in the orch. of the Johnny Carson *Tonight Show* until it was relocated to Los Angeles; also taught at various jazz clinics. In 1990 he was appointed a director for the new Thelonious Monk Inst. of Jazz at Duke Univ. in Chapel Hill, N.C.

tertia (Lat.). Interval of a 3rd.

Terz (Ger.; It. *terza*). Interval of a 3rd.

Terzett (Ger.; It. *terzetto*). Properly, a vocal trio; occasionally, an instrumental one.

terzina (It.). A triplet.

terzo rivolto (It.; Ger. *Terzquartakkord*). The 3rd inversion of the 7th chord; the ⁶/₄/₂ or ² chord.

terzo suono (It., 3rd tone). DIFFERENCE TONE (TARTINI TONE).

tessitura (It., texture). The proportionate use of high or low register in a given vocal range. If high notes are preponderant, the tessitura is said to be high, as in most coloratura soprano parts; if low notes are especially frequent, as in bass parts of some Russian songs, the tessitura is said to be low. In English a vocal part can "lie" high or low.

testa (It.). Head. *Voce di testa*, head voice.

Testament of Freedom, The. Cantata for chorus and orch. by R. Thompson, 1943. The text is taken from the writings of Thomas Jefferson. It was 1st performed at the Univ. of Virginia, of which Jefferson was the founder; Thompson's best-known work, it has had numerous subsequent performances.

testo (It., text). In Baroque oratorios and 20th-century works, the narrator (usually a recitative part).

testudo (Lat., turtle). An ancient Greek lyre, made with a tortoiseshell body; later applied to the lute.

tetrachord. 1. The interval of a perfect 4th. 2. The 4 scale-tones contained in a perfect 4th. In ancient Greek scales the tetrachord was treated invariably as a descending progression. However, the medieval tetrachord was counted upward, an ascent retained in subsequent centuries. As a result the names of the modes that developed from conjunct or disjunct tetrachords forming an entire diatonic scale were different from the Greek modes. The musical quality of the tetrachord was determined by the placement of the semitone in the diatonic progression; thus the Phrygian tetrachord was formed by the placement of the semitone between the 1st and the 2nd degrees; in the Aeolian and Dorian tetrachords the semitone was between the 2nd and 3rd degrees; in the Ionian and Mixolydian modes the semitone occupied the place between the 3rd and 4th degrees. The Lydian tetrachord is formed by whole tones only. 3. A set of 4 pitch classes, usually associated with a 12-note set.

tetralogy. A thematically connected series of 4 stage works or oratorios.

Teutscher (Tanz). DEUTSCHER TANZ.

text. Words to which music is set.

text-sound composition. A medium that germinated in the dadaist movement of the 1st quarter of the 20th century and was revived, making use of magnetic tape and other electronic devices in the 2nd half of the 20th century. Text-sound works emphasize the sonorous element independent from the meaning, if any, of the words recited; such compositions may hark back to prehuman cries through ritualistic incantation and pentecostal glossolalia or else may project into an absurd future with the aid of computers, synthesizers, and stereophonic sound engineering. The medium developed among modern poets, sound engineers, and composers in Sweden and was picked up by American composers. Among the former the best-known work is the *Ursonate* of the artist Kurt Schwitters (1922–32) Among the latter the works of Charles Amirkhanian achieved, in his own execution, a degree of true virtuosity.

texture. The musical parameter concerning the number and relationships of individual parts or lines in a piece; in essence, a vertical analysis of a work's external components. The most commonly described textures are: MONOPHONIC, 1 part (line) without accompaniment, performed solo or in unison; HOMOPHONIC 1, a primary part accompanied by rhythmically distinct music; the melody-and-accompaniment texture; HOMOPHONIC 2, better described as homorhythmic, having 2 or more parts moving more or less simultaneously, and with a distinct melody; typically found in vocal music; POLYPHONIC, when 2 or more parts are sufficiently independent that their role-playing is of little importance; includes the imitative forms of canon, fugue, and round; and HETEROPHONIC, mostly associated with non-Western music, where 2 or more parts approximate the same melodic line but with intentional "imprecisions" of attack, decay, time, and ornamentation.

texture music. Music in which timbral concerns in the form of atmospheric sound masses (characterized by their loudness, density, and/or instrumentation) are the primary feature.

Thaïs. Opera by Massenet, 1894, 1st performed in Paris. The libretto is drawn from the ironic novel by Anatole France (1890). A monk in Egypt is horrified by the depravity of the courtesan Thaïs and dreams of converting her. He succeeds rather well. He conducts Thaïs through the desert, where they reach the convent and she takes her vow as the bride of Christ. But the monk himself undergoes a reversal and now craves not the spirit but the flesh of Thaïs. To exorcise the obsession he flagellates himself violently but in vain. Meanwhile Thaïs attains spiritual perfection and dies a true Christian. The instrumental solo *Méditation* from the score is a perennial favorite.

Thanks for the Memories. Song, 1938, by Ralph Rainger (1901–42); a recipient of an Academy Award, it later became the theme song of comedian Bob Hope.

Thanksgiving (Forefathers' Day). Sym. poem by Ives, 1904, later incorporated into *Holidays, A Sym.* as the 4th movement.

That Old Black Magic. Song by H. Arlen, 1942, from the screen musical *Star-Spangled Rhythm.*

That'll Be the Day. The 1st number 1 hit for Buddy Holly and the Crickets, written by Holly and producer Norman Petty, released in 1957; Linda Ronstadt revived the song in 1976.

theater orchestra. A small, flexible ensemble for which arrangements are made, with separate instrumental parts cued into other parts when a particular instrument is not generally available; e.g., an English-horn solo might be cued in to the clarinet or even violin part. The piano part represents the harmonic skeleton of a theater arrangement.

theater set. A suite of instrumental pieces for small orch.; a term often used by Ives; akin to *orchestral set.*

thematic catalogue. An inventory of musical works by an individual composer arranged according to genre (operas, syms., chamber music, solo works) or chronologically (including opus number) and supplemented by incipits of the works catalogued. Such catalogues may be compiled by the composers themselves, their publishers, or subsequent scholars. Haydn entrusted his copyist with the job of compiling a thematic catalogue of his works, "which I can recall at present, from the age of 18 until my 73rd year of life." The Haydn catalogue contains errors of both omission and commission; at least 2 syms. are listed as having identical initial phrases. Mozart also began cataloguing his compositions, but a complete thematic catalogue of his works was 1st put together by a botanist named Köchel, who had a passion for inventories.

Thematic catalogues now exist for a majority of important composers, and a minority of unimportant ones. Some extensive catalogues include information about the provenance of the MSS, details concerning various editions, etc. In German catalogues of composers published after World War II the notation *verschollen* (disappeared, lost) makes its ominous appearance, alluding to the unconscionable looting of such manuscripts by the occupying armies, be they Allied or Axis.

thematic composition. Any compositional method based on the contrapuntal treatment or development of 1 or more themes. See CANON, INVENTION, FUGUE, SONATA FORM, etc.

theme. An extended and rounded-off subject with accompaniment, in period form, proposed as groundwork for elaborate development and variation.

theme and variations. A musical form, extant under this or other designations since the 16th century, in which the principal theme is clearly and explicitly stated at the beginning and then followed by a number of variations based on that theme. The pattern of development over the course of such a work is freely chosen, although the Classic period evolved a remarkably consistent structure, particularly in those works written for amateurs.

Theme and Variations: The Four Temperaments. A work for string instruments with piano by Hindemith, 1944, in which he set out to describe in musical terms the 4 temperaments of medieval medicine: melancholic, sanguine, phlegmatic, and choleric. The work was 1st performed in Boston; 2 years later it was performed as a ballet.

theme song. The most prominent song in a musical, or a movie, calculated to express the abiding sentiment of the entire production.

theme varié (Fr.). THEME AND VARIATIONS.

Theodorakis, Mikis (actually, Michael George), Greek composer; b. Chios, July 29, 1925. He studied at the Athens Cons. During the German occupation of his homeland he was active in the resistance; after the liberation he joined the left wing but was arrested and deported during the civil war. In 1953 he went to Paris and studied with Messiaen; soon after he began to compose. After returning to Greece in 1961 he resumed his political activities and served as a member of Parliament in 1963. Having joined the Communist party, he was arrested after the military coup in 1967 and incarcerated. During this period he wrote the music for the film *Z*, dealing with the police murder of the Socialist politician Gregory Lambrakis in Salonika in 1963. The film and the music were greatly acclaimed in Europe and America, and the fate of Theodorakis became a cause célèbre. Yielding to pressure from international public opinion, the military Greek government freed Theodorakis in 1970.

In 1972 he quit the Communist party and was active in the United Left; returning to the Communist party he served in Parliament in 1981 and again in 1985–86 before quitting it once more. In 1989 he became an ambassador of conservatism in Greece, going so far as to enter the race for the legislature on the New Democracy ticket; with 416 like-minded painters, writers, musicians, singers, and actors, Theodorakis signed his name to a manifesto condemning the divisive policies of the former Socialist government of Andreas Papandreou; he also ended 4 years of musical silence by appearing on an Athens stage before a crowd of 70,000 people, singing songs of protest and love in the name of national unity.

Theodorakis's works are usually programmatically inspired, whether instrumental or vocal; his favorite subjects are Greek mythology and personal liberation; he has written a ballet-opera, ballet, and film score for Kazantzakis's *Zorba the Greek*. Most of his works reflect a populist aesthetic.

Theorbo. A large, double-necked ARCHLUTE with 1 set of strings for the melody and another for the bass.

theory. The systematic study of basic musical principles, particularly as these relate to composition and analysis.

There's a Long, Long Trail. Western ballad by Zo (Alonzo) Elliott, 1913, written while he was a student at Yale University. Shortly afterward he went to England, where he had the piece publ. Eventually it became a standard song of World War I. President Wilson himself once sang it at a White House dinner.

There's No Business Like Show Business. Rollicking song by I. Berlin, 1946, from the musical *Annie Get Your Gun*. It became a wry but celebratory hymn to commercial American theater, especially among theatrical people themselves.

theremin (thereminovox). An early electronic melody instrument in which hand movements interface with electronic sound waves, allowing for the spatial control of pitch and dynamics; invented by Leon Theremin (see entry below).

Theremin, Leon (born Lev Termen), Russian inventor of the spatially controlled electronic instrument that bears his name; b. St. Petersburg, Aug. 15, 1896; d. Moscow, Nov. 3, 1993. He studied physics and astronomy at the Univ. of St. Petersburg; also cello and music theory. He continued his studies in physics at the Petrograd Physico-Technical Inst.; in 1919 he became director of its Laboratory of Electrical Oscillators. In 1920 he gave a demonstration there of his aetherophone, which was the prototype of the *thereminovox* (THEREMIN); also gave a special demonstration of it for Lenin, who at the time was convinced that the electrification of Russia would ensure the success of communism.

In 1927 he demonstrated his new instruments in Germany, France, and the U.S., where in 1928 he obtained a patent for the theremin. In 1930, at Carnegie Hall in N.Y., he presented a concert with an ensemble of 10 of his instruments, also introducing a space-controlled synthesis of color and music. In 1932, in the same hall, he introduced the 1st electrical sym. orch., conducted by Stoessel and including theremin fingerboard and keyboard instruments. Among his American students from the 1930s he especially commended Clara Rockmore, the best-known thereminist. He also invented the *rhythmicon*, capable of playing different rhythms simultaneously or separately (introduced by Henry Cowell), and an automatic musical instrument for playing directly from specially written musical scores (constructed for Percy Grainger).

With the theorist Joseph Schillinger, Theremin established an acoustical laboratory in N.Y.; also formed numerous scientific and artistic associations, among them Albert Einstein, himself an amateur violinist. Einstein was fascinated by the relationships between music, color, and geometric and stereometric figures; Theremin provided him a work space to study these geometries, but he himself took no further interest in these correlations, seeing himself "not as a theorist but as an inventor." More to Theremin's point were experiments made by Stokowski, who tried to effect an increase in sonority among certain instrumental groups in the Philadelphia Orch., particularly in the double basses. These experiments had to be abandoned, however, when the players complained of deleterious effects upon their abdominal muscles, which they attributed to the electronic sound waves produced by the theremin.

In 1938 Theremin returned (voluntarily or involuntarily) to Russia. He soon had difficulties with the Soviet government, which was suspicious of his foreign contacts; he was detained for a period, and speculations and rumors abounded as to his possible fate. Whatever else may have happened, he worked steadily in electronic research for the Soviet government, continuing his experiments with sound as a sideline. Upon his retirement from his work in electronics he became a prof. of acoustics at the Univ. of Moscow (1964). With the advent of more liberal policies in the USSR, he was able to travel abroad, appearing in Paris and in Stockholm in 1989. His return visit to the U.S. was documented in the film *The Electronic Odyssey of Leon Theremin* (1993).

Leon Theremin, c. 1930s

Thérèse. Opera by Massenet, 1907, premiered in Monte Carlo. Thérèse loves a French royalist who flees from Paris during the Terror. She marries a Girondiste who is no more acceptable to the revolutionary regime. He is arrested and sentenced to die on the guillotine; her exiled lover recklessly returns to Paris and is also seized. As the cart carrying them to execution passes by her window she shouts, "Vive le Roi," a suicidal outcry, and joins her husband and lover in death. The opera is not a major work of Massenet, but the score has enough vital elements to warrant occasional revivals.

These Boots Are Made for Walkin'. Number 1, protofeminist hit for Nancy Sinatra in 1966, penned by producer Lee Hazelwood.

Thésée. Opera by Lully, 1675, 1st performed in Paris. Theseus is the legendary hero who vanquishes the bull Minotaur in Crete, whose annual diet was 7 youths and 7 maidens. Although a hero in Crete, Theseus proves to be a reprobate when he abandons Ariadne, who had helped him find the way out of the Minotaur's labyrinth by giving him a thread ("Ariadne's thread") to guide him. Numerous epics and dozens of operas have been written with Theseus as the central character.

thesis (Grk., letting down). Orig. the strong beat in Greek prosody and therefore musical theory; now it is the unaccented beat, having exchanged meanings with ARSIS.

Thibaud, Jacques, celebrated French violinist; b. Bordeaux, Sept. 27, 1880; d. (in an airplane crash near Mt. Cemet, in the French Alps, en route to French Indochina) Sept. 1, 1953. He began his training with his father and made his debut at age 8 in Bordeaux; at 13 he entered the Paris Cons. as a pupil of Martin Marsick, graduating with the *premier prix* in 1896. Obliged to earn his living, he played the violin at the Café Rouge, where he was heard by the conductor Colonne, who offered him a position in his orch.; in 1898 he made his debut as a soloist (with Colonne) with such success that he was engaged for 54 concerts in Paris in the same season. Subsequently he appeared in all the musical centers of Europe, and from 1903 visited America numerous times.

With his 2 brothers, a pianist and a cellist, he formed a trio, which had some success; but this was discontinued when he joined Alfred Cortot and Pablo Casals in a famous ensemble (1930–35). With Marguerite Long he founded the renowned Long-Thibaud competition in 1943. His playing was notable for its warmth of expressive tone and fine dynamics; his interpretations of Beethoven ranked very high, but he was particularly authoritative in French music.

third. An interval embracing 3 degrees. Also, the 3rd degree of the scale; the mediant.

Third Stream. A compositional synthesis of cool jazz and classical techniques associated with the 1950s. The term itself was used 1st by Gunther Schuller at a lecture at the Berkshire Music Center in Tanglewood (1957). If the 1st stream is classical, and the 2nd stream is jazz, 3rd Stream is their Hegelian synthesis, which unites and reconciles the classical thesis with the popular antithesis. Instances of such synthetic usages are found in a number of modern works. Gershwin's *Rhapsody in Blue* is the most important precursor of 3rd Stream. In constructive application of 3rd Stream, ultramodern techniques, including serialistic procedures, can be amalgamated with popular rhythmic resources. The compositions of Schuller and John Lewis were notable in this style, and the Modern Jazz Quartet was a primary mover.

Third Symphony (Tchaikovsky). A sym. in D major, 1st performed in Moscow, 1875. The work is unusual in having 5 movements, unlike Tchaikovsky's other syms. The "interpolated" 2nd movement, marked ALLA TEDESCA, is a homage to Schumann.

thirteenth. An interval embracing an octave and a 6th; a compound 6th.

thirty-second note. Half of the value of a 16th note.

This Is the Army. Revue by I. Berlin, 1942. This patriotic revue was produced shortly after America's entry into World War II. Among the new songs were *I Left My Heart at the Stage Door Canteen*, *What the Well-Dressed Man in Harlem Will Wear*, and *I'm Getting Tired So I Can Sleep*; but the biggest hit of the show was *Oh! How I Hate to Get Up in the Morning*, a song from World War I days.

Thomas, (Charles Louis) **Ambroise,** noted French composer and teacher; b. Metz, Aug. 5, 1811; d. Paris, Feb. 12, 1896. He entered the Paris Cons. in 1828; his teachers there were Zimmerman (piano) and Dourlen (harmony and accompaniment); he studied privately with Kalkbrenner (piano) and Barbereau (harmony); subsequently studied composition with Le Sueur at the Cons., where he won the Grand Prix de Rome with his cantata *Hermann et Ketty* (1832). After 3 years in Italy and a visit to Vienna, he returned to Paris and applied himself with great energy to the composition of operas. In 1851 he was elected to the Académie; in 1856 he became a prof. of composition at the Paris Cons.; in 1871 he became director there.

As a composer of melodious operas in the French style he was 2nd only to Gounod; his masterpiece was *Mignon*, based on Goethe's *Wilhelm Meister* (Paris, 1866); this opera became a mainstay of the repertoire all over the world; it had nearly 2,000 performances in less then 100 years at the Opéra-Comique alone. Equally successful was his Shakespearean opera *Hamlet* (Paris, Mar. 9, 1868). In 1845 he was made a Chevalier of the Legion d'honneur, being the 1st composer to receive its Grand Croix in 1894. Thomas wrote 17 opéras-comique and 3 operas; 3 ballets; orch. music; string quartet; piano trio; string quintet; piano music; organ music; sacred vocal works, including a Requiem and Messe solennelle; secular vocal works.

Thomas, Michael Tilson, greatly talented American conductor; b. Los Angeles, Dec. 21, 1944. A grandson of Boris and Bessie Thomashefsky, founders of the Yiddish Theater in N.Y., he was brought up in a cultural atmosphere; he studied at the Univ. of Southern Calif., where he received instruction in composition with Ingolf Dahl; he also studied with the pianist John Crown and the harpsichordist Alice Ehlers; concurrently took courses in chemistry. He acquired his conductorial skill by practical work with the Young Musicians Foundation Debut Orch., which he led from 1963 to 1967. He served as pianist in the master classes of Heifetz and Piatigorsky at the Univ. of Southern Calif. in Los Angeles; also conducted at the Monday Evening Concerts, where he presented 1st performances of works by Stravinsky, Copland, Boulez, and Stockhausen.

In 1966 he attended master classes at the Bayreuth Festival; in 1967 he was assistant conductor to Boulez at the Ojai Festival; he conducted there also in 1968, 1969, and 1973. As a conducting fellow at the Berkshire Music Center at Tanglewood in 1968, he won the Koussevitzky Prize. The crowning point of his career was his appointment in 1969 as assistant conductor of the Boston Sym. Orch.; he was the youngest to receive such a distinction with that great ensemble. He was spectacularly catapulted into public notice in 1969 when he was called upon to conduct the 2nd part of the N.Y. concert of the Boston Sym. Orch., substituting for its music director, William Steinberg, who was taken suddenly ill.

In 1970 he was appointed associate conductor of the Boston Sym. Orch., and then was a principal guest conductor there with Colin Davis from 1972 to 1974. From 1971 to 1979 he was music director of the Buffalo Phil. Orch.; served as music director of the N.Y. Phil. Young People's Concerts (1971–76). He was a principal guest conductor of the Los Angeles Phil. Orch. (1981–85). From 1986 to 1989 he was music director of the Great Woods Performing Arts Center in Mansfield, Mass., the summer home of the Pittsburgh Sym. Orch.; served as artistic advisor of the New World Sym. Orch. in Miami (from 1987). In 1988 he became principal conductor of the London Sym. Orch. He has also appeared widely as a guest conductor throughout North America and Europe. His repertoire is exhaustive, ranging from the earliest masters to the avant-garde, with a special interest in American music; he is also an excellent pianist. Above all he is an energetically modern musician, pragmatically proficient, and able to extract the maximum value of the music on hand.

Thomas, Theodore (Christian Friedrich), re-nowned German-American conductor; b. Esens, East Friesland, Oct. 11, 1835; d. Chicago, Jan. 4, 1905. Taught by his father, a violinist, he played in public at the age of 6. In 1845 the family went to N.Y., where Thomas soon began to play for dances, weddings, and in theaters, helping to support the family; in 1851 he made a concert tour as a soloist, and in 1853 he joined Jullien's Orch. on its visit to N.Y., later touring the country with Jenny Lind, Grisi, Sontag, Mario, et al. He became a member of the N.Y. Phil. Soc. in 1854.

With the pianist William Mason, he founded a series of monthly matinee chamber concerts at N.Y.'s Dodworth Hall in 1855, which remained a vital force until it was disbanded in 1869. He 1st gained notice as a conductor when he led a performance of *La favorite* at the N.Y. Academy of Music (1859). In 1862 he led his 1st orch. concerts at N.Y.'s Irving Hall, which became known as the Symphonic Soirées in 1864; they were continued at Steinway Hall (1872–78). In 1865 he began a series of summer concerts in Terrace Garden, relocating these in 1868 to Central Park Garden. The influence of these enterprises on musical culture in N.Y. was enormous; Thomas's programs attained European celebrity. The 1st concert tour with the Theodore Thomas Orch. was made in 1869, and in subsequent years he led it on many tours of the U.S. and Canada.

In 1873 he established the famous Cincinnati Biennial May Festival, which he conducted until his death. He also founded the Cincinnati College of Music, of which he was president and director from 1878 to 1880, having given up his own orch. in N.Y. and the conductorship of the N.Y. Phil. Soc. (1877–78) to accept this post. After his resignation he returned to N.Y., where he immediately reorganized his own orch. and was reelected conductor of the Phil. Soc. Orch. and the Brooklyn Phil. Orch. (having been conductor of the latter in 1862–63, 1866–68, and 1873–78). Besides conducting these orch. bodies, he was at different times director of several choruses; from 1885 to 1887 he was conductor and artistic director of the American Opera Co.

In 1891 he settled permanently in Chicago as conductor of the Chicago Orch. In recognition of Thomas's distinguished services, a permanent home, Orch. Hall, was built by popular subscription, and formally opened in late 1904, with a series of festival concerts, the last directed by him. After his death the name of the orch. was changed to the Theodore Thomas Orch. in 1906; it became the Chicago Sym. Orch. in 1912.

The influence of Thomas upon the musical development of the U.S. has been strong and lasting. An ardent apostle of Wagner, Liszt, and Brahms, he also played for the 1st time in America works of Tchaikovsky, Dvořák, Rubinstein, Bruckner, Goldmark, Saint-Saëns, Cowen, Stanford, Raff, and R. Strauss. He likewise programmed many works by American composers.

Thompson, Randall, eminent American composer and pedagogue; b. N.Y., Apr. 21, 1899; d. Boston, July 9, 1984. He was a member of an intellectual New England family; studied at Lawrenceville School in N.J., where his father was an English teacher; began taking singing lessons and received his rudimentary music training from the organist Francis

Cuyler Van Dyck. When Van Dyck died, Thompson took over his organ duties in the school. Upon graduation he went to Harvard Univ., where he studied with Walter Spalding, Edward Burlingame Hill, and Archibald T. Davison (B.A., 1920; M.A., 1922). In 1920–21 he had some private lessons in N.Y. with Ernest Bloch. In 1922 he submitted his orch.1 prelude *Pierrot and Cothurnus*, inspired by the poetical drama *Aria da Capo* by Edna St. Vincent Millay, for the American Prix de Rome, and received a grant for residence in Rome; he conducted it there at the Accademia di Santa Cecilia (1923). Encouraged by its reception, he proceeded to compose industriously, for piano, for voices, and for orch.

He returned to the U.S. in 1925. From 1927 to 1929 he taught at Wellesley College, and again from 1936 to 1937; in 1929 he was appointed a lecturer in music at Harvard Univ.; in 1929–30 he held a Guggenheim fellowship. On 1930, his 1st Sym. had its premiere in Rochester, N.Y., with Howard Hanson conducting, and, in 1932, Hanson conducted in Rochester the 1st performance of Thompson's 2nd Sym., destined to become one of the most successful sym. works by an American composer; it enjoyed repeated performances in the U.S. and also in Europe. Audiences found the work distinctly American in substance; the unusual element was the inclusion of jazz rhythms in the score.

Equally American and equally appealing, although for entirely different reasons, was his choral work *Americana*, to texts from Mencken's satirical column in his journal, the *American Mercury*. There followed another piece of Americana, the nostalgic a cappella choral work *The Peaceable Kingdom*, written in 1936, and inspired by the painting of that name by the naturalistic fantasist Edward Hicks; for it, Thompson used biblical texts from the Prophets. Another piece for *a cappella* chorus, deeply religious in its nature, was the Alleluia (1940), which became a perennial favorite in the choral literature; it was 1st performed at Tanglewood, Mass., at the inaugural session of the Berkshire Music Center (1940).

In 1942 Thompson composed his most celebrated piece of choral writing, *The Testament of Freedom*, to words of Thomas Jefferson; it was 1st performed with piano accompaniment at the Univ. of Virginia in 1943 (a version with orch. was presented by the Boston Sym. Orch. 2 years later). With this work Thompson firmly established his reputation as one of the finest composers of choral music in America.

But he did not limit himself to choral music. His 1st String Quartet in D Minor (1941) was praised, as was his 1st opera, *Solomon and Balkis*, after Kipling's *The Butterfly That Stamped*, a parody on Baroque usages, broadcast over CBS in 1942. In 1949 Thompson wrote his 3rd Sym., presented in that year at the Festival of Contemporary American Music at Columbia Univ. in N.Y. Thompson's subsequent works were an orch. piece, *A Trip to Nahant* (1954), a Requiem (1958), an opera, *The Nativity According to St. Luke* (1961), *The Passion According to St. Luke* (1965), *The Place of the Blest*, a cantata (1969), and *A Concord Cantata* (1975).

During all this time he did not neglect his educational activities; he taught at the Univ. of Calif. at Berkeley (1937–39); the Curtis Inst. of Music in Philadelphia, where he served as director from 1939 to 1941; the School of Fine Arts at the Univ. of Virginia (1941–46); Princeton Univ. (1946–48); and Harvard Univ. (1948–65), where he retired as prof. emeritus in 1965. He also publ. a book, *College Music* (N.Y., 1935). In 1938 he was elected a member of the National Inst. of Arts and Letters; in 1959 he was named "Cavaliere ufficiale al merito della Repubblica Italiana."

In his compositions Thompson preserved and cultivated the melodious poetry of American speech, set in crystalline tonal harmonies judiciously seasoned with euphonious discords, while keeping resolutely clear of any modernistic abstractions. Thompson also composed the ballet *Jabberwocky* (1951); incidental music; chamber works, including 2 string quartets (1941, 1967); secular and sacred vocal works; solo songs.

Thomson, Virgil (Garnett), many-faceted American composer of great originality and a music critic of singular brilliance; b. Kansas City, Mo., Nov. 25, 1896; d. N.Y., Sept. 30, 1989. He began piano lessons at age 12 with local teachers; received instruction in organ (1909–17; 1919) and played in local churches; took courses at a local junior college (1915–17; 1919), then entered Harvard Univ., where he studied orchestration with E. B. Hill and became assistant and accompanist to A. T. Davison, conductor of its Glee Club; also studied piano with Heinrich Gebhard and organ with Wallace Goodrich in Boston.

In 1921 he went with the Harvard Glee Club to Europe, where he remained on a John Knowles Paine Traveling Fellowship to study organ with Nadia Boulanger at the Paris École Normale de Musique; also received private instruction in counterpoint from her. Returning to Harvard in 1922 he was made organist and choirmaster at King's College; after graduating in 1923, he went to N.Y. to study conducting with C. Clifton and counterpoint with R. Scalero at the Juilliard Graduate School.

In 1925 he returned to Paris, which remained his base until 1940; he established friendly contacts with cosmopoli-

COURTESY FRANK DRIGGS COLLECTION

Virgil Thomson

tan groups of musicians, writers, and painters; his association with Gertrude Stein was particularly significant in the development of his esthetic ideas. In his music he refused to follow any set of modernistic doctrines; rather, he embraced the notion of popular universality, which allowed him to use the techniques of all ages and all degrees of simplicity or complexity, from simple triadic harmonies to dodecaphonic intricacies; in so doing he achieved an eclectic illumination of astonishing power of direct communication, expressed in his dictum "jamais de banalité, toujours le lieu commun." Beneath the characteristic Parisian persiflage in some of his music there is a profoundly earnest intent.

His most famous composition is the opera *4 Saints in 3 Acts*, to a libretto by Stein, in which the deliberate confusion wrought by the author of the play (there are actually 4 acts and more than a dozen saints, some of them in duplicate) and the composer's almost solemn, hymnlike treatment, create a hilarious modern opera buffa. It was 1st introduced at Hartford, Conn., in 1934, characteristically announced as being under the auspices of the Soc. of Friends and Enemies of Modern Music, of which Thomson was director (1934–37); the work became an American classic, with constant revivals staged in America and Europe.

In 1940 Thomson was appointed music critic of the *N.Y. Herald-Tribune*; he received the Pulitzer Prize in music in 1948 for his score to the motion picture *Louisiana Story*. Far from being routine journalism, Thomson's music reviews are minor masterpieces of literary brilliance and critical acumen. He resigned in 1954 to devote himself to composition and conducting. He received the Légion d'Honneur in

1947; was elected to membership in the National Inst. of Arts and Letters in 1948 and in the American Academy of Arts and Letters in 1959. In 1982 he received an honorary degree of D.Mus. from Harvard Univ. In 1983 he was awarded the Kennedy Center Honor for lifetime achievement. He received the Medal of Arts in 1988.

thoroughbass. Basso continuo.

Three Blind Mice. This perennial popular children's song is probably the earliest printed nonreligious tune in music history. It was published in 1609 as a round for 3 voices, and it is still sung in English-speaking countries.

Three Musketeers, The. Operetta by Friml, 1928, based on the romance by Alexandre Dumas *fils*. Like the book, the operetta centers on the 4th musketeer D'Artagnan, a historical figure and guardsman of Louis XIII. His most notable exploit is the recovery of the Queen's jewels from a wily English duke. Among the best tunes are the *March of the Musketeers* and *With Red Wine*.

Three Mysteries. Sym. No. 3, 1950, by Paul Creston (b. N.Y., Oct. 10, 1906; d. San Diego, Aug. 24, 1985), 1st performed in Worchester, Mass., by the Philadelphia Orch. The 3 mysteries are the Nativity, Crucifixion, and Resurrection.

Three New England Sketches. An orch.l work by Piston, 1959, in which he portrays his impressions of the seaside, the summer evening, and the mountains, the parts of a landscape he as a New Englander knew so well. The suite was 1st performed in Worchester, Mass.

Three Places in New England. Orch.l set by Ives, 1903–14. The 3 places are the St. Gaudens Memorial in Boston Common, Putnam's Camp in Redding (Conn.), and the Housatonic at Stockbridge. The work, one of the most important in American music, evokes memories of the Civil War; characteristically Ives quotes fragments of popular American hymns and ballads in the music. The score itself represents a fantastic web of polytonal and polyrhythmic combinations. In 1930 Ives reduced the original score to the contingent of a chamber orch. at the request of the author, who conducted its 1st performance in N.Y., 1931, with his Chamber Orch. of Boston. This reduction became the standard of all subsequent performances of the work until the rediscovery of the original score for large orch., published posth. about 1980.

Three-Page Sonata. Piano piece by Ives, 1905, so entitled for the obvious reason that the MS has only 3 pages. Ives marked at the point of recapitulation: "Back to 1st Theme—all nice Sonatas must have 1st Theme."

Threepenny Opera, The. DREIGROSCHENOPER, DIE.

Three's a Crowd. Revue by A. Schwartz and others, 1930. The songs were mostly topical, but a few became perennial favorites: *Something to Remember You By*, and an interpolated John Green song, *Body and Soul*.

three-step. The ordinary (Vienna) waltz.

Threni. A cantata by Stravinsky, 1958, for solo voices, chorus, and orch., to the Latin text of the Lamentations of Jeremiah. As in *Canticum sacrum* and (to some extent) *Agon*, Stravinsky employed in this score some serial devices. *Threni* (tears) was 1st performed in Venice.

threnody (from Grk. *thrēnōdia*, lamentation). Poem or musical work expressing grief for the dead. The classical *thrēnos* was organized in ritornello form, a chorus alternating with solo passages. The work described in the next entry is a threnody in meaning if not structure.

Threnody to the Victims of Hiroshima. Sym. poem by Penderecki, 1959–61, for 52 solo strings. Compositional interest in microtonal clusters and fluctuating blocks of sound arose in the 1950s; this work made these experiments internationally known through a programmatic work that portrays the city of Hiroshima before, during, and after the dropping of the 1st atomic bomb in 1945. While the piece is a cornucopia of effects (the sound portrait of the airplane Enola Gay is particularly unnerving), the elegiac quality of the piece is the overwhelming one.

Through the Looking Glass. Orch.l suite by D. Taylor, 1923, inspired by the wonderful tale of Lewis Carroll. It is in 4 movements: *The Garden of Live Flowers*, *Jabberwocky*, *Looking Glass Insects*, and *The White Knight*. The music is romantic and effective. It was 1st performed in N.Y. and was quite popular for a while, until musical tastes changed, plunging it into oblivion. Another 20th-century composer, David del Tredici, was equally enamored by Carroll's whimsical tales and produced an entire series of so-called "Alice" works for amplified vocalist, orch., and various other ensembles (rock group and folk group). The tremendously popular

Alice works include *An Alice Sym.* (1969), *Adventures Underground* (1971), *Vintage Alice: Fantascene on A Mad Tea Party* (1972), *Final Alice* (1976), *Child Alice* (1980) and *Haddock's Eyes* (1986).

through-composed (Ger. *durchkomponiert*). A song with each stanza written to a different accompaniment, or composed in a developmental, quasi-symphonic manner; as opposed to the STROPHIC song or lied, with each verse set to the same music in each stanza.

thrush. Old slang for a female singer, especially of popular songs, named after a coloratura triller among songbirds. Spike Hughes declared, in a letter to the *Times* of London in the 1930s, that "all thrushes sing the tune of the 1st subject of Mozart's Sym. No. 40 in G Minor (K. 550), and phrase it a sight better than most conductors. The tempo is always dead right and there is no suggestion of an unauthorized accent on the 9th note of the phrase." However, it must be admitted that a conductor, however histrionic, is far less likely to fly away mid-piece. Another avian term with a similar meaning is *canary*.

thumb position. The high positions in cello playing, where the thumb passes the edge of the fingerboard.

thunder machine (Ger. *Donnermaschine*). A device used to imitate thunder by rotating a barrel with pebbles inside. It was 1st used by R. Strauss in the score of his *Alpine Sym.*, 1915. There are not many instances of its subsequent use, except for special effects in silent movie orchs.

Tibia (Lat.). The Greek AULOS, an ancient vertical flute. *Tibicen*, a flute player.

tie. A curved line joining 2 notes of like pitch which are to be sounded as 1 note equal to their total time value.

Tie a Yellow Ribbon Round the Ole Oak Tree. Annoying ditty recorded by Dawn (of Tony Orlando and . . .) written in a pseudo-1920s style by Irwin Levine and L. Russell Brown. It was a number 1 hit on its release in 1973. Later, when Americans were held hostage in Iran, yellow ribbons began appearing in remembrance of them; this practice has continued during other times of national strife.

tied notes. 1. Notes joined by a TIE. 2. Notes whose hooks (flags) are attached by 1 or more thick strokes (beams).

Tiefland (Lowlands). Opera by d'Albert, 1903, based on a Catalan play, 1st performed in German in Prague. A wealthy landowner who has his mansion in the highlands is tired of his mistress and lets her join her former suitor. When she confesses to him her past association with the landowner, the suitor strangles him. The couple then leaves the lowlands for the mountains. This VERISMO opera was quite successful and is the only d'Albert opera still occasionally performed.

tiento (from Sp. *tentar*, search). Musical form popular in Spain and Portugal in the late Renaissance and early Baroque, comparable to the Italian solo RICERCAR; the tiento is less elaborate but developmentally freer than the ricercar. The form was especially popular with composers of vihuela and keyboard music.

tierce (Fr.). 1. Interval of a 3rd. 2. In the organ, a mutation stop pitched 2 1/3 octaves above the diapason. 3. TERCE.

tierce de Picardi (Fr.). PICARDY THIRD.

Till Eulenspiegel's Merry Pranks (*Till Eulenspiegels lustige Streiche*). Sym. poem by R. Strauss, 1895, 1st performed in Cologne. The title bears an amplifying elucidation, *nach alter Schelmenweise* (After Old Rouges' Tales). Till Eulenspiegel is a hero of many medieval folk tales, blamed for a variety of practical jokes. In the score he is finally caught and pays the supreme penalty on the gallows; his angular mischievous motive is cut off at the drumstroke marking his hanging. This is followed by an epilogue repeating his original lyrical tune. The surname *Eulenspiegel* means "owl glasses."

Till the End of Time. A thing concocted in 1945 by a couple of unconscionable Broadway tunesmiths, using a truncated melody of Chopin's *Polonaise* in A-flat Major. It is an easy guess that the malefactors made more money on their thievery than Chopin made from all of his compositions during his entire lifetime.

timbale (*timballe*; Fr.; It. *timballo*). TIMPANI.

timbales. Pair of pitched, single-headed cylindrical drums of shallow diameter. The plastic heads are tuned by tension screws. Timbales are mostly associated with Latin American dance music but can be found in modern classical scores, sometimes in lieu of timpani, although their sonority is far less substantial.

timbre (Fr.). 1. TONE COLOR. 2. Small bell. *Jeu de timbres*, GLOCKENSPIEL.

timbré (Fr.). Sonorously.

timbrel (Hebr.). A TAMBOURINE.

time. The division of the measure into equal fractional parts of a whole, thus regulating the accents and rhythmic flow of music. The indication of musical time is the TIME SIGNATURE. There are 2 major classes of time: *duple* and *triple*. In *duple time* the number of beats per measure is divisible by 2; in *triple time*, by 3. There are also 2 subclasses, *compound duple time* and *compound triple time*; in the former each of the 2 beats contains a dotted note (or its equivalent) wholly divisible by 3; in the latter not only is each beat divisible by 3, but the number of beats in each measure is divisible by 3.

Time Cycle. Work for soprano and orch. by Foss, 1960, 1st performed by the N.Y. Philharmonic. The original version includes a small improvising group; in a revision for soprano and chamber ensemble, the improvising elements were eliminated.

time field. A topographical term used in structuralist modern music in which the temporal relationship is established spontaneously between the sounds as independent acoustical phenomena and the performer whose reactions to these sounds determine his or her next action.

time point. In serial music, a correlation of note value (duration in a pre-set time unit) with the melodic or harmonic interval counted in semitones; e.g., a major 7th would determine the duration of 11 note values (1 per semitone). Small intervals in melody and harmony would generate a fast tempo; large intervals, a slow tempo.

time signature. The indication of the number of a specific note value in a measure. This sign is always found at the beginning of the composition and at any point within the piece that the number of notes or the note value used changes. Thus, 4/4 indicates 4 beats (the 1st number, or numerator) at a quarter note per beat (the 2nd number, or denominator); the actual sign is written as a vertical fraction without the dividing line. The denominator is always a factor of 2 (2, 4, 8, 16, etc.), as the note values themselves. Although some traditional associations exist, the time signature does not determine the tempo, which requires a verbal or metronomic indication; for example, many Classic slow movements are written in extremely rapid values (at least 16th notes, sometimes 32nd, 64th, or even 128th notes); this probably saves paper but also conveys a visual sense of unusually long phrases.

Some alternate time signatures—**c** and **¢**—are remnants of mensural notation, when the 1st signature meant *tempus imperfectum*, and the 2nd referred to a proportional diminution further explicated by a figure. These symbols, in order, are now called *common time* (4/4) and *cut time* (2/2). There are 2 principal classes of time: *duple* and *triple* (see TIME).

time-bracket notation. A type of highly flexible notation developed by Cage in his mature works whereby time lengths are left to a large degree to the discretion of the performer. In the following example the performer is instructed to 1) begin playing the excerpt at any time between the 1st pair of bracketed times, and to 2) end playing the excerpt at any time between the 2nd pair of bracketed times: [00'00"-00'15"] [00'30"-01'00"].

Times They Are A-Changin', The. Quintessential social-protest song of the '60s, written by Bob Dylan in 1963.

timoroso (*timorosamente*; It.). With timidity, hesitation, fear.

timpani (It., kettledrums; sometimes spelled *tympani*; Fr. *timbales*; Ger. *Pauken*). A large orch.1 drum consisting of a hollow brass or copper hemisphere (the kettle) resting on a tripod; the top of the hemisphere was originally covered with a treated animal hide; now the head is made of vellum stretched by means of an iron ring and tightened by a set of screws, or by cords and braces. The instrument dates to the 6th century as a shallow *bowl drum* in the Middle East; it arrived in Europe in the late Middle Ages.

The timpani are the only standard membranophones in the orch. capable of producing a definite pitch. Orig. the drums were played in pairs, the larger drum yielding any tone from F_0 to c^0, and the smaller from B^b_0 to f^0. Its music is now written at actual pitch. In Classic syms. and

Timpani by Ludwig

overtures the timpani are usually played in pairs, tuned to the main tonic and dominant. In the older instruments the screws around the rim increase or relax the tension of the membrane so that the pitch can be regulated accordingly. Modern timpani are equipped with pedals that can change the pitch with greater precision; later developments led to the manufacture of a genuinely chromatic type of instrument.

In the 19th century the number of timpani in the orch. increased; Wagner's *Ring* requires 4; Berlioz, in his passion for grandiosity, scored the Tuba mirum in his *Grande Messe des Morts* for 16. Uncommon tuning is found in Beethoven's syms.; particularly remarkable is the tuning in an octave F to F in the scherzo of his 9th Sym., where it is applied antiphonally. A foreboding ostinato on the solo timpano occurs in the transition from the scherzo to the finale in the 5th Sym. The indication *timpani coperti* (covered) is synonymous with *timpani sordi* (muted); the desired effect is achieved by covering the head of the instrument with a piece of fabric.

Modern composers are apt to write timpani parts requiring acrobatic virtuosity in manipulating several instruments, playing on the rim, making a glissando with the chromatic pedals, retuning while performing a rapid trill, etc. Solo timpani occur in many modern works, and there are even timpani concertos. Alexander Tcherepnin composed a Sonatina for timpani and piano. The opening phrase of John Vincent's *Symphonic Poem After Descartes* opens with a timpani solo in the rhythm of the Cartesian maxim *Cogito ergo sum*. The American composer and percussion virtuoso William Kraft composed a Timpani Concerto which was premiered in Indianapolis in 1984.

tin ear. A lack of musicality or appropriate responsiveness to music.

Tin Pan Alley. A reference to the area along Broadway in N.Y. where popular songwriters worked in great numbers, hoping to produce the latest hit or successful musical; the term dates from the beginning of the century. The district moved geographically with the times, following the theaters' move uptown; beginning around Union Square (14th Street), it moved 1st to 28th Street and then, after World War I, to the Brill Building (50th Street, also a center of the advertising world). The term has come to be associated with anything connected with the commercial and assembly-line elements of popular song as late as the 1960s.

tin whistle. A small, high-pitched, end-blown whistle flute, made of metal; also called *pennywhistle*. It is used as a traditional melody instrument, notably that of the Irish-Scottish-British islands.

tinnitus. A sustained pressure on the auditory nerve, causing a persistent tintinnabulation in the cochlea in the inner ear. Schumann experienced it during the final stages of his mental illness; he heard a relentless drone on high A-flat. Smetana suffered a similar aural disturbance, but the note he heard was a high E, and he too eventually went insane. He introduced this high E in the violin part at the end of his 1st string quartet, significantly entitled *From My Life*.

Some clinically sane composers active in the last 3rd of the 20th century who never suffered from a pathologic tinnitus did experimentally create an artificial one. Morton Feldman wrote a violin part with an interminable F-sharp calculated to generate a psychic tinnitus in the outer and inner ears of performers and listeners alike. La Monte Young devised a tinnitus of a perfect 5th with a notation, "to be held for a long time." Other ways of affecting the listener is a tape recording of a dripping faucet, or a simulacrum of WHITE NOISE prolonged without a prospect of ever ending. Physical action may be added to a tinnitus, such as measured drops of lukewarm water on the occipital bone of the head held down by clamps, a device helpful to keep in subjection a particularly recalcitrant listener to a piece of avant-garde music. This method was widely practiced to subdue difficult patients in the 18th-century insane asylums.

tintement (Fr.). Jingling sound.

tintinnabulum (Lat.). Since antiquity, a single or set of graduated bells; also, the hammer it is struck with, or the clapper found in later exemplars.

tinto, con (It.). With shading; expressively.

Tiomkin, Dimitri, Ukrainian-born American composer of film music; b. Poltava, May 10, 1894; d. London, Nov. 11, 1979. He studied composition with A. Glazunov and piano with F. Blumenfeld and I. Vengerova at the St. Petersburg Cons.; in 1921 went to Berlin, where he studied with Busoni, Petri, and Zadora; was soloist in Liszt's 1st Piano Concerto with the Berlin Phil. (1924), and that same year gave several concerts with Michael Khariton in Paris. He appeared in vaudeville in the U.S. (1925); became a citizen (1937); made his conducting debut with the Los Angeles Phil. (1938), and later conducted his music with various U.S. orchs.; married Albertina Rasch, a ballerina, for whose troupe he wrote music.

From 1930 to 1970 he wrote over 150 film scores, including several for the U.S. War Dept. His film music betrayed his strong Russian Romantic background, tempered with American jazz. He received an honorary LL.D. from St. Mary's Univ., San Antonio, Tex.; was made a Chevalier and an Officer of the French Légion d'Honneur; also received awards of merit, scrolls of appreciation, plaques of recognition, 3 Oscars and a Golden Globe.

típico. Generic term for Latin American mestizo traditional music.

tiple (from Lat. *triplum*, treble). A general term for a high-pitched instrument, such as the *guitarillo* of the Canary Islands, a small Spanish guitar (also called *timple*); the Cuban BANDURRIA, a small plucked instrument of medieval Spanish origin; a treble *chirimía*, a Catalan shawm.

Tipperary. British song with uncertain authorship, *c.* 1912. It was long associated with World War I, but it may have originally referred to the endless spate of colonial wars that the U.K. was involved in. It is believed that a music-hall performer named Jack Judge helped compose the song.

Tippett, (Sir) Michael (Kemp)

〰〰 〰〰 〰〰 〰〰 〰〰

Greatly renowned English composer; b. London, Jan. 2, 1905. His family was of Cornish descent, and Tippett never refrained from proclaiming his pride of Celtic ancestry. He was equally emphatic in the liberal beliefs of his family. His father was a free-thinker, which did not prevent him from running a successful hotel business. His mother was a suffragette who once served a prison term; her last name was Kemp, which Tippett eventually accepted as his own middle name. He took piano lessons as a child and sang in his school chorus but showed no exceptional merit as a performer. He studied in London at the Royal College of Music (1923–28), where his teachers in composition were Charles Wood and C. H. Kitson; took piano lessons there with Aubin Raymar and attended courses in conducting with Boult and Sargent; studied counterpoint and fugue with R. O. Morris (1930–32). He subsequently held several positions as a teacher and conductor; from 1933 to 1940 he led the South London Orch. at Morley College; then served as director of music there (1940–51).

Tippett had difficulties with the social status quo from the beginning; he openly proclaimed extremely liberal political views, inalienable atheism, and strenuous pacifism. His best-known work, the oratorio *A Child of Our Time* (1939–41), was inspired by the case of Henschel Grynsban, a 17-year-old refugee Jew who responded to the persecution of his parents by assassinating a member of the Paris German embassy in 1938 (this act led to a major Nazi pogrom against Jews); Tippett's powerful, personal, and symbolic musical response to this event became the model for later compositions, particularly the eclectic yet archetypal use of Negro spirituals. As a conscientious objector Tippett refused to serve even in a noncombatant capacity in the British military forces; for this attitude he was sentenced to prison for 3 months (1943); he served his term in a Surrey County gaol with the suggestive name Wormwood Scrubs.

Because he was willing to stand for his beliefs (others simply left Britain until the war ended), he never lost the respect of the community. In 1951 he initiated a series of broadcasts for the BBC; from 1969 to 1974 he directed the Bath Festival. He received high honors from the British government; in 1959 he was named a Commander of the Order of the British Empire; in 1966 he was knighted; in 1979 he was made a Companion of Honour. He visited the U.S. in 1965, and thereafter was a frequent guest in America; his sym. works were often performed by major American orchs. Tippett's works have a grandeur of Romantic inspiration that sets them apart from the prevalent type of contemporary music; they are infused with rhapsodic eloquence and further enhanced by a pervading lyric sentiment free from facile sentimentality.

He excelled in large-scale vocal and instrumental forms; he was a consummate master of the modern idioms, attaining heights of dissonant counterpoint without losing the teleological sense of inherent tonality. Yet he did not shun special effects; 3 times in his 4th Sym. he injects episodes of heavy glottal aspiration meant to suggest the human life cycle.

A man of great general culture, Tippett possesses a fine literary gift and an interest in Jungian psychology; he writes his own librettos for his operas and oratorios. He publ. *Moving into Aquarius* (London, 1958); M. Bowen ed. *Music of the Angels: Essays and Sketchbooks of Michael Tippett* (London, 1980). His compositions include 5 operas, 4 syms. (1945; 1956–57; with soprano, 1970–72; 1977); concertos for double string orch. (1938–39; London, 1940, composer conducting), piano (1953–55; 1956), orch. (1963); violin, viola, and cello (1980); chamber works include: 5 string quartets (1935; 1943; 1946; 1979 ; 1991); Sonata for 4 horns (1955); *The Blue Guitar* for Guitar (1983). 5 piano sonatas: (1938; 1962; 1973; 1979; 1984). He also composed vocal works for groups and soloists.

tirata (It.; Fr. *tirade, coulade*). A ornamental scalar passage or arpeggio improvised to fill the distance between melody notes; thus a tirata spanning the interval of a octave was a *tirata perfecta*; that of a 4th or 5th, a *tirata mezza*; that of an interval greater than an octave, a *tirata aucta* (augmented).

tiré (Fr.). Down-bow in string playing.

tirolese (It.). In the manner of a Tyrol folk song.

Titan Symphony. Mahler's original name for his 1st Sym., 1883–88; Mahler later disavowed this title, taken from a 6-vol. Jean Paul novel (1800–1803). He also removed from the 5-movement work its 2nd movement (called *Blumine*); it was only put back in place for "completist" performances starting in the 1960s. The composer treated the 4-movement work as a sym. poem in 2 parts, the 1st part being described by Mahler as *From the Days of Youth* and the 2nd as *Commediate umana* (human drama, as opposed to Dante's *Divina commedia*). The main subject corresponds to the melody of the 2nd song of Mahler's cycle *Lieder eines fahrenden Gesellen* (Songs of a Wayfarer, 1883–85); the 3rd movement is a phantasmagorical funeral march. The sym. was 1st performed in Budapest, 1889.

titles. In classical music, titles of compositions usually describe the form and content of the work. Such genres and forms as *sym.*, *sonata*, *prelude*, *cantata*, and *opera* may have been changeable through the centuries of their evolution. Thus *sinfonia* meant any instrumental composition or an orch.l interlude in an opera; it is only in the 18th century that it acquired the meaning of a sym. in the modern sense of the word. But the advent of Romantic music made the problem of suitable titles acute. Time and time again composers would assign a programmatic title to a sym. or other work, only to repudiate it at a later time for fear that the music will be interpreted as ancillary to the story implied. What can be more explicit in its programmatic outline than Beethoven's *Pastoral Sym.*, with its realistic storm and 3 bird calls? Yet on 2nd thought Beethoven carefully marked the score *Mehr Ausdruck der Empfindung als Malerey* (more of an expression of feeling rather than painting).

Mahler's Romantic imagination prompted him to give all kinds of specific titles not only to his syms. in their entirety but also to individual movements; later, however, he denied any such programmatic implications. So violent was he in his renunciation that when he was questioned about the meaning of 1 of his syms. at a banquet he raised his glass as if for a toast and exclaimed, "Pereat den Programmen!" (Down with programs!).

Such repudiations are particularly baffling when a literary work lies at the foundation of a typically Romantic composition. Berlioz boldly transplanted his early overture *Les Francs-juges* into the *Sym. fantastique* where it became a *March to the Gallows*. To unify it with the rest of the *Sym.* he inserted a couple of bars of the IDÉE FIXE, the common theme of the work. He did even better: In order to save the labor of copying the old overture, he pasted on the idée fixe in the old MS, replacing a bar of rests. Mendelssohn's *Fingal's Cave*, inspired by his visit to northern Scotland in 1829, was originally entitled *The Solitary Island*.

A fascinating instance of a composer's decision to affix new programmatic titles is illustrated by Schoenberg's *5 Orch.l Pieces* of 1909. In the original they bore abstract titles without any programmatic content. But forty years later, yielding to the suggestion of his publisher to "humanize" the titles, Schoenberg agreed to change the title of the 3rd piece, *The Changing Chord*, to *Summer Morning by the Lake*. The titles that Scriabin selected for many of his works are mystical and theosophic, and he was often willing to listen to suggestions from his close intellectual associates. It was his brother-in-law, Boris de Schloezer, who suggested to him that the opening motive of his 3rd Sym., *Le Poème divin*, is a proclamation of self-assertion: "I am!" This notations appears in the final MS and in the published score. And it was Modest Tchaikovsky, the brother of the composer, who suggested the name *Pathétique* for his 6th Sym.

To what lengths will a composer go to eliminate an original programmatic intent? Stravinsky's *Scherzo Fantastique* (1909) was inspired by Maeterlinck's half-literary, half-scientific essay *Les Abeilles* (The Bees). Each section of the score corresponds to a beehive event: birth of the queen, nuptial flight, swarming, etc. The publishers quoted from the book in the score, and Maeterlinck, a hot-tempered poet, promptly sued Stravinsky for infringement of copyright. Fifty years later, in one of his conversation books with Robert Craft, Stravinsky denied ever intending to use the Maeterlinck book as a programmatic source; but his own 1907 letter to Rimsky-Korsakov plainly contradicts this.

To Anacreon in Heaven. Song by J. S. Stafford, 1st published in London, *c.* 1780. Originally a whimsical glorification of the Greek poet Anacreon, famous for his odes to love and wine, the melody was adapted to the poem *The Star-Spangled Banner* by F. S. Key (1st part written 1814) sometime later in the 19th century; it has been the official U.S. national anthem since 1931.

To Know Him Is to Love Him. A 1958 hit for the Teddy Bears, written by group member Phil Spector, who later enjoyed a successful career as the creator of "teen syms." for groups like the Ronettes. The title comes from Spector's father's tombstone.

toada (Port.). The equivalent of the Spanish TONADA.

toccata (from It. *toccare*, strike, touch; *toccatina*, short toccata). A virtuoso keyboard composition exploiting the articulated clarity possible with such instruments: free and bold in style, consisting of runs and passages alternating with fugued or contrapuntal work, generally in equal notes, with a flowing, animated, and rapid movement.

In the 16th century the term was understood widely as a prelude or an improvisation before the central section of a composition, particularly in organ playing. In the 17th century the toccata assumed a more precise definition as a keyboard composition in a rapid tempo, in steady rhythm (Frescobaldi, Froberger, Sweelinck, A. Scarlatti, Bach). In the 19th and 20th centuries, composers applied the term to a type of work that would otherwise be called a *moto perpetuo* (an alternate term). Schumann, Widor, Vierne, Debussy, Ravel, Prokofiev, Busoni, and Reger wrote toccatas marked by brilliant technical display.

toccato (It.). In the 17th century, the bass line of a trumpet fanfare, often "touched" (played) on the timpani.

Toch, Ernst, eminent Austrian-born American composer and teacher; b. Vienna, Dec. 7, 1887; d. Los Angeles, Oct. 1, 1964. His father was a Jewish dealer in unprocessed leather and there was no musical strain in the family; Toch began playing piano without a teacher in his grandmother's pawnshop; he learned musical notation from a local violinist and copied Mozart's string quartets for practice; using them as a model, he began to compose string quartets and other pieces of chamber music; at the age of 17 his 6th String Quartet, op. 12 (1905), was performed by the famous Rosé Quartet in Vienna. From 1906 to 1909 he studied medicine at the Univ. of Vienna.

In 1909 he won the prestigious Mozart Prize and a scholarship to study at the Frankfurt Cons., where he studied piano with Willy Rehberg and composition with Iwan Knorr. In 1910 he was awarded the Mendelssohn Prize; also won 4 times in succession the Austrian State Prize. In 1913 he was appointed instructor in piano at Zuschneid's Hochschule für Musik in Mannheim. From 1914 to 1918 he served in the Austrian army. After the Armistice he returned to Mannheim, resumed his musical career, and became active in the modern movement, soon attaining, along with Hindemith, Krenek, and others, a prominent position in the new German school of composition. He also completed his education at the Univ. of Heidelberg (Ph.D., 1921, with the diss. *Beiträge zur Stilkunde der Melodie*).

In 1929 he went to Berlin, where he established himself as a pianist, composer, and teacher of composition. In 1932 he made an American tour as a pianist playing his own works; he returned to Berlin, but with the advent of the Nazi regime he was forced to leave Germany in 1933. He went to Paris, then to London, and in 1935 emigrated to the U.S.; gave lectures on music at the New School for Social Research in N.Y.; in 1936 he moved to Hollywood, where he wrote music for films. He became an American citizen in 1940; in 1940–41 he taught composition at the Univ. of Southern Calif., Los Angeles; subsequently taught privately; many of his students became well-known, including Andre Previn. From 1950 until his death Toch traveled frequently and lived in Vienna, Zurich, the MacDowell Colony in New Hampshire, and Santa Monica, Calif.

Toch's music is rooted in the tradition of the German and Austrian Romantic movement of the 19th century, but his study of the classics made him aware of the paramount importance of formal logic in the development of thematic ideas. His early works consist mostly of chamber music and pieces for piano solo; following the zeitgeist during his German period he wrote several pieces for the stage in the light manner of sophisticated entertainment; he also composed effective piano works of a virtuoso quality, which enjoyed considerable popularity among pianists of the time. Toch possessed a fine wit and a sense of exploration; his *Geographical Fugue* for Speaking Chorus, articulating in syllabic counterpoint the names of exotic places on earth, became a classic of its genre.

It was not until 1950 that Toch wrote his 1st full-fledged sym., but from then on until his death of stomach cancer he composed fully 7 syms., plus sinfoniettas for wind and string orch. He was greatly interested in new techniques; the theme of his last String Quartet (No. 13, 1953) is based on a 12-tone row. In the score of his 3rd Sym. he introduced an optional instrument, the Hisser, a tank of carbon dioxide that produced a hissing sound through a valve. Among the several honors Toch received were the Pulitzer Prize for his

3rd Sym. (1956), membership in the National Inst. of Arts and Letters (1957), and the Cross of Honor for Sciences and Art from the Austrian government (1963). An Ernst Toch Archive was founded at the Univ. of Calif., Los Angeles, in 1966, serving as a depository for his MSS. His works include 3 operas, among them *Die Prinzessin auf der Erbse* (The Princess on the Pea; Baden-Baden, 1927); works for orch., including 7 symphonies; concerti for various instruments; chamber works including 13 string quartets; piano pieces; and vocal works.

Tod und Verklärung. DEATH AND TRANSFIGURATION.

Todesgesang (*Todeslied*; Ger.). A dirge; a musical composition commemorating the dead.

Tom Jones. Opera by F.-A. D. Philidor, 1765, 1st performed in Paris. The libretto is taken from the famous novel by Henry Fielding, *Tom Jones, The History of a Foundling* (1749). Tom is a scalawag who takes his pleasures where he finds them, but he loves Sophia Western in earnest. Her father, however, plans a rich marriage for her. It turns out in the end that Tom is really the nephew of a country squire and therefore belongs to nobility; as such he is qualified to marry Sophia. Byron called the character of Tom Jones "an accomplished blackguard," but in the opera he appears as a romantic lover.

tombeau (Fr., gravestone). An instrumental composition dedicated to the memory of a dignitary or a friend. In 1920 a number of French composers contributed memorial pieces to a collection entitled *Tombeau de Debussy*. A musical tombeau may also be found under other guises: *planctus* or *lachrymae* (Lat.), *dirge, threnody, elegy, dump,* or *tears* (Eng.); *déploration* or *apothéose* (Fr.), and *lamento* (It.). The same function of reverential remembrance is expressed by the term *homage*, as in *Hommage à Rameau* by Debussy and *Homage to Ives* by Copland. Ravel's *Le Tombeau de Couperin*, a tribute to François Couperin, is a fine 20th-century tombeau for piano; it contains 6 movements in 17th-century forms, with superinduced pandiatonic ornaments. Ravel orchestrated 4 of the movements, performed as such for the 1st time in Paris, 1920.

Tombeau de Couperin, Le. Piano suite by Ravel, 1914–17; 4 of the 6 movements were orch.l and presented in Paris, 1920. A tribute to François Couperin, the work uses Baroque suite movements as modes with superinduced

pandiatonic ornaments; as such it is a relatively early example of neoclassicism.

tom-tom. Generic term for Africa, Asian, or Latin American drums, of indigenous origin, of high but (usually) indefinite pitch. The instrument(s) may be played with hands or sticks; in addition to traditional music they are found in jazz, popular, and dance bands, as well as some percussion-oriented scores.

Ton (Ger.). A tone; key; mode; pitch; octave-scale.

tonada (Sp.). A Spanish song or dance song, in 3/4 or 6/8 time (or both), also adopted in Latin America. Several tonadas have been written by classical composers.

tonadilla (Sp.). A Spanish theater piece of a lighter character with folk melorhythms; originally a song (little tonada) placed in the interludes of spoken plays. It is an 18th-century predecessor of the ZARZUELA, a more ambitious, less folklike genre.

tonal. Pertaining to tones, or to a tone, mode, or key. *Tonal imitation*, imitation within the key of a composition; nonmodulating imitation.

tonal answer. An answer to the subject in a fugue, in which the tonic is answered by the dominant and the dominant is answered by the tonic, thus altering the intervallic content of the theme.

tonal aura. A coloristic hypertension created in modern technical innovations, such as playing below the bridge of stringed instruments, fluttertongue on the flute, glissando in the French horn, or a particularly unsettling borborygmus in the bass trombone. Aura is a medical term used to describe a premonitive sensation before an epileptic seizure. Schoenberg's score *Begleitungsmusik zu einer Lichtspielscene*, written for an unrealized abstract motion picture, contains striking instances of musical aura, beginning with the sections marked *Threatening Danger* and *Fear* and culminating in the finale, *Catastrophe*.

tonal tropism. An involuntary pitch orientation. By computing the frequency of recurrence of each particular note in an atonal work and finding which of the 12 notes of the chromatic scale has a marked preponderance over the others, it may be asserted that such a frequently recurrent note represents a tonal focus, and that other members of an atonal melody have a tonal tropism toward such a putative tonic. Other aspects of tonal tropism are: the approach to the most frequently occurring tone by a semitone from below, suggesting a leading tone; a preferential placement of a note in the bass; an extended duration of a certain tone; its appearance at the end of a musical fascicle; a simulated cadence or some other kind of privileged position at strategic points, at a strong beat of the measure, etc.

tonality. A cumulative concept that embraces all pertinent elements of tonal structure, including both melodic and harmonic juxtapositions that determine the collective tonal relations, i.e., a basic loyalty to a tonal center. The term itself is relatively new, having originated in France about 1820; it was universally adopted. Tonality does not determine a definite key; a composition may modulate widely from the outset and travel far from the original key, and yet it adheres to the sense of tonality as long as it follows the tonal structure. The antonym of tonality is ATONALITY, a type of composition in which tonality is rejected. The guardian of tonality is the key signature, and no matter how many times this key signature is changed during a given composition, the sense of tonality remains as long as each individual section is cast in a definite key.

tonante (It.). Thundering, thunderous.

tonarium. A catalogue of medieval chants; a complete tonarium was usually organized according to the principal 8 tones of Gregorian chant, including antiphons, communions, introits, and responsories.

Tonart (Ger.). Key (tonality).

Tonbild (Ger., tonal picture). SYMPHONIC POEM.

Tondichtung (Ger.). SYMPHONIC POEM; term preferred by R. Strauss. *Tondichter*, a Romantic term for composer.

tone. 1. Definite pitch, as opposed to pitchless NOISE. 2. Whole tone; major 2nd. *Half tone*, minor or chromatic 2nd; semitone. See also ACOUSTICS. 3. Timbre; TONE QUALITY.

tone clusters. A row of adjacent tones, diatonic, pentatonic, or chromatic. The technique was 1st demonstrated in public by Henry Cowell at the San Francisco Music Club (1912), on the day after his 15th birthday. The term itself

was invented by Cowell 6 years later. He applied them systematically in many of his compositions, such as *Amiable Conversations* for Piano, in which diatonic clusters are used in the right hand on white keys and pentatonic clusters are used in the left hand on the black keys. Small tone clusters can be performed on the piano keyboard with fists or the palm of the hand; extensive tone clusters of 2 octaves or more require the use of the entire forearm, from the fists to the elbow. Cowell notated tone clusters with a thick black line on a stem for rapid notes or a white-note rod attached to a stem for half-notes.

The idea of a cluster is not entirely new; composers of BATTAGLIA applied tone clusters using the palm of the hand, mostly in the bass, to imitate a canon shot; a curious piano piece called *Alpine Storm* by the German-American composer George Kunkel (1840–1923) specifies the use of the palm of the left hand to produce the effect of thunder. (The work is dedicated "to my son, Ludwig van Beethoven Kunkel.") Independently of Cowell, Charles Ives employed tone clusters to illustrate the "celestial railroad" in the *Hawthorne* movement of his *Concord Sonata*, produced by gently pressing a wooden plank down on the keys in the treble to create sympathetic vibrations. Bartók used tone clusters to be played by the palm of the hand in his 2nd Piano Concerto, a device that he borrowed expressly from Cowell, with permission.

tone color (timbre; Ger. *Klangfarben*). An often subjective description of musical sound quality, using adjectives as penetrating, dry, nasal, liquid, etc. As tonometric experiments and spectography demonstrate, the peculiar tone color of a musical instrument or human voice depends on the relative strength of harmonics produced by the fundamental tone. The same note produced on one instrument differs as much from one produced on another instrument as the tone color of the voice of one person differs from that of another.

The tone color of the flute is perceived as the purest of all instruments because its distribution of harmonics approaches a sine wave. The clarinet, on the other hand, generates a harmonic series characterized by odd-numbered harmonics. The oboe owes its penetrating sound to possessing harmonics of practically the same mutual strength. The harmonics of string instruments are also abundant in all registers. Schoenberg introduced the idea of a scale of tone colors, so that a succession of identical pitches on different instruments would form a scale he called the *Klangfarbe scale*. Recent theorists have proposed means of analyzing "sound color."

tone poem. SYMPHONIC POEM.

tone row. The fundamental subject in a 12-tone composition.

Tonfall (Ger.). Intonation.

Tongeschlecht (Ger., tonal gender). A modal structure, such as major or minor.

tongue. 1. (*noun*) A reed. 2. Use the tongue in producing, modifying, or interrupting the output of certain wind instruments. See TONGUING.

tonguing. The production of tone effects on wind instruments with the aid of the tongue. *Single tonguing*, the effect obtained by the repeated tongue thrust to the nearly inaudible consonant *t* or *d*; *double t.*, that obtained by the repetition of *t k*; *triple t.*, by *t k t*; etc.

tonic. The 1st note (keynote) of a scale. *Tonic accent*, in chant, unaccompanied cantillation, and recitation, a prosodic stress on a long vowel or syllable on a higher pitch; *tonic chord*, the triad on the keynote; *tonic pedal*, pedal-point on the keynote; *tonic section*, a complete sentence or longer passage in the opening key of the composition, with a cadence in that key before the work proceeds.

tonic sol-fa (Ger. *Tonika-do*). A method of teaching vocal music, invented by Sarah Ann Glover of Norwich, England, about 1812. Pupils are taught to recognize the tones of the scale by observing the mental impressions peculiar to each tone. It is based on the MOVABLE Do system, and uses the syllables Doh, Ray, Me, Fah, Soh, and Lah, adapted from the Guidonian alphabet (with Te added for the leading tone). This system, widely accepted in English-speaking countries, has the unfortunate consequence of divorcing the absolute sound from its adopted name. In all Latin countries and in Russia, the FIXED Do method is in use; in that system, Do is immovable and designates the sound of pitch class C.

Tonight We Love. Song, 1941, borrowed directly and unscrupulously from Tchaikovsky's 1st Piano Concerto; someone in Hollywood published a song in response entitled *Everybody's Making Money but Tchaikovsky.*

Tonkunst (Ger.). The art of musical composition. *Tonkünstler*, composer.

Tonleiter (Ger., tone ladder). Scale.

Tonmalerei (Ger.). Tone painting; musical illustration; the realization of programmatic ideas in sound.

tono (*tuono*; It.). 1. Tone, pitch. 2. Whole tone. 3. Key; mode. *Primo tono, secondo tono*, etc., designations of ecclesiastical modes.

tonolalia. Glossolalia is a preternaturally inspired manifestation of spontaneous and simultaneous multilingual intercourse. Tonolalia is an analogous verbal neologism, in that different instruments and voices disport themselves in a modernistic quodlibet. Particularly effective are antiphonal uses of tonolalia in which an improvised interlude is echoed by another instrument or a group of instruments.

tonotripsical impact. As a cephalotripsical blow crushes the skull, a tonotripsical impact is produced by an implosion of sonic matter calculated to stun into submission and psychically incapacitate the listeners to an ultramodern concert. At a HAPPENING in N.Y., a complete Sunday edition of the *N.Y. Times* was thrown on the floor of a chamber music hall and a power lawn mower was wheeled in and proceeded to chew up the newspaper with cephalotripsical effect. A literal example of tonocephalotripsical music is the *Concerto for the Hammer and the Skull*, by a French composer who performed it himself by striking different parts of the bones of his head, producing different tones, and opening his mouth as a resonator.

Tonsatz (Ger.). A composition.

Tonsetzer (Ger.). Composer.

tonus (1) (Lat.). Chant recitation. *Tonus ad introitum*, introit reciting tone; *tonus psalmorum*, psalm reciting tone.

tonus (2). In the Middle Ages, a mode. In the 16th century a system of 12 modes was established, comprising 6 authentic and 6 plagal modes. The Dorian mode, ranging from D to D, became the commonly accepted prototype and was called *primus tonus*; its plagal derivative, the Hypodorian, was called *secundus tonus*. The Phyrgian mode, from E to E, was called *tertius tonus*, and so forth.

The complete theory of the tonus was expounded upon by Glareanus in his treatise *Dodecachordon* (12 modes), 1547. The 11th tonus, Ionian, is equivalent to the modern C major scale. Zarlino changed the order of the modes in his *Istitutioni harmoniche*, 1558, placing the Ionian mode at the head of the list, thus anticipating the coronation of the C major scale as the fundamental tonal progression of modern times. To fill out the diatonic scale the Locrian and Hypolocrian modes were later added, with the range from B to B and F to F, respectively.

Tonus peregrinus (Lat., wandering mode), an irregular psalm tone whose recitation note changes in mid-chant; it is associated with Psalm 113, *In exitu Israel de Aegypto*, hence the name (referring to pilgrims). The wandering mode is 1st mentioned as the "9th mode" in the 10th century.

top. A child's toy in the shape of an inverse cone. When wound up and released it produces a humming noise of a fairly definite pitch. It is found in some 20th-century works, including *A Celtic Requiem* by John Taverner, which calls for "a top in E-flat."

Top Banana. Musical by J. Mercer, 1951. A former burlesque hoofer becomes the "top banana" of the new medium of television. His cronies fawningly sing the title song for him. When the sponsor of the show demands more love interest, a contrived romance between 2 singers is readily furnished. Naturally they become involved in earnest and sing the love duet *Only If You're In Love*. Also included is *A Word a Day*, which reeks intentionally with solecism.

topology in music. See TRANSLOCATION.

torch song. American slang for a ballad of despair and lovelorn lamentation, usually sung by a female singer with heartwrenching cadenzas; in musical terms, a song of the blues, if not always in blues mode. (Many Tin Pan Alley blues have as little to do with Bessie Smith as *Alexander's Ragtime Band* has to do with Scott Joplin.) The generic designation is taken from the expression "to carry a torch," i.e., to care for someone deeply. Torch songs evolved in the swing era as an outgrowth of urban blues; while attempts to revive them have often been stymied by changes in taste or mores, they have undergone a revival in the 1980s and 1990s, mostly in a soul context.

torculus (Lat., twisted). In mensural notation, a ligature indicating a rise and fall of 1 degree.

Toreador Song. The popular designation of Escamillo's entrance song from *Carmen* by Bizet, 1875. Alas, there is no such word as *toreador* in Spanish; a bullfighter is *torero*, and the correct term for the man who kills the bull in the ring is *matador*.

Torke, Michael, American composer and pianist; b. Milwaukee, Sept. 22, 1961. He studied composition with Joseph Schwantner and piano at the Eastman School of Music in Rochester, N.Y. (graduated, 1984); then completed composition studies with Martin Bresnick and Jacob Druckman at the Yale Univ. School of Music (1984–85); won the Prix de Rome and held a residency at the American Academy in Rome. His output reveals an effective blend of serious music, jazz, and rock elements.

He is best known for his "color works": *The Yellow Pages* for Flute, Clarinet, Violin, Cello, and Piano (1984); *Ecstatic Orange* for Orch. (N.Y., 1985); *Bright Blue Music* for Orch. (N.Y., 1985); *Verdant Music* (Green Music) for Orch. (Milwaukee, 1986); *Purple* for Orch. (N.Y., 1987); *Black & White*, ballet (N.Y., 1988); *Copper* for Brass Quintet and Orch. (Midland, Mich., 1988); *Ash* for Orch. or Chamber Orch. (St. Paul, Minn., 1989); *Slate* for Concertante Group and Orch. (as the ballet *Echo*, N.Y., 1989); *Rust* for Piano and Winds (1989); *Chalk* for String Quartet. Also important are: *Vanada* for Brass, Keyboards, and Percussion (1984); *Adjustable Wrench* for Chamber Ensemble (1987); and Saxophone Concerto.

Tormé (born Torme), **Mel(vin Howard),** American singer and composer of popular music; b. Chicago, Sept. 13, 1925. He was only 4 when he began singing with the Coon-Sanders band at a Chicago restaurant; studied piano and drums, then sang with various bands and acted in radio soap operas (1934–40). After touring as a singer, drummer, and arranger with the Chico Marx band (1942–43), he appeared

Mel Tormé, 1980

COURTESY FRANK DRIGGS COLLECTION

in films and with his own vocal swing ensemble, the Mel-Tones. Following World War II army service, he launched a prominent career as a pop and jazz vocalist; performed on radio, in nightclubs, on television, and on recordings. He won 2 successive Grammy Awards for best male jazz vocalist for his albums *An Evening with George Shearing and Mel Tormé* (1983) and *Top Drawer* (also with Shearing, 1984); appeared as soloist and conductor with a variety of sym. orchs., including those of San Francisco and Dallas. In 1980 Mayor Tom Bradley proclaimed Mel Tormé Week in Los Angeles in commemoration of his 50th anniversary in show business. His association with Judy Garland is recounted in his book *The Other Side of the Rainbow* (N.Y., 1970); he also wrote *Traps, the Drum Wonder* (1990), a biography of Buddy Rich. Among his more than 300 songs, *The Christmas Song* (1946) has become a holiday favorite.

Tormis, Veljo, Estonian composer; b. Kuusalu near Tallinn, Aug. 7, 1930. He studied organ and choral conducting at the Tallinn Music Instit. (1943–51), organ and composition at the Tallinn Cons. (1951), and composition with Shebalin at the Moscow Cons. (1951–56). He has taught at the Tallinn Music Inst. and consulted the Estonian Composers' Union. He is an expert in Estonian folk music and has often drawn upon it for his choral music; he has also drawn upon the traditional music of other Finno-Ugrian nations. His works range from simple, highly serious incantation to humorous parodies full of variety and buffoonery. Unaccompanied choral music dominates his output; his best-known work is *Forgotten Peoples.*

Torna a Surriento. Popular Neapolitan ballad by Ernesto de Curtis, 1904.

tornando (It.). Returning. *Tornando al primo tempo* or *tornando come prima*, returning to (resuming) the original tempo.

Torquado Tasso. Opera by Donizetti, 1833, 1st produced in Rome. The central character is the famous poet of the Italian Renaissance. The Duchess Eleonora falls in love with him when he reads poetry to her, but her brother, the reigning Duke of Ferrara, wants her to marry a Duke of Mantua and divests himself of Tasso by putting him in a madhouse. Torquado eventually succumbs to his new surroundings, especially after the Pope announces his intention to make him poet laureate.

torture organ. A political instrument used in Brazil to extract confessions by administering electric shocks from a large organ. According to reports from Rio de Janeiro in Nov. 1974, a keyboard apparatus, operating a system of electric currents, helped produce electric shocks varying in intensity and duration depending on the strength (*pp* to *ff*) of screams of the prisoner under torture; deafening sounds at close range were also available to the victims. No doubt the inventor was closely related to the Commandant of Kafka's *In the Penal Colony.*

Tosca. Opera by Giacomo Puccini, 1900, 1st produced in Rome. The libretto is derived from a semihistorical drama by Sardou. The action takes place during the turbulent events in Rome in the summer of 1800. Napoleon's army advances into Italy and is greeted by Italian patriots as liberators from the oppressive Austrian rule. Tosca is a famous opera singer; her lover, the painter Cavaradossi, shelters a political refugee and becomes the target of persecution by the sinister chief of the Roman police, Scarpia. Captivated by Tosca's generous feminine endowments, Scarpia seeks to bargain her favors against Cavaradossi's release from prison. In desperation she agrees to submit to him, whereupon Scarpia issues an order for a pretended execution of Cavaradossi, using blank cartridges, "As in the case of Palmieri," he adds ominously.

Confident of her lover's escape, Tosca takes advantage of Scarpia's amorous relaxation and stabs him to death. But Scarpia has outwitted Tosca: "In the case of Palmieri" was a code message to the soldiers to make the pretended execution real. Cavaradossi falls at the stake; after the soldiers are gone she rushes to him, but he does not rise. Distraught, Tosca hurls herself to her death from the prison's parapet. The score introduces many bold harmonic innovations—consecutive triads, unresolved dissonances, and whole-tone scales; at the same time, the exquisite art of Italian bel canto is beautifully exercised. Tosca's lament at the cruelty of fate (*Vissi d'arte*) and Cavaradossi's moving cavatina are among the finest arias in the operatic repertory.

Toscanini, Arturo

Great Italian conductor; b. Parma, Mar. 25, 1867; d. N.Y., Jan. 16, 1957. He entered the Parma Cons. at the age of 9, studying the cello with Carini and composition with Dacci; graduated in 1885 as winner of the 1st prize for cello; received the Barbacini Prize as the outstanding graduate of his class. In 1886 he was engaged as cellist for the Italian opera in Rio de Janeiro; one night he was unexpectedly called upon to substitute for the regular conductor, when the latter left the podium at the end of the introduction after the public hissed him; the opera was *Aida*, and Toscanini led it without difficulty; he was rewarded by an ovation and was engaged to lead the rest of the season.

Returning to Italy, he was engaged to conduct the opera at the Teatro Carignano in Turin, making his debut there in late 1886, and later conducted the Municipal Orch. there. Although still very young he quickly established a fine reputation. From 1887 to 1896 he conducted opera in the major Italian theaters. In 1892 he led the premiere of *Pagliacci* in Milan, and on 1896 the premiere of *La Bohème* in Turin. He also conducted the 1st performances by an Italian opera company (sung in Italian) of *Gotterdämmerung* (Turin, 1895) and *Siegfried* (Milan, 1899); he made his debut as a sym. conductor in 1896, with the orch. of the Teatro Regio in Turin.

In 1898 the impresario Gatti-Casazza engaged him as chief conductor for La Scala, Milan, where he remained until 1903, and again from 1906 to 1908. In the interim he conducted opera in Buenos Aires (1903–1904; 1906). When Gatti-Casazza became general manager of the Metropolitan Opera (1908), he invited Toscanini to be principal conductor; Toscanini's debut in N.Y. was in *Aida*. While at the Metropolitan Toscanini conducted Verdi's *Requiem* (1909) as well as 2 world premieres, Puccini's *The Girl of the Golden West* (1910) and Giordano's *Madame Sans-Gêne* (1915); he also brought out for the 1st time in America Gluck's *Armide* (1910), Wolf-Ferrari's *Le Donne curiose* (1912), and Mussorgsky's *Boris Godunov* (1913). Later that year he gave his 1st concert in N.Y. as a sym. conductor, leading Beethoven's 9th Sym.

In 1915 he returned to Italy; during the season of 1920–21 he took the La Scala Orch. on a tour of the U.S. and Canada. From 1921 to 1929 he was artistic director of La Scala; there he conducted the posthumous premiere of Boito's opera *Nerone*, which he helped complete for performance (1924). In 1926–27 he was a guest conductor of the N.Y. Phil., returning in this capacity through the 1928–29 season; then was its associate conductor with Mengelberg in 1929–30; subsequently was its conductor from 1930 to 1936; took it on a tour of Europe in the spring of 1930. He conducted in Bayreuth in 1930 and 1931. Deeply touched by the plight of the Jews in Germany, he refused to conduct there; he also acceded to the request of the violinist Bronislaw Huberman, founder of the Palestine Sym. Orch., to conduct the inaugural concert of that orch. at Tel Aviv (1936). During this period he also filled summer engagements at the Salzburg Festivals (1934–37) and conducted in London (1935; 1937–39).

He became music director of the NBC Sym. Orch. in 1937, a radio orch. that had been organized especially for him; he conducted his 1st broadcast on Christmas that year in N.Y. He took it on a tour of South America in 1940, and on a major tour of the U.S. in 1950. He continued to lead the NBC Sym. Orch. until the end of his active career; he conducted his last concert from Carnegie Hall, N.Y. (1954, 10 days after his 87th birthday), and then sent a doleful letter of resignation to NBC, explaining the impossibility of further appearances (apparently he suffered a memory lapse during that concert). He died a few weeks before his 90th birthday.

Toscanini was one of the most celebrated masters of the baton in the history of conducting; undemonstrative in his handling of the orch., he possessed an amazing energy and power of command. He demanded absolute perfection, and he erupted in violence when he could not obtain from the orch. what he wanted (a lawsuit was brought against him in Milan when he accidentally injured the concertmaster with a broken violin bow). Despite the vituperation he at times poured on his musicians, he was affectionately known to them as "The

Maestro" who could do no wrong. His ability to communicate his desires to singers and players was extraordinary, and even the most celebrated opera stars or instrumental soloists never dared to question his authority.

Owing to extreme nearsightedness, Toscanini committed all scores to memory; his repertoire embraced virtually the entire field of Classic and Romantic music; his performances of Italian operas, of Wagner's music dramas, of Beethoven's syms., and of modern Italian works were especially inspiring. Among the moderns, he conducted works by R. Strauss, Debussy, Ravel, Prokofiev, and Stravinsky, and among Americans, Samuel Barber, whose *Adagio for Strings* he made famous; he also had his favorite Italian composers (Catalani, Martucci), whose music he fondly fostered. In his social philosophy he was intransigently democratic; he refused to conduct in Germany under the Nazi regime. He militantly opposed Fascism in Italy, but he never abandoned his Italian citizenship, despite long years of residence in America. In 1987 his family presented his valuable private archive to the N.Y. Public Library.

tostamente (It.). Rapidly and boldly.

tostissimo (It.). Extremely fast.

tosto (It.). Almost; soon. *Allegro molto, più tosto presto*, very fast, nearly *presto*.

Tostquartette. A collective name for 12 quartets by Haydn, 1788–90, opp. 54, 55, and 64; he dedicated them to the amateur violinist and industrialist Johann Tost of Vienna. The 5th quartet (op. 55, no. 2) is nicknamed the *Razor Quartet*.

total music. A form of performance art in which the once autonomous art of music is again allied with other arts, albeit in an often ironic or oxymoronic manner. In ancient Greece, music was an inalienable part of drama and literature. In medieval universities it formed a division of the quadrivium that included also arithmetic, geometry and astronomy. In modern times, music lost this intimate connection with sciences and liberal arts. It maintained its proud independence until the middle of the 20th century when the avant-garde brought music out of its isolation into the condominium of MIXED MEDIA. The slogan of total music was launched, and the once exclusive art became (at various HAPPENINGS) an action to be performed on equal terms with conversation, consumption of food, sex, and sleep.

Performing musicians willingly surrendered even their physical separation from the audience, and invited the collaboration of the public on the stage. Formal attire that placed musicians on a higher plane was abandoned. Since nudity became admissible in the theater, musicians followed suit, notably the cellist Charlotte Moorman. Total music, which embraces all aspects of human behavior, is a counterpart of the French *roman total*, a fictional form that combines factual reportage with unbridled fantasy.

total serialism. See SERIALISM.

Tote Stadt, Die (The Dead City). Opera by Korngold, 1920, premiered in Hamburg and Cologne simultaneously. The libretto is Germanically morbid, the ending a dramaturgical smirk; but the score is one of the most effective operas of the post-Wagner era. A widower faithful to the memory of his wife is struck by a resemblance to her in a young dancer whom he learns to love (cf. Hitchcock's film *Vertigo*). In her desire to please him the dancer thoughtlessly makes a wig of his late wife's hair. Provoked by this act of sacrilege, he strangles the woman. But welcome relief is vouchsafed to him and the spectators: the whole sequence of events was but a dream. The *Mariettalied* is the best-known opera.

Toten Augen, Die (The Dead Eyes). An opera by d'Albert, 1916, 1st performed in Dresden, quite successfully. The libretto deals with a blind woman miraculously cured by Christ. But the miracle has its disadvantage, for as she regains her sight she realizes how ugly her husband is. Disappointed, she yields her favors to a Roman centurion. Her husband kills himself, and she too commits suicide.

Totenlied (Ger.). See TODESGESANG.

Totentanz (Ger., dance of death). A morbid but widespread topos cultivated during the Middle Ages, in poetry, painting, drama, and music. It evoked the image of death dancing with its prospective victim. Even in the songs of youth, expectation of death was often the principal motive, as in *Gaudeamus igitur*, warning the young to enjoy life before "nos habebit humus" (the earth will have us). Among the many works that quote the Dies Irae chant (from the Roman Catholic Requiem) is the work described in the next entry. Other pieces with a connection to the Totentanz topos are the final confrontation between Don Giovanni and the Commendatore in Mozart's opera; Schubert's lied *Tod und das Mädchen*, Saint-Saëns's *Danse macabre*, Rachmaninoff's *Isle of the Dead*, and the many settings and evocations of the poet Federico García Lorca.

Totentanz. Work for piano and orch. by Liszt, 1865, 1st performed in the Hague; it is also known under the French name *Danse macabre*. Liszt was inspired by the frescos in the cemetery of the town of Pisa, which represent Death mowing down indiscriminately both the rich and the poor, the old and the young. Throughout the composition the ominous strains of the Dies Irae chant are heard.

touch. 1. The method and manner of applying the fingers to the keys of keyboard instruments. 2. The amount and kind of resistance overcome by the fingers in depressing the kcys of an organ or piano; as a *heavy, light,* or *elastic* touch.

touche (Fr.). Fingerboard. *Sur la touche,* in string playing, bow on or near the fingerboard.

toucher (Fr., touch). Play a keyboard, with attention to the proper use of the fingers, as in Couperin's *L'Art de toucher le clavecin* (1716).

tourbillonant (Fr.). As if in a whirlwind.

tournebout (Fr.). CRUMHORN.

Tower, Joan (Peabody), American composer of instrumental music, pianist, and teacher; b. New Rochelle, N.Y., Sept. 6, 1938. She took courses in composition with Brant and Calabro and studied piano at Bennington (Vt.) College (B.A., 1961); completed her training with Luening, Beeson, Ussachevsky, and others at Columbia Univ. (M.A., 1964; D.M.A., 1978). In N.Y. in 1969 she cofounded the Da Capo Chamber Players, which became known for its promotion of contemporary music; she served as its pianist until 1984 and wrote many works for it. She taught at Bard College in Annandale-on-Hudson (from 1972) and was composer-in-residence of the St. Louis Sym. Orch. (1985–87). In 1976 she held a Guggenheim fellowship; held NEA fellowships in 1974, 1975, 1980, and 1984; received a Koussevitzky Foundation grant in 1982 and an American

Academy and Inst. of Arts and Letters award in 1983. In 1990 she received the Grawemeyer Award.

Tower practices different approaches to composition, but her central mode combines post-Debussy harmonic sensitivity with a Stravinskyian rhythmic freedom and drive, often producing evocative pictures of nature, not without wit. She has composed orch.l, chamber, and piano works.

Townshend, Pete(r Dennis Blandford). See WHO, THE.

Toy Symphony (*Kindersymphonie*). Toy syms. ostensibly written for children to perform were popular in the 18th century. This work, the most famous of them, was for a century and a half attributed to Haydn, but thanks to the labors of persistent musicologists it was found to be a movement in an instrumental suite by Leopold Mozart. The toys in the orch. are a rattle, a triangle, and several squeakers, to imitate the cuckoo, the quail, and the nightingale.

toye. Short piece for the virginal composed during the 16th and 17th centuries.

tract (Lat. *tractus*). A psalmodic or other biblical chant that replaces the ALLELUIA in the High Mass during penitential seasons (Lent) in the Roman Catholic liturgy.

Tragédie de Salomé, La. Sym. poem, 1907, by Florent Schmitt (b. Blâmont, Meurthe-et-Moselle, Sept. 28, 1870; d. Neuilly-sur-Seine, near Paris, Aug. 17, 1958), 1st performed in Paris. In this revision of the New Testament story, Salome throws the head of John the Baptist into the sea and the waters flow red like blood. A bolt of lightning strikes the palace and destroys it. The music dramatically illustrates these events in dark, dissonant harmonies.

tragédie lyrique (Fr.). Baroque and Classic French operas on classical subjects; the primary representatives of the genre are Lully and Rameau; Gluck also contributed to it during his activities in Paris. In the Romantic era, *drame lyrique* superseded the tragédie lyrique, as Classic subjects became rare in French opera.

Tragic Overture. Sym. overture by Brahms, 1880, 1st performed in Vienna. This is 1 of 2 such works by the composer, the other being the *Academic Festival Overture*. The *Tragic Overture* is in D minor, a tonality often having solemn and tragic connotations in romantic music. A number of commentators have exerted their verbal ingenuity to depict the music in terms of inexorable fate, sin and redemption, passion and purification, and the like—the kind of verbiage that requires no direct acquaintance with the music itself. The tragic element can easily be heard in the ominously sounding beats of the timpani and in the mighty blasts of the trombones. But there is a spirit of pastoral serenity in the 2nd theme and its development. Indeed, the overture is a diptych of contrasting moods.

Tragic Symphony (1). Mahler's 6th Sym., 1903–1905, in A minor. The tragic element is supplied in the orchestration by the inclusion of a large variety of percussion instruments, among them a hammer, whose blows seem to symbolize the end of hope. The nickname is not the composer's; the work is in 4 parts and was 1st performed in Essen, Germany, 1906.

Tragic Symphony (2). Schubert's Sym. No. 4, 1816, in C minor.

tragicamente (It.). Tragically.

Trail of the Lonesome Pine, The. Ballad by Harry Carroll, 1913, extolling the nostalgic beauty of the Blue Ridge Mountains in Virginia. Its melodic fidelity to traditional music was such that it was often taken for an authentic folk song.

trait de chant (Fr.). Melodic motion.

trait d'harmonie (Fr.). Harmonic progression.

Tramp, Tramp, Tramp, or The Prisoner's Hope. Civil War ballad by George Frederick Root, 1864. It describes the anguish of a Union soldier taken prisoner by the Confederate Army.

Trampler, Walter, eminent German-American violist and pedagogue; b. Munich, Aug. 25, 1915. He received his early musical training from his father; later enrolled at the Munich State Academy of Music; made his debut in Munich as a violinist in 1933 and in Berlin as a violist in 1935; from 1935 to 1938 he served as 1st violist in the Deutschlandsender Orch.; then emigrated to America. From 1947 to 1955 he was a member of the New Music String Quartet; also made appearances with the Yale, Emerson, Budapest, Juilliard, and Guarneri quartets and with the Beaux Arts Trio; was a member of the Chamber Music Soc. of Lincoln Center (from 1969). In 1962 he was appointed

prof. of viola and chamber music at the Juilliard School of Music in N.Y.; in 1971, was named prof. at the Yale Univ. School of Music; in 1972, became a member of the faculty at Boston Univ. One of the foremost masters of the viola, he appeared as a soloist with many of the leading orchs. of North America and Europe. He premiered works by several composers, including Henze, Berio, and Persichetti.

Tranfjädrarna (The Crane Feathers). Opera, 1957, by Sven-Erik Bäck (b. Stockholm, Sept. 16, 1919; d. there Jan. 10, 1994), from a Japanese Noh drama dealing with a bride who was really a bird. It was performed for the 1st time on Stockholm Radio.

tranquillo (It.). Tranquilly, quietly, calmly.

Transatlantic. Opera by Antheil, 1930, to his own libretto, 1st performed in Frankfurt. In it an American candidate for the presidency is searching for a suitable bride in various locales around N.Y. The tunes are jazzy, evoking the innocence of the eponymous transatlantic nation in search of elusive maturity; the divided staging with action occurring on several levels was revolutionary.

transcendental. The piano style of Liszt and his followers; so called because it surpasses the playing of former pianists and exceeds the limits of the piano by imitating the orch.

Transcendental Études. ÉTUDES D'EXECUTION TRANSCENDANTE.

transcriptions. The definition of terms such as transcription, arrangement, fantasia, and paraphrase became especially elusive during the 19th century, when every virtuoso bestowed upon the world his or her versions of other composers' music, whether strict, free, or in between, and no matter what medium the original composer had used. Perhaps the semantic distinctions made by the greatest practitioner of this art, Liszt, would be helpful. In his terminology the most literal arrangement was the *Übertragung* (note-for-note transfer from one medium to another; a vocal score). A more idiomatic transference was the *Bearbeitung* (ARRANGEMENT; a reworking of the original to fit the new medium more comfortably; Bach-Stokowski). Next in line was the more liberal *transcription* (some compositional freedom permitted; Bach-Busoni); then followed a FANTASIA (increasing structural improvisation), sometimes expanded even further (*free* or *romantic fantasia*).

Liszt liked to call an even more unrestricted type of free fantasia *reminiscences*, using selective memory to evoke the mood of the opera or sym. being recalled. (As an auxiliary category, Liszt introduced the term *illustrations* for recurring thematic allusion.) At the most extreme was the *paraphrase*, uniting any or all characteristics of the previous categories, with perhaps only a hint of the original. To indicate the publ. category of a given transcription, Liszt sometimes used the word *Klavierpartitur* (piano score). See also PARAPHRASES and ARRANGEMENTS.

Transfigured Night. VERKLÄRTE NACHT.

transient. Passing; not principal; intermediate. *Transient chord*, an intermediate chord foreign both to the key left and that reached; opposite of *pivot chord*; *transient modulation*, a temporary modulation, soon followed by a return to the original key.

transition. 1. Modulation, especially a transient one. 2. In TONIC SOL-FA, a modulation without change of mode.

translocation. By altering the intervallic structure of a given musical subject and by translocating its tonal constituents, it is possible to bring any melorhythmic figure into topological congruity with any other. The number of such changes—in which the intervallic unit is a semitone and the rhythmic unit is the smallest note value occurring in the subjects—will indicate the degree of affinity existing between such 2 subjects. In isometric melodies the index of rhythmic exchangeability will obviously be zero, so that only the index of the necessary intervallic changes measured by the number of semitones need be considered. In isotonal pairs only the rhythmic changes remain to be computed. The smaller the number of alterations required to transform the melorhythmic outline of one subject into that of another, the greater is the intrinsic similarity between the 2.

A cursive statistical survey indicates that virtually all principal leading motives in Wagner's music dramas are closely related. Thus we find that it requires but a few changes of intervals and rhythms to transmute the motive of erotic love in *Tristan und Isolde* to that of faith in Parsifal. The main motives of most tone poems of R. Strauss are also topologically similar, no matter what the programmatic design is. On the other hand the index of interchangeability of dodecaphonic tone rows is extremely high, characteristic of the numerical diversity of dodecaphonic themes. This result should not be surprising, for the works of Wagner and Strauss

(to take only these 2 composers as examples) are based on triadic formations with auxiliary chromatic notes, whereas serial music does not depend on tonality and the intervallic structure in the serial idiom is free of all restrictions.

A composer writing in any modern style, whether serial or nonserial, is in a position of selecting any desired table of approximations of main subjects in relation to intervallic, melodic, metric, and rhythmic parameters, planning in advance such incidental factors as repetition of thematic notes, lipogrammatic omissions, and thus achieving any degree of variety. Aleatory methods can be limited in advance by numerical parameters, thus imparting to the music an individual physiognomy. Intuition, being an aleatory mental state, may also enter this preliminary outline of substantive parameters. Ernst Krenek has pointed out that the German word *Einfall* (inspiration) connotes in its etymology a falling in as though by chance. The word *inspiration* itself has an aleatory connotation: the drawing in of breath. Once such a tabulation is set up, the composer can proceed to operate the field of desirable translocations, the topology of form, the degree of thematic cohesion or dispersion, etc. Thus the techniques of translocation and its cognate, that of computation of similarities, possess practical validity from both the analytical and synthetical viewpoints. A study of translocations may eventually become an integral branch of musical didactics in perfecting the skill of manipulating and coordinating a multiplicity of technical factors.

transpose. Perform or write out a composition in a different key than written.

Transposed Heads, The. Opera, 1954, by Peggy Glanville-Hicks (b. Melbourne, Dec. 29, 1912; d. Sydney, June 25, 1990), to her own libretto drawn from Thomas Mann's novel. It was 1st performed in Louisville, Ky. A Hindu woman, unsure of her choice between her genius of a husband and her handsome simpleton lover, proposes that they decapitate themselves and transpose their heads to their respective torsos. Bewildered by the resulting severed heads and decapitated torsos, she commits suicide. The score is rhythmically nervous and understandably dissonant.

transposing instruments. 1. Instruments whose natural scale is always written in C major, regardless of the concert pitch. Thus, for a clarinet in B♭, a written C-major scale will sound like the instrument's natural scale of B-flat major; to get the concert (sounding) scale of C major the music will have to be written in D major. 2. Instruments having some device by which the action or strings can be shifted so that higher or lower tones are produced than when they are in the normal position. Irving Berlin had a piano of this type, as he could only play in the natural key of F-sharp.

transposition. 1. Performance or notation of a composition in a higher or lower key than the original, in order to adjust to the range of an individual's vocal range or a more convenient and more effective tonality in an instrumental work. Most transpositions are made in song anthologies, usually from the original setting for a high voice to a lower range. Any singer can transpose a tune without training, but piano accompanists have to be quite adroit technically and musically to transpose a piece at sight. Transposing on sight can be especially difficult for persons with PERFECT PITCH; it is perhaps the only occasion when that particular talent is a curse. 2. One of 3 standard techniques in 12-note composition (retrograde, inversion, transposition).

transverse flute. The generic name for the cross FLUTE, held perpendicular to the nose and across the lips, as opposed to the vertical flute (e.g., recorder).

traps (trap set). Colloquial term for the jazz drum set.

traquenard (Fr.). A fast galop in 4/4 time with dotted rhythms; included in some Baroque instrumental suites.

trascinando (It.). Drawn out heavily; dragging, sluggishly.

trasporto, con (It.). With transport, ecstatically.

trattenuto (*tratto*; It.). Held back, drawn out, delayed.

Trauermarsch (Ger.). Funeral march.

Trauermusik (Ger.). Funeral music.

Trauersinfonie (Mourning Sym.). Haydn's Sym. No. 44, 1772, in E minor.

Träumerei (Ger., reverie). A quintessentially Romantic piano piece by Schumann, 1838, from his cycle of 14 character pieces entitled *Kinderszenen*, op. 15. The piece is in the Romantic key of F major, with hints of related major and minor keys; it was selected as a memorial to be played by Soviet military bands in place of the funeral march at the ceremonies for Soviet soldiers killed in World War II.

träumerisch (Ger.). Dreamy.

traurig (Ger.). Sad, melancholy.

Trautonium. Electronic musical instrument introduced by the German electrical engineer Friedrich Trautwein in 1930; Hindemith composed music for it.

Travers, Mary. See YARROW, PETER.

Traversflöte (Ger.). The cross flute; or a 4' organ stop resembling it in timbre.

travesty. See TROUSER ROLE.

Traviata, La. Opera by Verdi, 1853, 1st produced in Venice. The libretto is drawn from the French play *La Dame aux camelias* by Alexandre Dumas *fils*. The title is nearly untranslatable; while some choose "The Wayward One," this obviates the morally important point that the heroine was not wanton by nature; perhaps a more accurate if unwieldy translation is "The Woman Diverted from the Righteous Way" or "The Woman Led Astray." La Traviata is Violetta, a courtesan. She meets a dashing gentleman, Alfredo, who proclaims his ardent love for her. They take lodgings together near Paris without benefit of clergy. Alfredo's father Germont is dismayed by his son's misalliance and begs Violetta to let him go. She complies and contrives a way to end her affair with Alfredo. But, after a period of anger, he hears of her illness; he rushes to her side, finding her dying of consumption. After some bittersweet vocalizing and lots of guilt on Alfredo and Germont's part, Violetta dies in her lover's arms. (One wonders what librettists would have done if they had known that tuberculosis was contagious.)

La Traviata is one of the most tuneful of Verdi's operas. There is a famous scene of drinking a toast, the BRINDISI *Libiamo*; there are many poignant arias and duets. The subject of the opera shocked the sensibilities of some mid-19th-century operagoers. The London papers expressed outrage that "the ladies of the aristocracy" should be allowed to attend a production "to see an innocent young lady impersonate the heroine of an infamous French novel who varies her prostitution by a frantic passion." But *La Traviata* survived, an unusually contemporary opera for its composer; only *Stiffelio* (1850) takes place in Verdi's historical present; it was the major inspiration for VERISMO in general and Puccini's operas specifically.

tre (It.). Three. *A tre*, for 3 voices or instruments; *a tre voci*, for (in) 3 parts; *tre corde*, in piano playing, release soft pedal completely.

Treble. Voice with a soprano range, often sung by boys. Viol; soprano. *Treble clef*, the *G* clef; *treble recorder*, in U.K., the alto recorder in F; *treble viol*, soprano VIOLA DA GAMBA.

trecento. Italian designation for the 1300s (14th century), its art, literature, and music. Specifically, it refers to the period of polyphonic music from *c.* 1325 into the early 15th century. The style is characterized by efflorescent secular music with texts in the vernacular. The most important forms of the trecento are MADRIGAL and CACCIA; the best-known composers are Landini and Jacopo da Bologna.

Treemonisha. Opera, 1911, by S. Joplin, describing the life of an abandoned black baby girl found under a tree by a compassionate woman named Monisha and therefore christened Monisha of the Tree, or Treemonisha. It was performed in concert form in 1915, 2 years before Joplin's death; it did not receive its 1st stage performance until May 23, 1975 in Houston, orchestrated and conducted by Gunther Schuller.

Trees. Semiclassical song by Oscar Rasbach (1888–1975) to Joyce Kilmer's dendrological poem, which concludes that only God can make a tree. Despite awkward musical prosody and poorly managed tessitura, this song was once enormously popular on the concert circuit.

Tregian, Francis, English musician; b. 1574; d. London, 1619. He was a recusant and fled England to escape persecution; was attached to Catholic dignitaries in Douai and in Rome. Returning to England to settle his father's estate, he was convicted in 1609, remaining in prison until his death. His significance for English music lies in the fact that he was the scribe of the *Fitzwilliam Virginal Book* (ed. by J. Fuller Maitland and W. B. Squire, London and Leipzig, 1894–99) and of 2 MSS containing more than 2,000 motets, madrigals, etc., some of them of his own composition.

treibend (Ger.). Urging, hastening.

Treigle, Norman, remarkable American bass-baritone; b. New Orleans, Mar. 6, 1927; d. there, Feb. 16, 1975. He sang in a church choir as a child; upon graduation from high school in 1943 he served in the navy. After 2 years in service he returned to New Orleans and studied voice with Elizabeth Wood; made his debut in 1947 with the New Orleans Opera as Lodovico in *Otello*. He then joined the N.Y. City Opera, making his debut there in 1953 as Colline in *La Bohème*; he remained with the company for 20 years, establishing himself as a favorite with the public. Among his most successful roles were Figaro in *The Marriage of Figaro*, Don Giovanni, Boito's Mefistofele, and Boris Godunov; he also sang in modern operas, including the leading parts in the world premieres of 3 operas by Carlisle Floyd: *The Passion of Jonathan Wade* (N.Y., 1962), *The Sojourner and Mollie Sinclair* (Raleigh, NC, 1963), and *Markheim* (New Orleans, 1966). Treigle's other parts in contemporary operas were the title role in Dallapiccola's *The Prisoner* and that of the grandfather in Copland's *The Tender Land*. His untimely death, from an overdose of sleeping pills, deprived the American musical theater of one of its finest talents.

tremblement (Fr., trembling). Obsolete term for trill.

tremolo (It., quivering, fluttering). A popular embellishment consisting of a repeated alternation of 2 notes in rapid tempo, once regarded as a powerful device to produce dramatic tension; not synonymous with VIBRATO. In singing, a tremulous, somewhat unsteady tone is used; on bowed instruments the effect is produced by the very rapid alternation of down-bow and up-bow, written:

On a piano rapid alternation of the tones of a dyad or more serves the purpose. In his preface to the dramatic madrigal *Il combattimento di Tancredi e Clorinda*, Monteverdi describes the tremolo as the most expressive dynamic device of the *stile concitato*, illustrating as it does Tancred's unwitting fatal wounding of his beloved, Clorinda. The use of the tremolo for dramatic effect reached its greatest popularity in the 19th century, particularly in opera. Later it degenerated into melodramatic effect and soon vanished from serious composition altogether, except for comical effects. 2. The effect produced by the *tremolo stop*, or *tremulant* (organ).

tremoloso (It.). With a tremulous, fluttering effect.

tremulant. The tremolo stop in an organ.

trepak. A Russian dance in fast duple time.

très (Fr.). Very; *molto.*

Tretyakov, Viktor (Viktorovich), noted Russian violinist; b. Krasnoyarsk, Oct. 17, 1946. He studied at the Irkutsk Music School as a child, stoutly braving the Siberian cold; then moved to a more temperate climate in Moscow, where he studied at the Central Music School with Yury Yankelevich (from 1959), continuing with him at the Cons. (graduated, 1970) and as a postgraduate student. In 1966 he won the Tchaikovsky Competition, which automatically lifted him to the upper layers of the violinistic firmament, with applause-rich tours in Russia and later the enviable European and American engagements. A typical product of the Russian school of violin playing, Tretyakov combines the expected virtuosity in technical resources with a diffuse lyricism touched with melancholy in the Romantic repertoire.

triad. A chord consisting of 3 different notes (pitch classes); in tonal music, a chord made up of a given tone (the root), the note a 3rd above the root, and the note a 5th above the root, within the chosen scale. Modern music theory recognizes 4 types of triads: a *major triad*, consisting of a major 3rd superimposed by a minor (i.e., a perfect 5th above the root); a *minor triad*, consisting of a minor 3rd topped by a major 3rd (also a perfect 5th above the root); a *diminished triad*, which consists of 2 minor 3rds, one on top of the other (i.e., a diminished 5th above the root); and an *augmented triad*, comprising 2 conjunct major 3rds (the higher being an augmented 5th above the root). The major and minor triads are fundamental to the determination of a key; the diminished triad is regarded as a discord, since it contains a diminished 5th; the augmented triad is also a discord, because it contains an augmented 5th even though the augmented 5th is enharmonically equivalent to a minor 6th. In the 20th century some musicians attempted to deprive the triads of their specific connotations as consisting of 2 3rds and extended the notion of a triad to any chord containing 3 notes, even chromatically congested 3 notes; analogously, a group of 2 notes was described as a dyad.

triadic modulation. A common way to change keys in the middle of a piece without using the CIRCLE OF FIFTHS; in brief, a triad that belongs to both the keys that the music is in and modulating toward is chosen as a PIVOT CHORD and the change is accomplished by a kind of tonal overlapping or segue. In some cases only a note of the pivot chord need be shared by both keys. See also MODULATION.

Trial of Lucullus, The. Opera by Sessions, 1947, 1st performed in Berkeley, Calif. The libretto, by Brecht, was originally intended for a radio play as an allegorical indictment of Hitler. The Roman general Lucullus is dead, but before entering the Elysian Fields he must defend himself against the accusations of being a mass murderer. The jury is not impressed by his recital of military victories and unanimously condemns him. An adaptation of the same text was set by Dessau in German (1951).

triangle. A steel rod bent into triangular shape, with one corner left slightly open; it is struck with a metal wand.

trias (Lat., trinity). In old German treatises, the triad. *Trias harmonica major*, major triad; *trias harmonica minor*, minor triad.

tricesimorprimal temperament. A sesquipedalian if pedantically correct name for the microtonal division of the octave into 31 equal intervals, proposed by the 17th-century Dutch astronomer Christiaan Huygens, who was trying to find a way to use equal temperament to achieve something like JUST INTONATION. The system was championed by Adriaan Fokker in the 20th century and used in some works by Dutch composers.

trichord. A set of 3 pitch classes, usually a segment of a 12-note set.

trichord piano. One having 3 strings (unisons) to each tone throughout the greater part of its compass.

tricinium (Lat.). In 16th-century Germany, a 3-part vocal piece, as opposed to the usual piece for 4 (or more) parts. Collections of secular, sacred, and instrumental tricinia were published, primarily for didactic purposes.

tricotet. A type of melody improvised, sung, danced, and played on instruments by minstrels in the Middle Ages. It was completely free in form, rhythm, and character. French Baroque composers gave the title *tricotet* to fanciful sections of instrumental suites.

trill (Ger. *Triller*; It. *trillo*; Fr. *trille*). A melodic embellishment consisting of the even and rapid alternation of 2 tones a major or minor 2nd apart; the lower tone is the *principal note* (the 1 being ornamented), the higher tone the *auxiliary note* (the ornamenting one). The practice of trilling was cultivated in France in the 17th century and was sometimes picturesquely described as TREMBLEMENT, translated into English as SHAKE.

A graphic symbol for a trill is a wavy line, sometimes extending according to the duration desired; the abbrev. *tr* is also used. In modern instrumental writing the trill invariably begins on the principal note, but in the Baroque period the trill often began on the auxiliary note; interpretation of trill performance practice can differ from scholar to scholar and source to source. Vocal trilling now seems to emerge from the VIBRATO technique in constant use by opera singers; the technical danger is that one not be used when the other is called for.

trilletta (It.). Short trill.

trillo caprino (It.). GOAT'S TRILL.

Trinklied (Ger.). Drinking song; BRINDISI.

trio (It.). 1. A generic term for a composition employing 3 instruments or (less often) 3 vocal parts. The so-called piano trio is scored for violin, cello, and piano. A trio set for violin, viola, and cello is usually called a string trio; Beethoven wrote 5 such works. Haydn wrote a number of trios for 2 violins and cello and more than 100 baryton trios. Examples of the piano trio include those of Beethoven, Schumann, Mendelssohn, Brahms, and Tchaikovsky. Mixed trios are also found, such as those for piano, clarinet, and cello written by Mozart and Khatchaturian. 2. In minuets, marches, ragtime, etc., a 2nd dance or march, after which the 1st is repeated; sometimes the key is changed; in the Baroque, also known as an ALTERNATIVO. The term *trio* for the central (2nd) section of a Classic or Romantic sym. minuet or scherzo is a relic of the Baroque era, when it might actually be written for 3 instruments, such as 2 oboes and bassoon, or 2 horns and bassoon (cf. the finale of Bach's *Brandenburg Concerto No. 1*).

trio d'anches. Work for woodwind trio.

trio sonata. Important Baroque chamber music genre, written in 3 parts, the 2 upper (melody) parts supported by a basso continuo part realized by 2 instruments; hence the contradiction of seeing 4 persons perform a "sound piece for 3." The upper parts were usually played by violins, flutes, and/or oboes; the lower parts by cello or bassoon playing the bassline and harpsichord, the latter supplying the harmonic skeleton of the work. In pre-Classic music the upper parts were often taken over by viols and/or cornettos, and the lower parts by a viola da gamba and harpsichord. There are specimens of trio sonatas written for a considerably larger ensemble, but even in such cases the texture is in 3 principal parts; to emphasize this peculiarity the composer often added the words *a tre*. The trio sonata borrows from other standard genres structurally: the SONATA DA CHIESA, with its slow-fast-slow-fast arrangement; and SONATA DA CAMERA, with suite-like dance movements. Handel wrote 28 trio sonatas, including 6 scored for 2 oboes and bass; Vivaldi wrote 12; Bach's most famous trio sonata is in his *Musikalisches Opfer*, which he wrote for Frederick the Great. Toward the middle of the 18th century, trio sonatas circuitously evolved into piano trios (violin, cello, piano), with the piano part as *cembalo redivivus*, not only filling in the harmony but having an independent role melodically and contrapuntally, thus replacing one of the melody parts.

Triole (Ger.; Fr. *triolet*). Triplet.

trionfale (It.). Triumphal.

trionfante (It.). Triumphant.

Trionfi. Fortuitous triptych of scene cantatas by Orff, comprising *Carmina Burana, Catulli Carmina*, and *Trionfo di Afrodite*.

Trionfo dell'onore, Il (Triumph of Honor). Opera by A. Scarlatti, 1718, 1st performed in Naples. The antihero of the opera courts 2 ladies at once. When the honest suitor of 1 of them nicks him in a duel, he decides to marry the unattached lady. The opera is historically important as one of the earliest examples of the Neapolitan opera buffa.

Trionfo di Afrodite (The Triumph of Aphrodite). Scenic cantata by Orff, 1953, to his own libretto derived from Greek and Latin poems, 1st performed in Milan. In lieu of a dramatic plot, the work portrays the initiation into marriage according to the sacred rites of Aphrodite. The idiom is monodic, austere, and stylistically formalized so as to suggest an archaic ambience. This work is the 3rd part of the triptych *Trionfi*.

Trip to Chinatown, A. Musical farce by Percy Gaunt, 1893. The thin plot recounts a trip to San Francisco's Chinatown by a couple. The songs in the original score were very popular, including *The Bowery* and *Reuben, Reuben*. Many new songs were interpolated into the show during its run, including Charles Harris's classic *After the Ball*.

triple concerto. Concerto for 3 solo instruments and orch.

triple counterpoint. See COUNTERPOINT.

triple dot. Three dots placed to the right of a note head, augmenting its duration by 1/2 + 1/2(1/2) + 1/2 (1/2)(1/2) its value, each subsequent dot adding half the value of the preceding dot. Thus, a half note with a triple dot equals 1/2 + 1/4 + 1/8 + 1/16 = 15/16 (of a whole note). Triple dots are rare, as they can be translated into tied notes readily.

triple time. Meter containing 3 units, as in 3/4 or 3/8.

triple-croche (Fr.). Thirty-second note.

triplet. A group of 3 equal notes to be performed in the time of 2 notes of like value in the established rhythm; the most common, the 8th-note triplet, is written:

If quarter-note or half-note triplets are called for, a square bracket must be used, as follows:

triplum (Lat.). The 2nd added voice in medieval organum, resulting in a 3-part texture of cantus firmus (tenor), duplum, and triplum (the highest). The term is also used for medieval compositions in 3 voices without a cantus firmus.

triskaidekaphobia (from Grk. *tris + kai + deka + phobos*, fear of 13). Among musicians, Rossini and Schoenberg possessed it to an extreme degree. In addition to triskaidekaphobia, Rossini was afraid of Fridays; he died on Nov. 13, 1868, a Friday. Schoenberg was mystical about the sinister meaning of 13 in his own life; he was born on the 13th of the month and regarded it as an ill omen. Even in numbering bars in his compositions, he systematically omitted number 13. When he began to compose his opera *Moses und Aaron*, he realized that the number of letters in the title was 13. To exorcise triskaidekaphobia, he removed the 2nd "a" and came up with "Aron." He was seriously upset when he reached his 76th birthday, realizing that 7 plus 6 equals 13. He died on July 13, 1951, 13 minutes before midnight.

Tristan chord. A designation for the chord, comprising F–B–D♯–G♯, which occurs in the 2nd measure of the prelude to Wagner's *Tristan und Isolde*. To resolve, the upper voice ascends chromatically (G♯–A–A♯–B); the alto and bass descend chromatically (D♯–D♮; F–E); and the tenor drops a minor 3rd down (B–G♯). Thus the dominant-7th chord of the key of A is formed, establishing the Tristanesque connection with the opening note of the piece, which is A. The chord and its uncertain resolution are fundamental to melodic and harmonic transformations of the principal leading motives of the entire score. So unusual was it for the music of the middle of the 19th century that Wagnerophiles built a whole mystique about it in the theory of chromatic harmony. Even though the Tristan chord is closely associated with Wagnerian harmony, an almost identical anticipation of it is found in a transitional passage in the piano part of a little known song by Liszt. But then, the musical imaginations of Liszt and Wagner often ran in parallel lines. The notorious Wagnerophobe, the critic Hanslick, said that the chromaticism of the prelude reminded him of an old Italian painting representing a martyr whose intestines are being slowly unwound from his body on a reel.

Tristan und Isolde. Opera by Wagner, 1865, to his own libretto, 1st performed in Munich. The story is derived from an ancient Cornish legend. King Mark of Cornwall sends his nephew Tristan to fetch his chosen bride Isolde, a princess of Ireland. During a sea voyage, Isolde falls in love with Tristan so deeply that only death can save her from disgrace. She asks her lady attendant to give her poison, but she prepares a love potion instead. After drinking it both Tristan and Isolde become consumed with passion. Isolde marries Mark but continues to keep secret trysts with Tristan; their love duet is surpassingly moving in its chromatic sensuousness. Tristan, wounded by the King's henchman, is taken to his castle in Brittany. Isolde comes to visit him; a shepherd plays a tune on his wooden trumpet which is a signal that Isolde's ship is approaching. Tristan, still bleeding from his wound, rushes to meet her and expires lovingly. The concluding scene is Isolde's own *Liebestod* (love death), expressing a mystical belief that the deepest light of love can be fulfilled only in the deepest night of death.

Tristan und Isolde is the apotheosis of Wagner's system of leitmotivs. Wagner's annotators have painstakingly compiled the themes of love, death, day and night, love potion, and of soul states such as fidelity, suspicion, exaltation, impatience, and malediction. *Tristan und Isolde* is couched in a highly chromaticized idiom. The Vienna Opera House accepted the opera for performance, but after 53 rehearsals canceled the production. For some modernists the prelude to *Tristan und Isolde* is a prophetic vision of atonality; Berg inserted its opening measures in his atonal (and love-subsumed) *Lyric Suite*. On the other hand Debussy, whose attitude toward Wagner was ambivalent, made fun of the prelude in his whimsical *Golliwog's Cakewalk*.

Wagner chose to give the name Isolde to his illegitimate daughter born to him and Cosima von Bülow in Apr. 1865; during this time, Cosima's husband, Hans von Bülow, was conducting the strenuous rehearsals of *Tristan und Isolde*.

Tristano, Lennie (Leonard Joseph), famous American jazz pianist and teacher; b. Chicago, Mar. 19, 1919; d. N.Y., Nov. 18, 1978. He became blind in childhood but did not allow this handicap to deflect him from a study of music; he attended the American Cons. of Music in Chicago (B.Mus., 1943); after performing in Chicago clubs he settled in N.Y. in 1946; attracted wide notice with his own sextet in 1947; ran his own jazz school (1951–56) and then taught privately; also made occasional appearances as a performer, touring Europe in 1965 and the U.S. in 1968. He was a master at piano improvisations.

triste (Fr.). Sad, wistful (Sibelius, *Valse triste*).

tristo, -a (It.). In a style expressive of sadness or melancholy.

tritone. The interval of the augmented 4th, containing 3 consecutive whole tones, as F to B, or D to G-sharp; it is sometimes notated as a diminished 5th (e.g., F to C-flat, or D to A-flat). It was a forbidden progression in the building of tetrachords. Medieval theorists described the tritone as the DIABOLUS IN MUSICA (devil of music) and ejected melodic progressions using it from the body of church music wherever possible; while the ecclesiastical modes had the potential for a melodic tritone, *musica ficta* were employed automatically to avoid this interval. In German schools in Bach's time a music student who inadvertently made use of the augmented 4th was punished in class by a rattan blow on the knuckles of the hand.

The earliest suggestion that the use of the tritone may not be a *peccatum mortale* was made by Ramos de Pareja in

Musica practica (1482), but his leniency received little approbation. One of Bach's chorales begins with 3 whole tones in succession, to the words, "O schwerer Gang" (Oh, difficult step). It was in the natural course of events that the stone rejected by the medieval builders should become the cornerstone of modern music, in all its principal aspects—polytonality, atonality, and dodecaphony. The importance of the tritone is derived from the very quality that disenfranchised it before, namely its incompatibility with the tonic-dominant complex.

Two major triads at the distance of a tritone formed the bitonal *Parisian chord* (also called the *Petrouchka* chord) so popular in the 1st quarter of the century; complementary hexachords in major keys with tonics distanced by a tritone redound to the formation of a symmetrical 12-tone row; a series of intervals diminishing by a semitone beginning with a major 6th and ending with its inversion, the minor 3rd, forms a bitonal major chord with tonics at a tritone's distance; a chord containing all eleven different intervals is encompassed by 5 octaves and a tritone from the lowest to the highest note.

Trittico, Il (Triptych). A set of short operas by Puccini, 1918, premiered in its entirety at the Metropolitan Opera, N.Y. There is something for everyone in *Il Trittico*: verismo (*Il Tabarro*), sentimentality (*Suor Angelica*), and farce (*Gianni Schicchi*).

Trittico Botticelliano. Suite by Respighi, 1927, for chamber orch., premiered in Vienna. The 3 pieces focus on paintings by the great Florentine painter Botticelli (*c.* 1444–1510): *Spring, Adoration of the Magi*, and *The Birth of Venus*.

triumph cornet. Military cornet in B♭ with an especially brilliant tone; invented by Vaclav Červeny in 1862.

Triumph of Bacchus, The. Opera-ballet by Dargomyzhsky, 1867, 1st produced in Moscow. The libretto is based on a Pushkin poem that glorifies Bacchus as the god of wine and fertility. The music is strikingly reminiscent of Glinka's *Ruslan and Ludmila*.

Triumph of St. Joan, The, or The Trial at Rouen. Opera by Norman Dello Joio. The plot is the familiar one, in which the French maiden warrior is captured, tried and sentenced, and executed, but not without a great wave of spirituality and angelic conversation. What is far more complicated is this work's history. A Dello Joio opera entitled

The Triumph of St. Joan was premiered in Bronxville, N.Y. in 1950; he took some of the music and created *The Triumph of St. Joan Sym.* (which he at 1st entitled *Seraphic Dialogue)* the following year. In 1956 a new opera on the same subject was premiered on NBC Television under the title *The Trial at Rouen.* Finally, in 1959 the N.Y. Opera gave the 1st performance of a 2nd opera called *The Triumph of St. Joan,* but with new music (making it his 3rd Joan of Arc opera). In Dello Joio's eyes, there was no stopping the saint from Orléans.

trochee. In prosody, a foot consisting of one long (accented) and one short (unaccented) beat. In musical metrics, a trochaic meter would correspond to a leisurely waltz without accented upbeat.

Troilus and Cressida. Opera by Walton, 1954, after Chaucer (not Shakespeare), premiered in London. The story recounts the tragic love story between the Trojan prince Troilus and Cressida. When Troy is captured by the Greeks, Troilus is slain and Cressida is taken to the Greek camp as a slave; in desperation she stabs herself to death. In this work Walton succeeds in matching the classical theme with a dramatic modernistic technique.

Trois morceaux en forme de poire (Three pieces in the shape of a pear). A set of pieces for piano, 4-hands by Satie, 1903, written as a rebuttal to Debussy's reproach that his music lacked form. A color picture of a pear appeared on the title page of the published edition. Of course there are more than 3 pieces.

Trois petits liturgies de la Présence Divine. A work by Messiaen, 1945, scored for 18 sopranos, celesta, vibraphone, maracas, gong, tam-tam, piano, Ondes Martenot, and string orch. The text is drawn from religious writings of St. Paul, St. Thomas, the Apocalypse, and the Song of Songs, as well as from scientific writings in medicine, botany, geology, and astronomy. It was 1st performed in Paris.

Trois Véritables Préludes flasques (pour un chien) (3 Truly Flabby Preludes for a Dog). A piano suite by Satie, 1912, in which the title almost overwhelms the music. The adjective *flabby* is truly ill-suited to the music; perhaps Satie wanted a nonsensical rhyme for the alliterative "masques et bergamasques" from Verlaine's *Clair de lune,* so beloved of the French avant-garde; or perhaps the dog just liked preludes prepared in such a manner.

trois-quatre (Fr.). Three-quarter (waltz) time.

trojnice. Croatian triple flute, with 1 drone (left tube) and 2 playing tubes (melody on the right, secondary part in the middle).

Trolley Song, The. Song by Hugh Martin, 1944, for the musical film *Meet Me in St. Louis,* with an imitation of the jangling sound of the trolley car built in.

tromba (It.). Trumpet. *Tromba da tirarsi,* obs. for slide trumpet; *tromba spezzata,* slide trumpet.

tromba marina (It., trumpet marine; Ger. *Trumscheit;* Fr. *trompette marine*). A bowed monochord, with a single string stretched over a very long and narrow wooden box. The string was touched rather than stopped by the thumb, resulting in a long series of harmonics. The tromba marina dates from at least the 12th century, and may have been plucked rather than bowed at 1st. At one point, there was a 2nd string added (even more on occasion); but by the Baroque it was once again a monochord. During this period the body achieved a slightly more triangular shape, with a flared bottom and thinner neck; more spectacularly, instruments were built to reach 6 or 7 feet in height; the increased size amplified the instrument's tendency to buzz, and some makers invented devices to curb it. A variant added sympathetic brass strings for greater resonance.

For many centuries the instrument functioned as a monochord, useful in acoustic experiments with harmonics (e.g., Glarean's *Dodecachordon*); it was also popular with street musicians. The tromba marina seems to have become obsolete by the Classic period, although acoustically minded instrumental builders have experimented with the concept in recent years. Supposedly the instrument was used in convents, hence the name *Nonnengeige* (nun's fiddle). The seemingly absurd name for this bowed monochord is explained in part by its playing of the harmonic series, just as the natural trumpet did; presumably expert players could get around the string quickly and accurately enough to be comparable, especially without the vagaries of playing natural brass instruments. But "marina" remains a mystery, with no convincing explanation to date.

trombetta (It.). Small trumpet; mentioned in Dante's *Divina commedia.*

trombone (from It. *tromba + one*, big trumpet; Ger. *Posaune*). The tenor instrument of the brass group, pitched below the trumpet and horn, and above the (bass) tuba. The trombone is the only standard orch. instrument that utilizes a sliding tube (i.e., slide) to change pitch, rather than a shift of a finger, the closing or opening of a hole, or the pushing or releasing of a valve key. The trombonist draws the slide in or out, which changes the side of the tube that air travels through to produce notes. The more extended the slide, the larger the tube and therefore the lower the note; the opposite effect is produced by drawing the slide in toward the player; hence the instrument's colloquial name of slide trombone. Like for other brass instruments, manipulation of the lips replaces the reeds of woodwind instruments and determines the harmonic being used at any one time to generate the pitch.

The trombone is one of the oldest Western brass instruments, dating to the period when it was known as the SACKBUT. It has developed strong associations with things apocalyptic or hellish. No orch.l instrument can sound the Dies Irae more ominously. The trombone announces in doom-laden tones the entrance of the statue of the Commendatore in *Don Giovanni*, summoning the profligate protagonist to his own last supper. But the trombone can sound in triumph; Beethoven reserves the appearance of the trombone in his 5th Sym. for the glorious finale.

The range of the tenor trombone, the one most often used in the orch., is from E below the bass clef to C an octave above middle C (E_0 to c^2); the alto trombone is tuned a perfect 5th above, the bass a 4th lower. There is also a double trombone in B♭/F, in effect a tenor with an "F attachment" to shift to the bass range. Sometimes a pedal pump is attached to help the player to blow. R. Strauss makes use of it in the score of *Elektra*, as does Varèse in the score of *Arcana*.

Trommel (Ger.). Drum.

trompe de chasse (Fr.). A natural horn used for hunting calls.

trompette (Fr.). Trumpet. *Trompette à coulisse*, slide trumpet; *trompette à pistons*, a valve trumpet with pistons; *trompette marine*, TROMBA MARINA.

tronco, -a (It.). Cut off short; stopped abruptly.

trop (Fr.). Too, too much (as in amount), e.g., *pas trop vite*, not too fast.

16th-century trombone players

troparion. Byzantine hymn in its simplest form. Troparia were usually inserted between verses of psalms; the genre later evolved into the KONTAKION.

trope. In medieval chant liturgy, a musical insertion into any established piece, be it taken from the Ordinary, the Proprium, or the Divine Office. Originally the term applied to rhetorical figures of speech which Quintilian defined as "verbi vel sermonis a propria significatione in aliam mutatio" (a change from the proper meaning of a word into another). Initially these took the form of melismas, sometimes of great length; later these melismas had words fitted to them, creating the texted trope (e.g., the Kyrie *orbis factor*). Other tropes were dramatic in tone, leading to the liturgical drama (e.g., the Easter trope *Quem queritis*, dating to at least the 10th century). In the course of time the music of the tropes annexed all kinds of intrusive modalities, even secular tunes. This proliferation of unorthodox tropes and the supposed melismatic pollution of Gregorian chant caused the Council of Trent, held in the middle of the 16th century, to proscribe all such usages, allowing only those melodic figures that had become firmly ingrained into traditional ecclesiastical chants.

troppo (It.). Too; too much. *Allegro, ma non troppo*, fast, but not too much (fast).

Troqueurs, Les (The Tricksters). Opéra-comique, 1753, by Antoine Dauvergne (b.. Moulins, Oct. 3, 1713; d. Lyons, Feb. 11, 1797), 1st performed in Paris. Two young men try to outwit their girl companions who in turn outwit them by arousing unjustified jealousy. The piece is a trifle, but it made history as the opening of the famous literary and aesthetic squabble known as the GUERRE DES BOUFFONS. *Les Troqueurs* was the response of the nationalistic group of French men of the theater, supported by the King himself and his mistress Marquise de Pompadour to the proponents of Italian opera. *Les Troqueurs* was supposed to prove that the French could also write intermezzos *dans le goût Italien*, as opposed to the relatively tedious lyric operas of Lully and Rameau, full of Greek mythology and opaque allegory. The success of the opera gave impetus to the composition of light, short theatrical pieces with music. However, the director of the opera house, fearful that a purely French product would not attract the public accustomed to the Italian type of entertainment, did not reveal the name of the composer until *Les Troqueurs* became a definite success.

trotzig (Ger.). Stubborn, contrary (R. Strauss, *Symphonic Domestica*).

troubadour (Prov. *trobador, tropator*, composer of tropes; It. *trovatore*). The generic name for poet-musicians and singers who roamed the areas of southern France, northern Spain, and northwestern Italy in the 11th through 13th centuries. They wrote and performed in Provençal, the *langue d'oc*. The art of the troubadours gradually penetrated into northern France where a performer became known as a *trouvère*; in Germany was known as a Minnesinger. The troubadours originated many types of popular French songs, such as alba, aubade, pastourelle, and pastorela. A considerable number of the monophonic strophic songs composed by the troubadours have been preserved; the lack of rhythmic notation has led to decades of discussion and dispute.

Trouble in Tahiti. Opera by L. Bernstein, 1952, 1st produced at Brandeis Univ. in Waltham, Mass. The composer's own libretto describes a disgruntled wife, constantly squabbling with her uncongenial husband: she proposes that they go to a movie, about a quarreling couple on the Pacific island of Tahiti, as a form of therapy. The stratagem succeeds, and they live happily . . . for a few months. The score features Bernstein's customary jazz-inflected tonality. The entire opera was incorporated into the revised *A Quiet Place* (1984).

trouser role (travesty; U.K., breeches-part; Ger. *Hosenrolle*). In opera, a part sung by a female singer performing the role of a younger man or boy, e.g., Siebel in *Faust*, Cherubino in *The Marriage of Figaro*, Octavian in *Der Rosenkavalier*, Prince Orlovsky in *Die Fledermaus*. Double transvestiture is required of the singers performing Cherubino and Octavian; each put on maidservant's clothing in order to disguise themselves from an overbearing nobleman.

Trout Quintet (*Forelle-Quintett*). Piano quintet by Schubert, 1819, in A major, with violin, viola, cello, and double bass. The penultimate (4th) movement is a set of variations on Schubert's song *Die Forelle* (The Trout, 1819).

trouvère. A class of poet-musicians and singers who flourished in the 12th and 13th centuries, originating in northern France, domain of the *langue d'oeil*, so named to describe regions that used the word *oeil* for the affirmative particle, *oui*, as distinct from the Provençal *langue d'oc* for the TROUBADOUR, for whom the affirmative was *oc*. The songs of the trouvères created a profusion of literary and musical forms, known under the collective title of *chansons de geste* (songs of deeds); they also cultivated the forms of rondeau, ballade, and virelais, motets, and the instrumental estampes. Amazingly enough, thousands of trouvère songs have been preserved in medieval chansonniers. The word itself is probably derived from the French verb *trouver* (find). Fortunately many of the songs have been preserved; like the troubadour songs, no rhythmic notation is found in the MSS, thereby opening the way for discussion and dispute.

Trovatore, Il (The Troubador). Opera by Verdi, 1853, 1st produced in Rome. In a genre known for its absurd storylines, *Il Trovatore* probably takes the prize for the most ludicrous libretto in the history of opera; but the score contains some of Verdi's finest inventions, among them the celebrated *Anvil Chorus*. The troubadour Manrico leads the rebellion against the King of Aragon, whose army is commanded by Manrico's brother, the Conte di Luna. However, the brothers are not aware that they are kith and kin; to complicate matters further, they love the same woman, Leonora. (She chooses Manrico.) Enter a mysterious Gypsy woman named Azucena who tells Manrico the dreadful story that her own mother was burnt as a witch, so she decided to steal and slay the baby brother of di Luna. She informs Manrico that the baby killed was actually her own. (She doesn't mention that the other was saved, and that Manrico was that baby.)

Azucena is arrested as a spy and condemned to die the same fiery death as her mother. Manrico, who believes Azucena to be his mother, tries to save her life, but is captured by di Luna. Leonora begs di Luna to release him, and the unspeakable Count agrees provided she give herself to him. She submits, but takes a slow working poison to escape her unwelcome lover. She goes to the tower where Manrico is kept and brings him the message of his freedom. The poison begins to work, and she dies in his arms. At that moment di Luna arrives and orders Manrico executed after all. Just before she dies, Azucena reveals to di Luna that he has just executed his brother, and she dies avenged.

Troyens, Les (The Trojans). Grand opera by Berlioz, 1856–60, after the *Aeneid* of Virgil. The complete score was so long that, at Liszt's suggestion, Berlioz split it into 2 parts; only the 2nd part, *Les Troyens à Carthage*, was performed during his lifetime, in Paris (1863). The 1st part entitled *Le Prise de Troie*, was produced posthumously in Karlsruhe, Germany, 1890. While there were performances of both parts together with major cuts thereafter, the 1st uncut complete performances occurred as late as 1969 (Glasgow in Scot., London in Eng.). The libretto begins with the last days of Troy and ends with the suicide of Dido, the Queen of Carthage, after her abandonment by Aeneas. As so often happens with Berlioz's vocal works, the best known excerpt from *Les Troyens* is orch.l, namely, the *Royal Hunt and Storm* in the 2nd part, when Dido and Aeneas avoid a downpour by sheltering in a cave; the rest is mythology.

trüb(e) (Ger.).   Gloomy, dismal; sad, melancholy.

trumpet

〰〰 〰〰 〰〰 〰〰 〰〰

A brass instrument with cupped mouthpiece and small bell; the tone is brilliant, penetrating, and of great carrying power. At present the trumpet (Ger. *Trompete*; Fr. *trompette*; It. *tromba*) is a chromatic, transposing instrument in B♭ (standard or soprano trumpet) or other fundamentals, as well as upper-register trumpets (sopranino, piccolo). The sounding range of the B-flat trumpet is e⁰ to b♭² (written is f♯⁰ to c³).

In one form or another, the trumpet is one of the most ancient of human instruments; its principle, creating sound by blowing into a hollow object without the use of reeds (nor made of tusk or animal horn), finds fruition in trumpets made of conch shells, bamboo, cane, wood, bark, and ultimately metal. Its role in post-Classical Europe begins in the 8th century with the BUISINE and extends through to the natural trumpet of the 14th century; it in turn did not give way until the invention of the valve trumpet in the early 19th century. The Latin name for trumpet was *tuba*; in medieval hymns it was the "trump" of Judgment Day; however, when the Doomsday trumpet is represented in actual compositions, its part is usually given to the trombone, which is in fact a larger trumpet with an elongated body and a slide.

It is a dogma in books on orchestration that a single trumpet is equal in its sonority to the entire orch. The most obvious dramatic use of the trumpet is that of a military summons. In Beethoven's *Fidelio*, the trumpet announces the arrival of the new governor who is to establish justice. In *Carmen* the trumpet summons Don José to the barracks. In innumerable marches, operatic and orch., the trumpet sets the marching time for soldiers. But the trumpet can also be meditative and even philosophical, particularly when muted, as in *The Unanswered Question* by Charles Ives.

For centuries the trumpet was limited to natural harmonic tones and had to be tuned to the key of any work in which it was used. In order to effect a modulation to a lower key, the trumpet player had to insert extra tubing (a CROOK) into his instrument; to modulate to a higher key, the tubing had to be shortened. It was not until the 19th century that efficient trumpet keys (valves) were invented that made it possible to play an entire chromatic scale. As a result of this late discovery the trumpet parts in the works of Mozart, Haydn, and even Beethoven utilized mainly the tonic and the dominant of the principal key. Some audacious conductors revised the trumpet parts in Beethoven's syms. as Beethoven might have written them had he had a chromatic trumpet at his disposal (e.g., the beginning of the 2nd theme group in the 1st movement of the 5th Sym.), but such speculative tamperings are always dangerous and can be counterproductive to the intended purpose. Wagner wrote a part for a wooden trumpet in the 3rd act of *Tristan und Isolde*, but it is usually played by the English horn. Specially constructed trumpets are also required in Verdi's *Aida*, called, in French, *trompette thébaine* (trumpet of Thebes, the Egyptian city in which most of the action of *Aida* takes place) but in English, simply the *Aida trumpet*.

The standard type of trumpet was stabilized in the 2nd half of the 19th century, as a transposing instrument in B-flat, which sounds a major 2nd below the written note. The alto trumpet in F is used in many scores by French composers, among them *España* by Chabrier. In Germany, Russia, England, and the Netherlands the B-flat trumpet is used almost exclusively (in Germany it is in B). French and American composers increasingly used a trumpet in C, a nontransposing instrument. The trumpet plays a very important role in jazz; most jazzmen call it, with poetic nonchalance, a "horn," bringing about confusion in colloquies with classical musicians, to whom a horn is French. Some virtuoso trumpeters can overblow the range for several notes above high C. Louis Armstrong, the legendary jazz trumpeter, once hit high C (c^3) 280 times in succession. And it was the trumpet that brought down the walls of Jericho: "And it came to pass, when the people heard the sound of the trumpet, and the people shouted with a great shout, that the wall fell down flat" (Joshua 6:20). 2. In the organ, an 8' reed stop of powerful tone.

trumpet marine. Tromba marina.

Trumpet Voluntary. A celebrated march long and mistakenly attributed to Purcell; actually written by Jeremiah Clarke (b. London, *c.* 1673; d. there, a suicide, Dec. 1, 1707), a younger contemporary of Purcell with an even briefer lifespan. The original title of Clarke's piece was *The Prince of Denmark's March*, originally a harpsichord piece (by 1700), then scored for wind band with many a flourish, to glorify the arrival in England of Prince George of Denmark; consort of Queen Anne.

Trumscheit (Ger.). Tromba marina.

tuba. Brass instrument in the bass range of the orch., where it supplies a harmonic foundation for the trumpets and trombones above it; it replaced the SERPENT and OPHICLÉIDE. The tuba may be applied to the lowest members of the SAXHORN family. It has a wide conical bore, cupped mouthpiece, and flared bell held upright; it can have between 3 and 6 valves. In the 19th century there were 3 sizes—tenor, bass, and double-bass tuba—the last an octave below the tenor tuba, which is now obsolete (replaced by the BARITONE). The so-called WAGNER TUBA is smaller than the standard variety and more mellifluous sounding. In 2 sizes they were specially designed for Wagner's music dramas as performed at the Bayreuth Festival, thus they were also known as Bayreuth tubas. 2. The straight trumpet of the Romans; SALPINX. 3. In the organ, a reed stop (*tuba mirabilis*) on a heavy pressure of wind, of very powerful and thrilling tone.

Tubaphone. A glockenspiel in which the metal bars are replaced by metal pipes, with a sound approaching that of the xylophone. It is used in Khachaturian's *Sabre Dance* (from *Ganayeh*).

Tubb, Ernest (Dale), American country-music singer, guitarist, and songwriter; b. near Crisp, Tex., Feb. 9, 1914; d. Nashville, Tenn., Sept. 6, 1984. Following in the path of Jimmie Rodgers, he became a leading figure in the development of the "Western swing" or "honky-tonk" style of country-western music; his recording of *Walking the Floor over You* in 1941 established his reputation; from 1942 he made regular appearances on the *Grand Ole Opry* radio program in Nashville. In 1965 he was elected to the Country Music Hall of Fame.

Tubin, Eduard, Estonian-born Swedish composer and conductor; b. Kallaste, near Tartu, June 18, 1905; d. Stockholm, Nov. 17, 1982. He studied with A. Kapp at the Tartu Cons. and later with Kodály in Budapest. From 1931 to 1944 he conducted the Vanemuine Theater Orch. in Tartu; in 1944 he settled in Stockholm. In 1961 he became a naturalized Swedish citizen; in 1982 he was elected to the Royal Swedish Academy of Music. He was at work on his 11th Sym. at the time of his death. Tubin is best known for the syms. (1934; *Legendary*, 1937; 1942; *Lyrical*, 1943; 1946; 1954; 1958; 1966; *Sinfonia semplice*, 1969; 1973); concertos for violin (2), double bass, balalaika, and the piano concertino; sonatas (with piano) for violin (2), saxophone, viola, and flute; sonata for solo violin; 2 operas, a ballet, and the *Requiem for Fallen Soldiers* for alto, male chorus, solo trumpet, percussion, and organ (1979).

tubular chimes. An idiophone comprising metal bells made of long, hollow cylindrical tubes, arranged like a transmogrified keyboard and suspended from a frame; also called chimes, orch.l bells or tubular bells. The pitch is more definite than the church bells it sometimes imitates (Berlioz, *Sym. fantastique*); many modern scores use it, including Varèse's *Ionisation*.

Tucker, Richard (born Reuben Ticker), brilliant American tenor; b. N.Y., Aug. 28, 1913; d. Kalamazoo, Mich., Jan. 8, 1975. He sang in a synagogue choir in N.Y. as a child; studied voice with Paul Althouse; subsequently sang on the radio. His 1st public appearance in opera was as Alfredo in *La Traviata* in 1943 with the Salmaggi Co. in N.Y. In 1945, he made his Metropolitan Opera debut in N.Y. as Enzo in *La Gioconda*; he remained on its roster until his death, specializing in the Italian repertoire. In 1947 he made his European debut at the Verona Arena as Enzo (Maria Callas made her Italian debut as Gioconda in the same performance); he also sang at Covent Garden in London, at La Scala in Milan, in Vienna, and in other major music centers abroad. He died while on a concert tour. He was the brother-in-law of the American tenor Jan Peerce.

Tucker (born Abuza), **Sophie,** ribald popular American entertainer; b. in Russia, Jan. 13, 1884; d. N.Y., Feb. 9, 1966. She was taken to the U.S. in infancy; began her career as a singer in her father's restaurant in Hartford, Ct.; then sang in burlesque, vaudeville, and English music halls; gained fame during the World War I era, and remained a popular entertainer for some 60 years; she continued her professional appearances in nightclubs, in films, and on radio and television. She was well known for her rendition of *Some of These Days*, which became her theme song.

Tuckwell, Barry (Emmanuel), noted Australian horn player and conductor; b. Melbourne, Mar. 5, 1931. He was taught piano by his father and violin by his older brother;

was a chorister at St. Andrew's Cathedral in Sydney, and also acted as an organist there. At age 13 he began studying the horn with Alan Mann at the Sydney Cons.; making rapid progress, he played in the Sydney Sym. Orch. (1947–50). He then went to England, where he received valuable advice on horn technique from Dennis Brain; he also gathered some ideas about horn sound from listening to recordings by Tommy Dorsey. He filled positions as assistant 1st horn with the Halle Orch. in Manchester (1951–53), with the Scottish National Orch. (1953–54), and, as 1st horn, with the Bournemouth Sym. Orch. (1954–55); then served for 13 years (1955–68) as 1st horn player with the London Sym. Orch.

He subsequently launched a solo career, achieving recognition as one of the foremost virtuosos on the instrument. In the academic field he compiled a horn method and ed. horn literature. Several modern composers wrote special works for him: Thea Musgrave (a concerto that requires the horn to play quarter tones); Richard Rodney Bennett (*Actaeon* for Horn and Orch.); Iain Hamilton (*Voyage* for Horn and Orch.); Alun Hoddinott (a concerto); and Don Banks (a concerto). He also pursued a career as a conductor, making guest appearances in Australia, Europe, and the U.S. He was conductor of the Tasmanian Sym. Orch. (1980–83); was music director of the newly founded Maryland Sym. Orch. in Hagerstown (from 1982). In 1965 he was made an Officer of the Order of the British Empire.

Tudor, David (Eugene), brilliant American pianist and composer; b. Philadelphia, Jan. 20, 1926. At the age of 11 he encountered one of Messiaen's organ compositions, an occasion marking the beginning of his devotion to the music of his time. He studied piano with Josef Marin and Irma Wolpe Rademacher, organ and theory with H. William Hawke, and composition and analysis with Stefan Wolpe. His role as a pioneer performer of new music was established as early as 1950, when he gave the U.S. premiere of Boulez's 2nd Piano Sonata (N.Y., 1950). He also began a close association with John Cage, whose works he propagated in the U.S., Europe, and Japan. Tudor evolved imaginative and virtuosic solutions to the challenges of avant-garde works through a rigorous preparation process, distilling compositions that incorporated some degree of indeterminacy into more conventional notation for performance through the refining apparatus of measurements, calculations, conversion tables, and intricate computations. A special technique he applied in performing *5 Piano Pieces for David Tudor* by Sylvano Bussotti was to put on thick leather gloves for tone clusters. After mastering the problems unique to avant-garde music, Tudor moved gradually into another pioneer territory, live electronic music. In 1953 he became affiliated with the Merce Cunningham Dance Co., for which he produced numerous works, including *Rain Forest I* (1968), *Toneburst* (1974), *Forest Speech* (1976), *Weatherings* (1978), *Phonemes* (1981), *Sextet for 7* (1982), *Fragments* (1984), *Webwork* (1987), *5 Stone Wind* (with Cage and Takehisa Kosugi; 1988), and *Virtual Focus* (1990). He was also a member of the summer faculty of Black Mountain College (1951–53), and taught courses in piano and new music performance at the Internationale Ferienkürse für Neue Musik at Darmstadt (1956, 1958, 1959, 1961). He gave courses in live electronic music at the State Univ. of N.Y. at Buffalo (1965–66), the Univ. of Calif. at Davis (1967), Mills College in Oakland, Calif. (1967–68), and the National Inst. of Design in Ahmedabad, India (1969). In 1968 he was selected as one of 4 core artists for the design and construction of the Pepsico Pavilion at Expo '70 in Osaka.

Some of his biographers claim for him a direct descent, through a morganatic line, from Henry Tudor (Henry VII), and/or from one of the decapitated lovers of the beheaded Queen Anne Boleyn. Since Henry VII himself dabbled about in "aleatorick musick," Tudor's own preoccupation with tonal indeterminacy could be construed by people of easy imagination as a recessive royal trait. Among his other collaborators are Lowell Cross, Marcel and Teeny Duchamp, Gordon Mumma, Anthony Martin, Molly Davies, and Jackie Matisse, among whose creations were underwater kites.

tumultuoso (It.). Vehement, impetuous; agitated.

tune. An air, melody; a term chiefly applied to short, simple pieces or familiar melodies; its colloquial applications are practically boundless.

tuning. 1. The process of bringing an instrument into tune with itself or with other instruments. By universal convention, orch.l tuning begins with the oboe giving an A of the middle octave, which, in most orchs., is pitched at 440 cycles per second (cps). The rest of the orch. instruments then adjust themselves to this pitch. In the process, some sort of inchoate arpeggiating is spontaneously performed by the various instruments. A story is told that when an Asian potentate went to a concert in Paris and was asked which piece he liked best. "The beginning," he replied. "Just before the man with the stick came in." In piano tuning, it is necessary to reconcile the difference between the perfect 5th and 4th of the tempered pitch with the acoustical pitch derived from the series of overtones. On the piano 5ths and 4ths have to be altered to make the cycle of twelve 5ths equal to 7 octaves. The piano tuner arrives at this equation by making sure that tempered 5ths produce about 47 beats a minute, made audible by the slight increase and decrease of the loudness of the principal tone.

2. The *accordatura* of a stringed instrument. *Tuning cone*, a hollow cone of metal, for tuning metal flue pipes in the organ; *tuning crook*, a CROOK; *tuning fork*, a 2-pronged instrument of metal, yielding one fixed tone (usually a^1 or c^2); *tuning hammer*, a hand wrench for tuning pianos; *tuning horn*, a tuning cone; *tuning key*, a tuning hammer; *tuning slide*, a sliding U-shaped section of the tube in certain brass instruments, used to adjust their pitch to that of other instruments.

tuning fork. A metal fork giving the pitch of A above middle C (a^1), which, depending on the standard pitch in a given country, has anywhere from 435 to 450 cycles per second (most commonly 440 cps). By varying the thickness or the length of each prong, tuning forks can be manufactured in different sizes.

tupan. Double-headed cylindrical drum of the South Slavic region; the heads are tuned a 5th apart. The tupan is carried on straps over the body of the player, who strikes it with a drumstick in the right hand and a switch (whip) in the left hand, either together or in alternation.

Turandot (1). Opera by Busoni, 1917, 1st performed in Zurich with the composer conducting. In 1905, Busoni had composed incidental music for an imaginary production of Gozzi's commedia dell'arte "fable"; it had received its premiere in Berlin that year. He decided to turn this music into an opera after seeing a production of the play in London. Although the outline of Busoni's version is essentially the same as Puccini's, the earlier opera maintains the commedia dell'arte aspect of the original, with its comic and masked characters; crucially, there is no torture scene nor any suicide attempts (there are 2 unsuccessful attempts in the Gozzi, one successful attempt in Puccini). The opera is probably best known for an instrumental piece, *Turandots Frauengemach* (Turandot's Chambers), which is none other than the old English tune *Greensleeves*; the question comes down to whether Busoni knew what he was up to.

Turandot (2). Opera by Puccini, 1926, left unfinished at his death and 1st performed incomplete at the Metropolitan Opera in N.Y. by Toscanini ("At this point, the master lay down his pen, and died"); the next day, the work was performed with Franco Alfano's ending using Puccini's thematic material; and it is in this form that *Turandot* is usually performed. The score is remarkable in many respects; in it Puccini attempted bold experimentation, approaching polytonality and atonality. Since Turandot is a Chinese princess, Puccini made use of pentatonic scales supposedly oriental in their intervallic content. The libretto is based on an 18th-century play by Carlo Gozzi. Princess Turandot announces that she will marry only a man wise enough to solve 3 riddles proposed by her; the price of failure is death. Her palace begins to look like a mortuary, as one after another contender fails the quiz. But she meets her match in the person of Calaf, an exiled prince of Tatary, a Mongol group at war with China. He solves all her riddles, ludicrous as they are; she begs him to release her from the obligation to marry. He agrees if she can guess his own name by the next morning. The only person who knows his name is Liù, a Tatar slave girl who has followed Calaf and loves him secretly; she is tortured on Turandot's order and stabs herself to death to avoid the disclosure. After Calaf gives her a clue in the form of an embrace, Turandot guesses that his name is Love. This realization makes it possible for her to marry him, and the opera concludes with a sumptuous oriental celebration. Puccini's last completed music was the death of Liù; he spent many months trying to complete the opera, but the love duet and transformation of Turandot proved impossible for him to compose.

Turandot (3). Incidental music by Weber, 1809, for a Stuttgart production of Schiller's trans. of Gozzi's play (see above).

Turangalila-Symphonie (Hindi, love song). A grandiose sym. by Messiaen, 1949, in 10 sections inspired by Indian rāgas as a paean to love, conceived in a rhythmic idiom of tremendous complexity and scored for orch., Ondes Martenot, and solo piano. It was 1st performed by the Boston Sym. Orch., conducted by L. Bernstein.

turba (Lat., crowd). In Baroque oratorios, a piece for large chorus.

turco, -a (It.). Turkish. *Alla turca*, in Turkish style, i.e., with a noisy and somewhat static harmonic accompaniment.

Turco in Italia, Il. Opera by Rossini, 1814, 1st produced in Milan. The commander of a Turkish ship visiting Naples in the 18th century is attracted to a married Neapolitan woman. At a masked ball he mistakes a Gypsy woman for the object of his infatuation and urges her to elope with him. He soon discovers his error but finds his new companion pleasant and tractable; concurrently the Neapolitan matron discovers to her surprise that she really loves her husband; this double change of hearts results in a conveniently LIETO FINE. Not a major work by Rossini, *Il Turco's* popularity was helped by the fact that it was once banned in England as immoral.

Turina (y Perez), **Joaquín,** prominent Spanish composer; b. Seville, Dec. 9, 1882; d. Madrid, Jan. 14, 1949. He studied with local teachers; then entered the Madrid Cons. as a pupil of Trago (piano). In 1905 he went to Paris, where he studied composition with d'Indy at the Schola Cantorum and piano with Moszkowski. At the urging of Albéniz he turned to Spanish folk music for inspiration. Returning to Madrid in 1914, he produced 2 sym. works in a characteristic Spanish style: *La procesión del Rocio* and *Sinfonia sevillana*, combining Romantic and impressionist elements in an individual manner; the same effective combination is found in his chamber music of Spanish inspiration (*Escena andaluza, La oración del torero*) and his piano music (*Sonata romántica, Mujeres españolas*); he also wrote 5 operas and incidental music for the theater. In 1930 he was appointed a prof. of composition at the Madrid Cons.; also founded the general music commission of the Ministry of Education, serving as its commissioner in 1941.

Turken-Trommel (Ger.). Turkish drum; obsolete for bass drum.

Turkey in the Straw. American square dance tune identical to that of the song *Zip Coon*, published in N.Y., 1834. It was probably a variant of an Irish hornpipe, a popular genre early in the 19th century.

turkey trot. Another American "animal step" dance popular in the early 20th century; others include the grizzly bear, bunny hug, chicken flip, horse trot, and naturally the fox-trot.

Turkish March. Piece by Beethoven, 1812, from the incidental music to *The Ruins of Athens*. Its Turkish quality is nothing more here than a rhythmic march in 2/4 time.

Turkish music. JANIZARY MUSIC.

Turm-musik (Ger.). Tower music, played on brass instruments by STADTPFEIFER on top of the town hall to announce the hour.

turn. A melodic grace consisting (usually) of 4 notes, a principal note (struck twice) with its higher and lower auxiliary ∞.

Turn of the Screw, The. Opera by Britten, 1954, after the psychological novel of Henry James; it was 1st produced in Venice. A governess is placed in charge of a young boy and girl, in a dismal house in the English countryside. Two former servants, now dead, seemed to exercise a mysterious hold on the children's minds, and the governess herself entertains a neurotic belief in a strange posthumous influence. In questioning the boy she brings him to break his alliance with the ghosts; but in the process his heart gives way and he dies. The opera, like the novel, leaves the mystery of reality and superstition unsolved. The score is expressionistic; there is a modified application of dodecaphonic techniques. The thematic "screw" is turned in 15 interludes (variations on the opening thematic 4ths) connecting the opera's 8 scenes; the composer makes superb use of a chamber orch.

Turn, Turn, Turn. A 1965 folk-rock hit for the Byrds. Written by folksinger Pete Seeger, drawing the lyrics from the Book of Ecclesiastes.

Turner, Joseph Vernon "Big Joe," African-American blues singer; b. Kansas City, Mo., May 18, 1911; d. Englewood, Calif., Nov. 24, 1985. He 1st worked as a singing bartender in local nightclubs; then became associated with the pianist Pete Johnson; in 1938 they appeared at Carnegie Hall in N.Y. After moving to Calif., he sang with Duke Ellington's band; in 1945 he and Pete Johnson began appearing at their own club in Los Angeles; he later made tours in the U.S. and Europe. His *Shake, Rattle, and Roll* (1954) helped create the rock 'n' roll craze which swept the nation in the 1950s.

Turner, Tina (born Anna Mae Bullock), pulsating African-American soul and rock singer and actress; b. Brownsville, Tenn., Nov. 26, 1939. She joined Ike Turner (b. Clarksdale, Miss., Nov. 5, 1931) and his band, the Kings of Rhythm, in St. Louis in 1956; the 2 were married

Ike and Tina Turner, c. 1960s

COURTESY FRANK DRIGGS COLLECTION

in 1958 and toured as the Ike and Tina Turner Revue, accompanied by a female dance-and-vocal trio named the Ikettes. Tina made an explosive impact as a sexually provocative and intense singer, belting out such numbers as *I've Been Lovin' You Too Long* and *River Deep, Mountain High* (1966).

A 1969 tour of the U.S. with the Rolling Stones catapulted the Revue onto center stage; they won a Grammy Award for their recording of *Proud Mary* in 1971. While continuing to make appearances with her husband, she also made the solo albums *Let Me Touch Your Hand* (1972) and *Tina Turns the Country On* (1974). In 1975 she appeared as the Acid Queen in the rock-opera film *Tommy*, and that same year brought out the album *Acid Queen*. Having loved her husband too long, she left him in 1976 and obtained a divorce in 1978. She then pursued a solo career as a rock-and-soul songstress; after a few failures she finally produced the tremendously successful album *Private Dancer* in 1984; that same year she won 4 Grammy Awards, with *What's Love Got to Do with It?* being honored as best song and best record of the year. In 1985 she starred in the film *Mad Max beyond Thunderdome*. Her follow-up albums include *Break Every Rule* (1986) and *Foreign Affair*.

tusch (Ger.; Eng. obs., tuck, tucket). A usage, a complimentary fanfare played by orch.l musicians for an honored conductor or soloist.

tutta forza, con (It.). With all possible force.

tutte (le) **corde** (It., all the strings). In piano playing, release the soft pedal fully.

tutti (It.). Indication in an orch.l or choral score that the entire orch. or chorus is to enter; usually placed after an extended solo passage.

Tutti Frutti. Little Richard's joyous 1956 ode, whose cryptic lyrics were written in the studio when the original version was deemed too dirty to record by the producer. Perhaps the defining song of early rock; covered in whitebread style by Pat Boone later that year.

twelfth. 1. The interval of an octave plus a 5th; a compound 5th. 2. A mutation stop in the organ, pitched a 12th higher than the diapason.

twelve-note composition. DODECAPHONY.

twelve-tone music (Ger. *Zwölftonmusik*). An historically significant, ahierarchical method of musical organization, promulgated (1923) and most profoundly developed by Schoenberg, wherein all 12 notes of the chromatic scale are ordered and treated without undue concern for tonal and/or harmonic functions; in effect, all themes are composed of the 12 different tones of the chromatic scale. Schoenberg's own definition, which he regarded as the only correct one of the 12-tone system of composition, is "the method of composition with 12 tones related only to one another." The concept of 12-tone music was later incorporated in the generic category of SERIALISM, in which different intervals, different dynamics, and different instrumental timbres can be organized in a series.

24 Violins of the King. VINGT-QUATRE VIOLONS DU ROI.

Twilight of the Gods. GÖTTERDÄMMERUNG.

Twinkle, Twinkle, Little Star. A melody that 1st appeared in the middle of the 18th century; the tune is probably derived from a French folk song. The French text, *Ah, Vous dirai-je, maman*, is the earliest known version of the song. In an 1834 American collection, *The Schoolmaster*, the tune is set to the alphabet (A–B–C–D–E–F–G, etc.) and popularized in this alphabetical form in Russia and other countries. Mozart wrote a set of piano variations on this theme during his sojourns in Paris. The familiar English words were written by a Londoner named Jane Taylor and published in an 1806 collection, *Rhymes for the Nursery*.

Twist, The. Song by Hank Ballard, 1959, that helped launch the dance craze of the same name in 1960, as sung by Chubby Checker. Ballard, leader of a rhythm and blues group with previous successes, recorded the song 1st; but when he failed to show up to a live broadcast of Dick Clark's *American Bandstand* television show, Checker substituted and began his march to fame, with a number 1 record and other hits. The choreography itself continued an alarming new trend toward dances in which partners did not have to be synchronized and did not touch each other; more importantly, the twist proved a health hazard, as the constant counter-swiveling at the hips could easily put a back or knee out of joint; however, no Congressional committee was ever set up to investigate this element of rock 'n' roll's insidious effect on America's youth.

Twist and Shout. Isley Brothers' R&B rave-up of 1962, cashing in on the popular dance, which was itself covered by the Beatles 2 years later and became a major pop hit.

Two Guitars. Russian Gypsy song of uncertain origin, publ. 1912; in subsequent eds. it was preceded by an ingenious intro. for violin pizzicato. The text comments on the melancholy 2-guitar melody that evokes sadness in the soul of the listener.

Two Little Girls in Blue. Musical by V. Youmans, 1922. Two identical twins take turns at the captain's table on a steamship bound for India. The confusion persists when they meet 2 young men who are at a loss as to who's who. This contrived comedy of errors is resolved at the end of the voyage and the twins pair off with their chosen men. The title song made a dent on Tin Pan Alley.

two-step. American ballroom dance popular in the 1900s and 1910s, with a sliding step in 2/4 time.

Tye, Christopher, English organist and composer; b. *c.* 1505; d. *c.* 1572. In 1536 he received his Mus.B. from Cambridge; in 1537 he was made lay clerk at King's College there; in 1543 he became Magister choristarum at Ely Cathedral; in 1545 he received the D.Mus. degree from the Univ. of Cambridge. After becoming a deacon and a priest in 1560, he left his position at Ely Cathedral in 1561; held livings at Doddington-cum-Marche in the Isle of Ely (from 1561), and at Wilbraham Parva (1564–67) and Newton-cum-capella (1564–70). His son-in-law was Robert White (Whyte).

He described himself as a gentleman of the King's Chapel on the title page of his only publ. work, *The Actes of the Apostles, translated into Englyshe metre to synge and also to play upon the Lute* (London, 1553; it includes the 1st 14 chapters). The hymn tunes *Windsor* and *Winchester Old* are adaptations from this collection. Tye was an important composer of English church music; he left Masses, services, motets, and anthems. He was also an active composer of viol consort music, most notably his In Nomine fantasias.

tympani. An alternative English-language spelling of TIMPANI.

Typewriter, The. Novelty instrumental by L. Anderson, 1950, complete with the real thing clanking away; the piece became very popular.

tyrolienne (Fr.). A Tyrolian dance or dance song, based on that region's version of the LÄNDLER; a modern round dance in 3/4 time and easy movement, with a characteristic dotted rhythm on the 3rd beat. A peculiar feature of the dance song is the use of the YODEL, especially in the refrain. Rossini wrote a tyrolienne for his *William Tell*.

Tzigane. A rhapsody for violin and orch. by Ravel, 1924, written for the Hungarian violinist Jelly d'Aranyi. Stylistically the music is attenuated rather than forcibly imposed. Orig. Ravel wrote it for violin and *lutheal*, a piano with a mechanical attachment placed over the strings that makes it sound almost like an organ. It was performed for the 1st time in London, 1924, with Ravel at the lutheal.

Üben (Ger.). Practice.

über (Ger.). Over, above.

Übergang (Ger., going over). A transitional phrase; a modulation to a related key.

übermässig (Ger.). Augmented; applied to intervals a semitone larger than the standard type (major or perfect).

Übung (Ger.). Exercise; practice.

Uccelli, Gli. Orch.l suite by Resphigi, 1927, based on tunes from the works of Baroque composers, each concerning a different bird (pigeon, hen, nightingale, cuckoo). A ballet version of the suite was premiered in San Remo, 1933.

Uchida, Mitsuko, talented Japanese pianist; b. Tokyo, Dec. 20, 1948. She began training in childhood in her native city; at the age of 12 she became a pupil of Richard Hauser at the Vienna Academy of Music. In 1968 she won the Beethoven Competition, and in 1970 she received 2nd prize at the Chopin Competition in Warsaw. In 1982 she won particular notice in London and Tokyo for her performances of the complete piano sonatas of Mozart; during the 1985–86 season she appeared as soloist-conductor in all the piano concertos of Mozart with the English Chamber Orch. in London. In 1987 she made her N.Y. recital debut. Her repertoire also includes works by Debussy, Schoenberg, and Bartók.

'ūd (oud). Arab lute, known since the 7th century. It has gone through numerous subtle changes in construction and numbers of strings (always in pairs), but it has retained a fretless fingerboard. The instrument is plucked with a plectrum, and like the Spanish and classical guitars; tortoise shell or a similar material is glued to the body near the soundholes to prevent plectral damage. The 'ūd came to Spain during the Moorish occupation, and its introduction paved the way for the development of the European lute, vihuela, and guitar; it left with the Moors at the time of their expulsion. The modern 'ūd comes in various sizes and has a shorter neck than the European lute, with 4 to 6 pairs of strings and 3 soundholes. Historically it was played with the modern almond-shaped body (the older 'ūd was pear-shaped) higher than the pegbox; it can also be played with the body resting in the player's lap.

Ugo, Conte di Parigi. Opera by Donizetti, 1832, 1st performed in Milan. Ugo is Hugues Capet, who remains faithful to King Louis V (the Sluggard), the last of the Carolingians, despite the efforts of dissidents to install the house of Anjou on the throne of France. A love quadrangle complicates the libretto when the King's bride begs Ugo to give her his love. She drinks poison and expires when he marries her sister. In historical fact Louis V was France's nominal king only, and reigned for 1 year; Hugues Capet, already the Duke of France (and thereby holding the de facto power), was elected to replace Louis in 987; he ruled until his death in 996 as the 1st of the Capetian dynasty.

uguale (It., even). Equal, alike, similar. *Ugualmente*, equally, similarly, evenly; smoothly, tranquilly.

Uirapuru. Sym. poem by Villa-Lobos, 1935, 1st performed in Buenos Aires. Uirapuru is a legendary jungle bird who underneath his feathers is a handsome youth. He is fascinated by a jungle maiden but a jealous Indian kills him. In death he becomes a bird again. The score presents a colorful panorama of tropical birds of the Brazilian jungle.

ukulele (Hawaiian, flea; U.K., ukelele). Popular smaller guitarlike instrument with 4 strings. The instrument was originally imported by Portuguese sailors into Hawaii in the 1870s; it found its way to the continental U.S. in the early 20th century. It proved very popular, in part because the use of tablature allowed players to learn quickly without the ability to read music. Popular music of all kinds used the instrument, and it could be heard in vaudeville, musicals, and films. Its popularity died out after World War II, but it could be heard in unusual settings, e.g., as the accompanying instrument to the unusual vocal stylings of Tiny Tim (Herbert Khaury), who revived an endless number of Tin Pan Alley songs.

Ulisse. Opera by Dallapiccola, 1959–68, after Homer's *Odyssey*; its 1st performance was in German (Berlin, 1968); the Italian premiere followed a year later in Milan.

Ullmann, Viktor, Austrian composer; b. Teschen, Jan. 1, 1898; d. at the Nazi concentration camp in Auschwitz (Oświęcim), 17 Oct. 1944. He studied composition with Schoenberg in Vienna (*c.* 1918–21) and quarter-tone composition at the Prague Cons. (1935–37); was active as an accompanist and conductor at the New German Theater in Prague. He wrote music in the expressionistic manner, without renouncing latent tonality. In 1942 he was arrested by the Nazis and sent to the concentration camp in Theresienstadt (Terezín); there he composed a 1-act opera, *Der Kaiser von Atlantis,* depicting a tyrannical monarch who outlaws death but later begs for its return, to relieve humanity from the horrors of life. The MS was preserved, and the work was performed for the 1st time in Amsterdam (1975).

Of the many composers at Theresienstadt, Ullmann was the most prolific, composing 3 piano sonatas, a string quartet, and many songs and choruses. He was part of the Nazi plan to present a "model camp" to the International Red Cross; as such, it flourished under its false guise for a few years until the Nazis decided to end the musical activities and make way for new prisoners. They took the Terezín prisoners to Auschwitz, one of the death factories in the Nazi arsenal; unless Joseph Mengele decided to make someone a laborer there, he or she were sent immediately to their death; children, those with red hair or glasses, older people, or anyone who admitted to being at all artistic were doomed from the start. Other composers who perished at Auschwitz in 1944 were Pavel Haas (b. Brno, 1899; student of Janáček); Hans Krása (b. Prague, 1899; composer of the children's opera *Brundibár,* performed 55 times at Terezín); and Zikmund Schul (b. Kassel, 1916, a student of Alois Hába). Another active composer, Gideon Klein (b. Přerov, 1919) wrote chamber and vocal music at Auschwitz; he died at Fürtengrube in late January, 1945.

ultramodern music. In the early 1920s it became evident to composers using advanced techniques that the term *modern music* was no longer sufficiently strong to describe the new trends. In search of further emphasis, they chose the term *ultramodern music*—that is, music beyond the limits of traditional modernism. In announcing the publication of *New Music* magazine, Henry Cowell, its founder and editor, declared that only works in the ultramodern idiom would be acceptable for publication. Some decades later it was realized that ultramodern music, too, began to show unmistakable signs of obsolescence. Still, certain attributes of ultramodern music have retained their validity: dissonant counterpoint, atonal melodic designs, polymetric and polyrhythmic combinations, and novel instrumental sonorities.

Um Kalthoum (Oum Kolsoum; born Fatma el-Zahraa Ibrahim), Egyptian singer; b. Tamay az-Zahirah, 1898; d. Cairo, Feb. 3, 1975. During a career of more than 50 years, she was one of the most famous singers in the Arab world; she was particularly renowned for her renditions of nationalistic, religious, and sentimental songs, which resulted in her being dubbed the "Star of the East" and the "Nightingale of the Nile." Her influence was such that political figures such as King Farouk and Gamaliel Nasser courted her favor. Her death precipitated widespread mourning in Egypt and other Arab countries.

umano, -a (It.). Human. *Voce umana* (Lat. *vox humana*), an organ stop.

umore, con (It.). Humorously.

un, -e (Fr.). One; a(n). *Un peu,* a little; *un peu animé,* a little animated; *un peu plus lent,* a little slower.

un, -o, -a (It.). One; a(n). *Un poco,* a little; *un pochettino,* a little bit; *un poco meno,* a little less; *un poco più lento,* a little more slowly.

una certa espressione parlante, con (It.). With a certain speechlike expression (Beethoven, *Bagatelle*, No. 6, op. 33).

una corda (It., 1 string; abbrev. *U.C.*). An indication directing the player to use the soft pedal, which moves the entire keyboard, and with it the hammers, slightly to the right so that the hammers strike only 1 string instead of 2 or 3. When the composer wishes to restore full sonority, the indication is TRE CORDE (3 strings). Beethoven was the 1st to use these terms systematically in his piano works.

Unanswered Question, The. Chamber orch. work by Ives, 1908, sometimes subtitled *A Cosmic Landscape*. A solo trumpet propounds the "unanswered question" in an atonal setting, echoed in confusion by woodwinds, supported ethereally by strings. The score is remarkable because its components are written at different tempos in different meters. The work was not performed until nearly 50 years after its inception, at which point it became an instant classic.

unbestimmte Tonhöhe (Ger.). Indeterminate pitch; a form of improvisatory notation found in AVANT-GARDE MUSIC.

und (Ger.). And.

unda maris (Lat., wave of the sea). In the organ, an 8' flue stop pitched a trifle lower than the surrounding foundation stops; the interference of its tone with theirs produces acoustic beats and a wavy, undulatory effect of tone.

undecima (Lat.). Interval of the 11th.

undecuplet. A group of 11 equal notes to be performed in the time of 8 (or 6) notes of like value in the established rhythm.

Undertow: Choreographic Episodes for Orchestra. Ballet suite by Schuman, 1945, representing the case history of a psychopathic individual. It was 1st performed in Los Angeles.

Undine. Opera by Lortzing, 1845, 1st performed in Magdeburg. A water nymph marries a mortal by which act she is assured of gaining an immortal soul. But her husband betrays her with a human female. She avenges herself by enticing her husband to join her in her native watery realm, and he perishes. The opera was fairly popular in the 19th century. Another opera with the same title and a similar story was composed by the German fabulist E. T. A. Hoffmann, an amateur composer; it was 1st produced in Berlin, 1816. There are other works, operatic and nonoperatic, on this tale.

undulazione (It.). On bowed string instruments, the VIBRATO effect.

unequal temperament. See TEMPERAMENT.

unequal voices. Voices different in compass and quality; mixed voices.

unequivocacy. The absence of chance occurrences; a musical structure with a high degree of determinacy (as opposed to INDETERMINACY), precluding interchangeability of component parts, as found in Stockhausen's *Klavierstücke*. A similar goal pervades the late Romantic scores of Mahler and the modernist creations of Nancarrow. Ultimately the aim of unequivocacy is to reproduce as closely as possible an exact repetition of a composer's concept for a work; hence the invention of ELECTRONIC MUSIC.

Unfinished Symphony. Sym. No. 8 by Schubert, 1822, set in the melancholy key of B minor. A profoundly Romantic semi-sym., it has but 2 complete movements; despite its fragmentary condition the sym. became Schubert's most famous orch.l work. The MS also contains a few measures of the scherzo. While he never intended it to remain unfinished, there is a mystery as to why it was left incomplete. Schubert intended the work to be a token of acknowledgment of his election as an honorary member to the musical societies in Linz and Graz in 1822, when he was 25 years old. The manuscript eventually wound up in the cluttered Viennese room of Anselm Hüttenbrenner, a friend of the composer's, and received its 1st performance 37 years after Schubert's untimely death at the age of 31.

Like Schubert's memory, the *Unfinished Sym.* has been subjected to various atrocities. The lovely cello theme in the 1st movement is often sung to the phrase "This is the sym. Schubert wrote but never finished." According to a legend promulgated in a wretched movie, Schubert wrote the sym. for one of his high-born female students as an expression of his love for her. When she hinted to him that the disparity of their stations precluded any thought of marriage, Schubert declared that, like his love for her, the sym. would remain unfinished. On Schubert's death centennial in 1928, an international competition was held for the completion of the *Unfinished Sym.*; worldwide protests against this dese-cration of a musical monument changed the requirements to a work in the spirit of the master. The prize was given to the 6th Sym. of Kurt Atterberg, a Swedish composer who declared afterward that his score was a deliberate imitation of the style of the judges of the competition. In recent years, completions have been made of the scherzo; but the total lack of sketches for the finale render any attempt to perform the "entire work" completely absurd.

ungebändigt (Ger.). Irresistibly.

ungebunden (Ger.). Unconstrained. *Mit ungebundenem Humor*, with unconstrained humor; *burlando*.

ungeduldig (Ger.). Impatiently.

ungefähr (Ger.). Approximately.

ungestüm (Ger.). Impetuously.

ungherese (It.). Hungarian.

ungleicher Kontrapunkt (Ger., unequal counter-point). Fifth species counterpoint, in which the notes may be of different durations instead of being limited to 1 or 2 durations, as in species 1–4.

unhappy ending. An informal designation of any dra-matic work with 1 or more of the central characters dying violently or wasting away; the opposite of LIETO FINE.

Unicorn, the Gorgon, and the Manticore, The. Madrigal fable by Menotti, 1956, 1st performed in Washington, D.C., 1956. The story, by Menotti himself, tells of a poet who takes out on 3 successive Sundays a pet unicorn, a gorgon (Medusa was one), and a manticore (1/3 man, 1/3 lion, and 1/3 scorpion).

unison (sounded as one). 1. A tone of the same pitch as a given tone; also, a higher or lower octave of the given tone. Some texts use the term *prime* for unison; this term is no more misleading than *unison* (unified sound) to represent a noninterval (i.e., zero). Since the 1st note of a scale or inter-val is counted as 1, it follows that in present-day terminolo-gy the "zero note" or interval does not exist, just as there is no "zero harmonic." 2. Performing the same exact pitches on a polyphonic instrument or with 2 or more voices and/or

monophonic instruments. The description is often applied to playing octaves or even double octaves. 3. In the piano, a group of 2 or 3 strings tuned to the same pitch and struck by one hammer; a string in such a group is called a *unison string*.

unisono (It.). Unison. *All' unisono*, progressing in unison (or octaves) with one another.

unitamente (*unito, -a*; It.). Unified, together, joined.

uniti (It.). In orch.l music, an indication, after a *divisi* sec-tion, that instruments or voices should once again perform their parts in unison.

universal harmony. HARMONY OF THE SPHERES.

Universe Symphony. An unfinished project of Charles Ives for which he made sketches (1911–16), intended in his words to be a "contemplation in tones of the mysterious cre-ation of the earth and firmament, the evolution of all life in nature, in humanity, to the Divine." At least 2 attempts at completion have been made and performed.

unpremeditated music. Strictly speaking, no piece of music can be composed with an absolute lack of premedita-tion. Great improvisers of the past always had a proleptic image, in definite sounds, of what they were going to play. However, the composers of aleatory music in the 2nd half of the 20th century have made serious attempts to create music without a shadow of melody aforethought, or har-mony prepense.

unruhig (Ger.). Restlessly, excitedly.

Unsinkable Molly Brown, The. Musical by M. Willson, 1960. An ambitious Missouri girl makes it rich by marrying a lucky silver miner in Colorado, and subsequent-ly wows European royalty aristocracy. Molly proves her unsinkability when she sails on the *Titanic*, showing extra-ordinary mettle in directing the rescue when the ship hits an iceberg. In the end she returns to her mate in Colo. The theme song is *I Ain't Done Yet*; there is also a sentimental duet, *Dolce Far Niente*.

unten (*unter*; Ger.). Under, below, beneath.

Unterhaltungsmusik (Ger., conversation music). A broad category embracing all types of musical compositions designed to please and entertain rather than impress and impose, such as SALON MUSIC that proliferated so luxuriantly in the 19th century; music written for amateur performance; music to dine by; and light dance music.

Unterstimme (Ger., voice below). A lower voice, in performance or part-writing.

unvocal. 1. Not suitable for singing. 2. Not vibrating with tone; *unvocal air* is breath escaping with a more or less audible sigh or hiss, due to unskillful management of the voice.

unwasity. An etymological transliteration of the Russian word *nebylitsa* (fairy tale). This English neoterism may be used to describe a modernistic fairy tale, or a palingenetic form so dissimilar from its original that it becomes a literal unwasity, something that never was.

Up in Central Park. Musical by Romberg, 1945. A reporter for the *N.Y. Times* in the 1870s tries to expose the corrupt city machine, but he is in love with the daughter of one of the crooked ·politicians. Ambitious for a singing career, she marries an influential politico who ends up being killed in a brawl. His widow meets the reporter by chance in Central Park and they find that the flame of their old love is still burning brightly; there is a happy ending. Includes *Close as the Pages in a Book.*

upbeat (Ger. *Auftakt*). 1. The raising of the hand in beating time. 2. The last part of a measure, specifically just before the downbeat.

up-bow. The stroke of the bow in the direction from point to nut; the *up-bow mark* is ∨ or ∧ .

upright piano. A piano with its strings arranged crosswise (diagonally) along the vertical rectangular soundboard, as distinguished from a GRAND PIANO in which the strings and the soundboard are horizontal. The hammers are made to recoil by a spring. The upright piano became popular in the 19th century partly for economy of space and partly because of the proliferation of amateur pianism in middle-class society in Europe and America.

Upshaw, Dawn, American soprano; b. Nashville, Tenn., 1960. She studied at Ill. Wesleyan Univ. (B.A., 1982) and then pursued vocal training with Ellen Faull at the Manhattan School of Music in N.Y. (M.A., 1984); she

also attended courses given by Jan DeGaetani at the Aspen (Colo.) Music School. In 1984 she won the Young Concert Artists auditions and entered the Metropolitan Opera's young artists development program. She was cowinner of the Naumburg Competition in N.Y. (1985). After appearing in minor roles at the Metropolitan Opera in N.Y., she displayed her vocal gifts in such major roles as Donizetti's Adina and Mozart's Despina in 1988. She also pursued a notably successful career as a soloist with major orchs. and as a recitalist. Her remarkable concert repertoire ranges from early music to the most intimidating of avant-garde scores; she has added American popular song to her repertoire.

Uraufführung (Ger.). A world premiere; 1st performance.

urbanism. The music of the modern city. It derives its inspiration from urban phenomena, governed by the cult of the machine and comprising the art of the motion pictures, automobile traffic, newspapers, and magazines. Inter-urban machines (locomotives, airplanes) also enter the general concept of urbanism. One of the most durable musical manifestations of urbanism is Honegger's sym. movement *Pacific 231*, glorifying the locomotive. Luigi Russolo's suite for noise instruments, *Convegno d'automobili e d'aeroplani* (1913–14); it was the 1st work with a reference to airplanes in the title. The American composer Emerson Whithorne composed *The Aeroplane* for orch. in 1920. Sports (prize fights, football, rugby) attracted composers by their new urbanistic Romanticism.

Machine music received its greatest expansion in the 1920s; typical products were the operas *Jonny Spielt Auf* by Ernst Krenek and *Machinist Hopkins* by Max Brand, and the Brecht cantata *Der Lindberghflug* by Weill and Hindemith. In Russia musical urbanism coalesced with the development of proletarian music, in which the machine was the hero of the production; an example is *The Iron Foundry* by Alexander Mossolov; Prokofiev's ballet *Le Pas d'acier* (1927), representing life in a Soviet factory, is also urbanist in its subject matter. The ostentatious realism of urbanist music fell out of fashion after World War II, but as late as 1964 Aaron Copland wrote a sym. suite, *Music for a Great City*, descriptive of the sounds of N.Y.

Urlinie (Ger.). Schenkerian term for the imbedded structural melodic descent in tonal music, usually involving 3 steps, 5 steps, or, on rare occasions, a full octave. Sometimes this motion is *interrupted,* as in the Urline frequently associated with sonata-form movements in major: 5–4–3–2 (1st and 2nd theme groups; end exposition; interruption; development)–3–(return to tonic; recapitulation)–2–1 (completion of Urlinie; tonal coda may follow).

Exposition   Recapitulation
Development (Interruption)

Ursatz (Ger., primal movement). In Schenkerian analysis, the background structure of a tonal piece, a contrapuntal combining of the melodic URLINE and the I–V–I *arpeggiation* in the bass line; such a structure can theoretically be found in all tonal music.

Urtext (Ger.). Ideally, an edited score that claims to present the most authentic version of a musical work. The concept emerged in the early 20th century among German scholars, who reacted against the freestyle approach to editing that prevailed in the 19th century. The Urtext attempts to present the original MS as set down on paper by the composer.

Before the Urtext, editors treated the classics in a rather cavalier fashion, freely altering the notes and harmonies. Bach has been the favorite object of their unwelcome solicitude. There is the notorious case of an editor's adding a bar to furnish a transitional chromatic harmony in the C-major Prelude from the 1st book of *The Well-Tempered Clavier*; this bowdlerization was taken up by other editors, with the result that Bach's version had to be "rediscovered." Editions of Beethoven's piano sonatas by von Bülow and others handle the Urtext with little respect. On the other side of the spectrum, however, overly worshipful editors do not dare to correct even the most obvious of errors. Surely Beethoven's omission of an essential E natural in the traditional chordal passage of the final section of the *Appassionata* piano sonata cannot be treated as sacrosanct in publishing the work, but it is quite proper to publish a facsimile *à titre documentaire*.

Yet one can never be sure, in editing modern works, whether seeming errors were not intentional. A copyist tried to "correct" some "wrong" notes in a manuscript of Charles Ives, who notated in the margin: "Do not correct; the wrong notes are right." On the other hand, when a respectful copyist questioned a misplaced accidental in the proofs of Rimsky-Korsakov's sym. work, the great master of Russian music retorted on the margin: "Of course it is an error. I am not some person like Debussy or Richard Strauss to write wrong notes deliberately." But what if the composer changes his own Urtext? One has to decide whether to honor the composer's original authentic Urtext or to accept his later revision, not to mention the problems with the ever-insecure Bruckner.

Ussachevsky, Vladimir (Alexis)

〜〜 〜〜 〜〜 〜〜 〜〜

Innovative Russian-born American composer; b. Hailar, Manchuria, Nov. 3, 1911; d. N.Y., Jan. 2, 1990. His parents settled in Manchuria shortly after the Russo-Japanese War of 1905, at the time when Russian culture was still a powerful social factor there. His father was an officer of the Russian army; his mother was a professional pianist. In 1930 he went to the U.S. and settled in Calif., where he took private piano lessons with Clarence Mader; from 1931 to 1933 he attended Pasadena Junior College; in 1933 he received a scholarship to study at Pomona College (B.A., 1935). He then enrolled in the Eastman School of Music in Rochester, N.Y., in the classes of Howard Hanson, Bernard Rogers, and Edward Royce in composition (M.M., 1936; Ph.D., 1939); he also had some instruction with Burrill Phillips.

In 1942, as an American citizen, Ussachevsky was drafted into the U.S. Army; thanks to his fluency in Russian, his knowledge of English and French, and an ability to communicate in rudimentary Chinese, he was engaged in the Intelligence Division; subsequently he served as a research analyst at the War Dept. in Washington, D.C. He then pursued postdoctoral work with Luening at Columbia Univ., joining its faculty in 1947; was prof. of music (1964–80). At various times he taught at other institutions, including several years as composer-in-residence at the Univ. of Utah (from 1970), and was a faculty member there (1980–85).

His early works were influenced by Russian church music, in the tradition of Tchaikovsky and Rachmaninoff. A distinct change in his career as a composer came in 1951, when he became interested in the resources of ELECTRONIC MUSIC; to this period belong his works *Transposition, Reverberation, Experiment, Composition,* and *Underwater Valse,* which make use of electronic sound. In 1952 Stokowski conducted in N.Y. the 1st performance of Ussachevsky's *Sonic Contours,* in which a piano part was metamorphosed with the aid of various sonorific devices superimposed on each other. About that time he began a fruitful partnership with Otto Luening; with him he composed *Incantation* for tape recorder, which was broadcast in 1953.

Luening and Ussachevsky then conceived the idea of combining electronic tape sounds with conventional instruments played by human musicians; the result was *Rhapsodic Variations,* 1st performed in N.Y. (1954). The work anticipated by a few months the composition of the important score Deserts by Varèse, which effectively combined electronic sound with other instruments. The next work by Ussachevsky and Luening was *A Poem in Cycles and Bells* for tape recorder and orch., 1st performed by the Los Angeles Phil. (1954). In 1956 Ussachevsky and Luening provided taped background for Shakespeare's *King Lear,* produced by Orson Welles, at the N.Y. City Center, and for Margaret Webster's production of *Back to Methuselah* for the N.Y. Theater Guild in 1958.

In 1960 Leonard Bernstein conducted the N.Y. Phil. in the commissioned work by Ussachevsky and Luening entitled *Concerted Piece* for Tape Recorder and Orch. They also provided the electronic score for the documentary *The Incredible Voyage,* broadcast over the CBS Television Network (1965). Among works that Ussachevsky wrote for electronic sound without partnership were *A Piece* for Tape Recorder (1956) and *Studies in Sound, Plus* (1959). In 1968 Ussachevsky began experimenting with a computer-assisted synthesizer; one of the works resulting from these experiments was *Conflict* (1971); it is intended to represent the mystical struggle between 2 ancient deities.

In 1959 Ussachevsky was one of the founders of the Columbia-Princeton Electronic Music Center; was active as a lecturer at various exhibitions of electronic sounds; traveled also to Russia and in China to present his music. He held 2 Guggenheim fellowships, in 1957 and in 1960. In 1973 Ussachevsky was elected to membership in the National Inst. of Arts and Letters. In addition to purely electronic works and his collaborations with Luening, Ussachevsky composed several works for tape and acoustic instruments and/or voice, including *3 Scenes from Creation: Prologue "Enumu Elish"* for 2 Choruses and Tape, *Interlude* for Soprano, Mezzo-Soprano, and Tape (1960), and *Epilogue "Spell of Creation"* for Soprano and Chorus (1971); *Colloquy* for Solo Instruments, Orch., and Tape (1976); *Celebration 1981* for Electronic Valve Instrument, 6 Winds, Strings, and Tape (1981); *Dialogues and Contrasts* for Brass Quintet and Tape (1984).

Incidental music for tape: *To Catch a Thief* (sound effects for the film; 1954); *The Boy who Saw Through* (film; 1959); *No Exit* (film; 1962); *Mourning Becomes Electra* (sound effects for the opera by M. D. Levy; 1967); film score without tape: *Circle of Fire* (1940); chamber works. Vocal: *Jubilee Cantata* for Baritone, Reader, Chorus, and Orch. (1937–38); Psalm XXIV for Chorus and Organ, Organ and 5 Brass, or 7 Brass (1948); *2 Autumn Songs* after Rilke for Soprano and Piano (1952); and Missa Brevis for Soprano, Chorus, and Brass (1972).

Ut. 1. The 1st of the solmization syllables; the opening syllable of the hymn *Ut queant laxis* (That they might be relaxed) assigned by Guido d'Arezzo, to correspond with the tonic of the mode. Because *Ut* lacks a vowel at the end and is therefore difficult to sing, it was changed to Do(H), except in French nomenclature, where *Ut* remains in proper usage. *Ut* is the only syllable in Guido's hymn that constitutes an entire word; the rest of the lines begin with the initial voca-

bles of polysyllabic words. 2. Name of the note C in France. *Ut majeur,* C major; *Ut mineur,* C minor.

Utrecht Te Deum. Hymn by Handel, 1713, praising God and Queen Anne of England on the occasion of peace concluded in Utrecht, Holland, marking the end of the war of the Spanish succession. It was 1st performed along with another sacred work, *Jubilate.*

v. Abbrev. for VIDE, VIOLINO, VOLTI, and VOCE; *Vv.*, VIOLINI.

V Studni (In the Well). Opera, 1867, by Vilém Blodek (b. Prague, Oct. 3, 1834; d. there, May 1874), 1st performed in Prague. A village woman who enjoys a reputation for wisdom advises a young girl who is in a quandary as to whether to wed a rich widower or an impecunious but handsome youth, to look in the well to see whose face is reflected in the water. Both contenders find out about it, and both climb a tree next to the well to make sure that his face appears. The old widower falls into the well, but the youth keeps his balance and gains the girl's hand. The opera enjoyed much success in its day; in Germany it was given under the title *Im Brunnen* (1893).

va (It.). Go on, continuo. *Va crescendo*, go on increasing (in loudness).

vacillando (It.). Vacillating; the indicated passage is to be performed in a wavering, hesitating style.

Vagabond King, The. Operetta by Friml, 1925. It deals fictionally with the life story of the 15th-century French poet François Villon and his amorous exploits, which include being made King for a day so that he could tame a recalcitrant woman coveted by him. Villon also helps fight the Burgundians to save Paris. Includes *Only a Rose, Some Day, Love Me Tonight,* and *Song of the Vagabonds.*

vagans (from Lat. *vagari,* wander). A 5th part (*quinta pars*) or voice added to the standard 4-part texture of Renaissance sacred vocal music. Its name indicates that there was no set range for such a part.

vaganti (from Lat. *vagari,* wander). Medieval univ. students who roamed freely from school to school; hence the name, a cognate of *vagabond.* Even though the vaganti lived outside the framework of established society, they were divided into superior and inferior strata; the highest of them belonged to the *clericus,* an educated class, and the lowest to the nondescript *goliard* group. The distinctive characteristic of the vaganti was their dedication to poetry and music. Not being constrained by the strictures of the church, they indulged their fancy in songs glorifying the delight of the senses, drink, and secular games. The famous student song, still heard in European univs., *Gaudeamus igitur,* expresses this joy of living with the verse—typical of the spirit of the vaganti—"meum est propositum in taberna mori" (it is fated that I should die in a tavern). The most remarkable collection of songs by the vaganti is the *Carmina Burana,* discovered in 1803 in the monastery Benediktbeuren (Bura Sancti Benedicti) in Bavaria; many of the songs in this collection were popularized in an eponymous oratorio by Orff (1937).

vaghezza, con (It.). With charm.

vago (It.). Vague, dreamy.

Vaisseau fantôme, Le. FLYING DUTCHMAN, THE.

Vakula the Smith. Opera by Tchaikovsky, 1876, 1st produced in St. Petersburg. The story, after Gogol's fairy tale *The Night Before Christmas,* is a mixture of rustic merrymaking in the Ukraine, interfered with by unruly demons who wreak havoc on the lives and amatory pursuits of the peasants involved. Tchaikovsky later revised the opera as *Cherevichki* (The Little Shoes, 1887).

Valencia. Song by José Pailla, 1926.

Valkyries, The. WALKÜRE, DIE.

Vallee, Rudy (born Hubert Prior Vallée), popular American singer, saxophonist, bandleader, and actor. b. Island Pond, Vt., July 28, 1901; d. Los Angeles, July 3, 1986. He studied clarinet and saxophone in his youth; his admiration for the saxophonist Rudy Wiedoeft prompted him to adopt Rudy as his own 1st name. He was educated at the Univ. of Maine and at Yale Univ. (B.A., 1927); concurrently performed in nightclubs and vaudeville. In 1928 he gained fame when his band was engaged at N.Y.'s Heigh-Ho Club. His nasal-crooned rendition of *My Time Is Your Time*, a popular favorite, became his theme song. He struck a responsive chord with such numbers as *The Whiffenpoof Song* and *I'm Just a Vagabond Lover*. From 1929 to 1939 he was one of the leading performers on radio; starred in his own variety show; also appeared in many forgettable films. He made a remarkable comeback when he starred in the hit Broadway musical *How to Succeed in Business Without Really Trying* (1961), a title that aptly described his own lucrative career in show business; he also appeared in its film version (1967). He tried to persuade municipal authorities to name the street on which he lived after him, but without success.

valse (Fr.). Waltz. *Valse à deux temps*, a 2-step waltz, in 3/4 time, at a slightly faster tempo; *valse chantée*, sung waltz; *valse de salon*, a salon piano piece in waltz time.

Valse, La. Choreographic sym. by Ravel, 1919–20; an orch.l recollection of the Viennese waltz dreamily heard at the Austrian imperial court in the mid-19th century; 1st premiered in Paris. The waltz rhythm is purposely dimmed as though perceived through an acoustical fog, but gradually the oneiric shape becomes more and more dominant until it overwhelms the senses with a powerful explosion of sonorous matter. *La Valse* is Ravel's savage parody on the world of France's World War I enemies. The work was 1st performed as a ballet in Paris, 1928. There is a 2-piano version also (1921).

Valse Boston. HESITATION WALTZ; see also WALTZ.

Valse triste. Incidental music for strings by Sibelius, 1903, as part of the play *Kuolema* (Death) by Sibelius's brother-in-law, Arvid Järnefelt, produced in Helsinki. Next to *Finlandia*, this is the most popular work of Sibelius; it is lyric and full of natural grace. Yet there are interesting harmonic progressions not often found in traditional waltz movements. Sibelius later rescored the work for chamber orch. and conducted the 1st performance of this version in Helsinki, 1904.

Valses nobles et sentimentales. Piano suite by Ravel, 1911, inspired by Schubert's waltzes, 1st performed in Paris. Ravel orchestrated this suite the following year, when it was performed as a ballet, *Adélaïde, ou Le Langage des fleurs*, in Paris.

valtorna (Rus.; from Ger. *Waldhorn*, natural horn). Modern horn.

value. The time duration of a note or rest, as compared with (a) other notes in the same movement, or (b) the standard whole note or any fractional note.

valve. In brass wind instruments, a device for diverting the air current from the main tube into an additional side tube, lengthening the air column and therefore lowering the pitch of the instrument's entire scale. The valve system came into use about 1815; before that time, trumpets, horns, and other brass could play only natural (harmonic) tones above a single fundamental; in the orch.l scores of classical works, the parts of trumpets and horns—commonly set in a variety of pitches—compelled the player either to use several instruments in different keys or to insert extra tubing (CROOK) manually to change the air column. Modern instruments obviate this laborious procedure with the aid of 3 or more valves to lower or raise the pitch; as a result a full chromatic scale can be obtained. Since the tubes cannot be made proportionate in the precise mathematical relation required, some chromatic tones have to be rectified by combining several valves or adding special devices. Valves may be operated with piston or rotary mechanisms.

valve bugle. SAXHORN.

valve horn. A natural horn with valves added; developed in the 19th century. See HORN.

valzer (It.). Waltz.

vamp. In popular music and jazz, an improvised introduction or accompaniment usually consisting of a succession of chords against an ostinato figure in the bass, to set the rhythmic pace for the song or instrumental piece.

Vampyr, Der. Opera by Marschner, 1828, 1st produced in Leipzig. A Scottish lord is a vampire under his cloak, but he can maintain his existence only through an annual sacrifice of a young woman pure of heart. After dispatching 2 sopranos in succession, he is duly struck dead by lightning. The music is reminiscent of Weber's Romantic scores.

Van Beinum, Eduard. BEINUM, EDUARD VAN.

Vanessa. Opera by Barber, 1958, to a libretto by Menotti, 1st produced at the Metropolitan Opera, N.Y.

During a stormy night Vanessa awaits the return of her lover Anatol, as she has done for 20 years. A young man appears seeking shelter; it is the son of her lover, now dead, and his name is also Anatol. Over the chasm of a generation Vanessa falls in love with him and actually marries him. In the meantime Anatol spends a perilous night with Vanessa's niece, who subsequently suffers a miscarriage. As her aunt departs for Paris with her young lover, the niece settles down for long years of waiting for his return. The music is passionately Romantic, with a sophisticated modern technique.

Varèse, Edgard (Edgar) (Victor Achille Charles)

Remarkable French-born American composer who introduced a totally original principle of organizing sound, profoundly influencing the direction of 20th-century music; b. Paris, Dec. 22, 1883; d. N.Y., Nov. 6, 1965. Varèse's paternal grandfather was Italian; his other grandparents were French. He spent his early childhood in Paris and in Burgundy; in 1892 his parents went to Turin; there he took private lessons in composition with Giovanni Bolzoni, who taught him gratis. Varèse gained some performing experience by playing percussion in the school orch. He stayed there until 1903; then went to Paris. In 1904 he entered the Schola Cantorum, where he studied composition, counterpoint, and fugue with Albert Roussel, preclassical music with Charles Bordes, and conducting with Vincent d'Indy; then entered the composition class of Charles-Marie Widor at the Cons. in 1905.

In 1907 he received the *bourse artistique* offered by the City of Paris; at that time he founded and conducted the chorus of the Univ. Populaire and organized concerts at the Château du Peuple. He became associated with musicians and artists of the AVANT-GARDE; also met Debussy, who showed interest in his career. In 1907 he married a young actress, Suzanne Bing; they had a daughter. Together they went to Berlin, at that time the center of NEW MUSIC that offered opportunities to Varèse. The marriage was not successful, and they separated in 1913.

Romain Rolland gave to Varèse a letter of recommendation for Richard Strauss, who in turn showed interest in Varèse's music. He was also instrumental in arranging a performance of Varèse's sym. poem *Bourgogne*, which was performed in Berlin in 1910. But the greatest experience for Varèse in Berlin was his meeting and friendship with Busoni. Varèse greatly admired Busoni's book *Entwurf einer neuen Aesthetik der Tonkunst* (Trieste, 1907); he was profoundly influenced by Busoni's views.

He composed industriously, mostly for orch.; the most ambitious of these works was a sym. poem, *Gargantua*, but it was never completed. Other works were *Souvenirs, Prelude à la fin d'un jour, Cycles du Nord*, and an incomplete opera, *Oedipus und die Sphinx*, to a text by Hofmannsthal. All these works, in manuscript, were lost under somewhat mysterious circumstances, and Varèse himself destroyed the score of *Bourgogne* later in life. A hostile reception that he encountered from Berlin critics for *Bourgogne* upset Varèse, who expressed his unhappiness in a letter to Debussy. However, Debussy responded with a friendly letter of encouragement, advising Varèse not to pay too much attention to critics.

As early as 1913 Varèse began an earnest quest for new musical resources; upon his return to Paris he worked on related problems with the Italian musical futurist Luigi Russolo, although he disapproved of the attempt to find a way to new music through the medium of instrumental noises. He was briefly called to the French army at the outbreak of the 1st World War, but was discharged because of a chronic lung ailment. In 1915 he went to N.Y. There he met the young American writer Louise Norton; they set up a household together; in 1921, when she obtained her own divorce from a previous marriage, they were married.

Edgard Varèse, 1957

COURTESY OF THE NEW YORK PUBLIC LIBRARY

As in Paris and Berlin, Varèse had chronic financial difficulties in America; the royalties from his few publ. works were minimal; in order to supplement his earnings he accepted a job as a piano salesman, which was repulsive to him. He also appeared in a minor role in a John Barrymore silent film in 1918. Some welcome aid came from the wealthy artist Gertrude Vanderbilt, who sent him monthly allowances for a certain length of time.

Varèse also had an opportunity to appear as a conductor. As the U.S. neared its entrance into the war against Germany, there was a demand for French conductors to replace the German music directors who had held the monopoly on American orchs. In 1917 Varèse conducted the Requiem of Berlioz in N.Y. In 1918 he conducted a concert of the Cincinnati Sym. Orch. in a program of French and Russian music; he also included an excerpt from *Lohengrin*, thus defying the general wartime ban on German music. However, he apparently lacked that indefinable quality that makes a conductor, and he was forced to cancel further concerts with the Cincinnati Sym. Orch.

Eager to promote the cause of MODERN MUSIC, Varèse organized a sym. orch. in N.Y. with the specific purpose of giving performances of new and unusual music; it presented its 1st concert in 1919. In 1922 he organized with Carlos Salzedo the International Composers' Guild, which gave its inaugural concert in N.Y. that year. In 1926 he founded, in association with a few progressive musicians, the Pan American Soc., dedicated to the pro-

motion of music of the Americas; he also became a naturalized U.S. citizen in that year. He intensified his study of the nature of sound, working with the acoustician Harvey Fletcher (1926–36), and with the Russian electrical engineer Leon Theremin, then resident in the U.S. These studies led him to the formulation of the concept of ORGANIZED SOUND, in which the sonorous elements in themselves determined the progress of composition; this process eliminated conventional thematic development; yet the firm cohesion of musical ideas made Varèse's music all the more solid, while the distinction between consonances and dissonances became no longer of basic validity.

The resulting product was unique in modern music; characteristically Varèse attached to his works titles from the field of mathematics or physics, such as *Intégrales*, *Hyperprism* (a projection of a prism into the 4th dimension), *Ionisation*, and *Density 21.5* for solo flute, the last commissioned by Georges Barrère (1876–1944) and named for the atomic weight of platinum; the score of his large orch.l work *Arcana* derived its inspiration from the cosmology of Paracelsus. An important development was Varèse's application of electronic music in his *Déserts* and, much more extensively, in his *Poème électronique*, commissioned for the Brussels World Exposition in 1958. He wrote relatively few works in small forms, and none for piano solo.

The unfamiliarity of Varèse's idiom and the tremendous difficulty of his orch.l works militated against frequent performances. Among conductors only Leopold Stokowski was bold enough to put Varèse's formidable scores *Amériques* and *Arcana* on his programs with the Philadelphia Orch.; they evoked yelps of derision and outbursts of righteous indignation from the public and the press. Ironically it was left to the author, a mere beginner, to be the 1st to perform and record *Ionisation*. An extraordinary reversal of attitudes toward Varèse's music, owing perhaps to the general advance of musical intelligence and the emergence of young music critics, took place within Varèse's lifetime, resulting in a spectacular increase of interest in his works and the number of their performances; also, musicians themselves learned to overcome the rhythmic difficulties presented in Varèse's scores.

Thus Varèse lived to witness this long-delayed recognition of his music as a major stimulus of modern art; his name joined those of Stravinsky, Ives, Schoenberg, and Webern among the great masters of 20th-century music. Recognition came also from an unexpected field when scientists working on the atom bomb at Oak Ridge in 1940 played a recording of *Ionisation* for relaxation and stimulation in their work. In 1955 Varèse was elected to membership in the National Inst. of Arts and Letters and in 1962 in the Royal Swedish Academy. Like Schoenberg, Varèse refused to regard himself as a revolutionary in music; indeed, he professed great admiration for his remote predecessors, particularly those of the Notre Dame school, representing the flowering of the ARS ANTIQUA. On the centennial of his birth in 1983, festivals of his music were staged in Strasbourg, Paris, Rome, Washington, D.C., N.Y., and Los Angeles. In 1981 Frank Zappa, the leader of the modern school of rock music and a sincere admirer of Varèse's music, staged in N.Y. at his own expense a concert of Varèse's works; he presented a similar concert in San Francisco in 1982.

variable meter. Systematic oscillation of changing meters in consecutive measures; a metrical system introduced by Boris Blacher in his piano work *Ornamente*, composed in 1950. The device is deceptively simple: the 1st measure has 2 8th notes, the 2nd measure has 3 8th notes, etc., following the ascending arithmetical progression, then reversing the process to follow a descending progression. Other German composers adopted Blacher's variable meters, among them Karl Amadeus Hartmann in his concerto for piano, wind instruments, and percussion, and Hans Werner Henze in one of his string quartets.

Variaciones Concertantes. Chamber orch. work by Ginastera, 1953, 1st performed in Buenos Aires. The work has also been used as a ballet score.

variamente (It.). Variously, differently. *Variant* (Fr. *variante*), a variant; a different (optional) reading; OSSIA.

variation. One of a set or series of transformations of a THEME by means of harmonic, rhythmic, and melodic changes and embellishments.

Variations for Orchestra. Work by Schoenberg, 1928, op. 31, written in a consciously ordained method of composition with 12 tones; it was 1st performed in Berlin. In this work Schoenberg utilizes the familiar sequence of tones B–A–C–H (B♭, A, C, B♮), which is woven into the basic 12-tone subject.

Variations on a Nursery Song. Work for piano and orch. by E. von Dohnányi, 1914; the composer performed as soloist in its 1st performance in Berlin. The nursery song of the title is the French air *Ah, vous dirai-je maman*, celebrated as the alphabet song in all languages. The score is dedicated to "the enjoyment of lovers of humor and to the annoyance of others."

Variations on a Rococo Theme. Work for cello and orch. by Tchaikovsky, 1877, 1st performed in Moscow. Tchaikovsky was not sure of the meaning of the word ROCOCO and asked his friend Fitzenhagen, the cellist to whom the score is dedicated, to explain it. Fitzenhagen said *rococo* meant carefree enjoyment; there are 7 variations on the carefree (but hardly 18th century) theme.

Variations on a Theme by Frank Bridge. Work for string orch. by Britten, 1937, written as an act of homage to his teacher; it was 1st performed at the Salzburg Festival. The theme was taken from Bridge's *3 Idylls* for String Quartet (1907); there are 10 variations in all.

Variations sérieuses. Piano set by Mendelssohn, 1841, op. 54, in D minor, written of a virtuosic technique and yet never disrupts the harmonious web of the music.

Variations Symphoniques. Work for piano and orch. by Franck, 1886, 1st performed in Paris. The variations have 2 themes; the treatment is Romantic without an attempt to achieve external virtuoso effects.

variazioni (It.). Variations.

varié (Fr.). Varied. *Air* or *thème varié*, TEMA CON VARIAZIONI.

variety show. Theatrical entertainment that includes all kinds of popular presentations, from singing and dancing to magician acts, animal tricks, and comic skits. The variety show is the successor to vaudeville in that it became most popular in the radio and television media after live theatrical vaudeville had all but disappeared.

Värmland Rhapsody, A (*En värmlandrapsodi*). Orch.1 rhapsody by Atterberg, 1933, premiered in Stockholm, based on traditional motives of the Swedish province of Värmland.

Varsoviana (It.; Fr. *varsovienne*). A MAZURKA named after the city of Warsaw that became very popular in the middle of the 19th century in France and Germany, coincidental with a great upsurge of sympathy for the unsuccessful Polish rebellion against Russia in 1848. The tune again became popular among downtrodden masses and sympathetic intellectuals during the abortive revolution of 1905.

vaudeville. A word serving as an umbrella for several genres of French origin; all share a satirical, epigrammatic, or comic tone. These include: 1. *Vau de Vire*, named after a city in Normandy, a rural song incorporating the elements of daily life, from the 15th century; 2. *Voix de ville* (city voices), a 16th-century urban response to the earlier genre, with more courtly lyrics and simple tunes; much of the music was akin to the dances of the period, and influential on the chansons. 3. The term *vaudeville* became prevalent in the 17th century, representing simple strophic airs, continuing the traditional concerns with daily matters. The genre was very popular; the tunes were so well-known that they were not included in MSS. 4. The *comédie en vaudevilles* made the vaudeville a theatrical genre in the late 17th and early 18th centuries. These light, often parodic comedies alternated dialogue and pantomime with witty and satirical couplets, generally set to well-known popular airs. The genre gradually gave way to the newly composed OPÉRA-COMIQUE. 5. The *vaudeville final* applied 1 element of the comédie en vaudevilles to comic opera, German and Italian as well as French, in which all the characters of a work came onstage at the end and restored order to the proceedings, expressed their feelings, and gave a moral. Composers as early as J.-J. Rosseau and as recent as Stravinsky have used the form. 6. In the 19th century the musical comedy (separate from *opéra-comique*) evolved increasingly in the direction of a variety show, whether it be the Continental vaudeville, the English MUSIC HALL, or the American vaudeville and VARIETY SHOW.

Vaughan, Sarah (Lois), African-American jazz and popular singer and pianist; b. Newark, N.J., Mar. 27, 1924; d. Los Angeles, Apr. 3, 1990. She began to study music as a child; after winning an amateur singing contest at Harlem's Apollo Theater in N.Y. in 1942 she joined the Earl Hines band in the dual role of singer and pianist; then played and sang with the bands of Billy Eckstine (1944–45) and John Kirby (1945–46); subsequently pursued a successful solo career as a jazz and pop singer, appearing on radio, television, and recordings. A versatile musician, she also ventured to appear as a soloist with sym. orchs.

Vaughan Williams, Ralph

⌇⌇⌇ ⌇⌇⌇ ⌇⌇⌇ ⌇⌇⌇ ⌇⌇⌇

Great English composer who created the gloriously self-consistent English style of composition, deeply rooted in native folk songs yet unmistakably participant of modern ways in harmony, counterpoint, and instrumentation; b. Down Ampney, Gloucestershire, Oct. 12, 1872; d. London, Aug. 26, 1958). His father, a clergyman, died when Vaughan Williams was a child; the family then moved to the residence of his maternal grandfather at Leith Hill Place, Surrey. There he began to study piano and violin; in 1887 he entered Charterhouse School in London and played violin and viola in the school orch.

From 1890 to 1892 he studied harmony with F. E. Gladstone, theory of composition with Parry, and organ with Parratt at the Royal College of Music in London; then enrolled at Trinity College, Cambridge, where he took courses in composition with Charles Wood and in organ with Alan Gray, obtaining his Mus.B. in 1894 and his B.A. in 1895; he subsequently returned to the Royal College of Music, studying with Stanford. In 1897 he went to Berlin for further instruction with Max Bruch; in 1901 he took his Mus.D. at Cambridge. Dissatisfied with his academic studies, he decided, in 1908, to seek advice in Paris from Ravel in order to acquire the technique of modern orchestration that emphasized color. In the meantime he became active as a collector of English folk songs; in 1904 he joined the Folk Song Soc.; in 1905 he became conductor of the Leith Hill Festival in Dorking, a position that he held, off and on, until his old age.

In 1906 he composed his 3 *Norfolk Rhapsodies*, introducing the essential techniques and manners of his national style; he discarded the 2nd and 3rd of the set as not satisfactory in reflecting the subject. In 1903 he began work on a choral sym. inspired by Walt Whitman's poetry and entitled *A Sea Sym.* (Sym. No. 1); he completed it in 1909; there followed in 1910 *Fantasia on a Theme of Thomas Tallis*, scored for string quartet and double string orch.; in it Vaughan Williams evoked the polyphonic style of a 16th-century English composer.

After composing this brief but very popular work, he engaged in a grandiose score, *A London Symphony* (Sym. No. 2), intended as a musical glorification of the great capital city. Despite the inclusion of immediately recognizable quotations of the street song *Sweet Lavender* and of the Westminster chimes in the score, Vaughan Williams emphatically denied that the score was a representation of London life; he even suggested that it might be more aptly entitled "Symphony by a Londoner," finally declaring that the work must be judged as a piece of absolute or abstract music. Yet prosaically minded commentators insisted that *A London Sym.* realistically depicted in its 4 movements the scenes of London at twilight, the hubbub of Bloomsbury, a Saturday-evening reverie, and, in conclusion, the serene flow of the Thames River. Concurrently with *A London Sym.* he wrote the ballad opera *Hugh the Drover*, set in England in the year 1812 and reflecting the solitary struggle of the English against Napoleon.

At the outbreak of World War I in 1914 Vaughan Williams enlisted in the British army and served in Salonika and in France as an officer in the artillery. After the Armistice he was a prof. of composition at the Royal College of Music in London (1919–39); he also conducted the London Bach Choir (1920–28). In 1921 he completed *A Pastoral Sym.*, the music of which reflects the contemplative aspect of his inspiration; an interesting innovation in this score is the use of a wordless vocal solo in the last movement. In 1922 he visited the U.S. and conducted *A Pastoral Sym.* at the Norfolk (Conn.) Festival; in 1932 he returned to the U.S. to lecture at Bryn Mawr College. In 1930 he was awarded the Gold Medal of the Royal Phil. Soc. of London; in 1935 he received the Order of Merit from King George V. In 1930 he wrote a masque, *Job*, based on Blake's *Illustrations of the Book of Job*, which was 1st performed in a concert version in 1930 and then presented on the stage in London (1931). His 4th Sym., in F minor (1931–35), 1st performed by the BBC Sym. Orch. in London in 1935, presents an extraordinary deviation from his accustomed solid style of composition. Here he experimented with dissonant harmonies in conflicting tonalities, bristling with angular rhythms.

He always professed great admiration for Sibelius; in addition to the harmonious kinship between 2 great contemporaneous nationalist composers, there was the peculiar circumstance that each in his 4th Sym. had ventured into the domain of modernism; both were taken to task by astounded critics for such musical philandering. A peripheral work was *Fantasia on Greensleeves*, arranged for harp, strings, and optional flutes; this was the composer's tribute to his fascination with English folk songs; he had used it in his opera *Sir John in Love*, after Shakespeare's *The Merry Wives of Windsor*, performed in London in 1929. Vaughan Williams dedicated his 5th Sym. in D Major (1938–43) to Sibelius as a token of his admiration. In the 6th Sym. in E Minor (1944–47) Vaughan Williams returned to the erstwhile serenity of his inspiration, but the sym. has its turbulent moments and an episode of folksy dancing exhilaration.

Vaughan Williams was 80 years old when he completed his challenging *Sinfonia antartica* (Sym. No. 7), scored for soprano, women's chorus, and orch.; the music was an expansion of his soundtrack for the motion picture *Scott of the Antarctic* (1947–48) on the doomed 1912 expedition of Sir Robert Scott to the South Pole. Here the music is almost geographic in its literal representation of the regions that Scott explored; it may well be compared in its realism with the *Alpine Sym.* of R. Strauss. In *Sinfonia antartica* Vaughan Williams inserted, in addition to a large orch., several keyboard instruments and a wind machine; in the epilogue of the work he used quotations from Scott's journal. *Sinfonia antartica* was 1st performed in Manchester in 1953.

In the 8th Sym. he once more returned to the ideal of absolute music; the work is conceived in the form of a neoclassical suite, but faithful to the spirit of the times, he included in the score the modern instruments, such as vibraphone and xylophone, as well as the sempiternal gongs and bells. In his last sym., bearing the fateful number 9, Vaughan Williams at age 85 could still assert himself as a modern composer; for the 1st time he used a trio of saxophones, with a pointed caveat that they should not behave "like demented cats" but rather remain their Romantic selves. Perhaps anticipating the inevitable, he added after the last bar of the score the Italian word *niente*. The 9th Sym. was 1st performed in London in Apr. 1958; Vaughan Williams died later in the same year. It is a testimony to his extraordinary vitality that after the death of his 1st wife he married at age 80 the poet and writer Ursula Wood; in the following year he once more paid a visit to the U.S. on a lecture tour to several American univs.

The aesthetic and technical aspects of Vaughan Williams's style involves a distinctly modern treatment of harmonic writing, with massive agglomeration of chordal sonorities; parallel triadic progressions are especially favored. There seems to have been no intention of adopting any particular method of composition; rather he used a great variety of procedures integrated into a distinctively personal and thoroughly English style, nationalistic but not isolationist. Vaughan Williams was particularly adept at exploring the modern ways of modal counterpoint, with tonality freely shifting between major and minor triadic entities; this procedure astutely evokes sweetly archaic usages in modern applications; thus Vaughan Williams combines the modalities of the Tudor era with the sparkling polytonalities of the modern age.

In addition to the works mentioned above, Vaughan Williams composed the opera *Riders to the Sea*, after the drama by John Millington Synge (1925–32; London, 1937); incidental and film music; vocal music, including: *Songs of Travel* for Voice and Piano, to texts by R. L. Stevenson (1904); *Toward the Unknown Region* for Chorus and Orch., after Whitman (1905–1907); *On Wenlock Edge*, Song Cycle for Tenor, Piano, and String Quartet ad libitum, to poems from Housman's *A Shropshire Lad* (1909); *5 Mystical Songs* for Baritone, Optional Chorus, and Orch. (1911); *Flos Campi*, suite for Viola, Wordless Mixed Chorus, and Small Orch. (1925); *5 Tudor Portraits* for Mezzo-soprano, Baritone, Chorus, and orch. (1936); *Serenade to Music* for 16 solo voices and orch. (1938); *10 Blake Songs* for tenor and oboe (1958); other English songs; arrangements of English folk songs; Anglican choral music; hymn tunes; carols.

His orch.1 work includes: *In the Fen Country*, sym. impression (1904); *The Lark Ascending*, romance for Violin and Orch. (1914–20); *Fantasia on Sussex Folk-Tunes* for Cello and Orch. (1930); Suite for Viola and Small Orch. (1934); *5 Variants of "Dives and Lazarus"* for String Orch. and Harp (1939); Concerto Grosso for String Orch. (1950); concertos for violin, piano, oboe, and tuba. Among his chamber works are: 3 string quartets (1898; 1909; 1942–44); Piano Quintet in C Minor, with double bass (1905); Phantasy Quintet for 2 violins, 2 violas, and cello (1912); Double Trio for String Sextet (London); Violin Sonata in A Minor (1954). He also composed piano and organ pieces; made collections of religious song, including the well-known *The Oxford Book of Carols* (with P. Dearmer and M. Shaw; 1928); wrote lectures and articles, reprinted in *National Music and Other Essays* (London, 1963); and collected folk songs.

vectorialism. The modern preoccupation with mathematical factors in music has resulted in the formation of novel concepts and techniques, among them vectorialism, which specifies the angular value of the vector-radius from the center of the concert hall to musical instruments or electronic transmitters, so that each ingredient of a melodic or harmonic pattern receives its identifying index. Vectorialism of sonic sources is an aspect of spatial distribution.

veemente (*veemenza, con*; It.). Vehemently, passionately.

veil. A vocal tone that is not clear and bell-like, but somewhat obscured or covered.

velato, -a (It.). Veiled; sonorously dim.

veloce (It.). Rapid, swift; indicates that a passage is to be performed faster than those before and after, thus the opposite of RITENUTO.

velocità, con (It.). Rapidly, swiftly; *velocissimo*, very fast, with extreme rapidity.

velouté (Fr.; It. *vellutato*). Velvety; smoothly legato.

Velvet Underground

A rock group with a brief and relatively unnoticed existence (1965–70) but with a profound influence on emerging and later rock styles (metal, punk, new wave, grunge). (Members: Guitar/vocal/songwriter: Lou[is Alan] Reed, b. N.Y., Mar. 2, 1942; viola/bass/keyboards: John Cale, b. Garnant, South Wales, Dec. 3, 1940; guitar: Sterling Morrison, b. Aug. 29, 1942, East Meadow, Long Island; d. Poughkeepsie, N.Y., Aug. 30, 1995; drums: Maureen "Mo" Tucker, b. N.J., 1945; Nico, b. Christa Paffgen, Cologne, Germany, Oct. 16, 1939; d. Ibiza, Spain, July 18, 1988.)

After graduating from Syracuse Univ., Reed read books, wrote poetry, essayed journalism, vocalized to guitar accompaniment, and finally found his proper niche improvising variously with such psychedelically inclined groups as the Primitives and the Warlocks (not the same group from which the Grateful Dead developed). In 1966 he recruited Cale, and together they formed the Velvet Underground, projecting bizarre stage behavior and playing sophisticated numbers in dissonant harmony. The group revived the dadaistic, surrealistic type of old European MODERNISM, superadded with the screeching, screaming, sadomasochistic electronic sound to Reed's demoralizing anarchistic lyrics openly describing the psychedelic aspects of narcotics and totally emancipated sex play in such songs as *Heroin* and *Venus in Furs*.

The group was initially produced by the artist Andy Warhol as part of his N.Y. multimedia organization the Factory; it toured under the auspices of Warhol's Exploding Plastic Inevitable. The aesthetic of the Velvets was closer to the earthy films of Paul Morrissey rather than Warhol's deadpan irony, and it did not take long before the group separated from Warhol; the group produced 4 studio albums before its demise.

Another noteworthy performer with the Velvets was Nico, a German-Hungarian model and singer. Warhol convinced the group to take her on, and she contributed contralto vocals on their 1st album and tour; she later recorded several solo albums, some produced by Cale.

Other members of the Velvets were Agnus MacLise, a percussionist who joined and left early in the group's history; Maureen "Mo" Tucker, who replaced MacLise and remained with the group until 1969 (she has produced a few solo albums over the years); Sterling Morrison, guitarist, the only member to stay with the group during its entire history, but also the only one to quit music entirely (for an academic career); and the Yule Brothers—Doug, a bassist and guitarist who replaced Cale in 1968, and Billy, who replaced Tucker in 1969.

Two of its members had important careers after leaving the Velvets: John Cale was a vocalist, composer, instrumentalist, and producer; a classically educated musician, he worked with Copland and the avant-garde composer La Monte Young. He performed bass and viola on the Velvets' 1st 2 albums, *Velvet Underground and Nico* (1967) and *White Light, White Heat* (1968), which reveal the quintessentially dark world that the Velvets and their fans inhabited; Cale brought a modernist element to an essentially rock style. After leaving the group Cale's experimentation continued with his 1st solo album, *Vintage Violence* (1969); he subsequently collaborated with Terry Riley on *The Church of Anthrax* (1971) and *The Alchemy in Peril* (1972) and with Brian Eno (1974). Other albums include *Paris 1919* (1973), *Fear* (1974), *Helen of Troy* (1975), *Honi Soit* (1981), and *Caribbean Sunset* (1984). As a producer, he was an enigmatic but major influence on punk and proto-punk.

Reed left the group in 1970 and began exploring different sides of his musical personality; there was the accessible hard rock and balladry of *Transformer* (1972; including his biggest hit *Walk on the Wild Side*, a satire on life at the Factory), *Rock 'n' Roll Animal* (1974), *Coney Island Baby* (1976), *Blue Mask* (1981), *New Sensations* (1984), and *Magic and Loss* (1992); 2 brilliant concept albums, the harrowing *Berlin* (1973) and the streetwise *New York* (1989); and an unadulterated, utterly anarchistic display of uninhibited WHITE NOISE, *Metal Machine Music* (1975).

Reed and Cale reunited 20 years after Cale left to compose and perform the suite *Songs for Drella*, in memory of Warhol (1989); they in turn joined with Morrison and Tucker for a European reunion tour in 1993.

Vendredis, Les. Sixteen pieces in 2 sets for string quartet, 1899, by Russian composers, including Borodin, Rimsky-Korsakov, Glazunov, and Liadov, so named to observe the hebdomadal meetings on Fridays (*Vendredis*) held at the house of the publisher Belaiev in St. Petersburg in the 1880s and 1890s.

Venetian school. A style of composition that developed in Venice during the 16th century, with the participation of several important organists from northern Europe, specifically from the Low Countries. The center of the Venetian school was the cathedral of Saint Mark's (San Marco) with its magnificent architectural plan of symmetric enclaves, making it ideal for the performance of antiphonal choral works of a truly stereophonic quality. The 1st acknowledged master presiding over the principal organ at San Marco was Adrian Willaert, appointed maestro di capella in 1527; he was from Bruges. He instructed the great Italian madrigalist Andrea Gabrieli in the art of chromatic modulation, who in turn taught his nephew Giovanni Gabrieli to adapt choral techniques to the treatment of the orch., especially in the contrasting alternation of massive sonorities, popularizing the ECHO, in which a given melody is repeated softly.

A long series of great organists at Saint Mark's included Claudio Merulo and the theorist Zarlino. It has been claimed also that the great Flemish organist Sweelinck made a trip to Venice and became one of the builders of the Venetian school, but this contention has been refuted by documentary evidence; Sweelinck in fact never went to Venice. Undoubtedly the Venetian school of composition, orchestration, and choral treatment exercised a profound influence on composers in Germany, among them Hieronymous Praetorius, Michael Praetorius, and Hans Leo Hassler; it was also a powerful influence on Baroque instrumental and choral music at the same time that the Florentine DRAMMA PER MUSICA monopolized the development of opera.

Venezia e Napoli. Set of 3 piano pieces by Liszt, 1861, composed as a souvenir of his trip to Italy; the pieces are *Gondoliera*, *Canzona*, and *Tarantelle*.

Vengerova, Isabelle (Isabella Afanasievna). See SLONIMSKY, NICOLAS.

vent (Fr.). Wind. *Instruments à vent*, wind instruments.

Ventanas (Windows). Sym. poem by Revueltas, 1932, 1st performed in Mexico City. Despite the concrete title, the composer denied any programmatic content in the piece.

Ventil (Ger.). A piston valve. *Ventilhorn*, horn with piston valves; *Ventilkornet*, cornet with piston valves. *Ventilposaune*, trombone with piston valves.

venusto (It.). Graceful, elegant.

Venuti, Joe (Giuseppe), Italian-born American jazz violinist; b. Lecco, Apr. 4, 1898; d. Seattle, Aug. 14, 1978. He was taken to the U.S. as a child, and reared in Philadelphia. There he received a thorough classical training on the violin, but after meeting the jazz guitarist Eddie Lang he turned to popular music. After playing with Paul Whiteman he formed his own band in 1935, and led it until 1943; then went to the West Coast, where he became a studio musician in Hollywood. His great merit was to make the theretofore-suspect violin a respectable instrument among the swingers of Calif.

Vêpres siciliennes, Les. SICILIAN VESPERS, THE.

Vera Sheloga, Boyarynia. Opera by Rimsky-Korsakov, 1898, 1st performed in Moscow. The work was developed out of the prologue to *The Maid of Pskov* (1873) and helps to explain the relationship between the young Ivan the Terrible and a young married Pskov woman; she later gives birth to a natural daughter of Ivan's; this daughter is in turn a leading character in *The Maid of Pskov*, in which Ivan also figures.

Veränderung (Ger.). Variation; used by Beethoven.

verbalization. Karlheinz Stockhausen was probably the 1st to introduce the concept of verbalization in lieu of musical notation. One of his pieces represents a parabolic curve with the following inscription: "Sound a note. Continue sounding it as long as you please. It is your prerogative." John Cage has elevated verbalization to the degree of eloquent diction. Earle Brown and Morton Feldman are inventive verbalizationists. La Monte Young tells the player: "Push the piano to the wall. Push it through the wall. Keep pushing." Nam June Paik dictates: "Cut your left arm very slowly with a razor (more than 10 centimeters)." Philip Corner limits himself to a simple command: "One antipersonnel type CBU (Cluster Bomb Unit) will be thrown into the audience."

verbotene Fortschreitungen (Ger.). Forbidden progressions in harmony or melody.

verbunkos (Hung.; from Ger. *Werbung*, recruiting). Hungarian recruiting dance, performed by a group of hussars led by their sergeant, popular in the latter 18th and the 1st half of the 19th centuries (before involuntary conscription was imposed by the Austrians). The verbunkos essentially consists of a slow section (LASSU) and a fast section (FRISS); these will then alternate as necessary. The musical elements are embodied in Liszt's *Hungarian Rhapsodies* and works by composers from Beethoven and Schubert to Kodály and Bartók.

Verdi, Giuseppe (Fortunino Francesco)

Great Italian opera composer whose genius for dramatic, lyric, and tragic stage music has made him a perennial favorite of opera enthusiasts. b. Le Roncole, near Busseto, Duchy of Parma, Oct. 9, 1813; d. Milan, Jan. 27, 1901. His father kept a tavern, and street singing gave Verdi his early appreciation of music produced by natural means. A *magister parvulorum*, one Pietro Baistrocchi, a church organist, noticed his love of musical sound and took him on as a pupil. When Baistrocchi died, Verdi, still a small child, took over some of his duties at the keyboard. His father sent him to Busseto for further musical training; there he began his academic studies and also took music lessons with Ferdinando Provesi, the director of the municipal music school.

At the age of 18 he became a resident in the home of Antonio Barezzi, a local merchant and patron of music; Barezzi supplied him with enough funds so that he could go to Milan for serious study. Surprisingly enough, in view of Verdi's future greatness, he failed to pass an entrance examination to the Milan Cons.; the registrar, Francesco Basili, reported that Verdi's piano technique was inadequate and that in composition he lacked technical knowledge. Verdi then turned to Vincenzo Lavigna, an excellent musician, for private lessons, and worked industriously to master counterpoint, canon, and fugue. In 1834 he applied for the post of maestro di musica in Busseto, and after passing his examination received the desired appointment. In 1836 he married a daughter of his patron Barezzi; it was a love marriage, but tragedy intervened when their 2 infant children died, and his wife succumbed in 1840. Verdi deeply mourned his bereavement, but he found solace in music.

In 1838 he completed his 1st opera, *Oberto, conte di San Bonifacio*. In 1839 he moved to Milan. He submitted the score of *Oberto* to the directorship of La Scala; it was accepted for a performance, which took place in 1839, with satisfactory success. He was now under contract to write more operas for that renowned theater. His comic opera *Un giorno di regno* was performed at La Scala in 1840, but it did not succeed at pleasing the public. Somewhat downhearted at this reverse, Verdi began composition of an opera, *Nabucodonosor*, on the biblical subject (the title was later abbreviated to *Nabucco*). It was staged at La Scala in 1842, scoring considerable success. Giuseppina Strepponi (b. Lodi, Sept. 8, 1815; d. Sant' Agata, near Busseto, Nov. 14, 1897), a prominent soprano, created the leading female role of Abigaille; although she was in vocal decline, Strepponi became a great favorite of Verdi's.

Nabucco was followed by another successful opera on a historic subject, *I Lombardi alla prima Crociata*, produced at La Scala in 1843. The next opera was *Ernani*, after Victor Hugo's drama on the life of a revolutionary outlaw; the subject suited the rise of national spirit, and its production in Venice in 1844, won great acclaim. Not so popular were Verdi's succeeding operas, *I due Foscari* (1844), *Giovanna d'Arco* (1845), *Alzira* (1845), and *Attila* (1846). In 1847 Verdi produced in Florence his 1st Shakespearean opera, *Macbeth*. In the same year he received a commission to write an opera for London; the result was *I Masnadieri*, based on Schiller's drama *Die Räuber*. It was produced at Her Majesty's Theatre in London in 1847, with Jenny Lind taking the leading female role.

A commission from Paris followed; for it Verdi revised his opera *I Lombardi alla prima Crociata* in a French version, renamed *Jerusalem*; it was produced at the Paris Opera in 1847; the Italian production followed at La Scala in 1850. This was one of the several operas by him and other Italian composers where mistaken identity was the chief dramatic device propelling the action. During his stay in Paris for the performance of *Jerusalem* he renewed his acquaintance with Strepponi; after several years of cohabitation their union was legalized in a private ceremony in Savoy in 1859.

In 1848 he produced his opera *Il Corsaro*, after Byron's poem *The Corsair*. There followed *La battaglia di Legnano*, celebrating the defeat of the armies of Barbarossa by the Lombards in 1176. Its premiere took place in Rome in 1849, but Verdi was forced to change names and places so as not to offend the central European powers that dominated Italy. The subsequent operas *Luisa Miller* (1849), after Schiller's drama *Kabale und Liebe*, and *Stiffelio* (1850) were not successful. Verdi's great triumph came in 1851 with the production of *Rigoletto*, fashioned after Victor Hugo's drama *Le Roi s'amuse*; it was performed for the 1st time at the Teatro La Fenice in Venice in 1851, and brought Verdi lasting fame; it entered the repertoire of every opera house around the globe.

The aria of the libidinous Duke, *La donna e mobile*, became one of the most popular operatic tunes sung, or ground on the barrel organ, throughout Europe. This success was followed by even greater acclaim with the productions in 1853 of *Il Trovatore* (Rome) and *La Traviata* (Venice); both captivated world audiences without diminution of their melodramatic effect on succeeding generations in Europe and America, and this despite the absurdity of the action represented on the stage. *Il Trovatore* resorts to the common device of unrecognized identities of close relatives, while *La Traviata* strains credulity when the eponymous soprano sings enchantingly and long despite her struggle with terminal consumption.

Another commission coming from Paris resulted in Verdi's 1st French opera, *Les Vêpres siciliennes*, after a libretto by Scribe to Donizetti's unfinished opera *Le Duc d'Albe*; the action deals with the medieval slaughter of the French occupation army in Sicily by local patriots. Despite the offensiveness of the subject to French patriots, the opera was given successfully in Paris in 1855. His next opera, *Simone Boccanegra*, was produced at the Teatro La Fenice in Venice in 1857. This was followed by *Un ballo in maschera* (Rome, 1859), based on the original libretto written by Scribe for Auber's opera *Gustave III*, dealing with the assassination of King Gustave III of Sweden in 1792. But the censors would not have any regicide shown on the stage, and Verdi was compelled to transfer the scene of action.

Unexpectedly Verdi became a factor in the political struggle for the independence of Italy; the symbol of the nationalist movement was the name of Vittorio Emanuele, the future king of Italy. Demonstrators painted the name of Verdi in capital letters, separated by punctuation, on fences and walls of Italian towns (V.E.R.D.I., the initials of Vittorio Emanuele, Re D'Italia), and the cry "Viva Verdi!" became code for "Viva Vittorio Emanuele Re D'Italia!" In 1861 the composer received a commission to write an opera for the Imperial Opera of St. Petersburg; he selected the mystical subject *La forza del destino*. The premiere took place in St. Petersburg in 1862, and Verdi made a special trip to attend. He then wrote an opera to a French text, *Don Carlos*, after Schiller's famous drama. It was 1st heard at the Paris Opera in 1867, with numerous cuts; they were not restored in the score until a century had elapsed after the initial production. (Verdi wrote 3 versions in all, none of which contain all the music he wrote for the opera.)

In June 1870 he received a contract to write a new work for the opera in Cairo, Egypt, where *Rigoletto* had already been performed a year before. The terms were most advantageous, with a guarantee of 150,000 francs for the Egyptian rights alone. The opera, based on life in ancient Egypt, was *Aida*; the original libretto was in French; Antonio Ghislanzoni prepared the Italian text. It had its premiere in Cairo on Christmas Eve, 1871, with great éclat. Verdi stubbornly refused to join the caravan despite persuasion by a number of influential Italian musicians and statesmen; he declared that a composer's job was to supply the music, not to attend performances. The success of *Aida* exceeded all expectations; the production was hailed as a world event, and the work itself became one of the most famous in opera history.

After Rossini's death, in 1868, Verdi conceived the idea of honoring his memory by a collective composition of a Requiem, to which several Italian composers would contribute a movement each, Verdi reserving the last section, *Libera me*, for himself. He completed the score in 1869 but it was never performed in its original form. The death of the famous Italian poet Alessandro Manzoni in 1873 led him to write his great *Messa da Requiem*, which became known simply as the *Manzoni Requiem*, and he incorporated in it the section originally composed for Rossini. The Requiem received its premiere on the 1st anniversary of Manzoni's death, in Milan (1874). There was some criticism of the Requiem as being too operatic for a religious work, but it remained in musical annals as a masterpiece.

After a lapse of some 13 years of rural retirement, Verdi turned once more to Shakespeare; the result this time was *Otello*; the libretto was by Arrigo Boito, a master poet and composer who rendered Shakespeare's lines into Italian with extraordinary felicity. It received its premiere at La Scala in 1887. Verdi was 79 years old when he wrote yet another Shakespearean opera, *Falstaff*, also to a libretto by Boito, who used materials from *The Merry Wives of Windsor* and the 2 parts of *Henry IV*. *Falstaff* was performed for the 1st time at La Scala in 1893. The score reveals Verdi's genius for subtle comedy coupled with melodic invention of the highest order. His last composi-

tion was a group of sacred choruses, an Ave Maria, Laudi alla Vergine Maria, Stabat Mater, and Te Deum, publ. in 1898 as *4 pezzi sacri*; in the Ave Maria Verdi made use of the so-called SCALA ENIGMATICA.

Innumerable honors were bestowed upon Verdi. In 1864 he was elected to membership in the Académie des Beaux Arts in Paris, where he filled the vacancy made by the death of Meyerbeer. In 1875 he was nominated a senator to the Italian Parliament. Following the premiere of *Falstaff* the King of Italy wished to make him Marchese di Busseto, but he declined the honor. After the death of Strepponi in 1897 he founded in Milan the Casa di Riposo per Musicisti, a home for aged musicians; for its maintenance he set aside 2,500,000 lire. In Jan. 1901 Verdi suffered an apoplectic attack; he died 6 days later at the age of 87.

Historic evaluation of Verdi's music changed several times after his death. The musical atmosphere was heavily Wagnerian; admiration for Wagner produced a denigration of Verdi as a purveyor of "barrel-organ music." Then the winds of musical opinion reversed their direction; sophisticated modern composers, music historians, and academic theoreticians discovered unexpected attractions in the flowing Verdian melodies, easily modulating harmonies, and stimulating symmetric rhythms; a theory was even advanced that the appeal of Verdi's music lies in its adaptability to modernistic elaboration and contrapuntal variegations. By natural transvaluation of opposites, Wagnerianism went into eclipse after it reached the limit of complexity. The slogan "Viva Verdi!" assumed, paradoxically, an aesthetic meaning. Scholarly research into Verdi's biography greatly increased. The Istituto di Studi Verdiani was founded in Parma in 1959; an American Inst. for Verdi Studies was founded in 1976 with its archive at N.Y. Univ.

Verfasser (Ger.). Author; editor. As a postscript to the last unfinished fugue of Bach in his *Die Kunst der Fuge*, his son Carl Philip Emanuel wrote: "At this point *der Verfasser* died."

verges (Fr.). Slender drumsticks used to strike the suspended cymbals.

vergleichende Musikwissenschaft (Ger.). COMPARATIVE MUSICOLOGY.

vergnügt (Ger.). Cheerfully, entertainingly.

Vergrösserung (Ger.). AUGMENTATION.

verhallend (Ger.). Dying away.

verhalten (Ger.). Restrained. *Mit verhaltenem Ausdruck*, with restrained expressiveness (Mahler, 8th Sym.).

verismo (from It. *vero*, true). From the 1890s, a type of operatic naturalism exemplified by Mascagni's *Cavalleria Rusticana* and Leoncavallo's *Pagliacci*. Soon the vogue spread into France with the production of *Louise* by Gustave Charpentier. In Germany verismo assumed satirical and sociological rather than naturalistic forms (Weill, Krenek, Hindemith); in England Britten's *Peter Grimes* is veristic in its subject and execution. Verismo had no followers in Russia, where nationalistic themes preoccupied the interests of opera composers; however, the USSR's brand of socialist realism could be seen as a verismo of the proletariat.

Verklärte Nacht (Transfigured Night). String sextet by Schoenberg, 1899, based on the poem by Richard Dehmel (1863–1920), which Schoenberg wrote long before he initiated his 12-tone method of composing. It was 1st performed in Vienna, 1902. The poem describes the acceptance by a woman's lover of paternity of a child conceived by another man. The score is almost Wagnerian in its expansive harmonies; it was arranged for string orch. in 1917, and used as the score for the ballet *The Pillar of Fire* (1942).

Verkleinerung (Ger.). Diminution.

Verlag (Ger.). Publishing house, company, or imprint.

Verlobung in San Domingo, Die. Opera by Egk, 1963, 1st performed in Munich. The libretto, after Kleist, has historical foundation, as the action takes place on the island of Santo Domingo (now Hispaniola) in 1803 during the French occupation. A French officer has a love affair with a mulatto woman and proposes his intention to marry her, but he coldly orders her execution on suspicion of treason. The musical score is couched in a somewhat labyrinthine polyphony, but the principal vocal parts are singable.

verlöschend (Ger.). Dying away.

vermindert (Ger.). Diminished, as in an interval.

Veronique. Operetta, 1898, by André (Charles Prosper) Messager (b. Montluçon, Allier, Dec. 30, 1853; d. Paris, Feb. 24, 1929), 1st produced in Paris; one of the most successful Viennese-influenced French operettas.

Vers la flamme (Toward the Flame). Characteristic piano piece by Scriabin, composed in 1914. It expresses his esoteric ideas of a perpetual ascent toward the regenerating flame of the final ecstasy postulated in the theosophic doctrine. The music is extremely delicate and subtly nuanced; there is no set key signature nor tonality.

vers mesuré (Fr., measured verse). A movement in 16th-century French poetry where writers had their lyrics follow the rules of Greek and Latin prosody; the champion of this approach was Jean-Antoine de Baïf (1532–89). The music adaptation was created by doubling the basic note value for long syllables as a substitute for the tonal accent of speech. Orlando di Lasso, Claude Le Jeune (*c.* 1528–1600), and Jacques Mauduit (1557–1627) contributed to this genre of composition, known as *musique mesurée*.

Verschiebung, mit (Ger.). Use soft pedal. *Ohne Verschiebung*, release soft pedal.

verschwindend (Ger.). Vanishing, dying away (Mahler, 2nd Sym.).

Verschwörenen, Die, oder Der häusliche Krieg (The Conspirators, or The Domestic War). Singspiel by Schubert, 1823; produced posthumously in Vienna, 1861. The subject follows the plot of *Lysistrata* by Aristophanes; here the wives of the Crusaders announce a marital strike until their husbands formally repudiate war. It is not a major work of Schubert (opera was not his best medium), but anything by Schubert deserves attention.

verse. 1. In Gregorian chant, a scriptural portion for solo voice, introduced and concluded by a short choral passage. 2. A stanza, usually serving as the opening part of a popular song (followed by a refrain chorus or transitional bridge).

verse-anthem. One in which the verses (soli, duets, trios, quartets) predominate over the choruses. *Verse-service*, a choral service for solo voices.

verset. 1. A short verse, usually forming but one sentence with its response, for example:

> *Vers.* O Lord, save Thy people,
> *Resp.* And bless Thine inheritance.

2. A short prelude or interlude for organ, replacing a verse in the Mass. Composers began to compose versets that took advantage of organ registration and the technical opportunities of polyphonic writing. This greatly extended practice led to increasing domination over proper congregational singing, which alarmed the church authorities ever vigilant over the purity and simplicity of plainchant; the famous papal declaration *Moto proprio* (1903) specifically

warned against the spread of instrumental polyphony in church services.

Versetzung (Ger.). TRANSPOSITION.

versicle. An exhortation intoned by the celebrant in Roman Catholic or Anglican canonical hours, sung in litany style with congregational or choral responses. The best-known versicle is the Benedicamus Domino, used to close the service.

verstimmt (Ger.). Out of tune; out of humor, depressed.

vertatur (Lat.). Turn (the page) immediately.

vertical flute. Generic term for the end-blown flute (e.g., recorder, shakuhachi, tin whistle), as opposed to the TRANSVERSE FLUTE.

Verurteilung des Lukullus, Die (The Judgment of Lucullus). Opera by Dessau, 1951, 1st performed in Berkeley, Calif. The libretto, by Brecht, was originally intended for a radio play as an allegorical indictment of Hitler. The Roman general Lucullus has accumulated a fortune during his military exploits. After his death he is put on trial to decide whether he should go to Hades or the Elysian Fields. He is accused of uncounted murders but defends himself by claiming that he undertook his military actions in order to exalt Rome. The judges sentence him to total annihilation. An adaptation of the same text was set by Sessions in English (1947).

Verwandlungsmotiv (Ger.). A transformational motive, illustrating a magical change from one state to another.

verweilend (Ger.). Delaying, holding back.

Very Good Eddie. Comedy by Kern, 1915; the title was part of a catchphrase then current in vaudeville. The story is a comedy of errors in which 2 married couples take a trip on a Hudson River boat and the husbands accidentally switch their wives. Eddie heroically pretends he is married to his counterpart's wife, until the couples are disentangled at the end of the trip. Includes *Babes in the Wood.*

Verzierung (Ger.; Fr. *agréments*; It. *fioretti*). Ornamentation. Numerous treatises have been published in all languages dealing with the proper interpretation and uniform decoding of the multitude of signs and symbols indicating these "little flowers," but it is certain that complete scholarly agreement on the agréments or the indisputable organization of ornamentation will never be achieved.

Vespers (from Lat. *vespera*, evening; Angl. *evensong*). Orig., the 7th canonical hour of the Divine Office of the Roman Catholic daily liturgy, now the 5th hour, celebrated at dusk, about 6:00 in the afternoon. Vespers is the most important service in the Office insofar as its applicability to musical composition goes, for it includes a variety of chants, hymns, and a Magnificat. Secular forms are commonly admitted in the Vespers, and this dispensation encouraged composers to set Vespers and Magnificats as independent works in a polyphonic style. Monteverdi wrote several Vespers, and Mozart composed 2 Vespers for a large ensemble.

Vespri Siciliani, I. SICILIAN VESPERS, THE.

Vestale, La. Opera by Spontini, 1807, 1st produced in Paris. A Roman captain, Licinio, is busy conquering Gaul. In distress, his betrothed applies for a position as a vestal virgin; upon examination she is found to be a *virgo intacta* and is allowed to join the vestals. But Licinio refuses to guard her virginity and upon return to Rome invades the vestal premises, extinguishing the holy flame in the process. The poor bride is sentenced to death for her failure to protect the flame, but at the last moment before her execution, a bolt of lightning strikes the scene and relights the sacred fire. This celestial intervention is interpreted as of divine origin, and the lovers are reunited in unholy matrimony.

The opera was highly successful; Berlioz considered it a masterpiece in the Gluckian and Cherubinian traditions. It held the stage for over a century, before its harmonious and melodious flame, maintained mainly by arpeggios of the chord of the diminished-7th (ACCORDE DI STUPEFAZIONE), gave up its illumination. Ironically, *La Vestale* has been staged anew as part of the BEL CANTO revival begun in the 1950s, although its aesthetic is quite opposed to that of Bellini, Donizetti, and their contemporaries.

Vetrate di Chiesa. Orch.l suite by Respighi, 1927, depicting the images of 4 church windows; 1st performed in Boston.

Vexations. Piano piece by Satie, c. 1893, in which he stipulates that it should be repeated 840 times (the piece itself is brief). In 1963, in N.Y., a group of dedicated avant-garde musicians carried out Satie's instructions literally, using a 5-pianist tag-team. The total duration of this marathon performance was 18 hours and 40 minutes.

vezzosamente (It.). In a graceful, elegant style.

Viaggio a Reims, Il (The Journey to Rheims). Opera by Rossini, 1825, premiered in Paris on the occasion of the coronation of Charles X. The work aroused little interest, and Rossini made use of its materials in a better and more successful opera, *Le Comte Ory* (1828).

vibraharp. VIBRAPHONE.

vibrante (It.). With a vibrating, agitated effect or tone.

vibraphone. A percussion instrument, introduced in America early in the 20th century; in its popular form it consists of suspended metal bars in keyboard arrangement which, when struck with mallets, produce tones that are amplified by resonator tubes below the bars. A motor-driven propeller mechanism causes the vibrato that gives the instrument its name. Berg used it in his unfinished opera *Lulu*.

vibraslap. A shaker manufactured around 1970 to replace the Latin American instrument QUIJADA DEL BURRO. In the genuine jawbone the teeth rattled percussively when struck with the palm of the hand, or brushed with a stick, producing a dental glissando. The vibraslap is a wooden shell with small metal pieces inside.

vibrations. Periodic oscillations of a flexible sounding body, such as a string or a column of air, which produce definite pitches. The unit of vibration is a cycle covering the fluctuation of an acoustic body, 1st to one side, then to the other, returning it to its original position. The frequency of such units per second (also called cycles per second, or cps, and HZ) determines the sounding tone. The human ear is capable of perceiving vibrations from about 16 cps to several thousand cps. The lowest A on the piano keyboard has 27 1/2 vibrations per second, and the high C on the keyboard vibrates at 4,224 per second. The loudness of a tone depends on its AMPLITUDE, the width of the distance traveled by the sounding body from its original (at rest) position to its most extreme departure from it. The frequency (pitch) and amplitude (dynamic level) are independent of each other.

Vibrations are cumulative in their wave motion; unrelated objects can be set in motion by contact with *sympathetic vibrations* accrued in this manner; by trying to replicate the vibration pattern of the sound, the object is at risk. Suspension bridges, with their considerable flexibility, are notoriously vulnerable to accumulated sympathetic vibration; there are stories of bridges destroyed in this manner; soldiers are warned in army manuals not to maintain a steady rhythmic marching step when crossing such a bridge (a lesson also learned from sad experience).

Other flexible acoustical bodies will respond to a sympathetic tone by trying to resonate with it—objects such as candelabras, glass chimes, chandeliers, wall mirrors, and champagne glasses will break (as per a recording tape advertisement featuring Ella Fitzgerald). Caruso, a member of the Metropolitan Opera touring company that was in San Francisco for its 1906 earthquake, exclaimed, "I knew that high B-flat would cause trouble." Taking a cue from the undisputed phenomenon of sympathetic vibration, mystics and cultists claim to be in touch with astral bodies with which they communicate through vibration; more colloquially, a mood or relationship is often described as having good or bad "vibes."

vibrato (It.). 1. In singing, a timbral effect in singing by letting the stream of air out of the lungs about 8 times per second through the rigid vocal cords; ideally the pitch should remain the same to avoid an irrelevant trill. Wind instrument playing may also be affected by vibrato use. 2. On bowed string instruments, a widely used effect involving a slight oscillation of the pitch through a barely perceptible motion of the left hand and finger pressure on a sustained tone. In excess, vibrato becomes the baneful property of walking violinists in European sidewalk cafés. Vocal and instrumental vibrato assists in the projection of sound; it is the subject of great performance practice debates as to its proper use prior to the mid-19th century (much as temperament has been debated).

vicendevole (It.). Changeably, inconstantly.

Vicentino, Nicola, noted Italian music theorist and composer; b. Vicenza, 1511; d. Rome, 1575 or 1576. He was a pupil of Willaert in Venice; then became maestro and music master to Cardinal Ippolito d'Este in Ferrara and in Rome. In 1563–64 he was maestro di cappella at Vicenza Cathedral; by 1570 he was in Milan as rector of St. Thomas; he died during a plague. His book of madrigals for 5 voices (Venice, 1546), an attempt to revive the chromatic and enharmonic genera of the Greeks, led to an academic controversy with the learned Portuguese musician Lusitano; defeated, Vicentino publ. a theoretical treatise, *L'antica musica ridotta alla moderna prattica* (Rome, 1555), which contains a description of his invention, an instrument called the ARCICEMBALO, having 6 keyboards, with separate strings and keys for distinguishing the ancient *genera*—diatonic, chromatic, and enharmonic. It was followed by his treatise *Descrizione dell'arciorgano* (Venice, 1561). He also invented and described an ARCIORGANO. In chromatic composition he was followed by Cipriano de Rore and Gesualdo. His work paved the way for the monodic style and the eventual disuse of the church modes. His surviving works are madrigals and motets.

vicino (It.). Near. *Più vicino*, nearer (as of sounds coming nearer and growing louder).

Vickers, Jon(athan Stewart), eminent Canadian tenor; b. Prince Albert, Saskatchewan, Oct. 29, 1926. He sang in church choirs as a boy; engaged in a mercantile career to earn a living, and served as a manager in Canadian Woolworth stores; then was employed as a purchasing agent for the Hudson's Bay Co. and moved to Winnipeg. He won a scholarship at the Royal Cons. of Music of Toronto, where he studied voice with George Lambert; made his operatic debut in 1952 at the Toronto Opera Festival as the Duke of Mantua. In 1957 he sang Riccardo at Covent Garden in London; in 1958 he appeared as Siegmund in *Die Walküre* at the Bayreuth Festival; in 1959 he sang at the Vienna State Opera; in 1960 he made his debut at the Metropolitan Opera in N.Y. as Canio. He is particularly renowned as a Heldentenor in Wagner's operas, and he offered superb interpretations of Otello and Peter Grimes. In 1969 he was made a Companion of Honour of the Order of Canada.

Victoria, Tomás Luis de, great Spanish organist and composer; b. Avila, 1548; d. Madrid, Aug. 20, 1611. He was a choirboy at Avila Cathedral. In 1565 he went to Rome; to prepare himself for the priesthood he entered the Jesuit Collegium Germanicum; his teacher may have been Palestrina, who from 1566 to 1571 was music master at the Roman Seminary, at this time amalgamated with the Collegium Germanicum. Victoria was about the same age as Palestrina's 2 sons, Rodolfo and Angelo, who were students at the Roman Seminary; the Italian master is known to have befriended his young Spanish colleague, and when Palestrina left the Seminary in 1571 it was Victoria who succeeded him as maestro there.

In 1569 Victoria left the Collegium Germanicum to become singer and organist in the Church of Sta. Maria di Montserrato, posts he held until 1564; from this time on he also officiated frequently at musical ceremonies in the Church of S. Giaccomo degli Spagnuoli. He taught music at the Collegium Germanicum from 1571, becoming its maestro di cappella in 1573; it moved to the Palazzo di S. Apollinaire in 1574 and to the adjoining church in 1576, where he remained as maestro di cappella for a year. In the summer of 1575 he was ordained a priest; earlier that year he received a benefice at Leon from the Pope, and in 1579 he was granted another benefice at Zamora, neither requiring residence. In 1577 he joined the Congregazione dei Preti dell'Oratorio; served as chaplain at the Church of S. Girolamo della Carità from 1578 until 1585; this was the church where St. Philip Neri held his famous religious meetings, which led to the founding of the Congregation of the Oratory in 1575.

Though Victoria was not a member of the Oratory, he must have taken some part in its important musical activities, living as he did for 5 years under the same roof with its founder (St. Philip left S. Girolamo in 1583); he is known to have been on terms of the closest friendship with Juvenal Ancina, a priest of the Oratory who wrote texts for many of the LAUDI SPIRITUALI sung at the meetings of the Congregation. He served as chaplain to the King's sister, the Dowager Empress Maria, at the Monasterio de las Descalzas in Madrid from at least 1587 until her death in 1603; also was maestro of its convent choir until 1604, and then was its organist until his death. His last work, a Requiem Mass for the Empress Maria, regarded as his masterpiece, was publ. in 1605.

A man of deep religious sentiment, Victoria expresses in his music all the ardor and exaltation of Spanish mysticism. He is generally regarded as a leading representative of the Roman school, but it should be remembered that, before the appearance of Palestrina, this school was already profoundly marked by Hispanic influences through the work of Morales, Guerrero, Escobedo, and other Spanish composers resident in Rome. Thus Victoria inherited at least as much from his own countrymen as from Palestrina, and in its dramatic intensity, its rhythmic variety, its tragic grandeur and spiritual fervor his music is thoroughly personal and thoroughly Spanish.

Beginning with a volume of motets dedicated to his chief patron, Cardinal Otto Truchsess, Bishop of Augsburg (1572), most of Victoria's works were printed in Italy, in sumptuous eds., showing that he had the backing of wealthy patrons. A vol. of Masses, Magnificats, motets, and other church music publ. at Madrid in 1600 is of special interest because it makes provision for an organ accompaniment. He published 11 books of considerable variety, including motets, Masses, psalms, Magnificats, Propria for the saints, antiphons, hymns, and the Requiem for Empress Maria.

Victrola. Trademark for the phonograph made by the Victor Talking Machine Company, later considered a generic term (like GRAMOPHONE) for any 78-rpm record player.

Vida Breve, Il. Opera by de Falla, 1904–1905, 1st produced in French in Nice, 1913. The story is typical of the romantic preoccupation with bifurcated love. A young Gypsy woman loves a man, but he marries another. She curses him; her heart breaks; she collapses and dies. The opera is rarely performed in its entirety, but it has a couple of Spanish dances that have achieved universal popularity in numerous arrangements.

vidalita (Sp., little life). A popular Argentinian carnival song in a characteristically combined rhythm of 3/4 and 6/8; the name comes from the constant recurrence of the word *vidalista* at the end of every verse.

vide (Lat., see; It. *vedi*). Written in scores as *vi—de*, take a cut, skipping from the measure *vi-* to the measure marked *-de*.

vidula (*vitula*, etc.; Lat.). FIDDLE.

Vie en Rose, La. Song by Luis Guglielmi (pseud. Louisguy) and Edith Piaf, 1947, who popularized the song.

Vie Parisienne, La. Opera buffa by Offenbach, 1866, 1st performed in Paris. Two swains await the arrival by train of their mutual object of adoration, but she spurns them both. Frustrated, 1 of them tries to seduce a Swedish baroness; the other assumes the role of an admiral in the Swiss navy. Secret trysts are held; a traveling Brazilian sings an infectious MATCHICHE (maxixe); there are easily penetrable disguises, but at the end each swain finds a complementary damsel. *La Vie Parisienne* is an affectionate spoof on life under the emperor Napoleon III.

viel (Ger.). Much, great. *Mit vielem Nachdruck*, with great emphasis.

vielle. Obsolete French bowed chordophone, equivalent to the FIDDLE.

vielle à roue (Fr.). A medieval viol with a mechanical wheel attachment: a HURDY-GURDY.

vielle organisée (Fr.). LIRA ORGANIZZATA.

vielstimmung (Ger.). Polyphonic, many-voiced.

Viennese school. Historical designation of at least 2 styles of composition centered around the capital of Austria. The term was 1st proposed by the German writer and musician Christian Friedrich Daniel Schubart (1739–91), who defined the main characteristics of the Vienna school as "an organization without pedantry, graceful form, and an intelligent understanding of the nature of wind instruments." Aesthetically the *1st Viennese school* is distinguished from its contemporary Berlin school by its songful and attractive treatment of melodic material and harmonic formations. The Vienna school embraces the period between 1750 and 1830, with Haydn, Mozart, and Beethoven dominating the scene; ironically none of these Classic masters was born in Vienna, although they lived a good portion of their lives there. Some observers perceive a continuity to Schubert and even the Strauss family in the later 19th century.

The *2nd Viennese school* refers to the group of composers of the 1st half of the 20th century, mainly Schoenberg, Berg, and Webern and their disciples, who wrote in the dodecaphonic manner; their aim was, in the words of Webern, "to say in new terms something that was said before." Future musicologists may decide that the late-20th-century Viennese composers who helped pioneer the NEW SIMPLICITY (Schwertsik, H. K. Gruber) represent a 3rd Viennese school.

Viertelnote (Ger.). A quarter note.

Viertelton (Ger.). QUARTER TONE. *Vierteltonmusik*, quarter-tone music.

Vieuxtemps, Henri, celebrated Belgian violinist and composer; b. Verviers, Feb. 17, 1820; d. Mustapha, Algiers, June 6, 1881. His 1st teacher was his father, an amateur musician; continued his training with Lecloux-Dejonc. At age 6 he made his debut in Verviers; after performing in Liège in 1827, he gave several concerts in Brussels in 1828, where he attracted the notice of Bériot, who accepted him as a pupil; Vieuxtemps studied with Bériot until 1831. In 1833 his father took him on a concert tour of Germany; he continued his studies in Vienna, where he received lessons in counterpoint from Sechter. In 1834 he performed as soloist in the Beethoven Violin Concerto in Vienna, scoring a notable success. In 1834 he made his British debut with the Phil. Soc. of London. After training in composition from Reicha in Paris (1835–36) he set out on his 1st tour of Europe (1837).

During his constant travels he composed violin concertos and other violin works that became part of the standard repertoire, and that he performed in Europe to the greatest acclaim. He made his 1st American tour in 1843–44. In 1844 Vieuxtemps married the pianist Josephine Eder (b. Vienna, Dec. 15, 1815; d. Celle–St. Cloud, June 29, 1868). In 1846 he was engaged as a prof. at the St. Petersburg Cons.; he remained in Russia for 5 seasons; his influence on Russian concert life and violin composition was considerable. In 1853 he recommenced his concert tours in Europe; paid 2 more visits to America, in 1857–58 (with Thalberg) and in 1870–71 (with Christine Nilsson). He was a prof. of violin at the Brussels Cons. (1871–73); a stroke of paralysis, affecting his left side, forced him to end all his concert activities, but he continued to teach privately. He went to Algiers for rest, and died there; one of his most prominent pupils, Jenö Hubay, was with him at his death.

With Bériot, Vieuxtemps stood at the head of the French school of violin playing; contemporary accounts speak of the extraordinary precision of his technique and of his perfect ability to sustain a flowing melody; the expression "le roi du violon" was often applied to him in the press. As a composer Vieuxtemps is best known for his 7 violin concertos (1840; 1836; 1844; c. 1850; 1861, Grétry; posthumous, 1883; posthumous, 1883). Naturally he wrote much violin music with orch. or piano; also, 2 cello concertos (Paris, 1877, c. 1883); 3 string quartets (1871, 1884, 1884); and a Viola Sonata (1863).

He had 2 brothers who were musicians: (Jean-Joseph-) Lucien Vieuxtemps (b. Verviers, July 5, 1828; d. Brussels, Jan. 1901) was a pianist and teacher who studied with Edouard Wolff in Paris; made his debut at a concert given by his elder brother in Brussels (1845); devoted himself mainly to teaching there; also wrote a few piano pieces. (Jules-Joseph-) Ernest Vieuxtemps (b. Brussels, Mar. 18, 1832; d. Belfast, Mar. 20, 1896) was a cellist who appeared with his elder brother in London (1855); was solo cellist in the Italian Opera Orch. there before going to Manchester as principal cellist of the Hallé Orch. (1858).

vif (Fr.). Lively.

vigoroso (It.). With vigor, energy.

vihuela (Sp.). 1. A generic name for Spanish chordophones in the 15th century, both bowed and plucked, descendants of the Arab 'ūD. 2. A Spanish plucked chordophone of the 16th century, similar to the contemporaneous guitar but with between 6 and 7 courses of strings (the guitar had 4); there is a reference to a vihuela with 5 pairs of strings and 1 *chanterelle*, the short, high string found centuries later on the banjo. In the next century the vihuela was declining in favor of the guitar.

Village Romeo and Juliet, A. Opera by Delius, 1899–1901; premiered in Berlin as *Romeo und Julia auf dem Dorfe*, 1907.

Villa-Lobos, Heitor

Remarkable Brazilian composer of great originality and unique ability to recreate native melodic and rhythmic elements in large instrumental and choral forms; b. Rio de Janeiro, Mar. 5, 1887; d. there, Nov. 17, 1959. He studied music with his father, a writer and amateur cellist; after his father's death in 1899 Villa-Lobos earned a living by playing the cello in cafés and restaurants; also studied cello with Benno Niederberger. From 1905 to 1912 he traveled in Brazil in order to collect authentic folk songs. In 1907 he entered the National Inst. of Music in Rio de Janeiro, where he studied with Frederico Nascimento, Angelo Franca, and Francisco Braga.

In 1912 he undertook an expedition into the interior of Brazil, where he gathered a rich collection of Indian songs. In 1915 he presented in Rio de Janeiro a concert of his compositions, creating a sensation by the exuberance of his music and the radical character of his technical idiom. He met the pianist Artur Rubinstein, who became his ardent admirer; for him Villa-Lobos composed the transcendentally difficult *Rudepoema*. In 1923 Villa-Lobos went to Paris on a Brazilian government grant; upon returning to Brazil in 1930 he was active in São Paulo and then in Rio de Janeiro in music education; founded a cons. under the sponsorship of the Ministry of Education in 1942.

He introduced bold innovations into the national program of music education, with an emphasis on the cultural resources of Brazil; compiled a *Guia pratico* containing choral arrangements of folk songs of Brazil and other nations; organized the "orpheonic concentrations" of schoolchildren, whom he trained to sing according to his own cheironomic method of solfège. In 1944 he made his 1st tour of the U.S.; he conducted his works in Los Angeles, Boston, and N.Y. in 1945. In 1945 he established in Rio de Janeiro the Brazilian Academy of Music, serving as its president from 1947 until his death. He made frequent visits to the U.S. and France during the last 15 years of his life.

Villa-Lobos was one of the most original composers of the 20th century. He lacked formal academic training, but far from hampering his development, this deficiency liberated him from pedantic restrictions, so that he evolved an idiosyncratic technique of composition, curiously eclectic but all the better suited to his musical aesthetics. An ardent Brazilian nationalist, he resolved from his earliest attempts in composition to use authentic Brazilian song materials as the source of his inspiration; yet he avoided using actual quotations from popular songs; rather he wrote melodies which are authentic in their melodic and rhythmic content.

In his desire to relate Brazilian folk resources to universal values he composed a series of extraordinary works, *Bachianas brasileiras*, in which Brazilian melorhythms are treated in Bachian counterpoint. He also composed a number of works under the generic title *Choros*, a popular Brazilian dance form, marked by incisive rhythm and a balladlike melody. An experimenter by nature, Villa-Lobos devised a graphic method of composition, using geometrical contours of drawings and photographs as outlines for the melody; in this manner he wrote *The New York Skyline* (1939), using a photograph for guidance.

Villa-Lobos wrote over 2,000 works: 4 operas, including *Magdalena* (1948) and *Yerma*, after García Lorca (1953–56); and 7 ballets. *Bachianas brasileiras*: No. 1 for 8 Cellos (1932); No. 2 for Chamber Orch. (1933); No. 3 for Piano and Orch. (1934); No. 4 for Piano (1930–40); No. 5 for Voice and 8 Cellos (1939); No. 6 for Flute and Bassoon (1938); No. 7 for Orch. (1942); No. 8 for Orch. (1944; Rome); No. 9 for Chorus a Cappella or String Orch. (1944).

Choros: No. 1 for Guitar (1920); No. 2 for Flute and Clarinet (1921); No. 3 for Male Chorus and 7 Wind Instruments (1925); No. 4 for 3 Horns and Trombone (1926); No. 5, *Alma brasileira*, for Piano (1926); No. 6 for Orch. (1926; Rio de Janeiro, 1942); No. 7 for Flute, Oboe, Clarinet, Saxophone, Bassoon, Violin, and Cello (1924); No. 8 for Large Orch. and 2 Pianos (1925); No. 9 for Orch. (1929); No. 10, *Rasga o Coracao* for Chorus and Orch. (1926); No. 11 for Piano and Orch. (1928); No. 12 for Orch. (1929); No. 13 for 2 Orchs. and Band (1929); No. 14 for Orch., Band, and Chorus (1928).

Twelve syms (1916; 1917; 1919; 1920; 1921; 1944; 1945; 1950; 1591; 1952, with Vocal Soloists and Chorus; 1955; 1957); 2 sinfoniettas (1916, 1947); *Amazonas* (1917); *Momoprecoce* for Piano and Orch. (1929); *Erosion, or The Origin of the Amazon River* (1951); 5 Piano Concertos (1945; 1948; 1952–57; 1952; 1954); Guitar Concerto (1951); 2 cello concertos (1915; 1953); Harp Concerto (1953); Harmonica Concerto (1955). Chamber works, including 17 string quartets (1915; 1915; 1916; 1917; 1931; 1938; 1942; 1944; 1945; 1946; 1948; 1950; 1952; 1953; 1954; 1955; 1958) and 3 piano trios (1911; 1916; 1918); choral works; and piano pieces, including the 3 *Prole do Bebe* suites (1918, including the popular *Polichinello*; 1921; 1929).

villancico (Sp.). A term applied to different varieties of Spanish and Latin American vocal music, starting in the 15th century; originally the literary and musical forms determined inclusion in the genre. Spanish villancicos have included vernacular love songs with stanzas and a refrain; imitative polyphonic choral pieces, including the Christmas villancico, increasingly influenced by the madrigal; the Baroque religious villancico, with expanded formal structures tending toward the dramatic, later incorporating the recitative and aria; the genre was prohibited in the mid-18th century, although performances continued into the next century. In Latin America the genre is mentioned in the 16th century; villancicos of the 17th and 18th centuries are solely ecclesiastical and liturgical in purpose, incorporating instrumental music, song, and dance; Italian influences came into play in the 18th century. Many related genres evolved in Latin America; hundreds of villancicos have survived.

villanella (It.; Fr. *villanelle, villanesca*). A lighthearted secular song that originated in Naples in the 16th century. Its musical format was marked by a deliberately rustic style and was cultivated by educated composers who wished to combat the domination of the more refined madrigal type of vocal music. Often such villanellas were of topical content and regional in application; the term is used by some modern composers to refer to a kind of instrumental rustic dance.

Villi, Le. Opera by Puccini, 1884, 1st produced in Milan. The subject is Teutonically Romantic; in the tenebrous Black Forest, a villager intent on making a fortune in the city deserts his betrothed, who languishes and dies of the ever-present Romantic complaint, a broken heart. When he returns home her spirit reproaches him bitterly; worse still, a horde of willies (spirits of fiancéed women who die before their wedding) pursue him with their obscene mimicry until he collapses and dies. There is nothing in this score to presage Puccini's future dramatic power.

villotta. Song genre, related to the VILLANELLA, popular in Italy during the Renaissance. Its melodic and rhythmic structure combines elements of courtly dances and traditional refrains.

Vin Herbé, Le (The Magic Wine). Cantata by Frank Martin, 1942, on the Tristan and Isolde legend, premiered in Zurich; it differs from Wagner's opera in that the lovers drink the aphrodisiac potion by accident. The music is neoimpressionist in its style and idiom.

vīnā (S. Ind.; N. Ind *bīn*). 1. Generic term for Indian chordophones, orig. arched harps (up through the 1st millennium A.D.),

later more widely applied. 2. A highly developed stick ZITHER, now similar in shape to the more modern Indian lute (i.e., SITĀR), with a body replacing the stick and a gourd resonator at the upper end. The 7 strings comprise 4 melody and 3 drone strings, played with fingers or a plectrum; the vīnā is played seated, with the upper end resting on the player's shoulder.

Vingt-quatre Violons du Roi (24 Violins of the King). A string ensemble known as *la grande bande* that was attached to the courts of Louis XIII, Louis XIV, and Louis XV, comprising 24 violins and other string instruments. *La petite bande* had only 16 players. The ensemble was made famous by Lully, who conducted it for many years, until his accidental self-inflicted death of gangrene.

viol. A generic type of bowed string instrument that attained universal popularity in the 17th century. Its antecedents include the medieval fiddle. Viols differ from the violin family in having a fretted fingerboard, a variable number of strings (usually 6), and in the shape of the body. It was made in 4 sizes, like the violin, by which it was superseded in the orch., etc. At 1st 3 sizes of viols were in use, classified by their French names: *dessus de viole* (top viol, i.e., treble viol), *taille de viole* (tenor viol), and *basse de viole* (*bass viol*). The bass viol was called VIOLA DA GAMBA and was the precursor of the modern cello. An ensemble of viols was called in England a chest of viols, or consort of viols. The viols were tuned like the lute, in 4ths above and below the central interval, which was a 3rd. The bass viol was tuned D, G, C, E, A, and D; the tenor viol was tuned A, D, G, B, E, and A; the treble viol was tuned an octave above the bass viol. To these was added the *pardessus de viole*, tuned a 4th above the treble viol.

Viol player

viola (It.). The alto violin; a bowed string instrument with its 4 strings tuned C_0, G_0, d^1, a^1, a 5th lower than the VIOLIN. Physically the standard-sized viola is only 1/7 larger than the violin; its lower range is not properly accommodated in acoustical terms; thus its quality of tone lacks the brilliance of the violin and the deep singing quality of the cello. But the viola offers far more than a butt for endless jokes; its melancholy, philosophical sonority occupies a more subtle, less clichéd place in musical expressivity. Except for Berlioz's *Harold in Italy* (which has an important viola part but can't be considered a true concerto), few composers wrote viola concertos until the 20th century, when performers like Hindemith, Lionel Tertis, William Primrose, and Karl Doktor commissioned (or wrote) numerous works from leading composers.

viola bastarda (U.K. *lyra viol*). Viola da gamba sized between the bass and tenor viols, with 2 drone strings and 5 playing strings, tuned alternatively in 5ths or 4ths in the manner of the LIRA DA BRACCIO. Its strange name may derive from its shape or its tunings; it was popular in the early Baroque.

viola da braccio (It., viola for the arm). An obsolete bowed stringed instrument held at the shoulder; the precursor of the modern violin.

viola da gamba (It., viol for the leg). A family of bowed stringed instruments that evolved from the medieval fiddle around the beginning of the 2nd millennium A.D. The gambas, as they are known colloquially, are similar in shape to the violin family, with subtle differences—sloping shoulders, C holes, wider bridge and fingerboard, bow held with palm up—and not so subtle ones—being held vertically, supported on the lap or between the player's calves; 6 instead of 4 strings; frets. The gambas were commonly used in the late Renaissance and Baroque; there were 6 principal instruments: soprano, alto, tenor, and 3 basses of different sizes. There is much virtuoso solo music for gamba, and many treatises on its playing; the instrument was also featured in BASSO CONTINUO. The viola da gamba has been one of the leading instruments in the early music revival.

viola da spalla (It., shoulder viola). VIOLA DA BRACCIO.

viola d'amore (It., viol of love). A bowed chordophone in the middle range, for at least part of its history supplied with sympathetic strings. The viola d'amore, 1st reported in the early Baroque, is the size of the violin but lacks its perfect proportions. The number of strings varies from 5 to 7; in addition there are sympathetic metal strings under them, imparting a silvery resonance to its sound. The English diarist Evelyn commented on "its sweetness and novelty." The mysterious name of the viola d'amore may have the prosaic explanation that its scroll above the peg-box was often made in the shape of Cupid's face. The viola d'amore was very popular in Baroque music, and Bach used it in several of his works. In modern times the viola d'amore was mostly used for its evocative value, as in the *Sinfonia domestica* of R. Strauss; Hindemith wrote a chamber concerto for it.

viola di bordone (It., drone viol). BARYTON.

viola piccola (It., small viola). Obsolete instrument of the viola family.

viola pomposa (*violino pomposa*; It.). A viola with an extra string (usually e^2), used during the middle half of the 18th century. Despite later claims, Bach never invented nor scored for such an instrument, but it is found in scores of Telemann and Graun.

viole (Fr.). Viol; viola.

violento (It.). Violently, impetuously.

Violetera, La. A Spanish song composed by José Padilla, 1918.

Violetta (It.; Fr. *violette*). 1. Fiddle or small viola of the 16th century. 2. In the 18th century, the viola (alto violin).

violin

~~~ ~~~ ~~~ ~~~ ~~~

The best known, most expressive, and most artistic instrument of the string family. Poets and storytellers have extolled the violin (It. *violino*; Fr. *violon*; Ger. *Violine, Geige*) as the most human instrument, capable of an extraordinary variety of expression—merry and sad, boisterous and tranquil, frivolous and meditative.

The violin has an oval body modified by 2 elliptic depressions across its waist; there are 2 symmetrical soundholes in the shape of large cursive *f*s. The body of the violin has the function of a resonator box; the resonance is at its strongest at the vibrating center of the violin. There are 4 strings, tuned g^0, d^1, a^1, and e^2, that are held at the lower end (nearest the player) by a tailpiece and supported by a bridge above it. The strings are maintained in their tension by 4 pegs in a pegbox (at the end furthest from the player). A fingerboard is placed under the strings; there are no frets or other marks on the fingerboard to guide the violinist, as the guitar or viola da gamba player is guided on his or her instrument. The violinist must therefore develop a secure sense of the placement of the finger on the fingerboard to play in tune. The strings are activated into sound by a bow strung with horsehairs, or by being plucked with the fingers.

The 1st plausible ancestor of the violin was the Arab RABĀB, which penetrated into Western Europe, where it became known as the REBEC; in England the rebec was called the FIDDLE. The shapes of these instruments varied until the present form was fashioned by the great violin makers of Cremona in the late 17th century. The most celebrated of the Cremona masters was Antonio Stradivari (or Stradivarius). A genuine label marked "Antonius Stradivarius Cremonensis fecit anno" glued to the inner surface of the back of the violin and visible through the *f*-holes is a virtual guarantee of the excellence of the instrument. There are some 540 Stradivarius violins in existence, although the authenticity of some is still in doubt; while their monetary value depends on pedigree, some "Strads," as they are affectionately known, have fetched between half a million and a million dollars.

The secret of the art of Stradivarius and his workshop has been probed by generations of violin manufacturers, who sought the solution in the peculiar quality of the wood from the forests of the Cremona region, or the quality of the varnish. The drawings of violins and other string instruments which Stradivarius left behind do not shed light on his mysterious skill. Attempts have been made, using the most modern tools of analytical science, to create perfect copies of the Strads, but in vain.

The violin became a favorite instrument in the hands of early virtuosos of the 17th and 18th centuries. Its technique expanded through many ingenious devices such as

Simon Standage, violinist

COURTESY BYERS, SCHWALBE & ASSOCIATES, INC.

harmonics, double stops, and pizzicato. Violin virtuosity attained an apogee with Paganini, whose wizardry on the instrument was documented in detail by contemporary reports. The great era of violin virtuosity was attained in the 19th century, which numbered, besides Paganini, such illustrious artists as Joachim, Sarasate, and Ysaÿe. In the 20th century virtuoso violinists came increasingly from Eastern Europe, especially Russia. Later in the century ultramodernist composers demanded the execution of such antiviolinistic devices as quadruple stops under the bridge, indeterminate high notes beyond the fingerboard, pizzicato glissando, and quarter tones. But before declaring such usages an outrage to the spirit of Stradivarius, recall that the songful and stately violin concerto of Brahms was once described by a German music critic as "a concerto against the violin, rather than for it."

The violin is a patrician instrument that does not often participate in such exhibitions as jazz, swing, or rock (although there are notable performers in each field). There are two standard placements for the 2 violin sections in the orch.: either the 1st violins are in front, to the conductor's left, and the 2nd violins to the right, in front (the traditional layout until the 20th century, still used by some conductors); or the 2nds are also on the left, behind the 1sts (i.e., to the left). The 1st violinist, sitting nearest the audience at the 1st desk on the left of the conductor, is called leader in England, Konzertmeister in Germany, violon solo in French, and concertmaster in America. When the director of the Russian Imperial Orch. in St. Petersburg explained to a visiting Grand Duke that the 1st violins were placed to the left of the conductor and the

2nd violins to the right, the Grand Duke exclaimed, "Second violins? In the Imperial orch., all must be first!"

Orch. violinists, particularly concertmasters, often develop a yearning for conducting. Several famous conductors learned the art of conducting by playing in the orch. Charles Munch was a member of the Gewandhaus Orch. in Leipzig and did not launch his successful career as conductor until he was 40 years old. Eugene Ormandy was for several years concertmaster of a theater orch. in N.Y. before he received his 1st conducting engagement; Neville Marriner went from playing in London orchs. to leading the immensely successful Academy of St.-Martin-in-the-Fields. Virtually all concertmasters of large sym. orchs. served as associate conductors. It is not an accident of musical terminology that the British usage for concertmaster is leader.

violin clef. The G clef (). *French violin clef*, the G clef set on the lowest line of the staff.

violin diapason. Organ stop.

violin family. The familiar 4-stringed bowed instruments, constructed in 4 sizes, tuned as follows:

violina. A metal flue stop in the organ, of stringlike timbre, usually of 4' pitch.

Violinabend (Ger.). An evening of violin playing and music.

violinata (It.). 1. A piece for violin. 2. A piece for another instrument, imitating the violin style.

violin-conductor score. A particella or abbrev. score used in 19th-century theater orchs., particularly in Italian opera houses. It usually includes the 1st violin part, the harmony on the 2nd staff, and the bass line.

violini prima (It.). First orch. violins. *Violino primo*, 1st violin in a string quartet and other small ensembles.

Violoncello player

violini secondi (It.). Second orch. violins.

violino piccolo (It.; Ger. *Quartgeige, Halbgeige*). A small violin, tuned a perfect 4th above the standard violin, used to play in the upper registers. The instrument held sway during the Baroque era, but as Leopold Mozart reported, the improvement of technique made the piccolo instrument unnecessary; it continues to be used as a children's instrument.

Violinschlüssel (Ger.). VIOLIN CLEF; treble clef.

violon (Fr.). 1. Violin. 2. Violin diapason organ stop.

violon solo (Fr.). Concertmaster.

violoncello (It., cello; Fr. *violoncelle*). The most songful instrument in the lower range of the string family. The word *violoncello* is a diminutive of *violone*; thus, "little big viola." The cello has 4 strings, tuned as C_0, G_0, d^0, and a^0, an octave below the viola. The instrument is an enlarged version of the violin and viola; it resembles a viola da gamba without frets, and is also placed between the knees, but it is held in place by a floor spike and rests on the shoulder. Until the 20th century few cellists achieved the kind of worldly success had by Paganini and other wizards of the violin, but the names Casals, Piatigorsky, Feuermann, Rostropovich, Fournier, Starker, Harrell, Tortelier, Du Pré, Krosnick, and Yo-Yo Ma testify to the instrument's power of musical communication. As with orch. violinists, many orch. cellists have taken on a conducting role, such as Toscanini, Casals, Harnoncourt, and Barbirolli.

violoncello piccolo (It., small cello). A name attached to the 5-string cello used in some works by Baroque composers.

violone (It., large viola). 1. Synonym for the largest of the viola da gambas, the bass or double bass, with a bottom string tuned to D_0. It was a contemporary of and an influence on the instrument that eventually became the even lower-pitched double bass, but the violone usually had 5 or 6 strings, while the double bass had 3 or 4. 2. An organ stop on the pedal, of 16' pitch and violoncello-like timbre.

virelai (Fr., from *virer*, turn, twist). A medieval French fixed form, with the ballade and rondeau, that dominated French song and poetry in the late Middle Ages and early Renaissance. Although there were many variations on it, the basic formula for the virelai was in 5 parts: the principal A section, containing the refrain; the 2 B sections, with different but matching texts, plus 1st (*ouvert*) and 2nd (*clos*) endings; A, but with a matching text rather than the refrain; finally, a repetition of the 1st A. Its name incorporates both dance and poetic (*lai*) origins. Machaut was the greatest exponent of the genre, mostly composing monophonic examples.

virginal (virginals). 1. Keyboard instrument of the harpsichord family, extremely popular in the 16th and 17th centuries. The etymology of the name is uncertain; a natural surmise, that it refers to the unmarried British Queen Elizabeth I, is refuted by earlier German publications in which the term was already used. Other conjectures are that virginals possessed a virginal sound and a sweet voice; that it dates to an etymological error concerning eastern Mediterranean female players of the frame drum; or that the word is derived from the Latin *virga* (rod), by analogy to the jack, an essential part of the virginal's mechanism.

The virginal is a single-strung plucked keyboard instrument, strings placed within a rectangular shape running right to left, with some discretion as to design. Notable is

Virginal by Andreas Ruckers

COURTESY OF THE SMITHSONIAN INSTITUTION

the location of the relatively small keyboards (less than 4 octaves) at the left or right side of the virginal's playing area. Instruments were built throughout Europe, with particular skill in Flanders by the Ruckers family. While the virginal retained a role similar to the clavichord's, that of a home instrument, the louder harpsichord eventually replaced the virginal.

2. A term for all harpsichord family instruments, commonly in use in England at the same time of the particular instrument's vogue. Thus a collection of music published in 1611 bore a title that was revealing but at the same misleading: *Parthenia, or The Maydenhead of the First Musicke That Was Ever Printed for the Virginalls*. It included dances, mostly pavanes and galliards, by British composers of the time; however, they could be played on any plucked keyboard instrument (or arranged for lute).

virtuosity (from Lat. *virtus*, ability, value). A display of great proficiency by an instrumentalist or vocalist, called a *virtuoso*; the concept dates to the Baroque period, with the loss of religious restrictions on compositional excess and the new monodic textures. A virtuoso must possess above all else a superlative technique. The 1st virtuosos in this sense were church organists. Of these, Frescobaldi acquired legendary fame. His biographers claim that 30,000 people flocked to hear him at St. Peter's in Rome. In later centuries the term *virtuoso* was applied mostly to instrumentalists, particularly pianists and violinists.

Virtuosity reached its peak in the 19th century. Paganini was the 1st violin virtuoso in the modern sense; his own compositions of transcendental difficulty testified to his expertise, which was also described many times by professional musicians who heard his concerts. Liszt candidly declared that his aim in performance was to emulate Paganini in piano technique. Liszt's great rival was Anton Rubinstein, whose thundering octaves were, to believe reliable critics, overwhelming in their impact on the listeners. Other great pianists of the 19th century were Thalberg, C. Schumann, Henselt, Carreño, Tausig, Alkan, and Chopin, who partly modeled his compositions after the virtuosity of Italian bel canto. In terms of world acclaim, Paderewski was a true heir to Liszt and Rubinstein, but surviving recordings of Paderewski's playing raised doubts as to his place in the galaxy of great piano virtuosos. Busoni, Hofmann, Godowsky, Petri, Lhevinne, Rachmaninoff, and many other émigrés have enjoyed fame as a piano virtuoso. Pianists too numerous to mention continue the tradition to this day.

Among violinists 19th-century performers such as Vieuxtemps, Joachim, and Sarasate carried the tradition forward. In the 20th century Heifetz was the dominant figure; at present it is perhaps Itzhak Perlman who plays at an extraordinarily high technical level; but the apparent effortlessness of his playing illustrates the difference between Romantic and 20th-century virtuosos: the earlier embody the heroic attempts of humanity to attain godlike status, while the latter attempt to blend in as normal people who just happen to play an instrument incredibly well. Players of other instruments have demonstrated an ability to rise to the top of the virtuosic heap: viola (Primrose, Tertis), VIOLONCELLO (see entry), double bass (Koussevitzky), harp (Zabaleta), guitar (Segovia, Bream, Yepes, J. Williams), flute (Galway, Rampal), oboe (Holliger), clarinet (de Peyer, Stoltzman), saxophone (Harle), horn (D. Brain, Tuckwell), trumpet (W. Marsalis, André), percussion (Glennic), and harpsichord (Landowska). The term virtuoso is not limited to classical performers; jazz saxophonists and rock electric guitarists are often compared and analyzed as much as their classical counterparts.

Vocal virtuosity developed alongside the growth of opera, and certain skills have became professional necessities. Virtuosos singers must execute the most difficult passages in rapid tempo. Effortless trills in upper registers can be expected by prima donnas; on the other hand the bodily prepossessing bass should be able to hold his lowest notes with unwavering resonance. A tenor must be able to sustain a high C (actually c^2) at the climax of an aria. All singers must be able to perform execute flawless staccato and maintain a breathtaking pianissimo as well as a brilliant ff. An unusual (but not unique) example of the importance of the singer involves the male soprano castrato Farinelli, who spent years at the Spanish court and was paid a great deal for the task of singing the same 4 songs nightly to King Philip V, who suffered from manic depression.

Vishnevskaya, Galina (Pavlovna). See ROSTROPOVICH, MSTISLAV (LEOPOLDOVICH).

visible speech. A graphic method of translating spoken words or musical notes into a visual spectrum, in which the *abscissa* (horizontal coordinate) indicates duration and the *ordinate* (vertical coordinate) indicates frequency. Relative shadings indicate the amplitude; a 3-dimensional graph could denote this parameter more precisely.

Vision of Saint Augustine, The. Oratorio by Tippett, 1966, based on writings of Augustine of Hippo, in Latin, 1st performed in London; the work is scored for baritone soloist, chorus, and orch. The text focuses on the religious aspects of Augustine's life, particularly the moment in which he experienced conversion to Christianity.

Visions de l'Amen. Suite for 2 pianos by Messiaen, 1943, 1st performed in Paris. The 7 sections each invoke the blessing of material or spiritual entities.

Visitation, The. Opera by Schuller, 1966, after Kafka's *The Trial*, premiered in Hamburg. In his libretto Schuller changed the protagonist to an African-American student in the South. Accused falsely of a crime, he is pursued by a faceless bureaucracy; he is caught and lynched. The idiom of the opera ranges from popular ballads, jazz, and blues to dissonant harmonics and melodies in serial techniques. The opera has had greater success overseas than in the U.S.

vista (It.). Sight. *A prima vista* (at 1st sight), play at sight.

vistamente (It.). Briskly, animatedly.

vite (Fr.). Fast. *Pas trop vite*, not too fast.

Vitry, Philippe de (Philippus de Vitriaco), famous French music theorist, composer, poet, and churchman; b. Vitry, Champagne, Oct. 31, 1291; d. Meaux, June 9, 1361. There are 6 towns in Champagne named Vitry, and it is not known in which of these Vitry was born. He was educated at the Sorbonne in Paris, where he later was *magister artium*; was ordained a deacon early in life, and from 1323 held several benefices; was canon of Soissons and archbishop of Brie. He became a clerk of the royal household in Paris, and about 1346 was made counselor of the court of requests (*maître des requêtes*); from 1346 to 1350 he was also in the service of Duke Jean of Normandy (heir to the throne), with whom he took part in the siege of Aiguillon (1346); when Duke Jean became king in 1350, he sent Vitry to Avignon on a mission to Pope Clement VI, who appointed him bishop of Meaux (1351).

Vitry was known as a poet and a composer, but his enduring fame rests on his *Ars nova*, a treatise expounding a new theory of mensural notation, particularly important for its development of the principle of binary rhythm; it also gives the most complete account of the various uses to which colored notes were put. Of the 4 treatises attributed to Vitry in Coussemaker's *Scriptores III*, only the last 10 of the 24 chapters of *Ars nova* are now considered authentic. Most of Vitry's works are lost; another motet, with tenor only, is also extant.

viva voce (It.). In full voice; loudly.

vivace (*vivacemente, vivo*; It.; Fr. *vivement*). 1. Lively, animatedly, spiritedly, briskly. 2. As a tempo mark standing by itself, a movement equaling or exceeding ALLEGRO in rapidity. *Vivacetto*, less lively than vivace; ALLEGRETTO; *vivacissimo*, very lively; PRESTO.

Vivaldi, Antonio (Lucio)

Greatly renowned Italian composer; b. Venice, Mar. 4, 1678; d. Vienna, July 28, 1741. He was the son of Giovanni Battista Vivaldi (b. Brescia, *c*. 1655; d. Venice, May 14, 1736), a violinist who entered the orch. at San Marco in Venice in 1685 under the surname of Rossi, remaining there until 1729; was also director of instrumental music at the Mendicanti (1689–93). The younger Vivaldi was trained for the priesthood at S. Geminiano and at S. Giovanni in Oleo, taking the tonsure in 1693 and Holy Orders in 1703. Because of his red hair he was called *il prete rosso* (the red priest).

In 1703 he became *maestro di violino* at the Pio Ospedale della Pietà, where he remained until 1709; during this period his 1st publ. works appeared. In 1711 he resumed his duties at the Pietà, and was named its *maestro de' concerti* in 1716. In 1711 his set of 12 concertos known as *L'estro armonico*, op. 3, appeared in print in Amsterdam; it proved to be the most important music publication of the 1st half of the 18th century. His 1st known opera, *Ottone in Villa*, was given in Vicenza in May 1713, and soon thereafter he became active as a composer and impresario in Venice. From 1718 to 1720 he was active in Mantua, where the Habsburg governor Prince Philipp of Hessen-Darmstadt made him *maestro di cappella da camera*, a title he retained even after leaving Mantua.

In subsequent years Vivaldi traveled widely in Italy, bringing out his operas in various music centers. However, he retained his association with the Pietà. About 1725 he became associated with the contralto Anna Giraud (or Giro), one of his voice students; her sister, Paolina, also became a constant companion of the composer, leading to speculation by his contemporaries that the 2 sisters were his mistresses, a contention he denied. His *La cetra*, op. 9 (2 books, Amsterdam, 1727), was dedicated to the Austrian Emperor Charles VI. From 1735 to 1738 he once more served as maestro di cappella at the Pietà. He also was named maestro di cappella to Francis Stephen, Duke of Lorraine (later the Emperor Francis I) in 1735.

In 1738 he visited Amsterdam, where he took charge of the musical performances for the centennial celebration of the Schouwburg Theater. Returning to Venice, he found little favor with the theatergoing public; as a result he set out for Austria in 1740, arriving in Vienna in June 1741 but dying a month later. Although he had received large sums of money in his day, he died in poverty and was given a pauper's burial at the Spettaler Gottesacher (Hospital Burial Ground).

Vivaldi's greatness lies mainly in his superb instrumental works, most notably some 500 concertos, in which he displayed an extraordinary mastery of ritornello form and of orchestration. More than 230 of his concertos are for solo violin and strings, and another 120 or so are for other solo instruments (viola d'amore, cello, flute, oboe, bassoon) or multiple instruments and strings. In some 60 *concerti ripieni* (string concertos sans solo instrument), he honed a style akin to operatic sinfonias. He also wrote about 90 sonatas.

Only 21 of his operas are extant, some missing 1 or more acts; a few have been revived in recent years: *Tito Manlio* (1719); *Farnace* (1727); *Orlando (furioso)* (1727); *La fida ninfa* (1732); *Montezuma* (1733); *L'Olimpiade* (1734); 8 serenatas; 31 solo cantatas with basso continuo; 9 solo cantatas with instrument(s) and basso continuo.

Vivaldi composed 4 oratorios, including *Juditha triumphans devicta Holofernes barbarie* (1716); sacred vocal works include 7 Masses or Mass sections, psalms, hymns, antiphons, motets, etc.

In addition to those mentioned above, collections of concertos and sinfonias publ. during Vivaldi's lifetime (in Amsterdam unless contraindicated) include *La stravaganza*, op. 4 (2 books, *c.* 1714); 6 concertos *a 5 stromenti*, op. 6 (1716–17); Concertos *a 5 stromenti*, op. 7 (2 books, *c.* 1716–17); *Il cimento dell'armonia e dell'inventione*, op. 8 (2 books, 1725; including his most popular works *The 4 Seasons*, programmatic concertos with accompanying sonnets); 6 concertos, op. 10 (*c.* 1728); 6 concertos, op. 11 (1729); 6 concertos, op. 12 (1729). Sonata collections include: Chamber Sonata for 2 Violins and Violone or Harpsichord, op. 1 (Venice, 1705); Sonata for Violin and Harpsichord (Venice, 1709; publ. as op. 2, Amsterdam, 1712–13); 6 sonatas for violin or 2 violins and basso continuo, op. 5 (1716); 6 sonatas for cello and basso continuo (1740).

The difficulty of cataloguing Vivaldi's oeuvre chronologically has led to several attempts. Ryom edited *Verzeichnis der Werke Antonio Vivaldis: Kleine Ausgabe* (Leipzig, 1974) and *Repertoire des oeuvres d'Antonio Vivaldi* (vol. I, Copenhagen, 1986). See also M. Rinaldi, *Catalogo numerico tematico delle composizioni di Antonio Vivaldi* (Rome, 1945); M. Pincherle, *Inventaire thematique* (Paris, 1948); and A. Fanna, *Antonio Vivaldi: Catalogo numerico-tematico delle opere strumentali* (Milan, 1968).

Vive la Compagnie. Anonymous German military song, *c.* 1838, now known under its French title.

vivo (It.; Fr. *vivement*). Lively, spiritedly, briskly.

Vltava (Czech.). Original title of *Moldau*, the 2nd movement of Smetana's sym. cycle *Má vlast*, 1874.

vocal. Pertaining to the voice; suitable for the singing voice. *Vocal cords*, the 2 opposed ligaments set in the larynx whose vibration, caused by expelling air from the lungs, produces vocal tones; *vocal glottis*, the aperture between the vocal cords while singing; *vocal quartet*, chamber piece for 4 singers; group of 4 solo singers within a larger group.

vocal score. The arrangement of any work for voice(s) and ensemble (up to an orch.) as a score for voice(s) and piano reduction, for rehearsal purposes and, when resources are limited, actual performance.

vocalise (Fr.). A vocal étude or composition, sung on open vowels, without text. Vocal music sometimes uses vocalise as a technique for part of its duration, such as the *Bell Song* from Delibes's *Lakme* or *Bachianas Brasileiras No. 8* by Villa-Lobos. Other primarily orch.l pieces may include a passage for solo or choral vocalise, such as Debussy's *Nocturnes* (*Sirènes*), Holst's *The Planets* (*Neptune*), and Nielsen's 3rd Sym. (2nd movement).

vocalization. Singing exercise comprising a melody sung without words; scales and arpeggios are common vocalizations used to prepare the vocal cords for performance. When incorporated in actual composition, this technique is called a VOCALISE.

voce (It.). VOICE; part. *A due (tre) voci*, for 2 (3) parts or voices, in 2 (3) parts; *colla voce*, COL CANTO; *mezza voce*, see MEZZA; *sotta voce*, see SOTTO.

voce di gola (It.). Throat voice, produced gutturally.

voce di petto (It.). CHEST TONE (VOICE).

voce di testa (It.). HEAD TONE (VOICE).

voce intonata (It.). Pure voice.

voce pastosa (It.). Flexible voice.

voce rauca (It.). Raucous voice.

voces aequales (Lat.). Equal voices, i.e., those within the same gender or age category (men, women, children).

voces musicales (Lat.). Solmization syllables.

voci artificiali (It., artificial voices). An early term for the castrato sonority.

vodun (voodoo). A Haitian religious ritual, adapted from ancestor worship and mythology in West Africa, brought to the New World by the enslaved black population. In its present form vodun comprises a whole complex of songs, dances, and the heavy use of drums; there is also a notorious occult element that gives vodun its mystery for outsiders. Similar religious practice influenced African-Americans, especially in New Orleans, until Christianity became the primary belief for the black population.

Vogelquartett (Bird Quartet). String quartet by Haydn, 1781 (No. 3, op. 33), in the key of C major; nicknamed because some of the trills and mordents in its melodies sound like an aviary in mild turmoil. The quartet is part of a 6-work set known as *Gli Scherzi* for its use of scherzo (or scherzolike) movements instead of the older, statelier minuet.

Vogelstimme (Ger.). Bird singing or song. *Wie eine Vogelstimme*, like a bird singing (Mahler, 2nd Sym.).

voglia (It.). Wish. *A voglia*, at will, AD LIBITUM.

voice (It. *voce*; Ger. *Stimme*; Fr. *voix*). 1. Human vocal production of musical tone, divided into 6 principal ranges: soprano, mezzo-soprano, contralto (alto), tenor, baritone, and bass. Animal vocal sounds are considered voices; those of birds even called songs (although whale songs are not produced through the mouth); but all lack the facility and variety of the human voice. In contemporary scores, voice parts are written constantly for untraditional sounds; sometimes speech replaces musical production altogether (Toch, *Geographical Fugue*). See SINGING; individual ranges, genres, etc. 2. A part or line, vocal or instrumental.

voice exchange (Ger. *Stimmtausch*). 1. Medieval compositional technique in which 2 polyphonic voices take up a portion of each other's music immediately and in the same range, creating the effect of a repetition of the original material. 2. In Schenkerian analysis, an exchange of notes between 2 polyphonic voices over a span of time, not necessarily in the same range.

voice leading. The art of arranging the voices in a polyphonic composition, so that each part has a logical continuation without competing with the continuation in other voices. Depending on the harmonic (tonal, chromatic, atonal) context and the strictness of the contrapuntal "rules" in force at the time, voice leading is usually easier to describe as a series of prohibitions against consecutive perfect intervals, augmented and diminished intervals (melodic and har-

monic), balance of melodic skips by countervailing steps, range overlapping, etc.

voice production. A singing and pedagogical hypothesis that the human voice can be directed or projected physiologically from the head, the chest, or the epiglottis by conscious effort. Of course the only source of the human voice is the larynx, and the only resonator is the pharynx, but even serious professional singers are convinced that the lower notes travel from the vocal cords to the thoracic cavity and the head tone (voice) is monitored from the top of the head. With the invasion of the U.S. by Italian singing teachers late in the 19th century and by Russian singers after World War I, the mythology of voice production assumed the status of a science. One Russian singer who organized an American opera company urged his students to "exercise the muscles of the brain" and was quite unimpressed when he was told that the brain had no muscular network. There is no harm in using the terms *chest voice* and *head tone* (voice) if both the teacher and the student understand that they are using metaphors. It must be remembered, however, that great natural singers like Caruso and Chaliapin developed their glorious voices never knowing whether they sang from the chest, from the head, or from the epiglottis.

voicing. Instrument tuning, especially the balancing of multiple strings or pipes in keyboard instruments.

voilé (Fr.). Veiled; muted.

Voivoda, The. VOYEVODE, THE.

voix (Fr.). Voice; part. *À deux (trois) voix*, for 2 (3) voices, in 2 (3) parts.

voix blanche (Fr., white voice). Vocal production of a bland quality without distinctive timbre.

voix céleste (Fr., heavenly voice). An 8' tremulant organ stop.

voix de poitrine (Fr.). CHEST TONE (VOICE).

voix de tête (Fr.). HEAD TONE (VOICE).

Voix Humaine, La. Opera by Poulenc, 1959, to a libretto by Cocteau, 1st produced in Paris. This is a modern melodramatic monodrama, featuring a young woman speaking on the telephone to her lover, who has apparently just announced the end of their affair. The musical style is declamatory.

Vokalmusik (Ger.). Vocal music.

volante (It.). Flying; lightly, swiftly.

Volare. Alternate if better-known name for the Italian popular song *Nel Blu, Dipinto Di Blu* by Domenico Modugno, 1958, immensely popular then and over the years.

volata (It.; Ger. *volate*; Fr. *volatine*). A short vocal run or trill; a run or division; a light, rapid series of notes. *Volatina*, a brief volata.

Volga Boatmen's Song. A famous Russian folk song; its Russian title is *Burlaki* (boatman haulers), i.e., men who pulled boats upstream on the Volga River while singing a heaving strain. The Volga boatmen are also the subject of a celebrated painting by I. E. Repin (1844–1930). The Aeolian melody is associated with funerals, which, given its doleful character, requires no suspension of disbelief.

Volkslied (Ger.). Genuine folk song.

Volkston, im (Ger.). In the style of a folk song.

volkstümlich (Ger.). Like a folk song, but newly composed; neotraditional. *Volkstümliches Lied*, an ostentatiously simple German art song that emulates the melodic and rhythmic construction of a genuine folk song; *Lorelei* by P. F. Silcher is one example of a newly composed song that was and is often mistaken for a folk song. A neotraditional composer's goal would be that one of his or her songs is so popular that it, too, is mistaken for a genuine folk song, is often performed and recorded, and is thereby a substantial source of royalties. In the U.S. Kern's *Ol' Man River* or the songs of neotraditional musicians such as Bob Dylan are the equivalent of the German genre. Sometimes a composer incorporates the *volkstümlicher Geist* (spirit) into a composition without the limitation of pure imitation; Mahler's music, particularly his *Des Knaben Wunderhorn* works, exemplifies this style.

Volksweise (Ger.). Folk song or neotraditional melody.

voll (Ger.). Full. *Volles Orchester*, full orch.; *volles Werk*, full organ registration; *mit vollem Chöre*, with full chorus.

volles Zeitmass (Ger., full time measure). Strictly in time.

volltönend (volltönig; Ger.). Sonorously, resonantly.

Volo di Notte (Night Flight). Opera by Dallapiccola, 1940, premiered in Florence, based on the novel *Vol de Nuit* by St.-Exupéry. The protagonist takes a dramatic night flight over the Andes in a single-engine monoplane. The composer set the work in a dynamic atonal idiom, verging on dodecaphony; the score includes spoken dialogue and a wordless passage of a disembodied voice speaking to the pilot.

Volpone (The Fox). Opera by Antheil, 1953, 1st produced in Los Angeles. The libretto is taken from Ben Jonson's famous comedy, in which a sly Venetian miser spreads a rumor that he is dying, which encourages hopeful aspirants to his fortune to lavish attention, affection, and gifts on him. He then stages a miraculous recovery, leaving his would-be heirs in a state of chagrin and financial loss.

volta (*lavolta*; It., the turn). A dance of Provençal origin, popular in Western European courts between 1550 and 1650, described by Arbeau in *Orchésographie* (1588). The volta is in 3/4 or 3/2 time, at a relatively slow lilt. Unusual in its being a true couple dance; it features individual jumps by the dancers followed by a well-coordinated lift of the female by the male partner; each of the 3 jumps occur simultaneously with a three-quarter (280°) turn. It is mentioned in Shakespeare. Examples are found in lute, keyboard, and ensemble arrangements.

volta, -i (It.). A turn; time. *Prime volta* (or *Ima volta, Ima, Ia, I.,* 1.), 1st time or ending; *secunda volta* (or *IIda volta, IIda, IIa, II.,* 2.), second time or ending; *una volta*, once; *due volta*, twice.

voltare la pagina (It.). Turn the page.

volteggiando (It.). In certain keyboard passages, play with crossed hands.

volti subito (It.; abbrev. *v.s.*). Turn (the page) over immediately.

volubilmente (*volubile*; It.). Fluently, flexibly, flowing easily.

voluntary. A partly or wholly improvised organ piece used in Anglican church services. As the name indicates, such a piece is freely "volunteered," stylistically speaking. Traditionally it was written in a polyphonic idiom—containing elements of imitation—and was of a cheerful nature. English composers of the 17th and 18th centuries wrote many such voluntaries, not necessarily for organ or for religious settings. Eventually British organists applied the term to any kind of improvisation, particularly one using the loud cornet stop. The best known work of this genre is Jeremiah Clarke's *Trumpet Voluntary* (before 1700), long thought to be by Purcell; its subtitle (*The Prince of Denmark's March*) suggests its mood and milieu.

voluttuoso (It.). Voluptuous.

vom (Ger.). From the. *Vom Anfang*, DA CAPO.

Von Heute auf Morgen (From Day to Day). Opera by Schoenberg, 1930, 1st produced in Frankfurt. The score makes use of the full-fledged method of composition with 12 tones. The plot describes the daily effort of a housewife to retain the affections of her indifferent husband.

Von Stade, Frederica, remarkable American mezzosoprano; b. Somerville, N.J., June 1, 1945. She was educated at the Norton Academy in Conn.; after an apprenticeship at the Long Wharf Theater in New Haven she studied with Sebastian Engelberg, Paul Berl, and Otto Guth at the Mannes College of Music in N.Y. Although she reached only the semifinals of the Metropolitan Opera Auditions in 1969, she attracted the attention of Rudolf Bing, its general manager, who arranged for her debut with the company in N.Y. as the 3rd Boy in *Die Zauberflöte* (1970); she gradually took on more important roles there before going to Europe, where she gave an arresting portrayal of Cherubino at the opera house at the palace of Versailles in 1973.

In 1974 she sang Nina in the premiere of Pasatieri's *The Seagull* at the Houston Grand Opera. In 1975 she made her debut at London's Covent Garden as Rosina; subsequently attained extraordinary success in lyric mezzo-soprano roles with the world's major opera houses and also pursued an extensive concert career, appearing regularly with the Chamber Music Soc. of Lincoln Center. In 1988 she sang the role of Tina in the premiere of Argento's *The Aspern Papers* at the Dallas Lyric Opera, and in 1990 appeared in recital in N.Y.'s Carnegie Hall. Her memorable roles include Dorabella, Idamante, Adalgisa in *Norma*, Charlotte in *Werther*, Melisande, Octavian, and Malcolm in *La Donna del lago*. She has also proved successful as a crossover artist, especially in Broadway musical recordings.

voodoo. VODUN.

Vorausnahme (Ger.). ANTICIPATION.

Vordersatz (Ger., sectional antecedent). The 1st theme or subject of a musical PERIOD.

Vorgänger (Ger., one who goes 1st). Canonic subject or DUX.

vorgetragen (Ger.). Bring out. *Innig vorgetragen*, feelingly brought out.

Vorhalt (Ger.). A suspension.

vorher (Ger.). Before; previously.

vorig (Ger.). Preceding; previous. *Im vorigen Zeitmasse (tempo precedente)*, in the previous tempo.

Vorimitation (Ger.). In a fugal section, a preliminary imitation prior to the full exposition of the subject.

Vorschlag (Ger., forestroke). APPOGGIATURA.

Vorspiel (Ger.). A prelude, prologue, or overture. Wagner treated the Vorspiel as an introduction in a very broad sense and designated *Das Rheingold* as the Vorspiel to his tetralogy *Der Ring des Nibelungen*.

Vortrag (Ger.). Rendering, interpretation, performance, style, delivery, execution. *Vortragsstück* (performance piece), a composition calculated to appeal to the general public; *Vortragzeichen*, expression mark.

vorwärts (Ger.). Forward. *Etwas vorwärts gehend*, somewhat faster, *poco più mosso*; *vorwärts dringend*, driving forward.

Vorzeichnung (Ger.). Generic term for time or key signature.

votive mass. Roman Catholic Mass celebrated at the express wish of an individual votary.

vox (Lat., voice). 1. In medieval Latin nomenclature, a sound produced by any source. 2. In the theory of organum, *vox principalis* is the part with the cantus firmus; *vox organalis*, the added contrapuntal voice. *Vox angelica* (angelic voice), a 4' stop corresponding to the 8' vox humana; *vox harmonica*, human voice; *vox humana* (human voice), an 8' reed stop, with a (fancied) resemblance to the human voice; *vox organica*, wind instruments or organ.

Voyage of Edgar Allan Poe, The. Opera by Argento, 1976, his 3rd stage work, written in an expansively Romantic and ingratiating songful manner; it was 1st produced in Minneapolis. The libretto imagines a dream of Poe's in which he recapitulates the nostalgic and painful memories of his life, focusing mainly on his child bride who died before him.

Voyevode, The (The Voivoda). Sym. ballad by Tchaikovsky, 1891, 1st performed in Moscow. This work has no connection with Tchaikovsky's opera with the same name but is inspired by Pushkin's translation of a poem by Adam Mickiewicz (1798–1855). It has some merit, although Tchaikovsky himself referred to the score as "a piece of rubbish."

Voyevode, The (The Voivoda). Opera by Tchaikovsky, 1869, 1st performed in Moscow; the libretto is based on Ostrovsky's play *A Dream on the Volga*. The story deals with the attempt by the head of a Volga community to abduct a young woman engaged to another. He has a prophetic dream of his downfall, which comes true when he is dismissed from office by the Czar. His intended victim is now free to marry her beloved. Tchaikovsky destroyed the opera, but orch. parts were later discovered, and Pavel Lamm, the great restorer of fragmentary Russian operas, was able to reconstruct the work.

v.s. VOLTI SUBITO.

vue (Fr.). View. *À première vue* (at 1st sight), play À LIVRE OUVERT.

vuota battuta (It., empty measure). A general pause.

vuoto, -a (It.). Empty. *Corda vuoto*, open string.

Výlety pana Broučka. EXCURSIONS OF MISTER BROUČEK, THE.

Vysehrád. Sym. poem by Smetana, 1872–74, the 1st in the *Má vlast* cycle. The eponymous historic town is located on the Danube river.

Waart, Edo (Eduard) **de,** noted Dutch conductor; b. Amsterdam, June 1, 1941. He was a member of a musical family; his father sang in the chorus of the Netherlands Opera. He 1st studied the piano; at 13 he took up the oboe; at 16 he entered the Amsterdam Muzieklyceum, where he studied oboe and later cello (graduated, 1962); during the summer of 1960 he attended the conducting classes in Salzburg given by Dean Dixon. He played oboe in the Amsterdam Phil. (1962–63) and then joined the Concertgebouw Orch.; also studied conducting with Franco Ferrara in Hilversum, where he made his debut as a conductor with the Netherlands Radio Phil. in 1964.

He went to the U.S. that year and was one of the winners in the Mitropoulos Competition in N.Y.; in 1965–66 he was assistant conductor with the N.Y. Phil. Upon his return to Amsterdam in 1966, he was appointed assistant conductor of the Concertgebouw Orch., and accompanied it on a tour of the U.S. in 1967. He also organized the Netherlands Wind Ensemble, with which he established his reputation through extensive tours. In 1967 he became a guest conductor of the Rotterdam Phil.; from 1973 to 1979, served as its chief conductor. He toured with it in England in 1970 and 1974; in the U.S. in 1971, 1975, and 1977; and in Germany and Austria in 1976. In 1971, 1972, and 1975 he was a guest conductor of the Santa Fe Opera in New Mexico; in 1975 he also conducted opera in Houston. In 1976 he conducted at Covent Garden in London. In 1974, he made a successful debut with the San Francisco Sym.

In 1975 he was made its principal guest conductor and in 1977 its music director. In 1986 he became music director of the Minnesota Orch. in Minneapolis, and in 1988 was named artistic director of the Dutch Radio Phil. Orch. in Hilversum. De Waart represents the modern generation of sym. and operatic conductors; his objective approach to interpretation, combined with his regard for stylistic propriety and avoidance of ostentatious conductorial display, makes his performances of the traditional and contemporary repertory particularly appealing. He is tall, athletic-looking, and boasts a rich crown of hair; these attributes, topologically speaking, help him dominate the orch.

wachsend (Ger., growing). Crescendo.

Wacht am Rhein, Die. A rousing patriotic German hymn by Carl Wilhelm, 1840, which exhorted the Germans to keep "watch on the Rhine." It became famous during the Franco-Prussian War of 1870–71, when the Germans not only maintained their watch on the Rhine but actually crossed the river in Alsace and appropriated the city of Strasbourg, which became Strassburg in German, until its recovery by France after World War I.

Waffenschmied, Der (The Gunsmith). Comic opera by Lortzing, 1846, premiered in Vienna. In the city of Worms, the local gunsmith despises aristocracy; but a local count disguises and hires himself out as an apprentice to the gunsmith in order to woo his daughter. The two young people finally get married. The opera had success on the German stage.

Wagner, Cosima, daughter of Franz Liszt and the Countess Marie d'Agoult, 1st wife of Hans (Guido) von Bülow, 2nd wife of (Wilhelm) Richard Wagner; b. Bellagio, on Lake Como, Dec. 24, 1837; d. Bayreuth, Apr. 1, 1930. She received an excellent education in Paris; married von Bülow in 1857; there were 2 daughters of this marriage, Blandine and Daniela; the 3rd daughter, Isolde, was Wagner's child, as was the 4th, Eva, and the son, Siegfried.

A divorce followed (1870); the marriage to Wagner took place a few weeks later. A woman of high intelligence, practical sense, and imperious character, Cosima emerged after Richard's death as a powerful personage in all affairs regarding the continuance of the Bayreuth Festivals, as well as the complex matters pertaining to the rights of performance of Wagner's works all over the world. She publ. her reminiscences of Liszt: *Franz Liszt, Ein Gedenkblatt von seiner Tochter* (Munich, 2nd ed., 1911).

Wagner, Siegfried (Helferich Richard), German conductor and composer, son of (Wilhelm) Richard and Cosima Wagner; b. Triebschen, June 6, 1869; d. Bayreuth, Aug. 4, 1930. His parents were married in 1870, and Siegfried was thus legitimated. Richard Wagner named the *Siegfried Idyll* for him, and it was performed in Wagner's house in Triebschen on Christmas Day, 1870. He studied with Humperdinck in Frankfurt am Main and then pursued training as an architect in Berlin and Karlsruhe; during his tenure as an assistant in Bayreuth (1892–96), he studied with his mother, Hans Richter, and Julius Kniese. From 1896 he was a regular conductor in Bayreuth, where he was general director of the Festival productions from 1906. In 1915, he married Winifred Williams, an adopted daughter of Karl Klindworth. In 1923–24 he visited the U.S. in order to raise funds for the reopening of the Bayreuth Festspielhaus, which had been closed during the course of World War I. He conducted from memory, and left-handed. In his career as a composer, he was greatly handicapped by inevitable comparisons with his father. He wrote 12 operas, orch.l works, vocal pieces, and chamber music.

Wagner tuba. A brass instrument introduced by Wagner in *Der Ring des Nibelungen*, in two sizes, tenor and bass; its funnel-shaped mouthpiece helps to create a tone somewhere between the tuba and the trombone. Bruckner, Stravinsky, and R. Strauss also used the Wagner tuba.

Wagner, (Wilhelm) Richard

Great German composer whose operas, written to his own librettos, have radically transformed the concept of stage music, postulating the inherent equality of drama and sym. accompaniment, and establishing the uninterrupted continuity of the action; b. Leipzig, May 22, 1813; d. Venice, Feb. 13, 1883. The antecedents of his family, and his own origin, are open to controversy. His father was a police registrar in Leipzig who died when Wagner was only 6 months old; his mother, Johanna (Rosine), née Pätz, was the daughter of a baker in Weissenfels; it is possible that she was an illegitimate offspring of Prince Friedrich Ferdinand Constantin of Weimar.

Eight months after her husband's death, Johanna Wagner married the actor Ludwig Geyer (1814). This hasty marriage generated speculation that Geyer may have been Wagner's real father; Wagner himself entertained this possibility, pointing out the similarity of his and Geyer's prominent noses; in the end he abandoned this surmise. The problem of Wagner's origin arose with renewed force after the triumph of the Nazi party in Germany, as Hitler's adoration of Wagner was put in jeopardy by suspicions that Geyer might have been Jewish and that if Wagner was indeed his natural son then he himself was tainted by Semitic blood. Nazi biologists and archivists delved anxiously into Geyer's own ancestry, and much to the relief of Goebbels and other Nazi intellectuals it was found that Geyer, like Wagner's nominal father, was the purest of Aryans.

Geyer was a member of the Court Theater in Dresden, and the family moved there in 1814. Geyer died in 1821; in 1822 Wagner entered the Dresden Kreuzschule, where he remained a pupil until 1827. Carl Maria von Weber often visited the Geyer home; these visits exercised a beneficial influence on Wagner in his formative years. In 1825 he began to take piano lessons from a local musician named Humann, and also studied violin with Robert Sipp. Wagner showed strong literary inclinations, and under the spell of Shakespeare he wrote a tragedy, *Leubald*. In 1827 he moved with his mother back to Leipzig, where his uncle Adolf Wagner gave him guidance in his classical reading. In 1828 he was enrolled in the Nikolaischule; while in school he had lessons in harmony with Christian Gottlieb Müller, a violinist in the theater orch.

In 1830 he entered the Thomasschule, where he began to compose; he wrote a string quartet and some piano music; his overture in B-flat major was performed at the Leipzig Theater (also 1830), under the direction of Heinrich Dorn. Now determined to dedicate himself entirely to music, he became a student of Theodor Weinlig, cantor of the Thomaskirche, from whom he received a thorough training in counterpoint and composition. His 1st publ. work was a piano sonata in B-flat major, to which he assigned the opus number 1; it was brought out by the prestigious publ. house of Breitkopf & Härtel in 1832. He then wrote an overture to *König Enzio*, performed at the Leipzig Theater (1832); it was followed by an overture in C major, which was presented at a Gewandhaus concert (1832).

Wagner's 1st major orch.l work, a sym. in C major, was performed at a Prague Cons. concert (1832); in 1833 it was played by the Gewandhaus Orch. in Leipzig; he was 19 years old at the time. In 1832 he wrote an opera, *Die Hochzeit*, after J. G. Busching's *Ritterzeit und Ritterwesen*; an introduction, a septet, and a chorus from this work are extant. Early in 1833 he began work on *Die Feen*, to a libretto after Carlo Gozzi's *La Donna serpente*. Upon completion of *Die Feen* in early 1834, he offered the score to the Leipzig Theater, but it was rejected. In the summer of 1834 he began to sketch out a new opera, *Das Liebesverbot*, after Shakespeare's play *Measure for Measure*. That summer he obtained the position of music director with Heinrich Bethmann's theater company, based in Magdeburg; he made his debut in Bad Lauschstadt, conducting *Don Giovanni*.

In 1836 he led the premiere of his opera *Das Liebesverbot*, presented under the title *Die Novize von Palermo* in Magdeburg. Bethmann's company soon went out of business; Wagner, who was by that time deeply involved with Christine Wilhelmine (Minna) Planer, an actress with the company, followed her to Königsberg, where they were married (1836). In Königsberg he composed the overture *Rule Britannia*; in 1837 he was appointed music director of the Königsberg town theater. His marital affairs suffered a setback when Minna left

him for a rich businessman by the name of Dietrich. In 1837 he went to Riga as music director of the theater there; coincidentally, Minna's sister was engaged as a singer at the same theater; Minna became reconciled with Wagner. In Riga Wagner worked on his new opera, *Rienzi, der letzte der Tribunen*, after a popular novel by Bulwer-Lytton.

In 1839 Wagner lost his position in Riga; he and Minna, burdened by debts, left town to seek their fortune elsewhere. In their passage by sea from Pillau they encountered a fierce storm, and the ship was forced to drop anchor in the Norwegian fjord of Sandwike. They made their way to London, and then set out for Boulogne; there Wagner met Meyerbeer, who gave him a letter of recommendation to the director of the Paris Opéra. He arrived in Paris with Minna in 1839, and remained there until 1842. He was forced to eke out a meager subsistence by making piano arrangements of operas and writing occasional articles for the *Gazette Musicale*. In 1840 he completed his overture to *Faust* (later rev. as *Eine Faust-Ouvertüre*).

Soon he found himself in dire financial straits; he owed money that he could not repay, and later that year, he was confined in debtors' prison; he was released after 3 weeks. The conditions of his containment were light, and he was able to leave prison on certain days. In the meantime he had completed the libretto for *Der fliegende Holländer*; he submitted it to the director of the Paris Opéra, but the director had already asked Paul Foucher to prepare a libretto on the same subject. The director was willing, however, to buy Wagner's scenario for 500 French francs; Wagner accepted the offer (1841). Louis Dietsch brought out his treatment of the subject in his opera *Le Vaisseau fantôme* (Paris Opéra, 1842).

In 1842 Wagner received the welcome news from Dresden that his opera *Rienzi* had been accepted for production; it was staged there in 1842, with considerable success. *Der fliegende Holländer* was also accepted by Dresden, and Wagner conducted its 1st performance there in 1843. Later that year he was named 2nd Hofkapellmeister in Dresden, where he conducted a large repertoire of Classic operas, among them *Don Giovanni*, *Le nozze di Figaro*, *Die Zauberflöte*, *Fidelio*, and *Der Freischütz*. In 1846 he conducted a memorable performance in Dresden of Beethoven's 9th Sym. In Dresden he led the prestigious choral society *Liedertafel*, for which he wrote several works, including the "biblical scene" *Das Liebesmahl der Apostel*. He was also preoccupied during those years in working on the score and music for *Tannhäuser*, completing it in 1845. He conducted its 1st performance in Dresden in 1845. He subsequently revised the score, which was staged to better advantage there in 1847. Concurrently he began work on *Lohengrin*, which he completed in 1848.

Wagner's efforts to have his works publ. failed, leaving him again in debt. Without waiting for further performances of his operas that had already been presented to the public, he drew up the 1st prose outline of *Der Nibelungen-Mythus als Entwurf zu einem Drama*, the prototype of the epic *Ring* cycle; in 1848 he began work on the poem for *Siegfrieds Tod*. At that time he joined the revolutionary Vaterlandsverein and was drawn into active participation in the movement, culminating in an open uprising in May 1849. An order was issued for his arrest, and he had to leave Dresden; he made his way to Weimar, where he found a cordial reception from Liszt; he then proceeded to Vienna, where a Prof. Widmann lent him his own passport so that Wagner could cross the border of Saxony on his way to Zurich; there he made his home in July 1849; Minna joined him there a few months later.

Shortly before leaving Dresden he had sketched 2 dramas, *Jesus von Nazareth* and *Achilleus*; both remained unfinished. In Zurich he wrote a number of essays expounding his philosophy of art: *Die Kunst und die Revolution* (1849), *Das Kunstwerk der Zukunft* (1849), *Kunst und Klima* (1850), *Oper und Drama* (1851), and *Eine Mitteilung an meine Freunde* (1851). The ideas expressed in *Das Kunstwerk der Zukunft* gave rise to the description of Wagner's operas as "music of the future" by his opponents; they were also described as GESAMTKUNSTWERK by his admirers. He rejected both descriptions as distortions of his real views; he eventually rejected the term MUSIC DRAMA, which nevertheless has become an accepted definition for all of his operas.

In 1850 Wagner was again in Paris; there he fell in love with Jessie Laussot, the wife of a wine merchant; however, she eventually left Wagner, and he returned to Minna in Zurich. In 1850 Liszt conducted the successful premiere of *Lohengrin* in Weimar. In 1851 Wagner wrote the verse text of *Der junge Siegfried* and prose sketches for *Das Rheingold* and *Die Walküre*. In 1852 he finished the text of *Die Walküre* and of *Das Rheingold*; he completed

the entire libretto of *Der Ring des Nibelungen* in 1852, and it was privately printed in 1853.

In 1853 he began composition of the music for *Das Rheingold*, completing the full score in 1854. In 1854 he commenced work on the music of *Die Walküre*, which he finished in 1856. In 1854 he became friendly with a wealthy Zurich merchant, Otto Wesendonck (1815–96), and his wife, Mathilde (Luckemeyer) Wesendonck (b. Elberfeld, Dec. 23, 1828; d. Traunblick, near Altmünster on the Traunsee, Austria, Aug. 31, 1902; they were married in 1848). Her 1st meeting with Wagner took place in Zurich early in 1852; they soon developed a deep friendship.

Otto Wesendonck was willing to give Wagner a substantial loan, to be repaid out of his performance rights. The situation became complicated when Wagner developed an affection for Mathilde, which in all probability remained platonic. She wrote the famous *Fünf Gedichte* (*Der Engel, Stehe still, Träume, Schmerzen, Im Treibhaus*), which Wagner set to music as studies for *Tristan und Isolde*. The album was publ. as the *Wesendonck-Lieder* in 1857. In 1855 he conducted a series of 8 concerts with the Phil. Soc. of London. His performances were greatly praised by English musicians, and he had the honor of meeting Queen Victoria, who invited him to her loge at the intermission of his 7th concert.

In 1856 he made substantial revisions in the last dramas of *Der Ring des Nibelungen*, changing their titles to *Siegfried* and *Götterdämmerung*. Throughout these years he was preoccupied with writing a new opera, *Tristan und Isolde*, permeated with the dual feelings of love and death. In 1857 he prepared the 1st sketch of *Parzival* (later titled *Parsifal*). In 1858 he moved to Venice, where he completed the full score of the 2nd act of *Tristan und Isolde*. The Dresden authorities, acting through their Austrian confederates and still determined to bring Wagner to trial as a revolutionary, pressured Venice to expel him from its territory. Once more Wagner took refuge in Switzerland; he decided to stay in Lucerne; while there he completed the score of *Tristan und Isolde*, in 1859.

That autumn he moved to Paris, where Minna joined him. In 1860 he conducted 3 concerts of his music at the Théâtre-Italien. Napoleon III became interested in his work, and in 1860 ordered the director of the Paris Opéra to produce Wagner's opera *Tannhäuser*; after considerable work, revisions, and a trans. into French, it was given at the Opéra (1861). It proved to be a fiasco, and Wagner withdrew the opera after 3 performances. For some reason the Jockey Club of Paris led a vehement protest against him; the critics also joined in this opposition, mainly because the French audiences were not accustomed to the mystically Romantic, heavily Germanic operatic music.

Invectives hurled against him by the Paris press make extraordinary reading; the comparison of Wagner's music with the sound produced by a domestic cat walking down the keyboard of the piano was a favorite critical device. The French caricaturists exercised their wit by picturing him in the act of hammering a poor listener's ear. In Austria Hanslick used his great literary gift and a flair for a striking simile to damn him as a purveyor of cacophony. Oscar Wilde added his measure of wit. "I like Wagner's music better than anybody's," he remarked in *The Picture of Dorian Gray*. "It is so loud that one can talk the whole time without people hearing what one says." In an amazing turnabout, Nietzsche, a worshipful admirer of Wagner, publ. a venomous denunciation of his erstwhile idol in *Der Fall Wagner* (1888), in which he vesuviated in a sulfuric eruption of righteous wrath; Wagner made music itself sick, he proclaimed; but at the time Nietzsche himself was already on the borderline of madness.

Politically Wagner's prospects began to improve; in 1860 he was informed of a partial amnesty by the Saxon authorities. That year he visited Baden-Baden, in his 1st visit to Germany in 11 years. Finally, in 1862 he was granted a total amnesty, which allowed him access to Saxony. In 1861 Otto Wesendonck had invited Wagner to Venice; free from political persecution, he could now go there without fear. While in Venice he returned to a scenario he had prepared in Marienbad in 1845 for a comic opera, *Die Meistersinger von Nürnberg*. In 1862 he moved to Biebrich, where he began composing the score for *Die Meistersinger*. Minna, after a brief period of reconciliation with Wagner, left him, settling in Dresden, where she died in 1866.

In order to repair his financial situation, he accepted a number of concert appearances, traveling as an orch. conductor to Vienna, Prague, St. Petersburg, Moscow, and other cities (1862–63). In 1862 he gave in Vienna a private reading of *Die Meistersinger*. It is said that the formidable Vienna critic Hanslick was angered when he found out that Wagner had caricatured him in the part of Beckmesser in *Die Meistersinger* (the original name of the character was Hans Lick), and he let out his discomfiture in further attacks on Wagner.

Wagner's fortunes changed spectacularly in 1864 when young King Ludwig II of Bavaria (1845–86) ascended the throne and invited him to Munich with the promise of unlimited help in carrying out his various projects. In return, Wagner composed the *Huldigungsmarsch*, which he dedicated to his royal patron. The publ. correspondence between Wagner and the King is extraordinary in its display of mutual admiration, gratitude, and affection; still, difficulties soon developed when the Bavarian Cabinet told Ludwig that his lavish support of Wagner's projects threatened the Bavarian economy. Ludwig was forced to advise him to leave Munich. Wagner took this advice as an order, and late in 1865 he went to Switzerland.

A very serious difficulty arose also in Wagner's emotional life when he became intimately involved with Liszt's daughter Cosima, wife of Hans von Bülow, the famous conductor and an impassioned proponent of Wagner's music. In 1865 Cosima Bülow gave birth to Wagner's daughter, whom he named Isolde after the heroine of his opera that Bülow was preparing for performance in Munich. Its premiere took place with great acclaim, 2 months after the birth of Isolde, with Bülow conducting. That summer he prepared the prose sketch of *Parzival*, and began to dictate his autobiography, *Mein Leben*, to Cosima. In 1866 he resumed the composition of *Die Meistersinger*; he settled in a villa in Tribschen, on Lake Lucerne, where Cosima joined him permanently in 1868. He completed the full score of *Die Meistersinger* in 1867. In 1868 Bülow conducted its premiere in Munich in the presence of King Ludwig, who sat in the royal box with Wagner.

A son, significantly named Siegfried, was born to Cosima and Wagner in 1869. In 1869 *Das Rheingold* was produced in Munich. In 1870 *Die Walküre* was staged there. In 1870 Cosima and Bülow were divorced, and shortly thereafter Wagner and Cosima were married in Lucerne. Late in 1870 Wagner wrote the *Siegfried Idyll*, based on the themes from his opera; it was performed in their villa in Bayreuth on Christmas morning, the day after Cosima's birthday, as a surprise for her. In 1871 he wrote the *Kaisermarsch* to mark the victorious conclusion of the Franco-German War; he conducted it in the presence of Kaiser Wilhelm I at a concert in the Royal Opera House in Berlin in 1871.

Later that year, in Leipzig, Wagner made public his plans for realizing his cherished dream of building his own theater in Bayreuth for the production of the entire cycle of *Der Ring des Nibelungen*. In late 1871 the Bayreuth town council offered him a site for a proposed Festspielhaus; in 1872 the cornerstone was laid; Wagner commemorated the event by conducting a performance of Beethoven's 9th Sym. (this was his 59th birthday). In 1873 Wagner began to build his own home in Bayreuth, which he called *Wahnfried* (free from delusion). In order to complete the building of the Festspielhaus, he appealed to King Ludwig for additional funds. Ludwig gave him 100,000 talers for this purpose.

Now the dream of Wagner's life was realized. During the summer of 1876 *Der Ring des Nibelungen* went through rehearsals; King Ludwig attended the final dress rehearsals; the official premiere of the cycle took place in Aug. 1876, under the direction of Hans Richter; in all, 3 complete productions of the *Ring* cycle were given that month. Ludwig was faithful to the end to Wagner, whom he called "my divine friend." In his castle Neuschwanstein he installed architectural representations of scenes from Wagner's operas. Soon Ludwig's mental deterioration became obvious to everyone, and he was committed to an asylum. There, in 1886, he overpowered the psychiatrist escorting him on a walk and dragged him to his death in the Starnberg Lake, drowning himself as well.

The spectacles in Bayreuth attracted music lovers and notables from all over the world. Even those who were not partial to Wagner's ideas or appreciative of his music went to Bayreuth out of curiosity; Tchaikovsky was one such skeptical visitor. Despite world success and fame, Wagner still labored under financial difficulties. He even addressed a letter to an American dentist practicing in Dresden (who also treated Wagner's teeth) in which he tried to interest him in arranging Wagner's permanent transfer to the U.S. He voiced disillusionment in his future prospects in Germany and said he would be willing to settle in America provided a

Richard Wagner

sum of $1 million would be guaranteed to him by American bankers, and a comfortable estate for him and his family could be found in a climatically clement part of the country. Nothing came of this particular proposal. He did establish an American connection when he wrote, for a fee of $5,000, a *Grosser Festmarsch* for the observance of the U.S. centennial in 1876, dedicated to the "beautiful young ladies of America."

In the middle of all this Wagner became infatuated with Judith Gautier; their affair lasted for about 2 years (1876–78). He completed the full score of *Parsifal* (as it was now called) in 1882, in Palermo. It was performed for the 1st time at the Bayreuth Festival that year, followed by 15 subsequent performances. At the final performance, in 1882, Wagner stepped to the podium in the last act and conducted the work to its close; this was his last appearance as a conductor. He went to Venice in the fall of 1882 for a period of rest (he had angina pectoris). Early in 1883 he suffered a massive heart attack and died in Cosima's presence. His body was interred in a vault in the garden of his Wahnfried villa in Bayreuth.

Wagner's role in music history is immense. Not only did he create works of great beauty and tremendous brilliance, but he generated an entirely new concept of the art of music, exercising an influence on generations of composers all over the globe. R. Strauss extended Wagner's grandiose vision to sym. music, fashioning the form of a tone poem that uses leading motifs and vivid programmatic description of the scenes portrayed in his music. Even Rimsky-Korsakov, far as he stood from Wagner's ideas of musical composition, reflected the spirit of Parsifal in his own religious opera, *The Legend of the City of Kitezh*. Schoenberg's 1st significant work, *Verklärte Nacht*, is Wagnerian in its color. Lesser composers, unable to escape Wagner's magic domination, attempted to follow him literally by writing trilogies and tetralogies on a parallel plan with his *Ring*.

Wagner's reform of opera was incomparably more far-reaching in aim, import, and effect than that of Gluck, whose main purpose was to counteract the arbitrary predominance of the singers; this goal Wagner accomplished through insistence upon the dramatic truth of his music. When he rejected traditional opera, he did so in the conviction that such an artificial form could not serve as a basis for true dramatic expression. In its place he gave the world a new form and new techniques. So revolutionary was Wagner's art that conductors and singers had to undergo special training in the new style of interpretation in order to perform his works. Thus he became the founder of interpretative conducting and of a new school of dramatic singing, so that such terms as *Wagnerian tenor* and *Wagnerian soprano* became a part of the musical vocabulary.

In his many essays and declarations Wagner condemns the illogical plan of Italian opera and French grand opera. To quote his own words, "The mistake in the art-form of the opera consists in this, that a means of expression [music] was made the end, and the end to be expressed [the drama] was made a means." The choice of subjects assumes utmost importance in Wagner's aesthetics. He wrote: "The subject treated by the word-tone poet [*Worttondichter*] is entirely human, freed from all convention and from everything historically formal." The new artwork creates its own artistic form; continuous thematic development of basic motifs becomes a fundamental procedure for the logical cohesion of the drama; these highly individualized generating motifs, appearing singly, in bold relief, or subtly varied and intertwined with other motifs, present the ever-changing soul states of the characters of the drama, and form the connecting links for the dramatic situations of the total artwork, in a form of musical declamation that Wagner described as "Sprechsingen." Characters in Wagner's stage works become themselves symbols of such soul states, so that even mythical gods, magic-workers, heroic horses, and speaking birds become expressions of eternal verities, illuminating the human behavior. It is for this reason that Wagner selected in most of his operas figures that reflect philosophical ideas.

Yet this very solemnity of Wagner's great images on the stage bore the seeds of their own destruction in a world governed by different aesthetic principles. Thus it came to pass that the Wagnerian domination of the musical stage suddenly lost its power with changes in human society and aesthetic codes. Spectators and listeners were no longer interested in solving artistic puzzles on the stage. A demand for human simplicity arose against Wagnerian heroic complexity. The public at large found greater enjoyment in the realistic nonsense of Verdi's romantic operas than in the unreality of symbolic truth in Wagner's operas. By the 2nd quarter of the 20th century, few if any composers tried to imitate Wagner; all at once his grandeur and animation became an unnatural and asphyxiating constraint.

In the domain of melody, harmony, and orchestration Wagner's art was as revolutionary as was his total artwork on the stage. He introduced the idea of an endless melody, a continuous flow of diatonic and chromatic tones; the tonality became fluid and uncertain, producing an impression of unattainability, so that the listener accustomed to Classic modulatory schemes could not easily feel the direction toward the tonic; the prelude to *Tristan und Isolde* is a classic example of such fluidity of harmonic elements. The use of long unresolved dominant-9th-chords and the dramatic tremolos of diminished-7th-chords contributed to this state of musical uncertainty, which disturbed the critics and the audiences alike. But Wagnerian harmony also became the foundation of the new method of composition that adopted a free flow of modulatory progressions. Without Wagner the chromatic idioms of the 20th century could not exist. In orchestration, too, Wagner introduced great innovations; he created new instruments, such as the so-called WAGNER TUBA, and he increased his demands on the virtuosity of individual orch. players. The vertiginous flight of the bassoon to the high E in the Overture to *Tannhäuser* could not have been attempted before the advent of Wagner.

A less-known aspect of Wagner's was his many arrangements and editions: piano scores of Beethoven's 9th Sym. and Haydn's Sym. No. 103; vocal scores for Donizetti's *La Favorite* (1840) and *L'elisir d'amore* (1840); Halévy's *La Reine de Chypre* (1841) and *Le Guitarrero* (1841); new close to the overture and new trans. of Gluck's *Iphigénie en Aulide* (Dresden, 1847); Palestrina's Stabat Mater (Dresden, 1848); Mozart's *Don Giovanni*, version of dialogues and recitatives and partial new tr. (Zurich, 1850; not extant).

Wagner became the target of political contention during World War I when audiences in the Allied countries associated his sonorous works with German imperialism. An even greater obstacle to further performances of

Wagner's music arose with the rise of Hitler. Hitler ordered the slaughter of millions of Jews; he was an enthusiastic admirer of Wagner, who himself entertained anti-Semitic notions (see his essay *Judaism in Music*, 1850); *ergo*, Wagner was guilty by association of mass murder. Can art be separated from politics, particularly when politics become murderous? Jewish musicians in Tel Aviv refused to play the prelude to *Tristan und Isolde* when it was put on the program of a sym. concert under Zubin Mehta, and booed him for his intention to inflict Wagner on Wagner's philosophical victims.

Several periodicals dealing with Wagner were publ. in Germany and elsewhere; Wagner himself began issuing *Bayreuther Blätter* in 1878 as an aid to understanding his operas; this journal continued publication until 1938. Remarkably enough, a French periodical, *Revue Wagnerienne*, began appearing in 1885, at a time when French composers realized the tremendous power of Wagnerian aesthetics; it was publ. sporadically for a number of years. A Wagner Soc. in London publ., from 1888 to 1895, a quarterly journal entitled, significantly, *The Meister*.

Wagner devoted a large amount of his enormous productive activity to writing. Besides the dramatic works he set to music, he wrote several plays, librettos, scenarios, and novellas: *Leubald, Ein Trauerspiel* (1826–28); *Die hohe Braut, oder Bianca und Giuseppe*, 4-act tragic opera (prose scenario, 1836–42); *Mannerlist grosser als Frauenlist, oder Die glückliche Bärenfamilie*, 2-act comic opera (libretto, 1837; some music completed); *Eine Pilgerfahrt zu Beethoven*, novella (1840); *Ein Ende in Paris*, novella (1841); *Ein glücklicher Abend*, novella (1841); *Die Sarazenin*, 3-act opera (prose scenario, 1841–42; verse text, 1843); *Die Bergwerke zu Falun*, 3-act opera (prose scenario, 1841–42); *Friedrich I.*, play (prose scenario, 1846–48); *Alexander der Grosse*, sketch for a play (184?; not extant); *Jesus von Nazareth*, play (prose scenario, 1849); *Achilleus*, sketch for a play (1849–50; fragments only); *Wieland der Schmied*, 3-act opera (prose scenario, 1850); *Die Sieger*, opera (prose sketch, 1856); *Luther* or *Luthers Hochzeit*, sketch for a play (1868); Lustspiel in 1 act (draft, 1868); *Eine Kapitulation: Lustspiel in antiker Manier*, poem (1870).

Wagner also expounded his theories on music, politics, philosophy, religion, etc., in numerous essays. The 1st ed. of his collected writings, *R. Wagner: Gesammelte Schriften und Dichtungen* (9 vols., Leipzig, 1871–73; vol. 10, 1883), was prepared by Wagner himself. H. von Wolzogen and R. Sternfeld ed. the 5th ed. as *Sämtliche Schriften und Dichtungen*, adding vols. XI and XII (Leipzig, 1911); they also prepared the 6th ed., adding vols. XIII–XVI (Leipzig, 1914).

Wagneromorphism. An obsessive idolatry of Wagner, common among composers around the turn of the century, a mass genuflection before the unquestionable genius of Wagner, produced the phenomenon of Wagneromorphism. It is characterized by a total absorption of all familiar traits of Wagner's melody and harmony, particularly chromatic suspensions, triadic fanfares, modulatory sequences, and dynamic explosions followed by protracted recessions. Also called *Wagneromanticism*.

wait (wayt, wayte). A town watchman in the Middle Ages whose duty was to keep order in the streets at night and announce the time by playing a brass instrument. Waits often serenaded incoming travelers in their stagecoaches; they were also employed to provide music for ceremonial occasions. In Germany waits were called STADTPFEIFER, and a genre of urban folk music was collected under the designation TURM-MUSIK.

Waits, Tom, idiosyncratic and effective American songwriter and performer; b. Pomona, Calif., Dec. 7, 1949. He began his career playing in Los Angeles clubs as a singer, pianist, and guitarist, sometimes with his group Nocturnal Emissions. After being signed by Frank Zappa's manager in 1972, he produced his 1st record album, *Closing Time* (1973). He slowly rose from cultdom to stardom through such songs as *Ol' '55, Shiver Me Timbers, Diamonds on My Windshield*, and *The Piano Has Been Drinking*; noteworthy albums of this period include *Nighthawks at the Diner, Small Change, Foreign Affairs*, and *Heartattack & Vine*. He made a number of recordings for the Asylum label, then switched to Island; with *Swordfishtrombones* (1983) he expanded his accompaniment to include a broad spectrum of exotic instruments.

He wrote the score for Francis Ford Coppola's film *One from the Heart* (1982), and later made the album *Rain Dogs* (1985) and concert movie *Big Time* (1988). He also collaborated with his wife, Kathleen Brennan, on the stage show

Frank's Wild Years (1987), which includes the pastiches *Temptation* and *Innocent When You Dream*. In 1993 he created a performance work, *The Black Rider*, with the collaboration of William S. Burroughs. Among the artists who have performed his music are Bette Midler, Crystal Gayle, Bruce Springsteen, the Eagles, and the Manhattan Transfer; he also made frequent appearances as a film and stage actor.

Waits is a jazz songwriter who regards the beatniks of the 1950s as his primary inspiration; his imaginative lyrics are full of slang and focus on the sad flotsam of cheap bars and motels. He accompanies his gravelly voice and delivery with rough instrumentation or electronics, but always with sensitive musicianship and ironic pathos.

Wake Up Little Susie. Second single, 1st number 1 hit for the Everly Brothers in 1957. Lovers oversleep while parking in car; face trouble for breaking curfew. A '50s dilemma lined in perfect 2-part harmony. Written by Felice and Boudleaux Bryant.

Waldflöte (Ger.). An open metal flue stop in the organ, of 2' or 4' pitch and suave, full tone.

Waldhorn (Ger.). Natural or hand horn.

Waldstein Sonata. Nickname of Beethoven's piano sonata No. 21, op. 53, in C major (1803–1804). It is dedicated to Count von Waldstein, a friend and patron of Beethoven, hence the title. The opening movement is remarkable for its dramatic intensity in the low register.

Waldteufel (Ger., forest devil). FRICTION DRUM.

Waldteufel (born Lévy), (Charles-) **Émile,** famous French conductor and composer of light music. b. Strasbourg, Dec. 9, 1837; d. Paris, Feb. 12, 1915. His father, Louis (1801–84), and his brother, Léon (1832–84), were violinists and dance composers, and his mother was a pianist. In 1842 the family went to Paris, where he studied piano with his mother and then with Joseph Heyberger; subsequently was an auditor in L.-A. Marmontel's class at the Paris Cons., where he became a pupil of A. Laurent in 1853, but he left before completing his courses. He became a piano tester for the manufacturer Scholtus; also taught piano and played in soirées; when he had time he composed dance music for Paris salons. In 1865 he became court pianist to the Empress Eugénie and in 1866 conductor of the state balls.

His 1st waltz, *Joies et peines*, which he publ. at his own expense in 1859, was an immediate success, and he became known in Paris high society. In 1867 he publ. another successful waltz, with the German title *Vergissmeinnicht*. Then followed a series of waltzes that established his fame as a French counterpart to Johann Strauss (II): *Manola* (1873), *Mon Rêve* (1877), *Pomone* (1877), *Toujours ou jamais* (1877), *Les Sirènes* (1878), *Très jolie* (1878), *Pluie de diamants* (1879), *Dolores* (1880), and the most famous of them, *Les Patineurs* (1882). His dance music symbolized the "gai Paris" of his time as fittingly as the music of Strauss reflected the gaiety of old Vienna. Waldteufel lived most of his life in Paris, but he also filled conducting engagements abroad, visiting London in 1885 and Berlin in 1889.

Walk a Little Faster. Revue by V. Duke, 1932. The score presents a series, with action shifting from Alaska to N.Y. and Paris. The score includes his most celebrated hit *April in Paris*.

Walker, George (Theophilus), African-American pianist, teacher, and composer; b. Washington, D.C., June 27, 1922. He studied at the Oberlin College Cons. of Music (M.B., 1941); then entered the Curtis Inst. of Music in Philadelphia, where he studied piano with Rudolf Serkin, composition with Rosario Scalero and Gian Carlo Menotti, and chamber music with Gregor Piatigorsky and William Primrose (Artist Diploma, 1945); also took piano lessons with Robert Casadesus in Fontainebleau in France (diploma, 1947); obtained his D.M.A. from the Eastman School of Music in Rochester, N.Y., in 1957. In 1957 he received a Fulbright fellowship for travel to Paris, where he took courses in composition with Nadia Boulanger.

In 1945 he made his debut as a pianist, and subsequently appeared throughout the U.S. and abroad; was also active as a teacher; held appointments at Dillard Univ. in New Orleans (1953), the New School for Social Research in N.Y., the Dalcroze School of Music (1961), Smith College (1961–68), and the Univ. of Colorado (1968). In 1969 he was appointed a prof. at Rutgers, the State Univ. of New Jersey; was chairman of the composition dept. there in 1974; in 1975, was also named Distinguished Prof. at the Univ. of Delaware and adjunct prof. at the Peabody Inst. in Baltimore. In 1969 he received a Guggenheim fellowship; also held 2 Rockefeller fellowships for study in Italy (1971, 1975). In 1982 he was made a member of the American Academy and Inst. of Arts and Letters.

In his music he maintains a median modern line with an infusion of black folk idioms. He won a Pulitzer Prize in

1996. Among Walker's compositions are: Orch.: Trombone Concerto (1957); *Antiphonys* for chamber orch. (1968); Variations (1971); Piano Concerto (1975); *Dialogues* for cello and orch. (1975–76); *Overture: In Praise of Folly* (1980); Cello Concerto (N.Y., 1982); *An Eastman Overture* (Washington, D.C., 1983); Violin Concerto (1984). Chamber: 2 string quartets (1946; 1967); Cello Sonata (1957); 2 violin sonatas (1959, 1979); *Music (Sacred and Profane)* for brass (1975); 4 piano sonatas (1953, 1957, 1975, 1985); other piano pieces. Vocal: *3 Lyrics* for Chorus (1958); Mass for Soprano, Alto, Tenor, Baritone, Chorus, and Orch. (1978); *Poem* for Soprano and Chamber Ensemble, after T. S. Eliot's *The Hollow Men* (1986); choruses; songs.

walking bass. In jazz, a bass figure moving up and down in diatonic and chromatic steps in broken octaves in even 8th-note rhythms. It was 1st associated with piano boogie-woogie, but became principally associated with jazz double-bass playing in the swing era; it continues to serve that purpose.

Walküre, Die. The 2nd music drama of Wagner's cycle *Der Ring des Nibelungen*, 1876, premiered at the 1st Bayreuth Festival. *Die Walküre* begins with the meeting of Siegmund and Sieglinde, the long-separated mortal children of Wotan. Unaware of their kinship they feel a sensuous attraction toward each other. When Sieglinde shows Siegmund the magical sword Nothung, which Wotan drove deep into a tree and which can be pulled out only by a hero, Siegmund performs the task. Sieglinde becomes enraptured; she abandons her brutal husband, Hunding, and flees with her brotherly lover. But Wotan has to come to the aid of Hunding, and orders his 9 warlike daughters, the Valkyries, not to lend support to the lovers. Wotan's favorite Valkyrie, Brünnhilde, disobeys Wotan's orders by trying to help Siegmund, who is killed by Hunding when Wotan shatters the magic sword in Siegmund's hands. (Wotan rewards Hunding by killing him with a wave of his hand.) As Brünnhilde's punishment, Wotan takes her immortality away, places her on a high rock, puts her to sleep, and surrounds the rock by a ring of fire; only a hero can break through the fire and rescue her.

As the following opera of the *Ring* (*Siegfried*) relates, this hero will be Siegfried, son of Sieglinde, who died in childbirth. The most famous sym. episode from the opera is *The Ride of the Valkyries*, in which the sturdy Teutonic amazons disport themselves on top of cloud-covered rocks; Wagner's thematic use of the arpeggiated augmented triads here is notable. *The Magic Fire*, illustrating Brünnhilde's imprison-

ment by a fiery ring, is another popular tableau in the opera. In it the most important leading motives of the opera—including Wotan's imperious command, Brünnhilde's lament, the slumber motive, and the sparkling magic fire itself—are all combined in a gorgeous Wagnerian panoply.

Waller, "Fats" (Thomas Wright), noted African-American jazz pianist, organist, singer, bandleader, and composer; b. N.Y., May 21, 1904; d. Kansas City, Mo., Dec. 15, 1943. As a child he had private piano instruction and studied violin and double bass in school, but his most significant early lessons came from the player piano and nickelodeon pianists whom he studiously imitated; at 14 he was playing organ professionally in a Harlem theater; at 16 he received piano training from Russell Brooks and James P. Johnson; he claimed that he later had some lessons from Leopold Godowsky and studied composition with Carl Bohm at the Juilliard School of Music. In 1922 he began to make recordings, and in 1923 he made his 1st appearance on the radio; he subsequently made frequent broadcasts as a singer and pianist.

In 1928 he made his debut at N.Y.'s Carnegie Hall as a piano soloist. With the lyricist Andy Razaf, he composed most of the music for the all-black Broadway musical *Keep Shufflin'* (1928), and then collaborated on the shows *Load of Coal* and *Hot Chocolates* (1929), which includes the song *Ain't Misbehavin'*. He worked with Ted Lewis (1930), Jack Teagarden (1931), and Billy Banks's Rhythmakers (1932) before organizing his own band, Fats Waller and his Rhythm, in 1934; he was active on the West Coast and appeared in the Hollywood films *Hooray for Love* and *King of Burlesque* (both 1935). In 1938 he toured Europe, and again in 1939; in 1943 he appeared in the Hollywood film *Stormy Weather* leading an all-star band.

As a jazz pianist he was considered a leading exponent of stride piano, playing with a delicacy and lightness of touch that belied his considerable bulk of almost 300 pounds. Much of his popularity was due to his skills as an entertainer; he was especially effective in improvising lyrics to deflate the sentimentality of popular songs. A musical tribute to Waller, the revue *Ain't Misbehavin'*, was one of the great successes of the N.Y. theater season in 1978.

Wally, La. Opera by Catalani, 1892, premiered in Milan. The libretto is drawn from the morbid Teutonic tales dealing with strange calamities and unnatural passions in dark and isolated places. A maddened suitor tries to kill the lover of a young Swiss girl. They escape murder but perish in a mountain avalanche. The music is exceedingly mellifluous in the finest Italian manner. Toscanini admired Catalani and conducted *La Wally* often after Catalani died (1893).

Walpurgis Night (Ger. *Walpurgisnacht*). The feast day of St. Walpurgis, an 8th-century English abbess (May 1). Halloween-like Walpurgis Nights are celebrated at the reputed locale of the witches' sabbath, the peak of Mt. Brocken in the Harz Mountains. Faust attends one in Goethe's play; Mendelssohn based his secular cantata *Die erste Walpurgisnacht* (1833) on this scene. Berlioz presents a witches' sabbath in the final movement of his *Sym. fantastique*. Gounod includes a scene during Walpurgis Night in his opera *Faust*. Dies Irae is commonly used as a motto in virtually all musical representations of the Walpurgis Night.

Walter, Bruno

Eminent German-born American conductor; b. Bruno Walter Schlesinger, Berlin, Sept. 15, 1876; d. Beverly Hills, Calif., Feb. 17, 1962. He entered the Stern Cons. in Berlin at age 8, where he studied with H. Ehrlich, L. Bussler, and R. Radecke. At age 9 he performed in public as a pianist, but at 13 he decided to pursue his interest in conducting. In 1893 he became a coach at the Cologne Opera, where he made his conducting debut with Lortzing's *Der Waffenschmied*; in the following year he was engaged as assistant conductor at the Hamburg Stadttheater, under Gustav Mahler; this contact was decisive in his career, and he became in subsequent years an ardent champion of Mahler's music; conducted the premieres of the posth. Sym. No. 9 and *Das Lied von der Erde*.

During the 1896–97 season Walter was engaged as 2nd conductor at the Stadttheater in Breslau; he then became principal conductor in Pressburg, and in 1898 at Riga, where he conducted for 2 seasons. In 1900 he received the important engagement of conductor at the Berlin Royal Opera under a 5-year contract; however, he left this post in 1901 when he received an offer from Mahler to become his assistant at the Vienna Court Opera. He established himself as an efficient opera conductor; also conducted in England (1st appearance 1909, with the Royal Phil. Soc. in London). He remained at the Vienna Court Opera after the death of Mahler; in 1913 he became Royal Bavarian Generalmusikdirektor in Munich; under his guidance the Munich Opera enjoyed brilliant performances, particularly of Mozart's works.

Seeking greater freedom for his artistic activities, he left Munich in 1922 and gave numerous performances as a guest conductor with European orchs.; he conducted the series "Bruno Walter Concerts" with the Berlin Phil. from 1921 to 1933; from 1925 he also conducted summer concerts of the Salzburg Festival; his performances of Mozart's music there set a standard. He also appeared as pianist in Mozart's chamber works. In 1923 he made his American debut with the N.Y. Sym. Soc., and appeared with it again in 1924 and 1925. From 1925 to 1929 he was conductor of the Städtische Oper in Berlin-Charlottenburg; in 1929 he succeeded Furtwängler as conductor of the Gewandhaus Orch. in Leipzig, but he continued to give special concerts in Berlin. In 1932 he was guest conductor of the N.Y. Phil., acting also as soloist in a Mozart piano concerto; he was reengaged during the next 3 seasons as associate conductor with Toscanini. He was also a guest conductor in Philadelphia, Washington, D.C., and Baltimore.

With the advent of the Nazi regime in Germany in 1933, his engagement with the Gewandhaus Orch. was canceled, and he was also prevented from continuing his orch. concerts in Berlin. He filled several engagements with the Concertgebouw in Amsterdam, and also conducted in Salzburg. In 1936 he was engaged as music director of the Vienna State Opera; this was terminated with the Nazi annexation of Austria in 1938. Walter, with his family, then went to France, where he was granted French citizenship. After the outbreak of World War II in 1939 he sailed for America, establishing his residence in Calif.; he eventually became a naturalized American citizen. He was guest conductor with the NBC Sym. Orch. (1939); also conducted many performances of the Metropolitan Opera in N.Y. (debut in *Fidelio*, 1941). From 1947 to 1949 he was conductor and musical adviser of the N.Y. Phil.; returned regularly as guest conductor until 1960; made recordings with the Columbia Sym. Orch. created for him; also conducted in Europe (1949–60), giving his farewell performance in Vienna with the Vienna Phil. in 1960.

Walter achieved the reputation of a perfect classicist among contemporary conductors; his interpretations of the masterpieces of the Vienna School were particularly notable. He is acknowledged to have been a foremost conductor of Mahler's syms. He also composed his own music, including 2 syms., a string quartet, piano quintet, piano trio, and several albums of songs. He publ. the books *Von den moralischen Kraften der Musik* (Vienna, 1935); *Gustav Mahler* (Vienna, 1936); *Von der Musik und vom Musizieren* (Frankfurt am Main, 1957).

Walton, Sir William (Turner), eminent English composer; b. Oldham, Lancashire, Mar. 29, 1902; d. Ischia, Italy, Mar. 8, 1983. Both his parents were professional singers, and Walton himself had a fine singing voice as a youth; he entered the Cathedral Choir School at Christ Church, Oxford, and began to compose choral pieces for performance. Sir Hugh Allen, organist of New College, advised him to develop his interest in composition, and sponsored his admission to Christ Church at an early age; however, he never graduated; instead he began to write unconventional music in the manner that was fashionable in the 1920s.

His talent manifested itself in a string quartet he wrote at the age of 17, which was accepted for performance for the 1st festival of the ISCM in 1923. In London he formed a congenial association with the Sitwell family of quintessential cognoscenti and literati who combined a patrician sense of artistic superiority with a benign attitude toward the social plebs; they also provided Walton with residence at their manor in Chelsea, where he lived off and on for some 15 years. Fascinated by Edith Sitwell's oxymoronic verse, Walton set it to music bristling with novel jazzy effects in brisk, irregular rhythms and modern harmonies; Walton was only 19 when he wrote it. Under the title *Façade*, it was 1st performed in London in 1923, with Edith Sitwell herself delivering her doggerel with a megaphone; as expected, the show provoked an outburst of indignation in the press and undisguised delight among the young in spirit.

But Walton did not pursue the path of facile hedonism so fashionable at the time; he soon demonstrated his ability to write music in a Classic manner in his fetching concert overture *Portsmouth Point*, 1st performed in Zurich (1926), and later in the comedy-overture *Scapino* (1941). His biblical oratorio *Belshazzar's Feast* (1931) reveals a deep emotional stream and nobility of design that places Walton directly in line from Handel and Elgar among English masters. His sym. works show him as an inheritor of the grand Romantic tradition; his concertos for violin, for viola, and for cello demonstrate an adroitness in beautiful and effective instrumental writing.

Walton was a modernist in his acceptance of the new musical resources, but he never deviated from fundamental tonality and formal clarity of design. Above all, his music was profoundly national, unmistakably British in its inspiration and content. Quite appropriately he was asked to contribute to 2 royal occasions: he wrote *Crown Imperial March* for the coronation of King George VI in 1937 and *Orb and Sceptre* for that of Queen Elizabeth II in 1953. He received an honorary doctorate from Oxford Univ. in 1942; was knighted in 1951. He spent the last years of his life on the island of Ischia off Naples with his Argentine-born wife, Susana Gil Passo.

waltz (Ger. *Walzer*, from *walzen*, turn around; Fr. *valse*). The quintessential ballroom dance in 3/4 time, generated in Austria toward the end of the 18th century. Choreographically it consists of a pair of dancers moving around an imaginary axis, resulting in a movement forward. In the 18th century the waltz was regarded as a vulgar dance fit only for peasant entertainment. In 1760 waltzing was specifically forbidden by a government order in Bavaria. The waltz received its social acceptance in the wake of the French Revolution, when it became fashionable even in upper social circles on the continent. England withstood its impact well into the 19th century. A story is told about an English dowager who watched a young couple waltzing and asked incredulously, "Are they married?"

The 1st representation of a waltzlike dance on the stage occurred during a performance of the opera *Una cosa rara* by Martin y Soler in Vienna in 1786. The waltz attained its social popularity during the Congress of Vienna in 1815; at that time it was known under the name of *Wienerwalzer*. In France the *valse* assumed different forms, in 3/8, 3/4, or 6/8 time, as an andante (*sauteuse*), allegretto, allegro (*jeté*), or presto. In the 20th century an American waltz misnamed

Valse Boston (in reality, a HESITATION WALTZ) spread all over Europe about 1920.

As a musical form the waltz generally consists of 2 repeated periods of 8 bars each. The earliest printing of a waltz in this form was the publication of 12 concert waltzes by the pianist Daniel Steibelt in 1800; these were followed by a collection of waltzes by Hummel publ. in 1808. Such concert waltzes were extended by the insertion of several trios, multiple reprises, and a coda, lasting nearly half an hour in all. During the 19th century the concert waltz became a favorite among composers for piano, beginning with Weber and finding its greatest artistic efflorescence in the waltzes of Chopin. Beethoven canonized the waltz in his famous Diabelli variations (op. 120), based on a waltz tune.

The waltz grew into an industry in Vienna. Joseph Lanner and Johann Strauss (I) composed hundreds of waltz tunes to be played in Viennese restaurants and entertainment places. Johann Strauss (II) raised the waltz to its summit as an artistic creation which, at the time, served the needs of popular entertainment. He was justly dubbed "The Waltz King" (*Walzerkönig*). When Brahms was asked to autograph a waltz tune for a lady, he jotted the initial bars of Strauss's *On the Beautiful Blue Danube*, with a characteristic remark, "Unfortunately, not by me." Strauss wrote many other popular works, including *Tales of the Vienna Woods*, *Voices of Spring*, *Vienna Blood*, and *Wine, Women, and Song*. All these waltzes were really chains of waltz movements.

Gradually the waltz became acceptable in purely sym. dimension. Berlioz has a waltz movement in his *Sym. fantastique*; Tchaikovsky includes a waltz in his 5th Sym., and Mahler in his 9th Sym. Ravel parodied the Viennese waltz gloriously in his *La Valse*. Thus in less than a century the waltz, which began as a somewhat vulgar, popular dance tune, took its place next to the minuet as a legitimate concert form.

Waltzing Matilda. An Australian song, 1903; the words were fitted to an old Scottish tune (publ. 1818) and publ. in Sydney. Matilda is not a girl's name but Australian slang for knapsack; waltzing refers to bouncing, not dancing. Strangely, the song is in 4/4 rather than 3/4 time. The song became tremendously popular among Australian troops during the 2 world wars and has assumed the status of an unofficial national anthem (contrary to popular belief, *Waltzing Matilda* is not Australia's anthem). The song was placed in modern perspective by Eric Bogle, whose powerful antiwar song *And The Band Played "Waltzing Matilda"* describes the horrific battle of Gallipoli in World War I.

Walzer (Ger.). WALTZ.

War and Peace. Opera by Prokofiev, begun 1941; 1st complete stage production in Leningrad, 1948. Prokofiev did not specify the number of acts, and he emphasized that the production should be announced as being in 13 scenes. Originally he planned to have the opera presented in 2 parts on 2 consecutive evenings, but eventually he compressed it to fit a single evening. The cast of characters numbers 72 singing and acting dramatis personae. The score attempts with considerable success to embrace the epic breadth of Tolstoy's great novel, from which the libretto was extracted by Prokofiev and his 2nd wife, Myra Mendelson. The work went through more or less continuous revision until 1952; the last version of the opera opens with a choral epigraph summarizing the significance of Napoleon's invasion of Russia in 1812.

Interlaced with military events are the destinies of the Rostov family and the dramatic story of Pierre Bezuhov. The concluding words of the victorious Field Marshal Kutuzov, "Russia is saved," were unquestionably intended to echo the recent Russian experience in fighting off another invasion, that of Hitler. The musical idiom is profoundly Russian in spirit but there are no literal quotations from folk songs. The melodic, rhythmic, and harmonic realization is recognizably that of Prokofiev's own.

War of the Buffoons. GUERRE DES BOUFFONS.

War Requiem. Oratorio by Britten, 1962, written to commemorate the rebuilding of the Cathedral of Coventry, destroyed by bombing in World War II. The text includes 6 movements from the traditional Latin Requiem Mass and 9 wartime poems by Wilfred Owens, who was killed in action shortly before the 1918 armistice. The work is scored for soprano, tenor, baritone, chorus, boys' choir, organ, small ensemble, and full orch.

warble. See YODEL.

Warfield, William (Caesar), noted African-American baritone and teacher; b. West Helena, Ark., Jan. 22, 1920. He studied at the Eastman School of Music in Rochester, N.Y., graduating in 1942; sang in opera and musical comedy; gave his 1st N.Y. song recital in 1950, with excellent critical acclaim. He subsequently toured Europe in the role of Porgy in Gershwin's *Porgy and Bess*. He married the soprano Leontyne Price in 1952 (divorced, 1972). In 1974 he was appointed a prof. of music at the Univ. of Illinois.

Waring, Fred(eric Malcolm), famous American conductor of popular music and inventor of sundry kitchen appliances; b. Tyrone, Pa., June 9, 1900; d. Danville, Pa., July 29, 1984. He learned music at his mother's knee; a sense of moral rectitude was inculcated in him by his father, a banker who gave speeches at spiritual revivals and temperance meetings. He took up the banjo at 16 and organized a quartet that he called the Banjazzatra. He studied engineering and architecture at Pa. State Univ.; he retained his love for gadgets throughout his musical career, and in 1937 patented the Waring Blendor, for whipping food or drinks to a foam; another invention was a traveling iron.

He acquired fame with his own band, The Pennsylvanians, which played on national tours at concert halls, hotels, and college campuses; the group was particularly successful on radio programs sponsored by tobacco companies and the Ford Motor Co. His repertoire consisted of wholesome American songs, many of them composed by himself. Among his soloists on special programs were Bing Crosby, Hoagy Carmichael, Irving Berlin, and Frank Sinatra.

Waring had a natural streak for publicity; he once bet that he could lead a bull into a 5th Avenue china shop; he succeeded without breaking a single piece of crockery. He was a friend of President Dwight Eisenhower. In 1983 President Ronald Reagan awarded him the Congressional Gold Medal. He continued to lead youth choral groups, giving a concert at Pa. State Univ. a day before he suffered a stroke, and 2 days before his death.

Warlock, Peter. See HESELTINE, PHILIP (ARNOLD).

Wärme, mit (Ger.). With warmth, warmly. *Mit grosser Wärme*, with great warmth.

Warsaw Concerto. A semiclassical piece for piano and orch. by Addinsell, 1942, as part of the soundtrack for *Dangerous Moonlight* (U.K.; U.S., *Suicide Squadron*), a dramatic depiction of the Nazi destruction of the Polish capital. Surprisingly the *Warsaw Concerto* became enormously popular in the gray penumbra of concert fare in the U.S., perhaps due to its melodic and harmonic similarity to Rachmaninoff's 2nd piano concerto.

Warwick(e), (Marie) **Dionne.** See BACHARACH, BURT.

washboard (rubboard; Fr. *frittoir*). Traditional American instrument using a laundering board with a corrugated surface (usually metal); the board is scraped with a stick, like a guiro; it provides rhythmic support for jug bands, which included blown molasses jugs and broomstick bass.

Washington, Dinah (born Ruth Lee Jones), African-American singer of blues and popular music; b. Tuscaloosa, Ala., Aug. 8[?], 1924; d. (as a result of an overdose of drugs) Detroit, Dec. 14, 1963. She went to Chicago; won an amateur singing contest at the age of 15; made local appearances before singing in Lionel Hampton's band (1943–46); she soon established herself as a major rhythm-and-blues artist with such songs as *Blow Top Blues* and *Evil Gal Blues*. She was best known for her renditions of *What a Difference a Day Makes, Homeward Bound, Stormy Weather,* and *September in the Rain*.

Washington's Birthday. Poem for Small Orch. by Ives, 1909, 1st performed in San Francisco, 1931. It contains a barn dance in the rhythm of a square dance; it is the 1st movement of *Holidays, A Sym*.

Wasitodiningrat, (Ki) **K.R.T.** (Kanjeng Raden Tumengung), a title of honorary royal status, important Indonesian composer and performer; b. Yogyakarta, Java, Mar. 17, 1909. His former names are Wasitolodoro, Tjokrowasito, and Wasitodipuro. He was born in the Pakualaman Palace, one of 3 principal courts of central Java, where his father was director of musical activities. Wasitodiningrat studied dance from the age of 6, graduating from the SMA National High School in 1922. He became music director of the Yogyakarta radio station MAVRO in 1934 and remained there through the Japanese occupation, when the station was called Jogja Hosokjoku. In 1945 the station became RRI (Radio Republic Indonesia); he served as director there again in 1951.

Between 1951 and 1970 he taught dance at the Konservatori Tari and the Academy Tari, both in Yogyakarta, and music at the Academy Karawitan in Surakarta; he also founded and directed the Wasitodipuro Center for Vocal Studies in Yogyakarta. In 1953 he toured Asia, North America, and Europe; in 1961 he became associated with the new dance/theater form *sendratari*, later becoming music director for P. L. T. Bagong Kussudiardjo's troupe. He succeeded his father as director of the Pakualaman gamelan in 1962. In 1971 he joined the faculty of the Calif. Inst. of the Arts as master of Javanese gamelan; taught workshops at both the Los Angeles and Berkeley campuses of the Univ. of Calif. Wasitodiningrat is a leading performer and composer of central Javanese music; the

Pakualaman gamelan's recordings are considered exemplary; 1 is included in the 40 minutes of music installed in the spacecraft Voyager, intended to represent our planet's music to outsiders. His numerous awards include a gold medal from the Indonesian government honoring his devotion to Javanese music. He frequently performs with his daughter, Nanik, and her Balinese husband, Nyoman Wenten.

Watch Your Step. Musical by I. Berlin, 1914. This show was notable for Berlin's syncopated ragtime songs and the appearance of the popular dance team Vernon and Irene Castle. The most memorable song was the sentimental ballad *Play a Simple Melody*.

Water Music. Orch. divertimento by Handel, 1717, written for his royal patron King George I of England, to be played on an open barge during the King's sailing party on the Thames River. Three orch.l suites were subsequently drawn from *Water Music*, consisting of various aires, hornpipes, minuets, and other dances. The publishers seized on its success and printed numerous arrangements of it under the title *The Celebrated Water Musick*.

Waters, "Muddy" (born McKinley Morganfield), African-American blues singer, leading exponent of the Mississippi delta blues style; b. Rolling Fork, Miss., Apr. 4, 1915; d. Westmont, Ill., Apr. 30, 1983. His parents were separated, and he was reared by his maternal grandmother on a plantation near Clarksdale, Miss.; she called him "Muddy" because of his childhood habit of playing in the mud; his playmates called him "Waters," and he accepted the name "Muddy Waters" when he began to sing and play the guitar.

In 1941 Alan Lomax and John Work recorded his singing for the Library of Congress; this encouraged him to try his luck in commercial recording. In 1943 he moved to Chicago, where he made his 1st successes; indeed, he soon earned the sobriquet "King of Chicago Blues." Fortunately for him, his followers, and jazz historians, he totally lacked any vocal training and was forced to develop his own unrestricted lexicon of sounds, ranging from soft trembling moans to a ferocious animal-like roar. To make his mode of delivery even more physically stunning he used electric

Muddy Waters, c. mid-1960s

COURTESY FRANK DRIGGS COLLECTION

amplification on his guitar; soon he had assembled a band that brought the new technology to the blues for the 1st time; Waters was the most important of the acoustic rural blues musicians to make the transition to electric urban blues in the 1940s.

He played electric blues in England in 1958, which struck holy terror into the ears and hearts of purist British folk-song experts; but he recruited to his cause the young enthusiasts, among them Mick Jagger; in fact Jagger and his friends named their famous band the Rolling Stones after Waters's early hit song *Rollin' Stone*; the rock journal *Rolling Stone* also owes its name to Muddy's song; Bob Dylan created his own rock tune *Like a Rolling Stone* as an unconscious tribute to him. In his later years the Tex. blues guitarist Johnny Winter worked with him professionally as a performer, producer, and all-around champion. Waters died peacefully, in his sleep.

Watts, André, brilliant American pianist; b. Nuremberg, June 20, 1946. He was born in a U.S. Army camp to an African-American soldier and a Hungarian woman. His mother gave him his earliest piano lessons. After the family moved to the U.S. he studied with Genia Robiner, Doris Bawden, and Clement Petrillo at the Philadelphia Musical Academy. At the age of 9 he made his 1st public appearance playing the Haydn Concerto in D Major at a children's concert of the Philadelphia Orch. His parents were divorced in 1962, but his mother continued to guide his studies. At 14 he played Franck's *Symphonic Variations* with the Philadelphia Orch.; at 16 he became an instant celebrity when he played Liszt's 1st Piano Concerto at one of the televised Young People's Concerts with the N.Y. Phil., conducted by Leonard Bernstein, (1963).

His youth and the fact that he was partly black contributed to his success, but it was the grand and poetic manner of his virtuosity that conquered the usually skeptical press. Still, he insisted on completing his academic education. In 1969 he joined the class of Leon Fleisher at the Peabody Cons. of Music in Baltimore, obtaining his Artist's Diploma in 1972. In the meantime he developed an international career. He made his European debut as soloist with the London Sym. Orch. in 1966; then played with the Concertgebouw Orch. in Amsterdam. Later that year, 1966, he played his 1st solo recital in N.Y., inviting comparisons in the press with the great piano virtuosos of the past. In 1967 he was soloist with the Los Angeles Phil. under Zubin Mehta on a tour of Europe and Asia.

On his 21st birthday he played the 2nd Piano Concerto of Brahms with the Berlin Phil. In 1970 he revisited his place of birth and played a solo recital with sensational success. He also became a favorite at important political occasions; he played at President Richard Nixon's inaugural concert at Constitution Hall in 1969, at the last coronation of the Shah of Iran, and at a festive celebration of the President of the Congo. In 1973 he toured Russia. In 1976 he played a solo recital on live network television. He was also the subject of a film documentary. In 1973 he received an honorary doctorate from Yale Univ.; in 1975 he was given another honorary doctorate by Albright College. He celebrated the 25th anniversary of his debut with the N.Y. Phil. as soloist under Mehta in the Liszt 1st Concerto, the Beethoven 2nd Concerto, and the Rachmaninoff 2nd Concerto in a concert telecast live on PBS (1988); that year he received the Avery Fisher Prize.

wavelength. The length of a sound wave, marking the crests (or other corresponding points) of 2 successive waves. Lower sounds have longer wavelengths; higher sounds have shorter wavelengths. In other words, the wavelength is inversely proportional to frequency of vibrations of a given sound.

wa-wa (wah-wah). 1. A trumpet technique (placing the hand in the bell) or mute that produces a wavering amplitude effect used principally in jazz. 2. An electronic device producing a similar effect on the electric guitar and other instruments, usually manipulated by a foot pedal. Rock musicians such as Eric Clapton and John McLaughlin popularized the wa-wa sound in the 1960s.

Waxman (Wachsmann), **Franz,** German-American composer and conductor; b. Königshütte, Dec. 24, 1906; d. Los Angeles, Feb. 24, 1967. He studied in Dresden and Berlin; went to the U.S. in 1934 and settled in Hollywood, where he took lessons with Arnold Schoenberg; became a successful composer for films; his musical score for *Sunset Boulevard* won the Academy Award for 1950; also was active as a conductor; was founder-conductor of the Los Angeles Music Festival (1947–67). His other film scores include *Magnificent Obsession* (1935), *Captains Courageous* (1937), *The Philadelphia Story* (1940), *Stalag 17* (1953), *Sayonara* (1957), and *Sunrise at Campobello* (1960); he also composed orch. and vocal works.

wayte. WAIT.

We Are Coming, Father Abraham. Song by Foster, 1862, written in response to President Lincoln's call for more volunteers to join the Union forces in the American Civil War.

We Shall Overcome. Song of uncertain authorship that has served as the marching hymn of the black civil rights movement after World War II and has eventually been associated with other protests and struggles. The music has been traced to an 18th-century anthem, *O Sanctissima.*

Webber, Andrew Lloyd. LLOYD WEBBER, ANDREW.

Webber, Julian Lloyd. LLOYD WEBBER, JULIAN.

Weber, Carl Maria (Friedrich Ernst) von

〰〰 〰〰 〰〰 〰〰 〰〰

Celebrated German composer, pianist, and conductor; b. Eutin, Oldenburg, Nov. 18, 1786; d. London, June 5, 1826. His father, Franz Anton von Weber (1734[?]–1812), was an army officer and a good musical amateur who played the violin and served as Kapellmeister in Eutin. It was his fondest wish that Carl

Maria would follow in the footsteps of Mozart as a child prodigy (Constanze Weber, Mozart's wife, was his niece, thus making Carl Maria a 1st cousin of Mozart by marriage). Carl Maria's mother was a singer of some ability; she died when he was 11. Franz Anton led a wandering life as music director of his own theater company, taking his family with him on his tours. Although this mode of life interfered with Carl Maria's regular education, it gave him practical knowledge of the stage and stimulated his imagination as a dramatic composer.

Weber's 1st teachers were his father and his half-brother Fritz, a pupil of Haydn; at Hildburghausen, while with his father's company in 1796, he also received piano instruction from J. P. Heuschkel. The next year he was in Salzburg, where he attracted the attention of Michael Haydn, who taught him counterpoint; he composed a set of *6 Fughetten* there (publ. 1798). As his peregrinations continued he was taught singing by Valesi (J. B. Wallishauser) and composition by J. N. Kalcher in Munich (1798–1800). At the age of 12 he wrote an opera, *Die Macht der Liebe und des Weins*; it was never performed and the MS has not survived.

Through a meeting with Aloys Senefelder, the inventor of lithography, he became interested in engraving; he became Senefelder's apprentice, acquiring considerable skill in the method; he engraved his own *6 Variations on an Original Theme* for Piano (Munich, 1800). His father became interested in the business possibilities of lithography, and set up a workshop with him in Freiberg; however, the venture failed, and the young Carl Maria turned again to music.

Weber composed a 2-act comic opera, *Das Waldmädchen*, in 1800; it was premiered in Freiberg 6 days after his 14th birthday; performances followed in Chemnitz (1800) and Vienna (1804). In 1801 the family was once more in Salzburg, where he studied further with Michael Haydn; wrote another opera, *Peter Schmoll und seine Nachbarn* (1801–1802). He gave a concert in Hamburg in Oct. 1802, and the family then proceeded to Augsburg; they remained there from late 1802 until settling in Vienna in the fall of 1803; there Weber continued his studies with Abbé Vogler, at whose recommendation he secured the post of conductor of the Breslau Opera in 1804. He resigned this post in 1806 after his attempts at operatic reform caused dissension.

In 1806 he became honorary Intendant to Duke Eugen of Württemberg-Ols at Schloss Carlsruhe in Upper Silesia; much of his time was devoted to composition there. In 1807 he was engaged as private secretary to Duke Ludwig in Stuttgart, and also gave music lessons to his children. This employment was abruptly terminated when Weber became innocently involved in a scheme of securing a ducal appointment for a rich man's son in order to exempt him from military service and accepted a loan of money. This was a common practice at the Stuttgart court, but as a result of the disclosure of Weber's involvement he was arrested (early 1810) and kept in prison for 16 days. This matter, along with several others, was settled to his advantage, only to find him the target of his many creditors, who had him rearrested. Finally agreeing to pay off his debts as swiftly as possible, he was released and then banished by King Friedrich.

Weber went to Mannheim, where he made appearances as a pianist. He next went to Darmstadt, where he rejoined his former teacher, Vogler, for whom he wrote the introduction to his teacher's ed. of 12 Bach chorales. In 1810, Weber's opera *Silvana* was successfully premiered in Frankfurt; the title role was sung by Caroline Brandt, who later became a member of the Prague Opera and eventually Weber's wife.

Weber left Darmstadt in early 1811 for Munich, where he composed several important orch.l works, including the clarinet concertino, the 2 clarinet concertos, and the bassoon concerto. His clarinet pieces were written for the noted virtuoso Heinrich (Joseph) Bärmann (1784–1847). Weber's 1-act singspiel, *Abu Hassan*, was successfully given in Munich in the late spring of 1811. For the rest of that year Weber and Bärmann gave concerts in Switzerland; after appearing in Prague they went to Leipzig, Weimar, Dresden, and Berlin (attended by King Friedrich Wilhelm III), all in 1812. In late 1812 Weber was soloist at the premiere of his 2nd Piano Concerto in Gotha.

Upon Weber's return to Prague in early 1813 he was informed that he was to be the director of the German Opera there. He was given extensive authority; he traveled to Vienna to engage singers and also secured the services of Franz Clement as concertmaster. During his tenure Weber presented a distinguished repertoire that included Beethoven's *Fidelio*; however, when his reforms encountered determined opposition, he submitted his resignation (1816). In late 1816 he was appointed Musikdirektor of the German Opera in Dresden by King

Friedrich August III. He opened his 1st season in early 1817; that same year he was named Königlich Kapellmeister; he began to make sweeping reforms.

Weber and Brandt were married in Prague that year. About this time he approached Friedrich Kind, a Dresden lawyer and writer, and suggested to him the idea of preparing a libretto on a Romantic German subject for his next opera. They agreed on *Der Freischütz*, a fairy tale from the *Gespensterbuch*, a collection of ghost stories by J. A. Apel and F. Laun. The composition of this work, which was to prove his masterpiece, occupied him for 3 years; the score was completed in the spring of 1820; 2 weeks later Weber began work on the incidental music to Wolff's *Preciosa*, a play in 4 acts with spoken dialogue; it was produced in Berlin in 1821. A comic opera, *Die drei Pintos*, which Weber started at about the same time, was left unfinished. (A performing edition was later created by Mahler.)

After some revisions *Der Freischütz* was accepted for performance at the opening of Berlin's Neues Schauspielhaus. There arose an undercurrent of rivalry with Spontini, director of the Berlin Opera, a highly influential figure in operatic circles and at court. Spontini considered himself the guardian of the Italian-French tradition in opposition to the new German Romantic movement in music. Weber conducted the triumphant premiere of *Der Freischütz* (1821); the work's success surpassed all expectations and the cause of new Romantic art was won; *Der Freischütz* was soon staged by all the major opera houses of Europe.

Weber's next opera was *Euryanthe*, produced in Vienna (1823) with only moderate success. Meanwhile Weber's health was affected by incipient tuberculosis and he was compelled to spend part of 1824 in Marienbad for a cure. He recovered sufficiently to begin the composition of *Oberon*, a commission from London's Covent Garden. The English libretto was prepared by J. R. Planché, based on a translation of C. M. Wieland's verse-romance of the same name. Once more illness interrupted Weber's progress on his work; he spent part of the summer of 1825 in Ems to prepare himself for the journey to England.

He set out for London in early 1826, a dying man. On his arrival, he was housed with Sir George Smart, the conductor of the Phil. Soc. of London. Weber threw himself into his work, presiding over 16 rehearsals for Oberon. In the spring he conducted its premiere at Covent Garden, obtaining a tremendous success. Despite his greatly weakened condition he conducted 11 more performances of the score and also participated in various London concerts, playing for the last time a week before his death. He was found dead in his room, and was buried in London. His remains were removed to Dresden in 1844; later they were taken to the Catholic cemetery in Dresden to the accompaniment of funeral music arranged from motifs from *Euryanthe* for wind instruments as prepared and conducted by Wagner. The next day, Weber's remains were interred as Wagner delivered an oration and conducted a chorus in his specially composed *An Webers Grabe*.

Weber's role in music history is epoch-making; in his operas, particularly in *Der Freischütz*, he opened the era of musical Romanticism, in decisive opposition to the established Italianate style. The highly dramatic and poetic portrayal of a German fairy tale, with its aura of supernatural mystery, appealed to the public, whose imagination had been stirred by the emergent Romantic literature of the period. Weber's melodic genius and mastery of the craft of composition made it possible for him to break with tradition and to start on a new path, at a critical time when individualism and nationalism began to emerge as sources of creative artistry.

His instrumental works, too, possessed a new quality that signalized the transition from Classic to Romantic music. For piano he wrote pieces of extraordinary brilliance, introducing some novel elements in chord writing and passage work. He was himself an excellent pianist; his large hands gave him an unusual command of the keyboard (he could stretch the interval of a 12th). Weber's influence on the development of German music was very great. The evolutionary link to Wagner's music drama is evident in the coloring of the orch.l parts in Weber's operas and in the adumbration of the principle of leading motifs. Finally, he was one of the 1st outstanding interpretative conducting podium figures.

In addition to his 10 operas (some incomplete or lost) and works for solo wind instrument and orch., Weber wrote incidental and interpolated music for more than 25 dramatic works, including an overture and 6 numbers for Schiller's trans. of Gozzi's *Turandot, Prinzessin von China* (Stuttgart, 1809); 10 numbers and 1 song for unaccompanied mezzo-soprano for Müllner's *König Yngurd* (Dresden, 1817); 6 numbers for Moreto's *Donna Diana*, (1817); 8 numbers for Gehe's *Heinrich IV, König von Frankreich*, (Dresden, 1818); concert arias; 5 Masses and

2 liturgical related Offertories; secular cantatas. Orch.: including 2 syms. (1807, 1807); concertos and concerto-like pieces with flute, clarinet (3), bassoon (2), horn, viola (2), cello, piano (3), and harmonichord (a bowed keyboard instrument); concert overtures and other works; wind ensemble music. Chamber works, including the Piano Quartet in B-flat Major (1809); *6 Progressive Sonatas* for Violin (or Flute) and Piano (1810); *7 Variations on a Theme from "Silvana"* for Clarinet and Piano (1811); Clarinet Quintet in B-flat Major (1815); *Grand Duo Concertant* for Piano and Clarinet (1815–16); Trio for Flute, Cello, and Piano (1819).

Weber wrote prolifically for his own instrument, the piano, but relatively little of the music is played; the popular works are 4 sonatas (1812; 1816; 1816; 1822); *Momento capriccioso* in B-flat Major (1808); *Rondo brillante: La gaite* in E-flat Major (1819); *Aufforderung zum Tanze: Rondo brillante* in D-flat Major (1819; made even more famous by Berlioz's orchestration,

1861); *Polacca brillante L'hilarite* in E Major (1819); and some piano duets.

Weber's critical writings on music are valuable, if at times surprisingly conservative; like many of his day he had very mixed feelings about Beethoven's later music. Weber also left an autobiographical sketch, an unfinished novel, poems, etc. Editions of his writings include T. Hell, ed., *Hinterlassene Schriften von Carl Maria von Weber* (3 vols., Dresden and Leipzig, 1828; 2nd ed., 1850); G. Kaiser, ed., *Sämtliche Schriften von Carl Maria von Weber: Kritische Ausgabe* (Berlin and Leipzig, 1908); W. Altmann, ed., *Webers ausgewahlte Schriften* (Regensburg, 1928); K. Laux, ed., *Carl Maria von Weber:* Kunstansichten (Leipzig, 1969; 2nd ed., 1975); J. Warrack, ed., and M. Cooper, tr., *Carl Maria von Weber: Writings on Music* (Cambridge, 1982). Weber's compositions are catalogued according to the J. numbers established by F. Jähns in his *Carl Maria von Weber in seinen Werken: Chronologisch-thematisches Verzeichniss seiner sämmtlichen Compositionen* (Berlin, 1871).

Webern, Anton (Friedrich Wilhelm von)

～～～ ～～～ ～～～ ～～～ ～～～

Remarkable Austrian serial composer and innovator of Klangfarbenmelodie; b. Vienna, Dec. 3, 1883; d. shot and killed by an American soldier, Mittersill, Sept. 15, 1945. He received his 1st instruction in music from his mother, an amateur pianist; then studied piano, cello, and theory with Edwin Komauer in Klagenfurt; also played cello in the orch. there. In 1902 he entered the Univ. of Vienna, where he studied harmony with Graedener and counterpoint with Navratil; also attended classes in musicology with Guido Adler; received his Ph.D. in 1906 with a dissertation on Heinrich Isaac's *Choralis Constantinus II*.

In 1904 he began private studies in composition with Arnold Schoenberg, whose ardent disciple he became; Alban Berg also studied with Schoenberg; together

Schoenberg, Berg, and Webern laid the foundations of what became known as the 2nd Viennese school of composition. The unifying element was the adoption of Schoenberg's method of composition with 12 tones related only to one another. Malevolent opponents referred to Schoenberg, Berg, and Webern as a Vienna Trinity, with Schoenberg as God the Father, Berg as God the Son, and Webern as the Holy Ghost.

From 1908 to 1914 Webern was active as a conductor in Vienna and in Germany; in 1915–16 he served in the army; in 1917–18 he was conductor at the Deutsches Theater in Prague. In 1918 he removed the nobiliary particle *von* from his name when such distinctions were outlawed in Austria; he settled in Mödling, near Vienna, where he taught composition privately; from 1918 to

1922 he supervised the programs of the Verein für Musikalische Privataufführungen (Soc. for Private Musical Performances), organized in Vienna by Schoenberg with the intention of promoting modern music without being exposed to reactionary opposition (music critics were not admitted to these performances).

Webern was conductor of the Schubertbund (1921–22) and the Mödling Male Chorus (1921–26); he also led the Vienna Workers' Sym. concerts (1922–34) and the Vienna Workers' Chorus (1923–34), both sponsored by the Social Democratic Party. From 1927 to 1938 he was a conductor on the Austrian Radio; furthermore, he conducted guest engagements in Germany, Switzerland, and Spain; from 1929 he made several visits to England, where he was a guest conductor with the BBC Sym. Orch. For the most part, however, he devoted himself to composition, private teaching, and lecturing.

After Hitler came to power in Germany in 1933, Webern's music was banned as a manifestation of "cultural Bolshevism" and "degenerate art." His position became more difficult after the Anschluss in 1938, for his works could no longer be publ.; he eked out an existence by teaching a few private pupils and making piano arrangements of musical scores by others for Universal Edition. After his son was killed in an air bombardment of a train in early 1945, he and his wife fled from Vienna to Mittersill, near Salzburg, to stay with his married daughters and grandchildren. His life ended tragically when he was shot and killed by an American soldier after stepping outside his son-in-law's residence one evening; the circumstances were shrouded in secrecy for many years (for a full account, see H. Moldenhauer, *The Death of Anton Webern: A Drama in Documents*, N.Y., 1961).

Webern left relatively few works, and most of them are of shorter duration (the 4th of his *5 Pieces for Orchestra*, op. 10, takes only 19 seconds to play), but in his music he achieves the utmost subtilization of expressive means. He adopted the 12-tone method of composition almost immediately after its definitive formulation by Schoenberg (1924), and he extended the principle of nonrepetition of notes to tone colors, so that in some of his works (e.g., the Sym., op. 21) solo instruments are rarely allowed to play 2 successive thematic notes. Dynamic marks are similarly diversified. Typically each 12-tone row is divided into symmetrical sections of 2, 4, or 6 members, which enter mutually into intricate but invariably logical canonic imitations. Inversions and augmentations are inherent features; melodically and harmonically, the intervals of the major 7th and minor 9th are stressed; single motives are brief and stand out as individual particles or lyric ejaculations.

The impact of these works on the general public and on the critics was disconcerting, and upon occasion led to violent demonstrations; however, the extraordinary skill and novelty of technique made this music endure beyond the fashions of the times; performances of Webern's works multiplied after his death and began to affect increasingly larger groups of modern musicians; Boulez announced, "Schoenberg is dead! Long live Webern!" in 1952, referring to the greater influence Webern had than his mentor did; Stravinsky acknowledged the use of Webern's methods in his later works; jazz composers have professed to follow Webern's ideas of tone color; analytical treatises have been publ. in several languages. The International Webern Festival celebrated the centennial of his birth in Vienna (1983).

Webern's output includes 31 works with opus numbers and a few unenumerated works, mostly early in chronology and late Romantic in style; these include: Orch.: Passacaglia, op. 1 (Vienna, 1908, composer conducting); 6 Pieces for Orch., op. 6 (Vienna, 1913, Schoenberg conducting;); 5 Pieces for Orch., op. 10 (1911–13; Zurich, 1926, composer conducting); 5 Pieces for Orch., op. posthumous (1913; Cologne, 1969); Sym. for Chamber Ensemble, op. 21 (N.Y., 1929); Variations, op. 30 (1940; Winterthur, 1943). Choral: *Entflieht auf leichten Kähnen*, op. 2 (1908; Furstenfeld, 1927); 2 Goethe songs, op. 19, with Ensemble (1926); *Das Augenlicht*, op. 26, with Orch. (1935; London, 1938); 1st Cantata, op. 29, with Soprano and Orch. (1938–39; London, 1946); 2nd Cantata, op. 31, with Soprano, Bass, and Orch. (1941–43; Brussels, 1950). Solo vocal (with piano except where noted): 2 sets of 5 Stefan George songs, opp. 3 and 4 (1908–1909); 2 Rilke songs, op. 8, with ensemble (1910); 4 songs, op. 12 (1915–17); 4 songs with orch., op. 13 (1914–18); 6 Georg Trakl songs, op. 14, with instruments (1919–21; Donaueschingen, 1924); *5 Sacred Songs*, op. 15, with Instruments (1917–22; Vienna, 1924, composer conducting); 5 Canons on Latin texts, op. 16, with clarinet and bass clarinet (1923–24; N.Y., 1951); *3 Traditional Rhymes*, op. 17, with Instruments (1924–25; N.Y., 1952); 3 songs, op. 18, with clarinet and guitar (1925; Los Angeles,

1954); 3 songs, op. 23 (1933–34); 3 songs, op. 25 (1934); other early songs with piano.

Chamber: 5 Movements for string quartet (Vienna, 1910); 4 pieces for violin and piano, op. 7 (1910); 6 bagatelles for string quartet, op. 9 (1911–13; Donaueschingen, 1924); 3 Little Pieces for Cello and Piano, op. 11 (1914; Mainz, 1924); String Trio, op. 20 (1926–27; Vienna, 1928); Quartet for Violin, Clarinet, Tenor Saxophone, and Piano, op. 22 (Vienna, 1931); Concerto for 9 Instruments, op. 24 (Prague, 1935); String Quartet, op. 28 (1936–38; Pittsfield, Mass., 1938); Variations for Piano (Vienna, 1937); other early chamber works; arrangements of works by Schoenberg, Schubert, and Bach. W. Reich ed. *Der Weg zur neuen Musik*, transcribed from Webern's lectures (Vienna, 1933).

Wechseldominante (Ger., changing dominant). A term used by Riemann to designate the dominant of the dominant in a given key (V of V); e.g., D major is the Wechseldominante (V of V) of C major.

Wechselgesang (Ger., changing song). Antiphonal singing.

wechselnder Taktart, in (Ger.). In a changing tempo (R. Strauss, *Salome*).

Wechselnote (Ger., changing note). CAMBIATA.

Wedding in a Monastery, A. Opera by Prokofiev, 1946, after Sheridan's libretto *The Duenna* (1775), 1st premiered in Leningrad. The action transpires in Seville in the 18th century and treats a common dramaturgical theme: the intent of a socially ambitious father to marry his daughter off to a rich man twice or thrice her age and the subsequent foiling of the schemers by the daughter and her lover. The young couple find a willing ally in the person of the duenna, the girl's governess, who has plans to capture the wealthy suitor herself. The climactic wedding occurs in the refectory of a monastery, vouchsafing a happy ending for the lovers and an outraged frustration for the outwitted old men. The score is very much in the manner of *Love for 3 Oranges* and includes several farcical episodes.

Wedding, The. NOCES, LES.

wehmüt(h)ig (Ger.). Sadly, with melancholy.

weich (Ger.). Soft, tender; mellow, suave. *Weich gesungen*, sung softly (Mahler).

weiche Tonart (Ger., soft key). Minor key.

Weihe der Töne, Die (Consecration of Sounds). The 4th Sym. of Spohr, 1832, subtitled *A Characteristic Tone Painting in the Form of a Sym.* There are 4 programmatic movements: Largo, representing the stark silence of nature before the creation of sound, followed by an Allegro, portraying the actual sounds of nature; Andantino; March (War Music, Battle, and Return of the Victors); and Funeral: Consolation in Tears.

Weihnachtmusik (Ger.). Christmas music.

Weill, Kurt (Julian)

Remarkable German-born American composer; b. Dessau, Mar. 2, 1900; d. N.Y., Apr. 3, 1950. He was a private pupil of Albert Bing in Dessau (1915–18); in 1918–19 studied at the Berlin Hochschule für Musik with Humperdinck (composition), Friedrich Koch (counterpoint), and Krasselt (conducting). He was then engaged as an opera coach in Dessau and was also theater conductor at Lüdenscheid. In 1920 he moved to Berlin and became a student of Busoni at the Prussian Academy of Arts (1920–23); also studied with Jarnach there (1921–23). His 1st major work, the Sym. No. 1 (*Berliner Sinfonie*), was composed in 1921. However, it was not performed in his lifetime; indeed, its MS was not recovered until 1955, and it was finally premiered by the North German Radio Sym. Orch. in Hamburg in 1958.

Weill turned to the stage for his next large-scale work, the ballet *Zaubernacht* (with song; 1922), but under the impact of new trends in the musical theater he began to write satirical operas in a sharp modernistic manner: *Der Protagonist* (1924–25) and *Royal Palace* (1925–26). There followed a striking SONGSPIEL, *Mahagonny*, to a libretto by Bertolt Brecht, savagely satirizing the American primacy of money (1927); it was remodeled and was presented as the 3-act opera *Aufstieg und Fall der Stadt Mahagonny* (1929). Weill interrupted work on the opera to produce his success in this genre, a modern version of Gay's *The Beggar's Opera* to a pungent libretto by Brecht; under the title *Die Dreigroschenoper* (1928) it was staged all over Germany, and was also produced in translation throughout Europe.

Although Weill and Brecht grew apart over ideological differences, they produced 2 smaller works of great influence on later composers: *Der Jasager* (One Who Says Yes), a "school opera" with Marxist teachings (1930); and *Die Sieben Todsünden*, a sui generis dance-song cantata that encapsulates the Berlin of the 1920s and early 1930s (and indeed the world that Weill had to abandon).

After the Nazi ascent to power in Germany, Weill and his wife—the actress and singer Lotte Lenya, who appeared in many of his musical plays—went to Paris in 1933. They settled in the U.S. in 1935; Weill became a naturalized American citizen in 1943. Gradually absorbing the modes and fashions of American popular music, Weill adopted, with astonishing felicity, the typical form and content of American musicals; this stylistic transition was facilitated by the fact that in his European productions he had already absorbed elements of American popular songs and jazz rhythms. His musicals combine this Americanized idiom with a hint of early 20th-century advanced compositional techniques (atonality, polytonality, polyrhythms) and present the result in a pleasing and yet sophisticated and challenging manner.

Kurt Weill, 1920s

COURTESY FRANK DRIGGS COLLECTION

As Brecht, Georg Kaiser, and Caspar Neher had been his principal collaborators in Germany, Weill worked with such American literary luminaries as Paul Green, Maxwell Anderson, Moss Hart, Ira Gershwin, S. J. Perelman, Ogden Nash, Elmer Rice, Langston Hughes, and Alan Jay Lerner. Some works were too radical or offbeat for their audiences, others too operatic; his greatest successes were *Lady in the Dark* (1941), *One Touch of Venus* (1943), *Street Scene* (a "Broadway opera," 1947), and *Lost in the Stars* (1949). *Down in the Valley*, a 1-act "college opera," remains his most-performed English-language work.

For all Weill's success in American-produced scores, virtually all of his European works were unproduced in America at the time of his death. But 4 years after Weill's death, Marc Blitzstein made an English version of *Die Dreigroschenoper*, versified in a modern American vernacular; produced as *The Threepenny Opera* in 1954, it was a long-running N.Y. hit; its hit number, *The Ballad of Mack the Knife* (in German, *Die Moritat von Mackie Messer*), became tremendously successful. The production relaunched Lenya's career; she appeared in theatrical and film roles into the 1970s. At her death a Kurt Weill Foundation was established to help assist performances of his works, encourage scholarship, and produce a GESAMTAUSGABE.

Many of Weill's works have received 1st American productions or revivals; many new recordings have also been released. Weill's primary reputation as a theatrical composer has obscured attention to other valuable works, such as: 2 syms. (1921, *Berliner Sym.*; 1933, *Pariser Sym.* or *3 Night Scenes*); Divertimento (1922); Concerto for Violin, Woodwinds, Double Bass, and Percussion (Paris, 1925); *Kleine Dreigroschenmusik* for Winds, (1929).

Vocal: *Recordare* for Choir and Children's Chorus (1923); *Der neue Orpheus*, cantata for Soprano, Violin, and Orch. (1925; Berlin, 1927); *Vom Tod im Wald*, ballad for Bass and 10 Wind Instruments (Berlin, 1927); *Das Berliner Requiem*, cantata for Tenor, Baritone, Bass, Chorus, and 15 Instruments (Frankfurt Radio, 1929); *Der*

Lindberghflug, cantata after a radio score for Tenor, Baritone, Chorus, and Orch. (with Hindemith; Baden-Baden, 1929; rewritten by Weill as wholly his own work, Berlin, 1929; subsequent titles were *Der Flug des Lindberghs* and finally *Der Ozeanflug*, as a gesture of protest against Lindbergh's militant neutrality toward Nazi Germany). Chamber: 2 string quartets (1919; 1923); Cello Sonata (1920); film scores; radio and theater scores; some songs.

Wein, Weib, und Gesang. Waltz by J. Strauss (II), 1869, one of his most popular after *An der Schöne Blauen Donau.* The element of wine is represented by the short upbeat, suggesting a mild degree of intoxication; the element of woman is suggested by the flowing waves of accompaniment, and the concluding song unites both wine and woman under its irresistible melodic sway.

Weinberger, Jaromir. See SCHWANDA THE BAGPIPER.

Weir, Judith, important Scottish composer; b. Aberdeen, May 11, 1954. She studied in London with Tavener; computer music with Barry Vercoe; and with Robin Holloway, Schuller, and Messiaen. She has taught at Glasgow Univ. and held residencies. Weir's style represents an almost neoclassical approach to modern and non-Western techniques, with a unique deftness of touch. She is best known for theatrical works, including 3 operas: *A Night at the Chinese Opera* (1987); *The Vanishing Bridegroom* (1990); *Blond Eckbert* (1994); *Heaven Ablaze in His Breast*, dance-opera with Ian Spink and Second Stride (1995); *King Harald's Saga*, monodrama; incidental music. Orch.: *Music Untangled* (1991–92); *Heroic Strokes of the Bow* (1992); chamber music; piano music.

Weise (Ger.). Mode, manner; e.g., *Volksweise*, like a folk song; *Zigeunerweise*, in the Gypsy style.

Weisgall, Hugo (David), distinguished Moravian-born American composer and pedagogue; b. Eibenschutz, Oct. 13, 1912; d. Manhasset, N.Y., Mar. 11, 1997. He emigrated with his family to the U.S. and became a naturalized citizen in 1926. He studied at the Peabody Cons. of Music in Baltimore (1927–32); subsequently had composition lessons with Sessions at various times between 1932 and 1941; also was a pupil of Reiner (conducting diploma, 1938) and Scalero (composition diploma, 1939) at the Curtis Inst. of Music in Philadelphia; he pursued academic studies at Johns Hopkins Univ. (Ph.D., 1940, with a diss. on primitivism in 17th-century German poetry). After military service in World War II he was active as a conductor, singer, teacher, and composer.

He was founder-conductor of the Chamber Soc. of Baltimore (1948) and the Hilltop Opera Co. (1952); was director of the Baltimore Inst. of Musical Arts (1949–51); taught at Johns Hopkins Univ. (1951–57); was made chairman of the faculty of the Cantors' Inst. at the Jewish Theological Center in N.Y. in 1952. He taught at the Juilliard School of Music (1957–70) and at Queens College of the City Univ. of N.Y. (from 1961). He served as president of the American Music Center (1963–73); in 1966 he was composer-in-residence at the American Academy in Rome. He held 3 Guggenheim fellowships and received many prizes and commissions; in 1975 he was elected to membership in the National Inst. of Arts and Letters, and in 1990 became president of the American Academy and Inst. of Arts and Letters.

His music constitutes the paragon of enlightened but unstrident modernism; he was a master of all musical idioms, especially vocal. His intentions in each of his works never fail in the execution; for this reason his music enjoys numerous performances, which are usually accepted with pleasure by the audiences, if not by the majority of important music critics. He composed 10 operas, 4 ballets, orch.l works, vocal works, and songs.

Weiss, Silvius Leopold, lutenist and composer; b. Breslau, Oct. 12, 1686; d. Dresden, Oct. 16, 1750. He most likely was a pupil of his father, Johann Jacob Weiss, a lutenist and composer (b. *c.* 1662; d. Mannheim, Jan. 30, 1754); Silvius was in the service of Count Carl Philipp of the Palatinate in Breslau by 1706; then was in Italy with Alexander Sobiesky, Prince of Poland (1708–14). In 1715 he entered the service of the Hessen-Kassel court, and shortly thereafter went to Dusseldorf; in 1717 he joined the chapel of the Saxon court in Dresden, where his status was formalized in 1718. He also traveled as a virtuoso, appearing in Prague (1717), London (1718), Vienna (1718–19), Munich (1722), Berlin (1728), and Leipzig (1739), where he visited Bach.

Weiss was one of the foremost performers on and composers for the lute. His extant works number almost 600; he composed the largest corpus of solo lute works (mostly partitas and suites) by any composer; they are worthy of comparison with Bach's small number of works for this instrument. His brother was Johann Sigismund Weiss, lutenist, viola da gambist, violinist, and composer (b. probably in Breslau, *c.* 1689; d. Mannheim, Apr. 12, 1737). He became a lutenist at the Palatine chapel in Düsseldorf (*c.* 1708), following it to Heidelberg (1718) and to Mannheim (1720); in 1732 he was named director of instrumental music there, and later served as Konzertmeister and theorbo player. He was one of the finest composers of the early Mannheim school. Silvius's son Johann Adolf Faustinus Weiss (b. Dresden, Apr. 15, 1741; d. there, Jan. 21, 1814), was a lutenist and composer; served as chamber lutenist at the Dresden court from 1763 until his death; also traveled widely; composed lute and guitar music.

weite Lage (Ger.). Open harmony; wide disposition of voices in harmony.

weiter Entfernung, in (Ger.). In the far distance; played from behind the stage (Mahler, 5th Sym.).

Welk, Lawrence, popular American bandleader and accordionist; b. Strasburg, N.Dak., Mar. 11, 1903; d. Santa Monica, Ca., May 17, 1992. He began playing accordion in German-speaking areas of his native state as a youth; then performed with his own combos, gaining success as a self-described purveyor of "champagne music"; after touring and making numerous radio appearances, he launched his own television program in Los Angeles in 1951; it subsequently was featured on network television (1955–71). He owed his popularity to his skillful selection of programs containing a varied mixture of semiclassical pieces, western American ballads, and polkas and other dance tunes. His use of an accordion section in his arrangements, steadfast rhythmic beat, and sentimentalized tempos imparted to his renditions a rudimentary sound quality that made him a favorite with undiscriminating audiences.

well temperament. See TEMPERAMENT.

Well-Tempered Clavier, The (*Das wohltemperierte Clavier*). Collection of paired preludes and fugues by Bach, in 2 books (1722, 1742), often referred to as "the 48." Each book contains 24 preludes and 24 fugues in all major and minor keys arranged in chromatic order, alternating in major and minor keys. Consequently all odd-numbered preludes and fugues are in major keys, and all even-numbered ones are in minor; the 1st prelude and fugue in each of the 2 books is in C major; the last prelude and fugue in each of the

two books is in B minor. The complete German title of book I of the 48 is rendered into English as follows: "The Well-Tempered Clavier, or preludes and fugues through all tones and semitones, relating to the major 3rd, that is, Ut Re Mi, as well as those relating to the minor 3rd, that is Re Mi Fa. Compiled and prepared for the benefit and practice of young musicians desirous of learning, as well as for the entertainment of those already versed in this particular study, by Johann Sebastian Bach, Anno 1722."

The term "well-tempered" has often been interpreted to mean the use of equal temperament, but it is actually a late form of *meantone temperament* (see TEMPERAMENT), in which individual keys' characters are maintained. Bach's achievement was a triumph of tonal freedom within its Baroque context. Bach had a precursor in the person of J. C. F. Fischer, who published, a quarter of a century earlier, a collection of 20 preludes and fugues in 19 different keys, characteristically entitle *Ariadne musica neo-organoedum* (alluding to Ariadne, whose guiding thread helped Theseus to find his way out of the Cretan labyrinth). Bach must have known Fischer's work; in fact, some of Bach's fugal subjects are similar to Fischer's. The description *Clavier* is vague. In Bach's time the term was applied to all keyboard instruments; it could have been either a harpsichord or a clavichord.

A number of editors labored mightily over the publication of Bach's great work, trying to arrive at the proper understanding of various tonal and rhythmic ambiguities in the text. One editor had the temerity to insert a supernumerary bar in the C major prelude of book I, ostensibly to smooth down the uncomfortable transition between 2 unrelated diminished-7th chords; his unwarranted emendation is inexplicably adopted in most school editions. The English Bachologist Ebenezer Prout amused himself by setting the subjects of each one of Bach's 48 fugues to humorous verses, some of merit and wit. For fugue No. 7 of book II, he had this: "When I get aboard an ocean steamer/I begin to feel sick" (the last 2 words on a trill). The fugue No. 22 of book I, which is rather intricate, inspired him to write, "Oh, dear! What shall I do? It's utterly impossible for me to play this horrid fugue! I give it up!" And the chromatic countersubject of the same fugue is quite emotional: "It ain't no use! It ain't a bit of good! Not a bit, not a bit!"

wenig (Ger.). Little. *Ein klein wenig langsamer,* a little bit slower.

Werckmeister, Andreas, eminent German organist, organ examiner, music theorist, and composer; b.

Benneckenstein, Thuringia, Nov. 30, 1645; d. Halberstadt, Oct. 26, 1706. After his studies in Bennungen, Nordhausen, and Quedlinburg, he became organist in Hasselfelde, near Blankenburg (1664–74); after serving as organist and notary in Elbingerode (1674–75), he went to Quedlinburg as organist of the collegiate church of St. Servatius and of the court of the abbess and Countess of Palatine, Anna Sophia I; also was named organist of the Wipertikirche in 1677; in 1696 he settled in Halberstadt as organist of the Martinikirche. Werckmeister was highly influential as a music theorist; his exposition of number symbolism in music and its theological basis remains invaluable. But his work maintains its greatest relevance in the area of meantone temperament, as early music revivalists tackled keyboard tuning issues.

Among his numerous publications, Werckmeister's views can be found in 2 essays: *Musicalische Temperatur, oder Deutlicher und warer mathematischer Unterricht, wie man durch Anweisung des Monochordi ein Clavier, sonderlich die Orgel-Wercke, Positive, Regale, Spinetten und dergleichen wol temperirt stimmen könne* (Frankfurt am Main and Leipzig, c. 1686–87; not extant; 2nd ed., 1691); and *Hypomnemata musica, oder Musicalisches Memorial, welches bestehet in kurtzer Erinnerung dessen, so bisshero unter guten Freunden discursweise, insonderheit von der Composition und Temperatur möchte vorgangen seyn* (Quedlinburg, 1697).

Werfel, Alma Mahler. See MAHLER, GUSTAV.

Werk (Ger.). 1. Work, opus, composition. 2. An organ keyboard with its own set of pipes; *Orgelwerk*.

Werther. Opera by Massenet, 1892, 1st performed in Vienna. The libretto is extracted from Goethe's celebrated short novel *Die Leiden des jungen Werthers* (The Sorrows of Young Werther, 1774). Werther is a young man who is prey to a single overpowering passion for a young woman who reciprocates his affection on a philosophical level but marries a more pragmatic person. Werther does not cease to express his adoration for her. Then he borrows a pistol from her husband and shoots himself. She rushes to his side, and he has the ultimate satisfaction of dying in her arms while proclaiming the eternal validity of his deathless passion. A wave of suicides followed the publication of Goethe's novel among young males in the throes of unrequited love; in some countries the novel was banned as a result. In his melodious score Massenet extracted the last fluid ounce of tearful emotion afforded by the libretto.

Wesendonck, Mathilde (Luckemeyer). See WAGNER, (WILHELM) RICHARD.

West Side Story. Musical by L. Bernstein and Sondheim, 1957, 1st performed in Washington, D.C. It is an undisputed classic of the American musical theater, a score that convincingly demonstrates Bernstein's amazing duality of talent as composer of deeply earnest music and genius for creating original, authentically American musicals; many consider it his masterpiece. The idea was developed by choreographer Jerome Robbins jointly with Bernstein. The dramatic theme of the play is connected with the massive migration of Puerto Ricans in N.Y. and a formation of a cultural and racial enclave, principally in the Upper West Side of N.Y.

Two rival youth gangs, the Jets—composed of Italian and Irish boys—and the Sharks—recruited from the Puerto Rican population—fight each other tooth and nail, knife and switchblade, like latter-day Montagues and Capulets. Tony of the Jets is the counterpart of Shakespeare's Romeo, and Maria, sister of the leader of the Sharks, is Juliet. A dance in a school gymnasium sets the scene of mutual distrust between the 2 gangs. But Tony and Maria arrange for a clandestine meeting; their song *Tonight* is one of the most appealing love ballads in American musical theater; also remarkable is his invocation to *Maria*, and her vivacious confession, *I Feel Pretty*. The tension erupts in a savage fight ballet (*The Rumble*). In a climactic fight Tony's friend Riff is knifed to death. In revenge Tony kills Maria's brother Bernardo. After a tense cat-and-mouse chase Tony is inexorably shot by Shark, and dies in the arms of Maria.

Among other fine numbers are the ballad *Somewhere*; a group of Puerto Rican women debating the advantages of American life in the hemiola chorus *America*; and a classic comic song, *Gee, Officer Krupke*, a cynical commentary by the Jets on juvenile delinquency. The film version of *West Side Story*, released in 1961, received 10 awards for excellence. Shortly before his death Bernstein recorded a complete, almost operatic version of the work. Ironically, a goodly portion of the neighborhood in which *West Side Story* is set was demolished to make way for the Lincoln Center for the Performing Arts.

Westminster Chimes. Tune, c. 1794, attributed to William Crotch (b. Norwich, July 5, 1775; d. Taunton, Dec. 29, 1847). In 1860 the Big Ben tower clock at the Houses of Parliament was equipped with a mechanism for sounding the Westminster chimes. The opening 4 notes are identical with a phrase that occurs in *I Know That My Redeemer*

Liveth from Handel's *Messiah*, no doubt a coincidence. Countless arrangements have been made of the Westminster chimes. Vaughan Williams interpolated the Big Ben tune in his *London Sym.*

What Makes Sammy Run? Musical by Ervin Drake, 1964, based on a best-selling novel by Budd Schulberg centered on an utterly unscrupulous Hollywood producer. What makes him run is his total concentration on his own interests in reaching the highest power in moviedom, which he achieves at the price of eliminating his friends and associates and double-crossing his girlfriends. Includes *My Hometown.*

What's Goin' On? Turbulent social-protest anthem by Marvin Gaye released in 1971; also the title track of a highly influential album.

When Irish Eyes Are Smiling. Song by Ernest R. Ball, 1913, the best-known of his contributions to neo-Irish folklore, in the wake of the Celtic twilight era; other songs were *Mother Machree* (1910) and *A Little Bit of Heaven* (1914). Ball collaborated with the great Irish tenor John McCormack.

When Johnny Comes Marching Home. A Civil War song by Patrick Gilmore, 1863, under the pseudonym of Louis Lambert. It became a nostalgic ballad of Union soldiers returning home from the battlefields. Since Gilmore and bandmasters of the 19th century freely appropriated folk songs, or even songs by known contemporary composers (as Christy did in publ. Foster's Ethiopian songs under his own name), it may well be that *When Johnny Comes Marching Home* was an arrangement of a preexisting popular song; the modal character of the tune suggests Irish or Scottish origin.

When the Moon Comes Over the Mountain. Song by Harry Woods, 1931, and introduced by Kate Smith on the radio, to great acclaim.

When the Red, Red Robin Comes Bob, Bob, Bobbin' Along. Song by Harry Woods, 1926; its success led to its inclusion in several motion pictures.

When the Saints Go Marching In. Negro spiritual of unknown origins, publ. in 1908; it combines elements of a funeral hymn and a southern dance step. The tune became a standard for early New Orleans jazz bands and was further popularized by Louis Armstrong.

Where's Charley? Musical by F. Loesser, 1948, his 1st, and a major success. The plot is based on a farce by Brandon Thomas, *Charley's Aunt.* The impoverished father of an Oxford Univ. student wants his son to marry an eligible and rich Brazilian widow, while he has his own problem in getting a chaperone for his girlfriend. The dual problem is resolved when Charley dresses up in woman's attire to pretend to be his own aunt and acts as a chaperone. The Brazilian widow finally materializes; after meeting the impoverished father, she solves the financial problem by marrying him. Among the attractive songs in the score, the best known are *Once in Love with Amy* and *My Darling, My Darling.*

Whiffenpoof Song, The. Song of the Yale Univ. Glee Club, 1909. Whiffenpoof was a character in a famous comic strip (and Herbert's operetta *Little Nemo*, 1908). It was popularized by Rudy Vallee, himself a Yale man.

While Strolling Through the Park One Day. Song by Robert Ki, 1884, which became tremendously popular among young swains and shop girls in N.Y. Soft-shoe steps (tap dance) were usually interpolated during the refrain.

whip (Fr. *fouet*; Ger. *Peitsche*; It. *frusta*). A wooden percussion instrument having 2 sections joined at 1 end that are clacked together making the sound of a cracking whip. Ravel uses it in some of his scores, as does Varèse in *Ionisation.* Mascagni makes dramatic use of the whip in *Cavalleria Rusticana* to announce the entrance of the vengeful husband.

whipping bow. A form of violin technique in which the bow is made to fall with a certain vehemence on the strings. Chiefly employed when one wishes to mark sharply single tones in rapid tempo, as

Whispering. Popular song by John Schonberger, 1920. The opening line, "Whispering while you cuddle near me," gives an idea of the sentiment of the song, and the chromaticized harmony enhances the sentimentality to the point of saturation. The song sold millions of copies in sheet music and became a Romantic perennial.

whistle (from Old Eng. *hwistle*; Fr. *sifflet*; Ger. *Pfeife*). Family of short end-blown flutes, in numerous forms, dating to prehistory. In its basic form there are no fingerholes; the whistle is used as a decoy or signal.

Whistler and His Dog, The. A jiglike melody by Arthur Pryor, 1905. The front cover of the 1st edition shows a boy whistling at a dog standing near by, but in later editions the dog is sitting. The implications of this revision have yet to be understood by musical iconologists.

White Christmas. A ballad by I. Berlin, 1942, from film *Holiday Inn*, which became a hymn, an anthem, and a prayer for the G.I.'s in the Pacific islands, where Christmas is always green. By 1965, *White Christmas* had sold nearly 6 million copies in sheet music and over 50 million recordings. Bing Crosby made a career with this song but some 300 other performers also performed it.

white noise (sound). By analogy with the complementary colors of the visual spectrum, white noise can be described as a sonic continuum containing all available tones within a certain auditory range, or a complex consisting of prescribed intervals, a pandiatonic or panpentatonic tone cluster, a dodecaphonic or icositetraphonic cumulus, etc. White noise can be prismatically analyzed into a linear progression forming a scale of discrete tones.

white note. One with an open head: o or ♩.

White Peacock, The. Sym. poem by Griffes, 1919; originally a piano solo, 1915 (*Roman Sketches*, No. 1, op. 7). The piece is impressionist in style and idiom; its orch.l version was premiered in Philadelphia.

Whiteman, Paul, celebrated American conductor of popular music; b. Denver, Colo., Mar. 28, 1890; d. Doylestown, Pa., Dec. 29, 1967. He played viola in the Denver Sym. Orch. and later in the San Francisco People's Sym. Orch.; in 1917–18 he was conductor of a 40-piece band in the U.S. Navy. He then formed a hotel orch. in Santa Barbara, Calif.; and began to develop a style of playing known as *symphonic jazz*, which soon made him famous. In 1924, he gave a concert in Aeolian Hall in N.Y., at which he introduced Gershwin's *Rhapsody in Blue*, written for his orch., with the composer as piano soloist. In 1926 he made a tour in Europe. While not himself a jazz musician, he was popularly known as the "King of Jazz," and frequently featured at his concerts such notables of the jazz world as Bix Beiderbecke, Frank Trumbauer, and Benny Goodman; Bing

Crosby achieved his early fame as a member of Paul Whiteman's Rhythm Boys. Whiteman established the Whiteman Awards, made annually for symphonic jazz compositions written by Americans. He publ. the books *Jazz* (with M. McBride; N.Y., 1926), *How to Be a Bandleader* (with L. Lieber; N.Y., 1941), and *Records for the Millions* (N.Y., 1948).

Whithorne (born Whittern), **Emerson.** See LEGINSKA (LIGGINS), ETHEL.

Who? Song by Kern, 1925, from the musical *Sunny*; the full question is, "Who stole my heart away?"

Who, The. A popular and influential rock band, viewed by some to have been the leading 1960s British group after the Beatles and Rolling Stones. (Guitar/vocal/songwriter: Pete[r Dennis Blandford] Townsend, b. Chiswick, U.K., May, 19, 1945; vocals: Roger Daltrey, b. Hammersmith, Mar. 1, 1944; bass; John Entwistle b. Chiswick, Oct. 9, 1944; drums: Keith Moon, b. Wembley, Aug. 23, 1947; d. London, Sept. 7, 1978.)

In the early 1960s, Townsend began playing banjo in a Dixieland jazz group, in which Entwistle blew the trumpet; Entwistle would become the group's bassist, with occasional vocal and compositional contributions. They teamed with Entwistle's friend, vocalist Roger Daltrey and organized a group to which they 1st gave the name High Numbers. The drummer Keith Moon joined the group in 1964, at which point the group became The Who.

At the time, British youth culture was more or less divided between the Mods (middle-class scooter drivers wearing the cool style of Carnaby) and the Rockers (labor-class leather-jacketed motorcyclists). Anxious to project a Mod image for their fans as a statement in an alien world, they sported odd clothes, cultivated bizarre behavior, and indulged in maniacal conduct on the stage, which included physical destruction of their instruments at the end of each set, prescient of metal and punk performance practice. In 1965 the group released the single *My Generation*, their 1st major hit and soon a battle cry for youth rebellion. In 1966 they recorded *A Quick One While He's Away*, a mini-rock-opera that forecast the group's later development.

Although several well-produced and thoughtful singles had subsequent success in the U.K. and U.S., the Who did not reach worldwide success until the release of the "rock opera" *Tommy* (1969), composed mostly by Townshend, concerning spirituality in postwar England through a young boy who becomes deaf, dumb, and blind. In addition to its massive success as a recording, *Tommy* was long a staple of the Who's live performances; it has been recorded by superstar casts, released as a film, and many years later realized as a Broadway musical. The Who recorded a 2nd opera, the more evocative and less plot-driven *Quadrophenia* (1973), recalling the Mod phase of England's (and the group's) history.

In between these milestones they produced some fine recordings as a group and as solo artists, beginning in the 1970s, among them: The Who released *Live at Leeds* (1970), *Who's Next* (1971), and *Who Are You* (1978). Townshend produced *Who Came First* (1972), *Rough Mix* (with Ronnie Lane, 1977), *Empty Glass* (1980), (*All the Best Cowboys Have*) *Chinese Eyes* (1982), *White City* (video, 1985), *The Iron Man* (1989), and *PsychoDerelict* (1993); he has also released 2 collections of his demo recordings. Entwistle released solo albums with typically gothic titles as *Smash Your Head Against the Wall* (1971) and *Rigor Mortis* (1973). Moon recorded the idiosyncratic *Two Sides of the Moon* before his death. Daltrey recorded albums and acted in films (notoriously Ken Russell's *Lisztomania*, 1975). All 4 members participated in the film *The Kids Are Alright* (1979), a freewheeling documentary of the group's history, named after an early single. A tragic moment in their career occurred at a Cincinnati concert in late 1979 when 11 young people were trampled to death in a rush for the entrance gates. After Moon's death, the group took on Kenney Jones (like Lane a former member of the Small Faces) as drummer, made international tours, released 2 more albums, and called it a day. The Who has reunited for 1 subsequent *Tommy* tour and for benefit concerts.

whole consort. An old English term for an instrumental ensemble; consisting of either all wind or all string instruments (e.g., recorders, viols); the counterpart of BROKEN CONSORT.

whole note. The note o.

whole shift. See SHIFT.

whole step. 1. The step of a whole tone. 2. A whole tone.

whole tone. A major 2nd.

whole-tone scale

〰 〰 〰 〰 〰

A scale consisting entirely of consecutive whole steps, whether written as major 2nds or diminished 3rds. The whole-tone scale gained ephemeral popularity early in the 20th century as an exotic resource cultivated by the impressionist school of composers. The whole-tone scale is neutral in its polarity; it lacks modality; the intervallic progression in the whole-tone scale remains the same in melodic rotation. The perfect 5th and the perfect 4th, the cornerstones of tonality, are absent in the whole-tone scale; there is no dominant or subdominant, and no leading tone.

Analytically the whole-tone scale is atonal. It can also be regarded as the linear function of 2 mutually exclusive augmented triads; as 2 conjunct tetrachords comprised solely of whole steps; or as the intussusception of 3 mutually exclusive tritones at the distance of a whole tone from one another. Because of its association with the traditionally forbidden tritone (the DIABOLUS IN MUSICA), the whole-tone scale itself became a favorite device of early modernism to portray diabolical forces, menacing apparitions, and ineffable mysteries.

The earliest mention of an intentional employment of the whole-tone scale occurs in Mozart's comic divertimento *Die Dorfmusikanten*, subtitled *A Musical Joke*. But Mozart used the whole-tone scale here not to illustrate a malevolent agency, but to ridicule the incompetence of village musicians and their inability to play in tune. The whole-tone scale came into its own as an ominous symbol in Glinka's opera *Ruslan and Ludmila*, in which it is used as a motto of the magician Chernomor. Rossini made use of the whole-tone scale in a song written in 1864 entitled *L'Amour à Pékin*, in which it was described as "gamme chinoise." The possible reason for this reference is that an ancient Chinese panpipe contains 2 mutually exclusive whole-tone scales in symmetrically disposed tubes.

Liszt was fascinated with the whole-tone scale, and was greatly impressed by the *Fantastic Overture* (1859), which the Russian amateur composer Boris Vietinghoff-Scheel (1829–1901) sent him, and in which whole-tone scales were profusely employed. In his comment on the work Liszt described the effect as "terrifying to all long and protruding ears." Liszt himself made use of the whole-tone scale in his *Divina Commedia*, illustrating the Inferno; and he used it systematically in his posthumously published organ and late piano pieces.

The problem of harmonizing the whole-tone scale tonally was solved by Glinka in a sequence of modulations. Liszt harmonized a descending whole-tone scale that occurs in the bass. It is doubtful whether Puccini was aware of Liszt's application of this harmony, but he used a precisely identical triadic harmonization of the descending whole-tone scale in his opera *Tosca*, as an introduction to the appearance of Scarpia, the sinister Roman chief of police. The Russian composer Vladimir Rebikov (1866–1920) was probably the 1st to write an entire composition derived exclusively from the whole-tone scale and its concomitant series of augmented triads, his *Les Démons s'amusent* for Piano; its title suggests that Rebikov was fully aware of its demoniac association.

But it was Debussy who elevated the whole-tone scale from a mere exotic device to a poetic and expressive medium. Its Protean capacity for change and adaptability greatly attracted Debussy and his followers, as an alternative to a diatonic scale. A very interesting application of the whole-tone scale occurs in *La Mer*; the principal theme of the 1st movement is in the Aeolian mode; in the 3rd movement it appears isorhythmically as a progression of whole-tones. The 1st and the last sections of Debussy's *Voiles* for Piano (*Préludes*, book I) consist of whole tones with the middle section providing a contrast in the pentatonic scale. Berg used an alternation between the 2 distinct whole-tone scales (beginning on C and on D♭) in his *Nacht* (7 *Frühe Lieder*, 1907).

A whole catalogue can be compiled of incidental usages of the whole-tone scale. Even Tchaikovsky, not usually given to modern inventions, made use of the whole-tone scale in a modulatory sequence illustrating the appearance of the ghost of the old Countess in his opera *The Queen of Spades*. Rimsky-Korsakov filled the 2nd act of his opera *Le Coq d'or* with whole-tone scales and augmented triads to convey the impression of death and devastation of the battlefield. The entrance of Herod in *Salome* of R. Strauss is announced by a leading motive composed of whole tones. Holst characterized *Saturn* in his sym. suite *The Planets* by a series of whole-tone passages to evoke the mystery of Saturn's rings. Apart from astronomy, the whole-tone scale serves pure fantasy. In his sym. fairy tale *Kikimora* Liadov paints the mischievous sprite in whole tones. Paul Dukas introduces the hapless amateur magician in his *L'Apprenti Sorcier* in a series of whole-tones.

The English composer Edward Maryon (1867–1954) assigns the whole-tone scale to the changelings in his opera *Werewolf*, reserving the diatonic scale for normal children. Another English composer, Havergal Brian, has a chorus singing in whole-tone scales in his opera *The Tigers*, to illustrate the aerial bombardment of London by the zeppelins during World War I. There are bits of whole-tone figures in Menotti's children's opera *Help, Help, the Globolinks!* to describe the creatures from outer space; the earthlings in the opera overcome the invading globolinks in victorious C major. A remarkable demonstration of the perdurability of the whole-tone scale as a symbol of evil is provided by Stravinsky's *Elegy for J. F. K.* (1964), which contains within a 12-tone row two intervallically congruous groups of whole tones, each embanked in a tritone, itself a symbol of deviltry.

With the gradual decline of pictorial and sensorial programmaticism in contemporary music, the whole-tone scale sank into disuse and cliché. It found its temporary outlet and a stylistic rehabilitation in dodecaphonic usages in the form of two mutually exclusive hexachords. Eventually it joined the subculture of film music. Cinematic Nazis advance on the screen to the sound of whole-tone scales in the trombones. Mad scientists hatch their murderous schemes to blow up the world in mighty progressions of whole tones. Mentally disturbed maidens pluck whole-tone scales on the harp.

When Jean Harlow, in her screen biography, climbs up the ladder in the studio before her final collapse, she is accompanied by delicate whole-tone pizzicatos. The whole-tone scale is also used, wittily so, in satirical comment on pompous personages in animated cartoons.

Whoopee. Musical by Walter Donaldson, 1928. The plot concerns a man who has gone to Calif. to recuperate from hypochondria and gets involved with a young woman at an Indian reservation. She turns out to be of non–Native American stock, but it was love's labor lost anyway. The show's success was thanks to Eddie Cantor's presence in the cast; the best song was *Makin' Whoopee.*

Widmung (Ger.). Dedication (of a composition).

Widor, Charles-Marie (-Jean-Albert), distinguished French organist, pedagogue, and composer; b. Lyons, Feb. 21, 1844; d. Paris, Mar. 12, 1937. His father, an Alsatian of Hungarian descent, was organist at the church of St.-François in Lyons and was active as an organ builder. Widor was a skillful improviser on the organ while still a boy and became organist at the Lyons lycée when he was 11. After studies with Fétis (composition) and Lemmens (organ) in Brussels he became organist at St.-Francois (1860) and gained high repute via provincial concerts. In 1870–71 he held a provisional appointment as organist at St.-Sulpice in Paris, where he served as organist from 1871 until 1934. In 1934 he played his *Pièce mystique* there, composed at age 90. Around 1880 he began writing music criticism under the pen name "Aulétès" for the daily *L'Estafette.*

In 1890 he became prof. of organ and in 1896 prof. of composition at the Paris Cons. In 1910 he was elected a member of the Académie des Beaux-Arts, of which he became permanent secretary in 1913. He had many distinguished pupils, including Albert Schweitzer, with whom he collaborated in editing the 1st 5 vols. of an 8-vol. ed. of Bach's organ works (N.Y., 1912–14).

As a composer he wrote copiously in many forms but is best known for his solo organ music, especially the 10 "symphonies" (suites, 1876–1900). A master organ virtuoso, he won great renown for his performances of Bach and for his inspired improvisations. Other Widor organ works include the *Suite latine* (1927); *3 nouvelles pièces* (1934); 8 sonatas. He also composed 3 operas, 2 ballets, incidental music; 5 syms., including 3 with organ; 2 piano concertos, 1 cello concerto, other works; chamber and piano music; vocal works, both sacred and secular, with instrumental and orch.l accompaniment.

Writings (all publ. in Paris): *Technique de l'orchestre moderne* (1904); *Notice sur la vie et les oeuvres de Camille Saint-Saëns* (1922); *Initiation musicale* (1923); *Académie des Beaux-Arts: Fondations, portraits de Massenet à Paladilhe* (1927); *L'Orgue moderne: La décadence dans la facture contemporaine* (1928).

wie (Ger.). As, like. *Wie aus der Ferne,* as from a distance; *wie ein Naturlaut,* like a sound of nature; *wie oben,* as above; *wie vorher,* as before, as 1st; *wie wütend dreinfahren,* as if driving in furiously (Mahler, 6th Sym.).

Wieck, Clara Josephine. SCHUMANN, CLARA (JOSEPHINE) WIECK.

Wieck, (Johann Gottlob) **Friedrich.** See SCHUMANN, CLARA (JOSEPHINE) WIECK.

wieder (Ger.). Again. *Wiederhall,* echo; *Wiederholung,* repetition; *Wiederholungszeichen,* repetition sign (repeat mark).

wiegend (Ger.). Swaying, rocking.

Wiegenlied (Ger.; Fr. *berceuse*). A lullaby. The most famous is a song by Brahms, *Guten Abend, gut' Nacht* (1868; no. 4, op. 49).

Wienerwalzer. A fast-tempo waltz associated with Vienna; the standard version of this dance, made famous at the Congress of Vienna (1815).

Wieniawski, Henryk (Henri), famous Polish violinist, teacher, and composer, brother of Jozcf and uncle of Adam Tadeusz Wieniawski; b. Lublin, July 10, 1835; d. Moscow, Mar. 31, 1880. His mother, Regina Wolff-Wieniawska, was a talented pianist; he began training with Jan Hornziel and Stanislaw Serwaczynski in Warsaw; upon the advice of his mother's brother, Edouard Wolff, who lived in France, she took Henryk to Paris, where he entered the Cons. at the age of 8, 1st in Clavel's class, and the following year, in the advanced class of Massart. At the age of 11 he graduated with 1st prize in violin, an unprecedented event in the annals of the Paris Cons. After further private studies with Massart (1846–48), he made his Paris debut in 1848, in a concert accompanied by his brother at the piano; gave his 1st concert in St. Petersburg shortly thereafter, playing 4 more concerts there; then played in Finland and the Baltic provinces; after several successful appearances in Warsaw, he returned in 1849 to Paris, where he studied composition with Hippolyte Collet at the Cons., graduating with an *accessit* prize in 1850.

From 1851 to 1853 he gave about 200 concerts in Russia with his brother. He also devoted much time to composition, and by age 18 he had composed and publ. his virtuoso 1st Violin Concerto, which he played with extraordinary success in Leipzig that same year. In 1858 he appeared with Anton Rubinstein in Paris and in 1859 in the Beethoven Quartet Soc. concerts in London, where he appeared as a violist as well as a violinist. In 1860 he went to St. Petersburg and was named solo violinist to the Czar, and also concertmaster of the orch. and 1st violinist of the string quartet of the Russian Musical Soc.; likewise served as prof. of violin at the newly founded Cons. (1862–68). He continued to compose and introduced his greatly esteemed 2nd Violin Concerto in St. Petersburg (1862), with Rubinstein conducting. In 1872 he went on a tour of the U.S. with Rubinstein; one of the featured works was Beethoven's *Kreutzer Sonata*, which they performed about 70 times. When Rubinstein returned to Europe, Wieniawski continued his American tour, which included California. He returned to Europe in 1874, gave several concerts with Rubinstein in Paris, and in the same year succeeded Vieuxtemps as prof. of violin at the Brussels Cons., resigning in 1877 owing to an increasingly grave heart condition; he suffered an attack during a concert in Berlin on Nov. 11, 1878, but still agreed to play several concerts in Russia; made his farewell appearance in Odessa in Apr. 1879. His last months were spent in Moscow, where he was taken to the home of Nadezhda von Meck, Tchaikovsky's patroness, in 1880.

He was married to Isobel Hampton, an Englishwoman; their youngest daughter, Irene (1879–1932), wrote music under the pen name Poldowski. Wieniawski was undoubtedly one of the greatest violinists of the 19th century; he possessed a virtuoso technique and an extraordinary range of dynamics. He was equally distinguished as a chamber music player. As a composer he remains best known today for the 2 violin concertos and an outstanding set of etudes. He also composed numerous other orch.l works as well as pieces for solo or 2 violins.

Wildcat. Musical by Cy Coleman, 1960. Wildcat gets her nickname because of her reckless ways in prospecting for oil. When after much drilling she becomes convinced that there is no oil on her land, she blows up the riggings with a stick of dynamite; predictably an oil gusher erupts. She gains not only a fortune but a boyfriend. Includes *Hey, Look Me Over.*

Wildschütz, Der, oder Die Stimme der Natur (The Poacher, or The Voice of Nature). Opera by Lortzing, 1842, 1st performed in Leipzig. The poacher is a school teacher who accidentally kills an animal on the estate of a feudal aristocrat. He is threatened with dismissal from his job, and he sends his bride to plead with the lord of the manor, known for his lecherous inclinations. As a result of multiple transsexual changes of attire, a baroness takes her place. In the end class divisions are preserved, with aristocrats pairing up with their equals. The teacher regains his bride undamaged and is freed of accusations of poaching when it develops that the animal he shot was his own ass.

Will You Love Me in December as You Do in May? Song by Ernest R. Ball, 1905, with words by James Walker, destined to become the mayor of N.Y. Walker selected it as his theme song for his political campaigns; it was eventually played at his funeral.

William Tell. Opera by Rossini, 1829, his last stage work, 1st performed in Paris under the French title *Guillaume Tell*. The opera is rarely performed in its entirety, but its overture is an extremely popular concert piece, and its final section was the theme for *The Lone Ranger* radio and television series. The opera's subject is taken from a turbulent chapter in the history of Switzerland, as retold in Schiller's eponymous play (1804). William Tell is a Swiss patriot and a remarkable archer. The brutal governor of the province tests his marksmanship by ordering him to split an apple placed on the head of his small son with an arrow. William Tell passes the test, then turns the weapon on the tyrant and kills him with a single shot.

Williams, "Cootie" (Charles Melvin), African-American jazz trumpeter and bandleader; b. Mobile, Ala., July 24, 1908; d. N.Y., Sept. 15, 1985. He took trumpet lessons with Charles Lipskin; made his way to N.Y. and joined groups led by Chick Webb and Fletcher Henderson. From 1929 to 1940 he was a member of Duke Ellington's band; after working with Benny Goodman (1940–41) he led his own groups until rejoining Ellington's band in 1962; he left in 1975 but continued to perform until 1983. He was one of the leading jazz trumpeters of his era, equally adept at open and muted playing.

Williams, (Hiram) **Hank,** seeded American country-music singer, guitarist, and songwriter; b. Georgiana, Al., Sept. 17, 1923; d. Oak Hill, Va., Jan. 1, 1953. He sang church hymns and learned to play the organ at a very early age; then took guitar lessons from a black street singer. At 12 he won a prize in an amateur contest in Montgomery singing his own song, *W.P.A. Blues.* At 14 he formed his own band, Hank Williams and His Drifting Cowboys. In 1946 he went to Nashville; in 1949 he joined the famous Grand

Ole Opry there, and made an instant success with his rendition of *Lovesick Blues*; its recording sold over a million copies. In 1950 he put out several recordings of his own songs, *Long Gone Lonesome Blues, I Just Don't Like This Kind of Livin', Why Don't You Love Me?,* and *Moanin' the Blues,* which sold prodigiously. His subsequent releases, also magically successful, were *Hey, Good Lookin', Your Cheatin' Heart, Move It On Over, Cold, Cold Heart,* and *Jambalaya (On the Bayou),* but the nemesis of so many country singers—drugs, alcohol, women in excess—and a cardiac disorder killed him before he reached the age of 30. His son, (Randall) Hank Williams, Jr. (b. Shreveport, La., May 26, 1949), was also a successful country-western singer, guitarist, and songwriter; his career was also hampered by alcohol and drug problems; in 1975 he sustained severe injuries while mountain climbing, but eventually resumed his career. He has long been a legitimately popular and talented performer, not merely a son of his famous father. A television show on his life, *Living Proof,* was produced in 1983.

Williams, John (Christopher), remarkable Australian guitarist; b. Melbourne, Apr. 24, 1941. He 1st studied with his father, the guitarist Leonard Williams; when he was 14 he performed in London, then took guitar lessons with Segovia at the Accademia Chigiana in Siena (1957–59). In 1962 he made a tour of the Soviet Union; also played in America and Japan. In addition to classical music, he includes in his programs pieces of pop music and jazz; this egalitarian versatility makes him a favorite with the youth of English-speaking countries.

Williams, John (Towner), enormously successful American composer and conductor; b. N.Y., Feb. 8, 1932. He grew up in a musical atmosphere; his father was a film studio musician. He began to take piano lessons; later he learned to play trombone, trumpet, and clarinet. In 1948 the family moved to Los Angeles, where he studied orchestration with Robert van Epps at Los Angeles City College and composition privately with Mario Castelnuovo-Tedesco; he also took piano lessons with Rosina Lhevinne at the Juilliard School of Music in N.Y. He began his career as a composer, arranger, and conductor for films and television; wrote the film scores, rich in sounding brass and tinkling cymbals, for *Close Encounters of the Third Kind, Superman, The Empire Strikes Back, Raiders of the Lost Ark, E.T. The Extra-Terrestrial,* and *Return of the Jedi.* He won Academy Awards for *Fiddler on the Roof* (1971), *Jaws* (1975), and *Star Wars* (1977). The record albums for these background scores sold into the millions. He also wrote 2 syms., a violin concerto, a flute concerto, an essay for strings, and a number of chamber music pieces. In 1980 he was chosen conductor of the Boston Pops Orch., succeeding the late Arthur Fiedler, who had held that post for almost 50 years; Williams declared openly that no one could hope to equal Fiedler in charisma and showmanship, not to mention Fiedler's splendiferous aureole of white hair (as contrasted with his successor's alopecia), but he said he would try his best to bridge the gap. He largely succeeded, and diversified his appeal to Boston Pops audiences by playing selections from his own sparkling film scores.

Williams, Mary Lou (born Mary Elfrieda Scruggs), African-American jazz pianist, composer, and arranger; b. Atlanta, May 8, 1910; d. Durham, N.C., May 28, 1981. She began her career as a pianist in Kansas City with the saxophonist Andy Kirk (to whom she was married for a time); in 1931 she became pianist and arranger for Kirk's Twelve Clouds of Joy band, and provided him with such songs as *Walkin' & Swingin', Twinklin', Cloudy,* and *Little Joe from Chicago;* she then worked with Duke Ellington, Benny Goodman, and others. In 1945 she composed the bebop hit *In the Land of Oo-Bla-Dee* for Dizzy Gillespie; she also wrote *The Zodiac Suite,* which was performed by the N.Y. Phil. After becoming a Roman Catholic, she composed a number of religious works, including *St. Martin de Porres* and 3 Masses; her *Music for Peace* became popularly known as "Mary Lou's Mass." In 1977 she was named artist-in-residence at Duke Univ. in Durham. She was one of the leading figures in the jazz field for almost 60 years.

Williams, Ralph Vaughan. VAUGHAN WILLIAMS, RALPH.

Wills, Bob (James Robert), American country-music singer, fiddler, bandleader, and songwriter; b. near Kosse, Tex., Mar. 6, 1905; d. Fort Worth, May 13, 1975. He 1st took up the mandolin, then began to play the fiddle; through his association with local black musicians, he learned blues and jazz as well. In 1928 he organized his own group, the Wills Fiddle Band; subsequently he appeared on radio and made many recordings. After settling in Tulsa, Okla. (1934), he became a fixture on station KVOO with his Texas Playboys band. From 1942 he was active with the group on the West Coast; also appeared in films. He gained popularity with his composition *San Antonio Rose;* he was elected to the Country Music Hall of Fame in 1968.

Willson, (Robert Reiniger) **Meredith,** American flutist and composer of musicals; b. Mason City, Iowa, May 18, 1902; d. Santa Monica, Calif., June 15, 1984. He learned to play the flute as a child, then went to N.Y. and studied at the Damrosch Inst. (1919–22) and received instruction in flute from Georges Barrère (1920–29); also studied with H. Hadley (1923–24) and Julius Gold (1921–23). He was 1st flutist in Sousa's band (1921–23) and a member of the N.Y. Phil. (1924–29); then became a musical director for various radio shows. For the 30th anniversary of the San Francisco earthquake he wrote a sym., which he conducted in its 1st performance (San Francisco, 1936). His 2nd Sym. was 1st played by the Los Angeles Phil. in 1940; he wrote other sym. works, band pieces, and a choral work, *Anthem of the Atomic Age.* However, he devoted himself mainly to the composition of popular music, in which he revealed a triple talent as a performer, writer, and composer. He appeared as a comedian on a radio program, *The Big Show,* in which he engaged in a comic colloquy with Tallulah Bankhead, closing with an inspirational hymn, *May the Good Lord Bless and Keep You,* which became very popular as an anthem. Willson achieved his greatest triumph with his musical *The Music Man,* for which he wrote the book, the lyrics, and the music. It opened in late 1957, and became an immediate success, thanks to the satirical and yet somehow patriotic subject, dealing with a traveling salesman of band uniforms and instruments who sells them to small-town suckers, but gets a happy comeuppance; and to the sparkling score, containing the marching chorus *76 Trombones* and many other hits. His subsequent musicals were *The Unsinkable Molly Brown,* produced in late 1960, for which he wrote the musical score, and *Here's Love,* produced in 1963, an adaptation of the film *Miracle on 34th Street. The Music Man* and *The Unsinkable Molly Brown* were made into films. Willson was also active as an arranger and orchestrator in Hollywood; he helped Charlie Chaplin in arranging the score for his anti-Fascist film *The Great Dictator* (1940).

Wilson, Brian (Douglas). See BEACH BOYS, THE.

wind band. 1. A company of performers on wind instruments. 2. The wind instruments in the orch.; also, the players on, or parts written for, the same.

wind instruments. Instruments whose tones are produced by wind (compressed air) blown through a tube. In the Western classical orch., these are divided into the WOODWIND and BRASS families; in a score and onstage or in the pit, these instruments are grouped together, highest member of each family at the top (with the exception of the horn and saxophone, which are placed in the score between the two wind families). The organ is not usually considered a wind instrument, although it uses a hybrid wind-keyboard technology. While the modern woodwind family includes instruments made of metal and mouthpieces with zero, one, or two reeds, the brass family is more homogeneous: all are made of metal, have coiled tubing, a flared opening called a bell, and a cup or cup-like mouthpiece, and can use mutes; the only unusual feature is the trombone's having a slide rather than valves to change pitch. The loudest members of the families are the oboe and trumpet; care must be taken with balancing the winds' dynamic levels. Horns and bassoons match well with each other in chordal writing, and in pre-valve days the bassoons often stood in for the horns (Beethoven, 5th Sym., 1st movement). See also BRASS INSTRUMENTS; WOODWIND INSTRUMENTS.

wind machine (Ger. *Windmaschine*). An instrument comprising a large barrel covered with cloth, with a fixed piece of wood against which it rubs when the barrel is rotated manually with the aid of a crank. Pitch and dynamic level can be altered by the speed of rotation. Composers who have used the wind machine include R. Strauss (*Alpine Symphony; Don Quixote*), Ravel (*Daphnis et Chloé*), Milhaud (*Les Choéphores*), Schoenberg (*Die Jakobsleiter*), and Vaughan Williams (*Sinfonia antartica*).

Wings of the Dove, The. Opera by D. Moore, 1961, premiered in N.Y. The libretto, based on the Henry James novel (1902), deals with a rich young American woman dying in London of a debilitating disease. She falls in love with a young writer of dubious morality, and he is associated with a woman of even lower moral principles. At her suggestion he proposes to marry the dying woman in order to inherit her fortune. Although the intended learns about the plan, she bequeaths her fortune to him anyway; he is deeply struck by this demonstration of nobility, and becomes alienated from his scheming paramour. The opera follows the traditional division into set pieces, arias, choruses, and ensembles.

Winter Dreams. Title of Tchaikovsky's 1st Sym., 1868, in G minor, 1st performed in Moscow. The 1st two movements carry titles, *Dreams During a Winter Journey* and *Somber Land, Misty Land*; then follows a scherzo and finale.

Winternitz, Emanuel, Austrian-American musicologist and museum curator; b. Vienna, Aug. 4, 1898; d. N.Y., Aug. 22, 1983. He served in the Austrian army in World War I; after the Armistice, studied jurisprudence at the Univ. of Vienna (LL.D., 1922); then was engaged as a corporate lawyer in Vienna (1929–38). After the Anschluss in 1938, he emigrated to the U.S., where he devoted himself mainly to lecturing on art; served as Peripatetic Professor for the Carnegie Foundation. In 1942 he was appointed keeper of musical instruments at the Metropolitan Museum of Art in N.Y.; in 1949, was named curator of the Crosby Brown Collection of Musical Instruments of All Nations at the Metropolitan. He also administered the Andre Mertens Galleries for Musical Instruments (1971–73). In 1973 he became curator emeritus of the Metropolitan. Among his principal endeavors was musical iconography; he publ. a valuable reference work, *Musical Autographs from Monteverdi to Hindemith* (1955); other books were *Keyboard Instruments in the Metropolitan Museum of Art* (1961); *Die schönsten Musikinstrumente des Abendlandes* (1966); *Musical Instruments and their Symbolism in Western Art* (1967); *Leonardo da Vinci as a Musician* (1982).

Wirbel (Ger., chirping). Drumroll. *Wirbeltrommel,* tenor drum.

Wish You Were Here. Musical by H. Rome, 1952. The story concerns itself with young love in a camp in the Berkshire Mountains. The title song was a hit for a brief time.

Wittgenstein, Paul, Austrian-born American pianist; b. Vienna, Nov. 5, 1887; d. Manhasset, Long Island, N.Y., Mar. 3, 1961. His brother was the famous philosopher Ludwig Wittgenstein. Paul studied with Brée, Leschetizky, and Labor; made his debut as a pianist in Vienna (1913). Serving in World War I, he lost his right arm at the Russian front, was a prisoner of war, and was repatriated in 1916. Wittgenstein developed a superb left-hand technique, and played a work written by Labor for him. He then commissioned concertos from R. Strauss, Ravel, Prokofiev, Korngold, Britten, and others; he gave the world premieres for all except the Prokofiev, which he found unsuitable. After appearing in the major European musical centers and doing an American tour (1934), he emigrated to the U.S.

(1938), becoming a naturalized citizen (1946). He taught privately and at local colleges. John Barchilon's novel *The Crown Prince* (1984) is based on his career.

Wizard of Oz, The. Musical fantasy by Baldwin Sloane, 1903, based on the story by L. Frank Baum. The plot is superficially similar to that of the 1939 film, but the main action revolves around a magic ring given Dorothy by the witch of Oz to help her fulfill her desires. On the way she meets a brainless scarecrow and a heartless woodman; together the three go to find the wizard, succeed with the help of the ring, and get back what they lack. The musical did not long survive in the collective memory, so it was easy for the film to take its place, what with a far more dramatic plot, blockbuster production values, and excellent Arlen and Harburg songs, including the beautiful *Somewhere Over the Rainbow* as sung by Judy Garland.

Wizard of the Nile, The. Comic opera by V. Herbert, 1895. A Persian magician promises the king of Egypt to relieve the drought in the land. But then the Nile overflows and brings too much water. The magician is in trouble, but he finally escapes from Egypt. Includes *Am I a Whiz?*

Wohltemperiertes Klavier, Das. Well-Tempered Clavier, The.

wolf (tone; Ger. *Wolfton*). 1. Parasitic sound effects due to imperfect construction, produced in the course of playing an instrument in the usual manner. A particular pitch will sound much louder or softer than its neighbors, due to an irregularity of resonance that enhances or dampens the sound. String instruments are most likely to succumb to this effect; cellists offset the effect by playing slightly out of tune, squeezing the instrument between their knees, or by using a *wolf mute* behind the bridge. Other instruments susceptible to the wolf were the old bassoon, the early valve horn, and the pipe organ of any era.

2. The *wolf 5th* occurs at the point in the Pythagorean or meantone tuning systems that an apparent perfect 5th is much smaller or larger, resulting in an unpleasant dissonance written as a diminished 6th. In the days before equal temperament's acceptance, keyboard tuners would place the wolf in the most unlikely key areas for best sounding tuning all around.

Wolf, Hugo (Filipp Jakob)

Famous Austrian composer, one of the greatest masters of the lied; b. Windischgraz, Styria, Mar. 13, 1860; d. Vienna, Feb. 22, 1903. His father, Philipp Wolf (1828–87), was a gifted musician from whom Hugo received piano and violin lessons at a very early age; he later played 2nd violin in the family orch. While attending the village primary school (1865–69) he studied piano and theory with Sebastian Weixler. In 1870 he was sent to the Graz regional secondary school, but he left after a single semester and in 1871 entered the St. Paul Benedictine Abbey in Carinthia, where he played violin, organ, and piano; in 1873 he was transferred to the Marburg secondary school and remained devoted to musical pursuits; in 1875 he went to Vienna, where he became a pupil at the Cons.; studied piano with Wilhelm Schenner and harmony and composition with Robert Fuchs and later with Franz Krenn.

When Wagner visited Vienna in 1875, Wolf went to see him, bringing along some of his compositions; the fact that Wagner received him at all—and even said a few words of encouragement—gave Wolf great impetus toward further composition. But he was incapable of submitting himself to academic discipline, and soon difficulties arose between him and the Cons. authorities. He openly expressed his dissatisfaction with the teaching, which led to his expulsion for lack of discipline in 1877.

Wolf then returned to his native town, but after a few months at home decided to go to Vienna again; there he managed to support himself by giving music lessons to children in the homes of friends. By that time he was composing diligently, writing songs to texts by his favorite poets: Goethe, Lenau, and Heine. It was also about that time that the 1st signs of a syphilitic infection became manifest. An unhappy encounter with Brahms in 1879, who advised him to study counterpoint before attempting to compose, embittered him, and he became determined to follow his own musical inclinations without seeking further advice. That same year he met Melanie (née Lang) Köchert, whose husband, Heinrich Köchert, was the Vienna court jeweller. By 1884 she had become Wolf's mistress and a great inspiration in his creative work.

After serving a brief and acrimonious tenure as 2nd conductor in Salzburg in 1881, Wolf returned to Vienna in 1882, and in 1883 became music critic of the weekly *Wiener Salonblatt*. He took this opportunity to indulge his professional frustration by attacking those not sympathetic to new trends in music; he poured invective of extraordinary virulence on Brahms, thus antagonizing the influential Hanslick and other admirers of Brahms. But he also formed a coterie of staunch friends who had faith in his ability. Yet he was singularly unsuccessful in his repeated attempts to secure performances for his works. He submitted a string quartet to the celebrated Rosé Quartet, but it was rejected. Finally Hans Richter accepted for the Vienna Phil. Wolf's sym. poem *Penthesilea*, but the public performance was a fiasco, and Wolf even accused Richter of deliberately sabotaging the work; later he reorchestrated the score, eliminating certain crudities of the early version.

In 1887 Wolf resigned as music critic of the *Wiener Salonblatt* and devoted himself entirely to composition. He became convinced that he was creating the greatest masterpieces of song since Schubert and Schumann; he stated his conviction in plain terms in his letters. In historical perspective his self-appraisal has proved remarkably accurate, but psychologists may well wonder whether Wolf was not consciously trying to give himself the needed encouragement by what might have seemed to him a wild exaggeration. However, a favorable turn in his fortunes soon came.

In 1888 Rosa Papier became the 1st artist to sing one of Wolf's songs in public. Shortly thereafter Wolf himself played and sang several of his songs at a meeting of the Vienna Wagner-Verein; in late 1888 he made his public debut as accompanist in his songs to the tenor Ferdinand Jager, which proved the 1st of many highly successful recitals by both artists. Soon Wolf's name became known in Germany; he presented concerts of his own works in Berlin, Darmstadt, Mannheim, and other musical centers. He completed the 1st part of his great cycle of 22 songs, *Italienisches Liederbuch*, in 1891, and composed the 2nd part (24 songs) in 5 weeks, in the spring of 1896.

While Wolf could compose songs with a facility and degree of excellence that were truly astounding, he labored painfully on his orch.1 works. An early sym. was never completed, nor was a violin concerto; the work on *Penthesilea* took him a disproportionately long time. In 1895 he undertook the composition of his opera *Der Corregidor*, to the famous tale by Alarcón, *El sombrero de tres picos*, and, working feverishly, completed the vocal score with piano accompaniment in a few months. The orchestration took him a much longer time. *Der Corregidor* had its premiere in Mannheim (1896); while initially a success, the opera failed to find wide appeal and was soon dropped from the repertoire. Wolf subsequently revised the score, and in its new version *Der Corregidor* was brought out in Strasbourg (1898). He never completed his 2nd opera, *Manuel Venegas* (also after Alarcón); fragments were presented in concert in Mannheim in 1903, a week after his death.

In the meantime Wolf's fame grew. A Hugo Wolf–Verein was organized at Berlin in 1896, and did excellent work in furthering performances of Wolf's songs in Germany. Even more effective was the Hugo Wolf–Verein in Vienna, founded by Michel Haberlandt in 1897 (disbanded in 1906). As appreciation of Wolf's remarkable gifts as a master of lied began to find recognition abroad, tragedy struck.

By early 1897 he was a very ill man, both mentally and physically. According to Wolf, Mahler promised to use his position as director of the Vienna Court Opera to mount a production of *Der Corregidor*. When the production failed to materialize, Wolf's mental condition disintegrated. He declared to friends that Mahler had been relieved of his post and that he, Wolf, had been appointed in his stead. In the fall of 1897 he was placed in a private mental institution; after a favorable remission he was discharged (early 1898); he traveled in Italy and Austria. After his return to Vienna symptoms of mental derangement manifested themselves in even greater degree. In the fall of 1898 he attempted suicide by throwing himself into the Traunsee in Traunkirchen, but was saved and placed in the Lower Austrian provincial asylum in Vienna. (A parallel with Schumann's case forcibly suggests itself.) He remained in confinement, gradually lapsing into complete irrationality. He died at the age of 42, and was buried near the graves of Schubert and Beethoven in Vienna's Central Cemetery; a monument was unveiled in the fall of 1904. His mistress plunged to her death from the 4th-floor window of her home in Vienna (1906).

Wolf's significance in music history rests on his songs—about 300 in number—many of them publ. posth. The sobriquet "the Wagner of the lied" may well be justified in regard to involved contrapuntal texture and chromatic harmony, for Wolf accepted the Wagnerian idiom through natural affinity as well as by clear choice. The elaboration of the accompaniment, and the incorporation of the vocal line into the contrapuntal scheme of the whole, are Wagnerian traits. But with these external similarities, Wolf's dependence on Wagner's models ceases.

In his intimate penetration of the poetic spirit of the text Wolf appears a legitimate successor to Schubert and Schumann. Wolf's songs are sym. poems in miniature, artistically designed and admirably arranged for voice and piano, the combination in which he was a master. Wolf's operatic and instrumental works are largely fragmentary; a number of choral works have survived, including *Im stillen Friedhof* for Voices and Piano (1876); *Im Sommer* for Men's Voices (1876); *Geistesgruss* for Men's Voices (1876); *Mailied* for Men's Voices (1876); *Fröhliche Fahrt* for Voices (1876); *Grablied* for Voices (1876); *6 geistliche Lieder* for Voices (all 1881; rev. by E. Thomas, 1903); *Christnacht* for Solo Voices, Mixed Voices, and Orch. (1886–89; rev. by M. Reger and F. Foll, 1903).

Wolf usually grouped his lieder by poet or chronology; only 2 cycles have a programmatic concept: the *Spanisches Liederbuch*, 44 songs based on trans. of Spanish poetry by Geibel and Heyse (1889–90); and the *Italienisches Liederbuch*, 46 songs based on trans. of anonymous Italian poems by Heyse, in 2 books: 22 songs (1890–91) and 24 songs (1896). Individual collections are based on the poetry of Mörike (1889), Eichendorff (1889), Goethe (1890), Keller (1891), and others. About 90 lieder unpublished during his lifetime survive. *Hugo Wolf: Musikalische Kritiken*, R. Batka and H. Werner, eds. (Leipzig, 1911).

Wolff, Christian, French-born American composer and teacher; b. Nice, Mar. 8, 1934. He went to the U.S. in 1941 and became a naturalized citizen in 1946. He studied piano with Grete Sultan (1949–51) and composition with John

Cage (1950–51); then pursued training in classical languages at Harvard Univ. (B.A., 1955); after studying Italian literature and classics at the Univ. of Florence (1955–56) he returned to Harvard (Ph.D. in comparative literature, 1963). From 1962 to 1970 he taught classics at Harvard; in 1971 he joined the faculty of Dartmouth College to teach classics, comparative literature, and music; was made prof. of music and of classics in 1978; also was a guest lecturer at various institutions of higher learning; contributed articles on literature and music to many publications.

He evolved a curiously static method of composition, using drastically restricted numbers of pitches. His only structural resources became arithmetical progressions of rhythmic values and the expressive use of rests. He used 3 different pitches in his *Duo for Violinist and Pianist* (1961), 4 in the trio for flute, cello, and trumpet (1951), and 9 in a work called *For Piano I* (1952). Beginning in 1957 he introduced into his works various degrees of free choice, in the interest of Marxist dialectic and antiauthoritarianism; sometimes the players are required to react to the musical activities of their partners according to spontaneous and unanticipated cues.

Indeterminate works with a choice of instrumentation include *For 5 or 10 Players* for Any Instruments (1962); *For 1, 2 or 3 People* for Any Sound-Producing Means (1964); *Pairs* for any 2, 4, 6, or 8 Players (1968); *Prose Collection* for Variable Numbers of Players, Found and Constructed Materials, Instruments, and Voices (1968–71); *Changing the System* for 8 or More Instruments, Voices, and Percussion (1972–73). Chamber music: *Summer* for String Quartet (1961); *Wobbly Music* for Chorus, Keyboard, Guitars, and at least 2 melody instruments (1975–76); *Rock About, Instrumental, Starving to Death on a Government Claim* for Violin and Viola (1979–80); *Peace March* I–III for various instruments (1983–84). Piano works (solo unless indicated): *For Piano* I–II (1952, 1953); *Duo for Pianists* I–II (1957, 1958); *For Piano with Preparations* (1959); *Bread & Roses* (1976); *3 Studies* (1976); *Hay Una Mujer Desaparecida* (1979); Preludes (1981); *Piano Song, "I Am a Dangerous Woman"* (1983).

Wolf-Ferrari (born Wolf), **Ermanno,** famous Italian opera composer; b. Venice, Jan. 12, 1876; d. there, Jan. 21, 1948. His father was a well-known painter of German descent and his mother was Italian; about 1895 he added his mother's maiden name to his surname. He began piano study as a small child but also evinced a talent for art; after studying at the Accademia di Belle Arti in Rome (1891–92)

he went to Munich to continue his training but then turned to music and studied counterpoint with Rheinberger at the Akademie der Tonkunst (1892–95). In 1899 he returned to Venice, where his oratorio *La Sulamite* was successfully performed. This was followed by the production of his 1st major opera, *Cenerentola* (1900), which initially proved a failure; however, its revised version for Bremen (1902) was well received and established his reputation as a composer for the theater.

From 1903 to 1909 he was director of the Liceo Benedetto Marcello in Venice; then devoted himself mainly to composition; later was prof. of composition at the Salzburg Mozarteum (1939–45). He obtained his 1st unqualified success with the production of the comic opera *Le donne curiose* (Munich, 1903); the next opera, *I quattro rusteghi* (Munich, 1906), was also well received; there followed his little masterpiece, *Il segreto di Susanna* (Munich, 1909), a 1-act opera buffa in the style of the Italian verismo (Susanna's secret being not infidelity, as her husband suspected, but indulgence in surreptitious smoking). Turning toward grand opera, he wrote *I gioielli della Madonna*; it was brought out at Berlin in 1911 and soon became a repertoire piece everywhere; he continued to compose, but his later operas failed to match the appeal of his early creations, the most successful being *Sly, ovvero La leggenda del dormiente risvegliato* (1927) and *Il campiello* (1936).

Wolf-Ferrari also wrote popular orch.l works: Serenade for Strings (*c.* 1893); Kammersymphonie (1901); *Idillio-concertino* for Oboe, 2 Horns, and Strings (1933); *Suite-concertino* for Bassoon, 2 Horns, and Strings (Rome, 1933). Chamber: 3 violin sonatas (1895, 1901, 1943); 2 piano trios (*c.* 1897, 1900); Piano Quintet (1900); piano pieces. Vocal: *La vita nuova*, cantata (1901; Munich, 1903); other large and small choral works.

Wolpe, Stefan, significant German-American composer and pedagogue; b. Berlin, Aug. 25, 1902; d. N.Y., Apr. 4, 1972. He studied music theory with Paul Juon and Franz Schreker at the Berlin Hochschule für Musik (1919–24). After graduation he became associated with choral and theatrical groups in Berlin, promoting social causes; composed songs on revolutionary themes. With the advent of the anti-Semitic Nazi regime in 1933 he went to Vienna, where he took lessons with Anton von Webern; then traveled to Palestine in 1934; taught at the Jerusalem Cons. In 1938 he emigrated to the U.S., where he devoted himself mainly to teaching; was on the faculty of the Settlement Music School in Philadelphia (1939–42); at the Philadelphia Academy of

Music (1949–52); at Black Mountain College, N.C. (1952–56); and at Long Island Univ. (1957–68). He also taught privately.

Among his students were Elmer Bernstein, Ezra Laderman, Ralph Shapey, David Tudor, and Morton Feldman. He was married successively to Ola Okuniewska, a painter (1927), to Irma Schoenberg (1902–84), a Romanian pianist (1934), and to Hilda Morley, a poet (1948). In 1966 he was elected a member of the National Inst. of Arts and Letters. His last years were made increasingly difficult by Parkinson's disease. He contributed numerous articles to German and American music magazines.

In Wolpe's style of composition he attempted to reconcile the contradictions of triadic tonality (which he cultivated during his early period of writing proletarian music), atonality without procrustean dodecaphony, and serialism of contrasts obtained by intervallic contraction and expansion, metrical alteration, and dynamic variegation; superadded to these were explorations of Jewish cantillation and infatuation with jazz; the complex mixture is often contained within abstract, even dry titles. Remarkably enough, the very copiousness of these resources contributed to a clearly identifiable idiom.

He wrote theatrical works, the best known being the lyric scene *Anna Blume* for Musical Clown and Piano (after Schwitters; 1929) and the incidental music for 2 Brecht plays: *The Good Woman of Setzuan* (1953) and *The Exception and the Rule* (1960). Orch.: *The Man from Midian*, ballet suite (1942); Sym. (1955–56); Chamber Piece Nos. 1 and 2 for 14 players (1964; 1965–66). Wolpe was prolific as a composer of chamber music; most pieces are for between 1 and 4 instruments; larger works include the *Quintet with Voice* for Baritone, Clarinet, Horn, Cello, Harp, and Piano (1956–57); *Piece for 2 Instrumental Units* for flute, oboe, violin, cello, double bass, and percussion (1962–63); Piece for trumpet and 7 instruments (1971).

Wolpe's early piano works were quite vernacular in tone but the *4 Studies on Basic Rows* (1935–36) was his breakthrough to contemporary techniques; subsequent important works include *Toccata in 3 Parts* (1941); *Battle Piece* (1943–47); *Enactments* for

3 Pianos (1950–53); *Form* (1959); *Form IV: Broken Sequences* (1969). Wolpe's songs have a wide breadth of subjects and texts, setting Hölderlin, Fontaine, Tagore, Kokoschka, Mayakovsky, Becher, Albert Einstein, and biblical excerpts; they are unjustly neglected.

Wonder, Stevie (born Steveland Judkins Hardaway), phenomenally successful African-American soul singer, keyboardist, and songwriter; b. Saginaw, Mich., May 13, 1950. Other sources state that he was born Steveland Judkins or Steveland Morris. Blinded in infancy by insufficient oxygen in an incubator, he learned to play the drums and piano; improvised his 1st song, *Lonely Boy*, at the age of 10, and at 12 composed *Fingertips*, which became a hit. He signed with Berry Gordy, Jr. (Motown Records) in 1961. Possessed by that indefinable gift of song, he rapidly advanced in the rosters of popular success; his performances have become great attractions.

Wonder's music can be viewed stylistically. In his 1st recordings he was an apolitical hitmaker who took the Motown teenage formula to its heights; he recorded Dylan's *Blowin' in the Wind*, Tony Bennett's hit *For Once in My Life*, the Beatles' *We Can Work It Out*, and his own *Uptight*, *I Was Made to Love Her*, *My Cherie Amour*, and *Signed, Sealed, Delivered I'm Yours*; he also appeared in the films *Muscle Beach Party* and *Bikini Beach*.

At age 21 Wonder took a financial windfall and evolved a new approach based on synthesizers, complete control over his own work, and an interest in African-American experience. Beginning with the album *Music of My Mind* (1972), Wonder showed a greater maturity and musical sophistication; among the classic hits were *Superstition*, *Living for the City*, *You Are the Sunshine of My Life*, *You Haven't Done Nothing*, *Higher Ground*, *Boogie On Reggae Woman*, *Isn't She Lovely*, *I Wish*, and *Sir Duke* (an Ellington tribute).

After a nearly fatal automobile accident and the breakup of his marriage, he returned to form with songs in styles old (*I Just Called to Say I Love You* from the soundtrack *The Woman in Red*; *Part-Time Lover*) and new (*It's Wrong [Apartheid]* and the rap-influ-

Stevie Wonder, c. 1962

COURTESY FRANK DRIGGS COLLECTION

enced *Master Blaster [Jammin']*). *Happy Birthday* (1980) was part of Wonder's campaign to make Martin Luther King's birthday a national holiday. He collaborated with Paul McCartney on *Ebony and Ivory* (1982) and later with Michael Jackson on *Get It* (1987). He later wrote the soundtrack to Spike Lee's *Jungle Fever*. Wonder has devoted much time, energy, and money to social causes; added his voice to a campaign against drunk driving and donated to AIDS and cancer research; contributed to U.S. for Africa's charity record, *We Are the World* (1985).

Wonderful Town. Musical by L. Bernstein, 1953. Eileen comes to N.Y. from Ohio with her sister; they go through hilarious encounters with various men, including visiting sailors of the Brazilian navy. The nostalgic ballad *Ohio*, in which the sisters bemoan their decision to leave their home state, became a perennial favorite.

woodblocks. CHINESE BLOCKS.

Wooden Prince, The. Ballet by Bartók, 1917, 1st performed in Budapest.

woodwind. Group of instruments in the orch. orig. made of wood and played by blowing (flute, piccolo, oboe, English horn, clarinet, bass clarinet, bassoon, contrabassoon). In modern times flutes and piccolos are made of metal, but they are still included in the woodwind category. The saxophone, a hybrid metal wind instrument, has a reed and clarinet-style key system; it tends to be classified in the woodwind category. There are some special and rarely used instruments that belong to this group—the once popular recorder, the alto and bass flutes, the heckelphone (a baritone oboe). *Woodwind quintet*, a somewhat inaccurate name for an ensemble consisting of four woodwind instruments (flute, oboe, clarinet, bassoon) and the modern valve (French) horn, a brass instrument.

Woody Woodpecker. Song by Idriss, 1947, the theme song of a cartoon character created by Walter Lantz; Woody's rapid fanfare figure captures his zany character perfectly.

Work, Henry Clay, American composer of popular songs; b. Middletown, Conn., Oct. 1, 1832; d. Hartford, June 8, 1884. He was a printer by trade; was entirely self-taught in music; his 1st success was *We Are Coming, Sister Mary* (1853); other well-known songs were *Kingdom Coming* (1862), *Come Home, Father* (1864), *Wake,*

Nicodemus! (1864), *Marching through Georgia* (1865), and *Grandfather's Clock* (1876).

working out (Ger. *Durchführung*). Development section in SONATA FORM.

Worms Crawl In, The. Anonymous morbid vermicular ditty, publ. 1923, known to virtually everyone in the English-speaking world. The tune, in minor mode and jig time, is also called *The Hearse Song*. The idea that it originated with World War I British and American soldiers who, watching the coffins of their dead comrades being rolled out, speculated on what the worms were doing to their bodies, is psychologically absurd. The chances are that the song was the product of a drunk's ghoulish imagination after a long pub crawl.

Wouldn't It Be Loverly? Song by Lerner and Loewe, 1956, from the musical *My Fair Lady*. Sung by Eliza Doolittle before her Pygmalionesque transformation, the quasi-Cockneyisms in the song were taken up by the public and became temporary parts of the vernacular.

Wozzeck. Opera by Berg, 1925, 1st performed in Berlin. The libretto is extracted from *Woyzeck*, an unfinished play by Büchner, 1836. Wozzeck is a private in the German army, bedeviled by his cruel superiors. A drum major openly brags of his success in seducing Wozzeck's common-law wife, Marie. Provoked beyond endurance Wozzeck stabs Marie to death; he goes insane and, trying to wash the blood from his hands, walks into the pond and drowns. The opera concludes with a poignant scene when their child rocks on his wooden horse, uncomprehending of the tragedy. The opera is a milestone in the history of modern musical theater. It is a tour de force of formal organization; the entire score is programmed as a series of Baroque dance forms and variations. The idiom is tensely atonal.

Although *Wozzeck* is now acknowledged as a modern masterpiece, at its 1st performances German music critics described it as a cacophonous monstrosity. Curiously enough another composer, Manfred Gurlitt (1890–1972), chose the same subject independently from Berg for an opera; his *Wozzeck* was produced in Bremen, 1926, 4 months after Berg's masterpiece, but could not withstand the comparison and soon faded from the musical scene.

Wreck of the Old 97, The. Song by various authors, 1924, based on the melody of H. C. Work's *The Ship That Never*

Returned (1865). It became a famous railroad ballad, commemorating a tragic train wreck.

Wreckers, The. Opera by Smyth, 1896, premiered in Leipzig, 1906, in German as *Strandrecht.* A group of land pirates on the Cornish coast lives off the wrecks of ships. Being legally entitled to flotsam and jetsam, they contrive wrecks by giving wrong signals to ships in stormy weather. A woman villager, horrified by this, builds fires on the shores to guide imperiled ships. The pirates then chain her and her lover in a cave near the shore and they are drowned by the invading tide. The music is aggressively Wagnerian.

wuchtig (Ger.). Weighty, powerfully, ponderously; with strong emphasis.

Wunderbar. Song by C. Porter, 1948, from the musical *Kiss Me, Kate.* The song parodies the typical Viennese waltz, with plenty of extra schmaltz.

wunderkind. No art, no science is revealed at an age so early as that of musical talent. When an anxious and hopeful mother (less frequently father) notices that her darling child bangs on the keyboard of an upright piano (rarely a baby grand in such families), she perceives the breath of musical genius. The 1st symptom of *Wunderkindheit* is the possession of perfect pitch, the ability to name any note struck on the piano without a moment's hesitation; but the possession of this precious gift does not guarantee a successful musical career.

Most wunderkinder are taught piano or violin; there are few wunderkinder of the cello, and hardly any of a wind instrument. Wunderkinder are often exhibited by their parents as wonders of nature. They are kept chronologically young by cutting down their ages as they outgrow short pants. Mozart's father advertised his genius son as being 8 years old during several successive years. One of the most durable child prodigies was the violinist Jascha Heifetz. He made a sensational American debut at the age of 16 in Carnegie Hall, N.Y. The American Soc. for the Prevention of Cruelty to Children intervened against the exploitation of Josef Hofmann, who played a Beethoven piano concerto in N.Y. at the age of 11. He was forced to stop public appearances until the age of 16, but this hiatus did not prevent him from becoming one of the greatest master pianists of all time.

Child conductors are a great rarity, but at least 1 of them made a meteoric career early in the century: Willy Ferrero, an American-born Italian boy who toured Europe as a sym. conductor at the age of 8, arousing wonderment among audiences in France, Italy, and Russia. He ended his inglorious career as a provincial opera conductor. Another wunderkind conductor was Lorin Maazel, who led sym. concerts at the age of 9, eliciting invidious comparisons with a trained seal; he has since become one of the world's leading conductors.

Child composers are even more of a rarity than performing wunderkinder. Mozart was the greatest among them. Mendelssohn achieved a fantastic mastery of musical composition at a very early age. Schubert wrote inspired songs at the age of 17. But neither Beethoven nor Brahms were precocious composers; nor were Wagner, Tchaikovsky, or Stravinsky. Erich Wolfgang Korngold evinced comparisons with Mozart when he wrote a piano trio at the age of 12. He was introduced to Mahler, who exclaimed, "Ein Genie! Ein Genie!" He wrote operas at the age of 18. But his star set precipitously in the musical firmament as he grew older.

The number of talented wunderkinder who never made it big is large. Ineffable sadness surrounds the parade of red-cheeked little boys in velvet pants and little girls in white dresses whose pictures used to adorn the advertising pages of European and American music magazines of the fin de siècle. Whatever happened to them? Not even the most dogged efforts of musicological bloodhounds could trace most of them to their final retreats in some unknown home for the retired.

Wunderlich, Fritz (Friedrich Karl Otto), noted German tenor; b. Kusel, Sept. 26 1930; d. Heidelberg, Sept. 17, 1966. He received his musical education at the Freiburg Hochschule für Musik; then sang opera in Stuttgart (1955–58), Frankfurt (1958–60), and Munich (from 1960); in 1965 he appeared as Don Ottavio at London's Covent Garden. While still a young man he gained a fine reputation as a lyric tenor; his performances of Mozart roles were especially acclaimed for their expressive power. His untimely death (in a mysterious accident) deprived the opera stage of one of its finest and most promising artists.

Wuorinen, Charles, American composer and pianist; b. N.Y., June 9, 1938. His family roots originated in Finland; his father was a prof. of history at Columbia Univ.; the environment at home was highly intellectual. Wuorinen received a fine academic training; he began to play piano and to compose, so they say, at the incredible age of 5. He then took lessons in music theory with Beeson and Ussachevsky. He received the Young Composers Award from the N.Y. Phil. when he was 16 years old. At 18 he wrote his earliest orch.l work, *Into the Organ Pipes and Steeples*. In 1956 he entered Columbia Univ. as a student of Otto Luening; he composed, in quick succession, 3 full-fledged syms. (1958, 1958, 1959); received his B.A. in 1961 and his M.A. in 1963.

He cofounded the Group for Contemporary Music with Harvey Sollberger (1962). In 1964 he was appointed an instructor in music at Columbia; he taught there until 1971, when he resigned in a flurry of angry controversy, vesuviating in sulfuric wrath and ire about the refusal of the faculty to grant him tenure. He then taught at the Manhattan School of Music (1972–79). In 1968 and 1972 he held Guggenheim fellowships. In 1969 he received a commission from Nonesuch Records for a work using synthesized sound, titled *Time's Encomium*; it was awarded the Pulitzer Prize in music in 1970, an unprecedented honor for a work written expressly for a recording; later he rearranged it for a regular orch. In 1985 he was made a member of the American Academy and Inst. of Arts and Letters. From 1985 to 1987 he served as composer-in-residence of the San Francisco Sym.

From his very 1st essays in free composition, Wuorinen asserted himself as a true representative of the modernistic 2nd half of the 20th century. His techniques derived from Stravinsky's early period, when stark primitivism gave way to austere linear counterpoint; an even greater affinity in Wuorinen's music is with the agglutinative formations of unrelated thematic statements as practiced by Varèse; a more literal dependence connects Wuorinen's works with the dodecaphonic method of composition as promulgated by Schoenberg. These modalities and relationships coalesce in Wuorinen's writing into a sui generis complex subdivided into melodic, harmonic, and contrapuntal units that build a definitive formal structure.

The foundation of his method of composition is SERIALISM, in which pitch, time, and rhythmic divisions relate to one another in a "time point system" that lends itself to unlimited tonal and temporal arrangements, combinations, and permutations. Enormously prolific, Wuorinen finds it possible to explore the entire vocabulary of serial composition. Most of his works are instrumental, but he also wrote an opera entitled *The W. of Babylon, or The Triumph of Love* (alluding to the apocalyptic whore; 1975), a work he describes as a "baroque burlesque." Its dramatis personae includes a libidinous assortment of lascivious French noble and ignoble men and women of the immoral 17th century, spouting lewd declarations and performing lecherous acts.

As a helpful glossary to his music Wuorinen publ. a manual, paradoxically entitled *Simple Composition* (N.Y., 1979). Wuorinen has written 1 other opera, *The Politics of Harmony* (1967). His many orch.l works include 3 piano concertos; chamber works, including 3 string quartets (1971; 1979; 1987); solo instrumental works; vocal works; and electronic works.

würdevoll (Ger.). With dignity; loftily.

würdig (Ger.). In an imposing manner.

Wut (Ger.). Fury. *Mit Wüt, wüt(h)end*, furiously, frantically.

Wuthering Heights. Novel by Emily Brontë, 1848, basis for eponymous operas by 2 American composers: Bernard Herrmann, 1941–50, recorded 1966, premiered in Portland, Oreg., 1982; and Carlisle Floyd, premiered in Santa Fe, 1958.

Wynette, Tammy (real name, Wynette Pugh), American country-music singer; b. Red Bay, Ala., May 5, 1942. She taught herself to play the piano and guitar; after holding various jobs, including a position as a beauty operator, she decided to seek fame and fortune in Nashville, Tenn., as a singer of country music; in 1969 she joined the Grand Ole Opry. She struck a responsive chord with such songs as *Your Good Girl's Gonna Go Bad, Bedtime Story, Let's Get Together, D-I-V-O-R-C-E*, and her biggest hit, *Stand By Your Man*. She was married to the country-music star George Jones (1969–75).

Wyschnegradsky, Ivan (Alexandrovich), Russian composer, master of MICROTONAL MUSIC; b. St. Petersburg, May 16, 1893; d. Paris, Sept. 29, 1979. He studied composition with Nikolai Sokoloff at the St. Petersburg Cons.; in 1920 he settled in Paris. He devoted virtually his entire musical career to the exploration and creative realization of music in quarter tones and other microtonal intervals; had a quarter-tone piano constructed for him; also publ. a guide, *Manuel d'harmonie à quarts de ton* (Paris, 1932). In 1945 he presented in Paris a concert of his music, at which he conducted the 1st performance of his *Cosmos* for 4 Pianos, with each pair tuned at quarter tones.

Bruce Mather took interest in Wyschnegradsky's music and gave a concert of his works at McGill Univ. in Montreal that included 3 world premieres (1977). But with the exception of these rare concerts, Wyschnegradsky remains a figure of legend; few performances of his music are ever given in Europe or North America. He regarded his *La Journée de l'existence* for narrator, *ad libitum* chorus, and orch. (to his own text; 1916–17) as his germinal work, opening the path to microtonal harmony; he dated this "awakening to ultra-chromaticism" as having occurred in 1918. At his death he left sketches for a short opera in 5 scenes, *L'Éternel Étranger*, begun in 1939 but never completed; also unfinished was the ambitious *Polyphonie spatiale*.

Wyschnegradsky wrote quarter-tone works for piano(s), string ensembles (including quartet), voice and piano, chorus, ondes Martenot, and orch.; works for 3rd-, 6th-, 8th-, 12th-, and 31st (Fokker) tones, as well as works for standard equal temperament. *Ainsi parlait Zarathoustra* for Orch. (1929–30; arr. for 4 pianos, 1936) is considered his masterpiece. He also publ. several articles on ultrachromaticism and related topics.

Xenakis, Iannis

Eminent French composer and music theorist of Greek background whose training in engineering and architecture led him to derive a stochastic method of composition from scientific principles; b. Brăila, Rumania (of Greek parents), May 29, 1922. At the age of 10 he was taken by his family to Greece, where he began to study engineering, but he became involved in the Greek resistance movement against the Nazi occupation forces; he was severely wounded in a skirmish in 1945, and lost sight in 1 eye. Shortly thereafter he was captured, but he managed to escape to the U.S. In 1947 he went to Paris and later became a naturalized French citizen; studied architecture with Le Corbusier and became his assistant (1948–60); during the same period he took lessons in composition with Honegger and Milhaud at the École Normale de Musique in Paris and with Messiaen at the Paris Cons. (1950–53).

He aided Le Corbusier in the design of the Philips Pavilion at the 1958 World's Fair in Brussels; met Varèse, who was then working on his *Poème électronique* for the exhibit; he assisted Varèse and in return received stimulating advice on the creative potential of the electronic medium. During his entire career Xenakis strove to connect mathematical concepts with the organization of a musical

composition, using the theory of sets, symbolic logic, and probabilistic calculus; he promulgated the stochastic method, which is teleologically directed and deterministic, as distinct from a purely aleatory handling of data. He publ. a comprehensive vol. dealing with these procedures, *Musiques formelles* (Paris, 1963). He was founder and director of the Centre d'Études Mathématiques et Automatiques Musicales in Paris in 1966, and founder and director of the Center for Mathematical and Automated Music at Indiana Univ. in the U.S., where he served on the faculty from 1967 to 1972.

His influence on the development of advanced composition in Europe and America is considerable; several composers adopted his theories and imitated the scientific-sounding titles of some of his compositions. Xenakis uses Greek words for the titles of virtually all of his works to stress the philosophical derivation of modern science and modern arts from classical Greek concepts; in some cases he uses computer symbols for titles.

Among his most representative works are *Metastasis* for 61 Instruments, a harbinger of Penderecki's cluster pieces (1953–54); *Pithoprakta* for 50 Instruments (1955–56); *Syrmos* for 18 Strings (1959); *Duel*, musical game for 2 "antagonistic" Conductors and 2 Orchs. playing different material, mathematically based on game theory, with the audience determining the winning orch. (1959); *Orient-Occident* for Tape (1960); *Herma* for Piano (1960–61); *ST/48-1,240162* (1956–62; ST = stochastic; 48 = number of players; 1 = 1st work for this contingent; 240162 = 24 January 1962, date on which the work was finally calculated by the IBM 7090 computer in Paris as programmed probabilistically by Xenakis); *ST/10-1,080262* (1956–62; a string quartet version is entitled *ST/4*); *Morsima-Amorsima* (Fated-Not Fated) for Violin, Cello, Double Bass, and Piano (1956–62); *Atrées* for 10 Players (1956–62; written in homage to Blaise Pascal and calculated by the IBM 7090, with license); *Strategie*, musical game for 2 Conductors and 2 Orchs. (1959–62; Venice Festival, 1963; Bruno Maderna's orch. won over that of Konstantin Simonovic); *Bohor* I and II for Tape (1962, 1975); *Polla ta dhina* (Many Are the Wonders) for children's choir and small orch., to a text from Sophocles's *Antigone* (1962); *Eonta* (Ionian neuter plural of the present participle of the verb *to be*; the title is in Cypriot syllabic characters of Creto-Mycenean origin) for Piano, 2 Trumpets, and 3 Tenor Trombones (1963–64); *Akrata* (Pure) for 16 Wind Instruments (1964–65); *Terretektorh* for 88 Players scattered among the audience (1966); *Oresteïa*, incidental music for Aeschylus's tragedy, for Chorus and Chamber Orch. (1965–66); *Nomos Alpha* (Law Alpha) for Cello (1966); *Nuits* for 12 Mixed Voices

a cappella (1967); *Medea*, stage music for Male Chorus and Instrumental Ensemble (1967); *Kraanerg*, ballet music for Tape and Orch. (Ottawa, 1969); *Synaphai* for 1 or 2 Pianos and Orch. (1969); *Hibiki-Hana-Ma*, 12-channel electroacoustic music distributed kinematically over 800 loudspeakers, for the Osaka EXPO '70 (1969–70; also a 4-channel version); *Persepolis*, light-and-sound spectacle with 8- or 4-channel electroacoustic music (1971); *Mikka* for Violin (1972); *Evryali* for Piano (1973); *Gmeeoorh* for Organ (1974); *Psappha* for Percussion (1975); *N'shima* for 2 Horns, 2 Trombones, Cello, and 2 Mezzo-sopranos (1975); *Kphlegra hoai* for Chamber Orch. (1976); *Retours—Windungen* for 12 Cellists (1976); *Mikka "S"* for Violin (1976); *Akanthos* for Voice and Ensemble (1977); *Diatope* for 4- or 8-track Tapes (1977); *Pleïades* for Percussion (1979); *Aïs* for Baritone, Percussion, and Orch. (1979); *Palimpsest* for Ensemble (1979); *Chant des soleils* for Chorus, Children's Chorus, Winds, and Percussion (1983); *Tetras* for String Quartet (1983); *Thalleïn* for 14 Instrumentalists (1984); *Idmen A* for Chorus and 4 Percussionists (1985); *Keqrops* for Piano and Orch. (N.Y., 1986); *À l'ile de Gorée* for Harpsichord and Ensemble (1986); *Akea* for Piano Quintet (1987); *Jalons* for Orch. (1986); *AR (Homage to Ravel)* for Piano (1987); *Tracées* for Orch. (1988); *Plektó* for Chamber Ensemble (1993).

Xerxes. Serse.

Xochipilli. "Imagined Aztec music" by Chávez, 1940, for Wind Quartet and Mexican Percussion; he conducted the 1st performance in N.Y.

xylophone (from Grk., wood sound; Ger. *Xylophon*; It. *xilofono*). A keyboard percussion instrument with hardwood keys arranged and tuned like a piano; each key has a resonator tuned to it. The keys are fastened horizontally to 2 stretched boards and played with 2 or more sticks or mallets. Predecessors of the modern xylophone

Bamana tribe members, Mali, Africa with xylophone

PHOTOGRAPH BY ELIOT ELISOFON, COURTESY OF THE NATIONAL MUSEUM OF AFRICAN ART, ELIOT ELISOFON ARCHIVES, THE SMITHSONIAN INSTITUTION

are found in many parts of the world, consisting of a few wooden bars of different length producing different tones. They were usually laid out on straw, and therefore became known among explorers as *Strohfiedel* (straw fiddle).

The early xylophone reached its developmental height in Southeast Asia in the 14th century; the instrument had spread westward into Africa, then to the Americas; it arrived in Europe by the 16th century. Gradually assuming its modern form, the European-American xylophone was imported into Latin America and Africa and became domesticated there as kinds of pianos with wooden keys.

Saint-Saëns used the xylophone to great effect in his *Danse macabre* to suggest the bone rattling of disembodied ghosts. In the 20th century the instrument's use of straw finally gave way to a notch system to support the keys. Many composers of the 20th century included the xylophone in their sym. scores, including the *Sabre Dance* from *Gayané* by Khachaturian.

xylorimba (xylo-marimba). A hybrid keyboard instrument, developed in the early 20th century, with a 5-octave range encompassing that of the xylophone and marimba. Xylorimbas were used in popular music and vaudeville between the world wars (as the marimba-xylophone). It has been used by Berg, Stravinsky, Dallapiccola, Messiaen, Schat, and Gerhard.

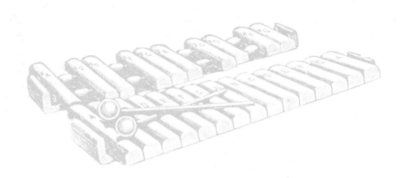

Yy

Yankee Doodle. American patriotic song of mysterious origin. A reference to the title is found in a libretto to an American ballad opera produced in 1767; the earliest printing of the tune itself was in 1794. During the American Revolution the song was already popular. For a long time the British believed that the tune was sung to mock the ragged American revolutionists, but Americans themselves played it as an expression of a certain swaggering confidence in their cause. Since the meaning of the word *doodle* in this context cannot be deciphered, the puzzle of the song's origin is fated to remain unsolved.

Yaravi. HARAWI.

Yasser, Joseph, Polish-born Russian-American organist, conductor, and musicologist; b. Lodz, Apr. 16, 1893; d. N.Y., Sept. 6, 1981. He studied at the Moscow Cons., graduating in 1917 as an organist; after several years of teaching organ in Moscow and Siberia he reached Shanghai in 1921 and conducted a choral society there; subsequently emigrated to the U.S. (1923); served as organist at Temple Rodeph Sholom in N.Y. (1929–60); held various positions in American musicological groups. His most important contribution to music theory was *A Theory of Evolving Tonality* (N.Y., 1932), in which he proffered an ingenious hypothesis as to the origin of the pentatonic and heptatonic scales and, operating by inductive reasoning, suggested that the next Western scale would contain 19 equally tempered degrees. He contributed several articles to *Musical Quarterly* (1937–38) dealing with QUARTAL HARMONY, which were publ. in a separate ed. (N.Y., 1938).

Yeoman of the Guard, The, or The Merryman and His Maid. Operetta by Gilbert and Sullivan, 1888, 1st performed in London. The merryman is a jester who expects to marry the beloved of a man sentenced to death. But the prisoner is unexpectedly reprieved, and the jester's plans are thwarted.

Yes, Sir, That's My Baby. Song by Walter Donaldson, 1925; it became a hit when Eddie Cantor sang it. The tune is something of a tour de force, for the 1st 16 syllables consist of only 2 different notes.

Yes, We Have No Bananas. American nonsense song by Silver and Cohn, 1923. The composers claimed that their inspiration came from a Greek fruit peddler who nodded his head to signify that yes, he did not have any bananas left. But Greeks nod their heads to signify the negative, and shake their heads for the affirmative, so the merchant had perfect ethnic logic on his side. Humorless musicologists point out that the 1st 4 notes are identical with the opening of the *Hallelujah Chorus* from Handel's *Messiah. Na und?*

Yeston, Maury. See NINE.

Yip! Yip! Yaphank! Revue by I. Berlin, 1918. Berlin himself took part in the show, which depicted the life of American doughboys (soldiers) in World War I. He made a sensation with his loud lament *Oh! How I Hate to Get Up in the Morning.* Berlin originally planned to include a 1st version of *God Bless America*, but it was cut from the show for reasons unknown and not revived until the 1930s.

yodel (Ger. *Jodel*). A type of rural singing in the European Alps, especially in Switzerland, characterized by the frequent alternation of falsetto tones with chest tones; a kind of expanded warble. The earliest yodel call is found in a collection entitled *Bicinia Gallica, Latina, Germanica*, publ. 1545. A similar technique is used by various groups in Africa. Yodeling is related to the *field holler* of the American South; it eventually found its way into country music through the singing of Jimmie Rodgers.

You Ain't Heard Nothin' Yet. Song by Al Jolson and others that he interpolated in his extravaganza *Sinbad*, 1918. The title was Jolson's catchphrase when addressing his audiences.

You Made Me Love You, I Didn't Want to Do It. Song by Jimmy Monaco, 1913, introduced by Al Jolson in *The Honeymoon Express*, the vaudeville show in which Jolson 1st assumed the character of a blackface comedian. The song became a Tin Pan Alley classic and was featured in several movies.

You Must Have Been a Beautiful Baby. Song by Warren and Mercer, 1938, included in the film *Hard to Get*. A great success, it was incorporated in several movie musicals.

Youmans, Vincent (Millie), American composer of popular music, including the perennial favorite of songs, *Tea for 2*; b. N.Y., Sept. 27, 1898; d. Denver, Apr. 5, 1946. He took piano lessons as a child but was apprenticed by his father to enter the business world; he served as a messenger in a Wall Street bank, then enlisted in the U.S. Navy; also played the piano in a Navy band; wrote a song, *Hallelujah*, which was picked up by John Philip Sousa, who performed it with his own bands; later it was incorporated by Youmans in his musical *Hit the Deck* (1927). After World War I Youmans earned a living as a song plugger for publishers in N.Y. He produced 2 musical comedies, *2 Little Girls in Blue* (1921) and *The Wildflower* (1923); both were moderately successful, but he achieved fame with his next production, *No, No, Nanette*; it opened in Detroit in the spring of 1924; then staged in Chicago; after a 49-week run there it moved to London, where it was produced in early 1925; it finally reached Broadway in the fall of 1925, where it proved to be one of the most beguiling and enduring American musicals; its hit song, *Tea for 2*, became

a perennial favorite all over the world (Shostakovich arranged it in 1927 for a salon orch. under the title *Tahiti Trot*).

There followed several other successful musicals: *A Night Out* (1925), *Oh, Please!* (1926), *Rainbow* (1928), *Great Day* (1929), and *Through the Years* (1932). In 1933 Youmans went to Hollywood to complete his score for the film *Flying Down to Rio*. Because of an increasingly aggravated tubercular condition, he retired to Denver in the hope of recuperation in its then-unpolluted environment; he remained there until his death. Among his songs the following were also hits: *Bambalina*; *I Want to Be Happy*; *Hallelujah*; *Sometimes I'm Happy*; *Great Day*; *Without a Song*; *Time on My Hands*; *Through the Years*; *Oh, Me, Oh, My, Oh, You*; *Carioca*; *Orchids in the Moonlight*; *Drums in My Heart*; *More Than You Know*; *Rise 'n' Shine*.

Young, La Monte (Thornton), influential American composer of the extreme avant-garde and early proponent of musical minimalism; b. Bern, Idaho, Oct. 14, 1935. He studied clarinet and saxophone with William Green in Los Angeles (1951–54); also attended Los Angeles City College (1953–56) and studied counterpoint and composition privately with Leonard Stein (1955–56); was a pupil of Robert Stevenson at the Univ. of Calif. at Los Angeles (B.A., 1958); pursued further training with Seymour Shifrin and Andrew Imbrie at the Univ. of Calif. at Berkeley (1958–60) and attended the summer courses in new music in Darmstadt; subsequently studied ELECTRONIC MUSIC with Richard Maxfield at the New School for Social Research in N.Y. (1960–61).

In 1963 he married the artist and illustrator Marian Zazeela, with whom he subsequently gave audiovisual performances in a series of Sound/Light Environments in Europe and America. In 1970 he visited India to study Eastern philosophy and train himself physically, mentally, and vocally for cosmic awareness, gradually arriving at the realization that any human, subhuman, or inhuman activity constitutes art; in his *Composition 1990* he starts a fire on the stage while releasing captive butterflies in the hall. In his attempt to overcome terrestrial limitations, he has decreed for himself a circadian period of 26 hours. He achieves timelessness by declaring, "This piece of music may play without stopping for thousands of years." Several of his

COURTESY FRANK DRIGGS COLLECTION

Vincent Youmans

works consist solely of imperious commands: "Push the piano to the wall; push it through the wall; keep pushing."

He ed. *An Anthology of Chance Operations, Concept Art, Anti-Art, etc.* (N.Y., 1963), which, with his own *Compositions 1960*, had primary influence on concept art and the FLUXUS movement; his own contribution to it was a line drawn in India ink on a 3 x 5 filing card. He has contributed extensively to the study of just intonation and to the development of tuning systems based on the set of rational numbers that make up the components of his periodic composite sound waveform environments; one goal was to create acoustic "clouds" of overtones. He received a Guggenheim fellowship and a grant from the N.E.A.

Among his ascertainable works are *Poem for Tables, Chairs, and Benches* (moving furniture about; Univ. of Calif., Berkeley, 1960); *The Well-Tuned Piano* (1964–81); *The Tortoise Droning Selected Pitches from the Holy Numbers of the 2 Black Tigers, the Green Tiger, and the Hermit* (N.Y., 1964); *The Tortoise Recalling the Drone of the Holy Numbers as They Were Revealed in the Dreams of the Whirlwind and the Obsidian Gong, Illuminated by the Sawmill, the Green Sawtooth Ocelot, and the High-Tension Line Stepdown Transformer* (N.Y., 1964); *Map of 49's Dream of 2 Systems of 11 Sets of Galactic Intervals Ornamental Lightyears Tracery* for Voices, Various Instruments, and Sine Wave Drones (Pasadena, Calif., 1968); *The Subsequent Dreams of China* (1980); *The 2nd Dream of the High-Tension Line Stepdown Transformer* for Trumpet Ensemble (1985).

He has created several pieces of conceptual music and tape recordings of his own monophonous vocalizing achieved by both inspiration and expiration, so that the vocal line is maintained indefinitely; also various physical exercises with or without audible sounds. His *Selected Writings* were publ. in Munich (1969).

Young, Lester (Willis), called Pres or Prez, remarkable African-American jazz tenor saxophonist; b. Woodville, Miss., Aug. 27, 1909; d. N.Y., Mar. 15, 1959. He studied trumpet, alto sax, violin, and drums with his father; then played in his family's band; turning to the tenor saxophone at 19, he began performing with various groups in the Midwest; was a member of Count Basie's band (1934; 1936–40; 1943–44). While serving in the U.S. Army, he was court-martialed for using drugs; upon his release in 1945 he resumed his career, which was plagued by his abuse of alcohol. All the same, he continued to perform until shortly before his death.

He made recordings with various jazz notables, including Billie Holiday, who dubbed him "Pres" (a contraction of "President") for his outstanding abilities. One of the great jazz saxophonists, he influenced numerous successors through his beautiful long melodic lines, fine phrasing, and inventive solos, among them *Lady Be Good, Shoe Shine Boy, Lester Leaps In, After Theatre Jump, These Foolish Things, All of Me* (with Holiday), *Pres Returns*, and *Easy Does It*.

Young, Neil, Canadian-born folk-rock singer, instrumentalist, and composer; b. Toronto, Nov. 12, 1945. After surviving childhood illnesses, he learned to play the banjo and guitar in his youth; moving to Los Angeles in 1966, he joined with Stephen Stills to form the Buffalo Springfield, which produced Young's hits *Nowadays Clancy Can't Even Sing, Broken Arrow, Mr. Soul,* and *I Am a Child.* He left in 1967 to begin a solo career, which he continued while performing and recording with (David) Crosby, Stills, and (Graham) Nash and scoring hits with their albums *Déjà Vu* (1970) and *4-Way Street* (1971). Young made the solo albums *Everybody Knows This Is Nowhere* (1969), *After the Goldrush* (with the backup group Crazy Horse; 1970), *Harvest* (his best-selling album; 1972), *Tonight's the Night* (1975), *Zuma* (1975), *Comes A Time* (1978), *Rust Never Sleeps* (1979), *Re-ac-tor* (1981), *Old Ways* (1985), and *Freedom* (1989). In his songs he creates an effective conglomeration of folk, country music, and hard rock; among his best are *The Loner, Cinnamon Girl, Down By The River, Southern Man, Only Love Can Break Your Heart, Ohio, Like a Hurricane, Heart of Gold, Country Girl, Helpless, Cortez the Killer, Hey Hey My My,* and *Vampire Blues.*

Young Person's Guide to the Orchestra, The. Orch. variations and fugue by Britten, 1945, premiered in Liverpool, 1946. The variation theme is taken from a piece of incidental music of Purcell; in its original form Britten's piece is part of an educational film entitled *Instruments of the Orchestra.* With an unpretentious narrative as support, Britten cleverly brought out orch. families and individual instruments one after another, so that the eponymous young person can really learn how orch.l instruments sound. The Purcell variations and fugue are often recorded and performed independently of the text.

Young, Victor, American pianist and composer; b. Bristol, Tenn., Apr. 9, 1889; d. Ossining, N.Y., Sept. 2, 1968. He studied piano with Isidor Philipp in Paris; toured in England and the U.S. as accompanist to prominent singers; held various teaching positions; was music director in Thomas A. Edison's Experimental Laboratory in West

Orange, N.J., conducting tonal tests and making piano recordings under Edison's personal supervision (1919–27). He wrote the musical score for one of the earliest sound motion pictures, *In Old California*; composed some 300 film scores altogether, including *Wells Fargo* (1937), *Gulliver's Travels* (1939), *For Whom the Bell Tolls* (1943), *Night Has a Thousand Eyes* (1948), *Rio Grande* (1950), *The Quiet Man* (1952), *Shane* (1953), and *Around The World in 80 Days* (1956; a posth. Oscar winner). He also wrote orch. works, piano music, and many popular songs.

Your Own Thing. Rock musical by various authors, 1968. The plot and song titles are loosely derived from Shakespeare's *12th Night*. Like *Hair* and other shows of its ilk, it was a tremendous success despite its unnerving of some sensitive or squeamish theatergoers. It was also the 1st in a string of musicals based on this particular play, most recently in RAP style.

You're A Good Man, Charlie Brown. Musical by Clark Gesner, 1967. The play is based on Charles Schultz's famous comic strip *Peanuts*, which combines simplicity with something like sophistication. Charlie Brown engages in all kinds of childhood adventures in the company of Snoopy (beagle and World War I flying ace), Linus (blanket-bearing genius), Lucy (bête noire and book reviewer), Patty (mystery woman), and Schroeder (Beethoven-worshipping toy pianist). Includes the title song, *Faithful Friends Always Near Me, Queen Lucy, My Blanket and Me,* and *Book Report.*

You're Driving Me Crazy. Song by Walter Donaldson, 1930; it was extremely popular.

You're the Cream in My Coffee. Song by Ray Henderson, 1928, from the musical *Hold Everything*. An all-time hit, it inspired a parody, "You're the fly in my coffee/you're the nail in my shoe."

Youth Symphony. Prokofiev's 7th Sym., 1951–52, his last, which he wrote to glorify the spirit of Soviet youth. Ostentatiously melodious and insistently harmonious, it provided a balm on Prokofiev's soul after the denunciation of his music hurled on him by the Soviet music functionaries in 1948. The 1st performance of the *Youth Sym.* took place in Moscow, 1952; a few months later Prokofiev was dead.

Yo-Yo Ma. MA, Yo-Yo.

Ysaÿe, Eugène (-Auguste), famous Belgian violinist, conductor, and composer; b. Liège, July 16, 1858; d. Brussels, May 12, 1931. At the age of 4 he began to study violin with his father, a theater conductor; at the age of 7 he was enrolled at the Liège Cons. as a pupil of Désiré Heynberg, winning 2nd prize in 1867; in 1869 he left the Cons. in a dispute with his mentor, but was readmitted in 1872 as a pupil of Rodolphe Massart, winning 1st prize in 1873 and the silver medal in 1874; then continued his training on a scholarship at the Brussels Cons. with Wieniawski; later completed his studies with Vieuxtemps in Paris (1876–79).

In 1879 he became concertmaster of Bilse's orch. in Berlin; appeared as a soloist at Pauline Lucca's concerts in Cologne and Aachen; in Germany he met Anton Rubinstein, who took him to Russia, where he spent 2 winters; he also toured in Norway. In 1883 he settled in Paris, where he met César Franck, Vincent d'Indy, et al., and gave successful concerts; he formed a duo with the pianist Raoul Pugno, and started a long series of concerts with him, establishing a new standard of excellence. In 1886 he married Louise Bourdeau; Franck dedicated his violin sonata to them as a wedding present; Ysaÿe's interpretation of this work made it famous. In 1886 he was named a prof. at the Brussels Cons. (resigned in 1898); in 1886 he also organized the Ysaÿe Quartet (with Crickboom, Léon Van Hout, and Joseph Jacob); Debussy dedicated his string quartet to Ysaÿe's group, which gave it its 1st performance at the Soc. Nationale in Paris on Dec. 29, 1893.

In 1889 Ysaÿe made successful appearances in England; in 1894 he made his American debut, playing the Beethoven Violin Concerto with the N.Y. Phil. and creating a sensation by his virtuosity. He revisited America many times, with undiminished acclaim. He began his career as a conductor in 1894 and established in Brussels his own orch., the Soc. des Concerts Ysaÿe. When the Germans invaded Belgium in 1914 he fled to London, where he remained during World War I. In 1918 he made his American debut as a conductor with the Cincinnati Sym. Orch., and also led the Cincinnati May Festival in that year. His success was so great that he was offered a permanent position as conductor of the Cincinnati Sym. Orch., which he held from 1918 to 1922. He then returned to Belgium and resumed leadership of the Soc. des Concerts Ysaÿe. After the death of his 1st wife he married an American pupil, Jeannette Dincin (1927).

Ysaÿe's style of playing is best described as heroic; but his art was equally convincing in the expression of moods of exquisite delicacy and tenderness; his frequent employment of "tempo rubato" produced an effect of elasticity without distorting the melodic line. He was known for an unorthodox bow grip, which excluded the little finger. His works include 8 violin concertos; 6 sonatas for solo violin (1924); other solo violin pieces; 9 sym. poems and concertolike works for violin and orch.; *Poème nocturne* for Violin, Cello, and Strings; *Les Harmonies du soir* for String Quartet and String Orch.; *Méditation* for Cello and String Orch. (*c.* 1900); *Trio de concert* for 2 Violins, Viola, and Orch.; *Amitié* for 2 Violins and Orch; a solo cello sonata; a duo-violin sonata; and other chamber music.

At the age of 70 Ysaÿe began the composition of an opera in the Walloon dialect, *Piér li Houïeu* (Peter the Miner), which was produced in Liège (1931); the composer, who was brought to the theater in an invalid's chair, was suffering from the extreme ravages of diabetes, which had necessitated the amputation of his left foot. He began the composition of a 2nd Walloon opera, *L'Avierge di Piér* (The Virgin of Stone), but had no time to complete it. In 1937 Queen Elisabeth of Belgium inaugurated the annual Prix International Eugene Ysaÿe in Brussels; the 1st winner was the Russian violinist David Oistrakh. Ysaÿe's younger brother, Théophile Ysaÿe (b. Verviers, Mar. 22, 1865; d. Nice, Mar. 24, 1918) was a pianist and composer; he participated in the Soc. des Concerts Ysaÿe as a rehearsal conductor.

Yun, Isang, important Korean-born German composer; b. Tongyong, Sept. 17, 1917; d. Berlin, Nov. 3, 1995. He studied Western music in Korea (1935–37) and in Japan (1941–43). During World War II he was active in the anti-Japanese underground; in 1943 he was imprisoned, and then spent the rest of the war in hiding until the liberation in 1945. He became a music teacher in Tongyong in 1946, and later taught in Pusan; in 1953 he became a prof. of composition at the Univ. of Seoul; then studied with Revel at the Paris Cons. (1956–57) and with Blacher, Rufer, and Schwarz-Schilling at the Berlin Hochschule für Musik (1958–59); also attended the summer courses in NEW MUSIC in Darmstadt. He settled permanently in Berlin; after a serialist phase he began producing music marked by a fine expressionistic and coloristic quality and written in an idiom of euphonious dissonance: *Bara* (orch., 1960); *Loyang* (chamber ensemble, 1962); *Om mani padme hum* (oratorio, 1964); *Réak* (orch., 1966); also his 1st opera, *Der Traum des Liu-Tung* (1965), and several chamber works.

Yun's career was dramatically interrupted when he and his wife were brutally abducted from West Berlin by secret police agents of South Korea (1967), forced to board a plane for Seoul, and brought to trial there for sedition; after a show trial he was sentenced to life imprisonment; his wife was given 3 years in jail. This act of lawlessness perpetrated on the territory of another country prompted an indignant protest by the government of West Germany, which threatened to cut off its substantial economic aid to South Korea; 23 celebrated musicians, including Igor Stravinsky, issued a vigorous letter of protest. As a result of this moral and material pressure, South Korea released Yun and his wife after nearly 2 years of detention, and they returned to Germany. In 1970 he was appointed lecturer in composition at the Berlin Hochschule für Musik, being made a prof. there in 1974; retired in 1985. In 1971 he became a naturalized German citizen.

In the years after his release from South Korean prisons, Yun composed 3 new operas, including *Die Witwe des Schmetterlings* (The Butterfly Widow), completed in his Seoul prison cell and produced *in absentia* in Bonn (1967). He also composed in certain genres for the 1st time, such as the 5 related syms. (1983; 1984; 1985; *Im Dunkeln singen*, 1986; with baritone, 1987) and concertos with full or string orch.: cello (1976); flute (1977); oboe and harp (1977); clarinet (1981); violin (1981; 1983–86; 1992); harp, *Gong-Hu* (1984); oboe/English horn and cello, *Duetto concertante* (1987); oboe/oboe d'amore (1990). Yun also composed other orch. and vocal works; chamber music, including 2 chamber concertos, 4 mixed quartets, 2 clarinet quintets (1984; 1994); 6 string quartets, 2 of which are withdrawn (1959–61; 1988; 1990; 1992); 3 mixed trios. His solo instrumental works are for recorder, flute(s), oboe, bass clarinet, bassoon, violin, cello, harp, piano, harpsichord and organ (the influential graphically notated *Tuyaux sonores*, 1967).

yurupari. A very long wooden trumpet used by the Amazon Indians in Brazil, which they considered taboo to women and strangers. Oscar Wilde mentions them in his novel *The Picture of Dorian Gray*, speaking of exotic and dangerous hobbies of his hero in whose collection there are "mysterious yuruparis of the Rio Negro Indians, that women are not allowed to look at." The reason for this proscription is not explicitly known.

Zz

Z mrtveho domu. From the House of the Dead.

Zabaleta, Nicanor, eminent Spanish harpist; b. San Sebastian, Jan. 7, 1907; d. San Juan, Puerto Rico, Mar. 31, 1993. He began his training in San Sebastian; after further studies in Madrid he went to Paris to study harp with Marcel Tournier and composition with Eugene Cools; then toured extensively in Europe, South America, and the U.S. He is noted for his efforts to increase the number of works available for the harp, both by bringing to light neglected compositions of early composers and by prompting modern composers to write harp music, including concertos by Ginastera, Milhaud, Piston, Villa-Lobos, Thomson, and Tal.

Zaïde. An unfinished opera by Mozart, 1779, to a libretto resembling that of *The Abduction from the Seraglio,* in which a heroic youth rescues his chosen bride from the Sultan's harem. It was not performed until 1866, in Frankfurt, in an arrangement made by various hands.

Zaira. Lyric tragedy by Bellini, 1829, based on Voltaire's tragedy, premiered in Parma. Orismane, sultan of Jerusalem, hopes to marry Zaira, a captive Christian woman now converted to Islam; this plan horrifies Muslims at court. In the prisons below the palace are captured Christian crusaders, including Zaira's father, unknown to her. A group of crusaders come to rescue the prisoners; among them is Zaira's brother, Nerestano, unknown to her. Eventually the 3 relations recognize each other, but the father dies. Nerestano gives Zaira the opportunity to escape; she is torn between freedom and her love for Orismane, who in ignorance has become suspicious of the relationship between the siblings. When he comes upon them in conversation he is convinced that they are lovers; he kills Zaira with his scimitar. When he is informed of his poor judgment, he turns the scimitar on himself.

zamacueca (*zambacueca;* Sp.). The national dance of Chile, also called *cueca,* a couple dance in rapid alternating 3/4 and 6/8.

zamba (Sp.). Popular Argentinian dance in 6/8 time, derived from the ZAMACUECA.

Zampa, ou La Fiancée de Marbre. Opéra-comique by Hérold, 1831. Camilla is to be married to a fine young man whose missing brother, Count de Monza, has disappeared after seducing and abandoning a young woman, Alice, who subsequently killed herself; her memory is honored by a marble statue in the hall where the nuptials are about to take place. But a pirate, Zampa, appears on the scene and announces his plans to abduct Camilla for his own. Seeing the statue, he mocks the memory of Alice, thus revealing his true identity as the missing Count; he adds insult to injury by placing a wedding ring on the statue's hand. In the meantime he receives an offer from the Viceroy that, if he leads a regatta into battle, Zampa would be pardoned for his crimes. Having accepted, he prepares to marry Camilla; when he goes toward the statue to retrieve the ring, the statue put her hands upon his shoulder. During the excitement, Camilla escapes from the hall; the statue then proceeds to crush Zampa to death. At this point Mount Etna erupts for a spectacular ending. The overture is very popular.

zampogna (*zampoña*). Italian traditional BAGPIPE.

zampoñas (Sp.). Chilean PANPIPES.

Zandonai, Riccardo, Italian composer; b. Sacco di Rovereto, Trentino, May 30, 1883; d. Pesaro, June 5, 1944. He was a pupil of Gianferrari at Rovereto (1893–98); then studied with Mascagni at the Liceo Rossini in Pesaro. He graduated in 1902; for his final examination he composed a sym. poem for solo voices, chorus, and orch., *Il ritorno di Odisseo*. He then turned to opera, which remained his favored genre throughout his career. His 1st opera was *La coppa del re* (*c.* 1906), which was never performed. After writing the children's opera *L'uccelino d'oro* (Sacco di Rovereto, 1907) he won notable success with his 3rd opera, *Il grillo del focolare*, after Dickens's *The Cricket on the Hearth* (Turin, 1908). With his next opera, *Conchita*, after the novel *La Femme et le pantin* by Pierre Louÿs (Milan, 1911), he established himself as an important Italian composer; the title role was created by the soprano Tarquinia Tarquini, whom Zandonai married in 1917.

Conchita received its American premiere in San Francisco in 1912; as *La Femme et le pantin* it was given at the Opéra-Comique in Paris (1929). Zandonai's reputation was enhanced by subsequent works, notably *Francesca da Rimini*, after Gabriele d'Annunzio (Turin, 1914; Metropolitan Opera, N.Y., 1916), but a previous opera, *Melenis* (Milan, 1912), was unsuccessful. During World War I Zandonai participated in the political agitation for the return of former Italian provinces; he wrote a student hymn calling for the return of Trieste (1915).

zapateado (*zabateado*; Sp.). Latin American dance in triple meter, characterized by heel stamping to emphasize the strong syncopation.

Zappa, Frank (Vincent)

Outspoken American rock artist whose compositions in both popular and serious forms—the latter influenced by the works of Varèse—teem with artfully dissonant counterpoint; b. Baltimore, Dec. 21, 1940, of Italian descent (Zappa means "hoe" in Italian); d. Los Angeles, Dec. 4, 1993. The family moved to Calif. From his school days he played guitar and organized groups with weird names such as the Omens and Captain Glasspack and His Magic Mufflers. In 1960 he composed the soundtrack for the film *The World's Greatest Sinner*, and in 1963 he wrote another soundtrack, *Run Home Slow*.

In 1965 he joined the rhythm-and-blues band the Soul Giants; he soon took it under his own aegis and thought up for it the name the Mothers of Invention. His recording of it, and another album, *Freak Out!*, became underground hits; along with *Absolutely Free* (with *Brown Shoes Don't Make It*), *We're Only In It for the Money*, and *Lumpy Gravy*, these works constituted the earliest concept albums, touching every nerve in a gradually decivilized Calif. lifestyle—rebellious, anarchistic, incomprehensible, and yet tantalizing. The band became a mixed-media celebration of total artistic, political, and social opposition to the Establishment.

In 1969 Zappa replaced the original Mothers with new musicians, a process he would undertake every few years; eventually he stopped using the Mothers name altogether. Moving farther afield, Zappa produced a film and score for *200 Motels*, glorifying itinerant sex activities (with Flo and Eddie, Ringo Starr, Theo Bikel, Keith Moon). He became a cult figure, and as such suffered the penalty of violent adulation. Playing in London in 1971, he was nearly killed when a besotted fan pushed him off the stage into an empty orch. pit. Similar assaults forced Zappa to hire an athletic bodyguard for protection. In 1982 his planned appearance in Palermo, Sicily, the birthplace of his parents, had to be canceled because the mob rioted in anticipation of the event.

Zappa deliberately confronted the most cherished social and emotional sentiments by putting on such songs as *Broken Hearts Are for Assholes*, and his *Jewish Princess* made the mistake of offending the sensitivity of American Jews. His production *Joe's Garage* contained Zappa's favorite scatological materials, and he went on analyzing and ridiculing urinary functions in such numbers as *Why Does It Hurt When I Pee?* (Ironically and tragically, Zappa died from prostate cancer that went undetected for a decade.) He managed to upset the members of his people's faith in the number titled *Catholic Girls*. Other less sharply directed satires included *Dancin' Fool* and *I Have Been In You*. In 1980 he produced the film *Baby Snakes*, which shocked even the most impervious senses.

Zappa's lyrical disdain and angry attitudes tend to disguise the remarkable development in his music. Having turned rock into a social and versatile medium, he moved into the greater complexities of jazz, with an interest in separating performance from recording. His *Hot Rats*, a jazz-rock release, gave the new fusion music a significant boost. Zappa recorded every performance he ever played, and over the years he released them, sometimes in large boxed sets (*Shut Up'n Play Yer Guitar*, 1981; *You Can't Do That On Stage Anymore*; *Beat the Boots*, 2 sets).

But Zappa astounded the musical community when he proclaimed his total adoration of the music of Edgard Varèse, gave a lecture on Varèse, and supported concerts of his music in N.Y. Somehow, without formal study, he managed to absorb the essence of Varèse's difficult music. This process led Zappa to produce truly astonishing full orch. scores reveling in artful dissonant counterpoint, *Bob in Dacron and Sad Jane* and *Mo' 'n' Herb's Vacation*, and the cataclysmic *Penis Dimension* for Chorus, Soloists, and Orch., with a text so anatomically precise that it could not be performed for any English-speaking audience.

An accounting of Zappa's scatological and sexological proclivities stands in remarkable contrast to his unimpeachable private life and total abstention from alcohol and narcotic drugs. An unexpected reflection of Zappa's own popularity was the emergence of his adolescent daughter, born Moon Unit, as a rapper on his hit *Valley Girls*, in which she used the vocabulary of growing womanhood of the San Fernando Valley near Los Angeles ("Val-Speak"). His son, Dweezil, is also a musician; his 1st album, *Havin' a Bad Day*, was modestly successful. In 1985 Zappa became an outspoken opponent of the activities of the PMRC (Parents Music Resource Center), an organization comprised largely of wives of U.S. Senators (and a future Vice President) who accused the recording industry of exposing the youth of America to "sex, vio-

Frank Zappa, mid–1970s

lence, and the glorification of drugs and alcohol." Their demands to the RIAA (Recording Industry Association of America) included the labeling of record albums to indicate lyric content.

Zappa voiced his opinions in no uncertain terms, 1st in an open letter published in *Cashbox*, and then in one to President Reagan; finally, in 1985, he appeared at the 1st of a series of highly publicized hearings involving the Senate Commerce, Technology, and Transportation Committee, the PMRC, and the RIAA, where he delivered a statement to Congress which began, "The PMRC proposal is an ill-conceived piece of nonsense which fails to deliver any real benefits to children, infringes the civil liberties of people who are not children and promises to keep the courts busy for years, dealing with the interpretational and enforcemental problems inherent in the proposal's design." Audio excerpts from these hearings can be heard, in original and Synclavier-manipulated forms, on his album *Zappa Meets the Mothers of Prevention*.

Later recordings which make extensive use of the Synclavier include *Francesco Zappa* (arrangements of works by the 18th-century Italian composer and cellist)and *Jazz From Hell*. Upon learning of his fatal illness, Zappa went through his entire recorded output, digitalized and remixed it, and sold it outright to the Rykodisc label. The last release before his death was *The Yellow Shark*.

Zar und Zimmermann. Opera by Lortzing, 1837, to his own libretto, premiered in Leipzig, 1837. The historical Peter the Great of Russia went to Holland as an apprentice to learn such Western trades as shipbuilding. The fictional plot has foreign diplomats gathering at the workshop, hoping to make profitable trade deals with him, but they mistake a mere carpenter for the czar. The music is unpretentiously melodious.

Zarlino, Gioseffo (Gioseffe), important Italian music theorist and composer; b. Chioggia, probably Jan. 31, 1517; d. Venice, Feb. 4, 1590. He received his academic training from the Franciscans; his teacher in music was Francesco Maria Delfico. In 1532 he received the 1st tonsure, in 1537 took minor orders, and in 1539 was made a deacon. He was active as a singer (1536) and organist (1539–40) at Chioggia Cathedral. After his ordination he was elected *capellano* and *mansionario* of the Scuola di S. Francesco in Chioggia in 1540. In 1541 he went to Venice to continue his musical training with Willaert; in 1565 he succeeded his fellow pupil Cipriano de Rore as maestro di cappella at San Marco, holding this position until his death; also was chaplain of S. Severo (from 1565) and a canon of the Chioggia Cathedral chapter (from 1583). His students included G. M. Artusi, Girolamo Diruta, Vincenzo Galilei, and Claudio Merulo.

Zarlino's historical significance rests upon his theoretical works, particularly his *Le istitutioni harmoniche* (1558), in which he treats the major and minor 3rds as inversions within a 5th, and consequently, the major and minor triads as mutual mirror reflections of component intervals, thus anticipating the modern dualism of Rameau, Tartini, Hauptmann, and Riemann; he also gives lucid and practical demonstrations of double counterpoint and canon, illustrated by numerous musical examples; while adhering to the system of 12 modes he places the Ionian rather than the Dorian mode at the head of the list, thus pointing toward the emergence of the major scale as the preponderant mode; he gives 10 rules for proper syllabification of the text in musical settings. His *Dimostrationi harmoniche* (1571) was publ. in the form of 5 dialogues between Willaert and his disciples and friends.

Zarlino's theories were attacked, with a violence uncommon even for the polemical spirit of the age, by Vincenzo Galilei, his former pupil, in *Dialogo della musica antica e della moderna* (Florence, 1581) and *Discorso intorno alle opere di Gioseffo Zarlino* (Florence, 1589). In reply to the 1st of Galilei's books, Zarlino publ. *Sopplimenti musicali* (1588). In the latter he suggests equal temperament for the tuning of the lute. As a composer Zarlino was an accomplished craftsman; he wrote both sacred and secular works.

zart (Ger.). Tender, soft, delicate, *dolce*; slender. *Mit zarten Stimmen*, with soft-toned stops.

Zartflöte (Ger.). A 4' flute organ stop of very delicate tone.

zärtlich (Ger.). Tenderly, caressingly.

zarzuela (from Sp. *zarza*, bramble bush). Spanish light opera characterized by dance and spoken dialogue. The name is derived from the Royal Palace La Zarzuela, near Madrid, where zarzuelas were performed before the royal court. The genre appeared in the 17th century. Performances of zarzuelas at the court were interspersed with ballets and popular dances fashioned after the spectacles at Versailles. With the massive intrusion of Italian opera into Spain in the 18th century, the zarzuela lost its characteristic ethnic flavor; but it was revived by nationally minded composers of the 2nd half of the 19th century, particularly Barbieri, Chapí, Bretón, Caballero, Valverde, and Chueca. In the early 20th century composers such as Giménez, Vives, Guridi, Usandizaga, Moreno Torroba, and Toldrá continued composing in a now dying genre. Classical composers such as Granados and de Falla contributed zarzuelas. The modern type of zarzuela, known as *genero chico*, embodied elements of the Viennese operetta, and still later annexed American jazz rhythms. Zarzuelas taking up an entire evening were called *zarzuela grande*; a *zarzuelita* is a small zarzuela. See also TONADILLA.

Zauberflöte, Die. MAGIC FLUTE, THE.

Zaubergeige, Die (The Magic Violin). Opera by Egk, 1935, 1st performed in Frankfurt. The libretto deals with a peasant who receives a magic violin from an earth spirit which has the power to fulfill any wish except love. When he meets the young woman of his heart he surrenders the violin in exchange for her love.

Zauberharfe, Die (The Magic Harp). Opera by Schubert, 1820, the only one performed during his lifetime, in Vienna.

Zauberoper (Ger.). A magic opera, in which supernatural forces intervene in human affairs. A typical example is Weber's *Der Freischütz*.

Zaza. Opera by Leoncavallo, 1900, 1st produced in Milan. A Paris café songstress who becomes embroiled in an affair with a married man. Abandoned by him, she finds happiness with her vaudeville partner. Although less successful than the composer's *Pagliacci*, the opera enjoys occasional performances.

zeffiroso (It.). Zephyr-like.

Zeit (Ger.). Time.

Zeitmass (Ger.). Tempo. *Im Zeitmasse*, in the original tempo.

Zeitmasse. Chamber instrumental work by Stockhausen, 1956, 1st performed in Munich. This serial piece experiments with constant metric and tempo modulations.

Zeitoper (Ger., opera of the times). German operas of the 1920s and early 1930s with distinct sociopolitical themes, driven by a generalized tendency of artists toward the creation of socially relevant art.

Zeitschrift (Ger.). Newspaper, periodical, magazine, publication, journal, etc.

zeloso (It.). Zealously, enthusiastically; with energy and fire.

Zelter, Carl Friedrich, eminent German composer and teacher; b. Berlin, Dec. 11, 1758; d. there, May 15, 1832. The son of a mason, he was brought up in the same trade, but his musical inclinations soon asserted themselves; he began training in piano and violin at 17; from 1779 he was a part-time violinist in the Doebbelin Theater orch. in Berlin; was a pupil of C. F. C. Fasch (1784–86). In 1786 he brought out a funeral cantata on the death of Frederick the Great; in 1791 he joined the Singverein (later Singakademie) conducted by Fasch, often acting as his deputy and succeeding him in 1800. He was elected associate of the Royal Academy of the Arts in Berlin in 1806; became a prof. in 1809. In 1807 he organized a Ripienschule for orch. practice; in 1809 he founded the Berlin Liedertafel, a pioneer men's choral society that became famous; similar organizations were subsequently formed throughout Germany, and later in America.

Zelter composed about 100 men's choruses for the Liedertafel. In 1822 he founded the Royal Inst. for Church Music in Berlin, of which he was director until his death (the Inst. was later reorganized as the Akademie für Kirchen- und Schulmusik). His students included Mendelssohn, Meyerbeer, Loewe, and Nicolai. Goethe greatly admired Zelter's musical settings of his poems, preferring them to Schubert's and Beethoven's; this predilection led to their friendship, which was reflected in a voluminous correspondence, *Briefwechsel zwischen Goethe und Zelter* (6 vols., Berlin, 1833–34). His songs are historically important, since they form a link between old ballad types and the new art of the lied, which found its flowering in Schubert and Schumann.

Zelter's settings of Goethe's *König von Thule* and of *Es ist ein Schuss gefallen* became extremely popular. He publ. a biography of Fasch (Berlin, 1801). He also composed a viola concerto (1779), keyboard pieces, and choral works.

Zémire et Azor. A pastorale by Grétry, 1771, 1st performed in Fontainebleau. In a plot reminiscent of *The Beauty and the Beast*, Azor is a royal prince transformed into a monstrous creature as punishment for his brutal behavior; he can only be restored to human shape by love. Zémire is the daughter of a merchant who has trespassed on the prince's lands and must sacrifice his life. Zémire voluntarily takes his place; the prince falls in love with her and risks letting her escape. Despite her family's pleas she returns to him; this breaks the spell, and Azor and Zémire live happily ever after as a lovely (human) couple.

Zemlinsky, Alexander (von), important Austrian composer and conductor of partly Jewish parentage (he removed the nobiliary particle "von" in 1918 when such distinctions were outlawed in Austria); b. Vienna, Oct. 14, 1871; d. Larchmont, N.Y., Mar. 15, 1942. At the Vienna Cons. he studied piano with Door (1887–90) and composition with Krenn, Robert Fuchs, and J. N. Fuchs (1890–92). In 1893 he joined the Vienna Tonkünstlerverein; in 1895 he became connected with the orch. society Polyhymnia and met Schoenberg, whom he advised on the technical aspects of chamber music; Schoenberg always had the highest regard for Zemlinsky as a composer and lamented the lack of appreciation for Zemlinsky's music. There was also a personal bond between them; in 1901 Schoenberg married Zemlinsky's sister Mathilde.

Zemlinsky's 1st opera, *Sarema*, to a libretto by his own father, was produced in Munich (1897); Schoenberg made a piano-vocal score of it. Zemlinsky also entered into contact with Mahler, music director of the Vienna Court Opera, who accepted Zemlinsky's opera *Es war einmal* for performance; Mahler conducted its premiere at the Court Opera (1900) and it became Zemlinsky's most popular production. From 1900 to 1906 Zemlinsky served as conductor of the Karlstheater in Vienna; in 1903 he conducted at the Theater an der Wien; in 1904 he was named chief conductor of the Volksoper; in 1910 he orchestrated and conducted the ballet *Der Schneemann* by the greatly talented 11-year-old wunderkind Erich Korngold. About that time he and Schoenberg organized in Vienna the Union of Creative Musicians, which performed his tone poem *Die Seejungfrau* (1903). In 1911 Zemlinsky moved to Prague, where he became conductor at the German Opera, and also taught conducting and composition at the German Academy of Music (from 1920). In 1927 he moved to Berlin, where he obtained the appointment of assistant conductor at the Kroll Opera, with Otto Klemperer as chief conductor and music director. When the Nazis came to power in Germany in 1933, he returned to Vienna, and also filled engagements as guest conductor in Russia and elsewhere. After the Anschluss of 1938 he emigrated to America, which effectively ended his career.

As a composer Zemlinsky followed the post-Romantic trends of Mahler and R. Strauss. He was greatly admired but his works were seldom performed, despite the efforts of Schoenberg and his associates to revive his music. How strongly he influenced his younger contemporaries is illustrated by the fact that Alban Berg quoted Zemlinsky's *Lyric Sym.* in his own *Lyric Suite.* In the latter 20th century a great number of Zemlinsky's works, both operatic and nonoperatic, have received revivals, bringing attention to a composer whose fine music was forgotten through the vicissitudes of music history. Among Zemlinsky's most popular works are 8 completed operas, 3 syms. (1892; 1897; *c.* 1903); *Lyrische Sym.* in 7 sections, after Rabindranath Tagore, for Soprano, Baritone, and Orch. (his best-known work; 1922–23; Prague, 1924); Sinfonietta (1934). He also wrote chamber works, including 4 string quartets (1895; 1913–15; 1924; 1936); and vocal works, including 3 psalms for chorus and orch.: No. 83 (1900); No. 23 (1910); No. 13 (1935); *Maeterlinck Lieder,* 6 songs for Medium Voice and Orch. (1910–13); *Sym. Gesänge* for voice and orch. (1929); 4 vols. of lieder to texts by Heyse and Liliencron (1894–97); also songs to words by Dehmel, Jacobsen, Bierbaum, Morgenstern, Ammann, Heine, and Hofmannsthal (1898–1913; 1929–36).

Zen. The philosophy of Zen is at once an infinitely complex and fantastically simple doctrine that accepts irrelevance of response as a legitimate and even elevating part of human discourse. This paradoxical liberating trait exercises a compelling attraction for composers of the avant-garde, eager to achieve a total freedom of self-expression combined with the precision of indeterminacy. The verbal and psychological techniques of Zen can be translated into music through a variety of means which may range from white noise of (theoretically) infinite duration to (theoretically) instantaneous silences. In the field of mixed media in particular Zen provides a rich vocabulary of gestures, facial expressions, inarticulate verbalization, ambulatory exercises, performance of physiological functions etc. In the composi-

tion of instrumental music Zen expands perception of the minutest quantities of sonic material and imparts eloquence to moments of total impassivity, in which the audible tones become interlopers between areas of inaudibility. Imagination and fantasy in the mind of a practitioner of Zen may subjectively become more expressive than the realization of the creative impulse in written musical symbols.

Zero Symphony. Unnumbered sym. by Bruckner, 1863–64, in D Minor; 1st complete performance in Klosterneuberg, 1924. This is the 2nd surviving early sym. of Bruckner; the 1st, 1863, in F minor, is nicknamed the *School Sym.* Bruckner actually named the D-minor work *Die Nullte* in retrospect; this is also trans. as the Sym. No. 0. Its music is in a pleasing Romantic vein, but the score lacks Brucknerian philosophical introspection.

zheng (cheng). A Chinese half-tube zither, dating from the 3rd century B.C. The zheng was a popular solo instrument of the people, while the QIN was reserved for scholars and officials in meditation. The number of strings was variable, with 14 as an average; modern instruments may have up to 24 or more; the strings are divided by movable bridges. The zheng is tuned pentatonically; in addition to harmonics, ornaments are performed by applying pressure to the non-playing side of the bridges (like the Japanese KOTO and Korean *kayago*).

Ziegfeld Follies. Series of spicy revues by Florenz Ziegfeld (b. Chicago, Mar. 15, 1867; d. N.Y., July 22, 1932), inaugurated in 1907, always decorated with a panoply of beautiful young women (he advertised his shows as "glorifying the American girl"). The Follies became cynosure of the American musical theater; the shows were produced annually until 1925; 3 more shows were produced during Ziegfeld's lifetime; 4 more revues of the Ziegfeld Follies were produced posth., the last in 1957. Songs and sketches were by various hands with topical subjects. Musically the most successful editions were the ones by Irving Berlin, who contributed one of his most enduring tunes, *A Pretty Girl is Like a Melody*, to the 1919 edition; he wrote the entire score and lyrics for the 1927 revue. Other famous participants included Nora Bayes (*Shine On Harvest Moon*), Bert Williams (*Nobody*), Fanny Brice (*I'm an Indian*), and Eddie Cantor. Ziegfeld was also an independent producer, with credits including *Show Boat, Rosalie, Whoopee,* and *Bitter Sweet.*

Ziehharmonika (Ger., pull harmonica). Accordion.

ziemlich (Ger.). Somewhat, rather. *Ziemlich bewegt und frei in Vortrag*, quite animated and free in delivery (style); *ziemlich langsam*, rather slowly.

zierlich (Ger.). Neatly, delicately; gracefully.

Zigeunerbaron, Der. GYPSY BARON, THE.

Zigeunermusik (Ger.). GYPSY MUSIC.

zimbalo(n). CIMBALOM.

Zimerman, Krystian, outstanding Polish pianist; b. Zabrze, Dec. 5, 1956. He commenced piano lessons at age 5 with his father; when he was 7 he became a pupil of Andrzej Jasinki, with whom he later studied at the Katowice Cons. In 1975 he won 1st prize in the Chopin Competition in Warsaw; then played with great success in Munich, Paris, London, and Vienna. In 1976 he was a soloist with the Berlin Phil. He made his 1st American appearance in 1978, and subsequently toured throughout the world to great critical acclaim. His performances of the Romantic repertory are remarkable for their discerning spontaneity.

Zimmermann, Bernd (Bernhard) **Alois,** important German composer; b. Bliesheim, near Cologne, Mar. 20, 1918; d. (suicide) Königsdorf, Aug. 10, 1970. He studied at the Cologne Hochschule für Musik and at the Univs. of Cologne and Bonn until he was drafted for military service during World War II; after his discharge he became a pupil of Lemacher and Jarnach (1942); later attended the summer courses in new music of Fortner and Leibowitz in Darmstadt (1948–50). He taught theory at the Univ. of Cologne (1950–52) and at the Cologne Hochschule für Musik (1957–70). Plagued by failing eyesight and obsessed with notions of death, he reflected these moods in his own music of the final period. His *Requiem für einen jungen Dichter*, a "lingual" for Narrator, Soprano, and Baritone Soloists, 3 Choruses, Tape, Orch., Jazz Combo, and Organ (1967–69) sets texts drawn from poems, articles, and news reports concerning poets who committed suicide; he killed himself less than a year after the premiere of this morbid score.

Zimmermann's idiom of composition is mainly expressionistic, with a melodic line of anguished chromaticism that does not preclude the observance of strict formal structures in his instrumental works; in a sense he realized the paths opened by Berg. The opera *Die Soldaten*, based on a play by J. M. R. Lenz (1958–60; rev. 1963–64; Cologne, 1965), took the atmosphere of *Wozzeck* several steps further; the explicit presentation of the molestation of innocent civilians by the military brought on a critical and societal storm of protest. Yet for all his manic depressive character, he held onto his senses of irony and humor, as evidenced by *Nobody Knows de Trouble I See*, a trumpet concerto (Hamburg, 1955) and *Musique pour les soupers du Roi Ubu*, "ballet noir" after Jarry (1966; Düsseldorf, 1968).

Zimmermann maintained strong religious beliefs; 5 days before his death he completed *Ich wandte mich und sah an alles Unrecht das geschah unter der Sonne*, "ecclesiastical action" after Ecclesiastes and Dostoyevsky, for 2 narrators, bass, and orch. (1970; Kiel, 1972), a moving final expression of hope. While in his lifetime he was primarily known to limited music circles in Germany, the significance of his music began to be realized after his death.

zingara, alla (*zingarese, alla*; *zingaresca*; It.). In Gypsy style.

Zingara, La. Opera by Donizetti, 1822, 1st performed in Naples. The eponymous young Gypsy woman defies traditional Neapolitan suspicion of Gypsies as thieves and villains by helping to reunite 2 separated lovers, foiling a dastardly duacide, etc. But, being so wonderful, could she really be a Gypsy? Alas, no—she is revealed as a missing daughter of an unjustly dungeoned nobleman; so much for breaking Romany stereotypes.

Zink (Ger.). CORNETT.

Zip Coon. Song from a blackface minstrel show, 1834, produced in N.Y.; the author is unknown. As its racist title suggests, the text portrays a Broadway dandy decked out in fine clothes and a silk hat. The melody used is the Anglo-Irish *Turkey in the Straw*, rather than any quasi-African-American tune.

Zirkelkanon (Ger., circle canon). PERPETUAL CANON.

Zither (Ger.). 1. An organological category for a simple chordophone, without resonator, or at most a nonintegral, detachable one. Most are plucked (PSALTERY type); some are idiophonic (struck with sticks or beaters; DULCIMER type) or heterophonic (plucked and struck). 2. A folk instrument popular in Bavaria and Austria, capable of considerable harmonic sonority. It is a shallow wooden resonating box with

32 or more strings stretched over it. It has a fretted finger-board on the side nearest the player, supporting 5 melody strings, plucked with the fingers and a metal plectrum worn on the right thumb; these are stopped with the fingers of the left hand to determine the pitch. In Finland the popular form of zither is called KANTELE.

zitternd (Ger.). Trembling, tremulous.

zögernd (Ger.). Hesitatingly.

Zopf (Ger., pigtail). An irreverent description of the type of music composed by wig-wearing Baroque musicians. The Zopf is familiar from the portraits of Bach, Handel, Haydn, and their contemporaries; Mozart even wore a Zopf as a child. The Zopf era came to a sudden end at the threshold of the 19th century. Beethoven's portraits show him with tousled hair, but he never wore a wig.

zoppa, alla (It., lame, limping). In a limpingly syncopated manner; in Hungarian 2/4 dances, a strong accent on the 2nd beat; *contrapunto alla zoppa*, an obs. Ger. expression for syncopated counterpoint.

Zorba. Musical by Kander and Ebb, 1968, based on Kazantzakis's novel *Zorba the Greek*. The action takes place around a sidewalk café in Athens and follows the fortunes and misfortunes of Zorba in his country. The songs imitate Greek traditional music, especially the sound of the *bouzouki*, a plucked chordophone; among the best songs are Zorba's ballads *The First Time* and *I Am Free*.

Zorn, John, innovative American composer and instrumentalist; b. N.Y., Sept. 2, 1953. He plays saxophone, keyboards, duck calls, and other semi-demi-musical instruments in dense, loud aural canvases that have been compared to the works of Jackson Pollock (and also to an elephant trapped in barbed wire). After a brief college stint in St. Louis and world travels, he became an active contributor to the downtown music scene in N.Y.; performed with a coterie of well-reputed avant-garde and rock musicians, including guitarists Bill Frisell and Fred Frith, bassist Bill Laswell, pianists Anthony Coleman and Wayne Horvitz, drummers Bobby Previte and David Moss, vocalist Shelly Hirsch, and the Kronos Quartet.

He has created separate entities for different facets of his music: *Naked City* (from late 1980s) and *Masada* (from 1994). His *The Big Gundown* (1987) uses the music of film compos-er Ennio Morricone (b. 1928) as material to be freely distorted and reworked. His major recordings include *Archery* (1981), *Cobra* (group improvisation, 2 vols.: 1986; 1994), *A Classic Guide to Strategy* (solo with overdubbing, 1987), *News for Lulu*, with Frisell and George Lewis, trombone (2 vols.: 1987; 1989), and *Spillane* (1988), *Spy vs. Spy*, playing the music of Ornette Coleman (1989), *The Book of Heads*, performed by guitarist Marc Ribot (1995), and *Kristallnacht* (1995).

zornig (Ger.). Wrathfully (R. Strauss, *Ein Heldenleben*, referring to his feelings toward his critics).

zortziko. A Basque song, melody, and dance type. Its most characteristic element is the 5/8 meter, with highly syncopated rhythms.

zu (Ger.). 1. Too, as *nicht zu schnell*, not too fast. 2. To; toward.

zufahrend (Ger.). Rushing headlong (Mahler, 4th Sym.).

Zugposaune (Ger.). Slide trombone.

Zukerman, Pinchas, outstanding Israeli violinist, violist, and conductor; b. Tel Aviv, July 16, 1948. He began to study music with his father, taking up the violin at age 6; he then enrolled at the Cons. in Tel Aviv, where he studied with Ilona Feher. With the encouragement of Isaac Stern and Pablo Casals, he became a scholarship student at the Juilliard School of Music in N.Y., where he studied with Ivan Galamian (1961–67). In 1967 he shared 1st prize in the Leventritt Competition in N.Y. with Kyung-Wha Chung, and then launched a brilliant career as a soloist with the major American and European orchs. He also appeared as both violinist and violist in recitals with Isaac Stern and Itzhak Perlman. He subsequently devoted part of his time to conducting, appearing as a guest conductor with the N.Y. Phil., Philadelphia Orch., Boston Sym. Orch., Los Angeles Phil., and many others.

From 1980 to 1987 he was music director of the St. Paul (Minn.) Chamber Orch. He was married to the flutist Eugenia (née Rich) Zukerman (b. Cambridge, Mass., Sept. 25, 1944) from 1968 to 1985; then married the American actress Tuesday Weld. His performances as a violinist are distinguished by their innate emotional élan and modern virtuoso technique.

Zukofsky, Paul, remarkable American violinist and talented conductor; b. N.Y., Oct. 22, 1943. His father Louis

Zukofsky was a poet who experimented in highly complex verbal forms; in 1970 he publ. a novel, *Little*, dealing with the trials and triumphs of a violin wunderkind. Paul began playing the violin at the age of 4 on a quarter-size instrument; when he was 7 he began lessons with Ivan Galamian; was soloist with the New Haven (Conn.) Sym. Orch. at the age of 8; he made his Carnegie Hall recital debut in N.Y. when he was 13. At 16 he entered the Juilliard School of Music. From his earliest years he was fascinated by ULTRA-MODERN MUSIC and developed maximal celerity, dexterity, and alacrity in manipulating special techniques, in effect transforming the violin into a multimedia instrument beyond its normal capacities.

In 1969 he inaugurated in N.Y. a concert series, Music for the 20th Century Violin, performing works often requiring acrobatic coordination. His repertoire includes all 4 violin sonatas by Charles Ives, the violin concertos by William Schuman and Roger Sessions, *Capriccio* by Penderecki, the solo violin works of John Cage, etc. As a violin instructor he held the post of Creative Associate at the Buffalo Center of the Creative and Performing Arts; also taught at the Berkshire Music Center in Tanglewood and at the New England Cons. of Music. In later years he became active as a conductor; served as conductor of the Contemporary Chamber Ensemble at the Juilliard School (from 1984), and also was director of chamber music activities there (1987–89). He directed the Schoenberg Inst. in Los Angeles, replacing Leonard Stein.

Zukunftmusik (Ger.). Music of the future; a term coined by Wagner. His opponents turned this lofty phrase into a derisive description of his music.

zummāra (Arab.). Arab double clarinet with parallel identical cylindrical pipes and a tremulant sound. It is a descendant of the Egyptian *memet*, dated to 2700 B.C.

zunehmend (Ger.). Increasing dynamic level; CRESCENDO.

Zunge (Ger.). 1. TONGUE. 2. Organ reed.

Zungenpfeife (Ger.). Organ reed pipe. *Zungenstimme*, organ reed stop.

Zupfinstrumente (Ger.). Plucked string instruments.

zurnā. Shawn family of wide geographic distribution, with conical bore, flared bell, 7 fingerholes, and several ventholes at the lower end. It is found under this and other names in Arab and Slavic regions, Turkey, India, and Indonesia.

zuruckgehend (Ger.). Returning (to a preceding slower tempo).

zuruckhaltend (Ger.). Holding back; RITARDANDO.

zusammen (Ger.). Together.

Zwei (Ger.). Two.

Zwei Herzen im Dreivierteltakt (2 Hearts in 3-Quarter Time). Operetta, 1933, by Robert Stolz (b. Graz, Aug. 25, 1880; d. Berlin, June 27, 1975), premiered in Zurich. This work, typically Viennese in style, is the best known of Stolz's 65 operettas and musicals.

Zweifacher (Ger.). Bavarian folk dance with alternating binary and ternary periods (e.g., 2 measures + 3 measures).

zweihändig (Ger.). For 2 hands.

zweistimmig (Ger.). For 2 voices; in or for 2 parts.

Zwilich, Ellen Taaffe, remarkable American composer; b. Miami, Apr. 30, 1939. She studied composition with John Boda and violin with Richard Burgin at Florida State Univ. (B.M., 1956; M.M., 1962); she then moved to N.Y., where she continued her violin studies with Ivan Galamian. After playing in the American Sym. Orch. there (1965–72), she enrolled at the Juilliard School in N.Y. and had sessions with Roger Sessions and Elliott Carter; she was the 1st woman to receive a D.M.A. in composition from that school (1975). In 1983 she received the Pulitzer prize in music for her Sym. No. 1 (originally titled *3 Movements for Orchestra*), 1st performed in N.Y. in 1982. Zwilich's music offers a happy combination of purely technical excellence and a distinct power of communication, while a poetic element pervades the melody, harmony, and counterpoint of her creations. This combination of qualities explains the frequency and variety of prizes awarded her from various sources: the Elizabeth Sprague Coolidge Chamber Music Prize; a gold medal at the 26th Annual International Composition Competition in Vercelli, Italy; N.E.A. grants; a Guggenheim fellowship (1980–81); the Ernst von Dohnányi Citation; and an award from the American Academy and Inst. of Arts and Letters (1984). Conductors in America, Europe, and Japan are also eager to program her works. During a 1988 tour of Russia Zubin Mehta and the N.Y. Phil. presented the world premiere of her *Symbolon* in Leningrad. She is best known for her instrumental works.

Zwischenfalle bei einer Notlandung (Incidents at an Emergency Landing). "Reportage in 2 phases and 14 situations" by Blacher, 1966, for instruments and electronic devices, 1st performed in Hamburg.

Zwischensatz (Ger.). Episode; in a fugue, a section in between thematic sections.

Zwischenspiel (Ger.). Interlude; intermezzo.

Zwölftonmusik (Ger.). See DODECAPHONY; SERIALISM.

Zymbel (Ger.). 1. Obsolete for CYMBALS. 2. Organ mixture stop.